Learn Office 2000 from the Experts

Platinum Edition Using Microsoft Office 2000 was written and edited by a team of Microsoft-certified experts—handpicked for their extensive Office knowledge. You'll find no other book that delves into the depths of Office as extensively as the one you are holding.

If you are the appointed Office guru at work or a longtime Office user who isn't afraid to get under the hood and tinker a little, this book is for you.

About the Author

Laura Stewart is an experienced technical writer and software instructor. She is a certified Microsoft Office Expert Specialist in Excel and PowerPoint and an award-winning Office 2000 beta tester. Laura has written five computer reference books for Que including *Using Microsoft Excel 97 (Second Edition)*, *Migrating to Office 95 & Office 97: A Corporate User's Quick Reference*, *Easy Microsoft PowerPoint 2000*, *Easy Microsoft PowerPoint 97*, and *Easy Microsoft Excel 97*. She also has been a contributing author on several other Que and Sams books, including *Special Edition Using Microsoft Project 98*, *Sams Teach Yourself Microsoft Project 98*, *Special Edition Using Microsoft PowerPoint 97*, and *Special Edition Using Microsoft Project 95*. Some of the books she has written have been under the name Laura Monsen.

About the Contributors and Editors

Kyle Bryant is the owner of Personal Computer Solutions, a PC-network integration/value-added reseller and authorized Microsoft OEM firm that serves the Dallas/Ft. Worth metroplex. His company specializes in Microsoft Windows-based local and wide area networks, network security, and Internet/intranet connectivity. Kyle has been a technical editor and author for Macmillan Computer Publishing since 1995—contributing to over three dozen titles about Windows 95, Windows 98, Windows NT, and Microsoft Office applications. Kyle was first awarded a Microsoft MVP designation in 1997 and has a Microsoft Certified Professional certification pending. Kyle has been an IT manager with two Fortune 500 corporations.

Ben M. Schorr is the Director of Information Services at Damon Key Leong Kupchak Hastert (a law firm) in Honolulu, Hawaii. He accepted this position after tiring of California's harsh climate where he started as a Certified NetWare Administrator and the Director of Operations at Watson/Schorr Consulting in Los Angeles. Ben is a Microsoft Outlook MVP and Microsoft Certified Professional. He was the technical editor of *Sams Teach Yourself Outlook 98 in 24 Hours*, and often teaches computer classes at Kapi'olani Community College.

Vincent Averello is a Microsoft Outlook MVP and Microsoft Certified Professional. Vince has extensive technical editing experience on a number of books, particularly on Microsoft Outlook, Windows 98, and Windows NT. In the few moments when he's not answering questions on the Outlook newsgroups and enjoying his family, Vince is a member of the Electronic Software Distribution team at Ernst & Young. You can reach Vince at `vince@maverick.com`.

Daryl J. Lucas is a Microsoft Office Connectivity Specialist for Ibbotson Associates in Chicago. Daryl has been a Microsoft Word MVP since 1987 and has been a programmer of WordBasic, Visual Basic, and VBA applications since 1992. He has authored seven books and contributed to more than a dozen others. Daryl graduated summa cum laude from Wheaton College.

Herb Tyson is an economist and a computer consultant in the Washington, D.C. area. He is the author of many computer magazine articles as well as over a dozen computing books, including the *Word for Windows Super Book*, *Sams Teach Yourself Web Publishing with Microsoft Word*, *Word for Windows Revealed*, and *101 Essential Word for Windows Tips*. Dr. Tyson has been awarded MVP status every year since the program's inception in recognition of his expertise in helping Microsoft Office users find solutions. Widely recognized for his expertise in applications and operating systems, his clients have included IBM, the Federal government, and the World Bank, as well as many of the most prestigious publishers in the U.S.

Tony Houston is a Microsoft Certified Systems Engineer, Microsoft Certified Product Specialist, and a Microsoft Certified Trainer. Tony is one of a handful of people participating with Microsoft in both product and courseware development for Windows 2000 (formerly Windows NT 5.0). He began as a computer programmer in the U.S. Air Force and became a Master Instructor, teaching all levels of programming, system administration, and microcomputer applications. Tony teaches Windows NT and networking classes throughout the United States.

Gordon Padwick is a consultant who develops applications mainly based on Microsoft's Office suite. Gordon is a Microsoft Outlook MVP and has authored and contributed to many computer application books including Que's *Special Edition Using Microsoft Outlook 2000, Using Microsoft Outlook 98,* and *Special Edition Using Microsoft Outlook 97*. Gordon is a graduate of London University, a Senior Member of the Institute of Electrical and Electronics Engineers, and a Member of the IEEE Computer Society. Gordon welcomes your questions and comments on Outlook-related subjects addressed to him at `gpadwick@earthlink.net`.

Robert L. Bogue is the Chief Operations Officer of AvailTek, Inc., a consulting company located in Indianapolis, IN. Robert is also a Microsoft Certified Systems Engineer, Novell Certified NetWare Administrator, and certified A+ service technician. Rob's been involved in over 75 book projects on topics ranging from Visual Basic to Windows NT to NetWare to Microsoft Office. He can be reached at `Rob.Bogue@AvailTek.com`.

Richard Bodien specializes in business-to-business marketing and technical communications. He has over 30 publications to his credit, including user manuals for the Arabic, Hebrew, and North African editions of Microsoft Word. As Webmaster for the IAM/Boeing Joint Programs in Seattle, he has produced several Internet and intranet sites using FrontPage, including `www.iam-boeing.com` and the "Career Explorer" career-development system for union-represented machinists and aerospace workers. Contact Richard at `bodien@rocketmail.com`.

Kevin Marlowe is a systems analyst with Computer Sciences Corporation at NASA's Langley Research Center in Hampton, VA, where he supervises a team of Web/database programmers and designs data-driven Web sites for NASA. He is the author of Que's *Using Microsoft Access 97, The Microsoft Office 97 Internet Developer's Guide,* and has contributed to and acted as technical editor for several other books, including *MCSD Training Guide: Microsoft Access*.

Using Platinum Edition

Using MICROSOFT® Office® 2000

201 West 103rd Street,
Indianapolis, Indiana 46290

Laura Stewart

Platinum Edition Using Microsoft® Office 2000

International Standard Book Number: 0-7897-1841-3

Library of Congress Catalog Card Number: 98-86836

Printed in the United States of America

First Printing: June 1999

01 00 99 4 3 2 1

Trademarks

All terms mentioned in this book that are known to be trademarks or service marks have been appropriately capitalized. Que Corporation cannot attest to the accuracy of this information. Use of a term in this book should not be regarded as affecting the validity of any trademark or service mark.

Warning and Disclaimer

Every effort has been made to make this book as complete and as accurate as possible, but no warranty or fitness is implied. The information provided is on an "as is" basis. The authors and the publisher shall have neither liability nor responsibility to any person or entity with respect to any loss or damages arising from the information contained in this book or from the use of the CD or programs accompanying it.

EXECUTIVE EDITOR
Jim Minatel

ACQUISITIONS EDITOR
Jill Byus

SENIOR DEVELOPMENT EDITOR
Rick Kughen

DEVELOPMENT EDITORS
Robert Bogue
Tom Dinse
Benjamin Milstead

TECHNICAL EDITORS
Vince Averello
Kyle Bryant
Daryl Lucas
Ben Schorr

MANAGING EDITOR
Thomas F. Hayes

PROJECT EDITOR
Sossity Smith

COPY EDITORS
Victoria Elzey
Kay Hoskin
Julie McNamee

INDEXER
Joy Dean Lee

PROOFREADER
Maribeth Echard

SOFTWARE DEVELOPMENT SPECIALIST
Jason Haines

INTERIOR DESIGN
Ruth Harvey

COVER DESIGN
Dan Armstrong
Ruth Harvey

LAYOUT TECHNICIANS
Tricia Flodder
Brad Lenser

Contents at a Glance

Table of Contents

II Visual Basic For Applications (VBA)—A Primer

IV Microsoft Excel

28 Auditing Worksheets and Resolving Errors 909

29 Sharing Excel Data with Other Users and Applications 929

V Microsoft Access

30 Migrating to Access 2000 953

31 Customizing Access 961

VII Microsoft Outlook

Chapters/Appendixes on the CD

About the Author

Laura Stewart is an experienced technical writer and software instructor. She is a certified Microsoft Office Expert Specialist in Excel and PowerPoint. Laura has written five computer reference books for Que including *Using Microsoft Excel 97 (Second Edition)*, *Migrating to Office 95 & Office 97: A Corporate User's Quick Reference*, *Easy Microsoft PowerPoint 2000*, *Easy Microsoft PowerPoint 97*, and *Easy Microsoft Excel 97*. She also has been a contributing author on several other Que and Sams books, including *Special Edition Using Microsoft Project 98*, *Sams Teach Yourself Microsoft Project 98*, *Special Edition Using Microsoft PowerPoint 97*, and *Special Edition Using Microsoft Project 95*. Some of the books she has written have been under the name Laura Monsen.

With more than seven years' experience as a professional instructor of computer application classes, Laura has become an expert at explaining difficult software application concepts. At the same time, her engaging teaching style keeps the classes interesting and fosters an interactive learning experience for her students. Laura teaches a wide variety of spreadsheet, project management, database, and graphic applications classes, primarily for Productivity Point International, a leader in computer software training solutions. Additionally, she frequently provides consulting expertise for Excel, Project, and PowerPoint.

Prior to getting into writing and instructing on computer software, Laura worked eight years for the Defense Intelligence Agency in Washington, D.C. During her career there, she was involved in upgrading more than 3,000 users to a new computer system and developing the courseware materials for these users. She was also responsible for initiating and chairing several long-standing user groups.

Laura has a B.A. in Economics from the University of the South, Sewanee, Tennessee. She can be reached at `stewart@fastol.com`.

ECCE QUAM BONUM

Contributing Writers and Technical Editors

The book you are holding—most assuredly with two hands—is the result of literally thousands of hours of work. We assembled an all-star cast, experts from every nook and cranny of Office. We would like to thank each and every one of these talented individuals for helping produce what you'll undoubtedly soon learn is one superb Office 2000 book.

Kyle Bryant is the owner of Personal Computer Solutions, a PC-network integration/value-added reseller and authorized Microsoft OEM firm that serves the Dallas/Ft. Worth metroplex. His company specializes in Microsoft Windows-based local and wide area networks, network security, and Internet/intranet connectivity. Kyle has been a technical editor and author for Macmillan Computer Publishing since 1995—contributing to more than three dozen titles about Windows 95, Windows 98, Windows NT, and Microsoft Office applications. Kyle was first awarded a Microsoft MVP designation in 1997 and has a Microsoft Certified Professional certification pending. Kyle has been an IT manager with two Fortune 500 corporations.

Ben M. Schorr is the Director of Information Services at Damon Key Leong Kupchak Hastert (a law firm) in Honolulu, Hawaii. He accepted this position after tiring of California's harsh climate where he started as a Certified NetWare Administrator and the Director of Operations at Watson/Schorr Consulting in Los Angeles. Ben is a Microsoft Outlook MVP and Microsoft Certified Professional. He was the technical editor of *Sams Teach Yourself Outlook 98 in 24 Hours*, and often teaches computer classes at Kapi'olani Community College. Despite all of this, his parents are proud of him.

Vincent Averello is a Microsoft Outlook MVP and Microsoft Certified Professional. Vince has extensive technical editing experience on a number of books, particularly on Microsoft Outlook, Windows 98, and Windows NT. In the few moments when he's not answering questions on the Outlook newsgroups and enjoying his family (the ever-patient Susan and kids—Vinnie and Jessica), Vince is trying to keep his job at Ernst & Young in the Electronic Software Distribution department. You can reach Vince at `vince@maverick.com`.

Daryl J. Lucas is a Microsoft Office Connectivity Specialist for Ibbotson Associates in Chicago. Daryl has been a Microsoft Word MVP since 1987 and has been a programmer of WordBasic, Visual Basic, and VBA applications since 1992. He has authored seven books and contributed to more than a dozen others. Daryl graduated summa cum laude from Wheaton College.

Kevin Marlowe is a systems analyst with Computer Sciences Corporation at NASA's Langley Research Center in Hampton, VA, where he supervises a team of Web/database programmers and designs data-driven Web sites for NASA. He is the author of Que's *Using Microsoft Access 97*, *The Microsoft Office 97 Internet Developer's Guide*, and has contributed to and acted as technical editor for several other books, including *MCSD Training Guide: Microsoft Access*.

Robert L. Bogue is the Chief Operations Officer of AvailTek, Inc., a consulting company located in Indianapolis, IN. Robert is also a Microsoft Certified Systems Engineer, Novell Certified NetWare Administrator, and certified A+ service technician. Rob's been involved in over 75 book projects on topics ranging from Visual Basic to Windows NT to NetWare to Microsoft Office. He can be reached at `Rob.Bogue@AvailTek.com`.

Herb Tyson is an economist and a computer consultant in the Washington, D.C. area. He is the author of many computer magazine articles as well as more than a dozen computing books, including the *Word for Windows Super Book, Sams Teach Yourself Web Publishing with Microsoft Word, Word for Windows Revealed*, and *101 Essential Word for Windows Tips*. Dr. Tyson has been awarded MVP status every year since the program's inception in recognition of his expertise in helping Microsoft Office users find solutions. Widely recognized for his expertise in applications and operating systems, his clients have included IBM, the Federal government, and the World Bank, as well as many of the most prestigious publishers in the U.S.

Tony Houston is a Microsoft Certified Systems Engineer, Microsoft Certified Product Specialist, and a Microsoft Certified Trainer. Tony is one of a handful of people participating with Microsoft in both product and courseware development for Windows 2000 (formerly Windows NT 5.0). He began as a computer programmer in the U.S. Air Force and became a Master Instructor, teaching all levels of programming, system administration, and microcomputer applications. Tony teaches Windows NT and networking classes throughout the United States.

Sharon J. Podlin is President of PTSI, a consulting firm specializing in the development and presentation of computer training courses. Sharon has over 15 years in the computer industry and has worked primarily in Fortune 100 companies including J.C. Penney, Hyatt International Hotels, and United Airlines. She is a Microsoft Certified Trainer for a wide range of products including Microsoft SQL Server, Excel, Visual Basic for Applications, Access, and Windows NT. She also teaches continuing education courses at Coastal Georgia Community College. Sharon is a graduate of the University of Texas.

David Karlins is a desktop publishing and Web publishing author. His recent books include *Sams Teach Yourself CorelDraw 9 in 24 Hours, Wild Web Graphics with Microsoft Image Composer, MCSD: Designing and Implementing Web Sites Using FrontPage 98*, and *How to Use Microsoft Publisher 97*. David co-authored *The FrontPage 2000 Bible*. You can visit his Web site at `www.ppinet.com`.

Susan Kucinkas Perry has extensive experience teaching Microsoft Office, especially Access and Word, for Productivity Point International (PPI) in San Antonio. She is also an IBM-qualified UNIX instructor and travels throughout North America conducting classes. Prior to her career in computer instruction, Susan developed proposals for The Psychological Corporation. She holds a bachelor's degree in Speech and Drama from Our Lady of the Lake University and a master's degree in English from the University of Texas at San Antonio. Susan can be reached at `sperry@texas.net`.

Judy A. Treviño has been a computer instructor since 1997. She is a Microsoft Certified Trainer with Productivity Point International where she specializes in teaching Windows NT, Microsoft Office, and A+ classes. Judy also teaches bilingual-application classes and is pursuing her MCSE. In her spare time, she co-wrote and edited an online instructional book on how to record, mass-produce, and distribute music CDs. Judy earned her B.A. in Education from Texas A&M University.

Gordon Padwick is a consultant who develops applications mainly based on Microsoft's Office suite. Gordon has authored and contributed to many computer application books including Que's *Special Edition Using Microsoft Outlook 2000, Using Microsoft Outlook 98*, and *Special Edition Using Microsoft Outlook 97*. Gordon is a Microsoft MVP and is a graduate of London University, a Senior Member of the Institute of Electrical and Electronics Engineers, and a Member of the IEEE Computer Society. Gordon welcomes your questions and comments on Outlook-related subjects addressed to him at gpadwick@earthlink.net.

Ron Stockdreher is a Training Manager at Productivity Point International—a computer solutions firm specializing in client-oriented customized technical and applications training. Ron is a Microsoft Certified Trainer in Visual Basic and Visual Basic for Applications. He has over 20 years' experience in training with the Air Force and private enterprise and also provides customized solutions using Microsoft Office products. He has extensive experience writing and editing applications courseware and has contributed to other Que books.

Richard Bodien specializes in business-to-business marketing and technical communications. He has over 30 publications to his credit, including user manuals for the Arabic, Hebrew, and North African editions of Microsoft Word. As Webmaster for the IAM/Boeing Joint Programs in Seattle, he has produced several Internet and intranet sites using FrontPage, including www.iam-boeing.com and the "Career Explorer" career-development system for union-represented machinists and aerospace workers. Contact Richard at bodien@rocketmail.com.

Brady P. Merkel is the Director of Internet Development for an international telecommunications company in Melbourne, Florida. Brady specializes in the technical aspects of Internet development, and has co-authored many Internet books, including *Web Publishing with Word for Windows*, *Web Site Administrators Survival Guide*, and *Building Internet Applications with Visual C++*. He hopes one day to move to a Caribbean island and begin a career installing Web-enabled navigation equipment on large yachts. Brady sends a special heartfelt thank you to his family who continue to love, support, and encourage him even though he doesn't visit them as often as they'd like. You can contact Brady at brady@merkel.net.

Molly Joss is a freelance writer and author who has written about the graphic arts and computer industries for more than a decade. Her articles have appeared in more than a dozen trade and computer-related business publications and she currently writes a monthly software column for *Computer User*. Look for her books in the computer and graphic arts sections of all major bookstores and specialty book stores.

Mike Bailey has 24 years' experience in the printing industry, working for Benwell Atkins in Vancouver, B.C., Canada. He is a regular contributor to the Microsoft Publisher newsgroup, and the HelpTalk page for Publisher users (http://www.helptalk.com/mspub/). His own Web site, http://www3.bc.sympatico.ca, is devoted to helping Publisher users work with copy shops and the commercial printing industry.

Helen Feddema earned a B.S. in Philosophy from Columbia and T.T.S. in Theological Studies from Harvard Divinity School. Helen co-authored *Inside Microsoft Access*, and co-authored *Access How-To* for the Waite Group Press. She is also a regular contributor to Pinnacle's *Smart Access* and *Office Developer* journals and *Woody's Office Watch* Newsletter.

Dedication

You watched over me as I learned
to laugh and cry,
and answered all my questions
that began with "Why..?"

You taught me to love
and live each day to the fullest,
to take each step
with renewed anticipation and interest.

You showed me the beauty
of an evening's twilight,
and the comfort brought
by warm firelight.

You helped me cope
with life's little ironies,
and amazed me with
your abundant generosity.

You became true friends,
companions in harmony,
and without you I feel lost
like a ship at sea.

So to you I dedicate
this book you see,
to my beloved and special
family.

—Laura Stewart

Acknowledgments

This is one of the largest computer reference books Macmillan Computer Publishing has ever produced. To coordinate the process from beginning to end requires a talented team of professionals who are experts at what they do. This enormous endeavor is primarily the responsibility of three key people. **Jim Minatel**, the Executive Editor, provided focus and guidance as we hashed out this book's detailed outline. His unique background and insight contributed greatly to the depth and scope of the topics covered here. **Jill Byus**, the Acquisitions Editor, singlehandedly assembled the team of highly qualified experts who assisted with creating this book. I am indebted to Jill for her integrity and perseverance. **Rick Kughen**, the Senior Development Editor, is responsible for ensuring the quality of the coverage from the first page to the very last. Rick possesses the rare and unique qualities necessary for this type of project—professionalism, humor, thoroughness, humor, patience, humor, tact, and did I mention abundant humor?

Several other individuals at Que were instrumental in developing this book and deserve my thanks: the copy editors **Kay Hoskin**, **Victoria Elzey**, and **Julie McNamee**; the formatters **Mandie Rowell**, **Melissa Pluta**, and **Katie Wise**; and the production team—all led by project editor **Sossity Smith**.

Tell Us What You Think!

As the reader of this book, *you* are our most important critic and commentator. We value your opinion and want to know what we're doing right, what we could do better, what areas you'd like to see us publish in, and any other words of wisdom you're willing to pass our way.

As an Executive Editor for Que, I welcome your comments. You can fax, email, or write me directly to let me know what you did or didn't like about this book—as well as what we can do to make our books stronger.

Please note that I cannot help you with technical problems related to the topic of this book, and that due to the high volume of mail I receive, I might not be able to reply to every message.

When you write, please be sure to include this book's title and author as well as your name and phone or fax number. I will carefully review your comments and share them with the author and editors who worked on the book.

Fax: 317-581-4666

Email: office_que@mcp.com

Mail: Executive Editor
Que
201 West 103rd Street
Indianapolis, IN 46290 USA

Introduction to *Platinum Edition Using Microsoft® Office 2000*

Who Will Get the Most Out of This Book?

Platinum Edition Using Microsoft Office 2000 is written for users who have mastered the basics of Office and want to take advantage of the inherent power in the advanced features. Because many people upgrade from earlier versions, you will find references or comparisons to features in Office 95 and Office 97.

This book is also written in such a way that system administrators and help-desk personnel will find useful information about what's going on behind the scenes. There are two chapters (and several appendixes) at the end of this book that are written specifically for anyone responsible for installing and supporting Office 2000 in a business environment.

The table of contents and index will help you locate the topics you are interested in learning about. Most sections within a chapter are designed so that you do not have to read the previous section(s) to follow the discussion. However, with some of the more complex topics there is a thread you need to follow and the text will indicate this. In each chapter, you'll find plenty of notes, tips, cautions, and sidebars that expand beyond the traditional numbered steps for performing tasks. Additionally, a new element has been added to this book—snippets of VBA code. To show you how easy VBA can be used in the Office applications, many of the chapters have short, easy-to-use code that will make working with the Office 2000 applications more efficient.

All the applications in Office 2000 are discussed in this book regardless of the version of Office 2000 you are using, with two exceptions: Small Business Tools and features unique to the Developer's version.

What Makes This Book So Special?

The single most important item that makes this book stand head and shoulders above any other Office 2000 book is the expertise of the people who contributed to it. A number of these people are certified by Microsoft as Microsoft Certified Systems Engineers, Microsoft Certified Product Specialists, and Microsoft Certified Professionals.

Additionally, each year Microsoft recognizes a handful of people who have been responsive to and accurate in answering users questions on the public newsgroups that Microsoft sponsors. These people are designated as Microsoft Most Valuable Professionals (MVP). Six Microsoft MVPs assisted in the writing and editing of this Office 2000 book:

- Ben Schorr
- Daryl Lucas
- Herb Tyson
- Kyle Bryant
- Vincent Averello III
- Gordon Padwick

All the writers and editors of this book have extensive experience using Office in a business environment. Several are software or networking instructors, including four Microsoft Certified Trainers.

How Is This Book Organized?

This book is divided into ten major sections: an overview, a primer for Visual Basic for Applications, sections for each of the Office applications, and a section devoted to planning, installing, and configuring Office 2000. In addition, there are several appendixes at the end of the book that provide information about managing system resources, working with the Registry, and a list of suggested references.

NOTE Although you will find some information about creating Web pages with Word, Excel, and PowerPoint, at this level we assume you will primarily be using FrontPage for your sophisticated Web-page creation needs.

Part I—Office 2000: Overview of New and Enhanced Features This section describes the new global and application features in Office 2000. Chapter 3 explains how to take advantage of the new Web-related features in Office 2000, such as Web Discussions and Web Components. Chapter 4 shows you how to customize Microsoft Office, including the Places Bar (new in the Open and Save dialog boxes) and the behavior of the personalized toolbars and menus.

Part II—Visual Basic for Applications (VBA)—A Primer The two chapters in this section will introduce you to creating VBA snippets, the VBA Editor, and understanding VBA terminology. In Chapter 6, you will learn how to take advantage of the snippets scattered throughout the book (and provided on the CD) in your own organization.

Part III—Microsoft Word This section begins with two chapters on migrating and customizing Word. If you are upgrading from previous versions of Word, you'll find an excellent discussion of what occurs when you bring templates and macros into Word 2000 in Chapter 7. Although applicable to other applications, Chapter 8 explains the new international usage features that enable users to set the language they want to work in without requiring them to purchase a copy of Office in that language.

The more sophisticated Word features are explained in the remaining chapters in this section including

- Using bookmarks as a quick placeholder tool while editing lengthy documents (see Chapter 9).
- Understanding the difference between character and paragraph styles and resolving conflicts that arise from using these styles.
- Working with local and global templates, and resolving template conflicts (see Chapter 10).
- Creating floating and inline images and controlling the flow of text around images.
- Effectively using fields in your Word documents, with emphasis on the top ten most useful fields.
- Exploring the enhancements made to table creation, including nesting and floating tables and formatting long or complex tables (Chapter 13).
- Choosing the correct type of form—FormField-based forms, ActiveX documents, or Web forms. Learning practical uses for forms and how to add controls such as Submit buttons, list boxes, and option buttons (see Chapter 14).
- Employing large document features such as tables of contents and indexes and using the tools built in to Word for managing lengthy document-like outlining and the improved Document Map.
- Performing advanced mail merges using data sources from Access, Excel, and Outlook. Printing and distributing form letters (see Chapter 17).
- Effectively collaborating with others using the new Web Discussions feature, email routing, embedded comments, and revision marks.

Part IV—Microsoft Excel If you are migrating from an earlier version of Excel to Excel 2000, see the first chapter in this section, Chapter 19. You not only learn about the changes in functionality between the versions, but changes to the interface and placement of commands. This is followed by a chapter on customizing how Excel starts and using the Shift key to take advantage of toolbar button shortcuts that are available only in Excel (see Chapter 20).

The section continues with discussions about

- Designing templates that automatically appear when you open Excel.
- Using formulas (instead of the cell values) as the criteria for conditional formatting.
- Understanding what array formulas are and when you want to use them (see Chapter 22).

- Creative ways to use some of Excel's functions, such as using the `OFFSET` and `COUNTA` functions to automatically update the range used to plot a chart, or using the `INDEX` and `MATCH` functions to look up data in multiple columns (see Chapter 23).
- Working with Microsoft Query to import data from external databases such as Access and FoxPro, and creating parameter queries that prompt you for values before executing the query.
- Learning about OLAP Cubes, an alternative to traditional relational databases, which allow you to query large stores of data and display the consolidated information in a PivotTable (see Chapter 24).
- Performing advanced filters, using database functions, creating custom outlines, and working with subtotals on worksheet lists.
- Exploring the enhancements made to PivotTables and designing PivotCharts—a new feature in Excel 2000 (see Chapter 25).
- Creating summary charts, using trendlines in charts, and other advanced graphic charting features.
- Analyzing worksheets through the use of Data Validation, scenarios, data tables, goal seek, and the Solver.
- Using the Exponential Smoothing feature in the Analysis ToolPak to generate forecasts (see Chapter 27).
- Taking advantage of Excel's auditing tools to locate formula precedents and dependents and to resolve worksheet errors.
- Collaborating with others on workbooks using the new Web Discussions feature, email, in-cell comments, and the sharing and merging workbook feature (see Chapter 29).

Part V—Microsoft Access In the first chapter of the Access section (Chapter 30), you will become acquainted with the retooled database window and the new object groups feature. You will read about the issues involved with converting databases, along with other topics that relate to upgrading from prior versions of Access.

You can alter the way Access starts by using the startup switches. To control the overall Access environment, you need to edit the Windows Registry. Both these topics are described in Chapter 31.

One of the new features you will enjoy is the capability to use the Print Relationships Wizard to print a report displaying the relationships between your tables (see Chapter 33).

The remaining topics in the section focus on exploring the advanced features of Access:

- Using the new Access 2000 feature, the Project, to connect to a SQL Server, expanding on the Access 97 client/server model to use Access as a front end to other database engines (see Chapter 32).
- Learning advanced methods for creating tables, queries, forms, and reports.

- Exploring the new Data Access Pages (DAPs) feature as a means of creating Web pages that you build from within Access, without having to export and convert the pages (see Chapter 38).
- Designing basic applications in Access which includes creating custom menus and toolbars, setting startup and security options, and distributing the application.

Part VI—Microsoft PowerPoint As with Access, the interface in PowerPoint has changed with the introduction of the new Normal view—a tri-pane view that combines the Slide, Outline, and Notes Pages views. Additionally, a detailed discussion of the version differences for users upgrading from previous versions of PowerPoint is included in the first chapter in this section.

Experienced PowerPoint users can perfect their presentations by reading Chapter 45 on advanced presentation formatting features. This chapter discusses the best slide transitions and colors to use to convey your message, as well as useful suggestions for customizing the presentation Masters.

Several new features, discussed in Chapter 43, include the changes to the way table slides are created and the ability to print two, three, four, six, or nine slides per page for your audience handouts.

Other PowerPoint topics in this section include

- Using picture, sound, and video clips effectively, both from the Clip Gallery and from other sources.
- Optimizing the PowerPoint Animation on text, charts, and drawn objects (see Chapter 46).
- Taking a complete set of slides and creating Custom Shows for different target audiences.
- Applying Action Settings and using hyperlinks to insert interactive features in a presentation, including creating automated and online slide shows (see Chapter 47).
- Avoiding problems when you take presentations on the road (see Chapter 47).
- Collaborating on a presentation by broadcasting a presentation online, conducting an online meeting, or copying a presentation to a Web server where others can post comments (see Chapter 48).

Part VII—Microsoft Outlook If you are new to Outlook, skip the first two chapters in this section and go directly to Chapter 51, "Installation and Integration Issues with Outlook." This chapter addresses integration with various operating systems, email products, PalmPilot, and WinCE. On the other hand, if you are upgrading to Outlook 2000 from Outlook 97 or 98, Chapters 49 and 50 will be very beneficial. You'll read about the issues surrounding and differences between these versions, as well as ways to customize Outlook. You'll also learn how Outlook 2000 makes switching between Corporate/Workgroup and Internet Mail Only modes far, far easier than it was in Outlook 98.

The section continues with discussions about

- Integrating Outlook with Exchange Server (see Chapter 52).
- Managing email with profiles and the Rules wizard (see Chapter 53).
- Modifying Outlook's email, contacts, and calendar forms to work the way you work; designing custom Outlook forms; adding fields to forms; setting form and field properties; working with actions; and publishing a custom form (see Chapter 55).
- Using Outlook Contacts in Word, importing and exporting whole folders, importing and exporting single items via the Personal Data Interchange (PDI) format standard, and synchronizing Outlook installations data (without an Exchange Server) (see Chapter 57).
- Configuring Outlook's security settings (Chapter 54) to ensure that your private information stays that way.
- Writing Visual Basic for Applications code specifically for Outlook. VBA is new to Outlook 2000 (see Chapter 56).

Part VIII—Microsoft FrontPage Even if you are familiar with FrontPage, you will want to read Chapter CD7, "FrontPage 2000—The Essentials," on the CD-ROM accompanying this book as it discusses a number of migrating issues along with explaining the FrontPage environment.

Because FrontPage is a Web site creation and management tool, as well as a Web page development tool, the remaining chapters in this section address both these topics:

- Chapter CD8 describes how you create, publish, and manage Web sites. You'll learn how to create online and offline Web sites, as well as sub-Webs.
- Through Chapters 58 and 60, you'll learn to develop Web pages from documents imported from other Office 2000 applications and from scratch directly in FrontPage. You'll create online forms, special effects, and connect your Web pages to databases.
- Additionally, you can use FrontPage to adjust images or, if you have the Office 2000 Premium version, you can experiment with a new application—PhotoDraw—to edit your images (see Chapters 59 and 61).

Part IX—Installing and Supporting Office 2000 This section is written primarily for people who have to install Office 2000 in a business setting. The chapters in this section discuss

- Chapter 62 describes the planning issues you need to consider before installing and deploying Office 2000.
- The installation options you can choose from and how to customize the installation for your particular needs, including how to use the Office Custom Installation Wizard (OCIW) and the Office Profile Wizard (OPW).
- The configuration requirements to support the unique Office 2000 Web tools, such as Web Discussions and the Office Server Extensions (see Chapter 63).

Part X—Appendixes At the end of the book, just before the Index, are two appendixes that provide supplementary information relating to Office 2000:

- Applications Found in Each Office 2000 Edition
- Suggested References

Special Features Used in This Book

Certain text formats, margin icons, and other conventions are used in *Platinum Edition Using Microsoft Office 2000* to help you use this book more easily. The following typefaces are used to distinguish specific text:

Table I.1 Typeface Conventions

Type Appearance	Meaning
italic	New terms or phrases when they are first defined. Some words are displayed in italic for emphasis.
`monospace`	Text or data you type.
UPPERCASE	Typically used to indicate items, such as function names, file format types, and cell references.
`monospace`	Visual Basic code.

Generally, keys appear in this book just as they appear on the keyboard (for example, Enter or Tab). When two keys are used together, a plus sign (+) will appear between them, such as Ctrl+Home.

Cross-References

An example of a reference to another part of the book will appear as follows.

▶ **See** "Unlocking the Power of PivotTables and PivotCharts," **p. 797**

Icons

Icons representing buttons on the applications' toolbars are displayed next to paragraphs which reference the button. The Chart Wizard button from the Standard toolbar in Excel appears to the left of this paragraph.

Tips

Additional, helpful information that makes a procedure easier to perform or a feature easier to use is displayed in this format.

Notes

NOTE Additional, useful information is displayed in this format.

Cautions

CAUTION

Warnings of potential problem areas are represented in this format.

Sidebars

Sidebars

Sidebars are designed to provide information that is ancillary to the topic being discussed. Read these if you want to learn more about an application or task.

PART I

Office 2000: Overview of New and Enhanced Features

CHAPTER 1

General Office Features at a Glance

In this chapter

New Features in Office 2000

In each new release of Office, Microsoft makes a number of improvements or enhancements to the way we use applications in our day-to-day work. At first glance, we embrace some of the new features, especially those that were long-awaited improvements. Other features leave us scratching our heads, wondering what Microsoft could possibly have been thinking when they included them in the new release. Office 2000 is no exception.

In Office 2000, Microsoft has expended a great deal of effort working on two areas: improving application interaction with Webs (intranets, extranets, and the Internet) and improving Office usability on a global level. The Web improvements include the integration of the HTML file format in Office and more alternatives for document collaboration online. To assist international companies, Office provides a single program executable and a number of multilingual-support features. In addition to these predominate areas, a large number of other features are designed to make it easier to work with the Office applications.

This chapter describes the most significant new features in Office 2000 and includes a number of references to sections in this book that explain, in detail, how to use each feature.

Integrating HTML in Office

One of the main areas Microsoft has concentrated on for improving Office is Web-productivity tools—tools that make exchanging data between Office 2000 applications and Webs (the Internet, intranets, and extranets) seamless. As more companies incorporate the use of Webs into their everyday business, users will want Web servers to provide the same tools and functionality that their network file servers provide. This makes it possible for anyone with a Web browser to view data created by Office 2000 applications.

HTML File Format

To accomplish this integration with Webs, Office 2000 has made *HTML (Hypertext Markup Language)* a file format you can save to and read from in most Office applications (the exception is Outlook, which doesn't allow much of its data to be saved in HTML). Users will be able to easily create and share rich Web documents with the same Office tools they use to create printed documents. Graphics created in the Office applications can be stored either in the native format of the application or in a format that Web browsers can display, such as GIF and JPEG. Editing graphics designed for Web documents is now as easy as editing graphics designed for non-Web documents.

In Office 2000, HTML is the default Clipboard format. When you copy (or cut) and paste, the data is typically pasted into the target document in the HTML format. This change was necessary to make it easier to share data between ***proprietary binary documents*** and Web documents.

NOTE The current Office file formats, such as .doc and .xls are referred to as proprietary binary file formats.

The most important benefit of this enhanced integration with the Web is that the content of your Office documents will be viewable by anyone with a browser. With this new emphasis on HTML, the trend away from printed output will continue as people discover the advantages of communicating and sharing information through publishing to a Web.

NOTE HTML files, unlike their binary Office cousins, cannot have passwords assigned to them.

Previewing and Saving in the HTML File Format

In most Office 2000 applications, several commands under the File menu can be used to preview and save a document in the HTML file format. The new File, Web Page Preview command displays your active document in HTML format in your default browser. There you can preview how the document will appear when saved in the HTML format and displayed as a Web page. This command is useful for making adjustments to the document prior to saving it in the HTML file format.

The File, Save As Web Page command displays a modified version of the Save As dialog box. Figure 1.1 shows the dialog box for an Excel document. From within this dialog box, you can either save the document in the HTML file format and store it in any folder you like, or you can use the Publish option to publish a copy of the document directly to a Web server.

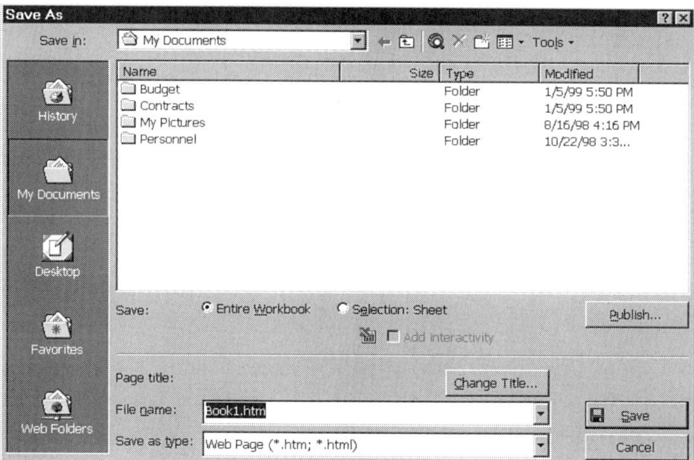

FIGURE 1.1
The file format is automatically selected for you.

NOTE You can also import Office documents into Microsoft FrontPage and take advantage of FrontPage's Web authoring features before publishing the document to a Web Server. See Part VIII, "Microsoft FrontPage," to learn more about FrontPage 2000.

Understanding How Office Stores HTML Files

When an Office document is saved, everything is saved in a single document. Because of the nature of HTML, when an Office document is saved in the HTML file format, separate files are created to store the various components of the HTML document. For example, a Word document that contains a table and a picture clip would actually save three files: a main HTML document and several supporting documents that contain the formatting information for the graphic and table. With a PowerPoint presentation, each slide would become its own file. To avoid problems with managing these multiple-document components, when you save an Office document in the HTML file format, Office creates a single HTML document in the folder you designate. Office then creates a subfolder to store the specific document components. The subfolder has the same name as the HTML document.

If you want to move an HTML document, you must move both the document and the subfolder containing the document components. Lengthy Office documents saved in the HTML file format typically have larger file sizes.

Cascading Style Sheets When Office documents that have been saved in the HTML file format are displayed in a Web browser, the closest browser layout and formatting equivalents (to those used in the original Office document) are used to display the document in the browser. *Cascading Style Sheets (CSS)* store the layout and formatting settings for the Office document so that as much of the formatting from the original Office document is preserved when the file is displayed in a browser. When a format from the Office document cannot be displayed in a browser, the CSS tracks the closest visual equivalent that will be used for that format in the browser.

Additionally, Web authors can edit the CSS and change the HTML text styles to quickly change the entire look of a Web site. Browsers that support CSS include Internet Explorer 3.0 (or later) and Netscape Navigator 4.0.

Extensible Markup Language (XML) Every document has information about it that is not actual document text or objects, but is nevertheless stored with the file. This information includes things such as the document properties, display settings, and how the HTML components relate to the document. When an Office document is saved in an HTML file format, this information is captured in *Extensible Markup Language (XML)* and stored with the document. When the HTML document is brought back into the Office application for editing, the information stored in XML is available to you and the application.

Another powerful use of XML is with OfficeArt objects. Downloading graphic objects from a Web site can sometimes be a time-consuming process. With XML, your browser reads an XML description of the graphic in the HTML document being downloaded, and your own browser draws the graphic instead of downloading it.

NOTE XML is a topic that goes far beyond the scope of this Office book. However, if you'd like to learn more about it, I suggest picking up a copy of *Platinum Edition Using HTML 4.0, XML, and Java 1.2*, also published by Que.

Vector Markup Language (VML) Two types of formats exist for storing graphic images: vector and raster. *Vector graphics* are stored as a single object and therefore can be resized without losing quality. They also take up less disk space than the raster format. Common vector file formats include WMF, CGM, and EPS. TrueType Fonts are in a vector format. *Raster graphics* are stored as bitmaps and often appear dithered (the stairstep look) when resized. Scanned images, such as photographs, are often stored in raster format. Common raster file formats include GIF, JPEG, PCX, BMP, and TIF/TIFF.

Vector Markup Language (VML) is a standard being proposed by Microsoft and other companies for displaying, editing, and sharing vector graphics on the Web. Office 2000 supports this standard, which is under consideration by the World Wide Web Consortium (W3C)). Today, applications save vector graphics in a raster format to display in browsers, increasing file sizes and download times. Office 2000 Art objects are created using VML so that, in the future, browsers and applications that support VML will be able to display and edit these graphics.

Editing HTML Files

Because of the way Office 2000 has implemented the HTML file format, documents originally created in an Office 2000 application can easily be edited. When you click the Edit button in Microsoft Internet Explorer, the Office application that created the HTML file is activated.

Improved Hyperlinks

Office 2000 has improved the way hyperlinks are created and modified in documents. One new feature is the capability to include spaces in Hyperlink URLs, which makes it easier to create links to documents that have spaces in the filename. Additionally, you can now assign hyperlinks to graphics and picture objects, in addition to creating textual hyperlinks.

NOTE Hyperlinks to other files are *relative links*; when a file is moved to another location or renamed, the hyperlink is automatically updated to reflect the new location or name. The hyperlinks are checked when a document is saved. If any of the files the hyperlinks point to have been moved, Office repairs the links. In FrontPage, you can access a Hyperlinks view to graphically see the links and identify any broken ones.

Web-Based Collaboration

Most organizations tend to collaborate on a document in one of three ways:

- A document is printed and distributed (or routed) to workgroup members, where written comments are added to the hard copy document.
- A meeting takes place in which workgroup members gather face-to-face to discuss and comment on a document.
- A document is placed in a shared location on a file server, where workgroup members view and insert comments into the document online.

With Office 2000, Microsoft has implemented several new alternatives to facilitate collaboration on documents, with a special emphasis on online collaboration using Web servers.

Office Server Extensions

Office 2000 includes a set of *Office Server Extensions (OSEs)*, software that enables users to take advantage of Web-based online collaboration. These OSEs are a superset of FrontPage extensions that reside on a Windows NT server. These extensions enhance the functionality of Office 2000 applications, Windows Explorer, and your Web browser.

The OSEs enable users to publish documents to Web servers, add and view annotations to Web documents, and receive notification when a Web document they are monitoring changes.

See "Office Server Extensions (OSEs)," **p. 1719**

Web Discussions

Instead of trying to get a team together for a face-to-face meeting, you can use Web Discussions as a way for people to collaborate on a document when it's convenient for each person to do so. The document to be discussed can reside in any location that all discussion participants have access to, including a Web server, a network file server, an intranet (or extranet) Web site, or an Internet Web site. Participants do not need write access to the document to participate in discussions because the discussions (which are added much like Word comments are added to Word documents) are stored in a database on the Web server instead of within the document.

NOTE It's important to note that all participants in a Web Discussion must be using the same Web server. Comments added by participants using other Web servers will not be visible to you, nor will your comments be visible to participants using another Web server.

The discussion participants can add comments, edit comments, and reply to existing comments when it's convenient for them, without having everyone available at the same time. Web Discussions can be used both with Office and HTML documents and can be added either directly from the Office applications or from within a Web browser. A special Discussions toolbar is added to the browser when the Office Server Extensions are installed.

The specific procedures for using Web Discussions vary slightly for each Office application:

NOTE Using Web Discussions with Word, Excel, and PowerPoint is covered more in depth in the following locations:

- Web Discussions in Word—Chapter 18
- Web Discussions in Excel—Chapter 29
- Web Discussions in PowerPoint—Chapter 48

Figure 1.2 shows a PowerPoint presentation to which discussions have been added.

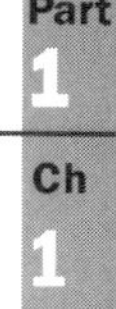

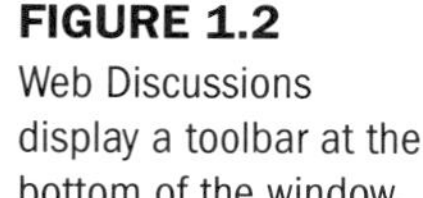

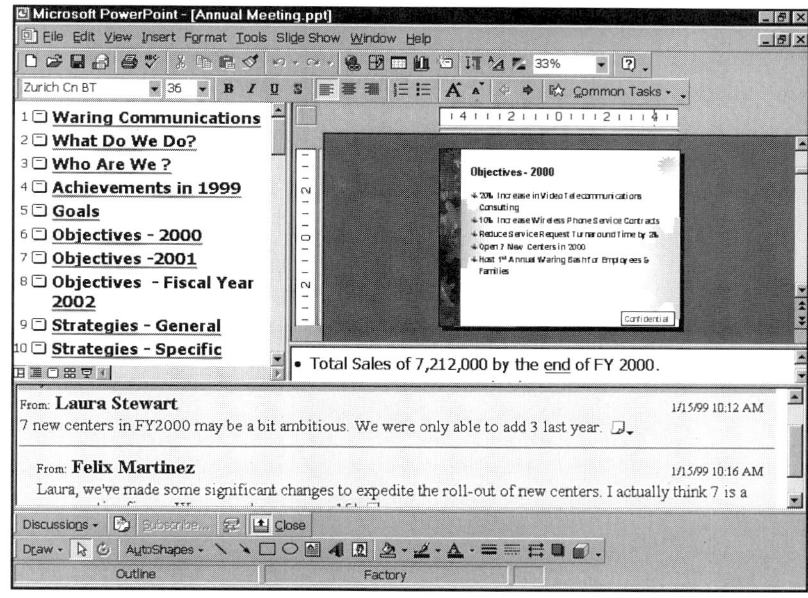

FIGURE 1.2
Web Discussions display a toolbar at the bottom of the window.

Web Subscriptions and Notifications

Web subscriptions and notifications enable you to *subscribe* to documents on a Web server and be *notified* (via email) when documents are created, changed, or deleted. You can choose from several notification alternatives: immediately, daily, or weekly.

Office 2000's Web subscription and notification feature can be used in conjunction with, or independent of, Web Discussions. You can subscribe to any document or folder to which you have at least read access; not just those to which Web discussions have been added. This includes documents that are Web pages on the Internet, such as a competitor's Web pages.

Online Meetings and Broadcast Presentations

When you want to get a team together to discuss a document, you can use Microsoft NetMeeting (which is part of Internet Explorer 5 and comes with Office 2000) to conduct a meeting online. NetMeeting provides the necessary data capabilities for you to share information with other people at different sites over your company's intranet, extranet, or the Internet, just as if everyone were in the same room. Microsoft NetMeeting includes a chat feature and a whiteboard feature, and is capable of transmitting both audio and video. Meetings can be scheduled through Outlook.

To use the NetMeeting feature, you need access to a directory server. Most corporations have a directory server, or you may be able to gain access to one through your Internet service provider. Additionally, to take full advantage of this feature, you should have speakers and a microphone.

▶ **See** "Choosing the Right Collaboration Method," **p. 1302**

NOTE Because this is an early attempt at video teleconferencing by Microsoft, NetMeeting is a little rough around the edges. Look for Microsoft to improve its functionality—and speed—in future versions.

PowerPoint 2000 also includes a feature called Presentation Broadcast, where you can deliver a presentation (including audio and video) over your company's intranet. The broadcast can be recorded and saved on a Web server and is available for playback at any time—a handy feature for archiving a presentation or if some people missed the original broadcast.

A few hardware and software requirements are necessary for a Presentation Broadcast. The presenter uses PowerPoint to show the presentation; to narrate, the presenter needs a microphone. A camera is not required, although video is supported. If more than 15 people are viewing the broadcast from different locations, a NetShow server is required. The Office Resource Kit contains detailed information on NetShow, using audio with a broadcast presentation, and information a system administrator needs to set up and support a NetShow server. Anyone wanting to view the broadcast must have a Web browser, such as Internet Explorer 4.0 or later or Netscape Navigator, and speakers to hear the narration. The presentation is broadcast in HTML and can be viewed on PCs, Macintoshes, or UNIX workstations.

▶ **See** "Setting Up Online Presentations," **p. 1289**

Web File Management

Documents stored on Web servers can be accessed just as documents stored on file servers—through Windows Explorer. You can create folders and move or copy documents the same as you would documents on your hard drive or a network file server.

Because of the Office Server Extensions, your browser can be used to display a directory listing of Web files and folders.

▶ **See** "Saving to a Web Server" **p. 60**

User Interface and Productivity

Microsoft has incorporated a number of new or enhanced features to increase productivity and adapt to user preferences. Among the most significant improvements are the *personalized menus* and *toolbars*, the Clipboard's capability to hold multiple items, the revamped Open and Save dialog boxes, and the access to open documents through the Windows taskbar.

NOTE During early development of Office 2000, personalized toolbars and menus were first known as adaptive toolbars and menus. You might hear them called by either name. Rest assured, however, that they are the same.

Personalized Menus and Toolbars

Two new features you will notice immediately in Office 2000 are the personalized menus and toolbars. When you first click a menu command, the menu initially displays a short subset of commands. As you use other commands, the menu automatically adjusts to show those commands you use frequently. Menus can easily be expanded with a double-click (rather than single–click) to show the entire set of commands.

To provide more space for displaying application data, the Standard and Formatting toolbars in each application share one row. Like the menus, toolbars also automatically adjust to display only those icons you use frequently. Buttons you use less frequently are hidden. You access the hidden buttons through the More Buttons drop-down list at the end of the toolbar (see Figure 1.3).

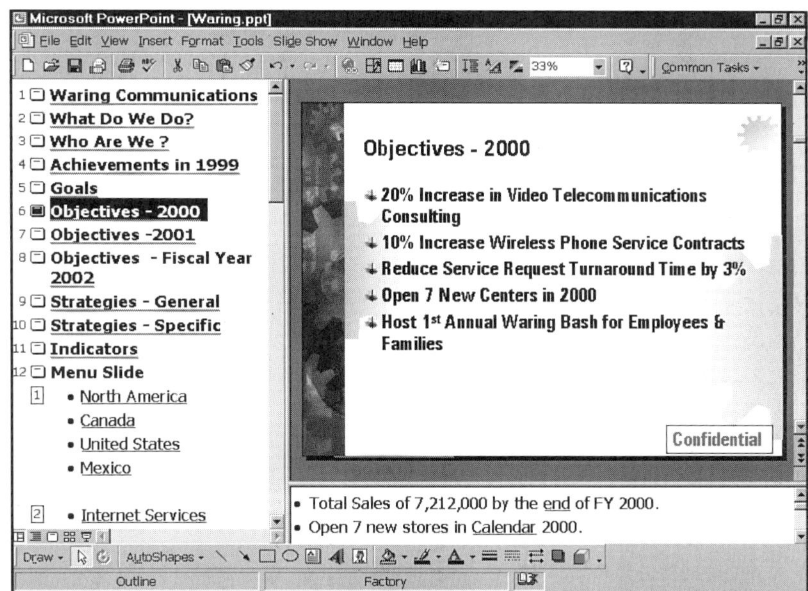

FIGURE 1.3
PowerPoint 2000—the new Normal view.

When you click a hidden button, the button is added to the toolbar. To make room for the button, one of the buttons that has not been used recently is placed on the More Buttons list. In addition to listing the active—but hidden—buttons, the More Buttons drop-down list also has an Add or Remove Buttons option to quickly customize a toolbar.

If you don't like the Standard and Formatting toolbars combined on one line, drag one of the toolbars to another line by using its move handle (refer to Figure 1.3). This changes the position of the toolbars in the active application; it does not affect the position of the toolbars in the other Office 2000 applications.

▶ **See** "Altering the Behavior of the Personalized Menus and Toolbars," **p. 86**

Collect and Paste

One of the most useful enhancements in Office 2000 is the capability to cut or copy multiple items to the Office Clipboard and selectively paste them into documents. When active, the Clipboard holds up to 12 items (or a maximum of 4 megabytes). This feature is particularly useful for holding data you want to paste repeatedly and for pasting data from one application to another. Items can be copied not only from Office applications, but from other Windows applications, email messages, and Web pages.

The Clipboard toolbar automatically appears when you cut or copy two items in a row, or you can right-click any toolbar to activate it. The toolbar is independently displayed in each active document, which means it can be docked in one document and floating in another—including documents in the same application.

Items placed on the Clipboard are represented by their application's icon—Word items display the Word "W" icon, for instance, and Excel items display the Excel "X" icon. When you position the mouse over an item on the Clipboard, a ScreenTip appears identifying the item. For example, a Word item displays the first few words of the clip. This makes it easy to distinguish each clip and select the correct one to paste.

When you dock the Clipboard toolbar, make sure all the tools, especially the Items drop-down button, can be seen.

▶ **See** "Clipboard Toolbar," **p. 189**

The Places Bar

The Open and Save dialog boxes now sport a bar on the left side of the screen that displays a set of "places" to help you locate files and folders quickly (see Figure 1.4). The five places are

- History—Displays the contents of the Recent folder, which lists shortcuts to the last 20 documents you accessed.
- My Documents—Lists the documents and subfolders in the My Documents folder, including the new My Pictures subfolder.
- Desktop—Displays the items on the Desktop that are used to hold or to locate documents. These items include My Documents, My Computer, Network Neighborhood, My Briefcase, and folders that are located on the Desktop.
- Favorites—Lists the same folders and sites that appear in the Favorites list in your Web browser.
- Web Folders—Displays a list of the folders on Web servers that you have access to, making it easy to retrieve and store intranet and Internet files.

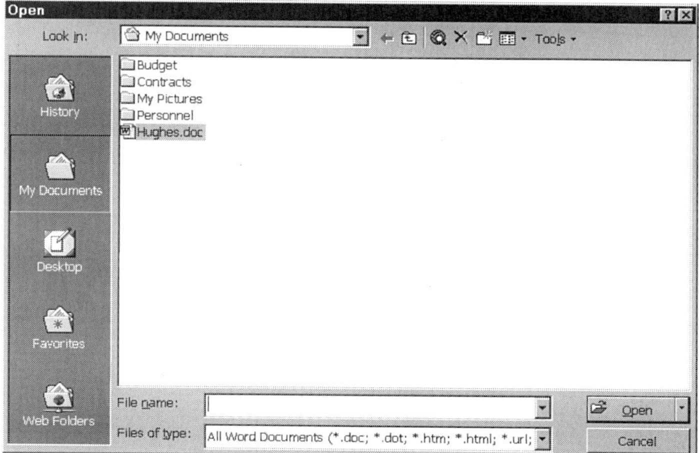

FIGURE 1.4
The Places Bar appears in both Open and Save dialog boxes.

NOTE The downside of the Places Bar is that it takes a change in the Registry to modify the locations listed on the Places Bar (such as a zip drive, a floppy drive, or a specific folder). See the PlaceBar Customizer utility included with WOPR 2000, included on the CD with this book. The PlaceBar Customizer enables you to change the Places Bar without using RegEdit.

See "Customizing the Places Bar," **p. 82**

In addition to the Places Bar, the toolbar in these dialog boxes has been altered. Some of the features that were on the previous toolbar have been moved either to the Views drop-down menu or Tools drop-down menu.

NOTE See Chapter 4 to learn how you can use VBA to change the buttons shown in the Places Bar. Also, see the PlaceBar Customizer utility included with WOPR 2000, included on the CD with this book. The PlaceBar Customizer makes customizing the Places Bar easy and convenient.

Switching Between Documents

In previous versions of Office, when several documents from the same application were open, they appeared in one program window. To switch between these documents, you would click the Window menu and select the document name. In Windows 95, a placeholder for each open application appeared on the taskbar. This method of handling documents was a standard established by Microsoft and is called *Multiple Document Interface* (MDI).

In Office 2000, Microsoft decided to implement the *Single Document Interface* (SDI) as a means of providing users with quick access to each open document. Each open document now displays a placeholder on the Windows taskbar. When you want to switch between documents, whether in the same application or different applications, you can now quickly do so through the taskbar. The exception here is Microsoft Access 2000, which still allows only one database open at a time. You can, if necessary, open several instances of Access and display different databases in each copy of Access.

This feature is supported only in Windows 95 (with Microsoft Internet Explorer 4.0 loaded), Windows 98, or Windows 2000.

As more and more documents are listed on the taskbar, the document names shrink. Rely on the ScreenTips that appear when the mouse is positioned over a taskbar item to identify documents.

Email Integration

Instead of having to launch email to attach an Office document to a message, you can send documents directly from the Office 2000 applications. Email functions are built into all the applications through the File menu. Although this capability was available in Office 97, the use of the HTML file format in Office 2000 means you don't have to worry whether the recipients will be able to read it. Any recipient with an HTML-compliant email reader will be able to view the data. Microsoft Outlook 98, Outlook 2000, Outlook Express, some Netscape products, some Lotus products, and Eudora are HTML-compliant email readers.

Office Help

Microsoft has enhanced the Help features in Office 2000 by making the Office Assistant less obtrusive, providing more interactive help, and improving the help provided over the Web.

Now when the Office Assistant appears, it is no longer displayed in its own window. Rather, it floats at the top of the screen and takes up less space. If you choose to turn off the assistant, it will stay turned off instead of popping up when it thinks you need it (as was the case in Office 97).

More of the help screens now include interactive help. Instead of just listing the steps necessary to accomplish a task or use a feature, the Show Me option actually displays the menu or dialog box being described in a step.

In previous versions of Office, a Help menu command called Microsoft on the Web listed topics such as Free Stuff, Frequently Asked Questions, and Product News. This Help command has been replaced by the command Office on the Web, which takes you to a Web site Microsoft promises will be more useful than the ones created for Office 97.

Improved Clip Gallery

When you access the Clip Gallery in Office 2000, you see a revised interface for the Gallery. Navigation buttons are at the top of the Gallery window, along with buttons for importing clips from your machine or network, and buttons for locating clips online by using Microsoft's Clip Gallery Live.

NOTE If you are upgrading from a previous version of Office, the clips from that version will be indexed and incorporated into Office 2000's Clip Gallery.

Toward the top of the window is the Search for Clips text box, along with copy and paste buttons. In addition to searching for clips, when you locate a clip you like, you can ask the Clip Gallery to find similar clips based not only on a keyword match, but clips that match in style and color.

The clip types and categories have been restructured as well. Clips are divided into three types: Pictures, Sounds, and Motion Clips. Pictures includes cartoons, line drawings, and photographs. In addition to the categories that come with the Clip Gallery, you can also create your own categories.

Several other useful features of the Clip Gallery include the capability to drag and drop clips from the Gallery onto your document and an option to resize the Clip Gallery window so that it can be kept onscreen as you are working.

▶ **See** "Working with the Revised Clip Gallery," **p. 1196**

Programmability

Visual Basic for Applications (VBA) version 6.0 is part of Office 2000. It is included in all Office 2000 applications except Microsoft Publisher and Microsoft PhotoDraw. Outlook 2000 now uses VBA instead of VBScript. This version of VBA includes Modeless Userforms and support for ActiveX Controls. The new exposed events (such as DocumentOpen and DocumentBeforeClose in Word, FollowHyperlink in Excel, and Dirty in Access) and the COM add-ins give developers greater programming control in creating solutions for Office users.

A number of features have been added or enhanced to assist developers in creating Office solutions for use in a browser on an intranet or the Internet. HTML scripts can now be authored in Office by using the script-editing features found in Visual Studio. Script anchors are available in Office documents, including programming control in a document using the Scripting Object Model. Full browser support exists for debugging.

Microsoft is offering a version of Microsoft Office especially for developers—the Microsoft Office Developers' Edition. This version of Microsoft Office contains the tools necessary for building and deploying desktop and Web solutions for Office users.

COM Add-Ins

Office Web components are a set of *COM (Component Object Model)* components that can be used in Internet Explorer (IE) and Visual Basic. By incorporating these Office Web components into Web pages, developers can create interactive Web pages to display a spreadsheet, a graphic chart, or a PivotTable. These interactive pages can be created in Excel or Access and are fully programmable with script, or they can be used in Visual Basic programs.

NOTE ActiveX is a marketing name for a set of technologies and services based on the Component Object Model (COM). Therefore, ActiveX controls are COM objects. Adding ActiveX controls to your Word documents is covered in more detail in Chapter 14, "Unleashing the Potential of Forms."

Virus Checking

To supplement Office's general macro warning, developers can now tie in to the Office File Open features to scan Office documents for viruses before the documents are opened. Using a virus-scanning *API (Application Program Interface)* provided with Office 2000, developers can use any antivirus software to scan the documents.

Digital Signatures

To help avoid spreading viruses, Office 2000 provides a way for developers to digitally sign their macros, certifying they are virus-free. A *digital signature* on a macro confirms that the macro originated from the macro developer who signed it and that the macro has not been altered. You can digitally sign macros from within the Visual Basic Editor. However, a digital signature does not guarantee the macro is free of viruses. Users must decide whether to trust a macro that has been digitally signed.

When a user opens a document that contains a digitally signed macro, a certificate displays naming the macro's source and provides additional information about the identity and integrity of that source. The user has the option of opening the document with or without the macros enabled.

Often users know a particular source and don't want to have to interrupt their workflow every time they open a document containing a macro from that source. Users can designate which signatures to include in their list of "trusted sources." When a document or add-in containing a macro is initially opened, Office 2000 looks at the digital signature. If the document creator is not on the list of trusted sources, or if the macro has been modified, Office displays the Macro Warning dialog box.

Users set up the trusted sources through the Tools, Macro, Security command.

NOTE To use this feature, the developer and user must have Internet Explorer 4.0 or later installed on their computers. This feature won't work with Internet Explorer 3.0, Netscape Navigator, or any other browser.

Installation and Administration Features

Office 2000 comes with several tools designed to make end-user installation easier and more intuitive, and to expedite deployment and maintenance of the software in a corporate setting. One of the key tools is the *Microsoft Windows Installer,* which enables you to select where Office 2000 program files will reside: on the user's desktop computer, on a server, or some files on the desktop and some on the server. The Microsoft Windows Installer also has a feature that can detect corrupted application files and repair them.

Another useful tool is the *Custom Installation Wizard*, which provides administrators more options for customizing Office 2000 features. The wizard assists administrators in creating installation profiles for end users, detailing the customized Office installation settings for that user or group of users.

Administrators can set up *roaming profiles* that can be implemented for users who travel to different corporate sites, or when several people share the same computer. These roaming profiles store the customizations made by the user to the Desktop and to the Office applications.

NOTE Part IX of this book is devoted to installing, configuring, and administering Office 2000.

Installation Options

Through the Office 2000 Microsoft Windows Installer, you can choose from four basic installation options:

- Run on a Terminal Server—Using a Windows-based terminal, Office 2000 is placed in a central server location rather than on an individual user's desktop computer. The applications actually run on the server and display the application screens on the user's computer. This is reminiscent of the early days of mainframe computers and "dumb" terminals. The advantage of this option is that it helps to reduce costs associated with desktop hardware management and software administration. The disadvantage is generally the slower response time from the server.
- Run from Network Server—Office applications are stored centrally on a network server, but the processing occurs on the desktop. The advantage with this option is that it reduces the requirement for a powerful server and keeps the software centrally controlled.
- Run from User Desktop—Office 2000 can be installed to run from a desktop or a laptop computer. This arrangement is ideal for laptops or desktop computers that are not always connected to a server—a big advantage when a network server is very active, is difficult to access, or for users who travel extensively. Additionally, it takes the load off the network servers and the applications tend to run a lot faster. Generally, this arrangement tends to increase time (and costs) associated with administering the software, but it's a trade-off most companies are willing to make.
- Install on Demand—Shortcuts, icons, and menu entries for not-yet-installed Office 2000 applications or components are displayed to indicate their availability, without requiring them to actually be installed on the user's computer. When the user selects a not-yet-installed component, the Office 2000 code is located and the component is installed. The IS administrator determines the code location (ranging from different server locations to the CD-ROM). Better resource management is achieved because the end user does not install features until they are needed. This option is often reserved for advanced features or less-frequently used features.

Corporate Customization Options

Replacing the Network Installation Wizard from Office 97, Microsoft created the *Custom Installation Wizard* (CIW). This wizard expands the capability of administrators to customize the Office 2000 applications at a more detailed level. Individual features, menus, and toolbars can be customized for the particular uses and needs of a corporation. This wizard guides the IS administrator through the process of creating installation profiles that are based on particular users' work requirements.

IS administrators can use the wizard to customize Registry entries, shortcuts, and files. They can also disable portions of the user interface through the System Policy Editor. For example, menu and toolbar options that corporations don't want users to have access to can be disabled.

Detect and Repair

The Microsoft Windows Installer also has the capability to determine whether essential files are missing when an application is started. It also automatically checks the Registry entries for missing or corrupted files. If files are missing, it reinstalls them. If files are corrupted, it repairs them. This self-repairing activity requires little or no intervention by you, but it does require that you have the Office CD loaded in your CD-ROM drive or that you have access to the program files online, such as on a company network server.

If you encounter problems while working in an application, try selecting Help, Detect and Repair. This feature scans the noncritical Office files and fixes discrepancies between the original installation and the current software setup.

File Format Compatibility

With the exception of Microsoft Access files, users running Office 2000 and Office 97 will be able to easily exchange documents. Office 2000 documents do not need to be saved in another format for Office 97 applications to open them. If you need to routinely exchange documents with users of Office 95 and 97, file formats exist that you can use to make the exchange work more smoothly. As with every new version, certain formatting options exist in Office 2000, however, that Office 97 and Office 95 will not recognize; it will either ignore them or use the options that most closely match the Office 2000 format.

The reason Access files do not share this compatibility is because Access 2000 now supports *Unicode*, a file format not previously supported in Access 97. You have to convert Access 2000 files to the Access 97 format to share them with Office 97 users. Likewise, when you want to use an Access 97 database in Access 2000, you have to convert it to Access 2000.

NOTE The first chapter in each application section of this book (except for Publisher and FrontPage, which are new to the Office suite) discusses specific issues about migrating from older versions of an application to Office 2000. ■

Roaming User Profiles

Roaming users are defined in three ways: users who move from computer to computer, users who share a computer, and users who roam with their computer (often a laptop). With Office 2000, IS administrators can track and manage their users' custom settings and make those setting available to the users when they roam, or in the case of several users sharing a computer, display the custom settings for each user during the logon. These user-specific settings are stored in a single and safe location on the server. When a user customizes a toolbar, that custom toolbar becomes available when he or she "roams."

▶ **See** "Roaming User Profiles," **p. 1722**

Multilingual-Support Features

As more companies do business on a global level, the need to simplify cross-language document sharing and system administration has increased. With Office 2000's multilingual-support features, companies will be able to easily deploy Office in multiple languages, using a single version of the program. End users can select the language interface they want to work in or can create documents in a different language than the one used for the application interface.

▶ **See** "International Support for Languages," **p. 1721**

Single Worldwide Executable

Office 2000 uses a single, worldwide executable for each application. Users around the world can enter, display, and edit text in all supported languages. These languages include the European languages, Arabic, Chinese, Hebrew, Korean, and Japanese. The language exceptions to the single executable feature are Thai, Vietnamese, and Indian languages.

Deployment and administration of Office 2000 in a multilingual corporation is made much simpler because only one set of files exists to manage for any system. All features, for all supported languages, are available in any version of Office 2000. A separate resource *dynamic link library* (DLL) holds the settings you implement locally.

Interface Language

Because all features of all languages are built into the single executable, the operation of the applications isn't affected by changing the interface language. Additionally, you can author documents in any language, independent of the interface. So if Office was installed with English as the interface language, end users can easily change the interface language to compose documents in other languages. IS administrators do not have to be involved in changing the interface language for end users. Changing the interface language includes the proofing tools, such as AutoCorrect, and the Help features.

NOTE To use this feature, you need to install the Office 2000 Multi-Language Pack. After it has been installed, the interface can be changed through the Programs option on the Windows Start menu. ■

CHAPTER 2

Application Features at a Glance

In this chapter

Application Level Changes to Office 2000

Microsoft has made a number of changes to each of the Office 2000 applications. You are bound to run across a number of small changes that are immediately apparent to experienced Office users (such as you) and don't require additional explanation. For example, in Word you can use pixels and percentages of a page as alternative units of measurements on the General tab of the Options dialog box (Tools, Options). When you select a group of cells in Excel, light shading is used to highlight the cells instead of inverse video. This see-through view feature ensures that none of the data or cell formatting is hidden by the highlight.

Although these are useful enhancements, there are other changes and new features that are not as readily apparent or easy to figure out. This chapter focuses on the *most significant* changes made to each application. You will find a succinct description of these important Office 2000 features in this chapter. Because many of the features are covered in more detail later in this book, there are cross-references to those sections in this chapter so that you can quickly locate the topics in which you are most interested.

If you are in a position where you provide assistance to Office users (such as a designated Office guru, instructor, system administrator, or help desk support person), the application help files are a great place to direct beginners. They can look up *each and every* change made to an application by using the Office Assistant and searching on the phrase "what's new."

Changes to Word 2000

In addition to the global changes to Office 2000 described in Chapter 1, "General Office Features at a Glance," you will find a number of significant changes and subtle enhancements in Word 2000. Among the most significant are the improvements to the way tables are created, Web and network features, and international ease-of-use features.

If you are upgrading from a previous version of Word, Chapters 7 and 8 will prove very useful to you.

▶ **See** "Migrating to Word 2000," **p. 185**

▶ **See** "Customizing Word," **p. 207**

Tables

Among the more significant changes is the greater ease with which you create and format tables. The way tables are created and formatted in Word 2000 has been improved, especially if you are upgrading from Word 95. A new toolbar, the Tables and Borders toolbar, was introduced in Word 97 and has been enhanced in Word 2000. You can create and customize tables as if you are drawing them with a pencil by using the Draw Table button on the toolbar.

Some of the key improvements to Word's table tools include

- Each table now comes with a move handle (see Figure 2.1) enabling you to more easily move the table to another position within the document.
- When inserting rows, you can designate the placement of the row—*above or below* the active row. When inserting columns, you can insert the column to the left or right of the active column.
- You can create *nested* tables (tables within other tables) and floating tables (text wraps around the table). Nesting tables provides you with many more options designing tables and makes creating tables for Web sites so much more flexible. Figure 2.1 shows an example of a nested table.
- Cells can be merged both vertically or horizontally in Word 2000. You no longer have to cut and paste to combine the data in separate cells, and merged cells provide a way to change the entire look of a table (as shown in Figure 2.1).
- Text can wrap around a graphic inside a table cell, just as it can outside a table cell.

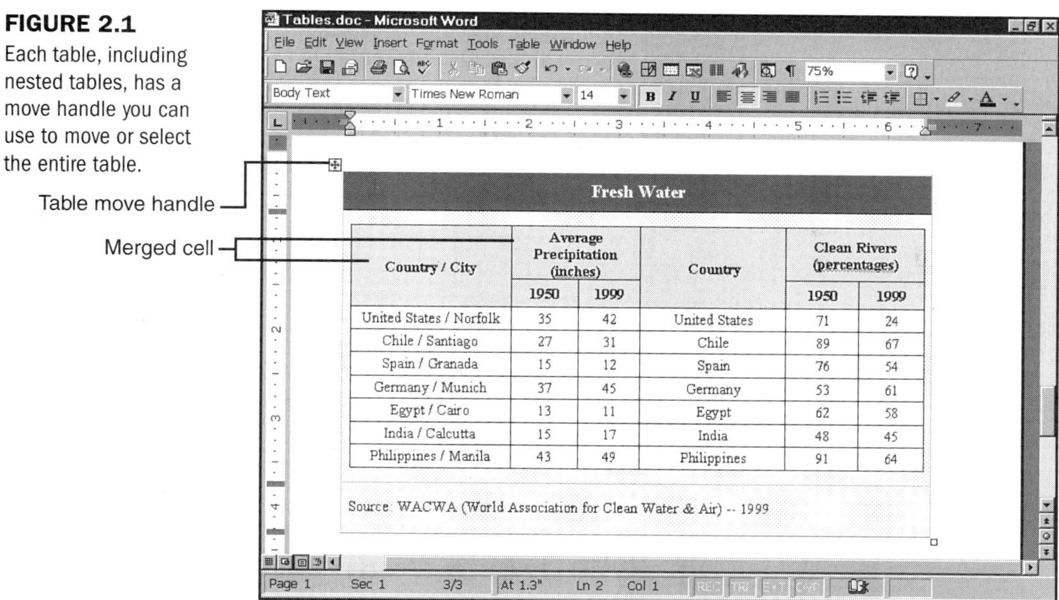

Fresh Water

Country / City	Average Precipitation (inches)		Country	Clean Rivers (percentages)	
	1950	1999		1950	1999
United States / Norfolk	35	42	United States	71	24
Chile / Santiago	27	31	Chile	89	67
Spain / Granada	15	12	Spain	76	54
Germany / Munich	37	45	Germany	53	61
Egypt / Cairo	13	11	Egypt	62	58
India / Calcutta	15	17	India	48	45
Philippines / Manila	43	49	Philippines	91	64

Source: WACWA (World Association for Clean Water & Air) -- 1999

FIGURE 2.1
Each table, including nested tables, has a move handle you can use to move or select the entire table.

▶ **See** "Unleashing the Potential of Tables," **p. 377**

Web and Network Features

Due to the enhanced integration with Web page creation and networks in Office 2000, several features have been added or improved in Word 2000. The inclusion of the HTML file format and the capability to use Word as your email editor are just a few of the Web and network features. Additionally, the Web Layout view replaces the Online Layout view (introduced in Word 97).

HTML File Format As discussed in Chapter 1, Office 2000 provides HTML as a file format that can be used with all Office applications. This means you can create a document in Word, save it in the HTML file format, reopen it in Word, and still use the features available in Word. This sequence of events is known as *round-tripping* or *roundtrip editing*. The only features that are not preserved when you round-trip a document are versions (introduced in Word 97) and passwords.

When an HTML file is opened in Word 2000, any HTML code Word does not understand is preserved to maintain the integrity of the original HTML file.

An *encoding* is a way to represent the text in an HTML file so that it can be read in different languages. Encoding converts text to a binary format. When an HTML file is opened in Word, the encoding used to create the file is determined and an appropriate font is applied to the text to display it properly.

▶ **See** "Integrating HTML in Office," **p. 12**

Themes A series of *themes* (see Figure 2.2) is available in Word 2000 to apply a quick overall design look to Web pages or to use with any of your Word 2000 documents. Themes include backgrounds, color schemes, bullets, and text formats. Themes are a great option when you don't have time to create your own design or you simply want to use a theme as a starting point for your design. Some of the themes are identical to the new design templates in PowerPoint. Themes are also compatible with Microsoft FrontPage 2000, which is included in Office 2000 Premium versions.

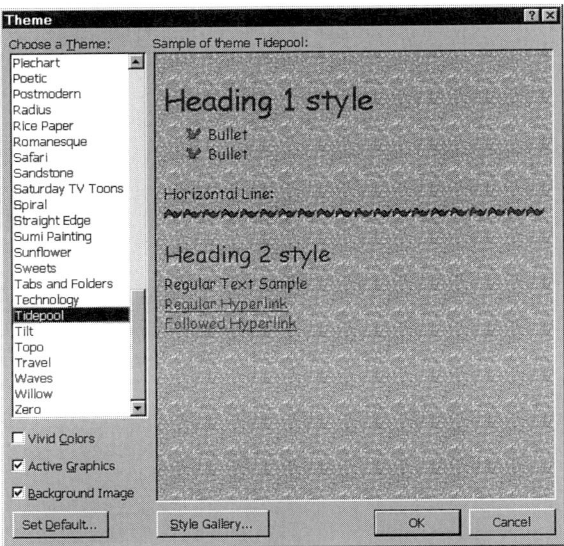

FIGURE 2.2
Not all themes are installed by default. You might need to access the Office 2000 CD or program files to use some of the themes.

▶ **See** "Using Themes," **p. 297**

Web Authoring Knowledge of HTML is essential when creating Web pages on a professional basis. Whether your goal is to create a personal Web site or a small business Web site, you'll very likely be able to get away with learning little, if any, HTML. Word 2000's enhanced Web-page tools provide a great starting place for novice Web authors.

In addition to Word's improved capability to convert your Word documents to HTML, Word also provides several other key Web authoring tools:

- Web Page Preview—You can use the File, Web Page Preview command to preview how a Word 2000 document appears in the HTML file format in a browser before saving the document in HTML.
- Browser Compatibility—If you are creating Web pages that are viewed in browsers other than the one you have, you can set the Web Options to disable features in Word 2000 that are not compatible with other browsers. You'll find Web Options on the General tab of the Options dialog box (Tools, Options).
- Frames Pages—Frames are a common way to display information in a Web page. For example, many Web sites use a vertical frame on the left side of the page. This vertical frame often contains navigational controls to key areas of the site, similar to a table of contents. While the information in the main area of the browser window changes depending on which hyperlinks the user chooses, the navigation frame remains unchanged.

Web Page Authoring in Office 2000

As an advanced Office user, we assume that you'll turn to FrontPage for Web page creation; therefore, we do not provide extensive coverage of creating Web pages with the other Office applications. If you want to learn more about FrontPage, see Chapters 58-61. If you need to learn more about the Web-authoring capabilities of each application, then I suggest picking up copies of the following books, all published by Que:

- *Special Edition Using Microsoft Word 2000*
- *Special Edition Using Microsoft Excel 2000*
- *Special Edition Using Microsoft PowerPoint 2000*
- *Special Edition Using Microsoft Access 2000*
- *Special Edition Using Microsoft Publisher 2000*

Email Editing with Word Word 97 included a feature called WordMail. You could use Word to edit email messages, but only people using WordMail could view the messages without concern about data being corrupted. In Word 2000, Microsoft Office Email has replaced WordMail. This makes it possible for you to create and edit email messages in Word. HTML is the file format used for email documents, so that any email reader capable of viewing HTML can view the message without fear of corruption.

- If you are using Outlook 2000 or Outlook Express 5.0 or later as your email editor, you can email a document directly or as an attachment.

- If you are using Microsoft Exchange Client or another 32-bit email program compatible with MAPI (Messaging Application Programming Interface), you can email a Word document as an attachment. You need to be sure the file Mapi32.dll is in the Windows System folder.
- If you are using Lotus cc:Mail or another 16-bit email program compatible with VIM (Vendor Independent Messaging), you can email a Word document as an attachment. You must make sure Mapivi32.dll, Mapivitk.dll, and Mvthksvr.exe are in the Windows System folder.

CAUTION

Not every email client supports HTML—most notably terminal-based systems, cc:Mail, and Telnet. Additionally, emailing and routing documents might not work across electronic mail gateways.

Additionally, you can create personal stationery (which includes themes, backgrounds, and font settings) to use for email messages created in Word 2000. Word 2000 also includes a tool that manages multiple AutoSignatures for use with email messages.

▶ **See** "Using Microsoft Word As Your Email Editor," **p. 1438**

International Features

Microsoft has implemented a number of changes in Office that assist users in composing documents across multiple languages. One of the biggest changes is the Single Worldwide Executable. As described in Chapter 1, Office 2000 integrates the more than 30-language versions in which Office is available—except for the Thai, Vietnamese, and Indian languages—into one worldwide executable version.

The advantage of this accomplishment is the ability to use proofing tools (such as spelling, grammar, and thesauri) in the language of your choice. If you have a version of Office 2000 that includes the Multilanguage Pack, you can also change the User Interface (UI) to display the menu commands and help in a language other than the language of the Office 2000 version you purchased.

NOTE There are a few exceptions here, particularly for right-to-left and Asian languages that come with both the native language and English.

Microsoft has developed separate tools that make this possible—the Microsoft Proofing Tools kit and the Office Multilanguage Pack.

- Each version of Office 2000 comes with proofing tools in languages that are typically used locally. For example, the English U.S. version includes English, French, and Spanish. The German version comes with German, English, French, and Italian.
- Should you need proofing tools in other languages, you can purchase the Office 2000 Proofing Tools on a single CD. It contains all proofing tools, fonts, and so on for the 37 languages Microsoft Office supports. This CD can be purchased by anyone.

- The Office 2000 with Multilanguage Pack contains a combined license of the English version of Office 2000, the Proofing Tools, the User Interface, and Help resources in all the languages Microsoft supports. The Multi language Pack is available only in this combined license form. It is not available separately.
- In addition to the full Multilanguage Pack, some language versions of Office 2000 include Mini language Packs that contain the main languages used in and around that country. For example, Korean, Simplified Chinese, Traditional Chinese, Hebrew, and Thai ship with an optional English interface. Arabic ships with English and French, and Hong Kong ships with Simplified Chinese, Traditional Chinese, and English.

You can buy the English version of Office 2000 with or without the Multilanguage Pack. When purchased together, they are licensed as a separate product from the regular English version of Office 2000. The Multilanguage Pack is not licensable separately, and is supported for use only with the Standard, Professional, and Premium versions of Office 2000. The Multilanguage Pack is available only to organizations that purchase five or more licenses of Office 2000. Contact your local retailer for information on how to purchase five or more licenses via the Open License program.

▶ **See** "Single Worldwide Executable," **p. 27**

Other improvements include the ability to save files written in any of the supported languages to earlier versions of Word, and enhanced ease of use for international users (especially for Asian users).

Using the Correct Keyboard with Other Languages

The Multilanguage Pack includes several features in support of international users, including the option to change the interface language and the language used for the editing and proofing tools. The interface language and the editing tools language are two separate, independent features. To effectively use other languages, it might be necessary for you to install the keyboard layout for the desired language. In the case of languages that do not use the Arabic alphabet, you need to identify the layout and actually exchange the keyboard used with the computer.

Many of the specifics detailed in the next few sections are provided so that advanced users and technical support personnel who need to describe these features to international users can do so.

Before you can use other languages, however, the Multi language Pack must be installed.

▶ **See** "International Support for Languages," **p. 1721**

Multilanguage Pack and AutoDetect Included with Office 2000 is a tool that enables users to select the language for the User Interface (UI) and the help files. Changing the UI language does not interfere with the operation of Word, but enables users to compose and edit in the language they prefer. The tool that makes all this possible is the Office 2000 Multilanguage Pack. Included in the Pack is the Microsoft Proofing Tools Kit, which installs the editing tools necessary to edit and format text in the supported languages.

After you enable editing of a language, you might need to install the correct keyboard layout so that you can enter characters specific to that language by using your existing keyboard. In some cases, you might need to configure Windows to work with additional keyboards to enter unique letters or for languages that do not use the same alphabet as your keyboard. The keyboard properties can be set in the Windows Control Panel. After the Proofing Tools from the Multilanguage Pack are installed, Word 2000 can automatically detect the language in a document you open or type into. You then have access to the proofing tools for that language, including

Spelling and grammar

AutoCorrect

AutoFormat

Punctuation rules

Sorting conventions

When you type text that has a unique format in the current interface language, Word can automatically format what you type in the formats used by the current language. Examples include document formats such as memos or letters, or formats for dates or the days of the week.

NOTE When Word detects a language, the name of the language is displayed on the status bar.

Importing Encoded Text Files When you receive text files from users in other countries, the files are typically encoded with a standard used in that country or language. Because Microsoft Word 2000 is based on the Unicode encoding standard, it can usually open text files that are encoded and will apply a default font to the text so that you can read it. For each encoding standard, Word has a default font it applies to the text. The encoding and fonts are defined in the Options dialog box (Tools, Options, General tab, Web Options button). The encoding does not translate the file if it is in another language, but makes it possible to *display* the document in its original language.

International Ease of Use Word's usability for international users has been improved in a number of ways:

- Lists and tables can now be sorted according to the practices of the current interface language. For example, if you have a list of dates, that list is sorted based on the date format commonly used for the active language, such as year/month/day.
- Word 2000 provides support for additional envelope and mailing label sizes found in Europe, Japan, Korea, and China.

€

- In Word 2000, you can enter the Euro currency symbol by pressing Ctrl+Alt+E (on a typical 101 keyboard), or by using the Insert, Symbol command. Although Microsoft indicates you can also get the symbol by pressing ALT+0123 (numeric keypad), I've not been able to get it to work. Regardless of the method, you must use a font that includes the symbol (such as Arial, Courier New, Tahoma, Times New Roman) in order for the Euro symbol to display. Your printer must also recognize this symbol; otherwise, a box prints in its place.

NOTE You need to contact the vendor of your printer about support if the Euro symbol does not print with your existing fonts.

- You now have a choice of Western, Hijri, or lunar calendar types (used for some Asian and right-to-left languages). Arabic month names can be displayed in the Western calendar type.
- When using the Find dialog box in Japanese, you can set the search to treat uppercase and lowercase letters the same or to search without distinguishing between Hiragana and Katakana characters.
- Line and character grids can be used for text layout in Asian text. You can specify the number of characters per line, the number of lines per page, and even the character pitch.
- There are typography options for line breaks and character spacing unique to Asian languages. For example, you can control the first and last characters by adjusting line-break control settings in the Format, Paragraph dialog box.
- For Asian languages, you can now create half-width and full-width characters. Only Latin letters, numbers, and Katakana can be changed to half-width characters. Hiragana can be changed to half-width Katakana characters.

Other New or Improved Features in Word

In addition to the major improvements discussed previously, you will encounter other new features in Word 2000:

- Click and Type—While in the Web Layout or Print Layout views, you can now position the mouse pointer on a blank part of a page, double-click, and start typing. The pointer displays a symbol that indicates the type of text alignment that will be applied to the text. Click and Type makes it easy to create center-aligned text, indent paragraphs, or display a single line with text positioned in different places. Click and Type isn't available in multiple columns, bulleted and numbered lists, next to floating objects, next to pictures with text wrapping, or next to indents.
- Spelling, Grammar, and AutoCorrect—A number of new words have been added to the dictionary in Word 2000 to reduce the number of words underlined in red as possible errors. As with earlier versions of spelling, you can right-click a word that is flagged and select a correct spelling from the list that appears. The grammar checker has been improved to reduce the number of false green grammar flags. AutoCorrect in Word 2000 looks for obvious spelling mistakes that might not be in the AutoCorrect list and automatically corrects.
- Multilingual Binary Converters—In previous versions of Word, users could not save a file in an earlier Word version in a different language, because only one binary converter could be installed at a time. Word 2000 allows multiple converters to be installed at the same time, which enable you to save files written in any of the 37 supported languages to earlier versions of Word.

- Graphics—Word 2000 includes several changes to make it easier to work with graphics in documents. Objects are easier to insert and you can quickly change between having a graphic float in a document or be anchored inline. Alignment, positioning, and text wrapping are more easily adjusted. By default, WordArt objects are now inserted as inline objects, but can be changed to floating objects. You can also more easily use WordArt objects for bullets and banners.

▶ **See** "Controlling the Text Around Inserted Objects," **p. 336**

- Multiple Pages per Sheet—You can scale pages of documents at print time and print more than one document page on a single piece of paper.

Changes to Excel 2000

As with all Office 2000, the improvements in Excel are primarily in the area of Web-based data sharing and collaboration. The two major exceptions include the enhancements to the way PivotTables are created and updated (along with the addition of PivotCharts), and the connectivity to OLAP (Online Analytical Processing) databases and other large server-based enterprise data. If you are upgrading from Excel 95 or earlier versions, take a look at Chapter 19, "Migrating to Excel 2000," before jumping into Chapters 20-29 on Excel.

▶ **See** "Migrating to Excel 2000," **p. 563**

Changes to PivotTables and the Introduction of PivotCharts

The PivotTable wizard in Excel 2000 no longer requires you to guess where to place fields in the PivotTable layout. Instead, the PivotTable wizard is simply used to identify the source of the data and the placement of the PivotTable. The layout is displayed in the worksheet, as shown in Figure 2.3. Selecting and changing the fields used in the PivotTable is easier with the embedded layout, which enables you to make the adjustments directly in the worksheet. Additionally, a new AutoFormat feature makes it easy to format a PivotTable.

Corresponding graphic charts, called *PivotCharts*, are a new feature added to PivotTables in Excel 2000. You must create a PivotTable to create a PivotChart. These charts are tied to the PivotTable data and layout. When the data is refreshed in the PivotTable, the corresponding PivotChart is updated. Changes to the PivotTable layout are reflected in the PivotChart and vice versa. Figure 2.4 shows a completed PivotChart.

▶ **See** "Unlocking the Power of PivotTables and PivotCharts," **p. 797**

Web-Based Enhancements

As described in Chapter 1, the ability to use HTML as a file format has brought with it several features for creating and publishing Web-based documents. By saving an Excel worksheet in the HTML file format, the worksheet can be viewed in a Web browser and then be brought back into Excel to use features and tools in Excel. This makes it easier for anyone to create a Web page from an Excel worksheet, rather than requiring users to learn HTML or to have someone else convert the document into a Web page. As more companies introduce intranets into their corporate network and expand their use of the intranet, this type of flexibility will be necessary.

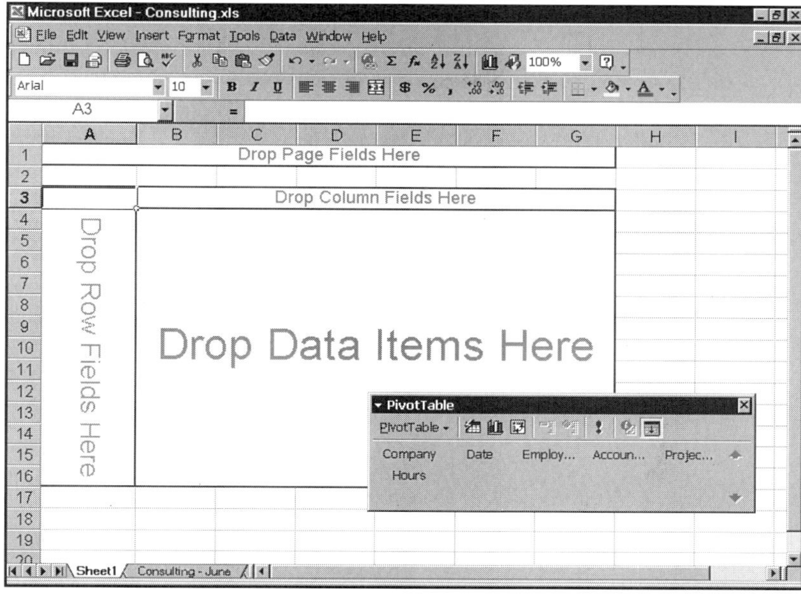

FIGURE 2.3
Drag the field name from the toolbar to the layout position.

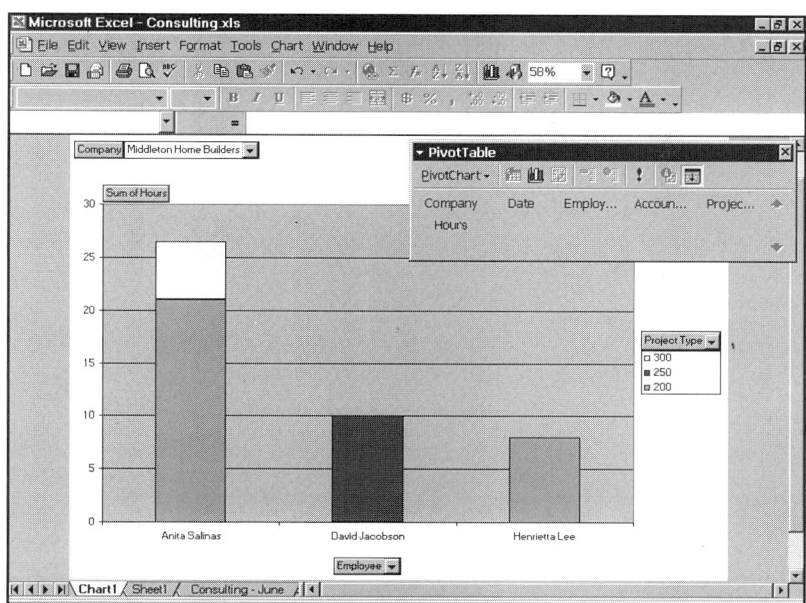

FIGURE 2.4
You can customize the data plotted on the chart by selecting items from the drop-down buttons.

Another very significant addition to Excel is the capability to save worksheets as interactive Web pages called *Office Web Components*. Office Web Components give users access to some of the analytical features in Excel. There are three types of Office Web Components: Spreadsheet

Component, Chart Component, and PivotTable Component. Data in a Component can be edited, sorted, and filtered from within a browser. The Chart Component can be set to provide live updates to the chart as the source data in the worksheet changes. Users can reorganize the data displayed in PivotTable Components by dragging fields to other areas of the PivotTable layout. So, for example, sales information is displayed in a PivotTable component on your company intranet. Anyone in the company who needs to generate internal or external reports can manipulate the PivotTable layout and fields to organize the sales information for the targeted audience. For a report to executives, the sales information might be broken down by country. A regional manager can display the sales information for just that region, broken down by sales representative.

The Office Web Components require a special configuration. For more information, see Chapter 3, "Unleashing the Office 2000 Web Tools."

▶ **See** "The Office Web Components," **p. 56**

Enhanced Database, Web, and Text Queries

Excel 2000 includes client software that enables you to work with *Online Analytical Processing* (OLAP) databases. OLAP is an alternative way to organize the data in very large databases to speed up data retrieval. Instead of arranging data into tables, the data is organized in levels, dimensions, and data values forming what are called *OLAP data cubes*.

The data retrieved from an OLAP cube can be returned to Excel only in a PivotTable or PivotChart report. OLAP cubes can be stored on a server or, in some cases, you can create offline cubes. An *offline cube* is a file that contains static data from the original database.

Server-based OLAP cubes have to be set up by a system administrator. However, you can create an offline cube from a relational database such as Access or FoxPro by using Microsoft Query and the OLAP client software included with Excel. You can also create offline cubes from the server-based OLAP cube.

▶ **See** "Using and Creating OLAP Cubes," **p. 749**

The process to import text or data from the Web has been enhanced. The process for importing text includes an option to refresh the text; the formatting and formulas are retained when the data is refreshed. In addition, the procedures to import data from the Web have been simplified, making it easy for anyone to import data.

Other New or Improved Features in Excel

In addition to the major improvements discussed previously, you will encounter other new features in Excel 2000:

- Graphic Charts—Several new formatting options are available to your Excel charts, including multilevel category axis labeling, timescale labeling, data point data labels, and the ability for you to define the units on the value axis.

- See-Through View—When a group of cells is selected, a light shading is used to highlight the cells instead of reverse video. In previous versions of Excel, the reverse-video highlight obscured the data or cell formatting.
- Year 2000 Date Formats—Additional data formats have been included to make it easier to display the four digits associated with the date year. There are two date settings in the System Policy Editor that system administrators can activate. One empowers users to enter their own rules for what century a two-digit year falls under, and the other ensures that dates entered with four-digit years are displayed with all four digits.
- List AutoFill—When the first few characters you type in a cell match an existing entry in the column, Excel fills in the remaining characters for you by using a feature known as *AutoComplete*. Similarly, the AutoFill feature extends any formatting and formulas. While the AutoComplete feature does not work on purely numeric or date entries, the AutoFill feature works on all types of entries.
- € Euro Currency—You can format numeric data with the new Euro currency format ([euro.tif]) in Excel 2000.

▶ **See** "Advanced Charting Techniques," **p. 815**

Changes to Access 2000

The most significant improvements in Access 2000 are the interoperability with back-end enterprise databases (such as Microsoft SQL Server), sharing databases by converting Access 2000 databases to earlier versions, the capability to print the Relationships window, and the restructuring of the Database Window.

Client/Server Interoperability

Access 2000 provides better integration with client/server databases, such as Microsoft SQL Server. Access provides the easy-to-use front-end (client) and SQL Server provides the scalable and reliable enterprise-level database back-end (server). To accomplish this, Access 2000 supports OLE DB, a standard for data access. As a result, you can connect directly to SQL Server without using the traditional default database engine in Access, the *Jet engine*.

Access Projects are a type of Access file that connects to the integrated data store in Office, SQL Server 6.5, or SQL Server 7.0. Access Projects use Access as the front-end client for a back-end data store.

▶ **See** "Creating Access Projects," **p. 977**

Convert Database to Prior Access Version

With Access 2000, you are able to save a database in a format for a previous version. This is particularly useful in an organization that has different versions active as the organization upgrades to Access 2000, or if your database solutions need to be available to clients with a wide variety of Access versions.

▶ **See** "Migrating to Access 2000," **p. 953**

Print Relationships Wizard

To see a visual diagram of your database table relationships, you can use the Print Relationships Wizard, instead of having to rely on the Relationships Window to see how the database is structured. The wizard automatically creates a report based on the relationships you have displayed in the Relationships Window. You still have to display the tables in the Relationships Window, and for those who do not have permanent links, you have to create temporary links between table fields.

Being able to print the Relationships Window is invaluable for complex databases that contain a large number of tables and links.

Database Window

With the introduction of new database objects, such as Data Access Pages (DAPs) and the database relationships diagram, the appearance of the Database Window has been revised (see Figure 2.5). On the left side of the window is an Object Bar that enables you to create and display different database objects, similar to the tabs used in the Access 97 database window. Fortunately, it doesn't shrink much when the window size is reduced.

The Database Window has an option called *Groups*, which you can use to place all the database objects relating to an item in the same group. For example, you could place tables, queries, and forms that relate to a particular report into one group.

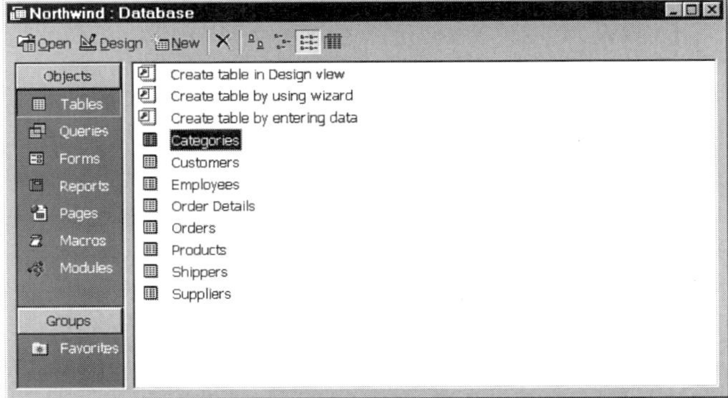

FIGURE 2.5
The wizards for creating new tables are listed in the same window with the existing tables.

Data Access Pages

One of the new features for information sharing via Webs is *Data Access Pages (DAPs)*. As with forms and reports, DAPs are database objects saved in the HTML format so that the data can be viewed and edited within a Web browser. However, DAPs are stored outside the database (.mdb) file, so they can be published on a Web site. Data Access Pages can be *bound* to source data that is to maintain an interactive link with the source data. Office Web components (discussed in the Excel section earlier in this chapter) can be included in Data Access Pages providing the opportunity to use the analytical features in Excel.

Although a design environment is provided to create DAPs, and DAPs use an object model that supports VBScript or JavaScript, most experienced Access users find the Data Access Pages feature lacking. No undo option exists in the design environment and the pages that are generated through the DAPs wizard are not as sophisticated as forms and reports created with wizards. As a result, they require a lot of time to customize.

▶ **See** "What Are Data Access Pages?" **p. 1100**

Other New or Improved Features in Access

In addition to the items discussed previously, there are other new features you might want to check out in Access 2000:

- Subdatasheets—When you open a table in the datasheet view that is linked to another table, you can view the linked data (by record) in a subdatasheet. By clicking on a plus sign (that automatically appears) next to a record, the subdatasheet displays.
- Name AutoCorrect—When you change the name of a field in a table, any report or form that uses that field is automatically updated with the new name. However, this feature does not change VBA code, replicated databases, or Access projects that employ the field name.
- Unicode Support—Data can be displayed in the language of your choice, because Access 2000 supports Unicode.
- Compact on Close—When you close an Access database, the database is automatically compressed if it will significantly reduce the file size. This helps save precious disk space.

▶ **See** "The Unicode File Format and Other Jet Changes," **p. 959**

Changes to PowerPoint 2000

The enhancements to PowerPoint 2000 increase your productivity when creating, coordinating, and delivering presentations. The new Normal view provides you with a single interface in which to create your presentations. There are several new alternatives you can use to coordinate with others on the development of the presentation, including conducting online meetings and adding comments to a presentation by using the new Web Discussions feature. The other significant change to PowerPoint is the revamped Clip Gallery, discussed in Chapter 1, "General Office Features at a Glance." If you are upgrading from PowerPoint 95 or earlier versions, Chapter 43, "Migrating to PowerPoint 2000," discusses some of the other new features you will encounter.

▶ **See** "Improved Clip Gallery," **p. 22**

▶ **See** "Migrating to PowerPoint 2000," **p. 1185**

The Normal View

The new tripane Normal view, shown in Figure 2.6, divides the screen into three panes—Outline, Slide, and Notes—placing most of the presentation information at your fingertips.

You no longer have to flip back and forth between each of the individual views, although they are still available, if you prefer.

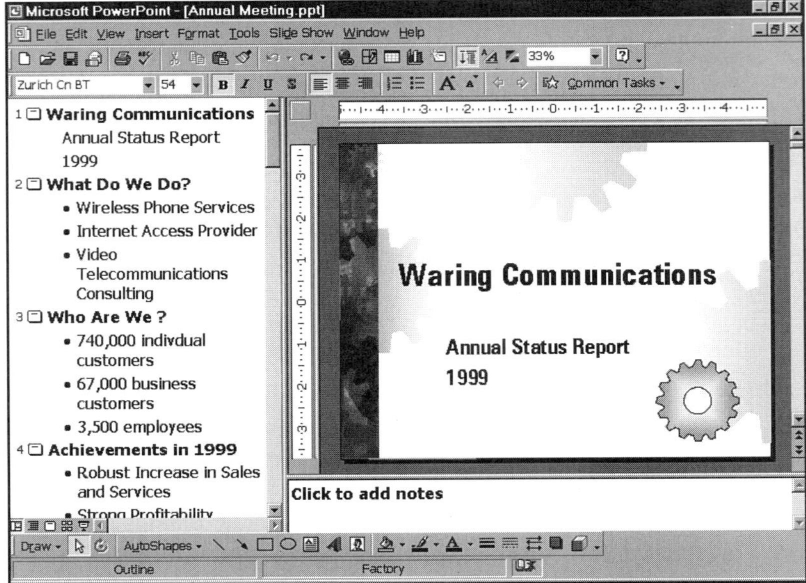

FIGURE 2.6
The panes in the Normal view can be resized by dragging the partition that divides the panes.

Online Collaboration

In all the Office 2000 applications, you can collaborate with other users online through online meetings (by using NetMeeting) or by copying documents to a Web server where others can post comments. However, in PowerPoint 2000, you can also collaborate with other people on a presentation by broadcasting a presentation online and even recording the presentation so that it can be run for people who missed the original broadcast.

Use the Presentation Broadcast feature to deliver a presentation to colleagues in different locations (using your company's intranet) or record the broadcast to archive for people who are unable to make the original broadcast. For more information, see "Setting Up Online Presentations," in Chapter 47, "Advanced Slide Show Features."

Microsoft NetMeeting is used to conduct online meetings. Use it to share and exchange information with other people at different sites in real-time over your company's intranet or the Internet, just as if everyone were in the same room. NetMeeting is a feature that Microsoft needs to polish before it becomes a significant benefit to most users. For more information, see "Setting Up an Online Meeting," in Chapter 48, "Sharing PowerPoint Data with Other Users and Applications."

When you can't get a group together for a presentation broadcast or an online meeting, a great alternative is to use Web Discussions. Individuals can access and add comments to slides in the presentation. They can also edit and reply to existing comments. For more information, see "Using Web Discussions," in Chapter 48.

Other New or Improved Features in PowerPoint

In addition to the items discussed previously, there are other new features you might want to check out in PowerPoint 2000:

- AutoFit Text—When there is not sufficient space in a bulleted list placeholder, AutoFit automatically adjusts the text. First, the line spacing is adjusted. If the text still won't fit, then the font size is reduced.
- Native Tables—The way tables are created and edited in PowerPoint has been changed. Previous versions of PowerPoint actually launched Word in the background to use the features in Microsoft Word to create and edit tables. Now, when you create slide with a table layout or insert a table into a slide, you use tools that are native to PowerPoint.
- Projector Wizard—The new Projector Wizard in PowerPoint helps you connect your computer to a projection system. This feature is located in the Set Up Show dialog box (Slide Show, Set Up Show).
- Audience Handouts—You now have the ability to print 2, 3, 4, 6, or 9 slides per page for your audience handouts.
- Multilingual Features—Companies that have multinational users find it easier to create and edit presentations in a wide range of languages. The language of the user interface can easily be changed, should employees traveling to other countries need to work in their native language. The help screens and editing/proofing tools also adjust to the language selected.

Changes to Outlook 2000

Unlike most of the other Office 2000 applications, Outlook had a major release in 1998. If you are upgrading from Outlook 97 or earlier, there are changes in Outlook 2000 that, although not technically new, are new to you.

One of the most significant changes, especially for those who like to customize views and forms in Outlook, is the inclusion of Visual Basic for Applications (VBA) in Outlook 2000, bringing it in line with the other Office applications. Other enhancements are outlined in the next few sections.

▶ **See** "Using VBA with Outlook 2000," **p. 1507**

Contact Management

There have been a number of improvements to Outlook's Contact Management features. You can create personal Distribution Lists that use a single distribution name for a group of contacts to repeatedly send messages to. These contacts can come from several sources including personal and shared contact folders and the Global Address List on an Exchange Server. Personal Distribution Lists can be forwarded to other users via email.

You can keep track of email, tasks, appointments, and journal entries that are related to a specific contact by using the new Contact Activity Tracking feature.

Another new feature in Outlook 2000 checks for duplicate entries when you add or move contacts.

The Rules Wizard

Previously available in Outlook 97 as an add-on, the Rules Wizard has been enhanced in both Outlook 98 and Outlook 2000. In Outlook 2000, the Rules Wizard is no longer an add-on, but is a built-in feature. You can now set up *rules* for handling your incoming mail in Outlook 2000 by using the Rules Wizard. Rules acts as a traffic cop. For example, you can create rules that move messages from specific people to specific folders, including the trash if you simply don't want to be bothered by mail from a particular sender. If you want to be alerted to the arrival of important email—from your boss, for example—you can have Outlook notify you with a dialog box or a sound or by marking the message in a different color in your inbox.

The new Run Rules Now feature enables you to activate a rule manually at any time.

▶ **See** "Using the Rules Wizard," **p. 1439**

Email

New in Outlook 98, and enhanced in Outlook 2000, is a feature that enables you to use Word (instead of the built-in editor in Outlook) to create and edit email messages. Messages can be sent in several formats: Plain Text, Rich Text, or HTML. But you still need to be cautious using Rich Text or HTML, as the recipient's email reader might not be able to interpret the message in those formats. Also enhanced in Outlook 2000 is the capability to switch between email formats at any time. Unfortunately, Outlook does not have the capability to designate the format based on the recipient.

▶ **See** "Managing Email," **p. 1421**

Switching Between Outlook Modes

Configuration is easier in Outlook 2000. There are basically three modes available in this version of Outlook. You can easily switch between these modes in Outlook 2000 as your contact and mail needs change.

- Corporate or Workgroup (CW) Mode—This mode utilizes the extended MAPI subsystem with its support for multiple transports. In this mode, you can send and receive mail via Internet and non-Internet mail servers (such as Microsoft Exchange, Microsoft MS Mail, or Lotus cc:Mail).
- Internet Mail Only Mode—This mode is capable only of collecting and sending mail through Internet standard mail servers.
- No Email Mode—This mode is used when you want to utilize the contact and other information management features of Outlook. It does not support sending or receiving mail or faxes.

For more detailed information about these three modes, see the sections "Three Flavors of Outlook" and "Changing Mail Modes" in Chapter 53, "Managing Email."

Other New or Improved Features in Outlook

In addition to the items discussed previously, there are other new features you might want to check out in Outlook 2000:

- Outlook Today—You can get a quick overview of the email messages you have recently received, upcoming meetings, and tasks due—all from within one view. Figure 2.7 shows an example of the Outlook Today window.

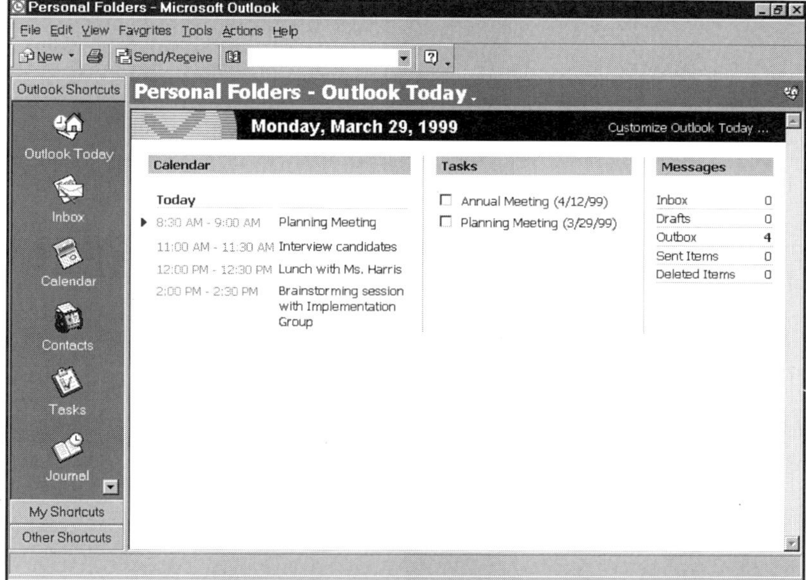

FIGURE 2.7
The Customize Outlook Today optioı is in the upper-right corner of the window.

- Remote User Enhancements—The synchronization of Offline Folders was disruptive in previous versions of Outlook. In Outlook 2000, the synchronization is performed in the background and you can schedule when the synchronization occurs. You now also have the ability to filter the items you want to synchronize from public folders.
- Personalized Email—Several features have been added to personalize email messages. You can create a variety of signatures to use. When you don't want to use the default signature, the Signature Picker enables you to designate a different signature on a message-by-message basis. Another option you have is to select a type of stationery to use as the background, font color, and styles for your email messages. While this feature might be popular for sending email inside your own organization, it might not be so palatable to Internet mail recipients, especially because it does increase the size of the email message.

Changes to FrontPage 2000

Microsoft FrontPage is a Web-site creation and management tool. Web pages can be created directly in FrontPage or imported from other Office 2000 applications into FrontPage. FrontPage 2000 is included only in the Premium version of Office 2000.

FrontPage was previously released as a separate application; the last version was FrontPage 98. Expanding on the changes in that version, FrontPage 2000 makes it even easier to create and manage Web sites. Freeing users from the dependence on Webmasters and HTML, FrontPage 2000 enables users to create the layout and navigational structure for the Web site. Users can save their Office 2000 documents directly to Webs based on FrontPage as effortlessly as they save documents to their hard drive.

Microsoft has improved FrontPage with further adherence to Internet standards and improved compatibility with other Office applications by incorporating standard Office features such as Visual Basic for Applications (VBA), personalized menus and toolbars, and common editing tools.

Integrated Editor and Explorer Environment

You no longer have to switch between the FrontPage Explorer and FrontPage Editor to view and edit pages. These environments are now integrated so that you can create and edit Web pages as well as perform site management tasks in one window.

Built-In Team Collaboration

If a team is working on a Web site, FrontPage has a page-level check-in and check-out feature to help manage the process of Web document collaboration. Users can reserve a file so that only they can edit it, preventing other users from saving edits on a document being worked on by someone else.

Additionally, Web pages can be assigned to a specific team member, including the option to set approval levels to track the progress of a page during the development process.

You can designate folders as subWebs, so they can be managed independently by team members.

▶ **See** "Creating, Publishing, and Managing Web Sites," **p. CD153**

Targeted Capabilities

You can preselect the environments (browsers and servers) your Web pages will be used with, to avoid adding features to pages that do not work in the targeted environments.

Other New or Improved Features in FrontPage

In addition to the items discussed previously, there are other new features you might want to check out in FrontPage 2000:

- Can open multiple Web sites at once—You no longer have to close the current Web site to open another one. FrontPage 2000 opens a new window for each Web site to which you want to connect.
- Create Web sites anywhere—FrontPage 2000 allows you to create Web sites in any folder, without connecting to a Web server. When the site is ready, you publish it to a Web server.
- HTML Editing—HTML documents created in other applications are not changed when brought into FrontPage. New features make it easy to insert HTML code directly in the HTML view.
- Reveal tags—You can see the underlying HTML tags for the different components of your Web pages. While in the WYSIWYG mode in the Normal view, you activate the Reveal Tags option. Figure 2.8 shows an example of a page with the tags revealed.

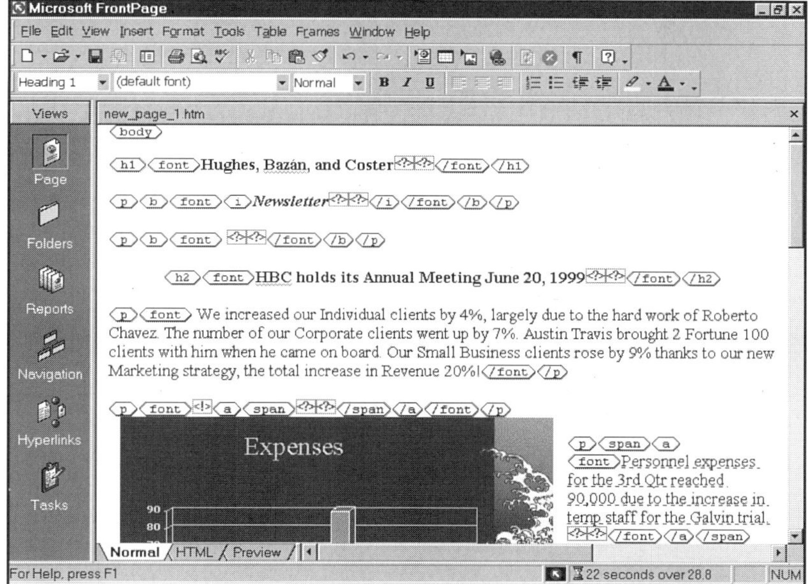

FIGURE 2.8
The Reveal Tags command is on the View menu, or you can press Ctrl+/ to toggle the HTML tags on and off.

- Themes—Microsoft has added more than 60 new themes. Use the themes to present a common design throughout your entire Web site. FrontPage 2000 has an integrated theme designer. If the standard themes don't provide the look you want, create your own. Choose the right styles, fonts, colors, images, and bullets for your Web site.
- Target browser and Web server capabilities—Choose the environments to target and FrontPage restricts you from using features that do not work on the targeted systems.
- Dynamic HTML effects—Add Dynamic HTML effects to your pages. The effects work with modern browsers and appear statically with version 3 browsers.

- Sitewide Cascading Style Sheets (CSS)—FrontPage now supports using style sheets applied to your entire Web site.
- Site Management—The views in FrontPage make it easy to manage the site. The new Reports view enables you to run reports listing important Web site information such as slow pages, broken links, and recent files.
- Multiple Language Support—Create and manage Web content in up to 15 different languages on the same Web site.

Changes to Publisher 2000

Microsoft Publisher is a desktop publishing application you can use to create professional-quality publications ranging from newsletters and pamphlets to invitations and banners. Publisher 2000 is available in three Office 2000 versions: Small Business, Professional, and Premium.

Wizards are an integral part of Publisher and the primary way you create publications. Publisher comes with a wide array of wizards to generate complex publications almost instantly. However, you can customize any of the publications to meet your particular requirements.

Although you can produce complex publications with Word and PowerPoint, Publisher provides some tools that are particularly suited to preparing documents for mass printing:

- You can design a newsletter, catalog, or brochure with many text files flowing through frames. You can apply complex backgrounds, including images and text that are applied to all pages in your publication.
- You can design and print a publication that does not fit on your office printer, ranging from a 10-foot-long banner to a folding invitation to an Open House for your business clients.
- If you don't want to tackle FrontPage, Publisher is a good choice for Web-page creation. Although there are some limitations to Publisher's usefulness as a Web-authoring tool, it does allow you to maintain a consistent look and feel between the printed publication and the Web site.

Commercial Printing Support

One the most significant new features in Publisher 2000 is the support it provides in preparing documents for commercial printing. It includes the capability to automatically convert between spot-color and four-color process (CMYK) with color separation. You can produce separated color plates for a commercial offset printer.

The Pantone® Process Color System is a standard ink-matching system that commercial printers use. When you prepare a publication in Publisher 2000, you can designate a specific color for the commercial printer to match during printing.

Trapping is the overlapping of the edges of different colors to compensate for minor variations in color registration on commercial printing presses. A publication can use trapping for the entire document or for specific objects in the publication. With Publisher 2000, you and the commercial printer have complete control over a publication's trapping settings.

Additionally, the fonts you designate for a publication are embedded in the Publisher document. This ensures that the commercial printer will not have a problem printing the publication with the fonts you intended.

▶ **See** "Working with Commercial Printers," **p. CD76**

Introducing PhotoDraw 2000

PhotoDraw is a photo-editing and illustration application. Using PhotoDraw, you can create custom graphics to use with any printed or online document including printed letters, newsletters, and brochures, as well as PowerPoint slides and Web pages.

NOTE PhotoDraw 2000 is included only in the Office 2000 Premium version.

Previous computer-imaging and illustration applications have been targeted to people with professional design experience, making them difficult to use for most Office users. PhotoDraw, on the other hand, has been built with the Office user in mind. Because it uses many of the standard Office interface features, experienced Office users find PhotoDraw intuitive and easy to use. PhotoDraw isn't anywhere as powerful as Adobe Photoshop, but as an experienced Office user, most likely you'll find its addition to the Office suite a welcome one, especially if you create graphics or manipulate images for Web pages.

PhotoDraw can manipulate clip art, scanned images, text, and user-drawn graphics. The tools to help you work with graphics include

- Templates
- Special effects tools
- Clip-art customization tools
- Photo-editing tools
- Painting and drawing tools
- Three-dimensional tools
- Interactive tutorial and online help

▶ **See** "Using Microsoft PhotoDraw," **p. 1661**

CHAPTER 3

Unleashing the Office 2000 Web Tools

In this chapter

Employing the Web Tools

More and more companies are exploring the use of the Internet and intranets as means of gathering and sharing information. Microsoft Office 2000 offers a number of features that integrate the productivity tools in the Office applications with the Web.

Today, many users take advantage of network file servers to store information that can be shared with others. However, file servers lack the interactive and dynamic interface found on the Web. To provide the information sharing requirements with a Web-like interface, Microsoft has enlisted the help of Web servers. So instead of having to use an interface similar to Windows Explorer to locate a document (and then display it in the appropriate application), users can locate and display a document in a Web browser, regardless of the application that created the original data. Using a browser interface enables users to combine the powerful document features of the Office applications with the interactive features of the Web.

Along with the Web servers, the new HTML file format and Office Server Extensions (discussed later in this chapter) make it possible to publish Office documents so that they can be displayed in Web browsers and enable you to collaborate with others online.

HTML File Format

To integrate the productivity tools in Office with the Web, and to provide the back-and-forth exchange necessary between Webs and the Office applications, Microsoft has incorporated the HTML file format into all the Office 2000 applications. This means you can create rich Web documents by using the same Office tools you use to create printed documents. Therefore, anyone with a browser can view documents created by Office 2000 applications when the document is saved in the HTML file format. The HTML file format is available in all Office 2000 applications.

▶ **See** "Integrating HTML in Office," **p. 12**

Office Server Extensions

Additionally, Microsoft has developed a dual set of features—Office Server Extensions (which are installed on a Web server) and Office Server Extension Supports (which are automatically installed with Office 2000 on your PC). These features work together to support several Office 2000 collaboration tools, including Web Discussions and Web Subscriptions.

The *Office Server Extensions (OSEs)* also make it possible for you to save documents to a Web server and view documents stored on the Web server with an Internet browser.

NOTE Office Server Extensions incorporate the Microsoft FrontPage extensions that live on a Windows NT-based HTTP server to provide additional Web publishing and document collaboration capabilities. Office Server Extensions do not replace existing Web server technologies. Rather, they enhance the way you work with Office in a Web-based environment.

▶ **See** "Office Server Extensions (OSEs)," **p. 1719**

Web File Management

Saving Office documents to a Web server is similar to saving documents to a file server on a network. You can create folders on the Web server, view document properties, and perform drag-and-drop operations directly from within Windows Explorer. *Web folders* are displayed in the left pane of Windows Explorer, at the same level as your local drives (hard drives, CD-ROM drives, removable storage drives, and floppy disk drives). You can create hierarchical folder structures on the Web servers just as you can other drives.

You can also create Web folders directly from within an application by clicking the Web Folders button on the Places Bar in either the Open or Save As dialog box. If you have Web folders, they will be listed in place of the Add Web Folder option. Additional folders can be created by clicking the New Folder button. A wizard appears to guide you through the creation process (see Figure 3.1).

NOTE You'll need to know the URL location of the Web server to create Web folders to it.

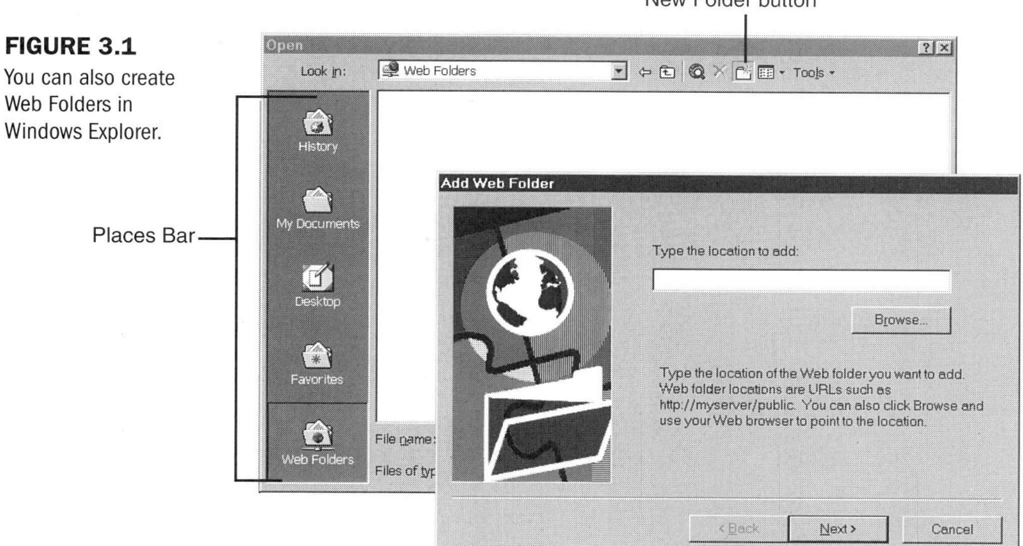

FIGURE 3.1
You can also create Web Folders in Windows Explorer.

You can also view the contents of a Web server in a browser. The Office Server Extensions enable you to see a display of Web directory listings and documents.

HTML Graphics Support

Because few HTML editors enable you to edit graphics, most people who use HTML editors to create Web pages are forced to save graphic files in two separate file formats—one format to display on the Web page and another format to use when they want to edit the graphic. Even then, you typically have to use a different program specifically for graphic editing. As a result, it's difficult to track the latest version of the graphic.

In Office 2000, when you save a document containing graphics, Office automatically saves those graphics in an appropriate file format. For example, photographs are saved as JPEG files and line art is saved as GIF files. Later, when you save the Office document in the HTML file format, Office 2000 stores graphics in both the original native format (for editing) and a format appropriate for use with a browser. This makes it easier to edit nonbitmap graphics. As a result, you don't have to keep track of a separate copy of the graphic for editing. You edit the graphic by using the appropriate tools and Office displays the format you need.

NOTE If your graphics are close together, they are automatically grouped for better display in HTML.

Office 2000 includes two tools for editing images. The Photo Editor is a good tool for manipulating scanned and bitmap images. A new application called PhotoDraw is also available for editing images, if you have Office 2000 Premium Edition.

▶ **See** "Using Microsoft PhotoDraw," **p. 1661**

For a detailed explanation of the other ways in which the HTML file format is integrated in Office 2000 features, see Chapter 1, "General Office Features at a Glance."

▶ **See** "Integrating HTML in Office," **p. 12**

The Office Web Components

Word processing and slide presentation documents are easy to convert into Web documents because they are comprised of static text or data. The power behind worksheets and databases, on the other hand, is the dynamic nature of the data. You can filter a worksheet list or create a PivotTable in Excel, both of which can be altered dramatically by revising the filter or changing the PivotTable fields. Likewise, a database table can be filtered or a report generated based on criteria you specify.

To provide this type of dynamic interaction with worksheet and databases while displayed on a Web page, Office 2000 includes the Office Web Components. The *Office Web Components* are a collection of COM controls for publishing data from worksheets, charts, and databases to an *interactive Web page*. Specifically, there are three Office Web Components—a Spreadsheet Component, Chart Component, and PivotTable Component. Data in a Worksheet Component can be edited, sorted, and filtered from within a browser. The Chart Component can be set to provide live updates to the chart as the source data in the worksheet changes. Users can reorganize the data displayed in PivotTable Components by dragging fields to other areas of the PivotTable layout. Additionally, the Office Web Components are fully programmable.

The Office Web Components can be useful to you and your company in many ways; here are just a few examples:

- Sales information is displayed in a PivotTable Component on your company intranet. Sales managers can manipulate the PivotTable layout and fields to organize the sales information by region or by sales representative.
- An Excel list of employees and their extensions can be displayed as a Worksheet Component on your company intranet. Employees can filter the list by department to see a list of everyone in a given department, or last name to locate a specific person.
- Clients can look up product information on your Internet Web site. They can sort the list by product name or number and filter the list to locate a particular product.

The user browsing the Web page does not need to have Excel installed on his computer to use the interactive features (but he must have at least some of Office 2000 installed).

NOTE The interactive Web Components are tied to Microsoft software, both on the client and on the server. Interactive Web Components run only on a Web server with OfficeMicrosoft 2000 Server Extensions. You can download and use the Extensions free, but they work only on a server running Windows NT 4.0 with Service Pack 3 or later, with IIS 4.0 or later.

On the client side, the user browsing the Web page does not need to have Excel installed on her computer to use the interactive features. But she must have Microsoft Internet Explorer 4.01 (or later) and Office Server Extensions Support features (on the Office 2000 CD) to use the Office Web Components.

When you save an Excel worksheet containing a list, a PivotTable, or chart as a Web Page, it is automatically saved in the HTML file format. In the Save As dialog box, there will be an option to Add Interactivity, as shown in Figure 3.2, when you indicate that just the selected sheets will be saved.

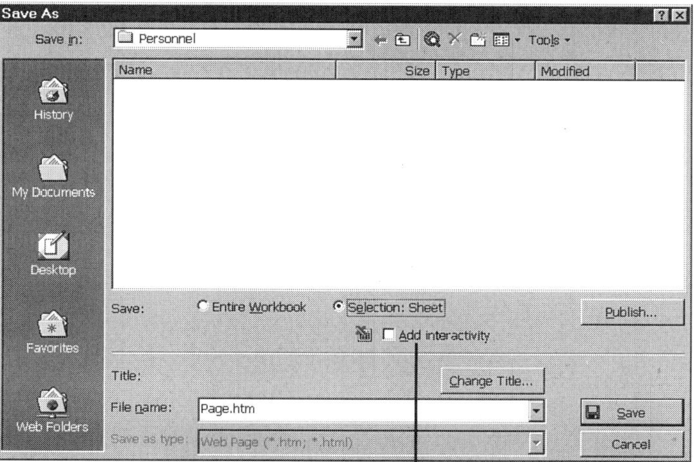

FIGURE 3.2
Interactivity is not available if the Entire Workbook option is marked.

Marking this option and saving the document to a Web server are all that's required to invoke the Office Web Components. When the document is displayed in Internet Explorer, the COM controls for the Web Components take over and provide the interactive features. Users can work interactively with the Web page to manipulate the data directly in the browser.

▶ **See** "Advanced Lists, PivotTables, and PivotCharts," **p. 773**

For example, with the Spreadsheet Component you can enter text and numbers, create formulas, sort, filter, and perform basic formatting. Figure 3.3 shows an Excel Worksheet Component. The Spreadsheet Property toolbox, activated by a button on the Worksheet Component toolbar provides a number of formatting features.

Some features are active only if they were in place before the worksheet was saved as a Web page. For example, if the spreadsheet is saved with frozen panes, header rows and columns will remain visible while scrolling through data.

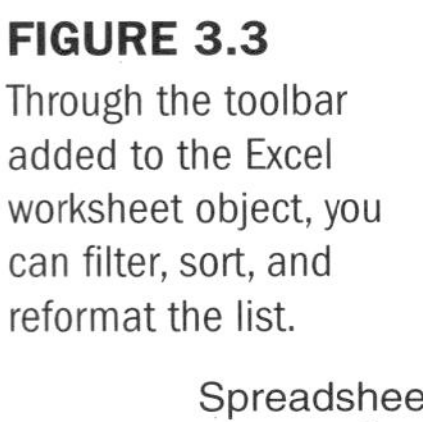

FIGURE 3.3
Through the toolbar added to the Excel worksheet object, you can filter, sort, and reformat the list.

Spreadsheet property toolbox button

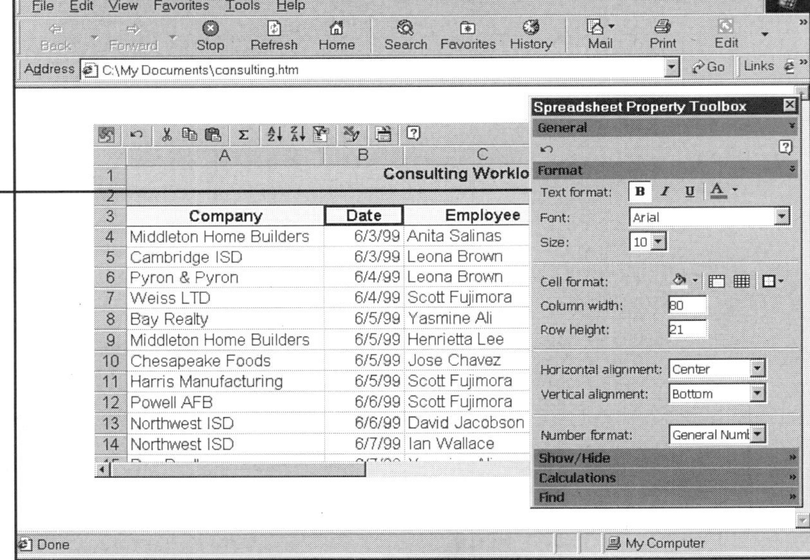

NOTE Your interaction with the component is limited to just the features available on the component toolbar. For example, in the Worksheet Component shown in Figure 3.3, there is no option to perform an advanced filter or create a PivotTable based on the list.

The Chart Component automatically updates when the underlying data changes.

The PivotTable Component can be created in either Access or Excel. You can view and analyze database information (from an Excel list or Access table) in a PivotTable, similar to the way you use PivotTables in Excel and the PivotTable Form in Access.

NOTE If you're familiar with previous versions of Access, PivotTables are similar to Crosstabs.

With this component, you can access the Field List to drag and drop the dynamically linked fields to the position you want on the PivotTable. You can also sort and filter the data, group data by rows or columns, and create totals. The PivotTable Component actually resides on a *Data Access Page (DAP)*, another new feature in Access 2000, because the PivotTable Component can be created in either Excel or Access.

▶ **See** "What Are Data Access Pages?" **p. 1100**

Authoring Web Pages

There are several approaches to creating Web pages in Office 2000. If you have Office 2000 Premium, I encourage you to use FrontPage 2000 to create Web pages. FrontPage is a Web *site* creation and management application and, it has the strongest Web *page* creation tools of all the Office applications. You'll find several chapters in the FrontPage section of this book that can help you create effective Web pages. Microsoft has also included a new image-editing application, Microsoft PhotoDraw, in the Premium version of Office 2000. All of these chapters are in the FrontPage section of this book.

▶ **See** "Web Page Development," **p. 1551**

▶ **See** "Creating Advanced Pages," **p. 1627**

▶ **See** "Using Microsoft PhotoDraw," **p. 1661**

If you don't have the Premium version of Office 2000, then you can take a document created in an Office application and generate a Web page by merely saving it as a Web page (discussed later in this section).

There are dozens of uses for Web pages on your company's Internet or intranet Web sites. These are just a few ideas for you to consider:

- You could create a database listing of all your products, product specifications, and pricing for customers to view on your company's Internet Web site. The listing could be generated in either Excel or Access and then saved in an HTML file format. Because of the Office Web Components, you can update the source data (when new products are added and other products are retired) and the Web page will reflect the changes. Naturally, if you want to get fancy you can add a search capability or index feature to provide your customers with a quick way to locate the product they are interested in. Another great addition would be the capability to order the product online, perhaps with an option to display the order form in other languages, an especially useful feature in today's international market.
- Instead of waiting for the annual meeting to share information on how the company is doing, you can post items such as gross sales or orders on an intranet Web page.

- A wide variety of personnel items can be placed on your company's intranet. For example, one page can list all the current positions you are looking to fill internally. Among other things, the site can list the qualifications, duties, and deadline for applying. You can even create an online form for employees to fill in and submit their applications through the intranet, rather than requiring a hardcopy form. On another page, you might list general travel information: mileage reimbursement rates, per diem rates to various cities, international travel information (medical shot requirements, travel warnings to areas of conflict), and so on.
- Other intranet uses include an interoffice telephone extension list; safety information; company human resource policies (and changes to those policies); and other activities, news, and information.

By placing this type of information on a Web site, you can provide valuable information to your customers and employees, which they can access when it's convenient for them. At the same time, you can take the burden off the offices within your company that are responsible for providing this type of information.

Formatting Web Pages

To provide the other Office applications with the same type of professional formatting features that are available in the PowerPoint presentation design templates, Microsoft has created *Themes*. Themes are a set of graphics and color schemes that include bullet styles, fonts, border styles, and backgrounds. The themes available in Office 2000 can be applied to Word documents and have been added as presentation design templates in PowerPoint. If you use FrontPage 2000 to create your Web pages, you can apply the themes to any document you create (or import into FrontPage from the other Office applications) and even customize the themes to suit your specific needs.

Saving to a Web Server

When a document is saved in an HTML file format, it is treated as a Web page. When saved to a Web server, it can be viewed by anyone with a browser who has access to that Web server.

Before you save a document as a Web page, use the new command File, Web Page Preview. This command enables you to see how your document will appear in a browser, before you actually save it. Previewing the document enables you to make changes to the document that will enhance its appearance in the browser.

Saving a document to a Web server is similar to saving a document to a folder on your hard drive. In most Office 2000 applications, you use the File, Save As Web Page command. The dialog box that appears varies slightly from application to application, but is similar to the Save As dialog box. Figure 3.4 shows the dialog box in PowerPoint.

In Access, you create Data Access Pages based on a component (such as a form or report) of the database. *Data Access Pages (DAPs)* are Web pages that you build from within Access. The easiest way to create a DAP in Access is to use the built-in wizards. After they are created, the DAP is stored in Access (and can be used in Access) natively, but you can use the File, Save As command to save the DAP to a Web server.

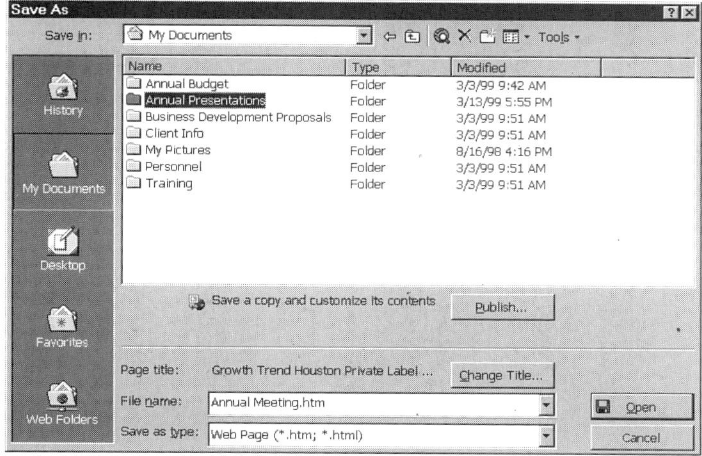

FIGURE 3.4
The Save As Type is automatically set to Web Page, the HTML file format.

▶ **See** "What Are Data Access Pages?" **p. 1100**

When you want to save a document to a Web server, consider creating Web Folders in Windows Explorer. Web folders are shortcuts to the Web server. Web folders were discussed in the section "Web File Management" earlier in this chapter.

Editing Web Pages

Each of the Office applications not only can save documents in the HTML file format, but they can view them as well. Because of the way Office 2000 has implemented the HTML file format, documents originally created in an Office 2000 application and saved in an HTML file format can easily be edited. When you want to edit a Web page, you have two choices:

- Open the Web page in the application in which it was originally created to edit it. For example, if the document was created it Word, open it in Word; if it was created (or finalized) in FrontPage, open it in FrontPage. You can then use the editing tools in that application to edit the document.
- Click the Edit button in Microsoft Internet Explorer and the Office application that created the HTML file will be activated.

See Chapter 1 for a detailed description of how object formats are handled when a document is saved in an HTML file format.

Online Collaboration

In previous versions of Office, when you needed to collaborate with others on a document, you had several choices. You could send a copy of the document to each of the people involved in the collaboration and then merge the comments into one document. You could route the document, in hard copy or electronically via email, giving each person the opportunity to edit and add comments to the same copy of the document. Or, you could save a copy of the document to a shared folder on a network server where others would add comments or make changes directly to the document.

Office 2000 provides several new ways for groups of people to collaborate on a document through the use of a Web server. Most companies have a Web server or an Internet Information Server (IIS) that is part of the company's internal intranet.

The collaboration method you choose largely depends on what time constraints you are under. You can schedule an online meeting (using NetMeeting) where collaboration participants get together online at a predetermined time. The advantage with this method is that participants do not have to be in the same room. Participants can be in offices at different sites; sites that are even in different cities or even countries.

When it's inconvenient (or impossible) to get everyone together at the same time, you can use the Web Discussions feature that enables participants to create and reply to comments about a particular document. Unlike the comments feature found in most of the Office applications (where the comments are embedded into the document), the Web Discussions comments are stored separately from the document on a Web server. By not attaching the comments to the document, this opens up the opportunity to make comments on virtually any document you can display on your monitor. For example, while viewing a competitor's Web site, people from your company can create Discussion comments about that site.

NOTE The NetMeeting feature is still in its infancy, meaning that it's not likely to work as you might expect. As more companies begin using this type of collaboration, Microsoft will expand its capabilities, reliability, and speed.

I *strongly* encourage you to test NetMeeting long before you decide to use it for an online collaboration session.

Another new Web tool that is often used in conjunction with Web Discussions is Web Subscriptions and Notifications. You can subscribe to a document and request that you be notified when changes are made to the document—for example, when someone else adds a Discussion comment to the document. Not only can the Web Subscriptions and Notifications feature be used with documents, but you can subscribe to folders as well. These features can be used from within the core Office applications to discuss a particular document, or you can use Internet Explorer to discuss intranet and Internet Web pages and application documents. Figure 3.5 shows a worksheet in Excel with Web Discussions taking place.

The following sections provide specific instructions for using these three new Web collaboration tools.

Using Web Discussions

The *Web Discussions* feature enables people to comment on any document that they can view; write access is not required. Web Discussions have a big advantage over other modes of collaboration—you don't have to assemble everyone at a set time to attend a meeting. People can review the document at their convenience.

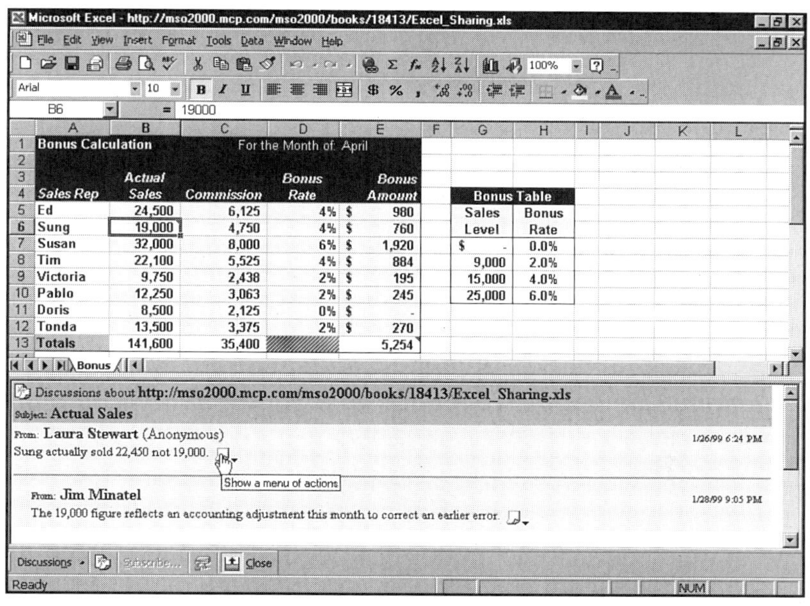

FIGURE 3.5
Excel allows discussions about the worksheet, not a particular cell. However, in Word, you can add inline discussions.

Web Discussion comments are usually created by documents. In Excel, the comments are by workbook; in PowerPoint, the comments are by presentation. Only Word enables you to create comments both by document and within the document text. There is a good example of Word's Web Discussion capabilities in Chapter 18. Besides adding comments about a document, you can also reply to comments, creating *discussion threads*.

▶ **See** "Web Discussions," **p. 536**

A Web server is used to store the comments. The document itself does not have to be stored on the Web server, but must reside in any location to which all discussion participants have access. This can be in a shared folder on a network File Server or on a company intranet, or even documents you access on the Internet. The discussions are stored in a database on a Web server and are displayed when you display the document. Think of the Web server as a discussion forum.

CAUTION

If you decide to save the document to a Web server, make sure the filename does not have a space in it, or you will not be able to open the file. Annual Report will be listed as Annual20%Report. You can use an underscore in the name, such as Annual_Report, to give the appearance of two separate words.

The Web Discussions tool is part of the standard Office installation. To use Web Discussion, you need access to a Web server that has been loaded with the Office Server Extensions (discussed earlier in this chapter). The first time you initiate Web Discussions, you may not have an automatic link to the Web server. You might be prompted to enter or confirm a user ID and password, depending upon how the system administrator set up security for the Web server. You may need to obtain the name of the Web server, a user ID, and a password from your system administrator to establish the link. For certain networks, you may also need a domain name. Figure 3.6 shows an example of the prompt you might see.

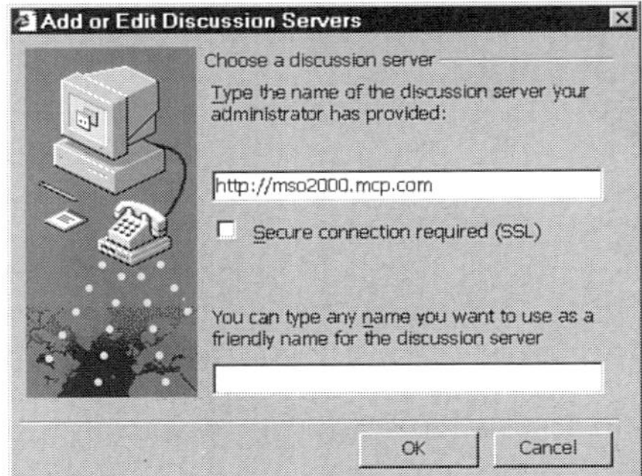

FIGURE 3.6
You must be actively connected to the Web server to use Web Discussions.

You can use the Web Discussions feature directly from within the Office 2000 applications. For example, you would open the document and then choose Tools, Online Collaboration, Web Discussions. The Discussions toolbar appears (which is supplied by the Office Server Extensions). Figure 3.7 shows Web Discussions active in Microsoft Word.

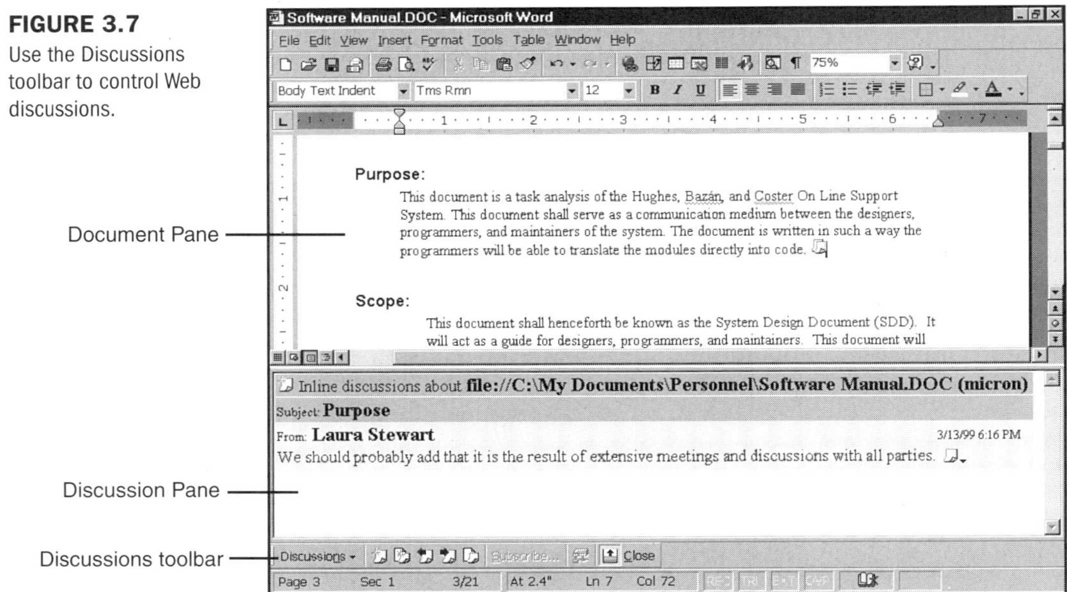

FIGURE 3.7
Use the Discussions toolbar to control Web discussions.

If the document you want to discuss is a Web page, first view the Web page in Internet Explorer (IE) and then activate the Web Discussions feature. You can activate Web Discussions in Internet Explorer by choosing View, Explorer Bar, Discuss or by clicking the double arrows on the far right of the Standard Buttons toolbar and clicking the Discuss option (see Figure 3.8). Web Discussions can be used with Internet Explorer version 4.0 or later (Internet Explorer 5.0 comes with Office 2000). It will not be available if you use Netscape Navigator as your Web browser.

Click double arrows to access the Discuss option.

FIGURE 3.8
The Web Discussions feature is available from within Internet Explorer.

After you access the Web server, the icons on the Discussions toolbar become active.

Through the Discussions toolbar you have access to all the Web Discussions features. You can insert new comments, view existing comments, edit comments, reply to comments, subscribe to a particular document or folder, and view or hide the Discussions Pane. These capabilities are described in the following sections.

CAUTION

If you access Web Discussions from within an application, the Discussions toolbar appears when you open or switch to any document in that application. It is not present in other applications. Be certain that discussion items are entered in the intended document.

Adding Discussion Items When convenient, participants turn on Web Discussions for a given document and enter or reply to *discussion items.* With the exception of Microsoft Word (which lets you create both document and inline discussions), each of the core Office 2000 applications, along with Internet Explorer, displays the discussions in a Pane—the Discussions Pane—in the bottom half of the window. If there aren't any discussions associated with a document, the Discussions Pane will not be visible when you initially activate the Web Discussions feature. After the first discussion is applied to a document, the Discussions Pane will always appear when you activate Web Discussions.

To enter a discussion item, click the Insert About the Document button on the Discussions toolbar. In the Enter Discussion Text dialog box that appears, type the subject and the text of the comment as shown in Figure 3.9 and click OK. The subject will be displayed in a gray banner to separate one discussion subject thread from another in the Discussions Pane.

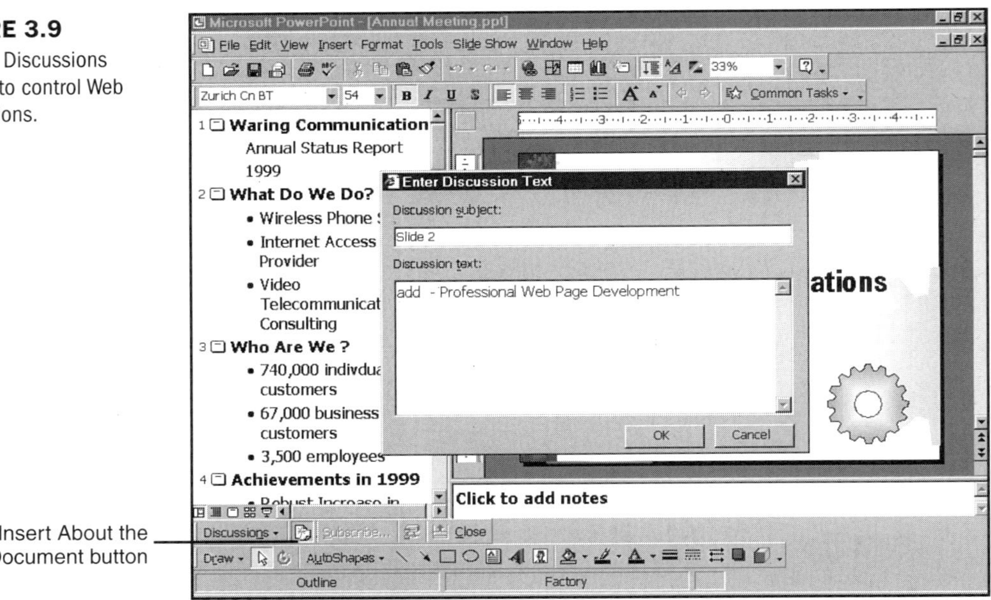

FIGURE 3.9
Use the Discussions toolbar to control Web discussions.

Discussion items show up in the Discussion Pane. Unless you are creating an inline discussion item in Word, it will be helpful to others if you identify which part of the document you are referring to in your discussion. For example, in Excel you can identify the cell, or in PowerPoint you can identify the slide number. A good place to identify the document part is in the subject or the beginning of the discussion comment.

After discussion items have been entered, additional buttons on the Discussions toolbar become available. Use the button ScreenTips to discover the purpose of each button.

Replying to, Editing, and Deleting Discussion Items Discussion items are not actually part of the document; they are stored on the Web server. When you activate Web Discussions, the discussions appear in the Discussions Pane. You can reply to or edit any of the comments in the thread, but you cannot edit an item directly in the Discussions Pane.

Instead, scroll to locate the item in the Discussions Pane. Then click the discussion item's icon to display a drop-down list of choices, as shown in Figure 3.10.

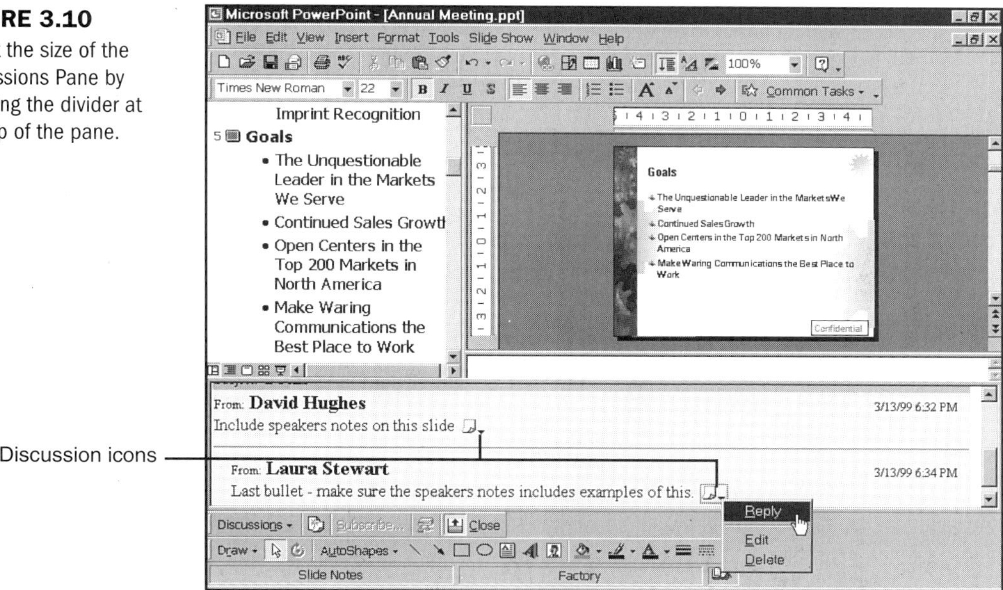

FIGURE 3.10
Adjust the size of the Discussions Pane by dragging the divider at the top of the pane.

When you select Reply or Edit, the Enter Discussion Text dialog box appears (refer to Figure 3.9) where you can reply to or edit the existing discussion. After you've entered the reply or made the edits, click OK. The Discussions Pane is updated, as shown in Figure 3.11.

You cannot delete or modify a discussion item by manipulating the icon in the document. If you delete a discussion item icon from a document—rather than using the Discussions Pane—it reappears the next time that document is opened.

To remove an item, select Delete from the drop-down list on the Discussion item. A confirmation message appears to confirm the removal.

Filtering Discussion Comments When a large number of people are commenting on a document or when discussion items are being added frequently, you can filter the discussions.

To filter the discussions, click the Discussions drop-down button on the Discussions toolbar and choose Filter Discussions. The Filter Discussions dialog box appears, as shown in Figure 3.12.

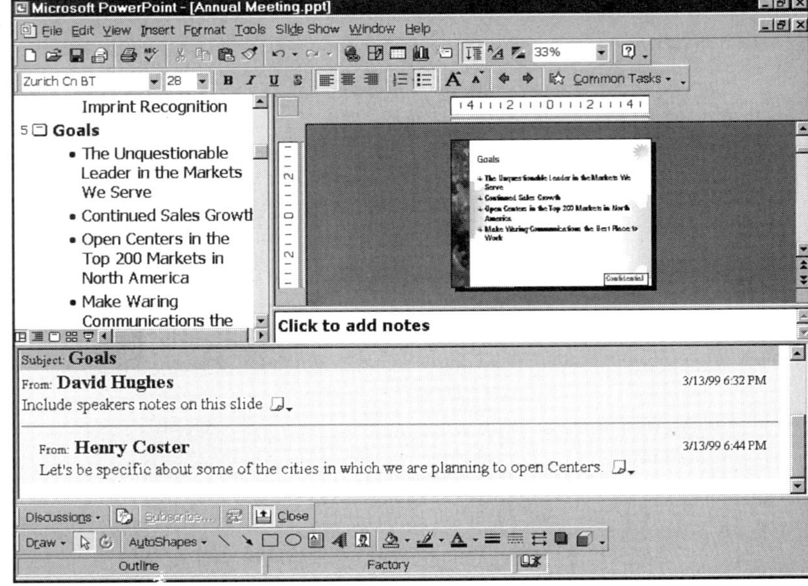

FIGURE 3.11
Replies appear slightly indented under the text to which they are associated.

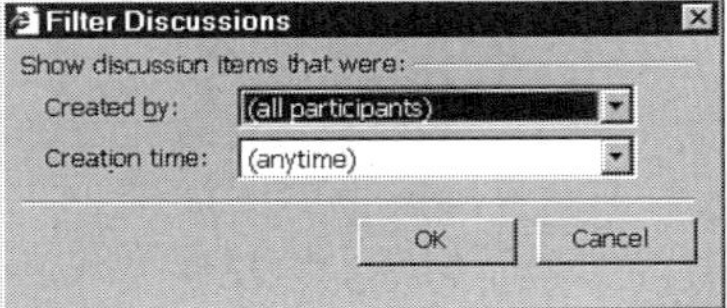

FIGURE 3.12
To see just the most recent comments, filter for comments made in the last 24 hours.

When you click the Created By drop-down list, a list of every person who has attached discussion comments appears. From the Creation Time drop-down list, you can choose to filter by hours, days, or months. For example, you can filter on the last 24 hours or the last 7 days. After you've made your filter section, click OK.

Using Web Subscriptions and Notifications

Collaboration on a document is much simpler with the Web Subscription and Web Notification features. You can *subscribe* to particular documents on a Web server and automatically be notified by email when the status of the document changes. The document does not have to contain discussion comments to use this feature, although you initiate it when Web Discussions is active.

To subscribe to a document or folder, click the Subscribe button on the Discussions toolbar. The dialog box shown in Figure 3.13 appears. You can subscribe to the active document or the folder in which that document resides. File is selected by default and the filename is displayed in the text box.

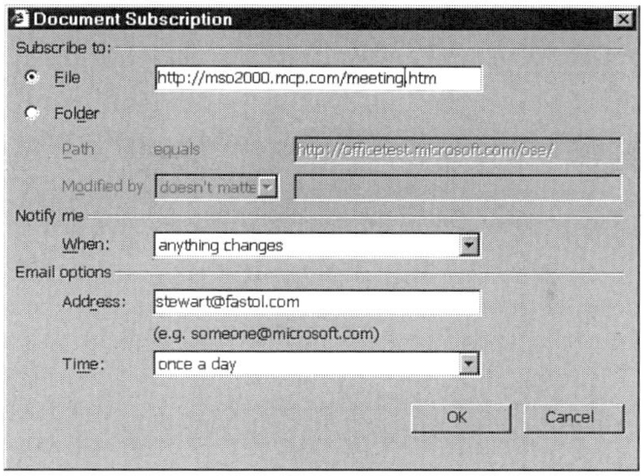

FIGURE 3.13
Subscriptions can notify you by email when changes occur.

For documents and folders located on a Web server, be sure you use the full Internet, intranet, or local network address (URL)—for example, `http://Webserver.jqsmith.com/FY2000/Budget.xls`. Office uses your network connection to access such addresses.

If you select Folder, you can even be *notified* when a person you specify makes a change to the folder. This is an excellent option if you are waiting for a green light from a client or boss. You activate this option by selecting Modified By.

You can monitor different types of modifications under the Notify Me When option:

- Anything changes—Choose this option to aggressively monitor every aspect of a Web Discussion server.
- A new document is created—This option is useful when you're anxiously awaiting a new document.
- A document is modified—This option can be useful when you've requested changes to a document.
- A document is deleted—This option and the following can alert you to changes in the overall contents of the Web server space.
- A document is moved—This option lets you know up-front when something moves, which beats scratching your head wondering what happened to it.
- A discussion item is inserted or deleted—This option is a useful way to monitor a specific discussion. This can be useful on servers that are very busy, where you don't want to get overwhelmed with information that is not relevant to your work.

Under the Email Option Address, include the address to which you want notifications sent. Of course, if you have several email accounts, you might consider setting up your email application to leave email on the server for remote addresses where you just want to see the mail (Outlook supports this feature).

You can select the frequency of the email notifications: When a Change Occurs; Once a Day; or Once a Week. If you're anxiously awaiting all input, the first option is an excellent choice. On the other hand, if you don't need immediate notification, consider one of the other options.

NOTE You're not actually notified every time a change occurs. The Web server can be set up to look for changes at specified intervals. So, your notification frequency would be only as often as the Web server is scheduled to check for changes. Often, this is hourly. So, when you get your notification by email, it might contain a record of all the changes that have occurred since the last notification.

Online Meetings

Online meetings are akin to conference calls, except they are conducted through your computer and make use of a number of network features, such as email and chat rooms. You can set up and participate in online meetings using Microsoft NetMeeting, which comes with Office 2000. NetMeeting is a separate application that requires Internet Explorer version 4.01 SP1 (or later) installed. It can be used from within Internet Explorer or any of the core Office applications. NetMeeting provides the necessary data capabilities that enable you to share and exchange information with other people at different sites in real-time over your company's intranet or the Internet, just as if everyone were in the same room. NetMeeting is capable of transmitting both audio and video.

CAUTION

Although the concept behind NetMeeting has great potential, the implementation of this feature falls short of the mark in Office 2000. You will find this feature very slow and may result in errors that quit the program unexpectedly. Look for enhancements to this feature in Office 2000 service releases.

That said, the following sections explain how NetMeeting is supposed to work.

Setting Up an Online Meeting

You can either host an online meeting or be invited to participate in one. The host has certain privileges that participants don't. As the host, NetMeeting lets you schedule a meeting ahead of time (where you invite others to participate) or you can start an impromptu meeting.

In the Office 2000 applications, you can set up a meeting using the scheduling features of Outlook. If your participants are using Outlook's Calendar feature to track their meetings and other scheduled activities, you can use that information to schedule and notify the participants. To schedule an online meeting, choose Tools, Online Collaboration, Schedule Meeting. An Outlook meeting request window appears. You can choose the participants, identify the day and time of the meeting, and even set up a reminder for the participants. Figure 3.14 shows an example of an Outlook meeting request for an Excel document.

To see all the options in the meeting request window, maximize the window.

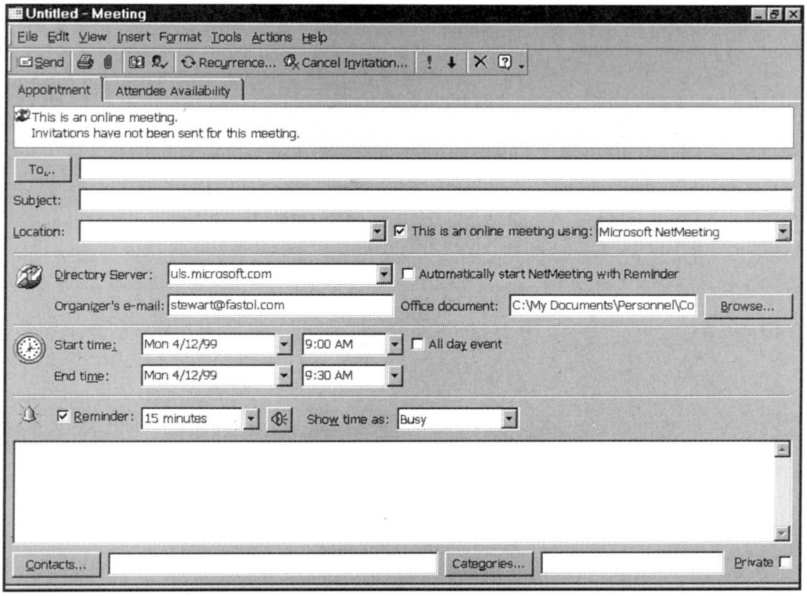

FIGURE 3.14
The name of your default Web server, your name, and the name of the active file are automatically filled in on the Outlook meeting request form.

Because the meeting request is generated by Outlook, you can specify a reminder that alerts the invitees that the meeting is about to start (assuming they accept the invitation, of course). When an invitation is accepted, it automatically gets entered into the invitee's Outlook Calendar. You can even choose an option to start NetMeeting automatically. The Automatically Start option is used in conjunction with the Reminder option. The invitees can enable the automatic option themselves, and reset the reminder to snooze until about five or ten minutes before the meeting's start time.

NOTE If your colleagues don't use Outlook, you can always coordinate a meeting through email or by phone, although you won't be able to take advantage of the group scheduling and notification features that are part of NetMeeting.

You can also conduct an impromptu online meeting by selecting Tools, Online Collaboration, Meet Now. NetMeeting asks you to identify the participants. For you to connect with these participants, they must be online with NetMeeting running on their computers. You can select the directory server you want to use (discussed in the next section) and select a person's name from the Web directory. If you get a message asking whether you want to open or save the file, choose Open File. If you cannot connect to someone by using his or her computer name, try using his or her IP address.

NOTE You can also start NetMeeting independently from your applications by clicking the Start button on the taskbar and choosing Programs, Microsoft NetMeeting.

Participating in an Online Meeting

To participate in an online meeting, choose Tools, Online Collaboration, Meet Now. You can also start NetMeeting independently from any application by clicking the Start button on the taskbar and choosing Programs, Microsoft NetMeeting.

The first time you start an online meeting, you may be prompted to select a directory server to connect to. You must have access to a directory server to participate in an online meeting. You can select any of the directory servers from the list in the Server name box under Directory; your system administrator can tell you whether there is a specific directory server to which you should connect.

The first time you start an online meeting, you are prompted to identify the directory server to which you want to connect. You are also prompted by the Audio Tuning Wizard to check your speaker and microphone volume.

NOTE A directory server is an Internet List Server (ILS) that contains the names of the users who are currently available online or who are using NetMeeting.

Microsoft maintains several directory servers on the Internet that you can use even if it does not appear in the list of servers you see onscreen:

ils.microsoft.com

ils1.microsoft.com

ils2.microsoft.com

ils3.microsoft.com

ils4.microsoft.com

ils5.microsoft.com

To change the directory server you log on to, choose Tools, Options, and select the Calling tab. Then change the Server Name. To log on to the directory server, choose Call, Log On To *[your directory server]*.

Collaborating During an Online Meeting At the start of an online meeting, the host (the person who called the meeting) controls the document while the other participants can see the Online Meeting toolbar and the document on their monitors.

The Online Meeting toolbar provides the host with options for activating and deactivating collaboration, adding and removing participants, displaying the Chat and Whiteboard windows, and ending the meeting. You can also click Microsoft NetMeeting on the taskbar to gain access to the NetMeeting program directly to alter the NetMeeting features.

Through the toolbar, participants have access to a chat room and whiteboard, which is similar to the Paint program. These windows can be used by the participants to make comments, regardless of who is controlling the document.

The Chat window (shown in Figure 3.15) floats on top of the application document. You can use the Tile options (available when you right-click the taskbar) to tile the windows so that you can see both. However, the Chat window is a fixed height window; you can change the window width, but there are constraints on the height.

You can save or print the contents of the chat window through the File menu in the Chat window.

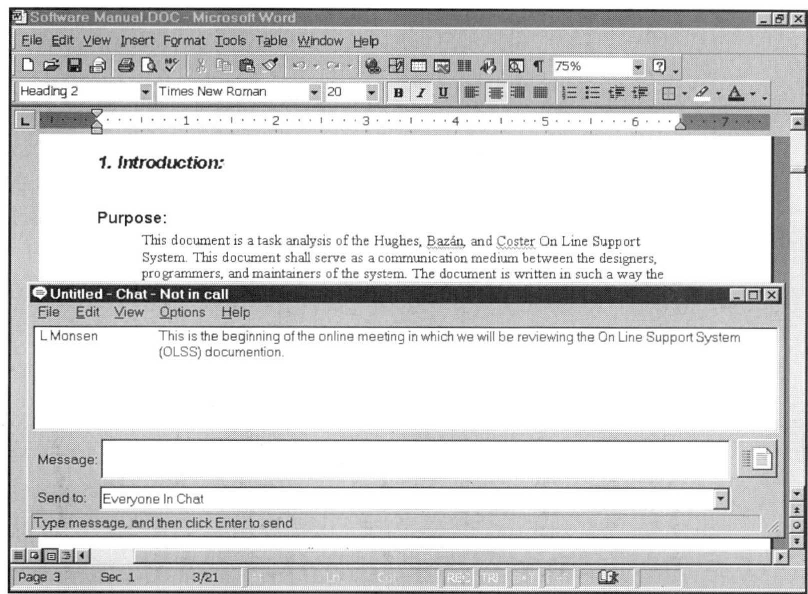

FIGURE 3.15
When the chat and whiteboard windows are active, the NetMeeting toolbar is hidden.

Like the Chart window, the Whiteboard window (shown in Figure 3.16) floats on top of the application document. It also has a fixed minimum size, both horizontally and vertically. You can save and print the contents of the whiteboard as a record of your discussions.

CAUTION

The whiteboard and chat features may not work properly between computers with different language settings and keyboard layouts. Again, it is in your best interest to thoroughly test these options before you conduct an important meeting.

The host can enable participants to make changes to the document by turning on collaboration. This enables the participants to take turns controlling and editing the document. When another user is in control of the document, his or her initials appear next to the mouse pointer onscreen. To turn on collaboration, the host clicks the Allow Others to Edit button on the Online Meeting toolbar.

NOTE You will not have the use of your mouse pointer for any purpose when someone else controls the document.

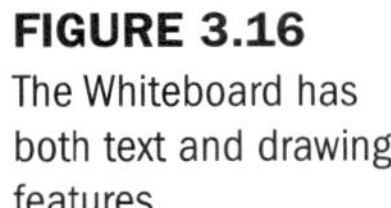

FIGURE 3.16
The Whiteboard has both text and drawing features.

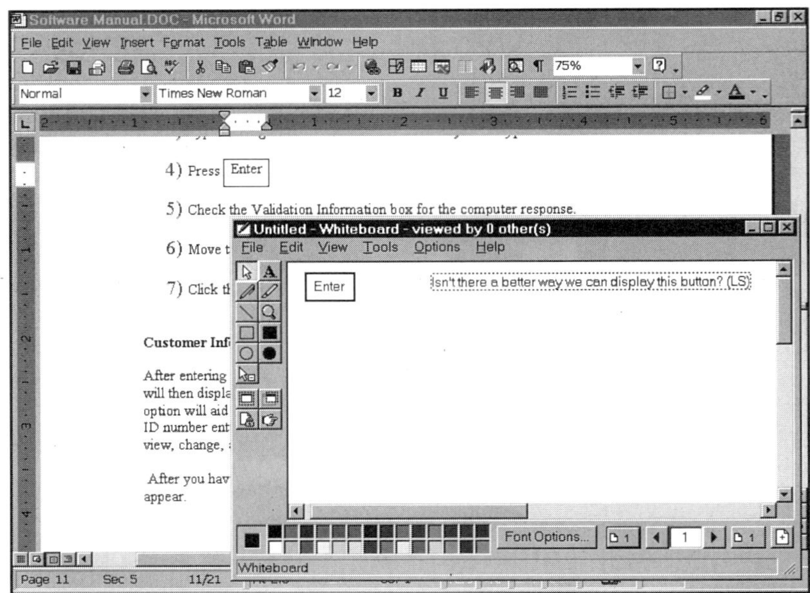

A participant can take control of a shared document after the host has turned on collaboration. It's a good idea to coordinate via audio or chat to discuss who will control the document next. The first time a participant wants to take control, they double-click anywhere in the document. After the first time, they need to just click once anywhere in the document to gain control.

The host can activate the Chat and Whiteboard windows from the Online Meeting toolbar. Participants can activate the window using the Microsoft NetMeeting program directly, by clicking Microsoft NetMeeting on the taskbar.

Members can use Chat to send text messages or use the online Whiteboard (similar to the Paint program) to make comments, regardless of who is controlling the document. Correspondence is faster in the Chat window if the host turns off collaboration. For participants to draw or type simultaneously on the Whiteboard, the host must turn off collaboration.

When collaboration is turned off, the participants cannot make changes to the document, but can work in Chat and use the Whiteboard. Only the host can turn off collaboration. If the host has control of the document, the host clicks the Allow Others to Edit button to turn off collaboration, If the host does not have control of the document, the host presses Esc.

Joining an Online Meeting If Outlook was used to schedule the online meeting, each participant receives a meeting reminder. If you're the host of the online meeting, click the Start This NetMeeting button in the meeting reminder. If you've been invited to participate in an online meeting, you can either click the Join This NetMeeting button to participate in the meeting or click the Dismiss button to decline the meeting request.

Participants can be invited to join an online meeting that is already in progress. The host is the only person who can invite other participants from within the Microsoft Office application. This is accomplished by clicking the Call Participant button on the Online Meeting toolbar. This displays the Place a Call dialog box. Select the name of the person you want to invite, and click Call.

A participant can invite others using the Microsoft NetMeeting program directly by clicking Microsoft NetMeeting on the taskbar.

NOTE Participants whom you invite to an online meeting must have NetMeeting running on their computers to receive your online meeting invitation. Remember, NetMeeting is part of Internet Explorer 5.

During the meeting, the host can click the Participant List drop-down list on the Online Meeting toolbar to see the list of people participating in the meeting.

The host is the only person who can remove a participant from an online meeting. To remove a person, select the person's name from the Participant List drop-down list on the Online Meeting toolbar. Then click the Remove Participants button.

Ending an Online Meeting The host of the online meeting is the only person who can end the meeting for the entire group. Participants can disconnect at any time by clicking Microsoft NetMeeting on the taskbar, and choosing Hang Up on the NetMeeting toolbar. When the host ends a meeting (by clicking the End Meeting button on the Online Meeting toolbar), others in the online meeting are automatically disconnected from one another.

For more information on using and troubleshooting NetMeeting, read the netmeet.txt file located in the following path:

C:\Program Files\NetMeeting\netmeet.txt

CHAPTER 4

Customizing Microsoft Office the Way You Want

In this chapter

Customizing Application Startup with Command-Line Switches

There are a number of reasons for customizing the way the Office applications start. You might want to start Word with a particular document template, rather than Normal.dot, or you might want to identify corrupt files that are preventing a proper startup of Excel, or you could have the Contacts folder display every time you open Outlook.

In these situations, you can use command-line switches to change the way an Office application starts. The phrase *command-line switches* is a holdover from the days of DOS when you typed a command to open a program. The switches (most of which start with a forward slash followed by a letter) were used in DOS, just as they are in Windows, to designate program startup alternatives. However, because Windows is a point-and-click operating system, the best way to invoke a startup switch is to create a shortcut to the application and enter the switch in the shortcut startup properties. You can even have multiple shortcuts that invoke different startup switches.

Basically, you create a shortcut to an application on the desktop and modify the properties of that shortcut. The command-line switches are added in the Target text box in the Properties dialog box.

Because the startup switches are unique to each application, you'll want to look at the chapters in this book that address the specific options you can customize. You'll find the startup switches discussed in these sections:

▶ **See** "Customizing Word," **p. 207**

▶ **See** "Customizing Excel 2000," **p. 577**

▶ **See** "Customizing Access," **p. 961**

▶ **See** "Customizing Outlook," **p. 1349**

Customizing the QuickLaunch Toolbar

The *QuickLaunch toolbar* (which, by default, appears just to the right of the Start menu) contains several default icons including shortcuts to Internet Explorer and Outlook Express. You can also add shortcuts to the desktop. The shortcut to the desktop is particularly useful when you have a lot of applications open. Instead of right-clicking a blank area of the taskbar and choosing Minimize All Windows, you can click the Desktop icon to immediately see the desktop. Another quick way to access your Desktop icons is discussed in the "The Office Shortcut Bar—For Power Users" section later in this chapter.

Like any other toolbar, icons (such as application shortcuts) can be added to and removed from the QuickLaunch toolbar. And you're not limited to just application shortcuts; shortcuts to folders and documents can be added as well.

Be selective about the icons you place on the QuickLaunch toolbar. Because of its limited space, reserve it for icons you must have access to all the time. Use the Office Shortcut Bar (discussed in the next section) for quick access to all your other shortcuts.

NOTE Shortcuts can be created on the desktop or within Windows Explorer and then dragged to the Start menu, the QuickLaunch toolbar, or the Office Shortcut Bar. If you are not familiar with creating and customizing shortcuts, see Appendix CDD, "Using the Power of Shortcuts and Desktop Icons," on the CD.

To add a shortcut to the QuickLaunch toolbar, you must create the shortcut either on the desktop or in Windows Explorer first. Then hold the Shift key down as you drag the shortcut to the QuickLaunch toolbar. A vertical insertion line appears (similar to when you are adding a button to an application toolbar) if you drag the icon in between other icons on the toolbar, to indicate the position of the shortcut. If you don't use the Shift key when you drag a shortcut onto the QuickLaunch toolbar, you will be creating a copy of the shortcut instead of moving it.

The Office Shortcut Bar—For Power Users

If you've never really used the Office Shortcut Bar, you might reconsider after reading this section. Although having shortcuts on the desktop and in the QuickLaunch toolbar can be useful, each has its practical limitations. The QuickLaunch toolbar has to compete with the open documents listed on the taskbar, and the desktop can quickly become cluttered with shortcuts to applications, folders, and documents. On the other hand, the Office Shortcut Bar has infinitely more space than either of these other areas—when you add toolbars to the Office Shortcut Bar.

NOTE In its original incarnation, several versions ago, the Office Shortcut Bar was a nuisance more than a help and most users turned it off. As a result, Microsoft decided not to install the Office Shortcut Bar by default for Office 2000. Instead, it is set to install on first use. To install and use it, click Start, Programs, Microsoft Office Tools, Microsoft Office Shortcut Bar. You must have either the Office 2000 CDs or know the location on your network where the installation files are stored.

The Office Shortcut Bar can be a floating window, such as an application window. You can also dock the Office Shortcut Bar on the side, top, or bottom of the screen. I prefer to dock it on the side of the screen.

You can begin customizing it by right-clicking the Office Shortcut Bar. From the shortcut menu (shown in Figure 4.1), you have several ways to adjust the Shortcut Bar:

- You can select other groups (referred to as toolbars) of icons to display, such as Desktop, Favorites, and Programs.

- You can remove the Auto Hide setting. By default, it is set to Auto Hide—when you move the mouse near the place onscreen where the Shortcut Bar is docked, the Shortcut Bar appears.
- You can access the Customize dialog box.

FIGURE 4.1
You can resize the Office Shortcut Bar (when it's floating) by dragging the window border.

By default, only the Office toolbar is displayed. Figure 4.2 shows the Office, Desktop, and Accessories toolbars available on the Office Shortcut Bar; Desktop is the active toolbar. The Desktop toolbar displays a list of the icons you have on the desktop, giving you yet another way to have quick access to shortcuts created on your desktop.

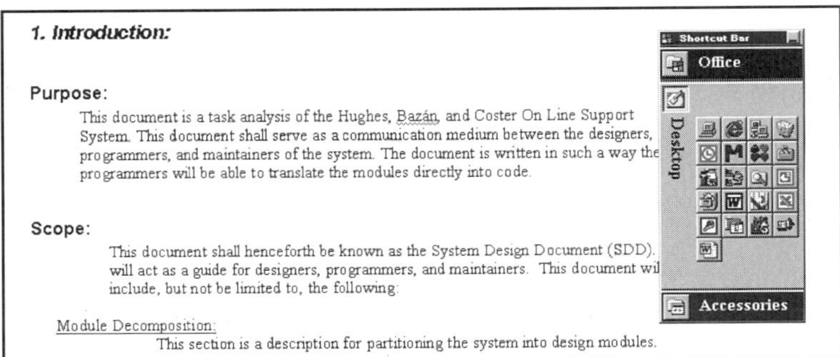

1. Introduction:

Purpose:

This document is a task analysis of the Hughes, Bazán, and Coster On Line Support System. This document shall serve as a communication medium between the designers, programmers, and maintainers of the system. The document is written in such a way the programmers will be able to translate the modules directly into code.

Scope:

This document shall henceforth be known as the System Design Document (SDD). will act as a guide for designers, programmers, and maintainers. This document wil include, but not be limited to, the following:

Module Decomposition:
This section is a description for partitioning the system into design modules.

FIGURE 4.2
When the Office Shortcut Bar is floating, it is listed as an open window on the taskbar.

Because only one group of icons can be active at any given time, click the name of the group on the Office Shortcut Bar to switch between the toolbars. When the Office Shortcut Bar is docked, the names of the toolbars are reduced to icons (see Figure 4.3).

If you want to modify the bar's appearance, add or remove buttons and other toolbars, or change the default locations for application templates, you need to customize the Office Shortcut Bar. Right-click the Office Shortcut Bar and choose Customize from the shortcut menu. The Customize dialog box appears, as shown in Figure 4.3. All the tools you need to customize the Office Shortcut Bar are in this dialog box.

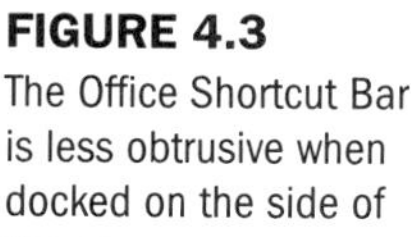

FIGURE 4.3
The Office Shortcut Bar is less obtrusive when docked on the side of the screen.

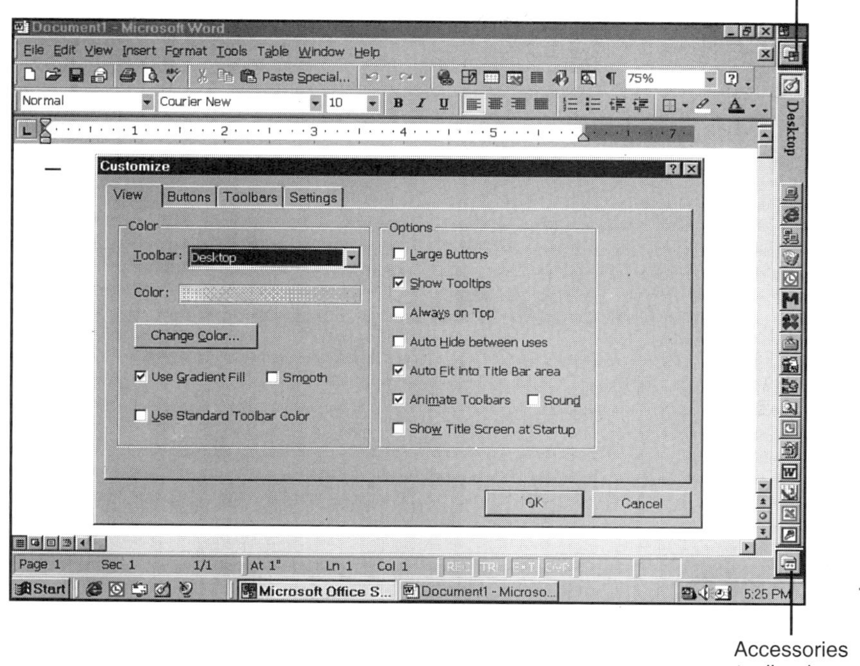

Click the Buttons tab to see a list of applications and other icons you can display on the Office Shortcut Bar (see Figure 4.4). You can rearrange the order of the icons and add spaces to separate the icons into groups. This tab also has options for adding shortcuts to specific files and folders to the Outlook Shortcut Bar.

FIGURE 4.4
The buttons on the Office Shortcut Bar; some are not active by default.

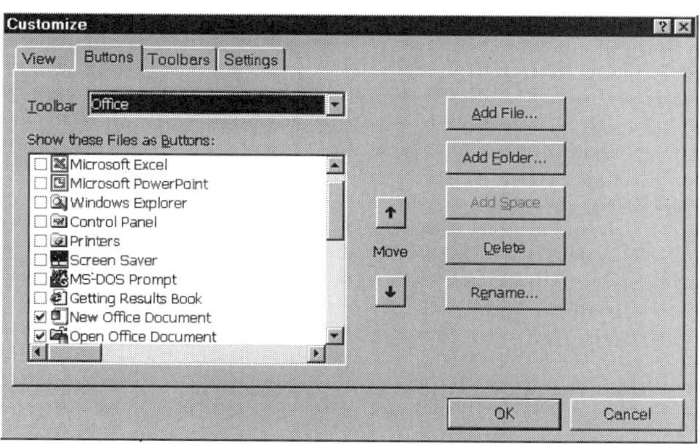

From the Toolbars tab, you can create other toolbars to use with the Office Shortcut Bar. One way to use this feature is to create shortcuts to folders and documents that you use on a frequent basis. For example, you can create a shortcut to the Templates folder for quick access to the built-in and custom templates, regardless of the application you are using. It is more convenient if you create a toolbar to a folder that does not have subfolders. When subfolders exist, clicking the folder on the Shortcut Bar displays a window displaying an icon for each file in the folder.

Another option is to create a toolbar that lists only those shortcuts from the other toolbars that you use most frequently.

Customizing the Places Bar

The Places Bar is a new feature in the Open and Save/Save As dialog boxes. It contains five default places—History, My Documents, Desktop, Favorites, and Web Folders—to access items quickly. Although you cannot modify the Places Bar directly, you can make a few simple changes to the Windows Registry to add your own places, such as a folder or drive you access routinely.

CAUTION

It's a *very* good idea to create a backup copy of your Registry before modifying it. Mistakes made to the Registry can disable your entire computer. To back up a copy of your Registry, access the Registry Editor (as described in steps 1–2 in the next section). Then from the Registry Editor menu bar (see Figure 4.5), choose Registry, Export Registry File command.

You can edit the Places Bar in several ways. You can replace one of the five default places with one of your own places, or you can expand the number of places to 10 by reducing the size of the places buttons.

In addition to the methods described in the next few sections, the CD accompanying this book contains a fully licensed version of WOPR 2000. WOPR 2000 contains a utility called "PlaceBar Customizer" that makes changing the buttons on the toolbar easy.

Replacing a Places Bar Button

To substitute a more useful place for one of the defaults on the Places Bar, you must first hide one of the default places and then create a new place:

1. Open Windows Explorer and navigate to the Windows folder.
2. Double-click the Regedit.exe file. The Registry Editor window opens, as shown in Figure 4.5.

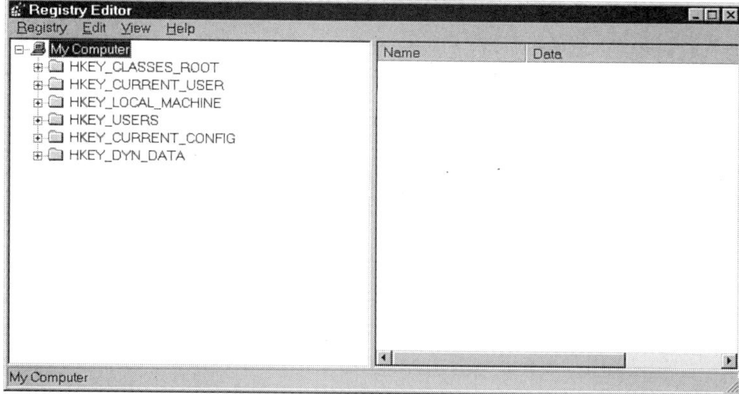

FIGURE 4.5
Each folder represents a Registry key.

3. Expand HKEY_ CURRENT_USER to show the following key:

   `HKEY_CURRENT_USER\Software\Microsoft\Office\9.0\Common\Open Find\Places\StandardPlaces`

4. To replace one of the default places, you must first hide one of the default places. Select one of the subkeys indented under the StandardPlaces key. Each subkey represents one of the five default buttons on the Places Bar:

   Desktop = Desktop button

   Favorites = Favorites button

   MyDocuments = My Documents button

   Recent = History button

   Publishing = Web Folders button

5. Choose Edit, New, DWORD Value.
6. Change the name of the new DWORD value to `Show` (see Figure 4.6). Leave the value of the *Show* DWORD at the default value.

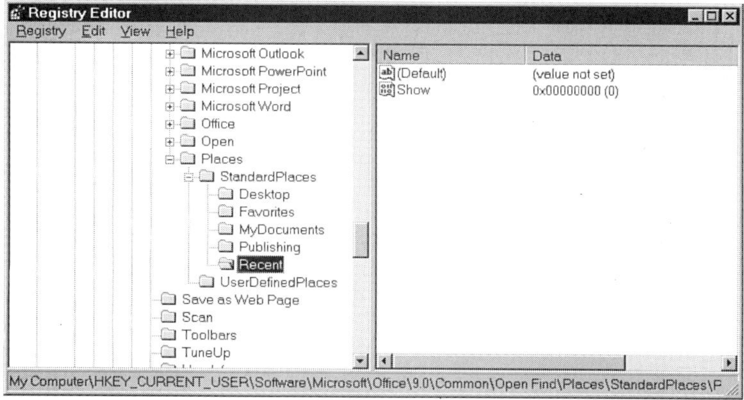

FIGURE 4.6
The Recent key, which represents the History places button, has been hidden.

7. After you have hidden one of the default places, you can add your own item on the Places Bar. First select the UserDefinedPlaces subkey.
8. Choose Edit, New, Key.
9. Change the name of this new key to `PlaceX`; where X is any value between 1 and 5. This *does not* set the position on the Places Bar of the key you are adding, but merely assists in keeping track of the keys you define.
10. With the *PlaceX* subkey selected, choose Edit, New, String Value.
11. Change the name of this string value to `Name`. With the *Name* subkey selected, choose Edit, New, String Value.
12. Double-click the string value and type the name you want displayed on the button for the new place you're adding to the Places Bar (see Figure 4.7).

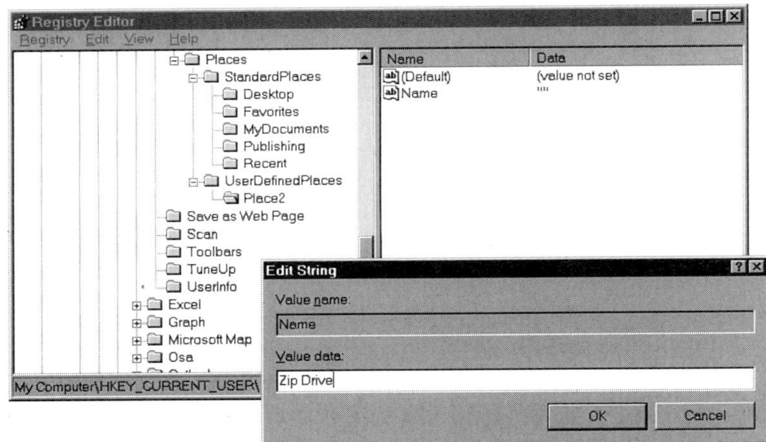

FIGURE 4.7
Name the button you are adding.

13. Select the new subkey, *PlacesX*, you created in step 9 and choose Edit, New, String Value.
14. Change the name of this string value to `Path`.
15. Double-click the *Path* string value and set the Data Value to the full path to any folder (see Figure 4.8).

Close the Registry Editor and access either the Open or Save As dialog boxes. You will see the changes to the Places Bar, as shown in Figure 4.9.

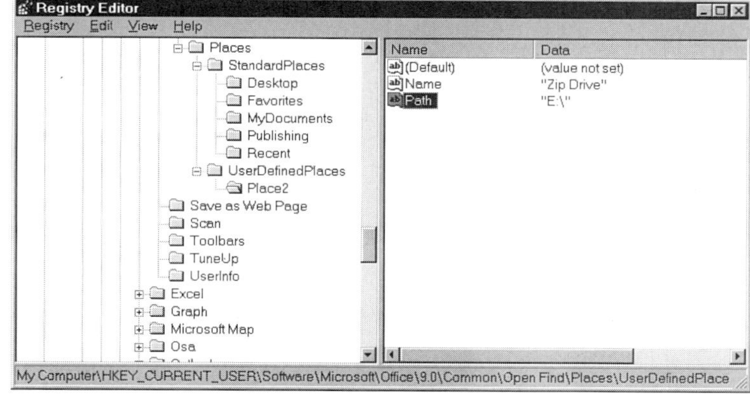

FIGURE 4.8
You can specify a path to a drive, a folder, or a URL. For example, the path to the annual budget folder would be c:\my documents\annual budget.

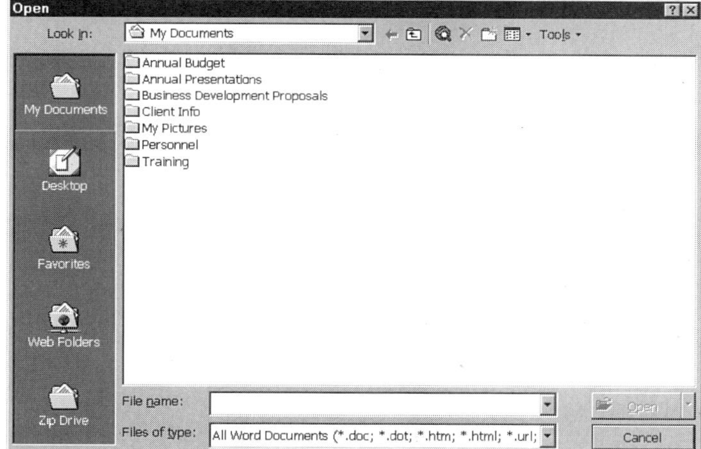

FIGURE 4.9
Standard places are always listed before user-defined places.

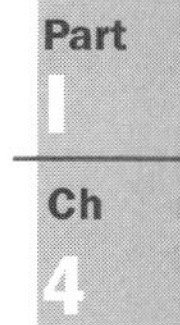

Doubling the Number of Buttons on the Places Bar

You can expand the number of buttons on the Places Bar from 5 to 10, by reducing the size of the buttons:

1. Open Windows Explorer and display the contents of the Windows folder.
2. Double-click the Regedit.exe file. The Registry Editor window opens.
3. Expand HKEY_ CURRENT_USER to show the following key:

   `HKEY_CURRENT_USER\Software\Microsoft\Office\9.0\Common\Open Find\Places`

4. Choose Edit, New, DWORD Value.

5. Change the name of the new DWORD value to `ItemSize`. Leave the value of *ItemSize* at its default value.
6. Repeat steps 8–15 from the previous section for each item you want to add to the Places Bar.

Close the Registry Editor and access either the Open or Save As dialog boxes. You will see the changes to the Places Bar, as shown in Figure 4.10.

FIGURE 4.10
The revised Places Bar with several new user-defined places added.

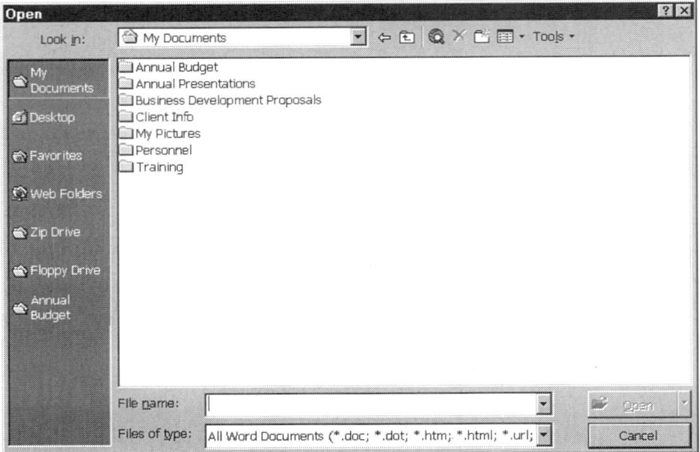

Altering the Behavior of the Personalized Menus and Toolbars

Realizing that people use a handful of commands frequently, other commands occasionally, and some commands not at all, Microsoft has revamped the behavior of the menus and toolbars in Office 2000.

Microsoft claims that the personalized menus and toolbars are designed with the increasing productivity of *all* users in mind. After avoiding them for quite a while, I have to grudgingly agree that for *advanced* users the new behavior of the menus will be useful. Because I'm a point-and-click type of Office user, I still prefer to see the full Standard and Formatting toolbars in each application. As for new users (and in most of the classes I teach), I encourage people to double-click the menus to see the full list of commands—at least until they become familiar with under which menu each command is located.

NOTE Microsoft uses a rather complex formula for determining when to promote and demote items from prominence in the personalized menus–the computation involves the number of times the application is launched and how many successive launches a given feature goes unused. As you use commands, the ones you use more frequently appear on the menu, and ones you don't use at all get suppressed. The end result is that what you use most frequently ends up on the abbreviated personalized menus.

Adjusting the Menu Behavior

If you want to see the full list of commands every time you click a menu, you can adjust the menu behavior in the Customize dialog box. Right-click a menu or toolbar, and choose Customize from the shortcut menu. In the Customize dialog box, click the Options tab, as shown in Figure 4.11.

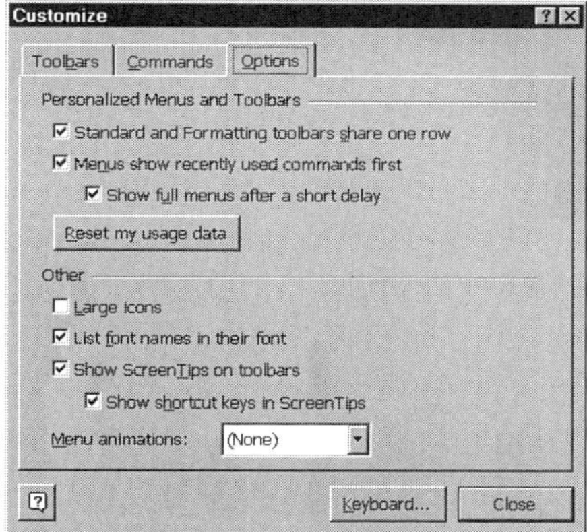

FIGURE 4.11
Personalized menus are turned on by default in Office 2000.

Remove the check from the Menus Show Recently Used Commands First option and click Close to turn off the personalized menus. Making this change affects the menu behavior in all applications, not just the application you are currently in.

NOTE You can also gain access to the Customize dialog box by selecting Tools, Customize or View, Toolbars, Customize.

You can also customize the items that appear on the application menus (discussed later in this chapter).

Adjusting the Toolbar Behavior

When you first open the Office 2000 applications, the Standard and Formatting toolbars share one line at the top of the window (see Figure 4.12). Initially, most of the Standard toolbar is displayed, and only a small part of the Formatting toolbar. There is a move handle in front of each toolbar with which you can move or adjust each toolbar. You can drag the Formatting toolbar move handle to the left to see more of the Formatting toolbar. However, to make room for these buttons, some of the buttons on the Standard toolbar will be hidden.

NOTE You can also use the move handle to reposition a toolbar. If you drag a toolbar to the edge of the application window or to a place next to another docked toolbar, it becomes docked at that position.

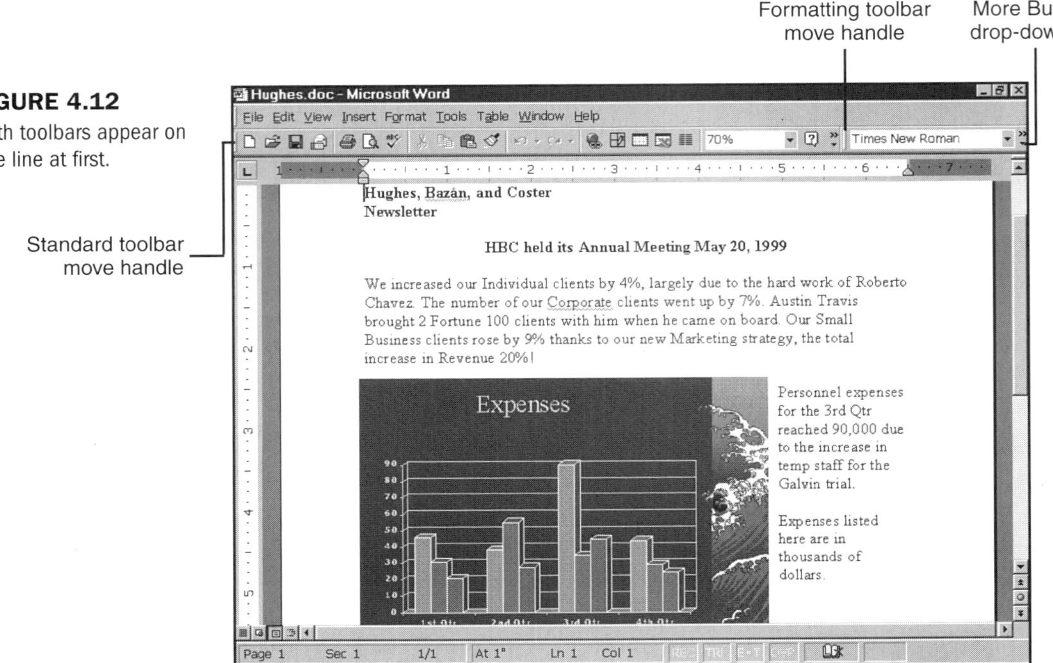

FIGURE 4.12
Both toolbars appear on one line at first.

Each toolbar has a set of default buttons that it displays. Although the Standard and Formatting toolbars share one line, there isn't enough space to show all the default buttons on both toolbars.

The buttons you use most frequently are displayed on the toolbar; the buttons you use least frequently are hidden—hence the name *personalized toolbars*. You access the hidden buttons through the More Buttons drop-down list at the end of the toolbar (refer to Figure 4.12). When you click a hidden button, that button is added to the toolbar. To make room for the button, however, one of the buttons that has not been used recently is placed on the More Buttons list.

If you want to see all the buttons on the Standard and Formatting toolbars, you can display the toolbars on separate rows. The easiest way to do this is to drag the move handle of the Formatting toolbar so that it is positioned below the Standard toolbar.

Alternatively, you can right-click any toolbar and choose Customize. On the Options tab remove the check from the Standard and Formatting Toolbars Share One Row option and click Close.

CAUTION

Except in Microsoft Word, this setting is application specific; it does not change the appearance of the toolbars in the other Office programs.

If you have multiple Word documents open and you manually drag a toolbar to a different position, such as from sharing one row to being docked one under the other, that toolbar setting is specific to that document during the active session.

Quickly Customizing Personalized Toolbars

If you have the Standard and Formatting toolbars sharing one line, then there is a quick way to customize those toolbars. In addition to listing the active, but hidden buttons, the More Buttons drop-down list also has an Add or Remove Buttons option to quickly customize a toolbar—a nice improvement in Office 2000.

When you click the Add or Remove Buttons drop-down list, the default buttons appear. There may be an arrow button at the top or bottom to see additional toolbar buttons. Figure 4.13 shows the list of buttons for the Standard toolbar in Word.

- Buttons with check marks are the current set of buttons appearing on the toolbar, from the default set of buttons associated with the toolbar.
- Buttons without check marks are not currently displayed on the toolbar. They are additional buttons you can add to the toolbar, from the default set of buttons associated with the toolbar.
- Buttons that are grayed out are *not* part of the default set of buttons associated with the toolbar. They are buttons that have been manually added to the toolbar through the Customize dialog box.

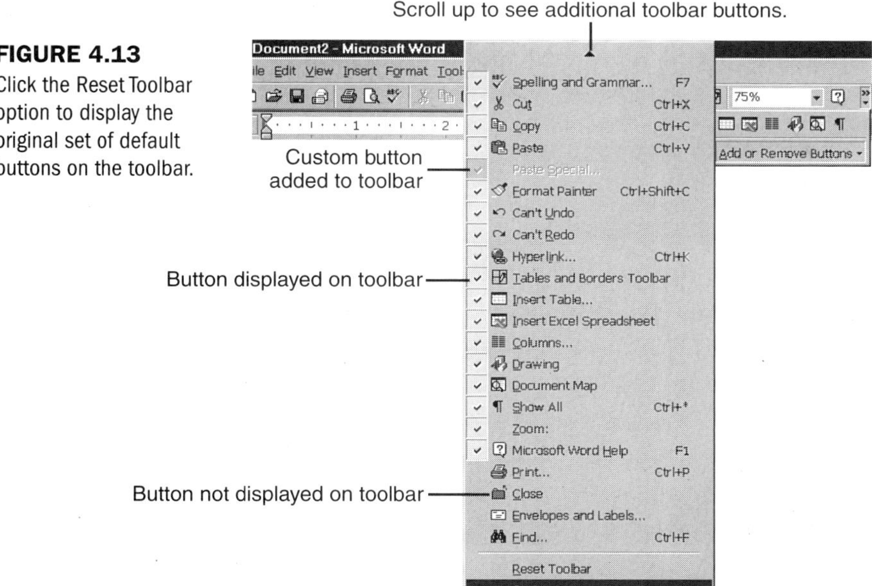

FIGURE 4.13
Click the Reset Toolbar option to display the original set of default buttons on the toolbar.

Customizing Application Toolbars

Toolbars are an efficient means for you to interact with your Office documents. Some of the toolbar buttons are vital to the way you work, although others are rarely used. In addition, you may find that there are tasks you perform frequently for which there are no toolbar buttons available. Likewise, if you've created macros to perform some action, you may want to add a toolbar button to execute the macro.

You can customize toolbars to remove the buttons you rarely use and replace them with buttons to help perform those tasks you use more frequently. You can also make the buttons more useful by

- Editing the design on button.
- Adding or changing the ScreenTip (formerly called ToolTip) associated with the button.

To create a new toolbar or customize an existing one, you must display the Customize dialog box. Right-click any toolbar and select Customize from the shortcut menu.

The Customize dialog box (shown in Figure 4.14) displays the custom choices on three tabs:

- Toolbars—You can choose to display or hide a toolbar by checking or unchecking the toolbar name. New toolbars can be created, renamed, or deleted, and toolbars you have customized can be reset back to display their original buttons.
- Commands—Using the button categories, you can add a tool to a toolbar (or a command to a menu).
- Options—From this tab you can change the behavior of the personalized menus and toolbars, enlarge the tool button size, display the font style in the Font drop-down list on the Formatting toolbar, control what is displayed in the toolbar button ScreenTip, or designate how the menus are animated.

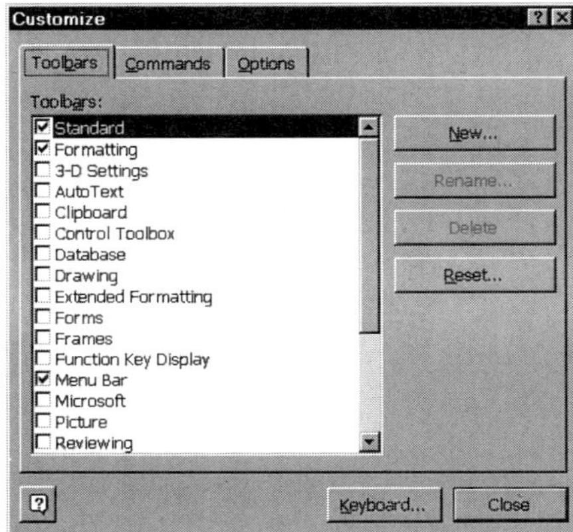

FIGURE 4.14
From the Customize dialog box, you can also resize combo box buttons and rearrange the order of the buttons on a toolbar.

Adding and Removing Toolbar Buttons

Before you can add or remove buttons from a toolbar, the toolbar must be displayed on the screen. If necessary, click the Toolbars tab in the Customize dialog box and display the toolbar you want to edit.

To add toolbar buttons, select the Commands tab. All application commands are grouped into categories. When you locate the command button that you want to add to a toolbar, drag the button from the Commands list onto the toolbar. By positioning the button between two existing buttons, the button drops into place and existing buttons move to the right to accommodate it.

One nice feature of the toolbars is that if you add more buttons than can be displayed on a single toolbar line, those buttons at the far-right end begin to wrap to a new line for the toolbar. The grouping of the buttons determines how many buttons wrap. Setting and changing groups is discussed later in this chapter.

NOTE Commands you add to the toolbars may or may not have icon buttons; those without icon buttons are displayed as text buttons.

To rearrange buttons, select a button (a heavy border indicates the button is selected) and drag it to another position. A thick capital I symbol indicates the position of the button when you release the mouse.

To remove a button from a toolbar, drag it off its toolbar and release it in the center of the screen away from other toolbars.

Anytime you want to quickly remove a button from a toolbar, hold down the Alt key and drag the button off the toolbar. You do not have to have the Customize dialog box displayed to remove buttons from toolbars.

Grouping Command Buttons

Command buttons on the toolbars are organized into groups. Vertical separator bars distinguish one group from another. When you right-click a button, a shortcut menu appears with a list of items you can adjust about that command button including one that enables you to add a separator bar in front of the active command button. Figure 4.15 shows the Copy command selected on the Standard toolbar and the items on the shortcut menu.

To add a separator bar, right-click the command button that is to the right of where you want the separator bar to appear. From the shortcut menu, choose Begin a Group. A check mark appears in front of the option to indicate a separator bar has been added. You can remove a separator bar from a button by selecting the button to the right of the separator bar and removing the check mark.

Resizing Combo Box Commands Combo box commands are two-part boxes that combine a text box with an entry list arrow used to select an option. The Formatting toolbar in most applications has at least two combo boxes—Font and Font Size. The width of the text box can be changed while the Customize dialog box is active.

To adjust the size of the combo box commands, select the combo box and position the mouse pointer over one side of the box. The mouse pointer changes to a four-headed dark arrow. Then drag the edge of the combo box to the desired size.

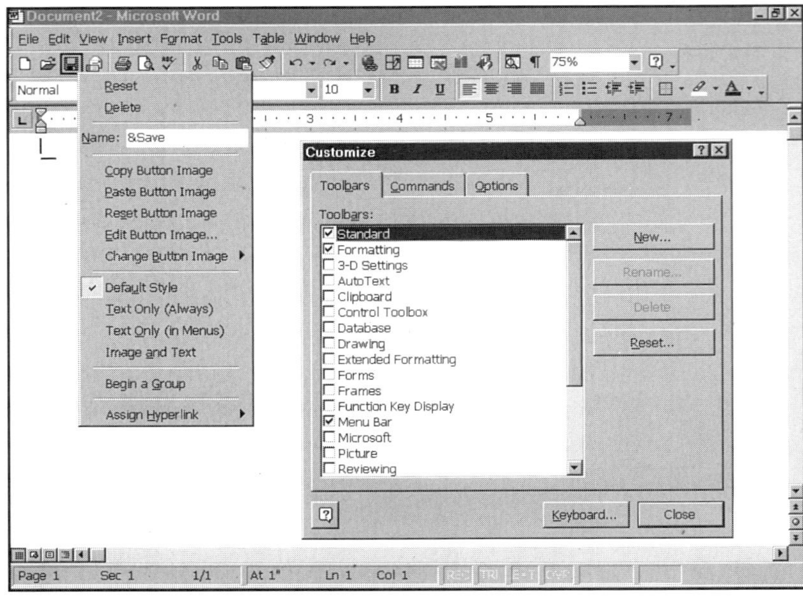

FIGURE 4.15
The shortcut menu enables you to change the display of command buttons on toolbars.

Restoring the Built-In Toolbars

Toolbars that install with the Microsoft Office applications remain a part of the application even after you customize them. As a result, they can be reset, but they can't be deleted. Resetting a toolbar restores the default buttons to a toolbar. The reset option is on the Toolbars tab of the Customize dialog box.

From the Toolbars tab in the Customize dialog box, select the toolbar you want to restore to its default settings and choose Reset. A warning message appears to confirm the action. Choose OK to restore the toolbar.

CAUTION

Resetting a toolbar removes *all* customized changes you have made to that toolbar–not just the most recent changes. If you have placed custom buttons on a toolbar that you plan to reset, you lose the custom buttons. Drag the custom buttons to another toolbar if you want to preserve them.

Creating New Toolbars

Sometimes the buttons you use most frequently are on several different toolbars. Instead of having four or five toolbars displayed—significantly reducing the space available on the screen to view your documents—you may want to have one or two toolbars that contain most (if not all) the command buttons you regularly use.

Creating a new toolbar from scratch creates an empty floating toolbar window that you must fill with the command buttons you need.

To build a new toolbar, follow these steps:

1. With the Customize dialog box active, click the Toolbars tab.
2. Choose New to open the New Toolbar dialog box. Office assigns a generic number sequentially to each new toolbar and identifies the toolbar name as Custom *number*, such as Custom 1.
3. Type the new toolbar name. Toolbar names must be unique and are limited to any combination of 50 characters and spaces.
4. Choose OK.

The new toolbar appears in the list on the Toolbars tab and the new empty toolbar appears beside the dialog box (see Figure 4.16). Select the Commands tab and drag command buttons onto the toolbar to create the collection you want. The toolbar enlarges as you add command buttons. You can dock the toolbar or leave it floating.

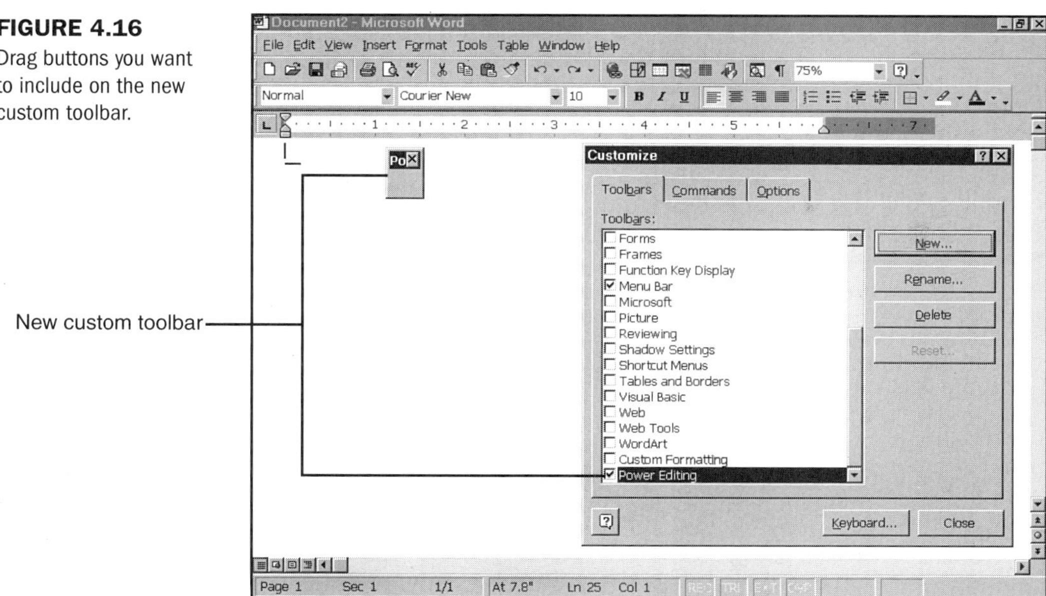

FIGURE 4.16
Drag buttons you want to include on the new custom toolbar.

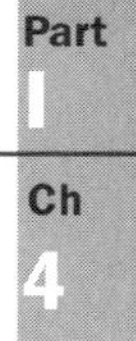

New toolbars you create can be deleted when you no longer want or need them. From the Toolbars tab in the Customize dialog box, select the toolbar you want to remove and choose Delete. A warning dialog box appears asking you to confirm the deletion of the toolbar. Choose OK to delete the toolbar.

Customizing Toolbar Command Buttons

Some of the commands available in the Customize dialog box have a blank button image associated with them. When these commands are added to a toolbar, only the name of the command is displayed.

Additionally, there will be times when no command button is available for a task you perform frequently, and it may be necessary for you to create a macro to record the steps of such a task. After you have created the macro, the name of the macro is listed on the Commands tab of the Customize dialog box. As with other commands, a blank button image is associated with the macro command. When the command is added to a toolbar, only the name of the macro is displayed.

▶ **See** "Planning Your Macro," **p. 108**

When you want to add a new command that will perform a custom function to a toolbar, you'll probably want the button image to carry a distinctive design so that you won't confuse it with other buttons on the toolbar.

Through the Customize dialog box, you can copy an existing design or access the Button Editor dialog box so you can customize the button design for blank buttons. If another button carries a design that resembles the one you want to use on the new button, you can copy the design from the button to the Clipboard and then paste it on the blank button. Copying the design does not copy the function of the original button to the new button. After you paste the design on the blank button, you can then modify the design to customize it for the new button.

Changing the Button Image One way to change a button image is to use an image from the set of images available through the Customize dialog box. Right-click the button you want to change and select Change Button Image. A palette of images appears, as shown in Figure 4.17 in the next section. Click an image from the list to apply it to the button.

Copying a Button Image To copy the design of an existing toolbar button to another button, right-click the button that contains the image you want to use and choose Copy Button Image from the shortcut menu. Then point to the button to which you want to apply the design and right-click. Choose Paste Button Image to place the design on the new button.

Designing or Editing a Button Image You can also design your own image or edit an existing image for a command button. Right-click the command button and choose Edit Button Image, the Button Editor dialog box displays as shown in Figure 4.18. In this example, the button design for the Paste button has been copied to the Paste Special button. To avoid confusing the two buttons, the Paste Special button needs to be edited.

The button design appears enlarged so that individual pixels can be identified in the Picture box. You can then change the location of each pixel in the picture by using the mouse to achieve the desired design.

The Colors box is your palette for selecting colored pixels for your design. The Move arrows help you position the picture on the button by moving it one row or column at a time. The Preview area shows you how the current picture looks.

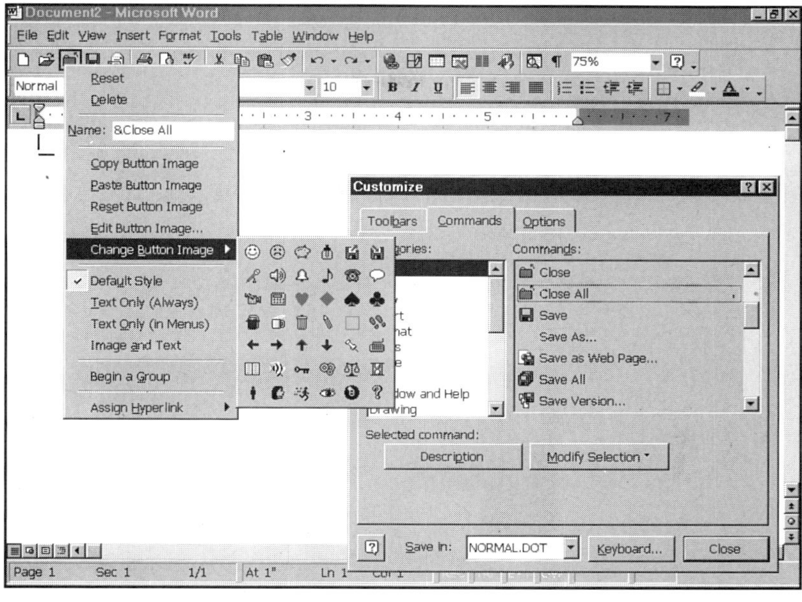

FIGURE 4.17
You can edit these images or design your own button image.

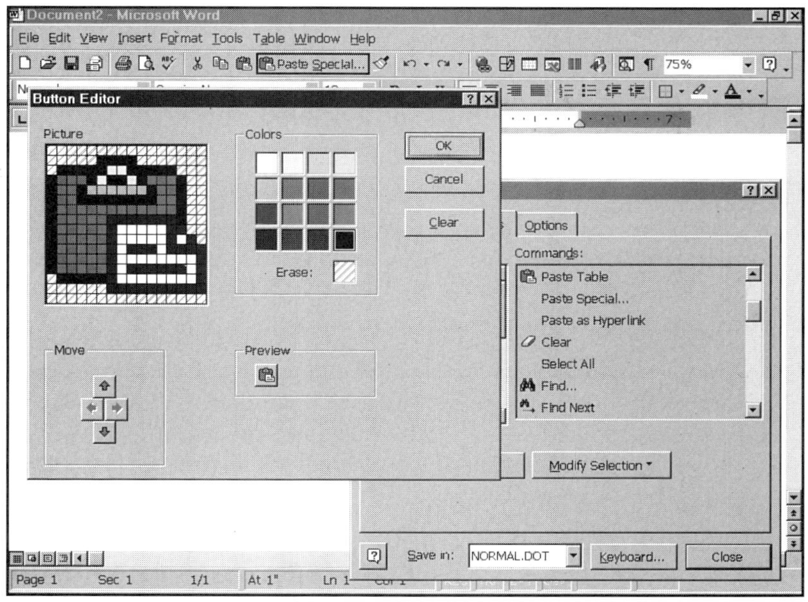

FIGURE 4.18
The Paste picture is selected as a template for building a new button.

To change the picture, use any of the following techniques:

- To change the color of any pixel, click a color in the Colors box and then click the pixel or drag the color across all pixels you want to color.

- To erase or clear pixels, click the erase box and then click all pixels you want to clear, drag the pointer across pixels you want to clear, or click a pixel a second time to clear the existing color.
- To reposition the picture on the button, clear an area along the edge toward which you want to move the design and then click the desired move button.
- To clear the picture canvas completely, choose Clear.
- To cancel changes to start over, choose Cancel or press Esc.

When the design appears as you want it, choose OK. The new design now appears on the new button. Figure 4.19 shows the finished picture that will be assigned to the Paste Special button.

FIGURE 4.19
The finished picture for the Paste Special button.

Creating Custom ScreenTips

The ScreenTips that appear when you rest your mouse over a toolbar button are actually the name assigned to that button command. To edit the ScreenTips, the Customize dialog box must be displayed.

Right-click the button and click Name on the shortcut menu; this highlights the current ScreenTip. Although it may look like only a short description is allowed, you can type lengthy ScreenTips (the text scrolls as you type). The ampersand (&) symbol is used when the button command is added to a menu and is not used when the button is on a toolbar. Type the new ScreenTip in the Name text box and press Enter. To check the new ScreenTip, you need to close the Customize dialog box.

Customizing Application Menus

Sometimes commands are buried so deeply on a menu that they aren't convenient to use. Or perhaps you've created macros that you want to access through the menus. In these situations, you will want to customize the application menus. As was the case with toolbars, existing menu bars displayed in Microsoft Office can be edited or you can create your own custom menu bar.

In Office 2000, the menu bar acts similar to the toolbars. By default, it is docked at the top of the screen, but like toolbars, it can be moved and docked at the side or bottom of the screen, or left floating in the middle of the screen. Additionally, the ways in which you customize a menu bar are similar to the ways you customize toolbars, described in the previous sections in this chapter.

In this version of Office, any command that has a pointing triangle is considered a menu. In Figure 4.20, the entire Table menu from Microsoft Word is active. Within the Table menu, there are five other built-in menus—Insert, Delete, Select, AutoFit, and Convert.

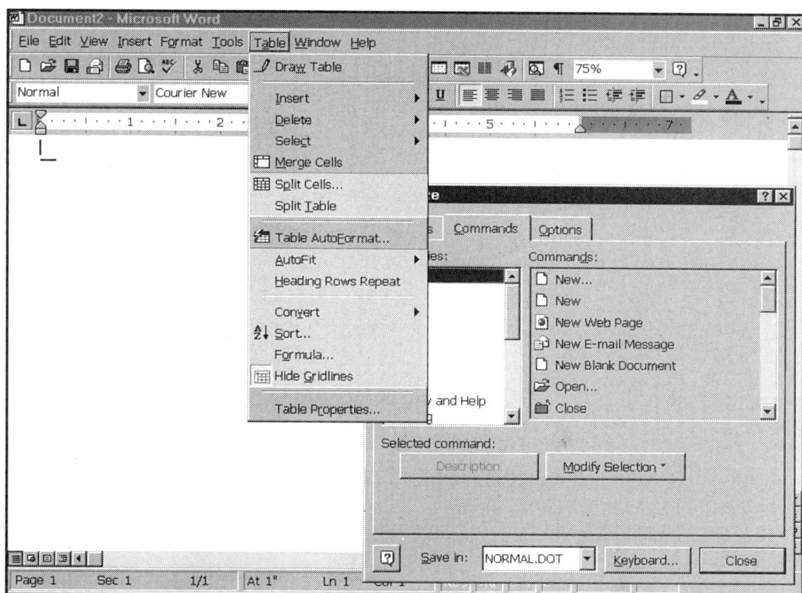

FIGURE 4.20
Built-in menus have a triangle.

As with the toolbars, you need to display the Customize dialog box to edit the menus. Right-click the menu bar and choose Customize to display the dialog box.

Adding a New Menu

You can add new menus to the main menu bar or embed them in an existing menu. To add a new menu, click the Commands tab in the Customize dialog box. Scroll to the bottom of the Categories list and choose the New Menu category. Drag the New Menu command to any position on the menu. When dragging the command onto an existing menu, the menu expands so that you can position the new menu where you want (see Figure 4.21).

When you create a new menu, you need to assign a name to it that reflects the special feature(s) attached to the menu. To name a menu, right-click the menu and click Name from the shortcut menu. This highlights the default name. Type the new menu name in the Name text box and press Enter.

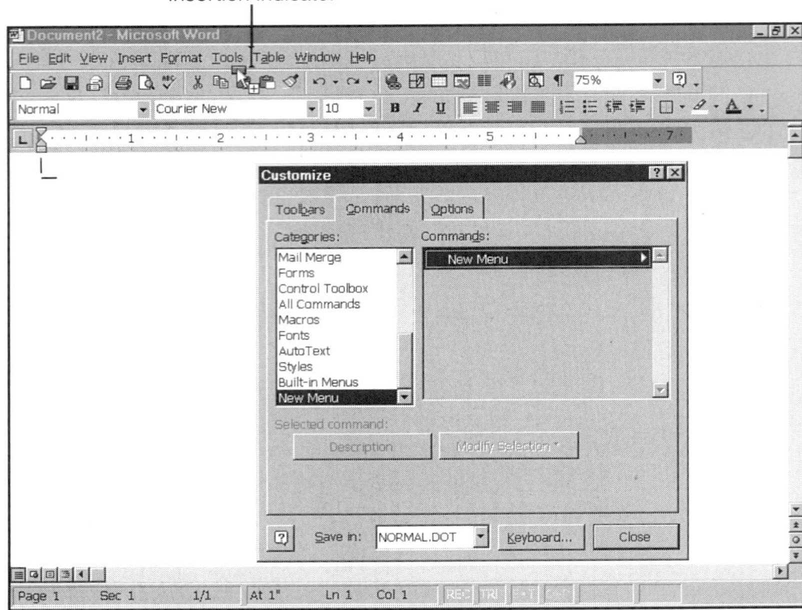

FIGURE 4.21
The position is indicated by a dark insertion indicator.

NOTE The ampersand (&) symbol is used in the Name text box to underline a letter in the name. This designates a keyboard shortcut if you typically use the keyboard (instead of the mouse) to activate and use menu commands.

Then proceed to add specific commands to the new menu, as described in the next section.

Adding and Removing Commands from a Menu

Adding items to the menu bar is identical to adding buttons to a toolbar. Select the category and item you want to add. Then drag the item onto the menu bar. By positioning the command between two existing commands, the new item drops into place.

To remove an entire menu or a command from a particular menu, drag it off the menu bar and release it in the center of the screen away from the menu bar and toolbars. You can also restore the menu bar to its original settings. Select the Toolbars tab and choose Menu Bar from the list of toolbars. Then click Reset. A warning message appears to confirm resetting the Menu Bar; choose OK.

CAUTION

Restoring the Menu Bar removes any custom menus you have created.

Moving and Grouping Menu Commands

The order of the menu commands on the menu bar can be rearranged by dragging the menu name to a different location. You can also reorder the commands within a particular menu. You select the menu name, and then the command within the menu you want to reorder. When rearranging the order of the menu commands, the Customize dialog box must be active.

As with the toolbars, command items on the menu bar can be ordered in groups. Horizontal separator bars distinguish one group from another. To add a separator bar, right-click the command above which you want the separator to appear. Then check the Begin a Group option from the shortcut menu.

Customizing Shortcut Menus

One of the new features in Office 2000 is the capability in most applications to customize the menus that appear when you right-click an object—*the shortcut menus.*

NOTE This feature is not available in Excel. When asked about this inconsistency, Microsoft indicated that "allowing menus to be available when they are not expected could, in some cases, cause Excel to crash." In other words, they couldn't isolate the problem that caused Excel to crash. If you want to see this (or any other) feature implemented in the next version of Excel, submit a request through Microsoft's Wish Web site–discussed in Appendix B, "Suggested References."

These menus are treated like other menus; to customize them you must have the Customize dialog box open. To display the Customize dialog box, right-click any toolbar and choose Customize from the shortcut menu. From the Toolbars tab, choose Shortcut Menus. A floating toolbar appears listing the shortcut menus you can alter in that application. Figure 4.22 shows the shortcut menus for Microsoft PowerPoint. You alter the shortcut menu in the same way you modify the toolbars and menu bar—by dragging commands from the Commands tab in the Customize dialog box to the menu.

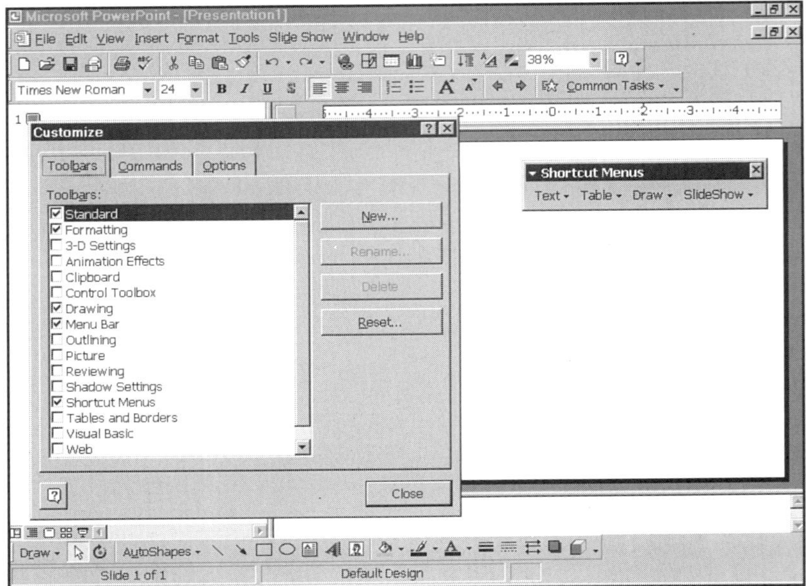

FIGURE 4.22
The shortcut menus automatically appear when you open the Customize dialog box in PowerPoint.

Editing Entries in the Custom Dictionary

Microsoft Office contains two dictionaries—one with all the words Microsoft thinks need to be part of its spellchecker, and another (aptly called custom) that contains any words you designate by clicking the Add button in the Spelling dialog box. All the Microsoft Office applications use these two dictionaries when you spell check a document.

If you have added a word mistakenly or have a lot of words you want to add all at once, you can edit the words in the custom dictionary. This can be accomplished only from within Microsoft Word. Choose Tools, Options and click the Spelling & Grammar tab. Click the Dictionaries button and the Custom Dictionaries dialog box appears, as shown in Figure 4.23.

Select the dictionary you want to edit (making sure you do not remove the check) and click Edit.

A warning message appears indicating that the automatic spell check feature will be turned off as a result of editing the dictionary. You will need to turn it back on after you complete editing the custom dictionary. Click OK.

The words in the custom dictionary are displayed in alphabetical order in a Microsoft Word document. To add words, click anywhere in the list and type the first word. Press Enter so that each word appears on a separate line. You can also edit or delete words, just as you would edit any other Word document.

After you have concluded editing the custom dictionary, save and close the file.

Turn the automatic spell checking feature back on by selecting Tools, Options and click the Spelling & Grammar tab. Mark the Check Spelling As You Type option and click OK.

FIGURE 4.23
You can create additional custom dictionaries by selecting New.

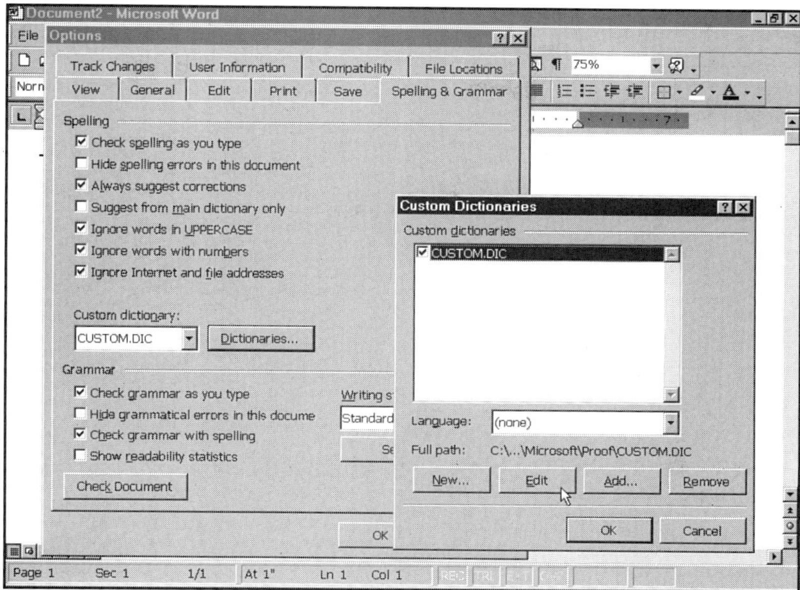

Customizing the Interface Language

Microsoft Office 2000 supports multiple languages on the same computer. A single workstation can be used by multiple people to create and edit documents in different languages. To use multilanguage support, you must have purchased and installed the Multilanguage Pack.

▶ **See** "International Features," **p. 34**

Creating Custom Help Screens

Office 2000 allows the information contained in many of the Office error messages, or alerts, to be customized. You can also selectively disable the built-in error messages. Because most error messages are pretty blunt, this provides a way to provide more information, instead of leaving users frustrated (or dialing the help desk phone number).

For example, instead of receiving the message `access denied` when a person attempts to delete a file to which they only have read permission, a customized error message could provide more information or point them to a Web page on your intranet with further information about the error message, and possibly some alternative actions they can take.

To customize these messages, you need to use a scripting tool to create or edit the message, such as Microsoft Visual Basic Scripting Edition or a CGI-based scripting tool. These messages are created using Active Server Pages (ASPs). An Internet Information Server (IIS) is also required. Chapter 63 provides more information about creating these messages.

PART II

Visual Basic for Applications (VBA)—A Primer

CHAPTER 5

Getting Acquainted with VBA

In this chapter

What Is VBA?

Visual Basic for Applications (VBA) is the programming language that has been used to create user-defined Microsoft Office applications since Excel version 5.0's release in 1993. It was the long-awaited fulfillment of a Microsoft goal to provide a rich development environment that is usable throughout the Office suite. Expanded in Office 97 to include Word, Access, and PowerPoint, it has been enhanced further in Office 2000 to include Outlook and FrontPage.

This chapter, along with Chapter 6, "Successful VBA Modules," shows how to harness the power of the Office applications. In every application, you reach a point where you think: "I really wish I could…" Well, you can! You can automate common tasks, eliminate some annoying features, and add needed functionality by using macros, building on those macros by editing them, or taking that "step beyond" and writing the code from scratch to meet your specific requirements. VBA is the programming language in all Office 2000 products: Word, Excel, Access, PowerPoint, Outlook, FrontPage, and even the Office Assistant. You won't find it, however, in PhotoDraw 2000 or in Publisher 2000.

Indeed, Microsoft has licensed the VBA environment to other companies such as Visio, to include in their programs. After you learn to develop procedures in one environment, you can quickly learn how to program in others.

▶ **See** "Converting Word Macros," **p. 200**

You Don't Have to Be a Programmer to Use VBA

It isn't necessary to be a programmer to fine-tune Office 2000 to be your workhorse. You just need to be willing to record a macro or type in a few lines of code (which looks more like English text than you might think) to pull in the benefits of the VBA snippets throughout this book. In fact, you can just cut and paste the code from the CD-ROM that accompanies this book! The code from the CD alone will give you a significant level of enhancement over the standard installation of Office 2000.

If you are willing to take yet a few more steps, you can control virtually every aspect of Office 2000. Indeed, even the features of the Windows operating system can be manipulated through your VBA code—code that you write in Access, Word, Excel, PowerPoint, Outlook, and FrontPage. The best part is if you start playing with macros and VBA code in one of the Office products, you've started the process that opens up the entire suite.

Because the structure and syntax of VBA is the same throughout, you can customize that program's features and even pull in the features of other Office 2000 programs. For example, from within Word you can create a spreadsheet in Excel, pull data from Access into the spreadsheet, analyze the data to provide your answer, and then place that answer in your Word document—all occurring behind the scenes, without even seeing the other programs and launched by an action as simple as placing a check in a check box.

NOTE Programming in VBA is similar to Object-Oriented Programming (OOP). That is to say, it manipulates objects, such as workbooks, worksheets, and ranges, in its code. It isn't a true Object-Oriented Programming language because some of the specifications for *true* object orientation are not fully met, as they are in C++ or Java. However, it is an object-using programming language and, for most purposes, VBA meets all the specifications you need. ■

From the start, Microsoft's plan was to incorporate Visual Basic into its other business-related products. For the end user and developer alike, this means that by learning how to create and edit Visual Basic procedures in Excel 2000, you can transfer those skills and that knowledge to other Office products, such as Word, PowerPoint, Access, the Binder, Outlook, and even the Office Assistant. VBA also extends the functionality of Microsoft Project 98 (not a member of the Office suite) and a number of products developed by other companies that have licensed the use of VBA in their programs.

Choosing Between Macros and Ready-Made VBA Code

This book provides two avenues toward learning and becoming proficient with VBA:

- Using the Macro Recorder to record the steps you take to complete a task—This method—which enables you to automate mundane, repetitive tasks—is covered in the next few pages. This method requires little knowledge of VBA because the VBA code is written for you as you record the macro. In many cases, you'll be able to record macros and have little or no involvement with the actual code.
- Type in or copy snippets of code in the Visual Basic Editor—This technique is covered in the next chapter. You will find ready-made snippets of code throughout the other chapters of this book and on the accompanying CD-ROM. This method requires some working knowledge of VBA, although we've written all the code for you. All you'll need to learn is how to copy and paste the code into the Visual Basic Editor and how to work with the basic controls.

NOTE Is it Visual Basic or is it Visual Basic for Applications? The answer is a qualified "yes." Both use the same core programming language, Visual Basic 6, but the difference between the two lies in the application–literally. The programming language Visual Basic is used to develop standalone applications–programs as independent as Word is from WordPerfect. Visual Basic for Applications is used only within the context of an application, that is, within Word, Excel, FrontPage, and so on. You cannot develop a standalone application with VBA. (It can and may look like one, but its core is one of the products that supports VBA.) The primary difference between the applications that support VBA is the object model used to manipulate the environment. Word has its own object model, as do Excel, PowerPoint, FrontPage, and so on. Each object model is unique to the tasks each must perform. ■

NOTE Another way to become proficient in VBA is to learn how to program with VBA from scratch. VBA is a powerful tool that can provide many benefits, but like any complex tool, it takes some time and a good reference to master. If this is something you want to pursue, I suggest *Special Edition Using Visual Basic 6*, published by Que.

Remember, relax! It's not like you're taking a hammer to your computer. If your macro or snippet doesn't work—your computer won't blow up and, with a small amount of preparation, you won't lose any data, either.

Your VBA experience starts with the Macro Recorder. The next section of this chapter explains the process of recording a macro. The steps that follow use Excel as the platform for recording your macro. These steps are virtually identical in Word and PowerPoint. Outlook and FrontPage do not provide any way to record a macro; in Access it is possible, although difficult.

▶ **See** "Using Macros and VBA in Access," **p. 1139**

Macros can also be created for Outlook and FrontPage by typing them out in the Visual Basic Editor.

Planning Your Macro

You should always plan the steps and commands that you want the macro to perform *before* you create the macro. If you make a mistake when you record the macro, your corrections are also recorded. Additionally, you need to consider the following items before recording a macro:

- Activating the macro—Consider how you plan to run the macro. You can run it from the menu, a button on a toolbar, a shortcut key, a graphic object in your file, or any combination of these choices. Base your decision on what your macro performs and how often you'll use it.
- Storing the macro—In Excel, you can store your macro in the currently active workbook, a new workbook, or the Personal Macro Workbook. The default location is the active workbook. In PowerPoint, all macros must be stored in the presentation. In Word, macros can be stored in templates or documents. Excel and PowerPoint place all newly recorded macros in a single module attached to the file; this module stores all macros recorded during that application session. Later sessions create new macro modules as needed (called Module1, Module2, and so on). Word places all newly recorded macros in a single module called NewMacros, even from session to session. In all cases, these module sheets are visible only in the Visual Basic Editor.

  Storing macros in the active file means you can use the macros only when that file is open. Storing macros in the Personal Macro Workbook (for Excel) or in the Normal Template (for Word) provides access to the macros whenever the program is open.

NOTE In Excel, the Personal Macro Workbook is open, by default, as a hidden workbook whenever Excel is open, and it is created the first time you store a macro in it. To Edit the Personal Macro Workbook, choose Window, Unhide... and then select Personal.xls from the list.

- Naming the macro—The first character of your macro's name must be a letter. Other name characters can be letters, numbers, or underscore characters. Spaces can't be used in a macro name. Name your macros so you know what function they perform when you want to run them. Using capital letters and the underscore character as a word separator make your macro names more readable. For example, you could name macros with simple names such as `ApplyCorporateHeading`.

Selecting Cells in Excel

If you select cells while recording a macro, the macro always selects the same cells every time it runs. It doesn't matter where the active cell currently is when you choose to run the macro.

If you want to select cells relative to the position of the active cell, set the Macro Recorder to use relative cell references. On the Stop Recording toolbar, select the Relative Reference toggle button. The Macro Recorder now records macros with relative cell references until you click Relative Reference again or close Excel. You can mix the use of relative and absolute references when you record the macro, by selecting the Relative Reference button when you want to use relative cell referencing and by deselecting it when you want to use absolute cell referencing.

Suppose you have a number of quarterly sales sheets for the various divisions in your company, such as the list displayed in Figure 5.1. Although the data is accurate, the worksheets don't have uniform, polished headings that you can use with a client. You want to change the style and background for each of the worksheets, but instead of formatting each worksheet separately, you decide to create a macro to speed up the process and to ensure consistency in your spreadsheets.

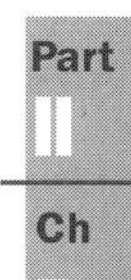

FIGURE 5.1
The worksheet is shown here, before the macro is created.

	A	B	C	D	E
1	Texas Division Sales				
2	Enterprise Software				
3		First Quarter	Second Quarter	Third Quarter	Fourth Quarter
4	TCP/IP Wizard	$4,500	$2,395	$6,720	$6,500
5	Evaluation Pro	$10,150	$8,000	$7,900	$11,900
6	Lizard Lan	$22,000	$24,000	$20,000	$23,500
7	Capacity Chart	$5,300	$3,000	$4,400	$5,000
8	Code Monitor	$2,500	$2,750	$3,100	$2,500
9	Total	$44,450	$40,145	$42,120	$49,400

Your first step is to plan the macro. Walk through the steps you want to record several times to make sure you know what to do and how to do it in the most efficient manner. Remember the recorder records mistakes as well as corrections; consider writing the steps out on a pad of paper. For example:

1. Select cells A1 through E2.
2. Change the font type and size, center across the columns, and change the background color to red.
3. Select cells A3 through E3.
4. Make the text bold and centered in the cells, and change the background color to blue.
5. Select cell A4.

After you identify the steps you want the macro to perform, you are ready to record the macro.

Recording a Macro

Recording a macro involves performing the exact steps you want the macro to perform. To record a macro, follow these steps:

1. Choose Tools, Macro, Record New Macro. The Record Macro dialog box appears, as shown in Figure 5.2.

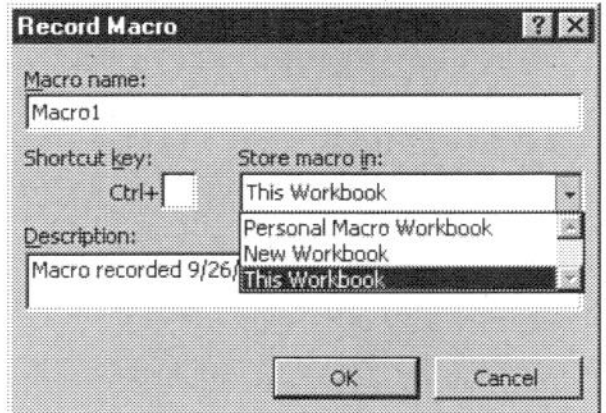

FIGURE 5.2
The default settings in the Record Macro dialog box are shown here.

2. In the Macro Name text box, type a descriptive name for the macro. The name must start with a letter and cannot contain spaces. Enter a description of the macro in the Description box. Be sure to describe what the macro does when run.
3. The Shortcut Key box lets you select a keyboard shortcut to run your macro. Type any letter into the box, except for numbers and special characters. Use the Shift key for uppercase. This results in the shortcut key being Ctrl+Shift+"*your letter.*" If no keyboard shortcut is entered, the macro is accessible by choosing Tools, Macro, Macros.

   In Word, there are two buttons available to assign the macro to a toolbar or to assign a shortcut key, rather than a small text box in the Record Macro dialog box. Selecting one or the other opens another dialog box that enables you to choose the keyboard stroke for your macro or to assign your macro to a button on a Word toolbar. In PowerPoint, no option exists for assigning a shortcut key.

▶ **See** "Assigning a Macro to a Toolbar Button," **p. 112**

NOTE Be careful when you choose the shortcut key. It overrides any default shortcut key during the time the macro is available. For example, if you choose Ctrl+S as your macro's shortcut key, it overrides the application's File Save shortcut key while your macro is available.

▶ **See** "Creating Keyboard Shortcuts" and "Customizing the Restricted Keys," **p. 222-223**

4. Select a location for the macro from the Store Macro In drop-down list. To make a macro available whenever you use Excel, store the macro in the Personal Macro Workbook in the XLStart folder, which typically is located in C:\Program Files\Microsoft Office\Office\XLStart. (This folder is machine-specific, not user-specific.)

NOTE On Windows 9x systems that have User Profiles enabled, Excel's startup folder also can be in C:\Windows \Profiles\<*User Name*>\Application Data\Microsoft\Excel\XLStart. This folder is user-specific, not machine-specific, and can be used by roaming user profiles. By default, the Windows NT equivalent to the Windows folder is Winnt. The <*User Name*> is the user's logon ID (such as dlucas, rkughen, and so on).

- In Word, select a location for the macro from the Store Macro In drop-down list. To make a macro available whenever you use Word, store the macro in the Normal.dot template.
- In PowerPoint, the macro can be stored only in an open presentation or template and is available only when that presentation/template is open.

5. The date you create the macro and the username listed on the General tab (Excel or PowerPoint) or the User Information tab (Word) of the Options dialog box (choose Tools, Options) are entered automatically into the Description text box. The description appears when you select the macro from the menu or when you assign a macro to a toolbar button. You can change the description as desired. This description gives you the opportunity to specify what your macro does. After you have recorded a dozen or so, you may forget exactly what some of them do. That's when you need that documentation.
6. Choose OK to begin recording the macro. The Stop Recording toolbar appears.
7. Follow the steps for the macro exactly as you laid them out; remember the recorder records every action you take.

8. To stop the recording process, click the Stop Recording button on the Stop Recording toolbar. If, during the course of recording your macro, the Stop Recording toolbar is removed, you can stop recording your macro by choosing Tools, Macro, Stop Recording.

CAUTION

Be aware of when you turn off the Macro Recorder, or you may get surprising results. For example, suppose you want to record a macro that creates a colorful default heading for your company, which you can insert on all your older workbooks. You planned everything and started the macro. When the last step finishes, you close the workbook and stop the recording. When you start using your macro, you discover that every time you use the macro, your workbook closes. Why? Because you recorded closing the workbook! Stop recording at the point where you want to be when the macro is finished running.

Running a Macro

After recording a macro, you should test it to be sure it performs the intended steps. You can run the macro in the Office program in which you recorded the macro or from the Visual Basic Editor. Test it first in the Office program. Typically, you run a macro from the Visual Basic Editor when you want to test it during an editing session. The Visual Basic Editor is discussed later in this chapter.

Before running your macro, be sure you are in the correct place in your file to run it. For example, if you are currently working in one of your charts, running a macro designed for a worksheet generates an error. To run a macro, follow these steps:

1. Open the workbook that contains the macro. If your macro is in the Personal.XLS workbook (Personal Macro Workbook), you do not need to do this.
2. Choose Tools, Macro, Macros to display the Macro dialog box, as shown in Figure 5.3.

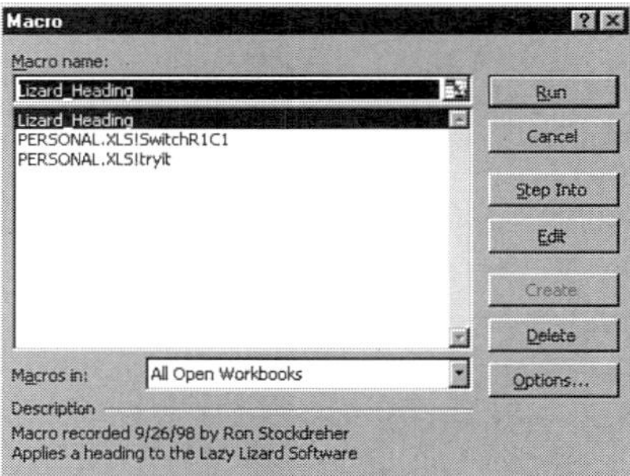

FIGURE 5.3
Be sure to select the correct macro by checking the description displayed at the bottom of the dialog box.

3. In the Macro Name box, select the name of the macro you want to run. In Figure 5.3, the macro Lizard_Heading is selected.
4. Click Run, and your macro runs exactly as you recorded it.

You can interrupt a macro before it completes its actions by pressing the Esc key.

Assigning a Macro to a Toolbar Button

Although the menu is a great place to *review* a complete collection of available macros, it's not the most convenient way to *run* a macro. Instead, you can improve access to your macro by assigning it to a toolbar button. The following steps show you how to assign a macro to a toolbar button:

1. Choose View, Toolbars, Customize.
2. In the Toolbars tab, select a toolbar to hold your macro. Because you can place your macro on any toolbar, choose one that matches the purpose of your macro and display it on the screen.

3. Select the Commands tab in the Customize dialog box. Scroll down in the Categories list and choose Macros. The only product that is different is Access; the category choice in Access is All Macros. The Customize dialog box appears as shown in Figure 5.4. Note that this dialog box appears with different options available for each of the Office applications.

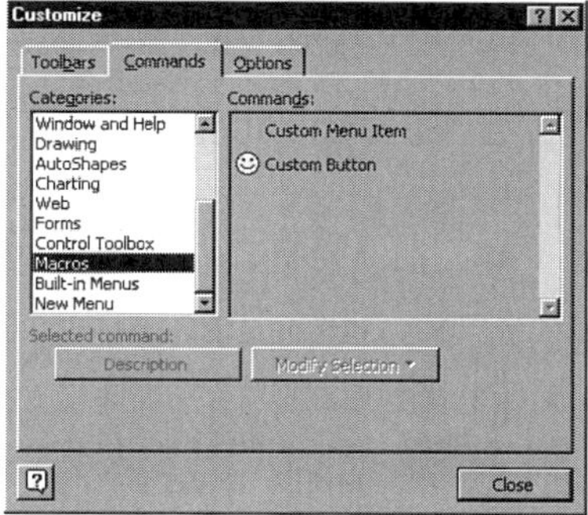

FIGURE 5.4
Use the Excel Customize dialog box to add macro buttons to your toolbars.

4. In Excel (refer to Figure 5.4), drag the Custom Button to the toolbar and drop it where you want to place it. In Word, Access, and PowerPoint, drag the selected macro to the toolbar and drop it where you want to place it.
5. After the custom button or macro name is on the toolbar, right-click the new button and choose how you want to display it. You can choose one of the following methods:
    - Default Style—For toolbar buttons, a button image that can be altered or replaced by using the Button Image commands on the shortcut menu (image only). For menu items, a button image together with text (image and text).
    - Text Only (Always)—Exclusively uses a text presentation. You can change the text by using Name on the shortcut menu. If you want to assign a hotkey to the name, place an ampersand in front of the letter you choose.
    - Text Only (In Menus)—Uses only the image when the custom button is on the toolbar and only text when you choose to place the command in a menu. Any hotkey assigned, of course, works with either the button or the text.
    - Image and Text—Displays the button and the text regardless of whether you choose to place the command on a toolbar or in a menu.
6. In Excel, with the Customize dialog box open, right-click the button and then select Assign Macro from the shortcut menu. The Assign Macro dialog box appears, as shown in Figure 5.5.
7. Select a macro from the Macro Name list in the Assign Macro dialog box, and click OK.

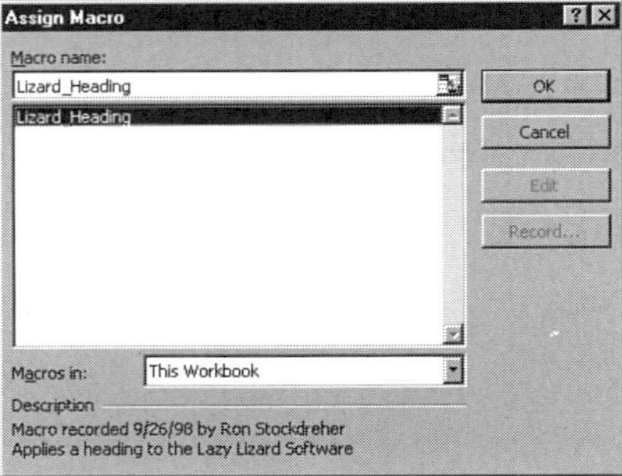

FIGURE 5.5
The description of the macro appears at the bottom of the Assign Macro dialog box.

NOTE Although you have the Customize dialog box open, you can edit the button image by right-clicking the image and selecting Edit Button Image. The image can't be changed unless the Customize dialog box is open. You can alter the standard buttons, too. Just right-click and express yourself.

8. Click Close to exit the Customize dialog box.

Assigning Macros to a Menu Command or Graphic Object

You can also assign a macro as a new menu command or to any graphic object. The following steps show you how to assign a macro as a new menu item:

1. Choose View, Toolbars, Customize.
2. Select the Commands tab in the Customize dialog box. Scroll down in the Categories list and choose Macros. (The only product that is different is Access; the category choice in Access is All Macros.) The Customize dialog box appears. Note that this dialog box appears with different options available for each of the Office applications.
3. In Excel (refer to Figure 5.4), drag the Custom Menu Item to the menu. An insertion point appears indicating where this new entry will be placed. If you place your mouse pointer over a menu command (for example, View), the list drops down and enables you to place your new entry on that list or any submenu's list. Drop it where you want to place it. In all other Office applications, you select the specific macro you want to use, drag it to the menu bar, and drop the command where you want to place it.
4. After the Custom Menu Item or macro name is on the toolbar, right-click the inserted object and choose how you want to display it. (See the options listed in the previous section on assigning a macro to a toolbar.)
5. In Excel, right-click the Custom Menu Item and select Assign Macro from the shortcut menu. The Assign Macro dialog box appears (refer to Figure 5.5).

6. Select a macro from the Macro Name list in the Assign Macro dialog box, and click OK.
7. Click Close to exit the Customize dialog box.

Assigning a macro to a graphic object in Office 2000 is done slightly differently in each application. Access and Word use ActiveX controls to accomplish this. For Access, this is covered in Chapter 41, "Using Macros and VBA in Access." In Word, you must add an ActiveX control to the document and use the Click event associated with that control.

▶ **See** "Using Events," **p. 165**

In Excel and PowerPoint, you can assign macros to graphic objects by following these steps:

1. Insert a graphic object. This can be a clip art object, a drawn item, or even an embedded chart.

NOTE If you want to create a hotspot in a particular graphic object, draw another graphic object over the first in the place where you want the hot spot. Set the fill and line properties to No Fill and No Line to make it transparent and assign the macro to this object.

   In Excel, right-click the object and choose Assign Macro from the shortcut menu. Choose the macro you want to assign from the Assign Macro dialog box and click OK. You can also record a macro from this point by creating a new, unique macro name and selecting Record Macro in the Assign Macro dialog box.

   In PowerPoint, right-click the object and choose Action Settings. When the Action Settings dialog box opens, click the Run Macro option button and choose the macro you want to run from the drop-down list to the right.

2. Click OK.

NOTE You can also use automated events on the Web pages you create in FrontPage, which use controls or graphics, but these pages are not developed using VBA. The Web pages use either Java, JavaScript, VBScript, or ActiveX controls.

Editing the Macro

If your macro doesn't do what you need it to do, you have two choices:

- You can record the macro again after reviewing the steps to be sure the steps for the task are correct.
- You can open the code and modify parts of your macro.

Keep in mind that a macro can do only so much. It's great for repeating the steps of a procedure—particularly mundane, repetitive tasks—exactly as you record them. But sometimes, you need more flexibility—flexibility you can add only by working directly with the VBA code. For example, after recording a macro, you might later decide that you want to edit the macro so only some of the recorded steps are executed. You also might decide you want to add a step to your macro. If the macro can be easily recorded a second time, it's usually best to do so, but if the macro involves many steps, it might be easier for you to edit the VBA code.

The editing process takes place in the *Visual Basic Editor,* which will be introduced in the next section. One of the Visual Basic Editor's primary uses is to write and edit macros that are attached to Office documents. The actual process of editing and writing code from scratch is covered in Chapter 6, "Successful VBA Modules." Chapter 6 covers the specific rules that you must follow and suggestions for improving the efficiency of your macros. The steps for entering the VBA code snippets you'll find throughout this book are located in Chapter 6 as well.

Starting the editing process for a particular macro depends on where the macro is stored. If you have stored the macro in an ordinary Excel workbook, Word document or template, or PowerPoint presentation, follow these steps:

1. Open the workbook, document, template, or presentation that contains the macro you want to edit.
2. Choose Tools, Macro, Macros. The Macro dialog box appears.
3. In the Macro Name box, select the macro you want to edit.
4. Select Edit. This launches the Visual Basic Editor, with which you can modify the code for your macro.

If you have stored the macro in Word's Normal.dot template, you do not need to open it first.

If you have stored the macro in Excel's Personal Macro Workbook, choose Tools, Macro, Visual Basic Editor. You cannot open this workbook directly in Excel via the Macros dialog box unless you unhide it first.

NOTE Chapter 6 explores the development process and provides a basis for modifying the code created when you record a macro. It also gives you a quick, no-frills tutorial on putting those chapter snippets to work—no muss, no fuss, just productivity. If you're ready for more in-depth customization, Chapter 6 discusses all the tools and conventions you need to get started with VBA programming.

Using the Visual Basic Editor

The Visual Basic Editor is a full-featured development environment for Excel 2000, Word 2000, PowerPoint 2000, and Access 2000 (although it is not used for Access macros). It provides the means to edit the macros you record and to create new procedures from scratch. Within this environment, you can create new procedures, edit existing ones, debug your code, and run all your code.

NOTE The Visual Basic Editor in Access is covered in more detail in Chapter 41, "Using Macros and VBA in Access."

NOTE Debugging code refers to the process of fine-tuning your macro code to remove any extra code, errors, and/or unintentionally recorded actions. You review your code line by line making certain that it does the tasks you require and nothing else. Most often it is a matter of editing the macro's text—similar to what you might do in a Word document.

Each product in the Office suite that supports the Visual Basic Editor (Word, Excel, PowerPoint, Access, Outlook, and FrontPage) has its own specific set of limitations. PowerPoint, for example, has a limited scope of programming options, although Word and Excel have a rich development environment that enables a programmer to modify the programs to fit their unique requirements.

The Visual Basic Editor screen, which looks the same in each Office program, is shown in Figure 5.6. Each program, however, has a separate and individual version of this editor.

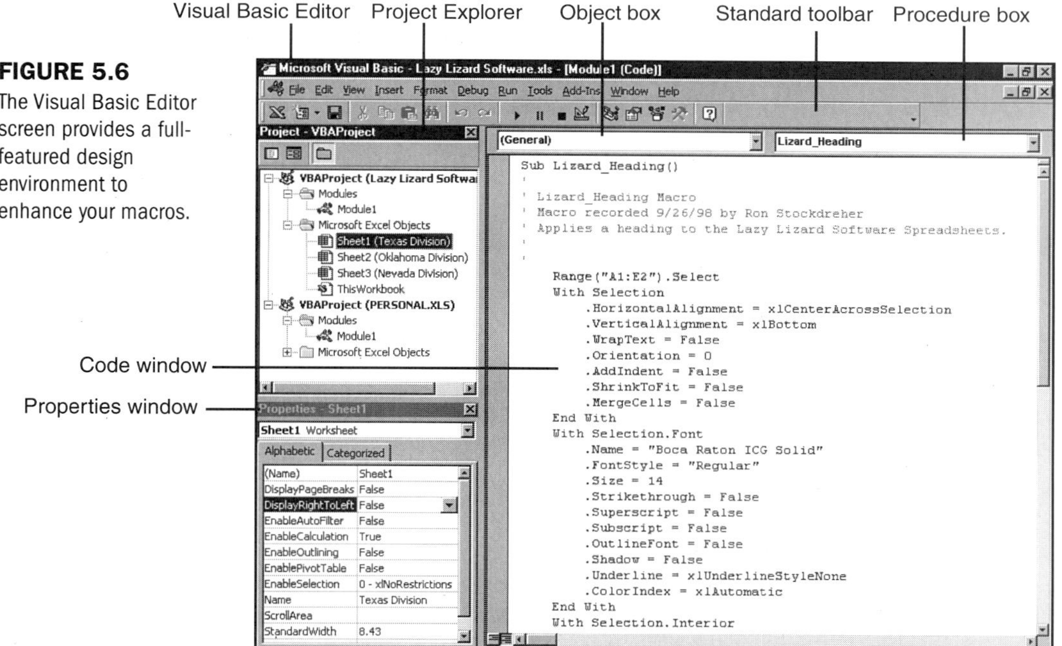

FIGURE 5.6
The Visual Basic Editor screen provides a full-featured design environment to enhance your macros.

The Visual Basic Editor has three main sections: the Project Explorer, the Properties window, and the Code window. These three sections are normally displayed the first time you open the Editor. Additionally, there are three other sections: the Immediate window, the Locals window, and the Watches window.

The following sections take a closer look at the Project Explorer, the Properties window, and the Code window.

The Project Explorer Window

The Project Explorer window, shown in Figure 5.7, displays the sections of your files that can be altered using VBA code. The application file itself is called the Project. Below that level you see the application's working files, such as workbooks and worksheets for Excel and documents and references to templates in Word—Code Modules, UserForms, and class modules.

NOTE Code modules are similar to text-based documents. They contain the actual code from your macros. Class modules are specialized code modules used to create new objects using VBA. Class modules, where they are used in Access coding, are described in Chapter 41.

▶ **See** "Designing `UserForms`," **p. 170**

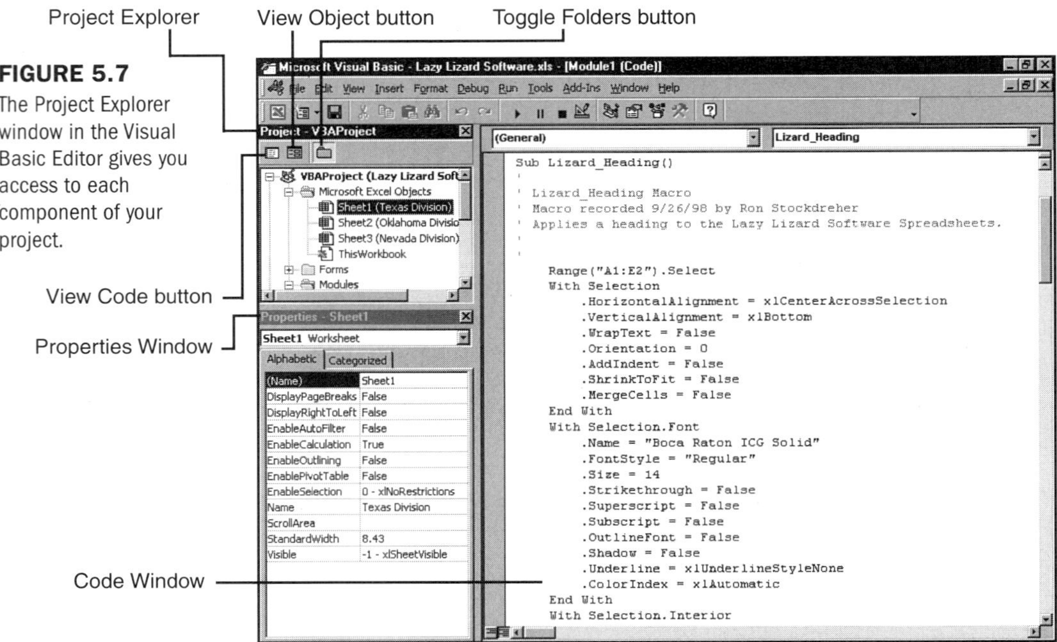

FIGURE 5.7 The Project Explorer window in the Visual Basic Editor gives you access to each component of your project.

If you open another file in the application (Word, Excel, PowerPoint, and so on), another project becomes available in the Visual Basic Editor. Selecting an item from one of the folders in this window automatically brings up the properties for that object in the Properties window. Selecting one of the two buttons at the top left of the Project Explorer displays either the code or the form for that object. If you recorded a macro, you will notice a Modules folder in this window. Each macro you record is stored in a module. To edit your code, select the module that contains it, and then click the View Code button (as previously shown in Figure 5.7). The Toggle Folders button changes how the folders in the Project Explorer window are displayed.

The Properties Window

The Properties window displays the characteristics of the object selected. You can set these properties to alter the behavior or presentation of the object. For example, the Worksheet object (listed by its Sheet name in the figure) has a DisplayPageBreaks property. If that property is set to True, page breaks are visible; if it is set to False, they are not visible. Each type of object has its own unique properties. Some objects have a number of properties, although others have just a few. Figure 5.8 shows the Properties window.

FIGURE 5.8
The Properties window in the Visual Basic Editor gives you an itemized list of each object's properties and their settings.

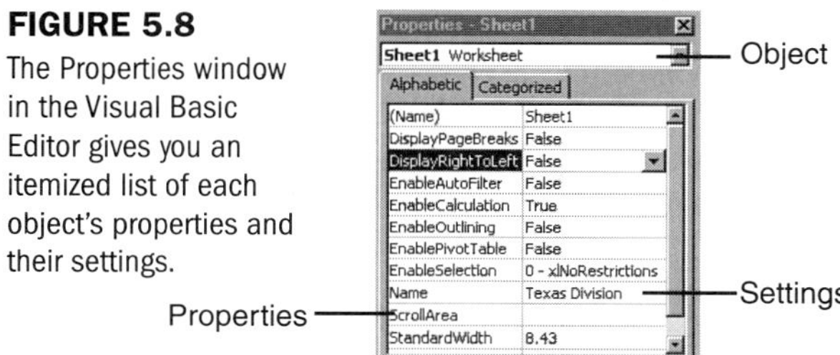

The Code Window

This window displays the code for your macros, and for any procedures that you create in your project. You enter the code snippets found in the other chapters of this book in this window. This window is used with the Project window. Select the module in the Project Explorer and click the View Code button at the top of the Project window. This displays the code for that module in the Code window. At the top of the Code window are two drop-down lists; one (on the left) identifies the object selected, and the other (on the right) identifies the name of your macro or the selected procedure. An example of the Code window is shown in Figure 5.9.

FIGURE 5.9
The Code window in the Visual Basic Editor displays the VBA code for the macros you write or record.

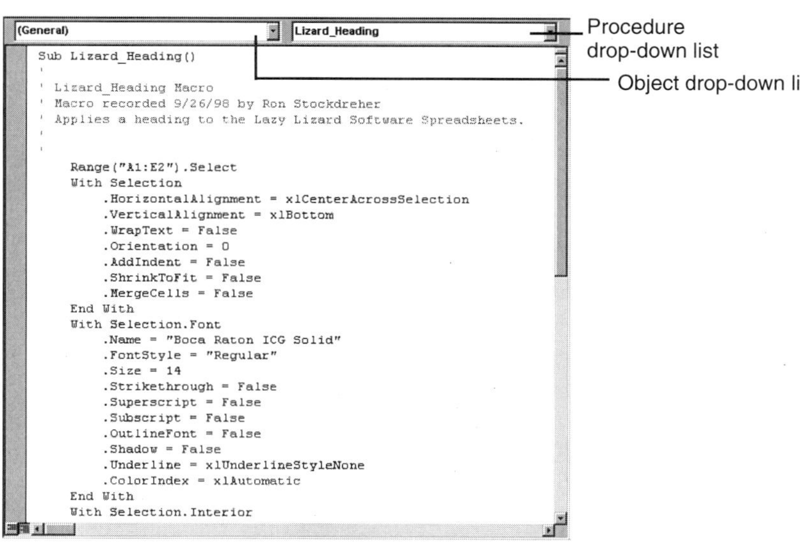

The Immediate, Locals, and Watches Windows

These three windows are not displayed as part of the default setting for the Visual Basic Editor. They have specific uses, primarily during the debug and evaluation phases of your project's development. You can see an example of these windows in Figure 5.10. Their use is covered in the following chapter's section on debugging your code. These windows are accessible through the View menu or the Debug toolbar.

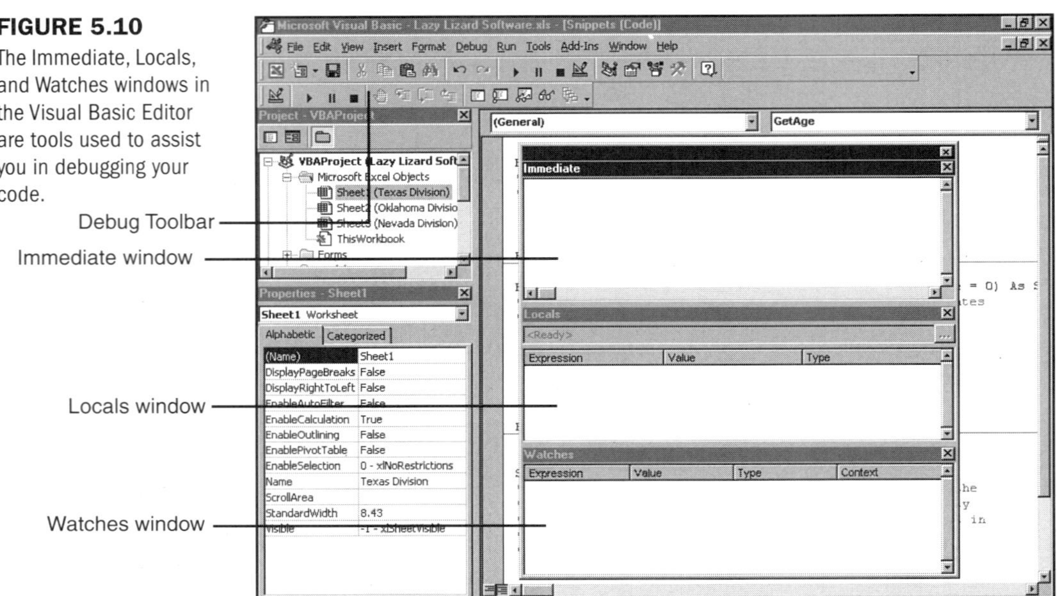

FIGURE 5.10
The Immediate, Locals, and Watches windows in the Visual Basic Editor are tools used to assist you in debugging your code.

Visual Basic Editor Toolbars

Four toolbars are associated with the Visual Basic Editor: Standard toolbar, Edit toolbar, Debug toolbar, and UserForm toolbar. Each provides a different set of tools to create and manipulate the objects and code in your project. To use any of these toolbars, click View, Toolbars and select the desired toolbar from the fly-out window.

Customizing the Visual Basic Editor

The Visual Basic Editor's environment can be adjusted to suit your needs. Because each Office program has its own Visual Basic Editor, each can be altered, based on the program and the desired result.

Docking Windows

Many windows are used in this design environment and although this provides many ways of looking at your project, it also clutters up the screen and makes it difficult to work. By moving, closing, and docking these windows, you can set up the environment that works best for you. The setup of your windows may also depend on the size of the screen on which you are working. The larger the screen (and finer the resolution), the easier it is to support more windows.

The View menu on the menu bar provides a listing of the different windows that are available in the Visual Basic Editor. Selecting one either makes that window appear or moves the focus to that window.

When it is docked, each window has a small window Close (X) button to close the window. Also, you can right-click the title bar of the window or in the main work area of the window and choose Hide or Dockable from the shortcut menu.

To make the window a free-floating window, grab its title bar, drag it to the open screen, and release. As a free-floating window, you will notice a small Close (X) window control in the upper-right corner of the title bar area. You can also right-click in the window and select Dockable. This will make the window a normal window in the VBE environment, similar to the code window. To dock it again, right-click in the window (not the title bar) and choose Dockable again. It is also a choice on the Options dialog box's Docking tab (Tools, Options, Docking).

Windows can be docked on all four sides of the Editor and in any relationship you choose with the other windows. Additionally, you can adjust the size of the docked windows. Place your mouse pointer on the border of the docked window and a double-headed arrow appears. Grab the border with your mouse and drag to make the window larger or smaller.

Maintaining the Screen Layout Between Sessions

Choosing Tools, Options opens up the user options dialog box so you can set the screen layout and other customization options. Four tabs are available: Editor, Editor Format, General, and Docking.

Options Dialog Box—Editor Tab The Editor tab has check boxes for code and window settings. The Code Settings are

- Auto Syntax Check—Checks each statement in the Code window for syntax errors, such as a misspelled keyword or missing separator, as you type. A dialog box alerts you if errors exist as soon as you end a line. This feature is turned on by default.
- Require Variable Declaration—Makes explicit variable declaration mandatory in modules. Selecting this adds the Option Explicit statement to General Declarations in any new module. This doesn't add the statement to existing modules.
- Auto List Members—Displays a list of terms that would logically complete the statement at the insertion point.
- Auto Quick Info—Displays syntax information about functions and their parameters as you type.
- Auto Data Tips—Displays the value of the variable over which your cursor is placed. This feature works only in Break mode.

- Auto Indent—Enables you to tab the first line of code. The lines of code that follow start at that tab location. With this feature, you can write your code so that its indentation structure matches its logical structure.
- Tab Width—The tab width can be set from 1 to 32 spaces. The default is 4 spaces.

The Window Settings are

- Drag-and-Drop Text Editing—Enables you to drag and drop text within the current Code window and from the Code window to the Immediate or Watches Windows. If you hold the Ctrl key down while dragging, it copies the code.
- Default to Full Module View—Sets the default for new modules to display procedures as a single scrollable list (see Figure 5.11) or only one procedure at a time. It does not change currently open modules.
- Procedure Separator—Displays or hides separator bars that appear at the end of each procedure (see Figure 5.11).

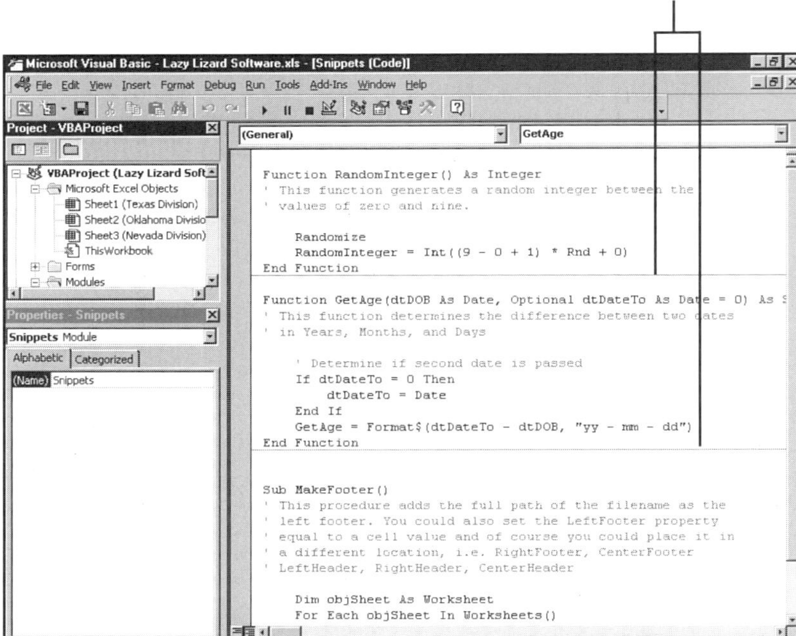

FIGURE 5.11
The Code window can display procedures individually or grouped together (such as in this example).

Options Dialog Box—Editor Format Tab The Editor Format tab has settings for Code Colors and Font, as well as a Size and Margin Indicator Bar:

- Code Colors—Colors for the foreground, background, text, and margin indicator can be changed to suit your preference. These colors assist in visually identifying different items in the Code windows. For example, if you have a syntax error, the default settings change the affected line of code to red.

- Font—Specifies the font used for all code.
- Size—Specifies the size of the font used for code.
- Margin Indicator Bar—Makes the margin indicator bar visible or invisible.

Options Dialog Box—General Tab The General tab has settings for the form grid, ToolTips, window display, notification of state loss, error trapping, and project compilation:

- Form Grid Settings—Determines the appearance of the form when it is edited. Options are available to display the grid (Show Grid), set the height and width of the grid (they can be set from 2 to 60 points), and automatically align the outer edges of controls on gridlines (Align Controls to Grid).
- Show ToolTips—Displays ToolTips for the toolbar buttons. Note that these are referred to as ScreenTips throughout the remainder of Office 2000.
- Collapse Proj. Hides Windows—Determines whether the project, UserForm, object, or module windows are closed automatically when a project is collapsed in the Project Explorer.
- Edit and Continue—Visual Basic enables you to make some editing changes to your code in Break Mode without resetting module level variables. Checking Notify Before State Loss provides a message notifying you that your action will reset all module level variables in the running project.
- Error Trapping—Determines how errors are handled in the development environment. Setting this option affects all instances of Visual Basic started from that application (Word, Excel, and so on) after you change the setting.
- Break on All Errors—Any error causes the project to enter break mode, whether or not you have designed an error handler and whether or not the code is in a class module.
- Break in Class Module—Any unhandled error occurring in a class module causes the project to enter break mode in the class module at the line of code that produced the error.
- Break on Unhandled Errors—If an error handler exists, the error is trapped and your project does not enter break mode. If no error handler exists, the error causes the project to enter break mode. An unhandled error in a class module, however, causes the project to enter break mode on the line of code that invoked the offending procedure. This is the least useful of the three during debugging because it does not identify the line of code that produced the error.
- Compile on Demand—Determines whether a project is fully compiled before it starts or whether code is compiled as needed, allowing the application to start sooner.
- Background Compile—Uses idle time during the project's runtime to finish compiling the project in the background. Background Compile can improve runtime execution speed. Compile on Demand must also be selected.

Options Dialog Box—Docking Tab The Docking tab enables you to choose which windows you want to be dockable. A window is docked when it is attached or "anchored" to one edge of other dockable or application windows. When moved, it snaps to the location. A window is not dockable when you can move it anywhere on the screen and then leave it there.

Select windows you want to be dockable and clear the rest. These settings remain set in the environment until you change them.

Customizing the Toolbars

Visual Basic toolbars are also customizable. You can right-click any visible toolbar to bring up a shortcut menu with the toolbar choices and a Customize option. Select the Customize option to open the Customize dialog box. This is also available by choosing View, Toolbars, Customize on the menu bar. The customization process works the same as other toolbar customization actions in Office by using the Toolbars, Commands, and Options tabs in the Customize dialog box.

▶ **See** "Customizing Application Toolbars," **p. 89**

The only major difference between the toolbar customization options in the Visual Basic Editor and other Office applications is that you cannot assign macros to the toolbar buttons. You can, however, edit the images on the buttons, move them between toolbars, and create your own custom toolbars that have the commands you choose.

Understanding Visual Basic for Applications Terminology

Computer languages are just like human languages. They have certain rules and conventions that must be followed to work correctly and get the task done. They also do not reveal themselves too readily. Some things seem right when you look at them; others don't seem to fit at all.

Don't expect to pick up the language in one sitting. It won't happen. Not any more likely than you could pick up Russian in one sitting. Concentrate on getting the feel of the language and understanding the concepts. The rest, in time, will fall into place. First, let's look at some terminology that you will see in the Code window and some core Visual Basic terminology.

NOTE The definitions you'll find in the following section are basic explanations designed to get you started. Digging deeply into each of these concepts is far beyond the scope of this book. These definitions, however, will give you a good starting place and will help you determine whether you want to learn VBA or whether you want to stick with recording macros and tinkering with the premade code you'll find throughout this book. In either case, getting comfortable with the terms will help you in the long run.

Procedures

A *procedure* is a named block of code that performs a task. Three different types of procedures are used: subprocedures, functions, and property procedures. The following sections examine each type of procedure.

NOTE No executable VBA code can be outside of a procedure. If you inadvertently place code outside of a procedure, an error occurs.

▶ **See** "The Differences Between Procedures and Functions," **p. 1149**

Subprocedures *Subprocedures* are the most common procedures. Each macro that you record is actually a subprocedure. If you choose to edit a macro, the Visual Basic Editor opens and your macro is displayed in the Code window. The name of your macro is the name of the subprocedure. A subprocedure starts with `Sub` and ends with `End Sub`. Following is an example of a Word subprocedure:

```
Sub MyFirstMacro()
     <<code>>
End Sub
```

The following "live" example creates an "instant bookmark":

```
Sub InstantBookmark1Drop()
    With ActiveDocument.Bookmarks
        .Add Range:=Selection.Range, Name:="Instant1"
    End With
End Sub
```

In this example, the following is happening:

- "`Sub InstantBookmark1Drop()`" begins the subprocedure (also called a macro). It also sets the name of procedure "`InstantBookmark1Drop`."
- "`With ActiveDocument.Bookmarks`" identifies which document gets the new bookmark and references a VBA collection called "`Bookmarks`." Numerous types of collections are in the VBA environment.
- "`.Add Range:=Selection.Range, Name:="Instant1"`" sets the bookmark in place. It adds a new bookmark at the insertion point, "`Range:=Selection.Range`," and gives it the name "`Instant1`."
- "`End With`" closes the reference to the Bookmarks collection.
- "`End Sub`" ends the subprocedure.

▶ **See** "Quick Editing with Temporary Bookmarks," **p. 244**

Functions A *function procedure* also performs a task, similar to a subprocedure, but with a couple of key differences. First, it must be written in the Visual Basic Editor. You cannot record a function procedure with the Macro Recorder. Second, and beneficial to you, a function procedure always returns a value. This value can be used to do a number of things in the programming environment. For example, you can use the returned value to determine whether an action (such as opening a file) took place or not. A function procedure starts with `Function` and ends with `End Function`. Following is an example of a function procedure:

```
Function NameOfTheFunction()
     <<code>>
     NameOfTheFunction = x
End Function
```

The following "live" example creates a random integer between 0 and 9:

```
Function RandomInteger() As Integer
    Randomize
    RandomInteger = Int((9 - 0 + 1) * Rnd + 0)
End Function
```

You might use this type of function to generate a random choice of scenarios in Excel, or perhaps a random series of templates in a PowerPoint presentation. In this example, the following is happening:

- "`Function RandomInteger() as Integer`" begins the function procedure. The phrase "`As Integer`" identifies what type of value is returned to the calling procedure. Functions always return a value. This one is an integer value so only whole numbers are returned.
- "`Randomize`" initializes the `Rnd` (used in the next line of code) function's random-number generator, giving it a new `seed` value.
- "`RandomInteger = Int((9 - 0 + 1) * Rnd + 0)`" sets the value that is returned equal to the equation after the equal sign. The key part is the `Rnd` function, which generates a random number between 0 and 1. The rest determines the range of random numbers.
- "`End Function`" ends the function procedure.

▶ **See** "Functions for Every Occasion," **p. 671**

Property Procedures You have already seen that Code Modules hold the code that is your macro. In VBA, Class Modules are also used by programmers to design program-specific Objects. For example, a programmer might design an Employee object for his or her program. Objects in VBA have certain properties (discussed later) and the *Property Procedure* is used to design unique properties for the class' objects. For example, the Employee object may have a Name or an EmployeeID property.

The use and creation of Class Modules and Property Procedures are beyond the scope of this book, but if you are interested, you can find out more about these wonderful features in *Special Edition Using Visual Basic 6*, published by Que.

Statements

A *statement* is a unit of code that defines an item or an action, or assigns a value to a variable. Normally, only one statement exists for each line of code. More statements can be placed on a line if a colon separates each statement, but this tends to get confusing. You can also use a continuation character, a space followed by an underscore, to allow you to use more than one line for a statement. This is normally done to make the procedure easy to read in the design environment.

Comments

Comments can be used to explain why a certain convention was used, or what a value needs to be. Comments do not execute with the other code. They also provide a way to test how a procedure might run without a certain statement, by letting you "comment out" the statement for testing purposes. The next chapter describes the use of comments.

NOTE Comments per se add nothing to the value of code. Whether they benefit the programmer depends greatly on whether the comments are accurate, necessary, well written, relevant, and meaningful. You'd be surprised how easily comments can fail to meet these criteria.

Keywords

A *keyword* is a word that describes an action or operation that the Visual Basic Editor recognizes as part of the VBA language. `Sub` or `Function` are examples of keywords. By default, the text color for these keywords is blue.

Variables

A *variable* is a place in memory that is set aside to store a unique value. This value can be changed while the procedure is running.

Constants

A *constant* is similar to a variable in that it is also a place in memory that is set aside to store a unique value. This value, however, is not changeable while the program is executing. Additionally, system and program constants are built in to the Office applications.

Objects

Virtually everything in the Visual Basic for Applications programming environment is an *object* or part of one. This is a common convention in modern programming that makes the programming process dynamic. Each application in the Office suite consists of objects. Documents are objects. Workbooks are objects. Even the words themselves are objects. Programming in VBA consists of manipulating those objects.

Properties

Each object has certain *properties*. Some have more properties than others, but all have properties. A document has a title or perhaps a subject; a spreadsheet has a background color; a font has a certain size or format, such as bold. These properties are set through your VBA code.

Methods

A *method* is an action that an object can perform. Just as in the properties, different objects have different methods. For example, the Document object has an Activate method that gives that document the focus. (This is like selecting the document's window with your mouse.)

Object Model

An *Object Model* is the entire collection of objects, methods, and properties that make up a given application. Word, Excel, PowerPoint, Access, Outlook, and even the Office Assistant each has a separate and unique Object Model that identifies the specific objects, methods, and properties of that application and their interrelationships.

CHAPTER 6

Successful VBA Modules

In this chapter

VBA—An Overview

Successful VBA modules take time to develop. You need to build them carefully and with a goal in mind.

This chapter examines a few guidelines that will help provide a sound structure to your VBA projects. You'll also explore the tools available in the Visual Basic Editor that enable you to test and fine-tune your code. This chapter also provides the information you'll need to create and display *UserForms*, which are user-designed dialog boxes on which you can place controls (text boxes, check boxes, option buttons, and so on). Essentially, UserForms are a method you can provide to make multiple choices in your project. For example, in Word, you will find a dialog box that changes all the font parameters. With VBA, you can employ UserForms to improve the functionality of your projects in the same way.

Also in this chapter, you'll learn how to use the snippets of prewritten VBA code found throughout this book. In many cases, that code is used to illustrate concepts integral to working with VBA. If you're interested in using only the premade code, skip ahead to "Putting VBA Code Snippets to Work." That's all you need to know to put these snippets of code to use.

However, if you want to get started building your own VBA code, keep reading. Keep in mind that a full discussion of VBA is beyond the scope of this book. If you have the time to tinker and learn as you go, you'll find a lot of advice here to get you started. If your goal is to thoroughly learn VBA, we suggest that you pick up a copy of the following Que books devoted to the Visual Basic programming language:

- *Special Edition Using Visual Basic 6*
- *Using Visual Basic 6*
- *Paul Sheriff Teaches Visual Basic 6*

You'll also examine an ongoing VBA Excel project that builds on a recorded macro. You'll edit the code to make it more efficient, add comments to the code to document the changes, and add a UserForm to make entries in the worksheet. Although this example focuses on a specific project to illustrate the process, it can work, with some modification, in all Office 2000 products that support VBA (Word, Excel, PowerPoint, Outlook, FrontPage, and Access).

The Development Cycle

As with any other project, developing a VBA project is a process. You wouldn't introduce a new compensation plan in your company without first looking at each facet and the ramifications of it. Likewise, developing a VBA project is a process. It involves planning, building the components, testing the code, debugging the code, documenting the procedures, delivering the module, and getting feedback on how it works. And here is where the beauty of using a structured programming environment, such as VBA, becomes most apparent. Because the project is modular and component-based, you can apply this process to any part of it at the same time, from the smallest procedures within it to the entire project.

It is possible to start at any point in the cycle, but the most common place is the planning stage (see Figure 6.1). Look at the scope of the project and decide what is needed to get it done. After that plan is written, start building the components of that project, such as the documents, macros, UserForms, and so on that are needed. Now test and debug your code. This should be done continually as your project moves toward completion. Write or record a procedure, test it, and debug the procedure. As you are writing, testing, and debugging, add comments to your code to help you through the process so that you can come back later and understand your methodology and reasoning. Deliver the project, put it to work, and get feedback from the users (or talk to yourself if it is just for you). Does it really do what you intended? Can it be better? If not, jump back into the cycle and start fine-tuning.

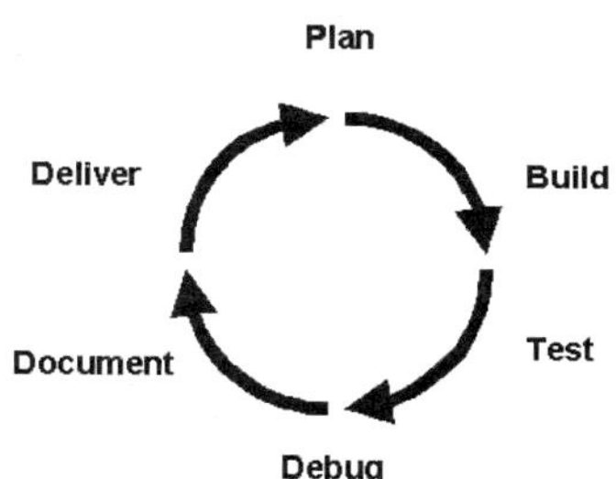

FIGURE 6.1
Use the Development Cycle to plan your project.

Plan the Project

Before writing any VBA code, plan the project on paper. Consider these key points:

- The people who will use the project
- The tasks the project should automate
- The data the project will manage

The more time you spend planning your project, the less time you will spend later rewriting VBA code. A well-planned module is more likely to meet your needs. Think about the key words to use in menus, dialog boxes, and help screens.

Understanding Object-Oriented Programming

Programming in VBA is similar to *Object-Oriented Programming* (OOP) in that it manipulates objects such as workbooks, worksheets, and ranges in its code. VBA isn't a true Object-Oriented Programming language because it does not meet some of the specifications for true object orientation, as do some other programming languages such as C++ and Java. But VBA uses objects heavily, and for most purposes, it will behave and allow design to follow a similar process.

What is an object? Loosely, it is any distinct *thing* or *process* in code that directly maps to a real-world thing or process. If you were to describe a task, the nouns, verbs, and adjectives would tell you what many of the programming objects, methods, and properties of your project would be.

continues

continued

For example, listen to what your users are saying about sales each month ("Does anybody know how sales are doing? We need a summary report each month!"). Now, look at the structure of their sentences. The nouns are the objects. "Create a summary report of sales each month" has at least one noun (and its modifying adjective) that could map to a corresponding VBA object—summary report. "Create" is a verb—a good candidate for one of this project's methods. "Sales" is another noun, so it could be an object, but it's also data for your report, making it a good candidate for a property of the report. On this level, "object-oriented" simply means that the software answer you are creating directly reflects the real-world problem you're trying to solve.

Build the Project

After you've planned your project, the first physical step is to start building the *programming objects* that form the foundation of the project. Usually a VBA project is built around objects, such as slides, text boxes, fields, workbooks, worksheets, UserForms, and so on. This can be as simple as creating a basic data entry form in Word or as complicated as building a customer database in Access. This part of the process depends solely on the complexity of the task at hand.

Next, it's also helpful to identify any external objects, such as remote databases, external files, or links to external programs, that you'll need before you start writing code. At this point, it is most helpful to create a list.

Fortunately, you can automate some of this programming by using the Macro Recorder to record your actions. Then you can edit the automatically generated code and add additional lines of code as needed. Be sure to test the code you've recorded before modifying it.

NOTE The steps of planning, building, and testing normally happen on an object-by-object basis. This is a feature of object-oriented application development that enables you to build the project one object at a time and make use of those finished objects immediately.

Making the transition from your idea to the actual code is often difficult. Here is an idea that might work the process.

Select a task to automate and follow these steps:

1. Write (in normal English, not code) what you want the program to accomplish. This pseudocode serves as an outline for your code-writing efforts later.
2. Break down complicated programs into several smaller procedures.
3. Select the task or process to be automated.
4. Determine whether you can record the VBA code or whether you need to type the procedure code.

How Do I Determine Whether to Record the VBA Code or Write It Out?

The easiest way to decide this is to identify what the dynamics of the process are. Ask yourself a simple question: "Is this a 'static' task that I am accomplishing or is it one that has changing parameters?" This is the key point.

If it is static—in other words, you want the same actions to take place each time the procedure is run and you want those actions to affect the same objects—definitely use the recorder. More often than not, recorder does all the work for you.

If the task is dynamic—for example, you need to select a varied number of cells in Excel and those determined by a user's input—then you need to write at least part of the procedure. Use the recorder as often as you can.

The macro recorder is a wonderful tool. With it you can record the essence of a task and then modify the code for your specific requirements. No muss, no fuss, and best of all—with fewer errors than you're likely to have if you write the code yourself. The recorder always gets the syntax of the code right.

Another benefit of using the recorder is that it identifies the objects necessary to do a task. Suppose you want to automate a certain task but don't know what objects to program. If you can do the task, or a similar one, turn the recorder on while you do it. The recorder records the procedure along with all the objects, methods, and properties you need to write the code yourself.

---

5. Record as much of the VBA code as possible.
6. Edit recorded code as needed to amplify the VBA code.
7. Add descriptive comments to document your work as you go.

Test the Project

Test your work as you go. Test each VBA procedure before moving on to the next procedure. If possible, test your work with realistic data.

Classify problems discovered as

- Programming errors (bugs) you need to analyze and correct
- Design flaws you need to fix
- Enhancements to implement now
- Enhancements to consider for the future

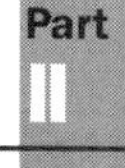

Debug the Project

Use the VBA *debugging* tools to determine the cause of programming errors. Correct the VBA code and retest the procedures involved. In some cases, you may need to retest more than one module or more than one set of interacting modules. In these complicated scenarios, it helps to have a written test plan. Identify and write down the steps and the order you want to go through to debug your project. Allow room to document this and keep track of the changes and revisions you made to the original code. This way, you can go back to an earlier point in the process if you run into a roadblock. See "Debugging Your Code," later in this chapter.

Document the Project

There are two types of documentation for you to consider—module documentation and user documentation. Module documentation helps future programmers—or you, for that matter—understand how the module works so that changes can be made quickly. I can't count the number of times I've looked back at a piece of code and wondered, "Why in the world did I do this that way?" Module documentation, through use of comments, answers those questions and can be used to explain interactions among objects, files, and other applications. See "Adding Comments to Your Modules," later in this chapter.

User documentation can be in the traditional form of printed text that explains what the system can do and how the user can best accomplish those tasks. You can also provide help in the form of ToolTips that you create for UserForm controls, MsgBoxes that contain simple instructions, and custom UserForms that list steps at appropriate points. You don't need to develop full-strength Windows Help to provide the guidance your users need. A little bit of help provided this way is far better than no help at all, and worlds easier to create than context-sensitive help or a link to the Windows Help system.

Deliver the Project

After the VBA project is tested, debugged, and documented, you are ready to deliver it. Whether you are creating this project for someone on your staff or just for your own use, there are considerations that should be taken to ensure it works correctly and can be installed where you want to install it. Consider these issues:

- Hard disk space and memory requirements
- The version of Microsoft Office currently installed
- Operating system and networking issues
- A medium to distribute the application (via floppy disk, network, email, or CD-ROM)

Gather Feedback

Incorporating feedback in every step of the development cycle, not just at the end, is best. Feedback at the end is usually news—usually bad. And if the feedback is bad enough, you may discover that your design doesn't solve the problem, which means going back to the drawing board. By the end, it's too late to do anything about all the hard work you've just completed. All you can do is plan for the next version.

Thus, look for ways to get feedback throughout the VBA project. Recruit someone, or several people, who can look at your project at every stage—especially the early planning and design stages, but also at every milestone. Let them critique it, comment on dialog boxes you have planned, run whatever code runs, comment on the dialog boxes that you actually created, and so on. Your finished product stands a much better chance of satisfying all the users eagerly awaiting your handiwork.

Then, after your VBA project is in use, get feedback from the people who are using it. Honest feedback can help you develop more efficient VBA modules in the future.

Putting VBA Code Snippets to Work

Throughout this book, we've included ready-to-use snippets of VBA code that provide speed and usability, and feature enhancements for the Office 2000 environment. These snippets of code are ready to use and are included on the CD included with this book.

Putting these snippets of code to use is a simple process:

1. Open the program (Word, Excel, Access, or PowerPoint) that will use the snippet.
2. Choose Tools, Macro, Visual Basic Editor to open the Visual Basic Editor (or press Alt+F11). This is the design environment that stores the VBA code. If this is the first time you have opened the editor, you will probably see three windows: the Project window, the Properties window, and the Code window (as shown in Figure 6.2).

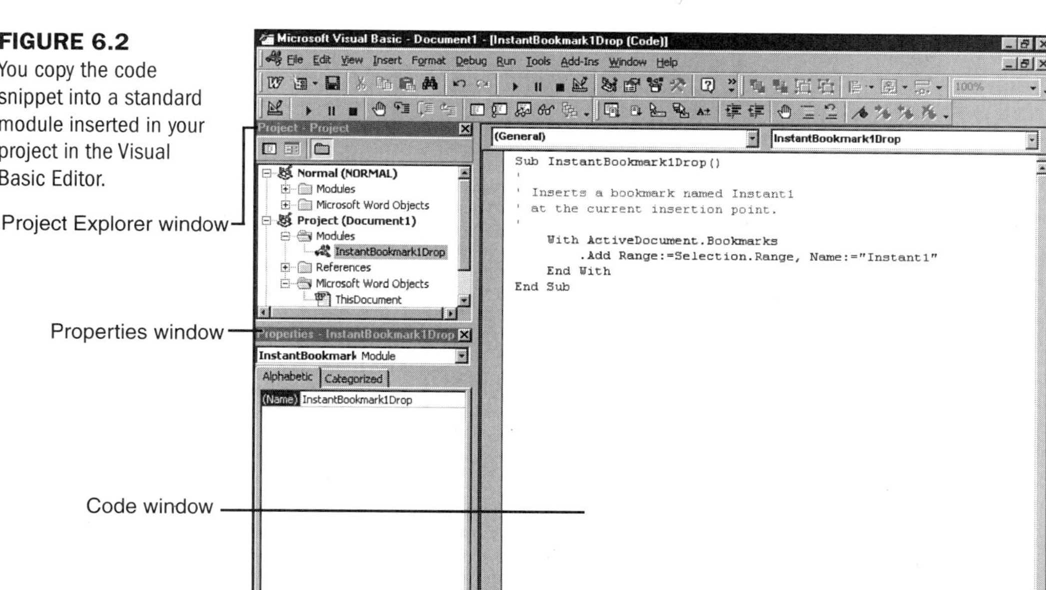

FIGURE 6.2
You copy the code snippet into a standard module inserted in your project in the Visual Basic Editor.

3. Select the project icon in the Project window that contains the snippet. One project is created for each open file and there also may be one for a template file. After selecting the project icon, choose Insert, Module. This inserts a VBA code module into the project and places the insertion point in the Code window of that module.
4. Here you have a choice; you can type the snippet code exactly as written in the book, paying close attention to punctuation and capitalization, or you can simply copy and paste the code directly from the CD included with this book.

NOTE Unless you want to get your hands dirty by actually typing the code yourself, your best bet is to copy the code from the CD and paste it in the code window.

5. To copy and paste—within the Office application in which you want to use the snippet—open the file on the CD that contains the VBA code. It is referenced in the text near the snippet in the book. Expand the directory tree in the Visual Basic Editor's project window for the project (file) you just opened from the CD. Locate the module with the code snippet you want to use and copy it as you would any text. Be sure to include the Sub and End Sub (or Function and End Function) statements. Now, double click the module you inserted in your document in step 3 and paste the copied snippet into your document.

That's it! You can now go back to the program window and put the snippet to work. An example of a completed snippet is shown in Figure 6.3.

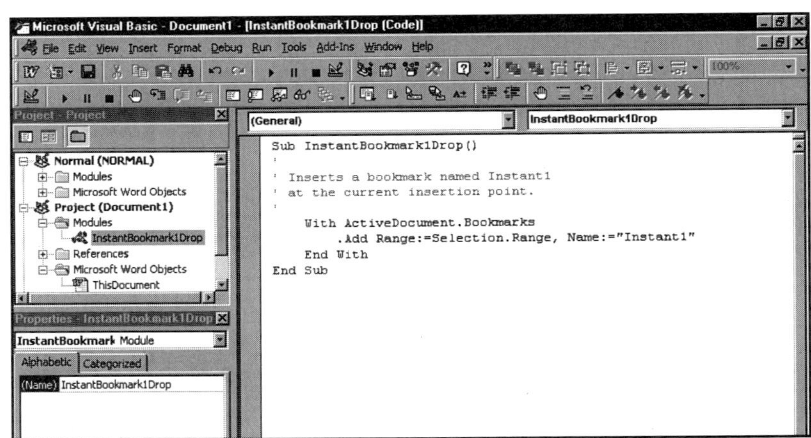

FIGURE 6.3
This completed snippet for creating instant bookmarks in Word is discussed in Chapter 9, "Power Editing and Formatting."

NOTE Some applications in Microsoft Office (PowerPoint, for example) have additional steps that need to be taken to implement the snippet code, especially when you want to activate the code for more than just the current file. See the instructions on the CD accompanying this book for activating VBA snippets.

Running a Macro

Before running your macro, make sure you are in the correct place in your file to run it. For example, if you are currently working in one of your Excel charts, running a macro designed for a PowerPoint presentation might generate an error.

To run a macro, follow these steps:

1. If necessary, open the document that contains the macro. If the macro is in the Personal.XLS workbook, for Excel, or the Normal template, for Word, you do not need to do this.

2. Choose Tools, Macro, Macros (or press Alt+F8) to display the Macro dialog box, as shown in Figure 6.4.

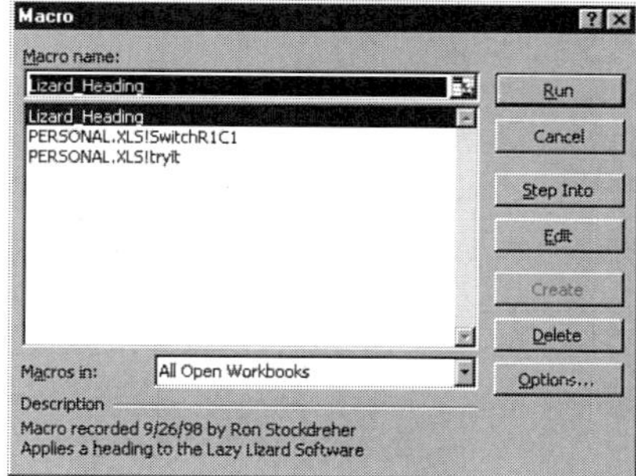

FIGURE 6.4
Be sure to select the correct macro by checking the description displayed at the bottom of the dialog box.

3. In the Macro Name box, select the name of the macro you want to run. In Figure 6.4, the macro Lizard_Heading is selected.
4. Click Run, and your macro runs exactly as you recorded it.

Creating Modules

What's the easiest way to create a module? Record a macro. That's right. Whether you record a macro in Excel, Word, or PowerPoint, a standard module is created. A *standard module* is the object in Microsoft Office VBA that holds the code for any macro procedure, whether recorded or written.

There are two types of modules:

- *Standard modules* that hold the code for subs and functions.
- *Class modules* that are used to create programmer-designed objects. These programmer-designed objects are beyond the scope of this book.

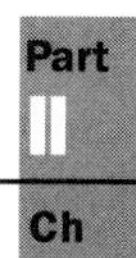

NOTE The topic of class modules can be a little overwhelming if you are a VBA beginner. To get started, I recommend that you visit Microsoft's Office Developer Web site (`www.microsoft.com/officedev`). This site contains plenty of beginner-level articles and tips, including links to other resources. After you have a better handle on the topic, I recommend that you pick up a copy of Que's *Special Edition Using Visual Basic 6*.

In this book, we focus on creating standard modules, as these are your primary tools for macros and other procedures.

In the VB Editor, Office 2000 refers to the combination of the file (that is, workbook, slide presentation, and so on) and any associated modules as a project. A project can have as many modules as you want and each module can hold any number of procedures. It is a good idea to organize procedures by module, so they're easy to find when you need them.

After you are in the VB Editor, you can add a new module by selecting Insert Module from the menu or clicking on the Insert Object button on the Standard Toolbar. The toolbar button has a drop-down arrow that enables you to choose among Modules, Class Modules, UserForms, or Procedures. The ToolTip text and the icon reflect which object was chosen last. The UserForm icon is displayed by default.

Because the easiest way to create a module is to record a Macro, you should start by creating a macro and then viewing the code in the Visual Basic Editor. Editing involves changing some of the recorded information to make your macro work faster and more efficiently.

Editing a Recorded Macro

Editing your macro involves the same skills that you use in word processing. You can cut, copy, and paste text by using the menu, toolbar, shortcut menu, or keyboard strokes. Inserting new code items is as simple as typing, or even using drag and drop within the code window. Before you start, look carefully at the code the recorder generates. Visual Basic for Applications is a language that requires a strict syntax for the construction of code lines. Each word, period, parenthesis, and quotation mark has a specific meaning to your macro. If you enter the wrong information, your macro may not run, or worse, it may run and cause some unexpected action in your project.

Be Careful with Using VBA to Apply Formatting

One common pitfall that every VBA beginner encounters is understanding that the Macro Recorder records every action, even actions you weren't aware that you'd taken. Take the code shown here, for example:

```
Range("A1:E2").Select
    With Selection
        .HorizontalAlignment = xlCenterAcrossSelection
        .VerticalAlignment = xlBottom
        .WrapText = False
        .Orientation = 0
        .AddIndent = False
        .ShrinkToFit = False
        .MergeCells = False
    End With
```

When you use a macro to format a selection, your macro records more than you might expect. Each selection has a default set of formats, and those defaults are recorded as part of the macro code.

This means that even though your actions were to change the font and font size of the selection, the macro also recorded all the default properties of that selection. If, for instance, the settings that control angling data and merging cells are not altered, the default settings for these items are recorded as part of the macro. If the macro is run on a worksheet where the data in cells A1 through E2 is angled or the cells merged, the macro makes the changes your macro was designed to do. However, it also removes the formats that angle and merge the cells because these default settings are included in the macro.

You can fix this by editing the macro and removing the default settings, which were automatically recorded, that were not part of the steps you wrote out before recording the macro.

The same snippet of code, after editing the lines you do not need, looks like this:

```
Range("A1:E2").Select
With Selection
    .HorizontalAlignment = xlCenterAcrossSelection
End With
```

Removing the unnecessary lines of code is as simple as highlighting the lines and pressing Delete.

Creating Procedures from Scratch

Although recording macros and tweaking the code is a viable solution to many problems, if your needs are more complex—say you want to gather and process form data from your co-workers—your only option is to write the code yourself. This is not as difficult as it sounds. In fact, the best way to do this, in most cases, is to use the Macro Recorder to set up the structure, by recording the basic steps. Then, you edit the macro to produce the final results. Every procedure has a certain syntax, or structure, that must be followed.

You identified the two main types of procedures—Function procedures and Sub procedures—in Chapter 5, "Getting Acquainted with VBA." Both types of procedures carry out tasks. The main difference between them is that Function returns a value, similar to the way a worksheet function in Excel returns a value.

NOTE You might notice that some information found in the following two sections is very similar to a section found in Chapter 5. This is intentional, as the explanation is helpful in both locations.

Subprocedures *Subprocedures* are the most common routines. Each macro that you record is actually a subprocedure. If you choose to edit a macro, the Visual Basic Editor opens and your macro is displayed in the Code window. The name of your macro is the name of the subprocedure. A subprocedure starts with Sub and ends with End Sub. Here is an example of a subprocedure:

```
Sub MyFirstMacro()
     <<code>>
End Sub
```

Here's a live example that creates an instant bookmark in Word:

```
Sub InstantBookmark1Drop()
    With ActiveDocument.Bookmarks
        .Add Range:=Selection.Range, Name:="Instant1"
    End With
End Sub
```

Here's what's happening in our example:

- `Sub InstantBookmark1Drop()` begins the subprocedure (also called a macro). It also sets the name of procedure `InstantBookmark1Drop`.

- `With ActiveDocument.Bookmarks` identifies which document gets the new bookmark and references a VBA collection called `Bookmarks`. There are numerous types of collections in the VBA environment.
- `.Add Range:=Selection.Range, Name:="Instant1"` sets the bookmark in place. It adds a new bookmark at the insertion point, `Range:=Selection.Range`, and gives it the name `Instant1`.
- `End With` closes the reference to the Bookmarks collection.
- `End Sub` ends the subprocedure.

▶ **See** "Quick Editing with Temporary Bookmarks," **p. 244**

Functions A *function* also performs a task, similar to a subprocedure, but with a couple of key differences. First, it must be written in the Visual Basic Editor. You cannot record a function procedure with the Macro Recorder. Second, and very beneficial to you, a function always returns a value. This value can be used to do a number of things in the programming environment. For example, you can use the returned value to determine whether an action (such as opening a file) took place. A function starts with Function and ends with End Function. Here is an example of a function:

```
Function NameOfTheFunction()
     <<code>>
     NameOfTheFunction = x
End Function
```

Here's another live example that creates a random integer between 0 and 9:

```
Function RandomInteger() As Integer
    Randomize
    RandomInteger = Int((9 - 0 + 1) * Rnd + 0)
End Function
```

You might use this type of function to generate a random choice of scenarios in Excel, or perhaps a random series of templates in a PowerPoint presentation. Here's what's happening in our example:

- "`Function RandomInteger() As Integer`" begins the function procedure. The phrase "`As Integer`" identifies what type of value is returned to the calling routine. Functions always return a value. This one is an integer value so that only whole numbers are returned.
- "`Randomize`" initializes the `Rnd` (used in the next line of code) function's random-number generator, giving it a new seed value.
- "`RandomInteger = Int((9 - 0 + 1) * Rnd + 0)`" sets the value that is returned equal to the equation after the equal sign. The key part is the `Rnd` function that generates a random number between 0 and 1. The rest determines the range of random numbers.
- "`End Function`" ends the function procedure.

▶ **See** "Functions for Every Occasion," **p. 671**

▶ **See** "Understanding Visual Basic for Applications Terminology," **p. 124**

Each procedure has a format, a header and footer, that must be followed to begin and end the procedure. Compare the following procedure with code from any macro that you have recorded.

```
Sub ToggleFull()
    'Toggles the Word window between full screen and normal views
    On Error Goto HANDLEERROR
    Const errCommandNotAvailable As Integer = 4248
    Dim cmdBar As CommandBar
    ActiveWindow.View.FullScreen = Not ActiveWindow.View.FullScreen
    If ActiveWindow.View.FullScreen = True Then
        For Each cmdBar In CommandBars
            If cmdBar.Name = "Full Screen" Then cmdBar.Visible = False
        Next
    End If
EXITHERE:
    Exit Sub
HANDLEERROR:
    If Err.Number = errCommandNotAvailable Then
        Resume EXITHERE
    Else
        Err.Raise Err.Number, Err.Source, Err.Description
        Resume EXITHERE
    End If
End Sub
```

NOTE The code shown here is a snippet that toggles the Word window between full screen and normal views without the annoying Full Screen toolbar. If you want to use it, skip back to "Putting VBA Code Snippets to Work" earlier in this chapter. The code is included on one of the CDs with this book. ■

▶ **See** "Customizing Word," **p. 207**

- The header begins with the Sub and then names the procedure (`ToggleFull`). After the name, there are open and close parentheses.
- Next, place comments identifying the purpose of the procedure and any explanatory information.
- On Error statements and variable declarations are placed in the next section I call the "preamble." This entry is located directly after your initial comments.
- After the preamble, enter the main body of the code. This is where the action takes place in your procedure. This can be as simple as one line of code or literally hundreds of lines. It all depends on what your procedure does. A little later in this chapter, we'll cover some of the programming tools you have at your fingertips to create the code to carry out your wishes—tools such as `If...Then` conditionals and `Do...Loop` loops.
- After accomplishing the tasks your code will handle, it starts the "post-amble" of your procedure. This part may not be necessary in some procedures, but if it is, this is where the error handler's code is placed.

- The start of this section is a statement to exit the procedure without running the error handler if no error exists. This is the `Exit Sub` statement. This statement quits the procedure without running any lines of code after that point.
- After the `Exit Sub` statement, a Label marks the place where the error handler begins. You can use any name you want for this Label (except a VBA keyword). Often it is "`ErrorHandler:`".
- Following this named location, place code to handle any errors that may occur.
- Last, the footer of the procedure, the `End Sub` statement. This is the last line of code for any sub procedure.

▶ **See** "Debugging Your Code," **p. 174**

The Syntax of the Sub or Function

The complete syntax for the `Sub` or `Function` statements has additional parameters that determine scope, how variables are used in the procedure, what, if any, arguments are passed to the procedure, and—if this is a Function—the type of data that it returns. These optional items are displayed in brackets, just as you find in Microsoft's help file.

The Sub procedure's syntax:

```
[Private | Public | Friend] [Static] Sub name [(arglist)]
     [statements]
     [Exit Sub]
     [statements]
End Sub
```

The Public, Private, or Friend inside the first set of braces determines the scope of the procedure. If not used, as in our case, the procedure's scope is Public by default. Only Class modules use Friend. The term Static is also optional and specifies that the Sub procedure's local variables be preserved between calls. *Arglist* is an optional list of variables representing arguments to be passed to the procedure when it is called. If the procedure takes more than one variable, you separate them in the list with commas.

After the first line, you will have any number of statements to be executed within the procedure. When the action is completed, you may have an Exit Sub statement, which may be followed by additional statements. These additional statements are normally located where code is designed to handle errors. The Function procedure's syntax:

```
[Public | Private | Friend] [Static] Function name [(arglist)] [As type]
     [statements]
     [name = expression]
     [Exit Function]
     [statements]
     [name = expression]
End Function
```

Most of the items in brackets are the same for both Function and Sub statements. Two main additions are [`As` *`type`*] and [*`name = expression`*]. [`As` *`type`*] sets the data type of the value returned by the Function; for example, it may be a Boolean, Integer, Long, or String variable.

▶ **See** "Determining the Scope of a Variable," **p. 159**

▶ **See** "Subprocedures," **p. 125**

▶ **See** "Functions," **p. 125**

The Functions that you write also have a specific header and footer. The header starts with the keyword Function, names the procedure, and has open and close parentheses. The footer has the keyword End Function.

Programming Methods

As with every other programming language, Visual Basic for Applications has keywords and conditional statements that enable you to build decision-making into your procedures. Decision-making is execution of code statements based on an evaluation of a condition. If the condition is met, one set of commands is executed. If the condition is not met, another set of commands may be executed.

If...End If The `If...End If` conditional statement is very similar to the Excel If function. It tests a condition and, depending on the results of that test, chooses one of two options. The `If...End If` statement is a commonly used decision-making tool in all programming languages. There are four different ways that this statement can be written, depending on how complex the condition or whether there are several conditions you are trying to test. The `If...End If` statement can be written as a single line of code. This is its simplest format.

NOTE Microsoft Help refers to the `If...End If` statement as an `If...Then...Else` statement. These are one in the same.

The syntax for the `If...End If` statement written as a single line of code is

```
If condition Then [statements] [Else else-statements]
```

Syntax Statements Are Optional

Syntax statements within brackets are optional for that statement. Items that are italicized in the syntax example may take several different formats or could be several lines of code. A couple of examples of the formats that italicized syntax items may take are

If X = 5 Then where `X=5` is the condition and, in this case, a variable named `X` that is being tested to see whether it is equal to 5.

"If MsgBox("Do you want to continue?", vbYesNo) = vbYes Then" where "MsgBox("Do you want to continue?", vbYesNo) = vbYes" is the condition and the MsgBox function is being tested to see whether it is vbYes.

The italicized words *statements* and *else-statements* refer to any code you want to use in the format you choose.

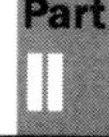

The main difference between this and the other variations is that when the `If...End If` statement is written as a single line of code, no need exists for the `End If`. This is because

everything is on one line and the program doesn't have to be notified when the `If...End If` statement is complete; the program assumes it is complete on that line.

The `If...End If` statement can also be written as a block of code with each branch of the conditional on a separate line. No difference is found in execution, just readability and the specific syntax of the statements. The following code is an Excel VBA example of using the `If...End If` statement on one line of code:

```
If Selection.Value >= 2000 Then Selection.Offset(0,1).Value = "Millennium
➥Solution"
```

The statement checks the value of a selected cell on the spreadsheet and compares it with a value of 2000. If the cell's value is greater than or equal to 2000, the rest of the `If...End If` statement executes. If the cell's value is less than 2000, the program goes to the next branch of the conditional. After the keyword `Then` is the code you want to execute if the condition is met. In this case, the value of the cell to the right of the cell whose condition you were testing is changed to read "Millennium Solution."

The syntax for the `If...End If` statement written as a block of code is

```
If condition Then
[statements]
[ElseIf condition Then
[elseif-statements]]
[Else
[else-statements]]
End If
```

For the most part, everything in this format is the same as the one-line version. Here are the differences. The first line of code must have the complete condition and the word "Then" on the same line. Next place as many lines of code as you need to execute if the condition is met. The next part, the `ElseIf` condition and the `[elseif-statements]`, enables you to add complex comparisons. Because they are in brackets, they aren't necessary, but there may be times when you need to use them. These two examples illustrate how this is done.

Here is an example of the `If...End` If statement written as a block of code without the "`[ElseIf]`" statements:

```
If Selection.Value >= 2000 Then
     Selection.Offset(0,1).Value = "Millennium Solution"
End If
```

This example is identical in result to the example used for the single-line `If...End If` statement. The style used to write it is the only difference.

Now the example using *else-if statements*:

```
If Selection.Value >= 2000 Then
     Selection.Offset(0,1).Value = "Millennium Solution"
ElseIf Selection.Value = "" Then
     MsgBox "There is no value in the selected cell."
End If
```

This also checks the value of the selected cell and determines whether it is greater than or equal to 2000. If it is then, once again, "Millennium Solution" is entered in the cell one column to the right of the active (selected) cell. If that condition isn't met, the program executes the `ElseIf` line of code. This is another condition check.

In this example, it happens to check the value of the same cell, but it could be something entirely different (another cell, a variable in your procedure, a property of the object you are using, and so on). In this example, it checks whether the selected cell is blank; if it is, a message box lets the user know that the selected cell has no value.

Alpha and Numeric Characters Are Interpreted Differently

If you run this conditional on a cell that contains an alpha value (such as "Y2K") instead of a numeric value, the `If` condition will return true. This is because Excel interprets alpha characters as being higher in value than numeric characters. To prevent this from happening, you can insert the entire `If...End If` conditional inside another one that tests for the proper kind of data:

```
If TypeName(ActiveCell.Value) = "Double" Then
    If Selection.Value >= 2000 Then
        Selection.Offset(0,1).Value = "Millennium Solution"
    ElseIf Selection.Value = "" Then
        MsgBox "There is no value in the selected cell."
    End If
End If
```

Now, the code first checks whether the cell contains numeric data ("Double" is a numeric data type). If it does, it continues and checks the cell's Value, knowing that it's safe to do so. Otherwise, checking the Value wouldn't make sense, because the data wouldn't be in the form we need for the test.

▶ **See** "Logical and Information Functions," **p. 722**

For Each...Next Another common programming action is running the same sequences of code a number of times. There are several different statements used to loop through records. Looping involves repeating a specified action, and can be accomplished a specific number of times, or it can be dependent on meeting a specified condition.

The `For Each...Next` statement enables the programmer to repeat a block of code once for each item in a group of items. For example, this can be done for each cell in an Excel worksheet range. You have a range of cells that have expiration dates that go from December 1997 to December 2002. You want to check each one to see whether the date is in the year 2000 or later. You could use the `For Each...Next` statement to programmatically move from cell to cell. Each time the program moves to a cell, your block of code that checks the date is executed. The following is the syntax of the `For Each...Next` statement:

```
For Each element In group
[statements]
[Exit For]
[statements]
Next [element]
```

Part II Ch 6

The following code example illustrates the use of the `For Each...Next` statement to loop through the collection of Command Bars. You also might note that the `For Each...Next` statement is nested within an `If` statement. The `For Each...Next` statement code loops once through the Command Bars collection. As it loops through the collection it checks each Command Bar looking for the "Full Screen" Command Bar. When the "Full Screen" Command Bar is found (once again, note that the check for that command bar is done with an `If` statement), the Visible property of that Command Bar is set to False.

This looping construction loops a specified number of times determined by the number of Command Bars in the Command Bar collection. That number is determined by the line of code `For Each cmdBar In CommandBars`.

```
Sub ToggleFull()
    Dim cmdBar as CommandBar
    ActiveWindow.View.FullScreen = Not ActiveWindow.View.FullScreen
    If ActiveWindow.View.FullScreen = True Then
      For Each cmdBar In CommandBars
        If cmdBar.Name = "Full Screen" Then cmdBar.Visible = False
      Next cmdBar
    End If
End Sub
```

You do not have to include the `cmdBar` portion of the Next line, but it is good practice to do so, because it documents what you are doing. If your `Next` line ever gets very far from the `For Each` line, it helps to know what kind of object comes `Next` in your loop.

Do...Loop The `Do...Loop` enables you to loop through a sequence of code based on whether a certain condition is met or changes. The code you want to make conditional is located between the `Do` and the `Loop`. There are two ways to write the `Do...Loop`. Which one you choose is dependent on when you want to check the condition.

NOTE This differs from the `For Each...Next` loop, which loops through a specific number of items in a collection. The number of items in that collection determines how many times the sequence goes through the loop.

The syntax of the `Do...Loop` statement with the condition checked before entering the loop is as follows:

```
Do [{While ¦ Until} condition]
[statements]
[Exit Do]
[statements]
Loop
```

The syntax of the `Do...Loop` statement with the condition checked after entering the loop is written like this:

```
Do
[statements]
[Exit Do]
[statements]
Loop [{While ¦ Until} condition]
```

With the condition checked before the looping action—for example, `Do While X = 5`—the program checks the condition first to see whether it is met. If it is met, the lines of code between `Do` and `Loop` execute until the condition is no longer met. If the condition is not met, the code inside the loop will not run.

For example, imagine you wanted an alarm clock that would tell you to take a break in ten minutes. You could use a `Do...Loop` construction to do the work. Just check whether ten minutes have passed since the procedure started and loop while the condition is false. As long as the current time is later than ten minutes from the start time, the loop will continue checking the condition. After ten minutes pass, the `While` condition enables the loop to exit, and you can display a message box to let you know it's time to take a break. Here is the example:

```
Sub TellMeWhenItsBreakTime()
    Dim datTime As Variant
    datTime = Now()
    Do While DateDiff("n", datTime, Now()) < 10
        '<<No need for any code here.>>
    Loop
    MsgBox "It's time for a break!"
End Sub
```

With the condition checked after entering the looping action—for example, `Loop While X = 5`—the program checks the condition after the code has run at least once. In this format, the code in the loop always executes at least once whether or not the condition is met. It repeats the loop only if the condition is met.

For example, you could use this `Do...Loop` syntax to display a login dialog box when it enters the loop. Then, if the user types an incorrect password, the `Loop While` line of code displays the login box again to give the user another chance to enter the password. It would continue repeating the procedure until the user types in the correct password. If he typed it correctly the first time, the code would not loop.

```
Do
    Answer = InputBox ("Enter the name of the Program User")
Loop Until Answer = Application.UserName Or Answer = ""
```

As well as being able to check the condition either at the start or the end of the loop, there are two ways of checking the condition. You can choose `Do While ...` or `Do Until ...` or you can choose `Loop While...` or `Loop Until...`. When you use `While`, you are waiting for a variable that normally remains constant to change. When you use `Until`, you are waiting for a variable to change into a certain value.

Useful Procedures

This section presents two sample procedures to give you a better idea of how Visual Basic for Applications can enhance your use of Microsoft Office 2000. Feel free to copy or alter these procedures to suit your particular situation. Some of the specifics, such as text entries and location references, must be changed to fit your requirements.

- Message boxes—Use this procedure to display a message to the user when the macro is run with this procedure.
- Input boxes—Use this procedure to display a box in which the user can type an entry.

Message Boxes The primary purpose for message box procedures is to let the user know something. For example, you might get a message box with an OK button when you finish downloading a file off the Internet. The message tells you that the download is finished. Your only option is to click the OK button.

There are two types of message box procedures that you can use—message box statements and message box functions.

Message Box Statements Use message box statements to display a message that does not require a decision by the user (for example, a message box that displays the message, "Word has finished spell checking the document" and an "OK" button). No decision has to be made; you just click the "OK" button to acknowledge the message. Notice that parentheses are not used to enclose the arguments. Parentheses are used only when a returned value is found, as in the Message box function that is covered in the next bulleted section.

The following procedure demonstrates the `MsgBox` statement in use. It has one mandatory argument—the message (prompt) for the user. The arguments in square brackets (buttons, title, and helpfile) are optional; if not specified, the `MsgBox` displays defaults of an "OK" button, the name of the application in the title bar, and no reference to a help file. The `MsgBox` syntax is

```
MsgBox prompt[, buttons] [, title] [, helpfile, context]
```

The procedure's code would be

```
MsgBox "Word has finshed spell checking the document."
```

Message Box Functions Message box functions also display a message, but they ask a question as well, which requires a choice by the user. For example, you might give the user a message box with the question, "Are you sure you want to delete this worksheet?" with "Yes" and "No" buttons from which to choose. Often an `If...Then` statement checks which button was chosen, and then executes code accordingly. In this example, it either deletes the worksheet or leaves the worksheet in place.

The following procedure demonstrates the `MsgBox` function being used to display a question for the user. It can be used in any other procedure. It has two mandatory arguments—the prompt for the user and a choice of buttons. Most often, the choice is a "Yes" or a "No" button. The arguments in square brackets (buttons, title, and helpfile) are optional and, if not specified, the title would be the name of the program and there would be no reference to a help file. The `MsgBox` syntax is

```
MsgBox(prompt[, buttons] [, title] [, helpfile, context])
```

Here is an example of how the `MsgBox` function can be used in a procedure.

```
Sub DeleteTheSheet()
    Dim intDelete as Integer
    intDelete = MsgBox("Are you certain you want to delete this worksheet?", _
        vbCritical + vbYesNo, ActiveSheet.Name)
    If intDelete = vbYes Then
        Application.DisplayAlerts = False
        ActiveSheet.Delete
```

```
        Application.DisplayAlerts = True
    End If
End Sub
```

In the previous example, the response from the user is stored in the variable `intDelete` (please note that there are several ways of doing this; only this one is discussed here). The second argument of the function is where the Yes and No buttons are added to give the user a choice and a "Critical" symbol is also added to emphasize the seriousness of the choice. The last argument used in this example is the title argument. The name of the `ActiveSheet` is used for the title.

To check which button the user presses—Yes or No—an `If...Then` statement is used to check the value of `intDelete`. If the value is "Yes," Excel's alert display is turned off, the worksheet is deleted, and the alerts are turned back on. If the value is "No," no action is taken.

Figure 6.5 shows the message box created from the previous procedure.

FIGURE 6.5
A `MsgBox` lets you provide information to the user.

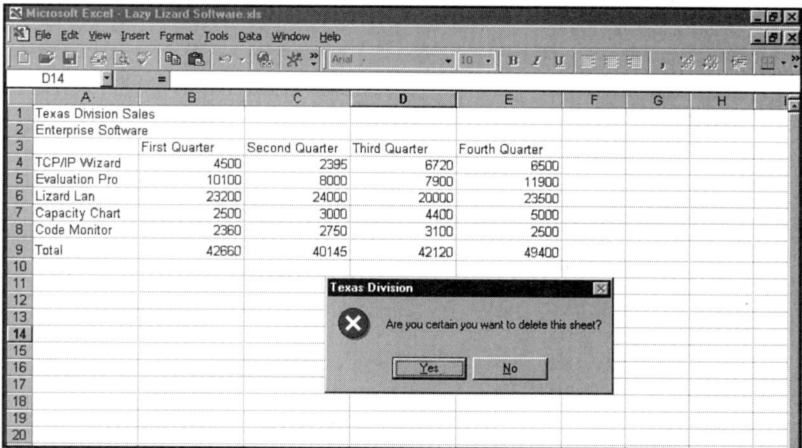

NOTE Whenever you see VBA code described as a *function*—whether a `MsgBox`, an `InputBox`, or any other procedure—you can count on that procedure returning a value. It is your choice whether or not to use that value. Most often, as in the message box function described earlier, you will use the returned value to decide how your procedure should proceed.

Input Boxes Another very useful procedure is the `InputBox` function, which is used to get information from a user beyond what can be determined by a push of a Yes or No button. The following example of the procedure uses an `InputBox` to ask for the user's name, and then places the name in the selected cell on the worksheet. The `InputBox` also has one mandatory argument, a prompt asking for information. The following is the `InputBox` syntax:

```
InputBox(prompt[, title] [, default] [, xpos] [, ypos] [, helpfile, context])
```

The prompt argument is required. The title, default, vertical (xpos) and horizontal (ypos) positions of the `InputBox`, and helpfile information all are optional.

The optional arguments used most often are the *title* and *default*. You can specify both either by typing literal text in quotes or by specifying a string variable, including the return values of built-in functions such as `ActiveSheet.Name`. (Note that when you use a variable or function call, you omit the quotes.) The default value is placed in the `InputBox` as highlighted text. If the user wants to keep the default value, she just clicks the OK button. If the user wants to enter a different value, she can type the entry over the default text, and then click the OK button (see Figure 6.6). Here is an example of the VBA code and resulting input box:

```
Sub ShowInputBox()
    Dim strName As String
    strName = InputBox("This is an example of an Input Box prompt. Please enter
➥your name.", "Example Title", "Default Value - John Q. Public")
    If strName <> "" Then
        MsgBox "Your name is " & strName & ".",,strName & "'s InputBox Result"
    End If
End Sub
```

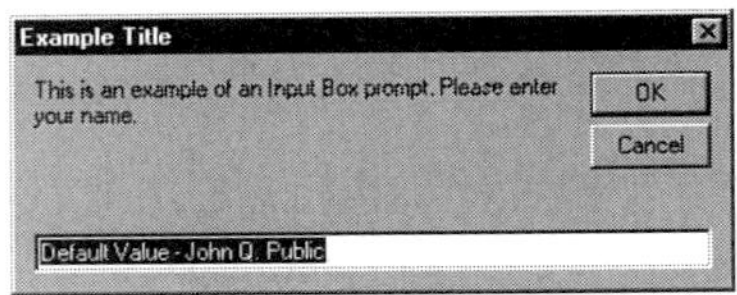

FIGURE 6.6
An `InputBox` lets you get information from the user.

Putting the Module Together

Suppose you want to find a faster way to create a common worksheet design to be used by your company every day. Instead of re-creating a new worksheet from scratch—applying formulas and formatting—consider creating a template that automatically applies your formulas, formatting, and input boxes for easy data entry.

The scenario is a standard Excel Worksheet with data in a predetermined number of rows and columns and with the columns added together. The worksheet is formatted to your design specifications. To make this usable as a template, delete the raw data from the cells and leave the formulas intact. The following macro makes it easier to enter the raw data.

This macro started out as a simple recorded cell selection and data entry macro. Then I added code to loop through the cells that needed data. I added an `InputBox` to ease the input.

```
Sub EnterDataInputBox()
'
' EnterDataInput Macro
' Macro written/recorded 11/3/98 by Ron Stockdreher
'
    Dim intRows As Integer
    Dim intCols As Integer
    Dim intRowCount As Integer
    Dim intColCount As Integer
    Range("B3").Select 'This was recorded. It selects the first cell in
    ' in the row of column headers.
    Range(Selection, Selection.End(xlToRight)).Select 'This was recorded. It
```

```
    ' selects all the contiguous cells with data, effectively selecting all the
    ' columns with data.
' The next line counts the number of columns used so the For/Next loop
' can cycle through a varied number of columns
    intColCount = Selection.Columns.Count
' Here is the first For/Next loop for the columns
    For intCols = 1 To intColCount
' Here is an If statement that checks if there is data in the target column
' If there is, the macro moves to the next column, if not data entry starts
        If ActiveCell.Offset(1, 0).Value = "" Then
            Range(Selection, Selection.End(xlDown)).Select 'This was recorded
' Here a count of the rows used is made to set the nested For/Next loop
            intRowCount = Selection.Rows.Count
            ActiveCell.Select
' Here is the nested For/Next Loop to cycle through the rows
            For intRows = 1 To intRowCount - 2
' The Offset method moves down one row at a time
                Selection.Offset(1, 0).Select
' There was a recorded line here that entered data into the cells. It was
' replaced with an InputBox
                ActiveCell.Value = InputBox("Please enter the data", _
                    ActiveWorkbook.Name)
' This line starts the next loop
            Next intRows
'When the loop is finished this line moves the active cell back to the top row
            Selection.End(xlUp).Select
        End If
' This line moves to the next column
        ActiveCell.Offset(0, 1).Select
' This line starts the next loop through the columns
    Next intCols
End Sub
```

There are a number of things happening in this small macro. I added two `For...Next` loops. One loops through the columns, while the other loops through the rows. The second `For...Next` loop is nested within the first. As it moves from cell to cell in a given column, an `InputBox` is displayed, enabling the reader to enter his data. After it works its way through all the rows in the columns, the macro stops.

Taking the macro apart helps you to understand the process:

```
Sub EnterDataInputBox()
'
' EnterDataInput Macro
' Macro written/recorded 11/3/98 by Ron Stockdreher
'
    Dim intRows as Integer
    Dim intCols as Integer
    Dim intRowCount as Integer
    Dim intColCount as Integer
```

This is a `Sub` procedure and carries out a task. It does not return a value, but it does make changes to the active worksheet. Comments identify the macro, the date when it was written, and the author. The next four lines declare the variables in the procedure that hold the row and column references so that the code can loop through the cells of the spreadsheet.

```
    Range("B3").Select 'This was recorded. It selects the first cell in
    ' in the row of column headers.
    Range(Selection, Selection.End(xlToRight)).Select 'This was recorded. It
    ' selects all the contiguous cells with data, effectively selecting all the
    ' columns with data.
' The next line counts the number of columns used so the For/Next loop
' can cycle through a varied number of columns
    intColCount = Selection.Columns.Count
```

Here the first cell in the main body of the spreadsheet is selected. It is the first cell with a column header in the row of column headers. After this cell is selected, the next line of code selects all the cells in that row (to the right) that contain data. With these cells selected, we can now count them to determine the total number of columns with data. That count is stored in the variable `intColCount`.

NOTE As is evident by the code and explanation of how it works, you need to plan ahead in the design of your project. This macro is heavily dependent on the spreadsheet being designed a certain way. For example, the initial cell with a column header is "B3." If you used this macro on a spreadsheet where that was not the case, the macro would not work correctly. This is why planning is the most important part of the development process.

```
' Here is the first For/Next loop for the columns
    For intCols = 1 To intColCount
' Here is an If statement that checks if there is data in the target column
' If there is, the macro moves to the next column, if not data entry starts
        If ActiveCell.Offset(1, 0).Value = "" Then
            Range(Selection, Selection.End(xlDown)).Select 'This was recorded
' Here a count of the rows used is made to set the nested For/Next loop
            intRowCount = Selection.Rows.Count
            ActiveCell.Select
```

By using the column count stored in `intColCount`, the first `For...Next` loop is started. It loops through each column up to the total number of columns one at a time. The next line of code is an `If` statement that checks to see where the data is found in the column. It looks at the cell immediately below the one it is currently in by using the `Offset` method (`ActiveCell.Offset(1,0)`) and checks the value. If it finds nothing (`ActiveCell.Offset(1,0).Value = ""`), it selects the total number of cells in that column down to the formula at the bottom of the column. Then the data is counted and stored in `intRowCount`. The variable `intRowCount` is used in another `For...Next` loop to loop through the rows in the column. The last line of code in the previous section selects the active cell, which is at the top of the column of cells selected to perform the count of rows.

```
' Here is the nested For/Next Loop to cycle through the rows
            For intRows = 1 To intRowCount - 2
' The Offset method moves down one row at a time
                Selection.Offset(1, 0).Select
' There was a recorded line here that entered data into the cells. It was
' replaced with an InputBox
                ActiveCell.Value = InputBox("Please enter the data", _
                    ActiveWorkbook.Name)
' This line starts the next loop
            Next intRows
```

This is the nested `For...Next` loop that loops through the rows. Note that the first line of code (`For intRows = 1 To intRowCount - 2`) loops from 1 to the total number of rows (`intRowCount minus 2`); the code subtracts two because it can skip the header row and the formula row (where totals are calculated). The next line moves down one row and selects the cell. The value of that cell is set to whatever the user enters in an `InputBox`. The `InputBox` function asks the user to enter the data, using the name of the active workbook as the `InputBox` title. After the user types the value and clicks OK, the code loops and does the exact same thing for the next cell in the column. This loop repeats until all the cells in the column are filled.

CAUTION

The code in this macro assumes that the user will enter only appropriate data into the cells—in this case, numbers. If the user enters text, that text will be entered into the cell and, of course, the formulas at the end of the columns will not work. You can make your code "bulletproof," or rather "user proof," by checking the value the user types in the `InputBox` before you enter that value into the cell.

```
'When the loop is finished this line moves the active cell back to the top row
            Selection.End(xlUp).Select
        End If
' This line moves to the next column
        ActiveCell.Offset(0, 1).Select
' This line starts the next loop through the columns
    Next intCols
End Sub
```

Here the loop through the rows has finished, but not the loop through the columns. To work on the next column, the selection first moves up to the top of the current column (`Selection.End(xlUp).Select`). Then the code exits the `If` statement that checked for missing data in the column. The active cell moves to the right and the next iteration of the loop through the columns starts. This continues until the last column passes the test and the procedure ends.

All you need now is a way to start this macro when the workbook opens and the sheet is activated. This is covered in the section "Using Events," later in this chapter. Before going on to automating this and other procedures, some other key points about VBA need to be covered.

Guidelines for Naming VBA Items

As you edit the macros that you recorded and as you begin writing code of your own, you will be doing a lot of naming. For example, you will need to give a name to every variable you declare. VBA enforces some basic rules for how you do this. (The rules are summarized in the online Help under "Visual Basic Naming Rules.") There are also some naming conventions that VBA will not enforce, but which will make your life easier. These rules and suggestions apply to all the names you give to all subs, functions, variables, constants, and arguments. The general rules are

- The first character of every name must be a letter; it cannot be a number or symbol.
- The name cannot include a space, period (.), exclamation mark (!), or the characters @, &, $, #.
- The name cannot exceed 255 characters in length.
- The name cannot conflict with a built-in (intrinsic) VBA statement, such as Sub, Stop, or Call. VBA statements are standalone commands that you execute in code. By contrast, VBA will let you use built-in property values and control names such as Left, Value, or Timer for names you create. However, in general, you should not, because it leads to confusion and forces you to qualify every call to the built-in name with its type library (`VBA.Minute`).
- You cannot repeat names within the same scope. For example, you can't declare two variables named "`strMyString`" within the same procedure. Although you can declare a module-level variable named "`strMyString`" and a procedure-level variable named "`strMyString`," don't do it. You end up by using one variable's value when you think you're using another's. Always use unique names and you'll never have to worry about this.

Naming Code Modules

Modules, such as all Office 2000 objects, must have unique names. When you first create a module, VBA gives it a unique name automatically (Module*x* by default) in the same fashion as Worksheet names in Excel. But you should always change the name to something more descriptive of its purpose. There's no reason not to, and it helps you organize your code.

Renaming a module is easy. Select the module's icon in the Project Window of the VB Editor and the Property Window displays its available properties, including its Name. To rename the module, click in the right side of the text box next to the property Name and type the name you want to use (see Figure 6.7). The name must be one word (no spaces) and can be up to 31 characters in length. Name your modules consistently and try to give them a meaningful relationship to the code in the module.

Avoiding Naming Conflicts

A naming conflict occurs when you try to create or use a name that was previously defined as something else. Naming conflicts that go undetected can result in bugs in your code that produce strange and erroneous results. This is particularly a problem if you do not require variable declaration.

The easiest way to avoid most naming conflicts is by understanding the scope of the variables and constants you create. A naming conflict occurs most often when a name is visible at more than one scoping level or has two different meanings at the same level.

Sticking to a specific naming convention can also help, because it gives you more names from which to choose. For example, most experienced programmers use prefixes to identify variables by data type and scope. The idea is to use a lowercase three-letter abbreviation as a simple and easy-to-read indicator that the variable is a String (str), an Integer (int), or a Variant (vnt). Following is an example of a variable using the prefix "int" to identify it as an Integer typed variable.

```
Dim intCounter As Integer
```

You can also use a prefix to indicate scope. For example, if you prefix every module-level variable with m or m_, you will always avoid a naming conflict with a like-named procedure-level variable.

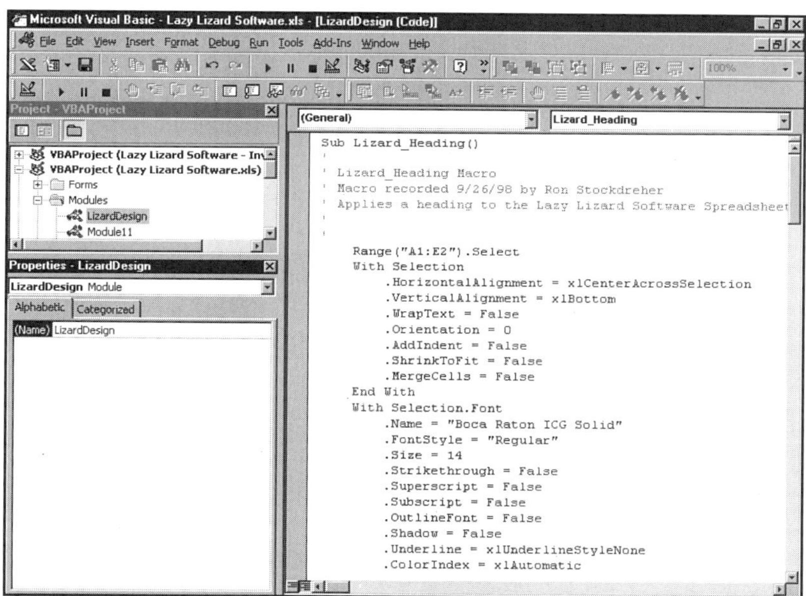

FIGURE 6.7
Use specific names for code modules to organize your macros.

Adding Comments to Your Modules

At the beginning of this chapter, you went over the development cycle. One of the steps in that cycle was documenting your code and using comments to accomplish this. Use comments to explain a procedure or a particular sequence of instructions, mark a position in the code text, temporarily indicate your location, or keep track of your thought process. Leaving your comments in the code lets anyone reading your code—you, in particular—know what in the world you were thinking six or eight months later when you want to make a modification.

VBA ignores comments when it runs code, which means it takes no longer to compile and run commented code than uncommented code. Comment lines begin with an apostrophe ('). They can be placed anywhere within the code window as a separate line or at the end of a line of code. To add a comment to the same line as a statement, insert an apostrophe after the statement, followed by the comment. To add a comment as a separate line, insert an apostrophe followed by your comment. Comments, by default, are displayed as green text.

You can also add comments by prefixing them with the `REM` keyword, but you should avoid doing so. Unlike the apostrophe, `REM` is a VBA statement (command) that executes—which means it does slow down your code.

Here is the syntax:

```
' comment goes here
```

The following example from the `EnterDataInputBox` macro uses comments at the end of lines and at the beginning of lines:

```
Sub EnterDataInputBox()
'
' EnterData Macro
' Macro recorded 11/3/98 by Ron Stockdreher
'
    Dim intRows as Integer
    Dim intCols as Integer
    Dim intRowCount as Integer
    Dim intColCount as Integer

    Range("B3").Select 'This was recorded
    Range(Selection, Selection.End(xlToRight)).Select 'This was recorded
' The next line counts the number of columns used so the For/Next loop
' can cycle through a varied number of columns
    intColCount = Selection.Columns.Count
' Here is the first For/Next loop for the columns
    For intCols = 1 To intColCount
' ///remaining macro code deleted for this example///
End Sub
```

Another great use for comments is to disable code that you want to avoid running during testing of a larger procedure. You don't want to delete the code; you just want to avoid running it during the test. Place apostrophes at the beginning of each line of code that you want to disable and VBA will ignore it. Be sure to comment out the entire sequence of code and not leave stray items that would affect the procedure.

Comment Block and *Uncomment Block* Commands

The `Comment Block` and `Uncomment Block` commands add and remove the comment character, an apostrophe, for each line of a selected block of text. These tools can be found only on the Edit Toolbar. If you do not have text selected and you use these commands, the comment character is added or removed in the line where the pointer is located.

Defining Variables

In Chapter 5, variables are described as a place in memory that is set aside to store a unique value that can be changed while the program is running. Before digging into the details of how to declare variables, there are two key points you should consider:

- Why bother to use variables at all?
- The two significantly different ways to declare variables in VBA.

Why Use Variables?

When you record a macro in any Office product, VBA dutifully records what steps you took to carry out the procedure and faithfully plays back those steps. This is wonderful, but what if you have some changing parameters you want to track and modify, such as counting the number of employees in the employee database and changing their seniority status based on their hire date?

The recorder would be a little weak, but using a variable in VBA lets you store and loop through values and test them as the loop progresses. Here are two samples of code that loop through a number of cells in an Excel spreadsheet and test those values. One works its way through the data one cell at a time and the other uses a variable to loop through the data.

This procedure comes from code that the macro recorder created:

```
Sub CycleThroughCells()
'
' CycleThroughCells Macro
' Macro recorded 10/15/98 by Ron Stockdreher
'    Range("A1").Select
    ActiveCell.FormulaR1C1 = "1"
    Range("A2").Select
    ActiveCell.FormulaR1C1 = "2"
    Range("A3").Select
    ActiveCell.FormulaR1C1 = "3"
    Range("A4").Select
    ActiveCell.FormulaR1C1 = "4"
    Range("A5").Select
    ActiveCell.FormulaR1C1 = "5"
    Range("A6").Select
    ActiveCell.FormulaR1C1 = "6"
End Sub
```

This procedure accomplishes exactly the same as the one shown earlier, except it uses a variable and a loop:

```
Sub LoopThroughCells()
' Loop through cells procedure
' Written 10/15/98 by Ron Stockdreher
'
    Dim intCurrentCell As Integer
    Range("A1").Select
    For intCurrentCell = 1 To 6
        ActiveCell.FormulaR1C1 = intCurrentCell
        ActiveCell.Offset(1, 0).Select
    Next intCurrentCell
End Sub
```


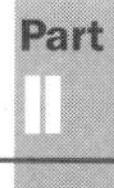

There are 12 lines of code in the top procedure and six in the lower one. Although this is not a huge difference with small programs, consider that the second procedure is half as long as the first. If you must create a 100-line procedure, you'll be glad when it doesn't end up being 200 lines of code.

Declaring Variables

To use variables in Visual Basic for Applications, you must declare them. There are two ways to do it—implicitly and explicitly. To declare a variable implicitly, all you have to do is use it. Here is an example:

```
Sub DeleteTheSheet()
    TheAnswer = MsgBox("Are you certain you want to delete this worksheet?", _
        vbCritical + vbYesNo, ActiveSheet.Name)
    If TheAnswer = vbYes Then
        Application.DisplayAlerts = False
        ActiveSheet.Delete
        Application.DisplayAlerts = True
    End If
End Sub
```

In this example, `TheAnswer` is declared implicitly. No `Dim` statement exists to explicitly allocate memory to it. VBA does it automatically the first time `TheAnswer` is used. The main reason to use implicitly declared variables is to avoid typing, but that's about the only benefit you can hope for. The much steeper, more frustrating price comes in two forms: bugs and inefficiency.

In the line,

```
TheAnswer = MsgBox("Are you certain you want to delete this worksheet?", _
        vbCritical + vbYesNo, ActiveSheet.Name)
```

VBA stores the user's response in the implicitly declared variable "`TheAnswer.`"

Then, in the line,

```
If TheAnswer = vbYes Then
```

VBA checks the variable to find out what that answer is.

What would happen if you mistyped "`TheAnswer`" as "`TheeAnswer`"? The program would not generate an error because it would assume you were declaring another implicitly declared variable, "`TheeAnswer.`"

The `If` statement that checks the value of "`TheeAnswer`" would find not the user's response, but an empty variable. The condition of the `If` statement would never do what you had intended.

Implicitly declaring variables also wastes a lot of time and resources, because all implicitly declared variables are of type Variant. Variants require more memory (16 bytes) than all other types except strings (which vary in size depending on the length of the string). They also have to convert their data to and from more specific types as the need arises, adding overhead to every operation that manipulates that data. For example, if you wanted to assign `TheAnswer` to another `InputBox`, VBA would first have to convert it to a String. If you do not explicitly declare your variables, your programs will take longer to execute and use more memory than needed.

To declare a variable explicitly, all you have to do is use a `Dim`, `Static`, `Private`, or `Public` statement to set aside memory for it. The following code snippet shows a very common use of explicit declaration.

```
Sub DeleteTheSheet()
    Dim intTheAnswer As Integer
    intTheAnswer = MsgBox("Are you certain you want to delete this worksheet?", _
        vbCritical + vbYesNo, ActiveSheet.Name)
    If intTheAnswer = vbYes Then
        Application.DisplayAlerts = False
        ActiveSheet.Delete
        Application.DisplayAlerts = True
    End If
End Sub
```

In this example, `Dim` tells VBA to set aside memory for a variable named `intTheAnswer`, and to make it an `Integer`. Now the procedure has an efficient data type to work with.

But this hasn't really solved the problem of implicit declaration, because VBA is still free to create new variables on-the-fly. You could still type "`If intTheeAnswer = vbYes Then`," and the code would not stop you.

If you want to prevent VBA from making implicit declarations, place the `Option Explicit` statement at the top of the module, before any procedures. This statement requires you to explicitly declare all variables within the module. If a module includes the `Option Explicit` statement, a compile-time error occurs whenever VBA encounters a variable name that has not been declared—which is what you'll have if you spell one incorrectly.

If you like this idea, you can set an option in the Visual Basic Editor to add `Option Explicit` to all new modules. Under Tools, Options, Editor tab, check the Require Variable Declaration check box. This does not change any existing code you have written, but you can type `Option Explicit` in any of those modules. Just set aside some time to catch all the compile-time errors that occur when you run any procedures in those modules.

VBA variable names aren't case-sensitive, but VBA does enforce the capitalization you specify in the variable declaration. This means that you can use capitalization to check your spelling. Declare your variables explicitly and type at least one letter of the name in uppercase. Then, whenever you use the variable in code, type the name in all *lowercase*. When you hit the enter key or move to the next line, the variable name capitalizes to match the declaration. If it doesn't, you know you've mistyped the name.

Determining the Scope of a Variable

The scope, or visibility, of a variable determines how often a procedure can use a variable, how many procedures can use the same variable, and how long the variable stays in memory.

NOTE The concept of scope also affects procedures, objects, and constants.

Scope exists at three levels:

- The procedure level (which is the lowest level)—allows visibility of a variable only within the procedure where the variable is declared. As soon as the procedure finishes, the variable is destroyed and its memory is freed. Different procedures can have identically named variables without conflict, because each exists only when that procedure is running.
- The module level—Variables declared at the module level are visible to any procedure within that module. They exist as long as that module is available. For example, if a document with a code module is open in Word, a module level variable is available until that document is closed. Identically named variables in this module would have a naming conflict if declared at the module level, but another module could have variables with the same name.
- The Public level—Variables declared as Public are visible to all procedures in all modules. They exist as long as the file is open.

Variables declared in a procedure are visible only within the procedure and lose their value between calls to the procedure. However, one exception exists—when variables are declared Static. You will examine Static variables in the section titled "The Static Statement," later in this chapter.

Entering a Declaration in Code

Having laid the groundwork, let's look at declaration statements. Declaration statements name external procedures, constants, or variables and define their attributes, such as data type. The statements `Dim`, `Static`, `Private`, and `Public` make declarations.

The *Dim* Statement The `Dim` statement is used to declare variables and allocate memory. Variables declared with `Dim` at the module level are available for use by all procedures within that module, just as with variables declared `Private` (covered in "The Private Statement," later in this chapter). If `Dim` is used at the procedure level, those variables are available only within that procedure.

In general, you should use `Dim` to declare procedure-level variables only, because the `Private` and `Public` statements now serve the module level. VBA won't force you to do this, though; Dim is kept as a means for backward compatibility with earlier versions of VBA where the `Private` statement was not available.

You also use the `Dim` statement to declare a variable's data type. If you do not declare a specific data type, the Variant data type will be assigned. See "How Data Types Affect Your Program," later in this chapter.

For example, the following statement declares a variable as an `Integer`.

```
Dim intRowCount as Integer
```

When the variable is first used in code, it is initialized. A numeric variable is initialized to 0 and a variable-length string is initialized to a zero-length string (`""`). Variant variables are initialized to Empty.

Common practice is to place the `Dim` statements in a procedure at the beginning of that procedure.

The *Static* Statement The `Static` statement is used at procedure level to declare variables and allocate storage space. It cannot be used at the module level. Variables declared with the `Static` statement retain their values as long as the code is running. Effectively, that means as long as the workbook, document, or presentation is open.

Use a `Static` statement within a procedure to declare a variable that retains its value between procedure calls. For example, the following statement declares an integer variable:

```
Static intCount as Integer
```

You could use this type of variable to count the number of times an event, such as the display of a login screen, happens. The procedure could start and stop several times as incorrect data is typed in and the user exits the Login. Normally, an integer variable declared with `Dim` within the procedure is reset to zero each time the procedure starts. If you use `Static` instead of `Dim`, the value is retained and you can keep track of the variable and shut down access to the program after a set number of attempts.

Common practice is to place the `Static` statements in a procedure at the beginning of that procedure just as with `Dim` statements.

The *Public* Statement The `Public` statement is used at module level to declare public variables and allocate storage space. It can be used only at the module level, not within a procedure.

Variables declared by using the `Public` statement are the most widely available variables. They can be used by all procedures in all modules in all applications. This can be a serious problem. For example, if you declare a variable "`intCostBasis`" as public in one document and you do the same in another document, you will have a naming conflict if both those documents are open at the same time. Also, that variable can be changed by code from any other document that is open. You can prevent this conflict by placing "`Option Private Module`" at the beginning of your module. Then, the variables are public only to the project in which they reside.

Here is an example of the `Public` statement used to declare a variable as an `Integer`:

```
Public intCount as Integer
```

The *Private* Statement The `Private` statement is used at module level to declare private variables and allocate storage space. The `Private` statement is used in the same way as the `Dim` statement, but never inside procedures. `Private` variables are available only to the module in which they are declared.

For example, the following statement declares a variable as an `Integer`:

```
Private intCount as Integer
```

Entering Declarations To enter procedure-level declarations:

1. Place your insertion point anywhere after the `Sub` or `Function` statement and before the first line of executable code.

2. Type `Dim` or `Static`. (`Private` and `Public` cannot be used at the procedure level.)
3. Name the variable. See "Guidelines for Naming VBA Items," earlier in this chapter.
4. Identify the variable's attributes. This is optional, but can be critical for efficient VBA modules. See Table 6.1, "VBA Data Types," later in this chapter.

To enter module-level or `Public` declarations:

1. Select the module you want to open in the Project window and click the View Code button.
2. In the Object box, select (General). In the Procedure box, select (Declarations).
3. Type `Dim`, `Private`, or `Public`. (Static cannot be used at the module level.)
4. Name the variable. See "Guidelines for Naming VBA Items," in this chapter.
5. Identify the variable's attributes. This is optional, but can be critical for efficient VBA modules. See Table 6.1, "VBA Data Types," later in this chapter.

The following example creates the variable `strMyString` and specifies the String data type.

```
Dim strMyString As String
```

If this statement appears within a procedure, the variable `strMyString` can be used only in that procedure. If the statement appears in the Declarations section of the module, the variable `strMyString` is available to all procedures within the module, but not to procedures in other modules. At the module-level, the `Dim` and `Private` keywords accomplish the same thing.

The `Dim` and `Private` keywords make the variable available to all procedures within the module, but not to procedures in other modules. When you use the `Static` statement instead of a `Dim` statement to declare variables at the procedure level, the variables retain their values as long as code in any module within that document is running. Here is an example of how the `Static` statement might be used:

```
Sub UserNameCheck()
    Static intCount As Integer
    Dim strUserName As String
    Do
        strUserName = InputBox("Enter your UserName.")
        intCount = intCount + 1
        If intCount > 3 Then
            IntCount = 0
            MsgBox "Please contact your System Administrator for access."
            Exit Sub
        End If
        If strUserName <> "Boss" Then
            MsgBox "I'm sorry, that UserName is incorrect. Try again."
        End If
    Loop While strUserName <> "Boss"
    MsgBox "Enter, Boss!"
End Sub
```

Variables can be declared as one of the following data types: Boolean, Byte, Integer, Long, Currency, Decimal, Single, Double, Date, String, Object, or Variant.

CAUTION

If you do not specify a data type, the Variant data type is assigned by default. Variables with Variant data types use up much more memory space and process more slowly than most other types (strings can be slower).

How Data Types Affect Your Program

The data type of a variable determines what kind of data it can hold. Variables that are strongly typed—declared as a specific data type—are more efficient in your program and make your code run faster. Here are two examples of strongly typed variables.

```
Dim strMyString As String
Dim intCounter As Integer
```

Most strongly typed variables are fast and efficient because VBA knows ahead of time how to handle the data and does not have to convert them from a Variant each time the variable is used. Additionally, specific data types use only the amount of memory required for that piece of data and do not waste as much valuable memory space as 16-byte Variants.

Probably the best reason to use specific data types, although, is that it makes your program less prone to errors. VBA does not let you place a string in an Integer variable, or an Integer in a Double. This eliminates some of the errors that can arise when a user tries to enter a name where an age ought to go. Without strongly typed variables, filtering out this kind of erroneous data can be difficult to do reliably, leading to problems in your code that are very difficult to identify and correct. The downside of using strongly typed variables (if it can be called a downside) is that you have to be more careful when you plan and code your project, determining exactly what type of data you will be using. Careful planning brings a lot of discipline to the process, so that tends to cancel out any disadvantage.

Table 6.1 shows the data types found in Visual Basic for Applications, the approximate amount of memory used for storage, and the range of values that a particular data type can hold.

Table 6.1 VBA Data Types

Data Type	Storage Size	Range
Byte	1 byte	0 to 255
Boolean	2 bytes	True or False
Integer	2 bytes	-32,768 to 32,767
Long (long integer)	4 bytes	-2.1 billion to 2.1 billion
Single	4 bytes	-3.4E38 to 3.4E38

continues

Table 6.1 Continued

Data Type	Storage Size	Range
Double	8 bytes	-1.8E308 to 1.8E308
Currency	8 bytes	-922.3 trillion to 922.3 trillion
Decimal	14 bytes	+/- 79 octillion **Or** +/-7.9 up to 28 decimal places
Date	8 bytes	Jan 1, 100 to Dec 31, 9999
Object	4 bytes	Any Object reference
String	10 bytes + string length	Up to 2 billion characters
Variant (with numbers)	16 bytes	Any numeric value of Double range
Variant (with characters)	22 bytes + string length	2 billion characters

VBA also lets you declare fixed-length strings, but these tend to be necessary only when accessing the Windows API directly. You won't need to do that in your macro projects.

Using Constants

Almost every procedure you record or write depends on some data values that do not change. A *constant*, short for *named* constant, is simply an unchanging data value that has been associated with a human-readable name.

You've already seen some in our samples—`vbYes` is a named constant with a value of `6`. Most named constants represent values that would be difficult to remember by themselves. You might be able to remember that a `MsgBox` answer of Yes equals 6, but how many such values could you remember? And would you be able to remember that `vbBlue` equals 16711680? The beauty of constants is that you can access them by their name rather than the value itself. This makes your code easier to write, easier to read, and easier to debug.

Constants bring another huge benefit to the macro-writing endeavor: code reuse. Let's say you are working on an Excel project that has two modules and three procedures each. Within this project, you have code that refers to several named ranges, some sheet names, and a few maximum values needed by calculations. You can save yourself a lot of work just by storing each of these values in named constants. At the module level, you might have this:

```
Public Const MyProjSalesRange As String = "TotalSales"
Public Const MyProjSubtotalRange As String = "Subtotal"
Public Const MyProjDataSheet As String = "Data"
Public Const MyProjMainSheet As String = "MainSheet"
Public Const MyProjThreshold As Integer = 600
```

Each time you need to use one of these values, just use the constant. The more often you need the value, the more you benefit. Even better, if you ever change any of these values (as is likely), you need to change your code in only one place—the constant declaration. All your other code automatically is assigned the new value.

As you've already seen in uses of the `MsgBox()` function, most constants don't come from you; they come from other sources. These constants are known as ***intrinsic*** constants. Intrinsic constants are built into the VBA language and into the Office-type libraries. Each Office application, `UserForm` control, and any other type libraries you have loaded have their own intrinsic constants. You can get a list of the constants available to you in the Object Browser. You open the Object Browser in the Visual Basic Editor by choosing View, Object Browser, by clicking on the Object Browser icon on the Standard Toolbar, or by pressing F2.

User-defined constants are declared using the `Const` statement, and they can be declared at any level of scope. Note the syntax of the constant declaration:

```
[Public ¦ Private] Const constname [As type] = expression
```

The Public and Private keywords are optional and are for module-level constants only; the `constname` is not case sensitive; the *type* is optional; and you declare the value when you declare the constant. Here is an example of an Integer constant:

```
Const intMYCONSTANT As Integer = 27
```

You may see some code listings put constants in all capital letters. That's a naming convention long used by many C and C++ programmers. But if you walk the VBA Object Browser, you'll see that all its constants use a mixed-case style (as in vbYes). Whether you follow one or the other matters less than that you have a consistent style. Choose one that helps you recognize constants for what they are so that your code stays easy to read.

Using Events

Every action you take in a Microsoft product is an event. You open files, close files, enter data into cells and documents, click buttons on slide shows, and double-click, right-click, change entries, and so on. In this example, we use an Excel Worksheet event to make the data entry macro start automatically.

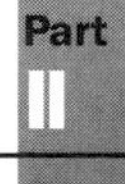

You can catch some of these events and run your procedures in response to them. For example, suppose you have a workbook that tracks monthly expenses, with each worksheet listing the expenses for a given month. In addition to the monthly worksheets, you also have a worksheet summarizing the year-to-date expenses. Suppose each time the year-to-date worksheet is activated, you want a particular VBA procedure to run, such as having a message or InputBox appear. The *event* is the activation of the year-to-date worksheet; the procedure can be any VBA procedure you create.

Table 6.2 lists several common events in Microsoft Office 2000. This list is not all-inclusive, but is meant to provide a sample of the possibilities.

Table 6.2 Common Events

Event	Location	Description
`Activate`	Excel Workbook	Occurs when the user activates the workbook.
`BeforeClose`	Excel Workbook	Occurs before the workbook closes.
`Deactivate`	Excel Workbook	Occurs when the workbook is active and the user activates a different workbook.
`Open`	Excel Workbook	Occurs when the user opens the workbook.
`Calculate`	Excel Worksheet	Occurs when the user recalculates the worksheet.
`Change`	Excel Worksheet	Occurs when the user changes a cell formula.
`SelectionChange`	Excel Worksheet	Occurs when the user selects a worksheet cell.
`DragOver`	Excel Chart	Occurs when the user drags data over the chart.
`MouseDown`	Excel Chart	Occurs when the user clicks a mouse button while the pointer is over a chart.
`MouseUp`	Excel Chart	Occurs when the user releases a mouse button while the pointer is over a chart.
`Open`	Word Document	Occurs when the user opens the document. This can replace the AutoOpen macro.
`Close`	Word Document	Occurs when the user closes the document. This can replace the AutoClose macro.
`New`	Word Document	Occurs when a new document based on this template is created.
`Close`	Access Report	Occurs when the user closes the report.
`NoData`	Access Report	Occurs when there is no data to display in the report; that is, the query produced no results.

NOTE The AutoOpen and AutoClose built-in macros have been around for a long time and are still supported. Using events can replace them; however, you can choose not to run AutoOpen or AutoClose macros based on a switch used with startup. You can keep both automatic macros and events from running by holding down the Shift key while opening or closing any document.

If you want more information on events in Microsoft Office, you can get a complete list through the Help program in the Visual Basic Editor. Ask the Office Assistant for directions by typing in "Events in Visual Basic" in the search box.

These events can be used to check values, initialize data, alter the view of the screen, remove screen items, disable toolbars, and much more. Next you'll see how a few of these events can be manipulated by using a few lines of code to illustrate Excel events in the Lazy Lizard Software spreadsheet.

▶ **See** "Useful Procedures," **p. 147**

In the Visual Basic Editor's Project Explorer (see Figure 6.8), select the object whose events you want to manipulate. For this example, select the Texas Division sheet in the Project Explorer window.

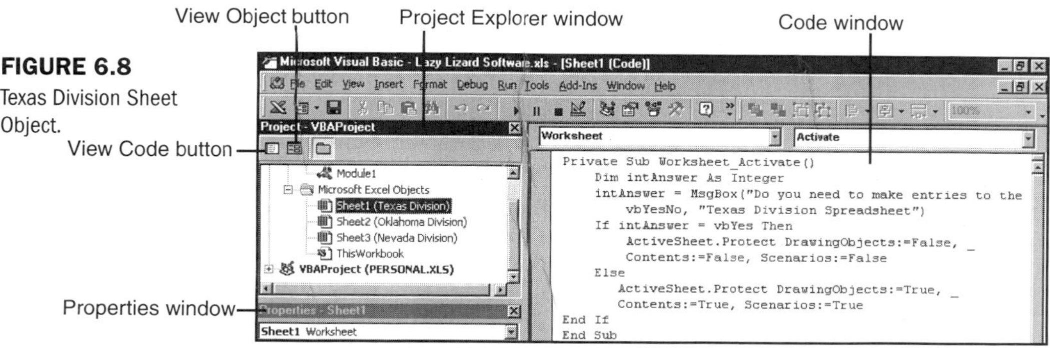

FIGURE 6.8
Texas Division Sheet Object.

Click the View Code button on the top left of the Project Explorer window. This displays the Code window (see Figure 6.9) for the Texas Division Sheet.

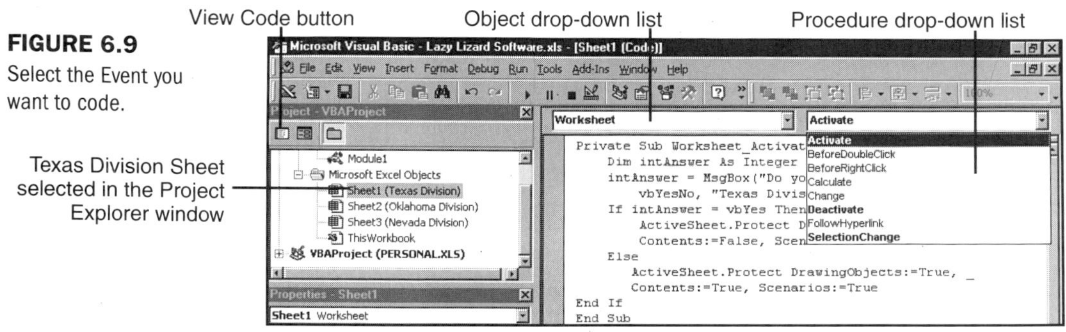

FIGURE 6.9
Select the Event you want to code.

As soon as you select the sheet in the Project Explorer, Word adds the Worksheet object to the Object drop-down list at the top left of the Code Window. Click the drop-down arrow to select the Worksheet object. This fills the Procedure drop-down list at the top right with all the Events that the Worksheet fires. Click the drop-down arrow on the Procedure drop-down list to select the event you want to use. For this example, the `Activate` event is selected (see Figure 6.10). As soon as you choose the event, Word inserts an empty Event procedure in the Code Window, ready for you to add code:

```
Private Sub Worksheet_Activate()

End Sub
```

Enter the following code in the `Worksheet_Activate()` event. This code adds a `MsgBox` function with Yes and No buttons, asking whether the user wants to enter data. (The `MsgBox` function is covered in "Useful Procedures," earlier in this chapter.) If the user chooses No, the code protects the worksheet; if the user chooses Yes, it unprotects the worksheet and runs the `EnterDataInputBox` macro. The finished code looks like this:

```
Private Sub Worksheet_Activate()
' Declare a variable to hold the answer to the question on data entry.
    Dim intAnswer As Integer
' Capture the answer
    intAnswer = MsgBox("Do you need to make entries to the data on the Texas
➥Division worksheet?", _
            vbYesNo, "Texas Division Worksheet")
 ' Check if the answer in intAnswer is yes.
    If intAnswer = vbYes Then
        ActiveSheet.Protect DrawingObjects:=False, _
            Contents:=False, Scenarios:=False
' Call the EnterDataInputBox macro to enter the data
        EnterDataInputBox
    Else
' Lock the worksheet if the answer to the MessageBox question was no.
       ActiveSheet.Protect DrawingObjects:=True, _
           Contents:=True, Scenarios:=True
    End If
End Sub
```

NOTE You might be wondering why the variable `intAnswer` is declared as an integer when the value stored is a Yes/No answer. It's true that a Yes/No condition can be handled as a Boolean value. But the answers the buttons return are integer values. The answer returned in this case is either `vbYes` or `vbNo`, both of which are Visual Basic constants and integer values (`vbYes` equals 6 and `vbNo` equals 7).

An additional event helps make this project more robust and foolproof. Use the `Deactivate` event to lock the worksheet whenever the user moves off the target worksheet:

```
Private Sub Worksheet_Deactivate()
    ActiveWorkbook.Worksheets("Texas Division").Protect _
        DrawingObjects:=True, _
```

```
        Contents:=True, _
        Scenarios:=True
End Sub
```

After you have coded the event, go back to Excel and select a different worksheet tab. Select the worksheet tab for the sheet you specified in the Visual Basic Editor's Project Explorer; in this example, that would be the Texas Division sheet. What happened? You should have seen a message box with the statement "Do you need to make entries to the data on the Texas Division worksheet?" Click the Yes button and the sheet is unprotected and the `EnterDataInputBox` macro starts; click the No button and the sheet is left protected. Try it again. Every time you come back to that sheet and make it the active sheet, your message box should come up to greet you.

This code runs only in this file because the event is tied to a specific sheet in this workbook. To have a procedure run in other worksheets, or in all the worksheets of a specific workbook, place the code outside of the event procedure, either in a standard module or in the declarations section of the workbook. You might, for example, place it in the `ThisWorkbook` object in a `Sub` procedure called `GenericDeactivate` (although you can call it whatever you like). Declare the procedure Public. Then, if you want to run this code every time someone activates a specific sheet, just place the name of your generic procedure in the `Activate` event for that sheet. It runs every time that sheet is activated.

If your sheet is the first sheet to come up when you opened the workbook, the message box does not display. The `Activate` event fires only when a sheet becomes the active sheet from within an open workbook. If you want your code to run when the workbook opens, place a call to the generic code in the `Open` event of the workbook.

The `SelectionChange` event fires whenever the user selects a worksheet cell (see Figure 6.10). Examples of how this event might be used include displaying messages, or changing formatting based on the data in the cell or cells that were selected. Because this event can be found in the Worksheet object, select the desired sheet in the Project Explorer and activate its code window.

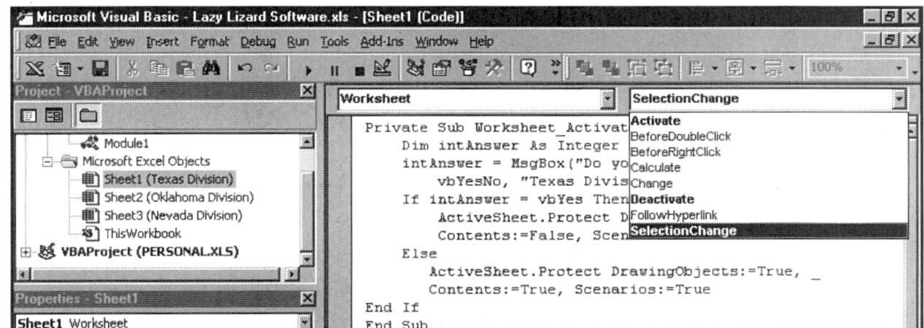

FIGURE 6.10
The `SelectionChange` event.

Choose the Worksheet object in the Object drop-down list of the code window, and then select `SelectionChange` in the procedure drop-down list. The following code should be displayed:

```
Private Sub Worksheet_SelectionChange (ByVal Target As Range)

End Sub
```

You can add some code to this event that tests an entry for its value. In our case, if that value is a formula, a warning message is displayed. To do this, add an `If...End If` statement. (The `If...End If` statement is covered in the section, "`If...End If`" earlier in this chapter.) The following is the code:

```
Private Sub Worksheet_SelectionChange(ByVal Target As Range)
' Check to see if the cell has a formula or simply data
    If Target.HasFormula = True Then
' If it has data display a message box to remind users.
        MsgBox "Please do not change formulas.", vbInformation, "Texas Division
➥Worksheet"
    End If
End Sub
```

The text between the parentheses, (`ByVal Target As Range`), identifies which cell or cells were selected. The default value would be the active cell:

- `ByVal`—Identifies how the cell reference is passed to the event.
- `Target`—Is a variable storing the name of the cell. This variable is declared as part of this `Sub` procedure when it is identified within the parentheses. The name of the variable is set to `Target` by default.
- `As Range`—Identifies what type of variable `Target` is.

Designing *UserForms*

The dialog boxes and forms that Office 2000 uses to enable you to set options and carry out actions in the program are quite interactive and user friendly. You can add these and make custom forms that enable you to focus on the specific tasks of your project.

The `EnterDataInputBox` macro gets the data on the spreadsheet, but it isn't very user friendly. It doesn't tell you what quarter you are entering data for or let you stop after one quarter. We'll design a `UserForm` that will fix this.

Select `UserForm` from the Visual Basic Editor's Insert menu or from the Insert Module button on the Standard Toolbar. The `UserForm` displays where the code window was and the controls Toolbox should become visible. If not, select the Toolbox from the View menu.

The `UserForm`'s default size and properties can be changed through direct manipulation of the graphic image, by entering new information in the Properties Box in the Visual Basic Editor, or through code when the project is actually run.

The Toolbox (see Figure 6.11) provides 15 standard controls to build your form. You can also open custom ActiveX controls through the Tools menu.

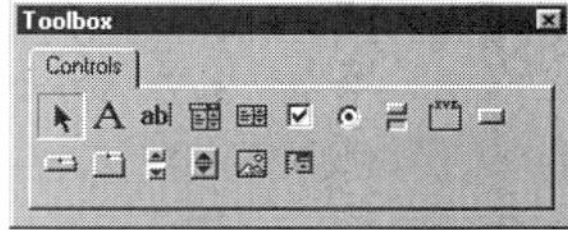

FIGURE 6.11
The Toolbox.

The Pointer is not a control; it is the tool you select to manipulate the controls on the form.

UserForm Controls

Adding controls to the `UserForm` (see Figure 6.12) is relatively simple. The hard part is designing the `UserForm` to fit your purpose. It is usually best to sketch a few layout ideas on paper first and then start building the actual form. Follow these steps to add controls to the `UserForm`:

1. Select a Control from the Toolbox.
2. Click once on the `UserForm`. The Control appears with default settings. You can also click, hold, and drag to specify a position and size.
3. Select the control and drag it to the position you choose on the `UserForm`. You can resize each control and set its properties to your specifications.

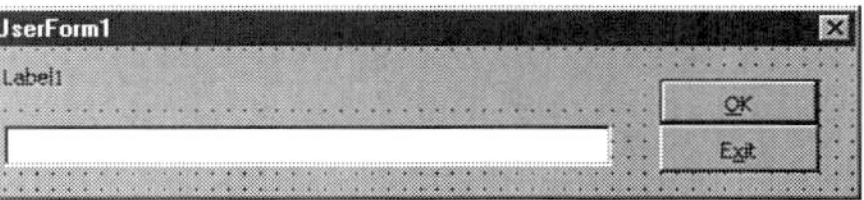

FIGURE 6.12
VBA `UserForm`—
InputBox Replacement.

If you've used a template in Word, you may know that you can have an `InputBox` generated to ask the user for input rather than have the user type directly on the document. Excel and other Office 2000 applications have this feature, also. This is a nice touch, but the `InputBox` has one major limitation. Except for setting the prompt, a default value for the answer, and the title, you cannot customize it. Designing a custom `UserForm` for this input keeps you in charge and lets you set any type of data entry you like.

First, design and draw the form—including labels, text boxes, buttons, and so on. Labeling form fields helps users enter the correct data. Text boxes can be used to provide a place for the user to add input. Buttons can be used as any standard dialog box button—OK and Cancel, for example.

Add a `UserForm` to the template you want to automate, and shape and add controls to match your design needs.

Before you add code to the `UserForm`, you'll need to set a few control properties. The properties we need to change are listed in Table 6.3.

Table 6.3 *UserForm* Property Settings

***UserForm* Object**	**Property Setting**
`UserForm1 Name`	`CustomInput` (Name your form to help you write code.)
`Caption`	Lazy Lizard Software (Provide a caption the user can understand.)
`TextBox1 Name`	`txtInput` (Name the TextBox control to help you write code.)
`CommandButton1 Name`	`cmdOK` (Name the command button to help you write code.)
`Accelerator`	O (enables keyboard control)
`Caption`	OK (to help the user identify the control)
`Default`	True (enables the user to activate by pressing the Enter key)
`CommandButton2 Name`	`cmdExit` (Name the command button to help you write code.)
`Accelerator`	x (enables keyboard control)
`Caption`	Exit (to help the user identify the control)
`Cancel`	True (enables the user to cancel action by pressing the Esc key)
`Label1 Name`	`lblPrompt`
`Caption`	Blank (Delete the default caption; you will set it in code.)

NOTE The Accelerator property of a control enables a hotkey of your choice. The only thing to watch for is duplicating a hotkey on the same `UserForm`. The Default property of a `CommandButton` enables the Enter key to act as if you clicked that button. Setting the Cancel property of a `CommandButton` enables the Esc key to act as if you clicked that button. Only one `CommandButton` on a `UserForm` can have its Cancel or Default property set to `True`.

Coding the *UserForm*

Now that you've created the `UserForm`, it's time to add the code that ties the `UserForm` to the project. To do that, you must add code to the `Worksheet_Activate` event that displays the form. And in the `UserForm`, you will add code that edits the worksheet.

With the `CustomInput` form selected in the Project Explorer, click the View Code button to display the `UserForm`'s Code Window. The code you'll need is as follows:

```
' This variable is checked to see if the user wants to stop entering data
' It is Public so other modules can "see" the value.
Public blnEnd As Boolean
Private Sub cmdExit_Click()
' This closes the UserForm and ends the procedure. Note that blnEnd
' is set to True which stops the EnterData macro.
```

```
    blnEnd = True
    End
End Sub
Private Sub cmdOK_Click()
' Enters the value of the UserForm's textbox into the active cell. Then
' it clears the textbox for the next input and hides the UserForm.
    ActiveCell.Value = txtInput.Value
    txtInput.Value = ""
    CustomInput.Hide
End Sub
Private Sub UserForm_Activate()
' This is the first code that runs when the UserForm starts
' We set the focus at the TextBox so the user can start
' typing immediately, name the UserForm after the active sheet
' and set blnEnd to False
    blnEnd = False
    CustomInput.Caption = ActiveSheet.Name
    txtInput.SetFocus
End Sub
```

When the `UserForm_Activate` event fires, it sets the `UserForm`'s Caption property, initializes the `blnEnd` variable, and sets the keyboard focus to the text box. All this happens before the form is displayed. After the form is displayed, the user can then type an entry in the `TextBox`. If he selects Exit, the `cmdExit_Click` event fires, the `UserForm` closes, and the variable `blnEnd` is set to True.

But if the user selects OK, the `cmdOK_Click` event fires and a series of events takes place. First, the text typed in the `TextBox` will be entered into the active cell of the worksheet. Then the `TextBox` will be blanked out for the next entry and the `UserForm` will be hidden.

How do we tie this code to the `Worksheet_Activate` event? First, we create a replacement for the `EnterDataInputBox` procedure that we stored in our standard module earlier. Type the following procedure into the same module or copy the code from the *Que's Platinum Edition Pack* CD accompanying this book.

```
Sub EnterData()
'
' EnterData Macro
' Macro recorded 11/3/98 by Ron Stockdreher
'
    Dim intColCount as Integer
    Dim intCols as integer
    Dim intRowCount as Integer
    Dim intRows as Integer
    Range("B3").Select
    Range(Selection, Selection.End(xlToRight)).Select
    intColCount = Selection.Columns.Count
    For intCols = 1 To intColCount
        If CustomInput.blnEnd = True Then
            Exit For
        End If
        If ActiveCell.Offset(1, 0).Value = "" Then
            CustomInput.lblPrompt.Caption = "Please enter date for " &
```

```
➥ActiveCell.Value & "."
            Range(Selection, Selection.End(xlDown)).Select
            intRowCount = Selection.Rows.Count
            ActiveCell.Select
            For intRows = 1 To intRowCount - 2
                If CustomInput.blnEnd = True Then
                    Exit For
                End If
                Selection.Offset(1, 0).Select
                CustomInput.Show
                CustomInput.txtInput.SetFocus
            Next intRows
            Selection.End(xlUp).Select
        Else
        End If
        ActiveCell.Offset(0, 1).Select
    Next intCols
End Sub
```

After you have created the `EnterData` procedure, edit the `Worksheet_Activate` event of the Texas Division worksheet so that it calls the `EnterData` procedure instead of the `EnterDataInputBox` procedure.

Now we have modified our project to use a custom form instead of the inflexible `InputBox`. Yes, it is more complex. But all we had to do to get this functionality was to add a `UserForm` and a few new lines of code. The rest of the structure remains the same—when the user selects the Texas Division worksheet, the `Worksheet_Activate` event fires, and the code in that event procedure displays a form. If the user chooses, edits are made to the worksheet.

Debugging Your Code

"Into every life a little rain must fall." Isn't that how the saying goes? Well, VBA is not immune. There will be times when programming errors crop up in your procedures. Luckily, VBA provides you with a broad array of tools to search out and correct those errors. Because this book is not devoted solely to programming, these will be covered rather lightly here. If you want to find out more about error handling in VBA, check out *Special Edition Using Visual Basic 6*, published by Que.

Types of Errors

There are four basic types of errors you will run into:

- Syntax Errors
- Compiler Errors
- Runtime Errors
- Logical Errors

Syntax errors result from typos and misspelling of keywords or missing punctuation. For example, the following line has two syntax errors in it:

```
MssgBox "Hello, world
```

The MsgBox statement is misspelled, and the prompt lacks a closing quotation mark. The VBA Editor can catch most of the syntax errors as you type them; incorrect lines appear red by default. The VBA Editor also displays a message alerting you to the error as soon as you type it. (You can disable this feature by choosing Tools, Options and on the Editor tab, clearing the Auto Syntax Check check box.)

Compiler errors are generated whenever you attempt to compile a procedure and one or more lines fails to compile for some reason. (All VBA code must be compiled before running; you can either force it to compile by choosing Debug, Compile *Projectname*, or you can simply try to run the code and VBA will compile it on-the-fly.) Compile errors can result from incorrect syntax, missing variable declarations, loops that are never closed, and other such mistakes. For example, the following procedure causes a compile error because the variable `intAnswer` was never declared and Option Explicit was included in the module declarations.

```
Private Sub AskWorldHowItsDoing()
    intAnswer = MsgBox("Are you OK, world?", vbYesNo)
End Sub
```

If VBA finds any discrepancies, it displays an Error dialog box and stops your code from executing.

Runtime errors result when VBA actually executes a line of code but runs into some other kind of problem. For example, a runtime error may occur because a filename does not exist at runtime, or an expression has evaluated to an invalid value such as division by zero.

Logic errors are mistakes in the concept or execution itself, not the code, and are the hardest programming errors to find. Flaws in logic result in code that does not perform the way you intended. For example, perhaps you performed multiplication instead of division. The code syntax is correct, compiles and runs without error, but the result is not correct. The Visual Basic Editor is very good at detecting some errors, but it just can't catch logic errors. These are in the mind of the programmer. As long as the code is clean, with no syntax, compiler, or runtime errors, it will run. This is where the programming saying goes "Garbage in, Garbage out." You have to work through these errors yourself.

Debugging Recorded Macros

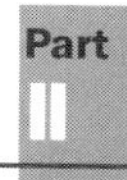

Debugging a macro is a tough process—one that every VBA programmer does differently. But recorded macros have their own set of hazards, and no matter how you prefer to debug, you have to watch out for them.

The following code contains a common error that is often made when using the code created by the Macro Recorder (see Figure 6.13).

```
Sub Lizard_Heading_Broken()
'
' Lizard_Heading_Broken Macro
' Macro recorded 9/26/98 by Ron Stockdreher
' Example of a Macro with errors applied to
' the Lazy Lizard Software Spreadsheets.'
'
```

```
    Range("A1:F2").Select
    With Selection
        .HorizontalAlignment = xlCenter
        .VerticalAlignment = xlBottom
        .WrapText = False
        .Orientation = 0
        .AddIndent = False
        .ShrinkToFit = False
        .MergeCells = False
    End With
    With Selection.Font
        .Name = "Boca Raton ICG Solid"
        .FontStyle = "Regular"
        .Size = 14
        .Strikethrough = False
        .Superscript = False
        .Subscript = False
        .OutlineFont = False
        .Shadow = False
        .Underline = xlUnderlineStyleNone
        .ColorIndex = xlAutomatic
    End With
    With Selection.Interior
        .ColorIndex = 3
        .Pattern = xlSolid
        .PatternColorIndex = xlAutomatic
    End With
    Range("3:3").Select
    With Selection
        .HorizontalAlignment = xlCenter
        .VerticalAlignment = xlBottom
        .WrapText = False
        .Orientation = 0
        .AddIndent = False
        .ShrinkToFit = False
        .MergeCells = False
    End With
    With Selection.Font
        .Name = "Arial"
        .FontStyle = "Bold"
        .Size = 10
        .Strikethrough = False
        .Superscript = False
        .Subscript = False
        .OutlineFont = False
        .Shadow = False
        .Underline = xlUnderlineStyleNone
        .ColorIndex = xlAutomatic
    End With
    With Selection.Interior
        .ColorIndex = 42
        .Pattern = xlSolid
        .PatternColorIndex = xlAutomatic
    End With
    Range("A4").Select
End Sub
```

FIGURE 6.13
This is a common error you can correct by debugging.

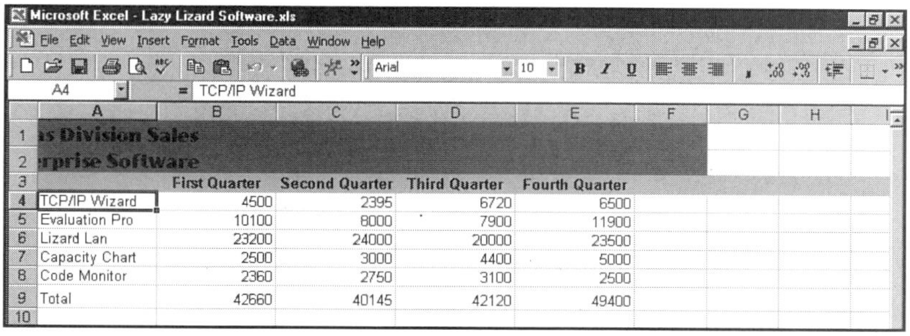

	A	B	C	D	E
1	as Division Sales				
2	erprise Software				
3		First Quarter	Second Quarter	Third Quarter	Fourth Quarter
4	TCP/IP Wizard	4500	2395	6720	6500
5	Evaluation Pro	10100	8000	7900	11900
6	Lizard Lan	23200	24000	20000	23500
7	Capacity Chart	2500	3000	4400	5000
8	Code Monitor	2360	2750	3100	2500
9	Total	42660	40145	42120	49400

Here are the places in the code that cause the problem:

```
Range("A1:F2").Select
```

and

```
Range("3:3").Select
```

Most of the actions taken in the procedure are acting on the Selection object. This object is determined in two places by the Select method of the Range objects listed in the preceding code. This is a common error in a recorded macro because all action is predicated on the selection of the right cells. If you do not select the right cells, the action will be taken on the wrong cells. Fixing this type of problem is relatively easy—just correct the range in the parentheses of the Range objects to reflect the cells you do want to select.

If you aren't sure where in the procedure things start to go wrong, step through your code line by line to watch what is happening. The following section details how to do that.

Stepping Through Your Code

The most effective way to find errors in your code is to step through it one line at a time. This enables you to execute your macro command-by-command and see what is happening at any moment during its execution and what the value of any variable or object setting is at the time.

To step through your code, enter Break Mode. You can go into Break Mode several different ways:

- From the main application window, choose Tools, Macro, Macros, select the macro you want to debug and then click Step Into. This starts the macro and stops at the first line of code. Press the F8 key or the Step Into button on the Debug Toolbar.

NOTE You want to rearrange the windows to display the Visual Basic Editor and the main application (see Figure 6.14). Keep the focus on the main application because some of the code refers to the active workbook. If the Visual Basic Editor has the Focus of the Windows environment, that is, the active window, an error may occur.

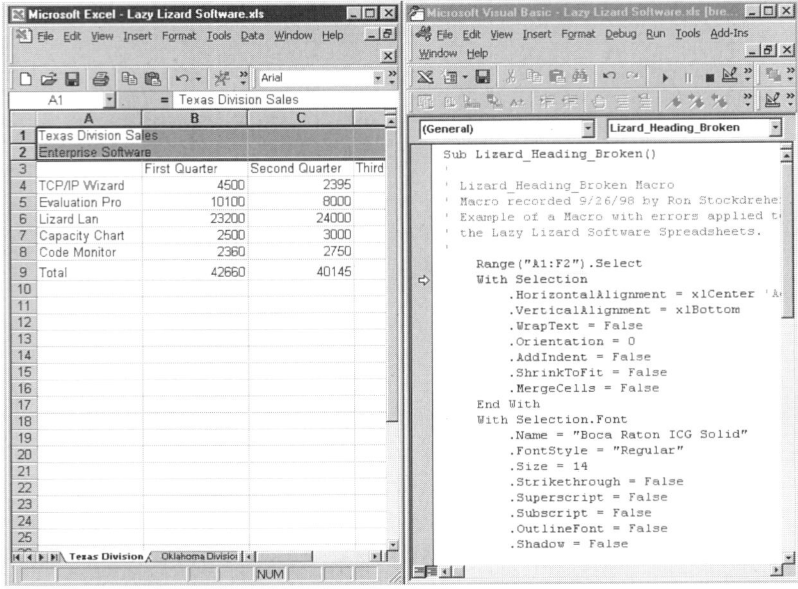

FIGURE 6.14
Arrange the windows on the screen to display both the Editor and your main application.

- Place the insertion point inside a procedure you want to step through and press the F8 key or the Step Into button on the Debug Toolbar.

NOTE The Visual Basic Editor has several tools to help you debug your macros, including a Step Into button. They are located on the Debug Toolbar and on the menu under Debug.

- Set a breakpoint on a line of code. This is done by clicking in the left margin of the code window next to the line of code you want to break on, clicking the Toggle Breakpoint button on the Debug toolbar, pressing F9, or choosing Toggle Breakpoint on the Debug menu. A maroon dot appears on the left margin of the code window and the entire line of code turns maroon. When you next run the macro, execution stops at this line of code. You then press F8 to move forward one line of code at a time (see Figure 6.15).
- If, when testing your macro, a runtime error occurs, a dialog box detailing the error displays. Select Debug and the Visual Basic Editor opens to your macro in Break Mode.
- Pressing Ctrl+Break while your macro is running displays a dialog box reading “Code execution has been interrupted.”

After you have entered Break Mode, you can press F8 (or use the Step Into button) to move one line at a time through your macro and watch the execution of your macro one command at a time. If you see something happen that should not, then the line of code that just executed may be the cause of the problem.

NOTE While in Break Mode, it is possible to add code to your macro or make changes to variables and code structure. Some changes cause your macro to stop running and the Editor warns you about this.

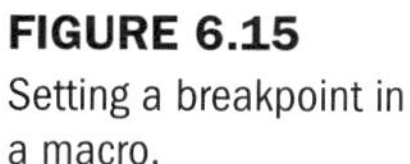

FIGURE 6.15
Setting a breakpoint in a macro.

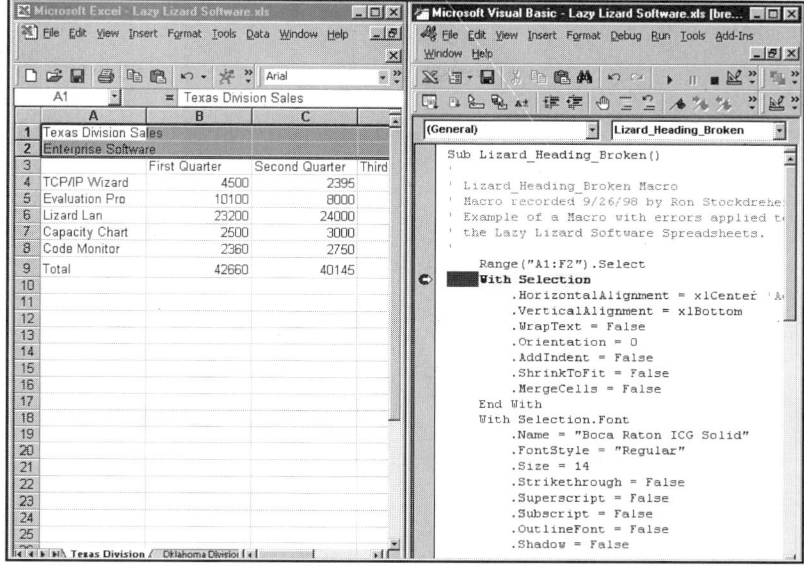

After you enter Break Mode, the Visual Basic Editor highlights each line of code before carrying out the instruction.

Handling User Interruptions

In addition to the possible errors that you may find in your macros, it is possible for someone running your macro to press Ctrl+Break and put it in Break Mode. You have three possible choices here:

You can let the user break into your macro, which will stop it and perhaps cause an irreconcilable problem if you are running a complex macro.

You can prevent the user from doing this by disabling any user input while your macro is running. This is easy, but unless you're very certain about your code, it may put the program in an endless loop. Correcting this would require the program to be shut down by using the operating system's controls.

You can choose when to allow and when not to allow user interruptions by programming areas of your code for this.

The following snippets disable user input in Word and Excel while a macro is running.

The Word version:

```
Sub WordDisableUser()
     Application.EnableCancelKey = wdCancelDisabled
End Sub
```

The Excel version:

```
Sub ExcelDisableUser()
     Application.EnableCancelKey = xlDisabled
End Sub
```

NOTE VBA automatically enables user input after the macro stops running.

Protecting Your Code

If you've worked long and hard to develop your procedures, you may consider taking some measures to protect your investment. Whether your code is to be distributed to others or used in a public context, it is often wise to prevent others from tampering with it.

In the Visual Basic Editor, open the Project Properties dialog box by choosing Tools, VBAProject Properties. On the Protection tab (see Figure 6.16), you can set the protection property for your project. The name reflects the Name property of the current project. For example, in Word, this dialog box for the Normal template will read Normal Properties on the Tools menu. (You can set this property in the Project's Properties window.) Place a check mark in Lock Project for Viewing to prevent others from viewing the code.

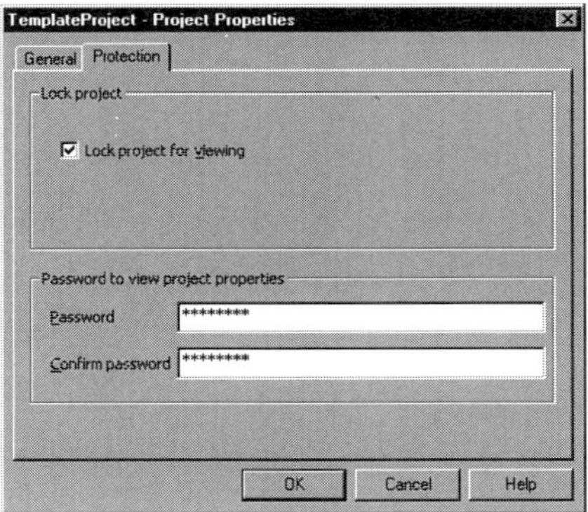

FIGURE 6.16
The Protection tab in the Project dialog box.

If you lock the project, you must also set a password to view protected project properties. If you do not check the Lock Project for Viewing option but set a password, you leave the project unlocked, but you need to enter the password to open the Project Properties dialog box again. All passwords that you enter must be confirmed. Do not forget your password. You cannot recover it later. After you set protection, you must save and close your project for the protection to take effect.

Guidelines for Distributing Your VBA Modules to Others

In most cases, your VBA modules can be distributed to anyone who has a copy of Office 2000. Most code does not operate without the application software—that is, the Microsoft Office products—to support them. It is not legal to distribute Microsoft software without permission from Microsoft, but there is no legal problem with distributing files that you have created with Microsoft Office products—except perhaps some reservations your company may have.

Microsoft Office 2000 is a highly customizable suite of software and can be altered in function and appearance to fit your needs. After the appropriate license issues are resolved (you or your company have purchased the requisite number of copies of this software), there are tools to deploy your customized applications. They can be found in Microsoft Office 2000 Developer. For a complete list of the tools in Office Developer Edition, see the Microsoft Office Developer forum Web site: `www.microsoft.com/officedev`.

Digital Signatures for Macros and Code

This feature is new to Microsoft Office 2000 and VBA procedures developed in Microsoft Office, but it is not new to the Internet and users of ActiveX controls. One of the long-standing problems with downloading controls, actually anything, from the Internet is the fear of getting a computer virus along with the item you download.

Microsoft established a system for providing a level of assurance to users who download ActiveX controls. The creator of the control can apply through Microsoft or an authorized third party for a Digital Signature that verifies the creator and provides a record that the user can access if a problem occurs. This has now been incorporated in Microsoft Office 2000.

VBA has come a long way and I would guess that every reader of this book has come across a macro virus at least once. It makes you reluctant to choose Enable Macros when that dialog box comes up on an unknown document, doesn't it? Now, the developer of those macros can apply to Microsoft for a Digital Signature Certificate that would be added to their development environment and they could choose to add that to any project they create.

You can add it by choosing Tools, Digital Signatures in the Visual Basic Editor. If you have more than one, select the Choose button and select the appropriate certificate and then click OK. It will be attached to your file and distributed with it. A more detailed explanation of this process can be found in *Special Edition Using Visual Basic 6*, published by Que.

Digitally signing your projects affects how they are treated when users try to run your code. Every Microsoft Office program that supports macros has a Security setting; choose Tools, Macros, Security, which opens the Security dialog box. See Figure 6.17.

Your choices are

- High—This enables only signed macros from sources that you have chosen as trusted sources to run. All others are disabled.
- Medium—Whenever you open a file that contains code, a dialog box displays giving you the option to disable it. Figure 6.18 shows an example of the dialog box that is displayed.
- Low—This setting allows all macro code to run, without giving you the option to disable it. You should choose this option only if you are sure that the files you open are safe.

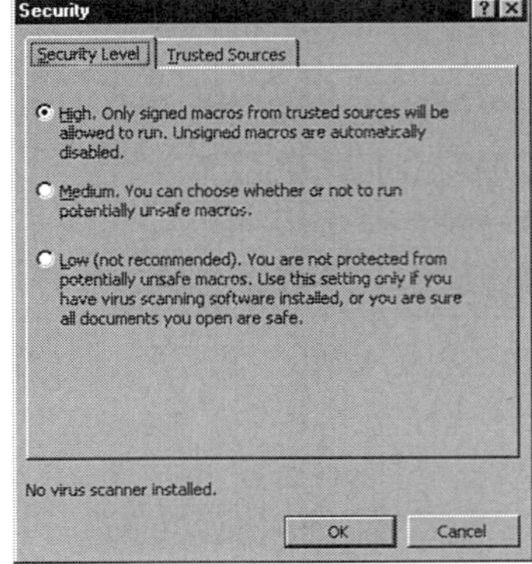

FIGURE 6.17
Choose which level of trust to use for macros in the Security dialog box.

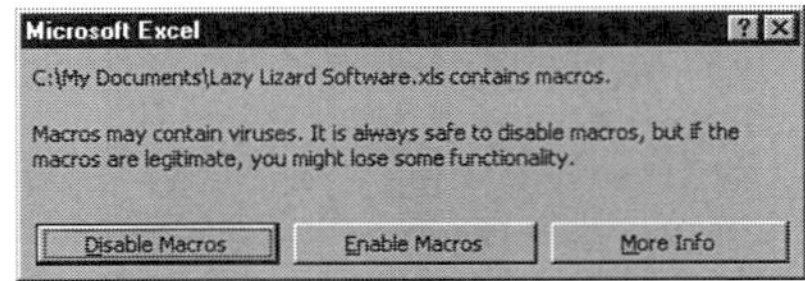

FIGURE 6.18
Choose to enable or disable macros attached to a document.

PART III

Microsoft Word

CHAPTER 7

Migrating to Word 2000

In this chapter

Personalized Menus

As discussed in Chapter 4, "Customizing Microsoft Office the Way You Want," the Office 2000 menus and toolbars can operate in a markedly different way, using what Microsoft has termed as "personalized." Office 2000 ships with this personalized feature enabled.

It's likely that you will find the personalized menus and toolbars to be somewhat irritating. If this is the case, you can easily disable this feature so your menus and toolbars operate just as they have in previous editions of Office. Choose Tools, Customize and deselect the Menus Show Recently Used Commands First option.

NOTE In this book, we'll assume that you have disabled personalized menus and toolbars. All figures showing a menu or a toolbar were captured with the personalized feature disabled.

If you choose to work with the personalized menus and toolbars enabled, you should be aware of a few tricks that will help you use these features properly.

First, click any of Word's menus and look at the bottom of that menu. You'll see a pair of downward-pointing arrows (also known as chevrons). These arrows indicate that the personalized feature is enabled. After clicking any of the menus, the rest of the menu appears after a short delay.

If your menus do not expand after a short delay, you can choose Tools, Customize and enable the Show Full Menus After a Short Delay option.

Deselecting the Show Full Menus After a Short Delay option means you'll have to click the arrows at the bottom of the menu to see all the contents of that menu. You also can press Ctrl+Down Arrow to see all the menu contents.

If you like the personalized menus, but occasionally need to see the full menu, double-click the main menu bar (such as File or Edit) item to immediately drop down the entire list.

Personalized Toolbars

Microsoft's attempt to unclutter the way we work with Office 2000 doesn't stop with the personalized menus. After all, within the scope of how Word works, the menu is also a toolbar. Of course, this means that you have the option to use personalized toolbars in Word 2000.

When you see Word 2000's toolbars for the first time, if you're familiar with Word 97 and Word 95, you'll immediately notice something missing or different—there's only one default toolbar!

Look more closely, because there are actually two. By default, however, now they're both displayed in the same row. Look even more closely and you'll see a set of double arrows or chevrons (») at the right end of each toolbar. Click the arrows to see additional tools.

If you jumped the gun and already turned personalized toolbars off, you won't see the arrows. You will, however, see a downward-pointing solid black triangle at the right end of each toolbar. Click the triangle to add or remove buttons–and to see a list of current and related tools.

As you use commands on the toolbars, the buttons displayed on the toolbar are modified depending on which tools you use most frequently. Tools you use most frequently appear onscreen. Tools you don't use as often get relegated to the hidden part of the toolbar. To access tools that aren't visible, click the double arrows (») at the right end of the toolbar.

If you prefer the good old ways of Word 97 and Word 95, choose Tools, Customize, and click the Options tab. Click to deselect the Standard and Formatting Toolbars Share One Row option. With that, toolbars suddenly are tamed and look a whole lot like they did in Word 97.

NOTE Most figures in this book were captured after the Standard and Formatting Toolbars Share One Row option was deselected. Therefore, your toolbars might appear differently than those shown in the figures used in this book.

For more information about how personalized menus and toolbars operate, see Chapter 4.

New Toolbar Buttons

Aside from the general differences owed to personalized menus and toolbars, some changes have been made to the Word toolbars, as shown in Figure 7.1. In its fully expanded configuration, the Word 2000 Standard toolbar is missing Word 97's Web Toolbar icon, and it sports a new E-Mail tool—Mail Recipient.

NOTE If you don't see the E-Mail (Mail Recipient) tool on your toolbar, you're not alone. You should be able to bring it out of hiding by setting Outlook or Outlook Express to be your default email handler. First, close Word. Next, launch Internet Explorer and choose Tools, Internet Options, Programs, and choose Outlook or Outlook Express for email. When you restart Word, the email tool should appear on the Standard toolbar.

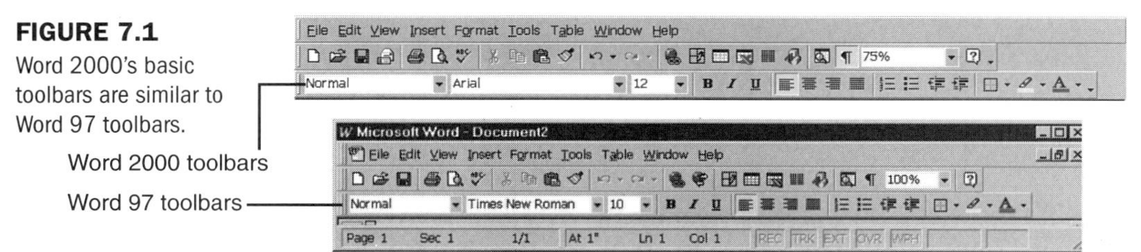

FIGURE 7.1
Word 2000's basic toolbars are similar to Word 97 toolbars.

The Web toolbar is still accessible; right-click any toolbar or menubar, and choose Web from the shortcut menu. Or, if you really liked having a Web Toolbar tool, you can add it to any toolbar easily enough. Choose Tools, Customize, and click the Commands tab. Under Categories, choose Web. Under Commands, scroll to the bottom of the list and find Web Toolbar. Use the mouse to drag the tool to whichever toolbar you prefer.

When you click the E-Mail (Mail Recipient) tool, Word sprouts To, Cc, Bcc, and Subject headers, as well as a set of email tools, as shown in Figure 7.2. Click the E-Mail (Mail Recipient) tool a second time, and the email paraphernalia goes away. The E-Mail (Mail Recipient) tool is equivalent to File, Send To, Mail Recipient, but is different from Word 97's identically named command. To replicate Word 97's behavior, choose File, Send To, Mail Recipient (as Attachment) instead. This brings up a message window from your default email program. The cool thing about the new command is that you can turn the email headers on and off at will, never having to deal with an Exchange, Outlook, or Outlook Express window.

FIGURE 7.2
Use the E-Mail (Mail Recipient) button to prepare the current document for sending.

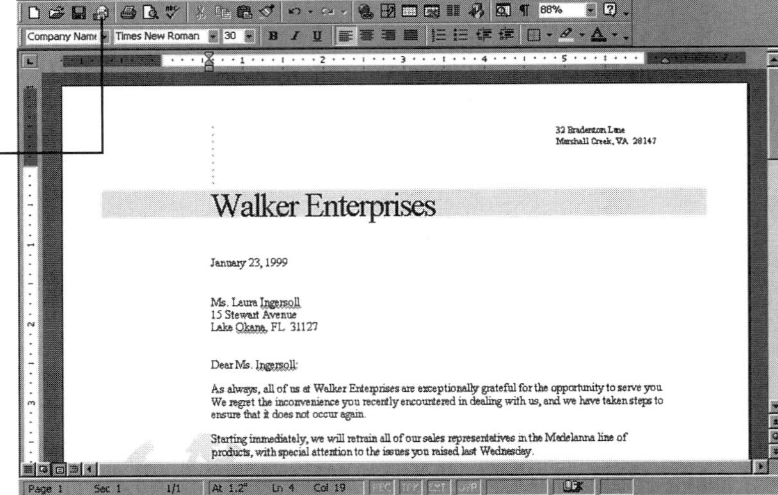

Another difference is that the new default puts the current Word document into the body of the email, although Word's old default made the document an attachment.

Right-click any toolbar or menu to see a list of the Word 2000 toolbars. The list includes three new toolbars:

- Clipboard
- Frames
- Web Tools

Clipboard Toolbar

The Clipboard toolbar is used to manage a brand-new feature known as *Collect and Paste.* When you copy or cut something to the Clipboard, Word uses a FIFO (first in, first out) stack of your 12 most recent clips. Let's say, for example, that you started copying words into the Clipboard, beginning with the first word of the current sentence. As you try to copy the second item to the Clipboard, the Clipboard toolbar pops up. At this point, each additional copy gets appended to the end of the list. At the 13th word, all the Clipboard's slots are full, and Word offers the option shown in Figure 7.3.

CAUTION

The Collect and Paste feature is one that sometimes causes Word to crash. To be safe, we recommend that you save your document before Collecting and Pasting.

FIGURE 7.3
The new Clipboard toolbar lets you paste any or all of the last 12 clips.

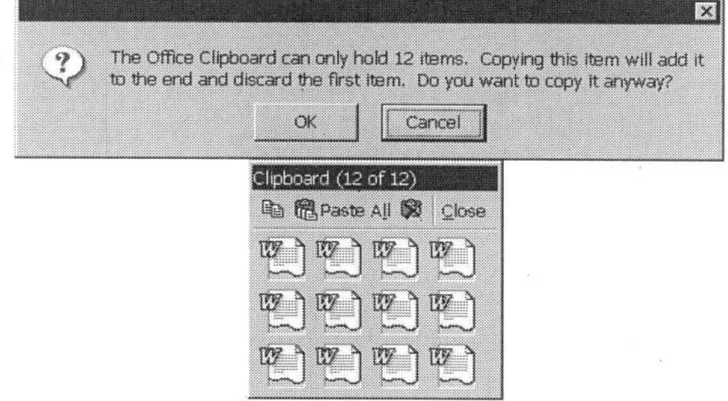

CAUTION

The stacking feature is enabled only when the Clipboard toolbar is displayed. This is good, in that when the toolbar isn't displayed, you won't be harangued each time you copy or cut to the Clipboard. However, it can be a nasty surprise if you have spent five minutes meticulously clipping items from 12 different documents so you could deposit them all into a single location—and then find out that each clip overwrote the previous. If the multiclip feature is adding clips, the Clipboard toolbar pops up when you add a clip. If the Clipboard toolbar does not appear automatically (when you need it to), then right-click a toolbar and turn it on.

If the default floating Clipboard toolbar gets in your way, move it to the main toolbar area. You can double-click the Clipboard toolbar's title bar to affix it to a window edge. However, if you have the Standard and Formatting toolbars displayed on separate rows at the top of the window, you can drag the Clipboard toolbar to the right of the Standard toolbar (where it fits perfectly) rather than have it take up an entire row by itself (as it does when you double-click its title bar). A new button (Items) is displayed with a drop-down list when the toolbar is docked. Use this button to see the complete list of clipped items.

To use the clips from the floating toolbar, hover the mouse pointer over the icons, and the contents display as ScreenTips, as shown in Figure 7.4. If you don't see the ScreenTips, choose Tools, Customize, and click the Options tab. Select the Show ScreenTips on Toolbars option. If you're using the multiple clips for a collect-and-dump operation, choose the Paste All button on the Clipboard toolbar. Unlike Word's ancient and semirevered Spike command, Paste All doesn't purge the clip stack—so you can reuse it if you like. To purge the stack, use the Clipboard toolbar's Clear Clipboard tool.

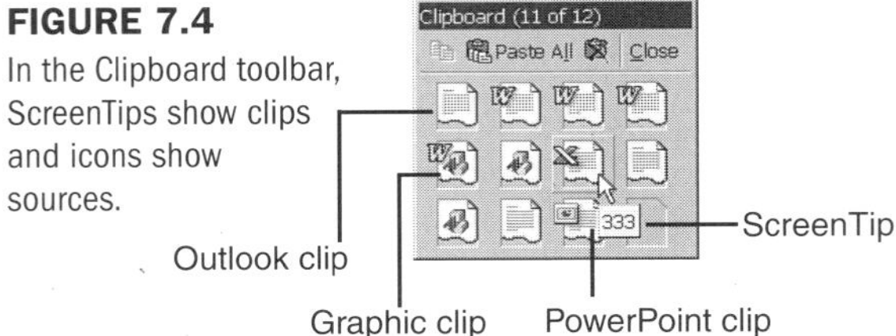

FIGURE 7.4
In the Clipboard toolbar, ScreenTips show clips and icons show sources.

The Clipboard toolbar has an additional useful facet, as previously shown in Figure 7.4—it displays distinct icons for different types of clips.

Notice that about half of these icons aren't from Microsoft Word. Not only does the Clipboard tool let you collect bits and pieces within Word, but also from within other applications, as well—even those that aren't part of Office. Each time you copy to the Clipboard in Windows, it gets added to the stack as long as the Clipboard toolbar is enabled in Word, Excel, Access, or PowerPoint. Outlook doesn't have a Clipboard toolbar, but can participate the same way Notepad does.

NOTE Although the ScreenTips for text clips display as text, nontext clips containing graphics or other nontext contents display as serialized descriptors. For example, Word drawing objects, clip art, and WordArt display as Picture 1, Picture 2, and so on. An Equation object's ScreenTip displays as Item#, where # is the position of the clip in the list of clips (for example, Item 6 means it's the sixth clip, not that it's the sixth equation). So, even though the contents ScreenTips are helpful, they won't always reveal exactly what's behind door number three.

Frames Toolbar

The Frames toolbar is used to create and edit frames in Web pages. Right-click the toolbar area and display the Frames toolbar. In a Web page, frames are windowed areas into which distinct content can be placed. Figure 7.5 shows three frames.

NOTE If the current document has ever displayed the WordMail envelope (by choosing File, Send To, Mail Recipient or by clicking the E-Mail/Mail Recipient tool on the toolbar), the Frames tools will be unavailable.

FIGURE 7.5
The Frames toolbar can create a table of contents for your Web page.

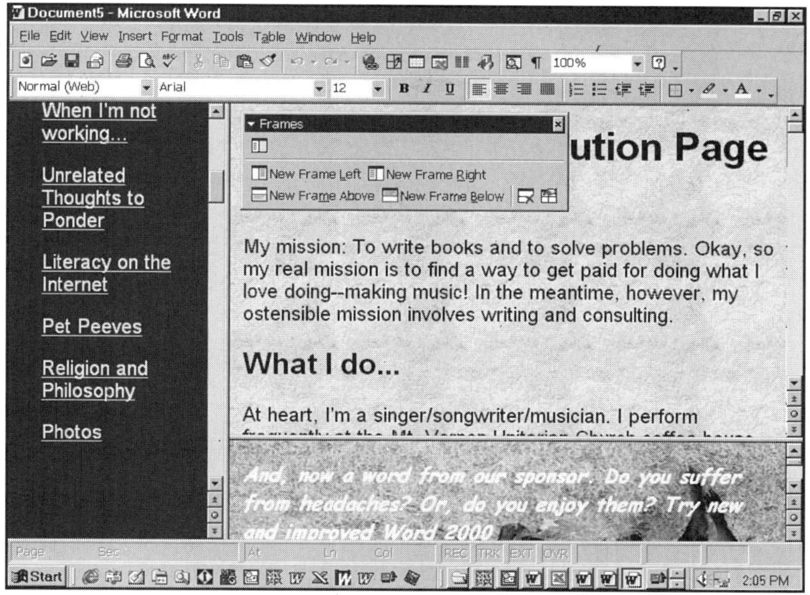

NOTE If you're a long-time Word user, you might at first confuse the Web page Frames concept with Word's Frames. In past versions of Word, it was necessary to *frame* graphics to accomplish some tasks. In recent versions of Word, including Word 2000, the older kind of frame is needed only for text boxes that contain comments, footnotes, and some fields (AUTONUM, AUTONUMLGL, AUTONUMOUT, TC, TOC, RD, XE, TA, and TOA). To access this kind of frame, select a text box, then choose Format, Text Box, and click the Text Box tab. Then choose the Convert to Frame option.

The capability to construct frames is a new feature for Word 2000. The basic idea of frames is to give the user as much content and control as possible in the opening page. Frames often contain site maps (a table of contents of what's on the site, usually—but not always—the left pane on framed Web page), advertising, and a display area for specific topics. This allows the site map to remain onscreen at all times for better navigational control.

Web Tools Toolbar

The Web Tools toolbar is used to design forms for receiving content over the Web. Shown in Figure 7.6, the Web Tools toolbar enables you to create check boxes, option buttons, drop-down boxes, list boxes, text boxes, submit buttons, password fields, and so on.

FIGURE 7.6
Use the Web Tools toolbar to develop user input Web forms.

The Script Editor button on the Web Tools toolbar displays the Script Editor, shown in Figure 7.7. Use this editor to develop scripts for handling information input over the Web, and to make Web pages more interactive.

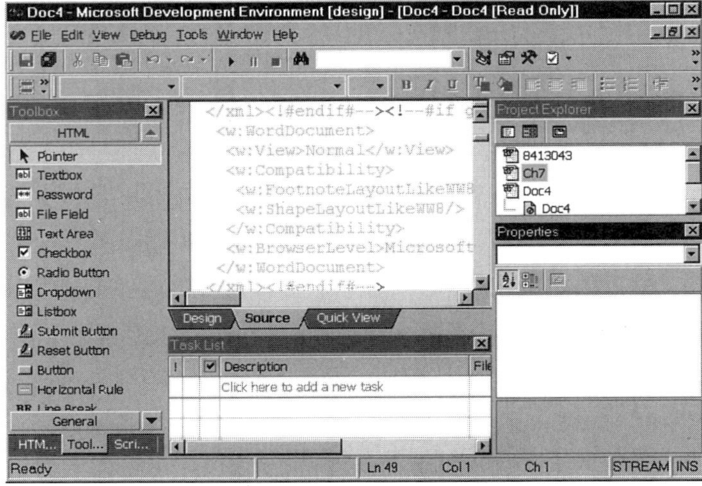

FIGURE 7.7
Use Microsoft Script Editor to make dynamic Web pages.

New Menu Commands

Aside from the drastically different personalized menus and toolbars, Word's menus have undergone some changes, too. At the on-the-surface level, you'll find the following changes from Word 97 in Table 7.1.

Table 7.1 New and Changed Word Menu Items (Between Office 97 and Office 2000)

Icon	Menu Location	Explanation
	File, Save As Web Page	New. Same result as File, Save As, Save As Type HTML Document (or File, Save As HTML).
	File, Web Page Preview	New. Opens the current Word document in the default Web browser.
	View, Web Layout	Former name Online Layout. Shows the document as it appears on the Web.
	View, Print layout	Former name Page Layout. Shows all formatting and page layout.
	View, Master Document	Gone; now only on Outline toolbar. Shows a master document and its subdocument components.

Icon	Menu Location	Explanation
	Format, Theme	New. Themes combine background, styles, color, and active graphics.
	Format, Frames	New. Creates and manages Web page frames.
	Format, Style Gallery	Gone, now in Format, Theme. Shows documents as they would be formatted using different templates.
	Tools, Online Collaboration	New. Activates NetMeeting.
	Tools, Macro, Security	Lets you set the conditions under which macros can run.
	Tools, Macro, Microsoft Script Editor	New. Use for designing dynamic Web Script Microsoft Script Editor pages.
	Table, Insert	New. All table Insert commands are located here.
	Table, Delete	New. All table Delete commands are located here.
	Table, Select	New. All table Select commands are located here.
	Table, AutoFit	New. Automatically resizes rows and columns to fit contents, window, fixed column width. This is also the new location for Distribute Rows Evenly and Distribute Columns Evenly.
	Table, Heading Rows Repeat	Former name was Headings. Repeats row headings across pages.
	Table, Convert	New. Contains Text to Table and Table to Text.
	Table, Table Properties	New. Master control for tables.
	Help, Detect and Repair	New. Finds and fixes problems with missing files and Registry settings for Word.

File, New, E-Mail Message

This is a new feature that's sure to be overlooked at first glance. Choose File, New, and click the General tab. For many users, a different icon is shown among the other templates—the E-Mail Message icon. Double-click E-Mail Message and Word starts a new email message, complete with text boxes for headers.

NOTE The E-Mail Message icon is present only if either Outlook or Outlook Express is set as the default mail client. In Internet Explorer, choose Tools, Internet Options, Programs, and choose Outlook or Outlook Express for email.

Enhanced Options

Some items on the surface might look unchanged, but have been enhanced to reflect growth in Internet communications. For example, new buttons—Web Options and E-Mail Options—have been added to the General tab of the Options dialog box.

As shown in Figure 7.8, the Web Options dialog box includes five tabbed settings areas, which enable you to control the form and content of Web pages published from Word. Yes, it's more to worry about, but it's more control, and that's what you need when publishing for distinct platforms, intranets, and audiences.

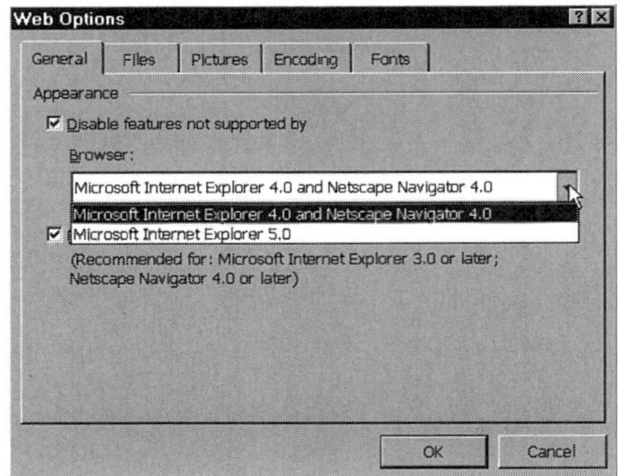

FIGURE 7.8
Word 2000's Web Options let you suppress features not supported by some browsers.

The E-Mail Options dialog box (see Figure 7.9) gives you control over the form and format of your email, as well as the format and content of email signatures. On the Personal Stationery tab, you can select specific themes and fonts.

CAUTION

Using stationery for email might make it more attractive–but the aesthetics come at the expense of speed and size. Stationery-laden emails require more space to store, take longer to download, and scroll slowly when viewing, depending on your correspondents' computing capabilities. Also, something that might look great to you might be barely legible to somebody else. Poorly contrasted backgrounds, fonts that are too small, and unnecessary graphics can quickly undermine otherwise businesslike communications. So, use stationery only when you know it's appropriate and won't put you on somebody's bad side.

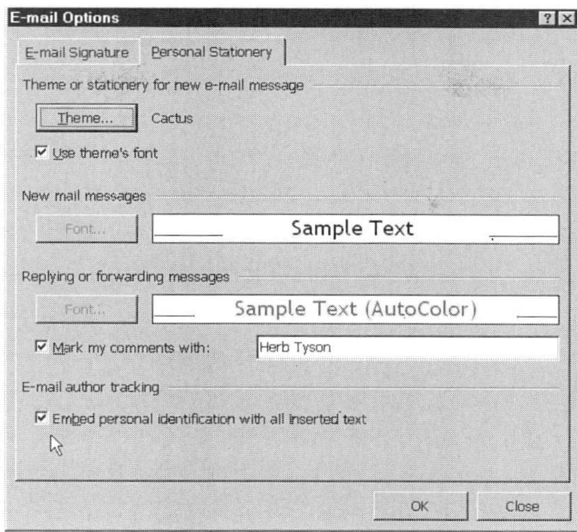

FIGURE 7.9
E-Mail Options lets you enable email author tracking.

File, Open Changes

One of the biggest changes to Word is in the Open dialog box (choose File, Open to get there). Shown in Figure 7.10, you'll notice a revamped approach to Look In (the drop-down list of resources you saw in Word 95 and Word 97, Desktop, My Computer, C:, Network Neighborhood, and so on). You can still use the traditional drop-down option. Or, you can click one of the areas (History, Personal, Desktop, Favorites, and Web Folders) on the Places Bar—Microsoft's name for the folder list at the left side of Word 2000's redesigned file dialog boxes. Gone, however, is immediate access to searching for text or property or last modified date. Instead, to access those features, you now need to click the Tools drop-down list and choose Find and use its more complicated and tedious dialog box.

TIP To activate Find within the Open dialog box, press Ctrl+F rather than choosing Tools, Find.

NOTE Office 2000's new Places Bar—which you'll see in file dialog boxes in Word, Excel, PowerPoint, and Access—resembles the customizable Outlook Bar you get in Outlook. The Places Bar, however, is not customizable the way Outlook's bar is.

The Places Bar can be changed, however, by editing the Windows Registry. The technique is described in Chapter 4.

▶ For additional information about changing the Places Bar, **see** "Customizing the Places Bar," **p. 82**

Gone also is the Add to Favorites tool at the top of the Open dialog box. To add the selected file or folder to the list of favorites, choose Tools, Add to Favorites.

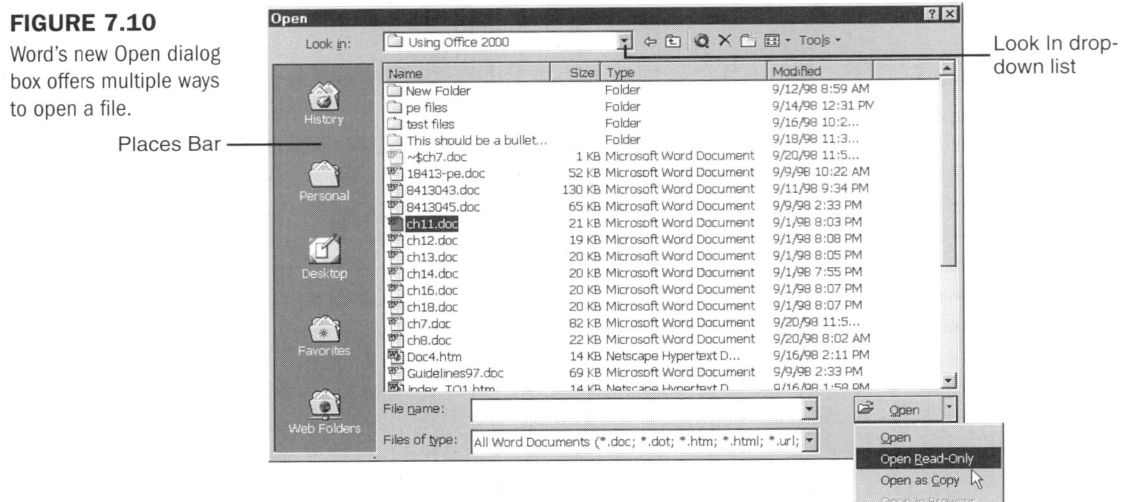

FIGURE 7.10
Word's new Open dialog box offers multiple ways to open a file.

Word 97's Commands and Settings button has been replaced by the Tools drop-down list. The Tools drop-down list is missing Word 97's Add/Modify FTP Locations control. Instead, this feature is now under the Look In drop-down list. Click the arrow to pull down the list of locations. FTP Locations and the Add/Modify option is at the bottom of the Look In list.

Page Setup and Printing Changes

Another noteworthy change, when you choose File, Page Setup, Margins tab, is shown in Figure 7.11. It's a subtle option you might not notice at first: 2 Pages per Sheet. Word has a built-in option that enables you to print two pages per sheet of paper as if you were printing to two virtual sheets of paper—headers, footer, and footnotes appearing correctly on each "sheet." Alas, this feature is not sophisticated enough to arrange the pages for a folding booklet. However, it's closer than it used to be. The Preview area gives you an idea of how this will print.

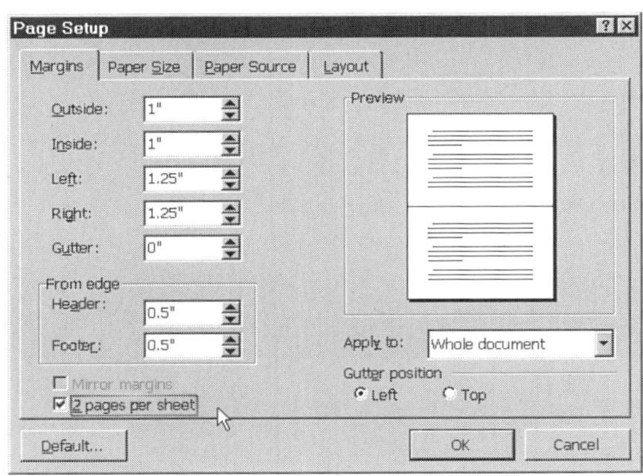

FIGURE 7.11

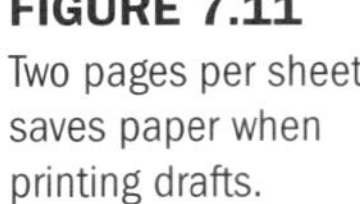
Two pages per sheet saves paper when printing drafts.

A related change also occurs in the lower-right corner of the Print dialog box. Two new options here are Pages per Sheet and Scale to Paper Size. The first of these options enables you to print a reduced size version of a document, with 2, 4, 6, 8, or 16 virtual pages per sheet of paper. This can be handy when you need a hard-copy view of what you normally see in Print Preview when you use the Multiple Pages tool, as shown in Figure 7.12. The second option resizes the whole page so it fits on the current size paper (like a reducing copying machine).

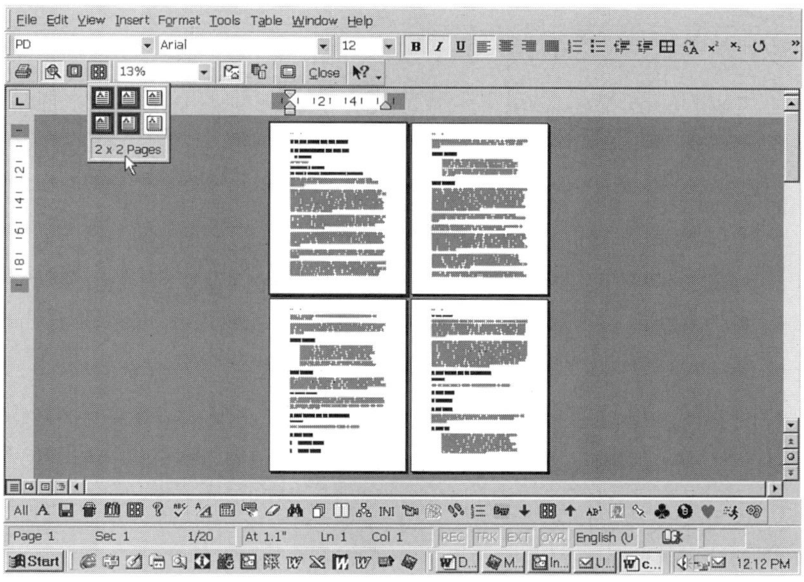

FIGURE 7.12
In the Print dialog box, the Pages per Sheet setting lets you print thumbnail views of multiple pages on a single sheet of paper.

Table Properties

At first sight, the new Table, Table Properties command just looks like a handy master control for tables. Indeed, it is that, but it's much more. For years, Word users have wanted the ability to wrap text around tables. It's here! Move the insertion point over a table, choose Table, Table Properties, and click the Table tab. Under Text Wrapping, you now have two options: None and Around.

To format a table so it sits inside a paragraph—with text wrapping around all sides, select the table or just click in any cell. Choose Table, Properties, and click the Table tab. Under Text Wrapping, choose Around. Click Positioning. Under Horizontal Position, choose Center.

Or, just grab the handle at the upper-left corner of a table and drag it where you want it to go. You can even drag multiple tables next to each other for side-by-side tables.

NOTE If you enable Word 2000 to be compatible with Word 97 (Tools, Options, Save, Disable Features Not Supported by Word 97 checked), this text-wrapping feature is unavailable.

Also new to Word 2000 is the capability to nest tables; in other words, embed tables within tables—a favorite organization technique used by many Web page designers. First, choose Tools, Options, and click the Save tab. Be sure Disable Features Not Supported by Word 97 is not checked. Use the Table tool to create a 4×4 table, and then click in any cell. Notice that—unlike Word 97—the Table tool on the toolbar does not change to an Insert Rows tool. Now, use the Table tool to create another 4×4 table inside any cells in the existing table.

▶ **See** "Creating Nested Tables," **p. 388**

If you create a nested table and later choose the option Disable Features Not Supported by Word 97, Word displays the warning shown in Figure 7.13. Also, if you already have Word 97 features disabled before attempting to nest a table, the nested tables option is unavailable to you.

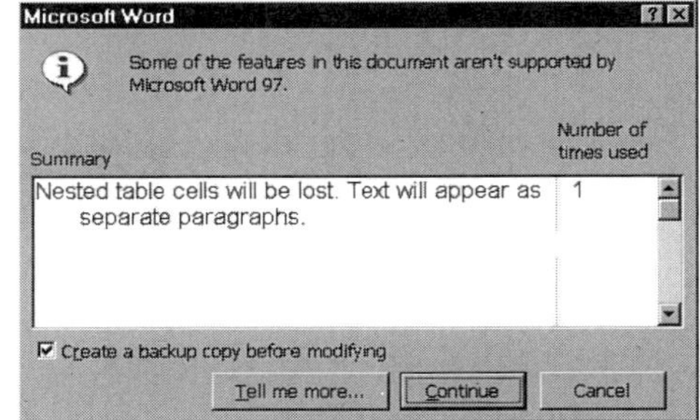

FIGURE 7.13
You have to choose between new features and backward compatibility.

Picture Bullets

The advent of the Web is responsible for yet another new feature—graphical bullets. To add picture bullets, choose Format, Bullets and Numbering, and click the Bulleted tab. Click the new Picture button at the bottom of the dialog box to open the Clip Gallery, which displays the Web Bullets category. On the Pictures tab, you'll find 60 or more graphics you can use as bullets. Use these graphical bullets the way you use ordinary bullets, but for Web pages, use them to create the kinds of snazzy designs frequently found on the Web.

NOTE Picture bullets are inserted differently than regular bullets. With regular bullets, using the built-in bullet feature, you cannot select the bullet itself. With picture bullets, to be Web-compatible, the bullets inserted actually are small graphical insertions. Be aware of this when editing, lest you accidentally delete your bullets.

Horizontal Lines

Another feature popularized by online documents is graphical horizontal lines. Choose Format, Borders and Shading, and click the Borders tab. Click the Horizontal Line button.

This starts the Clip Gallery (artgalry.exe) shown in Figure 7.14 and displays the clips in the Web Divider category.

FIGURE 7.14
The Clip Gallery applet displays only the clips available to you, based on the command used to access the gallery.

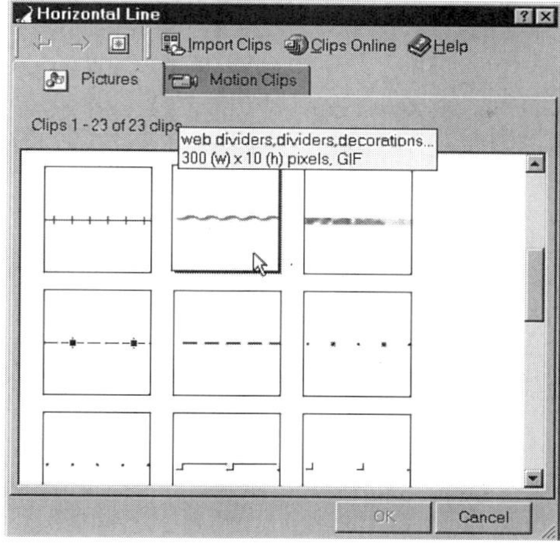

Because the Clip Gallery applet is not actually part of Word, it can remain onscreen at the same time as Word. Hence, if you need to insert a number of horizontal lines, use Windows' taskbar (or Alt+Tab) to switch between Clip Gallery and Word until you've created all the lines you need. Then close the Clip Gallery window.

Assign Hyperlink

The Assign Hyperlink feature is another that has been added in the wake of the Web. This new feature lets you associate any toolbar icon with a hyperlink to a picture, file, or Web address. Ordinarily, to assign a file or link to a toolbar icon, you must create a macro, and then make the corresponding assignments by choosing Tools, Customize. The new Assign Hyperlink feature enables you to take a shortcut.

Choose Tools, Customize, and click the Commands tab. Drag any icon to any toolbar. Now, right-click the new tool and choose Assign Hyperlink, Open (or Insert Picture). Navigate or browse to the desired link or file, and choose OK. Then Close the Customize dialog box.

Click the new icon. If you've linked to a picture, that picture is inserted into the current file. If you've linked to a file or URL, that file or URL is opened in the default viewer or browser for that type of file.

▶ **See** "Cross-References and Hyperlinks," **p. 459**

Considerations When Converting Documents

Word 2000 and Word 97 use the same file format. That does not mean, however, that they are identical. In effect, Word 97 contains a subset of Word 2000's features. You can open a Word 2000 document directly in Word 97—and vice versa.

The exception is that any Word 2000 features not recognized by Word 97 are ignored. This means that when a document originally created in Word 2000 is saved in Word 97, any Word 2000-specific features of the document are stripped.

Keep several things in mind when converting between Word 2000 and various earlier versions of Word: Pay particular attention to what happens with macros (and hence, templates) saved in Word documents, and what happens when converting documents to HTML.

Converting Word Macros

Word 2000's Visual Basic language is *supposed to be* identical to Word 97's, except for those additional features not supported by Word 97. Hence, macros written for Word 97 *should* work directly in Word 2000 without conversion.

In fact, most macros written for Word 97 do work fine in Word 2000. Some of the more involved macros, however, may require minor changes, either in the program or in the options you select.

▶ **See** Chapter 5, "Getting Acquainted with VBA."

▶ **See** Chapter 6, "Successful VBA Modules."

CAUTION

When loading Word 97 templates into Word 2000, no explicit conversion process exists. Sometimes, however, macros that worked fine under Word 97 don't work fine under Word 2000, and don't even give any error messages. Check macros carefully to make sure you're getting the results you expect. In the Visual Basic Editor, check both Tools, Options and Tools, References to be sure your settings are correct.

You might experience some difficulties when converting documents containing macros to Office 2000 from Word 95 or earlier versions. Even though Word attempts to automate the process, the resulting macros are not always useful and do not always work. The conversion process for Word 95 (and earlier) templates is initiated any time you open a template, attach a template to a document, open a document based on such a template, or make such a template global in Word 2000.

CAUTION

When using pre-Word 97 templates, any macros are automatically converted to Word 2000. Once converted (and the containing template has been saved), they will no longer work in the earlier version of Word, and you can't reverse the process. Therefore, we strongly recommend that you make copies of any pre-Word 97 templates, and then use the copies in Word 2000. This is especially true if users of those earlier versions of Word still need access to those templates.

If your macro doesn't work, however, and you are not familiar with Visual Basic, then prepare yourself for a little culture shock. It's different from what you're used to with WordBasic. Following is a simple Word 6 or Word 95 WordBasic macro that swaps two sentences:

```
Sub MAIN
SelectCurSentence
EditCut
SentRight
Insert " "
EditPaste
End Sub
```

When the Word 6 or Word 95 template that contained this macro was opened by Word 2000, the macro was immediately converted into the following, which makes heavy use of the WordBasic property:

```
Public Sub MAIN()
WordBasic.SelectCurSentence
WordBasic.EditCut
WordBasic.SentRight
WordBasic.Insert " "
WordBasic.EditPaste
End Sub
```

When converting simple macros from Word 95 or earlier, Word 2000 uses the WordBasic property (a set of WordBasic commands and functions), which is retained for compatibility purposes. However, the same macro written purely in Visual Basic becomes:

```
Sub SwapSent()
    With Selection.Sentences(1)
        .Select
        .Cut
        .MoveStart Unit:=wdSentence, Count:=1
        .Paste
    End With
End Sub
```

It's still not overly complex; however, it is different. The reason for the extra complexity is capability. Visual Basic provides far more power than WordBasic, and better integration among all Office components (often, modules developed for one Office application can also work for other Office applications).

Converting Documents from Other Versions of Word

The farther back in time (Word versions) you go, the more profound the differences between versions become. Word 97 and Word 2000 are similar. Word 6 and 95, which shared the same file format, is yet another generation away, and even more will be lost when saving to those formats. But, the good news is that when converting documents from earlier formats to Word 2000, nothing is lost.

On the other hand, if you edit a Word 97, Word 95, or earlier document using Word 2000, your documents are automatically saved in their original format, not in Word 2000 native format.

CAUTION

Saving in original formats does not apply to document templates. Word 2000 cannot save a document template in earlier Word formats. Document templates saved by Word 2000 are usable in Word 97 (albeit missing new features unique to Word 2000), but not in Word 95 or earlier.

For those who edit in a mixed environment—where documents travel back and forth between different versions of Word—this is a tremendous insurance policy.

A second line of defense in ensuring that documents travel in the formats you intend is to enable Word's capability to prompt to confirm file formats. Choose Tools, Options, and click the General tab. Enable the Confirm Conversion at Open option. At first, selecting this option might seem as if you're adding to your workload. Indeed, it does slow the saving process a little, but when you're working in a mixed environment, it pays to know the file format for any document you open and save.

Another point to consider is choosing the file format you want to use each and every time you save a document. One way to ensure that you always do this is to choose Save As, rather than just Save. Not only does that give you the opportunity to change the filename if you need to retain the original, but the act of using Save As shows you the default format, in the Save As Type drop-down list.

Swapping Shortcuts for Save and Save As

By default, the shortcut for Save is Ctrl+S and the shortcut for Save As is F12. If you really prefer to use Save As rather than Save—but are hopelessly addicted to pressing Ctrl+S—reassign Ctrl+S to Save As, and F12 to Save. Press Ctrl+Alt+[Number Pad Plus Sign]. A cloverleaf pointer appears. Press F12, and the Customize Keyboard dialog box appears with FileSaveAs already selected. Press Ctrl+S, and click Assign and Close.

Next, press Ctrl+Alt+[Number Pad Plus Sign] again. Use the cloverleaf pointer to choose File, Save from the menu bar. When the Customize Keyboard dialog box appears, press F12 to assign that key to save, and then click Assign and Close.

Now, F12 and Ctrl+S have been officially swapped. From now on, Ctrl+S does Save As and F12 does a Save.

If you want to revert to Word's default key assignments, you can, of course, do it by explicitly reassigning commands to original keystrokes. You can restore any given key's default assignment more simply, however. Display the associated command in the Customize Keyboard dialog box, click the keystroke shown in Current Keys, and click Remove. Clicking Reset All removes all custom key assignments.

▶ **See** "Customizing the Restricted Keys," **p. 223**

For those who plan to keep Word documents at a given pre-Word 2000 level for the time being, a third option is available. Choose Tools, Options, and click the Save tab. Set the Save Word Files As to the corresponding version, shown in Figure 7.15. This is tantamount to always doing Save As and always saving to the identical format (Word 2000, Word 97, Word 95, WordPerfect 5, and so on).

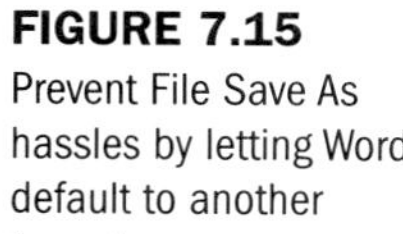

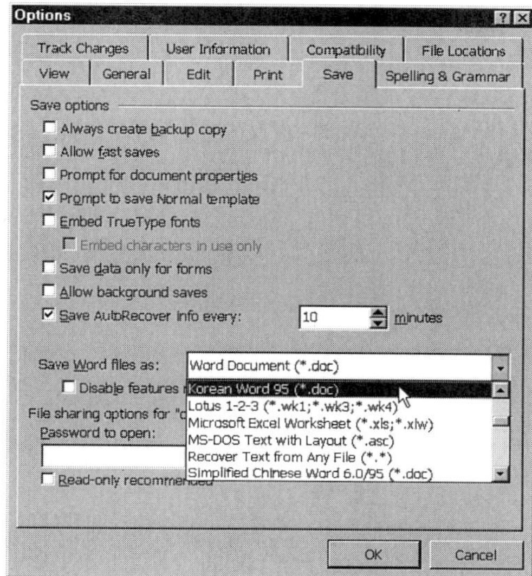

FIGURE 7.15
Prevent File Save As hassles by letting Word default to another format.

Be Careful When Saving Word 2000 Documents As Word 97 Documents

If you want to use Word 97 format, choose the option Disable Features Not Supported by Word 97, also in the Tools, Options, Save tab. If the file already has Word 2000 features in it, you will be warned that this option will cause a loss of formatting. The formatting loss occurs the moment you click Continue–not when you save. Furthermore, after you click Continue, you cannot Undo the change. If you then save the document under the same name, the Word 2000 formatting is lost permanently. To be on the safe side, you can use Save As to save it with a new name, or you can accept the dialog box's offer to make a backup copy. Of course, if you change your mind after disabling Word 2000 features, you can always close the file without saving changes and start again (unless the Word 2000 version has never previously been saved).

Saving Word Documents As HTML

Like Word 97 and the Internet Assistant-enabled Word 6 and Word 95, Word 2000 supports saving files in HTML format. Unlike previous versions, Word 2000 now supports more HTML controls than ever before, the most important of which is frames.

▶ **See** "Integrating HTML in Office," **p. 12**

First, the bad news. With Word 2000's extra capabilities come extra layers of complications in HTML files. Word now saves tons of extra stuff. Let's consider a simple HTML file created by FrontPage 2000. This page displays text reading, "Hello World!":

```
<html>

<head>
<meta http-equiv="Content-Language" content="en-us">
```

```
<meta name="GENERATOR" content="Microsoft FrontPage 4.0">
<meta name="ProgId" content="FrontPage.Editor.Document">
<title>Hello World</title>
</head>

<body>

<p>Hello World!</p>

</body>

</html>
```

FrontPage 2000 expands the simple 12-character, one-line message (Hello World!) to about 250 characters and 16 lines. If this file is opened with Word 2000 and saved as HTML from Word, the file grows to more than 2,000 characters and 94 lines of HTML code, most of which is absolutely unnecessary!

Keep this in mind before you choose Word as your HTML editor. As an aside, if you create the Hello World! Web page using Word from the outset, it could grow to between 3,000 and 12,000 characters of HTML (Word file sizes can be variable based on a variety of reasons).

Saving Web Pages for Use with the Right Browsers

Something else to keep in mind is the browser level or HTML version for which you're writing. If you're writing for the Internet in general, then you want to keep your features as mainstream as possible. All the polish in the world won't do any good if your average viewers can't access it.

Choose Tools, Options, and click the General tab. Then select the Web Options button to display the dialog box shown in Figure 7.16.

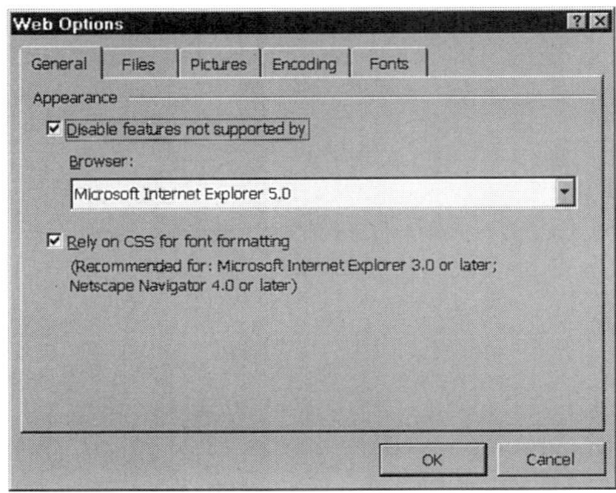

FIGURE 7.16
Customize Word's HTML for specific browser versions.

The first option lets you either not suppress any features, or selectively suppress features that are

- Not supported by Microsoft Internet Explorer version 5 (IE5)
- Not supported by Microsoft Internet Explorer version 4 and Netscape Navigator version 4

The second option lets you rely on CSS (Cascading Style Sheets) class definitions for font formatting, or not. The idea behind CSS is to separate formatting from content. Font definitions are established in a separate section of the HTML document (or even in a separate file), apart from the text. This lets you change the whole face of a Web site by changing the underlying style sheet rather than editing the content. When you think about it, this is precisely what Word does with document templates, styles, and themes.

▶ **See** "Cascading Style Sheets," **p. 14**

CSS is supported by Microsoft Internet Explorer 4 (IE4) and later, and by Netscape Communicator 4 and later. Even so, the implementation is not identical inside all browsers, and may depend additionally upon user settings and preferences in various browsers. Definitions that result in underlining in Communicator sometimes do not produce underlining in Internet Explorer.

Therefore, regardless of the settings you choose, you still need to review and proofread your online documents carefully using all available browsers before posting them publicly. This is true of documents posted on intranets, but especially for those posted to the Internet because you don't have any organizational control over what browsers and settings the general public uses.

Many Word features do not survive conversion to HTML. Your best bet in composing Web pages is to begin with HTML format whenever possible. That way, Word itself immediately denies access to features not supported by HTML—so you won't be lulled into wasting your time relying on such features.

For example, if the current document has already been saved as a Web page, Center Alignment in Table Properties doesn't work. If you choose Center Alignment, Word pops up a warning box that says the feature is disabled because it's not supported by some browsers compatible with IE or Netscape 4.

In the General tab of the Options dialog box (choose Tools, Options), select the Web Options button and explore the other settings. Under Files, you have the option to put everything Word saves into a single folder or to create subfolders for items such as links and graphics. If your Web server does not allow you to create new folders, keep this option in mind.

In the Pictures tab, you can choose whether to optimize for IE 5 by using VML (vector markup language) and PNG (portable network graphics). If you are designing a Web application for a specific workstation (for example, in a library, museum, or other intranet location), you can also optimize for a given monitor.

The Encoding and Fonts tabs are essential tools in effecting wide access for your Web applications. In all cases, find out the requirement of your Internet and intranet audiences so they'll see onscreen what you want them to see.

CHAPTER 8

Customizing Word

In this chapter

Word Startup Options

Users typically start Word in one of two ways: by opening/creating a new document or by double-clicking a Word shortcut icon. There might be times, however, that you would like Word to start differently. Users sometimes prefer to suppress the default blank Document1 that Word creates. You might want to start Word with a particular document template, rather than Normal.dot. Perhaps you have a project that requires that you run a particular macro each time you start Word for working on that project. You can accomplish these and other aims by creating and modifying shortcuts to Word, specifying different startup options.

Suppressing Macros and Events at Startup

When starting up, Word loads Normal.dot and any Startup templates. In the process, Word runs any AutoExec macros or VBA code tied to opening and closing events these templates might contain. Sometimes, however, circumstances can change causing errors to occur. For example, a critical folder might have been deleted. Or, perhaps a Word add-on installed an automatic macro that is defective in some way. Often, the quickest way to get to the root of the problem is to prevent Word from running any automatic macros or events, to see whether the problem goes away.

Understanding AutoMacros

Word provides five automatic macro names to facilitate automating Word. Macros with these names (sometimes called AutoMacros) run under varying conditions and circumstances. There are also events that occur that work similar to these AutoMacros. The five AutoMacro names are

- AutoExec—Effective only in global templates (Normal.dot and other global templates), macros named AutoExec run when a global template is first loaded (that is, when Word first starts, and when you load a global template from the Templates and Add-Ins dialog box). AutoExec macros typically perform initial setup, such as making a particular network location the current folder, setting up view and editing options for a general editing session, or initiating the File, New sequence for beginning a new document.
- AutoExit—Effective only in global templates, macros named AutoExit run when closing Word. AutoExit macros typically are used to perform cleanup chores, such as setting the default directory to the current directory.
- AutoNew—Macros named AutoNew are run when a new document is first created, based on a template containing an AutoNew macro. AutoNew macros typically are used for initial document setup such as inserting a date and signature into a newly created letter, activating an address book to insert an address, and prompting the user to enter one-time data for newly created documents. The event that occurs when a new document is created is the `Document_New` event. Code in this event also runs when a new document based on a template with this event is programmed.
- AutoOpen—Macros named AutoOpen are run when an existing template or any existing document based on that template is opened. AutoOpen macros typically are used to perform

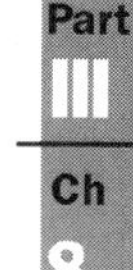

setup activities, such as displaying certain toolbars, setting view, edit, and other options, and so on. The `Document_Open` event can be programmed in the same fashion as the AutoOpen macro.

- AutoClose—Macros named AutoClose are run when an existing template or any existing document based on that template is closed. AutoClose macros typically are used to perform cleanup tasks when a document type is closed, such as updating links, printing, emailing updates to other users, and so on. The event that provides a similar functionality is the `Document_Close` event.

There is a simple startup option that prevents macros from running at startup. Better still is the fact that you don't have to modify any shortcuts to suppress the AutoMacros and events that carry out the same functionality. Simply hold down the Shift key when you start Word. The Shift key prevents any automatic macros or events from starting. This technique can be used not only when starting Word to suppress AutoExec, but also when opening or creating new documents to suppress AutoOpen/`Document_Open` and AutoNew/`Document_New`. The Shift trick can also be used when closing documents to suppress AutoClose/`Document_Close`, and when closing Word to suppress AutoExit.

NOTE Depending on your security settings (Tools, Macro, Security), Word will not run macros created by nontrusted sources (high security). Also dependent upon your security settings, Word can offer you the opportunity to disable macros (medium security). You can also instruct Word to enable all macros without warning you (low security). You would need to use the Shift-to-suppress approach only if you have selected low security, or if you have specific knowledge about an automatic macro you want to suppress.

▶ **See** "Programmability," **p. 23**

Using Windows Shortcuts to Start Word

Although the Shift trick discussed in the previous section is useful, its applications are limited. For controlling how Word starts, the most effective method is to create customized shortcuts. Using customized shortcuts, you can cause Word to open a particular document, create a new file based on a particular template, run a particular macro, and more.

One good way to begin is to create a shortcut to Word itself.

1. Choose File, New, Shortcut.
2. In the Create Shortcut wizard, click Browse. Navigate to the location where the Microsoft Office executable program files are stored. Usually, Microsoft Office is in the Program Files folder on the same drive where Windows itself resides. Word's executable file usually is found as

   ```
   C:\Program Files\Microsoft Office\Office\winword.exe
   ```

3. Select winword.exe (the executable program file for Word), and click Open, as shown in Figure 8.1. Figure 8.1 shows three windows:
   - The Browse window—Appears on top and lists the program executable files in the Office folder; the Word executable is selected.

- The Create Shortcut window—Appears in the middle and holds the command line that will be used for the shortcut.
- The Word Properties window—Appears at the back. This window does not normally display when you are creating a shortcut, but has been added to this figure so that you can see the Target for the command line.

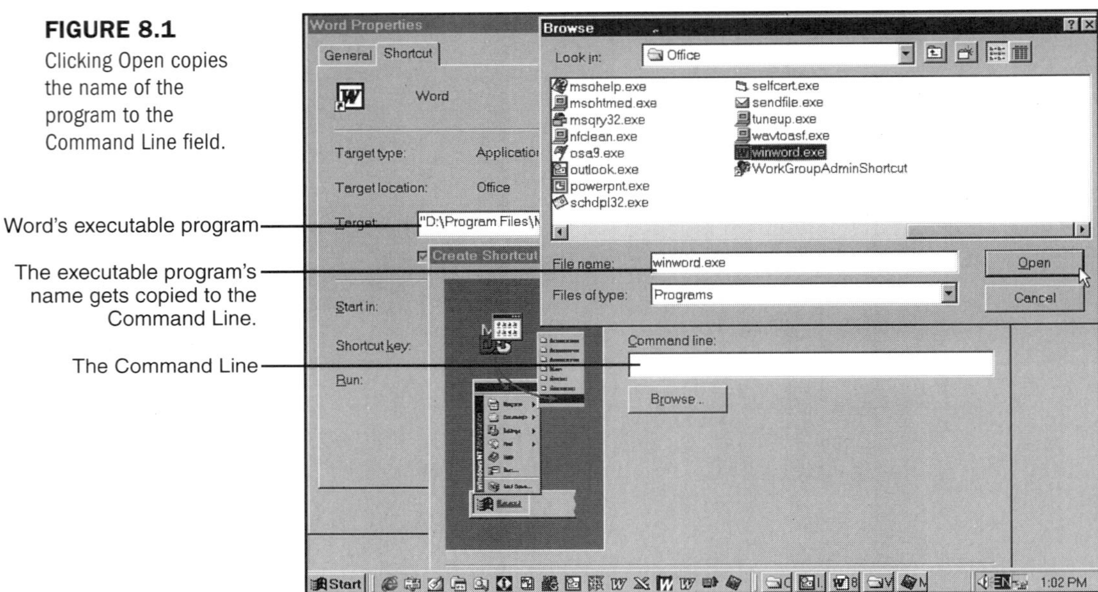

FIGURE 8.1
Clicking Open copies the name of the program to the Command Line field.

4. After you've located the file in the Browse window, you'll be returned to the Create Shortcut Wizard; click Next.
5. The next step requires a name for the shortcut. If you are creating a simple shortcut to Word (without any special switches), you'll most likely want to type `Word` to replace winword.exe. For special-purpose shortcuts, you'll want to use descriptive names.
6. Click Finish.

Avoid Creating Shortcuts That Begin with the Same Letter

When naming shortcuts—especially if you tend to be oriented more to the keyboard than to the mouse—avoid creating multiple shortcuts that start with the same letter. Microsoft's Setup programs create shortcuts such as Microsoft Word, Microsoft Excel, and so on.

If you're working in a folder and want to access a particular item, you can tap that item's first letter, and the first item beginning with that letter is selected. For a folder where everything is named Microsoft this and Microsoft that, tapping the M cycles you through the M items, but it won't take you directly to Word unless Microsoft Word is listed first. If, instead, you have names such as Word, Excel, Access, and PowerPoint—and nothing else beginning with those letters—then W takes you to Word, E takes you to Excel, and so on.

Moreover, these names take up less space on the screen, creating less visual clutter and displaying items that are easier to identify at a glance.

After the shortcut is created, you can clone it to save time. Using the right mouse button, drag a copy of the item you just created and drop the copy next to the item. Choose Copy Here, as shown in Figure 8.2. This creates a copy of the Word shortcut. Repeat this process as many times as necessary. Successive clones of the Word shortcut create additional copies of Word (Word(2), Word(3), and so on).

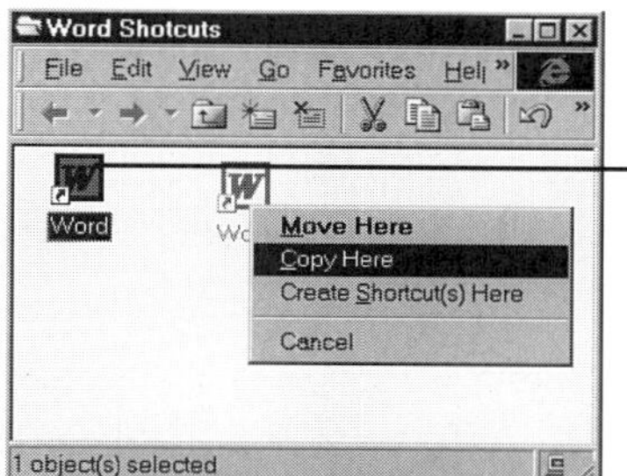

FIGURE 8.2
When cloning a shortcut, you can choose Create Shortcut(s) Here or Copy Here.

Using Switches to Alter Startup

After you've created a supply of Word shortcuts, you can modify their properties settings to include a variety of startup specifications. The technique is to add startup switches and filenames to the basic Word Target field (in the Properties settings for Word Shortcuts) depending on your needs, as follows:

Some of the switches are designed to help target the way you work—by loading specific templates, documents, or add-ins, or by running specific macros. Some help you work more efficiently, by automatically opening the last file you changed or by suppressing certain Word behaviors.

NOTE The switches introduced here are holdovers from the days of DOS and were called Command-Line Switches, because you entered them at the DOS command-line prompt as you typed the name of the program you wanted to open. Because the interface used with these applications is no longer DOS, in this book they are referred to as just plain switches.

Starting Word Without Add-Ins and User Settings—Using the /a Switch

From time to time—especially for diagnostic reasons—you may need to start Word without Normal.dot, without any other global templates and .wll Word add-ins, and without loading user options. This type of startup switch is particularly useful when the Normal.dot or other global add-in becomes corrupted, Word crashes immediately upon starting, or when you just want to see how Word works without any customizations. The idea is to run Word without these other items, in effect isolating the part of Word—winword.exe and the factory-installed files—from the templates, add-ins, and user settings to determine whether the application itself is damaged. By suppressing Normal.dot, other templates and add-ins, and user options, you effectively rule those out if the problem continues.

To create a diagnostic or raw Word shortcut, select the copy of the Word executable you created earlier in "Using Windows Shortcuts to Start Word"—Word (2)—and press F2 (Edit) to enter the edit mode, as shown in Figure 8.3. Change the name to Raw Word, and press Enter.

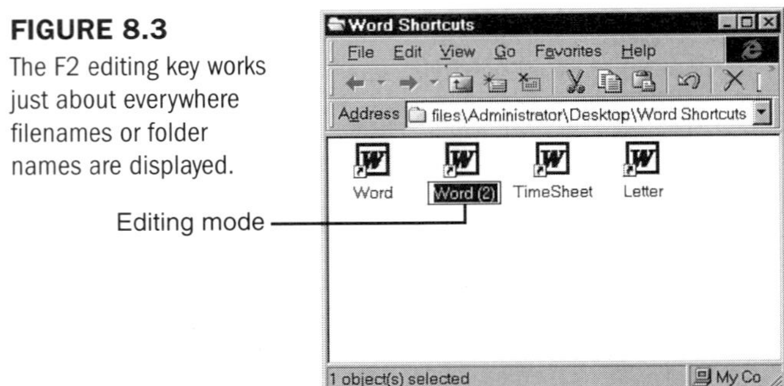

FIGURE 8.3
The F2 editing key works just about everywhere filenames or folder names are displayed.

Now, press Alt+Enter to edit the properties. The Properties dialog box (shown in Figure 8.4) has several important elements:

- Target—The Target text box is the instruction Windows uses to start the application. The Target includes the name of the executable program as well as any optional startup switches or files.
- Start In—The Start In text box specifies the default folder where the application begins. If the Target box includes the name of a document for the application to open—and omits the folder in the document specification—the application looks for the document file in the Start In folder.
- Shortcut Key—Use the Shortcut Key text box to designate a hotkey combination for starting the shortcut. Click in Shortcut Key and press the key combination you want to use to start that shortcut.
- Run—The Run drop-down list specifies the type of window the application starts in (Normal, Minimized, or Maximized).

In the Target field, add `/a` after the quoted startup command. When finished, it appears as

```
"C:\Program Files\Microsoft Office\Office\winword.exe" /a
```

It should look similar to Figure 8.4. Click OK.

FIGURE 8.4
Shortcuts are object-oriented equivalents to old-style DOS batch files.

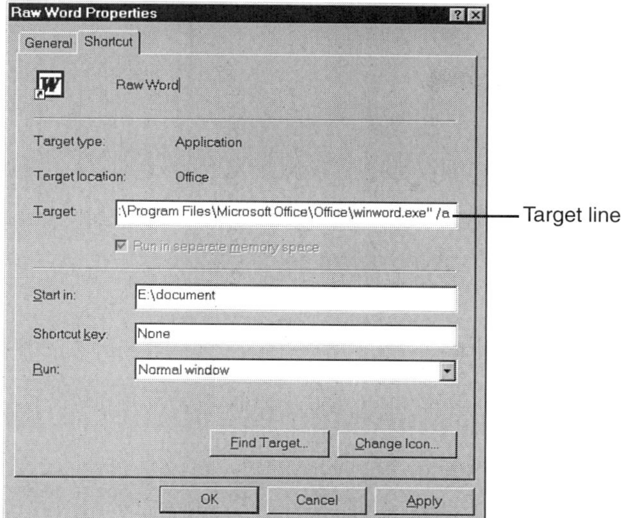

Starting Word with a Particular Document

If you want to start Word with a particular document, you have two options. The most obvious—if that document uses Word as its default Open application—is to create a shortcut to that document. Using Windows Explorer, find the document (or documents). Use the right mouse button to drag a copy to the desktop or to your Word Shortcuts folder, choosing Create Shortcut(s) Here.

CAUTION

Use the right mouse button when creating shortcuts. If you drag with the left mouse button, you'll be copying or moving the file from its original location. If you drag with the right mouse button, Windows prompts you for which action you want to perform, as shown previously in Figure 8.2.

The second option is to create a shortcut that uses a particular filename and location in conjunction with the specification for winword.exe. For example, suppose you have a timesheet that you want to be able to access from a given icon. Name the shortcut timesheet and then inscribe the file's folder and name into the shortcut's Target field, as shown in Figure 8.5:

```
"C:\Program Files\Microsoft Office\Office\winword.exe"
➥"e:\word docs\timesheet.doc"
```

The advantage of this approach is that you can specify multiple documents. Suppose, for example, that to work on a particular task, you usually have a number of documents open at the same time—various files containing notes, other files containing related reports, another file containing sources, and, of course, the document under construction. You can use this approach and have Word open all the files you need in one fell swoop.

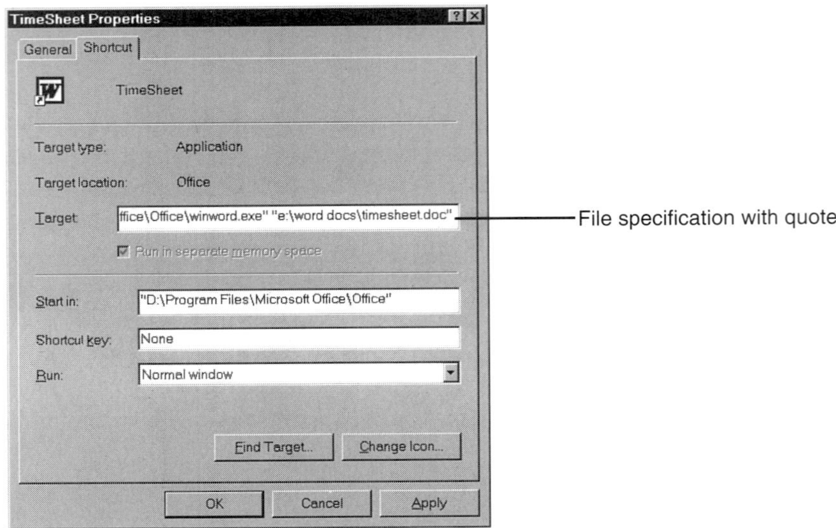

FIGURE 8.5
Use separate sets of quotes for the program and document files.

Specifying a half-dozen different fully qualified files can be a bit of a pain. If the files all reside in the same folder, an alternative is to modify the Start In: location to point to that folder. This allows you to specify just the filenames in the Target line. For this folder, you would set Start In: to `e:\report` (where e: represents the drive on which the folder resides), and then specify just the filenames in the Target line, as shown in Figure 8.6. The complete Target line might be

```
"C:\Program Files\Microsoft Office\Office\winword.exe" report11.doc notes12.doc
➥report12.doc
```

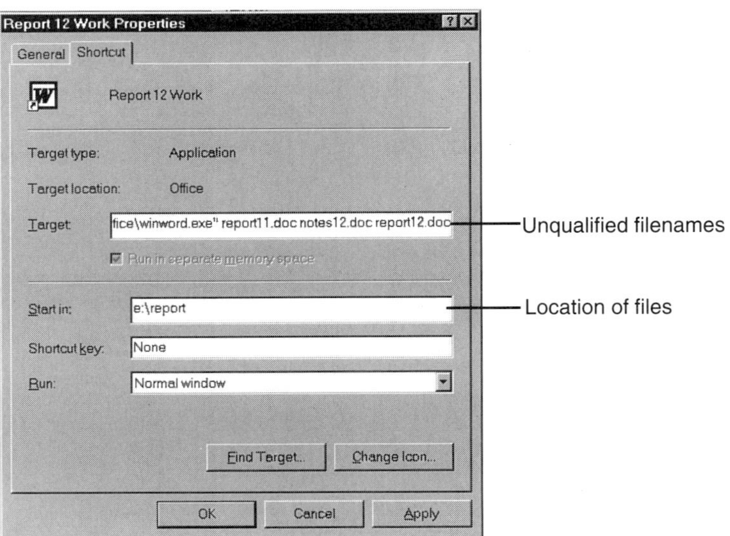

FIGURE 8.6
Save time by setting Start In: to the location of multiple files.

Using the /n Switch to Start Word Without Creating a Blank Document

There are times when you might want to start Word without creating the standard Document1 that Word automatically creates at startup.

To do this, start Word with the /n switch, using the following as Target in the properties setting for the shortcut, leaving the other properties settings unchanged:

```
"C:\Program Files\Microsoft Office\Office\winword.exe" /n
```

Using the /t Switch to Start with a Particular Template

Generally, when you start Word, you are presented with a blank document based on the Normal template. You can, however, instruct Word to start with another template of your choosing—such as a letter, fax, or memo template. You can create shortcuts named Letter, Invoice, Proposal, and so on, and use those shortcuts to start Word, and have a blank document based on the desired template ready and waiting. To start Word with the Professional Letter template that comes with Word, use this as the Target entry:

```
"C:\Program Files\Microsoft Office\Office\winword.exe" /t"C:\Program
➥Files\Microsoft Office\Templates\professional letter.dot"
```

NOTE Whenever a file or directory specification contains spaces, you need to include quotes. Otherwise, Windows divides the command line into pieces and processes those pieces separately. For example, if you have `winword.exe letter to grandma.doc`, Word first tries to open something called letter, then something called to, and finally something called grandma.doc. But in quotes, the string is passed in its entirety.

There should be no spaces between the /t and what follows it. But, why do you need /t? If you just have the file specification, wouldn't that work? Yes, it would. But, instead of creating a Document1 based on the template, it would open the template itself. You would then have to perform a File, Save As to avoid overwriting the template. Moreover, after you're editing a template itself, Word disables Save As, so you would be unable to convert it back into a document without ultimately performing a File, New operation using that template as a basis.

Use Caution When Using the /t Switch

There is one disadvantage to creating a new document with the /t approach, as opposed to using File, New, and selecting the template within Word while it's already running. When you use the /t approach, any automatic macros in the /t template are suppressed.

Hence, if you have an AutoNew macro that sets up a letter or does other chores, it does not run in the loading process. Instead, you would have to invoke it by some other means after the Document1 window has been created.

Note, however, that AutoExec macros in Normal.dot and other global templates (Tools, Templates and Add-Ins, Global Templates and Add-Ins) will run.

Using the /m Switch to Start with a Macro Other Than AutoExec or AutoOpen

By default, when you start Word, if Normal.dot contains a macro named AutoExec, that macro runs immediately when Word is opened. However, users sometimes have other macros they want to run at startup. Moreover, they want them selectively, so using AutoExec isn't an option. Instead of relying on AutoExec, you can use the /m switch to specify a macro to run at startup.

To run a macro named MyMacro, contained in Normal.dot, create the macro—giving it that name—and then use the following Target entry in a Word shortcut:

```
"C:\Program Files\Microsoft Office\Office\winword.exe" /mMyMacro
```

Note that there are no spaces between /m and MyMacro (and you don't need to capitalize mymacro, either). Note also that you can use multiple /m's and run several macros in consecutive order as Word starts up. This enables you to create different startup sequences for different Word shortcuts.

NOTE You cannot effectively combine the template and macro switches (/t and /m) in the same Target line. First, /m starts a macro only in Normal.dot. Second, even if you cleverly place your macro into Normal.dot instead of the template specified by /t, Word runs the /m macro *before* creating a new document based on the /t template. Third, as noted previously, the /t approach cannot run any automatic macros.

The /m switch can also be used to accomplish the same effect as holding down Shift while starting Word. Used without any macro name, the /m switch suppresses the running of all automatic macros when Word is started.

Using the /mfile1 Switch to Start Word with the Last Edited Document

A special but very useful case of the /m switch is in combination with built-in Word commands, such as File1. Word has nine built-in File# commands (File1 through File9) that correspond to the Recently Used File list at the bottom of the File menu.

The default number of files displayed in the Recently Used list is four. To display up to nine, choose Tools, Options, and click the General tab. Change Entries to any number between zero (blank) and nine.

The File1 command automatically opens the most recently edited file. Thus, you can have Word automatically open the most recent file by using the Target command line:

```
"C:\Program Files\Microsoft Office\Office\winword.exe" /mfile1
```

Better still, if you add a second /m command, you can have Word return to the last place in the document where editing occurred. The GoBack command (Shift+F5) toggles the insertion point among the last five places in the document where editing occurred. When executed upon first opening a document, the GoBack command returns the insertion point to the last place editing occurred the last time that document was saved (this is true only if there are no documents already open). This is good to know not only when you open that first document in Word, but as a useful appendage to the File1 command.

To reopen the last document you edited, right where you left off, use the Target command line:

```
"C:\Program Files\Microsoft Office\Office\winword.exe" /mfile1 /mgoback
```

Notice that you do need a space between /mfile1 and /mgoback.

Using the /l Switch to Start Word with a Specific Add-In

Another startup option is to load a specific add-in. Word automatically loads any .wll or .dot files located in Word's Startup folder set (using Tools, Options, File Locations). Sometimes, however, you might want other .wll or .dot files loaded for specific tasks. It would be tedious to move those kinds of files in and out of the Startup folder. It's equally tedious to have to choose Tools, Templates and Add-Ins each time to load them. By using the `/l` switch, however, you can create specialized Word startup shortcuts that initialize the Word environment as you see fit.

To automatically load the Macros9.dot (a sample macros file that comes with Word) upon startup, use the following Target entry:

```
"C:\Program Files\Microsoft Office\Office\winword.exe" /l"C:\Program
➥Files\Microsoft Office\Office\Macros\macros9.dot"
```

Note that there is no space between `/l` and the beginning of the file specification that follows. You can use the `/l` more than once within a given shortcut. To include a second add-in, insert a space at the end of the command shown previously, and add another `/l` specification.

Emergency Repair Startup Options

All the startup options discussed so far actually result in Word starting in a particular way. However, there are two startup options, for repairing damaged Registry entries, that are designed to start Word in a special maintenance mode, and then exit. Use these options with caution, however, because they can alter custom settings. Often, a user's only encounter with these options is when Microsoft support staff advises a user to use them to attempt repair.

Reregistration Using the /regserver Switch

You use the /regserver switch to reregister Word in the Windows Registry. The quickest way to do this usually is to modify an existing Word shortcut by adding the /regserver switch.

Reregistration can be useful for those times when you don't think you have time to run Help, Detect and Repair—which can be time-consuming. It's useful when you suspect the problem is caused by missing or corrupted registry entries rather than missing or corrupted files.

Unregistration Using the /unregserver Switch

You can use the /unregserver switch to clean up registration entries for Word. If you find that, despite reregistration, things are still messed up, you sometimes can restore order by using `winword.exe /unregserver` followed by `winword.exe /regserver`. This cleans up the server's entries, and then re-creates them correctly (hopefully). This one-two punch sometimes fixes matters and so can be a good alternative to more time-consuming Detect and Repair or removal/reinstallation.

NOTE Word is an OLE server. The /regserver and /unregserver switches can be used with most OLE servers compiled with current-generation Microsoft compilers.

Setting Word Options via the Word Interface

As shown, Word's behavior can be changed by modifying the way it starts up—by creating customized startup icons. After Word is running, a myriad of additional options can be changed using standard features in Word's interface.

Customizing the Screen for Quick Editing

The transition from plain Word for DOS to Word for Windows brought a number of improvements in ease of use. Much of that ease, however, has come at the expense of a lot of speed. You can, however, tweak some of Word's settings to reclaim some of the speed you exchange for a graphical front end. The factory-installed Word starts out in Print Layout view. That view is fine if you're concentrating on layout. However, while you're working on content, you don't need to have every little WYSIWYG bell and whistle rigged and waiting. To speed up screen display, there are a number of options you should set. Some other options don't speed up the screen display, but can enhance your editing power so that the net result is more effective speed.

Set the View to Normal This is the quickest display option available to Word users (choose View, Normal). Although you might consider displaying draft text (Tools, Options, View, Draft font), most users find that the light text employed by the draft font actually increases eyestrain, making Word more tedious, rather than less.

Set the Options on the View Tab To set these options, choose Tools, Options, click the View tab and click Picture Placeholders, Formatting Marks (All), Wrap to Window (see Figure 8.7). Checking Picture Placeholders substitutes a plain box instead of the actual pictures, speeding up screen display. Displaying formatting marks—such as spaces between words, tabs, and paragraph marks—prevents time-consuming editing mistakes. Showing the space character is a matter of taste. If you find the space characters distracting, you can turn them off. Leave paragraph marks on, however, because they're essential for some kinds of formatting and editing techniques.

Wrap to Window is a wonderful innovation that first appeared in Word 6.0. Prior to Word 6.0, users had to choose between horizontal scrolling and an onscreen display font that was too small to read comfortably. With Wrap to Window enabled, in Normal view, you can zoom to any magnification and still see both sides of the document. As an added bonus, after the zoom goes above a certain level, text automatically darkens, further enhancing onscreen readability.

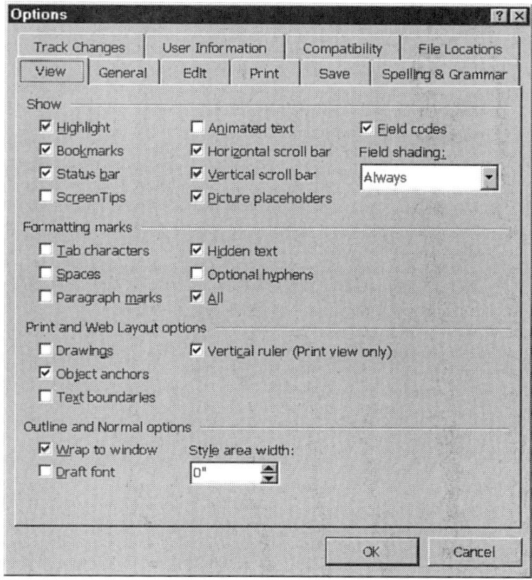

FIGURE 8.7
If you change options often, consider assigning a keystroke (for example, Ctrl+Alt+Shift+0) to display the Options dialog box.

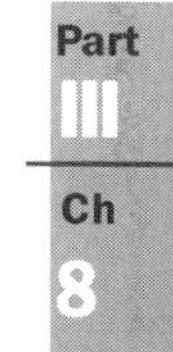

Turn On Background Repagination To enable background repagination, choose Tools, Options, click the General tab, and select Background Repagination. Background Repagination enables Word to repaginate in the background, rather than displaying the Wait icon. Repagination itself happens more slowly, but you can continue to use your computer while repagination occurs. Without this setting, especially in long documents, you lose the ability to work in Word until it completes repaginating.

Automatically Select Entire Word To direct Word to automatically select the entire word when highlighting text, choose Tools, Options, select the Edit tab, and check When Selecting, Automatically Select Entire Word. If you use the keyboard to select part of a word (Shift+Left or Shift+Right) instead of the mouse, the Options setting is ignored. If you use the mouse to drag-select part of a word, the selection expands to the complete word after you reach the left or right word boundary. Many Word users don't like that behavior, and opted to turn this feature off in previous versions of Word. In Word 2000, however, Microsoft has tied another behavior to this setting as well. If you put the insertion point in the middle of a word and click the Bold, Italic, Underline, or any formatting tool (or press the respective shortcut keys), and the Automatically Select Entire Word option is enabled, the whole word acquires the formatting. Without the Automatically Select option, however, this doesn't happen. So, grudgingly, to get this quick-formatting option, you have to enable Automatically Select—even if you don't particularly like it. On the positive side, if you use the keyboard to select, you'll never even notice the Automatically Select setting's effect on selecting text.

Turn On Background Printing To enable background printing, choose Tools, Options, select the Print tab, and check Background Printing. Background printing lets you continue working while Word prepares the document for printing (*spooling*). Otherwise, you lose the ability to work until spooling is finished.

Turn On Background Saving To enable background saving, choose Tools, Options, click the Save tab, and check Allow Background Saves. Background saving enables you to continue working while Word saves your document. Otherwise, you lose the ability to work until the save is finished.

Show ScreenTips on Toolbars To enable ScreenTips (formerly called ToolTips), choose Tools, Customize, select the Options tab, and check Show ScreenTips on Toolbars, Show Shortcut Keys in ScreenTips. On the surface, it might seem that ScreenTips would slow Word down—and perhaps they do. However, unless you know what an icon does, you can't use it. In addition, if you check the Show Shortcut Keys in ScreenTips option, ScreenTips can display shortcut keystrokes. Hover the pointer over the floppy disk icon on the Standard toolbar, for example, and it informs you that Ctrl+S is the shortcut for Save.

▶ **See** "Creating Keyboard Shortcuts," **p. 222**

Turn Off ScreenTips (in the View Tab), Animated Text, and Drawings Choose Tools, Options, click the View tab, and uncheck ScreenTips; Animated text; Drawings. Turning off animation and audible feedback keeps your CPU focused on the task at hand—writing and editing. Turning off the display of drawings also speeds up display and reduces CPU overhead.

What's the Difference Between ScreenTips in the Options Menu and in the Customize Menu?

The setting in the Tools, Options, View tab affects the display of comments in the Word document window, but does not affect toolbar tips. The need to have Word vigilantly aware of these can slow down Word's screen.

The setting in Tools, Customize, Options affects only the display of tips when the mouse moves over tools on toolbars. This, too, can slow things down, but only slightly and is so useful that it ends up saving time (unless you're dead-on sure what every tool does).

Set General Tab Options To set the General Tab options, choose Tools, Options, click the General tab, and uncheck Provide Feedback with Sound; Provide Feedback with Animation; Help for WordPerfect Users; and Navigation Keys for WordPerfect Users. The WordPerfect options redefine how the keyboard works. It's geared more to WordPerfect 4.2, however, and isn't terribly helpful even for diehard WordPerfect users.

Disable Check Spelling As You Type To disable this feature, choose Tools, Options, select the Spelling & Grammar tab, and uncheck Check Spelling As You Type; Check Grammar As You Type. Checking Spelling and Grammar As You Type—especially grammar—makes writing laboriously slow. Not only does it slow down how quickly words appear on the screen, but it often breaks your train of thought, forcing you to deal with spelling and grammar issues at a time when you really want to be focusing more on content.

Place Standard and Formatting Toolbars in Separate Rows To set this option, choose Tools, Customize, click the Options tab, and uncheck Standard and Formatting Toolbars Share One Row; Menus Show Recently Used Commands First; and List Font Names in Their Font. Set Menu Animations to (None).

The settings Standard and Formatting Toolbars Share One Row and Menus Show Recently Used Commands first come from Office's personalized features. Depending on how you use Word, they can slow you down or speed you up. Although I suggest turning them off, the bottom line is that you need to pay attention to how they affect your work, and then make a decision about whether they make sense for you.

▶ **See** Chapter 4, "Customizing Microsoft Office the Way You Want," **p. 77**

Toggling Word Options for Quick Editing

Here are two VBA snippets of code you can use to turn off (and then back on) some of the Word options that expedite editing documents. These snippets can be copied from the CD-ROM accompanying this book.

This code sets the options for quick editing:

```
Sub SpeedOptions()
     With ActiveWindow
          With .View
               .ShowAnimation = False
               .WrapToWindow = True
               .ShowPicturePlaceHolders = True
               .ShowAll = True
          End With
     End With
     With Options
          .CheckSpellingAsYouType = False
          .CheckGrammarAsYouType = False
     End With
     ActiveDocument.ShowGrammaticalErrors = False
     ActiveDocument.ShowSpellingErrors = False
End Sub
```

This code resets the options back to their original settings:

```
Sub ResetOptions()
     With ActiveWindow
          With .View
               .ShowAnimation = True
               .WrapToWindow = False
               .ShowPicturePlaceHolders = False
               .ShowAll = False
          End With
     End With
     With Options
          .CheckSpellingAsYouType = True
          .CheckGrammarAsYouType = True
     End With
     ActiveDocument.ShowGrammaticalErrors = True
     ActiveDocument.ShowSpellingErrors = True
End Sub
```

Speeding Up the Styles and Fonts Lists

One of the most annoying—perhaps *the* most annoying—features introduced with Word 97 was a revamped Styles list that displays the formatting of each style. Granted, it was a good idea, from an informational standpoint, but the cost in speed was dramatic. Even on a fast computer, this made using styles slow, but on slower computers, it was agonizing. Each time you called up the list of styles, it could take up to 20 seconds (sometimes longer) for the list to appear.

▶ **See** Chapter 10, "Using Styles, Templates, and Themes," **p. 267**

Thankfully, in Word 2000, not only is the styles list marginally faster to begin with, but this tiresome feature becomes an option you can turn off. Choose Tools, Customize, and select the Options tab. Then deselect List Font Names in Their Font, shown in Figure 8.8. You might not realize it at first, but this option controls not only the font list, but the style list as well. With this option checked, click the drop-down arrow next to the Style box on the Formatting toolbar; then click the drop-down arrow on the Font tool. Now, remove the check and try again. Relief at last!

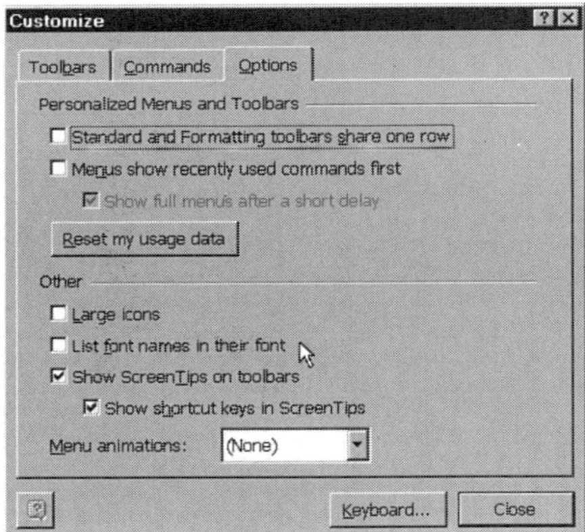

FIGURE 8.8
Turn off List Font Names in Their Font to speed up the font and style lists.

Creating Keyboard Shortcuts

Using Tools, Customize, Keyboard, you can assign keys to most Word commands as well as to any macros you create. You also can reassign most of Word's built-in shortcut keys. For example, if you prefer Ctrl+S (as in: *Search*) to be Find instead of Save, you can do it. If you prefer F11 to be Save, rather than NextField, you can do that, too. Just choose Tools, Customize, Keyboard to display the Customize Keyboard dialog box (as shown in Figure 8.9). To make the assignment, choose the desired command and click in the Press New Shortcut Key field, and tap the desired key combination. In Figure 8.9, the F11 key (NextField) is being reassigned to FileSave, in addition to the built-in Ctrl+S. When you click Assign, Word won't balk—it won't even warn you.

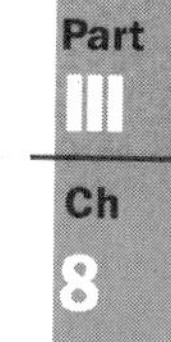

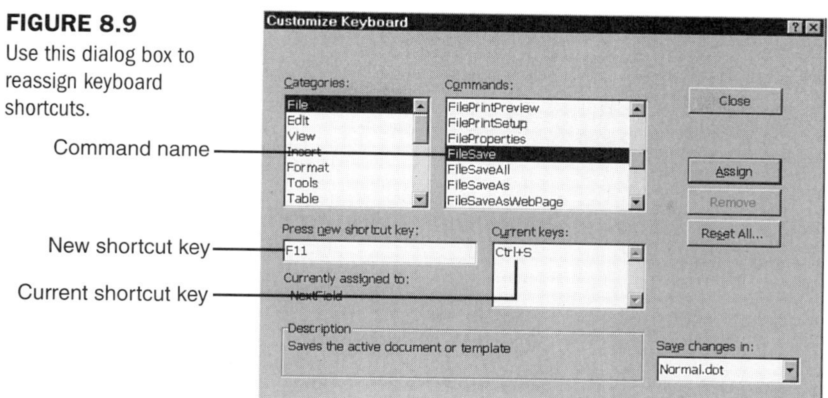

FIGURE 8.9
Use this dialog box to reassign keyboard shortcuts.

Restoring the Default Keyboard Shortcut Settings

After you've assigned a built-in key to something else, you can restore it to its default by assigning the key to the original command. Suppose you assigned F3 and now want to restore F3 to its original assignment. Press Ctrl+Alt+[Numeric Pad Plus]. Now press F3. The Customize Keyboard dialog box opens, with F3 in the Current Keys box. Click F3 and then click Remove. This not only removes F3's current assignment, but it restores its original assignment as well. Be careful, however; if you haven't assigned F3 to something else, Remove deletes all assignments to F3.

By the way, not only is the Ctrl+Alt+[Numeric Plus] trick good for helping remove key assignments, it's an excellent way to discover key assignments and to learn the exact name for any of Word's commands that are accessible by menu, toolbar, or keystroke. Press Ctrl+Alt+[Numeric Plus] twice, and you'll see that its command name is ToolsCustomizeKeyboardShortcut.

Customizing the Restricted Keys

There are *some* keys, however, you cannot assign using the Customize Keyboard dialog box. For example, with its default setting, pressing F1 prompts the Office Assistant. Without some serious trickery, Word won't enable you to reassign the F1 to any other function. The same goes for other keys such as Scroll Lock, Pause, and Esc.

The Customize Keyboard dialog box enables you to assign these keys with most combinations of Shift, Alt, and Ctrl—but never alone.

Similarly inaccessible are keys you'd probably never think of reassigning all by themselves—such as A, B, C, D, and so on (except possibly as an April Fool's prank, but we'd never encourage anything such as that).

The basic idea behind such restrictions is to prevent Word users from shooting themselves in the proverbial foot. And, that's fine—for *other* users. However, there are times when some users really would like to have access to other keys.

The good news is that most of the other keys *are* accessible. The bad news is that you have to indulge in a little bit of VBA to get at them. There are some unassignable keys that even VBA won't let you touch using the methods described here:

- PrintScreen
- Ctrl (alone)
- Shift (alone)
- Alt (alone)
- Caps Lock
- Num Lock

Also, some keyboards, such as the Microsoft Natural, have keys that are the equivalent to pressing Ctrl+Esc (displays the Start menu) and Shift+F10 (displays the current pop-up shortcut menu). Those keys do not appear to be accessible, either. Other than these, however, the rest of the keyboard is pretty much fair game.

Using VBA, there are two approaches to assigning keys. One is by number and the other is by name. The end result is the same (that is, the name ultimately stands for a number), but using the name approach usually is simpler for the user.

Using VBA to Reassign Keys

Using the name approach, however, is a lot more self-documenting and makes it harder to goof up. It's a lot easier to mistype 191 for 192 than it is to mistype wdKeyBackSingleQuote for wdKeySlash. The latter two are the key names corresponding to keycodes 191 and 192, respectively. If you make a mistake typing 191 instead of 192, you'll get a misassignment—pure and simple—with no error message. If you make a mistake typing wdKeyBackSingleQuote, you'll be warned *Invalid parameter*.

Word's keys, by and large, are logically named—their names are shown in Table 8.1. Armed with just a little more information, you can make just about any keyboard assignment you want (except for the unassignable keys noted earlier).

Table 8.1 Key Names for Customizing

Key	Key Name
Shift	wdKeyShift
Ctrl	wdKeyControl
Alt	wdKeyAlt
Enter	wdKeyReturn
Tab	wdKeyTab
Pause	wdKeyPause
Scroll Lock	wdKeyScrollLock

Key	Key Name
Esc	wdKeyEsc
F1 through F16	wdKeyF1 through wdKeyF16
0 through 9	wdKey0 through wdKey9
A through Z	wdKeyA through wdKeyZ
‘	wdKeyBackSingleQuote
,	wdKeyComma
.	wdKeyPeriod
/	wdKeySlash
;	wdKeySemiColon
‘	wdKeySingleQuote
[	wdKeyOpenSquareBrace
]	wdKeyCloseSquareBrace
-	wdKeyHyphen
=	wdKeyEquals
\	wdKeyBackSlash
Numeric Pad	
0 through 9	wdKeyNumeric0 through wdKeyNumeric9
.	wdKeyNumericDecimal
Enter	wdKeyReturn (Same as main Enter key)
-	wdKeyNumericSubtract
+	wdKeyNumericAdd
/	wdKeyNumericDivide
*	wdKeyNumericMultiply

In Word's VBA, you make key assignments with the KeyBindings collection, using the Add method. The following four-line VBA program assigns the Pause key to the RedefineStyle command:

```
Sub AssignKey()
CustomizationContext = NormalTemplate
KeyBindings.Add wdKeyCategoryCommand, "RedefineStyle",
➥KeyCode:=BuildKeyCode(wdKeyPause)
End Sub
```

Assigning an otherwise restricted key to a Word command is as simple as that. To create more complex assignments, include shifting key names (such as wdKeyShift, wdKeyAlt, and wdKeyControl) in the parentheses, along with the action key (for example, A, B, C, Pause, Scroll Lock, and so on). For example, to assign the save command to Alt+Shift+Pause, use

```
KeyBindings.Add wdKeyCategoryCommand, "RedefineStyle",_
KeyCode:=BuildKeyCode(wdKeyPause,wdKeyAlt,wdKeyShift)
```

Note that the KeyCode property uses a numeric value. Rather than trying to deal with the complexities of literal numbers (that involves a formula), this VBA line uses the BuildKeyCode method to calculate the needed keycode number. Thus, you get to work with nearly common-sense names, rather than having to insert the code to add 256+1,024+19 (the codes for Shift, Alt, and Pause). It's more typing this way, but it's a whole lot harder to make a hard-to-spot mistake!

Did the RedefineStyle command in the VBA example catch your eye? This truly wonderful command was added in Word 97. Did you ever use direct formatting to change a paragraph, and then decide that you want that formatting to become the new definition for a style? With most styles, you just reapply the current style, and Word pops up a dialog box asking whether you want to redefine the style, or reapply the style. When the current style is Normal, however, Word doesn't ask—it just rushes ahead and reapplies the Normal style—undoing your direct formatting. The RedefineStyle command immediately redefines the current style—including Normal—without prompting. It's a power-formatter's dream-come-true, giving you instant style-by-example.

If you want to assign other Word elements, such as macros, styles, AutoText, and so on, substitute the following key categories for wdKeyCategoryCommand:

- wdKeyCategoryAutoText
- wdKeyCategorySymbol
- wdKeyCategoryStyle
- wdKeyCategoryMacro
- wdKeyCategoryFont
- wdKeyCategoryPrefix

If you want to quickly reassign keys, there is a great user form (shown in Figure 8.10) that is included on the CD-ROM accompanying this book. There are two ways you can use this form. The easiest is to open the Customizing Restricted Keys document on the CD-ROM and start the AssignKeys macro from the Macros menu. This launches the form and all you need to do is follow the directions on the form. There is also an explanation of the UserForm and code on page one of the Customizing Restricted Keys document. The second way of using this form is to copy it to your Normal template. Instructions on how to do this are on page two of the Customizing Restricted Keys document.

You can do it piecemeal, using the simple VBA program as a starter, or you can go whole hog, using the full VBA program shown.

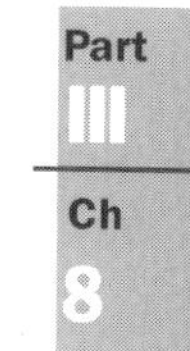

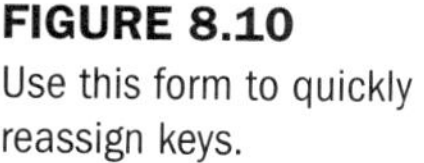

FIGURE 8.10
Use this form to quickly reassign keys.

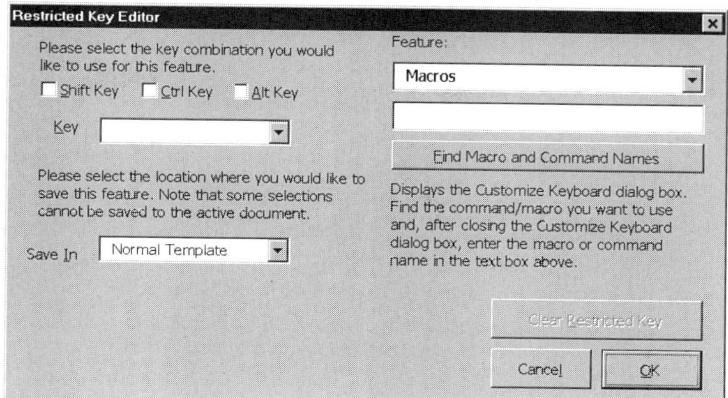

Using Prefix Keys

Each of the WdKeyCategory categories in the preceding bulleted list is self-explanatory, except for wdKeyCategoryPrefix, perhaps.

In Word, you can type many accented characters by pressing Ctrl+*accent* followed by the desired letter, where *accent* is ', `, ^, and so on. For example, for é, press Ctrl+' followed by e. For ò, press Ctrl+` followed by o. The accent keys used in this fashion are called *prefix* keys.

You can create your own prefix keys, if you like. Suppose, for example, that you often need Greek characters, but don't like using Insert, Symbol, and don't want to dedicate whole assignments to A, B, G, D, and so on for alpha, beta, gamma, delta, and so forth. You could create a prefix key setup instead.

By default, Ctrl+Shift+G isn't assigned to anything; that might make it a logical choice for a Greek prefix key. You could use the VBA method if you like, or, use Insert, Symbol, Shortcut Key, because the dialog box approach doesn't have any problem with this particular assignment series. To use a restricted key, such as Pause or Scroll Lock, as a prefix key, you would need a VBA approach.

Choose Insert, Symbol. On the list of symbols, click α, and then click Shortcut Key. In the Press New Shortcut Key box, press Ctrl+Shift+G, and then tap the A key, as shown in Figure 8.11. Click Assign and then Close. Repeat this for β, χ, δ (using B, C, D, and so on, respectively), and for as many Greek letters as you commonly need.

Now, back in a document, press Ctrl+Shift+G followed by A; then do it for each of the other letters to satisfy yourself that it works. Whether you're an econometrician, mathematician, or statistician, you might find your new shortcut to be a big timesaver!

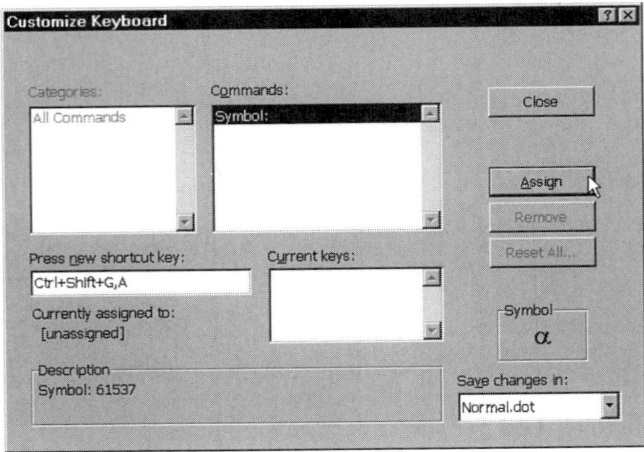

FIGURE 8.11
Creating prefix keys greatly expands the number of available keyboard shortcuts.

Setting Version Compatibility

As Word evolves, it acquires new features. Along the way, Word added Compatibility settings that enable the user to selectively turn some features on or off, depending on individual taste. Choose Tools, Options, and click the Compatibility tab to display the compatibility settings shown in Figure 8.12.

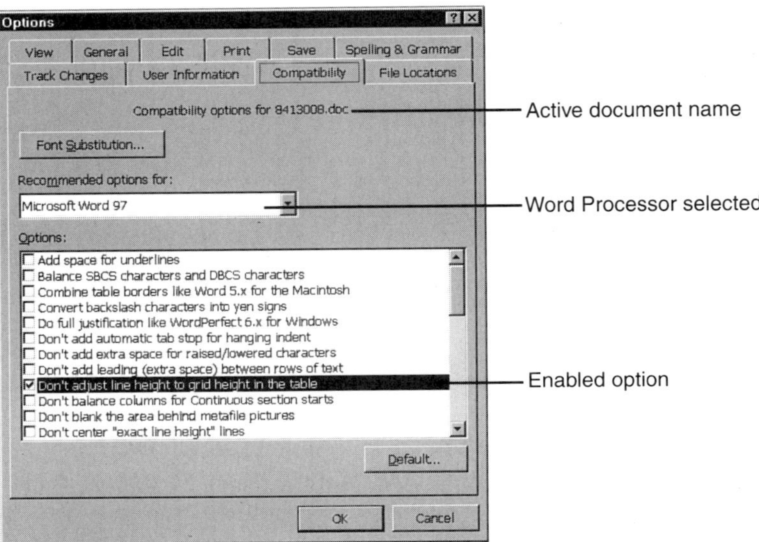

FIGURE 8.12
Compatibility settings are document-specific.

The compatibility settings covered include Font Substitution. Font Substitution provides a way to make a document compatible with a computer that does not have particular fonts available. The following sections describe Font Substitution as well as some of the more than 42 different compatibility settings you can select.

Substituting a Default Font

Font Substitution, shown in Figure 8.13, is used when the nominal font is not available on your computer. By default, Word uses Times New Roman.

If the basic font style of a document is sans serif, you might prefer to substitute Arial instead of Roman. Word then uses the substituted font in the document anytime the missing font is used to format text. The substitution is used for display and printing.

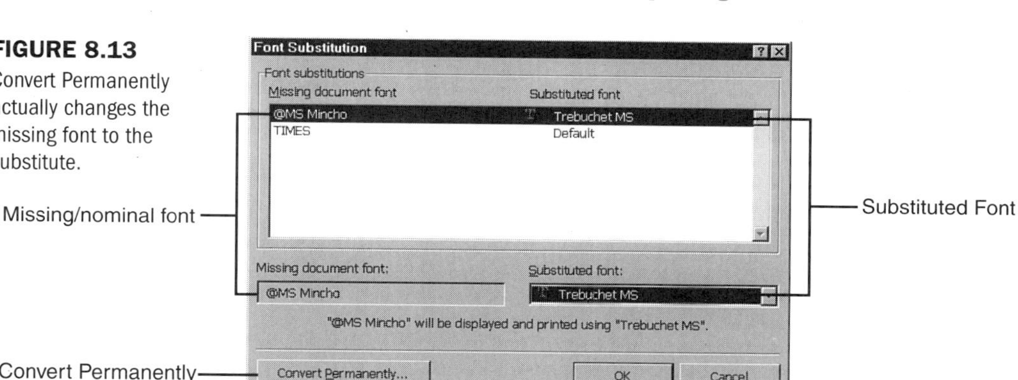

FIGURE 8.13
Convert Permanently actually changes the missing font to the substitute.

NOTE Word uses two types of fonts: DBCS (double-byte character set) and SBCS (single-byte character set). SBCS is typically used in Western European languages. DBCS typically is used by Eastern languages, such as Chinese and Japanese. If an odd unused font, such as MS Mincho, shows up in a document, you probably won't be able to make a substitution, unless you have installed extra DBCS fonts (with the Language Pack). You'll get an error message that says you can't substitute DBCS for SBCS or vice versa. That's because you probably don't have any DBCS fonts on your computer—and MS Mincho is a DBCS font.

▶ **See** "International Support for Languages," **p. 1721**

Font Substitution is document-specific. You can make it the default by opening the underlying template, and performing the substitution steps shown previously.

The Convert Permanently option is tantamount to performing a Find and Replace operation, wherein you replace the missing font with the substitution. Again, this affects only the current document, and would not be useful performed in a template, because it eliminates the missing font's name entirely.

Other Compatibility Settings

You might have noticed that Word doesn't wrap trailing spaces to the next line the way WordPerfect does. It's simply the way Word works—differently from WordPerfect. It was the result of decisions made by Microsoft and the WordPerfect Corporation years ago how their word processors would treat trailing spaces.

If you prefer to have Word wrap trailing spaces, choose Tools, Options, and click the Compatibility tab, shown in Figure 8.14. Wrapping trailing spaces is one of a number of options that is automatically selected when you choose any of the WordPerfect option sets (WordPerfect 5.x, WordPerfect 6.x for Windows, and WordPerfect 6.x for DOS).

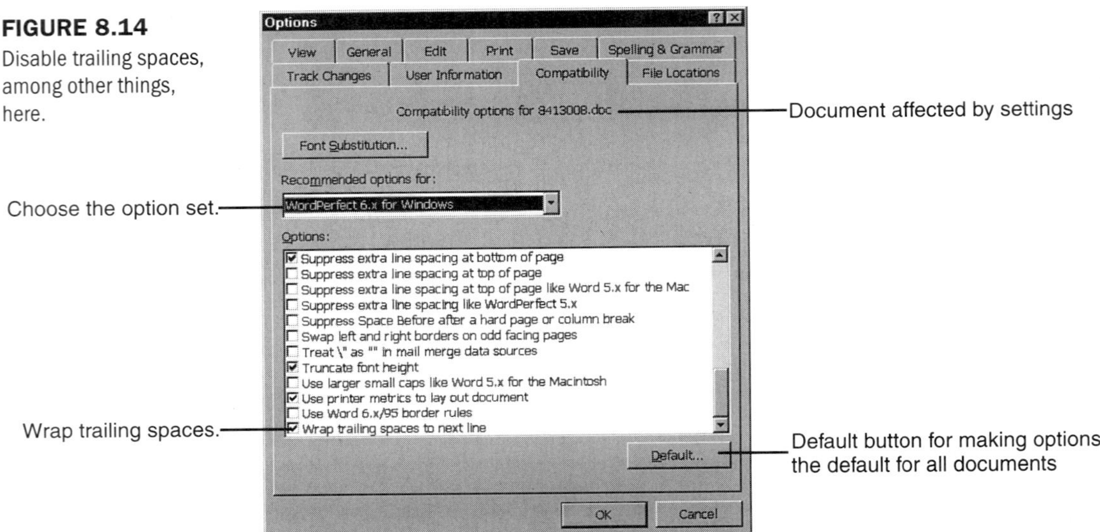

FIGURE 8.14
Disable trailing spaces, among other things, here.

When you use exact height line spacing (Format, Paragraph, Line spacing), Word by default centers the lines vertically, splitting any extra space equally between descenders and ascenders—the parts of letters that extend below and above the main part of the letter. If this is not the effect you want, you can use the compatibility options to tell Word *not* to center such lines, using the Don't Center Exact Line Height lines option.

Be careful with this setting, however. When using the Exact Height setting to more carefully control page size, the Don't Center setting often results in what you see in the bottom window in Figure 8.15. Where Don't Center is applied, descenders (for example, the bottom of a lowercase y) tend to get cut off. Where Don't Center is not applied, ascenders (for example, the dot on a lowercase i) might tend to get cut off. Keep this setting in mind if you have a clipped ascender or descender problem you cannot solve otherwise. This setting affects only paragraphs that have exact line spacing applied.

In fact, Word 2000 has more than 40 compatibility options for a number of different word processors, including all major versions of Word for Windows—versions 1 through 2000—Word for DOS, and several recent WordPerfect releases (but not the *most* recent).

If you're accustomed to using the compatibility features in prior versions of Word, check carefully when you make your selections. Word 2000 includes a number of additional settings—largely to accommodate backward compatibility with Word 97, just as Word 97 had settings to accommodate compatibility with Word 95 and earlier versions. Likewise, Word has changed the wording of

some longstanding options, dropping Don't from several and adding Don't to others. If you need backward compatibility with Word 97, also make sure you don't overlook the settings in Tools, Options, Save. To remain strictly compatible with Word 97, check the option Disable features not supported by Word 97, as well as the options in the Compatibility tab.

FIGURE 8.15
The Don't Center setting moves descenders down.

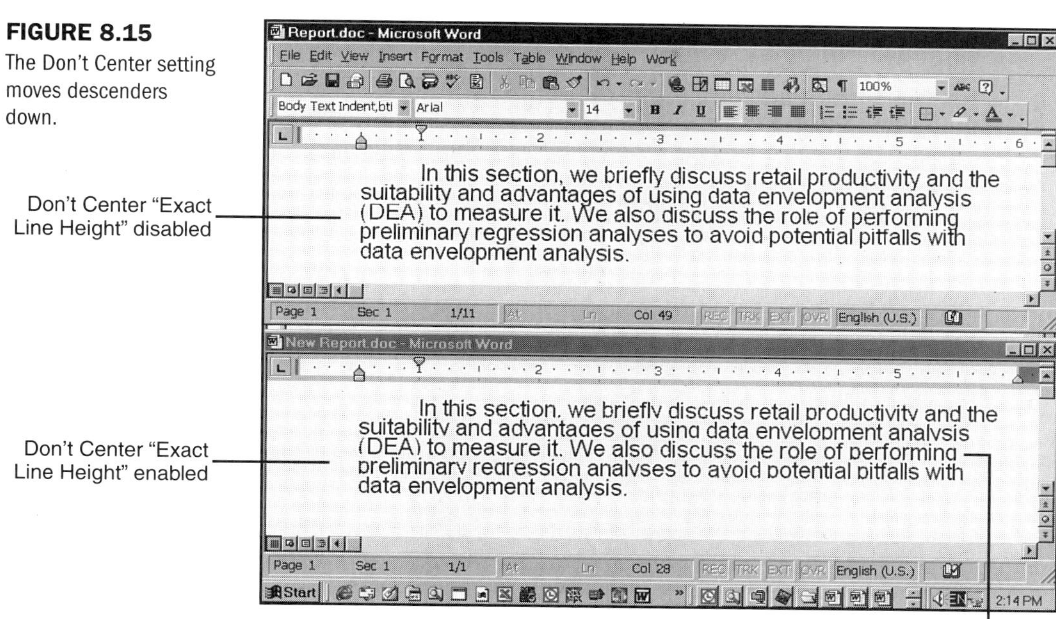

Letters get cut off (for example, the "p" and "g" in performing).

International Usage Features

In prior versions, Microsoft Office had language-specific editions. German users had one version, English users another, Japanese users another, and so on. Office 2000, however, takes a different approach, using the same core program for all languages. Different languages are installed using the Microsoft Office 2000 Multilanguage Pack (that isn't included with every edition of Office 2000).

There are tremendous advantages to this approach, especially for companies that do business on a number of different language platforms.

It also means that any given user can install support for multiple languages on the same computer, providing instant support for multilingual users as well as more versatile workstations that can be language-shifted to accommodate different users.

Global Interface and Proofing Tools Kit

The heart of Office's multilingual capabilities is the ability to install any combination of language support for interface, help, and proofing for supported languages.

NOTE The first release of Office 2000's Multilanguage Pack contains support for a limited number of major languages in which Word is used. Following initial release, Microsoft plans release of additional language elements as they become ready. If the language(s) you need weren't included in your package, check Microsoft's Web site to find out what's available (`www.microsoft.com`).

To use multilanguage support, you must have installed the Multilanguage Pack from CD.

If you haven't installed multilanguage support, open the Windows Explorer, insert the Multilanguage Pack CD, and run SETUP.EXE located in the root drive of the CD. Setup takes just a few minutes. If you are prompted for a language during this process, make sure you select the default language (usually English), and not the language to which you want occasional, but not default, access.

▶ **See** "International Support for Languages," **p. 1721**

The Multilanguage Pack provides the necessary infrastructure for multilanguage support, but does not install support for any particular languages. That's done using the Microsoft Office Language Settings control. Choose Start, Programs, Office Tools, Microsoft Office Language Settings, to display the dialog box shown in Figure 8.16.

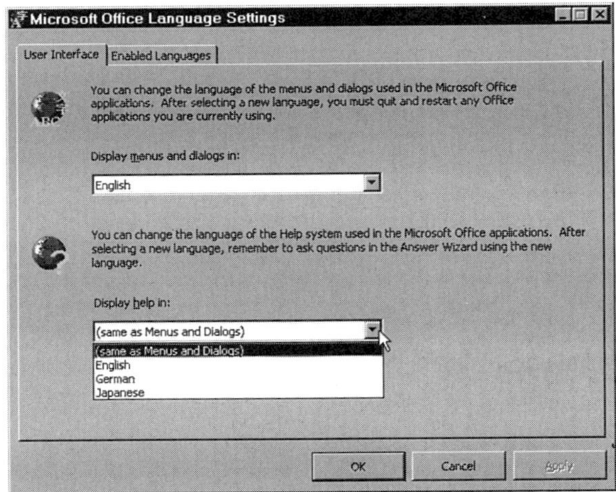

FIGURE 8.16
After you choose a language, settings take effect the next time you start Word.

To install support for a language, check the lists shown in the User Interface tab:

1. Click the drop-down arrow next to Display Menus and Dialogs In.
2. Click the drop-down arrow next to Display Help In.

Unless the language you want is listed, you cannot install support for that language. Visit Microsoft's Web site to see whether it is available.

If the language you want is listed, choose it from the list. You can choose the language for just the interface (menus and dialogs), just help, or both. International users sometime choose an English interface and a more comfortable language for the Help system. The help system provides local solutions.

Being literate in the English interface is more helpful, however, when trying to obtain assistance from others. When posting online questions on Microsoft's Usenet newsgroups, for example, directions and issues can be framed in more universal terms. Many Word power users probably wouldn't immediately recognize Tools, Options, File locations in German (Extras, Optionen, Dateiablage), and it could be more helpful if the English menu commands were used instead.

After selecting the interface and help languages, click the Enabled Languages tab, shown in Figure 8.17. If the language you selected is not on the list of enabled languages, scroll down the Show Controls and Enable Editing For list and place a check mark next to the language. Then click OK. If any Office applications are open, you'll be asked whether it's okay to shut them down and restart.

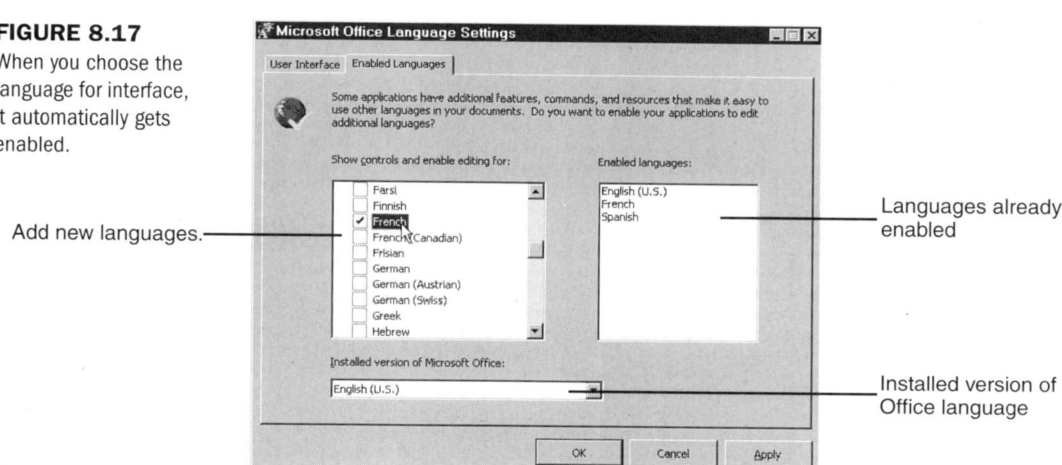

FIGURE 8.17
When you choose the language for interface, it automatically gets enabled.

CAUTION

On the Enabled Languages tab, do not change the Installed Version of Microsoft Office setting unless you really want to change the systemwide default language for Office.

After performing these steps, setup tells you that the change will take effect the next time you start a supported Office application. The next time you start Word, depending on which language(s) you installed in the preceding steps, you will be prompted to insert the Office 2000 and/or the Office 2000 Multilanguage Pack CD-ROMs.

TIP If you or your company has copied the CD-ROMs to a shared drive or folder, you won't have to keep the CD-ROMs handy; you can just designate the drive or folder when prompted.

Setup then copies the necessary files—but doesn't immediately copy support for proofing (spelling, thesaurus, and grammar). After the files have been copied, Word then starts up in the requested language. Thereafter, changing between installed languages becomes simply a matter of opening the Microsoft Office Language Settings control and choosing a language in the User Interface tab, as shown in Figure 8.17.

After support for certain languages has been installed, there will be certain changes to Word's interface, even when English is selected as the interface. For example, after Japanese has been added and is enabled, the Format menu acquires the extra commands seen in Figure 8.18. The Tools menu acquires a Japanese Postcard Wizard, and Tools, Language acquires a Japanese Consistency Checker.

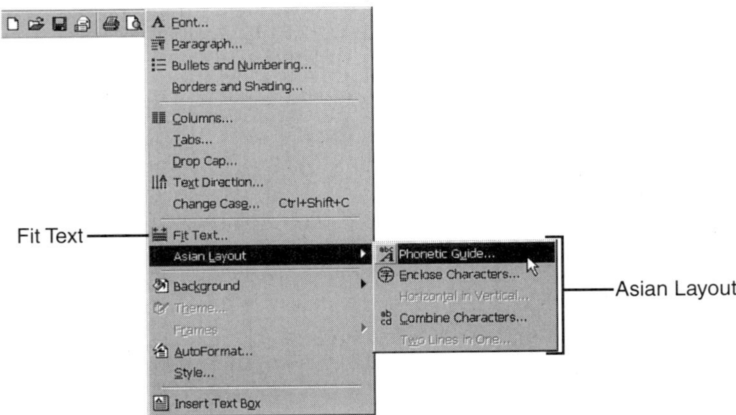

FIGURE 8.18
Japanese support adds Fit Text and Asian Layout to the Format menu.

You'll also find additions to the Tools, Options menu. Shown in Figure 8.19, enabling Japanese provides a Japanese Find tab and an Asian Typography tab.

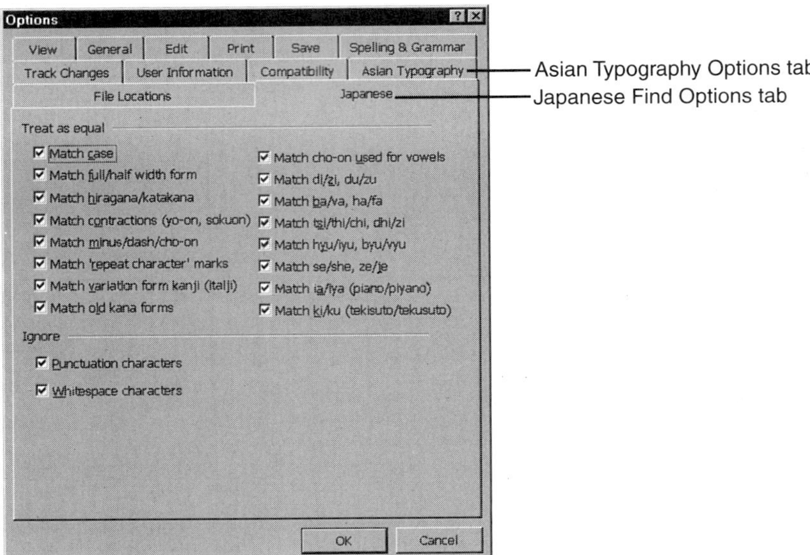

FIGURE 8.19
Enabling Japanese provides additional tools and settings.

Language AutoDetect

If you ever had to type multiple languages, you might sometimes see perfectly spelled words acquiring squiggly red lines. That's because previous versions of Word had to be told which language you were using before it could use the appropriate proofing tools. Word now automatically recognizes the language and formats the text with that language.

To use this feature, close any open Office programs. Next, choose Start, Programs, Office Tools, Microsoft Office Language Settings. In the Enabled Languages list, put a check mark by each of the languages for which you want to add AutoDetect support, and click OK.

NOTE If you have installed the Multilanguage Pack, the Language Settings control has two tabs (User Interface and Enabled Languages); if you have not installed the Multilanguage Pack, the control has just the list of enabled languages.

Now, in Word, choose Tools, Language, Set Language, click to enable Detect language automatically, and click OK. In a blank document, start typing something in English. After you type a sentence followed by some kind of sentence terminator (such as a period, question mark, or exclamation point), you should see English appear on the status bar—just to the right of OVR. Now, start typing in a different language that you've enabled. After a few words and some kind of terminator, the language indicator on the status bar should switch to that language, as shown in Figure 8.20. Then, switch back. Unfortunately, this feature usually mistakes my Visual Basic code for Portuguese!

The interpretation is on a sentence-by-sentence basis. When two languages are mixed in the same sentence, Word makes a decision about which language to use for the entire sentence.

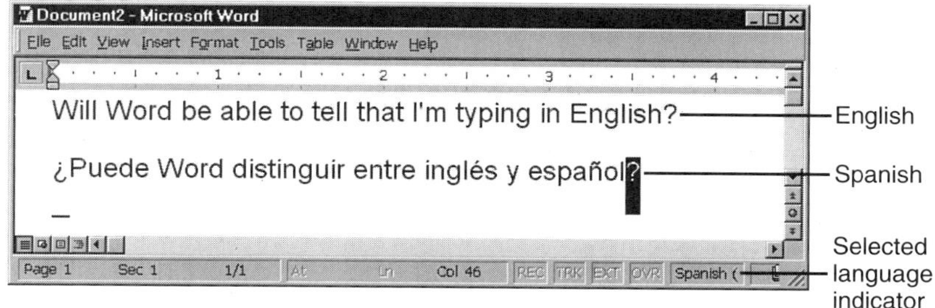

FIGURE 8.20
Double-click the language indicator to display the Language dialog box.

NOTE A downside of this feature is that the detection is sometimes wrong, especially when dealing with uncommon spelling and capitalization–the kind you routinely encounter in writing about new technology. Another downside is that language AutoDetect is CPU-intensive and slows down the computer. Like automatic spell checking, if you're a fast typist and have language AutoDetect enabled, you might find that word separators sometimes take a second or two to appear. This isn't a warning not to use the feature, but simply to reserve using it for documents in which language detection is needed.

International Language Features

Installing international support gives you the ability to display and write in most languages. For some languages, however, native entry can be accomplished only if you are using a localized version of Windows or Windows NT. For Japanese, Korean, Simplified Chinese, and Traditional Chinese, Microsoft provides the IME (Input Method Editor), which enables keyboard entry of characters using the standard keyboard.

Global Input Method Editor

Installing multilanguage support does not automatically install the Input Method Editor (IME). You can install that from the Multilanguage Pack. Insert the CD and, using Windows Explorer, drill down to the Extras\IME*language*\Global folder corresponding to the language you want to be able to input. For example, for Japanese, it's Extras\IME\Japanese\Global. In that folder, locate and run the executable program you find by double-clicking.

For each of the following languages, choose the indicated IME installation program shown in Table 8.2.

Table 8.2 Global Input Method Editor Language Options

Language	IME Installation
Japanese	Msjaime.exe
Korean	Mshaime.exe
Simplified Chinese	Msscaime.exe
Traditional Chinese	Mstcaime.exe

After the IME has been installed, you will need to shut down and restart Windows. Following that, a keyboard language indicator should now be visible in your Windows taskbar as shown in Figure 8.21.

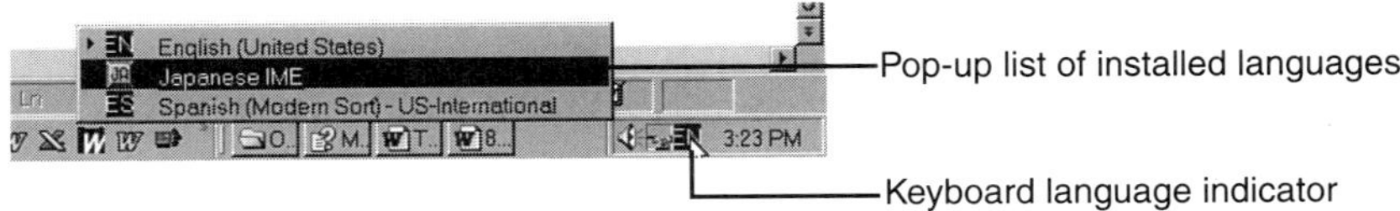

FIGURE 8.21
Click the Language control to switch languages.

To enter text using the IME, open Word. Click the language indicator, and choose the installed language—for example, Japanese. The IME toolbar should pop up, as shown in Figure 8.22.

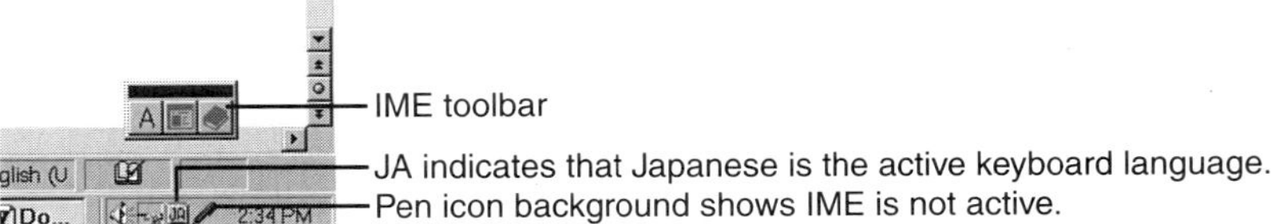

FIGURE 8.22
The pen icon shows that IME is enabled (but inactive); click and select the top option to turn IME on.

Notice the pen icon to the right of JA (Japanese) indicator. The plain background means that IME is toggled off. To toggle it on, press Alt+~. When it's on, a writing table background appears under the pen (as shown in Figure 8.22). The IME works by combining characters. Type a `k`, for example, and the dotted underlined letter k appears. Next, type an `a`, and the k and a are combined to produce the hiragana syllable *ka*, which is the left character shown in Figure 8.23. To continue typing hiragana, begin immediately with the next character. To type kanji, press the spacebar immediately after typing `ka`; this converts the hiragana character into the kanji character, shown as the second character. Typing `ti` produces the hiragana syllable *ti*, which is the third character shown in Figure 8.23, and the kanji symbol for *ti* is the fourth and last syllable shown.

FIGURE 8.23
Japanese syllables are formed by typing their sound with IME active.

An additional feature enables you to choose similar symbols from a pop-up list. After pressing a space to produce the kanji character, immediately press the Down or Up Arrow twice to pop up a list, as shown in Figure 8.24. Use this feature if the initial combination doesn't produce the expected kanji character. This facility works only with kanji.

Multilingual AutoCorrect

Word now supports AutoCorrect in multiple languages, assuming the correct language support has been added, and the necessary support files have been copied to your Office files.

Multilingual AutoCorrect can work in conjunction with automatic language detection. When Word recognizes that a given language is being used, it attempts to fix spelling errors it recognizes. Alternatively, you can assign the desired language to the text, and Word uses the corresponding proofing tools. As shown in Figure 8.25, Word's German AutoCorrect list is similar in scope to its English list.

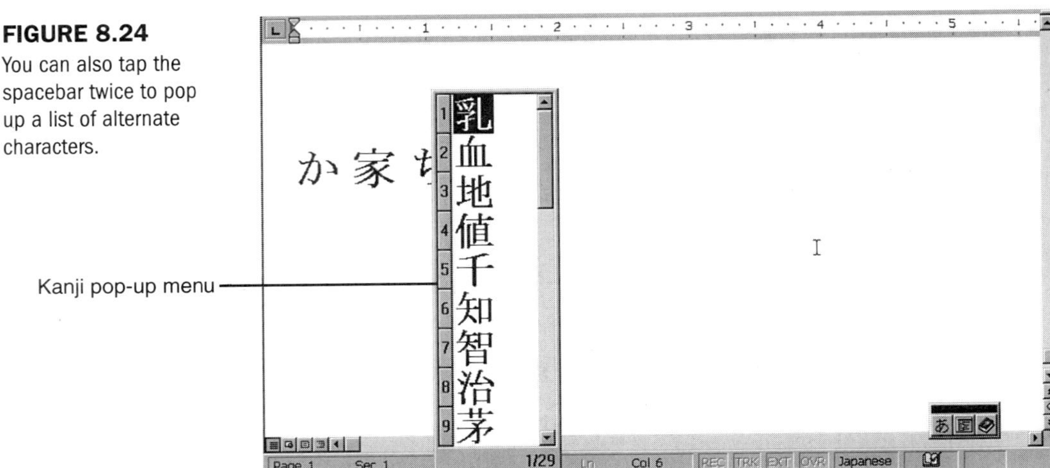

FIGURE 8.24
You can also tap the spacebar twice to pop up a list of alternate characters.

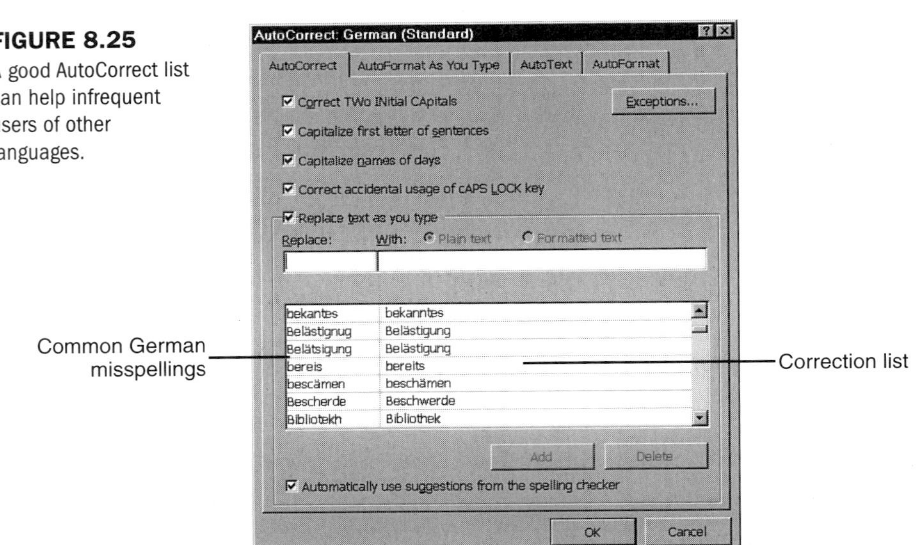

FIGURE 8.25
A good AutoCorrect list can help infrequent users of other languages.

The first time you come to an AutoCorrect situation while writing in another language—after the Multilanguage Pack base has been installed—Word prompts you to insert the Multi-language Pack CD-ROM so that it can copy the corresponding files to your system. After it is copied, you can continue working in Word without having to restart.

CHAPTER 9

Power Editing and Formatting

In this chapter

Displaying All Formatting Codes

Editing documents can be a long and laborious task. All the scrolling and searching can be quite tiresome. Word provides a few valuable tools to make this process much faster and much more tolerable. With these tools, the editing process becomes more manageable.

When using Word, it is often necessary to display formatting codes such as paragraph marks, tab marks, spaces, and bookmarks. Each of these formatting codes contain important information used by Word to control character attributes, tab stops, borders and shading, styles, text flow, line spacing, picture locations, bullets, numbering, and so much more. Unfortunately, Word does not automatically show these formatting marks.

The manner in which you display these characters depends upon two factors:

- Which formatting characters need to be displayed?
- Do you want the codes displayed temporarily on this document or will this be necessary for all documents?

For a quick way to display paragraph marks (hard and soft returns), spaces, and tab marks, click the Show/Hide button on the Standard toolbar. The button acts as a toggle to turn this feature on or off. This button is a great option if you want to see only some of the codes on the active document.

To show nonprinting characters on all Word documents, choose Tools, Options and click the View tab (see Figure 9.1). To display all formatting, including tab characters, spaces, paragraph marks, hidden text, and optional hyphens, select All from the Formatting Marks section of the tab.

For more information on the Tools, Options settings:

▶ **See** "Customizing Word," **p. 207**

After you display these characters, it will be easier to determine exactly how your document will be affected. For example, spaces in Word are represented by a dot while arrows represent tab marks. It's possible for someone to accidentally space text out rather than add tab marks or to even add extra spaces to a document. Although it may appear correct onscreen, problems arise when the document is actually printed or if the text is copied or moved to another location.

On a more advanced level, a common mistake occurs when adding stylistic borders to text. If the paragraph mark is not included in the selection when the formatting is done, the border will span only the length of the word, rather than the width of the page.

As you can see, nonprinting characters and their placement can have a profound effect on how a set of text or a document will behave when being copied, printed, or formatted.

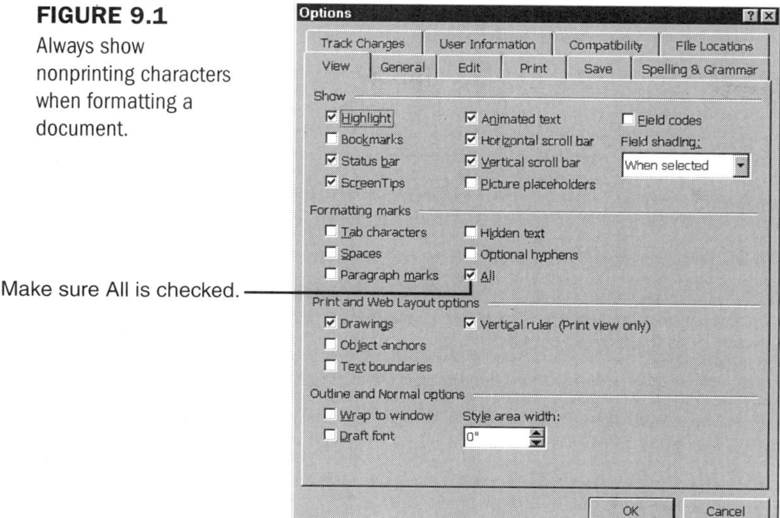

FIGURE 9.1
Always show nonprinting characters when formatting a document.

Unleashing the Power of Bookmarks

When working with larger documents, it is very likely that you will repeatedly return to various locations in your document for editing, formatting, or modifying. *Bookmarks* serve to mark these locations and provide for an easier, faster way of locating and navigating to them. Unlike other features in Word, bookmarks enable you to mark a specific set of text or a location rather than relying on page/section numbers or headings to revisit areas in your document.

In addition, Word uses bookmarks in combination with other features such as

- Indexes and Tables (TOC, Index, Table of Authorities, and Table of Figures)
- Cross References
- Fields (such as ASK)
- Hyperlinks

Word provides for two types of Bookmarks: bookmarks you create at your command, and those Word creates automatically when generating an index or table.

Location Versus Selected Text Bookmarks

User-created bookmarks can be broken down into two types.

- Empty bookmarks (I), which are bookmarks to a particular location.
- Bookmarks that enclose text or graphics [ ], which are bookmarks to specific text or graphics.

If you're using bookmarks for navigation, there is no need to select text, but rather a specific location in the document. A bookmark that can identify a specific location is known as an empty bookmark. A bookmark can also enclose selected text or graphics. Selecting text enables you to use the text elsewhere. For example, you can import it at another location, jump to it from another location, or work on it in a VBA macro. These are known as *non-empty bookmarks.*

As shown in Figure 9.2, location (empty) bookmarks insert an I-beam in the document, whereas selected text bookmarks (nonempty) place square brackets at the start and end of the selected text.

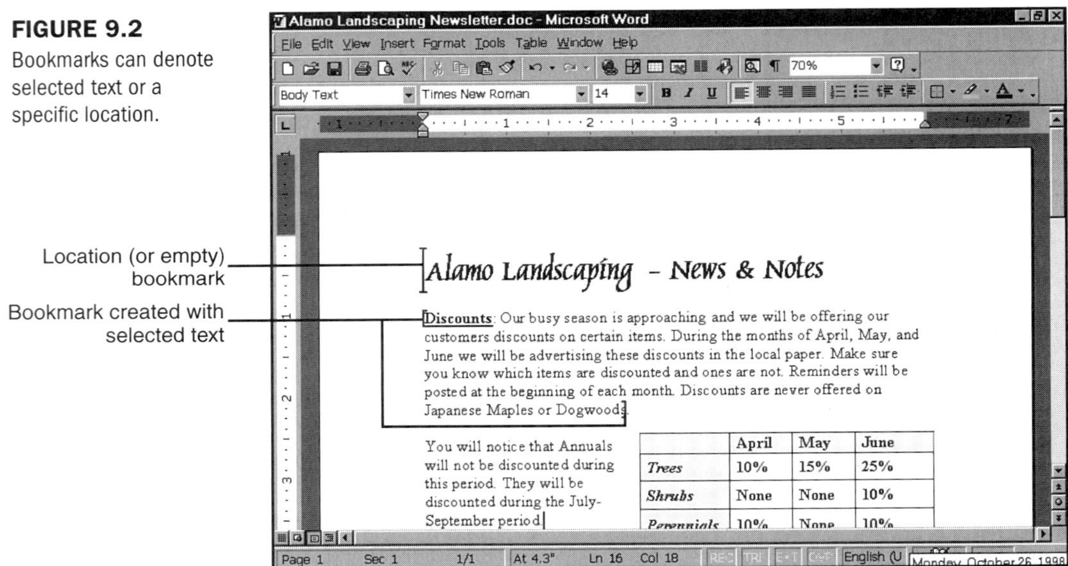

FIGURE 9.2
Bookmarks can denote selected text or a specific location.

Creating Bookmarks

Begin by ensuring that bookmarks will be displayed in your document. Choose Tools, Options and click the View tab. Then mark the Bookmarks check box and click OK.

The steps to create both location (empty) bookmarks and bookmarks that surround text or graphics (nonempty) are nearly identical and quite simple:

1. Select the text or location you want to reference with your bookmark.
2. Choose Insert, Bookmark to open the Bookmark dialog box (see Figure 9.3).
3. Enter a name in the Bookmark name text box.

NOTE Bookmark names must begin with a letter and must not contain spaces. They can however, include the underscore character (_) and numbers. A bookmark name can consist of up to 40 characters.

4. Then click Add.

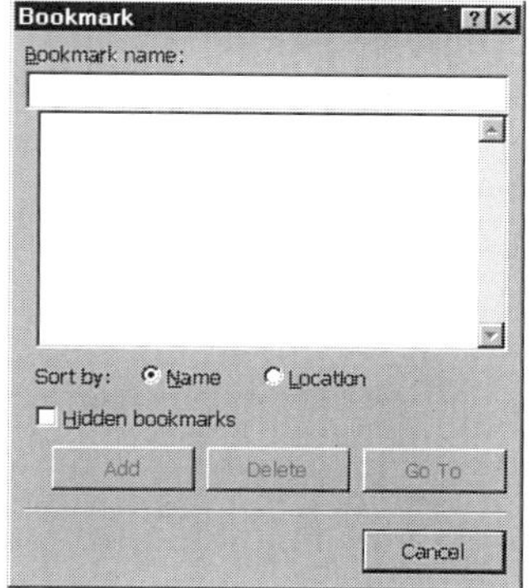

FIGURE 9.3
You can create and navigate to bookmarked locations in your document using the Bookmark dialog box.

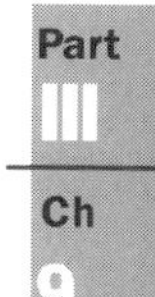

TIP Press Ctrl+Shift+F5 as a shortcut to display the Bookmark dialog box. From there, you can quickly insert, delete, or navigate to a bookmark.

Navigating with Bookmarks

There are two ways to navigate using bookmarks:

- You can display the Bookmark dialog box, select the bookmark you want to go to, and then click the Go To button (refer to Figure 9.3).
- You can display the Go To dialog box (Edit, Go To), choose Bookmark in the Go To What list box, and select the bookmark from the Enter Bookmark Name drop-down list (see Figure 9.4). Then click the Go To button.

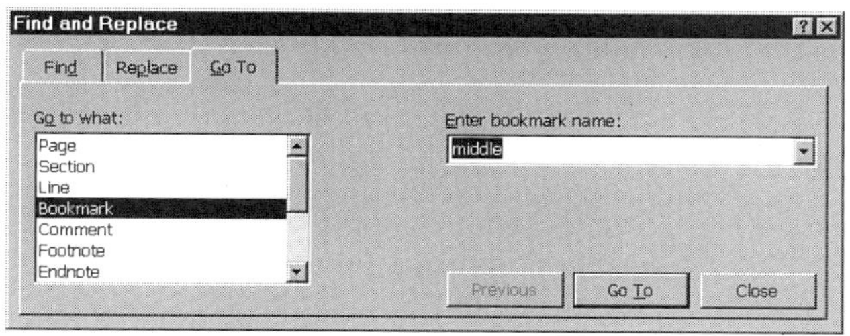

FIGURE 9.4
Navigate to bookmarks by pressing F5 to display the Go To tab in the Find and Replace dialog box.

It is important to note that you should always display bookmarks (through Tools, Options), especially when manipulating the text surrounding a bookmark. If you copy text associated with a bookmark, the bookmark will stay in place. However, if you move the text, the bookmark will also relocate. To delete a bookmark, choose Insert, Bookmark. Select the desired bookmark and click Delete.

NOTE You cannot delete a location (empty) bookmark with the Backspace or Delete key. If you delete the text associated with either a location or selection bookmark, the bookmark will also be deleted.

Using AutoText to Insert Bookmarks

Although inserting and manipulating bookmarks is easy, creating a series of all-purpose bookmarks can save even more time. This is accomplished by creating several AutoText entries containing bookmarks. The bookmark will be stored along with the AutoText entry and can be available for use in all documents. This prevents you from having to think of bookmark names and taking the time to insert them. Be sure, however, that each bookmark name is unique; otherwise, it will replace any existing bookmark with the same name with absolutely no warning.

Quick Editing with Temporary Bookmarks

Named bookmarks (bookmarks you create and name) work well to navigate in a document when editing for an extended period. However, within a single editing session, these permanent bookmarks may take longer to set up and use than the time they save. For this reason, you may want to add a kind of temporary set of bookmarks that you insert and return to with a single keystroke or click of a button. For example, while editing a document, you can mark a spot in the document that you know you will want to return to later. Another use would be to mark your current position, navigate to another part of the document to edit a section, and then return to your bookmarked position.

You create these "temporary" bookmarks with a pair of VBA macros (or snippets of code). The first of the pair sets the bookmark; the second enables you to return to that bookmark location. These macros represent ways to modify the existing book marking capabilities of Word and provide for a quick temporary way of adding bookmarks to a particular location. Here are two VBA snippets of code you can use to turn on and off temporary bookmarks. These snippets can be copied from the CD-ROM accompanying this book or you can manually type short snippets of code—like these—directly into the Visual Basic Editor.

This code sets the temporary bookmark:

```
Sub InstantBookmark1Drop()
    With ActiveDocument.Bookmarks
        .Add Range:=Selection.Range, Name:="Instant1"
    End With
End Sub
```

This code returns you to the temporary bookmark:

```
Sub InstantBookmark1GoTo()
    Selection.GoTo What:=wdGoToBookmark, Name:="Instant1"
End Sub
```

For quick access to these VBA snippets, assign the snippets to a keyboard shortcut or toolbar button.

▶ **See** "Assigning a Macro to a Toolbar Button," **p. 112**

One pair is sufficient for most people; however, you can create as many pairs as necessary. It is good practice to come up with a naming convention for these snippets and bookmarks. For instance, in our example, we referred to the first pair as `InstantBookmark1Drop()` and

`InstantBookmark1GoTo()`. You should then refer to the second pair as `InstantBookmark2Drop()` and `InstantBookmark2GoTo()`. The VBA code is identical for each pair except, of course, for the name and bookmark.

Making the Most of Bookmarks

Bookmarks can be used in conjunction with other features of Word such as fields, hyperlinks, and even cross-references. Using bookmarks with a field, such as the FILLIN field, within a Visual Basic Macro will allow you to make the most of bookmarks. Most of us have encountered less-experienced Word users in the workplace. It is helpful and sometimes necessary to simplify tasks for these beginners. Suppose a beginner can open up a document template (such as a memo) and have a dialog box prompt appear for each of the document's numerous fields. The user doesn't even have to worry about tab stops, spacing, or even where and how to click the mouse!

Experienced users will also benefit from the ease and speed of these "fill-in" templates. By comparison, a user using a normal template with fill-in fields must first navigate to each field's location and ensure that spacing and placement are correct.

This type of prompting can be added to your templates, by building a userform in the Visual Basic Editor with an OK and Cancel button, a text box, and a label, and then adding the code to the userform that fills specifically named bookmarks in a template. Finally, you must add a statement in the `Document_New` event of the template to open the form. For example:

```
CustomInput.Show
```

where "CustomInput" is the name of the userform created.

▶ **See** "Designing `UserForms`," **p. 170**

Included on the CD accompanying this book is a template, called Lazy Liz.dot, that includes these features. This template is designed to assist users in filling in a personal memo by automatically displaying prompting dialog boxes. The prompts fill in specifically named bookmarks in the template for the Company Name, the To line, the From line, and so on.

If you copy this template from the CD to the following folder on your computer, it will be available when you choose File, New and click the General tab in the New dialog box:

```
C:\Windows\Application Data\Microsoft\Templates
```

Customize the Lazy Liz.dot template and edit the bookmarks (Insert, Bookmark) to quickly create your own prompting templates.

To learn more about templates:

▶ **See** "Getting the Most Out of Word Templates," **p. 284**

Using Hyperlinks to Create Bookmarks

Going through the process of creating bookmarks, pulling up dialog boxes to navigate to them, and finally navigating back to your original location can be time-consuming. Instead, try using *hyperlinks* in conjunction with bookmarks to provide a quick way of getting around.

Hyperlinks can be used with bookmarks within the same document, between documents, or even in the World Wide Web.

To create hyperlinks to a specific location in a document:

1. Select text or location of your hyperlink.
2. Choose Insert, Hyperlink to open the Insert Hyperlink dialog box (shown in Figure 9.5).

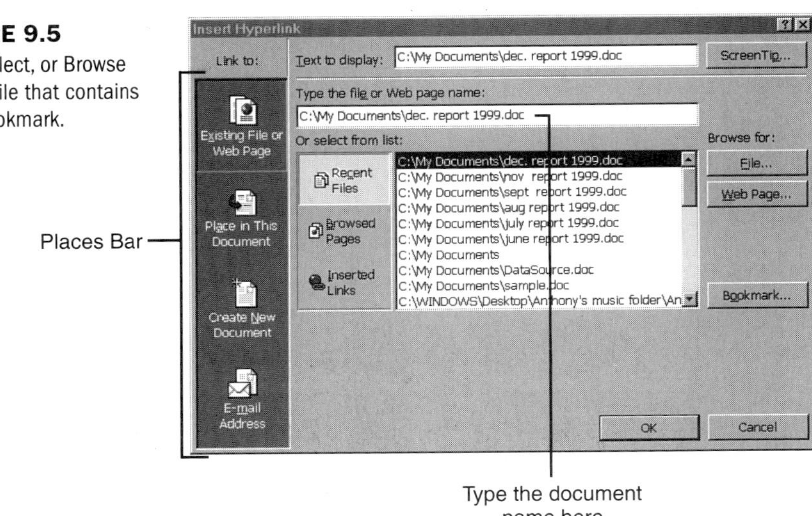

FIGURE 9.5
Type, select, or Browse for the file that contains your bookmark.

3. Choose or type the name of the file where the bookmark to be hyperlinked is located. You can use the Places Bar or Recent Files list to locate the file, or type the path and name in the Type the File or Web Page Name text box.
4. Click the Bookmark button to display the Select Place in Document dialog box, shown in Figure 9.6.

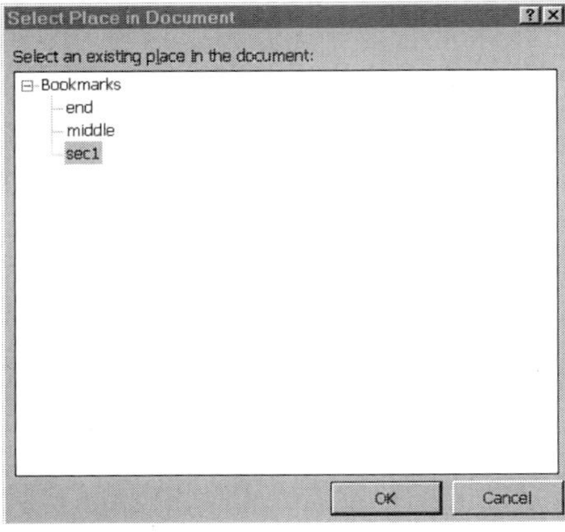

FIGURE 9.6
Selecting a bookmark allows you to navigate to a specific location in a document.

5. If necessary, expand Bookmarks by clicking the +, select the desired bookmark, and then click OK to close the Select Place in Document dialog box.
6. Click OK again to close the Insert Hyperlink dialog box. You should now see the underlined hyperlinked text in blue in your document.
7. When you place your mouse over the hyperlinked text, it changes to a pointer hand. Click this text to navigate to the bookmark.

Insert hyperlinks between two related topics in a document, so that you can navigate back and forth with a click. In addition, you can also add hyperlinks to Web pages and other documents being researched or compared, so that you can refer to them easily.

Hyperlinks can also be used in conjunction with cross-references to create bookmarks between related topics. In this manner, while working on electronic documents, a reader can simply click the cross-referenced text rather than try to navigate to the specific page and location named.

For more information on cross-references and hyperlinks,

▶ **See** "Cross-References and Hyperlinks," **p. 459**

Viewing and Using Hidden Bookmarks

User-created bookmarks are not the only bookmarks available for use. Word automatically creates *hidden bookmarks* whenever you insert cross-references, tables of contents, and other like items. These bookmarks cannot be accessed via the Go To tab of the Find and Replace dialog box (F5) because they are hidden.

Hidden bookmarks can be accessed only through the Bookmark dialog box. You can use these bookmarks to navigate to marked index entries, cross-references, or to heading levels reflected in a table of contents (this is helpful in navigating to sections of your document because you are navigating to the heading levels reflected in a table of contents).

To access these hidden bookmarks:

1. Choose Insert, Bookmark to display the Bookmark dialog box.
2. Check the Hidden bookmarks option (as shown in Figure 9.7) to show hidden bookmarks.
3. Select the desired bookmark and click the Go To button.

Although it is possible to use hidden bookmarks, the process is often clumsy. Word creates bookmark names that are meaningless to humans and it can be quite difficult to decipher which bookmark will take you to the desired location.

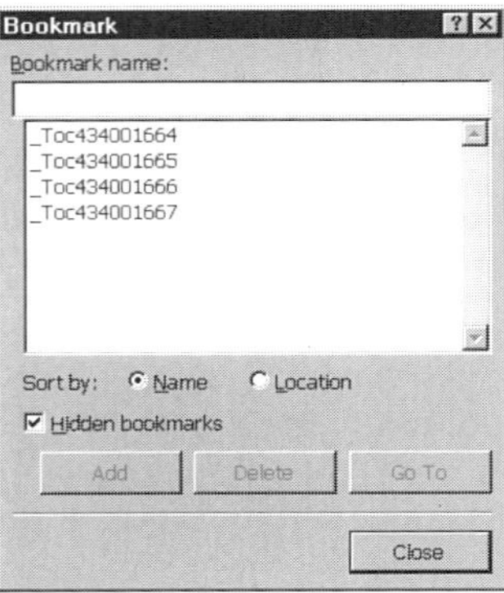

FIGURE 9.7
The Bookmark dialog box contains a check box that enables you to view hidden bookmarks.

Advanced Find and Replace Techniques

Most of us have used the Find and Replace feature to find a word or phrase we needed to change throughout a document. This is usually the extent of the average user's experience with Find and Replace. This feature, nonetheless, provides us with many more untapped utilities. From automating the Find Next option to using wildcards, Word's Find and Replace feature provides a number of search capabilities that most Word users—even advanced users—have never tried.

You can access the added functionality of Word's Find and Replace feature by clicking the More button in the Find and Replace dialog box. When you click the More button, it becomes the Less button (as shown in Figure 9.8) and the dialog box expands.

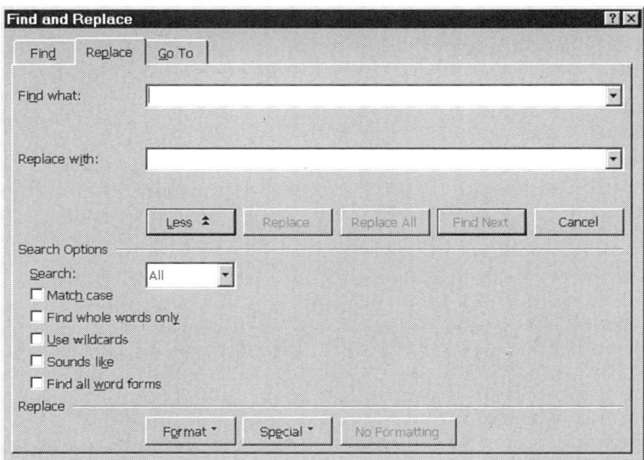

FIGURE 9.8
The Find and Replace feature provides for extensive search capabilities.

Automating the Find Next Option

Although the Find and Replace feature is a valuable tool, there are some aggravations. We have all experienced the minor annoyance of having to move the dialog box out of our way as we click the Find Next button during our searches. The following suggestion makes using Find and Replace more efficient.

To perform a Find, press Esc to close the dialog box and use the default keystroke Shift+F4 for RepeatFind. This reduces the time involved in clicking Find Next, moving the dialog box out of the way, making the changes and finally repeating the whole process. Using a keyboard shortcut also allows you to conduct text searches without the Find and Replace dialog box blocking your view of the text.

RepeatFind repeats the last browse operation and is incorporated with each of the three tabs in the Find and Replace dialog box. For example, if you last searched for a section break, the RepeatFind feature takes you to the next section, not to the last text search. Use the following VBA macro snippet to ensure you are using the Find Next feature for text searches only:

```
Sub FindNextText()
With Application.Browser
        .Target = wdBrowserFind
        .Next
End With
End Sub
```

You can copy this snippet from the CD that accompanies this book to your Normal template to make it available for all your Word documents.

The FindNextText macro is designed to search in only one direction—from the top of the document to the bottom. If you want the macro to search in the other direction, simply replace FindNextText() with FindPreviousText(), and then change .Next to .Previous. For quick access to this VBA macro snippet, assign the snippet to a keyboard shortcut or toolbar button.

▶ **See** "Assigning a Macro to a Toolbar Button," **p. 112**

Searching for Specific Formats Instead of Specific Text

Suppose that you want to locate a specific set of text, such as all the titles of books referenced in your document. If Word enabled you to perform a search in which you tried to locate only a specific string of text, Word's search capabilities would be useless. Fortunately, Word enables you to search by using a number of criteria—such as by using character and/or paragraph formatting. For example, if all book titles in your document were formatted with bold and italic, you could create a search that looked for all text containing both bold and italic formatting.

In the Find and Replace dialog box, the Format button shows a list of character and paragraph formatting by which you can search (see Figure 9.9).

Searching for Text by Character Formatting Attributes *Character attributes* can consist of anything found in the Format, Font dialog box (such as font style, color, and size). Although you can conduct your search by specifying which characters with these attributes you want to find, it is not necessary to detail the characters in your search. You can choose to search by using just the character attributes, rather than the specific word(s).

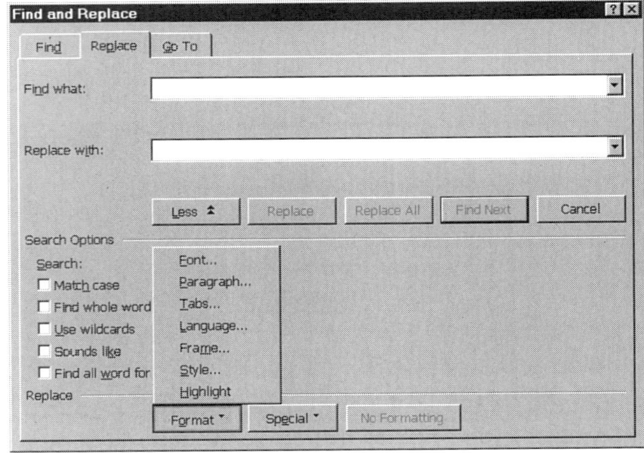

FIGURE 9.9
The Format button enables you to search for text by its character and paragraph formatting.

To conduct a character format text search:

1. Choose Edit, Replace to display the Find and Replace dialog box, and click in the Find What text box.
2. Click the More button to expand the dialog box if it is not already expanded.
3. Click the Format button, and choose Font to access the Find Font dialog box, as seen in Figure 9.10.

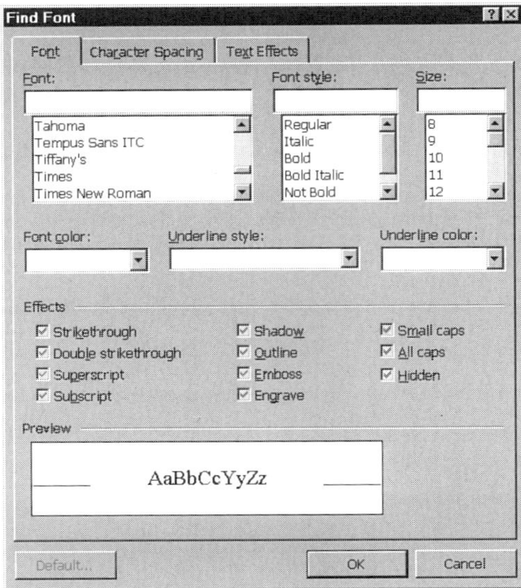

FIGURE 9.10
The Find Font option extends searching for text by character attributes.

4. Choose the attributes you want to search for and click OK.
5. If you want to replace the current formats with other formats, click in the Replace With text box and repeat steps 3 and 4 to identify the new formats you want to use.

6. To locate the first occurrence of the formats, click Find Next (see Figure 9.11). At each occurrence you would like to change, click Replace. To change all occurrences of that attribute with the new formatting, click Replace All. At this point, Word will tell you how many changes were made. Click OK to acknowledge the changes, and then close the Find and Replace dialog box.

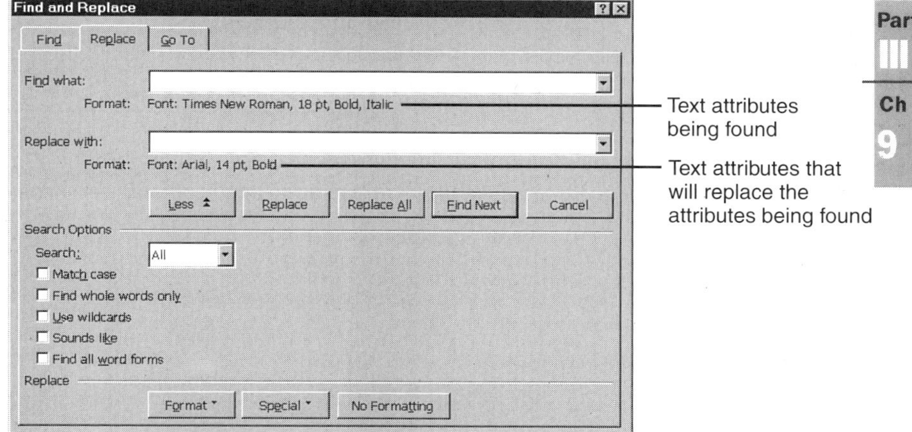

FIGURE 9.11
The Find and Replace dialog box allows you to replace all occurrences of a font style.

You can search for specific text formats such as italic or bold rather than text. You should now be able to use the FindNext command (or keyboard shortcut) to locate (or replace) all text with these character attributes.

Searching for Text by Paragraph Formatting It might become necessary to search for text according to its position on the page, such as text alignment. These attributes are referred to as *paragraph formatting*.

For example, suppose you need to locate all centered paragraph subtitles. In this case, you don't need to search for the character attributes of the subtitles, such as bold or size, but rather for text alignment—centering, in this example—a paragraph format.

Paragraph formatting can consist of the following features (the same as those found in the Paragraph dialog box):

- Indents and Spacing (Alignment, Indentation, Spacing, Line Spacing, and Outline Level).
- Line and Page Breaks (Widow/Orphan Control, Keep Lines Together, Keep with Next, and Page Break Before).
- Tabs (Tab Stop Position, Alignment, and Leader).

To search for text using paragraph formatting, display the Find and Replace dialog box and click the Format button (click the More button first to display the Search Options, if necessary). Choose Paragraph (or Tabs) from the menu. If you choose Paragraph from the menu, the Find Paragraph dialog box, as seen in Figure 9.12, displays.

Proceed by choosing the formatting you would like to search for and then click OK. Again, you should then be able to use the Find Next button to locate all text containing the selected formatting.

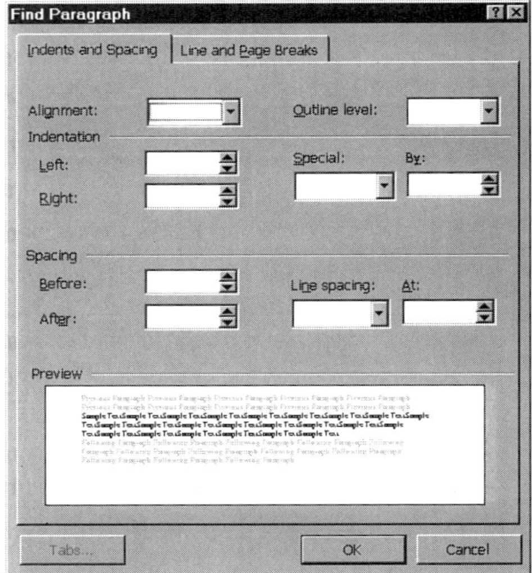

FIGURE 9.12
The Find Paragraph option enables you to search for text by paragraph formats.

Searching for Text Using Alternate Formatting In most instances, finding text using character attributes or paragraph formatting is sufficient. There are times, however, when you need to take your search a step further. Word's Find and Replace capabilities extend to searching by other attributes such as Language, Frame, Style or even Highlighting. You accomplish this in much the same manner as character and paragraph searches. From the Format menu in the Find and Replace dialog box, choose either Language, Frame, Style, or Highlight. When you select one of the items, a corresponding dialog box appears. Figure 9.13 shows the Find Style dialog box.

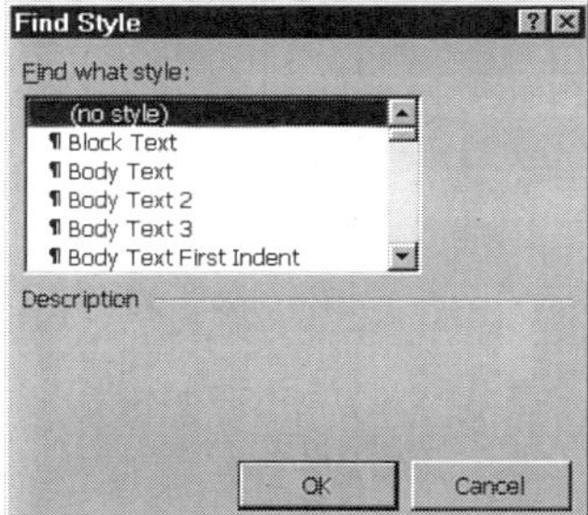

FIGURE 9.13
You can search for text with specific styles applied using the Find Style feature.

NOTE The Find Language option is available but will work only if you have installed Multilanguage Support.

It can then be used to locate text formatted in various languages and replace it with other text, typically in your own language.

For more information about Multilanguage Support:

- **See** "International Language Features," **p. 236**
- **See** "International Support for Languages," **p. 1721**

Locating Special Characters with Find and Replace

There are occasions when locating *special characters*, such as formatting or grammatical symbols, may be necessary. This is especially true when converting files from another text editor/word processor. A classic example occurs when converting DOS text files into Word. The conversion often places a hard return (or paragraph mark) at the end of every line. You could manually delete all of these—a process that takes valuable time—or you could use Word's Find and Replace tools to clear these characters out of your document in one stroke.

The Special button located in the Find and Replace dialog box enables you to search for special characters. The codes Word uses to identify each of the special characters have been included in the following list. These codes are automatically inserted when the item is chosen from the pop-up menu. It is not necessary, although it is possible, to type these into the Find What field.

You can search for the following special characters:

Paragraph Mark (^p)
Tab Character (^t)
Comment Mark (^a)
Any Character (^?)
Any Digit (^#)
Any Letter (^$)
Caret Character (^^)
Column Break (^n)
Em Dash (^+)
En Dash (^=)
Endnote Mark (^e)
Field (^d)
Footnote Mark (^f)
Graphic (^g)
Manual Line Break (^l)
Manual Page Break (^m)
Nonbreaking Hyphen (^~)
Nonbreaking Space (^s)
Optional Hyphen (^-)
Section Break (^b)
White Space (^w)

To locate or modify formatting characters from the Find and Replace dialog box:

1. Clear any previously searched for text or options.
2. Place the insertion point in the Find What box.
3. Click the Special button to display a pop-up list shown in Figure 9.14.

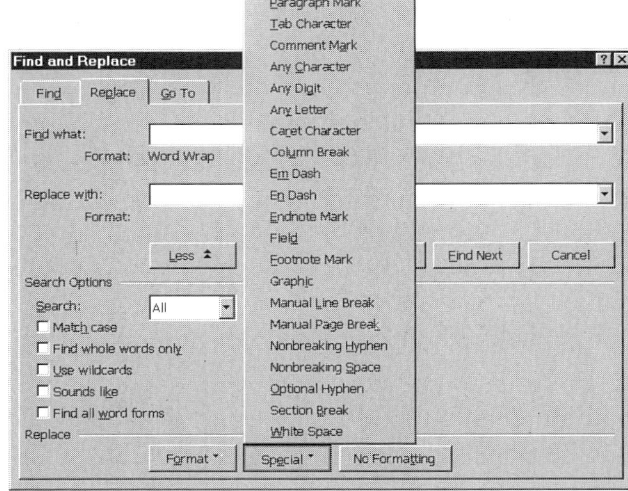

FIGURE 9.14
You can search for formatting characters and special symbols by using the Special option.

4. Select the formatting character for which you would like to search. (Word then automatically inserts the special code into the Find What box.)
5. If replacing the character, place the insertion point in the Replace With box. Click the Special button and choose the item you would like to use as the replacement from the pop-up menu. Figure 9.15 shows the Paragraph Mark (^p) being replaced with the Tab Character (^t). You can also replace a symbol with a space.
6. Click the Find Next or Replace button as required.

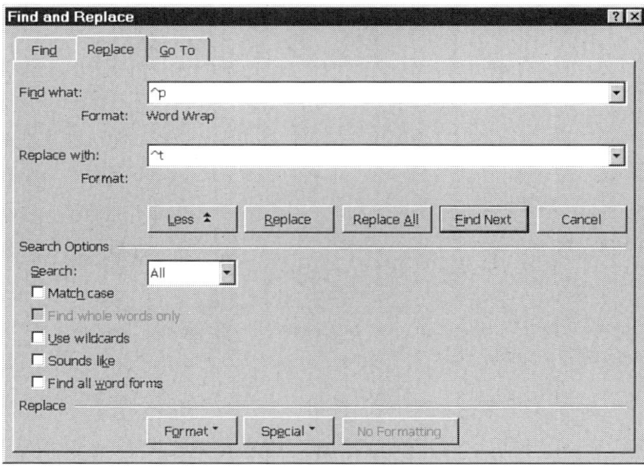

FIGURE 9.15
Word automatically inserts the codes necessary to perform special character searches.

In this manner, you can reduce finding and even replacing or deleting excessive formatting characters to a few clicks of the mouse.

Using Wildcards to Search for Text Entries

In card games, wildcards are cards that are allowed to be used in place of another specific card. Word's wildcards can be used in much the same way to assist you with pattern searches. As the name implies, *wildcards* are special characters that represent one or more characters when searching. Of course, they are invaluable when combined with standard characters.

CAUTION

When you use a wildcard in a Find or Replace search, the search is case sensitive. Word will search only for the exact characters you type in the Find What box. If you capitalize a word, the lowercase version of the word will not be found in the search.

Performing a wildcard search is not as complex as it would appear. Choose Edit, and either Find or Replace. Be sure the advanced options are visible by clicking the More button.

Next, check the Use Wildcards option to command Word to search using wildcards instead of searching for the actual character. By choosing Use Wildcards, you have also altered the options that will display in the Special pop-up menu.

NOTE You can use wildcards only in the Find What box, not in the Replace With box.

The following sections list wildcard operators and their functionality in Word searches, some of which you may not have seen before.

Using the Question Mark (?) As a Wildcard The question mark wildcard locates a single-text character. For example, typing in Defen?e will locate Defense and Defence (the U.S. spells defense with an "s," whereas the British spell it with a "c").

NOTE If you place a wildcard at the beginning of a word such as ?ill, it will find Bill, Jill, and surprisingly it will find "pill" in the words Spill, Spilled, or Spilling. To avoid finding these extra characters, use the less than (<) or greater than (>) wildcard symbols (discussed as follows).

Using the Asterisk (*) As a Wildcard The asterisk wildcard behaves very differently depending upon where the asterisk wildcard is positioned. If it is placed at the beginning of a word, for instance, it will find and highlight everything in front of the word you are searching for (every paragraph in your document before the word it finds), making your search pointless.

However, if you place the asterisk wildcard somewhere in the middle of the word, it will find any string of characters between the two characters on each side of the wildcard. For example, J*y will return January, Jeopardy, or Judy—any word that begins with a capital "J" and ends in a lowercase "y."

If you place the wildcard at the end of a word, it will help to find variations of that word. Invest, Investing, and Investment would all be found if you type in Invest*.

CAUTION

Because wildcard finds are case sensitive, be careful to indicate whether the word begins with a capital or a lowercase letter when using wildcards, such as the asterisk, in the middle or at the end of a word. Invest* would return Invest and Investing but not invest or investing (in lowercase).

CAUTION

Do not use the asterisk in a Find and Replace search along with the Replace All option. Because this wildcard finds multiple characters, you will end up replacing words and phrases you never intended to replace. Instead, step through each find and choose Replace only when you have confirmed the word found is correct. If it is not correct, simply choose Find Next to skip it. An alternative to this is discussed in the section "Using Wildcards to Find and Replace Text Entries" later in this chapter.

Using the Brackets ([]) As Wildcards The square brackets ([]) may be used to find any one character in a specified group. For instance, b[ia]t returns bit or bat, and not bet or but. This wildcard can also be used at the beginning of a word; however, it is important to note that [BS]at would find Bat and Sat, but not in their lowercase version.

Instead of finding a character listed within a particular group within brackets as in the previous example, you can specify a range by separating the beginning and ending of that range with a hyphen ([-]). For instance, [b-e]at would find bat, cat, and eat, but not fat, because it is beyond the alphabetical range created within the brackets.

You can exclude any one character by including an exclamation point before that character and enclosing them both within the square brackets ([!]). Consequently, d[!u]g will find dig and dog, but not dug.

Likewise, you can exclude a range of characters by incorporating the range-creating hyphen with the exclamation point. As a result, [!f-n]eat would find beat or seat, but not feat, heat, meat, or neat.

The square-bracket wildcard is not limited to alpha characters; it can also find numeric characters. For example, [1-3]00> will find 100, 200, and 300, but not 400, 101, or 1000. The greater than symbol limits the search to three-digit numbers. If you want to search for any number that is between 100 and 399, change the search to [1-3]??>; this will locate 101.

Using the Braces ({}) As Wildcards Several methods for using braces (sometimes called curly brackets) exist. They can be used to specify an exact number of occurrences of a particular character or range of characters. This wildcard can be used on alpha or numeric characters. You can also use braces to specify a minimum number of occurrences for a particular character or expression.

Enclosing a number within braces will find that exact number of occurrences of the character preceding the wildcard ({number}). For example, 19{2}8 would find 1998 but not 1999. It looks for a number that begins with one (1) followed by two (and only two) nines.

NOTE The previous example shows how this wildcard excluded 1999; however, it would not exclude 199802. It would highlight the 1998 portion of that expression. If you wanted to limit the number of digits, you could use the greater than or less than symbols, such as 19{2}8>, to get an exact match. However, if you know you are searching for 1998, why go through the trouble of using a wildcard at all? Do a find on 1998 without the wildcard and if you don't want to find 199802, do an Exact Match search.

A more useful Find and Replace option is to use wildcards to find a number of occurrences of a character or expression within a specified range ({n,m}) where n is the first character and m is the last character in the range. For instance, 10{1,3}18 would find 1018, 10018, and 100018, but not 1000018, because we specified from 1 to 3 zeros at this position in the number.

CAUTION

Be careful not to use the range at the end of the number because 10{1,3} would find 10, 100, 1000, and even 10,000. It would find and highlight the 100 thereafter regardless of how many zeros followed the one.

To find a minimum number of occurrences of a particular character or expression, use the {n,} wildcard combination. In this case, 1{3}7 would find 10007 and 100007, but not 1007 or 107.

Using the At Symbol (@) As a Wildcard The At symbol (@) wildcard is known as the *repeater* wildcard. It will find any number of occurrences of the preceding character. Fe@d would find Fed and Feed, and if it existed, Feeed.

Using the Less Than (<) and Greater Than Symbols (>) As Wildcards To find only words with the exact number of characters at the beginning of the word (including the wildcard placeholder), use the less than symbol (<) in front of the wildcard. For example, <?ill returns Jill and Bill, but not Spill, Drill, or Quill. However, it would find Billing. The entry in the Find What box should be <?ill> to avoid extra characters both before and after the word being searched for.

You can use the greater than symbol at the end of a word to limit the words it finds to only those ending with the specified number of characters. As a result, litigat?> would find litigate but not litigation or litigating.

Using the Backslash (\) to Find Characters Used As Wildcards Word includes a feature that enables you to use a backslash to search for wildcard characters while the Use Wildcards option is active. Placing a backslash (\) followed by a wildcard character in the Find What box allows you to search for characters normally reserved as wildcards. For example, you may want to search for any instance you used a question mark (?) so that you could find instances where you posed questions in your document. Unless you place the backslash before the question mark, Word will assume you want to use it as a wildcard.

Although you can use this feature, it may not be necessary. If you make sure that the Use Wildcards check box is deselected, you can search for these characters as you would any other text.

Using Wildcards to Replace Text Entries

Although wildcards can only be used in the Find What box, Word can be made to replace text using wildcards. Sometimes you may want to replace a portion of the word, and not the entire word. To accomplish this, you use parentheses to divide the Find What entry into segments that need to be replaced.

For example, Figure 9.16 shows a list of menu items that are changed daily. If you are a restaurant manager and you need to make global changes to your menu, you can use wildcards to locate every occurrence of part of a word and replace it with another. Consider, for example, a restaurant that serves fish. For today's menu, the only two fish items available are catfish and orange roughy. As the manager, you decide that you want to use catfish in every entrée except the poached orange roughy. Using wildcard searches, you can locate all text that contains the word "fish" such as Bluefish and Swordfish, and replace those words with Catfish.

NOTE If you're tempted to use an asterisk character to accomplish this, don't. As mentioned in the CAUTION earlier, using the asterisk in a Replace can result in incorrect, even disastrous results. It is much safer (and more accurate) to use the method discussed here.

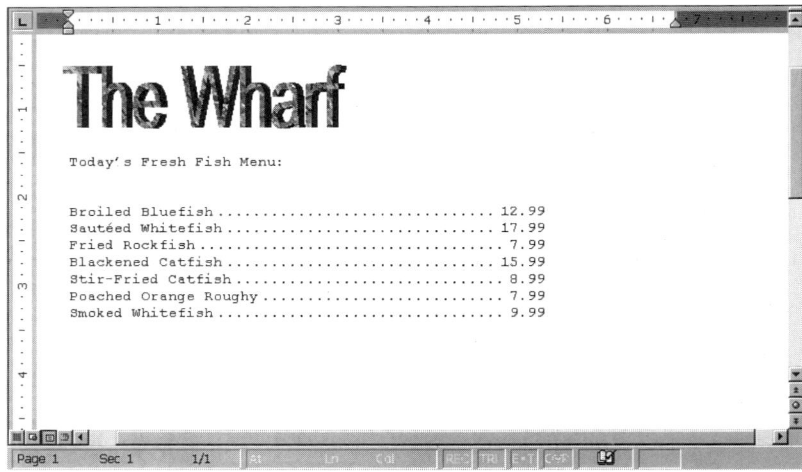

FIGURE 9.16
You can use wildcards to locate every occurrence of part of a word and replace it with another.

First, you need to divide the words into segments, and enclose each of the segments in parentheses. In this way, we partition off the part of the words we want to replace from the part we want to preserve—for example, (Blue)(fish) and (Sword)(fish). Because we don't care what the type of fish is, we can substitute the asterisk (*) wildcard for that segment—(*)(fish). To avoid the pitfalls of using the asterisk at the beginning of a word, add a segment at the beginning that looks for a space. The Find What entry becomes

( )(*)(fish)

CAUTION

In Figure 9.17, if you don't include the empty space as the first group when you use the asterisk (*), Word will assume you want to change everything in front of the word—including all words, spaces, and punctuation marks. For example, Broiled Bluefish becomes Catfish as opposed to Broiled Catfish.

Behind the scenes, Word assigns a number to each segment in the Find What box. The space in this example is 1, the asterisk is 2, and the word `fish` is 3.

Next, in the Replace With text box, you must enter a backslash (\) before the number of the segment you want to preserve. For this example, we want the space in segment 1 to remain, the word Cat to substitute for segment 2, and segment 3 to remain. Therefore, the entry becomes

\1Cat\3

When finished, your sample should resemble the one in Figure 9.17.

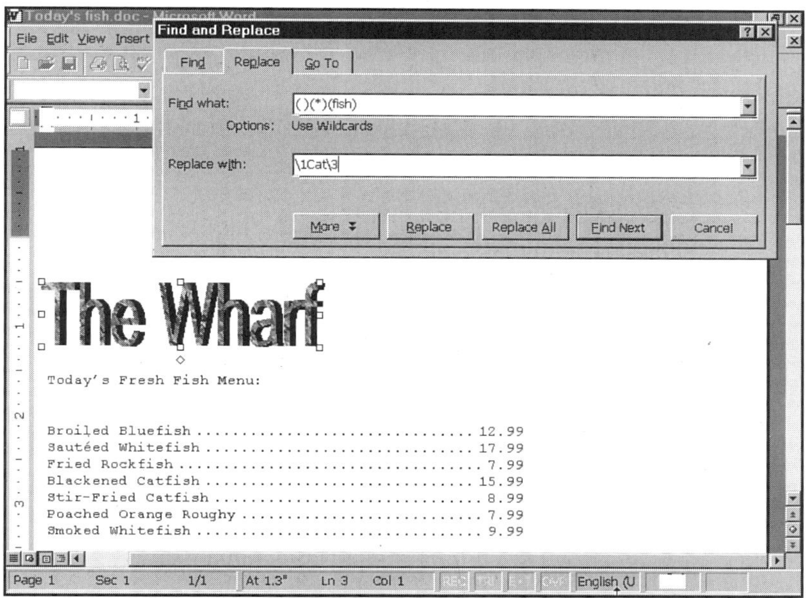

FIGURE 9.17
To use wildcards with the Replace feature, it is necessary to group the Find What text.

TIP If you want to change only a portion of your document, select the text you want to change before starting your wildcard search and replace.

CAUTION

If you see the a message indicating that the search item was not found, or that Word made zero replacements, chances are you may have forgotten to activate the Use Wildcard feature. Mark the Use Wildcard check box in the Search Options area of the Find and Replace dialog box.

This results in every form of fish (whether it was originally Swordfish or Whitefish), if it is preceded by a space, being converted to Catfish.

Using Wildcard Segments to Rearrange Text Order You can also use wildcards to reorder text in certain instances. For example, suppose you refer to Mrs. Ida Trevino-Sanchez throughout a document, and then you realize that it's supposed to be Ida Sanchez-Trevino! To reverse the text, simply use parentheses to separate each of the last names and the hyphen in the Find What box: (Trevino) (-) (Sanchez). In the Replace With box, enter \3\2\1 to rearrange the last name order (see Figure 9.18).

The text changes to read Sanchez-Trevino. Keep in mind, this same principle can be applied to more complex occurrences.

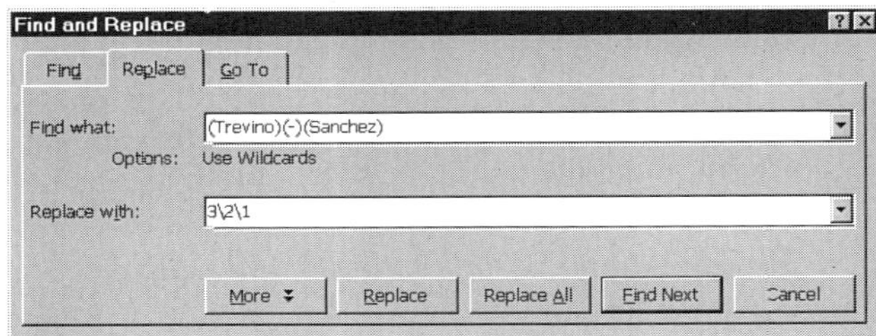

FIGURE 9.18
You can use wildcards to rearrange text order.

Making the Most of Tabs

In the ancient days of the typewriter, tab stops were used to align text or numbers. However, they were just not capable of flawless alignment (especially when working with numbers). In addition, table creation was next to impossible.

The advent of word processing brought a little relief, in the form of being able to correct onscreen rather than with the endless strips of correction tape or buckets of Liquid Paper. Nevertheless, early word processors still faced many of the same problems with alignment, as did their predecessors.

The functionality of tabs in early word processors extended to creating crude tables. This, however, doesn't compare to the powerful, easy-to-use table features in Word today. So, the question is if tables and column features have replaced tabs for most word processing requirements, when are tabs the best choice?

When Are Tabs the Best Choice?

Even though tables have taken up a bulk of the workload, there are still some tab features that cannot be substituted. For instance, only the Tab feature enables you to

- Align a column or row of numbers that contain decimal places.
- Align text to multiple horizontal locations on your page (unlike the alignment toolbar buttons, which allow for aligning over one horizontal location).
- Insert dot leaders that provide a visual connection between the text at the left margin and the text at the right.
- Insert line leaders to create offline, printable forms without having to use the underscore feature repeatedly.

Figure 9.19 shows an example of Word's capabilities for mixing different types of tabs all on the same line. You can even change your tab settings from one line to the next, if you like. Keep in mind, however, that all tabs are accessed in order from left to right.

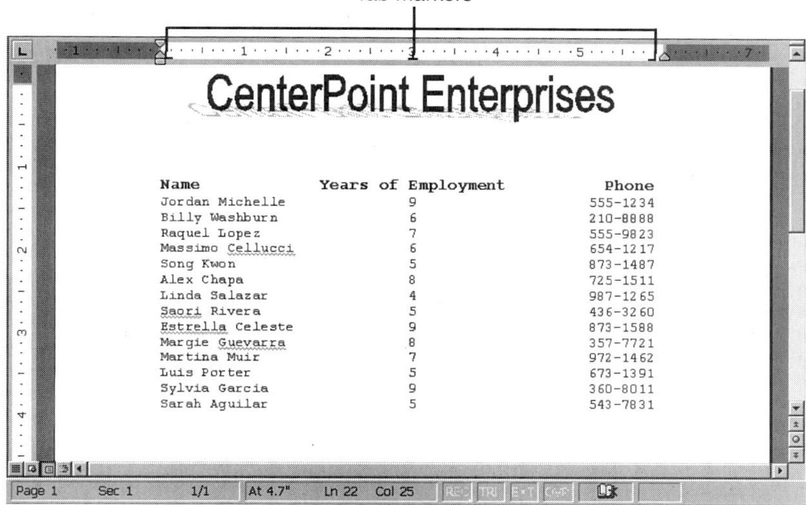

CenterPoint Enterprises

Name	Years of Employment	Phone
Jordan Michelle	9	555-1234
Billy Washburn	6	210-8888
Raquel Lopez	7	555-9823
Massimo Cellucci	6	654-1217
Song Kwon	5	873-1487
Alex Chapa	8	725-1511
Linda Salazar	4	987-1265
Saori Rivera	5	436-3260
Estrella Celeste	9	873-1588
Margie Guevarra	8	357-7721
Martina Muir	7	972-1462
Luis Porter	5	673-1391
Sylvia Garcia	9	360-8011
Sarah Aguilar	5	543-7831

FIGURE 9.19
Multiple tabs can be added on the same row and can be changed for any line within the same document.

There are times when tabs may not be the best choice. For example, many people still use tabs to create name, address, and phone number lists. In this instance, a table would be the best tool. A good rule of thumb to determine when tables or tabs should be used is to ask the question:

Does any one group of text extend beyond a single row (as in an address)? If so, tables are the best choice.

▶ For more information about tables, **see** "Unleashing the Potential of Tables," **p. 377**

If you decide that tabs are the way to go, Word provides you with two ways of creating them:

- Using the ruler
- Using the Tabs dialog box

Although the ruler is the faster way to create tab stops, some additional features are not available. In addition, tab stops can only be placed approximately and at designated places on the ruler.

The Tabs dialog box (Format, Tabs), on the other hand, provides for additional features, such as leaders and precise tab stop positions. Word 2000 provides you with five kinds of tabs (see Figure 9.20). They are listed as follows by Alignment type:

- Left—Text left aligns at this tab stop on the ruler.
- Center—As the name implies, all text centers upon this point on the ruler.
- Right—All text right aligns at this point on the ruler.
- Decimal—Use this tab to align numbers horizontally or vertically without regard to how many integer and decimal places they contain. All numbers align around their decimal point.
- Bar—These tabs are used to insert a vertical line at this point in the ruler and can span many rows.

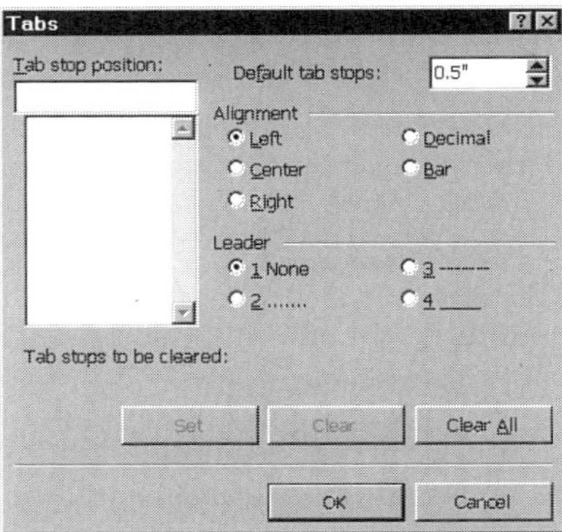

FIGURE 9.20
The Tabs dialog box features many options not available through the ruler.

Traditionally, the Tabs dialog box can be accessed in two ways: by choosing Format, Tabs or by double-clicking the tab area on the ruler. Another way to access the dialog box is to assign it a keyboard shortcut.

Calling the Tabs Dialog Box Instantly

To automatically summon the Tabs dialog box, you must create a custom keyboard shortcut. This shortcut needs to be created only once to work in all documents. To create a keyboard shortcut for the Tabs dialog box, follow these steps:

1. Choose Tools, Customize to display the Customize dialog box.
2. Click Keyboard to access the Customize Keyboard dialog box, shown in Figure 9.21.

3. In the Customize Keyboard dialog box under Categories, choose Format.
4. In the Commands scroll box, choose FormatTabs.
5. Place the insertion point in the Press New Shortcut Key box and press the desired shortcut on the keyboard (F6, F8, and F10 are good choices because they are currently assigned to rarely used features, although any combination you feel comfortable with will do).
6. Click Assign.
7. Click Close twice.

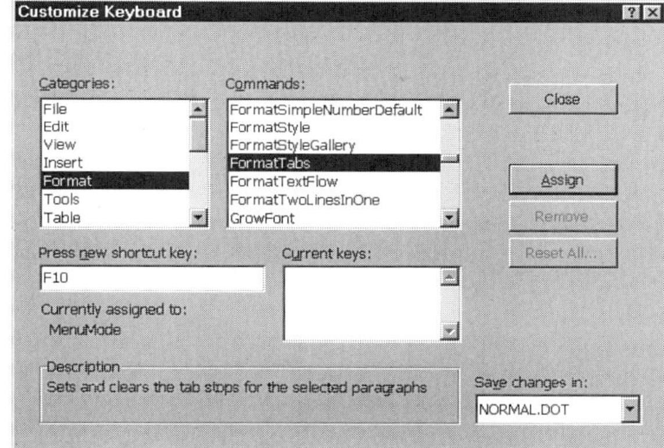

FIGURE 9.21
Most features, such as Tabs, can be assigned to keyboard shortcuts for efficiency.

You should test the keyboard shortcut by pressing the assigned button(s)—this should instantly call the Tabs dialog box in any document. Now that the dialog box is readily accessible, setting precise tabs is quicker than ever.

Setting Up Precise Tabs

Setting tabs from the Tabs dialog box is just as easy, yet more precise, than using the ruler. Just as with your ruler, you can add different kinds of tab stops in combination on the same line or paragraph. Create a precise tab as follows:

1. From the Tabs dialog box, enter the ruler position of the new tab stop in the Tab Stop Position box (refer to Figure 9.20).
2. Under Alignment, choose the type of tab you need (Left, Center, Right, Decimal, or Bar).
3. Click Set (at this point, you can add additional tab stops in the same manner).
4. Click OK.

You can repeat this process as many times as you need. Should it become necessary, you can clear tabs from the Tabs dialog box as well as the ruler. To clear them from the ruler, simply drag the tab mark off the ruler. To clear them from the dialog box, choose the tab(s) to be deleted and click the Clear button. To clear all tabs, access the Tabs dialog box and click Clear All.

Converting and Modifying Tab Types Instantly

You can move the approximate location of a tab by dragging it to a new location on the ruler. Unfortunately, there is no way to convert one type of tab to another by using the ruler. You must first drag the old tab mark off and replace it with a new one. This can be a frustrating and tedious job. There is an easier way through the Tabs dialog box.

If you need to convert a tab, open the Tabs dialog box (as shown in Figure 9.22) and select the desired tab. Its attributes (type and leader options) should display on the right. Simply select the new attributes and then click the Set button.

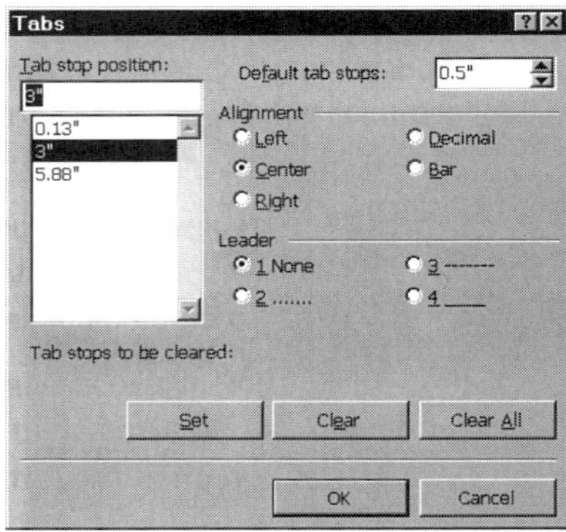

FIGURE 9.22
You can set, modify, and clear tabs from the Tabs dialog box.

Adding Leaders to Tabs

A *leader* is a repeated set of characters (such as dashes, dots, or underscores) that fills the space between a tab stop and text or margins. You can add a leader only through the Tabs dialog box.

You can use leaders in combination with any type of tab to create a visual straightedge that allows readers to follow a line of text across a page. There are three types of leaders available in Word—the Dot leader, Line leader, and Dashed leader. Tab leaders fulfill a couple of functions. They can lead the reader to the next tab stop position or margin. You usually find leaders similar to those in Figure 9.23 on menus, tables of contents, indexes, and phone lists, to name a few.

You can also use leaders to create printable forms and worksheets. Use the line leader to create a form similar to the one in Figure 9.24.

To add leaders to your tabs from the Tabs dialog box, simply

1. Enter the ruler position of the new tab stop in the Tab Stop Position box (refer to Figure 9.25).
2. Under Alignment, choose the type of tab you need (Left, Center, Right, Decimal, or Bar).
3. Under Leader, choose the leader you want to apply (dot, dashed, or line).

4. Click Set (at this point, you can add additional tab stops and/or leaders by repeating steps 1 through 3).
5. Click OK.

FIGURE 9.23
Tab leaders can create a visual straightedge for readers to follow.

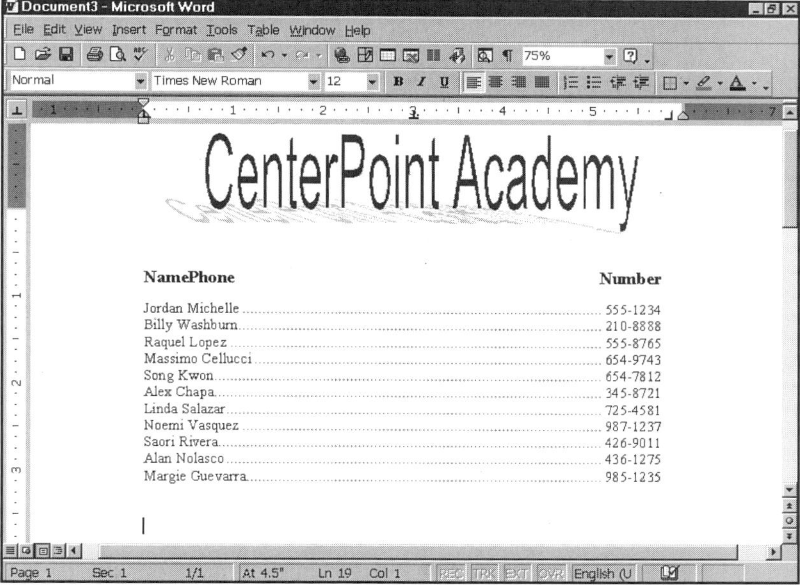

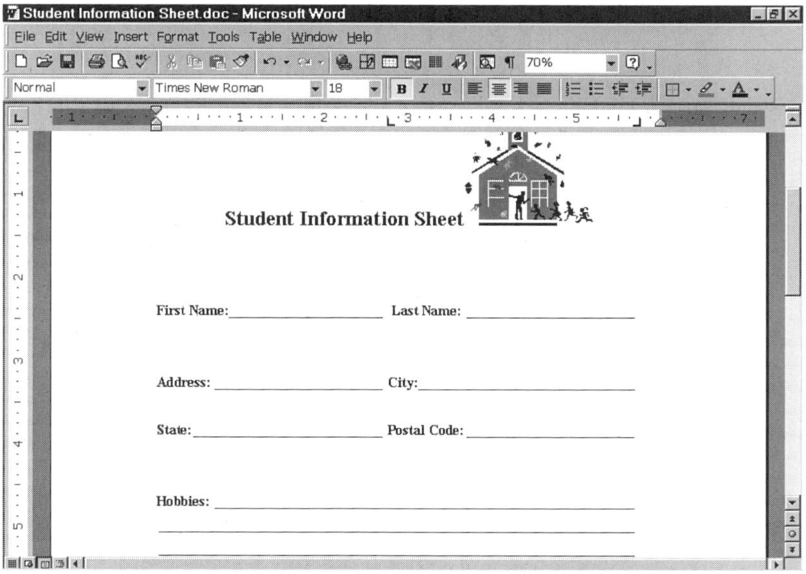

FIGURE 9.24
You can use line leaders to create offline, printable forms.

Student Information Sheet.doc - Microsoft Word

Student Information Sheet

First Name: ____________ Last Name: ____________

Address: ____________ City: ____________

State: ____________ Postal Code: ____________

Hobbies: ____________

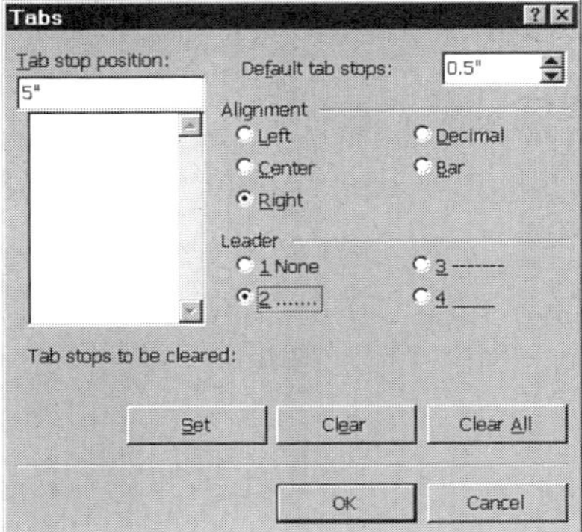

FIGURE 9.25
You can add tab leaders only from the Tabs dialog box.

Tabs, Find and Replace, and bookmarks are among the most useful power-formatting and editing tools. Most people never realize their potential. They may use them superficially but never unleash the power behind them. Master these techniques to become more efficient in your everyday use of Word.

CHAPTER 10

Using Styles, Templates, and Themes

In this chapter

Word's Formatting Features

Many people who use Word treat it as a glorified typewriter. One with extremely useful features to be sure, but generally they type text and then manually format the document. As you have already discovered, Word provides many features above and beyond the spelling and grammar checks. In fact, Word's architecture consists of three layers:

- The Word application that provides the standard menus, commands, and toolbars.
- Templates that are models from which you create new documents and which provide storage for such items as styles, themes, macros, AutoText entries, as well as custom menus, commands, toolbars, and keyboard assignments (shortcut keys).
- Documents that contain text, graphics, formatting, and settings for those documents.

This chapter explores the second of these layers, which contains styles, templates, and themes. *Styles* enable you to consistently format paragraphs or characters throughout a document. For example, if you manually format every heading in a document you risk leaving out elements of the heading formats: font, point size, indentation, and so on. On the other hand, when you create a style for each of the heading levels, you know that they are identical. Later, if you modify the style, that modification will be applied to all the headings or paragraphs with that style. Using styles also simplifies other tasks, such as creating tables of contents, figures, and so on.

▶ **See** Chapter 15, "Features Used with Complex Documents," **p. 441**

A *template* provides formatting for a document and stores custom features available during document creation. These custom features can include styles, AutoText, macros, themes, and custom toolbars. Each template has a filename with a .dot extension. You can easily modify the templates supplied with Word or you can create your own custom templates.

New in Word 2000, *themes* help you create unified, well-designed documents for electronic publication in Word, on the Web or in email. Themes are especially well-suited to Web page design since they help give your Web site a uniform appearance. Each theme provides a set of design elements and color schemes for background color or graphic, body and heading styles, bullets, horizontal lines, hyperlink colors, and table border color. If you are familiar with PowerPoint, themes are reminiscent of PowerPoint design templates.

Mastering Styles

Styles are the backbone of Word's text formatting. When you create a style, you standardize the formatting of specific text. Styles also provide a way of recognizing the text for other features, such as tables of contents, outlines, and so on. In this section, you will review style basics, create new styles, apply advanced features to your styles, and use styles for AutoFormat.

Fundamentals of Styles

As you recall, all documents in Word are based on a template. If you make no other choice (that is, if you click the New button or press Ctrl+N), then your new documents are based on

Normal.dot. This template provides access to all the built-in styles for Word. When you create a template, you define a set of styles that are available to that particular template in addition to the styles available in Normal.dot. Templates that you create contain built-in styles, any custom styles you've created. You can create as many styles and templates as you need.

Styles provide a way to store a series of formatting characteristics that can be used across documents. If you regularly create documents with headings and specifically formatted text, you would store the heading format in a paragraph style and the formatting for the text in a character style. The paragraph style could contain font characteristics, borders and shading, indenting, line spacing, and so on. The character style could include features available under the font, borders, and language menu.

▶ **See** "Getting the Most Out of Word Templates," **p. 284**

Following is a quick summary of some important points regarding Word styles:

- Word provides two types of styles: paragraph styles and character styles. A paragraph's appearance is controlled by a paragraph style. Formatting features include text alignment, tabs, line spacing, and borders, and can include character formatting. The built-in style, Heading 1, is a paragraph style. A character style is applied to text within a paragraph and controls formatting such as the font, point size, bold, and italic. Hyperlink is a character style.
- You apply paragraph styles to paragraphs to control the appearance of all (or most of) the text between one paragraph mark and the next.
- You apply character styles to individual characters to control the appearance of those characters. Character styles override text formatting specified in paragraph styles.
- Every template, including custom templates you create, contains the full set of styles provided with Word.
- You can add custom styles to any template.
- When you create a new document, Word copies into the document all the styles in the template on which the document is based.
- Any changes you make to a document's style do not affect the styles in that document's template.
- Any changes you make to styles in a template don't automatically affect documents based on that template (although you can update a document so that its styles match those in the template).

NOTE Style has several meanings in Word. In the context of styles and templates, a character style is the combination of all the factors that contribute to the appearance of characters. In the context of formatting characters by making choices in the Font dialog box, style is used for the choice made among Regular, Italic, Bold, and Bold Italic.

Two of the most important built-in styles are the Normal and Default Paragraph Font styles:

- Normal is the paragraph style Word applies to all paragraphs unless you choose a different paragraph style. So when you begin working in a new document, you will be working in the Normal style.
- Default Paragraph Font is a character style that formats characters according to the character formatting specified in the current paragraph style. You would apply the Default Paragraph Font style when you want to bring a paragraph back to the default settings before beginning work on it.

You can delete user-created custom styles, but Word doesn't enable you to delete any of its built-in styles, although, with the exception of the Default Paragraph Font style, you can modify them. The Default Paragraph Font style can't be modified from the Style dialog box. The only modification that can be made to this style is that you can change the default font through Format, Font command. The Default Paragraph Font style can be used to strip character formatting out of a paragraph or to standardize a paragraph. For example, if you are editing a paragraph in which the author has used italic, bold, underline, font size, and so on for emphasis, you can select that paragraph and apply the Default Paragraph Font style to strip the formatting changes out of the paragraph. The Default Paragraph Font style reflects the font you have chosen to be your default font.

Using Word's Built-In Styles

Word's templates already contain a large number of built-in styles that are useful for several reasons.

- Word is designed to look for certain styles for use in its other features. For example, by using the heading styles—Heading 1, Heading 2, and so on when you create a table of contents—Word automatically builds the table with the appropriate hierarchy.
- Word also has styles that are used in other tables as well. When you create a table of figures, Word searches for the caption style.
- If you have used Word's heading styles, when you apply AutoFormat the formatting changes are made consistently throughout your document.
- Word's built-in templates use Word's standard style names. So when you switch from template to template, all your styles change their appearance accordingly. If you have created styles with different names they won't be affected by a template change.
- Word has also created styles for almost every function including hyperlinks, lists, and captions. The disadvantage is that if you only use Word's styles, your documents run the risk of looking like every other document created in Word.

Normally, when you click the Style drop-down list (on the Formatting toolbar), you see a list of the styles that are used in the active document and a few other basic styles: Headings 1 through 3, Normal and Default Paragraph Font. This list is limited to the styles Word has deemed most useful. There may be other styles that are part of the template the document is based on that are not listed. To see the complete set of styles available, hold down the Shift key as you click the Style drop-down list.

Figure 10.1 shows some of Word's built-in styles available from the Styles drop-down list on the Formatting toolbar.

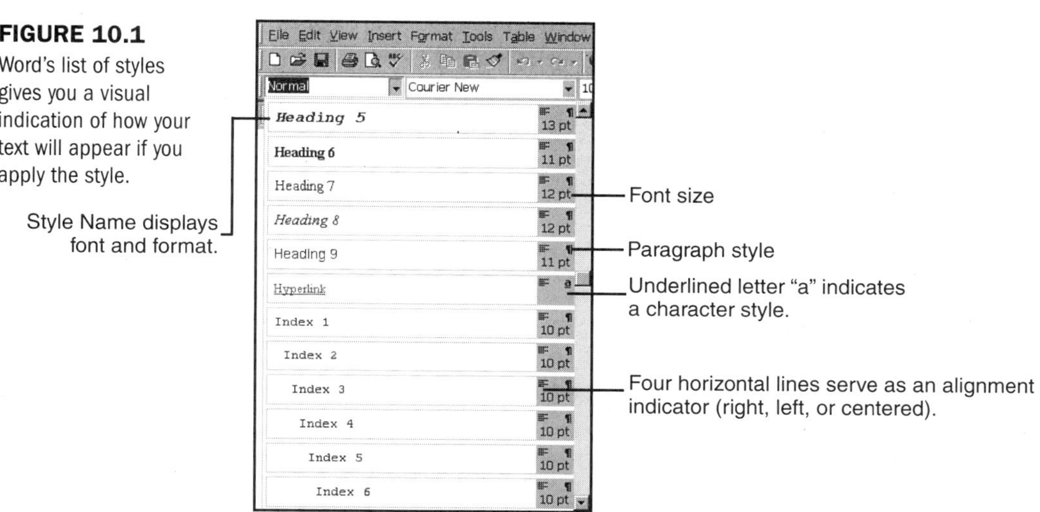

FIGURE 10.1
Word's list of styles gives you a visual indication of how your text will appear if you apply the style.

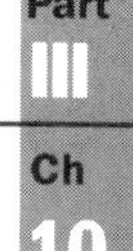

The list of styles shown in Figure 10.1 provides considerable information about each style. Some points to notice include

- The horizontal position (or indentation) of the style name shows any indentation from the left margin that is part of the style.
- The font used to display the style's name is the font specified in that style. The name also displays the formats (such as bold and italic) that the style will apply to the text.
- The size of the style's name is the same as the font size specified in the style, unless the specified size is smaller than 6 points (in which case the name is displayed in 6-point) or larger than 16 points (in which case the name is displayed in 16-point).
- The block at the right of each style name contains an underlined "a" to indicate a character style, or a paragraph mark to indicate a paragraph style.
- The four horizontal lines (at the right of each style) indicate whether the text is left-aligned, right-aligned, centered, or justified.
- The block also contains the size of the font, described in points, for all point sizes so that if the font is smaller than 6 points or larger than 16 points, that information is available.

The Differences Between Character and Paragraph Styles

A character style affects only specific characters within a paragraph. For example, the Hyperlink and Followed Hyperlink styles are character styles. They change the appearance of the characters, but do not affect any paragraph formatting such as indenting, line spacing, and so forth.

Paragraph formatting can contain any of the formatting options normally associated with paragraphs including borders and shading; indents and line spacing; and bullets and numbering. Figure 10.2 demonstrates a character style applied within a paragraph style.

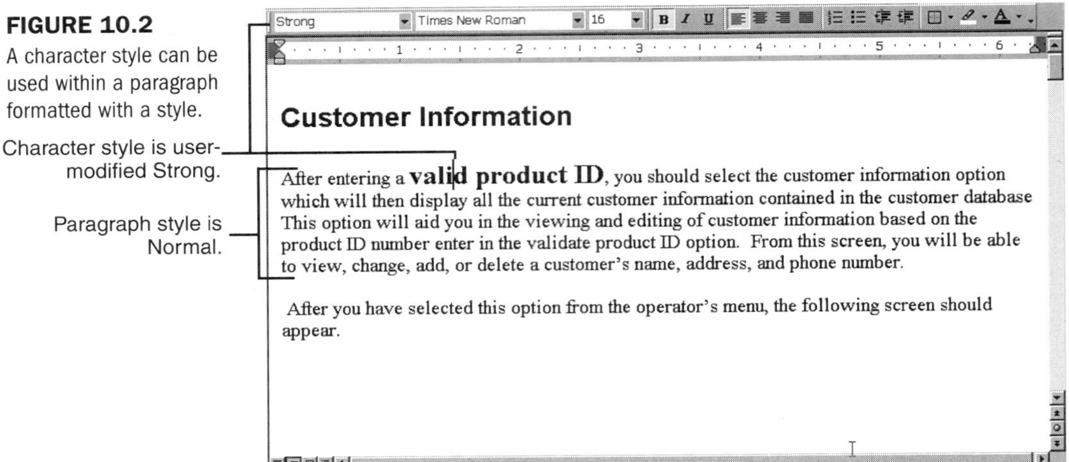

FIGURE 10.2
A character style can be used within a paragraph formatted with a style.

Applying Styles

If you ignore styles, Word automatically applies the built-in Normal paragraph style to all your paragraphs. To apply a different paragraph style to a paragraph, place the insertion point anywhere within that paragraph (you don't have to select all the text in the paragraph), open the list of styles, and select the paragraph style you want—make sure you don't select a character style (character styles are marked with an underlined letter "a"). Applying the Heading 1 style is an example of this. This style contains paragraph-level formatting that should be applied to the whole paragraph.

CAUTION

If you have text selected within a paragraph and apply a paragraph style, the selected text will accept the appearance of the style, but the style will not have been applied to the paragraph.

To apply a specific character style to certain characters within a paragraph, select those characters, open the list of styles, and select the character style you want.

One of the most useful ways to apply a style is by using a keyboard shortcut. For more information, see "Using Keyboard Shortcuts to Apply Styles" later in this chapter.

You can, if you want, select only some characters in the paragraph and then choose the Default Paragraph Font style. In this case, only the selected characters are affected.

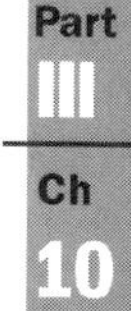

Creating a New Style

The easiest way to create a new paragraph style is to format a paragraph in the way you want, and then save that paragraph's format as a style. Remember that Word defines a paragraph as the text between two ¶ marks. Use these steps to create a new paragraph style:

1. Create a paragraph and then select the entire paragraph.
2. Use the Format menu to apply font, paragraph, and whatever other formatting attributes you want.
3. Place the insertion point in the Style Box at the left end of the Formatting toolbar.
4. Type a name for the new format and press Enter. Consider using a longer descriptive name for your style, so that you can more easily determine when it is appropriate to apply.

Now you have a new paragraph style.

CAUTION

If you try to name your new style with an existing style name, Word simply applies the old style over the existing paragraph.

Word doesn't provide a similar way to create a new character style based on a character style in a document. Instead, you must use the New Style dialog box to create a new character style.

To create a character style, or another way to create a new paragraph style, is by using the Format menu. Choose Format, Style to open the Style dialog box. Then choose New to display the New Style dialog box shown in Figure 10.3.

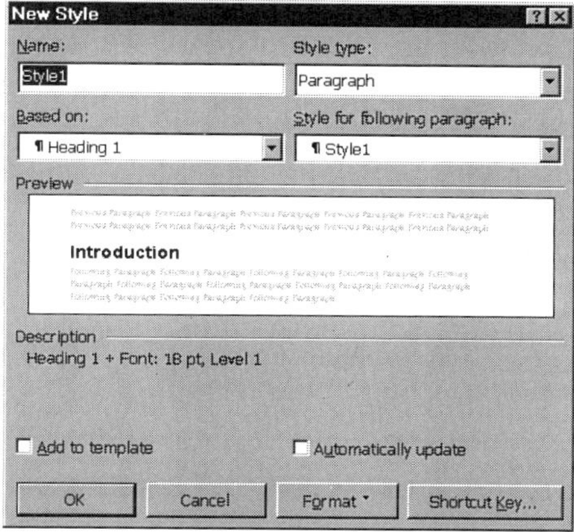

FIGURE 10.3
Use the New Style dialog box to begin creating a new paragraph or character style.

In this dialog box, enter a name for the new style, choose the Style type (Paragraph or Character), choose any existing style to base the new style on (you can choose No Style for paragraph styles), and choose a style for the paragraph. After you've supplied this basic information, proceed to specify whatever formats are appropriate for the new style.

NOTE The New Style dialog box is the only way to create the character styles .

Resolving Conflicts Between Paragraph and Character Styles

It's important to understand that character styles override paragraph styles. For example, in text with the Footnote Text style applied, you can also add a hyperlink. The Footnote Text style is a paragraph style and the hyperlink is a character style. If you were to change the paragraph style to Block Text, another paragraph style, your hyperlink would maintain its character style. In Figure 10.2 shown earlier, if the paragraph format were to change to reflect a different font, the characters formatted with the Strong style would retain their formatting while the text around them would change.

Also, most manual formatting you apply to text overrides paragraph styles. For example, in a short paragraph with the Normal style applied, one or two bold words or even a sentence or two will retain their bold formatting when another paragraph style is applied. Word decides what to do with manually formatted text with an algorithm. Generally speaking, if a majority of characters are formatted with bold, as an example, then if you apply a new paragraph style, Word treats the bold formatting as if it were a style and will override it, discarding the bold. If a minority of characters are bold, then they will retain that formatting through a paragraph style change. In a paragraph where each sentence is differently formatted—one bold, one italic, one underlined, and so on—each will retain its unique format.

If you want all the characters in the paragraph to match the new paragraph style's default character formatting, select the entire paragraph and choose the Default Paragraph Font style. This removes the effect of any character styles or manual character formatting in the paragraph. Then apply the new paragraph style.

Modifying Existing Styles

One of the disadvantages of using Word's built-in styles is that your document runs the risk of looking like other Word documents—possibly those created by your co-workers or competitors. One way to resolve this while maintaining the benefits of using Word's style names is to modify the built-in styles. Also, if you have created a custom style for your document, you may want to alter it as your work progresses.

One way to change an existing style:

1. Change the formats in a paragraph that currently uses the style.
2. When the paragraph reflects the changes you want, select the paragraph or just leave the insertion point there.
3. Click the Style drop-down list and select or retype the style name (be sure not to select a new name). Word displays the Modify Style dialog box shown in Figure 10.4.

TIP You can click into the Style box and type only the first character or two of the style name, and Word will jump to that section of the style list.

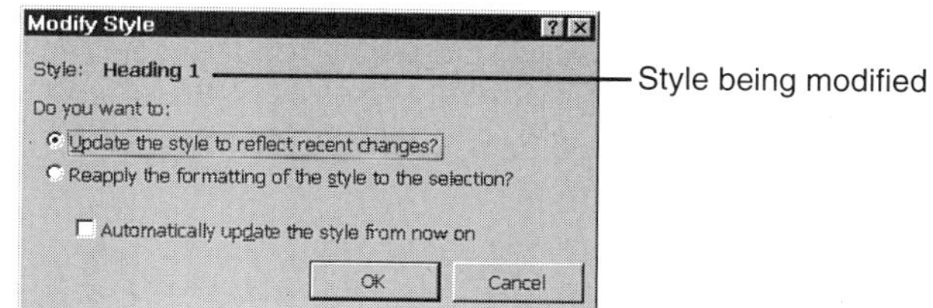

FIGURE 10.4
Word displays this dialog box when you make changes to an existing style and then click in the style box.

4. In the Modify Style dialog box, choose among the following options:
   - Choose Update the Style to Reflect Recent Changes? option to replace the original style with the new one.
   - Choose the Reapply the Formatting of the Style to the Selection? option to reapply the original style to the selected paragraph.
   - The Automatically Update the Style from Now On option affects what happens in the future. If you check this box, the next time you use this method of creating a new style, this dialog box doesn't appear; instead, the old style is immediately replaced with the new style—you will not be given an option.

TIP To restore access to the Modify Styles dialog box, choose Format, Style; select the style name and choose Modify. Then remove the check mark from the Automatically Update check box.

NOTE If you click Cancel in the Modify Style dialog box, the paragraph keeps the formatting changes you made manually without affecting the style.

The technique above is generally used when you decide while working on the document to make changes to the style. If you are setting the style up at the beginning of a project, it can be more convenient to use the Style dialog box:

1. Choose Format, Style to display the Style dialog box (shown in Figure 10.5) which provides additional options and features.
2. Click the List box drop-down list to choose among Styles in Use, All Styles, or User-Defined Styles; then select the style you want to modify. Notice that the Description panel contains a summary of what is defined in the selected style.
3. Click Modify to open the Modify Style dialog box shown in Figure 10.6.

NOTE You can't modify or delete the Default Paragraph Font style. You can modify any other built-in style, including the Normal style, but Word will not enable you to delete any of them.

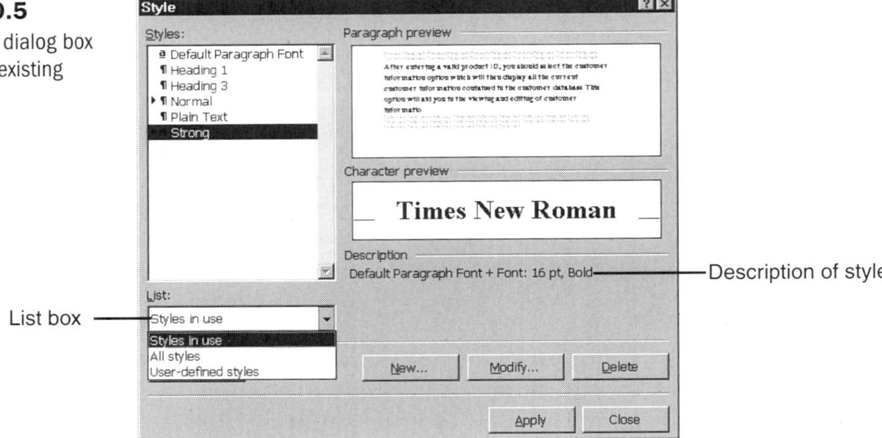

FIGURE 10.5
Use the Style dialog box to modify an existing style.

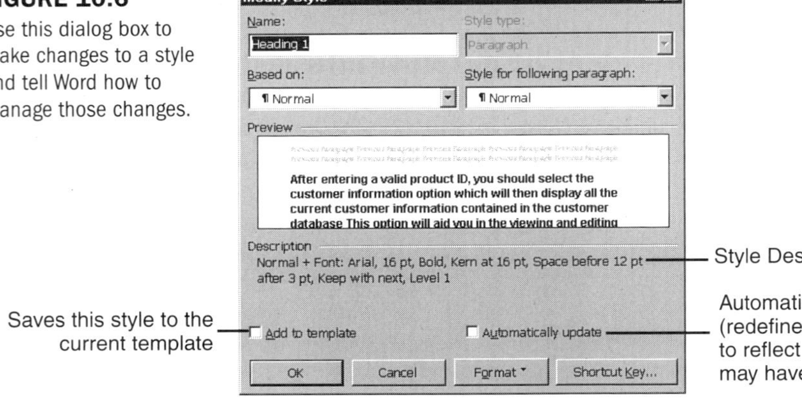

FIGURE 10.6
Use this dialog box to make changes to a style and tell Word how to manage those changes.

4. Click Format to proceed with your modifications. If you've chosen a paragraph style, you can display dialog boxes in which you can modify Font, Paragraph, Tabs, Border, Language, Frame, and Numbering; if you've chosen a character style, only Font, Border, and Language dialog boxes are available. Each of these dialog boxes is similar to those you work with when you directly modify text in a document. After you've modified a style, the Description in the Modify Style dialog box is automatically updated.

CAUTION

If you change a style that other styles are based on, that change cascades through the dependent styles. For example, many styles are based on the Normal style; if you change the default font, all the styles based on the Normal style will have their fonts changed. However, if a style already has a different font associated with it, that font remains unchanged.

5. After you've finished modifying the style, click OK to return to the Style dialog box.
6. Then click Apply to apply the changed style to the selected paragraphs, save the changed style, and close the dialog box. If you want to save your changes to the style without applying that style to the selected paragraphs, just choose Close.

Adding a Style to the Template

The Add to Template check box on the Modify Style dialog box (as shown in Figure 10.6) applies to how the modified style is saved.

- If you leave the Add to Template box unchecked, the modified style applies only to the active document. Select this option when you are making a style change that pertains only to the current document.
- If you check the box, the modified style is saved in the template that's attached to the current document. If you select this option, the style changes you make here will apply to any document you work with that uses the specified template.

Automatically Updating Document Styles

The Automatically Update check box as shown in Figure 10.6 can be a powerful friend or a cunning enemy. Think carefully before you check it. If you do check it, it becomes very easy (perhaps too easy) to modify the style. Here's what happens after you've checked this box and saved the style.

If you are developing a new template or a new document, choosing to automatically update your styles allows you to update your styles on-the-fly without confirmation. This is a very efficient way of making style changes, if you pay very close attention to what you are doing. The downside of this efficiency is that it is very easy to make unintended changes to styles you were already finished developing.

Suppose you've modified (or created) a style (call it the Manual style) and checked Automatically Update. Subsequently, you're working in a paragraph that's based on this style. You decide to make a change to the format of the paragraph. The change you make affects not only that paragraph, but also every other paragraph based on the Manual style. If that's what you want, okay. In many cases, though, you might not want a change you make in one paragraph to affect other paragraphs.

Usually, you will keep this option on during format development, the time you spend at the front end of a project creating a look for your document. After you have settled on the styles' format, turn this option back off. By turning Automatically Update off, you prevent other users from making inadvertent changes to your carefully created styles.

Seeing the Applied Styles

Word allows you to see all formatting associated with custom styles, even styles that were created by other users. For example, if you receive a draft of a business plan from a co-worker and find that he has created a custom style for all bibliographical references, you can easily see how the formatting comprises this style.

To see all the formatting associated with each style:

1. First select text in your document that uses the desired style.
2. Choose Format, Style and be certain that you are viewing Styles in Use as shown in Figure 10.7. The style you selected in the document will appear highlighted in the Styles: scroll box on the left of the dialog box. Samples of the style in a paragraph and the character preview are provided at the right. A description of the style is provided at the right, too.

Instead of first highlighting text in the document and then selecting Format, Style, you can simply open the Style dialog box and select the style from the scrollable list at the left. A description showing the style formatting appears at the right. This method is desirable because you can see the formatting used in a variety of styles simply by choosing styles in the Styles list at the left.

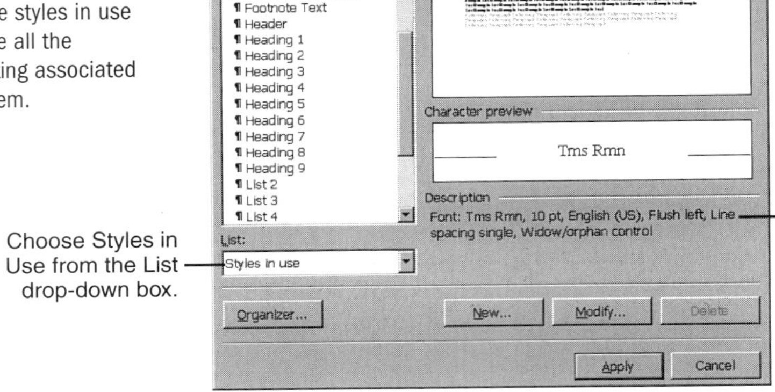

FIGURE 10.7
Use this dialog box to view the styles in use and see all the formatting associated with them.

If you want to know what formatting has been applied to text, you can choose Help, What's This and click on the text in question. The resulting pop-up box tells you both the paragraph and character formatting that is applied to that text. If you just want to know the style that is applied to the text, position your insertion point within the text in question and look at the style box. The name of the applied style will appear there.

Creating and Using Style Aliases

Most styles have descriptive names that may be long or complex. If you apply the style frequently, you may want to create an alias for it and cut down on the typing. If you create a style named "Margin Note 1," you may not want to type that many characters in the style box each time you apply that style. It's easy to create an alias:

1. Choose Format, Style and click the style for which you want to create an alias.
2. Click Modify.

3. In the Name box, add a comma and the alias to the end of the style name as shown in Figure 10.8.
4. Choose OK, and then Close to save your changes.

Now, whenever you want to apply the style, just click in the Style box (or press Ctrl+Shift+S), type the alias, and press Enter to apply the style. After you have created your alias, both the full name and the alias appear in the style box list.

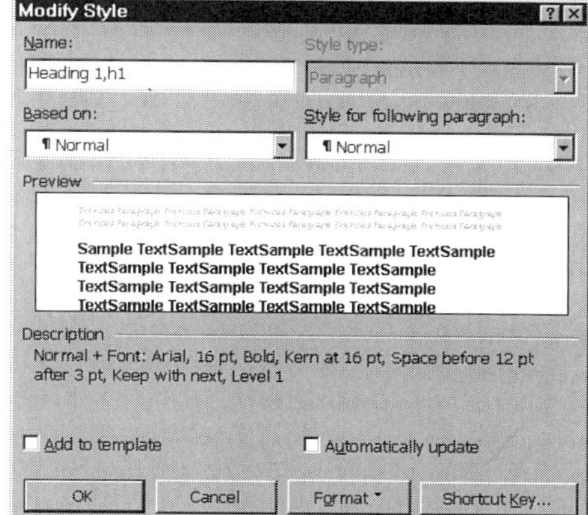

FIGURE 10.8
By adding the comma and the alias, you create a shortcut to reference the style when you use the style box.

Using Keyboard Shortcuts to Apply Styles

Assigning keyboard shortcuts to styles is particularly helpful if you work with a lot of styles or if you repeatedly assign the same styles to your documents. Instead of scrolling through the Styles drop-down list on the Formatting toolbar, you can simply arrow to the text you want to change and press the shortcut. Using this method for applying styles, you can format a long document in a very short time. If you're a touch typist, you'll wonder how you ever used styles before learning this simple trick.

In the Modify Style dialog box (choose Format, Style, Modify), you can click the Shortcut Key button to display the Customize Keyboard dialog box, shown in Figure 10.9, in which you can define a keyboard shortcut for a style.

Shortcut keys are key combinations created by holding down Alt, Ctrl, or Shift (or any combination of these) while you type an alphanumeric or punctuation character. The built-in shortcut keys in Word all have one part. Each shortcut is a single key combination such as Ctrl+F. Word doesn't limit you to one-part shortcut keys. You can also create two-part shortcut keys, something that's very useful when creating shortcuts for styles.

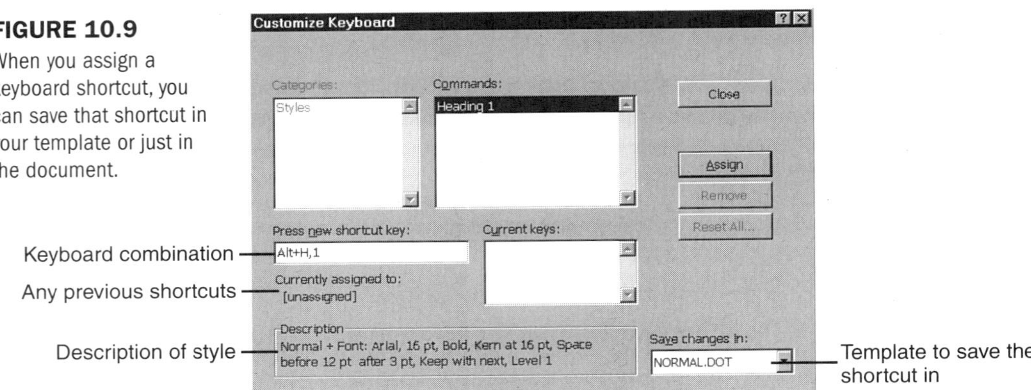

FIGURE 10.9
When you assign a keyboard shortcut, you can save that shortcut in your template or just in the document.

To create a two-part shortcut key, follow these steps:

1. Select a style (such as Heading 1) in the Style dialog box, choose Modify, and then click the Shortcut Key button.
2. In the Customize Keyboard dialog box (refer to Figure 10.9), place the insertion point in the Press New Shortcut Key box and press Alt+H; then press 1. The dialog box displays Alt+H,1 as the shortcut key.
3. Click Assign to save the shortcut key.
4. In a similar manner, create Alt+H,2 for the Heading 2 style, Alt+H,3 for the Heading 3 style, and so on. When you're finished creating shortcut keys, click Close, OK, and Close to save all your changes.

When you're working with a document, assign one of these styles to a paragraph by pressing Alt+H followed by a number (don't type the comma).

Word has already created several keyboard shortcuts for you. The top five most commonly used styles already have keyboard shortcuts associated with them, and are identified in Table 10.1.

Table 10.1 Predefined Shortcuts for Styles

Style	Shortcut
Heading 1	Alt+Ctrl+1
Heading 2	Alt+Ctrl+2
Heading 3	Alt+Ctrl+3
List Bullet	Ctrl+Shift+L
Normal	Ctrl+Shift+N

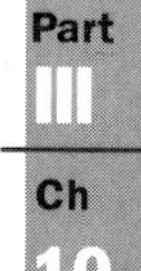

Setting a Style to Always Follow Another Style

Often, as you are working in a document, you'll find that you want one particular style to always follow another style. For example, perhaps your company frequently uses Heading 2 style for section headings and Body style for the text that follows. Instead of manually applying the body style every time you add the Heading 2 style, you can assign a following style so that Body style always follows Heading 2 style.

1. Select the text containing the style for which you want to add a following style.
2. Click Format, Style and press the Modify button in the Style dialog box. The Modify Style dialog box appears as shown in Figure 10.10.
3. Choose the style you want to follow the selected style from the Style for Following Paragraph drop-down list.
4. Click OK. Now, each time that you use a particular style (Heading 2, for example), it is followed by the style you assigned here (Body style, for example).

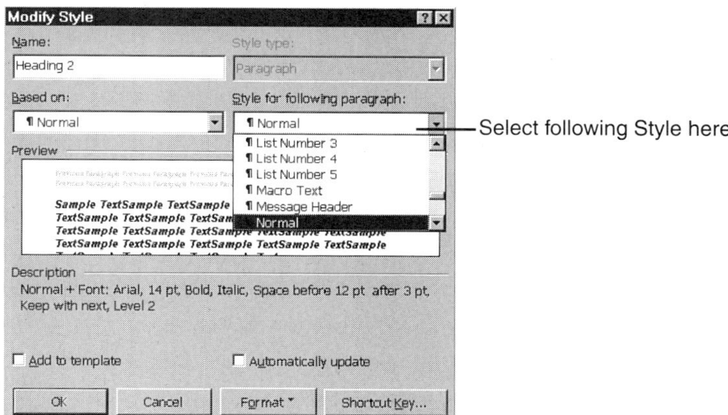

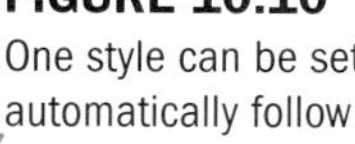

FIGURE 10.10
One style can be set to automatically follow another.

Saving Time with AutoFormat

Word's AutoFormat feature can save you time in two ways. The first way is to AutoFormat unformatted text such as text from email or an ASCII file. AutoFormat will apply the Word built-in styles to headings and text. Second, it can automatically make changes/corrections while you type. For example, it can change straight quotes to smart quotes, and 1/2 to ½.

Setting AutoFormat Options To define the AutoFormat options, choose Format, AutoFormat and click Options (or Tools, AutoCorrect, and then click the appropriate tab). Two tabs reference the AutoFormat feature: AutoFormat As You Type and AutoFormat.

The AutoFormat As You Type dialog box, shown in Figure 10.11, gives you control over what changes Word makes as you type. This is different from AutoCorrect in that AutoFormat focuses on symbol substitution and formats, and AutoCorrect is used primarily for word substitutions. By default, all the options are checked except for Headings. If you check Headings, when you enter text not followed by a period and press Enter twice, Word reformats that paragraph with the Heading 1 style. Of the other options here, some are routinely turned off by users. For example, if you leave Automatic Bulleted Lists and Automatic Numbered Lists turned on when you begin a paragraph with a bullet or number, Word begins the next paragraph with either a bullet or the next sequential number. If you have created a special style to deal with bulleted and numbered lists, you will want to turn this feature off. Many companies create documents that use straight quotes for the measurements inches and feet. To not have your straight quotes change into smart quotes, uncheck this option.

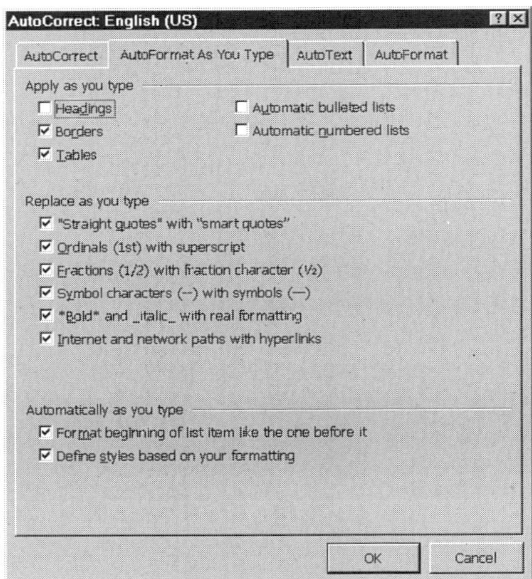

FIGURE 10.11
You can disable any of these features by deselecting them.

Applying an AutoFormat to an Unformatted Document Many times, you are faced with a document in which the author has used only Word default styles and you want to apply customized styles or a document that has no formatting at all such as a flat ASCII file. AutoFormatting such documents automatically applies styles and other features such as bulleted and numbered lists. Choose Tools, AutoCorrect to display the AutoCorrect dialog box. Click the AutoFormat tab to select the items you want Word to format automatically (see Figure 10.12).

If you are working on a document created by another user (especially one created in an application other than Word), these AutoFormatting options will not have been applied. Word, however, provides a simple way to format the document automatically.

To AutoFormat a document:

1. Choose Format, AutoFormat. The AutoFormat dialog box appears (see Figure 10.13).
2. Select General Document, Letter or Email from the drop-down list.
3. Choose to AutoFormat now or review each change. See the following section, "Accepting or Rejecting Each AutoFormat Change," for more details.
4. Click OK.

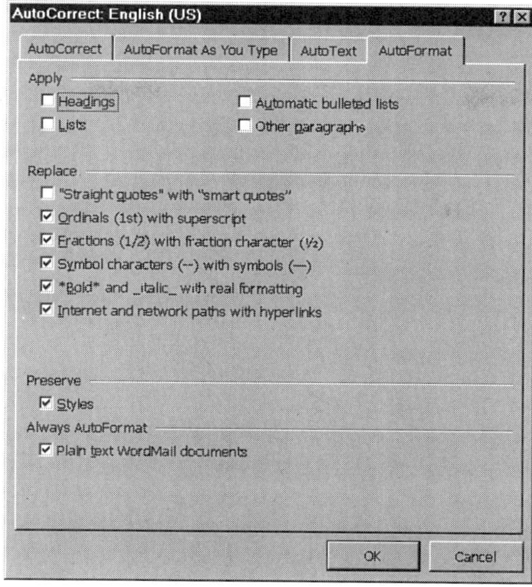

FIGURE 10.12
Control the behavior of the AutoFormat feature.

If you click the Options button in the AutoFormat dialog box, the AutoCorrect dialog will be displayed with the AutoFormat tab selected (as previously shown in Figure 10.12).

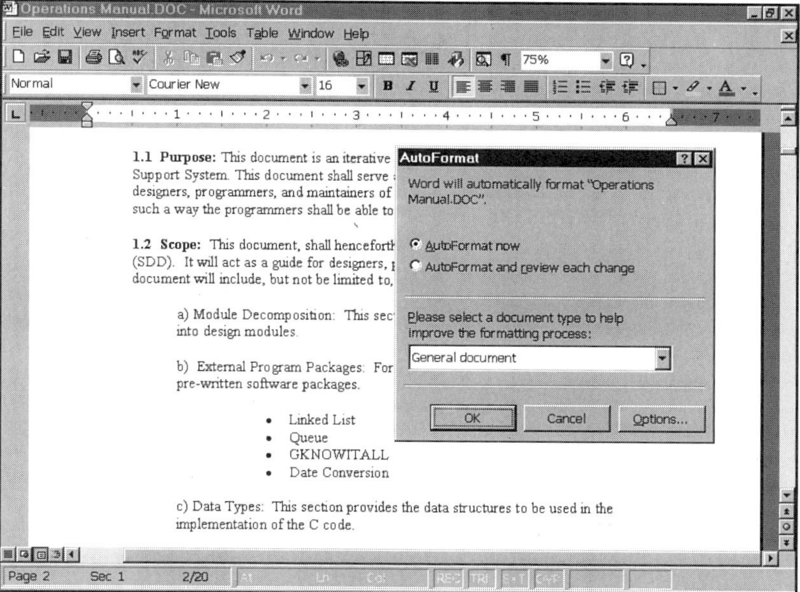

FIGURE 10.13
Select the behavior of AutoFormat here.

Accepting or Rejecting Each AutoFormat Change When you launch the AutoFormat feature, you have an opportunity to review each change that is made. All you have to do is check the AutoFormat and Review Each Change as shown in Figure 10.14.

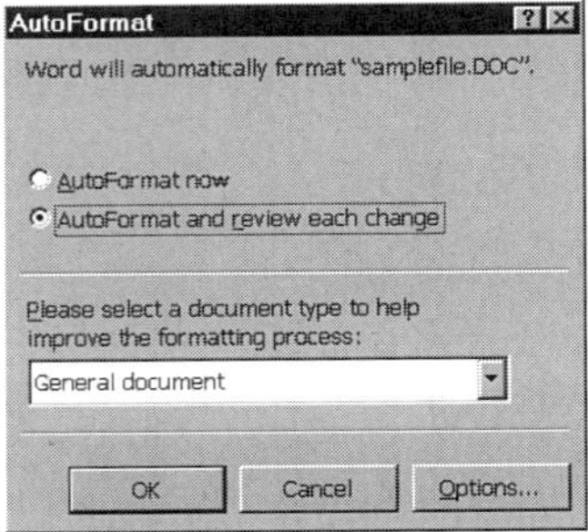

FIGURE 10.14
Reviewing changes gives you fine control over this feature.

After the AutoFormat is complete, you may go through the document change by change and accept or reject each one. The AutoFormat dialog box, shown in Figure 10.15, also gives you the option of rejecting all the changes or accepting all the changes.

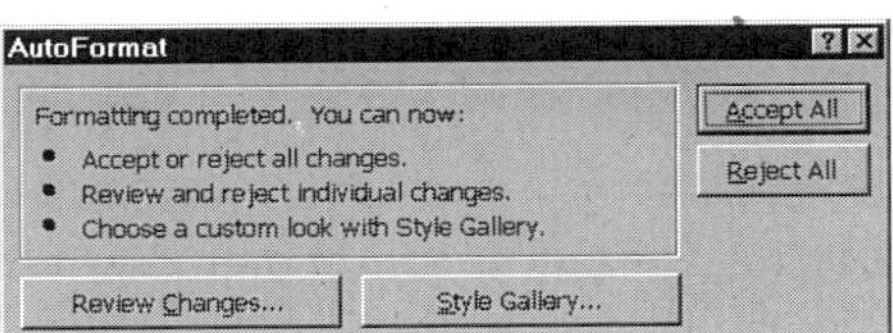

FIGURE 10.15
Your document is first reformatted, and then you choose to accept or reject each change.

If you cancel out of the AutoFormat dialog box, you reject all changes and your document is returned to its original state.

The AutoFormat dialog box is one of two places to reach the Style Gallery. The other place to access the Style Gallery is in the Themes dialog box. The Style Gallery used to be available through the Format menu, but has been moved in Word 2000 and is no longer in the Format menu. As you recall (if you are a longtime Word user), the Style Gallery provides a way of previewing the effects of applying a template to your document. For more details about the Style Gallery, see "Previewing a Template" later in this chapter.

Getting the Most Out of Word Templates

Templates are used to create a standardized look across a number of documents. Each built-in template contains formatting features specific to its use. For example, the memo templates contain the appropriate margins, tabs, address information for memo creation. If you want to create a report but don't want to spend the time to customize all of Word's styles yourself, you could apply one of the report templates and Word will have altered the appearance of the built-in styles for you. Templates provide you a place to store your own styles, toolbars, macros, and

AutoText. By storing these features in a template, can apply the template to any future documents you may create, saving you time when formatting and working in your document.

Local Versus Global Templates

Word has two types of templates: global and local. The key differences between the two types of templates are that

- Global templates—such as the Normal template—are available to every document. This means that styles, macros, toolbars, keyboard shortcuts, menus, and AutoText entries saved in the Normal template are available to all documents. The Normal template is the default document template.
- Local templates, on the other hand, are available only to those documents to which that template is applied. If you create a document based on any template other than the Normal template, the document has access to the styles and other components of that template and also (because the Normal template is global) to the contents of the Normal template.

NOTE Word's use of the word "Normal" is the cause of a great deal of confusion. There's a template named Normal and there's a style named Normal. Within the Normal template, and within all other templates, there's a style named Normal that defines the fundamental paragraph style used in a document. Unfortunately, you're stuck with these two uses of Normal. Just make sure when you come across the word, you understand whether it is a template or a style.

Local templates have precedence over global templates. This means that a document looks first for what it needs in the template to which it is attached; if it doesn't find what it needs there, it looks in any global templates that are loaded.

For example, suppose you've created a document based on the Elegant Report template that's supplied with Word. This template contains a Normal style that specifies the Garamond, 11-point font, whereas the Normal template (as supplied with Word) contains a Normal style that specifies the Times New Roman 12-point font. Because the local template (Elegant Report) takes precedence over the Normal template, the document uses Garamond as its Normal style font.

One very important point should be noted here—any change you make to the Normal (global) template has the potential of affecting all your documents based on Normal.dot. Because most documents are created based on Normal.dot and if you work within a workgroup, others may base their documents on Normal.dot. For this reason, you should base every document on a specific local template customized to your needs and, with few exceptions, modify only local templates. When you're tempted to modify your Normal template, do so only if you want that change to affect every document. For example, if you want to change your base font for all your documents from Times New Roman to Century Schoolbook, you would change the Normal template.

Although a document is typically based on a local template and has access to the Normal template, it can have access to other templates as well. To make any template temporarily global, so that all documents have access to it, you can load that template, as described in "Working with Global Templates" later in this chapter.

This technique is often useful when you need to run a macro that's in a template different from the one on which your current document is based.

Word's Built-In Templates

Microsoft provides a variety of special-purpose templates in addition to the Normal template. One way to create a document based on a specific Word template is to choose File, New. The New dialog box presents you with the options for creating both new documents and new templates. This dialog box will not be displayed if you just click the New button or use the keyboard shortcut. In fact, if you create document without going through the menu, your document will be based on Normal.dot. For example, after you choose the Letters & Faxes tab, the dialog box contains a list of templates, as shown in Figure 10.16.

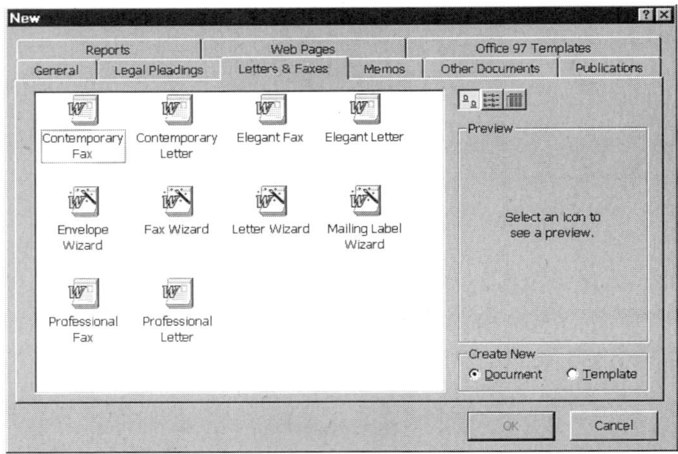

FIGURE 10.16
The Letters & Faxes tab of the New dialog box contains icons that access templates and wizards.

When you click any of the template or wizard icons, the Preview section of the dialog box shows you an example of what a document based on that template or wizard will look like. Double-click a template icon to begin creating a document based on that template. Depending on which template you choose, you'll probably see much more than just an empty Word page.

Additional templates are available through Help, Office on the Web.

Previewing a Template

To see what a specific document will look like if you attach a different template to it, choose Format, Theme and click Style Gallery. You might reasonably expect the choice to be named Template Gallery rather than Style Gallery because you actually use it to view the effect of templates. You also might reasonably expect the Style Gallery to be found under the format menu, or in a dialog box dealing with either style or templates, but instead you find the Style Gallery in the Theme dialog box (a change in Word 2000).

The Style Gallery dialog box shows a reduced version of the current document in the pane at the right and a list of templates at the left (see Figure 10.17). You can choose to view your document with the template attached or an example document. If you are selecting a template for a blank document, choose the Style Samples option.

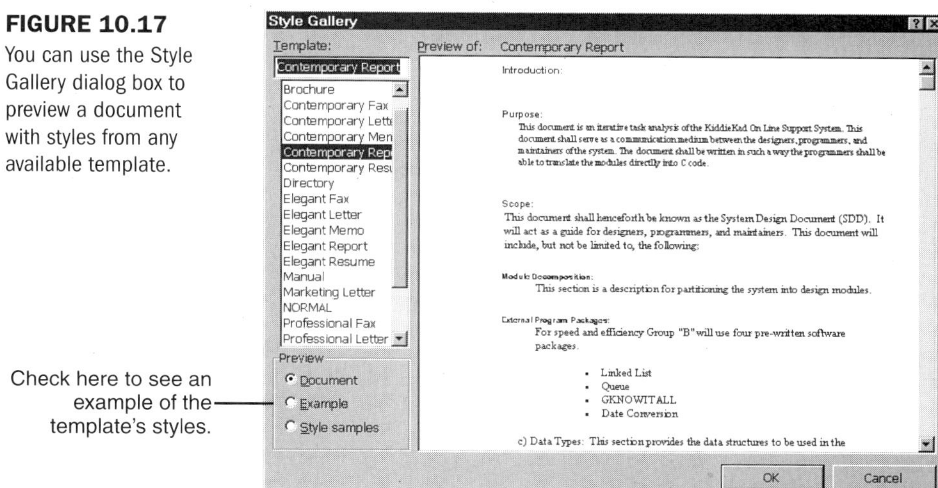

FIGURE 10.17
You can use the Style Gallery dialog box to preview a document with styles from any available template.

Check here to see an example of the template's styles.

If, in the Style Gallery, you like the sample document with styles attached from another template, click OK to use those styles.

Otherwise, click Cancel to close the dialog box without making any changes to the document.

Often you will want to start a document with a different template than Normal.dot. To see a sample document using the template styles, check Example at the bottom left of the Style Gallery dialog box.

Creating New Templates

Templates can be used for short documents as well as for long documents. Often a company will have two letterheads. On one, the company logo and information is placed at the top of the page. On the other, the logo and information run down the left side of the page. If the information is at the top of the page, it is easy enough to use Normal.dot and just press Enter enough times to make everything line up and type all the text from scratch each time. It's repetitious but not difficult. On the second letterhead, it's much more difficult to re-create the page for every letter. In both instances, creating a template will save you time. Because a template contains page setup information, styles, and Autotext, you don't have to re-create the same look each time.

You can create a template from scratch, or based on an existing template. The process is similar in each case.

To create a new template from scratch or based on another template, follow these steps:

1. Choose File, New to display the New dialog box.
2. Select either Blank Document or the template on which you want to base your new template.
3. In the Create New area, click Template and then click OK.
4. Word displays a blank screen; the left end of the Title bar contains Template1 - Microsoft Word.

   That's your clue to the fact that you're working with a template rather than with a document. With this screen displayed, you can add any of the template components listed previously in this chapter, such as boilerplate text.

To create a new template based on an existing document, open the document and choose File, Save As. Click the Save As Type drop-down list and choose Document Template (*.dot). Word automatically opens your Templates folder. Save the new template there or in a folder of your choice. See the next section for more information on storing templates in the Templates folder.

You should consider saving new templates in the default Templates folder, or in one of that folder's subfolders. To locate your templates, simply choose Tools, Options, and click the File Locations tab.

Where Templates Are Stored

On a typical single-user machine, templates are stored in C:\Windows\Application Data\Microsoft\Templates. If user profiles are set up through Windows at your worksite, your templates will be stored in C:\Windows\Profiles\<*username*>\Application Data\Microsoft\Templates. Custom workgroup templates are stored in the same folders but on a network-based machine. A network location can be set up to provide common templates for use throughout a company. Typically, workgroup locations allow for read-only sharing.

You can save custom templates you create in the Templates folder or one of its subfolders. If you do so, these templates are displayed in the New Office Document dialog box, so that you can easily choose them.

You can also create a subfolder for your custom templates. This separates the templates provided by Microsoft from those you create. It also makes it easier to locate your custom templates, because they are all stored in one location. To create a subfolder for your custom templates,

1. Choose File, Save As when you are ready to save your template.

2. Click the new folder icon and type the name of the folder you are creating.
3. Type a name for your new template and then click Save.

Now the folder appears as a tab in the New dialog box. If you create a new folder under the Templates folder and don't save your template, the new folder will not appear as a tab in the File, New dialog box.

If you are part of a Windows 98 and Windows NT workgroup, you can use the Systems Policy Editor to define default file locations–including those for templates–for all workgroup members. Refer to Que's *Platinum Edition Using Windows 98* for the steps to change these settings.

Word provides for storing two sets of templates: user templates and workgroup templates. *User templates* are usually stored in the default folders and subfolders on each user's computer. *Workgroup templates*, on the other hand, are stored on a network disk drive that is available to all workgroup members. Workgroup templates offer several advantages, such as

- Documents created by all workgroup members have a consistent format.
- All workgroup members have access to sophisticated templates created by experienced colleagues.

There is no default location for workgroup templates established in Word. To set that location, choose Tools, Options, File Locations. Select Workgroup templates, click Modify, and then use the Modify Location dialog box to navigate to the location of the workgroup templates as shown in Figure 10.18.

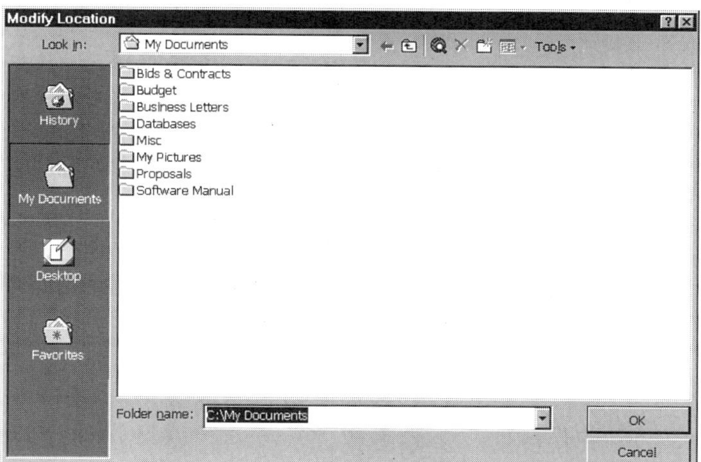

FIGURE 10.18
You can modify the default directories where your various files are stored.

Alternative Storage Locations for Template Contents

The preceding pages of this section have concentrated on what templates can contain and how Word uses the contents of templates. To complete the picture, you should understand that just because a template may contain certain items (such as AutoText entries and macros), those items are not necessarily stored only in the template; they may be stored elsewhere.

Although macros are usually stored in templates, they may also be saved in documents. Here's where a document accesses various items:

- Macros—These are stored in the document itself, in the attached local template, in the global Normal template, and in any loaded temporary global templates.
- AutoText Entries—These are stored in the attached local template, in the global Normal template, and in any loaded temporary global templates.
- Boilerplate Text and Graphics—These are stored in the template used to create the document. If you attach a template that contains text and graphics after you create a document, the text and graphics from the newly attached template are not inserted into your document.
- Custom Menus, Shortcut Keys, and Toolbars—These are stored in the attached local template, in the global Normal template, and in any loaded temporary global templates.
- Default Page Settings—These are stored in the template used to create the document. Page settings in a template that is subsequently attached to a document (and in any temporary global templates) are ignored.
- Document Text and Graphics—These are stored in the document file.
- Styles—These are stored in the document itself, copied from the template from which the document was created, and also from the global Normal template. If a different template is subsequently attached, you can choose between retaining the original styles or replacing them with the styles in the new template. Any styles in loaded temporary global templates are ignored.

Modifying Templates

There will be many times when you will want to modify a template. For example, you might want to modify a custom business letter template you've created if your company changes its letterhead or when you need to update some of the boilerplate text.

Templates are as easily modified as other files. Simply open the template and make any necessary modifications to it. There are, however, two important factors to keep in mind when you modify templates:

- First, any modifications to the formatting in the Template should be done at the style level. For example, if you want to increase the spacing between paragraphs to 6 points, change the Normal style in your template and all your new documents will reflect that change. If you make the same change to any boilerplate text in the template, that change affects only the boilerplate text. That change cannot be used retroactively, so only new documents reflect the change and the change will not be applied to any new text that is added to the document.
- Second, only style changes may be applied to previously created documents. The trick is to decide whether you want those style changes to affect only new documents created with the template or whether you want the template style changes to be reflected in files that were previously created with that template.

To determine whether style changes will apply to new documents created with the modified template or will be applied to all files that were created with the template before it was modified:

1. Choose Tools, Templates and Add-Ins (see Figure 10.19).
2. Confirm that the template displayed is the template you want to base your document on. If you want to attach a different template, click the Attach button and select the appropriate template from one of the folders listed. For more information on attaching templates, please see "Attaching a Different Template" later in this chapter.
3. If you want your style changes to affect previously created documents when those documents are opened, check the Automatically Update Document Styles check box. You would also check this box when you want a newly attached template's styles to override the styles currently being used.

If you check Automatically Update Document Styles as shown in Figure 10.19, all new documents will reflect the change and previously created files will reflect the changes as soon as you open them. Whether or not you use this feature is directly dependent on your work environment. For example, if you are archiving legally binding documents, you want them to be identical to the published copy when you retrieve them. You would not want to have the styles automatically update. On the other hand, if your company has distributed a modified version of a template you've been using to create a business proposal containing multiple documents, you would want those changes to appear in every document on which the modified template is based. This ensures that all the documents in the business proposal maintain a unified appearance.

FIGURE 10.19
Check Automatically Update Document Styles to have styles reflected in a previously created document.

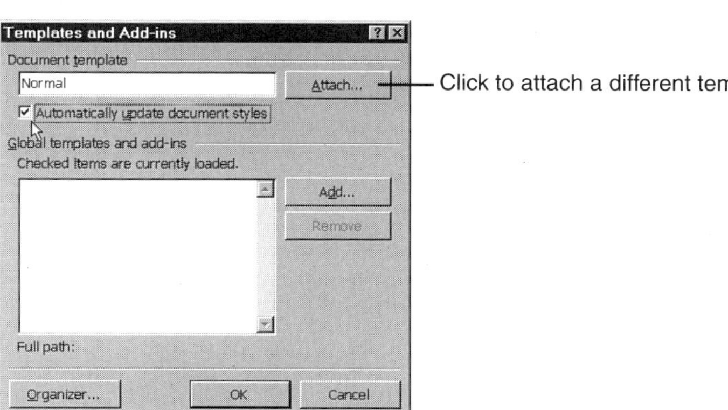

You can choose to have the styles update for only one document by going to the Templates and Add-Ins dialog box and checking Automatically Update Document Styles. Open the document. Return to the Templates and Add-Ins dialog box and uncheck Automatically Update Document Styles.

Attaching and Using Custom Templates

If you have been storing your custom templates in the default template folder, when you choose File, New your custom templates appear with the Word built-in templates. If you have stored your templates elsewhere, you must navigate to that folder and select the appropriate template. The following sections will explain how to do this.

Attaching a Different Local Template to a Document Suppose you start working on a document based on one template and then decide to use a different template. Choose Tools, Templates and Add-Ins to display the Templates and Add-Ins dialog box, such as that shown in Figure 10.19. A document can have one local template attached to it at a time.

To replace the current local template with another, you attach a different template to the document. When you do so, you can use styles, AutoText entries, macros, custom toolbars and menus, and shortcut keys in the new template; any boilerplate text and graphics, and any page settings (such as margins) in the new template, are not applied to the document.

1. Click Attach to open the Attach Template dialog box that lists several subfolders (each of which contains specialized templates and wizards) together with the Normal template and any other templates in your Templates folder as shown in Figure 10.20.

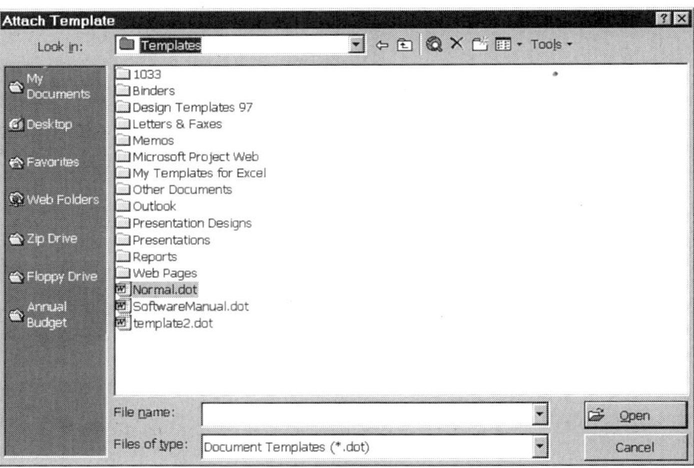

FIGURE 10.20
The Attach Template dialog box allows you to select a different template for your document.

2. Navigate to the template you want, and double-click that template (or click Open). The Attach Template dialog box closes and the Templates and Add-Ins dialog box reappears with the new template name in the Document Template text box.
3. At this point, you have a choice. Templates, as you know, contain styles that control paragraph and character formatting. Do you want the styles in the new template you're attaching to replace the styles in the original template (assuming they have the same names), or do you want to retain the styles from the original template? If you leave the Automatically Update Document Styles check box unchecked, styles in the new template don't affect the document. If you check this box, styles in the new template determine the format of existing text and any new text you subsequently add to the document.

NOTE The Organizer button at the bottom of the Templates and Add-Ins dialog box provides access to a dialog box in which you can copy styles, macros, AutoText entries, and toolbars from one document or template to another. For more details about the Organizer, please see "Copying Styles Across Documents" and "Copying Features Across Templates" later in this chapter.

4. Click OK to attach the new template to the document.

TIP If you forget to check the Automatically Update Document Styles check box before attaching the new template and want your styles to be updated with the styles from the new template, reopen the Templates and Add-Ins dialog box and check that option.

Figures 10.21 and 10.22 show the results of this process. Figure 10.21 shows a document with the Normal.dot attached. Figure 10.22 shows the same document with the user-created SoftwareManual.dot attached.

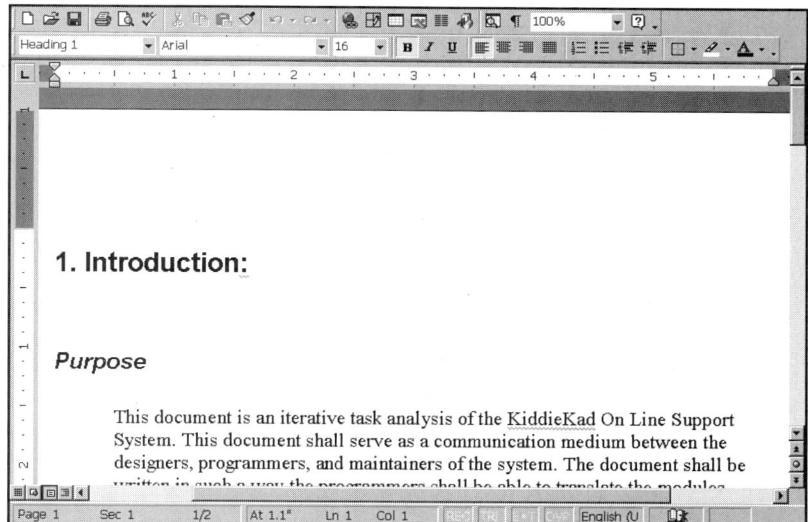

FIGURE 10.21
A document created with the styles in the Normal.dot.

Working with Global Templates

Although each document is based on one template and also has access to the Normal template, you may sometimes need to use macros, toolbars, or AutoText entries from other templates. For example, you are writing a client a letter that contains an informal proposal. You want to speed up your text entry by using the AutoText entries you have already set up in SoftwareManual.dot. You can do so by making SoftwareManual.dot temporarily global. Choose Tools, Templates and Add-Ins to display the Templates and Add-Ins dialog box shown in Figure 10.23. As before, the Document Template box shows the name of the template on which the document is based.

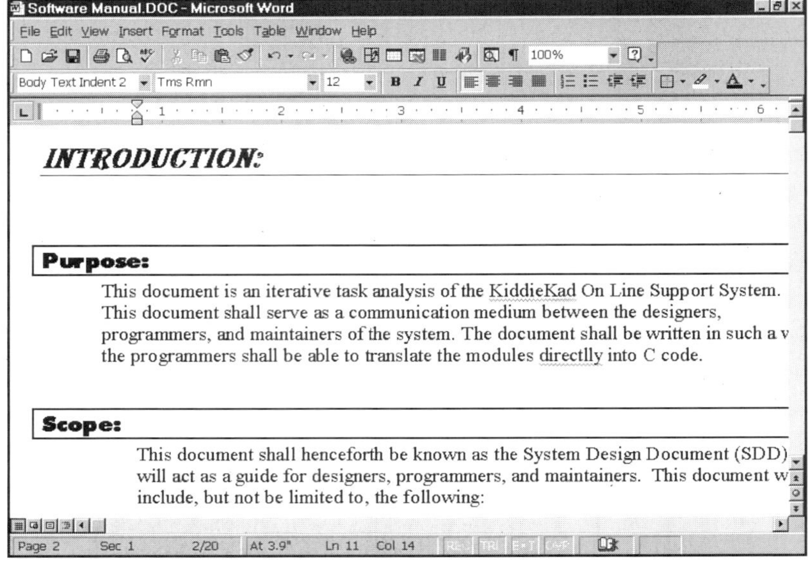

FIGURE 10.22
The same document after the SoftwareManual.dot was applied.

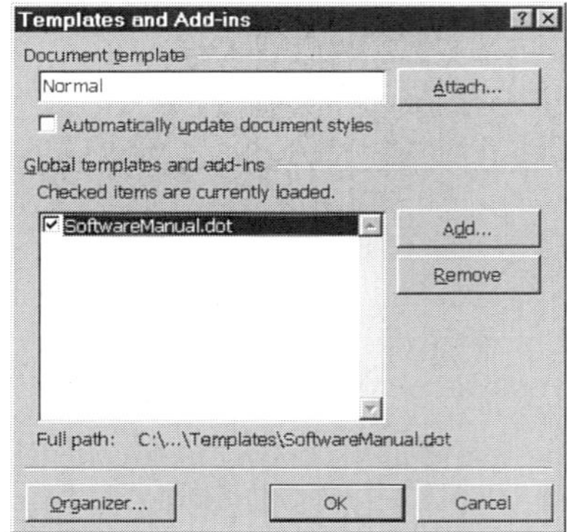

FIGURE 10.23
The Global Templates and Add-Ins list box shows the names of those templates and add-ins that are currently loaded.

All templates and add-ins in the Word Startup folder are loaded into memory automatically whenever you start Word. These templates and add-ins appear at the top of the Global Templates and Add-Ins list. The Word Startup folder is normally C:\Windows\Application Data\Microsoft\Word\STARTUP. You can locate your startup folder by choosing Tools, Options, and selecting the File Locations tab of the Options dialog box. You can make any of the templates and add-ins unavailable by unchecking their check boxes.

But what if the template you want to make global is not listed, as is the case in the preceding example? Follow these steps to locate it:

1. Choose Tools, Templates and Add-Ins.
2. Click Add to display the Add Template dialog box.

3. Navigate to find the required template, and then double-click to select it and return to the Templates and Add-Ins dialog box, which now contains the new template with its name checked.
4. You can add as many templates as you want to the list, and you can check and uncheck their names to select those you actually want to load as global templates.
5. You can remove a template or add-in from the list by selecting its name, and then clicking Remove (refer to Figure 10.23).

After you make a template global, all documents have access to macros, toolbars, and AutoText entries in that template during your current Word session.

CAUTION

Loaded global templates occupy memory. To avoid running low on memory, load only those templates you need to use globally. Unload global templates when you don't need them.

How Word Resolves Template Conflicts

As you've seen, a document is usually based on a local template, has access to the global Normal template, and may have access to several other temporary global templates. There may be conflicting settings or definitions in these templates; for example, an AutoText entry may be defined differently in two or more templates.

Word resolves such conflicts by looking in templates in the following order, and using the first entry it finds for the setting or definition:

1. The template on which the current document is based.
2. The Normal template.
3. Temporary global templates. If there are two or more global templates, Word looks at them in the order they're listed in the Templates and Add-Ins dialog box.
4. Add-ins.
5. The Word application layer (standard menus, commands, and toolbars).

For example, template XYZ and template ABC have customized toolbars. You create a document based on XYZ because that template has the boilerplate text you'll be working with. Template ABC has a few styles that you want to use, so you make it available globally. Your document has access to the toolbar from template XYZ. If you have a Heading 1 style in both XYZ and ABC, the heading from XYZ would be the one used in your document because the template that the document was based on (in this case, XYZ) has precedence over global templates (Normal and ABC) attached to the document.

Sharing Styles and Templates

To share styles and templates with other users, the styles and templates must be saved on a mutually accessible disk drive. Remember, styles are saved either with a document or in a template, so that document or template must be accessible to other users. As discussed earlier, choose Tools, Options and click the tab File Locations to set up a folder for Workgroup Templates. You could store shared documents in the same folder or a separate folder depending upon your organization's needs.

Copying Styles Across Documents

If you have been creating styles and saving them with the documents, you may encounter a situation in which you want to use a style you created for another document. Instead of reinventing the wheel, you can easily copy a style from one document to another by using the Organizer as shown in Figure 10.24.

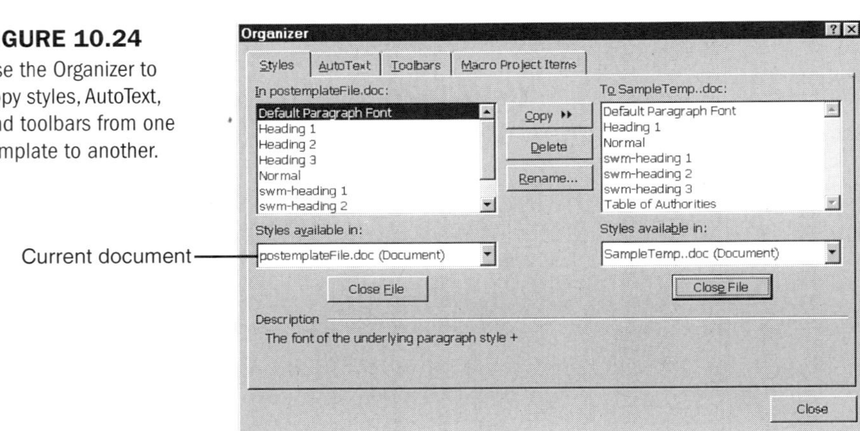

FIGURE 10.24
Use the Organizer to copy styles, AutoText, and toolbars from one template to another.

Use these steps to copy styles (and other items) between documents:

1. Choose Tools, Templates and Add-Ins.
2. Click the Organizer button. The Organizer dialog box appears (as shown in Figure 10.24).
3. On the left is the document you are working in. On the right is the document template. Click the right Close File button.
4. Now an Open File button is presented to you. Click it and select the document that contains the styles you want to use.
5. Back in the Organizer dialog box, select the styles you want to use in the right list box and click the Copy button to copy them to your current document.
6. Click Close when you have copied the styles that you need.

Copying Features Across Templates

The Organizer shown in Figure 10.24 can also be used to copy more than just styles from one template to another. It can also be used to copy AutoText, toolbars, and macros. To copy these additional features,

1. Choose Tools, Templates and Add-Ins.
2. Click the Organizer button.
3. On the left is the document or template you are working on. On the right is the document template or the base template. Click the right Close File button.
4. Now an Open File button is presented to you. Click it and select the template that contains the features you want to add.
5. Back in the Organizer dialog box, select the appropriate tab, the desired item in the right list box, and then click the Copy button to copy them to your current document.
6. Click Close when you have copied the features that you need.

Using Themes

Themes are a new feature in Word 2000. They are designed to help you create a unified look for documents destined for electronic publication. Themes coordinate the graphic elements of a document, such as background color, bullets and horizontal line, and the text-formatting elements that include heading and body text styles. Although templates provide such features as AutoText entries, custom toolbars, macros, menu settings, and shortcut keys, themes do not.

Exploring the Built-In Themes

Applying a theme to your document is similar to applying a template.

1. Choose Format, Theme. The Theme dialog box appears as shown in Figure 10.25.
2. Scroll through the list of Themes and choose one that is appropriate for your document. You can preview a Theme by selecting it and reviewing it in the Preview pane.

NOTE Not all of Word's themes are loaded during a standard installation. If you attempt to use a theme that is not stored on your computer, you will be prompted to install it from the Office CD.

3. If you want this theme to be the default for all new documents, click the Set Default button.

You can also choose to apply brighter colors, animate some backgrounds, or apply a background to your document by marking the check boxes in the lower-left corner of the Theme dialog box.

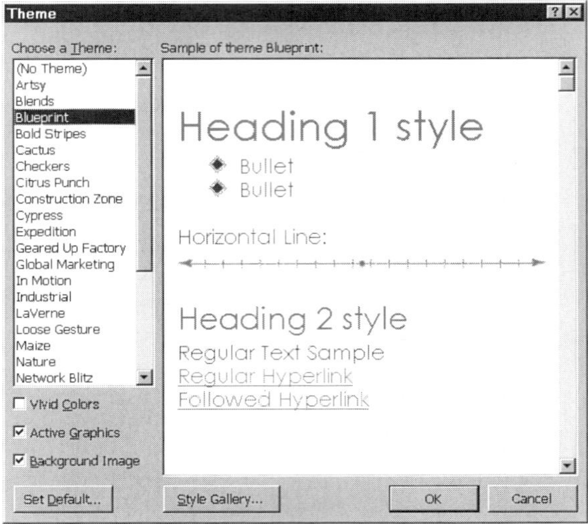

FIGURE 10.25
Themes are an easy way to apply color and animation to your electronic documents.

When to Apply Themes to Your Document

Because of their reliance on color and movement, themes are most appropriate for documents that will be viewed electronically. Themes provide a quick and easy way to dress up Web pages. However, Word does not support animation in Web graphics, so to see the animation of theme graphics you must view the document in a Web browser.

If you have FrontPage 4.0 or later installed, the FrontPage themes are available to your Word documents as well. Additional themes are available by choosing Help, Office on the Web or visiting `http://officeupdate.microsoft.com`.

Problem/Solution—Creating a Custom Template

Here is a real-world example of how to create a custom template. Suppose you have just joined the document development team in your company. Its primary function is to standardize all the documents produced by your company. Your task is to automate Word to make a lot of the mundane and time-consuming formatting tasks easier and faster.

First, review the types of documents you are responsible for and the formatting requirements of each document. What page settings are needed? What headings and paragraph styles does the company require on these documents? Are they the same for all documents or are there groups of documents that require unique formatting?

In this example, the first document to be tackled is the company's business proposal. Currently, each department has its own variation of the proposal and there is an urgent need to standardize this document throughout the company.

It's important that you determine the correct format for company business proposals. This includes the margin settings, headers and footers, font type and size, and so on. Then you need to determine whether there are any standard features, such as the company logo, or text, such as the company's mission statement, that need to be included in each proposal. After you've made a detailed list of the requirements, you are ready to create the proposal template:

1. Choose File, New and check Template in the Create New section of the New dialog box. If an existing Word template contains much of the formatting you require, select that template. Otherwise, select Blank Document. Then click OK. A template is created based on the document you select.
2. One of the first things you should establish are the page settings for the proposal. The easiest way to format the page settings, all at one time, is to use the Page Setup dialog box (choose File, Page Setup).
3. At this point, you may want to enter some preliminary text that will appear in each proposal, such as section headings or an outline of the major components found in each proposal.
4. You also might want to create any necessary headers and footers for the proposal—choose View, Header and Footer. You can create a single header and footer for the document, or apply headers and footers to each section of the proposal.

▶ **See** "Adding Custom Headers and Footers to Each Section," **p. 307**

Now you want to customize your styles so that the headings and text formats you intend to use are standardized. As discussed in the section "Mastering Styles" in this chapter, you need to decide whether you will be creating your own styles or modifying Word's built-in styles. The Style dialog box with modification options is shown in Figure 10.26.

Don't forget that you can assign a keyboard shortcut to your styles.

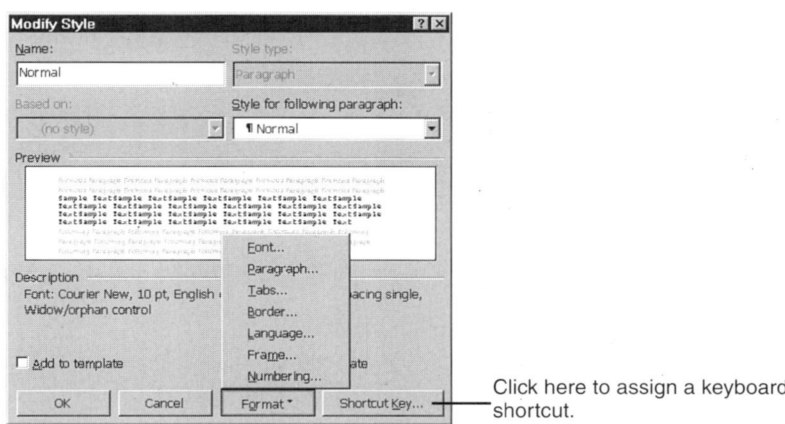

FIGURE 10.26
You can apply any of the paragraph-formatting features to a paragraph style.

After you have the formatting set up, you can start saving yourself keystrokes. Add any additional boilerplate text to your template. For example, if you always put your company's mission statement on the first page of a proposal, go ahead and add it to your template. When you create a new document based on this template, the mission statement will be there.

NOTE Just because you add text to the template doesn't mean you can't change it. You can edit the text for each client. And if a permanent change has occurred—maybe your company name has changed—you can edit the template to change it for all future proposals.

Another way to save keystrokes is to create AutoText entries. AutoText allows you to type a shortcut, and then press F3 and the full text appears. You can store plain or formatted text, tables, graphics, and other data in AutoText. To create AutoText, perform the following:

1. Type the text you want to save as AutoText.
2. Select the text.
3. Choose Insert, AutoText, AutoText. Now type the shorthand equivalent, click Add, and then OK.

TIP Remember that the AutoText entries you create are stored in this template. To use them from documents not based on this template, you must temporarily load this template as a global template.

Now continue to simplify your proposal creation. Note the repetitive tasks that you perform. Consider recording macros to automate those tasks and save the macros with the template.

▶ **See** "Getting Acquainted with VBA," to learn more about creating macros, **p. 105**

You may also want to create a custom toolbar for the features you use regularly during proposal creation. To create a custom toolbar, follow these steps:

1. Choose View, Toolbars, Customize.
2. Click the Toolbars tab and click the New button; the New Toolbar dialog box displays, as shown in Figure 10.27.

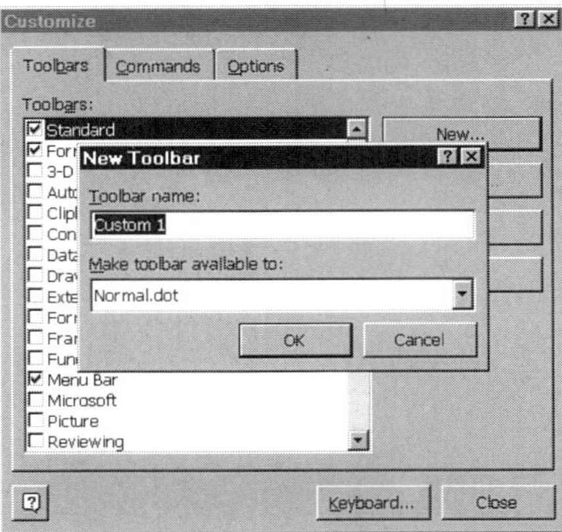

FIGURE 10.27
You can choose to which template the toolbar is saved.

3. Name your toolbar, and then click OK.

4. Add commands to your toolbar by dragging them from the Commands tab and dropping them on the toolbar.
5. Click Close.

At this point, you may want to add some graphics to your template. You can insert a picture clip from the Clip Gallery, add the company logo, incorporate a faint watermark behind the proposal text, or include some graphic chart in the template.

You can easily add a watermark to your template by using these steps:

1. Choose Insert, Picture, From File.
2. Navigate to the location of the picture and click Insert.
3. Right-click the Picture and choose Format Picture.
4. In the Picture tab, choose Color: Watermark.
5. In the Layout tab, choose Behind Text, and click the Advanced button.
6. In the Picture Position tab, turn off Move Object with Text; click OK; then click OK again to close the Format Picture dialog box.
7. As necessary, move and resize the picture so that it covers the text area of the page. Distortion is generally not objectionable in graphic watermarks.

Figure 10.28 shows the finished template.

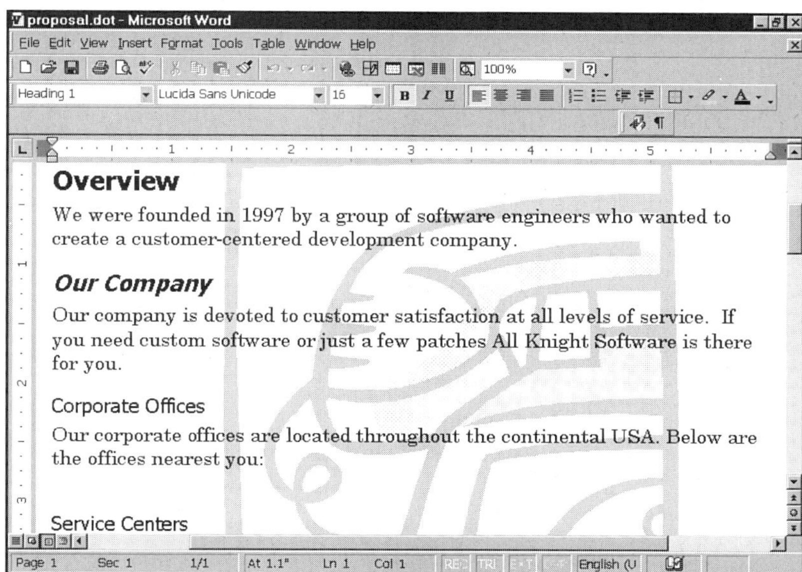

FIGURE 10.28
This template incorporates boilerplate text, modified Word styles, and a watermark.

Later, you realize that much of what you use on proposals is appropriate for corporate reports. You can copy styles, toolbars, macros, and AutoText from one template to another. You can create the corporate reports template using the same procedure you used for the proposal template. However, when you want to use something you've already created, access the Organizer to copy the features you want to incorporate:

1. Make either template the active document.
2. Choose Tools, Templates and Add-Ins.
3. Click Organizer. Close the Normal.dot template on the right side of the dialog box.
4. Open the other template on the right side of the Organizer dialog box.
5. Select an object you want to copy from the proposal template and click Copy to add the object to the corporate reports template. You'll need to repeat this for each item you want to use from the proposal template.

NOTE To remove styles, AutoText, toolbars, or macros from a template, click the Delete button in the Organizer dialog box.

CHAPTER 11

Making the Most of Your Page Layout

In this chapter

Word Document Building Blocks

A Word document can be thought of as being composed of basic building-block units. The smallest meaningful unit in Word is the *character*. Each character can have distinct font formatting, applied either directly or using a character style.

Font or character formatting includes font, point size, font style, font color, underline style, effects (strikethrough, superscript, and so on), character spacing, and text effects (blinking background, marching ants, and so on). Language, also, is a character-level format, although you'd never know it from where it shows up in Word's menus (Tools, rather than Format). You could, however, give each letter of a word a different language, although it is not clear why anyone would do that, except, possibly, in constructing ransom notes.

The next meaningful unit is the *paragraph*. There are some types of formatting that cannot vary within a paragraph, but each distinct paragraph in a document can differ. Included in this type of formatting are line spacing, alignment (left, center, right, and so on), outline level, indentation, paragraph spacing, widow/orphan control, line numbering, tabulations, hyphenation, and so on.

Paragraph formatting also includes formatting that's not accessible from the Paragraph dialog box, such as bullets and numbering, borders and shading (but not page borders), and paragraph style. See additional information about paragraph styles later in this section.

The next meaningful unit is the *section*. Section formatting is something many Word users are completely unaware of, quite simply because the most common document—the business letter—often needs just a single section. You won't find section formatting on the Format menu—at least not by name. Instead, section formatting attributes are assigned in selecting a variety of different formatting options. These include column formatting, margins, paper size, orientation (landscape versus portrait), headers and footers (which control page numbers), and more. Word users often are unaware that formatting they choose—such as page numbers (which are inserted in headers or footers)—actually is section formatting, as opposed to paragraph or document formatting.

The *document* level is located above the section level. Some attributes can vary *by* document, but not *within* a document. These attributes include document properties, file-sharing options, compatibility settings, track changes, merge-document status, some kinds of document protection, and so on.

Document Sections

Many users often are unaware that the formatting they apply to their documents is considered to be section formatting. In fact, some users are completely unaware of the sectional aspect of Word documents, and are often startled to find that applying three-column formatting results in the entire document adopting that format, rather than just the current paragraph. After you understand that the number of columns is a section format, then you know that everything in any given section of a Word document must have the same number of columns.

Section breaks contain section formatting. When you delete a section break, text above the break receives the section formatting of the section below the break. This is because a section break contains the formatting of the section that precedes it—much in the same way that each paragraph mark contains the formatting for the paragraph that precedes that mark. When you delete a section break, you are in effect merging two sections, and are giving the entire new section the formatting of the latter of the two sections.

In the previous section, we noted that paragraph formatting includes the paragraph style. As much as users might like the idea, you cannot embed section formatting into a style definition. To see the types of formatting that you can embed in a style definition, choose Format, Style, click the Modify button, and then click the Format button. The style definition includes all character (font) and paragraph formatting, but not section formatting. Therefore, you cannot create a two-, three-, or four-column format, and then assign it a style name, because columns are section attributes and not style attributes.

▶ **See** "Creating a Section 'Style,'" **p. 306**

Creating Sections Within a Document

Creating sections is simple. Choose Insert, Break, select any of the four different options under Section Break Types, as shown in Figure 11.1, and then click OK.

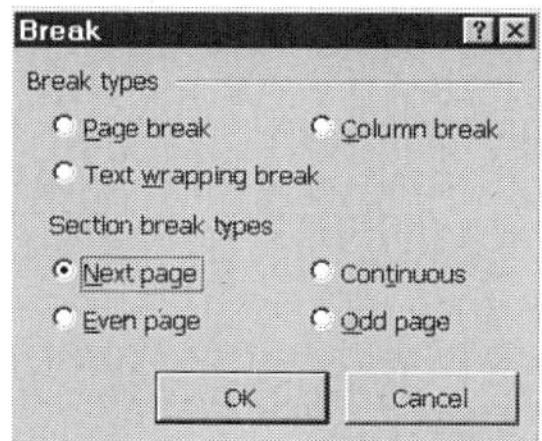

FIGURE 11.1
Don't use a section break when all you need is a regular page break.

Word has four different types of section breaks:

- Next Page—Ends the current page. Any numbering resumes on the following page with the next higher number.
- Continuous—Creates a new section that has no effect on page numbering.
- Even Page—Ends the current page. Page numbering in the next section jumps, if necessary, to the next higher even number.
- Odd Page—Ends the current page. Page numbering in the next section jumps, if necessary, to the next higher odd number.

The Next, Even, and Odd Page section breaks typically are used in multichapter documents with special page-numbering requirements.

▶ **See** "Page Numbering—Getting It Right," **p. 314**

The Continuous option typically is used when you have different section formatting within a single page—for example, when centering a heading across a multicolumn article.

Creating a Section "Style"

As previously mentioned, you cannot save section formatting as a style. However, if you want the utility of a section style, you can save a section break as an AutoText entry by following these steps:

1. Choose Tools, Options and click the View tab.
2. Turn on All Formatting Marks, and click OK.
3. Choose View, Normal.
4. Find the section break at the end of the section containing the formatting you want to reuse. Select the section break.
5. Choose Tools, AutoCorrect, AutoText tab. In Enter AutoText Entries Here, type a name for the format (for example, 2column, 3column, narrow margin, numbered, and so on), as shown in Figure 11.2.
6. Finally, click Add. The dialog box closes.

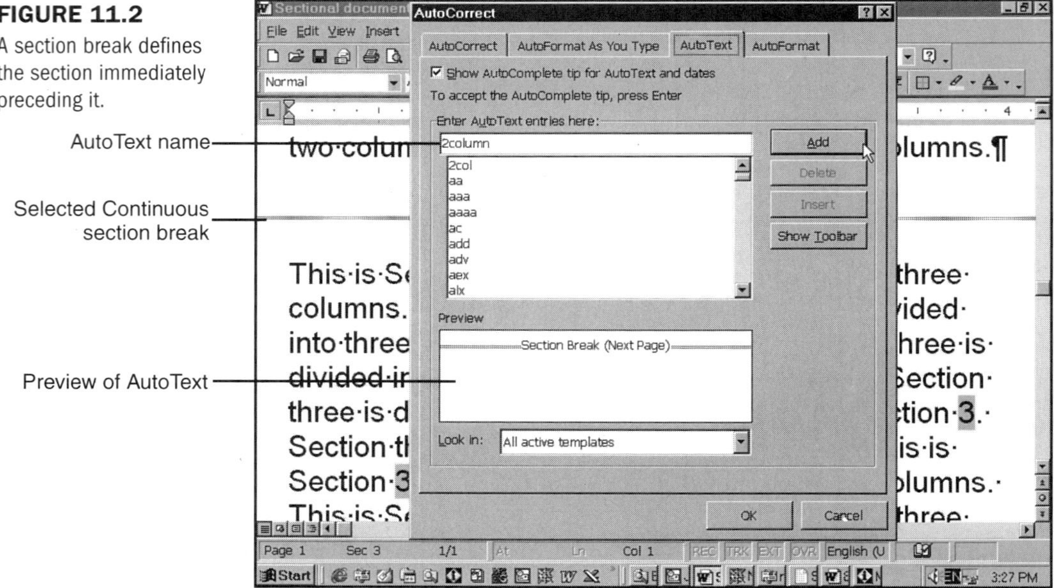

FIGURE 11.2
A section break defines the section immediately preceding it.

To use your new style, start by inserting a section break just above where you want the new formatting to take effect. The inserted section break prevents the formatting from affecting the text preceding the inserted style. Then follow these steps:

1. Move the insertion point to just below where you want the new section formatting to end.

2. Type the AutoText entry's name.
3. Press F3. If Word volunteers to complete the AutoText before you finish typing the name, you can press Enter instead of F3 the moment the AutoText ScreenTip appears.

Adding Custom Headers and Footers to Each Section

In many documents, uniform and identical headers and footers are exactly what you want. Sometimes, you might want different headers and footers, and sometimes, those differences cannot be accomplished using built-in options (for example, different first page or different odd/even pages). Creating separate document sections allows you to create unique headers and/or footers for individual sections.

Begin by choosing Insert, Break, Next Page (or Odd or Even, depending on your needs). Continuous is not a good choice for this exercise—when you have different headers and/or footers, the headers and footers for the later section show up on the page following the continuous section break. Insert a break at the end of each distinct section, recalling that a section break formats the text appearing before the break.

When you first insert a section break, the headers and footers for each new section are the same as the section that precedes it. To create different headers or footers for each section, you must first disconnect them. The best way to do this is to start at the end of the document and work your way to the top. Choose View, Header and Footer, which displays the Header and Footer toolbar.

Initially, each section's header and footer have Same As Previous turned on—except section 1, for which the Same As Previous button is grayed out (because there is no previous section).

Since this is a toggle (on/off) button, click the Same As Previous button to disconnect the displayed header or footer from the previous section's header or footer.

Next, click the Page Setup button and click the Layout tab, shown in Figure 11.3.

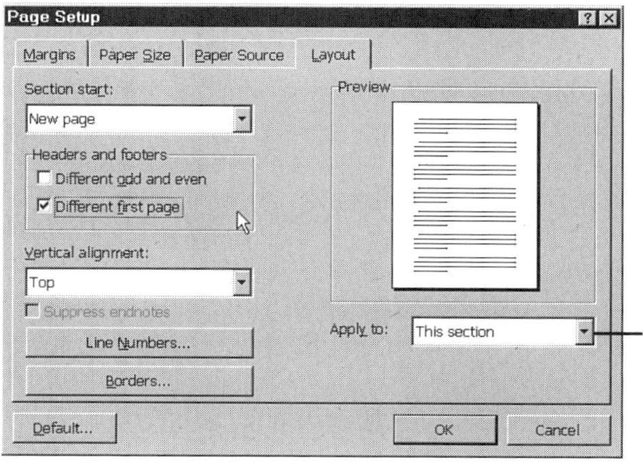

FIGURE 11.3
Page Setup Layout lets you determine how headers and footers, and therefore page numbers, flow.

You should consider a number of things when adding custom headers and footers:

- Do you want page numbers to flow continuously, or do you want numbering to start anew in each section? If you prefer the latter, do you want each section to begin on the next available page number (New Page), the next column (New Column), the next available odd page number (Odd Page), or the next available even page (Even Page)?
- Do you want headers and/or footers to be identical on every page of any given chapter or section? If so, then press Esc to close the dialog box.
- Do you want different headers and/or footers for odd and even pages? Some formats call for even page headers to be flush left, and odd page headers to be flush right. If you want different odd and even behavior, then choose the Different Odd and Even option (refer to Figure 11.3).
- Do you want to suppress headers and footers on the first page of each section? Or, perhaps you need to suppress the header and footer only on the very first page of the document—in which case, you need to remember to come back here and choose the Different First Page option when you get to section 1.
- If you want the same basic format for every section, then set Whole Document in the Apply To drop-down list, so you don't have to repeat this procedure for each and every header or footer.

When you're finished selecting the options for the current section, click OK. Then click the Show Previous button on the Header and Footer toolbar to move to the preceding section (remember you are working our way from bottom to top). Repeat the procedure—which consists of turning off Same As Previous, as needed, and enabling those Page Setup Layout features you need for this section.

NOTE Headers and footers can be disconnected separately. You can have the identical footer running throughout a document, and have distinct headers for each section. Therefore, if you want different headers *and* footers, you need to perform the disconnection for each header and footer.

After you have disconnected each header (or footer, or both), you should type the desired text into the header or footer area.

The Header and Footer toolbar offers additional resources for inserting page numbers, date, time, as well as a number of commonly used field codes. You also need to decide about alignment. Should your headers and footers be left, right, or center aligned? While in the header or footer areas, you can use normal formatting controls by using Word's regular toolbars and menus. You also can press Ctrl+A to select the entire header or footer.

▶ **See** "Ten of Word's Most Useful Fields," **p. 360**

Working with Section Page Numbering

For some kinds of documents—such as government reports—sections are numbered individually. For example, a common page numbering format is I-1, I-2, I-3, and so on, where the Roman numeral is the section or chapter number, and the number is the page number within that section. There are several techniques you can use to accomplish this kind of page numbering. An easy, low-maintenance approach is to tie numbering to the Heading style. This is a two-step process.

First, if you are using heading numbering, and have used a heading level as your section numbering component, you can tell Word to use that number in your page numbers. For example, assume that each section heading is formatted as Heading 1, and begins with

Section I

To obtain this result, choose Format, Style. Select Heading 1 from the Styles list and click the Modify button. Then choose Format, Numbering. Click the middle tab (Numbered), and select the format that shows I., II., III. (or whichever one is most similar), as shown in Figure 11.4.

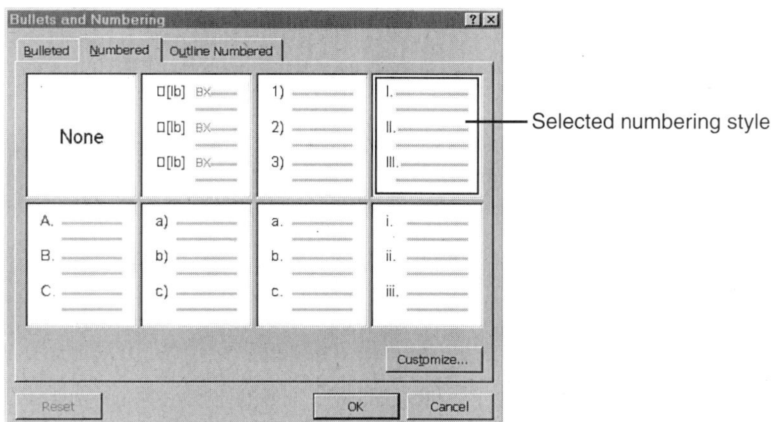

FIGURE 11.4
Assign a numbering style to Heading 1 to use for section numbering.

Click the Customize button. In the Number format field, delete the period after I. Move to before the I, and type `Section` (or `Chapter`, or whatever you prefer), for a result that looks similar to Figure 11.5. Choose a Number position and a Text position that you like, click OK twice, and then click Close.

Now, whenever you apply the Heading 1 style, you'll get the text `Section` followed by a Roman numeral. Be sure that you use Heading 1 style just once per section.

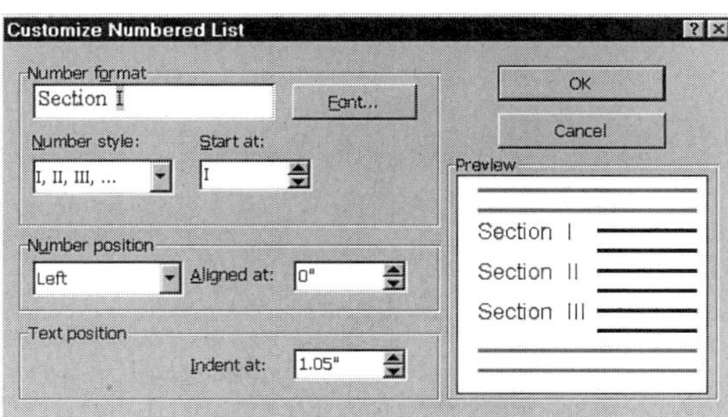

FIGURE 11.5
Use the Preview box in the Customize Numbered List dialog box to see what your Heading 1 headings will look like.

Now that you've created the proper section headings, follow these steps to create page numbers such as I-1, II-17, and so on:

1. Choose View, Header and Footer.

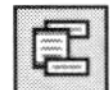

2. When you're working on a footer, click the Switch Between Header and Footer button on the toolbar. Find an appropriate spot in the footer, and type `Page 1` followed by a space.
3. Click the Insert Page Number button on the Header and Footer toolbar.
4. Choose Insert, Page Numbers from the menu toolbar, and click the Format button to display the Page Number Format dialog box shown in Figure 11.6.

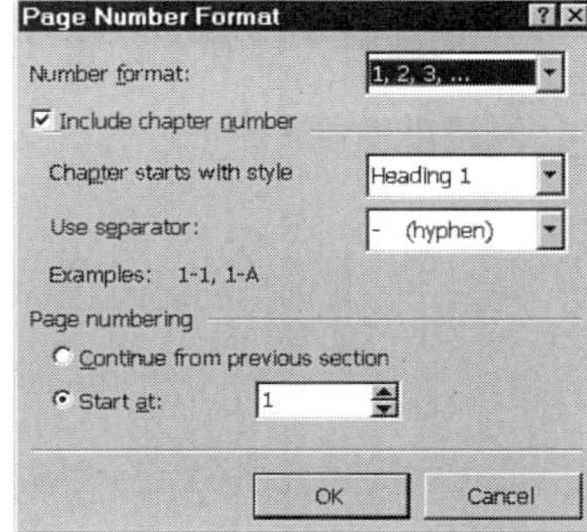

FIGURE 11.6
Use any of five separators between the section and page numbers.

5. Click the Include Chapter Number check box.
6. Use the Chapter Starts with Style drop-down box to select a heading level. Be sure that the setting you choose here matches the style name you use for chapter numbering (for example, Heading 1).
7. Select the desired separator and number format from the Use Separator drop-down list.
8. Set Start At to `1`.
9. Click OK and then choose Close in the Page Numbering dialog box. The page field you inserted into the header or footer should now display as `I-1` instead of `1`.

If you cannot use a heading style, you can use the section number field instead. Follow these steps:

1. Click in the header or footer in your document.

2. Click the Insert Page Number button on the Header and Footer toolbar.
3. Find an appropriate spot in the header or footer, and type `Page` followed by a space.
4. Rather than choosing Insert, Page Numbers, Format to include chapter numbers, position the insertion point just before the page number and type your separator (for example, -); then back up to just before the hyphen.
5. Choose Insert, Field.
6. In Categories, choose Numbering, and in Field Names, choose Section.
7. Click the Options button.

8. In the Formatting list, choose I, II, III, and then click Add to Field. Then type `\* ROMAN` in the field, as shown in Figure 11.7.
9. Click OK, and back in the Field dialog box, click OK again.

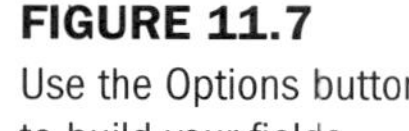

FIGURE 11.7
Use the Options button to build your fields.

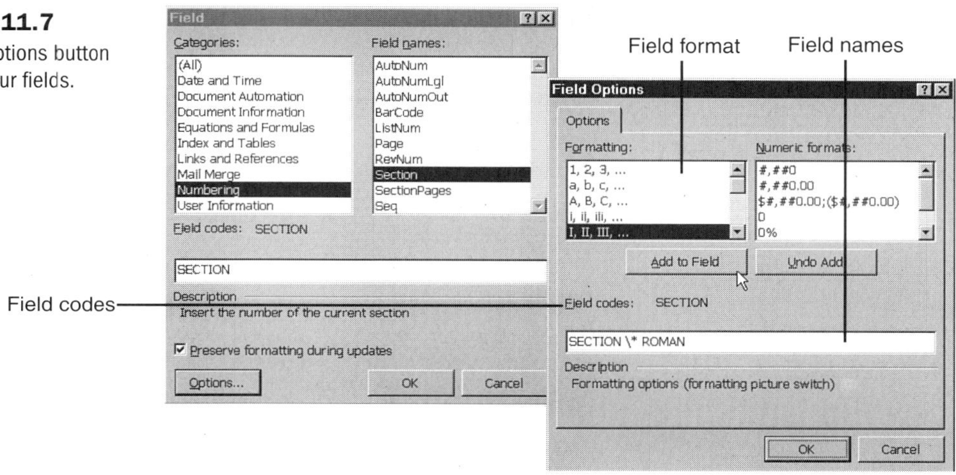

Part III
Ch 11

The result is a SECTION field inserted into the document header or footer.

Using the SECTION field approach means that you have to be careful about adding extraneous sections to your document. For example, suppose you have a landscape table in your document, which requires the insertion of two extra section breaks in the middle of a chapter or section. One section break is needed to begin the landscape section, and the second is needed to end the landscape section. This throws your section numbering off by two. You can compensate for this by performing a little bit of field math each time the section count is thrown off. This also requires separate headers/footers in different document sections each time the section number has to be adjusted.

Previously, the resulting section field code was

```
{ SECTION \* ROMAN \* MERGEFORMAT }
```

You would need to change the field so it looks similar to this:

```
{={ SECTION}-2 \* ROMAN \* MERGEFORMAT }
```

To change the field, follow these steps:

1. Press Alt+F9 to toggle the display of field codes.
2. Select the word `SECTION` and press Ctrl+F9 to insert field braces around it.
3. Type an equal sign between the two {{ opening braces.
4. Type `-2` after {SECTION}.
5. Select the entire new field and press F9 (to refresh or recalculate the field).
6. Press Alt+F9 to toggle back to display the field code results again.

Each time you find it necessary to insert additional sections—for landscape tables, for changing the number of columns, or whatever changes are required—you would need to perform an adjustment such as that shown. Now you can see why I referred to the Heading 1 style method as being low maintenance!

Working with Header and Footer Information in Different Document Sections

By default, Word's headers and footers in different document sections are the same—you have to explicitly divorce them by turning off Same As Previous, as shown earlier in this chapter in "Adding Custom Headers and Footers to Each Section." If you've created custom headers and footers for different sections in your document and now want to reconnect them, Word makes it simple.

If the header you want to keep is in the first section, the technique is simple. Choose View, Header and Footer, and use the Switch Between Header and Footer button, as necessary, to position the insertion point in the desired location.

On the Header and Footer toolbar, click Show Previous or Show Next buttons until you are in section 2. Click the Same As Previous button to turn that feature on; if it is already turned on, press it once to turn it off, then again to turn it on.

Click Yes to confirm that you want to delete the header or footer for the current section, and replace it with the header or footer from the preceding section.

Now, click the Show Next button on the Header and Footer toolbar, and repeat the procedure for each of the remaining sections in the document.

If the header or footer you want to keep is somewhere other than in section 1, follow these steps:

1. Choose View, Header and Footer and use the Show Next or Previous to move to the desired header or footer.
2. Press Ctrl+A to select the entire header or footer, and press Ctrl+C to copy the selection to the clipboard.
3. Click Show Previous to move to the section 1 header, and press Ctrl+A.
4. Press Ctrl+V to paste the copied header over the header in section 1.
5. Now, click Show Next, choose Same As Previous on the toolbar, and confirm that you want to replace the current header/footer with the one in the previous section.
6. Repeat this process until all subsequent headers or footers have been reconnected to the header or footer in section 1.

Repeating Graphic and Text Objects on All Pages

Using headers and footers allows you to include a graphic, company logo, or text on every document you create. For instance, your company might want to include the word CONFIDENTIAL along the bottom margin in all documents you create.

See "Adding a Watermark Graphic Behind Your Text," **p. 340**

To insert a picture clip in your header or footer:

1. First, create separate headers and footers for each section, as discussed in "Adding Custom Headers and Footers to Each Section," earlier in this chapter.
2. Choose View, Header and Footer. Use the Switch Between Header and Footer, Show Next, and/or Show Previous buttons, to navigate to the first header or footer you want to change.

NOTE Although the technique here describes inserting a picture clip, you can use the same technique with pictures, WordArt, or text boxes.

See "Working with Art, Images, and Graphics," **p. 331**

3. Choose Insert, Picture. If you have picture files (or other clip art) you want to use, choose From File. Otherwise, choose Clip Art to start the Clip Gallery.
4. Insert the picture into the header or footer. Resize the picture as necessary.

By default, an inserted picture is placed *inline* with your text, meaning that you cannot move it to another location in your header or footer without taking a few extra steps. To relocate the graphic:

1. Right-click the picture and choose Format Picture; click the Layout tab. The Format Picture dialog box appears as shown in Figure 11.8.

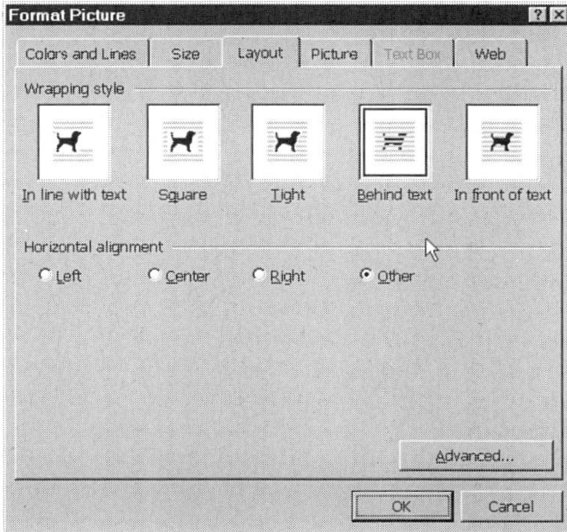

FIGURE 11.8
Avoid In Line with Text if you want to drag objects.

2. For best results, choose Behind Text or In Front of Text. These choices keep the object from being affected by the location and format of text in the header or footer.
3. Next, click the Advanced button to see the Advanced Layout dialog box as shown in Figure 11.9, and click the Picture Position tab.

FIGURE 11.9
Absolute positioning is best for objects you intend to drag.

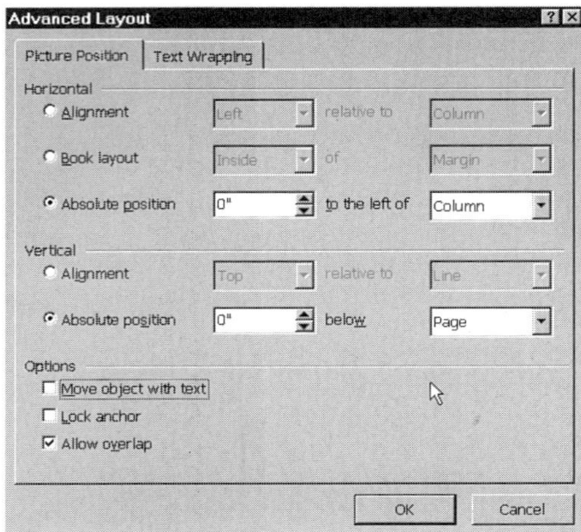

4. Remove the check mark next to Move Object with Text. This enables you to drag the object wherever you want.
5. Click OK, and then OK again to close the Format Picture dialog box. You can now drag the object (picture) anywhere on the page—even outside the header or footer.

You can now drag the object (picture) anywhere on the page—even outside the header or footer. Because you inserted the object into the header or footer, the object will appear on every page for which that header or footer is in effect.

Page Numbering—Getting It Right

Word users sometimes are confused by Word's default automatic way for inserting page numbers. Sometimes, automatic isn't best. The built-in defaults don't fit every situation. When you choose Insert, Page Numbers, Word shows you the built-in defaults, as shown in Figure 11.10. The default inserts page numbers at the bottom right, and includes a page number on the first page.

Adding to the potential confusion, if you use the Page Numbers dialog box to create your page numbers, you won't see any immediate result. However, if you switch into Print Layout view, zoom the view up to 200% or so, and scroll to the bottom-right edge of the page, then you will see that Word did insert a page number field into the document's footer. In fact, Word inserted a framed page number field—which is something you might not notice unless you enable the display of text boundaries (Tools, Options, View, Text Boundaries). The rectangular box around the number 1 in Figure 11.11 indicates a framed area within the document footer.

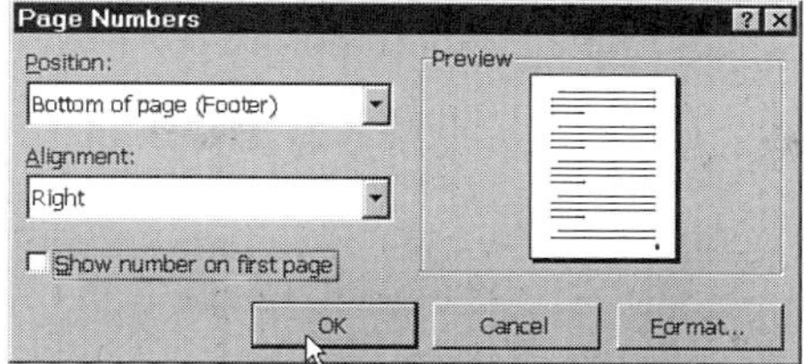

FIGURE 11.10
Remove the check mark to suppress page numbering on the first page.

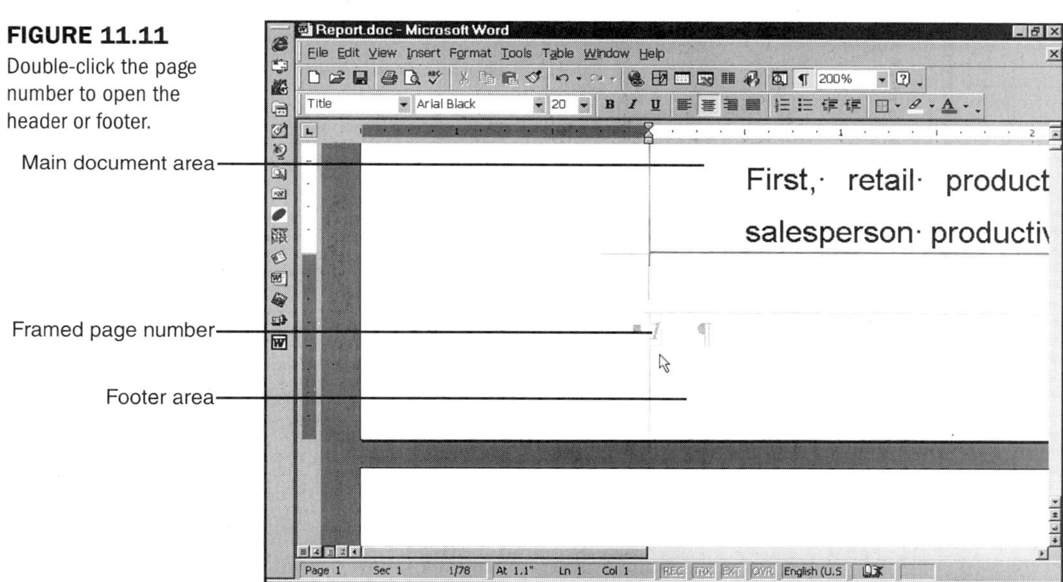

FIGURE 11.11
Double-click the page number to open the header or footer.

Automatic Page Numbering

When in Print Layout view, you can double-click the page number to open a header or footer area for editing. You might need to scroll horizontally to bring the page number into view. If you use Word's default technique for inserting page numbers, you should see a frame around the page number is a frame. The advantage is that the resulting frame can be dragged wherever you want it. The disadvantage is that frames can be confusing. Moreover, the resulting object can be difficult to work with if you want to add additional text.

Suppose you prefer "`Page 1`" instead of just "`1`." You can't just type "`Page`" beside the number. First, you have to widen the frame to accommodate the extra text. To widen the frame, you move your mouse pointer over the field until you see a four-headed arrow pointer; then click. This displays six sizing handles, as shown in Figure 11.12. You can drag the left, center sizing handle to widen the box that contains the number. Finally, you're now able to type the added text to the left of the page number.

Earlier, I said that Word inserted a page number field. You can confirm that what you see is a field by pressing Alt+F9 to toggle the display of field codes on and off.

FIGURE 11.12
Header/footer areas are one of the few places in Word where non-Web frames are used.

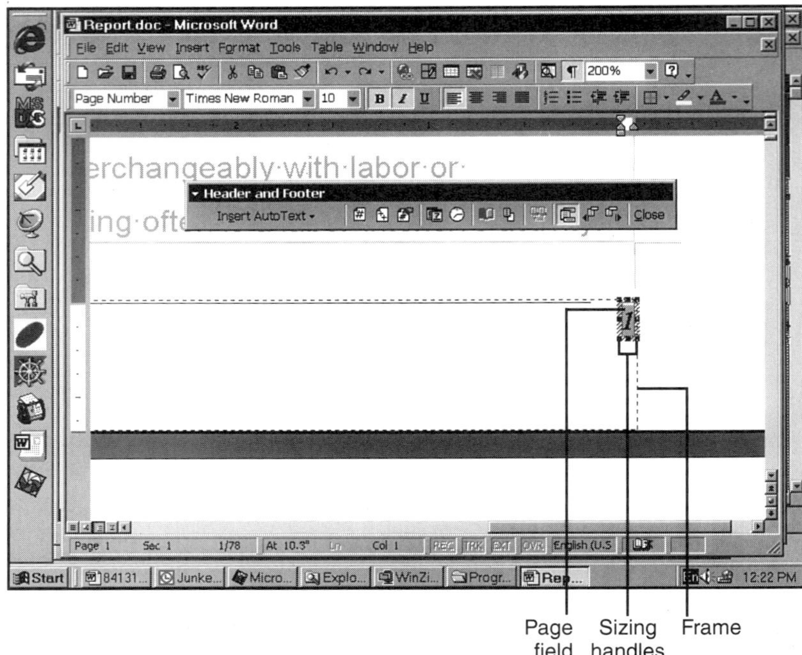

Changing the Numbering Style

If you need to change the numbering style, choose Insert, Page Numbers, and click the Format button. As shown previously in this chapter, you can choose the desired numbering style here. For example, in many documents, it's not uncommon to number front matter using lowercase Roman numerals. Using techniques described earlier in this chapter, you would establish separate sections, disconnect footers from each other, and then select different numbering format options for different sections.

Removing the Numbering Frame

You do not have to put your page numbers into a frame, however. If you prefer working with page numbers as ordinary text, which you can readily integrate into the surrounding footer or header, feel free to do so. To remove the frame, right-click the edge of the frame (not the interior), choose Format Frame, and click Remove Frame.

Or, don't use the Insert Page Number approach at all. Instead, choose View, Header and Footer, and use the buttons on the Header and Footer toolbar to insert page numbers. Done that way, the resulting numbers are not framed. If you don't need to drag the page numbers about, then don't use the frame approach. It'll mean less document overhead and something that's easier to understand.

Adding Line Numbers to Your Document

Many courts require that legal briefs, transcripts, and other legal documents have *line numbers* at the left edge of each page. Line numbers actually appear in the left margin rather than in the main part of the page. They provide a reference for a document without interfering with its flow. Line numbers are used in legal documents such as depositions and transcripts for cross-referencing testimony. For example, in examining a witness, a lawyer might say, "On page 1,206 of your deposition, line 27, you state..." Without line numbers, the attorney and witness would have to count, which would make trials even longer than they already are.

To add line numbers to a document, follow these steps:

1. Choose File, Page Setup, and click the Layout tab in the Page Setup dialog box.
2. Click the Line Numbers button, and check the Add Line Numbering option, as shown in Figure 11.13.
3. To number every line from 1 to the end of the page, accept the default options. To set the starting number (the numbering corresponding to the first line on the page) to something other than 1, use the Start At option.
4. To number every second, third, fourth, and so on line, change Count By to 2, 3, and so on.

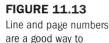

FIGURE 11.13
Line and page numbers are a good way to cross-reference text.

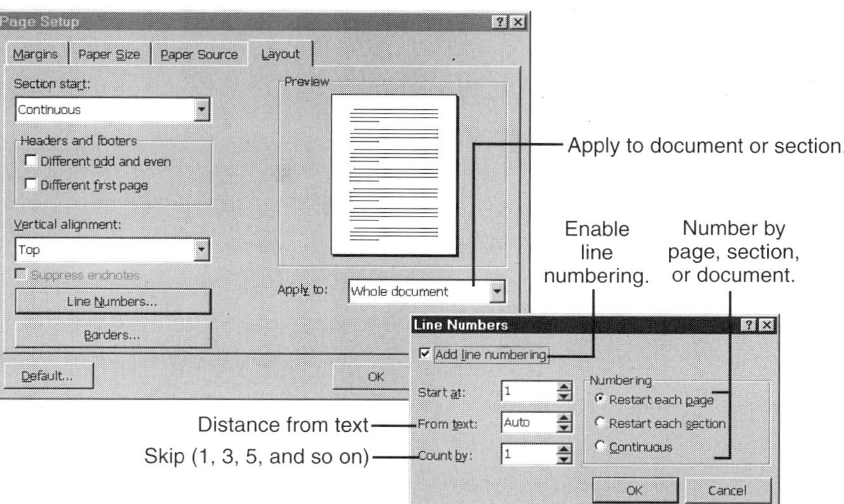

In the Numbering section of the Line Numbers dialog box, choose whether you want lines counted continuously through the whole document or section, or to restart on each page.

After you've made your decisions, click OK to close the Line Numbers dialog box, and OK again to close Page Setup. If you don't see any line numbers, switch to the Print Layout view or click the Print Preview button on the Standard toolbar to see the numbering.

Skipping Page Numbers

Another page numbering issue to consider is that of continuity. It's likely that you'll want to skip page numbers from time to time. For instance, most books don't start on page 1. Likewise, in a report, you might want to skip numbering for pages containing figures or charts.

Word gives you the ability to turn page numbering on and off, using two approaches that depend on the section formatting and line numbering you've chosen.

The first approach is useful if all other section formatting in the skipped parts is identical to the section formatting in the line-numbered parts.

1. After line numbering has been applied, select the paragraph(s) where you want line numbers skipped. For a single paragraph, selection isn't necessary; just click anywhere inside the target paragraph.
2. Choose Format, Paragraph, and click the Line and Page Breaks tab.
3. On the Line and Page Breaks tab, select Suppress Line Numbers, shown in Figure 11.14, and click OK.
4. Repeat this procedure for each paragraph (or for selected paragraphs) where you want line numbers suppressed.

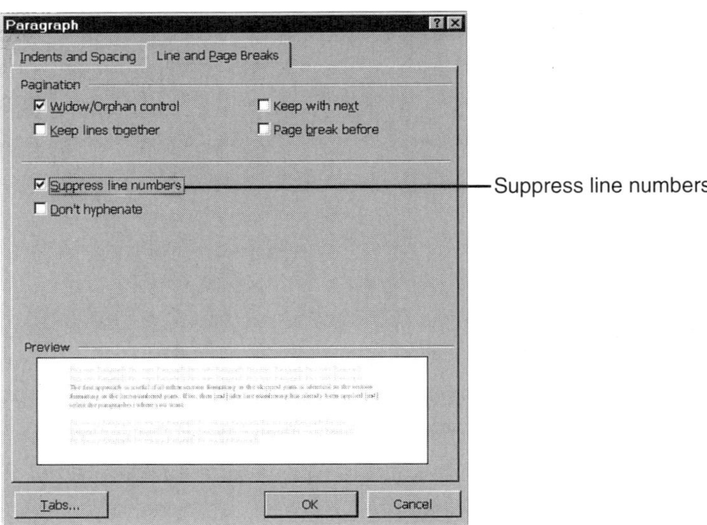

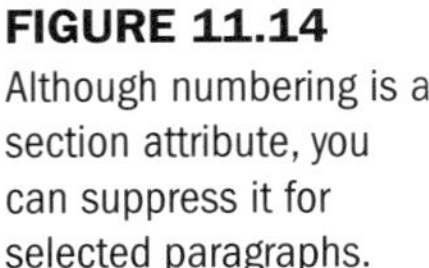
FIGURE 11.14
Although numbering is a section attribute, you can suppress it for selected paragraphs.

The second approach to "suppressing" line numbering is to insert section breaks into the document (Insert, Break), and to enable line numbering only in those sections where you want it.

Actually, this doesn't actually suppress line numbers—rather, it turns them off and then back on. This approach makes sense if the unnumbered and numbered sections will have different section-specific formatting, or if you want to suppress line numbering on any given page or set of pages (for example, you might want to skip numbering on pages that contain just graphics).

If you want line numbering only in part of the document, follow these steps:

1. Section off the part in which you want line numbers—choosing the desired kind of section breaks (Next Page, Continuous, and so on).
2. Move the insertion point to the section in which you want line numbers to resume.
3. Choose File, Page Setup, Layout, and click Line Numbers.
4. In the Line Numbers dialog box, choose the options you want, and click OK.
5. Back in the Layout dialog box, choose This Section from the Apply To drop-down list.

Using Line Numbers in Continuous Breaks

Another ostensible option is to select the section in which you want line numbers, and then set Apply To Selected Text. When you do this, Word automatically sets off the selection with section breaks.

However, Word varies its behavior depending on whether or not the newly created section is preceded by a continuous section break. If there is a continuous section break before the new section, then Word uses a continuous break at the beginning of the new section, and a Next Page break at the end. If there is no continuous section break before the newly created section, Word uses Next Page section breaks. So, if you know there is no continuous break before the new section you want to create, this approach is an ergonomic alternative for turning off line numbering on a page or range of pages.

Using Columns

Column formatting—sometimes called snaking text or newspaper columns—is common in newspapers, magazines, and newsletters. They're especially useful when you want to cover multiple topics or headings on a starter or cover page, with articles that continue on the interior pages. Another good but often-overlooked application of columns is in technical reading. Research shows that the eye can comprehend narrow columns better than wide columns that span an entire page. With technical matter that might be difficult to begin with, reducing the amount of horizontal sweep the eye has to perform makes reading less fatiguing and more comprehensible.

Using Columns Effectively

To create columns in an existing document that comprises a single section, click the Columns button on the Standard toolbar, and drag to the right to select the desired number of columns, as shown in Figure 11.15. To select more than four columns, press the left mouse button as you drag and the drop-down list expands.

On a standard 8 1/2-by-11-inch piece of paper, in a portrait layout, the maximum number of columns you can create using the Columns tool is six.

However, if you need more columns, you can squeeze out the most by choosing Format, Columns from the menu. Theoretically, by setting the paper width to 22" (the maximum), you can get up to 40 columns—should such a bizarre need ever arise.

NOTE The actual limit depends on the printer. If your printer will print on 22"-wide paper and allow your margins to be .5 inch, you can get 42 columns; 43 if you can print to the edge of the page.

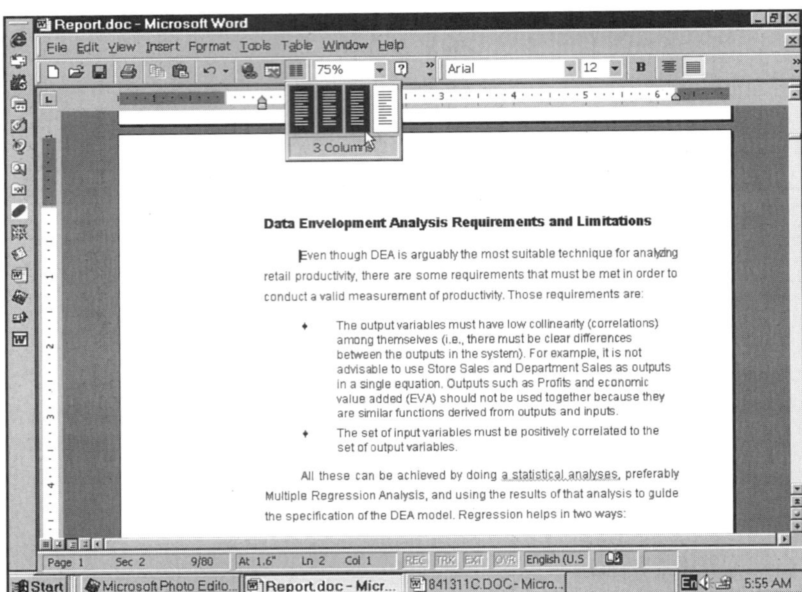

FIGURE 11.15
As you drag to the right, the number of columns you can highlight expands.

When you create columns by beginning in Normal view, Word switches the document into Print Layout view. This enables you to see the columns you created (otherwise, the page appears as having only one column at a time). You can switch back to Normal view for drafting purposes, if that suits your needs better.

For more custom column needs, choose Format, Columns. The Presets offer one through three equal-width columns, or two additional choices with narrow left/wide right, and the reverse (see Figure 11.16). A narrow left/wide right format often is used for newsletters, where the left column serves as a table of contents or key to the rest of the newsletter.

To create additional columns, use the Number of Columns control. You can also customize individual columns by setting the width and spacing directly. Use this approach when you have a precise layout to which you must adhere (for example, a made-to-measure document).

If you're winging it—creating a new format on-the-fly—then use either the Columns dialog box or the Columns toolbar button to insert the desired number of columns, and then use the Ruler to customize column spacing and width. To reduce spacing and increase the width of the right column, drag the right edge of a column divider to the left, as shown in Figure 11.17. With the mouse in this position, Word displays the ScreenTip *Left Margin*, because it corresponds to the left margin of the column to the right.

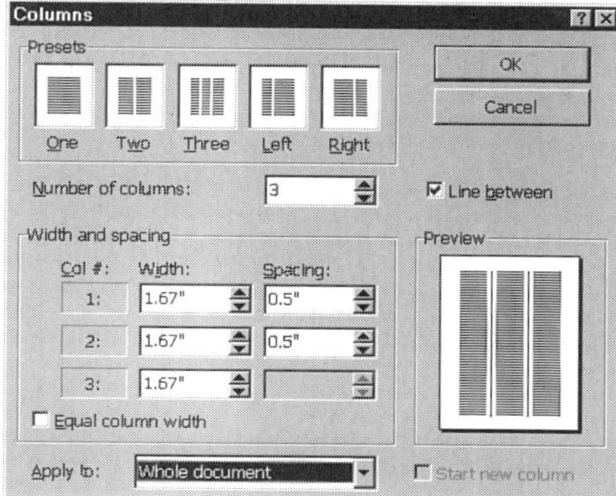

FIGURE 11.16
A line between columns has visual appeal.

Conversely, drag the left edge to change the spacing and the width of the left column. Note that you cannot change the spacing without simultaneously changing the width of a column.

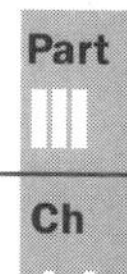

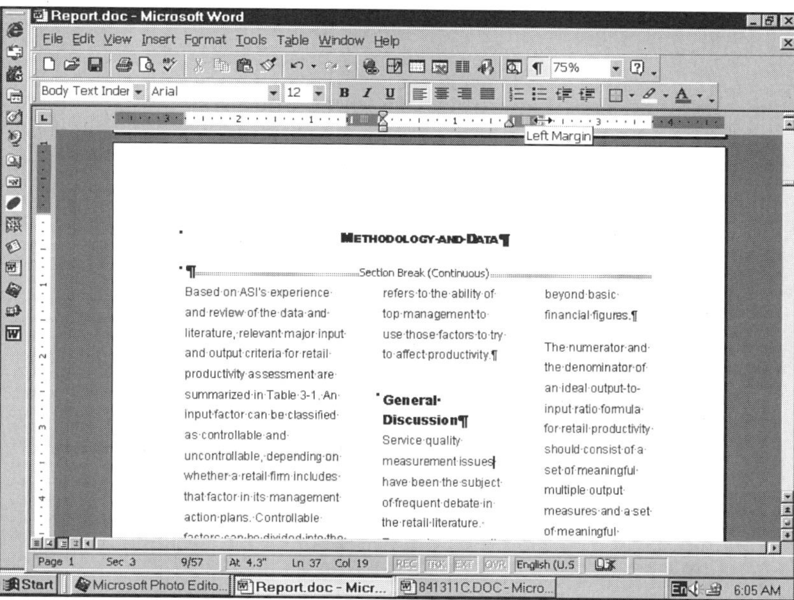

FIGURE 11.17
Use the Ruler to manipulate columns visually.

To change the relative widths of two adjacent columns simultaneously, while keeping the spacing the same, move the mouse over the center of the column divider, and drag the entire column divider to the left or right. To see the effect of dragging on the column dimensions, hold down the Alt key while dragging. Word now displays the dimensions, as shown in Figure 11.18.

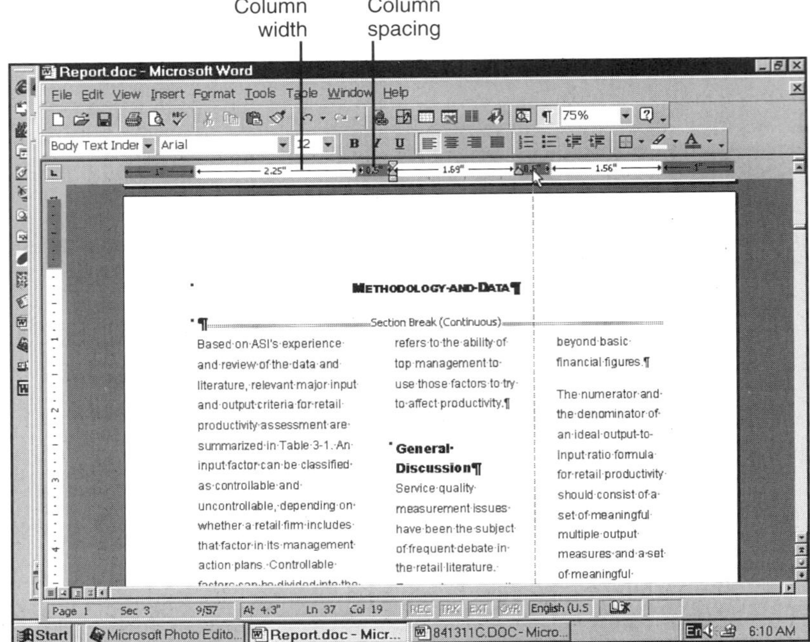

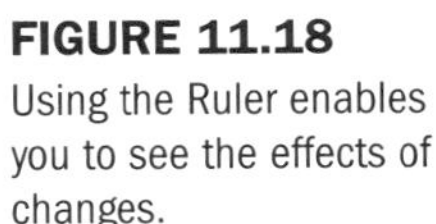
FIGURE 11.18
Using the Ruler enables you to see the effects of changes.

Varying the Number of Columns in a Document

Newsletters and other column-oriented documents sometimes have varying numbers of columns. For example, it's not uncommon for a newsletter to begin with three columns on the first page, with one or two columns on the inside. A varying style helps focus the reader's attention, but it also helps the author organize information more effectively.

Another common but sometimes elusive goal is centering a title over a multicolumn page, as shown in Figure 11.19. The title is in one column, but what follows on the page is in two columns. The trick lies in knowing that column formatting is a section-formatting attribute. You accomplish the desired goal by separating differently formatted columnar text with section breaks.

To center a title across a multicolumn article:

1. Move the insertion point to just before the first word in the article (below the title).
2. Choose Format, Columns.
3. Choose the number of columns you want. Choose This Point Forward from the Apply To drop-down list.
4. Click Start New Column. Click OK.

When you choose This Point Forward, Word automatically inserts a Continuous section break at the insertion point, leaving the material above at its current number of columns, and applying the new number of columns thereafter.

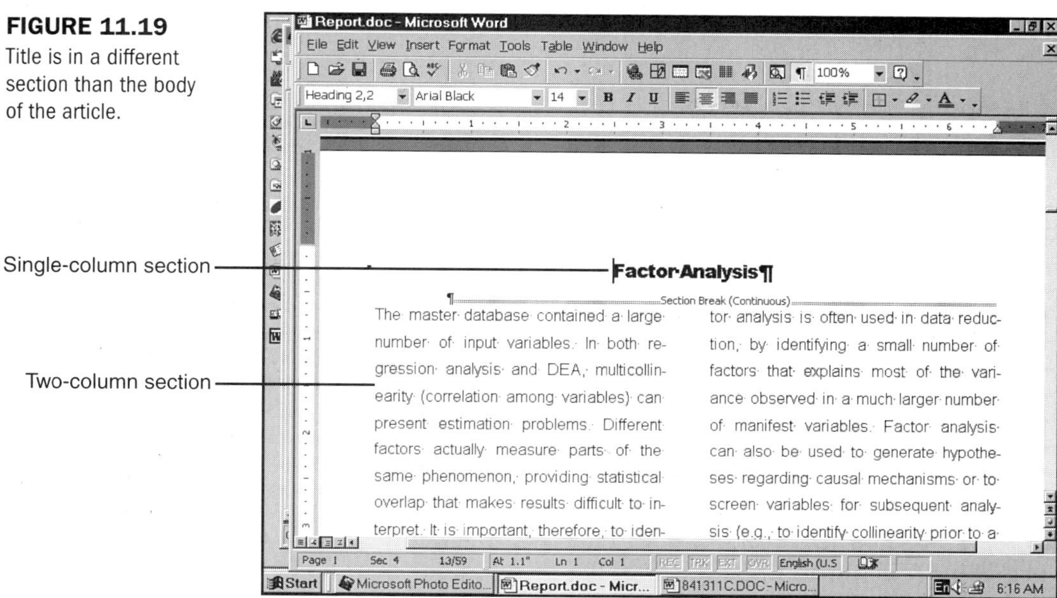

FIGURE 11.19
Title is in a different section than the body of the article.

NOTE In some formatting situations, Word inserts a Next Page section break instead of a Continuous break. If that happens, then you'll have to insert the section break manually (Insert, Break, Continuous), and then set the number of columns.

Sometimes, you might want to use more columns in one part of a document than you want to use elsewhere in the same document. Using sections, Word makes doing this easy:

1. Assuming you start with the entire document in one column, select the text you want to place in two or more columns.
2. Use the Column button on the toolbar to choose the desired number of columns.

Word automatically sets off the selected area with continuous section breaks, applying multiple columns to the selected area, and leaving the sections above and below at their original settings.

Forcing a New Column

Sometimes, you might want to force material in a column to the top of the next available column. Move the insertion point to just before the text you want to move into the next column. Choose Insert, Break, Column Break. This is analogous to a page break in single-column mode. Click OK to see the effect on your column.

Balancing Uneven Columns

Sometimes, columns end unevenly on the last page of a document. You can force them to appear more balanced. Move to the very end of the last column. Choose Insert, Break, Continuous to insert a continuous section break. This tricks the document into thinking a new section is beginning, and signals the need to conserve space by balancing (as much as possible) the text in the preceding section.

NOTE If you still have difficulty creating balanced columns, try choosing Tools, Options, Compatibility. Remove the check that's next to Don't Balance Columns for Continuous Section Starts. Keep this option in mind, also, if there are times when you *don't* want columns to balance when you're beginning an actual new section.

Bulleted and Numbered Lists

For years, Microsoft and most software trainers have been telling users that the best way to get the features they want is to use styles. Seemingly, Microsoft has given up—at least a little—and is now rewarding nonstyle users with intuitive new features: automatic multilevel bulleted and numbered lists. Word also sports new capabilities such as graphical bullets and the capability to underline bullets and numbers in a different color.

Automatic Bulleted and Numbered Lists

In Word 95 and Word 97, when you created bulleted lists or numbered lists, you were limited just to a single level of bullets or numbers. Word 2000 lets you create multilevel bulleted and numbered lists using the Numbering and Bullets tools on the Formatting toolbar.

You use the Bullets or Numbering tool to create the desired formatting. Then, you use Tab and Shift+Tab to increase or decrease the level.

To take best advantage of this feature, choose Tools, Options, and click the Edit tab. Make sure Tabs and Backspace Set Left Indent is checked. To create a multilevel bulleted list from scratch, click the bullet tool, type the first item, and press Enter. If the next item is at the same level, type it and press Enter again.

If the next item is at a deeper level, press the Tab key, type the item, and press Enter. If you accidentally go too deep, press Shift+Tab to promote the item to the previous level.

As shown in Figure 11.20, you can use this feature to create a bulleted outline. As a nice dividend, if you use Format, Bullets and Numbering to change the bullet style for any of the sublevels in the outline, all other items at that level will also acquire the changed bullet. Unfortunately, this does not work with the top level—only the bullet on the active line changes.

TIP Tab and Shift+Tab can be used to promote or demote outline levels–but only if the cursor is at the beginning of the line. From anywhere in the line, you can use Word's built-in outline to promote and demote keys in a multilevel bulleted list–even though it's technically not really a Word outline. Use Alt+Shift+Left arrow to promote, and Alt+Shift+Right arrow to demote.

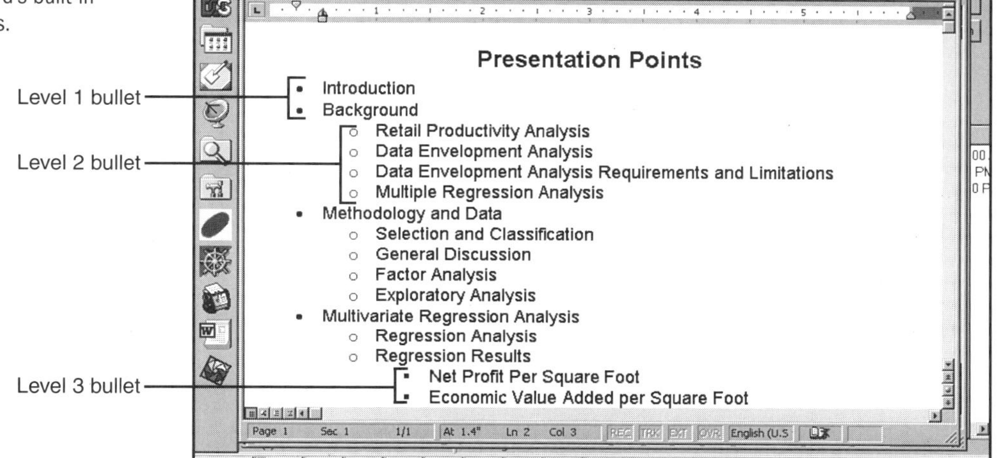

FIGURE 11.20
Use Format, Bullets and Numbering if you don't like Word's built-in defaults.

The identical techniques also work for numbering. Moreover, with numbering, Level 1 formatting works as you would expect. That is, create a multilevel numbered list, and then choose Format, Bullets and Numbering, Numbered, and change the numbering style. When you change the style at any level, all other items at that level also get changed—including Level 1.

TIP You can change a multilevel bulleted list into a numbered list, and vice versa, but you have to select the entire list. After the list is selected, click the Numbering tool. If you try changing just one item in the list, Word will continue to use bullets for lower levels until you change them all to numbers.

Bullets and Numbers: Underlining Enhancements

Another new and improved feature that could easily escape detection is Word's capability to add underline color. Simply choose Format, Bullets and Numbers, click the Bulleted tab and choose any style other than None. Next, click Customize and choose Font. Select an Underline Style and Underline Color.

The addition of enhanced underlining features isn't so much a suggestion that anyone would want to underline bullets and numbers, but a reflection of that new capability in the Format, Font dialog box. However, should the occasion arise, not only can you underline your bullets in a different color, but you can choose graphically from among 17 different underlining styles, as shown in Figure 11.21.

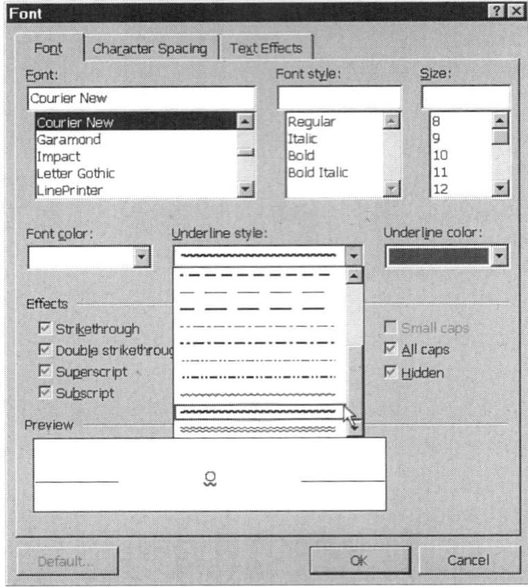

FIGURE 11.21
Now you can underline bullets and numbers in color.

Picture Bullets

For online content designers, Word now has graphical bullets. These bullets can include not only the built-in bullets that come with Word, but virtually any miniature picture you want to use.

HTML has long included tags for creating nongraphical automatic bulleted lists in HTML documents. On the plus side, they're simple and fast, and the user's browser gets to choose how to display them. On the negative side, however, they're simple and fast, and the user's browser gets to choose how to display them!

Many Web page designers want to control the entire presentation. Graphical bullets are pretty and impressive, despite the fact that they create extra logistics for the page designer—that is, making sure that bullet graphics get transferred to the Web site along with the main HTML document. However, the functional advantage is that graphical bullets can be used as hyperlinks.

To create graphical bullets:

1. Select the text you want bulleted.
2. Choose Format, Bullets and Numbering
3. Click the Bulleted tab.
4. Choose Picture. In the Picture Bullet dialog box (see Figure 11.22), choose the desired bullet. If you don't see the bullet you want, scroll to the bottom and click More Clips. If you still don't see what you want, or want to use your own, select Import Clips or Clips Online.
5. After you locate clip art you want, click it, and choose Insert Clip, as shown in Figure 11.22. This copies the clip into your document.

NOTE This bullet becomes the default bullet symbol for all future bulleted lists until you select a new bullet using Format, Bullets and Numbering.

▶ **See** "Working with the Revised Clip Gallery," **p. 1196**

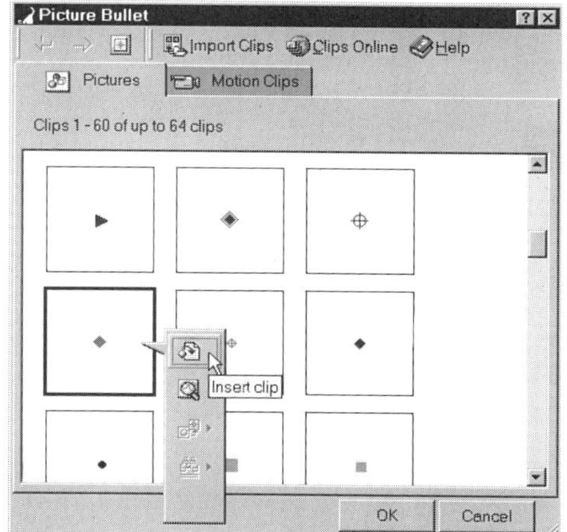

FIGURE 11.22
The Clip Gallery has Back and Forward navigation buttons—such as those on your browser.

Picture bullets are inserted differently than regular bullets. When using regular Word bullets, you cannot select the bullet itself. Word's regular bullets are created through formatting rather than through the use of characters or pictures—they display and print, but cannot be edited directly. For picture bullets to be Web-compatible, the bullets inserted must use actual characters or be small pictures. Be aware of this when editing, lest you accidentally delete your bullets.

Formatted Bullets

Word's regular bullets are created through an *overlay* process that can be controlled only through Word's Bullets tool and through the Bullets and Numbering dialog box (accessed either through the Format menu or through the Format, Style command). The process creates bullets (or numbers), tabs, and spacing (such as hanging indentation) that display onscreen and when printing, but which cannot be edited directly. Like right- and left-indentation, Word's bullets are part of the formatting, rather than created through the use of characters.

Users who migrated to word processing from typewriters recall a time when, if you wanted something block indented, you needed to insert spaces or press the Tab key to offset each line a set distance. Many users still press the tab key to indent the first line of a paragraph. By setting indentations through paragraph formatting, however, you avoid the hassle of creating those formatting effects manually.

The idea behind bullets (and numbering) as formatting, rather than bullets as symbols or characters, was to reduce the user's and the Help Desk's workloads. With a single click of the Bullets tool, you can apply or remove bullets from a selection containing many paragraphs. Microsoft's decision to implement bullets as formatting came with Word 6, following a tedious implementation of bullet symbols in WinWord 2 (which produced much confusion and lots of technical support issues). While still confusing (and mysterious!), the formatting approach usually works, and generates less need for technical support.

Using Picture Bullets As Hyperlinks

Picture bullets make ideal hyperlinks. After you complete your bulleted list, select the first bullet you want to use as a hyperlink. Choose Insert, Hyperlink. Navigate to or otherwise find the link you want to use (see Figure 11.23), and click OK.

▶ **See** "Cross-References and Hyperlinks," **p. 459**

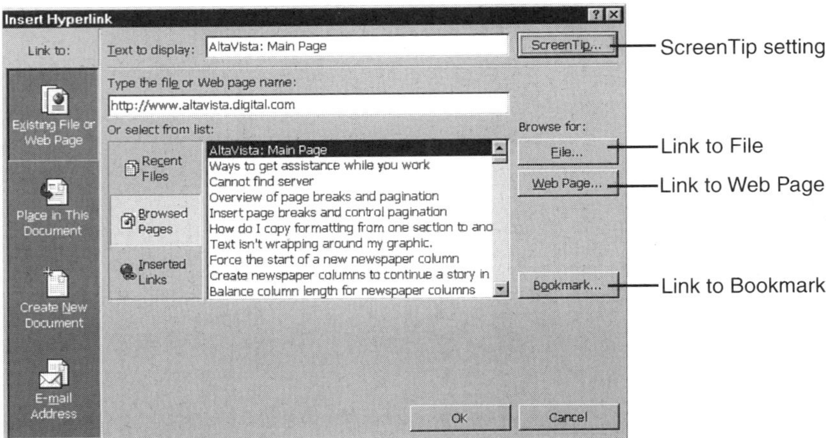

FIGURE 11.23
You can create ScreenTips for linked bullets.

> **CAUTION**
>
> Complete your bulleted list before you assign links to bullets. After a link has been assigned, you can no longer create the next list item simply by pressing Enter at the end of a bulleted line.

Using Text Boxes

Text boxes are useful ways to present information. A popular concept is to take a quote from the article and place it inside a text box, as shown in Figure 11.24. This serves as a *teaser* to entice the reader into finishing the remainder of the article. It's also known as a "pull quote."

There are two approaches to creating a text box.

- The easiest way is to select text you want in the text box, and choose Insert, Text Box, Horizontal. Word inserts a text box with the selected text already inside it. You can use the selection handles to shape the box as necessary and drag the box into the desired position.
- The other approach is *not* to select text, and, instead, choose Insert, Text Box, Horizontal. Taking this approach, the mouse pointer becomes crosshairs that you use to draw the text box in the desired location, as shown in Figure 11.25. After the box is formed, you then can type text into it or paste it from the Clipboard.

FIGURE 11.24
Selected text is automatically copied to the text box.

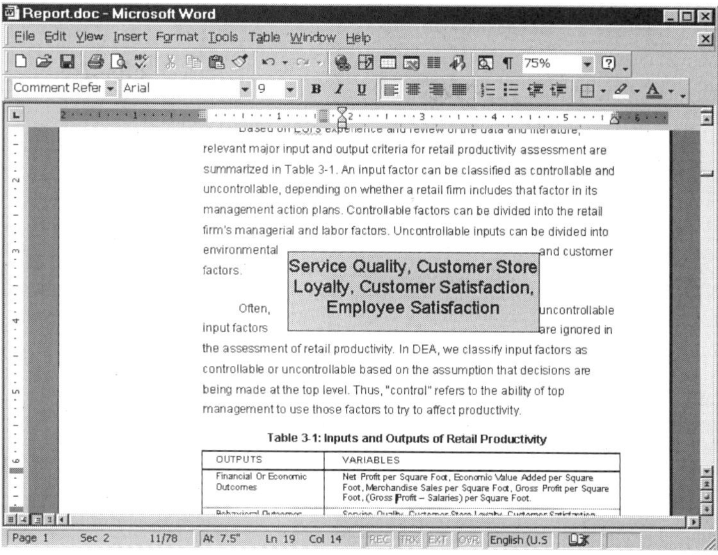

FIGURE 11.25
Drag down and to the right and release the mouse button.

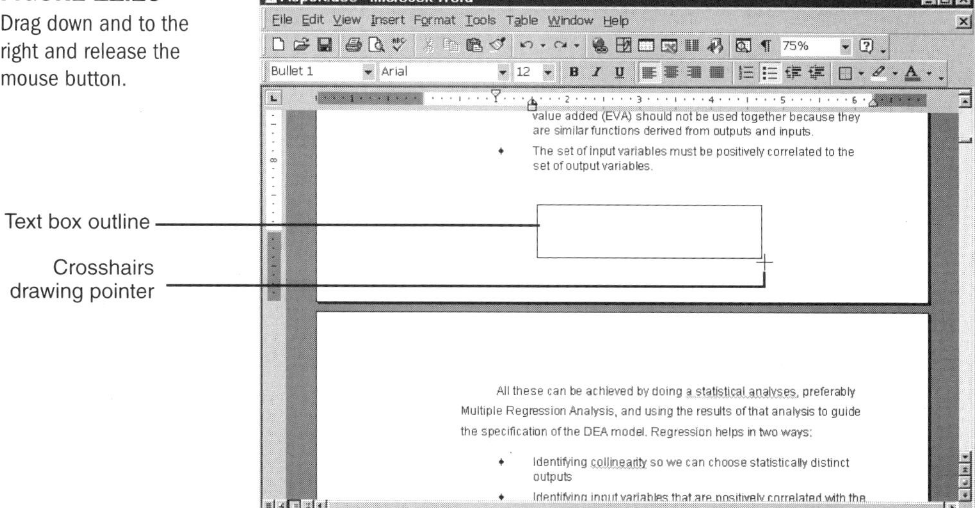

There are a couple reasons it's often easier to select text before inserting the text box. First, it saves the step of having to copy text to the Clipboard and paste it into the box. Second, you almost always end up having to drag and shape the text box anyway, which ends up negating the presumed advantage of being able to draw the box in the desired location.

▶ **See** "Controlling the Text Around Inserted Objects," **p. 336**

Creating Linked Text Boxes

Linked text boxes offer additional flexibility, especially in newsletters or other documents in which you want to control the flow of text in ways other than simple front-to-back style. Linked text boxes enable you to create a contiguous passage in multiple boxes that can be placed anywhere in the document. The boxes can then be moved about and shaped however best fits the document's overall layout—for example, to flow an article from page 1 to page 6.

To create a linked text box:

1. Choose Insert, Text Box, Horizontal.
2. Draw a text box of the approximate size and shape you want. You can position it now or later. Repeat this for as many text boxes as you will need to fit the entire passage.
3. Click to select the outside edge of the first text box in which you want to begin the passage. The Text Box toolbar should be visible, as shown in Figure 11.26. If not, then right-click any menu or toolbar and choose Text Box. Click the Create Text Box Link button, which displays the linking pointer (an upright pitcher), also shown in Figure 11.26.

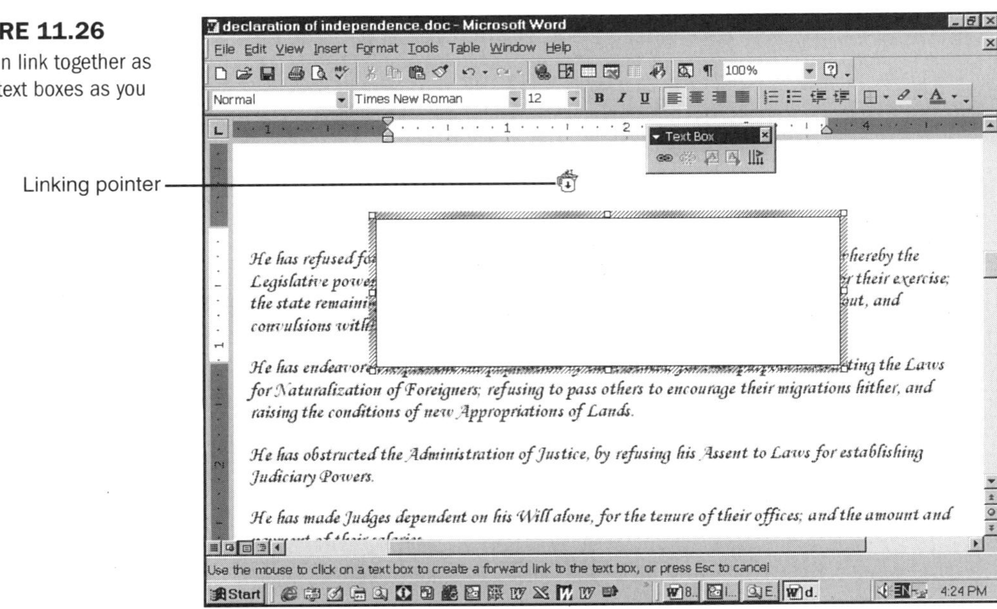

FIGURE 11.26
You can link together as many text boxes as you like.

4. Move the linking pointer over the second text box into which you want text to flow. As the pointer moves over a text box that can accept the flow of text, the pitcher tilts so you can *pour* the text into the text box.
5. Click in the text box to link to the original box.
6. If you have a third (fourth, and so on) text box in the series, click the outside edge of the second text box so that the Create Text Box Link button is again enabled on the Text Box toolbar. Now move the pouring pointer over the next text box in the chain, and click.
7. Repeat this for each additional text box.

To insert text into the linked boxes, you can type it directly or paste it from the clipboard. To insert text:

- Click inside the first box in the chain. If you're going to type it in, just start typing. When the first text box fills up, text automatically flows to the second, and so on.
- If the text is in the clipboard, paste it into the first text box in the chain. As it fills, text flows into each linked text box down the chain, as shown in Figure 11.27.

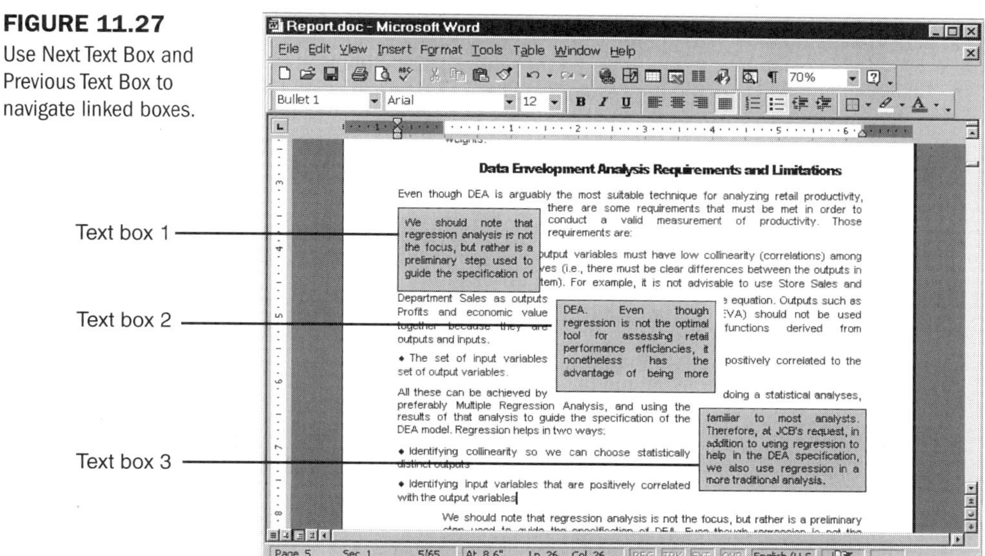

FIGURE 11.27
Use Next Text Box and Previous Text Box to navigate linked boxes.

Working with Art, Images, and Graphics

Compared to recent versions of Word, working with graphics in Word is now much easier and much more intuitive. Just a few versions ago, placing a picture on a page required tedious and meticulous attention to measurements in dialog boxes. Now, most of the same work can be done simply by dragging. Previously, users had to insert frames in order to have any dragging capabilities. Frames were cumbersome and confusing, however, adding an extra layer of work to tasks. Thanks also to OLE (Object Linking and Embedding), Word users have the editing power of their entire Office suite through Word, without necessarily having to know or care what application is doing what.

Some of this newfound ease of use can be attributed to the popularity of the Web and the need for Word to accommodate the creation of graphic-intensive Web pages. Here, we'll review Word's capabilities, pointing out new tricks and things to be aware of.

Linking Versus Embedding Art, Images, and Graphics

A general issue to be aware of is the difference between *linking* and *embedding* graphics into your documents. When you link to an object, you are creating a pointer from the active document (the *target* document) to the document in which the object resides (the *source* document). When you embed an object, you are placing a copy of the object in the target document; there is no link between the original object in the source document and the copy in the target document.

There are pros and cons for both linking and embedding. Which alternative you choose depends on your situation:

- Accessing the object—You should link to art and graphic objects when you will always have access to the source document (for example, if it resides on your computer or on a reliable network drive). Suppose, however, you decide to take the target document on a business trip. Unless you copy the source document onto your laptop (or to a floppy disk) and reset the link to the new path for the source document, you won't be able to see it when you display the target document. In this case, it would be simpler to embed the object into the target document and avoid hassling with the object link.
- Document size—Art and graphic objects are typically very large files. When embedded into a document (especially if you have several embedded objects), these objects can make your Word document size quickly become enormous. This becomes a problem typically when trying to transport or electronically transfer the document. Fortunately, with the advent of Zip disks and other high-capacity storage devices, as well as programs that will compress your files, this is becoming less of a problem. If document size is a concern, you're better off linking instead of embedding.
- Editing the object—Editing an embedded object is exactly like editing a linked one. You actually launch Excel when you edit an embedded Excel chart in a Word document. OLE hides this from you by making it look like you're using Word, but you're not. The only real difference between linking and embedding is the actual location of the object.

If you choose Insert, Picture, From File, and navigate to any picture file, you should see an Insert button at the lower-right corner of the Insert Picture dialog box, as shown in Figure 11.28.

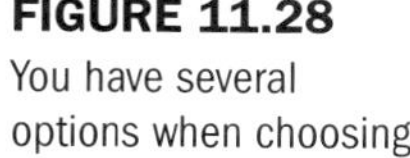

FIGURE 11.28
You have several options when choosing to insert a picture.

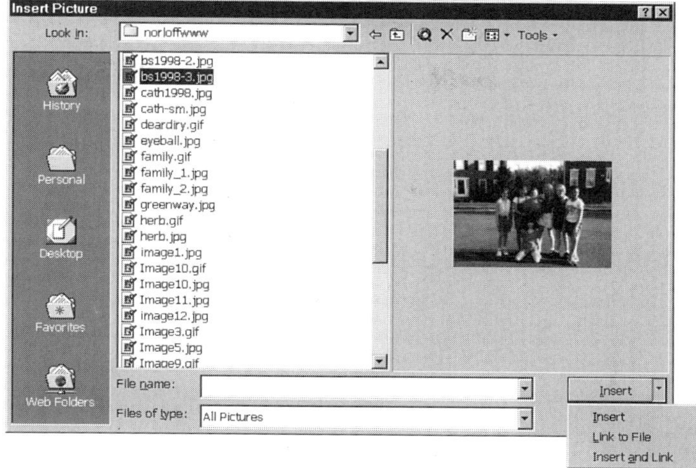

If you click the drop-down arrow to the right of the Insert button, Word displays three choices:

- Insert—This is the default. This embeds the picture into the document. Advantage: The picture becomes part of the document; you don't need two files (that is, the Word document *and* the picture file). Disadvantage: Inserted graphics make documents *much* larger.
- Link to File—This inserts a link to the picture in the document. Advantage: This contributes little to document size. If the picture is updated or improved, the document automatically uses the improved version. Disadvantage: You need to send a copy of the picture with the document, and the link can easily be broken if the path and filename of the source file change.
- Insert and Link—This inserts the picture *and* the link. Advantage: The document is portable and can benefit from updates, when available. Disadvantage: The document is *much* larger.

Word doesn't always give you a linking versus inserting (embedding) option. For Clip Art, for example, no choice is offered. However, for most objects, you have a choice.

The primary advantage to embedding is document portability—the capability of the document to stand alone without needing a lot of extra baggage. The primary advantages of linking are updatability and smaller document size. If size is not an issue, but portability and updatability are, then you can compromise and use the third option—Insert and Link. If you just click Insert—without dropping down the list—Word defaults to a plain insertion and embeds the picture.

When you choose Insert, the picture is inserted and becomes a part of your file. When you choose one of the link options, a Word field is inserted instead. The Link to File option and the Insert and Link option both insert an INCLUDEPICTURE field. You can see the field contents by pressing Alt+F9. This is what you would see:

```
{INCLUDEPICTURE "E:\\norloffwww\\bs1998-2.jpg" \* MERGEFORMAT}
```

The Link to File option also inserts the INCLUDEPICTURE field, but adds the \d switch. The \d switch tells Word not to store the graphics data with the file.

The easiest way to find out what a field switch does is to pretend that you want to insert that field. Choose Insert, Field, find the field of interest, and click the Options button—which lists and explains the switches. In this case, the INCLUDEPICTURE field can be found both in Links and References and in All.

Floating Images Versus Inline Images

The Word window can be thought of as existing in layers. Most of what you type goes into the text layer. There is, however, a layer that is beneath the text. If you insert a watermark, for example, it goes beneath the text into the bottom graphics layer. There is another layer that is on top of the text layer, which is used to store graphics that appear in your document. Word enables you to control which layer objects occupy.

NOTE There are other layers, as well. When drawing graphics, for example, Word enables you to select parts of the picture and send them behind or in front of other parts by using the Order options. Right-click any menu or toolbar and turn on the Drawing toolbar. Click the Oval tool and draw an oval. Now, right-click the oval and click the arrow next to Order, as shown in Figure 11.29.

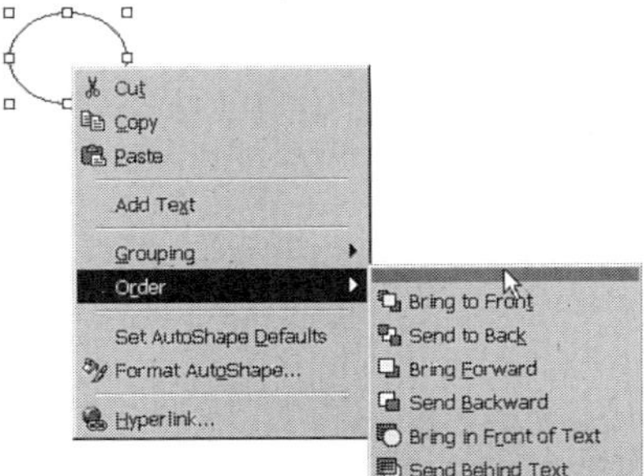

FIGURE 11.29
Drawings are inserted in one of the graphics layers.

When you insert an image, Word defaults to show the image inline. That means that the image is inserted into the text layer. Place the insertion point in any paragraph. Choose Insert, Picture, From File. Navigate to the location of any picture and Insert the picture. Try dragging the picture to the middle of a paragraph. You can't do it. That's because, by default, it can't be dragged. To float over text and to be drag-enabled, a picture cannot be in the text layer.

To move a picture outside the text layer:

1. Right-click the picture and choose Format Picture.
2. Click the Layout tab, to display the Layout section of the Format Picture dialog box shown in Figure 11.30. Note that In Line with Text is selected by default, which means that the picture is in the text layer. Choosing any of the other options (Square, Tight, Behind Text, In Front of Text) places the picture into the graphics layer.

3. Click the Advanced button, and then choose the Text Wrapping tab to display more choices. Here again, any of the options other than In Line with Text puts the picture into the graphics layer.

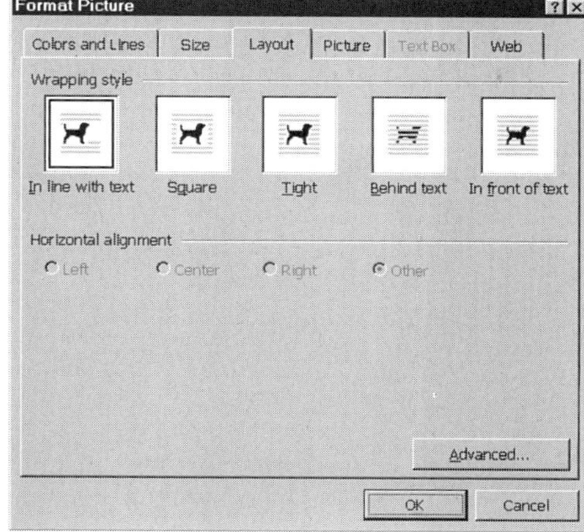

FIGURE 11.30
Don't overlook the Advanced button for additional options.

Inserting Scanned Images

If you have a Windows-compatible scanner, you can scan objects directly from within Word. Some scanners add a Scan button to the Standard toolbar. If you have a Scan button, click it to start your scanner. If you don't have a Scan button, then choose Insert, Picture, From Scanner or Camera.

If you don't have a Scan button on the toolbar, you can add one:

1. Choose Tools, Customize, Commands.
2. Under Categories, choose Insert.
3. Scroll down the Commands list to From Scanner or Camera.
4. Click the displayed command and drag it to the toolbar of your choice.
5. Click Close.

Depending on how scanning is installed on your system, after you click the Scan button or invoke the Insert, Picture, From Scanner or Camera command, you'll probably see a dialog box similar to that shown in Figure 11.31. If other options are available, make your selection, select the correct scanning device, and choose Custom Insert.

Next, your scanner driver software will *probably* take over. As shown in Figure 11.32, the Mustek driver is one that does. If Microsoft Photo Editor appears instead, then click its Scan button. Using the controls that appear, insert a picture into your scanner and instruct the scanner to scan it. Note, however, that depending upon the scanning software you use, the dialog box shown in Figure 11.32 will appear differently.

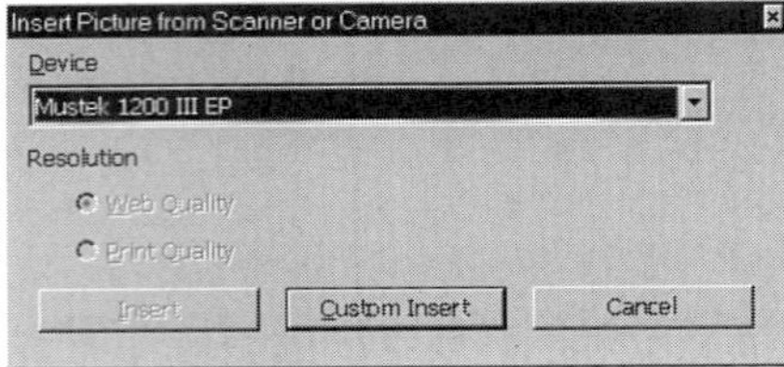

FIGURE 11.31
Some systems have multiple qualified devices.

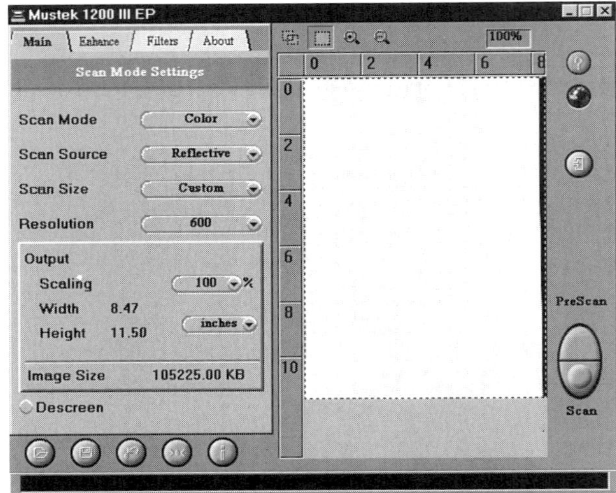

FIGURE 11.32
Don't set the resolution to 600—you'll regret it.

CAUTION

Note your scanning options carefully—especially size and resolution. The wrong settings can result in astronomically large files that can make your computer work in slow motion.

When the picture appears, it will be just the same as any other picture that was Inserted (not linked) into a Word document.

Now that you know it can be done, don't do it this way in the future. Instead, choose Start, Programs, Office Tools, Microsoft Photo Editor. Scan the picture in from Photo Editor so you can save the file in a suitable format (for example, .jpg). Also, it's rare that a scanner's preset options yield exactly what you want. In Photo Editor, you can perform actual cropping (which is different from masking cropping that Word performs) and reduce the size of the file. After that is done, use Insert, Picture, From File from within Word.

Controlling the Text Around Inserted Objects

Word provides a number of options for controlling the interaction between graphical objects and text. There are three basic choices, with variations:

- In line with text
- Text wrapping around
- Layered above or below the text

To see the full range of wrapping options, right-click a picture and choose Format Picture. Click the Layout tab, and then click Advanced. Click the Text Wrapping tab, to display the dialog box shown in Figure 11.33. You'll get the same basic set of options for other objects, as well, such as picture clips, WordArt, equation object, text boxes, Excel objects, and so on.

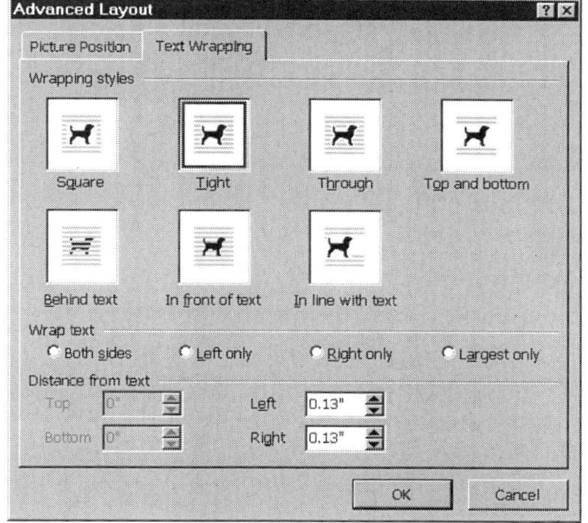

FIGURE 11.33
The Advanced Layout dialog box controls where wrapping can take place.

Figure 11.34 contains an equation object, which is formatted as square (Format Object, Layout tab, Advanced, and Square), with text wrapping only on the left side. When choosing square formatting, it helps if text is fully justified (Format, Paragraph, Alignment) and if hyphenation is enabled (Tools, Language, Hyphenation). If other options are selected, the edges can be unacceptably ragged.

The initial equation was too small, so it was resized by dragging a corner selection handle. If the sizing action is too granular or jumpy, hold down the Alt key as you drag. Without the Alt key, Word "snaps to" an invisible grid. Using the Alt key suppresses the gritty action.

With the Picture toolbar displayed, click the Text Wrapping tool and choose Behind Text.

CAUTION

When you plan to send a picture behind text, send it in front of text first for positioning. Often, the picture gets so lost behind text that you can no longer select it. Therefore, it is best to send it in front first, and then position it. Do not send it behind the text until it's in the correct position. If a graphic does get lost behind text–such that you cannot select it–one technique for getting a handle on it is to cut (to the Clipboard) some of the text that is covering it up, taking care not to accidentally delete the object itself. When the object is selectable again, send it in front of the text, and then restore the deleted text. When you get the graphic and document positioned just the way you want it, you can send it behind text again.

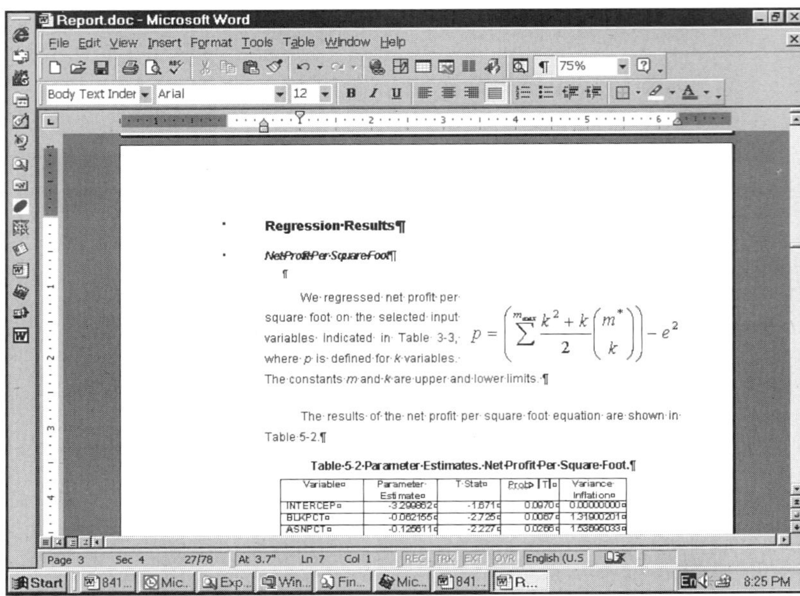

FIGURE 11.34
Equations typically are placed to the right or left of text.

Notice that the underlying image blocks out part of the text. You can try using the brightness and contrast controls to lighten or fade the picture. While the picture is selected, you can always undo your changes by clicking the Reset Picture button.

The Layout tab also includes a wrapping style called Tight. The Tight option places text wherever there is room. You can set the distance between the object and the text. Right-click the object and choose Format Object. Click the Layout tab, and then the Advanced button. As shown in Figure 11.35, the default right and left distance between the object and text is .13 inch. You can accept the default or enter your own distances. Click OK twice to apply your changes to the object.

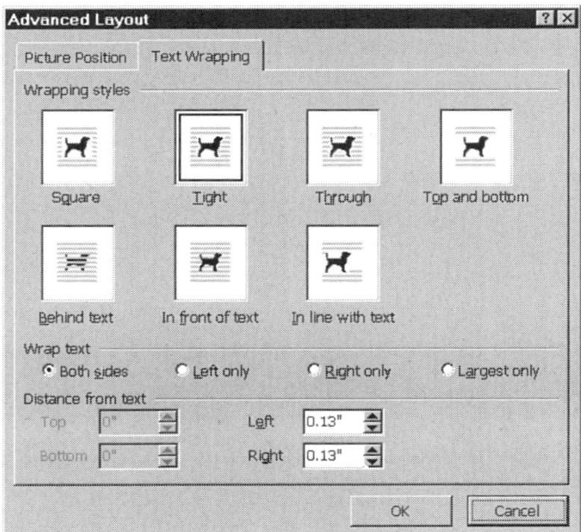

FIGURE 11.35
Don't set the distance from text too small.

Adding Headings or Captions to Inserted Objects

Word makes it easy to create captions for inserted objects. Captions help you keep track of objects by numbering them. This can be essential in long documents. Using Word's captioning also provides a built-in way to cross-reference inserted objects in other parts of the document. To insert a caption:

1. Move the insertion point to where you want the caption. Be sure to choose a blank paragraph, because the resulting caption will be formatted with the Caption style. If you choose an existing paragraph with text, that text will be formatted with the Caption style as well.
2. Choose Insert, Caption, and the Caption dialog box displays, as shown in Figure 11.36.
3. Choose the caption Label you want (if the defaults aren't adequate, click New Label and add new ones).
4. Click Numbering, choose the desired format, and then click OK.
5. Click in the Caption text box, and add a descriptive title for the object.
6. Click OK.

FIGURE 11.36
Create new labels if the pull-down menu doesn't meet your needs.

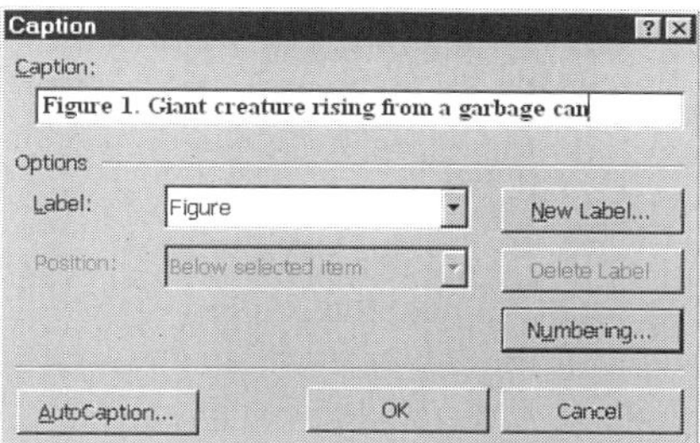

To create a shortcut for this procedure, choose Insert, Caption again. Click AutoCaption to display the AutoCaption dialog box shown in Figure 11.37. Go through the list of different object types and put a check mark next to each one you'll need, setting Use Label, Position, and Numbering as appropriate. Use New Label to create any new labels you need.

FIGURE 11.37
Word automatically creates captions for more than 50 object types.

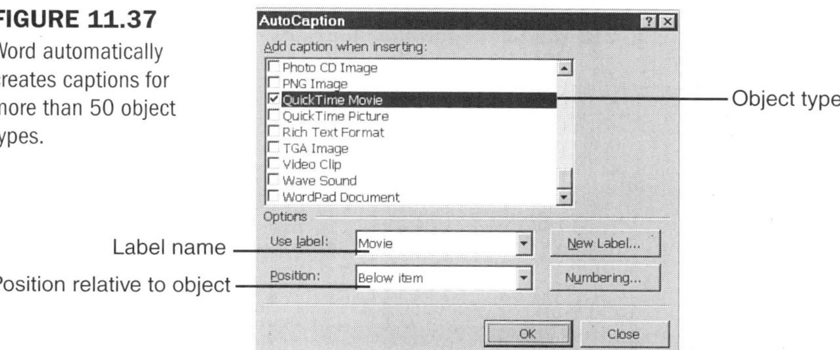

After you have set the AutoCaption options, anytime you insert an object of the checked type(s), Word inserts a caption automatically. You can annotate the caption, as needed, to add a descriptive title for the object.

Object numbers are inserted as a SEQ field, using the label name as the name of the SEQ field (for example, SEQ Table, SEQ Figure, and so on). SEQ fields are used to insert ***sequence numbers*** for figures, tables, equations, and so on. The first occurrence of a *{SEQ figure}* field resolves as 1, the second as 2, and so on. You can use these numbers as cross-references to refer to inserted objects from elsewhere in the document:

1. Choose Insert, Cross-Reference.
2. In Reference type, choose the type of object to which you're referring; labels you added using New Label will also appear in the list.
3. In Insert Reference To, select the reference you want (for example, entire caption, label and number, caption text, page number, the word Above or Below, depending on the position of the object in relation to the reference).
4. When referring to a page number, you can also include the word Above or Below by checking the check box.
5. In For Which Caption, choose the caption you're cross referencing.
6. For online documents, click Insert As Hyperlink.
7. Click Insert to insert as many cross-references as you need, and then click Close.

Adding a Watermark Graphic Behind Your Text

When inserting transparent graphics over or under text, text sometimes becomes difficult to read. To avoid this, you can turn the image into a watermark. For a graphic inserted into a document, you can use Image Control, Watermark from the Picture toolbar. This option washes out most or all the color in the picture, leaving behind a faded rendering of the original picture. You can also use text as a watermark, by using WordArt.

This alone, however, is not sufficient for a watermark as they typically are used—unless you want it just on one page. Instead, you need to insert the image into a *header or footer*, so that it repeats on every page. Common applications for watermarks include company logos, the word `Confidential`, or the word `Draft`.

You can create a watermark by using a variety of different sources for the image or artwork: a picture clip, WordArt, or a drawing object. To create one using WordArt, in a new document window, do the following:

1. Choose View, Header and Footer.
2. Choose Insert, Picture, WordArt.
3. Select a WordArt style, and choose OK.
4. In the Text area, replace Your Text Here with the text you want to appear as a watermark; in Figure 11.38, the word `Draft` will appear as a watermark. Then click OK.

5. Click the Zoom pull-down, and choose Whole Page.
6. Using the sizing controls on the WordArt object, shape or size it as desired—being careful to keep the image on the page.
7. On the WordArt toolbar, click the Text Wrapping tool and choose Behind Text.
8. Click Format WordArt on the toolbar, and choose Layout, Advanced, Picture Position. Turn off Move Object with Text. Click OK.
9. If the selected color is too dark, click the Color and Lines tab in the Format WordArt dialog box. Set Line Color to No Line; and Fill Color to a very light shade of gray. Click OK.
10. Click Close on the Header and Footer toolbar.

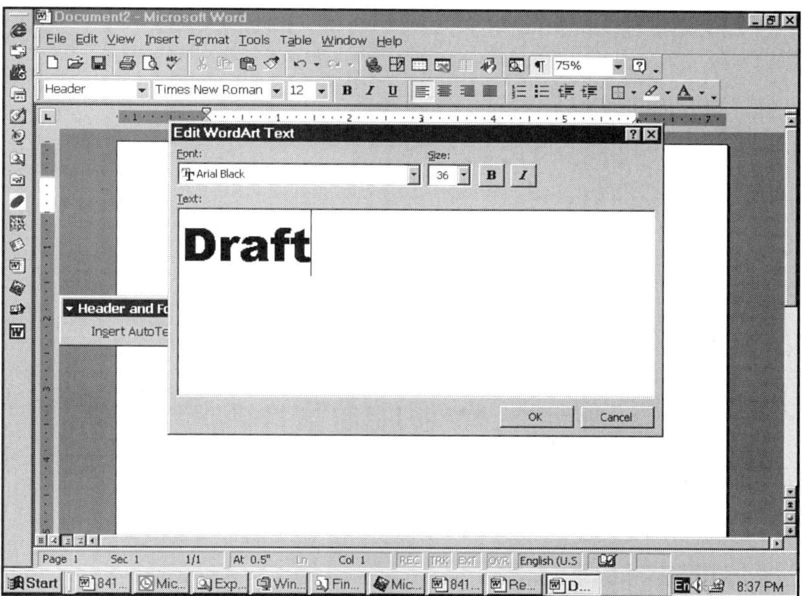

FIGURE 11.38
Choose an interesting Font for your watermark.

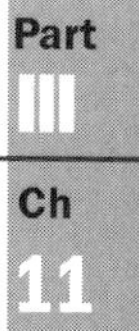

You should already be in Print Layout view, so you can see your handiwork. Try inserting some text to see how it looks. Print out a page. If you're satisfied with it, and would like to use it as stationery, choose File, Save As, and save it as a document template. You can use Tools, Templates and Add-Ins, Organizer to copy any needed styles. If this is a watermark you'd like to use in existing templates, save your watermark as an AutoText entry.

Choose View, Header and Footer, and redisplay the header or footer where you created the watermark. Press Ctrl+A to select the entire header or footer. Choose Tools, AutoCorrect, AutoText. In Enter AutoText Entries Here, type a name for the watermark, and click Add. Now, open any template in which you want to include that watermark, and choose View, Header and Footer. Type the watermark's name, press F3 (Insert AutoText).

The Watermark option is available only for pictures. There are specific lightening techniques for different kinds of graphics. If a graphic activates the Picture toolbar (which coincides with the presence of a Picture tab in the Format Object or Format Picture dialog box), then you can use the Image Control, Watermark button on the Picture toolbar (Format Picture, Picture tab, Color, Watermark) setting to get the desired effect. For Microsoft Drawing objects, use the File Color and Line Color controls on the Drawing toolbar. For an object that activates Microsoft Photo Editor, use Photo Editor's control to lighten and/or shape the picture.

Problem/Solution—Creating a Newsletter

You can use page layout tools described in this chapter to design and set up a professional-looking newsletter for your business or organization. To do this, you can make use of a number of different tools and techniques:

- Section breaks
- Different first-page header
- Click and type
- Linked text boxes
- Cross-references
- Watermarks

Title and Setup

In creating a newsletter, it's often useful to begin by creating a separate section for each page. This provides flexibility, giving you the advantage of different formatting on each page. To divide a blank document into sections, choose Insert, Break, Next Page to create a two-section document; then press F4 (Repeat) for each additional page you plan to have in the newsletter. Then, move the insertion point to the top of the document (the first section).

When doing initial document layout, it helps to be in Layout view (View, Print Layout). The vertical ruler is also a useful tool for laying out documents (choose Tools, Options, View tab, and click Vertical ruler under Print and Web Layout options). Also in the View tab, another useful layout aid is Formatting Marks, All.

Double-click the vertical ruler to summon the Page Setup dialog box. In the Layout tab, the following steps are often useful in setting up for creating a newsletter:

1. Check the Different First Page box.
2. From the Apply To drop-down menu, choose This Section.
3. On the Margins tab, widen the top margin to two inches or more—this will give ample room for a nice eye-catching title.
4. For better use of space, reduce the left, right, and bottom margins to .75".
5. Then click OK.

Move down to the second section (just after the first section break), and double-click the vertical ruler to invoke Page Setup again. In the Margins tab, set top, bottom, left, and right all to .75". Chances are, you won't need a large title area after the first page. Set Apply To to This Point Forward. This establishes narrow margins all around on the remaining pages.

Back at the top of your document, choose View, Header and Footer, and create your newsletter title. This is also a good place for the date, volume, and issue number (if desired). For the title, choose a font and point size appropriate for the target audience (see Figure 11.39).

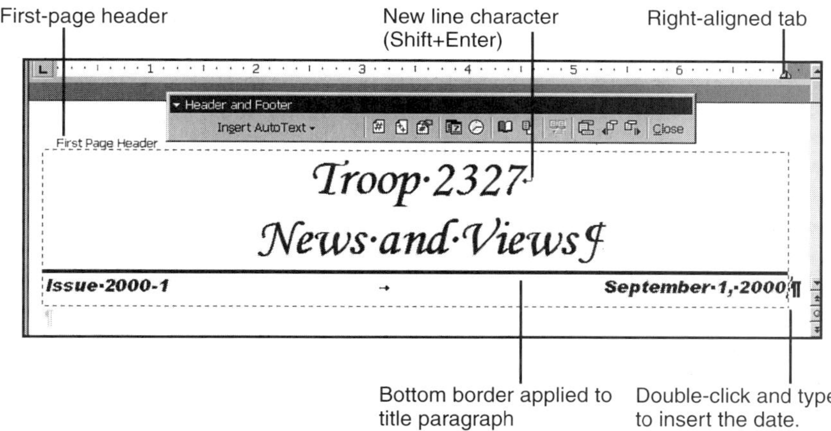

FIGURE 11.39
If color printing is an option, you can be creative with your title.

Part III Ch 11

To create the flush left and right effect for the issue number and date, the technique is to justify the entire line, separate the two items with a Tab, and set a right tab at the right indent. Here's a technique that uses Word's new [Double] Click and Type feature:

1. Click the Justify tool on the Formatting toolbar.
2. Type the item for the left half of the line, such as an issue number.
3. In the same line, double-click where you want the date to *end*—exactly under the ruler line's Right Indent slider. This should insert a tab character and cause a right-aligned tab to be set at the right margin.
4. Type the date, and format it as appropriate for the document you're creating.

A common option for newsletters is to include a line below the title and above the date. To create a line, click the last line of the title and choose Format, Borders and Shading. Under Style, Color, and Width, choose the type of line you want. Then, in the Preview box, click the bottom to apply those settings to the bottom line segment. Now the preview reflects your preferences, as shown in Figure 11.40. You may also need to click the left, right, and top segments to remove them. Then click OK. Click Close on the Header and Footer toolbar.

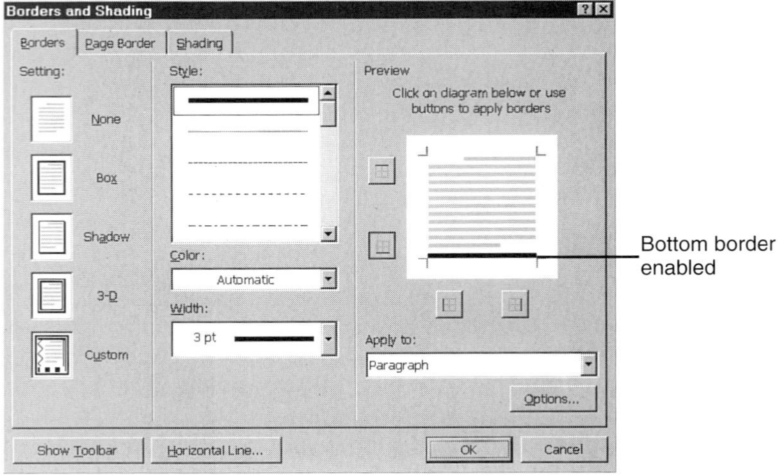

FIGURE 11.40
Choose the line style, size, and color before clicking the Preview box.

Adding the Watermark

Choose View, Header and Footer, and click Switch Between Header and Footer. Zoom to Whole Page. Decide what you want to use for the watermark and insert it. To use a graphic that's on your hard disk, follow these general steps:

1. Choose Insert, Picture, From file.
2. Navigate to the location of the picture; click Insert.
3. Right-click the Picture and choose Format Picture.
4. In the Picture tab, choose Color: Watermark.
5. In the Layout tab, choose In Front of Text (for now), and click the Advanced button.
6. In the Picture Position tab, turn off Move Object with Text; click OK; then click OK again to close the Format Picture dialog box.
7. As necessary, move and resize the picture so it covers the text area of the page, as shown in Figure 11.41. Distortion is generally not objectionable in graphic watermarks.

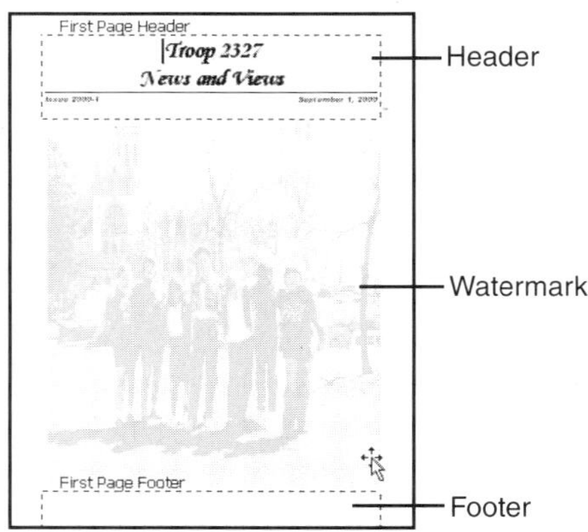

FIGURE 11.41
The normal page text area is the area between the header and footer.

8. Click Close on the Header and Footer toolbar when you're satisfied.

Designing the First Page

For a multicolumn newsletter, we could use column formatting. However, the logistics of starting multiple articles on one page and continuing them in the body of the newsletter can be complicated and time-consuming. Instead, it makes more sense to use linked text boxes—one set for each distinct item that extends across more than one page. Even if an item does not take multiple text boxes, using text boxes gives you enormous flexibility in doing paste-up layout. With each item in the newsletter—text and graphics—existing as an object, layout can be accomplished by dragging the pieces until you get exactly what you want.

To create linked text boxes, make sure you're in Print Layout view, and zoom the window to Whole Page. Choose Insert, Text Box, and draw a text box where you want the first item to reside. You could go ahead and draw additional items, but don't do it quite yet. Instead, format this *one* text box the way you want, and then copy *it* rather than drawing new ones. Choose Tools, Options, View, and click to enable Text boundaries—this enables you to see an outline of the text box after its outside border has been turned off. Click OK, and then proceed as follows:

1. Right-click the edge of the text box and choose Format Text Box.
2. In the Layout tab, choose In Front of Text, and click Advanced.
3. In Picture Position, turn off Move Object with Text so the text boxes stay in place. Write down the position for later reference (dragging can be imprecise and you might want to make a copied box exactly parallel to this one). Click OK.
4. Click the Colors and Lines tab. Under Fill, Color, choose No Fill (for now, but you can add fill later as needed), and under Line, Color, choose No Line. This turns off the text box's box. Again, you can selectively add boxes and fill (background shading) as needed to spruce up the newsletter or to highlight particular items. For now, however, just create a "vanilla" text box.
5. Click OK to apply the changes. Your document should now look similar to Figure 11.42.

Now, you're ready to copy the text box elsewhere. Move the mouse so the pointer displays as shown in Figure 11.42. Press and hold the Shift and Ctrl keys at the same time, hold down the left mouse button, and drag to the right. Adding Ctrl to a drag operation means Copy instead of Move. With the Shift key pressed, you can drag only straight to the right or straight down—depending on your initial movement, providing more precision in box alignment. When the box outline is in the desired position, release the mouse button. Reshape the copy as desired. Continue dragging off copies until page one has the desired layout. It might look similar to Figure 11.43.

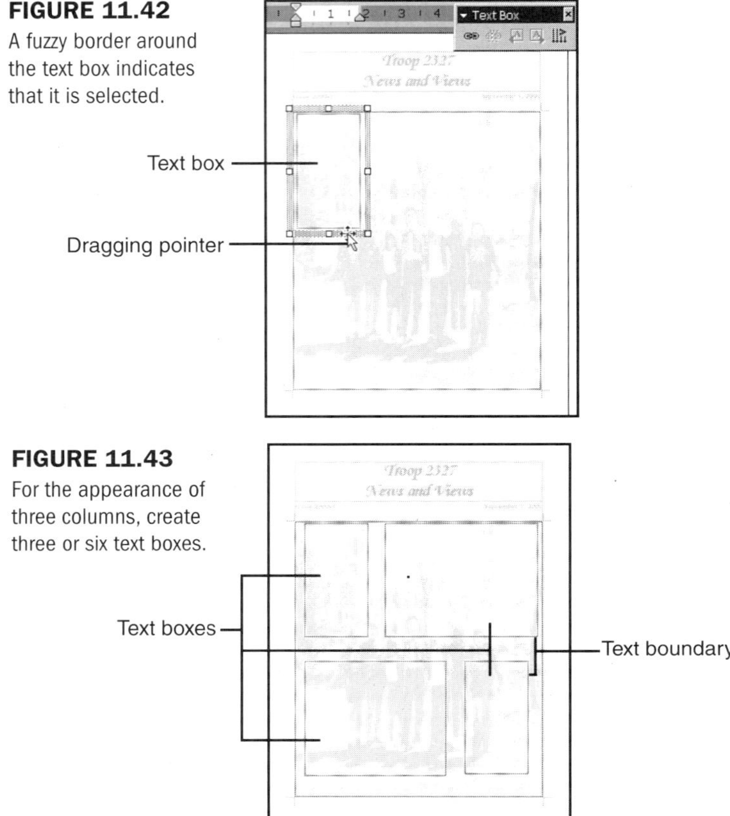

FIGURE 11.42
A fuzzy border around the text box indicates that it is selected.

FIGURE 11.43
For the appearance of three columns, create three or six text boxes.

Designing the Inside Pages

Now, page down to the next section/page and insert additional text boxes to define your layout. Repeat this on each page until the whole tentative layout is set. Keep in mind that you can change things as you go along. If you have an overall layout on any given page that you want to repeat, you can copy multiple text boxes by clicking on the first, and then using Shift+click on subsequent text boxes. Copy the whole group to the Clipboard and then paste them onto the page where you want to reuse that set.

Saving the Format As a Template

Now you're ready to insert your text—almost. Before you do that, if the format you've established is something you might want to use again, you should save the work you've done so far as a template. You could—if you like—first establish linkages between text boxes. You might, for example, link the lead story box to a box on the second page. Or, you can wait until you enter the text and link boxes as necessary. The key is to save the most likely scenario as your template to save work later.

To save the newsletter shell as a template, choose File, Save As. Set Save As Type to Document Template. This causes the Save In location to switch to the location of your templates. Choose a descriptive filename, and click Save. Then close the template. Now, choose File, New, select the template you just created (it should be on the General tab), and click OK.

Enter Text and Linking Boxes

Many newsletters are put together by pasting in items that already exist in other files. You can do it that way, or you can type directly into the text boxes. Let's assume you already have the text, but now want to copy and paste it into place. Open the source file for the first item, select the text, and copy it to the Clipboard. Now switch to the newsletter document you just began, and click in the text box where you want the item to go.

Choose Edit, Paste. Format the text and title as desired. Does the text fit inside one text box? If not, click the edge of the text box that contains the text. Then click the Create Text Box Link button on the Text Box toolbar; the pointer turns into an upright pitcher. Move to the page and text box that you want to receive the rest of the text and click in the next text box to dump the tilted pitcher of text into it, as shown in Figure 11.44.

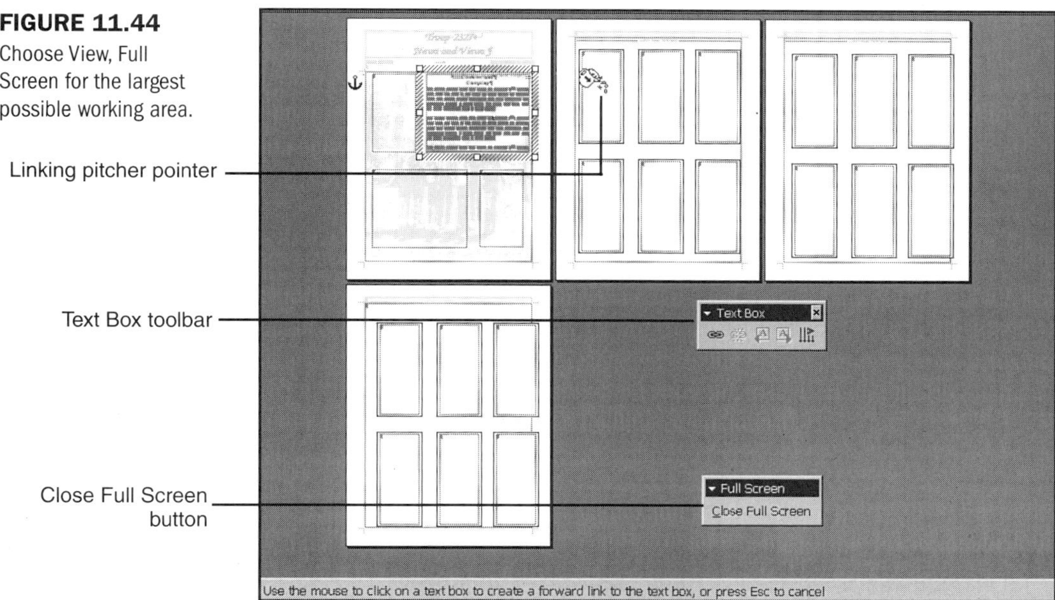

FIGURE 11.44
Choose View, Full Screen for the largest possible working area.

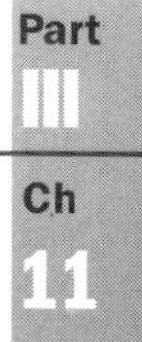

Rather than linking at this moment, you could instead paste text for all the items you want to include, and save the linking for later. When you get ready to link, choose View, Zoom, Many Pages, and try to select a view that enables you to see the entire newsletter.

From this aerial view, you should be able to get an idea of where things flow. Go ahead and link to populate the rest of the newsletter with text.

Creating the Finishing Touches

After depositing text, you can insert graphics or clip art as desired. To locate the rest of the story, go to the bottom of the first text box in a linked set. Find a good breaking point and type `See x on Page y`, where `x` is a continuation title on the continuation page, and `y` is the page number where the linked text box resides.

Press Enter so that the text that follows the continuation phrase is pushed into the next linked text box. At the top of the next text box, type and format a continuation title. Then select the title, choose Insert Bookmark, give the title a bookmark name, and click Add. Go back to the preceding page and text box and select the `x` (the continuation title). Now:

1. Choose Insert, Cross-Reference
2. Set Reference Type to Bookmark; set Insert Reference To to Bookmark Text; turn off Insert As Hyperlink (unless this is an online newsletter); select the bookmark name you gave to the title, and click Insert.
3. Without dismissing the Cross-Reference dialog box, select the `y` (the page number) in the text and set Insert Reference To to Page number; click Insert, and Close.

Now you have your continuation notice. Repeat this procedure for each continued item.

CAUTION

Possible bug alert—The page number may not resolve correctly. If the `y` page number looks like a 1 rather than the correct page number, then you'll need to replace `y` with the actual page number.

CHAPTER 12

Fields—Word's Hidden Functions

In this chapter

Using Fields in Your Everyday Documents

Fields are powerful tools that provide the engine for much of Word's word processing capability. In everyday use, fields provide the key to document automation that is the cornerstone of Word's popularity among power users. Understanding the ins and outs of fields can be essential to resolving problems that crop up from time to time. Often, adding or removing a simple switch makes the difference in getting precisely the effect you want.

Even without resorting to the Field command on the Insert menu, Word uses fields in a variety of ways. Word features that result in the creation of fields include

- Dates
- Cross-references
- Hyperlinks
- Linked files and pictures
- Embedded objects (inserted using Insert, Object)
- Formulas
- Mail Merge fields
- Forms
- Page numbers
- Some kinds of numbering

Adding a Field to a Document

As suggested in the previous section, fields are often created in the normal course of using Word (for example, choosing Insert, Date). To access all of any given field's features, however, it's sometimes necessary to insert the field directly by using the Field command from the Insert menu.

To insert a field in a document:

1. Choose Insert, Field.
2. From the Categories list, choose the type of field you want to insert. In this example, we'll choose Links and References as shown in Figure 12.1.
3. In the Field Names list, choose the specific field you want to insert. In this example, we'll use Ref.
4. Click the Options button for assistance in building the field code. As you can see from the Field Options dialog box that appears (see Figure 12.2), the options appear on separate tabs. This set of options includes tabs for General Switches, Field Specific Switches, and Bookmarks. The tabs may be different depending on which field you've selected. Setting these field options is discussed in more depth in the next section.
5. After selecting the desired options, click OK twice. The new field appears in your document.

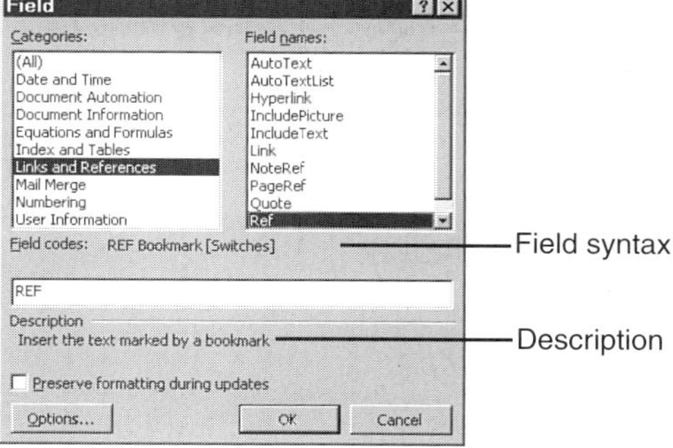

FIGURE 12.1
Under the Categories list, the Field Codes line shows the field syntax.

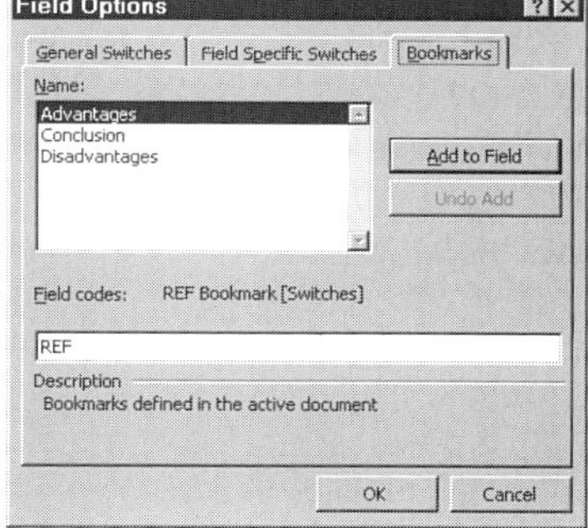

FIGURE 12.2
You can mix and match—typing or clicking Add to Field to build the code.

As shown in Figure 12.1, the Field dialog box contains a number of parts. It's useful to review what those parts are and how they can facilitate locating and building fields.

Categories The Categories section divides Word's fields into more manageable sublists to help you find fields more quickly. You should note, however, that the placement of items into categories isn't necessarily intuitive to every user. For example, not everybody would think of Numbering if they were looking for the Barcode feature. And, many people probably *would* look in Numbering for NumPages (the number of pages in the current document); NumPages is in Document Information, however—not Numbering.

If you don't see a field in the category you think most logical, then look in the All category. It's a longer list, but it contains everything, including two fields (BidiOutline and Private) that aren't in any of the other categories.

Field Names The Field Names list contains the field codes in each category. Sometimes, it's sufficient simply to locate the desired field and click OK. Other times, however, additional options are needed before the field code will perform the intended purpose.

Field Codes The Field Codes area shows a syntax model for the field. This gives you an overview of what the field must contain and what is optional. Items in brackets are optional. Items not in brackets are required for the field to work correctly. For example, for the Ref field selected in Figure 12.1, the field name Ref and the name of a bookmark are required elements. Switches that modify the basic behavior of the Ref field are optional.

Field The fill-in box just below the Field Codes syntax model is the "construction zone" for fields. If you know the syntax and options, you can type the field code directly. Or, you can click the Options button and have Word "build" the field for you through the selection of different options.

Description Area The Description area explains different options. The \h switch, for example, is used to create a hyperlink to referenced text.

Field Options For the Ref field, options are divided into three tabs: General Switches, Field Specific Switches, and Bookmarks. For inserting another passage into the current section of a document, you probably would not need any additional switches or options. For other effects—such as creating a hyperlink—choosing the correct switch is essential to having the field do what you want it to do.

Some fields, such as Ref, are used in conjunction with bookmarks. To include a bookmark in the field, you click the Bookmarks tab. Any bookmarks in the document are listed (refer to Figure 12.2). To complete bookmark selection for the Ref field, select the one that corresponds to the text to which you want to refer, and choose Add to Field. Clicking OK returns you to the Field dialog box.

Preserve Formatting During Updates The last option to consider is Preserve Formatting During Updates (refer to Figure 12.1). This option is useful when updating might undo any local formatting you apply. Suppose, for example, you use a field to insert selected paragraphs from another document into the current document, and the source document is formatted differently from the current document. You might prefer to reformat the inserted text so it conforms to the current document—while still retaining the link between the text and the original document—just in case the source text changes. The Preserve Formatting During Updates option is your insurance that you will be able to update the field without undoing your formatting changes.

When you know the field you want to insert, and you don't want to use the menu and dialog boxes, you can insert fields manually. Suppose, for example, that you want to insert a date field using the default date format. Press Ctrl+F9 to insert field braces–{ }–then type the field name, such as DATE, between the braces. It appears as { date }. You can use uppercase, lowercase, or mixed case–Word won't care. Then press F9 to update the field to the current date.

Inserting the Date and Time

One of the simplest fields you can insert in a Word document is a Date and Time field.

In a new document, choose Insert, Date and Time. Choose the date and time format from the Available Formats list and click OK. If you chose that Word should display both date and time, it might look like the following:

```
11/16/98 2:59 PM
```

You can copy, move, edit, or delete this text as you would any other text provided that the Update Automatically option was not checked in the Date and Time dialog box. That's because Word did not insert a field in this case. Rather, Word entered normal text that will not change unless you change it (in this example, a date stamp).

If you want the date and time to be updated each time the user opens the document, select the Update Automatically option. This inserts a traditional field that is updated each time the document is opened. Unless you've changed the default setting, Word also highlights fields so they appear with a light gray shading when the insertion point is placed within the field.

NOTE Word uses the Control Panel Date/Time to paste the date into the document. Word displays whatever date and time are set on the computer opening the document.

Setting the Field Highlighting Option

Generally, it's easy to tell whether you are working with field text or standard document text because Word's default setting is to display the field with gray shading whenever the user's insertion point is somewhere within the field. Many power users tell Word to add constant shading to fields so they always know when they're looking at fields rather than straight text.

To add full-time shading to your fields, choose Tools, Options, View, and then change Field shading from When Selected to Always.

To insert fields that never display shading, choose Tools, Options, View, and then change Field shading from When Selected to Always.

One instance when you might want field shading to never appear is if you want to insert bookmarked cross-reference text from another location in your document. A Word user might do this rather than retyping the text from another section. This ensures that if the text changes in the other section, the referenced quote changes, also.

First, select a paragraph in your document and bookmark it (choose Insert, Bookmark). Be sure to name the bookmark and choose Add. Now scroll to another location in the document and choose Insert, Cross-reference (see Figure 12.3).

Choose Bookmark from the Reference Type drop-down list and choose Bookmark text from the Insert Reference To drop-down list. Click Insert, then Close.

The text you bookmarked is replicated at the cursor's current location. With field codes not shaded, you might never know that what you're looking at is really a field, not just plain text.

CAUTION

You should be careful when setting field codes to never be displayed with shading because you could waste huge amounts of time changing text that appears normal but really is part of a field. Anything that updates fields—such as opening the document in Print Layout view or switching to Print Preview—however, will destroy all your work because the field refers to another section of text.

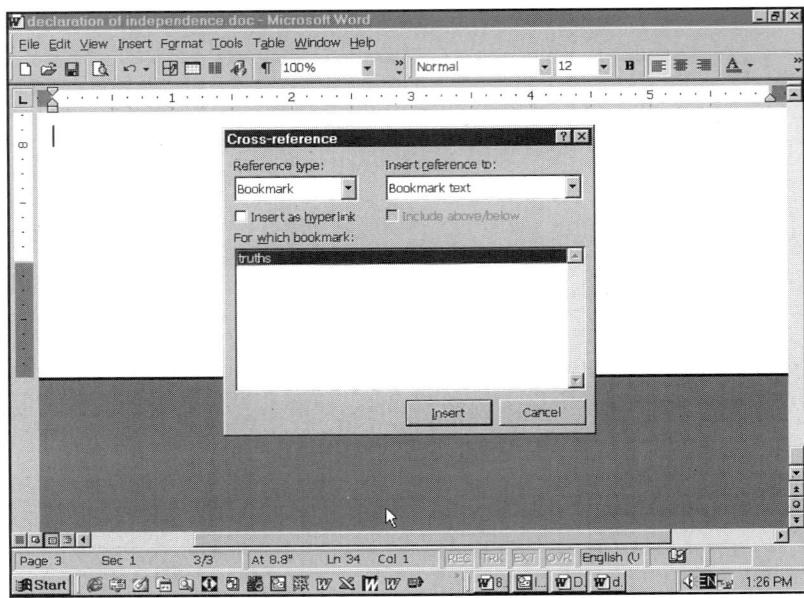

FIGURE 12.3
Whenever you insert a cross-reference, you are inserting a field code.

Switching Between Field Results and Field Code

Sometimes, as shown in Figure 12.4, a field goes awry. Often it's because something that the field depends on has changed. Perhaps a section of text containing a bookmark was deleted or a file was deleted or moved. When a field goes berserk, your best line of defense is to toggle the display of field codes (as opposed to seeing just field results). This lets you see the field code itself, so you can diagnose what the field code is trying to do, and determine what might be missing or different.

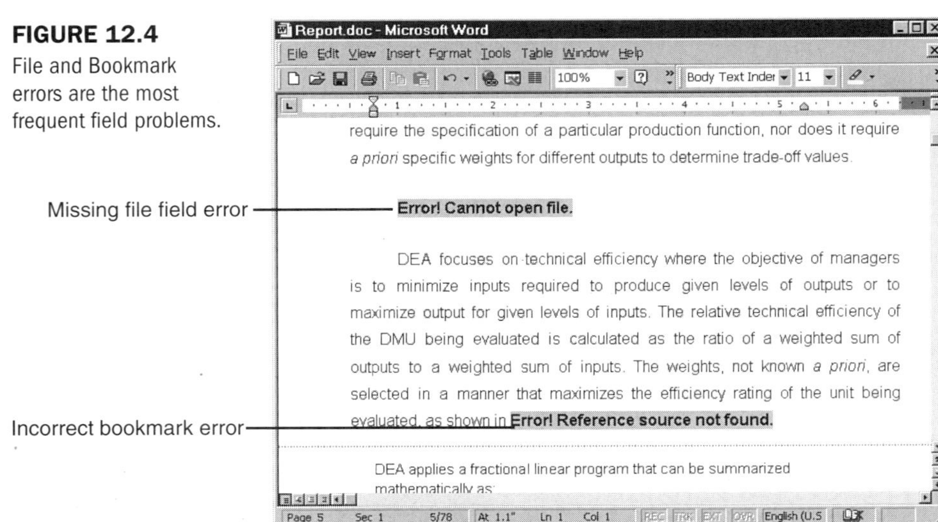

FIGURE 12.4
File and Bookmark errors are the most frequent field problems.

The easiest way to toggle field codes is to press Alt+F9. If you forget the keystroke, then choose Tools, Options, and click the View tab. Then check Field Codes. Remove the check to redisplay field code results.

Put a field toggle on your toolbar. Choose Tools, Customize, and click the Commands tab. In the Categories list on the left, choose View. Then find View Field Codes in the list of commands on the right. Drag the command to a toolbar and drop it there. Click Close. This button toggles between showing field results and field codes.

Converting Fields to Plain Text

After using a field to get precisely the result you want, you might want to convert the field result into plain text to prevent it from changing in the future. To do this, click anywhere in the field and press Ctrl+Shift+F9.

Updating Field Results

You already saw the most direct kind of field updating—pressing the F9 (Update) key. When you select a field (or a set of fields) and press F9, the field is updated or refreshed. The following options, actions, and events affect field updating:

- Tools, Options, General, Update Automatic Links at open. This option affects only links to files outside the current Word document.
- Tools, Options, Print, Update Links. This option affects the update of automatic links at the time the document is printed. Thus, if any changes have occurred between the time the document was opened and when you print, this setting determines whether or not those changes will be reflected in the printed version.
- Tools, Options, Print, Update Fields. This option affects the update of fields (not just automatic links) at the time the document is printed.
- Opening a document in Print Layout view updates all fields except for links to other documents (for example, IncludeText fields).
- Repagination causes fields in headers and footers to be updated.
- Switching to Print Layout or Print Preview updates all fields, except for links to other documents, in the current document.
- Printing a document updates all fields (unless Update Fields is turned off).
- Pressing Ctrl+A (Select All) and pressing F9 (Update Fields) updates all fields.

Why Did Word Automatically Update My Fields?

Some Word operations can update fields automatically, even when you don't want them updated. Suppose, for example, a letter contains a date field that shows when a letter was originally sent. If you need to produce a copy of that letter for the IRS, you probably don't want the date field updated.

continues

continued

Changing into Print Layout view could, however, automatically update the date without your even knowing it. When working with a document in which you want to preserve fields, you should avoid switching into a view that automatically updates fields, as well as avoid any operations (such as editing graphics) that result in the view being reset automatically. Also, keep in mind that Word automatically reopens a file in the same view in which it was last closed–so, if it was last saved in Page Layout view, fields (other than links) will be updated. Better still, lock the fields, as shown in the following sidebar, or, once a document is finished, replace fields with actual text to avoid the update hassle altogether.

Locking Fields to Prevent Unwanted Changes

You can lock fields so that they don't change. Most fields can be locked so that they cannot be updated–automatically or otherwise. Select the field and press Ctrl+3 (main keyboard–not the number pad) to lock. Use Ctrl+4 (main keyboard) to unlock fields. Suppose, for example, that you want to insert an Excel chart into a document and then lock the chart against updates. At the same time, you don't want to exclude the possibility of updating in the future. Rather, you just want full control of when and how updating occurs. Select the chart field and press Ctrl+3.

This locks the field so that it cannot be updated by opening, printing, pressing F9, and so on–even if various automatic update options are enabled. This is useful when your text refers to specific numbers in a chart, and you don't want the chart to change, rendering the text wrong. If you later decide to change the discussion and therefore change the chart, click the chart, press Ctrl+4 to unlock it, and then press F9 to update it. Then press Ctrl+3 again to relock it.

Understanding Field Syntax

Word's basic field syntax is

```
FIELDNAME [options] [switches]
```

Depending on the type of field, the exact specifications vary greatly. The best way to begin understanding field syntax is to choose Insert, Field, and take a look at the syntax models displayed there. Figure 12.5 shows the basic syntax model for the = field.

The parts not bracketed are required. The parts in [square brackets] are optional. Thus, at a minimum, an = field must contain some kind of formula. To see what these formulas can contain, press F1 to start Help, and then click Contents, Field Types and Switches. Help for the = field is shown in Figure 12.6.

If you see a useful example in the Help window, use the mouse to select it, copy it to the Clipboard (Ctrl+C), and then paste it into the Field Code text box in the Field dialog box.

The = field code is useful for performing math operations in Word documents—especially tables. In a table containing columns of numbers to be tallied, put the insertion point where you want the sum to appear. Then, choose Table, Formula, Sum(Above), as shown in Figure 12.7.

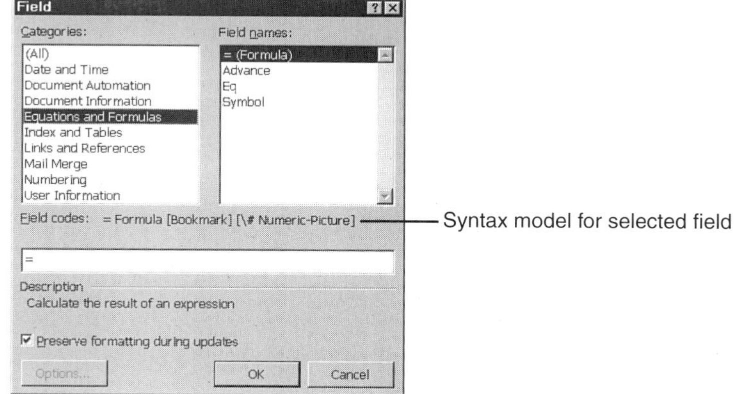

FIGURE 12.5
The Options button helps build some field codes–but not the = field.

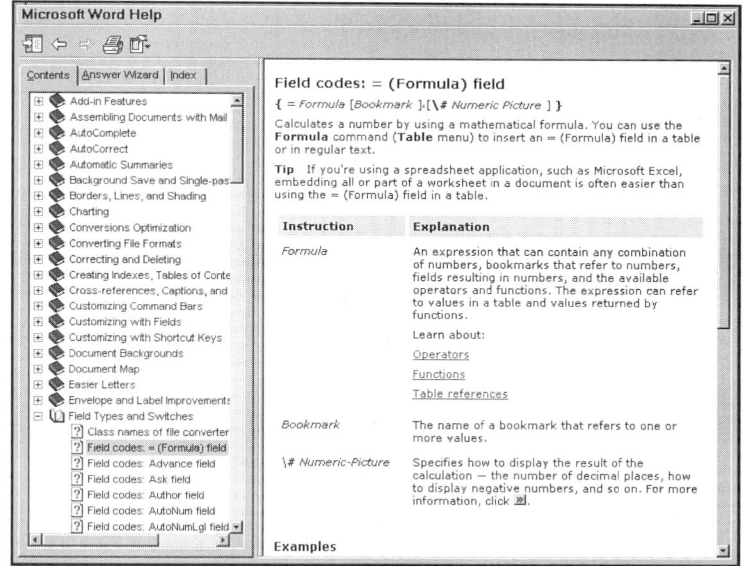

FIGURE 12.6
Help provides syntax and examples.

The dialog box shown in Figure 12.7 produces an = field that adds a column of numbers in a table. You can also bookmark text in and out of tables, and use bookmarks as variables in formulas. For example, suppose you have a table that displays NNP (Net National Product) in a table cell. You can bookmark that cell, naming it NNP. You can then use the NNP bookmark in = fields to perform calculations—anywhere in that document.

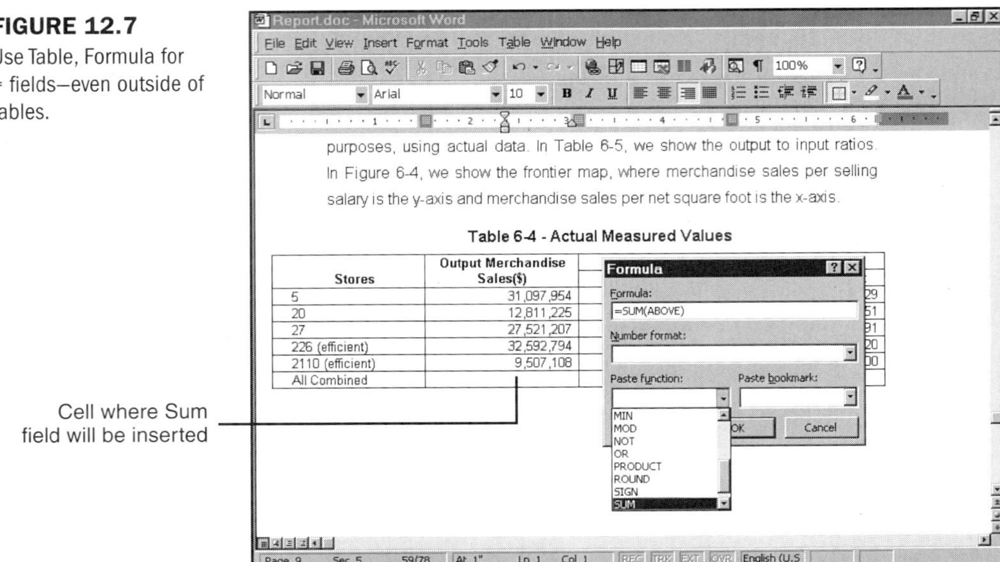

FIGURE 12.7
Use Table, Formula for = fields—even outside of tables.

Field Categories

Word has 73 different types of fields, most of which are listed in the All Category list in the Field dialog box (choose Insert, Field). If 73 seems a bit overwhelming, you can see Word's taxonomy by choosing one of Word's nine categories listed in the Field dialog box as described in the following sections.

Date and Time

This category includes not only the current date and time, but the date and time the current document was created, printed, or saved. For example, for critical time-sensitive documents, many users use the CreateDate field rather than Date for letters. This completely avoids the problem of inadvertently changing a letter's original date:

```
{ CreateDate }
```

Document Automation

This category includes fields useful for automating certain document functions. For example, the GoToButton field is used to create a hyperlink in a document. Unlike Web-style hyperlinks, GoToButton links must be double-clicked. The GoToButton is used in conjunction with a bookmark name that "tells" the GoToButton where to go, and user instructions. In this example, "form1035" would be a bookmark name, and "Double-click…" is the instruction:

```
{ GOTOBUTTON form1035 Double-click here to go to Form 1035 }
```

Document Information

This category includes information typically found when you choose File, Properties. A useful application here, for example, is to provide information about the current document. A useful piece of information to include is the name of the document author, which isn't always the same as the name of the current user. The author's name, which is set by choosing File, Properties, Summary, is displayed using the field:

```
{author}
```

Equations and Formulas

This category includes fields for creating special text effects (overprinting characters, equations without using the equation editor, and so on), offsetting text, table math, and inserting symbols by character number. For example, to create a 0 with a line through it, you could use the EQ field and the Overstrike (\O) switch:

```
{ EQ \O(0,/) }
```

Index and Tables

This category includes fields for creating tables of content, tables of authorities, and indexes. For example, the TOC field inserts a table of contents, such as

```
TOC \o "1-3" \h \z
```

The \h switch creates hyperlinks to sections listed in the table of contents, and the \z switch suppresses page numbers in Web Layout view.

Links and References

This category includes fields for inserting cross-references, AutoText, and several kinds of links (including hyperlinks). One particularly useful reference field is StyleRef. This field, most often used in headers or footers, displays the most recent occurrence of text formatted with a given style. This often is used to display the chapter or section title at the top of each page. To display the most recent ("current") Heading 1 text, use

```
{StyleRef "Heading 1"
```

Mail Merge

This category includes fields for handling Mail Merge data and logic. Many of these fields are inserted automatically when using Word's Mail Merge Helper tools. The Fill-In (FillIn) field is particularly useful in document automation. It provides a dialog box to prompt the user to enter information needed for the document. The Fill-In field sometimes is used for entering names or other information that might be missing from a mail merge database:

```
{FILLIN "Type Company Name""
```

The user's response is displayed at the field's location and is used in the merge. The Fill-In field can be useful in non-mail merge documents as well (for example, for setting up automatic letter templates).

Numbering

This category includes page numbers, section numbers, list numbering, sequence numbering, and paragraph numbering without using the numbering tool. The Seq field is especially useful in reports for numbering chapters, tables, figures, and other serial inserts. The following text and Seq field might be used in producing equation numbers:

```
Equation {SEQ chapter}.{SEQ equation}
```

Here, "chapter" is the name given to a field that numbers chapters, and "equation" is used for each individual equation. This number might display, for example, as `Equation 7.3`.

User Information

This category includes information such as name, initials, and address from the User Information tab in the Options dialog box (choose Tools, Options). If the address field is filled in, the following field might be useful as a return address field in an envelope template:

```
{UserAddress}
```

Ten of Word's Most Useful Fields

Fields are sometimes better than "hard-coded" text for a number of good reasons. One of the best reasons is that using fields enables you to create *variables* in your documents. By using a variable, information in your document can vary, depending on the circumstance of the particular user who opens that document. They're also useful in templates because they enable you to insert the date and the user's name, for example, without knowing the user's name in advance.

UserName

The UserName field displays the name listed on the User Information tab in the Options dialog box (choose Tools, Options). This is an extremely handy field to use in designing templates for an organization. For example, it's often useful to include the name of the person who created the document in the header or footer of certain kinds of reports—especially draft copies of reports. The UserName field often is appropriate as the signature line in letters or email.

CAUTION

If you haven't actually set your username by choosing Tools, Options, User Information, Word displays whatever happens to be there. Sometimes, it's "Current User" or even the name of the person who used to sit at your desk. So, before relying on this useful feature, be sure the username is correct.

To insert the UserName field:

1. Choose Insert, Field, and select the User Information category.
2. In the Field names list choose UserName.

3. Click OK to insert the username exactly as it appears in the User Information options tab. Or, click Options to force the field to always capitalize in a particular way.
4. Choose the desired Formatting option; click Add to Field; then click OK.

NOTE The Preserve Formatting During Updates option is irrelevant in this instance because the User Information option settings are unformatted (and hence, contain no inherent formatting that might override any manual formatting you might apply to the field results).

5. Click OK to insert the field.

As a special bonus, the other two UserInformation fields are also useful for constructing templates: UserInitials and UserAddress. UserAddress can serve as a return address and UserInitials can be used at the bottom of business letters.

FileName

The FileName field displays the name of the current Word document. Providing hard copy of Word documents, including the filename, can help steer readers toward the source of a document they're reading. By including the name as a field, it changes automatically if the document is renamed.

To insert the filename:

1. Choose Insert, Field.
2. In the Categories list, choose Document Information.
3. In the Field Names list, select FileName.
4. To include the full file path with the filename, choose Options, Field Specific Switches. The \p switch includes the path for the file—the drive and folder where the file resides. This information is useful in directing the reader to the location of the file. Click Add to Field if you want to include it.
5. The General Switches tab provides capitalization options.
6. Click OK to finish up with Field Options, and click OK to insert the field.

Note that Preserve Formatting During Updates is only useful when the underlying information source is formatted. For filenames, it is not.

NumPages

The NumPages field displays the total number of pages in the current document. Do you ever notice faxes, memos, or reports that include Page X of Y in the header or footer of each page, that is, Page 1 of 5? The x of y page numbering is important for some organizations and documents. For sheets coming off a fax machine, it's downright vital. Not only does it let you know how to reassemble the fax after someone invariably drops it on the floor, but it also lets you know whether the document you have is intact.

To add x of y page numbering to a document:

1. Choose View, Header and Footer.
2. Click the Insert AutoText drop-down button on the Header and Footer toolbar and choose Page X of Y. This inserts a page field for x and a NumPages field for y.

NOTE The NumPages field can also be inserted by clicking the Insert Number of Pages tool on the Header and Footer toolbar, or by choosing Insert, Field, Document Information, NumPages. Use the Insert, Field method when you want to insert the NumPages field outside of a header or footer. Use the Insert Number of Pages tool when you want to use the number of pages in a different context than "Page x of y."

NumWords

Professional writers often receive assignments to write a document that contains a set number of words. Some writers see it as a goal—while others see it as a limitation! Regardless, it's crucial for the writer to know how they're doing with respect to their target.

The NumWords field displays the number of words in the current document. To insert the NumWords field, choose Insert, Field, Document Information category, NumWords field, OK.

Insert a NumWords field at the end of your document. Then, click it and press F9 each time you want to see how you're doing. Or, better still, quickly assign the ToolsWordCount command to a keystroke. Press Ctrl+Alt+Add (plus sign on the number pad) to display the cloverleaf pointer. Then choose Tools, Word Count. When the Customize Keyboard dialog box appears, the ToolsWordCount command automatically appears in the dialog box. Press the shortcut key combination you want to use, and press Enter.

Date

The Date field inserts today's date. This field is useful in headers, footers, letters, and lots of other places. It's also handy to include in setting up templates. Word provides a number of formatting options. If the list of display options in the Date and Time dialog box doesn't display the type of display format you need, look at the date-time picture switches later in this chapter.

▶ **See** "Date-Time Picture Switches," **p. 374**

To insert a date field, choose Insert, Date and Time. Under Available Formats, choose the one you need, as shown in Figure 12.8. Select Update Automatically. Without this latter option, Word inserts just the date, rather than a date field. If you have multiple languages installed, then choose the desired language. Click OK.

▶ For more information using Word with other languages, **see** "International Usage Features," **p. 231**

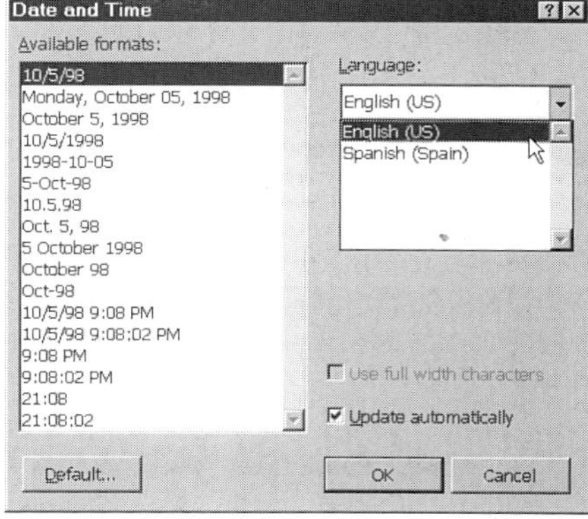

FIGURE 12.8
Default controls the date format of dates inserted with Alt+Shift+D.

CAUTION

Do you really want a Today's Date field? Sometimes you do, and sometimes you don't. If you want the date that a letter actually was sent, then you probably don't want the date to be updated after the letter has been sent. If you create and send letters on the same day, the CreateDate field might be more useful to you, or you might want to convert the date into normal text.

▶ **See** "Converting Fields to Plain Text," **p. 355**

Notice the Default button in the Data and Time dialog box (refer to Figure 12.8). Most users have a particular date format they usually want. If Word's default—10/5/99— isn't as useful as October 5, 1999 or some other format, then choose the preferred format and click the Default button. This does two things. First, it means that a simple DATE field—with no switches—will display in the preferred format from now on. Second, it means that the default Insert Date keystrokes (Alt+Shift+D) will now also insert the date in the new default format using a field code with the appropriate Date-Time Picture format switches.

TOC and TC

The TOC and TC fields are used in creating tables of content. The easiest way to create a table of contents in Word is to use the built-in Heading 1 through Heading 9 styles for heading levels. Then, inserting a TOC field automatically creates a table of contents for the document, listing each Heading # as a table of contents entry.

▶ **See** "Creating Tables of Contents and Similar Tables," **p. 442**

To insert a table of contents based on Heading # headings, choose Insert, Index and Tables, Table of Contents tab, to display the dialog box shown in Figure 12.9. By default, the Table of Contents shows three levels: Heading 1 through Heading 3. However, you can set up to nine levels.

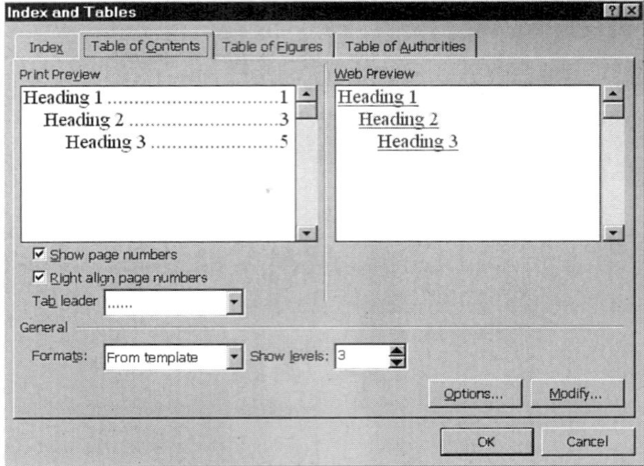

FIGURE 12.9
The default table of contents is keyed to outline level styles.

If you want to use styles to build your table of contents, but don't use Heading 1 through Heading 9, or perhaps start below level 1, you can choose Format, Style, Modify, Format, Paragraph, Outline Level to assign outlining levels to nonheading styles.

You can set a number of options in the Index and Tables dialog box.

- Show Page Numbers—Disabling the Show Page Numbers option is useful if you just want to create an overview for a document rather than a formal table of contents.
- Right Align Page Numbers—You can also choose whether page numbers are flush right or hug the table of contents entries.
- Tab Leader—For a tightly spaced table of contents, it's useful to have a tab leader to help the reader's eye move across from the entry to the page number.
- Formats—The Formats list lets you choose from a gallery of preset table of content formats. The default—From Template—uses the built-in TOC 1 through TOC 9 styles defined in the document or the underlying template.

Click the Options button to display the Table of Contents Options dialog box shown in Figure 12.10. This screen lets you choose whether to build your table of contents from styles, Table Entry Fields (more about these in a moment), or both.

Another option to consider is marking table of contents entries yourself. You might choose to do this either because you don't use any styles at all (for example, the entire document might be formatted as Normal, using direct formatting to achieve the desired layout). Or, perhaps you are using styles, but want to selectively include additional items in the table of contents on-the-fly.

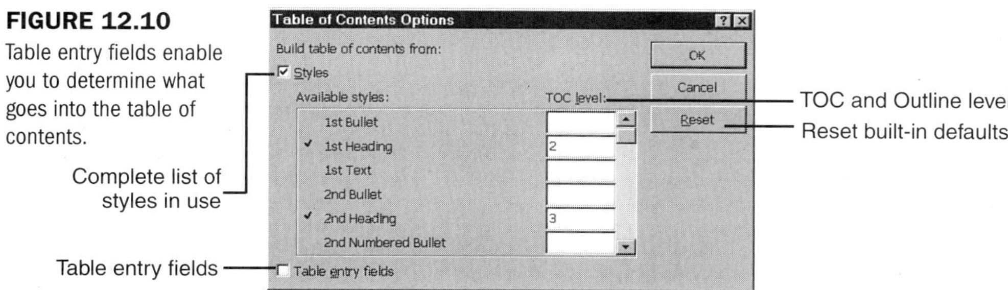

FIGURE 12.10
Table entry fields enable you to determine what goes into the table of contents.

To mark items for inclusion in the table of contents, you have two choices. First place the insertion in front of a line of text you want to use in the table of contents. You can choose Insert, Field and find the TC field in the Index and Tables category. Second, a much better way, is to press Alt+Shift+O to display the Mark Table of Contents Entry dialog box shown in Figure 12.11. Whether or not you select the item you want in the table of contents before pressing Alt+Shift+O, the selected text is automatically copied into the Entry field.

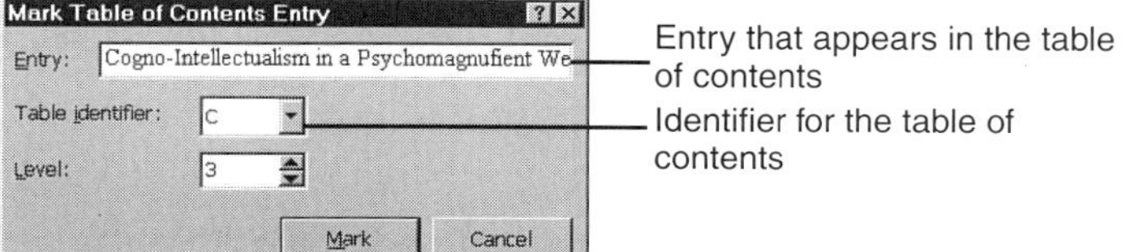

FIGURE 12.11
Press Alt+Shift+O to quickly insert TC fields.

NOTE The TC field does not resolve the way most other fields do. TC field codes are assigned the hidden text attribute. If hidden text display (choose Tools, Options, View) is turned on, the TC field code itself is displayed in your document to let you know it's there.

Part III Ch 12

The Table Identifier typically isn't needed unless you're collecting entries for a special kind of table. For example, suppose you are marking a group of common elements and are identifying them with the letter A. Further, you want to collect those items into a special table. You identify each item in that set with A. Then, to insert the table of contents field, choose Insert, Field, Index and Tables, TOC. In Options, find the /f switch, and add it to the field. Include the letter A after the /f. This tells the TOC field to collect only items with the A identifier.

▶ **See** "Creating Tables of Contents and Similar Tables," **p. 442**

IF

The IF field is used to display different text, depending on the result of an expression. This can be especially useful in invoices and forms. For example, the following field displays a different message for Vermont than for other states:

```
{IF state = VT "Vermont residents must pay ten cent deposit" "Deposit not
➥charged"}
```

The IF field is also commonly used to prevent blank lines from occurring in addresses when doing certain kinds of mail merges. For example, the following group of fields (based on bookmarks) would have a blank line if Company is missing or not applicable and the merge options are set to print blank lines:

```
{MERGEFIELD name}
{MERGEFIELD company}
{MERGEFIELD address}
{MERGEFIELD province}
{MERGEFIELD pcode}
```

You could, however, replace the company field with an IF statement:

```
{MERGEFIELD name}
{IF {MERGEFIELD company} <> "" "{MERGEFIELD company}
"}{MERGEFIELD address}
{MERGEFIELD province}
{MERGEFIELD pcode}
```

Here, the company field is not displayed unless it's nonblank.

NOTE When doing mail merge, Word provides an option not to print blank lines where data is missing. From inside the main merge document, click the Mail Merge Helper toolbar button, click Merge, and choose the option Don't Print Blank Lines When Data Fields Are Empty.

FileSize

The world of electronic mail is rapidly replacing the days when Office workers need to tuck a file onto a floppy disk for taking home to work over the weekend. Instead, they just email it to their home email address. Sometimes, however, when traveling to a remote location that has a computer but lacks an Internet connection, the old ways cannot be abandoned. When it comes time to put your document onto a floppy disk, you're faced with the eternal question: Will it fit?

Unlike the NumChars field (which tells you how many characters are contained in the text of your document), the FileSize field tells you the actual size of the file stored on the hard disk. So, without having to use the Windows Explorer, or without having to resort to File Open or other methods, you can quickly create a FileSize field in the current document, and use it to determine whether the current document will fit onto a given disk.

The FileSize field is also useful when graphics or other complicated elements are affecting file size. By including a FileSize field in the current document, you have a quick and easy way to assess the effects of different linking and embedding options on file size.

To quickly insert a FileSize field, press Ctrl+F9, type `FileSize`, and press the F9 key.

Section and SectionPages

The Section field inserts the current section number. This can be useful in setting up numbering that varies by section. Where you already have an existing page number field, you can pair it with a section field to get section/page numbering, such as Page VII-47. This can also be useful in numbering figures or tables by section. In a header, footer, or caption, set the insertion point in front of the existing page or item number. Choose Insert, Field. In Categories, choose Numbering, and in Field Names choose Section. Click the Options button. Under Formatting, choose the desired formatting and click Add to Field, as appropriate. Then click OK, and back in the Field dialog box click OK again.

NOTE In Chapter 11, "Making the Most of Your Page Layout," certain difficulties were pointed out with using section numbers rather than basing section/chapter numbering on the use of heading styles. The most significant drawback occurs where you need section breaks for other purposes—for example, to enable columnar or landscape/portrait changes. For more details, see "Working with Section Page Numbering" in Chapter 11.

The SectionPages field inserts the number of pages in the current section. You can achieve *Page x of y* page numbering within a given section. In a section header or footer, set the insertion point after the current page field; type `of` (that is, a space, "of," and another space). Choose Insert, Field. In Categories, choose Numbering, and in Field Names, choose SectionPages. Click the Options button. Choose the desired Formatting, and click Add to Field. Then click OK, and back in the Field dialog box click OK again.

If you use one section break for each logical section, this should give you precisely the result you want. If logical sections are interrupted by landscape or columnar interludes, however, you could have a problem with this approach.

Table 12.1 shows a hypothetical layout. Suppose you want to determine the number of pages in Chapter 1 of a document? Logically, it should be the sum of the pages in actual sections 1, 2, and 3. However, the SectionPages field resolves only in its current section. No built-in way exists to refer to the number of pages in Section 2 when you're in any other section.

Table 12.1 Layout of a Complex Document

Actual Section	Contents	Logical Section
Section 1	Chapter 1	Section 1
	Text	
	<Section break>	
Section 2	Landscape chart	
	<Section break>	
Section 3	Text	
Section 4	Chapter 2	Section 2

At this point, the best thing to do is to insert a bookmark at the end of each logical chapter, and then perform field math on the references to the resulting pages. For example, suppose we insert bookmarks named EOC1, EOC2, and so on, at the end of each chapter. Choosing Insert, Cross-Reference, To Page Number for each of those inserts the number of pages at each point in the book. This produces fields that look similar to this:

```
{ PAGEREF EOC1 }
{ PAGEREF EOC2 }
{ PAGEREF EOC3 }
```

The number of pages in Chapter 1 is `{ PAGEREF EOC1 }`. The number of pages in Chapter 2 is

```
{ PAGEREF EOC2 } - { PAGEREF EOC1 }
```

To perform the calculation, use an = field:

```
{ = { PAGEREF EOC2 } - { PAGEREF EOC1 }}
```

The real complication is not so much the field math, but rather setting up the headers or footers, because the PAGEREF fields are different within each logical section or chapter. This all seems complicated, and in fact it is, but there is a solution.

▶ For information on setting up distinct headers and footers, **see** "Document Sections," **p. 304**

XE

The XE field is used to create index entries. Index entries are items you want to appear in the index. Index entries can be inserted in the following way:

1. Select the text you want to index.
2. Choose Insert, Index and Tables, Index tab, Mark Entry (or press Alt+Shift+X), which displays the Mark Index Entry dialog box shown in Figure 12.12.
3. Selected text is displayed in the Main Entry box; use editing keys and formatting shortcut keys to change the text as necessary.
4. If you want, include a Subentry; this is a category within the main entry. For example, if the main entry is *risks*, a subentry might be *commodity futures*. Editing and shortcut keys work here as well.
5. Choose a reference option: *Cross-Reference* (to point the reader to a different entry category); *Current Page* (to include the page on which the item occurs); or *Page Range*. If you use the last, then you must select and bookmark the set of pages you want referenced, and then choose that bookmark.
6. Choose Bold, Italic, or both for the page number format.
7. To mark just this one entry, click Mark; to mark all words in the document that match this word, click Mark All. Mark All is not an option when choosing a page range.

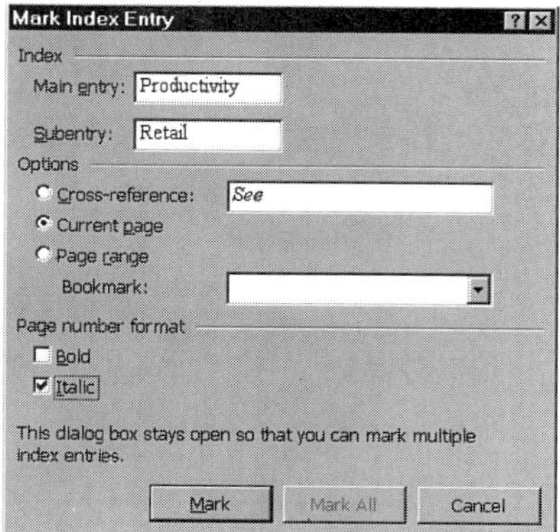

FIGURE 12.12
You can move between the Mark Index Entry dialog box and the text without dismissing the dialog box.

You can use shortcut formatting keys in the Main Entry and Subentry text boxes. Ctrl+B is bold, Ctrl+I is italic, and Ctrl+D opens the Font dialog box. You can select and format all or part of the text in the text box.

Like TC fields, XE fields are formatted as hidden text, and display only when Hidden Text Display is enabled (choose Tools, Options, View, Hidden text).

Use a Concordance File

Is it easier for you to meticulously mark each entry or to create a list of entries in a separate file? If the latter is easier, you might benefit by creating a concordance file. A concordance file is a table with two columns and one row for each distinct item you want marked in the text. Create a new Word document and insert a two-column table. The number of rows doesn't matter initially—you can insert new rows on-the-fly by pressing the Tab key in the bottom-right cell.

In column one, type the text you want Word to search for. In column two, type the index entry you want matching items listed under in the index. For example, in a book about the ocean, you might want to include any species of fish under an index label called Fish. Hence, you might have *shark* in column one, and *fish* in column two. For subentries, include a colon and the name of the subentry in column two. For example, you might have *fish:scary* as the column two entry for *shark*. After completing the column two entry, press the Tab key and continue, pressing Tab after each column one and column two entry.

When you're done, save the file and give it a name. Then, choose Insert, Index and Tables, and click the Index tab. Then choose AutoMark. Navigate to the concordance file and click Open. Word then performs a *search and mark* operation for each row in the concordance table, populating your document thoroughly with XE fields.

▶ To learn more about the XE field and a concordance, **see** "Creating an Index," **p. 463**

Modifying Fields with Formatting and Switches

Sometimes fields suddenly develop errors. Perhaps an underlying file location changed. Or perhaps you want to remove or change a field option. You could insert the field anew (choose Insert, Field); however, with a little *field training*, it might be faster and easier to edit the field to make the change you want.

To modify a field, use these general steps:

1. Press Alt+F9 to turn on field code display.
2. Make the desired change.
3. Press F9 to update the field.
4. Press Alt+F9 to toggle back to the field results.

Formatting the Field Results

A sometimes-overlooked feature is the Preserve Formatting During Updates option. It's upsetting to spend time reformatting a section of text, only to see it revert when you press F9, or when one of the automatic update mechanisms does the automatic equivalent.

CAUTION

The Preserve Formatting During Updates option adds the * MERGEFORMAT switch to fields. However, the MERGEFORMAT switch does not work with all fields. Notably, the Index and Table of Contents field's formatting cannot be preserved in this way–*even if you edit the field and add the MERGEFORMAT switch yourself.*

If you want to change the formatting of an index or table of contents, your best bet is to use the Index 1 through Index 9 styles or the TOC 1 through TOC 9 styles. By default, these styles have the Automatically Update (choose Format, Style, Modify, Automatically Update) option enabled. So, any formatting you perform to any complete line in the table of contents or index automatically causes the underlying style to be updated.

With this caveat in mind, you can use all Word's formatting resources to format most fields that display as text—paragraph, character, and font formatting. You cannot, however, insert paragraph, page, and section breaks on the interior of field results and have them survive an update. Only *formatting* is preserved. On the other hand, you can section off a field's displayed results and maintain formatting that way (for example, apply column formatting to text inside a section whose breaks are not within the field).

Using Switches to Control Formatting

Another way to control field formatting is through the use of switches. We've already looked at the MERGEFORMAT switch. Four types of general switches can be used with a number of different fields. These switches affect how the results of fields are displayed:

- Field locking
- Text format
- Number format
- Date format

Locking Fields Within Fields (\!) An important element to controlling fields sometimes is keeping them from changing until you're ready for them to change. When you use the REF or INCLUDETEXT fields, it's possible that the source text itself contains fields. For example, suppose a referenced block of text in another file—or in the same file—contains a date field. If you select the text where the field result is displayed and press the F9 key, the date field within that selection is updated, even if the date field in the source location has not been updated.

Suppose you have a passage of text in a document that contains a date. You bookmark that passage, and then use an INCLUDEDTEXT field to replicate that passage in another document. You can prevent fields within such areas from being updated in their own right by using the \! Switch. Consider the following field:

```
{ INCLUDETEXT contracts.doc grandfatherclause \! \* MERGEFORMAT }
```

Here, "grandfatherclause" is a bookmarked passage in a file named contracts.doc. That passage contains a date field that was January 24, 1997—the last time it was updated. By using the \! switch in the field, as shown here, the date displays as January 24, 1997 even after it's updated. If you remove the \! switch, and press F9, the date field will be updated to the current date—even though that's not the date in the original document! Using the \! switch ensures that the referenced section reflects exactly what is in the original document.

Text Format Switches Text format switches have the following syntax:

```
\* format keyword
```

These switches are used to affect how certain text displays. Format options can be any of 14 keywords:

- Alphabetic—This switch converts the numerical result of an expression into letters, producing an alphabetical numbering result. In other words, 1 becomes A, 2 becomes B, 27 becomes AA, and so on. For lowercase, use `alphabetic`; for uppercase, capitalize at least the first letter of alphabetic. For example,

  ```
  {Seq equation \* alphabetic}
  ```

  results in lowercase alphabetic sequence "numbers" for numbering equations.
- Arabic—This switch is the default and results in normal Arabic numbers. For example,

  ```
  {=2^16 \* Arabic}
  ```

  displays as 65536.
- Caps—Any text in the resulting expression is displayed in initial caps. For example,

  ```
  {subject \* caps}
  ```

  displays the current document subject with initial caps.

- Cardtext—This switch displays a numeric expression in cardinal form. For example,

  ```
  {=999999 \* cardtext}
  ```

  displays as "nine hundred ninety-nine thousand nine hundred ninety-nine." You can add the * caps switch for initial caps.
- Charformat—The Charformat switch affects the character format of text that's displayed. If *Charformat is specified, the displayed result will have the same character formatting as the first character in the field keyword or bookmark name. This lets you permanently fix the formatting of the displayed result. For example,

  ```
  {ref bookmark}
  ```

  displays the referred text in bold italic.
- Dollartext—The Dollartext switch is a variation of Cardtext. It produces the results you might want when writing the long amount form on checks. For example:

  ```
  {= 1017.95 \* Dollartext}
  ```

  produces "one thousand seventeen and 95/100."Again, the * caps switch can be added.
- Firstcap—The Firstcap argument capitalizes the first word. If other words in the resulting text are already capitalized, they remain so. For example,

  ```
  {ref cellcontents \* Firstcap}
  ```

  displays the text book marked as cellcontents with at least the first word capitalized.
- Hex—The Hex specification displays a number in hexadecimal notation. For example,

  ```
  {= 3528 \* hex}
  ```

  displays as "DC8."
- Lower—The Lower format argument displays text as all lowercase. For example,

  ```
  {quote http://www.mcp.com \* lower}
  ```

  ensures that the URL is displayed in the proper case.
- Mergeformat—The * Mergeformat switch, to the extent possible, preserves formatting of text when a field is updated. For example,

  ```
  {ref escapeclause \* mergeformat}
  ```

  safeguards the text against format changes when the field is updated.
- Ordinal—Ordinal adds th, nd, and rd endings to numbers. For example,

  ```
  {QUOTE \* ordinal "53"}
  ```

  results in "53rd."
- Ordtext—Ordtext is similar to ordinal, but displays in text. The following:

  ```
  {=66322 \* ordtext}
  ```

  displays as "sixty-six thousand three hundred twenty-second."

- Roman—Roman displays a number as a Roman numeral. For example,

  ```
  {=1999 \* roman}
  ```

  produces "mcmxcix," while

  ```
  {=1999 \* Roman}
  ```

  produces "MCMXCIX."

- Upper—Upper causes the field's text to display in all caps. For example,

  ```
  { quote "remember the maine" \* upper }
  ```

  displays as "REMEMBER THE MAINE."

Numeric Picture Switches Numeric picture switches have the following syntax:

```
\# format
```

These switches are versatile, allowing you to format numbers in almost any way imaginable.

CAUTION

Some confusion exists about the numeric picture switch because the switch itself, \#, can also use # as an argument. The field {=7 \#} generates the error message `Error! Switch argument not specified.` That's because \# is the switch itself, but as shown, there's no switch argument.

- # (Number)—The # parameter is used to reserve spaces for numbers in the display. The field

  ```
  {=5 \#$#.00}
  ```

  prints out as "$ 5.00." As a field argument, the # sign is used as a number space holder. The field

  ```
  {=5 \#$###.00}
  ```

  prints out with two spaces between the $ and the 5.

- 0 (Zero)—Zero is used as a 0 placeholder to guarantee an order of precision in numbers. For example, it's inappropriate to list the same statistic for different individuals using different precision:

Bob	6.5
Katie	6.4444
Karen	6.501
Mike	6.61111
Jan	6.49996

  If these are all the result of calculations, you can guarantee identical precision by using the same numeric switch in all the calculation fields, such as {=1/7 \#0.000}. This ensures that the result is always carried out to thousandths, with a leading zero, if necessary (for example, 0.143 instead of .143).

- X—When x is used at the left edge of any other arguments, Word truncates additional digits that don't fit in the reserved space. For example, {=98765 \#x#.00} displays as "65.00," because x# reserves only two places to the left of the decimal point.
- . (Decimal)—The decimal point is used in conjunction with number and 0 placeholders to specify the precision of the displayed result. For example, { =87654.356 \# #.00 } displays as "87654.36," with .356 rounded up to .36.
- , (Commas for Multiples of 1,000)—The comma is used to insert commas to separate three-digit series (thousands) to the left of the decimal point. For example, {=5386785343 \# #,} displays as "5,386,785,343."
- + (Force the Sign to Display)—The addition sign forces the positive or negative display of the number. No sign is displayed for zero. For example, {=5.78 \# +#} displays as +6. To display +5.78, use =5.78 \# +#.00. To display just the sign (without the number), omit the last #. This is useful in econometric tables when summarizing the results of an analysis wherein just the sign is needed.
- ; (Semicolon)—The semicolon is used to specify different formats for positive, negative, and zero. For example, the field { =45 \#[+###];(+###);{0.#} } yields [+ 45], (- 45), and {0.0}.
- ' (Single Quote)—Single quotes are used to insert literal text. For the most part, text is inserted verbatim with the quotes. Use quotes to prevent Word from interpreting verbatim text as a numeric switch argument; for example,

  ```
  {=4.5 \#"Please add #.0% 'sales tax'"}
  ```

  produces

  ```
  Please add 4.5% sales tax.
  ```

NOTE When you use single quotes, double quotes must surround the entire picture clause.

- SEQ Identifier—You can use the current value of a sequence number (SEQ field) in your field by enclosing it between grave accents (usually the lowercase complement to the tilde key). For example, if you have a SEQ series that uses the name tabno, then you can use the name as part of another field when referencing that table number. The field

  ```
  {= Sum(Sales[E5]) \# "$#,# 'total sales, shown in Table' `tabno`"}
  ```

  might display as

  ```
  $545,000 total sales, shown in Table 8.
  ```

Date-Time Picture Switches Date-time picture switches have the following syntax:

```
\@ format
```

and enable you to format dates in a variety of ways. You can set the default by clicking the Default button in the Date and Time dialog box (choose Insert, Date and Time).

The date-time picture switches can work with any dates—not just with date fields. If you have a date contained in a bookmark, for example,

```
{SET projectdate "11/25/99"}
```

You can print that date out in long format by using the field

```
{projectdate \@ "MMMM D, YYYY"}
```

The result would be November 25, 1999.

- Date and Format Components—Date formats use key letters to represent parts of dates and times, as shown in Table 12.2. These key letters affect only the component that gets displayed, not the capitalization. You must add the appropriate * switch to effect different forms of capitalization.

NOTE Case counts. In date and time formatting, capital M produces months, and a lowercase m produces minutes.

Table 12.2 Time and Date Picture Switch Format Specifiers

Format	Effect
AM/PM	AM and PM.
am/pm	am and pm.
A/P	A and P.
a/p	a and p.
d	Date, with no leading zero.
dd	Date, with a leading zero.
ddd	Abbreviated name of the day of the week (Mon, Sun, and so on).
dddd	Full name of the day of the week (Sunday, Monday, and so on).
h	Hour, 12-hour format, no leading zero.
hh	Hour, 12-hour format, leading zero.
H	Hour, 24-hour format, no leading zero.
HH	Hour, 24-hour format, leading zero.
M	Numeric month, no leading zero.
MM	Numeric month, leading zero.
MMM	First three letters of month (Aug, Sep, and so on).

continues

Table 12.2 Continued

Format	Effect
MMMM	Full month name (August, September, and so on).
m	Minutes, no leading zero.
mm	Minutes, with a leading zero for single-digit minutes.
s	Seconds, no leading zero.
ss	Seconds, leading zero.
y or yy	Year, two-digit format (93, 94, and so on).
yyyy	Year in four-digit format (1994, 1995, and so on).
'string'	You can supplement date and time text by adding additional text in single quotes.

CHAPTER 13

Unleashing the Potential of Tables

In this chapter

Creating Tables—A Quick Study

Word tables are designed to be easy to work with. With the myriad of features, however, it's sometimes easy to overlook the basics. For purposes of this chapter, we assume that you've worked with Word tables in other versions of Office and that you're comfortable inserting tables in your documents. Here, we offer a quick refresher on inserting and deleting cells, rows, columns, and data. The majority of this chapter, however, digs deeply into the power you can leverage by using tables in your Word documents.

NOTE For a more detailed introduction to tables, see *Special Edition Using Microsoft Word 2000*, also published by Que.

Inserting Cells in an Existing Table

To insert a given number of cells into a table, select an equal number of cells in your existing table. For example, to insert three cells, select three cells next to where the insertion is to be. To select cells, click in the starting cell and drag through the additional cells you want to select. Choose Table, Insert, Cells. Word displays the Insert Cells dialog box options. Choosing Shift cells right has the effect shown in Figure 13.1.

FIGURE 13.1
Select the number of cells you want to insert.

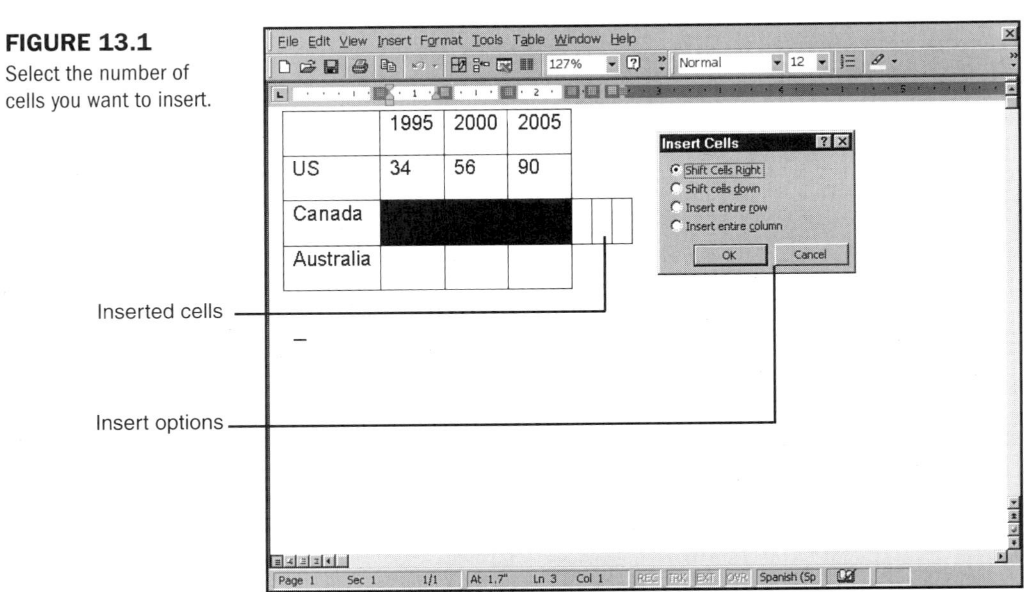

Inserting Rows in a Table

To insert one or more rows, select the number of rows you want to insert and choose Table, Insert, Rows Above (or Rows Below). To select rows, position the mouse pointer to the left of the row you want to select and press the left mouse button. Drag the mouse up or down to select additional rows. New rows can be inserted *above or below* the existing rows.

Inserting Columns in a Table

To insert one or more columns, select the number of columns you want to insert and choose Table, Insert, Columns to the Right (or Left) or click the Insert Columns tool on the Standard Toolbar.

To select columns, position the mouse pointer over the first cell in a column so that the column-selection pointer appears, as shown in Figure 13.2. Click and drag the mouse left or right to select the desired number of columns. New columns are inserted *to the left of* existing columns if you use the toolbar button. To insert to the right, choose Table, Insert, Columns to the Right.

FIGURE 13.2
The column-selection pointer lets you select right or left.

Column-selection pointer

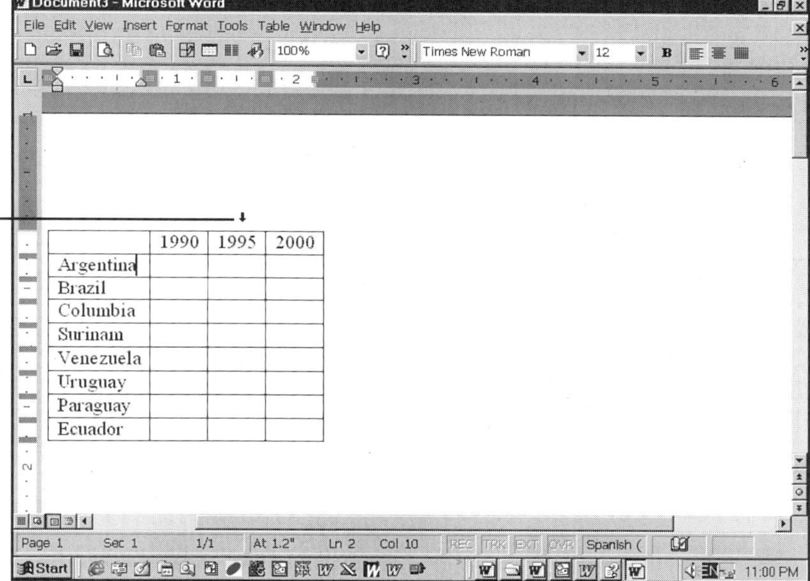

	1990	1995	2000
Argentina			
Brazil			
Columbia			
Surinam			
Venezuela			
Uruguay			
Paraguay			
Ecuador			

To make a quick column selection, Alt+Left-Click in any cell to select the entire column.

Deleting Data in Rows, Columns, and Cells

To delete data in a row, column, or cell (not to be confused with deleting the row, column, or cell itself), select the item and press the Delete key. To actually delete a row or column, select the entire row (including the end-of-row mark) or column, and press Shift+Delete (Cut).

If you prefer not to select first, click anywhere in the row, column, or cell and choose Table, Delete, and choose either Columns, Rows, or Cells.

Converting Text and Data into Tables

Word gives you the power to convert tables that are no more than a collection of tabs and paragraph marks into slick, well-organized Word tables. If the tabbed text is uniform, you usually can just select it and click the Insert Table button to convert the text to a Word table.

Another scenario in which converting text to a table is a powerful option is when you locate tables in Web pages that you want to drop into a Word document (giving credit to the original creator of the table, of course). Both kinds of conversions are possible; however, it might take a little maneuvering to get exactly the desired result.

Converting a Tab and Paragraph Table

Consider the text table shown in Figure 13.3. This table, which has been created by hand using tabs, has five columns and four rows.

Each row contains five items, separated by four tabs. As a text table, this one is perfectly balanced and does not present problems when converting into a table. Select the text, as shown, being careful not to select any extra paragraph marks above or below the table. Then click the Insert Table button on the Tables and Borders toolbar.

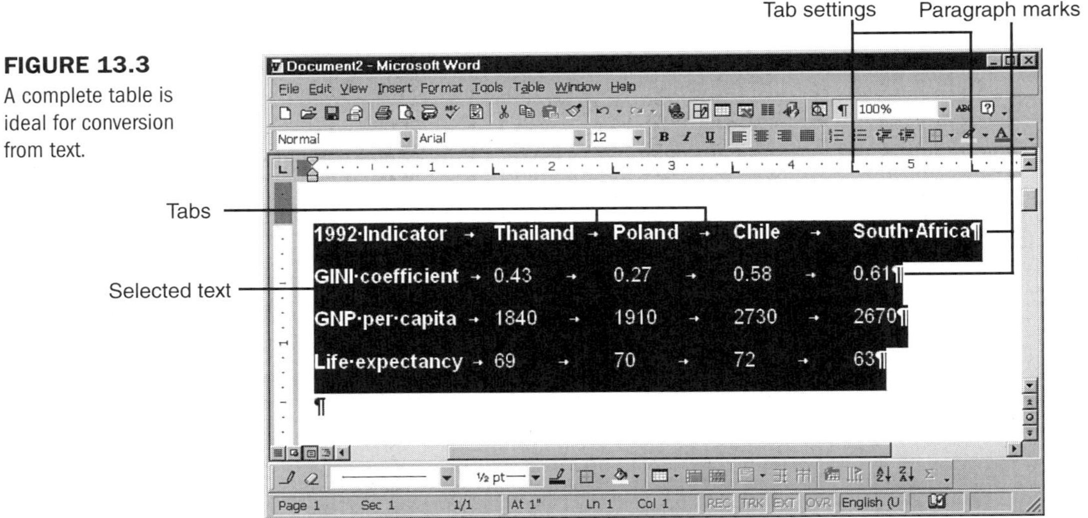

FIGURE 13.3
A complete table is ideal for conversion from text.

A Word table, something similar to that shown in Figure 13.4, should replace the tabbed text. Not bad for one click. If the table isn't exactly to your liking, you can always use the tools in the Table menu, the ruler line, or the Tables and Borders toolbar to touch it up.

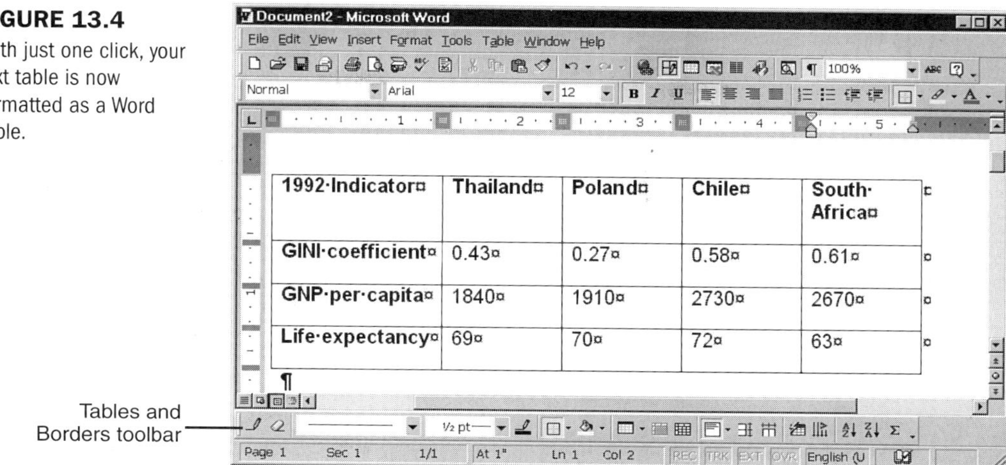

FIGURE 13.4
With just one click, your text table is now formatted as a Word table.

Not surprisingly, however, it's usually not this easy. If the table isn't consistently aligned with tabs or is missing data, converting text to a table becomes a little trickier. Figure 13.5 shows a text table more like the ones you're likely to encounter in real life. Simply highlighting the table and clicking the Insert Table tool now is likely to return results you weren't expecting, such as those found in Figure 13.6.

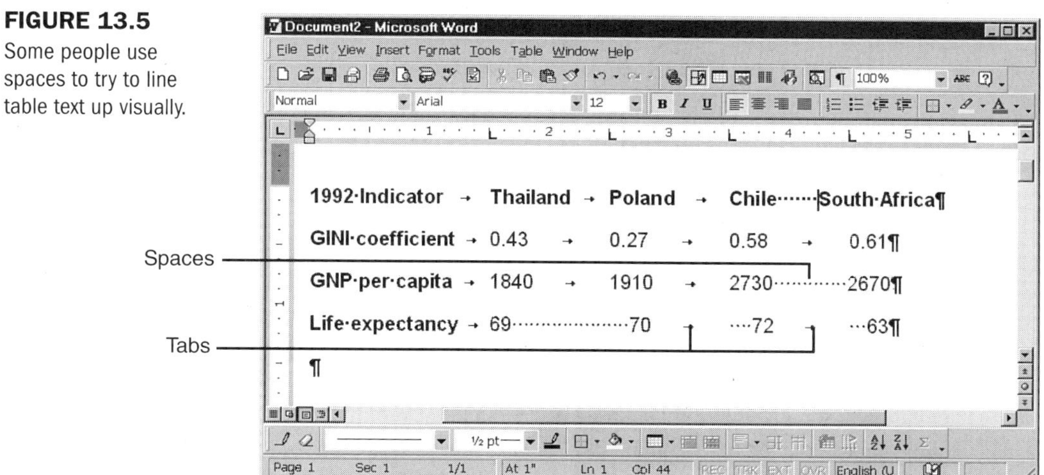

FIGURE 13.5
Some people use spaces to try to line table text up visually.

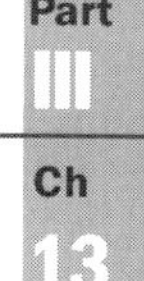

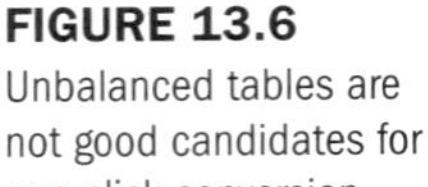

FIGURE 13.6
Unbalanced tables are not good candidates for one-click conversion.

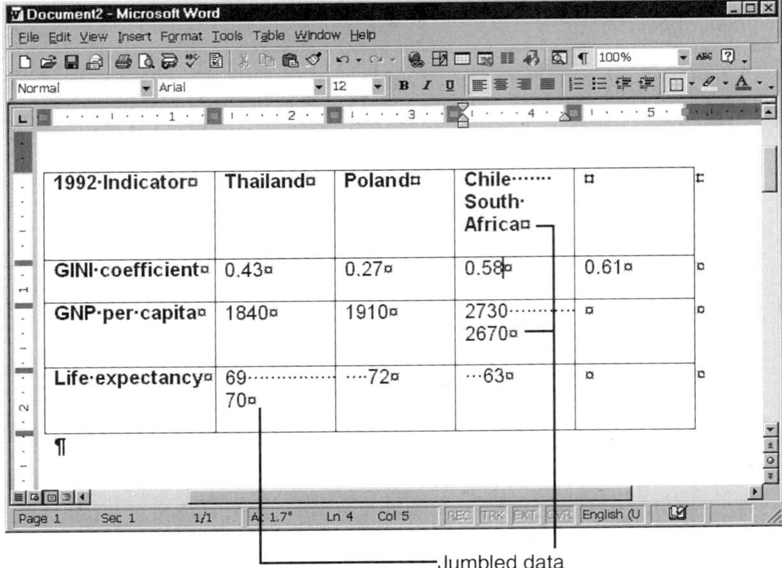

One way to avoid this problem is to manually touch up the table before converting it. You will find it helpful to display formatting marks by selecting Tools, Options, View, Formatting Marks, All. Without formatting marks displayed, the table shown previously in Figure 13.5 looks similar to the one seen earlier in Figure 13.3. However, they are quite different, as you can see when both text tables were converted to Word tables (see Figures 13.4 and 13.6).

With formatting marks displayed, you can do a little manual editing and replace the spaces with tabs and then convert the table with one click as before. Just be sure you end up with the same number of tabs in each row of the table.

Sometimes you might actually want tabs in a Word table cell. However, when you press the Tab key, Word moves you to the next cell. If you press the Tab key at the end of the bottom-right cell, Word adds a new row. To insert an actual tab into a cell, simply press Ctrl+Tab.

▶ For additional information on working with tabs, **see** "Making the Most of Tabs," **p. 260**

Converting Data into a Table

Other ways data imported from other sources or applications is formatted include data separated by spaces, semicolons, commas (comma-separated values or CSV), or other delimiters. For example, if you display the Contacts folder in Outlook and choose File, Import and Export,

Export to a File, one of the options is to export to CSV format. This format includes commas between data fields. The CSV format often also includes quotes around text items, but not always. Data files from older systems, however, sometimes use uncommon delimiters, such as those shown in Figure 13.7.

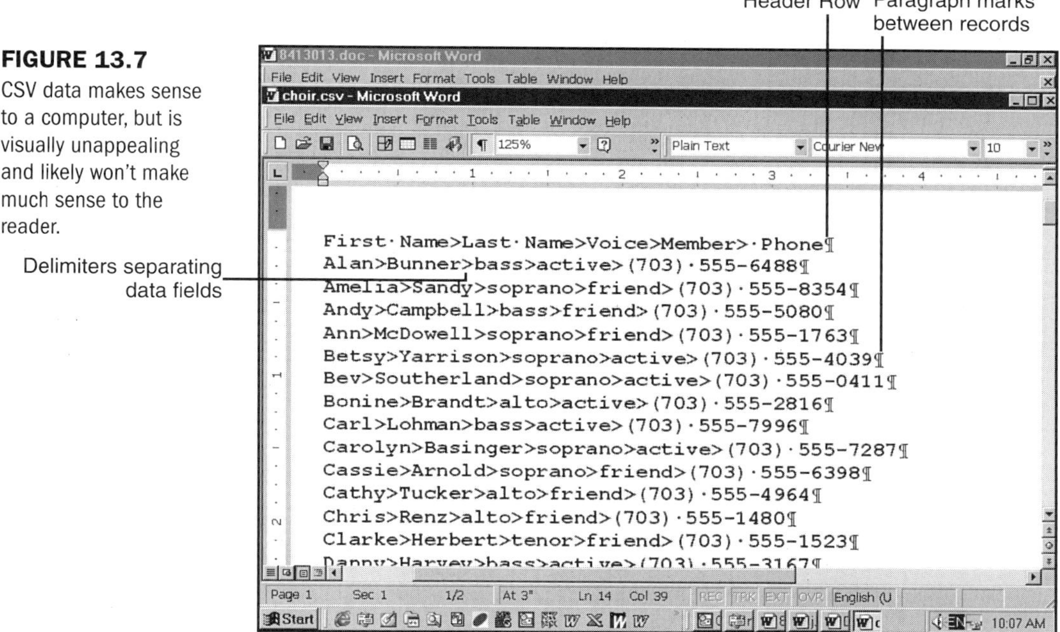

FIGURE 13.7
CSV data makes sense to a computer, but is visually unappealing and likely won't make much sense to the reader.

Usually, Word can convert this kind of data file the same way it handles a tabbed table. Select the text in the data file and click the Insert Table tool. Word generally manages to handle commas, tabs, semicolons, colons, slashes, and other common delimiters just fine.

The data file shown in Figure 13.7, however, cannot be handled using the Insert Table tool without training Word to recognize the greater than (>) character as a field delimiter or separator. If Word is not instructed to recognize > as a delimiter, using the Insert Table Tool simply places the data from each record in a single column instead of separating the data into definable table cells.

To properly convert the delimited data into a table by teaching Word to use the > character as a delimiter, you need to choose Table, Convert, Text to Table, which displays the Convert Text to Table dialog box shown in Figure 13.8. Click Other in the Separate Text At section of the dialog box. You can now add the > delimiter. Then click OK to start the conversion process.

Unfortunately, Word might not convert correctly the first time—even if you set the number of columns to the correct number. You usually get a result such as that shown in Figure 13.9.

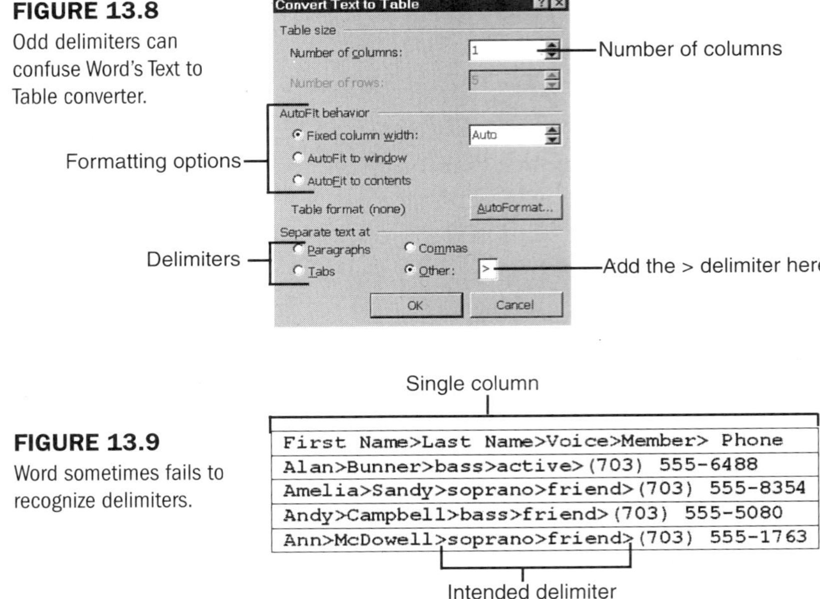

FIGURE 13.8
Odd delimiters can confuse Word's Text to Table converter.

FIGURE 13.9
Word sometimes fails to recognize delimiters.

If Word fails to recognize the delimiter you've set, press Ctrl+Z to undo the table conversion. Then promptly click the Insert Table tool. Examine the results. The trick is that Word has to be taught that the odd delimiter (>, in this instance) is acceptable. Unfortunately, you cannot teach Word to accept the odd delimiter without attempting an actual conversion. After it has made a conversion—even if that conversion had the wrong result—the next try using that delimiter suddenly works just fine.

Another common formatting problem you're likely to encounter when converting text to a table is when each record and field is separated by a paragraph mark as follows:

```
First Name
Last Name
Voice
Member
Phone
Alan
Bunner
bass
active
(703) 555-6488
Amelia
Sandy
soprano
friend
(703) 555-8354
Andy
Campbell
bass
friend
(703) 555-5080
```

In this instance, Word can't possibly sort out which is a field and which is a record. If you click the Insert Table tool, you'll get a table with one column and 20 rows.

If you select all 20 lines and choose Table, Convert, Text to Table, the Convert Text to Table dialog box shows columns as 1 and rows as 20. Notice that there are five heading fields:

1. First Name
2. Last Name
3. Voice
4. Member
5. Phone

Using the mouse or the up-arrow key, increase the number of columns to 5. At the same time, the number of rows goes down to 4. You still have 20 items, but it's now a 5×4 column-to-row table instead of 1×20 column-to-row table. Notice also that Separate Text At: option is set to Paragraphs (refer to Figure 13.8). Choose the desired AutoFit Behavior and click OK. Now Word converts the list into a nice-looking 5×4 table—with the first record being used as the header row.

Converting a Table from a Web Browser Increasingly, Internet users are finding useful data on the Web. Data does not always make the trip from the Net to Word gracefully, however. Consider, for example, the table shown in Figure 13.10. If you wanted to use this table in a report, you might be tempted to just take a screen shot and paste it into your report. However, this table isn't formatted perfectly—Square Miles and Percent headings are not aligned with the data columns. You also might want to update the data using new figures specifically for 1999 or 2000.

FIGURE 13.10
Misalignment of data makes using a screen shot reproduction unattractive.

Location text box in the Web browser

Misaligned headings and columns

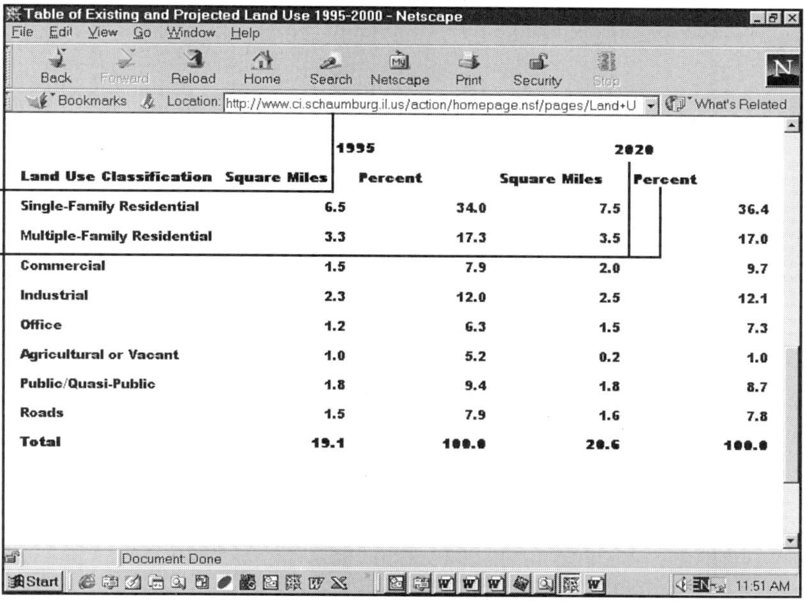

Table of Existing and Projected Land Use 1995-2000 - Netscape

http://www.ci.schaumburg.il.us/action/homepage.nsf/pages/Land+U

	1995		2020	
Land Use Classification	Square Miles	Percent	Square Miles	Percent
Single-Family Residential	6.5	34.0	7.5	36.4
Multiple-Family Residential	3.3	17.3	3.5	17.0
Commercial	1.5	7.9	2.0	9.7
Industrial	2.3	12.0	2.5	12.1
Office	1.2	6.3	1.5	7.3
Agricultural or Vacant	1.0	5.2	0.2	1.0
Public/Quasi-Public	1.8	9.4	1.8	8.7
Roads	1.5	7.9	1.6	7.8
Total	19.1	100.0	20.6	100.0

CAUTION

A common mistake users make when attempting to convert Web tables to Word tables is to select the table in the browser and then paste it into Word. When you do that, you are copying the data only, not the table structure. If the table contains empty cells, the result will be short rows or columns, with misaligned data and table headers. It takes only another minute or so to do it the right way. This can save lots of time you might otherwise have to spend reformatting and moving data around.

The easiest way to import table data from a Web page into Word usually is to use Word to read the URL directly from the Web. In your browser's Location text box (refer to Figure 13.10), select the URL and press Ctrl+C to copy it to the Clipboard. Then choose File, Open in Word, and press Ctrl+V to paste the URL into the Filename textbox; then click Open. Word opens the location as shown in Figure 13.11.

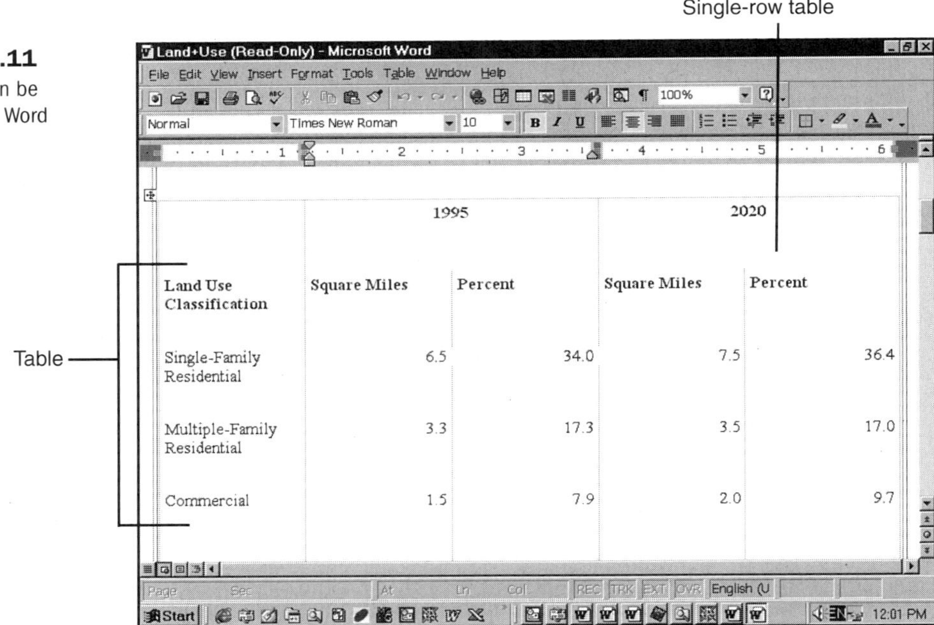

	1995		2020	
Land Use Classification	Square Miles	Percent	Square Miles	Percent
Single-Family Residential	6.5	34.0	7.5	36.4
Multiple-Family Residential	3.3	17.3	3.5	17.0
Commercial	1.5	7.9	2.0	9.7

FIGURE 13.11
Web tables can be converted into Word tables.

Now that you have the table in a Word window, select it (choose Table, Select, Table), copy it to the Clipboard, and paste it into the desired document. Often, all that remains is a little touch-up reformatting. In this case, the original table used a number of newline (Shift+Enter) marks to shove the text into place. You might want to strip them out using Find and Replace.

Often, the best way to format an imported table is to get rid of extraneous junk—such as extra spaces, tabs, and paragraph marks. If you select an area (such as a table), before choosing Edit, Replace, Word initially confines Replace All actions just to the selected area. To strip the newline marks out of this table, select the table, and choose Edit, Replace (Ctrl+H). In Find What type `^l`. Leave Replace With blank, and click Replace All. To remove extraneous paragraph marks, use `^p`.

▶ To learn more about using Replace to find and remove special characters, **see** "Advanced Find and Replace Techniques," **p. 248**

Next, select the table and choose Table, Table AutoFormat. The dialog box appears, as shown in Figure 13.12. Scroll through the Formats list until you find one you like, noting the additional settings in the Formats to Apply and Apply Special Formats To sections of the dialog box; click OK.

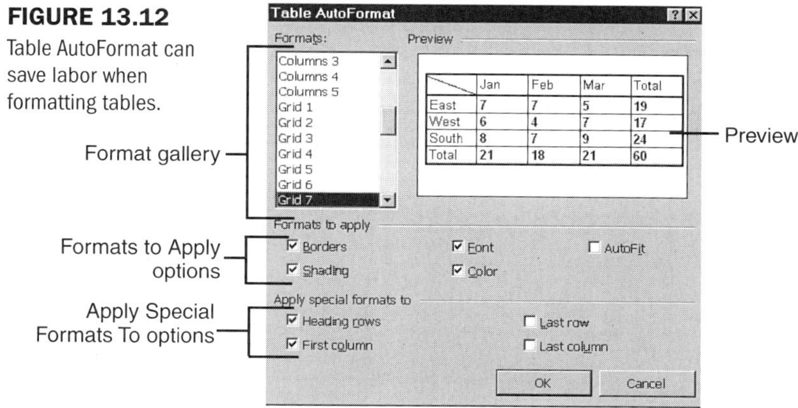

FIGURE 13.12
Table AutoFormat can save labor when formatting tables.

Drawing Complex Tables

Word's Insert Table tool makes it easy to create a traditional balanced grid table. Increasingly, however, users want additional flexibility to create uneven table shapes such as the one shown in Figure 13.13.

Tables no longer serve just as a way to organize data. They're a way to control layout—to give you places to put text without having to rely too heavily upon bandwidth-hungry graphics.

Drawing a customized table is easy:

1. With a new document window onscreen, right-click any toolbar area and display the Tables and Borders toolbar. Select the Draw Table tool.
2. Click and drag diagonally across the screen to create the basic table outline (the boundaries of the table); then release the mouse button. You've just created a one-cell table.

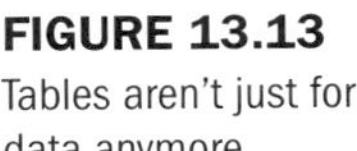

FIGURE 13.13
Tables aren't just for data anymore.

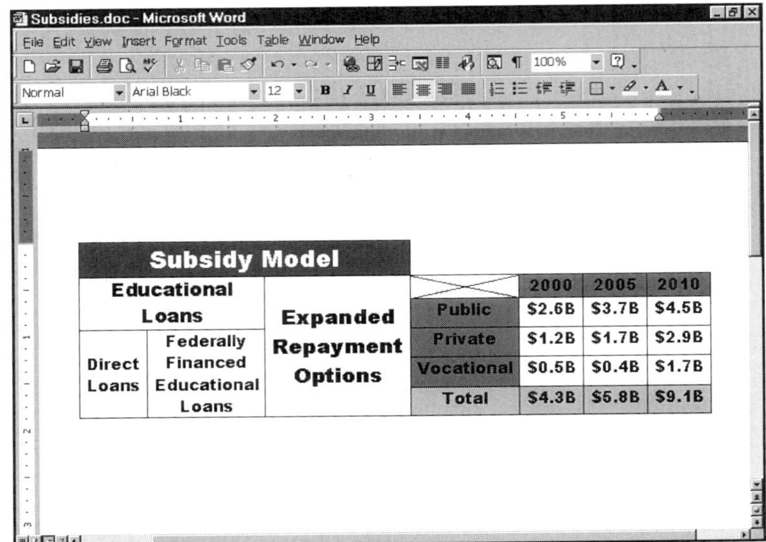

3. Now, use the drawing pointer to draw a horizontal or vertical line to divide the table into two parts—even or uneven. Continue drawing until you have exactly the shape you want. Imagine how long this all would take if you wanted to shape a table by dragging and manipulating using the menu tools.

To erase part of a table structure, you can click the Eraser tool. However, if you hold down the Shift key while dragging the Draw Table tool, it turns into an eraser! This lets you quickly fix any little mistakes you make.

Use the Draw Table tool to draw a diagonal line through a cell to denote that it is empty. Of course, you can draw two crossing diagonal lines to create an X.

NOTE Until Word is programmed to display text diagonally along the line, these diagonal lines are purely cosmetic. It does not create additional cells. If you simply need to show that a cell is empty, it's generally best to shade any empty cells instead. They will look much nicer. Your aesthetics committee will thank you.

After your custom table is created, you can insert text, graphics, bullets, and other content just as you would with a standard grid table.

Creating Nested Tables

One of Word 2000's brightest new features is the capability to nest tables: Create tables inside the cells of an existing table. The organizational implications are overwhelming. Suppose, for example, that you want to compare two sets of statistics from two different tables—side by side. Ordinarily, you would have to cut and paste the results to make the results part of the same table. With nested tables, however, you can actually paste whole tables into table cells.

To create a nested table:

1. Click the Insert Table tool on the Standard toolbar, and drag down and to the right to create the basic outer structure or framework of the outermost table.
2. Click inside the cell where you want to create a nested table and click the Insert Table tool on the Standard toolbar.
3. Drag down and to the right again to create a nested table as suggested in Figure 13.14. You can repeat this as many times as necessary—even creating nested tables within nested tables, as needed.

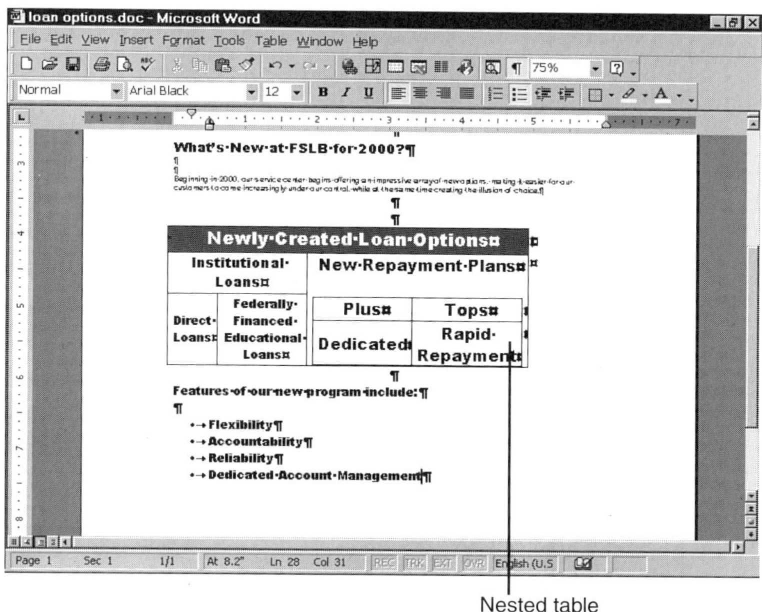

FIGURE 13.14
Pressing Tab in a nested table can insert new rows.

You can also create nested tables using existing tables. Suppose that you have tabular data from 1990 and 2000 and want to compare them side by side in the same table (such as the table shown in Figure 13.15). To create this type of table, follow these steps:

1. Start by creating a 2 by 2 table, and merging the top row's cells (choose Table, Merge Cells) to use for an overall table header.
2. Then copy and paste, or drag and drop, an existing table into the lower-left cell and another table into the lower-right cell.

You can now edit the data in the nested table just as you would any other table.

FIGURE 13.15
Nested tables can be created by pasting or by dragging.

Outermost table

Statewide Fish Consumption			
1990	Per Capita	2000	Per Capita
Salmon	10 kilos	Salmon	17 kilos
Red Snapper	5 kilos	Red Snapper	8 kilos
Atlantic Cod	25 kilos	Atlantic Cod	24 kilos

Nested tables

Creating Floating Tables

In previous versions of Word, you were limited to placing tables inline with text, meaning that they appeared in the text layer of the document.

In Word 2000, however, tables can be manipulated in the same manner as graphics. This gives you added flexibility for wrapping text around tables, or having a table actually appear in front of text or behind text.

To see table options, right-click a table and choose Table Properties from the shortcut menu (see Figure 13.16). To convert an inline table into one that can be manipulated in the same way as graphics, choose the Around wrapping option rather than None.

FIGURE 13.16
The Table Properties dialog box shows the settings for the inline table shown here; select Around to allow tables to float.

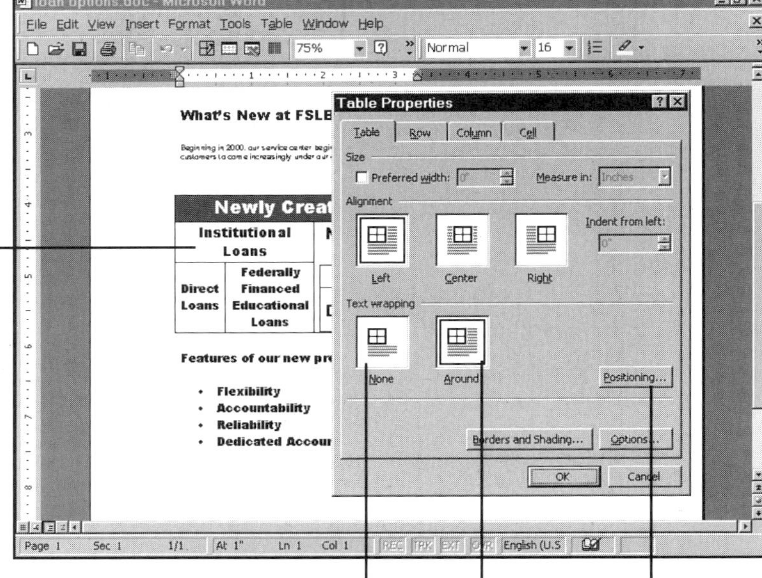

With text wrapping set to Around, the Positioning button becomes available. It's not necessary to display the Table Properties dialog box, however, to turn on text wrapping. First, make sure you are in Print Layout view or Web Layout view (choose View, Print Layout or View, Web Layout). Then, move the mouse pointer over a table and look at the upper-left corner of the table—it's not necessary to select the table. As shown in Figure 13.17, the table move handle appears.

Use the move handle to drag the table where you want it to go. When you move the table, Word automatically changes the text wrapping property from None to Around.

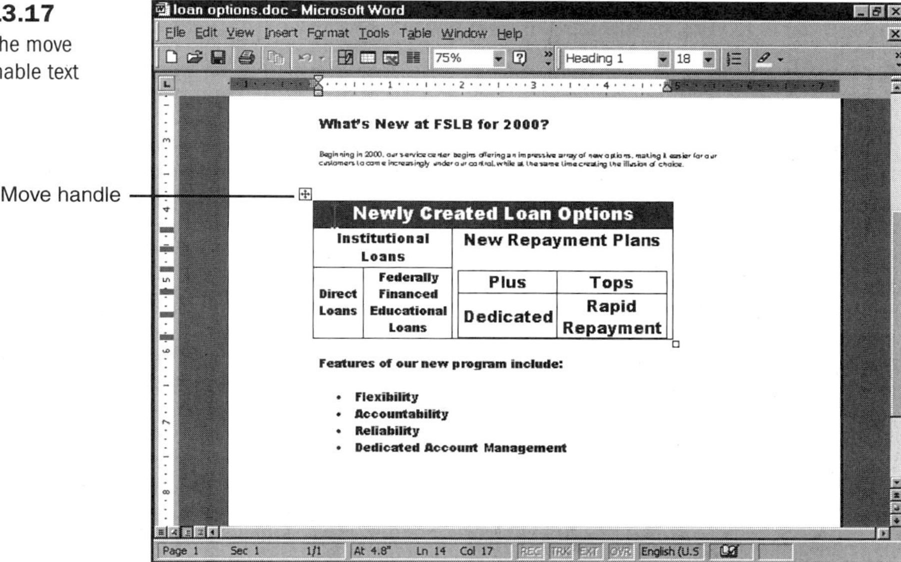

FIGURE 13.17
Drag using the move handle to enable text wrapping.

Optionally, you can cause a table to move with the text, rather than stay fixed in one position. To do this:

1. Right-click a table, choose Table Properties, and click the Table tab.
2. Set Text Wrapping to Around, if it's not already selected, and click the Positioning button.
3. In the Table Positioning dialog box, as shown in Figure 13.18, choose the Move with Text option.

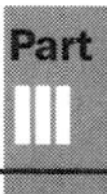

On the other hand, if you always want the table to appear on a particular page, regardless of the underlying text, uncheck the Move with Text option.

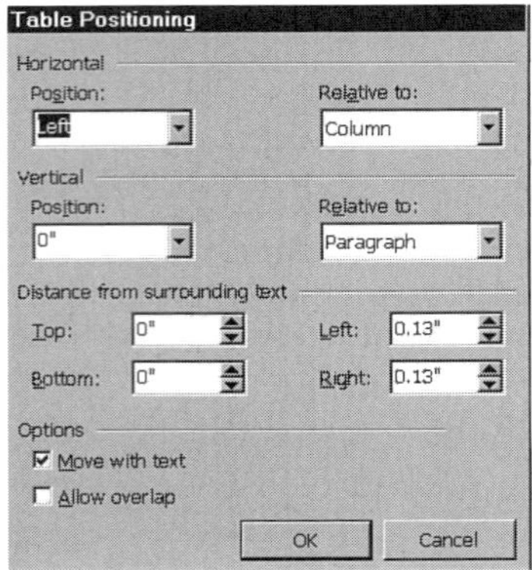

FIGURE 13.18
Allow Overlap enables the table to appear on top of other objects on the page.

Advanced Table Formatting and Manipulation

Word provides a number of important new capabilities for working with tables. Like many other new Word features, these capabilities are largely inspired by the Web. Because of widespread standardization, using tables in Web-page design is one way to ensure that users see onscreen what you want them to see. Increasingly, many other types of materials are appearing in tables—including graphics. In this section, you will look at Word's capabilities for formatting and manipulating tables to achieve precisely the right look.

Wrapping Text Around a Graphic in a Table Cell

Unlike previous versions of Word, Word 2000 lets you put graphics inside tables. Like many of Word's new features, this one exists because of the growing importance of the Web, and because of the importance of Word as a Web-page editor for many users. You can also wrap text around a graphic in a single table cell—depending on how the document is to be used.

To insert a picture into a table, click in the target cell. Choose Insert, Picture and find the picture, clip art, or other graphic you want, and insert it. Use the selection handles to resize the graphic, as necessary, so it fits as desired. To refine settings, right-click the graphic and choose Format, Picture. (If it's a different kind of graphic, such as WordArt, choose the appropriate Format counterpart. If it's a Picture or Clip Art, first choose Edit Picture from the shortcut menu.)

In the Format Picture (or other) dialog box, click the Layout tab, and then choose Advanced, Text Wrapping tab, shown in Figure 13.19.

To have cell text flow around the graphic, choose either Square or Tight. The Through, Behind Text, and In Front of Text options are useful for special effects, but not where you want to see both text and graphic distinctly in the same cell. Note that you can limit wrapping to just the left or right side, or you can have Word wrap to the larger side. The default is both sides—which actually means left, right, top, and bottom.

FIGURE 13.19
The Text Wrapping tab contains more wrapping options than the Layout tab.

In-cell graphic with text wrapping around

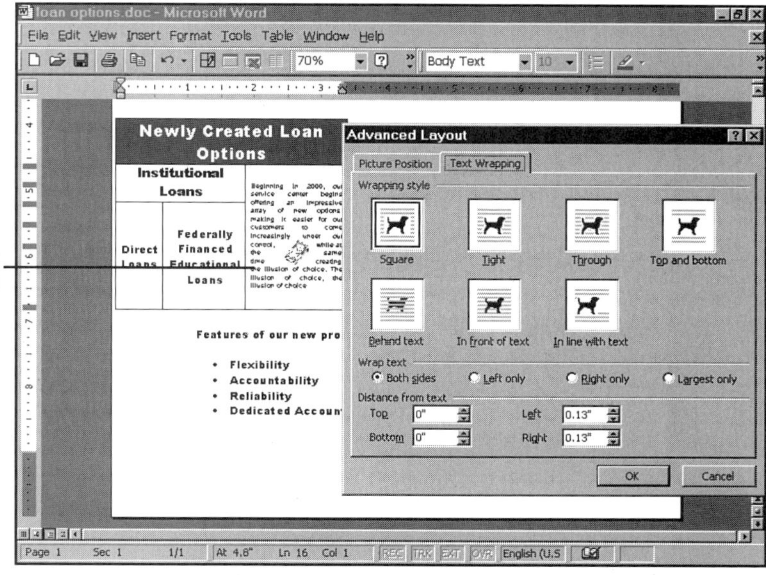

Click the Picture Position tab to display the dialog box shown in Figure 13.20. To make sure the graphic remains with the text in that cell, choose Move Object with Text and Lock Anchor. Move Object with Text causes the graphic to move as its associated text moves. Lock Anchor makes sure that the graphic appears on the same page as the paragraph mark to which it's anchored.

FIGURE 13.20
Turn off Move Object with Text to allow a picture to float anywhere.

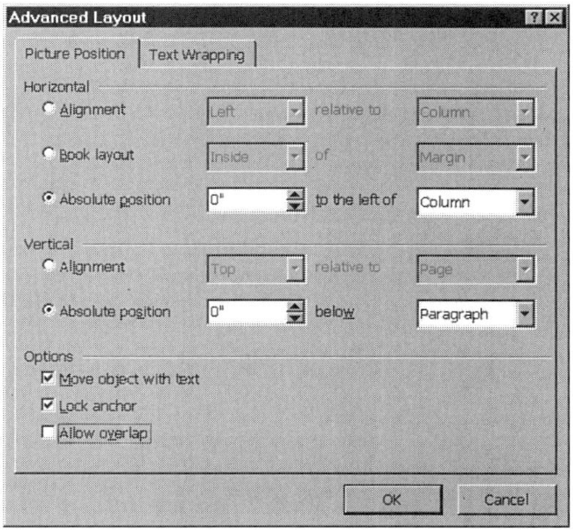

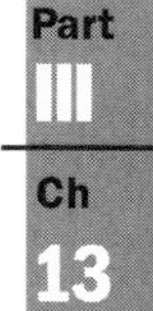

Quickly Rearranging Table Rows

Here's a quick way to rearrange rows in a table. Do you know your outlining keys? In an outline, Alt+Shift+Down and Alt+Shift+Up move the current paragraph (and its descendants) down and up in the document. Not down and up in level—rather, closer to the end and closer to the beginning of the document.

These keys also work in tables. Click in the row you want to change. Hold down Alt+Shift and use the Up key to move that row upward in the table. Use the Down key to move that row down. This is helpful for two reasons. First, it works from anywhere in the row. Second, you don't have to select the row—when you press the Up or Down key, the row automatically is selected.

You can move multiple rows by selecting the rows before moving them. In fact, you don't need to select the entire rows—just select cells that span the rows of interest. To move rows two through four (for example):

1. Click in any cell in row two.
2. Press Shift+Down to expand the selection to include cells in the same column in rows three and four.
3. Press Alt+Shift+Up or Down to move the three rows to a new location.

CAUTION

One word of caution, however. Sometimes, this trick doesn't work the way you expect it to. So, as you move rows around, verify that they actually end up where you expect before saving your changes.

After pressing Alt+Shift and Up or Down, you will reach the top or bottom of the table, yet the current row keeps on going. This enables you to instantly split that row into a new table. In fact, if you want to create a new table using several rows, use the Alt+Shift+Up or Down trick to move rows into the new table.

Tricks for Shifting Table Cells

Rows, cells, and columns can be dragged about in a table. Choose Tools, Options, Edit tab, and make sure drag-and-drop text editing is enabled. Now, select the row, column, or cell you want to move. Move the pointer over the selection and press and hold the left mouse button; drag the selection to the desired location and drop it. Figure 13.21 contains three blank columns (except for date headings). But they aren't contiguous because of an intervening blank column. To move the completely blank column in Figure 13.21 to the right of the 2000 column, drag as shown to the outside right edge of the last column and release the mouse button.

To copy rather than move, hold down the Ctrl key while dragging.

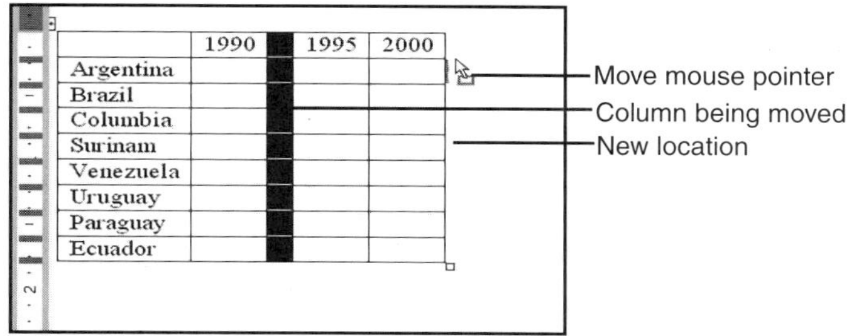

FIGURE 13.21
You can also drag columns, rows, and cells between different tables.

> **CAUTION**
> When copying or moving to occupied cells, the new material replaces the old. Sometimes this is what you want–sometimes not. If you inadvertently wipe something out, press Ctrl+Z to undo it and try again.

Numbering Cells in a Table

Users sometimes need to number cells in a table. This most often occurs in the leftmost column or in the top row, when numbering a list of items. Using a numbered table gives the user more formatting flexibility than trying to format a regular numbered list using multiple tabs.

There are several techniques for numbering cells in a table.

- To number a single row, group of cells, or column, as shown in Figure 13.22, select the target cells and click the Numbering tool on the Formatting toolbar.
- To number a complete table, select the whole table and click the numbering tool. If the cells already contain text, the numbering appears to the left—just as when you number existing normal paragraphs.
- A numbered table provides more formatting flexibility than an ordinary numbered list.

1. Select the first column and click the Numbering tool on the Formatting toolbar.
2. Now, select the second column and choose Format, Bullets and Numbering.
3. In the Bullets and Numbering dialog box, click the numbering pattern that matches column 1, and click Customize. The Customize Numbered List dialog box appears, as shown in Figure 13.23.
4. Set Start At to the next higher number, and click OK. Repeat this until the remaining columns are numbered.

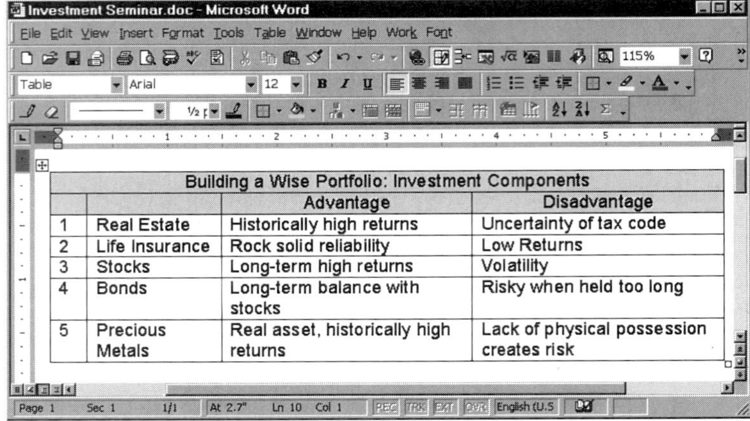

Building a Wise Portfolio: Investment Components			
		Advantage	Disadvantage
1	Real Estate	Historically high returns	Uncertainty of tax code
2	Life Insurance	Rock solid reliability	Low Returns
3	Stocks	Long-term high returns	Volatility
4	Bonds	Long-term balance with stocks	Risky when held too long
5	Precious Metals	Real asset, historically high returns	Lack of physical possession creates risk

FIGURE 13.22
Word can automatically number columns, rows, or both.

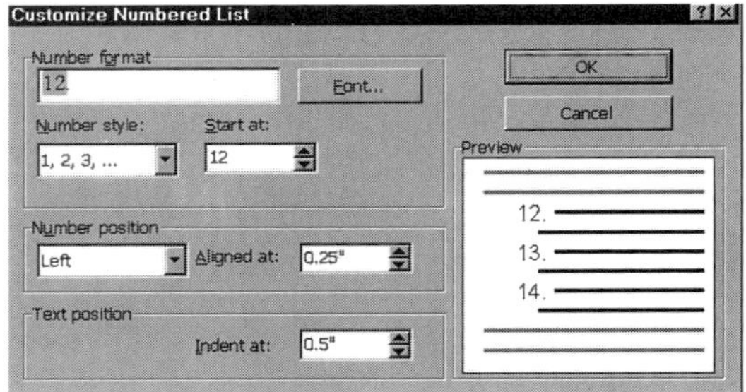

FIGURE 13.23
Numbering down requires more work than numbering across.

Positioning the Table on the Page

Word provides several options—fixed and variable—for positioning a table on the page. Choose Table, Table Properties from the menu.

In the Table Properties dialog box, click the Table tab. As shown in Figure 13.24, there are a variety of options. Under Alignment, you can choose Left, Center, or Right. If you choose Left and include an Indent from Left setting, the table is offset to the right by that additional amount. Indent from Left is unavailable if Center or Right is selected.

Notice also the Text Wrapping settings. If None is selected, the Positioning button is unavailable. Choose Around and click the Positioning button. Table positioning options, shown in Figure 13.25, enable you to set the horizontal and vertical position of the table.

The Table Positioning dialog box provides options for horizontal and vertical placement:

- Horizontal—If you haven't dragged the table anywhere, the Horizontal Position is usually Left. Although the drop-down choices say only Left, Right, Center, Inside, and Outside, you can also specify a measurement in the Distance from Surrounding Text section of this dialog box. Horizontal position and measurement can be relative to Column (the default), Margin, or Page. The Column choice is important if the table is going to be in a multicolumn document, and must appear in the same column as relevant text. Use Margin and Page settings for absolute positioning on the page—even in a multicolumn document.

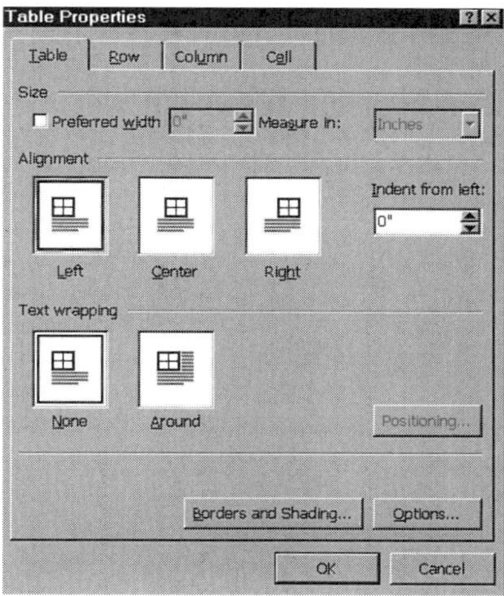

FIGURE 13.24
Preferred Width sets the width of the whole table.

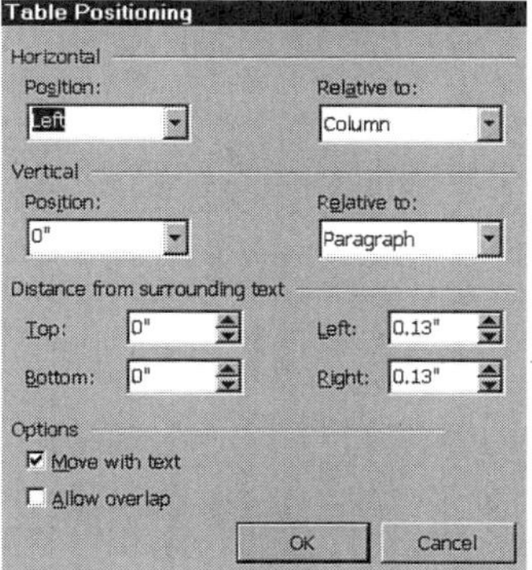

FIGURE 13.25
Use Move with Text for position-sensitive tables.

- Vertical—Similarly, Vertical Position can be specified directly by typing a measurement in the Distance from Surrounding Text section of this dialog box or relatively by choosing Top, Bottom, Center, Inside, or Outside. Inside and Outside refer to the location relative to the binding of a bound document. *Inside* is the part closest to the binding, and *Outside* is farthest away from the binding. Tables often work better visually and physically if they are toward the outside of the page in bound books.

- Options—Select Move with Text and make Vertical Position relative to Paragraph to ensure that tables remain with relevant text. On the other hand, informational tables that contain advertisements, phone numbers, or other less position-sensitive material, can be glued into an absolute position in a document (for example, always on a specific part of a specific page), by turning off Move with Text, and making both Horizontal Position and Vertical Position relative to Page.

Managing Long Tables

Long tables sometimes present formatting challenges. Adding or deleting text can change where and how a table breaks across different pages. Adding or deleting text in a table can change the optimal formatting. Word provides several features to help manage long tables:

- Repeating headings
- Automatically reformatting a table when text is added
- Prevent/Allow rows to break across pages

Repeating Headings in Multipage Tables Long tables with headings that must be repeated on each page present a formatting challenge. Many users often resort to breaking tables into multiple tables, which usually is not necessary. Click in the heading row of the table, and choose Table, Heading Rows Repeat. If the table contains multiple heading rows, such as the table under construction in Figure 13.26, then select all the heading rows before applying Heading Rows Repeat.

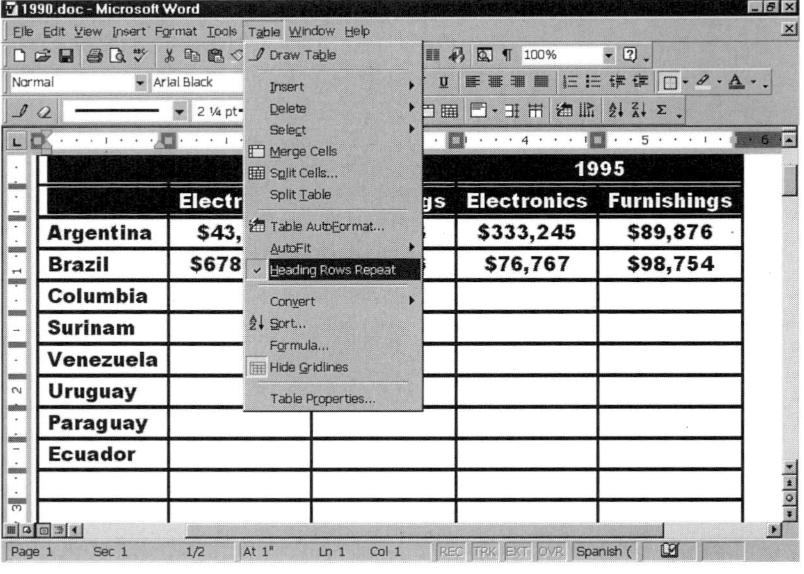

FIGURE 13.26
Heading Rows Repeat becomes an attribute of a table.

If you split a table that has repeating heading rows, the repeating attribute is not inherited by the new table. To create multiple tables from an existing table, it's usually faster and easier to copy the existing table and paste it into the new location, and then trim out the parts you don't want.

Automatically Reformatting a Table After Text Is Added Another problem often encountered with long tables is the fact that you don't know ahead of time how wide any given column ultimately will be until you input the data. A new Word 2000 feature—AutoFit—takes care of this problem. To see how this works, use the Insert Table tool to create a new 2×2 table. By default, Word arranges a new table to fill the available space between the margins. Right-click the table and choose AutoFit, AutoFit to Contents from the shortcut menu, as shown in Figure 13.27.

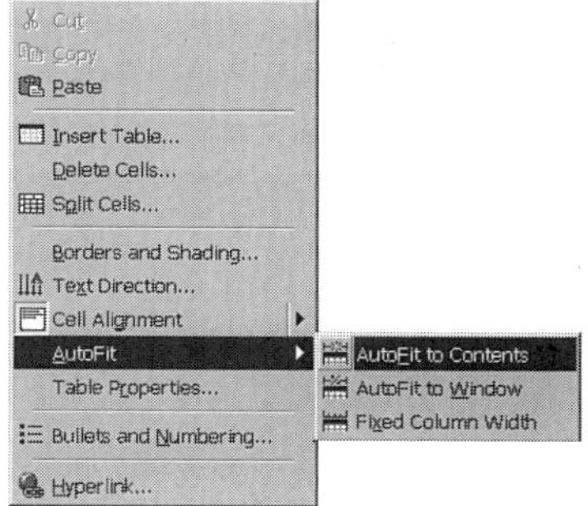

FIGURE 13.27
AutoFit to Window is great for online documents.

Now, click in the first cell and start typing. The table automatically expands as you type. As the other cells become populated, Word automatically adjusts the width. The result might not always be right for your purposes. You might still have to manually adjust the width. However, when it is right, it is a tremendous timesaver when working with a table that spans many pages.

Allowing or Preventing Rows from Breaking Across Pages By default, Word allows rows to break across pages. Sometimes, this behavior is exactly what you want. Allowing rows to break across pages makes more efficient use of paper and space. However, the logical or visual layout of some tables requires that certain rows be viewed intact, rather than spread over two pages.

To prevent one or more rows from breaking across pages, select the rows you want to affect. Then, right-click the selection and choose Table Properties. In the Row tab, click to remove the check next to Allow Row to Break Across Pages. To save paper, however, leave the option checked, as shown in Figure 13.28.

NOTE The Allow Row to Break feature does not work if the table is contained inside a text box. For example, suppose a table is displayed inside two linked text boxes. The table itself can break across pages, with part (whole rows) of the table in one text box and the rest in the other. However, Word will insist on placing only whole rows in any given text box.

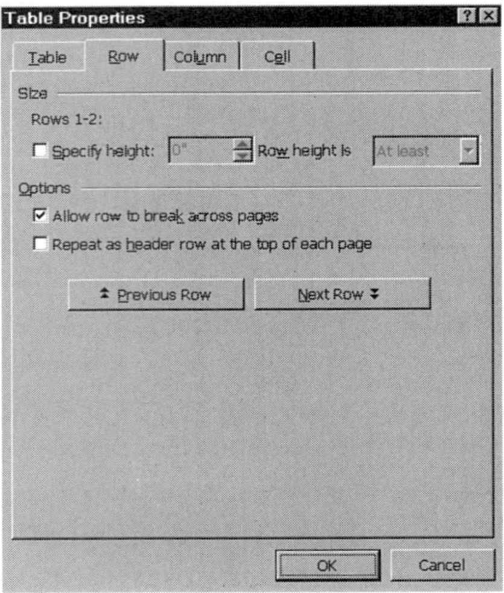

FIGURE 13.28
Allowing rows to break across pages can save paper.

Performing Calculations in a Table

Although Word isn't a good substitute for a full-featured spreadsheet program such as Excel, it does provide basic capabilities that enable you to perform calculations, create mini-spreadsheets, and prepare charts and graphs. For heavy-duty data work, you should consider using Excel or Access, as appropriate. However, for simple charts and graphs, adding up the numbers in an invoice, computing an average, or performing basic multiplication, you often can save time and trouble by using Word. The real trick is learning how to know when it might be more trouble to use Word, as opposed to resorting to more specialized applications.

▶ To learn more about performing calculations in Excel, **see** "Functions for Every Occasion" **p. 671**

Consider the table shown in Figure 13.29. This table shows scores for seven students for each of four semesters. With Word's basic calculation features, you could determine the average score for each semester, each student's total, as well as the average total.

	SEMESTER				
Student	**1st**	**2nd**	**3rd**	**4th**	**Year**
02103	**20.4**	**14.9**	**31.8**	**89.4**	
02104	**50.9**	**12.5**	**80.7**	**96.9**	
02105	**52.6**	**86.3**	**93.8**	**62.1**	
02111	**94.8**	**34.4**	**66.4**	**47.4**	
02312	**78.9**	**12.6**	**73.5**	**91.1**	
04332	**37.0**	**81.9**	**42.5**	**8.6**	
07893	**18.5**	**61.7**	**14.8**	**52.9**	
Average					

Total scores

Average total score

Average scores

FIGURE 13.29
Beware of using numerical headings such as 1st and 2nd, as they might become included in calculations.

To calculate the average score:

1. Click in the cell in which you want to place the result of the calculation.
2. Choose Table, Formula; the Formula dialog box appears (see Figure 13.30).

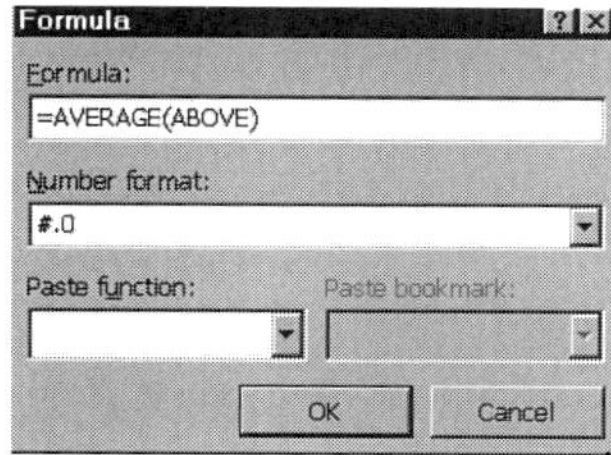

FIGURE 13.30
You can include bookmarks in formulas, too.

3. In the Formula field, replace the word `SUM` with `AVERAGE` (or, you can delete `SUM` and use the Paste Function drop-down to select a different function). Leave `ABOVE` as is, unless the column has a heading (see the caution following). If the column contains a heading, use spreadsheet references, where columns are lettered and rows are numbered. For example, column 2, row 3 would be b3; a range of seven cells (going down) beginning with b3 would be b3:b9. Going across, a range of seven cells would be b3:h3; for example, `=AVERAGE(b3:h3)`.
4. In Number Format, choose the desired format; for example, for a format with one decimal place, use `#.0` (Word automatically adds the `\#` switch for you).
5. Click OK.

CAUTION

Beware of headings in tables where you want to perform calculations. In step 3 you can use ABOVE provided that all the purely numeric entries above are supposed to be included in the calculation. As seen earlier in Figure 13.29, Word interprets 1st as 1, 2nd as 2, and so on. Even if we had pure text that included no numbers, Word would still interpret the cell as zero—a real problem with the average calculation!

After you click OK, Word inserts a formula field and performs the calculation. You can press Alt+F9 to display the field code Word used, for example:

```
{ =AVERAGE(ABOVE) \# "#.0" }
```

Pressing Alt+F9 again toggles the display back to field result. To replicate calculation fields, you can copy an existing field to the Clipboard and paste it into other locations. If `ABOVE` works, then the fields will work unmodified, but you would need to press F9 to recalculate the fields.

If cell references are used rather than `ABOVE`, you would need to press Alt+F9 to toggle the display of field codes and change the cell references to those appropriate for the copied calculation field(s). If copying to more than one location, it's quicker to make all of the edits at once, press Alt+F9 to toggle field results back on, select the modified fields, and press F9.

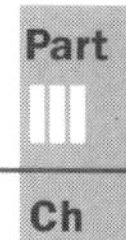

When you need to sum a row or column, the AutoSum tool, on the Tables and Borders toolbar, can be used. The AutoSum tool inserts a calculation field using the Sum function. Unlike the Average function, the Sum function yields correct addition results even if a heading is interpreted as zero. However, if you have a numerical heading such as a year, then AutoSum will produce incorrect results, and you will need to create the formula manually using cell references.

Word can also perform basic multiplication. Consider this simple table:

Item	Number	Price	Cost
Shirts	4	$39.95	$159.80
Slacks	2	$72.50	$145.00
Total			

Here, a user might want to multiply each number of items by the unit price. The total cost for shirts can be calculated using the field:

```
{=b2*c2 \# $#.00}
```

Similarly, the total cost for slacks would be

```
{=b3*c3 \# $#.00}
```

Finally, the total cost for all items can be calculated using the `=SUM(ABOVE)` formula, discussed earlier, which can be inserted by clicking the Tables and Borders' AutoSum tool while the insertion point is in the Total/Cost cell, although the result will not be formatted as the other totals are.

Creating Charts Based on Table Data

You can create graphs and charts directly from table data. Select the data—including row and column headings—and choose Insert, Object, Create New tab, Microsoft Graph 2000 Chart. Click OK. Word takes the selected data and creates a Microsoft Graph Datasheet, as shown in Figure 13.31. Word also opens Microsoft Graph.

Most of the time, Word correctly interprets your row and column headings as headings instead of data. Note that the Microsoft Graph menu replaced Word's. Word also creates a chart, as shown in Figure 13.32. If the default chart is not satisfactory, you can change the settings.

A common problem with the default chart is that the row and column orientation is reversed from what you want or expected. To change the orientation, choose Data, Series in Rows (or Series in Columns).

You can also change the chart type by choosing Chart, Chart Type and selecting from among 14 Standard Types, or 20 Custom Types. For the latter, Word uses your data to preview how the chart will look. Use Chart, Chart Options on the Microsoft Graph menu to customize the chart, choose labels, set up the legend, and so on.

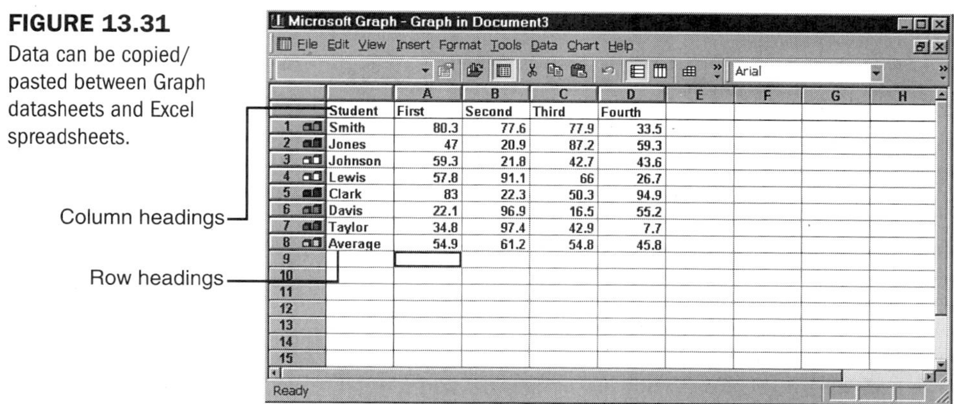

	Student	First	Second	Third	Fourth
1	Smith	80.3	77.6	77.9	33.5
2	Jones	47	20.9	87.2	59.3
3	Johnson	59.3	21.8	42.7	43.6
4	Lewis	57.8	91.1	66	26.7
5	Clark	83	22.3	50.3	94.9
6	Davis	22.1	96.9	16.5	55.2
7	Taylor	34.8	97.4	42.9	7.7
8	Average	54.9	61.2	54.8	45.8

FIGURE 13.31
Data can be copied/pasted between Graph datasheets and Excel spreadsheets.

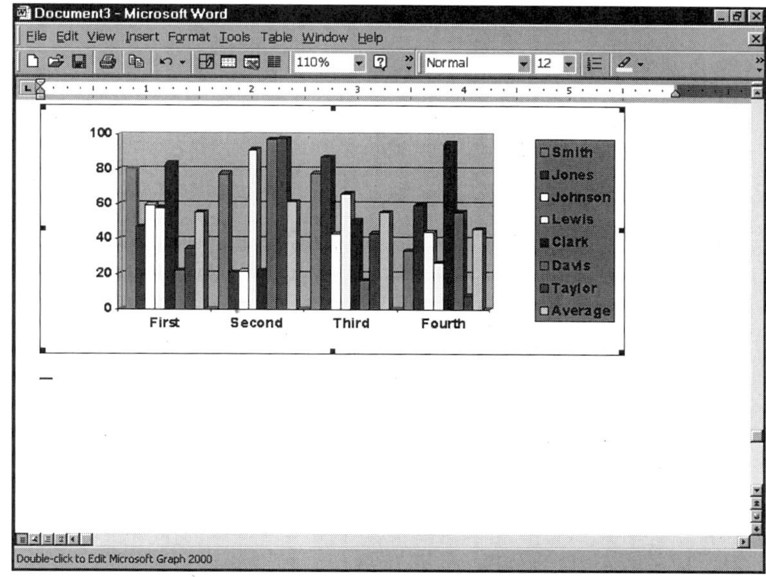

FIGURE 13.32
Microsoft Graph produces simple charts with few frills.

When you're finished, click anywhere outside the chart to return to Word. From within Word, right-click the chart and choose Format Object to set your preferences for layout, position, and text wrapping around the chart. Double-click the chart to edit the chart.

Problem/Solution: Moving Data Between Word and Excel

As shown in the preceding section of this chapter, Word has tools for performing basic calculations in tables. Sometimes, however, it is clear that Word's resources are too limited for some tasks. When resources permit and necessity dictates, the solution sometimes is to copy to Excel, perform the calculation, and then copy the results back to Word.

Consider the table shown in Figure 13.33. Suppose you have SAT scores for ten schools, and you want to compute the mean and standard deviation. As demonstrated earlier, the mean (average) and total are easy to compute from Word. And, if you worked at it a little, you could probably coax Word into computing the standard deviation, as well. But, why work so hard if Excel is available?

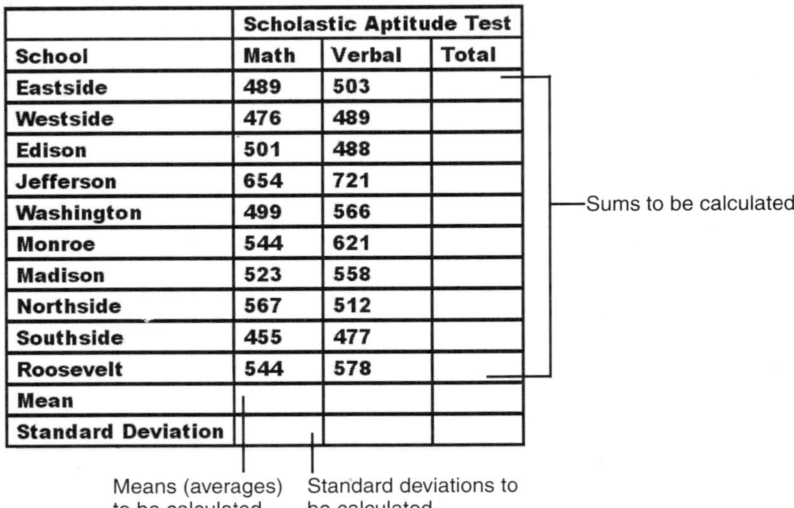

	Scholastic Aptitude Test		
School	Math	Verbal	Total
Eastside	489	503	
Westside	476	489	
Edison	501	488	
Jefferson	654	721	
Washington	499	566	
Monroe	544	621	
Madison	523	558	
Northside	567	512	
Southside	455	477	
Roosevelt	544	578	
Mean			
Standard Deviation			

FIGURE 13.33
Some calculations are easier for Excel.

Copying a Table into Excel

There are a number of ways to copy a table from Word to Excel. Which method you use should be determined by the purpose. To begin, you would select the Word table and copy it to the Clipboard. The different methods are then displayed in Excel when you choose Edit, Paste Special:

- Word document object—Pasting as a Word document object provides assurance that the table can continue to be edited using Word, and that the table will retain the identical appearance and formatting it has when viewed in Word. Use this option when the table will be printed and displayed from Excel, but you need to retain the ability to edit it.
- Picture (Enhanced Metafile)—Inserts the table as a picture. The resulting table can be formatted using Format, Picture from within Excel, but the contents of the table cannot be changed. Use this method when the table will not need to be edited, and when you plan to retain the table in Excel for display and printing.
- HTML—Inserts the table using HTML-level formatting. The table is formatted as in Word, but is editable within Excel and can be used for performing calculations. Use this method when you want the same formatting (borders, colors, fonts, and so on) that were used in Word, but you plan to retain the table in Excel for display and printing.

- Unicode text—Inserts the table using Unicode text formatting, retaining tabular structure. This ensures that international language characters are rendered properly. Depending on the user's local language settings, the Unicode option often is identical to the Text option.
- Text—Inserts the table as plain text, retaining tabular structure. This is the simplest method and often is the best approach to use when you want to use Excel to perform calculations and then return the results to Word.

▶ **See** "Importing Word Tables and Text into Excel," **p. 946**

In this example, because the purpose is to move a table to Excel for performing a calculation, the best option would be to paste the table as text.

Performing Calculations Using Excel

The next step is to use Excel's functions to perform the desired calculations. For example, to calculate the average or standard deviation, click in the cell where you want the computed result to be placed, and click the Paste Function button on the Standard toolbar. In the Paste Function dialog box, click the Statistical category and choose either AVERAGE or STDEV. Click OK and the Formula Palette appears and proposes the cell references it thinks you want to use in the formula. Adjust the cell range, if necessary, by highlighting the correct range of cells and then click OK. As shown in Figure 13.34, Excel sometimes incorrectly guesses which cells to use. So, don't automatically assume the suggested cell range is correct.

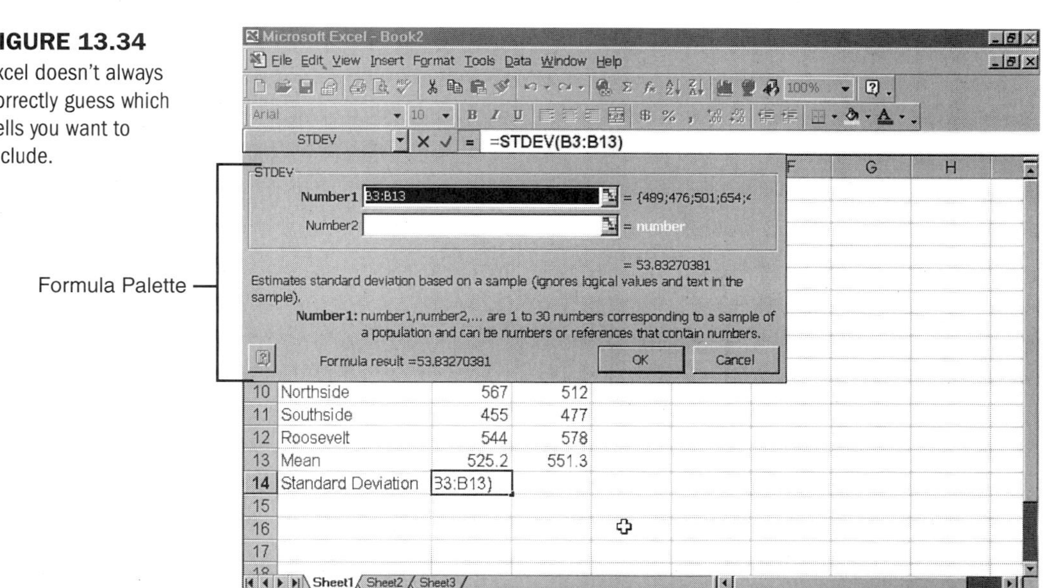

FIGURE 13.34
Excel doesn't always correctly guess which cells you want to include.

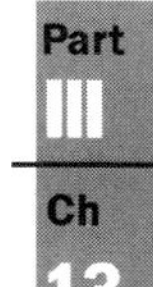

TIP Be a copycat. The real beauty of Excel is the extent to which you can copy formulas. Here, instead of inserting the formula anew for each column, copy the first one and paste it into place. Excel usually correctly adjusts the relative cell references to reflect the fact that the result is in a new row or column.

To calculate the total SAT scores, select the cells in which you want the totals to be placed (for example, D3 through D12); then click the AutoSum tool on Excel's Standard toolbar. Excel automatically fills in all the totals. Copy the mean and standard deviation formulas to the respective cells under Total.

▶ To learn more about performing calculations in Excel, **see** "Functions for Every Occasion" **p. 671**

Moving a Table from Excel Back to Word

Now, to move the table back to Word:

1. Select the table area in Excel, and press Ctrl+C to copy it to the Clipboard.

NOTE Important: The dimensions (numbers of rows and columns) selected in Excel must be identical to those of the original Word table.

2. Switch back to Word, where the original table is still selected. If the end-of-row marks are selected, reselect the table so that the end-of-row marks are not included in the selection.
3. Choose Edit, Paste Special, Unformatted Text, and click OK.

CHAPTER 14

Unleashing the Potential of Forms

In this chapter

Forms Background

From the beginning, Word has included strong forms creation tools, and with each version the tools have gotten stronger. But with Word 2000, the toolbox has begun to burst. Just a casual glance through Word's built-in toolbars will tell you that you can create Forms with special fields, place Controls on documents, and put together Web pages. But the presence of these toolbar buttons only hints at how they can help you create forms. The options you have for creating forms probably outnumber the uses you will ever have for them.

The Evolution of Form Controls

It all started way back in Word 2.0, where you could get a lot of mileage out of plain old tables and a combination of ASK and FILLIN fields. By placing these special fields in the right cells of a table, you could get the form to ask for input, act on user responses, and customize the resulting document. This was a small but significant step ahead of a static set of words and lines. It was also way too underpowered.

Word 6.0 advanced the state of the art with the introduction of special FORMFIELDs created specifically for electronic forms. These were not just additions to ASK and FILLIN; you could *program* these fields. You could tie them to macros, tell them to fire when the cursor entered or exited them, and even force formats on the user's input. The FORMTEXT, FORMCHECKBOX, and FORMDROPDOWN fields acted a little like the text boxes, check boxes, and drop-down list boxes in standard Windows dialog boxes with which users are so familiar. But these special form fields also lacked any graphical appeal and had limited flexibility. For the most part, they were useful only when you protected the document for forms, and that introduced all kinds of new problems, such as disabling most of the editing tools that are usually available in Word.

Advanced users longed for more, and they got it in Word 97. This version introduced Word's forms to ActiveX, the brand name for Microsoft's component technology, and its favored son, the COM component. COM stands for Component Object Model, and Office 2000 and the forthcoming Windows 2000 are built on it. The idea behind COM is that all Windows software should be—and for the most part is—built of reusable parts that are easily interchangeable, sharable, and reliable. Even Internet Explorer is a large COM component built of smaller COM components. ActiveX controls are COM components, and with Word 97 they became part of the Word user's forms toolbox.

This meant that for the first time, users could place command buttons, check boxes, and drop-down list boxes right on their documents. They could add controls that users had seen before in dialog boxes right where users were typing and entering data. This moved the user interface of online forms even closer to the point of use than ever before. Instead of having to display a dialog box so a user could run a macro, the dialog box could be built right into the form itself.

Form Controls Today

Word 2000 preserves all these options and adds one more: the Web form. Web pages, as you undoubtedly know, are built with HTML. But unlike ActiveX controls, the submit buttons, text boxes, list boxes, and option buttons that you see and use on the Web are nothing more than interpreted HTML tags and their corresponding code (properties, attributes, and script). That is, you can create these controls in any HTML editor, including Notepad, if you know the syntax. (Strictly speaking, you do not create the controls—you create the tags; the browser interprets the tags and generates or displays the controls when it displays the page.) You can create Web forms without Word. But Word lets you use a more graphical approach.

In other words, you can create three different kinds of forms with Word 2000:

- Old style, form field forms
- ActiveX forms
- Web forms

Form Types

Each kind of form serves a different purpose, and each one will suit you to a lesser or greater degree. It would make no sense to recommend one or the other over the rest on its merits alone. Creating and using forms has a lot of subjectivity to it, and you should use whichever kind works best for you and the problem you have to solve. You also may have to consider what the boss wants—maybe you do not have any choice. Or maybe you have to get the job done right now, and you do not have time to learn how to create ActiveX forms when you already know how to create form field forms.

But choosing the right kind of form will also depend on how well you know your options. You need to know about them well enough to know which one will solve your problems. Each one has strengths and limitations, as shown in Table 14.1.

Table 14.1 Form Strengths and Limitations

Form Type	Pros	Cons
Form field forms	1. Tools designed for forms 2. Mature toolset 3. Familiar to many creators and users 4. Forms protection	1. Lacks robust functionality 2. Cannot be hosted natively by browsers 3. Only two events
ActiveX forms	1. Very large, rich toolset 2. Familiar interface 3. Maximum programmability 4. Many events 5. Standard programming language	1. Cannot be hosted by most browsers 2. Lack of familiarity among Word users

continues

Table 14.1 Continued

Form Type	Pros	Cons
Web forms	**1.** Familiar interface **2.** Native functionality on intranets and in browser-based applications **3.** Standard programming language	**1.** Lacks standalone functionality (must be hosted by a Web server or client, such as a browser) **2.** Interface limited to HTML tags

Another way of looking at this is to think about the form's *purpose*. That is, the key to choosing the right kind of form is to understand the different kinds of forms available to you and how they are used.

Table 14.2 gives a summary of the different forms and their primary uses.

Table 14.2 How Forms Are Used

Form Type	Primary Uses
Form field forms	Data entry Interactive document creation Spreadsheet-style calculations
ActiveX forms	Data entry Application-like interactivity
Web forms	Web publishing Intranets

Keep in mind that the uses described in Table 14.2 are sweeping generalizations. You *can* use ActiveX documents for spreadsheet-style calculations, and you *can* use form field forms for application-style interactivity. The types overlap.

That is why you should start with what you know. If you have already created forms in Word 6.0, 7.0, or 97 using Word's form fields, you already know what to do. The tools you have come to know will still work and may still get the job done. Likewise, if you have ever programmed in Visual Basic or created UserForms in VBA, you already know *that* model, too, and it will work very well for your Word forms. Take advantage of inertia if you can.

Then move to purpose. If the form you must create will be hosted on a Web server, you'll have to create a Web form, even if you've never done it before.

Finally, if you can, push the limits. Whatever you don't know about, learn. You will find you soon have more options than ever before.

The following sections will discuss each option in greater detail.

Creating Form Field Forms

Most documents created with Word are designed to present information to the reader—letters, reports, memos, email, brochures, and so on. *Forms*, however, are interactive documents that are designed to collect information or data from the users. Sometimes the purpose is for data collection pure and simple—such as questionnaires or surveys. Other times, the purpose might be to organize information, so that it can be presented in a neat and consistent format—such as timesheets, invoices, and purchase orders.

Whether you know it or not, you already use forms every day because the entire Office interface is based on forms. For example, standard dialog boxes are forms because they are designed to collect input from you so that the application can respond accordingly. Even the Word window—where you type a document—is a kind of text form, with an expandable box for entering text. The forms you can create in Word fit well with the way you already work.

When creating a form field form, the basic idea is to create a template that provides two elements:

- Instructions or other explanatory content that solicits information from the user/reader of the form.
- Fields that provide a mechanism for the user to provide their response.

At its most simplistic, a printed form could be just a set of instructions and underlined areas for the user to respond. Word, however, provides the tools to create a wide variety of different kinds of forms, varying from simple fill-in-the-blank paper forms and forms with check boxes to online forms where the user can use drop-down controls to select responses.

Right-click any toolbar and click Forms, to display the Forms toolbar. To create a simple fill-in-the-blank form, you could type a label such as

```
Name:
```

Then, place the cursor to the right of the label—Name:—and click the Text Form Field tool on the Forms toolbar. This provides a fill-in area where the name can be entered as shown in Figure 14.1. If you have set Word to show bookmarks (Tools, Options, View, Show, Bookmarks), you will also see a pair of brackets at each end of the fill-in area.

Protecting Your Form

Before you can use the simple form described in the preceding section, it needs to be protected as a form. Otherwise, if you try to type in the field you created previously, you will either scroll the field to the right, or overtype the field entirely.

To protect the document as a form, choose Tools, Protect Document, and click the Forms option, as shown in Figure 14.2. Leave the Password field blank and click OK.

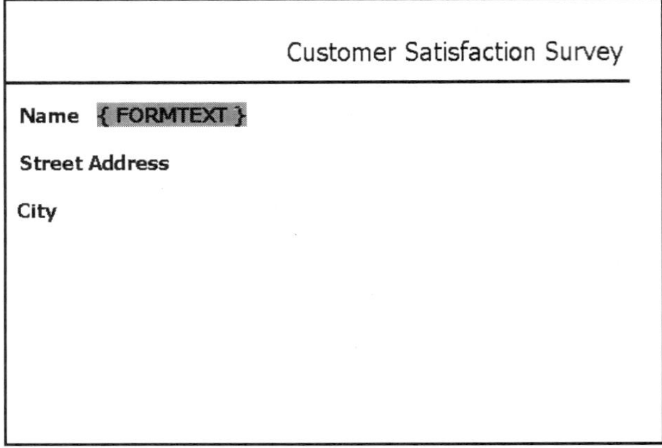

FIGURE 14.1
It's not a form until you protect it with Tools, Protect Document, Protect document for forms.

FIGURE 14.2
The Sections options are not available in single-section documents.

Be Careful with Passwords

Don't use passwords unless you really need them. If you lose your password, there is no built-in recovery method. If you do need passwords, establish a password list—which you would write down and put into a safe offline location—so you can refer to it as needed. Online lists can get corrupted, deleted, or otherwise lost, and often are easy targets for hackers.

There are some companies and individuals who will sell, or even enable you to download for free, password-cracker programs. If you really need password protection, you should know that your protection is very thin indeed. You're better off knowing that the protection isn't ironclad, however. Even so, there is no guarantee that you will be able to access a password cracker when you really need one. It's better to be conservative about using passwords, and to keep an offline list in a safe place.

Finally, passwords are case-sensitive. Case must match exactly. A common password failure scenario occurs when a password is set and confirmed while Caps Lock is turned on (as sometimes happens accidentally). Later, the user cannot figure out why the password does not work.

Now, with protection turned on, the user may only type in the fill-in areas. The nonform instructional part of the form is protected from modification, while at the same time form fields are enabled for data entry.

Add Form Protection to Word Documents

You can use *form protection*—even when you aren't creating a form. This is handy when you want to create documents using directives, dates, or other material that you don't want changed.

To add form protection to a document that you've not established as a form, insert continuous section breaks before and after the text you want to protect—unless it's at the beginning or end of the document. In this case, you just need a single section break to isolate the protected section. Choose Tools, Protect Document. Choose Forms. Click the Sections button. In Section Protection, remove the checks next to the sections you don't want protected, as shown in Figure 14.3, and click OK. If desired, use a password, and click OK; confirm the password, if necessary, and click OK again.

From now on, the protected section cannot be edited, deleted, or otherwise changed. It cannot even be selected and copied! Even Edit, Select All becomes unavailable. You can select the area before and after, but not the selected section. To remove protection, choose Tools, Unprotect, and supply the password (if necessary).

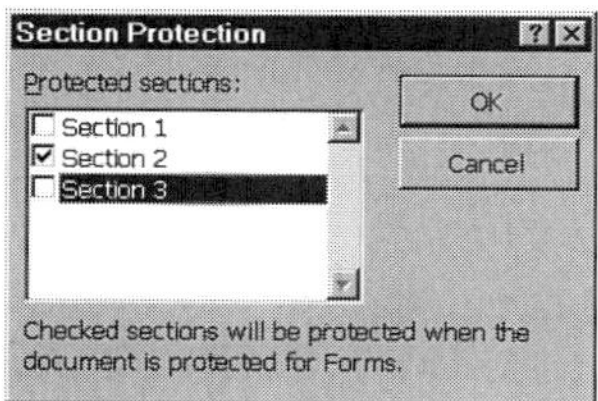

FIGURE 14.3
Uncheck sections you don't want protected.

Notice that you cannot select or edit any text in the template except for the form fields themselves. To insert your own company name or make other more substantial changes, you first need to unprotect the form template. Choose Tools, Unprotect Document.

Now, you can make any changes you want. Be careful not to delete any of the form fields—unless that's what you really want to do.

If you are working with a template created by another user, you might find that some form fields use other fields in their calculations; so, make sure you understand the underlying form and structure before you add or remove form fields.

After you make the desired changes, choose Tools, Protect Document, and click the Forms option to reapply protection.

To add the template to your User Templates location, choose File, Save As and give the template a unique name, and make sure that you are saving the template in the User Templates location (Tools, Options, File Locations, User Templates). Close the template.

Now the custom template will be one of your options when you choose File, New. With your company name and address in place, as well as any other modifications in text or form, you're now ready to fill in the blanks.

As previously noted, you're forced to unprotect if you want to change form labels or the nonform field portion of template.

CAUTION

After you've entered data into a new form, don't unprotect and reprotect the document. Unprotecting and reprotecting erases any data you might have entered. If you need to tweak the form, do it before you start entering data, not while entering data.

However, there is a workaround to make changes to your template and avoid losing data:

1. While the form is still protected, finish entering all the data—you won't be able to use the document as a form later on.
2. Then choose Tools, Unprotect Document to turn off forms protection.
3. Press Ctrl+A to select the whole document, and press Ctrl+Shift+F9. This is the Unlink Fields command—it converts fields into ordinary text.
4. Make any needed changes to the nonforms area.
5. Save the document.

Use Macros to Protect Field Data

There is another way that retains the fields–replace the Protect Document command with a macro that safely restores protection. It's a three-line macro, counting the `Sub` lines, that reprotects the document without destroying data:

```
Public Sub ReprotectDocument()
    ActiveDocument.Protect Type:=wdAllowOnlyFormFields, NoReset:=True
End Sub
```

▶ **See** "Assigning a Macro to a Toolbar Button," **p. 112**

▶ **See** "Assigning Macros to a Menu Command or Graphic Object," **p. 114**

Form Design Considerations

Forms are designed to collect information. In many ways, forms are similar to surveys, and should be open to the same kinds of design considerations. Here is a short list of essential rules to observe when setting up an interactive form, whether it be a form field form, an ActiveX form, or a Web form:

- Save the user's time—If you can anticipate all different possible answers to a question, present those answers for the user to choose from (using option buttons, check boxes, or drop-down lists).
- Don't make the user angry—Don't force the user to choose among options that don't encompass every possibility. When you have a list of options that isn't exhaustive, provide a place for Other.

- Don't overuse drop-down lists—Drop-down lists are great—sometimes. However, when you have a list of choices that can fit laterally on the computer screen, present them as option buttons or check boxes, whichever is more appropriate. When a user sees all the choices at once, filling out the form is easier and faster.
- Don't force the user to choose among nonexclusive choices—When the options aren't mutually exclusive, use check boxes rather than option buttons.
- Don't make the user read too much—Often, forms are for your convenience—not the user's. Explanatory text is useful, but don't go overboard, lest the user get over bored.
- Provide help—Use Word's form field Help facility to explain the kind of input needed. Provide a prompt on the Status Bar as well as help that responds to F1.
- Provide a place for comments—Provide space for users to include comments in case they need to explain or amplify a response.
- Use default text—Don't leave the default text blank. Embed either the expected answer or an invitation such as `Type your name here`.
- Provide a way for respondents to contact you—If something goes wrong with the form, you don't want it just sitting there collecting data incorrectly for hours or days on end.

Planning the Layout An ergonomic layout is useful in getting users to provide the needed information. Use the computer screen as a sketch pad; or, sketch your form design on a piece of paper. Get a good idea of where you want everything to go. By default, Word inserts form elements the same way normal text is inserted—inline. There are (at least) three ways to put form elements where you want them:

- Tables
- Click and type
- Frames

Each of these methods is described later in this chapter.

Testing the Design Testing is a vastly underused aspect of the design phase. After you have the form built, have some typical users work with it. Watch them carefully while they use it—take notes. Use your notes and their feedback to refine and rebuild as necessary. After the form is finished, field-test it. Make sure it works for the intended purpose.

Use open-ended forms to develop choices for other forms. Too often, form designers make up lists of options, believing they've covered all the bases. Instead of launching into a list of choices you think are important and relevant, it's sometimes useful to let the user decide. Start with open-ended questions. Then group and categorize the answers to develop selections for multiple choice form elements. If the list is exhaustive, that's good. If it's not, then make sure you include a place for Other.

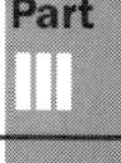

Using the Forms Toolbar

The Forms toolbar contains nine tools for working with form field forms. These tools provide the basics for creating many of the kinds of forms Word users often need—such as invoices, purchase orders, timesheets, ordering forms, and survey questionnaires.

The functionality of each of the Forms toolbar buttons is described in the following sections.

Text Form Field Button The Text Form Field button is used for creating fill-in-the-blank forms. Use this form for open-ended questions for which user input cannot reasonably be anticipated—such as names and places. Specific steps on creating this type of field are discussed later in this chapter. For more information on creating text form fields, see "Using Text Form Fields," later in this chapter.

Check Box Form Field Button Use Check Box Form Fields button to allow users a place to select among choices that are not mutually exclusive, such as lists that say Check All That Apply. For an online form for ordering pizza, you could have things that coexist on top of a pizza—pepperoni, mushrooms, sausage, olives, green peppers, and so on. For paper forms, you can add instructions that say Check Only One, which usually is easier than using option buttons from the Control Toolbox. You can try it for online forms, too, but it's impossible to enforce!

Drop-Down Form Field Button Use Drop-Down Form Fields for creating a list of mutually exclusive choices, especially if the number of items in the list may change later.

For an online pizza ordering form, mutually exclusive choices might be deep dish or thin crust; small, medium, or large; and so on. Specific steps on creating this type of field are discussed later in this chapter.

Form Field Options Button The Form Field Options button is context sensitive. Use this tool to display a dialog box that specifies the settings for the selected form field: Text Form Fields, Check Box Form Fields, or Drop-Down Form Fields. Refer to the specific discussion of each form field presented later in this chapter (for example, "Using Drop-Down Lists in a Form") for information about the options displayed when you click the Form Field Options button.

Draw Table Button The Draw Table button activates the Tables and Borders toolbar, and puts Word into table drawing mode. Tables often provide a useful format for designing forms. The Draw Table tool lets you sketch out the form design. Creating tables using this tool is discussed later in this chapter.

Insert Table Button The Insert Table tool button is the same tool that's on Word's Standard toolbar. Use it to create tables quickly.

See "Unleashing the Potential of Tables," **p. 377**

Insert Frame Button The Insert Frame tool button inserts a frame around the form field, allowing you to position the form field anywhere on the page. This kind of frame is a tool specific to Word, and has nothing to do with frames used on Web pages.

Form Field Shading Button Form fields—especially text form fields—sometimes are hard to see. The Form field shading button is used to shade the field so that you can better see with the text in the field.

Protect Form Button The Protect Form tool is a toggle that turns form protection on or off. This tool is different from choosing Tools, Protect Document. The latter provides access to options. However, when designing forms, it's often useful to briefly toggle protection on, so that you can test your settings. When doing that, it's much faster to click the Protect Form toggle than to go through the menu.

CAUTION

You can use the Protect Form tool to unprotect a passworded document (you must supply the password); however, if you click again to reprotect the document, passwording is not restored. You must choose Tools, Protect Document, Forms to enable passworded protection of the document.

Incorporating Advanced Elements in Form Field Forms

For many types of forms—especially paper forms— only underlined blank areas are needed, which allow the user to enter the necessary data. To create interactive form documents, or to be able to separate form data from the form itself (for example, for collecting data online, and then using Word to print just data to preprinted forms), you need to use form fields.

NOTE Word's Help file recommends that you use ActiveX controls for creating forms, and for good reason. ActiveX forms give you much more power and flexibility than form field forms do. (For more information on creating ActiveX forms, see "Creating and Using ActiveX Forms" later in this chapter.) Web forms are not really an option for your standard forms-creation needs, because Web forms require access to a Web server. (For more information on creating Web forms, see "Creating and Using Web Forms" later in this chapter.) But for most other forms, plain form fields work just fine.

For creating form field forms, Word relies upon the following three form fields:

- FORMTEXT
- FORMCHECKBOX
- FORMDROPDOWN

NOTE These three fields are different from the kinds of fields covered in Chapter 12. These fields take no switches. Properties for the form fields are stored internally by Word, and are not visible when you display field codes. These fields also cannot be inserted using Insert, Fields in the menu. Instead, you need to display the Forms toolbar and insert them from there.

Using Text Form Fields

Text form fields provide a way for users to input variable text data such as names, dates, times, numbers, cities, countries, or other text that you cannot predict. Working with form fields is easiest with the Forms toolbar displayed (right-click any toolbar and choose Forms).

It's usually a good idea to precede the text box with a plain text label describing the desired input (for example, Name, City, State, Zip, Telephone, Fax Telephone, Email Address, and so on). Then, click the Text Form Field tool on the Forms toolbar. This inserts a text form field into the document at the insertion point. Form fields are shaded by default, even if you set Tools, Options, View Show Field Shading to Never. This lets you more readily see form fields in a busy document. You also see bookmarks around every form field you insert if you have Tools, Options, View Bookmarks checked.

This is helpful if you display formatting marks and other unprintable characters. Press Ctrl+Shift+8 to toggle the display of all nonprinting characters.

Make sure you use the number 8 on the main portion of the keyboard—the number 8 on the numeric keypad does not work with this shortcut.

The form fields are now indicated with small circles, shown in Figure 14.4.

FIGURE 14.4
Text Form Fields default to unlimited length, although they initially display just five spaces.

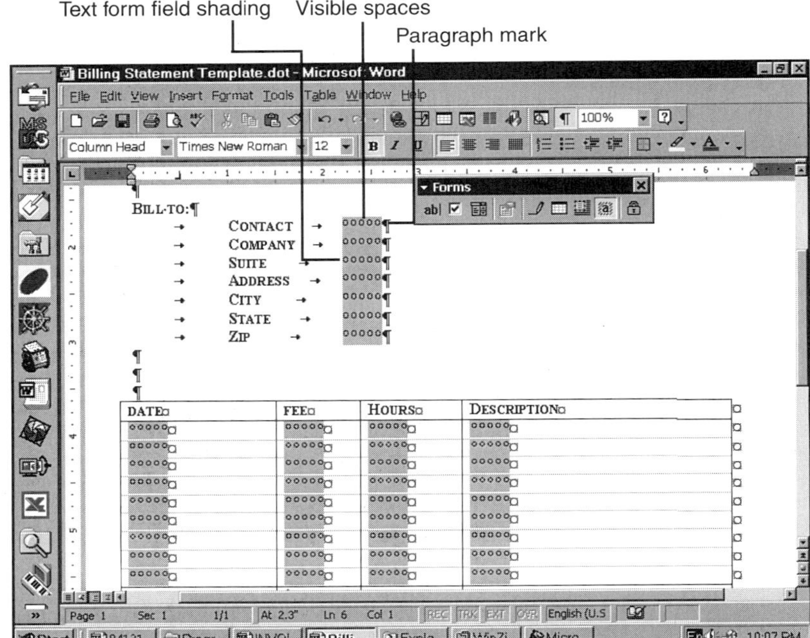

To specify settings, right-click the text form field and choose Properties, to display the Text Form Field Options dialog box as shown in Figure 14.5.

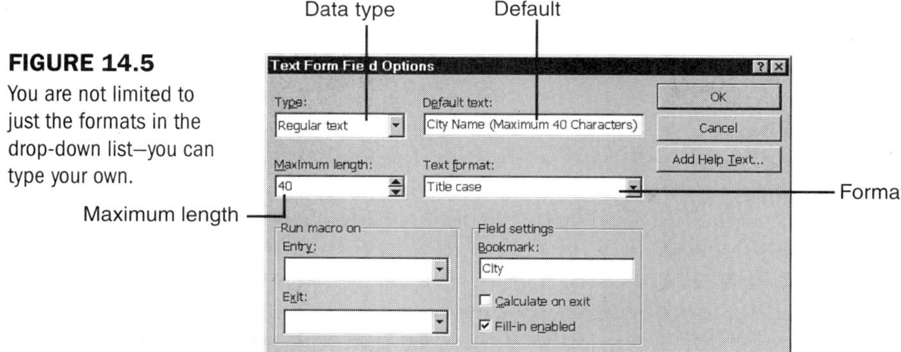

FIGURE 14.5
You are not limited to just the formats in the drop-down list–you can type your own.

Type Setting Under Type, choose a format that reflects the anticipated kind of entry. Use Regular Text for normal text, such as names of people, places, and things. Choose Number, Date, or Calculation, according to your needs.

For telephone numbers in the U.S., set Type to Number and set the format to `(###) ###-####`. This causes any 10-digit number to be formatted as a telephone number. Of course, if the user includes a 1 or excludes the area code, that can throw things off. However, that's what data-checking macros are for! See "Adding Macros to Forms," later in this chapter.

The other options in the dialog box change dynamically depending on the Type setting. For example, when you set Type to Number or Date, the Text Format option changes to Date Format or Number Format (for Number or Calculation). Choosing the appropriate format for dates and numbers can assist you in ensuring that user input is formatted in a way that is useful to you. Note that the default text you type will appear in the form, helping provide additional instruction to the form user.

Format Setting Choosing the correct format setting is particularly important for dates. If you want dates formatted as M/D/YY, for example, Word recognizes and automatically converts most user-entered dates to the desired format. By specifying YYYY, you can ensure that your forms data is year–2000-compliant.

For numbers such as dollar amounts, the correct choice of format ensures that the user entry has a dollar sign, decimal point, and commas (as appropriate).

Y2K Dates

In an effort to be Y2K-compliant, Word somewhat arbitrarily assumes that two-digit years from 00 through 29 mean 2000 through 2029, and that years from 30 through 99 are assumed to be 1930 through 1999. If your form includes dates before 1930 and after 2029, use YYYY rather than YY, so that the user immediately sees how their entry is interpreted.

For text entry, the format setting can assist you in making sure that the appropriate case is used. For names, for example, you typically might want title case. For email addresses or URLs, you typically would want to use lowercase.

Maximum Length Setting Another work saver is the Maximum Length setting. With most text entries, you either know or can reliably predict how long an entry is going to be. For example, state is always going to be two letters; zip code is always going to be five or nine digits. For others, such as names of people and places, you might have to guess. If you have sample data, find the longest entry and count the characters to come up with the length.

Macros Setting Running Macro On Entry and Exit options enable you to design control into your form. An Entry macro runs when the user tabs into or clicks a given form field (when the focus moves to that field). Entry macros typically provide information or check to ensure that other data required for that field has already been provided. Exit macros run when the focus leaves that field. Exit macros typically trigger calculations, perform consistency checks (for example, to ensure that data-entry error has not occurred), or provide conditional redirection (for example, sending the user to a different form or location in the same form depending on what answer is given).

Bookmark Setting Under Field settings, you can assign a bookmark name to the form field result. This is useful in performing calculations and in writing macros to parse entry as the form is being filled in. The bookmark becomes, in effect, a mathematical/programming *variable* you can use in calculations and other macro references.

Calculated on Exit Setting Calculate on Exit is a built-in facility that saves you from having to write a macro to calculate a given field. This facility is also useful when it's turned off. Sometimes, calculations are cumbersome or depend on other calculations. Under those circumstances, you might sometimes want to delay calculation or use a macro to control how numbers are calculated.

Fill-In Enabled Setting Fill-In Enabled is used to control user access to the field. Suppose you were designing a data form where some fields display the results of calculations based on data supplied by the user in other fields. You can embed a formula in a field and disable fill-in. This way, you get the advantage of forms automation (in seeing the calculation results), while protecting the field from manual entry.

Using Check Boxes

Another useful item is the check box. As indicated earlier, check boxes can be used for nonexclusive choices (for example, where the instructions say something such as *Check All That Apply*). They can also be used for mutually exclusive choices on paper forms. However, for mutually exclusive choices for online forms, using check boxes is not recommended. Use a drop-down list or option buttons, instead. Check boxes must be accompanied by text that says what the check corresponds to. Sometimes, however, forms are designed so tightly that it's easy to mistakenly check the wrong box. Consider the age items in the two forms shown in Figure 14.6. In the middle of the upper list, it would be very easy to mistakenly check the wrong number. The vertical lower list, however, is laid out clearly and logically.

CAUTION

Make sure your mutually exclusive items really are mutually exclusive. A 45-year-old client shouldn't be forced to choose between being 35 to 45 and 45 to 55.

FIGURE 14.6
Don't make check boxes too cluttered.

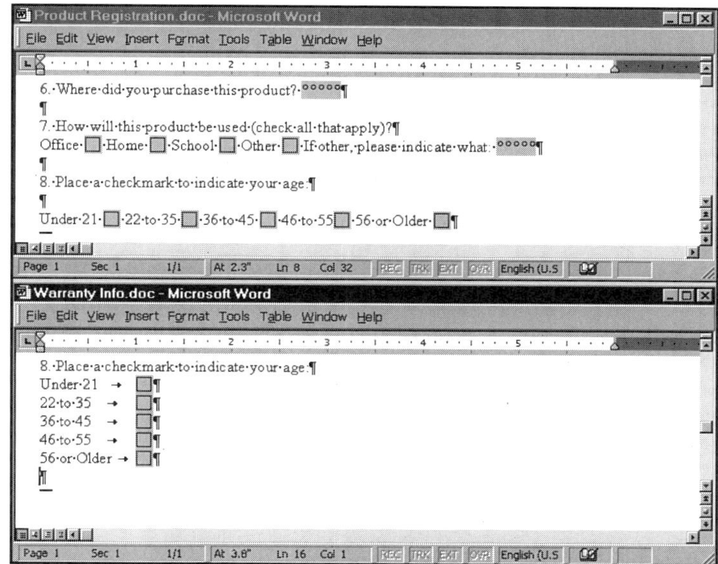

To insert a check box, enter the accompanying text or label and click the Check Box Form Field tool on the Forms toolbar. Setup and alignment often can be facilitated by using tabs or by putting text and check boxes into a table.

To set check box options, right-click the check box and choose Properties, as shown in Figure 14.7. See "Using Text Form Fields," earlier in this chapter.

FIGURE 14.7
It's sometimes useful to precheck boxes with the expected response.

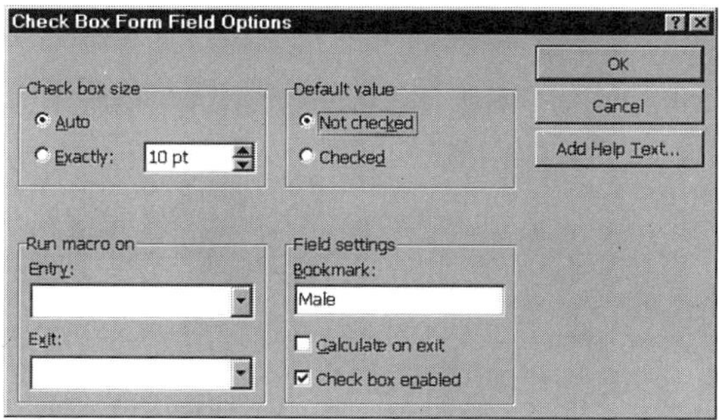

Check box size determines how large the check box is. By default, check boxes are the same size as the tallest letter in the current font.

For some forms, this might be too large. For others, it might be too small. Consider your audience carefully and make an appropriate size choice.

Use the Default value setting to force the initial setting to be checked or not checked. If you force it to be checked, you might be saving the user some work. However, you run the risk that the check you see was an oversight (just as an unchecked box can be an oversight).

Using Drop-Down Lists in a Form

Drop-down lists are useful for presenting a list of known mutually exclusive options. A common practice is to use drop-down lists for product categories, as shown in Figure 14.8.

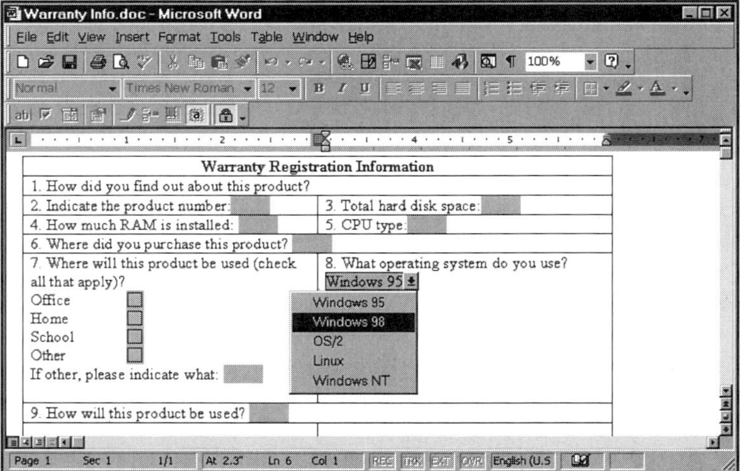

FIGURE 14.8 Drop-down fields are also called combo boxes.

Insert a drop-down list by clicking the Drop-Down Form Field tool on the Forms toolbar. Double-click the drop-down list to display the options, shown in Figure 14.9.

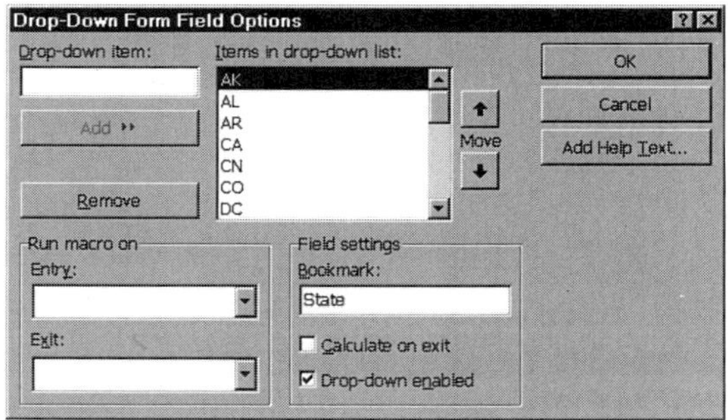

FIGURE 14.9 Save drop-down items as AutoText entries so that you can use them in other forms.

To populate a drop-down list, type the entries (one at a time) in the Drop-Down Item text box and click Add. Remove errant items with the Remove button. If the order of items is wrong, use the Move up/down arrows to reorganize. To learn more about other settings in the Drop-Down Form Field Options dialog box, see "Using Text Form Fields," earlier in this chapter.

Framing Form Fields

Word's form fields are inserted into the text layer of documents, and thus appear inline with text. That's not always where you want them. If you need additional positioning flexibility, you can use the Insert Frame tool button on the Forms toolbar to insert a frame around the form field and place it in the drawing layer. This allows you to position the form field anywhere on the page by dragging, or by using frame formatting (Format, Frame). As noted earlier, this kind of frame is specific to Word, and has nothing to do with frames used on Web pages.

To frame a form field:

1. Select the form field you want to frame and click the Insert Frame tool. A frame appears around the form field, as shown in Figure 14.10.
2. To position the frame, move the mouse pointer over the frame; drag the frame where you want it.
3. To format the frame, right-click the border of the frame and choose Format Frame.

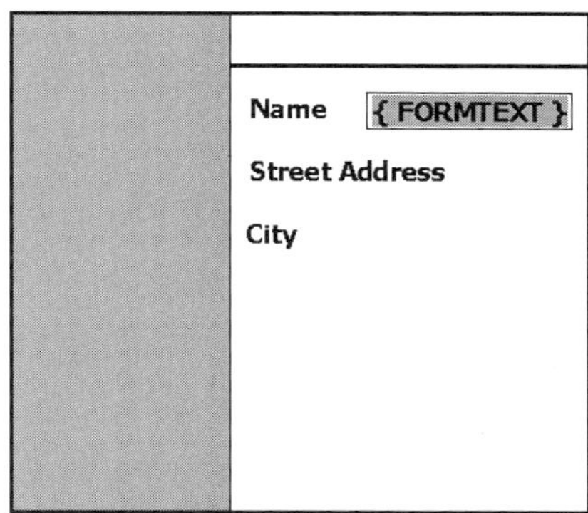

FIGURE 14.10
Frames can be positioned anywhere on the page.

To remove a frame, right-click the frame's border and choose Format Frame. In the Frame dialog box, choose Remove Frame.

Adding a Table to a Form

A good layout often enhances the likelihood that your form will collect the data you want, as well as lessening the chance of confusion on the part of the user. Tables can help to provide the needed organization. Consider Figure 14.11, a weekly timesheet. This form document consists of four tables: header (company name and title), employee information, timesheet data, and the signature block.

▶ **See** "Unleashing the Potential of Tables," **p. 377**

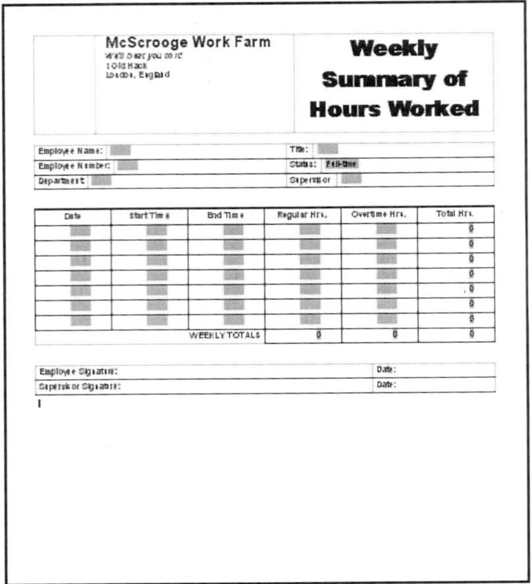

McScrooge Work Farm

1 Old Hack
London, England

Weekly Summary of Hours Worked

Employee Name:		Title:	
Employee Number:		Status:	Full-time
Department		Supervisor	

Date	Start Time	End Time	Regular Hrs.	Overtime Hrs.	Total Hrs.
					0
					0
					0
					0
					0
					0
					0
		WEEKLY TOTALS	0	0	0

Employee Signature:	Date:
Supervisor Signature:	Date:

FIGURE 14.11
Tables provide a sense of order.

This form didn't have to be created using four tables. It could have been created using one, two, or even no tables at all. Using tables, however, especially for data where calculations are needed, simplifies your work by letting you take advantage of built-in features such as table math.

▶ **See** "Performing Calculations in a Table," **p. 400**

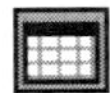

To use tables as the basis for your forms, start by sketching out the information blocks on scratch paper. Then, to create regular tables, use the Insert Table tool on the Forms toolbar.

To draw irregular tables, or to add irregular components to existing tables, click the Draw Table tool on the Forms toolbar. Using the mouse pointer, drag to draw table elements wherever needed. For additional facility, click the Tables and Borders tool on the Standard toolbar, which displays the Tables and Borders toolbar.

Choose View, Print Layout, and zoom to Whole Page view, so that you can see the whole page onscreen. In this view, use the table drawing tool to draw the basic framework for your form. Zoom back to normal levels to fill in the detail.

▶ **See** "Unleashing the Potential of Tables," **p. 377**

Inserting Fields in the Table Use tables to set up the working area. You can then insert form fields at will, wherever needed in tables. One problem with unlimited text form fields inserted outside a table is that you never know how large they'll get. When lengthy text is added to one of these fields, it is disconcerting to see the field overflow as you add text to a field. With each field in its own table cell, this won't happen.

Calculated Fields in a Form

Form fields can contain calculations. Consider the ordering form shown in Figure 14.12. Each of the entries in the Total column is the product of Quantity (QTY) and Unit Price. Notice that the Fill-In Enabled option in the Text Form Field Options dialog box is unavailable (Fill-In Enabled is automatically made unavailable when Type is set to Calculation).

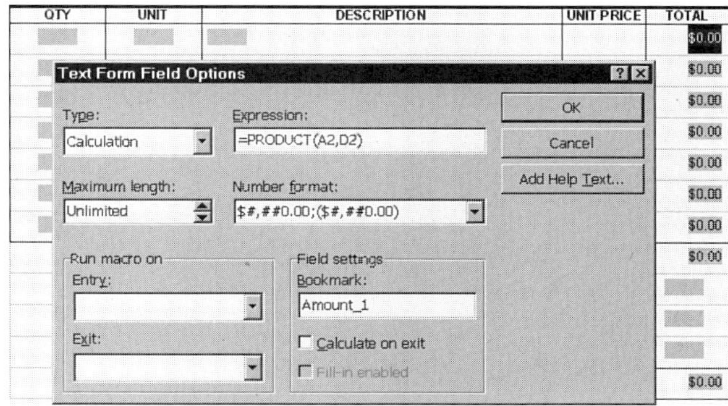

FIGURE 14.12
Total price is provided by the form—the user cannot edit that field.

To create a calculation form field:

1. Insert a text form field where you want the calculated result to appear.
2. Double-click the text form field; the Text Form Field Options dialog box appears.
3. Set Type to Calculation.
4. In Expression, type the formula for the calculation (for example, `=PRODUCT(A2,D2)`).
5. Choose the desired number format.
6. Click OK.

NOTE Note in step 4 that cell references are similar to those used in most spreadsheet programs, with rows numbered going down, and columns lettered going across. Note also that, unlike when using Excel, cell references are not automatically adjusted when you copy formulas from one cell to another. Instead, you would need to manually update the references. For example, when you copy a formula from column B to column C, you would have to change all the Bs to Cs.

▶ **See** "Fields—Word's Hidden Functions," **p. 349**

Using the *PRODUCT* Function The `PRODUCT` function multiplies the items in parentheses. You can use bookmarks, as well. Suppose the first Quantity value is bookmarked as Quantity_1, and the corresponding unit price is Price_1. The expression could instead be `=PRODUCT(Quantity_1,Price_1)` or `=Quantity_1*Price_1`.

NOTE The exponential operator, ^, is allowed, too. This lets you perform more complicated calculations—such as compound interest and amortization.

The Calculate on Exit option (refer to Figure 14.12) tells Word to recalculate any calculation fields that use a given field each time that given field is changed. For example, if the Quantity_1 form field has Calculate on Exit enabled, any form field that refers to Quantity_1 automatically is recalculated each time the value of Quantity_1 is changed (that is, when you exit that field after making a change). For most purposes, this lets you automatically recalculate forms without having to use macros, greatly simplifying form construction.

Adding Macros to Forms

Under some circumstances, you might want to include macros that run when a given field is entered or exited. Suppose, for example, that you want to be sure that data entered is within a certain range. Or, you might want to compare different entries and perform a logical consistency check. Whatever the reason, Word lets you pass control to entry and exit macros.

To associate an entry or exit macro:

1. Double-click the form field with which you want to associate a macro.
2. In Run Macro On, use the pull-down control by Entry or Exit (or both) to choose the desired macro(s).
3. Make any other desired changes, and click OK.

CAUTION

Unlike Tools, Macro, Macros, the macro list you see under Run Macro On includes all the macros in all the currently loaded templates (current template, Normal.dot, as well as any global templates). A macro that's available to you as you're developing a form template might not be available to others to whom you distribute the template. So, store any needed macros in the form template itself (just as you need to store any AutoText entries for Help or Status Bar messages in the form template, as well).

▶ **See** "Recording a Macro," **p. 110**

Sharing Your Forms with Other Users

In many offices, the idea underlying development of forms is to provide consistent enterprisewide solutions to everyday problems—such as recording hours worked, expense reports, invoices, helpdesk requests, problem reports, and so on. Before sharing a form with other users, it is useful to provide help on how to use the form.

Providing Help to People Using Your Forms

Double-click any form field to display the Form Field Options dialog box. Click the Add Help Text button to display the Form Field Help Text dialog box shown in Figure 14.13. There are two tabs in this dialog box. The tab you select depends on where you want the help information to appear—in the Status Bar or in a message box when F1 is pressed. You can have the same information appear whether the user looks at the Status Bar or presses F1, or you can display one message in the Status Bar and a different message when F1 is pressed.

Regardless, there are three alternatives from which to choose:

- None—Display no information.
- AutoText Entry—Use this option to display text from an AutoText entry. This is useful where the identical help text is used for multiple form fields. You might, for example, create AutoText entries for each of the different help messages you want to provide, and then refer to them by AutoText name, rather than typing each one individually (or using copy/paste). If you are going to use the same message more than once, it is generally more efficient to use the AutoText option.
- Type Your Own—Use this option for one-shot help items or for very short forms.

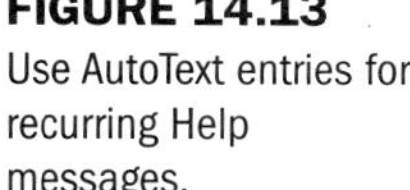

FIGURE 14.13
Use AutoText entries for recurring Help messages.

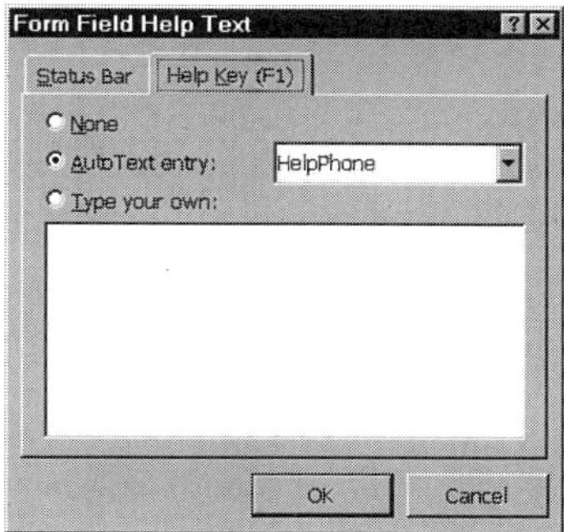

Creating AutoText Entries To create recurring text for help or Status Bar messages, use AutoText. At the bottom of your form, create a list of Help and Status Bar text messages. Select the first one and choose Tools, AutoCorrect, and then click the AutoText tab. Give the entry a logical name in the Enter AutoText Entries Here text box. Under the Look In drop-down list, set the location to the form template itself (which should be the name of the document template you are editing).

CAUTION

The AutoText entries must be stored in the form template itself, so that those entries are available to others to whom you distribute the form template.

Then click Add. Repeat this for each Help or Status Bar message you want to create. After you've completed all the entries, save the template.

Now, you can delete the list of text messages from the bottom of the document because they've been saved as AutoText entries. When you need Help messages or Status Bar messages in setting up form fields, you'll have a list of messages ready. In the Form Field Help Text dialog box, previously shown in Figure 14.13, you click the AutoText Entry option and choose the AutoText name from the drop-down list.

If you ever want to modify a help message, insert it into the template via AutoText—just as you would insert any other AutoText entry.

Make your change to the message, select it, and then choose Tools, AutoCorrect, AutoText, and re-create the entry. Then delete the text from the template. Use this procedure for all types of form fields.

Displaying Field Help in the Status Bar The Status Bar is useful for displaying short prompts indicating the type of entry or action the user is expected to perform, as shown in Figure 14.14. Status Bar options and settings in the Form Field Help Text dialog box are identical to those for the F1 key. Just remember that Status Bar messages are necessarily more succinct than F1 messages because there is a limited amount of space on the Status Bar.

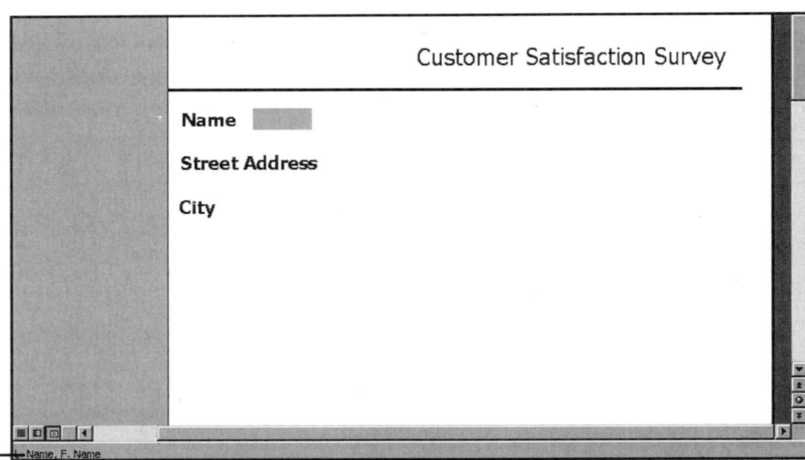

FIGURE 14.14
Be sure your messages fit on the Status Bar.

Creating and Using ActiveX Forms

Some of the forms you want to create need more functionality than form field forms can provide. For example, suppose your form needs a set of command buttons, such as the ubiquitous OK and Cancel. Or perhaps it needs some option buttons, such as the seven types of breaks in the Break dialog box (Insert, Break). If this is the kind of interface you need, form fields will not fill the bill. You need to use ActiveX controls.

A form that contains ActiveX controls is, in some ways, very similar to a Visual Basic form. You drag controls from a toolbox of available command buttons, list boxes, option buttons, and so on and place them right on the document. Then you write code behind the events that fire when the controls are pressed, clicked, typed in, and hovered over. Using this technique, you can create documents that look and work very much like standard Windows dialog boxes. In fact, it's best to think of them as dialog boxes—as tiny Windows applications.

But unlike dialog boxes (and like their form field-based cousins), ActiveX forms can have all the features of a real Word document—text, embedded graphics, tables, rich formatting, and so on. That gives them a lot more flexibility than a mere dialog box—perfect candidates for almost any application you care to create.

NOTE Don't confuse Word documents that contain ActiveX controls with so-called *ActiveX Documents*. ActiveX Documents are a special kind of COM control that can host other controls but also (more importantly) take over their host application. If you've ever seen a Word document or an Excel spreadsheet open in a Web browser and add Word's or Excel's menus and toolbars to the browser, you've seen an ActiveX Document in action. Merely putting ActiveX controls on a Word document does not make it an ActiveX Document. ■

Understanding the Pieces

To create and use ActiveX forms, you need three pieces:

- A document to host the controls and code; any Word document will work.
- One or more ActiveX controls to provide the user interface.
- VBA code to control what happens.

ActiveX Controls The heart of an ActiveX form is the ActiveX control. An *ActiveX control* is simply a software component—a device that you can program. While not every control in every dialog box you've ever seen is an ActiveX control, lots of them are. Many ActiveX controls don't even have visible interfaces. Somewhat like the plumbing in your house, ActiveX controls serve invisible purposes that don't require any user interaction. And the ActiveX controls you have installed on your system can be placed on your documents.

To work with these controls, display the Visual Basic toolbar and the Control Toolbox toolbar (right-click over any toolbar and select them, or choose View, Toolbars, and select them from the list).

NOTE You can also display the Control Toolbox by clicking on the Control Toolbox button on the Visual Basic toolbar. ■

Standard Controls The most commonly used controls appear as buttons on the Control Toolbox. Word 2000 ships with 11 standard controls: CheckBox, TextBox, CommandButton, OptionButtons, ListBox, ComboBox, ToggleButton, SpinButton, ScrollBar, Label, and Image.

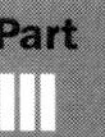

NOTE Word's Help file has a great overview of all 11 ActiveX controls and what they do. Press F1 and search for the topic "ActiveX Controls in Forms." ■

Figure 14.15 shows standard ActiveX controls as they appear by default on a Word page (except for Image). The left column shows the control name; the right column shows the control.

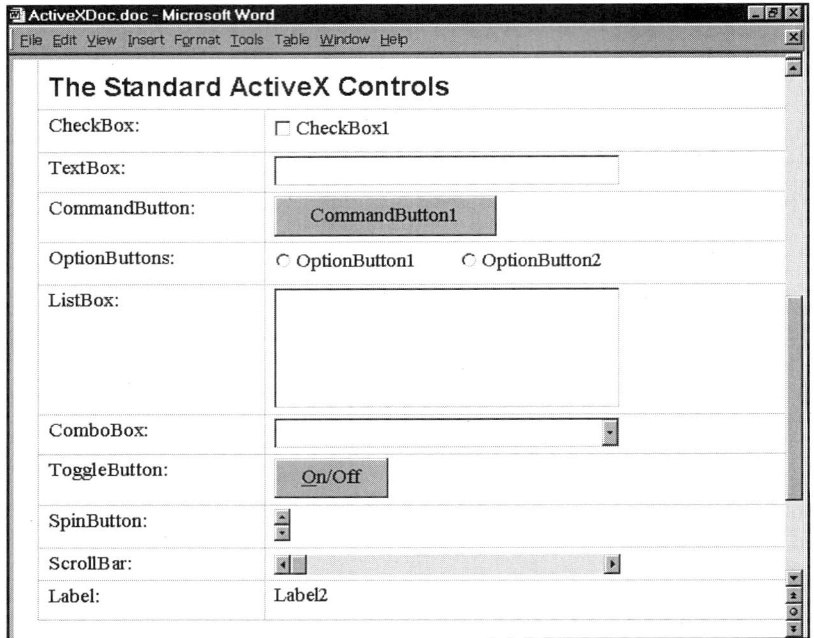

FIGURE 14.15
The standard ActiveX controls look just as at home in a Word document as they do in a dialog box.

Other Controls You can create most of your form elements with the workhorse controls in the Control Toolbox. But just in case you can't, you can always use other ActiveX controls. If you click the More Controls button, you will see a list of all the ActiveX controls registered on your system. You can probably use most of them in your ActiveX forms. Go ahead and experiment with different controls. See what you can do with them. The beauty of ActiveX controls is that they belong to a thriving community of component creators, distributors, and propagators. ActiveX controls are everywhere, often coming bundled with software that users download and install on a regular basis.

The dark side is that many of them will not be available for any form that you plan to distribute to others. This is because some require an additional license key; some require documentation that you do not have; and some are not installed on other machines that would use the form. So experiment as you will, but be careful about distributing what you use.

CAUTION

If you are creating a form that will be used by others and you want to use a nonstandard control, make sure all your target users have that nonstandard control or can easily install it. If your form uses a control that your users do not have, they will not be able to use your form.

Placing ActiveX Controls on a Form To place an ActiveX control in your document, follow these steps:

1. Place the insertion point where you want to insert the control.
2. Make sure the Control Toolbox is displayed (View, Toolbars, Control Toolbox).
3. In the Control Toolbox toolbar, click on the control you want to use. Word places the control at the insertion point and selects it.

4. Click the Properties button on the Control Toolbox. Word displays the Properties window for the selected control.
5. In the Properties window, give the control a Name (see Figure 14.16). Because you will use this name in code, use a name that tells you something about its function, such as cmdOK for an OK button. (Programmers often use a three-letter prefix that indicates the type of control it is.)
6. Change the control's Caption, if it has one, so that it describes the control's purpose. For example, if the control is an option button used to select a mode of payment, you might use Cash, Check, Credit Card, or COD.
7. Give the control an Accelerator, if it has one (a hotkey that activates the button when Alt+*key* is pressed; the key does not have to be in the Name).
8. Click the Exit Design Mode button on the Control Toolbox toolbar to exit Design Mode and return to normal document editing mode.

All controls have additional properties that you can set, some of which are specific to that type of control, and you can usually set most of them in the Properties window (see Figure 14.16). For example, option buttons have a Group Name property that associates related option buttons so that that only one option in the group may be selected. Image controls have a Picture property that stores the image it is to display. Most controls have Height and Width properties as well.

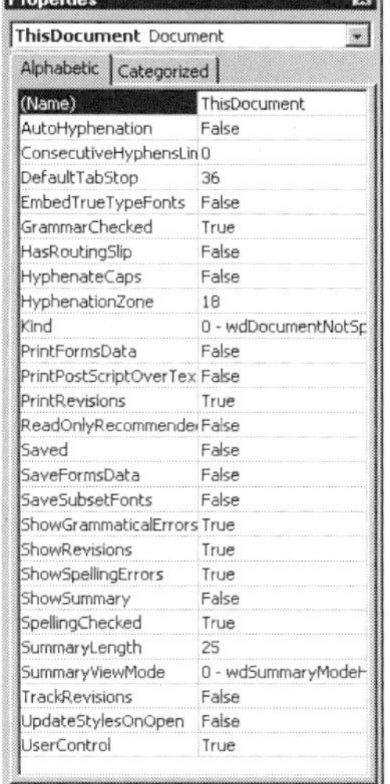

FIGURE 14.16
The Properties window lets you control many aspects of every control's appearance and behavior.

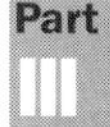

As soon as Word places the control, it switches to Design Mode so you can set its properties. You must be in Design Mode to set control properties in Word. As soon as you exit Design Mode, your form is ready to go—all ActiveX controls in the document respond as they normally would—all the events fire.

CAUTION

Whether your ActiveX form works will depend in part on the Security settings you have set (Tools, Macro, Security). Unless the code in the form has been digitally signed and trusted–a very rare situation at this point in computing history–you will have to set the Security Level to Medium or Low. The Security Level setting tells Word how much freedom to give to VBA code; if you don't set it to Medium or Low, you will not be able to use the automation features of any ActiveX forms because none of the VBA code will run.

Writing VBA Code The VBA code serves the same purpose as the On Entry and On Exit macros in form fields, except that it has many times more flexibility than form fields have. For example, a FORMTEXT form field fires two events, Entry and Exit. An ActiveX text box control (the equivalent), however, fires 14 events: `BeforeDragOver`, `BeforeDropOrPaste`, `Change`, `DblClick`, `DropButtonClick`, `Error`, `GotFocus`, `KeyDown`, `KeyPress`, `KeyUp`, `LostFocus`, `MouseDown`, `MouseMove`, and `MouseUp`. You can imagine how much more control that gives you over what your form can do. (ActiveX controls also have many more properties than form fields.)

The key to making your ActiveX form work is simply to write code that responds to the appropriate events and takes the appropriate action.

For example, suppose you want to create a form in which the user can enter a name and address, then add the information as a new Outlook Contact. You would start by creating a two-column table, and then insert ActiveX controls until you have the structure of a form that looks something like Figure 14.17.

NOTE As noted earlier, you do not have to put form controls in a table–you can place them anywhere you like. Because Word treats ActiveX controls as Shape objects, you can make them float over the text layer just like a picture or an AutoShape so you can drag the control to any spot on the page. This flexibility, however, also means you have to position each and every control manually. Using a table takes care of control positioning for you.

After you've finished placing the controls, you're ready to write the code. The general steps are as follows:

1. Open the Visual Basic Editor (VBE). You can do this by doing any of the following:
    - Press Alt+F11.
    - Choose Tools, Macro, Visual Basic Editor.
    -  Be sure you're in Design Mode by clicking the Design Mode button on the Visual Basic toolbar, and then double-click on the control for which you want to write code. Word launches the Visual Basic Editor and places the insertion point directly in the default event procedure for that control.

2. Be sure you have at least two windows displayed—the Project Explorer (Ctrl+R) and the Code window (F7). (The Visual Basic Editor displays these two windows by default.)
3. In the Project Explorer, expand the node that represents your form document. It will be named Project (*filename*).
4. Expand the Microsoft Word Objects node until you see a `ThisDocument` object.
5. Double-click on `ThisDocument`. Word takes you to the Code window.
6. Click the Object list box at the top left of the Code window (where "(General)" is displayed) and select the control for which you want to write code. The VBE loads the Procedure list box at the top right of the Code window with all the control's events.
7. Click the Procedure list box and select the event for which you want to write code. The VBE inserts the event-procedure stub and places the insertion point there.

FIGURE 14.17
A sample ActiveX form.

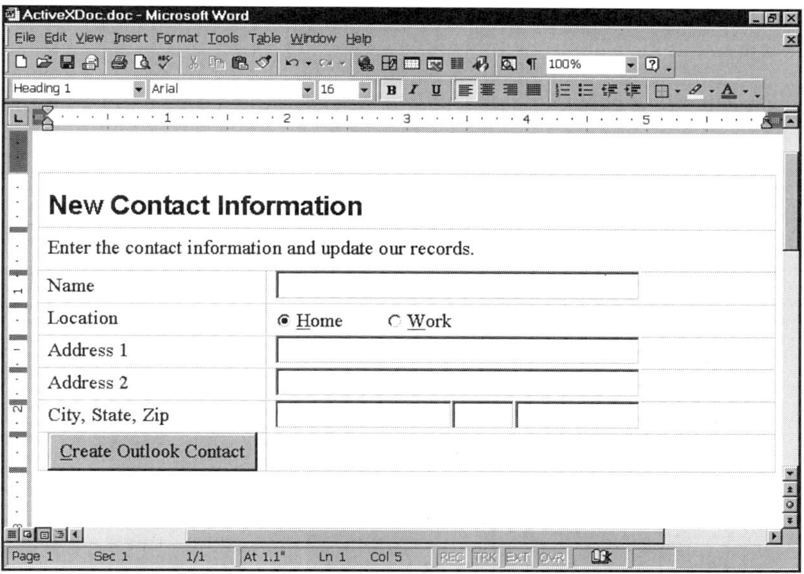

From here you can access all the ActiveX controls you just placed and all the events that they fire. For example, you could place code in the Create Outlook Contact button's Click event; this code would run every time a user clicks that button. Inside that event procedure, you could write code that checks the name and makes sure it is not blank, and then sends the information to Outlook if all is well (see Figure 14.18):

```
Private Sub cmdUpdate_Click()

    If txtFullName.Text <> "" Then
        CreateContactItem
        txtFullName = ""
    End If

End Sub
```

```
Private Sub CreateContactItem()

    Dim oOutlook As Outlook.Application
    Dim oNameSpace As Outlook.NameSpace
    Dim oFolder As Outlook.MAPIFolder

    On Error GoTo BOOM

    Set oOutlook = New Outlook.Application
    Set oNameSpace = oOutlook.GetNamespace("MAPI")
    Set oFolder = oNameSpace.GetDefaultFolder(olFolderContacts)
    With oOutlook.CreateItem(olContactItem)
        .FullName = txtFullName.Text

        ' Update other fields from your form
        ' as needed

        .Display
    End With

EXITHERE:
    Set oOutlook = Nothing
    Set oNameSpace = Nothing
    Set oFolder = Nothing
    Exit Sub

BOOM:
    Err.Raise Err.Number, Err.Description

End Sub
```

CAUTION

In order for this code to work, you must set a reference to the Outlook 9.0 type library. You do that in the VBE by selecting the project in the Project Explorer, then choosing Tools, References, and putting a check mark in "Microsoft Outlook 9.0 Object Library."

NOTE If you want to learn more about VBA, we suggest reading Chapter 5, "Getting Acquainted with VBA," and Chapter 6, "Successful VBA Modules," of this book. If you're interested in using this snippet of code, you'll find it on the CD accompanying this book. You'll also find directions for using this code snippet; see "Putting VBA Code Snippets to Work" in Chapter 6.

The sample code provided here just gets you started. To transfer all the data from the form to the new Outlook contact item, you will need to add code that sets the appropriate properties of the Contact item with the data stored in the ActiveX form's text boxes. Follow the pattern set in the `.FullName = txtFullName.Text` line.

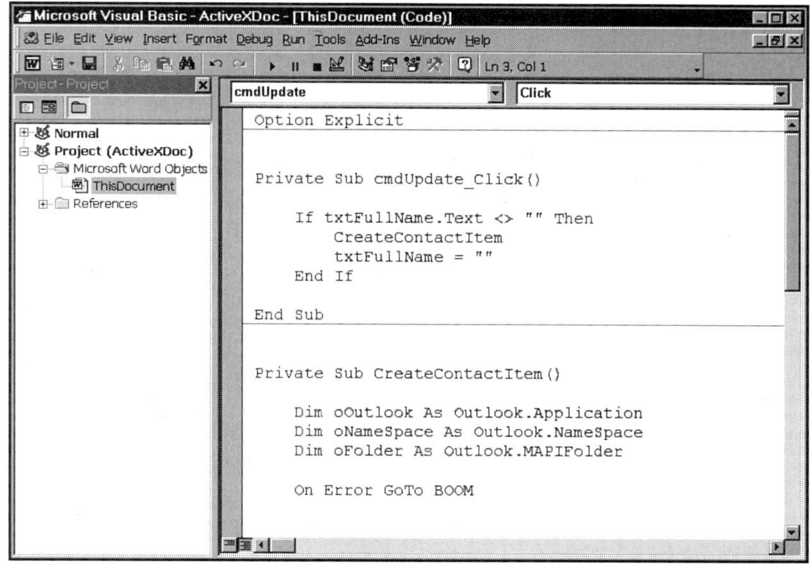

FIGURE 14.18
Write the code that automates your form here in the Visual Basic Editor.

You could add many more features to this form, too, just by adding code to the events to which you want to respond. For example, you could add a Label control to the bottom of the table, and then set that Label's caption each time the mouse moves over a text box. The message could contain a brief description of what to type in the text box. As you can see, you are limited only by your imagination.

If you've done Visual Basic programming before, this will be easy. If you are new to it, do not let it intimidate you. The best way to learn is dive right in, and if you consult the VBA Help files whenever you get stuck, you should be fine.

Protecting Your ActiveX Form You'll recall that form field forms require that you protect them before they can be used as forms. That is not true of ActiveX forms. You can type in ActiveX text boxes, make selections in list boxes, and choose from among options in option-button groups whether the document is protected for forms or not. However, you will probably want to protect the form anyway to keep the static parts of the form from being altered by mistake, and to enable Tab-key navigation. To protect an ActiveX form, follow the same procedure you use for form field forms.

▶ For details on how to protect a document for forms, **see** "Protecting Your Form," **p. 411**

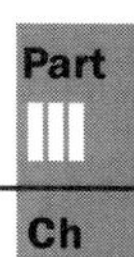

Creating and Using Web Forms

The third and final kind of form you can create in Word is the Web form. A *Web form* is an HTML page, a plain-text file constructed of HTML tags and scripting objects.

Web forms serve a different purpose from form field and ActiveX forms. Whereas form field and ActiveX forms are most commonly hosted by Word and used outside of a Web context, Web forms are almost always hosted by a browser and used to submit data to a Web server.

Unfortunately for Word, Office 2000 includes FrontPage, which is a much more capable HTML designer and editor. If you are going to create Web pages of any kind, and especially forms, you would be wise to consider using FrontPage first.

But if you are determined to use Word, the basic procedure is almost exactly the same as it is for ActiveX forms. You begin by creating a new HTML document; then you place controls.

Understanding the Pieces

To create and use Web forms, you need four things:

- An HTML document to serve as the host page
- One or more design elements to provide the content and the user interface
- Some code to control what happens
- A Web server to host the page

The fourth item is important. Unlike form field and ActiveX forms, Web forms depend greatly on the Web server that hosts them.

HTML Document An ordinary Word document will not do for a Web form; it has to be an HTML page. If you prefer to continue working in Word, you can use one of several techniques to create a Web page on which you want to base your Web Form:

- In Word, click File, New, General tab, Web Page, OK.
- Click the File New button on the Standard toolbar; then click File, Save As Web Page, give the file a name, and Save.
- Click File, New, Web Pages tab. Then select a template from the ones available and click OK. Word includes a Web Page wizard that can help you create rather complex Web pages. Unfortunately, Word 2000 ships with no Web form templates.

Although Word does sport some useful Web-page-creation tools, you'll find the tools in FrontPage 2000 to be far more flexible and sophisticated. If you need to create elaborate forms to gather information for your company's Web site, we recommend that you create your Web-based forms in FrontPage.

The Web Form Controls Web form controls are *not* ActiveX controls. They are standard HTML tags and their corresponding attributes, embedded in the Web page as plain text for the browser to interpret. Although programmers can create new ActiveX controls (and are doing so all the time), no one can create new HTML controls at will—only the World Wide Web Consortium can add controls by adding new tags to the HTML standard.

The controls Word lets you place directly on pages through the user interface appear on the Web Tools toolbar. Not all HTML controls available to you appear there, but most of the important ones do.

For an overview of the controls available on the Web Tools toolbar, launch Help from the Script Editor and search for "Form Controls You Can Use in a Web Page." This Help topic explains many of the basics of Web forms, why they're different, how they work, and what you need to do to get useful work out of them.

To display the Web Tools toolbar, right-click over any toolbar and select it.

To place a control in your Web page, follow these steps:

1. Place the insertion point where you want to insert the control.
2. Make sure the Web Tools toolbar is displayed (View, Toolbars, Web Tools).
3. In the Web Tools toolbar, click on the control you want to use. Word places the control at the insertion point and selects it.
4.  Click the Properties button on the Web Tools toolbar. Word displays the Properties window for the selected control. Note that the list of properties available for Web controls is much shorter than for ActiveX controls.
5. In the Properties window, give the control a Name. Because you will use this name in scripting code, use a name that tells you something about its function, such as cmdOK for an OK button. (Programmers often use a three-letter prefix that indicates the type of control it is.)

As you set the properties of Web controls, keep in mind that the Web server hosting your page will use the Name property of many controls when reading values from the form. Make them descriptive as you would for ActiveX controls.

Publishing to a Web Server At some point, your Web form will need to be published to a Web server. Word 2000 makes this much easier than ever before. To publish your form to the server, you simply choose File, Save As, navigate to a Web Folder, and save the file under the appropriate name. You do not need to go through FTP or a separate upload program (such as the Web Publishing Wizard found in Office 97).

Of course, you need to have write privileges on the Web server to be able to do this.

▶ **See** "Publishing Web Sites," **p. CD 159**

The Scripting Code After you've finished placing the controls, you're ready to write the scripting code. A Web form relies on scripting code to deliver its functionality. For example, if you build the form according to the model in Figure 14.17, you would replace the Create Outlook Contact button with a Submit button. You would then write scripting code that accessed the contents of each relevant control and sent it to the server for processing. This code serves the same purpose as the VBA code in ActiveX forms.

The general steps for writing script in Word are as follows:

1. Open the Microsoft Script Editor. You can do this by doing any of the following:
   - Press Alt+Shift+F11.
   - Click the Microsoft Script Editor button on the Web Tools toolbar.
   - Be sure you're in Design Mode by clicking the Design Mode button on the Web Tools toolbar, then right-click over any control, and select View Code from the shortcut menu. Word launches the Microsoft Script Editor and places the insertion point in the Source pane of the Code window.

2. In the Source pane of the Code window, add the scripting code you need.

NOTE If you want to learn more about VBScript, we recommend picking up a copy of *Inside VBScript with ActiveX*, published by New Riders; to learn more about JavaScript, see *Special Edition Using JavaScript*, published by Que.

The Script Editor lets you choose the scripting language you prefer for both client-side and server-side script. In the Script Editor, choose View, Property Pages (Shift+F4) to display the Properties dialog box for your form. In the General tab, set the Default scripting language by choosing either VBScript or JavaScript (you can specify different languages for both Client and Server). Click OK. Now whenever you double-click on an event procedure in the Script Outline (View, Other Windows, Script Outline, or Ctrl+Alt+S), Script Editor inserts an event procedure stub that specifies the appropriate language and uses the appropriate syntax.

Does it matter whether you choose VBScript or JavaScript? It can. Only Internet Explorer can interpret VBScript, but most major browsers—including Internet Explorer and Netscape Navigator—can interpret JavaScript. Unless you are developing a page for an intranet that uses only IE, choose JavaScript.

Publishing Forms in a Workgroup Environment

For forms to be useful, they must be available as templates. Of course, making Web forms available is easy—just publish them to the Web site. But Form field and ActiveX forms are another story. You have to go the extra mile to make them available to others.

First, you must do two things to the form document:

- Turn on form protection (applying a password, if needed).
- Save the form as a Word template in a location available to other users.

Protect the form as described under the section "Protecting Your Form," earlier in this chapter. After the form has been protected, the second step is to save it as a Word template. That way, users can create new documents based on the form. Those new documents can be printed or used online.

Your organization may already have a designated location for these Office-wide forms; check under Tools, Options, File Locations, and look for Workgroup templates. If nothing is listed here or there has not been a location decided upon, you should encourage them to set one up so that that everyone can have easy access to the forms templates you create.

To save a form as a template available to other users:

1. Choose File, Save As.
2. Be sure Save As type is set to Document Template.
3. Type a descriptive name.
4. Navigate to the location that your organization has designated for these template forms.
5. Click Save.

CHAPTER 15

Features Used with Complex Documents

In this chapter

Creating Tables of Contents and Similar Tables

Long or complex documents usually have a number of reference tables as part of their front matter. Best known of these tables is the table of contents, but the front matter may also contain tables of figures, equations, or other matter that lists specific content material. Each table consists of a list of headings, titles, or captions, and the page number on which those appear, allowing readers to quickly and easily reference specific sections and data within the document.

Word has incorporated features that automate creation of these tables. Tables of contents, figures, and tables of authorities can be created quickly and easily, with just a few mouse clicks. The way a section title, figure, or citation is formatted dictates how Word identifies and includes these items into tables. The table structure, text appearance, and even the actual table text entries can be customized, with a little additional effort.

Tables of Contents—The Basics

There are four ways to format your text to indicate to Word what text is to be incorporated into your table of contents:

- Standard or predefined Word heading styles (Heading 1, Heading 2 and so on).
- Custom heading styles (styles you or your company have created).
- Outline-level heading styles (you can use the outline headings, the predefined styles in Word, or ones you create for your table of contents).
- Embedded headings from your paragraphs (hidden text within a paragraph if you aren't using headings). You can also create a macro that looks for specific formats (predefined or custom) and places the table in a predetermined location, such as at the end of an introductory section or at the end of the document.

Using each of these text formatting options to identify items to include in the table of contents will be discussed in this chapter. To give you an idea of how simple it is to create a table of contents, a general overview to create a table of contents follows:

1. Identify the text to be included.
2. Position your cursor where you want the table of contents to appear in your document.
3. Choose Insert, Index and Tables. The Index and Tables dialog box appears.
4. Choose the Table of Contents tab (as shown in Figure 15.1) and make the appropriate selections.
5. Choose OK and give Word a moment to compile the table.

The actual text of the headings in the document becomes the entries in the table of contents. If you want to use abbreviated text to represent long headings, you can customize the table of contents entry. This is discussed in the section "Customizing a Table of Contents Entry" later in this chapter.

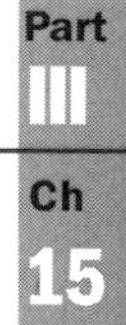

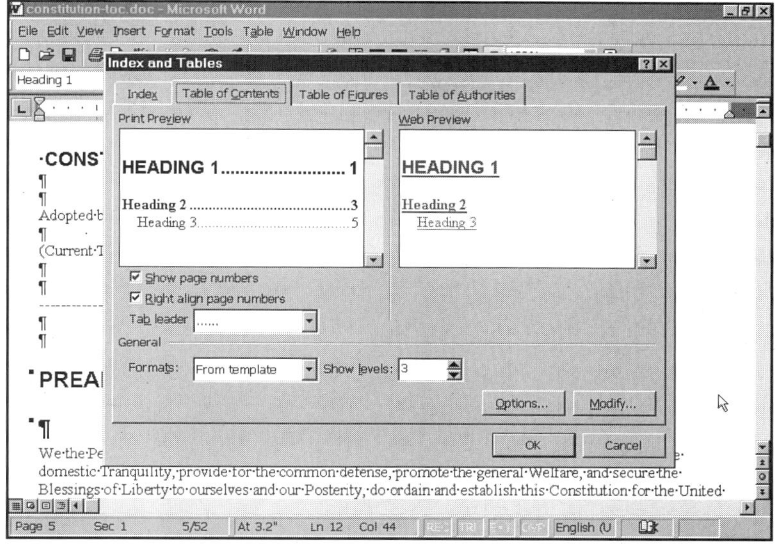

FIGURE 15.1
Use the Index and Tables dialog box to change the appearance of the table of contents.

CAUTION

If you continue to make changes and additions to your document, you will need to update your table of contents when the document editing is completed. See "Updating a Table of Contents," later in this chapter.

You can use a table of contents to move quickly to any heading in a document. After you've created a table of contents, click the page number in the table. Word acts as if the page number were a hyperlink, jumping immediately to the heading you chose.

The next few sections in this chapter discuss how to use various text-formatting alternatives to create tables of contents.

Using Built-In Headings to Create a Table of Contents

Generally, when you create a long document, you use some type of headings to indicate document structure or contents. If you used the headings from the Normal.dot template, all that remains is to define your table of contents. Word automatically assigns the appropriate hierarchy within the table to the built-in headings you have used in the document. For instance, Heading 1 is the highest level, Heading 2 the next lower level, and so on. Even if you have customized the headings within Normal.dot, this automation will be performed. The other advantage to using these headings is that Word provides you with keyboard shortcuts to quickly promote and demote heading levels.

If you want to promote a heading one level (from Heading 3 to Heading 2, for instance), press Alt+Shift+Left arrow. If you want to demote a heading one level (Heading 2 to Heading 3), press Alt+Shift+Right arrow. This works only if you have taken advantage of Word's heading names.

The key to this process is consistency. If you have consistently used the headings throughout your document and have used the heading styles only for headings, then Word will work the way you expect.

To create a table of contents using the built-in headings, follow these steps:

1. Position your cursor where you want the table of contents to appear in your document.
2. Choose Insert, Index and Tables and click the Tables of Contents tab.
3. Indicate the number of heading levels you want in your table of contents by changing the number in the Show Levels box (refer to Figure 15.1).
4. Choose OK and give Word a moment to compile the table. If you already have a table of contents, Word will ask whether you want to replace the existing one with a new one.

Using Custom Heading Styles to Create a Table of Contents

As discussed in Chapter 11, "Making the Most of Your Page Layout," you can create custom heading styles with titles other than the Word standard Heading 1, Heading 2, and so on.

To use your custom headings after you have applied them within your document:

1. Position your cursor where you want the table of contents to appear in your document; then choose Insert, Index and Tables.
2. Click the Table of Contents tab.
3. On the Table of Contents tab, choose Options. The Table of Contents Options dialog box appears as shown in Figure 15.2.

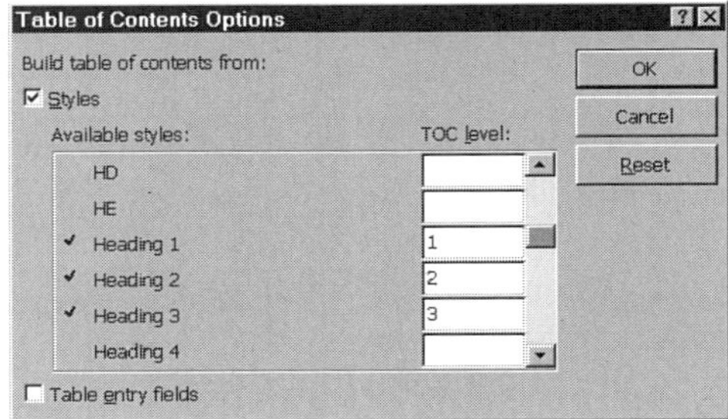

FIGURE 15.2
The styles currently used in the document appear in a column on the left side of the dialog box.

4. Use the scrollbar next to the TOC Level list to find the style names you have created under Available Styles.
5. Enter the number of the level you want that style to have in your table of contents.
6. Repeat these steps for each of the customized heading levels.

7. If you have headings that you don't want to appear in your table of contents, be sure to clear the number next to those headings.
8. Choose OK.
9. Make any other necessary selections on the Table of Contents tab.
10. Choose OK and give Word a moment to compile the table.

Using Outline-Level Heading Styles to Create a Table of Contents

The advantage of using outline-level styles for your table of contents is that you can choose to not change the appearance of your text. For example, you may be given a document that is fully formatted without styles. All you want to do is mark the existing formatted text. Assigning an outline style to a heading, which may or may not be formatted using a heading style, allows you to include that text in your table of contents without applying the heading style to the text. Although applying the standard Word styles changes the appearance of your document, the outline-level style format is not printed or viewed.

Outline levels enable you to take advantage of Word's outline feature. By using the outline feature, you can collapse a document in order to see only the outline headings. In outline view, you can then reorder your document and manipulate sections of text more easily.

To create a table of contents using outline styles, follow these steps:

1. Position your cursor in the heading (paragraph) you want to include in your table of contents.
2. Choose Format, Paragraph. The Paragraph dialog box appears; click the Indents and Spacing tab.
3. Click the heading level you want in the Outline level drop-down list, as shown in Figure 15.3. Click OK.

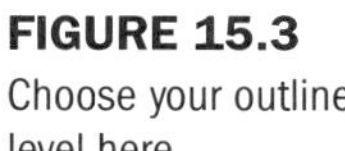

FIGURE 15.3
Choose your outline level here.

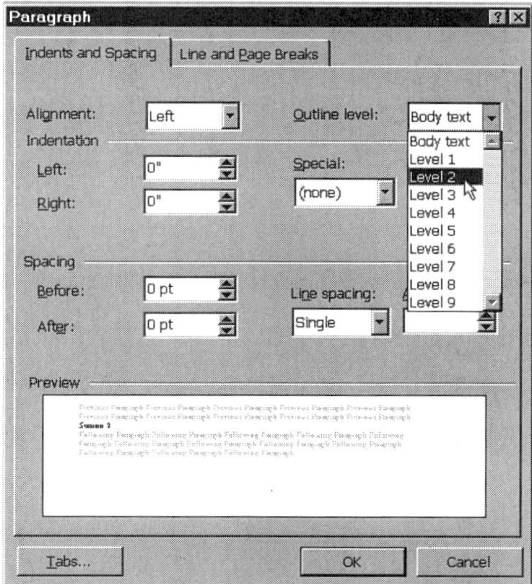

4. Click into the style list on the Formatting toolbar and type the name of your new style and press Enter. Repeat this step for each heading level you want to include in your table of contents.
5. Then position your cursor where you want the table of contents to appear in your document. If your table of contents already exists and you are adding only a new heading or style to your document, press F9. Choose Update Entire Table from the Update Table of Contents dialog box.
6. Choose Insert, Index and Tables.
7. Choose the Table of Contents tab and delete the table of contents levels assigned to built-in Word headings. Word automatically assigns the new styles the same hierarchy as the outline level.
8. Choose OK and give Word a moment to compile the table.

▶ **See** "Creating and Using Outlines Effectively," **p. 478**

▶ **See** "Creating a New Style," **p. 273**

Using Embedded Headings from Your Paragraphs to Create a Table of Contents

Although you can use an outline style discussed previously when you don't want to change the *appearance* of your text, or use field codes, you can use embedded headings when you don't want to change the text or have the headings appear in the document. Embedded headings enable you to insert the table of contents' text in the appropriate locations within your document, but not change the content of the document. For example, suppose you want to generate a table of contents for a document that has long, wordy headings without styles applied to them. You can create more succinct headings, apply Word's built-in heading styles to the headings you want to use, generate your table of contents, and then hide the headings you don't want to appear in your document. You can update the table of contents with the headings hidden, but you can't generate it initially with hidden text.

To create and use embedded headings in a table of contents that has not been previously generated, follow these steps:

1. Add the text you want to use for your table of contents and apply the appropriate heading levels to it.

2. Ensure that each heading is its own paragraph. To verify that each heading is its own paragraph, click the Show/Hide button on the Standard toolbar, and see that the paragraph symbol (¶) is present after each heading.
3. Position your cursor where you want the table of contents to appear in your document.
4. Choose Insert, Index and Tables.
5. Choose the Table of Contents tab and make the appropriate selections.
6. Choose OK and give Word a moment to compile the table.

7. For each heading you don't want to appear in your final document, select the paragraph and change the font characteristic to Hidden from the Font dialog box shown in Figure 15.4 (choose Format, Font). If all of the headings of a particular style are to be hidden, you can change the style characteristics to include hidden text (choose Format, Style, and click Modify).

If you are updating a table of contents, see the section "Updating a Table of Contents" later in this chapter.

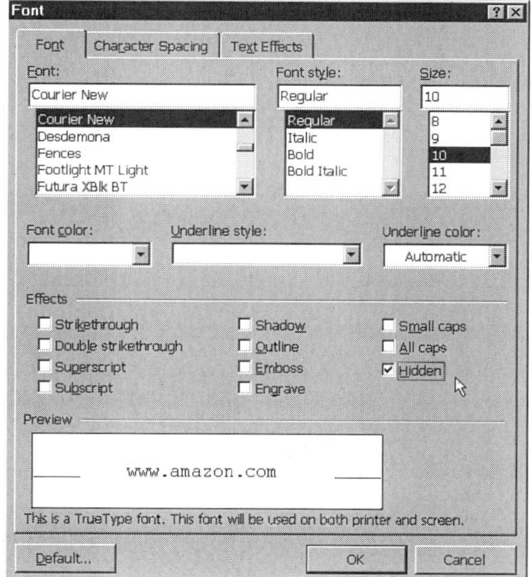

FIGURE 15.4
Choose Hidden to create embedded headings.

Creating a Table of Contents for a Multifile Document

For most documents, you create the table of contents as part of the document to which the table refers. However, in the case of a long document consisting of several files (for example, modular courseware), you have to create the table of contents as a separate file so it can include headings from all the document files (courseware chapters). This function does not require the use of a master document-subdocument relationship. The files can be freestanding and unrelated in any way. You must, however, have used your heading styles consistently. For example, if you use Heading 1 in one document for your table of contents, you want to be sure that you want Heading 1 to be used in the other documents for the table of contents as well.

1. Create a new document.
2. Display hidden text by clicking the Show/Hide button on the Standard toolbar.
3. Choose Insert, Field to display the Field dialog box shown in Figure 15.5.
4. In the Categories list, choose Index and Tables; in the Field Names list, choose RD, for Referenced Document.

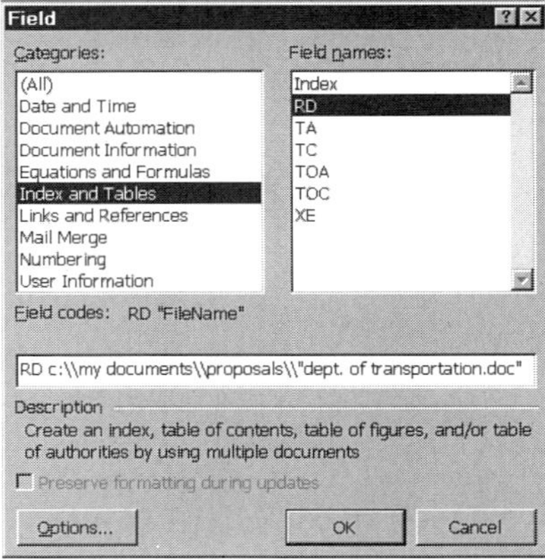

FIGURE 15.5
Use this dialog box to identify a document to be included in the table of contents.

5. In the Field Codes box, after RD, ensure that there is a space and the complete file path and filename of the first document to be included in the table of contents.
6. Click OK.

NOTE The file path must have double backslashes, as shown in Figure 15.5. If the folder or filenames contain spaces, the entire folder or filename must be enclosed within double quotation marks.

7. If you want to use any of the switches associated with this field, click the Options button for a list of available switches and an explanation of their uses (refer to Figure 15.5).
8. Unfortunately, you must repeat these steps (4 through 7) for each document you want to include in the table of contents.
9. Then position your cursor at either the beginning or end of the document to indicate where you want the table of contents to be placed.

CAUTION

If your cursor is positioned within one of the RD fields when you generate your table of contents, the table will be created as hidden text.

10. Choose Insert, Index and Tables.
11. Choose the Table of Contents tab and make the appropriate selections.
12. Choose OK and give Word a moment to compile the table.

Use the Show/Hide button to see the RD fields in the resulting document, as shown in Figure 15.6.

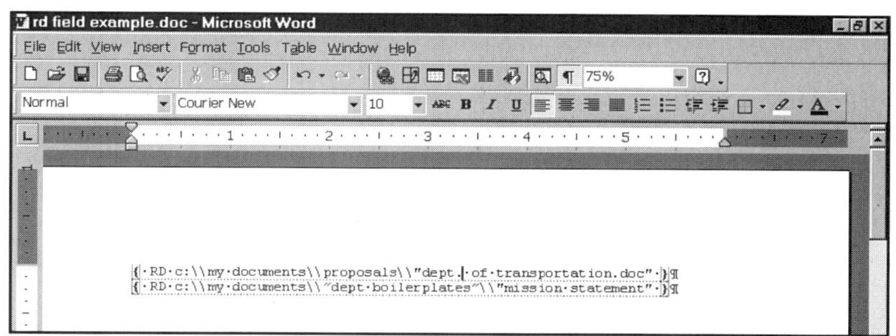

FIGURE 15.6
Two RD fields that reference separate documents for the creation of a table of contents.

Creating a Table of Contents in a Scrollable Frame

Another way to present a table of contents is in a scrollable frame. This frame can appear to the left, or right, or above or below the document text. The scrollable frame is most commonly used in HTML documents on the Web. The frame allows the hyperlink properties of the table of contents to be available from any point in the document text.

1. In your document, designate the text to be included in the table of contents by using heading styles.
2. Choose Format, Frames from the menu bar.
3. Choose Table of Contents in Frame.
4. Word closes your current document and creates a new document. An example of a resulting document is shown in Figure 15.7.

To reposition the table of contents into another frame, select the table of contents and copy and paste it to another frame.

CAUTION

You can't undo the creation of a new frame. You must place the cursor in the unwanted frame and click the delete frame button on the Frame toolbar.

Fortunately, after you have created your table of contents in any form, you can switch to Web Layout view (choose View, Web Layout) and your table of contents will maintain its hyperlink properties. If you have not used a scrollable frame, the Print Layout view of the table of contents appears in gray shading, while in the Web Layout view, the table of contents is a plain white Web page. In both views, the page numbers act as hyperlinks to that heading. You simply click on the page number and Word jumps to that page in the document.

NOTE Switching to the Web Layout view does not create a Web page. The view is used when you are creating a Web page or a document that is viewed on the screen.

For more information on designing Web pages, see the FrontPage section of this book.

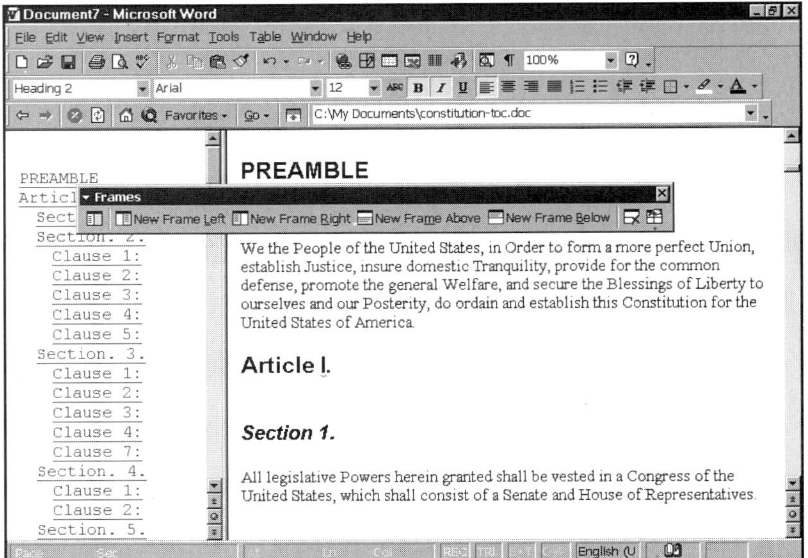

FIGURE 15.7
The Frames toolbar appears along with the new document.

Customizing a Table of Contents Entry

Regardless of how you've created the table of contents entry, you may still want to make changes to its wording. To do this, you must insert a `{TC}` field code in your document. The following technique also works if you want nonheading text in your table of contents. Word allows you to use both field codes and heading styles in creating the table.

Suppose you have a heading in your document that is not as descriptive as you would like. You can change the table of contents entry without changing the document text.

1. Select the heading text and press Alt+Shift+O to access the Mark Table of Contents Entry dialog box shown in Figure 15.8. If your headings consist only of numbers, position your cursor next to the heading number.
2. Your selected text will be highlighted in the text box. If you have no selected text, the text box will be blank. You may now add additional text or delete text you don't need. If the text you have selected is long, Home will move you to the beginning of your selection.

TIP You can use this technique to create tables of contents entries that can replace headings that are too wordy or too succinct. You can also create tables of contents headings that are not found in the text.

3. Leave the Table Identifier unchanged as C for a table of contents.
4. Select the appropriate heading level in the Level box. These heading levels correspond with the heading levels for the table of contents, not necessarily the heading style.

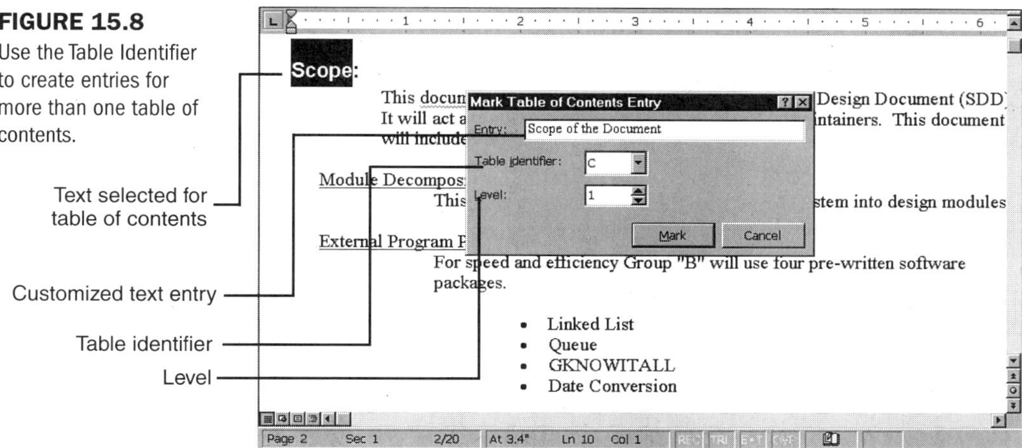

FIGURE 15.8
Use the Table Identifier to create entries for more than one table of contents.

5. Click Mark to insert a `{TC}` field code into the document. The actual field code will be inserted after the selected text.
6. Position your cursor where you want the table of contents to appear in your document.
7. Choose Insert, Index and Tables.
8. Choose the Table of Contents tab and make the appropriate selections.
9. Choose OK and give Word a moment to compile the table.
10. If you have used `{TC}` fields to edit heading style entries in the table of contents, you now have to remove any duplicate subject entries from your table of contents. Make this the last step in your document creation. If you update the complete table of contents, your changes to it will be lost.

CAUTION

If you use `{TC}` fields to customize your table of contents, you must be certain to check both the Table Entry Fields and Styles boxes when you create your table of contents if you are using both styles and field codes. If you are just using field codes and not styles, leave the styles check box blank (see Figure 15.9). If you do check the Styles check box and leave the table of contents level boxes, double entries will result for those headings that have `{TC}` fields—one from the heading and one from the `{TC}` field.

▶ **See** "Fields—Word's Hidden Functions," **p. 349**

You can also click the Office Assistant and type "`tc fields`" for more information.

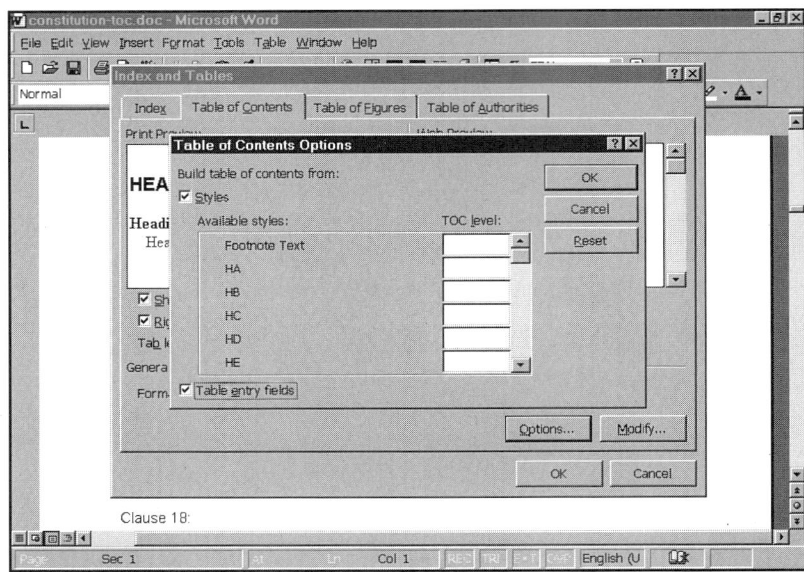

FIGURE 15.9
You can use both styles and table entry fields when you compile your table of contents.

Changing the Appearance of a Table of Contents

There are seven predefined formats for tables of contents available in Word. To preview the formats, choose Insert, Index and Tables, and click the Table of Contents tab. Click the Formats drop-down list in the General section to view its effect in the two Preview panes—Print Preview and Web Preview (refer to Figure 15.1). Select the format that best suits your needs.

If you require a specific format not predefined by Word, you can create it by using these steps:

1. While still in the Index and Tables dialog box, select the From Template Format. Then click Modify. The Style dialog box appears, as shown in Figure 15.10.

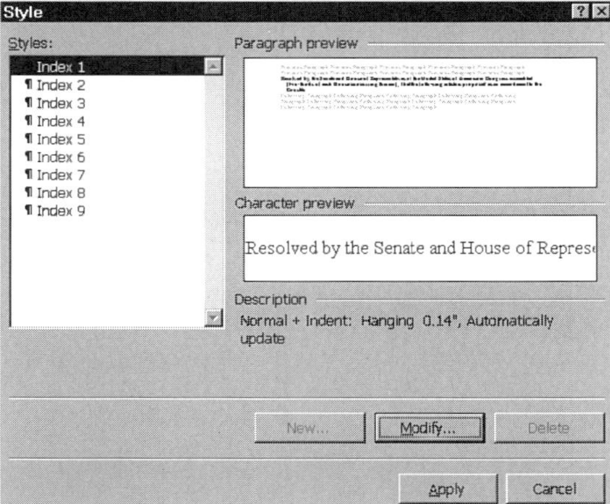

FIGURE 15.10
The current characteristics of the style are displayed.

2. Within the Style dialog box, you can modify an existing style. To modify an existing style, choose Modify. The Modify Style dialog box appears, as shown in Figure 15.11.
3. Choose the character and paragraph formats you want to use for the style, including font formats, borders, frames, and so on. Then choose any additional formatting that you want to apply. See the example in Figure 15.12.

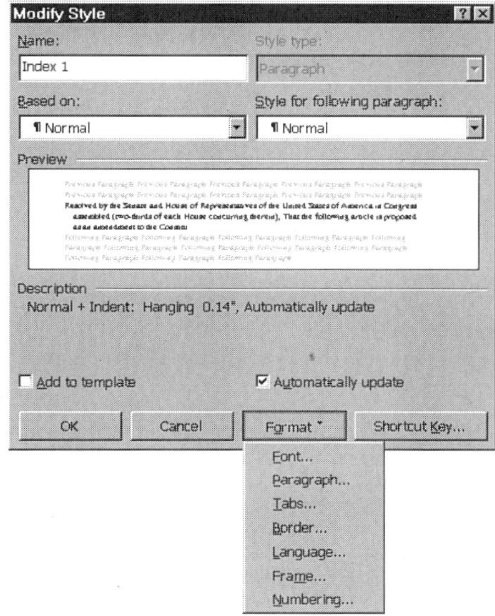

FIGURE 15.11
The standard formatting options are available here.

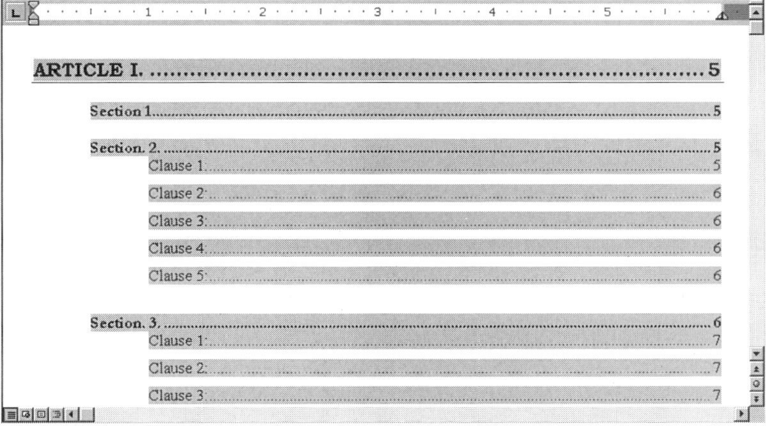

FIGURE 15.12
This table of contents has modified styles that include font changes, paragraph borders, and indenting.

You can also assign a shortcut key to your table of contents level by following the steps to modify a table of contents style and choosing Shortcut Key (in the Modify Style dialog box shown in Figure 15.11). This will allow you to assign table of contents styles from the keyboard.

Word lets you mark two or more styles with the same TOC level. Choose Indexes and Tables, and click options. Assign the appropriate levels to the appropriate styles. This may be useful, such as when you combine two or more documents in which different style names are used for headings.

CAUTION

Be consistent with your use of heading styles. If you have used a style for headings that you want in your table of contents, do not use that style for other text. If you have used those styles for something other than headings, your table of contents will contain unwanted items.

Word uses paragraph styles to identify headings for inclusion in the table of contents. Alternatively, Word can use table entry fields, or it can use styles and table entry fields to identify text for a table of contents. Table entry fields are those TC fields you may have added to customize your table of contents' text. The Table of Contents Options dialog box contains two check boxes: Styles and Table Entry Fields, as shown in Figure 15.13. By default, the Styles check box is checked so Word uses styles to identify text for inclusion in the table of contents. You can uncheck Styles and check Table Entry Fields to make Word use only table entry fields, those fields you created for customized entries. You can also check both boxes to make Word use styles and table entry fields if you have used a combination of the two.

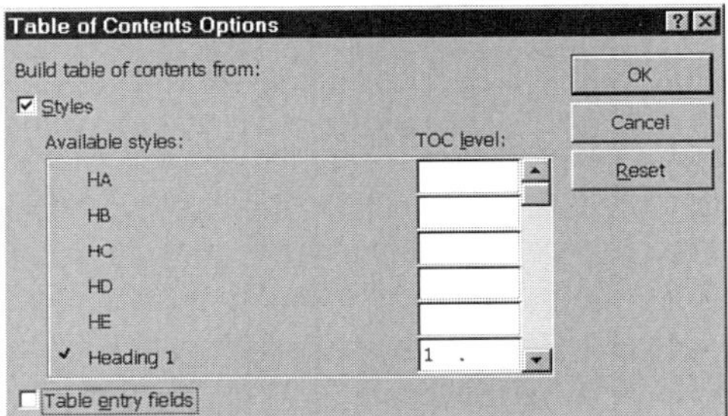

FIGURE 15.13
Remember to check Table entry fields if you have used {TC} fields as part of your table of contents.

Updating a Table of Contents

Word does not automatically update your table of contents as your work progresses or when you open the file or when you save the file. Because a table of contents is a *field*, you update it in the same way you update any other field. To do this, position your cursor in the table and press F9 to display the Update Table of Contents dialog box (shown in Figure 15.14). If your table of contents is in a scrollable frame, no page numbers are displayed, so this dialog box does not appear. Word updates the contents of the table of contents without looking for confirmation.

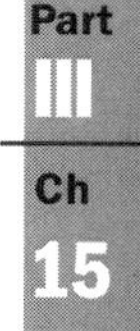

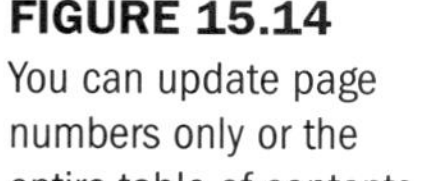

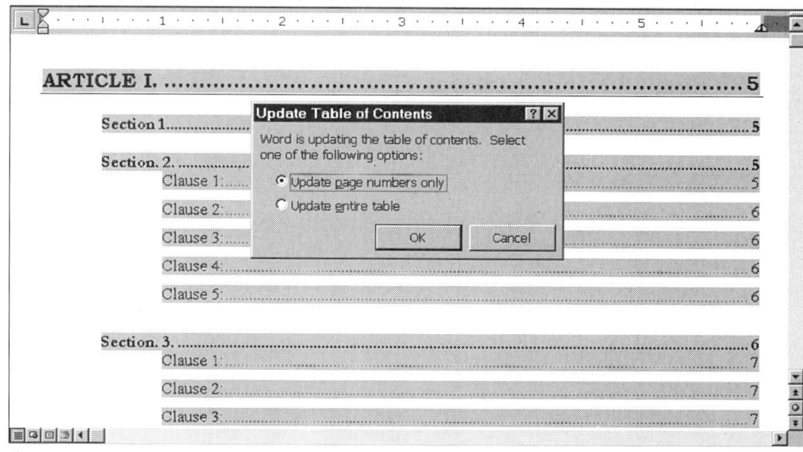

FIGURE 15.14
You can update page numbers only or the entire table of contents.

If you want to print an updated table of contents as part of your document, choose Tools, Options and then select the Print tab (as shown in Figure 15.15). In the Printing Options section, check the Update Fields check box. Subsequently, Word always updates the table of contents (as well as other fields such as {PAGE} and {DATE}) whenever you print the document. If you don't choose Update fields, you must remember to update each field by selecting it and pressing F9 before you print (or by selecting the entire document and pressing F9).

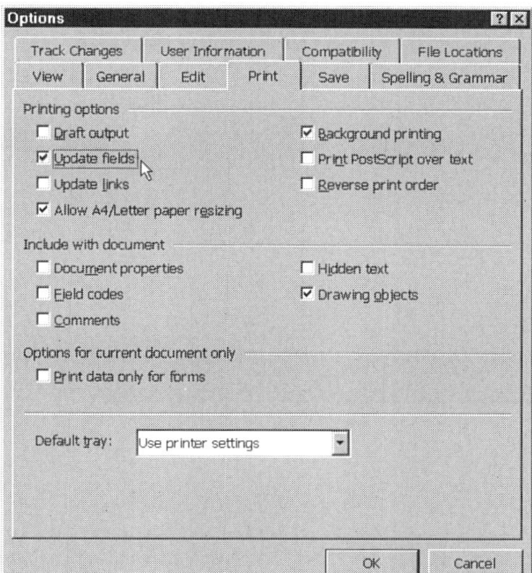

FIGURE 15.15
Update Fields updates all the fields in your document whenever you print.

Creating Tables of Figures and Other Tables

Many books and technical documents include a table of figures as part of their front matter. A table of figures allows the reader to reference a specific figure (chart, graph, picture, and so on) by page number.

Creating tables of equations, tables of figures, tables of tables, and other types of tables requires no special techniques. As with tables of content, the items you want to show in the table must be identified either by a specific character style or by table entry fields. To create these types of tables, select the Table of Figures tab in the Index and Tables dialog box shown in Figure 15.16.

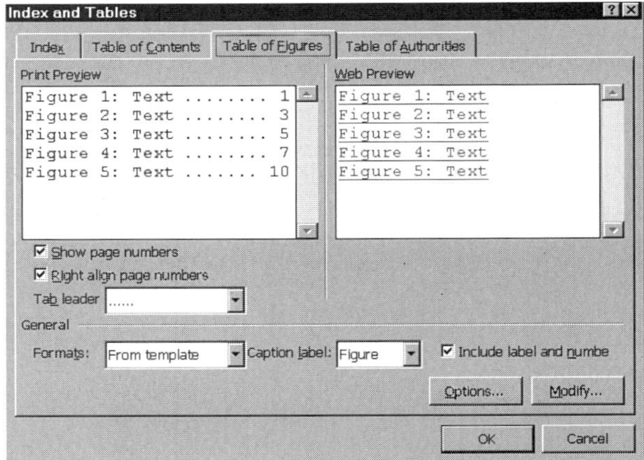

FIGURE 15.16
In this dialog box, choose the type of table and its format.

Click Options to display the Table of Figures Options dialog box in which you choose whether you want to create the table based on a style (and, if so, which one), table entry fields, or both. If you are using table entry fields, you must also select a table identifier character (Word suggests F for tables of figures). You can use this method to create as many additional tables as you need. Click OK when are done choosing options, or Cancel to dismiss them.

After you make your selections on the Table of Figures tab, click OK to create the table. The next two sections describe how to insert figure captions and how to create a specific table—a table of authorities.

CAUTION

You want to position your cursor where you want your table of figures to appear. If your cursor is positioned in your table of contents, Word will select the existing table of contents and ask whether you want to "replace the selected table of figures." If you choose Yes, Word will delete your table of contents and insert a table of figures in its place.

Inserting Captions for Tables of Figures and Other Tables

Word provides a caption style to make the creation of the tables of figures and others easier. To take advantage of the caption style and the automation it provides, you must add captions to your figures, tables, illustrations, and so on. Use these steps to insert captions:

1. Select your figure.
2. Choose Insert, Caption. The Caption dialog box appears, as shown in Figure 15.17.
3. Indicate whether you are labeling a Figure, Table, or Equation from the Label drop-down list.

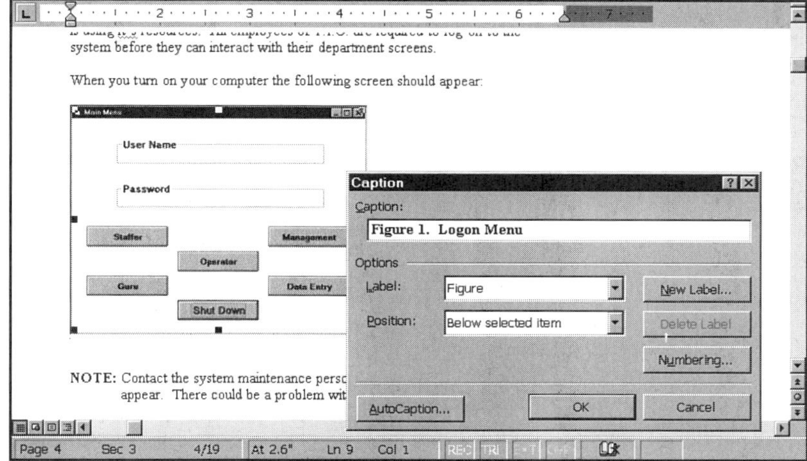

FIGURE 15.17
Here you can create and customize caption text.

4. If you are labeling something other than a Figure, Table, or Equation, click the New Label button to create another label.
5. To format the caption numbering, click the Numbering button. You can choose letters, numbers, Roman numerals, and so on.
6. The caption appears below the figure by default. You can choose to position the caption above the figure by selecting "Above selected item" from the Position list box. Click OK to accept the caption.

Creating a Table of Authorities

A table of authorities lists references to cases, statutes, rules, and so forth, and the pages they appear on in legal documents. As with all other text you want to be compiled into reference tables, you must indicate to Word what text you want to use.

1. For each citation, select the first long reference to it in your document.
2. With the text selected, press Alt+Shift+I to display the Mark Citation dialog box, as shown in Figure 15.18.

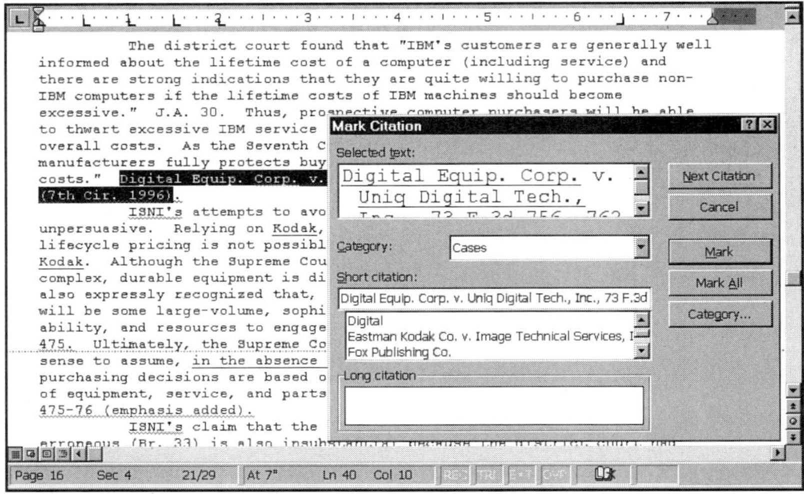

FIGURE 15.18
You can also display the Mark Citation dialog box through the Index and Tables dialog box.

3. Click the Category drop-down list to select the type of citation.
4. Use the Short Citation text box to indicate the short citation you will be using. Word will also mark the short citations and compile them into the table. The Long citation box merely holds the text you selected before you invoked the Mark Citation dialog box.
5. To mark this citation only, click Mark. To mark all the citations, long and short, that match this entry, click Mark All.

A finished table of authorities is shown next in Figure 15.19.

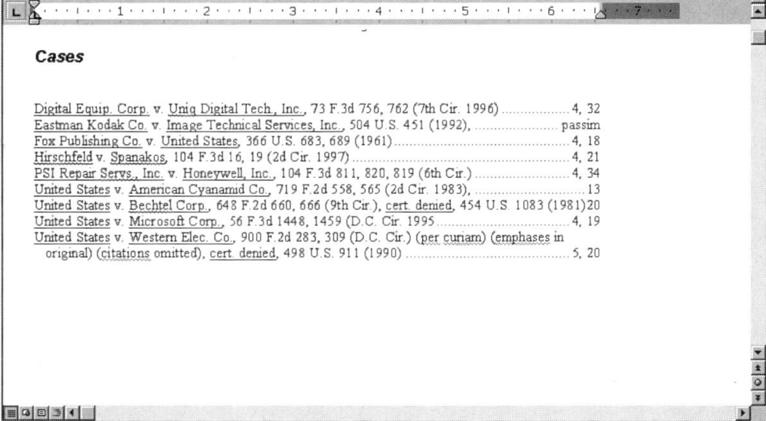

Cases

Digital Equip. Corp. v. Uniq Digital Tech., Inc., 73 F.3d 756, 762 (7th Cir. 1996) 4, 32
Eastman Kodak Co. v. Image Technical Services, Inc., 504 U.S. 451 (1992), ... passim
Fox Publishing Co. v. United States, 366 U.S. 683, 689 (1961) 4, 18
Hirschfeld v. Spanakos, 104 F.3d 16, 19 (2d Cir. 1997) 4, 21
PSI Repair Servs., Inc. v. Honeywell, Inc., 104 F.3d 811, 820, 819 (6th Cir.) 4, 34
United States v. American Cyanamid Co., 719 F.2d 558, 565 (2d Cir. 1983), ... 13
United States v. Bechtel Corp., 648 F.2d 660, 666 (9th Cir.), cert. denied, 454 U.S. 1083 (1981) 20
United States v. Microsoft Corp., 56 F.3d 1448, 1459 (D.C. Cir. 1995 .... 4, 19
United States v. Western Elec. Co., 900 F.2d 283, 309 (D.C. Cir.) (per curiam) (emphases in original) (citations omitted), cert. denied, 498 U.S. 911 (1990) 5, 20

FIGURE 15.19
Tables of authorities can be customized in the same way that tables of contents are.

Cross-References and Hyperlinks

Any long document that is to be read in electronic format can benefit from cross-references and hyperlinks. During document development, any long document, regardless of its published form, can also benefit from these features. A cross-reference is used within a document, creating a jump to another location within that document. It also can be used in print publishing, because the cross-reference presents the reader with the reference to a figure and the page number. A hyperlink can be used to reference a section in the current document, an existing file, a new file, an email address, or a Web site.

Word's automatic cross-referencing feature is a great timesaver and a valuable contribution to accuracy if you create long documents. Any printed document can benefit from cross-references. For example, if you want to reference your readers back to a figure or table presented earlier in a proposal, you can add cross-references back to it that contain just information about the figure or figure information plus a page number.

Figure 15.20 shows how cross-references and hyperlinks will appear in a printed document.

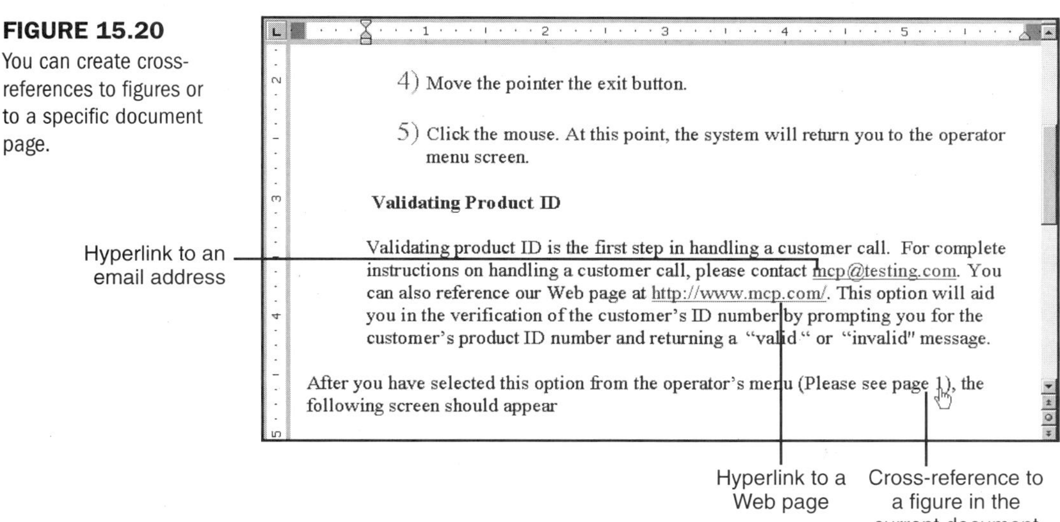

FIGURE 15.20
You can create cross-references to figures or to a specific document page.

The next few sections describe how to create cross-references and hyperlinks.

Cross-References Within the Current Document

Cross-referencing for either electronic or printed documents involves two steps: Identify the items to be referenced, and create the references.

The items to be cross-referenced can be identified as

- Numbered items
- Headings

- Bookmarks
- Footnotes
- Endnotes
- Equations
- Figures
- Tables

To make a reference to an item, type the introduction text such as `For more information, see` (including a space). Then choose Insert, Cross-Reference. In the Cross-Reference dialog box, shown in Figure 15.21, click the Reference Type drop-down list and choose the type of reference you want to make.

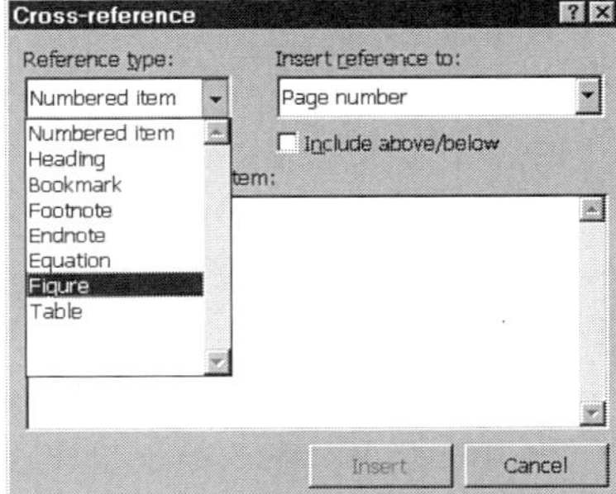

FIGURE 15.21
Specify the type of cross-reference you want to make.

The choices in the Cross-Reference dialog box vary according to the type of cross-reference you select. For example, if you choose Bookmark as the Reference Type, a list box displays all the bookmarks in your document so you can choose the one you want to use in the cross-reference.

Click the Insert Reference To drop-down list to choose how you want the reference to appear in your text: as text, as a page number, and so on.

If you're preparing a document to be printed, remove the check mark from the Insert As Hyperlink check box. However, if you're preparing a document to be viewed electronically, leave this box checked. This creates both a cross-reference and attaches a hyperlink to the cross-reference, so readers can click the reference to jump to the appropriate place in the document.

Cross-References to Other Documents

To build cross-references across documents, the documents must be subdocuments within a master document. If you want to create a hyperlink to another document without creating a master-to-subdocument relationship, use the hyperlink feature discussed in the next section, "Hyperlinks for Documents Published Onscreen."

▶ For a complete discussion of master and subdocuments, **see** "Using Master Documents to Handle Large Documents," **p. 487**

Hyperlinks for Documents Published Onscreen

Word's hyperlink feature allows your readers to click the hyperlink and jump to that position in the current document, another file, a new file, a Web page, or an email address.

You can create Web page and email links by typing an email address or Web site URL into your document. The AutoFormat tab in the AutoCorrect dialog box (choose Tools, AutoCorrect) contains an option to convert email addresses or Web sites into hyperlinks. This feature is turned on as a Word default.

If you want to reference a specific email address or Web site URL without creating a hyperlink, position the mouse pointer over the link until the hyperlink pointing hand appears. Right-click and choose Hyperlink. The next menu gives you the option to remove the hyperlink, thus turning the link back into normal text.

To create a hyperlink, follow these steps:

1. Position your cursor where you want the hyperlink to appear (typically after some introductory text such as `For more information, please see`).
2. Choose Insert, Hyperlink. Then click the Existing File or Web page button. The Insert Hyperlink dialog box appears, as shown in Figure 15.22.
3. Select the name of the file or Web site or type in the filename or Web site you want to link to. Provide the appropriate information: pathnames for files and URLs for Web pages.

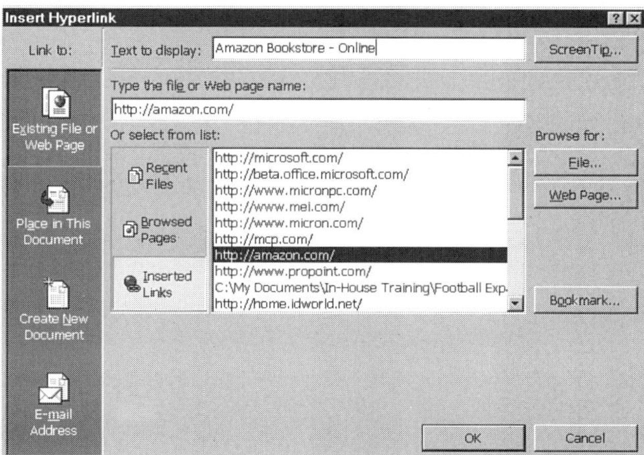

FIGURE 15.22
Use hyperlinks to create shortcuts for your readers to related material.

4. In the Text to Display text box, change the text that will appear in the document as the hyperlink if desired; otherwise, the file or Web site name will be inserted in the document.
5. Click ScreenTip to customize the text that will appear when the mouse is positioned over the hyperlink.

When you create hyperlinks to other files, you can use either relative or absolute pathnames. A relative pathname can be used if you are going to be moving the files at a later time. An absolute path references a file with a full pathname. You would use an absolute path to reference a file you don't expect to be moved. Examples of absolute and relative pathnames appear in Table 15.1.

Table 15.1 Absolute and Relative Pathnames As Used with Hyperlinks

Absolute Path	Relative Path	File Relationship
C:\documents*filename*.doc	*filename*.doc	Files share a folder
C:*filename*.doc	..*filename*.doc	*Filename*.doc in a higher-level directory

Absolute and relative paths apply only to documents saved on the same computer. If the files are being shared across a network or if the link is to a Web site URL, the reference is always considered to be absolute.

You can also copy and paste text from one document to another and one application to another as a hyperlink. First, copy the text you want from the source document or file to the Clipboard. Second, click where you want to insert the text in the destination document. Finally, choose Edit, Paste As Hyperlink. The text you copy from must come from a previously saved file. This technique will work only with text, not other data such as images.

You can edit hyperlinks after they have been created. Right-clicking a link gives you access to the Edit Hyperlink dialog box, as shown in Figure 15.23. Just choose Hyperlink, Edit Hyperlink on the pop-up menu.

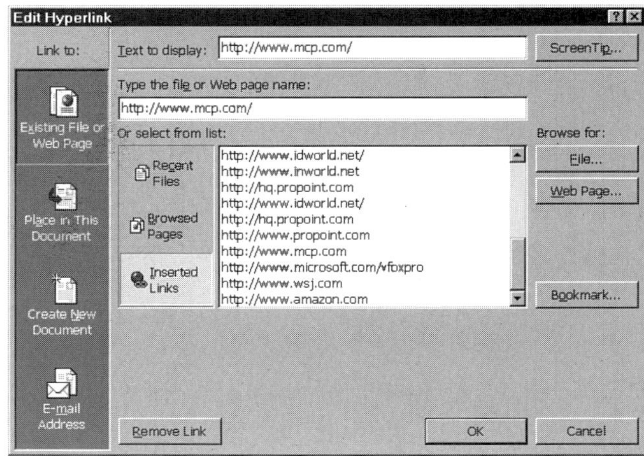

FIGURE 15.23
Here you can make any necessary changes to your hyperlink.

You can modify the hyperlink text that appears in the document using the Text to Display text box. You can change the file or Web site the hyperlink jumps to. You can even remove the link if you no longer want a hyperlink to appear in the document. This removes the link but leaves the text as it is in the document.

If you want to reference an email address or a Web site URL in your document without creating a link, type in the address. Go to the Edit Hyperlink dialog box and click Remove Link. The text remains in your document as you typed it without the link feature or color-coding associated with the link.

If you have just finished typing the hyperlink, press Ctrl+Z right after the formatting changes to that of a hyperlink. This undoes the autoformat command that Word uses to format hyperlinks. Now your hyperlink is plain text.

CAUTION

Word's hyperlinks do not work well with links that contain exclamation points, colons, semicolons, and closing parentheses. If your link contains these elements, you may have to edit the hyperlink, either by changing the text or adding a space after the offending element. Also the symbol # causes Word to truncate the filename and generate an error message. In this case, you will have to eliminate the symbol in the filename.

Creating an Index

Every nonfiction book that's worth buying contains an index. You can expect to use the index of a book to find the place in the book where a subject of interest to you is covered. Readers of any long document you create should have an index they can use to quickly find whatever information they're looking for.

The problem is that the person who creates the index has to list the subject and relate it to the words the author used when writing about the subject. For example, suppose you are creating an index for a software manual. You want your end users to be able to reference all the places you discuss logging client comments. Do you index under clients, comments, logging, or documenting?

There's no right answer to this question. You can't possibly list all the possible word combinations a reader might look for to find information about a particular subject. If you did, the index would occupy more pages than the subject matter of the document you're indexing.

What Is Indexing?

Indexing is an art—it's not mechanical. Although Word can help you create an index, it can't create an index automatically in the same way that it creates a table of contents. If you need to be convinced that there's a lot more to creating a good index than you might initially think, glance through the 47 pages about indexing in *The Chicago Manual of Style*, published by the University of Chicago Press. The comment in that book, "Indexing requires decision making of a far higher order than computers are yet capable of," is something to consider. Nevertheless, Word can provide valuable help in creating an index.

The process of creating an index consists of five principal stages:

1. Mark the places in the document to which the index should refer. For each place, designate the text to occur in the index. This is the stage that requires decision-making and detailed knowledge of the document and its subject matter.
2. Create the index. This is the part that Word does for you.
3. Examine the index carefully and mark any incorrect or missing entries.
4. Revise the index markings in the document to correct problems you noticed in step 3.
5. Re-create the index.

Be forewarned—You'll have to repeat steps 4 and 5 several times. The next few sections look at this process in more detail.

Marking the Document

Word marks items to be indexed by inserting {XE} (index entry) field codes into the document. You normally don't see these field codes, but you can reveal them by clicking the Show/Hide button on the Standard toolbar.

Word provides two ways for you to mark items to be indexed:

- Separately identify each place in the document by manually inserting the appropriate `{XE}` field code.
- Create a table, called a *concordance*, that contains the words and phrases to be indexed, together with the index text for each. Word can then search the document and insert the appropriate `{XE}` field code wherever the words and phrases you've listed occur.

NOTE Word calls this index entry table a concordance. A true concordance lists the location of every word in the document.

Creating a Concordance Using a concordance allows you to create an index quickly, but using it alone is not likely to result in an index that readers find useful. Therefore, it is often used in creating the index but rarely, if ever, included with the final document. Words often appear in combinations that make them candidates for more than one entry. For example, the word *representative* functions as both a noun and an adjective. An index generated with a concordance would find the word in any context and mark it. Your index then would have erroneous entries in it.

Because you can combine techniques, a concordance can be a great timesaver if you create a large number of similar documents. For example, if you write user manuals, you may use a concordance for standard index entries. After the concordance-generated entries are marked, you can go through your document and mark unique index entries.

To create an index using a concordance, you must first create the concordance.

1. Open a new document.
2. Create a two-column table.
3. Type the words and word combinations you want searched for in the first column, and the index entry you want them associated with in the second column. If you leave the second column blank, Word will use the entry from the first column.

CAUTION

If you leave the second column blank, the information from the first column will be present exactly as it appears in the first column. So, for example, if you are indexing "Operator" and "operator" for the index and the second column is blank for both entries, then both will appear in your index. However, if you have entered "Operator" in the second column for "operator," only "Operator" will appear in your index.

4. Check to be certain that you have included all case combinations and singular/plural combinations you want to be marked.
5. Save the file. The concordance is created, as shown in Figure 15.24. Consider using the word *concordance* and the file it references as part of the filename—for example, "manual concordance.doc."

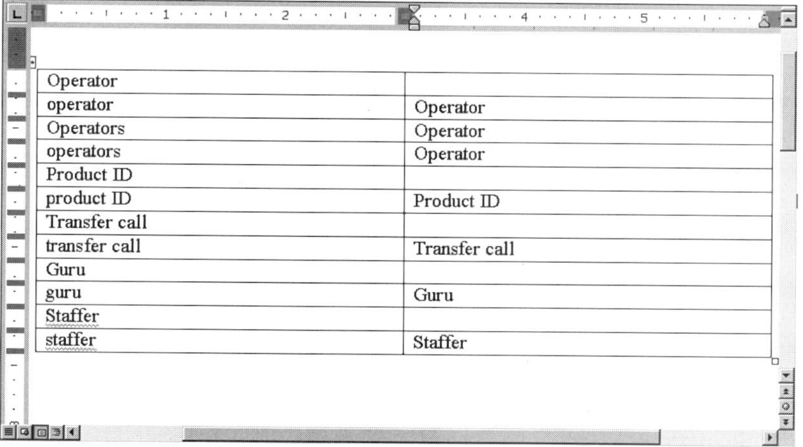

Operator	
operator	Operator
Operators	Operator
operators	Operator
Product ID	
product ID	Product ID
Transfer call	
transfer call	Transfer call
Guru	
guru	Guru
Staffer	
staffer	Staffer

FIGURE 15.24
A concordance allows you to use the AutoMark feature for indexes.

Inserting the *{XE}* Code After you have created your concordance, you are ready to mark your entries and compile your index:

1. Choose Insert, Index and Tables. Click the Index tab if necessary. Figure 15.25 shows the Index tab of the Index and Tables dialog box.
2. Click AutoMark to mark the entries listed in the concordance with `{XE}` codes. When the Open Index AutoMark File dialog box appears, supply the name of the file containing the concordance.

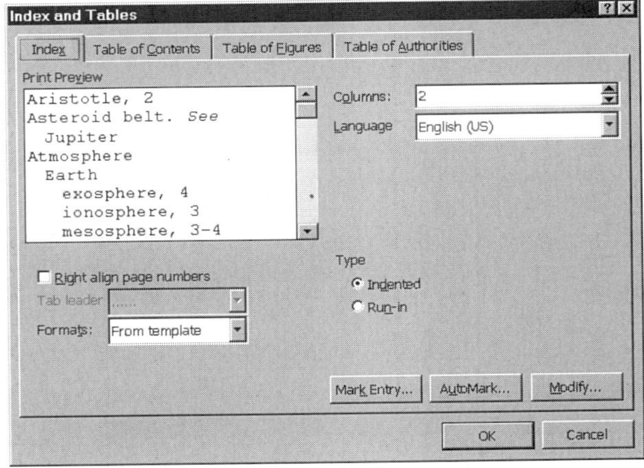

FIGURE 15.25
Use the AutoMark feature to automatically generate the index fields in your document based on your concordance entries.

You will save time if you AutoMark your index entries and manually mark any additional entries before you compile the index.

Even if you have used a concordance, chances are you will still want to manually mark a number of words and word combinations for your index:

1. Place the insertion point immediately before or after the text to which you want the index entry to refer.
2. Press Alt+Shift+X to display the Mark Index Entry dialog box, as shown in Figure 15.26.

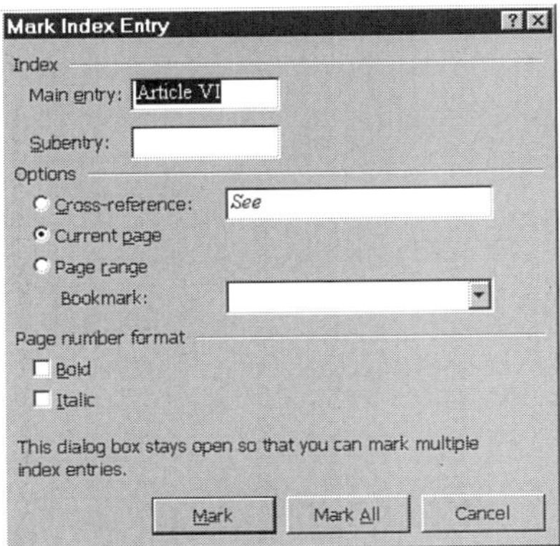

FIGURE 15.26
Use this dialog box to define the index entry.

NOTE Don't insert the {XE} field code between the letters of a word; if you do so, you won't subsequently be able to use the Find command to find that word. For example, if your document contains the word "taxes" and you place an {XE} field code within the word, your document will actually contain something like ta{XE "Funding"}xes; Word won't be able to find taxes. For the same reason, don't insert an {XE} field code anywhere within a phrase you're likely to want to search for.

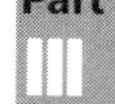

3. Type the Main entry for the index reference and, where appropriate, the Subentry. Of the three options offered, Word suggests the default Current page, which is normally what you want.
4. Click Mark to insert the `{XE}` field code. Quite often, you want more than one index entry for the same place in the document. For this reason, the dialog box stays open after you've inserted the field code so you can insert more `{XE}` field codes at the same place. Type any additional Main entries or Subentries that you want to refer to this spot in the document.

While you work, keep an updated list of the main entries and subentries you provide. By doing so, you can easily make sure that you consistently name subsequent items to be indexed. If you don't do this, you'll inevitably create index entry items that should be the same but are slightly different. Be particularly careful about consistently using the singular or the plural for index entries. Be consistent with capitalization; *The Chicago Manual of Style* recommends capitalizing main entries but not subentries.

After you insert an `{XE}` field code, you may not see it in your document. If you don't see it, click the Show/Hide button on the Standard toolbar to show the field. Examples of a main entry field and a main and subentry field are shown in Figure 15.27.

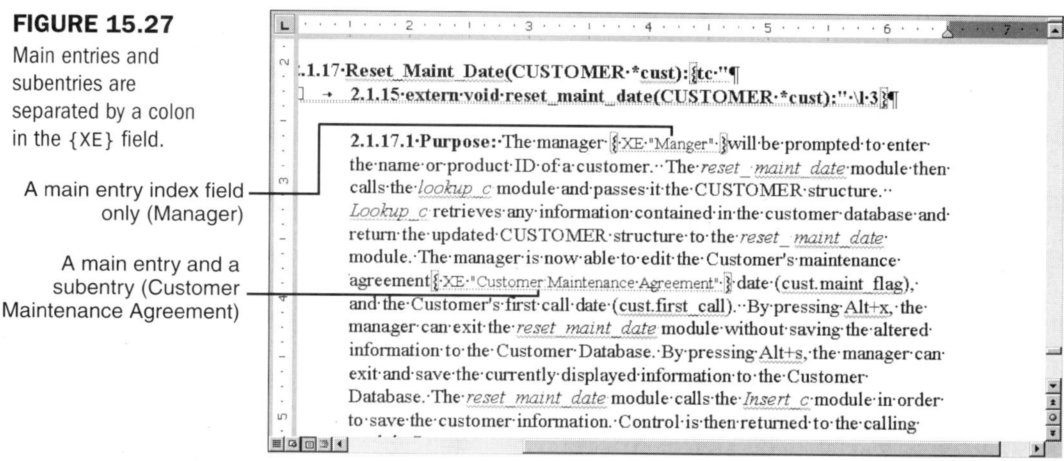

FIGURE 15.27
Main entries and subentries are separated by a colon in the `{XE}` field.

Insert `{XE}` field codes for each place in the document that's to be referenced in the index. This is a time-consuming, but necessary process.

To modify an index entry, go to the `{XE}` field and modify the field text. If you modify the actual index, when you update it your modification may be lost. Each time you update the fields in your document, the index is regenerated. If you edit the index directly, it will revert to its previous state upon updating. However, by editing the `{XE}` fields, your index will maintain those changes regardless of how often you update.

While you're writing the document and have each subject clearly in mind, it's a good idea to make a note of index entries as they come to mind, instead of leaving the indexing until the document is completed. Consider marking index entries while you write (if you subsequently change your mind, you can easily modify those entries, or even delete them).

Marking an Index for a Range of Pages Instead of referring to a specific page, you may want an index entry to refer to a range of pages. You can do this by first identifying the range of pages with a bookmark:

1. Select the range of pages to be included in your index entry.
2. Choose Insert, Bookmark and use the Bookmark dialog box (shown in Figure 15.28) to enter a bookmark name. Click Add to bookmark the selection.
3. Press Alt+Shift+X to display the Mark Index Entry dialog box. In the Options section, choose Page Range Bookmark, and then select the appropriate bookmark from the list.
4. In the Main Entry text box, give this range of pages an appropriate entry name. Do the same for the Subentry if necessary.
5. Click Mark to mark the entry, and Cancel to dismiss the dialog box.

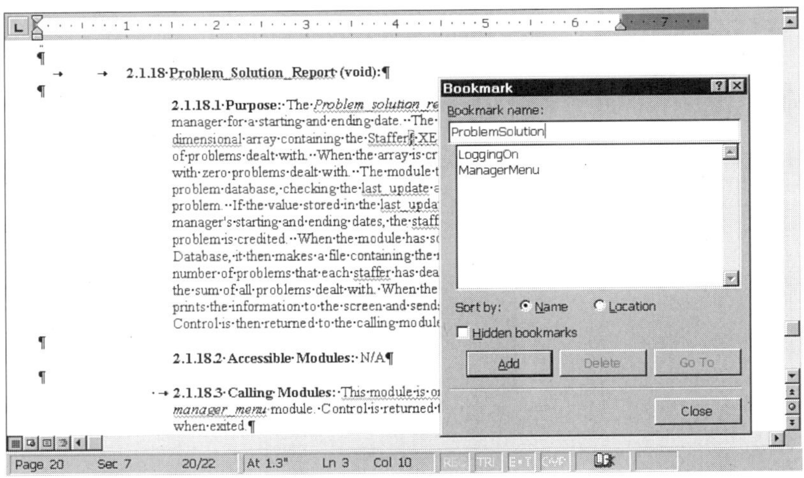

FIGURE 15.28
Use bookmarks to indicate to Word a range of pages for use in indexes, hyperlinks, and other features.

The index that Word subsequently creates refers to the range of pages on which the bookmarked text appears.

▶ **See** "Unleashing the Power of Bookmarks," **p. 241**

Compiling the Index

After you've inserted {XE} field codes at every place in the document that's to be indexed, the rest is easy. Place the insertion point where you want the index to start and choose Insert, Index and Tables to display the Index and Tables dialog box. If necessary, choose the Index tab, shown in Figure 15.29.

FIGURE 15.29
The Index tab of the Index and Tables dialog box is where you specify the format of the index.

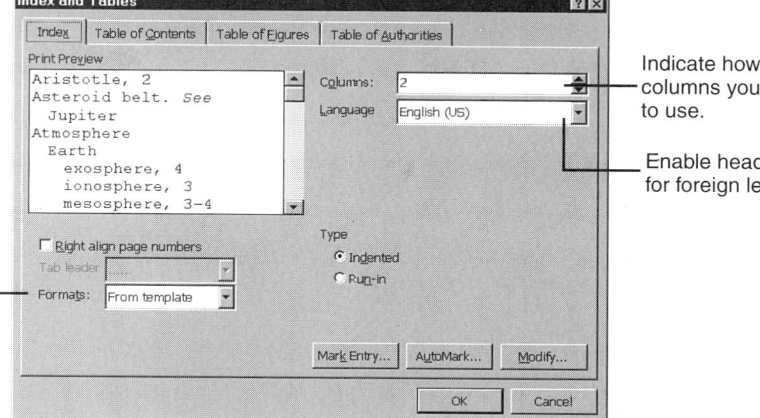

Make your choices among the options in this dialog box. Notice that you can change the number of columns. Also, if you are writing for an international audience, you can make use of any installed language set and have index headings from the other available alphabets. After you have made your choices, click OK and wait a few seconds for the index to appear. Although you see the index on your screen, Word actually inserts an *Index* field code. If you don't have your field codes toggled on, you can see this field code by placing the insertion point anywhere within the document and pressing Alt+F9, as shown in Figure 15.30. Press Alt+F9 again to go back to displaying the actual index.

FIGURE 15.30
If you want to see the index and not the field code, press Alt+F9.

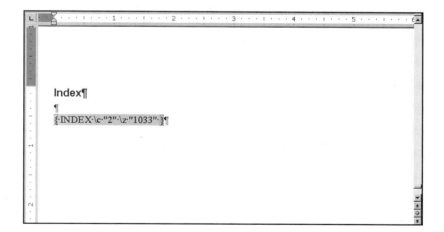

NOTE The \c switch in the Index field code tells Word to create an index formatted in more than one column; the number in quotes specifies the actual number of columns, two in this case. Word can create indexes with up to only four columns, even if you try to force Word by editing the field code with a greater number of columns. The \z switch defines the language id that Word uses to generate the index (in this case, 1033 represents English (U.S.)).

As already mentioned, you should carefully examine your first attempt at an index for a document, and note any places that require modification. Be sure you check for redundant entries from differing case or variations in wording; misspellings; and overall organization. Then go back to the document, make whatever changes are necessary to the `{XE}` field codes, and re-create the index.

CAUTION

Word lets you make changes to the actual index, but it's a very bad idea to do so. Any changes you make will be lost the next time you update the index. Always make changes to the `{XE}` field codes within the document and then update the index.

Modifying *{XE}* and *Index* Fields

Word provides many ways for you to tailor indexes to suit your specific needs. In addition to the choices offered in the Mark Index Entry dialog box and the Index and Tables dialog box, you can manually add a variety of switches to the `{XE}` and `{Index}` field codes. To see the available switches, click the Office Assistant. Type in either

- `XE Field`
- `Index Field`

The following section about creating multiple indexes contains an example of using switches.

Creating Multiple Indexes

Although most publications have a single index, some have two or more indexes. For example, a history book may contain an index of events, an index of people, and an index of places. The \f switch is the essence of multiple indexes. In `{XE}` and `{Index}` fields, \f is followed by a single alphabetic character enclosed within double quotation marks. By default, if an `{XE}` or `{Index}` field doesn't have an \f switch, the field behaves as if it had the default index switch "i." The i is the default identifier to indicate an index in the same way the c table is the default identifier for a table of contents.

As a result, you can identify all the event references with one switch (such as "e"), all the people references with another switch (such as "p"), and all the place references with yet another switch (such as "l" for location). Then you can create three separate Index fields, each with one of these switches. Each of the Index fields will then compile into its own index.

In summary:

- All `{XE}` fields that don't have an \f switch are included in the index without \f switch.
- All `{XE}` fields that have an "x" switch are included only in `{Index}` fields that have an "x" switch (here, "x" represents any alphabetic character other than "i").

Figure 15.31 shows an example of multiple indexes.

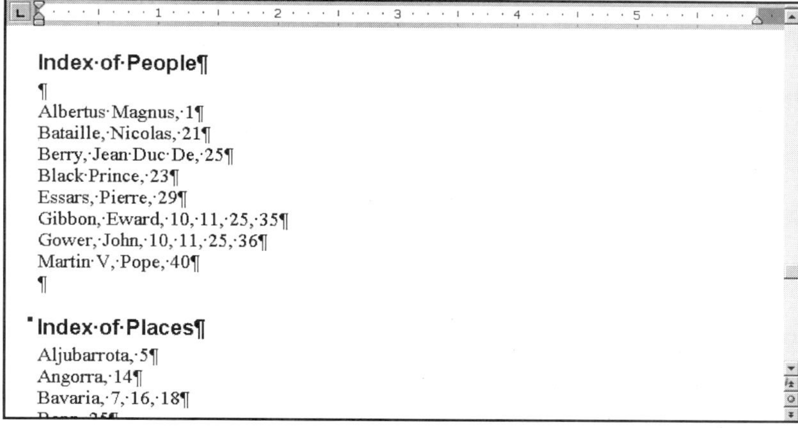

FIGURE 15.31
Multiple indexes are created using the /f switch in both the {XE} and {INDEX} fields.

Footnotes and Endnotes

Footnotes and Endnotes provide your reader with additional information about the text—either commentary or reference material. Whether you choose footnotes or endnotes depends entirely upon your publication policies or personal preference. The difference is that footnotes appear on the bottom of the page where they are indicated and endnotes appear at the end of the document. Thanks to Word's automation of these, one is just as easy to create as the other.

Creating Footnotes and Endnotes

In the days of typewriters, when you created footnotes you had to know how many lines the note would take, how many footnotes you would have on the page, and then count up from the bottom margin the number of lines you would need for the footnotes. In Word, you have a simple three-step process to insert a standard footnote:

1. Switch to Normal view.
2. Position your cursor where you want to reference the footnote.
3. Press Alt+Ctrl+F or choose Insert, Footnote.
4. Enter your footnote text into the footnote pane as shown in Figure 15.32 In Page Layout view, Word moves you to the bottom of the page into the footnote.

Word keeps track of the numbering and placement of your footnotes for you.

To insert an endnote, the process is identical except that you press Alt+Ctrl+D. The endnote pane opens and you can type your endnote text there as shown in Figure 15.33. Endnotes are numbered i, ii, iii, and so on, by default. See the later section "Customizing Footnotes and Endnotes" to change this pattern.

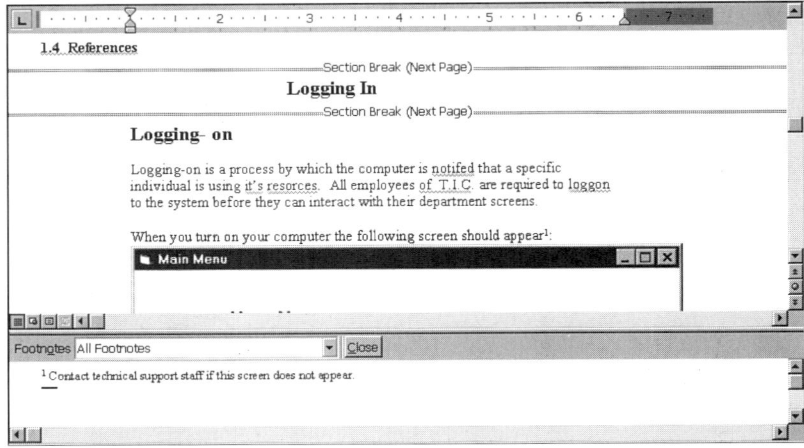

FIGURE 15.32
Word inserts the footnote reference mark and opens the footnote pane when you press Alt+Ctrl+F.

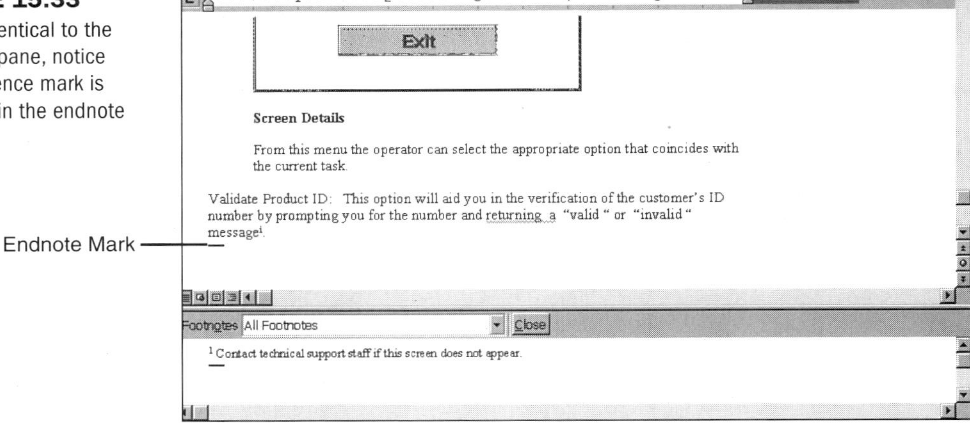

FIGURE 15.33
Nearly identical to the footnote pane, notice the reference mark is different in the endnote pane.

Editing Footnotes and Endnotes

If you are in Print Layout view, the footnote appears at the bottom of page where you can edit it. In Normal view, you can allow your mouse to rest on the reference mark and the footnote text pops up. If you want to edit the footnote, double-click the reference mark and the note pane appears.

You can resize the footnote pane by positioning your mouse on the border of the pane and then dragging the border to achieve the appropriate size.

To edit your endnotes, proceed as you would for footnotes; only when the footnote pane appears, choose endnotes from the drop-down list, as shown in Figure 15.34.

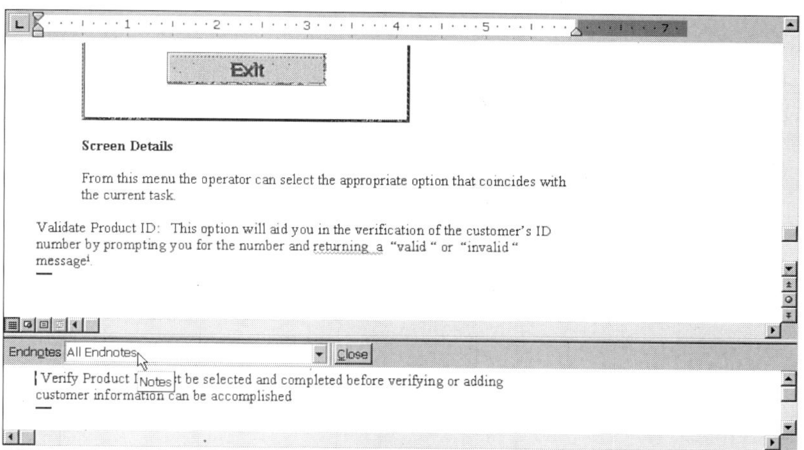

FIGURE 15.34
To edit your endnotes, choose endnotes in the drop-down list.

Customizing Footnotes and Endnotes

There are a number of ways to customize your footnotes and endnotes. You might want to use symbols instead of, or in addition to, a numbering system. You may need a different separator for your footnotes. Your style guide may require footnotes to be directly beneath the text and not at the bottom of the page.

In shorter documents, footnotes are often indicated with a symbol such as † or ‡. You can choose a symbol for the footnote reference mark instead of a number. Word allows you to intersperse symbols within a numbered footnote list. When you have a symbol as a footnote reference mark, Word does not include that footnote in the numbered list. The numbered footnotes continue in the correct sequence. To use a symbol in your footnotes instead of a sequential number, follow these steps:

1. Position your cursor where you want the footnote to be referenced.
2. Choose Insert, Footnote.
3. Click Symbol and choose the symbol you want to use.
4. Click OK twice and type your text into the footnote pane at the bottom of the screen.

To change the numbering sequence, position, and number system of the footnotes and endnotes, click Insert, Footnote, Options to display the Note Options dialog box as shown in Figure 15.35. Make the changes you need to make and click OK. Figure 15.36 shows the options available for endnotes.

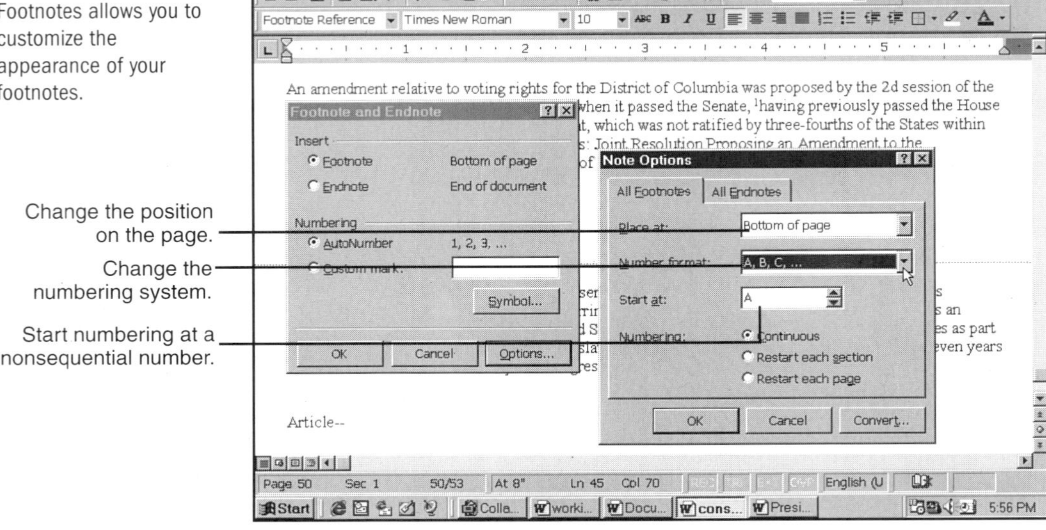

FIGURE 15.35
Note Options, All Footnotes allows you to customize the appearance of your footnotes.

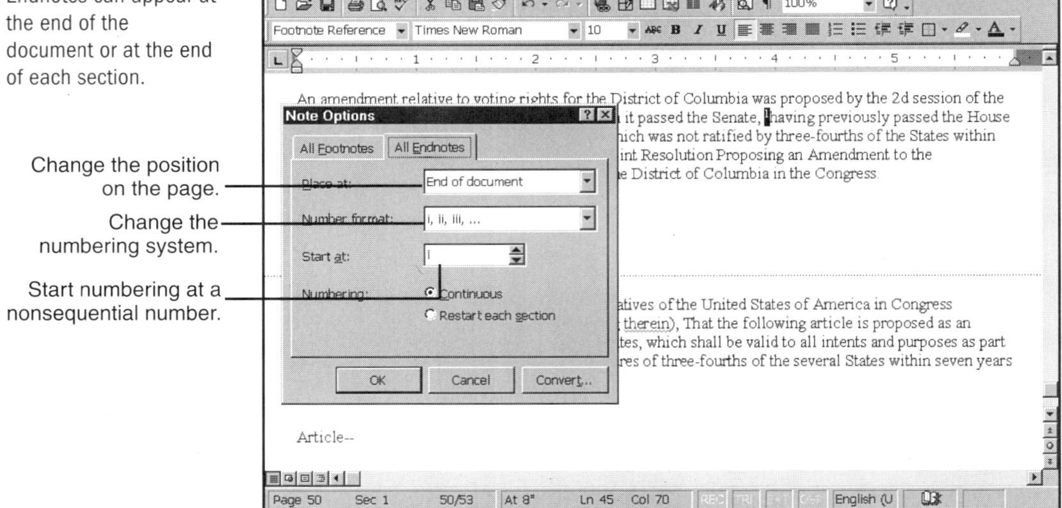

FIGURE 15.36
Endnotes can appear at the end of the document or at the end of each section.

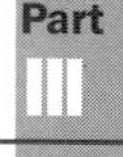

The separator line separates the footnotes from the text of the document. If a footnote flows onto the next page, a continuation separator separates the footnote from the body of the document. The separator line is a single line that extends one-third of the way across the page from the left margin. The continuation separator extends from margin to margin. To customize these lines, follow these steps:

1. Display the footnote or endnote pane. (Double-click the reference mark while in Normal view.)
2. Choose Footnote Separator from the drop-down list.
3. Make any changes you desire as you would to any other line or text.

Converting Footnotes to Endnotes and Back Again

Word makes it easy for you to change your mind. If you have carefully formatted all your notes as footnotes only to discover that you really needed endnotes, use these steps to convert the footnotes to endnotes:

1. Choose Insert, Footnote and click Options.
2. Click Convert. You are given a choice of all endnotes to footnotes, all footnotes to endnotes, and swap footnotes with endnotes. Make your choice and click OK to do the conversion; click Cancel to leave things as they are.

NOTE When you make changes in the Footnotes dialog box, you affect all the footnotes in your document—those that you have created previously and those that you will create.

CHAPTER 16

Working Effectively with Large Documents

In this chapter

Alternatives for Managing Large Documents

Word provides several approaches for managing large documents. One built-in approach is Master Document. This approach is designed for workgroups where you need the capability to control and lock documents while others are editing. At the same time, Master documents are flexible enough to enable multiple users to edit the same file simultaneously.

Another approach, sometimes called a compilation or multifile document, involves using the `INCLUDETEXT` field (from Insert, File, Insert as Link) to include different files in a main document.

Whatever the approach, document creation is made much easier by establishing a uniform method for working with documents. Using Word's built-in heading styles is perhaps the single best way to organize your documents—especially long documents. Using heading styles gives you easy and automatic access to some of Word's most powerful features, including outlining, Master Documents, Document Map view, and tables of contents.

Creating and Using Outlines Effectively

One of Word's most powerful and yet underused features, is outlining. Outlining lets you collapse a long document into a succinct view of just the headings—at any level you want. In the Outline view, you can move entire document sections around with ease. No cutting and pasting is necessary. Just move the headings around and all the subheadings and text within the headings are moved as well. Shuffling a 200-page document is as easy as clicking the mouse or pressing a few keys.

How Outlining Works

Outlining is underused because it requires that the user make use of heading styles. Far too many Word users populate their documents with a single style: Normal. They then use direct formatting to accomplish any variation they want.

NOTE Single-style formatting deprives the user not only of outlining, but tremendous formatting leverage as well. Using styles makes a writer fearless in the face of editors. If the editor wants all 250 of the third-level headings to use Arial Black, it's not a problem. Changing all 250 headings requires just a few keystrokes (for all 250—not apiece).

By default, Word's outlining is tied to the use of built-in Heading 1 through 9 styles. Using Word's Heading styles gives you the most flexibility—Word can do things with the built-in Heading styles that it cannot do by using styles you create.

Consider the document shown in full screen view in Figure 16.1. This document is 66 pages long and has seven level 1 (Heading 1) headings. With a document that contains Heading 1 through Heading 9 styles, you can view its outline by pressing Ctrl+Alt+O.

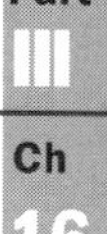

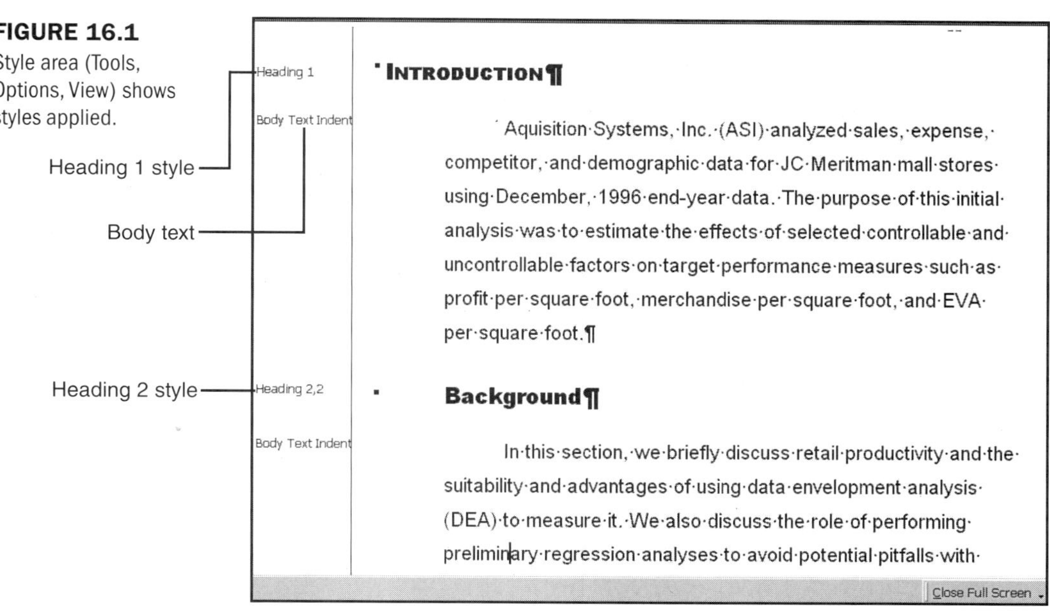

FIGURE 16.1
Style area (Tools, Options, View) shows styles applied.

Word displays documents in the outline level last used for that document. For example, Figure 16.2 displays only level Heading 2 and above. Headings formatted with Heading 2 are displayed as level 2, and headings formatted with Heading 1 are displayed as level 1. Not shown here are levels 3 through 9, which might also be in use.

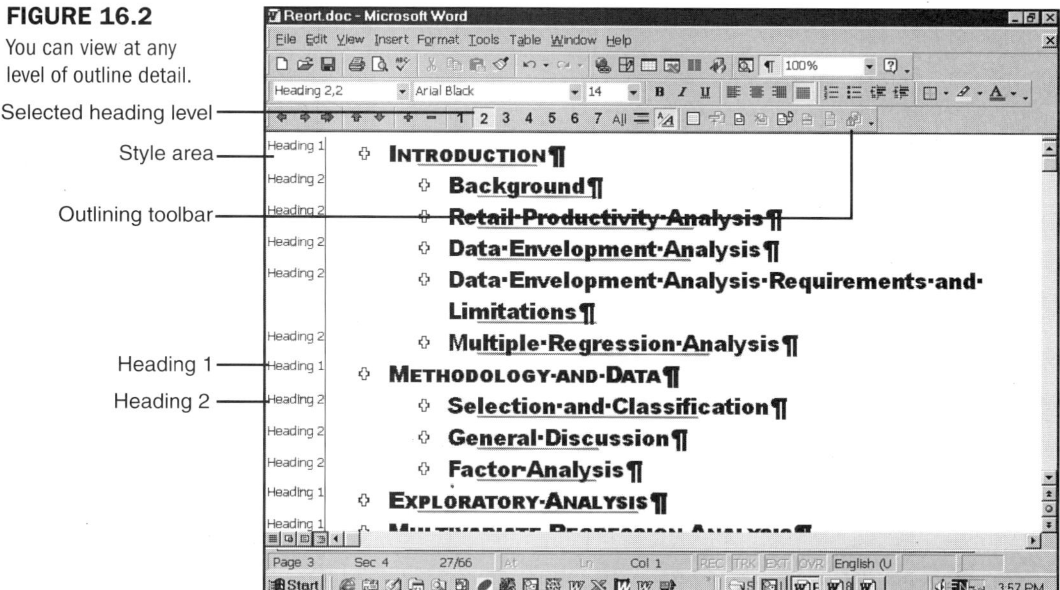

FIGURE 16.2
You can view at any level of outline detail.

If the heading levels use ostentatious formatting that takes up too much space, click the Show Formatting tool on the Outlining toolbar to toggle off the text formatting. Although the text is dimmer, Word usually can display much more of the outline at the identical zoom and resolution, as shown in Figure 16.3.

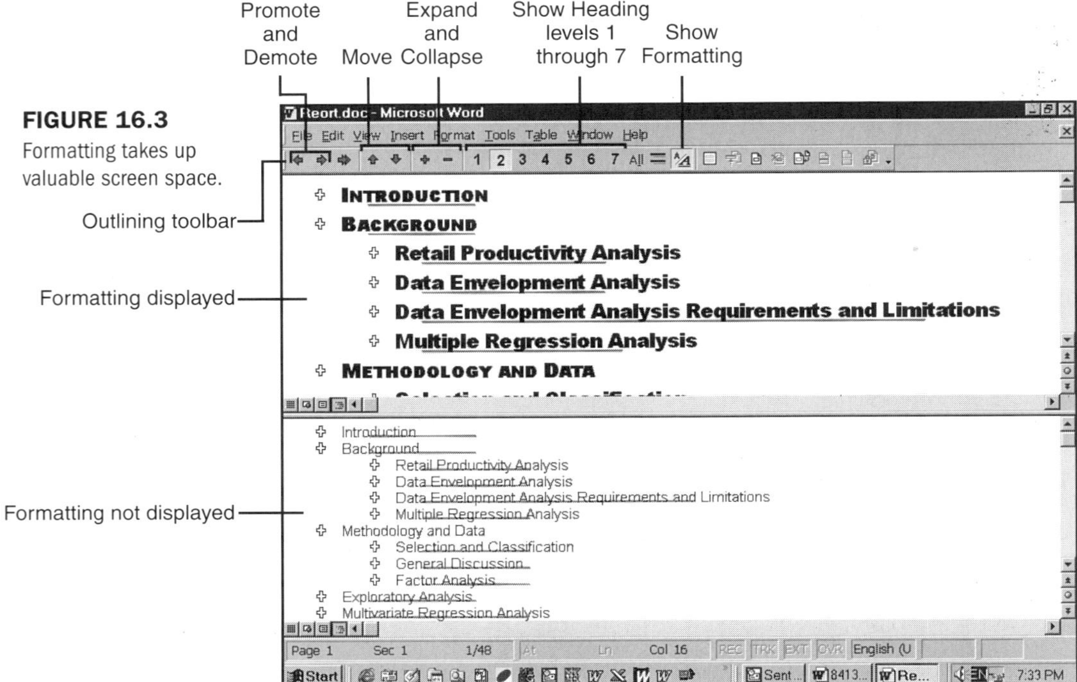

FIGURE 16.3
Formatting takes up valuable screen space.

Each of the buttons on the Outlining toolbar, except for the Show Formatting and Demote to Body Text buttons, has shortcut key equivalents.

- Promote (Alt+Shift+Left)
- Demote (Alt+Shift+Right)
- Move up (Alt+Shift+Up)
- Move down (Alt+Shift+Down)
- Expand (Alt+Shift+=)
- Collapse (Alt+Shift+ _)
- Show Heading 1 through 7 (Alt+Shift+1 through Alt+Shift+7)
- Show All Headings (Alt+Shift+A)
- Show First Line Only (Alt+Shift+L)

Although not displayed in the Outlining toolbar, Alt+Shift+8 and Alt+Shift+9 can be used to display heading levels 8 and 9 in Outline view.

Outline Collapse and Expand In Outline view, Collapse and Expand are used to reveal additional detail. You can expand any given level by clicking the Expand tool (Alt+Shift+=). If you expand a Heading 3 level, for example, that is not already expanded, any Heading 4s below that heading are then displayed. If you expand again, any Heading 5s are displayed. This pattern repeats through Heading 9. When level 9 headings are displayed, expanding again displays body text, as well.

Similarly, the Collapse tool (Alt+Shift+_) removes levels from display. Each click of Collapse removes the lowest current level from the display.

Outline Promote and Demote Outline Promote and Demote are used to raise or lower, respectively, the assigned heading level of the selected heading and all collapsed levels below that heading. For example, if the outline currently displays level 2 and above (Alt+Shift+2), you can promote any level 2 heading by clicking anywhere in the level 2 line and clicking the Promote tool. The Heading 2 text is promoted to Heading 1. Any subheadings—3 through 9—are also promoted to the next higher level. Therefore, Heading 3 becomes Heading 2, Heading 4 becomes Heading 3, and so on. Heading 1 levels are not affected by the Promote command.

Similarly, when you demote a level, all collapsed levels below that level also get demoted. For example, if you demote a level 3 heading, it becomes Heading 4. Any Heading 5s become Heading 6s, and so on. Heading 9 levels are not affected by the Demote command.

If you promote or demote at a time that subheadings are *not* collapsed, only the current heading is promoted or demoted. For example, if all outlining levels are displayed, and you promote a level 4 heading, then only that heading gets promoted. Levels 5 through 9, although logically below that level, do not get changed. To have the power to change all text below a given level, lower levels must be collapsed.

NOTE Promote and Demote work only when using Heading 1 through Heading 9 as the heading style names. If you use the Format, Paragraph dialog box to assign outlining levels to styles other than the Heading # styles, Promote and Demote will not work on those other styles.

Promote and Demote do in fact appear to change the relative position of headings in an outline based on other styles. However, if levels 1 through 9 correspond to styles named L1 through L9, then demoting an L2 style does not reformat that heading as L3. This is discussed in more detail under "Customizing the Outline Levels," later in this chapter.

Outline Move Up and Down Move Up and Down are used to move a heading level—and all text below it—in a document. For example, if a document is displayed in outline view at level 4, you could use the Move Up and Down tools or keystrokes to move any level 4 heading elsewhere in the document—even to under a different level 3 heading. For many users, the keystroke method works best. Click anywhere in the heading you want to move, and press Alt+Shift+Up (or Down) to move that heading elsewhere in the document. That heading, and all subheadings and text below it, gets moved in the document. This lets you quickly reorganize a document from within Outline view.

When you use Move Up or Move Down and the outline is not collapsed to the current level (for example, if you move a level 4 at a time that subheadings 5 and lower are displayed), only the displayed level moves.

Use Move Up and Move Down—Even When Not in Outline View

Move Up and Move Down also work when you're not in Outline view! That's why it pays to know your shortcut keys–because the Outlining toolbar isn't displayed when you're not in Outline view. In a document based on Heading # styles, click in the heading you want to move, and press Alt+Shift+Up to move the current heading–and its subordinate text–to a point earlier in the document. Alt+Shift+Down does the reverse. Note, however, that the collapsed level rule applies. Because you're not in Outline view, only the text below the immediate heading moves. Subordinate headings do not move.

This tip also works in nonheading text. Use Alt+Shift+Up and Down to reorganize items in bulleted and numbered lists.

Show Heading 1 Through 9 Use the Show Heading 1 through 7 tools to show the outline collapsed to the numbered level. For example, click 6 to display Heading 1 through Heading 6, with all headings and text below level 6 collapsed. Similarly, the keyboard shortcuts, Alt+Shift+1 through Alt+Shift+9, show the outline collapsed to the corresponding level number. Note that these keystrokes work only when in Outline view.

Show All and Show First Line The Show All Headings tool actually is a misnomer. It shows all the document—not just heading levels. However, it continues to show the document in Outline view. This can effectively be used in conjunction with Show First Line. With both Show All and Show First Line active, Word displays the document in Outline view with just the first line of body (nonheading) text revealed as well. If you're not entirely familiar with the underlying text, this view often gives you a quick sense of what a given heading title means.

Customizing the Outline Levels

Earlier, you noted certain advantages (for example, Promote and Demote) to using the built-in Heading 1 through Heading 9 styles for outlining. This suggests, however, that there is a way to use others. To cause any paragraph to be included in the outline, follow this general procedure:

1. In Normal view or Print Layout view, choose Format, Paragraph, Indents and Spacing tab.
2. In Outline level, pull down the control to associate the desired level with that paragraph.
3. Click OK.

This can also be useful if there are headings you want excluded from Outline view for whatever reason. Follow the preceding procedure, choosing Body Text rather than any particular level.

To be really effective, however, you should make the level assignments by using the style controls. Choose Format, Style. Choose the style you want to be displayed in the outline, and click Modify, Format, Paragraph. Here, use the Outline Level control to associate the desired level. Then, click OK twice to get back to the main style dialog box. There, choose the next style you want to change and repeat the procedure.

For example, some companies use heading styles named HA, HB, HC, and so on rather than Heading 1 through Heading 9. These style names can be traced back to Word for DOS. Some companies find it easier to continue using the two-letter mnemonic names rather than make the transition to the more descriptive names in Word for Windows. Using the Outline Level setting, however, such users can gain the use of outlining, albeit without the advantages of Promote and Demote.

Printing an Outline

When the document is displayed in Outline view, Word prints the outline rather than the document. Choose Outline view, use outlining keys or the toolbar to display the level you want printed, and choose File, Print.

NOTE If Word prints the entire document when you try to simply print the outline, try disabling the Reverse Print Order option in the Print dialog box.

Word does not provide a built-in way to get just the outline into a file. As a workaround, however, you can create a table of contents (TOC field) for the document, specifying the desired number of levels. Then use Ctrl+Shift+F9 to unlink the text in the table of contents, which converts the TOC into regular text. That text can then be copied and pasted into other documents.

Switching Between the Outline and Complete Text Quickly

Word provides a variety of tools for switching between Outline and various other views. Shown in Figure 16.4, Word has four view tools in the lower-left corner of the Word window. You can use the mouse to choose the desired view.

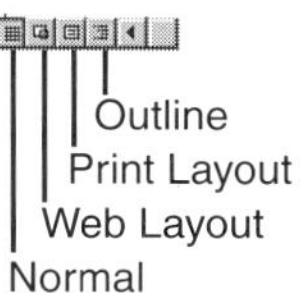

FIGURE 16.4
The view tools are one-way static tools, not toggles.

Word also has several default keystrokes for switching among Outline view and then back into Normal, Print Layout, and Print Preview view:

- Outline—Ctrl+Alt+O
- Normal—Ctrl+Alt+N

- Print Layout—Ctrl+Alt+P
- Print Preview—Ctrl+Alt+I

Note that none of these are toggles. If you would prefer, however, creating a Normal/Outline toggle is a fairly simple matter using Visual Basic. The following macro switches between Outline and Normal view. You could substitute one of the other views for Normal if something else better suits your style.

```
Sub ViewOutlineToggle()
    If ActiveWindow.ActivePane.View.Type = wdOutlineView Then
    ActiveWindow.ActivePane.View.Type = wdNormalView
    Else
    ActiveWindow.ActivePane.View.Type = wdOutlineView
    End If
End Sub
```

If your preferred default view isn't Normal, you might choose to substitute one of the following for wdNormalView:

- wdPrintView (Print Layout view)
- wdWebView (Web Layout view)
- wdPrintPreview (Print Preview)

You can either type this VBA code snippet into the VBA Editor, which is discussed in Chapter 6, or you can copy it from the book CD into the VBA Editor.

▶ **See** "Putting VBA Code Snippets to Work," **p. 135**

Using the Document Map

Document Map offers an additional navigation tool for Word documents. It can even provide a partial outline alternative for documents that don't use standard heading level styles, but, like Outline view, Document Map view works best for documents formatted using heading styles that are associated with specific outline levels.

NOTE Users upgrading from the original release of Word 97 should notice significant improvements in Document Map. In the first release of Word 97, Document Map often randomly displayed portions of the document text–headings and nonheadings–effectively making the feature useless. This previously buggy feature was improved substantially with Word 97's SR-2 (service release, number 2). The improvements have carried over to Word 2000.

To display Document Map view, choose View, Document Map. If you use headings with assigned outline levels (Format, Paragraph, Outline Level), such as Word's built-in Heading 1 through 9 styles, the document map appears immediately, as shown in Figure 16.5. Document Map view works equally well even with user-created styles other than Heading 1 through 9, just as long as the headings used have been assigned to specific outline levels.

FIGURE 16.5
An outline hierarchy is possible only with a hierarchy of heading levels.

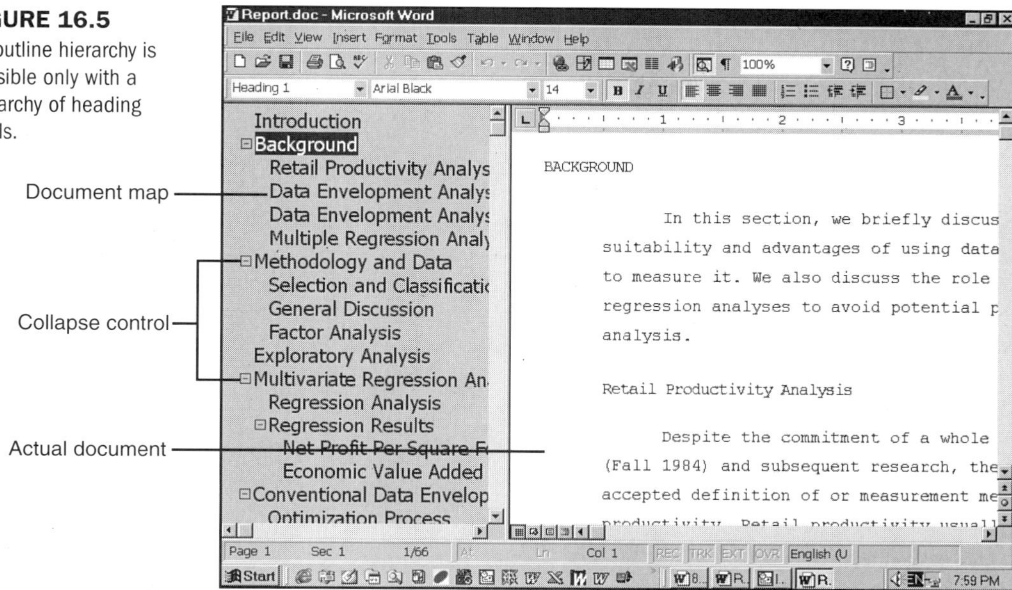

If the displayed document doesn't use heading styles with assigned outline levels, Word's behavior is different. When you choose View, Document Map, Word will advise you in the status bar that it is formatting the document. Actually, it's analyzing the formatting so that it can make a guess about what might and might not be headings. When done, the document map will appear at the left, but will not usually contain hierarchy levels unless different level headings are indented differently.

Even when you don't have a hierarchy of headings, Document Map view can still be useful for navigation purposes. Word generally is moderately successful in identifying important and useful headings in the document. This then allows you to use the Document Map panel almost as a table of contents for seeing the document's overall organization as well as a tool for jumping around. Unlike Outline view, however, you cannot use Document Map view for reorganizing a document.

Navigating Using Document Map View

In Document Map view, click a heading shown on the left to move the insertion point to that location in the document. Right-click the Map panel to see additional controls, as shown in Figure 16.6. The Expand (+) and Collapse (-) options work the same way as the + and – controls in the Document Map panel. Click + to display the next-lower tier of subheadings within the selected heading; click – to collapse all subheadings within the selected heading.

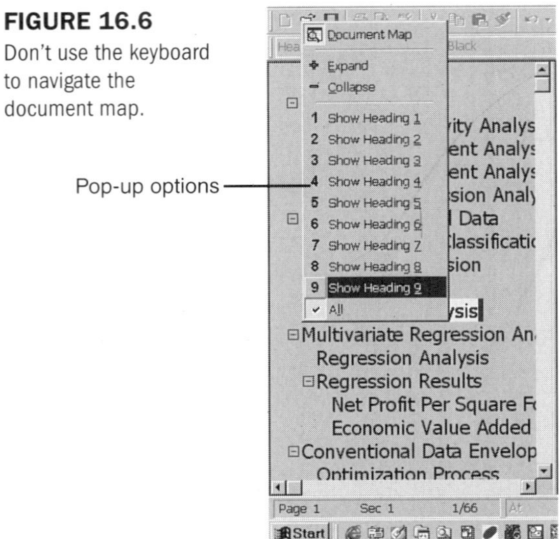

FIGURE 16.6
Don't use the keyboard to navigate the document map.

The Show Heading 1 through 9 commands are used to limit the display just to the level you click. Show All expands all levels, including Body Text. To move to a new location, click the desired heading in the left panel.

Changing the Document Map Pane

The Document Map pane can be widened or narrowed to suit your needs. Move the mouse pointer over the right edge of the Document Map pane until you see the Resize pointer shown in Figure 16.7. Using the left mouse button, drag to the left or right to narrow or widen the Document Map pane as desired.

Changing the Document Map Appearance

Users sometimes find the Document Map fonts and colors hard to deal with. Perhaps the fonts are too small and are unreadable, or, they are too large and take up too much space; the colors are wrong; or, the view is too cluttered. You can customize Document Map so that it suits your needs and eyesight.

Word provides a style called Document Map to control the formatting of the Document Map. Switch into Document Map view, and choose Format, Style. Find the Document Map style. Then choose Modify, Format, and change the attributes of style to match what you want.

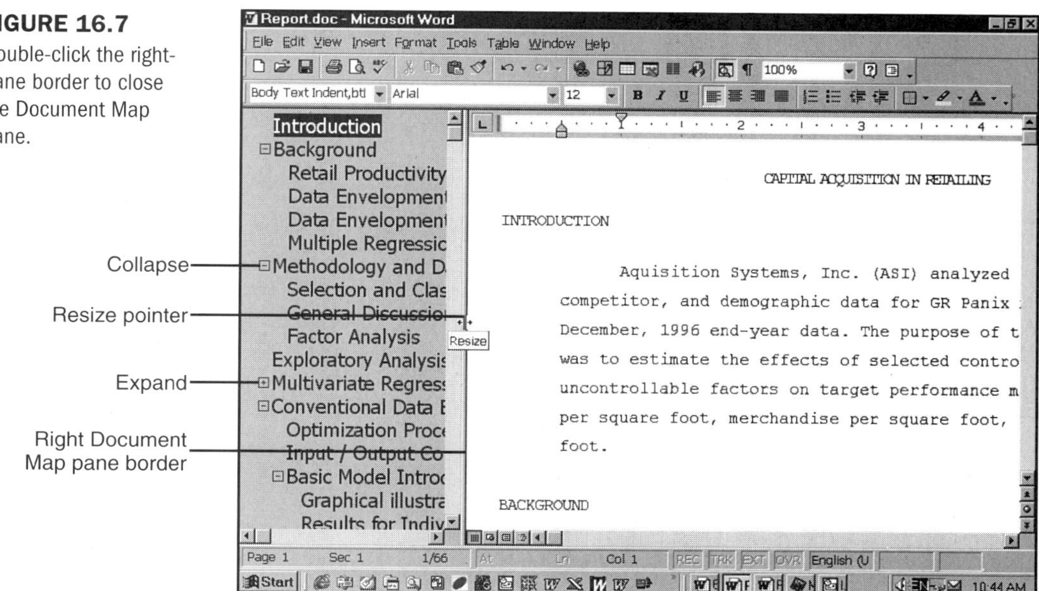

FIGURE 16.7
Double-click the right-pane border to close the Document Map pane.

Using Master Documents to Handle Large Documents

A Master Document is a single smaller document that is used to contain, organize, and manage a set of documents. The idea of Master Document is to make a long document more manageable by dividing it into smaller subdocuments, such as chapters. For example, a common use for Master Document is to organize and manage multichapter books.

CAUTION

Master Document is a wonderful idea. Unfortunately, it's also unreliable, and sometimes results in document corruption, especially with large documents—the very documents it was designed to facilitate! If and when Microsoft manages to bring it under control, the Master Document feature will be a big boon for workgroups who need simultaneous access to the same complex document. Until then, our best advice is to use this feature gingerly and with caution, making frequent backups.

In the spirit of eternal hope, this section describes the ideal use and methods for working with the Master Document feature. Given that the feature is considerably more stable than it was in Word 97, there's not as much cause for alarm. Given that it's still not 100% stable, however, it's better to be safe than sorry.

Master Document is a framework for a collection of related Word files. The Master Document itself typically contains very little text. It might contain a main title, header and footer settings, a table of contents, lists of figures and tables, and an index. It might also contain an introduction. Beyond that, however, Master Document contains references to subdocuments.

Taking advantage of Master Document is aided greatly if you use Word's Heading 1 through Heading 9 styles to organize your documents. You might also consider reserving the Heading 1 and possibly Heading 2 style just for use in Master Document itself, and using lower levels for the top level of any subdocuments. This gives you additional flexibility if you later need to divide your work into sections that comprise sets of chapters.

In a workgroup, you can store Master Documents centrally so that the different components can be worked on at the same time by different users.

Aside from management and sharing, using a Master Document can also simplify matters such as compiling indexes and tables of contents and creating cross-references. You can also use a Master Document to ensure consistency in formatting and style. Used properly, Master Document can also conserve resources by letting you (and others) work on subdocuments rather than having the entire document loaded into memory. Even if used by just a single user, there are benefits to be gained by working with just 20 pages, for example, instead of having a 400-page book all in the same document. Even without graphics, large files can quickly become so slow that working with them is a chore.

You can create a Master Document from scratch by creating a document outline or by converting an existing document. Or, you can create a Master Document by assembling a set of existing documents (for example, chapter files).

When you open a Master Document itself, the advantages of working with subdocuments becomes immediately clear—a Master Document assembled from many smaller subdocuments immediately takes on the behavior of a single long document. Loading a Master Document uses just as much memory as if all the subdocuments were contained in the same document.

There also are limits. Master Document cannot be used to exceed Word's built-in 32MB file-size limit. Also, Master Document theoretically is limited to 255 subdocuments. While these limitations might not seem important to some users, keep them in mind if you have bigger needs or plans.

CAUTION

While the theoretical maximum number of subdocuments is 255, the practical limit can be much lower. The exact number depends on the number and size of open files, number of running processes, the amount of virtual and physical memory, and the operating system as well as other factors. If you reach the limit when you try to save the Master Document, Word won't be able to save.

As a workaround, you can

- Cancel the save, close other files and programs, and try again.
- Convert groups of subdocuments into Master Document text (see "Removing Subdocuments" later in this chapter).
- Merge multiple subdocuments into a single subdocument.

Creating a Master Document from Scratch Using an Outline

Often, beginning with a new document helps you better understand the basic principles involved. That's certainly the case with Master Documents. Any document you create in Word has the potential for becoming a Master Document. You control what it becomes. A document becomes a Master Document the moment you use Master Document view to consign different sections into different physical files on your disk. This gives you a flexible tool for working with features (such as indexes and cross-references) that logically must use all the document components, as well as working on one component at a time.

You can use the following general procedure to create a Master Document from scratch:

1. Create a new blank document; press Ctrl+Shift+* to toggle the display of formatting marks on, if necessary.
2. Switch into Outline view, and click the Master Document View tool on the Outlining toolbar.
3. Using Heading # styles, create an outline for the document, specifying chapter titles that will serve as the top-level heading within individual subdocuments, as shown in Figure 16.8.

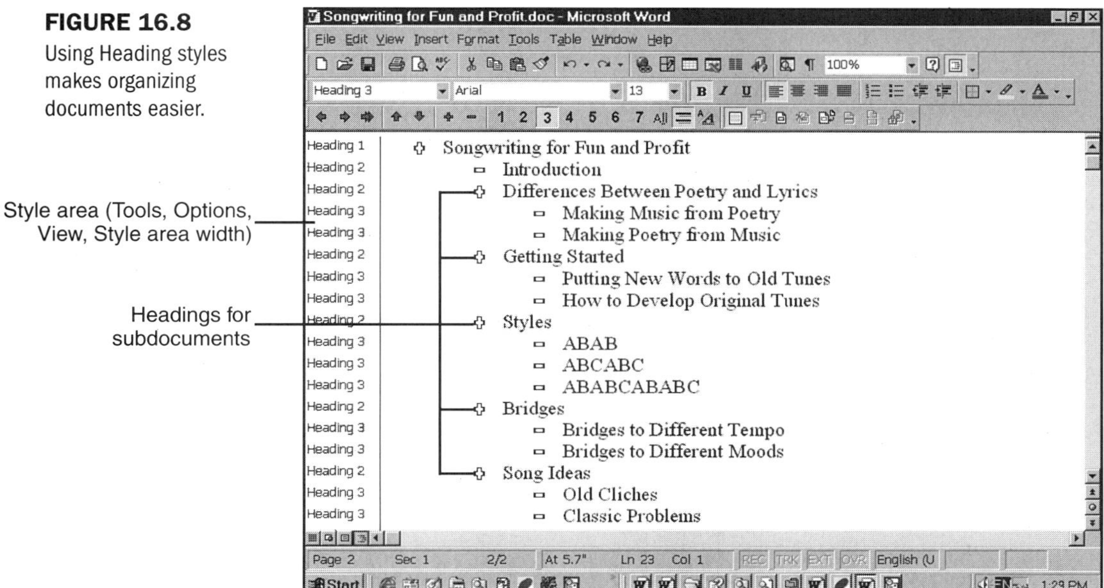

FIGURE 16.8
Using Heading styles makes organizing documents easier.

4. Click an outline level that displays just the top heading level for each subdocument (for example, Heading 2).

5. Select a heading that will form the basis for a subdocument (including the paragraph mark, to ensure that all subsidiary text is converted as well), and click the Create Subdocument tool; Word inserts a continuous section break and draws a box around each subdocument, as shown in Figure 16.9.

FIGURE 16.9
The + indicates that the heading level contains subheadings.

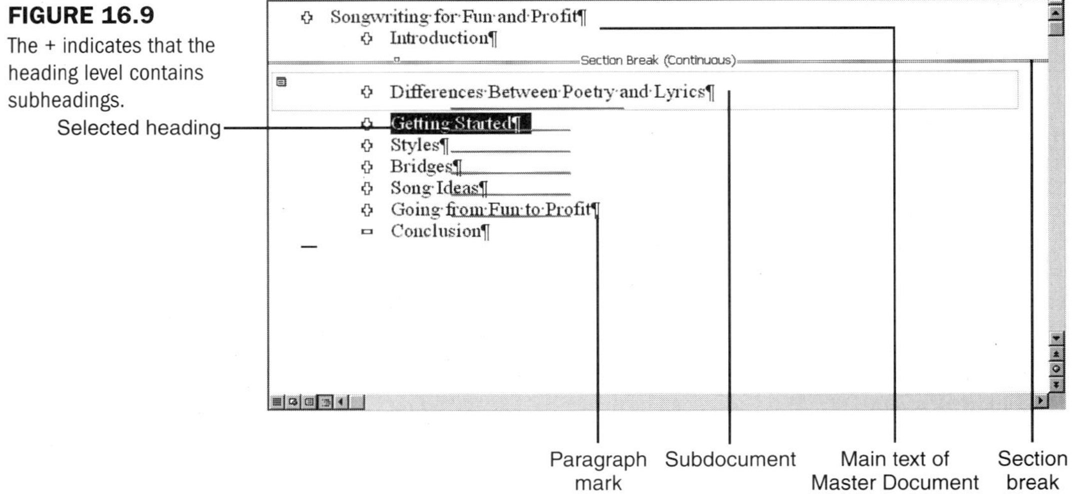

6. Repeat step 5 to create additional subdocuments.
7. Choose File, Save As, and name the Master Document; Word automatically creates files for each of the subdocuments, using the top-level subdocument headings as the titles for each, as shown in Figure 16.10.

FIGURE 16.10
The Open dialog box shows subdocuments created automatically.

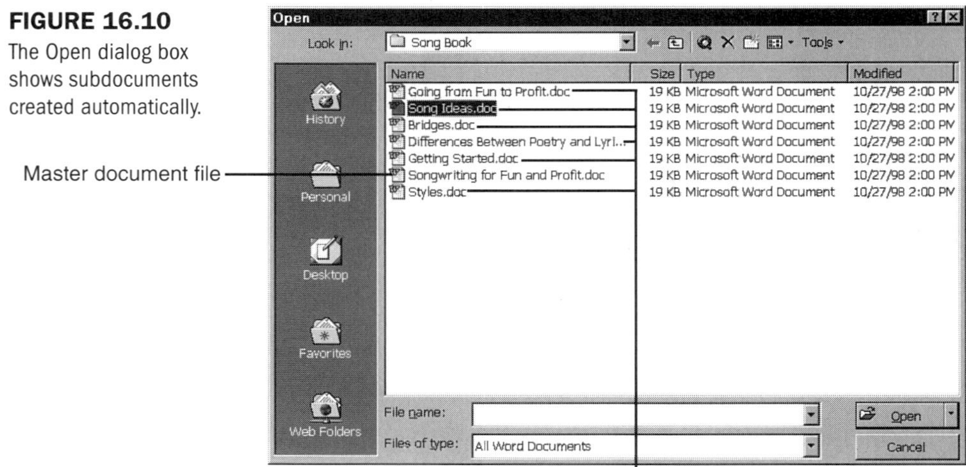

In lieu of step 5, after you've converted one heading into a subdocument, simply select the next heading (making sure you include the paragraph mark) and press F4. Word repeats the formatting and converts the selected heading (and all collapsed text within it) into a subdocument.

After the initial conversion, you have several choices. You can continue working in Master Document view, developing the outlines of the subdocuments. Any changes you make are automatically saved in each respective subdocument when you save the Master Document.

You can switch into Normal view, and work on the subdocuments from the Master Document. Again, all changes are saved in each respective subdocument, even though you're working at the Master Document level.

Or, you can double-click a subdocument icon, shown in Figure 16.11, and work just on the subdocument.

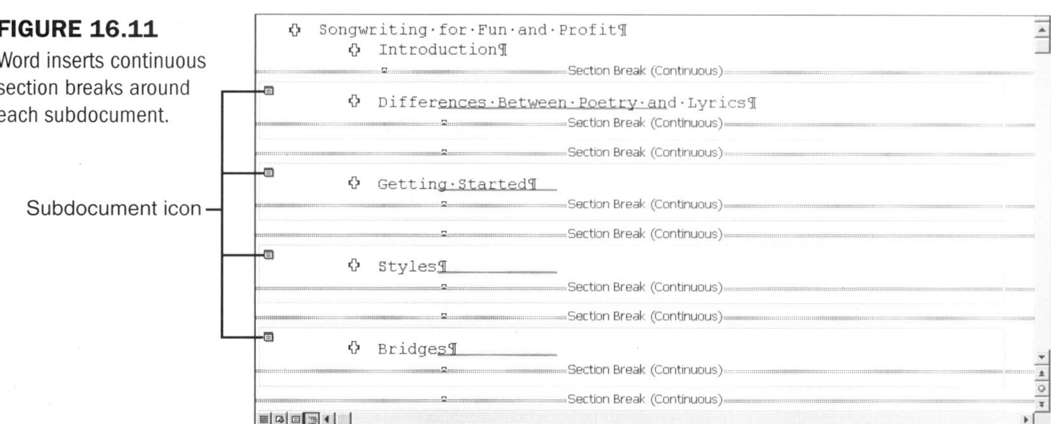

FIGURE 16.11
Word inserts continuous section breaks around each subdocument.

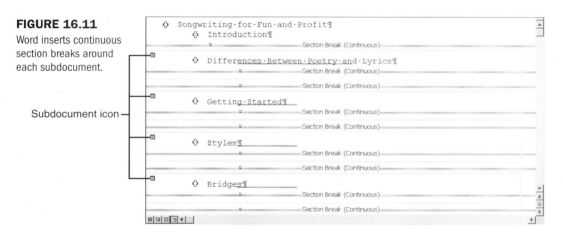

When you want to create cross-references, a documentwide table or index; perform a multifile find-and-replace operation; or otherwise perform an option that applies to all the subdocuments, use Master Document. Editing that applies just to a single subdocument can be done at the subdocument level. Master Documents can be viewed in Normal, Print Layout, Print Preview, Outline, or Master Document view—just like ordinary documents.

While you can work within the Master Document itself, it's often better not to. When focusing on a subdocument, Word is much faster if you work on the subdocument itself, rather than on the Master Document. When you save, for example, just the subdocument gets saved. When scrolling, working with graphics, updating fields, and so on, everything can be handled much more quickly if you don't have the overhead of the entire document in memory at the same time.

Creating a Master Document Using an Existing Document

You can also create a master document using an existing document. You might choose to take this step when a document begins to get too large to manage, or if different individuals need to take responsibility for different document sections.

Creating a Master Document from a document is always simplest if the document uses Heading styles. If it does, simply display the document in Outline view and use the same method described in the previous section. The only difference is that the sections in the existing document will already contain text and other substance.

CAUTION

When you convert an existing document into a Master Document, things sometimes can go wrong. In past versions of Word, the Master Document feature was not 100% reliable (and still does not appear to be 100% reliable), and users sometimes ended up with corrupted and unusable documents. So, if you plan to convert an existing document into a Master Document, make a backup copy of the whole document before you proceed.

If your document does not already use Heading styles, you can simplify your life (and that of your document) by taking the time to establish a heading hierarchy and using Word's built-in heading styles for the heading levels. If that is unfeasible due to document size or other considerations, the next best thing is to use Format, Style, Modify, Format, Paragraph, Outline level and assign whatever heading styles you *do* use to specific outline levels. If you haven't used styles at all, and using them is unfeasible for some reason, you can still use direct paragraph formatting (Format, Paragraph, Outline level), and assign levels to headings you use.

Another possibility is to use Format, AutoFormat and enable Word's AutoFormat feature. Word is sometimes accurate about guessing what your headings are. Depending on the structure of your document, AutoFormat can sometimes save time. Be prepared, however, to choose Edit, Undo.

If, for whatever reason, you cannot rework the document so that it is amenable to outlining, the task of converting it into a master document is a bit more tedious. The following general procedure can be used, however:

1. Open the document, display formatting marks (Ctrl+Shift+*), and switch into Outline view.
2. Click the Master Document View tool.
3. Select the first section you want to make into a subdocument, and click the Create Subdocument tool; make sure you include the final paragraph mark for each section so that subheadings under that section don't get separated.
4. Repeat step 3 for each section.

Creating a Master Document Using Subdocuments

You can also create a Master Document using several existing documents. This sometimes is a useful option when components of a document have been prepared by different authors who cannot, for whatever reason, access the same network. To create a Master Document from existing documents:

1. Create a new blank document to serve as the Master Document.
2. Go into Outline view, and click the Master Document View tool on the Outlining toolbar.
3.  Click the Insert Subdocument icon on the toolbar, to display the Insert Subdocument dialog box shown in Figure 16.12.
4. Select the file you want to insert, and click Open.
5. Repeat steps 3 and 4 for each subdocument you want to include.

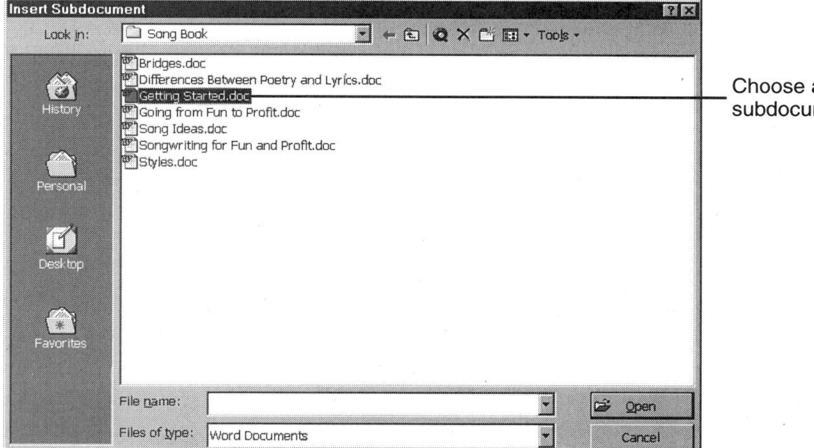

FIGURE 16.12
Word lets you insert only one subdocument at a time.

NOTE When inserting subdocuments, any differently defined styles that have the same name are homogenized according to the styles in the Master Document itself. For example, if the Master Document's definition of Normal includes a single-spaced 12-point Arial, and an incoming document's definition of Normal is double-spaced 10-point Times New Roman, the incoming document will be displayed according to the style definitions in the Master Document (that is, Arial, in this example). Note that the styles in the actual subdocument do not get changed. The override occurs only while displayed in the Master Document. Subdocuments retain their individual properties outside the Master Document.

Working with the Master Document

In many ways, working with a Master Document is like working with any other document, although extra effort is required in setting up a Master Document and ensuring that the formatting is correct when the document is used as a whole. Also, the larger the cumulative components of the Master Document, the slower it's going to be. Even so, the capability to work with components individually—until you need the whole document—provides benefits that make Master Document worth the extra effort.

Before opening Master Document, turn off background repagination unless you absolutely need it (Tools, Options, General). This feature can be a time-saver for small and medium-sized documents. For large documents–especially on slower computers–however, it's a real resource strain.

Formatting the Master Document

Master Document formatting is controlled by the main document itself, not by subdocuments. Proper planning, therefore, is important to ensure that the assembled subdocuments display and print correctly.

As previously noted, when subdocuments are inserted into a Master Document, the formatting of the Master Document takes priority. If the subdocument contains styles that are unique, those styles are added to Master Document's list of styles—just as happens whenever one document is inserted into another. Style dependencies, however, can make unexpected things happen. For example, if a unique style in an incoming subdocument is based on Normal, the Master Document's Normal then becomes the based-on style. This then changes how that unique style appears in the Master Document.

Subtle and not-so-subtle differences in formatting can render tables or other document elements less useful. When you have style-based formatting differences in your subdocuments, you often can save some reformatting time by using the subdocument with the most crucial formatting as the basis for creating your Master Document, rather than starting from scratch.

The easiest way to do this is to open that subdocument and save it under the intended name for the Master Document. Then, delete the contents. This leaves behind existing style definitions. When you use Insert Subdocument to populate the Master Document, the incoming documents will be formatted using familiar styles.

When you save the Master Document, included subdocuments maintain their individual styles.

Even so, it should be clear that if you have a collection of individual files that might someday be merged—either into a single regular file or used as a Master Document—you would be well advised to homogenize formatting as much as possible through proper planning. The following tips can help:

- Whenever possible, base all subdocument components of a given Master Document upon the identical document template (for example, when you plan to insert subdocuments into a Master Document).
- Use styles rigorously.
- Avoid direct formatting (that is, formatting that isn't part of a style's definition).

▶ For more information about Word Styles, **see** "Using Styles, Templates, and Themes," **p. 267**

Printing the Master Document

Printing a Master Document and its components must be performed using the Master Document. When you are working with very long Master Documents and you need only a single subdocument, it's tempting to open and print just the subdocument. However, if you do that, any cross-references, numbering, page numbers, or other dependencies will not be handled correctly. The subdocument will be printed independently of the rest of the Master Document and any other subdocuments. Bookmark references to other subdocuments, for example, will be displayed as error messages. Page numbering will begin with 1, rather than with the relative location in the Master Document.

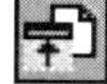

To print a Master Document, you need to open it. A Master Document opens in the same view it was last saved in—Outline view, Master Document view, or Normal view—except that the subdocuments are displayed in collapsed form, as shown in Figure 16.13. Subdocuments are collapsed as underlined links. To toggle the subdocuments into their expanded state, press Ctrl+\. If the Outlining toolbar is displayed, you can click the Expand Subdocuments tool on the toolbar instead.

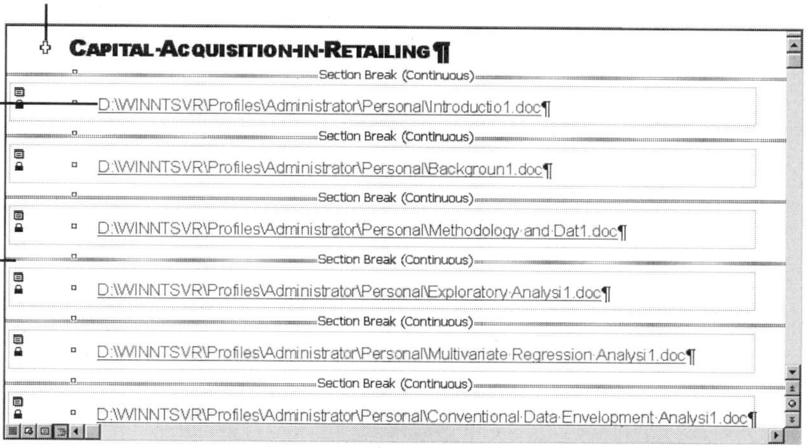

Outline level 1 from Master Document

Collapsed subdocument link

Section break

CAPITAL·ACQUISITION·IN·RETAILING¶
Section Break (Continuous)
D:\WINNTSVR\Profiles\Administrator\Personal\Introductio1.doc¶
Section Break (Continuous)
D:\WINNTSVR\Profiles\Administrator\Personal\Backgroun1.doc¶
Section Break (Continuous)
D:\WINNTSVR\Profiles\Administrator\Personal\Methodology·and·Dat1.doc¶
Section Break (Continuous)
D:\WINNTSVR\Profiles\Administrator\Personal\Exploratory·Analysi1.doc¶
Section Break (Continuous)
D:\WINNTSVR\Profiles\Administrator\Personal\Multivariate·Regression·Analysi1.doc¶
Section Break (Continuous)
D:\WINNTSVR\Profiles\Administrator\Personal\Conventional·Data·Envelopment·Analysi1.doc¶

FIGURE 16.13
Master Documents remember the last saved view, but subdocuments are collapsed.

Recall, also, that Word prints the currently displayed view. If the document is in Outline view, Word will print the outline. So, unless that's what you want, you should switch back into one of the various non-Outline views (Normal, Print Layout, Print Preview, and so on). If this is the first time you've printed the document, you should probably first try File, Print Preview to verify that headers, footers, footnotes, and such are displayed properly.

After the subdocuments have been expanded, the correct view has been chosen, and you've verified correct setup through Print Preview, you can now print the Master Document as you would any other document, by choosing File, Print. If you know all the settings and options are correct, you can, of course, just click the Print tool on the Standard toolbar. However, it often pays not to be in a rush, and to go the Print dialog box route instead. This enables you to choose options that can save you reprinting time and paper, as well as the work of manually sorting a badly collated document or reversed document.

When the Print dialog box is onscreen, click Options and ensure that the following options are enabled, as needed, as shown in Figure 16.14:

- Update fields
- Update links
- Background printing
- Reverse print order (for inkjet printers that stack page 2 on top of page 1, front side up)
- Drawing objects

FIGURE 16.14
Reverse Print Order can be a big manual-labor saver with HP DeskJet printers.

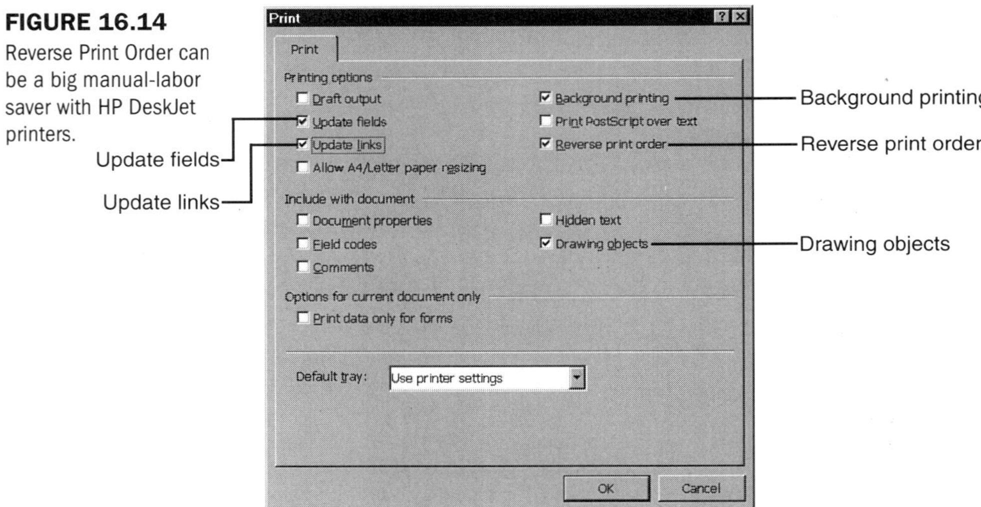

> **CAUTION**
>
> For very large Master Documents, you might be tempted to print without opening the document first. For example, if you choose File, Open and right-click the Master Document, one of the options is Print. What prints, however, is the collapsed view—not the whole document.

Sharing and Protecting Master Documents and Subdocuments

One of the biggest advantages of using Master Documents is that it allows multiple users to access different subdocuments simultaneously. This kind of use requires that the Master Document and all subdocuments be placed into a shared folder that is accessible over a network.

This use also requires a certain amount of care. Certain actions can wreak havoc on a well-crafted Master Document. For example, removing and then re-creating a subdocument the wrong way can create a brand-new file. It can become confusing if you have multiple subdocuments with similar names, especially if users try to edit subdocuments directly, rather than by first opening the Master Document.

Locking and Unlocking the Master Document The Master Document can be locked against editing. Locking happens automatically whenever a file is being edited by any user. For more assured control, however, you can lock the Master Document using the Lock Document tool on the Master Document portion of the Outlining toolbar. Click anywhere in the main part of the Master Document itself—rather than in a subdocument—and click the Lock Document tool. Locking provides the following protection:

- Disables editing in the main part of the Master Document; all access is read-only.
- Disables Create Subdocument.
- Disables Remove Subdocument.
- Disables Insert Subdocument.
- Disables Merge Subdocument.
- Disables Split Subdocument.

With a shared Master Document, it's often a good idea to lock the Master Document to prevent accidental and unauthorized changes to the main document structure. You can also password protect file locking, requiring a password to open or edit the document—or both. Choose Tools, Options, Save tab. In Password to Open, type a password that must be entered to even open the Master Document. In Password to Modify, type a password that must be entered to edit the document, as shown in Figure 16.15.

When you click OK, Word prompts you to reenter any passwords as a protection against the possibility of a typing error.

FIGURE 16.15

Word does not have a built-in way to override passwords.

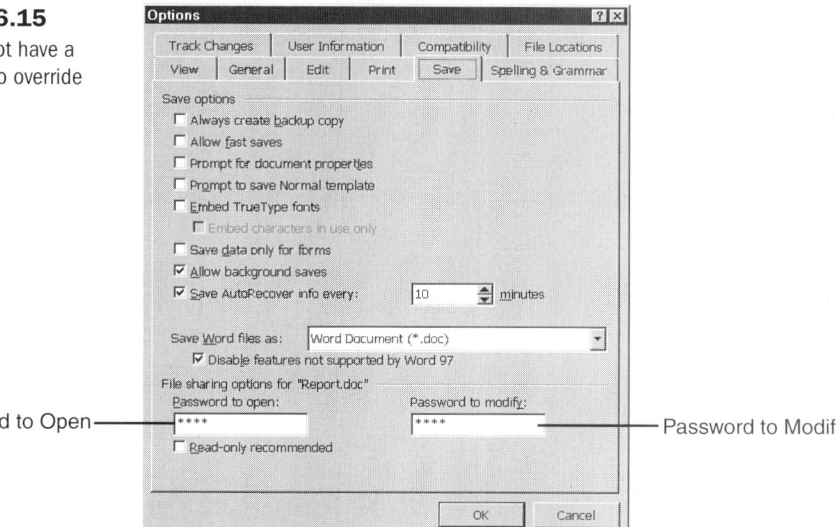

If you password protect the Master Document, you will be prompted to enter the passwords when you open the document. If you provide the Modify password when you open the file, a locked Master Document will automatically be unlocked. If you choose Read Only, shown in Figure 16.16, when the Master Document is opened, and later decide that you do want to make changes, click the Lock Document tool on the Outlining toolbar to toggle protection off, and Word will then prompt you to type the Modify password.

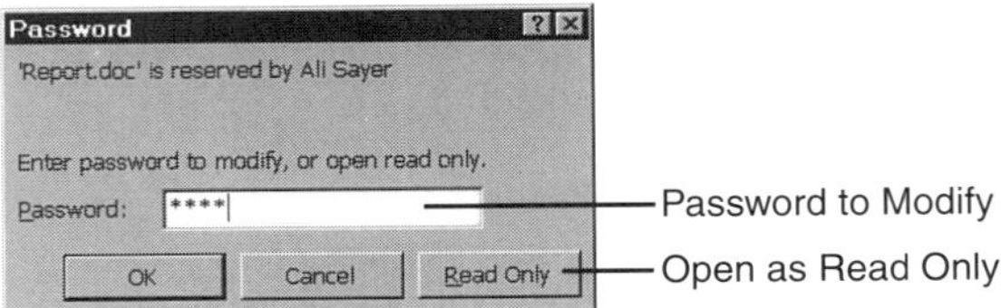

FIGURE 16.16
Leave the password blank and click Read Only to keep protection turned on.

Locking and Unlocking Subdocuments Protection also can be applied to individual subdocuments. When another user is editing a subdocument, it is already locked against write access (that is, the document can be edited in read-only mode, but changes cannot be saved into that file). From the Master Document, you can additionally lock a subdocument so that access is read-only, even if the subdocument is not already in use. This can be a useful option if you want to preserve the state of the document for some reason. Users can then open the subdocument in read-only mode, save the changes to a different file, and then incorporate the changed subdocument at a time that the Master Document is not locked.

To lock an individual subdocument, you must be in Master Document view. Go into Outline view and click the Master Document view tool on the Outlining toolbar. Click the Expand Subdocuments tool to enable the Lock Document tool. Click the subdocument you want to lock, and then click the Lock Document tool.

When a subdocument is locked, a lock appears at the left of the subdocument in Master Document view, as shown in Figure 16.17. Note that when the document is in collapsed form, all subdocuments appear with locks. Note also that when you save and close a Master Document, the individually locked status of any subdocument is not retained. When the Master Document is reopened, it will be in collapsed form, and all subdocuments will be locked. When you expand the subdocuments, however, they are unlocked, including any that might have been locked the last time the document was saved and closed.

You can also apply password protection to subdocuments. However, you must open the subdocument to apply password protection—you cannot password protect a subdocument from within the Master Document. Open the subdocument by double-clicking the subdocument icon at the left edge of the subdocument box, as shown in Figure 16.17. Choose Tools, Options, Save and type the desired Password to Open and Password to Modify, as shown earlier in Figure 16.15. Then save and close the subdocument.

FIGURE 16.17
Lock subdocuments to prevent changes.

With password protection applied to a subdocument, the procedure for accessing a Master Document becomes more complex. When you open the Master Document, you're prompted for any passwords for the Master Document itself. Then, when you go to expand the Master Document, you'll be prompted—one by one—for the passwords for any subdocuments that have passwords associated with them.

Additionally, if you attempt to unlock a passworded subdocument, Word will prompt you for the passwords. All this might seem a bit too cloak-and-dagger to some users. However, to anybody who has ever had a Master Document ruined by inappropriate or untimely editing, ample protection can be reassuring.

CAUTION

Don't be too reassured. Password-breaking software often is as close as the Internet for many users. At best, Word's password protection makes meddling inconvenient, but not impossible. Ultimately, protection can be assured only by having trustworthy employees and coworkers, a secure network, and careful attention to procedures.

Including Page and Chapter Numbers in the Master Document

Page and chapter numbers can be controlled from the Master Document, individual subdocuments, or both. When viewed from the Master Document standpoint, each subdocument occupies a distinct section in the document, separated by section breaks. As such, the same capabilities apply to the sections of a Master Document as apply to the sections of other Word documents.

If subdocuments don't specify their own headers and footers, any headers and footers in the main body of the Master Document itself take control. For example, if you use Heading 2 for the titles of subdocuments (chapters), and if you use numbering in the definition for Heading 2

(Format, Style, Heading 2, Modify, Format, Numbering), then you can create page numbers that use chapters in the numbering as follows:

1. With the insertion point at the beginning of the Master Document, choose View, Header and Footer.
2. On the Header and Footer toolbar, click Insert Page Number; then click Format Page Number.
3. Click to check Include Chapter Number; set Chapter Starts with Style to Heading 2 (assuming that's the style associated with the title for each chapter or subdocument).
4. Choose the desired separator and start number (use Start at 1 to have numbering begin afresh in each chapter).
5. Click OK.

Alternatively, you can create separate headers and footers for different sections, for example, whether you want text in the header or footer.

If you want to include the chapter name in headers or footers, you might not need to use separate headers and footers. Use the StyleRef field. For example, the field {StyleRef "Heading 2"} displays the most recent occurrence of text formatted as Heading 2.

▶ **See** "Document Sections," **p. 304**

Using Subdocuments with a Master Document

The key reason for using Master Documents is that it gives you additional leverage in dealing with long documents. When used with styled heading levels, the Master Document gives you the same organizing strength of outlining, but additional power in letting the overall document be worked on in smaller, more manageable chunks, by a single user or by multiple users.

Opening Subdocuments

You can open a subdocument in a variety of ways. All are appropriate depending on your work style:

- Open a subdocument as a normal document using File, Open.
- Open a recently used subdocument from the file list at the bottom of the File menu.
- Open a subdocument by double-clicking the subdocument icon in expanded Master Document view.
- Open a subdocument by clicking its hyperlink in collapsed view (for example, when the Master Document is first opened).

Subdocuments can be open for normal editing or in read-only mode. Open in read-only mode when you just need to see what's in it. Making unintended changes that have unforeseen repercussions is often all too easy. With a set of documents that is so heavily interdependent, you need to exercise caution.

In expanded Master Document view, if a subdocument is locked, it must be unlocked before you can open it for normal editing. Click the subdocument you want to open, and then click the Lock Document toggle on the Outlining toolbar.

Reordering the Subdocuments

Word's Help file describes a method for reordering subdocuments. Basically, you display the document in Master Document view, with subdocuments expanded. Then you use the Subdocument icon as a handle for dragging the subdocument where you want it. This method works—sort of—assuming you don't actually use section breaks for anything.

The problem is that this method does not take the section breaks with the moved subdocuments. As a result, if you have distinct headers or footers with special numbering or text, those headers and footers—which are attached to the section break immediately following each subdocument—are left behind.

A more certain method is to select the entire subdocument, as well as the section break that follows, cut it, and then paste it into the new location. Alternatively, you could save the changes to the subdocument you want to move, delete the entire subdocument from the Master Document, and then insert the subdocument in an alternative location. To delete a subdocument:

1. Switch into Master Document view.
2. Click in the selection bar area to select the entire subdocument you want to delete, and press the Delete key. Note that if the document is displayed in collapsed view, you cannot use Cut.
3. Move to where you want the subdocument to be.
4. Click Insert Subdocument on the Outlining toolbar and re-insert the subdocument at the new location.

CAUTION

How not to move subdocuments—don't use the outline Move Up and Move Down commands. They will move the heading, but will not move the subdocument structure. Suppose, for example, that all chapters of a 20-chapter book are divided into subdocuments. If you use Move Down to try to move chapter 10 to between old Chapters 15 and 16, the chapter will indeed move. However, the first press of the Move Down key removes the subdocument from the structure, and moves the content that *was* in the subdocument down into the next subdocument, or between existing subdocuments, depending on the outline level that's displayed.

Splitting and Merging Subdocuments

Sometimes it is useful to subdivide or to combine subdocuments. Responsibilities change, documents get reorganized—whatever the reason, the Outlining toolbar provides tools to do both.

Splitting Subdocuments The Master Document must be unlocked to split subdocuments; the subdocuments you want to split must be unlocked as well. You also need to be in Master Document view with subdocuments expanded. Setting the outline level so that you can see where you want to make the splits is useful.

To divide an existing subdocument into additional subdocuments, move the insertion point to where you want to make the split, and click the Split Subdocument tool. The split occurs at the insertion point. Beyond the simple mechanics, however, there are steps you can take to make the job of formatting the new subdocuments easier.

When splitting off a new subdocument, it's often useful to create headings that are parallel to the existing top levels for other subdocuments. Suppose that the top level for subdocuments currently is Heading 2, and you want to create new Heading 2s out of existing Heading 3s. For example, you might have a chapter that discusses Regression, and is divided into Heading 3 divisions for Analysis and Results, as shown in Figure 16.18.

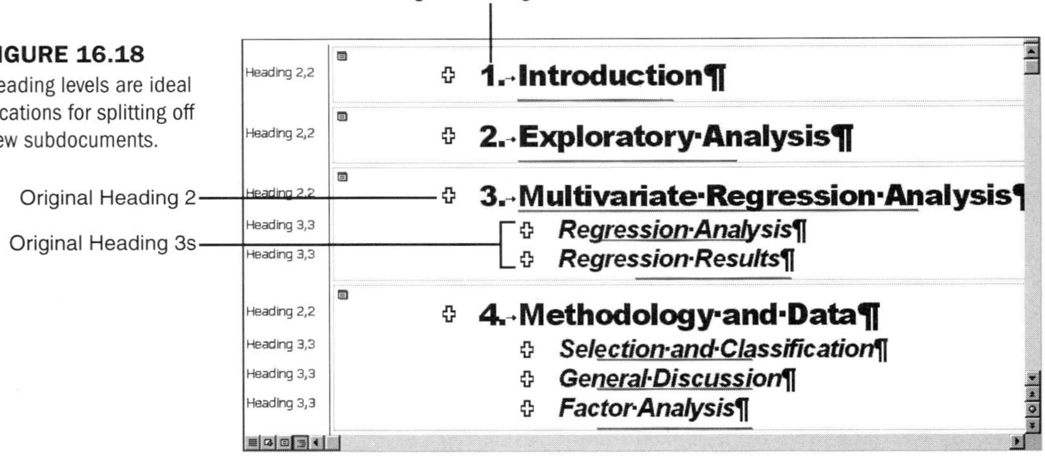

FIGURE 16.18
Heading levels are ideal locations for splitting off new subdocuments.

Now, you want a new Heading 2 for Analysis and a new Heading 2 for Results. In the Outline or Master Document view, find the first Heading 3, and Promote (Alt+Shift+Left) it to Heading 2. Do the same for the other Heading 3, which gives you what you see in Figure 16.19.

Next, move the insertion point to just in front of the first heading you want to split off, and click the Split Subdocument tool. Do the same for each heading you want split off. The result might appear as shown in Figure 16.20. At this point, depending on the structure of the text, you might need to do additional housekeeping. For example, you have the leftover introductory material from the old top level (the original heading). You need to think about whether the new subdocuments can stand alone or whether you might want to divide the old introductory text. More importantly, however, you now have additional section breaks to deal with. Deleting any unnecessary section breaks is generally a good idea; that is, one section break between chapters or subdocuments generally is adequate.

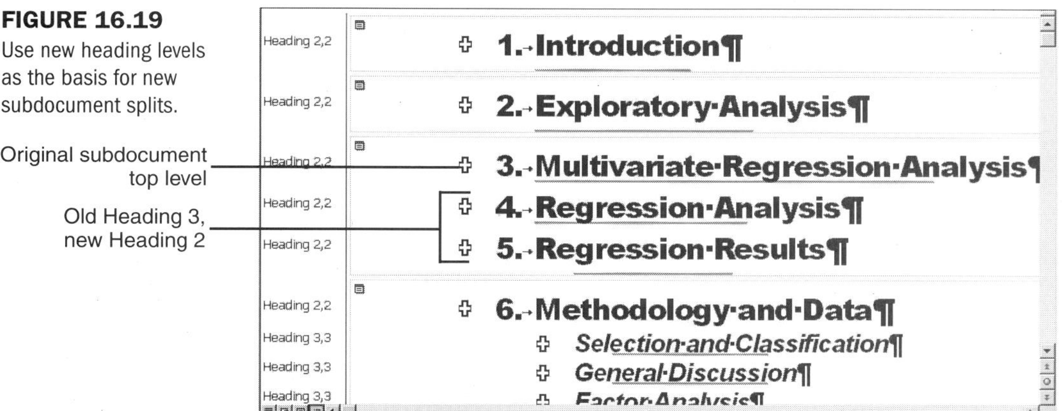

FIGURE 16.19
Use new heading levels as the basis for new subdocument splits.

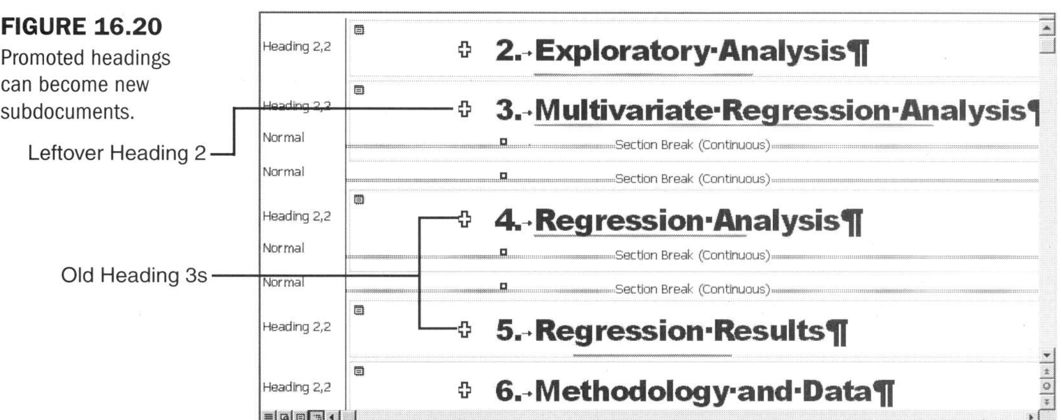

FIGURE 16.20
Promoted headings can become new subdocuments.

Merging (Combining) Subdocuments Merging subdocuments requires that the Master Document and subdocuments be unlocked. The Master Document also needs to be in Master Document view with subdocuments expanded. The general procedure is

1. Move the subdocuments so that they are adjacent to each other in the document.
2. Select the subdocuments you want to merge.
3. Click the Merge Subdocument tool on the Outlining toolbar.

CAUTION

Frustration alert! Trying to merge subdocuments is a real hair-pulling nightmare for some users. Whereas Word has a variety of ways to select parts of documents, the Merge Subdocument tool is extremely picky about what it takes before it enables you to merge.

The trick is in knowing how to select the subdocuments to make the Merge Subdocument tool available. You cannot select the subdocuments by dragging the mouse pointer over them. The Merge Subdocument tool becomes available only if the subdocuments are selected in a particular way.

Click the mouse on the first subdocument icon to select that subdocument. Now, hold down the Shift key and click the last subdocument icon to select the series. For example, if you have three subdocuments you want to merge, click the first, and then Shift+click the third. This then selects the group, as shown in Figure 16.21, making the Merge Subdocument tool come to life.

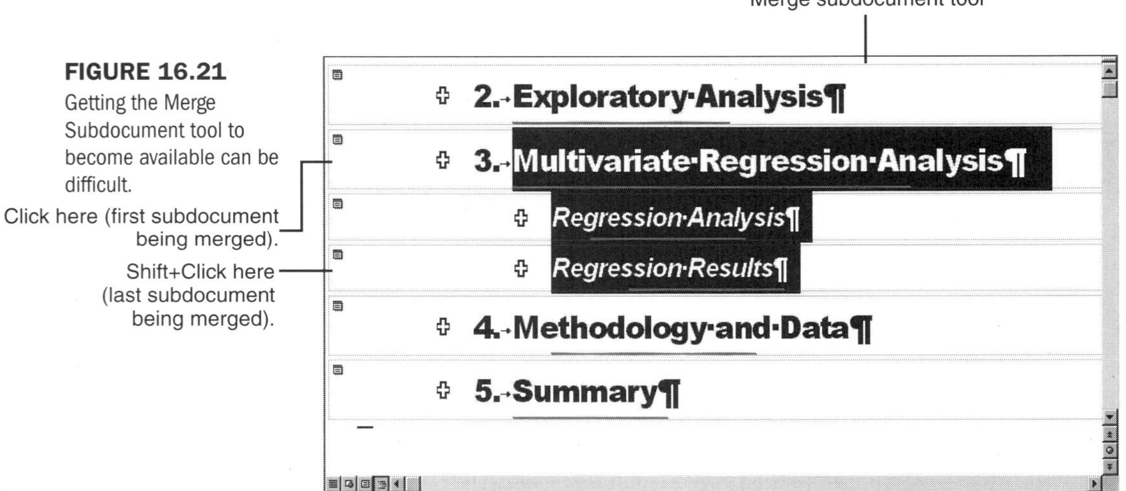

FIGURE 16.21 Getting the Merge Subdocument tool to become available can be difficult.

Removing Subdocuments

Sometimes it's useful to convert subdocuments back into Master Document text. You might want to do this, for example, if the need for having a Master Document has been served.

NOTE Some users find the term *removing* a subdocument a bit of a misnomer, and confuse it with *deleting* a subdocument. You're not actually removing the subdocument. Rather, you're changing its status from subdocument to actually being part of the Master Document. Removing subdocuments is also what you would do to convert a Master Document back into a regular document. To delete a subdocument, just select it and press the Delete key.

Removing subdocuments requires that the Master Document and subdocuments be unlocked. The Master Document also needs to be in Master Document view with subdocuments expanded. To remove a subdocument, click anywhere inside the subdocument and click the Remove Subdocument tool on the Outlining toolbar. The subdocument icon at the left end of the subdocument disappears, and the subdocument becomes part of the Master Document.

CAUTION

Just as removing a subdocument doesn't delete the subdocument from the Master Document, it doesn't delete it from the hard drive, either. After subdocument removal, the files corresponding to removed subdocuments remain on the drive. Some users keep them for backup purposes, while others prefer to delete them to get rid of clutter and prevent future confusion. Having leftover subdocument files can also make naming more complicated if you later need to reconvert removed subdocuments back into subdocuments. The presence of similarly named items not only is confusing, but also means that Word's automatic naming mechanism will add a number to newly created subdocuments.

Renaming Subdocuments

The process of removing and re-creating subdocuments often leaves you with subdocument names that have numbers. In cleaning up clutter and trying to improve organization, users sometimes prefer different names. For example, you might prefer your chapters to be named chapter1, chapter2, and so on rather than the names Word picks based on the first few words of a subdocument.

CAUTION

Do not use the Windows Explorer or other tools to rename subdocuments. If you do, Master Document will no longer be able to find the subdocuments.

To rename a subdocument, display the Master Document in Master Document view, with subdocuments collapsed (that is, so they display as hyperlinks). Unlock Master Document, if necessary. Click the link you want to change; this will open the subdocument for editing. Choose File, Save As, and give the subdocument a new name; then close the subdocument. When you return to the Master Document, the new name now appears as the hyperlink.

NOTE The subdocument file now exists under both old and new names. Delete the old file to avoid clutter and confusion.

Assembling a Large Document from Individual Files

The Master Document is one way to maintain a large document using individual files; but it's not the only way. If the Master Document approach doesn't fit your needs, an alternative is to use the `INCLUDETEXT` field.

NOTE When including individual files in a document, styles in the main document take precedence. For built-in styles, the definitions in the main document are used. Any user-created styles in the individual files are imported into the main document. If there are duplicate user-created styles, Word will offer to rename the incoming styles using numbers. For example, if the included document and the main document both have a style named WebText, Word will either use the main document's WebText style for incoming text that uses that style, or will offer to rename the incoming style as WebText2.

To include an individual file in a document, move the insertion point to where you want the document to appear. Choose Insert, File to display the Insert File dialog box, shown in Figure 16.22.

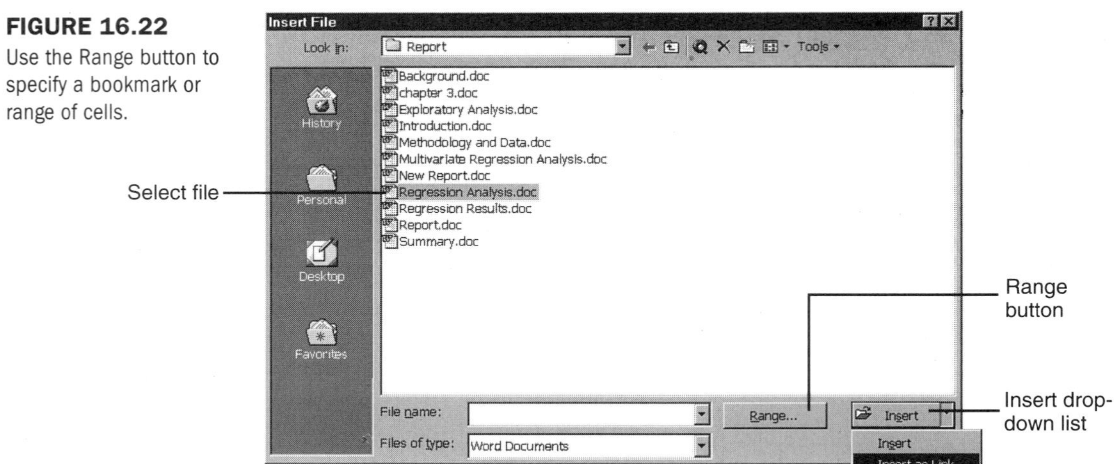

FIGURE 16.22
Use the Range button to specify a bookmark or range of cells.

Navigate to the location of the file you want to insert and select it. Click the Range button, if desired, to specify a bookmark or range of cells (for example, if the file is coming from Excel), as shown in Figure 16.23.

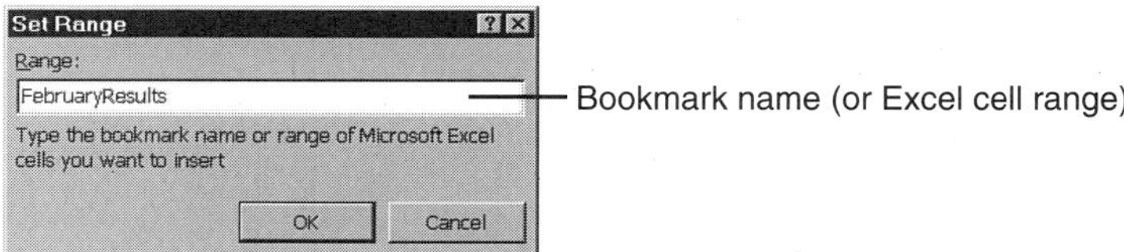

FIGURE 16.23
Range lets you select a part of the linked document.

Back in the Insert File dialog box, click the Insert drop-down list and choose Insert as Link to insert a link to the file, as shown previously in Figure 16.22. Or, if you simply want to merge the incoming file into the current document—rather than maintaining the file separately as a link—just click Insert.

Keep Field Shading Enabled

When working with inserted links—especially if field shading is not enabled (Tools, Options, View, Field Shading)—it's possible to sometimes forget that you're looking at a link rather than at actual text. In fact, you can make editing changes to a linked file.

However, the next time that link is updated, any changes you make will be replaced by the original contents of the linked file.

There is a solution. Actually, there are several solutions. One, of course, is to enable field shading as a reminder not to edit links from within the main document.

If you forget, however, there's a really easy solution: Ctrl+Shift+F7 (Update Source). When you press Ctrl+Shift+F7, any changes made to the link are written back into the actual linked file. Conceptually, this is the opposite of F9 (Update Fields), which instead updates what you see with the information in the linked file.

Numbering Pages and Chapters in Individual Files

When you include one Word document in another document—the document itself or a link to it—all formatting is controlled by the main document. This includes headers and footers where page numbers are stored.

If you need to maintain different page number styles in linked documents, however, you can do it. It just takes a little bit of effort, and you can't actually use the page numbers that are stored in the separate files.

Unlike subdocuments in Master Documents, when you insert a link to a file (using Insert, File), Word does not automatically insert section breaks. However, that's the key. Usually, it's easiest to insert section breaks before inserting the file—especially if the file is long—and then insert the file between the breaks.

You would choose Insert, Break from the menu, and choose the type of section break you want. For distinct headers, footers, and page numbering, use Next Page. You can press F4 (Repeat) to insert the second break. Then, click at the beginning of the second break, choose Insert, File, and insert the file or link. After this is done, setting up page numbers is identical to other section formatting, as explained in Chapter 11, "Making the Most of Your Page Layout."

▶ **See** "Document Sections," **p. 304**

Using Tables of Contents, Indexes, and Endnotes with Large Documents

For compilation documents—documents that consist of other linked documents—the basic procedures described in Chapter 15, "Features Used with Complex Documents," can be used. The main point to remember is that within the main document, with all parts displayed, that main document itself forms an integral whole. At any time, you have the option of unlinking any or all linked documents by selecting the link and pressing Ctrl+Shift+F9 (Unlink). The results you get will not be any different. Formatting in the main document controls how any linked subdocuments are displayed.

Table of Contents One option for creating a table of contents in a compilation document is to treat it as any other document. You can use built-in heading styles and/or custom heading styles—assuming that those styles are used in all the component documents—and use the techniques described in Chapter 15. Or, you can mark headings manually and again use standard techniques described in Chapter 15.

▶ **See** "Creating Tables of Contents and Similar Tables," **p. 442**

Alternatively, you can use a single file to compile a table of contents, as shown in Chapter 15.

▶ **See** "Creating a Table of Contents for a Multifile Document," **p. 447**

Indexes To create an index for a compilation document—including a Master Document—the Master Document itself must be displayed (not just a subdocument). This is essential for page references to be correct. Aside from this precaution, the indexing techniques and procedures described in Chapter 15 apply to multifile documents.

▶ **See** "Creating an Index," **p. 463**

Endnotes and Footnotes Endnotes and footnotes in linked individual-file components of a multifile document are handled as part of the flow of the whole document. You can number footnotes or endnotes separately within each section (choose Insert, Footnote, Options, and choose Restart Each Section, as shown in Figure 16.24). However, you can't have different numbering styles (for example, a mixture of Arabic and Roman numbering) within the same main document—even if the individual file components specify different numbering.

▶ **See** "Footnotes and Endnotes," **p. 471**

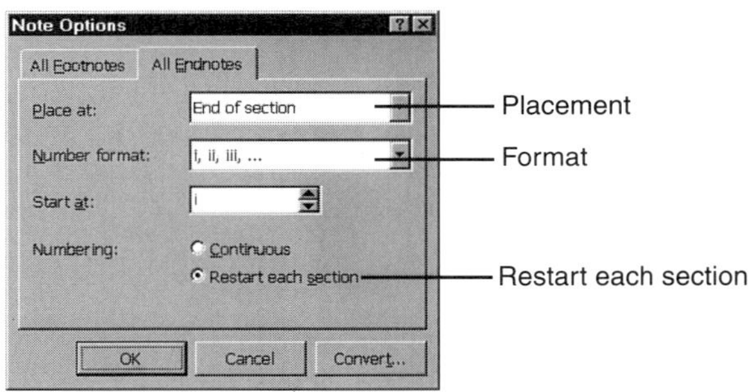

FIGURE 16.24
You can change footnote and endnote options without inserting a note.

CHAPTER 17

Advanced Mail Merge Features

In this chapter

Understanding How Mail Merge Works

The Mail Merge feature in Word enables you to create form letters, address envelopes, print labels, and create such items as catalogs and lists.

When writing form letters, memos, or other documents, it is often necessary to tailor each copy to suit the needs of every individual or group. If only a few people are going to be receiving a copy, very little time and energy is expended on manually editing the original document. However, in instances where two or three hundred people will receive a copy, it becomes a laborious task. With Word's Mail Merge capabilities, the workload is significantly reduced.

With Mail Merge, you can create form letters that contain conditional text that may be included in some letters but not in others. An additional Mail Merge feature facilitates creating catalogs and price lists that contain different information (such as prices or services) according to the areas or regions to which they are sent.

The use of Mail Merge requires two documents: the main document and the data source. The main document, or form letter, contains a set of fixed text that appears on all documents. In addition, any form letter may also contain text or fields specific to the individual copies of the document, such as name, address, and title. A second file, the data source, contains a database that will be used to merge information to the fields within the main document. The mail merge process can range from simple to complex. Let's begin by considering one of the simplest. Suppose your company is sending out a thank-you letter to each customer according to the item or service they have purchased. Figure 17.1 shows an example of such a letter.

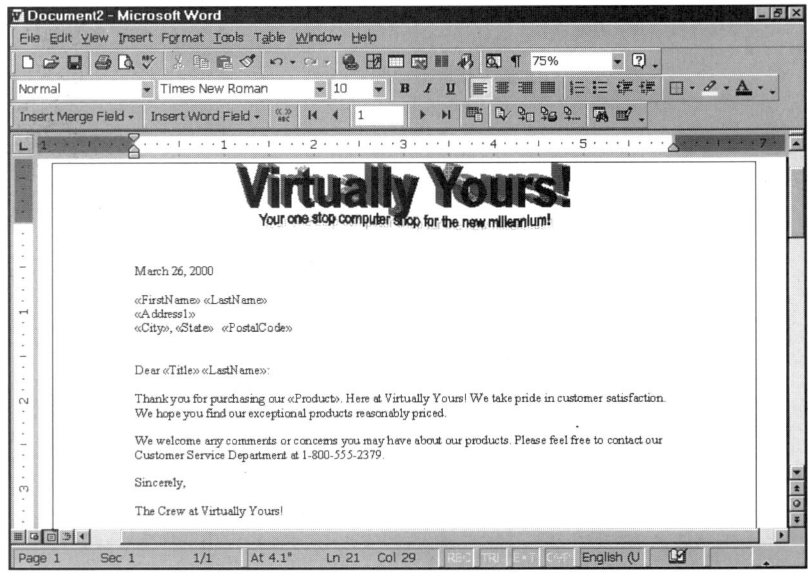

FIGURE 17.1
The main document contains text common to all merged documents and the field codes representing any unique data.

The letter contains eight fields specific to each person who receives the letter: The person's title (that is, Ms., Mrs., Mr., Dr.), their first name, last name, address, city, state, postal code, and the product purchased.

The Main Document

The main document (in this case, a form letter) contains all common text to be included in all the merged documents. In addition, a placeholder (or field code) represents any text unique to each letter. The letter shown earlier in Figure 17.1 actually contains eight field codes: <<Title>>,<<FirstName>> <<LastName>>, <<Address1>>, <<City>>, <<State>>, <<PostalCode>>, and <<Product>>. When the merged documents are created, the field codes are hidden, and the data they represent is displayed.

NOTE Word automatically encloses field names within chevrons (<< >>). It is not necessary to type these manually.

Figure 17.2 shows the Mail Merge main document with the field codes in chevrons. Unique values from a separate file, the data source, replace any field code text upon completion of the merge.

FIGURE 17.2
Mail Merge allows you to create a form letter that can be personalized for every individual.

Virtually Yours!
Your one stop computer shop for the new millennium!

March 26, 2000

«FirstName» «LastName»
«Address1»
«City», «State» «PostalCode»

Dear «Title» «LastName»:

Thank you for purchasing our «Product». Here at Virtually Yours! We take pride in customer satisfaction. We hope you find our exceptional products reasonably priced.

We welcome any comments or concerns you may have about our products. Please feel free to contact our Customer Service Department at 1-800-555-2379.

Sincerely,

The Crew at Virtually Yours!

The Data Source

A *data source* is a database table containing actual values to be substituted for the field codes in the main document.

One of the easiest data sources to use is a Word table, such as the one shown in Figure 17.3. This table contains eight columns, one for each field code in the main document. The first row of the table contains the names of the field codes—the header row. Each subsequent row contains information for individual merge documents.

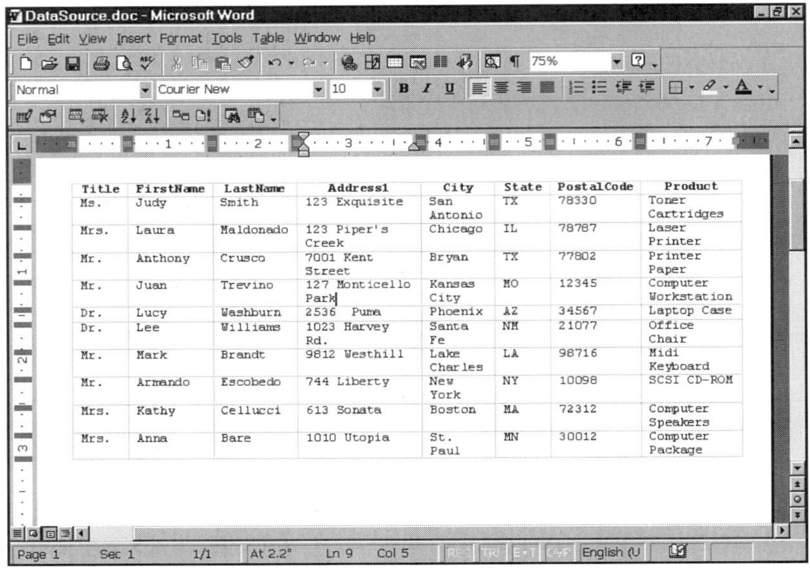

DataSource.doc - Microsoft Word

Title	FirstName	LastName	Address1	City	State	PostalCode	Product
Ms.	Judy	Smith	123 Exquisite	San Antonio	TX	78330	Toner Cartridges
Mrs.	Laura	Maldonado	123 Piper's Creek	Chicago	IL	78787	Laser Printer
Mr.	Anthony	Crusco	7001 Kent Street	Bryan	TX	77802	Printer Paper
Mr.	Juan	Trevino	127 Monticello Park	Kansas City	MO	12345	Computer Workstation
Dr.	Lucy	Washburn	2536 Puma	Phoenix	AZ	34567	Laptop Case
Dr.	Lee	Williams	1023 Harvey Rd.	Santa Fe	NM	21077	Office Chair
Mr.	Mark	Brandt	9812 Westhill	Lake Charles	LA	98716	Midi Keyboard
Mr.	Armando	Escobedo	744 Liberty	New York	NY	10098	SCSI CD-ROM
Mrs.	Kathy	Cellucci	613 Sonata	Boston	MA	72312	Computer Speakers
Mrs.	Anna	Bare	1010 Utopia	St. Paul	MN	30012	Computer Package

FIGURE 17.3
Mail Merge creates one merge document for each row in the data source table.

NOTE Mail Merge always creates only one document. The form letters that result may print as separate documents, and even function that way; however, they are in fact saved as one file.

TIP The data source table can be created through the mail merge dialog box or by using a previously created Word table.

▶ **See** "Unleashing the Potential of Tables," **p. 377**

Using the Mail Merge Wizard

To begin a mail merge, open a new Word document and choose Tools, Mail Merge. This opens the Mail Merge Helper Wizard shown in Figure 17.4.

Here is an example of how to use the wizard. Assume you're creating a form letter from scratch and have not yet created the main document or data source:

1. After opening the Mail Merge Helper Wizard dialog box, click Create. The wizard offers you a choice among Form Letters, Mailing Labels, Envelopes, and Catalog as shown in Figure 17.5. Choose Form Letters.
2. A pop-up window appears, giving you the choice of using the current document or a new Word document as your main document. If the Word document is already blank, click Active Window. Otherwise, you would click New Main Document. The pop-up disappears.

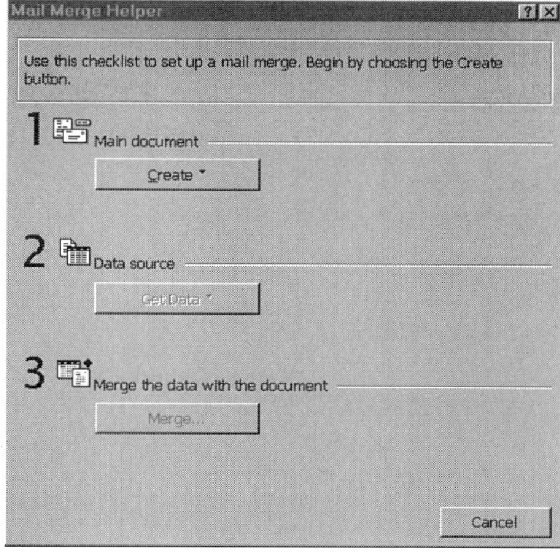

FIGURE 17.4
The Mail Merge Helper Wizard leads you through the three steps of creating Mail Merge documents.

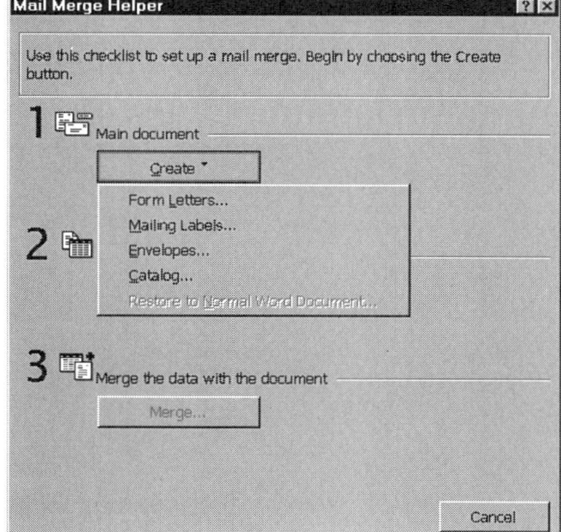

FIGURE 17.5
Mail Merge enables you to create Form letters, Mailing Labels, Envelopes, or Catalogs through the Create option.

3. Back in the Mail Merge Helper dialog box, you must now decide on the data source. Click Get Data. The wizard offers a choice between Create Data Source, Open Data Source, Use Address Book, and Header Options (see Figure 17.6). To create a Word table as your data source, click Create Data Source. The Wizard now leads you through creating the Word table that will become the fields and data for your main document.
4. The wizard displays the Create Data source dialog box in which you can choose any of 13 predefined field names or even create your own (see Figure 17.7). Follow the instructions in the dialog box to create a data source that contains the fields you require. Note the MS Query button in this dialog box. See Chapter 24 to learn more about creating a query to extract data from a database to use as your data source.

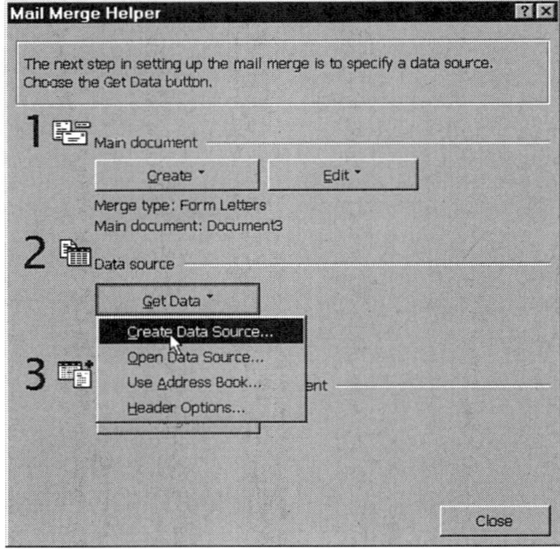

FIGURE 17.6
Mail merge allows you to merge your main document with a variety of data sources.

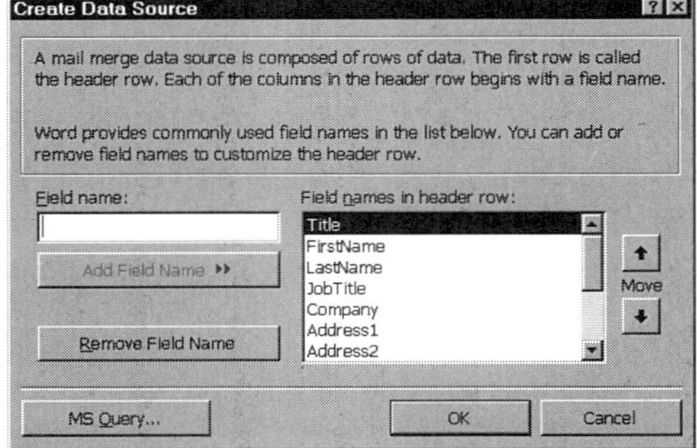

FIGURE 17.7
You can choose from 13 predefined field names or create your own for your data source document.

NOTE Field names can contain up to 40 characters, the first of which must be a letter. Subsequent characters may be letters, numbers, or the underscore character. There can be no spaces in the field names.

5. When you click OK to indicate you have finished defining the source document's fields, the wizard displays a Save As dialog box. Name the data source and save it as a Word document.
6. After you save the data source, a pop-up appears asking whether you want to edit the data source or edit the main document. Click Edit Data Source. The wizard displays the Data Form dialog box (shown in Figure 17.8) in which you enter data for the first merged letter. After you have completed the data for the first record, click Add New to add data for the second merged letter. Continue to add new records to the data source in this manner until you have entered data for several letters. You do not have to finalize the data at this time. It may be edited or added to later if necessary.

FIGURE 17.8
Use Word's Data Form to enter data into a Data Source Document.

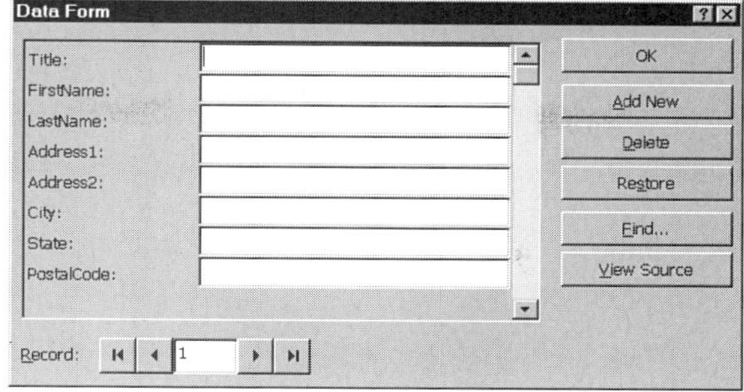

NOTE The data in each field can contain up to 255 characters.

7. Click OK to indicate that you have finished entering data. The wizard opens a new Word document with the Mail Merge toolbar displayed as shown in Figure 17.9. You are now ready to create the main document. The Mail Merge toolbar buttons will be grayed out until you insert your first merge field.

FIGURE 17.9
The Mail Merge toolbar contains 15 buttons to help you create merge documents.

Mail Merge toolbar

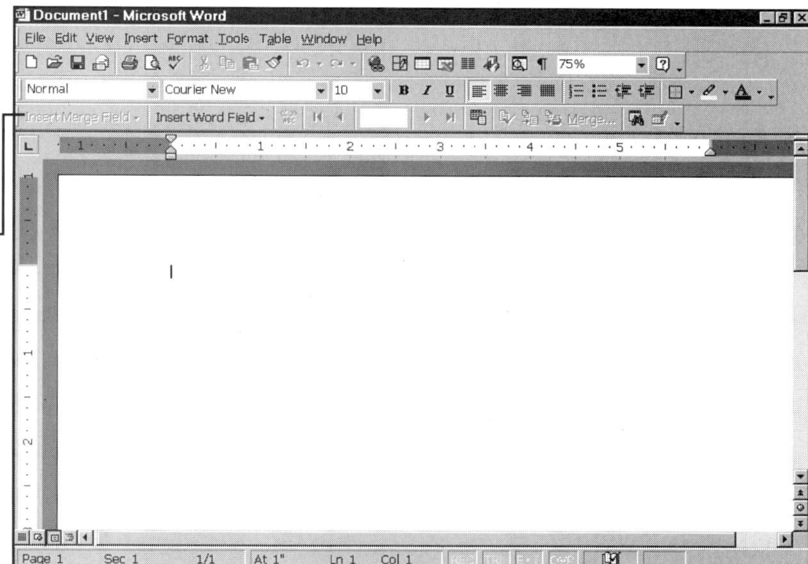

Creating the Main Document

A *main document* is the form letter or document you want to create and duplicate. The main document is similar to any other type of document with the exception of text, such as names or addresses, which may be customized for every document. To allow for customization, a main document contains field codes wherever text unique to each letter will be inserted from records contained in a data source document. The main document contains three types of elements:

- Items that appear in every copy of the letter, including characters you type, as well as imported, embedded, and linked items.
- Field codes that indicate where data from your data source should be placed.
- Word fields that control actions that happen during the merge process.

For the moment, consider only the first two elements.

Start typing the main document. When you come to a place where data from the data source should appear, click the Insert Merge Field drop-down button on the Mail Merge toolbar. This displays a list of fields from your data source from which you can choose. The field name, enclosed by chevrons, appears in the document.

If you see something similar to {MERGEFIELD FirstName}, instead of a field name enclosed by chevrons, press Alt+F9 or Shift+F9 to revert to the field name rather than the code.

Continue to create the main document, stopping each time to insert a merge field where necessary. Remember to insert any spaces or necessary punctuation between field codes. For example, you might want the resulting form letter to have a space between fields inserted consecutively such as between <<Title>> and <<LastName>>. Refer to Figure 17.2 for an example of a completed Mail Merge main document.

To see what the individual merge documents will look like, click the Check for Errors button on the Mail Merge toolbar. Word offers you the choice to

- Simulate the merge and report errors in a new document.
- Complete the merge, pausing to report each error as it occurs.
- Complete the merge without pausing, reporting errors in a new document.

The second of these, which you would normally use, is the default. Click OK to proceed. If there are no errors, word displays all your form letters in one document. A section break separates each letter from the next.

Switch back to the mail merge main document. To print the merged documents, click the Merge to Printer button in the Mail Merge toolbar.

Now that you've gone through a simple example to learn how mail merge works, take a more in-depth look at the mail merge process.

Using an Existing Document As a Mail Merge Main Document

You don't necessarily have to create all main documents and data sources from scratch. Quite often, you'll already have a document you want to convert to a Mail Merge main document. In addition, you may already have an address list, database, or spreadsheet you would like to use as a data source.

Preparing an Existing Document

Suppose you've previously written a document (such as a letter) and now you decide to use Mail Merge to personalize that letter for several individuals. Examine the document and make sure any element being personalized is clearly marked. Although it isn't necessary, it's sometimes helpful to replace these elements with a character set that won't actually print on the final letters. I use $$$$$. For example, if the original document starts with *Dear John,* I replace it with *Dear $$$$$*. This helps save time later when identifying locations for field code insertion.

Before continuing, ensure that you have your data source available by choosing Tools, Mail Merge. You should see the path for your data source listed under "Data Source." If not, click the Get Data button to display a drop-down list. Choose your data source type from the list.

▶ **See** "Creating a Data Source," if you do not have a data source already created; **p. 517**

Placing Field Codes in the Main Document

To place the field codes in a document you will be using as the main document, you need to access the Mail Merge Wizard. Choose Tools, Mail Merge to display the Mail Merge Helper Wizard dialog box. Click Create, Form Letters, Active Window to indicate that you are using the existing document as your form letter.

After you return to the Mail Merge Helper dialog box, choose Get Data, Open data Source. In the Open Data Source dialog box, select the existing data source and choose Open. The wizard automatically adds the Mail Merge toolbar to the original Word document. At this point, if you have not already added any merge fields to the document, Word alerts you to the fact that there are no merge fields in the main document. Click Edit Main Document to continue.

Now you are ready to add field codes to the main document. Move the insertion point to where you would like to place the first field code, click the Insert Merge Field drop-down button on the mail Merge toolbar and choose a field code from the list. Continue through the main document, inserting field codes wherever necessary. If you previously marked every place where field codes are needed, you should find them easily. When you have finished, click the Check for Errors button on the Mail Merge toolbar to see the merged documents and troubleshoot any problems.

Creating a Data Source

There are many ways to create a data source. The following sections describe several of these.

NOTE By default, Mail Merge creates one merge document for each record in the data source in that same order. For Form Letters, Mailing Labels, and Envelopes, each record is placed in a section. For Catalogs, all records are placed in the same section, one after the other. As explained in the section "Selecting Records in a Data Source" later in this chapter, you can select particular records from the source as well as reorder the way those records are used by Mail Merge. ■

Using a Word Table As a Data Source

When using the Mail Merge Wizard to create a main document from scratch, you are guided through a series of steps to create a Word table. Instead of following this process, you can create a Word table separately, or use one that already exists.

Without going into too much detail about creating a Word table, I'll provide you with a few hints. A Word table used as a Mail Merge data source has one column for each field code to be inserted into the main document. Usually, the top row of the table contains the names of the field codes; this is called the *header row*. Although a header is not necessary, it helps identify the fields and their purpose. Other rows of the table contain the data that replaces the field codes in each merged document. Do not be concerned with column widths and the way words wrap within the cells of the table. Be sure, however, that there are no spaces or text above the table and that there are no blank rows either above or throughout the table.

▶ **See** "Unleashing the Potential of Tables," **p. 377**

Unlike a Word table created by the Mail Merge Wizard, a table you create this way can contain spaces in the field code names, and the field code names can be longer than 40 characters. Word automatically changes each space in field code names to an underscore character when the table is accessed as a Mail Merge data source and any field names longer than 40 characters are automatically truncated to the 40-character limit in the Insert Merge Field option.

Save the table as a Word document. If you are using a table that already exists within a document, copy the table into a separate document and then save it. By default, Mail Merge assumes the top row of a Word table contains the names of the field codes. This row is known as the header row. You can, however, use a table that does not contain a header row—as long as you create a separate header file. This file consists of a table with only one row that contains field code names in the same order as the data in the source table.

NOTE If several people use the same table as a data source, they might prefer a table with no header row. Then they are each free to use any field names they want in their main documents.

To use a Word table that already contains a header row as your data source, access the Mail Merge Helper (Tools, Mail Merge). Then choose Get Data, Open Data Source. If the header information is stored in a separate file, you need to identify the header file before you identify the data source:

1. In the Mail Merge Helper, choose Get Data, Header Options, Open.
2. In the Open Header Source dialog box, select the header file and click Open.
3. Choose Get Data, Open Data Source, select the data source file, and click Open.

This process relates the columns in your data source table to the columns in the header file.

Using an Access Table As a Data Source

Sometimes your data source may be a non-Word document, such as an Access Database table. The steps involved in using an Access table as a data source are similar to those for a Word table. In the Mail Merge Helper, choose Get Data, Open Data Source. At the bottom of the Open Data Source dialog box, click the Files of Type drop-down list and select MS Access Databases (*.mdb) as shown in Figure 17.10. Navigate to and choose the Access file that contains your data source, and then choose Open. After a short delay, the Microsoft Access dialog box opens, displaying a list of tables (and queries, if any) in the selected file. Choose the table you want to use and click OK. Click Close to close the Mail Merge Helper wizard dialog box.

FIGURE 17.10
The Open Data Source dialog box allows for using non-Word files as data sources.

In the Mail Merge main document, click the Insert Merge Field button on the Mail Merge toolbar; you should see a list of the field names in the Access table. You can insert these field names as field codes in the main document.

Using an Excel Worksheet As a Data Source

Whereas an Access file contains tables, an Excel file contains worksheets and ranges. Unless the data source you want to use occupies an entire worksheet, you need to identify the data source as a *named range* in the worksheet. In addition, you should note whether the top row of the named range contains column names; if not, you need to create a separate header file, as explained in the previous section, "Using a Word Table As a Data Source."

When using an Excel file as a data source, you must use the entire worksheet or a named range within that sheet. To merge all or part of an Excel worksheet to your main document, choose Tools, Mail Merge. Click the Get Data button and select Open Data Source from the list to access the Open Data Source dialog box. Under Files of Type, choose MS Excel Worksheets from the drop-down list. Select the Excel file containing your data source. At this point, Word prompts you to select either the entire worksheet or any one of the named ranges in that workbook (as shown in Figure 17.11).

▶ **See** "Advanced Formulas" for more information on working with named ranges in Excel, **p. 629**

FIGURE 17.11
Word enables you to merge an Excel-named range with your main document.

Using Other Types of Data Sources

You can use virtually any source of organized data in a computer-readable file as a data source for Mail Merge. The Open Data Source dialog box offers several choices:

- All Word Documents
- Word Documents (*.doc)
- Web Pages (*.htm, *.html)
- Rich Text Format (*.rtf)
- Text Files (*.txt)
- MS Access Databases (*.mdb;*.mde)
- MS Excel Worksheets (*.xls)
- MS Query Files (*.qry; *.dqy)
- dBASE Files (*.dbf)

By installing the appropriate file converters that are supplied with Office 2000, you can also use data in other formats, including

- Earlier versions of Word for Windows as well as Macintosh and DOS versions of Word
- Earlier versions of Excel
- WordPerfect (Windows and DOS)
- Lotus 1-2-3
- ODBC databases

If you don't have the converters or drivers necessary to access data in a specific format, you may find that one of the other Office applications can translate data into a format suitable for Mail Merge. For example, Access can convert data from a Paradox file into an Access table; Excel can convert data from a Quattro Pro spreadsheet into an Excel workbook.

NOTE Most converters that come with Office 2000 are either automatically installed or are set to Install on First Use.

Using an Outlook Address Book As a Data Source

As mentioned before, just about any organized set of data may be used as a Mail Merge data source. This includes many of the address books available to us through email applications such as Outlook. You can use an address book created for use with Microsoft Exchange Server, Outlook, or Schedule+ 7.0 contact lists (any similar address lists created with a MAPI-compatible messaging system may also be used) as a data source.

To use an Outlook address book as your data source, access the Mail Merge Helper (Tools, Mail Merge). Then choose the appropriate source as shown in Figure 17.12.

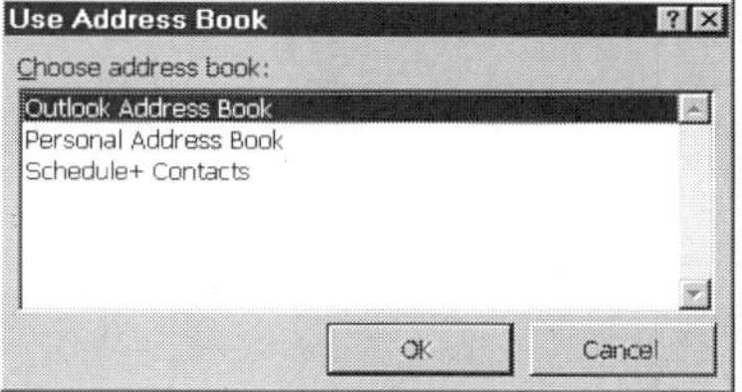

FIGURE 17.12
The Use Address Book dialog box offers a choice of address books.

Choose Outlook Address Book as your data source. When you select OK, you should see the Choose Profile dialog box. Choose the profile that accesses the address book you would like to use. There is a short delay while Word converts the address book into a format suitable for use with Mail Merge. Subsequently, when you click the Insert Merge Field drop-down button on the Mail Merge toolbar, you should see a list of all available fields from the Outlook address book. You can insert any of these fields into your Mail Merge main document.

Selecting and Ordering Records in a Data Source

The preceding sections of this chapter have assumed that you want to create form letters addressed to everyone listed in a data source in the same order as that source. It is likely, however, that you'll often want to create letters for only some of the people listed in the data source and that you want Mail Merge to create those letters in a specific order. For example, you might want your outgoing mail sent to only specific zip or postal codes or even sorted by those zip or postal codes for ease in mailing. This can be done in two ways:

- Create a customized data source. If your data source is in Access or Excel, you can easily extract the records you need and place them in an appropriate order for use in your Mail Merge, using the filter and sort features of Access and Excel.
- Use the tools within Mail Merge to select and order the records you want to use.

Because you are concentrating on Mail Merge features, let's focus on the latter method. Mail Merge enables you to select records, sort them, or do both simultaneously.

Selecting Records in a Data Source

Create a Mail Merge main document, and then click the Mail Merge Helper button on the Mail Merge toolbar. Next, click the Query Options button in the Mail Merge Helper dialog box to access the Query Options dialog box. A Filter Records tab, as shown in Figure 17.13, is displayed.

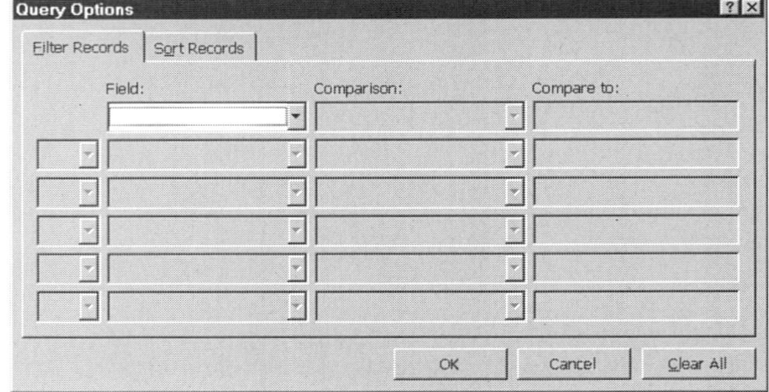

FIGURE 17.13
The Filter Records tab allows for selecting specific records from the data source.

To illustrate how to filter records, suppose the data source you've selected contains people's names and addresses, and you want to use only records for those people with the last name of Williams who live in the state of New Mexico.

When the Query Options dialog box first appears, only the Field box in the top row is enabled. Click the drop-down list in that box to show the names of all the fields in that data source. Choose the first field name you want to use. In this case, choose the LastName field.

After making an initial choice, the adjoining Comparison field becomes enabled with Equal To displayed. Although there are many comparison choices, in this case, we will accept the default. Next, you must decide what criteria the records must meet to qualify for mail merge. This is accomplished by typing in the last name (Williams) in the Compare To input field. You can include up to six sets of criteria that the record must meet in order to be merged with the main document. In this case, limit the example to two. In the second row, choose State for the field name, Equal To for the comparison, and then, in Compare To field, type the entry as it appears in the source document (in the example, the state abbreviation NM). Upon completion, your Query Options dialog box should look similar to the one shown in Figure 17.14.

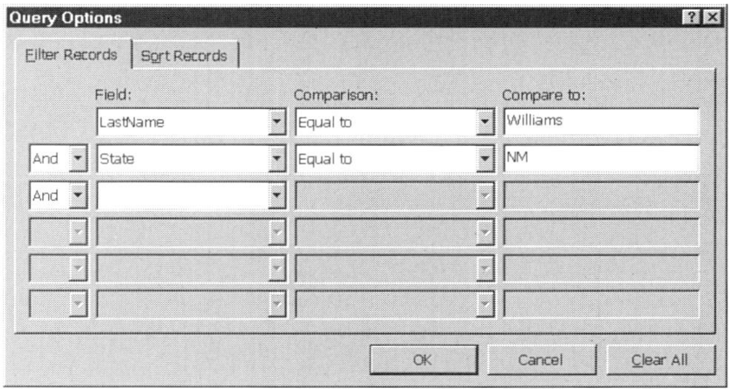

FIGURE 17.14
A filter allows you to determine restrictions for merging specific records from the data source.

Click OK to merge the main document with the filtered data source.

Earlier, you learned that up to six comparisons can be defined to create a filter in Mail Merge. Each may use the following conditions:

- Equal to
- Not equal to
- Less than
- Greater than
- Less than or equal to
- Greater than or equal to
- Is blank
- Is not blank

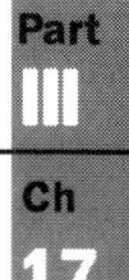

The first comparison is always used in a filter. The second comparison can start with either And or Or. If it begins with the And operator, only records that satisfy both conditions qualify. If it begins with the Or operator, data source records that satisfy either condition qualify for the merge. An example of the OR criteria is

LastName Equal to Williams OR

LastName Equal to Garza

The second through sixth comparisons, if used, can also be combined with the preceding conditions by the And/Or operators.

NOTE When fields contain alphanumeric information (any value that is not entirely numeric such as 1215 Warner Way), comparisons are made on the basis of the ASCII values of the alphabetic characters.

Sorting Records in a Data Source

By default, Mail Merge displays records in the order in which they occur in the data source. It is possible, however, to change the order based upon a maximum of three fields.

To sort the records from the data source, click the Mail Merge Helper button on the Mail Merge toolbar. Then click the Query Options button in the Mail Merge Helper dialog box to access the Query Options dialog box. Choose the Sort Records tab shown in Figure 17.15.

Begin by clicking the Sort By drop-down list and choosing the first field by which you want to sort. You may also choose to make your sort order ascending or descending at this point. Word uses the ASCII sort order, as outlined in Table 17.1. Symbols always take precedence in an ascending sort.

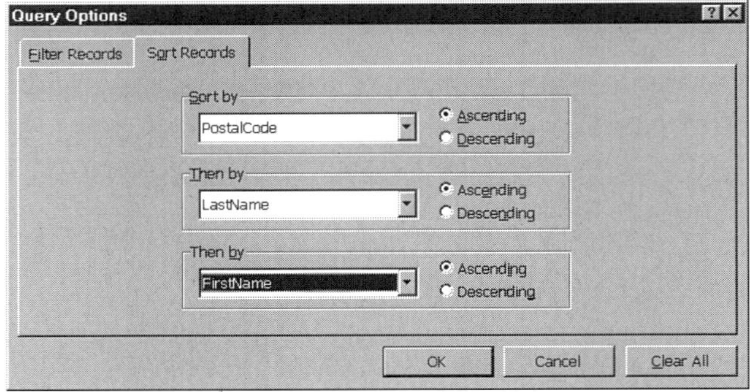

FIGURE 17.15
The sort feature allows you to sort by up to three fields.

Table 17.1 ASCII Sort Order

Ascending	Descending
Symbols	z-a (Lowercase Alpha)
0-9	Z-A (Uppercase Alpha)
A-Z (Uppercase Alpha)	9-0
a-z (Lowercase Alpha)	Symbols

Using Word Fields in a Main Document

You can add a great deal of flexibility to Mail Merge by incorporating Word fields in the main document. These fields are used to selectively add information to merge documents and control how data is merged.

To insert a Word field into a Mail Merge main document, click the Insert Word Field button on the Mail Merge toolbar to view the drop-down list.

▶ **See** "Fields—Word's Hidden Functions," **p. 349**

NOTE Three additional fields, described later in this section, are available by choosing Insert, Field from the Word menu bar.

Table 17.2 provides a brief explanation of the available Word fields. The field names used in the field dialog box (accessed by choosing Insert, Field) and in the Mail Merge toolbar drop-down list are slightly different.

Table 17.2 Available Word Fields

Field Name (Field Dialog Box)	Field Name (Mail Merge Toolbar)	Description
Ask	Ask	Provides a prompt for values placed at bookmark that apply to all merge documents (ask once option) as well as individual documents. A bookmark name represents your response.
Compare		Compares one value with another. Returns 1 if the comparison is true, O if it is false. The comparison can be used in an IF statement.
Database		Inserts the results of a database query in a Word table.
Fill-in	Fill-in	Provides customized text that applies to all (ask once option) or to individual merge documents as required by the user. This field is populated by a user's response to the fill-in prompt.
IF	If…Then…Else…	Chooses between two items of text depending on the value of a data source field or bookmark.
MergeField		Inserts the value of a data source field.
MergeRec	Merge Record #	Inserts into merge documents a number corresponding to the sequence number of the sorted data source record.
MergeSeq	Merge Sequence #	Inserts into merge documents the sequential number of successfully merged documents.
Next	Next Record	Goes unconditionally to the next record in the data source. This option merges the next data record in the current section of the Merge Document as opposed to defaulting to a new page.
NextIf	Next Record If	Goes to the next record in the data source if a specified condition is true.
Set	Set Bookmark	Assigns text to a bookmark.
SkipIf	Skip Record If	Skips the current data source record if a specified condition is true.

The following sections provide an introduction to Word fields. You can find additional information and examples in Word's online Help.

By default, Word fields are not displayed in Mail Merge main documents. To see Word fields, you must either

- Press Alt+F9 to display all field codes in detail for the current document.
- Choose Tools, Options, View; then check Field codes to display field codes for all Word documents.

Using the IF Field in Mail Merge Documents

The IF Word field is used to include text that may change or might be omitted per document, sometimes referred to as *alternative text*. This variation depends upon whether or not the conditions specified are met. It is important to think about an IF statement as containing three individual parts:

- The IF—This text can also be considered the test by which the merge inputs text.
- The THEN—If the test evaluates to true, the Then text is inserted.
- The ELSE (OTHERWISE)—If the test evaluates to false, then the Otherwise text is inserted.

Let's look at an example of this. Suppose you need to create a personalized thank-you letter for every customer. Adding to that scenario, you must now also extend an offer to those who have not previously purchased a specific product, such as toner cartridges. Those who have purchased the cartridges might be offered an alternative product so as not to offer something they have already ordered. To begin with, you must set up the conditions and results:

If a customer has purchased your featured product (toner cartridges) in the past, *then* offer those customers another product (printer paper). *Otherwise,* offer them the featured product of the month (toner cartridges).

In Mail Merge, it is possible to create an IF statement by completing the following steps:

1. At the appropriate place in the Mail Merge main document, type the lead-in to your IF statement: `Perhaps next time, you would like to try our .`
2. From the Mail Merge toolbar, click the Insert Word Field drop-down list and choose If...Then...Else. Word displays the Insert Word Field: IF dialog box shown in Figure 17.16.
3. Click the Field name drop-down list and choose the comparison field (Product) from the Field name drop-down list.
4. Choose the operator from the Comparison box (our example uses the default Equal to).
5. In the Compare To box, type the text that will be the qualifier, or test, for the merge (in the example, Toner Cartridges).

FIGURE 17.16
Define the IF field using this dialog box.

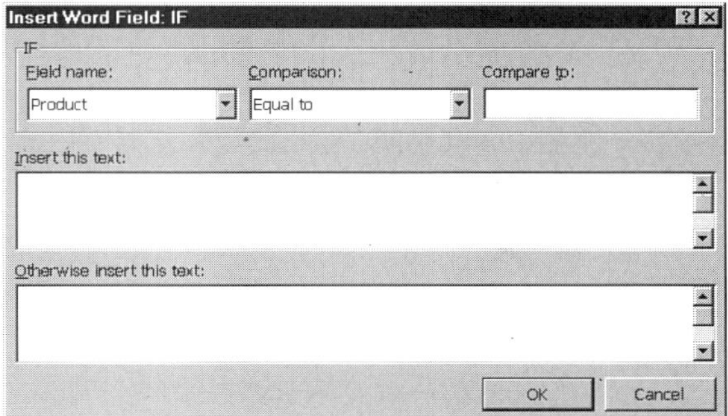

CAUTION

The Insert Word Field: IF dialog box is case sensitive. Be sure the data in the Compare To box matches the case from the criteria derived from your data source. In addition, the data source itself should have data with a consistent case format.

6. In the Insert This Text box, type the text that should be inserted if the results of the test are true. In the example, if the customer has already ordered the cartridges, you might want to offer them the printer paper, so type `Printer Paper`.
7. In the Otherwise Insert This Text box, type the text to be inserted if the results of the test are false. In the example, if the customer has not bought the cartridges, you want to let them know the cartridges are this month's special. So, type `Toner Cartridges`.
8. Click OK. The field is inserted in the main document after the lead-in text.
9. Type a period to end the sentence.

If you have opted to display field codes as mentioned in the previous section, your main document resembles the document featured in Figure 17.17.

▶ **See** "Ten of Word's Most Useful Fields," **p. 360**

In the example, documents based on data source records for which each Product field contains Toner Cartridges will return a Printer Paper value. Documents based on any other value for Product will contain Toner Cartridges in the IF field location. In this manner, you will not offer your featured product to the customers who have already bought toner cartridges. In other words, *IF* the test is true, *THEN* Mail Merge inserts the necessary text. *OTHERWISE*, the condition being false, merge inserts the alternate text.

NOTE When you want to include text if the condition is true, but have nothing inserted if the condition is false, leave the Otherwise Insert This Text box empty.

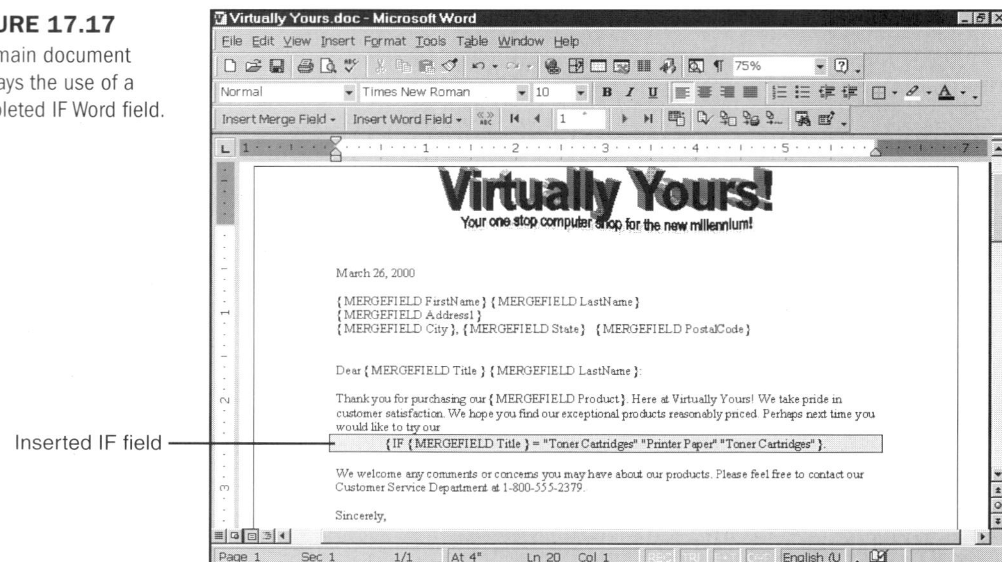

FIGURE 17.17
This main document displays the use of a completed IF Word field.

Using the ASK and IF Fields Together in a Mail Merge Document

Instead of using the value of a data source field to qualify text, you can decide upon those values interactively at the time Word creates each merge document. Suppose, for example, your data does not contain a Product field, but you still want to offer the featured product to some people and not to others. You can do this by using a bookmark instead of the value of a data source field in the IF statement. There are two distinct steps:

- Use an ASK field to provide a value for a bookmark.
- Use an IF field to select the text.

NOTE You can create a bookmark (using the Insert, Bookmark) prior to using an ASK field. The bookmark name appears in the ASK field dialog box for selection.

Seeing the Results from a Previous Search An ASK field is usually placed at or near the beginning of a Mail Merge main document. Move the insertion point to the beginning of the document. On the Mail Merge toolbar, click the Insert Word Field drop-down list and choose ASK to display the Insert Word Field: ASK dialog box shown in Figure 17.18.

Enter a name for the bookmark in the Bookmark box. If you have previously created bookmarks in the document, you will see their names in the list box. The names you enter must be different from the name of any existing bookmark. An example of a bookmark name might be `BkmkProduct`.

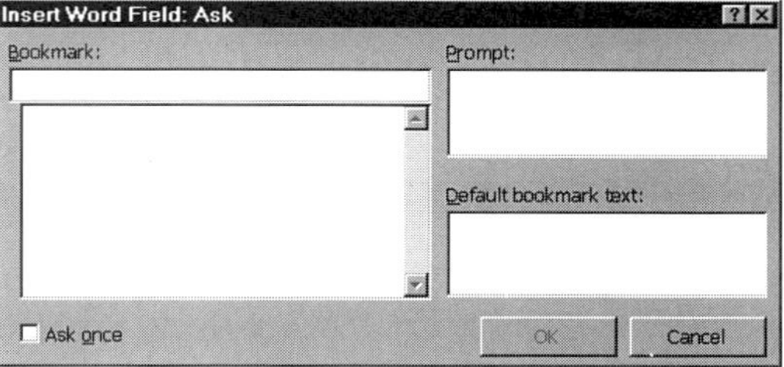

FIGURE 17.18
The ASK feature provides a bookmark name and prompt that are displayed when merging the main document with the data source.

The Prompt box is where you enter the prompt that appears on the screen as each merge document is created. Type something akin to Product Offer:Yes Or No? in the prompt box.

Enter a default value into the Default Bookmark Text box. This value automatically displays in the resulting prompt after you begin to merge your document.

Figure 17.19 shows the dialog box with the suggested entries completed.

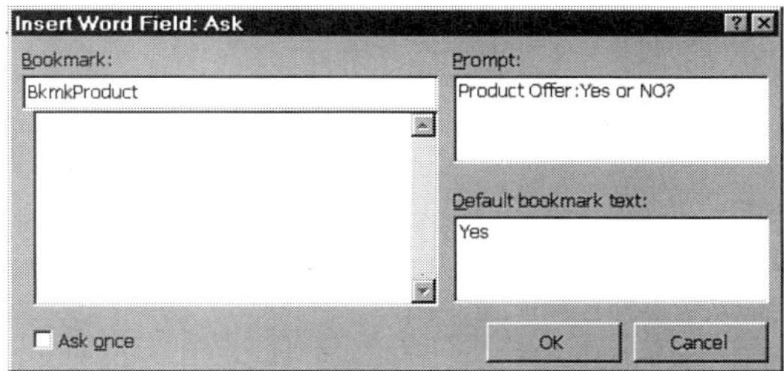

FIGURE 17.19
The Insert Word Field: ASK dialog box displays a typical prompt and default bookmark text entered.

When you click OK, Word displays a sample of the message box you will see when you create merge documents. Click OK to return to the Mail Merge Main document. You should see the ASK field (provided you have chosen to display the field codes). The ASK field in your document looks like

```
{ASK BkmkProduct "Product Offer: yes? Or no?" \d "Yes" }
```

in which the \d indicates that the quoted text that follows is the default response. For detailed information about the format of this field, refer to Microsoft Word Help under Field types and switches.

NOTE The Insert Word Field: ASK dialog box contains a check box labeled Ask once. By default, this box is unchecked. If it remains unchecked, Word asks you for a value for the bookmark as each merge document is created; the value you provide is available only while that merge document is being created.

If you check the Ask Once box, Word asks for a value for the bookmark only when the first merge document is created. This value is then applied to all subsequent merge documents being created.

After you have created the ASK field, you will not see any text display in your document. You must now insert the IF field and initiate the merge—as discussed in the following section—to complete this process.

Inserting the IF Field Move your insertion point in the main document to where you would like to place the IF field (the value dependent upon the ASK field results). If you need the full array of IF options available—do not create an IF field by choosing from the Insert Word Field drop-down list due to the limited field choices. This dialog box enables you to select only among the fields in your data source and not bookmarks. To correct this, go to the Word menu bar and choose Insert, Field to display the Field dialog box shown in Figure 17.20.

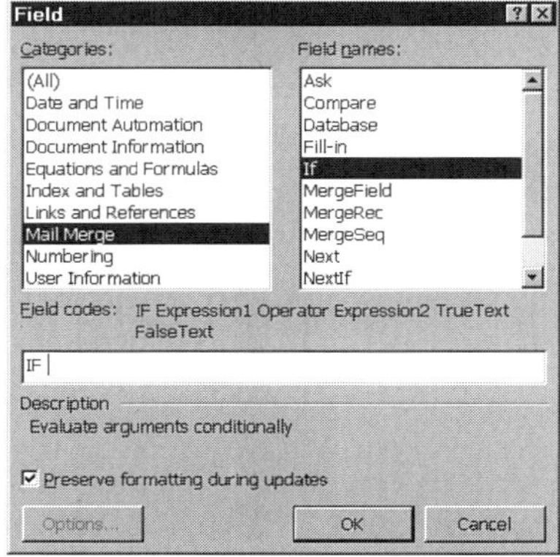

FIGURE 17.20
Use the Field dialog box to insert an IF field.

NOTE You can create an IF field by choosing from the Insert Word field drop-down box and temporarily choosing one of the available fields from the data source. Then, after inserting the IF field in the main document, you can edit it to replace the temporary field name with the name of the bookmark.

In the Categories list, choose Mail Merge to display the list of field names shown in Figure 17.20. Notice that the list contains more types of fields than are available in the Insert Word Field drop-down list.

Choose IF and notice that the text below the Categories and Field names lists summarizes the syntax of the IF statement. The text box below this summary already contains IF; it is up to you to complete this statement to suit your specifications. Figure 17.21 shows the dialog box with a completed IF statement.

CAUTION

Be cautious where you place your quotes in an IF statement. The conditional value for the bookmark is not enclosed within quotes. Any text provided whether the condition is true or false, however, is enclosed within quotes.

FIGURE 17.21
A completed IF statement includes a test and text to be included should the test prove true or false.

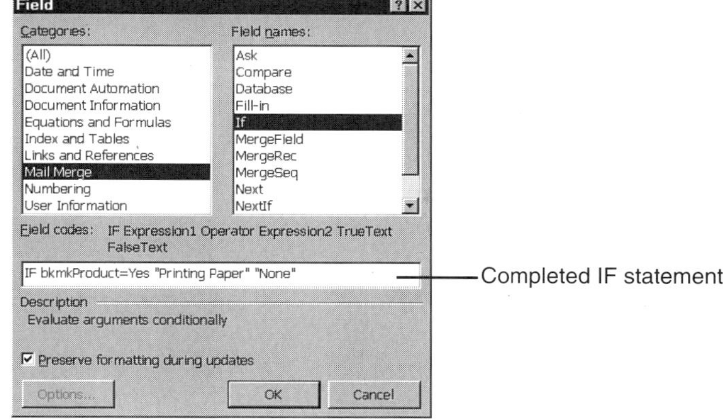

Providing Values for the Bookmark After completing the main document, or at least the part that contains the ASK and IF statements, you can run a trial merge by clicking the Check for Errors button on the Mail Merge toolbar. You will be prompted to choose between three error-checking options as listed in Figure 17.22. Choose this middle option and click OK. The merge process begins to create the first merge document and displays the message box shown in Figure 17.23.

FIGURE 17.22
When checking for errors, you have the option to simulate a merge before the actual merge takes place.

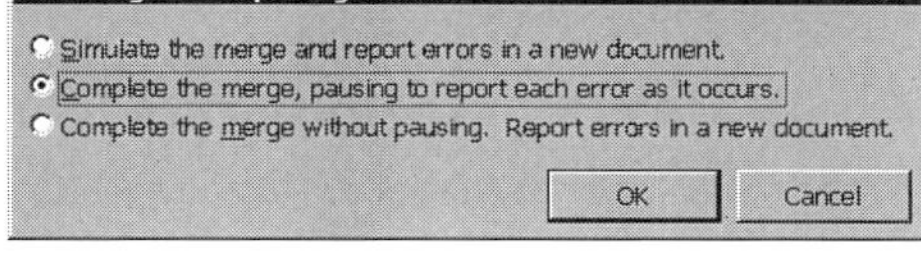

FIGURE 17.23
The default response you typed in the ASK statement appears in the message prompt.

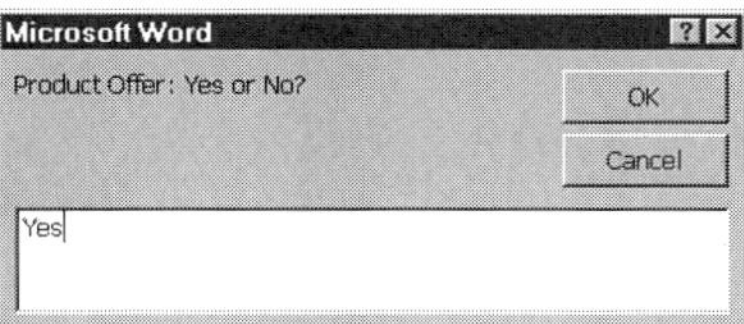

If the default value is the appropriate response, click OK. Otherwise, enter an alternative choice, such as No, and click OK.

When you click OK, Word uses the response from the ASK field as the qualifier for the IF statement you created. The results display at the location of the IF Fields throughout your merge documents. Word then continues to merge the second document. Again, you are prompted to accept the default or enter a different response. This procedure is now applied to all remaining merge documents.

You are given only one chance to provide a value for the bookmark. After you click OK, Word moves to the next document. See the section "Merging to a New Document" later in this chapter for information about correcting errors.

Filling In Text

The ability to choose between two words or phrases is often all you need; however, there are times when more flexibility is necessary. For example, you might be required to insert *personalized* text into each merged letter. You can use the Fill-In field to accomplish this task. In the Mail Merge main document, place the insertion point where you want to place personalized text. Click the Insert Word Field drop-down list on the Mail Merge toolbar and choose Fill-In. Word displays the Insert Word Field: Fill-In dialog box shown in Figure 17.24.

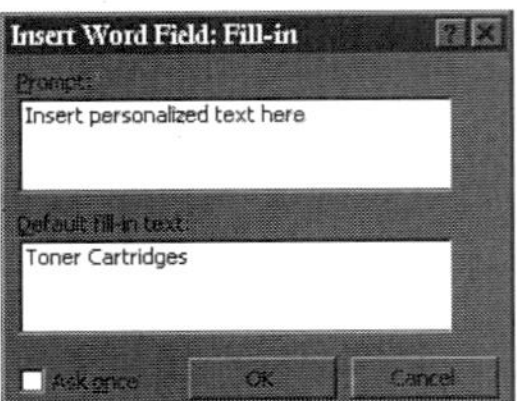

FIGURE 17.24
The Fill-In feature marks the place where you insert personalized text into each merge document.

Enter a prompt such as Insert Personalized Text Here in the prompt box. If there is a default value you would like to use on most of your documents, you may enter that value in the Default fill-in text box. After clicking OK, you will see a sample of the message box that appears for each merge document. Click OK again to return to the Mail Merge main document with the Fill-In field displayed.

NOTE Like ASK, the Insert Word Field: Fill-In dialog box contains an Ask Once check box.

Subsequently, as Word creates the merge document, the merging process stops at each document to allow you to add personalized text.

Printing and Distributing Form Letters

The preceding sections of this chapter have covered many aspects of creating a Mail Merge main document and providing for a data source. In those sections, you frequently used the Check for Errors button on the Mail Merge toolbar to see the results of your work on the screen. This does not produce merge documents you can actually send to individual people. You will now go over the actual process by which merge documents are produced.

Printing Directly

If you've created a simple Mail Merge document (and have great confidence in your work), you can print your merge documents directly and bypass merging them to screen. Click the Merge to Printer button on the Mail Merge toolbar to access the Windows Print dialog box. If you have ASK or Fill-In fields in the main document, printing pauses to allow you to provide the necessary information. In most cases, however, I recommend reviewing your work prior to sending it to print. This is achieved by merging to a new document.

Merging to a New Document

To review what the merge documents look like before you print them, click the Merge to New Document button on the Mail Merge toolbar. The merge process pauses whenever necessary to allow you to provide information in response to ASK and Fill-In fields. Upon completion, you can review all the merged records onscreen. This is particularly useful for reviewing your responses to ASK fields. Whatever action Word took as a result of your responses is shown in the merged records. If you did make a mistake, you can edit individual form letters instead of going back through the entire process.

When you are satisfied that all the form letters are correct, you can print them just as any other Word document.

After printing the merge document, save the merged file until you have checked the printed pages. It is possible you might have missed a couple of errors as you reviewed the file onscreen. If you do spot an error, you can correct it in the saved file and reprint that one page.

Distributing by Conventional Mail

In this chapter, you've concentrated on creating form letters. After creating those letters, it is often necessary to print companion mailing labels or envelopes. The process for creating these labels and envelopes is quite similar to producing a simple form letter.

To create labels and envelopes, open a new Word document. Start the Mail Merge Helper Wizard (Tools, Mail Merge) and choose Create. At this point, you are ready to choose whether you would like to print Mailing Labels or Envelopes. All subsequent steps are nearly identical to creating a form letter. Just follow the instructions provided by the wizard.

To automatically include your return address on printed envelopes, choose Tools, Options. Access the User Information tab and type your name and address in the Mailing address box.

CAUTION

You must create an envelope document type from scratch. It may not be converted from an existing Label document. If you attempt this, you may not get the proper formatting for an envelope.

Distributing by Email or Fax

Instead of spending time printing your merged documents, creating the envelopes, adding postage, and finally waiting for conventional mail to reach its destination, you now have the ability to send mail via email or fax almost instantaneously. Unfortunately, the process for sending merge documents electronically is by no means straightforward.

Suppose you have created a Mail Merge main document and have provided a data source that has email and fax address fields. The following steps help you address the issue of sending information electronically:

1. Display the Mail Merge main document and click the Mail Merge Helper button on the Mail Merge toolbar. When in the Mail Merge Helper dialog box, choose Query Options to display the query Options dialog box. Make sure the Filter Records tab is selected.
2. Click the Field drop-down list in the top row and choose the field that contains email or fax numbers.
3. Open the Comparison drop-down list and choose the Is Not Blank comparison. Leave the Compare To field empty and click OK.
4. In the Mail Merge Helper dialog box, click Merge. Then in the Merge dialog box, open the Merge To drop-down list, as shown in Figure 17.25.

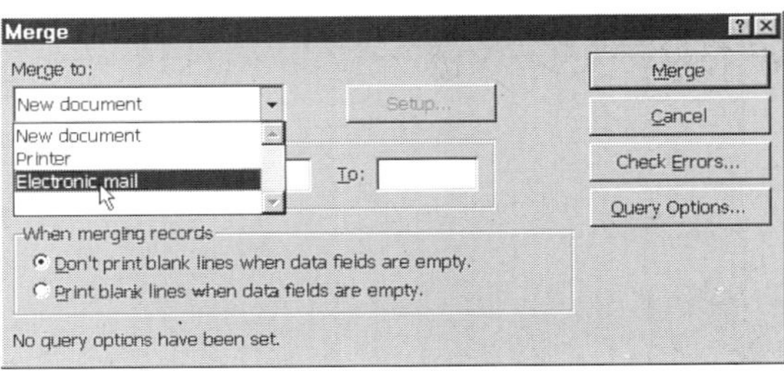

FIGURE 17.25
You can choose Electronic Mail or Electronic Fax as a means of distributing your merge documents.

5. If you chose a field that contains email addresses in step 2, choose Electronic Mail from the list. Alternatively, if you chose a field that contains fax numbers, choose Electronic Fax from the list.
6. Click Setup to display the Merge To Setup dialog box, shown in Figure 17.26. Open the Data field with the Mail/Fax Address drop-down list and choose the field that contains the appropriate email or fax indicator. Click OK to return to the Merge dialog box.

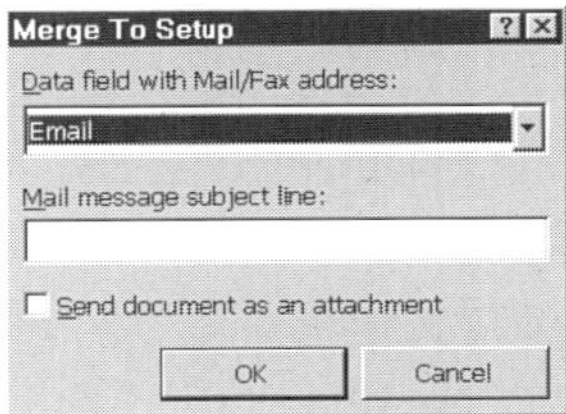

FIGURE 17.26
Choose the data source field that contains the email address or fax number.

7. In the Merge dialog box, click Merge to open your email or fax application (such as Outlook or Exchange).

What occurs after this step varies according to your email or fax application. If you are using Outlook, for example, and you have several email or fax addresses per person, you can choose from among the available addresses. After you have made these choices, Outlook places the messages in the Outbox and sends them in the conventional manner.

Learning the mail merge process might take some time. When internalized, however, you will see that it saves an incredible amount of time and expense. Keep in mind; it sure beats hand-typing tens, hundreds, or even thousands of individual letters.

CHAPTER 18

Sharing Word Data with Other Users and Applications

In this chapter

Choosing the Right Collaboration Method

Word provides a variety of ways to work with others. Which method you choose depends largely upon your resources (network, Internet, intranet, and so on), your work style, and your connectivity with those with whom you need to collaborate. Word's collaboration tools include the following:

- Web Discussion—Described in Chapter 3, Web Discussions enable users to conduct an organized Web-based discussion about an Office document without everyone having to be there at the same time. Users embed comments about and in documents, with comments (and sometimes documents) being deposited on a mutually accessible Web server that uses Office Web Extensions.

  ▶ **See** "Using Web Discussions," **p. 62**

- Routing—Described later in this chapter, routing combines email and optionally can enable document protection for tracking, comments, or forms, enabling you to route a document to a list of different recipients, either all at once or round-robin style.

  ▶ **See** "Routing Documents to Other Users," **p. 541**

- NetMeeting—Described in Chapter 3, online meetings take place in real-time, and enable users to share documents online using whiteboard, text, and audiovisual tools (depending on users' computer capabilities).

  ▶ **See** "Online Meetings," **p. 70**

- Comments—Comments, formerly called annotations in Word 95, are inserted much in the same way as endnotes, enabling collaborators to suggest changes or to otherwise comment upon a document. Comments can take the form of text and audio, and are marked with the commentator's initials and highlighting. Comments display as ScreenTips. The use of Comments is discussed later in this chapter.

  ▶ **See** "Getting the Most from Document Comments and Tracking Changes," **p. 544**

- Track changes—Formerly called Revision mode (in Word 95), and generically called redlining, the tracking option marks all changes that each user makes to a given document. Changes can be displayed and ScreenTips indicate the collaborator's name, type of change, and the time and date each distinct change was made. Tracking is discussed later in this chapter.

- Master Document—Described in Chapter 16, the Master Document feature enables multiple users to work on a multifile document at the same time.

  ▶ **See** "Working with the Master Document," **p. 493**

Web Discussions

Web Discussions provide a way that users can discuss a Word document using a Web server as a medium of exchange. Discussion items are kept on the Web server, rather than in the document. In fact, the document being discussed does not even have to reside on the Web server;

it just needs to be in a location that all users collaborating on the document have access to. Begin by opening the document you want to discuss. Choose Tools, Online Collaboration, Web Discussions. The Discussions toolbar appears as shown in Figure 18.1. You might also be prompted to enter or confirm user ID and password, depending upon how the system administrator has set up security.

FIGURE 18.1
Use the Discussions toolbar to control Web discussions.

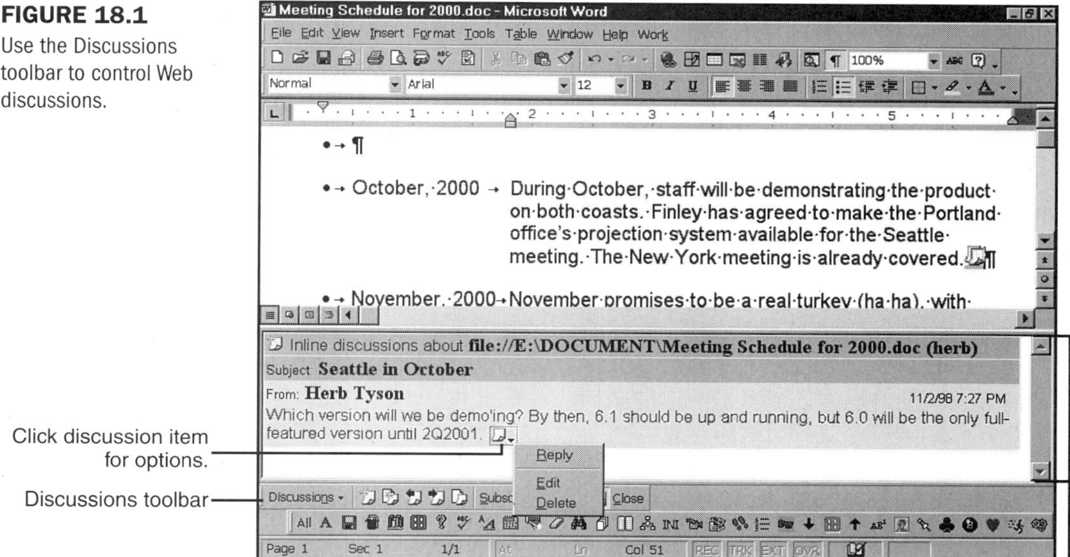

NOTE The first time you go online, you might not have yet specified a Web server for discussions. Obtain the name of the Web server, a user ID, and a password from the system administrator. For certain networks, you'll also need a domain name.

▶ **See** "Using Web Discussions," **p. 62**

After you are logged on, the icons on the Discussions toolbar become available.

The basic idea is to use the Web server as a discussion forum. The discussion forum takes place right in the document you open. The discussion takes place by discussants logging in (in effect by turning on Web Discussions for a given document), and entering and replying to discussion items.

In Word, there are two kinds of discussion elements:

- *Inline discussion elements* are displayed in the document as notes that resemble Word Comments. Use inline discussion items to refer to specific items in the document. To enter an inline item, position the insertion point in the document at the point you want to discuss, and click the Insert In the Document button on the Discussions toolbar.

- *General discussion items* are not displayed in the document, but do show up in the discussion pane. Use general discussion items to make general comments about the document—that is, when you don't really need a referenced point in the document itself. To enter a general item, click the Insert About the Document button on the Discussions toolbar.

To complete the discussion item—for general or inline—type the subject and the text of the comment into the Enter Discussion Text dialog box.

All actions are performed through the Discussions pane, which appears when you are working with the document in an online collaboration. To reply to, edit, or delete a discussion item, start by locating the item in the Discussions pane. Click the discussion item icon with the left mouse button (not the right) to drop down a list of choices (refer to Figure 18.1).

CAUTION

The Discussions toolbar gets turned on in all open document windows in Word–not just the current one. So, if you move back and forth between windows, make sure that any discussion items you enter are entered in the intended document.

One of the other Web Discussion features is *Subscription and Notification*. You can monitor a specific document or folder to which you have at least "read access." You have the option to be notified when a document is edited, discussion comments are added, or when items are added or removed from a folder. You can even be notified when a particular person makes changes to a folder.

Most of the subscription and notification options are self-explanatory. However, Chapter 3 contains specific descriptions of each option.

▶ **See** "Using Web Subscriptions and Notifications," **p. 68**

Using Email and Scheduling Features

Word provides built-in features that make online collaboration more fluid. As described previously, Word's list of collaboration features includes techniques that use network connectivity. Word enables you to initiate email messages without leaving the Word window, creating email from Word documents using the document as the text or as an attachment. Word also enables you to route the current document to others, automatically enabling tracking of changes, providing a built-in method to promote a useful flow and exchange of work on a shared document. And, when sharing and working on documents isn't enough, Word also provides an interface to Outlook's calendar, letting you schedule meetings with other Office users.

Creating and Editing Email Documents in Word

Word users often want the same editing and writing tools that are available when composing email. They do have them. You can create email using Word as the editor or you can tell Outlook to default to using Word for creating and editing email.

See "Using Microsoft Word As Your Email Editor," **p. 1438**

Creating Email Directly from Word To create email directly from within Word, start a new document and click the Email (Mail Recipient) tool on the Standard toolbar. Word displays standard email fields at the top of the current document window (just below Word's toolbars), as shown in Figure 18.2. These email fields are known as the email *Envelope*.

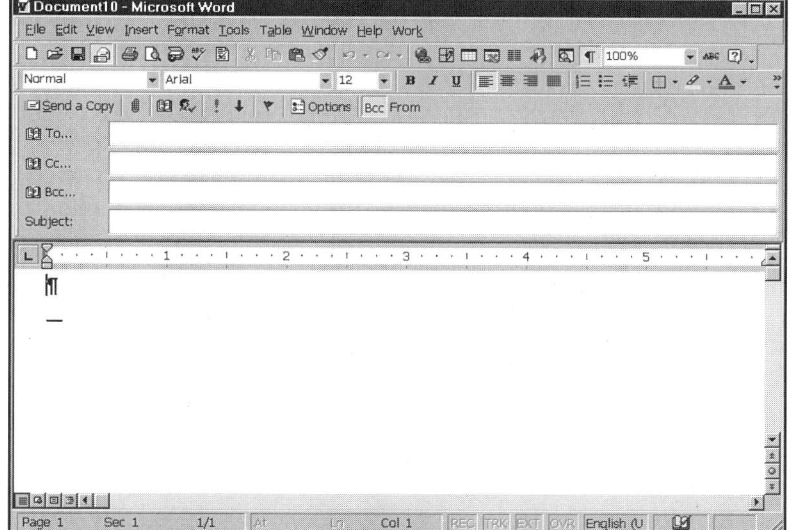

FIGURE 18.2
Sending email from Word provides access to Outlook features.

NOTE Depending on your setup, Word might not have the Email (Mail Recipient) icon on the Standard toolbar. For this option to work, Outlook or Outlook Express must be set as your default email client. In Internet Explorer, choose View, Internet Options, Programs, and choose Outlook or Outlook Express for Email.

Actually, the Email tool toggles the envelope on and off. If the email envelope is too obtrusive, simply click again to hide the envelope. When you've filled in the envelope for a given set of addressees, the information remains intact until the document is sent. If you close the document and later reopen it, it remembers the filled-in headers until the document has been sent as email (even if you toggle the envelope off).

CAUTION

If you accidentally toggle the email envelope on, Word remembers that document as an intended email until it actually gets sent. This can disable some features not available in WordMail (such as the tools on the Frames toolbar).

After the message has been composed, display the envelope (if it's hidden), supply the necessary addressing, and choose Send a Copy.

CAUTION

What you see is not necessarily what your recipients get. When sending email composed in Word, much of the Word formatting you've applied does not necessarily survive the journey. For example, a Word table might survive; but, if the table contains vertical text, it won't. And this assumes you're both using Outlook! If you're using different email programs, then you should send any formatting-dependent documents as attachments, rather than attempting to embed formatting in email messages.

Even if you and all of your correspondents for a particular message are using Outlook, before you include vital formatting, send a copy of the message to yourself so that you can get an idea how it appears to others. If essential formatting is lost, then send the document as an attachment rather than as the email itself.

Sending Email As an Attachment Word also enables you to attach the current document to an email message, rather than using the current file as the body of the email message. Choose this option when you want the file and all formatting to be preserved. Choose File, Send To, Mail Recipient (As Attachment). This causes the current document image (that is, even changes that have not been saved to disk yet) to be attached to an email message, using your default MAPI program. If your MAPI default is Outlook, the message window appears as shown in Figure 18.3.

What Is MAPI?

MAPI stands for *Messaging Application Programming Interface*. An *Application Programming Interface* (API) is a system of instructions that provides a standard way for individual applications programs to access features of the operating system.

MAPI provides a way for individual programs to handle messages. In Microsoft Windows, the default MAPI program is the program that handles mail transactions for the operating system. For many Office 2000 users, the default MAPI program is Outlook 2000. For some, it is Outlook Express. For others, it might be Eudora, Netscape, or some other third-party application. By programming using the MAPI standard, each of these programs achieves compatibility with Windows and with one another.

NOTE Plain Text in the window title bar refers only to the email message itself. The attachment is sent as a file, with all its formatting intact.

FIGURE 18.3
Word can use Outlook to send email.

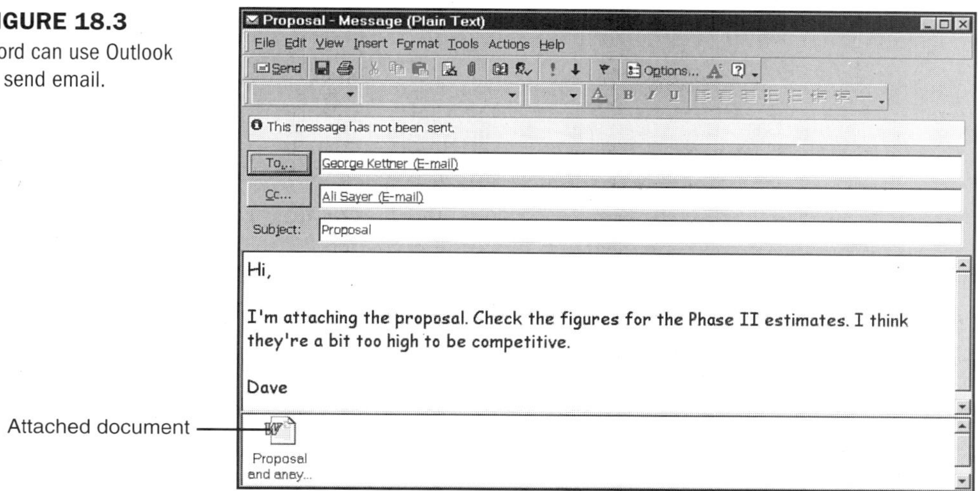

After sending a message from Word, a copy of the sent message is stored with your MAPI client. For example, if your MAPI client is Outlook, the messages are stored in your Sent Items folder within Outlook (unless you change the built-in default).

TIP When sending email directly from Word, the contents of the currently displayed document get sent—even if those contents have not been saved to disk. If you want to send modified versions of the same message to different people, this is a way you can do it. Just click the Email tool, add the addressing information and any changes to the body of the text, and click Send a Copy. The email headers disappear when the message has been sent. So, click the Email tool again, add a different address, change the message as you want, and click Send a Copy again.

Routing Documents to Other Users

One of Word's more useful but less-used features is electronic routing. In just about every multiperson office, it is routine to attach a paper routing slip to a document, and then pass it around to the people listed on the routing slip. Each person examines the document and does whatever is appropriate, and then passes it along to the next person on the list. Eventually, it finds its way back to the originator.

NOTE In order for Routing Recipient to appear in the Send To menu, you must have installed a MAPI-compatible email program. These include Outlook, Outlook Express, Microsoft Exchange Client, or any 32-bit email program compatible with the Messaging Application Programming Interface (MAPI). You should also verify that Mapi32.dll is in the Windows System folder.

You can do this electronically, via Word and your network. There are just a few basic steps:

1. Open the document you want routed, and choose File, Send To, Routing Recipient, which displays the dialog box shown in Figure 18.4.
2. Use the Address button to add addressees (or routees).
3. Choose the desired routing options—One After Another or All at Once; Return When Done, Track Status, and Protect (usually for Tracked Changes).
4. Choose Add Slip to add the routing slip, but defer sending until later; choose Route to begin routing immediately.

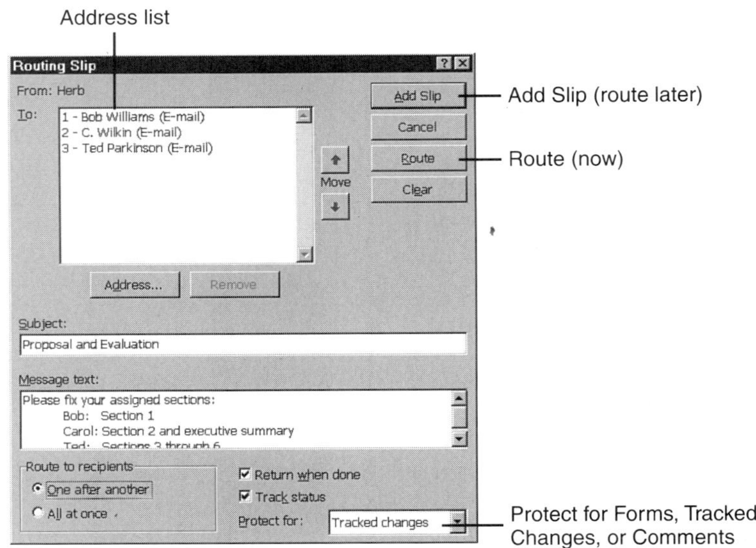

FIGURE 18.4
Any message you type is added to the default routing instructions that accompany every routed document.

If you choose Add Slip, you can route the document later by choosing File, Send To, Next Routing Recipient at any time; see Figure 18.5. Word automatically prompts, asking whether you want to send to the next recipient when you close the document.

Routing recipients receive the Word document as an attachment in an email message. They open the attachment by double-clicking, which opens the document in Word. When done editing, the recipient chooses File, Send To, Next Routing Recipient, and the document continues along its merry way. When the final recipient forwards the message, it simply returns to the originator.

Some users in some offices are notorious for turning off document protection. When you're trying to track changes or comments, this practice is infuriating. If the routed document is a protected form, turning protection off and then on again wipes out any user-entered data. If your routing recipients have that kind of notoriety, choose Tools, Protect Document, select the kind of protection appropriate, and supply a password. This generally deters users who don't like to play by the rules. Just make sure you keep a list of your passwords in a safe place.

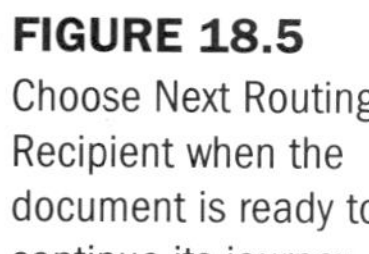

FIGURE 18.5
Choose Next Routing Recipient when the document is ready to continue its journey.

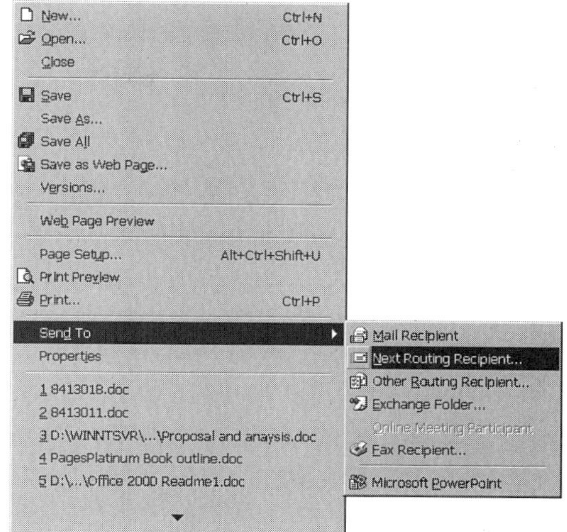

Scheduling Meetings with Other Users

Microsoft NetMeeting enables you to share and exchange information with other people at different sites in real-time over your company's intranet or the Internet, just as if everyone were in the same room.

Word 2000 provides a way for you to coordinate a meeting through Outlook. If you or any of the participants do not use Outlook, you can coordinate the scheduling of a meeting via email or by phone. Outlook is not required to participate in an online meeting. You can start a meeting anytime by selecting Tools, Online Collaboration, Meet Now.

To schedule an online meeting in Word, choose Tools, Online Collaboration, Schedule Meeting. This displays an Outlook meeting request dialog box. From within this window, you can specify the invitees (required, optional, and resources), the type of meeting (NetMeeting or NetShow), start and finish time, and so on.

Because the meeting request is generated by Outlook, you can specify a reminder that alerts the invitees that the meeting is about to start (assuming they accept the invitation, of course). When an invitation is accepted, it automatically gets entered into the invitee's Outlook Calendar. You can even choose an option to start NetMeeting automatically. Figure 18.6 shows an example of a meeting request created from within Word.

See "Online Collaboration," **p. 61**

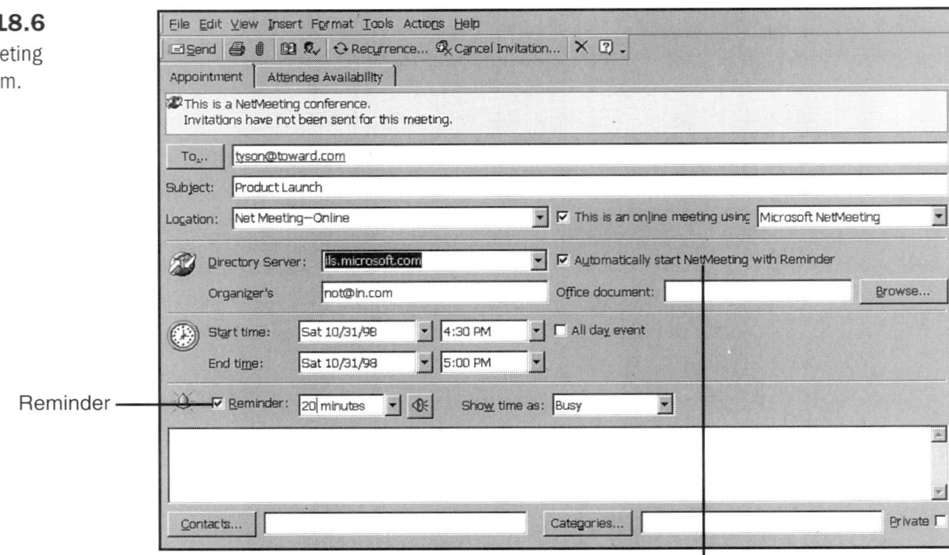

FIGURE 18.6
Outlook Meeting Request form.

Getting the Most from Document Comments and Tracking Changes

Word provides two features designed especially for workgroup collaboration on the same document:

- Comments
- Track Changes

Both of these features keep track of who said what. In a busy office setting, this information can be vital. Few things are more frustrating than fumbling with suggestions only to discover that they've already been integrated into the document. Also, Comments or other editing suggestions by the CEO will probably be treated differently than a comment made by somebody else in the organization.

Adding Comments to the Document

Comments, in effect, are self-tracking endnotes. They are entered very much like footnotes and endnotes—in an entry pane. Unlike footnotes and endnotes, however, Comments show you who inserted them and are highlighted so that you can see them more readily.

NOTE In Word 95, Comments were called Annotations.

When you insert a Comment, Word either highlights the word closest to the insertion point, or, if text is selected, Word highlights the selected passage.

NOTE Word highlights Comments in yellow. The color cannot be changed. If you use Word's highlighting button on the Formatting toolbar, apart from Comments, use a color other than yellow to avoid confusion.

To insert a comment, select any text you want highlighted, and choose Insert, Comment (or press Ctrl+Alt+M). Word responds by highlighting selected text and inserting the current user's bracketed initials and a sequential number into the text, and then by opening a Comment pane. You then type your comment into the pane as shown in Figure 18.7. The initials come from the settings on the User Information tab of the Options dialog box (Tools, Options). Each comment is numbered.

TIP If you use comments frequently and prefer toolbars to keyboard shortcuts, consider adding the Comment button to a toolbar. Choose Tools, Customize, Commands. In Categories, choose Insert. In Commands, find Comment, and drag the Comment icon to the desired toolbar location.

If resources are plentiful (memory and disk space) and a verbal comment would be especially useful, you can click the Insert Sound Object tool to record a comment. Click close (Alt+Shift+C) to close the pane.

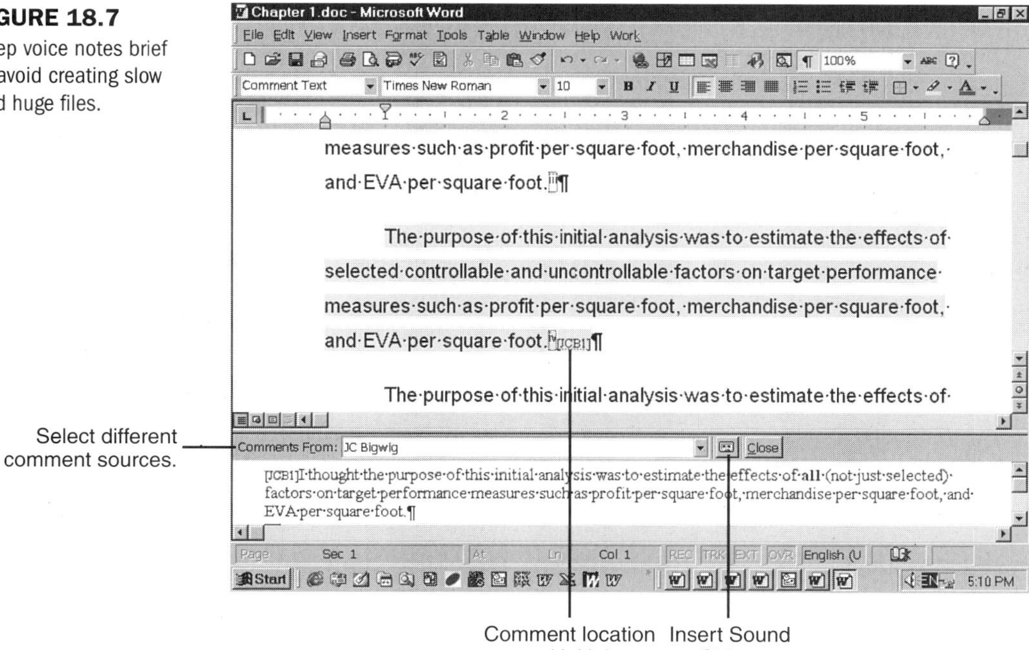
Chapter 1.doc - Microsoft Word
File Edit View Insert Format Tools Table Window Help Work
Comment Text
Times New Roman
10
measures·such·as·profit·per·square·foot,·merchandise·per·square·foot,·
and·EVA·per·square·foot.¶
The·purpose·of·this·initial·analysis·was·to·estimate·the·effects·of·
selected·controllable·and·uncontrollable·factors·on·target·performance·
measures·such·as·profit·per·square·foot,·merchandise·per·square·foot,·
and·EVA·per·square·foot.[JCB1]¶
The·purpose·of·this·initial·analysis·was·to·estimate·the·effects·of·
Comments From: JC Bigwig
Close
[JCB1]I·thought·the·purpose·of·this·initial·analysis·was·to·estimate·the·effects·of·all·(not·just·selected)·factors·on·target·performance·measures·such·as·profit·per·square·foot,·merchandise·per·square·foot,·and·EVA·per·square·foot.¶
Sec 1
Col 1
English (U
Start
5:10 PM
Select different comment sources.
Comment location and initials
Insert Sound Object

FIGURE 18.7
Keep voice notes brief to avoid creating slow and huge files.

NOTE Comment initials, which are set in Tools, Options, User Information, are inserted as hidden text. The bracketed initials are displayed while the Comment pane is open, but disappear when the pane is closed unless you have hidden text display enabled. Press Ctrl+Shift+* to toggle all formatting marks (including hidden text) on or off (or, choose Tools, Options, View, to enable just-hidden text to display).

The yellow highlighting that marks a comment location, however, is not toggled on and off with hidden text. If you ever come across highlighting that does not respond to the Formatting toolbar's Highlight tool, it's probably a comment.

Comments sometimes suggest replacement text. Rather than retyping it, display the comment (double-click the bracketed initials or choose View, Comments). In the Comment pane, copy the desired text to the clipboard. Then, close the Comment pane and paste the contents of the clipboard into the desired location.

Locating, Displaying, and Deleting Comments

Because of the highlighting, comments are generally pretty conspicuous. If you see a comment, the commentator's name and comment can be displayed in several ways. The easiest way usually is to hover the mouse pointer over the highlighted area, as shown in Figure 18.8. If the comment is especially long, or if you otherwise want to edit the comment, right-click the highlighted text and choose Edit Comment.

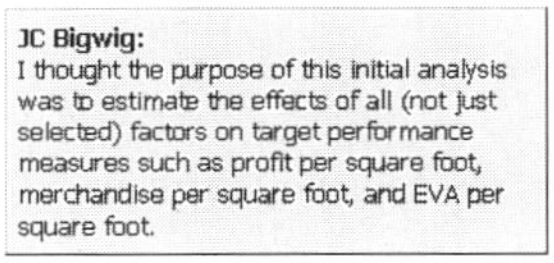

FIGURE 18.8
ScreenTips show the contents of comments.

JC Bigwig:
I thought the purpose of this initial analysis was to estimate the effects of all (not just selected) factors on target performance measures such as profit per square foot, merchandise per square foot, and EVA per square foot.

When the Comment pane is open, scrolling through the Comments changes the displayed area in the document to the location of the insertion point in the Comment area.

If you don't happen to be near any comments, you can open the Comment pane at any time by choosing View, Comments. You can also use the Previous/Next browse arrows at the bottom of the vertical scrollbar to navigate among comments. Click the Select Browse Object control, shown in Figure 18.9, and click Browse by Comment. Now, the browse control arrows become Previous Comment and Next Comment, rather than the normal Page-browsing defaults.

To delete a comment you can

- Right-click the comment and choose Delete Comment.
- Select the bracketed initial and press the Delete key.
- Chose Delete from the Reviewing toolbar.

FIGURE 18.9
Word has 12 different types of browse objects.

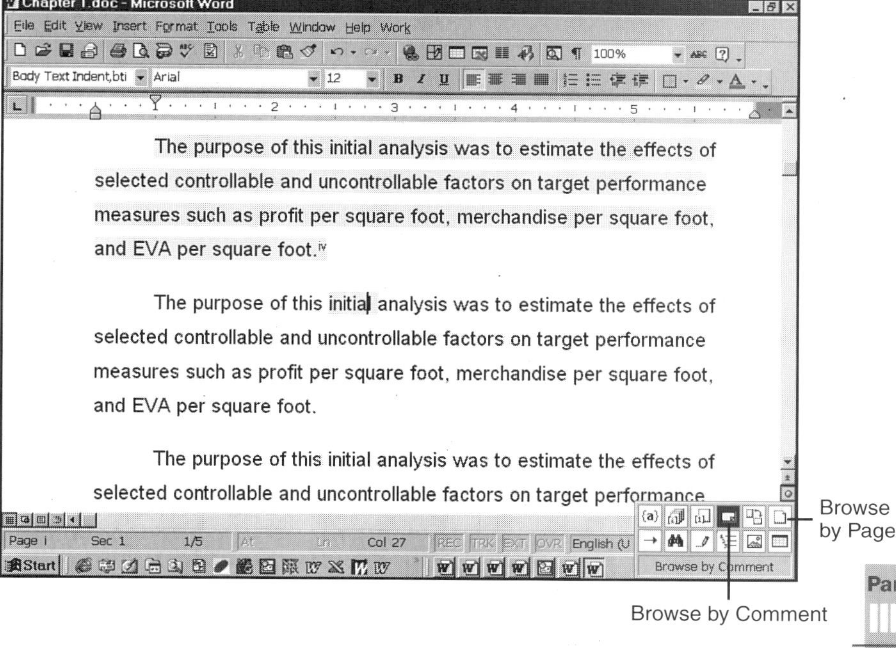

CAUTION

Users mistakenly sometimes try to delete comments from within the Comments pane. This deletes only the text of the Comment, not the Comment mark itself. To delete the whole Comment—mark and all—use one of the methods outlined previously.

Printing Comments

By default, Word does not print comments when you print a document. To tell Word to print comments when printing a document, choose Tools, Options, Print, and enable Comments in the Include with Document section. Comments are printed in a list at the end of the document.

NOTE Comments are not integrated into the document in the same way as endnotes.

To print just the comments—excluding the document text—choose File, Print. In Print What, click the drop-down arrow and choose Comments.

Tracking Changes with Revision Marks

Track Changes, formerly called Revision Marks and most often called redlining, lets you see additions, deletions, and other changes made to documents.

The Track Changes approach is preferred when the reviewer is actually editing the document. With the Track Changes feature, the user makes changes rather than merely suggesting them. The changes are *tracked,* however, so that the author and other reviewers can see the proposed changes, as well as who proposed them and when. When multiple users edit the document, using Track Changes often is the only way of maintaining a semblance of sanity in the process ("I didn't change that—you did!").

NOTE The alternative to Tracking Changes is the Comments feature, where you insert comments about the text, suggesting changes or additions. The Comments approach is preferred when the reviewer doesn't want to presume to edit the author's original words.

Word provides several tools for managing how tracked changes are displayed in the document. TRK on the Status Bar indicates the status of tracking. If tracking is not enabled, TRK is dimmed. Right-click TRK on the status bar to display the options shown in Figure 18.10—even if TRK is dimmed.

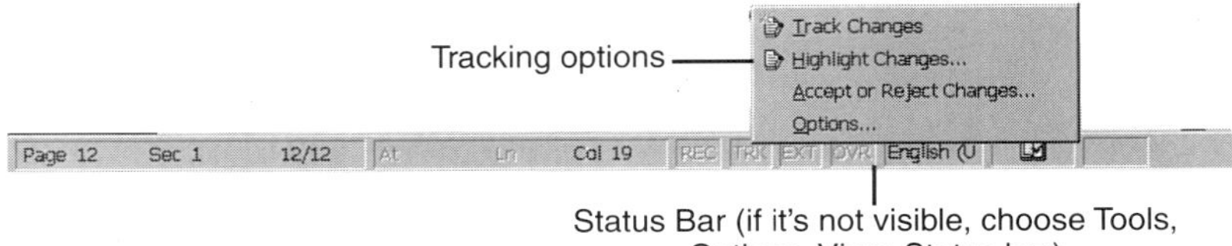

FIGURE 18.10
Double-click TRK to toggle Tracking on and off.

Track Changes toggles tracking on or off—the same as double-clicking TRK (or pressing Ctrl+Shift+E).

Highlight Changes displays the options shown in Figure 18.11. Highlight Changes on Screen toggles the display of tracked changes; Highlight Changes in Printed Document toggles the printing of tracked changes.

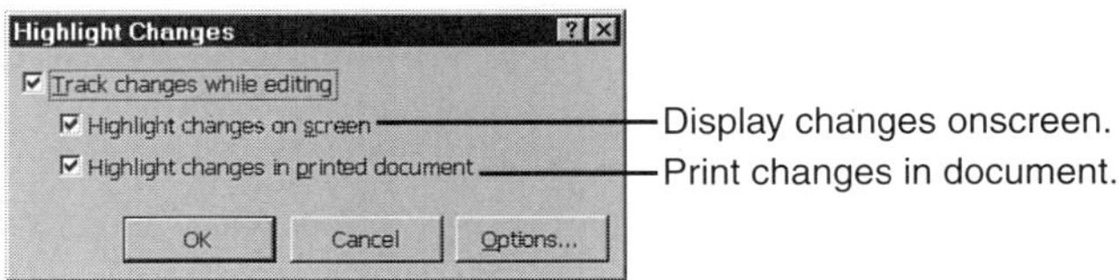

FIGURE 18.11
Printing and displaying of tracked changes are independent.

Click Options to display the dialog box shown in Figure 18.12. The Track Changes dialog box enables you to control exactly how tracked changes are displayed. You can choose among four different display attributes. Color enables you to choose a specific color; or, the default setting By Author tells Word to automatically choose one of 16 colors, assigning a different color for each author. Hopefully, you will never have more than 16 authors marking changes on a given document.

NOTE Don't take it personally if your comments show up in hot pink or seasick green. The default assignment is random. Closing and relaunching Word usually rewards you with a different color.

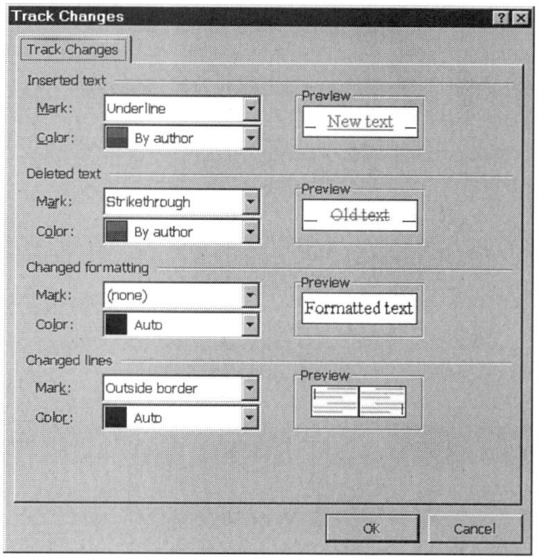

FIGURE 18.12
Word automatically assigns different colors for different authors.

Track Changes
Inserted text
Mark: Underline
Color: By author
Preview: New text
Deleted text
Mark: Strikethrough
Color: By author
Preview: Old text
Changed formatting
Mark: (none)
Color: Auto
Preview: Formatted text
Changed lines
Mark: Outside border
Color: Auto
Preview
OK Cancel

You can set the colors and attributes independently for inserted, deleted, or changed (formatting) text. The Changed Lines option enables you to display a vertical bar beside text that has any changes. By default, Word does not mark text with changed formatting. In some businesses, format changes are a hot topic—so, display them as needed.

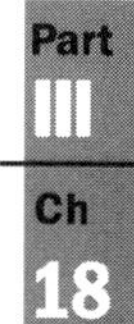

> **CAUTION**
>
> If changed formatting is denoted with double underlining, you might find it a little difficult to distinguish between any actual double underlining and tracked changes. Of course, the change lines in the margin would be a clue. For better results, if you choose to mark changed formatting, choose attributes and/or colors that are not part of the document's normal formatting.

Accepting or Rejecting Changes

Word provides a systematic way to review tracked changes. In a document containing tracked changes, right-click TRK on the Status Bar and choose Accept or Reject Changes, shown in Figure 18.13. If a change is selected, the author, time, and date are shown in the Changes section.

FIGURE 18.13
You can view the changed or the original text.

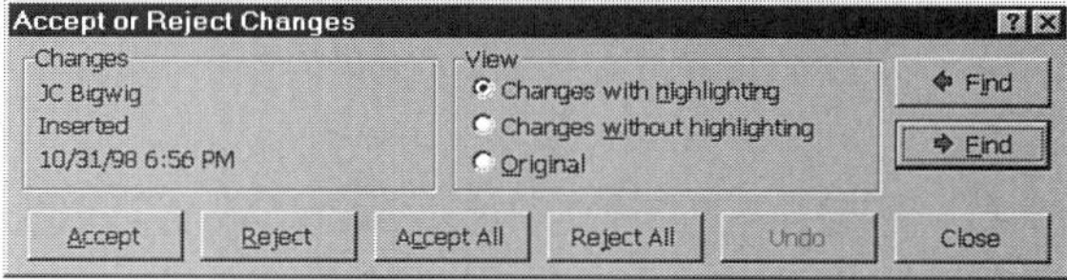

You can also use this dialog box to toggle the tracking displayed in the document. The view options are

- Changes with Highlighting—Displays changes with the selected attributes and colors.
- Changes Without Highlighting—Displays changed text without highlighting, letting you see how the changed text will appear.
- Original—Displays the unchanged text, enabling you to more easily determine the impact of the change.

With the Accept or Reject Changes dialog box onscreen, you can easily navigate forward and backward by using the Find arrows. Use the Reject, Accept, Reject All, and Accept All buttons to selectively or not-so-selectively issue a verdict on the changes; choose Undo for changes of heart.

Of course, if the document is swamped with unwanted, answered, and otherwise annoying queries, it's sometimes quicker to just turn tracking off and delete the unwanted material.

Reviewing Toolbar

An often overlooked alternative to the Comments and Tracking navigation methods discussed so far is the Reviewing toolbar. Users who discover the Reviewing toolbar usually find it more convenient than the Accept or Reject Changes dialog box. Simply choose View, Toolbars and select Reviewing to view the toolbar.

Comparing Two Documents

Sometimes, despite your best efforts, a changed document arrives in which the reviewer failed to track his or her revisions. Fortunately, Word enables you to compare two documents to find the changes. The end result is a "marked-up" version of the document that looks as if it were edited with tracking enabled.

To compare two documents, open the one that contains the changes. Choose Tools, Track Changes, Compare Documents. Navigate to the location of the original document, and choose Open. Word now compares the two, marking changes in the document as if the author had edited with Track Changes turned on.

CAUTION

Users frequently confuse Comparing documents with Merging documents. Comparing is for documents that do not contain tracked changes. Merging is for documents that already do contain tracked changes. Comparing inserts tracking into a document. Merging combines existing tracking from multiple documents.

Merging Changed Documents

Sometimes you might receive different copies of a document that contains different sets of tracked changes. Rather than going through them separately, you can merge them. To merge changes in multiple documents, open any document that contains tracked changes. Then, choose Tools, Merge Documents from the menu. Choose another version of the document that contains tracked changes. Repeat this until all documents containing changes have been merged. The resulting document contains all the tracked changes.

CAUTION

To merge, the only differences between documents must have occurred while Track Changes was enabled. If you attempt to merge a document containing unmarked changes, you will receive the warning:

```
The merged documents contain unmarked changes. Do you want to merge up to the
first untracked change?
```

The appropriate action at this point is to discontinue the merge (click Cancel), Compare the documents to mark the unmarked changes, and then try the merge again.

If the document already contains tracked changes, you should start by accepting all the tracked changes before beginning the Compare.

Working with Document Versions

The old-fashioned approach to dealing with different versions of the same document is to number them or to give them slightly differing names. With different document names, it's easy to get confused about exactly which version contains the latest changes.

The Version feature is also useful for saving slightly different versions of a document that have different purposes—such as letters, contracts, or boilerplate documents.

Word's Version feature enables you to save multiple versions of a document within a single file. To activate this feature, choose File, Versions to display the Versions control dialog box shown in Figure 18.14. Click Save Now. In the Save Version box, type comments that describe the version being saved, and click OK.

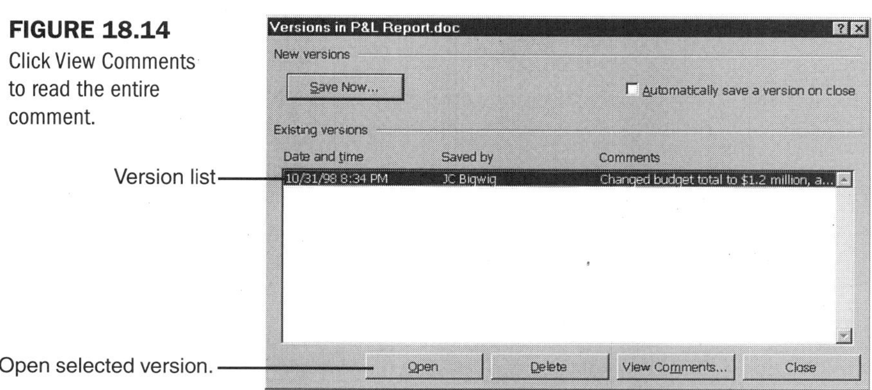

FIGURE 18.14
Click View Comments to read the entire comment.

When multiple versions exist, use the Versions dialog box to manage them. You can open, delete, and save. Each time you Save Now, a new version is added to the list.

Displaying Multiple Versions

You can display multiple versions of a file at the same time. Choose File, Versions, select the versions you want to open, and click Open. Word opens the selected versions, splitting the window horizontally so they can be seen at the same time.

You cannot, however, use Word's Compare feature to compare two different versions. To compare two different versions, save each version to a new filename and use the resulting files to perform the comparison. Alternatively, you can save the older version you want to compare to a new file. Then display the later version you want to compare (that is, using the multiversion document), run Compare Documents, and specify the newly named older version as the comparison file.

Importing and Exporting with Word

In years past, exporting and importing data between word processors and other programs have left users dreaming of the future—a time when everything would be compatible with everything else.

The first breakthrough for such dreamers came with the advent of *RTF*—rich text format. RTF was an attempt to provide a common document-formatting standard. To the extent that a number of office (that is, "office" with a little "o," which includes Corel WordPerfect and Lotus SmartSuite) application software programs adopted RTF as a supported format, RTF has served as a connectivity bridge between a number of applications offered by many different software publishers. By using a common set of formatting standards, the translation between different word processors is often better than when each tries to interpret the other's formatting.

The next major breakthrough to gain widespread acceptance came with *hypertext markup language* (HTML). Propelled forward by the success of the Web in making the Internet a household word, HTML has become a unifying principle. With Office 2000, HTML is now a common document language for all of Office, providing a rich vocabulary for presenting documents of increasing variety and complexity.

As you read this section, keep in mind that when all else fails, HTML and RTF usually provide a pathway for getting from here to there, and back again. So, without reading another word beyond this section of the book, you should be aware that you can transfer just about any data between Word and any other Office 2000 program by doing File, Save As and choosing either HTML or RTF format in one application. Then select File, Open, and setting Files of Type to HTML or RTF in the other application. You might want to do both, just so that you can use whichever gives you the better result for a given task.

There are, as it turns out, additional and often more efficient tools and techniques for getting Word to work with other Office applications. Rather than show you everything possible, the following sections lay out the quickest and easiest methods, knowing that you can always fall back on HTML and RTF in a pinch.

Importing an Access Table into a Word Document

Word offers several ways to import Access tables into a Word document. One way is to create a link to the Access table. Whenever data is updated in Access, it is updated in Word as well. Another way, that is less resource intensive, is to use the data in Word without a link. Use this approach if the database is unlikely to change. Copy the table to the Clipboard and paste it into Word. The approach you choose depends on your computing resources, how the document is to be used, and whether or not the data needs to be maintained just by Word.

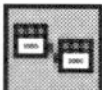

Position the insertion point where you want the table. In Word, display the Database toolbar, and click the Insert Database tool. Word displays the Database dialog box. Use the following general steps to open the desired Access table:

1. Click Get Data, set Files of Type to MS Access Databases, and navigate to and open the desired file.
2. If prompted, to Confirm Data Source, click OK.
3. Using the displayed Microsoft Access controls, select the desired table or query; when you complete that process, you are returned to the Database dialog box.
4. In the Database dialog box, choose Query Options.
5. Using Query Options, select the desired fields to build the table you want in the Select Fields tab (see Figure 18.15). Click OK when done.

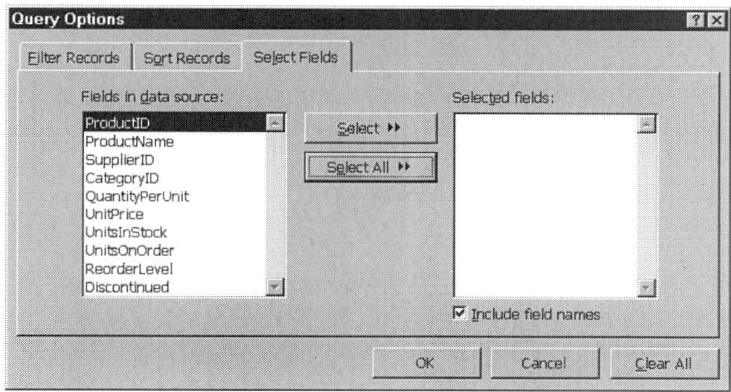

FIGURE 18.15
Use Query Options to select the desired table fields.

6. Again in the Database dialog box, if desired, click Table AutoFormat and choose an appropriate table style.
7. Click Insert Data; choose All or specify the records you want, as shown in Figure 18.16.

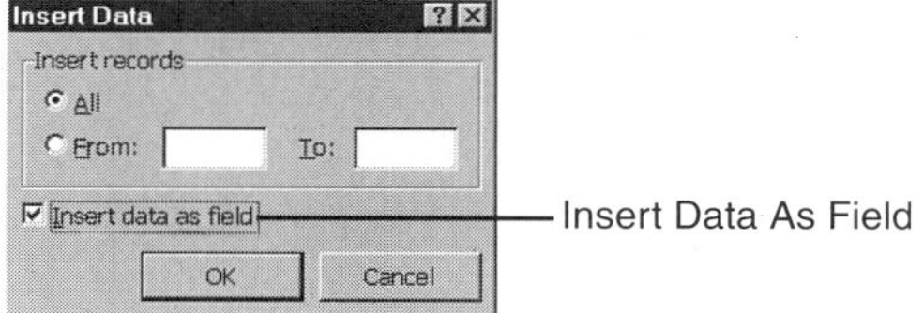

FIGURE 18.16
You can limit the table to specific records.

8. To create a link to the Access database, click Insert Data As Field. To insert the table without a link, leave the Field option unchecked. Click OK.

The selected data is now inserted as a Word table, as shown in Figure 18.17. From here, you can use standard table-formatting techniques to arrange the table as you want it to appear.

FIGURE 18.17
Shading indicates that the table cells are part of a Word field.

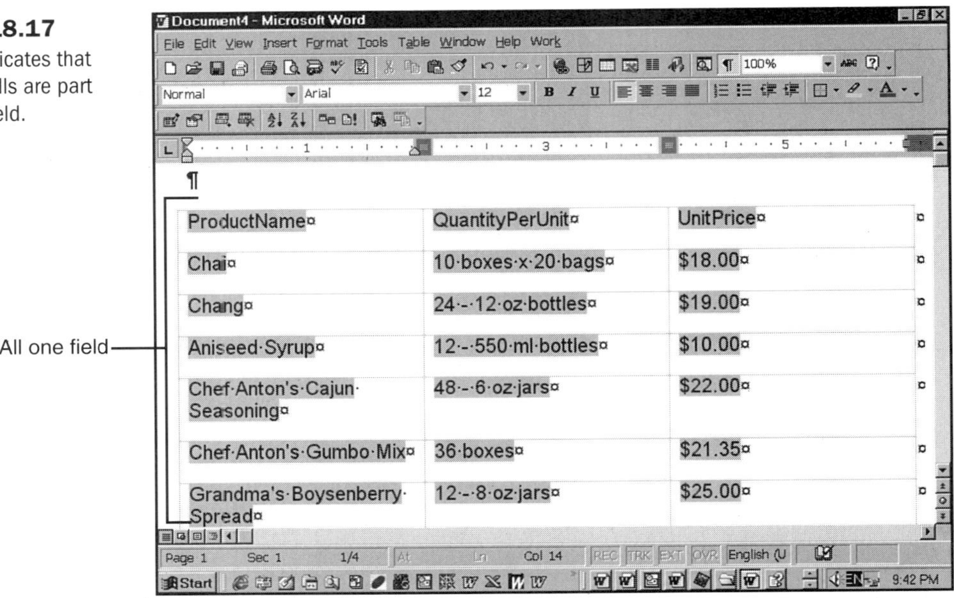

If you don't want a link to Access, and if the table is already displayed in Access, simply select the table and copy it to the Clipboard. Then, in Word, choose Edit, Paste Special, and insert the table as Formatted Text (RTF). Then reformat the table as desired.

Importing Access Data into a Word Table

You can also import Access data directly into an existing Word table. You might want to do this when some data has changed, but not all, and you don't want to go to the trouble of completely re-creating and reformatting a Word table.

In Access, display the table that contains the data you want to import. Select the data that you want to use and copy it to the Clipboard. If you're copying to an existing table, the shape of the copied data must exactly match that in Word. For example, if you're replacing a 5×4 section of a table, the selection in Access must also be 5×4. Word will not warn you if the shapes don't match. If the shapes don't match, the data will not fill the table correctly.

To copy to an existing table, select the cells you want to replace and choose Edit, Paste Special, Unformatted Text. This enables you to paste the new data over the old without reformatting the table. Note that while this preserves the table formatting itself, it does not preserve the paragraph formatting inside the table.

To create a new table, choose Edit, Paste Special, Formatted Text (RTF).

Sometimes you get different results from different paste operations—it's difficult to predict what works best for any given situation. It takes only a moment to try it several ways. Then choose the best technique, and make a note for next time.

Importing Excel Data into a Word Table

Bringing Excel data into a Word table is similar to exporting Access data into Word. In Excel, find the data you want to use in Word and copy it to the Clipboard. You can now paste that data into Word in several ways, depending on the objective:

- Paste as nonlink, unformatted—Replaces existing table or cells.
- Paste as link, Formatted Text (RTF)—Creates an updatable new table (that is, when the Excel source changes).
- Paste as link, Microsoft Excel Worksheet Object— Enables you to edit the table using Excel controls from within Word.
- Paste as hyperlink—Inserts the table as a clickable link that starts Excel.

To correctly paste into an existing table, the shapes of the two data areas must match exactly. Note that Word does not warn you if the shapes don't match. In Word, select the table area you want to replace and choose Edit, Paste Special. Choose Unformatted Text, and choose Paste—*not* Paste Link, as shown in Figure 18.18.

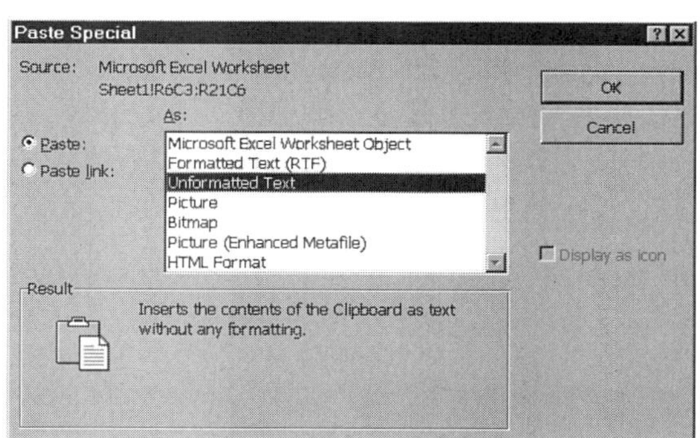

FIGURE 18.18
Unformatted text preserves table formatting at the destination, but not paragraph or font formatting.

NOTE If you're not sure whether the table shapes match, you can paste the Excel data into your Word document outside the table. Use the Edit, Paste Special command to ensure the data is pasted in the way you want.

You can also open an Excel worksheet directly from within Word—without using the Clipboard. Choose either Insert, File or File, Open—depending on whether you want to place worksheet data in a file by itself or insert it into an existing file.

In the Insert File or Open dialog box, set Files of Type to All (*.*). Use the Look In drop-down box to change to the location of the desired file. Click Insert or Open (depending on whether you're using Insert, File or File, Open).

In the Open Worksheet dialog box, shown in Figure 18.19, choose the desired options, and click OK. Use Open Document in Workbook to choose either Entire Workbook or the desired sheet. Use Name or Cell Range to specify a named range or a range of cells. For example, A1:C12 specifies a range that includes Columns A through C, and rows 1 through 12. The Format for Mail Merge option creates a table with column headings, set up for working with Word's mail-merge feature.

The incoming data is formatted as a Word table, rather than as an Excel object. This means that you can edit the table using Word's formatting and editing commands, rather than by using OLE to access Excel.

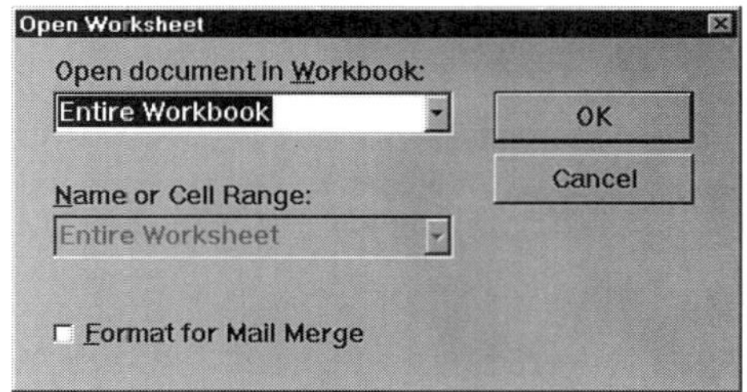

FIGURE 18.19
You can choose an entire worksheet, some of the worksheet data, or named ranges when importing Excel data.

CAUTION

When opening an existing Excel worksheet rather than inserting it, be careful not to save any work you do over the original Excel worksheet. Choose File, Save As, and save the file in Word format under a new name.

Exporting a Word Table to Excel Worksheet

You can send data from a Word table to Excel—and back again, if necessary. This sometimes is useful when it turns out that your computational needs exceed what you can comfortably do in Word. So, you might move a table into Excel, perform the desired computations, and then bring it back into Word.

To export a Word table into an Excel worksheet, copy it to the Clipboard in Word, and then paste it into Excel. That is, in Word, select the table (Table, Select, Table). Choose Edit, Copy to copy it to the Clipboard. Then switch to Excel and choose Edit, Paste.

A straight paste—that is, without resorting to Paste Special features—usually works well. Use this technique when you plan to export the data for calculation purposes and then bring it back into Word later.

To link the data pasted into Excel back to the Word table, in Excel, use the Edit, Paste Special, Paste As Link, Text command. This inserts the table's numbers into the Excel worksheet, using Excel's formatting. Because it's a link, however, change in the contents (in the originating Word document) can be updated in the Excel spreadsheet.

Or, if you want to control the table in Excel by using Word controls, paste it as a Microsoft Word Document Object, instead. When pasted this way, you edit the resulting table (in Excel) by double-clicking it. Excel creates a mini-Word window within Excel for you to modify the table.

Exporting Word Text to PowerPoint Presentation

There is a variety of ways to move text from Word to a PowerPoint presentation. The task works best, however, if you begin with an understanding of PowerPoint's relationship with Word. When you import a slide from a PowerPoint presentation into Word, the slide's titles, subtitles, and points are formatted as Heading 1, Heading 2, and so on styles in Word.

When you export text from Word to PowerPoint: Heading 1 becomes the title; Heading 2 and below become points (bullets) in the slides.

When PowerPoint sees a Heading 1 in the Word document, it creates a new slide and all headings underneath the Heading 1 become part of that slide. The next Heading 1 encountered triggers a new slide.

NOTE Only the outline headings get exported to PowerPoint. Text formatted with other styles, such as Normal, stays behind.

Suppose you have a report in Word, and you need to create supporting slides for it in PowerPoint. You have several options:

- Copy and paste (using Formatted RTF to preserve heading styles)
- Open directly from PowerPoint (File, Open, set Files of Type to All Outlines, navigate to the file, and click Open)
- Use HTML as an intermediary format (save as HTML from Word; open as HTML from PowerPoint)
- Use RTF as an intermediary format (save as RTF from Word; open as RTF from PowerPoint)
- Use Word's Send to PowerPoint option (File, Send To, Microsoft PowerPoint)

NOTE In the third bullet listed previously, if Word is your default HTML editor, then opening the file as HTML will invoke Word rather than PowerPoint.

Each of these methods provides varying degrees of success, depending on the formatting in the Word document. PowerPoint's first formatting efforts convert Heading styles into corresponding title, subtitle, and text levels. If the document does not use Heading styles,

PowerPoint next attempts to interpret the structure using paragraph indentation. This is not usually very satisfactory.

The most successful technique uses the following general steps:

1. Use Outline view in Word to create a document framework; use Heading 1 as the style for each major heading, keeping in mind that PowerPoint creates one slide for each Heading 1 it encounters. See Chapter 16 for additional information on how to use outlining in Word.
2. When the document is done, choose File, Send To, Microsoft PowerPoint. Word saves the file outline in RTF format, opens PowerPoint, and imports the RTF file.

Word doesn't provide a built-in way to get just an outline for an existing document—that is, with the text stripped out. You can use the technique just described to send an outline to PowerPoint. Then, in PowerPoint, immediately choose File, Send To, Microsoft Word, and just the outline is sent to Word.

For example, Figure 18.20 shows a seminar-planning document created in Microsoft Word 2000. Shown in Outlining view, this document contains a full complement of text below each heading level.

FIGURE 18.20
Word headings become PowerPoint titles, subtitles, and points.

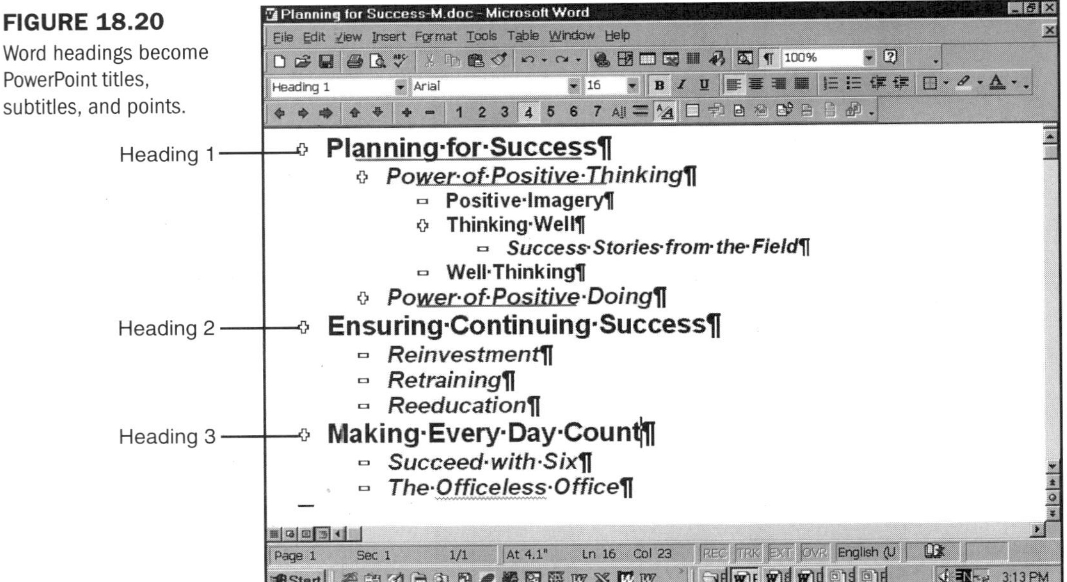

Choosing File, Send To, Microsoft PowerPoint creates a new PowerPoint presentation, as shown in Figure 18.21.

FIGURE 18.21
PowerPoint imports Word headings as titles, subtitles, and points.

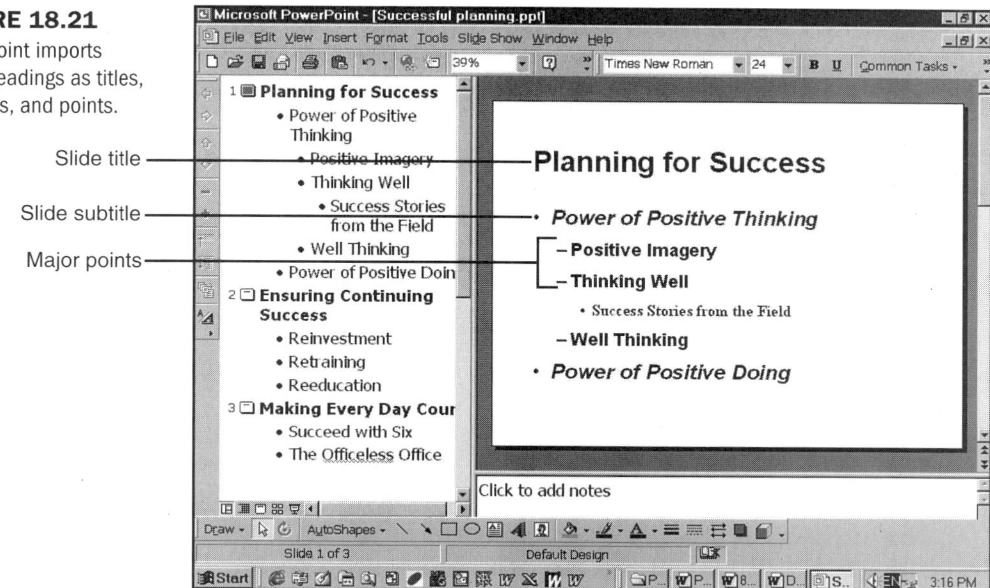

NOTE You cannot limit the levels that go over to PowerPoint. Thus, if your outline goes down to Heading 9, those headings go, as well. However, PowerPoint itself does not go beyond level 6. If the underlying text in Heading 6 through Heading 9 is formatted with different attributes (colors, italic, underlining, and so on) in Word, then those attributes will be sent into PowerPoint. However, the text size and indentation will be identical in PowerPoint for Heading 6 through Heading 9 levels. You'll be happy to know, however, that the same promote, demote, move up, and move down keystrokes that work in Word also work in PowerPoint.

See Chapter 16 for additional information on working with outlines.

PART IV

Microsoft Excel

CHAPTER 19

Migrating to Excel 2000

In this chapter

Upgrading from Excel 95

If you're upgrading from Excel 95 to Excel 2000, there are a number of features that were added in Excel 97. Although these are not technically new in Excel 2000, they will be new to you and are significant enough to warrant some discussion here. For example, starting in Excel 97 each worksheet now contains 65,536 rows, an increase from 16,384. This increase is very important for people who need to maintain extremely large worksheets. The number of columns—256—remains unchanged.

In a similar vein, the default number of sheets available when you create a new workbook has been reduced from 16 to 3. This was done to avoid storing a large number of empty worksheets. Of course, you can insert as many additional worksheets as you need. Likewise, cells can now contain 32,767 characters—an increase from 255 in Excel 95. The next few sections describe other important features added in Excel 97.

Creating and Editing Worksheet Functions

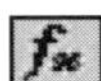

Several new enhancements were added in Excel 97 that make it easier to create and edit worksheet functions. The Function Wizard in Excel 95 has been replaced by the *Paste Function* command. This command expands on the features that were part of the Function Wizard, making it easier to use the built-in worksheet functions. Figure 19.1 shows the Paste Function dialog box.

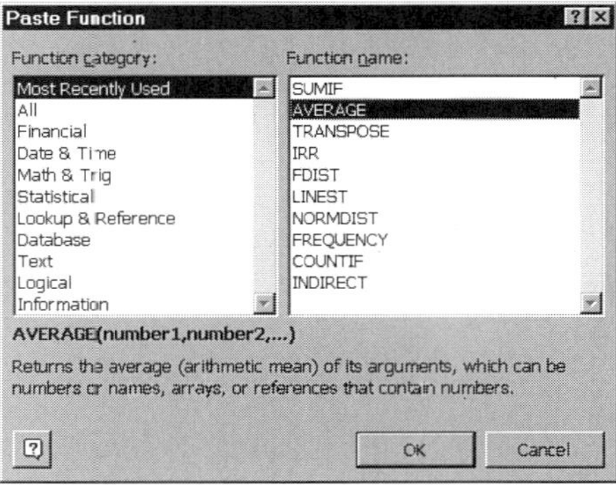

FIGURE 19.1
The Paste Function command in Excel 97 and 2000 is similar to the first step in the Function Wizard in Excel 95.

After you select a function to use, the Formula Palette dialog box appears as shown in Figure 19.2. Although it is anchored just below the Formula Bar, it can float in the middle of the screen if you drag it from any part of the gray background. The *Formula Palette* displays a description of the function and each argument. It also contains a new feature you will see in many dialog boxes, the *collapse/expand button*. Use this button when you need to select cells hidden by the dialog box. Click this button to toggle between collapsing and expanding the dialog box. When collapsed, just one line for the active argument is visible.

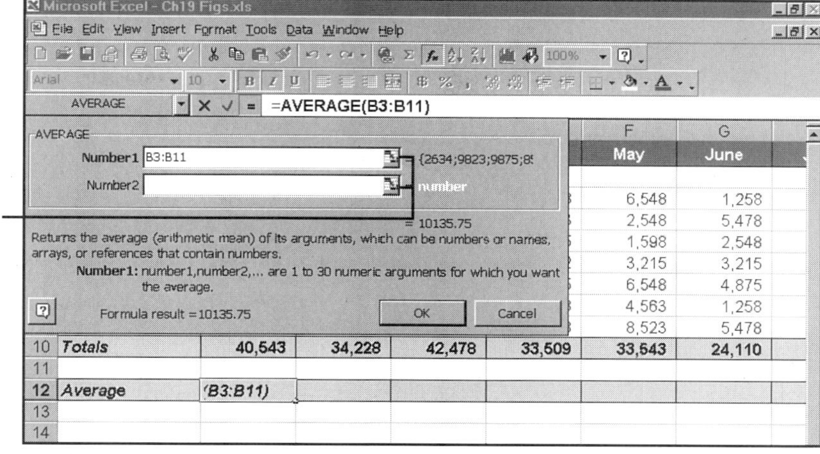

FIGURE 19.2
Use the Formula Palette to identify the arguments for the function you select.

NOTE The dialog box collapses automatically if you begin selecting cells in the worksheet.

If you are accustomed to selecting a range name from the Name Box to insert in a formula, this feature is no longer available—regardless of whether the Formula Palette is used to create the formula, or you simply type an equal (=) sign to start a formula. The Name Box is replaced by a drop-down option used to select other functions. This is designed to help build nested functions. To access the list of worksheet range names, press F3. The Paste Names dialog box appears from which you can select a range name.

▶ **See** "Advanced Formulas," **p. 629**

▶ **See** "Nesting Functions," **p. 677**

Improved Chart Wizard

One of the most significant improvements in Excel 97 was the revamping of Microsoft Graph, the charting program for Office applications. The Chart Wizard is easier to use and several new chart types have been added. Cylinder, pyramid, and cone charts are three-dimensional variations of column and bar charts. Bubble charts are a type of XY (scatter) chart used to compare sets of at least three values. In addition to these new chart types, there are now several useful variations of pie charts available, including pie-of-pie and bar-of-pie.

▶ **See** "Which Chart Type Do I Use?" **p. 816**

Editing Data and Validating Data Entry

The capability to perform multiple Undos was finally added to Excel in version 97, providing more flexibility in editing worksheets.

Another feature added in Excel 97 that you will find useful is *Data Validation*. Through this command, you have three options for controlling data entry:

- You can control the data that can be entered in a cell by displaying a list of choices or by placing restrictions on the entries.
- You can create input messages that instruct users on the appropriate data to be entered in a cell.
- You can display an error message if incorrect data is entered in a cell or have Excel draw circles around invalid entries in the worksheet.

These options can be used separately or in conjunction with one another. You access this feature by selecting Data, Validation.

▶ **See** "Validating and Analyzing Excel Data," **p. 860**

Conditional Formatting

A useful formatting enhancement added in Excel 97 is *Conditional Formatting*. This feature changes the appearance of the cell based on conditions (or criteria) you specify. The changes can be to the data in the cell (such as applying bold, italic, or font color) or to the cell itself (such as border style, border color, or background color).

The conditions can be based on the data in the cell where conditional formatting is applied, or based on the data in other cells. For example, you can have the worksheet display formula results differently if the results are above or below a certain number. You can have any number that is below the average number appear in a different color or format. Chapter 22, "Advanced Formulas" explores some advanced uses for Conditional Formatting.

▶ **See** "Conditional Formatting," **p. 630**

Merging Workbooks

Instead of sharing a workbook with other users, you can provide separate copies of a workbook to users and then merge the copies, along with any comments or changes, into one workbook file. This feature was added in Excel 97.

▶ **See** "Sharing and Merging Workbooks," **p. 937**

Merging Cells

In earlier versions of Excel, you could select several cells; and, by clicking a button on the Formatting toolbar, the data would be centered across the selected cells. This feature is still available in Excel, but the toolbar button is now used to merge the cells into one cell and center the data. Although these features may seem similar, they are in fact quite different.

Merging physically combines the several cells into one cell in the worksheet. You can merge cells across columns or across rows. The Center Across Selection option simply changes the display of the data; the cells remain unchanged. When cells are merged, the upper-leftmost cell reference becomes the reference for the merged cells. If the selected cells contain data, only the upper-left cell that contains data is retained when the cells are merged. Fortunately, Excel warns you before merging that several cells contain data and that data will be lost if you proceed with the merge.

To split cells that have been merged or to access just the Center Across Selection feature, choose Format, Cells and click the Alignment tab. To split cells that are merged, unmark the Merge Cells check box. To apply the Center Across Selection format, click the Horizontal alignment drop-down and choose Center Across Selection.

Indenting and Rotating Data

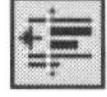

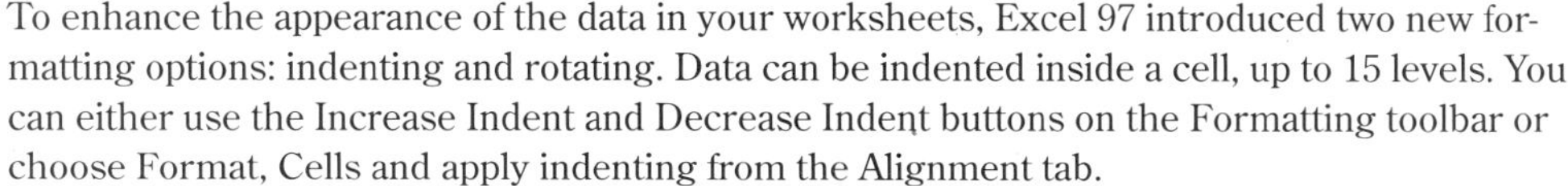

To enhance the appearance of the data in your worksheets, Excel 97 introduced two new formatting options: indenting and rotating. Data can be indented inside a cell, up to 15 levels. You can either use the Increase Indent and Decrease Indent buttons on the Formatting toolbar or choose Format, Cells and apply indenting from the Alignment tab.

You can rotate data in a cell from 90 degrees to –90 degrees, at 1-degree increments. Another option is change the orientation of the data to display vertically. This feature is also available through Format, Cells

New and Altered Features in Excel 2000

Excel 2000 offers a number of enhancements over Excel 97. The main areas include information sharing via webs, online collaboration, multilanguage support, and ease-of-use enhancements. These improvements have largely been designed for corporate users who do business on a national and international level.

You'll undoubtedly run into other minor enhancements and changes as you work in Excel 2000, but the next few sections discuss the most significant changes.

Web-Based Information Sharing

The new *Office Web Components* (described in Chapter 3, "Unleashing the Office 2000 Web Tools") are a set of COM controls for publishing interactive worksheet, charts, and PivotTables to a Web. Corporate data can be published to a company intranet where employees can not only view, but manipulate, the data directly in a Web browser. You can:

- Perform calculations on worksheet data
- Sort and filter worksheet data
- Change worksheet formatting
- Provide live updates as the data used to create charts is changed
- Adjust the chart options
- Alter the PivotTable sort and filter options
- Group the PivotTable data to generate different summaries

For example, international sales data provided in a PivotTable can be displayed in a number of useful ways—by geographic location, by sales representative, by type of product. This data is not only useful to the sales force, but can be used by many departments for budgeting and planning purposes. The manufacturing department can use the data to plan production cycles. The personnel department can use the data to determine whether additional bilingual sales staff is required for emerging markets and so on.

▶ **See** "The Office Web Components," **p. 56**

Online Collaboration

In previous versions of Excel you had several options for collaborating on a workbook with others. You could

- Provide individual copies of the workbook to others to edit and add comments to, and then merge the workbook versions into one file.
- Provide a single copy of the workbook for others to edit and add comments to, either setting up the workbook for workgroup sharing or routing the workbook to others via email.
- Hold a meeting and hope everyone involved would be able to attend.

Recognizing that businesses today require more flexible methods for collaborating, Microsoft provides several new ways to collaborate with colleagues online: You can hold online meetings using an applet called NetMeeting or you can use the new Web Discussions feature to collaborate on an Excel workbook. Both of these new features are introduced in Chapter 3. You find additional information about using these features in Chapter 29, "Sharing Excel Data with Other Users and Applications."

International Language Support

With Office 2000's commitment to multilingual support, companies that have multinational users will find it easier to create and edit worksheets in a wide range of languages. The language of the user interface can easily be changed, should employees traveling to other countries need to work in their native language. The help screens and editing/proofing tools will also adjust to the language selected.

▶ **See** "International Features," **p. 34**

Protecting Workbooks with Passwords

Excel includes the capability to protect a workbook from being opened or changed by requiring users to enter a password. To implement the password protection, the workbook must be saved using the File, Save As command.

In previous versions of Excel, there was an Options button in the Save As dialog box from which you accessed the password protection alternatives. With the new design of the Open and Save As dialog boxes, this button is no longer available. Instead, you will find this feature under the Tools drop-down menu in the Save As dialog box. From the Tools menu, choose General Options; the password protection options will appear, as shown in Figure 19.3. Although the wording has changed slightly, you can still require a password to open the file or a password to provide read/write access to the file, or both.

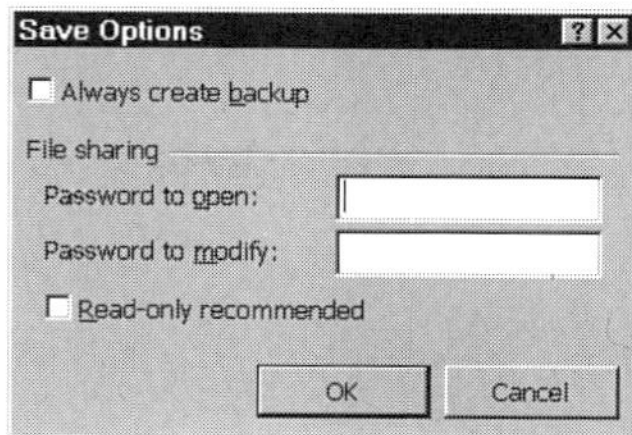

FIGURE 19.3
You can apply one or both password options to the workbook.

Toolbar Changes in Excel 2000

In addition to the new behavior of the personalized toolbars in Excel (described in Chapter 1, "General Office Features at a Glance"), there have been a few changes to the toolbars that you will encounter. When you right-click any toolbar, three new toolbars are now included on the list of Excel toolbars:

- 3-D Settings
- Shadow Settings
- Clipboard

In Excel 97, the 3-D Settings and Shadow Settings were only tear-off palettes buried in the Drawing toolbar under the 3-D and Shadows buttons. Although they are still available in that capacity, they are also now available independent of the Drawing toolbar as their own toolbars.

The Clipboard toolbar is used to manage a brand-new, and extremely useful, feature known as Collect and Paste. You can use the toolbar to gather a group of clips to be pasted at one time, or to hold a clip to paste in multiple locations. This feature is particularly handy for copying formulas to multiple locations in the active worksheet or to other worksheets and workbooks. The Clipboard toolbar will also be extremely useful when you need to copy data from Excel into other applications, such as a Word document or a PowerPoint slide. The Clipboard toolbar can hold up to 12 items.

CAUTION

Display the Clipboard toolbar before you begin copying the clips; otherwise, only the last clip is retained in memory. If you subsequently hide the Clipboard toolbar, the clip-stacking feature is still enabled until you exit Windows.

▶ **See** "Personalized Menus and Toolbars," **p. 19**

▶ **See** "Clipboard Toolbar," **p. 189**

PivotTable Toolbar Changes There have been a number of enhancements made to PivotTables in Excel 2000. You no longer have to access the PivotTable Wizard to add or remove fields from the PivotTable; you can make the adjustments directly in the worksheet. A new AutoFormat feature makes formatting a PivotTable effortless. In addition, corresponding graphic charts, called *PivotCharts*, have been added to the PivotTable report feature in Excel 2000. Like the new interactive PivotTable layouts, the PivotChart layouts let you adjust the data plotted directly in the chart.

As a result of these changes, the PivotTable toolbar has been revised. Figure 19.4 shows a PivotTable and the revised PivotTable toolbar.

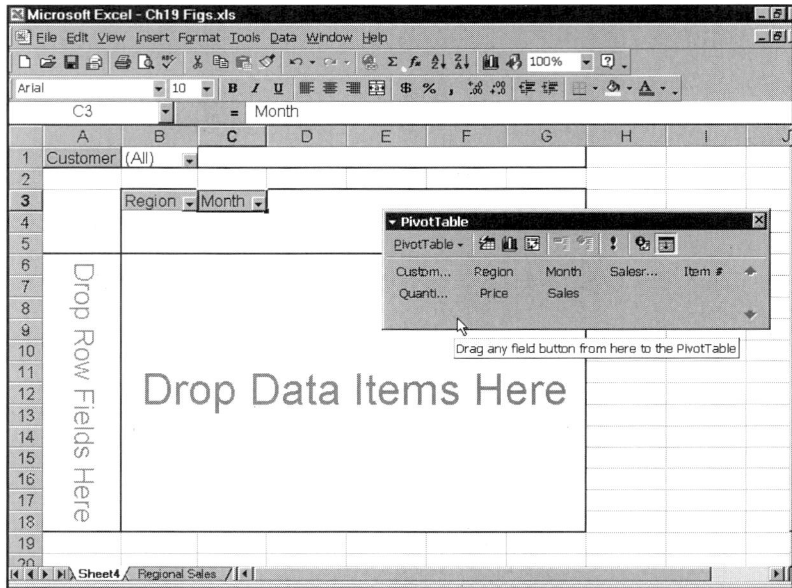

FIGURE 19.4
The list fields that can be used in the PivotTable automatically appear with the toolbar.

The following list describes the changes to the PivotTable toolbar from Excel 97 to Excel 2000:

- The Format Report button (new) displays predefined AutoFormats you can select for the PivotTable.
- The PivotChart option (new) creates a PivotChart based on the PivotTable data.
- The Client Server Settings option (new) is available under the PivotTable drop-down list. This option is used with offline OLAP cube files. Chapter 24, "Importing Data from Databases, Web Pages, and Text Files" discusses OLAP cubes.

- The Fields Dialog Box button was previously called the Fields button.

- The Display/Hide Fields button (new) shows the list fields you can use in your pivot table. The toolbar expands to show the list of fields. By default, fields are displayed.
- The Table Options were accessible only from the menu bar or PivotTable wizard in previous versions of Excel. Now you have quick access to the format and data options in the PivotTable options dialog box.
- The Show Pages button has been moved to the PivotTable drop-down list.

- There are no longer Select buttons directly on the toolbar; they have been moved to the Select option on the PivotTable drop-down list.

▶ **See** "Unlocking the Power of PivotTables and PivotCharts," **p. 797**

Visual Basic Toolbar Changes As with the PivotTable toolbar, the Visual Basic toolbar is not new, but there have been a few changes. This toolbar is often used when designing and testing new VBA code or macros. The toolbar provides a bit more control over the development process without having to assign the code to keyboard shortcuts or toolbar buttons.

The following list describes the Visual Basic toolbar changes from Excel 97 to Excel 2000:

- The Security option (new) lets you pick a security level and designate trusted sources.

- The Microsoft Script Editor option (new) launches the script editor where you can develop scripts for handling information input over the Web, and to make Web pages more interactive.
- The Resume Macro button that was previously on the toolbar has been removed.

Hidden Keyboard Shortcuts in Excel

In every Office program, keyboard shortcuts have been developed for many common actions, from formatting to printing. A handful of these shortcuts are listed when you click the menus—for example, Ctrl+C for Copy. However, there are dozens of shortcuts available that are not listed through the menus.

All of the Office 2000 programs—all except Excel—have a feature that will show keyboard shortcuts for toolbar buttons. When you position the mouse pointer over a toolbar button, the shortcut appears as part of the ScreenTip identifying the toolbar button. In the other programs, you turn this feature on through the Options tab in the Customize dialog box (Tools, Customize).

For whatever reason, Microsoft has neglected to implement this useful feature in Excel. However, if you are a diehard keyboard fan (or want to become one), you can learn about the hidden keyboard shortcuts through Help. Type `keyboard shortcuts` in the Office Assistant search box and press Enter. From the list of help topics that appears, choose `keyboard shortcuts`. From the help screen, shown in Figure 19.5, choose the type of shortcuts you want to learn about.

Ever hear of the "Squeaky Wheel Theory"? If enough of us request keyboard shortcuts be displayed with toolbar ScreenTips, perhaps we'll see this feature in the next release of Excel.

NOTE Microsoft provides an email address and Web site for users to make suggestions or requests for enhancements:

`mswish@microsoft.com`

`www.microsoft.com/mswish`

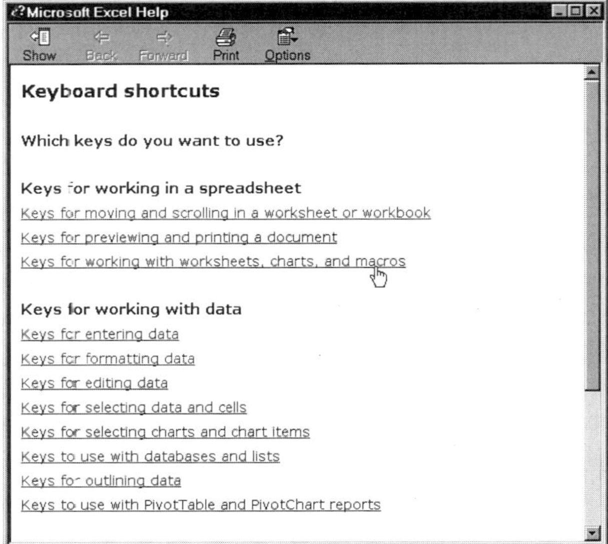

FIGURE 19.5
Excel's main help screen for keyboard shortcuts.

Menu Changes in Excel 2000

Aside from the new behavior of the menus (described in Chapter 1), none of the menu commands you used in Excel 97 has been moved in Excel 2000. However, some commands have been added to or modified on several of the menus:

- File menu—Save As Web Page replaces Save As HTML.
- File menu—Web Page Preview command added.
- Tools menu—Online Collaboration command added.
- Data menu—PivotTable and PivotChart Report command replaces the PivotTable Report command.
- Window menu—Next Pane command added.
- Help menu—Detect and Repair command added.

Considerations When Converting Excel Documents

You will have no trouble bringing Excel 97, 95, or even Excel 5.0 files into Excel 2000. Files created in earlier versions of Excel open easily in Excel 2000. When you open a workbook in Excel 2000 that was created in an earlier version, the file is not converted to Excel 2000. However, when you attempt to save the file (using the File, Save command or Save button), an alert displays reminding you the file was created in another version of Excel, and asks whether you want to save the file in Excel 2000 (see Figure 19.6).

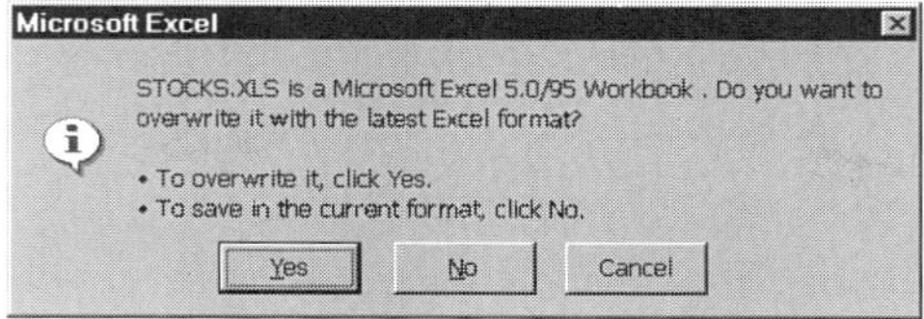

FIGURE 19.6
This alert gives you the option of saving the workbook as an Excel 2000 workbook.

Surprisingly, you can easily take Excel 2000 files into Excel 97, 95, and 5.0.

- When you want to open an Excel 2000 workbook in Excel 97, you do not have to save it in an Excel 97 format. You can open it directly in Excel 97.
- If you want to open an Excel 2000 file in Excel 95, 5.0, or an earlier version, you will need to save it in the earlier format using the File, Save As command. Figure 19.7 shows these options in the Save As dialog box.

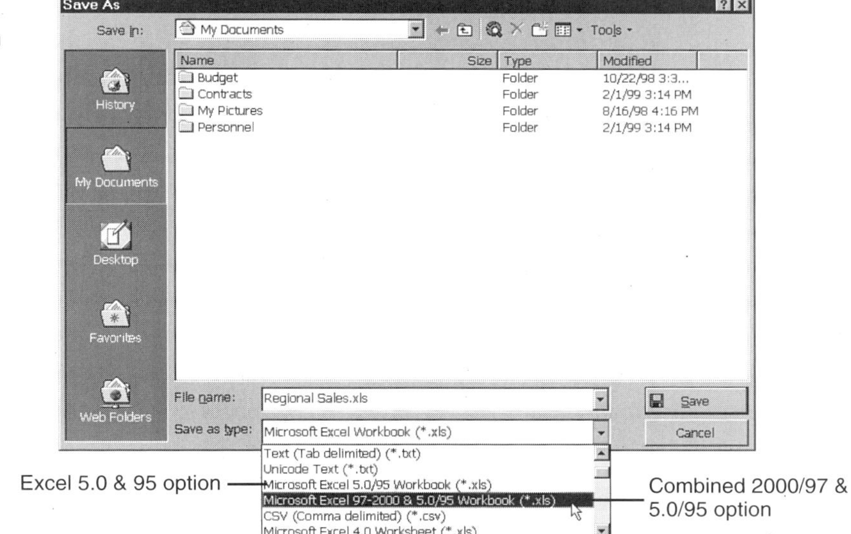

FIGURE 19.7
Choose the best option for your purposes from the Save As Type drop-down list.

When you open the Excel 2000 workbook in an earlier version, however, some of the Excel 2000 features use the earlier version's closest equivalent or simply will not function.

For example, suppose you create a PivotTable and PivotChart in an Excel 2000 workbook. The data plotted in the PivotChart is linked to the PivotTable data. When you open this workbook in Excel 97, the PivotTable is intact. The PivotChart is converted to a normal Excel chart. Additionally, the link between the data is broken—changing the data in the PivotTable will not change the data plotted in the chart. The good news is that when you open the workbook in Excel 2000 again, the link is reestablished.

If you routinely need to open a workbook in Excel 5.0, 95, 97, and 2000, there is a special dual file format option enabling you to do this (see Figure 19.7). When you choose a combination file format option, any new formatting or functionality that the earlier version of Excel does not recognize will be ignored by the earlier version.

NOTE When you use the Excel 2000-97 & 5.0/95 Workbook dual file format, the workbook is saved as a single file, but the 2000-97 formatting is saved separately from the 5.0/95 formatting. Therefore, the file size will be larger because it contains both sets of data.

CAUTION

When a workbook saved in the dual file format is opened in either Excel 5.0 or 95, a warning displays suggesting the file be opened Read Only. If the warning is ignored and the file is saved in the earlier version of Excel, the features and formatting available only in Excel 2000 or Excel 97 will be lost.

Additionally, Excel 95 and earlier versions allow fewer characters in a cell and have fewer rows in a worksheet. If your data extends beyond the limits in these versions, the data will be truncated.

A complete and detailed description of what happens when you save an Excel 2000 workbook in Excel 97, 95, or 5.0 is available through Excel help.

Converting Excel Macros

You should have very little trouble converting macros or VBA code created in Excel 97. Changes to the Excel architecture (expanded rows in worksheet and characters in a cell) may cause problems with macros written in Excel 95 and earlier versions.

If you are converting VBA and XLM macros from Excel 5.0, you should be able to run them in Excel 2000. However, you cannot record new XLM macros in Excel 2000. New macros can be recorded in Excel 2000 and edited in the Visual Basic Editor (VBE), or you can write them directly in the VBE (Tools, Macros, Visual Basic Editor).

NOTE Developers who design Excel application solutions that will be used across several versions of Excel typically write in the lowest-common-denominator code. Hence, some developers are still using Excel 4.0 macro functions. Help for these macros is not available through the Excel 2000 help screens. However, you can download the Macro Function Help files (Macrofun.hlp) from the Microsoft Knowledge Base article titled "XL:Macrofun.exe File Available on Online Services." You can see this article at the following Web location:

`http://support.microsoft.com/support/kb/articles/q128/1/85.asp`

If you used dialog sheets in Excel 5.0 and Excel 95, most dialog sheets should run in Excel 2000 without the need to change them. New custom dialog boxes, called *user forms*, are created in the VBE. After you are in the VBE, choose Insert, UserForm.

NOTE Visual Basic 6.0, the latest version of Visual Basic for Applications, is included with Office 2000. VBA 6.0 includes features such as modeless user forms and support for additional ActiveX controls.

▶ **See** "Getting Acquainted with VBA," **p. 105**

▶ **See** "Designing `UserForms`," **p. 170**

Converting Excel HTML Files from Previous Excel Versions

Likewise, files you saved as HTML files in earlier versions of Excel should convert seamlessly into Excel 2000. The File, Save As HTML command has been replaced by the File, Save As Web Page command and a new command—File, Web Page Preview—has been added so you can preview a worksheet as a Web page before you save it.

▶ **See** "Sharing Excel Data with Other Users and Applications," **p. 929**

CHAPTER 20

Customizing Excel 2000

In this chapter

Excel Startup Options

Sometimes you may want to start Excel and immediately display a specific document. Or perhaps you are working on an important project with a group and for the duration of the project you want to designate a particular folder as the default folder for opening and saving files. In these situations, you can use command-line switches to change the way Excel starts up. The phrase *command-line switches* is a holdover from the days of DOS when you typed a command to open a program. The switches (most of which start with a forward slash followed by a letter) were used in DOS, just as they are in Windows, to designate program startup alternatives. However, because Windows is a point-and-click operating system, the best way to invoke a startup switch is to create a desktop shortcut to the application and enter the switch in the shortcut startup properties.

- If the changes you want to make are temporary—for a set period of time—then the best approach is to create a shortcut on the desktop that starts Excel with the switches you want.
- If you want to have several startup alternatives, then create a folder on the desktop to store the shortcuts.

NOTE If you haven't already done so, change the setting in Windows to display file extensions. From either My Computer or Windows Explorer, choose View, Folder Options. Click the View tab and uncheck the setting Hide File Extensions for Known File Types and click OK. Not only will this help identify the program executable files (.exe) here, but will be handy in identifying file types when opening and saving files in all the Office applications.

Assuming you want to create several startup alternatives, you'll need to create a shortcut:

1. The first thing you need to do is create a folder on the desktop to store the Excel startup options. Right-click the desktop and choose New, Folder. Name the folder something like `Excel Shortcuts`.
2. Next, double-click the folder icon to open the new folder. Right-click anywhere inside the folder and choose New, Shortcut to create the first shortcut.
3. In the Create Shortcut dialog box, click Browse to locate the Excel program executable file (excel.exe). It is usually located in the Program Files folder; for example:

   C:\Program Files\Microsoft Office\Office
4. When you locate the excel.exe file, click Open, as shown in Figure 20.1. You are returned to the Create Shortcut dialog box and the path to the executable is displayed in the Command Line text box. Click Next.
5. Unless you already know what startup switch you want to use, just type a name that you'll remember later in the File Name: field. In this example, "`Excel`" is used to replace excel.exe. Then click Finish.

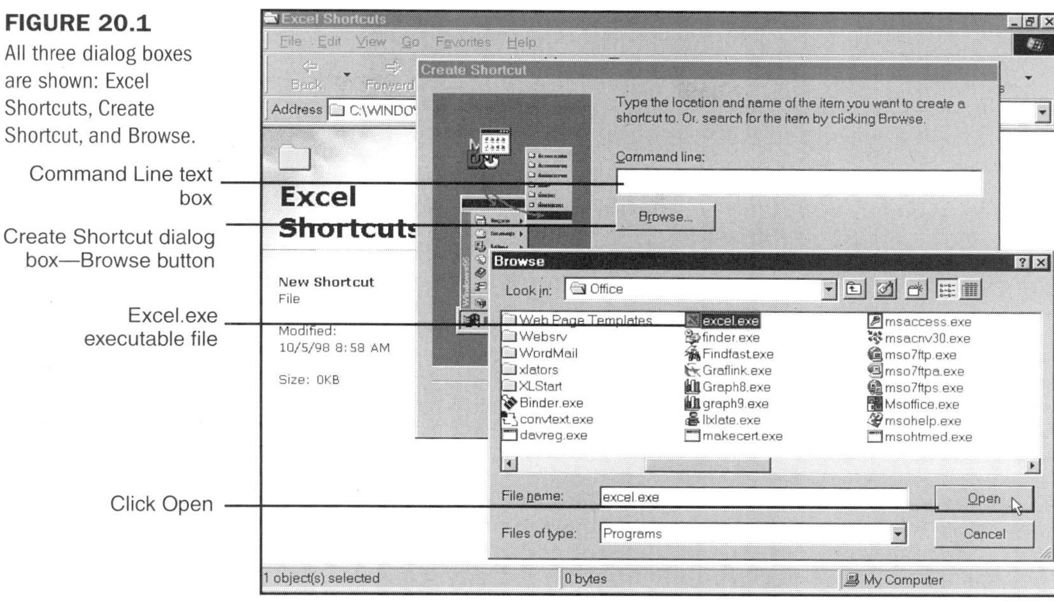

FIGURE 20.1
All three dialog boxes are shown: Excel Shortcuts, Create Shortcut, and Browse.

NOTE Later, when you want to assign a startup switch to the shortcut, you can change the name to help identify the type of startup being performed.

If you intend to create several startup alternatives, you can copy this shortcut. Press the *right* mouse button and drag; when you release the mouse button, choose Copy Here from the shortcut menu that appears. A copy of the new shortcut is created. Repeat this a few times until you have created as many shortcuts as you think you need for the various startup alternatives.

To assign a startup switch to a shortcut, you need to display the shortcut properties.

1. Right-click the shortcut icon and choose Properties from the menu. Then click the Shortcut tab of the Properties dialog box (see Figure 20.2).
2. Use the Target text box to add the startup switches. The text box already contains the path to the Excel program. Type a space after the program path and add the startup switches you want to use.

Table 20.1 briefly describes the startup switches. The following sections provide specific examples for each switch.

NOTE The folder path mentioned in several of the options in Table 20.1 is the complete file path to the specific workbook you want to open when Excel starts. For example, suppose the workbook name is Budget99 and it is located in the Planning folder, which is under the My Documents folder on your hard drive. The folder path and filename would be C:\My Documents\Planning\Budget99.xls.

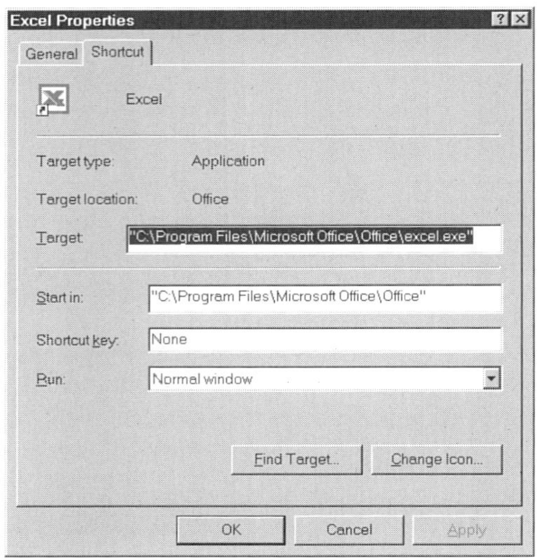

FIGURE 20.2
You can also use Alt+Enter to quickly edit the properties of a selected icon.

Table 20.1 Excel Startup Switches

Startup Switch	Startup Result
/automation	Starts Excel without loading any add-ins or templates. Ignores files listed in the XLSTART folder and the Alternate Startup File Location.
/s	Starts Excel in the Safe Mode. Ignores files listed in the XLSTART folder and the Alternate Startup File Location. Add-ins and templates are loaded as usual.
folder path\filename	Starts Excel and opens the specified workbook.
/r *folder path\filename*	Starts Excel and opens a read-only copy of the specified workbook.
/p *folder path*	Starts Excel and designates the default folder used for opening and saving files.
/e	Starts Excel, skips the startup window, and does not display a blank new workbook.
/m	Starts Excel and creates a new workbook with a single Excel 4.0 macro worksheet.

NOTE Aside from creating desktop shortcuts, you can apply these startup switches to other methods of starting Excel. If you use the Office Shortcut Bar to start Excel, you can assign a startup switch to the Excel button. Right-click the Excel button and choose Properties.

If you start Excel from the Start menu on the taskbar, you can assign a startup switch to the Microsoft Excel program. Using Windows Explorer, drill down to Windows\Start Menu and locate the Excel shortcut icon. Right-click the icon and choose Properties.

Using Startup Switches to Isolate Startup Problems

There are several switches you can use to troubleshoot problems starting Excel. For example, it is possible that corrupt files are preventing a proper startup. To help isolate the problem, use both the /automation switch and the /s switch.

The /automation switch starts Excel without any ancillary files and is referred to as a *clean boot*. Add-ins, files in the XLSTART folder, and files in the Alternate Startup File Location are not loaded. If Excel starts properly when this switch is used, then you have narrowed down the problem to one of these three items.

Use the /s switch to start Excel in the Safe Mode. The words Safe Mode actually appear in the Excel title bar. Several startup triggers are reset as if this were the very first time Excel has been started. You may be prompted to enter your workgroup name and initials, and the Office Assistant introduces itself to you. The files listed in the XLSTART folder and the Alternate Startup File Location are ignored. Add-ins, however, are loaded. If Excel does not start using this switch, then you have isolated the problem to the add-ins. You can determine which add-ins are loading by looking at the list under Tools, Add-Ins. By removing them one at a time and checking the startup again, you can determine which is the culprit. If Excel does start properly, then the problem lies in the files in the XLSTART folder or the Alternate Startup File Location. As with the add-ins, by removing the files one at a time, you should be able to locate the problem.

Using a Startup Switch to Open a Specific Workbook

There are several ways to open Excel and immediately display a specific workbook:

- *Desktop Document Shortcut*. You can create a shortcut on the desktop to a specific Excel file.
- *Documents List on the Start Menu*. You can use the Start menu and choose a file you have worked with recently from the Documents list.
- *Main Start Menu*. You can move the document to the C:\Windows\Start Menu folder. The document appears directly on the Start menu, at the top of the menu.
- *Desktop Excel Shortcut with Startup Switch*. You can use the *folder path\filename* startup switch with an Excel program shortcut.

NOTE You can also move documents to the XLSTART folder (C:\Program Files\Microsoft Office\Office\XLSTART). Any files that are in this folder will automatically be opened when Excel is opened. Placing workbooks in this folder does impact the way some of the startup switches normally behave. These anomalies are discussed in the sections later in this chapter that describe specific startup switches.

The advantage to using a startup switch is that you can designate more than one file to open when the program opens. You can use this approach and have Excel open all the files you need in one fell swoop. For example, suppose you are working on a payroll project and want to open three files: TimeSheet.xls, Payroll.xls, and Pay and Leave.xls.

Using the steps described in the previous section, create the Excel shortcut and access the Properties dialog box. The path to start the Excel program already appears in the Target text box. If the files are stored in separate folders, you have to type in the full path for each file to open all three files at once; for example:

```
"C:\Program Files\Microsoft Office\Office\excel.exe" "c:\my documents\dept
➥123\timesheet.xls" "c:\my documents\accounting\payroll.xls" "c:\my
documents\personnel\pay and leave.xls"
```

When entering the startup switch, keep these things in mind:

- Multiple paths are simply separated by a space.
- The startup entries are not case sensitive.
- Only where there are spaces in a folder or filename will you have to place quotes around the text.

Because the path for all three of these files in this example begins in c:\my documents, you can avoid having to type this lengthy entry by adding the common path to the Start In text box in the Properties dialog box. The entry in the Start In text box will be

```
"c:\my documents\"
```

The entry in the Target text box can then be changed to

```
"C:\Program Files\Microsoft Office\Office\excel.exe" "dept 123\timesheet.xls"
➥accounting\payroll.xls "personnel\pay and leave.xls"
```

If all three files are stored in the same folder, say Accounting, the Target entry is even shorter:

```
"C:\Program Files\Microsoft Office\Office\excel.exe" timesheet.xls payroll.xls
➥"pay and leave.xls"
```

Figure 20.3 shows an example of this last text entry.

FIGURE 20.3
Save time by setting Start In to the location of multiple files.

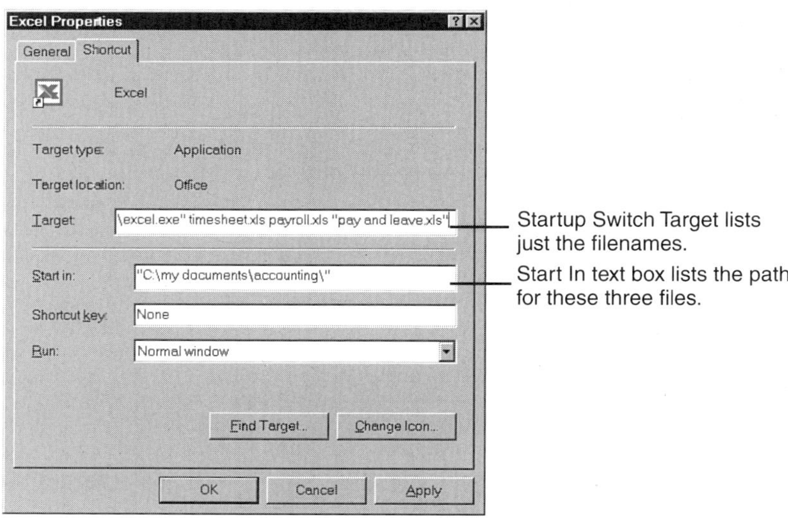

Using the /r Startup Switch to Open a Read-Only Copy of a Workbook

If you want Excel to open with a read-only copy of a specific workbook, use the /r *folder path\filename* startup switch. As with the *folder path\filename* switch, you can designate multiple files to open.

Using the steps described in the "Excel Startup Options" section, create the Excel shortcut and access the Properties dialog box. The path to start the Excel program already appears in the Target text box. As before, if the files are all in the same folder, you can enter the path in the Start In text box.

An example of the Target text box entry for files in the same folder is

```
"C:\Program Files\Microsoft Office\Office\excel.exe" /r timesheet.xls payroll.xls
➥"pay and leave.xls"
```

NOTE A space is required after the /r.

An example of the Target text box entry for files in different folders:

```
"C:\Program Files\Microsoft Office\Office\excel.exe" /r "c:\my documents\dept
➥123\timesheet.xls" "c:\my documents\accounting\payroll.xls" "c:\my
documents\personnel\pay and leave.xls"
```

NOTE Files that are placed in the XLSTART folder will also open, in addition to the files you designate to open read-only with the /r switch.

You can also combine startup switches. Suppose you want to open the TimeSheet.xls file to edit it, but want the Payroll.xls file opened read-only. The switch to use is

```
"C:\Program Files\Microsoft Office\Office\excel.exe" "c:\my documents\dept
➥123\timesheet.xls" /r "c:\my documents\accounting\payroll.xls"
```

Using the /p Startup Switch to Designate a Default Folder

When you open and save documents in Excel, the default file location is C:\My Documents. This default location is controlled through the Options dialog box (choose Tools, Options, General tab). However, suppose you're working on a special project for two months. The project files you want to access are located in another folder, perhaps one on a network drive. You can set up a startup switch to override the default location; the switch is /p *folder path\foldername*.

Use the steps described in the "Excel Startup Options" section to create the Excel shortcut and access the Properties dialog box. The path to start the Excel program already appears in the Target text box. Just add the switch.

An example of the Target text box entry is

```
"C:\Program Files\Microsoft Office\Office\excel.exe" /p "f:\office\projects\"
```

This switch, shown in Figure 20.4, starts Excel and designates the default folder for opening and saving files.

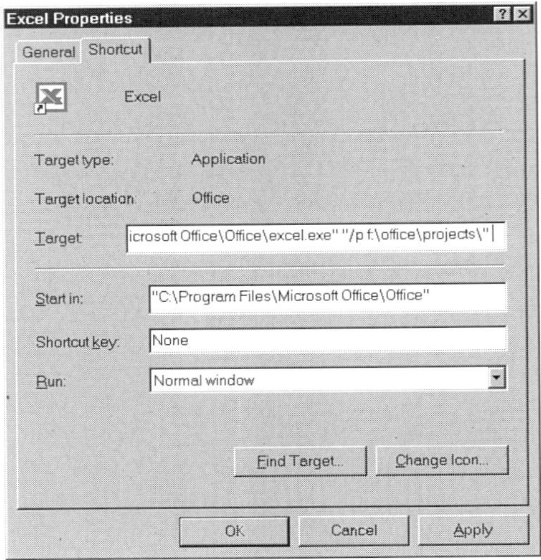

FIGURE 20.4
A space is required after the /p switch.

CAUTION

After you open Excel using this switch, if you open a file located in a different folder, that location becomes the default for opening and saving files.

Using the /e Startup Switch to Skip the Startup Window and Book1

If you want to skip the startup window (sometimes referred to as the *splash screen*) and the obligatory Book1 file, try the /e startup switch.

Use the steps described in the "Excel Startup Options" section to create the Excel shortcut and access the Properties dialog box. The path to start the Excel program already appears in the Target text box. Just add the switch.

The Target text box entry is

```
"C:\Program Files\Microsoft Office\Office\excel.exe" /e
```

This switch starts Excel without displaying the startup window or new empty workbook. If there are files in the XLSTART folder, they will be opened.

NOTE The /e switch was particularly useful in Excel 4.0. In that version, an initial workbook (Book1) opened when Excel started and remained open even after you opened other workbooks. By using this startup switch, users could avoid having to close Book1. Beginning with Excel 5.0 and continuing through Excel 2000, Book1 automatically removes itself when another workbook is opened (assuming changes have not been made to Book1). This switch now serves as a convenient way to remove the startup window when Excel is launched.

Using the /m Startup Switch to Create an Excel 4.0 Macro Worksheet

Some of the XLM codes from Excel 4.0 are not available in VBA. This startup switch is used when you are using Excel 4.0 Macros to create custom applications across many versions of Excel. The switch will start Excel 2000 with a new workbook containing only one sheet. The sheet is labeled Macro1.

NOTE This switch will not work if there are workbooks in the XLSTART folder.

Customizing the Settings in New Workbooks and Worksheets

Unless you have changed the Excel startup using the switches described in the previous sections, when you first start Excel a new empty workbook, called Book1, is displayed. New workbooks are based on the default Excel workbook.

A powerful way to customize Excel is to use autotemplates for new workbooks and worksheets. For example, suppose your company requires a specific header to appear at the top of each printed worksheet page. Instead of having to add this header to each sheet in every book you create or using a macro on each worksheet to add the header, you can create two autotemplates that already include the company header. Yes, two—one for the default workbook (and the sheets in that book), and one for new worksheets you add to workbooks.

Autotemplates can include built-in text such as sheet names, column and row labels, as well as other features such as cell formatting, formulas, macros, and print settings.

See "Creating Autotemplates," **p. 618**

Optimizing Toolbar Potential

Effectively designed toolbars can substantially increase your productivity while working in Excel. While the Standard and Formatting toolbars that come with Excel 2000 provide easy access to many common features and commands, as a proficient Excel user you should adjust them to maximize productivity.

Toolbar customization is performed in the Customize dialog box. You access this dialog box by right-clicking any toolbar and selecting Customize. Because toolbar changes affect the screen display, the changes you make are permanent changes until you alter them.

NOTE The menu bar is treated as a toolbar in all Office products.

General instructions on customizing the toolbar and menu settings (including the new behavior of the toolbars and menus) are discussed in Chapter 4. In this chapter, we focus specifically on getting the most from Excel toolbars and menus.

See "Customizing Application Toolbars," **p. 89**

Using the Shift Key to Display Alternative Toolbar Buttons

One of the best, and undocumented, toolbar features in Excel is the hidden toolbar opposites. Although not every button has an opposite, many of them do. So why should you care about button options? If you can use the same button, say the Right Align button, to either right or left align, you wouldn't need to have both buttons on the Formatting toolbar. You can remove the Left Align button, making room to add other buttons that are currently not on the toolbar, such as Cells (to quickly access the Format Cells dialog box).

When you press the Shift key and hold the mouse pointer over a button that has an opposite, the opposite displays. Release the Shift key and the original button displays.

Table 20.2 lists the opposites for buttons on the Standard and Formatting toolbars.

Table 20.2 Toolbar Button Opposites

Toolbar	Button	Opposite
Standard	Open	Save
Standard	Print	Print Preview
Standard	Sort Ascending	Sort Descending
Formatting	Underline	Double Underline
Formatting	Left Align	Right Align
Formatting	Center Align	Merge and Center
Formatting	Increase Decimal	Decrease Decimal
Formatting	Increase Indent	Decrease Indent

Imagine how many more buttons you could add to your toolbars if you used the Shift key to invoke the opposites. When you get ready to remove a button from a toolbar that has an opposite, be sure you leave the button you use most frequently. For example, I am constantly using the Decrease Decimal to remove decimals added by the Currency and Comma buttons. So I would leave that button and remove the Increase Decimal button, because I use it less often. Figure 20.5 shows an example of the opposite button for Decrease Decimal.

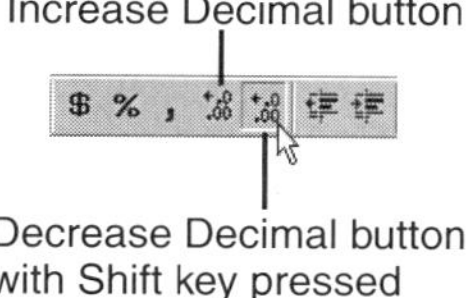

FIGURE 20.5
Release the Shift key to see the original button.

TIP To avoid actually executing the button command, drag the mouse pointer off the button.

When you customize the Standard and Formatting toolbars to remove buttons that have opposites, there will be room on these toolbars to include additional command buttons. Be aware that other buttons, not just the ones that appear on the Standard and Formatting toolbars, have opposites as well. You will save yourself precious toolbar space if you take the time to determine whether there is an opposite to a button—they are usually easy to figure out. Other opposites you might be interested in include

Insert Rows/Delete Rows

Insert Columns/Delete Columns

Paste Formatting/Paste Values

Clear Contents/Clear Formatting

Trace Dependents/Remove Dependent Arrows

Angle Text Upward/Angle Text Downward

NOTE These opposite shortcuts don't extend to the keyboard. For example, Ctrl+S saves the active file. The toolbar button opposite to Save is Open—you can't press Shift+Ctrl+S to Open.

The Auditing Toolbar

The Auditing toolbar is used primarily when you want to check for errors in calculations. It contains a number of useful buttons:

- To trace cell precedents and dependents.
- To trace error results, such as the `#DIV/0!` or `#VALUE` errors.
- To remove trace arrows.

- To attach embedded comments to cells.
- To circle invalid data (used in conjunction with the Data, Validation command).

▶ **See** "Auditing Worksheets and Resolving Errors," **p. 909**

▶ **See** "Validating and Analyzing Excel Data," **p. 860**

For whatever reason, Microsoft persists in keeping the Auditing toolbar buried under the Tools, Auditing command. I like to have more immediate access to this toolbar. So I create a simple macro that activates the Auditing toolbar. The macro steps are straightforward:

1. Create a new macro by selecting Tools, Macro, Record New Macro. The Record Macro dialog box appears, as shown in Figure 20.6.
2. Enter a macro name, assign a keyboard shortcut (if desired), and store the macro in the Personal Macro Workbook, so it will be available in all workbooks.
3. Click OK to start recording the macro.
4. Right-click any toolbar.
5. Choose Customize. The Customize dialog box appears.
6. On the Toolbars tab, check Auditing. The toolbar appears, floating in the Excel worksheet window. You can leave the toolbar floating, or dock it (I prefer docking it on the right side of the screen).
7. Choose Close.

Click the Stop Recording button on the Macro (Stop) toolbar.

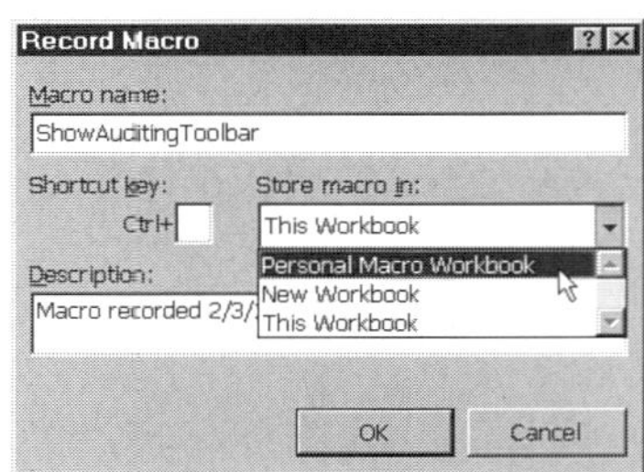

FIGURE 20.6
The Personal Macro workbook is created the first time you store a macro in it. It is then loaded each time you open Excel.

After the macro is created, you can use a keyboard shortcut (see step 2) or add a button to the Standard toolbar to run the macro.

▶ **See** "Assigning a Macro to a Toolbar Button," **p. 112**

Using the Shift Key to Display Alternative Menus

As with some toolbar buttons, you can use the Shift key to display alternative menu choices. Specifically, the File and Edit menus display slightly different menus if you press Shift before you activate the menu. You can also activate these alternative menus by using Shift+Alt+ the hotkey (the hotkey being the underlined letter). For the File menu, this would be Shift+Alt+F. Table 20.3 lists the opposites for menu commands.

Table 20.3 Menu Command Opposites

Menu	Command	Opposite
File	Close	Close All
Edit	Copy	Copy Picture
Edit	Paste	Paste Picture
Edit	Paste Special	Paste Picture Link

Using Pictures

You can create picture objects of worksheet data, charts, and other objects to use as illustrations in other Windows applications. Picture objects can be resized and moved like any drawn object. Worksheet pictures can be static or linked back to the original data. You can't link a picture of a chart. Instead, you have to copy the chart and use the Paste Special, Paste Link command to link the chart back to the source file.

There are advantages to using pictures instead of other object formats. When you copy a picture, you have the alternative of copying it in picture format or in bitmap format. The picture format uses less memory and disk space than the bitmap format. The picture format displays more quickly than the bitmap format. Images in picture format look good at any resolution and work well when you need a high-quality printout or display. Picture images should be used when you want to display Excel data in a PowerPoint presentation. Bitmap images change appearance based on the screen resolution.

Consider customizing the menus as well, especially if a command is buried under other commands. Suppose you routinely run the same query to extract data from an Access database. The steps to run the query are Tools, Get External Data, Run Saved Query. Consider copying the Run Saved Query command to the top of the Tools menu for easier access.

In previous versions of Excel, it made sense to rearrange the order of the commands on the menus to place frequently used commands near the top of the menu. However, if you give the new personalized (adaptive) menus a chance, I think you will find that, over time, this will automatically happen.

Like customizing toolbars, menu customization is accomplished through the Customize dialog box.

Speeding Up Data Entry

No doubt you are familiar with the AutoCorrect feature (on the Tools menu) that lists typical typing and spelling mistakes and automatically corrects these mistakes for you. Although this is a useful feature, of greater value in Excel is the capability to add short abbreviations or acronyms that will automatically be expanded by AutoCorrect.

So if you frequently need to type long text entries into your worksheets, you will save yourself quite a bit of time adding these entries. Because the AutoCorrect feature is shared among the Microsoft Office products, when you add a term in Excel it is available in Word, PowerPoint, Access, and Outlook.

Figure 20.7 shows the AutoCorrect dialog box with a sample abbreviation in the Replace text box and the full text in the With text box.

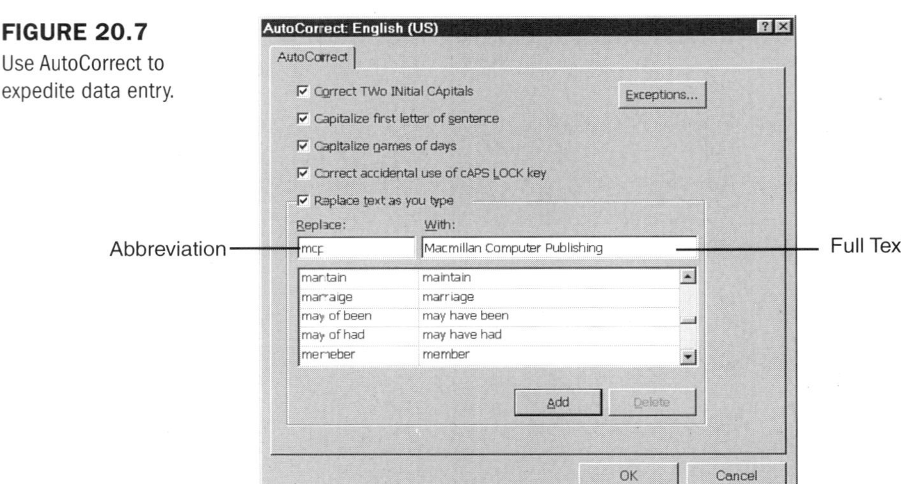

FIGURE 20.7
Use AutoCorrect to expedite data entry.

Speeding Up the Screen Display

Each new version of Excel adds powerful features that make it easier to work with your worksheet data. Unfortunately, this ease is typically accompanied by a decrease in speed, requiring faster computers with more RAM and larger hard drives. Big, intricate workbooks may take a long time to display or refresh. There are several options you can change to recapture some of the speed:

- *Tools, Options, View tab.* If your workbook contains a lot of charts, check the Show Placeholders option. A rectangular placeholder box displays instead of the chart. When you click the chart object, the chart appears.
- *Tools, Options, Calculation tab.* If your workbook contains a lot of formulas, check the Manual option. With this setting marked, formulas will calculate only when you click the Calc Now button in the Options dialog box or press F9.

If you change options a lot, either create a simple macro to display the Options dialog box, or create two macros that switch back and forth between your most common option settings. To have these macros available in all workbooks, they need to be saved in the Personal Macro workbook. You designate this workbook in the Record Macro dialog box when you record a new macro (Tools, Macro, Record New Macro).

▶ To learn more about creating macros, **see** "Planning Your Macro," **p. 108**

CHAPTER 21

Taking Control of Excel Templates

In this chapter

Taking Advantage of Excel Templates

A *template* is a special type of workbook file that is used as a master, or blueprint, for creating other Excel workbooks. There are two kinds of templates—ordinary templates and autotemplates. *Ordinary templates* are workbooks or worksheets that you create to serve as the basis for other similar workbooks. *Autotemplates* are used when you want to change the default formats for new, blank workbooks or worksheets. You can create workbook templates and worksheet templates (which include chart sheet templates).

When you create a workbook or worksheet based on a template, all the information and formatting in the template migrates to the new workbook or worksheet, including the

- Number and type of worksheets
- Text and data
- Formulas
- Cell formatting
- Range names
- Sheet names
- Print options
- Layout options
- Graphics
- Macros and Visual Basic modules
- Custom toolbars
- Worksheet controls

Templates are useful in many ways. You can create autotemplates that establish default settings, such as the default headers and footers you want to print on each worksheet.

You can create workbook templates that track periodic data. The workbook can be designed to store information for each month on separate worksheets, and consolidate the year-to-date data on a separate worksheet. If the necessary formatting and formulas are built in, all you need to do is add the appropriate data.

You can also use templates to create routine forms or reports—for example, company expense forms, client invoices, or budget reports. In a networked environment (where custom organization templates can be accessed by many users), templates become useful control mechanisms and data-gathering tools. For example, when 100 sales representatives submit their monthly sales reports, not only will all those reports have an identical structure, they can be designed to feed into a central database. The database can be a separate Excel workbook, or a database in another program such as Access or FoxPro. You can then use the database features to manipulate the data. Not only is this data-tracking feature available in network environments, it can be used on a standalone computer as well.

Using Excel's Built-In Templates

Excel includes three predesigned templates that you can customize to fit your specific requirements. Helpful notes and tips are embedded in the templates to assist you in working with and customizing the templates. Table 21.1 describes each built-in template.

Table 21.1 The Built-In Templates Included in Microsoft Excel

Template Name	Description
Expense	A form to track business expenses. Contains categories for accommodations, travel, fuel, meals, phone, entertainment, and other. Includes a feature to add data from each expense report to a database.
Invoice	A form to generate customer invoices. Contains fields to track shipping and handling charges, taxes, and payment method. Includes a feature to add data from each invoice to a database.
Purorder	A form to track purchase orders placed with vendors. Contains a field to ship the order to a separate address, as well as fields for shipping method, payment method, and sales rep. Includes a feature to add data from each purchase order to a database.

NOTE In addition to these built-in templates, you can download additional templates from Microsoft's Web site. Copy the templates to the Templates folder–C:\Windows\Application Data\Microsoft\Templates

To locate these templates, choose Help, Office on the Web, the Office Update Home page appears. Or you can type the following URL in your Web browser:

`http://officeupdate.microsoft.com`

Click the Excel hyperlink. Then click the Download hyperlink. You will see a list of items you can download, which includes several Excel templates.

If you are upgrading from Excel 95 or 97, the built-in templates from those versions will be replaced with the built-in templates in Excel 2000.

Accessing the Built-In Templates

To access the built-in templates, choose File, New. The New dialog box displays a series of tabs that identify the templates available in Excel 2000 (see Figure 21.1).

The General tab lists the Workbook template, which is used as the default template for new workbooks. Excel 2000 templates appear in the Spreadsheet Solutions tab, which contains the three most popular templates: Expense, Invoice, and Purorder. The marketing template—Village—is listed for Village Software, the company that created these built-in templates for Microsoft.

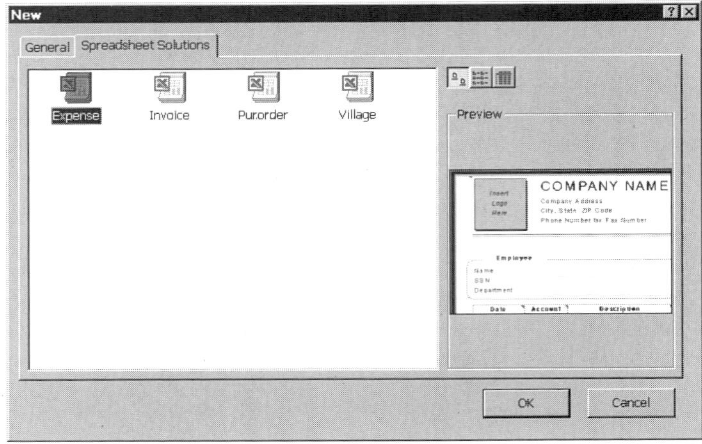

FIGURE 21.1
Excel templates supplied with Office 2000 appear on the Spreadsheet Solutions tab.

Double-click the template you want to use. Because each built-in template contains macros, the macro virus-warning message appears (see Figure 21.2). Whenever a file containing macros is accessed in Excel, this warning is displayed. The warning alerts you that the file contains one or more macros and reminds you that macros may contain viruses. Choose Enable Macros to proceed with creating the new workbook. A new workbook appears that is based on the template you selected.

NOTE Depending on how Excel was installed, the templates may not be installed on your machine. You will be prompted for the Office CD or the place on your network where the program files are stored.

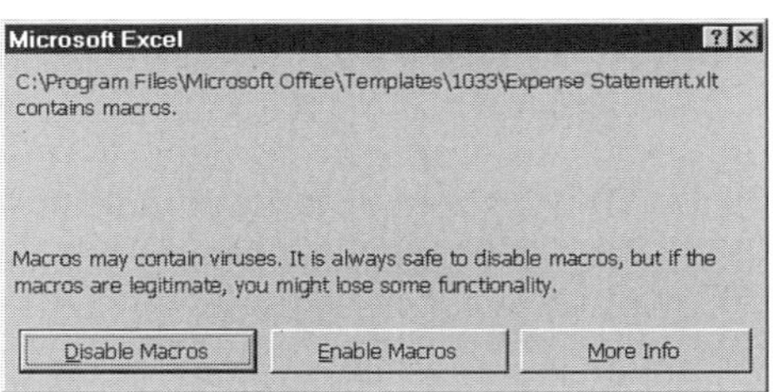

FIGURE 21.2
The virus-alert message appears whenever you attempt to open a file that contains macros.

NOTE Excel cannot detect viruses in your files. The virus alert message is just a warning, because many viruses are found in macros. To protect your computer and files from viruses, you should purchase software designed specifically to detect and remove viruses. I highly recommend Symantec Norton AntiVirus. Visit Symantec's Web site at `www.symantec.com`.

CAUTION

Any file that contains macros can potentially be carrying a virus. You should not open files that come from sources not known to you. To help identify sources that you trust and know, Microsoft has included a new feature in Office 2000 called Digital Signatures.

Built-In Template Features

The built-in templates have hidden the gridlines to make the worksheets appear similar to online forms. Each template has two worksheet tabs: the Document tab (the actual invoice, report, form) and a Customize tab. The Customize tab contains useful fields to help you quickly customize the document.

NOTE The Customize tab is hidden and appears only after you click the Customize button on the Document tab. When you click back on the Document tab, the Customize tab is hidden again.

The template toolbar includes the Template Help button. Whenever you create a new workbook based on a built-in template, this button explains how to use the specific template.

Each of the built-in templates has embedded comments to provide you with information about the parts of the template that require specific explanation. Position your mouse pointer near the triangular comment indicator to see the comment. In Figure 21.3 , the comment for the Logo is displayed.

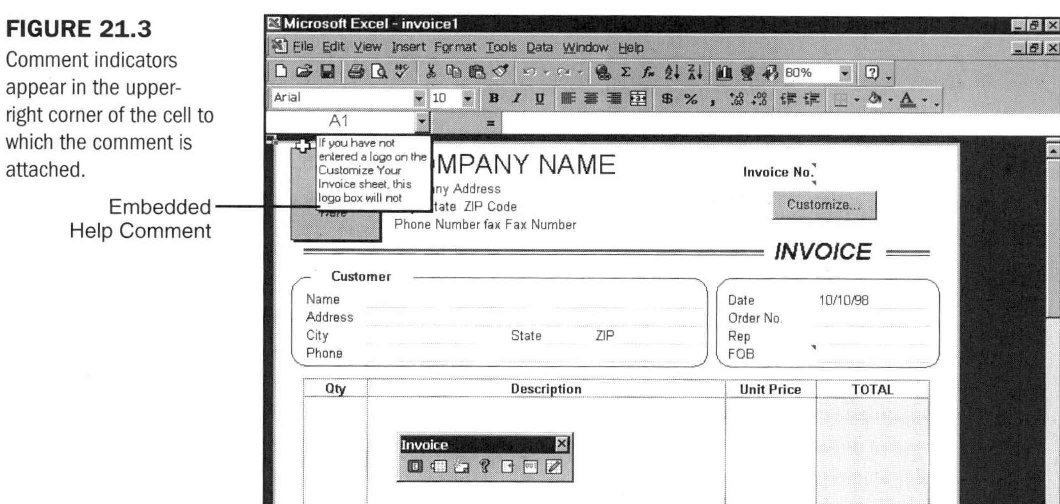

FIGURE 21.3
Comment indicators appear in the upper-right corner of the cell to which the comment is attached.

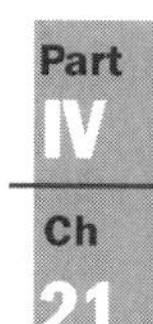

Sometimes the comment boxes are not large enough to display the entire comment, as is the case with the Logo comment in Figure 21.3. To view the entire comment, select the cell containing the comment indicator. Then right-click and choose Edit Comment from the shortcut menu. Use the keyboard arrow keys to scroll within the box to read the entire comment. Or you can resize the comment box by dragging one of the selection handles.

Customizing the Built-In Templates

Each of the built-in templates has an option to modify the template to include your company name and logo. You also can change the font attributes and add your own comments to template documents.

To modify a predefined template, follow these steps:

1. Display the template you want to modify.
2. Choose the Customize button, located in the upper-right corner of the template (refer to Figure 21.3). The Customize tab displays (see Figure 21.4).

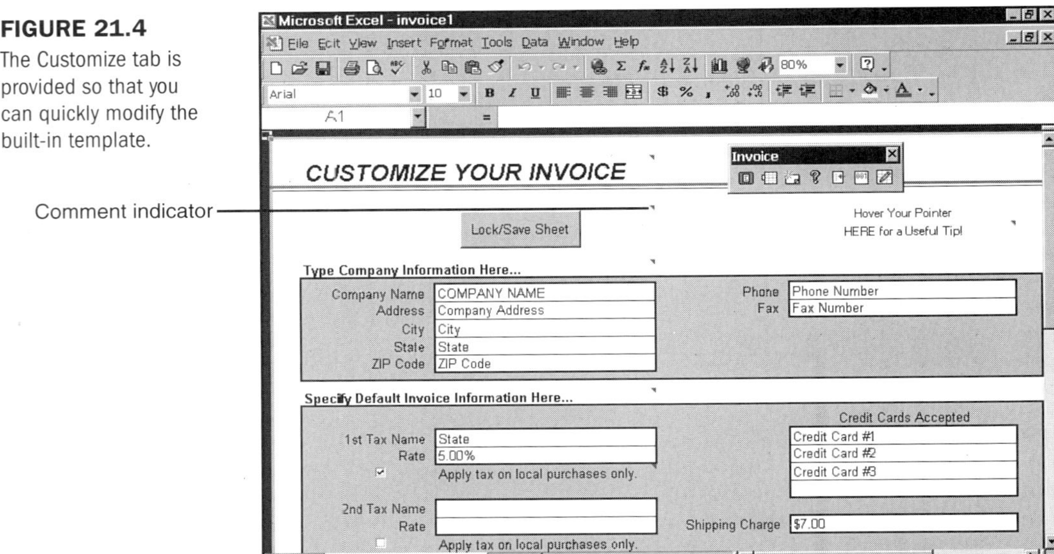

FIGURE 21.4
The Customize tab is provided so that you can quickly modify the built-in template.

3. Comments are embedded throughout the Customize tab to assist you in customizing the template document. It's best to start at the top and work your way down.
4. Make the desired changes to customize the template.
5. After all the changes have been made, click the Lock/Save Sheet button to prevent accidental changes to the customization you have made.

6. The Lock/Save Sheet dialog box appears. You have the choice of locking the template without saving or locking and saving the template.
   - Choose the Lock but Don't Save option to prevent accidental changes while remaining in the Customize tab of the template.
   - Choose the Lock and Save Template option if you have completed the customization and want to return to the Document tab.
7. Choose OK. If you select the Lock and sSave option, you will be prompted for a name and location for the new template. Be sure you save the template in the Templates folder for easy access, which is typically located at C:\Windows\Application Data\Microsoft\Templates.

These built-in templates include a feature that enables you to add data to a database each time you complete the template form. The data is added as a new record in a database that is associated with the template.

See "Feeding Template Data into a Database," **p. 619**

Use the Office Assistant to search for additional information pertaining to the built-in templates and the Template Wizard. Type `templates` or `template wizard` in the Office Assistant search box and press Enter to see a list of Help topics.

Drawbacks to Using the Built-In Templates

The built-in templates illustrate some good worksheet-formatting options that can be used with templates. If you need a template for an invoice, a purchase order, or an expense report in a hurry, one of the built-in templates is an adequate choice. However, if you have the time to design your own, do so. The predesigned templates are driven by macros that you cannot modify—they're saved as password-protected add-ins, which are not editable—and if you need to make any major change to the templates it's likely that the macros will not run as intended. The next few sections show you how to create Excel templates.

Creating Your Own Templates

You can design and create your own worksheet and workbook templates very easily in Excel. A *worksheet template* is a specific worksheet that you can add to a variety of workbooks. For example, you could create a worksheet that performs sales-analysis calculations or plots data on a special chart.

Workbook templates, on the other hand, contain a defined set of worksheets that you know you always want included in the workbook—for example, a workbook containing the five business reports you are required to produce every month.

Any worksheet or workbook you create repeatedly is a good candidate for a template. Although you have to invest some time up front, it's worth it. You'll be surprised how much time they save you down the road.

Templates provide several simple advantages in addition to merely modifying an existing workbook and saving it under a different name:

- You don't have to remove or type over the previous data. Thus, you avoid deleting the wrong thing (such as formulas) or worse, losing your place, and winding up with some previous data in your worksheet.
- Template files typically are stored together in one place; you don't have to remember where the former workbook is saved, or which workbook contains the worksheet you want to copy, or what you named it.
- By using a template file, you prevent accidentally saving your new data on top of your former data. Workbook template files create new workbooks, which always prompt you for a filename when you save them.

The following sections describe how to create several different types of worksheet templates (worksheets, forms, chart sheets), a workbook template, and how to finalize, save, and modify the templates.

Designing Worksheet Templates

You can design a template for just about any worksheet you have to create repeatedly. These templates contain everything you want to see on the final worksheet (except the data you type when you use the template). This includes any static text, formulas, cell formatting, and print settings that you want duplicated when you create a new worksheet based on the template.

Figure 21.5 illustrates a simple worksheet that needs to be created each month—a monthly expense sheet.

FIGURE 21.5
Any worksheet you have to create repeatedly is a good candidate for a template.

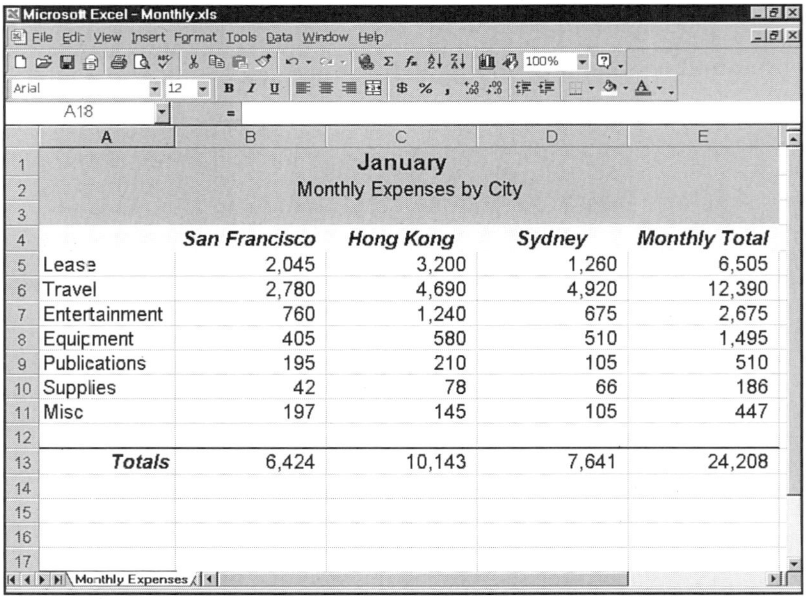

Microsoft Excel - Monthly.xls

January
Monthly Expenses by City

	San Francisco	Hong Kong	Sydney	Monthly Total
Lease	2,045	3,200	1,260	6,505
Travel	2,780	4,690	4,920	12,390
Entertainment	760	1,240	675	2,675
Equipment	405	580	510	1,495
Publications	195	210	105	510
Supplies	42	78	66	186
Misc	197	145	105	447
Totals	6,424	10,143	7,641	24,208

Monthly Expenses

Using an Existing Worksheet As a Template If you already have a worksheet that contains the type of calculations and formatting you want to use as the basis for a template—you're three-quarters of the way to having a template.

It is best if you use the File, Save As command and save the workbook under a different name, so you don't impact the original file. After it is saved under a new name, you will need to delete the other sheets in the workbook, because a worksheet template is a workbook with only one worksheet.

Skip to the section "Finalizing Your Templates" later in this chapter to complete the final steps before saving the worksheet as a template.

Creating a Worksheet Template from Scratch If you don't have a worksheet, but know what you want to include in the template, you'll have to start from scratch.

You create a worksheet template like you create any other worksheet. Start with a new workbook and remove all but one of the worksheets. Enter the text and data you want included in the template, and create the formulas you want calculated in the worksheet. If necessary, create any range names you need for the formulas.

▶ **See** "Using Range Names in Formulas," **p. 639**

Apply any cell formatting you want to see in the worksheet. Use the File, Page Setup command to select any specific print options—including page orientation, paper size, margins, centering, headers and footers, print titles, gridlines, or print area. If necessary, include any macros/VBA modules, custom toolbars, or controls in the worksheet.

Creating Workbook Templates

Workbook templates simply contain a series of template worksheets. The entire workbook is duplicated when you create a new workbook based on the template. Frequently, a workbook template is created when you have a series of worksheets that feed into a summary worksheet. Figure 21.6 illustrates a simple workbook that needs to be created weekly. It contains several worksheets tracking expenses by city (San Francisco, Hong Kong, Sydney) and a consolidated worksheet (labeled Weekly Summary) summarizing the weekly data and plotting the expenses on a chart.

The cumulative weekly expenses shown in Figure 21.6 are formulas summarizing data in the city worksheet (see the SUM formula in the Formula Bar). If you are not familiar with creating these types of formulas, turn to Chapter 22, "Advanced Formulas," for additional information.

▶ **See** "Consolidating Worksheet Data: Formulas That Cross Sheets and Books," **p. 646**

If you already have a workbook that you want to convert into a template, use the Save As command to save a copy of the workbook under another name. If you don't have an existing workbook, but know what you want in the workbook template, you'll have to start from scratch with a new workbook.

After you have created the worksheets, you are ready to finalize and save the workbook template. See the section "Finalizing Your Templates" later in this chapter to complete the last few steps.

Formula used to consolidate data from multiple sheets

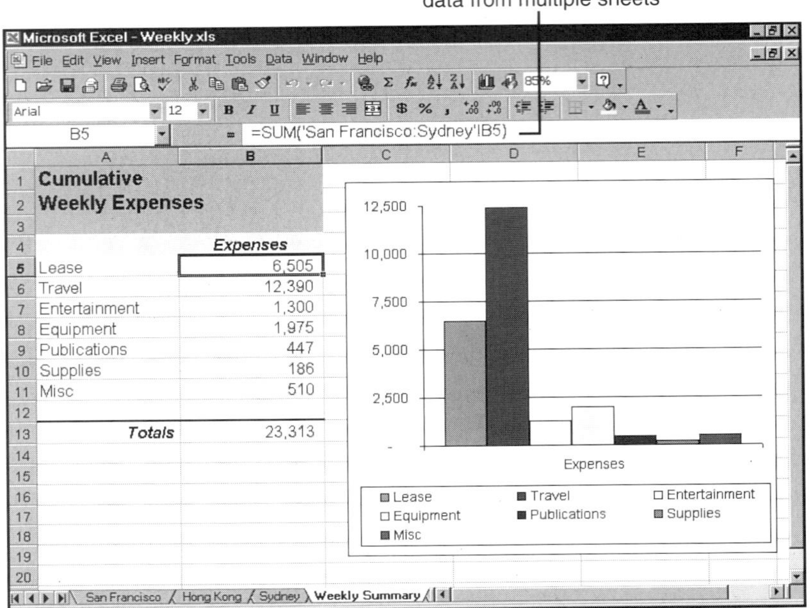

FIGURE 21.6
The data for each city is listed on separate sheets, and then consolidated on the Weekly Summary sheet.

Designing Form Templates

Creating a form to use as a template is slightly more time-consuming than using a simple worksheet. Because forms typically incorporate form controls—such as combo boxes, check boxes, and option buttons—you have to understand how to properly set up the controls. This is especially true if you plan to create calculations based on the items selected with the controls. As an example of design elements in this type of template, Figure 21.7 shows a template that is used to provide price quotes that include discounts and taxes in the quote. There are three controls in this form—two combo boxes and a spinner.

If you already have an Excel form created, use the Save As command to save a copy of the form under a different name and skip to the section "Finalizing Your Templates" later in this chapter. Otherwise, you have to start from scratch. As with a regular worksheet template, begin with a new workbook and remove all but one of the worksheets. Then add a worksheet title and other necessary labels you want to start with. You may also want to name the worksheet at this time. Figure 21.8 shows a form template worksheet that has been started.

Adding Controls to Forms

Adding controls to a worksheet is as easy as click and drag. Right-click any toolbar and click Forms to display the Forms toolbar.

FIGURE 21.7
Word templates provide an easy method to collect data.

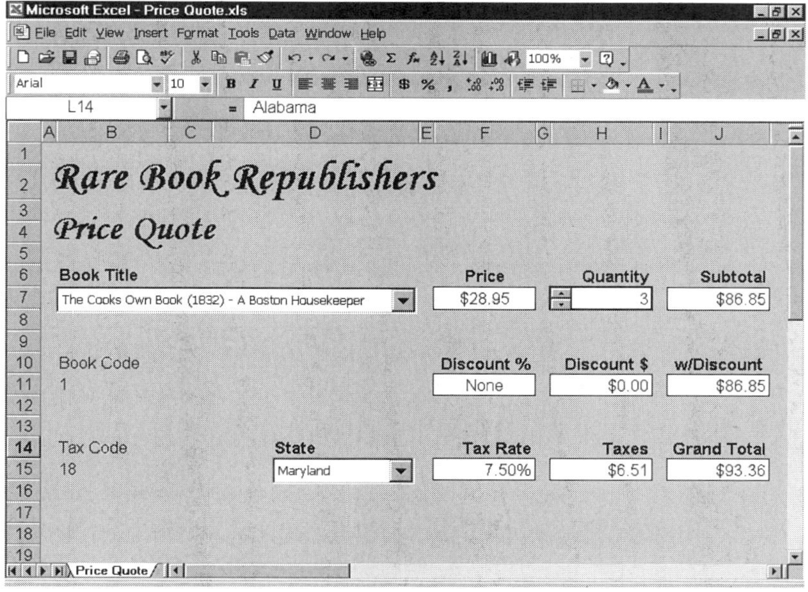

FIGURE 21.8
Add a form title and any other necessary headings.

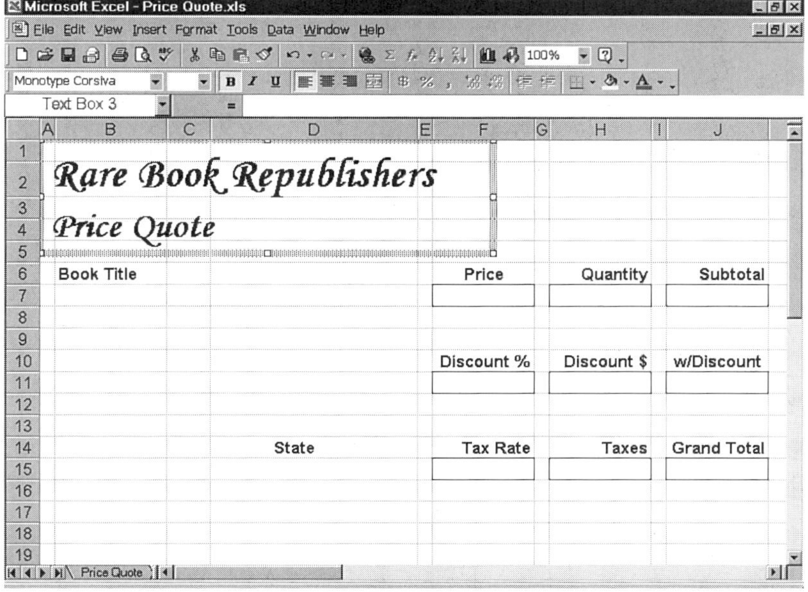

NOTE There are two toolbars that contain controls in Excel—the Forms toolbar and the Control Toolbox. Unless you are going to create a form that will be used in a VBA program that interacts with other Office applications or a Web site, you should use the controls on the Forms toolbar.

Probably the most common control added to a form is a *combo box*, also referred to as a drop-down list box. Combo boxes display one entry and a drop-down button that you click to see additional entries. If the entry list is long, when you click the drop-down button a scrollbar appears. To add a combo box, click the combo-box button (the mouse pointer changes into a crosshair) and drag to create a combo box, as shown in Figure 21.9

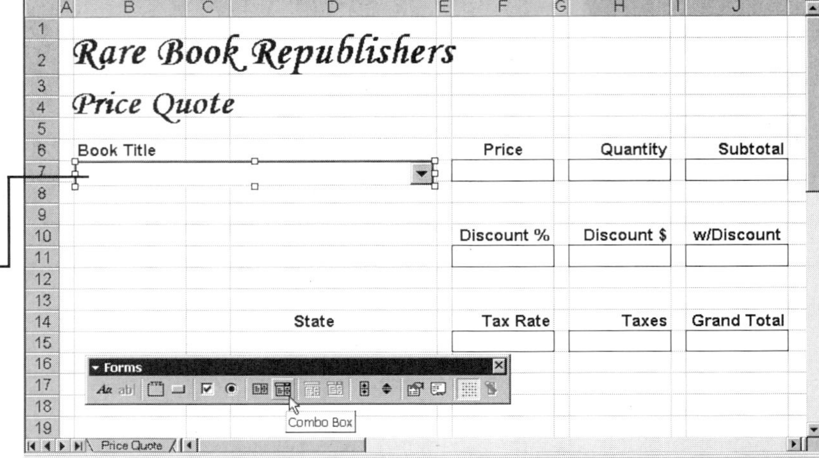

Combo-box control in the worksheet

FIGURE 21.9
Form controls don't fit into worksheet cells. They float on top of the worksheet, such as text boxes, WordArt, and other drawn objects.

That's all there is to adding a control. You can move and resize controls just as you would a text box or embedded chart. In order to select a control and not activate it, press Ctrl as you click on the control. Otherwise, the control will behave as it is designed; for example, a combo box will activate the drop-down list.

Now, for the time-consuming part—populating the drop-down list (if it's a combo box), formatting the control, and using the selected data in formulas. You can also assign macros to controls, which is discussed later in this chapter in the section "Using Option Buttons in Forms."

Populating a Combo Box List To see a list appear when the combo box is clicked, you have to create the list and tell the control where to find the list. The list can be located in one of three places:

- In the same worksheet as the form—This is a good choice for a form template where the list does not change much, because it will be the list that is used whenever a workbook is created based on the template. However, if you plan to print the form, make sure you either create a print area that encompasses just the form or create a range name that selects just the cells in the form for you to print. You will need to provide printing instructions to anyone who uses the template to explain how to print the form.
- In a separate worksheet in the workbook containing the form—This is also a good choice for a form template where the list does not change much. The advantage with this option is that the form can be printed separately from the list without having to create a print area or range name, and instructions on printing the form are not necessary, it will print like any worksheet.

- In a completely separate workbook—If the data in the list changes often or is updated by someone other than the person using the form template, then you should create and maintain the list separate from the form template.

To create a list that displays when you click the combo-box drop-down button, select the first cell in the worksheet where your list will begin and type the list. In the example shown in Figure 21.10, the list was added to an area just to the right of the form.

FIGURE 21.10

The list can be placed in the same worksheet or on a separate worksheet.

List of items to display in the combo box

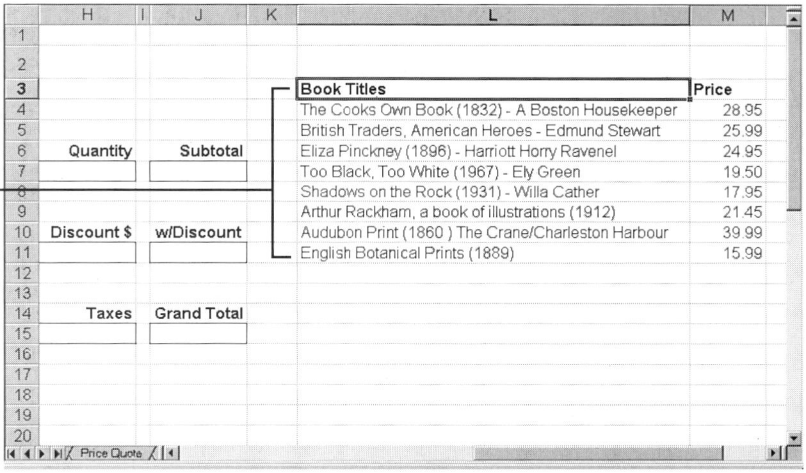

Book Titles	Price
The Cooks Own Book (1832) - A Boston Housekeeper	28.95
British Traders, American Heroes - Edmund Stewart	25.99
Eliza Pinckney (1896) - Harriott Horry Ravenel	24.95
Too Black, Too White (1967) - Ely Green	19.50
Shadows on the Rock (1931) - Willa Cather	17.95
Arthur Rackham, a book of illustrations (1912)	21.45
Audubon Print (1860) The Crane/Charleston Harbour	39.99
English Botanical Prints (1889)	15.99

Quantity | Subtotal | Discount $ | w/Discount | Taxes | Grand Total | Price Quote

Linking the combo-box list with the control is accomplished by formatting the control. You can either right-click the combo-box control and choose Format Control from the shortcut menu or select the control (by pressing Ctrl and clicking the control) and choosing Control from the Format menu. The Format Control dialog box appears.

In the Format Control dialog box, click the Control tab. There are three text boxes on this tab: Input Range, Cell Link, and Drop-Down Lines. The Cell Link option is discussed in the next section, "Displaying or Using Related Data in a Combo Box."

Click to place the flashing cursor in the Input Range text box. This is where you identify the cells that contain the combo-box list. Click the collapse/expand button to collapse the dialog box (see Figure 21.11).

Highlight the cells that comprise your list, making sure you don't highlight any list headings or extra cells. The cell references for the list appear in the Input Range text box. Click the collapse/expand button to show the Format Control dialog box.

CAUTION

If you have created a range name for the list, you must type the name into the text box. However, you will not be able to use Insert, Name, Paste or press F3 to see a list of the range names in the workbook.

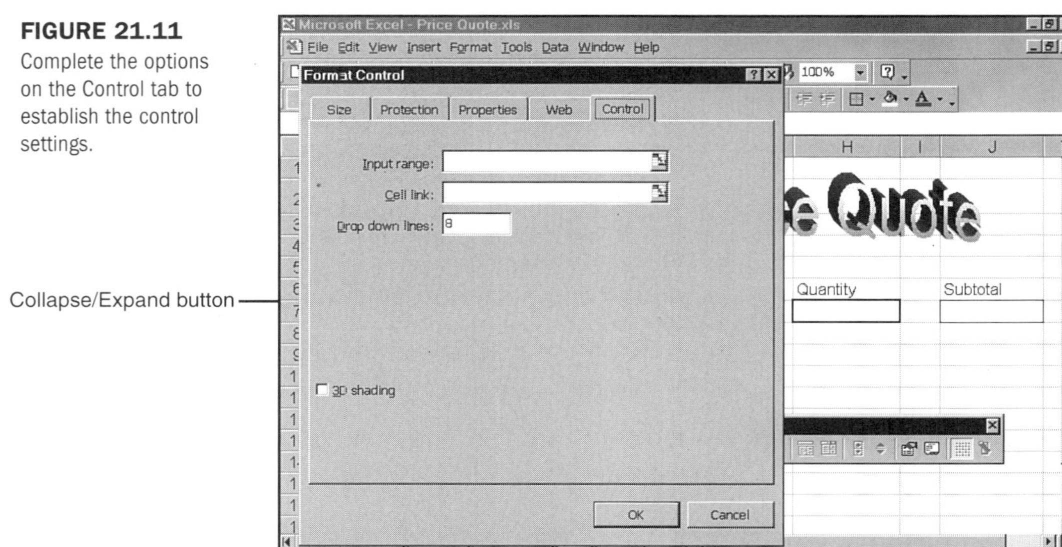

FIGURE 21.11
Complete the options on the Control tab to establish the control settings.

If you want a specific number of lines to appear when you click the combo-box control, change the number in the Drop-Down Lines text box. You can also have the combo-box control appear three-dimensional by selecting the 3D shading check box. After you've made these changes, click OK.

Now when you click the combo box in the worksheet, you can select an item from the list (as shown in Figure 21.12).

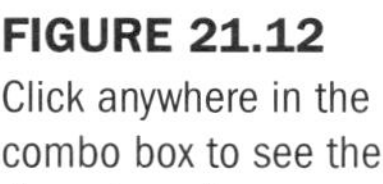

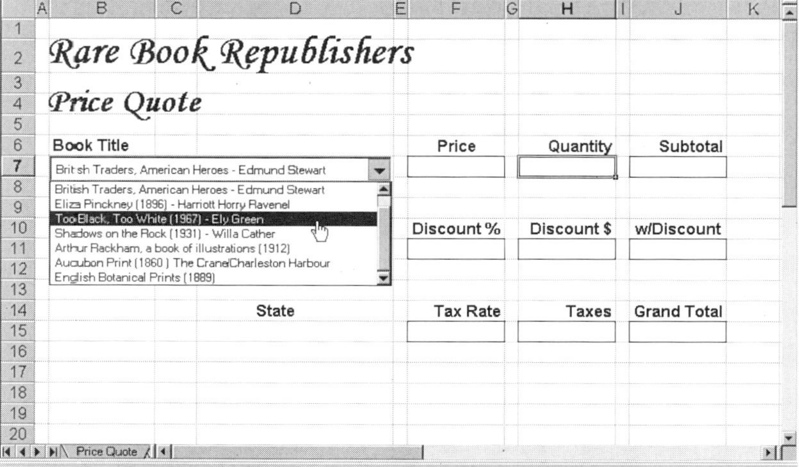

FIGURE 21.12
Click anywhere in the combo box to see the drop-down list.

Displaying or Using Related Data in a Combo Box Often when you choose an item from a combo box, you want related data to appear somewhere else in the worksheet form or you want to use related data in a calculation. For example, if the combo box shows product names, you might want to see the corresponding product number or product price. If the box shows a client's name, you might want to see the client's address, phone number, or purchasing preferences.

CAUTION

At first glance, you may be tempted to use a LOOKUP function to accomplish this. Don't—it doesn't work. The data in the combo box is not part of a cell and cannot be used in the formula. The INDEX function is a better choice (explained later in this section).

To display or use the corresponding data, you need to add the corresponding data next to your list. In this example, a list of corresponding prices will be added next to the book titles.

The data displayed in the combo box is not attached to a cell. So to look up the corresponding data (and use it in calculations), you need to use a cell in the worksheet that displays the relative position in the list of the item selected in the combo box. This cell is called the *Cell Link*. It sounds complicated, but in fact it is very easy.

You need to select a cell in your worksheet that will be used to display the relative position information. The cell does not have to be part of the form area. I suggest you type a label next to the cell that will help you remember what the cell data represents. Figure 21.13 shows the label Book Code. The cell directly below the label is where the relative list position information will appear.

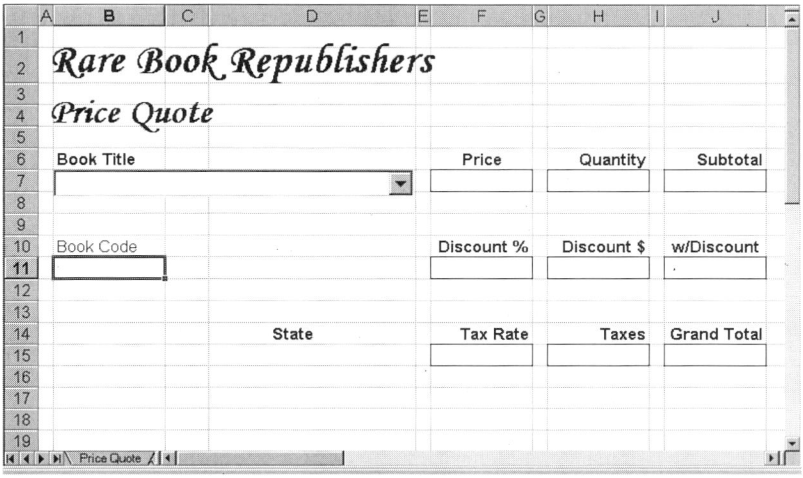

FIGURE 21.13
The relative list position information is needed to perform calculations in your form.

Then right-click the combo box and choose Format Control from the shortcut menu. In the Format Control dialog box, select the Control tab. Click to place the flashing cursor in the Cell Link text box; then click the collapse/expand button to collapse the dialog box.

Click the cell where the relative list position information will appear; the cell reference appears in the Cell Link range text box. Click the collapse/expand button to show the Format Control dialog box and choose OK.

Try selecting different items in the combo box. The corresponding position in the list appears in the Cell Link cell.

After you have the relative list position information displayed in the worksheet, you can use it to display the corresponding information or use the corresponding information in calculations.

The INDEX function has two possible syntaxes: an array syntax and a reference syntax. The array syntax always returns a value or an array of values. The reference syntax always returns a cell reference. In this example, we want a value returned (the book price) so we will use the array syntax:

```
=INDEX(array,row_num,column_num)
```

▶ **See** "Exploring the Power of Array Formulas," **p. 661**

The array argument is the list (in our example, the book price list). The row_num argument is the relative list position information, which we are displaying in the Cell Link cell. The column_num argument is the relative column number (not to be confused with the worksheet column letter) of the corresponding information in the list. If we select both the book titles and the book prices in the array, then the column_num is 2. If we just select the prices, the column_num is 1.

In this example (refer to Figures 21.10 and 21.13), the completed formula

```
=INDEX(L4:M11,B11,2)
```

`L4:M11` are the cell references for the book price list.

`B11` is the Cell Link cell reference.

`2` is the column in the book price list that contains the prices (because both columns of information in the array were selected).

After you've displayed the corresponding data in the form, you can use the information in formulas—the book price can now be used to calculate the subtotal (price times quantity).

Figure 21.14 shows the price quote form with two combo boxes— one for the book title and the other for the state name. By using the INDEX function with the book code and state code, the book price and state sales tax can be displayed. From these items, the form calculates the subtotal, discounts based on the quantity ordered, and determines the amount of tax to add to the grand total.

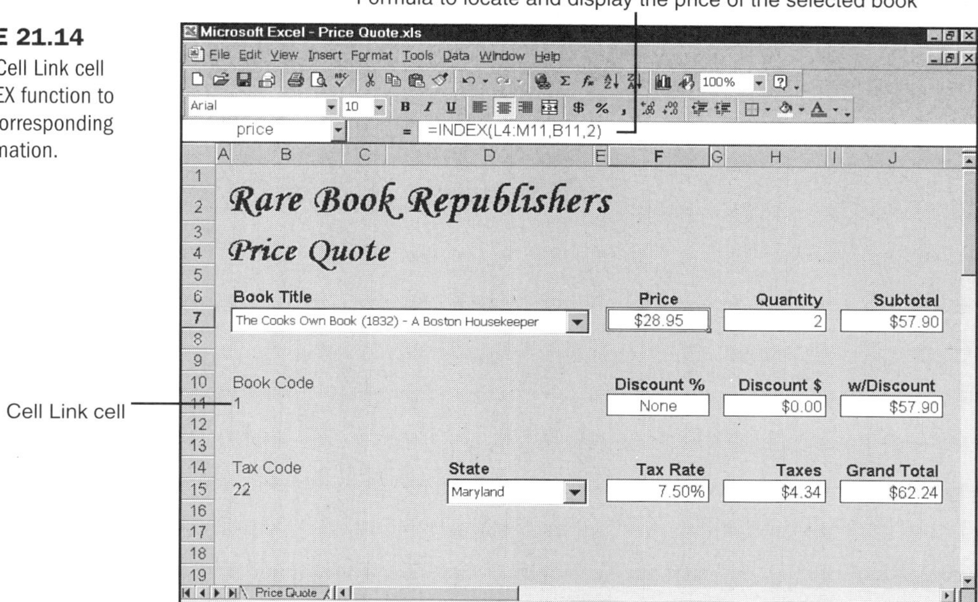

FIGURE 21.14
Use the Cell Link cell and INDEX function to display corresponding list information.

The section "Problem/Solution—Building Template Calculations" later in this chapter illustrates how these calculations were created.

Using Spinner Buttons in Form Templates *Spinner buttons* are used to change numerical data in regular increments. Often used to increase or decrease numbers one at a time, you can also set fractions or increments that skip numbers (5, 10, 15, and so on). Like other controls, you create a spinner by selecting the spinner button from the Forms toolbar and dragging in the cell where you want the spinner to appear.

- If you want the spinner to appear in the same cell as the number, position the spinner on the left side of the cell (because numerical data is right aligned).
- If you want the spinner to appear to the right of the number, you can either position the spinner in the cell just to the right of the cell that will display the numerical data or you can change the alignment of the numerical data to left aligned and position the spinner on the right side of the cell.

After you have created the spinner control, right-click the control and choose Format Control to display the Format Control dialog box (shown in Figure 21.15). Select the Control tab. Click to place the flashing cursor in the Cell Link text box. This is the cell you want the spinner to be linked to. Then click the collapse/expand button to collapse the dialog box and click the cell in the worksheet; the cell reference appears in the Cell Link range text box. Click the collapse/expand button to show the Format Control dialog box.

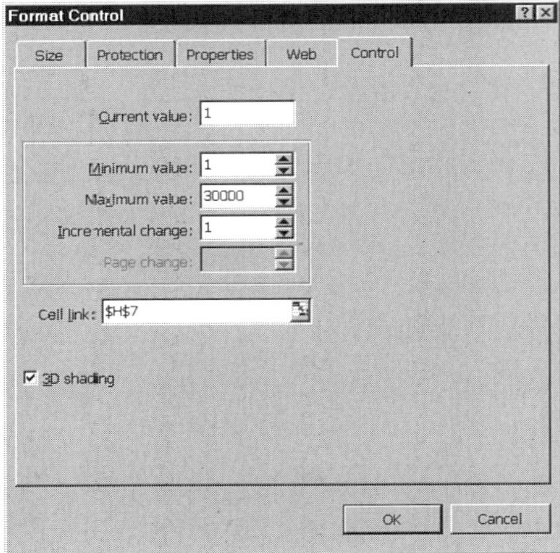

FIGURE 21.15
If you type the Cell Link cell reference, press F4 to make the reference absolute.

There are several other settings you need to choose on the Control tab. The Current Value is the default value you want to start with in the worksheet cell. You can also set the minimum and maximum values and the increment. After you have made these selections, click OK. The spinner button is now active.

Using Option Buttons in Form Templates Another type of control you can add to a form template is the *option button*, sometimes referred to as radio buttons. Option buttons are used in groups of two or more to provide a choice between alternatives; you can select only one option button. Figure 21.16 shows a worksheet form that calculates discount rates for computer equipment and software. The three option buttons on the right can be used to quickly change the allowable discount rates to Low, Medium, or High. Simple macros have been created to apply the corresponding discount rates (stored in another part of the worksheet) to the cells in the form.

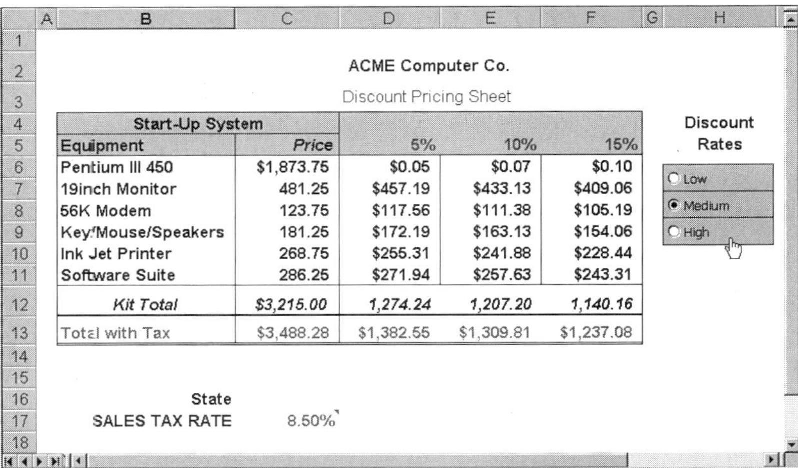

ACME Computer Co.
Discount Pricing Sheet

Start-Up System				
Equipment	Price	5%	10%	15%
Pentium III 450	$1,873.75	$0.05	$0.07	$0.10
19inch Monitor	481.25	$457.19	$433.13	$409.06
56K Modem	123.75	$117.56	$111.38	$105.19
Key/Mouse/Speakers	181.25	$172.19	$163.13	$154.06
Ink Jet Printer	268.75	$255.31	$241.88	$228.44
Software Suite	286.25	$271.94	$257.63	$243.31
Kit Total	*$3,215.00*	*1,274.24*	*1,207.20*	*1,140.16*
Total with Tax	$3,488.28	$1,382.55	$1,309.81	$1,237.08

Discount Rates
Low
Medium
High

State
SALES TAX RATE 8.50%

FIGURE 21.16
Option buttons have to be used in groups of two or more.

The best way to add a series of option buttons is to add one button, move and resize the button, apply the desired visual formats to the button, and then copy the button for as many options as you need. This way, all of the option buttons will appear identical. To add an option button to a form, click the option button control on the Forms toolbar and drag to create the control. The option button appears as shown in Figure 21.17.

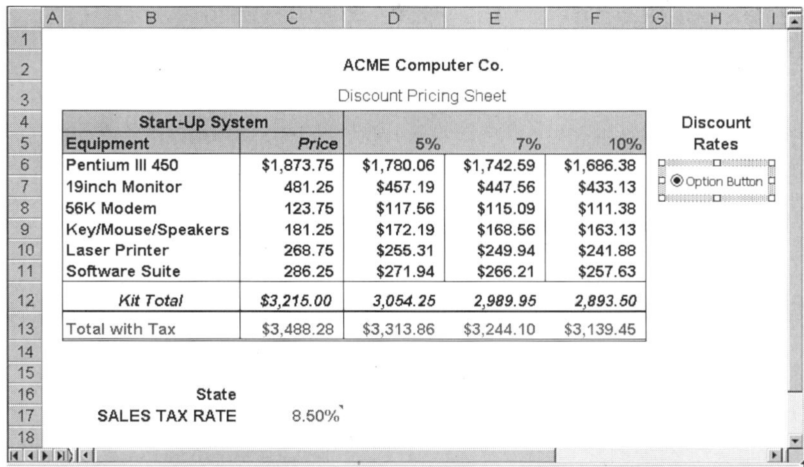

ACME Computer Co.

Discount Pricing Sheet

Start-Up System				
Equipment	Price	5%	7%	10%
Pentium III 450	$1,873.75	$1,780.06	$1,742.59	$1,686.38
19inch Monitor	481.25	$457.19	$447.56	$433.13
56K Modem	123.75	$117.56	$115.09	$111.38
Key/Mouse/Speakers	181.25	$172.19	$168.56	$163.13
Laser Printer	268.75	$255.31	$249.94	$241.88
Software Suite	286.25	$271.94	$266.21	$257.63
Kit Total	*$3,215.00*	*3,054.25*	*2,989.95*	*2,893.50*
Total with Tax	$3,488.28	$3,313.86	$3,244.10	$3,139.45

FIGURE 21.17
You can format the Option button to appear as a button or blend into the form background.

Formatting Option Button Controls By default, the label that appears on the control is Option Button followed by a number, as a way to provide a unique label to the control. You should replace this label with whatever you would like to display next to the control. You do this by highlighting the label and typing the replacement.

To format the appearance of the option button, right-click the control and choose Format Control from the shortcut menu. You can also choose Control from the Format menu. Click the Colors and Lines tab. Select a background color from the Color drop-down list. If you want a border around the button choose a color from the Lines drop-down list. For a truly professional look, apply 3D Shading, which you will find on the Control tab of the Format Control dialog box.

After you have applied the formats you want to the control, click OK. Now you can make copies of the control by pressing the Ctrl key as you click and drag the control. You will have to, of course, change the label for each control you have created.

You also might want to use the Align and Distribute features on the Drawing toolbar to make sure the control buttons line up. Press the Shift+Ctrl keys and click each control to select them. If the Drawing toolbar is not active, click the Drawing button on the Standard toolbar. Then choose Draw, Align or Distribute and select the alignment or distribution option you need.

One of the simplest ways to activate the option button controls is to assign a macro to the control.

Applying Macros to Option Buttons In the example shown in Figure 21.18, we want to create three separate macros, one for each option button control. These macros will copy the appropriate discount rates (listed in the table in cells L7:N9) to the cells in the Discount Rate table (cells D5:F5).

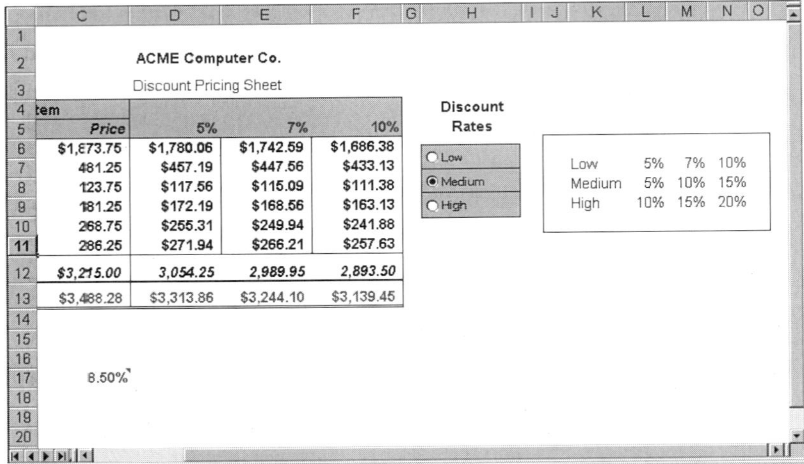

FIGURE 21.18
Create one macro first and test it to ensure it works properly.

To properly execute these macros, there are several things you should keep in mind:

- A list, such as the one that appears in cells L7:N9, needs to be created first. The list can appear in the same worksheet as the form, or in a different worksheet (including a worksheet in a different book). Because this is a form template, include the list in the same workbook as the form only if the list will remain relatively static. If the list will change regularly, place the list in a separate workbook.
- When a macro requires that cells be selected, create range names for the cells. For the example in Figure 21.18, use separate range names for the *source cells* (the cells to be copied) and the *target cells* (the cells where the data will be pasted). You can then use the Name box to select the range name as you are recording the macro.
- Because you want the formats in the form to remain intact, use the Edit, Paste Special command and select Values in the Paste Special dialog box. Do not use the Paste button on the Formatting toolbar or the Ctrl+V keyboard shortcut. This way, just the values, and not the formats, are pasted.

After you have the macros created, you can assign them to the option control buttons. Press Ctrl and right-click on the first option button. Choose Assign Macro from the shortcut menu. From the Assign Macro dialog box, choose the appropriate macro and click OK. Repeat for each option button. Now when you click on a option button, the form changes.

Formatting the Form Window

As with a worksheet template, you can format the cells in form template as well. However, for the worksheet to have the appearance of a form, there are some additional formatting elements to address:

- No row or column headers—Use Tools, Options and click the View tab. Then clear the Row & Column Headers check box.
- No gridlines—Use Tools, Options and click the View tab. Clear the Gridlines check box. You can use cell borders to make specific cells stand out.
- No scrollbars—Use Tools, Options and click the View tab. Clear the Horizontal Scrollbar and the Vertical Scrollbar check boxes.
- No sheet tabs—Use Tools, Options and click the View tab. Clear the Sheet Tabs check box.

The changes listed previously affect only the appearance of the sheets and window in this workbook. See the section "Finalizing the Template" later in this chapter to complete the last few steps required before saving the template.

NOTE With the added functionality of Excel user forms using VBA, you might think that this type of template is no longer needed. And you are right...and wrong. While VBA enables you to set the font and color characteristics of controls on user forms, there is one specific reason for using a form template–data tracking. The template can be designed to automatically move the data entered on the template into a database. You can find information on setting up this capability in the section "Feeding Template Data into a Database" later in this chapter.

Incorporating Charts in Templates

There are two ways to include charts in your templates: You can add a chart to a template workbook or you can create a custom default chart type to use anytime (whether in a template or not).

To have a chart automatically generated when you enter data in a template is an easy process. First, create the worksheet template as you would any worksheet being careful to include all data, formatting, formulas and so on (see Figure 21.19).

Select the sample data in the worksheet that you want plotted in the chart. Be sure to include the row and column labels but not the totals. Click the Chart Wizard button on the Standard toolbar. Proceed through the steps in the wizard to create the chart.

On the last step in the wizard, you have the choice of placing the chart in the worksheet (next to the data), or on its own sheet in the workbook. Choose whichever option is better for your circumstances. Then format the chart as needed.

After you finish creating and formatting the chart, you are ready to save the template. See the section "Finalizing Your Templates" later in this chapter to complete the last few steps required before saving the template.

Creating a Custom Default Chart Type

If you already have a chart you have customized that you use consistently, it's possible to save its design and formatting elements as the default chart type that Excel uses whenever you create a new chart.

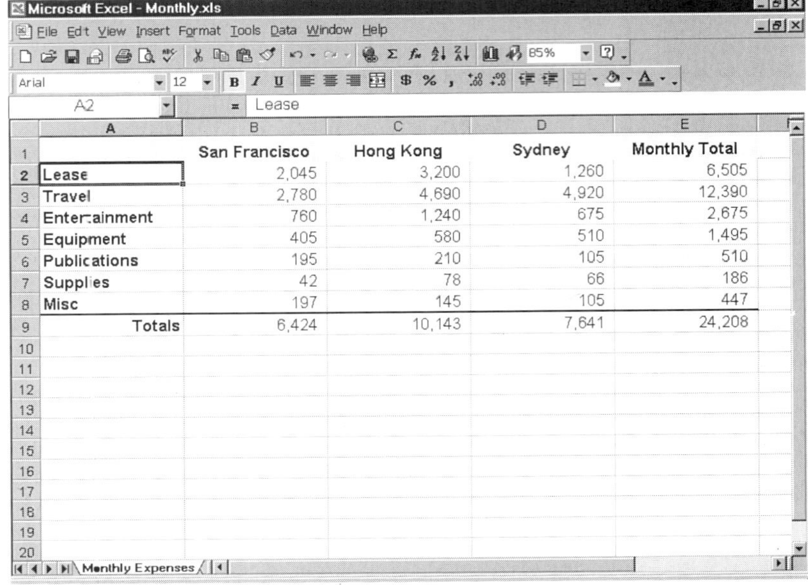

	A	B	C	D	E
1		San Francisco	Hong Kong	Sydney	Monthly Total
2	Lease	2,045	3,200	1,260	6,505
3	Travel	2,780	4,690	4,920	12,390
4	Entertainment	760	1,240	675	2,675
5	Equipment	405	580	510	1,495
6	Publications	195	210	105	510
7	Supplies	42	78	66	186
8	Misc	197	145	105	447
9	Totals	6,424	10,143	7,641	24,208

FIGURE 21.19
Be sure the data you want to plot is entered into the worksheet.

TIP Most chart formatting and chart options in the custom chart carry over into the default chart. So, unless you want the chart title you have in the custom chart to appear in all new charts, I'd suggest you remove it.

To designate a chart as the default chart type, select the chart and choose Chart, Chart Type. Click the Custom Types tab and choose the User-Defined option. Figure 21.20 shows the dialog box that appears.

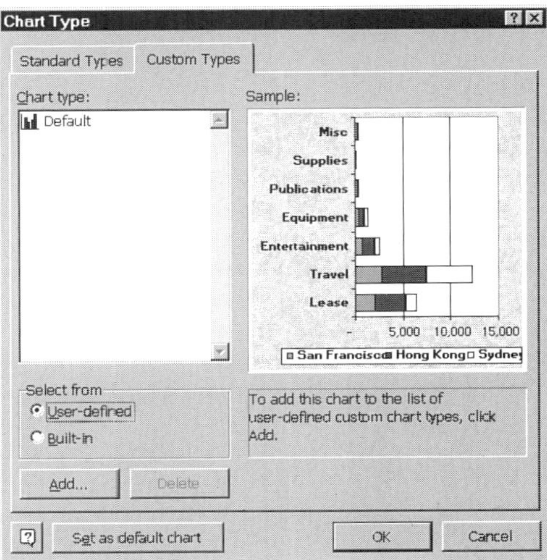

FIGURE 21.20
After you choose the User-Defined option button, the active chart appears in the Sample box.

CAUTION

Note that the current default chart format appears in the Chart Type list box. Do not select the default chart. If you do, the active chart disappears from the Sample box and you will not be able to get it back without canceling out of the dialog box.

Click the Add button. The Add Custom Chart Type dialog box appears, as shown in Figure 21.21.

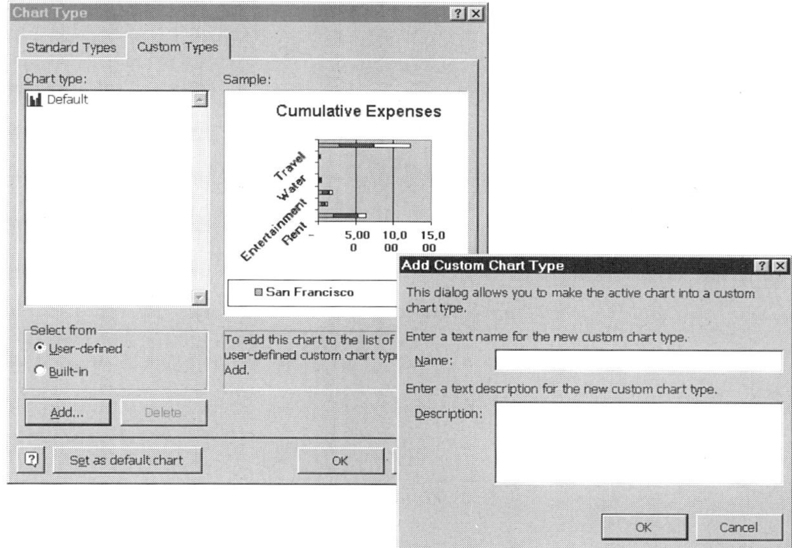

FIGURE 21.21
Provide a name and description here to make the template easier to use.

Using the Name edit box, assign a name to the new custom chart type. You should also type a description of the chart type in the Description edit box. After you save the chart type as a defined custom type, you will not be able to add or alter the description. Then choose OK to save the chart as a defined custom chart type. Figure 21.22 shows the appearance of the Custom Types tab after you add a custom chart type.

Now click the Set As Default Chart button. When the confirmation message displays, choose Yes. The custom chart is set as the default for new charts. Whatever built-in chart type (Line, Bar, Pie, Area, and so on) that was the basis for your custom chart is selected when the Chart Wizard starts. When it creates a new chart, Excel uses any custom formatting that you have added to the basic built-in chart.

CAUTION

Although the custom chart is the default, you can still create a chart based on a different built-in chart type. Any formats that are used in your custom chart type will be used in combination with the structure of the built-in type that is selected—the custom formats might not work well with a different built-in chart type.

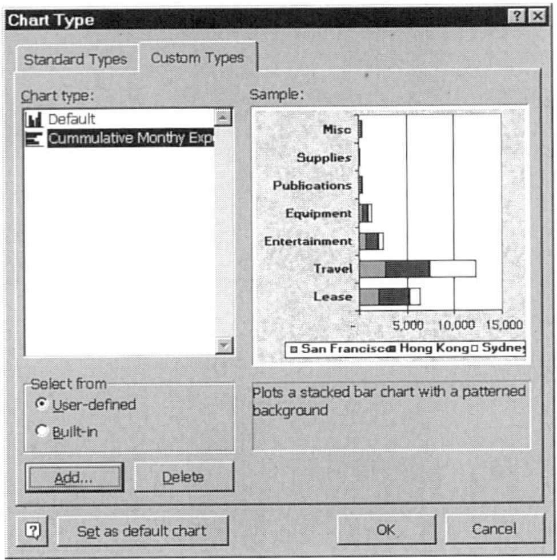

FIGURE 21.22
The name and description of your custom chart type are displayed in the Custom Types tab.

When you create a custom chart type, you're actually creating a template that the Chart Wizard uses to format new charts. The template is not stored in a standard .xlt template file, but in a file named Xlusrgal.xls (short for Excel User Gallery) in the folder (C:\Windows\Application Data\Microsoft\Excel), created the first time you save a custom chart.

If you want to alter some aspect of the chart template that you have created, you can do so by opening the Xlusrgal.xls file, finding the sheet tab that corresponds to the name you gave the chart type, and activating that sheet. Select some aspect of the chart (an axis, perhaps, or the chart title) and modify it as you would any other—usually, by means of the Format menu.

▶ For more information on creating graphic charts in Excel, **see** "Advanced Charting Techniques," **p. 815**

Finalizing Your Templates

Whether you are creating a worksheet template or a workbook template, there are a few things to consider as you finalize the template, before saving it:

- To preview the first page of a template in the New dialog box, you must set this up *before* you save the template. Choose File, Properties and on the Summary tab, mark the Save Preview Picture check box. Choose OK.
- Remove any unwanted, empty worksheets from the workbook *before* you save it as a template. Otherwise, these empty sheets will be included in each new workbook based on the template. This is especially important if you are creating a worksheet template. It should be the only worksheet in the workbook.
- Use the Delete key to remove any numerical data that was used to build and test the formulas and charts in the template file. Using the Delete key removes the data without removing any special formatting you applied to the cells.

- To avoid accidental changes made to the formulas or formatting, you should unlock the cells you want to be able to edit or enter data into. Select the cells and choose Format, Cells, and click the Protection tab. Unmark the Locked Cells check box. Then protect the worksheet (Tools, Protection, Protect Sheet).
- If your template contains macros, you should use a digital signature or let those who will be using the template know that it contains macros so that they will enable them as they open the template. To learn more about digitally signing macros, see the section "Digital Signatures for Macros and Code" in Chapter 6, "Successful VBA Modules."
- If your template will be used by others, consider adding text boxes or embedded comments that explain how to use the template.

Storing Templates Where You Can Find Them

When you save a custom template, you want to be able to access it in the New dialog box (shown in Figure 21.23) when you choose File, New. There are two tabs in this dialog box: General and Spreadsheet Solutions. The General tab contains the default Workbook template that is used to create new workbooks in Excel. The Spreadsheet Solutions tab contains the built-in Excel templates.

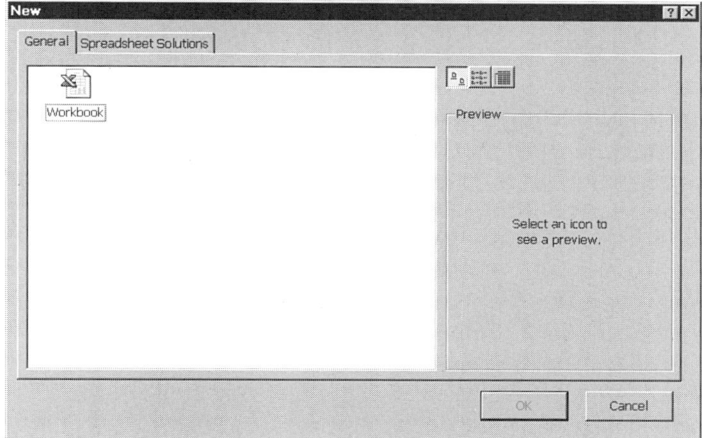

FIGURE 21.23
Create a separate folder for custom templates. The folder name appears as a tab in the New dialog box.

To have your custom templates appear in the New dialog box, you can either save it so the template appears on the General tab or, if you perform a few extra steps, you can create other tabs that will appear in the New dialog box.

If you save a template directly in the Templates folder (C:\Windows\Application Data\Microsoft\Templates), it will appear on the General tab of the New dialog box. If you create a folder under the Templates folder (such as Custom Books) and save your custom templates in that folder, a tab appears in the New dialog box with the folder name and the templates stored in that folder will be listed on the tab.

NOTE Don't try looking for the Spreadsheet Solutions folder; it isn't under the Templates folder. In Excel 2000, Microsoft has elected to hide this folder from users.

If you are using a network and need to make a custom template available to others, store the template in a shared area of the network. You (and others) can create a shortcut to the network location or template and place the shortcut in the Templates folder.

NOTE Template files are saved with an .xlt extension. Excel template file icons appear with a thick yellow band across the top of the icon image.

To save a workbook or worksheet template, choose File, Save As. The Save As dialog box appears.

Begin at the bottom of the dialog box and work your way up using these steps:

1. In the Save As Type box, choose Template (*.xlt). When you select Template (*.xlt) from the Save As Type box, the Templates folder is displayed automatically in the Save In drop-down list box. If you have upgraded from an earlier version of Office, there may be a folder, such as the one in Figure 21.24, listed under the Templates folder.
2. In the File Name text box, type the template name. In Figure 21.24, `Weekly` has been entered as the template name.

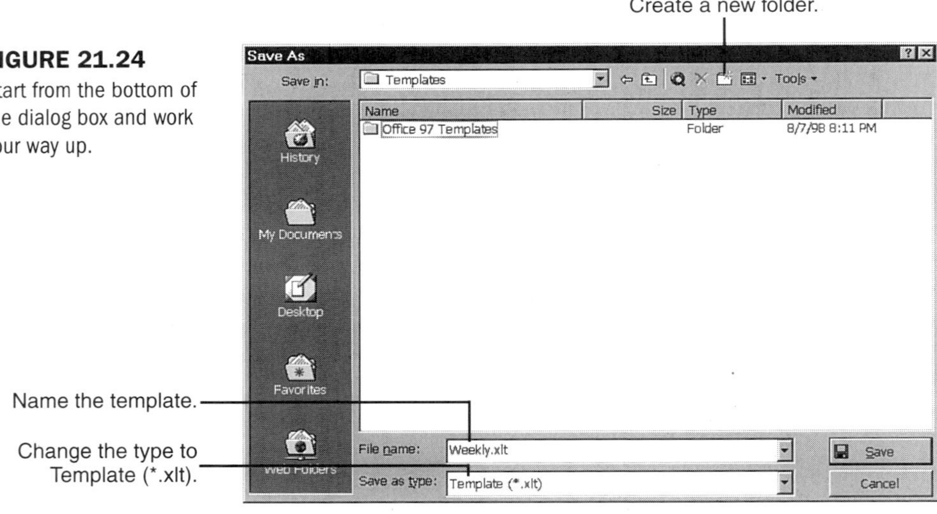

FIGURE 21.24
Start from the bottom of the dialog box and work your way up.

3. Decide where you want the template stored. To create a new folder in which to store your custom template, click the New Folder button on the Save As dialog box toolbar. If you store it in the Templates folder, it will appear on the General tab of the New dialog box.

4. Choose Save.
5. Close the template file.

After the template has been saved and closed, you can create new files based on the template or you can open the template to make any adjustments to the template file.

When you create a new file based on a template, a copy of the template appears—not the original template. The name of the template with a sequential number appears as a placeholder name—much the same way that new workbooks are named BOOK1, BOOK2, and so on.

Using and Modifying Custom Templates

After you have created custom templates, it's a good idea to test them before beginning to use them officially. This is especially true if you are sharing the templates with others. You may also discover things you want to change about the templates behavior or appearance.

Using Workbook Templates

To create a new workbook based on a template, choose File, New and select a template from one of the tabs in the New dialog box. A copy of the template appears—not the original template. As a placeholder name for the new file, the template name, with a sequential number, appears in the Title Bar.

NOTE You cannot use the New Workbook button on the Standard toolbar to access your list of template files. This button creates a new workbook based on the default template. See the section "Creating Autotemplates" for information on customizing the default workbook template.

Using Worksheet Templates

Inserting a worksheet template into an existing workbook must be done using a very specific set of steps:

1. Open or activate the workbook to which you want to add the worksheet template.
2. Right-click the worksheet tab name where you want to insert the new worksheet. The shortcut menu appears.
3. Choose Insert. The New dialog box appears.
4. Select the worksheet template you want to insert.
5. Choose OK. A copy of the worksheet template is added to the current workbook.

NOTE You cannot use the Insert, Worksheet command to insert a worksheet template. The Insert, Worksheet command inserts a new worksheet based on the default worksheet template. See the section "Creating Autotemplates" later in this chapter for information on customizing the default worksheet template.

Modifying Custom Templates

Modifying a template file is identical to modifying any other file. Choose File, Open to open a template file.

Periodically, you may want to revise your template files. Editing a template file is identical to the way in which you edit other workbooks:

- Open the template—Remember, templates are typically stored in C:\Program Files\Microsoft Office\Templates.
- Make the necessary modifications to the template.
- Choose File, Save or click the Save button on the Standard toolbar to update the template.

The changes you make affect only new workbooks or worksheets that you create *after* you update the template. It does not change any existing files that are based on the template.

Creating Autotemplates

Whenever a new blank workbook is created, it is based on the default *workbook autotemplate*. When a new blank worksheet is inserted into an existing workbook, it is based on the default *worksheet autotemplate*.

These autotemplates control the look and content of all new workbooks and worksheets—including the default font, cell and worksheet formatting, header and footer print options, and—for workbooks—the number of sheets in the book. You can change the format or content of the new workbooks and worksheets by modifying the existing autotemplates.

Creating a workbook autotemplate is identical to creating an ordinary template, with two exceptions—the autotemplate is saved in the XLStart folder and must be named **Book**. The worksheet autotemplate is saved in the XLStart folder and must be named **Sheet**.

Although the workbook autotemplate controls each new workbook created, any new worksheets added to a workbook will not have any of the formats or content you applied to the workbook autotemplate. This can be remedied by creating a worksheet autotemplate. If you want each new worksheet to have a specific header or footer that prints with the worksheet, add this header or footer to both autotemplates.

NOTE Of course, you might run into problems with sheet names when you use a worksheet template. Suppose that a worksheet in Sheet.xlt is named Sheet1, and that your open workbook also has a sheet named Sheet1. The worksheet that's inserted is automatically named Sheet1(2) to distinguish it from Sheet1. If you want it to have a different name, you have to rename it manually.

To create a workbook or worksheet autotemplate, follow these steps:

1. Begin a new workbook. Apply any formatting or settings you require. For a worksheet template, remove all but one sheet from the workbook.

2. Choose File, Save As. The Save As dialog box appears. To save the workbook as a template file, it is easiest to begin at the bottom of the dialog box and work your way up.
3. Choose Template (*.xlt) in the Save As Type text box. When you select Template (*.xlt) from the Save As Type box, the Templates folder is displayed automatically in the Save In drop-down list box.
4. For a workbook autotemplate, type `Book` in the File Name text box. For a worksheet autotemplate, type `Sheet` in the File Name text box.
5. Select the Save In drop-down list box and change the folder to XLStart, using the following path:

   ```
   C:\Windows\Application Data\Microsoft\Excel
   ```

6. Choose Save.
7. Close the template file.

To restore the original settings for new workbooks and worksheets, simply remove the Book.xlt and Sheet.xlt files you added to the XLStart folder.

Feeding Template Data into a Database

One of the features of Excel templates is its capability to automate saving the data from a workbook based on the template into a database, such as Access database, or Excel list.

This is accomplished through the Template Wizard, an add-in feature in Excel. The Template Wizard links cells in the template to fields in a database. This is particularly useful with templates that are input forms. When the data is entered and saved in the form, the information is automatically stored not only in the workbook, but a corresponding record is created in a database. The information in the database then can be manipulated using the features of the database.

For example, suppose you want to track the hours that employees worked each week on client projects. You would design a work log form on a worksheet and use the Template Wizard to create the template and links to a database. When the employee completes the work log form, the copy of the form can be saved or printed. The completed work log data is added as a new record in the database.

Additionally, you can use this feature with multiple sites that are connected by a network, where the form is linked to a central database. To store the template on a shared network drive to make it available to all users, you need to create a shortcut to the template and be sure the shortcut is copied to the Templates folder on each user's desktop.

Installing the Template Wizard

The Template Wizard is an Excel add-in. This feature is not installed automatically when you install Microsoft Office 2000, so you must install it.

1. Choose Tools, Add-ins. In the Add-ins dialog box, scroll down the list until you see Template wizard.
2. Click to check Template Wizard and choose OK.
3. Because it is not automatically installed, you will receive a message asking whether you want to install it at this time. Choose Yes. You need the Office CD or access to the location where the Office CD program files are stored.
4. Select the Template Wizard with Data Tracking check box and choose OK.

When the wizard has been added to your computer, the Template Wizard command appears in the Data menu. You can now use the wizard to set up the template.

Choosing a Database (and Driver)

Before moving on to the actual use of the Template Wizard, it's useful to consider which database you want to use. Let's compare the advantages of using an Access database and an Excel list.

NOTE You need to have Microsoft Access installed to create an Access database by means of the Template Wizard. You also need Access itself to be present if you want to examine or manage the data. However, after the database has been created, you do not need to have Access installed if all you want to do is store data by means of the template.

Unless you have some special reason to use Access, you should choose Excel. The reason is that the most valuable characteristic of a true database (such as Access) is its relational capability. But the Template Wizard does not take advantage of the relational capability.

Suppose that you created a template that tracks customer information. The Template Wizard was used to implement data tracking, and an Access database was selected as the place to store new data. You open a new workbook based on the template, enter the necessary information, and are ready to save the new record. When you do so, the entire record about the customer is written to one and only one table in the Access database. The record does not contain a unique identifier for each record, a feature of relational databases. Therefore, much of the strength of a relational database is lost. Therefore, you might as well direct the data to an Excel workbook, where you have access to Excel's data analysis, summary, and charting capabilities.

On the other hand, suppose that you have taken the trouble to set up your Excel template with a combo box. Using the Forms toolbar, place the combo box on the worksheet and assign it a Cell Link. The Cell Link contains the combo box's index value of the data, not the data itself. Customers can be selected from the combo box instead of typing the full customer name each time. You can use the Template Wizard to arrange the delivery of the numeric value in the Cell Link, rather than the customer name itself, to the Access database. So doing would set the stage for leveraging the database's relational capability.

There is a tradeoff of effort for efficiency. If you anticipate collecting large amounts of data and are willing to do the extra work in Excel of setting up the Cell Links and arranging the necessary lookups and links in Access, then, by all means, use the Access driver.

Otherwise, use the Excel driver. That way, when you open the workbook that stores all the data records, you can immediately start using Excel's tools and functions to analyze the data.

Setting Up the Template

Suppose that you have created an Excel workbook that you will use to calculate a price quote for product orders. An example is shown in Figure 21.25.

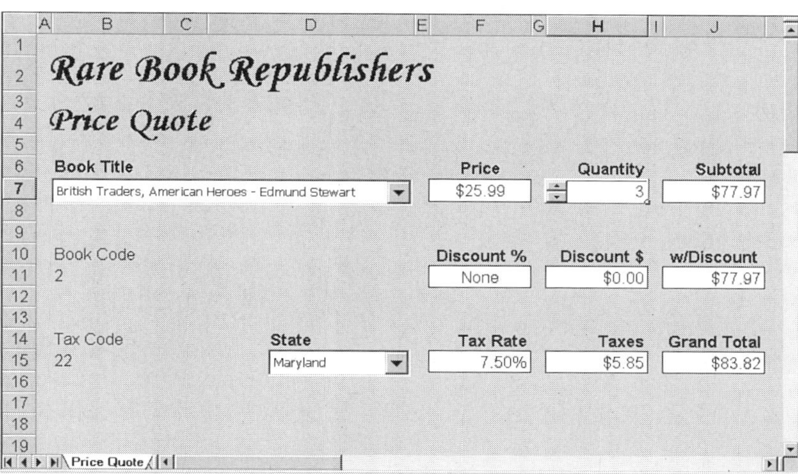

FIGURE 21.25
The price quote form is set up for ease of data entry.

After you have designed the form that you want, save it as a workbook—not as a template. The Template Wizard saves the .xlt file for you when it sets up the required connectivity information.

Structuring the Template After saving the workbook, and with the workbook still active, choose Data, Template Wizard. The Template Wizard dialog box shown in Figure 21.26 appears.

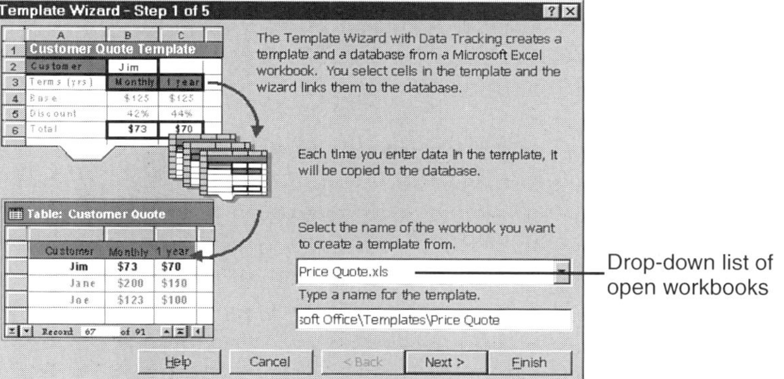

FIGURE 21.26
Step 1 of the Template Wizard—choose the workbook that will become the template.

The name of the workbook that is active when you start the Template Wizard appears in the dialog box's drop-down list. Verify that it is the workbook you want to use as the basis for the template, and, if necessary, use the drop-down list to choose another workbook.

The path to the Templates folder and the name of the active workbook appear in the Type a Name for the Template text box. You can accept this path and name, or type an alternative. If you want to store the template in a specific folder under the Templates folder, click in the Type a Name for the Template text box and press End.

Click Next to go to step 2 of the wizard (see Figure 21.27).

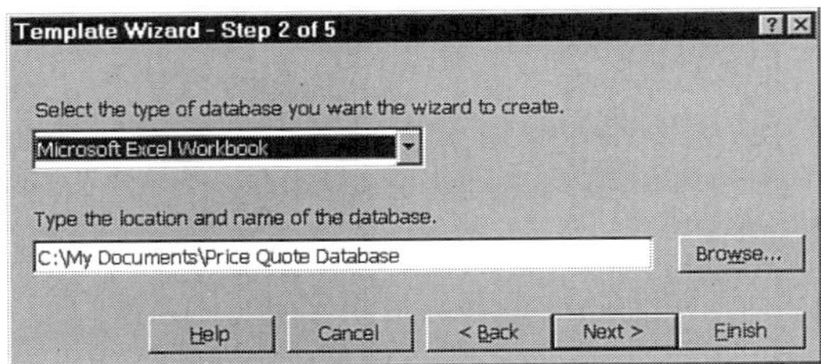

FIGURE 21.27
Select a database driver in step 2.

In step 2, select the database driver you want to use from the drop-down list. You also need to designate the name and location of the database. For a new database, type the path to and the name of the new database in the text box. To identify an existing database, click Browse to navigate to that database.

Then click Next to go to step 3 of the wizard as shown in Figure 21.28.

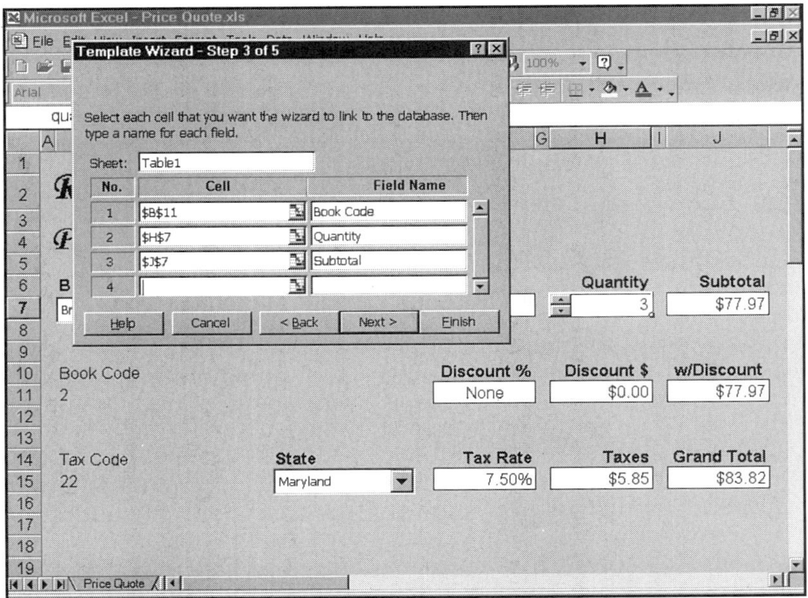

FIGURE 21.28
Use step 3 to identify the location of the data and the associated labels.

In step 3, type a name for the database table that will contain the data—or, if in step 2 you chose to store the data in an Excel workbook, the name you type must be that of a worksheet in that workbook.

The grid in step 3 is where you indicate the location of the data that is to be stored in the database. Click the cell in the worksheet that contains the first data value; its cell address appears in the Cell box for grid row 1. Then, click under Field Name in the same row of the grid.

What then appears in the associated Field Name box depends on how you have set up the worksheet. If there is a label in the same row and to the left of the data cell, Excel supplies that label as a default field name. If you have set up the data as a list, with header labels in the top row of the list, Excel supplies the header label as a field name. If there is no label in the same row or same column, you need to type a field name in the dialog box's grid.

Although you can overwrite the default label with another label, it's usually best to accept the default label. That way, you'll find it easier to determine the correlation between fields in the database and data in the worksheet form.

This step highlights the reason to use a template for the process of data entry. As new data is entered and collected in the database or worksheet, it's important that the information always be entered in the same location. The use of a template that establishes the worksheet's layout helps ensure that the data will always be found in the same locations.

After you have finished specifying the location of data and the field names, click Next to display step 4 in the wizard, shown in Figure 21.29.

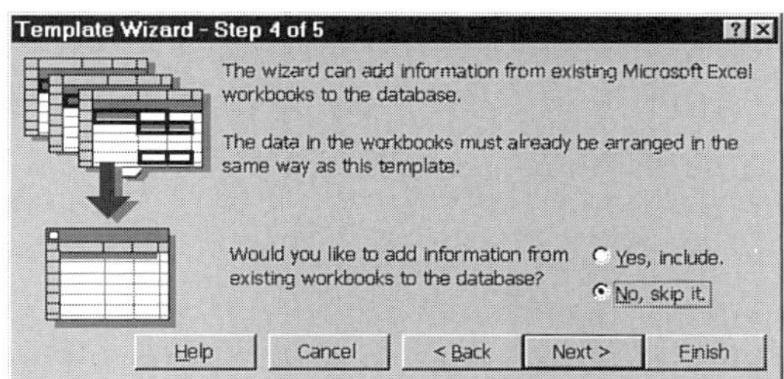

FIGURE 21.29
Step 4 gives you a chance to add data from existing workbooks to the database.

Suppose that you had been storing price quotes as worksheet files in a special folder for some time, but had not yet created the database to store the price quote data. You can add the information in those existing workbooks to the database. Step 4 is where you decide to do that.

To store the data correctly, the existing workbooks and this template workbook must be laid out identically. If you do have existing data laid out in the required fashion, you can choose the Yes, Include option button; otherwise, choose the No, Skip It option button. Choosing Yes, Include and then clicking Next displays the dialog box shown in Figure 21.30.

When you click the Select button, you will see a dialog box that is identical (except for its name) to the File, Open dialog box. Use it to navigate to the locations of the workbooks whose data you want to include in the database. As you locate them, select their names and then choose Open. Each file is added to the Files to Convert list.

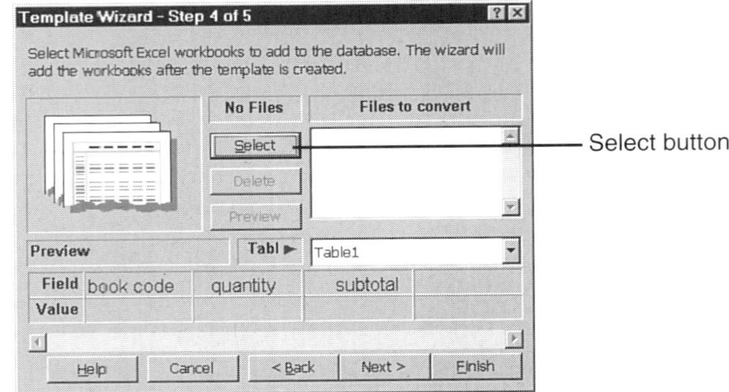

FIGURE 21.30
Although the dialog box contains different controls, the Template Wizard considers it to be part of step 4.

To preview a file, select it in the Files to Convert list and click the Preview button. The point, of course, is to enable you to verify that a file really does conform to the same cell addresses as in the template you are creating. If you add a few files, preview them; if you find that one or more have a layout that's even slightly wrong as to cell addresses, you can click Remove to take them off the list.

Click Next to display step 5 of the wizard (see Figure 21.31).

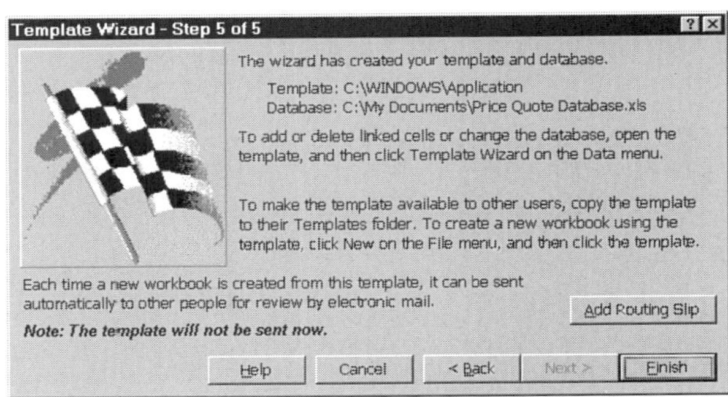

FIGURE 21.31
If you have installed Outlook or Exchange, you can automatically route new workbooks based on the template to addresses in the Personal Address Book.

You should note somewhere the summary information—the name and location of the template and of the Excel or database file that collects new data—for later reference.

After you click Finish, the database or Excel workbook that will store the data is created, and the workbook that was active when you started the Template Wizard is saved as a template with the .xlt file extension.

Entering New Data Based on the Template When you subsequently open a new workbook based on the template, enter data, and you choose either File, Close or File, Save, you see the dialog box shown in Figure 21.32.

Choose Create a New Record in the database in which to save the new data. Choose Continue Without Updating to omit the record from the database.

You will be prompted to save and name the workbook.

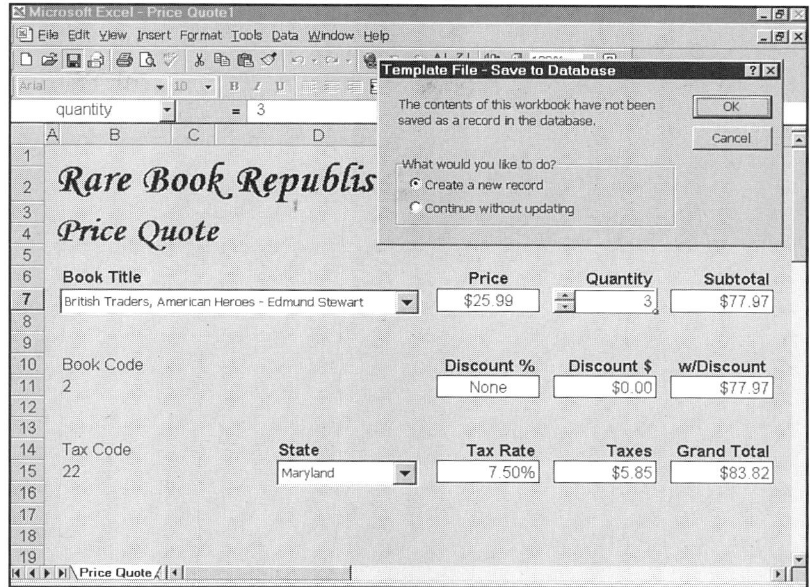

FIGURE 21.32
At this point, you can choose whether or not to add the data in the new workbook to the database.

Suppose that you have saved a workbook based on the template, and have selected Create a New Record when you did so. If you later open that workbook, you will see the message that warns you about existing macros. Choose Enable Macros.

That message is a little disconcerting, but the reason is that the template you created puts macros into new workbooks that are based on it. These macros help maintain the relationship between the workbook and the database.

NOTE If you click Finish in the Template Wizard, you might see a message that an Access database couldn't be created. Check first to see that you have Access installed. If you do, check the labels in the workbook you're using to create the template. If you want to create an Access database, the labels in the workbook must conform to Access naming rules. Therefore, your labels should not contain a period (.), exclamation point (!), accent grave (`), square brackets ([]), or leading spaces. You should also keep labels shorter than 64 characters–the shorter, the better–and unique with respect to one another.

NOTE The links referred to in steps 1, 3, and 5 of the Template Wizard are not links in the usual sense; they are not the same as, say, setting cell A1 in Book1 equal to cell A1 in Book2. Changing a value in one of the workbooks whose data is stored in the database does not result in an immediate change of value in the database.

Instead, if you change a value in an existing workbook based on the template, the macros take over. They change the value stored in the database to the new value.

Problem/Solution—Building Template Calculations

You can use the same types of formulas in templates as you can in other worksheets. Earlier in this chapter, we discussed form templates and used an example of a price quote (see Figure 21.33).

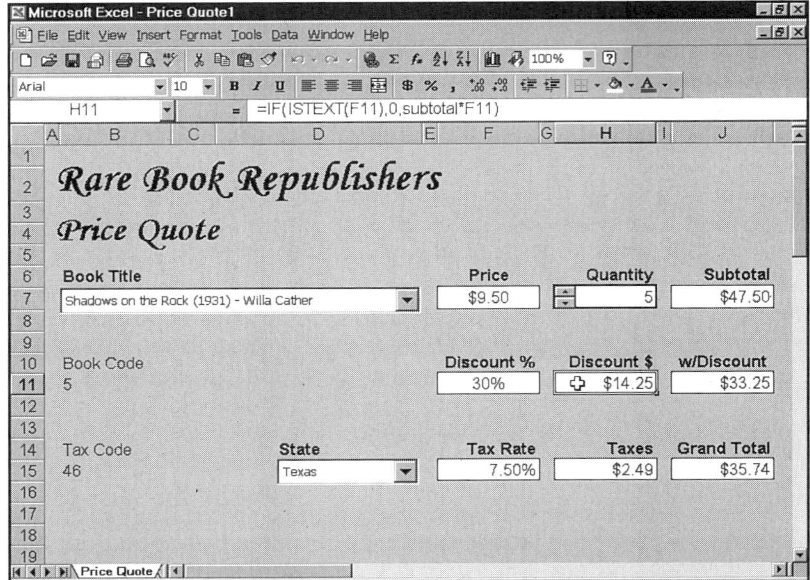

FIGURE 21.33
The Formula Bar displays the formula in the selected cell.

The INDEX function is used to list data—the book price and the tax rate—that corresponds to items selected in the combo boxes. Refer to the section "Displaying or Using Related Data in a Combo Box" for a complete discussion of using the INDEX function in forms.

An IF function is used to calculate the discount percent and discount amount. The basic syntax of an IF function is

```
=IF(Test,True,False)
```

The discount percent checks the quantity being ordered. Orders of fewer than 5 books do not receive a discount, and the text `No Discount` appears in the cell. Orders whose quantities are between 5 and 9 receive a 30% discount. Orders whose quantities are 10 or more receive a 50% discount. A nested IF statement is required to meet these conditions. The range name `quantity` is substituted for the cell reference H7. The formula for this calculation is

```
=IF(quantity<5,"No Discount",IF(quantity<10,30%,50%))
```

Normally, the discount amount would be the subtotal multiplied by the discount percent. However, because the discount percent cell displays a text phrase when the orders are for fewer than 5 books, an IF function (with an embedded IS function) is needed to calculate the discount amount (see Figure 21.33).

```
=IF(ISTEXT(F11),0,subtotal*F11)
```

The test in this formula is checking to see whether the cell F11 contains text. If it does, a zero is displayed in the discount amount cell. If the cell does not contain text, the subtotal is multiplied by the discount percent to calculate the discount amount.

▶ To learn more about IF and IS functions, **see** "Logical and Information Functions," **p. 722**

CHAPTER 22

Advanced Formulas

In this chapter

Conditional Formatting

Conditional Formatting is a feature that can apply up to three different formats to data in a cell or to the cell itself, based on conditions you specify. Conditional Formatting can be applied to a cell that contains a value, a formula, or text. This powerful formatting feature changes the visual appearance of the data or cell and draws attention to data that is in some way out of the ordinary. The font style, font color, cell borders, and cell background color or pattern can be changed to accentuate the data in the worksheet. It is particularly useful in performing data analysis.

With Conditional Formatting, you decide what the conditions are and how the data in your worksheet will appear that meets those conditions. Most people are familiar with using the most basic conditions. For example, if the value in a cell is greater than a specified amount, change the appearance. This type of condition is triggered by the value in a cell. However, you can also create a condition that uses a formula.

Consider the worksheet shown in Figure 22.1. Suppose you want the appearance of the state names to change when the total plant production reaches 75,000 units. Because the condition relies on the value in other cells, a simple formula is required.

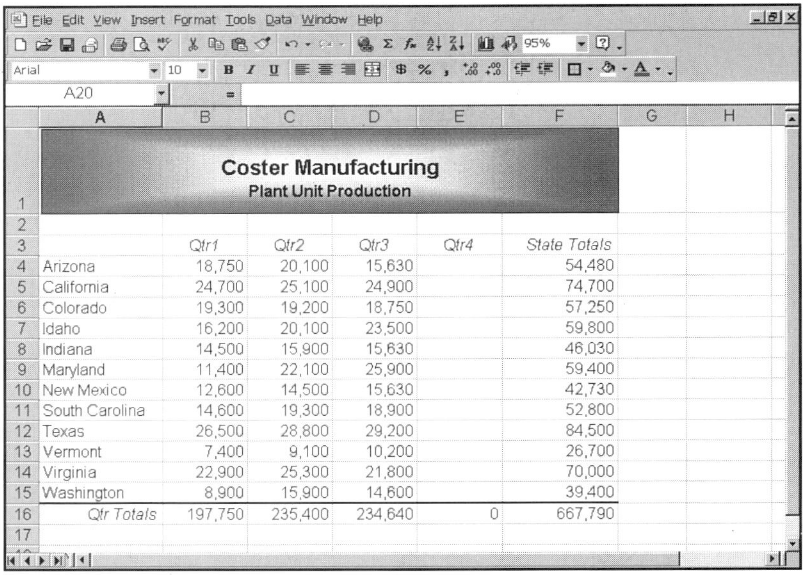

FIGURE 22.1
The fill-effect in the heading can be accomplished only if the heading is entered in a text box, rather than in the worksheet cells.

A20

Coster Manufacturing
Plant Unit Production

	A	B	C	D	E	F
3		*Qtr1*	*Qtr2*	*Qtr3*	*Qtr4*	*State Totals*
4	Arizona	18,750	20,100	15,630		54,480
5	California	24,700	25,100	24,900		74,700
6	Colorado	19,300	19,200	18,750		57,250
7	Idaho	16,200	20,100	23,500		59,800
8	Indiana	14,500	15,900	15,630		46,030
9	Maryland	11,400	22,100	25,900		59,400
10	New Mexico	12,600	14,500	15,630		42,730
11	South Carolina	14,600	19,300	18,900		52,800
12	Texas	26,500	28,800	29,200		84,500
13	Vermont	7,400	9,100	10,200		26,700
14	Virginia	22,900	25,300	21,800		70,000
15	Washington	8,900	15,900	14,600		39,400
16	*Qtr Totals*	197,750	235,400	234,640	0	667,790

With the data from the first three quarters filled in, only Texas meets the condition. However, when the data for the fourth quarter is entered, it is very possible other states will meet the condition. To accomplish this type of Conditional Formatting, follow these steps:

1. Start by selecting the first cell you want changed as a result of the condition; in this case, cell A4.

2. Choose Format, Conditional Formatting. The Conditional Formatting dialog box appears, as shown in Figure 22.2.

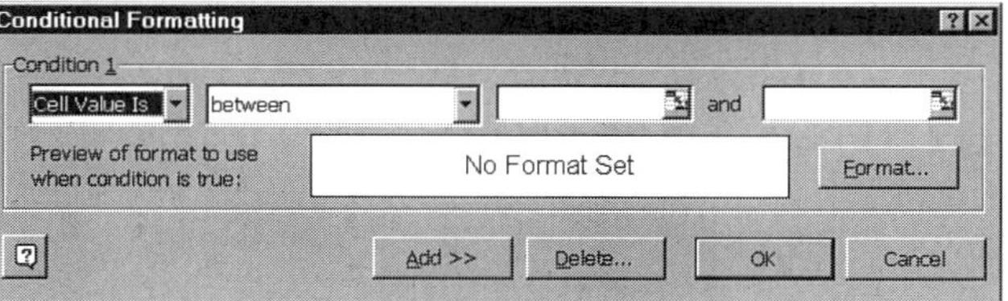

FIGURE 22.2
To create more than one condition, click Add and the dialog box will expand to show another condition.

3. The first drop-down box is used to indicate the type of condition. In this example, you need to change the type to Formula Is. If you were going to set a condition based on the value in the selected cell, you would leave the type set to Cell Value Is. When you change the type of condition to Formula Is, the dialog box changes, as shown in Figure 22.3.

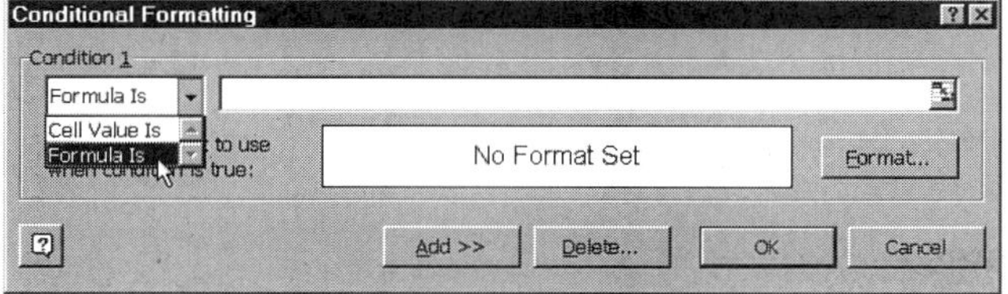

FIGURE 22.3
The Formula Is type provides a single box to enter the formula.

4. The formula is entered in the text box to the right of the condition type drop-down. As with all Excel formulas, start with an equal sign (=). Then enter the condition you are looking for. In this example, the condition is F4>=75000, so the formula entry is `=F4>=75000`.

NOTE When you need a cell reference in your formula, you can type it in, or select the cell with your mouse. When you use the mouse, an absolute cell reference is automatically displayed. Press the F4 key three times to change this to a relative cell reference.

▶ **See** "Using Absolute Cell References in Formulas," **p. 634**

5. Then click Format. The Format Cells dialog box appears, where you select the font style, font color, underlining, borders, shading, or patterns you want to apply when the condition is met.
6. Click OK to close the Format Cells dialog box. If you want to add another condition, click Add. The dialog box displays another condition for you to complete. You can specify up to three conditions.
7. After all the conditions and associated formats are specified, click OK.

There are two ways to copy the Conditional Formatting to other cells. You can use the Format Painter button on the Standard toolbar, but using this tool copies all cell formatting. To copy just the conditional formats, select the cell that currently has the Conditional Formatting and all the cells to which you want to apply the formatting. Then choose Format, Conditional Formatting. When the dialog box appears, simply click OK. The Conditional Formatting is applied to the selected cells; the formula adjusts for each cell in the range.

NOTE If more than one of the conditions you specify is present, Excel will apply only the formats of the first condition it matches to the worksheet.

In Figure 22.4, the Conditional Formatting has been applied to cells A4:A15. The data for the fourth quarter has been entered through cell E9 (Maryland). As the data is entered for each state, the condition is evaluated and the formats changed for those states that match the condition. As discussed earlier, Texas matched the condition with just the data from the first three quarters. Now California, Colorado, Idaho, and Maryland match the condition as well.

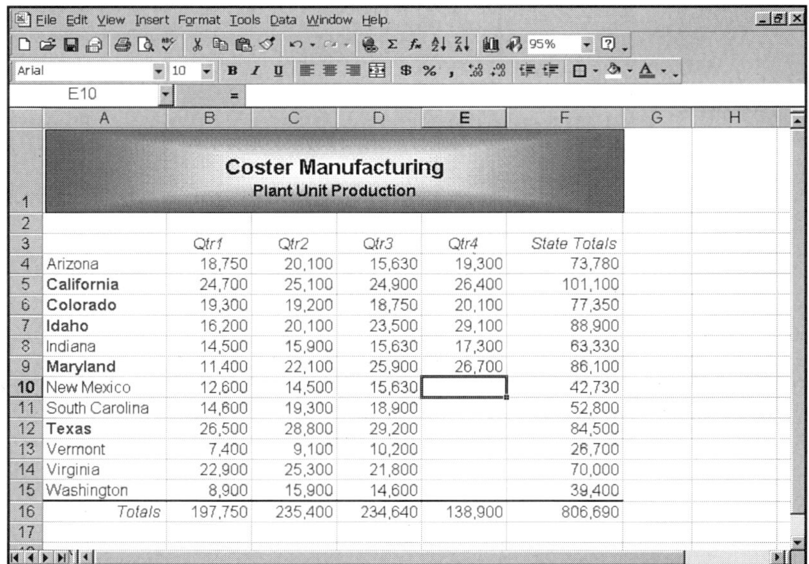

Coster Manufacturing
Plant Unit Production

	Qtr1	Qtr2	Qtr3	Qtr4	State Totals
Arizona	18,750	20,100	15,630	19,300	73,780
California	24,700	25,100	24,900	26,400	101,100
Colorado	19,300	19,200	18,750	20,100	77,350
Idaho	16,200	20,100	23,500	29,100	88,900
Indiana	14,500	15,900	15,630	17,300	63,330
Maryland	11,400	22,100	25,900	26,700	86,100
New Mexico	12,600	14,500	15,630		42,730
South Carolina	14,600	19,300	18,900		52,800
Texas	26,500	28,800	29,200		84,500
Vermont	7,400	9,100	10,200		26,700
Virginia	22,900	25,300	21,800		70,000
Washington	8,900	15,900	14,600		39,400
Totals	197,750	235,400	234,640	138,900	806,690

FIGURE 22.4
The formatting is applied only when the condition is met.

When the values in the worksheet don't match the conditions, the formatting is suppressed. If you want to determine which cells in a worksheet have conditional formats, choose Edit, Go To and click the Special button. In the Go To Special dialog box, choose Conditional Formats. Below the Data Validation option, choose All and then click OK. If you want to find only those cells with a particular conditional format, you must select a cell in the worksheet that has the conditional formatting you are looking for. Then in the Go To Special dialog box, after you select Conditional Format, click the Same option below Data Validation.

▶ **See** "Using the Go To Special Command," **p. 911**

Another way you can use formulas in Conditional Formatting is shown in Figure 22.5. This worksheet lists information regarding consulting work performed in June. You can use conditional formatting to highlight any work that was performed on a weekend—so the clients can be charged extra and the consultants given a bonus.

To evaluate whether the date is on the weekend, you use the `WEEKDAY` function and create two conditions. The first condition checks to see whether the date falls on a Sunday (where 1 is the first day of the week). The second condition checks to see whether the date falls on a Saturday (where 7 is the last day of the week).

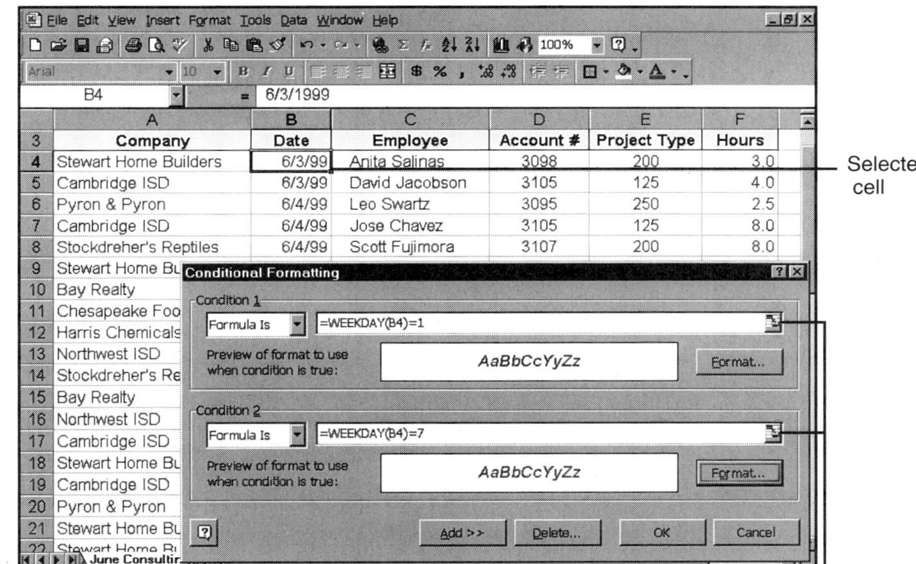

FIGURE 22.5
Click the Collapse/Expand buttons to shrink the dialog box whenever you need to select cells in the worksheet.

Figure 22.5 shows two conditions, one to evaluate the date for Sunday and the other to evaluate the date for Saturday. You need only two conditions if you want to format the results differently. If the formats are going to be the same, use one condition, such as:

```
=OR(WEEKDAY(B4)=1,WEEKDAY(B4)=7)
```

`OR` is a Logical function in Excel where the criteria (or in this case, the conditions) are separated by commas.

TIP It's a good idea to spend some time up front determining each condition you want to check and the formatting to be applied if the condition is met.

If you want to flag data entry errors, you can use conditional formatting. However, a more powerful option would be to use Excel's Data Validation feature. Data Validation can display error messages if an invalid entry is made.

▶ **See** "Validating and Analyzing Excel Data," **p. 860**

NOTE If you have conditional formats in a workbook, and then share the workbook, the conditional formats will continue to work. However, they cannot be modified and new ones cannot be added to the workbook while it is shared.

▶ **See** "Sharing and Merging Workbooks," **p. 937**

Using Absolute Cell References in Formulas

The flexibility behind worksheet functions lies in the use of cell references in formulas, instead of the actual worksheet values. By using cell references in a formula, when the worksheet values change, the formula results are automatically updated. Additionally, when you create a formula that contains cell references, the formula can be copied to other cells in the worksheet.

Using cell references in formulas can save you a tremendous amount of time creating and updating worksheets. There are three types of cell references you can use in formulas:

- Relative cell references
- Absolute cell references
- Mixed cell references

To get the most from your formulas, it is important you understand the differences and uses of each type of cell reference.

Relative Cell References

Formulas containing *relative cell references* adjust when copied to other locations. Figure 22.6 shows the difference between 1998 and 1999 sales. When the formula for calculating the sales for the Ultimate service in cell D6 is copied down the list, the cell references in the formula adjust relative to the location to which they are copied.

Think of it this way. Excel takes the cell references and remembers a *pattern* for the formula. When the formula is copied, Excel uses the pattern to calculate the formula. Using Figure 22.6 as an example, the pattern is—from the active cell—to take the data located one cell to the left of the active cell and subtract the data located two cells to the left of the active cell. The answer is placed in the active cell.

For example, the initial formula created in row 6 for the Ultimate service reads `=C6-B6`. When this formula is copied to the other rows, the cell references change to reflect the row they are copied to. Because the Standard service is listed in row 10, the formula for the Standard service is `=C10-B10`. Figure 22.7 shows the result of copying the formula in cell D6. The pattern is followed in each cell you copy the formula to.

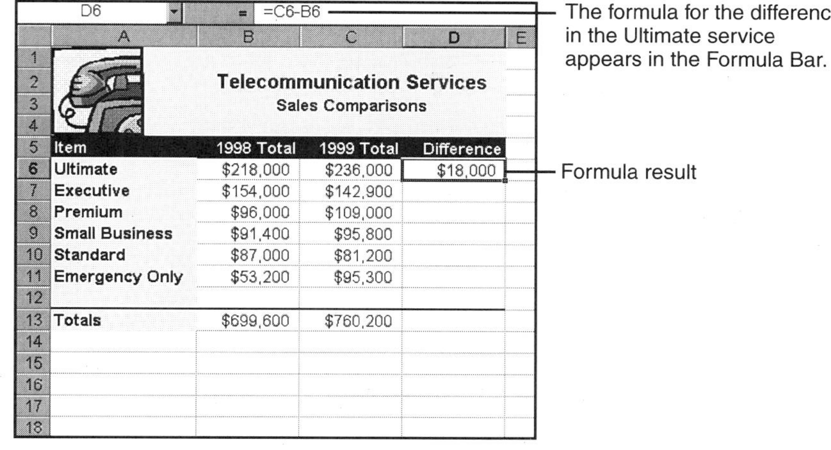
D6
=C6-B6
The formula for the difference in the Ultimate service appears in the Formula Bar.
Formula result

	A	B	C	D
2		Telecommunication Services		
3		Sales Comparisons		
5	Item	1998 Total	1999 Total	Difference
6	Ultimate	$218,000	$236,000	$18,000
7	Executive	$154,000	$142,900	
8	Premium	$96,000	$109,000	
9	Small Business	$91,400	$95,800	
10	Standard	$87,000	$81,200	
11	Emergency Only	$53,200	$95,300	
13	Totals	$699,600	$760,200	

FIGURE 22.6
A worksheet containing a relative cell reference formula that will be copied down the column.

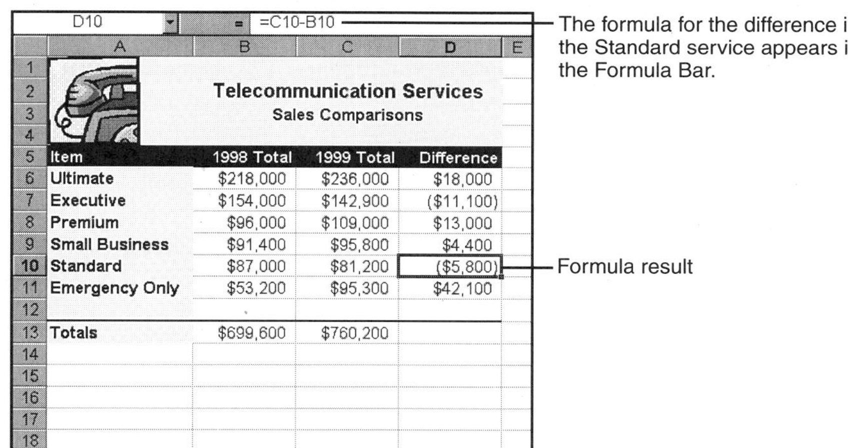
D10
=C10-B10
The formula for the difference in the Standard service appears in the Formula Bar.
Formula result

	A	B	C	D
2		Telecommunication Services		
3		Sales Comparisons		
5	Item	1998 Total	1999 Total	Difference
6	Ultimate	$218,000	$236,000	$18,000
7	Executive	$154,000	$142,900	($11,100)
8	Premium	$96,000	$109,000	$13,000
9	Small Business	$91,400	$95,800	$4,400
10	Standard	$87,000	$81,200	($5,800)
11	Emergency Only	$53,200	$95,300	$42,100
13	Totals	$699,600	$760,200	

FIGURE 22.7
When copied, the formula adjusts relative to its new position.

Absolute Cell References

However, there are times when you do not want the cell references to adjust. Occasionally, you will need one of the references in the formula to remain constant when you copy it to another cell or cells. In these situations, a code is used to tell Excel to freeze the cell reference so that it does not adjust when the formula is copied. This is known as *absolute cell referencing*.

Figure 22.8 shows a worksheet that contains a formula to determine what percentage each service's total sales comprise of the grand total for the year. In this example, the formula has determined the sales for the Ultimate service ($236,000) are 31% of the total sales for 1999 ($760,200). The formula for the Ultimate service is `=B6/B13`.

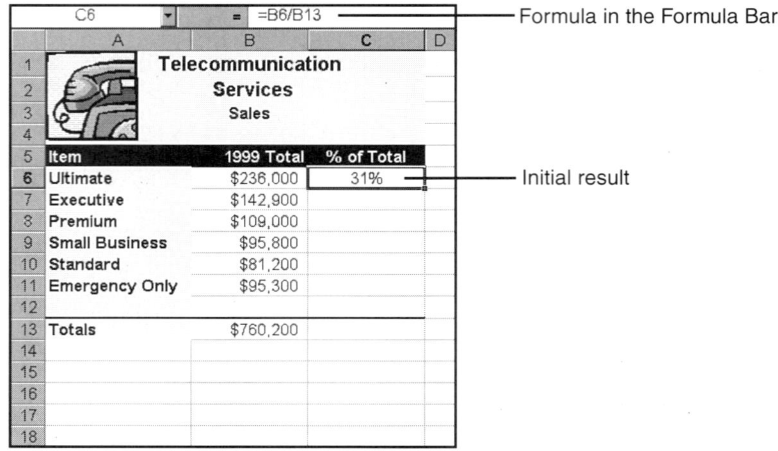

FIGURE 22.8
With relative cell referencing, the formulas won't be calculated properly in a Percent of Total calculation.

When the formula is copied, all the cell references adjust (as you would expect with relative cell referencing). So the formula for the Executive service becomes `=B7/B14`. The pattern is followed—take the data located one cell to the left of the active cell and divide by the data located one cell to the left and seven cells down from the active cell.

When the formula calculated for the Ultimate service is copied to the next row down, a message appears in cell C7 indicating a division-by-zero error. In Figure 22.9, the cell containing the error message is selected. The formula appears in the Formula Bar as `=B7/B14`. The first part of this formula, B7, is correct because that cell represents the Executive total sales figure for 1999. However, the second cell referenced is the empty cell below the grand total, B14, rather than the actual grand total. This happened because of relative cell referencing—the formula was copied down one row and the cell references in the formula adjusted accordingly.

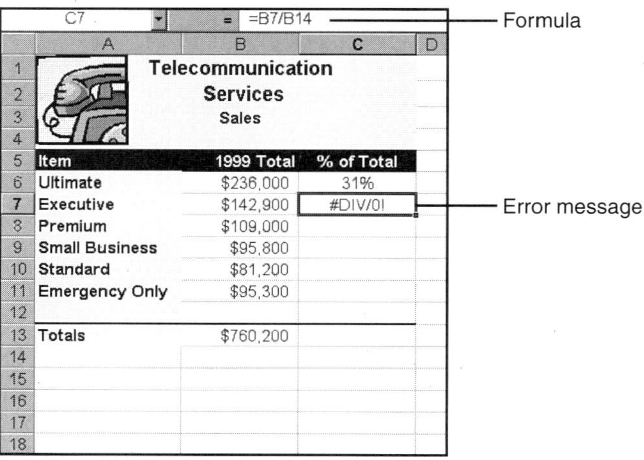

FIGURE 22.9
Relative cell referencing won't calculate the formulas properly in a Percent of Total formula.

To keep the reference to the grand total fixed on cell B13, you need to modify the original formula for the Ultimate service, making the reference to the grand total absolute. After this first formula has been changed, it can then be copied to the remaining cells in the % of Total column. To tell Excel these are absolute cell references, the dollar symbol ($) is added to the cell reference. In the previous example, the formula for the Ultimate service would appear as `= B6$B$13`.

To add the dollar symbols quickly, follow these steps:

1. Select the cell where the original formula was created—in Figure 22.9, that would be cell C6.
2. In the Formula Bar, click once in the middle of the cell that you want to freeze (B13).
3. Press the F4 function key once. It highlights the cell reference in the Formula Bar and adds a dollar symbol in front of both the row and column indicators (see Figure 22.10).
4. Press Enter or click the Enter button (green check) in the Formula Bar to complete the change to the formula.
5. Use the Fill Handle to copy the corrected formula to the remaining items.

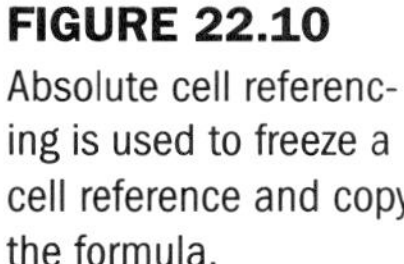

FIGURE 22.10
Absolute cell referencing is used to freeze a cell reference and copy the formula.

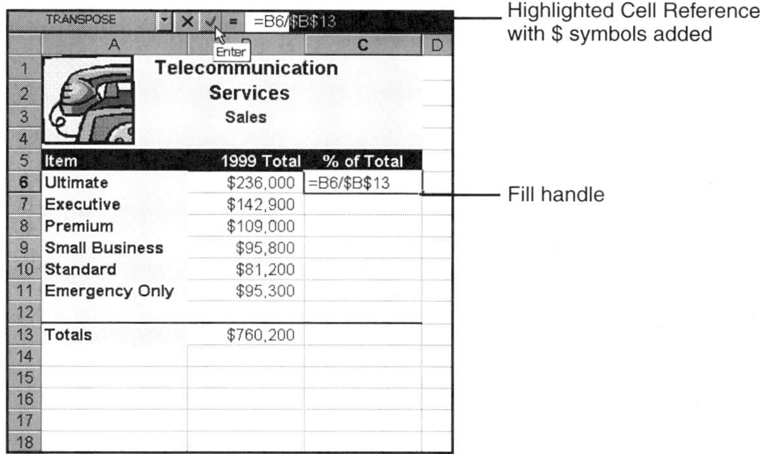

Absolute cell references are used quite often in advanced formulas that use range names and functions. The next section in this chapter discusses range names. You'll also see them in formulas that reference cells in other worksheets or workbooks.

▶ **See** "Consolidating Worksheet Data: Formulas That Cross Sheets and Books," **p. 646**

Mixed Cell References

You can mix absolute with relative references in the same cell reference—these are called mixed cell references. Mixed references are typically used to create a formula that you want to copy both down a column and across a row. Here's a simple example:

```
= A$5 + B$5
```

In this formula, the column references are relative and the row references are absolute. If you copy the formula into a cell in another column, to the right or left, in the same row, the column references adjust accordingly. If you copy it into another row, the absolute row references will not adjust. So, if you enter the preceding formula into cell C5, and then copy it into cell E7, the formula in cell E7 adjusts the columns but not the rows and becomes

```
= C$5 + D$5
```

Figure 22.11 shows a good use for mixed cell references. Here, a single formula has been created to calculate prices based on different markup rates. The formula is

```
= wholesale price + wholesale price * markup percent
```

The wholesale price * markup percent portion of the formula calculates the amount of the markup. This is then added to the wholesale price.

NOTE Remember that there is a priority (order of operations) in formulas that dictates which portion of the formula is calculated first. Multiplication and division are calculated before addition and subtraction.

FIGURE 22.11
A single formula using mixed cell referencing is all that's needed to create this price list.

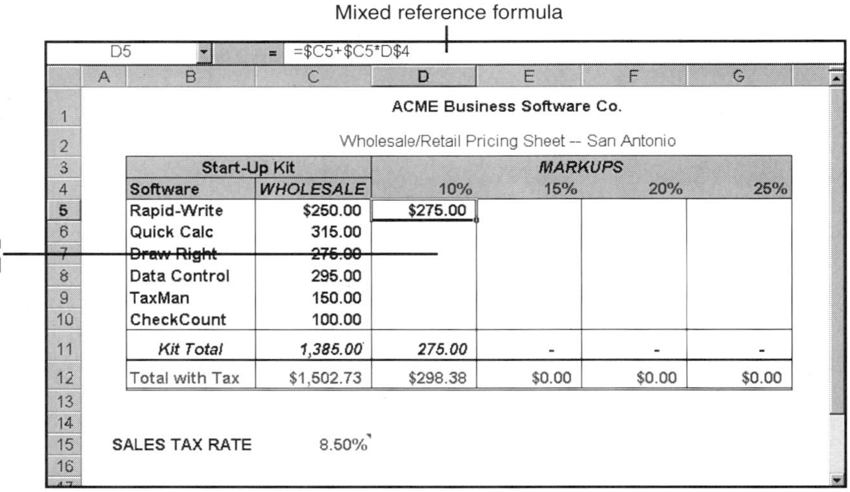

Mixed reference formula

Formula results in the active cell

D5 = =$C5+$C5*D$4

ACME Business Software Co.

Wholesale/Retail Pricing Sheet -- San Antonio

Start-Up Kit		MARKUPS			
Software	WHOLESALE	10%	15%	20%	25%
Rapid-Write	$250.00	$275.00			
Quick Calc	315.00				
Draw Right	275.00				
Data Control	295.00				
TaxMan	150.00				
CheckCount	100.00				
Kit Total	*1,385.00*	*275.00*	-	-	-
Total with Tax	$1,502.73	$298.38	$0.00	$0.00	$0.00

SALES TAX RATE 8.50%

When this formula is copied down the 10% markup column, it adjusts the row references (to the wholesale prices), but keeps the column reference (to the markup percent) fixed. When this formula is copied across a software row, it adjusts the column references (to the markup percents), but keeps the row reference (to the wholesale price) fixed.

It's inconvenient to manually type or remove the dollar signs. Instead, use the F4 key to cycle through the cell reference types. Suppose the cell reference is C5:

- Press F4 once to make both references absolute ($C$5).
- Press F4 again to display mixed references—with a relative column and absolute row (C$5).

- Press F4 again to display mixed references–with an absolute column and relative row ($C5).
- Press F4 again to make both references relative (C5).

If you press F4 once again, it cycles back to make both references absolute.

Most people use the A1 reference style in their worksheets. This reference style causes Excel to refer to columns by a letter and to rows by a number. There are times when it is handy to use the R1C1 reference style, which causes Excel to refer to both rows and columns by numbers. For example, you might want to set a VBA range object variable using the Cells (RowNumber, ColumnNumber) syntax. That's a lot easier to do if, on the worksheet, you see a number at the head of a column, instead of trying to figure out the number of column EH!

You select the R1C1 reference style by choosing Tools, Options and clicking the General tab. Then, choose the R1C1 style by selecting its check box.

Using Range Names in Formulas

Range names are textual names you give to one or more cell references that describe the cell or range. An astonishingly large percentage of otherwise competent Excel users neither understand nor make full use of ranges.

Range names can be used in many ways:

- To quickly move around to different parts of a large worksheet or workbook—Use F5 or the Name Box in the Formula Bar to jump from range to range.
- To designate a select group of cells for printing—This is similar to a print area, except you are not limited to just one range you can identify for printing.
- To make it easier to read and work with complex formulas—By default, range names are absolute cell references.

In this section, you'll focus on the last use for range names—formulas. A descriptive name in the formula makes it easier to understand the formula. Suppose you have a formula such as `=SUM(B2:B13)`, where cells B2:B13 represent your business revenue. For most people, the formula will be more meaningful if you created the range name Revenue for the cell references and substituted the name in the formula. The result would be `=SUM(Revenue)`. Range names make the meaning of a formula's result immediately apparent.

NOTE Moving the data around in a worksheet does not impact the formulas that use range names. Excel keeps track of the new location and the range name adjusts to point to the new location.

If you insert rows or columns in the middle of a range, the range expands to include the new cells when you use the range name. However, if you insert rows or columns at the beginning or end of a range, they will not be included when you use the range name. If you delete rows or columns in any part of a range, the range collapses to adjust for the cells that were removed. Deleting the contents of cell (with the Delete key) has no impact on the cells included in the range name, because you are merely clearing the contents of the cells and not removing the cells.

Naming the Range

Before you create a range name, it's important to understand the naming requirements. The following are guidelines you can use when creating range names:

- Use a letter or an underscore for the first character in a range name—the remaining characters can be letters, numbers, periods, and underscores.
- The maximum length of a range name is 255 characters.
- Range names cannot contain spaces. You can run the words together—for example, AmountDue or Sales1999. Or you can use a period or underscore to separate words—Amount.Due or Sales_1999.
- Names can contain uppercase and lowercase letters, although Excel does not distinguish between them. Therefore, you cannot create two names—Expenses and expenses—in a workbook, even if they are for different worksheets in the workbook.
- Range names that are the same as a cell reference, such as F111 or B52 (designating military aircraft), are not allowed. If you must have a name that is like a cell reference, use an underscore as the first character of the name (_F111).
- Range names are absolute cell references. An absolute cell reference is useful especially in formulas to freeze the cell references.

In Figure 22.12, the formula is calculating what percentage of total sales an individual item encompasses. For the first item, Ultimate, the formula is `=B6/$B$13`. Instead of this formula, you can give a name to cell B13, such as Total_Sales. The formula then becomes `=B6/Total_Sales`. Because range names are automatically absolute cell references, you can immediately copy the formula to the other cells in the % of Total column.

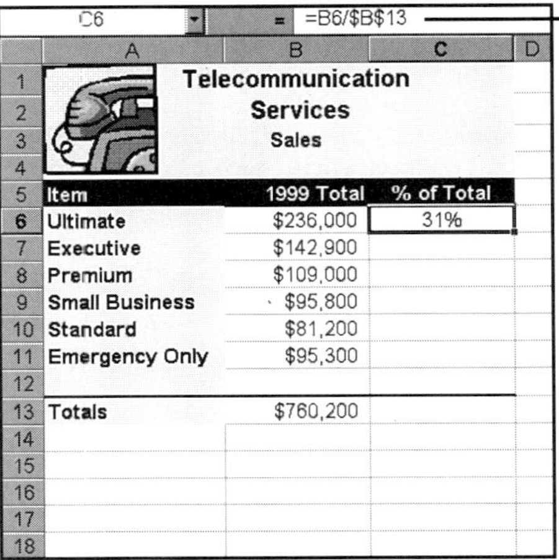

FIGURE 22.12
Use range names instead of absolute cell references.

There are several methods you can use to create range names. The two most common are using the Name Box on the Formula Bar, and using the Insert, Name command. The Name Box is by far the more convenient method. To create a range name using the Name Box, follow these steps:

1. Select the cell or cells you want to name.
2. Click in Name Box on the left side of the Formula Bar, as shown in Figure 22.13.
3. Type the range name (using the preceding guidelines) and then press Enter.

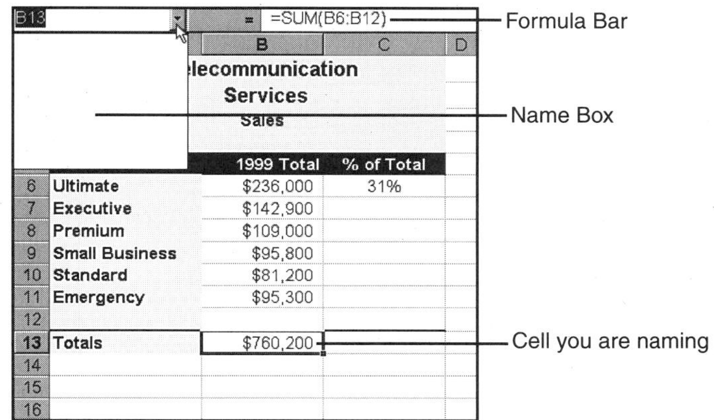

FIGURE 22.13
Range names cannot contain spaces; use the period or underscore to create the illusion of a space in the name.

If you have a worksheet that already contains labels you want to use for the range names, then use the Insert, Name, Create command to create the range names based on the worksheet labels. For example, Figure 22.14 shows a list of sales data for the Central American region. To create range names for each country's data (January through December), you would need to select the cells containing the labels (in column A) and the data (columns B through M).

FIGURE 22.14
Use worksheet labels for range names.

	A	B	C	D	E	F	G
1	Regional Sales	January	February	March	April	May	June
2	*Central America*						
3	Belize	2,634	8,523	4,875	6,548	6,548	1,258
4	Guatemala	9,823	4,563	6,542	8,523	2,548	5,478
5	Honduras	9,875	8,523	4,875	3,215	1,598	2,548
6	Nicaragua	8,523	1,258	6,548	6,542	3,215	3,215
7	El Salvador	3,215	1,598	9,875	4,875	6,548	4,875
8	Costa Rica	1,598	3,215	3,215	1,258	4,563	1,258
9	Panama	4,875	6,548	6,548	2,548	8,523	5,478
10	***Totals***	**40,543**	**34,228**	**42,478**	**33,509**	**33,543**	**24,110**
11							
12							
13							
14							
15							
16							
17							
18							

To create range names using worksheet labels, follow these steps:

1. Select the cells (including the labels) that you want to name.
2. Choose Insert, Name, Create. The Create Names dialog box appears as shown in Figure 22.15, asking where the labels are located in relation to the data. Excel looks for text in the selected cells and proposes the location.
3. Most of the time, Excel proposes the correct location. You can modify the selection if necessary.
4. After the correct location is selected, choose OK. The range names are immediately created.

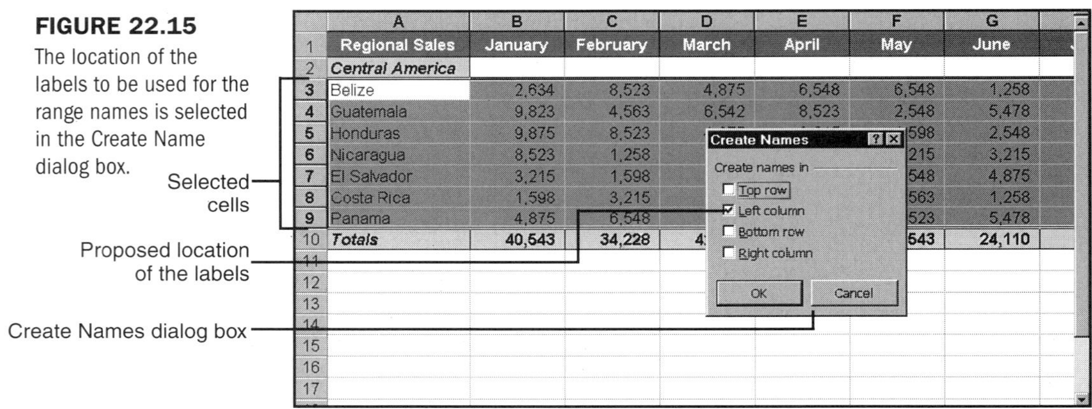

FIGURE 22.15
The location of the labels to be used for the range names is selected in the Create Name dialog box.

There is no limit to the number of range names you can create in a workbook.

NOTE To delete a range name, choose Insert, Name, Define. In the Define dialog box, select the range name you want to remove and click the Delete button. Then click OK.

Including Range Names in New Formulas

It's easy to define so many names that it becomes difficult to remember all of them. While you're building or editing a formula, you can use the F3 key to display the list of range names in the active workbook.

To insert a range name in a formula, use these steps:

1. Start the formula or function. For example, in Figure 22.16, a new formula has been started that calculates the average sales for Belize.
2. At the point you need the range name, press F3. The Paste Name dialog box appears, as shown in Figure 22.17. Choose the correct name from the list and click OK. The formula `=AVERAGE(Belize)` displays in the Formula Bar.
3. Click OK in the Paste Function dialog box to complete the formula.

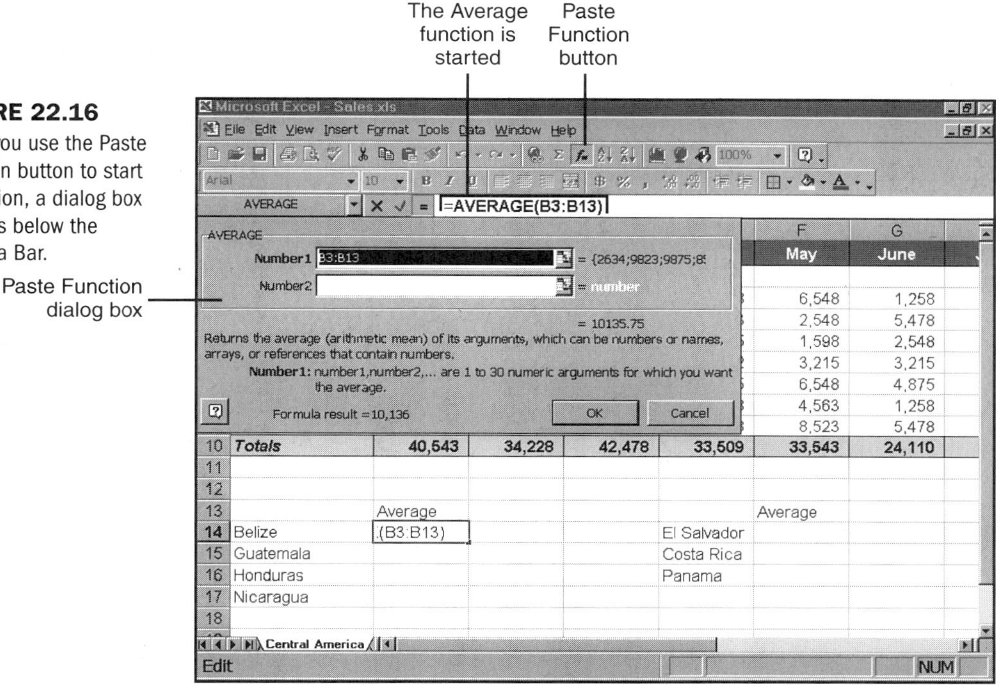

FIGURE 22.16
When you use the Paste Function button to start a function, a dialog box displays below the Formula Bar.

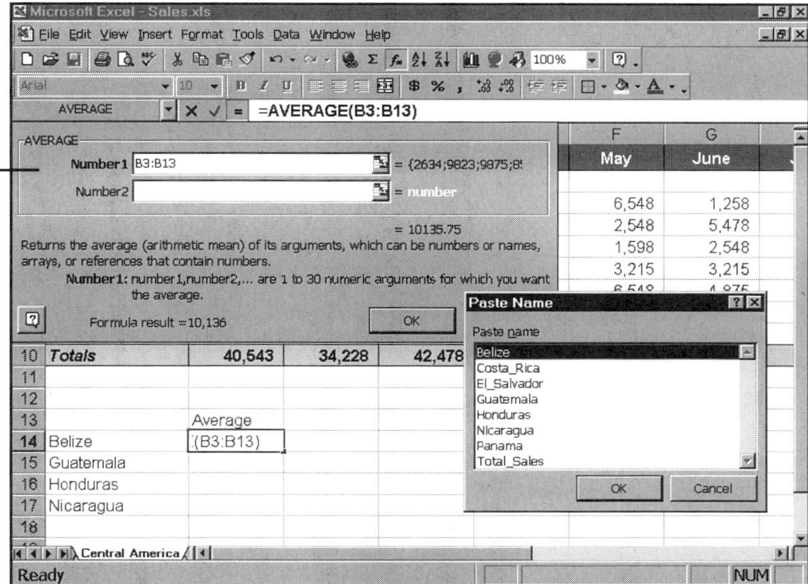

FIGURE 22.17
Press F3 to display the list of range names in the active workbook.

NOTE The Name Box on the Formula Bar is not active when you are creating or editing a formula. You either have to press the F3 key or choose Insert, Name, Paste.

Substituting Range Names for Cell References in Existing Formulas

Suppose that you have a number of formulas in a worksheet, and then you read this chapter and discover the wonderful world of range names. It's not too late to change existing cell references in your formulas to range names. Create the range names you want to use in your formulas. Then choose Insert, Name, Apply. The range names replace their associated cell references in all the formulas in your workbook. Pretty neat!

Understanding Sheet-Level and Book-Level Range Names

There are two broad classes of range names: sheet-level range names and book-level range names. When you create a range name in a worksheet, you are creating a book-level range name. For example, suppose you create a range name on Sheet1 called Expenses. On Sheet2, you create a range name called Revenue. Then on Sheet3, you can use the range names in a formula, such as `=Revenue-Expenses`. So, regardless of the sheet on which the range names are created, you can use them in formulas on any sheet in the book. These are book-level range names. Although not generally visible, the sheet the range refers to is part of the range name. To see which sheet is associated with a range name, choose Insert, Name, Define. Click any range name and look at the text box at the bottom of the Define Name dialog box (see Figure 22.18). The name of the sheet along with the cell references appears in the Refers To text box.

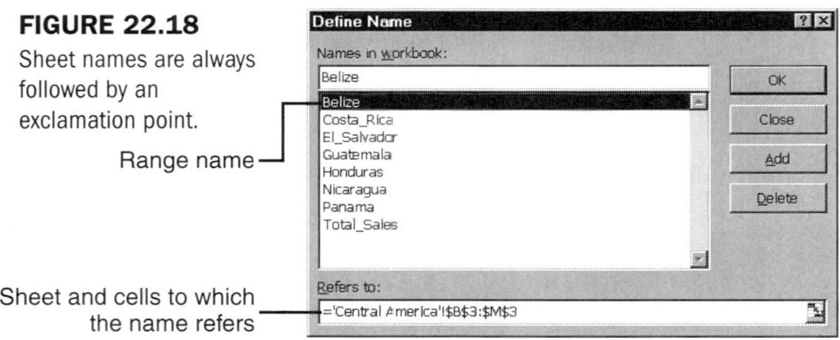

FIGURE 22.18
Sheet names are always followed by an exclamation point.

In addition to these book-level names, you can create sheet-level names. Why would you want to? Consider this. You have a large workbook that tracks monthly sales by region. You want to have a January range name for the Canada worksheet and a January range name for the Chile worksheet. If you create a January range name for Canada (using the methods described earlier in this chapter), when you try to create the January range name on the Chile worksheet, it will ignore it. Why? Because you created a book-level range name for the Canadian January figures, and you can't have two book-level range names with the same name.

To accomplish a January range name for Canada and a January range name for Chile, you have to create sheet-level range names instead.

Sheet-level names have these characteristics:

- The name begins with the name of the sheet it belongs to —for example, Sheet1!January. Sheet names are always followed by an exclamation point (!).
- Unqualified by its sheet name, the name is accessible from the sheet where it is defined, but only from that sheet.

NOTE The Name Box displays only workbook-level range names.

Suppose that you highlight B6:B12 on Sheet1, click the Names Box drop-down, and type the name `Sheet1!Expenses` into the Names Box. Now, if Sheet1 is the active sheet, you can enter

```
=SUM(Expenses)
```

to obtain the sum of the values in B6:B12. Notice that, although the sheet portion of the name is missing in the formula, it is implicit. When you refer to the name on its home sheet, you need not use the sheet portion of the name.

However, if you entered the same formula on Sheet2, it would return the `#NAME!` error value. Excel cannot interpret a sheet-level name when you use it on a different sheet. Instead, you have to enter

```
=SUM(Sheet1!Expenses)
```

to obtain the proper result anywhere other than on Sheet1.

This section discussed how to create and work with range names. Throughout this book, there are many features that employ the use of range names; here are a few you might want to take a look at:

- One especially interesting use of range names is with the `OFFSET` and `COUNTA` functions to automatically update a chart, when data is added to a worksheet outside the data series defined for the chart. See "Using `OFFSET` in Charts," in Chapter 23.
- To help consolidate information from multiple worksheets, use range names that identify cells across worksheets. See "3D Range Names," in Chapter 22.
- Range names can be used with many functions, such as `VLOOKUP`, as one or more of the function arguments. See "Using `VLOOKUP` with Lists," in Chapter 23.
- You can use range names to identify the database list and criteria ranges when performing advanced filters. See "Performing Advanced Filters," in Chapter 25.
- When creating PivotTables from nonadjacent groups of cells, use range names to make it easier to create and update the PivotTable. See "Unlocking the Power of PivotTables and PivotCharts," in Chapter 25.
- With the Data Validation feature, use a range name to identify a long list of entries or entries that will be changing often. See "Controlling Data Entry," in Chapter 27.

Consolidating Worksheet Data: Formulas That Cross Sheets and Books

One advantage of having multiple sheets in a book is the capability to create calculations across the sheets. For example, suppose you have a workbook devoted to expenses for the year, in which each sheet in the book lists the expenses for a single month. There is a sheet for January, another for February, and so on, for all 12 months of the year. In addition, there is another sheet that tracks the cumulative expenses for the year. To create the cumulative calculations, you will need to refer to cells in the other sheets. Through the calculations, the sheets are linked together. Changes made to the monthly expenses shown on one worksheet are reflected in the year-to-date cumulative expenses, which are shown on another worksheet.

When formulas and functions contain references to other sheets in the same book, the references include the worksheet name, followed by the cell reference. The worksheet name always appears with an exclamation point after the name. If multiple sheets are selected, the first and last sheet names are displayed, separated by a colon. Examples of the sheet references include:

SHEET!CELL

January!B12

January!B12:B15

January:December!B12

When formulas and functions contain references to other sheets in different books, the references include the workbook name, worksheet name, and then the cell reference. The workbook name always appears inside square brackets. For example:

[BOOK]SHEET!CELL

[Expenses99]January!B12

[Expenses99]January!B12:B15

[Sales]January:December!B12

NOTE If the book or sheet name is comprised of multiple words, you will see apostrophes (') surrounding the words. This is Excel's way of identifying that several words make up a name. For example:

'Jan 99'!B12

'Expense Info'!B12

'[International Sales]January:December!'B12

Creating Links Across Sheets

Although creating links between worksheets can be used in a variety of situations, the most common situation is that in which information from individual sheets is linked into a summary sheet.

Creating calculations that link data across multiple sheets is very similar to creating calculations in a single sheet.

- When the data is updated, the formulas are recalculated—regardless of where the data is located—on the same sheet as the formula or on a different sheet than the formula.
- As with calculations in a single sheet, the Formula Bar displays the calculation as each component of the formula is built.

When creating calculations across sheets and books, the manner in which the sheets are laid out impacts the way you approach creating the calculations. In some cases, using an identical design for every sheet can expedite building the calculations, saving you a significant amount of time. You can quickly create worksheets with the same layout by grouping the worksheets before you build them.

Figure 22.19 demonstrates a worksheet designed to show Net Income. Net Income is calculated as Sales minus Expenses. Because the sales and expense information is stored on other sheets in the book, a calculation will be created to link these sheets to the Net Income sheet.

FIGURE 22.19
To create calculations across multiple sheets in a workbook, start in the cell in which you want the answer to appear.

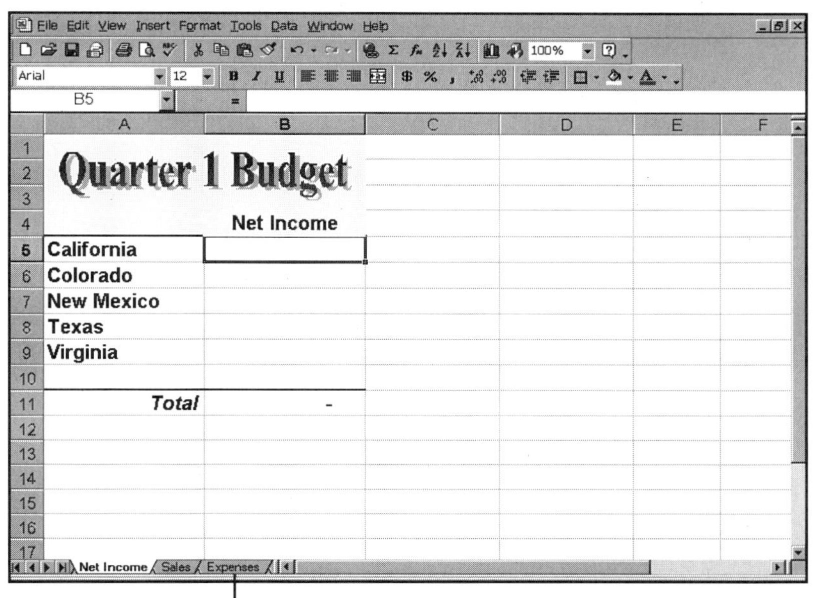

Separate worksheets store expense and sales information.

To create a simple calculation across multiple sheets, follow these steps:

1. Select the cell in which you want the answer to appear. In Figure 22.19, this is cell B5.
2. Begin the formula by typing an equal sign (=) or selecting a function by using the Paste Function button. In the example used in Figure 22.19, because a subtraction equation is being created, the formula begins by typing the equal sign (=).

3. Select the sheet tab that contains the first piece of data that you want to include in the formula. In this example, the Sales sheet is selected.
4. Select the required cell(s). In Figure 22.20, cell B5, the sales figure for California is selected. Notice that the name of the sheet and the cell reference appear in the Formula Bar.

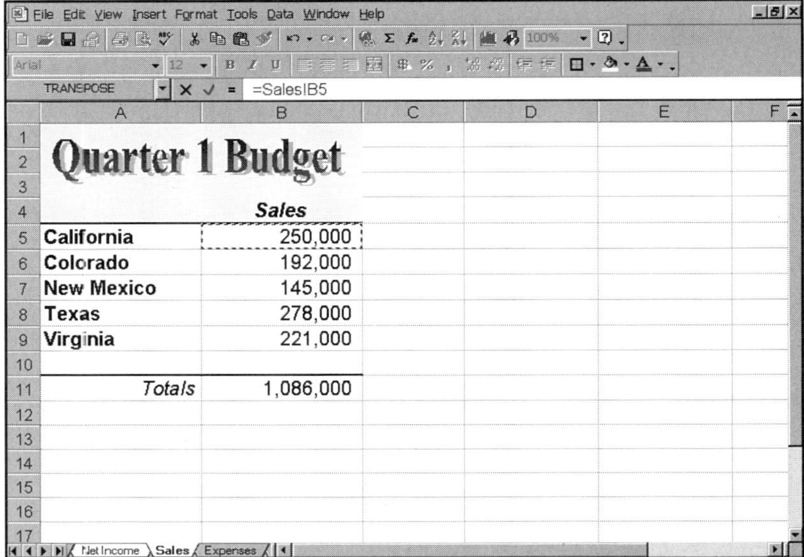

FIGURE 22.20
The sheet name is included in the formula to identify where the data was obtained.

5. Type the next component of the formula. In this example, it is a minus sign (–).
6. Repeat steps 3, 4, and 5 until the formula is complete. In this example, select the Expenses sheet and choose cell D4 (see Figure 22.21).
7. Verify the formula in the Formula Bar. The formula shown in Figure 22.21 is

```
=Sales!B5-Expenses!D4
```

8. Press Enter or click the Enter button (green check) in the Formula Bar to finish the formula. In this example, the formula is copied to the other cells in the Net Income worksheet.

Sometimes, you simply want the contents of a cell to appear in another sheet or book. The data can be copied by using the traditional copy/paste commands. However, if the data changes in the original location, it will not change in the destination location when you use copy/paste. If you want the data to change in the destination location when the original changes, the data has to be linked. To accomplish this, first select the cell in which you want the data to appear in the target worksheet. Type an equal sign (=) to begin the link. Select the cell in the source worksheet from which the data is to come and press Enter or click the Enter button (green check) in the Formula Bar.

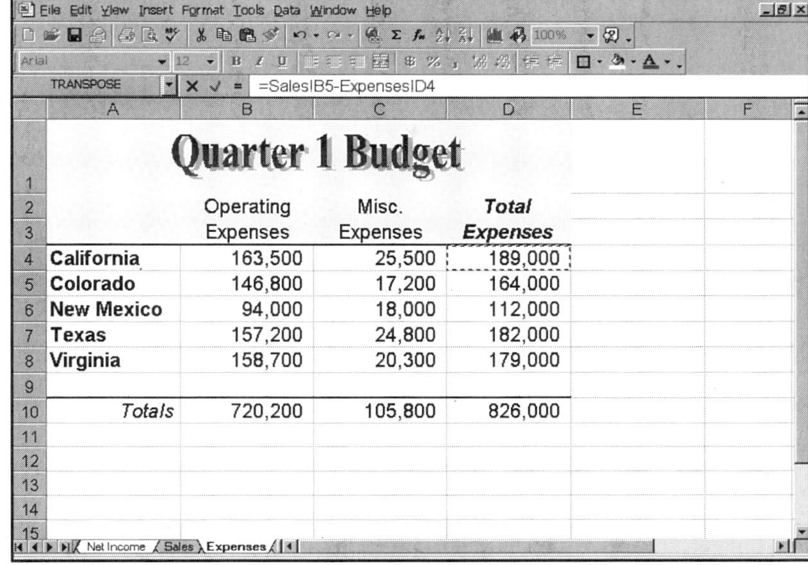

FIGURE 22.21
As you build the formula, use the Formula Bar to make sure you are building the formula you want.

Using 3D Ranges in Formulas

There are, of course, other more intricate examples of calculations being used across worksheets. *3 Dimensional,* or *3D, ranges* are simply ranges that extend across more than one worksheet. 3D ranges are used most often with worksheets that have the same layout. The most common and effective use of a 3D range is to consolidate information from multiple worksheets into one consolidation range on a single sheet.

Figure 22.22 shows a spreadsheet designed to track cumulative expenses for the year. Notice the sheet tabs; they begin with Jan (January) and end with Dec (December) and Year To Date.

In this example, a simple `SUM` calculation for Rent in Calgary will be created in the Year To Date worksheet. Each of the monthly expense worksheets is laid out identically, meaning that in each sheet, the Rent for the Calgary office is located in cell B3. The formula created is then copied to the other expenses and cities.

To identify the data from each of the monthly sheets for Calgary's Rent, you will create what's known as a 3D range.

To link multiple sheets that are laid out identically with 3D references, follow these steps:

1. Select the cell in which you want the result to appear. In Figure 22.22, this is cell B3 on the Year to Date sheet.

2. Begin the formula or select the function by using the Paste Function button. In this example, you are creating a SUM, so you would use the AutoSum button on the Standard toolbar. The Formula Bar displays `=SUM()`.

FIGURE 22.22
Information from the individual sheets is linked into a summary sheet.

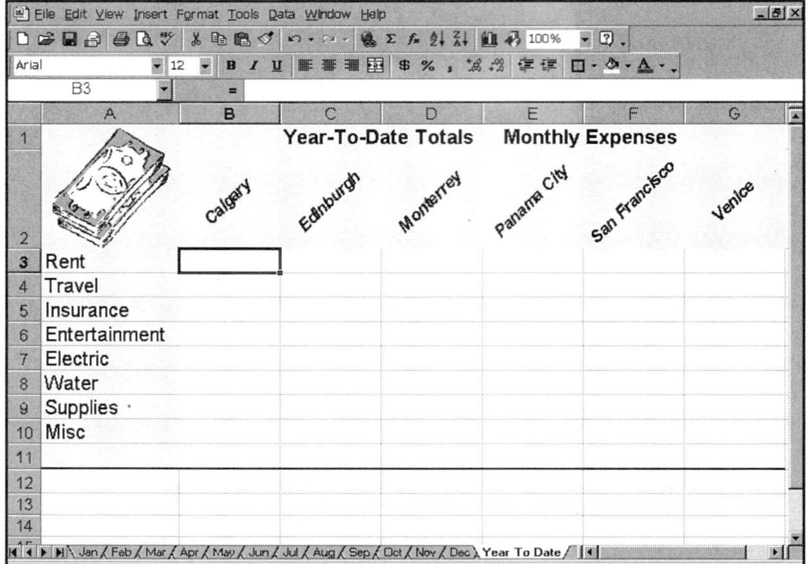

3. Select the first sheet tab to display the sheet that contains the cell or cells you want to include in your formula. For this example, select the Jan sheet. The Formula Bar displays the formula as it is built—in this case, it displays `=SUM(Jan!)`.

   Because the sheet layout is identical, you can select multiple consecutive sheets by holding down the Shift key and clicking the last sheet in the group. In this example, hold the Shift key and click the Dec sheet to include the January through December worksheets. The Formula Bar displays `=SUM(Jan:Dec!)`.

4. Select the required cell(s). In the present example, cell B3—Rent for Calgary—is selected. Notice the formula in the Formula Bar in Figure 22.23.

NOTE You don't have to select the sheets first. You can begin by selecting the cells and then selecting the sheets on the visible sheet. The end result is the same—the corresponding cells on the selected sheets are highlighted and will be included in the range.

5. Verify the formula in the Formula Bar. The formula in Figure 22.23 is

   `=SUM('Jan:Dec'!B3)`

   Notice the use of the range operator (the colon) between the sheet names in the 3D reference. Its effect is analogous to its effect in an ordinary cell reference—that is, it specifies everything between and including the two named worksheets.

6. Press Enter or click the Enter button (green check) in the Formula Bar to accept the formula and display the result.

FIGURE 22.23
The SUM function adds the contents of cell B3 from each of the 12 worksheets.

=SUM('Jan:Dec'!B3)

	A	B	C	D	E	F	G
1	**Monthly Expenses**						
	January						
2		Calgary	Edinburgh	Monterrey	Panama City	San Francisco	Venice
3	Rent	6,000	4,000	3,800	5,000	920	6,800
4	Travel	1,500	1,000	950	1,250	2,300	1,700
5	Insurance	1,350	900	855	1,125	2,070	1,500
6	Entertainment	675	450	428	563	1,035	765
7	Electric	375	250	238	313	575	425
8	Water	150	100	95	125	230	170
9	Supplies	245	162	187	210	322	214
10	Misc	300	200	190	250	460	340
11							
12		4,595	3,062	2,943	3,836	6,992	5,114

Jan / Feb / Mar / Apr / May / Jun / Jul / Aug / Sep / Oct / Nov / Dec / Year To Date

NOTE Whether you are using a function and the sheets are not laid out identically, or you need to select sheets that are not consecutive, you have to select each sheet and cell separately. After the first sheet and cell are selected, type a comma, which will appear after the cell reference in the Formula Bar. Continue to select the necessary sheets and cells, making sure you use a comma before continuing to the next sheet, until you reach the last sheet. After the last sheet and cell have been selected, press Enter or use the Enter button on the Formula Bar to finish the formula.

Continuing with this example, if you need to track a new city in these worksheets, the most efficient method of adding the city is to select all the sheets involved—Jan through Year to Date. When you insert the new column, it is added to all the sheets simultaneously. Right-click any sheet tab to ungroup the sheets. Add the data for the new city on each individual monthly sheet. On the Year to Date sheet, copy the formula from one of the other cities to the newly inserted city.

Incorporating New Sheets in 3D Ranges Another situation that often arises is the need to add another sheet to a book. The best way to ensure the new sheet has the same layout as the other sheets is to

1. Copy one of the other sheets. Make sure the copied sheet is placed between the other sheets, not at the beginning or end of the sheet tabs.
2. Rename the copied sheet as appropriate.
3. Replace the data in the copied sheet with data appropriate to the new sheet.

If you position the new sheet between the other sheets in the book, any formulas that use a 3D reference automatically include the new sheet.

You can use 3D references to refer to cells on other sheets, to define range names, and to create formulas by using the following functions: SUM, AVERAGE, AVERAGEA, COUNT, COUNTA, MAX, MAXA, MIN, MINA, PRODUCT, STDEV, STDEVA, STDEVP, STDEVPA, VAR, VARA, VARP, and VARPA.

3D Range Names Just as you use single-sheet named ranges in formulas, you can also use 3D ranges in formulas to roll up information across multiple sheets. There are, however, different procedures to create the 3D range names and several limitations to their use.

Suppose you work for a company that manufactures electric cars, and you have a group of worksheets that tracks the sale of each car. Each worksheet in the workbook has the same layout—that is, the sales figures for the sports coupe in January is in cell B6 in the California worksheet, and it's found in the same location in the Texas worksheet. This makes it very easy to define and use a 3D range named JanuaryCoupe. To create a 3D range name, use these steps:

1. From any worksheet in the workbook, choose Insert, Name, Define.
2. In the Names in Workbook text box, type the name you want to give the 3D range. In our example, this would be JanuaryCoupe.
3. Drag across the cell reference in the Refers To text box to highlight it. Click the first sheet tab to be included in the range and select the cells. The first sheet tab in our example is California, and the cell is B6.
4. If you are selecting consecutive sheets, hold down the Shift key and click the tab for the last sheet in the group. To select individual sheets, hold down Ctrl as you click each sheet tab. The range reference appears in the Refers To box—for example:

   ```
   California:Texas!$B$6
   ```

   You don't have to select the cells first. You can begin by selecting the sheets and then selecting the cells on the visible sheet.
5. Choose OK to create the range name.

The act of selecting more than one sheet is called *grouping* sheets. To ungroup sheets, right-click any of the selected sheet tabs and choose Ungroup from the shortcut menu.

CAUTION

You cannot use the Name Box to create 3D range names. When you try, a range is created for only the active sheet.

The 3D range is not listed when you click the Name Box. To use the 3D range in a formula, press F3 to see a list of all range names in the workbook.

Limitations with 3D Range Names When the worksheets are not laid out identically, you have to select each sheet and cell separately to create the range. Suppose that on the California worksheet, Coupe sales in January are in cell B6, but on the Texas worksheet, they are in cell C10. Then, the range name would refer to

```
California!B6,Texas!C10
```

You have to manually type the comma after you select each cell reference.

However, Excel is unable to evaluate this type of 3D range name (one created from sheets that are not laid out identically) when it's used in a function. This formula, for example:

```
=SUM(JanuaryCoupe)
```

returns the #VALUE! error value when the name refers to different cells on the comprising worksheets. Instead of using a range name for these cells, it is best if you just select the cells as you create the formula. In this case, the formula would be

```
=SUM(California!B6,Texas!C10)
```

There are a couple of other restrictions on the use of 3D references. You cannot use them as arguments to array formulas (discussed later in this chapter), nor can you use them as arguments to a formula that contains an implicit intersection. For example, if the name SalesTotal refers to A1:A22 on one sheet only, then this single-cell formula

```
=.5*SalesTotal
```

returns a valid result when it's entered in some cell in rows 1–22. The intersection of the row where the formula is entered with the column of values in SalesTotal is implicit in the formula (so, this sort of formula uses what's termed an *implicit intersection*).

But if SalesTotal is a named 3D range covering more than one worksheet, the formula fails and again returns `#VALUE!`.

Creating Links Across Books

Any advanced, real-world use of Excel involves multiple worksheets and workbooks. Budget rollups combine information from department budgets, usually found in different workbooks. Analyses of national sales grab data from regional workbooks. Quality analyses look to workbooks that contain manufacturing data, others that contain customer service and warranty information, and still others that detail the purchase of raw materials.

Whatever the application, the accuracy and the timeliness of the summary depend on its linkages to the details. You normally want live—not static—links between a budget rollup and departmental budgets. When a new position is created in the Information Systems department, you want to show the change to salary accruals in both the IS budget and the company budget—and you want this update to happen automatically. You manage this, of course, with links.

When linking workbooks, the workbook containing the original data is referred to as the *source*. The workbook that receives the linked data is called the *target*. The formula that creates the link is sometimes referred to as the *external reference formula*.

To ensure that the links made between books remain intact, the following guidelines should be used when working with linked books:

- Opening linked books—Source workbooks should be opened before target workbooks.
- Closing linked books—Source workbooks should be closed before target workbooks.

- Moving the source cell—If both the source and target workbooks are open, Excel adjusts the formula to reflect the new location when the source cell is moved. However, if only the source workbook is open when the source cell is moved, the target workbook will continue to use the old reference for the source cell. This results in incorrect calculations or error messages. The only exception to this result is if a range name is used for the source cell instead of a cell reference. When the target workbook is opened, it looks for the range name, which now refers to different cells.
- Renaming the source sheet or book—If both the source and target workbooks are open, Excel adjusts the formula to reflect the new name for the sheet or book when the source sheet or book is renamed. However, if only the source workbook is open when the source sheet or book is renamed, the target workbook will continue to use the old reference for the source sheet or book. This results in incorrect calculations or error messages.
- Deleting the source sheet or book—Naturally, this results in an error message in the target book.

As discussed previously, when you create a link to a cell in another sheet in the same workbook, the syntax is

```
Sheet!Cell
```

When you create a link to a cell in other book, the syntax is

```
[Book]Sheet!Cell
```

The steps used to create links between books are very similar to the steps for creating links across sheets, described in a previous section of this chapter. Follow these steps to create links between books:

1. Open both the source and target workbooks.
2. Make the target workbook the active file and select the cell in which you want the results to appear. Figure 22.24 shows the Monthly Totals workbook, with the cell B3 (January Mysteries) selected.

3. Begin the formula or select the function by using the Paste Function button.
4. At the point in the formula where you need the cell reference from the source workbook, choose Window and select the name of the workbook from the list of open files. If you have the two workbooks showing in tiled windows, you can just click the source workbook's window.
5. Select the worksheet and cells you want to include in your formula. You can see the formula being built in the Formula Bar. Figure 22.25 shows the SUM function with cell B3 selected on the Cancun sheet.

Whenever you include a cell reference from another workbook in a formula, the cell reference is automatically made absolute and displays the dollar sign ($) code in front of the column letter and row number. If you intend to copy the formula in the target book, the reference needs to be changed to a relative cell reference. Press the F4 key three times to convert the cell reference from absolute to relative.

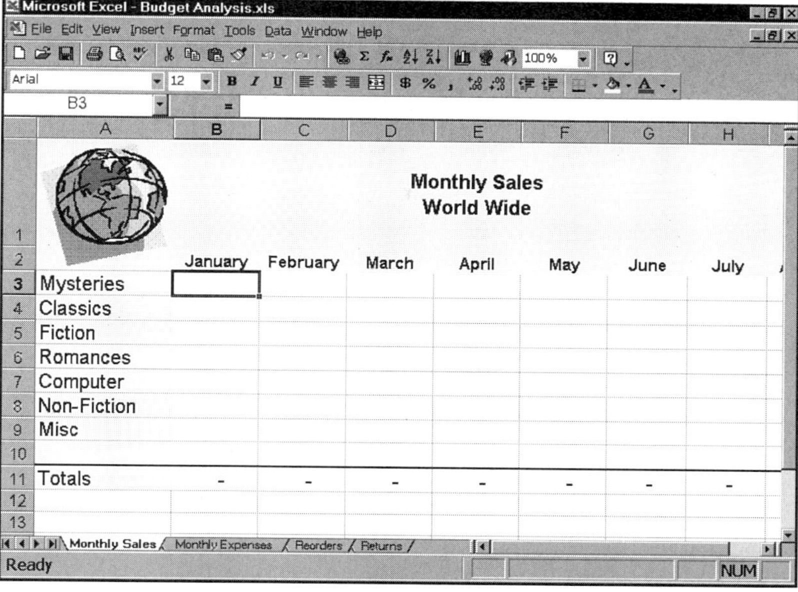

FIGURE 22.24
Always start in the target workbook.

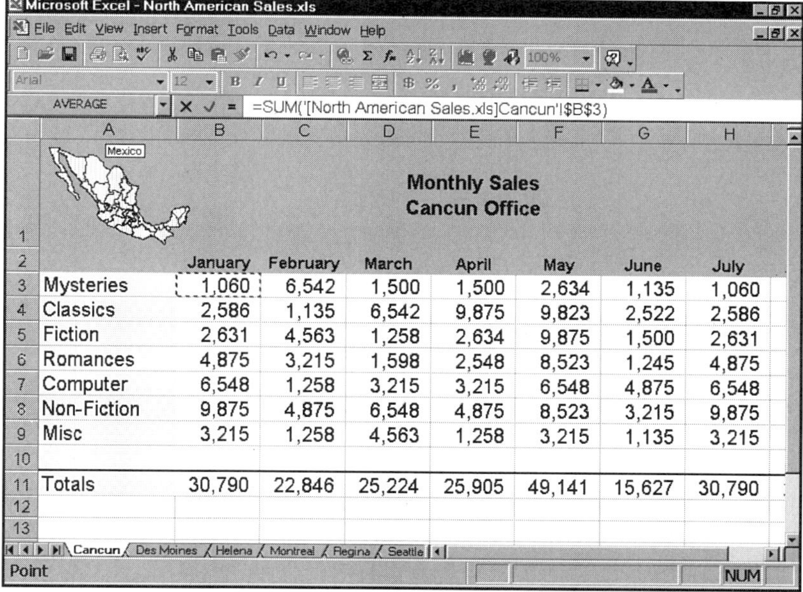

FIGURE 22.25
Initially, links across books are displayed as absolute cell references.

6. If you need to select multiple sheets in the source workbook, select the first sheet tab. If the sheets are laid out identically, you can select multiple consecutive sheets by holding down the Shift key and clicking the last sheet in the group.

   If the sheets are not laid out identically, or you need to select sheets that are not consecutive, you will have to select each sheet and cell separately. After the first sheet and cell are selected, type a comma, which will appear after the cell reference in the Formula Bar. Continue to select the necessary sheets and cells, making sure that you type a comma before continuing to the next sheet, until you reach the last sheet.

7. If you need to select data in another book, you must type a comma (which appears at the end of the formula) to signal you are going to designate data in another book.

8. If you need to select cells in other workbooks, repeat steps 4, 5, 6, and 7.

9. After the last sheet and cell have been selected, or you have typed in the last component of the formula, press Enter or use the Enter button (green check) on the Formula Bar to finish the formula. Figure 22.26 shows the sheets selected from the North American Sales workbook and the Pacific Sales workbook.

10. Assuming the sheets in each of the source workbooks have an identical layout, the formula can be copied to the other cells in the target workbook.

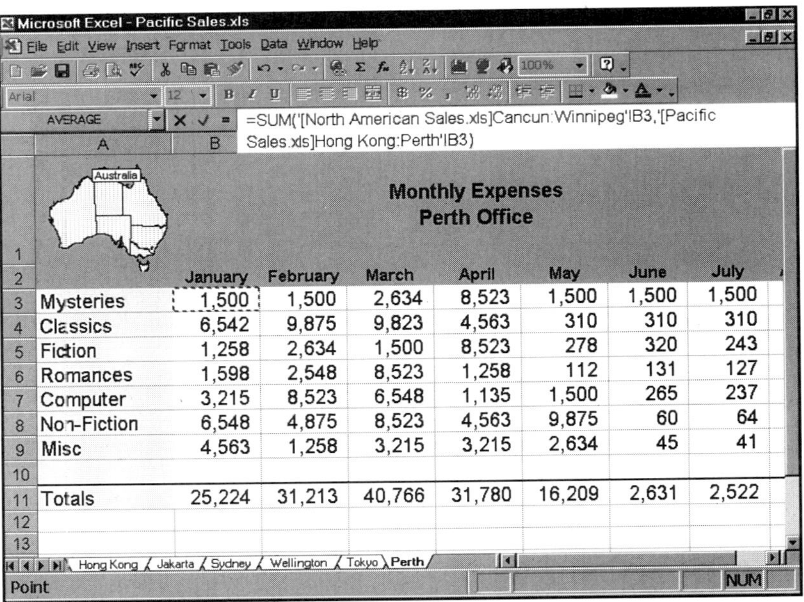

	January	February	March	April	May	June	July
Mysteries	1,500	1,500	2,634	8,523	1,500	1,500	1,500
Classics	6,542	9,875	9,823	4,563	310	310	310
Fiction	1,258	2,634	1,500	8,523	278	320	243
Romances	1,598	2,548	8,523	1,258	112	131	127
Computer	3,215	8,523	6,548	1,135	1,500	265	237
Non-Fiction	6,548	4,875	8,523	4,563	9,875	60	64
Misc	4,563	1,258	3,215	3,215	2,634	45	41
Totals	25,224	31,213	40,766	31,780	16,209	2,631	2,522

FIGURE 22.26
Remember that book names are displayed in square brackets and sheet names are followed by an exclamation point.

If you want to select more than a single value from the source, just drag across the source range that you want. If the source range is noncontiguous, use the Ctrl key to help select more than one range.

Cascading Links

When a series of links tie three or more workbooks together, they are sometimes referred to as *cascading links*. The cells in one workbook are linked to cells in a second workbook, which in turn are linked to cells in a third workbook.

For example, suppose a workbook summarizing national sales data contains links to several regional sales workbooks, which contain links to workbooks tracking sales by state, which contains links to sales data by city. Several cities have recently concluded promotional events and sales in these cities have soared. When the national sales workbook is opened, it is quite likely that it will not reflect the sales increases. Here's why. The links in the national sales workbook are only to the regional sales workbooks, not to the city sales workbooks. When you open the national sales workbook, the regional sales workbooks still contain the old data.

In order for the national sales workbook to have the current sales data, the workbooks have to be opened in hierarchical order, starting with the lowest level:

- City workbooks are opened and the new sales data is entered into the workbook.
- State workbooks are opened and automatically updated with the new city sales data.
- Regional workbooks are opened and automatically updated with the new state sales data.
- Finally, the national sales workbook is opened and automatically updated with the regional sales data.

The more cascading links you have, the greater the chance is that the most current data is not reflected in the workbook at the top of the hierarchy—in this case, the national sales workbook.

When Excel refreshes links, it goes no further than the workbook referenced in the linking formula. The eventual source might be several workbooks away, but Excel stops at the source specified in the link. When Excel checks a value in a regional workbook, for instance, it doesn't check whether that value is itself a link to yet another workbook.

The lesson here is that you should take one of these precautions:

- Ensure that your links go no further than one workbook away. This is usually impractical, but many national sales managers do it all the time.
- Include cell comments that remind you to open and update intermediate workbooks before opening the eventual target workbook.
- Open all the files involved and create a workspace, using the File, Save Workspace command. When you open the workspace, it opens all the files at one time and all the links are updated.

NOTE In addition to the problems associated with making sure the data is accurate, having a number of external links to other workbooks can significantly slow down the time it takes to open a file.

Opening Linked Workbooks

Whenever you open a file that has links to other workbooks, if the source workbook is open, the links are immediately updated. If the source file is not open, Excel will ask you whether you want to update the links (see Figure 22.27). If you select Yes when queried about the links, Excel will access the source file and perform any necessary updates. If you choose No, the data that was in the book when it was last saved appears in your target file. In either case, the source file does not open.

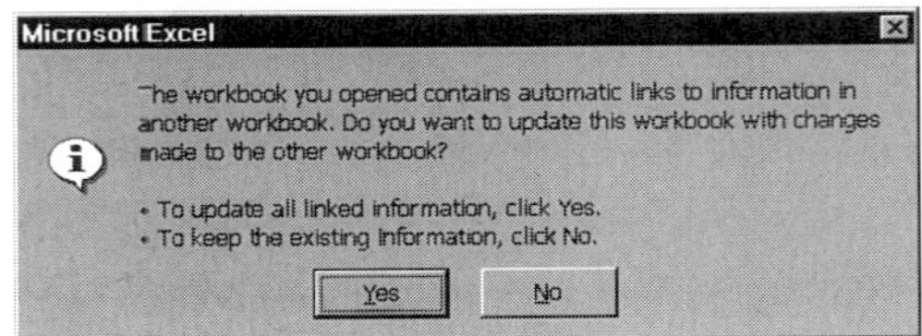

FIGURE 22.27
Excel displays this message when you open a file that contains links.

If there is a series of files that contain links, you should open these files in sequence. Suppose a Worklog file is the source file for a Payroll file, which in turn is the source file for the Monthly Budget file. The hours that employees have worked is entered into the payroll, where taxes and take-home pay are calculated. The taxes and payroll are fed into the budget for the month, which summarizes all the expenses for the month.

In this scenario, the Worklog file should be opened first, followed by the Payroll file, followed by the Monthly Budget file. If the Monthly Budget file is opened first, it will look only to the Payroll file (its source file) for any changes to the linked data. If changes have been made to the Worklog file, the Monthly Budget file will not see those changes because it is linked only to the Payroll file.

Changing and Updating Links

If a link to the source workbook is lost or needs to be changed, you do not have to re-create the formula. To reestablish links to a workbook or to link the target workbook to a different source, you can use Links dialog box. Open the target workbook and choose Edit, Links and the Links dialog box appears. A list of the workbook's source files is displayed (see Figure 22.28). If the source file is not open, the full path to locate the files is listed.

Use the Change Source button to select a different source file or to reestablish the link to the source file, when the source file has been renamed or moved.

Troubleshooting Links

It occasionally happens that an external reference's source disappears. When this occurs, it's usually because the reference contains a link to a workbook that's been deleted or moved to another location.

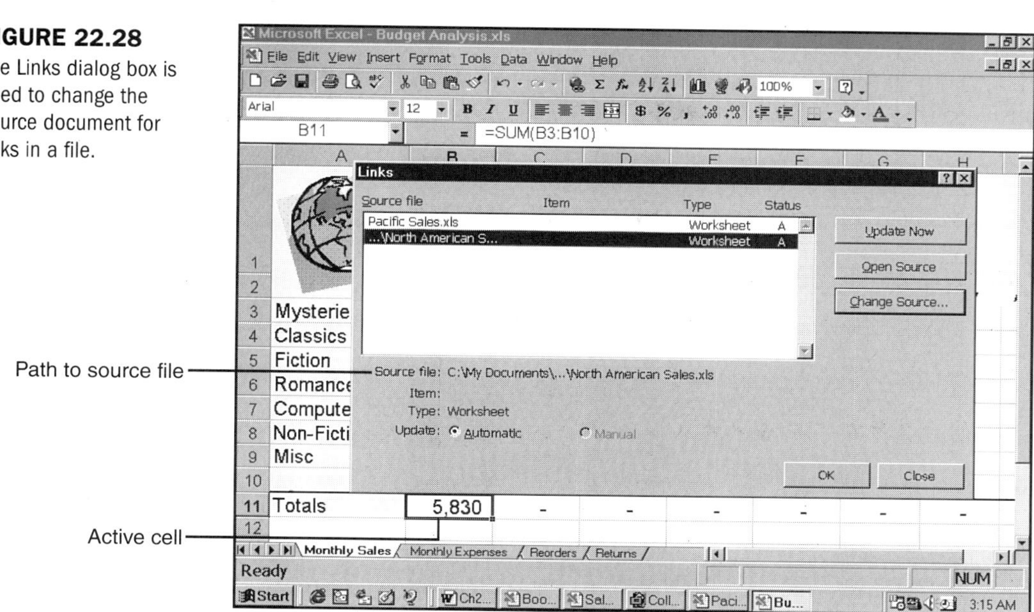

FIGURE 22.28
The Links dialog box is used to change the source document for links in a file.

If, for some reason, Excel cannot locate the file referenced in a link, it displays a File Not Found dialog box. From this dialog box, you can navigate to its new location. But what if someone has completely deleted the workbook? You can't navigate to a nonexistent workbook.

This problem is often easy to fix in a small, simple workbook. You just locate the cell with the linking formula and edit it as necessary. Perhaps the workbook has merely been renamed—then, you'd adjust the external reference in the linking formula. Or, it may be feasible to convert the formula to a constant value.

In a large, complicated workbook, the problem can be serious. There are many possible locations for the linking formula, and finding it can be tedious. The fact that Excel does not tell you the location of the link's target complicates the problem enormously. Here's how to resolve it more quickly.

Select, in turn, each worksheet in the workbook that contains the link that Excel cannot resolve. If you're not certain which sheets contain external links, you'll have to try each sheet, one at a time. Choose Edit, Find. In the Find What text box, enter a square bracket ([). Then make sure that the Find Entire Cells Only check box is cleared and that Formulas is selected in the Look In drop-down box. Click Find Next. Excel searches the worksheet for formulas that contain square brackets.

An external reference uses a square bracket to separate the name of the linked workbook from the name of the linked worksheet. Therefore, when Excel finds a square bracket in a formula, it's likely that you've located an external reference. Check that the reference is still valid.

If you cannot find the reference with this method, open any charts in the workbook. Select each data series contained in the chart and look in the Formula Bar to see whether the data series refers to a range in a different workbook.

Another place to look is in custom controls, such as buttons and scrollbars. Right-click the control and choose Format Control to check the object's control options. A scrollbar might, for example, have a cell link to another workbook.

Finally, you should check whether any defined names contain references to external workbooks. This is not simply a matter of using Insert, Name, Define to locate names in the workbook. Hidden names do not appear in the Names in Workbook text box, nor does a name that has somehow become corrupted.

Instead, put this VBA snippet into a module in the workbook. Then run the macro ListNames.

```
Sub ListNames()
Dim oName As Name
Dim i As Integer
Dim TempRefersTo As String
i = 1
        For Each oName In ThisWorkbook.Names
        TempRefersTo = "'" & oName.RefersTo & "'"
        Cells(i, 1) = i
        Cells(i, 2) = oName.Name
        Cells(i, 3) = TempRefersTo
        i = i + 1
        Next oName
End Sub
```

This subroutine writes the following items to the blank worksheet, as shown in Figure 22.29:

In column A, it writes the index number of each defined name (the integer i).

In column B, it writes the name of each range (the value you'd normally find in the Names in Workbook text box in the Name dialog box).

In column C, it writes the cells the range name refers to (stored as a string in the variable TempRefersTo).

Each link in Figure 22.29 that begins with `=#REF!` is an external link in this workbook that cannot be located. See Chapter 6, "Successful VBA Modules," to learn more about using VBA code snippets in this book.

NOTE When the subroutine writes TempRefersTo to a worksheet in column C, it does so as a string of text rather than as a reference. This prevents the subroutine from writing error values such as `#REF!` when it points to a cell that doesn't exist.

FIGURE 22.29
Use this list to help locate and resolve broken links.

=#REF! denotes an external reference that cannot be located.

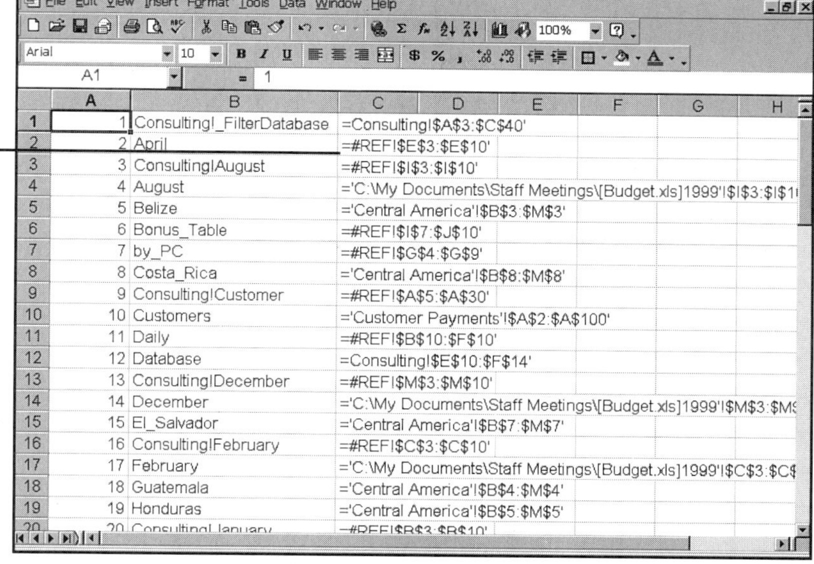

	A	B	C
1	1	Consulting!_FilterDatabase	=Consulting!$A$3:$C$40'
2	2	April	=#REF!$E$3:$E$10'
3	3	Consulting!August	=#REF!$I$3:$I$10'
4	4	August	='C:\My Documents\Staff Meetings\[Budget.xls]1999'!$I$3:$I$1
5	5	Belize	='Central America'!$B$3:$M$3'
6	6	Bonus_Table	=#REF!$I$7:$J$10'
7	7	by_PC	=#REF!$G$4:$G$9'
8	8	Costa_Rica	='Central America'!$B$8:$M$8'
9	9	Consulting!Customer	=#REF!$A$5:$A$30'
10	10	Customers	='Customer Payments'!$A$2:$A$100'
11	11	Daily	=#REF!$B$10:$F$10'
12	12	Database	=Consulting!$E$10:$F$14'
13	13	Consulting!December	=#REF!$M$3:$M$10'
14	14	December	='C:\My Documents\Staff Meetings\[Budget.xls]1999'!$M$3:$M
15	15	El_Salvador	='Central America'!$B$7:$M$7'
16	16	Consulting!February	=#REF!$C$3:$C$10'
17	17	February	='C:\My Documents\Staff Meetings\[Budget.xls]1999'!$C$3:$C
18	18	Guatemala	='Central America'!$B$4:$M$4'
19	19	Honduras	='Central America'!$B$5:$M$5'
20	20	Consulting!January	=#REF!$B$3:$B$10'

Exploring the Power of Array Formulas

An *array* is a rectangular arrangement of values in rows and columns, similar to a range of cells. In Excel, formulas that either use an array as an argument or generate an array as the formula result are called *array formulas*. Sometimes the array that is used as an argument in a formula is called an *array constant*. Sometimes the array that is returned as the formula result is called an *array range*.

NOTE Remember, an argument is what the formula operates on. If the formula is

```
=A1+B1
```

the two arguments are A1 and B1. If the formula is

```
=IF(B3>0,B3*C3,"")
```

there are three arguments: B3>0 is one argument, B3*C3 is another argument, and "" is the last argument. In a function, arguments are always separated by commas.

Two concepts are key to understanding when to use array formulas.

- When you want to use a single formula in multiple cells, and each of those cells should display a different value, use an array formula.
- When you want to supply an array as an argument to a function that doesn't normally expect one, use an array formula.

In this section, we'll explore how to create formulas that return an array range and that use arrays as arguments.

Using Functions That Return Arrays

Some of Excel's functions require that you use them in array formulas.

Most of the functions that require you to enter them as an array formula are used specifically for matrix algebra and statistical analysis. One function, `TRANSPOSE()`, has broad applicability. Figure 22.30 shows an example.

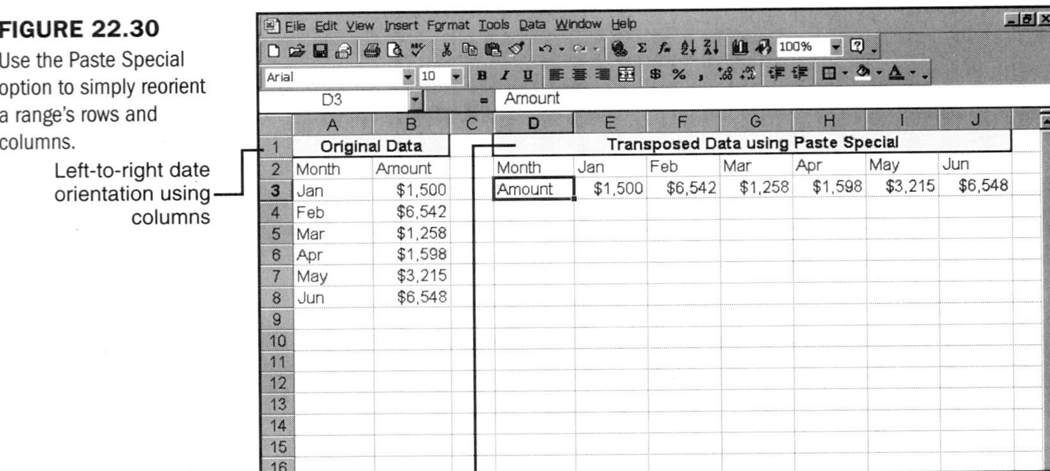

FIGURE 22.30
Use the Paste Special option to simply reorient a range's rows and columns.

There are many good reasons to show each month in a different row, as in A2:B8 of Figure 22.30. Worksheets have more rows than columns, and you might have too many data points to put each month in a different column. More likely, though, a text file created in a different application—one that orients the data with each month in a different row—has been opened in Excel to perform calculations on the data.

However, most formal worksheet reports normally show each month in a different column: The dates progress from left to right using columns instead of top to bottom using rows, as shown in cells D2:J3. Both orientations are also shown in Figure 22.30.

One way to reorient the data is to transpose the data, using the Paste Special command. The steps are

1. Select the cells you want to transpose (in this case A2:B8) and choose Edit, Copy.
2. Select the cell where you want the transposed list to start (in Figure 22.30, cell D2) and choose Edit, Paste Special.
3. In the Paste Special dialog box, select the Transpose check box. Then choose OK.

This method pastes the cell values. Unfortunately, if the data in the original cells change (A2:B8), the transposed copy of the data does not change; there is no link between the original and transposed copy.

Here's where the `TRANSPOSE()` function can help. You can create a link between the original cells and the transposed copy by creating an array formula using the following steps:

1. Select the cells where you want the transposed data to appear (in this example, we'll use cells D7:J8).
2. In the Formula Bar, type

   `=TRANSPOSE(A2:B8)`

   where (A2:B8) are the original cells you want to transpose.

If the original cells are on another worksheet, it is easier to use Paste Function rather than type the syntax for the worksheet reference. The `TRANSPOSE` function is in the Lookup & Reference category. You can then use the mouse to select the worksheet and cells.

3. Hold down the Ctrl and Shift keys, and, as you are holding them down, press Enter. This is called *array*—entering the formula. Figure 22.31 shows the result.

Array formula

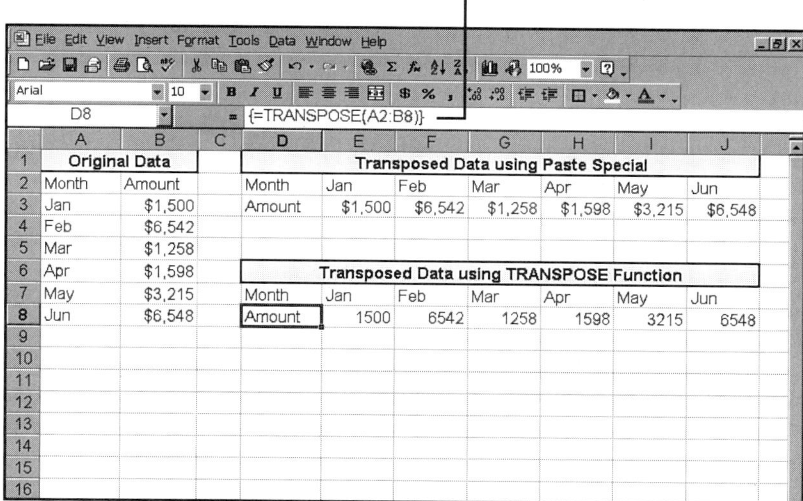

FIGURE 22.31
Use the `TRANSPOSE` function to maintain a link to the original data.

After you follow these steps, the cells in the range you selected before entering the formula now contain the transposed values. Curly braces surround the formula shown in the Formula Bar. The curly braces indicate that Excel is treating the formula as an array formula. The formula results in an array range. When you click on any of the cells in the transposed set, the same array formula appears in the Formula Bar.

CAUTION

Do not type the braces yourself. If you do, Excel treats the formula as a text entry. And when you edit an array formula, you must press Ctrl+Shift+Enter, instead of just Enter, to keep it as an array formula.

If you need to change a value in the original data, that change is reflected in the transposed data. Notice that each value in the array formula's range is different, even though you entered only one formula.

Prior to Excel 97, Excel's Function Wizard (now termed Paste Function) did not support array formulas. You could use it to help build an array formula, but after the wizard finished, you had to reenter the formula with Ctrl+Shift+Enter. In Excel 2000 (and 97) you can hold down Ctrl+Shift as you click the Paste Function's OK button to complete the array formula.

Using Arrays As Arguments to Array Formulas

The usefulness of array formulas isn't limited to returning arrays to a worksheet range. You also use array formulas when you want to use an array as an argument to a function that normally expects a single value.

Suppose that you have a worksheet range that contains a list of customers, and a corresponding range that contains the number of hours that you have worked for each customer (see Figure 22.32).

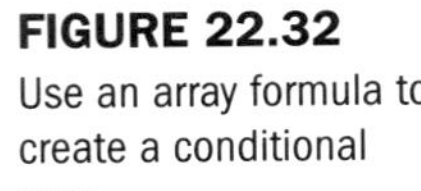

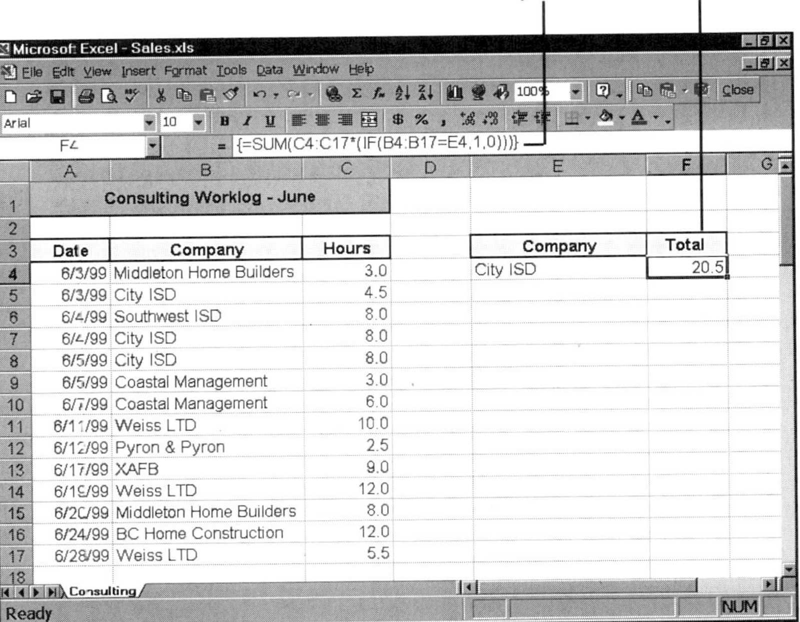

Date	Company	Hours
6/3/99	Middleton Home Builders	3.0
6/3/99	City ISD	4.5
6/4/99	Southwest ISD	8.0
6/4/99	City ISD	8.0
6/5/99	City ISD	8.0
6/5/99	Coastal Management	3.0
6/7/99	Coastal Management	6.0
6/11/99	Weiss LTD	10.0
6/12/99	Pyron & Pyron	2.5
6/17/99	XAFB	9.0
6/19/99	Weiss LTD	12.0
6/20/99	Middleton Home Builders	8.0
6/24/99	BC Home Construction	12.0
6/28/99	Weiss LTD	5.5

FIGURE 22.32
Use an array formula to create a conditional sum.

You'd like to get the total number of hours that you have worked for a customer, which you specify in cell E4. To do so, array-enter (Ctrl+Shift+Enter) this formula in cell F4:

```
=SUM(C4:C17*(IF(B4:B17=E4,1,0)))
```

As shown in the Formula Bar in Figure 22.32, this formula returns 20.5. Here's how Excel arrived at this result.

The IF function in the formula specifies that when a customer listed in E4:B17 is the same as the customer name in cell E4, return 1; otherwise, return 0. When evaluated, the IF returns an array of 1s and 0s.

After it has the 1s and 0s, the formula multiplies that array by the values in C4:C17. A value in C4:C17 multiplied by 1 returns that value; a value in C4:C17 multiplied by 0 returns zero.

Finally, starting the array formula with the `SUM` function returns the sum of the values in the array—20.5 total hours worked for the client listed in cell E4.

Why is it necessary to array-enter the formula? Because the IF function does not normally expect to receive an array as an argument. Pressing Ctrl+Shift+Enter, instead of just Enter, causes Excel to evaluate the entire array, perform the multiplication and summation, and return the complete result in the cell.

Using Array Constants

Usually, you supply a range of cells as an argument to an array formula, although, at times, it is handy to supply an array of constant values.

Suppose that you need to obtain the dates for your employees' 30-, 60-, and 90-day reviews. Figure 22.33 shows a sample list of employees.

FIGURE 22.33
Select the cells you want the array formulas to appear in.

	A	B	C	D	E	F	G	H
1		Employee Roster			New Hire Reviews			
2	DateHired	LastName	FirstName	Hired On	30 Days	60 Days	90 Days	
3	6/18/99	Michaels	Sylvia					
4	6/13/99	Salinas	Anita					
5	5/6/99	Rodgers	Marc					
6	4/25/99	King	Russell					
7	4/3/99	Lee	Henrietta					
8	3/17/99	Jacobson	David					
9	3/4/99	Chavez	Jose					
10	2/13/99	Parker	Judy					
11	1/15/99	Barretto	Rick					
12	1/13/99	Fujimora	Scott					
13	1/8/99	Stewart	Ian					
14	1/3/99	Webber	Edgar					
15	12/28/98	Miller	Peter					
16	12/14/98	Van Buren	Eric					
17	12/4/98	Ali	Yasmine					
18	12/2/98	Lee	Yung					

Instead of creating a separate formula for each review timeframe, you can create one formula (which contains an array of constants and a mixed cell reference) that can be used to calculate each review date for every employee. Here's how to get the results you're after:

1. Select a range of cells consisting of one row and four columns. In our example, cells D3:G3.
2. Array-enter (Ctrl+Shift+Enter) this formula in the selected range

   ```
   =$A3+{0,30,60,90}
   ```

   to return the four dates for the first employee, representing the dates for today, 30 days hence, 60 days hence, and 90 days hence.

The results are shown in cells E3:G3 of Figure 22.34. After you have verified the results, you can use the fill handle to copy the array formula to the other employees.

Array formula

D3 = {=$A3+{0,30,60,90}}

	A	B	C	D	E	F	G	H
1		Employee Roster			New Hire Reviews			
2	DateHired	LastName	FirstName	Hired On	30 Days	60 Days	90 Days	
3	6/18/99	Michaels	Sylvia	6/18/99	7/18/99	8/17/99	9/16/99	
4	6/13/99	Salinas	Anita					
5	5/6/99	Rodgers	Marc					
6	4/25/99	King	Russell					
7	4/3/99	Lee	Henrietta					
8	3/17/99	Jacobson	David					
9	3/4/99	Chavez	Jose					
10	2/13/99	Parker	Judy					
11	1/15/99	Barretto	Rick					
12	1/13/99	Fujimora	Scott					
13	1/8/99	Stewart	Ian					
14	1/3/99	Webber	Edgar					
15	12/28/98	Miller	Peter					
16	12/14/98	Van Buren	Eric					
17	12/4/98	Ali	Yasmine					
18	12/2/98	Lee	Yung					

FIGURE 22.34
Use array constants when the formula's arguments won't change.

The array of constants in the formula is {0,30,60,90}. By array-entering the formula in four contiguous cells that are in the same row, you add first 0, then 30, then 60, and then 90 days from today's date. The mixed cell reference ($A3) enables the array formula to be copied to the other rows.

The commas in the array of constants cause Excel to create an array in one row. If you want an array in one column, use semicolons instead of commas. For example:

```
=$A3+{0;30;60;90}
```

This technique is also useful when you want to re-create on a worksheet the values represented by a chart trendline. Suppose that you insert a second-order polynomial trendline in an XY (Scatter) chart. You're satisfied with the result, and you want to put the predicted trendline values on the worksheet. One way is to display the trendline's equation on the chart, and then to retype it into a range of worksheet cells. However, here's a better way.

Let your XY chart's x-values be in A2:A16 and its y-values in B2:B16. To get the values implied by the trendline into your worksheet, select a range such as C2:C16 and array-enter (Ctrl+Shift+Enter) this formula, as shown in Figure 22.35:

```
=TREND(B2:B16,A2:A16^{1,2})
```

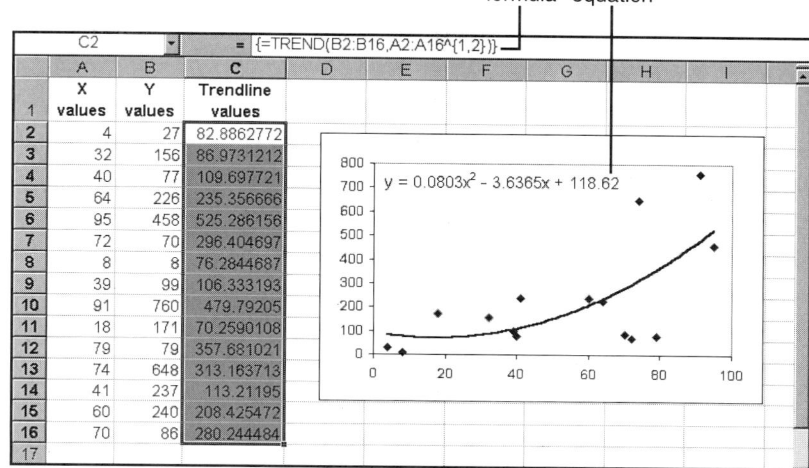

	A	B	C
1	X values	Y values	Trendline values
2	4	27	82.8862772
3	32	156	86.9731212
4	40	77	109.697721
5	64	226	235.356666
6	95	458	525.286156
7	72	70	296.404697
8	8	8	76.2844687
9	39	99	106.333193
10	91	760	479.79205
11	18	171	70.2590108
12	79	79	357.681021
13	74	648	313.163713
14	41	237	113.21195
15	60	240	208.425472
16	70	86	280.244484
17			

FIGURE 22.35
Use the array constant {1,2} to raise an array of values to the first and second powers.

A second-order polynomial trendline predicts y-values from the original x-values and from the square of the x-values.

You replicate the trendline on the worksheet by using the `TREND()` function. But you also need to tell the `TREND()` function to use the x-values raised to the first power (the original x-values), as well as the x-values raised to the second power (the squares of the x-values).

You do this in the `TREND()` function by means of the array constant {1,2}. The array formula raises the values in A2:A16 to the first, and then the second power, and predicts new y-values from the resulting arrays.

▶ **See** "Using Trendlines in Charts," to learn more about trendlines, **p. 833**

CAUTION

When you have entered an array formula into a range of cells, you cannot change those cells without first removing the array formula. Suppose you've entered an array formula in A1:C3. You now cannot make a new entry in cell C3 without removing the array formula. You cannot delete row 1, 2, or 3, or column A, B, or C. You cannot insert a new row between rows 1 and 3, or a new column between columns A and C.

Naming Array Formulas

When you create a formula that you use repeatedly, it is convenient to give that formula a name, just as you give a name to a cell or range of cells. Then, when you want to use the formula, you just type its name into the Formula Bar, preceded by an equal sign, and press Enter. This is far more sensible than typing a complicated formula over and over.

Suppose that you have a list of customers in A2:A100, dates when they paid you in B2:B100, and payment amounts in C2:C100 (as shown in Figure 22.36). The range A2:A100 is named Customers, B2:B100 is named PaymentDate, and C2:C100 is named PaymentAmount.

You want to know the total amount that the customer named Rick Barretto has paid you. One way is to array-enter (Ctrl+Shift+Enter) this formula:

```
=SUM(IF(Customers="Rick Barretto",PaymentAmount,0))
```

The name Customers refers to an array of values: those in A2:A100. Because the `IF()` function does not normally expect to receive an array as an argument, it's necessary to array-enter the formula.

The `IF()` function returns an array consisting of values in the PaymentAmount range when the associated value in Customers equals Rick Barretto and zero, otherwise. The `SUM()` function returns the total of this array: Rick Barretto's payment amounts, and zeros for all the other customers. This total, of course, is the sum of Rick Barretto's payments.

There is a way to make this formula a lot more flexible:

- For the argument that contains the name, you can use a cell reference where you would simply type the name instead of editing the formula each time. In this example, you'll use cell E2.
- You can give the entire formula a name such as TotalPayment.

The result is shown in Figure 22.36.

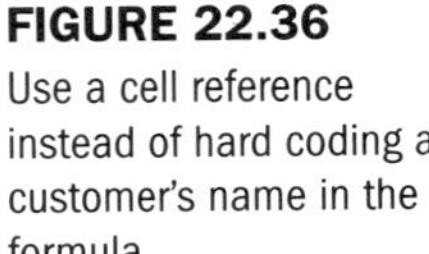

FIGURE 22.36
Use a cell reference instead of hard coding a customer's name in the formula.

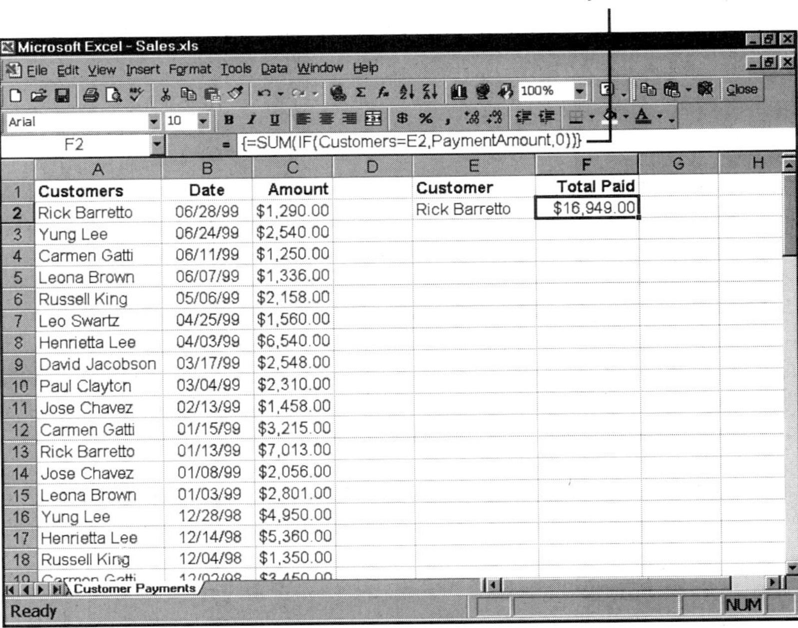

	A	B	C	D	E	F
1	Customers	Date	Amount		Customer	Total Paid
2	Rick Barretto	06/28/99	$1,290.00		Rick Barretto	$16,949.00
3	Yung Lee	06/24/99	$2,540.00			
4	Carmen Gatti	06/11/99	$1,250.00			
5	Leona Brown	06/07/99	$1,336.00			
6	Russell King	05/06/99	$2,158.00			
7	Leo Swartz	04/25/99	$1,560.00			
8	Henrietta Lee	04/03/99	$6,540.00			
9	David Jacobson	03/17/99	$2,548.00			
10	Paul Clayton	03/04/99	$2,310.00			
11	Jose Chavez	02/13/99	$1,458.00			
12	Carmen Gatti	01/15/99	$3,215.00			
13	Rick Barretto	01/13/99	$7,013.00			
14	Jose Chavez	01/08/99	$2,056.00			
15	Leona Brown	01/03/99	$2,801.00			
16	Yung Lee	12/28/98	$4,950.00			
17	Henrietta Lee	12/14/98	$5,360.00			
18	Russell King	12/04/98	$1,350.00			

Everytime that you want to check a particular customer's total payments, you simply type the customer's name in cell E2.

Here's the sequence to name and use the formula:

1. Choose Insert, Name, Define.
2. In the Names in Workbook box, type `TotalPayment`.
3. In the Refers To box, type:

   ```
   =SUM(IF(Customers=$E$2,PaymentAmount,0))
   ```
4. Click OK.

The formula returns the total of the payments made by the customer whose name is in cell $E$2. The absolute reference is needed, so that you can type the formula anywhere in the worksheet.

Now, enter any name in your customer list in cell E2. When you want the total of the payments a customer has made, select a cell on the worksheet (such as F2) and enter the named formula:

```
=TotalPayment
```

It happens that you can dispense with the `IF()` function in the TotalPayment formula. This is equivalent:

```
=SUM((Customers=E2)*PaymentAmount)
```

Here, the fragment `(Customers=E2)` returns an array of `TRUE` and `FALSE` values. When you multiply that array by PaymentAmount, which is an array of numeric values, Excel treats the `TRUE` values as 1s and the `FALSE` values as 0s. Therefore, the effect of the formula is the same as if you explicitly created an array of 1s and 0s by means of the `IF()` function. You can verify this in the usual way by highlighting in the Formula Bar and pressing the F9 key.

Defining Array Formula Names with Relative References You might wonder what would happen if you entered a relative, instead of an absolute, cell reference when you define the name as a formula. Well, magic happens.

When you use a relative cell reference in the definition of a name, the cell reference is relative to whatever cell is active when you define the name.

Suppose that you select cell D2 and choose Insert, Name, Define. You type the name `SameRowThreeColumnLeft` in the Names in Workbook box. In the Refers To box, you type `=A2`.

If you click cell A2 instead of typing it, Excel automatically supplies the dollar signs, making the reference `=$A$1`. To make the reference relative, you can either type it yourself, delete the dollar signs that Excel supplies, or highlight the reference in the box and press the F4 key (three times).

Suppose now that you have the value Anderson in cell A2. You select cell D2 and type an equal sign (=). Then press F3 and choose the range name SameRowThreeColumnLeft from the list. The value that's in the same row, three columns to the left of D2, appears in D2—that is, Anderson.

If you now select cell F12 and enter `=SameRowThreeColumnLeft`, whatever value is in cell C12 appears in F12. Excel evaluates the formula in terms of whatever cell is active when you enter it.

Back to the formula named TotalPayment used earlier (see Figure 22.35). Recall that column A contains customer names, column B contains payment dates, and column C contains payment amounts. If you now select cell D2 and define the name TotalPayment as

```
=SUM(IF(Customers=A2,PaymentAmount,0))
```

then the formula (since you've used a relative reference) uses the value found in the same row, three columns to the left, regardless of where on the worksheet you enter the formula.

Now, suppose that you're idly scanning this listing of customers and payments, and you happen to notice the name Henrietta Lee in cell A8. You wonder briefly how much Ms. Lee has ever paid you. You select cell D8 (same row, three columns to the right, as the value Henrietta Lee in A8) and enter this formula:

```
=TotalPayment
```

Your formula finds the name in the same row, three columns to the left, compares it to all the names in the Customers range, and returns the total of the payments for any instance of Henrietta Lee in the Customers range.

When you define a name as a formula with relative references, the formula's results depend on where you enter the formula's name.

This is much easier than trying to remember the proper syntax for the formula. As a bonus, if you have trouble remembering even the formula's name, you can paste it to a cell by choosing Insert, Name, Paste or pressing F3. Excel supplies the equal sign for you.

CHAPTER 23

Functions for Every Occasion

In this chapter

Understanding and Planning—Two Essential Precursors to Using Excel Functions

One of the most fundamental uses of worksheets is to perform calculations. The simplest calculations involve addition, subtraction, multiplication, or division. More complex calculations can be created from scratch or by using one of the 329 predesigned Excel worksheet functions.

Most books discussing Excel functions give you a list of the function names arranged by category, along with a one- or two-sentence description of the purpose of each function. Such a list is little more than the Paste Function command committed to paper.

The reason, of course, is that a full discussion of each of the worksheet functions would require a series of books. To make this book publishable as a single volume, and yet provide you with more information about the functions than you usually get, this chapter does some very specific picking and choosing. It discusses only a few of the functions that are available to you, but it does so by using some contexts and usages that you might not have seen before. Additionally, this chapter provides information up front on planning out your formulas and using Excel features to build your formulas, which can be applied to any function you choose to use.

Functions are formulas that perform specific calculations. Because there are so many functions in Excel, nine categories have been created to help you locate specific functions. The function categories are as follows:

Financial
Math & Trig
Lookup & Reference
Text
Information
Date & Time
Statistical
Database
Logical

There are many sources of information that can be used to look up the 320+ functions available in Excel 2000. Among the best are the following:

- Use the comprehensive online help to discover more about functions in Excel 2000. Type `functions` in the Office Assistant search box and press Enter. Choose Examples of common formulas from the results list.
- Excel 2000 comes packaged with several programs, called *Add-Ins*, which provide optional commands and features to Microsoft Excel. Because most of these features are not widely used, they must be added in to Excel. The Analysis ToolPak is an add-in program that includes a number of data-analysis tools such as Covariance, Exponential Smoothing, F-Test, Histogram, and Regression Analysis. To add the Analysis ToolPak to Excel, choose Tools, Add-Ins. Select Analysis ToolPak and choose OK. You will either need the Office CD or access to the location on your server where the Office 2000 program files are stored.

All functions have similar syntax:

```
= Function Name (Argument, Argument, ...)
```

The syntax begins with the equal sign and function name, followed by an opening parenthesis and the arguments for the function. The syntax concludes with a closing parenthesis. Arguments are separated by commas. Arguments can be

- A single cell reference.
- A range of cell references.
- Calculations (including functions).
- Range names.

For example:

```
=Sum(B2,B10:B17,D5*G5,January_Sales)
```

▶ **See** "Using Range Names in Formulas," **p. 639**

Some functions, such as SUM, don't care in which order the arguments appear. Other functions, such as PMT, require that the arguments be entered in a particular order. The function syntax is your clue, as seen by the syntax for these two functions:

```
=SUM(number1,number2,...)
=PMT(rate,nper,pv,fv,type)
```

Using the Paste Function Command

Instead of memorizing complex function syntax, Excel provides the Paste Function command, so that you can create functions rapidly, while avoiding syntax errors. The Paste Function command assists you in selecting a function and provides the Formula Palette to help in completing the necessary arguments. You can access the Paste Function command through a button on the Standard toolbar.

There are several advantages to using the Paste Function command instead of typing the function syntax:

- The Paste Function adds all the necessary function names and arithmetic symbols (equal, comma, and parentheses) for you—no more error messages about missing commas or parentheses.
- Anytime you need help with a particular function or argument, the Office Assistant is available to describe the function or argument.

Write Out Your Formula First

When creating any type of calculation, it is easiest if you first create the formula in words and then substitute the words with the appropriate cell references. For example, suppose you have to add sales tax for purchases by customers in Texas. If the customer is not from Texas, then no sales tax is charged. You would probably use the IF function, which contains three arguments: a test, what to do if the test is true, and what to do if the test is false. Using words, you would create this formula:

```
=IF (State = Texas, Sale Price * Tax Rate, Zero)
```

Using this method to create complex formulas makes it easier to understand what you are calculating. You then convert the text into cell references or range names. You will see this technique used throughout this chapter.

As mentioned earlier in this chapter, there are nine categories of functions in Excel. The functions are grouped by type. In addition to these categories, there are two other categories available under Paste Function—Most Recently Used and All. The Most Recently Used and All categories provide alternative ways to locate functions. When you first use The Most Recently Used category, it lists some of the most common functions because obviously you have yet to use a function. Thereafter, every time you use a function, that function appears at the top of the Most Recently Used list. In Excel 97, functions appeared in this list alphabetically.

The All category is an alphabetical list of every function in Excel. When you are uncertain to which category a function belongs, use the All category as a starting point in your search for the function.

To create a function by using the Paste Function command, follow these steps:

1. Select the cell in which you want the calculated answer to appear.

2. Click the Paste Function button on the Standard toolbar. The Paste Function dialog box appears (see Figure 23.1).

FIGURE 23.1
Use Paste Function to assist you in creating functions more quickly and with fewer errors than creating functions from scratch.

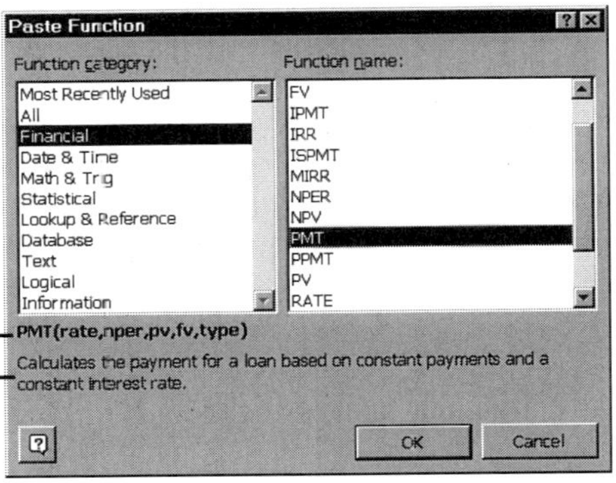

Syntax for the selected function

Description for the selected function

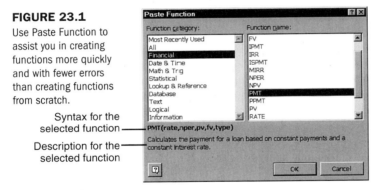

3. Choose one of the categories in the Function Category list box. In Figure 23.1, the Financial category is selected.
4. Choose a function from the names in the Function Name list box. The syntax and description for the selected function appear below the Function Category list box. In Figure 23.1, the PMT (payment) function is selected. A description of the selected function appears near the bottom of the dialog box.
5. Select OK and the Formula Palette appears, detailing the arguments for the function (see Figure 23.2). Arguments appearing in bold (Rate, Nper, and Pv) are required. Those not in bold (Fv and Type) are optional.
6. The first argument, Rate, is active—note the flashing cursor in the Rate entry box. A description of the function and the active argument appear near the bottom of the Formula Palette box.
7. Select the cell or cells in your worksheet that contain the data for the first argument, or manually type the cell references.

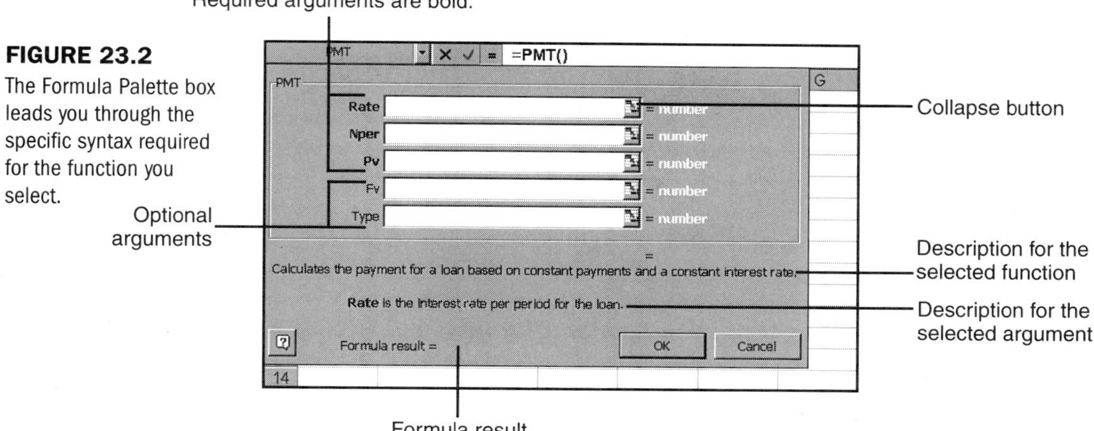

FIGURE 23.2
The Formula Palette box leads you through the specific syntax required for the function you select.

8. If necessary, select the next argument by pressing the Tab key or clicking with your mouse. Do not use your Enter key, as that is equivalent to selecting OK, which concludes creating the function.
9. After you have completed all the desired arguments, choose OK. The result of the function appears in the worksheet and the function appears in the Formula Bar.

If the Formula Palette box is blocking the data you want to select, click the collapse/expand button for the argument (see Figure 23.2) to temporarily hide most of the Formula Palette box while you are selecting cells. There is a collapse/expand button located at the far-right side of the entry boxes for each argument.

The collapse/expand button toggles between displaying the full Formula Palette and collapsing the dialog box to just the active argument (one line docked below the Formula Bar). You also can move the box out of your way—position your mouse pointer on any part of the gray background of Formula Palette box and drag.

When you need to edit a function in your worksheet, choose the Edit Formula button (an equal sign) located in the Formula Bar. The Formula Palette displays again.

Accessing Range Names from the Formula Palette

Range names are particularly useful when you are developing calculations using functions. By definition, range names are absolute cell references, something frequently needed with functions. Using range names in formulas can ease the process of creating and updating calculations.

▶ **See** "Using Range Names in Formulas," **p. 639**

▶ **See** "Using Absolute and Relative Cell References in Formulas," **p. 634**

The Name Box on the Formula Bar is used to create and select range names. Figure 23.3 shows the Name Box listing the range names already created for this worksheet.

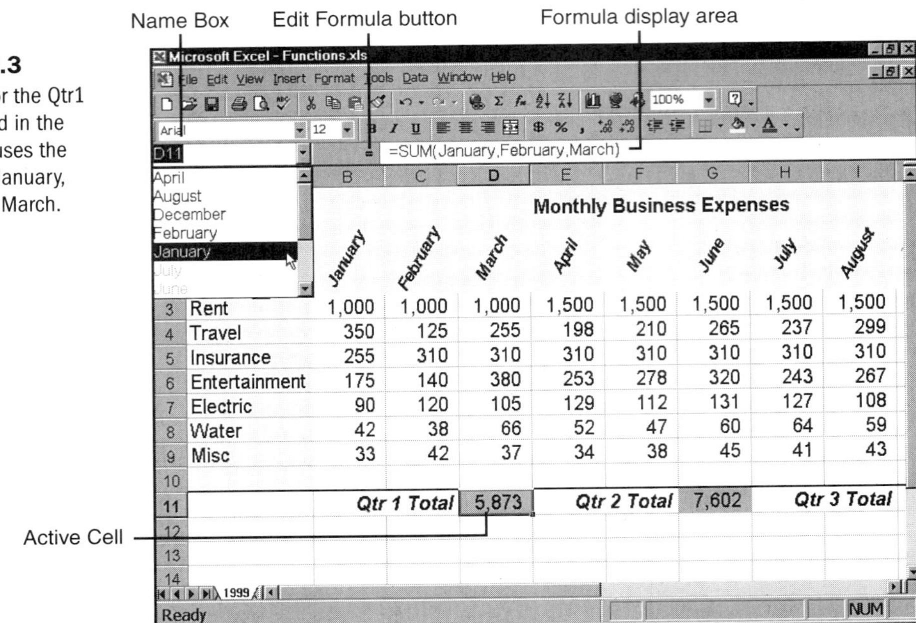

FIGURE 23.3
The formula for the Qtr1 Total, displayed in the Formula Bar, uses the range names January, February, and March.

The previous section discusses how to use the Paste Function command and Formula Palette to create functions in Excel. When Formula Palette is active, the Name Box is not available. A list of worksheet functions is substituted on the Formula Bar, as shown in Figure 23.4. This list is available to help you quickly select functions to nest inside other functions—a topic discussed in the next section.

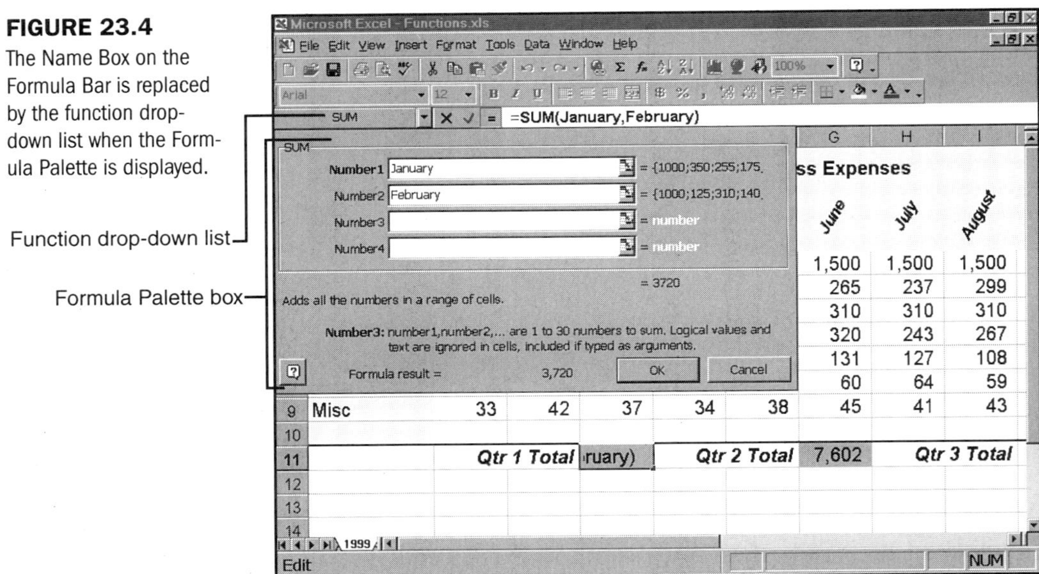

FIGURE 23.4
The Name Box on the Formula Bar is replaced by the function drop-down list when the Formula Palette is displayed.

Although you can use the traditional menu method (Insert, Name, Paste) to include range names in functions, it is not particularly convenient. If you plan to use range names frequently in your formulas, a quicker way to access the Paste Name dialog box is to press F3. Figure 23.5 shows how the Paste Name dialog box appears.

FIGURE 23.5
Use F3 to display the Paste Name dialog box.

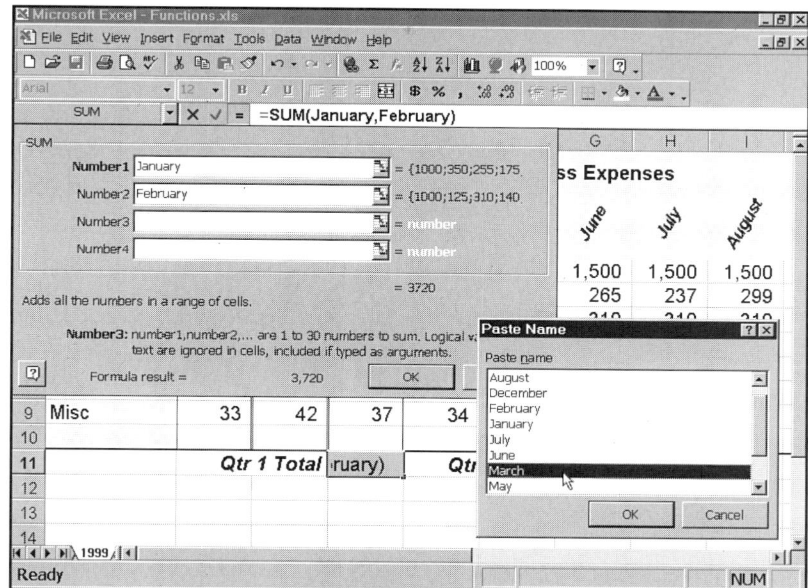

Nesting Functions

As you work with functions, you will probably find it useful to create functions that use other functions. When one function is used inside another function, it is referred to as *nesting functions*. A simple example of nesting functions is

```
=MAX(SUM(B12:B15),SUM(C12:C15))
```

This formula starts with the `MAX` function, which displays the argument that is the largest or maximum. There are two arguments (remember, arguments are separated by commas). The `SUM` function is used for both arguments—the `SUM` of cells B12 through B15 and the `SUM` of cells C12 through C15. So this formula will display whichever sum is larger; the larger sum appears as the answer to the `MAX` function.

Nesting is used in many of the examples you will see in this chapter. To read a formula containing nested functions, it is best to work from the inside out. Because each function uses parentheses, start with the innermost set of parentheses.

Math and Trig Functions

There are many mathematical and trigonometric functions included in Excel. The SUM and ROUND functions have several useful variations that aren't always fully understood. In this section you explore one of the variations of SUM—SUMIF—as well as the variations of ROUND—ROUNDUP and ROUNDDOWN.

Using the *SUM* and *SUMIF* Functions

As you probably know, the SUM function adds all the numbers in a designated range of cells. There can be up to 30 arguments in the SUM function and the arguments can be listed in any order.

The syntax for SUM is

```
=SUM(number1,number2,…)
```

You can use either the AutoSum or Paste Function buttons on the Standard toolbar to access the SUM function. The AutoSum is used to quickly total columns and rows of data. It can also be used to total multiple columns and multiple rows and provide a grand total. Access the SUM function through the Paste Function button when you want to total data that is not in consecutive rows or columns.

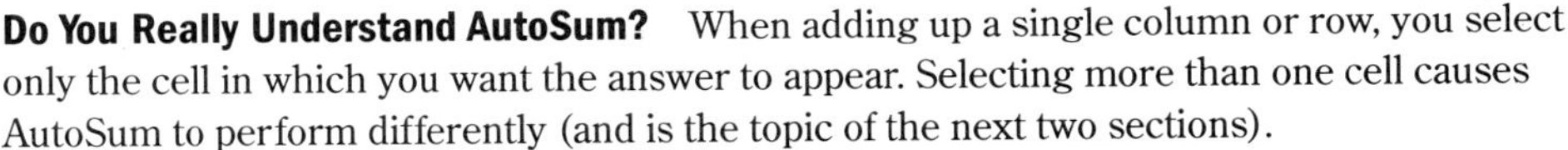

Do You Really Understand AutoSum? When adding up a single column or row, you select only the cell in which you want the answer to appear. Selecting more than one cell causes AutoSum to perform differently (and is the topic of the next two sections).

As with any other Excel calculation, you first select the cell in which you want the answer to appear. When you click the AutoSum button, it proposes a range of cells to add. If the cells are not the ones you want to add, you can select the correct cells with your mouse. To complete the AutoSum, press Enter or click the Enter button (green check) in the Formula Bar.

TIP A quick way to confirm the AutoSum, especially if it proposes the correct range you want, is simply to click the AutoSum button again.

Before you use the AutoSum button, it's important that you understand how it really works. By default, when you use AutoSum, the order in which it views your worksheet is as follows:

- AutoSum first looks above the active cell for numbers to add, when it finds an empty cell or text, it stops and displays the cell references it proposes to add.
- If there is an empty cell or text immediately above the active cell, AutoSum then looks to the left of the active cell for numbers to add; when it finds an empty cell or text, it stops and displays the cell references it proposes to add.
- If AutoSum encounters empty cells immediately above and to the left of the active cell, or if it encounters only one cell of numbers to the left of the active cell, it once again looks above the active cell in search of numbers to calculate.

- If there are multiple empty cells, AutoSum's priority is to continue to look above the active cell. For example, if AutoSum encounters only one empty cell to the left and multiple empty cells above, AutoSum proposes to calculate the sum of the cells above the active cell.

Using Figure 23.6 as an illustration, if the active cell is C14 (1997 Total by Year), AutoSum will encounter an empty cell (C13) above the active cell and text to the left of the active cell. AutoSum once again looks above the active cell (C14) and proposes to add cells C8 through C13.

If the active cell is D14 (1998 Total by Year), AutoSum will encounter an empty cell (D13) above the active cell and only one number to the left of the active cell (1997 Total by Year). AutoSum once again looks above the active cell (D14) and proposes to add cells D8 through D13.

If the active cell is E14 (1999 Total by Year), AutoSum will encounter an empty cell (E13) above the active cell, but finds two numbers to the left. It proposes to add C14 and D14, the totals for 1997 and 1998. This calculation does not provide the same answer that you would receive by adding the 1999 column. Thus, you would reject AutoSum's proposal by selecting the appropriate cells with your mouse.

FIGURE 23.6
The cells that AutoSum proposes depend on which cell is the active cell.

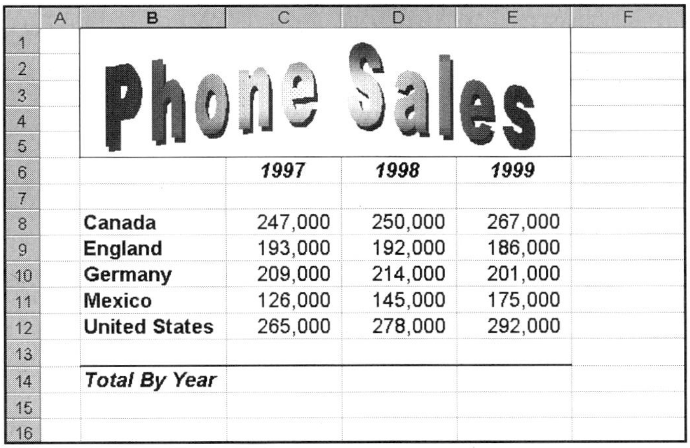

	A	B	C	D	E	F
1		Phone Sales				
2						
3						
4						
5						
6			*1997*	*1998*	*1999*	
7						
8		Canada	247,000	250,000	267,000	
9		England	193,000	192,000	186,000	
10		Germany	209,000	214,000	201,000	
11		Mexico	126,000	145,000	175,000	
12		United States	265,000	278,000	292,000	
13						
14		*Total By Year*				
15						
16						

CAUTION

If you use numbers for your column or row labels, such as the years (1998, 1999), Excel includes them in the range of cells it proposes to be summed. You can avoid this by placing an empty row between the labels and the data (as was done in Figure 23.6) or by including text in the labels (such as FY 1999 or 1999 Sales).

Totaling Multiple Columns or Rows When you select multiple cells and use the AutoSum button, Excel assumes you know what you're doing. AutoSum does not propose a range of cells to total—instead, it performs a sum immediately.

Using Figure 23.6 as an example, if you select cells C14 through E14 and click AutoSum, it calculates the total for the 1997 column, places the total in C14, and copies the formula to D14 and E14. If you select cells C8 through C14 and click AutoSum, it calculates a total in the 1997 column and places the total in the last empty cell—C14.

In Figure 23.7, by selecting the sales data and the cells in which you want the totals to appear (C8:F14), you quickly can perform all the calculations in your spreadsheet. You also can get a grand total at the intersection of the rows and columns that you have selected. In Figure 23.7, this grand total appears in cell F14. Because multiple cells are selected, these calculations are performed immediately.

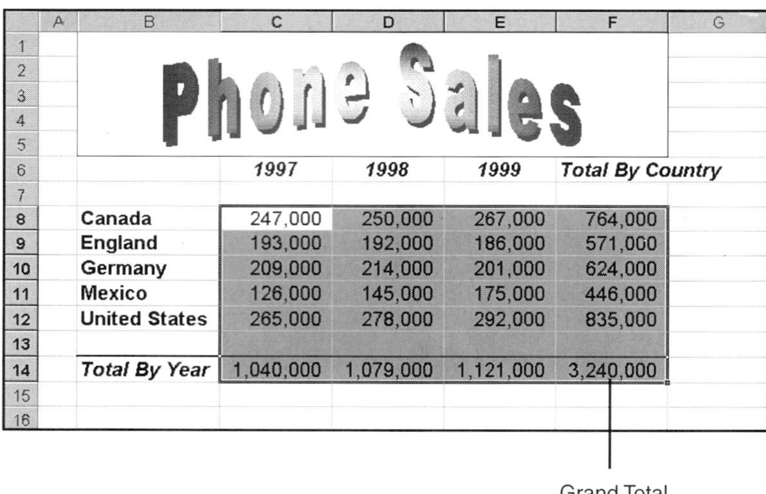

Phone Sales

	1997	1998	1999	Total By Country
Canada	247,000	250,000	267,000	764,000
England	193,000	192,000	186,000	571,000
Germany	209,000	214,000	201,000	624,000
Mexico	126,000	145,000	175,000	446,000
United States	265,000	278,000	292,000	835,000
Total By Year	1,040,000	1,079,000	1,121,000	3,240,000

FIGURE 23.7
AutoSum can quickly create the totals by year and country as well as a grand total.

Using *SUM* Through the Paste Function Command Figure 23.8 displays a monthly order list with quarterly totals. In this example, total orders for the year need to be determined. This can be accomplished by adding quarterly totals together. Because the cells that need to be summed are not in neat, consecutive cells, it's not as convenient to use AutoSum or to type the formula from scratch. Instead, it is easier to use the Paste Function command.

To calculate the total expenses for the year, select the cell in which you want the answer to appear. Click the Paste Function button. Choose the SUM function from either the Most Recently Used category or the Math & Trig category and click OK to display the Formula Palette (seen in Figure 23.9).

NOTE When the Sum function is accessed, it proposes a range of cells to total, just as the AutoSum button does on the toolbar. Simply select the first cell or range of cells, or press F3 to select a range name to replace the proposed cells in the first argument box in the Formula Palette.

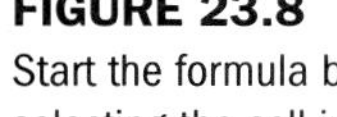

FIGURE 23.8
Start the formula by selecting the cell in which you want the answer to appear.

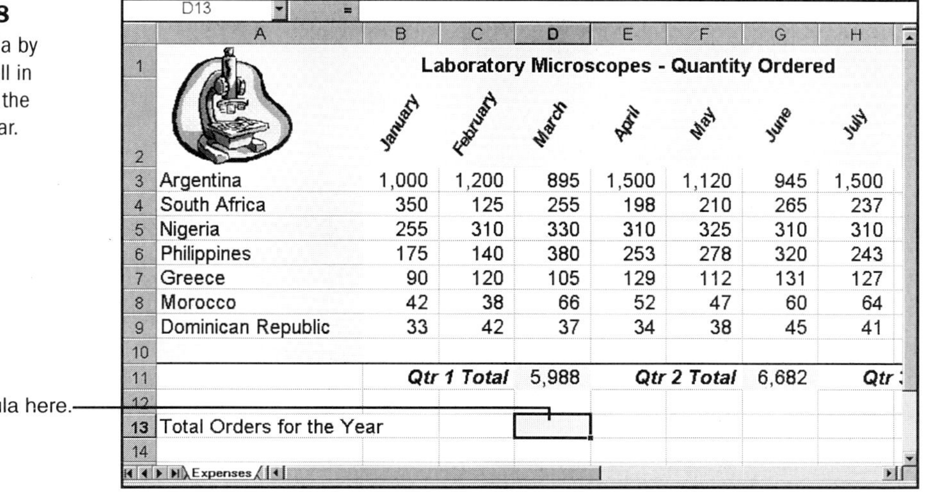

D13
Laboratory Microscopes - Quantity Ordered
January
February
March
April
May
June
July
Argentina 1,000 1,200 895 1,500 1,120 945 1,500
South Africa 350 125 255 198 210 265 237
Nigeria 255 310 330 310 325 310 310
Philippines 175 140 380 253 278 320 243
Greece 90 120 105 129 112 131 127
Morocco 42 38 66 52 47 60 64
Dominican Republic 33 42 37 34 38 45 41
Qtr 1 Total 5,988
Qtr 2 Total 6,682
Total Orders for the Year
Start the formula here.
Expenses

To insert the cell reference for the Qtr 1 total, select the cell containing the Qtr 1 total (D11) directly in the worksheet. Press the Tab key or click in the next argument entry box, and then choose the cell that contains the Qtr 2 total (G11), as shown in Figure 23.9. Continue until all four quarterly totals are selected. Choose OK to complete the function. In this example, it is necessary to use the scrollbars to select the remaining cells.

FIGURE 23.9
The Formula Palette for the SUM function.

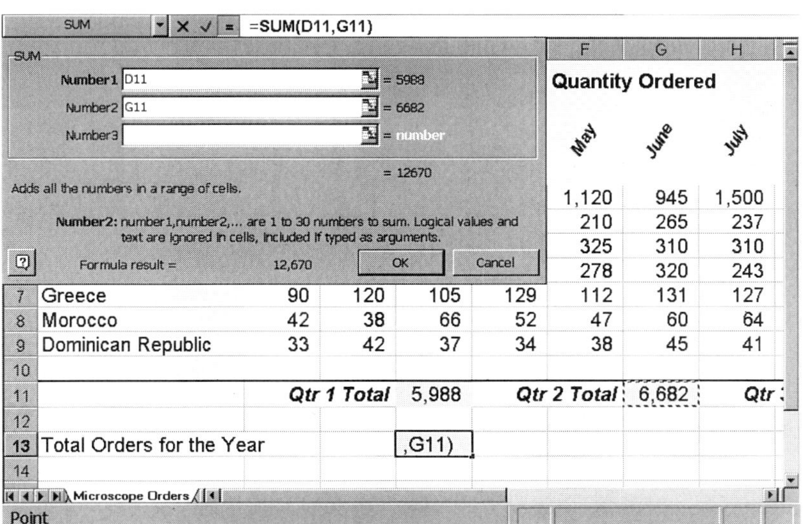

Using *SUMIF* to Create Conditional Totals The `SUMIF` function looks at a list and totals numerical data that meets criteria you specify. The syntax for `SUMIF` is

```
=SUMIF(range,criteria,sum_range)
```

The criteria can be a text string, a number, or a comparison (for example, >1500 or <=50%).

Figure 23.10 shows a list of hours spent on consulting for the month of June. The `SUMIF` function has been added to cell G4 to calculate the total hours for a particular customer (Pyron & Pyron). The *range* argument is the column of company names. The *Criteria* argument is the name of the customer. The *sum_range* argument is the column of hours.

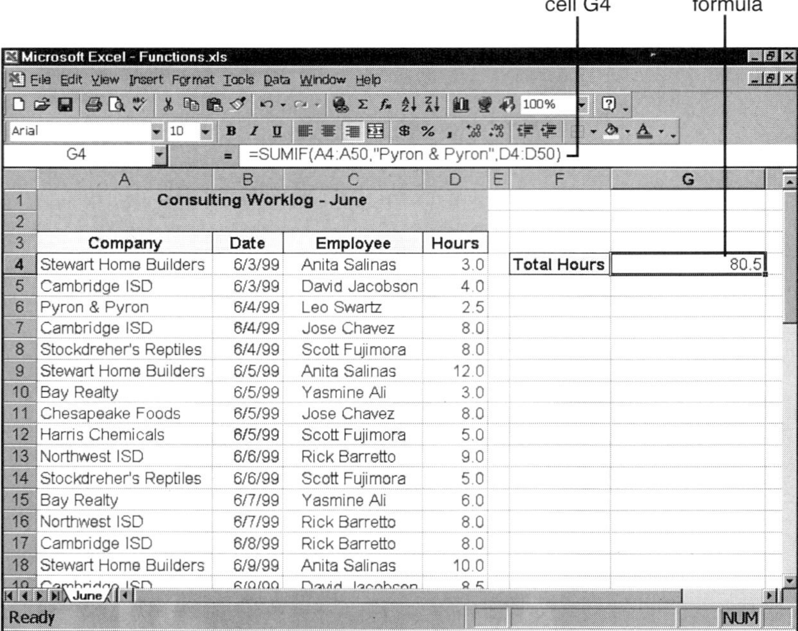

	A	B	C	D	E	F	G
1	Consulting Worklog - June						
2							
3	Company	Date	Employee	Hours			
4	Stewart Home Builders	6/3/99	Anita Salinas	3.0		Total Hours	80.5
5	Cambridge ISD	6/3/99	David Jacobson	4.0			
6	Pyron & Pyron	6/4/99	Leo Swartz	2.5			
7	Cambridge ISD	6/4/99	Jose Chavez	8.0			
8	Stockdreher's Reptiles	6/4/99	Scott Fujimora	8.0			
9	Stewart Home Builders	6/5/99	Anita Salinas	12.0			
10	Bay Realty	6/5/99	Yasmine Ali	3.0			
11	Chesapeake Foods	6/5/99	Jose Chavez	8.0			
12	Harris Chemicals	6/5/99	Scott Fujimora	5.0			
13	Northwest ISD	6/6/99	Rick Barretto	9.0			
14	Stockdreher's Reptiles	6/6/99	Scott Fujimora	5.0			
15	Bay Realty	6/7/99	Yasmine Ali	6.0			
16	Northwest ISD	6/7/99	Rick Barretto	8.0			
17	Cambridge ISD	6/8/99	Rick Barretto	8.0			
18	Stewart Home Builders	6/9/99	Anita Salinas	10.0			

FIGURE 23.10
Use `SUMIF` when you want to total values based on a criterion.

To provide more flexibility, you can replace the company name in the criteria with a cell reference. The formula becomes

```
=SUMIF(A4:A50,G2,D4:D50)
```

This way you don't have to edit the formula for each customer; simply type the company name in the cell G2.

If you want to count, rather than total, the number of occurrences of a string of text or a number within a range of cells, use the `COUNTIF` function. The syntax for the `COUNTIF` function is

```
=COUNTIF(range,criteria)
```

The range argument is the group of cell references you want to count. The criteria are the condition(s) that defines which cells will be counted.

Using the *ROUND*, *ROUNDUP*, and *ROUNDDOWN* Functions

If you're an accomplished Excel user, you might wonder why I've included a section on Excel's rounding functions. After all, Excel rounds digits for you when you specify the number of decimals to be displayed in a cell. And you are right, it does—but the results may not be what you expect.

A simple equation (seen in the Formula Bar) calculates Gallons * Markup and displays the results in the Unformatted Total column (see Figure 23.11). A grand total of 30.618 appears at the bottom of the Unformatted column.

FIGURE 23.11
No rounding is performed in the formula results.

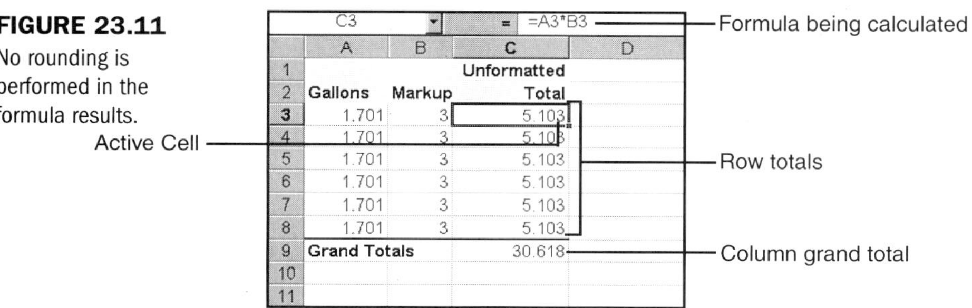

C3 = =A3*B3

	A	B	C	D
1			Unformatted	
2	Gallons	Markup	Total	
3	1.701	3	5.103	
4	1.701	3	5.103	
5	1.701	3	5.103	
6	1.701	3	5.103	
7	1.701	3	5.103	
8	1.701	3	5.103	
9	Grand Totals		30.618	
10				
11				

If you want to display the results in column C showing only two decimals, highlight the cells and click the Decrease Decimal button on the Formatting toolbar. Using the exact same formula, Figure 23.12 shows the difference between the unformatted and formatted results.

FIGURE 23.12
When formatting is applied, rounding occurs for display purposes but not for calculations.

D3 = =A3*B3

	A	B	C	D	E
1			Unformatted	Formatted	
2	Gallons	Markup	Total	Total	
3	1.701	3	5.103	5.10	
4	1.701	3	5.103	5.10	
5	1.701	3	5.103	5.10	
6	1.701	3	5.103	5.10	
7	1.701	3	5.103	5.10	
8	1.701	3	5.103	5.10	
9	Grand Totals		30.618	30.62	
10					
11					

Column does not appear to add up

Formatting the cells to display only two decimals hides the digits you don't want displayed. But the numbers are still part of the results and are reflected in the grand total (shown in cell D9). If the formatted column is the only one displayed on the worksheet, it appears as though the numbers don't add up. The row calculations in column D all end in zero, yet the grand total ends in two. Someone reading this worksheet would think there is an error, when in fact Excel is merely rounding the numbers for display purposes.

Some people accept this discrepancy, while others (especially Accountants) want the displayed numbers to add up. How can you resolve this? By using Excel's rounding functions.

The three rounding functions perform similarly—they take a number you designate and round to a specified number of digits. The syntax for each of the rounding functions is

```
=ROUND(number,num_digits)
=ROUNDUP(number,num_digits)
=ROUNDDOWN(number,num_digits)
```

The number argument is any number that you want rounded. The *num_digits* argument is the number of digits to which you want the number rounded.

When you specify the number of digits, keep this in mind:

- If the number of digits is greater than 0 (zero), then the number is rounded to the right of the decimal point. For example, ROUND(2390.149, 2) displays 2390.15, rounding to the second place to the right of the decimal.
- If the number of digits is 0, then the number is rounded to the nearest integer. For example, ROUND(2390.149, 0) displays 2390.
- If the number of digits is less than 0, then the number is rounded to the left of the decimal point. For example, ROUND(2390.149, -2) displays 2400.

The difference between the three rounding functions is, of course, the `ROUND` function rounds up numbers greater than or equal to 5 and rounds down numbers less than 5. `ROUNDUP` always rounds up. `ROUNDDOWN` always rounds down.

Using the worksheet shown in Figure 23.12, instead of the original formula in column C, such as

```
=A3*B3
```

incorporate one of the rounding functions into the formula, such as

```
=ROUND(A3*B3,2)
```

In Figure 23.13 each of the rounding functions has been used to calculate Gallons * Markup. You can see the differences between the results. Cell E3, which contains the `ROUND` function, is selected and the formula appears in the Formula Bar.

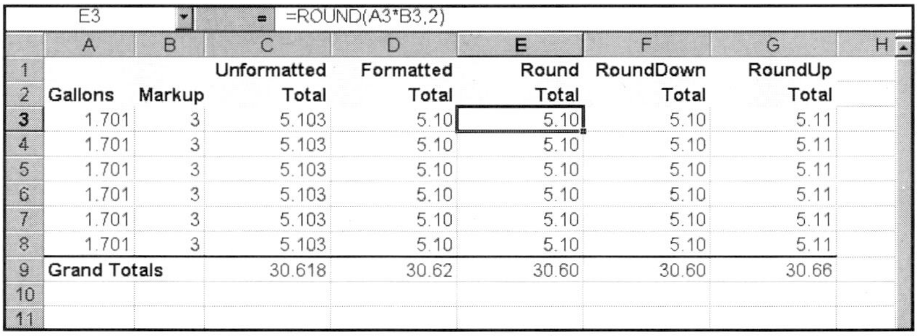

FIGURE 23.13

Compare the results to both the row and column totals when you use the rounding functions.

E3 = =ROUND(A3*B3,2)

	A	B	C	D	E	F	G	H
1			Unformatted	Formatted	Round	RoundDown	RoundUp	
2	Gallons	Markup	Total	Total	Total	Total	Total	
3	1.701	3	5.103	5.10	5.10	5.10	5.11	
4	1.701	3	5.103	5.10	5.10	5.10	5.11	
5	1.701	3	5.103	5.10	5.10	5.10	5.11	
6	1.701	3	5.103	5.10	5.10	5.10	5.11	
7	1.701	3	5.103	5.10	5.10	5.10	5.11	
8	1.701	3	5.103	5.10	5.10	5.10	5.11	
9	Grand Totals		30.618	30.62	30.60	30.60	30.66	
10								
11								

When Should You Use *ROUNDDOWN*?

There are several good instances when ROUNDDOWN should be used. Suppose you are performing calculations to track when employees are entitled to additional vacation days. At two years each employee gets two additional vacation days. If an employee has been with the company 1.6 years, formatting and the ROUND function would round this up to two years, making the employee eligible long before she is entitled. ROUNDDOWN, on the other hand, would round down the years until the employee actually reaches or surpasses the two-year mark.

Similarly, if you keep track of how many emergency medical kits are on hand and you have three full kits and two-thirds of another kit, how many do you want to officially record? Probably just three. No sense in taking chances—it would be just your luck to record four, wind up using the partial kit, and need the very items that are missing.

Lookup and Reference Functions

At first glance, some of Excel's Lookup and Reference functions don't appear to be particularly useful. For example, the ROW and INDEX functions seem particularly weak until you combine these functions with other functions. For example, you can use the INDEX and MATCH functions to dynamically look up the smallest or largest value in a list and return its corresponding label. Combining OFFSET with COUNTA to identify the data series plotted on a chart will automatically refresh the chart when new data is added to the bottom of your data series. Suppose you use the same worksheet to track monthly revenue figures. When you update the worksheet, you want the name of the product that has the greatest revenue automatically displayed. This can be accomplished by using the INDEX, MATCH, and MAX functions.

A number of Lookup functions enable you to create array formulas that return results that are otherwise very difficult to obtain.

Using Arrays with Functions

An *array* is a contiguous range of cells that Excel treats as single group. An *array formula* is a special kind of formula—one that either returns an array of values (called an *array range*) as the formula result, or one that uses an array as an argument (called an *array argument*).

With some Excel functions, several calculations must be performed to generate a single result. The power of an array formula is that it can perform multiple calculations and then return either a single result or multiple results (an array range). When used to return multiple results, array formulas can save computer memory; a single formula is stored even if the array affects many cells.

When you build an array formula, you must press Ctrl+Shift+Enter to complete the formula—you cannot press Enter or use any other confirmation method. This is called *array-entering* the formula. Excel automatically displays braces { } around the formula.

If you need to edit an array formula, select any cell in the array range and then click in the Formula Bar. When the Formula Bar is active, the braces { } do not appear in the array formula. Edit the formula and press Ctrl+Shift+Enter to have Excel accept the changes.

▶ **See** "Exploring the Power of Array Formulas," **p. 661**

Using *VLOOKUP* with Lists

Lookup functions are used to search for one value in a list, and to return another corresponding value from the list. Lookup functions can be used to find a product name in a price list and return the specific price, or find the tax rate for a particular salary range. Although there are several Lookup functions, VLOOKUP (Vertical Lookup) is most commonly used, as lists tend to be designed in columns rather than rows.

The syntax for VLOOKUP is

```
=VLOOKUP(lookup_value,table_array,col_index_num,range_lookup)
```

The specific arguments for the VLOOKUP function must appear in the order just shown.

Figure 23.14 illustrates a worksheet in which Sales Representatives earn a bonus based on the sales they make each month. The Actual Sales is looked up in the Bonus Table to find the appropriate Bonus Rate.

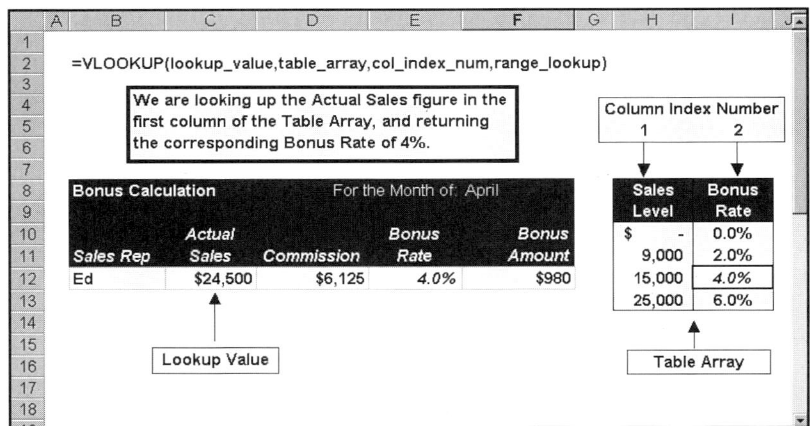

FIGURE 23.14
The arguments for a VLOOKUP function are identified in this figure.

The arguments for VLOOKUP are the following:

- lookup_value—The value being searched for in the first column of the table array. The lookup_value can be a number, a cell reference, or text. In Figure 23.14, the lookup_value is the Actual Sales figure.
- table_array—The list of information in which data is being looked up, commonly referred to as the table. Use a range name or absolute cell reference for the table , so that the VLOOKUP formula can be copied. Although Figure 23.14 shows the Bonus Table in the same sheet as the commission and bonus calculations, the table often is in another sheet or book. In Figure 23.14, the table shows various Sales Levels. Ed's Actual Sales are $24,500, which is higher than $15,000, but less than $25,000; therefore, he will earn a bonus of 4%.

NOTE The name of this argument (table_array) is unfortunate. It leads you to believe that this is an array argument, but it is not. A better name would be table_range, as it truly is just a range of cells.

- col_index_num—The column index number. Imagine that the columns in the table array are numbered. The column index number is the column number from which the matching value will be returned. In Figure 23.14, column 1 is the Sales Level and column 2 is the Bonus Rate. In this example, the column index number is 2.
- range_lookup—This argument is optional. If the range_lookup argument is omitted or TRUE, a range (approximate match) lookup is performed. If you enter FALSE for this argument, an exact match lookup is performed. In Figures 23.14 and 23.15 (shown in the next section), a range lookup is being performed. See Figures 23.16 and 23.17, later in this chapter, for examples of an exact match lookup.

Using *VLOOKUP* to Find a Range Match in a List The Bonus Table in Figure 23.15 lists levels of sales, rather than each possible sales amount. This is referred to as a *range lookup*.

When performing a range lookup, the table should account for the smallest possible value that can be looked up. The first column in the table also must be sorted in ascending order.

- If you are looking up numbers, ascending is from the smallest to the largest number.
- If you are looking up text, ascending is alphabetical from A to Z.

Figure 23.15 shows the completed formula for the first Sales Rep, Ed. The formula for looking up the bonus rate is displayed in the Formula Bar. The range_lookup argument is omitted because the default setting for the argument is TRUE.

FIGURE 23.15
The VLOOKUP function provides a convenient way to extract a value from a table.

Formula being calculated

D5 = =VLOOKUP(B5,Table,2)

	A	B	C	D	E	F	G	H	I
1	Bonus Calculation		For the Month of: April						
2									
3		Actual		Bonus	Bonus				
4	Sales Rep	Sales	Commission	Rate	Amount		Bonus Table		
5	Ed	24,500	6,125	4%	$ 980		Sales	Bonus	
6	Sung	19,000	4,750				Level	Rate	
7	Susan	32,000	8,000				$ -	0.0%	
8	Tim	22,100	5,525				9,000	2.0%	
9	Victoria	9,750	2,438				15,000	4.0%	
10	Pablo	12,250	3,063				25,000	6.0%	
11	Doris	8,500	2,125						
12	Tonda	13,500	3,375						
13	Totals	141,600	35,400		980				
14									
15	Commission Rate:								
16		25%							
17									

Result of the formula

The range name *Table* is used to identify the table_array. Because range names are automatically absolute cell references, this enables you to copy the formula to the other Sales Reps. To quickly access the list of range names, press F3. As an alternative, the absolute cell references $G$5:$H$8 could be used for the table_array argument.

▶ **See** "Using Absolute Cell References in Formulas," **p. 634**

Using *VLOOKUP* to Locate an Exact Match in a List Although the previous example works well for calculating bonuses, it does not work in every situation. Suppose you have a list of products that have been ordered and you want to look up the specific price for each item. If a given product does not appear in your price list, you want to be alerted to the fact that the product does not appear in the price list. This is an *exact match lookup.*

Unlike a range lookup, the table for an exact match lookup does not have to be sorted by the first column; it can be in any order. If an exact match is not found, the error value #N/A is displayed, indicating there is no match.

As discussed in the previous section, the range_lookup argument is FALSE when using an exact match lookup. It is omitted or TRUE when performing a range lookup.

Figure 23.16 shows a list of landscaping items that have been ordered. The prices for these items must be retrieved from the price list, which is on a separate worksheet in this workbook. Victorian Deco ordered the first item, Item #218. You need to look up the corresponding price in the Landscaping Price List displayed in Figure 23.17. The Item # is the *lookup_value* for your VLOOKUP function.

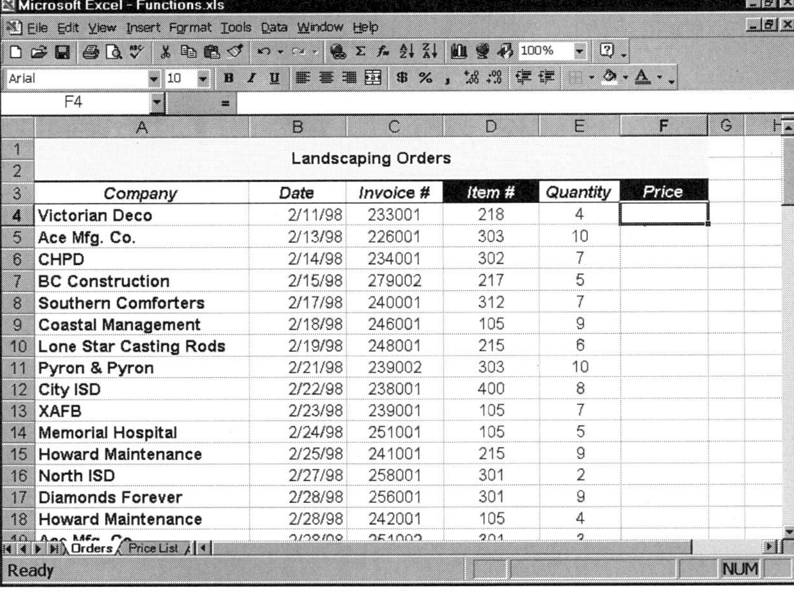

Landscaping Orders

Company	Date	Invoice #	Item #	Quantity	Price
Victorian Deco	2/11/98	233001	218	4	
Ace Mfg. Co.	2/13/98	226001	303	10	
CHPD	2/14/98	234001	302	7	
BC Construction	2/15/98	279002	217	5	
Southern Comforters	2/17/98	240001	312	7	
Coastal Management	2/18/98	246001	105	9	
Lone Star Casting Rods	2/19/98	248001	215	6	
Pyron & Pyron	2/21/98	239002	303	10	
City ISD	2/22/98	238001	400	8	
XAFB	2/23/98	239001	105	7	
Memorial Hospital	2/24/98	251001	105	5	
Howard Maintenance	2/25/98	241001	215	9	
North ISD	2/27/98	258001	301	2	
Diamonds Forever	2/28/98	256001	301	9	
Howard Maintenance	2/28/98	242001	105	4	

FIGURE 23.16
A VLOOKUP is used to locate the correct price for each of the landscaping orders.

Figure 23.17 shows the Landscaping Price List. Only part of this list is used in the table_array. The table_array in any VLOOKUP must have the lookup_value in the first column. Because you are looking up the Item # and returning the corresponding price, the table_array in this example is the Item # column through the Price column (C4:F16). In this table_array, the prices are in the fourth column of the array; therefore, the col_index_num, is 4.

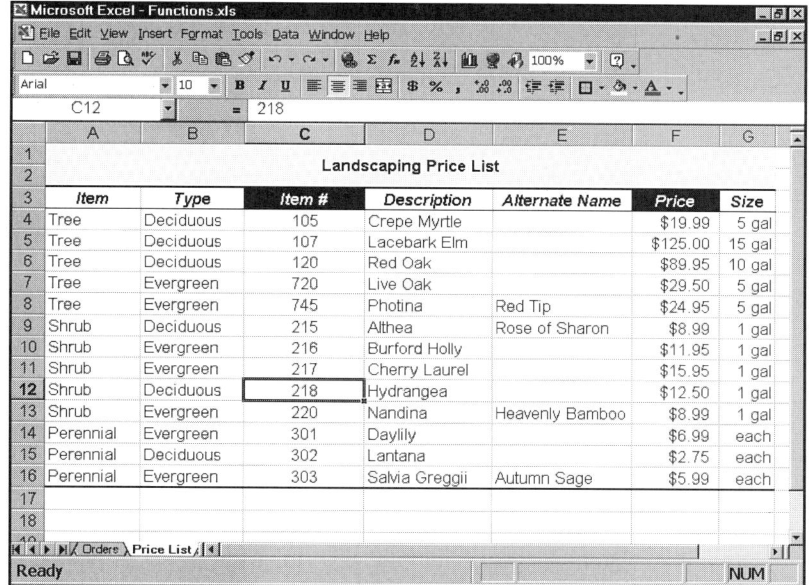

Landscaping Price List

Item	Type	Item #	Description	Alternate Name	Price	Size
Tree	Deciduous	105	Crepe Myrtle		$19.99	5 gal
Tree	Deciduous	107	Lacebark Elm		$125.00	15 gal
Tree	Deciduous	120	Red Oak		$89.95	10 gal
Tree	Evergreen	720	Live Oak		$29.50	5 gal
Tree	Evergreen	745	Photina	Red Tip	$24.95	5 gal
Shrub	Deciduous	215	Althea	Rose of Sharon	$8.99	1 gal
Shrub	Evergreen	216	Burford Holly		$11.95	1 gal
Shrub	Evergreen	217	Cherry Laurel		$15.95	1 gal
Shrub	Deciduous	218	Hydrangea		$12.50	1 gal
Shrub	Evergreen	220	Nandina	Heavenly Bamboo	$8.99	1 gal
Perennial	Evergreen	301	Daylily		$6.99	each
Perennial	Deciduous	302	Lantana		$2.75	each
Perennial	Evergreen	303	Salvia Greggii	Autumn Sage	$5.99	each

FIGURE 23.17
The price list for all landscaping products.

If you intend to copy the VLOOKUP function, either the table_array cell references need to be made absolute or a range name can be used to identify the table.

Remember, to make cell references absolute use the F4 function key on your keyboard, while the cell references are selected.

In Figure 23.18, the VLOOKUP function for the first order has been completed and copied to the remaining orders. The Formula Bar shows the formula for Victorian Deco. Because the price list was on another sheet, the name of the sheet (Price List) appears in front of the absolute cell references for the table_array. The Chapter 22 section, "Consolidating Worksheet Data: Formulas That Cross Sheets and Books," explains how to create (and interpret) calculations made across worksheets and workbooks.

Notice the error message (#N/A) in the orders for Southern Comforters and City ISD (see Figure 23.18). The item numbers for these orders do not exist in the Landscaping Price List (refer to Figure 23.17). Because the VLOOKUP is searching for an exact match, the error message alerts us to the fact that there is no match for Item #312 or Item #400.

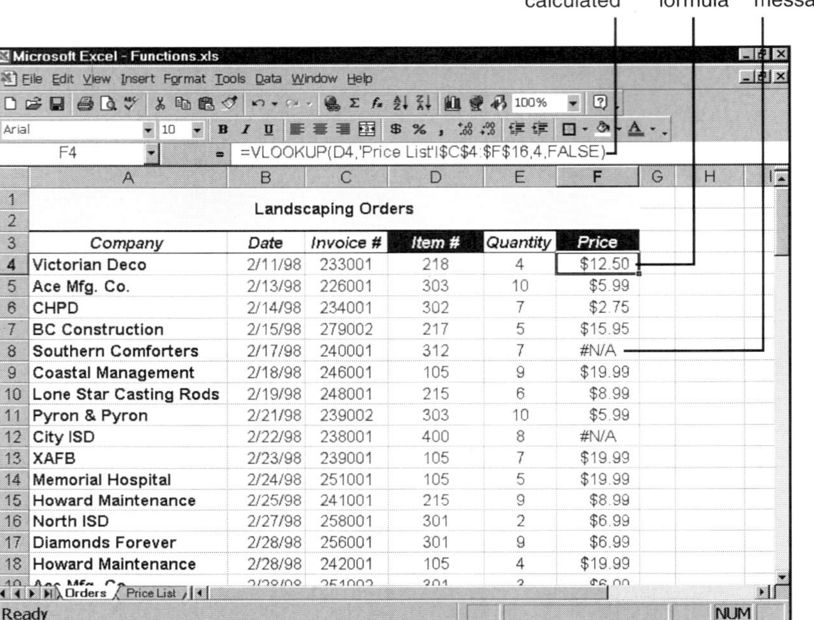

	Company	Date	Invoice #	Item #	Quantity	Price
4	Victorian Deco	2/11/98	233001	218	4	$12.50
5	Ace Mfg. Co.	2/13/98	226001	303	10	$5.99
6	CHPD	2/14/98	234001	302	7	$2.75
7	BC Construction	2/15/98	279002	217	5	$15.95
8	Southern Comforters	2/17/98	240001	312	7	#N/A
9	Coastal Management	2/18/98	246001	105	9	$19.99
10	Lone Star Casting Rods	2/19/98	248001	215	6	$8.99
11	Pyron & Pyron	2/21/98	239002	303	10	$5.99
12	City ISD	2/22/98	238001	400	8	#N/A
13	XAFB	2/23/98	239001	105	7	$19.99
14	Memorial Hospital	2/24/98	251001	105	5	$19.99
15	Howard Maintenance	2/25/98	241001	215	9	$8.99
16	North ISD	2/27/98	258001	301	2	$6.99
17	Diamonds Forever	2/28/98	256001	301	9	$6.99
18	Howard Maintenance	2/28/98	242001	105	4	$19.99

FIGURE 23.18
When an exact match is unavailable, an error message appears.

The section “Using ISNA to Avoid Error Messages” at the end of this chapter, discusses how to use the ISNA function with an IF to display text instead of the #N/A error message. You could place this VLOOKUP as the value_if_false argument in an IF function to produce a text message when performing an exact match lookup, instead of the error message.

NOTE If your table or list is designed horizontally instead of vertically, you should use the HLOOKUP function.

The syntax for HLOOKUP is

```
=HLOOKUP(lookup_value,table_array,row_index_num,range_lookup)
```

Using *MATCH* and *VLOOKUP* on Multiple Columns

You can use both the MATCH and VLOOKUP functions to return information about a value found in a list. The syntax for VLOOKUP and MATCH are

```
=VLOOKUP(lookup_value,table_array,col_index_num,range_lookup)
=MATCH(lookup_value,lookup_array,match_type)
```

The previous section described the arguments in the VLOOKUP function. The lookup_value in MATCH is exactly like the lookup_value in VLOOKUP—it is the item you are seeking. In the MATCH function, the lookup_array argument can be a contiguous range of cells, an array, or a reference to an array. The match_type argument can be -1, 0, or 1. This argument specifies how Excel matches lookup_value with values in lookup_array. If match_type is omitted, it is assumed to be 1.

If you want to find the largest value in the lookup_array that is less than or equal to the lookup_value, use 1 as the match_type. The lookup_array must be in ascending order. If you want to find the smallest value in the lookup_array that is greater than or equal to the lookup_value, use -1 as the match_type. The lookup_array must be in ascending order. If you want to find the first value in the lookup_array that is an exact match to the lookup_value, use 0 as the match_type. The lookup_array can be in any order. Match_type is like the range_lookup argument in `VLOOKUP`.

Besides the syntax differences, there are a few other differences between these functions you need to keep in mind:

- `VLOOKUP` returns a value from the list. `MATCH` returns the relative position or location of the value in the list.
- `VLOOKUP` is typically used on a list that has multiple columns. It looks up an item in one column and returns a corresponding item in another column. `MATCH` is used on a single column (or row) and will not work on multiple columns.
- `VLOOKUP` uses a range of cells as its list (the table_array argument). `MATCH` can use a range of cells or an array as its list (the lookup_array argument).

Consider the list and functions shown in Figure 23.19. The item being looked up is 8x CD Drive, as indicated in cell E1. `MATCH` returns the row this item is located in—row 10. `VLOOKUP` returns the corresponding value for this item—the price $6,752.48.

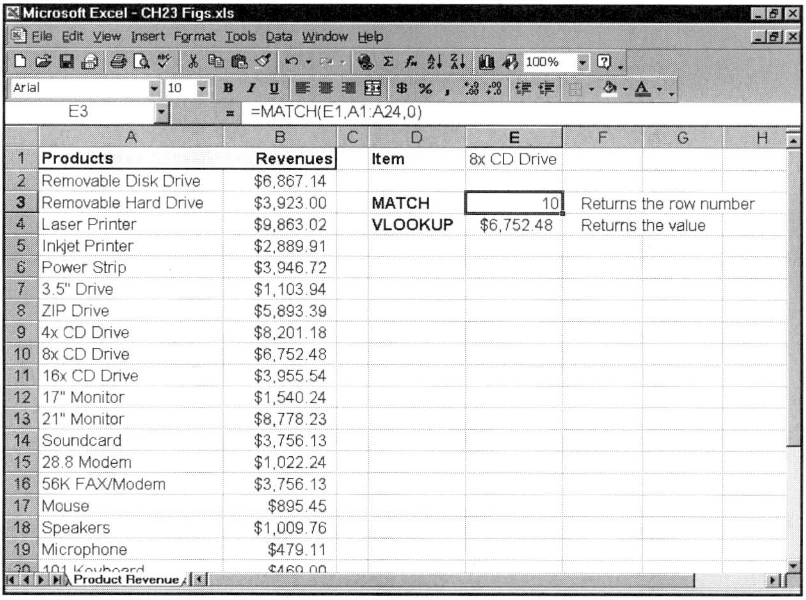

Microsoft Excel - CH23 Figs.xls

E3 = =MATCH(E1,A1:A24,0)

	A	B	C	D	E	F
1	**Products**	**Revenues**		**Item**	8x CD Drive	
2	Removable Disk Drive	$6,867.14				
3	Removable Hard Drive	$3,923.00		**MATCH**	10	Returns the row number
4	Laser Printer	$9,863.02		**VLOOKUP**	$6,752.48	Returns the value
5	Inkjet Printer	$2,889.91				
6	Power Strip	$3,946.72				
7	3.5" Drive	$1,103.94				
8	ZIP Drive	$5,893.39				
9	4x CD Drive	$8,201.18				
10	8x CD Drive	$6,752.48				
11	16x CD Drive	$3,955.54				
12	17" Monitor	$1,540.24				
13	21" Monitor	$8,778.23				
14	Soundcard	$3,756.13				
15	28.8 Modem	$1,022.24				
16	56K FAX/Modem	$3,756.13				
17	Mouse	$895.45				
18	Speakers	$1,009.76				
19	Microphone	$479.11				

Product Revenue

FIGURE 23.19
`MATCH` returns the position. `VLOOKUP` returns the associated value.

Cell E3 uses the `MATCH` function in this way:

```
=MATCH(E1,A1:A24,0)
```

Cell E4 uses `VLOOKUP` in this way:

```
=VLOOKUP(E1,A1:B24,2,FALSE)
```

In each case, the final argument (0 or `FALSE`) to the function specifies that it is to find in the list an exact match to the first argument. When an exact match is required, the list does not need to be sorted.

These two functions work well when you have unique values in the lookup column. Both these functions find just the first occurrence of the lookup_value. But what if it's a combination of two or more columns that, taken together, result in unique values? Figure 23.20 shows an example. A product along with its associated region makes these entries unique.

FIGURE 23.20
Individual cells are not unique and do not produce the correct results in the `VLOOKUP`.

A8 = ZIP Drive

	A	B	C	D	E	F	G	H
1	**Products**	**Region**	**Revenues**					
2	Removable Disk Drive	West	$6,867.14					
3	Removable Disk Drive	East	$5,893.39					
4	Laser Printer	East	$9,863.02					
5	Laser Printer	South	$2,889.91					
6	Laser Printer	West	$8,201.18					
7	3.5" Drive	South	$1,103.94					
8	ZIP Drive	West	$5,893.39					
9	ZIP Drive	East	$8,201.18					
10	8x CD Drive	East	$6,752.48					
11	8x CD Drive	North	$2,652.48					
12	16x CD Drive	East	$3,955.54					
13	16x CD Drive	North	$1,540.24					
14	21" Monitor	West	$8,778.23					
15	21" Monitor	North	$3,756.13					
16	28.8 Modem	North	$1,022.24					
17	56K FAX/Modem	South	$3,756.13					
18	56K FAX/Modem	West	$2,889.91					
19								

Product By Region

One possible solution is to concatenate—or merge—the values in A2:A18 with the values in B2:B18. To concatenate these columns, insert a new column in the list and use this formula:

```
=A2&" "&B2
```

This results in Removable Disk Drive West for the first row in the list.

The concatenation appears in column C of Figure 23.21. The concatenated values can now be used in the `VLOOKUP` formula.

To locate the revenue of an item, such as Zip Drive West, you can type the lookup_value directly in the formula, such as

```
=VLOOKUP("ZIP Drive West",C2:D18,2,FALSE)
```

But you'll provide greater flexibility in the formula if you designate a cell in the worksheet where you type a value from the first column and another empty cell where you type a value from the second column. In the example shown in Figure 23.21, cells G2 and G3 are used. The lookup_value then becomes the concatenation of these cells—G2&" "&G3. Setting up the worksheet this way enables us to type any product and any region. When the VLOOKUP function is entered in cell G4, it returns $5,893.39, the revenue for the designated lookup_value ZIP Drive West. The VLOOKUP function is

```
=VLOOKUP(G2&" "&G3,C2:D18,2,FALSE)
```

Formula being calculated

Result of the formula

G4 = =VLOOKUP(G2&" "&G3,C3:D19,2,FALSE)

	B	C	D	E	F	G	H
1	**Region**	Combined Columns	**Revenues**				
2	West	Removable Disk Drive West	$6,867.14		**Product**	ZIP Drive	
3	East	Removable Disk Drive East	$5,893.39		**Region**	West	
4	East	Laser Printer East	$9,863.02		**Revenue**	$5,893.39	
5	South	Laser Printer South	$2,889.91				
6	West	Laser Printer West	$8,201.18				
7	South	3.5" Drive South	$1,103.94				
8	West	ZIP Drive West	$5,893.39				
9	East	ZIP Drive East	$8,201.18				
10	East	8x CD Drive East	$6,752.48				
11	East	16x CD Drive East	$3,955.54				
12	North	16x CD Drive North	$1,540.24				
13	West	21" Monitor West	$8,778.23				
14	North	21" Monitor North	$3,756.13				
15	North	28.8 Modem North	$1,022.24				
16	South	56K FAX/Modem South	$3,756.13				
17	West	56K FAX/Modem West	$2,889.91				
18	East	Power Strip East	$479.11				
19							
20							

Product By Region

FIGURE 23.21
It's only by combining the Products with the Region that you get a unique value.

NOTE If you enter the formula =A2&B2 in cell C2 instead, the result is Removable Disk DriveWest. The VLOOKUP formula would then be =VLOOKUP(G2&G3,C2:D19,2,FALSE). The &" "& creates the space between Drive and West. If you don't particularly care how the results are displayed, you can leave off the literal space.

This solution can make the worksheet messy; you probably don't want to have to display the concatenated column in your worksheet. Although you can hide the column, an alternative solution uses the INDEX and MATCH functions and relies on a defined range name.

▶ **See** "Using Range Names in Formulas," **p. 639**

Suppose that you choose Insert, Name, Define and type ProductAndRegion in the Names in Workbook text box. Then, type the following into the Refers To text box:

```
=$A$2:$A$18 & $B$2:$B$18
```

This name performs the concatenation of columns A and B in the name, not in the worksheet, so as to keep the worksheet itself a little cleaner.

Remember, the MATCH function returns the position of the value in the list. The formula would result in 7, using the following syntax:

```
=MATCH(G2&G3,ProductAndRegion,0)
```

But we want to return the Revenue amount. This is where the INDEX function comes in. There are two syntax options with INDEX, the one needed here is

```
=INDEX(array,row_num,column_num)
```

where you can enter either the row_num or column_num argument. Since the MATCH function results in the row number, the row_num argument will be the MATCH function. All that's required is the array—the list cell references. Now, using the MATCH function in combination with the INDEX function

```
=INDEX(D2:D18,MATCH(G2&G3,ProductAndRegion,0))
```

returns the same value of $5,893.39. MATCH returns the row in the defined name that contains the combination of the Product and the Region, and then INDEX looks in that row in column D for the Revenues.

The concatenation shown in column C of Figure 23.21 need not exist on the worksheet at all. If column C is removed from the worksheet, the references in the preceding formula would have to change; references to column D become column C, references to column G become column F.

Why use INDEX and MATCH in this case instead of VLOOKUP? Because the columns are concatenated in the range name, you can't use the VLOOKUP function. VLOOKUP expects to locate the lookup_value in the first column of the designated range for the table_array argument. The first column in the list is just the products.

Use MATCH to find the correct row number, and use INDEX to return the corresponding value.

Using *INDEX* in Array Formulas

Both OFFSET and INDEX return a value in a range. The main difference between the two functions is that you normally use OFFSET to refer to a range that's removed from OFFSET's own range argument (see the example in the next section). In contrast, you use INDEX to refer to its own range argument. Both functions can return an array of values when you use them in array formulas.

INDEX becomes particularly useful when you use it with an array that's not visible on the worksheet. Suppose that the range A2:A100 contains the names of products, and that B2:B100 contains the revenue from each product. You update the revenue figures monthly, and would like cell D1 to contain the name of the product that has the greatest revenue. In addition to the INDEX function, you'll also need to use the MATCH and MAX functions.

The INDEX function has two syntax options, one for arrays and one for references. The array syntax is

```
=INDEX(array,row_num,column_num)
```

Begin by creating range names for the cells containing the product names and revenue values, such as Products and Revenues. By doing this, you can move those ranges around on the worksheet if you want, without wreaking havoc on the formulas that refer to the ranges.

Then, enter this formula in the worksheet:

```
=INDEX(Products,MATCH(MAX(Revenues),Revenues,0))
```

The result is shown in Figure 23.22.

FIGURE 23.22
You can achieve the same result with a data filter, but it does not recalculate automatically.

Microsoft Excel - Functions.xls

E3 =INDEX(Products,MATCH(MAX(Revenues),Revenues,0))

	A	B	C	D	E
1	Products	Revenues			
2	Removable Disk Drive	$6,867.14			
3	Removable Hard Drive	$3,923.00		Maximum revenue is from:	Laser Printer
4	Laser Printer	$9,863.02			
5	Inkjet Printer	$2,889.91			
6	Power Strip	$3,946.72			
7	3.5" Drive	$1,103.94			
8	ZIP Drive	$5,893.39			
9	4x CD Drive	$8,201.18			
10	8x CD Drive	$6,752.48			
11	16x CD Drive	$3,955.54			
12	17" Monitor	$1,540.24			
13	21" Monitor	$8,778.23			
14	Soundcard	$3,756.13			
15	28.8 Modem	$1,022.24			
16	56K FAX/Modem	$3,756.13			
17	Mouse	$895.45			
18	Speakers	$1,009.76			

Product Revenue

Ready NUM

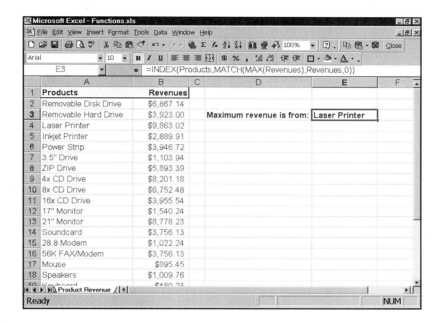

Because the formula occupies a single cell, and because the functions it uses expect to receive arrays as arguments, it's not necessary to array-enter the formula (Ctrl + Shift + Enter).

Work from the inside out to understand complex formulas that use nested functions. The `MAX` function returns the largest value in a specified range. In our formula, `MAX(Revenues)` returns 9863.02, which is the largest value in the Revenues range.

The `MATCH` function returns the relative position of an item in an array. The function syntax is

```
MATCH(lookup_value,lookup_array,match_type)
```

In the example shown in Figure 23.22, the `MATCH(MAX(Revenues), Revenues,0)` portion of the formula finds the relative position of the first instance of 9863.02 (the result of the `MAX` function). The result is 3—the third row within Revenues that corresponds to 9863.02.

Be certain you understand that this is not necessarily the worksheet row that contains the value 9863.02; rather, it's the relative position of 9863.02 in the list that matches 9863.02. This means that the Products range and the Revenues range could start in different worksheet rows, and the formula would return the same result.

After the formula has arrived at the `MATCH` number (in this example, 3) for the Revenues row that contains the maximum revenue value, `INDEX` takes over. At this point, the formula evaluates to `INDEX(Products,3)`. This is the third row within the Products range, or the product Laser Printer.

If you change the values in the Revenues range (for example, if revenue numbers are updated monthly), the formula automatically recalculates to locate the product that now has the maximum Revenue value.

If you have a list from which you want to extract the name corresponding to the smallest value, use the `MIN` function instead of `MAX`.

Using *OFFSET* in Charts

A common complaint about Excel charts goes like this: "After I've charted a data series, I'd like it to update automatically when I place additional data in the worksheet (outside the data series defined for the chart). I wish I didn't have to re-create the chart or edit the data series when I add a new row of data to the charted range."

If you use some imagination along with the `OFFSET` function, you can arrange to have your chart update automatically as you add new data to the worksheet. Suppose that you've created a line chart of the values in cells B3:B10. When you select the data series in the chart, here's what appears in the Formula Bar:

```
=SERIES(,,Sheet1!$B$3:$B$10,1)
```

Notice that the `SERIES` formula uses cell references, and that they're absolute. Given that setup, there is no way that the chart can update when you add new data. What you need is a chart series reference that is sensitive to new data. The solution involves using named ranges in combination with the `OFFSET` and `COUNTA` functions.

`OFFSET` takes one range or cell as an argument, and returns another range or cell, offset from the first one. Its other arguments specify how far to offset from the first range and the dimensions of the result. The `OFFSET` syntax is

```
=OFFSET(reference,rows,cols,height,width)
```

For example, this formula:

```
=OFFSET($A$1,3,5,2,4)
```

would return the values from the range \$F\$4:\$I\$5. This range starts in cell F4 (three rows down, five columns right from the offset cell A1). You've asked that the values (starting with cell F4) two rows high and four columns wide be returned (the range \$F\$4:\$I\$5). Because the offset range contains more than one cell, the formula would be array-entered in a two-row by four-column range, to match the height and width portions of the formula.

Remember, to array-enter a formula, you press Ctrl+Shift+Enter. See Chapter 22 for more details on working with array formulas.

You can make the number of rows returned by OFFSET depend on the number of values in a range of cells. You do so by using the COUNTA function, which returns the number of cells in a range that are not empty—COUNTA counts text and numbers. Assuming that each cell in the range $B$3:$B$10 contains a value, and the rest of column B is empty, then this formula:

```
=COUNTA($B:$B)
```

returns 8. (Notice that its cell references do not use rows. This is how you refer to a complete column.) You must be certain not to have any column headings, labels, or formulas in the column you are using. So, this formula:


```
=OFFSET($A$1,3,5,COUNTA($B:$B),4)
```

returns the values in a range that starts three rows down, five columns right offset from cell A1. The range returns with as many rows as there are values in column B and four columns wide.

As you saw in Chapter 22, "Advanced Formulas," you can define names that refer to entire formulas. Suppose that your active sheet is Sheet1. You choose Insert, Name, Define and type Sheet1!DataToChart in the Names in Workbook text box. Then, type the following into the Refers To text box:

```
=OFFSET($A$1,0,0,COUNTA($B:$B),1)
```

Now, open your chart and choose Chart, Source Data. Replace this SERIES formula:

```
=SERIES(,,Sheet1!$B$3:$B$10,1)
```

with this one:

```
=SERIES(,,Sheet1!DataToChart,1)
```

Now, when you insert a new value in column B, the name DataToChart recalculates to account for the new count of values in column B. The chart reevaluates what DataToChart refers to, and automatically redraws the charted series.

NOTE Be sure you don't have any stray values, labels, or formulas in the column you're charting. If your intention is to chart B3:B10, but you have a column heading in B2, then COUNTA($B:$B) will return 9 instead of 8.

The only way around this is to change the function to COUNTA($B$3:$B$100). In this case, you limit the chart's refresh to the second cell reference you enter.

Using *COLUMN* or *ROW* to Extract Strings of Text

The COLUMN and ROW functions are also part of the LOOKUP category of functions. The COLUMN function returns the numerical column position of a cell reference. The ROW function returns the row number of a cell reference. For example, COLUMN(B4) returns two (because B is the second column in a worksheet) and ROW(B4) returns four. You can enter a range of cell references in these functions, such as ROW(B4:B10). The results depend on how you enter the formula. If you enter this formula in one cell, it displays the first number. If you array-enter this formula in multiple cells, you will see a series of numbers. For example, if you enter this formula in a cell:

```
=ROW(A1:A5)
```

you'll see the number 1 in that cell. But if you click in the Formula Bar and press F9, you'll see this:

```
={1;2;3;4;5}
```

Fine, but are there practical applications for using these functions? Yes, indeed. As you have probably surmised, these functions don't have much applicability when used by themselves; their power comes when used as part of a formula or in combination with other functions. Both `COLUMN` and `ROW` can be used in array formulas when you need to get a sequence of numbers.

Suppose that you have a list of people's names, such as those shown in Figure 23.23, and you want to extract their last names from that list. It might first occur to you to use this formula on the name George Washington:

```
=RIGHT(A1,LEN(A1)-FIND(" ",A1))
```

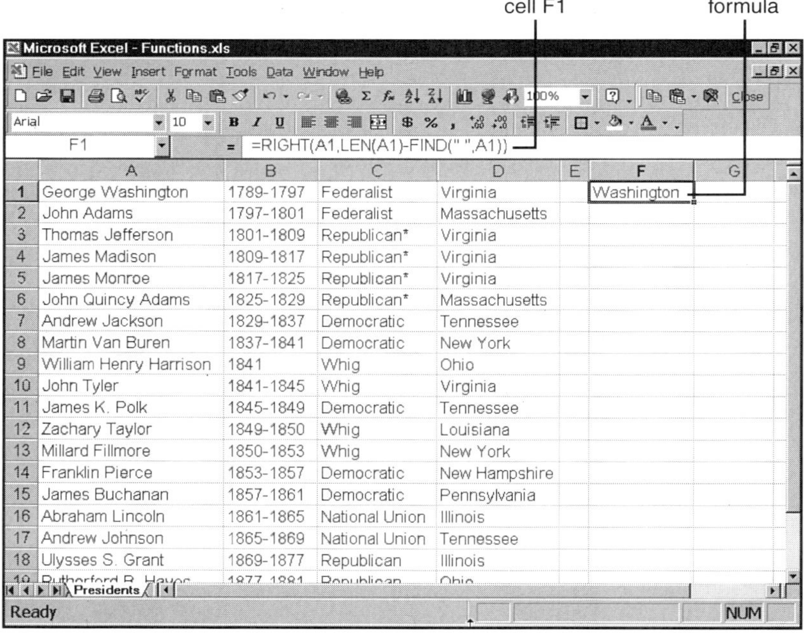

FIGURE 23.23
You can extract a group of characters from a text entry.

The `FIND` function locates the first space in the name—with George Washington that is the seventh character in the string. The `LEN` function determines the total string length. By subtracting the location of the space (7) from the length of the string (17 characters), you get 10.

The RIGHT function returns the number of characters you specify (in this example, 10) from the right end of the string of characters. The 10 rightmost characters for cell A3 returns the last name—Washington.

Perfect! So, you drag your formula from F1 down, and then in F6 you find that it returns not Adams but Quincy Adams. Unfortunately, the FIND function returns the first instance of a space, which comes between John and Quincy. What you need is a way to find the last instance of a space within a name. To do so, array-enter (Ctrl+Shift+Enter) this formula in F1:


```
=RIGHT(A1,MATCH(" ",MID(A1,LEN(A1)+1-ROW($A$1:$A$17),1),0)-1)
```

Again, working from the inside out, the ROW function returns the row number of a reference. So ROW($A$1:$A$17) returns this array, no matter where you use the function

```
{1;2;3;4;5;6;7;8;9;10;11;12;13;14;15;16;17}
```

Read on (it all becomes clear shortly). The length of the string in A1, plus 1, is 18. Subtract that from the row array numbers, so that this component of the formula

```
LEN(A1)+1-ROW($A$1:$A$17)
```

returns this array:

```
{17;16;15;14;13;12;11;10;9;8;7;6;5;4;3;2;1}
```

NOTE This component takes the length of the name plus 1 and creates a descending numerical array, up to 17 letters. So, for the name William Henry Harrison (which is 22 characters in length), 22 + 1 is 23. The resulting array will be

```
22,21,20,19,18,17,16,15,14,13,12,11,10,9,8,7,6
```

The assumption is that the longest last name is not greater than 17 characters. When you apply this formula to your own list, make sure you use the ROW range (to generate the sequence of numbers) that accounts for the longest possible entry.

To get to the last instance of a space in the name, this array of descending values is needed. Notice that the first value in the array is 17, the length of the string in A1. This is why the formula adds 1 to the length of that string; otherwise, the first value in the array would be 16.

Expanding one level further, this component:

```
MID(A1,LEN(A1)+1-ROW($A$1:$A$17),1)
```

returns this array:

```
{"n";"o";"t";"g";"n";"i";"h";"s";"a";"W";" ";"e";"g";"r";"o";"e";"G"}
```

which is, of course, the letters in George Washington in reverse order. Using the array of descending values, the MID function returns the 17th letter in the string, and then the 16th, followed by the 15th, and so on.

Now, use MATCH to locate the first instance of a space in the array of reversed characters. (You can't use FIND because it won't accept an array as an argument.) MATCH finds the final instance of a space in the original string. Here, for George Washington, that location is 11. To complete the formula, subtract 1 from 11 to eliminate the space itself, and return the 10 rightmost characters—Washington.

The result is shown in Figure 23.24.

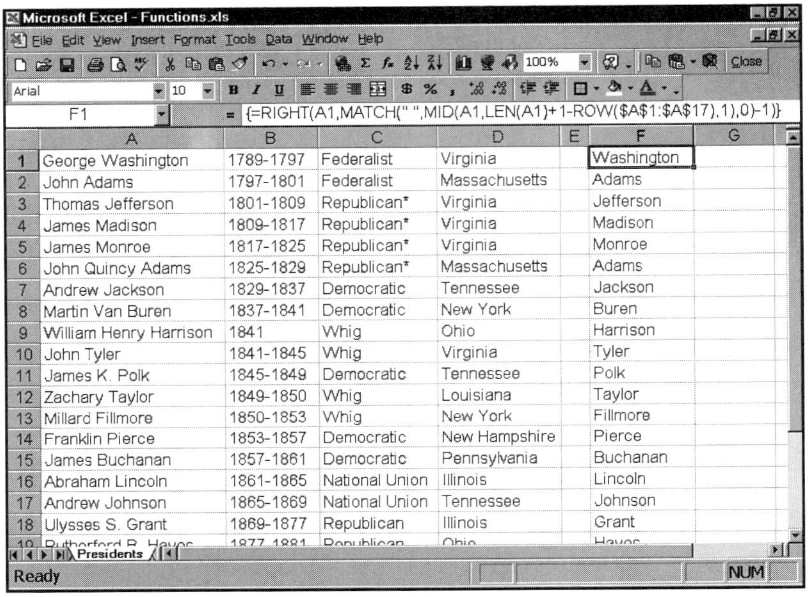

FIGURE 23.24
You can now sort the entire range on last name.

Microsoft Excel - Functions.xls

F1 = {=RIGHT(A1,MATCH(" ",MID(A1,LEN(A1)+1-ROW($A$1:$A$17),1),0)-1)}

	A	B	C	D	E	F	G
1	George Washington	1789-1797	Federalist	Virginia		Washington	
2	John Adams	1797-1801	Federalist	Massachusetts		Adams	
3	Thomas Jefferson	1801-1809	Republican*	Virginia		Jefferson	
4	James Madison	1809-1817	Republican*	Virginia		Madison	
5	James Monroe	1817-1825	Republican*	Virginia		Monroe	
6	John Quincy Adams	1825-1829	Republican*	Massachusetts		Adams	
7	Andrew Jackson	1829-1837	Democratic	Tennessee		Jackson	
8	Martin Van Buren	1837-1841	Democratic	New York		Buren	
9	William Henry Harrison	1841	Whig	Ohio		Harrison	
10	John Tyler	1841-1845	Whig	Virginia		Tyler	
11	James K. Polk	1845-1849	Democratic	Tennessee		Polk	
12	Zachary Taylor	1849-1850	Whig	Louisiana		Taylor	
13	Millard Fillmore	1850-1853	Whig	New York		Fillmore	
14	Franklin Pierce	1853-1857	Democratic	New Hampshire		Pierce	
15	James Buchanan	1857-1861	Democratic	Pennsylvania		Buchanan	
16	Abraham Lincoln	1861-1865	National Union	Illinois		Lincoln	
17	Andrew Johnson	1865-1869	National Union	Tennessee		Johnson	
18	Ulysses S. Grant	1869-1877	Republican	Illinois		Grant	

Presidents

Ready NUM

The same formula finds the final instance of a space in John Quincy Adams to return Adams. To keep the size of the arrays manageable, the formula uses `ROW($A$1:$A$17)`. If an array of 17 values isn't long enough to deal with the combined middle and last names, you could instead use `ROW($A$1:$A$50)`. But the next section discusses an even better approach.

▶ **See** "Exploring the Power of Array Formulas," **p. 661**

Using *INDIRECT* to Fine-Tune String Extractions

Normally, the `INDIRECT` function takes as its argument a cell that contains another reference. For example, if A1 contains C1 and C1 contains Washington, then `=INDIRECT(A1)` returns Washington. Note that A1 must contain a cell reference as text.

It is not immediately obvious why anyone would need to do this.

However, `INDIRECT` has a useful role to play in the problem of finding last names, detailed in the previous section. If you haven't read the previous sections, you need to do so in order to follow the discussion in this section. Referring to the list in Figure 23.24, suppose you entered

```
=INDIRECT("C1")
```

In that case, INDIRECT would still return the value it finds in cell C1 (Federalist) because the cell reference is enclosed in quotes. So, INDIRECT can evaluate cell references given as text values. In order to return the row number, array-enter this formula (using Ctrl+Shift+Enter):

```
=ROW(INDIRECT("1:17"))
```

in a range consisting of one column and 17 rows (such as cells G1:G17). It returns 1, 2, 3, and so on, through 17. Assuming that George Washington is in cell A1, this array formula

```
=ROW(INDIRECT("1:" & LEN(A1)))
```

returns the same 17 values. You use the length of each name itself to create the array of descending values. So, the complete formula becomes

```
=RIGHT(A1,MATCH(" ",MID(A1,LEN(A1)+1-ROW(INDIRECT("1:"&LEN(A1))),1),0)-1)
```


Using INDIRECT with the length of the name ensures that you have an array large enough to get all the characters in each name—and no larger. Because the cell reference A1 is relative, when you copy the formula from F1 down to F42, the LEN(A1) within the INDIRECT function changes to use the length of the string in cells A2, A3, and so on.

Okay, now if you apply this formula to the name Martin Van Buren, you get Buren.

Your only recourse is to make sure that these types of names are entered as VanBuren, or to manually go back and type the result you want displayed.

Statistical Functions

Be careful when you use Excel's statistical functions to help make real-world decisions. Because Excel's help documentation is not intended as a textbook, you can't expect much guidance there. Without the appropriate theoretical background or the advice of a statistician, it's all too easy to go wrong.

Nothing against Excel's statistical functions: Within the generous limits to arithmetic accuracy that are imposed by a PC's chip architecture, these functions are quite accurate. The problem is in knowing when it's appropriate to use one of the functions and when it's not.

For example, Excel's help documentation for *t-Tests* says that you use them to test whether the average values of two groups are different. It does not tell you that it is misleading to use three t-Tests to analyze the differences in the average values of three or more groups. The probabilities returned by the three t-Tests would be inaccurate, because you would have violated one of the assumptions underlying the mathematics of the t-Test. With three or more groups, you should use analysis of variance (ANOVA).

Similarly, Excel's trendlines and the worksheet functions LINEST and TREND make it easy to force a regression equation's constant (the intercept) to zero. When they notice that doing so normally increases the regression's R^2, users often choose that option. They do not realize that so doing changes the parameters of the sums of squares, which are no longer centered on the mean of the y-values. And then they're in trouble. If you're going to consult a statistician for guidance, choose a good one. Excel's Analysis ToolPak contains a tool named t-Test: Two Samples Assuming Unequal Variances. On the Internet, I have found people who are actually teaching statistics at universities but who do not realize that this tool adjusts the t-Test's degrees of freedom. Nor do they realize that it is supposed to do so. This information is usually discussed toward the end of an introductory course in inferential statistics, and yet two assistant professors of statistics did not know it. Be careful whom you listen to, and question authority.

This section briefly discusses a few statistical functions that you may already be using: `AVERAGE`, `COUNT`, and `COUNTA`. You also find out how to create normal curves on charts as a point of comparison for your data using the `NORMDIST` and `FREQUENCY` functions. Additionally, you will learn how to tell what kind of trendline you should use on your charts and use the `LINEST` and `FDIST` functions.

Using the *AVERAGE* Function

The `AVERAGE` function calculates the *arithmetic mean* of a list of numbers. For example, if the numbers being averaged are 10, 15, 20, and 35, Excel adds the numbers (totaling 80) and divides by the number of numbers (4) to derive an average, or mean, of 20.

There can be up to 30 arguments in the `AVERAGE` function, and the arguments can be listed in any order. If the term *argument* is unfamiliar to you, see the section titled "Understanding and Planning—Two Essential Precursors to Using Excel Functions," earlier in this chapter.

The syntax for `AVERAGE` is

```
=AVERAGE(argument,argument,…)
```

If a cell is empty, it is not included in the average. However, if a cell contains a zero, it is averaged in with the other values in the calculation.

In the worksheet displayed in Figure 23.25, the average number of hits for the Company Softball team needs to be calculated.

FIGURE 23.25
To determine the average number of hits for the team, you need to average both columns of numbers.

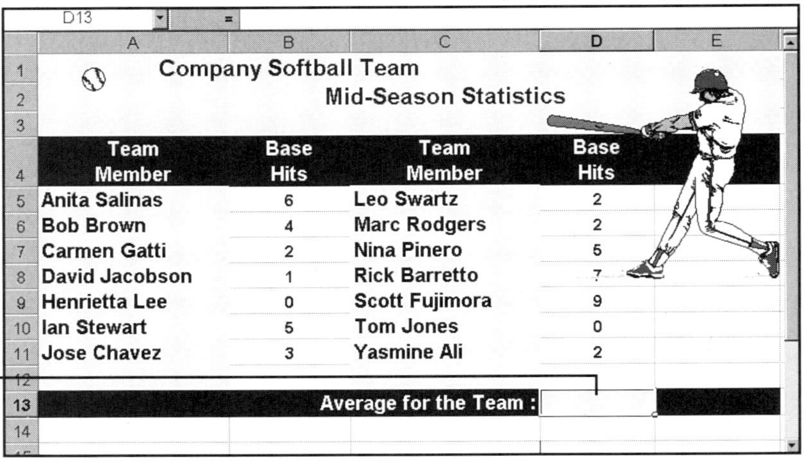

D13 =

	A	B	C	D	E
1	Company Softball Team				
2			Mid-Season Statistics		
3					
4	Team Member	Base Hits	Team Member	Base Hits	
5	Anita Salinas	6	Leo Swartz	2	
6	Bob Brown	4	Marc Rodgers	2	
7	Carmen Gatti	2	Nina Pinero	5	
8	David Jacobson	1	Rick Barretto	7	
9	Henrietta Lee	0	Scott Fujimora	9	
10	Ian Stewart	5	Tom Jones	0	
11	Jose Chavez	3	Yasmine Ali	2	
12					
13			Average for the Team :		
14					

The average will be displayed here.

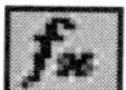

To calculate the average number of hits so far this season, begin the calculation by selecting the cell in which you want the answer to appear and then click the Paste Function button. Choose the AVERAGE function from either the Most Recently Used category or the Statistical category. Then select OK to display the Formula Palette (see Figure 23.26).

FIGURE 23.26
The Formula Palette for the AVERAGE function is shown here.

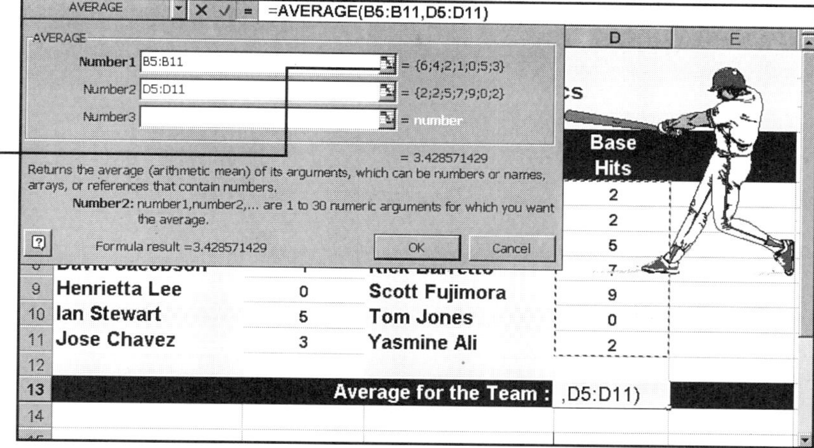

Select the cells for the first column of numbers by highlighting the cells directly in the worksheet. Press the Tab key or click with your mouse to select the second argument box and choose the second group of cells in the worksheet. Choose OK to complete the function.

Using *COUNT* and *COUNTA* Functions

Use the *COUNT* and *COUNTA* functions to count the number of entries in a group of cells. The COUNT function counts numbers and dates; COUNTA counts all nonblank cells including numbers, dates, text, and error values. There can be up to 30 arguments in either function, and the arguments can be listed in any order.

The syntax for COUNT is

```
=COUNT(argument,argument,...)
```

The syntax for COUNTA is

```
=COUNTA(argument,argument,...)
```

Neither COUNT nor COUNTA includes blank cells in their calculations. The COUNT function can usually be found in the Most Recently Used and Statistical categories. The COUNTA function is located in the Statistical category.

In Figure 23.27, the number of orders received so far this month is 24, as displayed in cell C2. The COUNTA function is using the range name Orders_Reveived, which are the cells in the Quantity column.

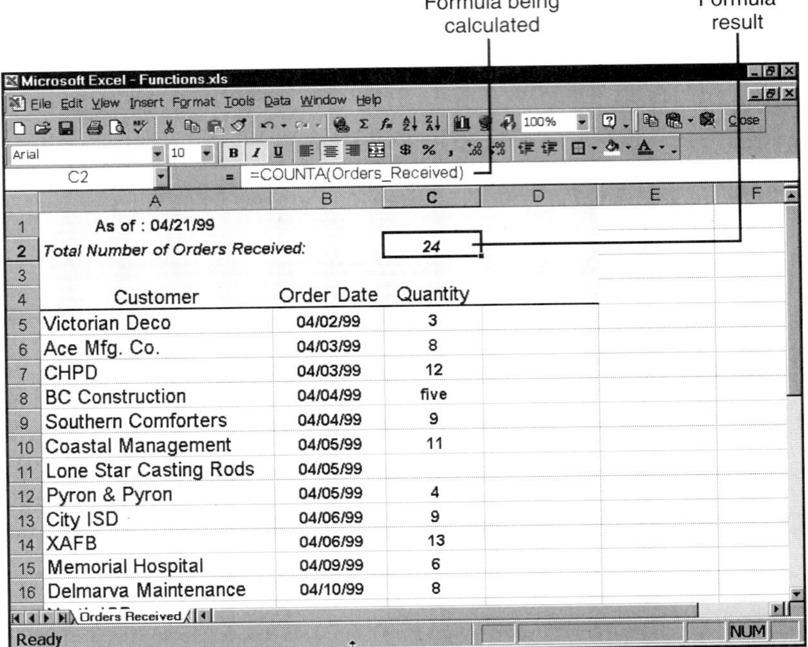

FIGURE 23.27
To determine the number of orders received, count the entries.

Because COUNTA counts all nonblank cells, whether the entry is a number or text, it will include the order from BC Construction in row 8. However, because there isn't a quantity listed for Lone Star Casting Rods, in row 11, that order is skipped.

▶ **See** "Using Range Names in Formulas," **p. 639**

There is also a COUNTIF function that can be used to count only those cells that match a criterion you specify.

Charting Normal Curves Using *NORMDIST* and *FREQUENCY*

There are many opportunities in business to employ statistics, especially in the areas of process control and quality improvement. Projects often need to know whether a set of observations at least roughly follows a normal distribution—that is, the famous bell curve. There are various statistical tests that return a probability that a set of numbers is normally distributed. Excel's CHIDIST function is useful in this context, if all you need is the numeric probability.

But nothing beats a visual analysis. It's usually informative to look at a chart that overlays actual observations onto a normal distribution curve. This section describes one way to do that.

Suppose that your observations are in A3:B22 (see Figure 23.28).

To assist in generating the values necessary to plot a normal distribution curve, it's necessary to calculate the average and standard deviation of the observed values. The *average*, or *mean*, is the center point of the observed values, and is calculated by taking the sum of the observed values and dividing by the number of the observed values. Use the AVERAGE function to calculate the average. The *standard deviation* tells how closely the values are clustered around the average. In general, the lower the standard deviation the closer the observations are to the average. The larger the standard deviation, the more spread out the observations are from the average. Use the STDDEV function to calculate the standard deviation.

The average and standard deviation calculations for the set of observations shown in Figure 23.28 have been derived by using these formulas:

```
=AVERAGE(B3:B22)
=STDDEV(B3:B22)
```

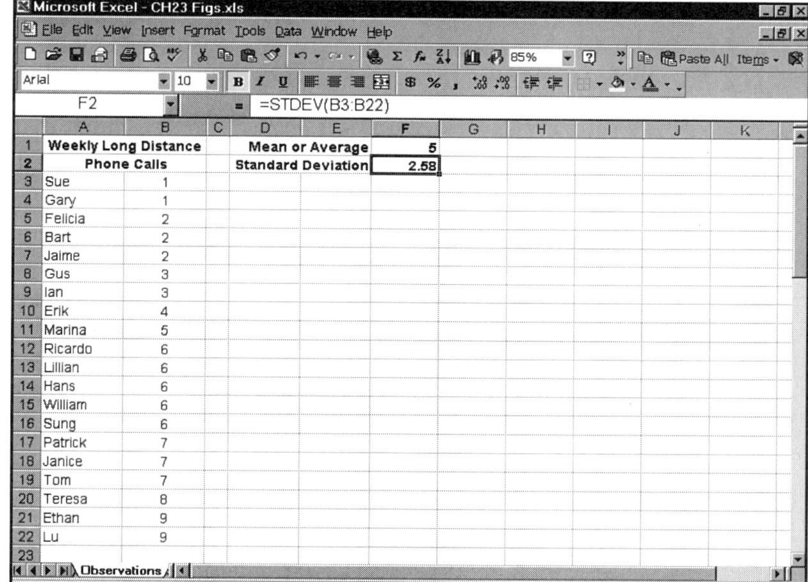

FIGURE 23.28
The larger the number of observations, the more precise the average and standard deviation.

In order to plot the observations overlaid with a normal distribution curve, we need to calculate several things: the x-values, the frequency, and the normal distribution.

Calculating the X-Values The *x-values* will be plotted along the horizontal axis of the chart. Creating these is a two-step process.

First, you need to generate the standard deviation interval points. In statistics, the Empirical Rules specifically apply to bell-shaped curves. One of the rules states that 99.7% of the observations lie within three standard deviations of the average. Therefore, on each side of the average, there will be observations that spread from –3 to +3 standard deviations. In order to produce a relatively smooth curve, the interval points need to be added to the worksheet.

To create these intervals, select a cell and enter the value –3. Then with the cell selected, choose Edit, Fill, Series. In the Series dialog box, choose Series in Columns, Type Linear, and set Stop Value to 3. Set Step Value to .1—this creates 61 values (-3,-2.9,-2.8, and so on). If you choose a Step Value of .01, you'll get a smoother curve, but you're also dealing with 601 values. In Figure 23.29, the intervals have been added in column D to cells D6:D66.

Next, the actual x-values need to be calculated. This adjusts the interval points in cells D6:D66 to have the average (mean) and standard deviation of your actual observations, rather than the generic standard-deviation interval points. The x-values for the normal distribution chart are always calculated by using the formula: x = average + (a particular deviation interval point * standard deviation).

In Figure 23.29, the formula

```
=$G$1+(D6*$G$2)
```

has been added to cell E6 and copied down as far down as the interval points extend. Remember, you can use the F4 key to change a relative cell reference to an absolute cell reference.

▶ **See** "Using Absolute Cell References in Formulas," **p. 634**

Calculating the Frequency The purpose of the `FREQUENCY` function is to count how often each value occurs within a range of values. For example, use `FREQUENCY` to count the number of test scores that fall within ranges of scores. `FREQUENCY` returns a vertical array of numbers. Because it returns an array, it must be entered as an array formula by using Ctrl+Shift+Enter.

The `FREQUENCY` function syntax contains two arguments—those that Excel calls its data array and its bins array:

```
=FREQUENCY(data_array,bins_array)
```

The data_array is the array of values for which you want to count frequencies (the observations). The bin_array is an array of intervals into which you want to group the values in the data_array (the x-values).

For the worksheet example shown in Figure 23.29, the cells F6:F66 were selected, and this formula was array-entered:

```
=FREQUENCY(B3:B22,E6:E66)
```

TIP You can use the same range for `FREQUENCY`'s data_array and its bins_array. If you do so, you obtain a count of each unique value in that range.

The frequency in column F indicates that exactly two of the values in the data array are 1. In the bins_array (x-values) there are two consecutive values—.88 and 1.14. In this example, the function returns the number 2 to cell F21. There are two values at the row in the bin_array that contain 1.14, which indicates there are two values in the observations that fall between .88 and 1.14 (see Figure 23.29).

Calculating the Normal Distribution The `NORMDIST` statistical function returns the height of the normal curve—a chart's *y-values*—at each of the values in a chart's x-values. The syntax for the `NORMDIST` function is

```
=NORMDIST(x,mean,standard_dev,cumulative)
```

where x is the x-value for which you want the distribution, mean is the average, standard_dev is the standard deviation, and cumulative is the True/False value that determines the form of the function. If cumulative is `TRUE`, `NORMDIST` returns the cumulative distribution function. If cumulative is `FALSE`, it returns a point distribution (sometimes called probability mass) function.

For the worksheet example shown in Figure 23.29, the formula

```
=NORMDIST(E6,$G$1,$G$2,FALSE)
```

has been added to cell G6 and copied down as far down as the frequency and interval points extend. Use F4 to change the relative cell reference to absolute cell reference.

There are two reasons to use the `NORMDIST` function instead of the simpler `NORMSDIST` function:

- You are not dealing with standard z scores for the x-values.
- `NORMSDIST` does not provide the choice between the cumulative distribution and point distribution (using `FALSE` as `NORMDIST`'s fourth argument gives the point estimate).

FIGURE 23.29
Cell F21 contains the number of values in B3:B22 that are between the values in E20:E21.

Microsoft Excel - CH23 Figs.xls

F21 = {=FREQUENCY(B3:B22,E6:E66)}

	A	B	C	D	E	F	G
1	**Weekly Long Distance**				**Mean or Average**		**5**
2	**Phone Calls**				**Standard Deviation**		**2.58**
3	Sue	1					
4	Gary	1		Interval	X-axis	Frequency	Normal
5	Felicia	2		points	values		distribution
6	Bart	2		-3	-2.73	0	0.00172098
7	Jaime	2		-2.9	-2.47	0	0.0023115
8	Gus	3		-2.8	-2.21	0	0.00307374
9	Ian	3		-2.7	-1.95	0	0.00404667
10	Erik	4		-2.6	-1.70	0	0.00527456
11	Marina	5		-2.5	-1.44	0	0.00680662
12	Ricardo	6		-2.4	-1.18	0	0.00869628
13	Lillian	6		-2.3	-0.92	0	0.011
14	Hans	6		-2.2	-0.67	0	0.01377555
15	William	6		-2.1	-0.41	0	0.01707978
16	Sung	6		-2	-0.15	0	0.02096586
17	Patrick	7		-1.9	0.11	0	0.02548004
18	Janice	7		-1.8	0.36	0	0.03065805
19	Tom	7		-1.7	0.62	0	0.03652129
20	Teresa	8		-1.6	0.88	0	0.04307295
21	Ethan	9		-1.5	1.14	2	0.05029448
22	Lu	9		-1.4	1.39	0	0.05814241
23				-1.3	1.65	0	0.06654612

Observations

Creating the Normal Distribution Chart All that's left is to create the chart. Select the columns containing the x-value, frequency, and normal distribution data. and use the Chart Wizard to create a combination chart. In the Chart Wizard's first step, click the Custom Types tab, and choose Line–Column on the 2 Axes in the Chart Type list box.

In the wizard's second step, click the Series tab. You should see the worksheet name and cell references in the Values edit box. By default, Excel is treating all three ranges as data series. However, the x-values are the x-axis labels and need to be moved. To do this, locate the x-values series and drag across the full reference in the Values box to highlight it. Choose Edit, Copy from the Menu Bar. Click in the Category (X) Axis Labels edit box, and choose Edit, Paste. Click the Remove button to remove that range as a data series. Click Next to proceed with the Chart Wizard.

In the wizard's third and fourth steps, choose any options that you want. Because there are only two data series (frequency and normal distribution), and because they are formatted differently, it usually makes sense to clear the Show Legend check box on the Legend tab and add these labels to the chart on the Titles tab. Frequency should be placed on the Value axis and Normal Distribution on the Second Value axis (if you forgot, select the Line—Column on 2 Axis chart type; you can add it on the Axis tab of the third step in the wizard).

When the wizard has created the chart, you have your actual counts overlaid on a normal curve. The top chart in Figure 23.30 shows this chart. It's a matter of personal preference, but you might consider making these format changes:

- Select the line series that shows the normal curve. Choose Format, Selected Data Series to set its Patterns as Line Automatic and Marker to None. Also, on the Patterns tab, set the Line, Weight to the thickest line.
- Select the plot area and choose Format, Selected Plot Area to set its Patterns as Border, Automatic and Area to None.
- Select the horizontal category axis. Choose Format, Selected Axis to set its Patterns for Major Tick Mark Type and Tick Mark Labels to None.
- Select each visible column in turn (you'll need two single-clicks, no double-clicking, to select a specific column). Choose Format, Selected Data Point and set its Data Label to Show Value. The reason you have to select them individually is that many of the frequency values are zero and you don't want those to appear, just the labels for the columns.

The bottom chart in Figure 23.30 shows the same chart with the suggested formats outlined previously.

Using *LINEST* and *FDIST* to Evaluate Polynomial Trendlines

When you want to determine how strong the relationship is between two items, you can plot those items on an XY (Scatter) chart and add a trendline. The items being plotted are called *variables*. The item on the x-axis is called the *independent variable* and the item on the y-axis is called the *dependent variable*. This type of comparison is known as *linear regression*. There are several different types of trendlines you can add in Excel, including Linear, Polynomial, and Moving Average.

▶ **See** "XY (Scatter) Charts," **p. 818**

▶ **See** "Using Trendlines in Charts," to learn more about the other types of trendlines, **p. 833**

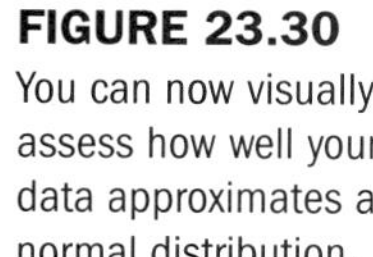

FIGURE 23.30
You can now visually assess how well your data approximates a normal distribution.

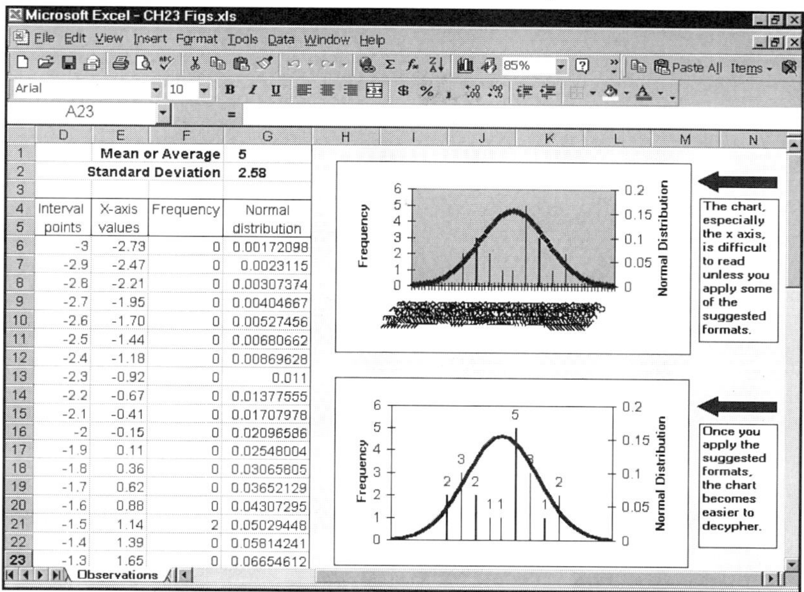

NOTE You can also apply trendlines to several other chart types, including area, bar, column, line, stock, and bubble. However, the chart must be unstacked and two-dimensional.

Generally, a *linear trendline* is used with simple data sets, where the pattern of the data points resembles a line. A linear trendline usually shows that something is increasing or decreasing at a steady rate. A *polynomial trendline* is a curved line that is used when data fluctuates. Fluctuations in the data or bends (hills and valleys) are characteristic of polynomial trendlines.

One indication of how closely your actual observed data (plotted points in the scatter diagram) and the predicted data (points on the trendline) match is through the R^2 value. R is the *correlation coefficient*, the measure of strength between two variables. However, just because two variables appear to have a strong relationship doesn't mean they actually do. For example, suppose we calculate the correlation coefficient between the price of a McDonald's hamburger and the average family size in the United States, using data over the past 25 years and discover a strong negative correlation. That is, over time, the price of a hamburger has increased and the family size has decreased. This finding does not mean that family size and the price of hamburgers are related. The R^2 value (called the *coefficient of multiple determination for polynomial trendlines*) factors in possible errors. The R^2 value always lies between 0 and +1. Typically the higher the value of R^2, the better the regression model; a greater portion of the total errors is explained by the included independent variable and a smaller portion of errors is attributed to other variables and randomness.

NOTE If you're a statistician, be advised that the R^2 value you display with a trendline is not an adjusted R^2 value.

Sometimes computer programs make things too easy for their users' own good. An example in Excel is a *polynomial trendline* in a chart.

The worksheet in Figure 23.31 lists the maintenance track record for a fleet of medium-sized delivery vans. Every time a van comes in for any kind of maintenance or check, that visit is recorded. The highest number of separate repair visits is 20. Therefore, the frequency of repairs ranges from 1 to 20. The average MPG for all the vans at each repair frequency is calculated and placed in an adjacent column. To see the visual relationship between the frequency of repairs (the independent variable) and the average MPGs (the dependent variable), an XY chart has been created. To see whether there is a relationship between the two variables, a linear trendline is added by selecting the chart and choosing Chart, Add Trendline. The R^2 value on the chart is displayed by selecting the Display R-Squared Value on Chart option in the Add Trendline dialog box. The value in this example is 0.3607. The closer R^2 is to 1, the better the relationship between the variables. This R^2 value isn't very high.

FIGURE 23.31

The R^2 value is in the upper-right corner of the chart.

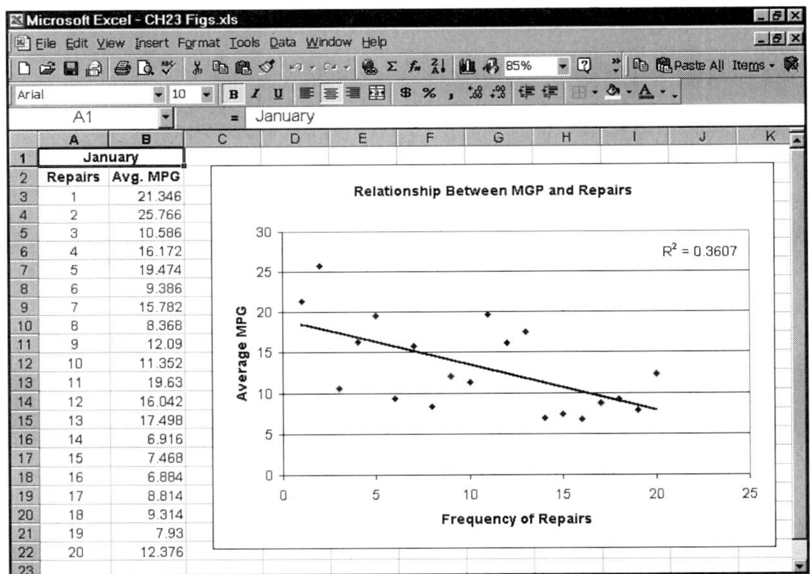

January	
Repairs	Avg. MPG
1	21.346
2	25.766
3	10.586
4	16.172
5	19.474
6	9.386
7	15.782
8	8.368
9	12.09
10	11.352
11	19.63
12	16.042
13	17.498
14	6.916
15	7.468
16	6.884
17	8.814
18	9.314
19	7.93
20	12.376

As stated earlier, polynomial trendlines are used when the data fluctuates. Typically, other factors (other variables) besides the dependent variable (x-values, repair frequency in this example) impact the independent variable (y-values, average MPG in this example). You can set the order to be used with the polynomial trendline to account for these other variables. The order can range from 2 to 6. So, when you increase the order of the trendline, you are adding another variable into the equation. So, an order of 4 has four dependent variables—the one plotted plus three more that are factored in.

Figure 23.32 shows the impact of different order settings on a polynomial trendline for the data shown in Figure 23.31. As you increase the order, the R^2 increases. In Figure 23.32, it has increased from 0.3607 to 0.5028, when the order is 4.

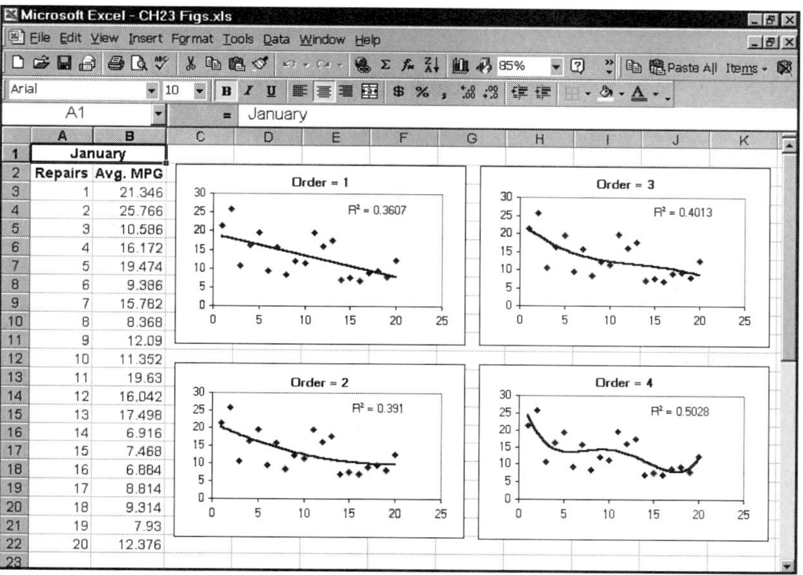

FIGURE 23.32
As you increase the order of the polynomial trendline, the R^2 almost always increases.

So, when you increase the order of a trendline, you are increasing the exponent of the charted x-values. A *linear trendline* shows the best-fit regression line of the y-values (the average MPG) against the x-values (the frequency of repairs).

A *second-order polynomial trendline* regresses the y-values against the combination of the x-values and the square of the x-values; a *third-order polynomial trendline* regresses the y-values against the combination of x-values, the square of the x-values, and the cube of the x-values; a *fourth-order trendline* regresses the y-values against the combination of the x-values, and the x-values squared, and cubed, and raised to the fourth power. You can remind yourself of this by using the trendline option that shows the equation on the chart.

But increasing the order to raise the R^2 of a trendline has other implications.

Understanding R^2 and Best Fit The larger an R^2 value, the stronger the relationship between the y-values and the x-values. In fact, you interpret an R^2 as the proportion of variance in the y-values that can be predicted from the x-values. So, in the data used to find a correlation between frequency of repairs and average MPG, an R^2 of 0.3607 means that 36.07% of the variance or fluctuation in average MPG can be predicted from the frequency of repairs—the linear trendline. The remaining 63.93% variance is attributed to other variables, not related to repairs. In this example, that might be road and weather driving conditions, octane level in the gasoline used, and so forth.

While all of this is true, it is also extremely misleading, and the reason is found in the phrase "best fit." All Excel trendlines, except Moving Average, are regression lines, and regression lines are lines of best fit. The math that underlies regression analysis has one goal: to minimize the squared differences between the actual y-values (plotted by the XY data points) and the predicted y-values (plotted on the trendline). Minimizing the squared differences (called the *least squares method* in statistics) generates the line that best fits the data.

In deriving the equation that provides this best fit, regression analysis relies heavily on the correlations among the individual x-variables and y-variables. It treats these correlations as though they were error-free, but in practice they never are. There is always some amount of sampling and measurement error due to chance circumstances. Because regression analysis seeks the best fit, it relentlessly fits not only the accurate part of the observations but their inaccurate part as well. This biases R^2 upward.

Choosing the Order of the Polynomial Trendline Every time you add another variable into the equation (which is what you do when you increase the order of the trendline), you add another opportunity for the equation to capitalize on chance and spuriously inflate the R^2 value.

There are various ways to avoid this situation. The best is always to have a good theoretical reason to increase the order of the trendline. But in the process of theory-development, which is what you're doing when you first investigate the relationship between your independent (repair frequency) and dependent (average MPG) variables, you don't yet have a mature theory to rely upon. You don't really know whether there is a correlation between these variables and it's premature to arbitrarily increase the order.

Another way to avoid inflating the R^2 value is to substantially increase the number of observations. Often, though, this is either too expensive or simply impossible.

A reasonable solution (not as good as basing your decision on your theory or increasing sample size, but still reasonable) is to run a statistical test on the change that occurs in R^2 as you increase the order of the polynomial trendline. Before performing that test (discussed in the next section), you need to perform a few simple calculations.

Excel's `LINEST` worksheet function is both a basic and powerful means of analyzing regression. The syntax for the `LINEST` functions is

```
=LINEST(known_y's,known_x's,const,stats)
```

where the known y- and x-values are the first two arguments. The `const` argument indicates whether the slope (b) of the line is calculated normally (that is, whether to force the constant b in line formula y=mx+b to be equal to 0). `const` is an optional argument; if omitted, it is assumed to be `TRUE`. If `const` is `FALSE`, b is set equal to 0 and the m-values are adjusted to fit the line formula y = mx. The `stats` argument indicates whether additional regression statistics will be returned as a result of the function. If `stats` is `TRUE`, `LINEST` returns the additional regression statistics. If `stats` is `FALSE` or omitted, `LINEST` returns only the m-coefficients and the slope (b).

Because this function returns an array of values, it must be entered as an array formula by using Ctrl+Shift+Enter.

When you set its fourth argument to `TRUE` and array-enter it in a range of cells one column wide and five rows down, it returns several statistics that are fundamental to evaluating the regression. In particular, the third row of the selected array contains the R^2 value (see Figure 23.33).

Using the data shown in Figure 23.32, array-entering this formula in the one column by five rows area:

```
=LINEST(B3:B22,A3:A23^{1,2,3,4},,TRUE)
```

returns the R^2 for the regression of the values in B3:B22 on the values in A3:A22 raised to the 1st, 2nd, 3rd, and 4th powers—the same R^2 displayed in the chart for the fourth order.

And this formula:

```
=LINEST(B3:B22,A3:A22^{1,2,3},,TRUE
```

returns the R^2 for B3:B22 on A3:A22 raised to the 1st, 2nd, and 3rd powers—the same R^2 displayed in the chart for the 3rd order. You would repeat that for each order you want to investigate.

After obtaining R^2 for each of the four trendlines, calculate the difference from one to the next by simple subtraction. By subtracting the third-order R^2 from the fourth-order R^2, you obtain the change in R^2 attributable to changing the trendline from a third-order polynomial to a fourth-order polynomial (displayed in cell E13).

FIGURE 23.33
By calculating the R^2 values using `LINEST`, you don't have to duplicate the charts, as shown in Figure 23.32.

Microsoft Excel - CH23 Figs.xls

F3 = {=LINEST(B3:B22,A3:A22,,TRUE)}

	A	B	C	D	E	F	G
1	January				LINEST Stats	-0.55669624	
2	Repairs	Avg. MPG				0.174693202	
3	1	21.346				0.360684401	← R^2 value for the linear regression line (order = 1)
4	2	25.766				10.15510843	
5	3	10.586				206.0906184	
6	4	16.172					
7	5	19.474					
8	6	9.386	Order	R^2 value	Change in R^2		
9	7	15.782					
10	8	8.368	1	0.3606	0.3606		
11	9	12.09	2	0.391	0.0304		
12	10	11.352	3	0.4013	0.0103		
13	11	19.63	4	0.5028	0.1015		
14	12	16.042					
15	13	17.498					
16	14	6.916					
17	15	7.468					
18	16	6.884					
19	17	8.814					

Change Tests

The change in R^2 for the first-order, or linear, trendline is the same as its R^2. In other words, a *zero-order* polynomial trendline would predict no values, and would therefore have an R^2 of zero; the first-order R^2 minus 0 equals the first-order R^2 (displayed in cell E10).

Creating the Statistical Test Before you can set up the statistical test, you need to determine the R^2 values and the change in R^2 (described in the previous section). If you haven't read the previous sections, it would be best if you do so before continuing with this section. Referring to Figure 23.33, the F ratios in column D were obtained by using the `LINEST` function to generate the stats for the different polynomials. For example, the formula for the fourth-order polynomial was

```
=LINEST(B3:B22,A3:A22^{1,2,3,4},,TRUE)
```

Column E contains the Change in R^2 from one polynomial to the next, obtained by taking the R^2 value from the larger polynomial and subtracting the R^2 value from the smaller polynomial.

For every independent variable noted on the x-axis, there is a predicted y-value (on the trendline) and an actual y-value (plotted by the data point marker). As noted earlier, R^2 is the proportion of predictable variance in the y-values that can be predicted from the x-values. In other words, R^2 tells you how much of the difference between the predicted and actual y-values can reasonably be attributed to the x-values. The remaining amount is attributed to other, undefined independent variables.

So, in the data used to find a correlation between frequency of repairs and average MPG, an R^2 of 0.3607 means that 36.07% of the variance from the dependent variable (the y-values for average MPG) can be predicted from the independent variable (the x-values for frequency of repairs). Because 1 (100%) is the highest value possible for R^2, $1-R^2$ is the proportion of unpredictable variance attributed to other independent variables. Therefore, 1 minus 0.3607 equals 0.6393 or 63.93% is the proportion of unpredictable variance that is attributed to other variables not related to repairs.

The next step is to create a statistical text, called the *F distribution* or *F test,* which evaluates ratios of the predictable and unpredictable variances and returns an associated probability. The smaller this probability, the more likely that the relationship between the two variances will stand up if you repeat the experiment. Put another way, the smaller this probability, the more likely that the change in R^2 is due more to something real than to chance.

In an F test you divide the proportion of predictable variance and the proportion of unpredictable variance by the degrees of freedom. The *degrees of freedom* is defined as the number of observations that can be chosen freely.

When you divide each proportion by the appropriate degrees of freedom, you obtain an expression of the predictable and the unpredictable variance. The ***predictable*** variance is the variance due to regression, sometimes called the ***mean square regression*** (MSR). The ***unpredictable*** variance is the residual variance, sometimes called the ***mean square error*** (MSE). Then, by taking the ratio of the predictable to the unpredictable variance (MSR/MSE), you can judge how large the predictable variance is relative to the unpredictable variance. This is called the *F ratio*.

So the F ratio is = MSR/MSE.

You calculate the MSR by dividing the proportion of predictable variance by the number of independent variables in the model. In Figure 23.34, because there is only one independent variable (the frequency of repairs), the changes in R^2 values are the MSR.

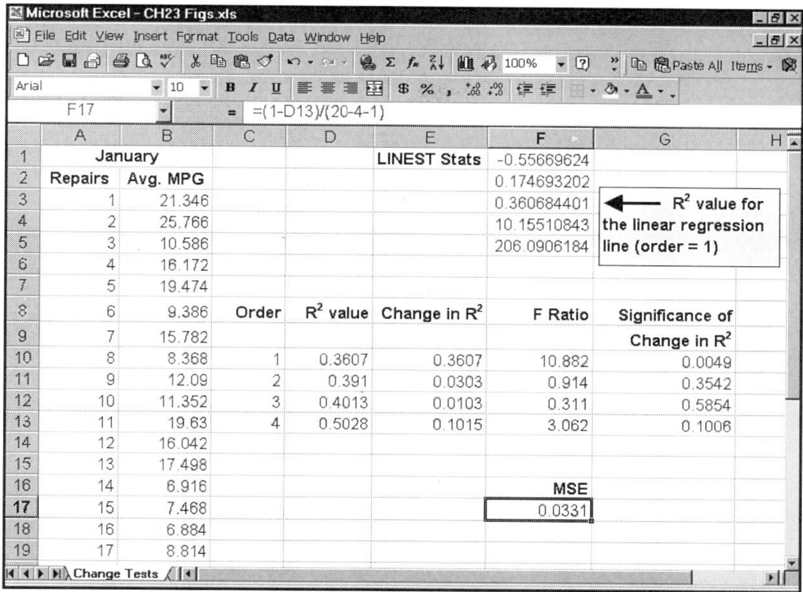

FIGURE 23.34

The F ratio is the F-test formula. The significance is the `FDIST` function.

Calculating the MSE is a bit more complex. The formula is

```
=(1-D13)/(20-4-1)
```

where (1-D13) is the same as (1-R^2) for the fourth-order polynomial: the proportion of variability that is not predictable. (20-4-1) is the degrees of freedom: the number of y-values, less the order of the polynomial, less 1. The value in F17 (the MSE) is the correct denominator for all four F ratios. For example, the F ratio in cell F11 is obtained by

```
=E11/$F$17
```

Finally, the probabilities associated with each F ratio are given in column G. The probability, often termed the significance of the F ratio, is obtained by using the `FDIST` worksheet function. For example, the formula in cell G10 is

```
=FDIST(F10,1,20-4-1)
```

`FDIST`'s first argument is the F ratio itself. The second argument is the degrees of freedom used to calculate the MSR, the number of independent variables (1, in this example). The third argument is the degrees of freedom for the MSE, the denominator in the F ratio calculation. That is, observations less order of the polynomial less 1, or (20-4-1)—the same value employed in cell F17.

How do you interpret these probabilities or significance levels? That's where you have to apply your judgment. Remember, the F ratio is a probability. The smaller the probability, the more likely that the relationship between the two variances (the R^2) will stand up if you repeat the experiment. The smaller the probability, the more likely that the change in R^2 is due to some other variable instead of chance.

The significance for the first-order (the linear trendline) is 0.0049 (see Figure 23.34). This means that if you repeated this experiment 100 times, and if there were no relationship between frequency of repairs and average MPG, you would obtain a change in R^2 as large as 10.879 less than one time (0.0049 * 100 = 0.5).

In contrast, consider the change in R^2 for the third-order polynomial. Its significance is .5854. If you repeat the experiment 100 times, in 59 of them you will get a change in R^2 as large as 0.103 (.5854 * 100 = 59), even if there were no relationship between average MPG and the square of frequency of maintenance.

Evaluating the Statistical Test Many people would regard a significance level of virtually zero (0.5) as important. They would believe that it is not rational to regard this experiment as one of the four out of 100 where an R^2 of 0.3606 would be obtained by chance, when in fact there was no relationship. They would believe that it is more rational to think that a relationship exists.

Many people would regard a significance level of 0.1006 for the change in R^2 from the third- to the fourth-order polynomial as marginally important at best, or even unimportant. When you can get a change in R^2 as large as 0.1015 10 times out of 100 purely by chance, they would prefer to regard this experiment as one of those chance 10, and would not employ a fourth-order polynomial.

So, you have to exercise your judgment. If you believe that the probability analysis means that only the linear component is important, back off your second-, third-, and fourth-order polynomials and stick with the linear trendline.

It may seem to be a lot of work, compared to clicking a spinner in the Trendline dialog box. But doing the spadework keeps some statistician from pointing at your chart and giggling at you.

Financial Functions

Most Excel users are familiar with some of its financial functions. There is a cluster of financial functions—RATE, PV, FV, NPER, and PMT—that work together to describe how you might pay for a house or a car. If you've ever purchased anything with a bank loan, you're familiar with the results of these functions and how they depend on one another.

It's when you encounter functions that address investment decisions and capital budgeting that things start to get complicated. In that context, two valuable functions are net present value (NPV) and internal rate of return (IRR).

Using Net Present Value (*NPV*) to Evaluate an Investment

The notion of net present value (NPV) is a powerful one. It tells you the value of an investment at some point in the future. In the process of calculating this value, it takes into account both the initial investment and the cash flow earned from the investment (this is the net part of NPV).

NPV also takes into account the time value of money: the fact that the value of a dollar bill today will be smaller at some future time (the present value part of NPV). The syntax for NPV is

```
=NPV(rate,value1,value2, ...)
```

where rate is the interest rate discounted over the length of one period. The value1 argument of future payments toward the investment is expressed as a negative number. The value2 (and other values) are the expected income from the investment, expressed as positive values. Suppose that you have $200 hanging around. You know that you don't want to just sit on it; a few years from now, it will buy much less than it can buy today. You know of an extremely generous bank that will pay you 10% annual compound interest if you deposit your $200 with them for five years. At the end of that period, how much has your $200 grown? This formula returns the value of your bank account after one year:


```
=1.1 * 200
```

If you entered that in cell A2, you could enter this in cell B2:

```
=1.1 * A2
```

and drag it to C2:E2. At the end of five years, cell E2 shows you that your account has grown to $322.10. The 1.1 in these formulas represents 100% of your initial investment plus the 10% interest, or 110%. If you do the algebra, you'll see that you could calculate the same end result by using just one formula (the rate raised to the fifth power):

```
=1.1^5 * 200
```

If you entered the numbers 1 through 5 in A1:E1, you could get your account balance at the end of each year by entering this formula in cell A2:

```
=(1.1 ^ A1) * 200
```

and dragging it through B2:E2.

A bank account, of course, isn't the only way you could use your $200. You could also spend it on equipment that would help you manufacture goods to sell. Over a five-year period, you would realize a net income from selling those goods. You estimate your annual revenue and cost of goods sold to arrive at the net income during each year, as shown in Figure 23.35.

An adjustment to net income is still needed. You need to subtract the cost of the equipment incurred in year 1. After you've done that, you have an estimated net cash flow for each year (shown in Row 8).

When you spend the $200 on equipment, you're foregoing the 10% interest you could earn at the bank. So, to get a more accurate picture of how much you're making from selling goods made by the equipment (versus putting the $200 in the bank), you adjust the net cash flow by this factor:

```
=(1+$B$10)^B1
```

As shown in Figure 23.36, this formula is entered in cell B11 and copied into C11:F11. (Notice that this formula is equivalent to the one used earlier to calculate the bank account interest.) The value in cell B10 is the interest rate you could earn at the bank, and is labeled the discount rate. The resulting values in B11:F11 are termed the annual discount factors.

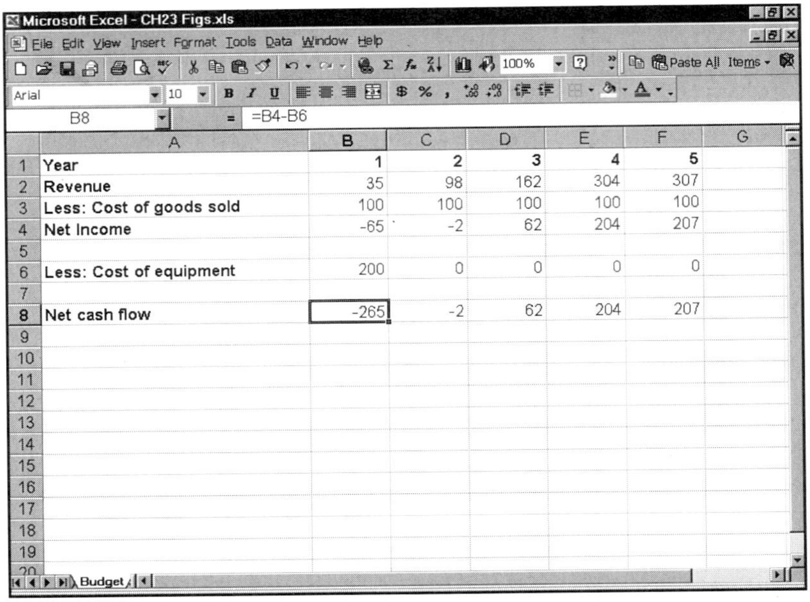

FIGURE 23.35
Early on, your net income is negative; you have to subtract expenses such as the cost of goods sold from the revenues.

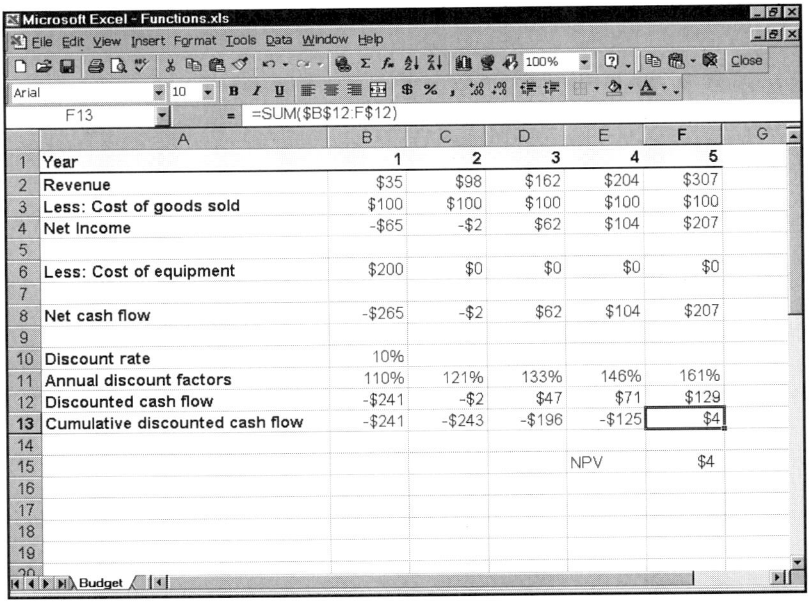

Microsoft Excel - CH23 Figs.xls

B8 = =B4-B6

	A	B	C	D	E	F
1	Year	1	2	3	4	5
2	Revenue	35	98	162	304	307
3	Less: Cost of goods sold	100	100	100	100	100
4	Net Income	-65	-2	62	204	207
5						
6	Less: Cost of equipment	200	0	0	0	0
7						
8	Net cash flow	-265	-2	62	204	207

FIGURE 23.36
Because your cumulative discounted cash flow turns positive in Year 5, the payback period is five years.

Microsoft Excel - Functions.xls

F13 = =SUM($B$12:F$12)

	A	B	C	D	E	F
1	Year	1	2	3	4	5
2	Revenue	$35	$98	$162	$204	$307
3	Less: Cost of goods sold	$100	$100	$100	$100	$100
4	Net Income	-$65	-$2	$62	$104	$207
5						
6	Less: Cost of equipment	$200	$0	$0	$0	$0
7						
8	Net cash flow	-$265	-$2	$62	$104	$207
9						
10	Discount rate	10%				
11	Annual discount factors	110%	121%	133%	146%	161%
12	Discounted cash flow	-$241	-$2	$47	$71	$129
13	Cumulative discounted cash flow	-$241	-$243	-$196	-$125	$4
14						
15					NPV	$4

Then, to arrive at a cash flow estimate that takes into account the interest earnings you forego, you divide the Net Cash Flow by the Annual Discount Factors. The results are in B12:F12 in

Figure 23.36. They tell you the value of your cash flow, discounted by the value of an alternative use of your original $200 capital.

So, given this discounted cash flow, how long does it take for your equipment investment to become profitable? As the Net Income row indicates, during the first two years, you're still in the red; you start showing a profit in the third year, but these profits are used to recoup your original investment. Figure 23.36 shows that you get back into the black in year 5.

The formula in cell B13 is

```
=SUM($B$12:B$12)
```

The formula is dragged through C13:F13. Notice that the formula makes use of a mixed reference, as discussed in Chapter 22, to create a running total.

After all that work, you arrive at the value in cell F13, which is $4 (actually $3.58 if you display two decimals). It is the NPV of your equipment investment at the end of five years. To get there, you took into account the revenues and the cost of goods sold, the cost incurred to obtain the equipment, and the value of an alternative use of your capital. Because you're foregoing that alternative use, you decrease the value of the net cash flow each year—you discount the net cash flow—by the earnings rate of the alternative investment.

Is there an easier way to calculate that $4 `NPV`? Yes. Cell F15 in Figure 23.36 contains the `NPV` function:

```
=NPV(B10,B8:F8)
```

The `NPV` function takes as its arguments the discount factor (in this example, 10%) and the net cash flow (in Figure 23.36, cells B8:F8).

Using Internal Rate of Return to Evaluate *NPV*

The *internal rate of return* (`IRR`) of an investment helps you compare the net discounted cash flow to the discount rate.

The example in the previous section resulted in an `NPV` of $3.58 (rounded to $4) at the end of the fifth year. This means that the investment in the equipment eventually performs better than the alternative investment with the bank—$3.58 better at the end of the fifth year.

You can convert this result to a rate: that is, a figure in the same metric as the discount rate. Using the data and the cell references in Figure 23.36, select cell F16 and enter

```
=IRR(B8:F8)
```

Like `NPV`, `IRR` works with the net cash flow. Here, the function would return 10% (actually 10.49%). Over the five-year period, the equipment investment performs slightly better (0.49%) than the discount rate (the rate of the alternative investment of putting the $200 in the bank) of 10%.

`IRR` uses an iterative algorithm to arrive at its result. In other words, `IRR` repeats (iterates) the formula up to a maximum of 20 times to get to the best estimate of the `IRR`. If the function doesn't get this best estimate by the 20th iteration, it returns the #NUM! error value. IRR starts out by assuming an initial value of 10%. Should this initial value be too far from an eventual best estimate, IRR could run out of iterations. So, if you use IRR and get #NUM!, you could try supplying your own estimate. For example:

```
=IRR(NetCashFlowRange, .2)
```

IRR requires at least one negative and one positive value to return a valid result. If the array that you present to IRR as its first argument contains fewer than two values, or if all the values in the array have the same sign (positive or negative), IRR will return #NUM!. Supplying your own estimate does no good in these cases.

Another way to conceptualize the IRR is that IRR is the discount rate that would result in an NPV of zero. In other words, it is the rate of return you would have to receive at the bank to equal the rate of return you will receive in manufacturing the goods over the same time period (see Figure 23.37).

FIGURE 23.37
Given the net cash flow in B8:F8, the IRR results in a net present value of zero.

Microsoft Excel - Functions.xls

F16 =IRR(B8:F8)

	A	B	C	D	E	F	G
1	Year	1	2	3	4	5	
2	Revenue	$35	$98	$162	$204	$307	
3	Less: Cost of goods sold	$100	$100	$100	$100	$100	
4	Net Income	-$65	-$2	$62	$104	$207	
5							
6	Less: Cost of equipment	$200	$0	$0	$0	$0	
7							
8	Net cash flow	-$265	-$2	$62	$104	$207	
9							
10	Discount rate	10%					
11	Annual discount factors	110%	121%	133%	146%	161%	
12	Discounted cash flow	-$241	-$2	$47	$71	$129	
13	Cumulative discounted cash flow	-$241	-$243	-$196	-$125	$4	
14							
15					NPV	$4	
16					IRR	10.49%	
17							
18	Annual discount factors using IRR	110%	122%	135%	149%	165%	
19	Discounted cash flow	-$240	-$2	$46	$70	$126	
20	Cumulative discounted cash flow	-$240	-$241	-$196	-$126	$0	

Budget

The annual discount factors shown in B18:F18 use 10.49%, the IRR in F16, instead of the 10% discount rate used in the NPV calculation. The formula in B18 is

```
=(1+$F$16)^B1
```

The net cash flow (in row 8) is divided by the new discount factors (in row 18) to return a new discounted cash flow in B19:F19. Finally, the cumulative discounted cash flow is shown in B20:F20; discounting a net cash flow by its own internal rate of return results in zero at the end of the fifth year. The mixed reference formula (as follows) is entered in cell B20 and copied across to F20:

```
=SUM($B$19:B$19)
```

Profitability Indexes

What if you had several different ways that you could use your capital of $200 to create income? If each investment is fairly sensible, it's quite possible that they have similar NPVs. But you might have one opportunity that requires your entire $200, and another that requires only $120 (the Cost of equipment).

If the two investments have identical NPVs, how do you choose between the two? There might, of course, be strategic reasons to prefer one investment to the other. If not, a *profitability index* can help put the choices into perspective. A profitability index indicates the potential for profit from your investment. You compare the profitability of one investment with another investment to determine which investment is better. Figure 23.38 shows two examples.

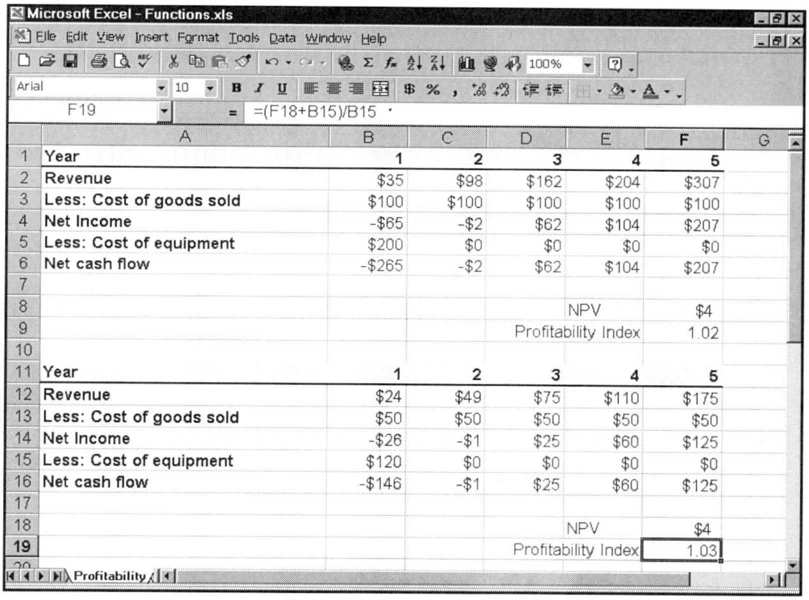

FIGURE 23.38
The profitability index helps to distinguish between two projects with the same NPV.

Microsoft Excel - Functions.xls

F19 = =(F18+B15)/B15

	A	B	C	D	E	F	G
1	Year	1	2	3	4	5	
2	Revenue	$35	$98	$162	$204	$307	
3	Less: Cost of goods sold	$100	$100	$100	$100	$100	
4	Net Income	-$65	-$2	$62	$104	$207	
5	Less: Cost of equipment	$200	$0	$0	$0	$0	
6	Net cash flow	-$265	-$2	$62	$104	$207	
7							
8					NPV	$4	
9					Profitability Index	1.02	
10							
11	Year	1	2	3	4	5	
12	Revenue	$24	$49	$75	$110	$175	
13	Less: Cost of goods sold	$50	$50	$50	$50	$50	
14	Net Income	-$26	-$1	$25	$60	$125	
15	Less: Cost of equipment	$120	$0	$0	$0	$0	
16	Net cash flow	-$146	-$1	$25	$60	$125	
17							
18					NPV	$4	
19					Profitability Index	1.03	

Profitability

The profitability index in cell F9 uses this formula:

```
=(F8+B5)/B5
```

In other words, add the initial investment (cost of equipment) to the NPV, and divide the result by the initial investment. An analogous formula is used to obtain the profitability index in cell F19 for the other investment. Both are formatted to display only two decimals. The higher the profitability index, which removes the effect of the amount of the initial investment from the comparison, the more attractive the investment.

Logical and Information Functions

Arguably, the most frequently used function in the Logical category is the `IF` function. The requirement to conduct conditional tests or comparisons seems to be prevalent among Excel users.

This section focuses on a variety of complex `IF` functions, which use other functions to extend the flexibility of the `IF` function. These other functions are nested inside the `IF` function.

▶ **See** "Nesting Functions," **p. 677**

As you probably know, the syntax for `IF` is

```
=IF(logical_test, value_if_true, value_if_false)
```

or more simply stated,

```
=IF(test,true,false)
```

Figure 23.39 illustrates a simple `IF` function. The countries whose percentage of change in sales is negative are marked with a reminder to contact the sales representative. The other countries are not marked. The formula has been prepared for the first country (Australia), and is ready to be copied to the other countries by using the Fill Handle.

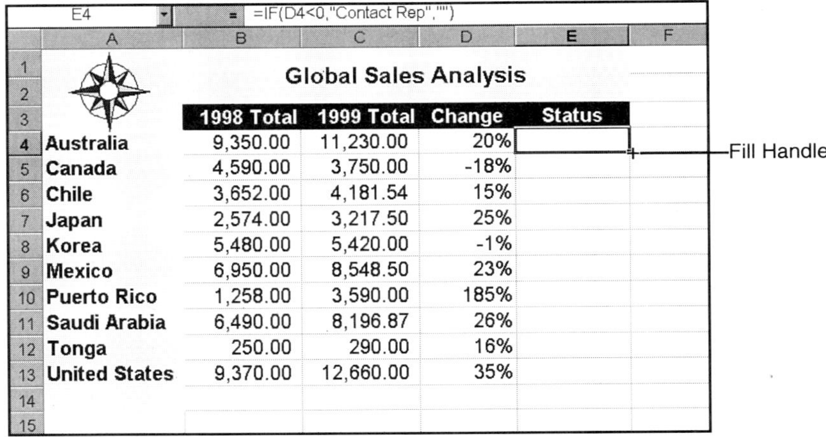

E4 = =IF(D4<0,"Contact Rep","")

Global Sales Analysis

	1998 Total	1999 Total	Change	Status
Australia	9,350.00	11,230.00	20%	
Canada	4,590.00	3,750.00	-18%	
Chile	3,652.00	4,181.54	15%	
Japan	2,574.00	3,217.50	25%	
Korea	5,480.00	5,420.00	-1%	
Mexico	6,950.00	8,548.50	23%	
Puerto Rico	1,258.00	3,590.00	185%	
Saudi Arabia	6,490.00	8,196.87	26%	
Tonga	250.00	290.00	16%	
United States	9,370.00	12,660.00	35%	

FIGURE 23.39
`IF` functions can be used to mark or flag specific cells.

When working with `IF` functions, there are a few things to keep in mind:

- With the Less Than or Equal To and Greater Than or Equal To operators, the equal sign (=) must always come second.
- If text is part of an `IF` function, it must be enclosed in quotation marks.
- `IF` functions can be nested inside of other `IF` functions. Up to seven nested `IF` functions are allowed in Excel 2000.

Using *IF* to Cross Check Summary Calculations

Formulas are an effective means of validating the summary calculations in a worksheet. In Figure 23.40, a list of personal computers sold is displayed. The list indicates the quantity and type of computers sold each day. The total number of PCs sold each day appears in row 10. The total number of each PC type sold for the week appears in column G. A grand total of computers sold for the week is calculated in cell G10. In this example, the sum of all daily totals (B10:F10) should equal the sum of all type totals (G4:G8). So, when the grand total is calculated, you can use either sum in cell G10. The amount currently displayed is 216, the sum of B10:F10.

By using an `IF` function, you can create a formula to check that both totals are the same. If they are not the same, you can design the formula to display a warning error message. This type of data-entry verification is known as a *cross-check*. There are several reasons why this error occurs. A constant value might have been accidentally typed over a formula, or a formula may be summing the incorrect cells. These types of errors are common in workbooks that are shared with other users.

FIGURE 23.40
Use formulas to automatically analyze worksheets.

G10 = =SUM(B10:F10)

	A	B	C	D	E	F	G
1	Stewart Computing - Weekly Sales						
2							Sales
3	Sales	Mon	Tue	Wed	Thu	Fri	by Type
4	Pentium II-400 Desktop	5	8	7	8	8	36
5	Pentium II-350 Desktop	10	6	11	9	10	46
6	Pentium II-333 Desktop	15	14	14	12	15	70
7	Pentium II-266 Notebook	8	8	12	8	7	40
8	Pentium MMX-233 Notebook	2	5	7	3	4	21
9							
10	Daily Totals	40	41	51	40	44	216
11							

The logical test to perform is the cross-check `SUM(B10:F10)=SUM(G4:G8)`.

If the test is true—meaning that the sums are equal—you simply display the results of one of the sums, such as `SUM(B10:F10)`.

If the test is false—meaning that the sums are not equal—you want to be warned that there is an error. This can be accomplished by entering the text you want displayed when the text is false. Text in Excel formulas is surrounded by quotes, for example "`ERROR`."

The `IF` function in cell G10 is

```
=IF(SUM(B10:F10)=SUM(G4:G8),SUM(B10:F10),"ERROR")
```

In Figure 23.41, the `IF` function is entered in cell G10. The warning message `ERROR` is in the cell to indicate a problem with the worksheet. To illustrate the problem, the totals are calculated below the worksheet and show the daily total is 216 and the total by type is 213.

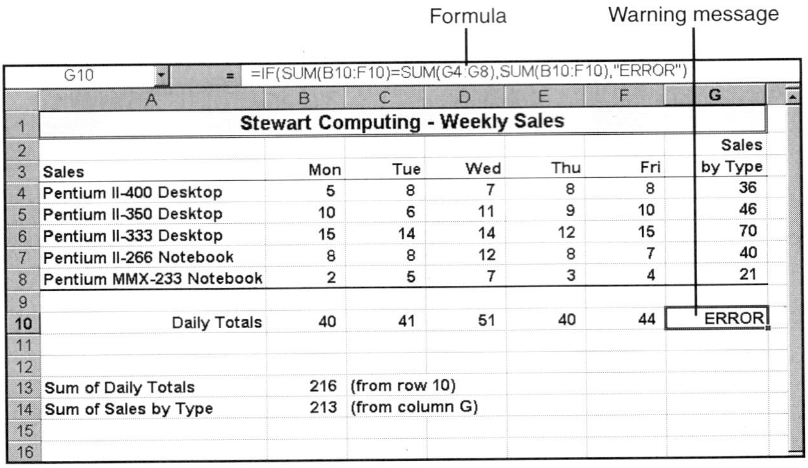

FIGURE 23.41
The cross-check formula flags you if there is an error in the worksheet.

	A	B	C	D	E	F	G
1	Stewart Computing - Weekly Sales						
2							Sales
3	Sales	Mon	Tue	Wed	Thu	Fri	by Type
4	Pentium II-400 Desktop	5	8	7	8	8	36
5	Pentium II-350 Desktop	10	6	11	9	10	46
6	Pentium II-333 Desktop	15	14	14	12	15	70
7	Pentium II-266 Notebook	8	8	12	8	7	40
8	Pentium MMX-233 Notebook	2	5	7	3	4	21
9							
10	Daily Totals	40	41	51	40	44	ERROR
11							
12							
13	Sum of Daily Totals	216	(from row 10)				
14	Sum of Sales by Type	213	(from column G)				
15							
16							

Whenever there is a cross-check error, the problem exists in one of the individual total calculations. In Figure 23.41 the totals are in row 10 or column G. Chapter 28, "Auditing Worksheets and Resolving Errors," describes how to quickly identify and correct the problem.

Using Nested *IF* Functions to Test Multiple Criteria

To test multiple conditions, you can insert `IF` functions inside other `IF` functions. A maximum of seven IF functions may be nested. An example of a nested `IF` function is

```
=IF(D4<0,"Contact Rep",IF(D4>=30%,"Bonus Due",""))
```

The logical_test is to determine whether cell D4 is negative. If it is negative, then the text Contact Rep is displayed. If it is not negative (then it must be zero or positive), another test is performed. This second `IF` function is the value_if_false of the first `IF` function. The second `IF` is checking to see whether D4 is 30% or greater. If it is, then Bonus Due is displayed. If it is not (D4 is between 0 and 29), then nothing is displayed.

To make it easier to understand this example, look at the following syntax:

```
=IF(Test1,True1,IF(Test2,True2,False2))
```

The second `IF` function is the False1 of the first `IF` function. When `IF` functions are nested inside other `IF` functions, write out the syntax, as shown in this example; then substitute the words for the syntax to make it easier to understand, for example:

```
=IF(PercentChange<0,"Contact Rep",IF(PercentChange>=30%,"Bonus Due",""))
```

You then substitute the cell references as necessary.

Nesting *OR* and *AND* Functions Inside *IF* Functions to Test Multiple Criteria

The AND and OR functions are Logical functions that return a TRUE or FALSE value, and are often used in the logical_test portion ofthe IF function. The syntax for the AND and OR functions is

```
AND(logical1,logical2,...)
OR(logical1,logical2,...)
```

With an AND function, all the logical arguments must be true to return a TRUE value. With an OR function, only one of the logical arguments must be true to return a TRUE value. The followimg formula illustrates the use of an OR function:

```
=IF(OR(B12="Tokyo",B12="Calcutta"),C12*5%,C12*4%)
```

In this formula, if B12 contains the text Tokyo or Calcutta, the value_if_true argument (C12*5%) is performed. If some other city name appears in cell B12, the value_if_false calculation (C12*4%) is performed.

Formulas that contain AND and OR comparisons work well when the entry is compared against a few alternatives. When the entry needs to be checked against a larger set of alternatives, listing each alternative in the formula is time-consuming and makes the formula unnecessarily complex. Instead, it is simpler to create a formula that compares the entry against a list of valid entries. You would use a lookup function (such as VLOOKUP) in the logical_test portion of the IF function. Here's an example:

```
=IF(B12=VLOOKUP(B12,Cities,1,false),C12*5%,C12*4%)
```

Cities is a range name for a list of valid cities. Because you want to compare only the name of the city and not return another value, the column_index_num argument in the VLOOKUP is one. Also, because you want to find only those cities in the list, the range_lookup argument in the VLOOKUP is set to false.

An example of nesting a VLOOKUP in an IF function is illustrated in the section "Using VLOOKUP to Look Up Values with an IF Function" later in this chapter.

Employing *IS* Functions Sometimes, calculations result in error messages such as #DIV/0! (when one of the cells contains a zero or is blank) or #VALUE! (when text is in one of the cells). Figure 23.42 illustrates this problem.

You can avoid the display of these errors by skipping the calculation for entries that contain a zero or text, or are empty.

The IS functions help you do this:

- To test for an empty cell, use ISBLANK. For example, ISBLANK(B4).
- To test for text, use ISTEXT. For example, ISTEXT(B4).
- To test for a zero, use the equal comparison operator. For example, B4=0.

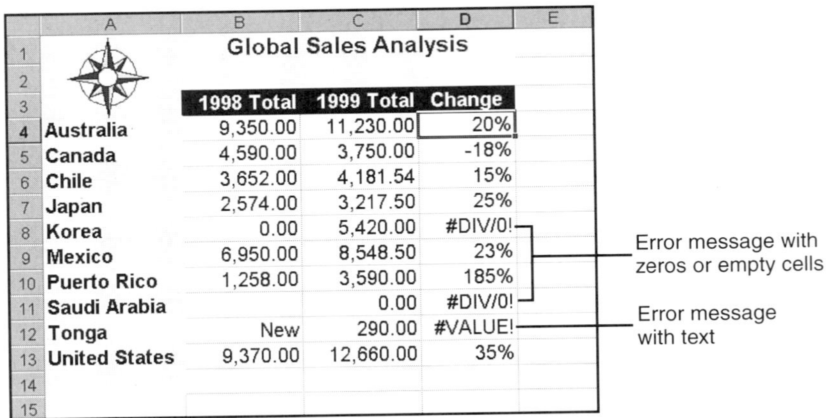

	A	B	C	D	E
1		Global Sales Analysis			
2					
3		1998 Total	1999 Total	Change	
4	Australia	9,350.00	11,230.00	20%	
5	Canada	4,590.00	3,750.00	-18%	
6	Chile	3,652.00	4,181.54	15%	
7	Japan	2,574.00	3,217.50	25%	
8	Korea	0.00	5,420.00	#DIV/0!	
9	Mexico	6,950.00	8,548.50	23%	
10	Puerto Rico	1,258.00	3,590.00	185%	
11	Saudi Arabia		0.00	#DIV/0!	
12	Tonga	New	290.00	#VALUE!	
13	United States	9,370.00	12,660.00	35%	
14					
15					

FIGURE 23.42
You can avoid these errors by using IS functions to test for the conditions you want to ignore.

You can combine all these with an `OR` function—here's an example:

```
=IF(OR(ISBLANK(B4),ISTEXT(B4),B4=0),"",(C4-B4)/B4)
```

If cell B4 is empty or contains text or a zero, nothing is entered in the results cell—otherwise, a division is calculated. Figure 23.43 shows the results.

FIGURE 23.43
You could display text such as New Account instead of leaving the cells blank in the value_if_true argument.

D4 = =IF(OR(ISBLANK(B4),ISTEXT(B4),B4=0),"",(C4-B4)/B4)

	A	B	C	D	E	F	G
1		Global Sales Analysis					
2							
3		1998 Total	1999 Total	Change			
4	Australia	9,350.00	11,230.00	20%			
5	Canada	4,590.00	3,750.00	-18%			
6	Chile	3,652.00	4,181.54	15%			
7	Japan	2,574.00	3,217.50	25%			
8	Korea	0.00	5,420.00				
9	Mexico	6,950.00	8,548.50	23%			
10	Puerto Rico	1,258.00	3,590.00	185%			
11	Saudi Arabia		0.00				
12	Tonga	New	290.00				
13	United States	9,370.00	12,660.00	35%			
14							
15							

Using Dates in *IF* Functions For Excel to perform comparisons on dates, the dates need to be converted into serial numbers. The `DATEVALUE` function is designed to convert dates into serial numbers. The syntax for `DATEVALUE` is

```
=DATEVALUE("date_text")
```

Suppose your company has implemented a price increase as of the 1st of June. Orders placed before the first are charged the old rates and orders placed on or after the first are charged the new rates. To check the date, it has to be converted to a serial number. Let's assume that cell C8 contains the first order you want to check, the logical_text of the `IF` function would be

```
C8<DATEVALUE("6/1/1999")
```

From this result you can have the formula look up the price in the correct price list. See the next section on how to express the rest of the formula by using `VLOOKUP` functions in the value_if_true and value_if_false arguments.

Using an `AND` function, you can also check to see whether a date falls within a range of dates, such as

```
AND(C8>=DATEVALUE("6/1/1999"),C8<=DATEVALUE("6/30/1999"))
```

Using *VLOOKUP* to Look Up Values with an *IF* Function

The `VLOOKUP` function can be used in any of the arguments in an `IF` function. In the example shown in Figure 23.44, `VLOOKUP` is used in both the value_if_true and value_if_false, with this formula

```
=IF(C4="Wholesale",VLOOKUP(D4,PriceList,2,FALSE),VLOOKUP(D4,PriceList,3,FALSE))
```

This formula checks to determine whether a transaction is wholesale or retail. If the type of transaction is wholesale, then the price for the product is looked up in the second column of PriceList (a range name for the list of products and prices). Otherwise (the type of transaction is retail), the price for the product is looked up in the third column of PriceList. The false argument is included to conduct an exact match lookup.

▶ **See** "Using VLOOKUP with Lists," to learn more about the VLOOKUP function, **p. 686**

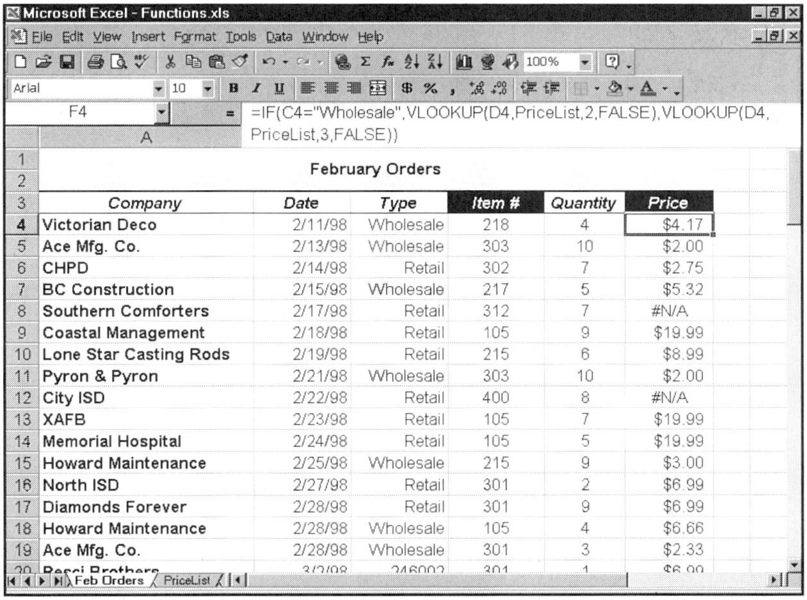

FIGURE 23.44
The `IF` function uses `VLOOKUP` to display the correct wholesale or retail price.

Microsoft Excel - Functions.xls

F4 = =IF(C4="Wholesale",VLOOKUP(D4,PriceList,2,FALSE),VLOOKUP(D4,PriceList,3,FALSE))

February Orders

Company	Date	Type	Item #	Quantity	Price
Victorian Deco	2/11/98	Wholesale	218	4	$4.17
Ace Mfg. Co.	2/13/98	Wholesale	303	10	$2.00
CHPD	2/14/98	Retail	302	7	$2.75
BC Construction	2/15/98	Wholesale	217	5	$5.32
Southern Comforters	2/17/98	Retail	312	7	#N/A
Coastal Management	2/18/98	Retail	105	9	$19.99
Lone Star Casting Rods	2/19/98	Retail	215	6	$8.99
Pyron & Pyron	2/21/98	Wholesale	303	10	$2.00
City ISD	2/22/98	Retail	400	8	#N/A
XAFB	2/23/98	Retail	105	7	$19.99
Memorial Hospital	2/24/98	Retail	105	5	$19.99
Howard Maintenance	2/25/98	Wholesale	215	9	$3.00
North ISD	2/27/98	Retail	301	2	$6.99
Diamonds Forever	2/28/98	Retail	301	9	$6.99
Howard Maintenance	2/28/98	Wholesale	105	4	$6.66
Ace Mfg. Co.	2/28/98	Wholesale	301	3	$2.33

Feb Orders / PriceList

Using *ISNA* to Avoid Error Messages The `VLOOKUP` shown earlier in Figure 23.44 is using an exact match lookup—when an exact match is not found, the `VLOOKUP` function returns the error

`#N/A` (as can be seen in cells F8 and F12 in Figure 23.44). Because the error message doesn't help you (or others) in correcting the entry, you will probably want to have some other more helpful message display.

The `ISNA` function can be used with the `VLOOKUP` function to determine whether the entry (in this case, the product name) is in the list of valid entries. If the entry is not in the list, you can display text instead of the error message.

To accomplish this, you would enter the following formula in cell F4:

```
=IF(ISNA(VLOOKUP(D4,PriceList,2,FALSE)),"Invalid Item#",
IF(C4="Wholesale",VLOOKUP(D4,PriceList,2,FALSE),VLOOKUP(D4, PriceList,3,FALSE)))
```

The results of this formula are displayed in Figure 23.45.

FIGURE 23.45
Use the `ISNA` function to display a more understandable error message.

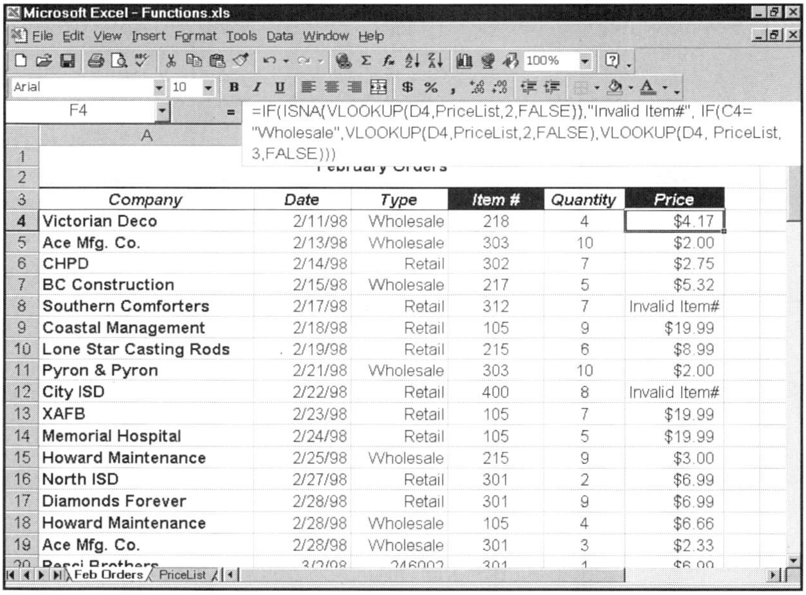

	Company	Date	Type	Item #	Quantity	Price
4	Victorian Deco	2/11/98	Wholesale	218	4	$4.17
5	Ace Mfg. Co.	2/13/98	Wholesale	303	10	$2.00
6	CHPD	2/14/98	Retail	302	7	$2.75
7	BC Construction	2/15/98	Wholesale	217	5	$5.32
8	Southern Comforters	2/17/98	Retail	312	7	Invalid Item#
9	Coastal Management	2/18/98	Retail	105	9	$19.99
10	Lone Star Casting Rods	2/19/98	Retail	215	6	$8.99
11	Pyron & Pyron	2/21/98	Wholesale	303	10	$2.00
12	City ISD	2/22/98	Retail	400	8	Invalid Item#
13	XAFB	2/23/98	Retail	105	7	$19.99
14	Memorial Hospital	2/24/98	Retail	105	5	$19.99
15	Howard Maintenance	2/25/98	Wholesale	215	9	$3.00
16	North ISD	2/27/98	Retail	301	2	$6.99
17	Diamonds Forever	2/28/98	Retail	301	9	$6.99
18	Howard Maintenance	2/28/98	Wholesale	105	4	$6.66
19	Ace Mfg. Co.	2/28/98	Wholesale	301	3	$2.33

Here, an `IF` function is checking to see whether the product is in the list (using a `VLOOKUP`). If the product is not in the list (which would display the `#N/A` error), then the text "Invalid Item#" is displayed instead. If the product is in the list, then the formula to locate the wholesale or retail price is performed.

CHAPTER 24

Importing Data from Databases, Web Pages, and Text Files

In this chapter

Creating Queries to Import Data from External Databases

To retrieve data from external sources, you use the Data, Get External Data command. This command includes options to create database queries, Web queries, and to import Text (.txt) files. As the name suggests, database queries are used to retrieve data from databases using an application called Microsoft Query. Creating Web queries and importing Text files are discussed later in this chapter.

Microsoft Query is an independent application that works with Excel to make it easy to retrieve data from databases and copy the data into an Excel worksheet. When you insert the data into a worksheet, it becomes a list—as if you typed it in yourself. You can then analyze and manipulate the data using any of the tools Excel provides to work with lists as discussed in Chapter 25, "Advanced Lists, PivotTables, and PivotCharts."

You might pull in data from an Access database that tracks company sales and then use the PivotTable and PivotChart features in Excel to summarize the sales data in ways the Access Crosstab queries can't hope to achieve. For example, suppose you create a PivotTable that summarizes the data by product and quarter, with the sales representatives field placed in the page area. Using the PivotTable Show Pages command, you can instantly create PivotTables for each sales representative. Another obvious reason for bringing data into Excel from a database is to take advantage of the built-in functions in Excel to perform complex calculations.

Examples of the databases from which you can retrieve data include Access, Visual FoxPro, dBASE, Paradox, SQL Server, and SQL Server OLAP Services. Microsoft Query can filter, sort, format, or edit the data before it is inserted into your worksheet.

Before attempting to retrieve data from an external database, it is important that you understand some of the terminology used with Microsoft Query and databases. The following list provides definitions for the terms you need to know.

- *Cube*—A data structure containing Online Analytical Processing (OLAP) data. The data cube consists of dimensions and data fields. Dimensions organize each type of data into hierarchical levels. Data fields measure the quantities at each dimension level. For example, a cube could have a geographic dimension (containing the levels Province/State, City, Area), a personnel dimension (containing the levels Medical Specialty and Experience Level), and the data field, Operations Performed. There are Operations Performed values in the cube for the intersection of each geographic and personnel level.
- *Data Source*—An address that Microsoft Query uses to locate the information in the external source. The data source may include information such as the name of the server, directory, and file in which the external data is located. You need to define a data source before you query an external source and retrieve information from it. The data source sometimes is referred to as the *query definition*.

- *Joining tables* (or *linking tables*)—The process of relating tables together based on a field that is common to both tables, such as an Account Number field or a Customer ID field.
- *ODBC (Open Database Connectivity) Driver*—A dynamic link library (DLL) file that Microsoft Query and Microsoft Excel use to connect to a particular database. Each database program, such as Access, FoxPro, or SQL Server, requires a different driver. Microsoft Query comes with many of the common ODBC drivers.
- *OLAP (Online Analytical Processing)*—In an OLAP database, data is organized hierarchically and stored in cubes instead of tables. OLAP data is organized for querying and reporting instead of processing transactions.
- *Returning Data*—Inserting data into an Excel worksheet that has been retrieved from a database.
- *Result Set*—The information, or data, retrieved from the external source.
- *Structured Query Language (SQL)*—A programming language that is used to retrieve, update, and manage data. Microsoft Query uses SQL to retrieve data from databases. You don't need to learn SQL, or any other programming or macro language, to use Microsoft Query. If you want to learn more about SQL, I suggest picking up a copy of *Special Edition Using Microsoft SQL Server 7.0*, published by Que.

To query an external source, you need to have an ODBC driver installed on your computer. Microsoft Query includes many common external source drivers. The drivers provided with Query include Access, dBASE, FoxPro, Visual FoxPro, Paradox, SQL Server, and Text. If the driver is not provided by Excel, you have to install the ODBC driver that you need before you can query the external source. The driver should be supplied by that external source.

After you retrieve data from an external source, you can rearrange, format, and sort the data with Query. When you are satisfied with the data and its formatting, the result set is returned to an Excel worksheet.

If you retrieve data regularly from a particular data source, consider creating a macro that runs the query, filters the data, pastes it into a specified worksheet, formats the data and sends it to the printer, and/or automatically distributes the worksheet via Office routing or standard email. Although this type of macro will require careful detailed planning, it would certainly turn a "tough day at the office" into a tremendous timesaver. See Chapters 5 and 6 to learn more about creating macros.

Starting Microsoft Query

You start Microsoft Query by choosing Data, Get External Data, New Database Query. However, Microsoft Query is an optional feature in Excel, and therefore may not be installed on your computer. If Query was already installed, the Choose Data Source dialog box appears (as shown in Figure 24.1).

If Query is not installed, a warning message is displayed when you select New Database Query. The warning message displays an option to install Microsoft Query; you need the

Office CD to complete the installation or you'll need to indicate the location on a network where the Office 2000 program files are located.

When the installation of Query is completed, the Choose Data Source dialog box appears (see Figure 24.1).

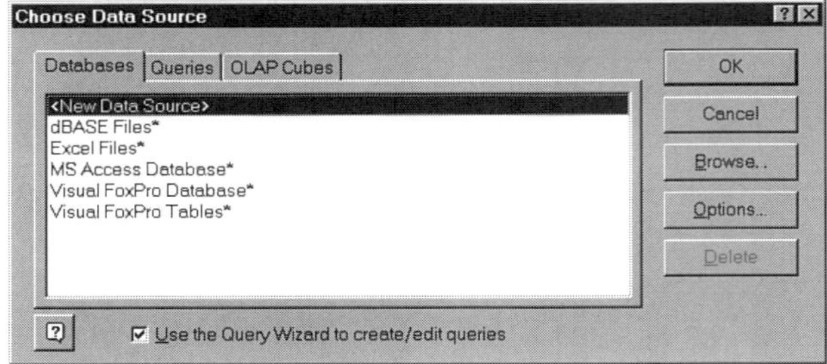

FIGURE 24.1
Use this dialog box to create a data source for each database you intend to query.

There are five default data sources listed in the Choose Data Source dialog box, as shown in Figure 24.1. If you created data sources in previous versions of Microsoft Query, they are also listed in the dialog box.

A *data source* provides the connectivity information necessary to connect to the database and select the data. The data sources listed in the Choose Data Source dialog box are called *Data Source Names* (DSNs). There are three types of DSNs: User, System, and File.

- A *User DSN* is a data source that is user specific. It is stored locally but is available only to the user who creates it. User DSNs are not used by Microsoft Query, but are used by ODBC, SQL (Structure Query Language) commands, and Microsoft Jet (a database engine included with Access).
- A *System DSN* is a locally stored DSN that is not user specific. System DSNs are required by Microsoft SQL Server and Microsoft Internet Information Server (IIS) and are often used in Microsoft Access to retrieve data from external sources.
- A *File DSN* is created locally and may be shared with others. This type of DSN is associated with a specific file. Microsoft Query uses File DSNs; Microsoft Jet and ODBC do not. When you create a new data source in Microsoft Query, you are creating a File DSN. These DSNs are stored in the Data Sources folder (Program Files\Common Files\ODBC\Data Sources).

Previous versions of Microsoft Query did not display User or System DSNs—Microsoft Query 2000 does. The five DSNs listed in the dialog box are User or System DSNs and are denoted by an asterisk. These are generic DSNs and do not point to any specific data source. Because this chapter covers creating your own File DSNs; you'll want to hide these while working through the examples in this chapter to avoid using them accidentally.

To hide the these DSNs, click the Options button in the Data Source dialog box and clear the Include Registry DSNs in List of Available Databases check box. Both User and System DSNs are stored in the Windows Registry, and are sometimes referred to as Registry DSNs.

You can create as many data sources as you need. I encourage you to create one for each database from which you plan to retrieve data. Because the five default data sources do not point to a particular data source, create your own data sources instead of using the built-in ones.

Creating the Data Source

Importing external data into Excel is a three-step process: setting up a data source, select the data (using the Query Wizard or the Microsoft Query Window), and returning the data to Excel.

A data source is a set of information that enables Excel and Microsoft Query to connect to the external database (such as an Access database). The data source information includes the name and location of the database or server, the type of database, the ODBC driver, and any necessary logon and password information. When created, the data source is then used to create a query that retrieves the data. You can use the same data source to create multiple queries.

To create a data source, follow these steps:

1. In the Choose Data Source dialog box (refer to Figure 24.1), select New Data Source.
2. Click OK. The Create New Data Source dialog box appears as shown in Figure 24.2.

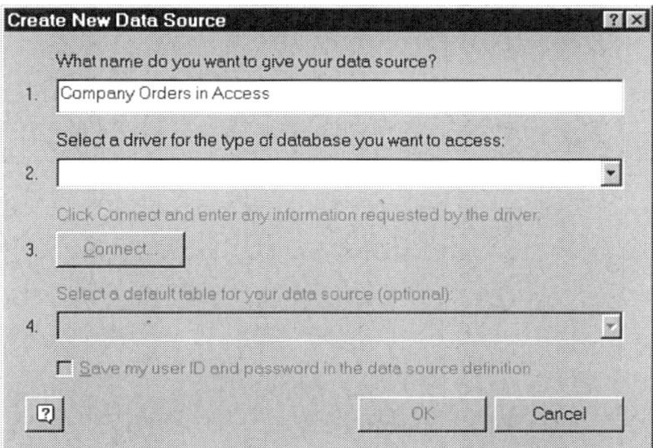

FIGURE 24.2
As you complete each step, the next step in the dialog box becomes active.

3. In Step 1 of the Create New Data Source dialog box, type a name that helps you to remember the source data you want to retrieve. Enter a name that identifies the database file or table and database application, such as `Company Orders in Access`.
4. In Step 2 of the dialog box, select a driver from the drop-down list for the type of data you want to retrieve. If the driver you need is not listed, you have to cancel the creation of the data source and install the driver.

NOTE Use the Office Assistant to find specific steps for installing ODBC drivers. Type `odbc` in the Office Assistant search box, and then press Enter to see a list of help topics. From the list, choose Install an ODBC Driver So That You Can Access an External Data Source. The step-by-step procedures guide you through the installation.

5. After you select the driver, click the Connect button in Step 3 (refer to Figure 24.2). The dialog box that appears requests different information, depending on the driver you selected. Figure 24.3 shows the dialog box for Access 2000, and Figure 24.4 shows the dialog box for FoxPro.

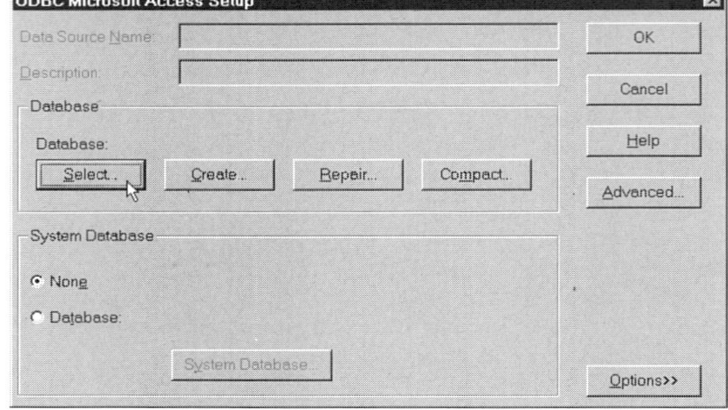

FIGURE 24.3
The ODBC Access 2000 setup dialog box.

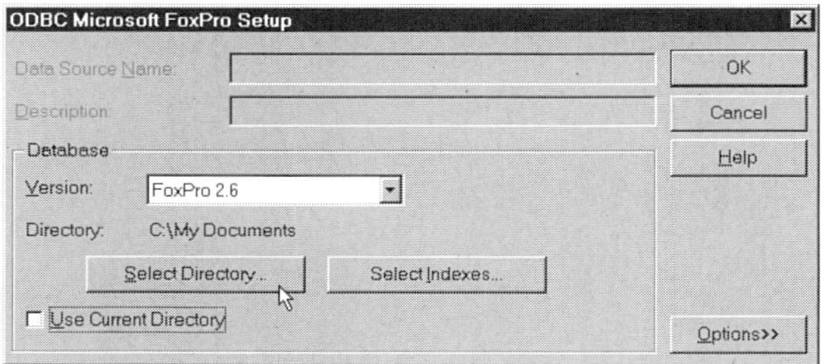

FIGURE 24.4
The ODBC FoxPro 2.6 setup dialog box.

6. In the ODBC Setup dialog box, enter the required information. For example, in the Access ODBC dialog box previously shown in Figure 24.3, click the Select button to designate the location of the Access database. In the FoxPro ODBC dialog box, remove the check from Use Current Directory, and then click Select Directory.
7. When you complete the ODBC Setup dialog box, click OK to return to the Create New Data Source dialog box. The path to the source data appears next to the Connect button.
8. Step 4 of the dialog box is optional. If the data you intend to retrieve comes from only one table in a database, use this box to identify it as the default table from which you plan to retrieve data. If the data you intend to retrieve comes from several tables in a database, leave this box blank. Figure 24.5 shows a completed Create New Data Source dialog box.
9. After you complete the Create New Data Source dialog box, click OK. The Choose Data Source dialog box is displayed. The data source name you entered in the first step of the Create New Data Source dialog box is listed on the Databases tab of the dialog box.

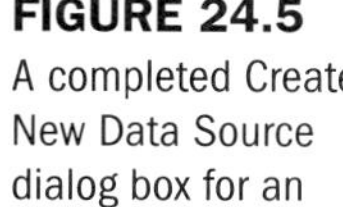

FIGURE 24.5
A completed Create New Data Source dialog box for an Access database.

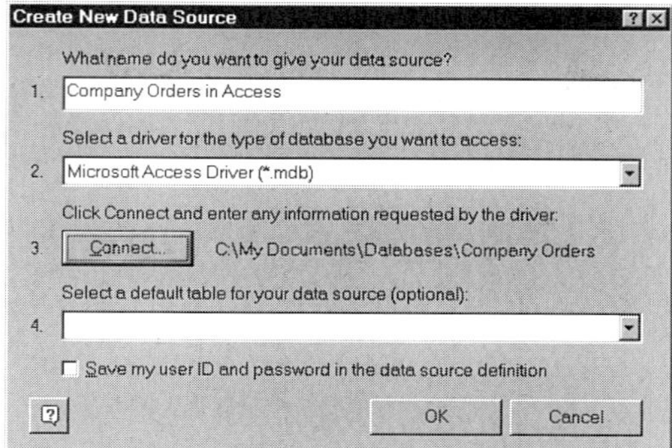

Now that the data source is created, you are ready to create your query. You have two choices for creating queries:

- Query Wizard—A tool provided with Microsoft Query that helps you create quick and simple query designs to retrieve data. Use the Query Wizard when you want to retrieve data from only one table in a database.
- Microsoft Query Window—If you want to retrieve data from multiple tables in a database, the Microsoft Query window enables you to work in more detail to customize and view your data retrieval. Use the Microsoft Query window when you want to merge data from multiple Excel lists into a single Excel list.

With either query-creation method, you can filter your data by specifying criteria, and reordering the data through sorting.

OLAP Data Sources

You can create a data source to an OLAP Cube through the Choose Data Source dialog box (OLAP Cubes tab). The Cube database must already exist either on a network server or on your hard drive.

Because accessing OLAP cubes is a new feature in Excel, it is discussed in detail in the section "Using and Creating OLAP Cubes," later in this chapter. This section addresses creating data sources, accessing cubes, and creating cubes.

Using the Query Wizard to Create a Query

The quickest and easiest way to create a query in Microsoft Query is to use the Query Wizard. It guides you through the basic steps to creating a query to retrieve data from a single database table. The wizard includes options to filter the data and sort the records before they are returned to Excel.

In the Choose Data Source dialog box, make sure the Use the Query Wizard to Create/Edit Queries box is checked. Then choose the data source from the Databases tab and click OK (see Figure 24.6).

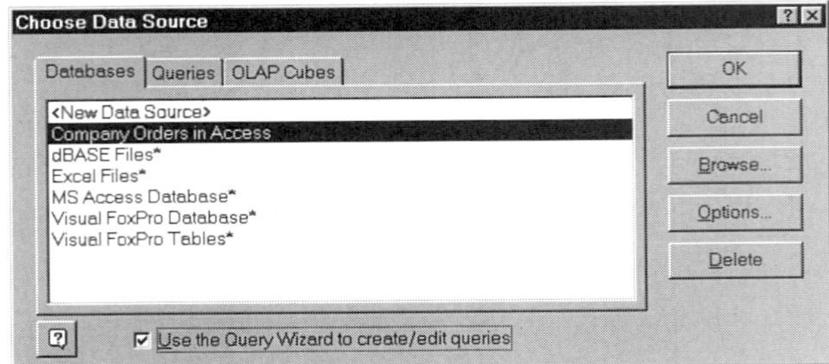

FIGURE 24.6
At the bottom of the dialog box, the check box indicates that the Query Wizard is used to create or edit queries.

In Figure 24.6, the Access data source is selected. When you click OK, the Query Wizard starts automatically and guides you through the process of creating a query. Figure 24.7 shows the Query Wizard—Choose Columns dialog box, the first step in the Query Wizard.

If you designate a table in the data source, the columns (fields) in that table are displayed automatically on the left side of the screen. If you did not designate a specific table, a list of the tables is displayed on the left side of the dialog box, as shown in Figure 24.7.

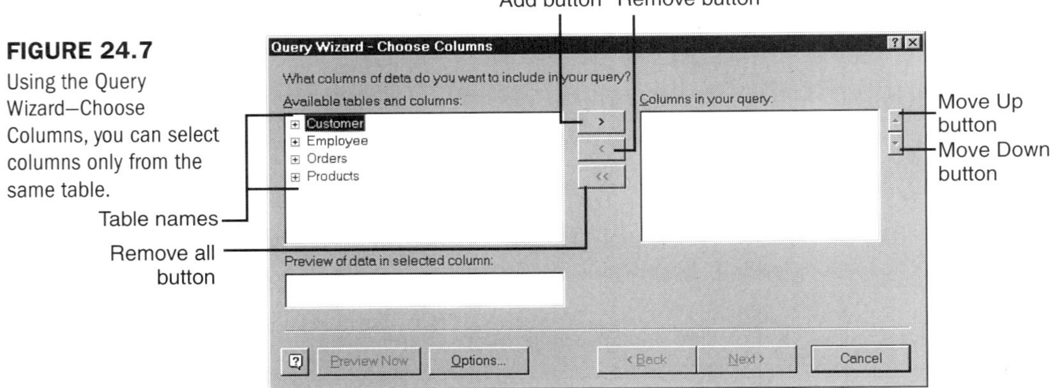

FIGURE 24.7
Using the Query Wizard–Choose Columns, you can select columns only from the same table.

To include all the columns in the table, select the table name and click the add button (>). All the column names are placed in the list on the right. To include individual columns, double-click the table name to display the column names. Then double-click the column name on the left (or click the Add button) for each column you want to add.

The order in which you select the columns is the order in which the columns are displayed when the data is returned to Excel. Use the Move Up and Move Down buttons on the far-right side of the dialog box to reorder the columns (refer to Figure 24.7).

After you select the columns you want and arrange them in the desired order, click the Next button to continue with the Query Wizard.

Filtering Data

The next step of the Query Wizard gives you the option of filtering the data. *Filtering* in Microsoft Query is not the same as filtering in Excel. In Excel when you filter data, you are hiding the data that does not match your criteria. In Microsoft Query when you filter data, you are excluding it from the result set—it will not be imported into Excel.

To retrieve only those records that meet your specifications, you specify criteria, similar to the way in which you use criteria to filter in an Excel list or in an Access query.

NOTE You can apply a filter only to one of the columns in the table. To filter on multiple columns, you need to use the Query Window, which you can access from the last step of the wizard.

Figure 24.8 shows the Query Wizard—Filter Data dialog box. To include all data, skip this step by clicking Next. To enter filter criteria, follow these steps:

1. Click the column name you want to filter from the list on the left side of the screen. The name of the column appears above the first filter box.
2. From the drop-down list in the first filter box, choose one of the comparison conditions, such as equals or is greater than or equal to. You can type the sample criteria or pick from the drop-down list of table entries in the corresponding box on the right side.
3. If necessary, enter another filter criterion. Be sure to select either AND or OR when you use multiple conditions. Although the dialog box shows only three criteria, you can add more. Each time you add a criterion, another criteria box becomes active. Scroll to see additional criteria boxes.
4. When you have entered all the conditions, click the Next button.

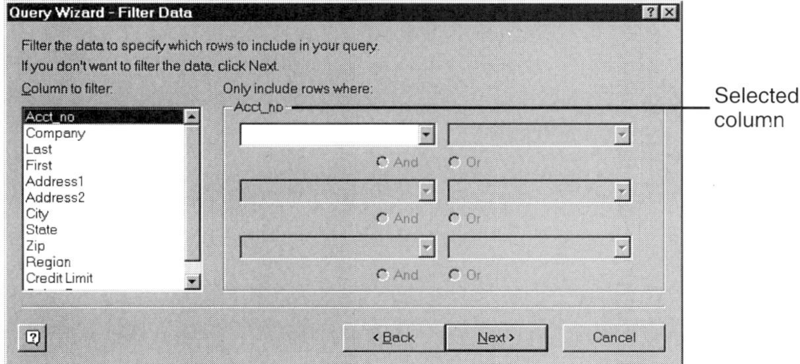

FIGURE 24.8
When you specify filters on multiple columns, the column names appear in bold type.

Sorting Records

The Query Wizard—Sort Order dialog box, shown in Figure 24.9, enables you to sort the data before placing it in the Excel worksheet. You can sort up to three columns of data, using either ascending or descending sorts.

As in filtering, sorting is optional in the Query Wizard. To skip the sorting option and display the records in the order they appear in the table, click the Next button. To specify a sort order for the records, use the drop-down list to choose the column by which you want the data sorted. Then select either ascending or descending order. In this example, the data is being sorted by the State column in ascending order. When you have entered all the conditions, click the Next button.

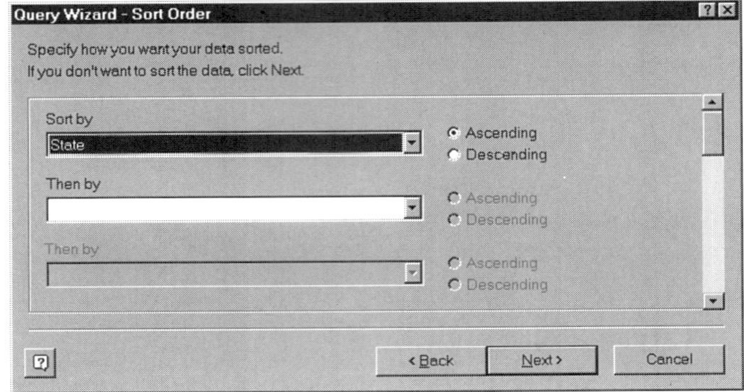

FIGURE 24.9
Using the Query Wizard—Sort Order, you can choose three columns by which to sort your data.

Finishing the Query

The last step in the Query Wizard (shown in Figure 24.10) contains several important choices. You can save the query if you believe you might want to run the query at a later date.

Regardless of whether you save the query, you have three choices as to what to do with the data. You can return the results immediately to Excel, display the Microsoft Query window to edit the query and view the results, or you can create an OLAP cube from the data.

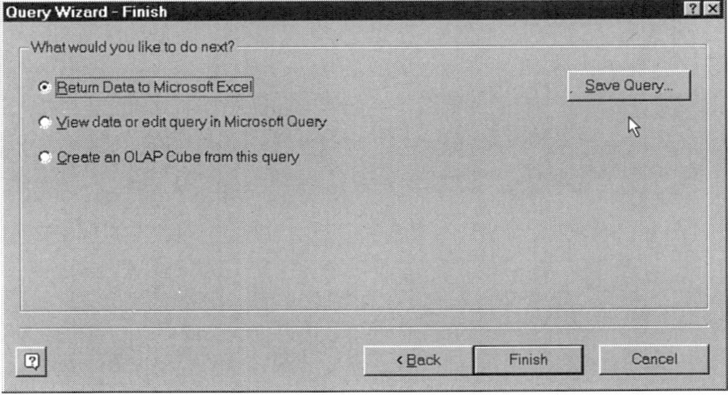

FIGURE 24.10
Saving your query before clicking Finish is always a good idea.

Saving the Query If you intend to (or think you might) use the query again, you should save the query. This avoids having to go through the wizard steps again. This option is independent of the other options; after the query is saved, you are returned to this dialog box to make a decision about the retrieved data.

Click the Save Query button to display the Save As dialog box. By default, the query is saved in a specific folder, which is located in the C:\Program Files\Microsoft Office\Queries folder. The default name displayed in the Save As dialog box uses the data source name on which the query is based.

Always give your query a name that helps you recognize the data it retrieves, instead of using the default name. After you type the name, click Save. The Query Wizard—Finish dialog box (shown in Figure 24.10) is displayed again.

Returning Data to Excel To place the data you retrieve into an Excel worksheet, choose Return Data to Microsoft Excel, and then click Finish. When returning the data to Excel, you are asked where the data should be placed, as shown in Figure 24.11.

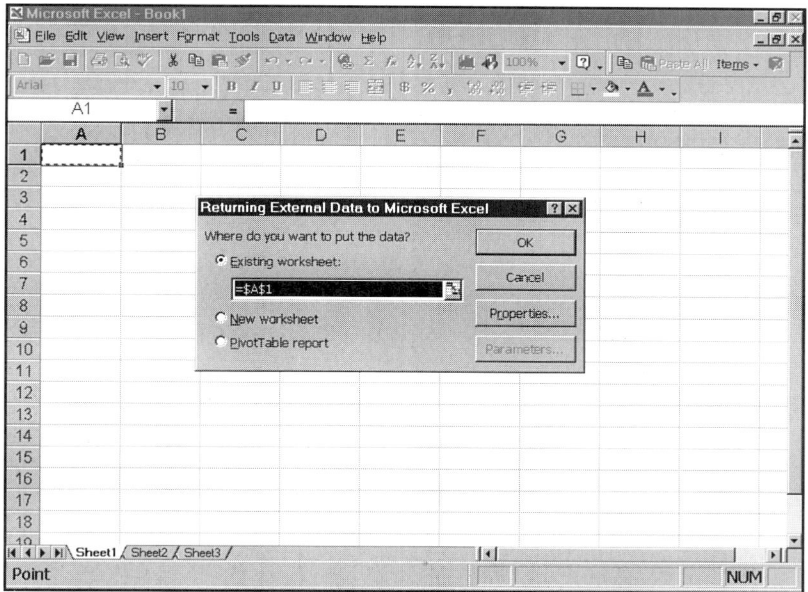

FIGURE 24.11
The data returned to Excel may be placed only in the active workbook.

You can place the data in the existing worksheet in the active workbook, in a new worksheet in the active workbook, or in a PivotTable report in the active workbook. Regardless, you must save the data in the active workbook.

If you select Existing Worksheet, click the Worksheet tab and select the cell where you want the list to start. If you select New Worksheet, a new worksheet is added to the active workbook and the list starts in cell A1. With either the Existing Worksheet or New Worksheet option, the columns in the worksheet are adjusted to fit the longest entry, and the column headings are formatted in bold.

If you select PivotTable Report, the last step of the PivotTable Wizard appears, giving you the choice of where you want the PivotTable placed.

▶ **See** "Unlocking the Power of PivotTables and PivotCharts," **p. 797**

Displaying the Query Window If you choose the View Data or Edit Query in Microsoft Query option in the final step of the Microsoft Query Wizard (refer to Figure 24.10), the Microsoft Query window opens showing the table columns and criteria in the upper half of the screen and the query results in the bottom half of the screen. Using the Microsoft Query window is discussed in detail in the following section "Using the Microsoft Query Window to Create or Edit a Query."

NOTE The Create an OLAP Cube from This Query option (refer to Figure 24.10) initiates the OLAP Cube wizard. Using this wizard to create an OLAP cube is discussed in detail in the section "Using and Creating OLAP Cubes" later in this chapter.

Using the Microsoft Query Window to Create or Edit a Query

While you can create a query using the Query Wizard, there are some limitations to that method, namely the limitation of selecting data from only one table in the source database. The other way to create a query is directly in the Microsoft Query window. Using the Query window, you can retrieve data from multiple tables. Additionally, the Microsoft Query window enables you to view on one screen all the components of a query such as tables, fields, and criteria. You will also see the data being retrieved in the Query window. With all of this at your fingertips, you have far greater control to make adjustments to the query before the data is placed in Excel than you do with the Query Wizard.

Before using the Microsoft Query window, make sure you have created the data source that identifies the location of the data that you want to retrieve. See the section "Creating the Data Source" earlier in this chapter for the steps to accomplish this. After you create the data source, you can use it to create a query to retrieve the data.

To display the Microsoft Query window, follow these steps:

1. Select Data, Get External Data, Create New Database Query. The Choose Data Source dialog box displays.
2. From the Databases tab, select the data source you want to use for your query.
3. At the bottom of the dialog box, remove the check from the Use the Query Wizard to Create/Edit Queries check box.
4. Then click OK to display the Microsoft Query window, shown in Figure 24.12.

The Microsoft Query window is similar to the query design window in Access. The query information is displayed in sections that are called *panes*. In Figure 24.12, two panes are displayed—the *table pane* (showing the database tables) and the *data pane* (which is blank because no table fields have been selected).

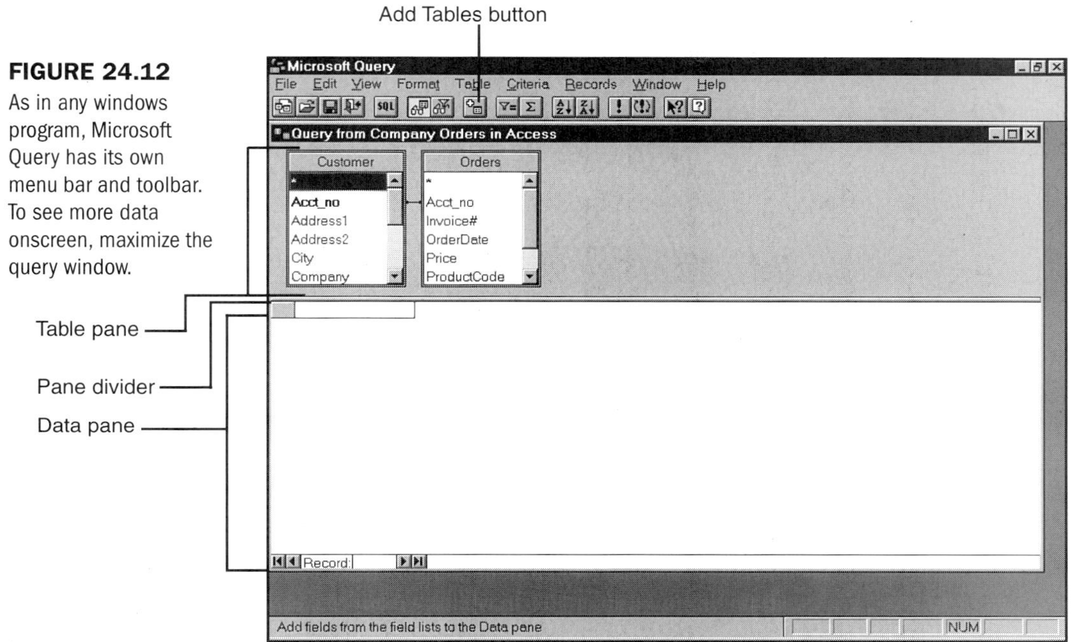

FIGURE 24.12
As in any windows program, Microsoft Query has its own menu bar and toolbar. To see more data onscreen, maximize the query window.

If you designated a default table in the source data, the table and the field names are displayed in the table pane at the top of the screen. If you did not designate a specific table when you created the source data, the Add Tables dialog box (shown in Figure 24.13) appears. Double-click the name of each table you want to add to the query window, and then click Close. To display the Add Tables dialog box, click the Add Tables button on the toolbar.

If you select more than one table, you need to join or link the tables on a common field to retrieve meaningful data.

Joining Multiple Tables

When you want to retrieve data from multiple tables, the tables must be joined using a field from each table that contains identical data. The field names do not have to be identical but the data in the field must be the same. For example, if one table contains a list of orders placed by customers and another table has a list of customer information, then they could be joined on a field such as customer number or account number.

If the tables have a permanent join in the source database, you should see a linking line appear automatically between the tables displayed in the upper pane of the Microsoft Query window (as shown in Figure 24.12). If you do not see a linking line, you will have to manually join the tables.

In Figure 24.14, two tables from an Access database are displayed in the table pane. The Sales Rep field in the Customer table is the same as the Emp# field in the Employee table.

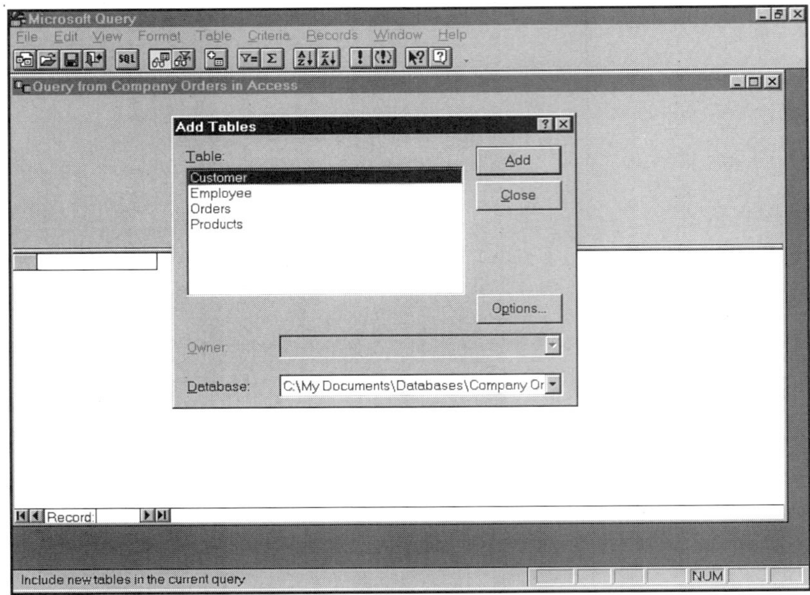

FIGURE 24.13
The Add tables dialog box lists all the tables available in the location specified in the data source.

NOTE One useful feature of Microsoft Query is the status bar. In Figure 24.14, notice the message displaying on the status bar in the lower-left corner. The status bar provides suggestions for the next step to take in the query process. In this instance, it indicates that you need to drag field from one table to related field in another.

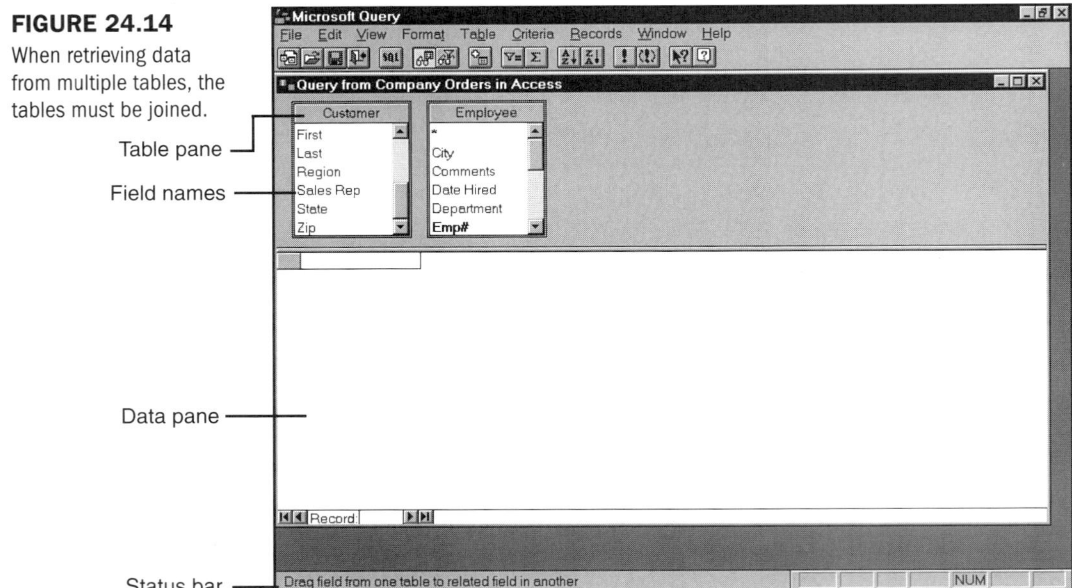

FIGURE 24.14
When retrieving data from multiple tables, the tables must be joined.

To join tables together in the Microsoft Query window, drag the field in the first table to the corresponding field in the second table. A line appears between the tables, as shown in Figure 24.15.

FIGURE 24.15
The linking line will appear automatically if the tables are already permanently joined in the source database.

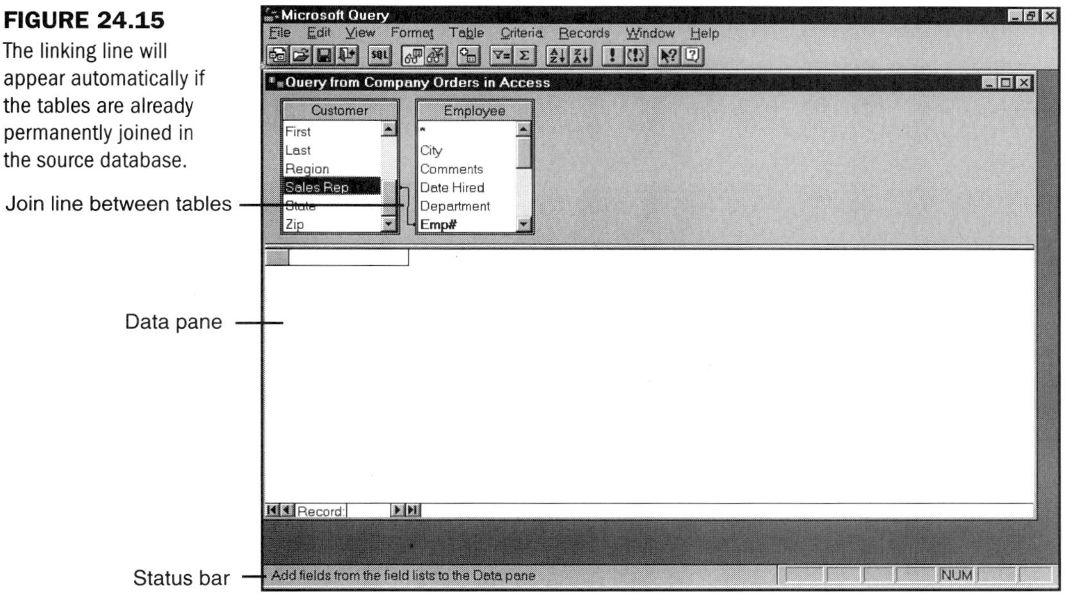

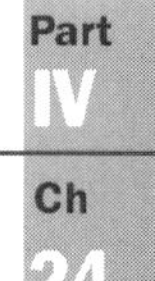

The status bar now displays a new message, recommending that you add fields to the Data pane. The next section provides instructions on how to do this.

Selecting and Ordering Columns

In the table boxes, the fields are listed alphabetically. To designate a field you want to retrieve from the database, you have to add it to the data pane in the bottom half of the screen. Double-click the field name to add it to the data pane area.

To reorder the fields in the data pane, position your mouse pointer over the name of the field you want to move. The mouse pointer changes into a black, down-pointing arrow; click once to select the field (see Figure 24.16). Your mouse pointer then changes into a white pointing arrow; hold and drag the mouse pointer to the new location. A thick black line indicates the location as you drag. Release the mouse when the thick line is at the desired position.

In Figure 24.16, the information listed in the data pane is coming from two different tables. Acct_no and Company are fields from the Customer table. ProductCode, OrderDate, and Quantity are fields from the Orders table.

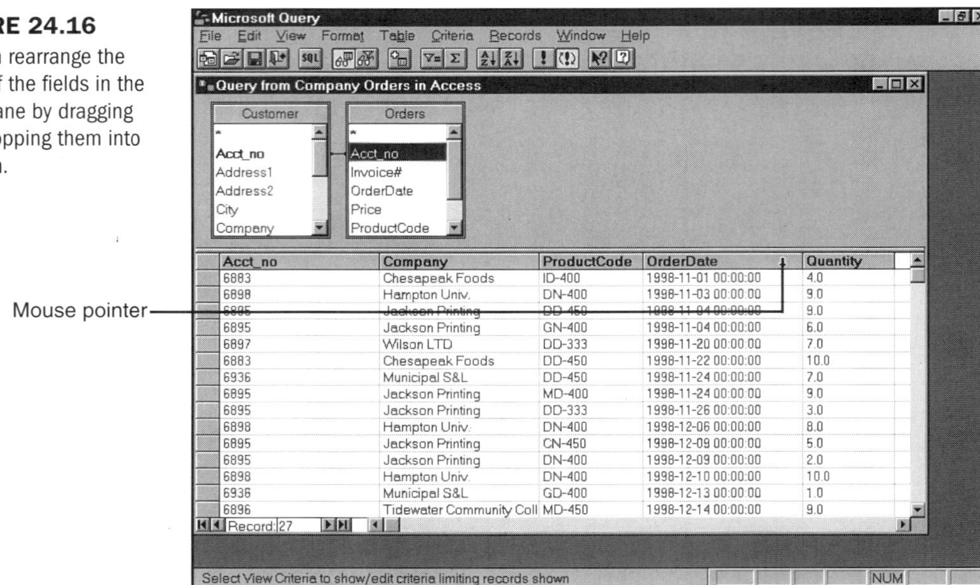

FIGURE 24.16
You can rearrange the order of the fields in the Data pane by dragging and dropping them into position.

Filtering Data

To filter out data that you don't want to retrieve from the databases, you must specify the criteria by which you want to filter. Microsoft Query uses another pane to display the filter criteria. Choose View, Criteria to display the criteria pane, or click the Show/Hide Criteria button on the Microsoft Query toolbar. The criteria pane is inserted between the table pane and the data pane, as shown in Figure 24.17.

The criteria pane displays the criteria you specify. Although you can use the criteria pane to enter the criteria, it is significantly easier to enter the criteria in the Add Criteria dialog box, which then places the criteria for you in the criteria pane. Choose Criteria, Add Criteria to display this dialog box, as shown in Figure 24.18.

To specify criteria in the Add Criteria dialog box, follow these steps:

1. Use the drop-down arrow in the Field box to display all the fields from the selected tables. Choose the field you want to filter.
2. In the Operator entry box, use the drop-down arrow to select one of the operators.
3. Click the Value entry box. Click the Values button to select from a list of existing values or type a value.
4. When you complete the criteria, click Add.
5. To specify another criterion, choose either the And or Or option button at the top of the Add Criteria dialog box. Then repeat steps 1-4.
6. After you specify all the criteria, click Close. Figure 24.19 shows two criteria selected for the query; Region equals MidAtlantic or Region equals West.

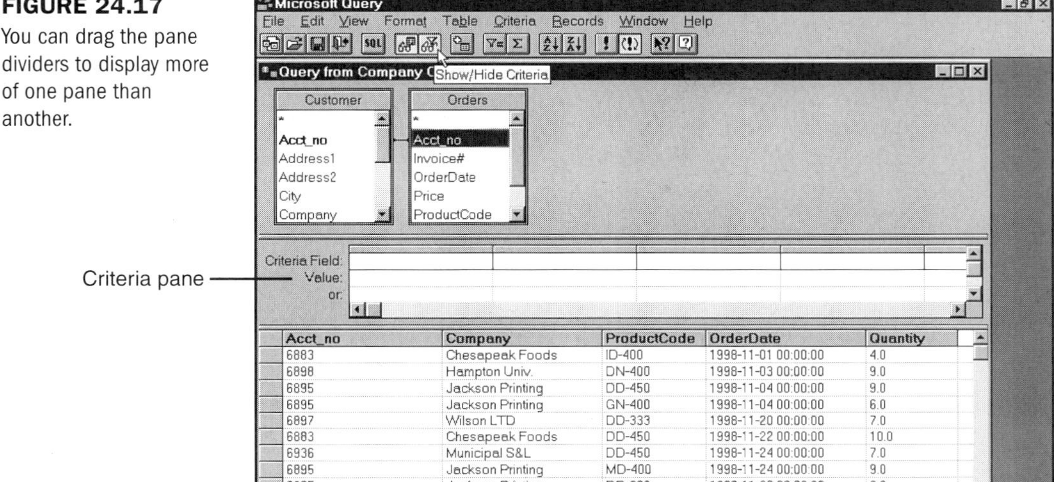

FIGURE 24.17
You can drag the pane dividers to display more of one pane than another.

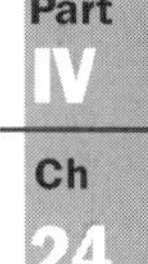

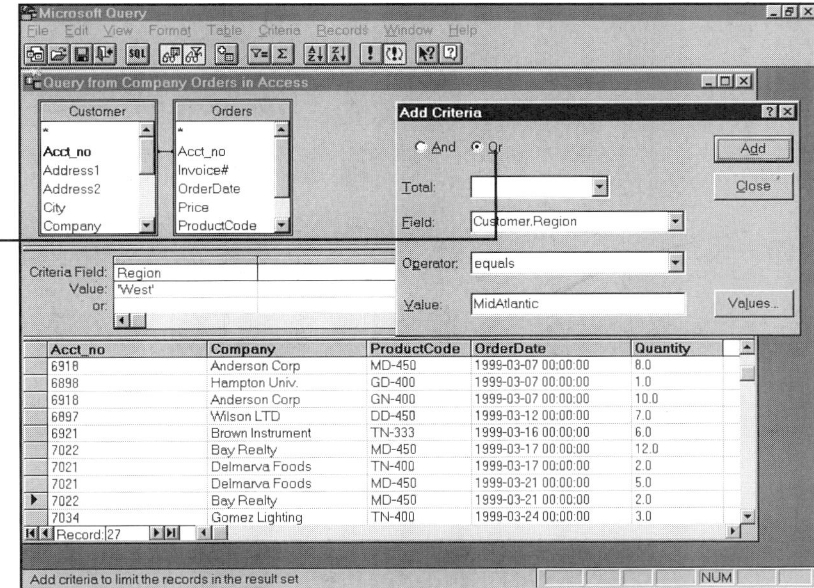

FIGURE 24.18
The results pane refreshes each time you add criteria.

By default, each time you add a field or specify criteria, Microsoft Query immediately searches for the records to display in the data pane. If you wait a long time for the screen to update, you can turn off the Auto Query button on the toolbar (refer to Figure 24.19). After you specify all the fields and criteria, select the Query Now button to retrieve the data.

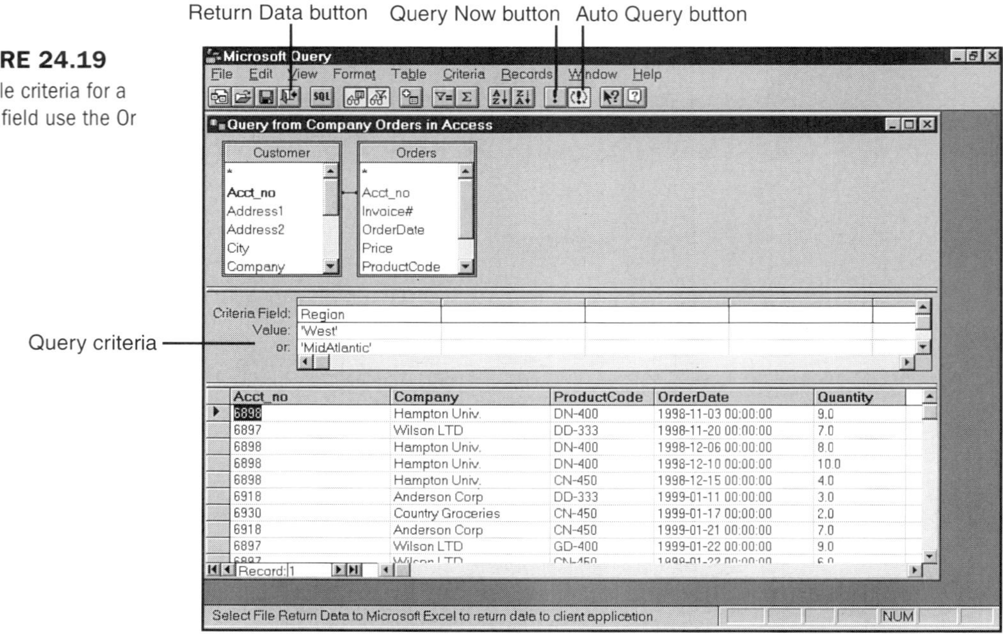

FIGURE 24.19
Multiple criteria for a single field use the Or rows.

The help screens in Microsoft Query provide additional examples of criteria. Use the Office Assistant to search for these help screens. Type `criteria examples` in the Office Assistant search box. Press Enter to see a list of help topics. Choose Examples of expressions. Look through each of the four types of expressions listed in the help screen.

Sorting Records

You can sort the list of records before returning them to Excel. Sorting records in Microsoft Query is similar to sorting a list in Excel. Before you sort the records, make sure Auto Query is turned off. It automatically runs the query again, whenever a change is made.

To sort the data based on one column, select the field in the data pane by clicking the field name in the data pane. Then use the Sort Ascending and Sort Descending buttons on the toolbar to sort the records.

Although you can sort on multiple columns in the Query window, I don't recommend it. Sorting on multiple columns in Query is similar to the way you sort in Access, and there are limitations. You must arrange the order of the columns from left to right in the data pane in the order by which you want to sort them. Then sort the columns and arrange them back in the column order you want them displayed in Excel. Furthermore, you cannot sort one column ascending and another column descending in Microsoft Query. Instead, return the list to Excel and perform the necessary sorting there.

Returning Data to Excel

If you think you might use the query again, you should save it by clicking the Save File button on the Microsoft Query toolbar. The Save As dialog box is displayed. By default, the query is saved in the Queries folder, which is typically located under the Application Data folder:

C:\Windows\Application Data\Microsoft\Queries

or, if profiles are active

C:\Windows\Profiles\<*username*>\Application Data\Microsoft\Queries

The default name displayed incorporates the source data name upon which the query is based. Always give your query a name that helps you recognize the data it retrieves, instead of using the default name. After you type the name, click Save.

To return the data resultset to Excel, click the Return Data button on the Microsoft Query toolbar (refer to Figure 24.19). The Returning External Data to Microsoft Excel dialog box is displayed, as shown in Figure 24.20.

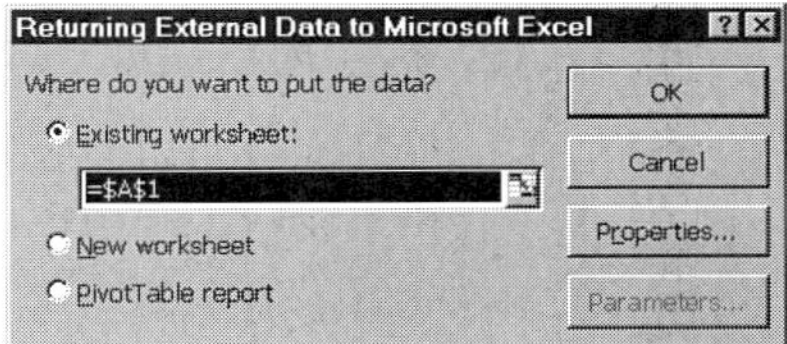

FIGURE 24.20
Select a destination for the result set.

You have several choices in which to store the data:

- The existing worksheet in the active workbook—You can specify a cell in the existing worksheet, marking the upper-left corner of the range where the data is to begin.
- A new worksheet in the active workbook—You can place the data in a new worksheet, which will be inserted in the active workbook. The data starts in cell A1.
- A PivotTable report in the active workbook—You can create a PivotTable based on the data.

If you select either Existing Worksheet or New Worksheet, the columns in the worksheet are adjusted to fit the longest entry, and the column headings are formatted in bold. Selecting the PivotTable Report option takes you directly to the final step of the PivotTable Wizard.

▶ **See** "Unlocking the Power of PivotTables and PivotCharts," **p. 797**

Creating Parameter Queries

Parameter queries prompt you for criteria when you run the query, adding a great deal of flexibility to your queries. Suppose, for example, that you want to query a table containing client information by state. Instead of a query for each state, you can create a parameter query that prompts you for the name of the state (or multiple state names if you want to be able to retrieve data on several states simultaneously). Likewise, if you want to query a table containing sales information by product code, you can create a parameter query to prompt you for the product code before the query is run. You can create parameter queries for most ODBC databases, such as Access, FoxPro, and SQL Server.

To create a Parameter query, follow these steps:

1. Start a query in the Microsoft Query window shown in Figure 24.21.
2. Turn off the Auto Query button so that data is not automatically retrieved as you are building the query. This button is a toggle button that is turned on by default.
3. Turn on the Show/Hide Criteria button so that the Criteria pane is visible. This button is a toggle button that is turned off by default.
4. Select the fields you want to retrieve. They appear in the Data pane.
5. Click the first cell in the Criteria Field row and select the field that you want to use as the parameter for the query.
6. Click the first cell in the Value row. Type a left square bracket followed by the prompt text to be displayed when the query is run. Then type a right square bracket—for example, `[Enter the Product Code]`. The prompt text cannot just be the field name.
7. Then save the query.

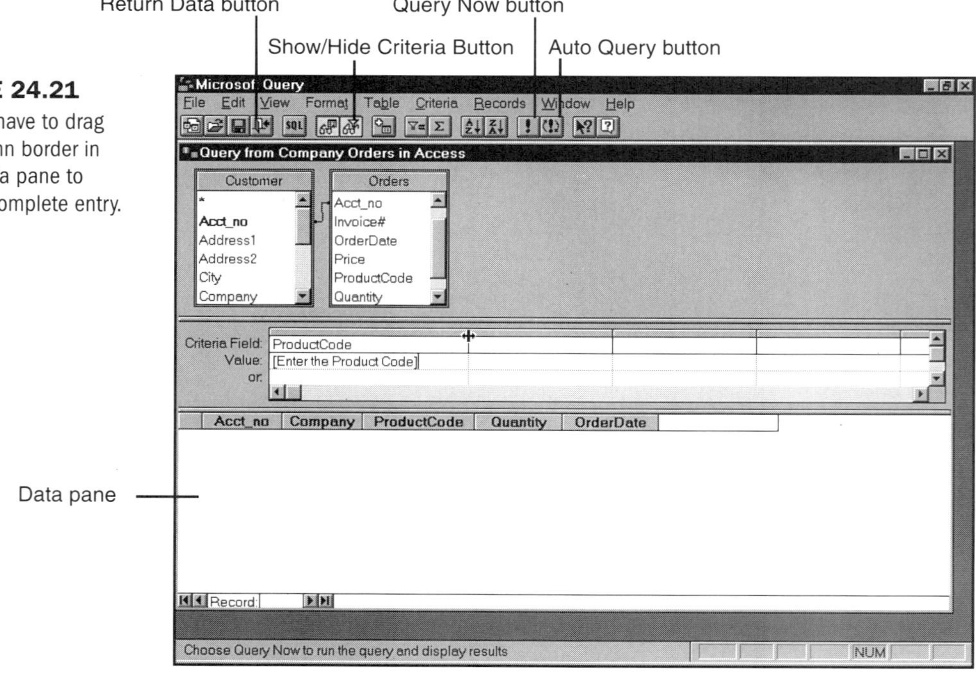

FIGURE 24.21
You may have to drag the column border in the criteria pane to see the complete entry.

Click the Query Now button to run the query. Click the Return Data button to return the result set to Excel. If you want to modify the prompt, open the saved query.

NOTE Parameter queries cannot retrieve data from OLAP databases.

Using and Creating OLAP Cubes

Excel 2000 includes client software that lets you work with *Online Analytical Processing (OLAP)* databases. OLAP is an alternative way to organize the data in very large databases to speed up data retrieval. Instead of arranging data into tables, the data is organized in levels, dimensions, and data values forming what are called *OLAP data cubes.*

Levels are hierarchical categories of data. For example, an international sales database might have separate fields identifying the country, region, city, and site of each sale. Each geographic field represents a level, with country at the highest level and site at the lowest level.

Dimensions are a set of levels that encompasses one aspect of the data; a group of geographic levels (country, region, city, and site) make up one dimension. Dimensions can have one or several levels. You can organize data in multiple dimensions, for example:

- By geographical location (country, region, city)
- By timeframe (year, quarter, month, day)
- By product type (category)

When dimensions are combined with data values, the result is an *OLAP data cube*. The data is summarized for each level in the dimension, sales by site, sales by city, sales by region, and sales by country. Examples of data values not only include sales figures, but could be units produced or quantity of inventory on hand.

There are four types of summary calculations that can be used in cubes: Sum, Count, Minimum, and Maximum.

By summarizing the data before it reaches Excel, it takes less time and effort to create the Excel reports you need. The OLAP server computes the summarized values, taking that burden away from Excel. And although Excel can import over 65,000 records, there are many databases that exceed that number. By creating OLAP cubes, it is possible for very large databases to utilize the PivotTable and PivotChart report features of Excel. In fact, that is the only way data retrieved from an OLAP data source can be displayed—in Excel PivotTable or PivotChart reports.

There are three ways that OLAP cubes get created:

- You can create an offline cube from a relational database such as Access or FoxPro using Microsoft Query and the OLAP client software included with Excel.
- You can create an offline cube from a server-based OLAP cube. You would also use Microsoft Query and the OLAP client software included with Excel to create the offline cube.

- A System Administrator can create an OLAP cube on a network server using a special OLAP software product. Microsoft has its own product, called Microsoft SQL Server OLAP Services 7.0, and there are third-party products that are available.

If the OLAP cube is on a server, you can access the OLAP cube directly to retrieve the data you want to use in an Excel PivotTable or PivotChart. However, you have to maintain the connection to the cube on the server while you are manipulating the Excel PivotTable or PivotChart.

An *offline cube* is a file that contains static data from the original database. The original database can either be a relational database or a server-based OLAP cube. Offline cube files have a .cub extension.

The advantage to creating an offline cube is that you don't have to maintain the connection to the server. Offline cubes can be stored on your local drive or placed on a network drive to share with others.

If you change your PivotTable or PivotChart reports frequently, using an offline cube will result in faster response time to changes made to the reports. This is especially true if your network connection to the server is slow.

NOTE Third-party OLAP products may not allow you to create offline cubes.

Using Existing OLAP Cubes

A server-based OLAP cube is created by a system administrator on network server using an OLAP Product, such as the Microsoft SQL Server OLAP Services 7.0 or using a third-party OLAP Product.

After the cube is created, an OLAP Provider is needed to access the data in a cube. OLAP Providers contain the client software and the data source drivers. Excel includes an OLAP Provider that can access cubes created by the Microsoft OLAP Product (Microsoft SQL Server OLAP Services 7.0).

If a third-party product was used to create the cube, the third-party OLAP Provider must be installed to provide the client software and drivers necessary to access the cube data. Any third-party OLAP Provider must be Office compatible and comply with the OLE-DB for OLAP standards.

Creating the OLAP Data Source for an Existing Cube If the OLAP cube already exists—for example, on an OLAP server on your network—you need to create a data source to the cube. You can either create the data source in Microsoft Query (as you do with other database data sources) or you can create the data source when you run the PivotTable and PivotChart Wizard. If you do not intend to retrieve the data immediately, use Microsoft Query to create the data source. Unlike other database data sources, you do not create a query to retrieve the data. Instead, you create a PivotTable report, which retrieves the data.

If you do want to retrieve the data at the same time you create the data source, you might as well create it as you create the PivotTable.

Although the following steps use Microsoft Query to create the OLAP Cube data source, they are virtually identical to the steps you'll encounter in the PivotTable Wizard:

1. Choose Data, Get External Data, New Database Query. The Choose Data Source dialog box appears.
2. Click the OLAP Cube tab and select New Data Source.
3. Click OK; the Create New Data Source dialog box appears (see Figure 24.22).
4. In the first step of the Create New Data Source dialog box, type a name that helps you remember the source data you want to retrieve—for example, the data source and cube name.
5. In the second step of the dialog box, select the OLAP Provider, as shown in Figure 24.22. The Microsoft OLE DB Provider for OLAP Services can be used for cubes that are created using the Microsoft OLAP Product—Microsoft SQL Server OLAP Services.

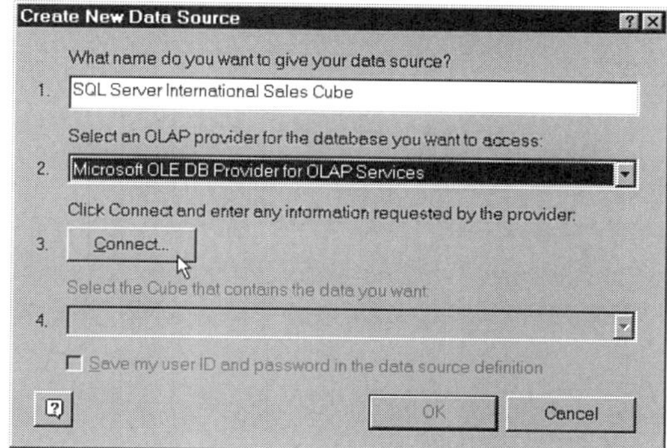

FIGURE 24.22
As you complete each step, the next step in the dialog box becomes active.

6. After you select the provider, click the Connect button in the third step. The Multi-Dimensional Connection dialog box appears, as shown in Figure 24.23.
7. If the cube is server-based, click the OLAP Server option button and identify the server. If the data source is an offline file-based cube, click the DCube File option button and identify the location of the .cub file.

NOTE If you create a data source to connect directly to an offline cube file, this data source may not give you access to the original server database from which the offline cube file was created. See the section "Creating OLAP Cubes" later in this chapter to learn more about offline cubes.

8. If you identified a Server, click Next to connect to the server.

   If you identified an offline cube file, click Finish to return to the Create New Data Source dialog box. The path to the source cube data appears next to the Connect button.
9. After you complete the Create New Data Source dialog box, click OK. The Choose Data Source dialog box displays. The data source name you entered in the first step of the Create New Data Source dialog box is listed on the Databases tab of the dialog box.

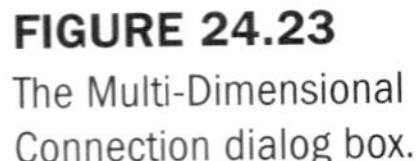

FIGURE 24.23
The Multi-Dimensional Connection dialog box.

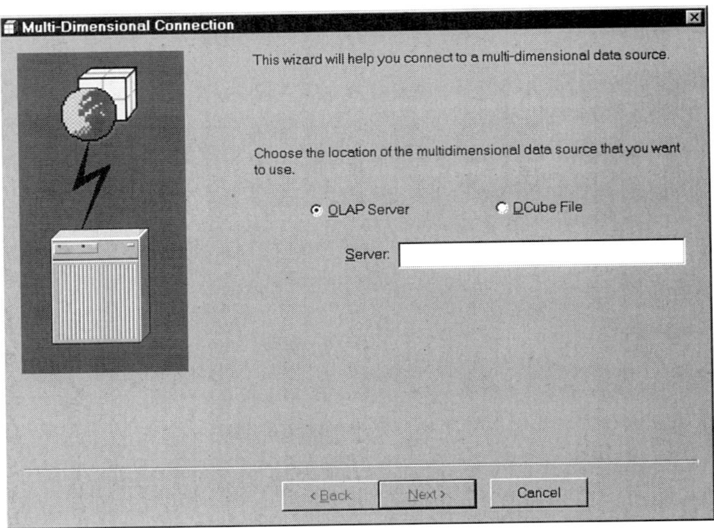

Creating Offline OLAP Cubes

Offline cubes can be a useful way of handling data from large relational databases, too large to be brought into Excel with a query. The limitation is that the data can be displayed only in Excel PivotTables or PivotCharts.

Offline cubes are also the best choice when you are retrieving data from an OLAP cube stored on a server where the connection with the server is slow or tenuous. You do not have to rely on the server availability or responsiveness. Because server-based OLAP cubes tend to be very large, you need to decide how much of the data should be placed in the offline cube file. It will be time-consuming initially to save a large offline cube file, but worth the effort for the time it will save you later on. Additionally, you can update the offline cube file when the server cube database changes.

NOTE You can create your own offline cubes, because Excel comes with an OLAP Provider, Microsoft OLE DB Provider for OLAP Services.

How you go about creating an offline cube depends on the source of the offline cube data:

- If the offline cube is going to be based on an existing cube on a server, you can create the offline cube after you've retrieved the data and created the PivotTable or PivotChart. From the PivotTable toolbar, there is a Client-Server Settings option you use to create the offline cube.
- If the offline cube is going to be based on a relational database (such as Access or FoxPro), you create a data source to the database and query through Microsoft Query. After the query is run, you create the offline cube using the OLAP Cube wizard in Microsoft Query.

Planning the Offline Cube Structure Before you create the cube, make sure you've decided which fields in the database you plan to use as dimensions and which fields as the data values to be summarized. The fields in a cube must be either dimension fields or data-value fields; when you create a cube, you identify each field as one of these two types. You should also plan out the levels for each dimension you create. For example, a sales dimension might have levels for country, region, and city—each of these fields must exist in the database before you create the cube. The data value fields can be summarized using the Sum, Count, Minimum, or Maximum functions.

NOTE If you want to sum and count a data field, you must add the field to your query or selection of source data twice, once for each type of summary you want.

Querying a Database to Create an Offline Cube Now that you have mapped out the cube dimensions and data fields, you're ready to retrieve the data. Use these steps to query the database:

1. Create a data source for the relational database as described earlier in this chapter.
2. Then create a query and retrieve the data you want to be part of the offline cube.
3. If you created the query using the Query Wizard, the final step of the wizard has an option to create the OLAP cube (as seen in Figure 24.24). Save the query (just in case), and then click the Create an OLAP Cube from This Query option and click Finish.

   If you created the query in the Microsoft Query window, choose File, Create OLAP Cube.

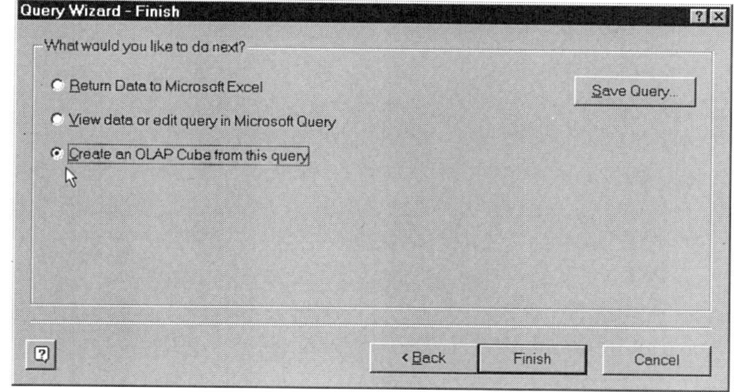

FIGURE 24.24
Because the wizard can work with only one table, OLAP cubes created from the wizard will contain fields from just one table.

4. The Welcome screen for the OLAP Cube wizard appears. Click Next to start the wizard.

Stepping Through the OLAP Cube Wizard With the OLAP Cube wizard, you can create two types of files—a cube definition file and an offline cube file. A *cube definition file* stores the information necessary to generate a temporary cube, similar to a data source. The cube definition is saved with an .oqy file extension. The *offline cube file* is a static file, a picture of the data from the database when you created the offline cube. Offline cubes can be stored in a shared network folder or on your local drive and have a .cub file extension.

With the cube definition, the offline cube is created when you use the cube definition, so that it always contains the latest data.

The OLAP Cube Wizard is a three-step process. Although not particularly complicated, it is important you complete each of the steps correctly to successfully create an OLAP cube.

The first step of the wizard, shown in Figure 24.25, is where you identify the data fields and choose the summary calculation you want for each data field. All other fields will be dimension fields.

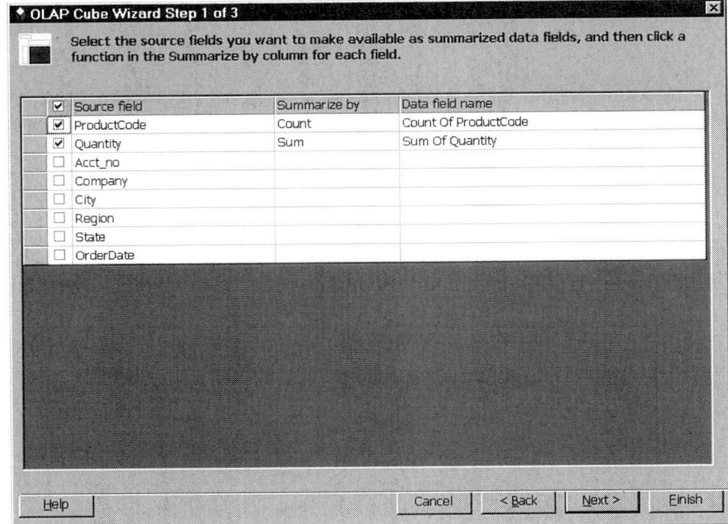

FIGURE 24.25
Only fields containing numeric values can be data fields. You can have more than one data field.

In the second step of the wizard, shown in Figure 24.26, you define the dimensions and the fields that make up the dimension levels. If one of your fields is a date or time, the wizard automatically inserts the levels for these fields, organizing the data by year, quarter, month (or hour, minute, second). If a field does not belong to a particular hierarchy, you can create dimensions that contain just one level.

Simply drag the fields to create the dimensions. Figure 24.27 shows a completed list of dimensions.

By default, the name of the first field in each dimension becomes the name of the dimension. To change the dimension name, click the name and press F2 to edit the name.

The third step of the wizard, shown in Figure 24.28, gives you the option to select the type of cube you want to create. Here you decide whether you want to build the cube in memory or save it as a cube file. Which of the three options you choose depends on the tradeoffs you're willing to make—how much data will be stored in the cube, what type of PivotTable reports will be created, and what memory and disk space resources are available.

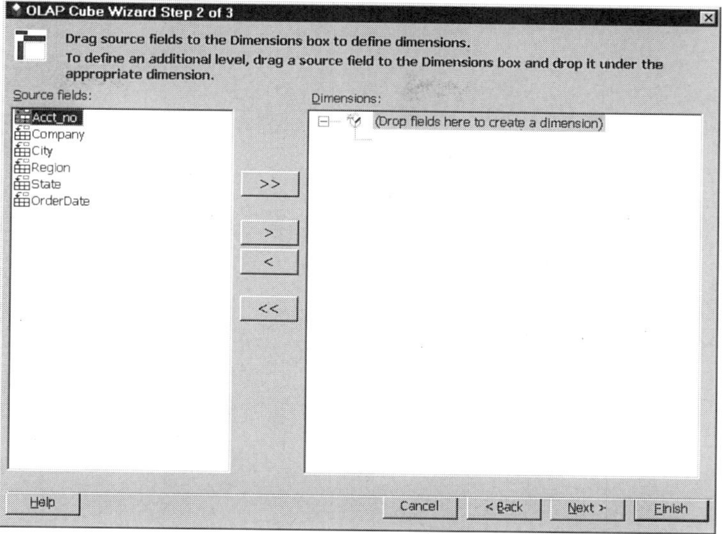

FIGURE 24.26
Dimensions can be one or multiple levels.

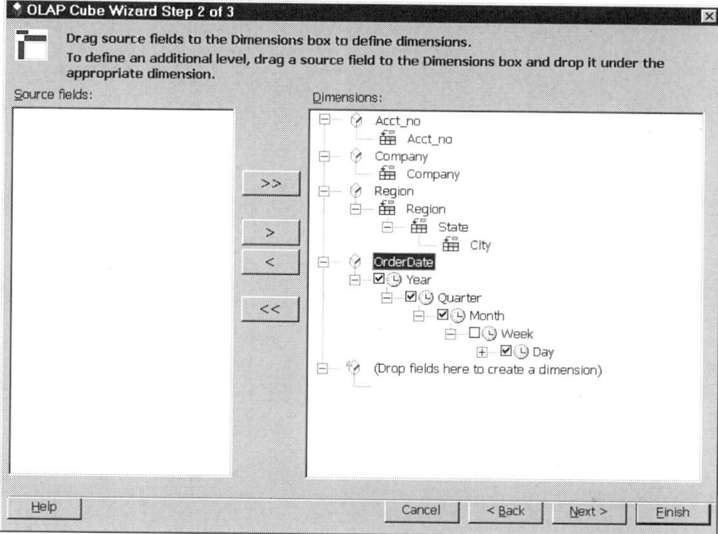

FIGURE 24.27
When you create a dimension based on a date field, the wizard automatically adds the timeframes. You can remove any levels you don't want by removing the check mark.

- Retrieving data as needed—Creates a cube definition that stores instructions for creating the cube. When you open the PivotTable report, the cube is created in memory. The cube retrieves only the data necessary to display the report. If you change the fields in the PivotTable report, the cube retrieves the necessary data to change the report. Use this option for reports that you rarely change, when memory and disk space are at a premium, and when you're not concerned about how long it takes to refresh the report when you make changes to the fields displayed.

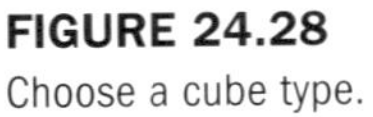

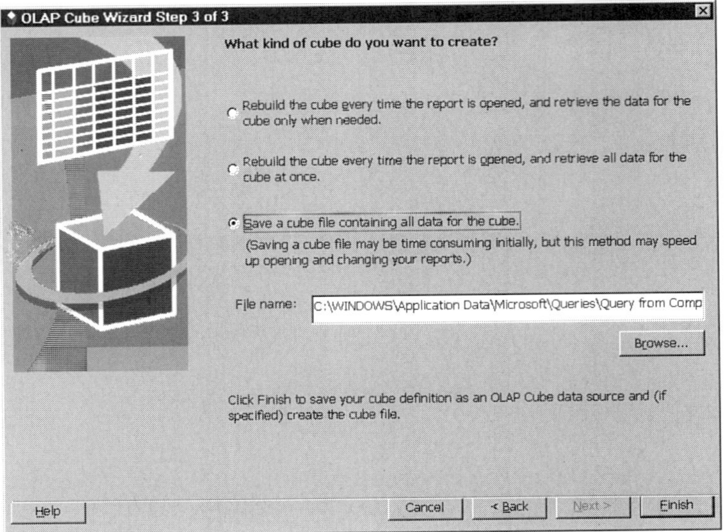

FIGURE 24.28
Choose a cube type.

- Retrieving the data all at once—Creates a cube definition that stores instructions for creating the cube. When you open the PivotTable report, the cube is created in memory. The cube retrieves all the data in the cube, not just the data necessary to display the report. When you change the fields in the PivotTable report, the data is immediately available to refresh the cube. Use this option for reports that will be changed frequently, but when you don't have the disk space to save the offline cube permanently. This option may require substantial memory and temporary disk space, especially for cubes that contain a lot of data.
- Saving a cube file—Creates an offline cube file that contains all the data. Use this option for reports that are changed frequently and at times when you have ample disk space to store the offline cube. This is also a good option when you want to store the cube on a network so that others can have access to it, especially if the source database contains confidential information that others should not have access to. This option takes longer to set up initially. The size of the cube affects the speed at which reports can be updated. If you choose this option, the cube file is not created when you click Finish. Instead, this file is created when you save the cube definition or create the PivotTable report based on the cube. When you select the Refresh button on the PivotTable toolbar, the cube will be re-created from the original source of the data.

NOTE Regardless of the option you choose, the wizard saves a cube definition (.oqy) file.

You don't have to create a separate data source to use the offline cube file. If you save the offline cube on a shared network location, other users can create data sources to access the file and base reports on it.

You can also create an offline cube from within the PivotTable and PivotChart Wizard. The steps are virtually identical to the steps outlined previously. Refer to the section "Unlocking the Power of PivotTables and PivotCharts" in Chapter 25.

Modifying Offline Cubes

If you find that you want to organize the cube differently or include different data in it, you can return to the OLAP Cube wizard to make changes.

After you create an OLAP cube, you cannot add more fields to it from the original database. You can, however, create a new OLAP cube from the same query. If you think you may need to do this, be sure to save a database query (.dqy). You can then open the query file and run the OLAP Cube Wizard to create a new cube that includes additional fields from the original database.

CAUTION

Do not use the same name for the revised offline cube; it is possible that incorrect data will be returned.

If you do find it necessary to create a new offline cube, either create a new PivotTable or change the existing PivotTable so that it points to the new cube.

Whenever you refresh a PivotTable report that is based on an OLAP cube, new and changed data from the original database is brought into the cube if the cube is built temporarily in memory. If the cube is an offline cube file, the file is rebuilt with the new data and the existing file is replaced.

Creating and Running Web Queries

Web queries are designed to retrieve data from intranet or Internet Web sites that use the HTTP or FTP protocols. If you used this feature in earlier versions of Excel, you'll notice the process has been enhanced in Excel 2000. There are several built-in financial Web queries included in Excel or you can create your own Web queries.

The built-in Web queries are designed to provide you with access to investment data. But you can create queries to any Internet or intranet Web page from which you want to routinely see the latest data. This includes a site that posts a table of home mortgage rates, a site that posts actuary tables, or a site that posts job descriptions.

Web queries retrieve only the data on a Web page, not the entire contents of the page. They can retrieve data in a table or text on a page. Because Web queries retrieve just the data, it is not recommended that you use them to copy information from a Web page to use on your own Web page.

Running Excel's Built-In Web Queries

The Web queries provided with Excel connect to the Microsoft Investor Web site and import data into a worksheet. The three built-in queries retrieve data about

- Currency Rates
- Stock Quotes
- Major Financial Indices

NOTE Microsoft Investor is a Web-based service providing tools and information to help personal investors track their investments, find new investing ideas, and research their next investment. Some of the services at this Web site are free and some require you to subscribe (for a fee) to the service. Investor offers portfolio tracking and analysis, editorial and market summaries, company and mutual fund research, email notifications and alerts, an investment finder, and access to online trading through brokers.

To run one of the built-in queries, use the following steps:

1. Choose Data, Get External Data, Run Saved Query. The Run Query dialog box is displayed, as shown in Figure 24.29. Select the query you want to run.

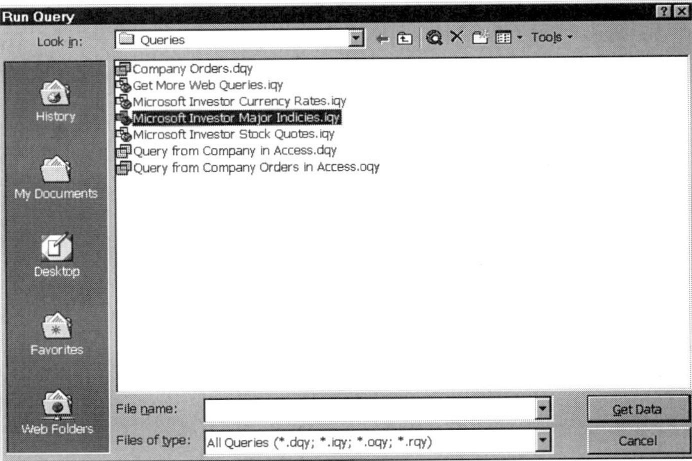

FIGURE 24.29
Web queries have the .iqy extension.

2. Then choose Get Data. Excel displays the Returning External Data to Microsoft Excel dialog box (shown in Figure 24.30).
3. Through this dialog box, you indicate where you want the data retrieved from the query to appear. You can select a worksheet and cell in any open workbook, or ask that a new worksheet be inserted into the active workbook. If you are working from within a PivotTable Report, you can select the PivotTable Report option.
4. Then click OK.

NOTE The next section, "Changing Web Query Properties and Parameters," discusses the property and parameter options that you can modify from this dialog box.

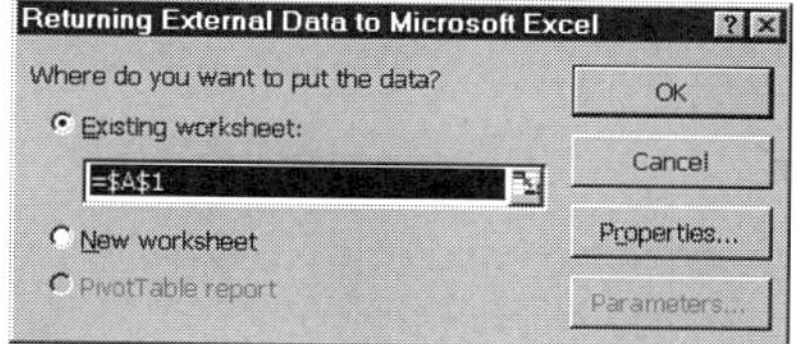

FIGURE 24.30
Choose the location for the query results.

If you select either the Currency Rates or Major Indicies queries, Excel establishes a connection to the Internet and displays the query results in your Excel worksheet. Figure 24.31 shows the result of running the Microsoft Investor Major Indicies query.

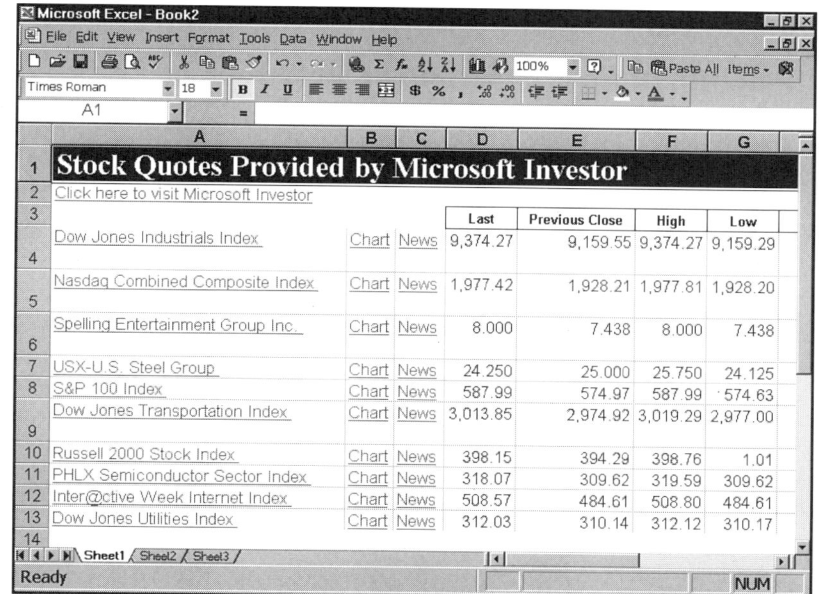

FIGURE 24.31
Indicate where you want the data to be returned from the query.

If you select the Stock Quote query, the Enter Parameter Value dialog box appears, as shown in Figure 24.32. Enter the appropriate stock symbols.

NOTE To look up a stock symbol, run either the Major Indices or Currency Rates query and scroll down when the results are returned. Below the data is a symbol search feature.

If you wanted to see the stock quotes for McDonald's, Hewlett-Packard, and Coca-Cola, you would enter the symbols `mcd, hwp, ko`. Select the Use This Value/Reference for Future Refreshes check box to avoid having to retype the symbols when you refresh the query. Then select OK to run the query and return the results to the Excel worksheet.

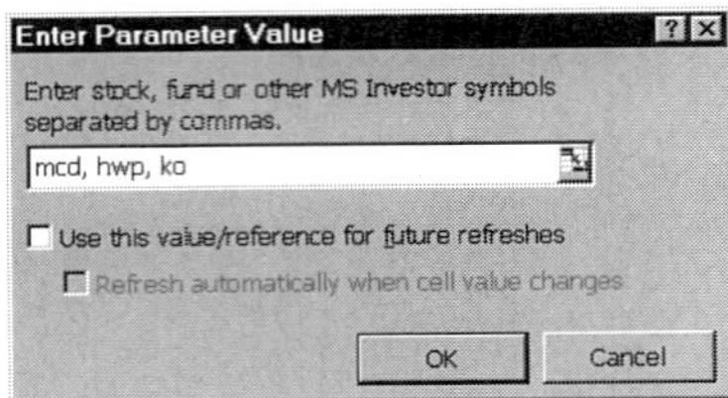

FIGURE 24.32
Make sure you enter the correct stock symbols.

In addition to the three built-in queries, another query has been designed to retrieve more Web queries. When you run this query, a list of additional sample queries appears in your worksheet. The list includes a description of each query and instructions on how to access these sample queries.

Creating Your Own Web Queries

Before you create your own Web queries, it may save you a lot of time (and headaches) to see the list of queries available when you run the built-in query, Get More Web Queries. This list has queries for stock market quotes, stock market reports, currency and exchange rates, commodities, money markets, and consumer information. Some of the queries included are

- Accutrade Quotes
- Money Magazine Quotes
- DBC Dow Jones Report
- CNN Commodities
- CNN Interest Rates

If you find that the data you want is on your local intranet or another Internet Web site, create your own Web queries. There are a number of things you need to take into consideration, however, before creating the query. For example, you need to have the correct address for the Web page; if the Web page uses frames you need to make sure the address is for the data and not the address of the frames page. If you want to retrieve only a table on the Web page, you need to identify the table. This may mean looking at the underlying HTML code for a Web page and identifying the table.

In the dialog box, you'll identify the Web address, what you want to retrieve from the site, and formatting options. The Advanced button provides additional formatting options for preformatted sections.

To create a new Web query, choose Data, Get External Data, New Web Query. The New Web Query dialog box appears, as shown in Figure 24.33.

In the first step, you have to identify the Web page that contains the data you want to retrieve. You can either type the URL or you can click the Browse Web button to locate the Web page. If the Web page uses frames, make sure you identify the page that contains the data and not the frames.

FIGURE 24.33
The Save Query button becomes active when you identify the Web page URL.

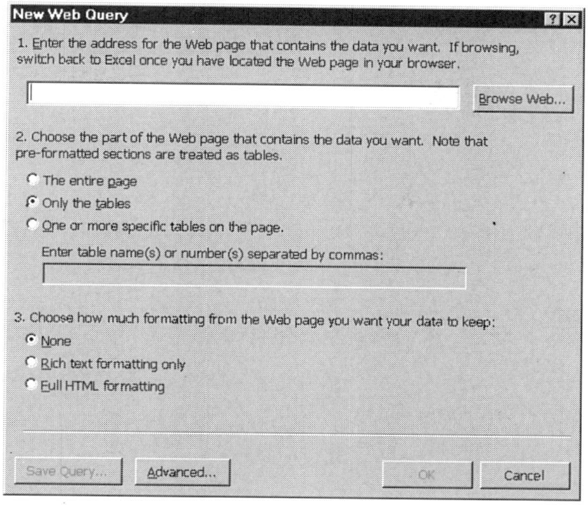

Next, you choose the data you want to retrieve:

- You can retrieve all of the data on the entire page.
- You can retrieve the data inside all tables or in all preformatted sections. A *preformatted section* is a section that can be used in other applications. For example, a Web page that contained a Web component such as a PivotTable is a preformatted section. These sections are typically formatted using tabs and spaces instead of HTML.
- You can retrieve the data in table and preformatted sections that you specify. To identify these items, you need to look at the underlying HTML code of the Web Page. Most browsers let you look at the underlying code. In Internet Explorer, you can right-click on a Web page and choose View Code from the shortcut menu to see the Web page code.

If you plan to specify a table or preformatted section, look for the HTML tags in the Web page code. For tables, look for the <TABLE> tab; for preformatted sections, look for the <PRE> tag. HTML codes typically come in pairs such as <TABLE> … </TABLE>. If the sections don't have names, you will have to count them and enter the item number in quotes, such as "2".

NOTE The order in which you specify the tables and preformatted sections is irrelevant; they are retrieved in the order in which they appear on the Web page.

After you have identified the Web page and what you want to retrieve, you need to decide how you want the data formatted. Data in tables will automatically be displayed in separate cells in the worksheet. Using the Advanced button, you can specify the formatting options for preformatted sections.

If you do not intend to share this Web query with others or use it with other workbooks, then you do not have to save it separately from the workbook. The query is automatically saved as part of the active workbook, when you save the workbook. You will be able to run the query, but only from the workbook with which it is associated.

If you do plan to share the Web query or want the option to use it in another workbook, you need to click the Save Query button in the New Web Query dialog box (refer to Figure 24.33). Web queries are saved with an .iqy file extension. The Web query will be saved in the Queries folder, which is typically located under the Application Data folder:

C:\Windows\Application Data\Microsoft\Queries

or, if profiles are active

C:\Windows\Profiles\<*username*>\Application Data\Microsoft\Queries

Editing a Web Query If the Web query does not retrieve what you expected, you can change it by clicking in any cell that contains the retrieved data and selecting Edit Query on the External Data toolbar. The Edit Web Query dialog box (similar to the New Web Query dialog box) appears from which you can make your changes.

Refreshing the Retrieved Data Periodically, you will want to retrieve the most current data from the Web page you have queried. You can have this done only when you click the Refresh Data button on the External Data toolbar or automatically when you open the workbook. To set the refresh to occur automatically, click the Data Range Properties button on the External Data toolbar and mark the option Refresh Data on File Open check box. Query properties and parameters are discussed in more detail in the next section.

Changing Web Query Properties and Parameters

There are several properties and parameters in Web queries over which you have control. To modify the properties, choose the Properties button in the Returning External Data to Excel dialog box when you first run a query, or select Data, Get External Data, Properties. The External Data Range Properties dialog box appears, as shown in Figure 24.34.

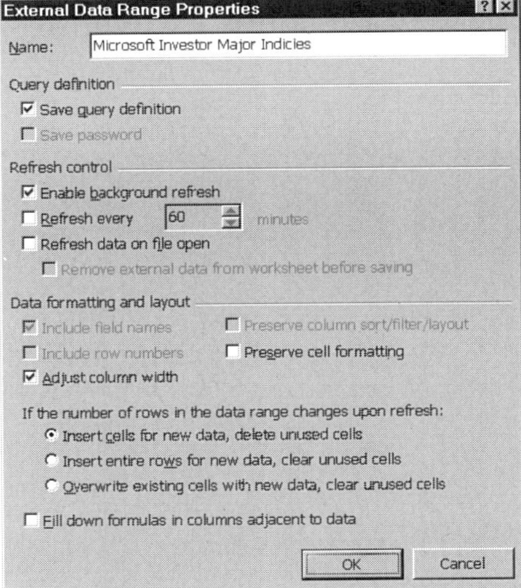

FIGURE 24.34
Options that are not available for the current query are grayed out.

The name of the query you are working with appears in the Name text box. The following list describes each option:

- Save Query Definition—Saves the query with the worksheet so that you can refresh the results directly from the worksheet.
- Save Password—If the query requires a password (which is requested the first time you run the query), the password is saved so that you won't be asked the password when you refresh the query results.
- Enable Background Refresh—Enables you to run query refresh behind the scenes, so you can continue to work in Excel.
- Refresh Data on File Open—Excel automatically refreshes the data for the query when you open the workbook containing query results.
- Remove External Data from Worksheet Before Saving—Removes the data returned from the external data source before the worksheet is saved. Data is refreshed when the workbook is opened again.
- Include Field Names—Used when you run queries against external databases, such as Access or FoxPro. Not applicable with Web queries.
- Include Row Numbers—Used when you run queries against external databases, such as Access or FoxPro. Not applicable with Web queries.
- Adjust Column Width—Automatically adjusts column widths for the widest entry in the column.
- Insert Cells for New Data, Delete Unused Cells—Inserts or deletes cells in the data range if the size of the data range changes when you refresh the data.
- Insert Entire Rows for New Data, Clear Unused Cells—Overwrites existing cells if the size of the data range changes when you refresh the data.
- Overwrite Existing Cells with New Data, Clear Unused Cells—Overwrites existing cells if the size of the data range changes when you refresh the data. Unused cells are cleared.
- Fill Down Formulas in Columns Adjacent to Data—If there are columns containing formulas adjacent to the imported data, the formulas are copied into the column to the right if the data range expands when you refresh the data.

If the query is a parameter query (such as the Microsoft Investor Stock Quotes query), you can adjust the parameters.

▶ **See** "Creating Parameter Queries," **p. 747**

To modify how the parameters for a query are obtained, choose the Parameters button in the Returning External Data to Excel dialog box when you first run a query, or select Data, Get External Data, Parameters.

The Parameters dialog box appears, as shown in Figure 24.35. Select the parameters you want to modify in the Parameter Name list box. In this instance, QUOTE is the only parameter. Choose an option for How Parameter Value Is Obtained from one of the following three options for the parameter:

- Prompt for Value Using the Following String—This option prompts the user for the value for the parameter, using the prompt entered in the text box. Refer to Figure 24.32 for an example of this parameter.
- Use the Following Value—Uses the value entered in the text box to run the query.
- Get the Value from the Following Cell—Uses the value in the specified cell as the input for the parameter.

When you have finished making changes in the Parameters dialog box, click OK.

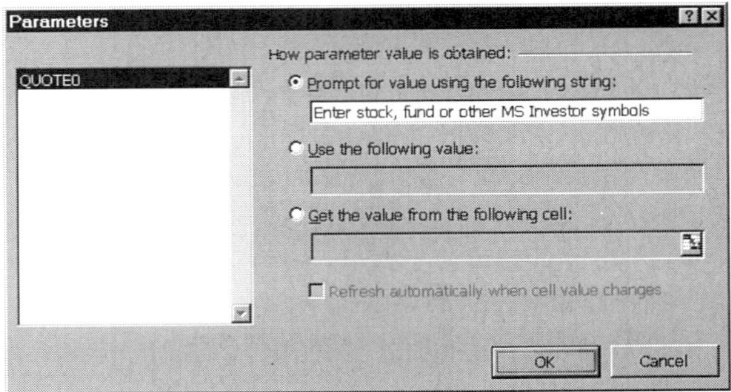

FIGURE 24.35
Choose one of the three parameter options.

Running Saved Queries

After you've created the query, you can run it anytime by selecting Data, Get External Data, Run Saved Query. The Run Query dialog box appears, as shown in Figure 24.36. You can distinguish the query types by their file extensions:

- .dqy—A database query.
- .iqy—A Web query.
- .oqy—An OLAP cube definition.

FIGURE 24.36
Double-click the query you want to run.

Importing Text Files

Text files are used when Excel cannot import a file type directly from another program, as most programs can save data to a text file. The three most common text file formats are Text (.txt), Formatted Text (.prn), and Comma-Separated Value (.csv):

- *.txt Tab-Delimited Files*—Columns of data are separated by tab characters. Each row of data ends in a carriage return. In some text files, commas or other characters may be used as delimiters. If a cell contains a comma, the cell contents are enclosed in double quotation marks. For example, if a cell contains 13,000, it appears as "13,000"; and Jackson, Tom appears as "Jackson, Tom". All formatting, graphics, objects, and other worksheet contents are lost.
- *.prn Space-Delimited Files*—Sometimes called *column-delimited* or fixed-width. Commas separate columns of data. Each row of data ends in a carriage return. When using this format, only visible text and values in the active worksheet are saved. You may need to adjust the column widths on the worksheet to ensure data is visible. Cells containing formulas are converted as text. All formatting, graphics, objects, and other worksheet contents are lost. If a row of cells contains more than 240 characters, characters beyond 240 are placed on a new line at the end of the converted file. For example, if eight rows of data are being converted, and rows 1 and 3 contain more than 240 characters, the remaining text in row 1 is placed in row 9, the remaining text in row 3 is placed in row 10, and so forth.
- *.csv Comma-Delimited Files*—Commas separate cell values. If a cell contains a comma, the cell contents are enclosed in double quotation marks. For example, if a cell contains 13,000, it appears as "13,000", and Jackson, Tom appears as "Jackson, Tom". All formatting, graphics, objects, and other worksheet contents are lost.

In Excel 97 and earlier versions, you imported text files either by opening the file (File, Open) or by creating a query in Microsoft Query. In Excel 2000, you can still open the file, but you no longer need to create a query to import a text file. Instead, a new option is now under the Data, Get External Data command—Import Text File.

There are a few differences between these two methods. When you use the File, Open method, the response by Excel depends on the file type you are attempting to open. If the file has a .txt or .prn extension, the Text Import Wizard begins. If the file has a .csv extension, the file is immediately opened. When you use the Get External Data methods, Excel looks only for files with the .txt extension. However, you can force Excel to look for all files and select a .prn or .csv file. Regardless of the file type, the Text Import Wizard begins.

Another benefit of the Get External Data method is that the original file is not opened. Rather, you get to designate the location in an active worksheet where the data will be inserted.

Using the Text Import Wizard

Unless you open a .csv file (File, Open), you will encounter the Text Import Wizard when you attempt to import a text file. This wizard contains only three steps, but incorporates a number of options for you to choose when importing these files. Figure 24.37 shows Step 1 of 3 of the wizard.

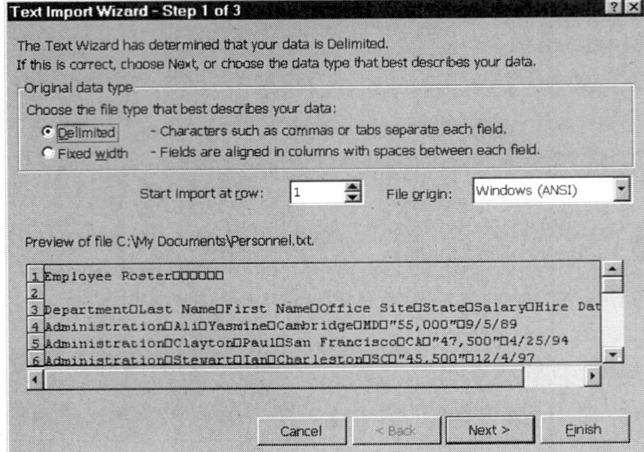

FIGURE 24.37
Step 1 in the Text Import Wizard.

In the Original Data Type area of the wizard dialog box, choose either Delimited or Fixed Width. Generally, you select Delimited if the text file you are importing is delimited with spaces, tabs, commas, or some other character (as most .txt or .csv files are). Select Fixed Width if the text file is space-delimited, column-delimited, or fixed-width. Most files using the Formatted Text file format (.prn) can be imported successfully by using the Fixed Width option.

NOTE Sometimes, when data is brought into Excel by using the Formatted Text format, an entire row of data must be placed in a single cell. To parse the data, Excel provides the Convert Text to Columns Wizard. Look ahead to the section "Parsing Text" for the procedures to separate the data.

In the File Origin drop-down list box, select the operating environment from which the file is coming—Macintosh, Windows (ANSI), or MS-DOS (PC-8). This tells Excel the type of character set the file is using. Text data from a mainframe computer most likely uses the PC-8 character set, although some mainframe text files may use the ANSI character set. At the bottom of the dialog box, a sample of the text file data is displayed in a preview window (refer to Figure 24.37).

NOTE If the data in the preview window contains odd-looking characters, or appears to be scrambled, you may not have selected the correct File Origin character set. Try using different character sets until the data in the preview window appears correctly.

In the Start Import at Row number box, select the row in the text file where you want the importing to start. Use the preview window at the bottom of the dialog box to assist you. If necessary, use the scrollbars in the preview window to scroll down to see more rows.

Because many text files contain titles (or other information) in the first few lines of the file, you can choose not to import these rows of data. In Figure 24.37, the first line contains a title and the second is blank. In this example, you would enter 3 in the Start Import at Row number box.

After you select the settings in Step 1 of 3 in the Wizard, choose Next. The Text Import Wizard displays a dialog box for the second step of the importing process. The exact dialog box that appears depends on whether you selected Delimited or Fixed Width in the first step. The next two sections in this chapter describe in detail the delimited text import options and the fixed-width text import options.

Choosing Delimited Text Import Options Selecting Delimited in Step 1 of the Text Import Wizard displays the dialog box shown in Figure 24.38.

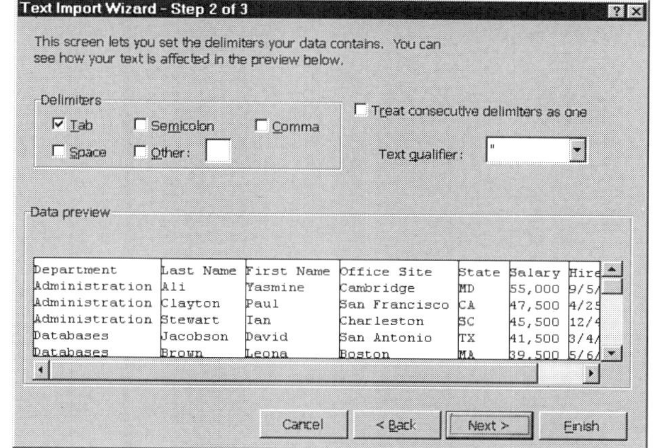

FIGURE 24.38
Step 2 of the Text Import Wizard, if Delimited is selected in Step 1.

To finish importing the text, follow these steps:

1. In the Delimiters section of the dialog box, indicate the delimiters in the text file by clicking the appropriate check box. More than one delimiter may be selected, if applicable.

   The wizard divides each row of text into columns, based on the location of the delimiters. The Data Preview window, at the bottom of the dialog box, indicates where each column begins and ends, with black vertical lines.

2. Select the Treat Consecutive Delimiters As One check box if you want to ignore empty columns of data as the file is imported. Usually, however, you should leave this check box empty.

3. Select the appropriate text qualifier from the Text Qualifier drop-down list.

   The text qualifier is used to enclose numbers or text that include the delimiting character, so that Excel can distinguish the delimiting character from the data containing the delimiting character. For example, if the delimiters are commas and the text qualifier is a double quote, any text that contains a comma is surrounded by double quotes. Excel ignores the comma inside the double quotes when it imports the data. The most common text qualifier is the double quotation mark.

   Use the Data Preview area at the bottom of the dialog box to verify that the column breaks appear in the correct locations. If they do not, alter the delimiter and text qualifier choice until they do. If you cannot align the columns, choose the Back button and choose Fixed Width as the Original Data Type.

4. Choose the Next button. The Text Import Wizard displays the final step. To finish the wizard, skip to the section "Completing the Text Import Wizard," following the next section.

Choosing Fixed-Width Text Import Options Selecting Fixed Width in Step 1 of the Text Import Wizard displays the dialog box shown in Figure 24.39.

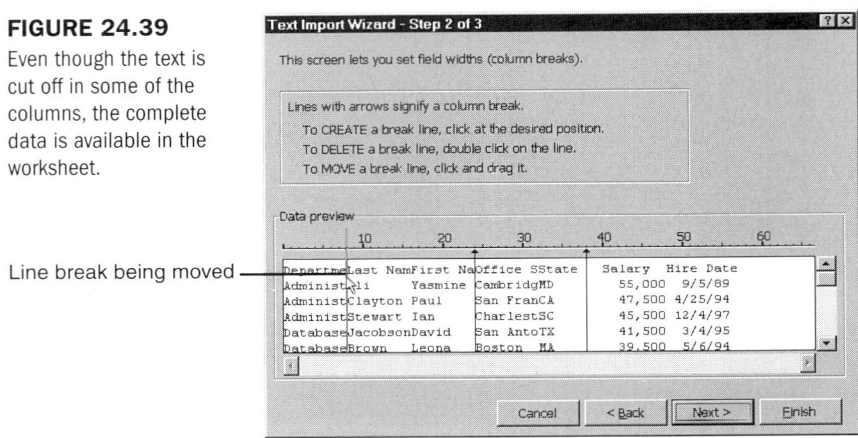

FIGURE 24.39
Even though the text is cut off in some of the columns, the complete data is available in the worksheet.

Follow these steps to finish importing the text:

1. The Data Preview at the bottom of the dialog box shows suggested column breaks, marked on the ruler above the preview window. If the column breaks are not correct, drag them to the correct positions. Create a new column break by single-clicking the ruler at the top of the Data Preview window; delete a column break by double-clicking it.
2. After the column breaks are established, click the Next button. The Text Import Wizard displays the final step. The steps to finish the wizard are described in the next section, "Completing the Text Import Wizard."

Completing the Text Import Wizard In the final step of the Wizard, shown in Figure 24.40, select the data format for each column of data.

To select a column, click the button (gray area) over each column. After selecting the column, choose the appropriate Column Data Format options. The options are summarized in the following list:

- General—Select this to have Excel convert numeric values to numbers, date values to dates, and all other values to text.
- Text—Select this to format all data in the column as text.

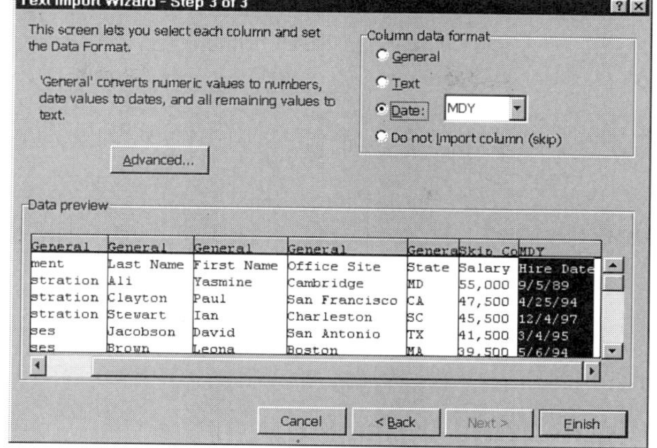

FIGURE 24.40
Step 3 in the Text Import Wizard.

- Date—Select this to format all data in the column as a date in the specified format.
- Do Not Import Column (Skip)—Select this if you do not want to import the data in the column. The Text Import Wizard skips the selected column when data is imported.

To import the data, choose Finish. You are then asked to select the worksheet and cell where the data is to be displayed.

Parsing Text

Occasionally, you may need to import a text file that is not properly delimited, or is improperly formatted as a fixed-length file. In these circumstances, you must import the file as a single column. In other situations, you may decide to paste a whole line of data into Excel from another application. Rather than making several copy and paste operations, it is sometimes easier to paste an entire line.

In either case, an entire row of data is entered into a single cell in your Excel worksheet. To separate the long lines of data into individual cells, you must *parse*, or separate, each line into its individual parts. Excel provides a wizard to help you parse text.

Figure 24.41 shows a worksheet that contains several lines of text. The first line of text is in cell A1, the second line of text is in cell A2, and so forth.

To parse text, use these steps:

1. Choose File, Save As to save the data in Excel format before you proceed to parse the data.
2. Select the cell or cells of text you want to convert to columns. If you select more than one cell, all cells you select must be in the same column.

   If your file is like the one in Figure 24.41, you cannot convert all the lines at once, because the text is not aligned in columns and does not have delimiters. In this situation, you must convert each line to columns individually. If at least some of the text is aligned in columns, you can select a range of rows to convert all at once.

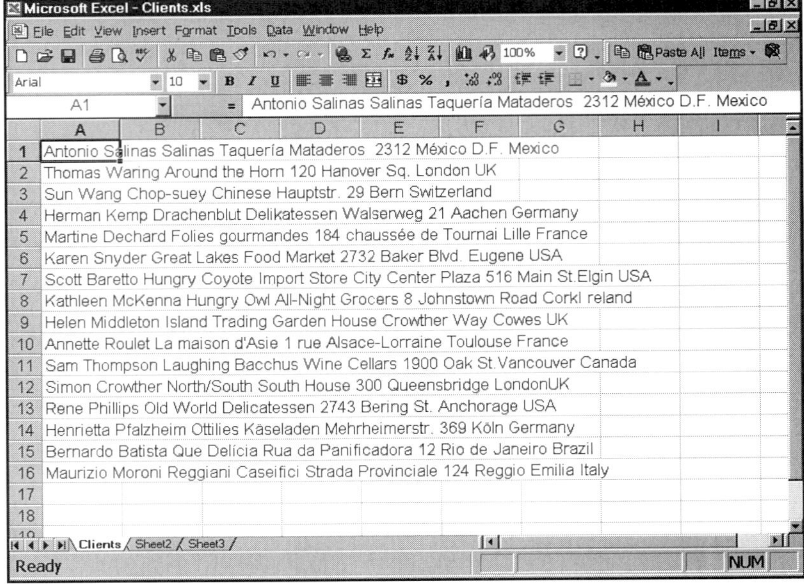

FIGURE 24.41
The data items are not delimited in any way.

3. Choose Data, Text to Columns. The Convert Text to Columns Wizard dialog box appears, as shown in Figure 24.42.

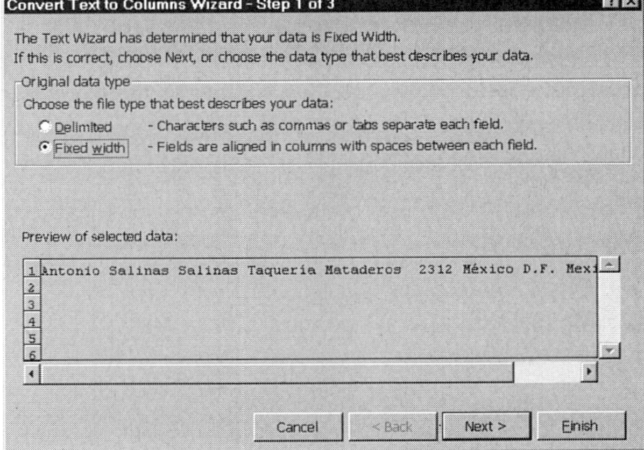

FIGURE 24.42
The Convert Text to Columns Wizard is used to separate data in text files.

The three steps of the Convert Text to Columns Wizard dialog boxes are exactly the same as the Text Import Wizard dialog boxes, discussed earlier—with one exception. In the Convert Text to Columns Wizard, the dialog box for Step 3 of the conversion has one additional option: the Destination text box.

Use the Destination text box to specify a destination for the parsed data other than the cell containing the line you are parsing. If you do not change the destination, the parsed data is inserted, beginning with the cell containing the line you are converting to columns. Follow the instructions in the previous section, "Using the Text Import Wizard," to fill in the other options in the Convert Text to Columns Wizard dialog boxes. Click the Next button after each step.

When you have completed the three steps in the Convert Text to Columns Wizard, click the Finish button. The text in the selected cell or cells is separated into individual columns.

Figure 24.43 shows the worksheet from Figure 24.41, with the first few rows parsed into columns, and the column widths adjusted to show the entire contents of the cells.

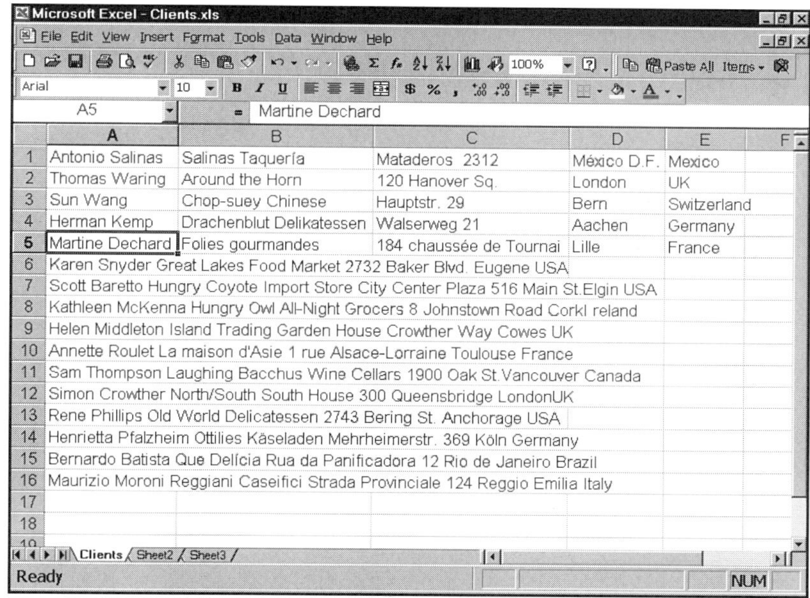

FIGURE 24.43
Parsing is a painstaking process because each line must be converted separately.

NOTE Be certain that sufficient blank columns exist to hold the parsed data. Parsed data overwrites cells to the right, with no consideration for their current contents.

CHAPTER 25

Advanced Lists, PivotTables, and PivotCharts

In this chapter

Structuring Lists

Most likely, many of the Excel worksheets you currently use are lists; any series of worksheet rows that contains information relating to a particular topic is a *list*. Using the techniques described in Chapter 24, you can import data from external sources such as databases, text files, and even Web pages. The data is imported into the worksheet as a list and can then be manipulated using the features described in this chapter. The only exception to this is OLAP cube data, which can be imported only into PivotTables or PivotCharts.

▶ **See** "Manipulating PivotTables Based on Data from OLAP Cubes," **p. 809**

There are four ways to manipulate data in lists: sorting, subtotaling, using database functions, and creating PivotTables. To take advantage of these list-manipulation tools, you need to verify that the worksheet is set up as a list by following these guidelines:

- Create one list per worksheet—Some of the tools used to manipulate information in lists, such as filtering, can be used on only one list at a time.
- Enter labels for each column—Excel allows only one row of labels in a list. Format the cells to word wrap for lengthy labels. Each label should be unique. Excel interprets "SALES" and "sales" as identical labels. Do not leave blank rows between the row of labels and the data in the list.
- Separate the row of labels from the worksheet title—Make sure there is at least one blank row between the worksheet title and the row containing the labels for the list.
- Avoid blank rows and columns in the list—Although there can be individual cells that are blank in a list, there should not be completely blank rows or columns in a list of data. To space out the data, enlarge the row height or column widths.
- Column calculations should be separated from the list—Calculations below your list should be separated from the list by using at least one blank row between the list and the calculations. Calculations to the right (or left) of your list do not need to be separated from the list, because list functions typically execute on rows of data.

CAUTION

If you use the Data, Form command to add data to a list, Excel places the data in blank rows at the bottom of the list. If there are calculations or other data in the rows below the list, a warning message stating—`Cannot extend list or database`—is displayed. You then have to close the form and insert additional rows (or move the data) below the list before you can enter new records using the form.

Custom Sorting

Occasionally, you need to *sort* a list according to something other than ascending or descending order. To accomplish this, you need to create a custom sort order for the list. Using the list in Figure 25.1 as an example, suppose you want to sort the list by department. But instead of an alphabetical listing of departments (the way it is currently sorted), you need the list sorted in a custom departmental order your company prefers to see.

FIGURE 25.1
Use a custom sort when the order you want displayed is not straight alphabetical or numerical.

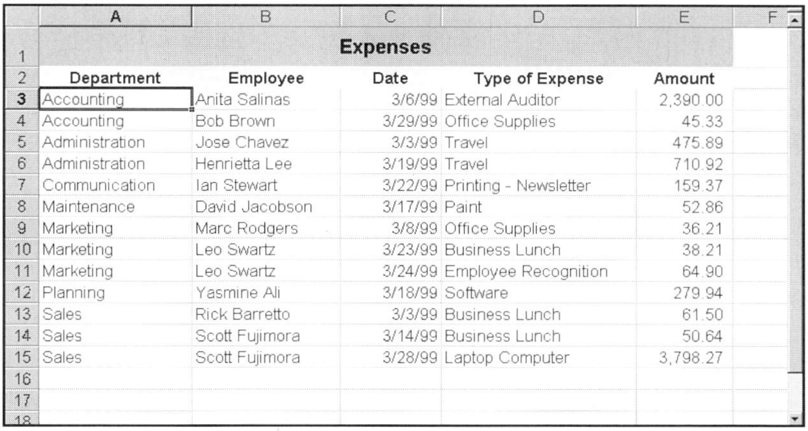

	A	B	C	D	E	F
1			Expenses			
2	Department	Employee	Date	Type of Expense	Amount	
3	Accounting	Anita Salinas	3/6/99	External Auditor	2,390.00	
4	Accounting	Bob Brown	3/29/99	Office Supplies	45.33	
5	Administration	Jose Chavez	3/3/99	Travel	475.89	
6	Administration	Henrietta Lee	3/19/99	Travel	710.92	
7	Communication	Ian Stewart	3/22/99	Printing - Newsletter	159.37	
8	Maintenance	David Jacobson	3/17/99	Paint	52.86	
9	Marketing	Marc Rodgers	3/8/99	Office Supplies	36.21	
10	Marketing	Leo Swartz	3/23/99	Business Lunch	38.21	
11	Marketing	Leo Swartz	3/24/99	Employee Recognition	64.90	
12	Planning	Yasmine Ali	3/18/99	Software	279.94	
13	Sales	Rick Barretto	3/3/99	Business Lunch	61.50	
14	Sales	Scott Fujimora	3/14/99	Business Lunch	50.64	
15	Sales	Scott Fujimora	3/28/99	Laptop Computer	3,798.27	
16						
17						
18						

To create a custom sort list, follow these steps:

1. Choose Tools, Options. The Options dialog box appears.
2. Select the Custom Lists tab and choose NEW LIST from the Custom Lists text box.
3. Type the values in the List Entries text box (see Figure 25.2). You can either press Enter after each entry or type a comma and a space to separate the entries.

Part IV
Ch 25

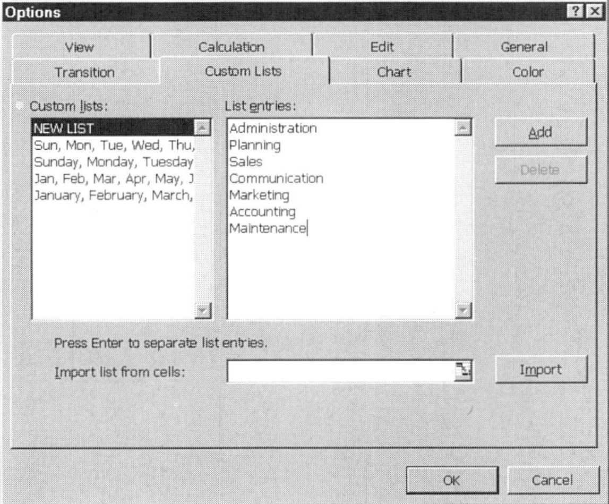

FIGURE 25.2
Excel has four built-in custom lists.

4. Choose Add. Your new list appears in the Custom Lists text box.
5. Choose OK.

The custom list can also be used in conjunction with the auto-fill (fill handle) feature to complete a series—just as the days of the week or months of the year can be auto-filled.

After you create the custom sort order, you must use the Sort dialog box (Data, Sort) to sort by the custom order. A custom sort list can be used only in the first criteria.

Suppose you need to perform custom sorts on two columns in your list, such as department and type of expense. The department is the primary sort, and type of expense is the secondary sort. You can accomplish this by first sorting the list only by the secondary custom order (type of expense). Then sort the list again, this time only by the first custom order (department).

Using the Sort Command to Rearrange Columns in a List

Most sorting is performed on the rows of a list (top-to-bottom sorting). You can also sort the columns in a list (left-to-right sorting). Choose Data, Sort and click the Options button in the Sort dialog box. Change the Orientation setting to Sort from Left to Right. Make sure you change it back when you complete the sort; otherwise, all future sorts will be columnar sorts!

Filtering Lists—Beyond the Basics

There are three methods in Excel for locating data in lists: the AutoFilter, the Data Form, and the Advanced Filter. The AutoFilter displays only the rows matching your criteria, while the other rows in the list remain hidden. You can use the Data Form to show rows matching your criteria, one row at a time, which provides a convenient way to edit the information. The Advanced Filter enables you to specify complex criteria, including calculations, to filter a list.

NOTE Excel does not distinguish between uppercase and lowercase letters in criteria.

Creating Custom Filters with the AutoFilter

After you've applied the AutoFilter to your list (Data, Filter, AutoFilter), you can take advantage of several features to customize your filters. The Top 10 filter is used to filter columns that contain numbers or dates. The Custom filter option is used when you need to use an OR condition, specify a range of numbers or dates, or include a wildcard in your search.

NOTE In the Custom Filter dialog box, you are limited to the asterisk (*) and question mark (?) wildcards. However, you can also select a criteria statement, such as Begins With or Is Greater Than, to create a custom filter.

To enter more than two criteria, you must use the Advanced Filter command, discussed in the section "Performing Advanced Filters," later in this chapter.

Taking Advantage of the Top 10 Filter Top 10 is a filter feature added in Excel 97, and is used to filter numbers and dates. By default, it displays the top 10 items that occur most frequently in a column—but it is capable of much more.

Instead of displaying the topmost items in a list, you can display the bottommost items. For example, suppose you have a list that tracks shrinkage (loss due to damage or theft) in every store your company owns in the country. You can display those stores that have the smallest shrinkage by selecting Bottom in the Top 10 AutoFilter dialog box.

And you're not limited to just the top (or bottom) 10 items. You can display any range from 1 to 500, either by number of items or percent (for example, the top 25 items or the top 25%). Figure 25.3 shows an example of a Top 10 filter and its results. There are four employees who earn salaries in the top 20 percent of all salaries.

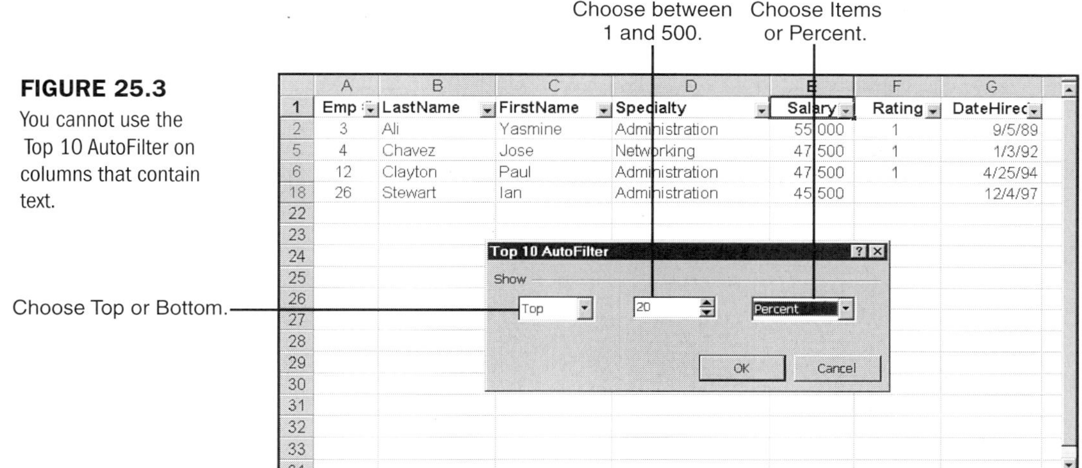

FIGURE 25.3
You cannot use the Top 10 AutoFilter on columns that contain text.

You access the Top 10 filter from the filter arrows supplied by the AutoFilter feature (Data, Filter, AutoFilter).

Using Custom AutoFilters To filter a column in your list based on two criteria or to use wildcards in your criteria, you use the Custom option from the AutoFilter drop-down arrows.

Let's say you have a list of consulting work performed during the month of June and you want to locate all rows for consulting performed between June 7 and June 13. You select Custom from the Date column's drop-down filter arrow. The Custom AutoFilter dialog box appears. Because you are looking for information in a range of dates, you need to make sure you use the Greater Than or Equal To and Less Than or Equal To comparison operators. Figure 25.4 shows an example of the criteria you would use.

The Custom AutoFilter dialog box also has an option that lets you filter for one item or another item. You simply select the OR option button displayed between the two criteria in the dialog box.

Finally, when you are looking for entries that are similar to each other, you can use asterisk (*) or question mark (?) wildcards. Using the data in Figure 25.4 as an example, if you wanted to display all the Independent School Districts (ISDs) for which consulting was provided, you would use the asterisk wildcard in front of ISD when you filter on the Company column.

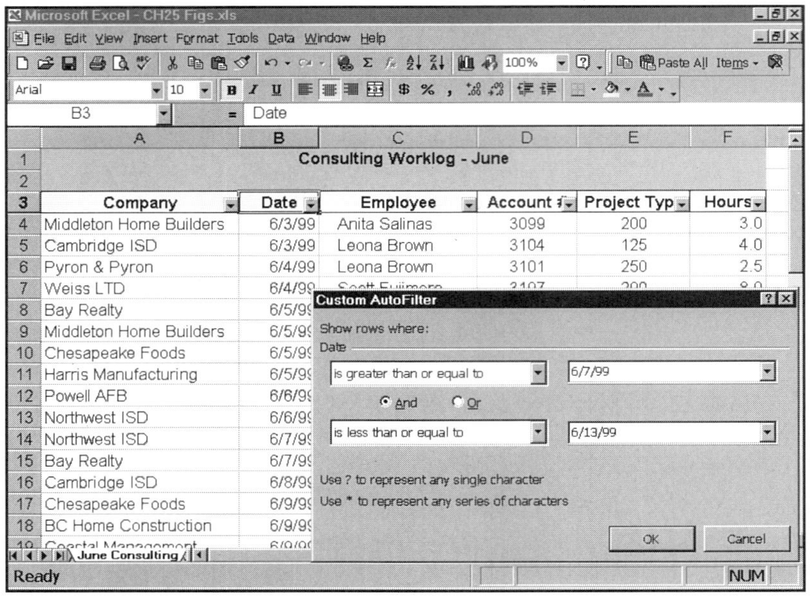

FIGURE 25.4
In the Custom AutoFilter dialog box, you can specify up to two criteria on which to filter.

If you need to find the asterisk (*) or question mark (?) symbols in a list, type a tilde (~) before the * or ?. The tilde indicates that you are not using the * or ? as a wildcard.

Performing Advanced Filters

The Advanced Filter enables you to search for data that matches complex AND and OR criteria. Although the custom AutoFilter is limited to two criteria, you can use the Advanced Filter to enter combinations of multiple criteria in the criteria range—for example, an OR condition that looks for three or more items within a single column.

In addition, you can specify a formula as a criterion in an Advanced Filter. The list is filtered based on the result of a formula. For example you might want to display records for every individual order where the quantity sold is greater than the average quantity sold. A formula comparing each quantity with the average is used for the criteria. Those records where the quantity is not greater than the average will be filtered out.

There are three components of advanced filters:

- The *list range*—This, of course, is the worksheet list. See the section "Structuring Lists" earlier in this chapter to verify that your list is set up properly before you begin the advanced filter.
- The *criteria range*—The group of cells in your worksheet that contains a copy of the column labels in your list. The criteria range also includes at least one row below the labels where you identify the criteria to be used in the filter.

- The *Copy To range*—The results of an advanced filter can be displayed in the list area (much the same way an AutoFilter displays results) or the results can be displayed in a separate area of the worksheet. If you decide to have the results displayed in another part of the worksheet, that location is known as the *results range* or *Copy To range*.

Preparing Your Worksheet to Use Advanced Filters

Before you can use the Advanced Filter, you must rearrange your worksheet so that it includes a criteria range. The easiest way to create the criteria range is to insert several rows above the list and copy the labels into one of the newly inserted rows:

- You do not have to include all the column labels in the criteria range that appear in the list, just the ones you intend to use. See Figure 25.10, later in this chapter, for an example of this.
- The labels do not have to be in the same order as the labels in the list. If you decide to type the labels, they must be spelled exactly the same as in the list, but the Advanced Filter is not case sensitive.

Figure 25.5 shows an example of a worksheet that includes the criteria range and a list.

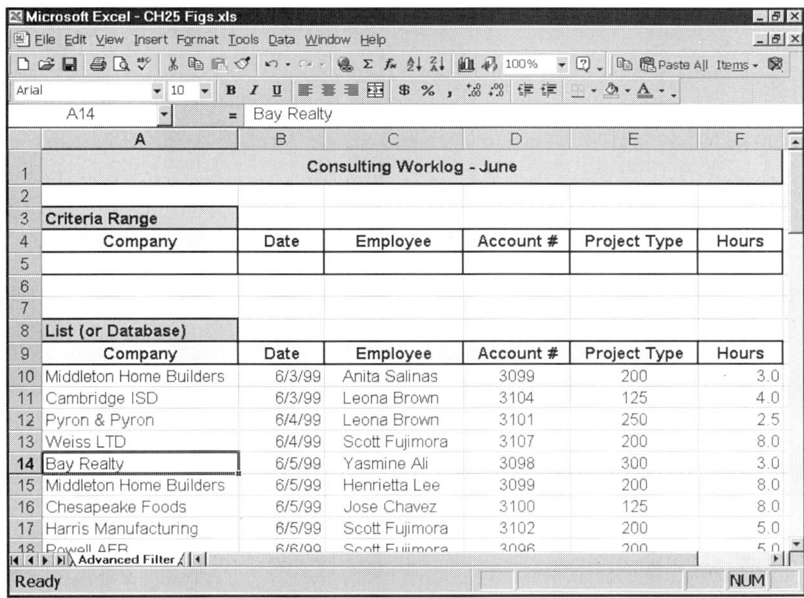

FIGURE 25.5
The criteria range in a worksheet is typically located above the list.

The labels Criteria Range and List (or Database) in Figure 25.5 are not required, but are used to make it clear what data is being displayed in each part of the worksheet.

Using Criteria Effectively

The second and subsequent rows in the criteria range are used to enter the specific criteria you are looking for. There are three things you should keep in mind when working with criteria in Excel lists:

- If criteria are entered into more than one column in the same row of the criteria range, an AND condition is assumed.
- If criteria are entered in different rows of the criteria range, an OR condition is assumed.
- You can use as many rows as necessary in the criteria range.

When you use text criteria, a wildcard is assumed at the end of the text. For example, suppose Smith is entered as the LastName criterion; any rows beginning with Smith (as well as Smithson, Smithfield, and any other person whose last name starts with Smith) will be displayed in the results. If you want only Smith you must enter `"Smith"` (with a space after the name inside the quotes) in the criteria range.

If a blank row is selected as part of the criteria range, all the rows in the list are displayed. This occurs because when you select multiple rows in the criteria range, the advanced filter creates an OR condition between the criteria in each row. The criteria specified in the first row OR the criteria specified in the second row. Suppose the first row has Smith in the LastName column and the second row contains no criteria. When you select both rows for the criteria, Excel expects two criteria. The criterion in the first row is— LastName begins with Smith. Because the second row is blank, the criterion in effect says—any row in the list. Put together, the criteria read "LastName begins with Smith" OR "any row in the list." The result is that every row in the list appears as the filter results.

If the range name "Database" is used for all or part of your list, Excel assumes the cells to which the name refers encompass the range to be filtered.

If the range name "Criteria" is not used in the worksheet, Excel automatically creates a range name Criteria for the cells. If the range name Criteria does exist, Excel assumes the cells to which the name refers are the range where the criteria appear.

Excel also automatically creates the range name "Extract" when you choose the Copy to Another Location option in the Advanced Filter dialog box.

NOTE The creation of the "Criteria" and "Extract" range names happens when you run the advanced filter for the first time.

Filtering the List In-Place

As mentioned before, you can display the results of the advanced filter where the list is displayed. Excel hides the rows in the list that don't match the criteria, similar to the way the AutoFilter command does.

To use the advanced filter this way, follow these steps:

1. Enter the criteria in the row(s) in the criteria range.
2. Select a cell in your list.
3. Choose Data, Filter, Advanced Filter. The Advanced Filter dialog box appears (see Figure 25.6).

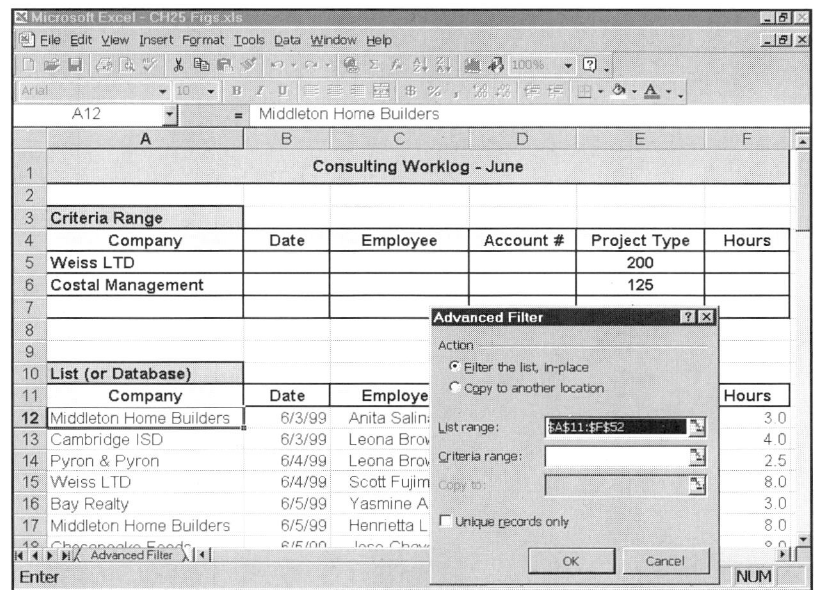

FIGURE 25.6
The criteria here locate all rows (records) that contain either the company Weiss LTD and the project type 200 or the company Coastal Management and the project type 125.

4. By default, the Filter the List, In-Place option is selected.
5. In the List Range entry box, Excel automatically selects the cells in your list, based on the cell you selected in step 3.
6. Click in the Criteria Range entry box. Then select the criteria range (the column labels and only the rows in which you entered criteria). Do not select any extra rows. The Advanced Filter dialog box collapses temporarily while you select the cells.
7. Choose OK. The rows matching your criteria are displayed where the list was originally located.

NOTE Undo does not reverse the effects of the filter. Choose Data, Filter, Show All to display the entire list.

Displaying the Filter Results in Another Location

Instead of filtering the list in-place, you can have the results copied to another location, either in the active worksheet or in another worksheet. This location is known as the results range or Copy To location.

Although setting up a results range is not strictly necessary, you should do so if you want data from only some of the columns to appear in the results range. Otherwise, data from all the columns is displayed. For example, suppose the columns in your list are

Company

Date

Employee

Account #

Project Type

Hours

Assuming this example, say you want only the data in the Company and Hours columns to appear in your results range. To do this, you would need to copy (or type) the labels from those columns in the results range. The results range can be in the active worksheet, or in another worksheet (including a worksheet in another workbook).

To use the advanced filter to copy the results elsewhere, follow these steps:

1. Enter the criteria in the row(s) in the criteria range.
2. If the results range is in the active worksheet, select a cell in your list.

   If the results range is in another worksheet, activate the worksheet that contains the results range and select a blank cell (not one that is part of the results range). This is the only way Excel allows you to copy filtered data to another worksheet.
3. Choose Data, Filter, Advanced Filter.
4. In the Advanced Filter dialog box, choose the Copy to Another Location option.
   - If you are copying the results to a place in the active worksheet, the cells in the list should already appear in the List Range text box.
   - If you are copying the results to another worksheet, click in the List Range text box. Then select the cells in the list, including the column labels. If you've created a range name for the list, you can enter the range name in the List Range text box. If the list is on another worksheet in the active workbook, you can use the Taskbar or Window command to switch to the file containing the list. The name of the worksheet appears in the List Range box. If the list is on a worksheet in another workbook, the name of the workbook and worksheet appear in the List Range box; for example, '[Consulting.xls]Worklog—June'!F7:F47

NOTE If you have already performed an advanced filter, the cells identifying the criteria range should already be listed in the Criteria Range entry box. If the Criteria Range text box is empty or if you need to change the range, type or select the correct cells. Make sure you include the column labels and only the rows in which you entered criteria. Do not select any extra rows.

If you have not set up a specific results range, click in the Copy To text box and then click in any cell in the worksheet where you want the display of filtered data to start. If you have established a results range, type or select the cells containing just the labels in the results range–do not select any extra cells (see Figure 25.7).

5. Choose OK. The filtered data matching your criteria is displayed in the results range.

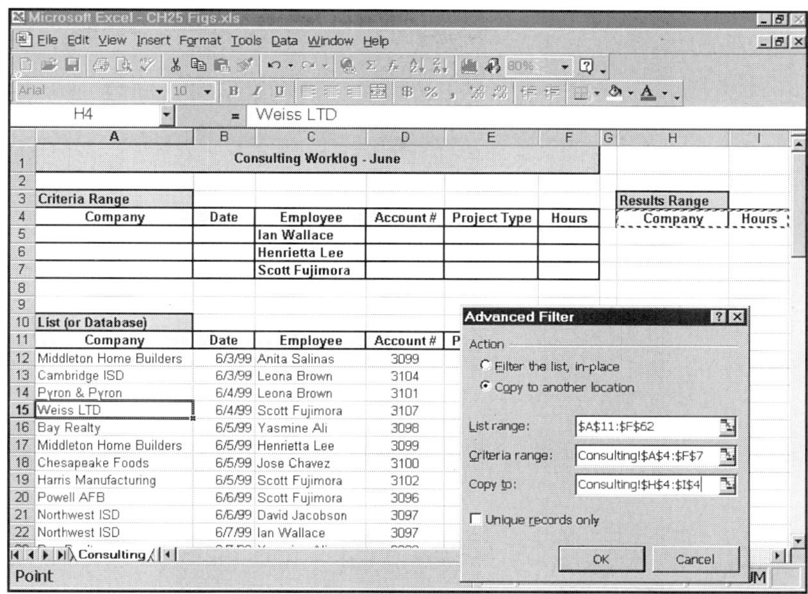

FIGURE 25.7
The cell references containing the results range labels must appear in the Copy To text box.

The criteria in Figure 25.7 filter out all the rows (records) except those that contain Ian Wallace, Henrietta Lee, or Scott Fujimora as the employees who performed the consulting. The companies to which they provided consulting, along with the specific hours, are displayed in the results area.

Using Calculated Values As Criteria

You can use a *calculated value*—the result of a formula—as your criteria in an advanced filter. In other words, the formula results become the criteria. For example, suppose you want to know which items in a particular column exceed the average of the items in the column. The formula for calculating the average, along with a greater than (>) comparison, is placed in the criteria area of the advanced filter. When the result of the average is calculated, the filter is performed and only those rows that contain items exceeding the average are returned.

Figure 25.8 shows a worksheet listing the hours worked on each consulting job in the F column. For verification purposes, the average hours worked

```
=AVERAGE(F12:F62)
```

has been calculated and placed in cell H5, the result being 7.9 hours.

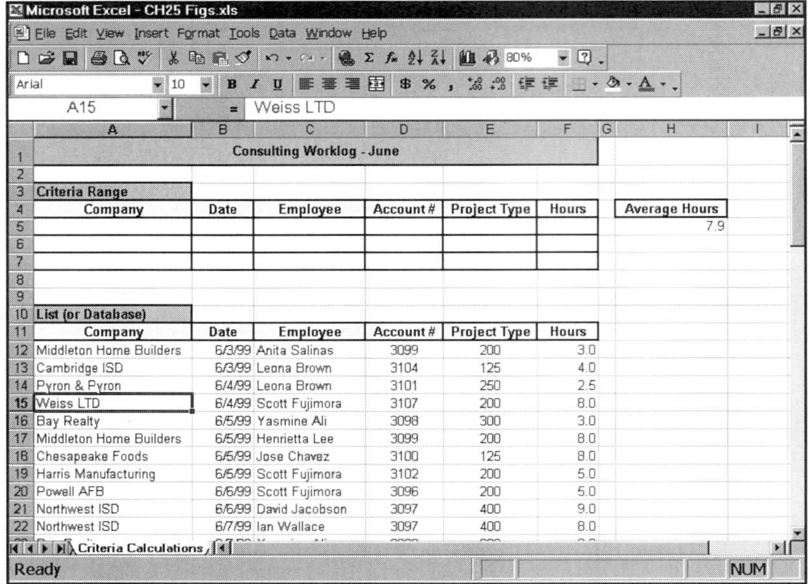

FIGURE 25.8
You can use calculations in your criteria if you follow a few simple rules.

Because you are comparing the hours worked in each row to the average, the basic comparison formula that will need to be placed in the criteria range is

```
=F12>AVERAGE(F12:F62)
```

where F12 is the first cell in the list.

For the filter to work properly, there are a few rules you must follow when using formulas in the criteria range:

- You must use a *relative cell reference* when identifying this first cell to which you will be making the comparison. In the example shown in Figure 25.8, the first cell in the list containing the hours worked, is cell F12. Because you want the filter to compare each of the hours worked with the average hours, F12 will remain a relative cell reference.
- The cell references used in the calculated portion of the criteria must be *absolute cell references*, so that the calculation remains static. In our example, the entire formula becomes `=F12>AVERAGE($F$12:$F$62)`.
- The column label in the list cannot be used as a label in the criteria range—otherwise, the calculation won't work. So, in Figure 25.8, the label Hours in cell F4 needs to be changed or left blank. In this example, change it to Hours Worked.
- Finally, the formula you use must evaluate to either TRUE (YES) or FALSE (NO). For the first record in the list, the formula asks: Are the hours in cell F12 greater than the average of the hours in cells F12 to F62? Because they are not, the formula evaluates to FALSE (NO).

▶ **See** "Relative Cell References," **p. 634**

▶ **See** "Absolute Cell References," **p. 635**

The formula that is placed in cell F4 is `=F12>AVERAGE($F$12:$F$62)`. Because the hours in F12 are not greater than the average, the result `FALSE` displays.

After you've entered the formula criteria, select a cell in the list and run the advanced filter. Figure 25.9 shows the results.

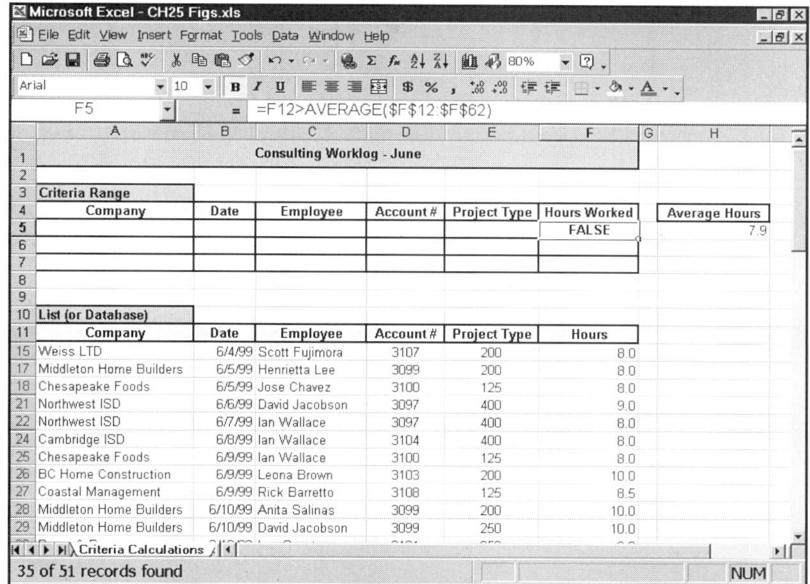

FIGURE 25.9
Make sure you change the column heading in the criteria area.

Part IV Ch 25

Using Filtered Data

Filtering a list is a powerful Excel tool. Besides merely viewing the filtered data, many of the actions that you can perform on the entire list also can be used with a filtered list.

- Use the sorting feature to change the order of your filtered data.
- The subtotaling command calculates totals and averages on just the data displayed onscreen. The section "Creating Subtotals and Grand Totals" later in this chapter provides more information on and examples of using the subtotal command.
- Create charts representing the filtered data; these charts automatically update when you change or remove the filter.

▶ **See** "Charts Based on Filtered Lists," **p. 842**

- Both the filtered list and charts based on the filtered list can be printed.

Using Database Functions with Lists

A *database* is a collection of information related to a particular subject or purpose. Databases are composed of one or more *tables*, or lists, of information. There are two types of databases:

flat file and relational. A *flat file database* is a database in which all the information is placed into one large table. Excel uses flat file type databases. A *relational database* is a database in which the information is divided into several smaller tables. In a relational database, when you need to display data from multiple tables, a relationship is established between the tables (the tables are joined or linked together). Access, FoxPro, and dBASE use relational type databases.

Deciding Which Database Application to Use—Excel or Access

There are several considerations you need to keep in mind when deciding whether to use Excel or Access to store your data. Are you going to be performing extensive or complex calculations on the data? If so, you will definitely want to keep the data in Excel. Although Access can perform basic calculations (SUM, AVERAGE, COUNT), it does not have the number-crunching power found in Excel.

The next issue to consider is design or ease-of-use, especially if the calculations you are performing are fairly basic. Database lists or tables are usually designed to hold the data associated with one topic. You might have a list or table for business expenses, another for employee personnel information, and a third for client information. Suppose you wanted to show a list of expenses and the employees who incurred the expense. In Excel, you would need to include the employees' names in the expense list. If you wanted to also see which department each employee belongs to, you would need to include that information in the expense list. In Access, on the other hand, to display information from more than one list, you can link (or relate) the tables together to retrieve the necessary data, rather than duplicating the information in multiple lists. With large databases, omitting the duplication saves a tremendous amount of time updating the information when it changes, such as when an employee moves to a new department. In Access, the information is changed in one location. In Excel, the information must be changed in each list in which it appears.

Another consideration is size. Until recently, Excel had a limitation of 16,384 rows. In Excel 97, the limit was raised to 65,536. For large corporations or businesses that track many transactions, the size of the Excel worksheets is not large enough to store the information they need to track. The size of most databases, such as Access, is limited only by the device being used to store the data.

In Excel, a database is a specific type of list to which new records routinely are being added.

Excel includes 12 powerful worksheet functions (described in Table 25.1) that are designed specifically to summarize the data in lists or databases. Excel's database functions are an alternative to generating subtotals in your list. Although the Subtotals command is an excellent choice when you need to print the subtotals and grand totals, using database functions is a terrific way to display the results onscreen.

Unlike the Subtotals command, the list does not have to be sorted to use the database functions. Of even greater importance is the fact that more complex criteria can be used with the database functions than can be used with subtotals.

Excel databases use a unique set of terminology, some of which is explained in the following list:

- *Database*—A database is a range of cells that make up the list. Because Excel uses flat file databases, which are composed of a single list (or table) of information, sometimes the terms database, table, and list are used interchangeably.

- *Records*—Each row of information in the list is a record.
- *Fields*—Each column of information in the list is a field.
- *Field Names*—The column labels are referred to as field names.
- *Criteria*—The range of cells listing the specifications of the search. The Criteria includes only those field names from the database that you intend to search.

The advantage to using these functions rather than the standard Excel functions is the capability of the database worksheet functions to perform calculations on part (a subset) of the list. You specify criteria that identify specific records (rows) in the list and the calculations are performed on those records (rows). Excel's standard functions (the nondatabase functions) perform the calculations on the entire list. Table 25.1 describes each database function.

Table 25.1 The 12 Database Functions Available in Excel

Function Name	Description
DAVERAGE	Averages the values in a column (field) that match conditions you specify.
DCOUNT	Counts the cells in a column (field) that contains numbers, based on conditions you specify.
DCOUNTA	Counts the nonblank cells in a column (field), based on conditions you specify. This function is useful when the column contains both text and numbers.
DGET	Extracts a single row (record) that matches conditions you specify.
DMAX	Returns the largest number in a column (field) that matches conditions you specify.
DMIN	Returns the smallest number in a column (field) that matches conditions you specify.
DPRODUCT	Multiplies the values in a column (field) that match conditions you specify.
DSTDEV	Estimates the standard deviation based on a sample from the selected list or database entries.
DSTDEVP	Calculates the standard deviation based on the entire population of the selected list or database entries.
SDUM	Adds the numbers in a column (field) in a list or database that match conditions you specify.
DVAR	Estimates the variance based on a sample from the selected list or database entries.
DVARP	Calculates the variance based on the entire population of the selected list or database entries.

Most of the functions are statistical calculations. Each function uses three arguments: database, field, and criteria. You need to be familiar with these arguments before you use the database functions:

- Database Argument—The range of cells that make up the list, including the column headings.
- Field Argument—The particular column in the database being searched. Each column of information in the list is a field. To search the Quantity # field in the worksheet displayed in Figure 25.10, "Quantity #" or 6 is entered as the field (column) in the database function. If the field (column) name is entered in the function, it must be enclosed in quotes. If a number is used, the number must correspond to the column in the database range. In this case, 6 indicates that Quantity # is the sixth column in the database.
- Criteria Argument—The range of cells listing the specifications of the search. As with filter criteria, database criteria often are placed in separate cells in the worksheet above the database. The Criteria is a range consisting typically of two rows—one row of labels that match the field (column) names and one row for the specific criteria being searched. In Figure 25.10, the criteria range is A4 to D5. The Criteria includes only those field (column) names from the database that you intend to search—a listing of all the column names is not necessary.

Figure 25.10 illustrates an Excel list using the database functions. Item # 450 is specified in the criteria range. The DSUM function is being used to determine the total quantity of Item # 450 ordered. The DCOUNTA function is used to determine the number of different orders that were placed for Item # 450.

FIGURE 25.10
The range name Database has been used in the DSUM formula.

I4 = =DSUM(database,6,A4:D5)

	A	B	C	D	E	F	G	H	I
1		ABC Display Rack Sales							
2									
3	Criteria					Database Statistics			
4	Customer	Date	Salesrep	Item #		Quantity Ordered =			236
5				450		Separate Orders =			49
6									
7									
8	Database								
9	Customer	Date	Salesrep	Invoice #	Item #	Quantity	Price	Sales	
10	Peter Rabbit Craft Supplies	10/4/98	Pinckney	220001	300	3	450	1350	
11	All-Night Gas	10/5/98	Lee	220003	200	4	325	1300	
12	StreetCorner Magazines	10/5/98	McGuire	220002	350	3	500	1500	
13	Johnson's Drug Store	10/6/98	Fujimora	220004	450	1	625	625	
14	Karate Academy	10/7/98	Abbott	220005	300	5	450	2250	
15	Campus Bookstore	10/8/98	Lee	220006	250	2	375	750	
16	Pets R Us	10/9/98	Horry	220007	400	6	575	3450	
17	All-Night Gas	10/9/98	Lee	220009	450	4	625	2500	
18	Gruene Donut Shoppe	10/9/98	Rodgers	220008	450	1	625	625	
19	Greer Drugstores	10/10/98	Felder	220010	200	5	325	1625	
20	St. Agnes School	10/10/98	Horry	220012	200	9	325	2925	

DSUM formula

Database Statistics using DSUM and DCOUNTA

Range names are used frequently in database functions to help identify the database and the criteria. The formula in Figure 25.10 uses the Range name "Database."

▶ **See** "Using Range Names in Formulas," **p. 639**

The criteria range can be located anywhere on the worksheet. If you add information to your list through the Data, Form command, you should not place the criteria range below your list. Excel attempts to add new information to the first row below the list when you use the Data Form. If the first row below the list is not blank, Excel cannot add the new information to your list.

To use the database functions, follow these steps:

1. Create your list and set up the criteria area in your worksheet.
2. Select the cell in which you want the calculated answer to appear.
3. Click the Paste Function button on the Standard toolbar. The Paste Function dialog box appears (see Figure 25.11).

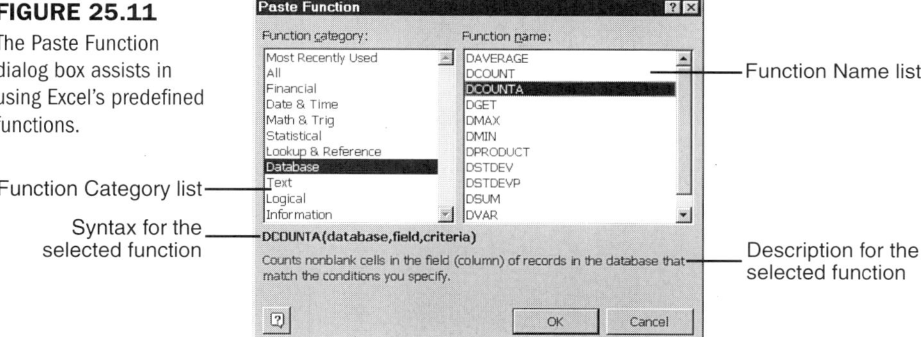

FIGURE 25.11
The Paste Function dialog box assists in using Excel's predefined functions.

4. Choose the Database category in the Function Category list box.
5. Choose the function from the names in the Function Name list box. The syntax and description for the selected function appear below the Function Category list box. In Figure 25.11, the DCOUNTA function is selected.
6. Select OK and the Formula Palette appears, detailing the arguments for the function (see Figure 25.12).

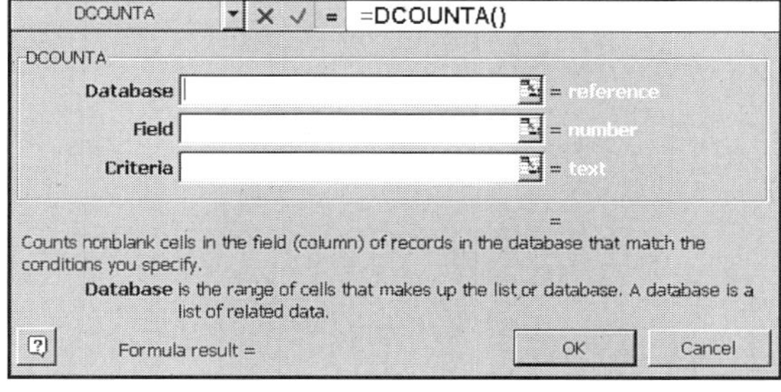

FIGURE 25.12
The Formula Palette box leads you through the specific syntax required for the function that you select.

7. The first argument, Database, is active in the Formula Palette. Select the cell or cells in your spreadsheet that comprise the database, including the column headings. If you have created a range name for the database, press F3. From the Paste Names dialog box, choose the range name from the list and select OK.
8. In the Field argument, enter either the column name in quotes or the corresponding column number. For example, if the list begins in column A and extends from column A to column E, the corresponding column number for column D is 4. However, if the list begins in column C and extends to column G, the corresponding column number for column D is 2.
9. In the Criteria argument, select the cell or cells in your spreadsheet that contain the criteria. If you have created a range name for the criteria, press F3 and choose the name from the Paste Names dialog box. Then select OK.
10. After you enter these three arguments, choose OK. The result of the function appears in the worksheet and the function appears in the Formula Bar.

If criteria are specified before the formula is created, the result of the specific criteria appears. If criteria are not specified, the calculation reflects all the records (rows) in the list. You can change the criteria at any time; the calculations are updated automatically.

Just as with advanced filters, you can use more complex criteria with the database functions. If two entries are placed in the criteria area (in the same row), Excel assumes an AND condition exists. For example, suppose you want to sum the quantity of a particular item that a company orders. You would enter both the company name and the item name or number in the criteria range. Only those records (rows) that match the criteria are summed.

To produce an OR condition between two criteria, you must use a second row in the criteria area. One criterion is placed in one row; the other criterion is placed in another row. For example, to sum the quantity ordered of two different items, one item name or number is entered in the first row of the criteria and the second item name or number is entered in the second row of the criteria.

Figure 25.13 shows the result of an AND condition in the criteria area.

FIGURE 25.13
The criteria specify the orders placed by the All-Night Gas company for Item # 450.

	A	B	C	D	E	F	G	H	I
1		ABC Display Rack Sales							
2									
3	Criteria					Database Statistics			
4	Customer	Date	Salesrep	Item #		Quantity Ordered =			36
5	All-Night Gas			450		Separate Orders =			6
6									
7									
8	Database								
9	Customer	Date	Salesrep	Invoice #	Item #	Quantity	Price	Sales	
10	Peter Rabbit Craft Supplies	10/4/98	Pinckney	220001	300	3	450	1350	
11	All-Night Gas	10/5/98	Lee	220003	200	4	325	1300	
12	StreetCorner Magazines	10/5/98	McGuire	220002	350	3	500	1500	
13	Johnson's Drug Store	10/6/98	Fujimora	220004	450	1	625	625	
14	Karate Academy	10/7/98	Abbott	220005	300	5	450	2250	
15	Campus Bookstore	10/8/98	Lee	220006	250	2	375	750	
16	Pets R Us	10/9/98	Horry	220007	400	6	575	3450	
17	All-Night Gas	10/9/98	Lee	220009	450	4	625	2500	
18	Gruene Donut Shoppe	10/9/98	Rodgers	220008	450	1	625	625	
19	Greer Drugstores	10/10/98	Felder	220010	200	5	325	1625	
20	St. Agnes School	10/10/98	Horry	220012	200	9	325	2925	

CAUTION

When using multiple criteria rows (for OR conditions), make sure you enter criteria in *both* rows. A blank row in the criteria range results in the calculation of *all* records in the list.

Outlining Worksheets

Excel's Outlining feature is designed to be used with worksheets that contain *groups*— detailed information with corresponding summary formulas at regular intervals. The formulas in each group are the basis for the outline. You can collapse the details to display just the formulas, providing a quick summary of the worksheet, or expand the outline to show all the detailed information. Groups can be outlined in both rows and columns.

Outlining a worksheet makes it easy to hide the detailed information in a large worksheet and quickly see the summary data. You can print the worksheet with the outline collapsed, to create a summary report. Additionally, charts can be created from a collapsed outline. Several Excel commands automatically outline your worksheet—subtotals, consolidation, and scenario reports.

▶ **See** "Charts Based on Subtotaled and Outlined Lists," **p. 844**

▶ **See** "Using Data Tables for What-If Analysis," **p. 867**

Figure 25.14 shows a worksheet that has its detailed information divided into quarters and regions. The columns are grouped by months, with January, February, March, and Qtr 1 comprising the first group. Likewise, the rows are grouped by regions, with Canada, United States, Mexico, and North America Totals comprising the first group in the rows.

FIGURE 25.14
Outlines can display up to eight levels of information.

	A	B	C	D	E	F	G	H
1	Regional Sales	January	February	March	QTR1	April	May	June
2								
3	*North America*							
4	Canada	6,521	5,478	9,823	**21,822**	4,563	6,542	8,523
5	United States	1,258	1,542	9,875	**12,675**	8,523	4,875	3,215
6	Mexico	2,548	4,563	6,542	**13,653**	3,215	3,215	6,548
7	**North America Totals**	**7,779**	**7,020**	**19,698**	**34,497**	**13,086**	**11,417**	**11,738**
8								
9	*Central America*							
10	Belize	2,634	8,523	4,875	**16,032**	6,548	6,548	1,258
11	Costa Rica	1,598	3,215	3,215	**8,028**	1,258	4,563	2,548
12	Panama	4,875	6,548	6,548	**17,971**	2,548	8,523	5,478
13	**Central America Totals**	**9,107**	**18,286**	**14,638**	**42,031**	**10,354**	**19,634**	**9,284**
14								
15	*South America*							
16	Ecuador	3,215	1,258	4,563	**9,036**	5,478	3,215	9,875
17	Peru	6,548	2,548	8,523	**17,619**	1,258	6,548	6,542
18	Chile	6,521	5,478	3,215	**15,214**	1,598	5,478	4,875

The background fill color in Figure 25.14 is used to accentuate the groups; it is not necessary to format cells with a background fill color to use the outline feature in Excel.

Part IV

Ch 25

NOTE A worksheet can contain only one outline.

Worksheets can be outlined either manually or automatically. To use the outlining feature in Excel, your worksheet has to meet the following conditions:

- The worksheet must contain rows or columns of formulas that summarize the detail data—summary formulas such as SUM or AVERAGE.
- The cell references in the formulas must point in a consistent direction, with summary rows placed consistently above or below their related detail data and summary columns to the left or right of their corresponding detail data. If the worksheet mixes the directions in which the data is summarized, you have to manually create the outline.

NOTE When rows and columns in an outlined list are hidden, the data in other parts of the worksheet that is not part of the outline is also hidden.

Creating Outlines Automatically

By default, the Auto Outline feature looks for summary formulas that appear to the right of the detail columns and below the detail rows. If the outline has the summary rows and columns in different positions (for example, above the detail rows) use the Data, Group and Outline, Settings command (which displayes the Settings dialog box) to modify these assumptions.

If the summary rows are above their corresponding detail rows, remove the check from the box in front of Summary Rows Below Details. If the summary columns are to the left of their corresponding detail columns, remove the check from the box in front of Summary Columns to Right of Detail. The formulas must summarize in the directions specified in the Settings dialog box for the outline to work correctly.

If you select a single cell in the worksheet and use the Auto Outline command, the entire worksheet is outlined. To outline a particular list in a worksheet, click any cell in the list and then use the keyboard shortcut Ctrl+Shift+* (asterisk). This shortcut highlights the current region until it reaches blank rows and columns.

If you have blank rows in your list, you need to select the cells manually.

To automatically outline a worksheet, follow these steps:

1. Select any single cell to outline the entire worksheet, or select a range of cells for which you want to create an outline.
2. Choose Data, Group and Outline. From the submenu, select Auto Outline.
3. Your worksheet will be reformatted to display outline symbols and numbers.
4. Use the outline symbols and numbers (described next) to collapse and expand the outline.

Use the following outline symbols to collapse and expand the outline:

- Level numbers—You can display specific levels of outline information by clicking these numbers. One set of numbers is for the row levels; the other is for the column levels. Clicking the row-level 2 number collapses the outline to display the regional totals, as shown in Figure 25.15. Specifically, you can see all the groups at levels 1 and 2 (but not 3) of the outline.
- Level bars—These bars span the ranges referred to in the formulas. One endpoint of the bar is over the formula itself. The other endpoint is over the last cell referred to in the formula.
- Hide details—The minus (-) signs are used to hide rows or columns of information, collapsing individual groups.
- Show details—The plus (+) signs are used to display hidden rows or columns of information, expanding individual groups.

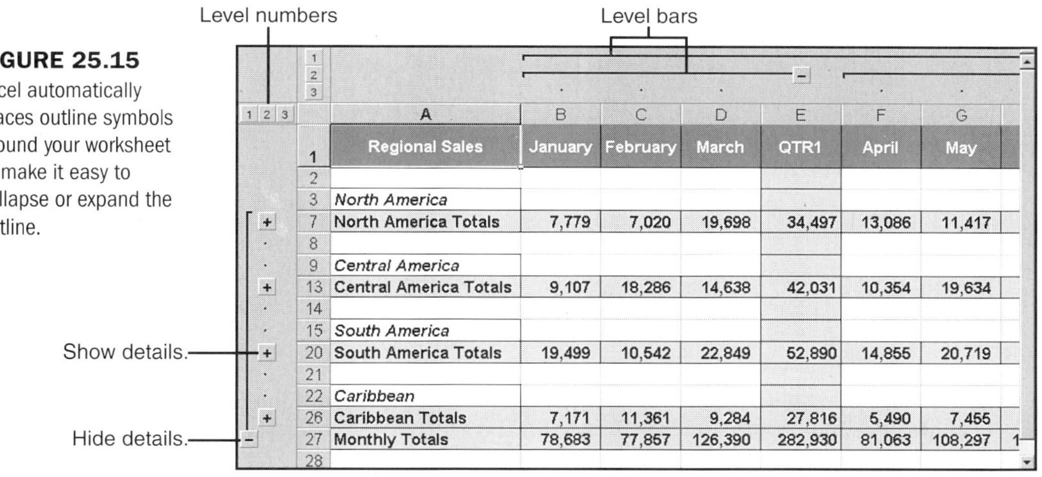

	A	B	C	D	E	F	G
1	Regional Sales	January	February	March	QTR1	April	May
2							
3	*North America*						
7	North America Totals	7,779	7,020	19,698	34,497	13,086	11,417
8							
9	*Central America*						
13	Central America Totals	9,107	18,286	14,638	42,031	10,354	19,634
14							
15	*South America*						
20	South America Totals	19,499	10,542	22,849	52,890	14,855	20,719
21							
22	*Caribbean*						
26	Caribbean Totals	7,171	11,361	9,284	27,816	5,490	7,455
27	Monthly Totals	78,683	77,857	126,390	282,930	81,063	108,297
28							

FIGURE 25.15
Excel automatically places outline symbols around your worksheet to make it easy to collapse or expand the outline.

To remove an outline from your worksheet, choose Data, Group and Outline, Clear Outline.

NOTE You can manually create or remove groups within your worksheets by using the Data, Group and Outline command, and then selecting either the Group or Ungroup options.

Creating Subtotals and Grand Totals

After a list is sorted, the Data, Subtotal command can quickly calculate *subtotals* and a *grand total* for the list. New rows are automatically inserted in your worksheet to display the subtotal and grand total calculations. You can choose from 11 common Excel functions for your subtotal calculations. Multiple subtotals can be calculated in a list at the same time.

NOTE The Subtotal command uses an outline to organize the list. See the previous section "Outlining Worksheets" if you are not familiar with Excel's outline tools.

Before using the Subtotal command, you must answer the following three questions:

- When do you want the subtotals to be calculated?
- What type of calculation do you want performed?
- Where do you want the calculation to appear?

Subtotals are calculated based on the order in which the list is sorted. Using Figure 25.16 as an example, if you want to generate subtotals by department, you would sort the list by the Department column. If you want to generate subtotals by expense type, you would sort the list by the Type of Expense column.

FIGURE 25.16

The only column in this figure that would not produce a meaningful list of subtotals is the Amount column.

	A	B	C	D	E	F
1			Expenses			
2	Department	Employee	Date	Type of Expense	Amount	
3	Administration	Jose Chavez	3/3/99	Travel	475.89	
4	Sales	Rick Barretto	3/3/99	Business Lunch	61.50	
5	Accounting	Anita Salinas	3/6/99	External Auditor	2,390.00	
6	Marketing	Marc Rodgers	3/8/99	Office Supplies	36.21	
7	Sales	Scott Fujimora	3/14/99	Business Lunch	50.64	
8	Maintenance	David Jacobson	3/17/99	Paint	52.86	
9	Planning	Yasmine Ali	3/18/99	Software	279.94	
10	Administration	Henrietta Lee	3/19/99	Travel	710.92	
11	Communication	Ian Stewart	3/22/99	Printing - Newsletter	159.37	
12	Marketing	Leo Swartz	3/23/99	Business Lunch	38.21	
13	Marketing	Leo Swartz	3/24/99	Employee Recognition	64.90	
14	Accounting	Bob Brown	3/29/99	Office Supplies	45.33	
15	Sales	Scott Fujimora	3/30/99	Laptop Computer	3,798.27	
16						

What the subtotal calculates is a separate issue. There are 11 functions that can be used as subtotal calculations in Excel, including SUM, COUNT, AVERAGE, MAX, MIN, PRODUCT, COUNTNUMS, SDTDEV, SDTDEVP, VAR, and VARP. Frequently, subtotals calculate the sum of a column of numerical data. You can also calculate averages, the standard deviation, and count items (including text) in the list.

Some of the calculations possible include the average amount for each type of expense (the list should be sorted by the Type of Expense column) and a count of the number of employees in each department submitting expenses (the list should be sorted by the Department column).

Where the subtotals appear in the worksheet is the final decision you must make. Often, the subtotals are displayed in the last column of the list, but you are not required to put the subtotals there. It would be logical to place the average type of expense subtotals in the Amount column. The number of employees submitting expenses can be placed either in the Department, Employee, Type of Expense, or even in the Amount column.

To create subtotals and grand totals, use these steps:

1. Sort the list by the column by which the data will be subtotaled.
2. Select a single cell in the list and choose Data, Subtotals. The Subtotal dialog box appears (see Figure 25.17).
3. From the At Each Change In drop-down list, select the column by which the list is sorted.
4. Select a function to calculate from the Use Function drop-down list.
5. In the Add Subtotal To list box, choose the column on which the function will perform the calculation. In Figure 25.17, the Amount column is selected. If there are several columns you want to subtotal using the same function, you can choose more than one column in the Add Subtotal To list box.

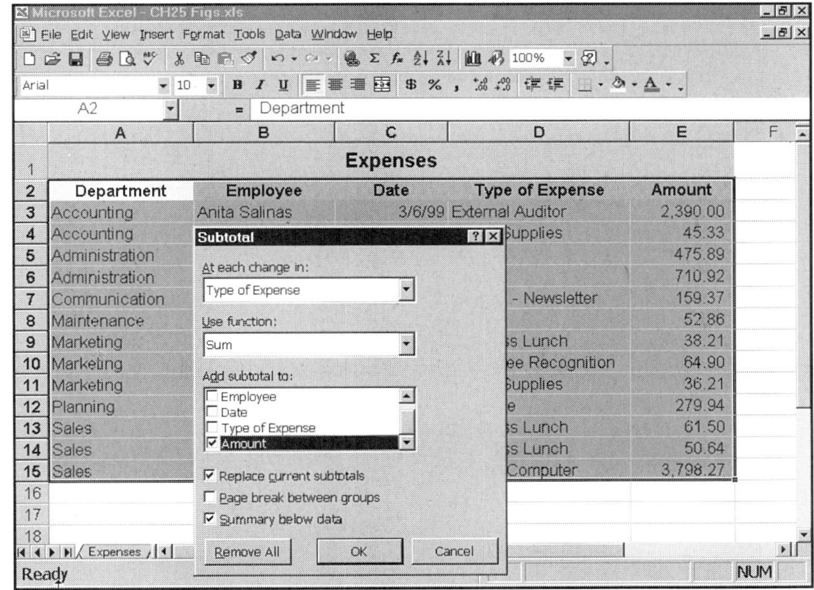

FIGURE 25.17
Common worksheet functions are used to calculate subtotals in a worksheet.

6. Choose OK. The subtotals and a grand total appear in your worksheet.

The worksheet is automatically outlined. You can use the outline symbols or number to collapse or expand the outline. Figure 25.18 displays the worksheet collapsed to display the subtotals and grand total.

One of the options in the Subtotals dialog box is to Replace Current Subtotals. This is used when you want to remove previous subtotals and replace them with new subtotals.

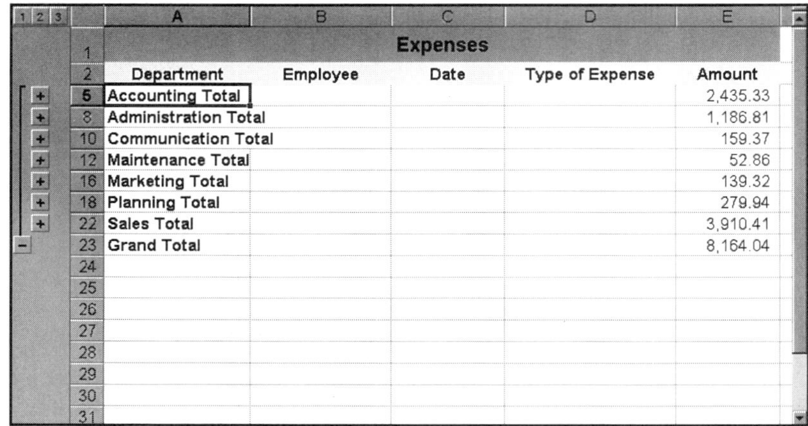

	A	B	C	D	E
1			Expenses		
2	Department	Employee	Date	Type of Expense	Amount
5	Accounting Total				2,435.33
8	Administration Total				1,186.81
10	Communication Total				159.37
12	Maintenance Total				52.86
16	Marketing Total				139.32
18	Planning Total				279.94
22	Sales Total				3,910.41
23	Grand Total				8,164.04
24					
25					
26					
27					
28					
29					
30					
31					

FIGURE 25.18
You can print the worksheet when the outline is collapsed. Only the data appearing onscreen will be printed.

Another option in the dialog box is to separate the groups by inserting a page break between each group. If you select this option, each group appears on a separate page when the worksheet is printed. This feature is particularly useful with long lists. For example, you might want to provide a list to each manager detailing his or her departmental expenses.

If you do not want to show a grand total beneath the list, remove the check from the Summary Below Data box (refer to Figure 25.17).

You can remove the subtotals, grand totals, and outline symbols from the worksheet through the Subtotals command. Select a cell in your list and choose Data, Subtotals. From the Subtotals dialog box, select the Remove All button.

Calculating Multiple Subtotals in a Worksheet

The Subtotals command enables you to create multiple subtotals using different functions. To accomplish this, you must remove the check from the Replace Current Subtotals box in the Subtotals dialog box. Only one function at a time can be calculated using the Subtotals command. You have to use the Subtotals command several times, once for each different subtotal to be calculated.

Figure 25.19 illustrates an example of two different subtotals: a count of the expense items per department, and a subtotal of the expenses grouped by department.

The first calculation you perform is listed last. Subsequent subtotals are listed above the first one. In this case, the Count was calculated first, and then the Total.

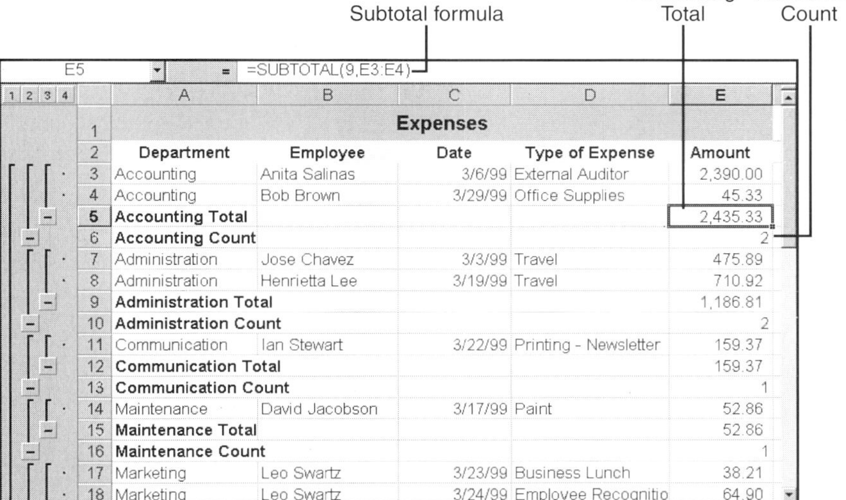

	A	B	C	D	E
1			Expenses		
2	Department	Employee	Date	Type of Expense	Amount
3	Accounting	Anita Salinas	3/6/99	External Auditor	2,390.00
4	Accounting	Bob Brown	3/29/99	Office Supplies	45.33
5	**Accounting Total**				2,435.33
6	**Accounting Count**				2
7	Administration	Jose Chavez	3/3/99	Travel	475.89
8	Administration	Henrietta Lee	3/19/99	Travel	710.92
9	**Administration Total**				1,186.81
10	**Administration Count**				2
11	Communication	Ian Stewart	3/22/99	Printing - Newsletter	159.37
12	**Communication Total**				159.37
13	**Communication Count**				1
14	Maintenance	David Jacobson	3/17/99	Paint	52.86
15	**Maintenance Total**				52.86
16	**Maintenance Count**				1
17	Marketing	Leo Swartz	3/23/99	Business Lunch	38.21
18	Marketing	Leo Swartz	3/24/99	Employee Recognitio	64.90

FIGURE 25.19
Make sure you sort the list on the column you want to subtotal. In this example, that's the Department column.

Unlocking the Power of PivotTables and PivotCharts

PivotTable reports, such as subtotals and database functions, are effective tools for summarizing lengthy lists of information. The difference is that PivotTables are a better tool for consolidating and analyzing data. They are called *PivotTables* because you can rotate, or pivot, the rows and columns in a PivotTable to see the data summarized differently. PivotTable reports can be created from Excel lists or from external data sources such as Microsoft Access, Microsoft FoxPro, Microsoft Project, and OLAP cubes.

▶ **See** "Using and Creating OLAP Cubes," **p. 749**

The procedure used in Excel 95 or 97 for creating PivotTable reports has been enhanced in Excel 2000. Selecting and changing the items used in the PivotTable are easier now that you no longer have to access the PivotTable Wizard to add or remove fields from the PivotTable. Instead, you can make the adjustments directly in the worksheet. Additionally, a new AutoFormat feature makes it easy to format a PivotTable.

Corresponding graphic charts, called *PivotCharts*, have been added to the PivotTable report feature in Excel 2000. These charts are tied to the PivotTable data and refresh when the items summarized by the PivotTable (or the data) changes.

To use the PivotTable reports effectively, the information in your worksheet must be organized in a list, as described in the section "Structuring Lists," at the beginning of this chapter. Additionally, before creating a PivotTable you should be aware of the following:

- Column Headings—Excel uses the data in the first row of the list for the field names in the PivotTable. Your list must contain column headings. If you are creating PivotTables from multiple lists, the column headings must be identical in each list.

- Range Names—Create a range name for each list you will be summarizing. It will be easier to refresh and update the PivotTable when the list data changes and it speeds up the creation of PivotTables based on multiple lists.
- Filters—If you have applied a filter to your list, Excel ignores the filter when it creates the PivotTable. All data in the list is included automatically in the PivotTable. To create a PivotTable from filtered data, use the Data, Filter, Advanced Filter command to copy a range of data to another worksheet location, and then base the PivotTable on the copied range. See the section "Performing Advanced Filters" earlier in this chapter for more information on advanced filters.
- Automatic Subtotals—Excel automatically creates grand totals and subtotals in the PivotTable. If you have created subtotals (using the Data, Subtotals command) in the list, you should remove them from the list before you create the PivotTable report.

Figure 25.20 shows a workbook containing a consulting worklog for the month of June. The list is sorted by Date.

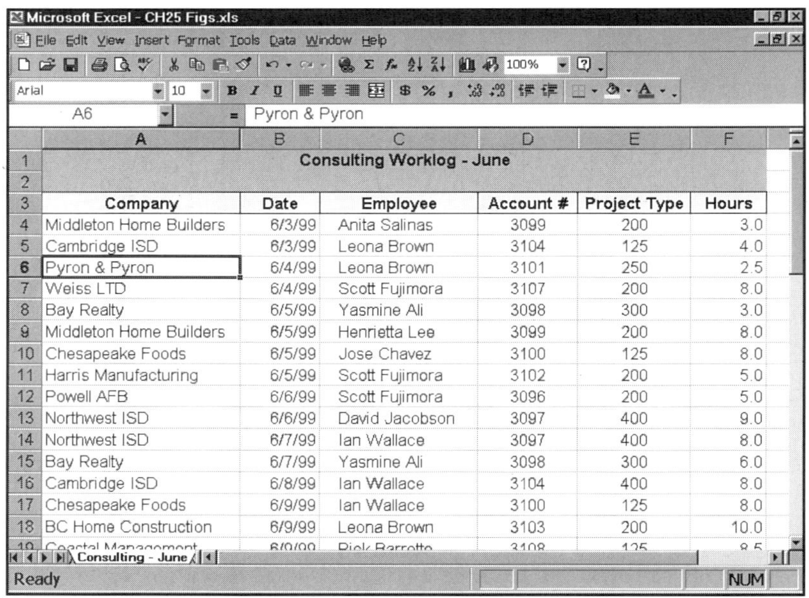

Consulting Worklog - June

Company	Date	Employee	Account #	Project Type	Hours
Middleton Home Builders	6/3/99	Anita Salinas	3099	200	3.0
Cambridge ISD	6/3/99	Leona Brown	3104	125	4.0
Pyron & Pyron	6/4/99	Leona Brown	3101	250	2.5
Weiss LTD	6/4/99	Scott Fujimora	3107	200	8.0
Bay Realty	6/5/99	Yasmine Ali	3098	300	3.0
Middleton Home Builders	6/5/99	Henrietta Lee	3099	200	8.0
Chesapeake Foods	6/5/99	Jose Chavez	3100	125	8.0
Harris Manufacturing	6/5/99	Scott Fujimora	3102	200	5.0
Powell AFB	6/6/99	Scott Fujimora	3096	200	5.0
Northwest ISD	6/6/99	David Jacobson	3097	400	9.0
Northwest ISD	6/7/99	Ian Wallace	3097	400	8.0
Bay Realty	6/7/99	Yasmine Ali	3098	300	6.0
Cambridge ISD	6/8/99	Ian Wallace	3104	400	8.0
Chesapeake Foods	6/9/99	Ian Wallace	3100	125	8.0
BC Home Construction	6/9/99	Leona Brown	3103	200	10.0

FIGURE 25.20
An Excel list must contain only one row of column headings. These headings are used as fields in the PivotTable.

A key element in a PivotTable is the information you want to summarize. Generally, only numerical information can be summarized. In the list displayed in Figure 25.20, the numerical column that logically needs to be summarized is the Hours column. Although the account numbers and project types are also numbers, they are numbers that are being used as labels. You're not likely to want Excel to calculate the sum of the account numbers or project types—that would be similar to asking for a sum of phone numbers or Social Security numbers. You might, however, want to count how many accounts or project types there are; the COUNT function is often used with labels. Some of the other calculations you can perform include AVERAGE, MIN, MAX, PRODUCT, STDDEV, and VAR.

Depending on the type of data in your worksheet, you'll generally have a number of PivotTable possibilities. For example, using the list displayed in Figure 25.20, a variety of different PivotTables can be created, including

- The total number of Hours worked by Employee
- The total number of Hours worked by Account number
- The total number of Hours worked by Date
- The total number of Hours worked for each Company on each Project Type
- The total number of Hours each Employee worked for each Company
- The total number of Hours each Employee worked on each Project Type

Using either the subtotal command or database functions, you can also derive the summaries in the first three examples. They summarize the hours by using one other column from the list. The last three examples can be created only by using PivotTables. These examples summarize the hours by using two other columns from the list, thus creating the PivotTable.

The data from one column is used as labels for the PivotTable rows (for example, Employee names). The data from another column is used as the labels for the PivotTable columns (for example, Project Types). The data (Hours) is summarized, or cross-tabulated, for the intersection of each row and column.

Each of the examples in the preceding bulleted list calculates totals, using the SUM function. However, this is not the only calculation that can be generated in a PivotTable report. You can calculate the average, standard deviation, variance, and count items in the list.

The first step in creating a PivotTable or PivotChart is to identify the source of the data you want to summarize. Sources include Excel lists, external data sources (such as Access and Project), consolidated ranges (multiple lists), and other PivotTables or PivotCharts.

Creating PivotTables Using a Single Excel List

If the source data is just one Excel list, the process is very easy. You select a cell anywhere in your list and choose Data, PivotTable and PivotChart Report. A wizard guides you through a three-step process.

The first step of the PivotTable Wizard is identifying the source of the data from which the PivotTable will be created. Because the default setting is Microsoft Excel list or database, click the Next button.

In the second step of the PivotTable Wizard, Excel is confirming the range of cell references for your list. If the incorrect cell range is selected, you can select the range of cells you want directly in the worksheet. You also can type a range name, if you created one. When the correct cell references (or range name) appears in the Range entry box, click the Next button.

The third step is designating the location where you want the PivotTable to be placed. The New Worksheet option inserts a new worksheet in the active workbook and places the PivotTable in this new worksheet. The Existing Worksheet option lets you place the PivotTable on a worksheet in the active workbook or in another workbook. If the other workbook is open, use the Window menu or Taskbar to display the target workbook. Then select the worksheet tab and cell where you want the PivotTable to begin. If the workbook is not open, you will have to type the entire path of the workbook—including drive, folder, workbook name, worksheet name, and cell reference. As you can see, it's a lot easier if you open the destination workbook before you start the wizard.

After you've identified the destination for the PivotTable, select Finish. The PivotTable layout is displayed along with the PivotTable toolbar, as shown in Figure 25.21.

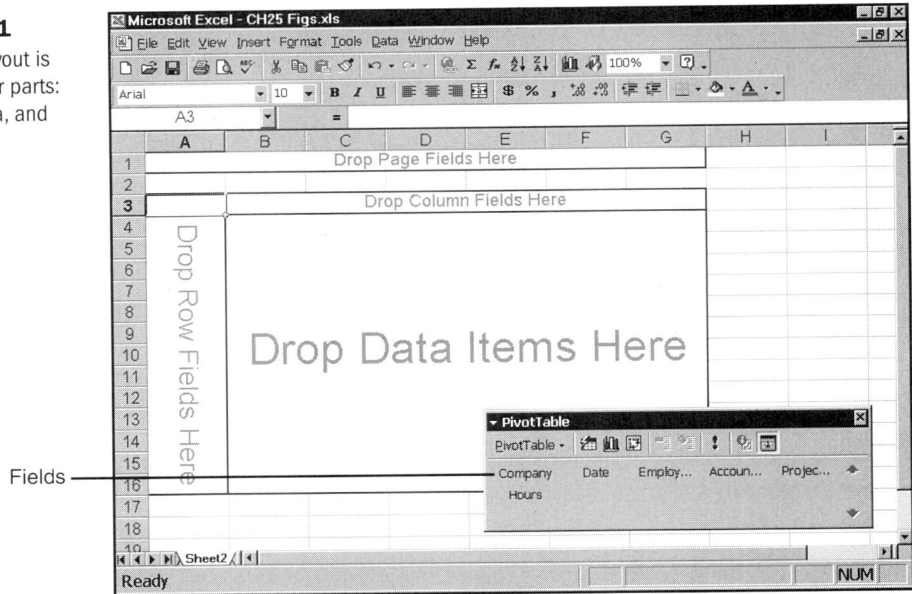

FIGURE 25.21
The PivotTable layout is composed of four parts: row, column, data, and page.

The list column headings become fields and appear as part of the PivotTable toolbar. You drag the field names from the toolbar to any of the four layout areas. You do not have to use all four areas, but you must use the Data area and at least one other area.

- Row—Drag the field containing the data you want to become the row labels in the PivotTable to the Row area. You can place more than one field in the row area.
- Column—Drag the field containing the data you want to become the column labels in the PivotTable in the Column area. You can place more than one field in the column area.
- Data—Drag the numeric field containing the data you want to summarize in the PivotTable in the Data area.
- Page—When you place a field in this area, it acts as a filter on the PivotTable.

Generally, it is best to place the field that has the fewest unique entries in the column area and the field that has the most unique entries in the row area. The exception to this would be entry length. If the field has very long entries, they should be placed in the row area, where you can see more of them at one time. Looking back at Figure 25.20, there are more employees than project types, so the project type field should be placed in the column area.

In Figure 25.22, the Employee field has been placed in the Row area and the Project Type field in the Column area. The Hours field has been added to the Data area. Initially, the Count of the Hours is calculated—this is not the same as the Sum of the Hours. In this example, the Count indicates how many times each employee worked on a particular type of project, not how many hours each worked.

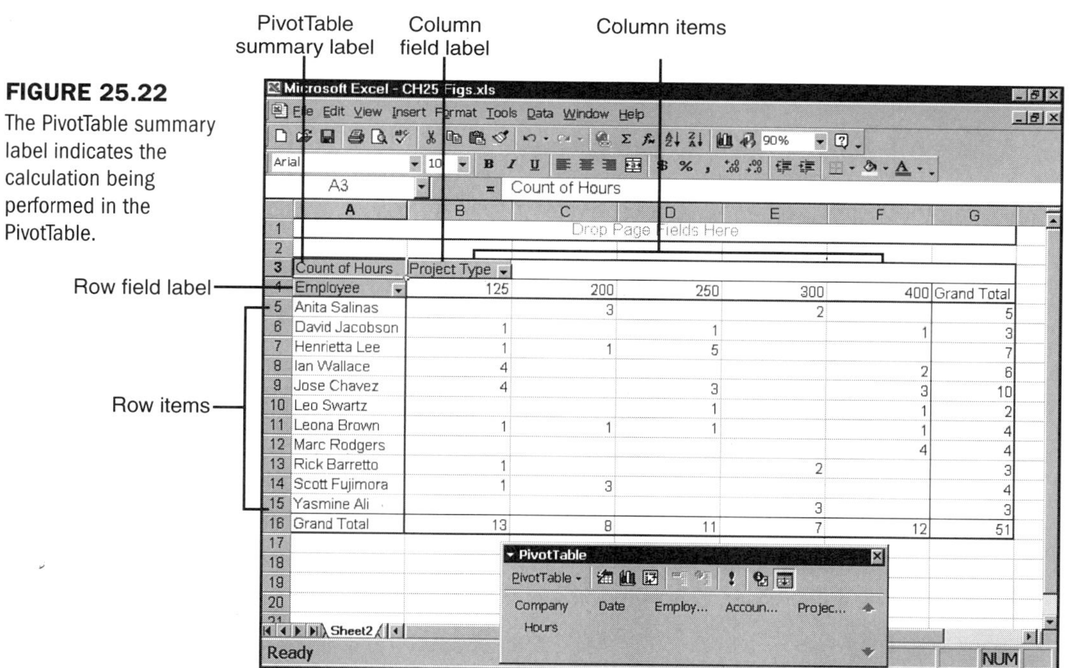

FIGURE 25.22
The PivotTable summary label indicates the calculation being performed in the PivotTable.

To change the fields used in the row, column, or data areas, simply drag the field off the PivotTable and replace it with another from the PivotTable toolbar until you get the summary you are looking for.

To change the type of calculation performed on the PivotTable, double-click the PivotTable summary label (in Figure 25.22, that would be the Count of Hours label). A dialog box appears where you can select a different calculation. You can also right-click on the label or anywhere in the data area (where the calculated results display) and choose Field Settings from the shortcut menu. Choose a different calculation from the Summarize By list in the PivotTable Field dialog box.

Formatting a PivotTable After a PivotTable has been created, there are several options you can use to format and edit the results. The PivotTable is designed to enable quick selection of various parts of the table through a selection arrow. Figure 25.23 shows the selection arrow positioned over the row field and all the row items selected. Although it may appear that Anita Salinas is not selected, she is. Remember, the first item selected in a range of cells has a transparent background.

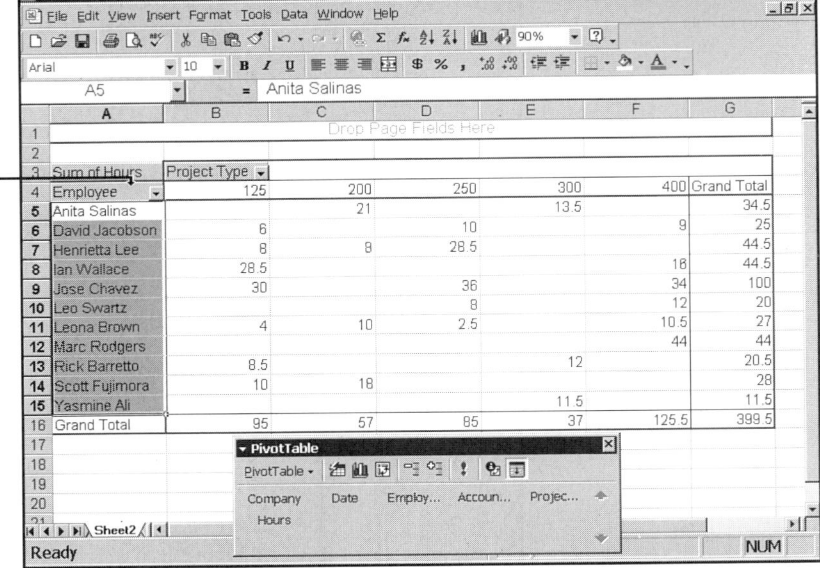

Selection Arrow

FIGURE 25.23
Look for the selection arrow to select parts of a PivotTable.

The PivotTable can be formatted easily to enhance its appearance. The fastest way to format a table is to use the AutoFormat command. Select any cell in the PivotTable and click the Format Report button on the PivotTable toolbar. If the PivotTable toolbar is not active, select Format, AutoFormat.

From the AutoFormat dialog box, choose one of the many predefined formats to quickly give your PivotTable a professional look.

To format individual parts of the PivotTable, select the cells you want to format, and use the buttons on the formatting toolbar or the Format, Cells command.

Updating a PivotTable When data in your list changes, the PivotTable isn't automatically updated to reflect the new data. To update your PivotTable, click anywhere in the PivotTable and select the Refresh Data command from the PivotTable toolbar. If the PivotTable toolbar is not displayed, choose Data, Refresh Data.

When you need to add new rows or columns to your list, adding the rows or columns in the middle of the list ensures the new data is reflected in the PivotTable. When you refresh the PivotTable, Excel automatically expands the range of cell references used to create the PivotTable.

However, if you add new data to the bottom of your list (by typing in the data or using the data form), Excel continues to use the original range of cell references for the PivotTable. The range is not expanded automatically when you refresh the PivotTable data.

To include these new rows or columns, you have to return to the PivotTable Wizard. When the wizard appears, by default, it displays step 3. Use the Back button to display step 2 of the PivotTable Wizard. The current range of cell references is listed. To quickly expand the range to include the new rows, use the Shift key and down arrow on your keyboard to select additional rows at the bottom of your list. Then click Finish to update your PivotTable.

Adjusting PivotTable Options There are several options over which you have control in your PivotTable. The PivotTable options can be selected when you initially create the PivotTable (from a button on the final step of the wizard) or anytime after the PivotTable has been created (by selecting Table Options from the PivotTable menu on the PivotTable toolbar). Figure 25.24 shows the PivotTable Options dialog box.

FIGURE 25.24
By default, row and column totals are added to PivotTables.

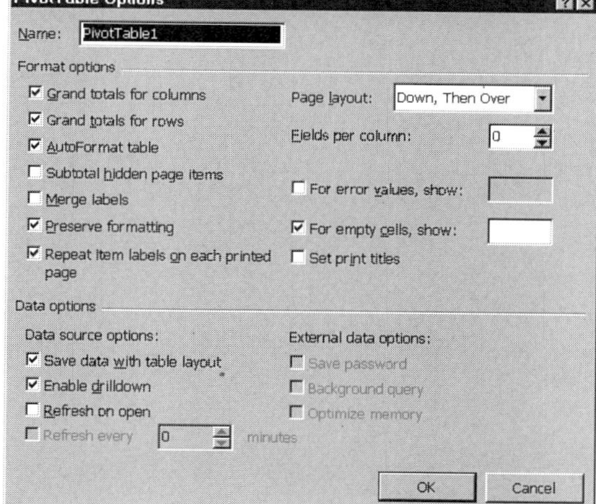

Figure 25.24 shows the default option settings for PivotTables. You can change these settings to modify the PivotTable. For example, empty cells appear blank in the PivotTable by default. You can specify a value such as 0 (zero) or a dash (-) to be displayed instead.

Workbooks containing PivotTables can be unexpectedly large. Excel creates a copy of the source data and stores it as hidden data, with the worksheet that contains the PivotTable. If your PivotTable references a large amount of data in another file, you are storing the same data twice—once in the original file, and again in the file that contains the PivotTable. This is an advantage when the data comes from a network server, which may not always be available.

You can avoid this duplication by deselecting the Save data with table layout check box in the Options dialog box (refer to Figure 25.24). When the file containing the PivotTable is saved, the hidden copy of the source data is not saved with it. When the PivotTable is refreshed, Excel updates it directly from the source data. Use this option when the data is coming from your own hard drive or other readily available source.

Grouping PivotTable Items for Greater Flexibility

There may be times you want to group row or column items in your PivotTable. Suppose you have a PivotTable that displays the sales for customer by year. If you have a field in the list that indicates the month of each sale, you can use the Show Detail button on the PivotTable toolbar to add that field to the PivotTable. But suppose you would rather see the yearly data displayed by quarter. Because you don't have a quarter field in the list, you'll have to create groups that represent each quarter. For example, you can group the first three months to create Quarter 1.

Grouping items in a PivotTable enables you to hide or show the items in the group. Figure 25.25 shows a PivotTable that displays monthly sales information, arranged alphabetically by sales representative. The Region field has been placed in the Page area, so the sales data can be viewed by region.

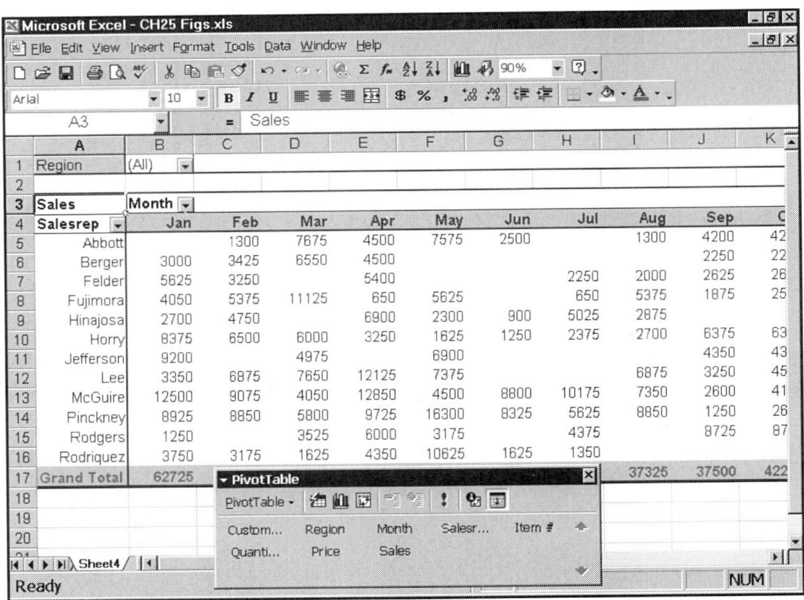

Sales	Month									
Salesrep	Jan	Feb	Mar	Apr	May	Jun	Jul	Aug	Sep	C
Abbott		1300	7675	4500	7575	2500		1300	4200	42
Berger	3000	3425	6550	4500					2250	22
Felder	5625	3250		5400			2250	2000	2625	26
Fujimora	4050	5375	11125	650	5625		650	5375	1875	25
Hinajosa	2700	4750		6900	2300	900	5025	2875		
Horry	8375	6500	6000	3250	1625	1250	2375	2700	6375	63
Jefferson	9200		4975		6900				4350	43
Lee	3350	6875	7650	12125	7375			6875	3250	45
McGuire	12500	9075	4050	12850	4500	8800	10175	7350	2600	41
Pinckney	8925	8850	5800	9725	16300	8325	5625	8850	1250	26
Rodgers	1250		3525	6000	3175		4375		8725	87
Rodriquez	3750	3175	1625	4350	10625	1625	1350			
Grand Total	62725							37325	37500	422

FIGURE 25.25
The PivotTable has been formatted using the Format Report button.

To group items, select them and choose Data, Group and Outline, Group. Above the items, a group name will be inserted, called Group1. Select the label Group1 and type the name you want to display for the group (for example, Quarter 1). As you add groups, not only is a label added for each group created, but another field label is added to the PivotTable. Figure 25.26 shows the groups Quarter 1 and Quarter 2 created and the additional field label "Month2" added to the Row area of the PivotTable. You rename this label by typing a new name in the label cell.

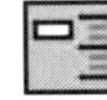

You can hide the detailed data and display just the group totals several ways. You can select the cell containing the new label and click the Hide Details button on the PivotTable toolbar. To display the detailed data, click the Show Details button on the PivotTable toolbar. Figure 25.27 shows data from Quarter 1 displayed using this method.

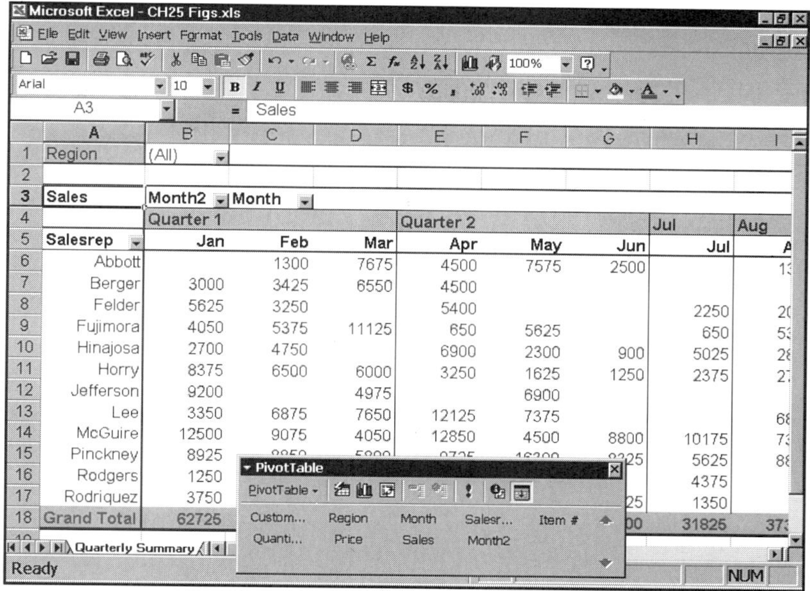

FIGURE 25.26
The new field has also been added to the PivotTable toolbar.

FIGURE 25.27
The field label can be renamed—here it has been changed to Quarters.

Microsoft Excel - CH25 Figs.xls							
Region	(All)						
Sales	Quarters	Month					
	Quarter 1	Quarter 2			Jul	Aug	Sep
Salesrep		Apr	May	Jun	Jul	Aug	Sep
Abbott	8975	4500	7575	2500		1300	4200
Berger	12975	4500					2250
Felder	8875	5400			2250	2000	2625
Fujimora	20550	650	5625		650	5375	1875
Hinajosa	7450	6900	2300	900	5025	2875	
Horry	20875	3250	1625	1250	2375	2700	6375
Jefferson	14175		6900				4350
Lee	17875	12125	7375			6875	3250
McGuire	25625	12850	4500	8800	10175	7350	2600
Pinckney	23575						1250
Rodgers	4775						8725
Rodriquez	8550						
Grand Total	174275						37500

PivotTable: Custom... Region Month Salesr... Item # / Quanti... Price Sales Quarte...

New field added to toolbar

Alternatively, you can move the new field label to the Page area of the PivotTable. Then use the drop-down list on the label to filter the PivotTable and display the data by group—in this example, by Quarter.

Using Custom Calculations in PivotTables

There are a number of other summary calculations that can be displayed in a PivotTable. Additionally, you can create custom calculations, such as Running Total In, which displays the data as a running total for each item, or % of Total, which displays the data as a percentage of the grand total of the PivotTable.

You can create custom calculations for the PivotTable data for each item in a field, or for all items in a field. In some of the custom calculations, you must specify a field and an item or value by which all other items are compared. This field and value are referred to as the *base field* and *base item*. Table 25.2 lists the custom calculations you can perform.

Table 25.2 Custom Calculations That Can Be Used in the PivotTable Data Field

Calculation Name	Description of the Calculation
Difference From	Calculates the difference between the data and a specified base field and base item (value).
% Of	Calculates the percentage a value constitutes of a specified base field and base item (value).
% Difference From	Calculates the difference between the data and a specified base field and base item, but displays the difference as a percentage of the base data.
Running Total In	Calculates the data for successive items as a running total.
% of Row	Calculates the data in each row as a percentage of the total for that row.
% of Column	Calculates the data in each column as a percentage of the total for that column.
% of Total	Calculates the data as a percentage of the grand total of all the data in the PivotTable.
Index	Calculates each data item as an index, based on the grand totals, using this formula: ((value in cell)×(Grand Total of Grand Totals))/((Grand Row Total)×(Grand Column Total)).

To change the type of calculation performed on the PivotTable data, double-click the PivotTable summary field. The PivotTable Field dialog box displays. The built-in Excel functions are listed in the Summarize By list box. Click the Options button to create a custom calculation. In Figure 25.28, the data will be shown as a percent of the grand total. After you've selected the calculation you want, click OK. The PivotTable will be revised.

Creating PivotTables from Multiple Excel Lists

Don't be fooled by the option in the PivotTable Wizard for consolidating multiple lists—it does not produce the same flexibility as a PivotTable created from one list. This is especially true if some of your data is text or numbers used as labels, such as an account number, part number, or Social Security number.

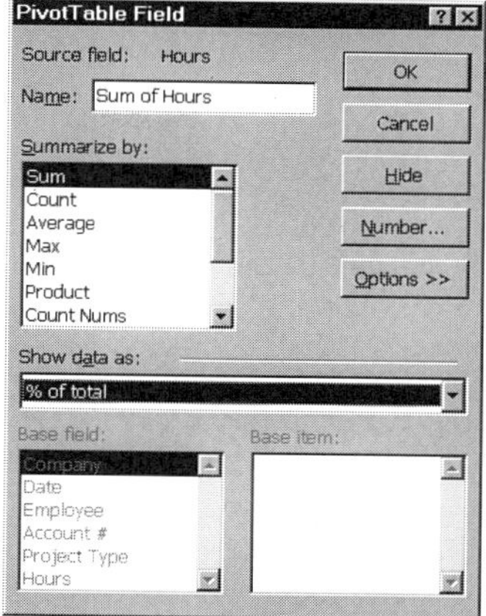

FIGURE 25.28
The built-in Excel functions are listed in the Summarize By list box.

With this option, you will not have a choice as to which fields are placed in the row area and which are placed in the column area. Excel always places the data in the first column from the list in the row area and, all the remaining fields are placed in the column area. Additionally, the same calculation is performed on all fields, whether it makes sense to perform the calculation or not—for example, the sum of the dates work was performed or the sum of the account numbers. If you use this feature, you will spend a great deal of time tweaking the results in order for them to make sense.

Like the Data, Consolidate command, this option is best when used to consolidate lists composed of numerical data, rather than lists that contain a mix of text, numbers used as labels, and numerical data.

If your lists contain columns of text or numbers used as labels, I recommend that you combine the data (using Copy/Paste) into one big list to take advantage of the PivotTable features.

Creating PivotTables Using Data from Other Programs

In addition to being able to use an Excel list as your data source, you can use external sources for the data. An *external data source* could be a database, a text file, or sources on the Internet. Examples of external sources include Microsoft Access, Microsoft FoxPro, dBASE, Oracle, SQL Server, Microsoft Project, and OLAP cubes.

Usually, you specify the external data source when you run the PivotTable Wizard—on step 1 of the wizard.

To use data from an external source, you will need to extract the data using a *query*. With the PivotTable Wizard, you can open query files you have already created, or create new queries from within the PivotTable wizard.

▶ **See** "Creating Queries to Import Data from External Databases," to learn about creating data sources or queries, **p. 730**

To create a PivotTable or PivotChart from external data, follow these steps:

1. Choose Data, PivotTable or PivotChart Report.
2. In step 1 of the wizard, select External Data Source and choose Next.
3. In step 2 of the wizard, click the Get Data button.
4. The Choose Data Source dialog box appears. From the Databases tab, you can create a new data source and query. From the Queries tab, you can select an existing query. From the OLAP Cubes tab, you can create a data source or select an existing query for extracting the data.

   ▶ **See** "Using and Creating OLAP Cubes" to learn more about OLAP cubes, **p. 749**

5. If you decide to create a new database query using the Query Wizard, select the option Return Data to Microsoft Excel in the final step of the Query Wizard (see Figure 25.29) and choose Finish.

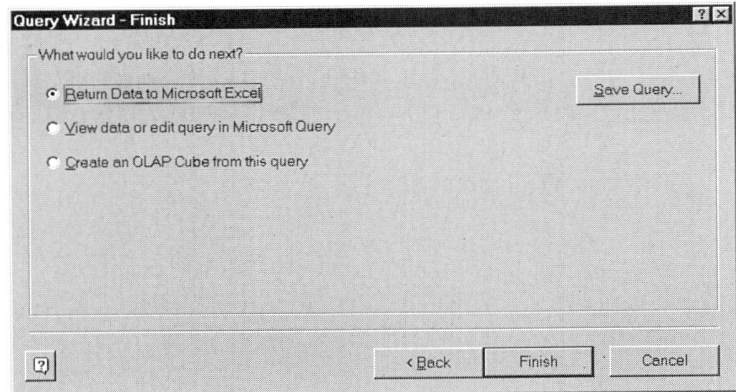

FIGURE 25.29
Using the default option will take you back to the PivotTable Wizard.

   - If you create a database query using the Query window, or if you run an existing query (which opens the Query window), click the Return Data button (in the Query window) to identify the data and proceed with the PivotTable Wizard. The Return Data button appears as a closing door on the Query window toolbar.
   - If you decide to use an existing OLAP source or run an existing OLAP query, click the OK button in the Choose Data Source dialog box.

6. Regardless of your choices in step 5, the PivotTable Wizard reappears indicating the data fields have been retrieved, as shown in Figure 25.30; click Next.

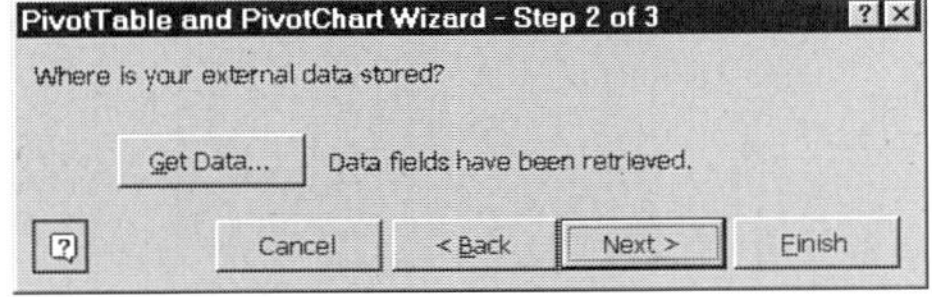

FIGURE 25.30
The dialog box indicates that the data has been retrieved.

7. On the third and final step of the PivotTable Wizard, indicate where you want the PivotTable to appear and click Finish.
8. The PivotTable structure appears. Drag and drop the fields to the desired Page, Row, Column, and Data positions.

Manipulating PivotTables Based on Data from OLAP Cubes

When you import data from relational databases into Excel, the data is returned to Excel as a list. You can then use any of the tools described in this chapter to manipulate the list data. However, when you import data from OLAP cubes, the data can be returned to Excel only in a PivotTable or PivotChart. Chapter 24, "Importing Data from Databases, Web Pages, and Text Files," describes how to create OLAP cubes and several methods for extracting the data from these cubes to manipulate in Excel.

Figure 25.31 shows the structure of an OLAP cube.

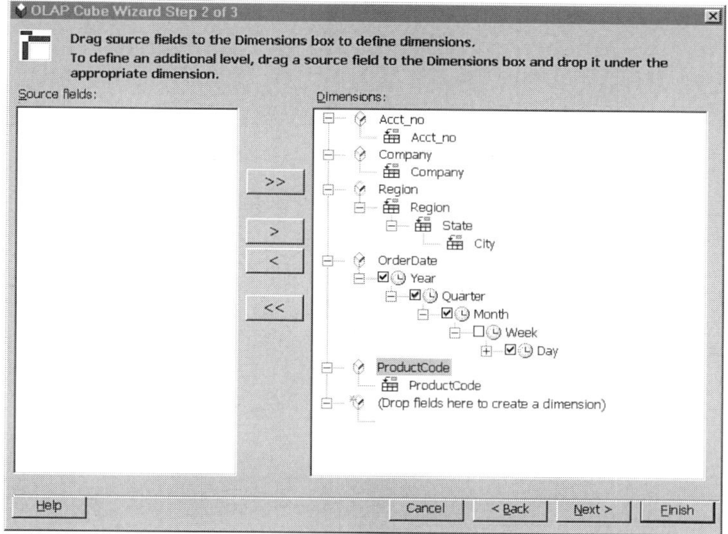

FIGURE 25.31
You define the structure in the OLAP Cube wizard.

There are several ways to bring the data from an OLAP cube into a PivotTable or PivotChart. You can run the PivotTable report (Data, PivotTable and PivotChart Report) and select External Data Source in step 1 of the PivotTable Wizard, as described in the previous section.

You can accomplish the same thing by simply running the OLAP cube definition file, which stores instructions for creating the cube. Choose Data, Get External Data, Run Saved Query. In the Run Query dialog box, shown in Figure 25.32, double-click the cube definition file. All cube definition files have the .oqy file extension.

FIGURE 25.32
Web, database, and OLAP queries are stored in the Queries folder.

The final step of the PivotTable Wizard appears where you identify the location for the PivotTable. You then proceed to drag the fields to the desired locations in the PivotTable (see Figure 25.33). The fields that appear are the cube dimension names (refer to Figure 25.31).

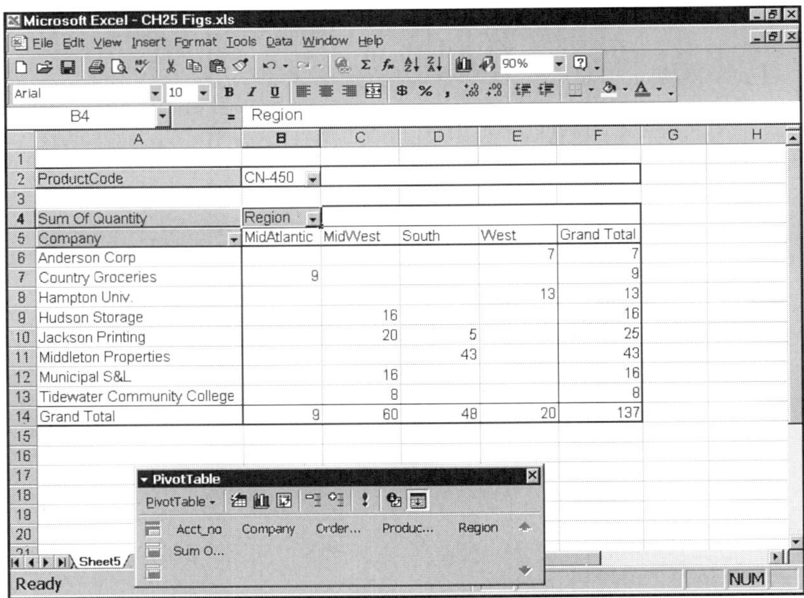

Company	MidAtlantic	MidWest	South	West	Grand Total
Anderson Corp				7	7
Country Groceries	9				9
Hampton Univ.				13	13
Hudson Storage		16			16
Jackson Printing		20	5		25
Middleton Properties			43		43
Municipal S&L		16			16
Tidewater Community College		8			8
Grand Total	9	60	48	20	137

FIGURE 25.33
The page drop-down list was used to display a specific product code.

To see the data from a specific level in a dimension, you need to select the field in the PivotTable and click the Show Detail button on the PivotTable toolbar, as shown in Figure 25.34 (for example, to see the State field under the Region dimension).

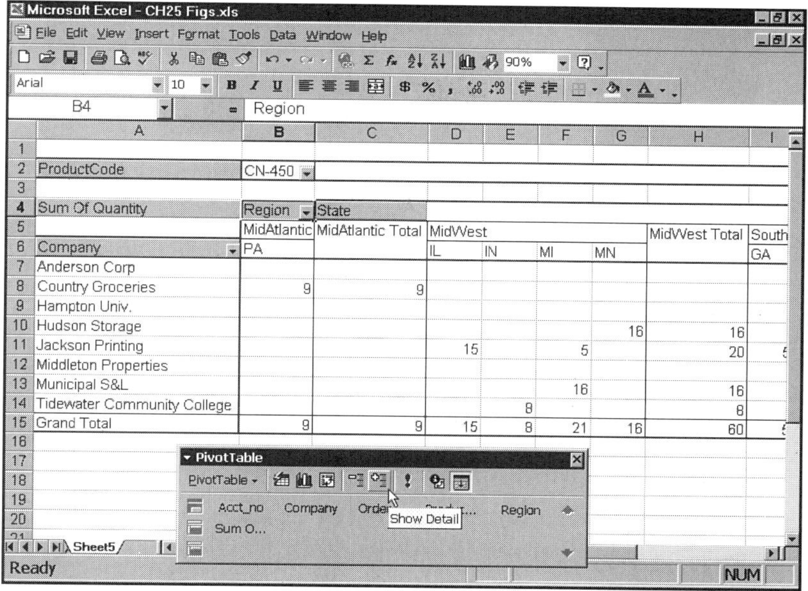

	A	B	C	D	E	F	G	H	I
2	ProductCode	CN-450							
4	Sum Of Quantity	Region	State						
5		MidAtlantic	MidAtlantic Total	MidWest				MidWest Total	South
6	Company	PA		IL	IN	MI	MN		GA
7	Anderson Corp								
8	Country Groceries	9	9						
9	Hampton Univ.								
10	Hudson Storage						16	16	
11	Jackson Printing			15		5		20	5
12	Middleton Properties								
13	Municipal S&L					16		16	
14	Tidewater Community College				8			8	
15	Grand Total	9	9	15	8	21	16	60	5

FIGURE 25.34
Each level is summarized in the PivotTable.

Creating PivotCharts

PivotChart reports are a new feature in Excel 2000. They provide a graphical representation of the PivotTable data. PivotCharts can be created simultaneously with a PivotTable or after you have created and adjusted a PivotTable.

To create a PivotChart from an existing PivotTable, select a cell in the PivotTable and click the Chart Wizard button on the PivotTable toolbar. Figure 25.35 shows a PivotTable summarizing sales data by region for each sales representative. Figure 25.36 shows the PivotChart created from this PivotTable.

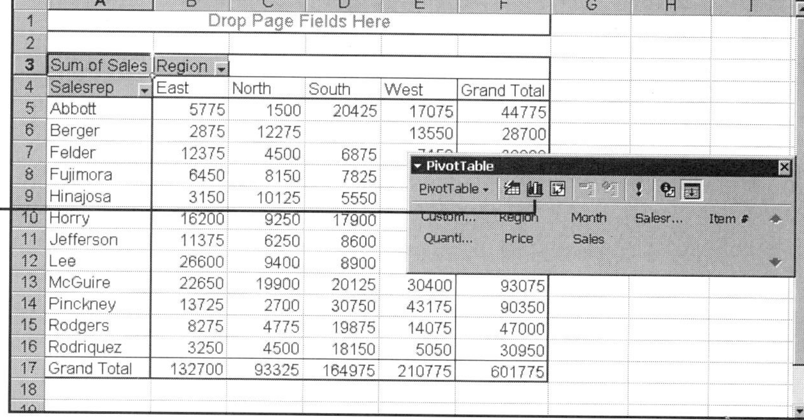

	A	B	C	D	E	F
3	Sum of Sales	Region				
4	Salesrep	East	North	South	West	Grand Total
5	Abbott	5775	1500	20425	17075	44775
6	Berger	2875	12275		13550	28700
7	Felder	12375	4500	6875		
8	Fujimora	6450	8150	7825		
9	Hinajosa	3150	10125	5550		
10	Horry	16200	9250	17900		
11	Jefferson	11375	6250	8600		
12	Lee	26600	9400	8900		
13	McGuire	22650	19900	20125	30400	93075
14	Pinckney	13725	2700	30750	43175	90350
15	Rodgers	8275	4775	19875	14075	47000
16	Rodriquez	3250	4500	18150	5050	30950
17	Grand Total	132700	93325	164975	210775	601775

FIGURE 25.35
Make sure you click inside the PivotTable before you click the Chart Wizard.

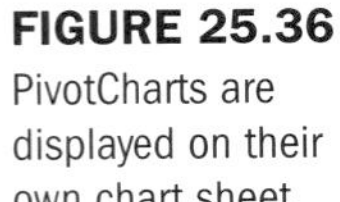

FIGURE 25.36
PivotCharts are displayed on their own chart sheet.

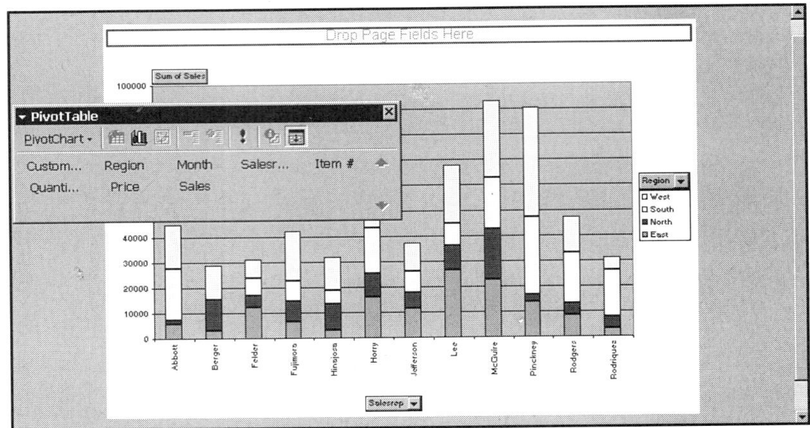

The PivotTable and PivotChart are linked. Changes you make in the PivotTable are reflected in the PivotChart and vice versa. For example, if you use the Page drop-down field in the PivotChart to filter the data displayed in the chart, the PivotTable adjusts to reflect the change as well.

To create the PivotTable and PivotChart at the same time, select a cell anywhere in your list and choose Data, PivotTable and PivotChart Report. In the first step of the wizard, you identify the source of the data and the type of report you want to create. If the source data is Microsoft Excel list or database, you simply need to select the PivotChart option and click the Next button.

In the second step of the PivotTable Wizard, Excel confirms the range of cell references for your list. Click the Next button.

PivotCharts are always placed on a separate worksheet. You can, however, in the third step of the wizard, designate the location where you want the PivotTable to be placed. You can place the PivotTable in a new worksheet or in a worksheet in the active workbook or any other workbook. If you intend to place the PivotTable in another workbook, it is best if the other workbook is open. Otherwise, you will have to type the entire path of the workbook, including drive, folder, workbook name, worksheet name, and cell reference.

After you've identified the destination for the PivotTable, select Finish. A new worksheet for the PivotChart is added to the active workbook and the PivotChart layout is displayed along with the PivotTable toolbar, as shown in Figure 25.37.

As with a PivotTable, you drag the field names from the toolbar to any of the four layout areas in the PivotChart:

- Category—The data in the field you drag to the Category area becomes the labels along the x-axis of the chart.
- Series—The data in the field you drag to the Series area becomes the plotted groups in the chart and the labels in the legend.

FIGURE 25.37
The PivotChart layout is composed of four parts or "drop-zones": category, series, data, and page.

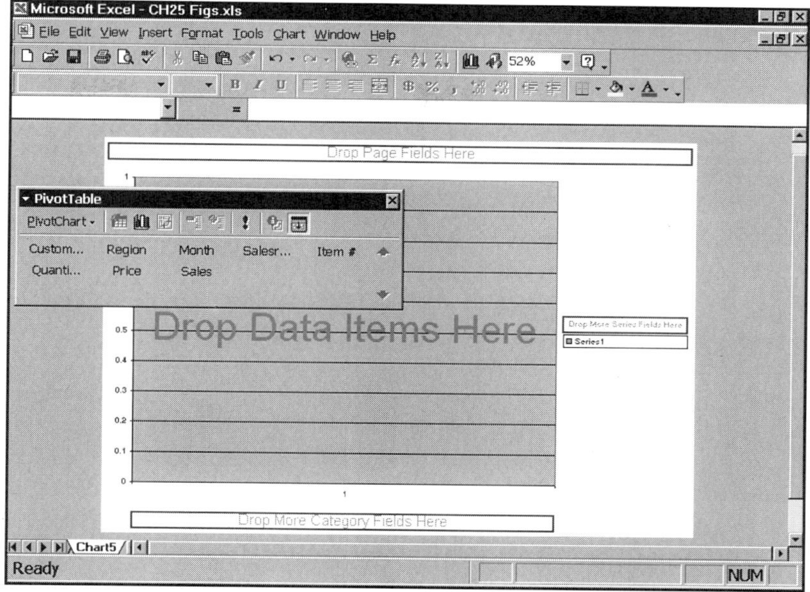

- Data—The numerical data in the field you drag to the Data area is plotted (grouped by series) in the chart.
- Page—Although you do not have to place a field in this area, it acts as a filter on the PivotChart when you do.

In Figure 25.38, the SalesRep field has been placed in the Category area and the Year field in the Series Area. The Sales field is being summed in the Data area. The Customer field is in the Page area.

FIGURE 25.38
The PivotChart summary label indicates the calculation being performed in the PivotChart.

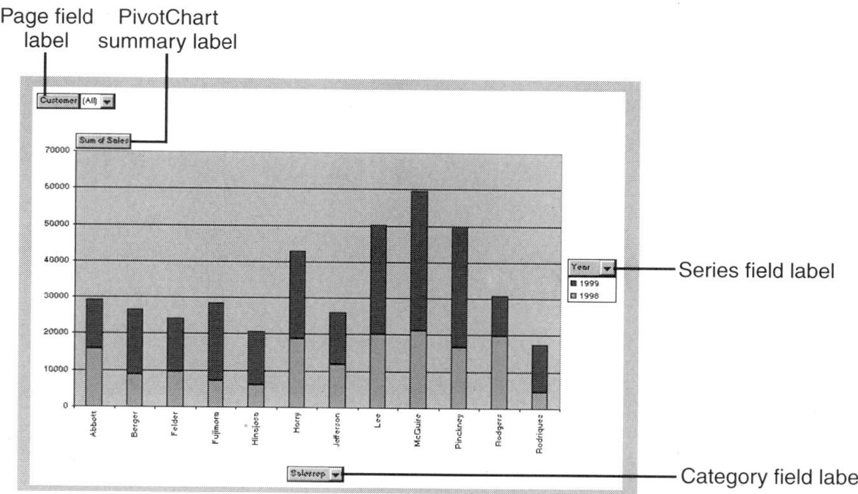

Manipulating PivotCharts

Notice that Customer is the Page field in Figure 25.38. To display the data for a particular customer, click the drop-down arrow next to the Page field and choose the customer name from the list and click OK. Figure 25.39 shows the chart filtered to display only the data for Johnson's Drug Store. Because the PivotChart and PivotTable are linked, if you display the PivotTable, it will also reflect only the data for Johnson's Drug Store.

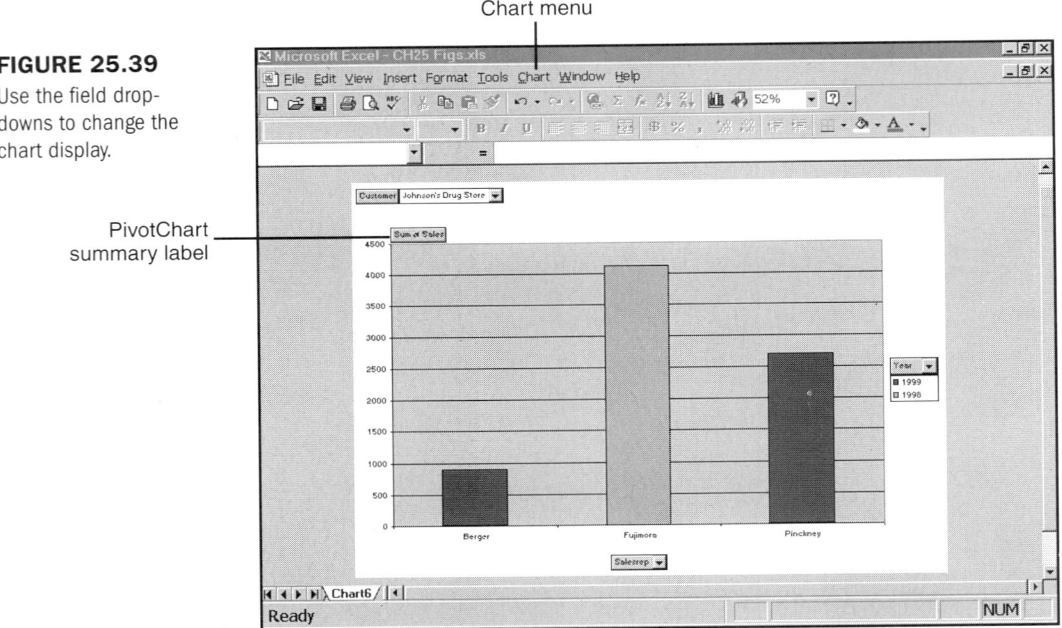

FIGURE 25.39
Use the field drop-downs to change the chart display.

To change the type of calculation performed on the PivotChart, double-click the PivotChart summary label. The PivotTable Field dialog box appears so that you can select a different calculation.

Formatting a PivotChart is similar to formatting any other Excel chart. Click an area of the chart and use the Format or Chart menus on the Menu Bar. Although you can right-click areas of the chart and choose an option from the shortcut menu, some options that normally appear on the shortcut menu are not listed when the chart is a PivotChart. So, it's best to use the Chart menu commands to format a PivotChart.

NOTE You cannot move most of the elements in a PivotChart, including the title, plot area, or axis labels. You can move the legend by using the Legend tab of the Chart Properties dialog box, but you can't manually drag the legend as you can in standard Excel graphic charts.

CHAPTER 26

Advanced Charting Techniques

In this chapter

Which Chart Type Do I Use?

Choosing the best chart type is critical to illustrating your worksheet data. The people reading the chart need to be able to rapidly decipher what the chart represents. The column chart, by far, is the easiest chart for people to read (which is why it is the default chart type). However, depending on what you are plotting, another chart type might be more appropriate. Excel has eleven basic chart types, and variations, or subtypes, are available for each one. Some have two-dimensional and three-dimensional variations; for bar or column charts, you can use the distinctive cone, cylinder, and pyramid variations. Other common variations include stacked charts, exploded charts, and 100% charts. Additionally, you can mix chart types to create what are called *combination charts*.

▶ **See** "Mixing Chart Types," **p. 826**

Category Axes Versus Value Axes

Most charts have two axes, the *category axis* and the *value axis*. It is important that you understand the difference between the chart axes. The value axis is easily identifiable—it always displays numerical data, such as currency amounts, quantity, percents, temperature, and so on. Frequently, the category axis displays text labels, such as months or years, regions or cities, sales representatives or factories. The category axis is called the x-axis and is often, although not always, the horizontal axis. For example, in a bar chart, the category axis is the vertical axis.

To confuse the matter even further, some 3D chart types add a third axis called the *series axis*. Where this axis is placed depends more on the angle you are viewing the chart than on the chart type (although the type is a factor).

Because of this confusion, Microsoft refers to the axes as category, value, and series in both the Chart Wizard and on the Help screens, rather than as the x-, y-, and z-axes. This is also how they are referred to in this book.

Area Charts

These charts are often used to plot the continuous change in volume over time, especially with multiple data series. The best variations to use are the two-dimensional stacked or the 100%; they show how each data series contributes to the total volume. Area charts are good for sales and production volume—units produced, ordered, shipped, or sold. Area charts plot a continuous line, connecting data point to data point, and are similar in that way to a line chart (see Figure 26.1). Unlike the line chart, however, they do not display data markers to show the precise data points. They are best to use when you want to display the data values in a general way.

Column Charts

Column charts are the default chart type because they are very easy to read and are a good starting point if you're not sure which chart type to use. These charts are used for side-by-side comparison of items that have distinct (noncontinuous) measurements made at regular intervals. If the number of items or intervals is relatively small—ranging from one to eight—column charts are a good initial choice.

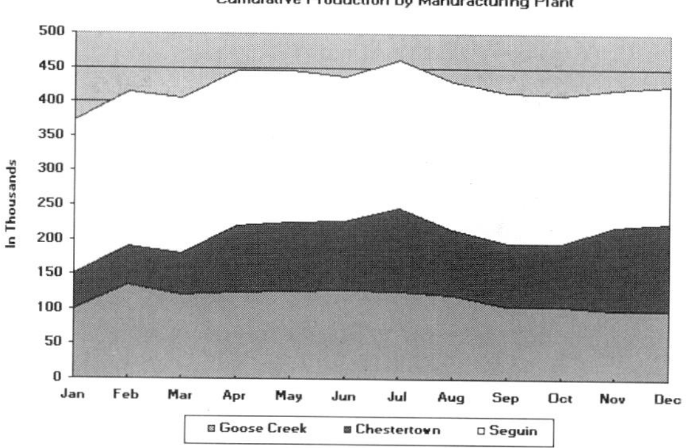

FIGURE 26.1
A two-dimensional area chart.

When a lot of category labels are in a column chart, Excel automatically displays the labels at an angle or skips every other category label. If you must have a column chart, you can reduce the font size of the category axis labels or abbreviate the labels in the worksheet. Otherwise, try using a bar chart instead.

Bar Charts

Bar charts (like column charts) are used for side-by-side comparison of items that have distinct (noncontinuous) measurements made at regular intervals. This chart type focuses more on the value axis (which is displayed horizontally) and less on the category axis. It is a good choice when you want to show positive or negative variation from a center point (as shown in Figure 26.2), to show cumulative totals (using the stacked variation), or when the category labels are very long and appear cluttered in a column chart.

Take advantage of the formatting options. In Figure 26.2, the labels on the category axis were placed to the left of the chart by selecting the Low option for Tick Mark Labels in the Format Axis dialog box (Pattern tab). By default, the categories are plotted from the bottom of the chart upward; if your worksheet data is in alphabetical order, then when the data is charted, it appears in reverse alpha order. You can change this either by selecting Categories in Reverse Order (Scale tab of the Format Axis dialog box), which also places the value axis at the top of the chart, or you can reorder the data in your worksheet. When you add data labels to your charts, they appear at the top end of the bar. You can change the placement of the labels by selecting an option from the Data Labels tab of the Format Data Series dialog box.

When you have a large number of items to plot, try a column or bar chart first. If the number of columns or bars makes the chart look overly cluttered, switch to a line chart. A line chart is a good choice when you are plotting more than six to eight categories or series.

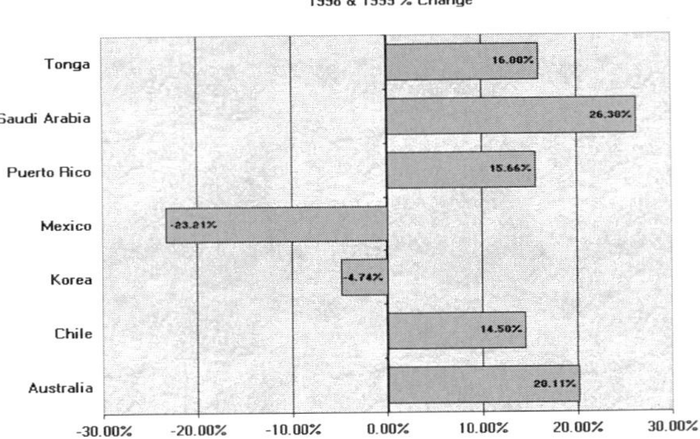

FIGURE 26.2
A two-dimensional bar chart.

Line Charts

Line charts show trends over regular intervals and are a good choice when a lot of data points exist. Use line charts when the category time intervals are evenly spaced or when the categories are text (and spacing is irrelevant). Use line charts to show trends in business or financial data, such as production, sales, costs, or the stock market over time.

If the time intervals in your categories are uneven intervals, use an XY (Scatter) chart instead.

▶ **See** "Using Trendlines in Charts," **p. 833**

XY (Scatter) Charts

XY or scatter charts are used to compare trends over uneven time intervals or other measurable increments. Use XY charts to plot survey responses or sampling data that was randomly gathered to display patterns or clusters of data points. Scientific, engineering, and marketing data is often charted with XY scatter charts. An XY chart can also plot two groups of numbers as one series of XY coordinates—that is, when both the categories and data series are numerical values. When you arrange your data, place x values in one row or column and then enter corresponding y values in the adjacent rows or columns. XY (scatter) charts cannot be used for PivotChart reports.

▶ **See** "Unlocking the Power of PivotTables and PivotCharts," **p. 797**

If you are plotting two groups of numbers, Figures 26.3 and 26.4 illustrate the difference when data is plotted with a Line chart and an XY chart. The line chart plots the category axis values at regular intervals. The XY (scatter) chart plots the category values at intervals that show groupings or concentrations.

NOTE The exception–the line and XY (scatter) charts plot identically when the category axis values are dates. The line chart shows concentrations just as the XY (scatter) chart does. This occurs because Excel recognizes time values and creates a special scale for time on the category axis.

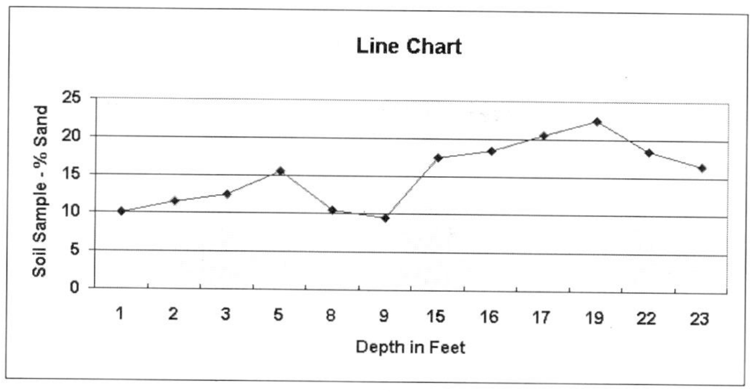

FIGURE 26.3
The line chart does not give an accurate plot with intermittent category (x) values.

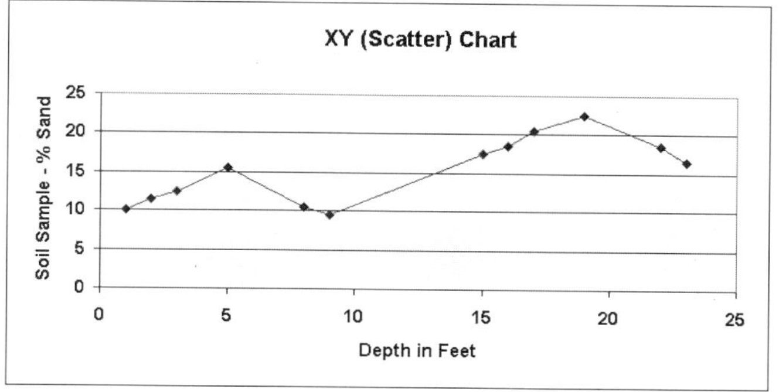

FIGURE 26.4
The XY (scatter) chart was expressly designed to plot intermittent values on the category axis.

Stock (High, Low, Close) Charts

Stock charts are typically used to plot stock market data. This chart can also be used for scientific data; for example, to indicate temperature changes. To use this type of chart, the data must be organized in the correct order in the worksheet, starting with the date, followed by the high, low, and close. Several variations measure volume; they have two value axes (one for the volume and the other for stock prices, as shown in Figure 26.5). Stock charts cannot be used for PivotChart reports.

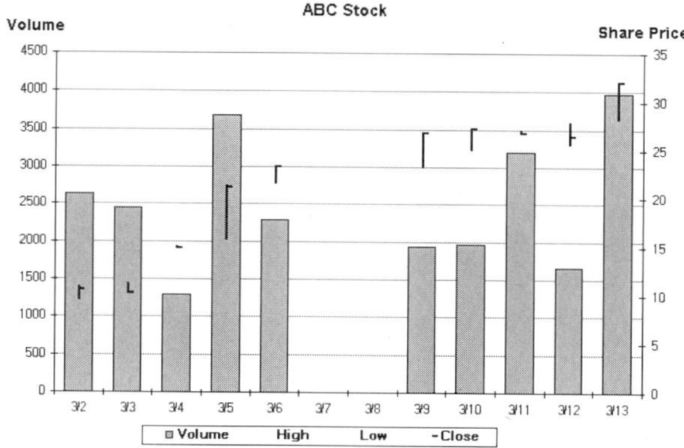

FIGURE 26.5
The Volume-High-Low-Close variation of the stock chart.

The data series markers and high-low lines are easier to see if you increase their size/weight through the Format dialog box.

Pie Charts

Pie charts are used to compare the ratio (percentage) of each wedge or piece to the whole pie. A single data series is plotted, and each data point becomes a pie piece. If you select multiple data series, only the first data series is plotted as the pie. Pie charts typically display percentages instead of exact values and work well to show the percentage mix of items, such as products shipped, marketing expenditure, tax dollars, and target populations. It becomes difficult to make accurate comparisons when more than six or eight pieces are in a pie. When you have a lot of pieces in a pie, you can either use the Pie-of-Pie or Bar-of-Pie variations or change to a column chart. See the section "Creating Effective Pie Charts" later in this chapter for examples of these pie chart variations.

Doughnut Charts

Doughnut charts are used like pie charts to compare the ratio (percentage) of each segment or piece to the whole doughnut ring (see Figure 26.6). The difference between a doughnut chart and a pie chart is that doughnut charts can show more than one data series; each series becomes a ring. Read each ring separately, comparing segment portions. It is a little more difficult to compare the same segment item between rings; therefore, doughnut charts are best displayed with only a few data series (two or three).

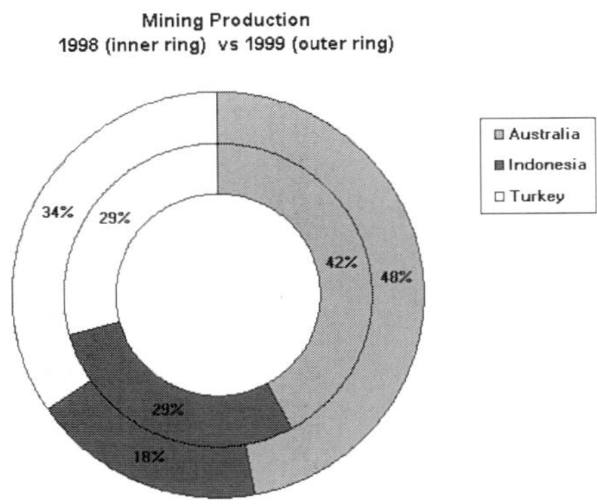

FIGURE 26.6
Doughnut charts are a great alternative to multiple pie charts.

If you need to make precise distinctions between percentages or values, use a chart that has a value axis (such as a column chart) instead of a pie or doughnut chart. A value axis can display percentages or values.

Radar Charts

Radar charts can be used to compare specific values in a data category and to compare one entire data series with another entire data series. Each category has its own axis radiating from the center point, like a spoke on a wheel. Data points for a category are plotted along the spoke. Lines connecting the data points form the data series and define the area covered by the items. Radar charts can be difficult to understand; be sure your audience is accustomed to radar charts (or be sure you have the time to explain the chart thoroughly).

The chart in Figure 26.7 plots the percentage of defects in the same product manufactured on three separate assembly lines. You can use this radar chart to compare the rate of defects for each component. If every assembly line has a high rate of defects in the same component, the culprit might be the assembly process. You can also use this chart to see how each assembly line performed overall. The smaller the area plotted, the better the line's performance. Line C has the smallest plot area overall. The other assembly lines can be challenged to match that record, and Line A should be encouraged to improve its record.

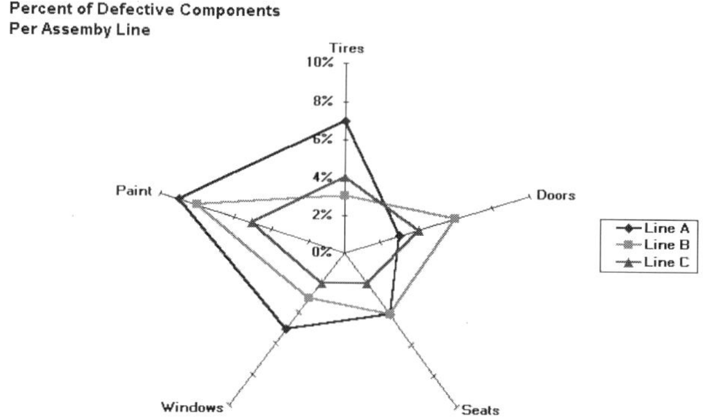

FIGURE 26.7
The lines connecting the series data points are easier to see if you increase their weight (Format dialog box).

Surface Charts

Surface charts are like topographical maps. They show high and low points along a surface and are an excellent way of visually locating high and low points resulting from two changing variables. These charts are often used to plot scientific data. Several variations exist for surface charts, including contour, which displays a side view of the surface.

Suppose a paint manufacturer uses two drying agents in a brand of paint. The drying time is dependent on the amount of each of the drying agents. The Research and Development department for the paint company needs to determine the optimal mix for its "quick-dry" paint. Its goal is to look for the lowest amount of drying agents that yield the fastest drying time. In Figure 26.8, the amount of drying item is plotted for each 1% increase in the drying agents.

Bubble Charts

Bubble charts are a type of XY (scatter) chart that displays bubble markers for each data point. They are used to compare sets of at least three values. Each data point has at least two values, and the size of the bubble represents the value of the third. The size of the data marker indicates the value of a third variable. To arrange your data, place the x values in one row or column and enter corresponding y values and bubble sizes in the adjacent rows or columns. Use bubble charts to plot product information, such as the number of products, sales, and market share percentage. Bubble charts cannot be used for PivotChart reports.

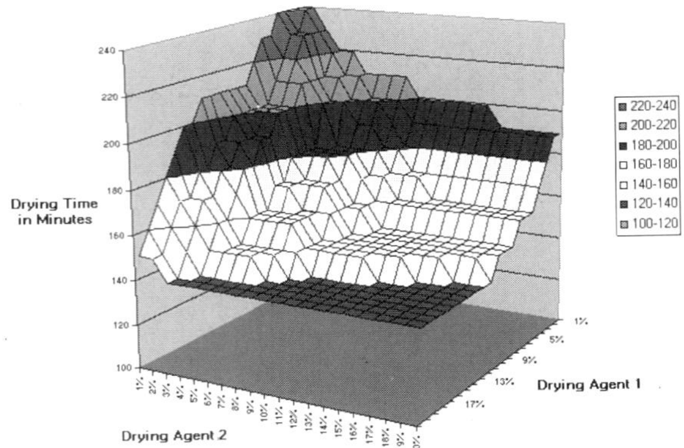

FIGURE 26.8
To adjust the perspective from which you view the chart, choose Chart, 3D View, and rotate the chart.

In a sense, a bubble chart has three value axes. It is like an XY (scatter) chart because both the horizontal and vertical axes are value axes. In addition, the size of the chart's bubbles, the third axis, can represent some third, continuous variable.

Suppose that you wanted to chart some summary information on the sales of your company's products. Specifically, you're interested in the relationship between the total sales, the quantity sold, and the number of unique products (the product mix) that each sales representative markets. Unlike most charts, instead of having two variables, you have three. To plot this on a chart, you can use the size of the bubbles as a visual indicator of the product mix.

For this type of chart, it is easiest if you organize your data with

- The category (horizontal x-axis) data in the first column.
- The value (vertical y-axis) data in the second column.
- The data for the bubble sizes in the third column.

Figure 26.9 shows an example of a bubble chart.

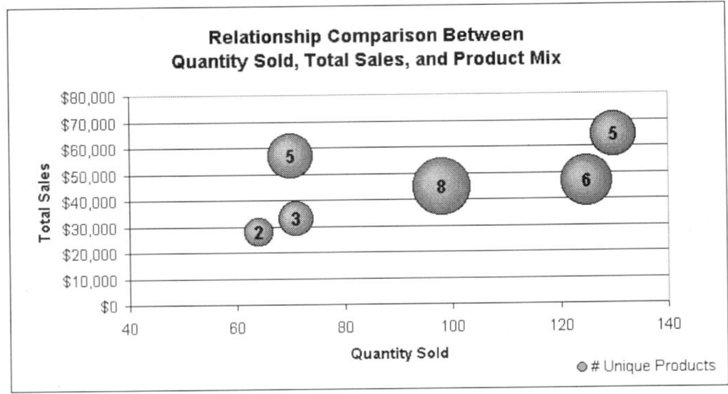

FIGURE 26.9
The larger the bubble, the greater the product mix.

To create a bubble chart, it's best if you select only the data (no labels) and use the second step of the wizard to identify whether the data series is in the rows or columns and which cell contains the name of the data series. You can also use this step to adjust the role of each set of data. You may also want to use the third step of the wizard to place titles and data labels in the chart.

▶ **See** "Working with Chart Data Series," **p. 829**

Creating Your Own Custom Charts

Although Excel contains a number of interesting chart types with their subtypes or variations, at times you need something a little more, a little different. One place to start is the Custom Types tab in the Chart Wizard dialog box shown in Figure 26.10. It contains 20 built-in custom chart types.

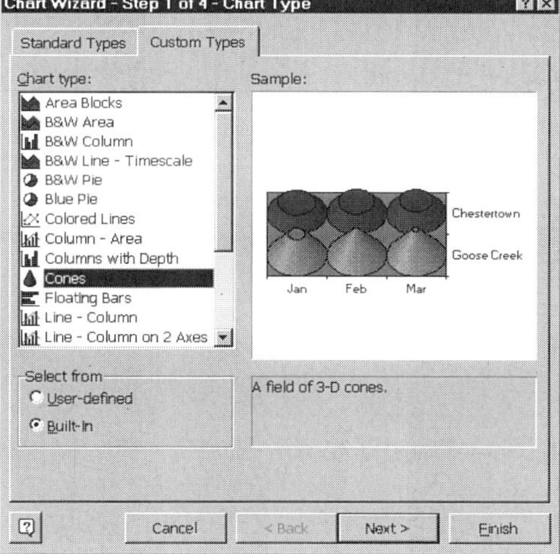

FIGURE 26.10
The Custom Types tab is on step 1 of the Chart Wizard.

Some of these are merely standard charts to which some interesting formatting has been added, or they have been modified by the selection of certain chart options. Others are quite distinctive, including the mixed chart types and the logarithmic chart type. If none of these are appealing, you can create and save your own custom chart types.

3D charts and flashy series fill options are eye-catching. However, the most important question to ask yourself when creating charts is—Does the chart clearly communicate the data? Creating an elaborate graph is pointless if your audience is distracted instead of enlightened by it.

If you find that you use the same chart type over and over, you can either set that chart type as the default chart type (replacing the column chart as the default) or you can establish a user-defined custom chart type.

Setting a Default Chart Type

If you typically use a specific chart type when you graph worksheet data, or if you spend a lot of time changing the settings on the default column, you will save a lot of time if you make that chart type (or those settings) the default. You can use one of the charts you have already created as the basis for the new default chart type. This is especially useful if you have specific chart options or formatting that you usually want to appear on the chart.

To change the default chart type, follow these steps:

1. Display the chart that you want to use as a sample for the default chart type. If the chart is an embedded chart, click the chart to select it. If the chart is on a chart sheet, make it the active sheet.
2. Right-click in a blank area of the chart, away from the chart objects. From the shortcut menu, choose Chart Type. In the Chart Type dialog box select the Custom Types tab (see Figure 26.11).
3. Click the Set As Default Chart button. A message appears confirming that you want to change the default chart type. Choose Yes. The Add Custom Chart Type dialog box may appear. If it does, enter a name and description for your new default chart. Choose OK to accept the name and description.
4. Choose OK to complete the default chart type change.

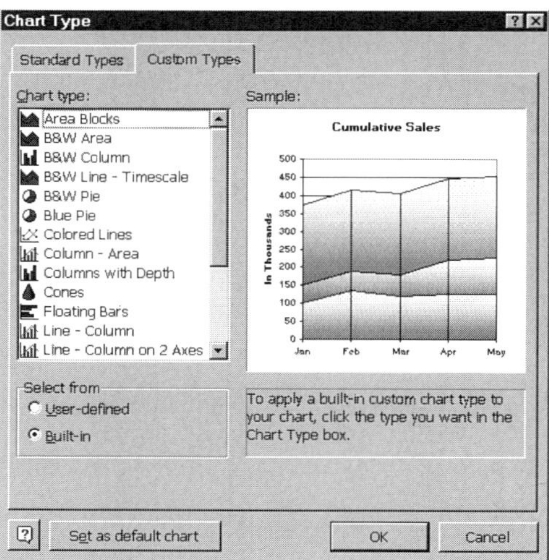

FIGURE 26.11
Use the Chart Type dialog box to change the default chart type.

The Custom Types tab lists the built-in custom chart types. If you select the User-Defined button, the list changes to display the default chart type and any custom chart types you have added. Displaying the User-Defined list is not a requirement for changing the default chart type, but you can use it to verify the change.

Designing Your Own Custom Charts

Suppose that you have agonized over a chart (customizing the data series, the axis scale, the data labels), and you know your boss is going to want you to use the same settings for other charts you routinely create. You can try to re-create the chart based on a hard-copy printout (not smart), or you can save the chart and settings as a user-defined custom chart type (smart) and just tell your boss how time-consuming it is to create those charts (very smart).

To create a custom chart type based on an existing chart, follow these steps:

1. Display the chart that you want to use as a custom chart type. If the chart is embedded in a worksheet, select the chart. If the chart is on a chart sheet, make it the active sheet.
2. Choose Chart, Chart Type from the menu. In the Chart Type dialog box, select the Custom Types tab.
3. Click the User-Defined option button; then click the Add button.
4. The Add Custom Chart Type dialog box appears. Enter a name and description for the new custom chart (see Figure 26.12). Then choose OK.

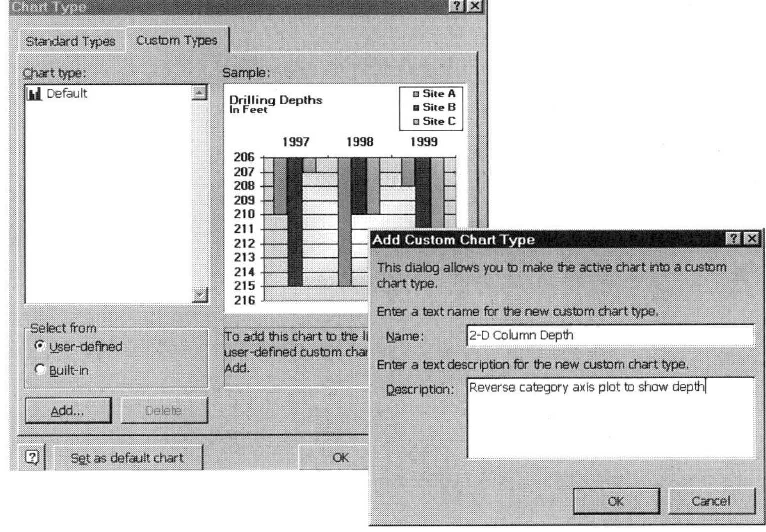

FIGURE 26.12
Type a name and a description that clearly defines the custom chart.

5. The new chart is added to the User-Defined chart list and the description appears in the lower-right corner when that chart type is selected.
6. Close the dialog box.

Sharing Custom Chart Types with Others After you've created a custom chart type, you can share it with other people so that it can be used as a template. All user-defined custom chart types are stored in the `xlusrgal.xls` file, which is located in the Windows folder in Office 2000:

```
C:\Windows\Application Data\Microsoft\Excel\xlusrgal.xls
```

Part IV
Ch 26

Before you share these custom chart types, you should be aware of the following:

- You are, in fact, replacing the `xlusrgal.xls` file on someone else's machine with the one from your machine. Any custom chart types they had will be lost. If they have not created custom chart types, then this does not present a problem. However, if they want to preserve any custom charts they have created, it would be better to create a sample workbook containing the custom charts you want to give them. Using the steps outlined in the previous section, they can add your custom charts to their existing files. When working with less-experienced Excel users, consider creating a macro that performs these steps and adding a macro button to the sample workbook.
- Use Windows Explorer to copy the `xlusrgal.xls` file to the appropriate folder (listed previously). Because you are replacing the existing file, a dialog box appears, confirming the replacement.
- Although Excel can be open when you copy the `xlusrgal.xls` file to your machine, it's better to close it. If Excel is open and you have created a chart during the active session, you won't be able to copy the `xlusrgal.xls` file. When you create a chart, the `xlusrgal.xls` file is automatically opened, and you can't copy over an open file. Even if you close the Excel workbook that contains the chart, the `xlusrgal.xls` file remains open until you terminate the active Excel session.

NOTE You can also share the `xlusrgal.xls` with users who still have Excel 97. However, it is located in a different folder:

`C:\Program Files\Microsoft Office\Office\`

Mixing Chart Types

Although they are not part of the 11 basic chart types, combination charts are a powerful charting alternative—when used properly. *Combination charts* are created by placing one chart type over another chart type and are used to compare different types of data, or data that needs different axis scales. Combination charts are used to look for possible interactions between the types of data. These charts can be used to display how close the actual results are to a goal or a projection. You might use a column chart to plot sales data and overlay a line chart to plot profit.

Combination charts are also frequently used to prove/disprove a correlation between two disparate items. For example, do people buy more of your product during the warmer months? If a relationship exists between sales and the weather, should you increase your production in the warmer months? A combination chart can illustrate whether a correlation exists between these two kinds of information.

▶ **See** "Creating Effective Multiple-Combination Charts," **p. 472**, in *Special Edition Using Microsoft Excel 2000* (Chapter 16).

Using the Built-In Combination Charts

The Custom tab in the Chart Wizard dialog box has four custom combination chart types available for you to choose from, or you can create your own combination chart. Follow these steps to create a combination chart using one of the built-in custom chart types:

1. Select the cells containing the data to be charted.
2. Click the Chart Wizard button on the Standard toolbar.
3. In step 1 of the Chart Wizard, select the Custom Types tab.
4. Choose one of the four custom combination charts: Column – Area; Line – Column; Line – Column on 2 Axes; or Lines on 2 Axes. See Figure 26.13.

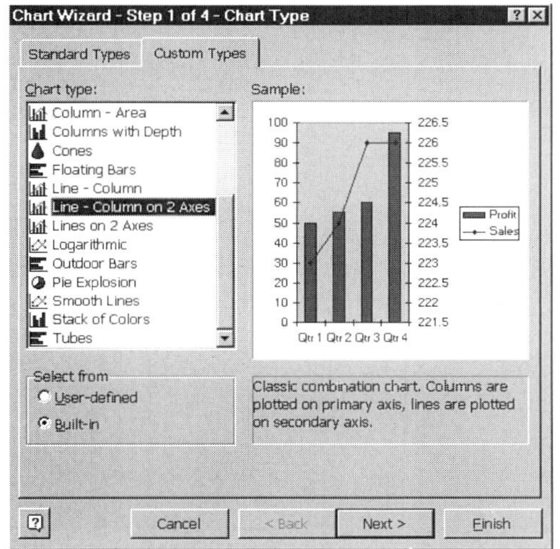

FIGURE 26.13
The most common combination chart is Line - Column on 2 Axes chart type.

5. Proceed through the remaining steps of the Chart Wizard.

Figure 26.14 shows a simple combination chart. A line represents the goal for the number of telemarketing calls to make each day and a column displays the *actual* number of calls that were made. It is easy to see whether you exceeded, met, or fell short of your goals by using this chart.

A combination chart depicting the number of car loans approved each month and the average monthly interest rate is shown in Figure 26.15. Because loans and interest rates are different types of data, two value axes are used.

When you're creating combination charts, keep the following items in mind:

- It is important that you label each value axis to make the chart easier to read (refer to Figure 26.15). You can use the Chart Options command to add titles or create text boxes to label the axis.
- 3D chart types cannot be used in combination charts.

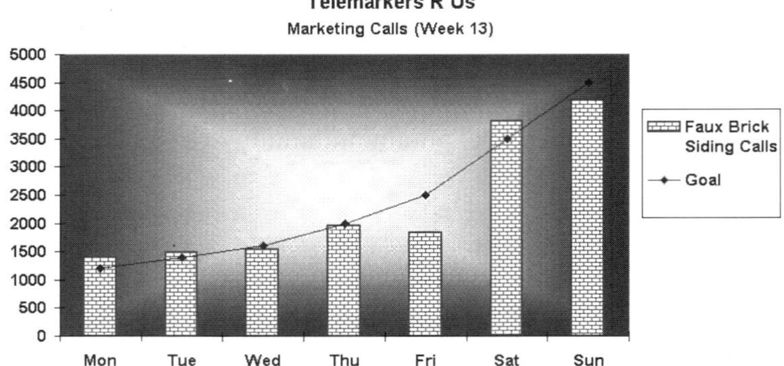

FIGURE 26.14
A Line - Column combination chart, using one axis.

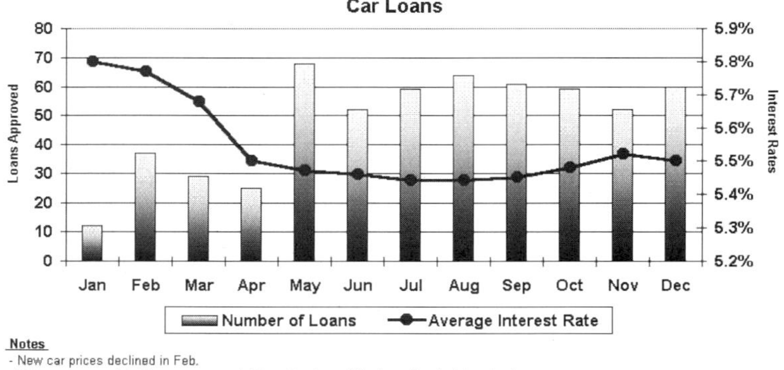

FIGURE 26.15
A Line - Column combination chart using two axes.

Understanding Data Series in Combination Charts

When you use one of the built-in combination chart types, Excel automatically determines which of the data series becomes the first type of chart and which becomes the second type of chart. An even number of data series is handled differently than an odd number of data series.

If an even number of data series exists, the first half of the data series becomes one chart type, and the remaining half becomes the other chart type. If an odd number of data series exists, the first half of the data series plus one more of the data series becomes one chart type, and the remaining data series becomes the other chart type. So if you have five data series and you create a Line – Column chart, the first three series become columns and the remaining two series become lines.

Manually Creating Your Own Combination Charts

To overlay one type of chart on top of another type, you can manually designate the data series for each chart type. If all the data series already appear on an existing chart, it is just a matter of changing one or more of the series to the desired chart type.

Changing the chart type used by one of the data series is easy:

1. Right-click the series you want to change and then select Chart Type from the shortcut menu.
2. Pick the type of chart you want to apply to the selected series from the Chart Type dialog box and then choose OK.

If you need to add a data series to use as part of a combination chart, first add the data and then designate the chart type for the newly added series. Select the chart and choose Chart, Add Data from the menu. Highlight the data you want to add and click OK. After the new data series is added, use the steps outlined previously to change the chart type of the new series.

Adding a Second Value Axis to Your Chart If you create your own combination chart, you might want to add another value axis so that you can see the distinct values of the data plotted by each chart type. Refer to the line-column chart in Figure 26.15 for an example of a chart with two value axes. The following are the steps to add a second value axis to a chart:

1. Select the data series you want to appear on the second value axis.
2. Right-click the series and choose Format Data Series from the shortcut menu.
3. From the Axis tab, choose Secondary Axis.

Working with Chart Data Series

Let's clear up one common misconception about how charts are plotted—data in worksheet columns is *not* always plotted as the chart categories, and data in worksheet rows is *not* always plotted as the chart series. Many people (including authors of other books on Excel) have stated, or perpetuated, this notion. In fact, the *number* of rows and columns of data you select dictates how Excel plots the data:

- If the number of columns is greater than or equal to the number of rows, then Excel plots the data in the rows. The column headings are used along the category axis and the row headings become the legend labels designating the data series.
- If the number of rows is greater than the number of columns, then Excel plots the data in the columns. The row headings are used along the category axis and the column headings become the legend labels designating the data series.

Modifying the Data Series Used in a Chart

You can use several methods to add or remove data in an existing chart. If the chart is embedded in a worksheet, you can use your mouse to drag and drop data from your worksheet into the embedded chart. This method is convenient only if the chart and data are both visible.

If you have to scroll or zoom out to see the data and the chart, it is probably easier to use the Add Data command. As with the drag-and-drop method, the Add Data command is convenient when you simply want to include another row or column of worksheet data in the chart.

The Source Data command should be used when you need to add and remove data at the same time or when you want to use a completely different set of data for the chart. The Source Data command is the best way to remove data from a chart.

NOTE If the data you want to add is in another workbook, that workbook must be open to add the data.

Using the Add Data Command

Use the Add Data command when you want to add small amounts of data to your chart, such as one or two new data series. If you are adding data to an embedded chart, select the chart. If you are adding data to a chart sheet, make it the active sheet. In Figure 26.16, the 1999 data is going to be added to the chart.

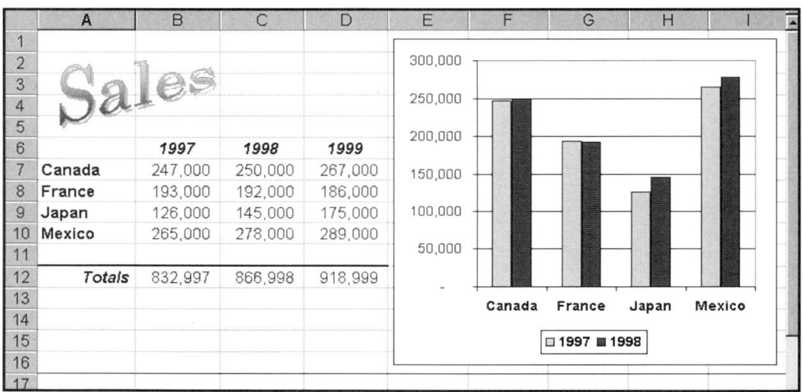

	1997	1998	1999
Canada	247,000	250,000	267,000
France	193,000	192,000	186,000
Japan	126,000	145,000	175,000
Mexico	265,000	278,000	289,000
Totals	832,997	866,998	918,999

FIGURE 26.16
The embedded Sales chart reflects the figures only for 1997 and 1998, but the 1999 figures need to be added.

Then choose Chart, Add Data. The Add Data dialog box appears (see Figure 26.17). The Range entry box is active. Select the data in the worksheet that you want to add to your chart, being sure to include the corresponding labels. If the data is on another worksheet, activate the worksheet and then select the data.

If you don't see the Add Data command on the Chart menu, double-click the Chart menu to see the complete list of commands.

After you have selected the additional data, confirm the cell references in the Range entry box. If you used the Collapse/Expand button to shrink the dialog box, click the button again to expand the dialog box, and then choose OK. Your chart should update immediately.

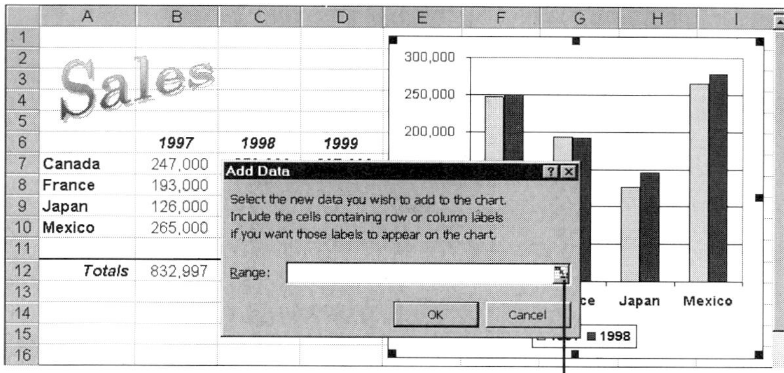

FIGURE 26.17
The Collapse/Expand dialog box button helps to shrink the dialog box so that you can see more of your worksheet.

Using the Source Data Command

Use the Source Data command to add or remove groups of data from your chart or to select an entirely different set of data to plot. If you are adding data to an embedded chart, select the chart. If you are adding data to a chart sheet, make it the active sheet. Then right-click in a blank area of the chart, away from the chart objects. From the shortcut menu, choose Source Data. The Source Data dialog box appears (see Figure 26.18).

Two methods are available for adding or removing data using the Source Data dialog box. You can select an entirely new set of data to plot (such as data on another worksheet) by using the Data Range tab. By using the Series tab, you can select individual series to add to or remove from your chart.

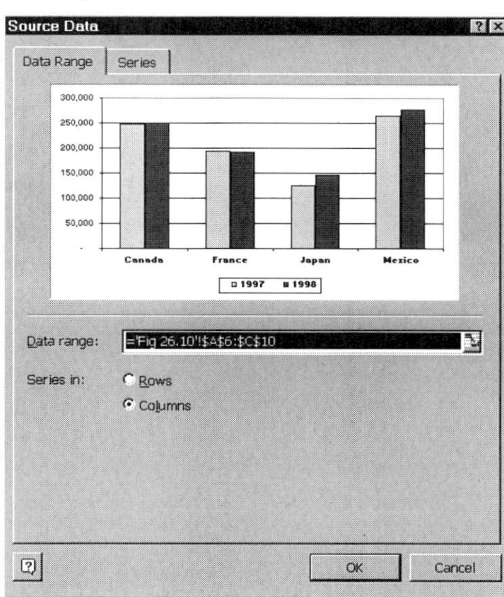

FIGURE 26.18
Use the Data Range tab to select an entirely new set of data.

To select an entirely new set of data, click in the Data Range entry box on the Data Range tab. Then select the cells in your worksheet containing the new data to be plotted, including the corresponding labels. The worksheet name and cell references appear in the Data Range entry box. Above the Data Range entry box, the sample chart revises to reflect the new data you selected. Choose OK to confirm your change.

You can use the Series tab in the Source Date dialog box to add or remove individual series of data from your chart. In the Series tab, click the Add button at the bottom of the dialog box. In the Series text box, a placeholder for the new series titled Series# is listed. In Figure 26.19, Series3 is the placeholder. Use the Name and Value boxes (which appear to the right of the Series box) to identify the label and data for the new series. Click in the Name box and choose the cell in your worksheet that contains the label you want to use for this series. The label replaces the placeholder in the Series text box.

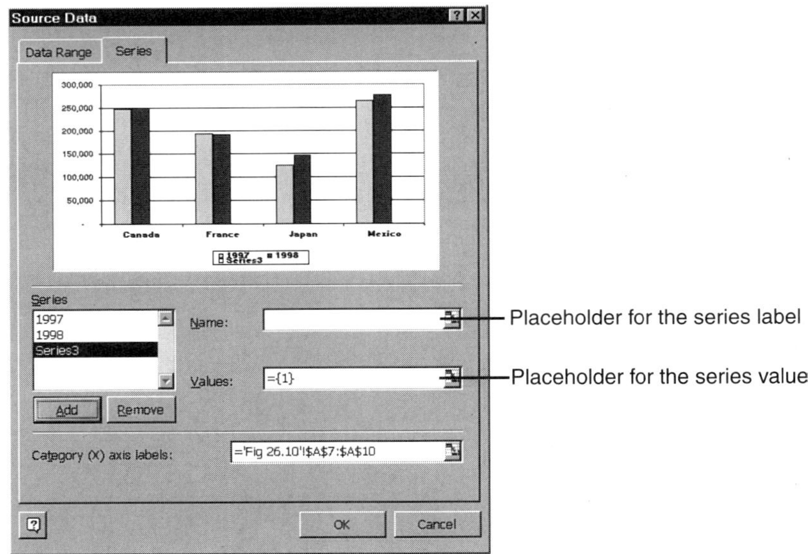

FIGURE 26.19
The Series tab in the Source Data dialog box controls the data plotted in your chart.

Activate the Values box and select any data that appears there. Choose the cells in your worksheet that correspond to the data you want plotted for this series.

> **CAUTION**
>
> If you use the mouse to click in the Values box, you need to select the entry in the box. By default, Excel uses a placeholder, typically ={1}, for the series data. If you do not select the placeholder, Excel attempts to plot this entry along with the data you select in your worksheet. An error results. However, if you use the Tab key to activate the Values box, it automatically selects the entry in the box.

The sample chart at the top of the dialog box shows the revised chart. Choose OK to confirm your change.

Removing Data Series from a Chart

To remove a series from a chart, activate the Source Data dialog box. From the Series tab, click the series name in the Series box that you want to remove. Then select the Remove button (refer to Figure 26.19).

Using Trendlines in Charts

Trendlines are used to show trends within your series data. Trendlines can be created only for specific 2D charts: area, bar, column, line, stock, XY (scatter), and bubble. You cannot use the stacked variation of these chart types with trendlines. If you decide to change the chart type for a chart that contains a trendline, use one of the chart types listed earlier. Otherwise, you will lose the trendline. You often see trendlines used with XY (scatter) or line charts.

The trendlines generated by Excel use a statistical model called *regression analysis*. This type of analysis is typically used to show the relationship between two variables. For example, suppose you want to know the relationship between revenue and advertising expenditures. What factors or *variables* does a business consider when deciding how much money should be spent on advertising every week or every month? Certainly the company's revenue is one factor. However, many other variables also affect advertising expenditures. For instance, some of the variables that influence your advertisement expenditure decisions might include

- How your competitors advertise their products
- The time of year the ads will run
- The medium used to advertise (periodicals, radio, TV)
- The markets in which you choose to advertise
- The frequency of the advertisements
- The number of products you choose to advertise

These variables are called *independent variables* because they all vary independently, and they explain why different amounts of money are spent on advertising, rather than a steady amount. The advertising expenditure is called the *dependent variable* because it depends on the independent variables. Only one dependent variable is used. Studying the effect of two or more independent variables on a dependent variable using regression analysis is called *multiple regression*. However, if you choose only one (usually the most important) independent variable and study the effect of that single variable on a dependent variable, it is called a *simple regression*.

The trendlines are based on mathematical equations. A simple straight line, called a *linear trendline*, uses the equation y = mx + b (the multiplication of *m* times *x* is implied in this mathematical equation).

> Y is the dependent variable and is plotted on the value (y) axis. In the example described previously, *y* is the advertising expenditure.
>
> X is the independent variable and is plotted on the category (x) axis. In the example described previously, *x* is the revenue.

M is the slope of the line (sometimes called the coefficient of x). The *slope* is the amount of change in *y* due to a one-unit change in *x*. In the example, the change is in advertising expenditures with a unit increase in revenue.

B is the y-intercept of the line (sometimes called the constant term). The *y-intercept* is the value of *y* when *x* is zero, the point where the trendline crosses the y-axis.

To draw a straight line, you need two points. In an XY (scatter) chart, a large number of straight lines can be drawn, given any two points. Each line gives a different value for the slope and the y-intercept. In regression analysis, the idea is to find a line that best fits the points in the XY (scatter) chart—a line that provides the best possible description of the relationship between the dependent and independent variables. This is known as the *best fit* or *least squares method* because it minimizes the difference between the points plotted on the trendline and the points plotted that are the actual values.

In Excel, you can also forecast trends outside the existing series data. These forecasts are predictions of what a series will do in the future or what it may have done in the past. The trendlines are extended beyond the actual data to predict future (or past) values. For example, if you don't have data from the previous period but want to plot a general trend of what probably happened in the past to reach the point where you are now, you would plot a trendline that forecasts backward. Trendlines can also predict values where data is missing from the data series. So if you have gap for which no data is available, the trendline can predict what the data might have been.

CAUTION

Be careful in using trendlines to forecast or predict values. As mentioned earlier, you are factoring in only one independent variable, and many other items can influence the dependent variable. Any time you extrapolate a data point outside the bounds of your known data, you need to be sure you have some concrete evidence that the extrapolation is valid. Although Excel plots a value in the future based on the existing data, it doesn't mean the prediction is valid. You should be able to offer arguments as to why it is a valid prediction.

If you do use trendlines to predict future values, be sure that you clearly identify these as predictions in the chart so that you do not mislead anyone who sees the chart. Use trends only to forecast into the near future. Take the stock market, for example. Although it is useful to plot the past performance to see a general trend, the market is influenced by many unpredictable factors. You certainly wouldn't want to forecast what it will do far into the future.

Excel can plot six trendlines: linear, polynomial, exponential, power, logarithmic, and moving average. Each of the trendlines is determined by a mathematical equation. If you use a trendline, you need to at least be able to explain in some terms why this equation fits your data and what each of the variables represents. For example, a logarithmic trendline is a curved line that increases or decreases quickly and then levels out. This type of line might be explained by an initial product launch, followed by growth in sales, then a leveling-off period as the market and channels become saturated. In this logarithmic trendline example, you should be able to relate the logarithmic equation to the size of the population for your product, the number of stores, sales reps, and channels selling your product, and so on. If you can't make any logical connection between the equation you fit to the data or the variables and constants in the data, it might be a good idea not to use the trendline until you can explain it.

CAUTION

Be sure that you understand the theory behind the trendlines before you use trendlines to analyze the data in your charts. It is very easy to apply a trendline to data that doesn't necessarily have any statistical validity.

For example, you often see charts where some unit of time (months, quarters, years) is used as the independent variable plotted on the x-axis to plot quantities sold over time, expenditures over time, or the number of employees over time. Although it certainly is useful to see general trends over time, units of time may not be the most significant independent variable influencing the dependent variable. Other factors, such as availability of raw materials, business expansion, and even weather, may have had a greater impact on the dependent variable rather than time.

Understanding Trendline Alternatives

Six types of trendlines can be displayed on Excel charts: linear, logarithmic, polynomial, exponential, power, and moving average. The type of data you have determines the type of trendline you should use.

NOTE One indication of how closely your actual data and the predicted data (points on the trendline) match is through the R-squared (R^2) value. R is the measure of strength between two variables (the *correlation coefficient*). However, although two variables may appear to have a strong relationship, that doesn't mean they actually do. When you square R, the possible errors are factored in. The higher the value of R^2, a greater portion of the total errors is explained by the included independent variable, and a smaller portion of errors is attributed to other variables and randomness. The R^2 value always lies between 0 and +1, and a trendline is most reliable when its R^2 value is at or close to 1. When you apply a trendline to your chart, Excel calculates the R^2 value, which you can display on your chart. For logarithmic, power, and exponential trendlines, Microsoft Excel uses a transformed regression model.

See "Understanding R^2 and Best Fit," **p. 711**

Part IV Ch 26

Linear Trendlines Use a linear trendline when the data is generally increasing or decreasing at a steady rate. A straight line is plotted with this type of trendline. Linear trendlines use the following equation:

$$y = mx + b$$

where m is the slope and b is the y-intercept. This equation is sometimes shown as y = a + bx, where a is the y-intercept and b is the slope.

When you're not sure which trendline to use, start with a linear trendline. This type of trendline is often used with data you are plotting over time, where units of time (months, quarters, years) are displayed on the x-axis. Sometimes, variations in the data can be explained by other factors. For example, you might have spent a year expanding your business, which throws off your trendline and lowers the R^2 value for a chart depicting the trend in business expenses over a 10-year period. Consider creating one chart with all the data plotted and a second chart without the data for the year you expanded. Naturally, you will want to explain to anyone viewing the chart what the differences in R^2 values and the trendline position represent.

Polynomial Trendlines Simple regression analysis uses one dependent variable and one independent variable. A linear trendline uses the simple regression equation. Multiple regression analysis uses one dependent variable and multiple independent variables. A polynomial trendline uses the multiple regression equation. A *polynomial trendline* is used when data fluctuates in hills and valleys. The hills and valleys are the influence of separate independent variables on the dependent variable.

A curved line is plotted with this type of trendline. The number of *fluctuations* in the data—the hills and valleys—dictates the order you select for the polynomial curve. An Order 2 polynomial trendline has only one hill or valley. Order 3 generally has one or two hills or valleys. Order 4 generally has up to three. The highest order Excel can calculate is Order 6. The equation used by polynomial trendlines is similar to the linear trendline, but it has been rearranged to account for multiple orders. Because an Order 1 polynomial trendline (no hill or valleys) is the same as a linear trendline, the orders available to you in Excel are 2 through 6. Table 26.1 shows the equations for each of the orders.

Table 26.1 The Polynomial Trendline Equations

Order	Equation
1	$y = b + c_1x_1$
2	$y = b + c_1x_1 + c_2x_2$
3	$y = b + c_1x_1 + c_2x_2 + c_3x_3$
4	$y = b + c_1x_1 + c_2x_2 + c_3x_3 + c_4x_4$
5	$y = b + c_1x_1 + c_2x_2 + c_3x_3 + c_4x_4 + c_5x_5$
6	$y = b + c_1x_1 + c_2x_2 + c_3x_3 + c_4x_4 + c_5x_5 + c_6x_6$

Y is the dependent variable and is plotted on the value (y) axis.

X_1 is the first independent variable and is plotted on the category (x) axis. X_2 through x_6 are the other independent variables and are not plotted on the chart.

C_1 is the slope of the line that would be created based on the first independent variable. C_2 through c_6 are the slopes for the lines that would be created for the other independent variables.

B is the y-intercept of the line, the point where the trendline crosses the y-axis.

If you decide to use a polynomial trendline, make sure you can justify the order that you use. That is, you need to be able to specify what the other independent variables are in the equation. So, if you use an Order 3 polynomial, the equation ($y = b + c_1x_1 + c_2x_2 + c_3x_3$) accounts for three independent variables. The y-axis depicts one of the independent variables. The trendline will have one or two hills or valleys indicating the other two independent variables you need to identify.

Excel provides statistical functions that you can use with polynomial trends.

▶ **See** "Using LINEST and FDIST to Evaluate Polynomial Trendlines," **p. 708**

Logarithmic Trendlines Use a *logarithmic trendline* when the data increases or decreases quickly and then levels out. This type of trend occurs in several situations:

- With the introduction of a new popular product or service in the marketplace. Sales increase at a fast rate and then level off as other companies introduce similar products or services.
- With the production of a new item on an assembly line. The production line gets more efficient as the workers master their tasks, and it then levels off when they hit maximum efficiency.

A curved lined is plotted with this type of trendline. A logarithmic trendline can use negative or positive values (or both). Logarithmic trendlines use the following equation:

$$y = c\ln x + b$$

Y is the dependent variable and is plotted on the value (y) axis.

C is the slope of the line based on the independent variable.

Ln is the natural logarithm function.

X is the independent variable and is plotted on the category (x) axis.

B is the y-intercept of the line, the point where the trendline crosses the y-axis.

Exponential Trendlines Use an exponential trendline when the rate of change in the data increases or decreases over time. A curved line is plotted with this type of trendline. Exponential trendlines should not be used if your data contains zero or negative values. Exponential trendlines use the following equation:

$$y = ce^{bx}$$

Y is the dependent variable and is plotted on the value (y) axis.

C is the slope of the line based on the independent variable.

E is the base of the natural logarithm.

B is the y-intercept of the line, the point where the trendline crosses the y-axis.

X is the independent variable and is plotted on the category (x) axis.

Power Trendlines Use a *power trendline* when you want to compare measurements that increase at a specific rate. This type of trendline is a special case of the polynomial trendline where all the c_i (slopes) except one are zero. A curved line is plotted with this type of trendline.

Power trendlines should not be used if your data contains zero or negative values. Power trendlines use the following equation:

$y = cx^b$

Y is the dependent variable and is plotted on the value (y) axis.

C is the slope of the line based on the independent variable.

X is the independent variable and is plotted on the category (x) axis.

B is the y-intercept of the line, the point where the trendline crosses the y-axis.

Moving Average Trendlines Use a *moving average trendline* to smooth out fluctuations in data in order to plot trends by a set time period. This type of trendline is often used when you have a large data set (such as daily or weekly sales figures) with a number of fluctuations. The group of data points in the period are averaged, then this period average becomes a point on the moving average trendline. For example, if Period is set to 3, then the average of the first three data points (periods) is plotted as the first point in the trendline. The average of the fourth, fifth, and sixth data points is used as the second point in the trendline.

Excel Help contains samples that will help you understand trendlines better. Type `trendlines` in the Office Assistant search box and press Enter. Then choose `Choosing the Best Trendline for Your Data` to see the examples.

Adding Trendlines to Charts

To add a trendline to a chart, you first need to create the chart. Then select the chart and choose Chart, Add Trendline. The Add Trendline dialog box appears (as shown in Figure 26.20). Two tabs are in this dialog box—Type and Options.

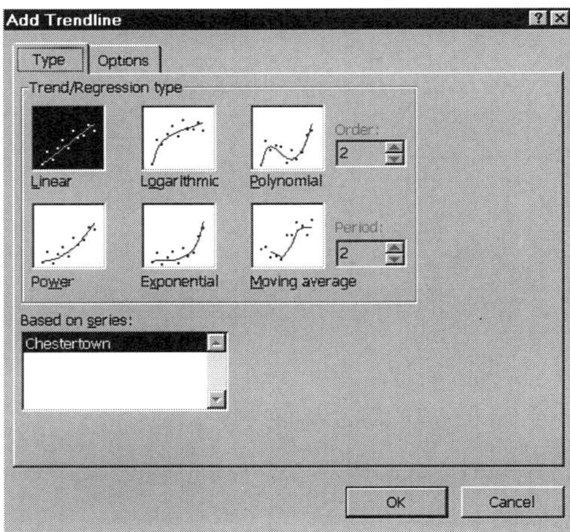

FIGURE 26.20
The most commonly used type is Linear.

On the Type tab, choose one of the trendline types and choose the series for which the trendline will be drawn. After you've selected the trend type, click the Options tab (see Figure 26.21).

- If you want to forecast into the past or future, choose the direction and number of periods that you want the trend to forecast.
- If you are plotting a polynomial trendline, select the Order number.
- If you are plotting a moving average trendline, select the number of periods averaged.

NOTE A trendline is calculated for a specific data series. If you want to add trendlines to each series in the chart, you'll need to add each one separately.

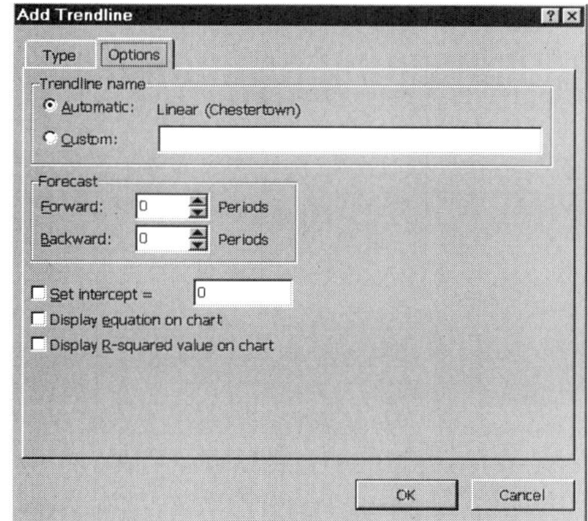

FIGURE 26.21
The choices on the Options tab depend on the type of trend you select on the Type tab.

Part IV Ch 26

You can also choose to have the formula and/or the R^2 value on the chart from the Options tab. After you've made your selections, click OK. Figure 26.22 shows the plot of a linear trendline.

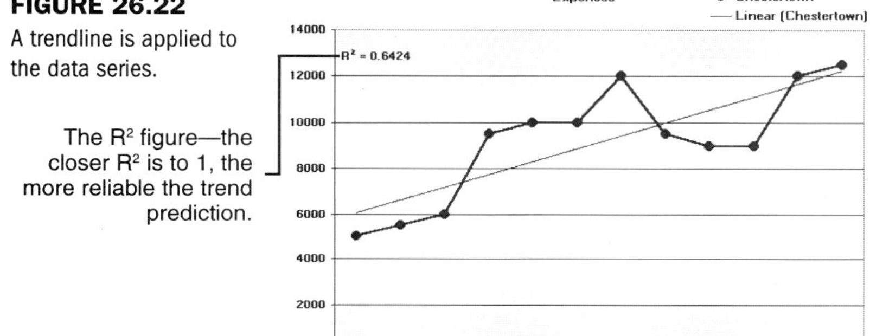

FIGURE 26.22
A trendline is applied to the data series.

To change the type of trendline or the trendline options, right-click the trendline and choose Format Trendline from the shortcut menu. Figure 26.23 shows a trendline forecasting into the future.

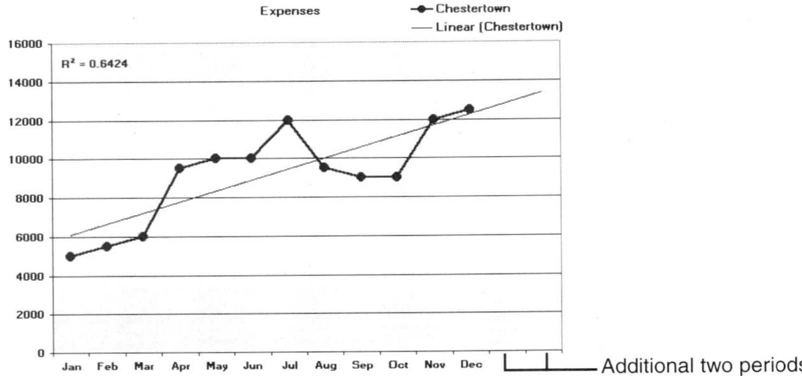

FIGURE 26.23
This trendline forecasts the expenses for the next two months.

Displaying Trend Data in the Worksheet

You can also generate the trend data directly in a worksheet (without creating a chart) by using a Fill Handle. To predict a linear trend, select the worksheet cells that contain the known data. Then position the mouse pointer on the Fill Handle (see Figure 26.24) and drag the mouse to the right. The values for the extended series are generated, as shown in Figure 26.25.

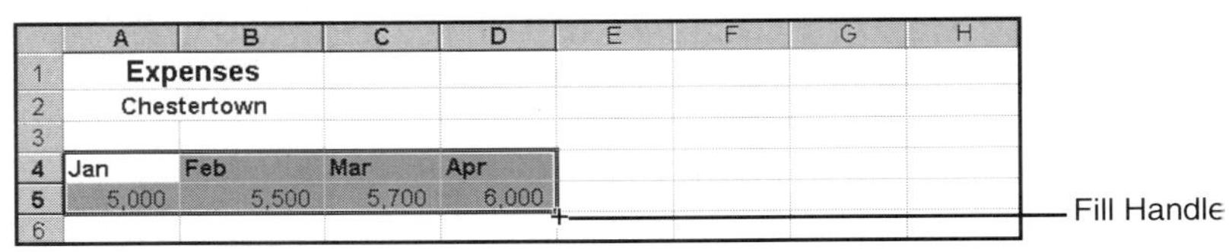

	A	B	C	D	E	F	G	H
1	Expenses							
2	Chestertown							
3								
4	Jan	Feb	Mar	Apr				
5	5,000	5,500	5,700	6,000				
6								

FIGURE 26.24
You can also use the Edit, Fill, Series command to create linear forecasts.

	A	B	C	D	E	F	G	H	I
1	Expenses								
2	Chestertown								
3									
4	Jan	Feb	Mar	Apr	May	Jun	Jul	Aug	
5	5,000	5,500	5,700	6,000	6,350	6,670	6,990	7,310	
6									

FIGURE 26.25
The Fill Handle completes the series of months and projects the series of expenses.

If you want to create an exponential growth trend, drag with the right mouse button instead. When you release the button, a special shortcut menu appears, as shown in Figure 26.26, from which you can select Growth Trend.

Suppose you have been asked to project the sales for your company for the next two years. Your research indicates that sales will continue to increase at approximately the same rate. You can create a linear trend estimate using the `=TREND` statistical function. The syntax for this function is

```
=TREND(known_y's, known_x's, new_x's,const)
```

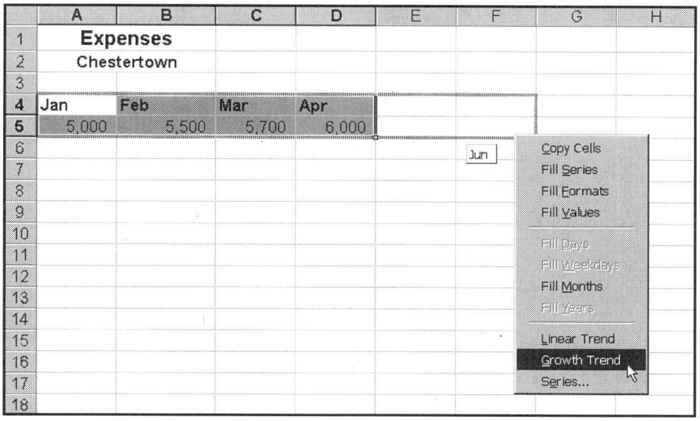

FIGURE 26.26
You can also use the Edit, Fill Series command to create growth forecasts.

Jan	Feb	Mar	Apr
5,000	5,500	5,700	6,000

Figure 26.27 shows the sales figures for 1996 to 1998. Using this figure as an example, the known *y* values (the sales figures) are dependent variables. The known *x* values (the years 1996-1998 that correspond to the sales figures) are the independent variables. The new *x* values are the existing values (1996-1998) plus the next two years (1999-2000). The `const` is a `TRUE/FALSE` argument used to indicate whether the y-intercept (b) is to be calculated normally (in the y = mx +b equation) or forced to be set at zero. If the `const` argument is omitted or set to `TRUE`, the y-intercept is calculated normally. If set to `FALSE`, the y-intercept is set to zero.

Using this function, a new set of *y* values are created based on the new *x* values. To use the Trend function, select the cells where you want the trend projection to fill (the new *y* values); this should be a set of cells separate from the original values, as shown in Figure 26.27.

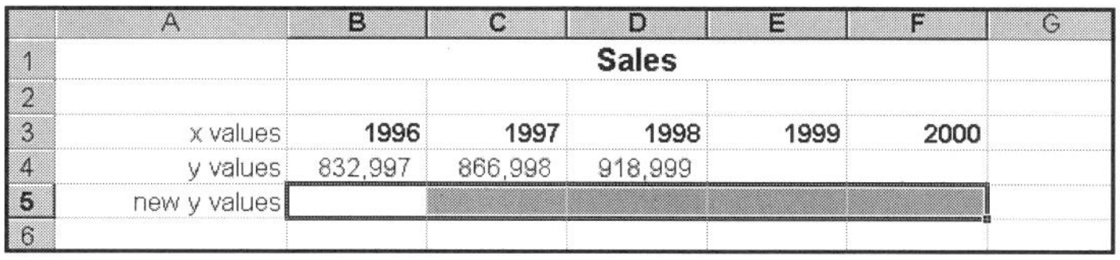

FIGURE 26.27
Select all the cells necessary to project new y values.

	Sales				
x values	1996	1997	1998	1999	2000
y values	832,997	866,998	918,999		
new y values					

Click the Paste Function button on the Standard toolbar and select the `TREND` function from the Statistical category. Then click OK. In the Formula Palette dialog box, complete the function by selecting the known y values (the sales data) and the known *x* values (the labels 1996 through 1998). The new *x* values are the existing *x* values plus the additional *x* values you want predictions for (the labels 1996 through 2000). After you've completed the formula, hold down Ctrl+Shift and press Enter to array enter the formula.

Excel calculates new *y* values for each *x* value (see Figure 26.28). You'll notice the new *y* values don't exactly match the original *y* values. This is because the `=TREND` function calculates the new *y* values based on the trend equation.

B5	= {=TREND(B4:D4,B3:D3,B3:F3)}					
	A	B	C	D	E	F	G
1				Sales			
2							
3	x values	1996	1997	1998	1999	2000	
4	y values	832,997	866,998	918,999			
5	new y values	829,997	872,998	915,999	959,000	1,002,001	
6							

FIGURE 26.28
Curly brackets in the formula indicate that it was array entered.

▶ To learn more about using arrays in formulas, **see** "Exploring the Power of Array Formulas," **p. 661**

NOTE If you see the #VALUE error as the result of your formula, you are probably using labels such as January or Quarter 1 as the x values. The x values must be values; that is, they must be numbers. Simply substitute 1 for January, 2 for February, and so forth.

▶ **See** "Statistical Functions," **p. 701**

Creating Summary Charts

Chapter 25, "Advanced Lists, PivotTables, and PivotCharts," describes several ways to manipulate Excel lists, including using filters, generating subtotals, applying outlines, and creating PivotTables. You can take the data displayed in these lists and create very useful summary charts.

Charts Based on Filtered Lists

Although you can create charts based on filtered lists, it may be more trouble than it's worth. Take the filtered list in Figure 26.29, for example. Suppose you wanted to create a chart based on the sales (by customer) of a particular Salesrep, Berger. To create a meaningful chart, you must summarize the data (by customer).

▶ **See** "Filtering Lists—Beyond the Basics," **p. 776**

The problem is that Excel won't produce subtotals on a filtered list—and allow you to collapse the list to the subtotals—in the same way that you can when the list is not filtered. Instead, you would have to use the Advanced Filter feature and copy the filter results to a separate range in your worksheet. Once copied, the filtered results could then be subtotaled to summarize the data, and finally, you could create a chart from the summarized data.

Instead of going through all that effort, consider creating a PivotTable to summarize the data and using a PivotChart to plot the summarized data. Using the preceding example, you would place the customers in the PivotTable Row field area, the Salesreps in the Page field area, and then use the Page field to filter on a particular Salesrep, as shown in Figure 26.30.

After you have the data in the PivotTable, you can click the Chart Wizard button on the PivotTable toolbar and a PivotChart is immediately created based on the PivotTable. The best part is that the chart is interactive. You can use the Page field to select any Salesrep, and both the PivotTable and the PivotChart display the data for that Salesrep.

FIGURE 26.29
An Excel list, filtered on the Salesrep column.

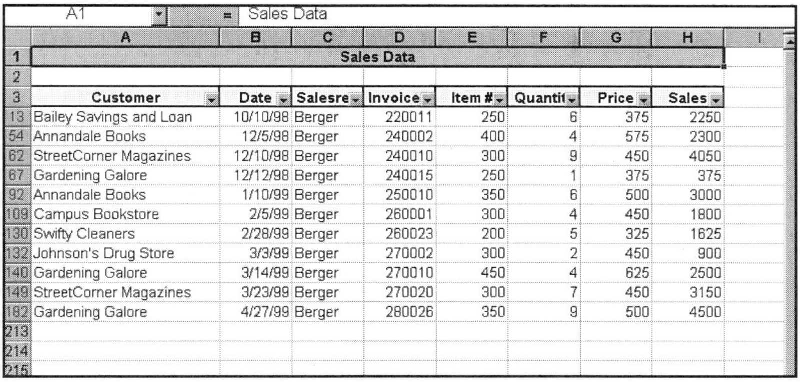

A1 = Sales Data

	A	B	C	D	E	F	G	H
1	Sales Data							
2								
3	Customer	Date	Salesre	Invoice	Item #	Quantit	Price	Sales
13	Bailey Savings and Loan	10/10/98	Berger	220011	250	6	375	2250
54	Annandale Books	12/5/98	Berger	240002	400	4	575	2300
62	StreetCorner Magazines	12/10/98	Berger	240010	300	9	450	4050
67	Gardening Galore	12/12/98	Berger	240015	250	1	375	375
92	Annandale Books	1/10/99	Berger	250010	350	6	500	3000
109	Campus Bookstore	2/5/99	Berger	260001	300	4	450	1800
130	Swifty Cleaners	2/28/99	Berger	260023	200	5	325	1625
132	Johnson's Drug Store	3/3/99	Berger	270002	300	2	450	900
140	Gardening Galore	3/14/99	Berger	270010	450	4	625	2500
149	StreetCorner Magazines	3/23/99	Berger	270020	300	7	450	3150
182	Gardening Galore	4/27/99	Berger	280026	350	9	500	4500
213								
214								
215								

FIGURE 26.30
Drag and drop the fields from the PivotTable toolbar to the PivotTable area.

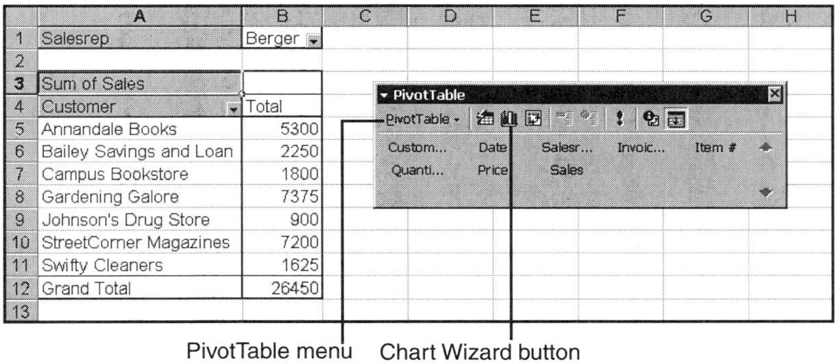

	A	B
1	Salesrep	Berger
2		
3	Sum of Sales	
4	Customer	Total
5	Annandale Books	5300
6	Bailey Savings and Loan	2250
7	Campus Bookstore	1800
8	Gardening Galore	7375
9	Johnson's Drug Store	900
10	StreetCorner Magazines	7200
11	Swifty Cleaners	1625
12	Grand Total	26450
13		

PivotTable
PivotTable ▾
Custom... Date Salesr... Invoic... Item #
Quanti... Price Sales

PivotTable menu
Chart Wizard button

PivotCharts have the same chart type and formatting options as regular charts, except you must select the chart object you want to format and use the menu commands. The shortcut menu will not display when you right-click a chart object in a PivotChart. Figure 26.31 shows a PivotChart based on the PivotTable shown in Figure 26.30.

Part IV Ch 26

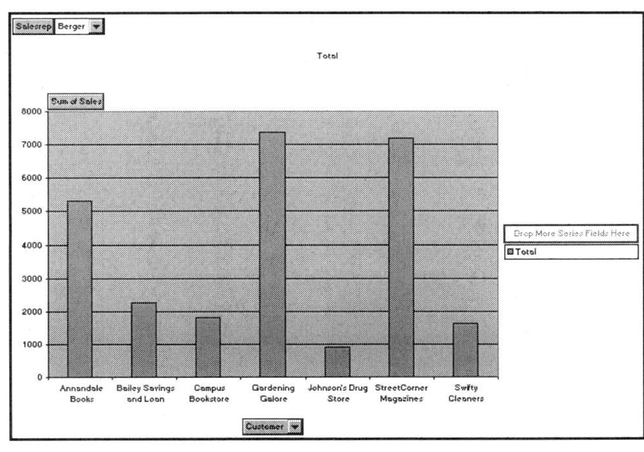

FIGURE 26.31
PivotCharts cannot be embedded next to worksheet data as other charts can. They must appear on their own Chart Sheet.

If you need individual charts for each Salesrep, select the PivotTable menu on the PivotTable toolbar and choose Show Pages. A separate worksheet containing a PivotTable for each Salesrep is added to the workbook. Click anywhere in the PivotTable for the first Salesrep and click the Chart Wizard button on the PivotTable toolbar to create the PivotChart for that Salesrep. Then click anywhere in the PivotTable for the second Salesrep and repeat the procedure until all the charts are created.

▶ **See** "Unlocking the Power of PivotTables and PivotCharts," **p. 797**

Charts Based on Subtotaled and Outlined Lists

It is often useful to create a chart using data from an outlined list, where the list has been collapsed to display only the formula results. This could include situations where an outline has been applied to a list or where an outline has been generated as a result of creating subtotals in a list. When you create a chart from an outlined worksheet, the chart reflects the data visible in the worksheet. When you collapse or expand the outline in the worksheet, the chart changes to reflect the data visible in the worksheet.

▶ **See** "Outlining Worksheets," **p. 791**

▶ **See** "Creating Subtotals and Grand Totals," **p. 793**

Figure 26.32 shows an outlined worksheet with the outline collapsed to display only the regional, quarterly, and grand totals. The chart in Figure 26.33 is based on the selected cells shown in Figure 26.32.

	A	E	I	M	Q	R
1–6	Regional Sales					
7		Qtr 1	Qtr 2	Qtr 3	Qtr 4	*Grand Total/Country*
11	North American Total	32,803	43,659	45,406	38,457	282,193
15	Central American Total	42,310	35,109	38,411	44,495	276,155
20	South American Total	43,998	53,677	52,188	52,044	351,770
24	Caribbean Total	45,406	31,126	44,800	34,776	277,440
25	*Grand Total/Month*	164,517	163,571	180,805	169,772	1,187,558
26						

FIGURE 26.32
An outlined worksheet with the third level collapsed to show only the totals.

You can create a chart based on an outlined worksheet and force Excel not to adjust the chart when the outline is collapsed or expanded. To create the chart, follow these steps:

1. If necessary, collapse the outlined list so that only the cells you want to plot are visible.
2. Select the cells in the outlined list and choose Edit, Go To, and select Special. The Go To Special dialog box appears (see Figure 26.34).

3. Select the Visible Cells Only option. (You can accomplish the same thing by selecting the first cell to be plotted, then using the Ctrl key to select subsequent cells. The method described in these steps, though, is probably *much* faster!)
4. Choose OK.

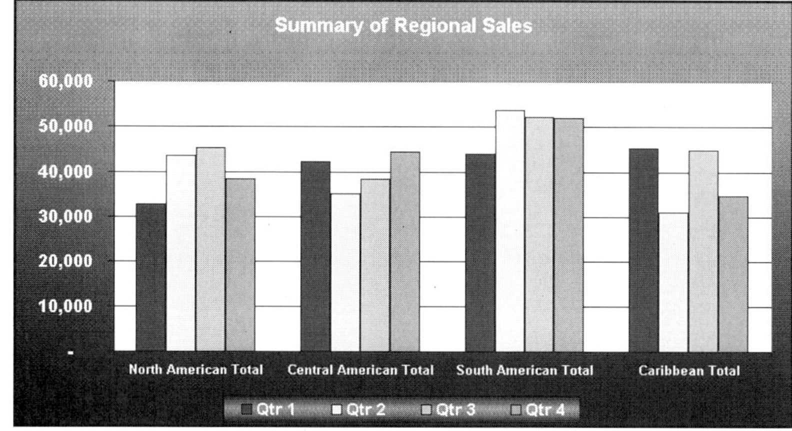

FIGURE 26.33
The chart based on the data selected in Figure 26.32.

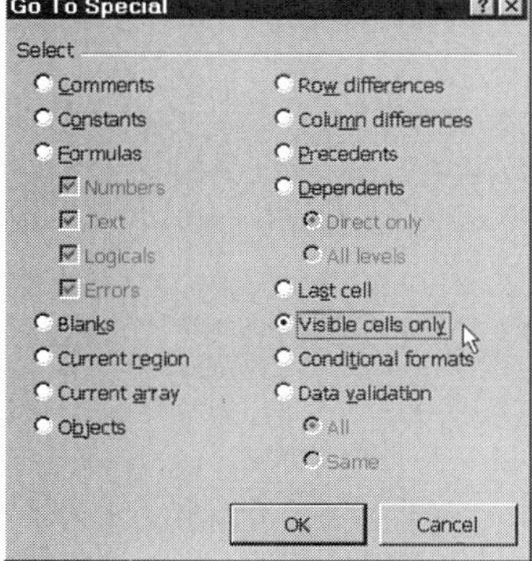

FIGURE 26.34
The Go To Special dialog box.

5. Proceed with creating the chart. When the outlined worksheet is collapsed or expanded, the chart continues to display the summarized worksheet data that was originally plotted.

Creating Effective Pie Charts

Pie charts are designed to display only one series or category of data, usually to show what percentage of the whole pie each item constitutes. Figure 26.35 shows a simple pie chart plotting monthly expenses, showing what percentage each expense is of the total expenses. Because some of the expenses are very large and some are very small, many of the smaller data points are difficult to interpret.

FIGURE 26.35
A simple 2D pie chart.

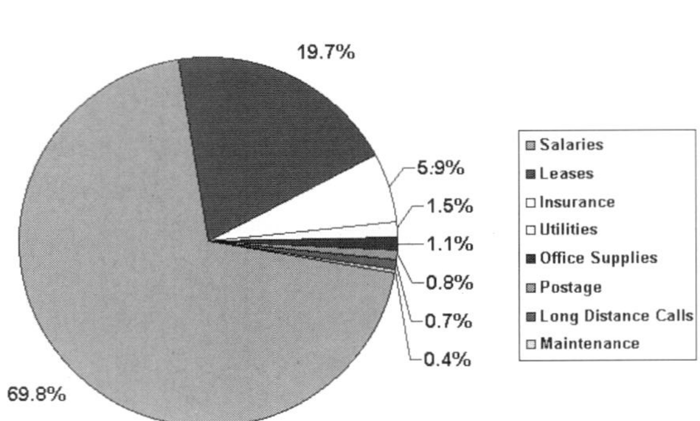

In Excel 97, Microsoft introduced two new subtypes of pie charts that can help to make this data easier to read: Bar of a Pie and Pie of a Pie. Figure 26.36 illustrates the Bar of a Pie variation. Some of the minor expenses are grouped into one slice, referred to as Other, which collectively represents 4.5 percent of the expenses. This pie slice is linked to a bar, which allows these smaller expenses to be seen more clearly. In Figure 26.36, the Other slice is selected and the ChartTip provides information about the data point.

TIP To create this type of chart, you need to organize all the data series you want to appear in the bar at the end of the worksheet list.

FIGURE 26.36
A Bar of a Pie, a subtype variation of the pie chart.

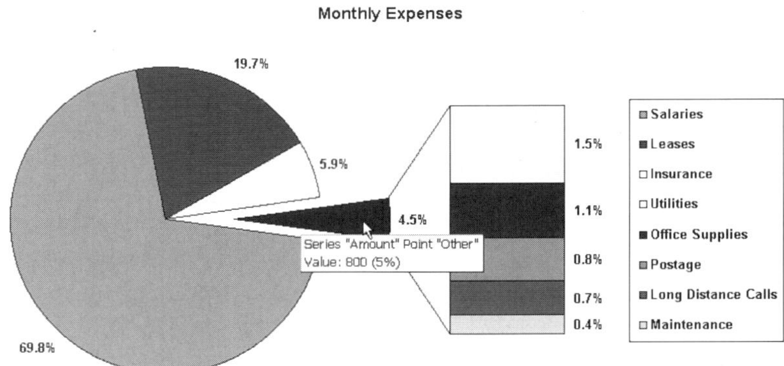

Another pie chart variation is the Pie of a Pie subtype, as shown in Figure 26.37. The Other slice and all the secondary plotted pie slices have been manually exploded to make the chart easier to read.

Either of these two variations can also be used to show a group of related data points. For example, suppose you have a list of expenses for Airfare, Lodging, Food, and Car Rental. If these expenses are small fractions of your total expenses, they may be lumped together under an umbrella expense—Travel. With Bar of a Pie or Pie of a Pie, you can show each of the specific travel-related expenses.

FIGURE 26.37
A Pie of a Pie, a subtype of the pie chart.

Monthly Expenses

Leases
Insurance
Postage
Long Distance Calls
Office Supplies
Maintenance
Utilities
Salaries
Miscellaneous expenses make up 4.5% of total monthly expenses.

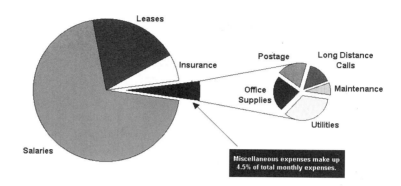

To create either one of the pie chart subtypes shown in Figures 26.36 and 26.37, follow these steps:

1. Select the cells containing the data to be charted. Be sure to include the row and column headings if you want them to appear in the chart as category and legend labels. Do not include blank rows in your selection.
2. Click the Chart Wizard button on the Standard toolbar; the Chart Wizard dialog box appears.
3. In step 1 of the Chart Wizard, select Pie from the Standard Types tab. Choose either the Bar in a Pie or the Pie in a Pie subtype (see Figure 26.38).
4. Proceed through the remaining steps of the Chart Wizard.

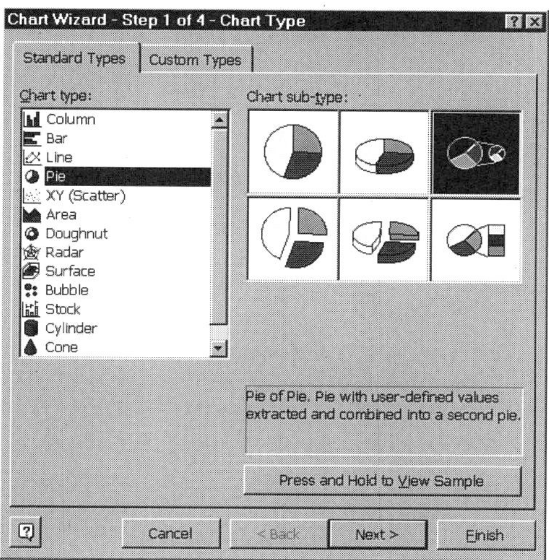

FIGURE 26.38
The six standard subtypes that are available with a Pie chart.

An existing chart can also be changed to one of the new pie chart variations. Right-click an empty area of the chart, away from the chart objects, and choose Chart Type from the shortcut menu. Select Pie from the Standard Types tab, pick a subtype, and select OK.

Once created, a number of features in these charts can be customized. It is helpful to people who view your chart if some type of data label is displayed on the pie charts. Refer to Figure 26.36 for an example of percentages displayed next to each pie slice. Figure 26.37 displays an example of labels next to each slice, eliminating the need for a legend.

If a particular data label is too long and you want part of the label to appear on a second line, you can force part of the text to a new line in the label. First click the data labels–this selects all data labels. Then click the label you want to change–this places a selection border around the selected data label. Click once inside the label to edit the label. To force a particular word to a second line, position the flashing cursor in front of the word and press Enter. This forces the text to the right of the cursor to move to a second line.

The Options tab of the Format Data Series dialog box contains specific choices for customizing Bar in a Pie or Pie in a Pie charts. The following list describes each of these options:

- Split Series By—The drop-down list provides four methods that Excel can use to determine which data points appear in the second plot: Position, Value, Percent Value, and Custom.
    - Position—The last *x* number of data points is plotted in the second plot. You can indicate the number of data points. With this option, these data points must be listed together at the bottom of the cells selected from the worksheet so that Excel can plot them together.
    - Value—The data points less than a specific amount are listed in the second plot. You can indicate the amount. Regardless where the data points are located in the worksheet, if they are less than the amount you enter, those data points are displayed in the second plot.
    - Percent Value—Those data points less than a specific percent are listed in the second plot. You can indicate the percent. Regardless where the data points are in the worksheet, if they are less than the specified percent, the data points are displayed in the second plot.
    - Custom—You can use the mouse to drag data points between the first plot and the second plot.
- Second Plot Contains—This option varies depending on the selection you make in the Split Series By option.
- Size of Second Plot—The second plot can be larger, the same size, or smaller than the first plot. The range is 200 to 5. Selecting 200 makes the second plot twice the size of the first plot. Choosing 100 makes the second plot equal to the size of the first plot. Choosing 5 makes the second plot one-fifth the size (20 percent) of the first plot.

- Series Lines—Display or remove connecting lines between the slice in the first plot to the bar or pie in the second plot. The default displays the lines.
- Vary Colors by Slice—Use different or identical colors for each data point. The default uses different colors.
- Gap Width—Distance between the slice in the first plot and the bar or pie in the second plot. You may decide to widen the gap to provide additional room for data labels.

Advanced Chart Formatting Options

Chart Options are common chart objects that you elect to include or exclude from your chart. If you've used the Chart Wizard, the Chart Options are the same options available in the third step of the Chart Wizard. Right-click in a blank area of the chart, away from the chart objects. To modify these objects, choose Chart Options from the shortcut menu. The Chart Options dialog box appears. The formatting options vary from chart object to chart object. This dialog box typically includes the following tabs: Titles, Axes, Gridlines, Legend, Data Labels, and Data Table.

NOTE If you are modifying a PivotChart, you will not be able to use the shortcut menu (by right-clicking) to modify the chart objects. Instead, select the object you want to modify and choose Chart from the Menu bar.

Using Clip Art As Fill Patterns and Data Markers

One way to add pizzazz to your charts is to create picture charts. Although pictures can be used with several chart types, they work best in two-dimensional line, bubble, column, and bar charts. Use pictures from Excel's clip art library, graphics from other windows program, or scanned images, or create your own picture in PhotoDraw or the Paint Accessories program.

▶ **See** "Using Scanned Pictures," **p. 1207**

▶ **See** "Using Microsoft PhotoDraw," **p. 1661**

An example of using a picture as a marker in a line chart is shown in Figure 26.39. Because the pictures are larger than ordinary markers, a data table is added to the bottom of the chart to provide the precise values for the sales in each country.

Figure 26.40 illustrates how pictures can be used as a fill for a bar chart. Bar charts created with pictures are often easier to read than column charts created with pictures. The pictures appear side by side rather than stacked one on top of another.

The easiest way to create picture charts is to paste the picture into the data series. Follow these steps:

1. Select an empty area in a worksheet. Insert a picture into the worksheet by using the Insert, Picture command. Clip art is a good place to find pictures.
2. Resize the picture to about half an inch. Be sure that you drag one of the corner selection handles to keep the picture proportional as you resize it.

3. Use the Format, Picture command to remove the border surrounding the picture before including it in your chart. Change the Line Color to No Line on the Colors and Lines tab of the Format Picture dialog box. To get the bar background-color effect in Figure 26.40, choose a Fill color in the Format Picture dialog box. Then select OK.
4. With the picture selected, click Copy.
5. In the chart, select the data series you want to display as a picture and click Paste. By default, the picture is stretched in the bar or column.
6. To have the picture repeated instead of stretched to fill the bar, as shown in Figure 26.40, right-click the data series and choose Format Data Series from the shortcut menu.
7. In the Format Data Series dialog box, choose the Patterns tab and select the Fill Effects button. The Fill Effects dialog box appears.
8. In the Fill Effects dialog box, choose the Picture tab (see Figure 26.41).

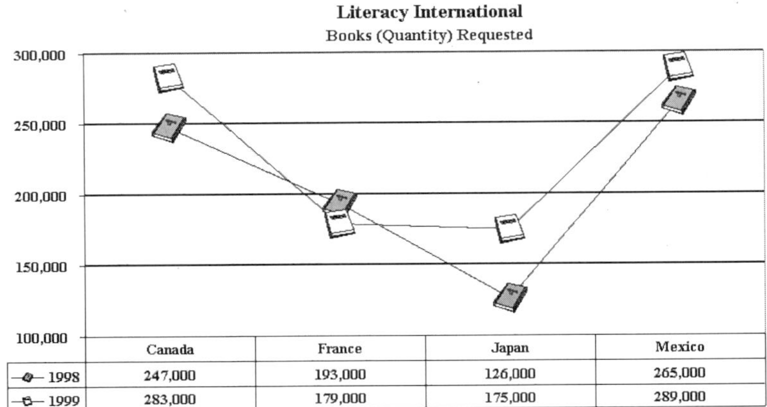

FIGURE 26.39
A 2D line chart with pictures marking the data points and a data table providing precise values.

FIGURE 26.40
A 2D bar chart with a repeating picture filling the bars.

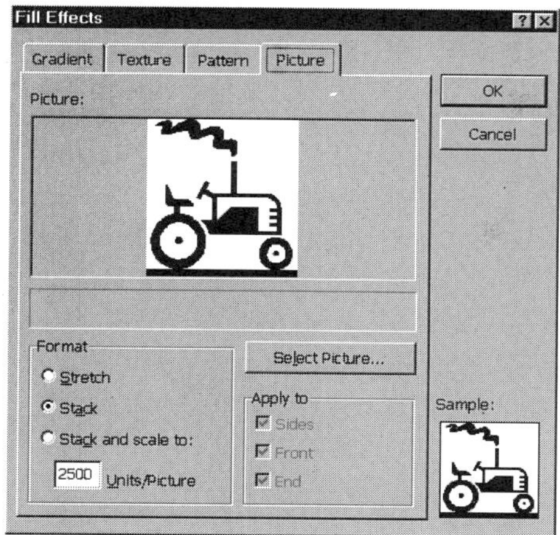

FIGURE 26.41
The Picture tab of the Fill Effects dialog box controls how the picture appears in your chart.

9. Three choices as to how your picture will be displayed are the following: Stretch, Stack, and Stack and Scale To x Units/Picture. Stretch resizes the picture so that it completely fills the area of the data series. Stack displays repeated copies of your picture until the area of your data series is filled, based on the original size of the picture. Stack and Scale To x Units/Picture also displays repeated copies of the picture, but at increments you choose.

   In Figure 26.40, for example, for every 2,500 tractors sold, the picture repeats. When you use this option, the picture may be expanded or contracted slightly to adhere to the unit you select. You may want to add a text box indicating the increment each picture represents.

10. Choose OK to accept your fill changes. Choose OK again to accept your data series format changes.

Using Data Labels and Data Tables

The tick-mark labels on a chart's axes are the usual way to tell what each data marker represents. A Column chart that shows monthly expenses per department usually shows each department's name on the horizontal category axis. Figure 26.42 shows an example.

At times, however, you need to display additional information that better identifies each data marker. For example, the relative height of each column makes it easy to compare departments' operating expenses. But to determine the actual expense figures, you need to refer to the value axis. It can be useful to display the expense value along with the data marker. You might also want to display data labels purely for formatting reasons. You might want to modify the horizontal axis to gain space in a report. You would select the horizontal axis; choose Format, Selected Axis; click the Patterns tab; and set Tick Mark Labels to None. Then, display each department's name as a label on its own column marker.

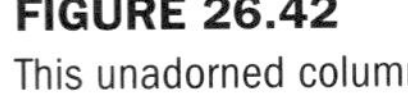

FIGURE 26.42

This unadorned column chart provides basic information about departmental expenses.

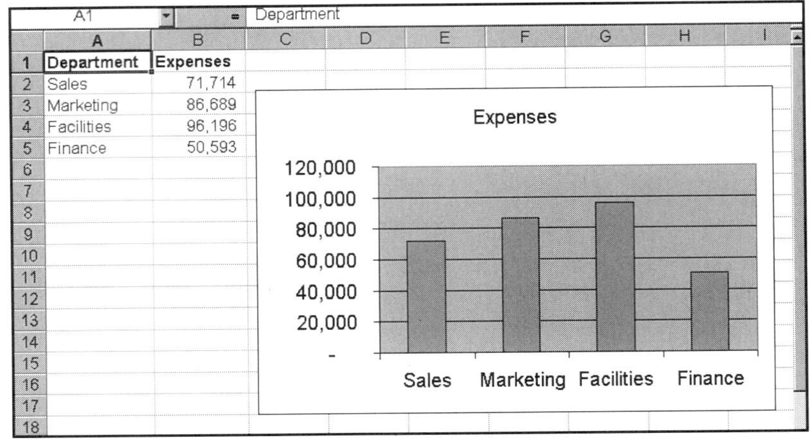

Adding Data Labels Excel makes it very easy to put two types of data labels on a chart. To label each column with the actual expense value, you would select the chart and choose Chart, Chart Options. From the Data Labels tab, you can include the data values, percentages, or labels next to a series. With pie charts, you can also choose to display *leader lines*—lines that point from the data label to the specific piece of pie (refer to Figure 26.35). The options vary depending on the chart type.

FIGURE 26.43

Data Label options for a two-dimensional column chart.

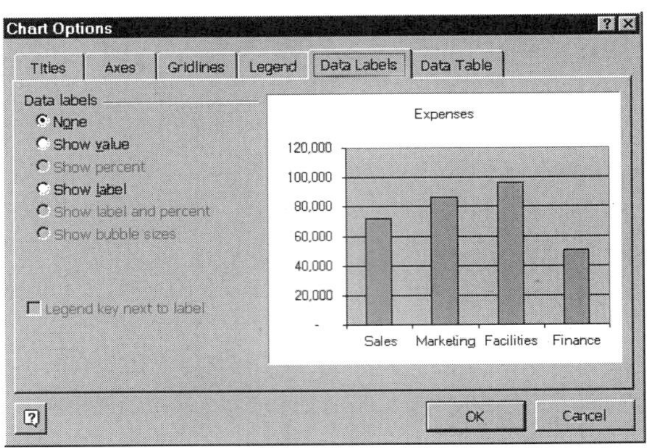

If the chart type is one that has a category and a value axis, such as a column or bar chart, you have the choice to Show Labels or Show Values in the data labels. Selecting the Show Labels option takes the category axis labels and places them in the chart.

NOTE Remember, the Category Axis typically plots labels from the worksheet. In Figure 26.42, the category labels are the department names. In most charts, the category axis is the horizontal axis. The exception is a bar chart where the category and value axes are swapped and the category axis is the vertical axis.

If the chart type is an XY (scatter) in which there is no category axis, you have the same choice. However, choosing to Show Labels shows the horizontal axis values you are displaying, not labels, but true quantitative values. Choosing to Show Values shows the vertical axis values.

But what if you wanted to indicate whether each department's expenses for the current year are greater or less than its expenses for the prior year? To do so, you would like to show a label that says Increase or Decrease on each column. The problem is that Increase and Decrease exist on neither the chart's value nor its category axis.

Many situations exist in which you want to attach data labels, but you want neither the category label nor the value axis as the data label. Perhaps you have created an XY (scatter) chart of staff salaries and length of employment. You would like to label each point with the name of the associated staff member, but because you didn't include employees' names in the chart, you can't attach their names as labels. The usual solution to this problem is to attach data labels to the series, choosing to show either Labels or Values. When the labels have been created, select the first data label and type a new entry in the Formula bar. Then when you press Enter, the new text appears in the selected data label on the chart (see Figure 26.44). Data labels are actually text, regardless of the type of label you chose.

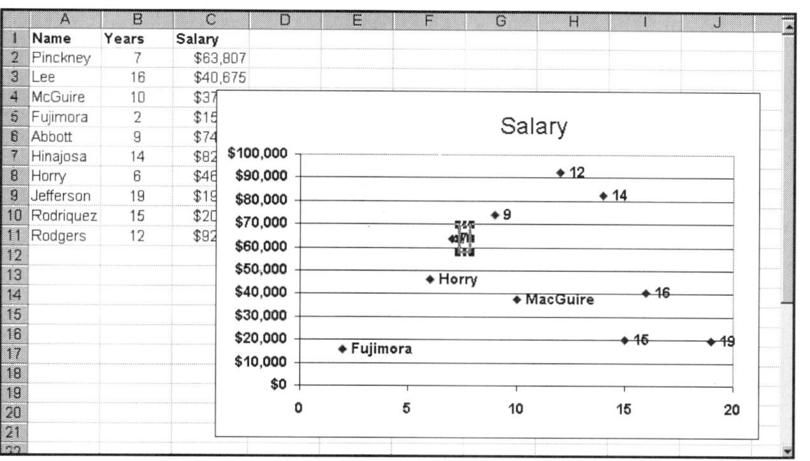

FIGURE 26.44
Unless you type a new value for a data label, the label's value is linked to the chart's source data.

Adding a Data Table You have an alternative to including data labels on a chart. You can add a data table beneath the chart to display the series values. However, a data table is more than a glorified list of values. This table combines the labels on the category axis and the legend into the table along with the precise data being plotted.

From the Data Table tab (shown in Figure 26.45), select the Show Data Table option. Because the data table includes the legend information, whenever you add a data table to a chart you should remove the legend.

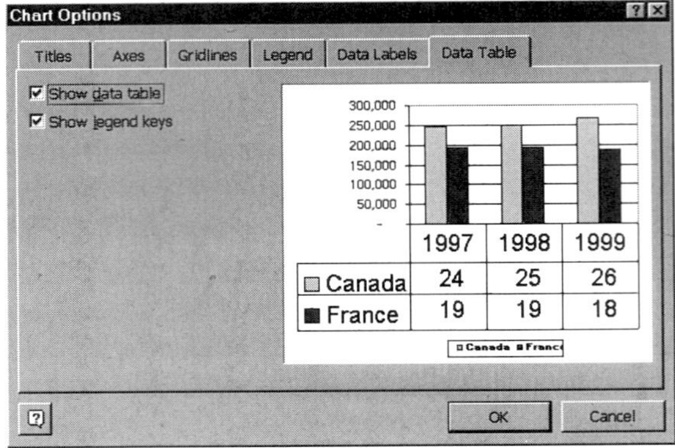

FIGURE 26.45
Data tables provide a great way to combine the worksheet data and the chart.

Using Chart Axes Effectively

Most charts have two axes: the category axis and the value axis. The category axis displays labels from the worksheet data and is typically the horizontal axis. Timeframes are common category labels, including January, February, …Quarter 1, Quarter 2, …1997, 1998. The value axis plots data values from the worksheet and is typically the vertical axis. Among the types of values plotted on this axis are currency, quantity, size, and temperature.

Excel calls the values that are charted on the category axis the X (Category) Axis Labels. The values on the value axis are called Values. The actual data points—the columns on a column chart, the bars on a bar chart, the points on a line chart, and so on—are called *data markers*.

You may be surprised to discover that a pie chart has both category and value axes. The slices represent the category axis and the size of each slice represents the value axis.

Using Two Value Axes The XY (scatter) chart is fundamentally different from other chart types because it has two value axes (see Figure 26.46). Both the horizontal and vertical axes space the values according to their magnitude. For a chart that has two value axes, Excel calls the values on the horizontal axis the X Values and the values on the vertical axis the Y Values.

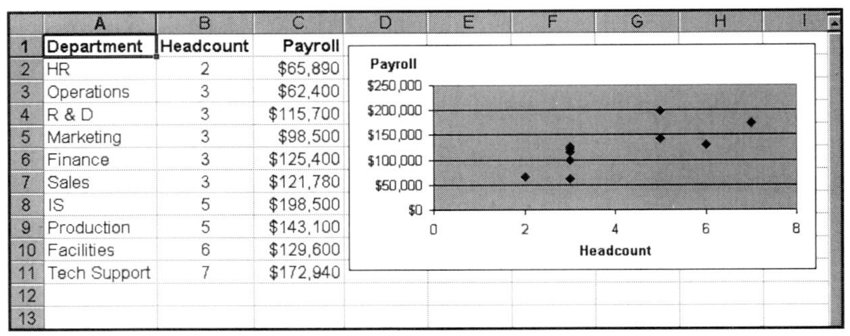

Department	Headcount	Payroll
HR	2	$65,890
Operations	3	$62,400
R & D	3	$115,700
Marketing	3	$98,500
Finance	3	$125,400
Sales	3	$121,780
IS	5	$198,500
Production	5	$143,100
Facilities	6	$129,600
Tech Support	7	$172,940

FIGURE 26.46
Notice that both the horizontal and vertical axes space the values according to their magnitude.

A line chart, like a column chart, has a horizontal category axis and a vertical value axis. Because line charts resemble XY (scatter) charts so closely, many people get themselves into trouble by using a line chart when an XY (scatter) chart is needed, and vice versa.

Figure 26.47 shows how a line chart and an XY (scatter) chart would display payroll information and the employee headcount per department. Compare the two charts shown in Figure 26.47 and notice that the line chart gives the employee values equal spacing—ignoring the quantitative differences between the values. In contrast, the XY (scatter) chart reflects the magnitude of the values on its horizontal axis.

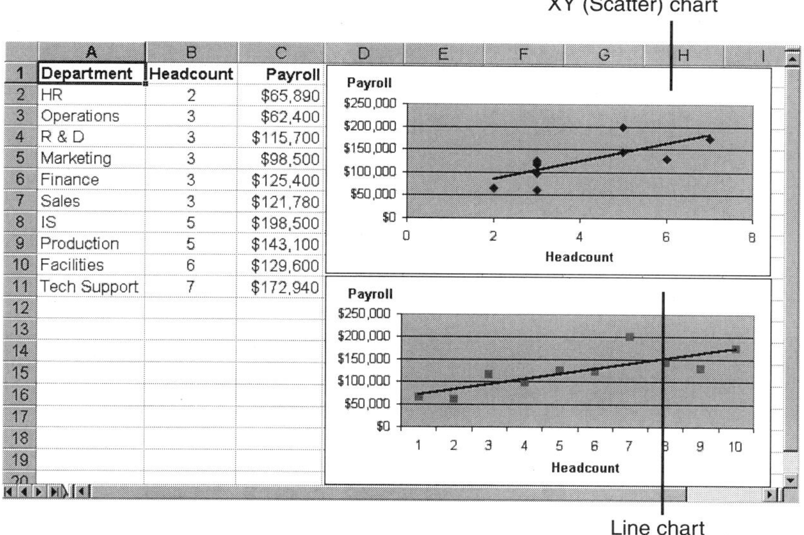

Department	Headcount	Payroll
HR	2	$65,890
Operations	3	$62,400
R & D	3	$115,700
Marketing	3	$98,500
Finance	3	$125,400
Sales	3	$121,780
IS	5	$198,500
Production	5	$143,100
Facilities	6	$129,600
Tech Support	7	$172,940

FIGURE 26.47
Although both charts use the same source data, the horizontal-axis spacing and the trendlines are different.

In the line chart, the category axis isn't assigning values to data points according to their numeric magnitude. Instead, it assigns the first category a value of 1, the second category a value of 2, and so on. In other words, the value of a category is its ordinal position with respect to the other values. And that, of course, is a function of each data point's placement on the worksheet.

In any chart, a trendline depends on the relationship between the sets of values on the two axes. In the XY (scatter) chart, the trendline depends on the relationship between the actual values of Employees and Payroll. But in the line chart, the trendline depends on the relationship between the actual values of headcount and the ordinal value (1, 2, 3, and so on) of each payroll measurement. Unless you're sure that you want to trend a continuous variable against a series of equally spaced integers, use an XY (scatter) chart for your trendlines.

A major exception exists to the general rule about how Excel treats values on a category axis. When the category values are formatted as *dates* on the worksheet, Excel 2000 adjusts the scale of the category axis accordingly (see Figure 26.48).

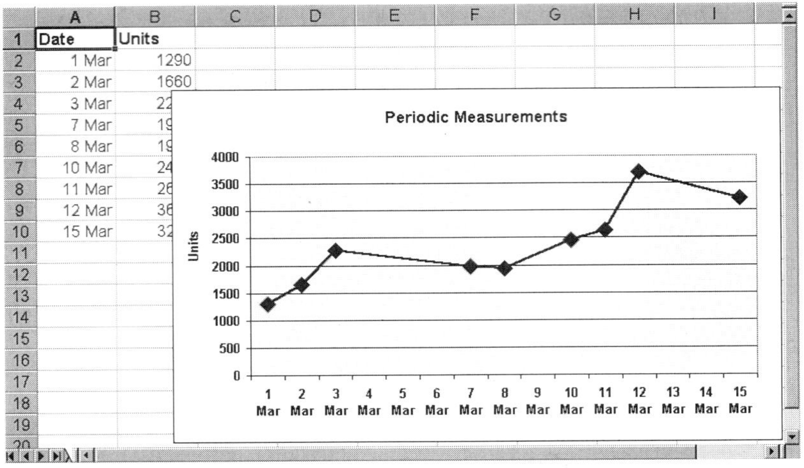

FIGURE 26.48
The line chart spaces the date values properly on the category axis.

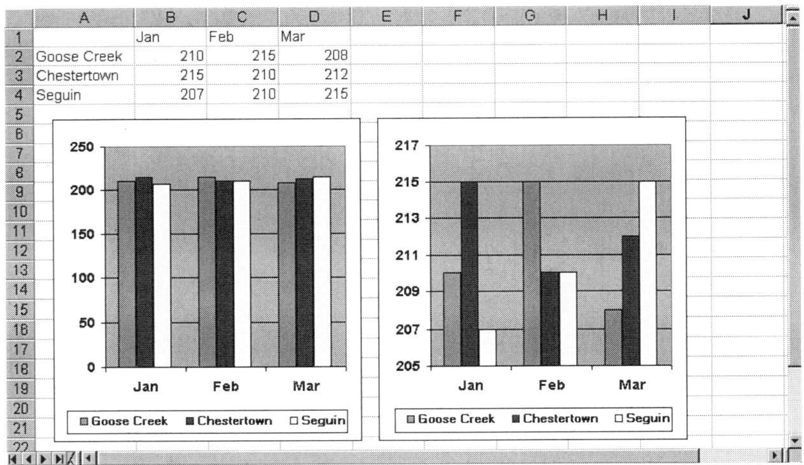

FIGURE 26.49
Choose Chart, Chart Options to alter the scale.

You will find that the same effect occurs in other chart types when you place values formatted in date units on the category axis. That format causes Excel to use the actual date values on the category scale instead of their ordinal values.

Modifying the Value Axis Scale

The chart scale is the numeric increments marked along the value axis. By default, the low end of the scale is zero and the high end of the scale is typically one numeric increment mark higher than the largest number plotted. You can, of course, change the scale that appears on a chart. With numbers that are close together, you may want to change the minimum value to better show the difference between the values plotted. Consider Figure 26.49. The chart on the left shows the default scale from zero to 250 with increments of 50. The chart on the right shows the scale from 205 to 217 with increments of 2.

CAUTION

Resetting the axis scale so that the x-axis crosses the y-axis above (or below) zero exaggerates the change or difference in the y values. Although this makes it easier to see smaller changes, it does distort the chart. When it is used with an audience who is knowledgeable about charting and who has adequate time to analyze the chart and scale, it's a safe technique. However, when it is used with an audience less familiar with charts or who gets only a fleeting glimpse of the chart, the visual difference in the size of the bars will be what the audience remembers. One bar that is twice the height of another will lead the audience to think an item has doubled (or has been cut in half) when, in fact, the percentage change is much smaller.

Other alternatives exist on the Scale tab of the Options dialog box, including an option to plot the values in reverse order. This option might come in handy when plotting depths, such as the drilling depths shown in Figure 26.50 or when marking depths underwater.

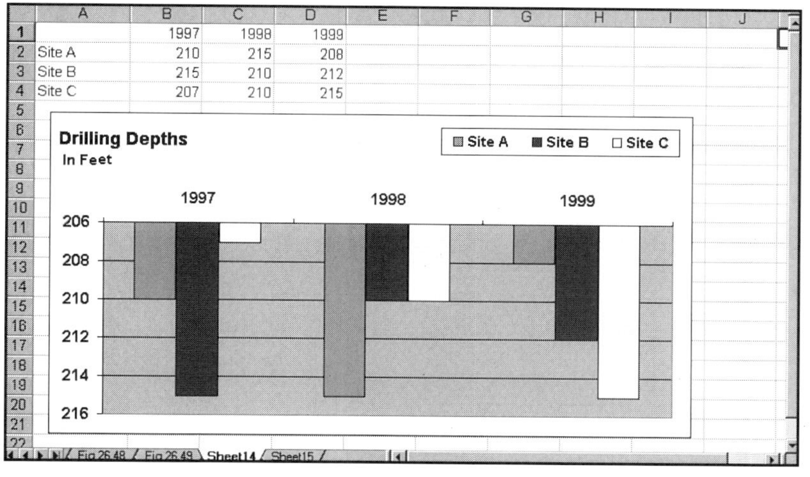

FIGURE 26.50
A standard column chart with the axis displayed above instead of below the chart.

Using Error Bars in Charts

The margin of error or degree of uncertainty in a data series can be plotted on a chart using error bars. Error bars graphically express potential error amounts relative to each data marker in a data series. For example, you could show 5% positive and negative potential error amounts in the results of a scientific experiment. Statistical and engineering data often displays error bars as an indication of the reliability of the data being displayed. The greater the uncertainty associated with the data points in a series, the wider the error bars. Figure 26.51 shows a chart with error bars inserted.

You can associate error bars with any data series of a two-dimensional area, bar, column, line, or XY (scatter) chart type. Because XY (scatter) and bubble charts have two value axes, you can display error bars for the x values, the y values, or both. If you change the data series to any three-dimensional, pie, doughnut, or radar chart, the error bars will be permanently lost.

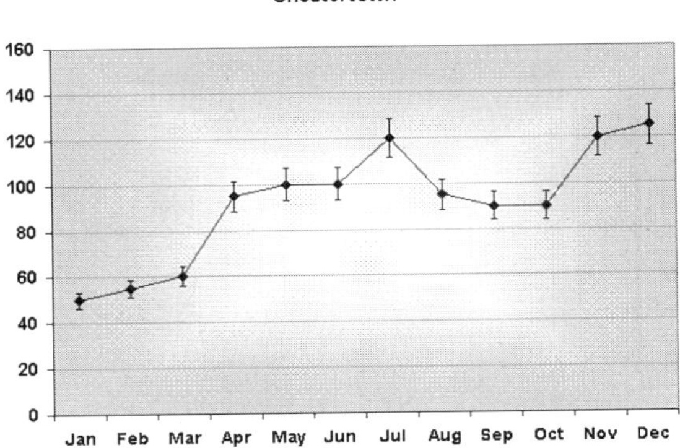

FIGURE 26.51
Error bars on each side of the data points.

To apply error bars to a data series, use the following steps:

1. Right-click the data series to which you want to add error bars.
2. Choose Format Data Series from the shortcut menu. The Format Data Series dialog box appears.
3. Click the Y Error Bars tab and select the type of error bars you want from the Display options (see Figure 26.52).
4. Then select the method you want Excel to use for calculating the error amounts from the Error Amount options: Fixed Value, Percentage, Standard Deviation, Standard Error, or Custom. Use the Custom option if you want to specify different error amounts for each data point from error data already in your worksheet.
5. Choose OK.

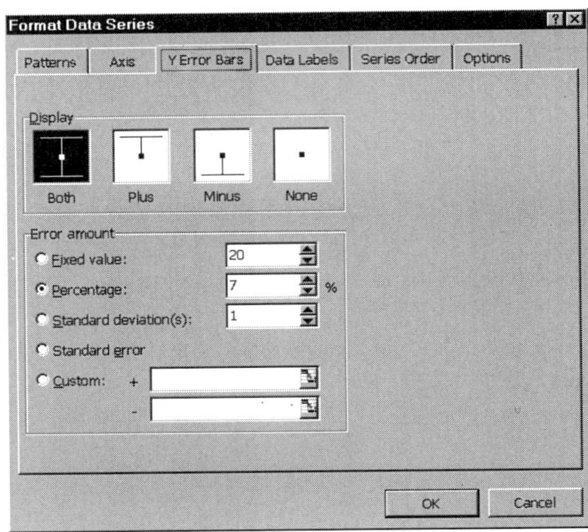

FIGURE 26.52
You can enter your own error amounts, except for the Standard Error option.

If the values for the data points change, the error bars are automatically recalculated.

CHAPTER 27

Analytical Tools

In this chapter

Validating and Analyzing Excel Data

You can use a number of tools to validate and analyze data in Excel worksheets. With the Data Validation command, you can display a list of valid entries for the user to choose from, insert prompts with notes on data entry, place limits on the entries to ensure the appropriate data is entered in the worksheet, and have Excel draw circles around invalid entries. The Data Validation command can be used prior to, during, and after data entry to ensure the correct data is entered into a worksheet.

Excel also provides a variety of other tools you can use to perform "what-if" type analysis on your worksheet data. The tool you choose largely depends on how you want the analysis displayed in your worksheet:

- Data Tables—This feature creates a table of results based on variables you want to compare side by side.
- Scenarios—Creating scenarios enables you to propose different values and monitor the impact on the results of your worksheets. You can display each set of values, or scenarios, to see the impact each scenario makes on your data. A consolidated report can be produced to compare the various scenarios.
- Goal Seek—The Goal Seek command is effective in calculating what needs to change so that you reach a target or goal. With the Goal Seek command, you enter a target goal amount, such as actual sales, and Excel calculates what needs to change in your worksheet to reach this goal.
- Analysis ToolPak—One of the Excel add-ins. It provides a number of analytical tools that include Exponential Smoothing, ANOVA, F-Test, Histograms, and Covariance.
- Solver—Like Goal Seek, the Solver can perform calculations to help you determine what is necessary to reach a specific goal. However, with the Goal Seek command, you can specify only one precedent, whereas the Solver can accommodate many precedents. In addition, the Solver lets you set conditions, or constraints, on the solution.

Controlling Data Entry

The Data Validation command (introduced in Excel 97) is a powerful feature for controlling data entry. The validation can take place before or after data is entered in a cell.

To use the Data Validation command, you must first select the cell (or groups of cells) to which you want to apply the validation. Using the worksheet displayed in Figure 27.1 as an example, suppose you want to restrict the dates typed in column A to the days in the month of June. Because you want to apply the validation to all cells in the column, you'd select the entire column.

After you have the cell(s) selected, choose Data, Validation. The Data Validation dialog box appears. You use the three tabs in the dialog box to establish the data entry validation: Settings, Input Message, and Error Alert. You can use these three options separately or in conjunction with one another.

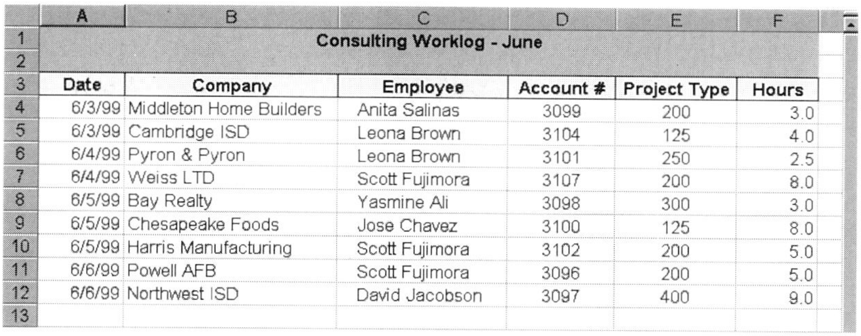

FIGURE 27.1
A list of consulting jobs performed in June.

	A	B	C	D	E	F
1	Consulting Worklog - June					
2						
3	Date	Company	Employee	Account #	Project Type	Hours
4	6/3/99	Middleton Home Builders	Anita Salinas	3099	200	3.0
5	6/3/99	Cambridge ISD	Leona Brown	3104	125	4.0
6	6/4/99	Pyron & Pyron	Leona Brown	3101	250	2.5
7	6/4/99	Weiss LTD	Scott Fujimora	3107	200	8.0
8	6/5/99	Bay Realty	Yasmine Ali	3098	300	3.0
9	6/5/99	Chesapeake Foods	Jose Chavez	3100	125	8.0
10	6/5/99	Harris Manufacturing	Scott Fujimora	3102	200	5.0
11	6/6/99	Powell AFB	Scott Fujimora	3096	200	5.0
12	6/6/99	Northwest ISD	David Jacobson	3097	400	9.0
13						

Establishing the Validation Criteria Settings

Use the Settings tab to specify the type of data a cell will accept. The options displayed on this tab change depending on what type of restriction you select. A generic message displays when the incorrect data is entered. You can create a message on the Error Alert tab that is tailored to the options you select on the Settings tab. A variety of restrictions can be placed on the data entered in a cell:

- Any Value—This is the default setting; no restrictions are placed on the entries.
- Custom—You can enter a formula to determine valid entries. The custom option must be a formula that produces a True or False result, such as—Is cell G2 greater than 50? The formula for this question is, of course, `=G2>50`.
- Date—Allows only date entries. You can specify a range of valid dates (1/1/99 through 12/31/99), or specify a set date that an entry must occur before or after (any date after 6/1/99).
- Decimal—Allows numbers with decimals. You can specify a range of numbers (10.00-10.99), or numbers that are larger or smaller than a number you specify (greater than 10.50).
- List—You can specify a list of the valid entries. The list can either be entered into the dialog box (separated by commas), or you can use a range name or cell references to identify a list that exists in a worksheet. A drop-down arrow appears, displaying the list of valid entries.
- Text Length—You can specify the number of characters for text entries. You can specify a minimum length, a maximum length, or both.
- Time—Allows only time entries. You can specify a start time, an end time, or both.
- Whole Number—Allows only numbers that are integers. You can specify a range of numbers (1–100) or numbers that are larger or smaller than a number you specify (greater than 25).

The Settings tab, shown in Figure 27.2, is where you select the type of restriction you want on the selected cell(s). In Figure 27.2, the Date restriction is selected. By default, the criteria operator is `between`, and a start date and an end date are expected. The dates you use with the `between` operator are included in the criteria, so the `between` operator is greater than or equal to the start date and less than or equal to the end date. Select the Data drop-down arrow to see other operators, such as `greater than` or `greater than or equal to`. The Ignore Blank check box allows blank entries in the cell. Clear the Ignore Blank check box to indicate that blank entries are not valid.

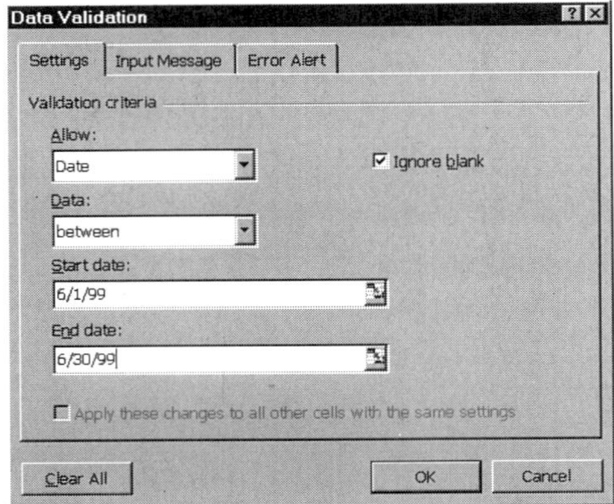

FIGURE 27.2
The options in the Data drop-down list vary depending on what restriction and operator you choose.

NOTE Specifying the type of data allowed in a cell does not change the cell formatting. You will have to apply the appropriate format to the cell. For example, choosing a date restriction does not apply a date format to the cell. Choose Format, Cells to select the desired format.

Another useful restriction is the List option. If the list of valid entries is short or won't be changing very much, you can type the list of choices directly in the Data Validation dialog box. However, if the list is long or will change regularly, it is best to create the list in a worksheet and assign a range name to the list.

Figure 27.3 shows an order form that includes a place to indicate the Item Number. To avoid mistakes in data entry, you can use the Data Validation command to identify a list of valid Item Numbers. To make this process easier to follow, the list is visible in the worksheet displayed in Figure 27.3—but the list doesn't have to be. However, it must be in the active worksheet. You cannot use a list in another worksheet.

If a list already exists in another worksheet or workbook, try using a Combo Box control to restrict data entry. This is discussed in the next section.

To use the list restriction, select the cell you want use and choose Data, Validation. On the Settings tab, choose List from the Allow drop-down box. Click in the Source drop-down box. If you have created a range name for the list, press F3 and choose the range name from the Paste Name dialog box (as shown in Figure 27.4). Otherwise, highlight the cells that compose the list directly in the worksheet. Click OK.

▶ **See** "Using Range Names in Formulas," **p. 639**

FIGURE 27.3
Use the List option to produce a drop-down list from which users can select an entry.

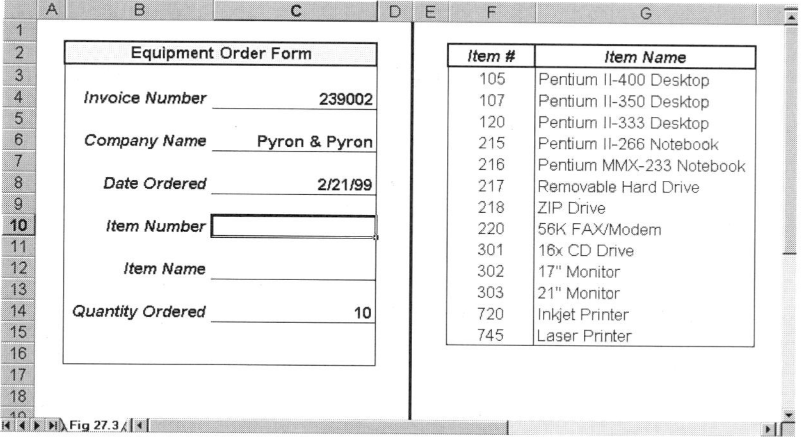

FIGURE 27.4
Using range names makes it easier to identify ranges within the active workbook.

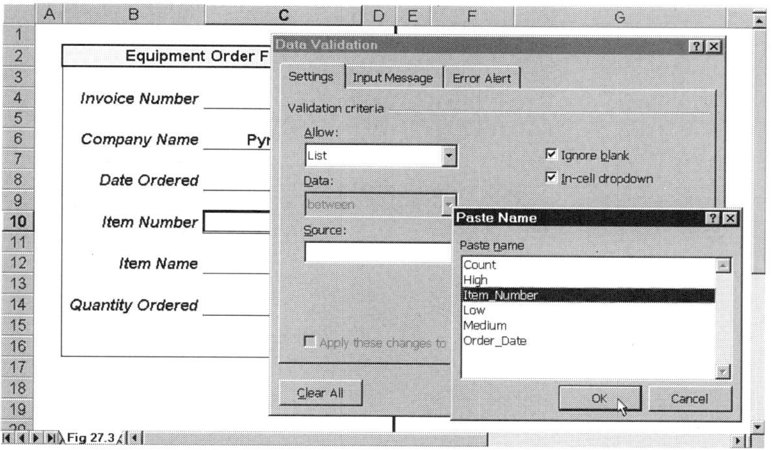

When you click the cell that contains the list restriction, a drop-down arrow appears from which you can select an entry (see Figure 27.5).

Instead of using the Data Validation command for the Item Name (refer to Figure 27.3) you can use a VLOOKUP function (discussed in "Using VLOOKUP with Lists" in Chapter 23, "Functions for Every Occasion") to automatically display the corresponding name.

Use the Input Message tab to create a message telling the user what data can be entered in a cell, before the user types it in. Creating an Input Message does not validate the entry; it merely helps the user before entering data. Select options on the Settings tab to control the data entry. Figure 27.6 shows an example of an Input Message. When the user clicks a cell that contains this data validation input message, a pop-up (similar to an attached comment) appears with the message.

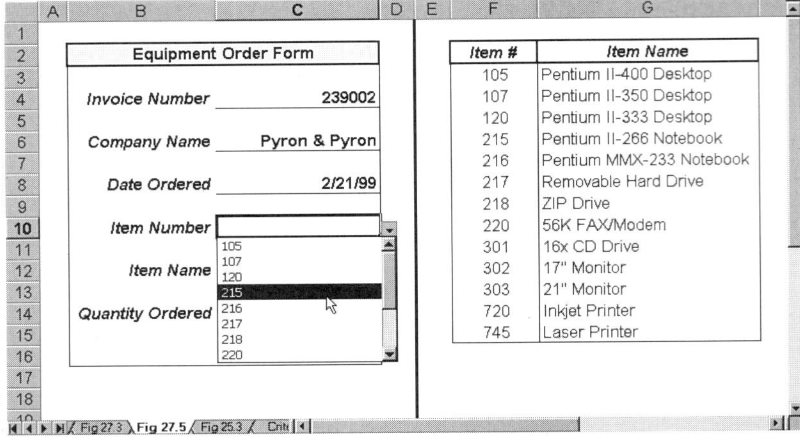

FIGURE 27.5
The order of the items in the drop-down list is the order in which they appear in the source list.

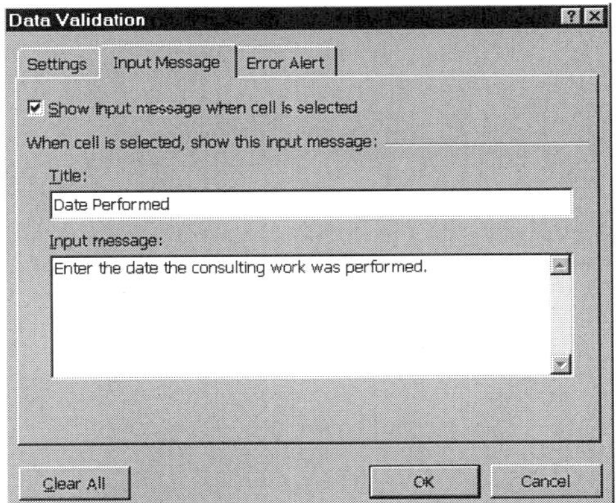

FIGURE 27.6
Use the Input Message tab to provide the user with helpful information about what data is allowed in the cell.

Use the Error Alert tab to create a custom error message that displays when incorrect data is entered in a cell. This is a very useful way to tailor messages to your users. Figure 27.7 shows the Error Alert tab of the Data Validation dialog box. You can create three types of error messages:

- Stop—This type displays the error message you create and provides the option to Retry or Cancel the entry. An entry that does not meet the validation criteria settings is not accepted.
- Warning—Although it displays the error message you create, the Warning type does allow an entry that does not meet the validation criteria settings. A message asks whether the person wants to continue and provides the options Yes, No, and Cancel; No is the default.
- Information—Like the Warning type, the Information type displays the error message you create but allows the entry. It provides the OK and Cancel buttons; OK is the default.

The Stop error message is the default message, preventing an invalid entry. The Warning and Information messages can be used to accept valid entries that are higher or lower than expected. For example, if the actual sales are a designated percentage (15%, for example) lower than the projected sales, you might want to use an Information error message to alert the person editing the worksheet.

The type is selected from the Style drop-down box. In addition to the different behavior of the error messages, three distinct symbols appear in the dialog box to alert readers as to the type of dialog box they are viewing.

Regardless of the type you select, you can enter a title and message for the error you want to display. The Title field in this dialog box is where you specify the title of the error message box that displays to the user.

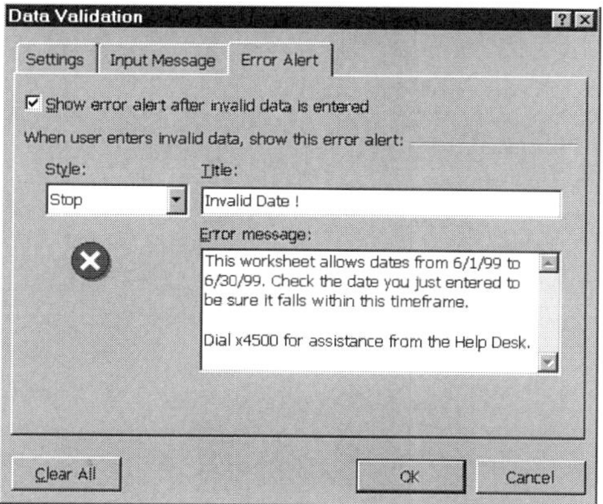

FIGURE 27.7
Give the user suggestions on how to resolve the error.

Figure 27.8 shows how the Error Alert appears to a user. The Retry button highlights the cell and provides an opportunity to type another entry. The Cancel button clears the entry.

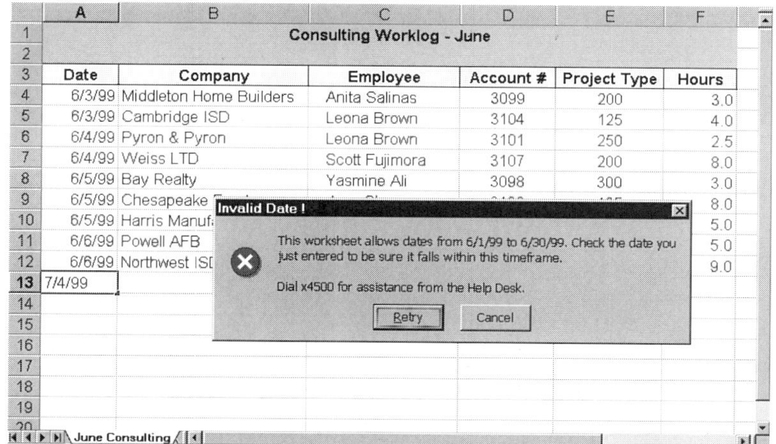

FIGURE 27.8
The Error Alert message is similar to other Windows Caution/Error messages.

Circling Invalid Entries

To complement the Warning and Information error message options in the Data Validation dialog box, you can have Excel draw circles around invalid entries in the worksheet. To use this feature, you must establish Data Validation criteria in the worksheet cells, as described in the previous sections.

To draw circles around cells in the worksheet that do not match the data validation criteria, you need to display the Auditing toolbar. This toolbar can be accessed using only the Tools, Auditing, Show Auditing Toolbar command; it is not listed, as are the other Excel toolbars, when you right-click a toolbar. To draw the circles, click the Circle Invalid Data button on the Auditing toolbar. Red circles appear around cells that have Data Validation applied, where the entry does not match the validation criteria. You can remove the circles by selecting the Clear Validation Circles button on the Auditing toolbar.

Using Worksheet Controls to Control Data Entry

You can also use *controls* like combo boxes to restrict data entry. Unlike the List option in the Data Validation command, you are not limited to where the source of valid entries is stored. The source can be in the active worksheet, in another worksheet in the active workbook, or in another workbook entirely.

To add a Combo Box control to a worksheet, right-click any toolbar and click Forms to display the Forms toolbar. Then click the Combo Box button (the mouse pointer changes into a crosshair) and drag in the worksheet to create a Combo Box control. Form controls don't fit into worksheet cells. They float on top of the worksheet, like text boxes. You can move and resize the Combo Box controls the same as you would a text box or embedded chart. To select a control and not activate it, press Ctrl as you click the control. Otherwise, the control will behave as it is designed; for example, a combo box activates the drop-down list.

To see a list appear when the combo box is clicked, you have to create the list and tell the control where to find the list. The list can be located in one of three places: in the same worksheet, in a separate worksheet in the same workbook, or in a completely different workbook.

Linking the Combo Box list with the control is accomplished by formatting the control. You can either right-click the Combo Box control and choose Format Control from the shortcut menu, or select the control (by pressing Ctrl and clicking the control) and choose Control from the Format menu. The Format Control dialog box appears.

In the Format Control dialog box, click the Control tab. Two text boxes that you need to use are available on this tab: Input Range and Drop-Down Lines. Click to place the flashing cursor in the Input Range text box. This is where you identify the cells that contain the Combo Box list. Highlight the cells that compose your list, making sure you don't highlight any list headings or extra cells. The cell references for the list appear in the Input Range text box.

If you want a specific number of lines to appear when you click the Combo Box control, change the number in the Drop-Down Lines text box. You can also have the Combo Box control appear three-dimensional by selecting the 3D Shading check box. After you've made these changes, click OK. Now when you click the combo box in the worksheet, you can select an item from the list.

To learn more about using controls in worksheets, such as performing calculations using the data selected from a control or adding option or spinner buttons to your worksheets, see Chapter 21, "Taking Control of Excel Templates."

▶ **See** "Designing Form Templates," **p. 600**

Using Data Tables for What-If Analysis

Businesses routinely ask the question, "What if ...?" For example, "What if we increase production? What if the return on our investment is higher than expected? What if we cut costs?" Many tools in Excel help analyze the impact of these what-if questions—one of these tools is the *data table.*

Consider the calculation in Figure 27.9. It shows a future value calculation of a monthly investment of $200 at 6.5% interest over a 10-year period. This calculation has three variables you can change: interest rate, timeframe, and contribution. When you change one of these variables, the future value is recalculated.

NOTE Financial functions require a negative number to record a debit. In the future value calculation in Figure 27.9, the contribution needs to be a negative number. The contribution is actually the payment (PMT) argument of the `FV` function: `=FV(RATE,NPER,PMT)`. Financial functions are explained in more detail in the "Financial Functions" section in Chapter 23.

FIGURE 27.9
Place labels next to the cells to identify what component of the formula they compose.

	A	B	C	D	E	F	G	H
1	Investment Plan							
2								
3	Interest Rate	6.50%	annual %					
4	Timeframe	10	years					
5	Contribution	-$200	dollars per month					
6								
7	Future Value	$33,680.63	based on the above assumptions					
8								
9								
10								
11								

Suppose you want to know how much the future value will be for different timeframes. Although you can change the timeframe and note the revised future value, that isn't the best approach to use for making comparisons of multiple timeframes. Instead, set up a data table like the one shown in Figure 27.10. When you set up a *data table*, you see the calculated results side by side. Because you are displaying multiple results for one of the variables—namely, timeframe—you will need to alter only one of the other variables (interest rate or contribution) to see the revised future value results.

FIGURE 27.10
A one-variable, column-oriented data table.

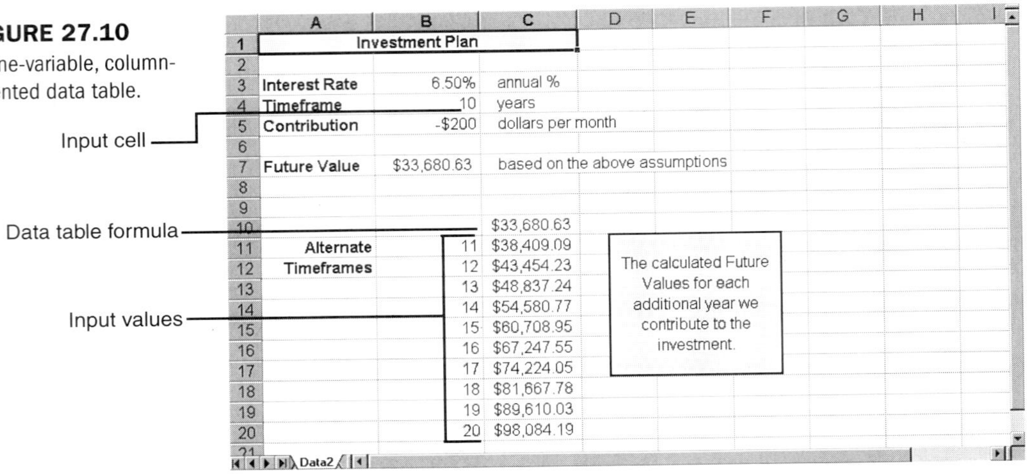

	A	B	C	D
1	Investment Plan			
2				
3	Interest Rate	6.50%	annual %	
4	Timeframe	10	years	
5	Contribution	-$200	dollars per month	
6				
7	Future Value	$33,680.63	based on the above assumptions	
8				
9				
10			$33,680.63	
11	Alternate	11	$38,409.09	
12	Timeframes	12	$43,454.23	The calculated Future Values for each additional year we contribute to the investment.
13		13	$48,837.24	
14		14	$54,580.77	
15		15	$60,708.95	
16		16	$67,247.55	
17		17	$74,224.05	
18		18	$81,667.78	
19		19	$89,610.03	
20		20	$98,084.19	

Input cell

Data table formula

Input values

You can create two types of data tables in Excel: one that displays the calculations based on one variable, or one that displays the calculations based on two variables. To create these two types of data tables, you need to follow specific steps. These steps are discussed in the next few sections.

However, before you create a data table, it's useful to understand these terms:

- Input cell—The cell in the worksheet that contains the variable you want to display in the data table. In Figure 27.10, the input cell is the timeframe in cell B4.
- Input values—The alternative values you want to use in the data table. In Figure 27.10, the input values are the other timeframes in cells B11:B20.
- Data table formula—The formula you want to calculate for each of the Input Values. In Figure 27.10 the formula is entered in cell C10. In this example, this is the same formula that is being calculated in cell B7. Data tables require that the formula be adjacent to the table.

Creating One-Variable Data Tables

To create a data table, you need to start by creating a worksheet like the one shown in Figure 27.9, which contains the initial data and calculation you want to appear in the data table. Properly labeling and entering of the variables for the formula you are calculating will make it easier to create the data table.

One-variable data tables can be either *column-oriented* or *row-oriented*; that is, the input variables can be listed down one column or across one row. After you've typed in the list of input values in a column or row, you need to enter the appropriate formula. The data table formula is always offset from the cell containing the first input value:

> If the input values are listed down a column, type the formula you want calculated one row up and one cell to the right of the first input value.

If the input values are listed across a row, type the formula you want calculated one cell down and one column to the left of the first input value.

After you have created the worksheet, entered the input values, and created the table formula, you're ready to calculate the results for each input value. Select the cells that compose the table. In Figure 27.11, that would be cells B10:C20. Then choose Data, Table; the Table dialog box appears. If the data table is column-oriented, click in the Column Input Cell text box. If the data table is row-oriented, click in the Row Input Cell text box. Then click the input cell in the worksheet (see Figure 27.11). The cell reference appears as an absolute cell reference.

▶ **See** "Using Absolute Cell References in Formulas," **p. 634**

FIGURE 27.11
The text box you select in the Table dialog box depends on the orientation of your data table.

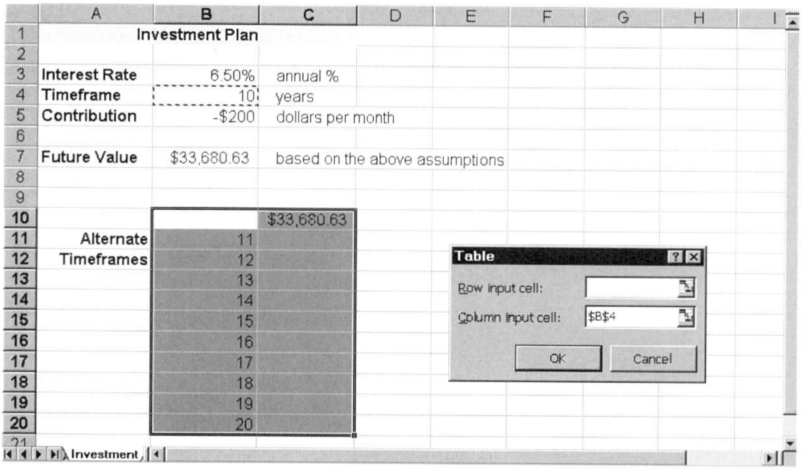

	A	B	C	D
1		Investment Plan		
2				
3	Interest Rate	6.50%	annual %	
4	Timeframe	10	years	
5	Contribution	-$200	dollars per month	
6				
7	Future Value	$33,680.63	based on the above assumptions	
8				
9				
10			$33,680.63	
11	Alternate	11		
12	Timeframes	12		
13		13		
14		14		
15		15		
16		16		
17		17		
18		18		
19		19		
20		20		

Table
Row input cell:
Column input cell: $B$4
OK Cancel

Investment

When you click OK, the formula is calculated for each input value, and the data table is completed. When you change one of the other formula variables (in this example, Interest Rate or Contribution), the calculated results are automatically updated.

NOTE The calculations in the table are part of an array. Although you can change one of the input values, you cannot delete an individual calculated result in the table. You must clear all calculated values. Select only the calculated values and choose Edit, Clear, Contents. If you select the input values, you'll be clearing the entire data table.

▶ **See** "Exploring the Power of Array Formulas," **p. 661**

The advantages to using a data table are that they make it easier and quicker to create these types of tables, and if you change the data table formula (cell C10 in Figure 27.11), all the results in the table immediately update. If you attempt to create a table by entering a formula and copying it, you will need to design the original formula so that it can be copied; if you change the formula, you will have to copy the revised formula to the cells that comprise your table.

In a small table, there won't be much difference in the effort. But in a large table or in a two-variable table, it requires a significant amount of additional effort. The main function of data tables is to save you the trouble of designing the complex formulas, which must use absolute and mixed references in order to be copied.

Creating Two-Variable Data Tables

You can also create a two-variable data table. Consider the table in Figure 27.12. It contains calculations based on two variables—timeframes and contributions. With this type of table, the data table formula is always placed at the intersection of the two variables.

FIGURE 27.12

The formula is calculated for the input values at the intersection of each row and column.

	A	B	C	D	E	F	G
1	Investment Plan						
2							
3	Interest Rate	6.50%	annual %				
4	Timeframe	10	years				
5	Contribution	-$200	dollars per month				
6							
7	Future Value	$33,680.63	based on the above assumptions				
8							
9				Alternative Contributions			
10	(formula)	$33,680.63	-$100	-$150	-$200	-$250	-$300
11		11	$19,204.55	$28,806.82	$38,409.09	$48,011.36	$57,613.64
12	Alternate	12	$21,727.11	$32,590.67	$43,454.23	$54,317.78	$65,181.34
13	Timeframes	13	$24,418.62	$36,627.93	$48,837.24	$61,046.55	$73,255.87
14		14	$27,290.39	$40,935.58	$54,580.77	$68,225.96	$81,871.16
15		15	$30,354.48	$45,531.72	$60,708.95	$75,886.19	$91,063.43
16		16	$33,623.78	$50,435.66	$67,247.55	$84,059.44	$100,871.33
17		17	$37,112.03	$55,668.04	$74,224.05	$92,780.06	$111,336.08
18		18	$40,833.89	$61,250.84	$81,667.78	$102,084.73	$122,501.67
19		19	$44,805.01	$67,207.52	$89,610.03	$112,012.54	$134,415.04
20		20	$49,042.09	$73,563.14	$98,084.19	$122,605.23	$147,126.28

Data Table

To create a two-variable data table, set up the worksheet with necessary data, enter in the column and row input values, and create the table formula. Then select the cells that compose the table. In Figure 27.12, the cells are B10:G20. Then choose Data, Table; the Table dialog box appears. With the flashing cursor in the Row Input Cell text box, click the input cell for the row variable. Then click in the Column Input Cell text box and click the cell input for the column variable. Figure 27.13 shows the completed dialog box.

When you click OK, the formula is calculated for the intersection of each pair of input values. When you change the third formula variable (Interest Rate), the calculated results are automatically updated.

You can change the input values in the data table to calculate different results. For the table shown in Figure 27.13, you could change the timeframes to every other year or the contribution to reflect $25 increments. If you have created a very large table, use the Fill Handle to complete the series of new input values.

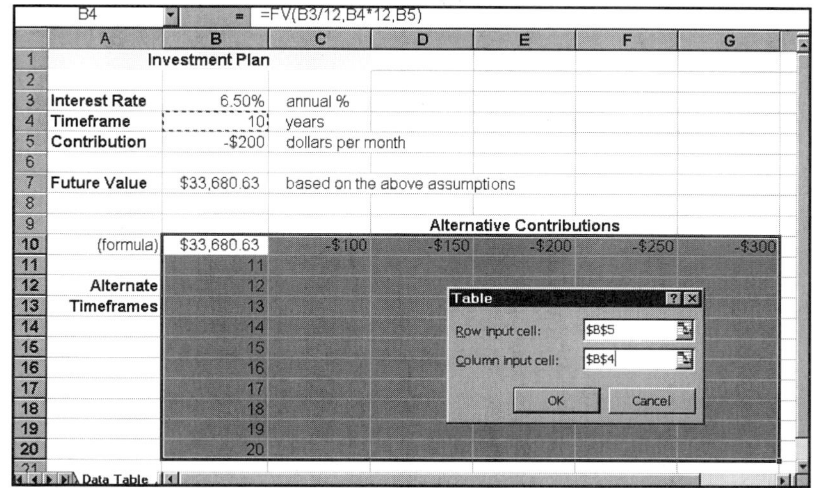

FIGURE 27.13
Because two variables are used, the table formula is entered at the intersection of the row and column input values.

You could, in effect, create a three-variable data table by adding a Combo Box drop-down list for the third variable (in this case, Interest Rate). By placing a text box that contains the text "Click here to choose a different interest rate" next to the Combo Box drop-down list, the worksheet becomes easier for even inexperienced users to use.

Creating and Managing Scenarios

A *scenario* is nothing more than a group of values that are associated with certain worksheet cells. By storing the values in a scenario instead of in the cells themselves, you are able to

- Change the cells' values on the worksheet, and subsequently recall the values that you stored in the scenario.
- Define several scenarios, each with a different set of values for the cells. Then switch between the scenarios to see their different effects on dependent formulas, one scenario at a time.
- Summarize multiple scenarios, including the resulting values of dependent formulas, in a report or in a PivotTable.
- Employ various scenario management tools, such as tracking changes that have been made to scenarios and merging scenarios from different worksheets into one location.

NOTE Scenarios are worksheet specific. They are saved as a part of the workbook.

Chapter 23 described the meaning and use of the NPV (Net Present Value) function by means of an analysis of cash flows from an investment. That analysis is repeated here in Figure 27.14; the formula calculating the NPV appears in the Formula bar.

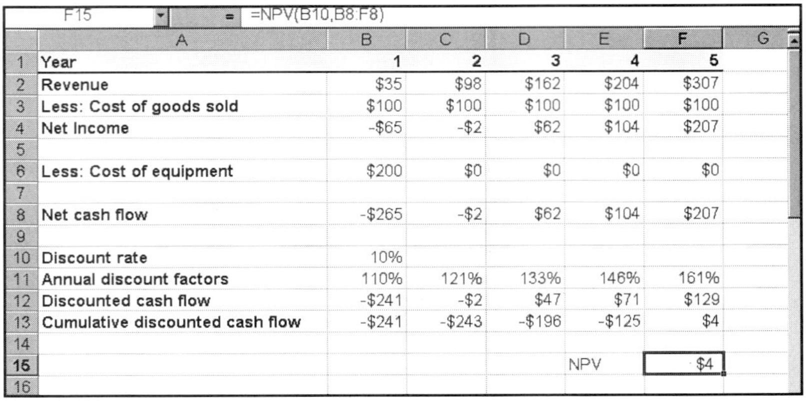

FIGURE 27.14
The NPV for the investment depends on various assumptions, including the sales dollar amounts and the discount factor.

F15 = =NPV(B10,B8:F8)

	A	B	C	D	E	F	G
1	Year	1	2	3	4	5	
2	Revenue	$35	$98	$162	$204	$307	
3	Less: Cost of goods sold	$100	$100	$100	$100	$100	
4	Net Income	-$65	-$2	$62	$104	$207	
5							
6	Less: Cost of equipment	$200	$0	$0	$0	$0	
7							
8	Net cash flow	-$265	-$2	$62	$104	$207	
9							
10	Discount rate	10%					
11	Annual discount factors	110%	121%	133%	146%	161%	
12	Discounted cash flow	-$241	-$2	$47	$71	$129	
13	Cumulative discounted cash flow	-$241	-$243	-$196	-$125	$4	
14							
15					NPV	$4	
16							

Suppose that you wanted to check the NPV of this investment opportunity under different conditions—for example, with a different discount factor or with different projections for annual sales revenue. The Scenario Manager is an ideal tool for this sort of analysis.

Creating Scenarios

Begin with the existing values shown previously in Figure 27.14. Perhaps they represent the initial estimate. Before you create scenarios with other values, it's important that you save the initial or original settings—if you don't, you will lose them when you apply a scenario containing different values. Using the data shown in Figure 27.14 as an example, here's how to set up the scenario.

Select the cells you want to change with each new scenario. If necessary, use the Ctrl key to select cells that are not adjacent to one another. In Figure 27.14, for example, cells B2:F2 and then (using the Ctrl key) cell B10 would be selected. After you have the cells selected, choose Tools, Scenarios. The Scenario Manager dialog box appears, as shown in Figure 27.15.

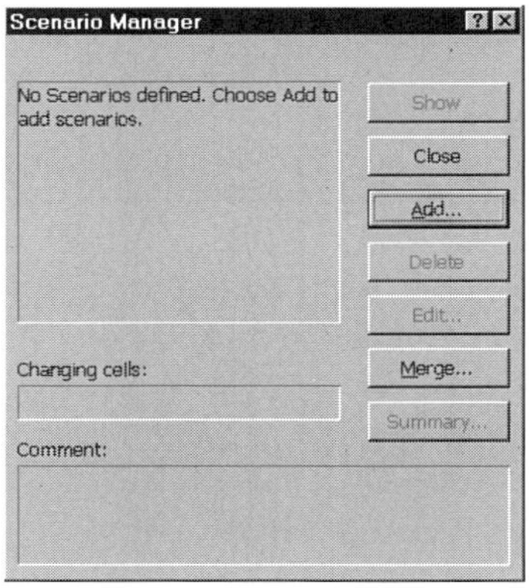

FIGURE 27.15
Until at least one scenario is defined on the active worksheet, you can only Close the dialog box, Add a scenario, or Merge other scenarios.

Scenario Manager

No Scenarios defined. Choose Add to add scenarios.

Show
Close
Add...
Delete
Edit...
Merge...
Summary...

Changing cells:

Comment:

Choose Add to create a new scenario. When you do so, the Edit Scenario dialog box appears, as shown in Figure 27.16.

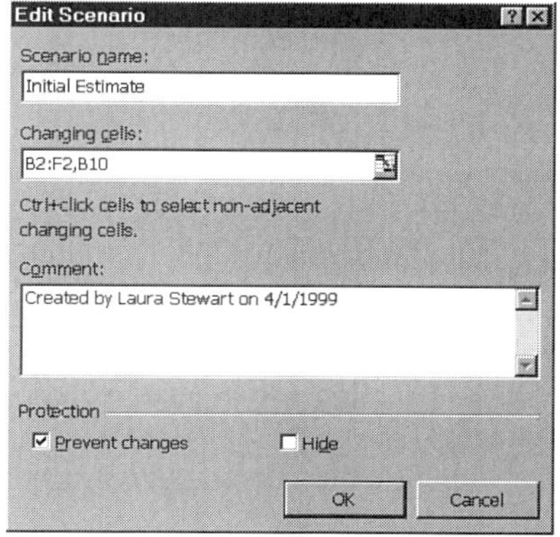

FIGURE 27.16
If you choose to protect or to hide a scenario, you must then choose Tools, Protection, Protect Sheet, and check Prevent Changes.

In the Scenario Name edit box, enter a descriptive name, such as Initial Estimate. When you later retrieve a scenario, you select it by the name you give it here.

Because you began by selecting B2:F2 and B10, these cell references appear in the Changing Cells edit box. If you selected the incorrect cells, use this edit box to modify your selection. The term "changing cells" refers to the cells in the worksheet whose values are saved in the scenario. Because the values of the cells are usually changed when you switch from scenario to scenario, they are called *changing cells*. For consistency, this term is also used by the Goal Seek tool and by the Solver tool (both are discussed later in this chapter).

The Comment typically displays the name of the person creating the scenario and the date it was created. This information is handy when you later need to edit a scenario or manage scenarios created by other people. Unless this data is not accurate or you want to supplement the information, it's a good idea to keep the default comment. The name that appears in the comment comes directly from the User Name text box on the General tab of the Options dialog box (Tools, Options). If this does not reflect your name, change the comment.

Protecting a scenario makes it impossible to modify the values of its changing cells after you have finished defining it. You and other users can view the scenario but cannot modify it. Hiding a scenario prevents anyone from viewing it—and therefore, from modifying it. However, neither of these choices has any effect until the worksheet that contains the scenario has been protected, perhaps with a password. To modify the changing cells in a protected scenario or to view a hidden scenario, first unprotect its worksheet (Tools, Protection, Unprotect Sheet).

When you have finished entering information in the Add Scenario dialog box, choose OK. The Scenario Values dialog box appears as shown in Figure 27.17.

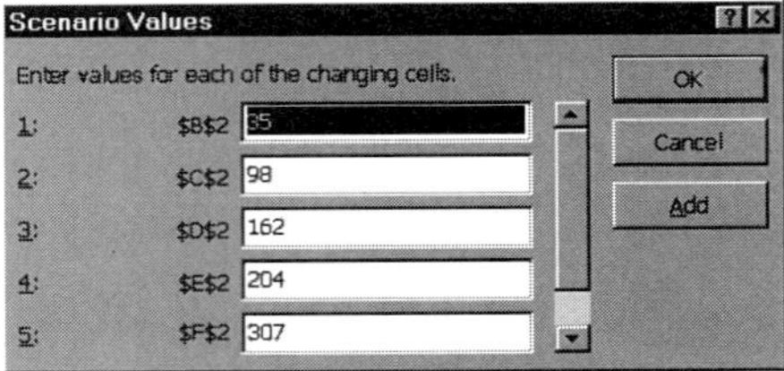

FIGURE 27.17
If you have identified more than five changing cells, use the scrollbar to display them.

Because you're simply capturing a scenario for the current values, you accept the values shown for the changing cells by clicking OK.

When you create additional scenarios, this dialog box (Add Values) is where you change these values. Choosing Add takes you back to the Scenario Name dialog box (refer to Figure 27.16), where you can create additional scenarios. When you finish creating all the scenarios you need, choose OK in this dialog box to return to the Scenario Manager dialog box (refer to Figure 27.15).

At this point, you would define other scenarios, perhaps one for a conservative estimate and another for an optimistic estimate. A conservative estimate would probably reduce the assumed revenues in B2:F2 to very pessimistic values, and it might increase the discount factor in B10 so that competing investment alternatives become more attractive.

After the alternative scenarios are defined, it's very easy to switch among them from the Scenario Manager dialog box (see Figure 27.18).

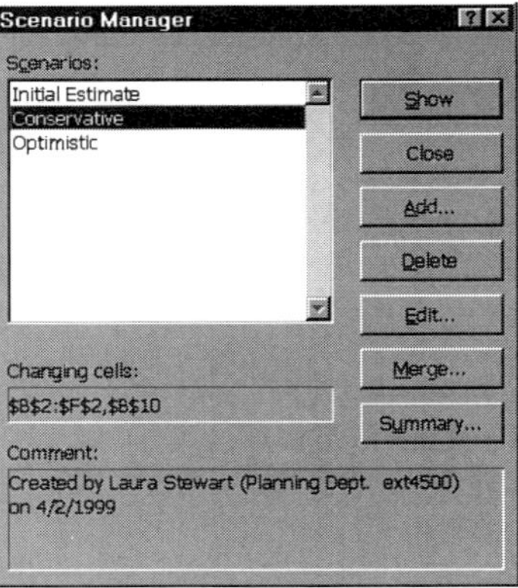

FIGURE 27.18
A list of all the scenarios in the active worksheet.

To use a particular scenario, access the Scenario Manager dialog box (Tools, Scenarios). Then from the Scenarios list box, click a defined scenario name and choose Show. The values for the changing cells that are associated with that scenario are placed into their worksheet cells, and the dependent formulas recalculate accordingly.

When you choose the Close button in the Scenario Manager dialog box, it does not remove the scenario applied to your worksheet. To return to the original values, you must apply that scenario containing the original values—the first scenario you created.

The Conservative scenario appears in Figure 27.19; contrast it with Figure 27.14. Notice, in particular, the effect on the NPV in cell F15: It recalculates from $4 in the Initial Estimate scenario to -$219 in the Conservative scenario.

FIGURE 27.19
Scenarios don't have to contain only numeric values; they can also contain text.

F15 = =NPV(B10,B8:F8)

	A	B	C	D	E	F	G
1	Year	1	2	3	4	5	
2	Revenue	$31	$75	$99	$123	$145	
3	Less: Cost of goods sold	$100	$100	$100	$100	$100	
4	Net Income	-$69	-$25	-$1	$23	$45	
5							
6	Less: Cost of equipment	$200	$0	$0	$0	$0	
7							
8	Net cash flow	-$269	-$25	-$1	$23	$45	
9							
10	Discount rate	14%					
11	Annual discount factors	114%	130%	148%	169%	193%	
12	Discounted cash flow	-$236	-$19	-$1	$14	$23	
13	Cumulative discounted cash flow	-$236	-$255	-$256	-$242	-$219	
14							
15					NPV	($219)	
16							

Comparing Scenario Results

One of the ideas behind scenarios is that they enable you to change several values on a worksheet in one stroke. Because the alternative values of the changing cells are stored in scenarios, they are out of the way, yet immediately accessible.

Without scenarios, it would be necessary to store all the information shown in Figure 27.19 three times, each time using a different set of values for the changing cells. You might then store the results of using each set of values on a different worksheet. This is a wasteful and inconvenient way to store and switch between different sets of input assumptions.

Although the scenario approach has obvious benefits, the drawback is that you can't view the results of all defined scenarios simultaneously. However, you can create a scenario summary:

1. With a worksheet active that contains scenarios, choose Tools, Scenarios to open the Scenario Manager dialog box.
2. Choose Summary. The Scenario Summary dialog box appears, as shown in Figure 27.20.
3. Select either Scenario Summary or Scenario PivotTable.
4. Excel proposes one or more cells to use as result cells. The result cells are cells containing formulas that change when each scenario is applied to the worksheet; they are dependent on the changing cells you selected to create the scenarios. You can accept the cells Excel proposes or select a different group of cells. In this example, we need to add the NPV cell to the result cells. Hold down the Ctrl key as you click additional cells.
5. After you have the results selected, choose OK.

If you choose a Scenario PivotTable in the Scenario Summary dialog box, Excel creates a PivotTable on a new sheet that shows the relationships between each scenario's changing cell values and its result cell values (see Figure 27.21). The last column is the NPV.

FIGURE 27.20
The Scenario Summary dialog box enables you to choose between a Scenario Summary and a Scenario PivotTable.

F13 = =SUM($B$12:B$12)

	A	B	C	D	E	F
1	Year		2	3	4	5
2	Revenue		$75	$99	$123	$145
3	Less: Cost of		$100	$100	$100	$100
4	Net Income		-$25	-$1	$23	$45
5						
6	Less: Cost of		$0	$0	$0	$0
7						
8	Net cash flow		-$25	-$1	$23	$45
9						
10	Discount rate					
11	Annual discount factors	114%	130%	148%	169%	193%
12	Discounted cash flow	-$236	-$19	-$1	$14	$23
13	Cumulative discounted cash flow	-$236	-$255	-$256	-$242	-$219
14						
15					NPV	($219)
16						

Scenario Summary
Report type
Scenario summary
Scenario PivotTable
Result cells:
B13,C13,D13,E13,F13
OK
Cancel

FIGURE 27.21
In a Scenario PivotTable, you can set options, such as number formats, after the PivotTable is created.

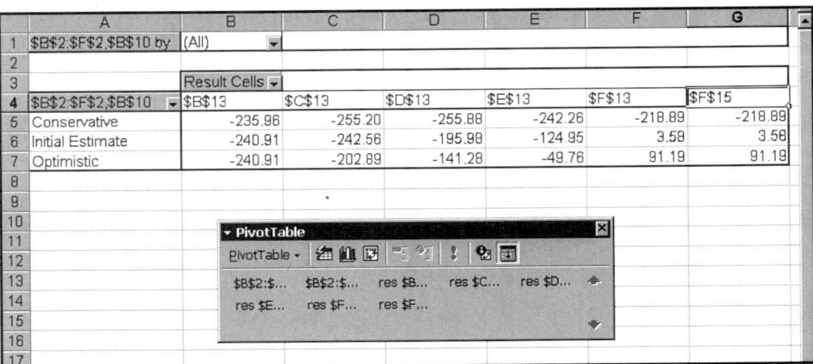

	A	B	C	D	E	F	G
1	$B$2:$F$2,$B$10 by	(All)					
2							
3		Result Cells					
4	$B$2:$F$2,$B$10	$B$13	$C$13	$D$13	$E$13	$F$13	$F$15
5	Conservative	-235.96	-255.20	-255.88	-242.26	-218.89	-218.89
6	Initial Estimate	-240.91	-242.56	-195.98	-124.95	3.58	3.58
7	Optimistic	-240.91	-202.89	-141.28	-49.76	91.19	91.19

Notice the following aspects of the PivotTable shown in Figure 27.21:

- The result cells are shown as items in the Column field.
- Each scenario is shown as a different item in the Row field. The collective address of the changing cells is used as the Row field's name.
- The original number formats in the PivotTable's data source are not preserved in the PivotTable itself.

Another aspect of the PivotTable, although not visible in Figure 27.21, is that each result cell is a different Data field. The creator of each scenario is a different item in the Page field. And, if your different scenarios use different sets of changing cells, each set of changing cells is represented in a different Row field. Each Row field then has its own set of items.

You can, as usual, use the controls on the PivotTable toolbar to modify the PivotTable's layout and format so that it's easier to interpret and use. However, you cannot refresh the PivotTable's data cache. If your scenarios change, you need to create a new Scenario PivotTable to summarize their results correctly.

▶ **See** "Unlocking the Power of PivotTables and PivotCharts," **p. 797**

If you prefer to create a Scenario Summary, choose that option in the Scenario Summary dialog box. You are again asked to identify the result cells. An example of the resulting report appears in Figure 27.22.

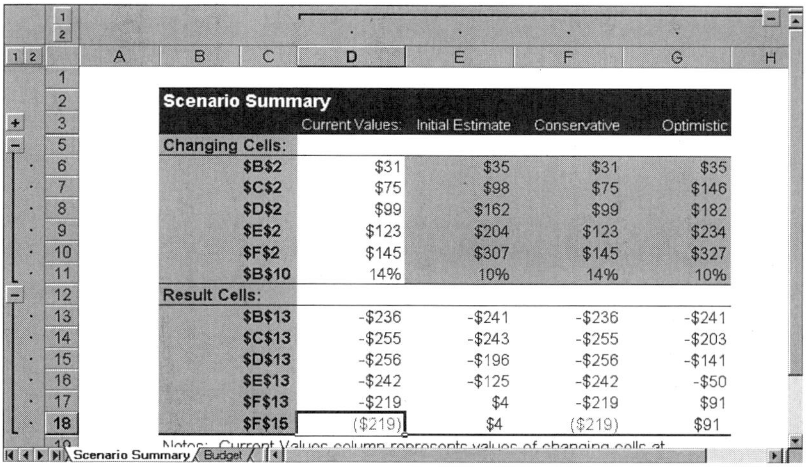

FIGURE 27.22
Use the Outline buttons to group or ungroup levels of the Scenario Summary.

Scenario Summary	Current Values:	Initial Estimate	Conservative	Optimistic
Changing Cells:				
$B$2	$31	$35	$31	$35
$C$2	$75	$98	$75	$146
$D$2	$99	$162	$99	$182
$E$2	$123	$204	$123	$234
$F$2	$145	$307	$145	$327
$B$10	14%	10%	14%	10%
Result Cells:				
$B$13	-$236	-$241	-$236	-$241
$C$13	-$255	-$243	-$255	-$203
$D$13	-$256	-$196	-$256	-$141
$E$13	-$242	-$125	-$242	-$50
$F$13	-$219	$4	-$219	$91
$F$15	($219)	$4	($219)	$91

Scenario Summary / Budget

Using either the Scenario Summary or the Scenario PivotTable, you can judge the sensitivity of the result cells to changes in the input assumptions—that is, in the changing cells.

You can also use this information to evaluate how well you have specified the values of the changing cells. For example, if you find a wildly aberrant result cell for a particular scenario, that's a good clue that the changing cells for that scenario have unrealistic values. One way to obtain a more realistic value for a changing cell is to use Goal Seek.

Exploring Goal Seek

The fundamental approach taken by any spreadsheet application is to apply input values to formulas: You supply an input value and a formula, and the application supplies the result of the formula. Goal Seek turns this sequence around. By using Goal Seek, you specify the formula and its result, and Excel supplies the input value.

Suppose that you have $1,000, and you wonder how long it would take to turn it into $1,200 at a 6% compound annual interest rate. You can manually predict the goal by entering the necessary information into a worksheet, as shown in Figure 27.23.

B3 = =B1*(1+B2)^B4

	A	B	C	D	E	F	G	H
1	Starting Principle	$ 1,000						
2	Annual Interest Rate	6%						
3	Goal	$ 1,226						
4	Years to Goal	3.5						
5								
6								
7								

FIGURE 27.23
Setting up a simple Goal Seek example.

Cell B1 contains the $1,000 value that you have at present; B2 contains the 6% interest rate, and B4 contains your guess as to the length of time needed to earn $200 in interest. Cell B3 contains the formula:

```
=B1*(1+B2)^B4
```

This formula returns the result of earning 6% on an original investment of $1,000 for as many years as are entered in cell B4. When you try out different values in B4, the goal in B3 changes. You continue trying out values in B4 until you close in on $1,200 in cell B3. This is the essence of goal seeking.

However, it's a lot faster and usually more accurate to use Excel's Goal Seek tool. To use the Goal Seek command, select the cell containing the formula and choose Tools, Goal Seek. The Goal Seek dialog box appears (see Figure 27.24). The following are the three parts of the Goal Seek command:

- Set Cell—Select the cell that is to show the target or goal. This cell must contain a formula. In our example, this is cell B3, the Goal formula.
- To Value—Type the goal, target, or end result that you want to achieve—for example, $1,200.
- By Changing Cell—Select the cell containing the value that you want to adjust to reach the goal you've specified. The Years to Goal, cell B4, is the value that will be changed.

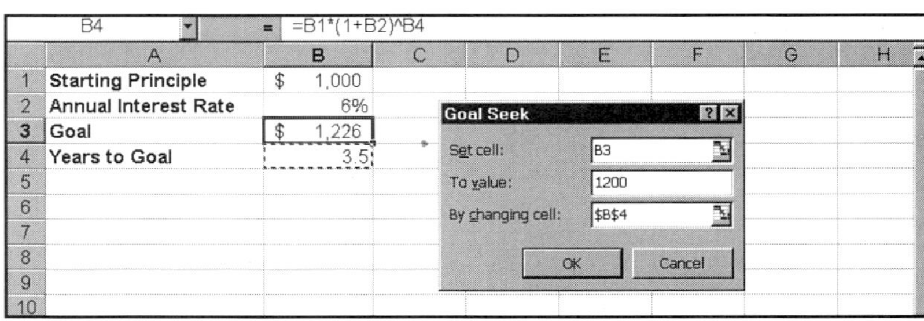

FIGURE 27.24
The Goal Seek dialog box requires three entries.

Goal Seek then iterates through different values in cell B4 until cell B3 contains the value of 1200.

For some formulas, Goal Seek might encounter difficulty in reaching the solution that you specify. For example, if you were to specify -1200, instead of 1200, Goal Seek would be unable to reach a solution.

TIP The default number of iterations for Goal Seek is 100. The default maximum change per iteration is 0.0001. Sometimes Goal Seek needs additional iterations or a smaller maximum change number to solve the problem. You can change these defaults by choosing Tools, Options, and selecting the Calculation tab. Increase the value shown in the Maximum Iterations edit box or lower the value shown in the Maximum Change edit box.

Goal Seek is more valuable when given more complicated problems to solve. Consider the commission and bonus rate worksheet shown in Figure 27.25. The commission calculations in column C are the result of multiplying the actual sales for each sales rep by the commission rate in cell B16. The bonus calculations are based on the actual sales and the level achieved in the bonus table. This calculation uses the `VLOOKUP` function.

▶ **See** "Using `VLOOKUP` with Lists," **p. 686**

Suppose Victoria wanted her total compensation to be $4,000. This problem is complicated by the fact that both the commissions and the bonus amount make up the total compensation. However, these items are tied to actual sales. Therefore, the question is—What actual sales would she need to reach this goal?

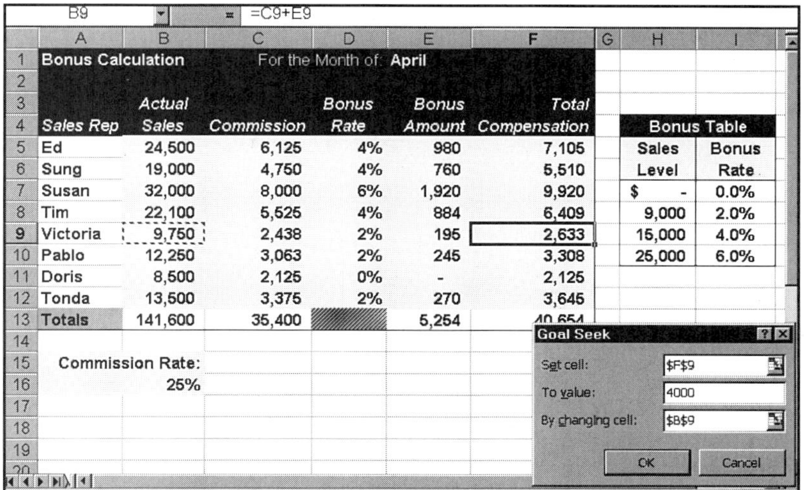

FIGURE 27.25
The goal is to have Victoria's total earnings equal $4,000.

Remember, you need to identify three cells with a Goal Seek: the Set Cell (the goal cell which contains a formula), the To Value (the goal or the end result you want to achieve), and the By Changing Cell (the one cell you want Goal Seek to change in the worksheet to reach the goal). In this example, the Set Cell is cell F9 (Victoria's total compensation); the To Value is $4,000; and the By Changing Cell is cell B9 (Victoria's actual sales). Goal Seek will iterate through the actual sales until the combination of the commission and bonus amount reach $4,000.

The investment analysis discussed in "Creating Scenarios" earlier in the chapter and shown in Figure 27.26 presents a more difficult problem. The Initial Estimate scenario resulted in an NPV (Net Present Value) of $4, achieved during the fifth year of the investment. In other words, the break-even point—the date when you have recouped the original investment and subsequent expenses—occurs during Year 5. The cumulative discounted cash flow amount turns from negative to positive in Year 5 (see row 13 in Figure 27.26). However, suppose you need to break even during Year 4 instead of Year 5.

FIGURE 27.26
The goal is to have a positive number appear in cell E13.

F15 = =NPV(B10,B8:F8)

	A	B	C	D	E	F	G
1	**Year**	**1**	**2**	**3**	**4**	**5**	
2	**Revenue**	$35	$98	$162	$204	$307	
3	**Less: Cost of goods sold**	$100	$100	$100	$100	$100	
4	**Net Income**	-$65	-$2	$62	$104	$207	
5							
6	**Less: Cost of equipment**	$200	$0	$0	$0	$0	
7							
8	**Net cash flow**	-$265	-$2	$62	$104	$207	
9							
10	**Discount rate**	10%					
11	**Annual discount factors**	110%	121%	133%	146%	161%	
12	**Discounted cash flow**	-$241	-$2	$47	$71	$129	
13	**Cumulative discounted cash flow**	-$241	-$243	-$196	-$125	$4	
14							
15					NPV	$4	
16							
17							
18							

One way to break even in Year 4 is to increase your revenues during the first four years. How much of an increase would you need?

It's possible that the best way to answer this question is to use another Excel tool, the Solver, which is covered in detail later in this chapter. One reason is that Goal Seek lets you specify one changing cell only, but the Solver lets you specify multiple changing cells. However, a way exists to use Goal Seek on this problem, and you might want to do so for a preliminary analysis or because it's desirable to change only one cell.

In this example, the Set Cell is the cumulative discounted cash flow in Year 4 and the To Value is $0. The By Changing Cell is where things get complicated. Goal Seek allows you to change only one cell to determine the goal. We know that an increase in revenues will provide us with the desired results. It would be artificial to simply change the revenues in one year; each of the yearly revenues needs to change. To accomplish this, we need to tie the revenue numbers together, by creating formulas that link the yearly revenues back to the revenues for Year 1. By taking the ratio of change between the years and using that ratio in a formula, we can create the necessary links to use Goal Seek. For example, Year 2 revenue divided by Year 1 revenue results in the ratio of increase between Years 1 and 2. That ratio multiplied by whatever the revenue is in Year 1 will generate the revenue for Year 2. Likewise, the Year 3 revenue divided by Year 2 revenue results in the ratio of increase between Years 2 and 3. That ratio multiplied by whatever the revenue is in Year 2 will generate the revenue for Year 3. The end result is that

Goal Seek can use the Year 1 revenue for the By Changing Cell because the revenues for the other years are indirectly linked to the Year 1 revenue.

To use Goal Seek in this example, follow these steps:

1. In cell C18, type `=C2/B2` and copy this formula from C18 into D18:E18. In C18:E18, you now have the ratios of the second, third, and fourth years' revenue to that of each prior year.
2. Select C18:E18. Choose Edit, Copy, and then choose Edit, Paste Special, Values to convert the formulas to values so that the ratios stay fixed.
3. In cell C2, enter `=B2*C18` and copy this formula in C2 into D2:E2. This gives you the original revenue estimates in C2:E2, but as formulas instead of values. Each of these formulas is now based, in part and indirectly, on the value in cell B2, Year 1 revenues.
4. Select cell E13, which contains the cumulative discounted cash flow for Year 4 and choose Tools, Goal Seek.
5. The Set Cell edit box contains E13. In the To Value edit box, enter `0`. This specifies the break-even point during Year 4.
6. In the By Changing Cell edit box, enter B2 and choose OK.

Goal Seek now iterates through values in B2. As it does so, the formulas in C2:E2 recalculate in response, and the cumulative discounted cash flow in cell E13 eventually reaches $0 (see Figure 27.27).

FIGURE 27.27
The values in B2:E2 are required to bring about a break-even point in Year 4.

E13 = =SUM($B$12:E$12)

	A	B	C	D	E	F	G
1	Year	1	2	3	4	5	
2	Revenue	$47	$131	$216	$272	$307	
3	Less: Cost of goods sold	$100	$100	$100	$100	$100	
4	Net Income	-$53	$31	$116	$172	$207	
5							
6	Less: Cost of equipment	$200	$0	$0	$0	$0	
7							
8	Net cash flow	-$253	$31	$116	$172	$207	
9							
10	Discount rate	10%					
11	Annual discount factors	110%	121%	133%	146%	161%	
12	Disc		$25	$87	$118	$129	
13	Cum		-$205	-$118	$0	$129	
14							
15					NPV	$129	
16							
17							
18			2.8	1.653061	1.259259		
19							

Goal Seek Status
Goal Seeking with Cell E13 found a solution.
Target value: 0
Current value: $0
OK
Cancel
Step
Pause

It is probable that the Solver would return a different result. By constraining cells C2:E2 to maintain particular ratios to B2, you make it possible for Goal Seek to solve this problem. In contrast, the Solver can reach a solution without those constraints because it can change more than only one cell.

But that's not necessarily a virtue. It's possible—even probable—that you would want the projected revenues to take on a specific growth rate, such as an annual 10% increase. You would edit the formulas in C2:E2 accordingly: For example, C2 might equal 1.1 * B2, D2 might equal 1.1 * C2, and E2 might equal 1.1 * D2.

Something such as this is likely to occur if you obtain revenue estimates from the sales force. Given a choice between spending time with a customer and spending time making sales projections, a good sales rep will opt for the former every time. The result is that sales forecasts are frequently a straight-line guess based on the prior year's actuals.

In that case, you would not want the Solver to change cells C2:E2. You would want to change the first year's revenue only, and, in that case, you might just as well use Goal Seek.

Of course, neither Goal Seek nor the Solver is able to change actual sales results. That's up to the sales force, the marketplace, and your product line. But this technique can tell you what the sales results need to be to reach break-even during different years.

NOTE Goal Seek may stop and say it has not found a solution. This problem is most frequently caused by incorrectly specifying the Changing Cell. If the Set Cell's formula is not dependent on the Changing Cell, then Goal Seek could iterate forever and not change the Set Cell's value. The Set Cell must depend, directly or indirectly, on the value in the Changing Cell.

It's also possible that Goal Seek ran out of iterations before it reached a solution. You can change the maximum number of iterations by choosing Tools, Options, and clicking the Calculation tab. Often, though, it's more practical to start with a value in the Changing Cell that's closer to the one you expect Goal Seek to return.

Using the Analysis ToolPak to Predict the Future

Suppose that you've been hired to replace the national sales manager who was fired several months ago. One of your responsibilities is to project next year's sales revenue. One way to do so is to check the rate of growth between last year's results and this year's, and apply that growth rate to estimate next year's results. But if you have several years' worth of data at hand, you can probably do better. Excel provides several methods, such as the TREND function, that help you forecast from a baseline of data. The TREND function is discussed in Chapter 26, "Advanced Charting Techniques."

▶ **See** "Displaying Trend Data in the Worksheet," **p. 840**

Another alternative is to use an Excel add-in, the Analysis ToolPak (ATP), that provides a tool it calls *Exponential Smoothing*. This is a pretentious term for a fairly simple technique that's very similar to a moving average. Using it along with a reasonable amount of data can give you an objective forecast of the next, as yet unobserved, value in a series. And its assumptions are nowhere near as restrictive and sensitive as those used in regression approaches.

To use the ATP's tools, the add-in must be installed. To determine whether it is installed, choose Tools, Add-ins. If a check mark appears next to Analysis ToolPak, then it is already installed and you can close the dialog box. If no check mark is present, place one there and click OK. A warning message appears, asking whether you'd like to install the add-in. You need access either to the location where the Office 2000 installation files are stored or to the Office 2000 CD to install this add-in.

After it is installed, you will find the Data Analysis command on the Tools menu. Selecting that command is how you get to the Exponential Smoothing feature.

Before actually using the feature, however, you need a baseline of data.

Setting Up the Baseline

In the context of forecasting, *baseline* means a series of observations (such as actual sales figures) in a time sequence; for example, 1988 sales, 1989 sales, …, 1998 sales.

A useful baseline has a few additional characteristics:

- No missing data. You shouldn't try to use a baseline of data that includes all years from 1988 through 1998, but that is missing 1990.
- Each time period should be equally long. Don't intersperse, for example, the average of three days' worth of data with other observations that are all daily. Slight deviations, such as 31 days in January versus 28 days in February, are permitted.
- The observations all come from the same point in a time period. If your data includes monthly observations, for example, then all observations should be as of the end of the month, or halfway through, or on the first of the month. Avoid getting data from January 1, February 27, March 7, and so on.

Making use of the list structure that's so handy in Excel, your baseline might look like the one shown in Figure 27.28.

FIGURE 27.28
The data complies with the requirements for a valid baseline.

	A	B
1	Date	Actual Sales (in $K)
2	1/31/98	$199
3	2/28/98	$189
4	3/31/98	$222
5	4/30/98	$191
6	5/31/98	$195
7	6/30/98	$235
8	7/31/98	$257
9	8/31/98	$108
10	9/30/98	$197
11	10/31/98	$166
12	11/30/98	$156
13	12/31/98	$90
14	1/31/99	$120
15	2/28/99	$67
16	3/31/99	$71
17	4/30/99	$169
18	5/31/99	$217
19	6/30/99	$155
20	7/31/99	
21		

Forecast

Creating the Forecast

After you've set up your data as shown in Figure 27.28, you're ready to make the forecast. When you track data over time, invariably the data contains *noise*—factors that influence the data values. These factors include a number of things: weather, unplanned inventory reduction sales, promotional sales conducted by competitors, and so forth. The noise in the data distorts trends and makes cyclical repetitions difficult to detect. The Exponential Smoothing tool provides a way to smooth out the random variations to see the underlying trends more clearly. It does this by using a formula based on both the observed and the forecasted values for the prior time period, adjusted for the error in that prior forecast, to determine the forecast for the next time period.

Suppose you forecast sales of $16,000 for February. At the end of February, you find that your sales were only $10,000. The error was $6,000. To predict a more accurate forecast for March, you would use the actual sales figure for February ($10,000), the predicted sales figure ($16,000), and factor in the error (the $6,000 difference). Using the actual sales figure from the prior period doesn't factor in the noise, so instead of using 100% of the prior actual value, you might use 70% or 80%. This then factors in 30% or 20% for error of the previous forecast. The 70% to 80% of the prior actual value is called the *smoothing constant*. The remaining 30% to 20% accounts for the error and is called the *damping factor*.

Excel's Exponential Smoothing formula is

= Smoothing Constant * Prior Actual + Damping Factor * Prior Forecast

Both the smoothing constant and the damping factor are used to indicate the confidence level, or weight, that should be given to each of the values. The higher the smoothing constant, the more weight is put on the actual value from the prior period, and the less responsive the current forecast is to the value forecast for the prior period. The smoothing constant is denoted by the letter *a* in the Exponential Smoothing formula, and the damping factor is *(1-a)*.

When you use the Exponential Smoothing tool, you indicate the damping factor rather than the smoothing constant. If you enter .2 as the damping factor, then .8 is the smoothing constant.

To create the forecast, follow these steps:

1. Choose Tools, Data Analysis. Click Exponential Smoothing and choose OK. The dialog box shown in Figure 27.29 appears.
2. The Input Range is the cell references for the data you want to analyze. The range must be a single column or row with four or more cells of data. Make sure you include one extra cell so that you can generate the forecast for the next time period. Referring to the data ranges shown in Figure 27.27, enter `$B$1:$B$20` as the Input Range. This creates the values for the existing data as well as the forecast for the next month, July 1999.
3. The Damping Factor is the value that minimizes the instability of data collected across a population. The default damping factor is .3. In this example, a damping factor of .2 is entered.
4. If the first row (or column) of your input range contains a label, mark the Labels check box.

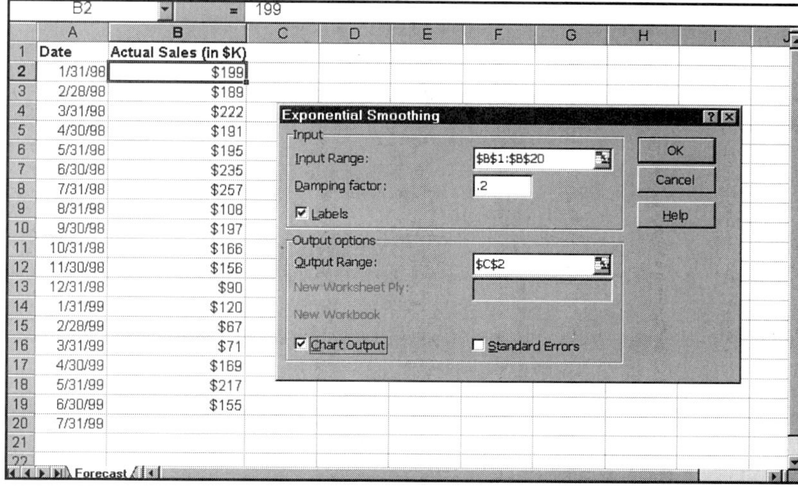

	A	B
1	Date	Actual Sales (in $K)
2	1/31/98	$199
3	2/28/98	$189
4	3/31/98	$222
5	4/30/98	$191
6	5/31/98	$195
7	6/30/98	$235
8	7/31/98	$257
9	8/31/98	$108
10	9/30/98	$197
11	10/31/98	$166
12	11/30/98	$156
13	12/31/98	$90
14	1/31/99	$120
15	2/28/99	$67
16	3/31/99	$71
17	4/30/99	$169
18	5/31/99	$217
19	6/30/99	$155
20	7/31/99	

FIGURE 27.29
In Exponential Smoothing, the output range must be in the active worksheet.

5. For the Output Range for the forecast values, you select the first cell of the range. The cell must be empty, with a blank area below and to the right of the cell (such as cell C2).
6. To generate an embedded chart displaying the actual and forecast values, select the Chart Output check box. The Standard Errors are discussed in the following sections. Initially, leave this box unchecked.
7. Choose OK to create the forecast and the chart. The results appear in Figure 27.30.

NOTE Because the first forecast sales value doesn't have a prior actual or forecast value to use in the formula, the #N/A error value is displayed, as shown in cell C2 in Figure 27.30. The second forecast (cell C3) is the first actual value. The Exponential Smoothing formula begins in the third forecast value in cell C4.

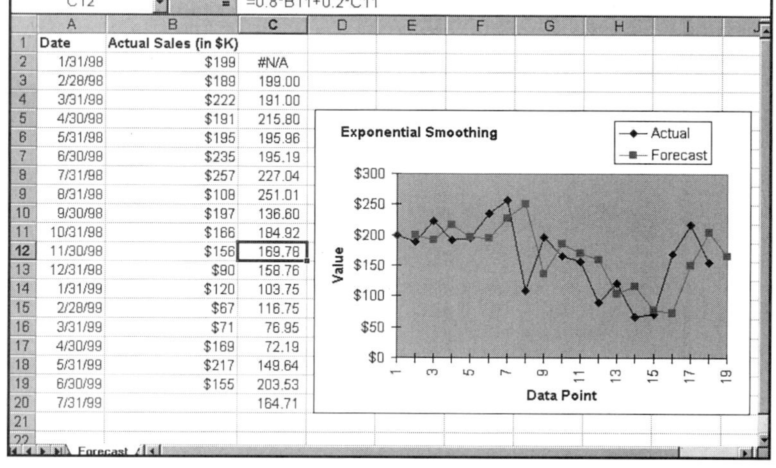

	A	B	C
1	Date	Actual Sales (in $K)	
2	1/31/98	$199	#N/A
3	2/28/98	$189	199.00
4	3/31/98	$222	191.00
5	4/30/98	$191	215.80
6	5/31/98	$195	195.96
7	6/30/98	$235	195.19
8	7/31/98	$257	227.04
9	8/31/98	$108	251.01
10	9/30/98	$197	136.60
11	10/31/98	$166	184.92
12	11/30/98	$156	169.78
13	12/31/98	$90	158.76
14	1/31/99	$120	103.75
15	2/28/99	$67	116.75
16	3/31/99	$71	76.95
17	4/30/99	$169	72.19
18	5/31/99	$217	149.64
19	6/30/99	$155	203.53
20	7/31/99		164.71

FIGURE 27.30
The forecasts appear both in the chart and in cells C2:C20.

Understanding the Forecast

The fundamental idea behind smoothing is that each forecast is composed of two components: the prior forecast and the error in the prior forecast.

The *error component* is just the difference between the prior observation and the prior forecast. It's used to adjust the new forecast in a direction that would have improved the accuracy of the old forecast. This is where the *smoothing constant* comes into play. Excel uses its value as part of the adjustment to the prior forecast.

Suppose that in January, you forecast sales of $16,000 for February. At the end of February, you find that your sales were only $10,000. The error was $6,000. Using a smoothing constant of .7, your forecast for March would be

= Prior Forecast + (Smoothing Constant * Error)

= 16000 + (.7 * (10000-16000))

= 16000 - 4200

= 11800

Notice that the adjustment to the prior forecast is negative. In making the new forecast, the prior forecast of $16,000 is reduced by $4,200 because $16,000 was an overestimate.

If, on the other hand, you forecast sales of $10,000 for February, but had sales of $16,000, then the forecast for March would be

= 10000 + (.7 * (16000-10000))

= 10000 + 4200

= 14200

In this case, the adjustment to the prior forecast is positive. In making the new forecast, the prior forecast of $10,000 is increased by $4,200 because $10,000 was an underestimate.

In each case, smoothing "pulls" the new forecast in the direction that would have improved the prior forecast. The amount of pull—*the smoothing constant*—in the prior two examples is .7, or 70%.

A little algebra shows how the previous equations turn into the equations used by Excel for the Exponential Smoothing. Given that

- *y[t]* is a forecast of the series at time *t*. *y[t]* is the prior forecast value.
- *Y[t]* is an observation made at time *t*. *Y[t]* is the prior actual value.
- *a* is the smoothing constant.

To forecast the value for the next period, *y[t+1]*, the formula evolves from

= Prior Forecast + (Smoothing Constant * Error)

*y[t+1] = y[t] + a * (Y[t] - y[t])*

*y[t+1] = y[t] + a * Y[t] - a * y[t]*

$$y[t+1] = a * Y[t] + y[t] - a * y[t]$$

$$y[t+1] = a * Y[t] + (1 - a) * y[t]$$

to

= Smoothing Constant * Prior Actual + Damping Factor * Prior Forecast

The prior discussion focused on the smoothing constant because it clarifies the definitional aspects of smoothing. Choosing a damping factor of .3 in the Exponential Smoothing dialog box results in a smoothing constant of .7.

The last preceding equation is what you get on your worksheet after you have run the Exponential Smoothing tool. For example, in Figure 27.30, the forecast for 11/30/98 uses this formula:

=0.8*B11+0.2*C11

The prior observation (or *Y[t]*) is in cell B11. The prior forecast (or *y[t]*) is in cell C11. The analysis in Figure 27.30 used a damping factor of .2, and therefore, a smoothing constant of .8.

Why might exponential smoothing be superior to some other method, such as a TREND function or (equivalently) a linear trendline on a chart? The reason has to do with *recency*; that is, the emphasis in Exponential Smoothing on the most recent data. Using smoothing, the greatest influence on a new forecast is the prior observation: directly via the smoothing constant and indirectly via the error associated with the prior forecast.

In contrast, a regression-based forecast places equal weight on all the values in the baseline so as to create the regression equation. That means that an observation taken 20 years ago has as much influence on the regression equation as one taken last year. That approach might or might not be appropriate.

Suppose that you are tracking and forecasting inventory levels. Last month you made a major purchase of raw materials to take advantage of relatively low pricing from your suppliers. Does it make sense to forecast inventory for next month by giving equal weight to the inventory level two years ago and to the inventory level last month? Probably not. By using smoothing, you give more weight to recent observations and less weight to older observations.

Smoothing doesn't throw out those older observations. Each forecast is based in part on the prior forecast, which itself was based on the prior observation. You can backtrack in a similar fashion all the way to the beginning of the baseline. The very first observation has an effect on each subsequent forecast. It's just that for a given forecast, the older the observation, the smaller its effect.

Most regression approaches require that you use some other variable—for example, the value of the year or month itself, or the ordinal value of each observation in the baseline—as the equation's x-values. (An exception is an autoregressive model—not available in Excel—that regresses each value onto prior values.) With smoothing, you're always forecasting from the baseline itself.

But there are plenty of drawbacks to smoothing. One is that you're limited to a one-step-ahead forecast. That is, you can't forecast farther than one time period into the future because you run out of prior observations. With regression, you can always add another x-value and compute the resulting y-value. Other drawbacks are more theoretical in nature; if you're interested, you should consult an intermediate-level text on forecasting.

Choosing the Damping Factor

The Excel Help documentation suggests that you use a smoothing constant of .7 to .8, resulting in a damping factor of .3 to .2. This is a reasonable suggestion, but it's just a rule of thumb. The documentation also notes correctly that the larger the smoothing constant, the more closely the forecast tracks the actual baseline. The smaller the smoothing constant, the less the forecast tracks noise in the baseline—but the more slowly it responds to real changes in the baseline.

One good way to select the damping factor, and thus, the smoothing constant, is to use the one that minimizes the square of the forecast errors. This approach uses the Solver to identify the best damping factor.

NOTE Don't worry if you're not familiar with the Solver. We'll be discussing it in detail later in this chapter; this section's use of the tool is very basic.

The Solver is used instead of Goal Seek because Goal Seek requires that you specify a particular value as its goal. The problem of minimizing the square of the forecast errors requires finding some unknown minimum value; because it's unknown, you can't specify it beforehand. In contrast, the Solver lets you search for a minimum, a maximum, or a specified value.

To minimize the square of the forecast errors, we'll use the SUMXMY2 function. This function calculates the differences of corresponding values in two ranges or arrays (the baseline and the forecast) and then returns the sum of squares of the differences.

Begin by entering the formula whose result the Solver will minimize. As shown in Figure 27.31, enter this formula in cell D1:

```
=SUMXMY2(B3:B19,C3:C19)
```

The SUMXMY2 function we've created takes the difference between each value in B3:B19 and the corresponding value in C3:C19, squares the difference, and returns the sum of the squared differences. It's this amount that the Solver minimizes.

Then, to create starting values for the smoothing constant and the damping factor, follow these steps:

1. In the cell where you want to display the initial value for the smoothing constant (in our example, that is cell G1), type

   ```
   .8
   ```

2. Then in the cell where you want to display the initial value for the damping factor (in our example, that is cell G2), type

   ```
   =1-G1
   ```

   (where G1 is the cell reference for the initial smoothing constant).

FIGURE 27.31
After the Exponential Smoothing tool has returned forecasts, replace the actual values in the formulas with cell references.

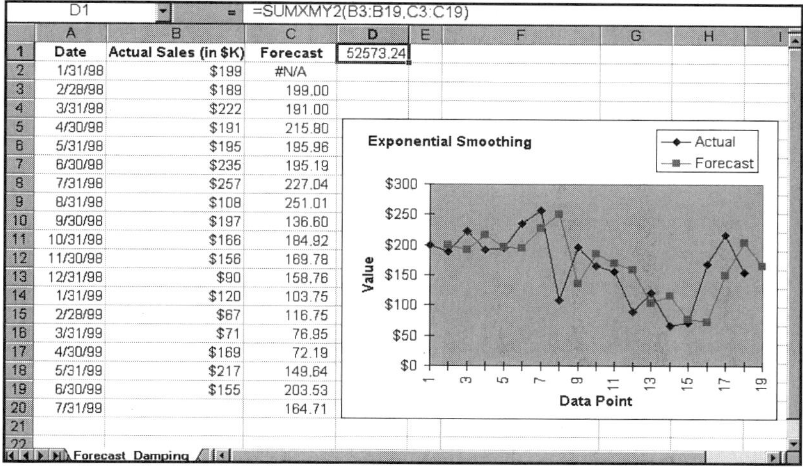

D1 = =SUMXMY2(B3:B19,C3:C19)

	A	B	C	D
1	Date	Actual Sales (in $K)	Forecast	52573.24
2	1/31/98	$199	#N/A	
3	2/28/98	$189	199.00	
4	3/31/98	$222	191.00	
5	4/30/98	$191	215.80	
6	5/31/98	$195	195.96	
7	6/30/98	$235	195.19	
8	7/31/98	$257	227.04	
9	8/31/98	$108	251.01	
10	9/30/98	$197	136.60	
11	10/31/98	$166	184.92	
12	11/30/98	$156	169.78	
13	12/31/98	$90	158.76	
14	1/31/99	$120	103.75	
15	2/28/99	$67	116.75	
16	3/31/99	$71	76.95	
17	4/30/99	$169	72.19	
18	5/31/99	$217	149.64	
19	6/30/99	$155	203.53	
20	7/31/99		164.71	

3. Select the cell containing the second forecast value. In our example, that is cell C4. It currently has the formula `=.08*B3+.02*C3` (the smoothing constant times the actual sales of the previous timeframe, plus the damping factor times the forecast for the previous timeframe). We're simply going to substitute the cell references that contain the calculated smoothing constant and the damping factors.
4. Edit the formula and substitute the cell references for the smoothing constant and damping factors (for example, `=$G$1*B3+$G$2*C3`). Use the F4 key to make the cell references absolute. Then copy the new formula down the list of forecast values (through C5:C20). You have now replaced the actual values for the smoothing constant and the damping factor with cell references. The purpose is to enable the formulas to recalculate as the Solver iterates through different values for the smoothing constant.
5. Select the cell containing the `SUMXMY2` formula (D1) and choose Tools, Solver (if you do not see the Solver in the Tools menu, refer to the section "Using the Solver" later in this chapter for instructions on installing it). Cell D1 appears in the Set Target Cell edit box. See Figure 27.32.
6. Choose the Min option button. Click in the By Changing Cells edit box and select the cell reference for the smoothing constant (G1). The Solver displays it as an absolute cell reference.
7. Click the Add button. In the Add Constraint dialog box (see Figure 27.33), enter G1 as the Cell Reference, >= as the operator, and 0.0 as the Constraint. This tells the Solver that the smoothing constant must be a positive number. Choose the Add button to add that constraint. When you do so, the edit boxes clear but the Add Constraint dialog box remains.

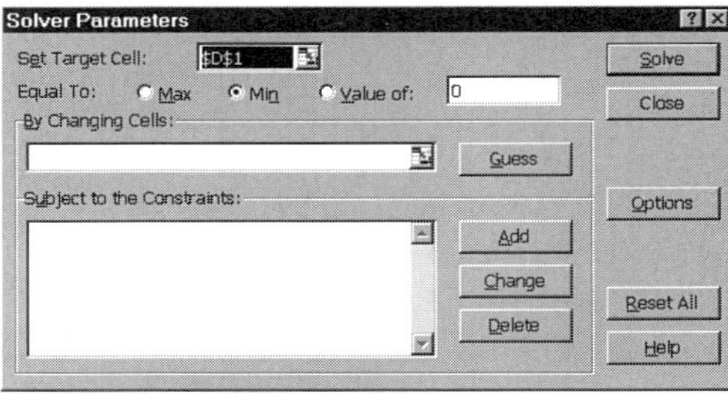

FIGURE 27.32
You need to set only four options in the Solver dialog box to complete this analysis.

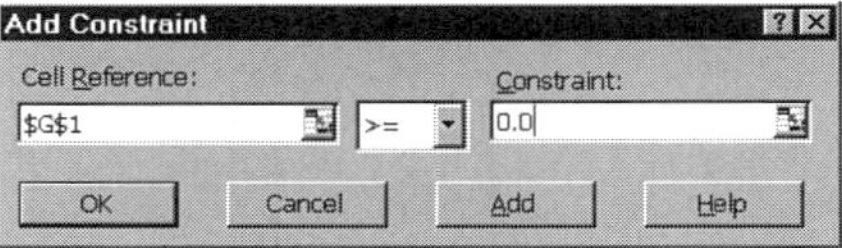

FIGURE 27.33
By adding constraints, you set limits to the possible solutions that the Solver can reach.

8. Enter G1 as the Cell Reference, <= as the operator, and 1.0 as the Constraint. This tells the Solver that the smoothing constant must be less than or equal to 1.
9. You have now established a range of possible values—0.0 to 1.0—for the smoothing constant. Choose OK to close the Add Constraint dialog box and return to the Solver dialog box. (If you accidentally chose Add, the dialog box is waiting for another constraint; click Cancel to close the dialog box.)
10. The Solver Parameters dialog box reappears with the constraints added (see Figure 27.34). Choose Solve. The Solver iterates through different values for the smoothing constant (G1) until it finds the value that results in the smallest result in the sum of the squared forecast errors (D1).

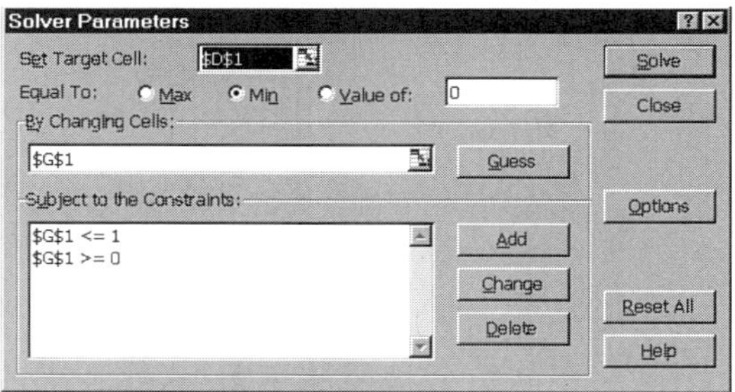

FIGURE 27.34
The Solver Parameters dialog box after constraints have been added.

When it reaches a solution, the Solver notifies you, and you then have the choice of keeping its solution or restoring the original values (see Figure 27.35). Given the target that you called for, the solution that the Solver reaches will be the one that minimizes the sum of the squared forecast errors. By this criterion, you have reached the best forecast for the next time period at the end of the baseline.

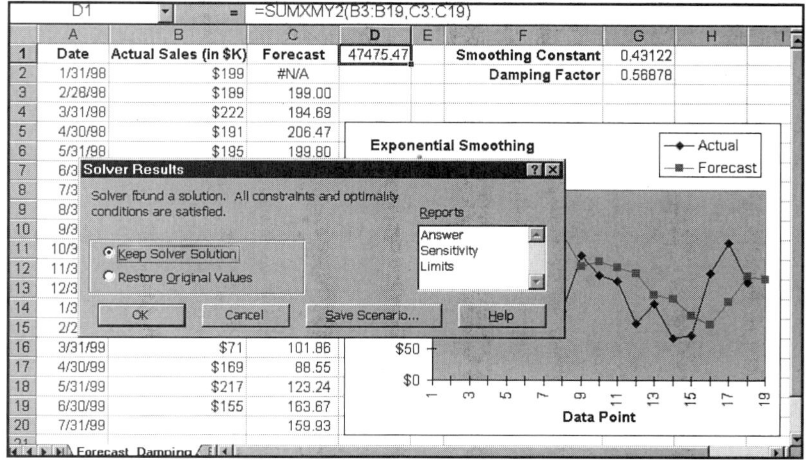

FIGURE 27.35
Based on the solution reached, the smoothing constant is changed—and therefore the damping factor, all the forecast values, and the chart.

For 7/31/99, instead of the forecast value in cell C20 being 164.71 (see Figure 27.31), it is now 159.93 (see Figure 27.35). This process must be repeated for each new time period. So, to reach the best forecast for 8/31/99, you need to expand the sum of the squared differences (the `SUMXMY2` function) to include July, and then run the Solver again to minimize the errors for the expanded ranges. This produces a new smoothing constant. The damping factor and all forecasts will change again in response.

Dealing with Autocorrelation

All baselines have a characteristic called autocorrelation. The *autocorrelation* is the correlation between each point in the baseline and the next point. If the autocorrelation in the baseline is large, the Solver won't be of much help in finding the best smoothing constant.

For the data in Figure 27.35, you estimate the autocorrelation by entering the following formula into some blank cell:

```
=ABS(CORREL(B2:B19,B3:B20))
```

Using the `ABS` function with the `CORREL` function returns the absolute value of the correlation. The result must be between 0.0 and 1.0 because of the way that a correlation and an absolute value are defined. If the result is at all large—for example, greater than 0.5—then substantial autocorrelation exists in the baseline data.

In that case, using the Solver to determine the best smoothing constant would often result in a value of 1.0, which is equivalent to a damping factor of 0.0. This means that the best forecast is identical to the prior observation. The forecast would track too much noise and not enough signal.

If you do encounter a situation such as this, subtract each observation, starting with the second one, from its prior observation. By subtracting the observations, you are left with the difference between the two values. This is called *first-differencing*, and its effect is almost always to remove the autocorrelation from the data. As a result, you will have a better smoothing constant and damping factor for your forecasts.

Use the Exponential Smoothing tool, and subsequently the Solver, with this differenced series instead of with the original series. The differenced series will have one observation fewer than the original.

After you have completed the analysis, replace the differenced series with the original. The forecast values recalculate accordingly, and you will now have your forecasts in their original scale of measurement.

This section has explored the use of a fairly simple tool, Exponential Smoothing, to forecast a new value from a baseline of values. After the initial forecast is complete, you can use the Solver to find the optimum value for the smoothing constant and circumstantially, the damping factor. This use of the Solver only scratches the surface. The next section goes into detail on how you can use the Solver to develop more complex models.

Using the Solver

The Solver resembles the Goal Seek command. Both backtrack to a precedent value that satisfies a dependent value that you specify. A precedent value is a value on which that formula is directly or indirectly based. In Goal Seek, the precedent value is the By Changing Cell option. But the Solver also differs from the Goal Seek command—you can specify only one precedent in Goal Seek, whereas the Solver can accommodate many precedents.

In addition, the Solver enables you to set conditions, or constraints, on the solution—that is, you use the Solver to specify that certain values and formulas must satisfy your conditions before a solution is judged to be acceptable.

Setting the Solver Parameters

The Solver is an add-in supplied with Office 2000, so you must install it specifically before you can use it. The easiest way to do so is to choose Tools, Add-Ins. If a check mark appears next to Solver Add-In, then it is already installed and you can close the dialog box. If there is no check mark, place one there and click OK. A warning message appears, asking whether you'd like to install the add-in. You need access either to the location where the Office 2000 installation files are stored or to the Office 2000 CD to install this add-in. After it is installed, you will find the Solver command on the Tools menu.

The steps and the considerations involved in defining the problem for the Solver are described in the next three sections.

Structuring the Problem for the Solver Suppose that you are a publisher who is considering the publication of a new book on a suite of software applications named Cubicle 2000. The shelf life of such books is fairly short because the book product line must keep current with new software releases. Given the short shelf life, your decision is an important one: You will incur significant costs in development, printing and binding, marketing, and getting the book through the distribution channel.

You sit down with your Excel worksheet and start to input some timelines, costs, and revenue projections. After a few minutes, you come up with the rough estimates shown in Figure 27.36.

FIGURE 27.36
The eventual goal is to optimize the cumulative net cash flow at the end of the fourth quarter.

B2 = =600000*(1+3*F10)

	A	B	C	D	E	F
1	**Quarter**	1	2	3	4	
2	**Revenues**	$645,000	$429,257	$285,677	$190,122	
3	**Uncontrollable Costs**					
4	Market Research	$60,000				
5	Lost Value of Existing Book	$150,000				**Quarterly**
6	**Controllable Costs**					**Percent**
7	Advertising @ 9.00 %	$58,050	$38,633	$25,711	$17,111	9.00%
8	Production @ 45.17%	$291,347	$193,895	$129,040	$85,878	45.17%
9	Salaries @ 14.00%	$90,300	$60,096	$39,995	$26,617	14.00%
10	Commissions @ 2.50%	$16,125	$10,731	$7,142	$4,753	2.50%
11	**Total Costs**	$665,822	$303,356	$201,888	$134,359	
12	Revenues less Total Costs	-$20,822	$125,901	$83,789	$55,763	
13	Less Depreciation	$14,000	$14,001	$14,002	$14,003	
14	PreTax Income	-$34,822	$111,900	$69,787	$41,760	
15	Taxes @ 34.00%	-$11,839	$38,046	$23,728	$14,198	34.00%
16	**Net Income**	-$22,982	$73,854	$46,059	$27,561	
17	Plus Depreciation	$14,000	$14,001	$14,002	$14,003	
18	Net Cash Flow	-$8,982	$87,855	$60,061	$41,564	
19	Cumulative Net Cash Flow	-$8,982	$78,873	$138,934	$180,499	

Book Model

Your estimates are educated guesses. Some of them are based on solid empirical information, such as the costs associated with salaries and taxes. Some are based on nothing more quantifiable than your own current sense of the market. And some blend real data, such as sales of earlier books, with guesses—for example, how aggressively the publisher will market the new software release.

Using these data sources, you arrive at the estimates in Figure 27.36. The firm will incur many costs that are not shown, of course, but the ones in the figure are those that are relevant to the business decision.

The revenue for Quarter 1 is dependent on the commission rate—the more you pay the sales reps, the more books they are able to get on bookstore shelves initially. The formula is

```
=600000*(1+3*F10)
```

The revenue for the other quarters is dependent, in part, on the previous quarter's sales and the percentage spent on advertising. Because sales naturally decline over time, a logarithmic function is used in these formulas. The expenditures on advertising slow down the natural decline. The formula for Quarter 2 is

```
=(B2/2)+B2*LN(1+2*$F$7)
```

Specifying the Target Cell The revenues and costs flow through the model to result in a cumulative cash flow, net of the relevant costs, of $180,499 in cell E19. Your first reaction on seeing this figure is that it is an inadequate return on the costs you will incur. You believe that to make going ahead with the book worthwhile, that value must be closer to $300,000.

You decide to make cell E19 the Solver's Target Cell. When you choose Tools, Solver, the Solver Parameters dialog box appears, as shown in Figure 27.37.

If you selected cell E19 prior to starting the Solver, its address appears in the Set Target Cell reference edit box. Otherwise, drag across whatever address appears there and click in cell E19.

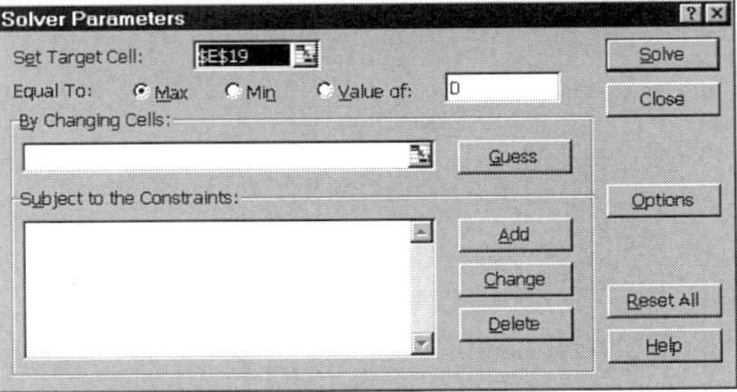

FIGURE 27.37
Although the Solver can handle many Changing Cells, it solves for just one Target Cell.

As with the Goal Seek command, the target cell that you specify for the Solver must contain a formula. Otherwise, if that cell contains a value, the Solver could change the values of other cells repeatedly and the target's value would never change.

In the Solver example in the "Choosing the Damping Factor" section earlier in this chapter, the goal was to minimize a particular value, and the Min option button was chosen. In this example, you are seeking to maximize a particular value—so, choose the Max option button.

Each of the choices you make is capable of causing the Solver to fail, and one of the most important choices concerns setting the goal for the target cell. When the Min option was chosen in the "Choosing the Damping Factor" example, it was possible to arrive at a minimum value. The target cell contained a formula that totaled the squares of other values. Because of the way that the second power of a value is defined, a square can never be a negative value. Because zero is a true minimum possible value for any square (and thus is a true minimum for the total of a set of squared values), it is possible for the Solver to find a minimum target value.

Not so in the present example. If you were (perversely) to set the target value for the cumulative net cash flow to a minimum, you would make it impossible for the Solver to reach a solution. Any one of several outcomes is possible:

- The Solver might return a message that it could not find a feasible solution.
- You might see a message that an internal error had occurred, or that the Solver ran out of memory.
- The Solver might exceed the number of permissible iterations.
- Exceptionally, the Solver might find a minimum value that's legal but completely ridiculous—for example, a negative $184,538,962.

So, before you specify a target cell goal for the Solver to find, make sure that the formulas on the worksheet support the goal you specify.

Specifying the Changing Cells In the model shown in Figure 27.36, many cells are precedent to the result in cell E19, the final cumulative net cash flow.

The percentages in F7:F10, however, are the real drivers. The revenues are dependent on the percentages of the Advertising, Salaries, Production, and Commissions. For example, the revenue expected for the first quarter is $645,000, based on the formula

```
=600000*(1+3*F10)
```

A revenue base of $600,000 is expected, plus an additional $45,000 as a result of the threefold increase in commissions offered to the sales reps for advance sales.

Likewise, the advertising spent on each of the other quarters is expected to increase revenue as well.

The formula for the 2nd, 3rd, and 4th quarters takes the sales from the previous quarter and multiplies it by the logarithm of double the percent spent on advertising. The formula is

```
=(B2/2)+B2*LN(1+2*$F$7)
```

The percentages you use for advertising and commissions are controllable. It's possible for you to make decisions about the advertising budget, for example, that will raise or lower the total quarterly costs. Because they actually are under your control, the percentages that drive these costs are good candidates for Changing Cells.

By Changing Cells, the Solver means values that it can adjust to reach the goal that you specify for the Target Cell. Just because the Solver can change them, however, doesn't mean that it necessarily will do so. Several factors determine whether the Solver will change the value of a particular cell as it searches for a solution.

For example, you might establish a constraint (see the next section for information on constraints) that establishes very narrow bounds on the values a Changing Cell can take on. The Solver might not change that cell's value if doing so has a negligible impact on the Target Cell value.

Or it might be that some other Changing Cell has such a strong relationship to the Target Cell's value that the Solver reaches its target before it has even gotten around to changing some other cell by more than a very small amount.

The point is that it occasionally takes some experimenting before you reach the right mix of values, formulas, and constraints. If the Solver makes a huge change in one Changing Cell and leaves another completely alone—and if this isn't what you want—you'll have to make some adjustments to the constraints, to the formulas, or both.

Two costs, that of market research and that of the lost value of the existing book, are constant values. Your market research firm charges a fixed fee of $60,000, and you know that you still have $150,000 worth of the existing book about the former software version in your inventory. Although you could use the Solver to alter these two values in pursuit of a higher cash flow, to do so would be irrelevant. In the Solver, you would have control over those values, but in reality, you do not—so they are poor candidates for Changing Cells.

Although you can't control these costs, it doesn't mean that they don't belong in the model, however. They have an effect on the Target Cell both in reality and in the model, and so they remain on the worksheet as actual costs.

Both the controllable and the uncontrollable costs, along with taxes, investment dollars, and depreciation, are subtracted from the revenue figures to reach eventual net cash flow figures. The cumulative net cash flows are the running total of the net cash flows.

You decide that you want Solver to modify the percentages that determine the controllable costs and revenues. You note, though, that even if each of those costs dropped moderately, you would still not have reached your goal of $300,000 cumulative net cash flow at the end of the fourth quarter. You can't reduce the costs too far or no resources would be available to produce the book.

In the Solver dialog box, click the By Changing Cells reference edit box and drag across F7:F10 to capture the cost percentages. The dialog box, with both the Target Cell and the Changing Cells identified, now appears as shown in Figure 27.38.

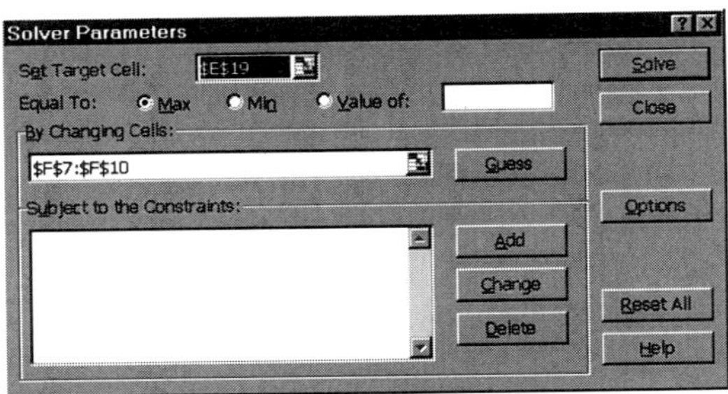

FIGURE 27.38
You still need to set some constraints to keep the Solver from assigning unrealistic values to the Changing Cells.

Instead of specifying the Changing Cells yourself, you could leave the By Changing Cells reference edit box empty and choose the Guess button. If you do, the Solver does its best to determine which cells are the precedents to the Target Cell. In the process of doing its best, the Solver can set up a situation in which too many cells, or the wrong cells, are identified as Changing Cells. With the model set up as in this example, using the Guess button would return this range of Changing Cells:

$B$13:$E$13,$B$4:$B$5,$B$2:$E$2,$F$7:$F$10

That range uses some cells unnecessarily. As discussed previously, the market research and lost inventory costs in B4 and B5 should not enter the analysis because they aren't under your control. When you can't change these costs in reality, why allow the Solver to change them in the worksheet model?

CAUTION

Occasionally, and with a very simple model, you might find it convenient to use the Guess button. But be aware that when you do, you relinquish control of the model, and Solver's best guess for the Changing Cells might well be different from what you intend.

By specifying the percentages used in F7:F10, you completely specify all the other controllable costs: advertising, production, salaries, and commissions, and you indirectly specify the revenue values as well. To arrange for the Solver to change, for instance, the advertising costs in B7:E7 would be redundant.

Suppose that you identified the advertising costs in B7:E7 as Changing Cells, in addition to the cost percentages in F7:F10. Apart from the redundancy and inefficiency of doing so, you do not want the Solver to alter B7:E7. Those cells contain formulas. When the Solver changes a cell, it changes its value. If a cell starts out with a formula, the Solver replaces the formula with the value that helps get to the target. Then you've lost your formulas.

Specifying the Constraints To turn the Solver loose on the model as specified in Figure 27.38 would be to tell the bull where the china shop is. It might decide to turn the cost percentages in F7:F10 into negative values. This would change the costs from reductions to the revenue into contributions to the revenue (that is, subtracting a negative $30,000 from a positive $100,000 results in $130,000). So, you still need to provide some boundaries, or *constraints*, for the Solver to use as it modifies the values in the Changing Cells.

Begin by clicking the Add button. The Add Constraint dialog box appears, as shown in Figure 27.39.

FIGURE 27.39
Use constraints to control the values the Solver can use in the Changing Cells option.

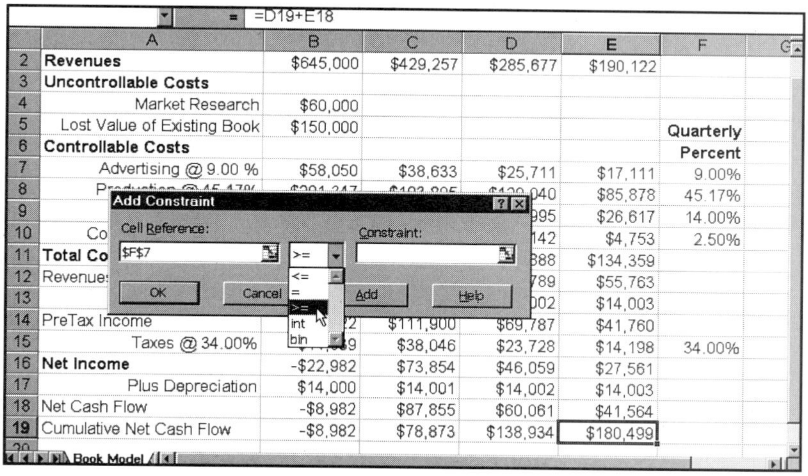

To add a constraint to the model, click the Cell Reference box, and then click a cell in the worksheet. This is the cell whose value the Solver will constrain. Click the drop-down arrow to choose from among the available operators; as shown in Figure 27.39, you can choose from three comparison operators and two special operators (int and bin).

If you choose one of the comparison operators (less than or equal to, equal to, and greater than or equal to), then you also specify in the Constraint box a number, a cell reference, or a formula that returns a number.

For example, you might decide to prevent the Solver from reducing the value 9% in cell F7 below 5%. You would do so if you believed that you could not allow advertising costs to fall below 5% of estimated revenue without jeopardizing the marketing effort. You would choose >= as the comparison operator. Then, in the Constraint box, you could enter

- The number .05
- The address of some worksheet cell that contains the number .05
- The address of a cell that contains a formula whose result is .05
- The formula 0.1/2

Any one of these, in combination with the >= operator, prevents the Solver from setting the associated cost percentage to a value lower than 5%.

The int operator restricts the constrained cell's value to an *integer*. For example, suppose you were using the Solver to establish a business budget that included finding the optimal number of employees for a given project or department. It's unrealistic to have fractions for the number of employees, and you should constrain that value to take on only integer values.

The bin operator restricts the constrained cell's value to 1 or 0: The term *bin* is short for binary. Use this operator when you develop a model in which a value is either present or absent, on or off, or some other situation that can take on two values only.

Suppose, for example, that you are analyzing a model that involves switching logic—perhaps to predict the mean time between failures in an electrical system. Then the value that represents the state of the switch should be 1 or 0, and you would constrain it to one of those two values by means of the bin operator.

If you choose a comparison operator, the cell that you're constraining can be anywhere on the active worksheet. It need not be one of the Changing Cells that you have identified. In the book model used in our example, cell B8 contains the total production costs for the first quarter. It is not one of the Changing Cells, but it is completely determined by the combination of the first quarter revenue and the cost percentage for production—and both of these are Changing Cells. You might want to be sure that the cost of production during the first quarter does not exceed $300,000. If so, you would enter B8 as the Cell Reference, <= as the comparison operator, and 300000 as the Constraint.

In contrast, when you use either the integer or the binary operator, the Cell Reference edit box must contain one of the Changing Cells. Neither operator is legal with a cell outside the range of Changing Cells, even if that cell changes value during the process of reaching a solution.

In either case, the Solver fills in the Constraint edit box for you, displaying integer if you choose int, and binary if you choose bin.

After specifying a constraint, click Add in the Add Constraint dialog box. The constraint is added to the list of constraints in the Solver dialog box, and the edit boxes in the Add Constraint dialog box are cleared. Continue until you have added all the constraints you want, and click OK. If you have finished adding constraints but the edit boxes have been cleared because you clicked OK, just click Cancel. Both the OK and the Cancel button return you to the Solver dialog box, with the constraints identified in the Subject to the Constraints list box.

For the current example, suppose that you choose to keep the advertising, production, salaries, and commission cost percentages from falling below 7%, 40%, 10%, and 2%, respectively. When you return to the Solver Parameters dialog box, it appears as shown in Figure 27.40.

FIGURE 27.40
The constraints you specify in the Add Constraint dialog box are listed in the Subject to the Constraints list box.

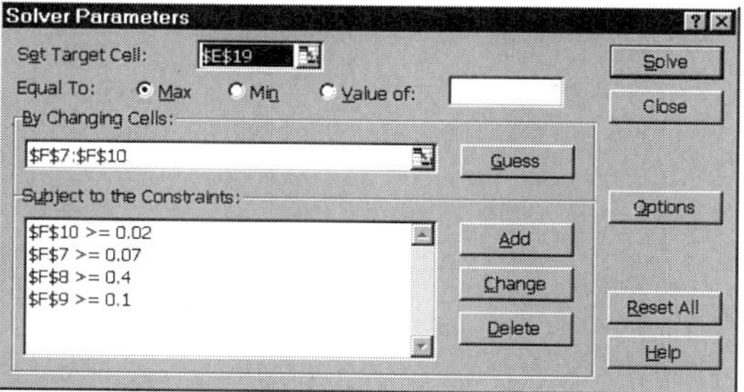

You now have a chance to change your mind about a constraint. To remove any constraint, click it in the list box and choose Delete. Or if you want to modify a constraint, click it and choose Change to display the Change Constraint dialog box. The Change Constraint dialog box is identical to the Add Constraint dialog box. There you can change the Cell Reference, the operator, and the constraint value itself.

Using the Solution

After identifying the Target Cell, Changing Cells, and Constraints, you are ready for Solver to find a solution. When you click the Solve button, the Solver tries different values in the Changing Cells until it reaches the target value that you specified. You can watch the Solver's progress in the status bar, where it displays information about the current trial solution.

If the Solver reaches a solution that conforms to the target value and that complies with the constraints you specified, you see the dialog box shown in Figure 27.41.

FIGURE 27.41
You might choose to Restore Original Values if you don't want to lose them.

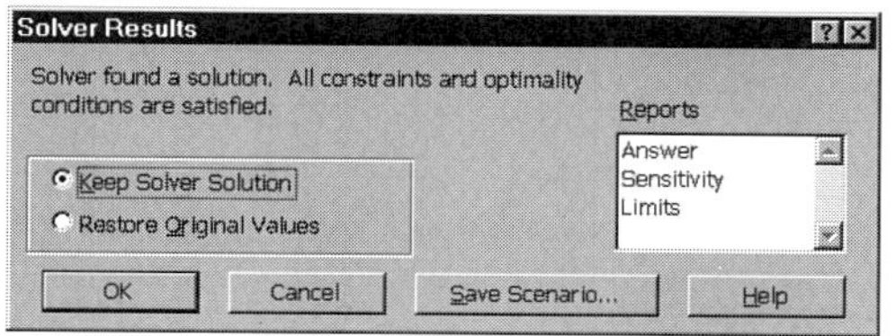

You will want to be careful at this point. Suppose that you choose Keep Solver Solution. If you do, the new values for the Changing Cells stay on the worksheet, and you will have lost their original values. Keeping in mind that the Solver puts values only (not formulas) in the Changing Cells as it seeks a solution, notice that any formulas or values that were in the Changing Cells when you started the Solver will be lost.

For this reason, among others, it's a good idea to create a scenario, perhaps named Initial Values, before you start the Solver. If you do, you can retrieve the original values (not formulas:

Scenarios don't save formulas) that were in the Changing Cells whenever you want. Scenarios were discussed earlier in this chapter.

▶ **See** "Creating and Managing Scenarios," **p. 871**

Notice that one of the options shown in Figure 27.41 is Save Scenario. If you choose that option, the Solver displays a dialog box where you can type a name for the scenario. After you enter the name and click OK, the Solver creates a scenario for you and returns to the Solver dialog box. The Changing Cells that you specified for the Solver are used as the Changing Cells for the scenario.

Taking this approach means that you can later use the Scenario Manager to switch back and forth between a scenario that uses the original values for the Changing Cells and scenarios created by the Solver that represent different solutions. Those different solutions might include some that use different target values, some that use different Changing Cells, and some that use different sets of constraints. Be sure to give each scenario a descriptive name so that you can tell how it differs from other scenarios.

The solution returned by the Solver for the current example is shown in Figure 27.42. The solution is based on the target of maximizing the cumulative net cash flow at the end of the fourth quarter and cost percentages that were identified as the Changing Cells, and on the constraints that were specified, as shown in Figure 27.40.

FIGURE 27.42
After a solution is reached, be sure you evaluate it. Is the solution realistic?

E19 = =D19+E18

	A	B	C	D	E	F
1	**Quarter**	1	2	3	4	
2	**Revenues**	$682,229	$436,821	$279,690	$179,081	
3	**Uncontrollable Costs**					
4	Market Research	$60,000				
5	Lost Value of Existing Book	$150,000				**Quarterly**
6	**Controllable Costs**					**Percent**
7	Advertising @ 9.00 %	$51,372	$32,893	$21,061	$13,485	7.53%
8	Production @ 45.17%	$272,892	$174,728	$111,876	$71,632	40.00%
9	Salaries @ 14.00%	$68,223	$43,682	$27,969	$17,908	10.00%
10	Commissions @ 2.50%	$31,166	$19,955	$12,777	$8,181	4.57%
11	**Total Costs**	$633,653	$271,259	$173,683	$111,206	
12	Revenues less Total Costs	$48,576	$165,562	$106,007	$67,875	
13	Less Depreciation	$14,000	$14,001	$14,002	$14,003	
14	PreTax Income	$34,576	$151,561	$92,005	$53,872	
15	Taxes @ 34.00%	$11,756	$51,531	$31,282	$18,316	34.00%
16	**Net Income**	$22,820	$100,030	$60,723	$35,555	
17	Plus Depreciation	$14,000	$14,001	$14,002	$14,003	
18	Net Cash Flow	$36,820	$114,031	$74,725	$49,558	
19	Cumulative Net Cash Flow	$36,820	$150,852	$225,577	$275,135	

Book Model

Examining the solution might suggest to you that you shouldn't publish the book. To return a final cumulative net cash flow of $275,135, the Solver had to increase the percentage paid on commissions to 4.57% and decrease the percentages for advertising, production, and salaries.

The model suggests, then, that to reach your target, you would have to reduce the advertising budget, presumably bringing the book to the attention of a smaller audience. You would have to reduce the production budget, possibly binding the book in a soft cover instead of a hard cover. And you would have to reduce the salary budget, perhaps assigning fewer editors to the development process.

Any one of these actions could make it more difficult to sell the book to bookstores, thus reducing the potential revenue. But the Solver's solution also suggests that you need higher revenues than you initially estimated in the first three quarters to reach the target. Therefore, you might well decide that it would be a bad decision to publish the book.

Equally, you might decide to go ahead with it. Suppose that you started out with initial values that were very conservative as to estimated revenues, and values that were very pessimistic as to cost percentages. You could now evaluate the Solver's solution and judge whether it's realistic.

Given the conservative initial revenue estimates, are those suggested by the Solver attainable? Given the pessimistic cost percentages, are those suggested by the Solver feasible? If so, you might decide in favor of publishing the book. All depends on how you regard the initial values that you supplied. A blind acceptance of the Solver's results changes artificial intelligence into artificial stupidity.

This section has warned you about allowing the Solver to overwrite the initial values for the Changing Cells with the values that bring about your target result. Although you can make your life easier by saving in Scenarios both your initial values and the values that are returned by the Solver, you can make things easier yet by keeping each Changing Cell as simple as possible.

Consider the cost percentages in the current example. Each one was set out separately in cells F7:F10. The percentages are used in the quarterly cost formulas. For example, the formula in cell B7 is

```
=B2*$F$7
```

which multiplies the first quarter's revenue estimate by the advertising cost percentage.

You could, of course, specify cell B7 (and, for that matter, the remainder of the cells in B7:E9) as one of the Changing Cells. But if you do so, the Solver replaces the formulas with values. You then lose the capability to modify the cells by changing a cost percentage. Furthermore, you lose the entire logic of the model, which implies that expenses and revenues are directly related.

Therefore, whenever possible, you should set up the worksheet so that the Changing Cells contain values that are used by formulas. These formulas, in turn, control the value in the Target Cell.

This approach is followed in the sample worksheet. The Changing Cells each contain a single value—one that is easy to recapture by means of the Scenario Manager—and no violence is done to the intermediate formulas in B7:E18.

The Proper Use of Solver The example outlined in the previous sections can be used as a guide when you go through the process of using the Solver to analyze your worksheet problem. Regardless of the problem, you will need to determine three things before starting the Solver:

The Target Cell

The By Changing Cells

The Constraints

The Target Cell must contain a formula. If the Target Cell contains a value, the Solver could change the values of the By Changing Cells repeatedly and the target's value would never change. For the Solver to find the goal you specify for a Target Cell, be sure that the formulas on the worksheet will support the goal you specify.

The By Changing Cells are cells that contain values that the Solver can adjust to reach the goal that you specify for the Target Cell. The Solver changes only the value of a particular cell if the change will have an impact on the Target Cell. If one Changing Cell has a stronger relationship to the Target Cell's value than another Changing Cell, the Solver may reach the goal before it has changed a cell. Therefore, whenever possible, you should set up the worksheet so that the Changing Cells contain values that are used by formulas. These formulas, in turn, control the value in the Target Cell.

Use Constraints to control the values the Solver can use in the Changing Cells option. The Constraints can set a minimum value, a maximum value, or both for the Changing Cells. You can also specify that the Changing Cell value be a whole number (an integer) or a Yes/No or True/False number (a binary).

After identifying the Target Cell, the Changing Cells, and the Constraints, you are ready for Solver to find a solution. When you click the Solve button, the Solver tries different values in the Changing Cells until it reaches the target value or goal that you specified.

It may take some experimenting before you reach the right mix of values, formulas, and constraints. If the Solver makes a huge change in one Changing Cell and leaves another completely alone —and if this isn't what you want—you'll have to make some adjustments to the constraints, to the formulas, or both.

Understanding the Solver's Reports

When the Solver reports that it has found a solution, you can direct the Solver to create three additional reports: an Answer Report, a Sensitivity Report, and a Limits Report (refer to Figure 27.39). Choose any or all reports by clicking them in the list box. When you then choose OK, the Solver creates a new worksheet for each report. The first portion of the Answer Report is shown in Figure 27.43.

The Answer Report is a convenient way to view information about the initial and the final values for the Target Cell and the Changing Cells. Below that information is a section on the constraints you specified (see Figure 27.44).

FIGURE 27.43
The Solver uses the terms Changing Cells and Adjustable Cells interchangeably.

Microsoft Excel 9.0 Answer Report
Worksheet: [solver.xls]Book Model (2)
Report Created: 2/20/99 6:29:19 PM

Target Cell (Max)

Cell	Name	Original Value	Final Value
$E$19	Cumulative Net Cash Flow	$180,499	$275,135

Adjustable Cells

Cell	Name	Original Value	Final Value
$F$7	Advertising @ 9.00 % Percent	9.00%	7.53%
$F$8	Production @ 45.17% Percent	45.17%	40.00%
$F$9	Salaries @ 14.00% Percent	14.00%	10.00%
$F$10	Commissions @ 2.50% Percent	2.50%	4.57%

Constraints

Book Model | Answer Report 1 | Sensitivity Report 1 | Limits Report 1

FIGURE 27.44
The Cell Values in the Constraints section of the Answer Report are their final values.

Adjustable Cells

Cell	Name	Original Value	Final Value
$F$7	Advertising @ 9.00 % Percent	9.00%	7.53%
$F$8	Production @ 45.17% Percent	45.17%	40.00%
$F$9	Salaries @ 14.00% Percent	14.00%	10.00%
$F$10	Commissions @ 2.50% Percent	2.50%	4.57%

Constraints

Cell	Name	Cell Value	Formula	Status	Slack
$F$7	Advertising @ 9.00 % Percent	7.53%	$F$7>=0.07	Not Binding	0.53%
$F$8	Production @ 45.17% Percent	40.00%	$F$8>=0.4	Binding	0.00%
$F$9	Salaries @ 14.00% Percent	10.00%	$F$9>=0.1	Binding	0.00%
$F$10	Commissions @ 2.50% Percent	4.57%	$F$10>=0.02	Not Binding	2.57%

Book Model | Answer Report 1 | Sensitivity Report 1 | Limits Report 1

The Constraints section identifies the constrained cells, their final values, and the constraint that you established for each. It also shows whether the final value for the constrained cell equals the bound for the constraint, and the difference between the two. *Binding* means that the solution value is at the constraint's bound—the maximum or minimum limit you set in the constraint. *Not Binding* means that it is not at its bound—that slack exists between the constraint value and the final value reached.

The Slack value is the absolute value of the difference between the final value of the constrained cell and the constraint's bound or limit. You can use this information to judge whether the constraints you established are too rigorous.

In Figure 27.44, the percentages used for Advertising and Commissions are Not Binding; they contain some slack. The Solver reached a solution with 7.53% for Advertising. Because the constraint was for no less than 7%, the difference, .53%, is the slack. The Limits Report is shown in Figure 27.45.

FIGURE 27.45
The Limits Report displays information about the Target Cell value for each constraint's upper and lower limits.

	A	B	C	D	E	F	G	H	I	J
1	Microsoft Excel 9.0 Limits Report									
2	Worksheet: [solver.xls]Book Model (2)									
3	Report Created: 2/20/99 6:29:20 PM									
4										
5										
6			Target							
7		Cell	Name	Value						
8		$E$19	Cumulative Net Cash Flow	$275,135						
9										
10										
11			Adjustable			Lower	Target		Upper	Target
12		Cell	Name	Value		Limit	Result		Limit	Result
13		$F$7	Advertising @ 9.00 % Percent	7.53%		7.00%	27507532.00%		#N/A	#N/A
14		$F$8	Production @ 45.17% Percent	40.00%		40.00%	27513530.00%		#N/A	#N/A
15		$F$9	Salaries @ 14.00% Percent	10.00%		10.00%	27513530.00%		#N/A	#N/A
16		$F$10	Commissions @ 2.50% Percent	4.57%		2.00%	27332297.00%		#N/A	#N/A
17										
18										
19										

Book Model / Answer Report 1 / Sensitivity Report 1 / Limits Report 1

Notice in Figure 27.45 that you can evaluate the target value (labeled Target Result) associated with each constraint's lower and upper limits. If a constraint was not given one limit or the other, the Limits Report displays `#N/A` as the Target Result.

Notice also that the Limits Report erroneously uses the cell format for the constraint cell as the format for the Target Result. For example, the advertising cost percentage is formatted as a percent; the Target Result associated with that constraint is also formatted as a percentage. You can correct the formatting in the reports the same as you would any Excel worksheet.

The Solver's Sensitivity Report for this example appears in Figure 27.46.

FIGURE 27.46
When a solution satisfies the specified target value and the constraints, the reduced gradient is zero.

	A	B	C	D	E	F	G	H
1	Microsoft Excel 9.0 Sensitivity Report							
2	Worksheet: [solver.xls]Book Model (2)							
3	Report Created: 2/20/99 6:29:20 PM							
4								
5								
6	Adjustable Cells							
7				Final	Reduced			
8		Cell	Name	Value	Gradient			
9		$F$7	Advertising @ 9.00 % Percent	7.53%	0.00%			
10		$F$8	Production @ 45.17% Percent	40.00%	-104136206.25%			
11		$F$9	Salaries @ 14.00% Percent	10.00%	-104136206.25%			
12		$F$10	Commissions @ 2.50% Percent	4.57%	0.00%			
13								
14	Constraints							
15		NONE						
16								
17								
18								
19								

Book Model / Answer Report 1 / Sensitivity Report 1 / Limits Report 1

You will see a Constraints section in the Sensitivity Report only if you have constrained cells that are not among the Changing Cells.

Some understanding of the gradients mentioned in Figure 27.46 is useful if you want to manipulate the Solver options described in the next section. The Solver works by substituting new values in the Changing Cells and observing the effect—both the direction and the magnitude—of those changes on the value of the Target Cell. In a formal mathematical sense, the value of the Target Cell is said to be a function of the Changing Cells.

The Solver finds the first derivative of that function; the *first derivative* measures the rate of change of the function in response to modifications in the Changing Cell values. In a case such as the current example where more than one Changing Cell exists, there is not only one derivative, but several partial derivatives—each measuring the rate of change in the function as a result of modifying the value in each Changing Cell.

That set of partial derivatives is called the *gradient* of the function, and the partial derivatives associated with a particular Changing Cell constitute a partial gradient. At the point in the solution process that the Solver has found values that result in the target value you specified, the partial gradient for each Changing Cell equals zero. This is shown in the Reduced gradient column on the Sensitivity Report for a problem that does not assume a linear model.

How this process is affected by Solver options you might choose is described in the next section.

Setting the Solver's Options

Choosing the Options button on the main Solver dialog box displays the dialog box shown in Figure 27.47.

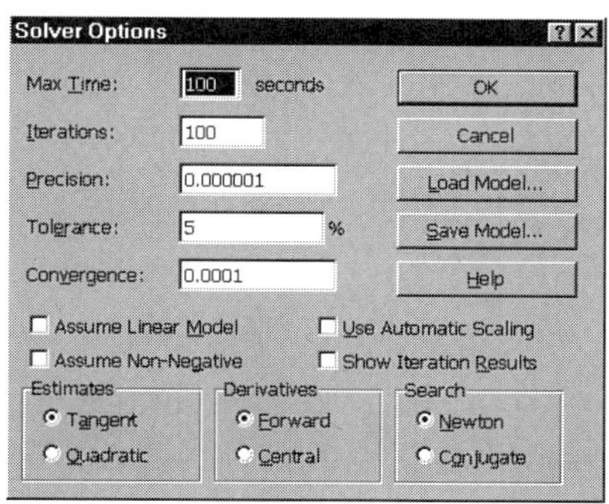

FIGURE 27.47
The Solver Options dialog box enables you to control the amount of work the Solver does and how it goes about reaching a solution.

In many cases, you do not need to even look at these options, much less change them. On occasion, though, you will find it necessary to make some adjustments.

Controlling the Precision The default value of 100 for both the number of seconds and the number of iterations that the Solver uses is fairly generous. But for a very complicated problem, and especially when a nonlinear model is involved, the Solver might return to the Solver

Results dialog box with a message that it could not find a solution. If it seemed to you that the Solver took a long time before it displayed the Solver Results dialog box, you might try increasing the Max Time and Iterations values. Doing so gives the Solver more opportunity to converge precisely on the target value that you specified. The maximum permissible value for Max Time and for Iterations is 32,767.

You can give the Solver some flexibility by increasing the value in the Precision edit box. When the Solver evaluates the current value of a constrained cell or of the target cell, it does so in terms of the value of the Precision option. The precision value must be between 0 and 1. The smaller the number, the higher the precision.

The Tolerance option is another way of saying "close enough." It applies only to models that have constraints using the int operator. In other words, you have constrained at least one cell to be an integer. When a constrained cell cannot take a fractional value—when that cell is constrained to integer values only—it might not be possible to reach the exact value that you specified for the Target Cell. By increasing the Tolerance to, say, 10%, you indicate that a solution as much as 10% higher or lower than your target value is acceptable.

Suppose that you have $100,000 to spend on the purchase of several cars. You have set up a model that Solver will use to arrive at an average purchase price of $17,000. One of the constraints is the number of cars to purchase. You cannot purchase a fractional number of cars, so you constrain that cell to integer values.

But to arrive at an average purchase price of $17,000 on a total purchase of $100,000, you must purchase 5.88 cars. That conflicts with the integer constraint. Therefore, set the Tolerance to 15%, allowing a result somewhere between 85% and 115% of $17,000. Doing so enables an average purchase price based on either five or six cars—both integer values.

The Convergence option comes into play when the Solver is nearing a solution. The Solver continually examines the most recent five solutions it has calculated as it varies the values in the Changing Cells. If 1 plus the ratio of the amount of change—not the values themselves, but the change in values—from solution to solution is less than the Convergence value for five consecutive solutions, the Solver concludes that it's not going to get any closer to your target value. Make the Convergence more precise by providing a smaller number—any fractional value between 0 and 1.

Defining the Search The Solver Options dialog box also enables you to establish some control over how the Solver will go about seeking a solution to the problem you set for it.

If you check the Assume Linear Model check box, you make a fundamental change in how the Solver goes about evaluating the problem. Recall from the prior section "Understanding the Solver's Reports" that the Solver proceeds by modifying values in the Changing Cells and by observing the resulting differences in the function's gradient.

You prevent this from occurring by assuming a linear model. With a linear model, the Solver can simply calculate a linear equation that fits different Changing Cell values to Target Cell values. In effect, the Solver backtracks from a specified solution to a set of requisite Changing Cell values by means of that equation. This speeds up the solution process dramatically because it's not necessary to evaluate a series of trial solutions.

If there is no exponentiation in any of the Changing Cells, in the Target Cell, or (more typically) in any of the formulas that come between the Changing Cells and the Target Cell, then it's quite possible that the model is a linear one.

It can happen, though, that nonlinearity exists in the model, not immediately apparent to you, that's induced by the relationships among the Changing Cells and between the Changing Cells and the Target Cell. If so, you may be setting the Solver an impossible task by telling it to assume a linear model. You might get an error message that the conditions for a linear solution aren't met. Or it's possible that the Solver will return the correct solution to the wrong problem.

Although a nonlinear search is slower, in a time when many users are running Excel with processors whose clock speed exceeds 200MHz, you can probably afford to assume a nonlinear model. If your model turns out to be linear, its linearity is unlikely to make a difference in the solution.

So when the difference in solution time is a matter of a few seconds and when you're likely to obtain the same result, it's sensible to leave the Assume Linear Model check box in its default cleared state.

It can help to select the Use Automatic Scaling check box when the scale of measurement of the Changing Cells and that of the Target or Constraint cells are very different. In this chapter's example, the Changing Cells use both percentages (to derive costs) and hundreds of thousands of dollars (to represent revenue estimates). The automatic scaling option can speed up calculation in this and similar situations.

The Assume Non-Negative option is a good shortcut when you have Changing Cells that should not be assigned negative values. In the current example, if you were willing for any cost percentage to be zero but not negative, you could dispense with the Constraints and select the Assume Non-Negative check box instead.

It can be useful to select the Show Iteration Results check box. Doing so causes the Solver to pause after each iteration. This gives you an opportunity to examine the current values of the Changing Cells and the Target Cell and to save the current solution as a scenario. Subsequently examining the differences among the temporary solutions can give you some insight into the relationships among the Changing Cells and the Target Cell.

Influencing the Calculations When the Solver establishes a gradient of partial derivatives, it extrapolates from that gradient to choose the next set of values that it assigns to the Changing Cells. It can do that on either a linear or a nonlinear basis. If you keep the default value, Tangent, for Estimates, the Solver lays a straight line that's tangential to the gradient. It then extrapolates along that line to reach the next set of values it will try for the Changing Cells.

If you choose Quadratic instead of Tangent, the Solver lays a curve against the gradient. In nonlinear problems, this can speed up performance because it's not necessary to repeatedly create straight-line tangents to extrapolate to the next set of Changing Cell values. Again, though, because of the speed of today's microprocessors, the option will usually be irrelevant to you.

When the Solver is in the midst of evaluating a current solution and trying to figure out the next set of Changing Cell values it should try, it does so by altering each Changing Cell slightly and keeping track of the combined effect on the rate of change, the derivative, of the Target Cell value. This is how the default option for Derivatives, Forward Differencing, works.

If you choose Central Differencing, the Solver makes two estimates at each iteration, instead of just one. It does this by selecting values for the Changing Cells that cause the two estimates to lie in different directions along the gradient from the current estimate. This results in more accurate calculations at each step, but it also results in more calculations.

The Search option specifies the algorithm used at each iteration to determine the direction to search: Newton or Conjugate. The default is Newton. The choice between the Newton and the Conjugate methods is difficult to understand. Very briefly, the *Newton method* calculates analytic derivatives at each iteration. The *conjugate gradient method* constructs each iteration's estimate by means of a minimization procedure. It takes longer per iteration and requires more iterations than the Newton method. You'll usually do fine by accepting the default Newton option.

Troubleshooting Solver Errors

If you use the Solver on a data set and get one solution, another colleague may use the Solver on the data set and get a different solution. Most often, this occurs when two users have some Solver option set differently. But it can happen even when both users have set the Solver options identically. Very small differences in the starting values of the Changing Cells can exert an apparently disproportionate influence on the results returned by the Solver. Try copying the starting values from one user's worksheet to the other user's worksheet, and then running the Solver again.

If you set the constraint for a range of cells to Integer, when the Solver finished, you might find that the cells weren't integers. The Solver comes as close as it can to integer values for integer-constrained cells. It can happen, however, that slight variances from the integer value occur. When this happens, the variances tend to be beyond the tenth decimal place; for example, instead of 3, the Solver returns 3.000000000594. For most purposes this is close enough. But if not, use the TRUNC function on the Changing Cells in question, copy the results, and paste them as values over the original Changing Cells. Then compare the new value for the Target Cell with the one that the Solver returned.

CHAPTER 28

Auditing Worksheets and Resolving Errors

In this chapter

Auditing Worksheet Data

Over time, a workbook can become more and more complex. This is particularly true of workbooks used for financial and accounting purposes; the ongoing growth and diversification of a business is mirrored by the growth and diversification of its financial records. When more data and categories of data are added, structures that were originally kept on one worksheet are given their own sheets or even their own workbooks. Formulas that once were simple become sophisticated as further refinements are made. As new accountants and analysts join the business, the labor is divided among them, and so are the workbooks.

Eventually, this process results in formulas that refer to multiple cells and ranges—references that, through linking, point to locations in other worksheets and workbooks (sometimes two and even three or more workbooks) from the worksheet containing the formulas referencing these cells.

Inevitably, a mistake occurs. Sometimes it's obvious—you see an error message—and sometimes it's not as obvious—a formula returns an erroneous result. This chapter discusses ways to *audit* your worksheets to locate and resolve both of these types of errors.

The key to locating, troubleshooting, and avoiding errors in worksheets is to regularly audit your files. Most auditing consists of verifying that your formulas are making the correct calculations by looking at the formulas' *precedents*—the cells used by the formula to calculate the result. Several ways to do this exist. When you edit a formula, the Range Finder feature distinguishes the precedents by color-coding the cells. Another option is to check the worksheet to make sure a formula hasn't been replaced with a constant value or an incorrect formula. You do this with the Go To, Special command by highlighting cells that contain constant values or formulas or by uncovering formulas that are not using the correct cell references.

It is important that you learn to interpret and correct worksheet error messages such as reference errors, division-by-zero errors, and circular references. Excel includes several methods for tracing precedents, dependents, and errors. *Dependents* (the flip side of precedents) are the formulas that are dependent upon the data in a particular source cell.

You can also do several things to avoid errors. For example, you can use formulas to help check for errors or add cell comments to documents—notes or messages that will avoid worksheet errors.

Auditing Formulas

Errors may occur in worksheets that don't display error messages but that cause incorrect calculations to occur. Sometimes these erroneous results are not obvious; you have to perform routine auditing to catch these errors. At other times, the results clearly aren't correct. Then begins the laborious process of tracing the references used in the formula to their destinations, checking at each intermediate point until the problem is found and corrected.

Several ways exist to find the cells that may be causing these types of errors in your formulas. If you are performing routine auditing, you might try using some options available through the

Edit, Go To, Special command. If the error is obvious, tracing the cells the formula references (the precedent cells) is the first step.

Using the Go To Special Command

Excel worksheets typically consist of data and formulas, which are often linked to other worksheets or workbooks. The Go To Special command provides a beneficial, yet simple way to analyze your worksheets. This command helps find cells that meet criteria you specify. For example, you can locate all cells that contain comments, formulas, or error messages.

Suppose, for instance, you have a worksheet such as the one in Figure 28.1. Although there aren't any error messages, this worksheet contains several incorrect calculations.

FIGURE 28.1
Audit worksheets to find the less obvious errors.

	A	B	C	D	E	F	G
1		ACME Computer Co.					
2		Wholesale/Retail Pricing Sheet -- Maryland					
3		Start-Up System		MARKUPS			
4		Equipment	WHOLESALE	15%	25%	30%	40%
5		Pentium II 400	$1,499.00	$1,723.85	$1,873.75	$1,948.70	$2,098.60
6		17inch Monitor	385.00	$442.75	$481.25	$500.50	$539.00
7		56K Modem	99.00	$113.85	$123.75	$128.70	$138.60
8		Key/Mouse/Speakers	145.00	$166.75	$181.25	$557.00	$203.00
9		Ink Jet Printer	215.00	$247.25	$268.75	$279.50	$301.00
10		Software Suite	229.00	$247.25	$286.25	$297.70	$320.60
11		*Kit Total*	*2,572.00*	*2,941.70*	*3,215.00*	*3,712.10*	*3,600.80*
12		Total with Tax	$2,790.62	$3,191.74	$3,488.28	$4,027.63	$3,906.87
13							
14		SALES TAX RATE	8.50%				
15							

To locate the errors, start by using the Go To Special feature. A quick way to display the Go To dialog box is to press the F5 key once. Choosing Edit, Go To, or pressing Ctrl+G are the alternative methods of displaying the dialog box. Selecting the Special button displays the Go To Special dialog box, as shown in Figure 28.2.

If a single cell is selected when an option from the Go To Special command is used, the entire active workbook is searched. If a range of cells is selected when the command is used, only the cells in the selected range are searched.

The options in the Go To Special dialog box help locate specific cells in your workbook. The following options are used to analyze your worksheets:

- Constants—Identifies all cells that do not contain formulas. By default, all cells that contain constants are selected. However, you can specify only cells with numbers, text, logical values (True or False), errors, or any combination of these options. This is useful in identifying cells where there should be constants, not formulas.

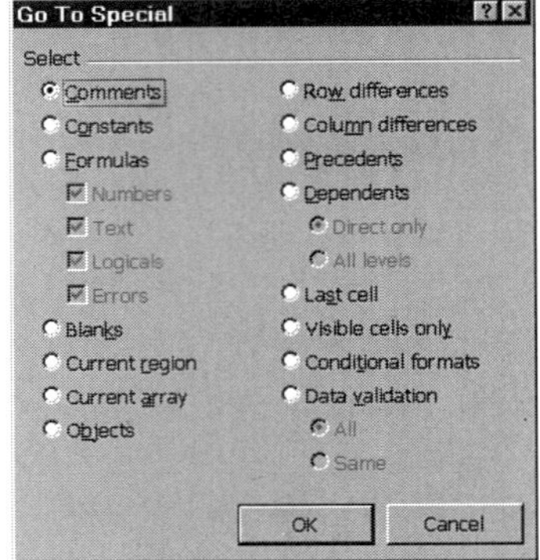

FIGURE 28.2
Select criteria for Excel to use in the Go To Special dialog box.

NOTE The check boxes under Formulas in the Go To Special dialog box are actually linked to both the Constants and Formulas options, even though they appear indented under Formulas.

- Formulas—Identifies all cells that contain formulas. By default, all cells that contain formulas are selected. However, you can specify formulas in which the results of the formulas are numbers, text, logical values, error messages, or any combination of these options. This option is useful in identifying cells that should have formulas, not constant values.
- Row Differences and Column Differences—Compares a formula pattern in one cell to the relative formulas in other cells in the same row or column. This option is useful in identifying errors in a series of formulas.
- Precedents and Dependents—Selects cells that the active cell refers to (precedents) or selects cells that refer to the active cell (dependents). Cells that are directly or indirectly linked to the active cell can be selected. This option is useful in identifying errors in formulas.

NOTE The Direct Only and All Levels options in the Go To Special dialog box are actually linked to both the Precedents and Dependents options, even though they appear indented under Dependents.

- Conditional Formats—Identifies cells that contain formats based on the type of data in the cells. All cells containing conditional formatting or just those that contain the same formatting as the active cell can be selected.

NOTE The All and Same options in the Go To Special dialog box are actually linked to both the Conditional Formats and Data Validation options, even though they appear indented under Data Validation.

- Data Validation—Selects cells that have imbedded data validation (established through the Data Validation command). You can select All Cells data validation or just those that contain the same validation as the active cell.

▶ **See** "Conditional Formatting," **p. 630**

▶ **See** "Controlling Data Entry," **p. 860**

The other options in the Go To Special dialog box are not used explicitly for analysis but are useful for selecting items in your worksheets.

To check whether the formulas have been overwritten by constant values, mark Formulas in the Go To Special dialog box and click OK. All formulas in your worksheet are highlighted, as shown in Figure 28.3. Of course, the first cell in any group of highlighted cells appears with a transparent background, as seen in cell D5. However, cell F8 clearly does not contain a formula, and it should—the wholesale price plus markup amount (the wholesale price times the markup percent).

NOTE Because Excel found an exception in the group of formulas, it highlights the cells in groups, like ranges. This creates highlighting that appears to have borders around certain cells, but it is merely a function of the way Excel highlights the cells.

FIGURE 28.3
The cells that are not highlighted contain constants, not formulas.

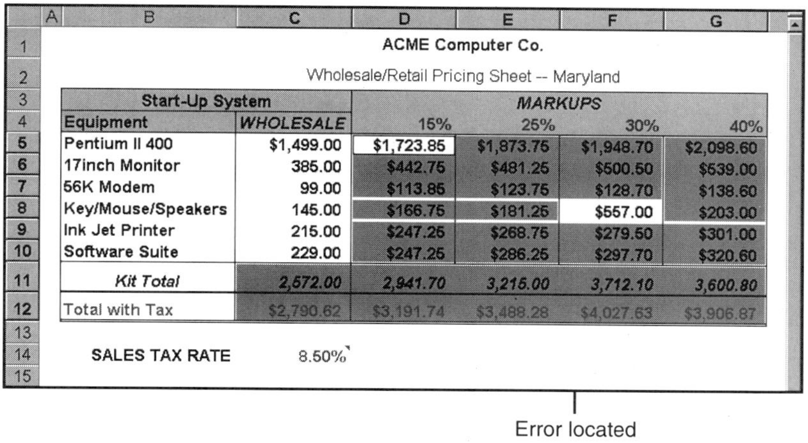

	A	B	C	D	E	F	G
1				ACME Computer Co.			
2				Wholesale/Retail Pricing Sheet -- Maryland			
3		Start-Up System		MARKUPS			
4		Equipment	WHOLESALE	15%	25%	30%	40%
5		Pentium II 400	$1,499.00	$1,723.85	$1,873.75	$1,948.70	$2,098.60
6		17inch Monitor	385.00	$442.75	$481.25	$500.50	$539.00
7		56K Modem	99.00	$113.85	$123.75	$128.70	$138.60
8		Key/Mouse/Speakers	145.00	$166.75	$181.25	$557.00	$203.00
9		Ink Jet Printer	215.00	$247.25	$268.75	$279.50	$301.00
10		Software Suite	229.00	$247.25	$286.25	$297.70	$320.60
11		Kit Total	2,572.00	2,941.70	3,215.00	3,712.10	3,600.80
12		Total with Tax	$2,790.62	$3,191.74	$3,488.28	$4,027.63	$3,906.87
13							
14		SALES TAX RATE	8.50%				
15							

Error located

If you have formulas in a row or column that follow the same pattern, you can compare each formula to the first formula to ensure they all follow the same pattern. For example, in Figure 28.1, the row of retail prices for the Pentium II 400 computer follows the same pattern for their formulas—they each take the wholesale price in cell C5 and add the markup amount based on the percentages in row 4. By comparing the pattern of the other formulas in row 5 against the first formula in cell D5, you can audit the formulas and perhaps uncover an error that is not obvious. In most cases, you are checking one row or column of data. Because this example is a series of formulas, we can check for patterns in all the rows by selecting all the cells to be checked (cells D5:G10).

After you have the cells selected, press F5 and click the Special button to display the Go To Special dialog box. In the Go To Special dialog box, choose Row Differences and click OK. Figure 28.4 shows the result. The error in F8 we already knew about. But the formulas in row 10 are highlighted, all except the first one—meaning none of the formulas in that row match the pattern used on the first formula. Often when you see this, it is the first formula that has an error. Because this example is a series of formulas, we'll also check column differences on the same set of cells; the result is shown in Figure 28.5. Figure 28.5 confirms that the error in row 10 is in cell D10, not E10:G10.

TIP If a lot of cells are highlighted, use the Enter key to cycle through the highlighted cells as you look at the contents in the Formula bar.

FIGURE 28.4
Checking row and column differences can uncover hidden errors.

	A	B	C	D	E	F	G
1				ACME Computer Co.			
2				Wholesale/Retail Pricing Sheet -- Maryland			
3		Start-Up System			MARKUPS		
4		Equipment	WHOLESALE	15%	25%	30%	40%
5		Pentium II 400	$1,499.00	$1,723.85	$1,873.75	$1,948.70	$2,098.60
6		17inch Monitor	385.00	$442.75	$481.25	$500.50	$539.00
7		56K Modem	99.00	$113.85	$123.75	$128.70	$138.60
8		Key/Mouse/Speakers	145.00	$166.75	$181.25	$557.00	$203.00
9		Ink Jet Printer	215.00	$247.25	$268.75	$279.50	$301.00
10		Software Suite	229.00	$247.25	$286.25	$297.70	$320.60
11		*Kit Total*	*2,572.00*	*2,941.70*	*3,215.00*	*3,712.10*	*3,600.80*
12		Total with Tax	$2,790.62	$3,191.74	$3,488.28	$4,027.63	$3,906.87
13							
14		SALES TAX RATE	8.50%				
15							

FIGURE 28.5
If the formulas are in a row, check row differences. If they are in a column, check column differences.

	A	B	C	D	E	F	G
1				ACME Computer Co.			
2				Wholesale/Retail Pricing Sheet -- Maryland			
3		Start-Up System			MARKUPS		
4		Equipment	WHOLESALE	15%	25%	30%	40%
5		Pentium II 400	$1,499.00	$1,723.85	$1,873.75	$1,948.70	$2,098.60
6		17inch Monitor	385.00	$442.75	$481.25	$500.50	$539.00
7		56K Modem	99.00	$113.85	$123.75	$128.70	$138.60
8		Key/Mouse/Speakers	145.00	$166.75	$181.25	$557.00	$203.00
9		Ink Jet Printer	215.00	$247.25	$268.75	$279.50	$301.00
10		Software Suite	229.00	$247.25	$286.25	$297.70	$320.60
11		*Kit Total*	*2,572.00*	*2,941.70*	*3,215.00*	*3,712.10*	*3,600.80*
12		Total with Tax	$2,790.62	$3,191.74	$3,488.28	$4,027.63	$3,906.87
13							
14		SALES TAX RATE	8.50%				
15							

After you've identified a problem formula, you can use the Range Finder or trace the formula's precedents to locate the error. These techniques are discussed in the next few sections in the chapter.

Using the Range Finder to Audit Your Formulas

Range Finder (introduced in Excel 97) helps to quickly identify the cells used by a formula. When you double-click to edit a formula, each cell reference, range of cells, or range name used in the formula is changed to a different color. The borders of the corresponding cells in the worksheet are colored to match the cells in the formula. This makes it easier to find each of the formula's precedent cells.

So when you double-click the formula in Figure 28.5 (cell D10) identified as a possible error, the results are displayed as shown in Figure 28.6.

FIGURE 28.6
You can also press F2 or click in the Formula bar to edit the formula.

One color code points to the markup percentage.

The other color code points to the wholesale price for the Ink Jet Printer—the wrong product.

FV | =$C9+$C9*D$4

	A	B	C	D	E	F	G
1				ACME Computer Co.			
2				Wholesale/Retail Pricing Sheet -- Maryland			
3		Start-Up System			MARKUPS		
4		Equipment	WHOLESALE	15%	25%	30%	40%
5		Pentium II 400	$1,499.00	$1,723.85	$1,873.75	$1,948.70	$2,098.60
6		17inch Monitor	385.00	$442.75	$481.25	$500.50	$539.00
7		56K Modem	99.00	$113.85	$123.75	$128.70	$138.60
8		Key/Mouse/Speakers	145.00	$166.75	$181.25	$557.00	$203.00
9		Ink Jet Printer	215.00	$247.25	$268.75	$279.50	$301.00
10		Software Suite	229.00	=$C9+$C9*D$4		$297.70	$320.60
11		*Kit Total*	*2,572.00*	*2,941.70*	*3,215.00*	*3,712.10*	*3,600.80*
12		Total with Tax	$2,790.62	$3,191.74	$3,488.28	$4,027.63	$3,906.87
13							
14		SALES TAX RATE	8.50%				

Use the Range Finder's color coding in a simple worksheet where most, if not all, of the data is visible. This color coding does not appear if the cell references data in other worksheets or workbooks—a serious limitation. Instead, use the tracing feature in Excel to locate cells in complex worksheets. Tracing arrows indicate the data is in another worksheet or workbook.

Tracing Precedents and Dependents in Formulas

Several ways exist to trace precedents and dependents: You can use the Go To Special dialog box or you can use the Tools, Auditing commands.

NOTE Remember, precedents are the cells used by the formula to calculate the result. Precedents can be constant values or other formulas. Dependents are the formulas that are dependent on the data in a particular source cell.

When you select a cell that contains a formula, you can look in the Formula bar to see the precedents. If the precedents are cell references, it's fairly easy to locate them. On the other hand, if the cell references are range names, using the tracing tools in Excel speeds up the process.

The one advantage to using the Go To Special dialog box is that you can ask to see precedents and dependents at all levels, not just the direct ones. For example, suppose cell B4 is used in a formula in cell B12, and the B12 is used in another formula in cell G19. If B4 is the active cell, choosing to see the direct-only dependents would select only cell B12. But choosing to see all levels of dependents would select both B12 and G19.

Using the Auditing commands, you have to repeat the command to see the next level because these commands display only the direct precedents and dependents. This can be useful as a way to step through all the cells involved, one level at a time. However, it can also be very time-consuming on large, intricate worksheets.

The advantage to using the Auditing commands to trace precedents and dependents is the indicators that display when a precedent or dependent is on another worksheet or workbook. The Go To Special dialog box options identify the cells by highlighting them, as if you dragged the mouse across and highlighted them yourself. The Auditing commands, on the other hand, draw arrows from the selected cell to the precedents and dependents. The trace arrows provide a nice visual link to the precedents and dependents.

We'll use the worksheet shown in Figure 28.7 to trace the precedents for the formula in cell B8 using both the Go To Special dialog box options and the Auditing trace commands. This worksheet was introduced in Chapter 23, "Functions for Every Occasion," and discussed again in Chapter 27, "Analytical Tools." The worksheet calculates the Net Present Value (NPV), and cell B8 is the Net Cash Flow for Year 1.

FIGURE 28.7

You can trace errors on any worksheet that contains formulas.

F15 = =NPV(B10,B8:F8)

	A	B	C	D	E	F	G
1	Year	1	2	3	4	5	
2	Revenue	$35	$98	$162	$204	$307	
3	Less: Cost of goods sold	$100	$100	$100	$100	$100	
4	Net Income	-$65	-$2	$62	$104	$207	
5							
6	Less: Cost of equipment	$200	$0	$0	$0	$0	
7							
8	Net cash flow	-$265	-$2	$62	$104	$207	
9							
10	Discount rate	10%					
11	Annual discount factors	110%	121%	133%	146%	161%	
12	Discounted cash flow	-$241	-$2	$47	$71	$129	
13	Cumulative discounted cash flow	-$241	-$243	-$196	-$125	$4	
14							
15					NPV	$4	

Tracing the Precedents from the Go To Special Dialog Box If you use the Go To Special dialog box (Edit, Go To, Special) and select Precedents (direct only) from the dialog box, the result is the highlighting of the precedent cells in the worksheet (see Figure 28.8). Cells B4 and B6 are highlighted when tracing the precedents for cell B8. You can use the Enter key to switch between the highlighted cells.

In some cases, the cells containing the error are in cells indirectly associated with the formula. Figure 28.9 shows the precedents traced back all levels (using the Go To Special dialog box) from cell B8. Now, cells B2 and B3 are highlighted in addition to B4 and B6, which means that B2 and B3 must be precedents for B4 or B6—the direct precedents for B8 were shown in Figure 28.8. This makes B2 and B3 indirect precedents for B8.

FIGURE 28.8
The cell you started with is not part of the highlighted group.

B4 = =B2-B3

	A	B	C	D	E	F	G
1	Year	1	2	3	4	5	
2	Revenue	$35	$98	$162	$204	$307	
3	Less: Cost of goods sold	$100	$100	$100	$100	$100	
4	Net Income	-$65	-$2	$62	$104	$207	
5							
6	Less: Cost of equipment	$200	$0	$0	$0	$0	
7							
8	Net cash flow	-$265	-$2	$62	$104	$207	
9							
10	Discount rate	10%					
11	Annual discount factors	110%	121%	133%	146%	161%	
12	Discounted cash flow	-$241	-$2	$47	$71	$129	
13	Cumulative discounted cash flow	-$241	-$243	-$196	-$125	$4	
14							
15					NPV	$4	

FIGURE 28.9
All cells in the active worksheet that are the precedents of cell B8 are highlighted.

B6 = ='C:\My Documents\[Equipment.xls]Sheet1'!$G$26

	A	B	C	D	E	F	G
1	Year	1	2	3	4	5	
2	Revenue	$35	$98	$162	$204	$307	
3	Less: Cost of goods sold	$100	$100	$100	$100	$100	
4	Net Income	-$65	-$2	$62	$104	$207	
5							
6	Less: Cost of equipment	$200	$0	$0	$0	$0	
7							
8	Net cash flow	-$265	-$2	$62	$104	$207	
9							
10	Discount rate	10%					
11	Annual discount factors	110%	121%	133%	146%	161%	
12	Discounted cash flow	-$241	-$2	$47	$71	$129	
13	Cumulative discounted cash flow	-$241	-$243	-$196	-$125	$4	
14							
15					NPV	$4	

Although this appears complete, in fact, it is not. Both cells B2 and B6 are linked to other worksheets. B2 is linked to another sheet in the active workbook and B6 is linked to another workbook entirely. To really see this, you must use the Auditing command.

Tracing Precedents Using the Auditing Trace Commands The most efficient way to use the Auditing commands is to display the Auditing toolbar. This toolbar does not appear on the shortcut menu when you right-click other toolbars. Nor does it appear on the list when you choose View, Toolbars. The Auditing toolbar can be displayed either by choosing Tools, Auditing, Show Auditing Toolbar or by activating it in the Customize dialog box (Tools, Customize). As with other toolbars, the Auditing toolbar can be docked or floating (as shown in Figure 28.10).

Then when you want to use one of the trace commands, you select the cell and click the appropriate button on the toolbar. Unlike the Go To Special method, the Auditing commands method of *tracing* actually displays tracing arrows, as shown in Figure 28.10.

FIGURE 28.10
The trace arrows point to the precedent cells, one level back.

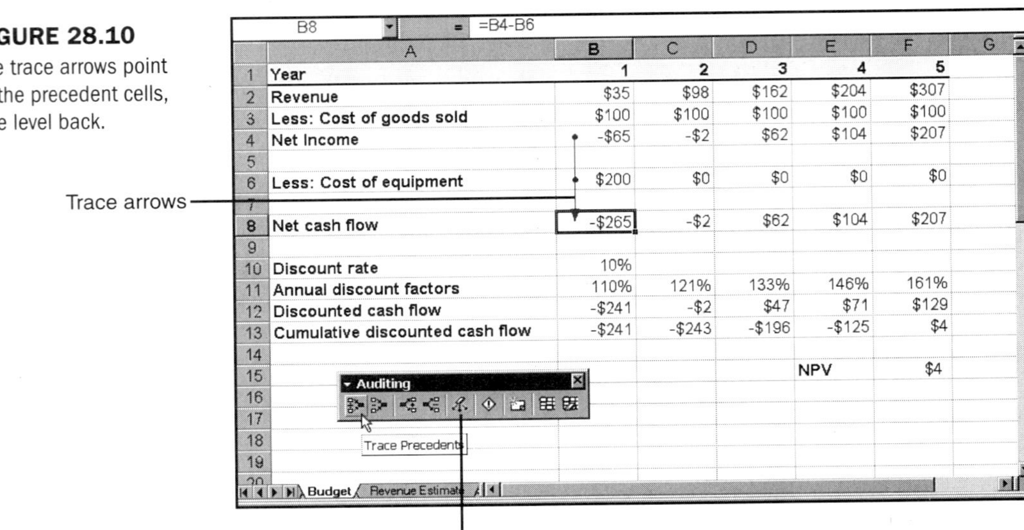

	A	B	C	D	E	F
1	Year	1	2	3	4	5
2	Revenue	$35	$98	$162	$204	$307
3	Less: Cost of goods sold	$100	$100	$100	$100	$100
4	Net Income	-$65	-$2	$62	$104	$207
5						
6	Less: Cost of equipment	$200	$0	$0	$0	$0
7						
8	Net cash flow	-$265	-$2	$62	$104	$207
9						
10	Discount rate	10%				
11	Annual discount factors	110%	121%	133%	146%	161%
12	Discounted cash flow	-$241	-$2	$47	$71	$129
13	Cumulative discounted cash flow	-$241	-$243	-$196	-$125	$4
14						
15					NPV	$4

To trace all levels, you may need to click the trace precedents button several times. Each time, Excel traces back one level. When there are no further levels, you'll hear a beep. Figure 28.11 shows the result.

FIGURE 28.11
You may need to trace back several levels to locate all cells the formula directly or indirectly uses.

	A	B	C	D	E	F
1	Year	1	2	3	4	5
2	Revenue	$35	$98	$162	$204	$307
3	Less: Cost of goods sold	$100	$100	$100	$100	$100
4	Net Income	-$65	-$2	$62	$104	$207
5						
6	Less: Cost of equipment	$200	$0	$0	$0	$0
7						
8	Net cash flow	-$265	-$2	$62	$104	$207
9						
10	Discount rate	10%				
11	Annual discount factors	110%	121%	133%	146%	161%
12	Discounted cash flow	-$241	-$2	$47	$71	$129
13	Cumulative discounted cash flow	-$241	-$243	-$196	-$125	$4
14						
15					NPV	$4

Trace arrows locate all precedent (or dependent) cells, whether in the active workbook or in other workbooks. If a trace arrow points off the screen, this indicates the precedent (or dependent) is in the active worksheet but not currently visible. If the trace arrow points to a worksheet symbol, this indicates the precedent (or dependent) is either on another worksheet in the active workbook or in another workbook entirely. To help clarify that these arrows are connected to worksheet symbols and not other cells, arrows indicating precedents (or dependents) not in the current sheet are also indicated by dashed lines instead of solid lines, as shown in Figure 28.11.

If the precedent (or dependent) is indicated by a linking line to a worksheet symbol, double-click the trace line. The Go To dialog box appears, indicating the path to the link. Select the path and click OK. If the link is to another worksheet in the active workbook, that sheet displays with the linked cell selected.

If the link is to another workbook—and the workbook is open—the workbook is activated and the sheet containing the linked cell is displayed. However, if the workbook is not open, the Go To dialog box remains active. You will be able to see the path to the workbook. Close the dialog box and open the necessary workbook. Then double-click the linking line again.

Figure 28.12 shows the result of double-clicking the first linking line indicated in Figure 28.11.

FIGURE 28.12
The source of the data in cell B2 of the Budget worksheet.

C18 = =SUM(C4:C17)

	A	B	C	D	E	F	G	H
1	Revenue Estimates							
2			1	2	3	4	5	
3								
4		North America	$3.7	$12.5	$19.3	$25.4	$36.9	
5		Central America	$0.3	$3.5	$12.2	$15.9	$21.2	
6		Caribbean	$0.2	$2.2	$7.9	$10.2	$18.6	
7		South America	$3.4	$10.8	$13.2	$16.8	$26.1	
8		Western Europe	$2.9	$11.1	$17.1	$22.5	$31.3	
9		Eastern Europe	$4.1	$10.9	$11.9	$13.2	$21.1	
10		Northern Africa	$3.9	$5.5	$9.2	$11.7	$19.6	
11		Central Africa	$0.6	$4.3	$7.4	$9.1	$13.4	
12		Southern Africa	$0.9	$5.1	$10.2	$14.6	$23.5	
13		Middle East	$2.6	$4.6	$9.1	$11.9	$17.2	
14		Russia	$3.2	$9.9	$17.3	$21.2	$27.9	
15		India/Pakistan	$1.7	$4.1	$7.6	$9.4	$14.7	
16		Asia	$4.9	$7.8	$11.5	$12.7	$22.3	
17		Australia	$2.6	$5.7	$8.1	$9.4	$13.2	
18		*Totals*	$35.0	$98.0	$162.0	$204.0	$307.0	
19								

Budget | Revenue Estimate

To remove trace arrows, click the Remove All Arrows button on the Auditing toolbar (refer to Figure 28.10) or choose Tools, Auditing, Remove All Arrows.

Understanding Excel Error Messages

Error messages display when the result of a formula cannot be calculated. These messages display for several reasons—when a cell used in a formula is blank or contains text, or when cells referenced by a formula are deleted or cannot be located.

The error may be in the formula or in one of the cells to which the formula refers. The next few sections describe each error and show you how to find the cause and resolve the error.

Resolving Circular Reference Errors

A *circular reference* occurs when a formula refers back to its own cell. When a circular reference is made, Excel displays a warning message, as shown in Figure 28.13. You have a choice of resolving the reference by selecting OK or ignoring the circular reference by choosing Cancel.

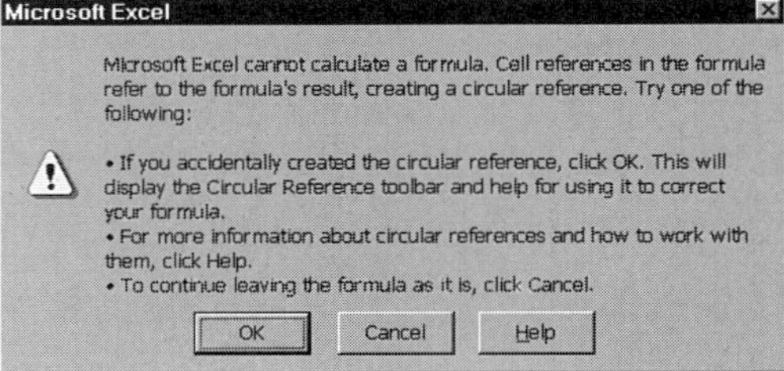

FIGURE 28.13
A warning message displays when a circular cell reference is made in a formula.

If you select OK, the Circular Reference toolbar is displayed (see Figure 28.14). The toolbar helps to identify each cell in the circular reference.

The status bar displays the word "Circular" and one of the cell references contained in the circular reference. If no cell reference with the word "Circular" is in the status bar, the circular reference is not in the active worksheet.

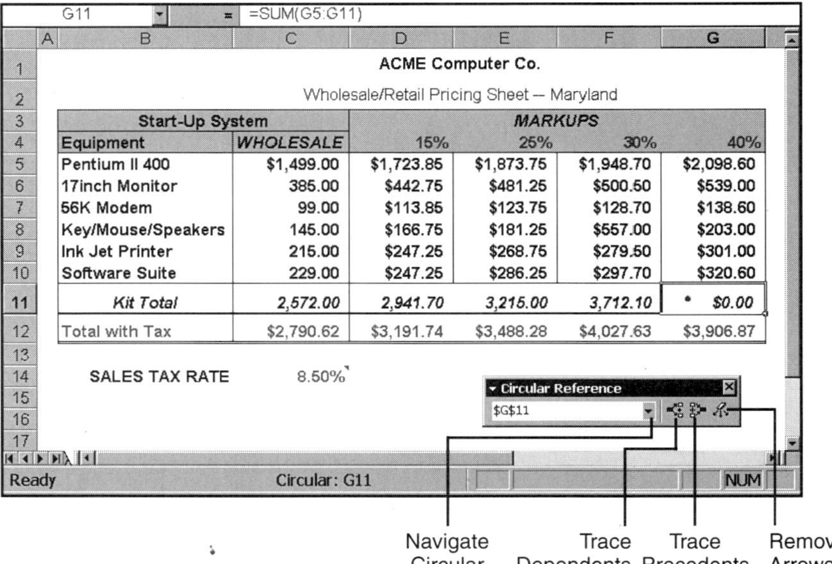

Start-Up System		MARKUPS			
Equipment	WHOLESALE	15%	25%	30%	40%
Pentium II 400	$1,499.00	$1,723.85	$1,873.75	$1,948.70	$2,098.60
17inch Monitor	385.00	$442.75	$481.25	$500.50	$539.00
56K Modem	99.00	$113.85	$123.75	$128.70	$138.60
Key/Mouse/Speakers	145.00	$166.75	$181.25	$557.00	$203.00
Ink Jet Printer	215.00	$247.25	$268.75	$279.50	$301.00
Software Suite	229.00	$247.25	$286.25	$297.70	$320.60
Kit Total	*2,572.00*	*2,941.70*	*3,215.00*	*3,712.10*	*$0.00*
Total with Tax	$2,790.62	$3,191.74	$3,488.28	$4,027.63	$3,906.87

FIGURE 28.14
Excel displays the Circular Reference toolbar to help you trace the error.

Circular References Required by Some Excel Functions

Some of Excel's scientific and engineering functions require circular references. To calculate a circular reference formula, Microsoft Excel must calculate each cell involved in the circular reference one time by using the results of the previous iteration. By default, Microsoft Excel calculates either up to 100 iterations or to the point that all values in the circular reference change by less than 0.001 between iterations, whichever comes first.

You may need to change the number of iterations if your formula is one that requires a circular reference. To change the number of iterations, choose Tools, Options. In the Options dialog box, select the Calculation tab. Check the Iteration box and indicate the maximum number of iterations and degree of change you want Excel to use.

Most engineering and scientific functions are available in the Analysis ToolPak add-in. Choose Tools, Add-Ins to install the Analysis ToolPak.

Resolving *#VALUE!* Errors

The `#VALUE!` error indicates that the formula contains an unacceptable argument. Examples include the following:

- When one of the cells referenced in a formula contains text instead of a number
- When a formula expects a single cell reference and a range is entered instead
- When you create (or edit) an array formula and press Enter instead of Ctrl+Shift+Enter (as is required by array formulas)

Figure 28.15 shows an example of a `#VALUE!` error message in the Sales calculation. A look at the Formula bar indicates the `DSUM` function is being used. Database is a range name for the sales list.

FIGURE 28.15
To display the toolbar, choose Tools, Auditing, Show Auditing toolbar.

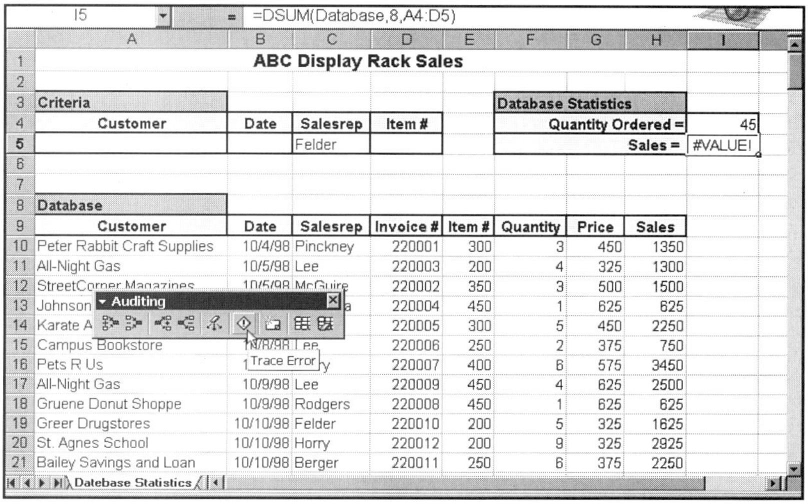

I5 = =DSUM(Database,8,A4:D5)

ABC Display Rack Sales

Criteria			
Customer	Date	Salesrep	Item #
		Felder	

Database Statistics	
Quantity Ordered =	45
Sales =	#VALUE!

Database

Customer	Date	Salesrep	Invoice #	Item #	Quantity	Price	Sales
Peter Rabbit Craft Supplies	10/4/98	Pinckney	220001	300	3	450	1350
All-Night Gas	10/5/98	Lee	220003	200	4	325	1300
StreetCorner Magazines	10/5/98	McGuire	220002	350	3	500	1500
Johnson			220004	450	1	625	625
Karate A			220005	300	5	450	2250
Campus Bookstore		Lee	220006	250	2	375	750
Pets R Us			220007	400	6	575	3450
All-Night Gas	10/9/98	Lee	220009	450	4	625	2500
Gruene Donut Shoppe	10/9/98	Rodgers	220008	450	1	625	625
Greer Drugstores	10/10/98	Felder	220010	200	5	325	1625
St. Agnes School	10/10/98	Horry	220012	200	9	325	2925
Bailey Savings and Loan	10/10/98	Berger	220011	250	6	375	2250

Auditing

Trace Error

Datebase Statistics

To locate this error, select the cell containing the error, display the Auditing toolbar, and click the Trace Error button. Arrows are drawn to the problem cells, and the worksheet scrolls so you can see the cells, as shown in Figure 28.16.

▶ **See** "Exploring the Power of Array Formulas," **p. 661**

▶ **See** "Using Database Functions with Lists," **p. 785**

FIGURE 28.16
The arrows indicate all precedents that are involved in the error.

H22 = =F22*G22

	A	B	C	D	E	F	G	H	I
3	Criteria					Database Statistics			
4	Customer	Date	Salesrep	Item #				Quantity Ordered =	47
5			Felder					Sales =	#VALUE!
6									
7									
8	Database								
9	Customer	Date	Salesrep	Invoice #	Item #	Quantity	Price	Sales	
10	Peter Rabbit Craft Supplies	10/4/98	Pinckney	220001	300	3	450	1350	
11	All-Night Gas	10/5/98	Lee	220003	200	4	325	1300	
12	StreetCorner Magazines	10/5/98	McGuire	220002	350	3	500	1500	
13	Johnson's Drug Store	10/6/98	Fujimora	220004	450	1	625	625	
14	Karate Academy	10/7/98	Abbott	220005	300	5	450	2250	
15	Campus Bookstore	10/8/98	Lee	220006	250	2	375	750	
16	Pets R Us	10/9/98	Horry	220007	400	6	575	3450	
17	All-Night Gas	10/9/98	Lee	220009	450	4	625	2500	
18	Gruene Donut Shoppe	10/9/98	Rodgers	220008	450	1	625	625	
19	Greer Drugstores	10/10/98	Felder	220010	200	5	325	1625	
20	St. Agnes School	10/10/98	Horry	220012	200	9	325	2925	
21	Bailey Savings and Loan	10/10/98	Berger	220011	250	6	375	2250	
22	StreetCorner Magazines	10/10/98	Felder	220013	350	six	500	#######	
23	Moore Music	10/11/98	Rodgers	220014	300	4	450	1800	

Resolving *#DIV/0!* Errors

The `#DIV/0!` error indicates the formula is dividing by a cell that is blank or contains a 0 (zero). For example, in Figure 28.17, it is clear what the cause of the error is—no number exists for Italian Sodas sales in 1998.

FIGURE 28.17
No need to trace the error, but you can use the `IF` function to display more desirable results.

D10 = =(C10-B10)/B10

The Reading Room
Sales Comparisons

	A	B	C	D
5	Item	1998 Total	1999 Total	Percent Change
6	Espresso	$21,800.00	$23,600.00	8.3%
7	Cappuccino	$15,400.00	$14,290.00	-7.2%
8	Soft Drinks	$9,600.00	$7,900.00	-17.7%
9	Latte	$8,700.00	$9,580.00	10.1%
10	Italian Sodas		$9,120.00	#DIV/0!
11	Fresh Fruit Drinks	$4,910.00	$9,530.00	94.1%
12				
13	*Total*	$60,410.00	$74,020.00	$13,610.00
14	*Average*	$12,082.00	$12,336.67	$254.67

NOTE If Italian Sodas were just introduced in 1999, then the cell (B10) can remain blank. If Italian Sodas were offered in 1998 and no one purchased them, then the cell (B10) should contain a zero (because this needs to be factored into the calculation, especially AVERAGE). Either way, the `#DIV/0!` error message appears.

In the first situation, you can also enter text in the cell; for example, "not available." However, you will be presented with the `#VALUE!` error message.

To avoid this, you can employ an `IF` function (along with the help of a few other functions) to account for all the possible situations. The function would be created in the cell containing the first percent change formula and then copied to the other cells. The formula looks like this:

```
=IF(OR(ISBLANK(B6),B6=0,ISTEXT(B6)),"",(C6-B6)/B6)
```

This `IF` statement checks to see whether the 1998 sales cell is empty, contains a zero, or contains text. If it does, then nothing is displayed in the corresponding percent change cell. Otherwise, the calculation is performed.

▶ **See** "Logical and Information Functions," **p. 722**

Resolving *#NAME?* Errors

The `#NAME?` error indicates the formula includes text, usually a range name or nested function, that Excel cannot recognize. The range name may have been deleted, or the range name or function may be misspelled. A space between the function name and the open parenthesis, or the lack of a colon between a range of cell references, can also result in the `#NAME?` error.

These types of errors are easy to avoid. To include a range name in a formula (or check to make sure a range name exists), press F3 to see a list of available range names instead of typing in the range name. If the range name has been deleted, you can re-create it and the error will disappear. To nest functions inside one another, don't type them in. Instead, click the Functions drop-down list in the Formula bar at the point you need the function, and then select it from the list.

▶ **See** "Using Range Names in Formulas," **p. 639**

Resolving *#N/A* Errors

The `#N/A` error indicates a value is not available to a formula or refers to a cell that contains `#N/A`. This may occur for several reasons—when an exact match cannot be found using a lookup function, when an argument is missing in the formula, or when not all the necessary data used by the formula is entered into the worksheet.

Lookup functions, such as `VLOOKUP` and `MATCH`, that search for exact matches and do not find them return the `#N/A` error message as an indication there wasn't a match. You can use an `IF` function and the `ISNA` function to display text in the cell instead of the `#N/A` error.

Consider the worksheet shown in Figure 28.18. It is a list of orders. A `VLOOKUP` function (see the Formula bar) looks up an item number in a price list that is maintained on another worksheet. The `VLOOKUP` formula has been copied to the other cells in the worksheet and several `#N/A` errors have occurred, meaning the item number could not be found in the price list.

FIGURE 28.18
An exact match lookup is expected to return `#N/A` if no match is found.

F4 = =VLOOKUP(D4,PriceList,4,FALSE)

	A	B	C	D	E	F
1			Product Orders			
2						
3	Company	Date	Invoice #	Item #	Quantity	Price
4	Middleton Home Builders	4/3/99	233001	218	4	$12.50
5	Cambridge ISD	4/3/99	226001	303	10	$5.99
6	Pyron & Pyron	4/4/99	234001	302	7	$2.75
7	Weiss LTD	4/4/99	279002	217	5	$15.95
8	Bay Realty	4/5/99	240001	312	7	#N/A
9	Middleton Home Builders	4/5/99	246001	105	9	$19.99
10	Chesapeake Foods	4/5/99	248001	215	6	$8.99
11	Harris Manufacturing	4/5/99	239002	303	10	$5.99
12	Powell AFB	4/4/99	238001	400	8	#N/A
13	Northwest ISD	4/4/99	239001	105	7	$19.99
14	Northwest ISD	4/7/99	251001	105	5	$19.99
15	Bay Realty	4/7/99	241001	215	9	$8.99
16	Cambridge ISD	4/8/99	258001	301	2	$6.99
17	Chesapeake Foods	4/9/99	256001	301	9	$6.99
18	BC Home Construction	4/9/99	242001	105	4	$19.99
19	Coastal Management	4/9/99	251002	301	3	$6.99
20	Middleton Home Builders	4/10/99	246002	301	1	$6.99

Price List / Orders

To display something else in those cells, you can build an `IF` function that checks for the `#N/A` result and displays a text response instead. The formula looks like this:

```
=IF(ISNA(VLOOKUP(D4,'Price List'!$C$4:$F$16,4,FALSE)),"Invalid Item#",
➥ VLOOKUP(D4,'Price List'!$C$4:$F$16,4,FALSE))
```

This `IF` statement checks to see whether the result of the `VLOOKUP` will be `#N/A`. If it will, the text `invaliditem#` is displayed instead. Otherwise, the `VLOOKUP` calculation is performed.

▶ To learn more about using the `VLOOKUP` and `MATCH` functions, **see** "Lookup and Reference Functions," **p. 685**

Resolving *#REF!* Errors

The `#REF!` error indicates the formula refers to a cell that is not valid. This usually occurs when cells have been deleted, or if the reference is to an external workbook and the path to the workbook has been changed or the workbook deleted. The best way to approach this error is with the tracing arrows discussed in the section "Tracing Precedents and Dependents in Formulas" earlier in this chapter.

Resolving *#NUM!* Errors

The `#NUM!` error indicates a number in a formula either is not valid or calculates an invalid result. Edit the function and make sure the arguments used in the function are the correct type of arguments.

Resolving *#NULL!* Errors

The `#NULL!` error usually occurs when a cell range or series of references is entered incorrectly. For example, if a function contains the references `(B6:B16D6:D16)`, the `#NULL!` results. A comma is needed between B16 and D6 to separate the ranges.

This error is easy to avoid by using the Paste Function command to build a formula instead of typing it in from scratch. That said, however, if you prefer to type in your formulas, you can resolve this error by editing the formula and checking for typing errors in the reference to the ranges.

Avoiding Errors

Although checking for errors and responding to errors as they arise is one method of auditing your worksheets, preventing the errors in the first place certainly reduces the errors you will have to resolve! Excel provides several alternatives to help you avoid errors—Data Validation and Cell Protection. Chapter 27 explains rather extensively how to take advantage of the Data Validation feature in Excel. Through this tool, you can designate the types of values acceptable in cells, as well as display input messages when a user selects a cell and display error alert messages when an incorrect entry is added to a cell.

Locking Cells Another option for preventing accidental errors in worksheets is to lock cells that contain formulas. By default, all cells in worksheets are locked, but the "locking" is not active until you protect the worksheet. To protect the worksheet, you should *unlock* the cells you want to be able to change, which typically are cells that contain constant values—everything but formulas. Use the Format, Cells command to unlock cells. Then use the Tools, Protection command to protect the worksheet. For more information, use the Office Assistant. Type in `protecting cells` in the Office Assistant search box. Choose Limit What Others Can See and Change in a Shared Workbook from the results list.

Adding Comments to Worksheets A tool that is frequently overlooked when auditing worksheets is the use of *embedded comments* in your worksheets. Comments are especially useful in forms or templates in which other people will be inputting data. Comments can be attached to any cell. Excel places an indicator (a red triangle) in the upper-right corner of each cell that contains a comment. When the mouse pointer is positioned over the cell, the comment automatically appears on the screen.

To attach a comment to a cell, right-click the cell and choose Insert Comment from the shortcut menu. A small box appears. The title is the User Name defined in the Options dialog box. Enter the text you want to appear in the comment. Resize the box by positioning the mouse pointer on one of the selection handles and drag to reshape the comment box. Press the Esc key or click in an area away from the box to complete the comment.

After comments have been entered into a worksheet, you can edit, delete, or display the comment through the shortcut menu.

Several of the comment settings are controlled through the Options dialog box. Choose Tools, Options to access the dialog box. On the View tab, you can choose not to display the comment or indicator, to display the indicator only, or to display both comment and indicator. By default, only the indicator appears. In the User Name text box on the General tab, you can enter the text you want to display as the title in the comment box. Any comments created before the change in the User Name text retain the former title.

Using Functions to Build In Error Checking

Formulas are an effective means of validating the summary calculations in a worksheet. In Figure 28.19, a list of personal computers sold is displayed. The list indicates the quantity and type of computers sold each day. The total number of PCs sold each day appears in row 10. The total number of each PC type sold for the week appears in column G. A grand total of computers sold for the week is calculated in cell G10. In this example, the sum of all daily totals (B10:F10) should equal the sum of all type totals (G4:G8). So, when the grand total is calculated, you can use either sum in cell G10.

You'll notice that below the worksheet, the calculations for the sum of the daily total and the sum of the sales by type have been added, and that they do not match.

By using an `IF` function, you can create a formula to check that both totals are the same. If they are not the same, you can design the formula to display a warning error message. This type of data-entry verification is known as a *cross-check*. There are several reasons why this error may occur. A constant value might have been accidentally typed over a formula, or a formula may be summing the incorrect cells. These types of errors are common in workbooks that are shared with other users.

FIGURE 28.19

Use formulas to automatically analyze worksheets.

G10 =SUM(B10:F10)

	A	B	C	D	E	F	G
1	Waring Computing - Weekly Sales						
2							Sales
3	Sales	Mon	Tue	Wed	Thu	Fri	by Type
4	Pentium II 450 Desktop	5	8	7	8	8	36
5	Pentium II 400 Desktop	10	6	11	9	10	46
6	Pentium II 450 Notebook	15	14	14	12	15	70
7	Pentium II 400 Notebook	8	8	12	8	7	40
8	Pentium II 266 Notebook	2	5	7	3	4	21
9							
10	Daily Totals	40	41	51	40	44	216
11							
12							
13	Sum of Daily Totals	216					
14	Sum of Sales by Type	213					

The syntax for an `IF` function is

```
=IF(logical_test, value_if_true, value_if_false)
```

The *logical test* that will be performed is the cross-check: `SUM(B10:F10)=SUM(G4:G8)`.

If the test is true—meaning that the sums are equal—you simply want to display the results of one of the sums, such as `SUM(B10:F10)`.

If the test is false—meaning that the sums are not equal—you want to be warned that an error exists. This can be accomplished by entering the text you want displayed when the test is false. Text in Excel formulas is surrounded by quotes—for example, `"ERROR"`.

The `IF` function in cell G10 will be

```
=IF(SUM(B10:F10)=SUM(G4:G8),SUM(B10:F10),"ERROR")
```

In Figure 28.20, the `IF` function is entered in cell G10. You can see it in the Formula bar. The warning message `ERROR` is in the cell to indicate a problem with the worksheet. To illustrate the problem, the totals are calculated below the worksheet and show the daily total is 216 and the total by type is 213.

FIGURE 28.20
The cross-check formula flags you if an error occurs in the worksheet.

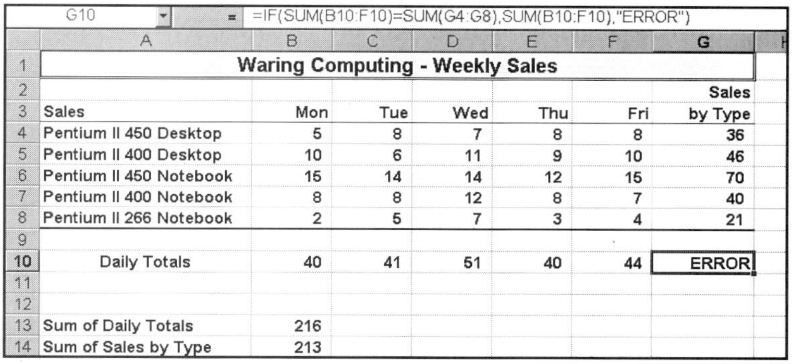

G10 = =IF(SUM(B10:F10)=SUM(G4:G8),SUM(B10:F10),"ERROR")

	A	B	C	D	E	F	G
1	Waring Computing - Weekly Sales						
2							Sales
3	Sales	Mon	Tue	Wed	Thu	Fri	by Type
4	Pentium II 450 Desktop	5	8	7	8	8	36
5	Pentium II 400 Desktop	10	6	11	9	10	46
6	Pentium II 450 Notebook	15	14	14	12	15	70
7	Pentium II 400 Notebook	8	8	12	8	7	40
8	Pentium II 266 Notebook	2	5	7	3	4	21
9							
10	Daily Totals	40	41	51	40	44	ERROR
11							
12							
13	Sum of Daily Totals	216					
14	Sum of Sales by Type	213					

Whenever a cross-check error occurs, the problem exists in one of the individual total calculations. In Figure 28.20, the totals are in row 10 or column G. When a cross-check error occurs, the problem is in one of the row or column calculations.

To check to see whether a value has been accidentally typed over a formula, use the Go To Special dialog box and select either the Constants or Formulas to highlight those cells in your worksheet. Then look for inconsistencies—for example, constants where formulas should be. You can also use both the Row Differences option and Column Differences option to be sure the formulas are totaling the correct cells.

See "Using the Go To Special Command," **p. 911**

In Figure 28.21, we used the Go To Special dialog box (Edit, Go To, Special) and the Constants option was selected to identify all cells with constant values in the entire worksheet. Those cells that contain constant values (anything but a formula) are highlighted. Notice that cell G7 is selected, indicating that it contains a constant. This cell should be a formula totaling the sales for Pentium II 400 Notebooks.

FIGURE 28.21
Use the Constants option in the Go To Special dialog box to quickly identify cells that are constants but should be formulas.

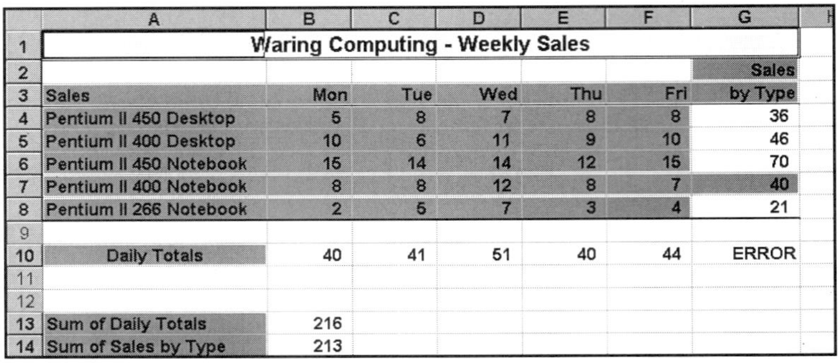

	A	B	C	D	E	F	G
1	Waring Computing - Weekly Sales						
2							Sales
3	Sales	Mon	Tue	Wed	Thu	Fri	by Type
4	Pentium II 450 Desktop	5	8	7	8	8	36
5	Pentium II 400 Desktop	10	6	11	9	10	46
6	Pentium II 450 Notebook	15	14	14	12	15	70
7	Pentium II 400 Notebook	8	8	12	8	7	40
8	Pentium II 266 Notebook	2	5	7	3	4	21
9							
10	Daily Totals	40	41	51	40	44	ERROR
11							
12							
13	Sum of Daily Totals	216					
14	Sum of Sales by Type	213					

CHAPTER 29

Sharing Excel Data with Other Users and Applications

In this chapter

Choosing the Right Collaboration Method

You can choose several ways to work with others to revise and refine Excel workbooks. The collaboration method you choose depends largely on the resources you have available (network, Internet, intranet, and so on) and what time constraints you are under. Excel's collaboration tools include the following:

- Web Discussions—Members of a workgroup can add comments, edit, and reply to existing comments at their convenience—they do not all have to be available at the same time. Additionally, if the workbook is changed or if discussion comments are added, you can be notified by email.
- NetMeeting—You can hold online meetings where workgroup members can collaborate online together, just as if they were in the same room.
- Embedded Comments—Comments (called Notes in Excel 95 and earlier versions) can be attached to cells within a worksheet. To provide others the opportunity to collaborate on the workbook, they can be routed via email, saved to a floppy disk or zip disk, or saved on a network server to which all workgroup members have access.
- Routing—A workbook can be attached to an email message while you're working in Excel. The message can either be sent simultaneously to all workgroup recipients, or you can use a routing slip to specify the order of the recipients.
- Sharing and Merging Workbooks—By sharing a workbook, workgroup members can edit simultaneously. Features include establishing a history of changes, highlighting changed data, and accepting or rejecting changes. The shared workbook feature replaced the shared list feature that was available in Excel 95. Instead of sharing a single workbook, you can merge the comments and changes from multiple copies of a workbook into one workbook.

If you use the email routing and embedded comments to collaborate on a workbook, you either have to merge everyone's individual comments into one file or wait until the workbook is routed through all the recipients before you can see (and begin responding to) comments being made on the workbook. You can avoid having to manually consolidate individual comments by using the workbook sharing and merging features. However, if you have the resources to use either the NetMeeting or Web Discussions features, it expedites receiving feedback on a workbook and consolidating comments.

The next few sections describe how to use some of these collaboration options.

Web Discussions

When it's inconvenient to gather everyone together for a meeting to collaborate on a workbook, use the Web Discussions feature. Workgroup members can review the workbook at their convenience and can be notified by email when a workbook has been modified or comments have been added.

The way you access and use the Web Discussions feature in Excel (and the other Office 2000 applications) is identical. You open the document you want to discuss and choose Tools, Online Collaboration, Web Discussions. The Discussions toolbar appears in the bottom-left corner of the Excel screen. Through this toolbar you can insert new comments, view existing comments, edit or reply to comments, subscribe to a particular workbook or folder, and hide the Discussions pane. Figure 29.1 shows an Excel worksheet with Web Discussions enabled.

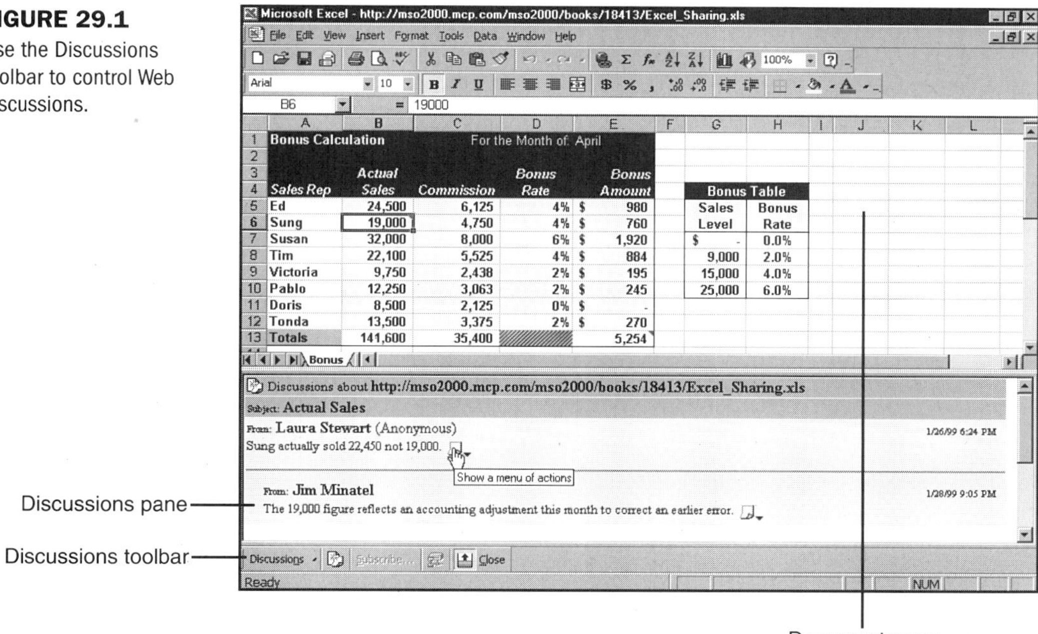

FIGURE 29.1
Use the Discussions toolbar to control Web discussions.

To use the Web Discussions features, you must have access to a Web server and the workbook must be stored in a location accessible by all members.

NOTE Chapter 3, "Unleashing the Office 2000 Web Tools," describes the resources necessary to take advantage of Web Discussions. That chapter also explains the basic steps required to add and reply to discussion comments.

▶ **See** "Online Collaboration," **p. 61**

When working with Web Discussions in Excel, keep these things in mind:

- Adding Discussion Items—Because Web Discussions are added on a worksheet-by-worksheet basis, it is important to identify the cell reference or area of the worksheet you are writing about.
- Replying to Discussion Items—Make sure you locate the correct item to which you want to reply. To add a comment to the overall discussion, reply to the first item in the

discussion thread. A reply is always slightly indented underneath the discussion item you select when replying.

One of the other Web Discussions features is *Subscription and Notification*. You can monitor a specific workbook or folder to which you have at least "read access." You have the option to be notified when a document is edited, when discussion comments are added, or when items are added or removed from a folder. You can even be notified when a particular person makes changes to a folder.

Most of the subscription and notification options are self-explanatory. However, Chapter 3 contains specific descriptions of each option.

Scheduling and Conducting Online Meetings with NetMeeting

Microsoft NetMeeting enables you to share and exchange information with other people at different sites in real-time over your company's intranet or the Internet, just as if everyone were in the same room.

NetMeeting includes a scheduling feature that works with Outlook; a chat feature so that you can have open, written discussions; a whiteboard feature; and the capability to transmit both audio and video (assuming the participants' machines have that capability).

You can either schedule an online meeting ahead of time or start an impromptu meeting (choose Tools, Online Collaboration, Meet Now).

The first time you start an online meeting, you may be prompted to select the directory server to which you want to connect. You can select any of the directory servers from the list in the Server Name box under Directory; your system administrator can tell you whether you should connect to a specific directory server.

Chapter 3 describes the resources necessary to take advantage of Microsoft NetMeeting, describes how to create a meeting request, and discusses the interaction between the meeting host and the participants.

▶ **See** "Online Collaboration," **p. 61**

Getting the Most from Document Comments and Revisions

Attaching notes to cells is a feature that has been available for some time. In both Excel 95 and Excel 97, this feature was enhanced, and in Excel 97 it was renamed Comments. Embedding comments in a worksheet is another way to collaborate—but at the cell level instead of the worksheet level provided with Web Discussions. You can use this Excel feature with other collaborative options, such as email routing or workbook sharing and merging. Comments can be attached to any cell. Excel places an indicator in the upper-right corner of each cell that contains a comment. The indicator is a red triangle. When you position the mouse pointer in the cell, the comment automatically appears on the screen.

Figure 29.2 shows a worksheet where embedded comments have been used by several people to collaborate on the data and formulas in a worksheet.

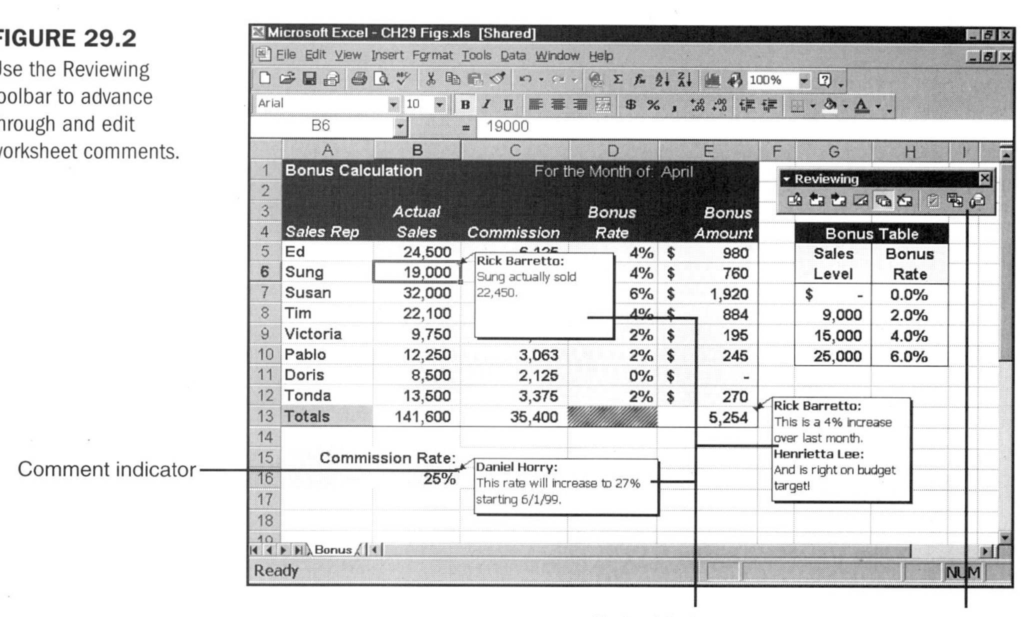

FIGURE 29.2
Use the Reviewing toolbar to advance through and edit worksheet comments.

To attach a comment to a cell, right-click the cell and choose Insert Comment from the shortcut menu. A small box appears. The title is the User Name as defined in the Options dialog box. Enter the text you want to appear in the comment. Resize the box by positioning the mouse pointer on one of the selection handles and drag to reshape the comment box. Press the Esc key or click in an area away from the box to complete the comment.

The bold title in the comment is taken from the User Name box on the General tab in the Options dialog box. You can edit the text directly in the comment in the worksheet, making each title unique to that particular comment.

After comments have been entered into a worksheet, you can edit, delete, or display the comment through the shortcut menu.

Several of the comment settings are controlled through the Options dialog box. Choose Tools, Options to access the dialog box. On the View tab, you can choose not to display the comment or indicator, to display the indicator only, or to display both comment and indicator (as shown in Figure 29.2). By default, only the indicator appears. In the User Name text box on the General tab, you can enter the text you want to display as the title in the comment box. Any comments created before the change in the User Name text retain the former title.

To print worksheet comments, choose File, Page Setup, and select the Sheet tab in the Page Setup dialog box (see Figure 29.3). Choose At End of Sheet to print the comments separately from the worksheet. To see how they will appear when printed, click the Print Preview button in the Page Setup dialog box.

You can also print the comments embedded in the worksheet. However, you must first display the comments on the worksheet. This obscures some of the worksheet data, and if adjacent cells have comments, the display of one comment may hide part of another. To specify individual comments, right-click the cell containing the comment and choose Show Comment from the shortcut menu for each comment you want displayed. To display all comments, access the Options dialog box (Tools, Options) and select the Comment and Indicator setting on the View tab.

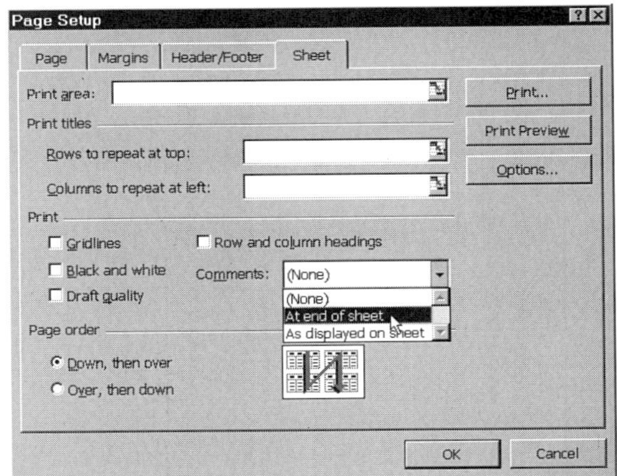

FIGURE 29.3
The Page Setup dialog box must be accessed from the File menu, not through the Print Preview screen, to choose one of the Comment print options.

Using Email to Share Data with Others

When you want to provide people with a copy of a worksheet or workbook to review, you can send it to them as an email message. You can initiate email messages while remaining in Excel. You have the choice of sending the current worksheet in the body of an email message or adding the entire workbook as an attachment to an email message. You can send these messages simultaneously to everyone involved or route them in a sequential order.

NOTE Depending on your setup, Excel might not have the Email (Mail Recipient) button on the Standard toolbar. For this button to appear, Outlook or Outlook Express must be set as your default email client.

Sending the Active Worksheet

When you want to provide people with a copy of a worksheet or workbook to review, you can send it to them while remaining in Excel. To send the active worksheet in the email message body, the sender needs Excel 2000 and Outlook 2000. Recipients need a Web browser or Outlook 98 or later. Click the Email button on the Standard toolbar or choose File, Send To, Mail Recipient.

NOTE The first time you do this, a pop-up message may appear asking you to choose between attaching the workbook to an email message or sending the active worksheet as the message body. Make your selection and proceed with the remaining steps.

The email message and routing lines appear just below the Excel toolbars where you can address the message.

Although the workbook name appears in the Subject line, you can replace it with another subject if you prefer. After you've completed the message header information, click the Send This Sheet button.

The Email button on the Standard toolbar acts as an on/off button. If you accidentally activate it for the wrong worksheet, click the Email button to hide the message header. The File, Send To, Mail Recipient command can be used this way as well.

Sending an Entire Workbook

To send an entire workbook, you need to email or route the workbook as an attachment. The sender must have Excel 2000 and either a 32-bit email program compatible with the Messaging Application Programming Interface (MAPI), such as Outlook and Outlook Express, or a 16-bit email program compatible with Vendor Independent Messaging (VIM), such as cc:Mail. To view the attached workbook, recipients must have Excel 97 or later.

If you want to use a routing slip instead of sending the file to everyone simultaneously, you must send the entire workbook as an attachment.

To send the entire workbook as an attachment, start by choosing File, Send To, Mail Recipient (As Attachment). A separate window appears, as shown in Figure 29.4. The name of the active workbook is listed either in an Attach line beneath the email To and Subject lines or at the bottom of the window below the area where you enter the message text.

After you've completed addressing the message, enter the message text and click Send.

NOTE If the workbook has been saved in an HTML file format, when you send it as an attachment, Excel automatically converts it back to an .xls file.

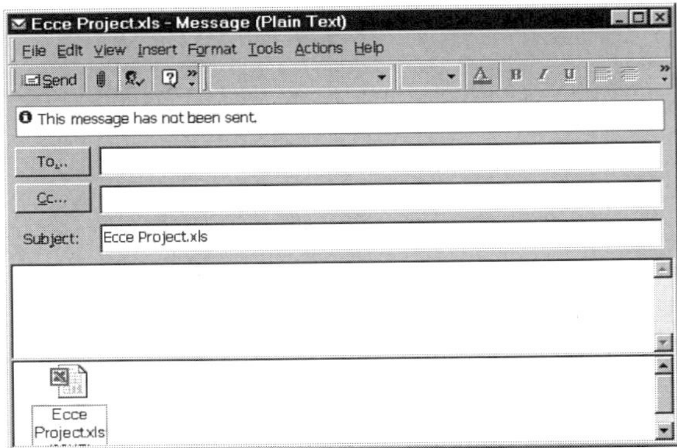

FIGURE 29.4
Maximize the message window to increase the message text area.

Routing a Workbook Through Several Recipients

When you want workgroup members to review a workbook, one after another, you can route the workbook through email. You can track the file as it is routed consecutively from one recipient to another so that you always know where it is. After all recipients have reviewed and routed the workbook, it is automatically returned to you.

If you're the originator of the routed workbook, you must create a routing slip. Display the workbook you want to send and choose File, Send To, Routing Receipt. The Add Routing Slip appears, as shown in Figure 29.5.

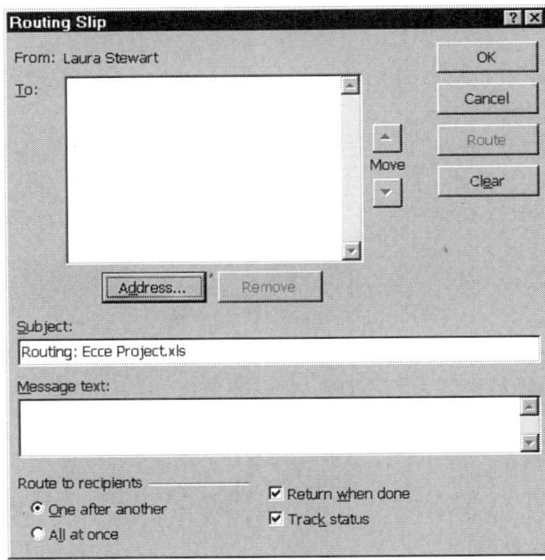

FIGURE 29.5
Any message text you type is added to the default routing instructions that accompany every routed workbook.

Address the routing slip and type comments or instructions in the Message text box. Several routing options exist—One After Another or All at Once, Return When Done, and Track Status. After you've completed the routing slip, click Route to send the message with the workbook attached.

NOTE Excel automatically adds text to every routed workbook that tells the recipient how to route the workbook to the next person.

Sharing and Merging Workbooks

One of the most productive features in Excel is the capability to share and revise workbooks with groups of people. Sharing a workbook is a great alternative to routing a workbook because it enables users to edit the file simultaneously. Most projects involve several people inputting or verifying data in the same documents. Although previous versions of Excel flirted with this notion, it wasn't until Excel 97 that people could truly share a workbook. One person can edit one worksheet in a workbook, and someone else can edit another worksheet simultaneously. You can even have different people access and modify data in adjacent cells in the same workbook. The shared workbook feature replaced the shared list feature found in Microsoft Excel 95.

Before you can take advantage of these features, the workbook has to be set up as a shared workbook. Then, multiple users can view and modify it simultaneously. When one user saves the workbook, the other users who are sharing it will see the changes made by that user.

NOTE If some users in your group are still working with Excel 95 or earlier versions, they will not be able to open the shared workbook.

To set up a shared workbook, follow these steps:

1. Open the workbook you want to share.
2. Using the File, Save As command, save the workbook to a shared network drive.

   ▶ **See** "Mapping a Network Drive in Windows 95/98 and NT," **p. 193**

3. Then choose Tools, Share Workbook. The Share Workbook dialog box, as shown in Figure 29.6, appears.
4. On the Editing tab of the dialog box, mark the check box titled Allow Changes by More Than One User at the Same Time.
5. Choose OK.

After a workbook has been set up to be shared, users can open the shared workbook as they would any other file, by using the File, Open command. When a workbook is shared, the word [Shared] displays in the title bar for the workbook window. Users save changes to a shared document the same as they save changes to any other file, by using the File, Save command.

NOTE If the workbook contains links to other workbooks or documents, make sure these links are intact after you save the workbook to the network drive. Click Edit, Links to confirm and correct the links.

▶ **See** "Troubleshooting Links," **p. 658**

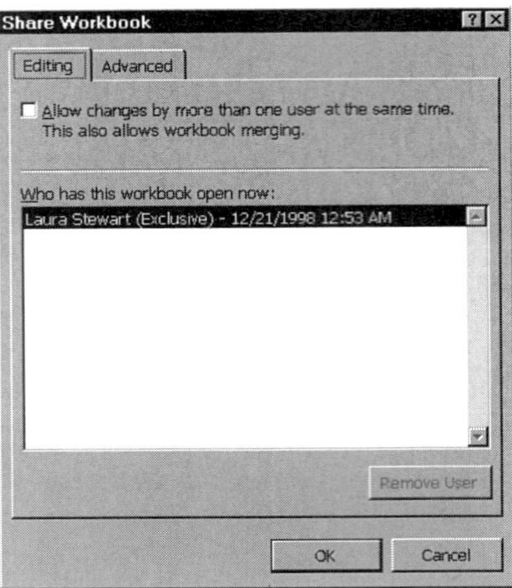

FIGURE 29.6
From the Share Workbook dialog box, you can set up the workbook to be shared.

Any user who has access to the network location where a shared workbook is stored has access to the shared workbook. You can do several things to protect the workbook:

- Password protecting the workbook requires that a password be entered before the workbook is opened or modified (two separate settings). Attaching a password to a file is accomplished through the Options button in the Save As dialog box.
- Unless you want others to be able to change the workbook structure, it is a good idea to protect the workbook. Structural changes include adding, moving, renaming, hiding, unhiding, and deleting sheets. Workbook protection is accomplished by choosing Tools, Protection, Protect Workbook.
- You can also protect the cells you don't want edited in the workbook. Cell-level protection is a two-step process. By default, all cells are protected; the cell protection is not implemented until you protect the worksheet. To prevent people from making inadvertent edits to a worksheet, you have to select the cells you want them to edit and unprotect the cells (Format, Cells, Protection). After this first step is accomplished, the second step is to protect the worksheet (Tools, Protection, Protect Sheet).

If you want to implement any of these protections, do so before the workbook is placed on the shared drive. If the workbook is already shared, then you must remove the workbook from shared use before you change the protection.

Another setting that you should consider is to protect the workbook from being removed from shared use. This is set by choosing Tools, Protection, Protect and Share Workbook. You can turn on protection for sharing while the workbook is shared.

Shared Workbook Options

When you share workbooks with others, you need to make several decisions. The Advanced tab of the Share Workbook dialog box, shown in Figure 29.7, and the Highlight Changes dialog box, shown in Figure 29.8, work together to control how changes to the shared workbook are tracked.

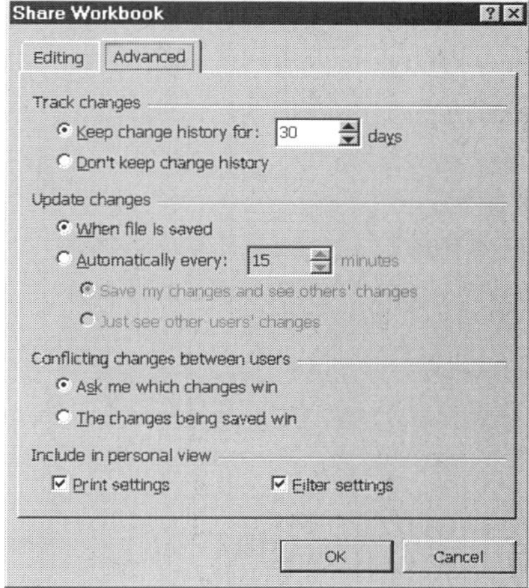

FIGURE 29.7
The default settings for sharing your workbooks with other users are displayed in this figure.

The following list outlines the options on the Advanced tab of the Share Workbook dialog box:

- Track Changes—By default, Excel keeps a history of all the changes made, for up to 30 days. The history can be viewed by highlighting the cells in the worksheet. When you rest the mouse pointer over a modified cell, the changes are listed. You also can see the changes displayed in a list on a separate worksheet. The settings in the Highlight Changes dialog box control the specifications of when and how you see the changes. Look ahead to the next list for descriptions of the settings in the Highlight Changes dialog box.
- Update Changes—You have two options to specify when changes to the file are updated: when the file is saved or after a specified period of time. By default, you will see changes to the file when the file is saved. You can view other users' changes more frequently by setting a time interval in the Automatically After (15) Minutes box. To save the workbook each time you get an update—so that other users can see your changes—select Save My Changes and See Others' Changes. The other option, Just See Other Users' Changes, does not save the workbook.
- Conflicting Changes Between Users—The Ask Me Which Changes Win option displays the Resolve Conflicts dialog box if changes you are saving conflict with changes saved by another user. You can elect to save your changes or keep the changes made by others. The Changes Being Saved Win option always saves your changes automatically, without viewing the proposed changes made by others.
- Include in Personal View—Each user of a shared workbook can set independent view and print options. Whenever a user views the workbook, that user's settings are displayed. These settings include page breaks, print areas, headers, footers, and other options selected in the Page Setup dialog box. Additional settings that are saved include zoom percent and options marked on the View tab of the Tools, Options dialog box.

After a workbook has been set up as a shared workbook, you can allow other users to view and edit a workbook—all at the same time—and see one another's changes. Each user of a shared workbook can set independent options for highlighting changes.

In the shared workbook, Excel identifies who made what changes and when, based on the name of the user. To ensure accurate tracking, each user should establish a username before working on the shared book. Instruct each user to choose Tools, Options, and click the General tab, and then type his or her username in the User Name box.

The Highlight Changes dialog box, shown in Figure 29.8, works with settings on the Advanced tab of the Share Workbook dialog box to control how changes to the shared workbook are tracked.

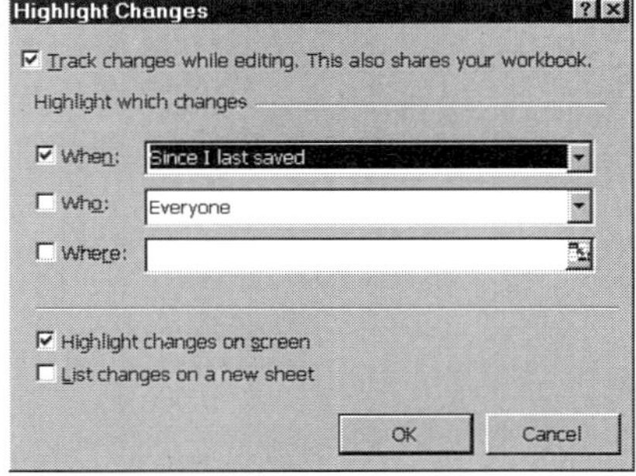

FIGURE 29.8
Changes to a file can be highlighted on the screen, listed in a separate worksheet, or appear in both places.

Figure 29.9 shows a shared workbook with changes and comments added. When a change has been made to a cell, a blue triangular change indicator appears in the upper-left corner of the cell, and a thin blue border is added to the cell.

Each time you view the shared workbook, you need to specify how you want to review the changes in the Highlight Changes dialog box. The settings are established only for the working session; the next time you view the file, you have to specify your choices again. The change indicators appear (and disappear) based on the settings you made in the Highlight Changes dialog box (refer to Figure 29.8) and are described next:

- Track Changes While Editing—This setting must remain on for the workbook to be shared. Changes made to cell contents, and inserted or deleted rows and columns, are highlighted. Changes to worksheet names are listed on the History worksheet when you select List Changes on a New Sheet. New or additional comments are displayed when you rest the mouse pointer over the cell.

  Certain changes are not highlighted: cell formatting, hidden and unhidden rows and columns, and inserted or deleted worksheets. In addition, some changes can't be made to a shared workbook—a list is provided later in this section.
- When—By default, this setting shows only those changes made to the file since you last saved the file. Alternatives in the drop-down list include seeing all changes, seeing changes not yet reviewed, or seeing changes since a specified date.

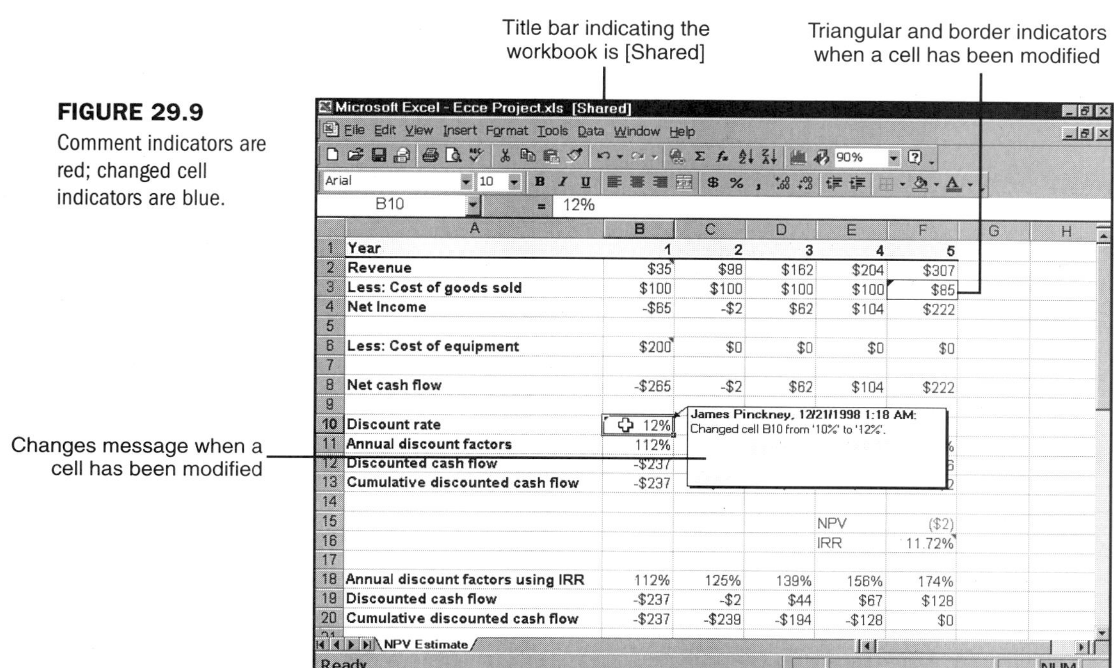

FIGURE 29.9
Comment indicators are red; changed cell indicators are blue.

- Who—By default, you see changes made by everyone. Alternatives in the drop-down list include changes made by everyone except you or changes made by a specific person.
- Where—This option is blank so that you can see changes made to the entire file. If you want to see the changes made only to a few specific cells, mark this option and identify the cells. Select nonadjacent cells by using the Ctrl key. You can also designate a range name. Press F3 to see a list of range names in the workbook.
- Highlight Changes on Screen—By default, changes are noted on the worksheet. Cells that have been changed are identified several ways: a triangle in the upper-left corner of the cell, a thin border surrounding the cell, and the row and column headings display a different color to note that changes exist in that row or column.
- List Changes on a New Sheet—If you want to see a list of the changes on a separate worksheet in the workbook, choose this option. The list is based on the settings you have made in the When, Who, and Where options of this dialog box. The name for the new worksheet is History. The History worksheet displays a complete list of changes, including the names of the users who made the changes, data that was deleted or replaced, and information about conflicting changes. The list displays with the AutoFilter turned on. After you save the workbook, Excel removes the History worksheet. To display it again, you have to mark this option in the Highlight Changes dialog box.

The History worksheet shows only the changes that have been saved. To include all changes on the History worksheet from your current session, save the workbook *before* you display the History worksheet. The History worksheet does not automatically update during your working session. You have to save your workbook and redisplay the History worksheet.

When you remove a workbook from shared use, the history of changes is erased. When you share the workbook again, a new list of changes is created. For information on saving the history list of changes before you remove the workbook from shared use, see the section "Discontinue Workbook Sharing" later in this chapter.

Limitations When Workbooks Are Shared

Some Excel commands are not available when a workbook is shared. In some cases, if you implement a feature before sharing the workbook, it is then available while the workbook is in the [Shared] mode. For example, you can't add or change data validation while the workbook is shared, but you can see the effects of any settings that were established *before* the workbook was shared. The commands impacted by workbook sharing are

- Inserting—Blocks of cells cannot be inserted, although you can insert new rows and columns.
- Deleting—Entire worksheets or blocks of cells cannot be deleted. You can delete entire rows or columns.
- Formatting—You cannot apply conditional formats or merge cells after a workbook has been shared.
- List Manipulation Commands—The Group and Outline, Subtotals, Table, PivotTable and PivotChart Report commands cannot be used when a workbook is shared.
- Linked or Embedded Objects—Charts, pictures, objects, or hyperlinks can't be inserted or modified in a shared workbook.
- Macros—You can run macros that were created only before you shared the workbook. New macros cannot be created.
- Password Protection—While a workbook is shared, you cannot create, modify, or remove passwords that protect the worksheets or the entire workbook. Any protection that is assigned to a worksheet or workbook prior to sharing the file remains in effect while the workbook is shared.
- Scenarios—This command can't be used while the workbook is shared.
- Data Validation—You can't modify or create data-validation restrictions while the workbook is shared. Any restrictions that are set up prior to sharing the workbook remain in effect.
- Drawing—The drawing tools can't be used while a workbook is shared.

Discontinue Workbook Sharing

When you no longer need to permit others to have access to your workbook, or if you want to use an Excel command or feature that is not supported by shared workbooks (see the previous list), you need to stop sharing the workbook. One thing to be certain of before removing a workbook from shared use is that you are the only user who has the workbook open. Otherwise, the other users may lose their work. To stop sharing a workbook, follow these steps:

1. Choose Tools, Share Document. The Share Workbook dialog box is displayed.
2. Select the Editing tab. If you are the only one listed in the Who Has This Workbook Open Now list box, then you can safely remove the workbook from being shared. If other users are listed, notify them to save and close the file so they don't lose their work.
3. After you have verified that you are the only one with access to the workbook, clear the Allow Changes by More Than One User at the Same Time check box.
4. Choose OK to stop sharing the workbook.

CAUTION

When you remove a workbook from shared use, the history of changes is erased. When you share the workbook again, a new list of changes is created.

If you plan to remove a workbook from shared use but want to retain the change information, display the information about all changes on the History worksheet by marking the List Changes on a New Worksheet box in the Highlight Changes dialog box. You then can copy the information on the History worksheet to another worksheet in the workbook, print the History worksheet, or save a copy of the shared workbook.

Merging Workbooks

Sometimes it is more convenient to distribute multiple copies of a workbook and have users make changes to their copy. To merge the copies, each copy of the workbook must maintain a history of changes. The history has to extend from the day the copies were created to the day you merge the copies.

In fact, you actually have to specify the number of days you expect the copies to be reviewed. If the actual number of days exceeds the specified days, you will not be able to merge the copies. Therefore, it's a good idea to specify a high number of days, such as 1,000.

If you anticipate that people will attach comments to cells, encourage them to check (or set) their username in the Options dialog box (choose Tools, Options, General tab) to help track comments. Comments are merged when the worksheets are merged. The username helps distinguish one comment from another when more than one person has attached a comment to a cell.

To set up the workbook for merging, choose Tools, Share Workbook. On the Editing tab of the Share Workbooks dialog box, mark the Allow Changes by More Than One User at the Same

Time check box to enable workbook sharing. Then click the Advanced tab. Select the Keep Change History For option and type the number of days you want the Change History to be active. Click OK and save the workbook. Then use the File, Save As command to make copies, giving each copy a different name.

When you are ready to merge the various copies, follow these steps:

1. Open the copy of the shared workbook into which you want to merge changes from another workbook.
2. Choose Tools, Merge Workbooks. You may be prompted to save the shared workbook. The Select Files to Merge into Current Workbook dialog box appears.
3. Locate the copy of the shared workbook that contains the changes to be merged. To merge more than one workbook at a time, select all the workbooks by pressing the Ctrl key as you click each workbook name. Then click OK.
4. Repeat steps 2–4 until all copies of the shared workbook are merged.

Exchanging Data with Other Applications

In addition to sharing Excel data with other people, you may also need to exchange data between Excel and other applications. Importing and exporting data saves you the time (and trouble) of re-creating data that already exists elsewhere. Excel offers several techniques to accomplish this:

- Copy and Paste—You can use the Copy and Paste (including Paste Special and Paste Link) commands to import or export data. You can also drag and drop data from one application to another or store scraps of data on the desktop that you routinely need to insert into documents.
- HTML—Hypertext Markup Language is a file format universally accepted by all Office 2000 applications. You can save a file in HTML format and insert the contents of that file into other Office applications with ease.
- Built-In File Format Conversions—When you want to share information with applications that are not part of the Microsoft Office suite, you use the built-in file format converters to import and export the data. For example, you can import spreadsheets created in Lotus 1-2-3 (through .WK4 format) or Quattro Pro (.WQ1 format) and databases created in dBASE (through .DBF dBASE IV format).

As mentioned in the preceding list, Excel can read from and write to many application file formats. For those file formats that Excel cannot directly read from or write to, several generic file formats exist, such as .txt and .csv, that can be used to exchange data between applications.

These generic text file formats use spaces, commas, tabs, or other characters to separate, or delimit, the values in a file so that the values can be placed in individual cells or database fields. In some cases, especially with mainframe programs, the file may contain values arranged so that each field or cell has a certain width. These file formats are referred to as *fixed-width* files, or sometimes as *column-delimited* files.

If you're interested in importing delimited text files (including parsing text) or data from databases (such as Access), OLAP cubes, or intranet and Internet Web pages, see Chapter 24.

▶ **See** "Importing Data from Databases, Web Pages, and Text Files," **p. 729**

Importing and Exporting in the HTML File Format

Microsoft has made converting documents to the HTML format as easy as saving files to your hard drive. You have the option of saving the entire workbook or selected worksheets.

Using this format makes it easier for Excel data to be incorporated into other documents and to publish Excel data on a Web. You can then post these files to your company's intranet server, taking the burden off the IS department. Because this process is so easy to do, it aids in keeping the posted information more current.

To save a workbook or worksheet in the HTML format, activate the workbook. If you want to save just several sheets in the book, you need to select those sheets:

To select a series of consecutive sheets, click the first sheet tab and press the Shift key as you click the last sheet tab you want to select.

To select individual sheets, click the first sheet tab and press the Ctrl key as you click the other sheet tabs you want to select.

Then choose File, Save As Web Page. The Save As dialog box appears, as shown in Figure 29.10. From this dialog box, you can select the option to save the entire workbook or just the selected sheets.

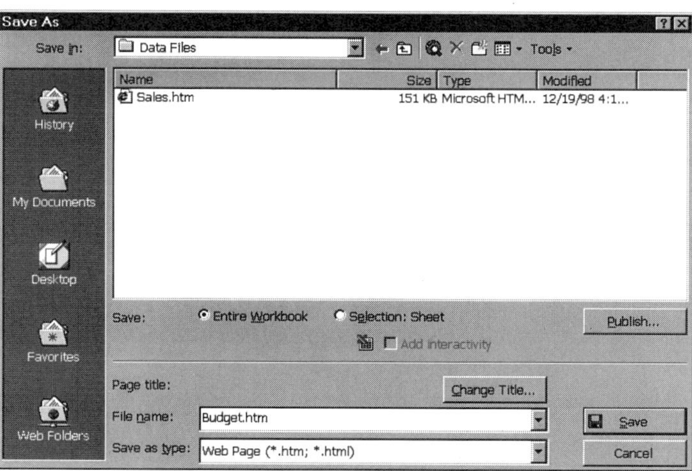

FIGURE 29.10
This dialog box also appears when you choose File, Save As and change the Files of Type to Web Page.

Mark the Add Interactivity option only if you want people to be able to change and manipulate the data when the worksheet displays as a Web page. This does not link the changes back to the original file; it merely allows people to modify the HTML copy of the worksheet.

▶ **See** "The Office Web Components," **p. 56**

Importing an Access Table into an Excel Worksheet

Data from Access is often brought into Excel to take advantage of Excel's powerful PivotTable and other list and database features, which are discussed in Chapter 25, "Advanced Lists, PivotTables, and PivotCharts." Two approaches exist to bringing Access data into Excel. You can import an entire table or you can create a query to import selected records.

If you need to bring in an entire table, you can export the table from within Access. The steps to do this are fairly straightforward:

1. From the Access Database Window, select the table to be exported and choose File, Export. The Export window appears.
2. Choose .xls from the Save As Type drop-down list box at the bottom of the window, and type a name in the File Name.
3. Use the Save In drop-down box and the Up One Level button to select the location to which you want to save the table.
4. Then click Save. You can then open the file in Excel the same as you would any workbook.

Remember, Excel has a limit of 65,536 rows and 256 columns. Although, in many situations, Access tables don't exceed these numbers, each row (record) in the Access table takes up a row in an Excel worksheet. Large Access tables will not fit into an Excel worksheet. In those cases, you must create a query in Excel to import the Access data. You can also use a query when you want to import a group of records, or if you aren't familiar with Access. Creating queries is discussed in detail in Chapter 24.

▶ **See** "Creating Queries to Import Data from External Databases," **p. 730**

Importing Word Tables and Text into Excel

Probably the easiest way to import a Word table into Excel is to simply copy the Word table and paste it into an Excel worksheet. If you use the copy-and-paste tools (or their keyboard equivalents), the imported data retains the formatting it had in Word. Should you want to import the data without the formatting, you can use the Paste Special command and choose the Text option.

In either case, the data is not linked to the original Word table. To create that link, you must choose Paste Link in the Paste Special dialog box (shown in Figure 29.11).

Generally, text is brought into Excel to provide notes or comments about the worksheet data or a chart. The best place to add Word text is in a text box, as shown in Figure 29.12. To create a text box in Excel, click the Drawings button on the Standard toolbar to display the Drawings toolbar. Then click the Text Box button on the Drawing toolbar and drag to create the text box. You're now ready to copy the text from Word and paste it into the text box in Excel.

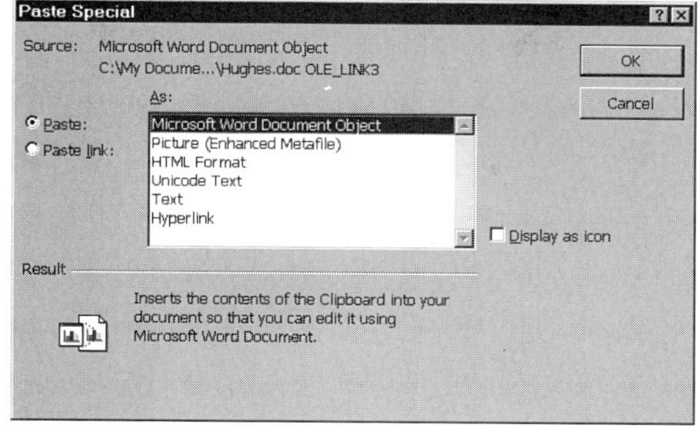

FIGURE 29.11
When you select an option in the As list box, the Result description, at the bottom of the dialog box, explains what happens when the data is pasted into the target file.

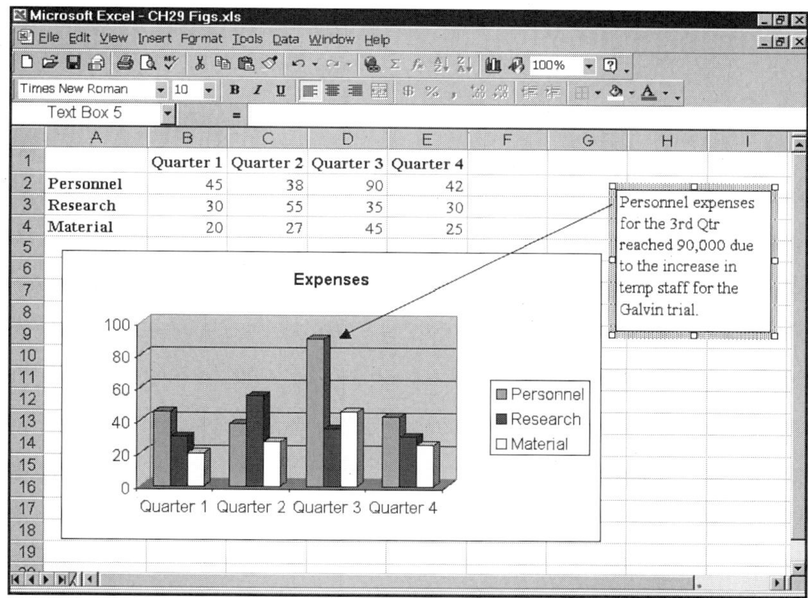

FIGURE 29.12
You can add text boxes to a worksheet or chart sheet.

Move or resize the text box as necessary. You can format the text inside a text box just as you would other text. To format the text box (background color, border width), right-click anywhere in the text box and choose Format Text Box from the shortcut menu.

If you paste Word text (that is not part of a table) into Excel, the entire text selected in Word is inserted into one cell. If you need to bring in a lot of information from Word, such as a list of names and addresses, save the Word text in the Text Only (.txt) file format and then open it in Excel. The Text Import Wizard, discussed in Chapter 24, guides you through importing the data.

▶ **See** "Importing Text Files," **p. 765**

Exporting Excel Worksheets and Charts into Word Documents

When you use the Clipboard, worksheet data that you copy to another application is pasted in using the HTML format so it can be edited in the target application. For example, Excel worksheet data is pasted into Microsoft Word as a Word table, and the HTML format converts the Excel cell formatting to Word table cell formatting.

Using the Paste Special command, you can change how the data appears in Word. If you choose to paste the data as unformatted text, the Excel data appears in Word separated by tabs. If you choose to paste the data as an Excel Worksheet Object, the Excel data appears in Word as an object, similar to WordArt.

An Excel chart, on the other hand, is automatically pasted in as an Excel Chart Object. If you want to link the pasted chart to the original chart in Excel, use the Edit, Paste Special command instead. The Paste Special dialog box, shown in Figure 29.13, lists the options for pasting an Excel chart into Word.

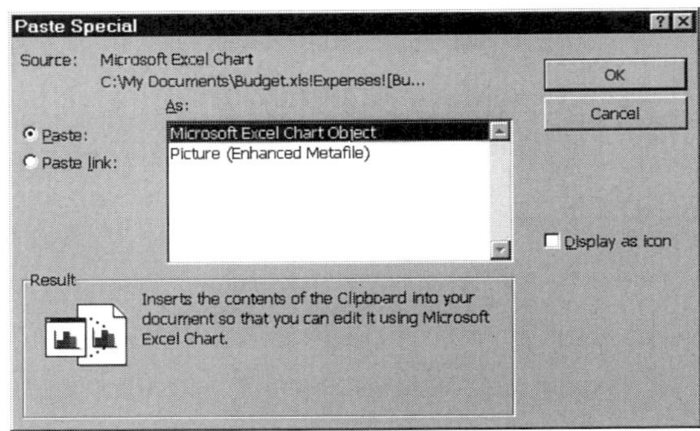

FIGURE 29.13
Changes made to the chart in Excel are reflected in the linked chart in Word.

NOTE If you need to resize the chart pasted into Word, position your mouse on a corner selection handle and then drag to adjust the image. If you do not enlarge from a corner, the object may appear distorted. Using a corner ensures that the object resizes proportionally.

Exporting an Excel Worksheet into an Access Table

Sometimes you start a simple database in Excel, and then after a while realize you need to use the relational database capabilities of Access. To copy worksheet data from Excel into Access, the worksheet must be organized as a list. The first row in the worksheet should contain the field names that you want to use in Access.

▶ **See** "Structuring Lists," **p. 774**

The "Using Database Functions with Lists" section in Chapter 25 describes some of the differences between the database features in Excel and Access and offers some suggestions on how to decide which to use.

After you have the worksheet data in list format, it's easiest to use the tools in Access and import the Excel data through Access. You create or display the table in Access, where the Excel data will be copied. Then, from within Access, choose File, Get External Data, Import. Follow the steps to copy the data from Excel into Access. The Access section of this book contains more information on importing worksheet data.

▶ **See** "Importing, Exporting, and Linking Spreadsheets," **p. 1177**

Exporting an Excel Worksheet into a PowerPoint Slide

You can copy or link data from an Excel worksheet into a PowerPoint slide. The data is pasted in as a slide object, similar to a picture clip. Slides that contain linked Excel data are updated when the Excel data is changed.

Figure 29.14 shows data from an Excel worksheet pasted into a PowerPoint slide. Position your mouse pointer in the middle of the data and drag to move it. As you can see, the data is displayed very small. Position your mouse on a corner selection handle and drag to enlarge.

CAUTION

Always resize the Excel object from a corner selection handle; otherwise, the data may become distorted. Using a corner ensures the object enlarges proportionally.

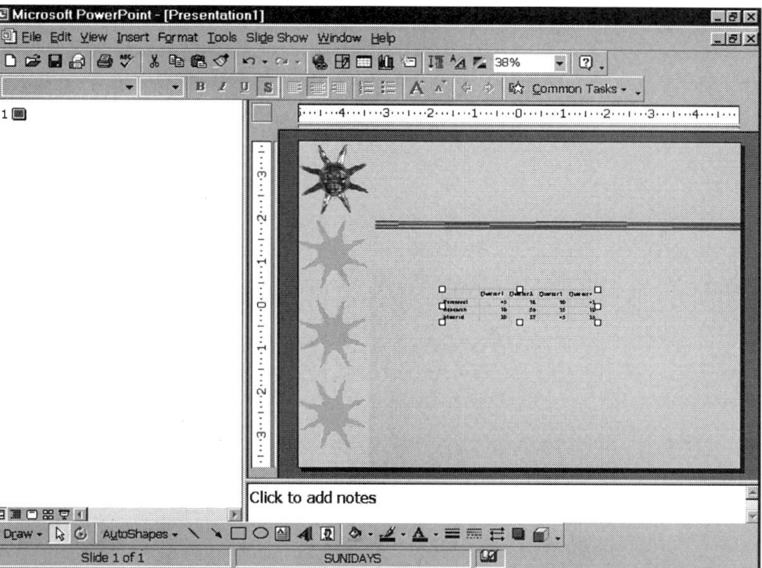

FIGURE 29.14
The Excel data is pasted to the center of the PowerPoint slide.

The data and cell formatting are carried over to the PowerPoint slide, including the cell gridlines. Changing the gridline color in Excel will change their appearance in the PowerPoint slide. Alternatively, you can apply borders to the cells you want to copy and format the border color to complement the PowerPoint slide and background. Borders provide a cleaner look to the Excel data.

Because the default format of pasted data is HTML, you no longer have to go back into Excel to change the appearance of the data—you can edit it directly in PowerPoint by double-clicking the object.

Exporting Excel Data into a PowerPoint Chart

PowerPoint charts are created using the same program Excel uses—Microsoft Graph. However, you can export the Excel data into PowerPoint's datasheet and create the chart in PowerPoint. You will probably find it much easier to export an Excel chart into a PowerPoint slide. For one thing, it is much easier to manipulate the data in Excel than it is to work in PowerPoint's datasheet. Additionally, Excel provides the Chart Wizard to guide you through the process of creating a graphic chart.

When you paste an Excel chart into PowerPoint, it becomes an embedded PowerPoint chart object. The pasted chart appears quite small, so you'll probably want to resize it. As with Excel data that has been pasted into a PowerPoint slide, drag from the chart's corner selection handles to resize it. Otherwise, the chart becomes distorted.

To edit an embedded Excel chart, simply double-click the chart object. All the chart-editing features you are used to in Excel become available—the Chart command appears on the menu bar, ScreenTips identify parts of the chart, and you can right-click to edit a chart component.

▶ **See** "Importing Excel Data into a PowerPoint Slide," **p. 1319**

PART V

Microsoft Access

CHAPTER 30

Migrating to Access 2000

In this chapter

New Features in Access 2000

If you're not new to Access, you'll find Access 2000 an incremental change from Access 97 or Access 95. Although Microsoft has added a host of new features to improve Access's Web-specific and workgroup features, many of the other changes are cosmetic or incremental. So you shouldn't expect any difficulty adapting to the new features. In fact, you may find no difficulty at all in using the features that you've already come to know and rely on in Access.

Several additional features exist that experienced users of any relational database will find helpful, and Access still provides the best user interface to powerful database engines on any platform.

On the other hand, if this is your first foray into full-featured relational databases, you'll probably find that you can use the basic features of Access (with the help of the wizards) intuitively, but need some coaching to design customized applications and code. Access 2000 improves on its predecessors in that the number of features made easily available to the new user is considerably greater than ever before, with step-by-step help for a myriad of functions and applications.

This section assumes some familiarity with Access and relational database techniques, such as using table relationships and creating queries. Your experience with relational databases such as Access 95/97, Paradox, dBASE, Microsoft SQL Server, Sybase, Oracle, and/or Informix will provide a basis for the techniques and features discussed here. If you believe that your database experience is limited and that these topics are too advanced, you might consider reading one of the following books, also published by Que.

- *Special Edition Using Microsoft Access 2000*
- *Platinum Edition Using Microsoft Access 2000*

Upon starting Access 2000, the first change you'll notice is the design of the familiar Database Window (see Figure 30.1). Following in the Outlook 97 tradition, the familiar object tabs at the top of the window have become a Shortcut bar on the left. The functionality is the same, with the welcome addition of the capability to add *object groups*. Although the Tables, Queries, Reports, and other object windows contain objects only of the named type (that is, only tables are visible in the Tables window, and so forth), the customizable object groups each can contain shortcuts to objects of any type.

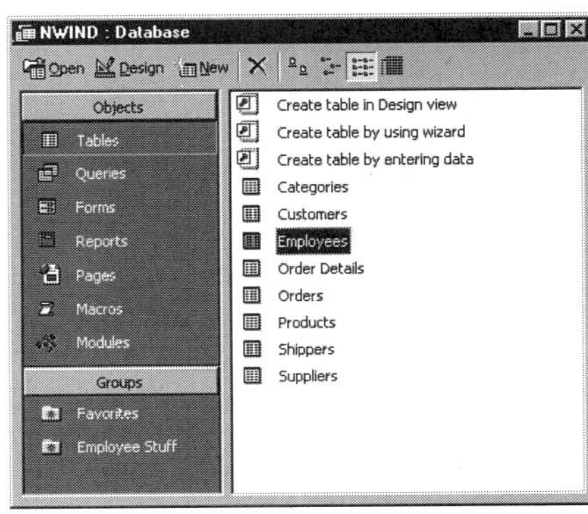

FIGURE 30.1
The Database window in Access 2000 displays database objects as icons or with property details, and the Shortcut bar replaces the old-style tabs.

You might, therefore, create an object group for logical pieces of an application. For example, in a sales application such as the Northwind sample database (slightly updated for Access 2000), you might create one group for the tables and queries that make up the employee functions (as in the "Employee Stuff" group in Figure 30.2), another group for customer functions, another for inventory, and so on. To create a new group, right-click in the Shortcut bar, select New Group and name your group, and then drag objects from the other views onto your new group to create shortcuts to them. Delete or rename a custom group by right-clicking its name and selecting the appropriate menu option.

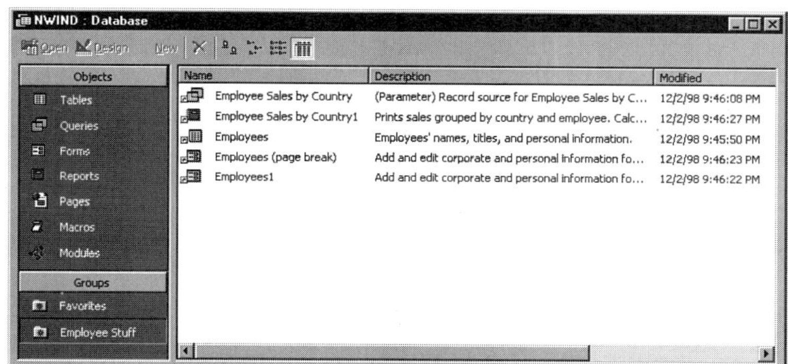

FIGURE 30.2
A custom group containing shortcuts to related objects. Note that deleting the group or shortcut doesn't affect the object(s) pointed to.

One new object type, Data Access Pages, is used for making your Access database accessible via the World Wide Web. This new feature is covered in depth in Chapter 38, "Access and the Web."

Also new to the Database window is the capability to arrange the objects in it as if each view were a listing of files in a folder. Database objects can be sorted within their type by name, creation or modification date, or by object subtype (most useful for queries of different types). Regardless of the sort order chosen, any wizards in a group always appear at the top of the list.

You'll notice few changes to the design interface first implemented in Access 95; the design interfaces for tables, queries, reports, and forms are changed very little. However, the design environment for code modules is very different—Access now uses the Visual Basic design environment. By default, separate development windows monitor the code currently being developed, as well as the properties of the current module and a hierarchical view of the project as a whole.

Several new features are hidden in the toolbars or operate invisibly. These include:

- The capability to convert an Access 2000 database back to Access 97.
- Object consistency checking, which changes all occurrences of an object name in code, queries, reports, and so on when it is changed in one.
- The Print Relationships Wizard (see Figure 30.3), which sends a graphical representation of the relationships between tables to the print device of choice.

- Compact on Close, which reorganizes the database to save disk space whenever the database is closed and the database engine can shrink it below a user-defined threshold.
- Microsoft Access Projects, which permit the experienced user to choose a database engine (integrated store) other than the default Jet engine.

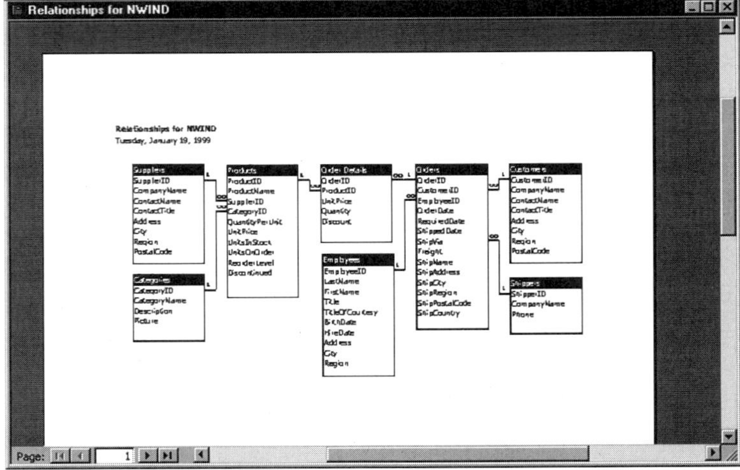

FIGURE 30.3
The Print Relationships Wizard sends a graphical representation of the database structure to a printer.

Changes to the Access 2000 Interface

You can rest assured that almost everything you could do in earlier versions of Access can be done in Access 2000, and more. However, the locations of some of these commands have changed to provide better compatibility with other Office applications, and for ease of use.

Noticeably absent is the Publish to the Web Wizard, which Microsoft insists is made unnecessary by Data Access Pages (DAPs). DAPs, however, include none of the useful features of the old Publish to the Web Wizard, such as the remote server support and built-in FTP.

Menu and Toolbar Changes

The most significant change to the menus and toolbars in Access 2000 is the implementation of the personalized menus and toolbars, which remember what menu and toolbar selections you make and hide features until you use them once, adapting to display only the Access commands you use most frequently.

To see all selections in a given menu, you can double-click the menu (such as File), click and pause the mouse (without making a selection), or select the double arrow at the bottom of the current menu to make hidden selections appear. After you use a hidden selection, it is visible by default the next time that menu is used.

To permanently show all menu options, right-click the menu bar, select Customize, then Options, and deselect Menus Show Recently Used Commands First.

▶ **See** "Personalized Menus and Toolbars," **p. 19**

▶ **See** "Altering the Behavior of the Personalized Menus and Toolbars," **p. 86**

The default menu selections have been moved around a little and have been added to considerably since Access 97. A list of the Access 97 menu selections that have had their locations changed and a cross-reference to their location in Access 2000 is shown in Table 30.1. If the function is the same but the name is slightly different and obvious (such as Access 97's New Database versus Access 2000's New), the difference isn't listed. As you might expect, most of the changes are in the module design environment, which now uses the same VBA Editor that the other Office applications use.

Table 30.1 Access 97/Access 2000 Command Cross-Reference

Access 97 Menu	Access 2000 Menu
Database Menu	
File, Save as HTML	deleted; use File, Export
Tools, Repair Database	Tools, Database Utilities, Compact and Repair Database
Add-Ins, Database Splitter	Tools, Database Utilities, Database Splitter
Add-Ins, Linked Table Manager	Tools, Database Utilities, Linked Table Manager
Add-Ins, Switchboard Manager	Tools, Database Utilities, Switchboard Manager
Help, Contents and Index	deleted; use Help, Microsoft Access Help
Module Design Menu (Now VBA Editor)	
Edit, Delete	Edit, Clear
View, Debug Window	View, Immediate Window
Debug, Compile <various>	Debug, Compile <*databasename*>
Run, Go/Continue	Run, Run Sub/UserForm
Run, End	Run, Break
Tools, ActiveX Controls	deleted from this menu
Tools, Add-Ins	deleted from this menu
Window, Hide/Unhide	deleted

Customize your Access menus to include your favorite options by creating a new command bar (see Chapter 40, "Building Basic Applications") and adding commands to it that you find particularly useful or difficult to locate.

Considerations When Converting Databases

Unlike every other Office 2000 application, Access has again changed its file format (this time to accommodate *Unicode* characters; see the following section on Unicode). The change in format necessitates the conversion (or accommodation) of databases in earlier formats so that they will work correctly in Access 2000, and it may present problems in a mixed-version environment.

A few general rules exist for database conversion as it applies to Access databases:

- First, the version of the database can be no greater than the installed version of Access on any user's desk. If someone on your office network is running Access 2.0, you're stuck with developing and distributing an Access 2.0 database. Although you can purchase the Microsoft Office 2000 Developer Edition (ODE) and distribute your application along with a runtime version of Access, the runtime executable is notorious for causing problems when it's installed over an existing, complete (not runtime), earlier version of Access; it is not a good idea.
- Second, you must develop in the version of Access in which you intend to distribute. You can't develop an application in Access 2000 and expect people running Access 95 to run it.

However, these rules can be relaxed slightly for Access 2000 users because Access 2000 can (for the first time) save databases in the format of an earlier version. By clicking Tools, Database Utilities, Convert Database, To Prior Access Database Version, you can save an Access 2000 database in Access 97 format. This is a great help for simple databases without any complex or Access 2000-specific features; they'll generally convert OK. Note that you must have Access 97 (and Access 2000) installed on your conversion PC to correctly resolve the differences in library file versions, and new features in Access 2000 (such as Data Access Pages) won't be converted.

Access 2000 can read databases written in any prior version of Access (this is called *enabling* the database), but it won't allow you to modify their design unless you convert them to the Access 2000 format first. This enables you to upgrade networked machines gradually, converting a shared application to Access 2000 only after all the clients have been upgraded. It also enables you to use an application written in an earlier version; you just can't modify its design elements. In short, you'll want to design new applications in Access 2000 only after you're sure that everyone who will use it has a copy of Access 2000.

You can assume that all noncode objects (forms, reports, queries) will convert properly and automatically. For the most part, Access correctly converts your macros and VBA to the Access 2000 if you're converting from Access 97. Conversion from earlier versions may not be as simple; some language elements from Access 2.0 and earlier may not be supported in Access

2000, but these are usually quickly discovered and manually corrected. Significant conversion issues were involved in migrating Access 2.0 databases to Access 95 or 97, but considerably fewer exist when moving from Access 97 to Access 2000.

A few properties and methods have changed from Access 97 to Access 2000; some of the more common ones are summarized in Table 30.2. Access 2000 continues to support the Access 97 syntax, however, so it's not strictly necessary to convert code calling these methods or properties. In most of these cases, the values of the properties have changed as well.

Table 30.2 VBA Object and Method Changes in Access 2000

Access 97 Syntax	Access 2000 Syntax	Example
`Form.AllowEditing,` `Form.Default Editing`	`Form.AllowAdditions,` `Form.AllowDeletions,` `Form.AllowEdits,` `Form.DataEntry`	`Me.AllowAdditions=True;`
`Control.` `BorderLineStyle`	`Control.BorderStyle`	`myComboBox` `Borderstyle=acThin;`
`Form.MinButton,` `Form.MaxButton`	`Form.MinMaxButtons`	`me.MinMaxButtons=` `acBothEnabled;`

Macro conversions are similarly straightforward, with all unsupported Access 97 (and earlier) statements replaced by their Access 2000 equivalents. The most significant of the changes is the replacement of the `DoMenuItem` command (a staple in pre-Access 2000 macros) with the `RunCommand` action. This conversion is automatic for all macros but is not implemented for VBA code (the `DoMenuItem` is obsolete but still supported in VBA). If an old `DoMenuItem` statement in a macro or VBA calls a menu item that no longer exists, the command will not convert correctly and you'll see a runtime error (in macros) or a compilation error (in VBA).

Databases that use Access security can be converted as well, but Microsoft recommends that you compact them after conversion. After the database is converted, you should join a different workgroup long enough to compact the Workgroup Information File containing the security information for the database you're converting. You can't compact the Workgroup Information File for the workgroup you currently belong to—the file is in use.

The Unicode File Format and Other Jet Changes

The database engine that underlies the Access graphical interface is called *Jet*. The version included with Access 2000 is Jet 4.0. The changes from Jet 3.5 to 4.0 are practically invisible to the casual user and are well-hidden even from the experienced database developer, but they are significant and of interest if you've developed applications with earlier versions of Access.

Access also ships with another database engine based on Microsoft's SQL Server product, which is called MSDE. MSDE is discussed in Chapter 32, "Databases and Projects."

The Implementation of Unicode

Earlier versions of Access were dependent on the operating system to provide support for non-English languages, and it expected non-ASCII characters to be contained in one byte for storage. Unfortunately, this scheme (called *Multi-Byte Character Format*, or MBCF) severely limited the support Access could provide to languages with hundreds of characters, including Asian languages. The implementation of Unicode provides two bytes of storage to all nonnumeric characters, providing ample room to support most non-English languages.

It should be noted that this change directly affects only character, not numeric data. Although the internal implementation of numeric data in some cases has changed (primarily to ease the transition of Access data to SQL Server), the Unicode conversion has no effect on numeric data.

As a welcome side-effect to the conversion to Unicode, Access databases are no longer limited to 1GB; this limit was hard and fast in earlier versions. The maximum theoretical size of an Access 2000 database is now slightly more than 2GB.

Although the Unicode data format actually requires twice as much storage space per character as pre-Jet 4.0 databases, Jet 4.0 databases may actually be somewhat smaller because of the implementation of data compression in Text fields. During the compression process, data in text fields is analyzed for the presence of repeating or predictable character sequences. Once identified, these fields are then replaced by tokens for storage. Because tokens require only a few bytes but may replace much longer strings, the total size of the database may be reduced. To start the compression process, choose Tools, Database Utilities, Compact and Repair Database.

Relatively little compression is possible in Memo fields because of the way they are processed. Furthermore, Text fields that are left to their default, unlimited length, are interpreted as Memo fields, essentially disabling compression in those fields. You can improve the storage efficiency (but not necessarily the speed) of your tables by making sure that you use Text fields instead of Memo fields wherever possible and that you assign a finite length to your text fields.

One additional enhancement in the current release of the Jet engine is the implementation of *row-level locking*, which permits multiple users to make changes in the same table at the same time, as long as they are not working in the same record. In earlier versions of Jet (and Access), the engine locked a 4KB page of data whenever a user was active in that page, and a page might include many rows from a variety of tables. A potential complication of this enhancement is that performance may be degraded in certain situations where many users are working in the same table at the same time; the row-locking option can be disabled by clicking Tools, Options, Advanced tab, and marking Default Record Locking.

CHAPTER 31

Customizing Access

In this chapter

Altering Access Startup with Command-Line Switches

Starting Access is no great mystery. You double-click the Access icon on the desktop or you start Access from the Start menu. Access starts and the Startup dialog box displays. But what if you want a particular database to automatically open for you? Or what if you don't like using the Startup dialog box?

Access, like most Office applications, has a series of *command-line switches* that are used to control how Access starts. For example, you can use a command-line switch to open a particular database when you start Access. This can be useful if you do the majority of your work in the same database. You can also control how the database opens. You can open a database, using switches, for exclusive use or read-only use.

The use of switches isn't limited to the control of databases. Using switches, you can control the behavior of Access. For example, you can use a switch to hide the Startup dialog box.

Command-line switches are set through your Access shortcut property window by using the following steps:

1. Add a shortcut for Access to your desktop.

To create a shortcut, right-click your desktop. From the menu, select New, Shortcut. The Create Shortcut dialog box displays. Select the Browse button. From the Browse dialog box, locate and select the application for which you want to create a shortcut and click Open. For Access, the application file is MSACCESS.EXE located in c:\program files\microsoft office\office. Click the Next button. Click Finish.

2. Right-click the Access shortcut to display the shortcut menu.
3. Click Properties to display the Microsoft Access Properties.
4. Click the Shortcut tab.

On the Shortcut sheet, you see the Target text box. The Target setting determines Access' startup behavior. The target is the complete path of the application. The switches go after the complete path of the application. The current contents of your Target text box might have quotes around the database name. These quotes are required if a space exists anywhere in the database or path name.The following sections discuss the switches you can enter for the Target text box.

Opening a Database When You Start Access

If you work primarily with one database, you might want to save yourself the step of always opening the database after Access starts. To open a database automatically, use the following syntax in the Target text box:

```
"\path\msaccess.exe" "\path\database_name"
```

"\path\msaccess.exe" is the path and executable filename for the Access application. This information is entered into the Target field when you create the shortcut. At the end of the text that already resides in the Target text box, you'll enter the path and name of the database file in quotes. *"\path\database_name"* is the complete path and name of the database you want to open when starting Access. Be sure to place a space between the existing text in the Target text box and your entry for "\path\database_name" entry. If you want to open the Northwind database with a switch, you would create the following entry for the Target field:

```
"C:\Program Files\Microsoft Office\Office\MSAccess.exe"
➥"C:\Program Files\Microsoft Office\Office\Samples\Northwind.mdb"
```

If you work with two or three databases frequently, you might want to create multiple shortcuts and set their Targets to different databases. Be sure to include the name of the database in the shortcut's name to avoid confusion.

Opening a Database As Exclusive Using a Switch

Certain database tasks are best done in *exclusive access* for performance reasons. When you open a database in exclusive access, you prevent other users from opening that database. If you are deleting large numbers of records, adding several rows to a large, indexed table, or updating key information, you might find that it is more efficient to be the only person using a particular database. You can open a database for exclusive use when starting Access by using the /excl switch after the name of the database. If you created a shortcut to Access with the Target set to open Northwind, you would have the following value:

```
"C:\Program Files\Microsoft Office\Office\MSAccess.exe"
➥"C:\Program Files\Microsoft Office\Office\Samples\Northwind.mdb"
```

To open Northwind with exclusive access, you would add /excl as shown:

```
"C:\Program Files\Microsoft Office\Office\MSAccess.exe"
➥"C:\Program Files\Microsoft Office\Office\Samples\Northwind.mdb" /excl
```

If you sometimes need to open your startup database for exclusive use and other times you don't need exclusive use, you can create two shortcuts, each with the appropriate Target setting.

Opening a Database for Read-Only Access Using a Switch

As a power user, you probably don't have a need to open a database for read-only access, but what if you are setting up a database for use by a less-experienced user who shouldn't do anything but read from a database? One way to deal with this situation is to set up security through Access' own security mechanism. Another way is to create a shortcut that opens a database for read-only access using the /ro switch. For example, to open the Northwind database for read-only access using the /ro switch, you would enter the following for the Target:

```
"C:\Program Files\Microsoft Office\Office\MSAccess.exe"
➥"C:\Program Files\Microsoft Office\Office\Samples\Northwind.mdb" /ro
```

Obviously, this isn't the most secure way to open a database for read-only access. Operating system, network, and Access' security are much more sophisticated and secure, but the /ro switch does provide a quick way to automatically open a database for read-only access.

There are other reasons to open the database as read only. If you put a database on a read-only medium, you open the database as read only and exclusive to prevent Access from trying to write to a lock file. This is often used to ship access databases on CD-ROMs.

Using Switches with Database Security

If you have elected to use Access' built-in security features to secure a database, you can still use switches to open the database. Two switches that come in handy when security has been implemented are /user and /pwd. The /user switch enables you to pass your username to Access for the database you are opening. The /pwd switch is used to provide the appropriate password for the database. If you needed to open the Northwind database and you had a username of *north* and a password of *wind*, you would use the following value for the Target:

```
"C:\Program Files\Microsoft Office\Office\MSAccess.exe"
➥"C:\Program Files\Microsoft Office\Office\Samples\Northwind.mdb"
➥/user north /pwd wind
```

CAUTION

The /pwd switch does not work with the database password. It's for user-level security only.

NOTE If you used the Security Wizard to set up your security, you probably need to include the /WRKGRP switch. For example, if you created a database named expenses1 and set up security using the Security Wizard, you would need to use the following command line to log on as a user named junk with a password of junk:

```
"C:\Program Files\Microsoft Office\Office\msaccess.exe"
➥"C:\expenses1.mdb" /WRKGRP "C:\Secured.mdw" /user junk /pwd junk
```

Using a Switch to Avoid the Startup Dialog Box

When you start Access, without using a command-line switch to open a database, you see two dialog boxes. The first dialog box is the Access logo (also referred to as a splash screen) and the second is the startup dialog box, which enables you to either create a new database or open an existing database. You have the option of not displaying the Startup dialog box. One way to turn off the Startup dialog box is by using the Tools, Options menu to display the Options dialog box. Using the View tab, you can elect not to display the Startup dialog box. You can also elect not to view the Startup dialog box by using the /nostartup switch.

Performing Database Maintenance with Switches

Some switches enable you to perform maintenance tasks such as compacting, repairing, and converting databases. There are two approaches for using these specialized switches. One is to create a separate shortcut that is only used to perform these tasks. Another is to create a batch file that accesses the database and executes the desired switch. One of these switches is /compact databasename. This switch compacts and repairs the Access database. Another switch is /convert databasename. The /convert switch converts a previous-version Access database to an Access 2000 database with a new name, and then closes Access.

Customizing Access Using the Options Dialog Box

You've seen in other chapters that the easiest way to customize Office applications is using the Options dialog box. Access is no exception. Using the Options dialog box, you can control how the Access interface is viewed, including the editing features, keyboard behavior, datasheet settings, and form and report settings, as well as query and table-design settings. To access the Options dialog box, select Tools, Options.

After the Options dialog box displays, you see that it contains eight tabs (see Figure 31.1). These tabs organize the options that you can set:

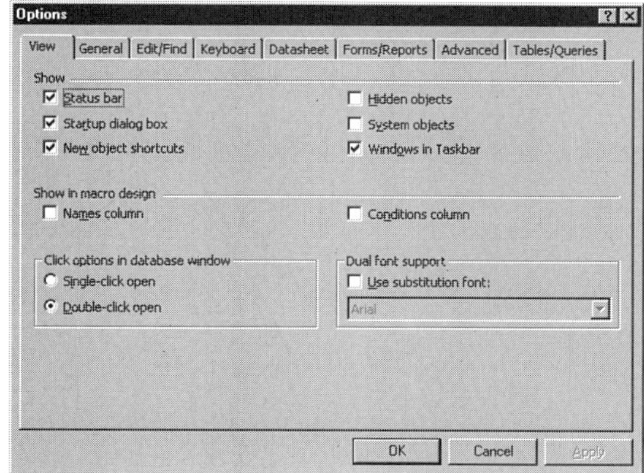

FIGURE 31.1
The Options dialog box enables you to customize the look, feel, and behavior of the Access environment.

- View—The items found on the View tab control various elements of Access' visual interface. Notice that you can control the display of the Startup dialog box from this tab and it is an alternative to using the command-line switch discussed earlier in this chapter.
- General—The General tab contains settings that don't apply specifically to Access objects. Using the General tab, you can set AutoCorrect options, set your default database folder, control sort order, assign default print margins, and control the number of files listed in the recently used file list.

- Edit/Find—The settings on the Edit/Find tab control Find/Replace, Confirm, and Filter by Form operations.
- Keyboard—One area that many users like to customize is keyboard behavior. Using this tab, you can control where you are moved to in a table or recordset when you press Enter. You can also control how your arrow keys behave, whether they are to move character to character or field to field. Depending on the type of data entry you do, you might want to change the setting for behavior entering a field. As a default, this is set to select entire field. If you typically replace the value of the field, leave this setting as is, but if you typically add to the information in a field, then you might want to change this to go to the end of the field.
- Datasheet—The Datasheet tab enables you to control the colors, fonts, default column width, gridlines, and cell appearance on your datasheets. You might, for example, want to change the default font used by your datasheets or elect not to display gridlines on your datasheets.
- Forms/Reports—Use the Forms/Reports tab if you want to change the default templates used by your forms and reports.
- Advanced—The Advanced tab contains many settings. DDE, timeout intervals, and record-locking behavior are set through this tab. You can also set whether shared or exclusive mode is used when a database is opened.
- Tables/Queries—The settings of the Tables/Queries tab control the options for table and query design. One setting you might want to change is the default field type. When you install Access, the field type defaults to text. If you find that when you design tables the majority of fields are of another type, such as number, you might want to change your default field type to save time when creating tables. Another setting on this tab is the default size for text fields. This is initially set to 50. You might want to increase or decrease this default size based on your needs.

Optimizing Access by Altering the Windows Registry

In the previous section, you saw how to customize Access using command-line switches. Although command-line switches control the startup behavior of Access, there are a couple of ways to control the overall Access environment.

One way is to use the Access Options dialog box. Another way is to modify the settings for Access found in the Windows Registry. The Registry is the single location where all system and application settings are stored. When you make a change to Access using the Options dialog box, you are actually making a change to the Registry.

CAUTION

Before you start modifying the entries in the Registry, you should know that incorrectly modifying the Registry can mean that you might damage Access, or your Windows installation, to the point of not being able to run it. And, in some cases, uninstalling and reinstalling Access doesn't always correct the problem. Always use extreme care when working with the Registry!

If you find a way to set an option using the Option or other dialog box, do it that way. The Registry is not something to play with just for fun!

For an advanced user, modifying the Registry does provide a benefit over the settings available through the Options dialog box. You are able to directly work with the settings of the database engine. To state it simply, you can optimize the database engine for your environment. In large organizations with large amounts of data moving across networks, engine optimization can become important. If, for example, your users are complaining of not being able to open records and you determine that it is because of a record-locking issue, you can adjust the record-locking settings.

You are probably wondering how to edit the Registry. You use the Registry Editor. Use the following steps to start the Registry Editor:

1. Click the Start button on the taskbar.
2. Select Run. The Run dialog box displays.
3. Enter regedit and press Enter. The Registry Editor starts as shown in Figure 31.2.

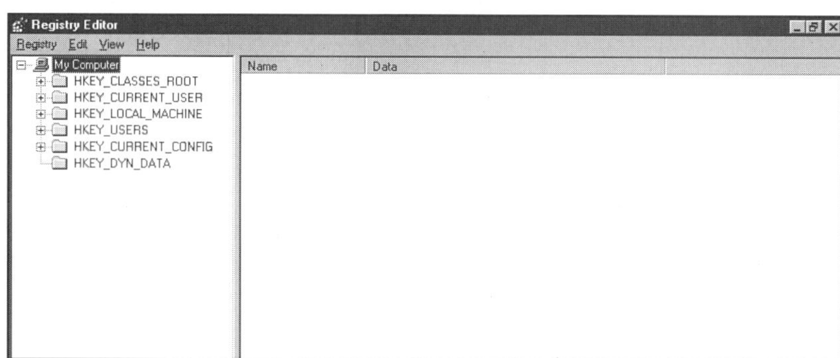

FIGURE 31.2
The Registry Editor is a tool for editing the Registry's settings.

In the left pane of the Registry Editor, you see a series of folders. These folders are called *keys*. The Registry's information is divided by type of information into the keys that you see listed. Traversing a key's structure is just like maneuvering through a directory listing in the Windows Explorer. When you click the expand button (+ sign) for a key, you'll see a list of subfolders. You'll continue to open folders until you get to your final destination.

You are now ready to make changes to the Registry. When you make a change, it does not take effect until the next time you start Access.

Before you begin editing the Registry, it is highly recommended that you back it up. To do this, choose Registry, Export Registry File when you first open the Registry Editor.

NOTE To learn more about working with the Windows Registry, see Appendix CDC (on the CD-ROM accompanying this book), "Working with the Registry." Also, we recommend reading a copy of *Using the Windows 98 Registry* or *Special Edition Using the Windows 95 Registry*, both published by Que.

Customizing Jet 4.0 Database Engine Settings

The majority of users access their data in one of two ways when working with Access, either with the Jet engine or by using ODBC. Using the Registry, you can control the way the Jet engine performs by adding entries. Typically, on a machine that has recently had Access installed, you might not find the actual subkey that you need and you might have to add it yourself. Complete the following steps to add the needed subkey:

1. Click the expand button for HKEY_LOCAL_MACHINE.
2. Continue through the key structure until you are at \HKEY_LOCAL_MACHINE\SOFTWARE\Microsoft\Office\9.0\Access\Jet\4.0\Engines.
3. With the Engines key selected, select Edit, New, Key. A new key is added.
4. Type Jet 4.0 and press Enter to name the key (see Figure 31.3).

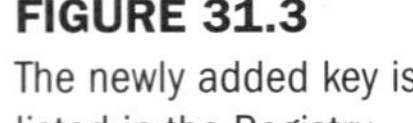

FIGURE 31.3
The newly added key is listed in the Registry.

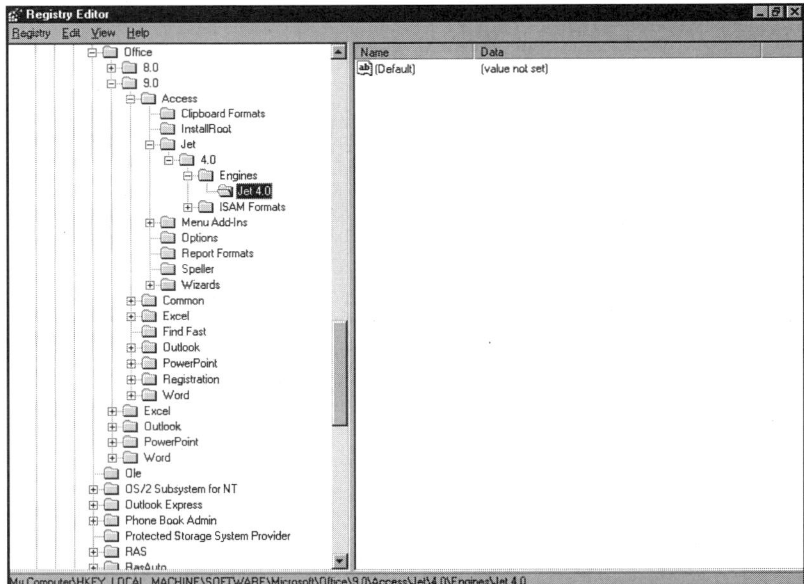

NOTE Making changes to this subkey affects only Access. On your machine, you might have several programs that use the Jet 4.0 database engine, including Excel and Visual Basic 6.0. If you want the changes you make to affect all applications that use the Jet 4.0 database engine, make changes to the settings in the \HKEY_LOCAL_MACHINE\SOFTWARE\Microsoft\Jet\4.0\Engines\Jet 4.0 subkey.

After you have the Jet 4.0 key added to the Registry, you can add values to it. To add a value, use the following steps:

1. Select the key to which you want to add values.
2. Select Edit, New.
3. Select the type of value you want to add: string, binary, or DWORD.
4. Enter a name for the value and press Enter.
5. Double-click the value. A dialog box displays.
6. Enter the appropriate data for the value and press Enter.

Table 31.1 lists some of the values you set for the Jet 4.0 database engine. This table doesn't list all the available values but lists the ones you are most likely to use. Remember, Access works fine without setting any of these values. Set these values only if you are having performance issues. Another word of caution—I highly recommend that you set one value, exit the Registry Editor, start Access, and make sure it works before setting another value. I know that it is tedious to set one value at a time and test Access after each value, but it is a lot easier to troubleshoot using this method. If you enter ten values and Access won't start, then you would have ten places to look for errors.

Changes to the Registry apply to all databases all the time. If you want to just change Registry settings for a single session, you can use the Application.DBEngine.SetOption method in a VBA procedure. The values set using the Application.DBEngine.SetOption method remain in effect until either the Application.DBEngine.SetOption method is executed again or until the current session is closed.

Table 31.1 Jet 4.0 Database Engine Registry Values

Value Name	Value Type	Description
LockRetry	DWORD	This value sets the maximum number of times Jet should attempt to access a locked page before returning a lock-conflict message. The default setting for this value is 20. You might want to increase this if you have a high-volume database and users are frequently receiving lock-conflict messages.
MaxLocksPerFile	DWORD	You might want to set this value if you are running Access on a NetWare 3.1 network. If the locks in a Jet transaction attempt to exceed the assigned value, the transaction is split into two or more parts and then each part is committed. Refer to your NetWare documentation for information on NetWare's lock limit. You might also notice a performance increase in Access when setting this value if you are running Access on a NetWare network.

continues

Table 31.1 Continued

Value Name	Value Type	Description
PagesLockedToTableLock	DWORD	If you perform bulk insert, delete, or update operations to your tables, you might want to consider setting this value to a nonzero value. The default setting for this value is 0. When set to 0, Jet never automatically changes from page locking to table locking. You can specify the maximum number of pages that are locked before Jet escalates to table locking. In a multiuser environment, it is recommended that you use this setting carefully because when a table is locked, your users are not able to use it. I recommend using this value only if your bulk operations are always performed after hours.
Threads	DWORD	The Threads value is used to control the number of background threads available to the Jet database engine. By increasing the number of available threads, you can gain performance. However, assigning more threads to Access can decrease the performance of other applications running on the same machine. The default setting for this value is 3. If you are running Access on a dedicated machine or if you are running Access on a Windows NT machine with multiple processors, you might want to use this value. You might also want to change this value if Access is running in the foreground.

Customizing ODBC Driver Settings

In the previous section, ODBC (Open Database Connectivity) was mentioned as one of the more common data access methods used with Access. And, like Jet 4.0, ODBC can be customized via the Registry. The subkey you'll be working with in this case is \HKEY_LOCAL_MACHINE\SOFTWARE\Microsoft\Office\9.0\Access\Jet\4.0\Engines\ODBC. You might find that the ODBC subkey does not exist and needs to be created using the technique described in the previous section.

After you have navigated to this subkey, you are ready to set the values found in Table 31.2. This table doesn't list all the available values, but it does list the ones you are most likely to use.

NOTE Making changes to this subkey affects only Access. On your machine, you might have several programs that use the ODBC driver, including Microsoft SQL Server and Visual FoxPro. If you want the changes you make to affect all applications that use the ODBC, make changes to the settings in the\HKEY_LOCAL_MACHINE\SOFTWARE\Microsoft\Jet\4.0\Engines\ODBC subkey. ■

TIP The Application.DBEngine.SetOption method discussed in a previous tip can be used to set ODBC driver Registry values for a single session.

Table 31.2 Jet 4.0 Database Engine Registry Values (ODBC)

Value Name	Value Type	Description
ConnectionTimeout	DWORD	This value controls how long a connection can be idle before it is timed out. The default setting for this value is 600. If your users are frequently being timed out, you might want to increase this value. On the other hand, if you have the problem of people staying logged on when they are not using the connection, then decrease this number.
DisableAsync	DWORD	This value is used to control the type of query execution used. The default setting for this value is 0, meaning the asynchronous execution is to be used if possible. Setting DisableAsync to 1 forces synchronous query execution. Setting this to 1 can increase speed when performing query execution but is recommended only for single-user environments, not for multiple-user environments. Basically, what this value does is increase query performance at the expense of processor cycles on the local machine.
QueryTimeout	DWORD	The meaning of this value is dependent on the setting of the DisableAsync value. If DisableAsync is set to 0, then the QueryTimeout value is the number of seconds to wait for a response from the server between query-completion polls. If DisableAsync is set to 1, then the QueryTimeout value is the number of seconds of total processing time that a query can run before timing out. The default setting for this value is 60. If users are frequently getting timed out while performing queries, increase the setting for this value.
TraceSQLMode	DWORD	By default, this value is set to 0. When set to 0, Jet does not trace SQL statements to the ODBC data source in the SQLOUT.txt file. If this is set to 1, then it writes the statements to SQLOUT.txt. The advantage of setting this to 1 is that it performs an audit trail of SQL statements that are performed through Jet to an ODBC data source. The downside of setting this value to 1 is that you are increasing the overhead associated with these operations and can degrade performance. This is also a debugging flag.

Remember that any changes you make do not take effect until the next time you start Access.

CHAPTER 32

Databases and Projects

In this chapter

The Client/Server Nature of Access 2000

Access 2000 expands on the desktop database paradigm by permitting Access to act as a *front-end* to any of several database engines that may or may not reside on the local computer. This is an evolutionary step forward from the Access 97 client/server model, which encouraged developers (via the Database Splitter Wizard, still available in Access 2000) to store interface components (forms, reports) in a different database file from the underlying data structure elements (tables, queries). In Access 97, one could create forms and reports that operated on remote data sources that were linked to the interface via Open Database Connectivity (ODBC); this required the database engine to support ODBC and the operating system on the client to be configured specifically for that server.

▶ **See** "Database Splitter," **p. 1115**

In Access 2000, the Jet database engine that has always shipped with Access is somewhat improved (as discussed in Chapter 30, "Migrating to Access 2000") and is still the default tool for storing Access data. For most users, it is invisible, and the concept of selecting a different integrated store is unnecessary to consider. But Jet is somewhat limited, as database engines go. It is physically limited to a little more than 2GB of storage; its practical limit is only a few megabytes; and Jet isn't intended to support more than 20 or 30 concurrent users.

Microsoft has positioned its enterprise-class database engine, SQL Server, to handle large databases, but SQL Server doesn't ship with a graphically oriented development environment. Thus, the invention of the Access 2000 *Project*: the Access GUI links integrally to an underlying database engine other than Jet (usually SQL Server), permitting the convenience of Access for users and developers and the power of an enterprise DBMS for business use.

One surprise in Access 2000 is the inclusion of the Microsoft Data Engine (MSDE), which can be used instead of Jet by Access 2000 Projects to ensure complete compatibility with SQL Server 7.0. A Project using MSDE can be migrated immediately to a Windows NT Server PC running SQL Server 7.0 with no conversion issues (or so the promise goes). This eliminates even the minor issues typically encountered when converting Access (Jet) databases to SQL Server.

This is a welcome step for business databases that the developer anticipates may need to move to SQL Server someday, but not yet. It's not clear yet whether any performance advantages or disadvantages exist in using MSDE instead of Jet.

There's no requirement that Access databases be developed as Access Projects, and only one reason to create a Project file: to eventually use it in conjunction with SQL Server. If your application is small enough to remain on Access, or if it uses a different database engine (via ODBC), no need and no advantage occurs in using Access Project features.

Moving Objects from One Database to Another Database

Occasions exist when it's convenient to copy or move database objects from one Access database file to another. These include the following:

- When reusing code or designs
- When making minor customizations while maintaining a pristine copy of a database
- When troubleshooting database corruption problems

The simplest way to accomplish this, assuming that all the objects to be moved are in a single database file, is simply by copying the originating database using the file system, and then working on the copy. This method has the added advantage of creating a backup of the source file where one didn't necessarily exist before.

If the objects to be moved are in several database files, a couple of other options are available. The easiest—and perhaps most surprising—is to use OLE drag and drop to move the objects between databases, as shown in Figure 32.1. Access, unlike the other Office applications, doesn't allow you to open more than one document (database, in this case) in the same instance of the application. However, you can open multiple instances of Access at the same time, and each instance can contain a different database. After you have the source and destination databases open in different instances of Access, you can simply drag each object to be copied from one instance to the other.

NOTE Some Office 2000 applications enable you to open more than one document at the same time. A new window is opened for each (technically violating Microsoft's own coding standards, which require that applications support multiple data files in the same window). Access enables only one database to be open at a time. However, it enables you to start multiple instances of the Access environment, each open to a different database. Each database is listed on the Windows taskbar, but you can see that they're not the same by starting the Windows Task Manager (press Ctrl+Alt+Delete; if running Windows NT, select Task Manager), which indicates that two copies of Access are running. In this case, one of the taskbar entries is different because the Inventory Control database has an entry in the Name field in the Database Properties dialog box (File, Database Properties).

A more involved technique for moving objects between databases involves the use of intermediate file types. Although more difficult, this method works with almost any database; however, you need to ensure that objects with unusual data types or attributes are accounted for in the process.

By using the File/Export function, any database object can be saved in any of several formats. Of all these formats, the most useful is comma-delimited text, which can then be imported by nearly any modern application. However, data objects that do not readily convert to text (OLE objects, for example) or objects that are Access-specific (such as memos) do not always benefit from this technique.

▶ **See** "Data Sharing with Other Applications," **p. 1161**

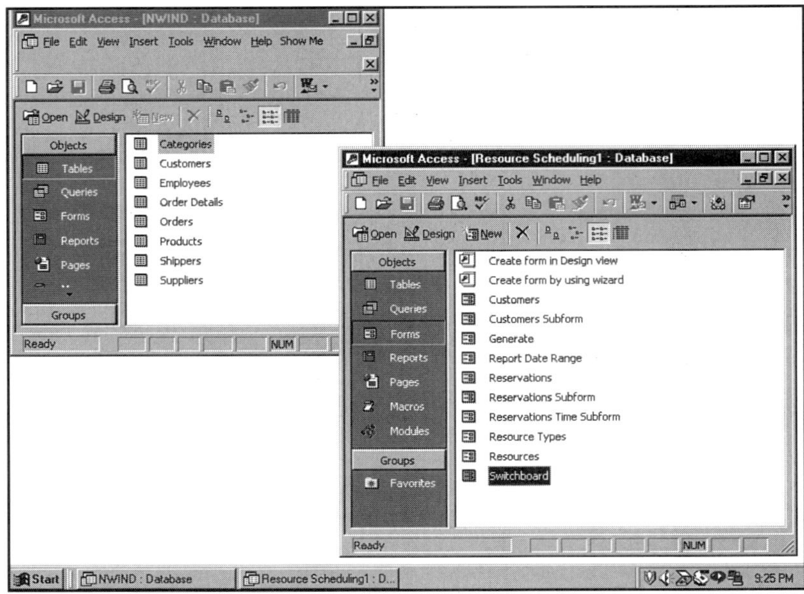

FIGURE 32.1
You can have multiple instances of Access open at the same time, and you can drag and drop objects among them.

Using the Built-In Database Templates

Access includes 10 templates for business and home databases. They're relatively complete databases and are easy to customize if you're familiar with the Access programming environment. Don't try to modify the wizards, however; they're supplied in compiled form and aren't modifiable.

To create a new database using the templates, follow these steps:

1. From the Windows Desktop, start Access. On the startup dialog box, choose Access Database Wizards, Pages, and Projects and click OK. The file selection dialog box shown in Figure 32.2 appears (in Detail view).
2. Select one of the templates and click OK. In the File New Database dialog box that opens, name the new database and click Create.
3. The wizard for the database you chose opens and typically includes a description page. To navigate the wizard, click Next in each dialog box, after answering the relevant questions posed. Most of these databases include several tables and enable you to choose certain fields to include (or not include) for each table.
4. When asked to select a style for the onscreen display and for printed reports, choose a background and typeface option that suits you and click Next.
5. You're asked to name the database and whether you want to include a logo or picture. If you choose to, you can select from almost any graphic on your computer. This image is included in the reports your database prints.
6. Click Finish to save your work and create the database. Note that most database reports won't work until you enter some data values.

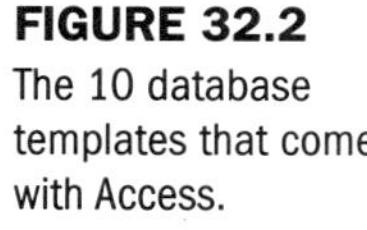

FIGURE 32.2
The 10 database templates that come with Access.

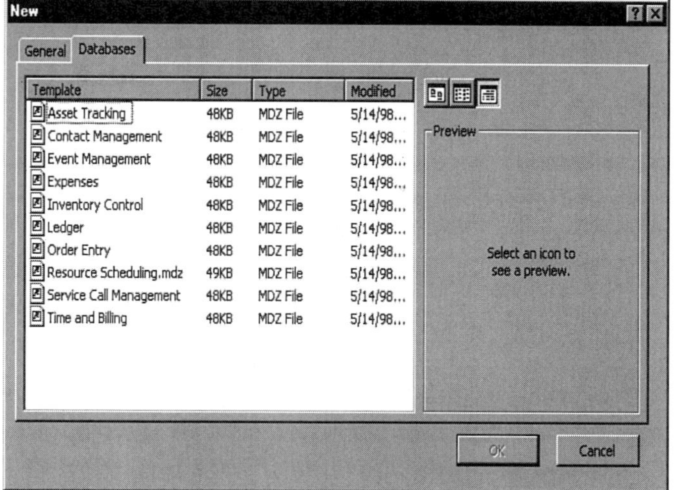

Creating Access Projects

Most Access databases use the Jet database engine that is installed with Access. To the casual user, no difference exists between the database engine (Jet) and the database interface (the Access GUI); they are one and the same. The query and table operations available in Access seem to be Access-specific. In fact, they're Jet-specific. In previous versions of Access, no way existed to distinguish between the two.

It's certainly possible to create an Access database that is entirely composed of linked tables from another database, such as dBASE, Paradox, or an ODBC database. In this case, the Access interface still provides the same functions as when the data was stored in a Jet database. The data is filtered through Jet before it's made available to the user. Still, no obvious distinction is made between Jet and Access.

In Access 2000, advanced users can finally completely detach the Access interface from the Jet engine. The concept of an Access project (with a file extension of .adp) is very similar to that of an Access database with linked tables, but, in this case, the Access interface is closely coupled with either a SQL Server engine or the new Microsoft Data Engine (MSDE). MSDE is essentially a one-user version of SQL Server, and it can be installed from the Microsoft Office 2000 Premium Edition CDs.

The obvious question is "Why not use Jet?" Surprisingly, a couple of good answers exist. One is size-related. Even though the maximum size of a Jet database has increased in Jet 4.0 to more than 2GB, it may still be too small for some applications, especially those creating several temporary tables. In this case, it might be nice to work with a database that could grow somewhat larger over a period of time.

Another good answer, and the one Microsoft prefers to emphasize, is that you may want to someday migrate your Access database to Microsoft SQL Server. Doing so adds considerable robustness and security, and effectively removes the built-in limits on database size. Although a significant number of low-level changes were made to Jet 4.0 to make it more compatible with SQL Server, the Upsizing Wizard still has to deal with some incompatibilities. By using MSDE, you eliminate all potential incompatibility between the two applications. This is made inescapably apparent by the changes that occur in the Access interface after the decision to use MSDE or SQL Server as a back-end is made when creating an Access Project.

Finally, if you're accustomed to the way SQL Server (and some of the enterprise-level databases) operates, you may want to take advantage of features that MSDE provides that Jet doesn't, such as stored procedures and event triggers. These features are undocumented in the Access environment, but they should work as they do in SQL Server.

One caveat to using MSDE: Microsoft has imposed an artificial 2GB size limit on MSDE databases, and a few esoteric limits exist to the ways you can use transaction processing in MSDE. These features prevent you from using MSDE as a single-user version of SQL Server. For details, look up "MSDE" in Access Help.

Installing MSDE

To create an Access project, you'll either need to have local or network access to a SQL Server database (either version 6.5 or 7.0), or you'll need to install MSDE. MSDE is on CD #1 of the Microsoft Office 2000 Premium Edition in the directory \SQL, and no option is provided to install it as part of the Office installation process.

To install MSDE, insert the Office 2000 CD, click Start, Run from the Windows Desktop, and enter `D:\SQL\X86\SETUP\setupsql.exe` (assuming your CD drive is D:). You can generally accept all the defaults for the prompts, restarting your machine after installation is complete.

At restart, MSDE will be installed but not started, by default. To start the MSDE process from the Windows Desktop, click Start, Programs, MSDE, Service Manager. The Service Manager opens and gives you the option of starting, stopping, or pausing the MSDTC, MSSQLServer, and/or SQLServerAgent services. Choose MSSQLServer (which should be the default service) and click the Start button to start the service. You may choose to check the Auto-Start Service When OS Starts box, if appropriate.

MSDE is now installed and ready to use with an Access Project.

To create an Access project and a new back-end database, use these steps:

1. Start Access. From the Access startup dialog box, choose Access DatabaseWizards, Pages, and Projects. The New window appears (refer to Figure 32.2); click the General tab and click the icon marked Project (New Database). Click OK to continue.
2. Choose a name and folder location for the project database and click Create to generate the project file. After creating the database, Access opens the SQL Server Database Wizard (see Figure 32.3) in the Database window for your use in specifying the database engine for this project file.

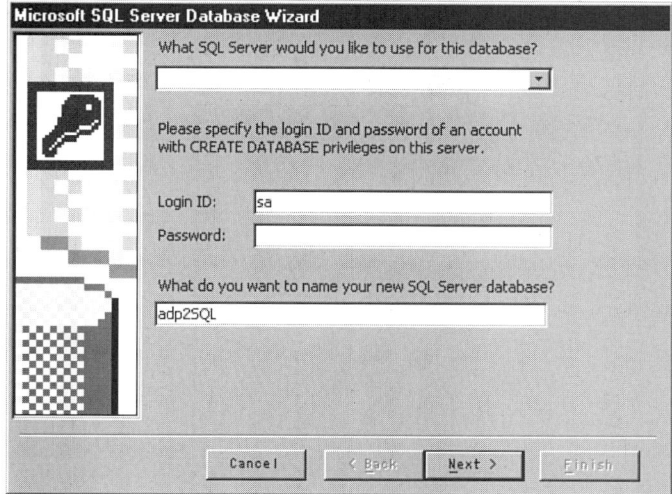

FIGURE 32.3
The SQL Server Database Wizard applies to both MSDE and SQL Server back-end databases.

3. If you're planning on using a SQL Server database engine, follow the instructions in the first bullet as follows. For MSDE, follow the instructions found in the second bullet.
   - SQL Server—Select a database server by typing the name of a SQL Server machine on the local network. Previous selections, if any, are visible in the drop-down list. Enter a login name and password on the SQL Server with privileges to create a new database, and change the name of the database on the remote machine, if desired. Click Next to continue.
   - MSDE—Type the name of the PC running MSDE in the Which SQL Server box. (To find out the name of the local PC, go to Control Pane, Networks, Identification.) Previous selections, if any, are visible in the drop-down list. Unless you've configured user accounts for MSDE, use "sa" as the Login ID and leave the password blank. Enter a new name for the database, if required, and click Next.
4. If an error message appears, it's likely either that you entered an incorrect username or password or that the SQL Server or MSDE is not running. For SQL Server, contact your administrator. For MSDE, check the applet tray to ensure MSDE is running and start it (see the previous sidebar) if it's not. Click Finish to complete the creation of the database.

To create an Access Project using an existing database, use these steps:

1. From the Database Window, click File, New. The New dialog window appears; click the General tab and click the icon marked Project (Existing Database). Click OK to continue.
2. Choose a name and directory for the project database and click Create to generate the project file. After creating the database, Access opens the Data Link Properties dialog box (see Figure 32.4) in the Database window for your use in managing your connection to MSDE or SQL Server.

NOTE You'll need to have Service Pack 5 or later installed on your copy of SQL Server 6.5 for this to work. It will also work with SQL Server 7.

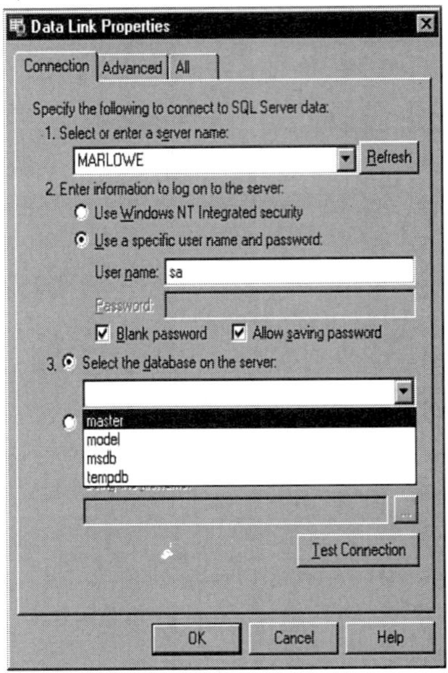

FIGURE 32.4
Use the Data Link Properties dialog box to specify the location and properties of the database for which you want to create a Project.

3. Click OK to finish creating the Access Project based on the database you selected. You're returned to the Database window with the objects in the remote database displayed in the appropriate tabs.

After you've created a Project file, you can start working with it the same as you would a regular Access database, except that you'll use design tools custom-tailored to SQL Server (and MSDE). It's worth mentioning that you can import tables, forms, and so on from other Access databases (or other data sources, as appropriate), but you can't use the Link feature to dynamically link remote data sources to your MSDE or SQL Server database. You can't import Access queries. Also, Access VBA code may not compile when it's imported into a SQL Server or MSDE database.

Working with Access Projects

It should be completely transparent to the user whether the back-end database is MSDE or SQL Server. It is immediately apparent, however, that this isn't an Access database because the design environments are very different from their Access equivalents, and even the tabs on the Database window (see Figure 32.5) are different.

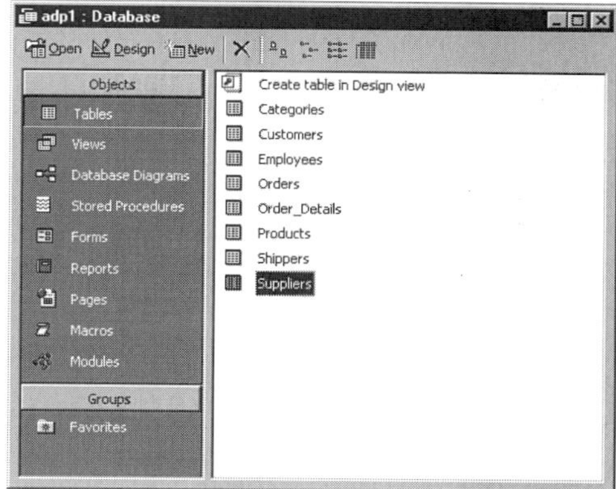

FIGURE 32.5
The Database window for an Access Project. The Create <object> in Design View selection is visible only if a valid connection exists to an MSDE/SQL Server data source.

- The Views tab is analogous to the Queries tab in Access. However, SQL Server Views have some additional features, including the capability to encrypt individual views.
- The Database Diagrams tab contains objects that represent various arrangements and relationships between the tables in the remote database, such as the Relationships window in Access. However, you can do much more in the Database Diagrams environment than you can in the Relationships window, including creating and deleting tables, relationships, and indices.
- Stored Procedures are similar to both Access Modules and Queries; they are written procedures written in SQL that perform operations directly on the database. The SQL language used here is considerably richer than the SQL used in Access queries, and stored procedures are callable from external programs and other ODBC-compliant applications.

Getting used to the SQL Server/MSDE environment can be challenging unless you're already familiar with the Access development tools. The Access Project design tools are presented here for familiarization using imported Northwind database objects; you'll see immediately that the Project environment is different.

For more information on SQL Server objects and the MSDE/SQL Server design environment, consider the following books:

- *Special Edition Using Microsoft SQL Server 7*, published by Que
- *Using Microsoft SQL Server 7*, published by Que

Table Designer

The *Table Designer* in an Access Project (see Figure 32.6) is somewhat more complex than its Access Database equivalent because of the larger number of properties and constraints that can be set in SQL Server/MSDE. The differences include an entirely different set of data types, some of which are generally equivalent to Access data types (`datetime = Date`) and some of which are not ("bit"). Additionally, the user can specify precision and scale for some data types, and several other properties are directly available in the Designer.

Note that imported tables from Access databases generally lose their key and relationship properties upon import. You'll need to reestablish keys in the Table Designer (select the key fields and click the Primary Key icon on the toolbar) and relationships in the Database Diagrams environment (discussed later in this chapter).

NOTE The Table Designer may not be installed by default in your copy of Access 2000; if not, you'll be asked to insert the installation CD (or select the network path for a network installation).

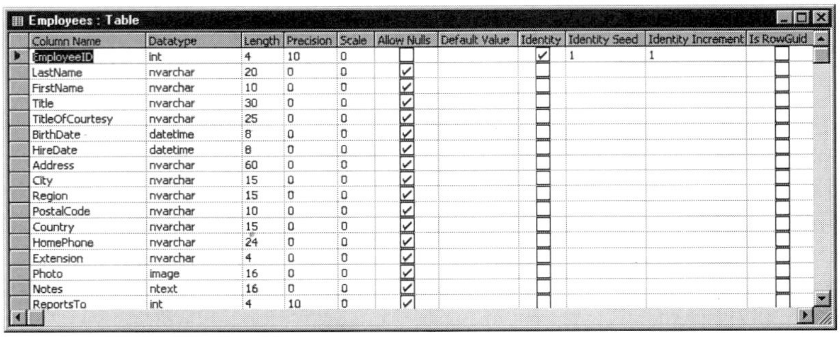

Employees : Table

Column Name	Datatype	Length	Precision	Scale	Allow Nulls	Default Value	Identity	Identity Seed	Identity Increment	Is RowGuid
EmployeeID	int	4	10	0	☐		☑	1	1	☐
LastName	nvarchar	20	0	0	☑		☐			☐
FirstName	nvarchar	10	0	0	☑		☐			☐
Title	nvarchar	30	0	0	☑		☐			☐
TitleOfCourtesy	nvarchar	25	0	0	☑		☐			☐
BirthDate	datetime	8	0	0	☑		☐			☐
HireDate	datetime	8	0	0	☑		☐			☐
Address	nvarchar	60	0	0	☑		☐			☐
City	nvarchar	15	0	0	☑		☐			☐
Region	nvarchar	15	0	0	☑		☐			☐
PostalCode	nvarchar	10	0	0	☑		☐			☐
Country	nvarchar	15	0	0	☑		☐			☐
HomePhone	nvarchar	24	0	0	☑		☐			☐
Extension	nvarchar	4	0	0	☑		☐			☐
Photo	image	16	0	0	☑		☐			☐
Notes	ntext	16	0	0	☑		☐			☐
ReportsTo	int	4	10	0	☑		☐			☐

FIGURE 32.6
The Table Designer in an Access Project includes many more properties than can be directly set for an Access table.

Views Designer

Because you can't import Access queries into the Views tab of the Access Project window, you'll have to create your queries from scratch by using the *Views Designer* (shown in Figure 32.7). It's largely the same as the Access Query Designer, except that you must either drag field names from the Diagram (the top portion) to the Grid, or check the box to the left of their name; double-clicking doesn't work. You should also notice that the grid is laid out 90 degrees rotated from the Query Designer grid for Jet databases.

Database Diagram Designer

You'll use the *Database Diagram Designer* to establish relationships between tables (see Figure 32.8). You can also create new tables and table elements directly from this window. Available options include the capability to automatically resize and position the table representations. You'll notice that relationships in MSDE/SQL Server are named, giving the capability to deal with them directly in stored procedures. You can modify the relationship names by double-clicking the line connecting the related tables and editing it in the dialog box that appears.

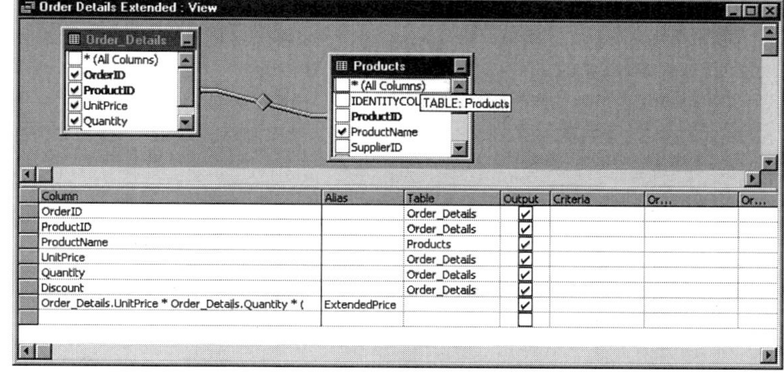

FIGURE 32.7
The Views Designer in an Access Project has a slightly different syntax for expressions; compare this query with the Northwind query "Order Details Extended."

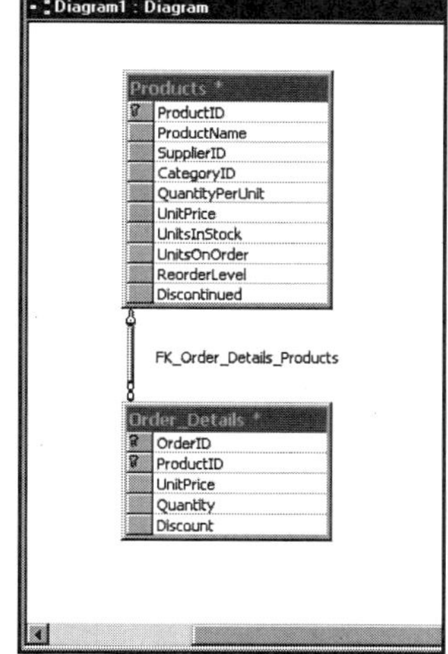

FIGURE 32.8
The relationship line in the Database Diagram environment refers to the relationship between the tables and provides no direct information on the particular fields related.

CHAPTER 33

Advanced Tables

In this chapter

Advanced Methods for Creating Tables

You have probably created tables by using a couple of methods at this point. One way that most Access developers have used to create tables is via a Wizard. You may have also created a table by using the Design view. These are not the only ways to create a table. You can create a table by importing data from another source such as a SQL Server table or an Excel worksheet. You can also create a table by using a SQL (Structured Query Language) Select statement, which selects records from one table and creates a new table with those records.

There are two other methods to create tables that are frequently used. You can create new tables based on the contents of another table by either importing data or linking to a table. *Importing data* is the process of making a copy of data located in one data source and creating a table by using the copied data. *Linking* is the process of connecting to data from another database without importing it. This allows you to view and edit the data both in its original location and in your Access database.

NOTE In previous versions of Access, linking was called attaching.

Users often wonder when they should import data and when they should link to a table. If you need to do extensive querying or reporting on the data you are working with, you probably need to import the data for performance reasons. If the data resides in the current database, it is faster to work with. The downside to importing is that importing data results in copying data to your database. This means you are supporting data in two locations—the location where the data originated and the new location in your Access database. This may not be an optimal solution for your situation, particularly if the original data is updated frequently. If you need to be able to view frequently changing data and have your updates available in both your database and the database where the data originates, then create a link to it.

Access provides two ways of creating a table using imported data. One way is to open the destination database and select File, Get External Data, Import. The other way is to use the File, Open command to open an external database such as dBASE, Paradox, or Visual FoxPro. When you open an external database, Access automatically creates a new database based on the existing database and creates links to the tables in the external databases' tables. Links are discussed in more detail in a later section of this chapter.

Importing an Access Object After creating a table, query, report, and so on in one Access database, you may find that you want that same object in another Access database. This is easily done with the Import menu. You can import the following objects from one Access database to another:

- Tables
- Forms
- Queries
- Reports

- Pages
- Macros
- Modules

You can't import the following objects from one Access database to another:

- Views
- Stored procedures
- Database diagrams

To import database objects, access the Import dialog box by using the following steps:

1. Select File, Get External Data, Import. The Import dialog box displays (see Figure 33.1).

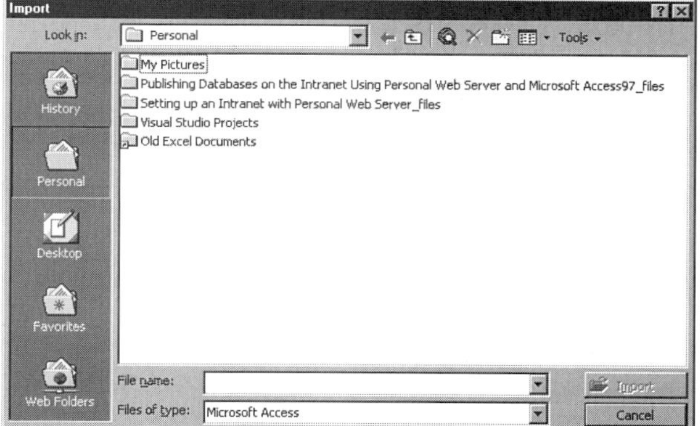

FIGURE 33.1
The Import dialog box enables you to import data from a variety of sources.

2. With Microsoft Access selected in the Files of Type drop-down list box, locate and select the database from which you want to import the object.
3. Select Import. The Import Objects dialog box displays (see Figure 33.2).

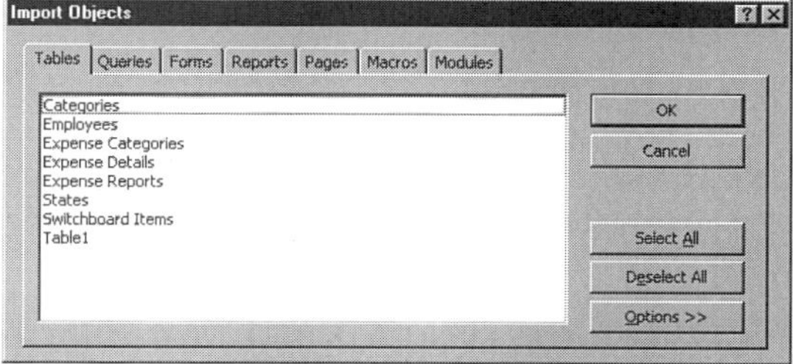

FIGURE 33.2
The Import Objects dialog box contains tabs, which organize database object types.

4. Select the tab for the database object type you want to import.
5. Continue to select objects until all desired objects are selected.
6. Click OK. The objects are added to the current database.

The imported objects are immediately available for use in the current database. Remember that some objects are based on other objects. For example, queries are often based on tables. Therefore, you may need to import the parent tables of a query to make the query work in its new location.

Importing Data from a Data Source Other Than Access You are not limited to just importing data from other Access databases. Access makes it easy to import data from a wide range of data sources. How you complete the import process is dependent on the type of data being imported. Access comes with several predefined filters for use with importing. These filters are as follows:

- dBASE III
- dBASE IV
- dBASE 5
- dBASE 7
- Microsoft Excel
- Exchange
- HTML Documents
- Lotus 1-2-3 for DOS
- Lotus 1-2-3 for Windows
- Outlook
- Paradox
- Text Files

However, you are not limited to these data sources. You can import data from any ODBC data source as long as you have its driver installed on your system. Examples of ODBC databases are Oracle and Microsoft SQL Server. To import data using one of Access' built-in filters, complete the following steps:

1. Select File, Get External Data, Import. The Import dialog box displays.
2. Select the appropriate file type from the Files of Type drop-down list box.
3. Locate and select the database from which you want to import the data.
4. Click Import. After a few moments, a message displays letting you know that your data was successfully imported.
5. Click Close.

The steps described are the basic steps for importing data. Depending on the type of data, you may be prompted for additional information.

Importing Data from an ODBC Source In today's world it is becoming less and less frequent that data is located in just one place. Some data is found locally on your system, some may reside on your network, and still more data may be on your mainframe. Because of these varied database formats and platforms, Microsoft and other manufacturers implemented an interface for data access called *ODBC (Open Database Connectivity)*. ODBC provides a common standard for transferring data between databases and applications. A wide variety of databases can be accessed via ODBC including

- Access
- Visual FoxPro
- Microsoft SQL Server
- Sybase
- Oracle
- Btrieve
- DB/2

The basic steps for importing data using ODBC are similar to the ones discussed in the previous section. The difference comes into play when you select ODBC Databases as your file type to import. At this point the Select Data Source dialog box displays. This dialog box allows you to select from a defined data source name or create a new one. A ***data source*** is a collection of named connection information that is used by the ODBC driver to access a database. Data source information may include database name, database location, database file type, username, password, and so on. To import data from an ODBC data source already defined, use the following steps:

1. Select File, Get External Data, Import. The Import dialog box displays.
2. Select ODBC Databases from the Files of Type drop-down list box. The Select Data Source dialog box displays, as shown in Figure 33.3.

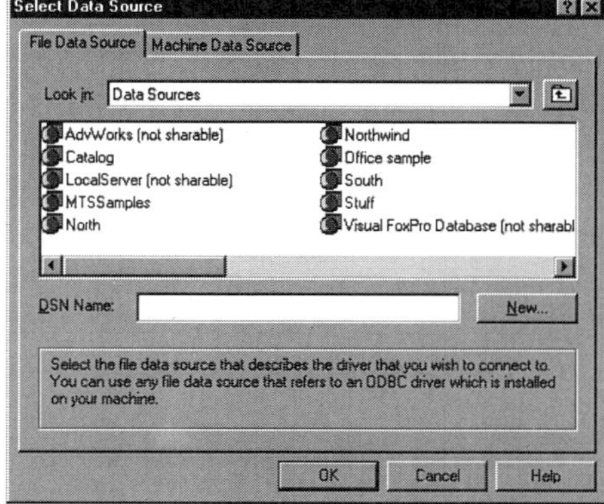

FIGURE 33.3
Select Data Source allows you to select from an existing data source or define a new data source name.

3. Select the name of the data source you want to import from in the list box.
4. Click OK. The SQL Server Login dialog box displays.
5. Enter your login ID and password, and then press Enter. The Import Objects dialog box displays (see Figure 33.4).

FIGURE 33.4
The Import Objects dialog box allows you to select the tables you want to import.

6. Select the table(s) you want to import. Click OK. The tables are imported to the current Access database.

If you do not see a data source defined for the ODBC database that you need to import from, you can define one yourself. To import data from an ODBC data source that does not have a *data source name* (DSN) defined, use the following steps:

1. Select File, Get External Data, Import. The Import dialog box displays.
2. Select ODBC Databases from the Files of Type drop-down list box. The Select Data Source dialog box displays (refer to Figure 33.3).
3. Click New. The Create New Data Source dialog box displays (see Figure 33.5).

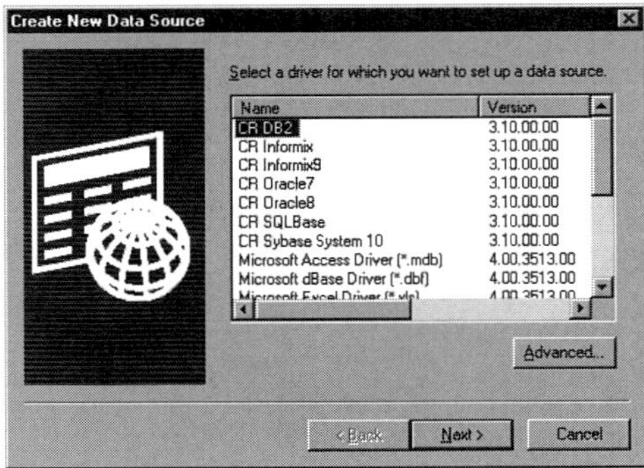

FIGURE 33.5
To create a new DSN, you must have the appropriate ODBC driver installed.

4. Select the driver that matches the data source you want to use and click Next.
5. The next dialog box prompts you for a name for your data source. Enter the name and click Next.
6. At this point you are asked to review the information you entered. After you are through reviewing it, click Finish.

Depending on the driver you selected, you may be prompted for additional information. For example, if you create a DSN for SQL Server, you'll be prompted for additional information such as a description for the connection, the default database used by the connection, password information, and so on.

Importing Data from Excel In the "Importing Data from a Data Source Other Than Access" section of this chapter, you saw the basic steps for importing data. In that section, it was pointed out that when you import from some data sources, you might need to provide additional information to complete the import. Such is the case with importing data from Excel. If the file you have selected from the Import dialog box is an Excel workbook, the Import Spreadsheet Wizard automatically starts when you click the Import button. Excel workbooks are three-dimensional and, as such, each sheet in the workbook is viewed as a table by Access. The Import Spreadsheet Wizard lets you tell Excel from which sheet in your workbook you want to import data. You also can import a sheet or a named range.

If you are planning to import data from an Excel file, you need to keep a couple of things in mind as to the design and layout of the Excel sheet where the data is located. The first row of the sheet should contain the name or title of the column's data. This is because Access allows you to use the first row of worksheet as the name of the fields for the imported data. As an example, pretend you have a worksheet with three columns of information and those columns have the following entries in the first row: First Name, Last Name, and Phone. Then the records in the table created when you imported the Excel data would have fields named First Name, Last Name, and Phone. Another thing to remember when naming the columns in your Excel worksheet is to use Access' field-naming rules to avoid import issues. The last thing to keep in mind when designing an Excel worksheet that is to be imported to Access is that the sheet should contain only rows that are to be imported to Access. In other words, the sheet shouldn't contain rows with totals, summaries, or other additional information. To import data from an Excel workbook, use the following steps:

1. Select File, Get External Data, Import. The Import dialog box displays.
2. Select Microsoft Excel from the Files of Type drop-down list box.
3. Locate and select the workbook file from which you want to import the data.
4. Click Import. The first dialog box of the Import Spreadsheet Wizard displays (see Figure 33.6).

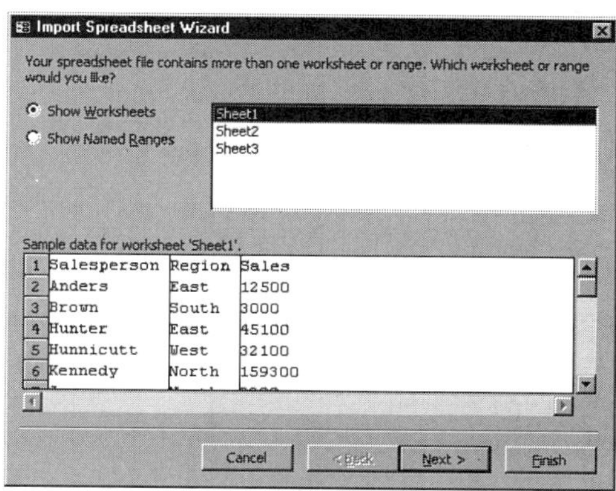

FIGURE 33.6
The first dialog box of the Import Spreadsheet Wizard asks you to select the sheet in the selected workbook from which you want to import data.

5. Select the sheet (or named range) with the data to be imported from the list box. A sample of the data on that sheet displays in the preview area.

The Jet database engine may have problems interpreting certain characters—such as apostrophes—allowed by Excel in sheet names. Before importing data from an Excel file, you may want to simplify your sheet names so that they contain only letters, numbers, and spaces.

6. Click Next. The second dialog box of the Wizard displays (see Figure 33.7).

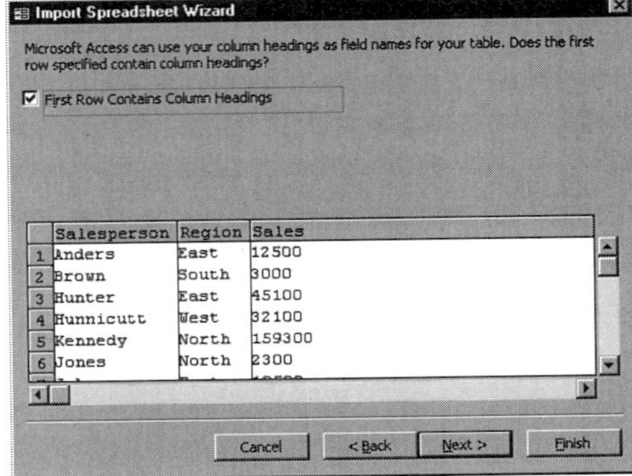

FIGURE 33.7
The next step in import Excel data is to let the Wizard know whether your data contains column headings.

7. If your data has column headings, place a check in the First Row Contains Column Headings check box. Click Next. The next dialog box of the Wizard displays.
8. You are prompted for the location in which you want to store the imported data. You can either store it in a new table or an existing table. If you elect to store it in a new table, the Wizard creates a new table. The name of the table is based on the name of the sheet in which the data was located. If you want to import the data to an existing table, you need to provide the Wizard with the name of the table. Click Next. The next dialog box of the Wizard displays, as shown in Figure 33.8.

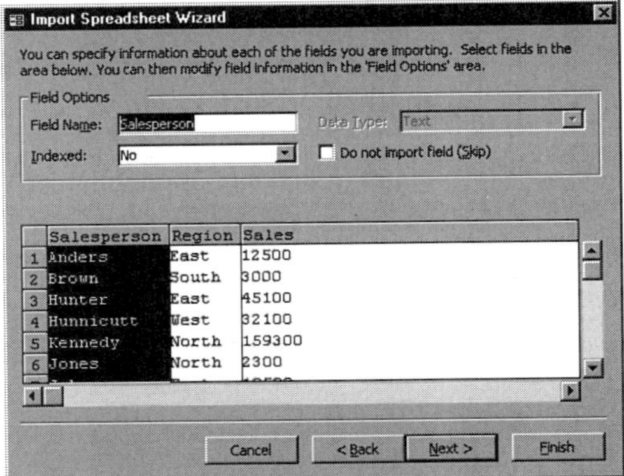

FIGURE 33.8
This part of the import process allows you to set field options.

9. You are now ready to set field options for your imported data. You can assign a different field name, change the field type, and decide whether you want the field to be indexed or whether you want to skip the field altogether. To work with the different fields you are importing, select the field from the fields area at the bottom of the dialog box and then set its options. When you have completed setting options, click Next.
10. The next step in importing your data is to select a primary key. You can let Access assign a primary key for you. In this case Access adds a field to your data. The added field contains a unique number for each record in the table. If one of the fields in your data should be used as the primary key, select the Choose My Own Primary Key option. If you don't want to have a primary key, select No Primary Key. Click Next.
11. The final dialog box of the Wizard allows you to name the table if you are importing to a new table. Access assumes that you want the table's name to be the same as the name of the sheet you are importing from. You can keep this name or enter a new one. Click Finish.
12. In a moment a message box displays letting you know that the data was imported successfully. Click OK.

Importing a Text File There are times when you need to import data but you don't see a file type listed in the Import dialog box for the application you are importing from. In this case you probably need to import from a text file. Most applications can save to or export to a text file. This includes many spreadsheets, word processors, and older DOS databases. This option is also often used if you are importing data from a mainframe or UNIX system.

NOTE This is not the case for all mainframe and UNIX systems. If, for example, you want to import mainframe data from DB2 or UNIX data from Oracle and you have a gateway from that system to your network, you may be able to import data using ODBC.

Text data is formatted in one of two ways. *Delimited* means that a certain character such as a tab or semicolon separates each field. *Fixed width* means that each field is assigned a certain number of characters. Although you can use just about any character as a delimiter, there are certain characters typically used. Common delimiter characters are

- Tab
- Semicolon
- Comma
- Space

When you import a text file, the Text Import Wizard steps you through the process. Use the following steps to import a text file:

1. Select File, Get External Data, Import. The Import dialog box displays.
2. Select Text Files from the Files of Type drop-down list box.
3. Locate and select the file you want to import.
4. Click Import. The first dialog box of the Import Text Wizard displays (see Figure 33.9).

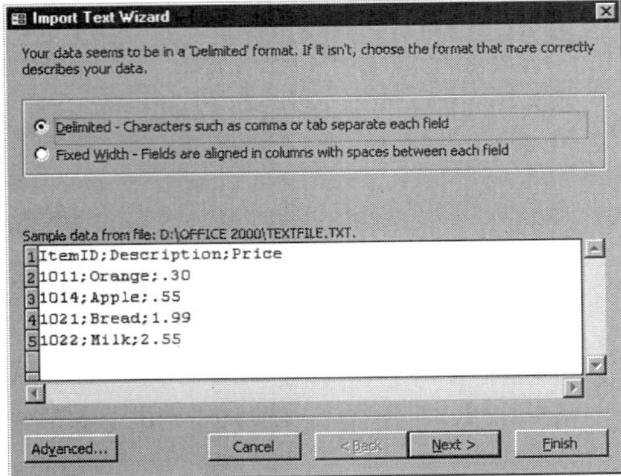
Import Text Wizard

Your data seems to be in a 'Delimited' format. If it isn't, choose the format that more correctly describes your data.

- (•) Delimited - Characters such as comma or tab separate each field
- ( ) Fixed Width - Fields are aligned in columns with spaces between each field

Sample data from file: D:\OFFICE 2000\TEXTFILE.TXT.

```
1 ItemID;Description;Price
2 1011;Orange;.30
3 1014;Apple;.55
4 1021;Bread;1.99
5 1022;Milk;2.55
```

Advanced... | Cancel | < Back | Next > | Finish

FIGURE 33.9
The first dialog box of the Import Text Wizard displays a sample of the data to be imported.

5. The Wizard attempts to interpret your data and determine whether it is delimited or fixed. In case it misinterprets the layout of your data, you are given the opportunity to select the appropriate format. After the correct format is selected, click Next.
6. If you have delimited data, the next step is to verify that the Wizard has correctly determined the delimiter character. If it hasn't, select the correct delimiter character. If the first row of your data contains field names, place a check in First Row Contains Fields Names. Depending on your data, you may also need to select a Text Qualifier. A *text qualifier* is a character that denotes a field as a text field. Placing a character such as a quote or apostrophe before text is done by some older spreadsheet applications. If you have fixed width fields, the next step is to confirm that the Wizard correctly interpreted the field breaks. Make any necessary adjustments.
7. Click Next.
8. After the Wizard knows how to interpret your text data, it can place it into a table. You have the option of either placing the data into a new table or an existing table. If you opt to place it into an existing table, you'll need to provide the table name. Click Next.
9. If you are importing to an existing table, the next dialog box displayed is the Finish dialog box. If this is the case, click Finish.

   If you are importing to a new table, the next dialog box allows you to set field options. You can assign a different field name, change the field type, and decide whether you want the field to be indexed or whether you want to skip the field altogether. To work with the different fields you are importing, select the field from the fields area at the bottom of the dialog box and then set its options. When you have completed setting options, click Next.
10. If you are importing to a new table, the next step in importing your data is to select a primary key. You can let Access assign a primary key for you. In this case Access adds a field to your data. The added field contains a unique number for each record in the table. If one of the fields in your data should be used as the primary key, then select the Choose My Own Primary Key option. If you don't want to have a primary key, select No Primary Key. Click Next.

11. The final dialog box of the Wizard allows you to name the table if you are importing to a new table. Access assumes that you want the table's name to be the same as the name of the file you are importing from. You can keep this name or enter a new one. Click Finish.

Linking Data to Create a Table

Creating a link to a table is very much like importing a table. As a matter of fact, the database types from which you can import are the same ones that you can link to. To link to data, use the following steps:

1. Select File, Get External Data, Link Tables. The Link dialog box displays.
2. With Microsoft Access selected in the Files of Type drop-down list box, locate and select the database you want to link to.
3. Select Link. The Link Tables dialog box displays.
4. Select the tables you want to create a link to.
5. Click OK. The objects are added to the current database.

NOTE To create an updatable link to a dBASE 7 table, you must have the Borland Database Engine (BDE) version 4.*x* or later installed on your system. If you do not have BDE 4.*x* or later installed, you have three options:

- Install dBASE 7 or Delphi on your system.
- If you have an older version of the BDE that does not support dBASE 7 file format, then you can upgrade your engine from the Inprise's (formally Borland) Web site at `http://www.inprise.com`.
- Save the table to dBASE III, IV, and 5.0 file format.

The preceding steps illustrate how similar linking is to importing. Linked tables are denoted in the Database window with a small arrow to the left of their icon.

Using a Query to Create a Table

Another way to create a table is to use a SQL query. Using a `SELECT...INTO` statement, otherwise known as a make-table query, you can choose fields and records from one or more tables and create a new table. For more information on make-table queries, see Chapter 35, "Advanced Queries."

Advanced Table Settings

Now that you have the tables you created, you are ready to fine-tune their settings. There are a variety of options that you can set to make your tables better fit your data and needs. Most of the settings you'll be working with have to do with the fields of your tables. By setting various field properties, you can control not only the appearance and type of data used by the field, but you can even control how data is entered into the field.

Setting Field Properties

Setting field properties is done through a table's Design Windows. When viewing a table's design, you are actually viewing the properties of the table's fields. The properties that you can set for a field are dependent on the data type that has been assigned for that field. For example, if the data type of a field is Currency, you can set the number of decimal places to display for that field. There are some properties that most data types share:

- Format—The Format property enables you to customize the way data is displayed and printed. There are predefined formats for dates, time, numbers, currency, and yes/no data types. You can use one of the predefined formats or you can create your own.
- Input Mask—Whereas the Format property controls the appearance of data, the Input Mask property controls the entry of data. An *input mask* forces a user to input values in a certain way. For example, if you had a field for Social Security number, you would want an input field of 000-00-0000 where the 0 represents a number. This way the user would always enter the correct number of characters for a Social Security number and could not accidentally enter in an alpha character. Using an input mask has two advantages. One is for your user. Input mask makes data inputs easier because the format, as well as any special characters such as hyphens or parentheses, is entered for them. The other advantage has to do with the data itself. By using an input mask with your data, you reduce the possibility of input errors by forcing your user to enter data in a specific way.
- Caption—The Caption property is actually the field's label when displayed on a form. The Caption property's setting defaults to the field's name, but if you want to display a more descriptive name or shorter name on forms for the field, enter a value in the Caption property. This if often used when you want to display a space in the name but don't want the field name to have a space in it.
- Default Value—Some fields naturally lend themselves to having a default value. For example, if you are creating a table for your client information and the majority of your clients reside in the same state, you'll want to enter that state's name for the Default Value property of the field. This makes inputting faster for your users and reduces input errors. If the user doesn't want to accept the default value, he simply types over it.
- Validation Rule—You can control the data input into your field by using the Input Mask and Default Value properties. But there are times when neither of these properties adequately controls or limits the data that can be entered into the field. Access provides you with another property to limit data values for a field, called the *Validation Rule* property. Using the Validation Rule property, you can, for example, set a rule that allows only values less than 50 to be entered for a particular field. A validation rule can be up to 2,048 characters in length.

NOTE The MSDE data engine supports another tool that can be used for data validation, called *triggers*. Triggers are a special kind of stored procedure used to enforce data integrity. A trigger is automatically executed when a user accesses or attempts to change the specified data-modification statement on the specified table. The three types of triggers supported are insert, update, and delete.

- Validation Text—You can customize the error message that appears when a user's input violates the validation rule by entering a value for the Validation Text property. A validation text can be up to 255 characters in length.
- Required—If the Required property is set to Yes, then a valid value must be entered in the field or the record will not be saved.
- Indexed—An *index* is used by Access to speed up queries that use the indexed fields. Indexes also speed up sorting and grouping operations. When you are selecting fields to index, look for fields that contain multiple unique values such as last name or city. Often you won't need to create an index on, for example, a field of Yes/No data type or if a field can contain only a few possible values such as the case would be with salutation. If you plan to update the table frequently, use indexes sparingly as they may slow updates. There are three possible settings for this field. The default is No, which means no index. If you want to set the field as an indexed field, select either Yes (Duplicates OK) or Yes (No Duplicates).

There is a reason to index a yes/no field. If the field is used for an open/closed flag and most of your reports use only records that are open, the index helps limit the records reviewed by the query.

These properties can be set either by using the Design Windows or using VBA code. Following is an example of setting a property using VBA:

```
'This sets the ValidationRule property for the DiscountAmount field of the
'Discounts table in the current database
CurrentDb.TableDefs("Discounts").Fields("DiscountAmount").ValidationRule =
➥"<=.50"
```

One of the previously discussed properties does not follow the format of the code illustrated. To set an index for a field via VBA code, you need to execute the `CREATE INDEX` statement.

Defining an Input Mask

Earlier in this chapter, an input mask was defined as a way to force a user to input values in a certain way. For example, if you had a field for Social Security number, you would want an input field of 000-00-0000 where the 0 represents a number. Input mask makes data inputs easier because the format, as well as any special characters, such as hyphens or parentheses, is entered for them. Also, by using an input mask with your data, you reduce the possibility of input errors by forcing your user to enter data in a specific way. To define an input mask, you use a series of characters shown in Tables 33.1 and 33.2. If you were defining an input mask for a phone number in the United States, you would use the following mask: (000)000-0000. This requires that the user enter the phone number with the three-digit area code. The parentheses and the hyphen are automatically provided in the field and the user does not have to enter them. You can enter the input mask characters directly into the Input Mask property, or if you are working with a field that is a text or date data type, you can use the Input Mask Wizard to create your input mask. Clicking the build button that displays when you select the Input Mask property field accesses the Input Mask Wizard.

Table 33.1 Input Mask Definition Characters

Character	Entry	Description
L	Required	Letter A through Z
?	Optional	Letter A through Z
A	Required	Letter or number
a	Optional	Letter or number
0	Required	Number 0 through 9; + and – signs not allowed
9	Optional	Number 0 through 9 or space; + and – signs not allowed
#	Optional	Number or space; blanks converted to spaces; + and – signs allowed
&	Required	Any character
C	Optional	Any character

Table 33.2 Input Mask Special Characters

Character	Description
.	Decimal placeholder.
,	Thousands separator.
: ; - /	Date and time separators.
<	Characters that follow this symbol are converted to lowercase.
>	Characters that follow this symbol are converted to uppercase.
\	Characters that follow this symbol are displayed as a literal character. For example, \0 would display as 0.
Password	Using Password as the setting for the input mask creates a password entry text box. Any character that is typed into the box is displayed as an asterisk.

Moving a Field to a Different Location in the Table

After creating or importing a table, you may find that you need to rearrange the order of the fields in the table. Dragging fields to a new location is easily done by using the following steps:

1. With the table open in Design view, select the field or fields you want to move. To select one field, click the field's row selector. To select several fields, highlight the row selectors of the fields.

2. Drag the selected row or rows to their new location by clicking the highlighted row selector(s) and holding down your mouse button while moving the mouse. A thin horizontal bar displays to show you where the field(s) would be relocated if you released the mouse button.
3. When you have reached the new location for the field(s), release your mouse button.

When you move a field in the table Design view, you are changing the order in which the field is stored in the table. You are also changing the order in which the field displays in the datasheet. You aren't changing the location of the field in any forms or reports that have been created prior to the move.

Using Multiple Fields to Create a Primary Key

Usually when you create a table, you define a primary key. A *primary key* field contains a value for each record that is unique, such as an employee ID number or a Social Security number. This avoids the problem of duplicate data in your table. A primary key is typically defined when you are creating a new table. If you create a table using a wizard, you are given the option of either letting Access create a field to be used as a primary key or to select a primary field yourself to be used as the primary key. If you are creating a table using the Design window, select the field you want to use for your primary key and click the Primary Key toolbar button.

You are not limited to using a single field as your primary key. There are times when a combination of fields would make a better primary key than a single field. One of the classic examples of this is a catalog item number. In this situation you may want the first three characters to represent the catalog issue in which the item originated, the next three digits to be the department number, and the final four digits to be the inventory ID. You can enter a ten-digit catalog item number, but this is harder to input and leaves more room for error in the data.

You can also break it into three fields. This makes it easier to input and two of the fields, catalog and department, become candidates for lookup fields. And you can still use the information from all three fields combined as your table's primary key. Another name for a primary key that is created using multiple fields is a *composite key*. To create a primary key using multiple fields, complete the following steps:

1. Open the table in Design view.
2. Select the first field to be used as part of the multifield primary key.
3. Hold down the Ctrl key and click the remaining fields to be used as part of the multifield primary key (see Figure 33.10).
4. Click the Primary Key toolbar button.

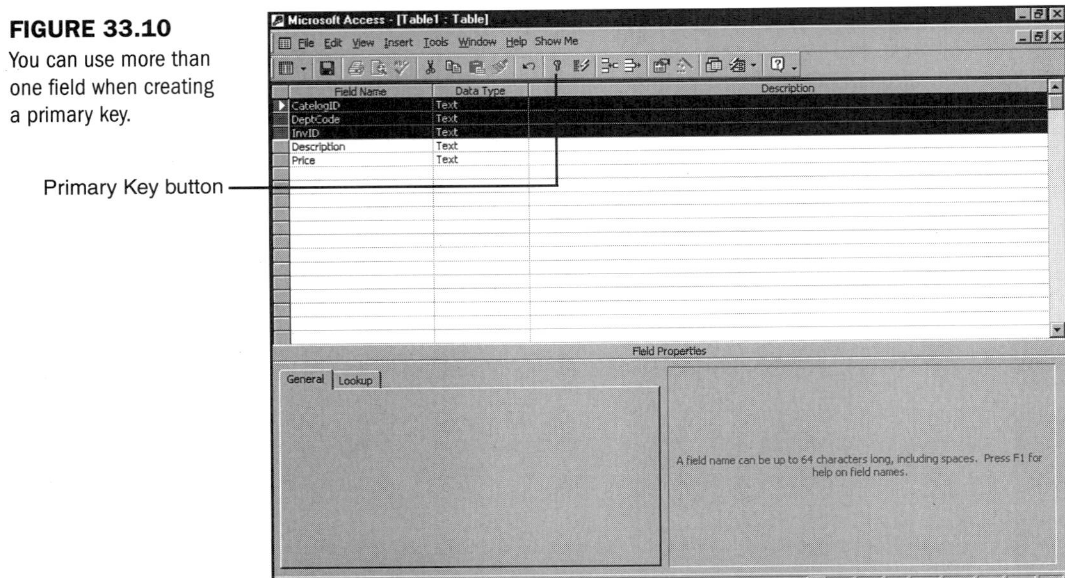

FIGURE 33.10
You can use more than one field when creating a primary key.

Understanding Table Relationships

Access is a relational database management system making table relationships essential to its functionality. Tables relate to one another through *key fields*. Key fields act as connections between tables. For example, you have a table named Stores that has a field named Store ID in it. You also have a table in the same database named Employees. Because employees work in stores, you need to know in which store they work and therefore you would like to relate an employee to a store. Relating the two tables via a common field can do this. If, for example, both the Stores table and the Employees table have the field Store ID in them, then they have a relationship. By having a relationship between these two tables, you can use them in queries. Because of the relationship, you create a query that retrieves fields from both tables.

An example of the type of query you may want to create is one that retrieves all the employees that work in a certain city. Although the location of the store they work in isn't stored in the Employees table, it is available through a query because of the relationship that the table shares with the Stores table, which would contain the location information.

Accessing the Relationships Window

To review and modify relationships between tables you use the Relationships window. The Relationships window presents table relationships in a graphical format. Use the following steps to access the Relationships window:

1. Close any Table views you may have open.
2. If necessary, switch to the Database window.

3. Click the Relationship toolbar button. The Relationships window opens, as shown in Figure 33.11.

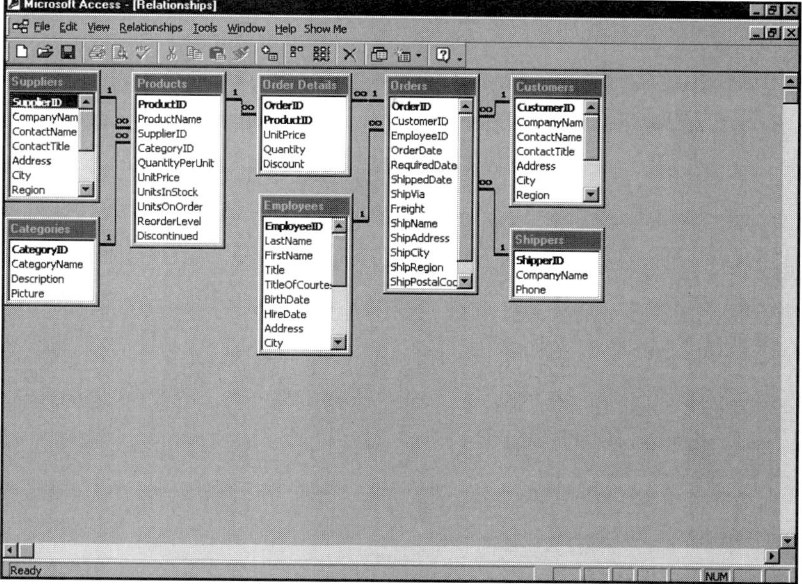

FIGURE 33.11
The Relationships window is used to view, create, and modify table relationships.

If you created the database using a wizard, then you'll find the relationship layout has been created and saved for you. If you created your tables from scratch, you may need to define the relationships yourself. If this is the case, you'll need to add your tables to the window and then build the table relationships. To add tables to the window, select Show Tables from the Relationships window. Double-click the names of the table you want to relate and close the Show Table dialog box. To define a relationship between two tables, drag the field that you want to relate from one table in the Relationships window to the related field in the other table. A line appears between the related tables.

Printing the Relationships Window

Many Access developers like to document their work to make the database easier to support in the future. The Relationships window makes documenting relationships easy to do. Using the New Print Relationships Wizard, you can print a report that displays the relationships between your tables. To generate a report about your table relationships, select Print Relationships from the File menu while the Relationships window is open. The report that is generated is similar to the one shown in Figure 33.12.

Using Lookup Fields

When you create your tables, you may find repeating fields in your tables. For example, if you created a database to track your company information, you would find a field to store State (as in Georgia, Florida, California, New York, and so on) in tables such as Stores, Vendor Detail, Employees, and Customers. Because State data is very static and is used in multiple locations, you may want to create a table that includes state information. Now you can define the State fields in your various tables as lookup fields. A *lookup field* displays values looked up from an existing table or query. Lookup fields are yet another use for table relationships.

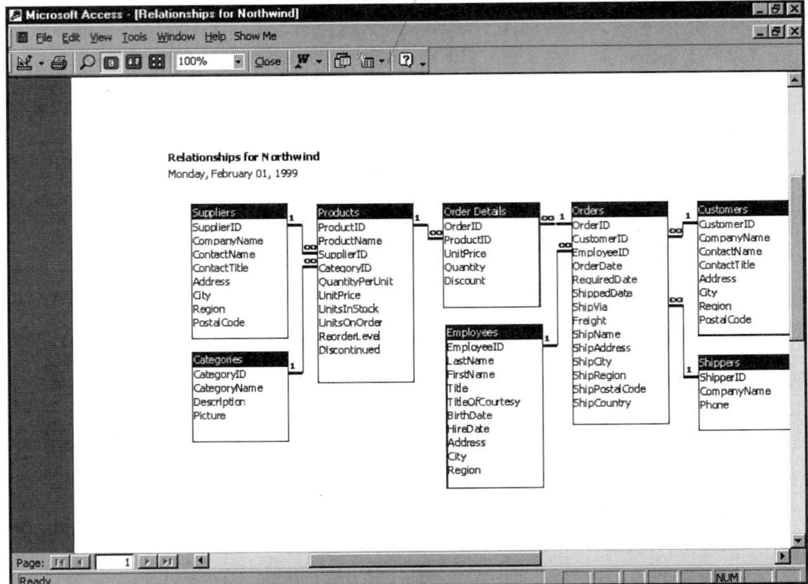

FIGURE 33.12
You can print or save the generated report for future reference.

You aren't limited to creating lookup tables for fields used by multiple tables. You can create a lookup table for any field that has a limited set of acceptable values. For example, you can create lookup fields for expense codes, employee types, departments, or regions. You may want to consider doing this for two reasons. One reason is for data integrity. If the user has to pick from a list of values for a field, then they can't input an invalid value. It is beneficial to provide a pick list to your user as well. They don't have to memorize codes and categories because they are listed for them.

Although not required by Access, it is considered good database design to build a relationship between the table containing the lookup field and the lookup table itself. This is done through the Relationships window. Setting a field as a lookup field is done through the field's properties. To set a field as a lookup field, complete the following steps:

1. Open the table where the field is located in Design view.
2. Select the field.
3. Select the Lookup tab from the Properties box.
4. Select List Box or Combo Box from the Display Control property. The Lookup tab displays additional properties, as shown in Figure 33.13.
5. Select Table/Query for the Row Source Type property.
6. Select the Row Source property. Click the down-arrow button for that property. A list of tables and queries displays.

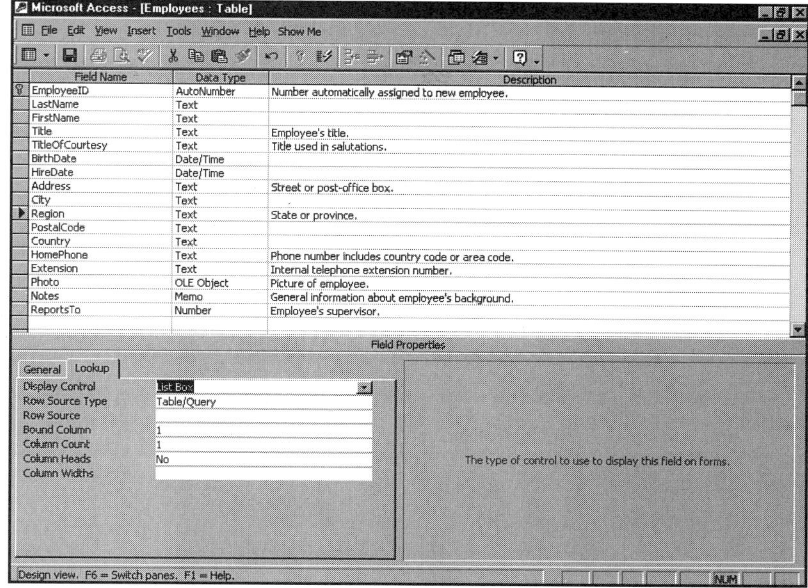

FIGURE 33.13
After you set the Display Control property to List Box or Combo Box, you are ready to select the source of the lookup.

7. Select the table or query you want to use for your lookup values.
8. Close the Design window. Save your changes.

Now, when users enter data into a Datasheet and they come to the lookup field, they are able to select from a series of values, as shown in Figure 33.14.

Part V
Ch 33

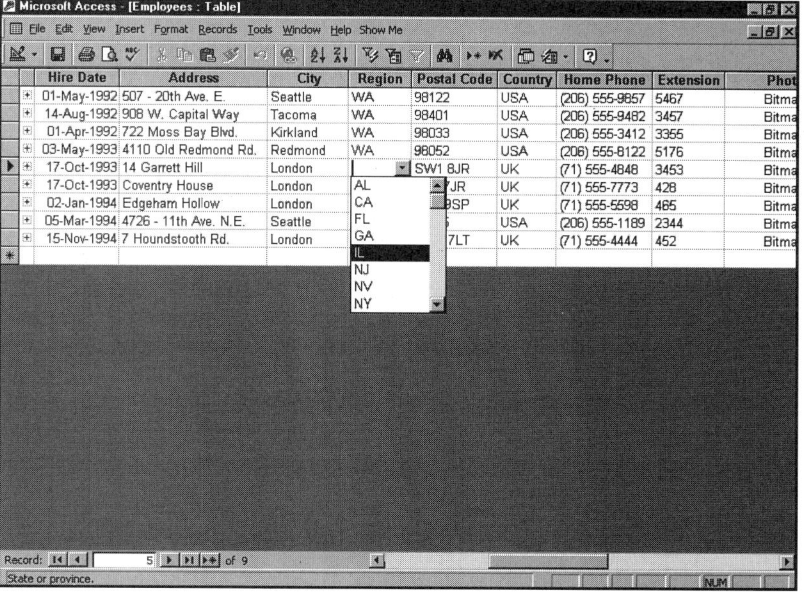

FIGURE 33.14
By clicking the down-arrow button associated with the field, a user can pick from a list of values.

Understanding Referential Integrity

The relationship between tables is based on the fact that the field in one table has data that matches the field in another table. Say that you have an inventory table that contains a field named DepartCode. The DepartCode field relates to the Departments table's primary key, which is also named DepartCode. What if someone accidentally deletes a row from the Departments table? Then you have a problem with the relationship between the two tables because the Inventory table has entries for DepartCode that don't have a matching value in the Departments table. This is where referential integrity comes into play. *Referential integrity* is a system of rules that Access uses to make sure that relationships between records in related tables are valid and remain valid. This means that you can't accidentally delete or change related data. To set referential integrity, there are three conditions that have to be met:

1. The matching field from the primary table is a primary key or has a unique index. Using the example of Inventory and Departments, the Departments table's DepartCode would need to be the table's primary key.
2. The related fields have to be the same data type. This means that if Department's DepartCode field is text, then Inventory's DepartCode field needs to be text.

NOTE There are two exceptions to the rule. One is that an AutoNumber field can be related to a Number field as long as its Field Size property is set to Long Integer. The other exception is that an AutoNumber field with a Field Size property of Replication ID can be related to a Number field with a Field Size property set to Replication ID.

3. Both tables must reside in the same Access database. If the tables are linked tables, then they must be tables in Access format. In the case of linked tables, you must open the database in which they are stored to set referential integrity. In other words, referential integrity can't be set for linked tables from databases in other formats.

After you set up referential integrity for tables, you can't enter a value in the foreign key field of the related table that doesn't exist in the primary key of the primary table. Going back to the example of Inventory and Departments, you can't enter a value into the Inventory's DepartCode field that doesn't exist in the Departments' DepartCode field.

After you have elected to enforce referential integrity, you can't delete a record from a primary table if matching records exist in a related table. For example, you can't delete a record from the Departments table if the Inventory table has a record in it that matches an entry in the Departments table. You also can't change a primary key value in the primary table if that record has related records. This means, for example, that you can't change a DepartCode in the Departments table if there are inventory items already listed for that DepartCode in the Inventory table.

To set up referential integrity, you need to be in the Relationships window. When you create or edit a relationship and you want to enforce referential integrity, click the Enforce Referential Integrity check box found on the dialog box that displays.

If referential integrity is enforced and a user breaks one of the rules with related tables, Access displays a message to alert the user and won't allow the change.

CHAPTER 34

Functions and Expressions

In this chapter

Working with Expressions

The primary reason that you store data on a computer is to make your work easier and to utilize the power of the computer. This is definitely the case with using Access. Storing data is just part of its job. The other thing that Access enables you to do is analyze your data. To analyze data you often need to perform calculations using the values in your table. For example, if you had a table with your inventory information in it, you could multiply the quantity of an item times its cost to get a cost of goods on hand.

The great thing about using *expressions* is that you don't have to add a field to your table to store the calculated information. You simply display the result of the calculation in queries, tables, and reports. You can create your own formulas or you can use the built-in functions provided by Access.

When you are working with expressions, there are a few terms that you need to be familiar with. Expressions contain *operators*. Operators refer to the arithmetic symbols used in an expression such as =, -, *, /, <, and >.

In conjunction with operators, you often use *literals*. Literals are values. For example, you may have the expression `Price>100`. In this case 100 is a literal. In the expression `Price>100` you have another element, the name of a field. In expressions, field names are called *identifiers*.

The name of any object in Access (tables, forms, controls, field, and so on) used in an expression is called an *identifier*. The final term that you'll encounter when working with expressions is *function*. A function calculates and returns a value. For example, the `Date()` function returns today's date.

Access' Operators

Access organizes its operators into five categories:

- Arithmetic—This category is probably the one that you are most familiar with. Its operators perform addition, subtraction, multiplication, and division.
- Comparison and Assignment—When working with queries one of the most useful sets of operators are the comparison and assignment operators. These are used for testing certain conditions such as whether the price of an item is greater than $100.

NOTE These operators are not just for use with queries, forms, and reports. They are also for use with VBA code.

- Logical—Logical operators are used to build on assignment and comparison operators. For example, you would need a logical operator to find out which products have a price of more than $100 and are in the toys department.
- Concatenation—Concatenation operators are used to combine string values. If you want to combine the value in the Last Name field with the value in the First Name field and display it on a report, you would need to use a concatenation operator. There are two concatenation characters in Access—the ampersand (&) and the plus sign (+).

TIP When creating VBA code it is highly recommended that you use the & concatenation character as the + concatenation character sometimes leads to unexpected results.

- Identifier—Identifier operators are used in conjunction with object names to form an object's hierarchy. For example, to specify the Price field in the Inventory Table, you would enter Inventory!Price. Identifier operators are also used to separate object names from properties in code.

Arithmetic Operators Arithmetic operators include old favorites, such as addition (+) and subtraction (–). Of course, there are arithmetic operators for multiplication and division, but they aren't the ones you learned in school. And there are arithmetic operators available that you may not be familiar with. Table 34.1 lists Access' arithmetic operators.

Table 34.1 Arithmetic Operators

Operators	Description
+	Addition
–	Subtraction
*	Multiplication
/	Division
\	Integer Division
Mod	Modulus—returns the remainder of division by an integer
^	Exponentiation

NOTE All the arithmetic operators in the preceding table are probably familiar to you, except perhaps Integer Division and Modulus. They are both used for integer division. Integer Division returns the maximum number of times a number can be fully divided into another number. Modulus returns the remainder after those divisions.

For instance, using integer division, 15 divided by 6 equals 2—with a remainder of 3, which is the modulus.

Comparison and Assignment Operators The *comparison operators* are used to test conditions. If the condition is met, then the condition tests true. If the condition is not met, it is said to have tested false. Comparison operators are used extensively in queries, and are useful tools when seeking records that match specific criteria.

The *assignment operator*—the equal sign—is used to assign a value to an Access object, variable, or constant. The equal sign is also used as a comparison operator to test whether something is equal to a particular value. Table 34.2 lists the comparison and assignment operators.

Table 34.2 Comparison Assignment Operators

Operator	Description
<	Less than
<=	Less than or equal to
>	Greater than
>=	Greater than or equal to
=	Equal to
<>	Not equal to
Like	Used to find string value similar to another string value. Used with the * and ? wildcard characters. For example, `Like "John*"` could return values like John, Johnson, Johnston, and so on.
In	Used to determine whether a specified string is a member of a list of values. For example, you could enter `in("Toys", "Mens", "Sports")`.
Between	Used to determine whether a numeric value falls within a given range of values. For example, you may want to evaluate Between 10 and 100.
Is	Used with Null to determine whether a value Is Null or Is Not Null.
=	Assigns a value to an Access object, variable, or constant.

NOTE When a variable contains no valid data, it is said to have a Null value.

Logical Operators Logical operators, also referred to as *Boolean operators*, are used to combine two or more comparison expressions into a single expression. Table 34.3 lists the logical operators and provides you with their possible results. The Results column of this table assumes that you have two expressions combined using the logical operator. As an example, look at the following expression:

```
Price > 100 And Department = "Toys"
```

If this expression were used as part of a query and the price were more than $100 and the item were part of the toys department, then expression would evaluate as true and the record would be included as part of the resultset. However, if the price wasn't more than $100 or the item wasn't in the toy department, then the record would be included in the resultset.

Table 34.3 Logical Operators

Operator	Description	Example	Result
And	Logical And False And True True And False False And False	True And True False False False	True

Operator	Description	Example	Result
Or	Inclusive Or	True Or True	True
	False Or True	True	
	True Or False	True	
	False Or False	False	
Not	Logical Not	Not True	False
	Not False	True	
Xor	Exclusive Or	True Xor True	False
	True Xor False	True	
True Xor False	True		

Functions can be implemented in one of two ways. One way is by entering the function directly as a property value for a report or form or as criteria in a query. The other way is to create an expression using the Expression Builder.

Using the Expression Builder

The Expression Builder is a tool that aids you in creating expressions by providing you with a list of operators, functions, and object names that are used to literally paste together an expression. You can start the Expression Builder from most places in which you enter expressions including property sheets, criteria cells in the Query Design Grid, and the Macro window.

Accessing the Expression Builder is dependent upon what are you are doing in Access:

- If you are working in the Query Design Grid, right-click the field or criteria cell to display a shortcut menu. Select Build from this menu.
- If you are in a property sheet or the Macro window, select the property or argument box in which you want to create the expression and then click the Build button that displays next to the property or argument.

Figure 34.1 shows the Expression Builder.

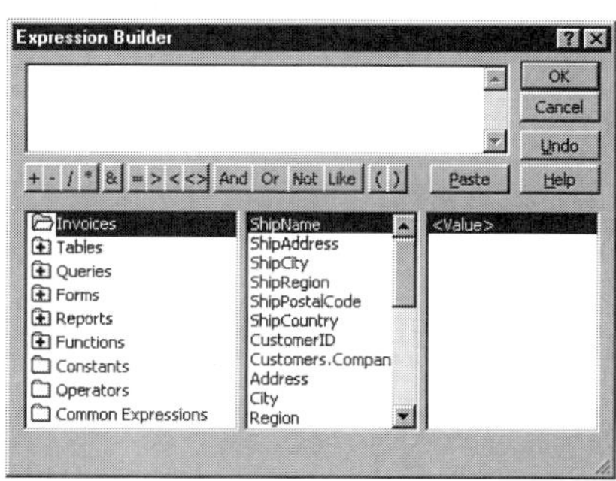

FIGURE 34.1
The Expression Builder enables you to create an expression using click and paste.

The upper section of the Expression Builder is called the expression box. This is where you actually build the expression using the elements found in the remainder of the builder. The components of your expression are created by either pasting builder elements into the expression box or by typing directly into the expression box.

Under the expression box are the operator buttons. There is a button for each of the commonly used operators. When you click an operator button, that operator displays in the expression box.

The lower section of the builder is broken into three areas. The left box displays folders that group expression elements. The following folders can be found in this box:

- Tables
- Queries
- Forms
- Functions
- Constants
- Operators
- Common Expressions

The middle box contents are dependent on the folder open in the folders box. For example, if you open the Functions folder, you'll see two subfolders listed. If you then open the Built-in Functions folder, the middle box lists the different categories of functions.

The right box is dependent on the selection made in the middle box. If you have the categories of built-in functions listed in the middle box and you select Financial, then the financial functions list appears in the right box. At this point you can select the function you want from the right box and click Paste to see the function added to the expressions box.

Continue pasting and entering any operators, objects, elements, and values you want in the expression. When your expression is complete, click OK. The expression is copied to the location where you started the Expression Builder.

Functions

Rather than creating a formula from scratch, you may want to see whether a function is available for you to use instead. A function returns a value to its name. Access and VBA support more than 100 functions. Functions can perform a variety of tasks including

- Retrieve system date and time
- Extract parts of dates and times
- Perform financial calculations, including calculating depreciation, internal rate of return, payments, and so on

- Perform string manipulation, including text-manipulations functions; can be used to format strings, remove spaces from strings, convert strings to uppercase, and so on
- Convert one data type to another
- Perform mathematical and trigonometric operations

Functions can be used in a variety of areas in Access including reports, forms, queries, and VBA code.

Arithmetic and Aggregate Functions

Access provides you with the ability to use arithmetic expressions on forms, reports, and Data Access Pages. For example, you may want to create an expression that multiplies the value in the Quantity field by the value in the Price field. Or you may need to calculate a sales tax:

```
=[Quantity]*[Price]
=[Price]*[Sales Tax]
```

Access provides a series of aggregate functions designed to summarize a set of records. These functions, referred to as ***domain aggregate functions***, enable you to display information about the sum, average, count, and so forth, on a domain or set of records. Domain aggregate functions can be used in macros, queries, or calculated controls. The domain aggregate functions share the same basic syntax:

```
Daggregate_Name(expr, domain[,criteria])
```

The required *expr* argument is an expression that identifies the field containing the numeric data you want to average. The expression is typically a field name. It can also be an expression that performs a calculation on data in that field.

The *domain* argument is also required and is a string expression that identifies the set of records, such as the domain. The *domain* can be a table name or a query name. The *criteria* argument is optional and is a string expression used to restrict the range of data used by the function. The domain aggregate functions include

- `DAvg`—The `DAvg` function calculates the average of a set of values in a domain. The `DAvg` function can be used to calculate a wide range of averages including average shipping cost, average test score, average number of years employees have been with your company, and the average age of employees. Records with Null values are not included in the calculation of the average.
- `Dcount`—The `DCount` function is used to determine the number of records that are in a domain. `DCount` can be a particularly useful function when used with the criteria argument. For example, you could use `DCount` to find out how many employees are in a particular department.
- `DMin` and `Dmax`—The `DMin` and `DMax` functions are used to find out the minimum and maximum values in a domain. Records with Null values are not included in the determination of a min or max value. Using `DMin` and `DMax` you could, for example, find out your largest and smallest sale.

- DStDev and DstDevP—DStDev and DStDevP are used to estimate the standard deviation across a set of values in a domain. DStDev is used to evaluate a population sample and DStDevP is used to evaluate a population. The classic use of DStDev is to determine the standard deviation for a set of test scores or results. If domain has fewer than two records in it or if fewer than two records satisfy the criteria argument, then these functions return a Null, letting you know that a standard deviation can't be calculated.

The following is an example of using the DAvg function. In this case the field being averaged is named Sales Total and resides in the Sales table:

```
=DAvg("[Sales Total]", "Sales")
```

This would give you the average sale for all your sales. If you wanted to get the average sale for a particular store, use the following expression:

```
=DAvg("[Sales Total]", "Sales", "[StoreID] = '1111'")
```

Date and Time Functions

Probably the easiest functions to use and understand are the date and time functions. Some of the functions in this group are used to retrieve system date and time information. Others are used to extract parts of dates and time.

***Date* and *Now* Functions** One of the most commonly used date and time functions is Date(). The Date function is used to retrieve the current system date. The date is retrieved in mm-dd-yy format.

The Date function is nice to use in conjunction with a field's Default Value property to Date(). Each time a new record is created the default value for the field is set to the current date.

If you need both the current system date and time, use the Now() function. The date and time is returned as mm/dd/yy hh:mm:ss AM/PM.

For example, if you wanted to use the Date() function as criteria for a query, you would open the query in Design view and in the Criteria cell of the appropriate field, enter Date(). This would use the current system date for the criteria.

***DateAdd* Function** If you need a calculated field in a report or form that performs a calculation on a date, you may want to use the DateAdd or DateDiff function. The DateAdd function is used to add days, weeks, months, or years to a specified date. Its syntax is as follows:

```
DateAdd(interval, number, date)
```

The *interval* argument is required and contains a string that represents the interval of time you want to add. The following string values can be used for the interval argument:

- yyyy—Sets the interval of time to year.
- q—Sets the interval of time to quarter.
- m—Sets the interval of time to month.
- y—Sets the interval of time to the day of the year.

- d—Sets the interval of time to day.
- w—Sets the interval of time to weekday.
- ww—Sets the interval of time to week.
- h—Sets the interval of time to hour.
- n—Sets the interval of time to minute. N is used instead of m because m is used for month.
- s—Sets the interval of time to second.

The next required argument is *number*. The number argument represents the number of intervals you want to add. To get future dates, use a positive number. To get past dates, use a negative number.

The final argument, *date*, is also required. This argument contains the date to which the interval is being added.

If you want to add a week from the order date to get the shipping date in a report, add a text box to the report and set the text box's `ControlSource` property to the following expression:

```
=DateAdd("ww", 1, [Order Date])
```

The `DateAdd` function makes working with date calculations very easy. It deals with moving a date to the next month, year, and so on and handles leap year date adjustments.

***DateDiff* Function** If you need to subtract two dates, then use the `DateDiff` function. `DateDiff` returns the number of time intervals between two specified dates. The time intervals that can be returned by `DateDiff` are the same ones used by `DateAdd: ww` for week, d for day, and so on. The syntax for the `DateDiff` function is

```
DateDiff(interval, date1, date2)
```

The required *interval* argument is a string expression that is the interval of time you want use to calculate the difference between *date1* and *date2*.

date1 and *date2* are also required and are the two dates to use in the calculation. For example, if you want to find out how many years an employee had been with the company, use the following expression:

```
=DateDiff("yyyy", [Start Date], Date())
```


Text Manipulation Functions

To find values in part of a field, use the `Left`, `Right`, or `Mid` functions. The syntax for these functions is

```
Left(stringexpr,n)
Right(stringexpr,n)
Mid(stringexpr,start,n)
```

The required *stringexpr* argument can be either a field name or a text expression. The *n* argument is the number of characters you want to extract from the string. The `Mid` function has an additional argument called *start*, which is the position of the first character you want to extract.

Table 34.4 illustrates the use of these functions. The first column gives an example of the function, the second column provides a sample value to manipulate, and the third column is the result returned.

Table 34.4 String Manipulation Function Examples

Example	Value Manipulated	Result Returned
=Left([ItemNum], 3	199-TOYS-1234	199
=Right([ItemNum], 4	199-TOYS-1234	1234
=Mid([ItemNum], 5,4	199-TOYS-1234	TOYS

Format()

If you want to control the appearance of a value returned by an expression, then use the `Format` function. Values can be formatted using a named format or a user-defined format. The syntax of the Format function is

```
Format(expression, [format])
```

The *expression* argument is required and can be any valid expression. The *format* argument, though optional, really should be included as part of the expression. It can be any valid named or user-defined format expression. If no value is provided for the *format* argument, a string is returned from the expression.

The following examples illustrate the use of the `Format` function. The first example illustrates using a named format with the function. The second example illustrates using a user-defined function:

```
=Format([Order Date], "Long Date")
=Format([Price], "##,##0.00")
```

Concatenation

Another thing that you may need to do with string values is manipulate them with concatenation. *Concatenation* enables you to combine string values. If you wanted to combine the value in the one field with the value in another field and display it on a report, you would need to use a concatenation. The concatenation character is the ampersand (&). The classic example of a use for concatenation is combining values in a First Name field with those in a Last Name field. Your first guess at how to do this may be as follows:

```
=[First Name] & [Last Name]
```

Although this works, it isn't going to return the result you are looking for. If the value of the First Name field in this example is John and the Last Name field value is Smith, the result of this expression is JohnSmith. Access isn't smart enough to know that you want a space between the two names. You have to tell it to add the space using the following expression:

```
=[FirstName] & " " & [LastName]
```

This expression adds a space between the two names. As you can see, you can concatenate literal text as we did in this example with the space.

IsNull()

The `IsNull` is used to determine whether a field or expression contains valid data. If the field or expression does not contain valid data, and therefore is null, then the result of the `IsNull` function is True. The syntax of the `IsNull` function is

```
IsNull(expression)
```

Only one argument exists for the `IsNull` function. The *expression* argument is required and contains a field name or other expression. Often the `IsNull` function is used in conjunction with other functions, as you'll see in the next section on the `IIf` function.

IIf()

The `IIf` function is used to evaluate an expression and return a value depending on whether the expression tested true or false. This is a useful function for use with forms and reports. It would enable you, for example, to place text on a form letting a user know whether a discount has been applied to an order or whether the order has shipped. The syntax for the `IIf` function is

```
IIf(expr, truepart, falsepart)
```

The *expr* argument is required and is the expression you want to evaluate. The required *truepart* argument is the value or expression you want returned if the *expr* is true. The *falsepart* argument is also required; it is the value or expression returned if *expr* is false.

Let's say that your company has no shipping fee when an order is more than $30; otherwise, you charge five dollars. To use the `IIf` function to place the current amount in the Shipping text box on a form, you would use the following as the value of the `ControlSource` property for the field:

```
=IIf([Total] > 30, "0.00", "5.00")
```

The `IIf` function is often used with the `IsNull` function. For example, if you want the result of an `IIf` function to determine whether an employee was still with your company, use the following expression:

```
=IIf(IsNull([Termination Date]), "Still here!", "No longer with company")
```

This expression would test to see whether there is a value in the Termination Date field. If there isn't a date in the field—in other words, it was Null—then the employee was still with the company. If there was a date in the field, then they had left the company.

CHAPTER 35

Advanced Queries

In this chapter

Making the Most of Access Queries

The vast majority of database queries used in any database application are record selection queries (also called SELECT queries), which return some value or set of values from the database depending on criteria set by the author. This makes sense; after all, a database is of little use if data isn't being retrieved from it, and a data element is typically retrieved many times after it is stored. Running a close second are data insertion queries (INSERT queries) and data update queries (UPDATE queries). Data insertion queries insert additional data into a table while data update queries change data already in a table. Many database applications consist of examples of only these three query types. This book assumes that the reader is familiar with these basic query types.

However, there are many more actions that can be performed with queries. Database queries can directly summarize data, anticipate parameters and act as if they were dynamic tables. Access includes an unusually rich set of query types, including queries that create new tables, queries that summarize data in rows and columns, and queries that merge the results of other queries and tables. Access even stores and passes queries written in dialects specific to other database engines to those engines as required.

The Access dialect of Structured Query Language (SQL) is well hidden from the user for most query types through the use of the graphical Query By Example (QBE) interface. Any query designed in QBE can be viewed in plain-text SQL by selecting SQL View from the View menu, and queries can be designed in SQL and viewed in the graphical view as well.

The ability to switch between views is invaluable when debugging queries and when migrating database objects from one database engine to another, as different databases invariably implement their own version of SQL. Fortunately, familiarity with one dialect of SQL facilitates reading other dialects, and converting one dialect to another usually means figuring out the differences in syntax between the two, because most underlying functions are the same.

Multiple Table Queries

Good database design requires that each data element be stored in as few places in the database as necessary and that data with like characteristics are grouped together. In many cases, this means that a single database may have many tables, some with as few as two fields. The more tables in a database, the more likely it is that a query will need to extract data from more than one of those tables at a time.

To maintain some semblance of order in the database, we usually design tables so that each table includes a field or fields that uniquely identify each record in the table. This field (or combination of fields, considered together—a *composite key*) is called a *primary key field* (or just *key*), and every different value of the key identifies a different record in each table. Keys can be explicit (identified as keys by the developer to the database), or implicit (doing the job without the title), but every table should have a key field.

When we use more than one table in a query, it's important that there be some sort of relationship between them, so Access knows how a record in one of the tables relates to a record in another. Access can do this automatically whether you define your tables with keys having the same name and data type, or whether you can identify these relationships explicitly by using the Relationships Window.

▶ **See** "Understanding Referential Integrity," **p. 1004**

When you open the QBE editor, you're given the opportunity to select as many tables and queries as you need; as you select them, they appear above the QBE grid (in the Query Design window) in the order selected. Access draws lines between the tables to represent the relationships between them that it can infer, either from previously defined relationships, or by comparing the names and data types (fields in different tables with the same names and compatible data types are assumed to be related).

Working with Table Joins in the Query Design Window

Establishing a relationship between tables in the Query Design window causes them to act as one data source for the duration of the query. In almost all cases, all tables in any query should be related in some way, either automatically by Access or manually by you.

The act of relating tables is also called *joining* them, and Access defaults to creating *inner joins*. *Inner joins* include only the records whose key value appears in both tables joined. For example, consider the Order Details and Products tables in the Northwind database. A unique key—a Product ID—links them, as shown in Figure 35.1. If a product in the Products field has not been ordered by anyone (and therefore does not appear in the Order Details table), it is not shown in a query with both tables joined in this way.

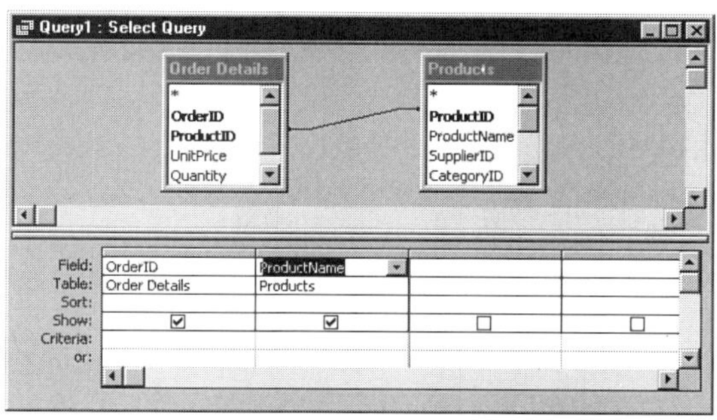

FIGURE 35.1
Each of these tables has an identifying key value–in this case, the Product ID.

There are probably records in the Products table that are not represented by records in Order Details; a query based on an inner join between these tables returns only the records that appear in both tables.

Access denotes an inner join in a query by a line connecting the tables by their key values, with small dots on each end. After the QBE grid is open and both tables are visible in the Query Design window, you can drag the key field(s) from one table onto the other, thus informing

Access that you want to create an inner join between the two tables on they key field(s) selected. A simple query using the Products and Order Details tables discussed earlier might appear as in Figure 35.2.

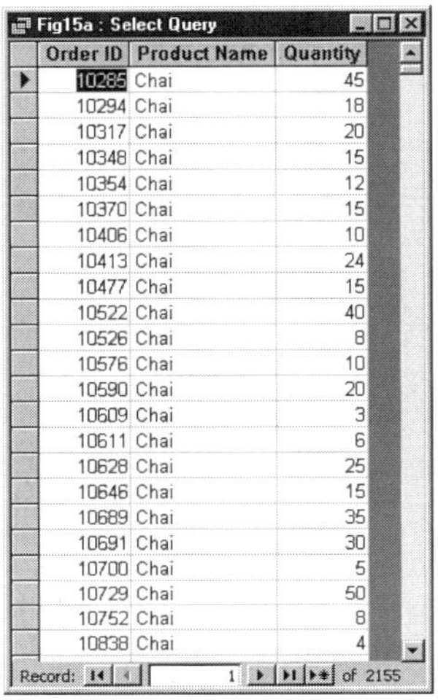

FIGURE 35.2
These two tables are joined and act as one data source.

Fig15a : Select Query

Order ID	Product Name	Quantity
10285	Chai	45
10294	Chai	18
10317	Chai	20
10348	Chai	15
10354	Chai	12
10370	Chai	15
10406	Chai	10
10413	Chai	24
10477	Chai	15
10522	Chai	40
10526	Chai	8
10576	Chai	10
10590	Chai	20
10609	Chai	3
10611	Chai	6
10628	Chai	25
10646	Chai	15
10689	Chai	35
10691	Chai	30
10700	Chai	5
10729	Chai	50
10752	Chai	8
10838	Chai	4

Record: 1 of 2155

To remove a join after it has been established, right-click the line between the two tables representing the join and select Delete from the menu that appears.

NOTE Because a relationship has already been established between these two tables in the Relationships Window (click Tools, Relationships), Access shows the relationship automatically in the Query Designer. It's still an inner join.

You can add more tables or queries to the Query Designer at any time by clicking the Show Tables button on the toolbar. You can even add the same table or query more than once, but the times when that would be necessary are very rare (and are probably limited to many-to-many relationships). For an example of a really big multitable query, see Northwind's Invoices query. After you understand it in the Query Designer window, switch to SQL View (View, SQL View) and see for yourself what a wonderful tool the Query Designer window really is.

Tables included in a query, but not part of any relationship, almost always produce undesirable results. If two tables in a single query are not related, Access assumes that all records in both tables should be included, and that every record in one table should match every record in the other. This results in the number of records returned equaling the product of the number of records in each of the tables in the query. This product is called a *Cartesian product* and the data returned is probably incorrect, matching data from records which have no logical relationship with one another.

Altering Table Join Options for Desired Results

Not all joins are inner joins. Most relational databases, including Access, also allow for *outer joins*, which return all the records from one of the constituent tables (regardless of whether there's a matching record in the other table) and only the records that match the key value in the other. In Access, outer joins are referred to as *left outer joins* or *right outer joins* depending on the position of the tables in the Query Design window.

To create an outer join, first create an inner join by dragging the key field(s) from one table to the other. Access draws a line between the tables, indicating that an inner join has been established. Then double-click the join line and the Join Properties dialog in Figure 35.3 appears.

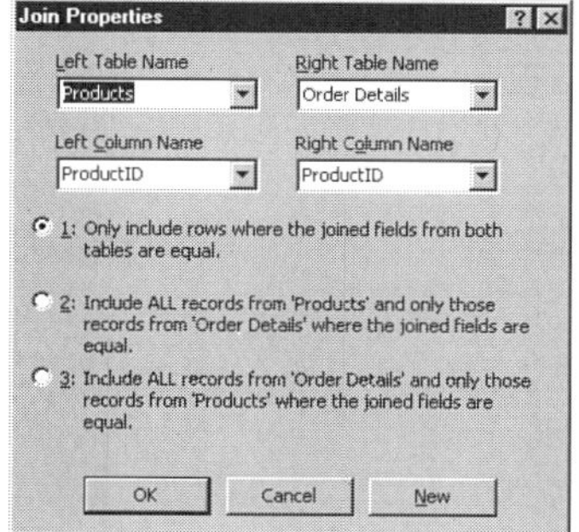

FIGURE 35.3
The Join Properties dialog box allows you to specify the type of join between the two tables noted.

Select the appropriate option and click OK to return to the QBE grid. Option 1 represents an inner join (the default), option 2 is a left outer join, and option 3 is a right outer join. The boxes containing the names of the tables and fields aren't particularly useful; it's easier to double-click the line in the Query Design window to ensure you chose the correct relationship to modify. You'll notice that the line connecting the tables has changed; the arrow at one end denotes the table that supplies only matching records, and points left or right depending on the position of the tables in the Query Design window.

This is not a technique you'll use every day. However, this technique is especially useful for troubleshooting the data in tables. It ensures that all data in one table is also represented in another. The Find Duplicates and Find Unmatched wizards (from the Query View of the Database Window, select New from the toolbar) make good use of outer joins.

In queries where more than two tables are involved, outer joins can sometimes become *ambiguous*. When the query is executed, Access returns an error (as shown in Figure 35.4) because the results of the query depend on which outer join is executed first, and the database engine can't decide which. This is usually a sign of poor query design; you can minimize the chance of creating ambiguous queries by keeping all outer-join arrows going in the same direction, whether left-to-right or right-to-left; see Figure 35.5 for an example of the right way to design this query.

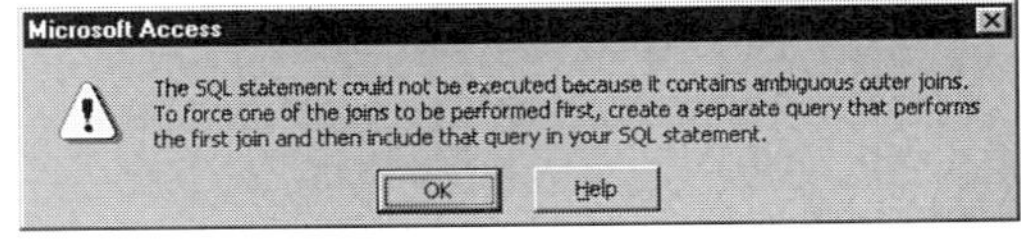

FIGURE 35.4
The error occurs because different results would come from executing the Orders-Order Details outer join before executing the Order Details-Products outer join, but neither order is necessarily correct.

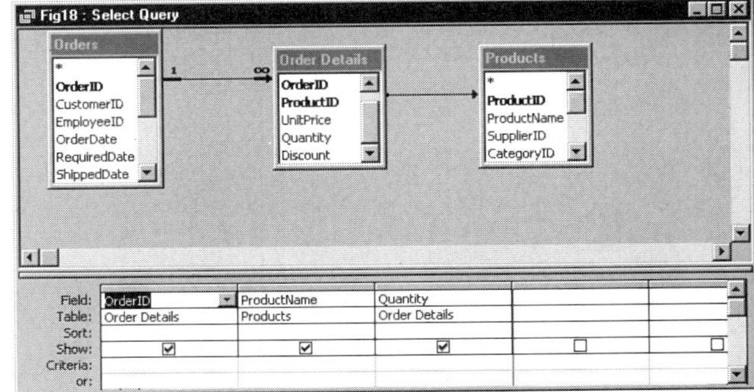

FIGURE 35.5
To avoid ambiguous errors, rearrange the tables so that the join lines all point in the same direction.

The example shown previously in Figure 35.5 ensures that all the people listed in the Orders table, and no others, are included in the result set. It would be equally correct (as far as Access is concerned) to create a left outer join from Orders to Products, but the result set would be different. You can create multiple joins on the same table.

Using Queries to Change Records

The familiar SELECT query is useful for viewing data in a database table, but you can't modify tabular data using a select query. SQL (and Access, by extension) provides several SQL constructs that change the data in a data source; queries that use these constructs are called ACTION queries. By selecting the appropriate action query type in Access' design environment, you can delete, change, or extract sets of records in Access tables.

The Access query designer interface provides a simple method for choosing the right query type for the operation at hand. After the QBE grid is opened and a data source is selected, a query of any type can be configured by selecting the appropriate type from the Query menu selection shown in Figure 35.6. Some of the types displayed in this list require additional input, and all modify the display of the query designer in some fashion specific to the type selected.

NOTE Open the QBE grid either by selecting Create Query in Design View from the database window or by selecting New, Design View from the database window toolbar.

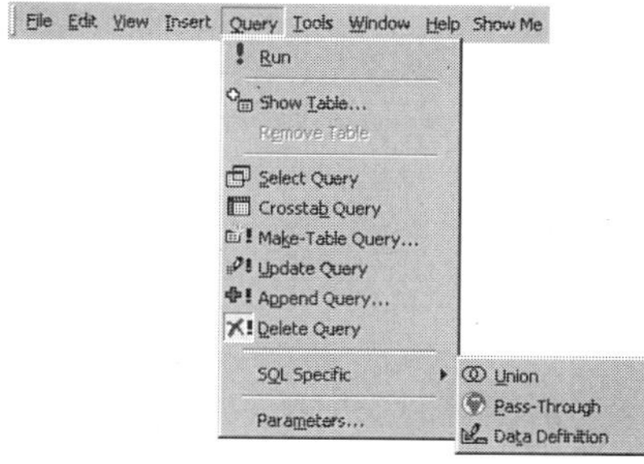

FIGURE 35.6
The various query types available in Access. The SQL-Specific query types don't use the GUI development environment at all.

All queries except SELECT queries make irreparable changes to the database. There's no undo command for database changes, and it's always a very good idea to back up your work periodically to avoid disasters. You can delete forever every record in any table with as few as four mouse clicks after the table is selected in the QBE (see Figure 35.7).

You can back up your Access data in several ways. Two fast and easy ways to prevent a disaster when working with data in local tables:

- Saving to a different file (File, Save As)
- Copying a critical table to a backup table (Edit, Copy, Edit, Paste)

Fortunately, you can usually preview the results of action queries before committing them to the database by executing the query in Datasheet View (by selecting View, then Datasheet View from the menu). This gives you, in effect, a preview of the records that are affected by the query you're designing.

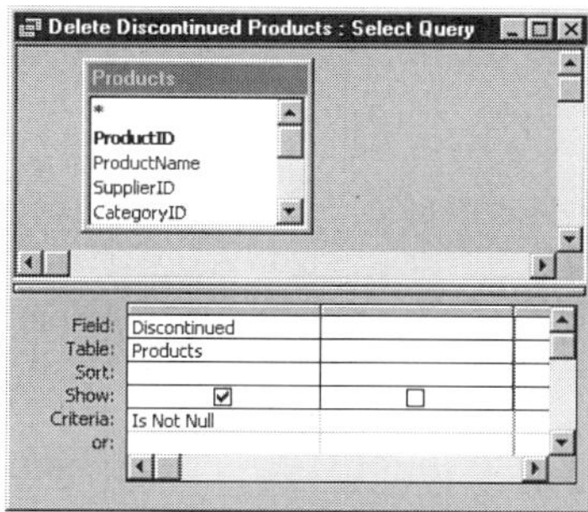

FIGURE 35.7
A DELETE query in Datasheet View, before executing it. All of the records that meet this criterion (the value in the "Discontinued" field is not null) will be deleted when this query is run, and there's no getting them back.

For database operations where the ability to undo actions is critical (often the case in financial databases), the use of database transactions is highly recommended. Queries executed in a transaction are logged and can be undone, or rolled back. Unfortunately, Access doesn't support transactions from the GUI; you have to write Visual Basic for Applications (see Chapters 5 and 6 for an introduction to VBA) code to create the transactions, execute the queries, and commit the completed transactions to the database. For more information, see transactions in Access Help.

Creating a Table with a Query

Most of the time, you can use a SELECT query as if it were a table itself, referencing it in other queries and using it as the basis for reports and forms. This has the effect of making a query act like a table without actually creating a new table. For example, consider the following query, which selects all Italian customers of the Northwind Co. who ordered products in January, 1998:

```
SELECT CompanyName, Country, OrderDate FROM Invoices
WHERE Country="Italy"
AND OrderDate Between #1/1/98# And #1/30/98#
```

NOTE This query, if created in the QBE grid and viewed in SQL View, would appear as follows:

```
    SELECT DISTINCT Invoices.Customers.CompanyName, Invoices.Country,
➥Invoices.OrderDate FROM Invoices
WHERE (((Invoices.Country)="Italy") AND ((Invoices.OrderDate) Between #1/1/98#
➥And #1/30/98#));
```

Access is entirely too conservative in its use of parentheses and table names, adding unnecessarily to the complexity of QBE-designed queries.

This query is based on another query, Invoices, which combines information from six tables (many of which are unnecessary to view the information being extracted). You don't need to re-create the "Invoices" query to take advantage of the results it returns; because SELECT queries typically return rows and columns of tabular data (called a "dynaset"), you can base queries on the results of other queries. A SELECT query, therefore, can act like a table when it's referenced by another query.

This query is largely self-documenting, because the names of the tables and fields they reference are sufficiently descriptive that almost anyone reading it can tell what it's supposed to do.

The preceding query displays the data selected, but doesn't save it anywhere. There are times when you'll want to create a whole new table based on query results. These typically include when debugging code, when preparing to export data from Access to another format, and when saving intermediate results of very long queries for display. Access includes a MAKE-TABLE query type, which combines the features of a SELECT query, the SQL commands to create a new table, and an INSERT query to save the results in the new table.

To create a new table from query results using the make-table type of query, follow these steps:

1. Select the Queries menu item from the database objects pane of the Database Window. From this, the Query view of the database window, select Create Query in Design View. Choose a data source and click Close.
2. Select the fields to be included and enter any criteria necessary in the appropriate boxes in the QBE grid as whether creating a SELECT query. You can even run the query (Query, Run) to see the results without affecting the data in the database or creating any new tables.

3. From the menu select Query, Make-Table Query (which may not be immediately visible in your personalized menu; hold the pointer in the menu drop-down list for a few seconds to make it appear). The dialog box in Figure 35.8 appears.

FIGURE 35.8
The Make Table dialog box. Selecting a table name from the drop-down list overwrites the table chosen.

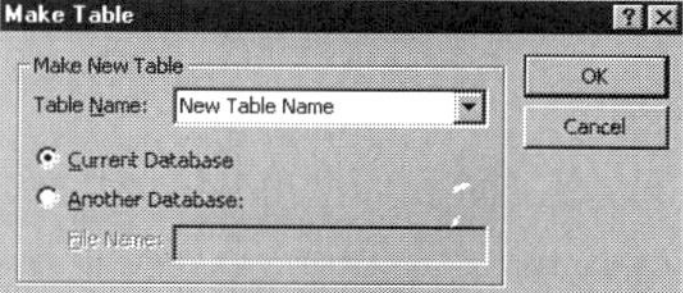

4. Enter a name for the new table. If you want the table created in another Access database, enter its filename in the box. Note that the remote database must already exist. Click OK to continue.
5. Save your new query, if desired, by closing it and choosing to save the design. If this is a one-time operation, you can simply execute the query by choosing Query, Run.

NOTE You can't change the name of the new table dynamically when using the GUI environment. However, you can create a Make-Table query in code and have the name change as required. The syntax of a Make-Table query is

```
SELECT <field1>[,field2...] INTO <tablename> FROM <source> [WHERE <where clause>]
```

The value of the tablename variable (the predicate for the INTO clause) can be any legal string value.

Note that using a MAKE-TABLE query deletes any records that may be in the table named. If you want to add new records to any existing records, use an Append query.

Deleting Records with a Query

An Access DELETE query is really a SELECT query, followed by the deletion of the selected records. Designing one is as easy as defining the records to be deleted (using a SELECT query) and then letting Access delete them.

CAUTION

There is no way to undo a DELETE query. Save a copy of your database or the specific tables you're working with before beginning the development of DELETE queries.

Use the Datasheet View of the QBE grid liberally during the design of DELETE queries to see what you'll be deleting without actually doing it. At any point in query design, and especially just before executing the query, select View, Datasheet View and ensure that the records displayed are the ones you want deleted.

To delete records from the database using a DELETE query, use these steps:

1. From the Query view of the database window, select Create query in Design View. Choose a data source and click Close.
2. Select criteria necessary to identify the records to be deleted in the appropriate boxes in the QBE grid as if creating a SELECT query. There's no need to select any fields other than those necessary to identify deletion criteria; all of the records selected by the query will be deleted regardless of what fields you've added to the QBE grid.
3. From the menu select Query, Delete Query. The QBE grid changes slightly, replacing the Sort and Show rows with a Delete row. Every cell in the Delete row contains the word Where, indicating that records are deleted where each field equals the criteria listed for it.
4. Preview the records to be deleted by choosing View, Datasheet View. To return to the QBE Grid if desired, select View, Design View.
5. Save your new query, if desired, by clicking the Save icon on the toolbar. If this is a one-time operation, you can simply execute the query by choosing Query, Run. You are then prompted to confirm the deletion, and then the records selected will be deleted.

To stop any query in progress, press Ctrl+Break.

To delete all records from a table, you can create a DELETE query with no fields selected. Because no criteria are specified, all records match and all records are deleted.

To turn off the dialog boxes asking you to confirm your deletions, select Tools, Options, Edit/Find, and toggle Confirm Action Queries off.

Updating Records with a Query

A critical skill in query design is the capability to write queries that modify data already in a database table. This process starts with selecting the records to be modified, making changes as required, and then rewriting the records with the new data included. Note that this is different from appending new data; the UPDATE query requires that the data already be in the database.

Update operations can modify records in several ways:

- By replacing all values in a field with another constant value. For example, a table containing information about customers may require that certain customers' telephone area codes be changed from one value to another.
- By replacing all values in a field with a variable value. For example, a table containing information about employees might need to be changed to reflect a percentage increase in everyone's salary to reflect a cost-of-living increase. The value updated may be different for every record, but a single formula describes the change (the specified percentage) required.
- By replacing all values in a field with a value based on another query. For example, a financial database might require that individual customer records be updated with values

retrieved from another table depending on the performance of their investments for a certain period.

When updating records, it's important to realize that any changes made are permanent; however, you can use the Datasheet View to preview the changes before they're written to the database. Consider backing up your data before starting work on any query that will modify or delete values.

To update records in the database by using an UPDATE query, follow these steps:

1. From the Query view of the database window, select Create Query in Design View. Choose a data source and click Close.
2. Select criteria necessary to identify the records to be updated in the appropriate boxes in the QBE grid as if creating a SELECT query. There's no need to select any fields other than those required to identify the records to be changed or the fields to be changed.
3. From the menu select Query, Update Query. The QBE grid changes slightly, replacing the Sort and Show rows with an Update To row.
4. In the Update To row of each column representing fields to be modified, enter the new value. For example, if the title of all Sales Representatives in the Employees table of the Northwind Database is to be changed to Account Executive, you would enter Account Executive in the Update To row and Sales Representative in the Criteria row of the Title column.
5. Preview the records to be deleted by choosing View, Datasheet View. To return to the QBE Grid, if desired, select View, Design View.
6. Save your new query, if desired, by selecting File, Save. If this is a one-time operation, simply execute the query by choosing Query, Run.

To delete the contents of a particular field in the selected records, enter `Null` in the Update To row. Altering all the fields that you use to define the criteria for the update is not necessary; that is, you don't necessarily need to have values in both the Criteria and Update To rows of any column.

You can update records based on formulas as well as literals. For example, you can give everybody a 5% raise by using a formula as shown in Figure 35.9.

FIGURE 35.9
The value updated in every row is different, but all are based on the same formula.

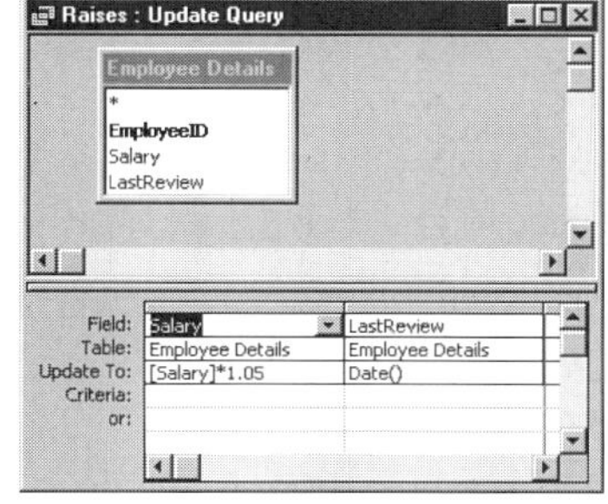

You can also use aggregate functions and even the results of other queries to calculate the new value.

Appending Records with a Query

The APPEND query copies records from one table to another based on the criteria entered. As many records are created as the criteria specified require; these are typically all or some of the records from another table. APPEND queries (from the QBE grid) aren't very useful for creating new records out of thin air, because there's no way to create more than one record unless the record source is another table or query.

To add records to a table by using an APPEND query, follow these steps:

1. From the Query view of the database window, select Create Query in Design View. Choose a data source (which provides the records to be appended) and click Close.
2. Select criteria necessary to identify the records to be extracted in the appropriate boxes in the QBE grid as if creating a SELECT query. Select all the fields that are to be copied to the destination table by double-clicking their names in the source table.
3. From the menu, select Query, Append Query. The QBE grid changes slightly, replacing the Sort and Show rows with an Append To row. A dialog box appears, asking the name of the table to receive the new records. Type it and click OK.
4. In the Append To row of each column representing fields to be modified, enter the name of the field in the destination table to receive the data. Access fills in the name automatically if a field in the destination table has the same name and data type as a field in the source table.
5. Preview the records to be appended by choosing View, Datasheet View. To return to the QBE Grid, if desired, select View, Design View.
6. Save your new query, if desired, by closing it and choosing to save the design. If this is a one-time operation, you can simply execute the query (Query, Run).

Using Functions and Expressions in Queries

You can use Access functions and expressions in queries to specify criteria or to change table values wherever needed. With expressions, you can even define criteria based on combinations or subsets of fields, and you can include any expression from simple addition to a detailed subquery in the QBE grid where appropriate. This capability permits the Access developer to describe relatively complex operations in the context of the simple QBE grid.

Because functions are really stored expressions, the use of the term expression in this chapter can be considered to include all Access built-in functions.

Expressions are appropriate in either the Field or Criteria rows of the QBE grid for all types of queries. In UPDATE queries, expressions can be used in the Update To row as well. For a list of all Access functions, see Function Reference in Access Help. To see some real-world uses of functions and expressions, take a look at Chapter 34.

▶ **See** "Functions and Expressions," **p. 1005**

For simple aggregate functions (the SQL aggregate functions), the Totals row of the QBE grid can save some time in development. Normally hidden, it can be viewed by clicking the Totals button on the Design toolbar when the QBE grid is open or by selecting View, Totals. The Totals line contains a drop-down palette of various functions that can be applied to the field for that column. For example, to quickly determine the average price of an item in Northwind's inventory, you can create a Select query on the Products table, selecting only the UnitPrice field and choosing Avg on the Totals row, as shown in Figure 35.10. Note that the Category Name appears even though the Category ID was selected, because Category ID is defined as a Lookup field in the Products table.

FIGURE 35.10
You could add criteria to limit the number of products considered.

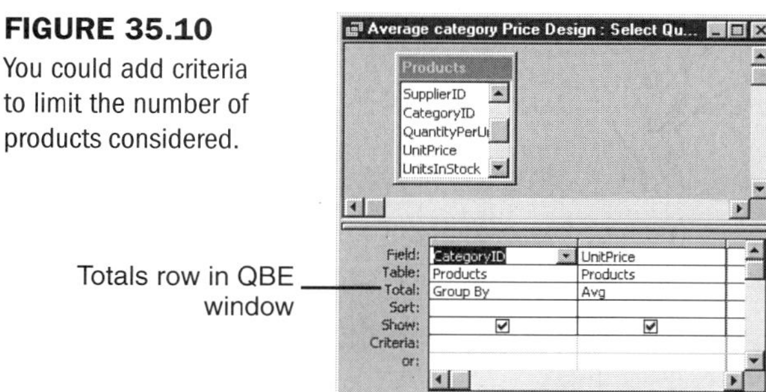

The functions available in the Totals Row are shown in Table 35.1.

Table 35.1 Aggregate Functions Available on the Totals Row

Name	Description
`GroupBy`	Denotes a field to group by, creating a sort break
`Sum`	Result of adding all of the values in this field
`Avg`	Average of the values in this field
`Min`	Smallest of the values in this field
`Max`	Greatest of the values in this field
`Count`	The count of the number of records returned where the value isn't NULL.
`StDev`	Standard Deviation of values in this field
`Var`	Variation of values in this field
`First`	First (oldest) stored value in this field
`Last`	Last (newest) stored value in this field
`Expression`	Denotes that the field name contains an expression, but no other aggregate is to be performed on that field

In addition to the aggregate functions listed previously, you may also use `Where` in the totals line. `Where` is used to determine which records are included in the query, and is not displayed in the results.

NOTE Note that using an aggregate function on any field that contains Null values will result in the aggregate ignoring the Null. However, when Null is used in an expression, the value of the expression becomes Null. For example, the sum of three fields containing the values 1, 2, and Null will return Null. This caveat applies to all arithmetic functions in Access.

If this isn't desirable (and it almost never is), you can use the `Nz()` function to change nulls to zeros for the duration of the calculation. For example, instead of averaging a column called "Cost" (if it might contain nulls), enter "Calc_Cost: Nz(Cost)" in the first row of the QBE grid and average that.

The Expression Builder It is often convenient to use the Expression Builder (see Figure 35.11) to construct complex expressions; this ensures that the expression is syntactically correct and minimizes debugging time. The Builder is available from the toolbar whenever the QBE grid is open; clicking the toolbar icon (or pressing Ctrl+F2) opens the Builder for editing. Whether the cursor is in a Field, Criteria, or Update To row of the QBE grid, the Expression Builder contains any value already in that cell and updates to it when closed.

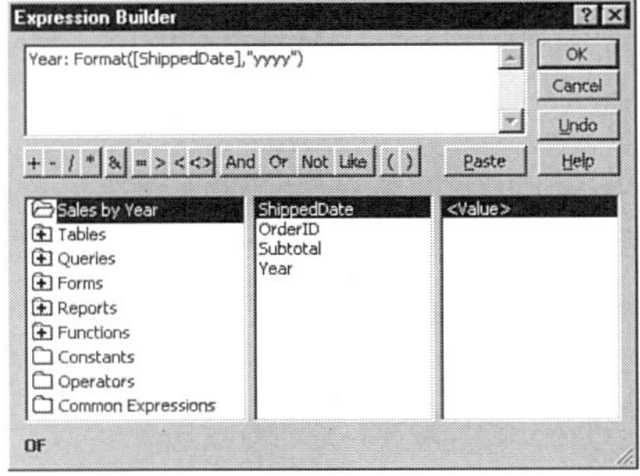

FIGURE 35.11
The Expression Builder serves as a handy function and database object reference, listing all valid expression elements in one place.

Using Expressions in Criteria Using expressions to qualify data for query criteria is often helpful. For example, a Select query to extract all instances of a specific area code from the Northwind Customers table, where area codes and phone numbers are stored in one string, would use a *substring expression* (`Mid` works well in this case) to qualify the records selected.

The `Mid(string,n,m)` function returns the characters of a string from character number `n` (starting with 1) for `m` characters. In this example, the Phone field is in the string. We're starting from the second character to account for the parenthesis in front of the area code, and locating all records where the next three characters (the second, third, and fourth) are 503 (See Figur 35.12).

Using Expressions in Field Names In an APPEND or UPDATE query, you can use an expression in the name of the field to assign calculated values to that field. You can take the result of two different fields, or one field and a constant. In a SELECT query, you can perform calculations on a field to display the results without saving them anywhere.

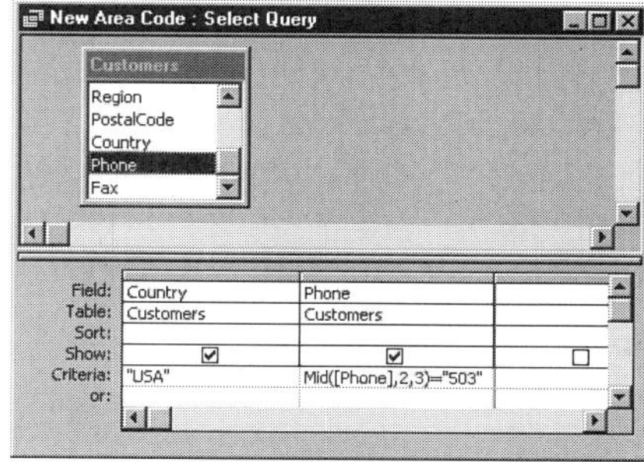

FIGURE 35.12
The Country criterion is necessary in this example because countries other than the USA format their phone numbers differently.

You can assign a name to the result of your calculation by entering the name you want for the expression and a colon before the expression in the QBE grid. For instance, if you want to get the extended price for an invoice line item, and have the field named ExtendedPrice, you could use the following in one of the QBE grid columns:

```
ExtendedPrice:UnitPrice*Units
```

There's an excellent example of this technique in the Order Details Extended SELECT query in the sample Northwind database, shown in Figure 35.13. The ExtendedPrice field is calculated on-the-fly for each record the query returns, multiplying the unit price by the quantity ordered and subtracting the discount amount. There's no need to store this value in the database literally, because it can always be calculated when needed. The expression used,

```
ExtendedPrice: CCur([Order Details].[UnitPrice]*[Quantity]*(1-[Discount])/
➥100)*100
```

includes the `CCur()` function to convert the result to the data type Currency and several simple arithmetic operations.

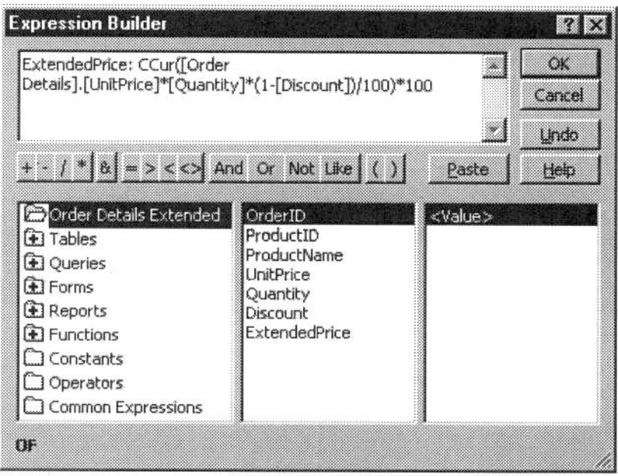

FIGURE 35.13
You can enter expressions in the field name row of the QBE grid (shown here in the Expression Builder for clarity) to calculate data for display.

NOTE In Figure 35.13, the [UnitPrice] field needs to be qualified with its table name because that field appears in both tables in the query; this duplication often indicates inefficient database design, but it may be intentional in this case for clarity.

The QBE grid doesn't provide a lot of space for entering functions, and you may not want to use the Expression Builder if you know the syntax of the command you want to enter. You can pop up a larger working box by pressing Shift+F2 ("Zoom") while your cursor is in the window you want to edit.

Queries That Prompt for Information Before Executing

When developing forms and reports, it's often useful to use as a record source a query that changes based on the data the current user is interested in. For example, a query against a Customer table that shows the details of all the customers in the database is helpful, but you may be interested in only one specific customer. If the query criteria include some identifying information about that one customer, you'll have to manually modify the query every time you want to see another customer.

The solution to this problem is to use a PARAMETER query, which prompts the user for input when it is run. This allows the developer to create queries that enable their criteria to be modified when running, instead of requiring that the criteria be known during development.

Consider the Sales By Category query in the Northwind database. When run, this query lists all product categories and totals the sales of each item in that category, shown in Figure 35.14. But suppose you're only interested in one category, and you don't know at design time which category this is. The solution is to add a parameter to the criteria for the Category Name.

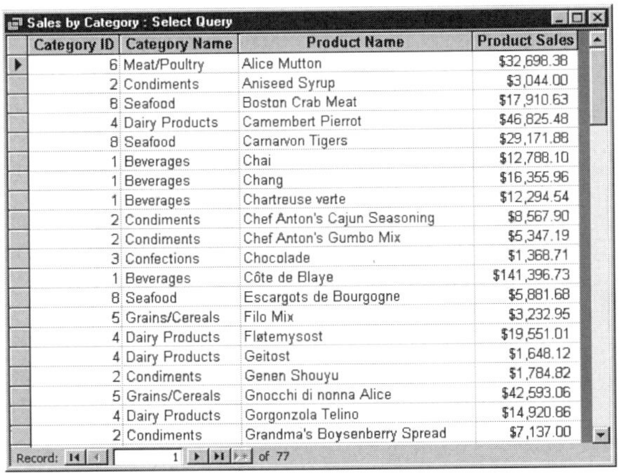

FIGURE 35.14
This query has no criteria, so it lists all records in the database in the format described. You can prompt the user for criteria at runtime by including a prompt in the criteria row, enclosed by square brackets.

Sales by Category : Select Query

Category ID	Category Name	Product Name	Product Sales
6	Meat/Poultry	Alice Mutton	$32,698.38
2	Condiments	Aniseed Syrup	$3,044.00
8	Seafood	Boston Crab Meat	$17,910.63
4	Dairy Products	Camembert Pierrot	$46,825.48
8	Seafood	Carnarvon Tigers	$29,171.88
1	Beverages	Chai	$12,788.10
1	Beverages	Chang	$16,355.96
1	Beverages	Chartreuse verte	$12,294.54
2	Condiments	Chef Anton's Cajun Seasoning	$8,567.90
2	Condiments	Chef Anton's Gumbo Mix	$5,347.19
3	Confections	Chocolade	$1,368.71
1	Beverages	Côte de Blaye	$141,396.73
8	Seafood	Escargots de Bourgogne	$5,881.68
5	Grains/Cereals	Filo Mix	$3,232.95
4	Dairy Products	Fløtemysost	$19,551.01
4	Dairy Products	Geitost	$1,648.12
2	Condiments	Genen Shouyu	$1,784.82
5	Grains/Cereals	Gnocchi di nonna Alice	$42,593.06
4	Dairy Products	Gorgonzola Telino	$14,920.86
2	Condiments	Grandma's Boysenberry Spread	$7,137.00

Record: 1 of 77

Parameters for queries are entered by enclosing a prompt for the user in square brackets in the criteria row for the field to be evaluated. When the query is run, the prompt entered in the query design appears in a dialog box and waits for user input. After that input is received, the value you enter is substituted into the query and the query executes.

In the Sales by Category example, you can enter a simple prompt in the criteria row for the Category Name field:

```
[Enter Category Name]
```

When the query is executed, Access prompts the user for the value of the parameter [Enter Category Name], and returns the data for the category entered. If the value entered isn't found in the field designated, no rows are returned; for this reason, it's usually better to develop a form that enables users to choose a valid category from a combo box, as described in Chapter 36, "Advanced Forms."

NOTE What's actually happening here is that Access looks for a variable called Enter Category Name at runtime, doesn't find one, and prompts the user for a value. The same thing happens if you misspell or type the incorrect field name in a criterion, such as [Products].[Categories]—because there's no such field, Access prompts for user intervention.

There are a few special cases when you need to tell Access the data type of the parameters you intend to use in your query:

- When the data type is not known by Access (as in the case of a SQL PASS-THROUGH query).
- When the parameter type affects the display of the dialog box (a Yes/No parameter).
- When the parameter type affects the display of the results (a parameter to a CROSSTAB query).

For these cases, list the parameters to be entered in the Parameters window, displayed by selecting Query, Parameters. Make sure you enter the parameter name(s) exactly as listed in the QBE grid. If you use the same parameter name in more than one place in a query (or in more than one query underlying a form or report), Access will prompt only once for it.

You can get creative with parameters, using them as you would any expression in any query. For example, you could use parameters in the context of the Like function:

```
Like [Enter beginning of category name] & "*"
```

where entering just the letter C matches both Condiments and Confections.

NOTE Access prompts only once for a parameter although it may appear within several subqueries. Access uses the same value for all of the parameters as was entered by the user the one time the prompt appears. Be careful when naming parameters so that the parameter names don't duplicate one another in queries that might be called from one another.

Summarizing Data with Crosstab Queries

Many Access users are familiar with the way data is displayed in Excel worksheets—with column headers representing field names and rows each representing a data record. Access takes this concept one step further by including the CROSSTAB query, which summarizes the tabular data stored in the database (as opposed to simply listing the data as it appears in the table). Crosstabs provide a convenient way to make data values appear as column headers, adding or averaging some other field based on the value of the field selected as the column header. They are particularly useful for analyzing financial data and evaluating numeric values over time. Readers familiar with Excel PivotTables find Crosstab queries very familiar.

▶ **See** "Unlocking the Power of PivotTables and PivotCharts," **p. 797**

As an example, consider the Orders and Order Details tables in the Northwind database. A simple Select query that takes advantage of the relationship between the two tables can produce a matrix listing all sales, the salesperson, and the date of the sale as shown in Figure 35.15. Access has provided a linkage, or join, between these two tables as a result of their relationship on the OrderID field. You don't have to explicitly create this relationship.

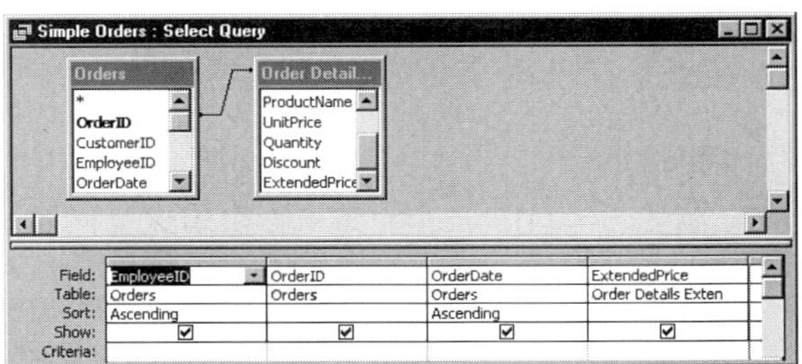

FIGURE 35.15
This listing of all product orders in the database doesn't summarize them in any useful way.

By adding a Totals row (View, Totals), summarizing the ExtendedPrice amounts, removing the individual OrderIDs, and extracting the year and month from the Order date (using the `Year()` and `Month()` functions), you can sum all orders for each employee by month, as shown in Figure 35.16.

This is the type of data often used for financial reporting, but the format is unusual. Most accountants would list the months across the top and the employee names in a column on the left and a summary of the activities at the intersection of each employee and each month. There's no easy way to do that using a single Select query, but it's the type of presentation that a Crosstab query handles easily.

Crosstab queries have three elements not found in other query types: Row Headers, Column Headers, and Values. The Row Header field denotes the values to appear in a column on the left side of the results grid, and the Column Header field(s) appear at the top. The Values field is summarized in the grid in spreadsheet fashion.

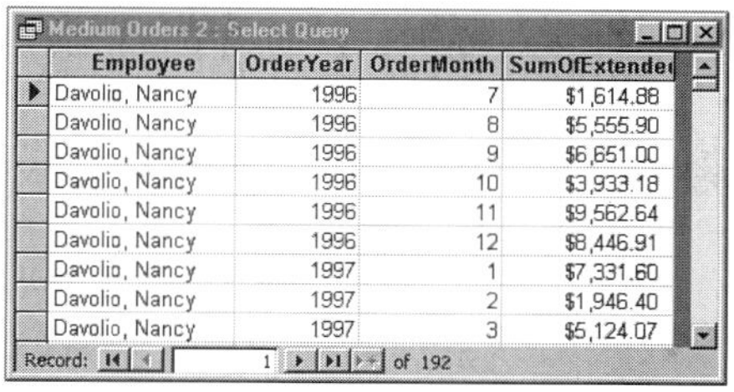

FIGURE 35.16
Now the sales are summarized by employee and month, but the presentation is lacking. It would be nice to see the months across the top.

Medium Orders 2 : Select Query

Employee	OrderYear	OrderMonth	SumOfExtende
Davolio, Nancy	1996	7	$1,614.88
Davolio, Nancy	1996	8	$5,555.90
Davolio, Nancy	1996	9	$6,651.00
Davolio, Nancy	1996	10	$3,933.18
Davolio, Nancy	1996	11	$9,562.64
Davolio, Nancy	1996	12	$8,446.91
Davolio, Nancy	1997	1	$7,331.60
Davolio, Nancy	1997	2	$1,946.40
Davolio, Nancy	1997	3	$5,124.07

Record: 1 of 192

To change a SELECT query to a CROSSTAB query, choose Query, Crosstab Query. A new row labeled Crosstab appears in the QBE grid, and you can select the fields to act as the Row and Column Headings and the Value. Making this simple change to the query in Figure 35.16 gives the much more readable results of Figure 35.17.

NOTE Unfortunately, there's a problem with this simple example. A crosstab query can have only one data value designated as the column heading, which means that either the OrderMonth or OrderYear column (from Figure 35.16) can be retained in the crosstab. Retaining only the year loses the granularity of the monthly information, but retaining only the month combines data from different years into the OrderMonth sums. One way around this problem would be to use a pretty complicated calculated value for the column headers; it would probably take advantage of the `DatePart()` and `CStr()` functions.

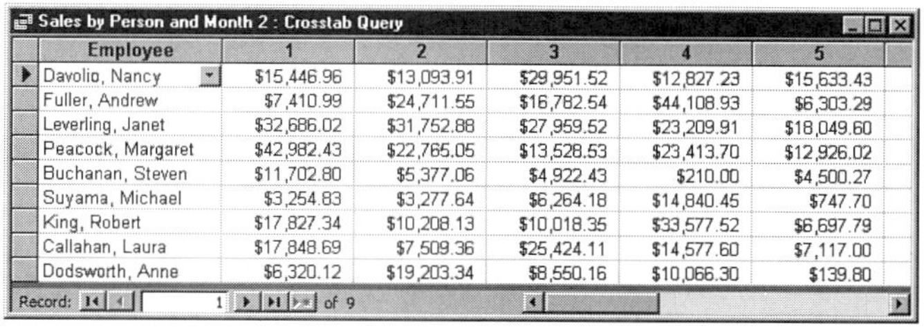

FIGURE 35.17
Orders summarized by month for each employee. Column numbers represent the months—that is, 1 = January.

Sales by Person and Month 2 : Crosstab Query

Employee	1	2	3	4	5
Davolio, Nancy	$15,446.96	$13,093.91	$29,951.52	$12,827.23	$15,633.43
Fuller, Andrew	$7,410.99	$24,711.55	$16,782.54	$44,108.93	$6,303.29
Leverling, Janet	$32,686.02	$31,752.88	$27,959.52	$23,209.91	$18,049.60
Peacock, Margaret	$42,982.43	$22,765.05	$13,528.53	$23,413.70	$12,926.02
Buchanan, Steven	$11,702.80	$5,377.06	$4,922.43	$210.00	$4,500.27
Suyama, Michael	$3,254.83	$3,277.64	$6,264.18	$14,840.45	$747.70
King, Robert	$17,827.34	$10,208.13	$10,018.35	$33,577.52	$6,697.79
Callahan, Laura	$17,848.69	$7,509.36	$25,424.11	$14,577.60	$7,117.00
Dodsworth, Anne	$6,320.12	$19,203.34	$8,550.16	$10,066.30	$139.80

Record: 1 of 9

The CROSSTAB query presents this summary in a very readable, spreadsheet-like fashion. In fact, this would be a very useful table to export to Excel by selecting File, Export; Excel would have no trouble reading it for the benefit of the office accountant. It's worth noting that you could accomplish similar results by exporting the results of the SELECT query to Excel and using the PivotTable feature there to do the summary.

▶ **See** "Data Sharing with Other Applications," for more information on importing and exporting data from Access; **p. 1161**

The preceding example shows the use of a CROSSTAB query to sum values, but you can use any aggregate function to summarize the Value field. CROSSTAB queries typically include averages, percentages, and record counts as well as sums.

The Access Crosstab Query Wizard is very helpful if you're new to designing CROSSTAB queries. To start it, select New from the database window while in the Query view, and then choose Crosstab Query Wizard. The Wizard walks you through the steps involved in creating a CROSSTAB query using graphical examples, and you can always open the resultant query in the QBE grid later to modify it.

NOTE Selecting Create Query by Using Wizard from the Query View of the database window opens the wizard for creating SELECT queries, not Crosstabs.

Uses for Queries Based on Other Queries

In most implementations of Structured Query Language (SQL), including Access', it's permissible to nest queries inside one another. Rather than build enormous, monolithic joins (as in the Invoices query in Northwind), it's often preferable for a complex query to be thought of as the final result of several smaller queries—they're easier to debug and easier for others to understand. Alternatively, you may find it advantageous to create a library for simple queries to collect information you need frequently for other, more complex queries.

The Groups feature in Access 2000 makes it easier than ever to create libraries of related code, including queries. It might be convenient to create queries that answer commonly asked questions, such as, "What were our sales for a specific month?" and "What are our least-selling products?" Storing shortcuts to them in a custom group (maybe called FAQ, short for Frequently Asked Questions) makes them easily accessible for later queries, forms, and reports.

Alternatives for Handling Query Results

Running a query (other than an ACTION query) interactively results in the selected data being displayed on the screen in table-like fashion. That's fine for developing queries and inspecting data, but it's not very useful for complete applications and it's unfriendly to database users. After a query is run, there are several other possible destinations for query results.

Saving Query Results to a File

The Save command, when used with query results onscreen, actually saves any changes made to the query design, not the result set. There's a good reason for that; a query is usually much more useful when it is dynamic and can incorporate changes to the data in its underlying tables. A query's result set isn't a query anymore; it's a table, so the Save command is inappropriate.

NOTE Actually, it's a table-type recordset, and the distinction is important when accessing query results using Visual Basic for Applications. From the graphical interface, however, the distinction is semantic. An overview of VBA can be found in Chapter 41, "Using Macros and VBA in Access."

The Save As command is equally unhelpful, because it still tries to save some dynamic representation of the query to the database. You can save as a query (same as save, but with the opportunity to rename the query), as a form, or as a report. None of these preserve the data in the resultset.

The only way to directly save the actual results of a given query execution is to Export them to a file. Selecting File, Export displays the Export Query To dialog box (see Figure 35.18), which allows you to select the folder and filename for the output. The Save As Type drop-down box at the bottom of the window enables you to specify the format of the output. The default, Microsoft Access (*.adp, *.mdb, *.mdw) works only if you select the name of an existing Access database, in which case the query results are saved as a query in that database, defeating the purpose for exporting the results in the first place. Some 20 or so other options should be available (depending on the filters you selected when installing Access), and most of these save the actual query results to a file.

You have a couple of other options when you want to save query results, if you don't mind using other Office applications to do some of the work. Office Links (Tools, Office Links) will quickly transfer the results of a query to Word (as a mail-merge data source or as an embedded table) or to Excel with a single operation. You could also select some or all of the rows in a result set, and use the Clipboard (Edit, Copy; Edit, Paste) to move them to another application that can save them to a file.

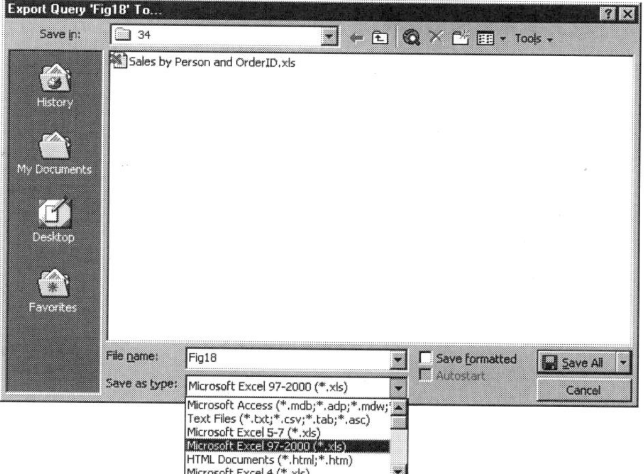

FIGURE 35.18
The Export Query To dialog box, showing some of the file types available.

Printing Query Results

One way to ensure that a record is made of the query results is to print the result set. Selecting File, Print from the default menu bar while the result set is displayed creates a nicely formatted columnar report (see Figure 35.19) containing the query results and sends it to the selected printer. The report created includes a title (the title of the query), the date printed, and is nicely paginated. Interestingly, this is a different-looking report than the report created when selecting Save As, Report (described as follows).

FIGURE 35.19
A print preview (File, Print Preview) of the results of Northwind's Invoices query.

Invoices 1/16/99

Ship Name	Ship Address	Ship City
Island Trading	Garden House	Cowes
Island Trading	Garden House	Cowes
Island Trading	Garden House	Cowes
Island Trading	Garden House	Cowes
Reggiani Caseifici	Strada Provinciale 124	Reggio Emilia
Reggiani Caseifici	Strada Provinciale 124	Reggio Emilia
Reggiani Caseifici	Strada Provinciale 124	Reggio Emilia
Ricardo Adocicados	Av. Copacabana, 267	Rio de Janeiro
Ricardo Adocicados	Av. Copacabana, 267	Rio de Janeiro
QUICK-Stop	Taucherstraße 10	Cunewalde
QUICK-Stop	Taucherstraße 10	Cunewalde
Split Rail Beer & Ale	P.O. Box 555	Lander
Split Rail Beer & Ale	P.O. Box 555	Lander
Lehmanns Marktstand	Magazinweg 7	Frankfurt a.M.
Lehmanns Marktstand	Magazinweg 7	Frankfurt a.M.

Using File, Print Preview can be a very effective tool in data analysis, because you can zoom in and out of the preview at will by clicking in it. Selecting the Multiple Pages icon from the Print Preview toolbar causes as many as six pages to be displayed at one time on the screen.

Creating a Report from Query Results

The Save As dialog box (shown in Figure 35.20) that appears when you select File, Save As while a result set is visible is useful for saving the query in several different formats. None of these actually save the query results, but all can be used as first steps to more detailed development of customization.

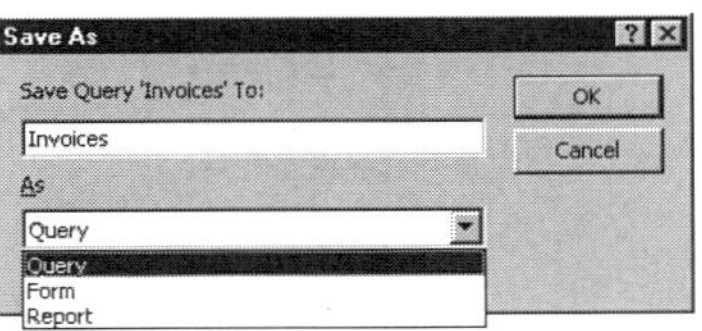

FIGURE 35.20
The Save As dialog box gives a few options for saving a query, whether the query is in Design view or in Datasheet view (executed).

Most of the time, when generating a report, you will want to create a new report and select the query as the data source. This will enable you to utilize all of the report wizards and standard report formats. To find out more about creating reports, see Chapter 37, "Advanced Reports."

Creating a Form from Query Results

You can Save As a form the same way you Save As a query or report: Simply select File, and then Save As and choose Forms from the drop-down list in the dialog box that appears. Assuming you don't already have a form with the same name as that query, a dynamic form is created, which can be used later to review and change the query results.

Although you can directly save a query to a form, just like you can save it to a report, you may find it easier to develop the form based on the query by creating a new form and selecting the query as the datasource. To find out more about creating forms from queries, see Chapter 36, "Advanced Forms."

Using the SQL-Specific Query Types

Access includes several special-case query types that are used only rarely. These queries are supported either to enhance compatibility with SQL-compliant databases in general (such as the UNION and DATA-DEFINITION queries), or to enhance Access' usability in the marketplace (such as the SQL PASS-THROUGH query). While rarely used, these query types can be quite useful.

None of these queries use the familiar QBE grid, relegating the hardy user to the SQL View instead. That's because the QBE grid isn't suited to the types of operations these queries perform. There are several good cut-and-paste examples of each of these types of queries in Access help.

UNION Queries

UNION queries are useful for those situations when you have several tables (or queries) with exactly the same fields, in the same order, and you want to combine them. You can often do the same thing with a complicated join, of course, but that can become cumbersome and inefficient after about three tables, and the query is difficult to write. UNION queries simply append the contents of each of the component queries into a new recordset, which can be used as a table.

This use sounds esoteric, but it is not as unusual as it sounds. For example, suppose you have several copies of the same database running on different machines on a network and want to periodically combine the tables in them for consolidated reporting. Or consider the case of Web server logs, which typically start a new file daily. If you can write a routine to import the data from the files, you can use a UNION query to combine data from different days.

You create a UNION query by first creating and saving as many component queries as required. Then copy them to the Windows clipboard, create a new UNION query, and paste them into the editor as shown in Figure 35.21. Alternatively, you can write the SQL yourself; it's not complicated.

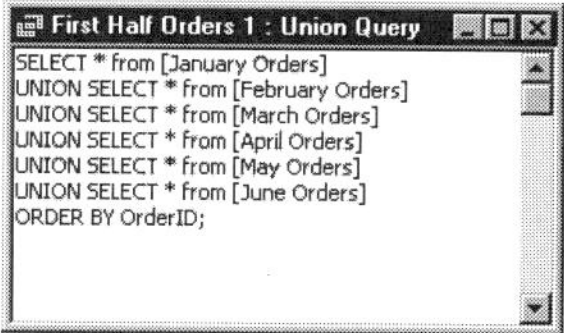

FIGURE 35.21
A simple Union query. The QBE grid isn't available, but it really isn't needed.

> **CAUTION**
>
> You must ensure that the component queries contain the same fields, in the same order, before combining them this way. Access tells you whether the number of fields is different, but it won't check for the order of the fields, and very strange results can be obtained from mismatched data sources.

DATA-DEFINITION Queries

Some database management tasks don't act on the fields in tables, but rather on the tables themselves. All these functions are handled by the GUI in some fashion, but are also enabled via SQL to provide an application-programming interface (API) to these functions for when the GUI is unavailable or inconvenient.

The following SQL functions are available as DATA-DEFINITION queries:

ALTER TABLE: modifies the design of a table

CREATE INDEX: designates fields for indexing

CREATE TABLE: creates a table

DROP TABLE: deletes a table

DROP INDEX: deletes an index

These commands are critical to manage a database in most languages, but their use is rare in Access. Other than through VBA code, there's no way to manually create indices other than through a CREATE INDEX query, but Access does a pretty good job of that if keys are chosen appropriately, and Access databases aren't usually so large that creative indexing makes much difference in query execution.

PASS-THROUGH Queries

Access can be used as a front-end to any ODBC-compliant database, thus providing a GUI for some very non-GUI commercial database engines. When an Access database is created that takes advantage of linked ODBC tables, any queries created are executed in the host environment using default options.

However, it sometimes may be helpful to utilize extensions in the host system's language to make sure that the query executes quicker. Additionally, you may want to take advantage of stored procedures, which aren't available unless you're using a PASS-THROUGH query.

NOTE VBA modules (see Chapter 41) are similar to stored procedures in that they are precompiled collections of statements that perform processing on the local database, but they do not qualify in the traditional sense because they cannot be referenced by applications other than the currently open database. True stored procedures don't require that the database be opened, because database engines supporting them are usually running all the time in the background.

Another important difference is that a stored procedure generally returns a recordset, such as a query, whereas VBA modules generally return no value or only a single value.

The key to using PASS-THROUGH queries effectively is to understand how to configure the property settings for the PASS-THROUGH query being defined. The property settings are obscure and easily overlooked, but the query will not run without configuring them properly. To view the properties for a PASS-THROUGH query, select View, Properties. The unusual property sheet for the PASS-THROUGH query being edited appears, as shown in Figure 35.22.

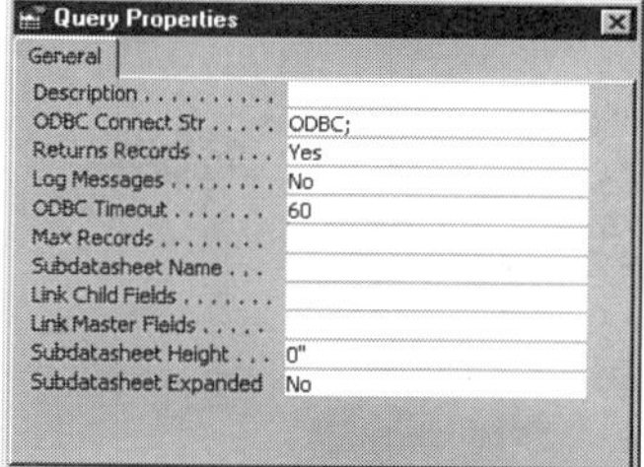

FIGURE 35.22
The property sheet for a PASS-THROUGH query is unlike that for any other kind of query. For information on setting these properties, see Access help.

CHAPTER 36

Advanced Forms

In this chapter

Types and Uses for Forms

Access forms are typically used in one of three ways:

- To view and modify records one at a time.
- To work with groups of records.
- To provide information and/or navigation.

Forms are the most visible part of an Access application to the end user, and choosing the correct type of form for a given situation is critical to the success of the development effort.

Consider an application that tracks inventory and processes orders, such as the Northwind database included with Access 2000. Detailed information about the products that Northwind sells changes from time to time and needs to be updated. This is probably best done one product at a time, because the changes are likely to affect only a few products, whatever they are. And there may be a dozen pieces of information stored about each particular product. Fitting all that on the screen for more than one product might be impossible. A form that displays and permits the updating of one product at a time might be best for this application; the Products form (shown in Figure 36.1) works well.

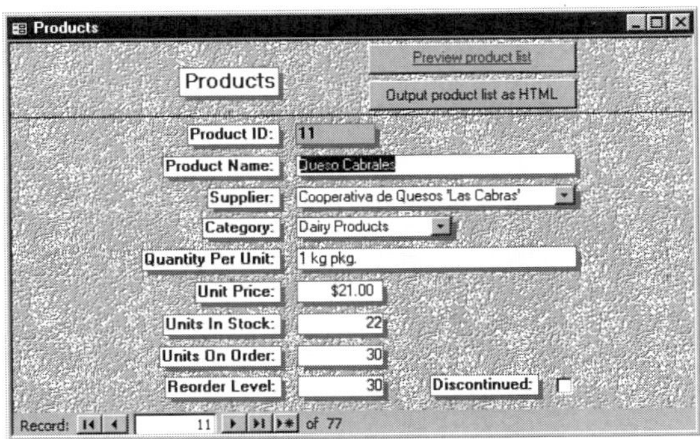

FIGURE 36.1
The Products form in Northwind packs a lot of information about one product into each page of the form.

For customer orders, however, little information about each product must be displayed. A whole myriad of customer information may be considered, but all you need to know about the products at order time is the name, quantity, and total price. Using separate forms for each item ordered would be slow and cumbersome, so you can create a form of the second type, such as Northwind's Orders form, shown in Figure 36.2. This form pulls data from several tables.

Because forms are the user's interface to an application, they're often used to provide information and navigation. They can do this without having any interaction with data at all. Instead, they use command buttons and other specialized controls combined with underlying code to allow the application to work as a cohesive whole rather than as a group of unrelated forms, tables, queries, and reports. In the Northwind database, the Main Switchboard and Startup forms (see Figure 36.3) are examples of information/navigation forms.

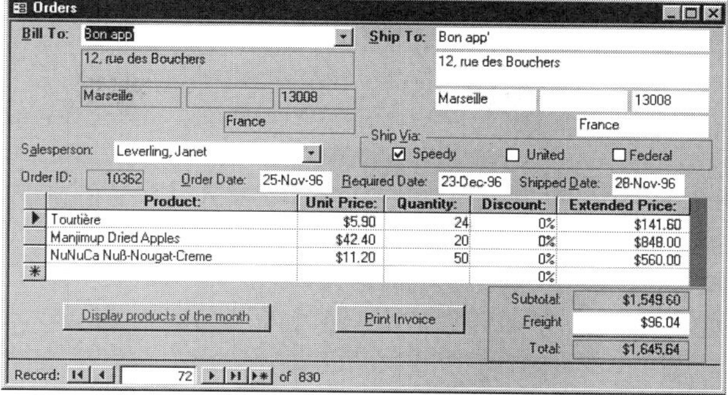

FIGURE 36.2
Northwind's Orders form. You can deal with as many orders as necessary on one form because only a few data elements need to be tracked at a time for each order.

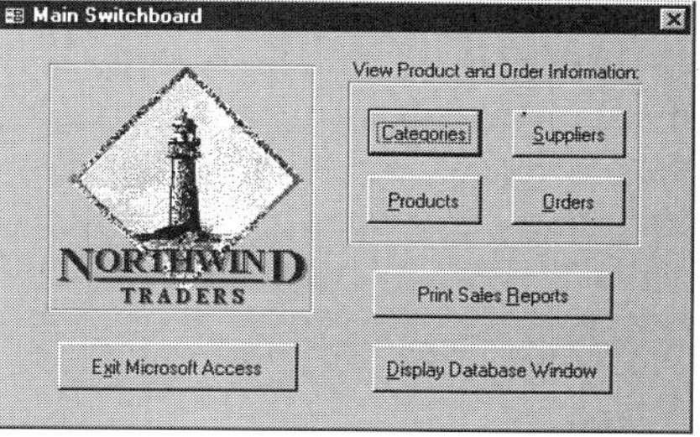

FIGURE 36.3
Information and Navigation forms make use of modules and macros to pull an application together into a cohesive whole.

Applications that do not take advantage of all three of these common uses for forms are rare. When designing a database application and considering each element of its interface, ask yourself whether the operation in question is best-suited to a single-record form, a multi-record table form, an informational/navigational form, or a combination of more than one of these. If you consider all the options, one is likely to stand out as the best for the particular circumstance at hand.

Form Data Sources

Access uses the term *binding* to describe how forms relate to data. Information/navigation forms are often *unbound*, meaning that there's no data for them to query or update. Single and multirecord forms are almost always *bound*, married to a data source of one sort or another, and having direct access to that data source's records.

In the simplest sense, forms are interfaces to tables. The datasheet you use to enter data directly in Access tables (from the Database Window in Table view, select a table and click Open) acts as a simple form. Double-clicking a Select query in the Database Window opens a datasheet that you can use to modify data in the query's data source; the query passes through the changes you make to the tables that comprise it. As long as there's no ambiguity about exactly which table originally supplied the data, the query acts as a table for this purpose.

▶ **See** "Multiple Table Queries," **p. 1018**

When you create or edit a form, you select a data source for it (if desired) by making a selection in its Record Source property (see Figure 36.4). Access provides a drop-down list of all the tables and queries in the current database for you to choose from.

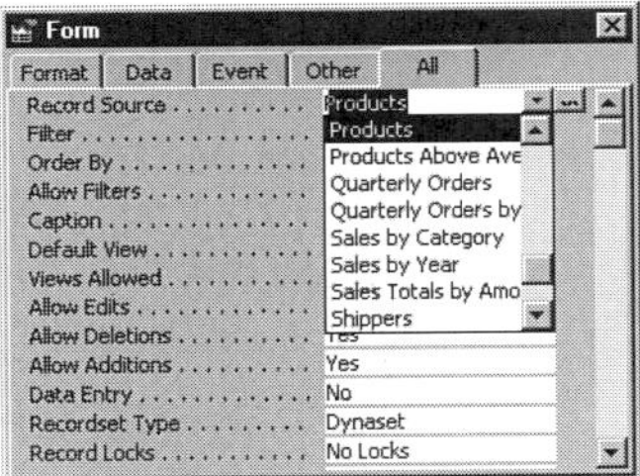

FIGURE 36.4
The Record Source for a form is limited to any table or query in the database or SELECT statement.

Binding forms to data sources other than simple tables or queries in the current database requires a little creativity. One way to create a form that draws data from more than one table is to create a query that joins the tables you need. Queries can even join other queries together, and there's nothing wrong with creating a customized query that contains just what you need for a specific form; in fact, it's a good practice. Northwind's Quarterly Orders form is bound to the Quarterly Orders query, which joins the Orders and Customers tables.

▶ **See** "Advanced Queries," **p. 1017**

Forms can also be bound to SQL Select statements. If your form's Record Source changes as the application is run, it might be more convenient to assign a SQL statement to the Record Source property and change it in code. Admittedly, anything you can do this way you can also do with stored queries, but it's good to know that it's possible, especially for debugging complicated forms.

Using non-Access data sources as the basis for forms requires making them look like Access data sources. Depending on the options you selected when installing Access, you can create live links to more than a dozen different potential data sources directly from Access, including Excel spreadsheets, Paradox, and dBASE databases, and Microsoft Outlook and Exchange datasets. When you create these links (File, Get External Data, Link Tables), they appear to Access as if they were native tables, and you can write queries using them and use them as the basis for forms and reports (see example in Figure 36.5). After the external data source is linked, it appears in the list of Record Sources available to the form and you can view and (usually) edit the records in it as you would any local (Access) table.

You can extend this concept further by using Open Database Connectivity (ODBC) to link external data sources that may not even lie on the same computer. Figure 36.6 shows a form based on a query that incorporates an Informix table on a Sun (UNIX) workstation. The actual source of the data is invisible to the user, except for a (hopefully) slight delay for the request to travel across the network, be processed, and return.

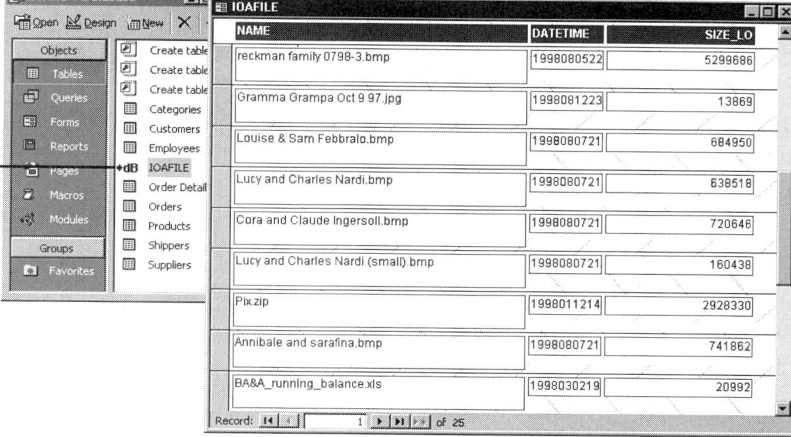

FIGURE 36.5
This linked dBASE IV file looks a little different in the Database Window, but Access uses it as a record source just the same.

Linked dBASE table

Informix Raw Data

org	projectid	project_name	ıasa_required	ıther_required	ıasa_available
GM	L0016-A -1998-I6-GM -GM	STI - LEAD CENTER OPS	5	0	0
GM	L0016-A -1998-I6-GM -GM	STI - LEAD CENTER OPS	5	0	0
GM	L0016-A -1998-I6-GM -GM	STI - LEAD CENTER OPS	5.300083	0	5.300083
GK	M0025-CC-1996-I5-GK -GKC	CERES	1.250024	0	1.250024
GK	M0025-CC-1996-I5-GK -GKC	CERES	0.8480769	0	0
GK	M0025-CC-1996-I5-GK -GKC	CERES	0.8480769	0	0
GF	M0031-G -1997-I7-GF -GF	INDIRECT (MGT.)	0.2288461	0	0
GF	M0031-G -1997-I7-GF -GF	INDIRECT (MGT.)	1	0	0
GF	M0031-G -1997-I7-GF -GF	INDIRECT (MGT.)	0.2140426	0	0.2140426

FIGURE 36.6
Any data source you can link to can be the Record Source for a form.

Of course, it's most useful if the remote server permits updating records as well as viewing them; otherwise, you may as well write a report instead of a form.

The bottom line is that you have to make the data source look like a table in the current database to Access (or it won't appear in the list), but it doesn't need to be one itself.

▶ **See** "Data Sharing with Other Applications," **p. 1161**

Customizing Forms

Access provides several easy ways to create simple forms: the Form Wizard (double-click Create Form by Using Wizard from the Database Window); the columnar, tabular, and datasheet AutoForms; and the new Chart and PivotTable Wizards. To the extent that these tools create forms that work as advertised, they're helpful, but all have limitations that you can get around only by modifying them manually or by creating the form you need from scratch. Access includes a lot of form-building features that the wizards and built-in tools don't take advantage of.

Using Form Sections Effectively

Access forms are typically divided into one or more *sections*, each of which has its own properties and customary uses. Simple forms may use only one section, whereas complex ones may include up to five. Understanding when and how to use form sections correctly is critical to the proper operation of a form, as each section is responsible for certain form functions that other sections may not be able to provide.

The Detail Section When you create a new form in Design view (usually the best way to start designing a new form), only one section is visible: the Detail section. This section typically contains data elements (called *controls*, and described later in this section) that display and usually permit changing data in the form's data source. The Detail section, by default, includes navigation buttons that enable users to move among records; these buttons are visible only in Form view. When you assign a Record Source to the form, the Detail Section's appearance is dictated by the Default view property of the report (Edit, Select Form, View, Properties). You have three options:

- Single Form—the default, forces the display of only one data record at a time in the Detail Section, as shown in Figure 36.7.

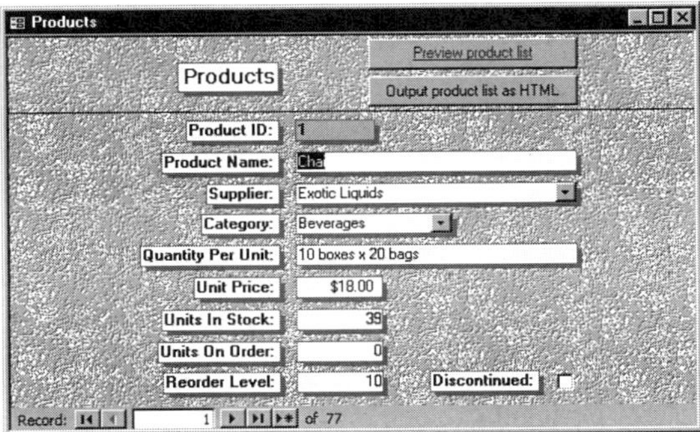

FIGURE 36.7
The Single Form setting shows only one record, no matter how the form is resized.

- Continuous Forms—allows the display of as many records as can fit in the current window (see Figure 36.8). A vertical scrollbar appears if there are more records in the bound data source than can fit.
- Datasheet view—displays records in an unformatted, rigid spreadsheet-like grid (see Figure 36.9). This view is rarely used, because a continuous form can be developed that looks like a datasheet but is much more flexible.

The Form Header and Footer If you select View, Form Header/Footer while designing a form, new sections appear above and below the Detail section. These sections are intended to contain information that needs to appear only once per form (such as header graphics or footnote information), regardless of the number of detail records returned. You can change the size of either section by setting its Height property or by dragging the header of the section below it (for the Form Header) or the bottom of the page (for the Form Footer) as required.

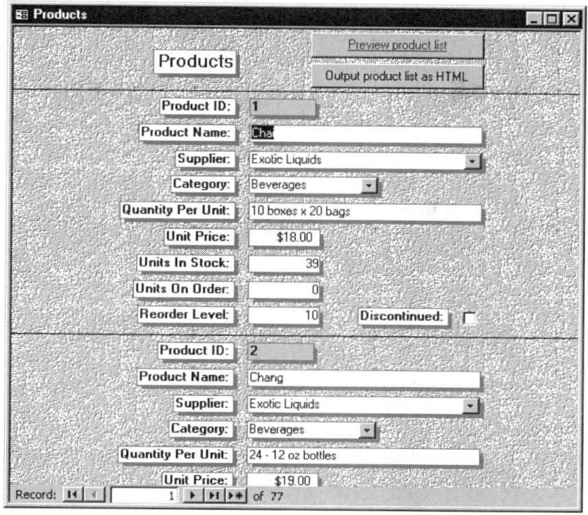

FIGURE 36.8
The Continuous Forms setting shows as many copies of the Detail Section as can fit.

Products

Product ID:	Product Name:	Supplier:	Category:	Quantity Per Unit:
1	Chai	Exotic Liquids	Beverages	10 boxes x 20 bags
2	Chang	Exotic Liquids	Beverages	24 - 12 oz bottles
3	Aniseed Syrup	Exotic Liquids	Condiments	12 - 550 ml bottles
4	Chef Anton's Cajun Seasoning	New Orleans Cajun Delights	Condiments	48 - 6 oz jars
5	Chef Anton's Gumbo Mix	New Orleans Cajun Delights	Condiments	36 boxes
6	Grandma's Boysenberry Spread	Grandma Kelly's Homestead	Condiments	12 - 8 oz jars
7	Uncle Bob's Organic Dried Pears	Grandma Kelly's Homestead	Produce	12 - 1 lb pkgs.
8	Northwoods Cranberry Sauce	Grandma Kelly's Homestead	Condiments	12 - 12 oz jars
9	Mishi Kobe Niku	Tokyo Traders	Meat/Poultry	18 - 500 g pkgs.
10	Ikura	Tokyo Traders	Seafood	12 - 200 ml jars
11	Queso Cabrales	Cooperativa de Quesos 'Las Cabras'	Dairy Products	1 kg pkg.
12	Queso Manchego La Pastora	Cooperativa de Quesos 'Las Cabras'	Dairy Products	10 - 500 g pkgs.
13	Konbu	Mayumi's	Seafood	2 kg box
14	Tofu	Mayumi's	Produce	40 - 100 g pkgs.
15	Genen Shouyu	Mayumi's	Condiments	24 - 250 ml bottles

Record: 1 of 77

FIGURE 36.9
The Datasheet option ignores all formatting.

For unbound forms, creating the entire form in the Form Header and shrinking the Detail and Form Footer sections to their minimum height is usually preferable. This is because the Detail section, when seen in Form view, includes record selectors and navigation buttons by default, and it's easier to work in the Form Header for the Information/Navigation type forms rather than to change all the defaults for the Detail Section appropriately. Of course, the Form Footer would work as well.

Some controls, such as the Tab Control (see Specialized Form Controls and Objects later in this chapter) incorporate their own record-navigation mechanisms. They're also good candidates for inclusion in the Form Header, because they don't need the Detail Section's navigation controls anyway.

The Page Header and Footer Page Headers and Footers, as parts of forms, come into play only when the form is printed. When the form is displayed on the screen, the contents of these sections are invisible. For this reason, they're very different from the Report Header and Footer, which are visible onscreen as well as on paper.

Users seldom print forms directly, but if they do, you may want to provide some kind of summary information in the Page Footer to identify what they printed. A record ID of some type and the date and time the form was printed (use the Date and Time functions in a text box control) can help determine what was happening when a form was printed. Reports are covered in depth in Chapter 37, "Advanced Reports."

Form Controls and Properties

Access provides a Toolbox that contains commonly used controls for placement on forms. This is really a standard toolbar that appears detached from the application window by default.

In most cases, you'll want to use the Control Wizard—a toggle button that is enabled when pressed on the Toolbox. When the Control Wizard toggle is enabled and certain controls (the option-box control, combo-box control, list-box control, subform control) are placed on the design canvas, different Control Wizards kick in to help you configure the control appropriately. Unless you're an expert at creating a particular kind of control, the wizard is a good idea.

Most form controls are relatively self-explanatory (the label control, the line control, the text box), but some are a little more complicated. The more complex controls are detailed in the following sections.

The Option Group Control The Option-Group Control contains one or more option-button controls, check-box controls, and/or toggle-button controls (but not mixed together). You can bind an option-group control to a field in a data source and have it return any value you want depending on which of the controls within it have been selected. Only one control in an option group can be toggled on, so only one value is returned. Remember, the bound control is the option group, not the button or box inside it.

NOTE You'll almost always want to put option buttons inside an option group, because the other types of buttons imply that more than one can be selected at a time. In an option group, you can select only one button at a time, but Access permits the different appearance given by the other button types if you desire.

The List Box and Combo Box Controls A list box is almost exactly like a combo box, except that one or several values from the list are displayed all the time. List boxes take up more screen real estate than do combo boxes and are generally not preferred except in special cases.

The venerable list box and combo box Controls (sometimes called a drop-down list or drop-down combo box) date back to the earliest versions of Access and give most Access applications a distinctive "Access feel." Both use a query or a typed-in list to populate a list of options from which the user can select one (or more, in the case of the list box if the MultiSelect property is set). In both cases, the values in the list are determined by the records returned by the query in the control's Row Source property.

In a list box, the valid values appear when the user starts typing in the control; Access completes the entry being typed with the first matching entry in the list. In a combo box, the user clicks the drop-down arrow on the right of the text box, which displays several of the values in the list; one can then be selected with the mouse or arrow keys. The value selected is stored in the field to which the box is bound. Combo boxes have some advantages over list boxes in that they can be made to accept values that are not in the list.

Both are especially useful because the query or list need have nothing at all to do with the data source for the form. For example, a combo box might contain a list of employees (generated by a query from the Employees table) to store in the Orders table when they make a sale. Using a combo box to provide a list of possibilities, rather than forcing a user to type values, enhances the integrity of the database by ensuring uniformity of data values and alleviates confusion by prompting a user to select one of an appropriate list of options.

The Object Frame Controls The Bound and Unbound Object Frame Controls insert OLE objects registered with Windows into your Access form. OLE objects available on most systems include graphs, music and video clips, MIDI sequences, and others, depending on what other applications are installed on your system. The difference between the bound and unbound variants of this control is that the bound control expects to find the object in the form's data source (in an OLE Object field); the unbound control looks for the object on the file system or in the control itself. For an example, see the Northwind Employees form, which includes a bound object control displaying a photo of the employee described by the current record.

The Page Break Control The Page Break Control forces a page break when a form is printed. It also provides a navigation feature; if a form is very long and extends vertically off the page, inserting a page break causes Access to reposition the form at the break when the PageUp and PageDown keys are pressed. This feature works only when a form is in Single Form view, and there are several other options to consider when using the page break control this way; see Access Help for details. In any case, this use isn't usually intuitive and you're usually better off breaking your form into several if it becomes much larger than the display.

The Tab Control The Tab Control creates a set of overlaid pages that can be individually selected by clicking on a tab that extends from each page. The pages can have entirely different designs, giving an application a notebook feel, and the controls on each tab can be individually configured. Using this control is an effective way to maximize the amount of data that can be displayed on a small computer display. Northwind's Employees form includes a tab control that effectively doubles the amount of information that can be displayed on the form at a time.

Form and Control Properties

Each type of control has properties specific to it, and forms and form sections themselves have properties you can use to customize them. For any control, you can view and modify its properties by selecting it and clicking the Properties button on the toolbar. To view a form's properties, first select the form itself by clicking the Form Selector in the top-left corner of the form (see Figure 36.10), and then click the Properties button. For a form section, click the section's header bar before clicking the Properties button.

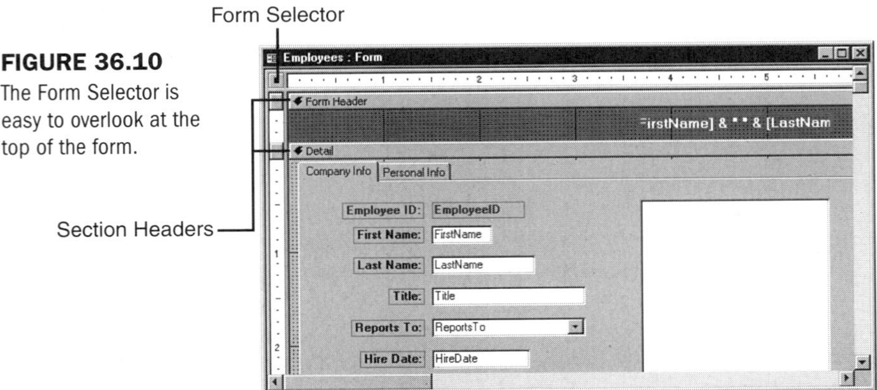

FIGURE 36.10
The Form Selector is easy to overlook at the top of the form.

There are hundreds of properties that you can set, but some of the more commonly modified properties are listed in the following sections.

Allow Edits, Allow Deletions, Allow Additions The Allow Edits/Deletions/Additions properties control the types of activities that users can perform on records visible in this form. The Data Entry property, when set to Yes, limits form activities to adding new records only; it's like setting Allow Additions to Yes and the other two Allow properties to No, except that it also doesn't allow for browsing of records.

Record Locks The Record Locks property is useful in multiuser databases, where someone else may be editing the same record that you are, at the same time. The options for this property are No Locks (the default), All Records, or Edited Record. The Record Locks property determines what constraints the database should put on other users while one is working in this form. Note that locks applied in a particular form lock the data source, not the form, so other users using different forms or queries will be affected by locks if they are set in those forms.

Pop Up and Modal The Pop Up and Modal properties control how this form should interact with other forms displayed at the same time. If this form should always appear on top of other forms (as in an informational or cautionary form), you should set Pop Up to Yes. If this form should require that it be closed before input can continue on any other forms, set Modal to Yes. These properties can be used together (as in Northwind's Startup form) to display a form that is particularly important and must be seen and dealt with immediately.

Allow Design Changes The new Allow Design Changes property controls whether users should be able to change the design of the form in Form view, instead of requiring that the changes be made in Design view. For applications to be distributed to users (where Design view is often disabled), the fact that Access 2000 now permits users to modify forms directly should be reason for caution; set this property to Design View Only to prevent tampering with your forms.

CAUTION

Leaving the Allow Design Changes property set to All Views, the default, can quickly result in users destroying their forms by clicking in the wrong places. Be careful with this property.

Grouping Controls Form controls can now be grouped to enable several to be modified (moved, have properties changed, and so on) together. To group controls, place them on a form in the correct positions relative to each other. Then select all the controls to be grouped (hold down Shift while clicking within the boundaries of each control in turn) and select Format, Group. They now act as one until ungrouped (select Format, Ungroup after selecting the grouped controls).

One advantage to this feature is that you can now essentially lock the position of any control relative to its neighbors. This makes it easier to design well-aligned forms and to move entire groups of controls to another place on a form while designing it.

Changing Field Properties from the Form View

As alluded to previously, Access 2000 now permits users to modify form elements while running the form in Form view. Microsoft's "Enhancement Guide for Access 2000" illuminates this feature by saying, "for example, a user could select a field on a form and change the background color, size, and border while in browse mode and immediately see the effects of the work." This is true.

A user could also select a field on a form and change the filter (permitting viewing of otherwise unauthorized records) or underlying code (permitting other kinds of mayhem) if this option is left to the default.

Consider this scenario: An Access programmer who doesn't realize that this feature is now in Access copies the Employees form from the Northwind database for use in an Executive Information System (EIS) for their company. The Access programmer modifies the form to include salary and raise information, and adds a password form and filter to permit employees only to view their own data and not change it. Unfortunately, the programmer forgets to change the Allow Design Changes property to Design View Only before distributing the application. In a matter of seconds, a disgruntled employee displays the property sheet for the form, removes the filter, and changes the Allow Edits property to enable changes. The rest is history.

Using Command Buttons

When you use forms to provide navigation, options, or other nondata-related services to your users, you generally use buttons on the active form to do it. Users recognize buttons as a standard part of the interface, and expect something to happen when they press one. Of course, the programmer decides what each button should do when pressed.

While users expect buttons to do something only when the button is pressed, there are several more events that Access can trap and for which you can add code. For example, you can make a button change its appearance when the mouse moves over it, or when it's double-clicked.

You should take care not to rock the boat too much, though; the extra events that buttons support can be used to initiate background processes, but users get confused if buttons start doing things when they're not clicked on.

Whenever a user clicks a button, the following chain of events is executed:

```
Enter
GotFocus
MouseDown
MouseUp
Click
```

You can create code that executes whenever any (or all) of these events occur. The most commonly used event, by far, is the `On Click` event.

You can attach three different kinds of code to command button events: macros, modules, and user-defined functions. The last is not commonly used and isn't recommended.

To attach a macro to an event, create the macro in the Macro editor, save it, and enter its name in the property box for the event for which you want to trigger the macro.

For modules, click the Builder button after clicking in the event property box, choose Code Builder, and enter the module code in the VBA Editor window that opens. Using module code with command buttons is by far the most flexible and capable way to customize a button's actions.

For simple buttons performing common actions (opening another form, selecting a record, printing, and so on), you can use the Command Wizard. When you place a command button (or one of several other types of controls) on a form, the Command Wizard begins. If it doesn't, make sure the Control Wizards are enabled (the Control Wizards button appears pressed). You'll be given a choice of several common actions and designs for your button and Access inserts the necessary code (as a module) in the `On Click` event of the button. The code created by the Command Wizard is stored as VBA; you can certainly manually create a macro that executes in response to an event on a command button if you choose.

As examples of command buttons, let's consider command buttons in Northwind that use macros and modules as their event actions. First, the form Employees (page break), shown in Figure 36.11, consists of two pages. Only one page is visible at a time when the form is displayed in Form view. Each page contains a single command button at bottom center. This command button is bound to a macro group also called Employees (page break); the button on the first page calls the Personal Info macro, and the button on the second page calls the Company Info macro.

Because the macro is bound to the `On Click` property of each button, it is executed when the primary mouse button is pressed while the pointer is over the control button.

NOTE Access takes care of some event processing behind the scenes. In the case of command buttons, Access takes care of making the button appear to depress during the `Mouse Down` event and extend during the `Mouse Up` event. Another example is in check box controls, which appear to have a graphic check mark in them when their value is True. The programmer doesn't have to worry about these trivial things, even though they significantly enhance the user experience.

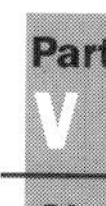

FIGURE 36.11
The macro group Employees (page break) can contain any number of individual macros, each of which is addressed by using a period between the macro and macro group names.

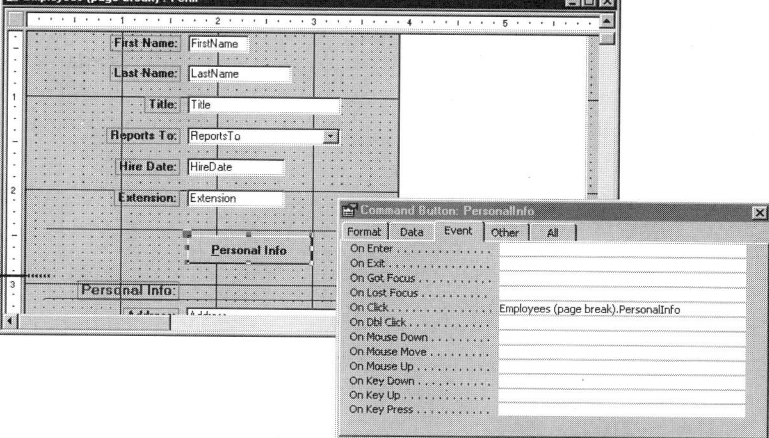

These simple macros take care of switching the Employees (page break) form back and forth between its two pages. The macro titles in the left column are referred to in the Property sheets for the command buttons, and the action taken in each case is simply to GoToPage 1 or 2, depending on the button pressed. Because there's a page break in the form and the form is sized only large enough to display one page at a time, the buttons become the only way to switch between the pages.

Advantages to Page Switching

This technique easily could be used to create the illusion of a lot of different forms on the screen, when in fact there's only one. The advantage of doing page switching this way is that it's very fast when the button is pressed. However, the entire form is loaded before the first page is displayed, so this may take a few seconds if the form is large. If it's likely that users traverse all or most of the pages in order, though, it's a good way to facilitate navigation.

A similar technique uses the tab control to accomplish the same thing. It's also particularly useful when you don't know the order in which the user accesses the pages.

If users aren't likely to use more than half of the pages, it is often better to use separate forms to minimize the startup delay. Tabs are an option if you are concerned about the delay between steps.

▶ **See** "Procedures and Functions," **p. 1149**

Using VBA modules instead of macros isn't much more difficult and is often easier to debug and document. Furthermore, module code runs slightly faster than macro code (because macro code must be interpreted every time it is run). This isn't likely to make a big difference in the performance of your command buttons, but it's a good rule of thumb.

To create code modules that run when a command button is pressed, you have two choices:

- You can create a function in the VBA Editor, save it as a module, and call the function from the Property sheet of the command button by listing the function name in the event box, as in `=gotopage(2)`.

- You can create a *class module* (a module that is an intrinsic part of a form or report), which becomes part of the command button itself and isn't visible in the module window, by clicking in the event box you want (probably `On Click`) in the Property sheet for the command button and selecting the Builder button that appears on the right. You can then select the Code Builder from the dialog box that appears and write your new module directly in the VBA Editor.

No example of the first method exists in Northwind, but it's rarely used anyway. If code applies only to a specific form or report, it's better to localize it within that form or report to ease debugging. You can see the second method on the Products form, in the Output to HTML button, shown in Figure 36.12:

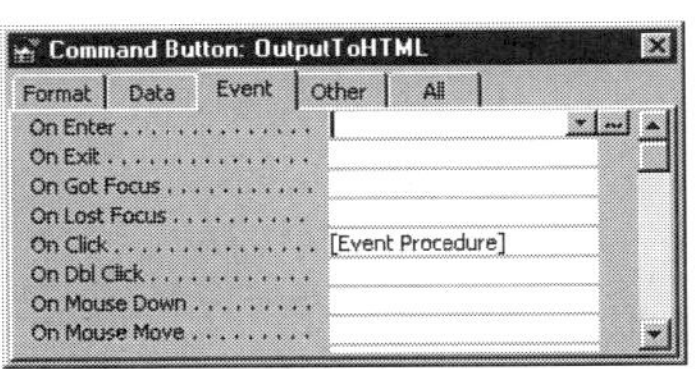

FIGURE 36.12
The property sheet for the Products form shows that there's an [Event Procedure] behind the `On Click` event for the Output to HTML command button.

Clearing the dummy phrase [Event Procedure] from this dialog box disables the procedure, but doesn't delete it. View the code behind this button by clicking in the box marked [Event Procedure] and selecting the Builder button. Because there's a class module already behind this button, the VBA Editor automatically appears with the event code visible in the Code Window at right (see Figure 36.13).

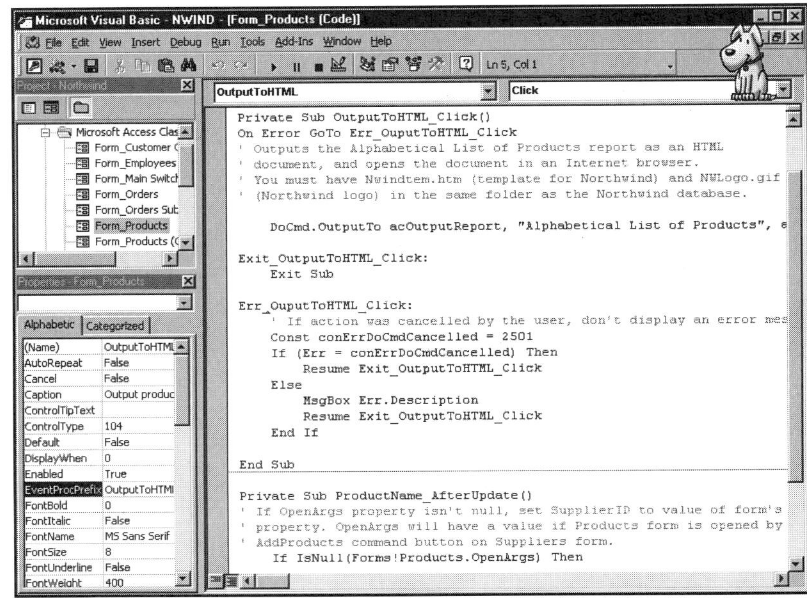

FIGURE 36.13
The Visual Basic for Applications (VBA) Editor, showing the project hierarchy, object properties, and class module code attached to the Products form. Note that all code behind a particular form or report appears in the same class module.

Of all the code in that module, only one line is critical:

```
DoCmd.OutputTo acOutputReport, "Alphabetical List of Products",
acFormatHTML, "Products.htm", True, "Nwindtem.htm"
```

This VBA command says to output the report called Alphabetical List of Products in HTML to the file Products.htm, using the style template Nwindtem.htm. The keywords beginning with "ac" are VBA constants, represented as words instead of numbers for readability. All remaining code in that procedure is for error handling and is necessary only if your application needs to be bulletproof.

Anything you can do in a macro you can do in code. The converse is not true. For more information on using macros and modules, see Chapter 41, "Using Macros and VBA in Access."

Creating and Modifying Menus and Toolbars

In Access 2.0, creating menus was complicated. You had to create a specially formatted macro (there was a tool to help) that generated the menu when it was run. Since Access 95, though, menu creation has been simplified somewhat, and menus and toolbars lost their distinction from each other in Access 97. Menu bars and toolbars are now slightly different manifestations of the same object type, and you can create and/or modify these objects just as any other Access object. This capability makes toolbars and menu bars dynamic, giving them the potential to change based on data or circumstances.

Because menu bars and toolbars are really the same thing in Access 2000 (toolbars usually show icons for commands, and menu bars show words), we'll use the generic term command bars for the remainder of this section to refer to both. You can create or modify command bars either interactively or programmatically. Changes made interactively to the Access default command bars are saved with the Access client, and are not part of the database itself; if you modify a standard command bar and give a copy of your database to a friend, they won't see the changes. Custom command bars created from scratch, however, are stored in the database.

There are times when you'll want to import a command bar from one database into another. You can't—they're not accessible from the Import menu. The only thing you can do is copy the database containing the command bar to a new file, delete all its objects (tables, forms, and so on), and import the objects from the destination database. Then save the imported objects with the new command bar. There's no Save As option in Access that applies to the whole database, either, so you'll have to save it and rename it in the operating system.

Using and manipulating command bars in code greatly increases the flexibility of your application; in addition to using command buttons (which take up valuable screen space), you can use menus to control navigation and even process data. Users don't typically expect command bars to do anything but navigation, but your application may benefit from other creative options for other uses.

To create a command bar in code, create a new module (from the Database Window, switch to Modules View and click New) and use the Add method of the CommandBars collection to instantiate an empty command bar. You can then use the Controls property of the newly created command bar to add a command button and give it an action to perform. The code in Listing 36.1, copied and slightly modified from Visual Basic help, does just that:

Listing 36.1 VBA Code to Create a Command Bar and Place a Control Button in It

```
Sub Create_Menu ()

Dim MyCommandBar As CommandBar
Dim MyControl As CommandBarControl

Set MyCommandBar = Application.CommandBars.Add("MyCommandBar")
Set MyControl = MyCommandBar.Controls.Add(msoControlButton)
MyControl.Caption = "I'm a button!"
MyControl.Style = msoButtonCaption
MyCommandBar.Visible = True

End Sub
```

NOTE This VBA code snippet is included on the CD with this book. To learn how to use this cut-and-paste code, see "Putting VBA Code Snippets to Work" in Chapter 6, "Successful VBA Modules."

This looks complicated if you don't have much experience with VBA, but it's not too bad. Lines 1 and 9 (Sub and End Sub) begin and end the procedure and are required. Lines 2 and 3 declare a couple of variables: the new command bar itself and one button for it. After all, they have to have names so that you can refer to them later. Line 4 adds a new command bar with the name `MyCommandBar` to the Application (which is also an object itself) and makes the name `MyCommandBar` refer to it. Line 5 creates a button (the constant `msoControlButton` causes a button to be added instead of a separator line or other object) and makes the name `MyControl` point to it. Line 6 sets that button's caption and Line 7 uses the constant '`msoButtonCaption`' to force the text (instead of an icon or icon/text combination) to be displayed. And Line 8 makes the whole thing visible.

To execute this code, create a new module, copy and paste it in from this book's CD, and press the Run button on the VBA standard toolbar to run it. The new command bar appears on the screen. Note that you cannot run the code twice without getting an error, because it will try to re-create a command bar with the same name. Delete the new one before running the code again, and experiment with different options. For more information, look up command bars in VBA Help (not Access Help; select Help while you're editing the module in the VBA Editor).

Specialized Form Controls and Objects

Forms can make use of several sophisticated controls that are unavailable to reports because forms are interactive, whereas reports are not. All these controls (sometimes called OLE custom controls or *ActiveX controls*) have special unique properties and methods that you'll be able to discover only through a little digging, but most are well worth the effort for the pizzazz they add to your application.

Calendar Control

The *calendar control* is a fully functional, multiyear calendar that you can place in a form. When a user selects a date in the calendar, the value of the calendar object changes to the date selected. You can bind code to the `AfterUpdate` property of the control to check the value selected and do something with it, such as filter a set of records. The form in Figure 36.14 shows the Calendar Control in action. You can customize its appearance by inserting it (Insert, ActiveX Control, Calendar Control 9.0) into a form, right-clicking on it, and choosing Calendar Object, Properties from the menu that appears.

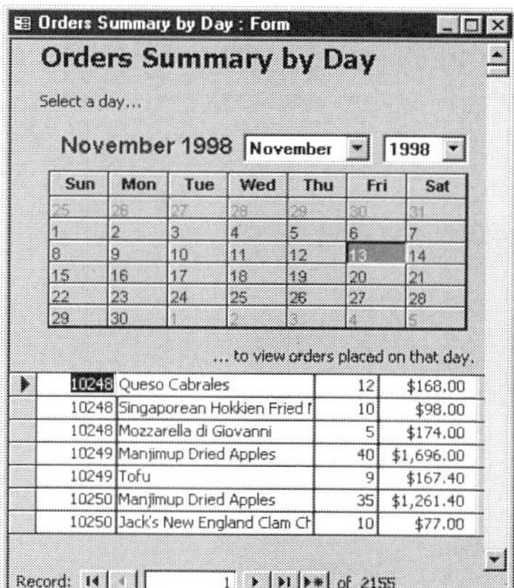

FIGURE 36.14
The Calendar Control in a form, filtering records.

Common Dialog Control

Sometimes you want users to input a filename, perhaps to specify data to import or a destination for an output action. You could provide a simple text box for typing, but Windows users are accustomed to selecting from the standard Explorer-type folder hierarchy. If you have the Office 2000 Developer Edition, you can provide it to them via the *common dialog control*. This control remains invisible on the form until it's called from code, usually triggered by a command button. When triggered, the familiar Windows file-selection box appears, and users can select a file or folder, whose name is returned as the value of the control, when they press OK.

Status Bar Control

Actions that take a long time can make users think that the system is hung. You can help alleviate their worries with the *status bar control,* which shows a progressively filling rectangle as some counter (which you specify) increments.

NOTE Earlier versions of this control have been known to overflow if the incrementing variable exceeded the maximum set for the control. There's not usually any detrimental effect from this bug except for the counterintuitive appearance of an overfull status bar.

OLE Objects

Any valid Windows OLE object can be embedded in a form. Clicking Insert, Object displays a dialog box (see Figure 36.15) containing the names of all registered objects on your system; the list you see depends on what applications you have installed and what objects they've registered with Windows.

Selecting one of these objects and clicking Create New and OK executes the object's controlling application so that you can create an object of that type. Clicking Create from File changes the appearance of the selection dialog box to enable you to select a file whose extension identifies it as one of the types in the first dialog box. After you embed the object of choice, you can modify its properties as necessary to achieve the desired effect.

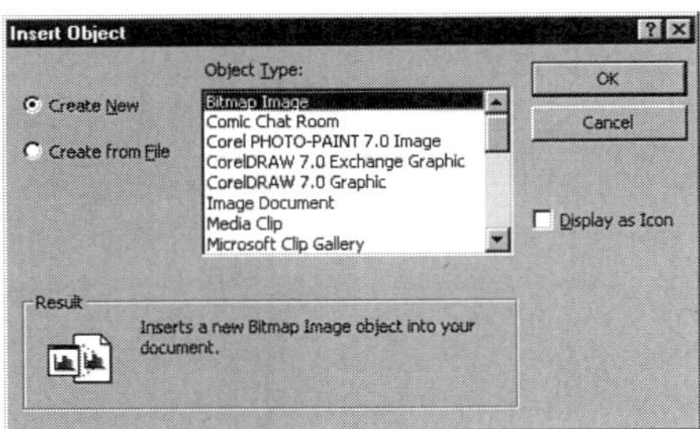

FIGURE 36.15
Application objects available for embedding in a form.

You're not even limited to the objects and controls currently on your computer. Object definition files (.ocx) are available from various Web sites (not always for free), and some come with Office 2000, Developer Edition (the ODE). If you obtain an .ocx file and want to use the control it contains, you must first register the control with Windows.

To do so, select Tools, ActiveX Controls, Register, and select the .ocx file from the dialog box that appears. Don't worry about copying it to the right place; the act of registering it automatically copies it to \windows\system (or wherever the system files directory of your installation is) and makes it available for your use.

Remember that the control is registered to your individual Windows installation and does not work on another PC unless you copy and reregister the control there first using the same process or by creating a distribution package and self-executing installation program using the ODE.

Creating Subforms

Access forms are designed to display flat data; that is, data where a one-to-one relationship exists between all data elements on a given form.

A single table makes a good candidate, because all the records in a table have a one-to-one relationship with all other records in the same table. Even in the case of a query that joins several tables, the resulting dataset is made up of discrete records, usually with identifying unique fields, each of which can stand by itself.

The real world isn't flat, however. Most data that describes situations and environments in human society has a one-to-many or many-to-many relationship with other data.

Examples of this are everywhere: You're an individual, but you have a one-to-many relationship with the members of your family. They, in turn, have one-to-many relationships with their relatives, who may not be related to you.

Therefore, you have a many-to-many relationship with your family's family, and it gets more complicated from there. The textbook example of a many-to-many relationship (which many people find difficult to understand) is that of a school, with students and classes. Many students, many classes, different students in each class. A real nuisance to model in a data structure, and not well-suited to an Access form at all.

The manmade world is usually a little less convoluted, perhaps because many-to-many data structures are hard to model and to automate. Consider the Northwind company's inventory. There are categories, and there are products in those categories. Many categories, many products. But any given product is in one and only one category, so the relationship of any one category to the products in that category is unique. For any given category, you can figure out exactly what products are in it. This is pretty easy to show on an Access report, but it's not so easy to do on a form.

▶ **See** "Using the Group Feature Effectively," **p. 1082**

You could create a query that combines the Categories and Products table and display it on a report as in Figure 36.16 (an AutoReport—Tabular of the query described). It does the job, but it's annoying that the category name has to be repeated on every line. If you want to show added information about the category, in addition to the product information, this form becomes very crowded.

What you need is a way to display the category information once, maybe at the top of the form, and then see a list of all the products in that category below it. You'll need a mechanism to move from category to category, changing the list of products as you go. Such a form exists; look at the Categories form in Northwind (see Figure 36.17).

FIGURE 36.16
A simple report showing the Categories and Products tables joined. Every data field in the Categories table is repeated for every product.

Categories and Products

CategoryName	ProductName	UnitPrice	UnitsInStock
Beverages	Chai	$18	39
Beverages	Chang	$19	17
Beverages	Guaraná Fantástica	$5	20
Beverages	Sasquatch Ale	$14	111
Beverages	Steeleye Stout	$18	20
Beverages	Côte de Blaye	$264	17
Beverages	Chartreuse verte	$18	69
Beverages	Ipoh Coffee	$46	17
Beverages	Laughing Lumberjack Lager	$14	52
Beverages	Outback Lager	$15	15
Beverages	Rhönbräu Klosterbier	$8	125
Beverages	Lakkalikööri	$18	57
Condiments	Aniseed Syrup	$10	13
Condiments	Chef Anton's Cajun Seasoning	$22	53

Record: 1 of 77

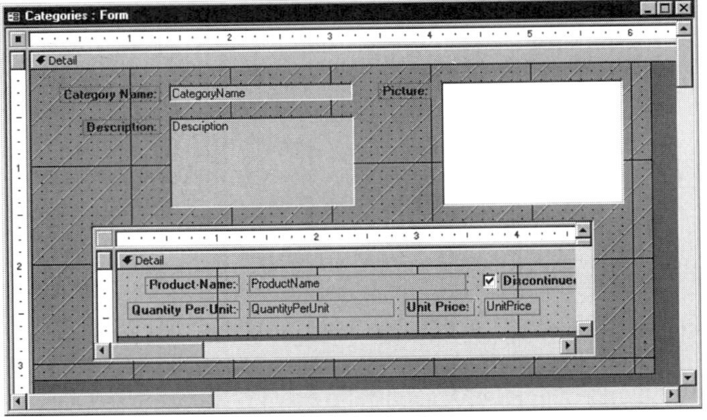

FIGURE 36.17
The Categories form in Northwind, in Design view. The capability to see and modify the design of a subform within its parent is new in Access 2000.

There are two forms here: a parent form (Categories), and a child form (Product List). The child form is what Access calls a *subform*. The record source for the parent is the Categories table, and all the form controls are in the Detail section; this means that Access shows the Detail section once for every record in the Categories table.

If you display the Product List form in Design view, you'll see that it's a simple Detail section-only form displaying all the products. By placing it as an object in the Detail section of the Categories form, you probably expect to see the same data in the Product List subform no matter which category is displayed. But that's not the case, and that feature is what makes subforms useful.

Take a look at the property sheet for the Product List subform (click the border of the subform and select View, Properties; it's shown in Figure 36.18). Forms, when used as subforms, have two additional properties that limit the data visible in the subform: Link Child Fields and Link Master Fields.

In this case, the field CategoryID is listed in both places, and the field CategoryID is carried in the underlying data sources for both forms. Access automatically realizes that these fields have the same name and data type and it creates a dynamic link between the two forms based on that field. As the CategoryID changes in the parent (Master) form, it's synchronized in the child so that only records with that CategoryID are displayed. This ensures that only the products for the currently selected category are shown.

As an exercise, try clearing the linked field properties in the Product List subform. The form works as before, except that all products are displayed for every category, which is exactly what you should expect.

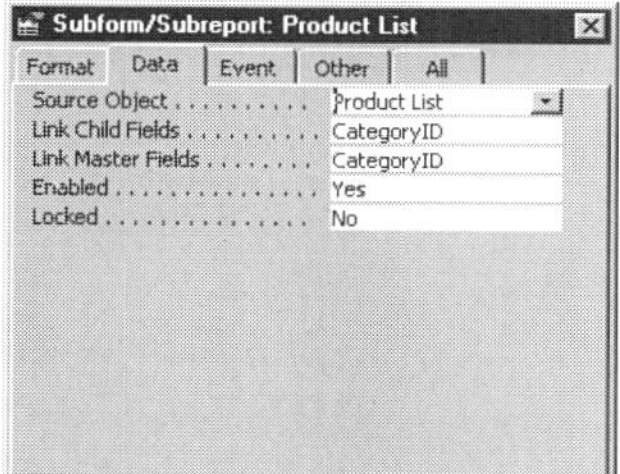

FIGURE 36.18
The Property Sheet for the Product List subform shows the Link Child and Link Master fields, which limit the records displayed in the subform.

In order for this technique to work, you must ensure that there is a field (or fields) that the data sources for the two (or more) forms have in common, and that field must be entered in the Linked properties. If more than one field should be linked, separate them by a comma in the property sheet, and make sure they're in the same order in both properties. If the relationship between the two forms is obvious (as when their data sources have a relationship already established), Access fills in these properties for you. This can sometimes be a hindrance if the form/subform behavior is not what you're looking for.

When creating this kind of form from scratch, you have to create the form and subform separately, and then merge them together. You'll notice that the subform in the previous example, Product List, is a form in its own right. Also, forms and reports are so closely related that you can embed a report in a form and vice versa; Access converts the behavior of the embedded object as necessary on-the-fly. This can be convenient when you have a perfectly formatted report that would be nice to use as a subform.

Some very creative programming can be done with subforms, such as changing the embedded subform based on a selection made in the parent or causing one subform to change based on a selection in another subform. Northwind includes an example of this kind of behavior in the form Customer Orders (see Figure 36.19).

Here, the parent form is based on the Customers table, and the two subforms (Customer Orders Subform1 and Customer Orders Subform2) are based on the Orders and Order Details Extended queries. Changing the Customer record forces a change in Customer Orders Subform1 because the CustomerID field links them. The magic occurs because Customer Orders Subform2 is linked to the currently selected order number in Customer Orders

Subform1, not the parent form. When the current order number changes in Customer Orders Subform1 (as happens when the customer is changed in the parent or when the user clicks on an order), the link causes the Customer Orders Subform2 to show a different list of products.

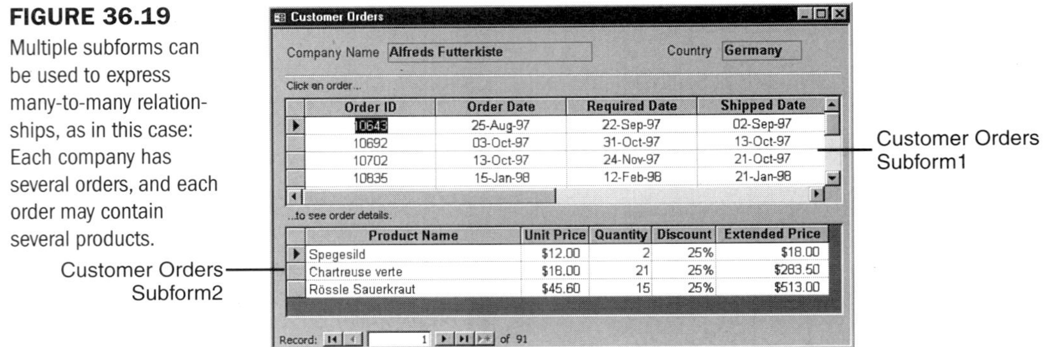

FIGURE 36.19
Multiple subforms can be used to express many-to-many relationships, as in this case: Each company has several orders, and each order may contain several products.

NOTE There's one more trick here, and it's so poorly coded in Northwind that it's hard to figure out. The `On Current` property of Customer Orders Subform1 forces a requery of Customer Orders Subform2 after the link element is changed. This is necessary because the modification of a linked element forces a reevaluation of the data in the subform only in a parent-child relationship, not a child-child relationship.

Few programmers would realize this when designing a form such as this, but experience teaches that a requery is sometimes necessary to remind Access to recalculate which records should be displayed when it seems recalcitrant.

Forms in Applications

When creating an application in Access, you should carefully consider the flow of information throughout. Some of the issues you should consider include

- What should users see when they start the application?
- How can you minimize the number of clicks they need to perform to get where they want to go?
- Can you arrange your forms so that the most-needed information is immediately visible and draws the eye?
- What happens if someone enters invalid data, and can you minimize the number of places where that's possible?

There are dozens more considerations, of course, but many well-intentioned applications don't even go this far, creating consternation among users and a maintenance disaster.

Startup Options

When a user double-clicks your application file in Windows Explorer, Access starts and loads your database. Unless you take certain precautions, however, that user is dumped into the Database Window and needs to figure out what to do next.

There are a couple of options for controlling the execution of the application at startup. An antiquated method is via the use of an Autoexec macro. If a macro with the name Autoexec exists in a database, Access runs it as soon as the database is loaded. In Access 2.0 and earlier, this was the only way to control the flow of the program at startup. Since Access 95, however, Access has provided a Startup options dialog box (click Tools, Startup) as shown in Figure 36.20.

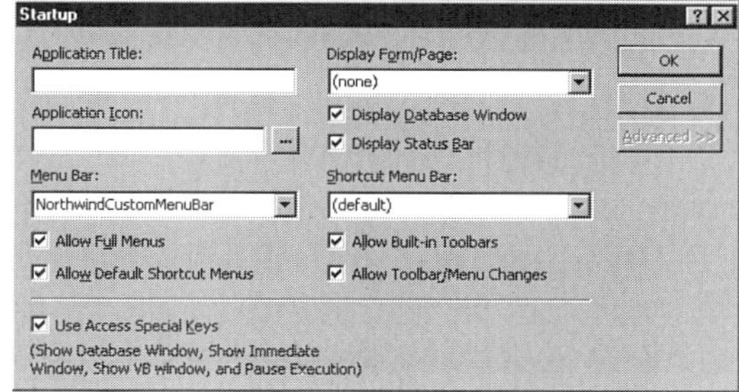

FIGURE 36.20
The Startup Options dialog box permits customization of the Access environment for standalone applications.

The most important element in this dialog box is the Display Form/Page combo box, which allows selection of any form in the database to pop up when the application is started. The Display Database Window check box runs a close second; disabling it hides the Database Window, effectively removing a user's ability to see database objects except as they're presented through your navigation system. Finally, consider building your own command bar for your application and unchecking the Allow Built-In Toolbars option; this makes it hard for users to get to the Design view for any of your database objects.

Holding down the Shift key while starting your application bypasses the startup options (and Autoexec macro, if any).

Creating Effective Navigation

Earlier versions of Access included a feature called the Switchboard Wizard. This wizard created a hierarchical series of forms containing command buttons that eventually opened the form the user was looking for in the first place. The Main Switchboard form in Access 2000's Northwind is a remnant of that feature, streamlined and simplified.

A switchboard was good navigation design when it was the only way available to perform form-to-form navigation. In recent versions of Access, however, there are too many other good ways to manage the flow of information through forms to rely on switchboard-like mechanisms. As a rule of thumb, you should strive to require no more than two mouse clicks to get from any form to any other form. The difficulty is in making that goal work.

There are three relatively straightforward ways to facilitate navigation through a series of forms:

- Command buttons on forms
- Command bar elements
- Tabs

As an example, you can see each of these mechanisms applied to the Northwind database to show their values relative to one another. First, look at the Main Switchboard in Northwind in Figure 36.21. The four grouped buttons go directly to forms; one (Print Sales Reports) opens up another form for report selection, and the last two take care of system operations. In no case does it take more than two clicks to reach any form or report, and the display is uncluttered. However, there are several forms in the database that are completely inaccessible from this interface (Employees, Customer Orders, and so on). This approach is well-suited to an application with only four forms, but it rapidly gets unwieldy as the number of forms increases.

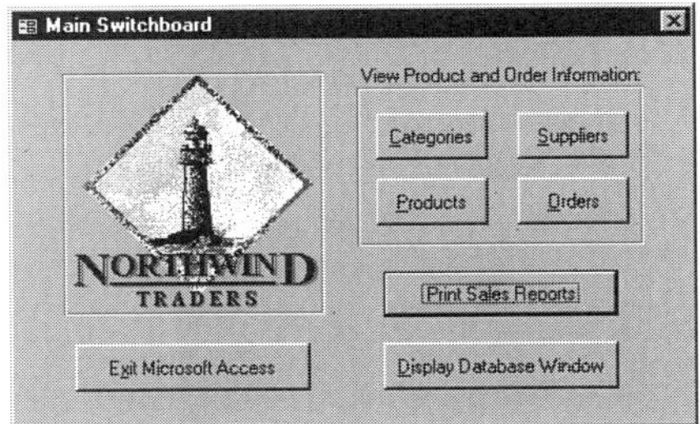

FIGURE 36.21
Northwind's Main Switchboard looks great, but it doesn't get you to every form in the database.

Creating a new command bar for Northwind that includes every form and report, hierarchically arranged, takes about five minutes. By including the File and Help menus, the developer can disable the built-in command bars completely, minimizing any chance of damage to the forms and reports themselves. A simple example is shown in Figure 36.22; this command bar includes every report and form in the database.

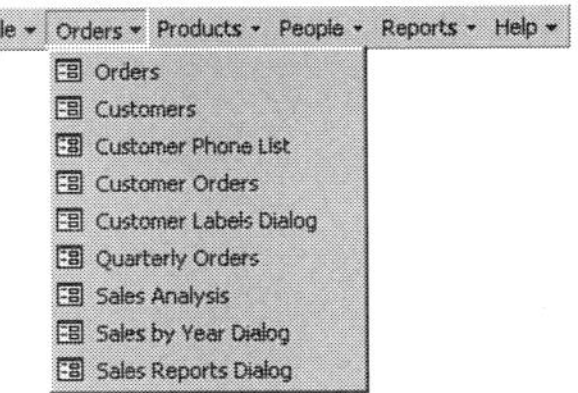

FIGURE 36.22
A command bar for Northwind gives quick and easy access to every object in the database.

The problem with using a command bar for navigation is that it doesn't enforce any order in the process. Users can flit from one form to any other; this can be good or bad. If you need to recommend an order of operations without making it mandatory, consider using the tab control with the forms appended to the tab pages in order (see Figure 36.23). Users tend to work from left to right across the tabs, especially if you number them that way.

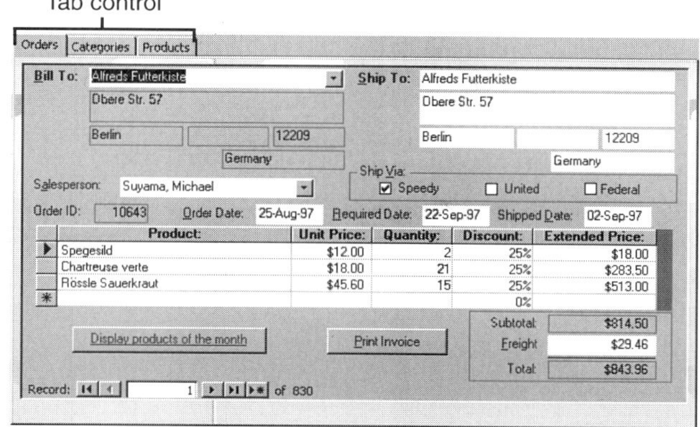

FIGURE 36.23
The tab control is useful for grouping related forms together and making them instantly available without wasting screen space.

Form Design and AutoFormat

There's nothing more important to the user experience than to enforce some kind of consistent formatting on your application. An application that looks like a hodgepodge of different styles, shapes, and colors is distracting and tiring. Few people would consider Windows a work of interface design excellence, but consider how consistent it is: The menus are standardized, with File and Edit always on the left and Help on the right; the color scheme is maintained from dialog window to dialog window; text boxes and lines are the same size and in the same position wherever possible.

Now consider Northwind: a hodgepodge of differing styles and formats, with absolutely nothing in common (see Figure 36.24). Northwind is supposed to be a sample database, so some diversity can be explained away as demonstration, but don't make the mistake of thinking you should design a production system this way.

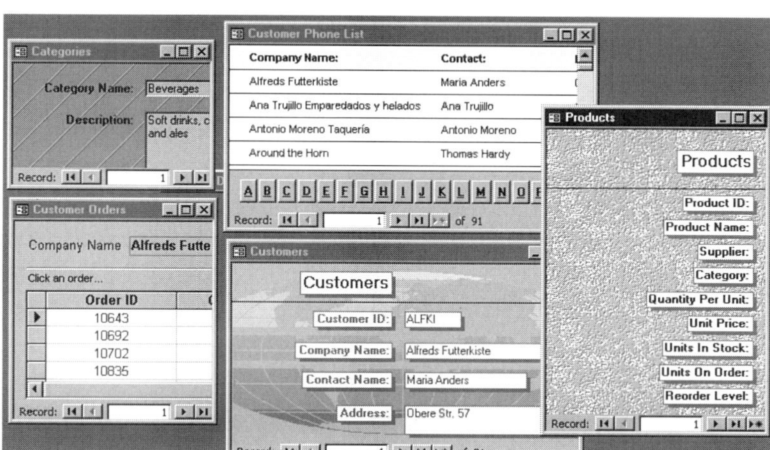

FIGURE 36.24
Several forms from the Northwind database, with all different backgrounds, navigation methods, and typefaces.

You can save yourself a lot of heartache by designating standard typefaces and page layouts at the beginning of a project for all programmers to follow. However, don't forget Access' AutoFormat tool (from Form Design view, choose Format, AutoFormat), which permits you to define some of the more visible elements of a form's style and then apply them to any and all forms in the database. This won't solve navigation and layout problems, but it makes things look consistent and may be good enough in a small system.

Problem/Solution—Customizing Forms

The holiday season around the Northwind plant has been pleasant, and the boss has a new toy: a digital camera. He really wanted it to take pictures of the grandkids, but needs to come up with a business use to get the tax write-off. So he's decided to add pictures of each product in the line to the company catalog. Problem is, how do you get them into the database?

This is a good opportunity to modify an existing form to do more. You already have the Products form, which lists product details and permits changing them. Maybe it can be modified to include a picture.

The first thing to decide is whether the pictures are to be stored in the database or on the file system. Depending on the camera software, it may be easier to go either way, but working from the file system is a slightly more generalized way of getting the image into the database, so let's try to do it that way.

Some parts of this problem are easy to solve:

1. Add a picture field to the Products table. From the Database Window, switch to Table view, select Products, and click Design. Add a field called Picture, using the OLE Object type, and save the table design.
2. Add a bound object control to the Detail section of the Products form (switch to Form view, select Products, and click Design). Widen the form by dragging the right edge out a couple of inches. Select the Bound Object Control in the toolbox and click the form in the empty space you just created. Open the Property Sheet for the new control if it's not already open (View, Properties). Name it Picture, change the Control Source to the new field Picture, and change the Size Mode property to Zoom to maintain the image's proportions.

This causes any image in the database to be displayed on the form. Using the camera's own software and/or Microsoft PhotoDraw (included with Office 2000 Premium), you can save the images from the camera onto the file system in a convenient directory. Now you have to provide a way to get the image from the file and into the form.

One way to accomplish this is to provide a field for users to enter the filename; when they press a command button, you assign that file to the bound object control via its Source Document property and save the record. Add a text box and appropriate label to the form by selecting them in the toolbox and clicking in the form where they belong. When on the form, change the name of the text box to PictureFile in its Property Sheet. Make sure the Command Wizards are turned off and add a command button to the form; caption it Get Picture.

If you run the form as is, you will see that the text box allows typing, and the button presses, but nothing happens. You need some code behind the button. In Design view, select the new command button, open its Property Sheet if not already open, and click in the `On Click` event box. Select the Builder button at the right edge of the box and choose Code Builder when prompted. The VBA Editor opens, and you can paste the code in Listing 36.2 into the new module window:

Listing 36.2 ***Sub GetPictureButton_Click()***

```
With Me!Picture
     .SourceDoc = Me!PictureFile
     .Action = acOLECreateLink
End With
Me!PictureFile = ""
```

Lines 1 and 4 provide a kind of shorthand; they mean that every line between them can be assumed to have to do with the object Me!Picture, which is the bound object frame you created. The term Me! refers to the current form, and is shorthand for Forms!Products in this case. Line 2 sets the source for the object to the value of the text box PictureFile, line 3 creates a live link to the image file (which is fine as long as you don't intend to delete the file; otherwise, use the constant `acOLECreateFromFile`), and line 5 clears the typed text from the box—ready for the next entry.

Save the class module you just created (when prompted, select a name) and exit the VBA Editor. Switch to Form view and enter the name of a file, press the button, and (assuming the file is in a format the control can parse, such as BMP or GIF) watch it appear in the bound object frame as in Figure 36.25.

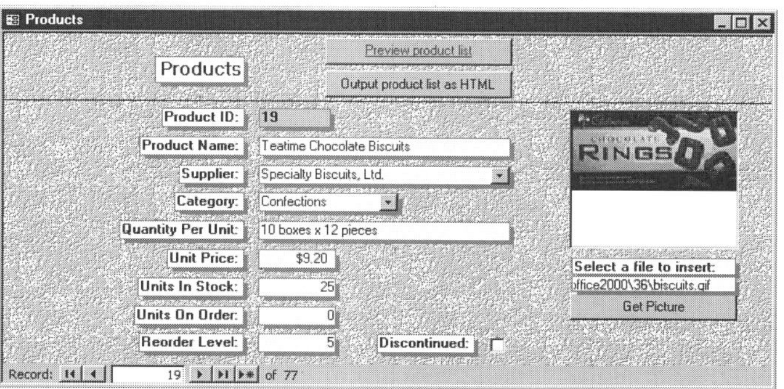

FIGURE 36.25
The Products form modified to include a picture.

This method is easy and works great as long as the name is typed correctly. But what if the name is unknown or likely to be misspelled? Try it—it creates a runtime error and your code halts. You could (and should) build in error-checking to inform the user that the name typed is invalid. If you have the Office 2000 Developer Edition, you can use the common dialog control in it to display a file-selection box and pass the filename back to a procedure that uses the same techniques as in the preceding paragraph. This eliminates any possibility that the filename could be mistyped.

CHAPTER 37

Advanced Reports

In this chapter

Reports Versus Forms

Access reports provide a means for printing information retrieved from the database. With a few exceptions, their use should be limited to paper. For onscreen display, *forms* are much more capable and flexible. *Reports* are like forms in that they retrieve data from a data source and display it (prior to printing); they differ in that they don't permit modification of the data in the database. In fact, forms and reports are so similar that converting from one to the other is trivial; for a report that lets you change data, simply create the report and save it as a form.

In practice, however, most developers use forms and reports very differently. Forms are typically used to provide a means to input or edit data, with a few exceptions for forms optimized for analyzing data. Reports are collections of data, meant to be examined by a user as a whole. Consider this—it's not at all unusual to create a form that displays only one record at a time. But a report that shows only one record is a waste of paper.

We expect reports to contain certain elements that forms don't need, such as pagination, page and column headers, and totals. A well-designed report is useful both as a means to inspect a single record in a sea of others, but also as a tool to see the flow and trend of data as a whole. A good report design takes into account the display of data such that it's equally effective showing a few records as it is showing hundreds. Good luck doing that with a form.

This chapter assumes that you know how to create basic reports, using Design view and the Report Wizards. You should be familiar with the mechanics of adding and deleting controls, and most of their functions. Reports allow quite a bit of flexibility as to their data sources and you should be comfortable with multiple-table queries and table relationships as well.

▶ **See** "Advanced Queries," **p. 1017**

▶ **See** "Advanced Forms," **p. 1043**

Creating Multiple-Table Reports

If the data that you want to report on is in more than one data source, you have the following two options:

- Create a single query that combines the disparate data sources (tables or queries) and use it as a single data source for your report. The query can be saved (as a query), or the query itself (in SQL) can be entered as the record source property of the report.
- Create subreports for each data source and place them on a single, omnibus report.

NOTE For clarity, we'll use the term *table* wherever possible from here on to represent *data sources*; you should understand that data sources could be tables or queries.

Which option you choose depends on the data you're trying to present. If the data is easily considered as a cohesive whole, or if data in one table needs to be compared with data in one or more of the other tables, you should create a single query joining the tables. Queries are well suited to managing the relationships between tables, when there's something to relate.

On the other hand, if there's no relationship between the data at all, you may be better off creating subreports. That way, you can get data from several wholly unrelated subjects (such as employees and products, or orders and product categories) onto one report.

Creating and Using Subreports

When one report is placed in the Detail Area of another report it becomes a *subreport*. The report that contains the subreport is called the *main report*. When you use subreports, you're creating a bound control in the main report; the control designates the subreport. Access enables you to specify linked fields that control the display of data in the subreport. The data on the subreport is filtered depending on what's being displayed (printed) on the main report it's contained in.

The subreport is repeated once for every record in the main report's data source. Because you probably don't want the same exact data repeated in the subreport for every record in the main report, you use these linked fields to specify how the data in the subreport should be limited.

The process of actually creating a subreport is quite simple:

1. Create a report in Design view or by using the Report Wizard. Keep in mind as you create it that it will eventually be embedded in another report, so you don't need to worry about page numbering or too much header and footer information. Save this report (File, Save).
2. Create a main report, remembering that you intend to insert a subreport into it. Leave some room in the Detail section of the main report about the size of the subreport to be inserted.
3. While the new main report is open in Design view, arrange the windows so you can see both the Database Window and the design canvas for the main report. Drag the subreport from the Database Window to approximately the place in the main report where it should appear (you can resize and move it later). The subreport appears in Design view at the point where you drop it.

As an example, consider the Catalog report in the Northwind database, part of which is shown in Design view in Figure 37.1 and in Print Preview in Figure 37.2. It makes good use of several design elements:

- A Report Header with embedded page breaks.
- A header and footer for the major sorting field, Category Name.
- A Page Footer with a footer title and page number.
- A Report Footer containing additional information.

NOTE Even though the example here uses two data sources that are related, and could be assembled using a single query, and thus without subreports, the real power of the subreports feature is the ability to show more than one type of data on a single report as mentioned earlier.

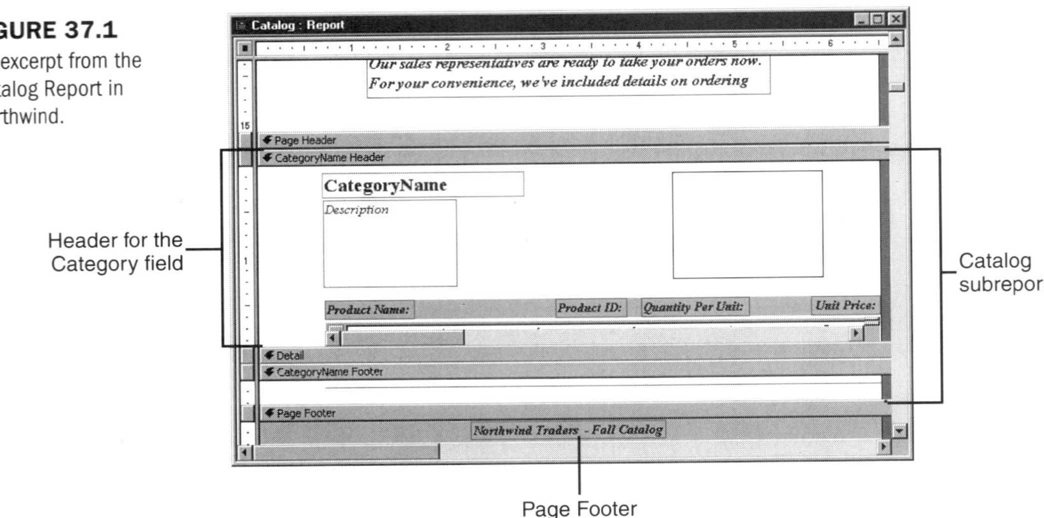

FIGURE 37.1
An excerpt from the Catalog Report in Northwind.

The detail section in Figure 37.1 is minimized because the record source for the report (Categories) is also set up as a group (View, Sorting and Grouping), giving it a Page Header and Page Footer section of its own.

▶ **See** "Using the Group Feature Effectively," **p. 1082**

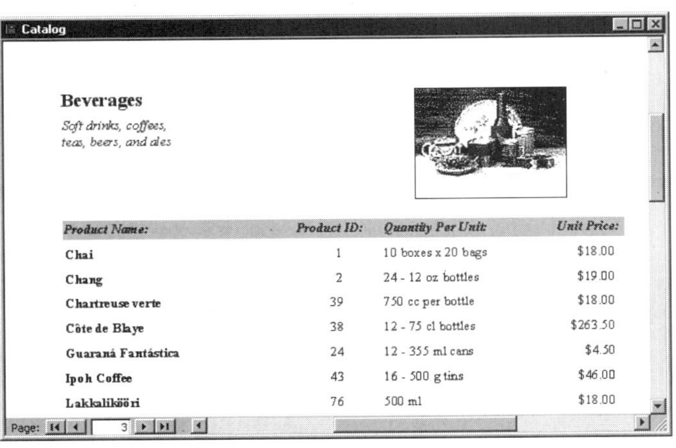

FIGURE 37.2
The same Catalog Report shown in Figure 37.1, in Print Preview. The subreport is indistinguishable from the main report, except that it contains data from a different source.

There's a lot to learn from this report, but the key feature is the inclusion of a subreport in the middle of the CategoryName Header section. This detail report, containing product-specific information from the Product table, is embedded in this section so that the one-to-many relationship between Categories and Products can be exploited. For every CategoryID in the Categories table, there can be any number of records in the Products table, which includes a CategoryID field.

The behind-the-scenes details that make this work are the establishment of CategoryName as a group with a header section and the linking of the CategoryID field in Categories (on the main form) to the CategoryID field in Products (on the subform). The first of these is done in the Sorting and Grouping dialog box (see Figure 37.3); the second in the Group Properties dialog box for the subform.

FIGURE 37.3
The Sorting and Grouping dialog box.

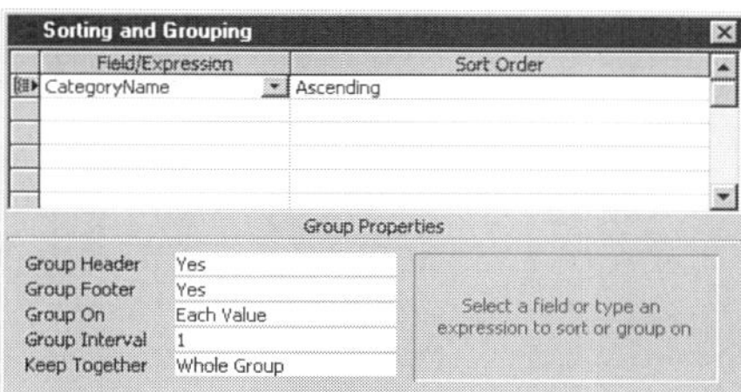

The appearance of this report, if these options were not set as shown, is worth considering. The Category Name group ensures that the categories are presented alphabetically. In this example, they're stored that way in the table, so removing the group and moving all the controls in the CategoryName Header to the Detail section works fine.

Eliminating the linked fields, however, is disastrous, because doing so causes the entire contents of the Products table to be displayed on every category page.

Creating Custom Mailing Labels

The Label Wizard provides a quick and easy way to create a report formatted as mailing labels. It automates the tedious task of figuring out label sizes and margins, formatting the data on the label, figuring out how to print the correct number of labels across the page (Access reports typically print down, not across), and dealing with page breaks.

To use it, select New, Label Wizard from the Database Window toolbar in Report View. After selecting a data source (the Customers table in Northwind is a good example) and clicking OK, you're escorted through several self-explanatory dialog boxes, prompting you for the label size, font, label fields, and so on. Saving the report this generates is a good idea, so that you can easily modify it later without going back through the Wizard.

NOTE Most label manufacturers include an Avery-equivalent label number on the box, simplifying this process considerably, but Access 2000 now includes information for several manufacturers' labels.

One feature in the Label Wizard is worth mentioning specifically because you may not stumble upon it naturally: the process used to create new label templates, which is invaluable for creating custom labels for gifts, nametags, and so on.

From the first screen of the Wizard, click Customize, New. The fantastic New Label dialog box appears, allowing you to specify every dimension of the label down to hundredths of a centimeter, and including the option to specify the number of labels across the page. Best of all, your custom settings are saved for future use.

This report works because of the well-hidden Columns property dialog box for the printed page (select File, Page Setup, Columns and you'll see the dialog box shown in Figure 37.4). On this property sheet, you can choose the number of columns your report should print, and the spacing between iterations of the report. Obviously, the sum of the column width and column spacing times the number of columns specified shouldn't exceed the distance between the margins, and you should perform the same analysis on the height. There are no special formatting or controls needed in the report to print in columns; this feature simply enables you to print the pages of your report across as well as down.

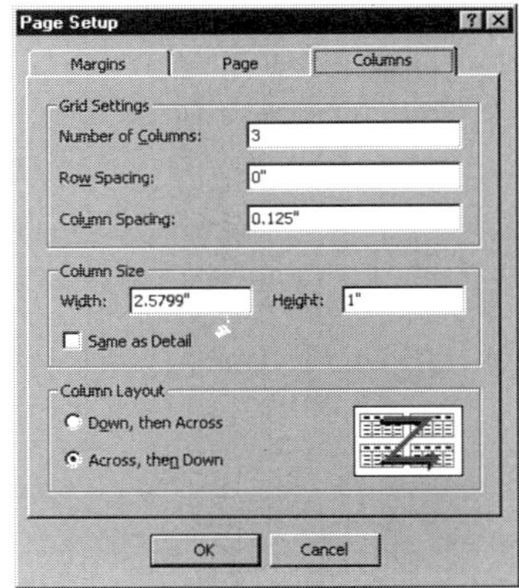

FIGURE 37.4
The row and column spacing displayed here refers to the spacing between iterations of your report across and down the paper, not within the report.

NOTE Using columns in a subreport while the main report prints one column across won't work—the page setup settings apply to the entire report. So you can't have part of your report printing in two-column format and another part printing in one-column format.

Customizing Reports

Before you start tinkering with reports, you should get comfortable with the automatic reports Access can create. Although they're not fancy, the various report wizards create passable reports that are relatively easy to customize, and (most importantly) take care of the drudge work of lining up columns, inserting graphic lines where appropriate, choosing reasonable typefaces, and so on. When and if you set out to create a brand-new report from scratch, ask yourself whether there's an automatic report (or an existing report in one of the sample databases) that you can modify faster than you can write a new one yourself.

Although Access 97 came with only two sample databases (and only one installed by default), Access 2000 ships with four (not counting the SQL sample database): Northwind, a household inventory application, a contact manager, and an address book. These are full of good examples and ideas and the effort saved by familiarity with the techniques they illustrate is worth the time that it takes to explore them.

That said, when you do start customizing and creating complex reports, remember to periodically test your report with a full range of production data. A report that looks good with sample data may not work at all with production data. For instance, you may find that your totals in production become six digits and your report format allows for only five-digit totals. It is also a good idea to frequently save backup copies (more than one) of your reports as you go along.

Manipulating the Appearance of a Report

When you create a new report in Design view, Access automatically creates the report with three sections: Page Header, Page Footer, and Detail. The Page Header and Footer appear only once per printed page, and the entire Detail section is repeated for every record in the report's data source. You can turn the headers and footers off by clicking View, Page Header/Footer.

You can add several other sections to a report. These include the following:

- A *Report* Header and Footer, which become visible when you select View, Report Header/Footer. These sections are printed only once per report, at the beginning and end. You might include a Report Header to create a cover sheet for the entire report.

- Group Headers and/or Footers for every field in the underlying data source that you choose to sort on. These are enabled by selecting View, Sorting and Grouping, selecting a field to use as a sort break, and changing the Group Header and/or Footer options to Yes. These sections appear every time the value in the field chosen changes (in special cases, see "Using the Group Feature Effectively" later in this chapter).

Office 2000's personalized toolbars don't always show all the options available to you when you first click them. Some lesser-used options are hidden unless you wait a few seconds, click the double-down arrow at the bottom of each menu, or double-click the menu (View). An example of this is the Header/Footer options in the View menu, which do not appear by default. If you use either of the commands once, however, they become part of the personalized menu (until you don't use them again for a long time, which causes them to become hidden again). Of course, you can disable personalized toolbars if you prefer. See Chapter 4 for more details.

You can create up to ten grouping sections as necessary, but more than two makes for a very cluttered report. The sections can be resized by dragging their title bars up and down as necessary; you can't resize a section smaller than is necessary to accommodate the controls included in it. Dragging a section until its title bar touches the next section's title bar makes it invisible without disabling it (useful for times when you want a group footer but not a group header, and so on).

To make the report look like something other than a blank page, you add *controls* to it. Each object on a report is a control. Controls display data (labels, text boxes), perform actions (command buttons, hyperlinks), or are used for decoration (logos, lines, rectangles). You can choose controls from the Toolbox by clicking once on the control you need and then clicking in the report designer where you want it to go. The Toolbox appears in a window of its own by default. Drag it to any side of the Access window to dock it there and get it out of the way.

Seventeen controls are available in the default Toolbox, and their functions are well described in Access Help.

NOTE If you'd like a more detailed description of the controls available in the default Toolbox, see *Special Edition Using Microsoft Access 2000*, also published by Que.

Two of the buttons in the Toolbox are not controls at all:

- The Select Objects icon is pressed when you can use the mouse cursor to select controls in the report designer, and pops up when you have another control selected for insertion.

- The Control Wizards button is pressed when Control Wizards are enabled, and pops up when you press it to turn Control Wizards off. Controls Wizards assist with the setting of properties for the more complicated controls, especially the Combo Box and Command Button controls.

Don't forget that you have a whole myriad of other controls available to you by selecting the More Controls button in the Toolbox. Most of these are more appropriate for forms than reports, and many can't be used in Access at all (such as controls added to the list by other commercial applications for that application's use only), but there may be a winner or two in there. Several more controls are available in the Insert menu; see the Chart object in Northwind's Sales by Category report for an example.

The Toolbox is just another toolbar. You can add buttons to it by right-clicking anywhere in it, choosing Customize, and dragging any of the command icons in the Customize dialog box onto the Toolbox in the position you want it. Similarly, you can delete buttons from it by selecting Customize as previously and dragging any of the buttons out of the Toolbox and into oblivion. (Don't worry—you can always get them back, as they're always available from the Customize dialog box.)

Getting controls to line up on a form can be a trial. You have several tools available to you:

- The grid can be viewed, snapped to, or both. It appears as a pattern of dots on the background of the form, which you can use visually to line up objects and forms. The grid can be made visible or invisible by toggling View, Grid. This tool is much more useful when used in conjunction with its Snap property (Format, Snap to Grid). This forces objects to be placed on a grid boundary, causing the top-left corner of the object to land on a grid intersection. You can usually eyeball controls to the same vertical or horizontal grid position when Snap To is on. You can temporarily disable Snap to Grid by holding down the Ctrl button while dragging a control.

Turning Snap To on also constrains the sizes of controls to the grid. If that causes problems (that is you're forced to make a control an inconvenient size), you can either change the grid spacing (see the following Tip), turn off Snap To, or hold down the Ctrl key long enough to resize the control appropriately.

- The alignment of controls can be adjusted by selecting more than one control and choosing the appropriate alignment option from the Format, Align menu. You can select multiple controls simultaneously in several ways: by holding down the Shift key while you click the controls, by dragging a marquee box around them (start the box outside of any control boundaries), or by dragging on the horizontal or vertical ruler to select all controls within that ruler position range.

- The spacing of controls can be adjusted with the Format, Spacing menu. However, use this command carefully because altering the spacing of overlapping controls (which may be intentionally overlapped) causes them to be placed side by side.
- You can group controls that are correctly placed relative to one another by selecting all of them and clicking Format, Group. They then move as if they're one object. To select a group for moving, you have to click within the boundaries of one of the controls in that group. You can still edit the properties of any control in the group by right-clicking it. You can group groups together, but ungrouping the grouped groups ungroups all its component groups as well. Some changes you make to objects within a group, such as changing the type of a control in a group, will cause the affected control (only) to become ungrouped.
- The rulers at the top and left side of the report design window show the maximum extent of the currently selected control, while the mouse button is pressed, relative to the current report section (see Figure 37.5). If you select multiple controls and hold down the button, the area shown represents the full left-to-right and top-to-bottom extent of the combined controls. This isn't the best way to align and space controls relative to one another, but it's invaluable when the precise layout of controls relative to the paper is critical, as on a paper form.

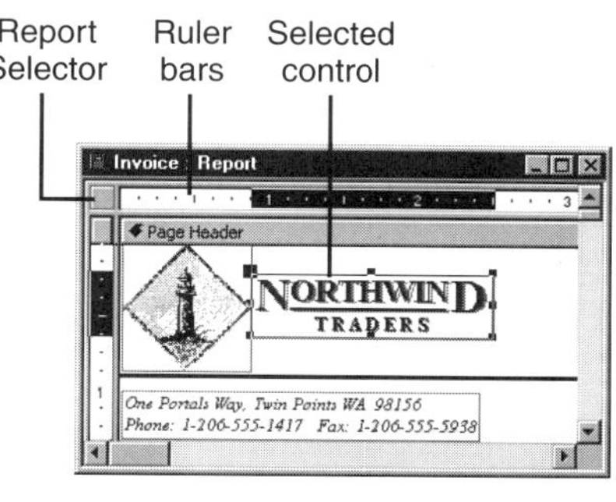

FIGURE 37.5
The dark bars in the ruler areas denote the extent of the control selected as long as the left mouse button is pressed. You can show/turn off the Rulers by clicking View, Ruler.

Change the spacing of the grid lines (dots) by changing the GridX and GridY properties of the report itself. Smaller numbers cause more dots per unit of measure, and therefore align elements closer together. You can view the report's properties by clicking Edit, Select Report and then View, Properties, or by double-clicking in the Form and Report Selector box at the top-left corner of the report design window.

Using Conditional Formatting in a Report

Understanding the data types and values to be included in a report can help you make decisions as to how to design the report itself. For example, if a data element is sometimes null, you may want to prevent a header and/or footer section of a report from printing. If a financial figure is outside some acceptable range, you may want to make it more apparent, perhaps by printing it in bold, red print or by adding a flag somewhere on the page. You'll use Visual Basic for Applications (VBA) to make the controls change their appearance based on the data.

▶ **See** "Using Macros and VBA in Access," **p. 1139**

VBA procedures are executed in response to *events*, which are defined by Access and typically include a database object's opening, closing, being clicked in or moved, and so on. All objects of the same type have the same events, and different object types have different events. For example, a report has an On No Data event, which is triggered when the report is executed and the underlying data source returns no records. You can see that it may be preferable to attach a procedure to the On No Data event of a report to inform the user that no records have been returned, rather than printing a blank report.

In reports (unlike forms), the controls (including subreports) on the form have no events of their own. Instead, events are assigned to each report section, and to the report as a whole. To execute code that affects the entire report or whole sections, you'll usually attach it to one of the report's events; for code that affects one control or a set of controls in a single section, use that section's events.

Access reports and sections include the events shown in Tables 37.1 and 37.2; most are self-explanatory, but are discussed in detail in Access help:

Table 37.1 Report Events

Object	Event Description
On Open	Triggers just before opening
On Close	Triggers just before closing
On Activate	Triggers after opening
On Deactivate	Triggers before On Close
On No Data	Triggers when data source is empty
On Page	Triggers before each page prints
On Error	Triggers when a runtime error occurs

Table 37.2 Report Section Events

Object	Event Description
On Format	Triggers before a section is formatted
On Print	Triggers when a section is printed or previewed
On Retreat	Triggers when the report processor has to back up during printing to recalculate position or size

The Employee Sales by Country report has three groups set up (select View, Sorting and Grouping while the report is open in Design view), two with headers; note that the second group is an expression ([LastName] & ", " & [FirstName]) rather than a simple field value. In the expression group, a label control and a line control are found—the label exclaiming Exceeded Goal! is in bright red. It should be clear that there's not much sense in putting a statement such as that on a report unless it's true in every detail record, and if that's the case, why repeat it on every salesperson's page?

The key is to change the Visible property of both of these controls based on the value of some field in the data source. In this case, the report makes the controls visible only if the employee's total sales ([Salesperson Total]) are greater than 5,000. The evaluation is performed by code bound to the On Format property of the group header itself, causing it to be executed before that section is formatted for every record in the data source. You can quickly verify that the group header has code behind it by selecting it (click the horizontal Heading bar above the design section for that group) and clicking View, Properties. It's easy to overlook VBA modules (called *class modules*) hidden behind structural objects such as report sections and the report itself, but using code in this way is critical to precise operation of a report in response to the data displayed in it.

The procedure itself is pretty straightforward:

```
Private Sub GroupHeader2_Format(Cancel As Integer, FormatCount As Integer)
' Display ExceededGoalLabel and SalespersonLine if salesperson's total
' meets criteria.

    If Me!SalespersonTotal > 5000 Then
        Me!ExceededGoalLabel.Visible = True
        Me!SalespersonLine.Visible = True
    Else
        Me!ExceededGoalLabel.Visible = False
        Me!SalespersonLine.Visible = False
    End If


End Sub
```

The code on line 5 refers to the object Me; any object operating on itself (in this case, the report operating on the report) can use the keyword Me in code. An exclamation point separates the parent object (Me) from the child object (the SalespersonTotal) control.

Lines 6 and 7 change the value of the Visible property of the line and label depending on the result of the comparison in line 5. Lines 9-10 act as toggles for the changed controls; if the else clause (lines 8-10) in this code were not there, the controls would stay visible forever after they were made visible the first time.

NOTE The parameters listed on line 1 are specific to the On Format event; most events have parameters that can be used by the programmer or ignored, as they are here. In this case, the value of Cancel is False unless otherwise specified by some other calling program, and Access increments the value of FormatCount once for every time the On Format event occurs for each record in the data source. If a record's header extends across a page break, for example, the On Format event would occur twice for each record and the value of FormatCount would be 2 the second time it was executed.

Enter the name of an event (such as On Format) in Access Help for specific details on that event's parameters.

Using the Group Feature Effectively

On your reports, you may want to provide certain information or summaries only when the values of certain fields in the underlying data source change. This is most easily accomplished through use of group headers and footers. The Sorting and Grouping dialog box (View, Sorting and Grouping) also provides some more esoteric options that can greatly enhance the appearance of your report if used correctly.

Every report can contain Page and Report headers and footers. When first added to a report (through the View menu) both the header and footer are added to the report. If you want only the header and not the footer (or vice versa), drag the vertical height of the section you don't need to 0", making it invisible. The section band is still visible, but will not print.

Placing controls in the report sections makes them appear only once per page (for Page sections) or once per report (for Report sections).

TIP Want to make a header or footer disappear, but it won't let you drag it any smaller? You probably can't see some of the controls in that section. To select them, drag the mouse through the entire range of the vertical ruler for that section. That selects all controls in the section, and you can press Del to delete them, enabling the section to resize smaller.

To create a header and/or footer based on data contained in a field (or calculated from several fields), you need to create a *group section*. With a report open in Design view, click the Sorting and Grouping icon on the Reports toolbar. The Sorting and Grouping dialog box appears, enabling you to choose up to ten fields (or ten expressions), and to specify a sort order for each field. If all you need to do is specify a sort order, it's usually better to do that in the underlying query. But some additional options are available in this dialog box that aren't available in the Query Editor.

Group Header Option Setting this option to Yes (the default is No) creates a header section above the Detail section. Whenever the value of the field placed in this section changes, your report displays the records associated with the value. This is an excellent place for titles that include that field, such as CategoryName in the Products by Category report.

Group Footer Option Like the Group Header, the default for the Group Footer is No. but the Group Footer section is placed below the Detail section. You usually put summaries and column totals in a group footer. Look at the CategoryName Footer in the Products by Category report for an example.

Group On Option The default, Each Value, causes the group section to occur every *n*th time the value changes in that field, where *n* is the value set in the Group Interval field, described as follows. The alternative, Prefix Characters, tells Access that the break occurs when a certain number of characters (counting left to right) change in the entered field. You use this option when you don't want a header/footer to appear after every different value in this field. For example, you might use this option for the printing of a relatively short telephone directory—breaking on every different last name would be useless, but breaking every time the first letter changed would nicely group the A's, the B's, and so on.

Group Interval Option This box contains either (1) the number of different data values to skip before creating another group section, if "Group On" (described previously) is set to "Each Value," or (2) the number of characters to check in each record before deciding whether to create a new group section, if "Group On" is set to "Prefix Characters." The default, 1, forces a break only when the first letter (or number) in the field selected changes ("Prefix Characters") or on every discrete value in the field noted ("Each Value").

Keep Together Option This box controls the pagination of the report. It refers to the entire group for which it's set—the group header and footer (if both are enabled), and the associated detail section. Three options are available:

- None:—Access should make no effort to keep the group together on a page. This is the default.
- Whole Group:—If possible, Access should try to keep the entire group together on one page. If the group is too long for one page, this setting is ignored.
- With First Detail:—Access should try to print the group header and the first record in the detail section together. If either the header or first record is too long to make that happen, this setting is ignored.

You can accomplish the same thing as the Group Interval option by using an expression for your group. For example, to create a report of all Northwind's customers, with a title every time the first letter of the CustomerName field changes, you could create a group on the CustomerName field. Then set the Group On option to Prefix Characters, and set the Group Interval to 1. Or you could just create the group on the expression

```
=Left([CustomerName],1)
```

to accomplish the same thing. Why bother? Because the report design is self-documenting if you do it this way. A person looking at the report design doesn't need to view the Sorting and Grouping dialog box and select that particular group to know how it works–it's clearly visible in the Report Designer.

Adding Title and Summary Pages

When most people create reports in Access, they usually design them such that the data is the central item of the report, the element that draws focus. Consider the example in Figure 37.6:

FIGURE 37.6
A typical Access report, full of useful information, and formatted nicely. The formatting is effective, but unexciting.

Sales by Year

08-Nov-98

1997 Summary

Quarter:	Orders Shipped:	Sales:
1	92	$143,703
2	92	$145,655
3	105	$144,320
4	109	$175,169
Totals:	398	$608,847

1997 Details

Line Number:	Shipped Date:	Order ID:	Sales:
1	01-Jan-97	10392	$1,440
2	02-Jan-97	10397	$717
3	03-Jan-97	10393	$2,557
4	03-Jan-97	10394	$442
5	03-Jan-97	10395	$2,123
6	06-Jan-97	10396	$1,904
7	08-Jan-97	10399	$1,765

For many types of information, such as financial reports and ad hoc reports that summarize data for one-time use, this is fine. But programmers rarely have an eye for graphic design, and Access' report features allow for a lot of eye-catching creativity in reports that often goes unused. For some applications, a little style isn't necessary and draws disdainful sneers, such as being too flashy! But sometimes a little flash makes the difference between ho-hum and wow.

For an excellent example of a well-designed report with a little bit of panache, consider the Catalog report in Northwind (shown in Print Preview in Figures 37.7 and 37.8). Not only does it make good use of full-color graphics, but it also includes some elements that are decidedly unusual in Access reports.

FIGURE 37.7
The first page of the Catalog report in Northwind. The catalog label, *Fall,* is hard-coded, but could certainly be calculated instead so that the report could be easily reused.

A Two-Page Header Section Any header or footer can be as long or as short as you like, and there's no requirement that any data be in any particular section. This example makes good use of the Report Header to print ancillary information before the data starts appearing. The page break is forced by the Page Break control (on the Toolbox toolbar) in the report design. Other excellent design features include the use of two horizontal lines of differing widths to continue the graphic line in the Northwind logo across the page.

FIGURE 37.8
Some of the detail page in the Catalog report. The background shading on the column headers (which are actually in the ColumnName group header) and lines in the footer makes it clear where the data starts and ends.

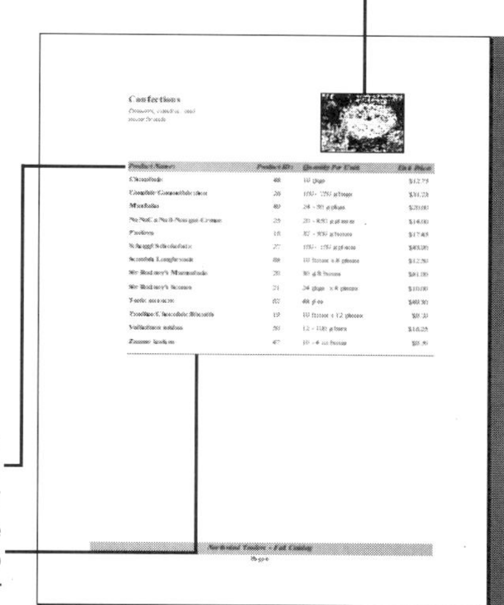

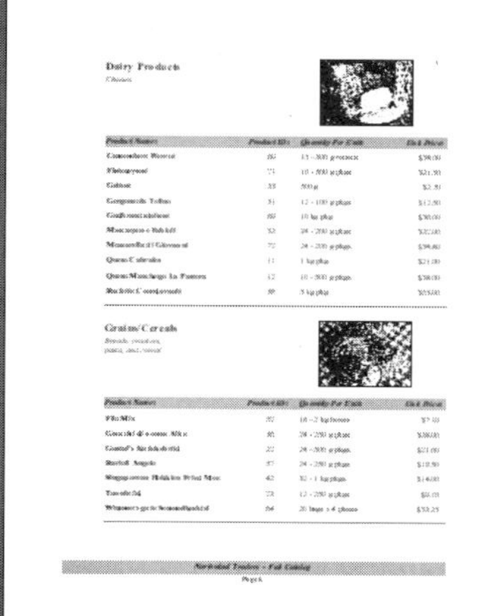

Right-aligned graphic

Background shading in the ColumnName group header

Line in the ColumnName group footer

Off-Center Controls Most custom report designs look like the Access report wizards: left-justified titles, centered data. This design right-justifies the graphic illustrating the food category, which draws the eye across the page.

Use of White Space Even on the pages where two categories appear together, these pages don't look cluttered because plenty of spacing is built into the headers and margins. Many report designs try to fit too much information on a page and end up looking cluttered and are hard to read.

The order form in the Catalog Report gets a page to itself because it is entirely enclosed in the report's Report Footer, and that section's Force New Page property is set to Before Section, which causes a page break before it prints.

TIP Forcing a page break before the report footer causes the report footer to start a new page, and is excellent for keeping totals on one page, or as shown here, for creating standard pages at the end of a report.

Control Borders and Fonts The How to Order paragraph (refer to Figure 37.9) is a single Label control with its Border Style property set to Solid. This makes it stand out a little on the page. The header elements are in a different font (choose the Font pull-down in the Report Formatting toolbar after selecting the control), causing them to jump out a little from the rest of the text.

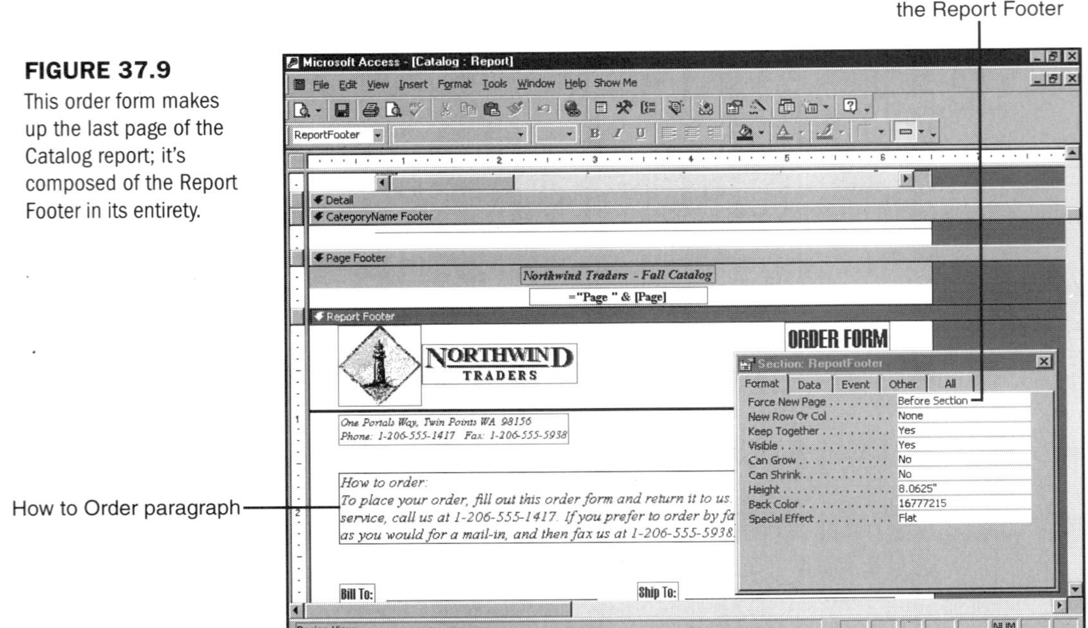

FIGURE 37.9
This order form makes up the last page of the Catalog report; it's composed of the Report Footer in its entirety.

The horizontal and vertical lines are tedious to create, but not too tricky. If you create a line and copy it (Edit, Copy), you can then paste a line of the same dimensions next to it (Edit, Paste). Even better—when you put the pasted line where you want it, clicking Paste again creates a third line spaced proportionately to the way you placed the second one. Every time you paste a new copy of the same object, it is positioned proportionately to the previous paste.

Using Section Properties Report and group headers and footers have several properties that can be manually set to improve their appearance, including some options on whether to force a page break before or after the section (Force New Page), to begin a new row or column in multiple-column reports such as labels (see the section "Creating Mailing Labels" earlier in this chapter for more information on the New Row or Column property), and an option to force Access to keep the header/footer together on one page if possible. The report itself has several special-case formatting options, including one to ensure that the page headers don't print on the Report Header and/or Footer pages.

Figure 37.10 shows a report that exists entirely in the report header, using subreports, images, and labels to keep the reader's eyes moving. There's no reason to use the Detail section, because the main report doesn't need a data source (which means that the Detail Section won't show up at all on the printed report). The design is sufficiently interesting that there's some element of expectation as to what's on the next page. This is certainly more effective than raw data in a table, or even the graphs and text presented vertically as usual. This kind of report is well suited to Access because the designer has pixel-level layout control for each element of the report and because the subreports can be dynamic and data-driven depending on the data in the Access database (without going through the hassle of ODBC).

FIGURE 37.10
A report that makes good use of the Report Header to display data and maintain interest.

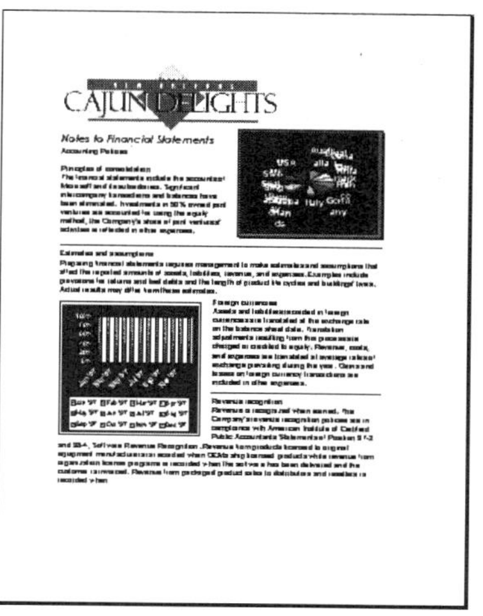

Creating Summary Calculations in Reports

To summarize report data, you can create an aggregate expression in the group footer that acts on all the records in that group or all the records printed so far. This technique enables you to print either totals for any group in the report or running totals for all data displayed.

Summary Calculations in Footers When you create a group footer, you generally do so because you intend to include some kind of summary information in it. This summary information is often a sum or average of numeric data contained in data columns in the Detail section, but can include any information available in the underlying data source.

To create the expressions that summarize data in a footer section, use the standard aggregate expressions and functions available in Access (that is, "Sum([ExtendedPrice])"). Almost every calculated footer includes the `Sum()` function, and many take advantage of the `DCount()` function or calculation of percentages by simple division (as in ([Qty]/[ExtendedPrice]).

You need a text box control in the footer section to display the summary data your expression calculates. To add a calculated control to a footer region, follow these steps:

1. Select the Text Box control from the toolbox. Place the control in the position desired in the footer.
2. Right-click on the new control and select Properties from the drop-down list. In the Name property field, enter a name for the control.
3. In the Control Source property field, enter a summary expression. You can click the Build button to the right of the Control Source property field to use the Expression Builder, if you like, or press Shift+F2 to open the Zoom window for a little more space in typing an expression.

Right-clicking in a property field opens a menu that includes the Expression Builder ("Build") and the Zoom window ("Zoom"), as well as Cut, Copy, and Paste. It may be easier to remember to right-click than to remember the keyboard shortcuts for these commands.

By default, a calculation performed on a detail field in a group footer operates only on those records that have been printed since that group's header was last printed.

▶ **See** "Functions and Expressions," **p. 1005**

An example helps illustrate how to use summary controls. The Employee Sales by Country report in the Northwind database makes use of several layers of summaries in footers. In addition to simple Page and Report footers, there are two footers for the group sections, and every footer except the Page Footer includes at least one summary calculation. The Page Footer is no slouch, either; it includes a calculated expression worth looking at (see Figure 37.11).

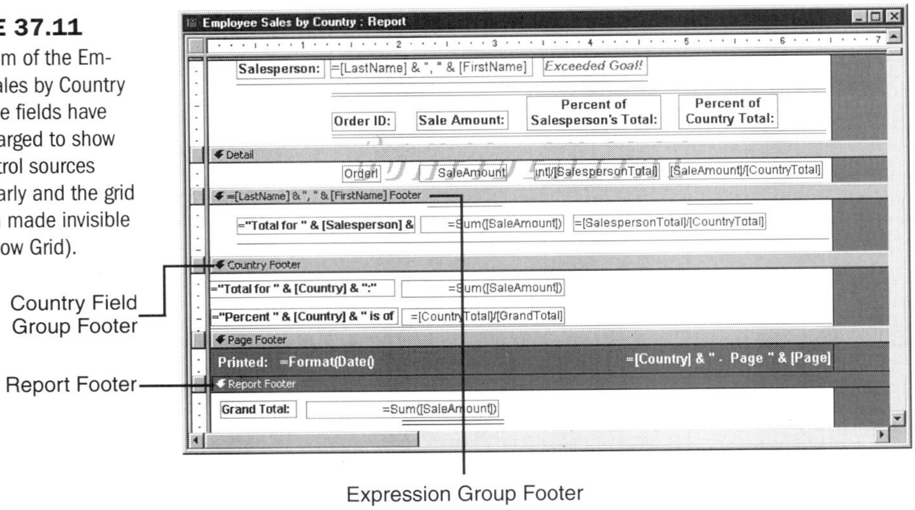

FIGURE 37.11
The bottom of the Employee Sales by Country report. The fields have been enlarged to show their control sources more clearly and the grid has been made invisible (View, Show Grid).

Country Field Group Footer

Report Footer

Expression Group Footer

Take a look at the elegantly named =[LastName] & ", " & [FirstName] Footer. It includes two summary fields: one that sums the values in the field SaleAmount in that group and another that calculates the aggregate percent sales per country for each salesperson. The function in the first field,

```
=Sum([SaleAmount])
```

tells Access to report the sum of the values of SaleAmount in that group. As soon as the group footer is printed, the values that comprise this calculation are reset for the next group. The same holds true for the two calculations in the Country Footer and the single calculation in the Report Footer. The controls in the Country Footer are executed only for each change in the value of the field Country, and the Report Footer is calculated after all records have been processed.

Viewing this report in Print Preview (Figure 37.12) shows the effects of these calculations. Even though the identical expression Sum([SaleAmount]) is used in three different footers, the value it calculates is different in every case because the range over which it operates is different. Each iteration of that calculation applies only to the group in whose footer it is placed.

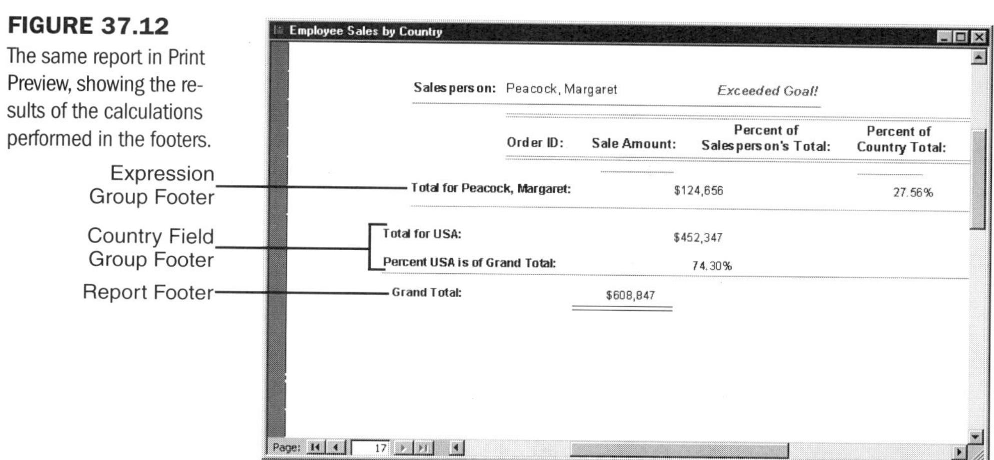

FIGURE 37.12
The same report in Print Preview, showing the results of the calculations performed in the footers.

Part V Ch 37

For this figure, the Force New Page property of the Country Footer was changed from After Section to None, so the results of all three footers with summaries could be seen on the same page.

NOTE It's important to realize that Access actually makes at least two passes through a report to correctly calculate the values included on it. In the previous example, each of the detail records includes a calculated field at the end of each row:

```
=[SaleAmount]/[CountryTotal]
```

The field [CountryTotal] doesn't appear anywhere in the database. It's actually calculated on this report in the Country Footer section as =Sum([SaleAmount]). The only way Access can know how to calculate this expression is to first process the group footer (to find the values of [CountryTotal]) and then to go back and process each of the detail sections. Realizing this allows you to create expressions that depend on the values of other expressions (perhaps later) in your report.

Summary Calculations Elsewhere Summary calculations aren't limited to footers. They can appear anywhere on a report, but placing them in footers is convenient because Access is responsible for limiting their scope, not the designer of the code.

Generating calculated totals in footers is a good idea, because the calculation to generate them in the Detail section or in a header is relatively complicated. But there are times when you need to print a calculation based on the fields in the current record, or when you want to print a running sum. These operations are well suited to the Header and Detail sections.

To create a calculation based on the current record, remember that you need to write an expression that calculates the value only once. Access replicates the calculation across all the records in the report for you if you include it in the Detail section. You can create any calculation you like by placing a new text box control anywhere on the report and entering an expression as its Control Source. A calculated control in the Detail section is evaluated only once per record, and a calculated control in a header is evaluated over that group.

Access makes it easy to calculate an aggregate of values in a section with the Running Sum property of text boxes in forms. For any text box, the Running Sum property can be set as follows:

- No—This control does not contain a running sum. If it's in the Detail section, it applies to the current record only; in a group header or footer, it applies to the group.
- Over Group—This control should be additively aggregated until the end of the current group, when it should be reset. For example, a control bound to the field [SaleAmount] in the Employee Sales by Country report would add the values of each record's sale to the previous record's until the value of the [SaleAmount] field changes is encountered.
- Over All—As the preceding, except that the value does not reset, accumulating with every record until the report completes.

A common use for running sums is to generate line numbers for records on reports. You can accomplish this by creating a text box control in the Detail section and setting its Control Source to the expression

```
=1
```

which has the effect of initializing the variable at 1. Set the Running Sum property of that control to Over Group or Over All as appropriate, and it increments with every record, creating sequentially numbered lines in the report.

Using Functions and Expressions in Reports

Simple controls in reports contain references to single data fields in the underlying data source. These references are the simplest of expressions, and expressions of reasonable complexity can be embedded in controls as Control Sources, performing calculations on-the-fly as the report is generated. Expressions may be based on data fields, or they may generate data unrelated to the data source (page numbers, for example).

The Northwind sample database is full of reports containing expressions and functions (which are also expressions). Some of the expressions are very straightforward, such as this example from the Employee Sales by Country report:

```
=[SaleAmount]/[SalespersonTotal]
```

▶ **See** "Functions and Expressions," **p. 1005**

This expression, found in the Detail section, computes the percentage of a salesperson's total sales that is represented by the current record. The field [SalespersonTotal] is actually calculated as the sum of all the individual sales by the report in the group footer for each salesperson; note that this value must be calculated in the footer before the values of controls in the earlier Detail section can be generated.

This expression from the Page Footer of the same report makes use of an Access built-in function:

```
=[Country] & "— Page " & [Page]
```

The Country field is drawn from the data source, but the [Page] field is computed by Access when the report is previewed or printed. Because this is a text box, it's best to have the expression evaluate to a string, thus the use of ampersands to concatenate the data elements and quotes around the literal string in the middle. Access includes a myriad of built-in functions (easily accessible from the Expression Builder) that are useful for reporting but don't require any interaction with the data source, including

- Date (and Day, Month, Year, Hour, Minute, and numerous date calculation functions).
- Dir (and FileDateTime, FileLen, CurDir) for information about the file system.
- Choose, Iif, and Switch provide program flow control features within other functions and expressions.
- Page returns the current page of the report.

Using these functions with empty parentheses after the name is customary if no parameters are being passed to them to make it clear to other readers that they're functions. Access interprets them correctly regardless.

Printing Reports

Access provides several options for printing reports, many new since Access 97. In general, reports are either printed from the Print Preview window (by clicking the Print icon on the toolbar or selecting File, Print) or from the Database Window (File, Print). Several other options are available as well.

You can view a report in three ways: in Design view, in Print Preview, and in Layout Preview (which is rarely used). Layout Preview is the same as Print Preview except that it operates with a small subset of the dataset, making the report preview appear very quickly. This is very useful for reviewing report formatting where the dataset is large, because Access evaluates every record when Print Preview is selected, and that can take a long time. So unless you have a relatively small dataset, use Layout Preview.

After a report is designed and is ready to be printed, other printing options can be considered. The File, Page Setup menu is key in formatting reports for the printer. The Margins tab in the Page Setup window enables setting the page margins to infinitesimal precision. The Print Data Only toggle eliminates lines, boxes, and other nondata items from the previews and the final printed report, making it useful for completing forms (when preprinted form stock is available) and printing the form as well as the data (when stock is not).

The Page tab of the Page Setup window is used for choosing the orientation and paper source for the report. Access 2000 adds an option to select a specific printer for the current report, regardless of the default printer set in Windows. This option would be useful for printing tractor-fed labels to a dot-matrix printer, or for sending invoices to a remote customer-service desk without changing the printer setting every time the report is printed.

The Columns tab controls how many instances of the report are printed across and down each physical page. These are discussed earlier in this chapter in the section titled "Creating Mailing Labels with a Report."

Problem/Solution—Creating Complex Reports

To create a relatively complex report, it's helpful to keep in mind the ultimate intended destination—paper—and to maintain a perspective considerate of the reader. In this Problem/Solution example, we'll work through the creation of Northwind's Catalog report, concentrating on the steps it took to create it and paying special attention to the steps that are somewhat less than obvious. Refer to Figures 37.7, 37.8, and 37.9 for an example of this report.

The ultimate format of this report is pretty straightforward, because it's easy to imagine what a printed catalog should look like. In this case, the last thing you want to worry about is the product data, which comes from the database. In many reports, the layout task is harder and more critical, and this report falls in that category.

To start, create a new report (from the Database Window in Report view, select New, Design View, OK). The resulting window has three sections: Detail, Page Header, and Page Footer. We'll use all of them.

The mental image of a catalog you're working to create should remind you that a catalog includes information that's neither data-related nor belongs at the top and bottom of every page, so you'll want to turn on a Report Header and Footer by clicking View, Report Header/Footer. Remember that the Page Header/Footer and Report Header/Footer options may not be visible by default (if personalized menus are active); double-click the View menu and they'll appear.

Turn on the Toolbox (View, Toolbox) and Properties dialog box (View, Properties) when working with report controls. You can move them out of your way, or even dock the Toolbox to any side of the design window.

The Report Layout

You should concentrate on the graphic layout requirements first, because it always takes longer than you expect. First, make the Report Header section large enough to work in, because you will want to insert the report title and an appropriate logo in this section of the report. Click the gray Report Header bar in the design window, change the Properties dialog box to either the Format or All tab, and change the Height property to 15". This property appears in both tabs; the All tab includes all properties.

NOTE You could also enlarge the section by clicking and holding on the Page Header bar, but enlarging something to that large an area is tricky, since it will probably extend off your screen.

Scroll back to the top of the section if you need to. A width of 6.5" fills the page nicely; drag the right edge of the paper until it intersects the 6.5" mark on the horizontal ruler at the top of the page.

Next, place a Northwind logo on the Report Header by clicking the Image icon in the Toolbox, and then click in the middle of the window near the top of the Report Header. A file selection box opens; you can select any file you want to display on the report's first page. To insert the Northwind logo, choose the file C:\Program Files\Microsoft Office\Office\Samples\nwlogo.gif (assuming you installed Access in the default location).

A small Northwind logo appears on the page. We want it to be about 2.5" on a side, so change its Height and Width properties accordingly. You'll notice that the box containing the image gets bigger, but the image remains small; change the Size Mode property from Clip to Zoom to make the image proportionally larger. There's no good way to center it on the page except for a little math: 6.5"-wide window minus 2.5" image leaves four inches—two inches on each side. You can set the Left property of the image to 2" to place it perfectly.

Next, add the label that titles the catalog. Click the label tool, and place it under the logo image by dragging a box about the same width as the logo and about an inch tall. You do not need to be precise at this point. The blinking cursor tells you it's your turn to type, so enter `Fall Catalog` and click outside the label box.

TIP Label boxes can't be empty. If you don't type something (anything), the control disappears. Most controls don't care what you put in them, but this one does.

Chances are that the text you entered is tiny and boring. Change the label box properties by clicking anywhere in it to select it, and then choose options from the Formatting toolbar at the top of the screen. Try centering, italicizing, and changing the font to about 22 points and maroon.

You'll want to make sure that the title is perfectly centered on the logo image. Because you already centered it in its control, you should make the image and label controls the same size. Select them both (hold down Shift and click inside both controls), and choose Format, Size, To Widest from the menu. While they're both still selected, click Format, Align, Left. The title should be perfectly centered under the image.

Add a level horizontal line (using the Horizontal Line tool in the toolbox) the full width of the page across the top of the bottom half of the logo. Click it to select it, and then copy it (Ctrl+C) and paste the copy (Ctrl+V). The copy appears just below the original.

You can easily duplicate any object by copying it (Ctrl+C) and pasting it (Ctrl+V), and the duplicate will appear in the proximity of the original object. If you move the duplicate and paste again, another duplicate will appear spaced proportionately from the first duplicate as the first duplicate is from the original. If any keystrokes or mouse clicks intervene between the copy and paste operations, the pasted object will appear in the top-left corner of the current section of the report, and you can drag and drop it from there. Lines can be very difficult to see in the corner, so drag a selection box (using the selection tool) around where you think the object is to find it if it's lost.

Change the width of the pasted line to four points by changing its Border Width property appropriately. The two lines on top of the logo don't look so great, so select the control containing the logo and click Format, Bring to Front to make it opaque over the lines. Figure 37.13 shows what the product should look like at this point.

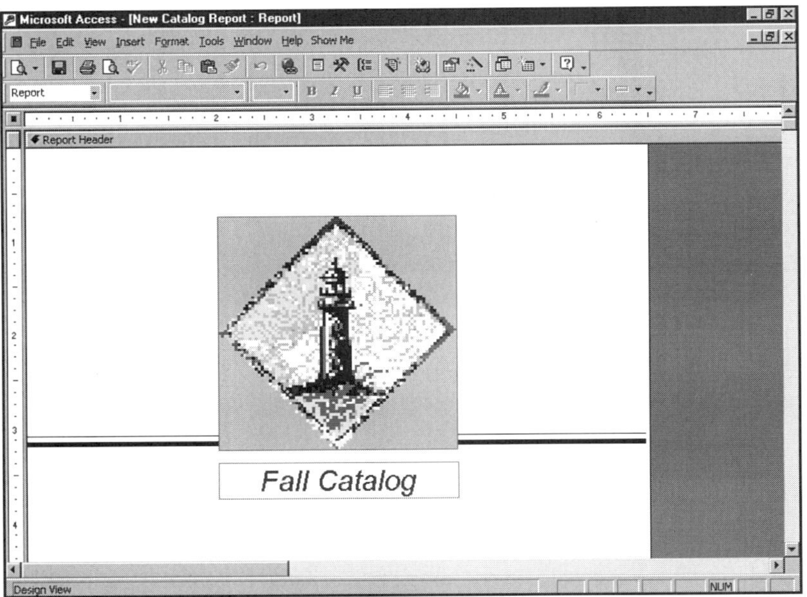

FIGURE 37.13
A very nice-looking report header.

You can improve the appearance of zoomed images either by using large bitmapped images (.pcx, .gif, .tif) or by using vector images (.wmf, .cgm, .cdr), which can be enlarged infinitely.

The rest of the Northwind Catalog header and footer are created similarly. They are composed almost entirely of lines and labels, with a few images thrown in. Turning the Grid on (View, Grid) makes creating tables from lines, as in the order form, much easier than estimating it.

There's one more trick in the header section. This header spans two pages, and it's important to start the second page in the right place. You could carefully place the controls such that the natural page break occurs just before the controls that belong on the top of Page 2, but it's easier to use a Page Break control, placed anywhere on the canvas in the vertical position where the page should break. It forces the printer to perform a page feed when that point is reached. Also, change the Force New Page property of the Report Header to After Section to ensure that the first data record starts on a new page, and change the same property of the Report Footer to Before Section to force a break before the order form prints. If your page text is longer or wider than the printed page can fit, you may end up with extra pages. Be sure that your text regions fit inside the page area, remembering to compensate for the margins (which aren't visible in Design view).

As for the Page Header and Footer, it would be nice to include some promotional text (such as *Northwind Traders* and a phone number) and page numbers in one of them. The sample database does so in the Page Footer, with the Page Header shrunk to 0" height to make it invisible. Remember, unlike group headers and footers, it's all or nothing with the Page and Report headers and footers—you have to have both or neither. The expression in the footer to create the page numbers makes use of Access' Page function in a straightforward manner.

Creating Groups

After the marketing stuff is done, it's time to get some data in this report. Suppose the powers-that-be have decided that the catalog will include each product's name, ID code, quantity per packaging unit, and unit price. Furthermore, the report should be sorted by product category. One way to create this report is as a report/subreport combo, binding the parent report to the Categories table and the subreport to the product data in the Products table. This allows you to include some information about the Categories that isn't in the Products table.

NOTE The obvious way to write this report is as a simple report based on the Products table, with the data fields in the Detail section and grouped on the CategoryName. This method doesn't include the category descriptions and pictures, though. Most people would create a new query joining the Categories and Products tables and base the report on the query. However, that method causes a category image to be replicated once for every record in the query, and the resulting dataset could be pretty big. Therefore, the report/subreport method is probably the best way to do this.

Select the entire report by clicking on the gray square in the top-left corner of the report design window (or by clicking Edit, Select Report). In the Properties dialog box, change the Record Source property to Categories. Then create a group on the CategoryName field by clicking on the Sorting and Grouping icon, choosing the CategoryName field, and selecting an Ascending sort order.

You'll want to turn on a group header and footer, and change the Keep Together property to Whole Group to force the details to stay with the header and footer if possible. Close the Sorting and Grouping dialog box and scroll through your report until you can see the CategoryName header and footer.

You can drag the Detail section to its minimum height for this report, because you're going to use a subform to hold the data records. You need to use the CategoryName header to hold information specific to each category. You can place the subform in the header, footer, or detail section in this case with the same effect. Make the CategoryName Header about 2" tall.

Adding Fields to the Report

If the Field List isn't visible, click the Field List icon to make it so. You'll want to drag several fields from the Field List to the CategoryName Header: CategoryName, Description, Picture. In each case, Access creates a label titling the field by default; select the labels and delete them. Arrange the three controls in a pleasing way; the Northwind report places the CategoryName field directly over the Description field near the left margin (use Format, Align, Left) and the picture on the right.

Change the size and color of the CategoryName field to 14 points, blue. You'll want to resize the text box after changing the font of its contents; you can do so quickly by double-clicking any of the corners or sides causing them to expand (or contract) to optimal size. You'll probably want to shrink the Picture field and change the Size Mode to Zoom to ensure that the picture is resized proportionally.

Turn off the automatic labeling of text boxes by clicking the Text Box button in the toolbox, then setting the Auto Label property for the Default Text Box (on the Format and All tabs of the Property sheet) to "No."

Your report should look something like Figure 37.14.

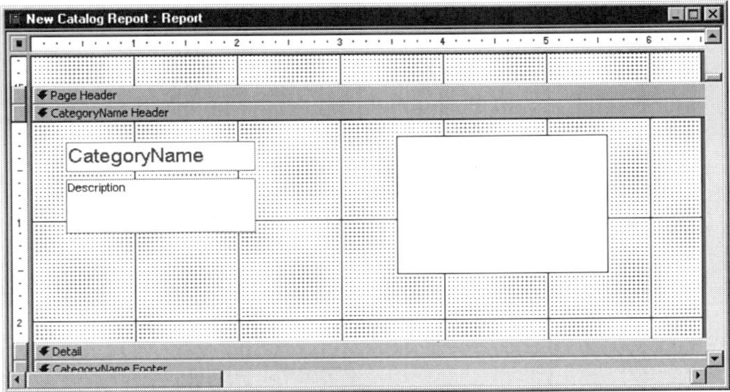

FIGURE 37.14
The Catalog report in Design View, before the detailed subreport is added.

Creating and Including the Subreport

For the product data (in the subreport), minimize the main report and create a new report for the data, based on the Products table. You can do this very quickly by using the Report Wizard: In the Database Window click Report, Create Report using Wizard and select the Products table. Select only the fields you need (ProductName, ProductID, QuantityPerUnit, and UnitPrice). Choose a sort order (Ascending, on the ProductName field is nice) and specifying a Tabular report. You won't need a style, and you should name the subreport something descriptive.

NOTE For hard-code coders, there exists a standard notation for naming objects in Access. It's called "Hungarian Notation," after the nationality of the Microsoft developer (Charles Simonyi) who devised it, and it specifies ways to name objects by including an indication of the type of object in the name. A valid name for a subreport like this one might be "rptCatalogSub," where the main report might be "rptCatalog." A relatively complete list of Hungarian prefixes is at `http://support.microsoft.com/support/kb/articles/q173/7/38.asp`. Using this scheme makes sharing code with other developers easier, because your object names aren't arbitrary, but it takes some getting used to. Microsoft recommends its use in C++ and Visual Basic projects, but (obviously) doesn't adhere to it in Northwind.

The resulting report is pretty close to what you need. Delete the page numbers Access creates, and change the column headers to more descriptive titles. Turn off the Report Header and Footer, deleting all controls in those sections, and save this report; Access calls it Products automatically.

Now for the tricky part. Arrange and resize the windows for your new main report (which has the Category information) and the Database Window so that both are visible. Drag the new Products report from the Database Window to the CategoryName Header section on the new report. Access realizes that the two data sources for these reports have a preexisting relationship (Tools, Relationships) already established, so it links the CategoryID in the parent report to the CategoryID in the child report for you. Move the new subreport as necessary to line it up under the CategoryName and Description fields. You'll want to delete the label Access adds to identify the Products subreport.

That's it. The fact that the subreport is within the CategoryName group limits the records displayed in it to the records in each category, and you've created a catalog.

CHAPTER 38

Access and the Web

In this chapter

What Are Data Access Pages?

In the "good old days" of the World Wide Web (circa 1995), if you wanted to create a Web page that allowed you to read and write data to a database, you had to write custom software that intercepted the data sent to and received from browsers in HTML forms.

You'd interpret the form's data elements, query the database appropriately, and return the data requested to the user. It was tedious, and the tools of the day were limited in their capability to display data in anything but simple tabular formats.

Around 1996, several companies began marketing commercial products that worked in conjunction with the Web server to handle the database connectivity issue. Their products worked well, but they required certain configuration settings in the server and required the person developing the Web pages to understand some special HTML syntax that they supported. If you didn't have access to the Web server or didn't want to learn HTML, you were out of luck.

Access 95 and 97 brought Web/database connectivity a little closer to the end user by implementing several variations on a "save as HTML" theme. These options created rudimentary reports and forms that anybody who could run a wizard could create. However, they were limited either in functionality or in application because the most capable variant of these (Active Server Pages) could be run only on a Microsoft Web server; most pages that Access 97 generated included Microsoft's ActiveX controls and could be viewed only in Microsoft's Internet Explorer Web browser.

▶ **See** "Importing, Exporting, and Linking to HTML Files," **p. 1169**

These options are still available in Access 2000 (and still have the same limitations), but now there's another option to consider. With Data Access Pages, Microsoft has brought HTML one level closer to the graphical Access development environment. Now an object type exists that can be developed directly in Access without exporting and conversion. Data Access Pages support a rich set of tools, including a dozen or so controls, relatively precise positioning of those controls, sorting, grouping, filtering, and the capability to take advantage of event execution in the pages developed.

Data Access Pages are Web pages that you build from within Access. They're stored in Access (and can be used in Access) natively, but they can as easily be saved on the file system in HTML. Microsoft has brought Access one step closer to the Web by including a graphical Web page editor within Access 2000—it's not as good as the better commercial editing environments (including FrontPage and even Word), but it's functional and customized for use in Access. With Access, you can create and edit any HTML page, regardless of whether it was generated from within Access.

However—and this is a big however—all this is implemented via Microsoft's proprietary ActiveX object model. That means that Data Access Pages will appear correctly only in version 5 or later of Microsoft's Internet Explorer (IE) Web browser.

It's impossible to tell how many Internet Explorer 5 browsers will be deployed at any point in time, but the distribution curve has shown that it takes a year or so for a majority of users in the general public to migrate to a new version. Even then, the market saturation will probably be far less than you'll need to generate pages that most people can use. On the other hand, at least you don't need to install the ASP extensions on the Web server anymore, so maybe this is a step in the right direction.

Other shortcomings exist, such as the almost unbelievable absence of an Access Form-to-Data Access Page converter tool in this release of Access 2000. You can, however, create Data Access Pages based on another Web page—a nice feature. When working with Data Access Pages, you'll be alternatively amazed at how intriguing this idea is—to view an Access data object from a browser—but equally nagged by the feeling that this isn't quite ready for prime time yet.

One of the things that makes Data Access Pages so difficult to get accustomed to is that they do things that the Web just hasn't been used for before. Where have you ever seen an Access-type record navigation bar on the Web? How about expanding and collapsing sections of a Web page based on the data underlying it? Experienced webbies recognize that these tricks aren't part of standard HTML and they must be done with complicated coding behind the scenes.

They're right. But because you haven't seen them before or been involved in writing the code, the Data Access Page development environment is a little like a toy chest filled with baubles written in Visual C++. You won't know what the toys do until you play with them.

In any case, Data Access Pages (which we'll abbreviate as DAPs throughout this chapter) are the first really new feature in Access in several versions and have a whole new learning curve associated with them. Adding controls, manipulating controls, handling grouping and sorting options, properties, and so on—it's all new. Even the venerable Field List window has changed for DAPs. It will make you wonder how we'll design forms and reports in the next version of Access after Access 2000.

Ways to Create Data Access Pages

So much is new in DAPs that you'll need to try a few and examine how they are built before you can really understand just how different this technique is from the other Access intrinsics. A good place to start is with the Page Wizard, which generates passable DAPs that you can modify easily (unlike most Wizard-created objects, which may generate difficult-to-read code).

▶ **See** "Multiple Table Queries," **p. 1018**

▶ **See** "Creating Multiple Table Reports," **p. 1072**

Start by navigating to the Pages tab of the Database window in the Northwind database. Three options are available for creating Data Access Pages:

- Create a Data Access Page in Design View—This opens the DAP editor in a PowerPoint-like fashion, ready to create a page based on a standard template. This method is covered later in this chapter.

- Create a Data Access Page by Using a Wizard—The Page Wizard starts after you double-click this entry.
- Edit a Web Page That Already Exists—This option opens the DAP Editor on any Web page you specify, either on your local file system or somewhere on the Web. Of course, you can save back only to your file system.

NOTE The Publish to the Web Wizard seems to have passed away and is not available in Access 2000.

One more option exists, available only from the New button: AutoPage:Columnar creates a DAP that aligns the fields from the underlying data source in columns.

Using the Page Wizard

Creating your first DAP is likely to be a frustrating experience as you discover all the new controls and techniques available to you, especially if you already have experience writing Web pages or creating Access forms and reports. It's a whole new world. A good place to start is the Page Wizard, which will expose you to some of the features at your disposal.

NOTE Data Access Pages will not work in Access 2000 unless you have Internet Explorer 5 installed on your system. The DAP features will be grayed out in the Pages tab. Internet Explorer 5 or later is required to create or modify DAPs.

CAUTION

DAPS save representations of your pages in both the Database window and on the file system. If you delete or move the page in the file system, however, the icon in the Database view will not be updated, causing an error should you try to edit or open the page later from within Access. Access gives you the option of trying to find a moved DAP on the file system, but if you delete the HTML file, the remaining icon in the Pages tab of the Database window will be useless.

Surprisingly, if you try to delete the icon in the Database window, you are given the option of deleting the HTML files as well, if you desire.

NOTE If you create DAPs using the Page Wizard and intend to apply a decorative theme to the page (see steps 4 and 5 as follows), you'll need to be sure you have the Theme Wizard installed before beginning the design process. Unlike most Office 2000 add-ins, you can't install the Theme Wizard after you've already started the Page Wizard. You can, however, install more themes in the middle of the process.

To create a DAP using the Page Wizard, activate the Pages tab of the Database window and follow these steps:

1. Double-click Create Data Access Page by Using Wizard. After a long delay, the Page Wizard opens, asking which fields you want on your page, as shown in Figure 38.1. The

admonishment that you can choose from more than one table or query is no different from Forms or Reports, but the way this is implemented in DAPs is a little different, as we'll soon see. Select a data source and some fields. Click Next to continue.

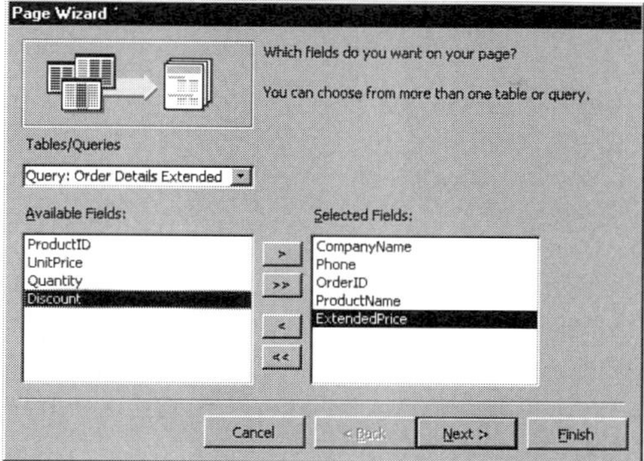

FIGURE 38.1
The first dialog box of the Page Wizard looks just like the first step in a form or report wizard.

Part V Ch 38

2. The second dialog box of the Page Wizard, shown in Figure 38.2, displays which fields should be dominant and which fields should be set off in a related subpage. It offers the option of adding another group header, but advises that this option, if chosen, creates a read-only page. This is due to the way joins are executed in DAPs; they depend on existing relationships between data objects, and adding another grouping level implies that a data issue exists (such as an ambiguous or unenforced relationship) that the DAP doesn't know about. If the grouping doesn't look right, think about the relationships already established for the data objects involved in the page and press Next to continue.

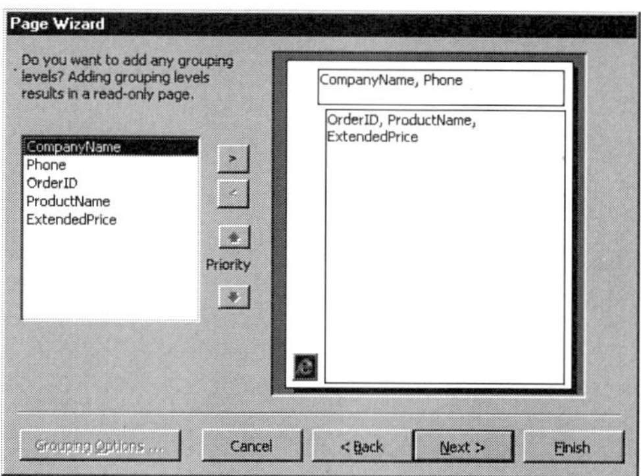

FIGURE 38.2
Access chooses a default grouping scheme for the DAP automatically based on the existing relationships among the data.

3. You're asked to select a sort order for the detail records in the third dialog box, shown in Figure 38.3. You can reverse the default order, if desired, by clicking the button to the right of the field name. Notice that Access allows you to select sorting options only for the data fields in the detail section of the page. Press Next to move on.

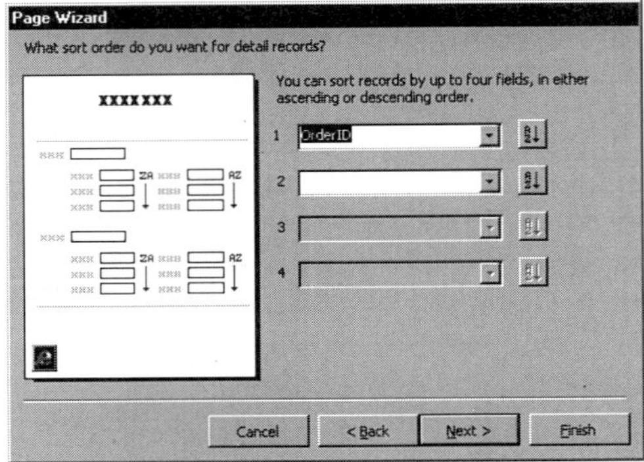

FIGURE 38.3
Access chooses a default sort order for the DAP automatically based on the existing relationships among the data.

4. The final dialog box of the wizard, like most, offers to name the page and to let you open it in Design view or in its default state, as do most wizards. Additionally, this wizard offers the option of applying a "theme" to your page. Most wizards don't offer the option of applying formatting at this point, although other ways exist to include custom formatting in forms and reports. Using themes is fun, so click next to "Do you want to apply a theme to your page?" (indicating agreement) and click Finish.
5. After whirring and clicking for several seconds, Access creates your data access page and minimizes it; while it's minimized, a new dialog box appears (see Figure 38.4) for you to use in selecting a *theme* for your page. The nearly 70 themes listed are borrowed from Microsoft FrontPage 2000. They contain information on the default background for pages, font styles and colors, and field defaults. Most reside on the Office Premium Edition CD and are not installed by default, so have your CD (and a big hard drive) ready if you want to go through all of them. Select a theme and click OK.

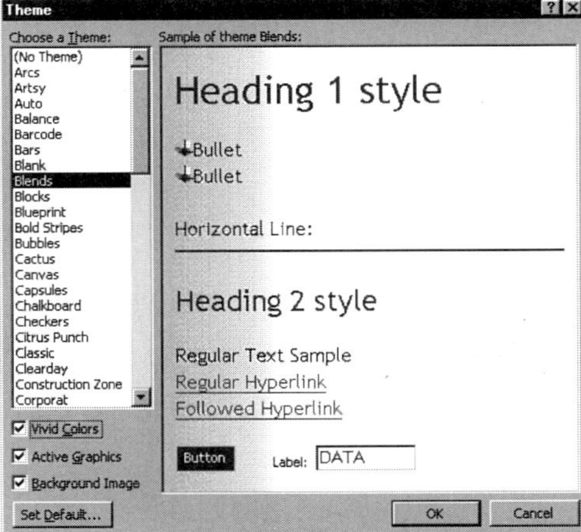

FIGURE 38.4
The Theme dialog box enables you to choose a prepackaged look for your DAP.

6. You're returned to Design view to edit your page and add finishing touches. Typical DAPs include modifiable labels ("Click here and type title text") that are invisible in the final product if ignored. You can add additional controls or HTML elements in this view, if required. Save your work (File, Save); you'll notice that the DAP is saved in two places: in the Page tab of the Database window and outside of the database in an HTML file. You can switch to Page view (also called the Web Page Preview) in Access (View, Page View) to get a preview of the page (see Figure 38.5), or view your page in Internet Explorer (File, Open), as shown in Figure 38.6.

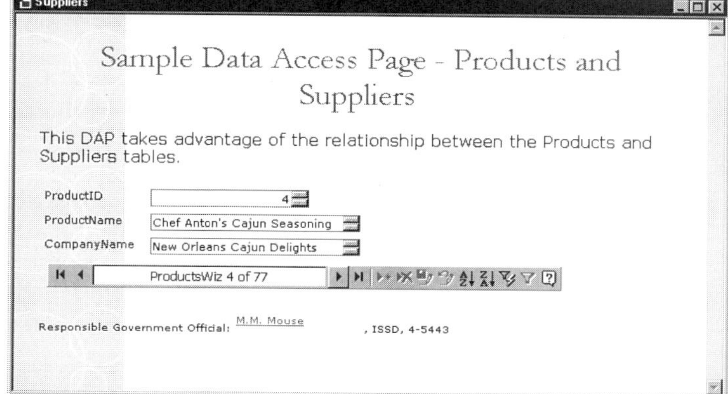

FIGURE 38.5
Switch to Page view to see the finished DAP.

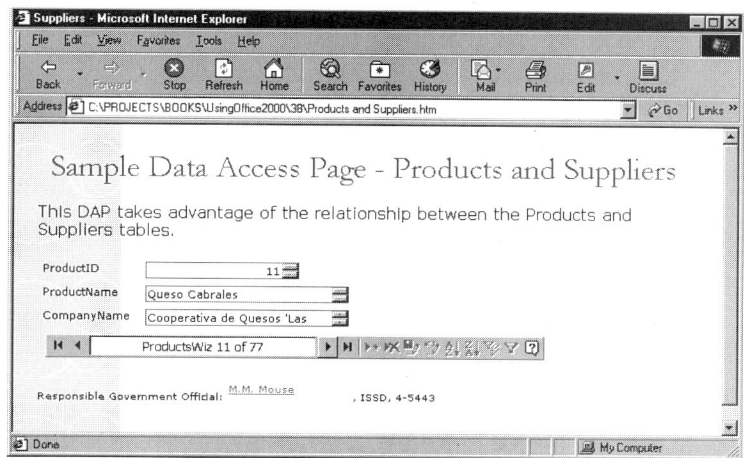

FIGURE 38.6
The same DAP in Internet Explorer 5. This works correctly even if no Web server is installed on your PC.

After your page is finished, you can modify it extensively by reopening it in Design view from the Database window and applying additional controls, editing the HTML, and so on. You have full control over the size and properties of each data element control, but some techniques you may have used in the Form or Report Design views may not work in the HTML Editor (such as selecting multiple objects with the Ctrl key, for example). A number of new properties are available for DAP controls; these are adequately described in the online help system.

DAP Design View

Now that you have an idea of how a DAP looks when the Page Wizard designs it, you should build it from scratch to get intimate with the design elements required to successfully complete a task such as this. This discussion creates the same page as the previous one via the Design view instead of the Page Wizard.

To build a DAP in Design view, start at the Database window, Page view. Double-click the option Create Data Access Page in Design view. Several windows should open, all shown in Figure 38.7. These windows include the following:

- The Page window acts as the design canvas on which you'll place, move, resize, and modify page objects.
- The Field List presents a hierarchical view of the data objects in the database (including related objects) for you to drag and drop onto the Page window.
- The Property Sheet contains all the modifiable properties for each object on the page (and the Page itself). Note that some object features, such as a hyperlink associated with a label, can't be changed with the Property Sheet—they must be changed in the GUI.
- The Alignment and Sizing window contains standard alignment controls for making your page elements line up.

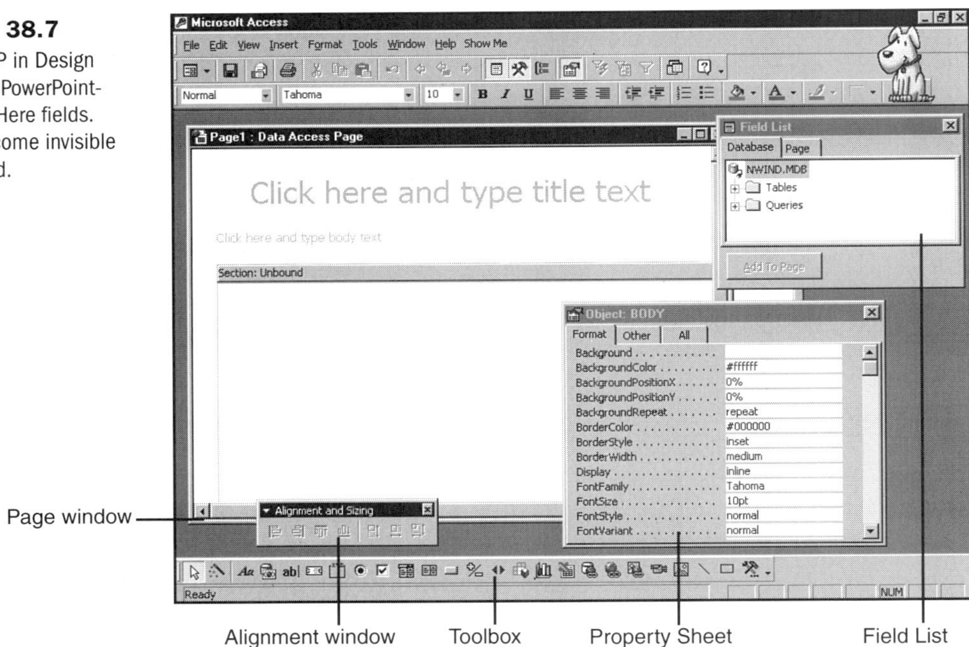

FIGURE 38.7
A new DAP in Design view, with PowerPoint-like Click Here fields. These become invisible if not used.

NOTE Some of these windows may not be visible, depending on the way Access was closed last time. If you can't see any of the default windows (and want to), click View and the name of the window you want to see. Windows that are already visible have check marks next to them.

It's also worth noting that the default toolbox (shown in Figure 38.5 docked to the bottom of the window) is somewhat different for DAPs than for forms, indicating that the controls that can be included are different as well. The controls that are different include the following:

- The Bound HTML control references a text field in a data source that contains HTML text. This enables you to show formatted text, images, hyperlinks, and other HTML objects that change with every record displayed.

- The Scrolling Text control creates a marquee-style area that contains the text you specify. Various properties control how the text is displayed, but it's generally used to make text move across the screen repeatedly.

- The Expand control gives a user the capability to "roll up" the detail records under a particular group header on a DAP. Including an Expand control in the header creates a visible control in the client browser that toggles detail expansion on or off.

- The Record Navigation control works just like the navigation buttons in an Access form, moving the current record marker forward or back. It also includes filter and sorting options.

- The Office PivotTable control includes a PivotTable in your DAP. PivotTables are analogous to Crosstab queries in that they rearrange tabular data into rows and columns and allow calculations based on the organization and contents of each row or column.

See "Summarizing Data with Crosstab Queries," **p. 1034**

- The Office Chart control embeds a chart in your page. Upon placing this control in your page, the Chart Wizard starts and helps you identify the data sources for your chart.

- The Office Spreadsheet control embeds a spreadsheet reminiscent of Excel in your page.

- The Bound Hyperlink control references a text field in a data source that contains a URL. This enables you to include a link to an external Web page that changes with every record.

- The Hyperlink control contains a single URL for display on your page. When clicked, this object opens the URL displayed in the same browser window.

- The Hotspot Image control places an image in your page that acts as a hyperlink when clicked, loading a specified URL in the browser. This differs from a picture embedded in a Bound HTML control in that it includes a facility for pop-up ScreenTips and initiates a cursor change when the mouse cursor passes over it.

- The Movie control embeds a Windows movie (.mov or .avi) on the page. The movie plays back in both Design and Page views.

After the Page window is open, you'll want to start adding data controls to it. Open the Field List window (see Figure 38.8) large enough to see its current contents and to expand those contents considerably. If you've used the Field List in any of the other object design environments, you'll notice immediately that this one is different. Instead of a flat list of the data fields in the currently selected data source, you're given a hierarchical, folder-based list of all the data sources (tables and queries) and fields in the database.

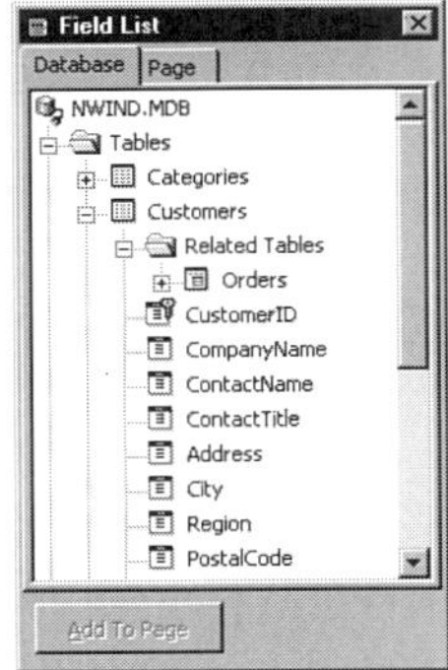

FIGURE 38.8
The new Field List enables you to see all the database's data sources in one place and to expand and collapse them at will.

In the Field List, open the Tables folder and double-click a table to see the fields in it. Drag a field to the "Section: Unbound" area of the Page window and drop it. You'll immediately see that the caption on that section changes to "Header:<*tablename*>," and a Navigation section is created with a Navigation bar control included. By adding a field from any table to the page, you've created a header and detail region for the data and made the record sources for those sections of that table.

It's instructive to switch to Page view at this point (Figure 38.9) to see how these controls work together. The DAP created so far has only one data control, so there's not a lot to see, but you'll notice that the Navigation bar at the bottom of the data area is fully functional, enabling you to move between records, to add and delete records, and to change the sort order. If you were to export the page as is to HTML (File, Export), you'd find that it looks the same in Internet Explorer 5. This is functionality not typically found in browsers.

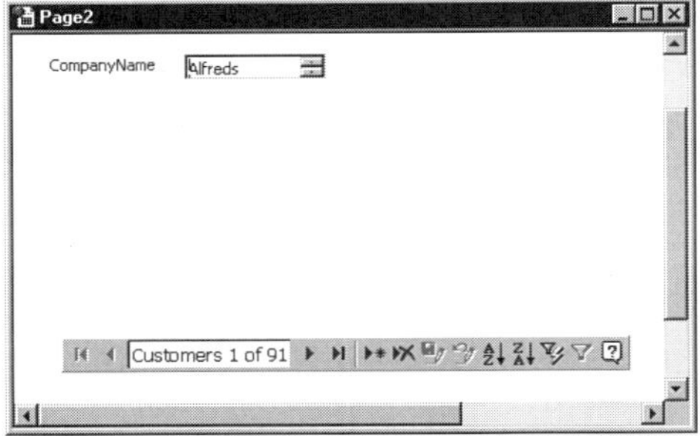

FIGURE 38.9
A very simple DAP includes a fully functional Navigation bar and the usual features of an Access datasheet, all in a browser window.

Switch back to Design view (View, Design View) to add more controls. You may need to hover the pointer on the View menu for a few seconds for those options to appear. If a relationship exists between tables, you can click the Related Tables folder in the Field List and select fields from it, if desired. You can also go to the Queries folder in the Field List, open it, select a field from an existing query, and drag a field onto the canvas. Finally, you can drag an entire table or query onto the canvas; if you do, the Layout Wizard opens, asking whether you prefer to see the detail records including the Order ID in a PivotTable or as individual controls. Make a selection and click OK.

If you created a simple page with information from one table or query, you can use the toolbox controls to format the page as you desire and skip ahead.

If you included field(s) from a related table or query, you'll want to try "promoting" a field from one of the data sources to implement a report-like grouping. For example, consider a DAP containing information from both the Customers table and Orders table (which are related by the field OrderID). It might be nice to see each customer name only once and all of that customer's orders listed under it, instead of an instance of customer name and order info for each order (the default behavior). To promote the Customers field(s), select one of them and click the Promote button on the toolbar. All the fields from the same data source as the promoted field are elevated to a new group heading and an Expand button is placed next to them for use in the browser. This example is shown in Figure 38.10, with one of the Company Name sections expanded by clicking the Expand button in the browser.

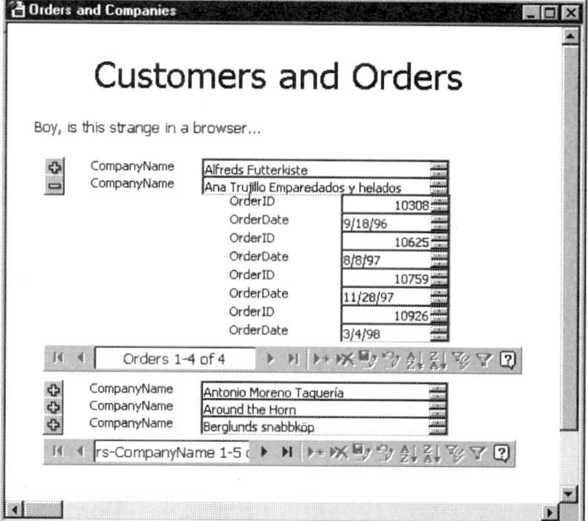

FIGURE 38.10
A DAP that takes advantage of grouping, built in a few minutes using the Design view.

Note that navigation bars are provided for both the detail and group header sections. You can delete or move them as required in Design view. To return the DAP to the flatter, prepromoted look, select one of the fields in the header and click Demote on the toolbar.

To complete the DAP's look, apply a theme, if desired (Format, Theme).

Then save your work. You'll notice that Access saves a copy of the DAP outside of the database as an HTML file when it prompts you for a filename, which you should provide. It's still available from the Database window for editing, however, and deleting the version in the file system doesn't affect the one stored in the database.

That's a lot of work, and you'll find as you work through the preceding steps that you'll rarely get the data source defined correctly the first time, or you'll promote or demote a section and you won't be able to get it back. It can be frustrating to create DAPs from scratch, giving the impression that this environment is some kind of a technology demonstration—as though Microsoft is saying, "You'll create all your forms this way someday, but maybe not quite yet." The hierarchical Field List is a great tool, and the ActiveX controls provided for DAPs make it a lot easier to create data-driven Web pages. This is probably a step in the right direction, but it's still pretty cumbersome.

Editing an Existing Web Page

You can open an existing Web page in Access as a DAP for editing and adding or modifying data elements or other controls.

CAUTION

Remember that DAPs are viewable only in Internet Explorer 5 or later; you'd be ill-advised to create a DAP for public viewing at this date because very few people would be able to view it.

That warning aside, Access makes a passable WYSIWYG (what you see is what you get) HTML editor, including (not very good) support for HTML tables and all the usual elements of HTML with a very "Access" feel.

To edit a saved DAP or to edit an existing Web page as a DAP, follow these steps:

1. From the Database window, select File, Open. A file selection dialog box appears. After you have made your selections (taking the following items into account), click OK to continue.
    - If the page you want to edit is stored on the local file system, you can select it there after choosing Web Pages in the Files of Type box. Otherwise, enter the URL as the filename.
    - If you enter a URL, Access may ask you for a username and a password that is a valid FrontPage user on the server.
    - If you don't intend to edit the document directly, you should save a copy from Internet Explorer first, and then work from that copy.

NOTE Access assumes that you want to select a different data source for the page you're editing, and it closes any database you had open. The Data Link Properties dialog box is displayed for you to enter SQL Server or MSDE connection information as appropriate.

If you want to obtain the data elements from an Access database, click the Provider tab and select the Microsoft Jet 4.0 OLE Provider option and click Next. The Connection tab window changes to allow you to select an Access database on the local machine and to specify a username and password if necessary (use "Admin" with a blank password unless Access security is enabled on that database).

▶ **See** "Creating Access Projects," **p. 977**

NOTE Access allows you to have more than one DAP open at a time, which do not need to have the same data source.

2. Access displays the page and all the usual DAP design controls for you to use in modifying it. You'll want to be careful and save often; the controls sometimes appear and disappear unexpectedly when you press Delete or change the alignment of another control. As HTML editing goes, this is not a convenient way to work; however, it's an intriguing way of spicing up a Web site. When you're done editing, save your work and view your page in Internet Explorer.

CHAPTER 39

Using the Add-In Features

In this chapter

Add-Ins and Utilities

Several features exist in Access that most people use infrequently, if at all. Instead of integrating them with the built-in toolbars, Microsoft chose to set them aside slightly, placing them off the beaten path but still available to users should they be needed. This set of functions is also a kind of trial area for the Microsoft developers; with every release of Access, the functionality in this set of features seems to change more than the core functions you find in the middle of the more typically used toolbars.

In general, you can get by just fine as an Access developer without ever using any of these functions. Almost everything they do can also be done in code or manually; these features just provide an easy way to implement some functions that may make your life a little easier.

Add-In Manager

In one context, *Add-ins* are small programs provided by Microsoft for your use while creating database applications in Access. Most of the wizards and helpers described in this chapter are add-ins in that sense. However, Microsoft's Visual Basic (not VBA) line of programming tools includes an interface that can be used for third parties to write software that is intended to be used in conjunction with Microsoft Office products, all of which include an interface (a "hook") to tell the Office application that a third-party helper program is available for it—this interface is usually called an "Add-In Manager."

Without add-ins (either Microsoft's or somebody else's), there's no reason to use the Add-In Manager. The Office installation program takes care of installing and uninstalling most of the standard add-ins. But an entire industry is centered on creating "helper applications" for Access; these applications are frequently created as add-ins.

To obtain these add-ins, usually you download a demo copy from a development company's Web site and give them a try, paying for them if they do what you need. When you receive an add-in file, it is usually an .mde or .mda file; both of these represent compiled Access-compatible applications (they're compiled so you can't see or modify their source code).

You load and unload these products into Access by using the Add-In Manager. After you receive an add-in program, follow these steps to install it using the Add-In Manager:

1. From the Database window, select Tools, Add-Ins, Add-In Manager. You may be prompted to install the Add-In Manager from the Office 2000 CD. The Add-In Manager window appears, as shown in Figure 39.1.
2. Click Add New. The Open dialog box appears, enabling you to select the add-in file and click Open.
3. Assuming the add-in file is compatible, its name appears in the Add-In Manager window, indicating that it's loaded. Most add-ins add custom entries to the Access menu to enable you to use its functions.

NOTE Remember—many add-ins designed for earlier versions of Access won't work with Access 2000.

4. Click Close to terminate the Add-In Manager.

To uninstall an add-in, open the Add-In Manager, select the add-in, and click Uninstall.

Database Splitter

Most beginning Access programmers create their databases as if they were building a skyscraper: It's one enormous structure with a bunch of interconnecting pieces, all or most of which need to be present for the thing to work as a whole. Unfortunately, databases aren't buildings, and sometimes it makes a lot of sense to separate like functions from their cousins to improve performance or maintainability.

It's pretty easy to see, for example, how it is probably better to place several VBA procedures with similar functions (mathematical, string manipulation, database utility, and so forth) in one code module to make managing them less arduous. It's harder to see how *splitting* a perfectly good database into two can improve its performance. But it certainly can, given the right environment. Furthermore, the capability in Access to decouple the *interface* (forms, reports, queries) from the data store (tables) makes it an unusually versatile application, well-suited to use in office networks and in prototyping.

When you create a database that includes tables and at least one of the interface elements mentioned previously, you create a *monolithic* database—one that can stand alone. For developing code and for learning, this is certainly the best structure for a database. It's extremely fast because all the data is stored on the local file system, and it's easy to manage because little or no possibility exists that someone else will muck with any of the database while you're developing it.

But after a database is ready for release to the general public, a monolithic design begins to present problems. For example, Access can support up to 30 concurrent users. If you save an all-in-one database to a network server and tell the entire company where it is, you risk bringing your network to a screeching halt, depending on the network and the size of the company.

Every time someone on the office network loads your database, a significant portion gets transported over the network lines—the data tables, the forms, everything. As users make changes to the data, only the changes are sent back (so they're really sharing a central data store). So network traffic isn't really an issue at that point.

A better answer exists for network-enabled databases. If you can detach the data store (the tables) from everything else, store the tables alone on the network, and let users install the interface components alone on their local hard drives, the network traffic becomes limited to data passing back and forth. In the case of the Northwind database, the data alone comprises about 800KB, but not all of that is sent over the network. If the remote tables are linked in the distributed interfaces to the centralized data store, only the data requested is sent, limiting traffic somewhat.

As the number of users and the size of the database increases, the amount of traffic increases as well, but adding code to a local copy of the interface (new reports, forms, and so on) has almost no direct effect on network traffic. At this point, you'll probably need to use a dedicated database server running Microsoft SQL Server or a similar server-based database. These databases have the capability to process some queries themselves, without sending all the data across the network.

To split a database this way, you have two equally good options:

- Do it yourself by exporting the tables from the monolithic database to a new database, and then linking them back in.
- Using the Database Splitter add-in, which does it for you.

It's a good idea to save your database before running the Database Splitter (just in case). After it is saved, follow these steps to use the Database Splitter:

1. From the Database window, choose Tools, Database Utilities, Database Splitter. A confirmation window appears, advising you to save a copy of the database first; click Split Database to continue.
2. A standard Open/Save window opens, asking for the name of the database to contain the data store. The recommended name, <*databasename*>`_be.mdb`, should work for most installations. If you want to place the back end (the data store) on the network, now would be a good time to save it to the fully qualified UNC network path where it will reside, so the links in the interface point to the correct path. After the file is saved, click Split.
3. The database is split, and a confirmation dialog box appears. Click OK to continue.

If you look at the Tables tab of the Database window, you'll see that all the Table objects are now links to tables with the same names in the back-end database you created. If you saved the back end to a network path, you can now distribute the interface (the front end) to anyone on your local network (assuming their permissions are appropriate), and the linked tables will point to the correct data source.

Remember that even more scalability exists in Access. If using the database splitter doesn't help performance enough, or if you're beginning to see a slowdown, you can use a Microsoft SQL Server or other similar database engine to handle all the data.

Linked Table Manager

If you discover after creating your split database that you didn't, in fact, save the back-end database file to the correct network path, or if you decide later that you want to change where it lives, you can use the Linked Table Manager to change the locations of one or more linked tables with just a few keystrokes. This feature is one of those that is an absolute necessity to use in normal work. Without this tool, the only way to modify a link is via VBA code or by dropping (deleting) and relinking each linked table.

The Linked Table Manager shows a simple window (see Figure 39.1) that contains all the linked tables in the current database, along with the network path to their source. After you see the list of tables available for relinking, you can select one or all of them and modify the network path as necessary. Of course, the data source must already exist in the destination directory; you can't create a new data source by linking to a previously nonexistent database. You also can't create a new link via the Linked Table Manager.

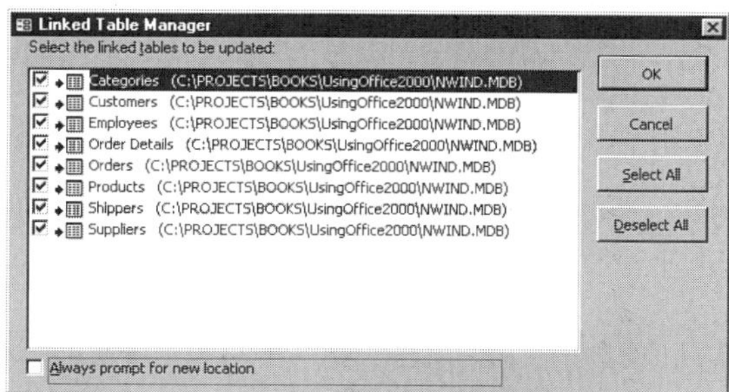

FIGURE 39.1
The Linked Table Manager enables you to select one, many, or all linked data sources to modify.

You can, however, use the Linked Table Manager to update the design of linked tables manually. If you know that the design of a remote data source has changed since it was originally linked, you can update the link without changing it, importing the new design information to your local Access database.

NOTE It isn't necessary to use the Linked Table Manager to update data stored in the remote sources—that's automatically done whenever the sources are accessed. Linked tables store no data locally.

To modify the paths to or update the design of linked data sources via the Linked Table Manager, use these steps:

1. From the Database window, select Tools, Database Utilities, Linked Table Manager. The Linked Table Manager opens, showing all linked data sources in the current database.
2. Select those data sources for which you want to change the location or update. To choose all of them, click the Select All button.
3. If you want to modify the location of the linked tables, check the Always Prompt for New Location box at the lower left. This does not, in fact, "always prompt"; it prompts you once for the location of all checked data sources.
4. Click OK to execute the update. If the update is unsuccessful (for example, a table has been deleted since the link was created), an error dialog box appears. Otherwise, a confirmation that the refresh operation was successful is shown.

NOTE To link to different databases, select the links in only one individual remote table (or view) at a time. Then update them and choose the next link to change.

Database Documenter

One of the more apt criticisms of modern relational database management systems (DBMSs) is that they're difficult to document. Unlike standard procedural languages where all the code is stored in text files that can easily be printed and read, much of the design of a relational database is stored in formats that can't easily be exported to text. Access is worse than most DBMSs for documenting, for the same reason that it's often better for development—because so much of it is graphical in nature.

Consider the Relationships window, for example. Until Access 2000, no way existed to print this efficient, easy-to-understand graphical interpretation of the relationships between the tables in the database. Fortunately, in Access 2000 you can choose Tools, Relationships, then File, Print Relationships to print this window. Or what about forms? You can print a list of the controls on a form and their properties, but you need graphics to show the layout in a format that a human can quickly comprehend.

Unfortunately, the fact that DBMSs are hard to document doesn't mean that they shouldn't be documented. Access includes an add-in called the Database Documenter. It inspects every element in the database and creates a text report that describes every object as clearly as text can describe it. If your database and all the copies you so carefully stored on tape in a safe, offsite location were somehow trashed, you could do a reasonable job of putting the whole thing back together (exclusive of the data, of course) with a preapocalypse printout from the Database Documenter.

It's a useful tool, but it isn't really enough to completely describe an Access database. If you're set on getting a paper description of your work, run the Documenter as described in the following set of steps. Then print out every form, report, and the Relationships window as well, and send the whole stack to your grandmother for safekeeping.

To create a database description report using the Database Documenter, follow these steps:

1. From the Database window, select Tools, Analyze, Documenter. Note that this is not the usual menu location for add-in tools.
2. The Documenter window (see Figure 39.2) opens. There are eight tabs—one for each Access object type. The exception is Data Access Pages, which aren't supported by the Documenter. In addition, a tab marked Current Database includes the database properties and table relationships defined in the database itself. Another tab is the All Object Types tab, which includes every object in the database. With one click on the Select All button, you can select individual objects to document or all the objects in the database.

   If you click the Option button, the dialog box at the bottom right of Figure 39.3 (or one similar to it) appears. Depending on the object type visible on the current tab, you can choose to print various properties of each object type. All the object types except Current Database have an additional dialog box (accessed through Options) that enables you to refine the information provided even further.

   Select the objects, properties, and options you want to document and press OK.

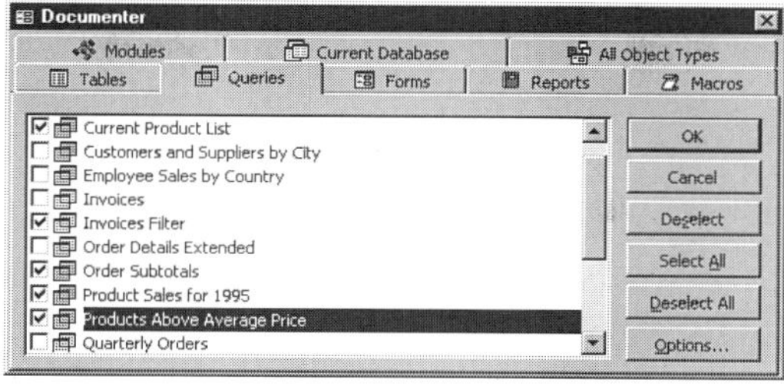

FIGURE 39.2
The Documenter window includes tabs for each object type and one for the database itself, new in Access 2000.

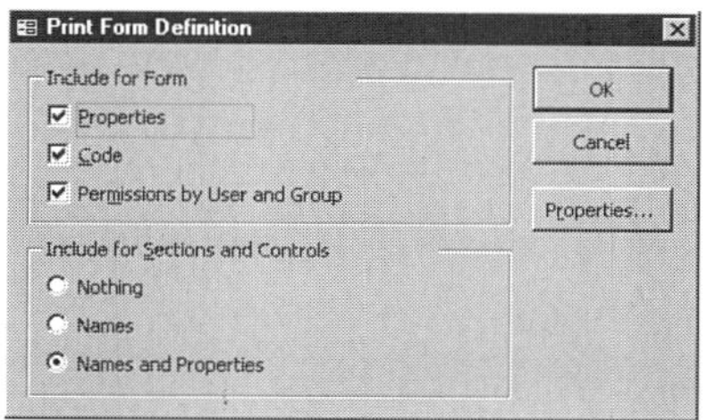

FIGURE 39.3
You can refine the documentation by selecting the appropriate options for each object type.

3. Access whirrs and clicks as it examines the objects you selected, and it eventually produces a report that looks something like Figure 39.4. You can then save and/or print the report, as desired.

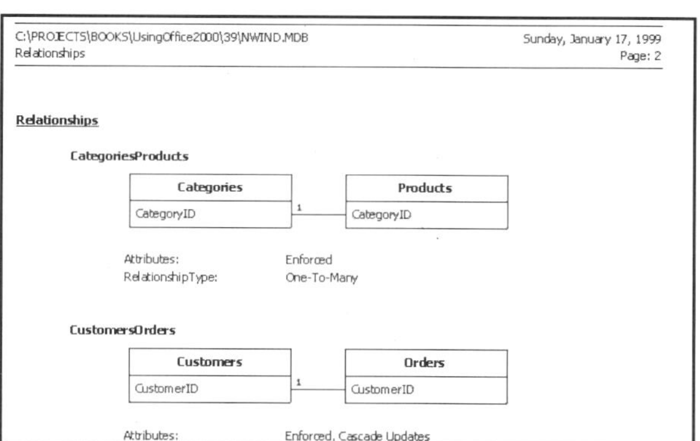

FIGURE 39.4
A Documenter report for a portion of the Catalog report object.

These reports don't take long to generate, but they can grow very large; the Northwind database, with all objects selected and the default properties and options chosen, runs to about 150 pages. Which options you choose depend on why you're generating the report. If you're seeking to create a paper record from which the database could be reconstructed, choose all the options and prepare to sacrifice a few trees. If you need to create a report containing only the SQL versions of several queries, then choose only those queries and only the SQL option.

Performance Analyzer

One of the most useful utilities included in Access is the Performance Analyzer. This tool analyzes the objects in your Access database and makes recommendations as to how to optimize them to improve performance of the database as a whole. Better yet, the Analyzer will implement its own recommendations in many cases.

To run the Performance Analyzer, use these steps:

1. It's best to close any open objects before proceeding because they can't be analyzed if they're open. From the Database window, select Tools, Analyze, Performance.
2. An object selection dialog box appears (see Figure 39.5); you'll probably want to select the All Object Types tab and click Select All. Then click OK to continue.

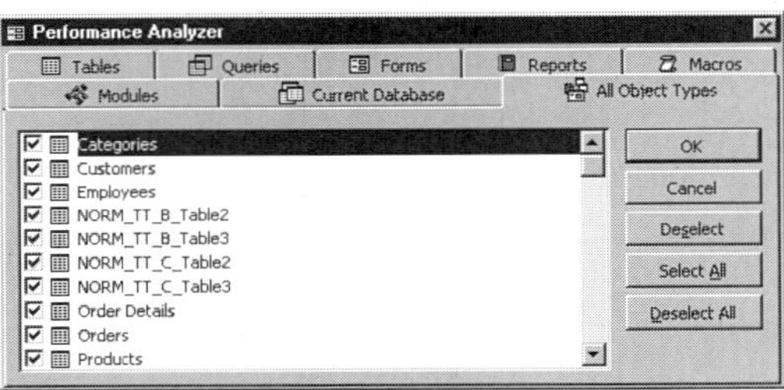

FIGURE 39.5
Select the objects to be analyzed.

3. After going through all the database objects selected, a dialog box appears (see Figure 39.6), containing the results of the analysis.

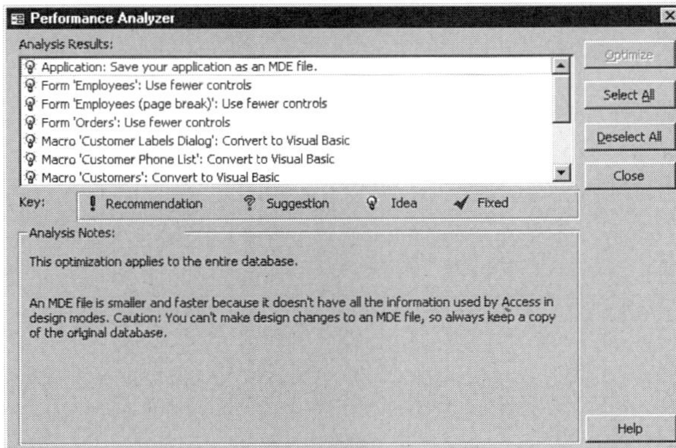

FIGURE 39.6
The results of an analysis of the Inventory sample database that comes with Office 2000.

To see more information about any particular analysis result, click it and read the text that appears in the Analysis Notes window below. In many cases, the Optimize button is enabled after selecting a suggestion or recommendation (or all of them); clicking it implements the changes Access believes will enhance performance. Analysis results of the idea class can't be implemented automatically. After making the modifications you request, they appear as Fixed in the Analysis Results pane.

Table Analyzer

When you create a database, you typically concentrate on making your table design efficient and logically organized. In the Northwind sample database, for example, the Customers table is comfortably granular, breaking up the data elements into different fields and following all the usual rules of good table design.

After the data is applied to the design, though, some problems may start to arise. Consider the Country field. When only a few data elements are present, that data in this field doesn't typically duplicate (although the County field in most customer databases would; you have to know your data pretty well to optimize it), and a quick look at the datasheet (or a report) quickly reveals any misspellings or errors made in data entry. But as the number of records increases, the likelihood of a duplication or misspelling increases as well. This duplication increases database size and creates the possibility that the same data element (such as a country name) could be entered in error.

These common design problems can be solved by creating *related tables* that contain data likely to be duplicated. You could do this manually by examining the data, determining which data is duplicated (or is likely to be duplicated), and creating new tables for that data (and the necessary relationships). Or you can use the Table Analyzer to do it for you.

The Table Analyzer evaluates the data in the tables you select, and based on what it discovers, recommends either no action or creating a new table for each data element that's frequently repeated. Although this creates more tables, it can reduce the size of the database as a whole by cutting down on duplicate data elements, all of which would otherwise have to be stored separately.

To use the Table Analyzer, follow these steps:

1. From the Database window, select Tools, Analyze, Table. The Table Analyzer starts.
2. Two dialog boxes explain what the analyzer is about to do and provide an opportunity to examine examples of tables that would benefit from analysis and splitting. Click Next in each of these dialog boxes to continue.
3. The third dialog box asks you to choose a table to analyze. Select one and click Next.

TIP Unchecking "Show Introductory Pages?" on this dialog box makes the previous two dialog boxes go away and not come back the next time you run the Analyzer.

4. The Analyzer asks whether you want to decide which fields are likely to contain duplicate information, or whether it should. If a reasonable amount of data is already in the table selected, the Analyzer will make reasonable choices. If not, you'll have an opportunity to select the fields to break out on the next window.

5. Regardless of the choice you made in step 4, you're taken to the window shown in Figure 39.7 to approve or complete the recommended design changes (if any). Dragging any of the fields from the source table to the design canvas creates a new table containing only that field and a key field to link back to the original table. If you disagree with a recommendation Access made, you can drag any of the fields Access moved into new tables back into the master table. Double-clicking any new table or selecting the Rename Table icon gives you an opportunity to rename it. If you didn't choose to have Access analyze the table for you, you can also choose a field to be the primary key in the new tables. After you've created and/or deleted tables and renamed them, click Next to continue.

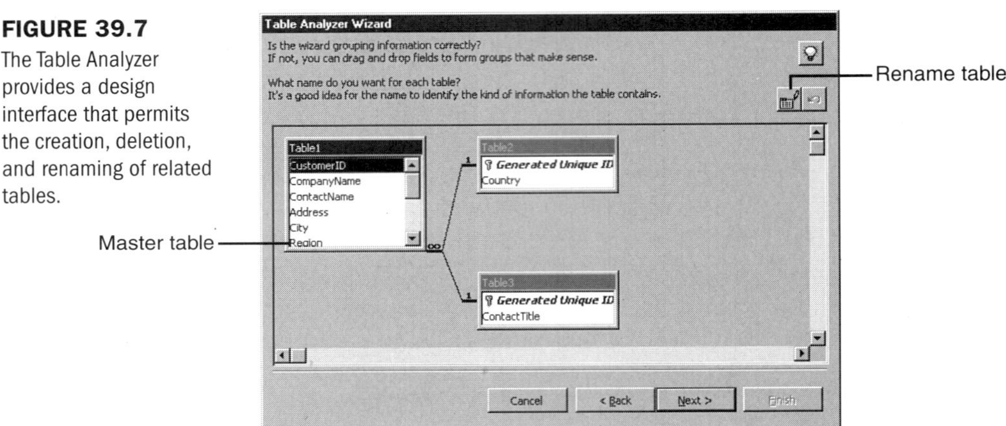

FIGURE 39.7
The Table Analyzer provides a design interface that permits the creation, deletion, and renaming of related tables.

6. If you don't rename any of the new tables, Access asks you to verify that this is what you intended. Regardless of your choice, the next dialog box (which looks exactly like the previous one) asks whether the bold fields uniquely identify each record in the proposed tables. This is necessary because the bold fields will become primary keys. Click Next if they do, or click Back to modify the table contents.
7. If Access detects that certain data values in the new related tables are similar (and may therefore be intended to have the same value, but include a misspelling), it displays the dialog box shown in Figure 39.7 to enable you to manually reassign values that may be incorrect to correct ones. If you see a value that's not right, clicking in the pull-down box of the Correction column displays a list of other possible values; if you choose one, Access modifies the data values as indicated in the table. Of course, incorrect data may still be in the table—you'll have to examine it manually to make sure everything's been cleaned up. Furthermore, Access recommends changes that may well be incorrect, as shown in Figure 39.8; you'll want to change these to Leave As Is, if warranted. After you've made corrections, click Next to continue.

FIGURE 39.8
Some of the recommended changes aren't correct, as shown here. You need to change these to Leave As Is to avoid changing the data.

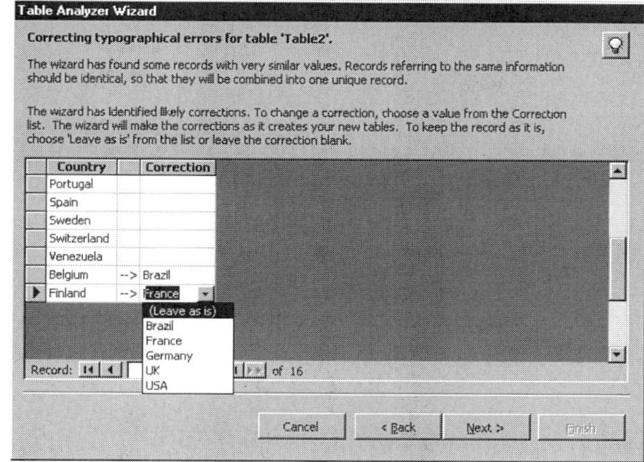

8. Finally, Access offers to create a query with the same name as your original table that takes advantage of the newly added tables and the relationships among all of them. You'll usually want to select the default (to create the query) and click Finish to do all the hard work.
9. Access displays the query it created so you can see the results of the table-splitting operation.

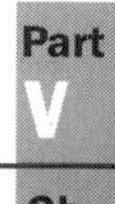

CHAPTER 40

Building Basic Applications

In this chapter

Application Design in Access

Access is unlike any of the other Office applications in that it is uniquely qualified to form the basis for professional applications that can be easily distributed. Unless you want to make the jump to Visual Basic or Visual C++, Access is the environment of choice for building an application that is consistent and flexible, taking advantage of all the power of a relational database in the context cf a rich Windows-based application framework.

With the possible exception of Outlook, Access offers more functionality in one package than any of the other Office components. The primary driving force behind this functionality is the richness of Access' *object model*, the elements that make up an Access database. In Word, everything is based on the document as a framework. In Excel, the worksheet is the least common denominator. In PowerPoint, you have a presentation composed of slides. In Access, the combination of forms (for data input and output) and tables to store records of any type (from user data to application state information) makes it a much more powerful environment for application development. There's no rule that says that an Access application must be based on traditional database techniques, either; anything you can do with an ActiveX control on a form can become an Access application.

More than any other programming discipline, developing coherent applications requires experience and patience to perfect. Easy-to-use applications are difficult to create; they require careful planning and design, detailed documentation, extensive testing, and comprehensive error-checking and data-integrity controls.

Conversely, simple applications based on the built-in design wizards often lack consistency and a sense that all the pieces fit together smoothly. They may or may not incorporate data checking, and nobody writes documentation for a wizard-created form—after all, who knows exactly what it does behind the scenes? You will quickly find that a good application is a lot of work to create, but the pride of authorship is significant.

The task of learning to write good applications is too broad to cover in a short chapter such as this one, but some excellent examples exist that you already have access (no pun intended) to, and others that you can obtain without a lot of effort. When designing a new application from scratch, think about all the applications you have seen that perform similar tasks:

- Are they organized similarly?
- Do you like that, or are there things that you want to do differently?
- What about application paradigms in dissimilar software—are there ideas you've seen in other applications that you like?

Of course, love it or hate it, the paradigm that Access best fits into is the Windows feature set—menu bars and toolbars, File menu on the left and Help on the right, drop-down boxes and command buttons.

Unfortunately, Access makes bad user-interface design trivially simple, and makes you work to develop truly elegant solutions. Access applications tend to look blocky and disjointed, with buttons and menus all over the place. That's because the tools that Access provides for application development are intended to get the job done quickly and easily, with not a lot of emphasis on style. One example is the Switchboard Manager, an Access Wizard that helps build a simple navigation system for an Access database. Access Switchboards are pedestrian in design (although you'll see how to spruce them up a bit), but they provide an easy way to quickly create an interface that ties disparate parts of your database together.

Creating the Switchboard Startup Form

Let's assume you've already created many of the forms and reports you intend to use in your application (not generally the way applications are built, but that's the operating assumption here). You can use the Access Switchboard Manager to create a simple front-end for your forms and reports, allowing users to get to them with one or two mouse clicks. You can even nest switchboards, so that a main switchboard includes a button that opens a second switchboard, and so on.

You can use the Switchboard Manager to edit switchboards that you've already created, and because the switchboards are implemented as one form with attributes modified in code, it's probably best that you do. Any modifications you make to the Switchboard form (adding control, pictures, and so on) risks making the underlying code inoperable.

The Northwind sample database does not include a switchboard, but all the included Database Wizards create customized switchboards for their applications. As an example, the Inventory Control Wizard (File, New, Databases, Inventory Control) creates the simple switchboard shown in Figure 40.1. It has been slightly modified from the default Switchboard Manager version by adding a bitmap graphic on the left.

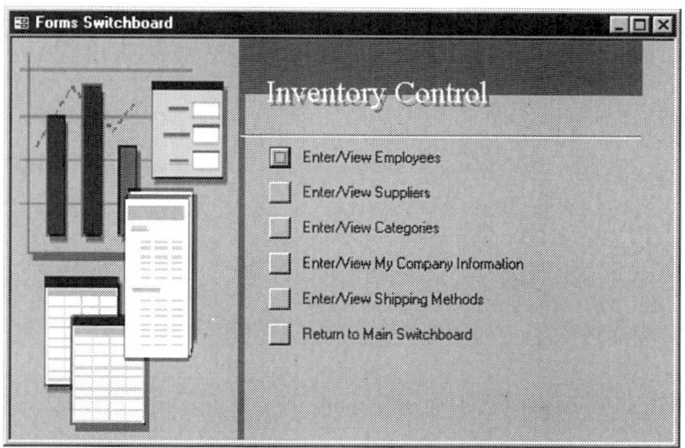

FIGURE 40.1
A sample switchboard created by a Database Wizard. You can enhance the plain switchboards created with the wizards by adding graphics.

To create a switchboard for your database, use these steps:

1. From Database View, select Tools, Database Utilities, Switchboard Manager. The Database Utilities and Switchboard Manager menu options may not be visible initially; if they're not, just hold the mouse pointer over the menu for a few seconds and they'll appear.

2. If this is the first time you've run the Switchboard Manager in your database (including Northwind), you'll be asked to confirm that you want to create a new switchboard. Click Yes to continue.
3. Access creates a form called Switchboard in the background and the Switchboard Manager window appears. The Main Switchboard page (really the Switchboard form) appears in the list of valid Switchboard Pages, and five buttons appear on the right:
   - Close makes the Switchboard Manager disappear. This isn't a cancellation, because the Main Switchboard form has now been created.
   - New creates a new switchboard page in the list.
   - Edit opens an existing switchboard form for editing in a view of the Switchboard Manager called "Edit Switchboard" (not in Design view).
   - Delete removes a page from the switchboard. Because switchboard pages are not physically separate forms in the database (and the Delete button won't remove the default switchboard page), you're not deleting database objects with this button. Of course, if you delete a switchboard page, there's no way to get it back.
   - Make Default makes the currently selected switchboard page the main page for the application.
4. To add buttons to the Main Switchboard, select it and click Edit. The Edit Switchboard Page opens. Until you create some buttons for this page, your only options are Close and New; Close returns to the Switchboard manager, and New opens the Edit Switchboard Item dialog box as shown in Figure 40.2. Click New to add an item.

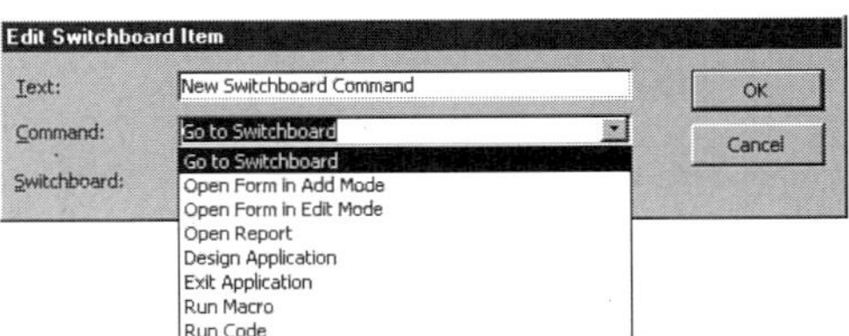

FIGURE 40.2
The Edit Switchboard Item dialog box lets you configure the buttons on a switchboard page.

5. Three boxes are in the Edit Switchboard Item dialog box; the first two are always labeled Text and Command. The third field appears, disappears, and changes depending on the selection you make in the Command field. Enter the text you want to appear next to the command button in the Text box and choose a Command from the drop-down list (refer to Figure 40.2). Commands available include
   - Go To Switchboard—opens the switchboard named in the third field.
   - Open Form in Add Mode—opens the form named in the third field with its Data Entry property set to Yes, so records in it can be added, but not edited or viewed.
   - Open Form in Edit Mode—opens the form named in the third field with its Data Entry property set to No, so records in it can be viewed, edited, or added.
   - Open Report—opens the report named in the third field in Print Preview view.

- Design Application—creates a button that opens the Switchboard Manager.
- Exit Application—closes the current database.
- Run Macro—runs the macro named in the third field.
- Run Code—executes the function named in the third field. Note that you can't enter a Sub procedure name here; only functions work. The return value (all functions return values) is ignored.

For example, if you wanted to edit employee information, you could enter Edit Employees in the Text field, select Open Form in Edit Mode from the Command field, and select Employees in the Form field that appears. Click OK after you've made your selections to return to the Edit Switchboard Page window.

As with menu buttons, entering an ampersand (&) character in the text field will make it appear underlined in the Switchboard and it will act as a hotkey in your application. For example, entering "E&xit" will make the "x" appear underlined, and a user pressing Alt+X will make the code behind the "Exit" button execute.

6. Repeat step 5 for as many buttons as you want on your switchboard. When you've added all the buttons you need, click Close to return to the Switchboard Manager.
7. If you want to add additional switchboard pages, click New on the Switchboard Manager and repeat steps 5 and 6 until the page is complete. For example, you could create a page containing only reports (call it Reports) and add a button (using the Go to Switchboard command) on the Main Switchboard to open it. This creates a cascade of switchboard pages as deep as you like. Don't forget to include navigation on each page to return to the previous page and/or the main switchboard page.

Creating menu structures more than three deep is not a good idea. The navigation quickly becomes too difficult for users to follow.

8. Open each of your switchboard pages (using the Edit button) and arrange the buttons in a sensible order by selecting each button and clicking either Move Up or Move Down as necessary. Alphabetical order is best if no other arrangement seems right. After closing the pages to return to the Switchboard Manager, select Close to return to the Database Window.

Your switchboard exists in the database as a generic form called Switchboard, with quite a bit of code underlying its `On Current` and `On Open` properties. Each generic button calls a function in the class modules generated by the Switchboard manager. Editing this code is not for the squeamish. However, you can modify the design of the Switchboard form itself if you're careful not to delete any of the elements the code requires to execute. Figure 40.3 shows a default switchboard form and Figure 40.4 shows one that's enhanced a bit.

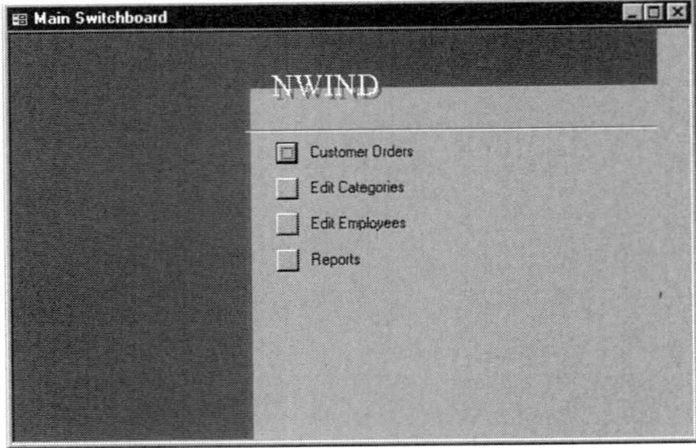

FIGURE 40.3
The default Switchboard form is legible but boring.

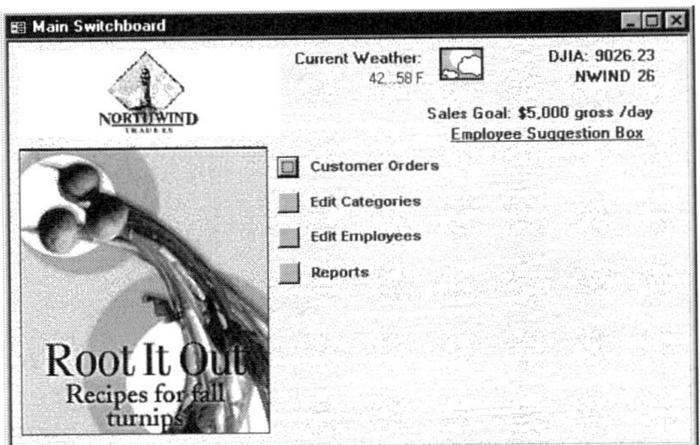

FIGURE 40.4
You can move and add elements in a standard switchboard to make your application a little less cookie-cutter, if you're careful.

Setting Startup and Security Options

Access' capability to act as an application framework is strengthened by the inclusion of a myriad of startup and security options that control access to your application and affect the way the Access environment appears to the user before the user gains control of the application.

Startup Options

In earlier versions of Access, you had to use a special macro called AutoExec to customize the appearance of the application; Access ran a macro with that name before it did anything else. That method still works, but in Access 2000 you have a better tool for managing the environment: the Startup window (Tools, Startup; see Figure 40.5).

The functions of most of these options are immediately apparent; if you want Cajun Pizza Orders Database to appear at the top of the active window when running your application, enter it as the Application Title. To cause a particular form or Data Access Page to appear on startup, select it in the Display Form/Page field. Of critical importance are the Display Database Window and Allow Toolbar/Menu Changes options; if you leave these checked, users have the ability to view and modify your database's design via the Database Window. Turn them off and users are limited to the menu commands you provide for them in custom command bars.

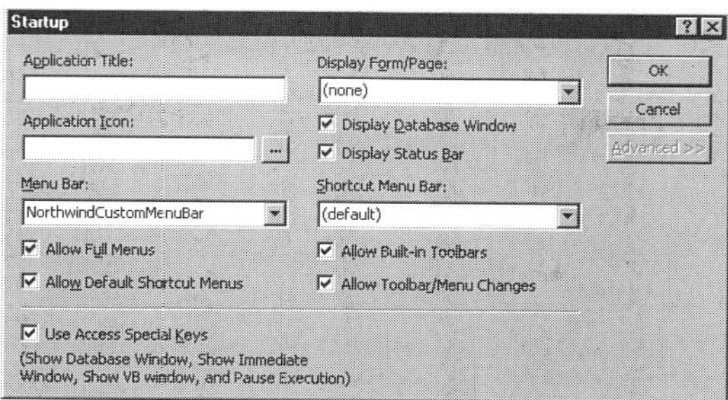

FIGURE 40.5
The Startup window allows you to specify exactly how the application will appear when it's started.

Using Database Security

Access provides two types of security for your application: user-level password protection and encryption. Both are easy to implement, difficult to bypass or defeat, and quite dangerous to use unless certain precautions are taken.

Whenever implementing security options other than the defaults in Access, you should make sure that you save an unencrypted, unsecured version of the database somewhere safe. A copy on a 3.5-inch floppy disk (1.54MB), LS-120 (120MB) or Zip Disk (100MB) locked in a safe gives you a clean backup to restore from if the secured version fails, stored on a medium that is widely readable. If you don't make an unsecured backup copy, you will be completely out of luck the day you forget the administration password on the secured copy.

Access 2000 improves on the Access security model by including a vastly improved User-Level Security Wizard that automatically performs some of the techniques that had to be performed manually in earlier versions of Access, such as creating a new workgroup information file. By forcing the adoption of security techniques that used to have to be manually implemented, Access 2000 is a much more secure database than its predecessors.

You should note that password protecting or encrypting an Access database protects it from access by unauthorized users, but does not necessarily protect it from modification. An easy way to prevent users from modifying database objects without implementing password-style security is available; for more information, see "Protecting the Application" later in this chapter.

Every Access installation includes a special file called a *workgroup information* file (sometimes ambiguously called a system file; we'll call it a WIF for brevity). Even if you haven't secured any database on your computer, a file called system.mdw exists in your Microsoft Office directory; it contains the default permissions for Access. Every Access database is, in fact, password-protected; until you change the database password, every user is presumed to be Administrator and has a null password. One of the steps the User-Level Security Wizard takes is to create a new WIF for your database, eliminating this security hole.

The User Level Security Wizard contains nine relatively complex dialog boxes and could comprise a chapter all to itself. In the interest of readability, this discussion concentrates on the defaults and recommended settings. You should explore the many other available options on your own.

To implement password-style security for an Access database, use these steps:

1. From the Database Window, select Tools, Security, User-Level Security Wizard. The first screen of the wizard asks whether you want to create a new WIF or modify the existing one, but the only option available the first time it's run is to create a new file. Click Next.
2. The wizard proposes creating a WIF called Secured.mdw in the current directory. You have two options: to make this new WIF apply to all databases on this computer or for Access to create a shortcut on the Desktop to the current database using the new WIF. Unless you're very comfortable with Access security, the option to create a shortcut (the default) is safer. Click Next.

NOTE The command line for the shortcut this command creates is

```
"C:\Program Files\Microsoft Office\Office\msaccess.exe" [cc]
"<database filename>" /WRKGRP "<WIF filename>"
```

3. You're prompted to select the database objects that should be secured. If you're going through the trouble of implementing security, you may as well secure everything, which is the default. Press Next.
4. Access' new integration with the Visual Basic for Applications model for Office 2000 means that you need to choose a password to secure all the code in modules and behind forms and reports in your application. There's no reason why this can't be the same password you'll use for the database administrator or developers, if they're different people. You can also choose a null password. Enter a password (if desired) and press Next.
5. You can establish groups (to which users will be assigned later) that share permissions among other members of the group. Access suggests some reasonable user groups, which you can choose to use if you like by clicking next to the group name. Turn on any groups you may want to use and click Next.
6. The next dialog box (see Figure 40.6) asks whether you want to assign any permissions to the default Users group, to which all database users belong. If you select No, you're saying that every user will be assigned to a group and that every group will have explicit permission set. If that sounds like too much work, select Yes, choose the types of objects that you want to assign permissions to, set the appropriate permissions, and press Next.

If you intend to distribute this application to users on a different network, make sure you assign permissions to the Users group, because the user IDs on the destination machines are different from the development machine, and you are not able to assign individual passwords.

7. Every user of the database should be individually identified (unless you're using the Users group described in step 6) in this window, which allows you to select from all the users defined on your system and assign individual passwords. You can add user names not currently defined if you like and delete users that have machine accounts but do not have database permissions. Press Next to continue.

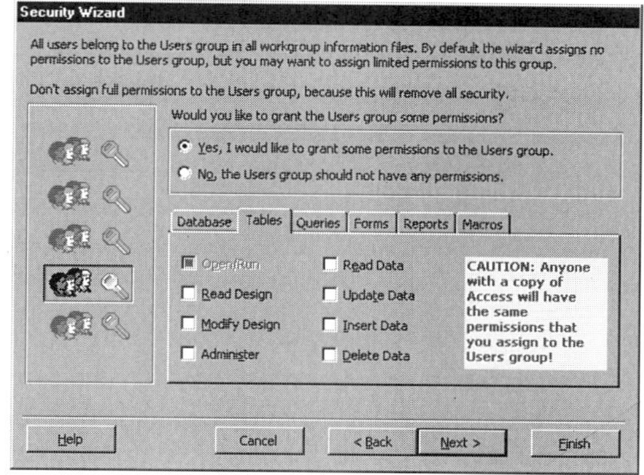

FIGURE 40.6
The CAUTION is in bright yellow and red for good reason. Use the Users group with care.

8. The eighth dialog box of the wizard enables you to assign the users you created to the groups you authorized. You can also assign the groups to users, a minor distinction. When you're finished, press Next.

If you don't assign yourself to an appropriate group, you'll find that you're unable to do anything in the database after the wizard finishes running. Don't forget.

9. Finally, you're asked to name the backup, unsecured version of the database. The default is the current name with a .bak extension in the same directory. Choosing a different name is not a bad idea. Append a string such as unsecured to it, and use the usual Access .mdb extension instead. Press Finish.

After you complete the wizard's interrogation, it helpfully creates a report (see Figure 40.7) that contains all your security settings and the identifying strings you chose (or Access supplied) during the process. This report, with its information, is as important to keep as the unsecured copy of the database. Should the workgroup file ever get deleted or become corrupted, the only way you are able to get into the secured database is by re-creating the WIF with the exact same settings and ID strings.

Access also gives you the option of saving a snapshot image of the report; however, doing that is probably not very useful. The report is then deleted so that users can't re-create it without the hard copy.

If you've used the wizard to set security, you can use the other tools (Tools, Security, User and Group Permissions and Tools, Security, User and Group Accounts), or the wizard later to modify your settings.

You can do two more things to make your database a little less susceptible to predators. One is to add a database password (Tools, Security, Set Database Password). Anybody trying to open the database is asked for this password, regardless of the other security options set.

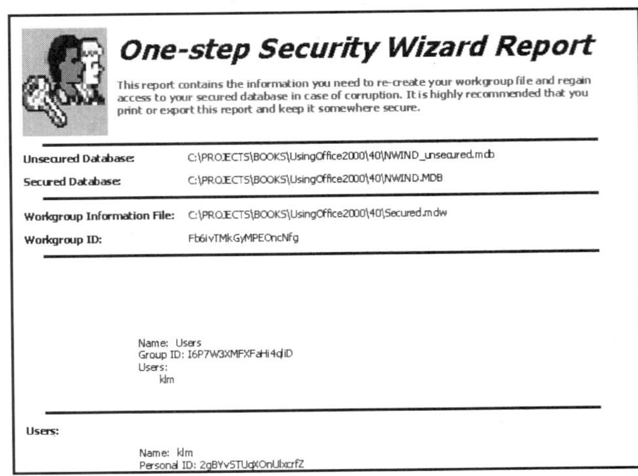

FIGURE 40.7
Access records all your WIF settings for you in a helpful report if you use the wizard to set them.

Finally, you can encrypt your databases so that no program other than Access can read them. This prevents disk analysis programs from scanning the physical disk on which your database resides for data in your tables, but does not limit access by anyone running Access. Note that encryption and decryption require processing time and that your machine may slow noticeably when working with an encrypted database.

Distributing Your Application

When you are ready to make your application available to others, you can usually just give a copy of the .mdb file to anyone who has a copy of Access 2000. If you have a copy of the Office 2000 Developer Edition, you can use the new Package and Deployment Wizard (replacing the Setup Wizard) that creates a custom Setup program and includes tools to create distribution floppy disks and other, professional-looking features. Regardless of how you distribute your application, you should consider some issues to make sure it's ready for distribution.

NOTE Access 2000 uses a new file format, so people with Access 97 and earlier are not able to read it. You can convert an Access 2000 database to Access 97, however, by selecting Tools, Database Utilities, Convert Database, To Prior Access Database Version. Note that any Access 2000-specific features are disabled.

Splitting the Database for Network Use

Access 2000 is even more client/server oriented than its predecessor. It has become *de rigueur* to separate the client functions (interface) from the server functions (data management) in distributed applications written in Access; there are several good reasons for doing so:

- Ease of manageability—Keeping the interface separate from the data enables you to create smaller incremental updates when form and report designs change and makes it easier to create custom interfaces for different users if required.

- Network health—If your database is placed on a central server for remote users to access, giving each a copy of the interface and leaving the data on the server significantly decreases the impact the database places on the network, because users send and receive traffic only when accessing the back-end tables.
- Ease of upgrade—If you want to migrate the database to SQL Server or another enterprise database management system, you may be able to do so without replacing the interfaces users have already installed.

You could build your database and then separate the tables from the forms, queries, and reports manually, but Access provides a tool to do this for you. The Database Splitter is easy to use and does a good job. To start it, select Tools, Database Utilities, Database Splitter. Access creates a new database called <*databasename*>_be.mdb (*be* stands for back end), exports all the tables from the master table to the new back-end database, deletes them from the original, and creates links to all the exported tables. You can then distribute just the interface to users and place the back end in an appropriate place on the network. Be sure you include instructions (or, better yet, a module using the TransferDatabase action) to link to the new location of the back-end database after you move it.

▶ **See** " Importing, Exporting, and Linking with VBA," **p. 1153**

▶ **See** "Database Splitter," **p. 1115**

Replicating the Database for Network Use

Database replication is a technique that's useful for providing separate copies of a database to people who may be separated in such a way that a full-time network connection isn't available or is slow. It also works with good network connections, but it's unclear whether the extra effort it requires to manage is worth the benefits in that case.

When you replicate a database, you really create copies of it for remote use. The original, called the *Design Master*, is maintained to consolidate changes made to the data in the copies and for making changes to the interface if necessary. The copies, called *replicas*, are distributed and used by others elsewhere on the network.

Periodically, a person in charge of the Design Master synchronizes all the replicas, one by one. Any changes made to the data in the replicas are also made in the master, and then the master's synchronized dataset can be sent to each replica. You can easily see that a full synchronization, where all the replicas update the Design Master and the Design Master updates each replica, can take several passes through the synchronization routine.

There's another problem with synchronization. If replicas make changes that conflict with one another, a conflict, design error, or data error occurs that must be adjudicated by a human. These terms have precise meanings:

- A *conflict* occurs when two replicas change the same record in different ways.
- A *data error* occurs when a change is made in one replica that affects the referential integrity of another.

- A *design error* occurs when a change is made in the Design Master that causes a loss of data in a replica.

▶ **See** "Understanding Referential Integrity," **p. 1004**

Managing synchronized databases, then, includes not only managing the synchronization schedule, but also handling conflicts and errors that may occur. Although managing synchronized databases is a daunting job, synchronization works particularly well in some situations (as with a mobile work force) and it may be worthwhile to pursue.

Creating Replicas If you want to use synchronization to manage an Access database, you need to create a Design Master and as many replicas as are required (and no more).

NOTE You can't change a database with a password into a Design Master. Remove any database password (select Tools, Security, Unset Database Password) before proceeding.

To make a database into a Design Master and create one replica, follow these steps:

1. Select Tools, Replication, Create Replica.
2. Access confirms that you want to proceed and asks whether you want a copy made; you should always select Yes, because there's no way to change a Design Master back into a normal database.
3. You're asked to confirm the name of the replica. The original database is closed (after asking you to confirm that it can be—it's required), the Design Master and one replica (called Replica of <*databasename*>) are created, and the Design Master is reopened in Access.

When the database reopens as a Design Master, you'll notice small yin-yang symbols next to each of the objects, indicating that this is a Design Master. You can give the replica to whoever needs to use it, but don't copy it directly to make more replicas. To create more replicas, select Tools, Replication, Create Replica. Each replica is uniquely identified by information not accessible from the interface, and copying a replica in the file system copies the identifiers as well, which prevents correct synchronization.

CAUTION

Each replica is uniquely identified by a field in a hidden table. If you copy a replica, that field is copied directly and the copy has the same identifier as the replica that it was copied from, which will wreak havoc when synchronizing. Make sure you always create new replicas from the Design Master.

Synchronizing Replicas After the replicas have been distributed, you'll need to synchronize the replicas and the Design Master periodically. Of course, you need access to the replica database file to do this, so you'll need the remote user to be logged in to the network (with the directory containing the replica shared appropriately) or to have provided you with a floppy copy first. To synchronize a replica, use these steps:

1. Select Tools, Replication, Synchronize Now. The Synchronize Database dialog box appears.
2. You are presented with several choices. However, unless you're running the Office 2000 Developer Edition, only the default (Directly with Replica) is relevant. Use the Browse button to find the replica file on the network (or on a floppy disk).
3. After the replica has been located, an option appears to make this replica the Design Master. You should use this option only if the original Design Master has been destroyed. Click OK to continue.

You can repeat steps 2 and 3 with as many replicas as you need to synchronize. If conflicts occur, you'll be notified; you can then click Tools, Replication, Resolve Conflicts to see the conflicts and follow the instructions provided in several dialog boxes to resolve them.

On subsequent replications, you'll be able to select the files to synchronize from the drop-down list in the Synchronization dialog box. Remember to synchronize each replica twice—the first time to migrate design changes out from the master to the replicas and data changes from each replica to the master, and the second time to ensure that every replica's changes (now incorporated in the Master) are sent to all replicas.

The process of manually synchronizing all replicas is tedious and inefficient. In the Office 2000 Developer Edition, the Replication Manager takes control of this task, automatically scheduling synchronization tasks and alerting you only when there's a problem. If you're going to use synchronization in a production environment, the ODE is worth owning.

Other Replication Issues There are a few more relatively uncommon situations you may encounter when using replication that you should be aware of:

- If you need to change the design of the database, be sure you do so in the Design Master, not in a replica. At the next synchronization, the changes will be replicated along with the data to all of the replicas.
- If your Design Master becomes corrupt or is lost, you have a couple of options for recovering it. The easiest way is to open a replica, manually synchronize it with all of the other replicas (Tools, Replication, Synchronize Now for each replica in the replica set), and then select Tools, Replication, Recover Design Master. This will create a new copy of the Design Master. Alternatively, you can promote a replica to be the new Design Master (which is useful if constructive changes have been made to its structure by accident) by selecting Tools, Replication, Synchronize Now, selecting the current Design Master, and clicking Make '*<filename>*' the Design Master.
- In certain circumstances, you may want to create a replica that has only a subset of the records available in the Design Master. You can do that by creating a *partial replica*, which filters records in a particular replica according to rules you set. In Access 97, you would use the Partial Replica Wizard, available on Microsoft's Web site, to help create these; this tool has not yet been published for Access 2000 (and it's not clear whether it will be). Because the only other way to create a partial replica is through complicated VBA (really DAO) coding, you may expect that the wizard will be updated for Access 2000.

Protecting the Application

There's one way to ensure that no changes occur to your application's forms, reports, or code after it has left the development machine. It's easier than implementing user-level security and securing the database design against changes. It's easier than creating a Design Master and only giving out replicas. It's called creating an MDE file, a version of the database that contains no design information. If you distribute an MDE file, there's no way to change forms, reports, or code, because the design structures for those elements aren't included in the database to modify. Upon opening an MDE, users immediately discover that the Design view doesn't exist, so there's no way to change forms, reports, or code. They can, however, modify and create new macros, queries, and tables. As an added bonus, MDE code usually runs a little faster than the same code in a standard Access database file.

To make an MDE file of your application:

1. Select Tools, Database Utilities, Make MDE File.
2. You'll be asked to name the new file; the .mde extension is required.
3. Click Save and the MDE file is created.

There's no way to change an MDE file back into something you can modify, so be sure to save a copy of the original.

CHAPTER 41

Using Macros and VBA in Access

In this chapter

Macros Versus VBA

A normal progression occurs that most Access developers follow as they gain experience working in a relational database. The first element most people learn to work with is the Access table. Next come queries and forms. Reports follow, and macros come into vogue at about the same time as budding developers start to want to control the state of the application—it becomes desirable to make the application perform differently depending on some variable or condition in the database.

Forms, queries, and so forth all behave the same regardless of what else is happening in the custom application, but macros impart some intelligence to the database, permitting the developer to force certain things to happen depending on other things happening.

Access is different from other Office applications, however, in that its implementation of macros is independent of its programming language, Visual Basic for Applications (VBA). In Word, Excel, and PowerPoint, macros are really VBA procedures that can be generated automatically from the interface, usually by recording keystrokes. In those applications, you can record a macro without any knowledge of VBA, but the macro is stored as VBA code, and it's edited in the VBA Editor. In Access, macros are unrelated to VBA except in function (see Figure 41.1). And they're probably doomed for just that reason.

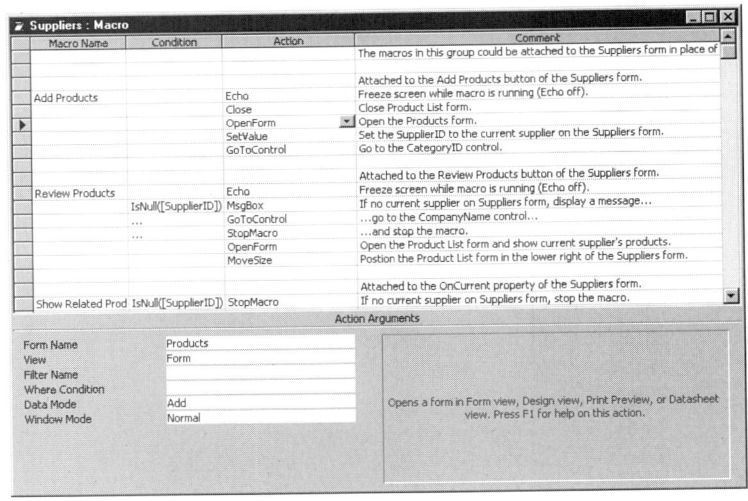

FIGURE 41.1
A macro library from Northwind, showing names, conditions, actions, and comments. Access macros have nothing in common with macros in the other Office applications.

Starting with Access 95, the Access programming language (used for modules) began to be called VBA, even though it was somewhat incompatible with the VBA in other Office applications. Because Microsoft has long made its intentions clear—that the Office applications should share a common programming interface—it seems reasonable to expect that it won't be long until Access macros, those white elephants of the Office community, are no longer supported. In fact, since Access 97, there's nothing you can do in a macro that you can't also do in VBA, but VBA does a lot of things macros can't handle.

So why use a macro for anything at all? For one thing, the macro interface is somewhat simpler than VBA's, because so many fewer options exist. For developers with no programming experience, the macro coding environment may seem friendlier and less overwhelming. But it's not clear that becoming a good macro programmer eases the transition to VBA at all. The Office object model and terminology can be confusing, as can any programming language, but insulating users from it by encouraging the development of macros is often counterproductive because the learning curve is just as great when they need to use VBA later. Macros can't perform error handling; they can't make use of variable scope; and whole planets of the VBA object environment are unavailable to the macro programmer to manipulate. Lastly, they're usually slower-executing than modules, which should be the last nail in the coffin.

Converting Macros to VBA

So what do you do if you have a database full of macros? You convert them to VBA, of course. You can easily convert any macro to VBA by opening it in the Macro editor, selecting File, Save As, and choosing Module in the As drop-down list. Access gives you the options of adding error handling and keeping the comments, if any, and a VBA module is quickly created from the macro. Figure 41.2 shows the result of converting the macro in Figure 41.1 to a module.

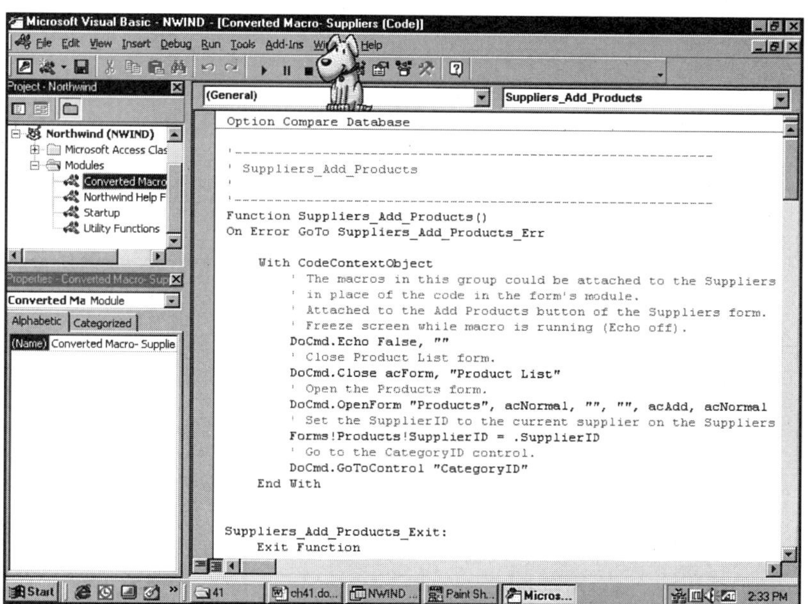

FIGURE 41.2
The macro in Figure 41.1 converted to a module, with error handling added automatically.

The `CodeContextObject` mentioned in the code window is added to all converted macros; it means "the code in this module applies to the object that has the focus when this code is run." In this case, though, most of the commands are context-independent and pretty easy to figure out: `DoCmd.Echo False` turns off the screen echo so that the screen doesn't update while the code is running; `DoCmd.Close acForm, 'Product List'` closes the form called Product List, and so on. After you know the keywords (`Echo`, `Close`, `OpenForm`, `GoToControl`), the code practically writes itself (and Access provides hints for completing the VBA methods if you have Auto List Members turned on—Tools, Options, Editor in the VBA Editor).

Most macro commands are directly related to equivalent VBA commands. Many macro commands that perform actions (`OpenForm`, `CancelEvent`, and so on) are replaced by the syntax `DoCmd.<command>` in VBA (`DoCmd.OpenForm`, `DoCmd.CancelEvent`, and so forth) Some are replaced by VBA statements (the macro command `MsgBox` becomes the VBA action `MsgBox`).

Just creating or converting some VBA code doesn't make it run. To execute the code, it needs to be "attached" or bound to an object, or called from another VBA module. You typically bind code to objects by entering the name of the function or module you wrote in one of the object's *event properties*, properties that Access "triggers" when certain things happen (such as opening a form or clicking a button). Events and event properties are discussed in the section "Writing Class Modules to Handle Events" later in this chapter. The point of this exercise is to show that anything you can do with a macro can be done in VBA, with a lot more flexibility.

The VBA Editor Interface

With Access 2000, the module editor finally falls into sync with all the other Office applications' macro languages, Visual Basic for Applications, and with Microsoft's commercial programming language, Visual Basic.

Although this interface is familiar to people who have written VBA code for other Office applications, it's a strange new beast to veteran Access programmers. When you edit a code module in Access 2000, you're transported out of Access and into an entirely separate application. Experienced Access programmers will find themselves closing module code windows and wondering what happened to the Database window more than once.

The VBA Editor is a separate application that is, by default, made up of three window panes: The Project Explorer, the Properties window, and the Code window (see Figure 41.3). Depending on the situation, you may want to make visible the Immediate, Locals, and Watches windows and the Call Stack. Discussions of all these windows, when they're useful, and why you would use them follow in the next few sections.

The Code Window

The Code window is probably the most important of all. It's where you do your editing, and your code is color-coded to help you tell comments from declarations and statements from breakpoints. If one good reason exists to have big color monitors on programmers' desks, it's to support color-enabled code editors, which really do ease and speed the development process. The two drop-down boxes at the top of the Code window, the Object and Procedure boxes, enable you to quickly find any *class module* (a code module that is part of an Access object; see "Writing Class Modules to Handle Events" later in this chapter) within a different object in the current form or report, if you know the object it refers to.

FIGURE 41.3
The VBA Editor, showing a class module (discussed later) in the Employees form. Each pane is resizable and can be made invisible.

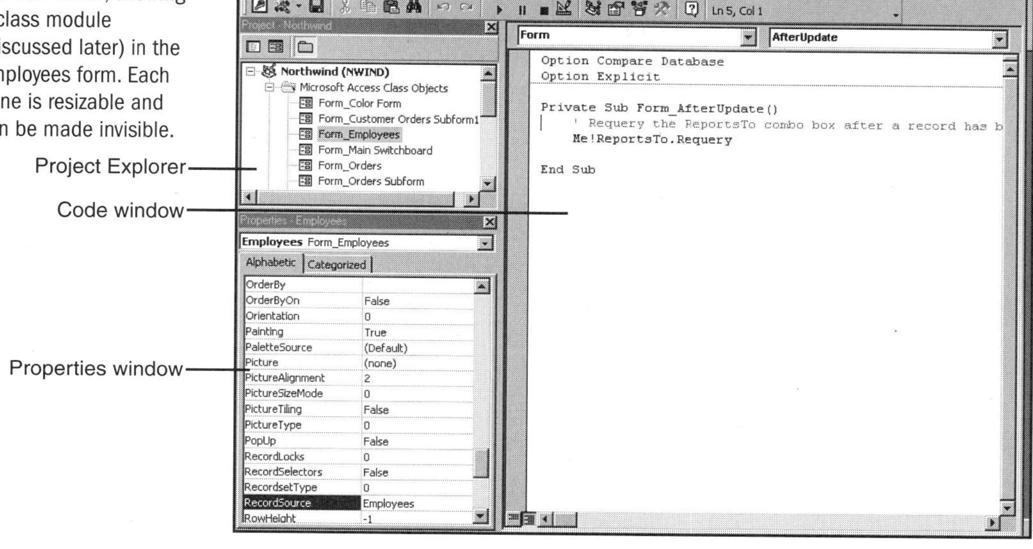

The Code window supports several debugging features that make your life easier when testing code. These include the following:

- *Breakpoints*, which halt code at the line you specify so you can inspect variables or watch the progress of execution from that point on (until you don't want to watch anymore). Pressing F9 or selecting Debug, Toggle Breakpoint makes the current line turn burgundy, adds a marker icon (a ball) in the left margin, and stops execution before that line is interpreted as the procedure runs. If it's not already visible, the VBA Editor comes to the foreground when the breakpoint is reached. Pressing F9 on a breakpoint clears it.
- When a breakpoint is reached, it may be useful to *step* through the code, line by line. The Code window supports four step commands, all accessible from the keyboard or Debug menu:

  - *Step Into* (F8)—Advances one line, "stepping into" called functions and procedures as necessary.

  - *Step Over* (Shift+F8)—Advances one line, "stepping over" functions and procedures and maintaining the focus in the current procedure.

  - *Step Out* (Ctrl+Shift+F8)—Advances to the next line in the next-higher procedure (nice for getting out of loops or jumping out of a procedure you meant to step over).
  - *Run to Cursor* (Ctrl+F8)—Advances the code to the cursor position.

All these commands execute the code as they advance.

- To skip code and designate the next line to be executed, place the cursor on the next line to be run and select Debug, Set Next Statement (Ctrl+F9). This ignores any intervening code; it is useful when a value didn't get set correctly, so the preceding statement didn't do what was intended. You can use the Immediate window to change the variable, and then reset the execution to the preceding statement.

The Project Explorer shows all the objects in the current file (project). This hierarchical list typically includes any forms or reports that already have class modules attached to them, any standard modules (code modules visible from the Database window), and any objects included in add-ins, such as Access Wizards (as is the case with the Northwind database but is unlikely otherwise). Double-clicking any object in the Project Explorer opens it in the Code window for editing. The command bar buttons at the top determine whether the VBA Editor or Access should be in the foreground and whether the object list should be flat or hierarchically arranged in folders.

The Properties Window

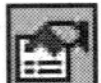

The Properties window shows the properties of the currently active object in Access (or any other Office application). Just clicking an object in the Project Explorer doesn't necessarily show its properties in the Properties window; the object must be visible in Design view (View, Design View) or otherwise open for editing (as is possible in some subforms in Form view) in its native application to view and change properties here (refer to Figure 41.3). To change an object's property, click in the right column of the Properties window and type or select an appropriate value. The drop-down list at the top of this window displays the names of all objects that are currently open for editing, and the tabs enable you to choose an alphabetical or categorical list of properties, not unlike the Property Sheets in Access's design environments.

Veteran Access programmers may prefer to work with the Project Explorer and Properties window closed and the Code window maximized to mimic the environment to which they're accustomed.

The Immediate Window

Several old Access favorites are available in the VBA editor on demand. They include the Immediate window, the Locals window, and the Watch window. The Immediate window permits interactive entry of commands and code for immediate evaluation. To open the Immediate window, click View, Immediate Window.

In the Immediate window, type

```
Print DCount'("'EmployeeID","'Employees")
```

and you'll get a count of all the employees in the Employees table without having to create a procedure or function to do it. Better still, as you type an expression, the Auto List Members and Auto Quick Tips features of the editor prompt you for the next logical entry in the expression you're typing (as shown in Figure 41.4), unless you turn them off in Tools, Options.

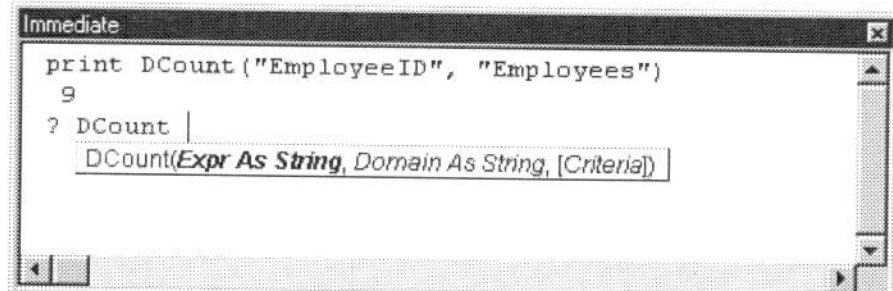

FIGURE 41.4
The Immediate window, including a helpful Quick Tip on the DCount function.

VBA sometimes shows its roots in traditional BASIC; you can use the character "?" to represent the word "print," as in "? CurrentDB.Name."

The Locals Window

The Locals window, if viewed while code is executing (as often happens when using breakpoints), shows the names, values, and types of all variables local to the current procedure (see Figure 41.5). You don't have to guess as to the value of a loop counter because it's always visible in the Locals window if you choose to display it (View, Locals Window). Instead of the Locals window, you can hold the pointer over the name of any variable in the Code window while the code is executing (or is stopped at a breakpoint) to see the variable's current value.

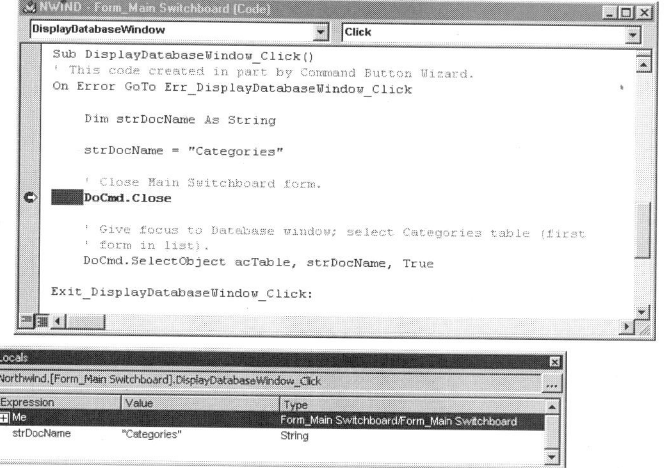

FIGURE 41.5
The Locals window shows the values of the variables within scope in the code currently executing (and stopped at a breakpoint). The small plus sign to the left of a variable name means that you can expand it to view its properties.

The Watches Window

The Watches window shows the names, values, types, and context of any variable in any module that you select (see Figure 41.6). Add a variable to the watch list by opening the window (View, Watches Window) and right-clicking anywhere in it, or by selecting Debug, Add Watch. Choose Add Watch from the menu and type the name of the variable you want to watch. Select its context (the object and procedure the variable is created in), and it will be followed through the execution of all modules, regardless of its scope. This is useful because a variable may not be local in the currently executing module (that is, it's neither global nor defined in the current routine), but you still may need to know its value. Edit or delete a watched variable by right-clicking it and choosing Edit or Delete from the menu that appears.

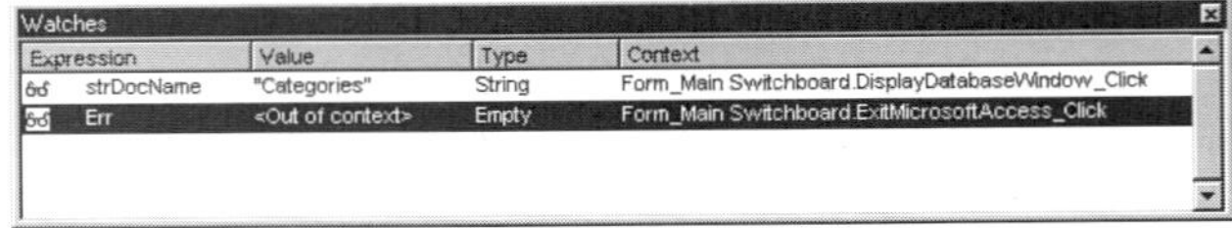

FIGURE 41.6
The Watches window shows the value of variables selected for tracking and the contexts in which they have values.

Add a watch quickly by highlighting a variable name or entire expression and selecting Debug, Quick Watch.

The Call Stack

The *Call Stack* pop-up can be made visible only when code is currently executing (see Figure 41.7). It shows the sequence of procedure calls that have transpired to get the application to the current point, usually a breakpoint in a module. It's useful for tracing back how you got here from within a large application.

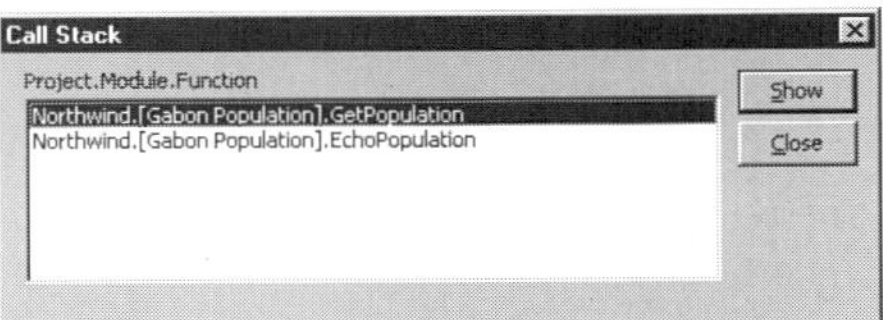

FIGURE 41.7
The Call Stack, showing the names of the code modules that have called the current module.

Writing Class Modules to Handle Events

You can create two types of modules in Access: *standard modules* and *class modules*. Standard modules stand alone and may contain functions, procedures, and other programmatic entities that can be called from any other procedure or function and usually do not depend on a specific, internally detected event to execute. For example, you might create a standard module to contain a library of commonly used functions, as in the Utility Functions module in Northwind. Or you may develop a standard module specifically to contain code to perform a specific kind of data manipulation. Standard modules may act only on certain objects or data, but they're stored independently of that data and they don't depend on an event occurring in the database (other than their name being called) to execute.

Class modules are actually parts of the objects they support and are usually executed in response to a specific event occurring in the database. This kind of programming is called "event-driven," and it depends on the application (the database, in this case) being able to detect that certain things (events) are happening.

NOTE Objects without code are called *lightweight objects*, and they often work a little faster as a result. You can make a small improvement in the efficiency of your database application by ensuring that forms and reports that don't require class modules have no code behind them at all (left over from debugging, copied from another object, and so on). An easy way to do this is to set the `HasModule` property of the form to False. Be careful—setting this property to False deletes any class modules the object may contain.

These events vary depending on the object currently active in the database. For example, if a form is active, more than 30 different events (which are intrinsic to forms) are monitored, including the insertion of records (before and after), the movement of the mouse and pressing of its buttons, its loading, unloading, and closing, and dozens of others. In addition, each control on a form supports several events depending on the control type. Finally, certain changes to the data itself cause events to occur. As a rule of thumb, just about anything that a user does or any task that the database performs can be detected, and code can be run at that instant.

Access class modules follow a strict naming scheme. The name of a class module is always a concatenation of the name of the object type, an underscore, and the name of the event the code is bound to. For example, a module set to run when a form is opened will always be called "Form_Open" and is stored with the form definition (not in a separate module) in the database. Because every control in a form or report must have a unique name, this scheme guarantees that every class module in a given form or report will have a unique name.

Class modules are bound to events through the Property Sheet for that object. The list of events supported for that object is visible in either the Event or the All tab of the Property Sheet, and if code is bound to an event, the symbol [Event Procedure] is shown in the property box (see Figure 41.8). Clicking in that box and selecting the Builder button opens the VBA editor and makes that class module visible in the Code window.

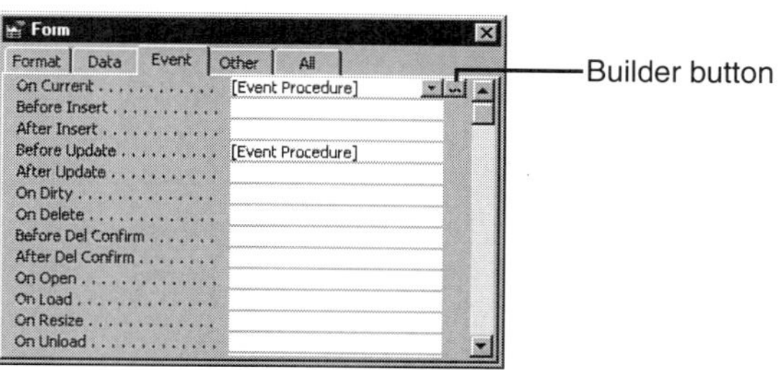

FIGURE 41.8
A Property Sheet for a form with bound class modules.

To create a new class module, click in the property box next to the event you want to act upon and select the Builder button, Code Builder, OK from the dialog box that appears. The VBA Editor opens and names your class module for you according to the object and event you selected.

NOTE It's possible to create a class module and not bind it to an event. In this case, clearing the symbol [Event Procedure] from the Property Sheet unbinds the procedure created for that event but does not delete the procedure. Any other events using that procedure will still be able to call it, but the event it was created for will not trigger it until the [Event Procedure] symbol is reentered in the Property Sheet.

Code in class modules sometimes becomes unbound from events inadvertently when the object containing the modules is renamed. In this case, simply changing the Property Sheet to reflect the existence of class modules reenables them correctly.

To write class modules to handle events, it's important to understand the order in which events happen. The events specific to every type of object in a database differ, and the order in which the events occur differs as well. To determine which events occur in which order, you'll need to make use of Access Help. Type `events occur` in the Office Assistant search box and press Enter. Then select the topic "Find out when events occur." It contains links to the event orders for each type of database object.

After you determine which event you want to trap, you can create a new class module as previously described and add code to perform the action desired. For example, command buttons trap the `OnClick` event, which occurs whenever the preferred mouse button is pressed while the pointer is over the command button. You can create a command button on a form and attach whatever code you like to its `OnClick` event by creating a new class module as previously described. For example, when the code in Listing 41.1 is attached to the `OnClick` event of a command button on a form with a header region, it changes the form header's background color to a random value every time the command button is pressed.

Listing 41.1 Code to Change a Form Header's Background Color Randomly

```
Private Sub Command0_Click()
Randomize
Me.FormHeader.BackColor = Int(Rnd() * 100000)
End Sub
```

NOTE The Randomize function initializes Access's random-number generator so the `Rnd()` function on the next line generates a reasonably random number. If you leave out the Randomize statement, Access chooses the same sequence of random numbers every time it's restarted.

Note that the name of the routine in the previous example changes automatically depending on what you name your command button. Access names command buttons "Command0," "Command1," and so on, by default.

This is an example without much basis in real practice, but it should be clear that the event of pressing the command button causes the code to execute. Writing code for class modules is generally easier than figuring out exactly what event to write them for; that takes experience and a careful reading of the event order documentation in Access Help.

Procedures and Functions

Your Access modules are either *procedures* (easily recognized by the keyword `Sub` in the first line of the procedure) or *functions* (called `Function`). The difference between the two is subtle: Procedures don't need to return a value to the calling procedure (if any), although they may; functions always return a value, although the calling procedure may not use it. The reason for the difference is historical; functions typically have performed mathematical calculations, and their return values are important to the caller, but procedures have stood alone. However, third-generation procedural languages (such as C and C++) assign values to subprograms (procedures) as well as functions, and that's carried over into VBA.

The Differences Between Procedures and Functions

Think of a function as shorthand for a set of calculations that would otherwise make the code difficult to read. Functions are also usually concise, general (so they can be used by many other procedures and functions), and are named so they can easily be understood. For example, Northwind includes the function `IsLoaded` (see Listing 41.2) in the standard module Utility Functions:

Listing 41.2 This Function Returns a Value Consistent with Its Name; It's Also Potentially Useful in Many Applications

```
Function IsLoaded(ByVal strFormName As String) As Boolean
  ' Returns True if the specified form is open in Form view or Datasheet view.
    Const conObjStateClosed = 0
    Const conDesignView = 0
    If SysCmd(acSysCmdGetObjectState, acForm, strFormName) <> conObjStateClosed
    Then
        If Forms(strFormName).CurrentView <> conDesignView Then
            IsLoaded = True
        End If
    End If
End Function
```


To use this function in code, you'd probably create a conditional statement that called it, such as

```
If IsLoaded("Orders") Then DoCmd.OpenForm "Orders"
```

This causes Access to evaluate the function `IsLoaded` and to replace its name in the calling procedure with its value; if `IsLoaded()` evaluates to True, the conditional statement would open the form "Orders." If the function evaluated to False, the rest of the conditional would not be executed. The value of the function is set by assigning the function name to a value in the code, as is done on line seven of this example.

NOTE This function has a flaw, however; it doesn't explicitly set its value to False when the conditions listed are not met (refer to Listing 41.2). In Access, this will execute properly, but writing ambiguous code isn't a good habit to get into. A better way to write the core of this function might be as follows:

```
    If SysCmd(acSysCmdGetObjectState, acForm, strFormName) <> conObjStateClosed
    Then
        If Forms(strFormName).CurrentView <> conDesignView Then
            IsLoaded = True
        Else
            IsLoaded = False
        End If
    Else
        IsLoaded = False
    End If
```

or like this:

```
IsLoaded = False
If SysCmd(acSysCmdGetObjectState, acForm, strFormName) <> conObjStateClosed Then
        If Forms(strFormName).CurrentView <> conDesignView Then
            IsLoaded = True
        End If
    End If
```

This forces the function to return False if the form is not loaded and doesn't depend on Access to assume False unless told otherwise.

One way to keep the traditional dichotomy between functions and procedures clear is to consider Access's built-in functions and the kinds of operations they perform: mathematical calculations, single-command SQL lookups, returning system values such as the date and time, and so forth. Functions are typically used as shortcuts to accomplish a general, well-defined action. If you're familiar with the use of arithmetic functions in Excel, such as `=SUM(A3:D3)`, then you'll see that Access functions are very similar.

Procedures, on the other hand, may be long and complicated, and their return values (if any) are generally ignored. The concept of *modular coding*, which most modern programmers aspire to, requires that every program be written as a group of procedures, which are called in sequence. Modular code is easy to understand, easy to debug, and VBA is an easy environment in which to write modular code.

NOTE Veteran programmers often like to have procedures return the value 0 if execution finished properly, and -1 if it did not. The calling code can then check the value of the procedure to see whether it worked correctly, as in

```
If (procEnsureEnoughLifeboatsForEverybody <> 0) Then
    procCallCelineDion
Else
    procAbandonShip
End If
```

This is a fine convention in general, but Access's robust error-handling mechanisms make it unnecessary. A properly written procedure will catch and handle its own errors without returning control to the calling procedure.

Except for the way they're used, procedures look exactly like functions except for the keyword `Sub` on their first and last lines.

Declarations, Arguments, and Scope

Both procedures and functions can accept variables passed from the calling procedure or object, modify them, and return them to the caller. Alternately, passed variables (known as *arguments*) can be modified locally without changing their value in the caller. Understanding the difference between these two methods (referred to as *passing by reference* and *passing by value*) is critical to making procedures and functions work correctly. Finally, it's often important to tell Access what kind of value can be stored in a particular variable; the statements that do this are referred to as *declarations*, and they're often used in conjunction with arguments.

Before you use a variable for the first time, it's good practice to declare it in a special kind of statement called a declaration. Declarations are, by convention, grouped at the beginning of modules (procedures and/or functions) so they're easy to find. A typical declaration statement might look like the following:

```
Dim country_name As String
```

This statement tells Access that the variable `country_name` is a string anywhere that it's used in the current module. Other data types that you can use in declarations include Integer, Single (for single-precision decimal numbers), Double (for double-precision decimal numbers), Date, and a host of others. Look up `Dim` in VBA Help (which you'll have to install from Office Setup) for details about the data types you can declare in `Dim` statements. After a variable is declared as being of a certain type, generally you can't change it in the same module.

Variables are, by default, visible only to the module in which they're declared; that is, their scope includes only the current module. If a procedure or function outside of the current one needs to change a variable, you can pass it by reference in the call to the new procedure or function. Because Northwind doesn't include any useful examples of this type, consider the snippet of code in Listing 41.3:

Listing 41.3 Simple Sample Code to Illustrate Parameter Passing and Variable Scope

```
Sub EchoPopulation()

Dim country_name As String
Dim population As Long

country_name = "Gabon"
population = GetPopulation(country_name)
MsgBox "The population of " & country_name & " is " & population

End Sub

Function GetPopulation(ByRef country As String) As Long
```

continues

Listing 41.3 Continued

```
If country = "Gabon" Then
    GetPopulation = 1190159
Else
    GetPopulation = 0
End If

End Function
```

This example declares two variables (lines 2-3; "Long" means "long integer"), calls a function (line 5), and pops up a message box displaying the result of its calculation (line 6). The call to the function `GetPopulation` includes the argument "`country_name`," which points to the same place as country in the function, meaning they are the same variable. Notice that the function declaration (line 8) gives the expected type of the incoming argument; this serves to declare the placeholder variable that will be used in the function.

Also note that the function declaration must list the data type of the function itself, and the type listed must be compatible with the declared type of the variable to which its value is assigned. You can pass any number of arguments to functions and procedures in this way, separating them with commas in both the calling statement and the procedure declaration.

Arguments passed by reference can be modified in the called procedure, even if their name is different; in this case, if the `GetPopulation` function changed the value of the local variable `country`, the value of `country_name` in the calling procedure would change as well. This is because arguments passed by reference actually pass their location in the computer's memory, not their value. Passing by Reference is the default method in VBA. To pass by value, you should add the word `ByVal` to the argument declaration in the called procedure:

```
Function GetPopulation(ByVal country As String) As Long
```

This protects the value of the variable from being changed in the calling procedure, even if it's changed in the called procedure.

Variables declared within the bounds of a procedure or function, such as those in Listing 41.3, are visible only within those procedures or functions. Most of the time, that's good coding procedure. However, VBA recognizes that it may sometimes be convenient to make variables visible among all procedures and functions in a module—or even across an entire project. To make variables visible to all procedures in a module, simply declare them before the beginning of the first procedure:

```
Dim country_name As String
Dim population As Long

Sub EchoPopulation()

country_name = "Gabon"
```

The VBA editor recognizes that their scope is now intended to include the entire module and draws a line between the declarations and the code; the section above the line is often called the declarations section. Any variable declared in a declarations section will be visible to all procedures and functions in the current module. Of course, if one procedure changes the value of a variable declared this way, it changes for all procedures in that module.

Although we used the `Dim` keyword here, you will learn in the following paragraphs about the two preferred ways of declaring variables outside of procedures.

To declare the scope of a variable to be *global* (visible to all procedures) across all modules in a project, declare it in the declarations section and use the keyword `Public` in the declaration:

```
Public country_name As String
Public population As Long
```

These variables will be visible in all procedures in this database after one of the procedures in that module is called.

You will sometimes see the keyword `Private` used in a variable declaration:

```
Private country_name As String
Private population As Long
```

This form indicates that the scope is local to the current procedure and is the preferred method of declaring module scope variables, rather than the `Dim` statement previously described.

One additional declaration keyword you should consider is `Const`, which declares your variable to be not variable at all—the value you assign to it at declaration time is the value it holds throughout its *life* (the time it remains in scope). The syntax is pretty self-explanatory:

```
Const variablename [As datatype] = value
```

You can also use the keywords `Public` and `Private` in conjunction with `Const` (as in `Public Const`) to change a constant's default scope.

Importing, Exporting, and Linking with VBA

To use data from other applications from within Access, you need to either import it or link to it. Importing data makes a copy, so any changes you make in Access don't affect the original data source; linking data maintains it in its original application and location, so any changes you make to the data in Access are actually made in the serving application. When you link external data, Access acts as a client, a front end, to the remote data source. For more information about sharing data, see Chapter 42, "Data Sharing with Other Applications."

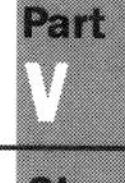

It's usually convenient to set up this kind of relationship between applications from the Access graphical interface, where you can use the menu commands and follow the step-by-step instructions Access provides to create the linkages you need. But at times, it's more convenient to use VBA, such as when the remote data source may not be known during the design of the application or may change during execution.

The key to using VBA to connect to remote data sources is the use of the Transfer set of VBA methods: `TransferText`, `TransferSpreadsheet`, and `TransferDatabase`. Depending on the source and format of the data to be imported or linked to, one of these methods should suffice.

TransferDatabase

The `TransferDatabase` method of the `DoCmd` object takes the following syntax:

```
DoCmd.TransferDatabase [transfertype], databasetype, databasename[,
objecttype],source, destination[, structureonly][, saveloginid]
```

The only required arguments are the `databasetype`, `source`, and `destination`. Valid `databasetypes` are strings representing recognized external databases, such as "Microsoft Access," "dBASE III," "ODBC Databases," and several more enumerated in VBA Help for the `TransferDatabase` method. Make sure the filter for any `databasetype` you choose has been installed on the client machine before executing this code, or an error condition will be generated.

The `source` and `destination` arguments are string expressions that name the source and destination database and/or table. Note that the method for exporting a database object is the same as the method for importing one, except that the source and destination names are reversed and the optional `transfertype` argument `acExport` is used.

In this command more than most, the optional arguments are practically required to eliminate ambiguity in the command. The `transfertype` argument determines whether the desired action is an import (the default), export, or link. The `objecttype` argument is useful only when working with two Access databases; otherwise, you can transfer only table-type objects. The `structureonly` argument is convenient if you're interested in copying the table structure, not the included data.

The following simple example illustrates the basic use of this command:

```
DoCmd.TransferDatabase , "Microsoft Access",  "Nwind.mdb", , "Employees",
➥"Employees"
```

Because the transfer type is not specified, an import is assumed. Note the use of the commas to mark the places of arguments not used; they're required if you don't specify optional arguments in the middle of the command. You should omit the extra commands at the end, however. This command imports the Employees table from the file `Nwind.mdb` in the current directory into the current database.

The use of `TransferDatabase` can get quite complicated, as in this example:

```
DoCmd.TransferDatabase acLink, "ODBC Database",
"ODBC;DSN=OracleDBs;UID=marlowe;PWD=mypassword;
LANGUAGE=us_english;DATABASE=myDB", acTable,
"sourceTable", "destTable"
```

Here, we connect to a preexisting Oracle database (called `'myDB'`) via ODBC and link the local table `'destTable'` in Access to the source table `'sourceTable'`. Changes made to data in `'destTable'` will actually change values in `'sourceTable`.'

TransferSpreadsheet

`TransferSpreadsheet` is a little less complicated than `TransferDatabase`; its syntax is

```
DoCmd.TransferSpreadsheet [transfertype][, spreadsheettype], tablename,
filename[, hasfieldnames][, range]
```

The only required arguments are the name of the table to be imported to or exported from and the spreadsheet filename. The `transfertype` argument, as in the `TransferDatabase` method, specifies whether this is an import, export, or link (import is the default); the `spreadsheettype` argument assumes that the spreadsheet in question is Excel, but several variants of Excel and Lotus 1-2-3 are supported (with some limitations for linking to 1-2-3 spreadsheets) through the use of various constants for this argument. The `hasfieldnames` argument specifies whether the names of fields are to be imported or replicated as the headers of columns in the spreadsheet, and the range is a valid range of cells to be imported (you can't specify a range to export to).

NOTE It's worth noting that the `spreadsheettype` argument in the `TransferSpreadsheet` method uses integer constants (which Access predefines as `acSpreadsheetTypeLotusWK1`, `acSpreadsheetTypeExcel8`, and some others), but the `databasetype` argument in `TransferDatabase` requires a string ("`Microsoft Access`, "`dBASE III`", and so on).

The following example imports the range A1 through J400 (which includes fieldnames) of the Excel 2000 spreadsheet stored in the file `Products.xls`:

```
DoCmd.TransferSpreadsheet acImport, acSpreadsheetTypeExcel9,
➥"Products","products.xls", True, "A1:J400"
```

TransferText

The `TransferText` command reads or writes data that is stored in a flat text file. The syntax is

```
DoCmd.TransferText [transfertype][, specificationname],
tablename, filename[, hasfieldnames][, HTMLtablename][, codepage]
```

The required arguments `tablename` and `filename` refer to the table and file to be imported, linked, or exported, as desired. Various `transfertypes` support importing or exporting delimited, fixed-width HTML tables or lists, or mail-merge files; note that linking to a text file doesn't permit writing to it, but changes in the text file are reflected in Access. The `specificationname` argument is used to name an import or export specification that was created with the Import/Export Wizard in Access (selecting File, Get External Data, Import or Link, and then selecting a file starts the wizard, which permits the saving of a specification). Using a specification is required when working with a fixed-width file.

The `hasfieldnames` argument works the same as in the `TransferSpreadsheet` method, specifying whether columns of text should have field names at the top. The `HTMLtablename` argument specifies the name of a table or list in the HTML file referenced, and the `codepage` argument represents a language `codepage` pertinent to the file in question.

An example illustrates how a flat text file can be imported into an Access table:

```
DoCmd.TransferText acImportDelim, , "Employees", "employees.csv"
```

Improving Module Performance

Access loads modules "on demand," that is, when procedures in those modules are requested by the application. Because this loading almost always occurs during application execution (while users are sitting in front of the screen, waiting for something to happen), sluggish modules can cause the appearance of a sluggish application (and programmer, by extension). You can take some positive steps, however, to make sure that your VBA code is as speedy as possible:

- Write efficient code—Try to keep related statements in one procedure and/or module if possible. It's helpful to write modularly, but that doesn't mean that every module should have three or four lines of code; each procedure call is another executable statement that must be run to continue. Use `SELECT` statements instead of nested `IF` statements, if possible, because `IF` statements are notorious CPU hogs (and `IIF` statements are doubly so). Use SQL aggregate functions (`DLookup`, `DCount`, and so on) instead of `DoCmd.RunSQL` commands, which have to be interpreted at runtime.
- Compile your code—Access doesn't really "compile" code in the way a C or FORTRAN compiler does—it doesn't convert the text-programming language to machine-language object code. But it does perform a one-pass optimization and reduction to an intermediate form called p-code, and p-code runs a whole lot faster than uncompiled VBA. Compiling your code at design time (by selecting Debug, Compile) does two useful things: It error-checks your code for obvious errors and it takes care of the first step of interpretation, performing the p-code conversion while you watch it instead of while your user watches it.
- Dimension your variables—It takes time to figure out what data type your variables should be, and that time is expended while the code is running if you haven't declared them earlier. Using the Option Explicit command (or setting the VBA Require Variable Declaration option by clicking Tools, Options, Editor, Require Variable Declaration) not only improves database performance, but it lessens the chance that a misspelled variable name will wreak havoc in your application.
- Help VBA out—Use techniques that lessen the amount of work the engine has to do. Use the `Me` keyword to refer to controls in and properties of the current form or report to prevent VBA from searching the whole application for the referenced object. Declare and use constants (typed appropriately) instead of variables that never change value. Remember that calculations performed on integers are much faster than calculations on floating-point numbers, so declare your variables as integers (`Int` or `Long`) if possible. You can implement a more efficient two-decimal floating-point number by declaring it as `Currency`. Finally, make sure the `HasModule` property of forms and reports is set to `No` if they have no class modules; this makes them "lightweight" and allows the runtime interpreter to avoid inspecting the form or report's properties looking for any modules that might be there.

One other technique that you might consider is intentionally controlling when your modules execute. If you need to do a lot of back-end calculation and setup (creating temporary tables), it may be advantageous to create a module that runs immediately after the application is started, rather than after the user has begun working in it. It's often more forgivable to force a startup delay (look at how long it takes to boot Windows) rather than interrupt the user as he or she works.

Error Handling Using Modules

When you're writing and testing code, you generally want errors to stop everything and show a descriptive message on your screen. This helps you figure out what isn't working right so you can fix it. But after you distribute an application to users, the last thing you want is for an error to pop up in all its naked glory right after your user has entered a few dozen data elements into a form. It's practically impossible (and theoretically impossible, for most kinds of procedural code) to guarantee error-free code, and you can never assume that you've handled every possible outcome of a user's actions. The only way you can protect yourself (and your application) is by *trapping errors* and dealing with them gracefully. Code you write to manage trapped errors is called an *error handler*. Error handlers are useful even after you think you have all the bugs worked out, because they can be used to detect certain program conditions that may not have been predictable or anticipated at coding time.

By default, Access passes all detected runtime errors to the screen along with the error number and a simple description of the error. Figure 41.9 shows a representative error caused by typing "print 4/0" in the Immediate window. Of course, you'd never allow a user to do that, but what if you prompted a user for a value that was used somewhere else as a divisor, and they entered zero? It would not be helpful for the application to stop executing at that point and to display this helpful error message.

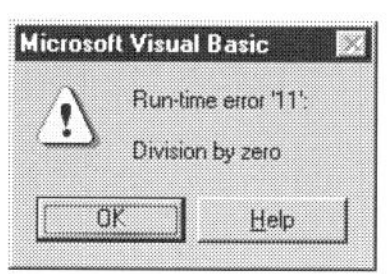

FIGURE 41.9
A friendly error message to remind your user that you didn't implement an error handler in your code.

It's not overkill to include a few lines of error handling in every procedure in your code. When you use the Command Wizard to create a simple command button on a form, Access includes an error handler, even though most command button operations are usually one statement long and are practically impossible to break. You can never be too careful.

The message box in Figure 41.9 generates the error number and description it displays by querying a system object called `Err`. `Err` is created automatically for every database and has two important properties: `Number` and `Description`. These are populated automatically by Access when a runtime error occurs, and you can take advantage of them in your error-handling code. In the preceding example, Err.Number = 11 and Err.Description = "Division by zero." To create an error handler, you insert a line containing an `On Error` statement at the very top of every procedure or function. Code that doesn't include an `On Error` statement doesn't handle errors, and any runtime error during its execution will halt it. The `On Error` statement can be used in one of three ways:

- The *On Error Go to Label* tells Access to redirect control to the line with the named label when an error occurs. Statements after this label can then deal with the error condition and/or exit gracefully, insulating the user from the Access error message. This is the most common error-handling method, and an example appears as follows in Listing 41.4.
- *On Error Resume Next* tells Access to ignore the error and continue processing at the line immediately following the one that caused the error. This is useful in cases where the programmer is sure that an error may occur that won't affect execution, as in the case of a statement that tries to delete a database object that doesn't exist. You could check for its existence and then delete it if it's there, but it's faster and more concise to nuke it and ignore the protestations of the database engine.
- *On Error Go to 0* does not go to a line labeled "0," even if one exists; it simply disables all error handling in the current procedure. It's rarely used, and you'll probably see it only in conjunction with another error handler, disabling the dominant handler for a short stretch of code.

The code in Listing 41.4, from Northwind's Main Switchboard form, is a classic example of Command Wizard error handling:

Listing 41.4 A Typical Error Handler. Manually Generated Handlers Should Follow This General Format

```
Sub ExitMicrosoftAccess_Click()
' This code created by Command Button Wizard.
On Error GoTo Err_ExitMicrosoftAccess_Click

    ' Exit Microsoft Access.
    DoCmd.Quit

Exit_ExitMicrosoftAccess_Click:
    Exit Sub

Err_ExitMicrosoftAccess_Click:
    MsgBox Err.Description
    Resume Exit_ExitMicrosoftAccess_Click

End Sub
```

A few elements are worth noting here. The `On Error` statement immediately follows the procedure heading, before any errors have time to get generated. It specifies that, upon detecting an error, Access should jump to the line labeled `Err_MicrosoftAccess_Click` (line 8). If no error exists, the code executes the `DoCmd.Quit` statement on line 5, ignores the line label `Exit_MicrosoftAccess_Click` on line 6, and exits the procedure at line 7. If an error exists (presumably in lines 1-5, before the code exits), control passes immediately to line 8, the label specified in the `On Error` statement. It's important to note that no error message is returned to the user by Access because an error handler is in place. Of course, this isn't much better, because line 9 pops up a message box containing the error description (from the `Err` object, the same as the Access internal error handler does). Control then passes to line 10, which resumes execution at the label on line 6. It then exits gracefully at line 7, with Access' internal handler never invoked.

Typically, you'll do something more useful than pop up an error message in your error handlers, such as show a more descriptive interpretation of the error. This example is also limited in that it makes no attempt to figure out what caused the error; you could as easily implement a `Select` statement on `Err.Number` to show different messages (or even perform different actions), depending on the type of error detected. You certainly don't have to exit the code after a trapped error if you can handle it and prevent it from recurring.

One more item of interest: The `Err` object is reset (to 0) by the execution of a `Resume` statement. The `Resume line` statement can restart execution at any named *line*; you can use `Resume Next` to pick up after the statement that created the error, or simply `Resume` to retry the statement that caused the error.

CAUTION

Using a simple `Resume` without eliminating the problem that caused the error will send Access into an infinite loop, which you can break out of with Ctrl+C.

NOTE The `Clear` statement also clears the `Err` object without leaving the error handler; it's rarely used except during debugging.

You could write an error handler that didn't contain a `Resume` statement, but the error would regenerate as soon as control left the negligent procedure. In this case, Access will look for an error handler in the calling procedure, cascading up the line until it either leaves the code stack out the top or finds a suitable error handler. This kind of cascading error can be devilish to debug (hint: make use of the `Source` property of the `Err` object) and is best avoided by always including a `Resume` statement in the error handler.

CHAPTER 42

Data Sharing with Other Applications

In this chapter

Importing, Exporting, and Linking Other Databases

One of the nice things about working with Access 2000 in an office environment is that it's a good neighbor. Access includes a powerful suite of data conversion tools that enable it to read and write data formats from nearly any other modern database on the planet, from simple text files, and even from HTML (World Wide Web) files that are formatted in reasonable ways.

Access is so versatile as a "middleman" between other databases, experienced database designers often use it to convert data from one full-powered enterprise database (Microsoft SQL Server, Oracle, Sybase, Informix, and so on) to another. It's also useful for throwing together "prototypes" of databases that will eventually be moved to more powerful engines. All this is possible primarily because Access speaks so many database languages.

Open Database Connectivity (ODBC)

Microsoft invented *ODBC* as part of its plan to create protocols to allow the sharing of data between disparate data providers of several types, including electronic mail systems, telephony applications, and databases. After several iterations of development, the 32-bit variants of ODBC (versions 3.0 and 3.5) ship with every Microsoft operating system and connect to nearly every commercial database on the market.

Access is a fully ODBC-compliant database, which means that it can both read and write data across an ODBC connection to another ODBC-compliant database (that is, it can act both as an ODBC server and as an ODBC client). Some implementations of ODBC support only one-way communications (although this is rarer than it used to be); check with your ODBC vendor to find out. In addition, some companies specialize in creating ODBC interfaces for other companies' applications, such as MicroFocus (formerly Intersolv) at `http://www.microfocus.com/products/data.htm`. Your noncompliant DBMS might, in fact, have a third-party driver available for it. It's important to use only 32-bit drivers with Windows 95, 98, NT 4.0, and Windows 2000; older 16-bit drivers can cause significant system problems.

NOTE Access can natively link to Borland's Paradox and dBASE database products up to version 5 of dBASE and version 5 of Paradox. It can also write in Paradox versions 7-8. To link to newer versions of dBASE and/or Paradox, you'll need the Borland Database Engine, which is included in Borland Delphi and newer versions of Paradox. After that driver is installed, Access will be able to link to the latest versions of dBASE and Paradox. For details, see Access Help.

Even though Access happily reads files from many DBMS file systems, it's almost always better to use ODBC, if possible. Here's why:

- Going through the file system usually forces you to import or export an entire file (created by another DBMS) at a time. Most DBMSs store more than one data object in each physical file, and you might just want to work with one particular table or view.
- Access's interpreter of the other DBMS's data format might not be perfect; in any case, the manufacturer's own knowledge of its data format and internal hooks to ODBC are likely to be faster and more reliable than Access's.

- Linking to ODBC databases is usually seamless; after the initial connection is made, little difference exists between a table in any ODBC DMBS and in Access, and you can use live links to ODBC databases on several remote servers at the same time.

Of course, some good reasons exist not to use ODBC. If your network connection is spotty, you might want to grab (or put) data while you can before the line drops again. You might not have access rights to use the database engine, but you can read the file system. Maybe you're writing code for distribution and don't want to assume that the client computers on which your application will run will have ODBC configured properly.

One case to consider in which you can't use ODBC, even though drivers are available, is using ODBC to link to certain other PC databases, including FoxPro and Paradox. That's because Access includes internal hooks to those applications that make ODBC unnecessary. Drivers for these applications are included for non-Microsoft applications that might need to use ODBC to talk to Microsoft applications.

To install a driver for ODBC on your system, follow the documentation that came with the remote database. ODBC drivers generally are not available for download from manufacturers, but your system database administrator (DBA) can probably help you. Windows typically installs ODBC drivers for many popular PC databases; you can check to see what drivers you have on your system by clicking Start, Settings, Control Panel, ODBC, and selecting the Drivers tab. A typical Windows 98 installation is shown in Figure 42.1.

FIGURE 42.1
ODBC drivers installed by default in Windows 98 with Office 2000 Premium.

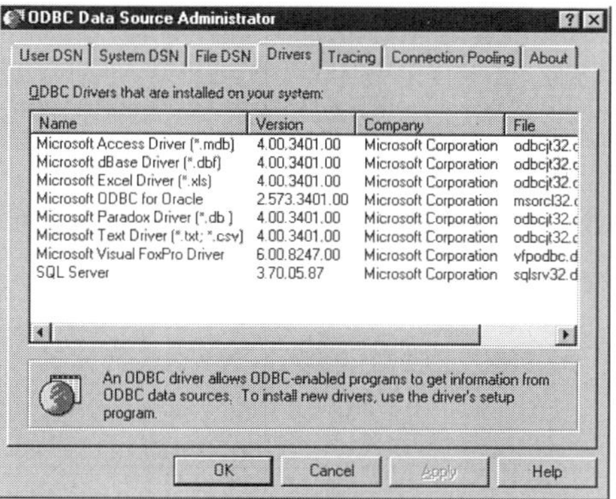

After the driver is installed, you'll need to connect to the remote data source. This process is database-dependent; some DBMSs permit direct connection to their database files (the database engine gets involved after you choose the database file), and some require you to log on, specify protocols, and so on. In some cases, the import/export process also creates the connection to the database; you'll have to try it with your database engine to find out. The following examples should give you some idea of what to expect.

Importing from ODBC The process of importing a static table from any ODBC data source is largely the same, regardless of the source. ODBC supports only importing and exporting tables and queries, and not all implementations support the query elements (sometimes called *views*).

To import a remote ODBC database object, use these steps:

1. From the Database window, select File, Get External Data, Import.
2. The Import window opens. At the bottom, click the Files of Type drop-down list and scroll all the way to the bottom. You'll see `ODBC Databases()`. Select it and the Import window disappears; the Select Data Source window opens.
3. This window has two tabs: File Data Source and Machine Data Source. A *File Data Source* is a file containing the connection information to a database, which can be copied from one machine to another. A *Machine Data Source* (which includes user data sources and system data sources) uses the appropriate ODBC driver to take advantage of particular quirks or features of that database type. Select the appropriate tab:
   - If you're connecting to a File Data Source, either select the appropriate data source from the list shown (if it was created earlier, it should be visible in the list; occasionally, you might have to browse the file system) or create a new data source by entering its name in the DSN Name box and clicking New. After you click New, you'll be asked to specify the type of data source to create and the name of a file to store the data. Click OK to continue.
   - If you're connecting to a Machine Data Source, select a data source from the list under the Machine Data Source tab and click OK. To create a new Machine Data Source on-the-fly, click New, decide whether you want a User Data Source (visible only to the current user) or a System Data Source (for any user of this machine), choose a data type, and choose a name for the DSN. Click OK to continue.
4. The Link Tables window appears (see Figure 42.2), listing all the tables in the remote database. You can select all of them to import by clicking the Select All button, or you can select the tables you're interested in by clicking them. You don't need to use the Ctrl or Shift key to make multiple selections. When you're finished, press OK.

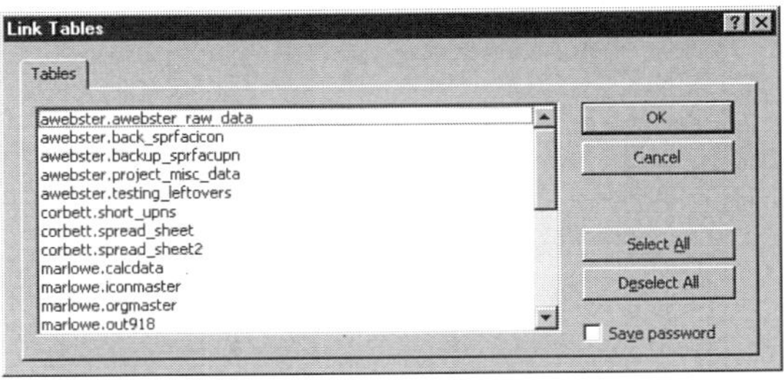

FIGURE 42.2
This list of tables is from Informix, which appends the name of each table's author to its name. You can rename imported objects after importing them.

ODBC connections can take much longer to make than standard local or network file system connections, so depending on the number and size of the tables you've asked to import, Access might require several minutes to import everything. When it's done, you'll see the new table added to your Database window and a message box saying `Successfully imported` *`<table>`*. Or `Successfully imported` *`<number>`* `of tables`.

Exporting to ODBC Access exports tables and queries to another ODBC database, but how the recipient database treats the object received is up to it. Typically, if a remote ODBC database doesn't know how to import a certain object type, you'll get an "illegal call" error from the ODBC driver after you try to execute the export. Queries are typically exported either as "views" in enterprise databases or as tables.

To export an Access object to an ODBC database:

1. From the Database window, select the object to be exported, then File, Export. The Export window appears, titled Export *<objecttype>* '*<tablename>*' to....
2. Select ODBC Databases in the Save As Type list box at the bottom of the window. The Export *<objecttype>* window disappears; the Export window opens (see Figure 42.3).

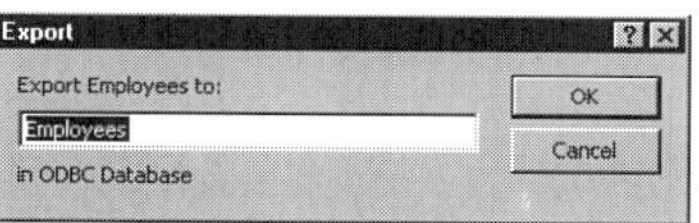

FIGURE 42.3
The Export window enables you to change the name of the object exported in the remote database.

3. You're given an opportunity to rename the exported object in the external database; do so, if needed, and press OK.
4. In the Select Data Source dialog box, select the appropriate data source type tab (File Data Source or Machine Data Source) and choose a data source in the list under that tab. Click OK to continue.
5. Depending on the remote database, a dialog box might appear for you to complete connection information or a password. Enter it if necessary and choose OK. The object is copied to the remote database.

Linking to ODBC The process for linking to an ODBC database is the same as for importing one, except that you'll start by selecting File, Get External Data, Link Tables instead of File, Get External Data, Import. The intermediate prompts and options are the same.

Linking to ODBC databases is a great way to harness the power of a large external database without losing the ease of the Access interface. After remote tables are linked, you can write and execute queries against them, use them as the sources for reports and forms, and do anything else you can do with a native Access data source. Of course, if you're using a remote ODBC data source, you're dependent on your network to send all the traffic that Access usually gets off your local hard drive, so using linked, remote ODBC databases is usually not a very fast way to work.

A linked ODBC database appears in the Database window as a distinctive globe with an arrow next to it, as shown in Figure 42.4.

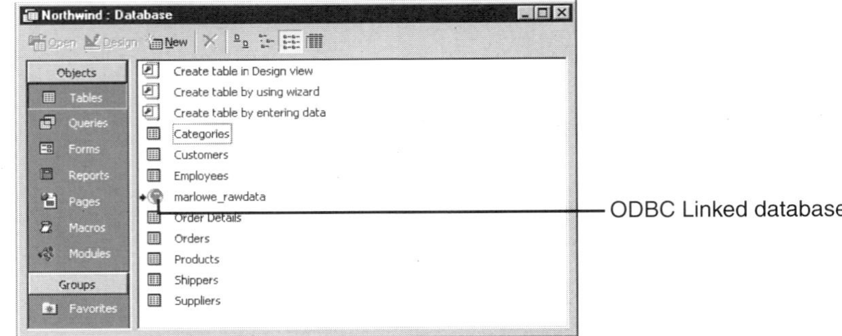

FIGURE 42.4
All linked tables have arrows next to them in the Database window; the icon next to the arrow tells you something about the source of the data. In this case, it's a linked ODBC table.

Non-ODBC Databases

Working with non-ODBC databases is really a matter of finding a way to read from and write to their file formats because Access is interacting with the file system directly. Office 2000 includes interpreters for the following data file formats (some of which are discussed later in this chapter):

- Text files
- Microsoft Excel
- MAPI data sources (such as Exchange)
- Lotus 1-2-3
- Paradox
- Hypertext Markup Language (HTML)
- dBASE III, IV, and V

Note that some of these data types might have multiple file extensions (for example, Access interprets files with four different extensions to be text files, all delimited differently), and that some database types (dBASE, for example) might require more than one file to compose a single dataset. If that's the case, Access prompts you for additional information.

Importing from Non-ODBC Databases In general, the only kind of data structures you can import from non-ODBC data sources are tables and similar entities. Depending on the data type, this might be tabular data in rows and columns, native data tables, or constructs that are designed to emulate tables when displayed or printed.

You cannot use ODBC to import or export from a Microsoft data source (such as Excel) or from Paradox because Access includes native support for their data files. If you try, you'll get an error message. Treat these formats as non-ODBC databases, even though they support ODBC.

To import tabular data from a non-ODBC database, use these steps:

1. From the Database window, select File, Get External Data, Import. The Import window appears.

2. In the Files of Type drop-down list box at the bottom of the window, select the data type of the file containing the table(s) to be imported.
3. Navigate through the file system using the Look In list box and the Up One Level button until you find the directory containing the file you want to import. Select it and press Import.

If Access can successfully import the table, you'll see a notification dialog box. Access might prompt you for additional information before completing the import, such as the name of index files (dBASE) or the designation of key fields in the imported tables (Informix). Importing from nondatabase applications (such as Excel) might require more intermediate steps, such as specifying a data range. If a table already exists with the name of the imported file, a sequential integer is appended to the end of the imported table's name.

Access tends to be conservative with the data types of imported tables. It almost always sets the data type of numerical data as Double and character data as Text. You might want to modify the table design appropriately after the import is complete to use more efficient or appropriate data types.

Exporting to Non-ODBC Databases Access can export to all the database types that it can import, including the following:

- Four versions of Microsoft Excel (3, 4, 5-7, and 97-2000)
- Three versions of Lotus 1-2-3 (1, 2, and 3)
- Four versions of Paradox (3, 4, 5, and 7-8)
- dBASE III, IV, and 5
- Microsoft Word Merge (.txt) and Rich Text Format (.rtf)
- Microsoft HTX/IDC
- Microsoft Active Server Pages

Depending on the type you choose, different options might be available (named columns, delimiters, and so forth); you'll be prompted for them if necessary. The results obtained by exporting to some formats (especially the Web formats) might be less than satisfactory upon exporting, and it will probably require some editing to make them presentable.

You can export tables and Select queries (which export as if they were tables) to any other database format; you can also export macros to a new Access database and export modules to Access or to text files—a great way to document your code.

To export an Access object to a non-ODBC database, use these steps:

1. From the Database window, select the object to be exported, then File, Export. A window titled Export *<objecttype>* '*<objectname>*' appears.
2. Choose a file type option (the type of file you want to save to) in the Save As Type drop-down list box at the bottom of the window. Enter a filename in the File Name box if the default name (which is the same as the object to be exported) isn't satisfactory. Navigate the directory structure by using the Save In drop-down box and the Up One Level button until you arrive at a suitable directory.

3. Press Save. Access might prompt for additional information; follow the instructions in the dialog boxes that appear.

You won't receive confirmation that your save was successful, but you will receive an error if it fails.

Linking to Non-ODBC Databases In most cases, you can successfully *link* (attach for reading and writing) database files from non-ODBC data sources. If the linked data source is a database engine (for example, Microsoft Access, SQL Server, FoxPro, dBASE, or Paradox), you should have no trouble actively using the remote table as if it were an Access table. Any changes you make to the data in linked tables will be replicated in the original data file format. Linking to non-ODBC data sources that are not generated by database engines (such as text files and HTML files) generally results in a link with less functionality; typically, these connections do not permit writing to the original data store.

The inability to write back to the original data source might not be a show-stopper, however; for example, it's possible that you need to use Access to monitor or convert data from a legacy system or a Web site that continually updates the original data source or file. In that case, linking the remote data instead of importing it would enable you to use Access always to see the latest changes, without needing to modify the source.

You can link only to table-type data in any data format.

To link a data source from a non-ODBC database, use the following steps:

1. From the Database window, select File, Get External Data, Link Tables. The Link window opens.
2. In the Files of Type drop-down list, select the data type of the file to which you want to link.
3. Use the Look In and the Up One Level button to select the directory containing the file on the file system. When it's visible in the main window, select it and click Link.
4. In the case of dBASE and Paradox databases, after you select the data file, another window appears, asking you to Select Index Files. These index files typically have an .ndx (dBASE) or .px (Paradox) extension. If the index file is accessible, select it and click Select. If not, Access will still make the linkage, but performance might be affected; click Cancel.
5. In some cases (certain databases provide more information to ODBC than others), a window appears and asks you to designate fields that uniquely identify records. If you do, Access denotes them as primary keys. If you do not, performance might be impacted, but the database will still link. Press OK to continue.

▶ **See** "Using Multiple Fields to Create a Primary Key," **p. 999**

6. Access links the database file if it's readable and in the appropriate format. No law says that any particular file extension can be used only by a particular database engine, so it's possible you might try to import a file, thinking it's of one type, and find out it's not when Access displays a helpful error message at the end of the process, as shown in Figure 42.5.

FIGURE 42.5
Access displays an error message when you try to link to a file in an unsupported format. It found the "object," contrary to the message, but it didn't like what it found.

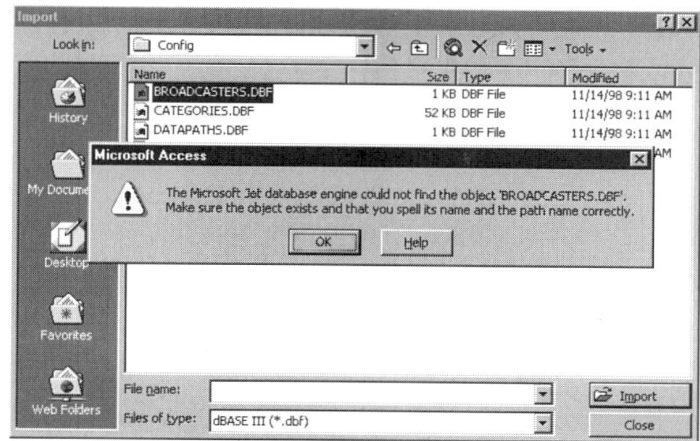

The Link window doesn't disappear after you successfully link to an external file, assuming that you might want to link more. Click the Close or Cancel buttons to close the window.

Importing, Exporting, and Linking to HTML Files

Access provides a wizard to assist in the importing, exporting, and linking of Hypertext Markup Language (HTML) documents. HTML documents are designed for presentation on the World Wide Web (or intranet Web sites) and often contain frequently changing data from which Access can read. As with other data sources, Access can

- Import from HTML—Copy the current data into an Access table.
- Link to HTML—Connect to an HTML data source on demand and update a table based on what's out there.
- Export to HTML—Write a file in HTML format that contains Access data.

It performs these actions with varying degrees of success, as described in the sections that follow.

Importing from HTML

Access 2000 can import data from HTML tables and lists. That said, the process is fraught with potential problems. These include the following:

- Trying to import or link to a page containing frames will link only to the tables and lists (if any) in the main (frameset) page. Because most frameset pages don't contain any data except the names of the files that will appear in the frames, you'll probably not be able to import or link any data from pages with frames.
- Files with funny characters in the names (brackets, for example) confuse the HTML Wizard. You'd probably never find a page called `myfile[1].htm`, or `myfile(1).htm` in a URL, but it's not at all uncommon in a file saved on disk from Internet Explorer—the bracketed number is part of Internet Explorer's default filename if you view a page's source HTML and save it.

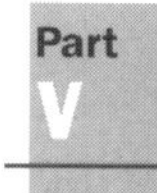

- Access imports or links only to data in HTML tables or lists. It makes interesting decisions about what to do with data that's not strictly tabular. For example, data that spans table columns (common in HTML) is repeated in each column. This is OK, but Excel's Import HTML method does it a little differently, leading to surprise results. Also, Access guesses as to the data type of imported data. If the first several rows of license plate numbers are all numeric, Access assumes that they're all numeric, and it starts generating errors when the first nonnumeric license plate number comes along.

All those caveats aside, suppose you still want to import an HTML file. You've determined that it's not a frameset; it includes tables and/or lists; it doesn't have any funny characters in the URL; and you can live with whatever Access decides to do with the data in the file. To import an HTML file, use the following steps:

1. From the Database window, select File, Get External Data, Import. The Import window appears.
2. At the bottom of the list, select HTML Files from the Files of Type drop-down box. If the data source is local to your file system, browse your disk drives and the Network Neighborhood with the Look In box and Up One Level button at the top of the window. If you know the URL, enter the full URL in the File Name box. Press Import to continue.
3. What appears next depends on the content of the page. If your selected HTML file contains only one table or list, skip ahead to step 4. If the page you selected contains more than one table and/or list, you'll see a dialog box from which you select one of the Show option buttons to display a list of the tables and/or lists in the page. If the table or list is named, its name will appear; otherwise, a not-very-descriptive name will show in the list along with a preview of the data at the bottom of the dialog box.

   An Advanced button is available at the bottom of the window (which is available from this dialog box through the end of the process); pressing it displays the Import Specification dialog box (see Figure 42.6). This dialog box enables you to make some decisions about the data types of the items to be imported in the currently selected table or list. Select a table or list, set the Import Specifications options if you desire, and press Next.

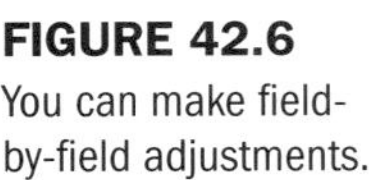
FIGURE 42.6
You can make field-by-field adjustments.

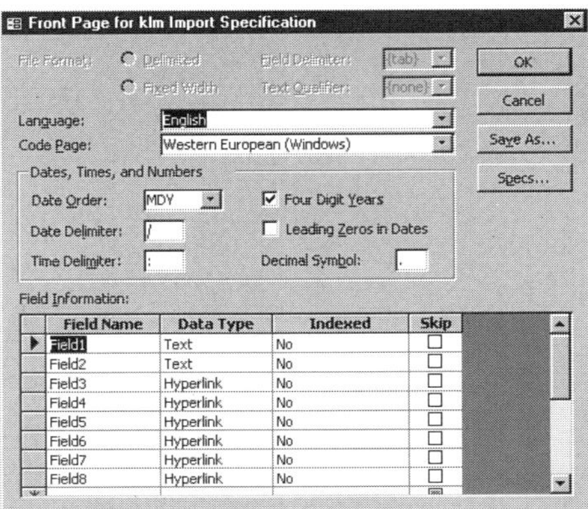

NOTE If you use the Advanced button and expect to perform this particular import again sometime, you can save your settings in an Import Specification file by clicking Save As in the Import Specification dialog box. You can retrieve your settings later by opening the Import Specification dialog box and pressing the Specs button; this displays a list of saved specifications. If importing via code, you can (and should) use the specification you create and save here to be sure it works correctly. See the section "Linking with VBA" in Chapter 41.

4. In the next step of the Import HTML wizard, Access asks whether the first row of the table contains column headings. If it does and you click First Row Contains Column Headings, the fields will be assigned those names. Click Next to continue.
5. You're asked whether you want to store your data in a new table or in an existing one. Make a choice and press Next.
6. Access takes you through the data field-by-field so you can specify a field name, a data type, an index if desired, and whether to skip a particular column, as shown in Figure 42.7. If you created an import specification by using the Advanced button earlier in the process, your choices are reflected in each field's properties. Set properties for each field as necessary, clicking in each field you want to modify.
7. After you approve the settings for the final field, you're asked whether you want Access to add a primary key field to the table, whether you want to specify a field in the import as the primary key, or to continue without a key. If you have Access add a primary key field, it adds an AutoNumber field as the first column in the table. The Advanced dialog box appears if the Advanced button is pressed. Make your choice and press Next.
8. Finally, Access confirms your choice of a table name, shows the Advanced button one more time, and offers to run the Table Analyzer or to display Help after the import process is over. These options are better selected manually, if needed, so you will probably leave them unchecked. Press Finish to complete the import.

Access imports your data and displays a message box advising you that it's finished. If errors occur during the import, the message box says so, and Access creates a new table with the words `Import_Errors` appended to its name; you can inspect that table to see exactly which rows of the source data were not imported and why not.

Import errors are common and are often caused by too-restrictive import specifications for individual fields. If you're having trouble, try creating an import specification that imports every field as Text, which is completely nonrestrictive.

Save the specification. If that import works, start choosing more restrictive data types (Integer, Single, and so on) field by field until you find the one with the errant data. Often, you'll discover a space character in a numeric field or a line of dashes used as a separator (and imported as data).

Saving and reusing the specification saves time in re-creating the specification every time you perform the import.

Figure 42.7 shows the source HTML page and Figure 42.8 shows its representation as an Access table. Note that Access correctly interprets the hyperlink information in the original table and creates fields with the hyperlink data type in the imported table. If the imported column contains a mix of hyperlinks and plain text, Access usually (depending on the order of the elements) imports the column as text, and the hyperlinks will look quite ugly.

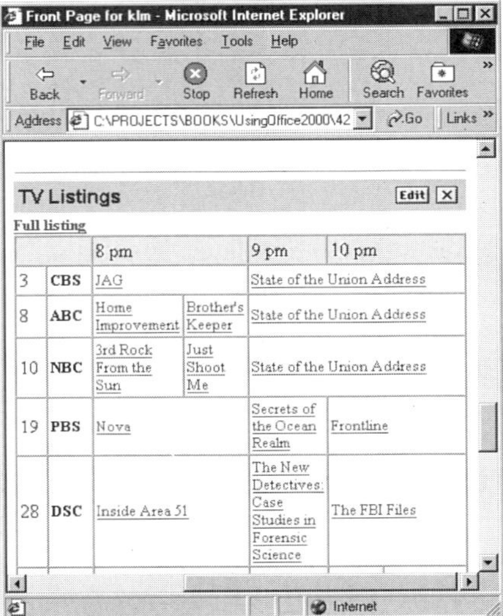

FIGURE 42.7
An HTML table in Internet Explorer.

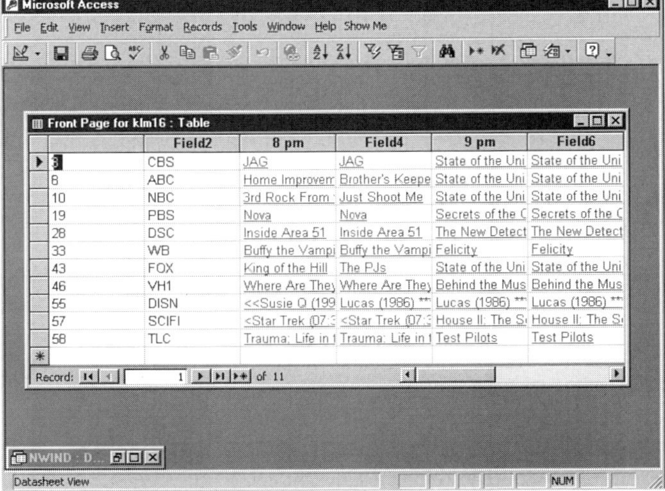

FIGURE 42.8
The same HTML table's representation as an Access table.

Exporting to HTML

One would hope that the process of exporting to HTML would be as simple as pressing a couple of buttons; then a nicely formatted HTML representation of an Access data object appears. Such is not the case. You can export Access tables, Select queries, forms, and reports to HTML. Tables, queries, and reports export reasonably well, as long as they don't contain embedded graphics. Forms export poorly in two of the three formats Access supports, and the third is of limited use.

NOTE Creating Web pages with Access is complicated and many variations exist; for more information on creating Web pages with Access without using Access 2000's new Data Access Pages, see *Special Edition Using Microsoft Access 2000*, and *Platinum Edition Using Microsoft Access 2000*, both published by Que.

If you want to learn more about Web-page creation in general, we recommend *Special Edition Using Microsoft FrontPage 2000* and *Platinum Edition Using HTML 4.0, XML, and Java 1.2*, also published by Que.

Access permits you to save Access objects in one of three formats:

- As static HTML (tables, queries, forms, and reports)—The form is converted to a report and is saved in a flat, noninteractive style. Simple forms export to this format reasonably well (see Figures 42.9 and 42.10).

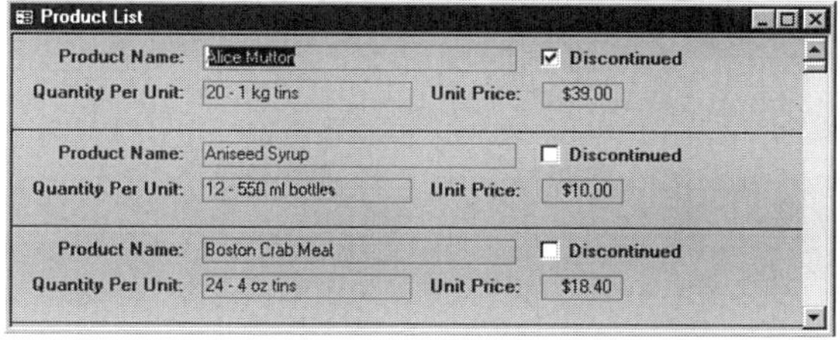

FIGURE 42.9 The Product List form in Access.

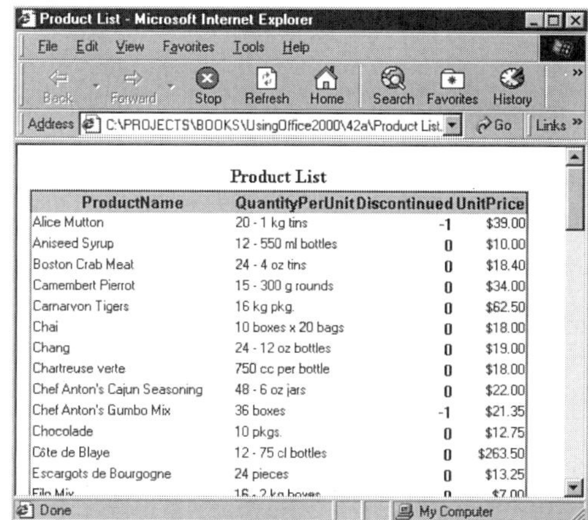

Product List

ProductName	QuantityPerUnit	Discontinued	UnitPrice
Alice Mutton	20 - 1 kg tins	-1	$39.00
Aniseed Syrup	12 - 550 ml bottles	0	$10.00
Boston Crab Meat	24 - 4 oz tins	0	$18.40
Camembert Pierrot	15 - 300 g rounds	0	$34.00
Carnarvon Tigers	16 kg pkg.	0	$62.50
Chai	10 boxes x 20 bags	0	$18.00
Chang	24 - 12 oz bottles	0	$19.00
Chartreuse verte	750 cc per bottle	0	$18.00
Chef Anton's Cajun Seasoning	48 - 6 oz jars	0	$22.00
Chef Anton's Gumbo Mix	36 boxes	-1	$21.35
Chocolade	10 pkgs.	0	$12.75
Côte de Blaye	12 - 75 cl bottles	0	$263.50
Escargots de Bourgogne	24 pieces	0	$13.25

FIGURE 42.10 The Product List form in Internet Explorer after saving as static HTML.

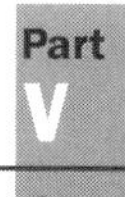

More complex forms, such as Northwind's Employees form, don't fare so well when saved in HTML, as illustrated in Figures 42.11 and 42.12.

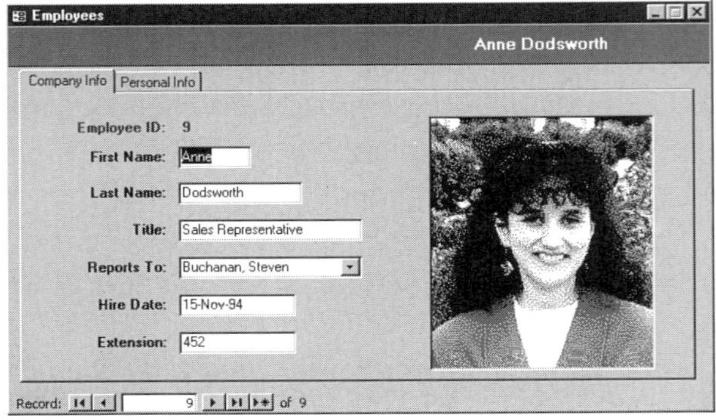

FIGURE 42.11
The Employees form in Access.

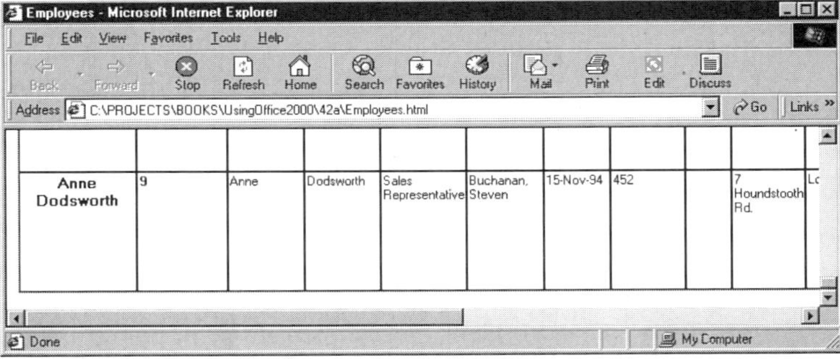

FIGURE 42.12
The Employees form exports to static HTML as if no form layout exists at all.

- As Internet Data Connector (HTX/IDC) files (tables, queries, and forms)—Access provides a way for you to create Web pages that change dynamically as data in the underlying database changes. This style, called HTX/IDC, really creates two Web pages for every table, query, or form you export—one with an .htx extension and one with an .idc extension. The former of these contains the layout information for the pages, and the latter takes care of connecting to the database and returning the required data. You can't create HTX/IDC files for reports.

  These pages look like the static HTML pages in Figures 42.9 and 42.10, but the data is up-to-the minute when the page is requested. Note that these pages look right in any Web browser, but the Access database must be configured as a System Data Source and the Web server must be running Microsoft's Internet Information Server (or one of its variants for Windows 95/98 or NT Workstation) software for this to work.

- As Active Server Pages (.asp) (tables, queries, and forms)—For pages that accept user input as well as output, you can create Active Server Pages from tables and forms. Active Server Pages created by Access depend on unusual processing by the Web server (only Microsoft's Internet Information Server and variants will work) to interpret them correctly, and they work only in Microsoft's Internet Explorer browser because they use ActiveX components. Those problems aside, tables, queries, and simple forms can be created as ASPs, and users will be able to enter data into them. For all practical purposes, however, you're better off building Data Access Pages from scratch than you are trying to export existing forms and tables as ASP—the configuration and maintenance issues are too detailed for almost all sites.

▶ **See** "What Are Data Access Pages?" in Chapter 38, **p. 1100**

A few options are different for each HTML format, depending on the result you desire. In general, to export a table, query, or report to HTML, you would use these steps:

1. From the Database window, select the table, query, or report to be exported, and then select File, Export. The Export window appears.
2. Enter a name for the exported file in the File Name box if the default name isn't suitable. In the Save As Type drop-down box, choose HTML Documents to save as static HTML, Microsoft IIS 1-2 to create Internet Data Connector pages, or choose Microsoft Active Server Pages. Navigate the directory structure with the Save In and Up One Level buttons to locate the folder where you'd like to export the file.
3. Press Save. A dialog box appears, asking the name of an HTML template file, if any. HTML templates provide all the formatting and visual interest of the exported data object, which is pretty plain otherwise. Leave the box blank or select a file and press Next.
4. Access saves an HTML representation of the table, query, or report.

NOTE You'll want to create HTML Templates for your data if you intend to use HTX/IDC to the maximum extent of its capability, which isn't much. They specify how to format the data being output, and they give some flexibility in formatting if you're already comfortable in HTML. They're not hard to write; look up "About HTML Templates" in Access Help for details.

Figure 42.13 shows the result of saving the Northwind Sales by Year report as HTML without a template. Notice that the lines around the tables are missing. This is a multipage report, and Access adds rudimentary hyperlinks at the bottom of the page to help you navigate from page to page.

If you choose to save a table, query, or form as an HTX/IDC page, a different dialog box appears in step 3 of the previous list. In addition to specifying the name of a template file, you have the opportunity to enter a data source name (DSN), a username, and a password (neither of which might be required depending on the data source). You create data sources through the ODBC applet in the Control Panel; HTX/IDC pages require a system data source (a file or machine data source created with the Control Panel's ODBC applet) to work correctly. The entries you make on this page are embedded in the IDC file, which controls how the pages connect to the data source when executed.

FIGURE 42.13
A simple Access report, saved as HTML.

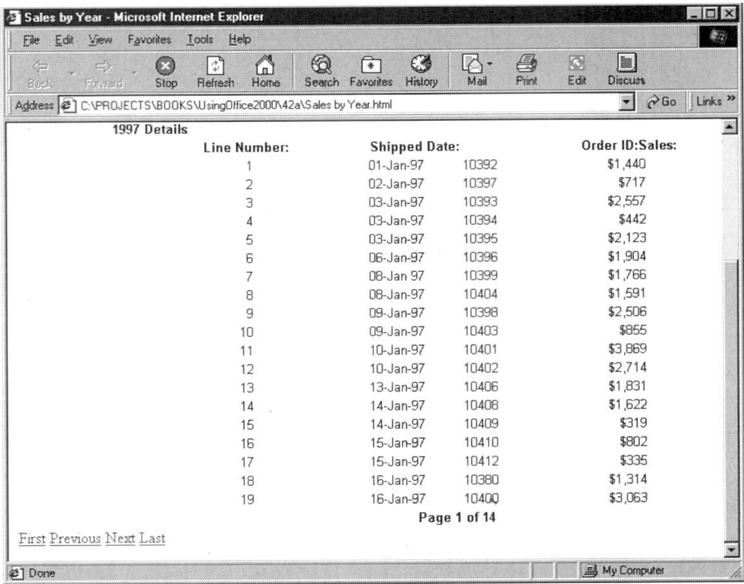

NOTE The contents of IDC files are trivial, but seeing how they're laid out might help you understand the HTX/IDC concept better. Here's a sample IDC file created by exporting the Employees form to HTX/IDC:

```
Datasource:mydatasource
Template:Employees.htx
SQLStatement:SELECT * FROM [Employees]
Password:
Username:
```

When exporting to an Active Server Page, you're promoted for all the options listed previously for Internet Data Connector pages, along with the Server's root URL and an option to time out the connection after a certain number of minutes. Access uses this information to build a relatively complex HTML representation of the object you're exporting.

Linking to HTML

The process for linking to an HTML page is the same as for importing one, except that you'll start by selecting File, Get External Data, Link Tables instead of File, Get External Data, Import. The intermediate prompts and options are the same.

The sole advantage to linking to HTML rather than importing is to provide your Access database real-time data from the linked page if it changes. Of course, the change to the Web page can't change the structure of the table or list, just its data. Also, you should consider that Access needs to go across the network and get the updated HTML page every time the linked table is used; this might make database operations involving the linked table seem slow if the network connection is slow or unavailable.

Importing, Exporting, and Linking Spreadsheets

Access treats spreadsheet files in both Excel and Lotus 1-2-3 formats as tabular data sources. Any named range or worksheet can be considered a table; it's unusual that entire worksheets are formatted appropriately for import (most contain extraneous headers and elements that make the Access interpreter very unhappy), but because it's sufficiently easy to create a named range in a spreadsheet, using a spreadsheet for importing or linking is a worthwhile skill to acquire. Similarly, Access is capable of exporting in either Lotus 1-2-3 or Excel format.

Importing from Spreadsheets

Spreadsheets are often configured in a manner that makes them easy to work with, unlike many of the other file types that Access imports. Most spreadsheets group similar data in columns, with records breaking on row boundaries. Importing spreadsheets, then, is as simple as traversing column-by-column and row-by-row to populate an Access table. The resulting table in Datasheet view should look very much like the spreadsheet that spawned it.

CAUTION

Access can import from different worksheets in Excel files, but the worksheet name must contain no special characters or spaces. Otherwise, it won't appear in the Import dialog box.

To import a spreadsheet, follow these steps:

1. From the Database window, select File, Get External Data, Import. The Import window appears.
2. Change the Files of Type drop-down box to reflect the type of spreadsheet you want to import: Lotus 1-2-3, Lotus 1-2-3/DOS, or Excel. Using the Look In and Up One Level controls at the top of the window, traverse the file system until you see the file you want to import. Select it and press Import.
3. If the file selected includes more than one worksheet or named range, the Import Spreadsheet Wizard appears and gives you the option of selecting from the available named ranges or worksheets. A preview of the data in each range or worksheet helps you find your data. Press Next to continue.
4. The next dialog box asks whether you want to use the data in the first row of the imported spreadsheet as field titles. If so, check the First Row Contains Column Headings box; after your choice is made, press Next.
5. Access asks whether you want to import the data into a new table or to append to an existing one. Make your selection, choose a table name if necessary, and click Next.
6. Access enables you to review the settings for each column so you can specify a field name, a data type, an index, if desired, and whether to skip a particular column. Set properties for each field as necessary, clicking in each field you want to modify.

7. After you approve the settings for the final column, you're asked whether you want Access to add a primary key field to the table, whether you want to specify a field in the import as the primary key, or to continue without a key. If Access adds a primary key field, it adds an AutoNumber field as the first column in the table. Make your choice and press Next.
8. Finally, Access confirms your choice of a table name and offers to run the Table Analyzer or display Help after the import process is over. These options are better selected manually, if needed, so you will probably leave them unchecked. Press Finish to complete the import.

Figures 42.14 and 42.15 show an Excel spreadsheet and its appearance in Access after importing.

Investment Projections.xls

	A	B	C	D	E	F	G	H	
1									
2			What if the annual rate of return is....						
3			5%	8%	11%	14%		6%	
4	Year	Annual Contribution	Gift Trust Bal	Gift Trust Bal	Gift Trust Bal	Gift Trust Bal		1yr Tuition	4yr T
5	1997		$950	$950	$950	$950		$10,700	$4
6	1998	$3,000	$4,148	$4,266	$4,385	$4,503		$11,342	$4
7	1999	$3,000	$7,505	$7,847	$8,197	$8,553		$12,023	$4
8	2000	$3,000	$11,030	$11,715	$12,428	$13,171		$12,744	$5
9	2001	$3,000	$14,732	$15,892	$17,126	$18,435		$13,509	$5
10	2002	$3,000	$18,618	$20,404	$22,339	$24,436		$14,319	$5
11	2003	$3,000	$22,699	$25,276	$28,127	$31,277		$15,178	$6
12	2004	$3,000	$26,984	$30,538	$34,551	$39,075		$16,089	$6
13	2005	$3,000	$31,483	$36,221	$41,681	$47,966		$17,054	$6
14	2006	$3,000	$36,207	$42,359	$49,596	$58,101		$18,077	$7
15	2007	$3,000	$41,168	$48,987	$58,382	$69,655		$19,162	$7
16	2008	$3,000	$46,376	$56,146	$68,134	$82,827		$20,312	$8
17	2009	$3,000	$51,845	$63,878	$78,958	$97,843		$21,531	$8
18	2010	$3,000	$57,587	$72,228	$90,974	$114,961		$22,822	$9
19	2011	$3,000	$63,617	$81,247	$104,311	$134,476	Dan 18	$24,192	$9
20	2012	$3,000	$69,947	$90,986	$119,115	$156,722		$25,643	$10
21	2013	$3,000	$76,595	$101,505	$135,548	$182,083		$27,182	$10
22	2014	$3,000	$83,575	$112,866	$153,788	$210,995	Dan 21	$28,813	$11

TSP Chart / TSPData / Dan Trust Chart / TrustData

FIGURE 42.14
An Excel spreadsheet before importing.

TrustData : Table

Field1	Field2	Field3	Field4	Field5	Field6
		What if the annu			
		5%	8%	11%	14%
Year	Annual Contribu	Gift Trust Bal	Gift Trust Bal	Gift Trust Bal	Gift Trust B
1997		$950	$950	$950	$950
1998	$3,000	$4,148	$4,266	$4,385	$4,503
1999	$3,000	$7,505	$7,847	$8,197	$8,553
2000	$3,000	$11,030	$11,715	$12,428	$13,171
2001	$3,000	$14,732	$15,892	$17,126	$18,435
2002	$3,000	$18,618	$20,404	$22,339	$24,436
2003	$3,000	$22,699	$25,276	$28,127	$31,277
2004	$3,000	$26,984	$30,538	$34,551	$39,075
2005	$3,000	$31,483	$36,221	$41,681	$47,966
2006	$3,000	$36,207	$42,359	$49,596	$58,101
2007	$3,000	$41,168	$48,987	$58,382	$69,655
2008	$3,000	$46,376	$56,146	$68,134	$82,827
2009	$3,000	$51,845	$63,878	$78,958	$97,843
2010	$3,000	$57,587	$72,228	$90,974	$114,961

Record: 1 of 22

FIGURE 42.15
Spreadsheets import very well; the Access Datasheet view mimics the spreadsheet's native appearance.

Exporting to Spreadsheets

As you might expect, Access does a creditable job of exporting tabular data to spreadsheet format. By default, you have the option of creating spreadsheet files in either Excel 97-2000 format or in Excel 5-7 format. If you want to export to a spreadsheet type not listed in your Export dialog box, run Office Setup and be sure you've installed the appropriate converter for the spreadsheet version you want to write to.

Exporting tables and reports doesn't preserve any formatting except for the color and font of text fields. Otherwise, the exported data looks like the equivalent Access datasheet for the form or record's data source. Information in subforms or subreports is not exported.

To export from an Access table, query, report, or form to Excel, follow these steps:

1. From the Database window, select the object to be exported, then File, Export. The Export window appears.
2. Choose either Microsoft Excel 97-2000 or Microsoft Excel 5-7 in the Save As Type drop-down list box and enter a filename in the File Name box if the default name (same as the object to be exported) isn't satisfactory. Navigate the directory structure by using the Save In drop-down box and the Up One Level button until you arrive at a suitable directory.
3. Press Save.

You won't receive confirmation if your save was successful, but you will receive an error message if it fails.

Linking to Spreadsheets

To link to an Excel spreadsheet (you can't link to Lotus 1-2-3 spreadsheets), follow the same process as if you were importing it, except that you should click File, Get External Data, Link Tables instead of File, Get External Data, Import.

This feature permits both reading from and writing to an Excel spreadsheet in real-time, ensuring that your database always contains the most up-to-date information and permitting the two applications to remain synchronized. In office environments where some people might be intimidated by database applications, you can consider this method to create simple databases that use Excel as an interface.

Importing, Exporting, and Linking to Text Files

Access' capability to read and write text files is both a great boon and a serious limitation. When no other method of sharing data exists between Access and almost any other data-driven application ever devised, a simple text file usually works. However, text files can display only text, and the graphical (really binary) nature of data today makes it likely that a great deal of information will be lost when using this facility. Reports exported as text lose all formatting, except for spacing, and are limited to standard alphanumeric characters (so exporting the

Northwind Catalog report, which contains non-ASCII characters in nearly every product name, produces a particularly poor text file). This also means that you can't export or import binary objects, such as bound OLE objects (pictures, sounds, and so on) via text files. Alphanumeric data transfers very well this way, but nothing else does.

To comprehend the data in a text file, some scheme must be agreed upon to separate data elements (fields and records) from one another. The de facto standard record delimiter is a carriage return; Access doesn't even give you the option of choosing another way to mark the end of records in text files. Marking field boundaries is another matter. Access first permits you to choose whether fields in text files are *delimited*, meaning that a certain ASCII character(s) separates one field from another, or *fixed-width*, meaning that every field has a certain width as measured in number of characters. Not all fields have to have the same width in fixed-width text files, but figuring out where the boundary falls can be quite tricky with some kinds of data.

If you choose to export or import delimited data, Access enables you to choose any character you like to mark the end of one field and the beginning of another. The character chosen is almost always a comma or a tab. You can also specify a character to mark the beginning and ending of text fields in case the text includes your delimiter (as often happens with commas); the default is a double quotation mark ("). Of course, even the defaults are not foolproof; a quotation mark in the middle of a text string will confuse the Import Wizard terribly. Sometimes it's best to break with tradition and use characters that you're sure don't appear in your data, such as curly braces ({}), tildes (~), backquotes (`), vertical bars (|), or backslashes (\).

Importing from Text Files

To import a text file into an Access table, follow these steps:

1. From the Database window, select File, Get External Data, Import. The Import window appears.
2. In the Files of Type drop-down list box at the bottom of the window, select Text Files.
3. Navigate through the file system using the Look In list box and Up One Level button until you find the directory containing the file you want to import. Select it and press Import.
4. The Import Text Wizard shows a preview of your data and asks you to decide whether it looks delimited or fixed-width. For most data, the choice is obvious: If it appears that fields are separated by a delimiting character, choose Delimited. Otherwise, choose Fixed Width. Press Next to continue.
5. Depending on your choice in the previous step, you'll be asked either to identify the field and text delimiters or to mark the boundaries between the fields in a fixed-length dataset. In either case, you can click the Advanced button and perform a detailed specification on each field in the file to be imported. After you've chosen a delimiting option, click Next.

These specifications can be saved and reused (click Save As from the Advanced dialog box); if you intend to perform this import via VBA code someday, a saved import specification is critical. Take advantage of this if you ever intend to import this file again.

6. Access asks whether you want to import the data into a new table or to append it to an existing one. Make your selection, choose a table name if necessary, and click Next.
7. Access enables you to review the settings for each column so you can specify a field name, a data type, an index, if desired, and whether to skip a particular column. Set properties for each field as necessary, clicking in each field you want to modify.
8. After you approve the settings for the final column, you're asked whether you want Access to add a primary key field to the table, whether you want to specify a field in the import as the primary key, or to continue without a key. If Access adds a primary key field, it adds an AutoNumber field as the first column in the table. Make your choice and press Next.
9. Finally, Access confirms your choice of a table name and offers to run the Table Analyzer or display Help after the import process is over. These options are better selected manually, if needed, so you will probably leave them unchecked. Press Finish to complete the import.

Exporting to Text Files

To export from an Access table, query, report, or form to a text file, follow these steps:

1. From the Database window, select the object to be exported, then File, Export. The Export window appears.
2. Choose Text Files in the Save As Type list box and enter a filename in the File Name box if the default name (same as the object to be exported) isn't satisfactory. Navigate the directory structure by using the Save In drop-down box and the Up One Level button until you arrive at a suitable directory.
3. You have the option of saving formatting—underscores and bars masquerading as datasheet lines—between rows and columns of the exported table. Almost no good reason exists to do this, and it makes subsequent use of the exported text file nearly impossible; but the option is yours if you click the Save Formatting box at the bottom of the window.
4. Press Save. The Export Text Wizard appears and shows a preview of your data and asks you to decide whether you'd prefer to save it delimited or fixed-width. Make a choice and press Next to continue.
5. Depending on your choice in the previous step, you'll be asked either to identify the field and text delimiters or to mark the boundaries between the fields in a fixed-width dataset. In either case, you can click the Advanced button and perform a detailed specification on each field in the file to be imported. After you've chosen a delimiting option, click Next.
6. The filename you chose earlier appears in a box for confirmation, and you can press Finish to continue.

Linking to Text Files

Linking to text files gives Access a way to retrieve the contents of the file on demand, rather than as it was when the file was first accessed (as would be the case if the file were imported). The linked table always has current information, which is useful if another program is regenerating the text file periodically. Access can't write to linked text files, however, so the sharing is only one-way. Of course, Access could process the data, export a text file, and the other application could link to it—if it were capable and the developer so desired.

The linking process is the same as the importing process, except that it begins with File, Get External Data, Link Table rather than File, Get External Data, Import.

PART VI

Microsoft PowerPoint

CHAPTER 43

Migrating to PowerPoint 2000

In this chapter

Upgrading from PowerPoint 95

If you're upgrading from PowerPoint 95 to PowerPoint 2000, you will find a number of new and enhanced features added to PowerPoint in version 97 that will be new to you—although not technically new in PowerPoint 2000. The next few sections describe the features that were added in PowerPoint 97 and are included in PowerPoint 2000.

Enhanced Charting

One of the most significant improvements in PowerPoint 97 was the revamping of Microsoft Graph, the charting program for Office applications. The Chart Wizard steps have been improved and several new chart types have been added. Cylinder, pyramid, and cone charts are three-dimensional variations of column and bar charts. Bubble charts are a type of XY (scatter) chart used to compare sets of at least three values. In addition to these new chart types, there are now several useful variations of pie charts available, including pie-of-pie and bar-of-pie.

▶ To learn more about each chart type and its uses, **see** "Which Chart Type Do I Use?" **p. 816**

Office Art

The Drawing toolbar was altered in Office 97 to provide a common set of tools in all Office applications. Located at the bottom of the PowerPoint screen, you will find the Insert Clip Art button, as well as many new or enhanced drawing options. A large list of AutoShapes was added in Office 97 (and expanded in Office 2000) that make drawing common shapes effortless. Also included on this toolbar are 3D and shadowing effects that can be added to drawn objects.

Hyperlinks and Action Settings

You can create links from your PowerPoint slides to other slides in the same presentation or to other presentations, documents in other programs, or Web sites on your company's intranet or the Internet. These links can be accessed while you're running a slide show.

The Action Settings command under the Tools menu can be used to set up actions that occur when you click on or move your mouse pointer over slide objects. This is particularly handy when you want to play sound or video clips during a presentation.

▶ **See** "Using Hyperlinks in Presentations," **p. 1275**

▶ **See** "Incorporating Action Settings in Presentations," **p. 1284**

Building and Running Presentations

In PowerPoint 97, Microsoft added the Slide Finder feature (activated when you choose Insert, Slides from Files) which lets you locate and preview the slides in other presentations and insert these slides into your active presentation.

The Custom Shows command was also added in PowerPoint 97. Found on the Slide Show menu, this command lets you create versions of a presentation. This feature is invaluable for tailoring a presentation to different audiences or building versions based on specific discussion topics. All of this is accomplished without creating separate files. All the slides are contained in one presentation; the Custom Shows are simply lists of slides that you want to show to a particular audience.

See "Working with Custom Shows," **p. 1272**

PowerPoint 97 improved the options you have for creating self-running and interactive presentations for conventions, conferences, trade shows, and kiosks. These presentations can loop automatically with built-in timing for each slide, or can rely on interaction with passersby. Looping presentations are set up through the Slide Show, Set Up Show command. Interactive presentations usually contain Action Buttons that viewers select to move through a presentation.

See "Creating Automated Slide Shows," **p. 1284**

Embedded Comments

To expand the options for collaborating on presentations, you can use the Insert, Comment command to embed comments in slides. Comments appear like Post-it notes and are attached to individual slides. When a comment is inserted into a slide, the Reviewing toolbar automatically appears. From this toolbar, you can insert, review, edit, and hide comments.

See "Working with Embedded Comments," **p. 1303**

Programming with VBA in PowerPoint

Another feature added to PowerPoint in the 97 version is the capability to use Visual Basic for Applications (VBA) to create custom features, dialog boxes, and add-ins for PowerPoint. You can also create presentations that use ActiveX controls, such as drop-down lists and check boxes.

New and Altered Features in PowerPoint 2000

The improvements in PowerPoint 2000 can be separated into four main areas: information sharing via the Web, online collaboration, multilanguage support, and ease-of-use enhancements. These improvements have largely been designed for corporate users who do business on a national and international level.

You'll undoubtedly run into other minor enhancements and changes as you work in PowerPoint 2000, but these next few sections discuss the most significant changes.

Web-Based Information Sharing

Through the use of Hypertext Markup Language (HTML) as a file format, document sharing is expanded to include sharing data via the Web—including company intranets, extranets, and the Internet. As businesses embrace Web technology, it has become necessary for users to have the capability to create presentations in Office applications and take these files back and forth between PowerPoint and a browser for editing and viewing. Presentations can be saved in an HTML format and published to a Web server directly from within PowerPoint.

See "Publishing a Presentation on a Web," **p. 1316**

Online Collaboration

There are several ways to collaborate with other people on a presentation: You can broadcast a presentation online, you can set up an online meeting, or you can copy a presentation to a Web server where others can post comments.

With the Presentation Broadcast feature, you can deliver a presentation to colleagues in different locations, using your company's intranet. Additionally, you can record the broadcast to archive it for people who are unable to make the original broadcast.

▶ **See** "Setting Up Online Presentations," **p. 1289**

Microsoft NetMeeting is an applet that comes with Office 2000, and is used to conduct online meetings. When you want to get a team together to discuss a document, a chat feature and a whiteboard feature help to facilitate discussions. NetMeeting is also capable of transmitting audio and video. Use it to share and exchange information with other people at different sites in real-time over your company's intranet or the Internet, just as if everyone were in the same room. You access the NetMeeting feature through the Tools, Online Collaboration command.

▶ **See** "Conducting Online Meetings," **p. 1313**

When you can't get a group together for an online meeting or presentations broadcast, a great alternative is to use Web discussions. Individuals can access and add comments to slides in the presentation. They can also edit and reply to existing comments. In order to use this feature, a Web server is required.

▶ **See** "Using Web Discussions," **p. 1314**

International Language Support

With Office 2000's commitment to multilingual support, companies that have multinational users will find it easier to create and edit presentations in a wide range of languages. The language of the user interface can easily be changed, should employees traveling to other countries need to work in their native language. The help screens and editing/proofing tools will also adjust to the language selected. PowerPoint 2000 supports separate AutoCorrect lists for each language.

Interface and Ease-of-Use Improvements

A number of changes were made to PowerPoint to increase productivity. The interface changes include the addition of a new view, the Normal view, and a revolutionary (or perhaps evolutionary) change in the way menus and toolbars function, known as *personalized* menus and toolbars. Other improvements include the capability to create tables by using PowerPoint tools and a revised Clip Gallery.

View Changes in PowerPoint 2000 Probably the most obvious new feature in PowerPoint 2000 is the implementation of a new view—the *Normal view*—a welcome addition to PowerPoint. This view divides the screen into three panes: Outline, Slide, and Notes. Instead of flipping back and forth among each of the individual views (which are still available), you will probably use the Normal view to perform about 90% of your PowerPoint activities. This new tri-pane view, shown in Figure 43.1, places most of the presentation information at your fingertips.

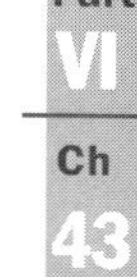

FIGURE 43.1
Click or press F6 to change panes in the Normal view.

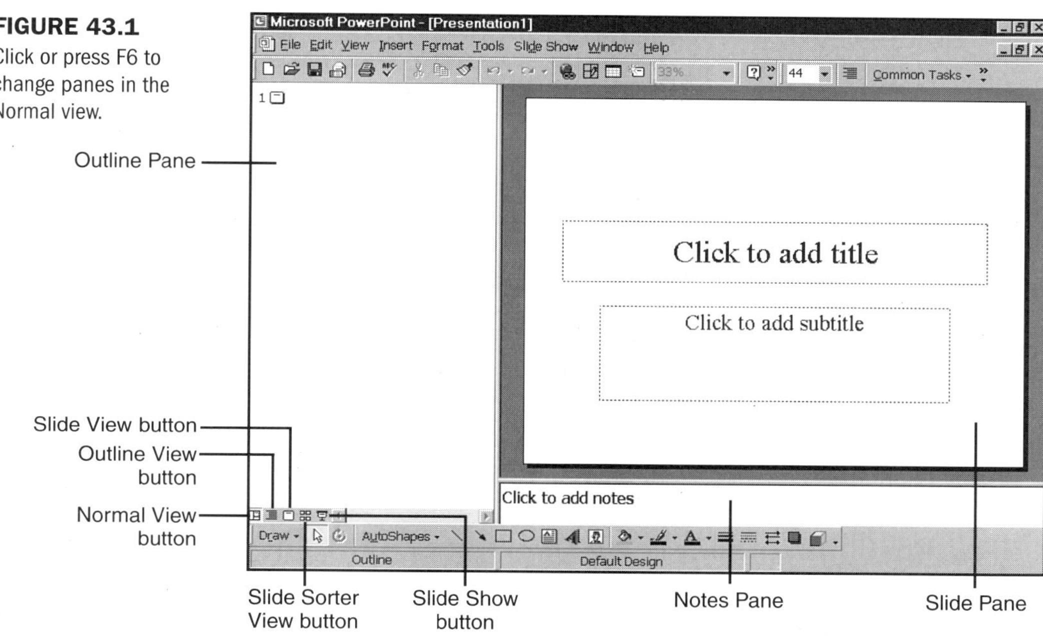

Focusing on increased productivity, Microsoft has made a few changes to some of the other views:

- When you display the Outline view, the Slide Pane and Notes Pane remain onscreen but are reduced to much smaller sizes.
- When you display the Slide view, the Outline Pane is collapsed to the left side of the screen and the Notes Pane is collapsed to the bottom of the screen. You can display these panes by dragging the pane border (the mouse pointer appears as two parallel lines when positioned on a pane border).
- The View buttons located at the bottom-left corner of the screen no longer include Notes Page view. You can still access this view from the View menu.
- The View menu no longer contains options to display the Outline view or Slide view; you have to access these views through the view buttons.

CAUTION

If you use Notes Pages, make sure you look at them in the Notes Page view rather than relying on the Notes Pane. Bullets typed in the Notes Pane appear to have a space between the bullet and the text—yet when printed, the bullets will have no space. Use the Notes Pages view as a way to "preview" exactly how the speaker's notes will print.

Personalized Toolbars and Menus in PowerPoint Another interface change you'll see in PowerPoint 2000 is the implementation of personalized menus and toolbars.

When you first open PowerPoint, there are three toolbars on the screen: Standard, Formatting, and Drawing. The Standard and Formatting toolbars share one line at the top of the screen. The Drawing toolbar appears at the bottom of the screen (see Figure 43.2).

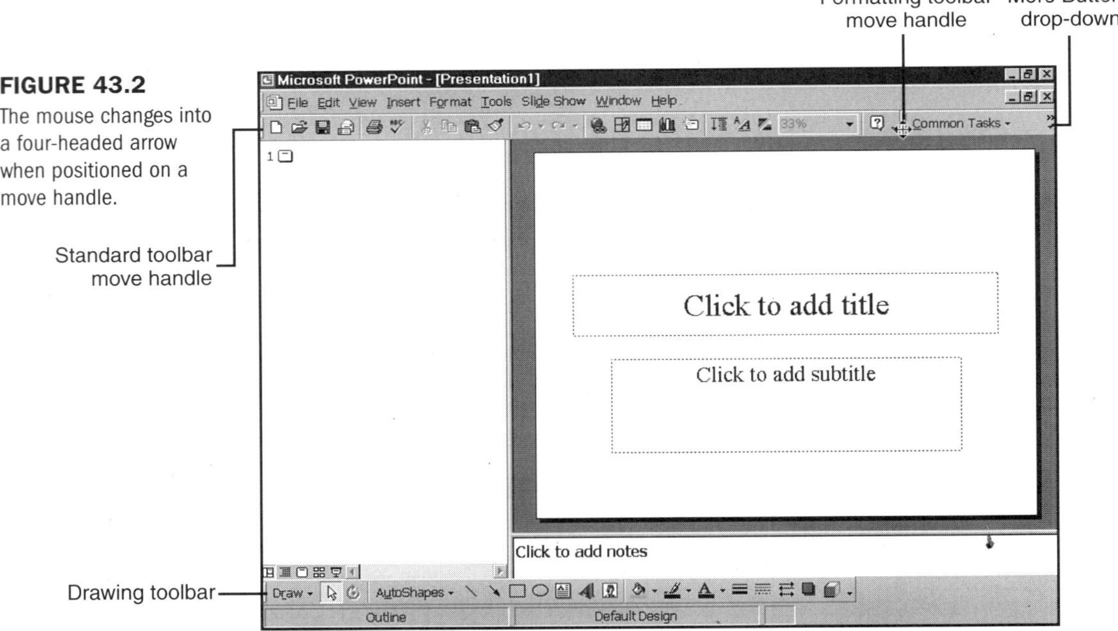

FIGURE 43.2
The mouse changes into a four-headed arrow when positioned on a move handle.

If you don't like the Standard and Formatting toolbars combined on one line, drag a toolbar from its move handle to another line. This changes the position of these toolbars in PowerPoint only, and does not affect the position of the toolbars in the other Office 2000 applications.

The new interactive menus initially display the most frequently used commands on a short menu list (see Figure 43.3). If you double-click the menu or pause a moment, the menu will expand to show all the commands. After an entire menu has been displayed, moving the mouse right or left to another menu displays the other menus in their entirety.

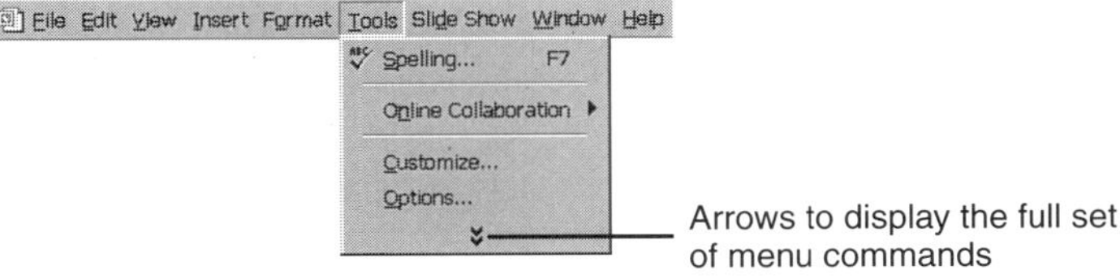

FIGURE 43.3
You can also click the double arrows at the bottom of a menu to expand it.

The menus initially display a default set of commands. As you use other commands, the menus automatically adjust to only those commands you use frequently (hence the name "personalized menus"). If you don't like the behavior of the menus, you can force PowerPoint to always show the full set of commands when you click a menu. Choose Tools, Customize and in the Customize dialog box, click the Options tab. Remove the check from the Menus Show Recently Used Commands First check box.

Designed to display only the menu commands and toolbar buttons you use frequently, the personalized menu and toolbar feature take a little getting used to. However, in time, you'll discover they will actually save you time.

▶ **See** "Altering the Behavior of the Personalized Menus and Toolbars," **p. 86**

Toolbar Button Changes In addition to the changes in menu and toolbar behavior, a few buttons have been moved or added to the PowerPoint toolbars:

- The Insert Clip Art button has been moved to the Drawing toolbar.

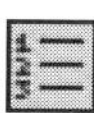

- If you want to create a numbered list, use the new Numbering button on the Formatting toolbar.

- A button to create a Summary Slide appears on the Outlining toolbar.

Native Tables Another significant improvement is the way tables are created and edited in PowerPoint. Previous versions of PowerPoint actually launched Word in the background to use the features in Microsoft Word to create and edit tables. Now when you create a slide with a table layout or insert a table into a slide, you use tools that are native to PowerPoint. The most frequently used tools for creating Word tables have been replicated in PowerPoint, including the Tables and Borders toolbar and the Draw Table feature.

AutoFit Text When text is typed into a slide placeholder, it will now automatically be adjusted if the text won't fit into the placeholder. AutoFit first adjusts the line spacing to fit the text. If the text still won't fit, then the font size is reduced to make the text fit. This feature happens automatically. If you don't want the AutoFit adjustments, you can press Ctrl+Z (Undo) to return the text to its previous settings. This reverses only the most recent adjustments. AutoFit can be deactivated on the Edit tab of the Options dialog box.

Other Changes A number of other changes have been implemented in PowerPoint 2000:

- The View on Two Screens option has been replaced by support for using multiple monitors. You can display a slide show on one monitor, while viewing the presentation outside the slide show on another monitor. This enables you to see the speaker's notes, look ahead to the next slide, or even edit slides before showing them to the audience. Unfortunately, this functionality requires hardware that supports dual video output, and either Windows 98 or Windows 2000.

NOTE If you use a laptop to give PowerPoint presentations, PowerPoint 2000 now disables the Windows screensaver and your laptop's low-power screen mode during the presentation to avoid interruptions.

- You can now record voice narration that is truly synched to individual presentation slides (including slide transitions and build animations). Previous versions of PowerPoint required users to record narration for the entire presentation. If a mistake was made, the entire recording had to be repeated. PowerPoint 2000 allows rerecording of narration on a slide-by-slide basis.
- PowerPoint Central (introduced in PowerPoint 97) has been removed from the Tools menu. Access to additional clips is now available through the revised Clip Gallery.

  See "Working with Picture, Sound, and Motion Clips," **p. 1195**
- Numbered bullets will automatically renumber when you insert new bullets.

Considerations When Converting PowerPoint Documents

You will have no trouble importing PowerPoint 97, 95, or even PowerPoint 4.0 presentations into PowerPoint 2000. What's surprising is how easily you can open PowerPoint 2000 presentations with PowerPoint 97 and PowerPoint 95.

If you save a PowerPoint 2000 presentation in an earlier version, however, some of the features will be converted to the earlier version's closest equivalent or will no longer work. A complete and detailed description of what happens when you save a PowerPoint 2000 presentation in PowerPoint 97, 95, and 4.0 is available through PowerPoint Help.

When you open a PowerPoint presentation created in an earlier version of PowerPoint, a dialog box displays to alert you that the presentation is being updated from a previous version of PowerPoint (see Figure 43.4).

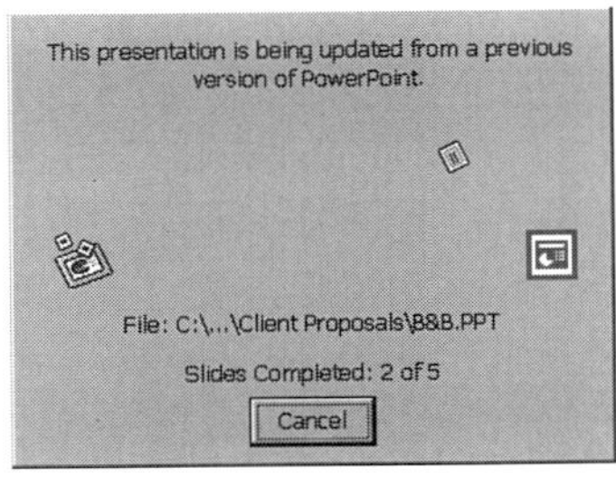
This presentation is being updated from a previous version of PowerPoint.
File: C:\...\Client Proposals\B&B.PPT
Slides Completed: 2 of 5
Cancel

FIGURE 43.4
The bottom of the dialog box provides status information.

The presentation has not been converted into PowerPoint 2000. When you save the file, PowerPoint asks whether you want to save the presentation in PowerPoint 2000 (see Figure 43.5).

FIGURE 43.5
If the Office Assistant is active, the message will be displayed by the Assistant instead of in this pop-up.

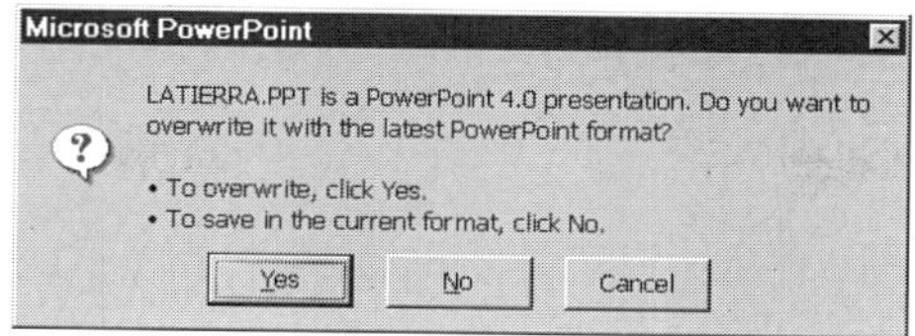

When you want to open a PowerPoint 2000 presentation in PowerPoint 97, you do not have to save it in a PowerPoint 97 format. You can open it directly in PowerPoint 97. If you want to open a PowerPoint 2000 presentation in PowerPoint 95 or PowerPoint 4.0, you will need to save it in the earlier format by using the File, Save As command.

TIP If you need to routinely open a presentation in PowerPoint 95, 97, and 2000, a special file format option (PowerPoint 97-2000 & 95 Presentation) enables you to do this.

CHAPTER 44

Working with Picture, Sound, and Motion Clips

In this chapter

Working with the Revised Clip Gallery

The difference between a good presentation and a great presentation is the effective use of clips and animation. Let's face it, slides containing succinct bullets or color-coordinated column charts aren't sufficient to pique and keep the attention of today's audiences. Using clips and animation to captivate your audiences will help them focus on the details of the topics presented. In this chapter, we will concentrate on using and animating clips in presentations. See Chapter 46, "Unleashing the Power of Animation," to learn how to animate drawn objects, text, and graphic charts.

Several sources of clips are available to you. PowerPoint itself comes with a large variety of clips located in the Clip Gallery. If you have access to the Internet, you can tap into a plethora of clips on Microsoft's Clip Gallery Live Web site, including clips that were available in previous versions of PowerPoint. If you need more clips, you can purchase clips in many stores where you buy software or from sites on the Internet. You can even scan in images, record sounds and music, or use segments from videos as clips in your presentations.

The best place to start looking for clips is in the Clip Gallery. From there, you have access not only to the clips in the Gallery, but you can also quickly locate clips on your PC, clips on your company's network, and clips on the Internet. The revised Clip Gallery (shown in Figure 44.1) divides clips into three groups: Pictures, Sounds, and Motion Clips.

- Pictures—This group contains drawings, photographs, and bullet symbols. The Clip Art and Picture groups used in previous versions of PowerPoint have been combined into this one group in Office 2000. Common picture file types include Windows Metafile (.wmf) and Graphics Interchange Format (.gif).
- Sounds—Individual sounds and longer clips of music are found in this group of clips. Sound and music clips tend to be .wav files.
- Motion Clips—In earlier versions of PowerPoint, these were called Video clips. Because this group includes both animated and live-action video clips, Office 2000 uses the more generic name—motion clips. .avi and .mov are the most common types of motion clips.

Although the categories appear when you click the Sounds and Motion Clips tabs, these clips are in fact not loaded with the typical installation of Office 2000. You need to add these from the Office 2000 program files, either directly from the Office 2000 CD or wherever your company has stored the program files on your network.

On the upper-left side of the Gallery dialog box are three navigation buttons, similar to the type of buttons you use in a Web browser. Use these to move backward and forward through Clip Gallery screens, and to quickly get back to viewing all categories of clips.

On the upper-right side of the dialog box is a button used to reduce the size of the Clip Gallery window. This makes it easier to see your presentation slides when you want to add multiple clips to a presentation.

FIGURE 44.1
Copy clips into the Favorites Category to store clips you use frequently.

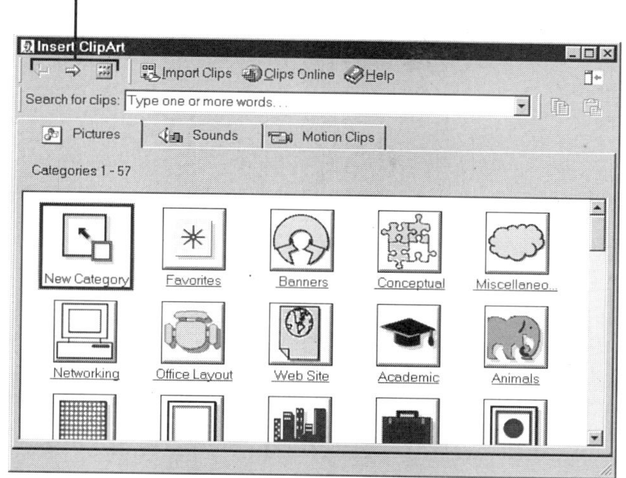

NOTE You can no longer double-click a clip to insert it into a slide. When you click a clip, a pop-up menu appears with the options to insert the clip, to preview the clip, to add the clip to the Favorites (or other) category, or to find more clips like it. Inserting the clip does not close the Clip Gallery dialog box; you have to manually close it, which makes it easier to add multiple clips.

Clip Gallery Dialog Box Is Context Sensitive

The method you use to access the Clip Gallery dictates the tabs that appear. If you have a slide layout that contains a placeholder for a clip, only the clips appropriate for the placeholder appear. For example, if you have a Clip Art placeholder, when you double-click the placeholder, only the Pictures tab appears in the Clip Gallery dialog box. If you have a Media Clip placeholder, only the Sounds and Motion Clips tabs appear in the Clip Gallery dialog box.

If the slide does not have a clip placeholder, PowerPoint doesn't know what type of clip you want to insert when you click the Insert Clip Art button, so all three tabs (Pictures, Sounds, Motion Clips) appear in the Clip Gallery dialog box. (The Insert Clip Art button was located on the Standard toolbar in PowerPoint 95 and 97 and is now located on the Drawing toolbar at the bottom of the PowerPoint window.)

Likewise, when you use the menu commands to access the Clip Gallery, it shows only the appropriate tabs. For example, if you choose Insert, Movies and Sounds, Sounds from Gallery, only the Sounds tab in the Clip Gallery appears.

Locating Clips in the Clip Gallery

In Office 2000, the changes to the Clip Gallery are more than merely cosmetic; the approach you use to locate and insert clips has changed as well. Searching for clips is the best way to navigate the myriad of categories.

To locate a clip, make sure you have the correct tab selected for the clip type you are attempting to locate. For example, click the Pictures tab to locate drawings, photographs, and bullet symbols. Each clip stored in the Clip Gallery has several keywords associated with it. When you type a word in the search text box and press Enter, the keywords are used to retrieve the correct clips.

To perform another search, click in the Search for Clips text box and start again. You can use the navigation buttons to go back to the results of a previous search or to see all the clip categories.

CAUTION

When you begin to type a word in the search text box, AutoComplete sometimes suggests a word for you to use. For example, when you type "`buil`", AutoComplete suggests "`builders`". To accept the AutoComplete suggestion, press Tab. To ignore the suggestion, continue to type the remaining letters of the word you want to use in the search.

Interestingly enough, the word that AutoComplete suggests may result in no clips being found (as is the case with `builders`). This AutoComplete feature is a function of the Clip Gallery, not PowerPoint, and you can't disable it.

NOTE If you want to repeat a search (even if the search was conducted during a previous working session), click the drop-down arrow on the right side of the Search for Clips text box and choose a term from the list.

When you see the clip you want to use, click the clip. A pop-up menu of options appears (see Figure 44.2).

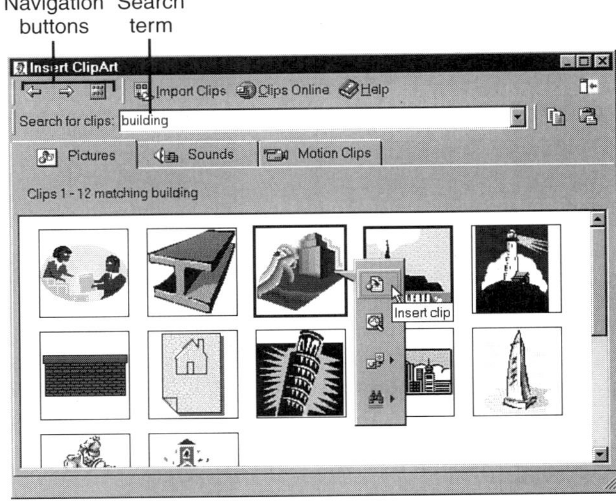

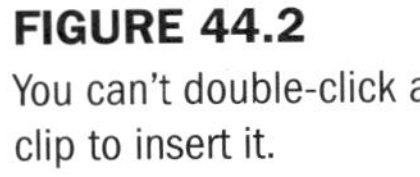

FIGURE 44.2
You can't double-click a clip to insert it.

Click the first button to insert the clip into a slide. Use the second button to enlarge the clip so that you can see it better. If you plan to use the clip regularly, you can click the third button to add the clip to the Favorites, or another, category. When you click the last button, the display expands to give you the opportunity to locate similar clips, as shown in Figure 44.3.

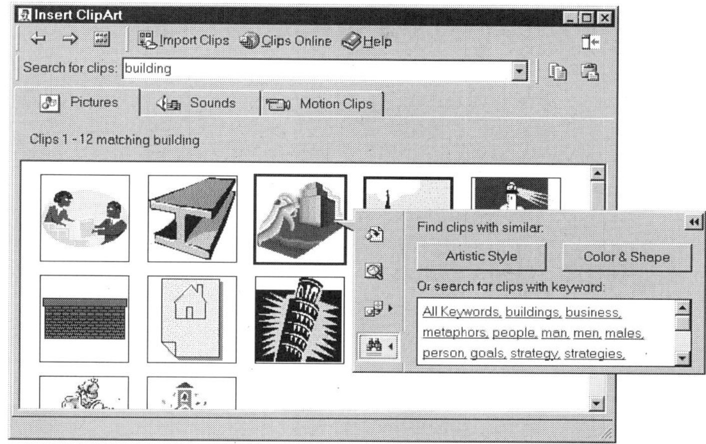

FIGURE 44.3
Use this feature to search for similar clips based on design, color, style, or a specific keyword.

Adding Clips to the Clip Gallery

The Clip Gallery provides a convenient means of accessing clips. Although it already includes a large number of interesting clips, you will periodically want to add other clips to the Gallery—such as a company logo or music theme, drawings you've created in PowerPoint, clips you find on the Internet, or images you have scanned in.

Adding clips to the Gallery is a quick and straightforward process. Clips are added in one of two ways. Clips can be imported from a disk drive such as floppy drives, Zip drives, CD-ROM drives, or network drives. Clips also can be imported from the Internet. As you add clips, it may become necessary to create new categories or move clips from one category to another.

Follow these steps to import clips from a disk or network drive into the Clip Gallery:

1. Open the Clip Gallery and click the Import Clips button.
2. The Add Clip to Clip Gallery dialog box displays as shown in Figure 44.4. Use the Look In drop-down list, the Up One Level button, or type the full path in the File Name text box to display the folder where the clip is located. If you prefer, you can type full path (with the filename) to select the clip.

NOTE If the Files of Type drop-down list isn't displaying the type of clip file you are attempting to locate, choose another file type from the drop-down list.

3. At the bottom of the Add Clip to Clip Gallery dialog box, choose one of the Clip Import Options. You can copy, move, or link to the clip.

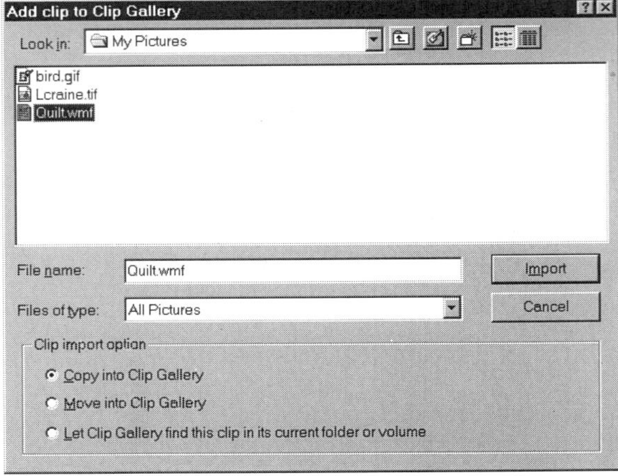

FIGURE 44.4
You can copy, move, or link clips to the Clip Gallery.

CAUTION

The Let Clip Gallery Find This Clip in Its Current Folder or Volume option creates a link to the clip. A thumbnail of the clip appears in the Clip Gallery. If you link to a clip on a drive that is not always available, you will not be able to access this clip. Suppose, for example, you have a laptop you dock at the office and take with you on business trips. You have used the Let Clip Gallery Find This Clip in Its Current Folder or Volume option to link to a clip on a drive on your company's network. When you take your laptop on the road, you won't be able to insert the clip into a slide, because the clip is not actually stored in the Clip Gallery.

4. When you've selected the file you want to add to the Clip Gallery, click the Import button. The Clip Properties dialog box appears, as shown in Figure 44.5.

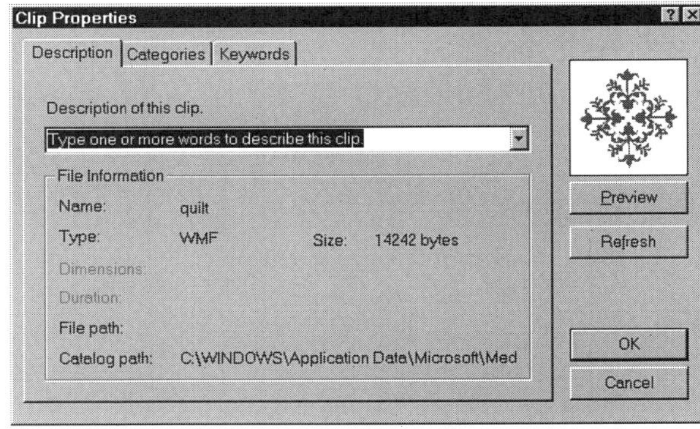

FIGURE 44.5
Don't press Enter until you've completed the options on all three tabs!

5. On the Description tab, add a description that will appear when you point to the clip in the Clip Gallery. This tab includes property information about the clip, such as file type, size, and duration.

6. On the Categories tab, choose one of the existing categories, or create your own. Clips can be added to multiple categories.
7. On the Keywords tab, click the New Keyword button and type a keyword that can be used by you (or others) to search for this clip. Repeat this step for each keyword you want to add to the clip. You can select from a drop-down list of previous keywords you have typed in.
8. After you have completed the options in the Clip Properties dialog box, choose OK.

In addition to importing clips from disk and network drives, hundreds of great-looking clips are available through Microsoft's Web site called Clip Gallery Live.

To import a file from Clip Gallery Live, follow these steps:

1. Open the Clip Gallery and click the Clips Online button.
2. A message appears to confirm if you have access to the World Wide Web. If you don't want to see this message each time you select the Clips Online button, you can mark a check box to avoid seeing this message in the future. Choose OK.
3. PowerPoint opens your browser and attempts to connect you to the Internet and the Clip Gallery Live Web site.

NOTE Depending on the configuration of your Web browser, you may need to manually connect to the Internet—not all configurations will automatically dial and connect for you. ■

4. The first screen of the Clip Gallery Live Web site is an agreement regarding the use of the clips. Read the agreement, and then click the Agree button.
5. In the Clip Gallery Live site shown in Figure 44.6, select the type of clips you want to retrieve from the tabs toward the top of the page. You can search for clips or display clips by category using the text boxes on the left side of the Web page. On the right side of the Web page, Microsoft also includes links to the latest clips as well as clips that relate to the time of year, upcoming holidays, and so on.
6. Regardless of the method you use to locate clips, thumbnails of available clips appear on the right side of your browser window (as shown in Figure 44.7). The file size, a download icon, and a check box appear below each clip.
7. Typically, the thumbnails are displayed in groups of 12. Click the More arrow to see additional clips. When you click a thumbnail, an enlargement of the clip displays on the left side of the Web page, along with a set of links to similar clips.
8. Click the download icon under the thumbnail to immediately download the clip or mark the clip's check box if you want to download several clips (or just browse other clips). If you've marked several clips, click the Selection Basket hyperlink to see the clips and download them.
9. The clips are automatically added to the Downloaded Clips category in the Clip Gallery, and may be added to other categories as appropriate. Clip Gallery Live remains active in your browser until you close the browser window or access another Web site.

FIGURE 44.6
The Selection Basket tracks how many clips you've marked to download.

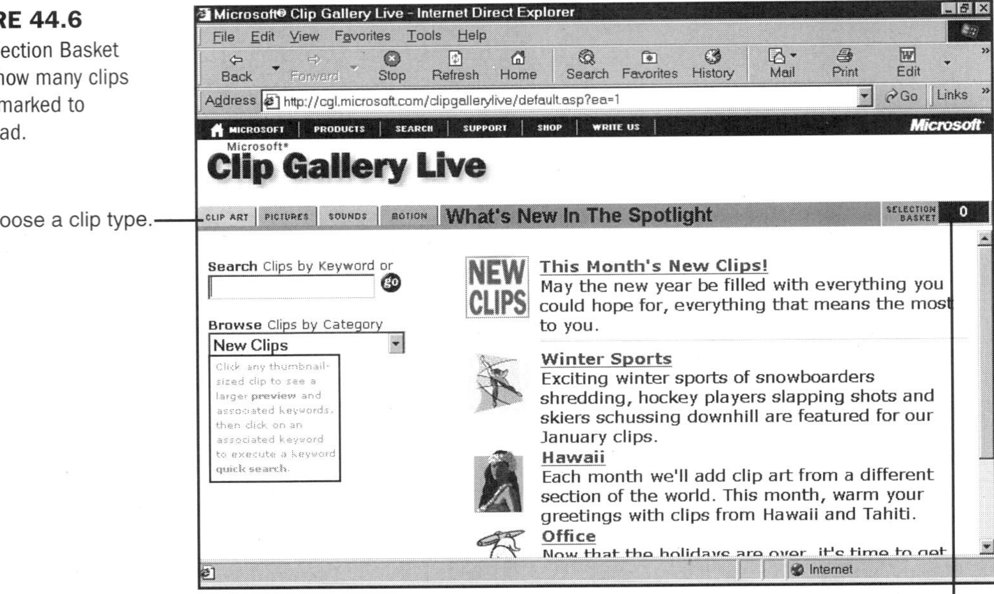

Choose a clip type.

Selection Basket

FIGURE 44.7
The preview on the left side of the page displays when you click a thumbnail.

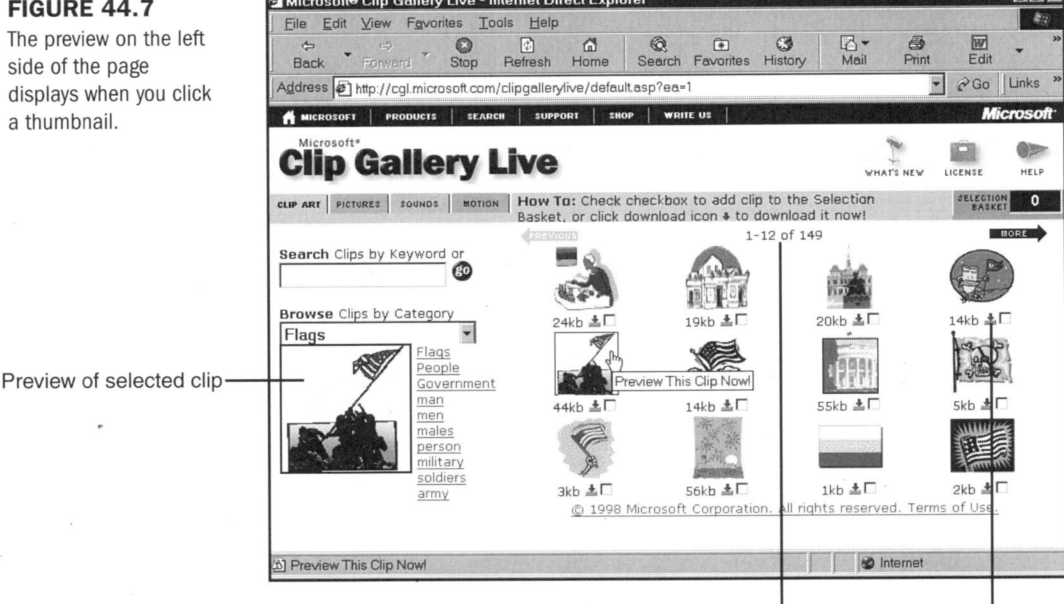

Preview of selected clip

Total number of clips in the selected category

Download icon

NOTE Other sources for clips on the Internet are generally people or organizations that are in the business of selling clip packages or graphic services. Many offer free sample clips you can download. Search for "Clip Art" or the particular file format (such as .wav) using any Web search engine to locate these sites.

Adding PowerPoint Drawings to the Clip Gallery

You can create your own drawings in PowerPoint using clips from the gallery, AutoShapes, WordArt, text boxes, and the other drawing tools. These drawings can be added as clips to the Clip Gallery.

Follow these steps to add PowerPoint drawings to the Clip Gallery:

1. Activate the slide containing the drawing and select the drawing you have created.

NOTE If there are several objects that compose the drawing, select all the objects and group them as one object. To group objects, click the Draw button on the Drawing toolbar and choose Group.

2. Right-click the object and choose Copy from the shortcut menu, or select the object and click the Copy button on the Standard toolbar.

3. Click the Insert Clip Art button on the Drawing toolbar.
4. Right-click in a blank portion in the Categories area of the Clip Gallery dialog box, and choose Paste Clips.

NOTE If you right-click a category, that category is automatically selected in the Clip Properties dialog box as a destination for the clips.

5. The Clip Properties dialog box appears, as shown in Figure 44.8.

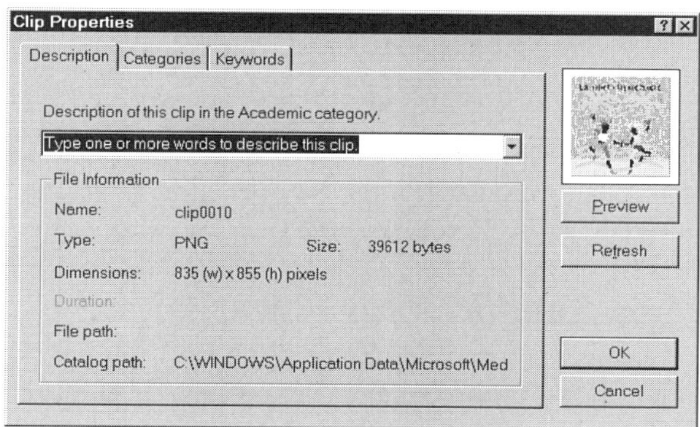

FIGURE 44.8
Click the Preview button to see an enlargement of the clip.

6. On the Description tab, insert a brief description that will appear when you point to the clip in the Clip Gallery.

7. On the Categories tab, choose one of the existing categories, or create your own. Clips can be added to multiple categories.
8. On the Keywords tab, click the New Keyword button and type a keyword that you (or others) can use to search for this clip. You can also select a previously typed keyword from the drop-down list.
9. After you have completed the options in the Clip Properties dialog box, choose OK.

Creating New Clip Categories

When adding clips to the Gallery, you might want to create new categories for the imported clips. As you use the Clip Gallery more and more, you may want to modify the clip categories or specific clip properties.

To add a new category to the Clip Gallery, access the Clip Gallery and click the New Category icon in the upper-left corner of the category portion of the dialog box. A dialog box appears permitting you to name the new category.

Type in the name for the new category and press Enter or click OK. Try to use no more than 12 characters for a category name. Longer names are accepted, but only the first few words are displayed as the title underneath the category icon.

NOTE The icon used for the new category is similar to the Favorites category icon and cannot be modified.

Working with Picture Clips

Picture clips, sometimes referred to as *clip art* or *graphics files*, are composed of a wide variety of clips, including drawings, line art, photographs, and bullet symbols. Using picture clips is one of the best and easiest ways to enhance a slide. They are often used on slides containing bulleted or numbered lists. In fact, PowerPoint has two slide layouts that have placeholders for text and picture clips.

You can insert picture clips into PowerPoint slides in three ways: You can use the clips in the Clip Gallery, insert a clip located in a specific file, or scan an image into a slide.

If you plan to insert clips from a specific file, or add clips into the Clip Gallery, you need to be familiar with the types of clips PowerPoint accepts.

Graphics File Types Supported by PowerPoint

Many types of graphics files can be inserted directly into a presentation by choosing Insert, Picture, From File. Most popular graphics file types can also be added to the Clip Gallery, including

- Enhanced Metafile (.emf)
- Graphics Interchange Format (.gif)
- Joint Photographic Experts Group (.jpg)
- Portable Network Graphics (.png)
- Windows Bitmap (.bmp, .rle, .dib)
- Windows Metafile graphics (.wmf)

However, some types of clips do require special filters so that you can add the clips to the Gallery. These filters are included on the Microsoft Office 2000 CD. Use the Add/Remove option in the Setup Wizard to select and install the filters from the CD. The graphics file types that require special filters are

- AutoCAD Format 2-D (.dxf)
- Computer Graphics Metafile (.cgm)
- CorelDRAW (.cdr)
- Encapsulated PostScript (.eps)
- FlashPix (.fpx)
- Hanako(.jsh, .jah, and .jbh)
- JPEG File Interchange Format (.jpg)
- Kodak Photo CD (.pcd)
- Macintosh PICT (.pct)
- Micrografx Designer/Draw (.drw)
- PC Paintbrush (.pcx)
- Tagged Image File Format (.tif)
- Targa (.tga)
- WordPerfect Graphics (.wpg)

To learn more about the support and limitations PowerPoint provides for specific graphics file types, activate the Office Assistant. Type `File Formats` in the search box and select `Graphics File Types PowerPoint Can Use` from the list of help topics. Then click the file type you are interested in.

Animated GIF files play only while a slide show is running or when you publish your presentation as a Web page and view it in a Web browser. You cannot use the Picture toolbar in PowerPoint to crop or group animated GIF pictures, or to change the fill, border, shadow, or transparency of an animated GIF. You need to make these changes in an animated GIF editing program before you import it into PowerPoint. It is recommended that you use screen settings of 1024×768 and 256 colors with Animated GIF files. Depending on the graphics card you are using, Animated GIFs may become static after they run once while in the Slide Show view.

Inserting Picture Clips into PowerPoint Slides

You can insert a picture clip into a slide in two ways:

- Inserting Clips through the Gallery—You can use a slide layout that contains a Clip Art placeholder; click the Insert Clip Art button on the Drawing toolbar; or choose Insert, Picture, Clip Art to access the Clip Gallery.

  ▶ **See** "Locating Clips in the Clip Gallery," **p. 1197**

- Inserting Clips from Other Sources—You can use the Insert, Picture, From File command to access clips located on your hard drive or a network drive.

When you use the Insert, Picture, From File command, the Insert Picture dialog box appears, as shown in Figure 44.9.

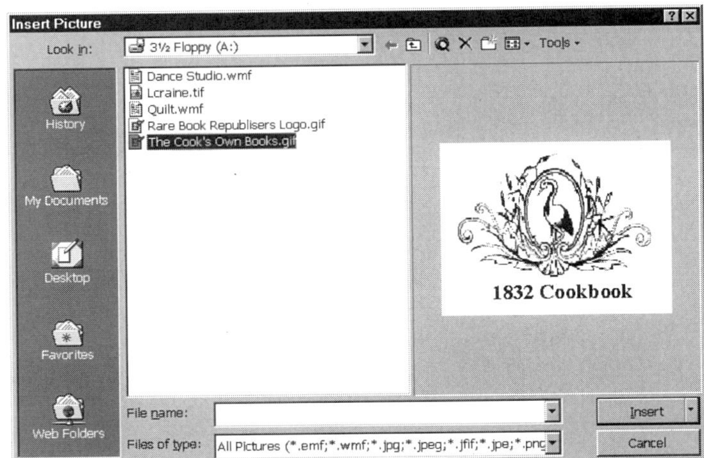

FIGURE 44.9
Use the Files of Type drop-down list to display only a specific type of picture file, such as only .wmf files.

Use the Look In field or the Up One Level button to select the drive and folder in which the picture clip is located. To make sure you insert the correct clip, click the filename and check the preview of the clip that appears on the right side of the dialog box.

When you have the correct clip selected, choose Insert.

A hidden option to link to the clip (rather than insert the clip) is available in the Insert Picture dialog box. Notice the drop-down button on the right side of the Insert button in Figure 44.9. When you click the drop-down button, you will see the link option.

Remember, there are advantages and disadvantages to linking to clips. The advantage is that the file size of your presentation remains low. The disadvantage is that you may lose the link if the location of the presentation or clip changes.

The Clip Gallery will sometimes accept files that cannot be inserted using the Insert, Picture, From File command. If you get an error message while inserting a file, try importing the file into the Clip Gallery instead.

To insert picture clips from the Internet, it is best to insert them into the Clip Gallery.

▶ **See** "Adding Clips to the Clip Gallery," **p. 1199**

Using Scanned Pictures

Another way to add pictures to slides is to use scanned pictures. Frequently, companies scan their logo into PowerPoint so it can be added to presentation slides.

Your computer must be attached to the scanner before you begin. Follow these steps to save a scanned image or to insert a scanned picture directly into a slide:

1. Display the slide where you want to insert the scanned picture.
2. Choose Insert, Picture, From Scanner or Camera. PowerPoint may display a message that the Scanner and Camera Add-In is not installed. You need access to the Office CD or to the Program Files on a network drive to install the Add-In.
3. The dialog box shown in Figure 44.10 appears. Choose Device and then, depending on the device, you may need to select the resolution you want to use.

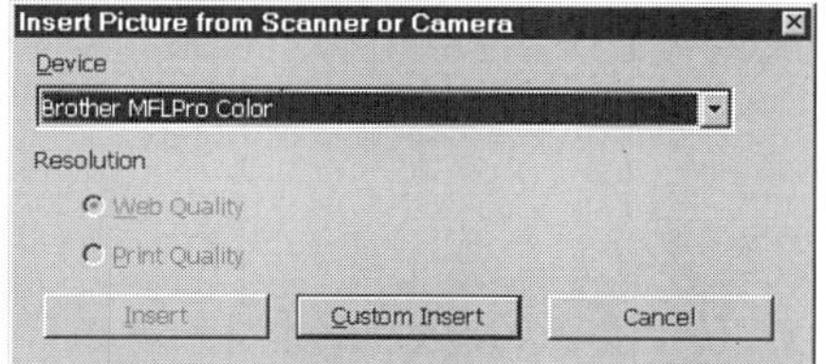

FIGURE 44.10
This dialog box provides capture options based on the device you are using.

4. Scan the picture according to the directions that came with your scanner.
5. Once scanned, the Microsoft Photo Editor window appears with the scanned image. Use the Photo Editor to make changes to the image, such as cropping the picture, or adjusting the color, contrast, and brightness.

To learn about the editing features in Microsoft Photo Editor, click Help.

6. If you intend to use the image repeatedly, choose File, Save to save the image in a file format PowerPoint supports. Then import the image into the Clip Gallery. From there you can add it to any slide.

   If you will not be using the image often, choose File, Exit and Return to insert the image directly into your slide.

Recoloring Picture Clips

Even though PowerPoint includes a large number of interesting Picture images, sometimes you'll find a clip you like, but would prefer it to display in different colors. Most picture clips can be customized by changing the image colors. Recoloring pictures is accomplished through the Format Picture dialog box.

NOTE Some of the picture clips are merely grouped shapes. If the command on the shortcut menu is Format Object, or if the Picture tab in the Format Object dialog box is grayed out (step 3 in the following list), the clip you have is just a group of drawn objects. You can ungroup the object to recolor individual shapes.

To recolor a Picture clip, follow these steps:

1. Select the picture clip that you want to recolor; selection handles appear around the selected object.

2. If the Picture toolbar is displayed, click the Recolor Picture button on the toolbar.
3. Otherwise, right-click the picture and choose Format Picture from the shortcut menu. The Format Picture dialog box appears with the Picture tab active. Choose the Recolor button at the bottom of the dialog box.
4. The Recolor Picture dialog box appears (see Figure 44.11). The colors used in the image are displayed on the left and a preview of the picture appears on the right of the dialog box.

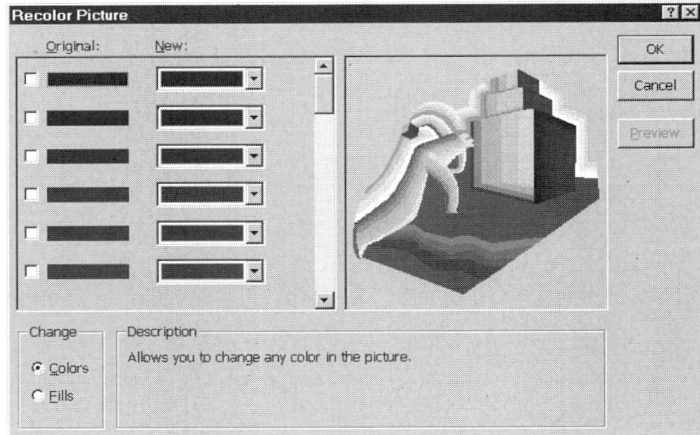

FIGURE 44.11
You may have to scroll to see all the colors used in the picture.

5. Locate the color you want to change. You may need to scroll down to locate the color.
6. To change a color, click the drop-down button next to the color in the New column, as shown in Figure 44.12. The eight colors that are part of the active presentation's design template are listed. Choose one of the presentation default colors or click More Colors for additional color choices.

   ▶ **See** "Working with Slide Color Schemes," **p. 1229**

7. If you select More Colors, the Colors dialog box appears as shown in Figure 44.13. Choose a color from the Standard tab and click OK.

   ▶ **See** "Customizing Slide Color Schemes," **p. 1230**

8. The clip image in the preview window is updated automatically to show the new color you selected.

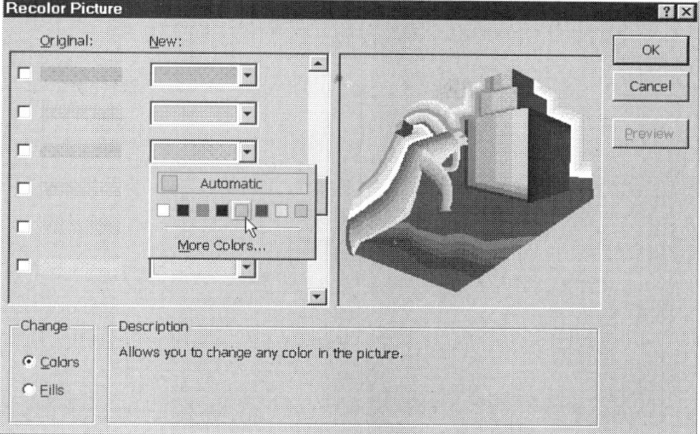

FIGURE 44.12
Additional colors used in the presentation are displayed below the eight default colors.

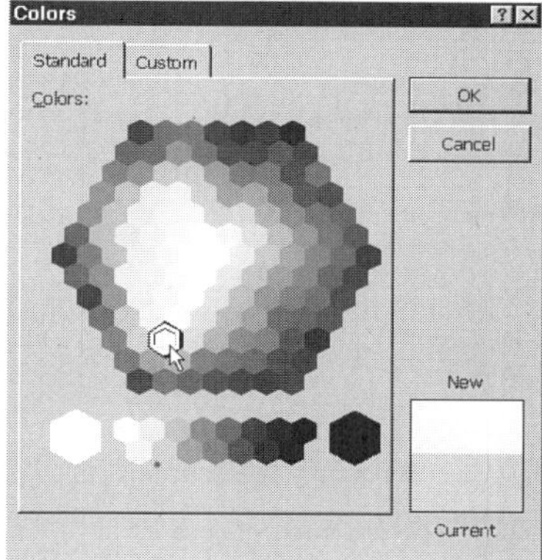

FIGURE 44.13
The quickest way to recolor is to select one of the Standard colors.

9. Click OK to exit the Recolor Pictures dialog box. (If you accessed the Recolor Pictures dialog box through the Format Pictures dialog box, you will need to click OK to change the picture image in your presentation.) The picture displays with the new colors.

If you decide at some later time to restore the original colors to a picture clip, access the Recolor Pictures dialog box as described in the previous steps . Then remove the check marks that appear in the row displaying the Original and New colors (refer to Figure 44.12). Without the check mark, the original color is restored to the picture.

Editing Picture Clips

Pictures are images or photographs that you can insert into PowerPoint slides or other application documents. These pictures are not PowerPoint objects, such as the arrows and rectangles that you draw in PowerPoint. Pictures are typically .wmf (Windows Metafile) or .gif (Graphics Interchange Format) files. When you insert a picture, you are actually importing the image into the PowerPoint slide.

Let's use the picture in Figure 44.14 as an example. Suppose you want to remove or duplicate the cattail or some of the grass under the crane, or perhaps you want to display some of the image components at different angles. If these seem like the types of changes you want to make to pictures, then you need to learn about editing picture images.

NOTE You cannot edit photograph clips in PowerPoint. Use Photo Editor or PhotoDraw instead. You can access these applications through the Programs option on the Start menu.

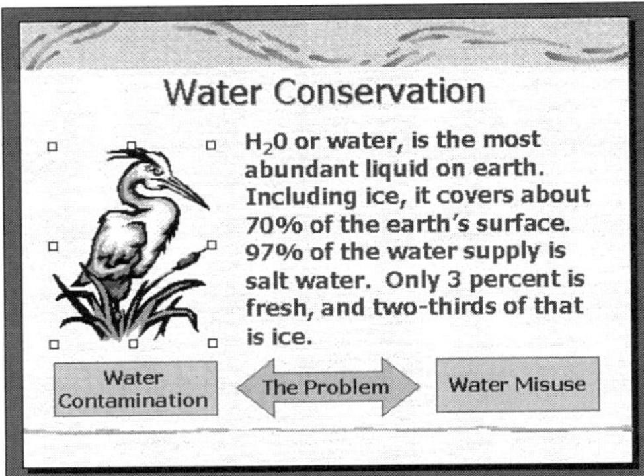

FIGURE 44.14
The crane clip can be found in the Animals category of the Clip Gallery.

To edit these images, you must convert them to PowerPoint objects. This is easily accomplished by ungrouping the picture. However, there are a few things you should know before you ungroup any picture:

- When an image is ungrouped, it is converted into a series of objects, some of which may need to be ungrouped further to get to the part of the image you want to change.
- After the image is ungrouped, any recoloring you performed before you ungrouped is lost. The original colors for the object reappear when you ungroup a clip art picture.
- After it is ungrouped, you cannot recolor an image, as described earlier in this chapter. Although you can change the color of individual parts of the image, it is tedious to do so.

To edit a picture clip, double-click the clip. A message appears indicating the object is an imported picture and asks whether you want to convert it to a Microsoft Office drawing. Choose Yes.

The clip is ungrouped and converted to a series of drawn objects. The additional sets of selection handles around the clip identify each object that now makes up the clip. Figure 44.15 shows the crane image ungrouped. Use the drawing tools in PowerPoint to edit the image.

If the only reason you ungrouped the clip was to rotate or flip it, immediately click the Draw button on the Drawing toolbar and choose Group. Don't be confused: This merely groups the clip as a single PowerPoint object; it does not convert it back into an imported picture. Grouping the picture objects into a single PowerPoint object prevents you from accidentally pulling one of the picture objects away from the others and messing up the picture. Trust me on this!

FIGURE 44.15
You can move, copy, resize, rotate, or flip ungrouped picture clips.

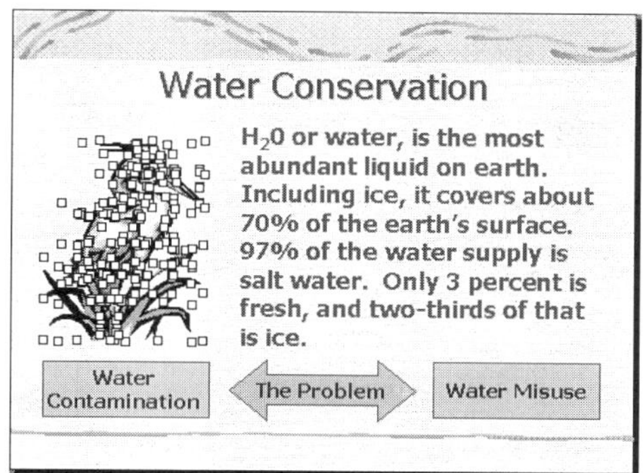

This short little snippet of VBA code will automatically ungroup and then regroup a picture clip so that you can quickly rotate or flip the picture.

```
Sub Ungroup_ReGroup_Picture()
    On Error Resume Next
    ActiveWindow.Selection.ShapeRange.Ungroup.Select
    ActiveWindow.Selection.ShapeRange.Group.Select
End Sub
```

The title of the snippet is Ungroup_ReGroup_Picture, and can be found on the CD accompanying this book. To learn more about working with VBA snippets and macros, see Chapters 5, "Getting Acquainted with VBA," and 6, "Successful VBA Modules."

NOTE In PowerPoint, you can copy VBA snippets from one presentation to another. But unlike Word, where you can copy a VBA snippet to the Normal.dot template, there isn't an easy way in PowerPoint to make a snippet available to all presentations. The only way to accomplish this in PowerPoint is to turn the snippet into an Add-In. The CD accompanying this book includes instructions on how to create an Add-In for the PowerPoint VBA snippets.

To edit one of the objects in the picture, click away from the picture so none of the objects is selected. Then click the specific object you want to change. After the object is ungrouped, you can edit it as you would any PowerPoint object; you can copy, move, and resize the object as desired. It will be easier to edit the object if you zoom in on the object by changing the zoom percent on the Standard toolbar.

NOTE It may be necessary to ungroup an object further so that you can select the specific item you want to change. Click the Draw button on the Drawing toolbar and choose Ungroup.

After you finish editing the object, select all of the objects that make up the picture and group them. This will make it much easier to resize, move, and copy the entire picture, keeping each component in proportion with the other objects.

Animating Picture Clips

After you've added a picture clip to a slide, you should decide whether or not to apply animation to the clip.

Animation is a special visual effect or sound that is applied to text or an object, and seen (or heard) when the presentation is in the Slide Show view.

NOTE Animation is sometimes referred to as *build*—for example, "building objects on the slide..." These terms are used interchangeably in this book.

There are only three reasons you should use animation:

- To focus your audience's attention on important points.
- To control the flow of information in your presentation.
- To add interest to your presentation.

Generally, you apply animation to picture clips only for the last reason—to add interest to your presentation.

Use animation sparingly. Too much animation can be distracting to your audience. The audience will focus on the interesting animation or sound effects and may miss the point of your presentation altogether.

In PowerPoint, you can either use Preset Animation or Custom Animation on slide objects. You can apply Preset Animation to slide objects; however, I don't recommend it. Preset animation includes both visual effects (how the object will appear on the screen) and sound effects (what sound is played as the object appears). You have no control over which sounds are paired with the visual effects or the timing associated with the animation.

▶ **See** "Understanding Preset Animation," **p. 1250**

Instead, I suggest you explore the Custom Animation options for complete control over all aspects of the animation of a clip. There are a number of animation options you can apply to picture clips. Here is a list of the options, with a brief description of each:

- Set a time when the object appears—The clip can appear when you click the mouse or press Enter, or you can set a specific time interval between animation events.
- Use a visual effect to display the object—As with slide transitions, you can apply a visual transition effect to picture clips. Visual transitions include the type of animation and the direction from which the clip will appear.
- Play a sound bite as the clip appears on the slide—There are 16 sound effects available, including two types of clapping, a drum roll, and a ricochet.
- Control what happens after the animation—You can choose to change the color and hide or dim the picture clip after it has animated on the screen.

To animate a picture clip, select the clip and choose Slide Show, Custom Animation. The Custom Animation dialog box appears, as shown in Figure 44.16. The upper-left corner of the

Custom Animation dialog box lists the objects in the current slide. Check the object you want to animate. A set of selection handles appears around the object in the preview window.

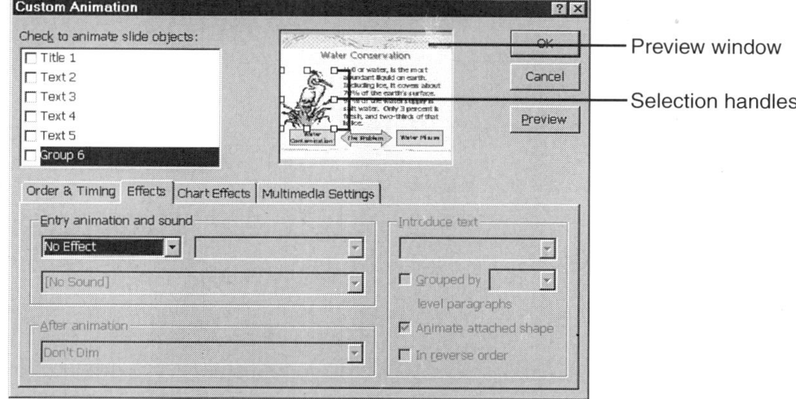

FIGURE 44.16
Picture clips that have been converted to PowerPoint objects are identified as Group in the list of slide objects.

There are four tabs in the dialog box that contain animation options—Order & Timing, Effects, Chart Effects, and Multimedia Settings. The only two tabs you need for picture clips are Order & Timing and Effects. Effects is the default tab.

Applying Visual and Sound Effects to Picture Clips As with slide transitions, you can apply a visual transition effect to a clip. The visual effect is composed of two things: type of animation and the direction of the animation appearance. For example your clip can Fly into the slide and appear From Left. There are 17 unique types of animation. The animation direction options depend on which type of animation you select.

NOTE The Random Effects type of animation picks a different visual effect each time you run the Slide Show.

On the Effects tab, select the type and direction of the animation from the top two drop-down boxes. Figure 44.17 shows the Zoom animation type and the In from Screen Center direction selected. To see how the effect will appear on your slide, choose Preview. The slide miniature displays the animation effect.

In addition to (or instead of) animating the picture clip, you can have a sound play as the clip appears. Use sound to really draw your audience's attention to the clip or slide you are displaying. There are 16 sound bites listed in the drop-down box on the Effects tab, including an explosion, a music chime, and even the sound a slide projector makes. As with the visual animation, choose Preview to hear the sound before you apply it to the clip.

NOTE The default installation of Office 2000 does not install the sounds. You will need the Office 2000 CD (or the location on your network where the Office 2000 program files are stored) to install the sound effects.

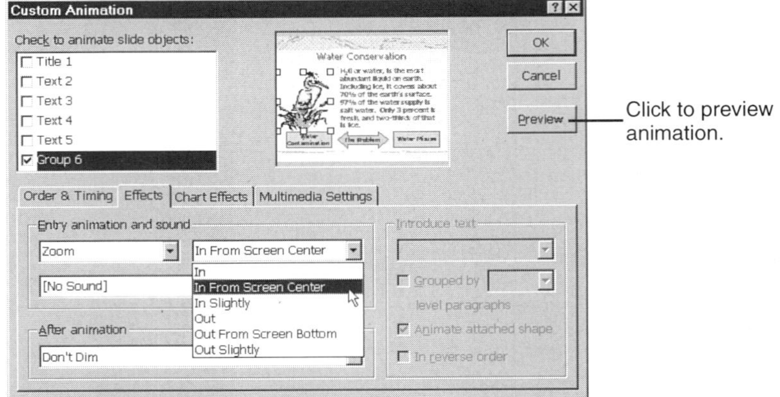

FIGURE 44.17
The list of direction options depends on the type of animation you choose.

In addition to the 16 built-in sounds, you can also apply other sounds to your slides. Scroll to the bottom of the sound drop-down list and click Other Sound. To find all the sounds used by the various programs on your computer, choose Tools, Find in the Add Sound dialog box. Search your entire hard drive and all subfolders to locate files with a .wav extension.

After the animation effect is complete, PowerPoint leaves the object on the screen. However, you can hide the clip by selecting either Hide After Animation or Hide on Next Mouse Click from the After Animation drop-down box (refer to Figure 44.17).

NOTE The color option in the After Animation drop-down box does not work with picture clips. However, the color option is particularly useful with bulleted or numbered lists; it helps the audience focus on each item you're discussing. The after-animation effect does not display in the Preview box; you have to run the Slide Show to see it.

▶ **See** "Applying Custom Animation to Text," **p. 1255**

After you've selected the animation effects, you need to set the animation order and timing.

Selecting the Animation Order and Timing Most slides have several objects on them—a title, a bulleted text, and clip or drawing objects. Objects that are not animated will automatically appear on the screen when the slide is displayed. To set the order of objects you have animated, use the Order & Timing tab in the Custom Animation dialog box.

Figure 44.18 shows a slide that contains four objects. When the Order & Timing tab is activated, you see that two of the objects have been animated—the text and the picture object. The current animation order has the text animated before the picture object.

To reorder the list, select the item you want to reorder and click the Move up or down arrows until the item is in the desired order.

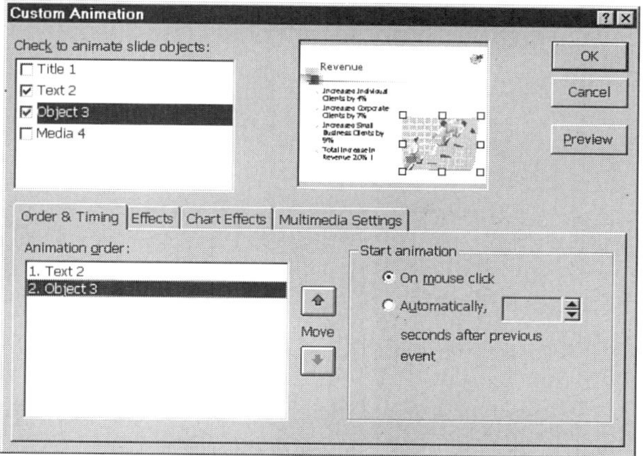

FIGURE 44.18
Picture clips are identified as Object in the list of slide objects.

In addition to establishing the order in which objects will appear on the screen, you need to decide the timing—when the object will appear. By default, objects will appear when you click the left mouse button (or press Enter, Page Down, the Down Arrow, or the Right Arrow keys). You can, however, set the object to animate a specific amount of time after the previous object has animated.

To set the timing for an animated object, select the object in the Animation Order box (refer to Figure 44.18). Then choose Automatically, __ Seconds After Previous Event, and type in the number of seconds you want to wait before the selected picture object appears.

After you select the effects, order, and timing for your animated objects, choose OK to apply the custom animation settings.

Using Sound Clips, Music Tracks, and Narration

You can use sounds, music, or narration in a variety of ways in your PowerPoint presentations. You can have a long music clip play as the audience for your presentation enters the conference room and gets settled. Self-running presentations, used in kiosks and trade shows, often include narration to guide viewers through the topics and to indicate when to display the next slide.

Sound clips can be added to your PowerPoint slides either by inserting a sound icon or by attaching a sound to an object. You can also set a music track or sound clip to play during all or part of your presentation, not just on the active slide.

▶ **See** "Configuring the Playback Options for Sound and Music Clips," **p. 1220**

Although both of these methods work well, and are described in this chapter, you will probably prefer to use the second method. See the section "Attaching Sound Clips to Objects," later in this chapter.

Sound File Types Used in PowerPoint

Most sound clips are wave (.wav) audio files, which are digitally recorded sounds. Wave audio files are sound effects, slide transition sounds, and all recorded sounds such as voice or music. The advantage to using wave audio sounds is that they can be recorded using a microphone or a line input source. The disadvantage is the file size. Wave files tend to be large.

NOTE You can reduce the size of wave audio files by either limiting the fidelity or compressing the file while recording. However, you will have to sacrifice sound quality.

Another audio file type is MIDI, Musical Instrument Digital Interface. These files use electronic musical instruments, such as synthesizers, and consist of commands that tell MIDI hardware what notes and instrument sounds to play. The advantage to using MIDI audio files is that the size of these files is quite small compared to wave audio files. The disadvantage is that they play electronic music and the quality of the sound can be poor, depending of the type of sound card on your machine. MIDI audio is used almost exclusively to play instrumental musical scores, such as background music in a presentation.

In this book we will concentrate on using wave audio files.

Inserting Sound Clips into PowerPoint Slides

You can insert sound clips into a slide in two ways:

- Inserting Clips through the Gallery—You can use a slide layout that contains a Media Clip placeholder; click the Insert Clip Art button on the Drawing toolbar; or choose Insert, Movies and Sound, Sound from Gallery to access the Clip Gallery.
- Inserting Clips from Other Sources—You can use the Insert, Movies and Sound, Sound from File command to access clips located on your hard drive or a network drive.

You insert sound clips from the Clip Gallery in the same way you insert Picture clips. If the slide to which you want to add a sound clip contains a media placeholder, double-click the placeholder to access the Clip Gallery. If the slide does not have a media placeholder, click the Insert Clip Art button on the Drawing toolbar.

In the Clip Gallery, activate the Sounds tab and choose a clip category. Thumbnails of the clips appear. When you click a clip, a pop-up set of button icons appears. Select the second button to play the clip. Select the first button to insert the clip into the current slide.

NOTE Depending on how Office 2000 was installed on your computer, no sound clips may be loaded in the Clip Gallery. Using the methods described earlier in this chapter, you can add clips to the gallery from the CD or from Microsoft's Clip Gallery Live Web site.

When you insert a sound clip this way, a sound icon and a pop-up window appear in your slide. In the pop-up window, choose Yes to play the sound automatically in the Slide Show, or choose No to have the sound play only when you click it. The small sound icon is always placed in the center of your slide by default. You can move it anywhere on the slide.

For a better way to insert sound clips into a slide, see "Attaching Sound Clips to Slide Objects" later in this chapter.

If the clip you want to add is not located in the Clip Gallery, you can insert an icon on your slide that will play the sound clip from a file you specify.

Choose Insert, Movies and Sounds, Sound From File. The Insert Sound dialog box appears, as shown in Figure 44.19.

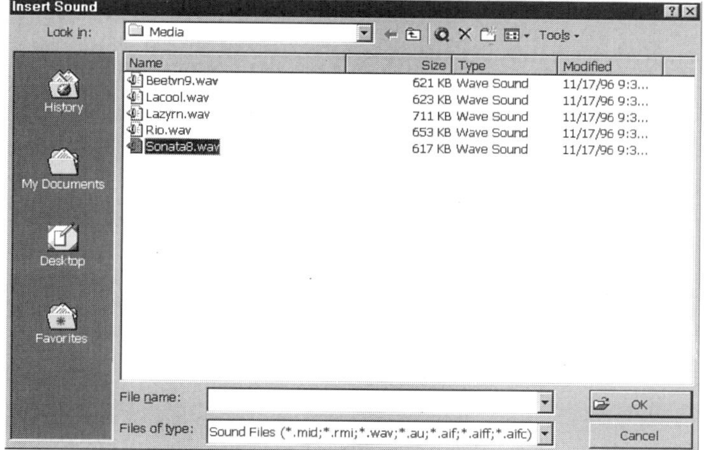

FIGURE 44.19
The types of sounds PowerPoint can import are listed in the Files of Type drop-down list.

Use the Look In field or the Up One Level button to select the drive and folder where the sound clip is located.

After you have the desired clip selected, choose OK. A sound icon is inserted in the slide and a pop-up window appears in which you choose Yes to play the sound automatically in the Slide Show, or choose No to have the sound play only when you click it.

You can move or resize the sound icon just as you would any PowerPoint object.

Attaching Sound Clips to Slide Objects

With the Clip Gallery and Insert command methods described previously, a sound icon appears in the slide when you insert a sound clip. Personally, I think having these icons displayed in slides is, well, just really tacky.

A more subtle way to add a sound clip to a slide is to attach the clip to one of the slide objects—such as a picture clip, drawing, or even a text box. However, sound clips cannot be attached to click placeholders such as the slide title.

Using this method, you can set the sound clip to play either when you click or point to the slide object.

Use the following steps to attach a sound clip to a slide object:

1. If necessary, add an object, such as a picture clip or AutoShape, to a slide to which you want to attach the sound clip.
2. With the object selected, choose Slide Show, Action Settings. The Action Settings dialog box displays, as shown in Figure 44.20.

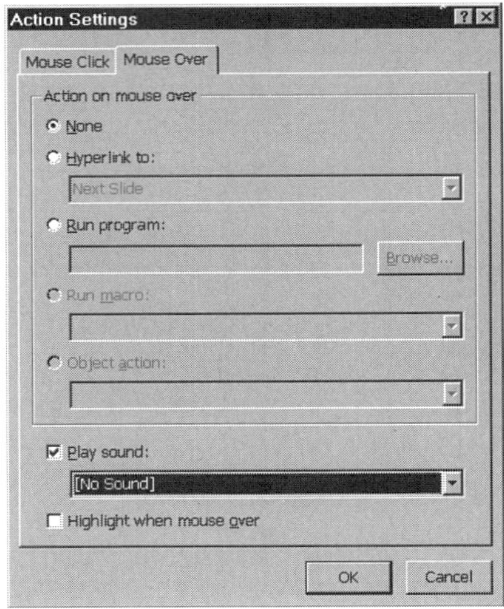

FIGURE 44.20
When you select a tab, you are selecting the method of activating the sound clip.

NOTE The Action Settings dialog box allows you to choose one action when you click the object and a different action when you point to the object.

3. If you select the Mouse Click tab, the clip will be set to play in the Slide Show view when you click the slide object.
4. If you select the Mouse Over tab, the clip will be set to play in the Slide Show view when you use the mouse to point to the slide object. The options on these two tabs are identical.
5. Regardless of the tab you choose, click the Play Sound check box.
6. Scroll down in the drop-down list and choose Other Sound at the bottom of the list.
7.  The Add Sound dialog box appears (see Figure 44.21). Use the Look In field or the Up One Level button to locate the sound clip you want to use.
8. Choose OK in the Add Sound dialog box.
9. Choose OK in the Action Settings dialog box.

Inserting a CD Music Track on a Slide

Instead of using a sound clip, you can set up a music track from a CD to play on a slide. First, display the slide to which you want to add a CD music track. Then choose Insert, Movies and Sounds, Play CD Audio Track.

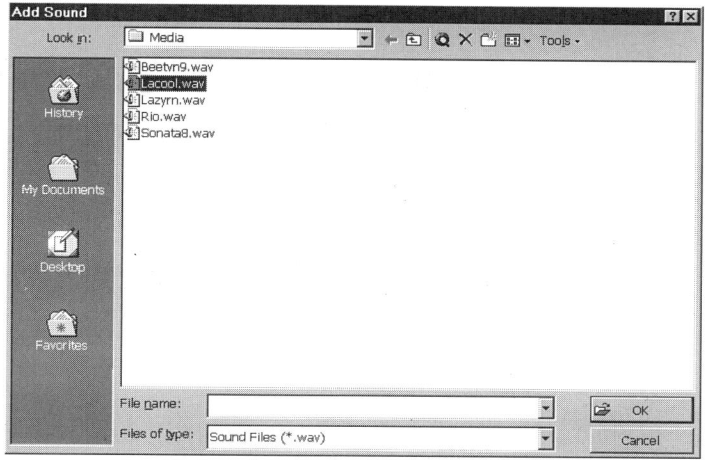

FIGURE 44.21
Locate the sound you want to use.

In the Movie and Sound Options dialog box, shown in Figure 44.22, select the music tracks you want to start with and end with. Then click OK.

FIGURE 44.22
The total playing time for the tracks you select is listed at the bottom of the dialog box.

A CD icon and a pop-up window appear in your slide. In the pop-up window, choose Yes to play the CD track automatically in the Slide Show, or choose No to have the CD track play only when you click it.

TIP Hide the CD icon behind another object, such as a picture clip, if you don't want your audience to see it.

In the next section, you'll learn how to set a music track to play during all or part of your presentation, not just on the active slide.

Configuring the Playback Options for Sound and Music Clips

After you've added a sound clip to a slide, you should choose the playback settings. Select the clip and choose Slide Show, Custom Animation.

The Multimedia Settings tab in the Custom Animation dialog box (see Figure 44.23) is active. The upper-left corner of the dialog box lists the objects in the current slide. A set of selection handles should appear around the sound object in the preview window (upper-right corner of the dialog box).

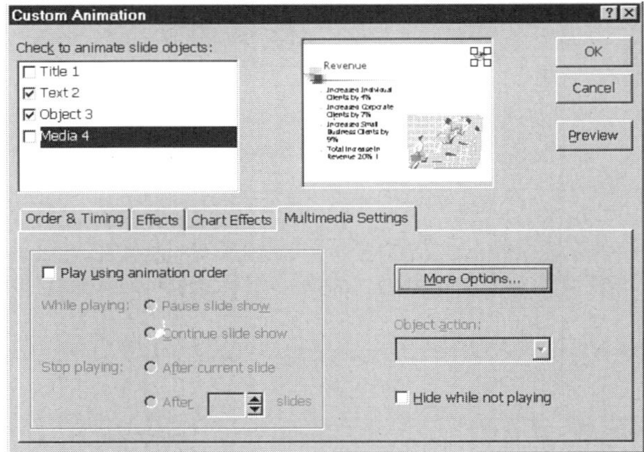

FIGURE 44.23
Choose Preview to play the sound clip.

On the Multimedia Settings tab, click the Play Using Animation Order option button. To play a music track or sound clip across multiple slides choose While Playing, Continue Slide Show. Then choose the Stop Playing, After __ Slides option. Click in the text box and type the number of slides across which you want the music or sound to play.

If the music or sound clip is short, click the More Options button. The Sound Options dialog box appears where you can set the clip to loop continuously until you press Esc. The dialog box also displays the clip playing time and location.

Then use the Order & Timing tab in the Custom Animation dialog box to set the animation order.

After you have selected the multimedia settings, order, and timing for your sound objects, choose OK to apply the custom animation settings.

Adding Narration to a Presentation

There are many reasons why you might want to record narration for your presentations:

- For self-running slide shows on the Web, at kiosks, or at trade shows.
- To record a presentation for individuals who are not able to attend.
- To document the comments or questions made by presentation attendees.

Narration can be recorded for the entire presentation, or for individual slides.

NOTE Voice narration overrides all other sounds inserted in a presentation. If you run a presentation that includes both narration and other sounds, only the narration will be played.

To add voice narration to your slide show, follow these steps:

1. Choose Slide Show, Record Narration. The Record Narration dialog box appears, and displays the amount of free disk space and the number of minutes you can record. See Figure 44.24.

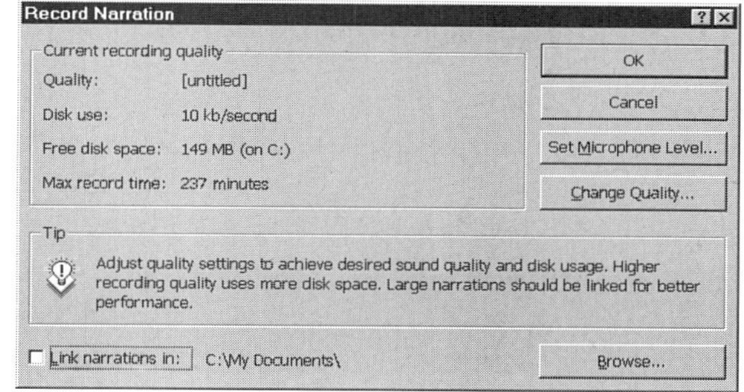

FIGURE 44.24
You must have a microphone to record narrations.

2. Click the Set Microphone Level button and follow the directions to set your microphone volume level.
3. Click the Change Quality button and set the recording quality you want from the Name drop-down list.
4. To embed the narration on your slides, choose OK and begin recording. To create a separate narration file and link the narration to the presentation, click the Link Narrations In check box, located in the lower-left corner of the dialog box. Then choose OK to begin recording.
5. Proceed through the slide show as you would normally, narrating as you go.
6. At the end of the slide show, a confirmation message will appear. Choose Yes to save the slide timings along with the narration. Choose No to save only the narration and ignore the slide timings.
7. An icon will be displayed in the lower-right corner of each slide that includes narration.

By default, the narration will play automatically when you run the slide show. To run the slide show without the narration, choose Slide Show, Set Up Show. Then click the Show Without Narrations check box.

CAUTION

You cannot play narration and other sound clips at the same time. Narration takes precedence over sound clips.

To record a sound or comment on a single slide, display the slide and choose Insert, Movies and Sounds, Record Sound. Click the Record button, represented by a circle. A meter tracks the length of your recording. Click the Stop button, represented by a square. To hear what you recorded, click the Play button (right-pointing triangle). Then enter a name for the recording and click OK. A sound icon appears in the slide.

You can use this feature to record all or part of a song from a music CD, using the CD-ROM on your computer. Play the CD and when the part of the music you want to use begins, click the Record button.

Using Video and Animated Clips

As presentations have become more sophisticated, the need to show motion or video clips has increased. Most video clips typically include both motion and sound, and, as a result, video clips are often referred to as movies or motion clips. These terms are used interchangeably in this book. There are two ways to import video clips. You can insert a clip from the Clip Gallery or from a separate file.

Video clips are usually large files; a clip lasting only three seconds has a file size that is three quarters of a megabyte—five times the size of a 50-page Microsoft Word document! As you can see, video clips require a significant amount of system resources.

For digital video to play on a PC, it must be in a format Windows can recognize. Typically, video clips are in either Audio Visual Interleave (.avi), Apple® QuickTime (.mov), or Moving Pictures Experts Group - MPEG (.mpg) file formats.

Inserting Motion Clips into PowerPoint Slides

As with the other types of clips, you can insert motion clips into a slide in one of two ways:

- Inserting Clips through the Gallery—You can use a slide layout that contains a Media Clip placeholder; click the Insert Clip Art button on the Drawing toolbar; or choose Insert, Movies and Sound, Movie from Gallery command to access the Clip Gallery.
- Inserting Clips from Other Sources—You can use the Insert, Movies and Sound, Movie from File command to access clips located on your hard drive or a network drive.

If the slide to which you want to add a video clip contains a media placeholder, double-click the placeholder to access the Clip Gallery. If the slide does not have a media placeholder, click the Insert Clip Art button on the Drawing toolbar.

In the Clip Gallery, activate the Motion Clips tab and choose a clip category. Thumbnails displaying the first frame of each clip appear. You can right-click a clip and choose Clip Properties to find out the length and size of the clip.

Left-click a clip and a pop-up set of button icons is displayed. Select the second button to play the clip. Select the first button to insert the clip into the current slide.

NOTE Depending on how Office 2000 was installed on your computer, no motion clips may be loaded in the Clip Gallery. Using the methods described earlier in this chapter, you can add clips to the gallery from the CD or from Microsoft's Clip Gallery Live Web site.

The video clip and a pop-up window appear in your slide. In the pop-up window, choose Yes to play the video automatically in the Slide Show, or choose No to have the video play only when you click it.

If the clip you want to add is not located in the Clip Gallery, you can insert the video by choosing Insert, Movies and Sounds, Movie from File. The Insert Movie dialog box appears, as shown in Figure 44.25.

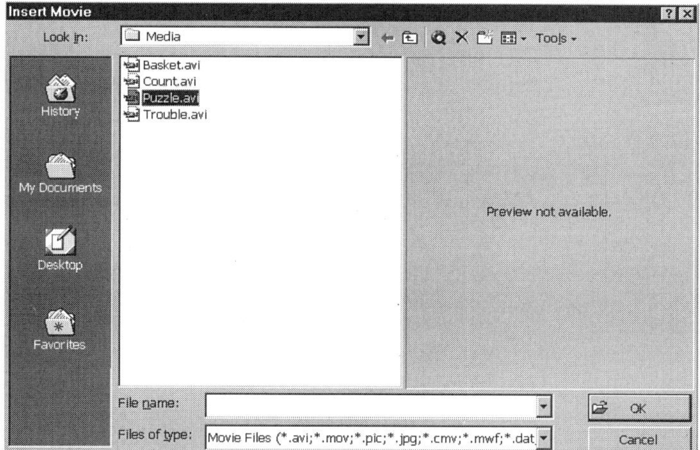

FIGURE 44.25
If you plan to use the clip over and over, consider adding it to the Clip Gallery.

Use the Look In field or the Up One Level button to select the drive and folder where the video clip is located.

After you have the correct clip selected, choose OK. The video and a pop-up window appear in your slide. In the pop-up window, choose Yes to play the video automatically in the Slide Show, or choose No to have the video play only when you click it.

You can move or resize the video object just as you would any PowerPoint object.

NOTE To create your own video file from commercial or home movies, you'll need a video capture card and video-editing software. Microsoft Office includes the Microsoft Media Player, which can be used to capture and play video and audio. Sophisticated video editing may require separate software such as Adobe Premiere© or Ulead VideoStudio Pro©.

Configuring the Motion Animation Playback

After you've added a video clip to a slide, you should decide how and when you want the clip to play during your presentation—the playback.

Animation playback can include a special visual effect for the motion clip to appear on the screen, looping the clip to play over and over and deciding when the clip plays.

To set the animation playback for a motion clip, select the clip and choose Slide Show, Custom Animation. The Custom Animation dialog box appears, as shown in Figure 44.26.

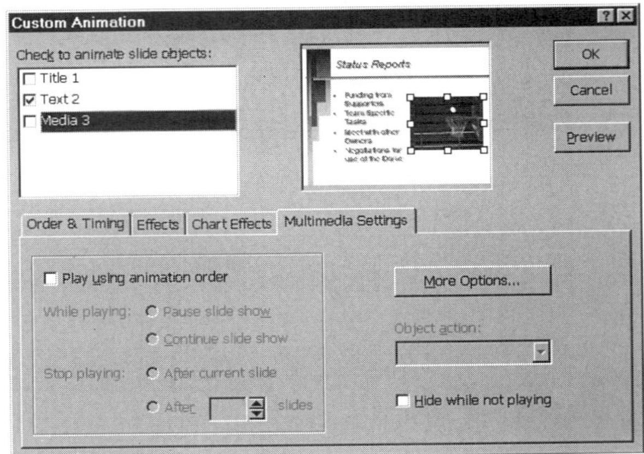

FIGURE 44.26 Motion clips are identified as Media in the list of slide objects.

There are four tabs in the dialog box that contain animation options—Order & Timing, Effects, Chart Effects, and Multimedia Settings. The default tab is Multimedia Settings.

Animation controls how and when the motion clip appears on the screen. It does not control how and when the clip plays. You do not have to animate a video clip to set other playback options. Objects that are not animated will automatically appear on the screen when the slide is displayed and will play based on the option you selected when the clip was added to the slide (immediately or on a mouse click).

If you do want to animate the motion clip, click to check the clip in the list in the upper-left corner of the Custom Animation dialog box. You will then want to use the Order & Timing tab in the Custom Animation dialog box to set the animation order.

Setting the Animation Order and Timing Most slides have several objects on them—a title, a bulleted text, and media (motion) clips. Figure 44.27 shows a slide that contains three objects. When the Order & Timing tab is activated, you see that two of the objects have been animated, the text and the media clip. The current animation order has the text animated before the media clip.

To reorder the list, select the item you want to reorder and click the Move up or down arrows until the item is in the order you want.

In addition to establishing the order in which objects will appear on the screen, you need to decide the timing—when the objects will appear. By default, objects will appear when you click the left mouse button (or press Enter). You can, however, set the object to animate a specific amount of time after the previous object has animated.

FIGURE 44.27
The numbers in front of the objects indicate animation order.

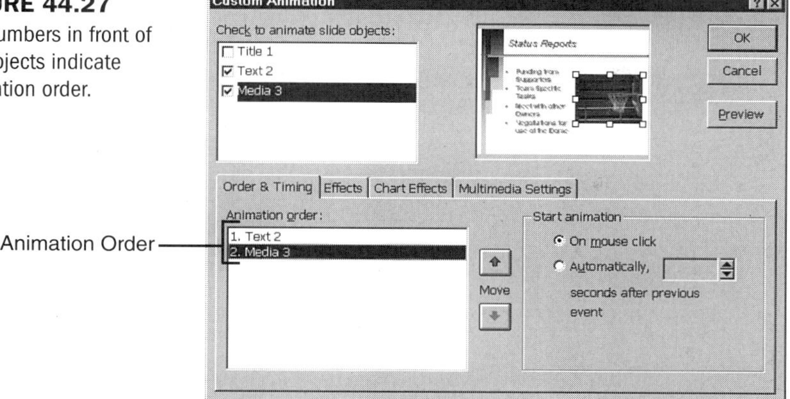

To set the timing for an animated object, select the object in the Animation Order box. Then choose Automatically, __ Seconds After Previous Event, and type in the number of seconds you want to wait before the selected motion clip appears.

Applying Visual Effects to Animated Motion Clips If you have decided to animate a motion clip, you may want to apply a visual transition effect to the clip. The visual effect is composed of two things: type of animation and the direction of the animation appearance. For example, your clip can Fly into the slide and appear From Left. There are 17 unique types of animation. The animation direction options depend on which type of animation you select.

To set the animation effects, click the Effects tab. This list identifies the Effects options:

- Entry Animation and Sound—Select the type and direction of the animation from the top two drop-down boxes. To see how the effect will appear on your slide, click the Preview button. The slide miniature displays the animation effect. Although you can have a sound effect play as the clip is animated on the screen, it is not recommended, because many of the motion clips include sound.
- After Animation—Controls what should happen to the clip after the animation effect is complete. Because you want the motion clip to play, keep the Don't Dim default setting.

Setting the Multimedia Options The options you use on the Multimedia tab depend on whether you decided to animate the motion clip.

If you animated the clip, the Play Using Animation Order option button will be selected, as shown in Figure 44.28. By default, any timing associated with changing slides will be paused as the motion clip plays.

Regardless of whether you animated the clip, the More Options button activates the Movie Options dialog box. It displays the clip playing time and location, and contains a setting to have the clip loop continuously until you press Esc.

Finally, choose the Hide While Not Playing check box to have the motion clip remain hidden until it plays and then hide again after it has played.

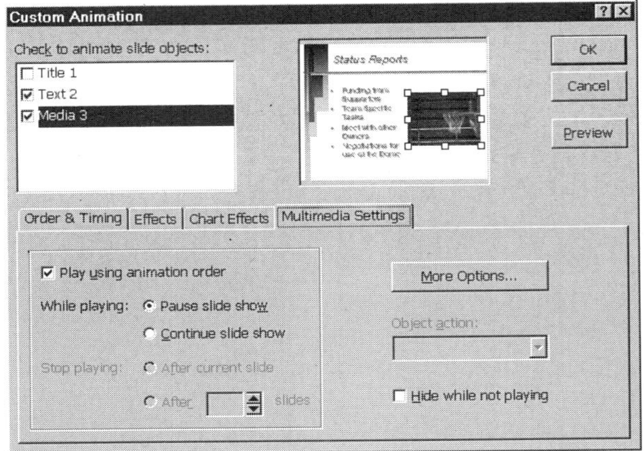

FIGURE 44.28
The default settings on the Multimedia Settings tab are displayed in this figure.

After you have selected the multimedia settings, order, timing, and effects for your motion clips, choose OK to apply the custom animation settings.

Look at the PowerPoint presentation examples on the CD that accompanies this book to see how picture, sound, or motion clips can be used to enhance your presentations.

CHAPTER 45

Advanced Presentation Formatting Features

In this chapter

Choosing the Right Slide Transition

Slide transitions are a subtle way to reinforce (psychologically) the message of a slide. Transitions should not be applied at random, but with deliberate, conscious purpose. Generally, you should use a positive transition for most of your slides and apply a special transition on the slides whose message you want to reinforce.

Another reason for using different slide transitions is to denote a change in topic. For example, if your presentation has three major sections, you might consider using a different transition for each section.

Table 45.1 provides you with a guide for choosing a slide transition.

Table 45.1 Use Slide Transitions to Convey Your Message

Message	Direction	Slide Transitions
Positive, Progression Moving Forward	Right or Up	Cover Right Cover Up Cover Right-Down Cover Right-Up Strips Right-Down Strips Right-Up Uncover Up Uncover Right-Down Uncover Right-Up Wipe Right Wipe Up
Negative, Regression Moving Backward	Left or Down	Cover Down Cover Left Cover Left-Down Splits Left-Down Strips Left-Down Strips Left-Up Uncover Down Uncover Left-Down Uncover Left-Up Wipe Left Wipe Down
Positive Transition Opening a Window (of opportunity)	Out	Blinds Horizontal Blinds Vertical Box Out Checkerboard Fade Through Black Split Horizontal Out Split Vertical Out

Message	Direction	Slide Transitions
Starting Over Closing a Window (on old, negative news) Removing (the competition)	In	Box In Dissolve Random Bars Split Horizontal In Split Vertical In
Quick Pace		Cut Cut Through Black

A few additional notes about transitions you should know:

- Any transition whose name includes “Out” generally equates to opening, such as Box Out.
- “In” usually equates to closing, such as the Split Vertical In transition.
- The Cut Through Black transition is not as smooth a transition as just plain Cut.
- “Out with the old and in with the new” is the message the Starting Over set of transitions (identified in Table 45.1) conveys.
- The Random transition should not be used for formal presentations; save it for informal, in-house presentations where you don’t care about aligning the message with the transition.

Working with Slide Color Schemes

Slide Color Schemes are one component of the presentation design templates; the other component is the presentation *Masters*.

Color Schemes control eight default colors:

- Title Text—The Slide Title.
- Background—The main color in the background behind the text and other slide objects.
- Text and Lines—Text in click placeholders and text in text boxes; also the color of drawn lines and the border color around drawn objects.
- Shadows—The shadow color displayed on drawn objects, but not the shadow color on text.
- Fills—The color inside drawn objects and the color used for the first data series in charts.
- Accent—The color used for the second data series in charts.
- Accent and Hyperlink—The color used for the third data series in charts and for hyperlinks that have not been clicked.
- Accent and Followed Hyperlink—The color used for the fourth data series in charts and for hyperlinks that have already been clicked.

Every presentation has a default color scheme attached to it, including new presentations.

When you click the Fill Color, Line Color, or Text Color button on the Drawing toolbar, you see these eight default colors (the colors displayed match whatever scheme you've selected for your presentation). By displaying these colors, these buttons make it easy for when you add text and objects to the slides to color coordinate them with the Color Scheme that is attached to your presentation. In this way, any text or other objects added to your presentation will blend in with the existing objects. Click the More Font Colors button to choose from a wider range of colors.

Customizing Slide Color Schemes

Built into each color scheme are the *default color scheme* and a set of *alternative schemes*. The alternative schemes will also complement the Design Template, and the designs and images on the Title Master and Slide Master.

▶ **See** "Customizing Presentation Masters," **p. 1240**

To take a look at the default and alternative slide color schemes, choose Format, Slide Color Schemes. The Color Scheme dialog box appears. There are two tabs in this dialog box: Standard and Custom. The Standard tab in the Color Scheme dialog box (shown in Figure 45.1) displays the default color scheme and several predesigned alternative color schemes. The default color scheme is usually in the top row and has a heavy dark border. The other schemes offer you color-coordinated alternative looks you can apply to your slides.

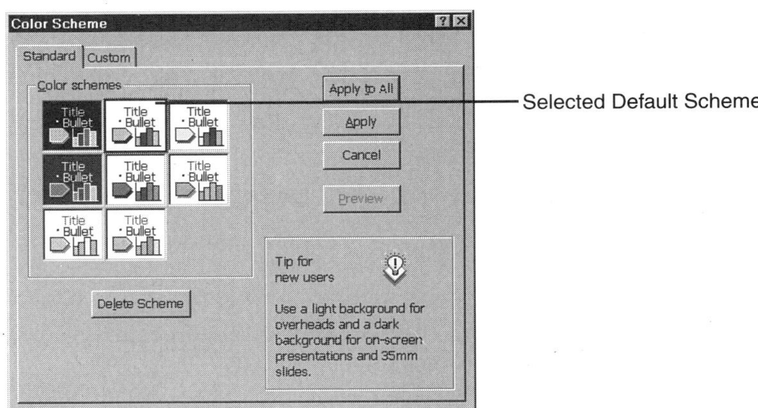

FIGURE 45.1
See the Tips in the lower-right corner for helpful hints.

The Custom tab (shown in Figure 45.2) displays the eight colors for the active color scheme, and the slide components those colors apply to. Through the Custom tab, you can change a specific color in the scheme and apply that new color to the active slides or the entire presentation.

Before applying a different color scheme or changing one of the scheme's color components, you need to decide if you want to apply the color scheme changes to just one slide, a group of slides, or the entire presentation.

FIGURE 45.2
Use this tab to change the slide component colors.

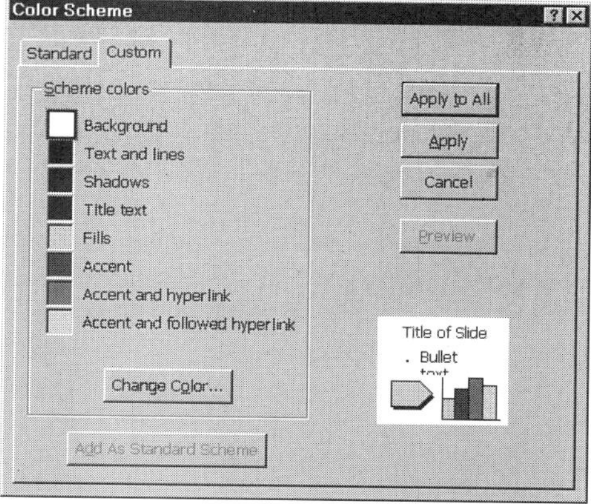

Changing a Group of Slides

One way to keep your audience's attention during a long presentation is to alter the color scheme for each major section of the presentation. There are several approaches to changing the color scheme for a group of slides. You can apply the color scheme changes to one slide and, using the Format Painter, copy the scheme to other slides. Alternatively, you can select the slides before displaying the Color Scheme dialog box and then apply the color scheme changes to the groups of slides all at one time. Regardless of the approach you choose, you need to use the Slide Sorter view.

If you changed only one slide, double-click the Format Painter button on the Standard toolbar and click each slide to which you want to apply the custom scheme.

If you want to change several slides at the same time, switch to the Slide Sorter view to select the slides. Click the first slide, and then press Ctrl as you click the remaining slides. Then access the Color Scheme dialog box to make your changes.

If you change the background color for a group of slides using the Format, Background command, you will not be able to revert to the original color through the Color Scheme dialog box. You must use the Format, Background command again and click the Automatic option in the Color drop-down list to revert to the original scheme.

Likewise, suppose you change the font color for a slide title using the Format, Font command or the Font Color button on the Drawing toolbar. You need to select the text and click the Font Color drop-down button next to the Drawing toolbar, and then click the Automatic option to revert to the original color.

The reason you are not able to use the Color Scheme dialog box is that PowerPoint considers these changes to be "exceptions" to the original color, thereby overriding the original color. Because you went to the trouble of changing the color, PowerPoint assumes you want to keep the changes no matter what. You can even change the Design Template and the "exception" colors will remain unchanged.

Using the Alternative Color Schemes To apply one of the alternative color schemes to your slides, follow these steps:

1. Switch to the Slide Sorter view and select the slides whose colors you want to change. If you want to change all the slides in the presentation, you need select only one slide.
2. Choose Format, Slide Color Scheme.
3. Click the Standard tab and choose a color scheme (refer to Figure 45.1).
4. Choose Apply to change only the selected slides. Choose Apply to All to change all slides in your presentation.

Modifying Individual Colors in the Color Schemes The Custom tab in the Color Scheme dialog box shows each of the eight default colors, and provides you with the opportunity to change individual colors.

To change the colors used with a particular color scheme, follow these steps:

1. Switch to the Slide Sorter view and select the slides whose colors you want to change. If you want to change all the slides in the presentation, you need select only one slide.
2. Choose Format, Slide Color Scheme.
3. To change the current color scheme, click the Custom tab. To change one of the alternative schemes, select the scheme on the Standard tab, and then click the Custom tab.
4. Choose the specific slide component you want to change and click the Change Color button (refer to Figure 45.2). A dialog box appears from which you can choose a built-in color or create your own custom color. Figure 45.3 shows the color wheel on the Standard tab.

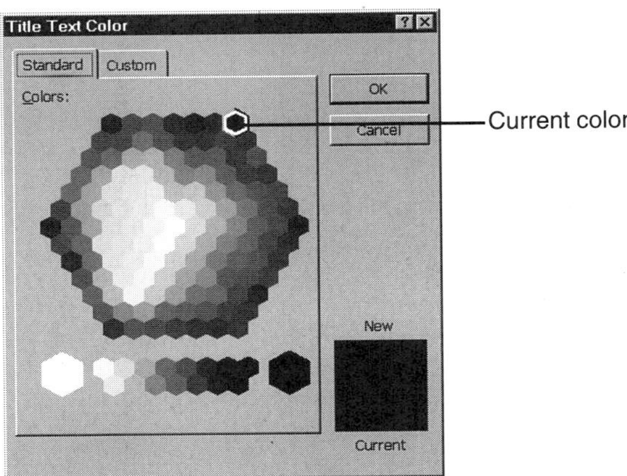

FIGURE 45.3
The lower-right corner displays a comparison of the new and current colors.

5. Click the new color you want to use.
6. Choose OK. The thumbnail of the slide on the Custom tab of the Color Scheme dialog box enables you to preview the change (see Figure 45.4).

FIGURE 45.4
If you don't like the appearance, click Change Color button again to select another color.

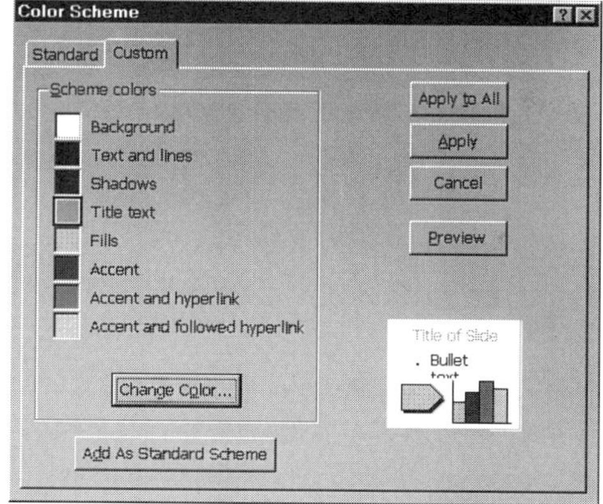

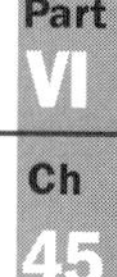

7. After you select the colors you want to change, choose Apply to change only the selected slides. Choose Apply to All to change all slides in your presentation.

NOTE You can click the Preview button in the Color Scheme dialog box to see the change applied to the selected slides in the Slide Sorter view. You will, however, need to move the dialog box to clearly see the change.

Adding and Deleting Schemes If you have altered a color scheme, you can add the revised scheme to the set of schemes on the Standard tab of the Color Scheme dialog box. This is particularly handy when you have spent a lot of time customizing the color scheme and know you will be using the modified scheme on other slides in the presentation.

NOTE Adding a color scheme to the active presentation makes it available only in the active presentation. If you want to add a color scheme to a Design Template (so that it is available whenever you use that Design Template), you need to add it directly to the Design Template. This procedure is discussed in the next section.

In the Color Scheme dialog box, click the Add As Standard Scheme button on the Custom tab. You then have to click the Standard tab to confirm that the scheme was added. Figure 45.5 shows the new scheme added to the end of the list.

NOTE Although it appears that only nine schemes can be stored on the Standard tab, you can add more. A scrollbar appears when the number of schemes exceeds nine.

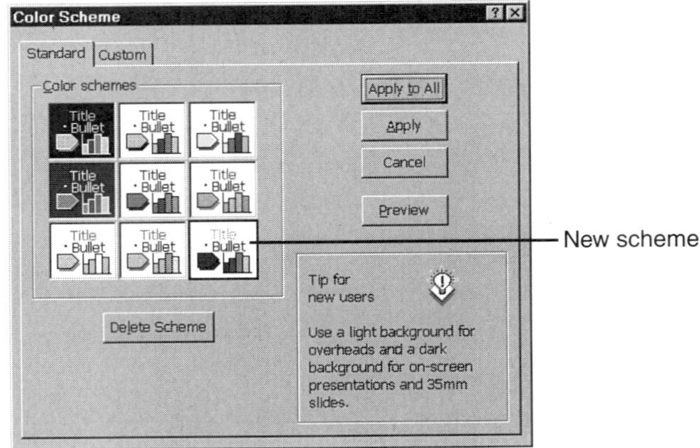

FIGURE 45.5
The added scheme has a dark border around it, indicating it is the selected scheme.

If you no longer want a scheme on the Standard tab, you can remove it by selecting the scheme and clicking the Delete Scheme button (refer to Figure 45.5).

TIP If you accidentally remove a scheme, click Cancel. This closes the dialog box and ignores any changes, including the action of deleting schemes.

Distributing Custom Color Schemes

Changes to Color Scheme apply only to the current presentation. If you want to make a custom Color Scheme available when you use the same Design Template on other presentations, you need to open the template and change the color schemes directly on the Design Template.

Before you open and modify the Design Template, consider these issues:

- If an open presentation is using the Design Template, the Design Template file is opened as a Read-Only file. You are forced to save the Design Template under another name.
- If the Design Templates are stored on a network server, you may be allowed to open the Design Template only as a Read-Only file. You'll again be forced to save the Design Template under another name and you may not be allowed to save the modified Design Template in the folder on the network server. Your Network Administrator controls the permissions for files on the network server.
- Even if you can open the Design Templates without the "Read-Only" caveat, you may prefer to save the modified Design Templates under a different name and leave the original Design Template alone.

Follow these steps to save the modified Design Templates:

1. Click the Open button or choose File, Open. In the Open dialog box, use the Look In drop-down list to switch to the Presentation Designs folder. If PowerPoint is installed on your PC, the location is

   ```
   C:\Program Files\Microsoft Office\Templates\Presentation Designs
   ```

If you cannot find this folder, it may be because the folder resides on a network drive. You can locate the Presentation Designs folder by clicking the Tools drop-down list in the Open dialog box, and choosing Find to search for the folder.

2. After you locate the folder, double-click the Presentation Designs folder and a list of the templates is displayed, as shown in Figure 45.6. Design Template names all have a .pot file extension.

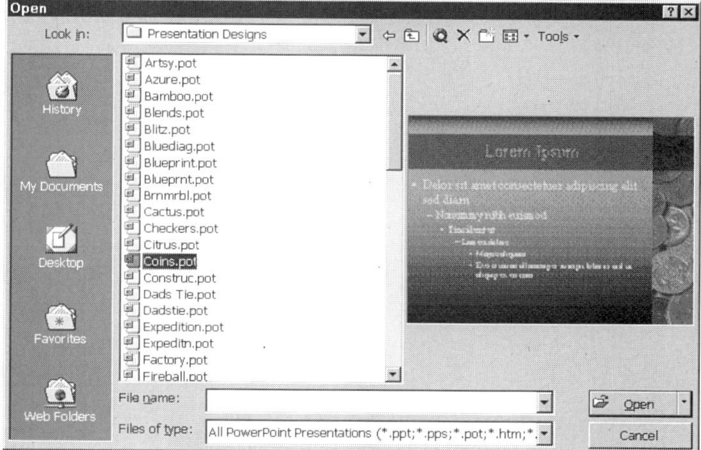

FIGURE 45.6
Template files always display a yellow band across the top of the file icon.

3. Click the name of the design you want to change. A preview of that design appears to the right of the list. If the preview does not display, click the View drop-down list and choose Preview.

4. Choose Open. The file is open, but no slide appears. You cannot change the Color Schemes from here, as you would in a presentation.

5. Choose View, Master, Slide Master. When the Slide Master opens, the Design Template is displayed (see Figure 45.7).

6. Now make the Color Scheme changes you want. Refer to the "Altering Colors in the Color Schemes" section earlier in this chapter for specific steps.

CAUTION

After you add the custom scheme in the Color Scheme dialog box, you must choose Apply to save the scheme. Selecting Cancel or closing the dialog box will not save the scheme. If you don't want the custom scheme to be the default scheme when you apply the Design Template to a presentation, display the Color Scheme dialog box again, select the original scheme, and click Apply.

7. After you have made the changes to the Design Template, save the file.

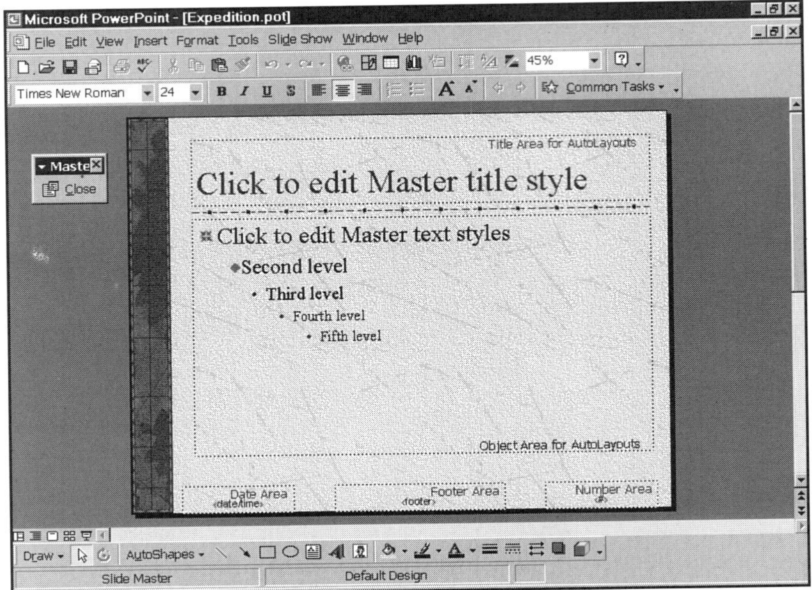

FIGURE 45.7
Most of the commands and toolbar buttons are available in the Master.

8. If you decide (or are forced) to save the file under a different name, make sure you change the file type from Presentation to Design Template in the Save As Type drop-down list. Click in the File Name box and type an appropriate name. To distinguish custom Design Templates from the originals that come with PowerPoint, it's a good idea to start the name with Custom, such as Custom Coins. Because the templates are listed alphabetically, this method groups all the templates you change together.
9. If you want to save the template back in the Presentation Designs folder, make sure that is the folder name displayed in the Save In drop-down box. Step 1 shows the correct path. Otherwise, select the folder in which you want to save the template.

CAUTION

Always check the file location *after* you change the file type. The destination should be Presentation Designs, not Templates. If you've upgraded from a previous version, PowerPoint has a sneaky habit of changing the destination folder. It may say Presentation Designs *before* you change the file type and then Templates *after* you change the file type. It's not that you can't store Presentation Designs in other folders; it's just more convenient to have them all in one location.

10. Click Save.

You can now share the Design Template file with others, so they can use the custom color scheme you created.

Making the Most Effective Font and Color Choices

The font and color choices you make can enhance or degrade the information you are presenting. Legibility is essential—blank space, text case, font type, and color are critical elements that go into making your slides legible.

Choosing the Right Fonts for Your Presentation

One common mistake in PowerPoint is to add too many objects to slides. Avoid too much text or too many picture clips. Some blank space on a slide is desirable; too much is stark or boring. When in doubt, remember this—fewer or less is better.

Another common error is to use only uppercase letters. Did you know it takes an audience longer to read slides that are in all uppercase? Instead, use uppercase sparingly, as a way to emphasize specific text in your slides. To quickly change the font from uppercase to mixed case, select the text and choose Format, Change Case, Sentence Case.

The font type you select is yet another area essential to legibility. Serif fonts are formal fonts, and are noted by the "feet" at the bottom of letters. They were designed to resemble cursive for a more fluid movement of the eye from one letter to the next. Serif is used a great deal in printed materials, such as in this book and in novels. However, serif fonts tend to be somewhat difficult to read quickly from a distance—a poor choice for presentations in a large room. Times New Roman is a serif font.

Sans serif fonts are less formal; some might even say plain. They do not have the feet at the bottom of letters—hence the name *sans*, meaning *without*. Sans serif fonts are a better choice if your presentation is given in a large room or auditorium. Arial is a sans serif font. In printed text, serif fonts are frequently used for body text, and sans serif is a popular choice for headings. Of course, there are no hard-and-fast rules, other than you should pick a font scheme and stick to it throughout your presentation.

Take a look at Figure 45.8. Note the difference in the letter F in the word Font; Times New Roman displays the feet and Arial does not.

FIGURE 45.8
Be careful when you use mixed font types. The font sizes often vary between fonts.

Choose the Right Colors for Your Presentation

In addition to font and text issues, it is important that you choose the right colors. Your first consideration should be your audience—what would appeal to them? If you're not certain, a good choice, especially for slide background, is blue. Blue is perfect for formal business meetings, as it is universally liked and invokes a positive image.

Although it may sound strange, I suggest you take your color ideas from your everyday environment. For example, when I think of where I see the color blue, two places instantly come to mind: the sky and the ocean. When I think of these two important components of our world, I recall phrases people use to describe them, such as clear and clean. These are positive responses, making blue an excellent choice for presentations.

Now, when I think of where I see the color green, I immediately think of three things: plants (grass, trees), money, and stoplights. Therefore, I would use green to denote the environment, financial information, or a positive sign to move forward.

On the other hand, colors such as yellow, cyan (aqua), orange, and magenta (pink) are often found as accent colors in our everyday life. You'll find these colors frequently in flora and fauna (especially flowers and birds). As in nature, these colors should be used as accents, not as your primary slide color.

Red tends to be thought of as an angry or negative color. We usually associate this color with fire (danger), and stoplights/signs (stop, quit). You should also use red primarily as an accent color.

What text color shows up better on a dark background—yellow or white? If you said yellow, you'd be wrong. From a distance, the eye is drawn to white text quicker than to yellow text. Now, if we could just get the folks who design the sports ticker at the bottom of one popular news channel to see that...

Should you decide to change the text color, or colors used to plot chart data, make sure you choose contrasting colors. Avoid using similar colors next to each other, such as black with blue, or yellow with white. For example, yellow or cyan text on a white slide background is difficult to see. Similarly, dark blue and black columns should not be displayed next to each other in a graphic chart.

People who suffer from color blindness typically cannot distinguish red from green. Therefore, it is not advisable to use these colors side by side in a presentation.

Adding Headers and Footers to Slides, Note Pages, and Handouts

Much like headers and footers in Word documents, PowerPoint enables you to add *headers* and *footers* to slides. Headers and footers are useful when you want to insert the same text (dates, page numbers, or filenames, for instance) at the top or bottom of all slides in your presentation.

If you want to apply a footer to just a group of slides, switch to the Slide Sorter view. Select the first slide; then press Ctrl and select the remaining slides.

To access this command, choose View, Header and Footer. Figure 45.9 shows the Header and Footer dialog box.

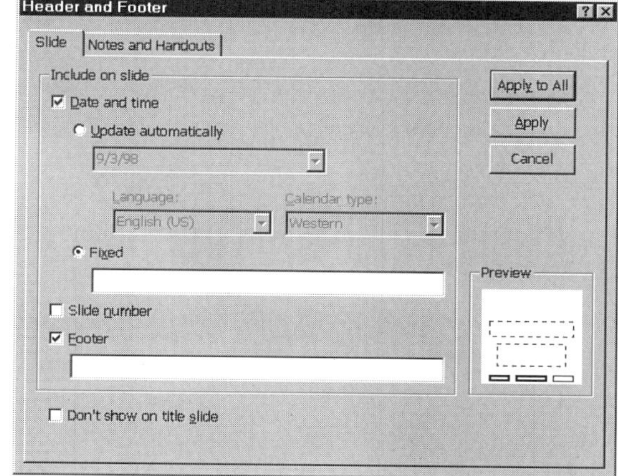

FIGURE 45.9
If an item in the preview has a heavy border, it is an active (although perhaps empty) header or footer option.

The dialog box contains two tabs, one for Slide settings and the other for both Notes pages and Handouts settings. Many of the options are the same on these tabs. Exceptions on the Slide Tab are

- Includes an option to apply the settings to just the selected slides—the Apply button.
- Includes an option to omit the settings from Title slide layouts—the Don't Show on Title Slide check box.
- Does not include a text header option—You can use the Slide Master to add header text to all slides. To add a header to one or a few slides, you can add a text box to one slide, and if necessary, copy it to the other slides.

Exceptions on the Notes and Handouts Tab are

- Includes a text header option—the Header check box.
- Does not include an option to apply the settings to just the one page. Settings are applied to all printed pages—the Apply to All button.

If you want to set a fixed date—for example, the date you are delivering the presentation—click the Fixed option button and type the date (and time) exactly as you want them to appear on the slides, notes pages, or handouts.

If you want the date or time to change automatically, there are many format choices listed in the Update Automatically drop-down list.

The placement and font of the header and footer items are controlled on the presentation Masters, which are discussed in the next section.

CAUTION

You cannot alter the slide footer objects directly on the slide, even if you apply them to only one slide. You must alter them on the Master. Therefore, you cannot have different placements for each slide; changing a footer object placement or properties on the Master changes it for all slides.

Customizing Presentation Masters

There are four *presentation Masters* in PowerPoint. They control the placement of the background objects (such as company logos, page numbers, and dates) on your slides, handouts, and note pages.

- Title Master—This Master is used only with presentation Design Templates that have a unique layout for Title slides.
- Slide Master— This Master is used to control all slide layouts, except where there is a unique Title slide layout in a presentation Design Template.
- Handout Master—This Master is used to control the page layout when printing slide handouts where multiple slides are printed per page. It also includes a layout for the Outline view.
- Notes Master—This Master is used to control the page layout for printed speaker's notes pages.

The next four sections describe how to customize each of these Masters.

Customizing the Title Master

Title slide layouts are great not only for the first slide in a presentation, but they also provide a nice segue from major topic to major topic, such as chapter pages in a book.

The only way to access the Title Master is to choose View, Master, Title Master. If Title Master is grayed out, you either have the Default Design Template applied to your slides, or the presentation Design Template does not have a unique layout for Title slides.

The Title Master, shown in Figure 45.10, contains placeholders for Slide Title, Subtitle, Date, Footer, and Page Numbers. Additionally, there may be background drawings or objects on the Master. The Title and Subtitle placeholders are used to modify the style of the text and background for these objects. You don't actually type text in these two placeholders.

You can modify any of the placeholders and background objects as you would objects in regular slides. Additionally, you can add objects to the Master including logos, picture clips, drawings, Action Buttons, and WordArt that you want to display on slides using the Title slide layout. You can even add a sound object to the Title Master that plays the company theme song or jingle. Anytime you use a Title slide layout, you'll have access to these objects.

FIGURE 45.10
Each Master displays a floating Close toolbar.

Figure 45.11 shows a modified Title Master whose Subtitle area has been resized and the page number placeholder moved.

FIGURE 45.11
Select an object to change it.

TIP To select a text object, click inside a text object (which puts you in the Edit mode with a flashing cursor) and press Esc to select the object, or click the text object border.

Customizing the Slide Master

To access the Slide Master, choose View, Master, Slide Master or press Shift and click the Slide View button.

As you can see from Figure 45.12, the Slide Master contains placeholders for Slide Title, Bulleted or Numbered Text, Date, Footer, and Page Numbers. Additionally, there may be background drawings or objects on the Master.

As with the Title Slide Master, you don't actually type text in the Title and Bulleted List placeholders. You can only modify the text styles and background formats for those particular placeholders.

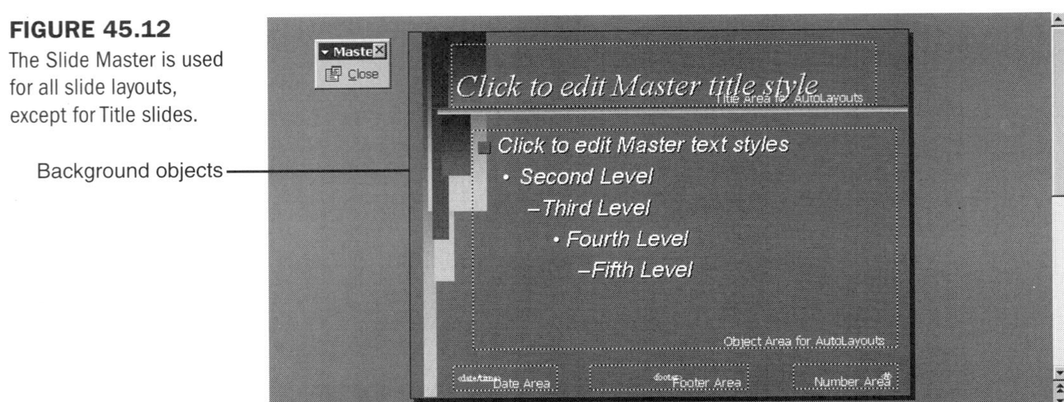

FIGURE 45.12
The Slide Master is used for all slide layouts, except for Title slides.

The placeholder for Bulleted Text also acts as a placeholder for the Body object in other slide types, such as Graphic Charts, Organization Charts, and Tables. The Body object is the actual chart or table. Use the Bulleted Text placeholder to resize or move the Body object placeholders on all slides.

You can modify any of the placeholders and background objects as you would objects in regular slides. Additionally, you can add objects to the Master, including logos, picture clips, drawings, Action Buttons, and WordArt that you want to display on all slides, except those using the Title slide layout.

Figure 45.13 shows a modified Slide Master whose color scheme has been changed, bullet symbols have been modified, and the background objects adjusted.

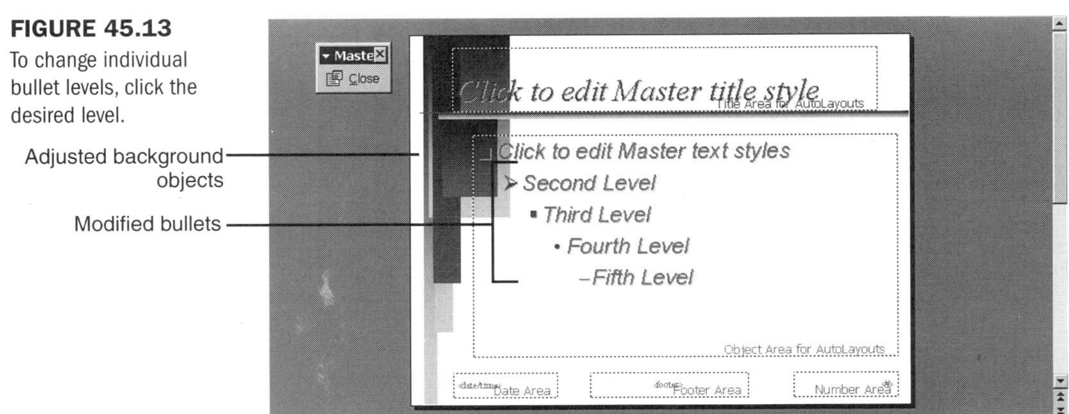

FIGURE 45.13
To change individual bullet levels, click the desired level.

Customizing the Handout Master

To access the Handout Master, choose View, Master, Handout Master or press Shift and click either the Outline View button or Slide Sorter View button.

The Handout Master, shown in Figure 45.14, contains placeholders for Page Header, Page Footer, Date, and Page Numbers. Additionally, there is a Handout Master toolbar which includes five arrangement buttons for the number of slides per printed page: two slides, three slides with lines for notetaking, four slides, six slides, and nine slides. Surprisingly, the miniaturized slides (including three, four, and six per page) are legible when the handouts are printed!

The toolbar also includes a layout for the Outline view. Figure 45.14 shows the Handout Master with the three slides with lines layout. This layout is particularly useful when your audience will be taking detailed notes. (The lines don't appear here, but they will print.)

FIGURE 45.14
Use the Zoom button on the Standard Toolbar to zoom the screen in and out.

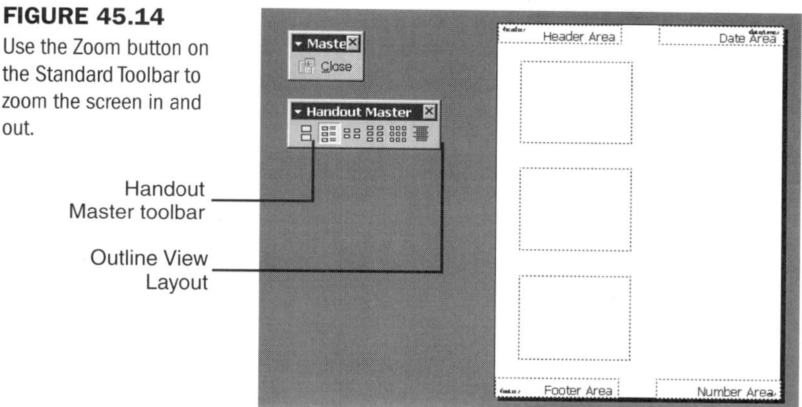

Figure 45.15 shows the Handout Master with the Outline layout. The Footer Area has been expanded and the Page Number Area reduced.

TIP Use this layout to print the Outline view. You can even collapse the Outline view to print just each slide title, such as a Table of Contents for your slides.

Use the Print dialog box (choose File, Print) to print just one of the handout pages before you print the entire presentation, just in case.

Customizing the Notes Master

The only way to access the Notes Master is to choose View, Master, Notes Master. The Notes Master contains placeholders for a miniature of the slide, Note Text, Page Header, Page Footer, Date, and Page Numbers. Figure 45.16 shows the Notes Master.

You can modify any of the placeholders and the slide miniature object as you would other objects. Resizing the miniature slide object will make room for you to expand the Notes Body Area placeholder. Figure 45.17 shows a modified Notes Master.

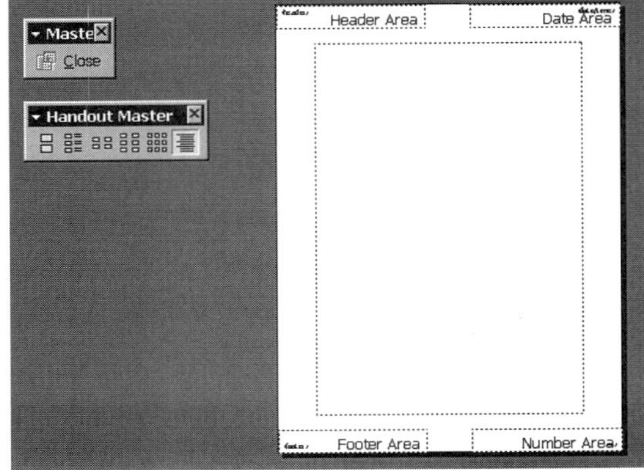

FIGURE 45.15
As with the other Masters, you can rearrange the placeholders as you need to.

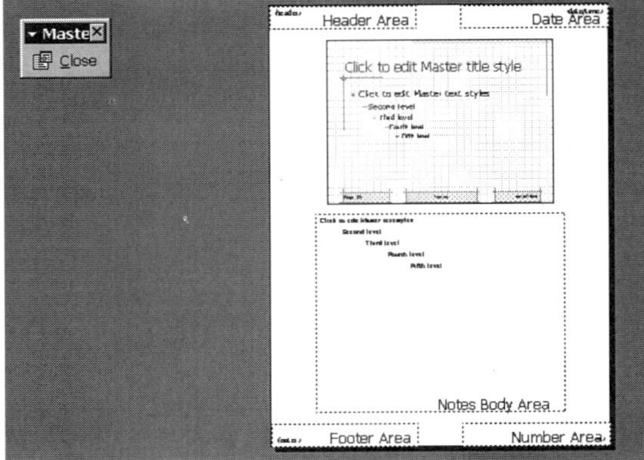

FIGURE 45.16
The Notes Body Area controls the size of the font used for your printed notes.

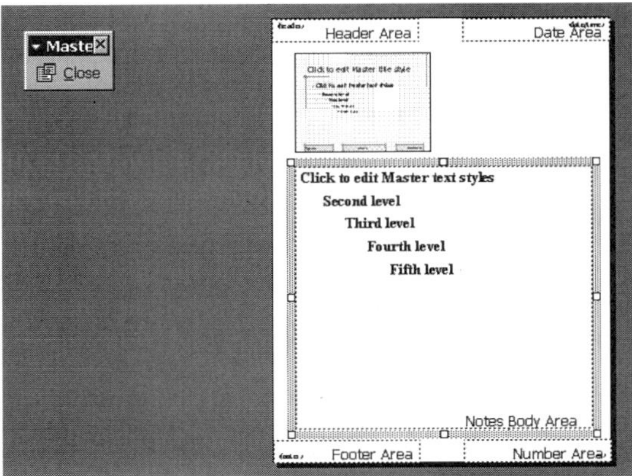

FIGURE 45.17
Enlarging the Notes Body Area and font size comes in handy when your presentation is in a dark room.

Creating Summary Slides

If you have a presentation that is divided into sections or major topics, several techniques can be used to alert your audience that you are starting a new section or topic. One way is to place a Title Slide at the beginning of each section that lists the section topic. Another technique is to use a different slide transition for each section. A third method is to create a summary slide.

When a summary slide is created, the titles used in the section slides are copied into a bulleted list in the summary slide. With lengthy presentations, this can be a real timesaver.

Use these steps to create a summary slide:

1. Switch to the Slide Sorter view.
2. Click the first slide whose title you want to use in the summary slide; then press Ctrl as you click each additional slide. Figure 45.18 shows several slides selected.

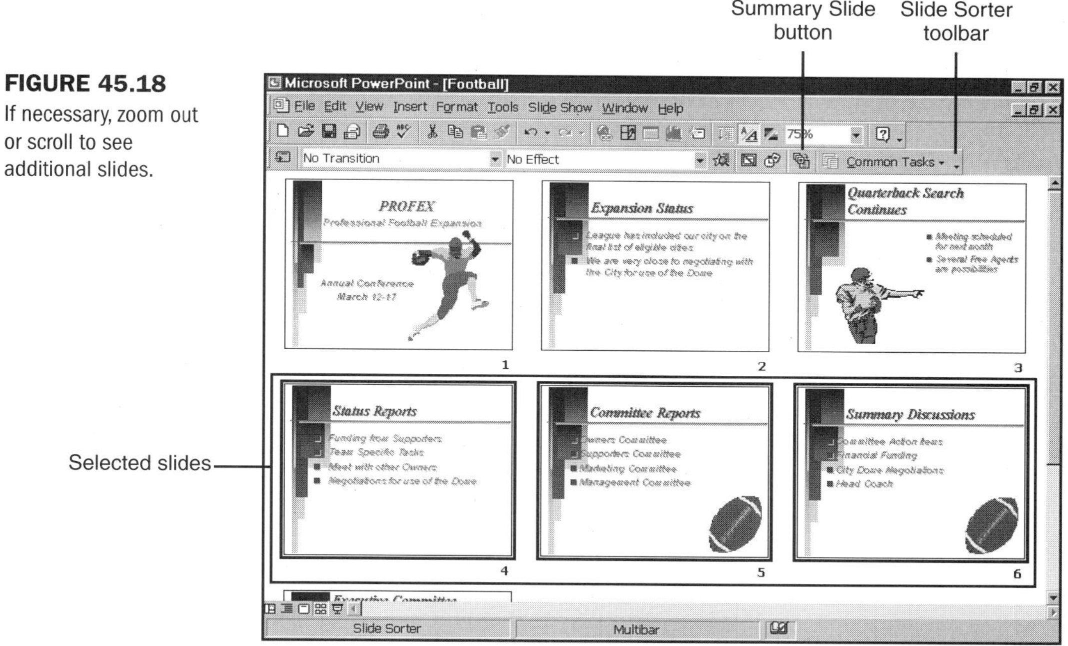

FIGURE 45.18
If necessary, zoom out or scroll to see additional slides.

3. Click the Summary Slide button on the Slide Sorter toolbar (refer to Figure 45.18).
4. A new slide, as shown in Figure 45.19, is inserted in front of the first slide you selected. Each of the titles from the selected slides is a bullet on the summary slide.

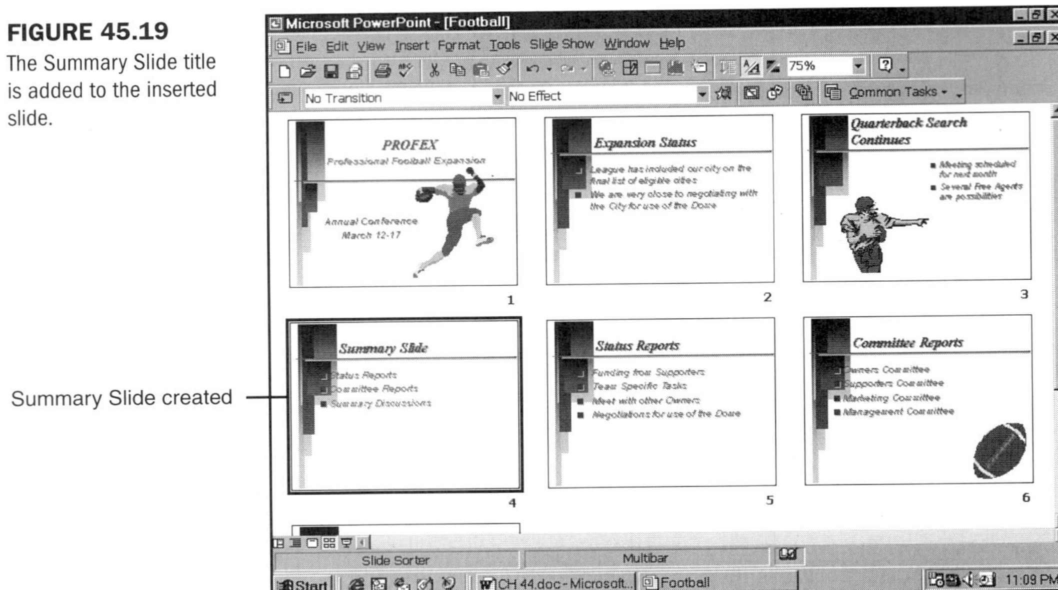

FIGURE 45.19
The Summary Slide title is added to the inserted slide.

If you want to create hyperlinks that will take you from the Summary Slide directly to a specific section, then at the end of the section return you to the Summary Slide, you need to use the Custom Show and Hyperlink features.

▶ **See** "Problem/Solution—Creating and Using Branch Presentations," **p. 1297**

Editing Complex Diagrams

Sometimes the slide you need to create in PowerPoint is a diagram that does not fit into the prescribed slide layouts. Figure 45.20 shows a slide that was created using a series of text boxes.

A number of tools in PowerPoint can help you create, copy, and align objects on a slide:

- Rulers—Through the View menu you can display a horizontal and vertical ruler.
- Guides—Through the View menu you can display a set of straight lines, one horizontal and one vertical. Initially, they display in the middle of your slide, but you can drag them to other positions on your slide. Using the Ctrl key, you can create additional guidelines.
- Ctrl, Shift, and Alt Keys—Use the Ctrl key to copy a slide object. Use Ctrl+Shift to copy an object and move it in a straight line. Use the Alt key to move an object more precisely, overriding the slide grid.

FIGURE 45.20
Use the Ctrl key to copy text boxes.

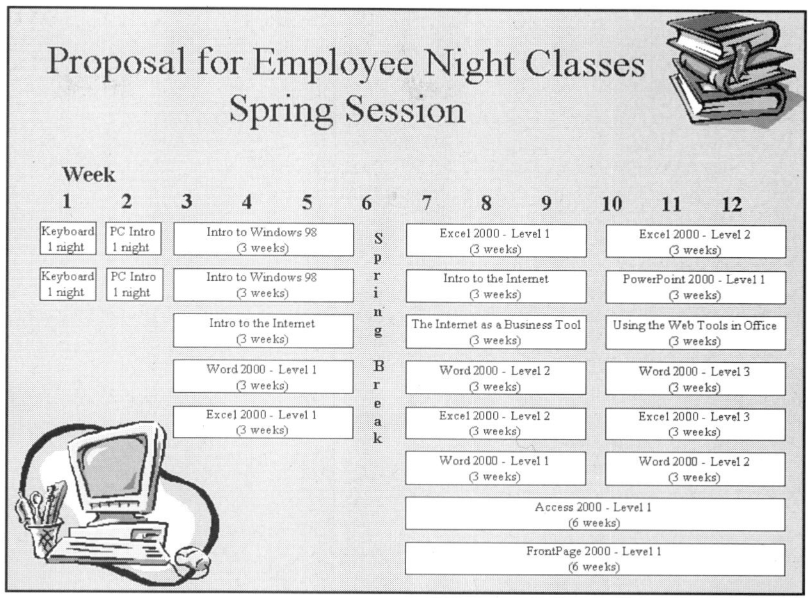

- Group Command—Grouping slide objects is a great way to move or resize multiple slide objects that you want to keep displayed together proportionally. Grouping is usually done when you know you will be moving or resizing the objects again. Generally, to edit a single object in the group, the entire group must be ungrouped. PowerPoint 2000 does have a few exceptions, including the capability to edit text while an object is part of a group.
- Selecting Multiple Objects—Using the Shift key, you can randomly select multiple objects. To select all the objects in a given area of the slide, you can drag a selection box around the objects (position the mouse pointer outside the objects and drag to create a box around the objects you want selected). To select all the objects on the slide, choose Edit, Select All or press Ctrl+A. Typically, you select objects to apply the same formats to them all at once, or to move or resize them. Selecting, not grouping, is used when you want to group the objects temporarily and do not anticipate needing to group them with the same formatting.

If you need to select all the text boxes on a slide, use this snippet of VBA code. It selects all the text boxes on a slide that are not part of a grouped object. Don't be daunted by the length of the code; you can copy this snippet from the CD that accompanies this book. The title of the snippet is Select_Shape.

```
Public Sub SelectTextBoxes()
Dim objSheet As Object
Dim lngCount As Long
Dim shp As Shape
Set objSheet = ActiveWindow.View.Slide
 For Each shp In objSheet.Shapes
    If shp.Type = msoTextBox Then
        lngCount = lngCount + 1
    End If
Next shp
If lngCount = 0 Then
    MsgBox "There are no Text Box shapes on slide '" _
    & objSheet.Name & "'.", vbInformation, "Text Box Select"
    Exit Sub
End If
lngCount = 0
For Each shp In objSheet.Shapes
    If shp.Type = msoTextBox Then
        If lngCount = 0 Then
            shp.Select msoTrue
        Else
            shp.Select msoFalse
        End If
        lngCount = lngCount + 1
    End If
Next shp
End Sub
```

▶ **See** "Using the Visual Basic Editor," **p. 116**

▶ **See** "Putting VBA Code Snippets to Work," **p. 135**

CHAPTER 46

Unleashing the Power of Animation

In this chapter

Using Animation in PowerPoint

Animation is a special visual entry effect or sound applied to slide objects. It is seen (or heard) when you run the presentation in the Slide Show view. Animation is sometimes referred to as *build*; for example, "building objects on the slide…." The terms animation and build are used interchangeably here.

You should consider using animation for several reasons:

- To focus your audience's attention on important points.
- To control the flow of information in your presentation.
- To add interest to your presentation.

CAUTION

Be careful with animation. Use it only when the slide warrants it. For example, don't animate every graphic chart in your presentation, only the few important ones where you need to focus your audience's attention.

You can apply animation to objects in your slide show in one of two ways:

- Preset Animation—PowerPoint has built-in, preset animation effects designed to help you quickly enhance your presentation.
- Custom Animation—If you want to have complete control over the entry animation and sound options, you should customize the animation effects.

This chapter concentrates on animating drawn objects, WordArt, text, and graphic charts. See Chapter 44, "Working with Picture, Sound, and Motion Clips," to learn how to animate clips—pictures, music, and motion (video).

Action Settings allow PowerPoint to play a sound when you point to a drawn object in your slide show. Action settings also make it possible to launch an Excel spreadsheet when you click a chart, or edit the same chart while in the middle of running a slide show.

▶ **See** "Using Action Settings in Presentations," **p. 1283**

Understanding Preset Animation

Preset animation attaches an entry effect to a slide object, and usually includes other animation settings. For example, if you apply the Drive-In preset animation to an object, it will Fly from the Left and the sound of screeching brakes will be heard. If you apply the Drop In preset animation, the object will Fly from Top, and if the object is a bulleted list, the text will appear one word at a time to build each bullet item.

You can work with preset animation in several views—the Slide pane of the Normal view, the Slide view, and (if you are animating a list of bullets or numbers) the Slide Sorter view.

To apply preset animation, select the object you want to animate and choose Slide Show, Preset Animation. There are 14 text animation effects. See Table 46.1 for a breakdown of these effects.

Table 46.1 Preset Animation Effects

Animation Name	Visual Effect	Sound Effect
Drive-In	Fly from Right	Screeching Brakes
Flying	Fly from Left	Whoosh
Camera	Box Out	Camera
Flash Once	Flash Once Medium	No sound
Laser Text	Fly from Top -Right	Laser
Typewriter	Wipe Down	Typewriter
Reverse Order	Wipe Right	No sound
Drop In	Fly from Top	No sound
Fly from Top	Fly from Top	No sound
Wipe Up	Wipe Up	No sound
Wipe Right	Wipe Right	No sound
Dissolve	Dissolve	No sound
Split Vertical Out	Split Vertical Out	No sound
Appear	Appear	No sound

Some effects are available only for certain types of objects. As with other menu commands, when an option is not available, it will be grayed out. For instance, the Wipe Up Preset Animation is active only if a graphic chart is selected.

Avoid Preset Animation

Although you can apply Preset Animation to slide objects, I personally don't recommend it. Some preset animation includes both a visual entry effect and a sound effect. If you are animating a bulleted or numbered list, the preset animation also includes how the text will appear—one line at a time, one word at a time, and some preset animation introduces the text one letter at a time (such as Laser Text and Typewriter). You have no control over which sounds are paired with the visual effects or the timing associated with the animation.

Instead, I suggest you explore Custom Animation, as discussed in the remaining sections in this chapter. Custom Animation gives you complete control over all aspects of the animation settings.

Applying Custom Animation to Drawn Objects

Drawn objects include virtually any shape you draw with the tools on the Drawing toolbar. This includes any of the AutoShapes, WordArt, text boxes, lines, arrows, rectangles, and circles.

For example, instead of creating a bulleted list, you might draw a group of arrows using a style from the AutoShapes list. Add text to the arrows and then animate each arrow with the Swivel or Fly from Left effect.

NOTE You can add text to most drawn objects just by typing the text when the object arrow is selected. By default, the text is centered in the object, but you can use the Format, AutoShape command to alter the alignment or force the text to word-wrap in the object.

The options you have available for animating drawn objects are identical to those for animating picture clips:

- Set the animation timing—If you set manual timing, the object appears only when you click the mouse or press Enter. Automatic timing involves setting a specific time interval between animated objects.
- Use a visual effect to display the object—As with picture clips, you can apply a visual transition effect to other slide objects. Visual effects include the type of animation and the direction the object will appear from.
- Play a sound bite as the object appears on the slide—There are 16 built-in sound effects available, including the "whoosh" sound of something moving very fast and the sound of a typewriter. If you have sound effects from other sources, you can use the Other option to add the effect.
- Control what happens after the animation—You can choose to change the color, and hide or dim the object after it has animated on the screen.

To animate a drawn object, select the object and choose Slide Show, Custom Animation. The Custom Animation dialog box appears, as shown in Figure 46.1.

The upper-left corner of the Custom Animation dialog box clearly identifies each object in the current slide. A set of selection handles appears around the object in the preview window. Check the object you want to animate.

The four tabs in this dialog box contain animation options—Order & Timing, Effects (the default tab), Chart Effects, and Multimedia Settings. The only two tabs you'll need for drawn objects are Order & Timing and Effects.

Adding Visual and Sound Effects to Drawn Objects

Visual effects are composed of two things: type of animation and the direction of the animation appearance. For example, the object can Stretch into the slide and appear From Right. There are 18 unique types of animation. The direction options vary, depending on which type of animation you select.

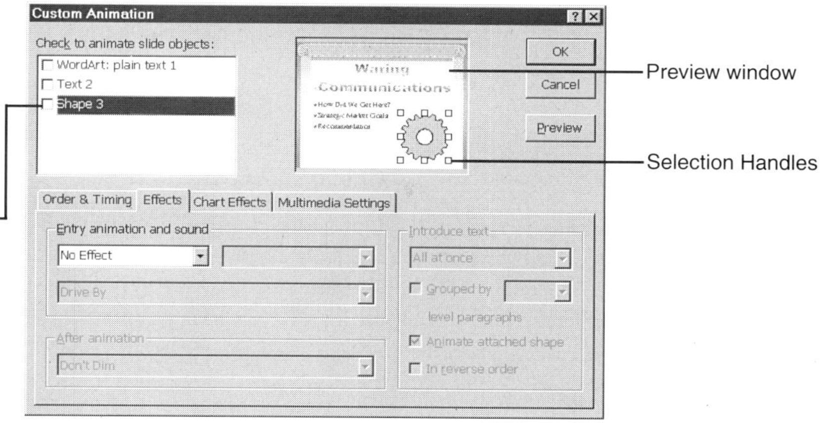

FIGURE 46.1
The object identification includes the numerical order in which it was added to the slide.

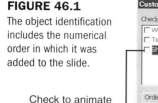

Check to animate the object.

Preview window

Selection Handles

Suppose at the end of discussing a slide, you want to have a statement appear, such as Great Work or Good Job Team. One way to use animation and sound is to draw an object, such as a star or starburst, from the Stars and Banners group of AutoShapes. Add your text to the object and then animate the object. Perhaps you could have the Applause or Clapping sound play as the object animates.

NOTE The Random Effects type of animation picks a different visual effect each time you run the Slide Show. This type of effect is best for informal presentations.

On the Effects tab, select the type and direction of the animation from the top two drop-down boxes. Figure 46.2 shows the Fly animation type and the From Left direction selected.

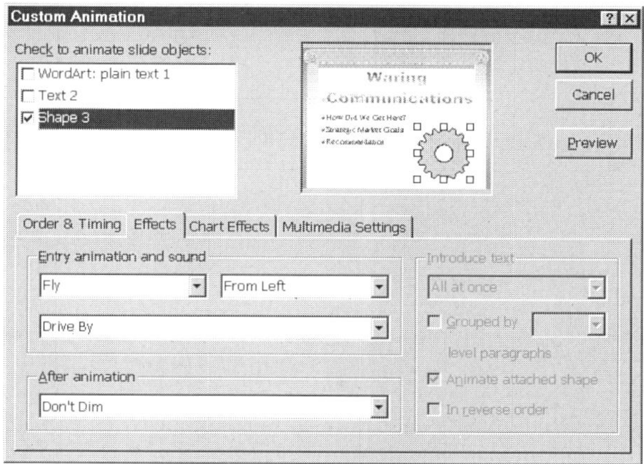

FIGURE 46.2
Choose the animation type first, then the animation direction.

In addition to animating the object, you can have a sound play as the object appears. There are 16 built-in sound effects listed in the drop-down box on the Effects tab, including clapping, ricochet, and even the sound an old-fashioned cash register makes. To add a sound effect without any obvious animation effect, use the Appear animation effect.

NOTE The default installation of Office 2000 does not install the sounds. You will need the Office 2000 CD (or the location on your network where the Office 2000 program files are stored) to install the sound effects.

TIP In addition to the 16 built-in sounds, you can also apply other sounds to your slides. Scroll to the bottom of the sound drop-down list and click Other Sound. To find all the sounds used by the various programs you have on your computer, choose Tools, Find in the Add Sound dialog box. Search your entire hard drive and all subfolders to locate files with a .wav extension. Sound files are also widely available on the Internet.

To see (and hear) how the effect will appear on your slide, choose Preview. The slide miniature displays the animation effect and plays the sound.

After the animation entry and sound effects are complete, PowerPoint leaves the object on the screen. However, you can hide or recolor the object by choosing an option from the After Animation drop-down box (see Figure 46.3).

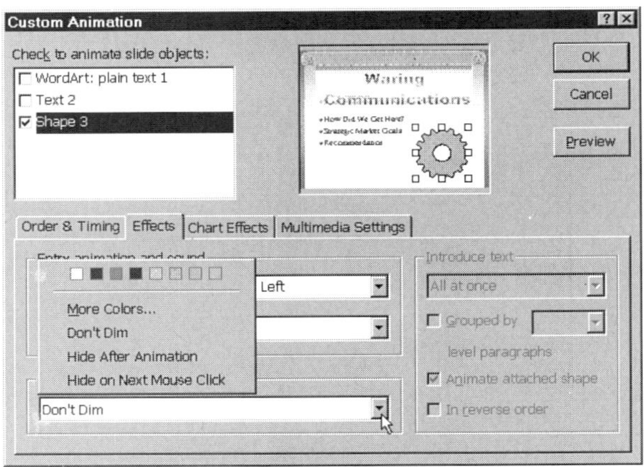

FIGURE 46.3
The default setting is Don't Dim.

After you've selected the animation effects, you need to set the animation order and timing.

Selecting the Animation Order and Timing

Most slides have several objects on them—a title, a bulleted list, and clip or drawing objects. Objects that are not animated will automatically appear on the screen when the slide is displayed. To set the order of objects you have animated, use the Order & Timing tab in the Custom Animation dialog box.

Figure 46.4 shows a slide that contains four objects. When the Order & Timing tab is activated, you see that two of the objects have been animated—the picture and the WordArt object. The current animation order has the picture animated before the WordArt object. To reorder the list, select the item you want to reorder and click the up- or down-Move arrows until the item is in the order you want.

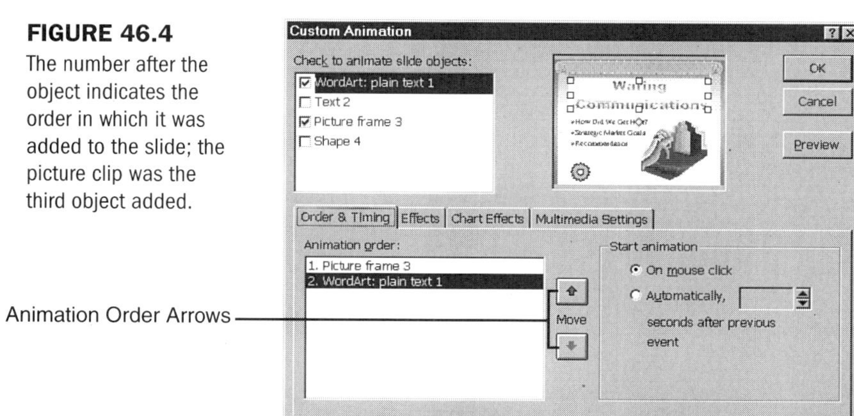

FIGURE 46.4
The number after the object indicates the order in which it was added to the slide; the picture clip was the third object added.

In addition to establishing the order objects will appear on the screen, you need to decide the *timing*—when the object will appear. By default, objects appear when you click the left mouse button (or press Enter). You can, however, set the object to animate a specific amount of time after the previous object has animated.

To set the timing for an animated object, select the object in the Animation Order box (refer to Figure 46.4). Then choose Automatically, __ Seconds After Previous Event, and type in the number of seconds you want to wait before the selected drawn object appears.

After you have selected the effects, order, and timing for your animated objects, click OK to apply the custom animation settings.

Applying Custom Animation to Text

Slide text includes text in the slide title, text in a bulleted or numbered list, or even text in a text box. Most presenters don't animate the slide title, but frequently animate a bulleted or numbered list. This is an especially useful technique when you want to address one topic at a time. It leaves the control of a discussion in your hands. The audience isn't asking you about the information in topic 5 while you're still addressing topic 2. Then, when you and the audience are ready to move on, you display the next topic in the list.

You can also animate text in a text box. One example of how this might be used is with a graphic chart. Suppose you want to highlight a particular data point in the chart, such as a fantastic sales figure in the third quarter. You can draw an arrow to the data point and add a text box with some appropriate description or comment. Then animate both the arrow and text box with the Appear effect.

There are a number of animation effects you can implement to build your slide text. As with drawn objects, you can select a visual entry effect, play a sound bite, recolor or hide the previously animated text, and choose the animation order and timing. However, there are several animation effects unique to text:

- Apply timing to build the text—You can set a specific time interval between the bullets or numbers. For example, you might have 10 seconds between the appearance of each bullet. If more time is needed, you can pause the presentation and resume whenever you are ready.
- Select the level of the build—By default, the text appears all at once. You can have the text appear one word or character at a time. If you have a bulleted or numbered list, groups of bullets can be displayed together or each level can appear separately.

To animate a text object, select the object and choose Slide Show, Custom Animation. The Custom Animation dialog box appears, as shown in Figure 46.5.

The upper-left corner of the Custom Animation dialog box identifies each object in the current slide. A set of selection handles appears around the selected text in the preview window. Check the text object you want to animate.

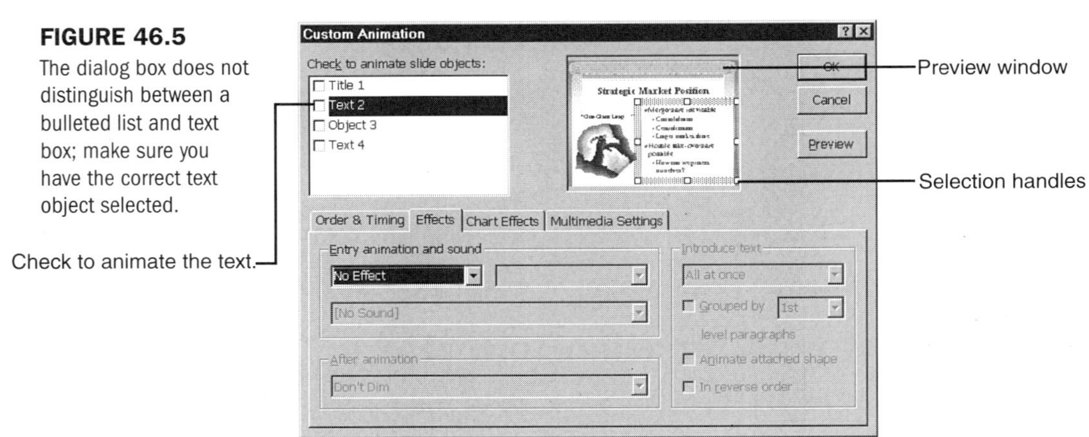

FIGURE 46.5
The dialog box does not distinguish between a bulleted list and text box; make sure you have the correct text object selected.

Use the Effects tab to designate the animation for the selected object. Use the Order & Timing tab to set the order in which the object will be animated and to apply a timeframe between the appearances of text objects.

Adding Visual and Sound Effects to Text Objects

Visual effects are composed of two things: type of animation and the direction of the animation appearance. For example, the object can Peek into the slide and appear From Bottom. There are 18 unique types of animation. The direction options vary, depending on which type of animation you select.

By default, text in a slide title or text box is introduced all at once. You have the option of introducing the text one word or character at a time. These options are typically used in an informal presentation, when you have a special title or phrase you want to emphasize. For instance, text that reads "Costs Reduced 25%!" or "Every Milestone Reached!" is a good candidate for by-word or by-character animation.

If you are animating a list of bullets or numbers, each main bullet (along with its sub-bullets) is animated separately. The same entry effect is used to build all the bullets on the slide. The only exception is the Random Effects animation, which, of course, selects effects at random to build each main bullet. In formal presentations, you want the entry effect to be subtle. Fly, From Left, From Bottom, From Bottom-Right, or Box, Out are good choices in these situations. The more casual the presentation and topic, the more creative you can be. Spiral and Swivel are less formal entry effects. See the next section, "Selecting the Text Introduction Settings," to pick how the text is introduced and at what level.

NOTE PowerPoint sometimes refers to bullets as paragraphs. The main bullets are the first-level paragraphs; the indented bullets under the main bullet are second-level paragraphs, and so forth.

If you are creating formal business presentations, it is best to consistently use the same entry effect on most of your bulleted text, and then use a different effect (or add sound) to emphasize the points on a particular slide.

On the Effects tab, select the type and direction of the animation from the top two drop-down boxes. Figure 46.6 shows the Box animation type and the Out direction selected. To see how the effect will appear on your slide, choose Preview.

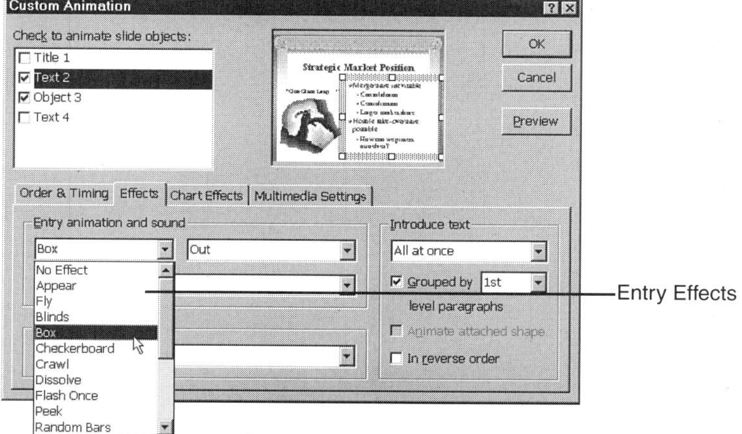

FIGURE 46.6
The slide miniature displays the animation effect.

Sound is best used with slide titles, text boxes, drawn objects, and picture clips. The same repeating sound each time a bullet appears will become annoying to your audience. Instead of a repeating sound, consider playing a long sound clip or music during the slide or the entire presentation.

See "Using Sound Clips, Music Tracks, and Narration," **p. 1215**

After an object has animated on the screen, you can leave it there, hide it, or change its color by selecting an option from the After Animation drop-down box (refer to Figure 46.6).

Changing the previous text to a lighter color will help focus your audience's attention on each specific item as you are discussing it. Previous items are still visible, just not as noticeable.

Selecting the Text Introduction Settings

When you animate text, the initial setting is to introduce the text all at once. In most cases, this is the best setting to use. On rare occasions, however, you might introduce the text word-by-word or letter-by-letter. A slide title or text box with the words "We Did It!" will have more impact on your audience if the words are animated individually, rather than all at once.

On the right side of the Effects tab in the Custom Animation dialog box, there is an Introduce Text area, as shown in Figure 46.7. Click the drop-down list and select how you want the text introduced on the screen.

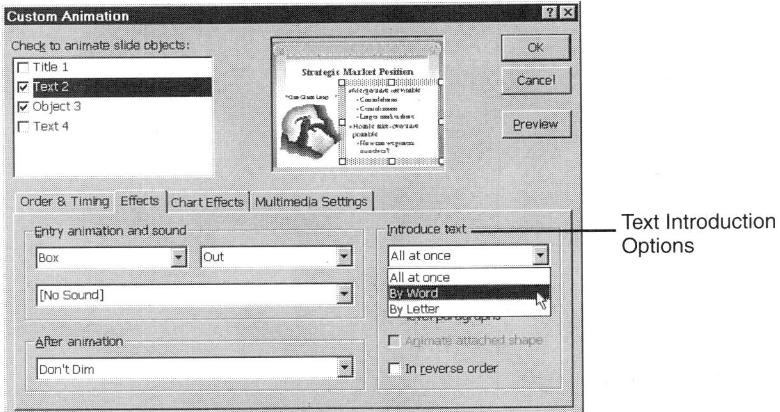

FIGURE 46.7
The default setting is All at Once.

In addition to deciding whether the text should be animated incrementally, there are several other alternatives when you animate text. Many of these settings are especially useful with bulleted or numbered lists:

- Animate by Paragraph Level—PowerPoint treats each bullet in a list as a separate paragraph. There are five paragraph levels you can have in bulleted or numbered lists. To change the paragraph level, select the Grouped by Level Paragraphs drop-down list and choose the desired level (see Figure 46.8).

- Animate the Attached Shape—This option is available only when there are both a shape and text. Examples include a text box or placeholder that you have formatted with a border or background fill color, or when you've added text to an AutoShape. PowerPoint identifies two objects—the text and the shape. By default, the shape is animated with the text. You can elect to have only the text animate, and not the shape.
- Animate in Reverse Order—A unique alternative to a traditional build, the text builds from the bottom up (refer to Figure 46.8). One great use for the In Reverse Order option is when you have a ranking or a hierarchical order of some kind, such as the Top Ten Sales Reps or Top Ten Reasons to Buy Your Product. To foster excitement and anticipation in the audience, you can present the tenth item first and work your way up the list to the first or highest ranking.

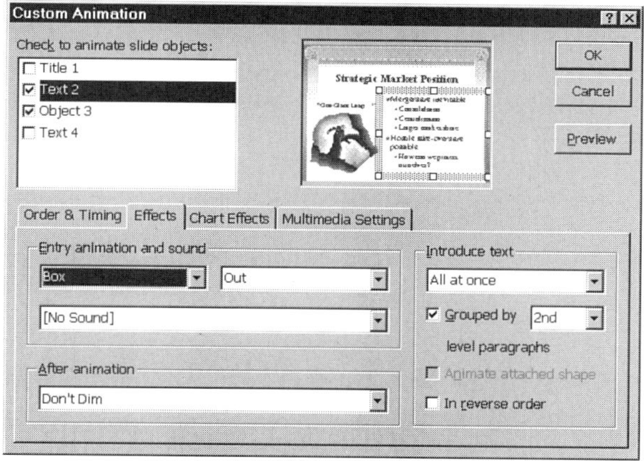

FIGURE 46.8
Additional text animation settings.

After you've selected the animation effects, you need to set the animation order and timing.

Selecting the Animation Order and Timing

Most slides have several objects on them—a title, a bulleted list, and clip or drawing objects. Objects that are not animated automatically appear on the screen when the slide is displayed. To set the order of objects you have animated, use the Order & Timing tab in the Custom Animation dialog box. Figure 46.9 shows a slide that contains three objects. When the Order & Timing tab is activated, you see two of the objects have been animated—the picture object and the bulleted list. The current animation order has the text list animated before the picture. To reorder the list, select the item you want to reorder and click the up or down arrows until the item is in the order you want.

In addition to establishing the order objects will appear on the screen, you need to decide the timing—when the object will appear. By default, objects appear when you click the left mouse button (or press Enter). You can, however, set the object to animate a specific amount of time after the previous object has animated.

FIGURE 46.9
A picture clip is always identified as Object in the Custom Animation dialog box.

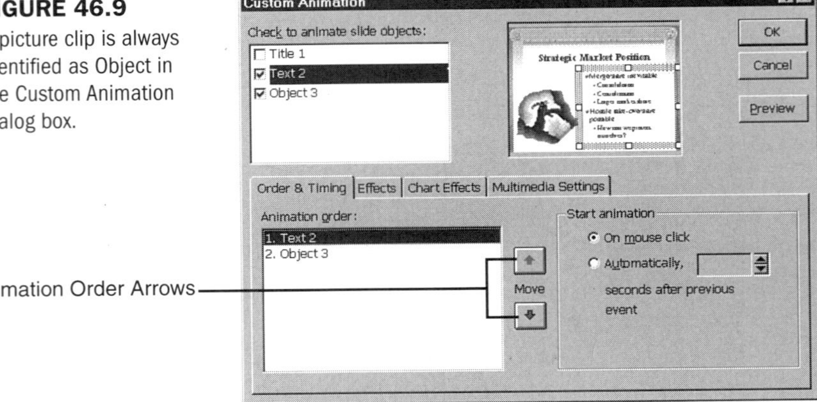

The time you add will depend on how you intend to animate the bullets. If you plan on showing the text all at once, your time interval should be set long enough for you to discuss the entire list. However, if you plan on building the bullets, the time you set here is the interval between the display of each of the components.

To set the timing for an animated object, select the object in the Animation Order box (refer to Figure 46.9). Then choose Automatically, __ Seconds After Previous Event and type in the number of seconds you want to wait before the selected text object appears.

TIP If you find in the course of delivering your presentation that you need additional time to discuss a topic, you can pause the presentation. Press the letter S to stop the presentation. To continue with the presentation, press the letter S again. You can also use the Spacebar, Enter key, or click the left mouse button to resume the presentation.

Choose Preview to see how the effects you've selected will look on your slide. Only the animation effect appears in the Preview; run the slide show to see both the animation and timing. After you have selected the effects, order, and timing you want, click OK to apply the custom animation settings.

Applying Custom Animation to Charts

One of the more exciting animation options in PowerPoint is the ability to animate graphic charts. Similar to building bulleted text, chart animation can build a pie chart one piece at a time. Or, you can animate a bar chart by the data series, data categories, or data points. This can be very useful when you want to discuss each chart component separately.

For example, suppose you have a slide such as the one shown in Figure 46.10. You could animate the chart by displaying just the Revenue columns for all four quarters, and then animating the columns for Expenses. This is animating by the data series. Alternatively, PowerPoint can show both Revenue and Expenses for Quarter 1, adding the remaining quarters one at a time. This is animating by the data categories. And, if you're really ambitious, PowerPoint can display each and every column separately! This is animating by data points.

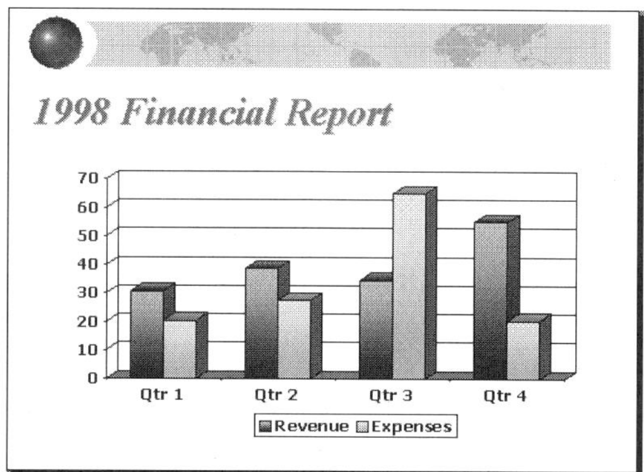

FIGURE 46.10
Be creative when thinking about adding animation to a chart.

Unless you are providing a very detailed presentation, you will probably not animate each and every chart in your slide show. On some slides, you might build the slide title separately from the chart, and then show the entire chart all at once. On other slides, you may need to discuss each series or category of the chart as it appears on the screen. Planning ahead on what you want to emphasize in your presentation is important.

There are a number of animation effects you can implement in conjunction with building a chart. Here is a list of the effects with a brief description of each:

- Use a visual effect to animate chart components—You can apply an entry effect to the chart components. Visual effects include the type of animation and the direction the object will appear from. Chart components can appear to Box Out or Wipe Up.
- Select the level of the chart build—Choose to build the chart by data series, data category, or element (which are the series or category data points). You can also animate the chart grid (frame and gridlines) and legend. Remember, the data series is identified in the chart legend.
- Play a sound bite as each item builds on the slide—A variety of sounds can be played when your chart components appear. 16 sound effects are available including sounds made by a camera click, a laser, and a typewriter.
- Control what happens after the animation—You can choose to change the hide the chart component after it has animated on the screen.
- Set the animation order and timing—Determine the order in which the chart animates, relative to the other slide objects. You can set manual or automatic timing for the chart components.

To animate a chart, you must be in either the Normal, Outline, or Slide view. Then choose Slide Show, Custom Animation from the menu bar. The Custom Animation dialog box appears (see Figure 46.11).

Of the four tabs in the dialog box that contain animation options, the only two tabs you'll need for animating graphic charts are Order & Timing and Chart Effects. The default tab is Chart Effects.

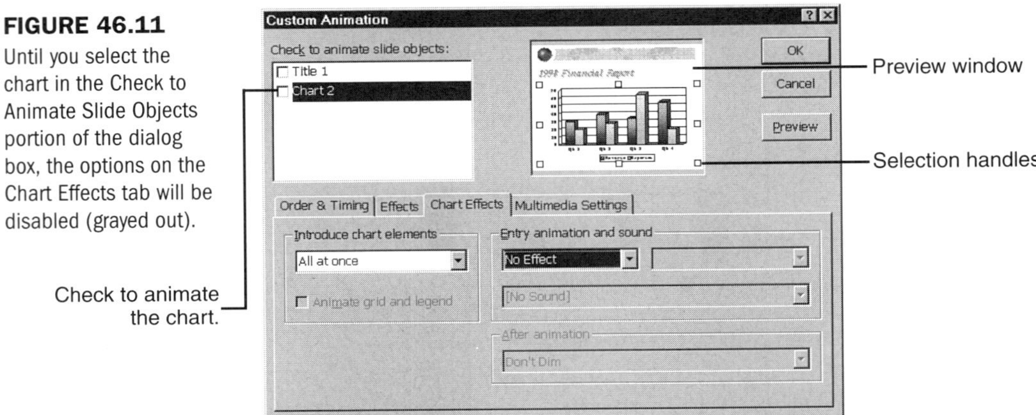

FIGURE 46.11
Until you select the chart in the Check to Animate Slide Objects portion of the dialog box, the options on the Chart Effects tab will be disabled (grayed out).

The upper-left corner of the Custom Animation dialog box identifies each object in the current slide. Click the object labeled Chart. A set of selection handles appears around the chart in the preview window and the settings on the Chart Effects tab become active.

Adding Visual Effects to Charts

You can apply a ***visual entry effect*** to build a chart, just as you can build a list of bullets. Chart elements can Wipe Up or Appear on the screen. As with any animation, you choose the type of animation (Wipe) and then the direction of the animation (Up).

As with animating other slide objects, use less-distracting animation for formal presentations. The effect you select depends on the type of chart you are animating. For column charts, choose Appear, Wipe Up, Strips Right-Up, or Strips Left-Up. These last three effects give the illusion of growth; the columns are rising up from the category axis. Likewise, in a bar chart you use any effect that comes from the left (Wipe Right, Strips Right-Up, or Strips Right-Down). Avoid using effects that do not display smoothly, such as Blinds, Checkerboard, and Random Bars.

Choose one of the 18 unique types of animation. The direction options vary depending on which type of animation you select—and some of the animation types do not have animation directions.

CAUTION

You should *always* select the chart entry animation before selecting the chart introduction settings. Why? Because when you select an entry effect, the introduction setting automatically reverts to the default—All at Once—even if you had another introduction setting selected first.

Also, certain entry effects can be used only with the default introduction setting; they are Fly, Crawl, Peek, Spiral, Stretch, Swivel, and Zoom. So, if you had visions of each data series "swiveling" into your slide, you are out of luck!

For formal business presentations, I recommend you use the same entry animation on most, if not all, of your charts. If a particular chart needs to be emphasized further, then use different chart animation to make it stand out from the others.

To select a chart entry animation, click the Entry Animation and Sound drop-down list on the Chart Effects tab (see Figure 46.12).

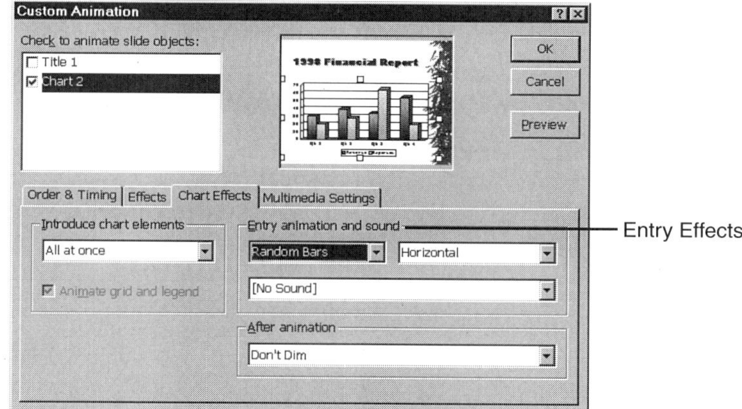

FIGURE 46.12
Scroll down the list to see additional effects.

NOTE The Random Effects transition does not work the same way with chart elements as it does with text. If the Random Effects option is selected, the first time you run the slide show, PowerPoint selects a transition and all elements of the chart then appear using that one transition. The next time you run your slide show, a different transition is selected and all the elements of the chart appear using the new transition.

Choose Preview to see how the effects you've selected will look on your slide. Next, you need to decide whether you want the chart components to appear on the slide incrementally.

Selecting the Chart Introduction Settings

After the entry effect is selected, you have to decide how you want to build or introduce the chart components. Use Figure 46.13 with Table 46.2 to understand your choices.

Table 46.2 Animating Chart Elements

Introduction Setting	Description
All at Once	The default setting. In effect, this shows the entire chart at one time. No "building" of the chart takes place.
By Series	The items represented in the legend are the "series" in the chart. In Figure 46.13, there is a 1997 and a 1998 series.
By Category	The groups along the Category axis (sometimes called the x-axis) are the "categories" in the chart. In Figure 46.13, each quarter is a category.
By Element in Series	Each component in a series is displayed one at a time. The 1997 column in Quarter 1 of Figure 46.13 displays first, followed by the 1997 column for Quarter 2. When all the 1997 columns have appeared, the first 1998 column comes up on the screen.
By Element in Category	Each component in a category is displayed one at a time. The 1997 column in Quarter 1 displays, followed by the 1998 column for Quarter 1. The columns for the remaining quarters appear in the same order, first 1997 and then 1998.

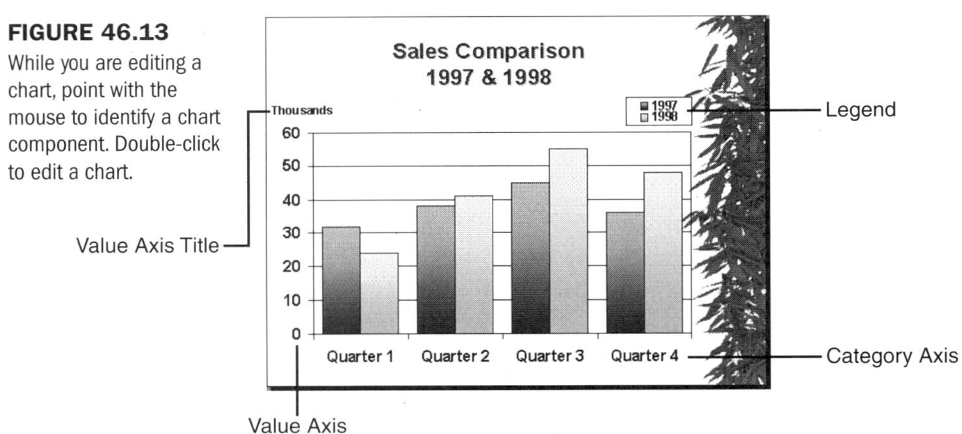

FIGURE 46.13
While you are editing a chart, point with the mouse to identify a chart component. Double-click to edit a chart.

The chart introduction options are tied to the entry effects. If you select the All at Once option, the entry effect you have chosen will be applied as the chart appears on the screen. If you select one of the other introduction options, the entry effect will be applied to each element that is built.

Also, certain entry effects can be used only with the All at Once introduction setting: Fly, Crawl, Peek, Spiral, Stretch, Swivel, and Zoom. If you select a different introduction setting with these entry effects, the entry effect will change to Appear.

From the Introduce Chart Elements drop-down box, select a level of introduction you want to use to animate the chart (see Figure 46.14). The default setting when you choose something other than All at Once is to also animate the chart frame, gridlines, and legend before animating the chart data. If you want to have the chart frame and so on already displayed when the slide appears, uncheck the Animate Grid and Legend option.

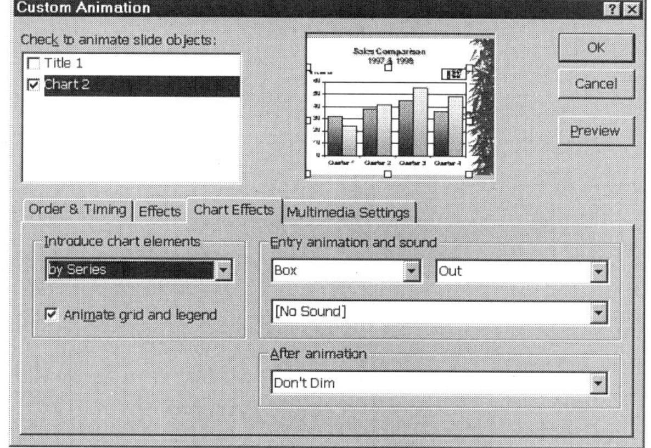

FIGURE 46.14
Click the Preview button to see the chart build using the animation options you've selected.

If, while running the slide show, you discover there isn't enough time between the build of the last chart component and the transition to the next slide, you need to lengthen the slide transition time. Choose Slide Show, Slide Transition from the menu bar to change the amount of time the slide displays before transitioning to the next slide.

Sound and After-Animation Effects with Charts

Sound bites and after-animation settings have their place in PowerPoint presentations, but animated charts is not one of them. You should avoid this for two key reasons:

- The sound you apply is heard each time a chart component appears. This can become very annoying to your audience, especially if they hear the same sound over and over on the same chart. Think about it: screeching brakes or a whoosh again and again. And, you cannot apply a sound only to a particular element—for example, to a great Revenue number in the Third Quarter.
- Although the After Animation options are available for charts, it is not likely you will often apply them to charts. How often do you want the chart to appear, then disappear? And changing color does not appear to change anything on the slide.

However, if you insist on having sound with your chart slide, I suggest you apply the sound to the slide transition or the slide title, or play music or the longer sound clips instead of applying the sound to the chart itself.

Selecting the Animation Order and Timing

After you have selected the animation effects, you may want to look at the settings on the Order & Timing tab. If you are working with a typical chart slide layout, there are two objects on the slide—the slide title and the chart. If the chart was inserted into another slide layout, there may be other objects on the slide.

Because you have already animated the chart, it will be listed in the Animation Order text box on the Order & Timing tab (see Figure 46.15). If you also want to animate the slide title, check the box in the upper-left corner of the Custom Animation dialog box.

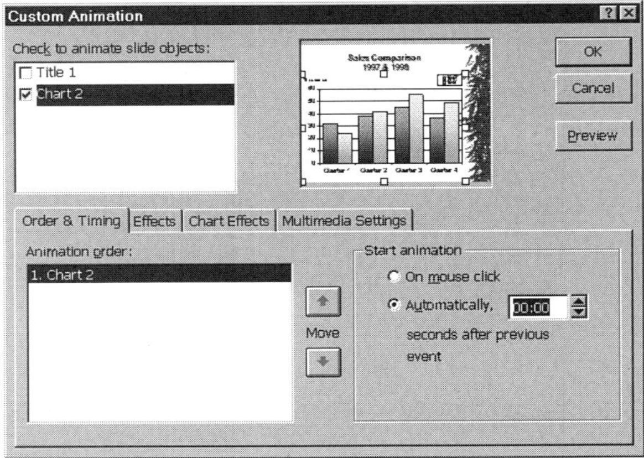

FIGURE 46.15
The timing is tied to the chart introduction options you selected on the Chart Effects tab.

By default, charts animate when you click the left mouse button (or press Enter). You can set the chart to appear a specific amount of time after the previous object has animated.

The time you add will depend on how you intend to animate the chart. If you plan on showing the chart all at once, your time interval is the amount of time between the last event and when you want the chart to appear. For example, if the last event was the transition to the slide containing the chart, you might want only two to three seconds' delay before the entire chart appears onscreen. However, if you plan on building the chart by the data series or categories, the time you set here is the interval between the display of each of the chart components; two to three seconds doesn't give you much time between events to discuss each chart component! Personally, when I am building the chart, I don't add timing to it. Instead, I use the mouse (or a remote device) to display each animated element.

To set the timing of the chart, choose Automatically, __ Seconds After Previous Event and type in the number of seconds you want to wait before the chart animates (refer to Figure 46.15).

Choose Preview to see how the animation effects you've selected will look on your slide. If you've applied timing, run the Slide Show to see both the animation and timing together. After you have selected the effects, order, and timing you want, click OK to apply the custom animation settings.

Animating Organization Charts

Organization charts can be animated with timing, entry effects, and sound. However, unlike graphic charts, organization charts cannot be built. Rather, PowerPoint treats organization charts as objects (similar to drawn objects) rather than graphs and so they are animated differently. See the "Applying Custom Animation to Drawn Objects" section earlier in this chapter, for the options to animate organization charts.

Automating Chart Animation

To help you quickly animate a column, bar, or pie chart, use the snippets of VBA code provided here. All you need do is select the chart you want to animate and run the appropriate macro. Custom animation is automatically applied to the chart.

The first snippet animates either a bar or column chart by data series using the Wipe Up entry effect. The animation timing is set to occur when you use a mouse click. The chart background and legend are not animated. The title of the snippet is StdColBarChartAnimation.

```
Sub StdColBarChartAnimation()
On Error Resume Next
    With ActiveWindow.Selection.ShapeRange.AnimationSettings
        .Animate = msoTrue
        .EntryEffect = ppEffectWipeUp
        .ChartUnitEffect = ppAnimateBySeries
        .AnimateBackground = msoFalse
    End With
End Sub
```


This next snippet animates a pie chart by data category using the Box Out entry effect. The animation timing is set to occur when you use a mouse click. The chart background and legend are not animated. The title of the snippet is StdPieChartAnimation.

```
Sub StdPieChartAnimation()
On Error Resume Next
    With ActiveWindow.Selection.ShapeRange.AnimationSettings
        .Animate = msoTrue
        .EntryEffect = ppEffectBoxOut
        .ChartUnitEffect = ppAnimateByCategory
        .AnimateBackground = msoFalse
    End With
End Sub
```

You can copy these snippets to your presentation from the CD that accompanies this book. See Chapters 5, "Getting Acquainted with VBA," and 6, "Successful VBA Modules," for more about working with VBA snippets and macros.

NOTE To learn how to turn these snippets into an Add-In so that it can be used in all presentations, see the CD accompanying this book. It contains instructions on how to create an add-in for PowerPoint VBA snippets.

CHAPTER 47

Advanced Slide Show Features

In this chapter

Rehearsing Your Presentation

Although you can practice your presentation by running the slide show, there are several reasons why you might want to use PowerPoint's presentation-rehearsing feature. Perhaps you have a set time limit in which to deliver a presentation. Or maybe you want to assign specific, practiced transition times to each slide. Regardless of the reason, this built-in feature is handy.

The best place to start is the Slide Sorter view. Click the Rehearse Timings button on the Slide Sorter toolbar (as shown in Figure 47.1) or choose Slide Show, Rehearse Slide Timings.

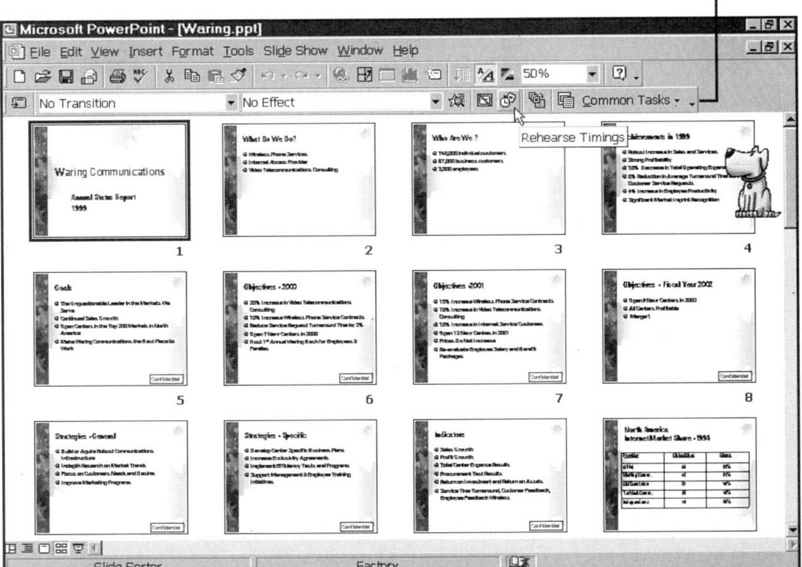

FIGURE 47.1
Time assigned to each slide appears next to the slide number in the Slide Sorter view.

The first slide in your presentation and a Rehearsal toolbar appear, as shown in Figure 47.2. The following list explains the toolbar buttons:

- Next Button—Advances to the next slide in the presentation, just as a left click does.
- Pause Button—This on/off button pauses both the slide time and total presentation time. This is especially handy when you are gathering your thoughts, or even if you are interrupted as you are rehearsing.
- Slide Time—Indicates how long you are taking to discuss the current slide.
- Repeat Button—Starts the timing over for the current slide.
- Total Presentation Time—Indicates how long, up to this point in the presentation, it has taken you to discuss the slides.

NOTE When you click the Repeat button, only the time starts over; any animated objects that have already been displayed remain on the screen. However, when you just click the mouse (not on the Repeat button), the animation repeats on top of the existing objects.

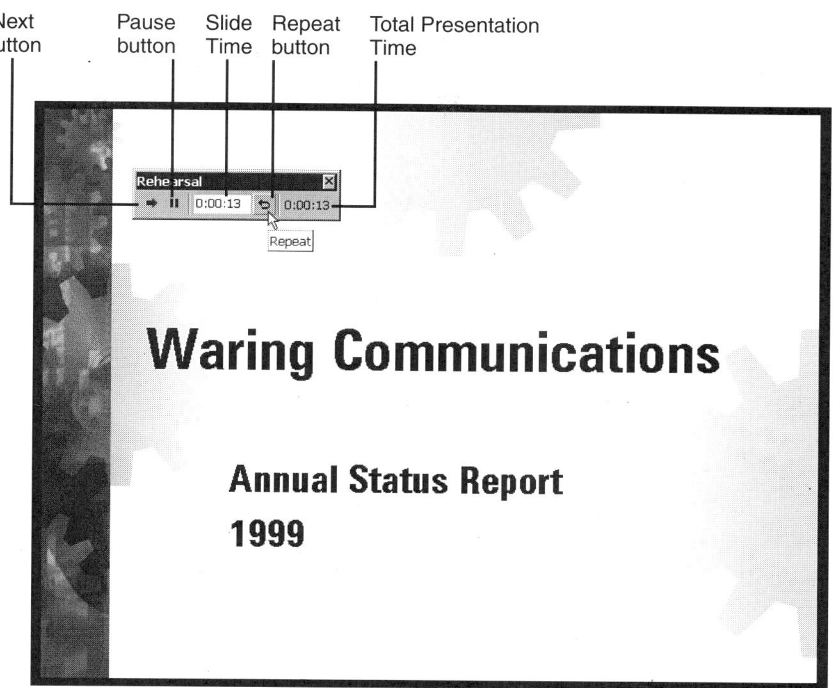

FIGURE 47.2
ScreenTips identify the Rehearsal toolbar buttons.

To stop the rehearsal, click the Close (X) button (refer to Figure 47.2) or press Esc. A dialog box appears, indicating the total presentation time, and asks whether you want to apply the specific slide timings to each slide. Click Yes to accept the new slide timings. Click No to keep the existing (if any) slide timings.

If you click Yes, you are creating a presentation that will run automatically (instead of on a mouse click) using the slide timings. As with all slide timings, if you click the mouse before the end of the designated display time, the slide will advance—the mouse click overrides any preset timings.

Two kinds of timing are used in PowerPoint presentations—the length of time a slide displays on the screen (slide timing) and the length of time between animated slide objects (animation start timing).

Resolving Timing Conflicts

Suppose you have a bulleted list that you have animated to appear using the options in the Custom Animation dialog box. There are 10 bullets and you have set a 15-second interval between the bullets. The total time to animate the bulleted list is 135 seconds (9×15).

Then when you rehearse the presentation, it takes you only 120 seconds to discuss the bullets on the slide. If you click Yes in the dialog box, the time assigned to the slide is 120 seconds.

continues

continued

When there are conflicting timings, PowerPoint uses whichever time is longer; in this example it's the animation time for the bulleted list. You need to be aware however, that after the last bullet appears, PowerPoint immediately transitions to the next slide. There won't be any time to discuss this last bullet.

If the situation were reversed (bullet animation at 120 seconds and slide timing at 135 seconds) there would be 15 seconds after the last bullet appears before the transition to the next slide.

If you apply timings to your slides, you can always pause the presentation by pressing the S key on the keyboard. Press the S key again to resume the presentation. Here's a great way to remember this–S is for Stop and Start.

Working with Custom Shows

If you have to tailor a presentation for different audiences, this is the feature for you. Think of Custom Shows as versions of the same presentation for different audiences—without having to create separate files. Custom Shows can be built based on target audience or based on discussion topic. For example, you can give an overview presentation to one audience and a detailed version of the same presentation to another audience. Or, if your presentation includes slides devoted to three specific topics, you can create Custom Shows for each topic while still having the full presentation when you need it.

The basic premise is that all the slides are contained in one presentation. Custom Shows are lists of slides that you want to show a particular audience. Figure 47.3 illustrates this concept.

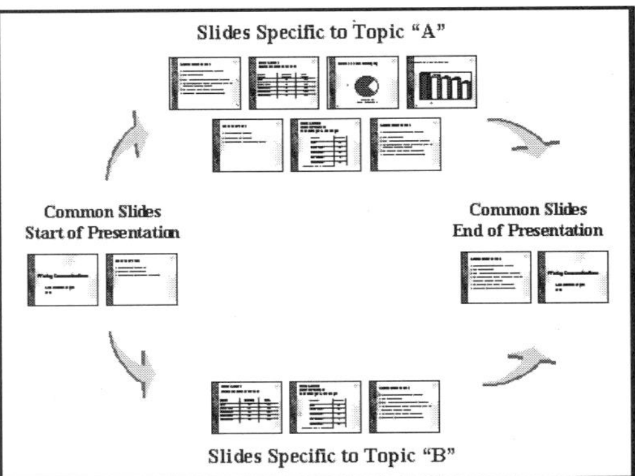

FIGURE 47.3
The slides can be flagged for more than one Custom Show.

Creating and Modifying Custom Shows

When creating a Custom Show you should include every slide you want to use. Using the examples illustrated in Figure 47.3, the first Custom Show includes the common slides at the start of the presentation, the slides specific to topic "A," and the common slides at the end of the presentation. The second Custom Show includes the common slides at the start of the presentation, the slides specific to topic "B," and the common slides at the end of the presentation.

To create a Custom Show, follow these steps:

1. Display the Presentation and choose Slide Show, Custom Shows.
2. Click New to start a new Custom Show. The Define Custom Show dialog box appears (see Figure 47.4).

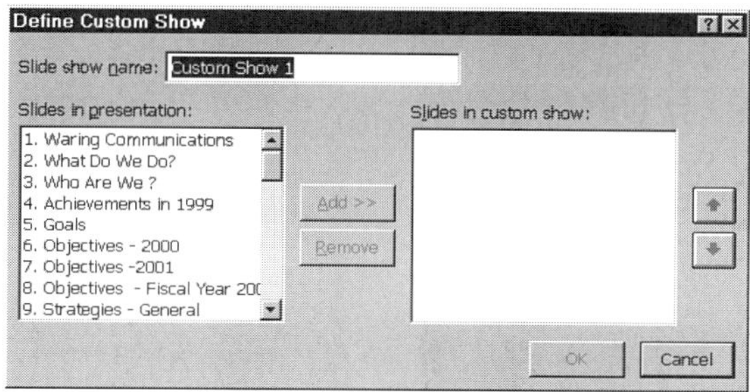

FIGURE 47.4
The slide titles are used to identify each slide.

3. At the top of the dialog box is the Slide Show Name text box. Type an appropriate name for this Custom Show. The maximum length for a name is 30 characters.
4. On the left side of the dialog box is a list of the titles of each slide in the current presentation. Double-click each slide you want to be part of the Custom Show. The slide titles are copied to the right side of the dialog box, as shown in Figure 47.5.

NOTE The trick to identifying slides to be part of a Custom Show is the slide title. If all your slide titles start with your company name, it will be difficult to distinguish one slide from another.

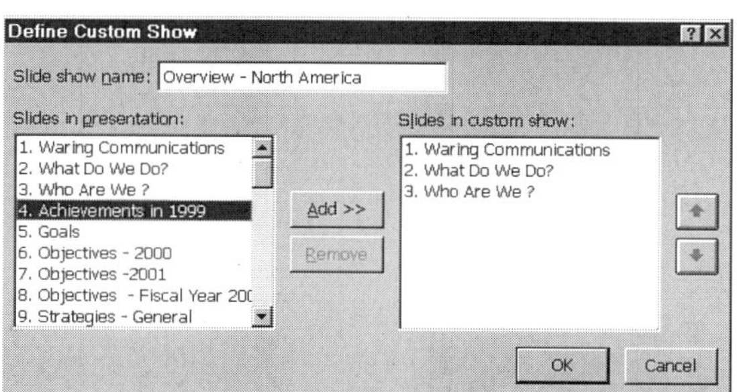

FIGURE 47.5
Double-click or use the Add button to copy slides to the right side of the dialog box.

5. You can select a group of slides at once. If the slides are consecutive, click the first slide, hold down the Shift key, and click the last slide. If the slides are not consecutive, click the first slide, hold down the Ctrl key, and click each slide title. Then click the Add button to copy the names to the Slides in Custom Show text box.

6. To reorder the slides in the Custom Show, select the slide you want to move and click the up- or down-arrow button to move the slide in the list. You cannot select multiple slides in the Slides in Custom Show list. You must move the slides one at a time.
7. After you have copied the slide titles and ordered the list, click OK.

The Custom Shows dialog box appears again. Figure 47.6 has two Custom Shows listed in the dialog box. To preview a Custom Show, select the name and click Show. Other buttons in the dialog box include

- Edit—Displays the Define Custom Show dialog box (refer to Figure 47.4). You can add, remove, or reorder the slides flagged for a Custom Show.
- Remove—Deletes a Custom Show. Only the list of slides for the Custom Show is deleted, not the actual slides.
- Copy—You can copy an existing Custom Show to use as a starting point for a new Custom Show.

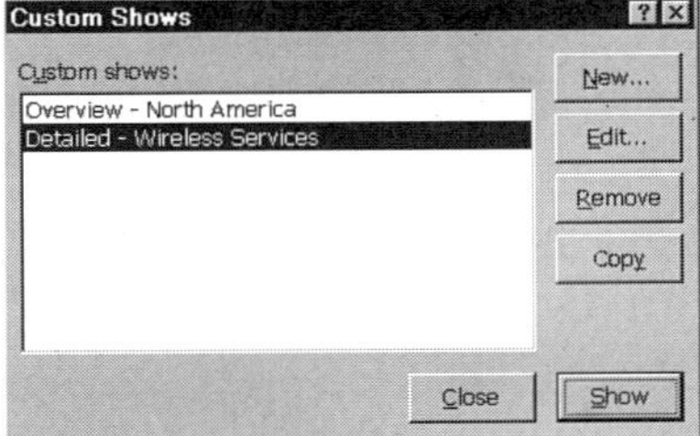

FIGURE 47.6
To preview the Custom Show, click the Show button.

Running a Custom Show

Now that the Custom Show has been created, you can run the show by choosing Slide Show, Set Up Show. In the Set Up Show dialog box, click the Custom Show drop-down arrow and select the Custom Show you want to use (see Figure 47.7).

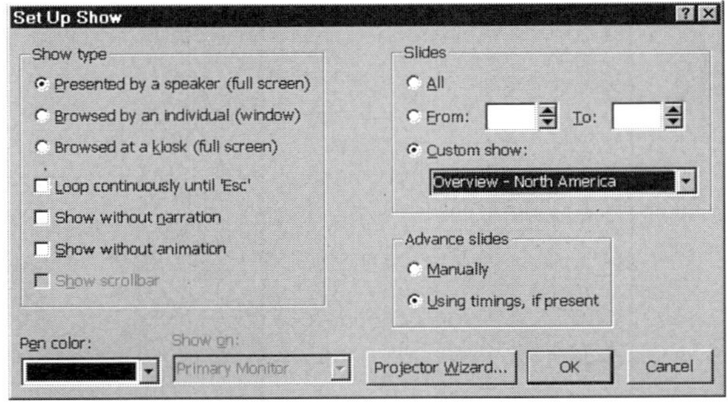

FIGURE 47.7
You can also run a Custom Show as a hyperlink, which is discussed in the next section.

Click OK; the dialog box closes. Then click the Slide Show button to run the show.

CAUTION

It's a good idea to change the Set Up Show option back to All after you are finished with the Custom Show (refer to Figure 47.7). Otherwise, each time you attempt to run the presentation, only the slides in the Custom Show will be displayed.

Custom Shows can also be launched from within a presentation as a hyperlink. Using Action Settings, Action Buttons, and hyperlinks, you can create a presentation that will run any number of Custom Shows you've created.

▶ **See** "Problem/Solution—Creating and Using Branch Presentations," **p. 1297**

Using Hyperlinks in Presentations

Hyperlinks are pointers to other files, objects, or locations. They are used to quickly jump from one place to another. If you use the Internet or an intranet, you've seen and probably used hyperlinks—colored and underlined text. But did you know that in PowerPoint, you can create a hyperlink that is attached to a slide object? The object can be a picture clip, a text box, an AutoShape, or even a placeholder object such as a graphic chart or table.

You can use a hyperlink in a presentation to go to a variety of places:

- To another slide in the current presentation
- To a different presentation
- To a Custom Show
- To a file in a different program, such as a Microsoft Word document or a Microsoft Excel spreadsheet
- To an Internet or intranet site
- To an email address

Typically, hyperlinks are one-way trips. You may need to create another hyperlink to return to the original slide. Only the Custom Shows have a built-in "round-trip" option to run the show and return to the slide from which the show was launched.

Text Hyperlinks Versus Object Hyperlinks—Planning Ahead

You can create two types of hyperlinks: text hyperlinks and object hyperlinks. *Text hyperlinks* are one or more words in a slide that are used to jump to the hyperlink destination. *Object hyperlinks* are objects in a slide that are used to jump to the hyperlink destination.

Text hyperlinks are underlined and displayed in a special color. The hyperlink color is determined by the color scheme associated with the Design Template applied to the presentation. The text color changes after you click a hyperlink, indicating you have viewed the hyperlink.

▶ **See** "Working with Slide Color Schemes," **p. 1229**

Object hyperlinks are created using objects such as shapes, picture clips, charts, or tables. They do not have special markings or colors.

Before you create a hyperlink, it's important that you decide which type you plan to use. Generally, text hyperlinks are used for online or self-running presentations, or to show the audience explicitly the hyperlink you are accessing. Object hyperlinks are more common in presentations that you control, because they provide a subtle place to hide a hyperlink. The audience usually isn't aware you are using hyperlinks.

To create a hyperlink, you must first do one of the following:

- Select a word or phrase—This can be text selected in a placeholder (slide title or bulleted list), text selected in a text box, or text selected in a shape. The hyperlink is attached to the selected text.
- Click inside a text object—The flashing cursor must appear in the text object. The hyperlink inserts text at the point of the flashing cursor. The inserted text identifies the hyperlink destination.
- Select an object—Including shapes, picture clips, charts, tables, or text boxes. This does not include text placeholders such as slide titles and bulleted lists. The hyperlink is attached to the object.

Figure 47.8 illustrates both text and object hyperlinks.

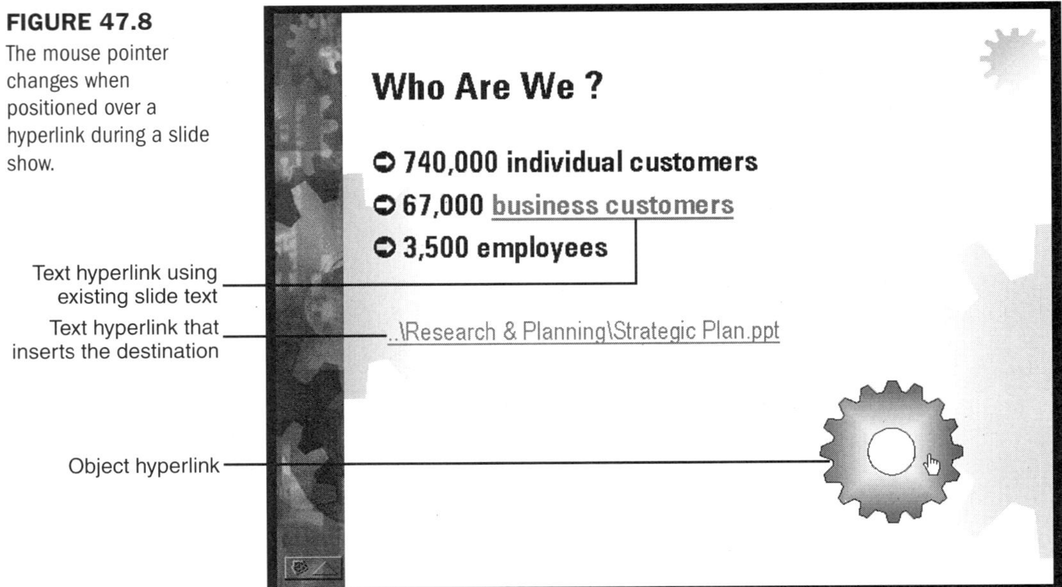

FIGURE 47.8
The mouse pointer changes when positioned over a hyperlink during a slide show.

Regardless of the type of hyperlink you create, hyperlinks are active only when you run a slide show.

Navigating the Insert Hyperlink Dialog Box

After you have decided which type of hyperlink to create, you need to access the Insert Hyperlink dialog box and identify the hyperlink destination.

Click the Insert Hyperlink button on the Standard toolbar, or choose Insert, Hyperlink from the menu bar to access the Insert Hyperlink dialog box (see Figure 47.9).

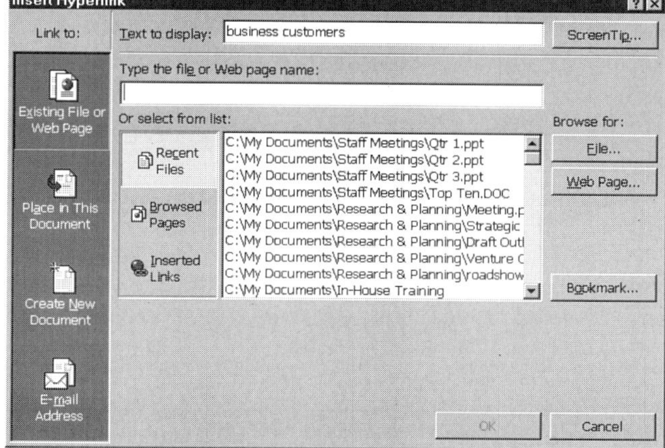

FIGURE 47.9
Start by choosing a Link To option.

The left side of the dialog box contains four Link To choices, representing the destinations you can select from for your hyperlink:

- Existing File or Web Page
- Place in This Document
- Create New Document
- E-Mail Address

The next few sections describe the specific steps for creating hyperlinks.

Creating Hyperlinks to Slides or Custom Shows in the Current Presentation

To create a hyperlink to another slide in the current presentation or to a Custom Show in the current presentation, follow these steps:

1. Click the Place in This Document option on the left side of the Insert Hyperlink dialog box; the dialog box changes (see Figure 47.10).
2. Click one of the destinations in the Select a Place in This Document list. Use the Slide Preview window to verify you've selected the correct slide.

   If you select a Custom Show, the Show and Return option becomes active. This option runs the Custom Show and returns to the current slide. If you don't check this option, when the Custom Show has concluded, the slide show ends.
3. After you've selected the file or site, click OK to create the hyperlink.

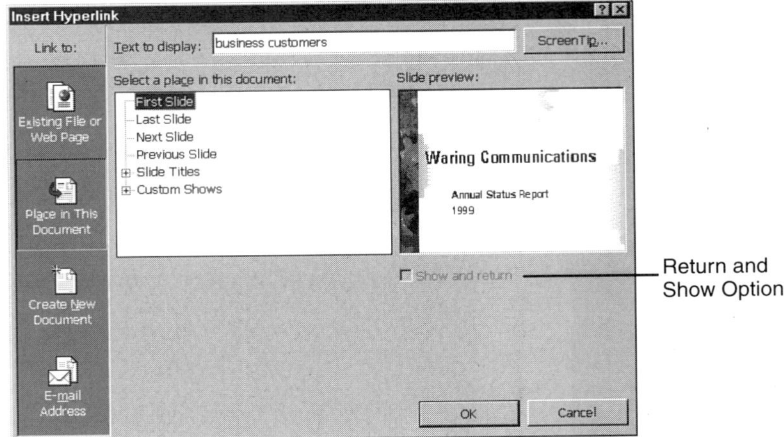

FIGURE 47.10
Expand the Slide Titles and Custom Shows lists by clicking the plus (+) sign.

Creating Hyperlinks to Other Presentations, Files, or Web Pages To create a hyperlink to another presentation, to any file (typically, you'll want to hyperlink to Word and Excel files), or to an Internet or intranet Web site, follow these steps:

1. Click the Existing File or Web Page option on the left side of the Insert Hyperlink dialog box; the dialog box display changes (see Figure 47.11).

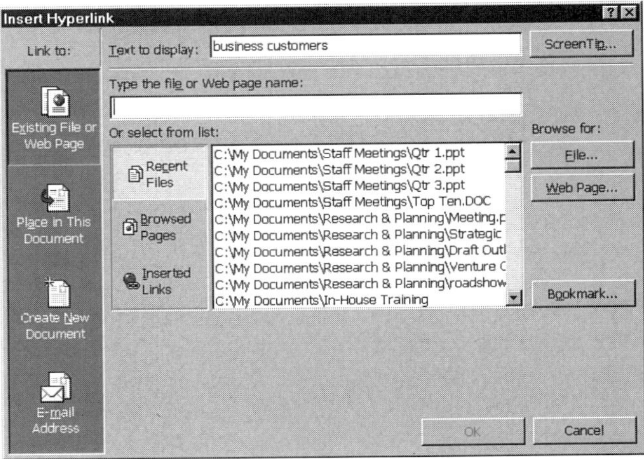

FIGURE 47.11
You can also create links to other slides in the active presentation.

2. If you want to link to a file you have used recently, click the Or Select from List buttons to locate the file. Figure 47.11 shows the list of recently used files (regardless of their location). Figure 47.12 shows the list of Browsed Pages you've recently viewed.

   You can also use the File or Web Page buttons to search for a file or Web site.

To create a hyperlink to a specific slide in another presentation, locate and select the presentation name. Then click the Bookmark button. Select the title of the slide you want to link to. You might also want to create a hyperlink on that slide to return back to the original presentation.

FIGURE 47.12
Browsed Pages include Internet sites and Help screens.

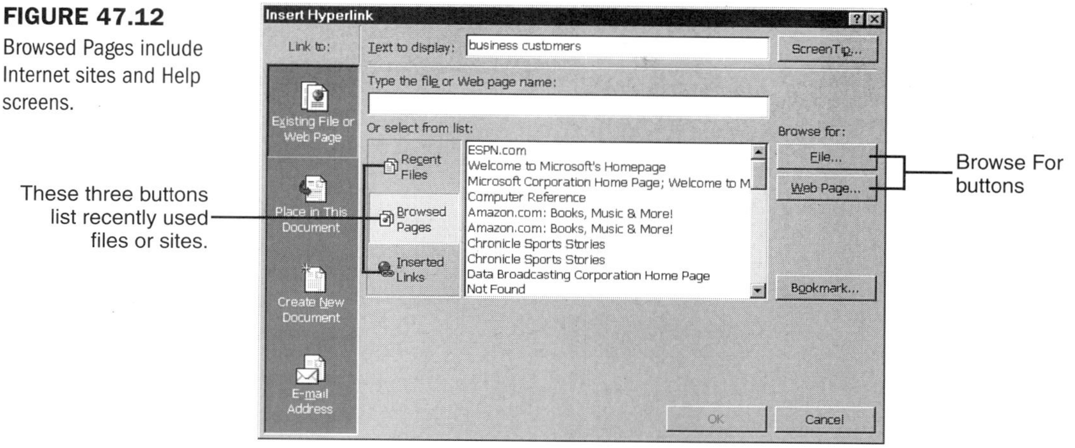

These three buttons list recently used files or sites.

Browse For buttons

3. When you click the file or site name, it appears in the Type the File or Web Page Name text box.
4. After you've selected the file or page, click OK to create the hyperlink.

You can also create a hyperlink to an existing Web site by typing the URL directly in a text object on a slide or in the Outline pane.

Creating Hyperlinks to New Files If you know you want a hyperlink to a file, but the file needs to be created, you can create both the file and hyperlink at the same time. Follow these steps:

1. Click the Create New Document option on the left side of the Insert Hyperlink dialog box; the dialog box display changes (see Figure 47.13).

NOTE Remember, the text in the Text to Display box at the top of the Insert Hyperlink dialog box is the text selected in the active presentation to which the hyperlink will be attached.

2. Type a name for the document in the Name of New Document text box. You must specify the file type by including the file extension in the new document's name, if you want to create something other than a PowerPoint file.

   If you want the new file to be located in a destination other than the default path, click the Change button to select a new destination.

FIGURE 47.13
This option enables you to create a document on-the-fly.

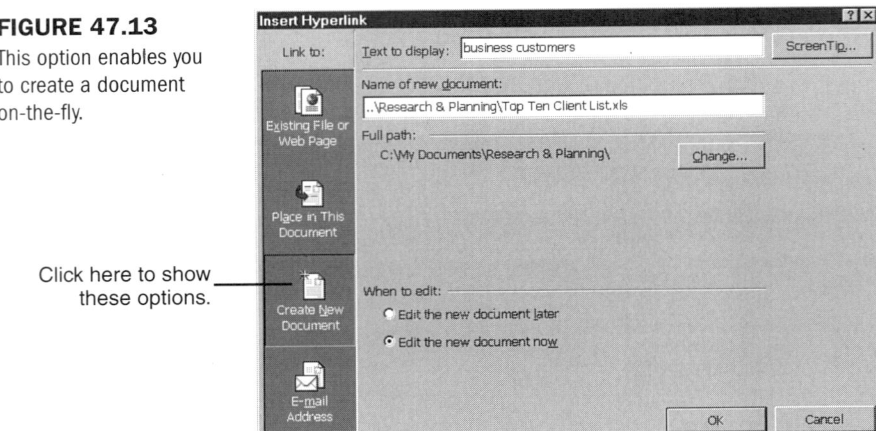

3. At the bottom of the dialog box, you have the choice of creating the new document now or later. Selecting the Edit the New Document Now option starts the appropriate application and creates a new document for you. Selecting the Edit the New Document Later option creates a new, empty file. You'll have to remember to fill it in later.
4. After you've typed in a filename and made your other selections, click OK.

Creating Hyperlinks to Email Addresses This type of hyperlink is used generally in online or automated presentations. To create a hyperlink to an email address, follow these steps:

1. Click the E-Mail Address option on the left side of the Insert Hyperlink dialog box; the dialog box displays changes (see Figure 47.14).

FIGURE 47.14
Use this type of hyperlink for feedback from people who see this presentation on a Web site.

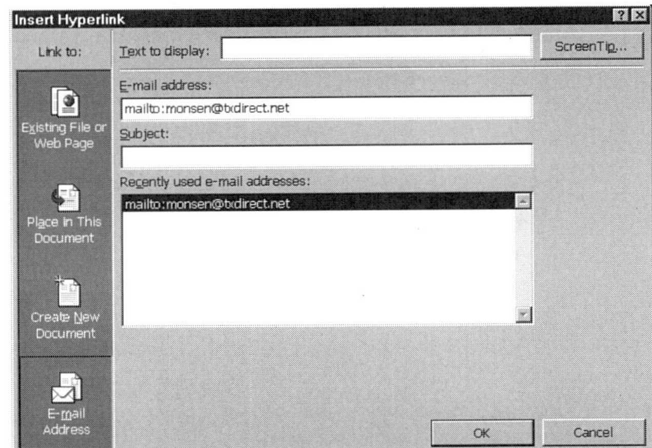

2. Type an email address or select one from the Recently Used E-Mail Addresses list. Use the Subject line to create a fixed subject for all email messages sent through this hyperlink.
3. Click OK to create the hyperlink.

TIP You can also create a hyperlink to an email address by typing the address directly in a text object on a slide or in the Outline pane.

Adding a ScreenTip to a Hyperlink

ScreenTips are useful for identifying or explaining the hyperlink and are useful in online or automated presentations.

NOTE Hyperlinks to other files, Web sites, or email addresses automatically include a ScreenTip identifying the path or URL. Hyperlinks to slides or Custom Shows in the same presentation do not automatically have ScreenTips.

To create a ScreenTip, click the ScreenTip button in the Insert Hyperlink dialog box. Figure 47.15 shows a ScreenTip example in the Set Hyperlink ScreenTip dialog box. Figure 47.16 shows how the ScreenTip will appear in the slide show.

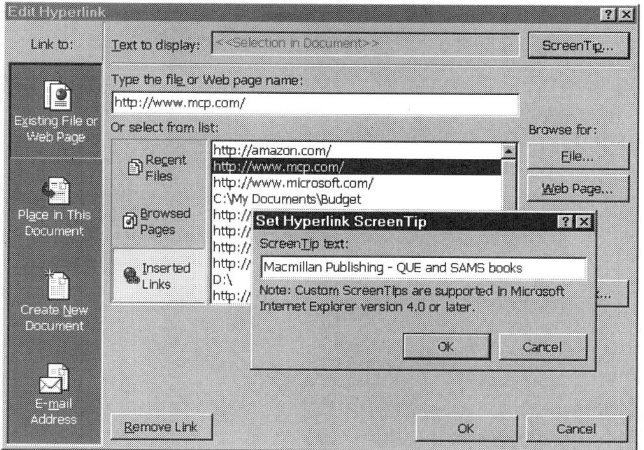

FIGURE 47.15
Use ScreenTips to describe the hyperlink, instead of using the file path.

Removing a Hyperlink

If you want to remove a hyperlink from a slide, you must first select the text or object representing the hyperlink. Then click the Insert Hyperlink button on the Standard toolbar, or choose Insert, Hyperlink from the menu bar to access the Edit Hyperlink dialog box (see Figure 47.17).

FIGURE 47.16
ScreenTips appear when you point to the hyperlink.

NOTE If you select only part of the hyperlink text, you will just be removing the hyperlink from that portion of the text. You must select all the hyperlink text to remove the hyperlink completely.

Click the Remove Link button and click OK to remove the link from the slide.

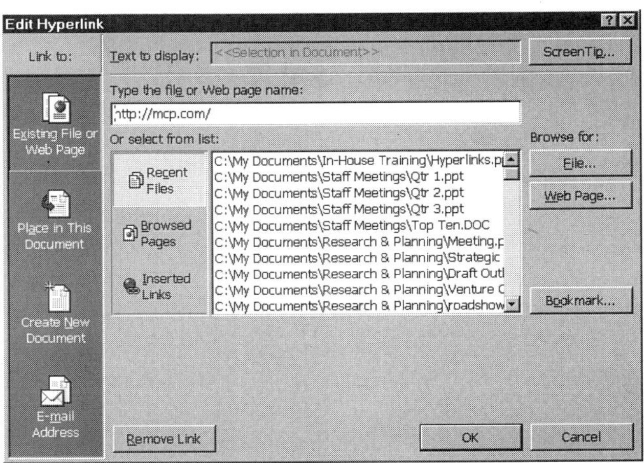

FIGURE 47.17
The Remove Link button appears only in the Edit Hyperlink dialog box.

Using Action Settings in Presentations

Like hyperlinks, actions take place only during slide shows. You can set an action to occur when the mouse pointer is positioned over a slide object, or when you click a slide object. You can even have one action occur when the mouse is over an object and a completely different action occur when you click the object.

Some useful examples of actions include

- Activating a hyperlink to other slides or Custom Shows in the current presentation, other presentations, other files, or Web site URL addresses.
- Playing a sound bite, music clip, or recorded narration when you point to or click a picture clip object in a slide.
- Launching an Excel spreadsheet when you point to or click a chart.
- Starting MS Graph to edit a chart, while you are still in the middle of running a slide show.

To create an action, select the object to which you want to apply the action. Then choose Slide Show, Action Settings. The Action Settings dialog box appears, as shown in Figure 47.18.

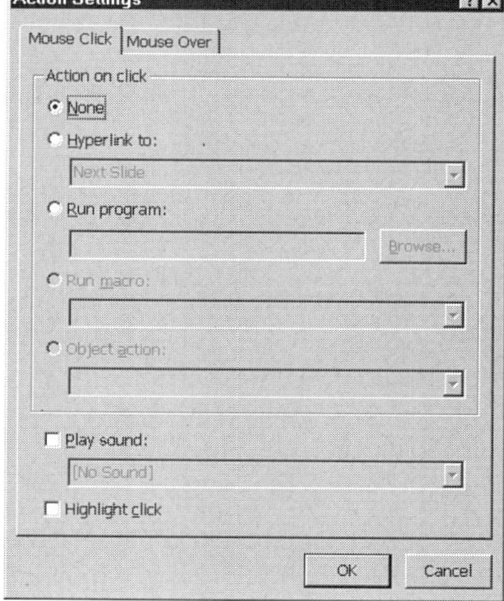

FIGURE 47.18
Options in the dialog box become active based on the object you selected.

By choosing a tab in the Action Settings dialog box, you are selecting when the action will take place. The specific options on the tabs are identical. Click the Mouse Click tab to create an action when you click the object during the slide show. Click the Mouse Over tab to create an action when the mouse is moved over the object during the slide show.

The options in the Action Settings dialog box are described as follows:

- Hyperlink To—Creates a hyperlink to another slide in the current presentation, to a Custom Show in the current presentation, to another PowerPoint presentation, to a file in another program, or to a site on an intranet or the Internet. You cannot hyperlink to an email address.

- Run Program—Starts another program. You must know the name of the executable (.exe) program you want to launch. This option does not display a specific file, as the Hyperlink To option will; however, you can use the Browse button to locate the file.
- Run Macro—Starts a macro that you have created and stored with the current presentation.
- Object Action—Enables you to play a motion clip, open an embedded object in the program in which it was created, edit a graphic chart, or edit an organization chart while still running the slide show. You cannot use this option to edit a PowerPoint table. However, you can use this option to edit an embedded Word table.
- Play Sound—Plays a sound bite, sound clip, music, or voice narrative. This option can be in addition to, or instead of, the other options in this list.
- Highlight Click—The selected object will change color or otherwise be highlighted. This occurs either when the mouse pointer is over the object or when you click the object, depending on the tab in which you activate this option.

CAUTION

It can be hazardous to create a hyperlink on the Mouse Over tab. You might inadvertently rest the pointer on a hyperlink and launch the hyperlink accidentally during your slide show. Create hyperlinks on the Mouse Click tab to avoid this problem.

After you've selected the options in the Action Settings dialog box, click OK to invoke the Action Settings.

Creating Automated Slide Shows

There are many reasons why people create automated slide shows. You might want to publish them on an Internet or intranet Web site. You might want to have an informational presentation—called kiosk presentations—available in your company's lobby where visitors can look up information about your company or employees. You might need a presentation for a trade show or convention that runs automatically or through interaction with passersby.

PowerPoint has several tools to help you create automated presentations. You can include action buttons in the slides to help viewers move from slide to slide, you can designate the presentation to be self-running, and you can include hyperlinks and Custom Shows in the presentation.

Incorporating Action Buttons in Presentations

PowerPoint contains 12 prebuilt *Action Buttons* that can be inserted into slides to aid in moving around in an automated presentation. These buttons are used with Action Settings, described earlier in this chapter. Most of the buttons have a default hyperlink setting. When you add the button to a slide, you will have the opportunity to accept the default or change the hyperlink destination.

The prebuilt buttons are

- Home—By default, creates a hyperlink to the first slide in the presentation.
- Help—No predefined action. You can create a link to a Word document, Web URL, or other file that contains helpful information.
- Information—No predefined action. You can create a link to a Word document, Web URL, or other file that contains additional information.
- Back or Previous—By default, creates a hyperlink to the previous slide in the presentation.
- Forward or Next—By default, creates a hyperlink to the next slide in the presentation.
- Beginning—By default, creates a hyperlink to the first slide in the presentation.
- End—By default, creates a hyperlink to the last slide in the presentation.
- Return—By default, creates a hyperlink to the last slide you viewed before the current slide.
- Document—Prompts you to specify a program to launch.
- Sound—Prompts you to specify a sound to play.
- Movie—No predefined action. You have to specify a hyperlink to a motion clip.
- Custom—No predefined action. You have to specify the action you want the button to perform.

You can add a set of common Action Buttons to every slide in a presentation by adding them to the Slide Master. Adding an Action Button to a slide is like drawing a shape. You can format, resize, and move the buttons just as you would any other shape or object.

To add a set of Action Buttons to your slides, follow these steps:

1. Open the presentation to which you want to add Action Buttons.
2. Choose View, Master, Slide Master.
3. Choose Slide Show, Action Buttons. A pop-up menu appears.
4. Position your mouse pointer at the top of the pop-up menu and drag the Action Buttons menu off to the side of the screen. This makes it easier to add multiple buttons.
5. Click the button you want to add; the mouse pointer becomes a crosshair.
6. Position the mouse pointer and click; the button is created using a predefined size.

   The Action Settings dialog box appears, as shown in Figure 47.19. Most of the Action Buttons automatically propose actions "on a mouse click." You can accept the default action or change to another action.

   ▶ **See** "Using Action Settings in Presentations," **p. 1283**

FIGURE 47.19
Click to create a button instantly.

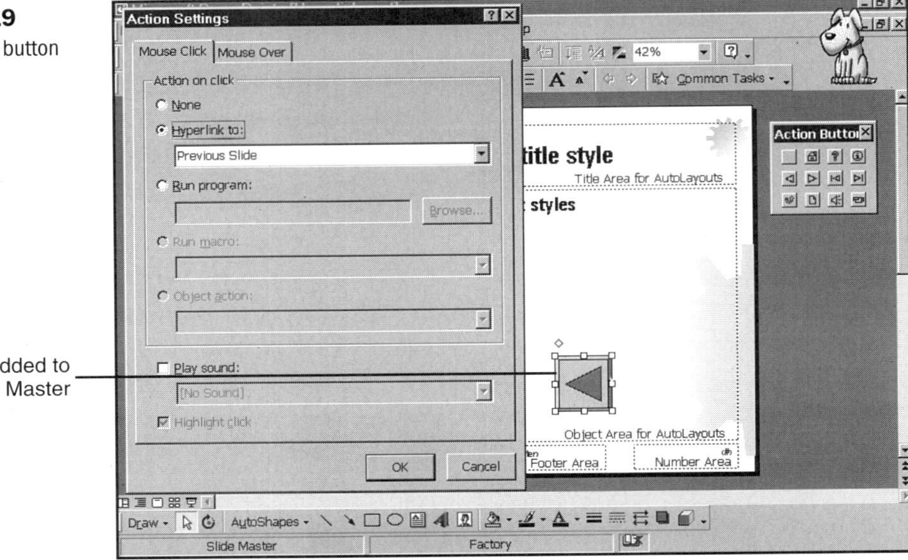

Create as many buttons as you need. Figure 47.20 shows several buttons created at the bottom of the Slide Master.

FIGURE 47.20
Use the Distribute Horizontally command on the Draw menu (on the Drawing toolbar) to space the buttons evenly; choose Draw, Align or Distribute, Distribute Horizontally.

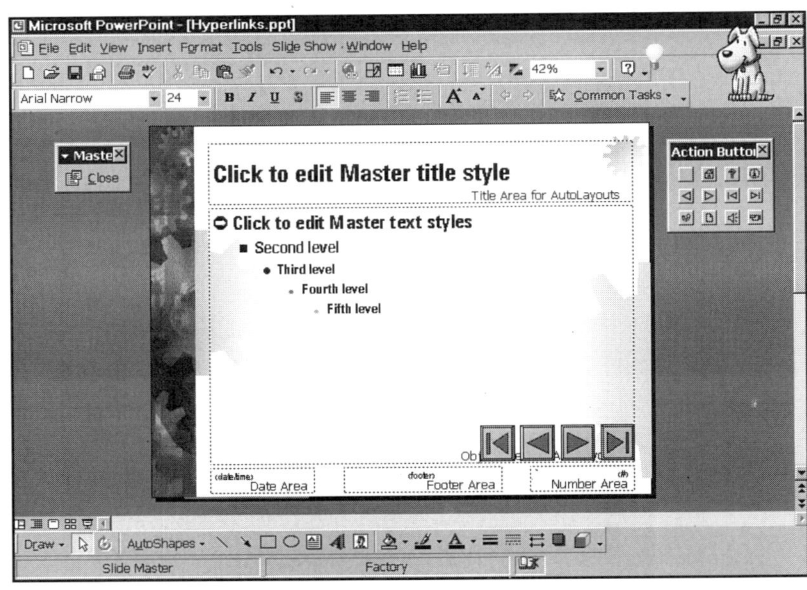

7. Move and resize the buttons as necessary. You can select the buttons and align them through the Align and Distribute options on the Draw menu of the Drawing toolbar.

CAUTION

Be careful where you place the Action Buttons. If you are adding these buttons to an existing presentation, they may display behind existing slide objects. If you can't click directly on the Action Button, you may end up just advancing to the next slide. Try adding these buttons to the Slide Master early on in the presentation-development process. You can then add slide objects around the Action Buttons. Alternatively, you might try making the Action Buttons very small initially to see where they conflict with existing objects.

To add text to an Action Button, right-click the button and choose Add Text from the shortcut menu. Text is centered on the button. To place the text at the bottom of the button, move the flashing cursor to the beginning of the text and press the Enter key a few times to force the text down.

8. You can format Action Buttons by double-clicking the button. The Format AutoShape dialog box appears (see Figure 47.21).

FIGURE 47.21
Change the Fill and Line colors.

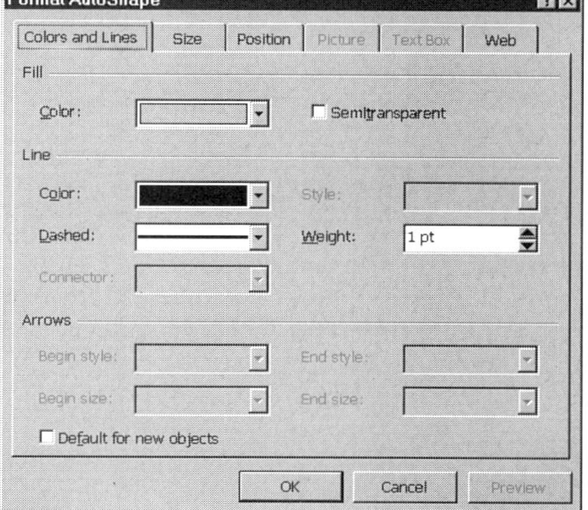

9. Alter the color or apply a gradient or texture fill effect to the buttons. Figure 47.22 shows examples of buttons that have been formatted.
10. After you've added and formatted the Action Buttons, close the Slide Master. The buttons will appear on all your presentation slides, except those using the Title Slide layout.

Action Buttons that need to be added to only a few slides can be added directly to the slides. The steps you take to create and format buttons on individual slides are identical to the steps outlined in this section.

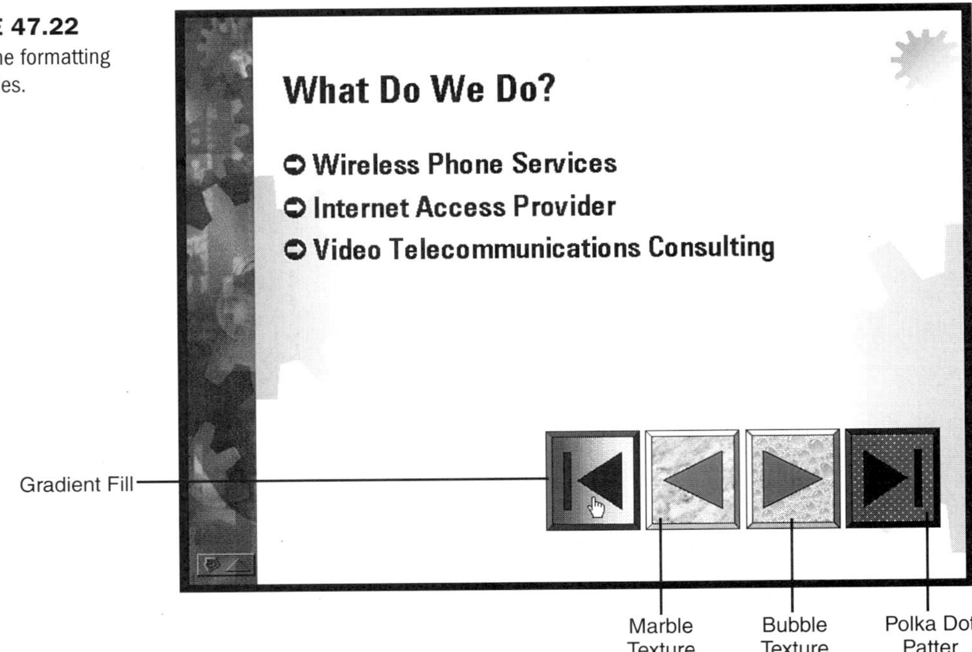

FIGURE 47.22
Explore the formatting possibilities.

Setting Up a Self-Running Presentation

Before you make a presentation a self-running presentation, you must decide whether you want it to advance automatically or have the viewer advance the presentation. If you want the presentation to run automatically (much like a kiosk), you need to add timing to the slides. You can apply slide timings through the Slide Show, Slide Transition command sequence or as a result of rehearsing a presentation.

▶ **See** "Rehearsing Your Presentation," **p. 1270**

If you want the viewer to advance the presentation, you must add Action Buttons to each slide.

After you've decided how you want the presentation to advance, the rest is easy. Choose Slide Show, Set Up Show. The Set Up Show dialog box appears, as shown in Figure 47.23.

NOTE If you are interested in designing a self-running presentation from scratch, see *Special Edition Using Microsoft Office 2000*, Chapter 39, "Creating Self-Running Presentations for Kiosks and the Web."

Click the Browsed at a Kiosk (Full Screen) option. Choose the method you want to use to advanced the slides—Manually or Using Timings, If Present. Then click OK. When you run the slide show, it runs using these settings. Kiosk presentations display full screen and are set up to loop continuously. If a person doesn't activate the presentation first, it automatically restarts after being idle five minutes. Viewers cannot edit kiosk presentations.

FIGURE 47.23
Click the Projector Wizard to get assistance from PowerPoint for setting up the presentation to work with a projector.

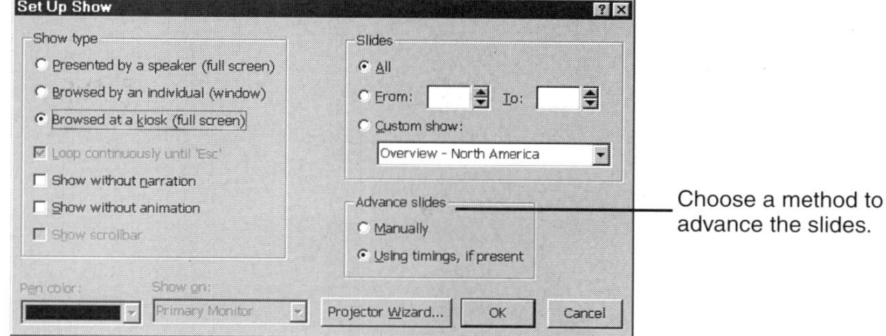

CAUTION

If you choose to advance the presentation manually, you must have Action Buttons on all slides. You cannot advance the slides with the usual keyboard (Enter or Page Down) or mouse (left-click) methods. A mouse click on an Action Button is the only way to manually advance a kiosk-type presentation. You can also use hyperlinks to move around the presentation.

Setting Up Online Presentations

Using PowerPoint's Presentation Broadcast feature, you can deliver a presentation, including audio and video, over your company's intranet. *Broadcasting* a presentation is particularly useful when your audience is coming from different locations.

Additionally, the broadcast can be recorded and saved on a Web server and be available for playback at any time—a handy feature for archiving a presentation or if some people missed the original broadcast.

▶ **See** "Publishing a Presentation on a Web," **p. 1316**

▶ **See** "Using Web Discussions," **p. 1314**

There are a few hardware and software requirements for a Presentation Broadcast. As the presenter, you need Internet Explorer 4.0 or later. To narrate the presentation, a microphone is required. A camera is not required, but video is supported if used.

NOTE If more than 15 people will be viewing the broadcast, a NetShow server is required. NetShow uses streaming multicast technology to distribute a live or recorded audio and/or video broadcast over an intranet. The Office 2000 Resource Kit contains detailed information on NetShow, using audio with a broadcast presentation, and information a system administrator needs to set up and support a NetShow server.

The presentation is broadcast in HTML. Your audience needs a browser, such as Internet Explorer or Netscape Navigator, to view the presentation, and speakers to hear your narration. The broadcast can be viewed on PCs, Macintosh computers, or UNIX workstations.

Scheduling a Presentation Broadcast

To schedule a Presentation Broadcast, you must first open the presentation you want to broadcast. Then choose Slide Show, Online Broadcast, Set Up and Schedule. The Broadcast Schedule dialog box appears, as shown in Figure 47.24. Choose Set Up and Schedule a New Broadcast and click OK.

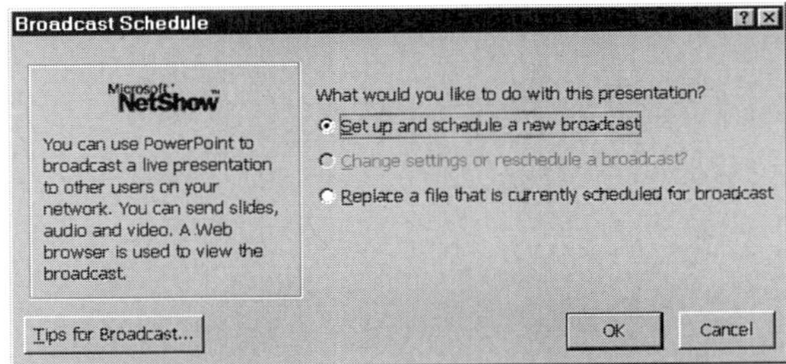

FIGURE 47.24
This is the starting point for scheduling a broadcast or modifying broadcast information.

The Schedule a New Broadcast dialog box appears as shown in Figure 47.25. The information you fill in on the Description tab is displayed on a Web-like page, called the Lobby Page. The Lobby Page provides information to your audience about the Presentation Broadcast.

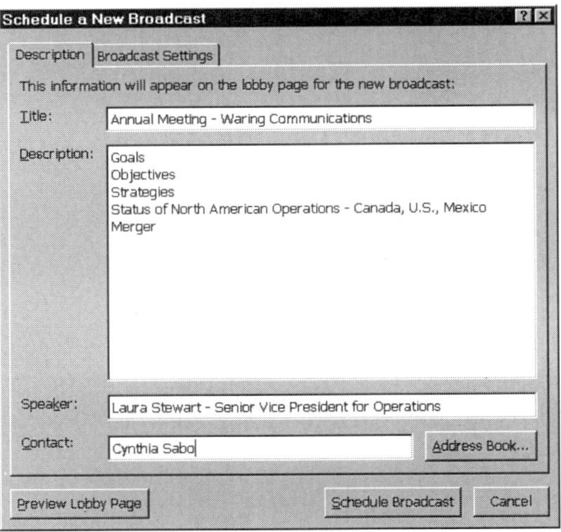

FIGURE 47.25
Provide any information you think the audience would like to know about the upcoming presentation.

NOTE You can preview the Lobby Page in your Web browser by clicking Preview Lobby Page. In the default installation, this option is not installed. You need access to the Microsoft Office 2000 CD-ROM or program files to install this feature.

The Broadcasting Settings tab, shown in Figure 47.26, contains options for the Presentation Broadcast. After you have established the Broadcast Settings, you should not have to change them for future broadcasts. Select or verify the options on the Broadcast Settings tab. These options enable you to

- Include audio and video in the broadcast.
- Allow audience feedback, via email or chat text, during the broadcast.
- Allow the audience to view the speaker's notes during the broadcast.
- Record and archive the broadcast.

FIGURE 47.26
Servers are required for video, chat, and audiences greater than 15.

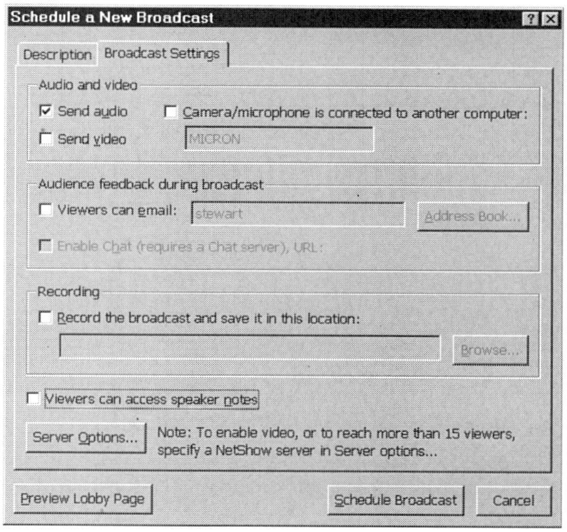

NOTE If you want to use video or you anticipate an audience size of more than 15, you must use a NetShow server on a LAN. Click Server Options to set options for the NetShow server location.

After you have completed the options on both tabs, click the Schedule Broadcast button. If you are using Outlook as your email program, Outlook opens automatically and you schedule the presentation as you would any other meeting in Outlook. If you or your recipients are using some other email program, the URL of the broadcast site will be embedded in your mail message.

Viewing a Presentation Broadcast

When you schedule a Presentation Broadcast, "invitations" are sent to participants as email messages. The broadcast time and date are included in the message. A reminder is sent to each participant 15 minutes prior to the broadcast start time. The reminder contains a Join button that the participants click to view the Lobby Page.

The Lobby Page (shown in Figure 47.27) contains the information the presenter added to the Description tab in the Schedule a New Broadcast dialog box (refer to Figure 47.25).

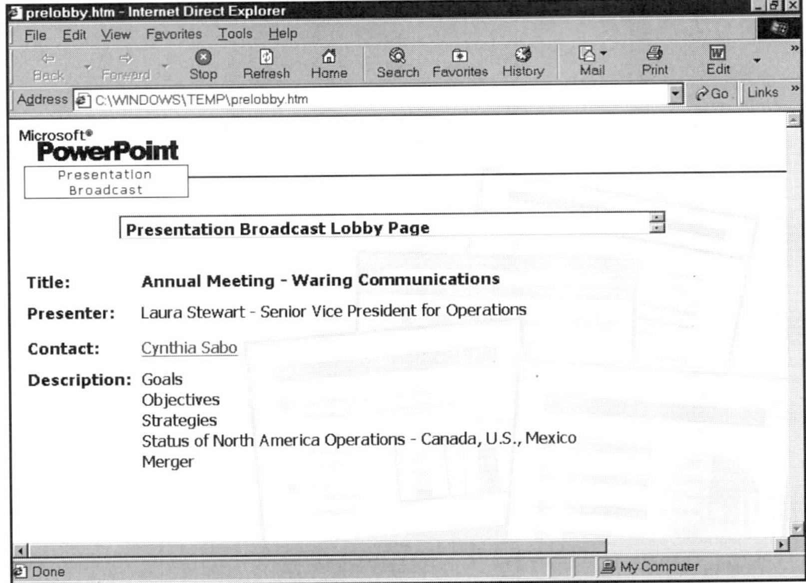

FIGURE 47.27
The Lobby Page opens in your Web browser.

The presenter starts the broadcast from his machine using the Slide Show, Online Broadcast, Begin Broadcast command sequence. The presentation is saved in HTML format and copied out to the specified server location. When the presenter begins, a separate multicast stream with audio, video (if present), and the slide navigation commands is sent to the participants; the slides appear in the participants' Web browser windows.

Avoiding Problems on the Road

When you run a presentation using equipment that was not used to create the presentation, such as a computer or overhead projector, you can run into problems. This includes presentations you deliver in your own company's conference room or at a client's site.

The majority of the problems arise with either equipment differences or trying to access the files or objects you have created links to as part of the presentation.

Suppose you plan to play music or sound clips and you arrive at the site only to discover the machine you will run the presentation on doesn't have speakers.

Perhaps you've created links in your presentation to your company's Web site on the Internet. What if the machine doesn't have a browser installed? What if the room doesn't have access to the appropriate server needed to connect to the Internet? What if the connection requires a username and password?

Maybe your presentation has links to other files that were on your hard drive or a zip drive. Will the presentation be able to find these files when you click the link?

There are several things you can do to avoid these and other problems before they arise:

- Plan ahead—Make sure you ask about the facility and equipment you will be using before you arrive. Try to anticipate possible problems and decide ahead of time what you are going to do if things don't go as planned.
- Arrive early—Test the equipment and every link in your presentation. Make sure you have access to the Internet if you need it and that you've already connected before the presentation starts.
- Use the Pack and Go Wizard—This PowerPoint feature can really help avoid embarrassing problems that can occur with linked objects or files.

Using the Pack and Go Wizard

The Pack and Go Wizard walks you through a quick process of selecting the items you want to take with your presentation. It places a copy of your presentation and supporting files on a floppy disk or other portable storage device. You can even include the PowerPoint Viewer, a piece of software that enables you to run a presentation on a computer that doesn't have PowerPoint.

To use the Pack and Go Wizard, follow these steps:

1. Open the PowerPoint presentation you want to pack up.
2. Choose File, Pack and Go.
3. The initial screen, as displayed in Figure 47.28, provides you with a roadmap of the steps in the wizard. Click Next.

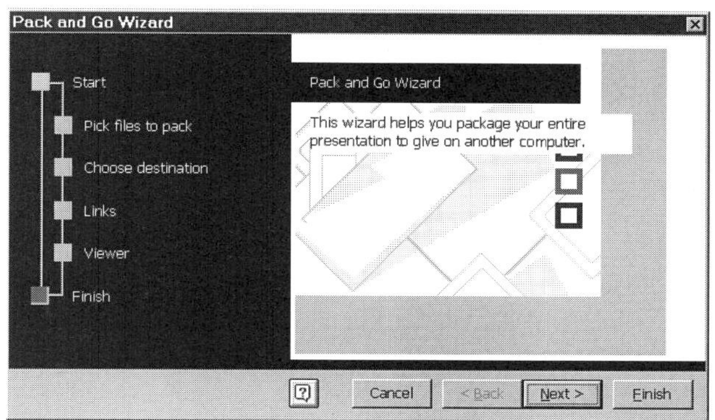

FIGURE 47.28
You can skip to any step in the wizard by clicking the gray button in front of the step.

4. On the first step (pick files to pack), choose Other Presentation(s) if you need to pack other presentations in addition to (or instead of) the current one (see Figure 47.29).

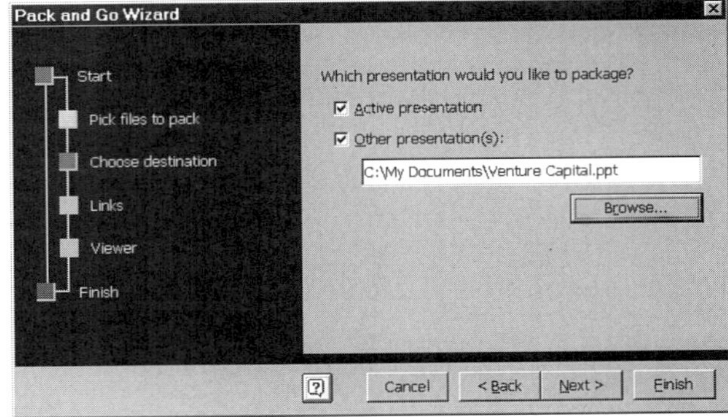

FIGURE 47.29
It is not necessary to pick the files you have links to at this step.

5. Click Browse, and select the other presentations in the Select a Presentation to Package dialog box (which is similar to the Open and Save dialog boxes). Click Select to return to the Pack and Go Wizard. Then click Next. The Choose Destination dialog box appears, as shown in Figure 47.30.

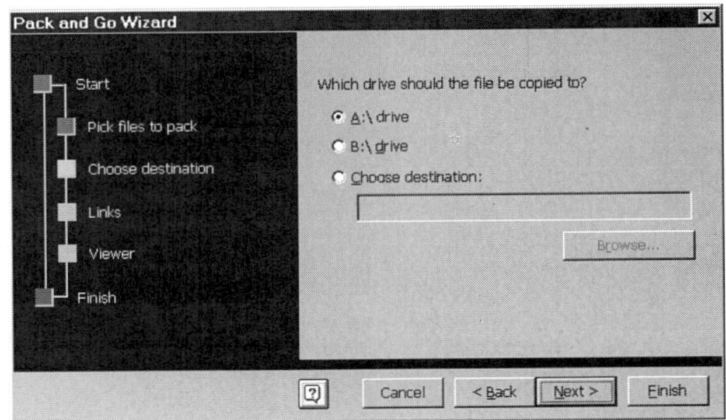

FIGURE 47.30
Choose a floppy disk, zip drive, or other portable media; use the Choose Destination option to pack a presentation to a destination not listed in the dialog box, such as a location on your hard drive.

You can also pack the presentation to a directory on the hard drive. Use this option for presentations that you want to put on multiple floppy disks to distribute—for example, as a handout to the attendees to take back to their offices with them.

6. On the second step, choose the destination you want the files to be packed to. Then click Next.
7. On the third step, shown in Figure 47.31, check to include any linked files and special TrueType fonts that you need to run and display in your presentation. Then click Next.
8. If you anticipate running the presentation on a machine that does not have PowerPoint, make sure you include the PowerPoint Viewer. Then click Next.
9. The final screen of the wizard, shown in Figure 47.32, confirms that you want to copy the files to the destination you selected in step 6. Click Finish.

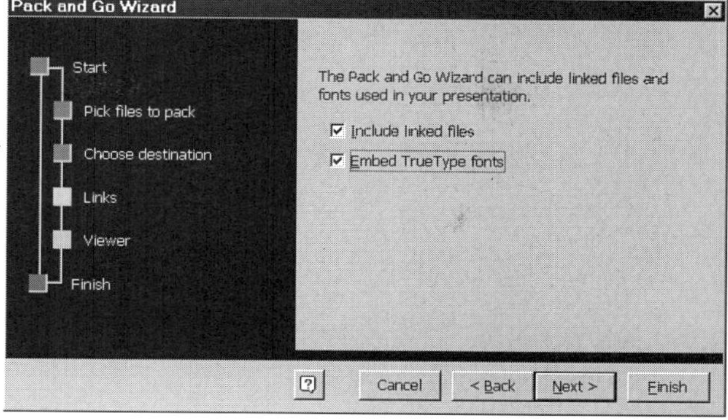

FIGURE 47.31
It's a good idea to check both options.

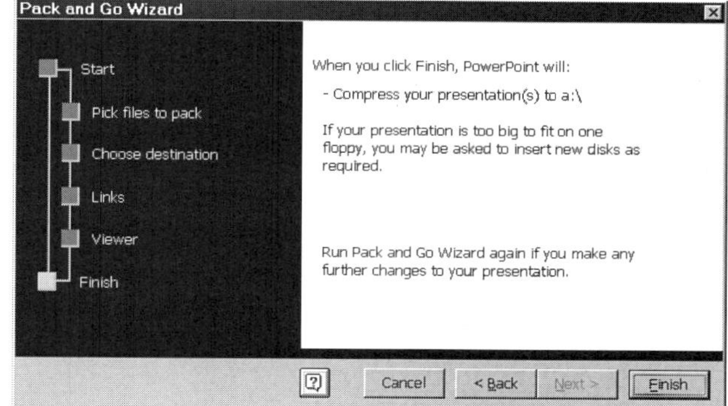

FIGURE 47.32
You can run the Pack and Go Wizard again if you modify the presentation or hyperlinks.

If you make changes to your presentation after you use the Pack and Go Wizard, you can run the wizard again to update it.

Unpacking the Presentation

When you arrive at the site where you will be delivering the presentation, one of the first things you should do is unpack the presentation and test it.

CAUTION

You should unpack and test a presentation long before your presentation is scheduled to start—if possible, the day before. If you are going to be giving an important presentation, consider unpacking it on another machine at work or home before you travel. This way you can work out any problems beforehand.

To unpack a presentation, start by displaying Windows Explorer. Insert the floppy disk (or other storage device containing the packed presentation) and display the contents of the floppy disk. Figure 47.33 shows the contents of the A:\ drive where a packed presentation is stored.

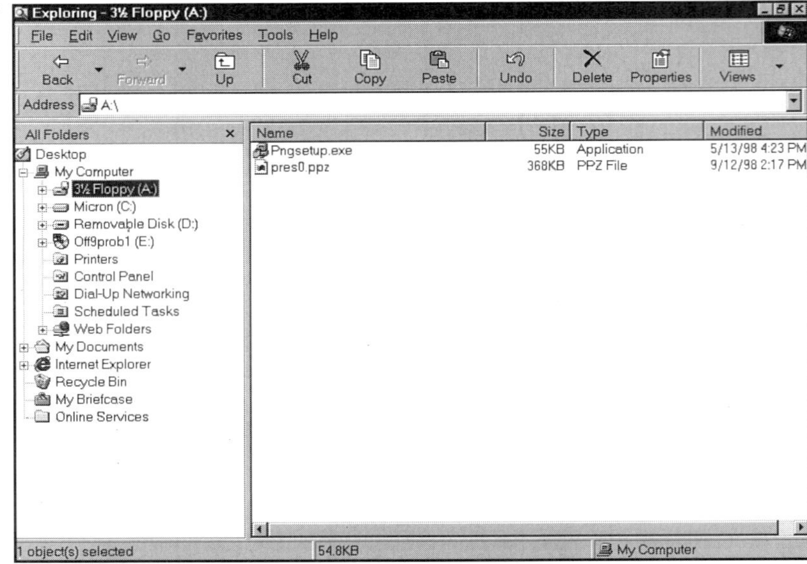

FIGURE 47.33
The Pack and Go Setup application and compressed presentation files are shown in the Explorer window.

Create a temporary folder on the destination drive, with a folder name not longer than eight characters, and without using spaces (see the Note later in this section).

Then double-click the Pack and Go setup application—pngsetup.exe—in the Explorer window. The first screen of the unpack window appears (see Figure 47.34).

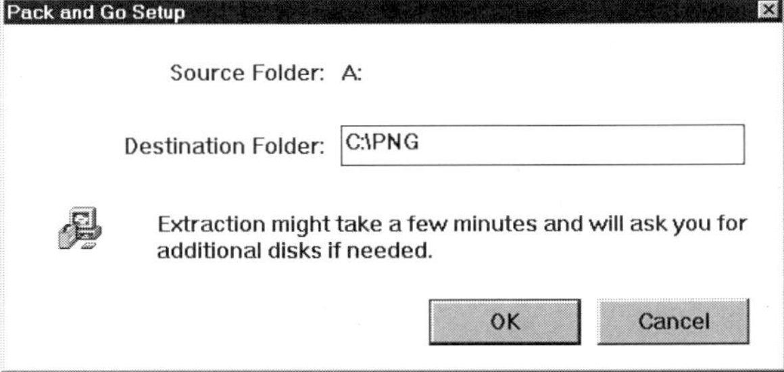

FIGURE 47.34
The default destination is *C:*.

Enter the drive and folder destination where you want the presentation to be unpacked. Click OK. The wizard unpacks the presentation, clips, and hyperlink files in a destination folder you created.

NOTE There is an awkward warning message that displays when you enter the long name for a destination folder, such as My Documents. The wizard accepts only destination names that are a maximum of eight characters, no spaces.

NOTE If you selected a destination folder instead of creating a new one, a warning appears indicating there are files in the destination folder and that any file having the same name as the files you are unpacking will be overwritten.

Then run the presentation to verify the appearance of the slides and the behavior of the hyperlinks.

Problem/Solution—Creating and Using Branch Presentations

You can create a slide that acts as a menu of the topics, or sections, of your presentation. With a menu slide, you can branch off to view the slides in each topic in your presentation; when you reach the end of a topic, you can set up the slides to automatically return to the menu slide.

To create a menu slide that branches to various sections or slides in a presentation, you need to combine several PowerPoint features:

- Custom Shows.
- Action Settings.
- Summary Slides—discussed in Chapter 45, "Advanced Presentation Formatting Features."

Figure 47.35 shows an example of a menu slide that contains hyperlinks to sections or topics in the presentation.

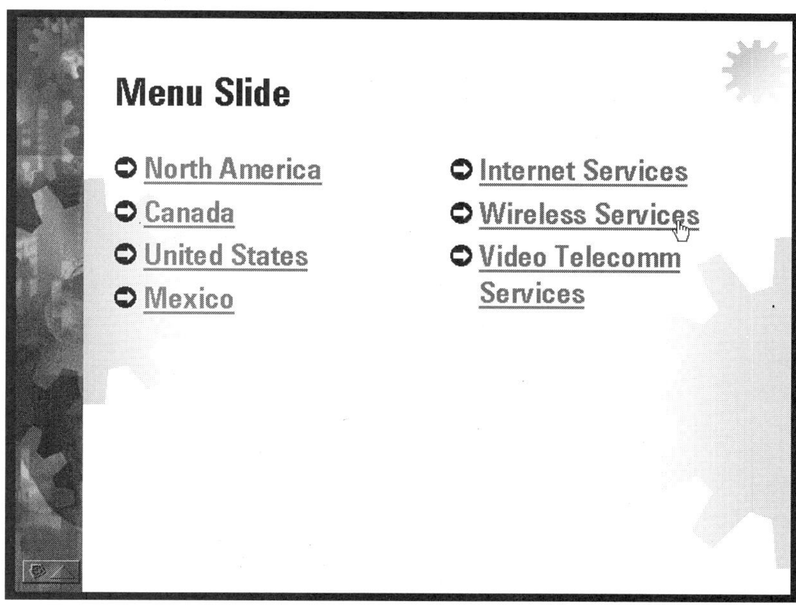

FIGURE 47.35
Text hyperlinks are always underlined and formatted with a special color.

Use the following steps to create a menu-type slide:

1. Open the presentation in which you want to insert a menu slide.

2. Switch to Normal or Outline view. If the titles are unique to each slide, click the Collapse All button to display only the titles of each slide. Otherwise, leave the full slide text displayed in the Outline pane or view.
3. Choose File, Print (do not click the print button on the Standard toolbar). In the Print dialog box, click the Print What drop-down list and select Outline View (see Figure 47.36).

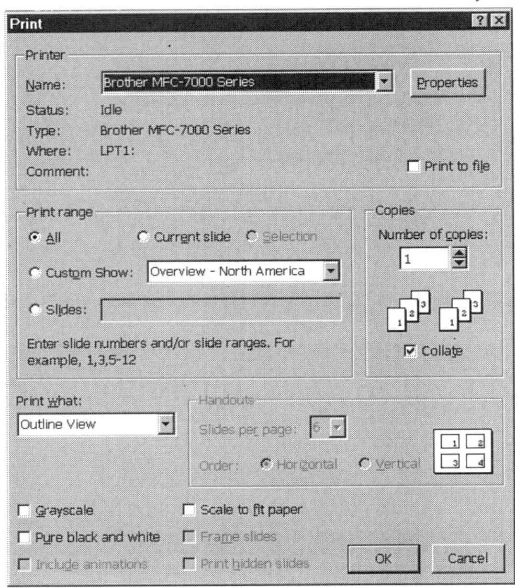

FIGURE 47.36
Use the presentation outline to help create the menu slide.

4. Use the Outline view printout to plan the sections and/or topics to which you want to create branches. It's a good idea to decide exactly which slides will be included in each branch.
5. Create separate Custom Shows for each section and/or topic to which you want to branch in your presentation. Refer to the "Working with Custom Shows" section earlier in this chapter for specific steps on creating Custom Shows.

6. After you have created the Custom Shows, switch to the Slide Sorter view.
7. Select the first slide used in each Custom Show you just created. Remember to press the Ctrl key as you click multiple slides (see Figure 47.37).

8. After all the necessary slides are selected, click the Summary Slide button on the Slide Sorter toolbar.
9. The summary slide is created; a bulleted list displays the slide titles to each of the selected slides.
10. Drag to move the summary slide to the desired position in the presentation.

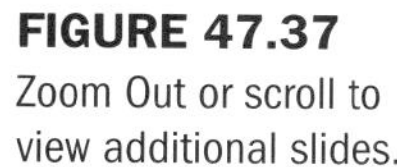

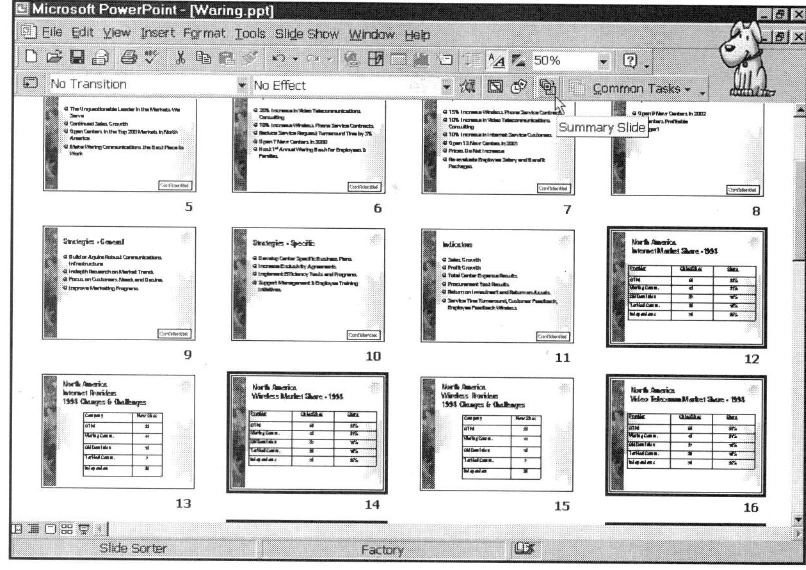

FIGURE 47.37
Zoom Out or scroll to view additional slides.

11. Double-click the summary slide. The Normal view or Slide view appears, depending on which view you were in before you switched to the Slide Sorter view.
12. If necessary, change the text of the bullets to reflect the topic or section name you want to use for each branch. Figure 47.38 shows the modified summary slide.

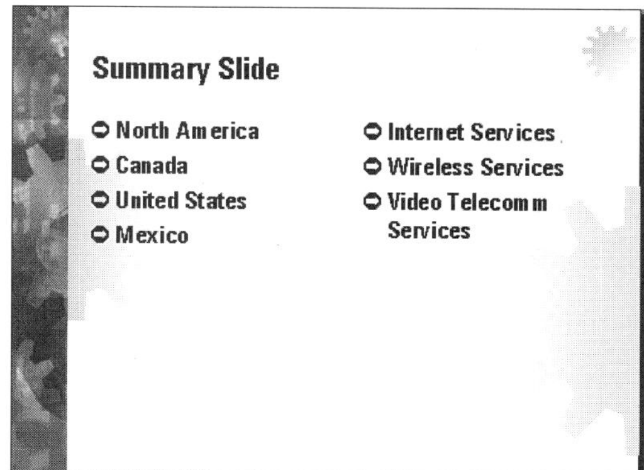

FIGURE 47.38
A two-column bulleted list slide layout was applied; the text was changed to parallel the names of the Custom Shows.

13. Select the text for the first bulleted topic. Then choose Slide Show, Action Settings.
14. In the Action Settings dialog box, create a hyperlink to the Custom Show for that topic, by choosing Custom Shows from the Hyperlink To drop-down list, as shown in Figure 47.39.

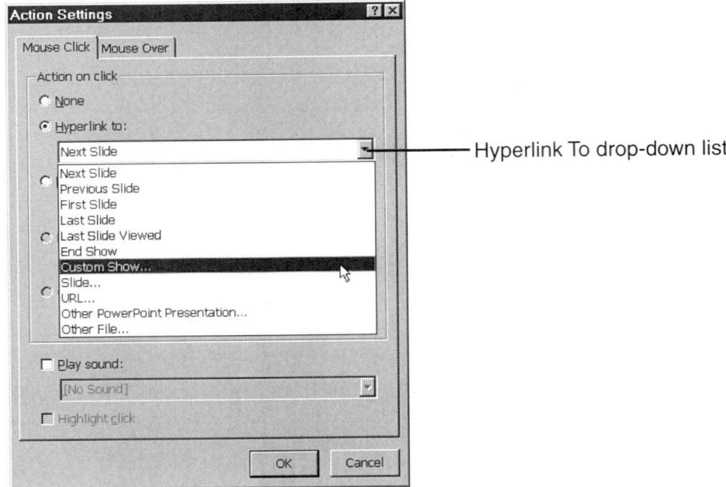

FIGURE 47.39
The Custom Show must be created before you reach this step.

15. Select the Custom Show to which you want to branch from the list and click the Show and Return check box to return to the menu slide after the last slide of the Custom Show (see Figure 47.40).

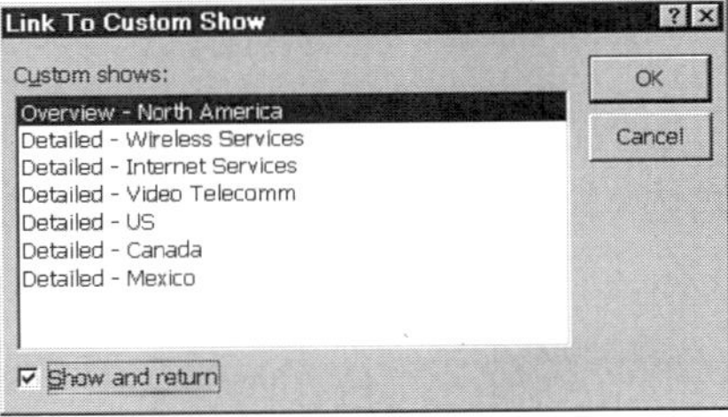

FIGURE 47.40
Always check the Show and Return option for menu slides.

16. Click OK in the Link to Custom Show dialog box, and again in the Action Settings dialog box to create the hyperlink.
17. Select the text for the next branch and repeat the steps to create the hyperlinks to the remaining Custom Shows.

▶ To change the hyperlink color, **see** "Working with Slide Color Schemes," **p. 1229**

CHAPTER 48

Sharing PowerPoint Data with Other Users and Applications

In this chapter

Choosing the Right Collaboration Method

There are several ways to work with others on developing and finalizing a presentation. The collaboration method you choose largely depends on the resources you have available and what time constraints you are under. The following list describes your collaboration options in PowerPoint:

- Embedded Comments—Workgroup members can attach their comments to slides in a presentation. The presentation can either be routed via email, routed via a Zip disk, or saved on a network server to which all members have access. The Reviewing toolbar can be used to show or hide comments and to quickly move from comment to comment in a presentation.
- Email—You can attach a PowerPoint presentation to an email message. The message can be sent simultaneously to all workgroup recipients or you can specify the order of the recipients by using a routing slip. Workgroup members can display the presentation to edit or add comments as necessary.
- Placed on a Zip disk—If the group needing to review the presentation is within close proximity, using a Zip disk is particularly advantageous. Today's presentations often include picture clips, sound, and video files and are usually too large to fit on a single floppy disk. The capacity of the Zip disks makes this an attractive medium to use. Of course, other types of removable media your workgroup uses—such as Jaz or LS-120 cartridges—will work just as well.
- Using a Shared Folder or Drive—A copy of the PowerPoint presentation can either be saved in a folder that is on your PC (to which you give members of the workgroup access) or saved on a shared network drive (to which members of the workgroup already have access). Members can then edit or add comments to the presentation.
- Broadcasting a Presentation—New to PowerPoint 2000 is the capability to show a presentation online and invite workgroup members to discuss the presentation by using audio transmissions, Chat text, or by sending in email comments. The host controls the presentation throughout the broadcast.

  ▶ **See** "Setting Up Online Presentations," **p. 1289**

- Conducting an Online Meeting—During an online meeting, the host allows other members of the workgroup to control the presentation. All members use Chat to send text messages or use the online Whiteboard to make comments, regardless of who is controlling the presentation.

  ▶ **See** "Setting Up an Online Meeting," **p. 70**

- Using Web Discussions—Workgroup members can add comments when it's convenient for them; they do not have to make time to participate in an online meeting. Additionally, if the presentation is changed or if discussion comments are added, you can be notified by email.

  ▶ **See** "Using Web Discussions," **p. 62**

The disadvantage to using email, Zip disks, and embedded comments is that you have to merge everyone's individual comments into one file or you have to wait until the presentation is routed through all the recipients before you can see (and begin responding to) comments being made on the presentation. If you have the resources to use any of the online collaboration options, it expedites feedback on a presentation.

The next few sections describe how to use some of these collaboration options.

Working with Embedded Comments

Anyone who has write-access to a presentation can embed comments in it. Having read-access will not display embedded comments. Comments are attached to individual slides and appear as Post-it notes within the slide. It is a good idea to establish some standards, or ground rules, for a workgroup when using embedded comments:

- The name of the person or, if appropriate, the name of the organization making the comment should appear in the comment box.
- The date of the comment should appear in the comment box.
- Members should be reminded how to move and resize slide objects, as it may be necessary to move or change the size of the comment boxes on the slides.

There are several ways to provide to workgroup members the opportunity to add comments to a presentation. You can attach a presentation to an email message. You can give members access to a folder on your PC in which the presentation is stored. You can save the presentation to a floppy or Zip disk. You can save a copy of the presentation in a folder on a shared network drive. These options are discussed later in this chapter.

Adding Comments to Presentation Slides

To embed comments in a presentation, follow these steps:

1. Open the presentation and display the first slide to which you want to attach a comment.
2. Choose Insert, Comment. A new comment box appears in the upper-left corner of the slide. The Reviewing toolbar appears underneath the other toolbars at the top of the screen (see Figure 48.1).

NOTE The name that appears in the comment box comes from a setting on the Tools, Options dialog box. The name can be changed on the General tab of the dialog box. However, if you are sitting at someone else's computer, you can simply edit the text in the comment box.

3. Type the comment; the text wraps as necessary. To force a new line, press Enter.
4. To add a comment to another slide, display the slide and click the Insert Comment button on the Reviewing toolbar (refer to Figure 48.1).

Encouraging workgroup members to date their comments is a good idea. This way, if several people add comments to the same slide, you can see the chronology of the comments.

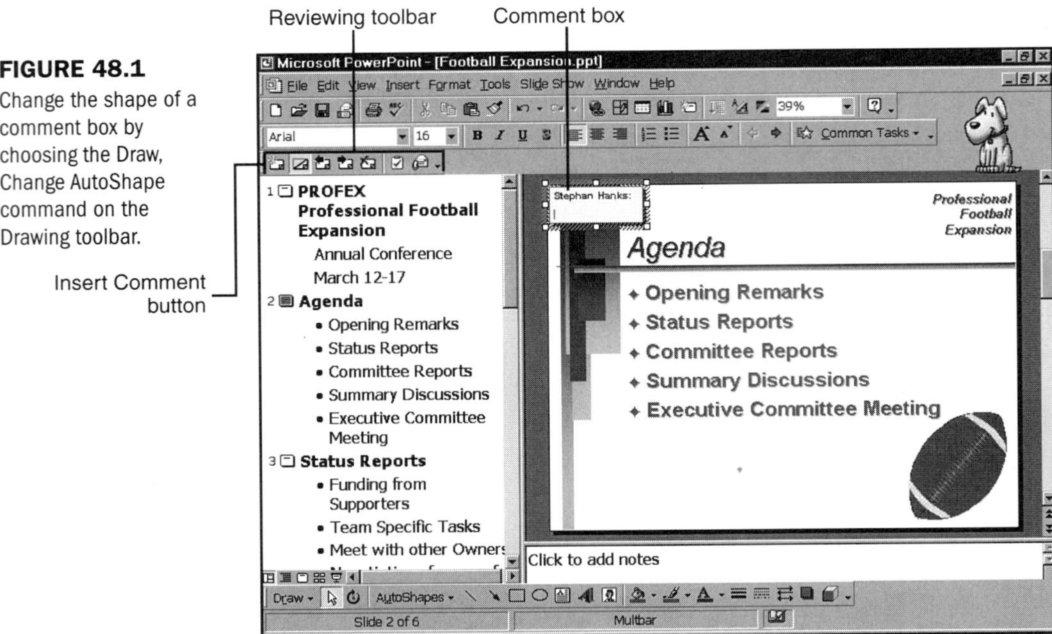

FIGURE 48.1
Change the shape of a comment box by choosing the Draw, Change AutoShape command on the Drawing toolbar.

If more than one person places a comment on a slide, they begin to pile up in the upper-left corner of the slide, as seen in Figure 48.2.

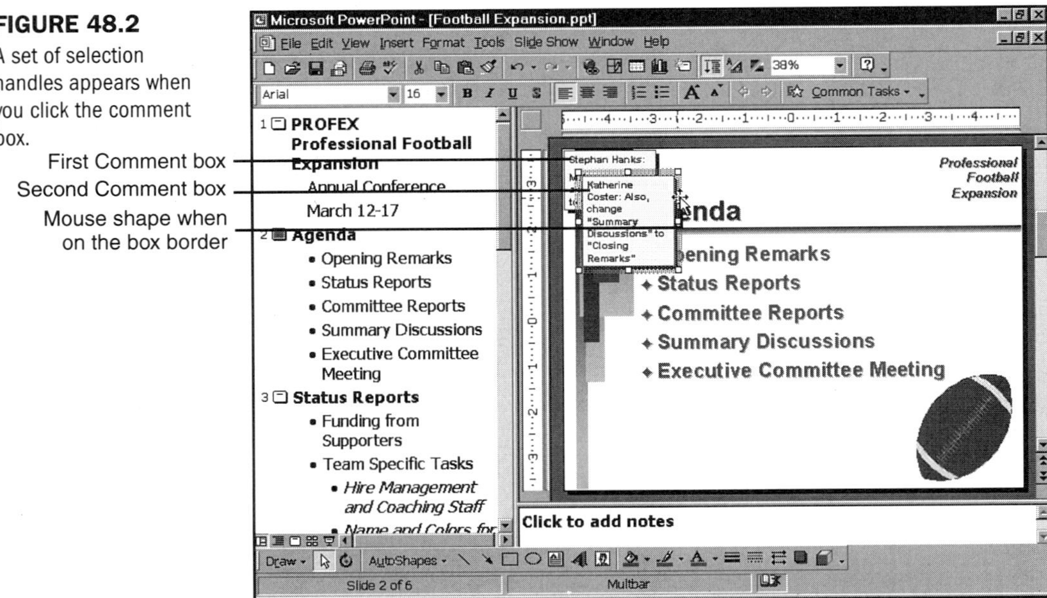

FIGURE 48.2
A set of selection handles appears when you click the comment box.

Encourage workgroup members to move the boxes out of the way. Comment boxes can be moved and resized, just as you would other text boxes. The mouse pointer becomes a four-headed arrow when positioned on the comment box border. Drag the border to move the box. Use the selection handles to resize the box.

Reviewing Comments on Presentation Slides

The Reviewing toolbar contains several useful buttons you can use when going through presentation comments. To display the Reviewing toolbar, right-click any toolbar and choose Reviewing. Typically, the toolbar appears underneath the other toolbars docked at the top of the screen.

This toolbar has buttons for displaying or hiding slide comments, inserting or deleting comments, and moving to the previous or next comment. It also has options to create an Outlook task or attach the presentation to an email message.

NOTE If you're not familiar with Microsoft Outlook Tasks, I recommend that you pick up a copy of *Using Microsoft Outlook 2000*, also published by Que.

Sharing a Presentation with Embedded Comments

There are several ways you can share a presentation with other members of a workgroup.

- You can give them access to a folder on your PC.
- You can send a single slide or an entire presentation through email.
- You can save the presentation to a floppy or Zip disk.
- If you want the presentation reviewed by workgroup members one after the other, you can attach a routing slip to the presentation before sending it through email.
- Finally, you can copy the presentation to a shared network folder where members of the workgroup can view and comment on the slides.

NOTE To attach a presentation to an email message, your email system must be compatible with the Messaging Application Programming Interface (MAPI) or Vendor Independent Messaging (VIM). Microsoft Exchange uses MAPI. Lotus cc:Mail uses VIM.

The next few sections describe how to use these options for sharing presentations with embedded comments.

Giving Others Access to a Presentation on Your PC

One way you can get a group to collaborate on a presentation is to give them access to a folder on your computer that contains the presentation. This option assumes you are on a network.

CAUTION

It is a good idea to consult your IS department or system administrator before giving others access to a folder on your hard drive. It is too easy to inadvertently give others access to your entire hard drive, not give the proper read-write access, or alter one of the other network settings that impact network interaction, such as printing to a network printer.

Use these steps to allow others access to your computer:

1. Click the Start button on the Taskbar and choose Settings, Control Panel.
2. Double-click the Network icon. The Network dialog box appears.
3. On the Configuration tab, click the File and Print Sharing button (see Figure 48.3).

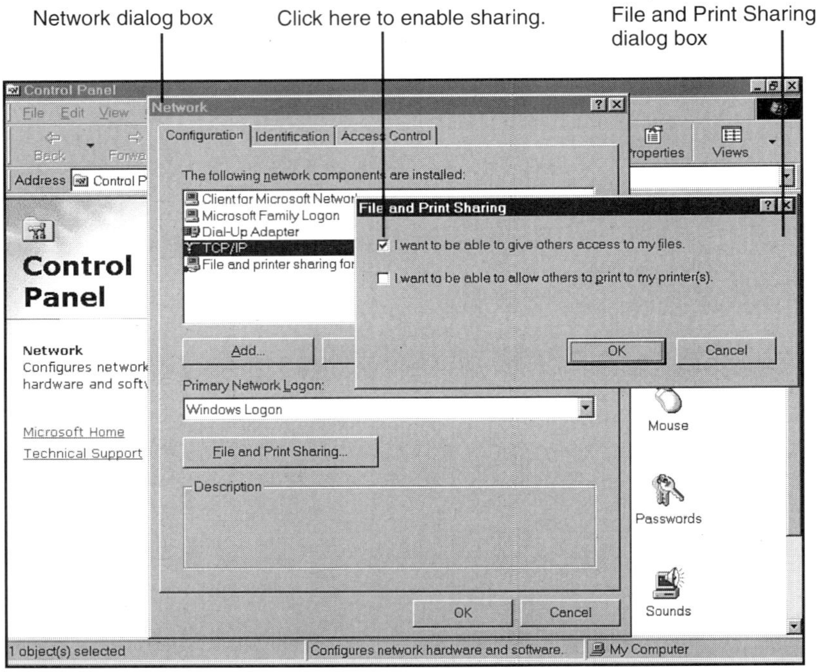

Network dialog box — Click here to enable sharing. — File and Print Sharing dialog box

FIGURE 48.3
Before you can share your folders, you have to change this setting.

4. Select the I Want to Be Able to Give Others Access to My Files check box option.
5. Click OK to close the File and Print Sharing dialog box. Then click OK to close the Network dialog box.
6. You may be prompted to restart your computer or insert the Windows CD to complete this change.

Access to files is given on a folder-by-folder basis. If you don't already have one, use Windows Explorer to create a new folder for sharing files. Then move or copy the presentation to that folder. Using Windows Explorer, right-click the folder that contains the presentation you want to share and choose Sharing from the shortcut menu.

On the Sharing tab of the dialog box, click Shared As. The folder name appears in the Share box. You can change the name of the folder and type a description of the folder in the Comment box. To specify the people you are giving access to, click Add and select the names. You can also specify the type of access you want to give. Choose OK to accept the changes.

Sending Slides or Presentations Through Email

You can send a copy of an entire presentation or just a single slide through email. There is an email button on the Standard toolbar and an email as attachment button on the Reviewing toolbar (see Figure 48.4). Both of these buttons are new to PowerPoint 2000.

NOTE Depending on your setup, PowerPoint might not have the Email (Mail Recipient) icon on the Standard toolbar. For this option to work, Outlook or Outlook Express must be set as your default email client.

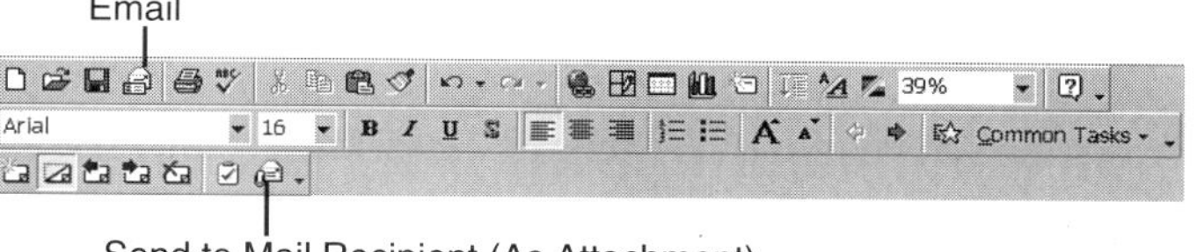

FIGURE 48.4
You can dock or float the Reviewing toolbar, just as with any Office toolbar.

When sending a single slide, the slide is part of the body of the message, not an attachment. The slide is sent in HTML format; recipients must be using an email program that can read messages in HTML format. Outlook 2000 is HTML-compliant. If a recipient is not using Office 2000, it is better to send the presentation as an attachment, rather than in the body of the message.

To send just the current slide, click the Email button on the Standard toolbar. The first time you use this button in a presentation, a message appears asking whether you want to send the entire presentation or just one slide. It also may take a very long time for the message header to appear the first time you use this feature.

Choose Send Single Slide in Message Body. The email message header is displayed in PowerPoint where you can address the message and set message options.

After the slide is sent, the message header disappears. The list of recipients and the message options are saved with the presentation. If you need to send recurring updates of the slide, the message header information previously used is automatically displayed in the message header when you click the Email button.

NOTE PowerPoint remembers whether you have previously sent a single slide from the active presentation. When you click the Email button, PowerPoint assumes you only want to send a single slide (the active slide) again and does not give you the option to send the entire presentation as an attachment. If you want to send the entire presentation, you should use the File, Send To, and choose either the Mail Recipient (As Attachment) or the Routing Recipient command instead of the Email button.

TIP The Email button on the Standard toolbar acts as an on/off button; you can click it to hide the message header.

If you click the Send to Mail Recipient (As Attachment) button on the Reviewing toolbar, a new email message appears in a separate window, and the entire presentation is automatically attached to the message. To view an attached presentation, the recipient needs PowerPoint 97 or PowerPoint 2000.

Routing a Presentation

When you want workgroup members to review a presentation, one after another, you can route the presentation through email. You can track the presentation as it is routed consecutively from one recipient to another, so that you always know where it is. After all recipients have reviewed the presentation, it is automatically returned to you.

To route a presentation to a series of recipients, follow these steps:

1. Display the presentation you want to send.
2. Choose File, Send To, Routing Receipt. The Add Routing Slip appears as shown in Figure 48.5.

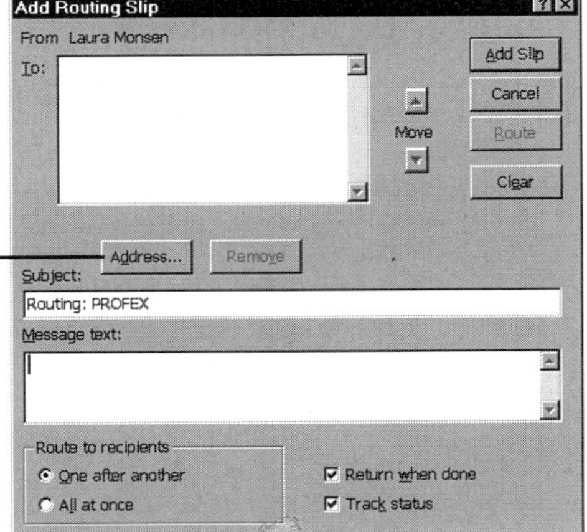

FIGURE 48.5
To remove all recipients, click Clear.

Click Address to add recipients.

3. Click the Address button to add the recipients to the routing slip.
4. Use the Move buttons to change the order of the recipients.
5. Edit the Subject as desired.
6. Enter any comments in the Message text box.

PowerPoint automatically adds text to every routed presentation that tells the recipient how to route the presentation to the next person, so there is no need for you to provide routing instructions in the Message text box.

7. After you've completed the routing slip (Figure 48.6 displays an example), click Route to send the message with the attached presentation.

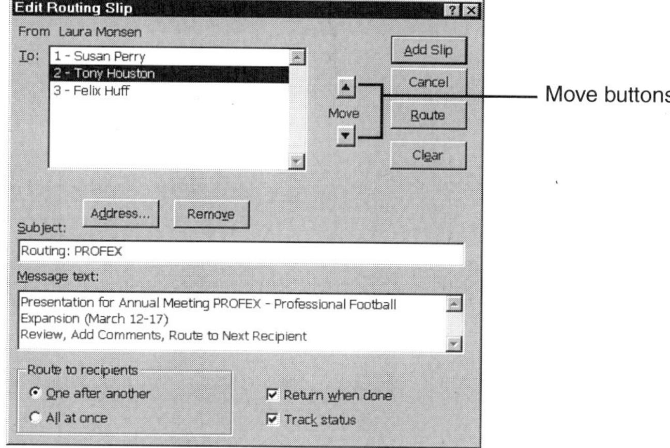

FIGURE 48.6
By default, the presentation is routed back to you when the last person on the list completes their review.

If you do not want to send the message immediately, you can select the Add Slip button instead. This attaches the routing slip to the presentation. You can edit the list of recipients by choosing File, Send To, Other Routing Recipient. When you are ready to send the presentation, choose File, Send To, Next Routing Recipient.

Adding a Presentation to a Microsoft Exchange Public Folder

PowerPoint has a built-in option to copy presentations to Microsoft Exchange public folders. You can also use Windows Explorer to copy presentations to a shared folder listed under Network Neighborhood.

To copy a presentation to a Microsoft Exchange public folder, choose File, Send To, Exchange Folder. A list of folders appears. Select the folder to which you want to copy the presentation.

To copy a presentation to a shared network folder, follow these steps:

1. Open Windows Explorer.
2. Display the folder in which the presentation is currently stored on the All Folders (left) side of the window; the presentation should be listed on the right side of the window.

3. Right-click the presentation name and choose Copy from the shortcut menu.
4. If you already have a drive letter already mapped to a network drive, double-click the drive letter to display a list of folders on that drive. Otherwise, scroll to display Network Neighborhood on the All Folders (left) side of the window and double-click to locate the drive on which the shared folder is located.
5. Select the shared folder to which you want to copy the presentation.
6. Right-click the folder and choose Paste from the shortcut menu.

Creating Web Pages from Your Presentation Slides

PowerPoint 2000 enables you to save a presentation in an HTML (Hypertext Markup Language) format, which allows the presentation to be viewed with a Web browser. Saving a presentation as a Web page is necessary if you plan to take advantage of the Broadcast Presentation feature or you want to publish the presentation on an intranet Web site or an Internet Web site.

▶ **See** "Setting Up Online Presentations," for more information on using the Broadcast Presentation feature, **p. 1289**

Preview Before You Save

Before saving a presentation as a Web page, you can use PowerPoint's preview feature to see how the slides appear in a browser. When you choose File, Web Page Preview, PowerPoint starts your Web browser program and displays the first slide of the presentation. Figure 48.7 shows a presentation in PowerPoint and Figure 48.8 shows the same presentation being previewed in a Web browser.

A navigation bar (similar to the outline pane in the PowerPoint Normal view) is displayed in a frame on the left side of the browser window. The navigation bar acts as a table of contents for the presentation, derived from the titles from each slide in the presentation. Just as with the outline pane, you can move sequentially or randomly through the slides. If you want to hide the navigation bar, click the Outline button in the bottom-left corner of the window.

If there are notes on the presentation slides, they will appear in a frame at the bottom of the browser window (see Figure 48.8). Click the Show/Hide Notes button to toggle the display of the notes. This is similar to the notes pane in the PowerPoint Normal view.

NOTE If you have added animation effects and timing to your presentation slides, the animation is active in the Web Page preview, just as if you were running the presentation in the Slide Show.

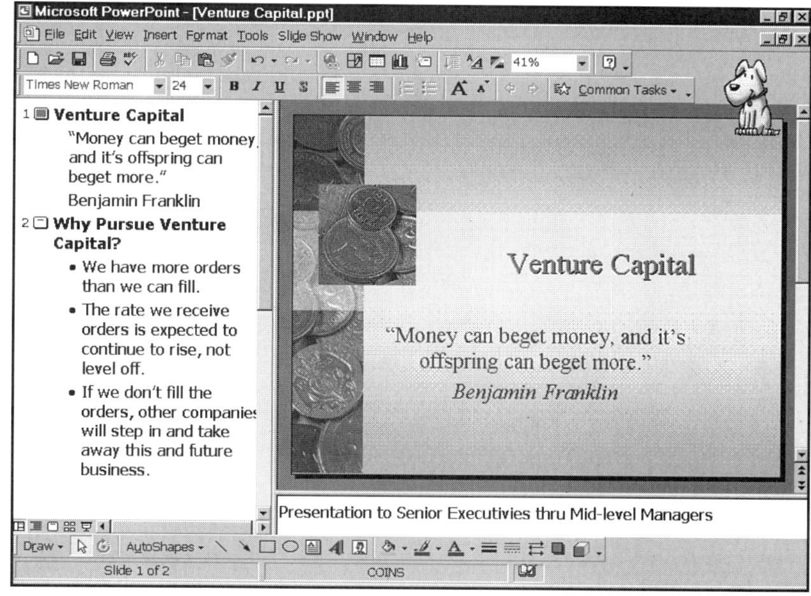

FIGURE 48.7
A presentation displayed in PowerPoint.

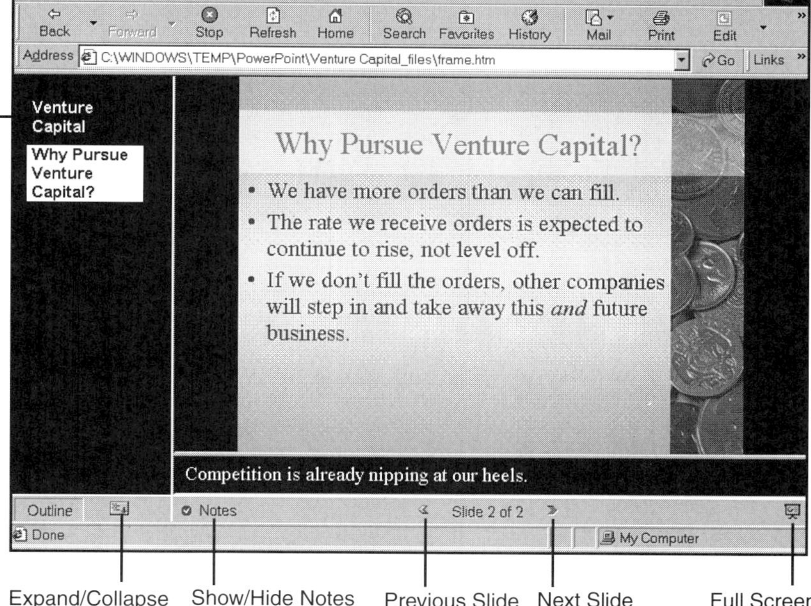

FIGURE 48.8
The HTML version of the presentation displayed in a Web browser.

Saving a Presentation As a Web Page

After you have previewed the presentation as a Web page, you can save it in the HTML file format. When you save a presentation in the HTML format, PowerPoint creates a single HTML document in the folder you designate. It also creates a subfolder (with the same name as the document) to store the components of the document. In PowerPoint, each slide is considered a component and saved as separate files in the subfolder.

▶ **See** "Understanding How Office Stores HTML Files," to learn more about saving files in the HTML format, **p. 14**

Use these steps to save a presentation in an HTML format:

1. Choose File, Save As Web Page. The Save As dialog box appears (see Figure 48.9).
2. Use the Save In drop-down list or Places Bar to locate the folder in which you plan to save the presentation.
3. Click the Change Title button if you want to type a different Title for the presentation HTML file. This title appears in the Title Bar in your Web browser when you display the presentation.
4. If you want to save the presentation with a different name, type the new name in the File Name text box. The Web file type (.htm) automatically is added as the file extension.
5. Click Save to save the presentation as an HTML file.

FIGURE 48.9
Supporting files are saved in a separate folder.

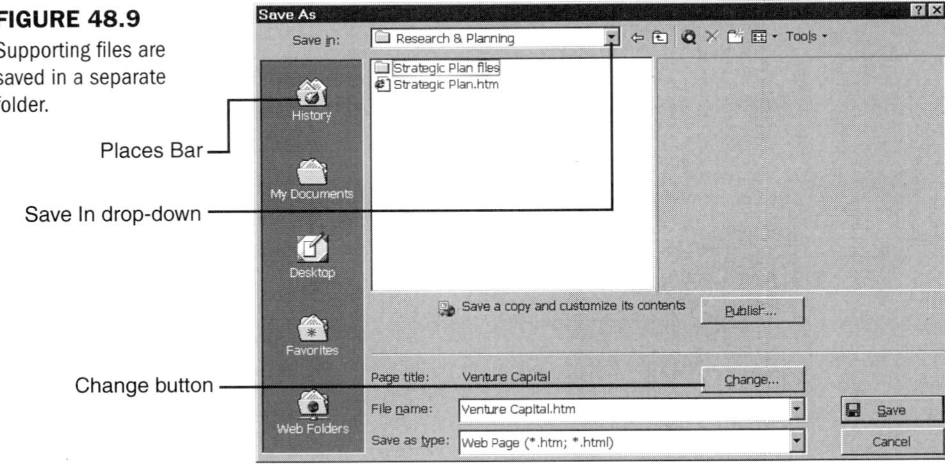

After you have saved the presentation as a Web page, you should confirm its appearance in the browser window.

▶ **See** "Publishing a Presentation on a Web," **p. 1316**

If your Web page doesn't appear as you expect, use PowerPoint's help screens to find out how to correct the problem. In the Office Assistant Search box, type `web pages`; then press Enter or click Search. From the list of help topics, choose Troubleshoot Web Page Options.

Conducting Online Meetings

Online meetings are akin to conference calls, except they are conducted through your computer and make use of a number of network features (such as email and chat rooms) and are capable of transmitting video. Online meetings are conducted using Microsoft NetMeeting, which comes with Office 2000. NetMeeting is actually part of Internet Explorer 5.0, but can be used from within all the Office applications.

You can either host an online meeting or be invited to participate in one. You can schedule a meeting ahead of time (where you invite others to participate) or you can start an impromptu meeting from within the PowerPoint presentation you want to discuss.

In PowerPoint you can set up a meeting using the scheduling features of Outlook. To schedule an online meeting, choose Tools, Online Collaboration, Schedule Meeting. An Outlook meeting request window appears (to see all the options in the meeting request window, maximize the window). You can choose the participants, identify the day and time of the meeting, and even set up a reminder for the participants. Figure 48.10 shows an example of an Outlook meeting request for a PowerPoint presentation.

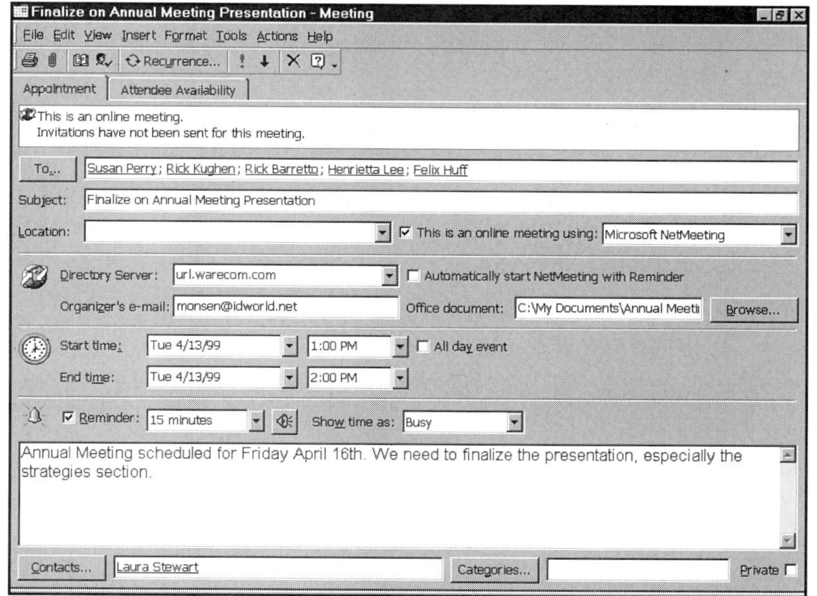

FIGURE 48.10
The name of your default Web server, your name, and the name of the active file are automatically filled in the Outlook meeting request form.

Most of the options in the meeting request window are easy to decipher. However, if you need more information on an option, use the Help, What's This feature command.

NOTE If your colleagues don't use Outlook, you can always coordinate a meeting through email, although you won't have any of the group-scheduling features available to Outlook users. ■

You can also conduct an impromptu online meeting by selecting Tools, Online Collaboration, Meet Now. NetMeeting asks you to identify the participants. In order for the participants to receive your invitation, NetMeeting must be running on their computers. If the participants are available and accept your invitation, the online meeting begins.

NOTE You can also start NetMeeting independently from PowerPoint by clicking the Start button on the Task Bar and choosing Programs, Microsoft NetMeeting. ■

To learn more about participating in an online meeting, see Chapter 3.

▶ **See** "Setting Up an Online Meeting," **p. 70**

Using Web Discussions

If you can't get a group together for an online meeting, a great alternative is to use Web Discussions. Web Discussions are a new feature in Office 2000 that enables people to comment on any document to which they have read access. In PowerPoint, this can include presentations in a shared folder on network server, presentations on a company intranet, or even presentations you access on the Internet. Presentations do not need to be saved in the HTML file format in order to use Web Discussions; you also can comment on presentations stored in the .ppt format.

Discussion comments are not embedded or stored with the presentation. They are stored on a Web server and displayed when you display the presentation.

Chapter 3, "Unleashing the Office 2000 Web Tools," describes the resources necessary to take advantage of Web Discussions. That chapter also explains the basic steps necessary to add and reply to discussion comments.

▶ **See** "Online Collaboration," **p. 61**

Web Discussions have some big advantages over other modes of collaboration:

- Convenience—You don't have to assemble everyone at a set time to attend a meeting. Workgroup members can review the presentation at their convenience.
- Notification—You can subscribe to a document. When the presentation is modified, such as when comments are added to it, you will be notified by email.

Besides adding comments about a presentation, you can also reply to comments, creating *discussion threads*. The comments are not attached to any particular slide, but appear regardless of the slide you have displayed.

To add a discussion comment, click the Insert Discussion About the Presentation button on the Discussions toolbar. The Enter Discussion Text dialog box displays (see Figure 48.11). The Discussion Subject is displayed in a gray banner to separate one discussion thread from another.

Since Web Discussions are added on a presentation-by-presentation basis, it is important to identify the slide and topic on which you are commenting.

FIGURE 48.11
The discussion subject will appear at the top of the discussion thread.

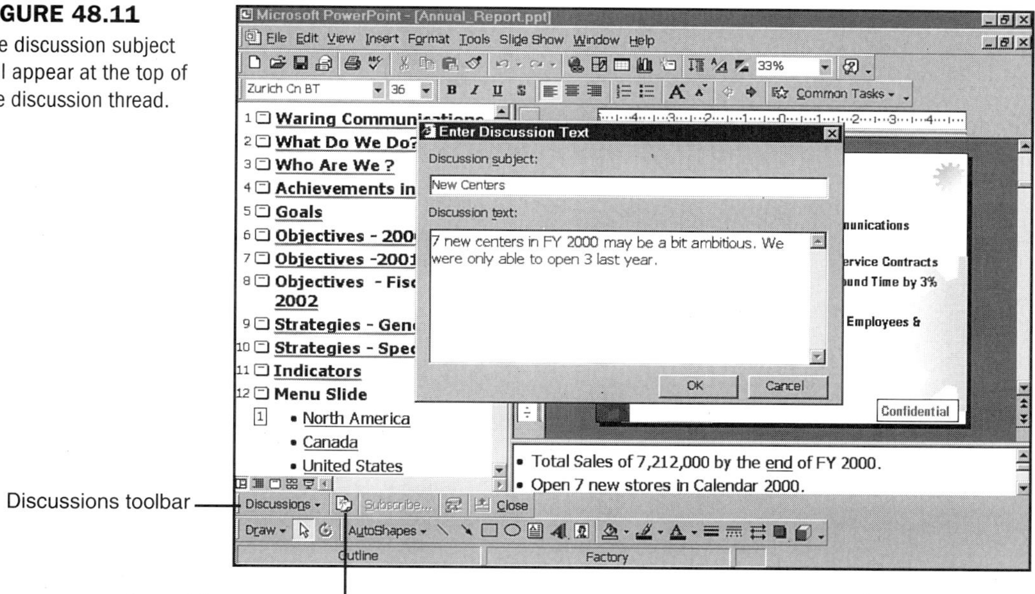

When replying to discussion items, make sure you locate the correct item you to which you want to reply. To add a comment to the overall discussion, reply to the first item in the discussion thread. A reply is always slightly indented underneath the discussion item you select when replying.

One of the other Web Discussion features is Subscription and Notification. You can monitor a specific presentation or folder to which you have at least “read access.” You have the option to be notified when a document is edited, discussion comments are added, or when items are added to or removed from a folder. You can even b e notified when a particular person makes changes to a folder.

Most of the subscription and notification options are self-explanatory. However, Chapter 3 contains specific descriptions of each option.

Publishing a Presentation on a Web

Saving a presentation as a Web page to a Web server is known as *publishing* a presentation. Unlike just saving a presentation as a Web page, when you publish a presentation you have the choice of saving just the active slide, a group of consecutive slides, a Custom Show, or the entire presentation. Regardless, the slides are saved in an HTML format and given an .htm file extension.

NOTE Before you can save a presentation on a Web server, you must have access to a server. Your system administrator will be able to tell you which Web server supports the use of Web Folders.

To publish a presentation to a Web server:

1. Display the presentation that contains the slides you want to publish.
2. Choose File, Save As Web Page. A modified version of the Save As dialog box appears.
3. Click the Places Bar to locate on the Web server the Web folder in which you plan to save the presentation.

   ▶ **See** "Saving to a Web Server," **p. 60**

4. Click the Publish button. The Publish As Web Page dialog box appears, as shown in Figure 48.12.
5. In the Publish What? section (at the top of the dialog box), choose one of the options to indicate what you want to publish. You can publish your entire presentation or selected slides. By default, the Speaker Notes are included with the published slides.

CAUTION

Unless you really want to share Speaker Notes with others, you should remove the check in the Display Speaker Notes box. It might be really embarrassing to have someone read notes like "Smile when you deliver the bad news" or "Don't let the discussion stray here."

6. The Web Options button displays a separate dialog box (see Figure 48.13) for the output options for the HTML Web Page. These options include slide transitions and other animation, scaling of slides and graphics, and resolution. After you make your selections in the Web Options dialog box, click OK to return to the Publish As Web Page dialog box.

NOTE PowerPoint 2000 is the first application to generate HTML that scales automatically for different screen resolutions and window sizes.

7. In the Browser Support section of the Publish As Web Page dialog box (refer to Figure 48.12), choose which browser (Netscape Navigator, Internet Explorer, or both) your presentation supports. The last option creates a dual-output format, which checks the browser type and version and displays only the presentation information that the browser used by your viewer(s) can support.

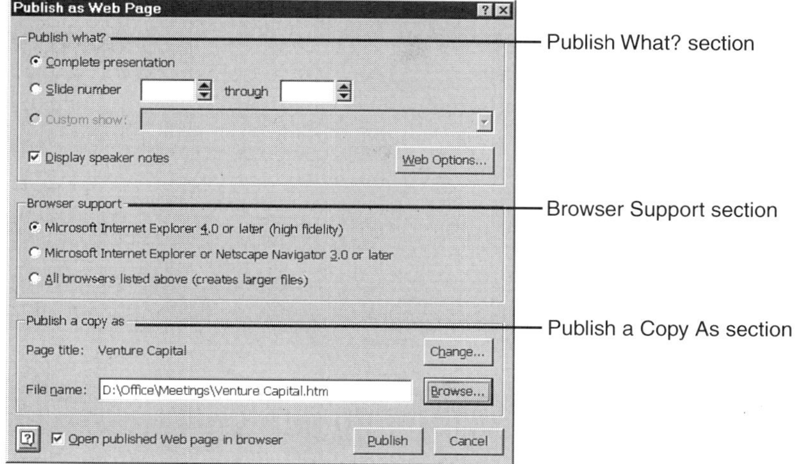

FIGURE 48.12
After you click Publish or press Enter, a copy of the presentation is saved as an HTML file to the Web server you designated.

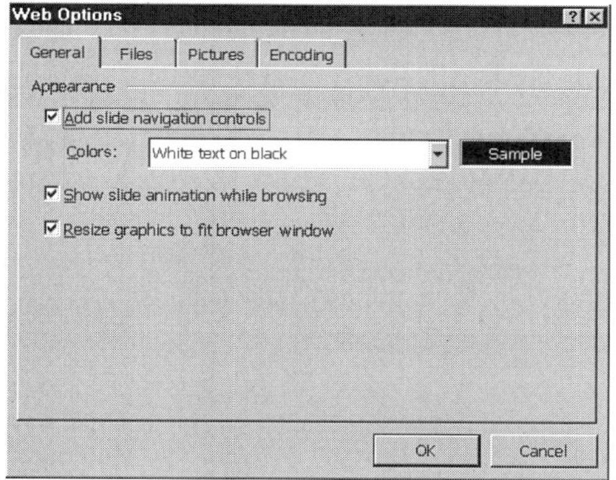

FIGURE 48.13
After you click Publish or press Enter, a copy of the presentation is saved as an HTML file to the Web server you designated.

8. The Publish a Copy As section is where you designate the location and title of the presentation you are publishing. You can click the Change button to alter the text that appears in the Title bar when this file is displayed in the browser.
9. The location you selected in the Save As dialog box (see step 3) should appear in the File Name text box. If you've changed your mind about where you want to save this file or if you want to save the file with a different name, click the Browse button.
10. If you want to have the Web Page displayed immediately in your browser, leave the Open Published Web Page in Browser checked at the bottom of the dialog box. Otherwise, uncheck the option.
11. After all the settings have been selected in the dialog box, click Publish to save a copy of the presentation as an HTML file on the Web Server.

If you left the default setting to Open Published Web Page In Browser, the slide(s) or presentation immediately displays in a browser window. Figure 48.14 shows an example of a published Web Page. A Navigation bar is displayed on the left side of the window. It contains a list of each slide title and acts as a table of contents for the Web page. Additionally, if Speaker Notes were attached to the slides, there is an option at the bottom of the browser window that lets you display a Notes frame.

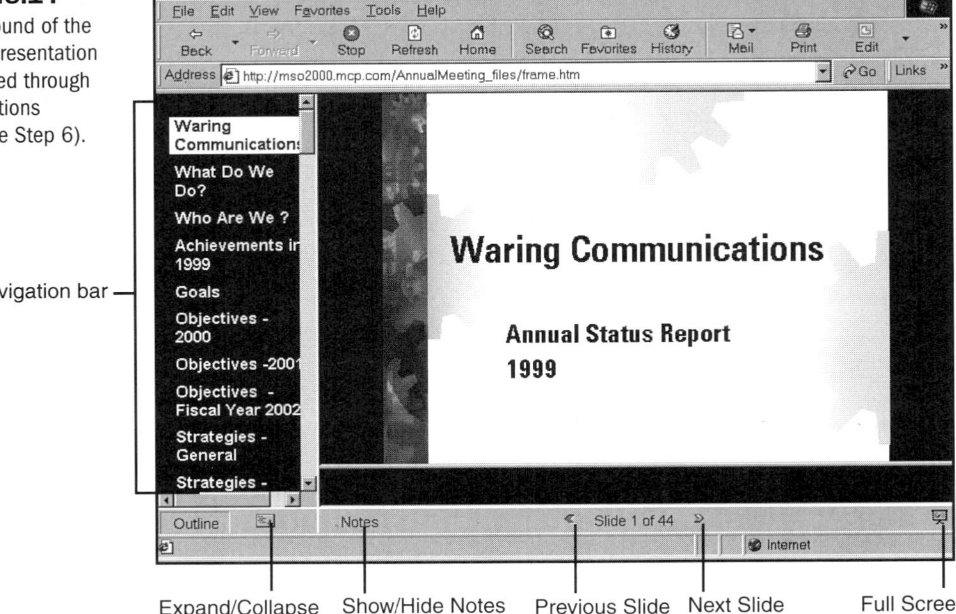

FIGURE 48.14
The background of the published presentation is established through the Web Options settings (see Step 6).

Importing and Exporting Data

Importing and exporting data simply saves you the time and trouble of re-creating data that already exists elsewhere.

When you want to share information with another Microsoft Office application, you can use the copy and paste commands to import or export data. In some circumstances you can open a file to import data into PowerPoint. PowerPoint also has a built-in option to send presentation information to Word by using the Send To command.

When you want to share information with applications that are not part of the Microsoft Office suite, you use the built-in file format converters to import and export the data. You can import presentations created in Lotus Freelance or Harvard Graphics. You can save the presentation text in Rich Text Format (.rtf) file format, or save the slides as graphic images, which can then be opened in other programs.

There are many ways you can share information among Office applications. The technique you choose depends on several things: how the information is displayed in PowerPoint, whether the information updates in the target document when it changes in the source document, and with whom you want to share the information.

The most common techniques for sharing information among PowerPoint and other Windows applications are

- Copy and paste—Information is copied from one program and pasted into another program. This technique adds the information to the target document. Unless the Paste Link or Paste Special commands are used, the information in the target document is static. It is a "picture in time" or snapshot of the information at the moment it is pasted.
- Drag and drop—Used to copy or move information between two open documents. This technique is useful only for small pieces of information and if you display both documents onscreen at the same time. Using the Ctrl key as you drag creates a copy rather than moving the information.
- Hyperlinks—A link (typically represented by colored or underlined text) is created to information in another application. This technique provides access to the most current data with having to add it to the presentation.
- Opening and saving in other file formats—To share large amounts of information, you can use this technique to open a document created in another application or save a PowerPoint presentation or slide in another file format. Converters accompanying Office 2000 make it possible to share information with many other applications, including other Office and non-Office applications.

Importing Excel Data into a PowerPoint Slide

You can copy or link data from an Excel worksheet into a PowerPoint slide. The data is pasted in as a slide object, similar to a picture clip. Slides that contain linked Excel data are updated when the Excel data is changed. Follow these steps to copy or link data from Excel:

1. Select the data in Excel you want to show in PowerPoint.
2. Click the Copy button or choose Edit, Copy.
3. Switch to PowerPoint and display the slide you want the data to appear on.
4. To copy or link the data into the slide, you should choose Edit, Paste Special (see the following sidebar about using the Paste command). The Paste Special dialog box appears, as shown in Figure 48.15.
5. To copy the data into the slide, choose Microsoft Excel Worksheet Object.

   To link the data into the slide, click the Paste Link option button. Then choose Microsoft Excel Worksheet Object.
6. Choose OK. The data is pasted into the slide. Figure 48.16 shows examples of the same Excel data pasted in using the HTML file format and pasted in using the Paste Link option.

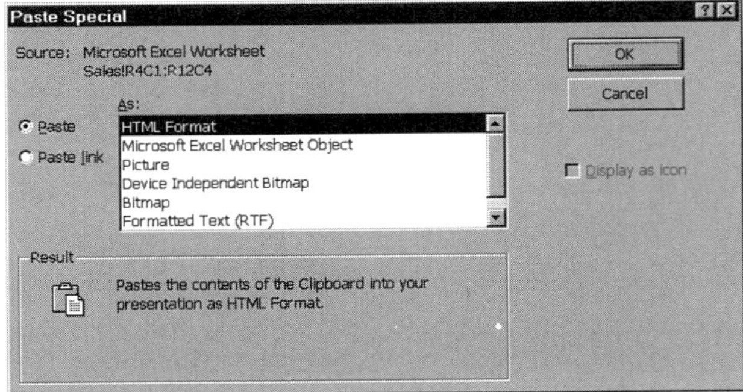

FIGURE 48.15
The Result section of the dialog box provides information about the selected Paste option.

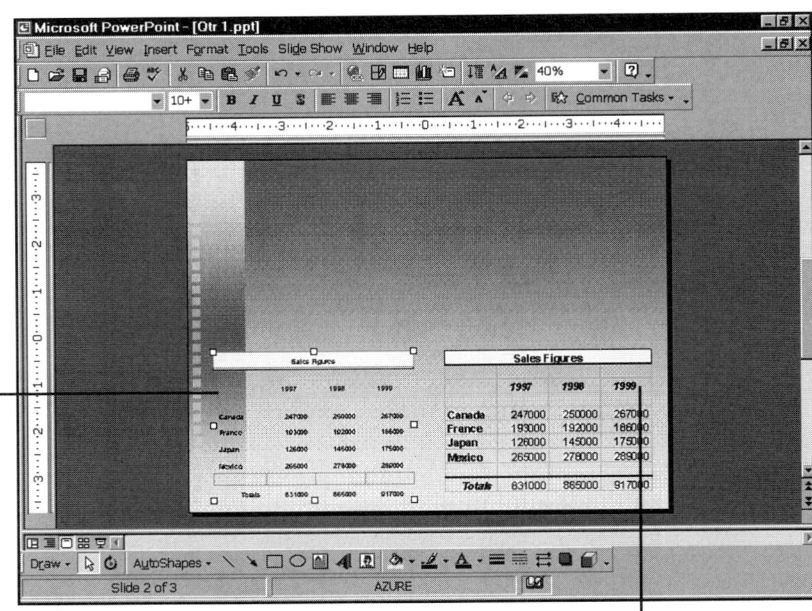

FIGURE 48.16
Excel data pasted in using the HTML file format.

Avoid the Paste Command

When you paste data into PowerPoint using the Paste command or the Paste button on the Standard toolbar, the data will be pasted in using the HTML format and may appear distorted in the slide or display awkwardly.

The HTML format pastes the data in as separate components, similar to a grouped object. You can select and edit the components individually. And, in theory, you can move and resize the entire object. But when you resize the data, the font does not resize. The Excel data that appears on the left side of the PowerPoint slide in Figure 48.16 was pasted in and resized; as you can see, the font did not increase proportionally and there is a stray set of gridlines between the last row of data and the totals.

You can select the object and use the Font Size drop-down on the Formatting toolbar to change the data font size. To remove the stray gridlines, you will have to ungroup the object and delete the cells showing gridlines.

In addition to these problems, when you use the Paste command, you do not have the option of linking data to the original source. If the data changes in Excel, the PowerPoint slide will continue to reflect the old data.

You can avoid these types of problems by using the Paste Special command as described in the preceding steps.

CAUTION

Always resize the Excel object using a corner selection handle; otherwise, the data may become distorted.

Any formatting on the Excel worksheet cells is copied into PowerPoint. Notice the gridlines in the linked example in Figure 48.16. To darken the gridlines, apply borders to the cells you want to copy and format the border color to complement the PowerPoint slide and background. You have to hide the gridlines in the Excel worksheet if you don't want them to show up on the linked data in the PowerPoint slide.

When you open a presentation that contains linked data, a message asks whether you want to update the links as the file opens. Sometimes you have to manually update the linked data. This usually occurs when you have both the Excel worksheet and PowerPoint presentation open at the same time and have been making changes to the Excel data. In PowerPoint choose Edit, Links, Update Now to update the linked data.

Importing Spreadsheet Data into a PowerPoint Chart

When you create charts in PowerPoint a separate program, Microsoft Graph, is used. The data for the chart is stored on the Microsoft Graph Datasheet. Before bringing spreadsheet data into the Datasheet, you need to clear the sample data. Select the gray cell in the upper-left corner of the Datasheet to select all the cells and press Delete. Click the first cell in the Datasheet that is not gray, at the intersection of the row and column used for the data labels (see Figure 48.17). This indicates where you want the data being imported to begin.

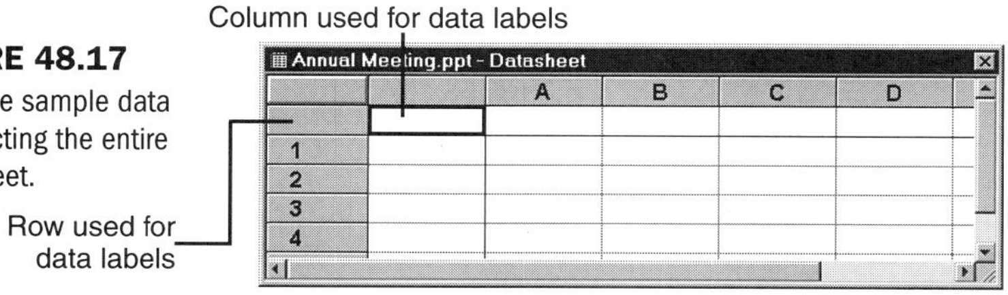

Column used for data labels

Annual Meeting.ppt - Datasheet

		A	B	C	D
1					
2					
3					
4					

Row used for data labels

FIGURE 48.17
Clear the sample data by selecting the entire Datasheet.

There is an Import File command in Microsoft Graph that can copy data from Excel or Lotus 1-2-3 into the Microsoft Graph datasheet. However,

- You have to know the specific cell references of the data you want brought in or you have to import the entire sheet.
- A copy of the data is brought into the Microsoft Graph datasheet; you cannot link to the spreadsheet data.

To use the Import File command in Microsoft Graph, choose Edit, Import File. The Import File dialog box appears. Locate and select the file whose data you want to import. When you click Open, the Import Data Options dialog box (shown in Figure 48.18) appears. Select the sheet or type the cell references you want to import, and then choose OK.

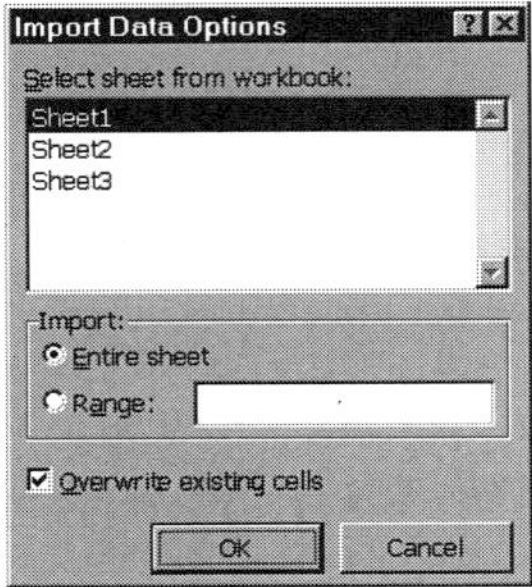

FIGURE 48.18
If the sheets have been named, the names appear in the dialog box.

To import spreadsheet data and create a link to the data, follow these steps:

1. Open the spreadsheet program and select the cells you want to import.
2. Click the Copy button or choose Edit, Copy.
3. Switch to the Datasheet in PowerPoint and choose Edit, Paste Link.
4. A warning message appears to let you know that the imported data replaces any existing data in the Datasheet. Click OK. The data is pasted into the Datasheet.

Importing Text to Create a New PowerPoint Presentation or Slide

PowerPoint can import text stored in several different formats—including Word documents (.doc), Rich Text Format (.rtf), plain text format (.txt), or HTML format (.htm). The imported text can be used to create a new presentation or to create slides in an existing presentation.

PowerPoint looks for styles in the text document to create slides. First-level headings become slide titles, second-level headings become main bullets, and other headings become indented bullets. If the document contains no styles, PowerPoint uses the paragraph indentations or tabs as the basis for a presentation outline.

If you have a Word outline, you can quickly create a PowerPoint presentation by using the File, Send To command.

To create a new presentation based on a text outline, follow these steps:

1. Choose File, Open. The File Open dialog box appears.
2. Click the Files of Type drop-down, and choose All Outlines from the list.
3. Use the Look In drop-down or Places bar to locate the file you want to use.
4. Double-click the filename. New slides are added to the presentation based on the text file.

To create slides in an existing presentation based on a text outline, follow these steps:

1. Open the presentation you want to add the slides to.
2. Choose Insert, Slides from Outline. The Insert Outline dialog box appears.
3. Use the Look In drop-down or Places bar to locate the file you want to use.
4. Double-click the filename. New slides are added to the presentation based on the text file.

Converting Lotus Freelance and Harvard Graphics Presentations into PowerPoint Presentations

PowerPoint can open Lotus Freelance and Harvard Graphics presentations and save them as PowerPoint presentations. Using special file converters, PowerPoint can retain most of the content and formatting from the original files.

PowerPoint can convert Lotus Freelance 4.0 for DOS or Freelance Graphics for Windows 1.0-2.0 file and Harvard Graphics 2.3 or 3.0 for DOS presentations. If the files you want to convert are more recent versions, you must save them into one of the formats listed here before you will be able to open them in PowerPoint. After the files are opened in PowerPoint, to complete the conversion you must save them as PowerPoint files, using the File, Save As command.

You can convert multiple files at one time by selecting all the files in the Open dialog box. After PowerPoint converts each presentation, you'll have to save each file separately.

If there are presentations created in other programs, for which PowerPoint has no converter, it may be possible to convert the presentation text. You can save the presentation in a text file format, such as .rtf or .txt, or graphics file format, such as .wmf, and then open the file in PowerPoint.

▶ **See** "Working with Picture Clips," for more information if there are graphic files you want to use in PowerPoint, **p. 1204**

Exporting a PowerPoint Slide into a Word Document

You can easily copy or link a PowerPoint slide to a Word document. The key is starting in the Slide Sorter View:

1. Open the presentation that contains the slide you want to use.
2. Switch to the Slide Sorter view.

3. Select the slide and choose Edit, Copy.
4. Switch to the Word document and place the flashing cursor where you want the slide to appear.
5. To copy the slide, click the Paste button.

   To link the slide, choose Edit, Paste Special. Click the Paste Link option button and select Microsoft PowerPoint Slide Object. Then click OK.
6. The slide is inserted into the Word document. Figure 48.19 shows an example.

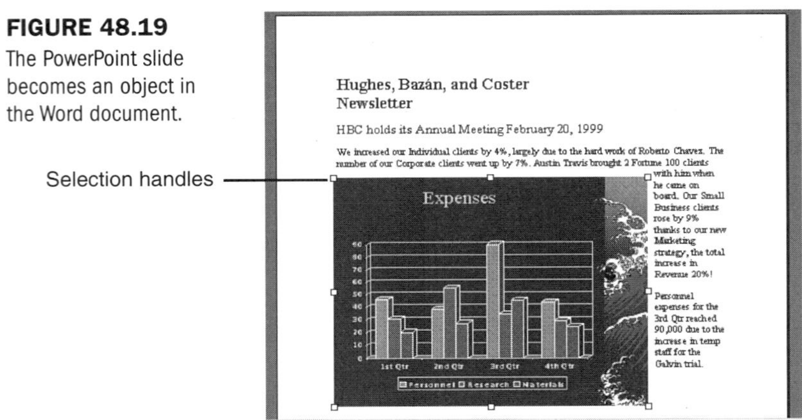

FIGURE 48.19
The PowerPoint slide becomes an object in the Word document.

Treat the slide as a clip object. If you want to resize the slide, use the corner selection handles to keep the slide proportional.

Exporting PowerPoint Presentation Notes, Handouts, or Text Outline to Word

The File, Send To command has an option to send presentation information to Microsoft Word. Figure 48.20 shows the Write-Up dialog box.

You have the option to paste or paste link the PowerPoint data into Word. Remember, the Paste Link option will automatically update the Word document when changes are made to the PowerPoint data. After you've made your selections, choose OK.

Exporting PowerPoint Presentations into Text or Graphic File Formats

If you need to share the data in a PowerPoint presentation with a program that cannot read PowerPoint files, you can save the presentation in a text or graphic file format. Text formats don't preserve graphics elements, such as charts and picture clips, but presentation and word processing programs can open them. Saving a PowerPoint presentation in a graphic format converts each slide to a separate (and large) graphic image.

FIGURE 48.20
Use this option when you want to include a slide and its notes in a Word document.

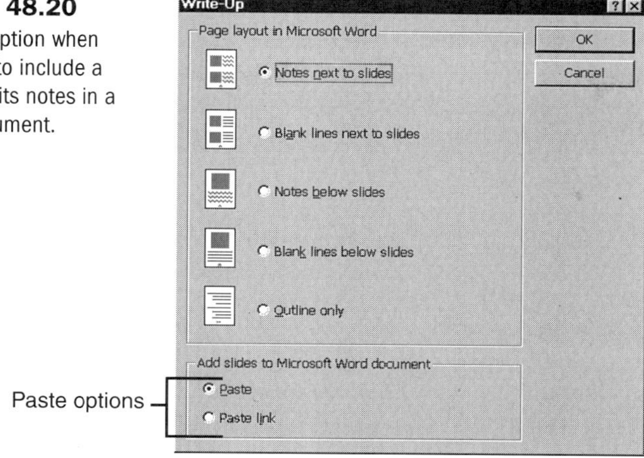

To convert the PowerPoint presentation, you simply choose File, Save As and select a different file type from the Save as Type drop-down list. Use .wmf to save a slide as a graphic. Use .gif or .jpg to save a slide as a graphic for use on Web pages. Use .rtf to save the text of the presentation as an outline. Use .htm to save the presentation so that it opens in a Web browser.

PART VII

Microsoft Outlook

CHAPTER 49

Migrating to Outlook 2000

In this chapter

Deciding to Upgrade to Outlook 2000

You wouldn't be reading this book if you weren't considering replacing Office 97 with Office 2000 or, perhaps, have already done so. However, you might be wondering whether you might as well stick with your old friend, Outlook 97 (or Outlook 98), something you know and, despite its quirks, does what you need. The purpose of this chapter is to give you enough information about the enhancements in Outlook 2000 that you'll come to the conclusion that you should upgrade. If you decide to stay with Outlook 97 or Outlook 98, at least you'll know what you're missing.

You should upgrade from Outlook 97 or Outlook 98 to Outlook 2000 for many reasons. Your biggest concern is probably compatibility, so let's put your mind to rest about that first. All Outlook items—messages, contact information, calendar data, tasks, and journal items—you've been working with in Outlook 97 or Outlook 98 are completely compatible with Outlook 2000. This compatibility works both ways. After you've switched to Outlook 2000, you can export Outlook items from Outlook 2000 into Outlook 97 or Outlook 98.

With the compatibility problem out of the way, let's look quickly at the advantages, and one possible disadvantage, of switching to Outlook 2000. Some of the advantages of switching from Outlook 97 are

- Outlook 2000 is integrated with the other Office 2000 applications.
- Outlook 2000 has a similar user interface to the other Office 2000 applications.
- Outlook shares the Web-based design philosophy with the rest of the Office 2000 suite.
- Outlook 2000 has improved and expanded support for Internet standards.
- Outlook 2000's overall performance is significantly improved.
- Outlook 2000's object model provides greatly enhanced access from other Office and Office-compatible applications.
- Outlook 2000 fully supports Visual Basic for Applications (VBA).

The same benefits apply to switching from Outlook 98 to Outlook 2000, although in most cases, to a lesser degree. An exception is support for VBA. Neither Outlook 97 nor Outlook 98 supported VBA, which Outlook 2000 does.

NOTE In Outlook 97 and Outlook 98, as well as in Outlook 2000, you can use Visual Basic Script (VBScript) to programmatically control Outlook's forms. Outlook 2000 adds the capability to use VBA to programmatically control the total Outlook application from within Outlook, as well as from other applications, and also to control other Office applications from within Outlook. You can also use VBScript to control Outlook 2000. ■

When you switch from Outlook 97 to Outlook 2000, you'll notice a greatly simplified user interface. After switching from Outlook 98 to Outlook 2000, you won't see such a significant change, although you will notice some slight changes. This brings up a possible disadvantage to switching—users have to become accustomed to a new interface. This isn't likely to be much of a problem for people who switch from Office 97 (or an earlier version of Office) to Office 2000 because the new Outlook 2000 user interface is similar to that of the other Office 2000 components. However, those people who've been using Outlook 97 or Outlook 98 and don't use the other Office applications might not find the improvements in Outlook 2000 have enough value to justify learning a new interface.

Understanding Outlook's Service Options

Service Options were introduced in Outlook 98 and are retained in Outlook 2000; Outlook 97 doesn't have service options. The service options in Outlook 98 and Outlook 2000 are

- No Email
- Internet Mail Only (IMO)
- Corporate or Workgroup (C/W)

Microsoft introduced these service options so that users could install just those Outlook capabilities they need in order to minimize the disk space required and to optimize Outlook's performance.

The No E-Mail Service option is appropriate if you want to use Outlook as a Personal Information Manager (PIM) and not use it for email or faxes.

The Internet Mail Only service option is appropriate if you want to use Outlook as a PIM, to send and receive email by way of the Internet or an intranet that supports Internet protocols, or to send and receive faxes.

NOTE Throughout this chapter, I'll abbreviate references to Corporate or Workgroup service as C/W, and Internet Mail Only service as IMO.

The Corporate or Workgroup service option is necessary if you want to use Outlook to communicate in any environment that depends on the Messaging Application Programming Interface (MAPI). This includes using Outlook as a client for messaging systems based on a Microsoft Exchange Server, Microsoft Mail, or Lotus cc:Mail. You can use this service option as a PIM, to send and receive Internet or intranet email, and to send and receive faxes.

NOTE Lotus cc:Mail relies on Vendor Independent Messaging (VIM) protocols, not on MAPI. However, Microsoft provides Outlook compatibility with cc:Mail by including an add-in licensed from Transend Corporation.

Although Microsoft doesn't provide Outlook support for Lotus Notes, Lotus supplies an Outlook add-in that gives Outlook the capability to act as a client for Lotus Notes.

The remaining pages of this chapter contain detailed information about many of the new and enhanced capabilities in Outlook 2000.

Outlook 2000's New and Enhanced Capabilities

Outlook 97 appeared first as a component of Office 97. It was Microsoft's first attempt to integrate the Microsoft Messaging (previously known as Exchange) client in Windows with Schedule+, an Office component. Many people who started using Outlook 97 were less than pleased with many aspects of it and they let Microsoft know. As a result, Microsoft quickly made some patches available for downloading and subsequently offered Outlook 98 as a free upgrade to Outlook 97 owners. Many people, this author included, think Outlook 98 was close to what Outlook 97 should have been when it was first released.

Despite the availability of Outlook 98, many people continued to use Outlook 97. That was particularly the case in large organizations that don't want to spend resources and money on retraining and supporting users on a regular basis.

Now that Office 2000 has arrived, it's likely that organizations will switch from using Office 97 to Office 2000 applications, Outlook 2000 included. Many people will, therefore, see Outlook 2000 as an upgrade to Outlook 97, instead of as an upgrade to Outlook 98. That's why the rest of this chapter covers the differences between Outlook 97 and Outlook 2000, although it does mention Outlook 98 where appropriate.

NOTE The Outlook enhancements described in the subsequent pages of this chapter are grouped according to the functional part of Outlook where they're most useful. Many of the enhancements apply to Outlook areas other than those within which they are listed.

Improved Usability

One of Microsoft's prime objectives in Outlook 2000 was improved usability. Some of the places where you'll see this improvement are described in the next few sections.

Outlook Today

Outlook Today (first introduced in Outlook 98) provides a summary of your current activities that, by default, is displayed when you start Outlook. Figure 49.1 shows a typical Outlook Today window.

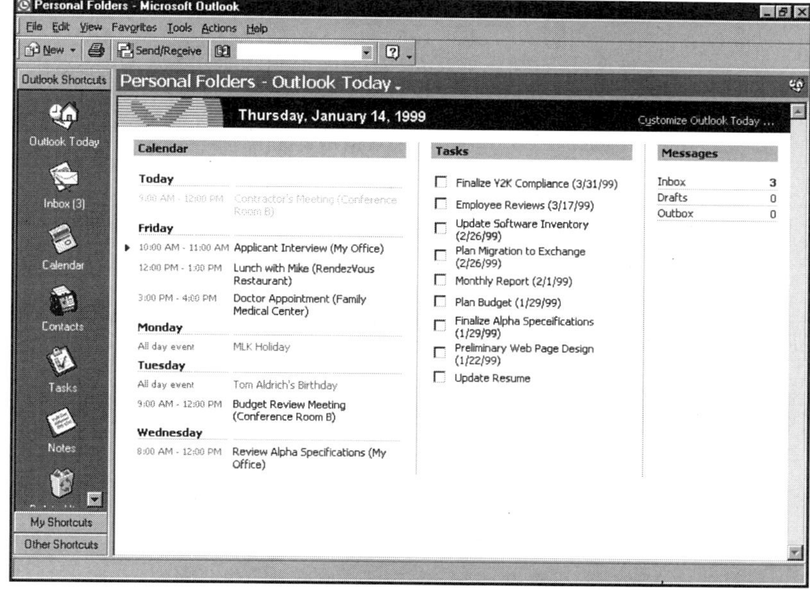

FIGURE 49.1
A typical Outlook Today window displays your calendar activities for the next few days, your current tasks, and any messages that are waiting for your attention.

The Outlook Today window is defined by HTML code. You can customize the window to display anything that's accessible by HTML code.

Simplified Menus and Toolbars

The many capabilities in Outlook 97 led its designers to create rather complicated and difficult-to-understand toolbars. Outlook 98 simplified the toolbars and Outlook 2000 has simplified them even more. Most of the buttons in Outlook 2000 toolbars contain words that make their purpose obvious. For example, instead of having to remember which icon to choose to create a new Outlook item, now you choose the word New. Also, in Outlook 2000, if you move the pointer onto a toolbar button and pause, Outlook displays a ScreenTip to identify that button.

In addition, Outlook fully supports the personalized menus and toolbars that are a shared feature in Office 2000 applications. As with other Office applications, you may disable personalized menus and toolbars if you prefer.

▶ **See** "Altering the Behavior of the Personalized Menus and Toolbars," **p. 86**

Expanded Use of InfoBars

InfoBars are status banners that appear at the top of many forms to draw your attention to something important about the information displayed in a form, such as that shown in Figure 49.2.

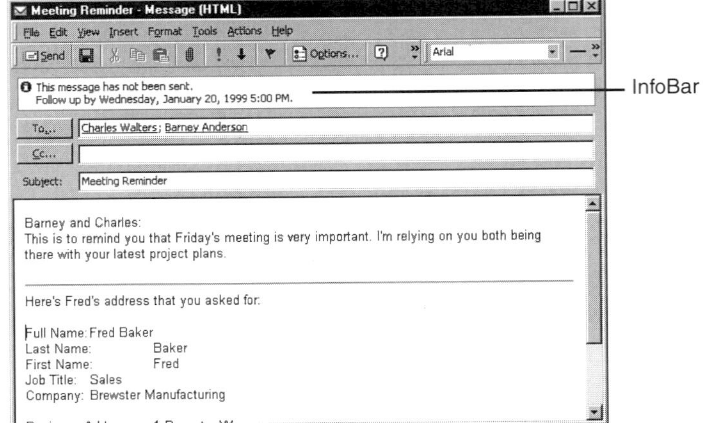

FIGURE 49.2
The InforBar near the top of this form makes it clear the message hasn't been sent and that a follow-up is included.

Although Outlook 98 displayed some InfoBars, they could easily be missed. Not only does Outlook 2000 make more extensive use of InfoBars, it makes them easy to see by displaying them with a bright yellow background.

Finding and Organizing Messages

One of the purposes of Outlook is to save messages so that those items can subsequently be displayed, something that isn't always easy to do in Outlook 97. The Find Tool, introduced in Outlook 98 and retained in Outlook 2000, provides an easy-to-use solution to this problem. When you choose Find in the toolbar, the pane shown in Figure 49.3 opens at the top of the Inbox or Sent Items Information viewer.

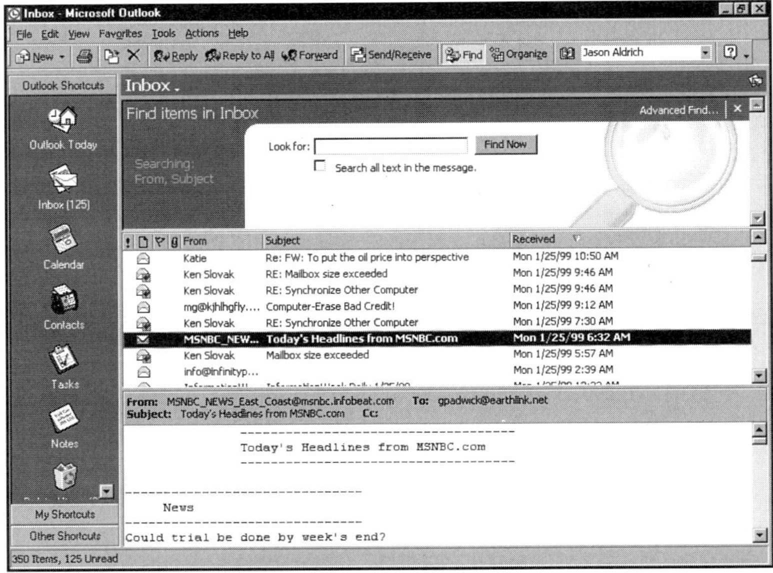

FIGURE 49.3
The Find tool shown here is used to locate messages received from a certain person or to locate messages that contain certain words.

You can use this tool to find messages from a certain person, or messages that contain a certain word or phrase.

If you want to find messages or other Outlook items based on more extensive criteria, you can use Advanced Find, as you could in Outlook 97.

The Organize tool is somewhat similar to the Find tool. You can use this tool for various purposes, such as to move selected messages into specific Outlook folders, automatically color messages from specific people, or detect junk email and automatically place it in a folder for subsequent disposal.

Quickly Finding a Contact

Outlook 2000 provides a quick way for you to find information about a contact, something you can't do in Outlook 97 and Outlook 98.

No matter which Outlook Information viewer you have open, you can enter the name of a contact in the box near the right end of the toolbar. Outlook immediately displays information about that contact in a form.

Searching in Public Folders

If you use C/W Outlook as a client for an Exchange server, you can use Outlook 2000's capability to search for information in public folders in the Exchange store. This is something you can't do in Outlook 97 and Outlook 98.

More Versatile ScreenTips

Outlook 2000 uses ScreenTips more extensively than did Outlook 98 and much more extensively than Outlook 97. For example, if you don't remember the purpose of a column in an Information viewer that's only identified by a symbol, point to that symbol and pause; Outlook displays a ScreenTip to tell you what the symbol means.

Outlook also uses ScreenTips when the text in a box is truncated because there isn't room for all of it. When you point to the box and pause, Outlook uses a ScreenTip to display the entire text in the box.

Archiving in the Background

Because the space occupied on your hard drive can grow rapidly, you should use Outlook's AutoArchiving capability to regularly move old items to an archive (or delete them). This is somewhat inconvenient in Outlook 97 because you can't use Outlook for anything else while archiving is taking place. In Outlook 2000 (also in Outlook 98), AutoArchiving can take place in the background while you're using Outlook for other purposes.

Installing and Configuring Outlook

Installing and configuring Outlook 2000 is improved over Outlook 98, and very significantly improved over Outlook 97.

The Outlook 2000 installation process automatically detects whether you have previously installed an earlier version of Outlook and, if so, uses the settings from within that installation. The installation process also detects the presence of accounts, folders, and address books in such applications as Outlook Express, Netscape Messenger, and Eudora and offers the choice of copying that information into the new Outlook 2000 installation.

NOTE You can subsequently import PIM information from such applications as Ecco Pro, Lotus Organizer, and ACT!. ■

Selecting a Service Option

As mentioned earlier in this chapter, Outlook 98 and Outlook 2000 both have service options (Corporate or Workgroup and Internet Mail Only), so you can install Outlook with only the communications capabilities you require.

Switching from one service option to another is less than convenient in Outlook 98. In Outlook 2000, you can easily switch between service options.

▶ For information about switching between service options in Outlook 2000, **see** "Switching to a Different Service Option," **p. 1366**

Improved Compatibility with Internet Standards

The support for Internet standards in Outlook 97 is greatly enhanced in Outlook 98, and is even more enhanced in Outlook 2000. Table 49.1 lists the Internet standards supported in Outlook 98 and Outlook 2000 that were not supported in Outlook 97. Unless otherwise noted, the standards are supported in both Outlook 98 and Outlook 2000.

Table 49.1 Supported Internet Standards

Standard	Purpose
POP3/SMTP	Internet (and intranet) email with support for multiple accounts.
IMAP4	High-performance Internet (and intranet) email with support for multiple accounts (available only for IMO Outlook).
LDAP	Internet directory access, including the capability to search for and check names, with support for multiple accounts. This is enhanced in Outlook 2000.
NNTP	Internet news reader (shared with Internet Explorer).

Standard	Purpose
HTML and MHTML	Send and receive HTML-formatted messages.
S/MIME	Authenticate and encrypt messages (shared with Internet Explorer).
MDN	Generate and receive Internet Message Disposition Notifications (read receipts). This is new in Outlook 2000.
vCard	Send and receive contact information in the Internet vCard format.
iCalendar	Permits group scheduling by way of the Internet or an intranet.

Email Enhancements

Outlook 98 contained many email enhancements over Outlook 97, some of which are further enhanced in Outlook 2000.

Faster Email Downloading

Outlook 2000 shares with Outlook 98 the capability to download email messages considerably faster than Outlook 97. Also, as in Outlook 98, IMO Outlook 2000 displays the progress of sending and receiving Internet email messages.

Downloading Email in the Background

Although you couldn't use Outlook 97 for other purposes while email was being downloaded, in Outlook 98 and Outlook 2000, you can download messages in the background while you're working with Outlook.

Previewing Messages

In Outlook 98 and Outlook 2000, you can split the Inbox Information viewer into two panes, something you couldn't do in Outlook 97. The lower pane, called the Preview pane, displays the contents of the message, the header of which is selected in the upper pane, as shown in Figure 49.4. This gives you the capability to quickly read messages without opening them.

Independently Selecting a Mail Editor and Message Format

The matter of choosing between Outlook's native editor and Word for creating and editing messages, and selecting a format in which to send a message is, to put it kindly, somewhat confusing in Outlook 97. Outlook 98 removed some of this confusion, but didn't go all the way. Outlook 2000 completely solves the problem. In Outlook 2000, you deal with selecting an editor and selecting a message format completely separately.

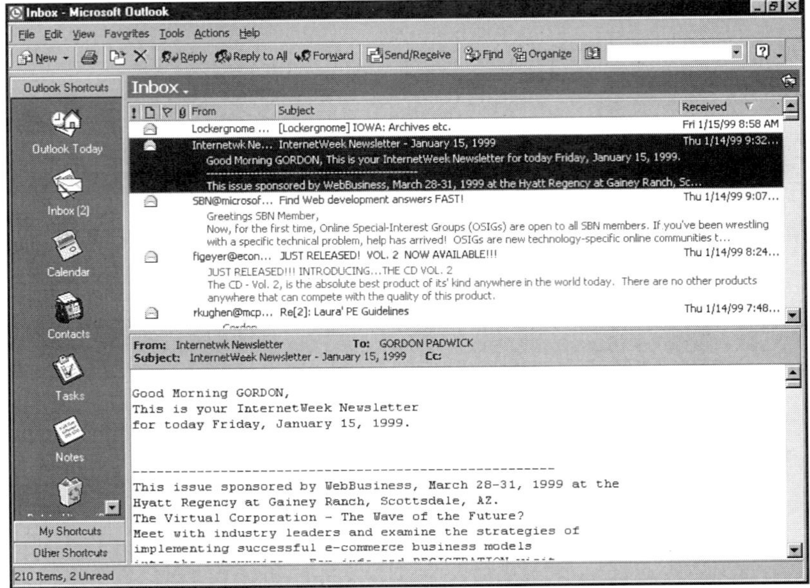

FIGURE 49.4
The Preview pane below the list of message headers displays the selected messages, attachments to them, and HTML links.

In Outlook 2000, you use the Options dialog box, shown in Figure 49.5, to select an editor. After you've done that, Outlook always uses that editor. You use the same Options dialog box to select HTML, Microsoft Outlook Rich Text, or Plain Text as your default message format. Subsequently, when you create a message, Outlook proposes to use that format; you can, however, select a different format for individual messages. When you receive a message, Outlook automatically detects its format so that you use the same format when you reply to, or forward, the message.

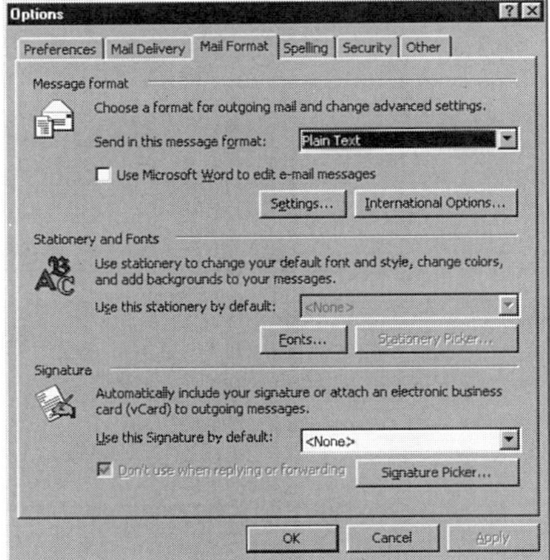

FIGURE 49.5
Use the Message Format section at the top of this dialog box to choose your editor and your default message format.

Displaying Conversation Threads

A conversation thread is a sequence of related messages. The thread starts with an original message; the subject of that message becomes the subject of the thread. The person who receives the original message can reply to it and forward it to other people; although that person can change the subject of the message, the name of the thread remains the same. In Outlook 98 and Outlook 2000, but not in Outlook 97, you can use a single click to find all the messages in a thread. That's much more convenient than having to hunt through your Inbox and Sent Items folders to find the individual related messages, as you had to do in Outlook 97.

Tracking Messages

If you use Outlook C/W as a client for an Exchange server or Microsoft Mail, you're probably familiar with being able to request delivery and read receipts.

NOTE A delivery receipt is a notification you receive when a message you send arrives in the recipient's mailbox. A read receipt is a notification you receive when the recipient opens the message. ■

Prior to Outlook 2000, you couldn't request receipts for messages you sent by way of the Internet. With Outlook 2000, you can request a read receipt because Outlook 2000 supports the Internet Message Disposition Notifications standard.

Calendar Enhancements

Outlook 98 adds several enhancements to the way Outlook 97 handles date-related information. Outlook 2000 improves what was already enhanced in Outlook 98, and also provides additional functionality to handling calendar-related information

Seeing Calendar Notes in the Preview Pane

You can add notes to a Calendar item such as an appointment. In Outlook 97, if you want to see those notes, you have to open the item to display it in a form. In Outlook 98 and Outlook 2000, you can display a Preview pane that contains the notes for a selected Calendar item, as shown in Figure 49.6.

Publishing Your Calendar on a Web Page

Publishing your calendar as a Web page is new in Outlook 2000. With the Calendar Information viewer displayed, you can choose File, Save As Web Page to display the dialog box shown in Figure 49.7.

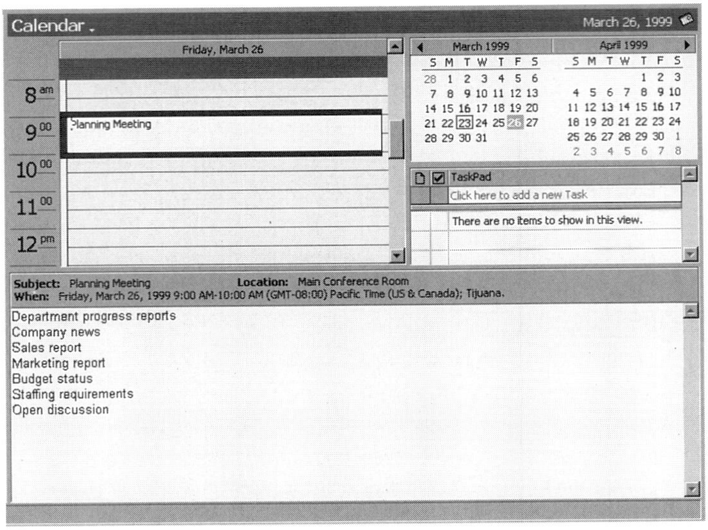

FIGURE 49.6
The Calendar Information viewer's Preview pane contains the notes for a selected Calendar item.

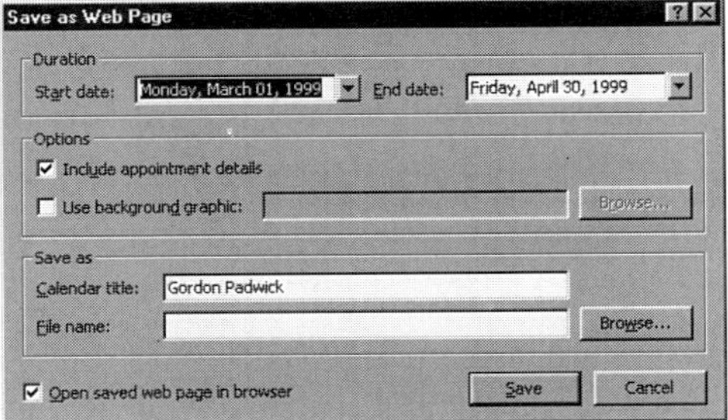

FIGURE 49.7
Use this dialog box to publish your calendar as a Web page.

In this dialog box, you can specify the range of dates you want to publish, whether you want to publish details of your appointments, and, of course, a filename or URL in which you want to publish the calendar.

Group Scheduling by Way of the Internet

If you've used Outlook as a client for an Exchange server, you've probably discovered the value of being able to share calendars so that you and other people can easily schedule meetings at times when all the intended participants are available. You can't do that in Outlook 97 if you don't have an account on an Exchange server.

Outlook 98 offered some capability to share calendars by way of the Internet and this has been enhanced in Outlook 2000. Now, using the Internet, you and other people can make information about free/busy time available so that scheduling meetings is simplified. Because Outlook 2000 supports the Internet iCalendar standard, you can share free/busy information among people who use Outlook or another application that supports iCalendar.

Using ScreenTips to Display Calendar Information

In Calendar Information viewers, particularly the week and month views, limited space is provided to display the details of appointments and events. In Outlook 97, it's necessary to double-click an appointment or event to see the details in a form. Outlook 98 introduced the capability (enhanced in Outlook 2000) to point onto a Calendar item in the Calendar Information viewer and pause so that Outlook displays all the information in a ScreenTip.

Selecting a Calendar Background Color

In Outlook 97 and Outlook 98, the background color for the Calendar Information viewer is a uniform white for times within the workweek and a uniform gray for other times. In Outlook 2000, you can select a different background color so that times reserved for appointments (white) stand out more clearly.

Enhanced Calendar Printing

In Outlook 97 and Outlook 98, a printed calendar contains only as much information as is displayed within the Calendar form. Outlook 2000 automatically expands each item to print information in full (much like a ScreenTip).

Outlook 2000 also offers the option to omit Calendar items marked as Private from the printed calendar. It can also print exactly one month per page.

Direct Resource Booking

When planning meetings, you have to schedule resources (meeting rooms and equipment) in addition to people. In Outlook 97 and Outlook 98, it's necessary to treat every resource as a person, each with a computer and an email account. Outlook 2000 removes this limitation to make it much easier to plan meetings that require resources.

Accessing Other People's Calendars

Outlook 2000 simplifies accessing other people's calendars. Outlook users can make their calendars available to specific other people.

As you probably already know, Outlook 97 and Outlook 98 let you mark certain items as private so that when you share your calendar with other people, they see only that you are busy at the times marked private—they don't see any information about that busy time. C/W Outlook 2000 takes this one step further. If you're using Outlook as a client for an Exchange server, you can designate one or more people as delegates. When you assign permissions to delegates, you can choose whether or not to give each delegate permission to see your private items, as shown in Figure 49.8. Assigning delegates is useful if you have an assistant who manages your schedule.

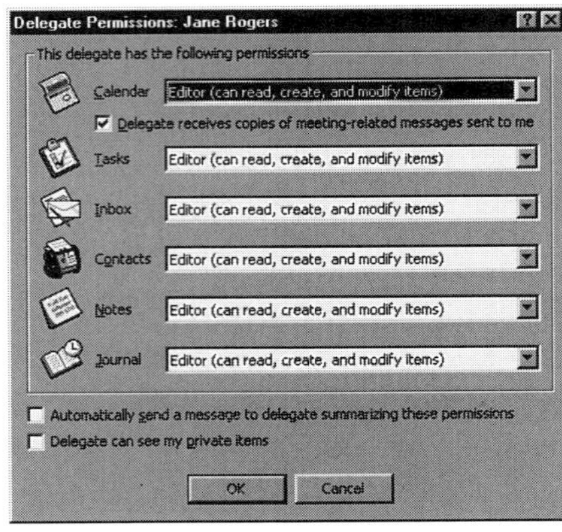

FIGURE 49.8
Check Delegate Can See My Private Items at the bottom of this dialog box if you want the delegate to be able to see items you've marked as private.

Contact Enhancements

Managing information about contacts—people and organizations—is one of the core components of Outlook. You'll notice several new capabilities in Outlook 2000 as well as numerous improvements over Outlook 97 and Outlook 98.

Creating Distribution Lists

Outlook 2000 greatly simplifies creating and using distribution lists. In Outlook 97 and Outlook 98, creating distribution lists was somewhat awkward—the recommended way is to create a Personal Address Book, copy items from your Contacts folder into that, and create distribution lists in the Personal Address book.

In Outlook 2000, you can easily create distribution lists within your Contacts folder. To do so, choose File, move the pointer onto New, and choose Distribution List to display the dialog box shown in Figure 49.9.

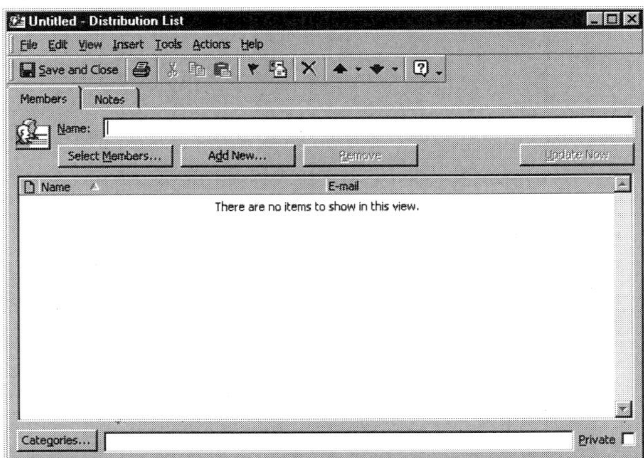

FIGURE 49.9
You can use this dialog box to select items from your Contacts folder to create a distribution list.

Outlook 2000 saves a distribution list as an item in your Contacts folder. The distribution list can contain items from your Contacts folder and, if you're using Outlook as a client for an Exchange server, from shared Contacts folders in the Exchange store and from the Exchange Global Address List.

If you've previously used Outlook 97 or Outlook 98 and have used a Personal Address Book for the principal purpose of creating distribution lists, you probably won't need a Personal Address Book after you switch to Outlook 2000. The first time you run Outlook 2000, you are asked whether you want to import the contents of the old Personal Address Book into your Contacts folder.

Contact Activity Tracking

Contact activity tracking is new in Outlook 2000; it enables you to automatically track activities relating to a contact.

You relate an Outlook item to a contact by entering the contact's name in the Contacts box on an Outlook form, as shown in Figure 49.10.

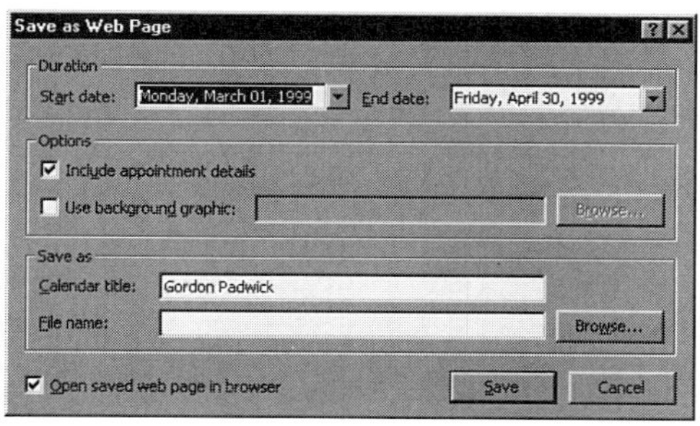

FIGURE 49.10
Choose Contacts at the bottom of the Task form to display a list of contacts. Then select the contacts you want to link to the task.

NOTE With the exception of the Message form, each of the forms in which you create Outlook items has a similar Contacts box. To link a message to a contact, choose Options in the toolbar to display a dialog box that contains the Contacts box.

After you've linked contacts to items in this way, you can see the activities relating to a contact by selecting the Activities tab in the Contact form as shown in Figure 49.11.

Adding Senders' Names to Your Contact Folder

In Outlook 97, if you want to create Contact items from your incoming email messages, you must do so manually. In Outlook 98 and Outlook 2000, you can do that automatically. Open the Message, then right-click the sender's name to display a context menu, and choose Add to Contacts. If a Contact item for that person already exists, Outlook warns you so that you don't create a duplicate item, as described in the next section.

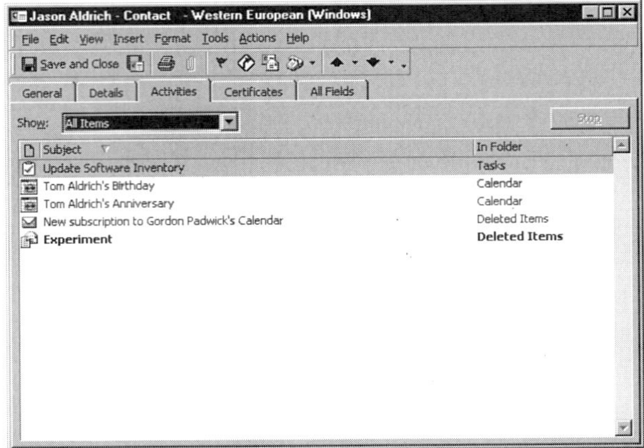

FIGURE 49.11
The Contact form's Activities tab is where you see activities relating to a contact.

Avoiding Duplicate Contacts

You can add contacts to your Contacts folder manually by creating an item based on the name of a person who has sent you a message, or by accepting a vCard that's been sent to you. If the new Contact item appears to be a duplicate of an existing one, Outlook 2000 displays a dialog box in which you choose whether to add a new contact, even though it is a duplicate, or to update the existing contact with the new information.

Exchanging Contact Information with Other People

In Outlook 98 and Outlook 2000, but not in Outlook 97, you can exchange information about contacts with other people by way of the Internet, using vCard files. The people you send vCard files to, or receive vCard files from, don't necessarily have to use Outlook; they can use any messaging client software that supports the Internet vCard format.

NOTE vCard is an Internet standard format for providing information about a person or organization—it's an electronic business card.

Creating Custom Contact Forms

Although you might find the Contact form supplied with Outlook suitable for your needs, you might prefer to create a custom Contact so that you can easily provide different information about contacts. For example, when you enter information about family members and friends, it's convenient to have a place to enter a spouse name (without having to go to the Contact form's Details tab).

You can't modify the Contact form's General tab in Outlook 97. In Outlook 98 and Outlook 2000, you can modify this tab, so it's easy to customize the form.

Using Contact Items for Form Letters

Outlook 2000 includes enhanced integration with Word's Mail Merge capability. You can individually select items in your Contacts folder, or you can use Outlook's filter to select contact items based on the contents of any field (such as the Category field), and use the selected contacts as the data source for a form letter created in Word.

Showing a Contact's Location on a Map

It's one thing to know a contact's street address; it's another matter to be able to drive to that address. Outlook 98 introduced the capability to display and print a map showing a contact's location, as shown in Figure 49.12. Outlook 2000 has the same capability.

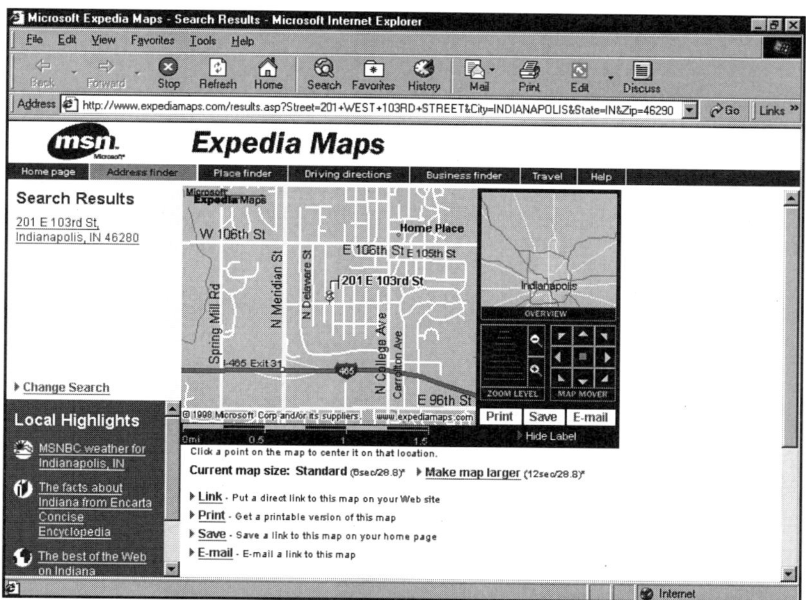

FIGURE 49.12
Outlook automatically uses Internet Explorer to access Microsoft's Expedia Web site, find a contact's location, and display a map with that location marked.

Microsoft claims that this capability works for any location in the United States.

CAUTION

Mapping technology such as that provided by Outlook is fallible. There are times when maps generated by Outlook will get you into the general vicinity but will leave the details to you. Other times, it works like a charm.

Integration with the Web

In common with other Office 2000 applications, Outlook 2000 has several new capabilities for integrating with the Web.

Creating Outlook Bar Shortcuts

In Outlook 2000, you can create Outlook Bar shortcuts that give you immediate access to Web pages as well as to Outlook folders and Windows files. To do so, display the Web page and Outlook side by side on your screen, as shown in Figure 49.13. Then drag the icon at the left of the site's URL into the Outlook Bar.

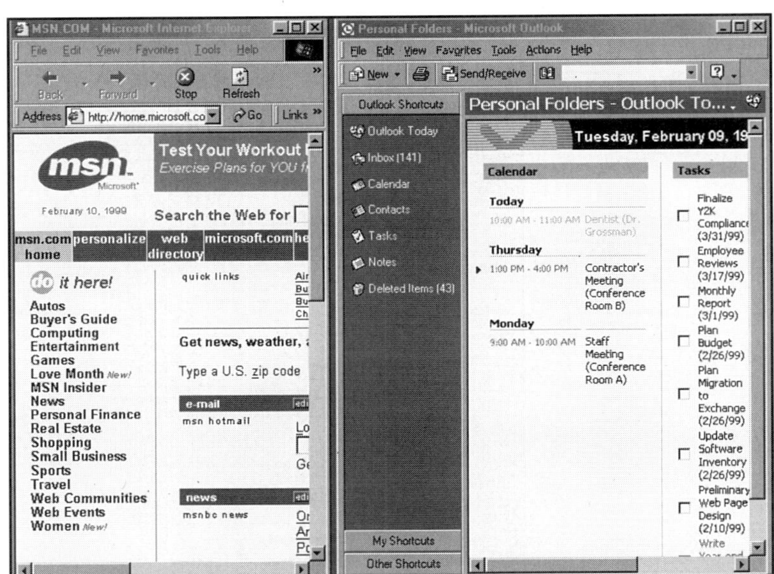

FIGURE 49.13
With the Web page Outlook displayed side by side on your screen, drag the icon at the left of the Web page's URL into the Outlook Bar.

After you've done that, you can click the Web page's icon in the Outlook Bar to display it. Outlook uses HTML rendering and security services in Internet Explorer to safely display the Web page where an Information viewer is normally displayed.

Outlook includes the basic Web navigation capabilities in the standard Office 2000 Web toolbar. However, Microsoft doesn't intend you to use Outlook as your primary Web browser.

Folder Home Pages

In Outlook 2000, you can associate a Web page with any Outlook folder in your local Personal Folders file or in the Exchange store. You won't normally want to do this for the standard Outlook folders, but you can create custom folders and use those folders to display either Outlook items or the associated Web page.

Synchronization Enhancements

Synchronization is the process of comparing information in two places and copying the most recent from one to the other so that both have the most recent. When you use Outlook as a client for an Exchange server, you synchronize information between the Exchange store and your offline folders. Outlook 98 offers improved synchronization over Outlook 97; Outlook 2000 offers even more improvements.

Improved Synchronization with Exchange

Quick synchronization with Exchange is new in Outlook 2000. In Outlook 97 and Outlook 98, you have to choose between synchronizing all folders or synchronizing individual folders one at a time. In Outlook 2000, you can create Synchronization Groups and subsequently use one command to synchronize any group of folders.

Also, in Outlook 2000, you can specify the maximum size of messages to be synchronized. When you are using a slow connection, this can save a lot of time if you don't need to synchronize large messages.

Another improvement in Outlook 2000 is the capability to combine synchronizing the Exchange Global Address List (GAL) with folder synchronization, instead of separately synchronizing the GAL as before.

Making Folders Available for Offline Use

In Outlook 97 and Outlook 98, you have to open the Properties dialog box for each folder in the Exchange store that you want to make available for offline, synchronized use. Outlook 2000 makes this process considerably more convenient by offering a single dialog box in which you can specify which folders are to be available for offline use.

Sharing Outlook Folders

Outlook 98 and, even more so, Outlook 2000 place emphasis on sharing information. Two of the enhancements you'll notice are integration with Pocket Outlook and the capability to share folders by way of the Internet.

Integration with Pocket Outlook

Outlook 98 and Outlook 2000 both support integration with Pocket Outlook running under Windows CE on palmtop computers. You can synchronize between Outlook 2000 and Pocket Outlook by way of an infrared or cable connection.

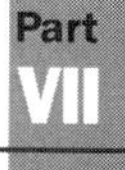

Sharing Information by Way of the Internet

Outlook 98 introduced the concept of Net Folders which you can use to share Outlook folders by way of the Internet, much like you can use Public Folders when Outlook is a client for an Exchange server. The performance and reliability of Net Folders are enhanced in Outlook 2000.

CHAPTER 50

Customizing Outlook

In this chapter

Nearly everyone likes to leave their mark on things to make them their own. A house becomes a home after you put something of yourself into it. Outlook is no different. There are a myriad of ways to add the little touches to Outlook that make it a truly personal information manager.

Adding Folders

When you start Outlook for the first time, you have access to a basic folder set. The set includes the Calendar, Contacts, Inbox, Journal, Notes, Outbox, and Tasks folders. After using Outlook for a time, you might find the need to create different folders to sort items the way you find best. Outlook makes it simple to create new folders to hold any sort of item. To create a new folder:

1. Select the File, New, Folder command. The dialog box shown in Figure 50.1 appears. Click the "+" symbol next to Personal Folders to view the entire folder tree.
2. Enter a name for the folder in the Name field.
3. Choose the item type that the folder will contain from the Folder Contains drop-down list.

NOTE To create a new calendar folder, choose Appointment Items from the Folder Contains list.

4. Select the location for the folder in the folder tree shown in the dialog box. Your folder will be created under the location you've selected.
5. Click the OK button to create the folder.

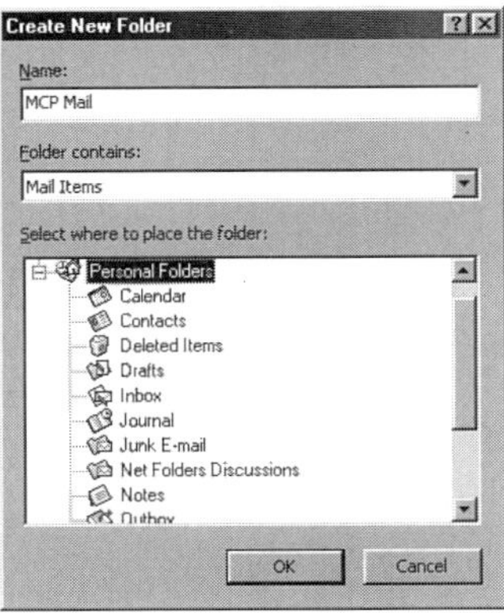

FIGURE 50.1 The Create New Folder dialog box lets you create what you need, where you need it.

Customizing Outlook's Appearance

The most noticeable changes you can make to Outlook are those that modify the manner in which it presents itself. From the View menu, you can toggle the three major interface elements: Outlook Bar, Folder List, and Preview Pane (see Figure 50.2). In addition to simply toggling among them, you can change the appearance of each of these features.

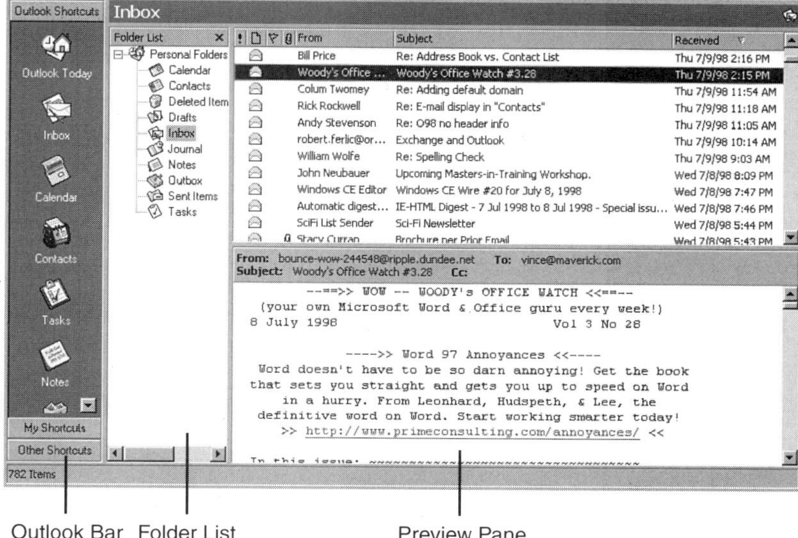

FIGURE 50.2
The main Outlook window is shown with all three elements displayed.

Customizing the Outlook Bar

The Outlook Bar, when enabled, runs down the left side of the main Outlook window. It provides quick access to Outlook folders, file folders (whether local or remotely located on other machines), and shortcuts to Web pages. Simply click a folder or shortcut in the Outlook Bar to display its contents in the information viewer pane.

When Outlook is initially installed, the Outlook Bar contains three groups. The first two (Outlook Shortcuts and My Shortcuts) consist of shortcuts to the default Outlook folders, whereas the third (Other Shortcuts) contains shortcuts to filesystem locations. If you're using Outlook's Corporate/Workgroup mode (see Chapter 51, "Installation and Integration Issues with Outlook," for more information about the modes of Outlook 2000) and you're attached to an Exchange Server, the Other Shortcuts section will also contain a shortcut to Public Folders.

To create a new shortcut on the Outlook Bar, follow these steps:

1. If it's not visible, display the Outlook Bar by selecting View, Outlook Bar.
2. If the group you want to add your shortcut to isn't expanded, click that group's header.
3. Right-click in a blank area of the Outlook Bar.
4. Choose Outlook Bar Shortcut from the context menu that appears.
5. The Add to Outlook Bar dialog box (shown in Figure 50.3) displays. Set the Look In field to either Outlook or File System.
6. Use the tree view of the chosen location to find the folder you want to add.

FIGURE 50.3
The Add to Outlook Bar dialog box is displayed.

NOTE You cannot add shortcuts to files nor can you add single Outlook items to the Outlook Bar—only to folders.

7. Click OK to add the shortcut.

In addition to the three groups shown on the initial Outlook Bar, you can add, delete, or rename groups at will. Right-click on a blank area of the Outlook Bar to display the same context menu that was used for the shortcut operation.

You can mix filesystem and Outlook folder shortcuts in the same group. With the addition of filesystem items to the Outlook Bar, you can add another hat, that of Windows Explorer replacement, to the pile that Outlook already wears. Outlook can become the linchpin of your computing environment because it can help you manage most forms of information on your system.

In addition to controlling whether the Outlook Bar is displayed or not, you can also fine-tune its appearance. You can control the width of the Outlook Bar by clicking on the right border and dragging it until the Outlook Bar is the size you want. You can also control the size of the icons by right-clicking in a blank area of the Outlook Bar and choosing either Large Icons or Small Icons from the context menu.

The Folder List

Serving a function very similar to that of the Outlook Bar is the Folder List (enabled by choosing the Folder List item on the View menu). There are some major differences, however, between the two. The Folder List

- Displays only Outlook item folders.
- Displays all folders, not just the ones that you choose.
- Uses a Windows Explorer-style tree interface that always lists folders in alphabetical order.

The Preview Pane

Available as an add-in for Outlook 97, and later as an integral part of Outlook 98 and 2000, the Preview Pane can be a very useful and productivity-enhancing part of your Outlook interface. By selecting an item in the upper pane of the information viewer, you can quickly view the major details of any standard Outlook item (such as From, To, Subject, and the first portion of the document) without having to open it. It also supports all three mail formats (Plain Text, Rich Text, HTML), so that you can see the item as the sender intended. If you use a Microsoft IntelliMouse, quick zooming of the content in the pane is supported by holding down the Ctrl key while rolling the mouse wheel down (to increase the font size) or up (to decrease the font size).

The Preview Pane has some helpful configuration options (as outlined in Table 50.1). To access them, choose Tools, Options, Other tab, and click the Preview Pane button.

Table 50.1 Preview Pane Options

Option Name	Description
Mark Messages As Read in the Preview Window	Causes highlighted message to be marked as read after the number of seconds entered in the next field
Mark Item As Read When Selection Changes	Causes highlighted item to be marked as read when you select another item
Single Key Reading Using Spacebar	Enables you to scroll the content in the preview pane one screen at a time by pressing the Spacebar
Preview Header Font	Allows you to set the font used in the shaded header portion of the preview pane

NOTE The options Mark Messages As Read in Preview Window and Mark Item As Read When Selection Changes are mutually exclusive.

There are several ways to alter the size of the Preview Pane:

- You can click and drag the top border of the pane.
- You can hide the shaded header portion of the pane by right-clicking in the shaded area and uncheck the Header Information option in the context menu that is displayed.
- You can also hide the header by double-clicking on it. If you want to show it again, double-click the thin gray top border of the pane.

Enhancing Outlook's Performance

Outlook has some great features that exact a price in performance from your machine. Thankfully, these features can be either fully or partially deactivated. The two biggest features that fall into this category are the Journal and using Microsoft Word as your email editor (also referred to as WordMail).

NOTE One of the biggest blights in the category of performance hindrances, the Find Fast Indexer, is no longer installed by default as it was in Office 95 and Office 97. The Find Fast Indexer was ostensibly designed to speed file searches in Open dialog boxes by pregenerating content indexes. You now have to specifically choose to install the module (which has proven to be of little help and much harm to most users).

Configuring Journal Options

The capability to keep track of all the Office documents you've worked on is a great feature to have in a PIM but it can cause a drain on your machine. Outlook can track every opening and closing of these files to determine the amount of time a document was used. It also tracks Outlook items you've created in association with your contacts. If you don't need all this tracking, or if you want to reclaim the disk space this feature uses, you can recover some of the performance by limiting the scope of journaling.

NOTE Originally conceived to be a universal tracking feature, the Journal turned out to be less useful because it doesn't track all the activities that you might do in Outlook and it also is limited to recording in a user's Journal folder (it can't add records to an Exchange Server public folder, for example). To alleviate/eliminate this limitation, Microsoft added the Activities feature to Outlook (discussed in detail in Chapter 55, "Creating and Using Custom Forms"). Microsoft appears to be encouraging the use of Activities while de-emphasizing the use of the Journal.

1. Choose Tools, Options and click the Journal Options button on the Preferences tab of the Options dialog box.
2. Uncheck any of the Outlook item types you don't want to track from the Automatically Record These Items section of the Journal Options dialog box (shown in Figure 50.4).
3. Uncheck any of the file types you don't want to track from the Also Record Files From section of the dialog box.

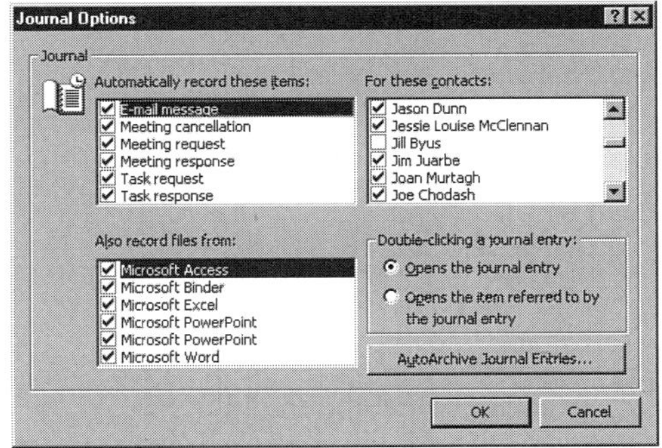

FIGURE 50.4
The Journal Options dialog box enables you to fine-tune exactly what you want to track.

Performance and the Use of Word as Email Editor

Another feature that takes its toll on your machine is using Word as your email editor. This enables you to use many of Word's features while sending mail. New to Outlook 2000 is the use of Word as your editor for HTML (Hypertext Markup Language) mail. Of course, loading Word in addition to Outlook does result in a loss of performance. It's up to you to decide whether the speed loss is worth the feature gain. To turn this option on or off, use the Use Microsoft Word to Edit Email Messages box on the Mail Format tab of the Options dialog box.

Using Command-Line Switches to Control Outlook

One of the quickest ways to change the face of Outlook is to alter the command line used to start the program. You can change what folder Outlook opens in, what parts of Outlook's interface show, and, in some cases, fix problems through the use of command-line modifications. Some of the problems involved using this way of altering Outlook are finding where to change the command line that you use to start Outlook and what to add to the line to make the changes you want.

There are four ways to start Outlook (each of which can be modified with a command-line switch so that Outlook will open as your prefer):

- Double-click a Windows shortcut (this could be the Outlook shortcut in the Start menu or a custom shortcut you've placed in a convenient location).
- Double-click the special Outlook icon on your desktop (this icon is placed on your desktop during installation of Office).
- Select the Mail item on Internet Explorer's Go menu.
- Enter a command line in the Open field of the Start Menu's Run command.

NOTE A full discussion of all the command-line options you might want to use in each of these situations is contained in the "Command-Line Options" section later in this chapter.

After you've decided which switch or switches you want to use and where you want to use them, you might want to know how to use them. You've got to construct a command line that begins with the full path to the Outlook.EXE file (typically C:\Program Files\Microsoft Office\Office\Outlook.EXE) encased in quotes (because the path contains embedded spaces) followed by the switches you've chosen to use.

Locating and Changing a Windows Shortcut

You can place a shortcut to Outlook in a variety of locations. These include the Desktop, Start Menu, and QuickLaunch toolbar. No matter where you place a shortcut on your system, the manner to change it is the same:

1. Right-click the shortcut.

NOTE The only time this does not work on a Start Menu shortcut is when you are running Windows 95 or Windows NT 4.0 without the Internet Explorer (4 or 5) Desktop update. If you are using such a system, you'll need to open Windows Explorer and navigate to the directory containing the Start menu shortcuts on your system.

2. Choose Properties on the context menu that appears.
3. Click the Shortcut tab, if it's not already selected.
4. Change the command line in the Target field as shown in Figure 50.5.

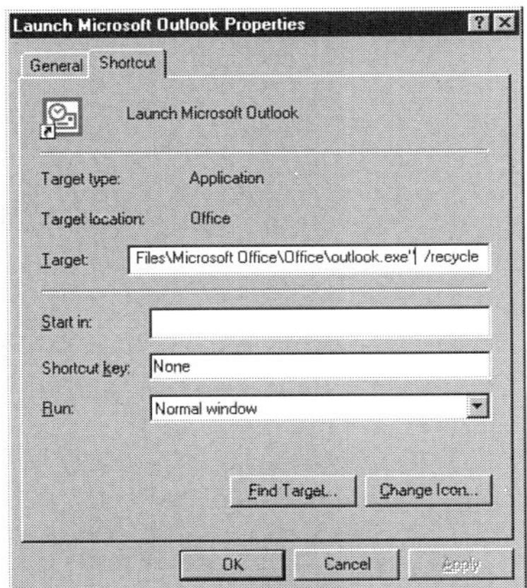

FIGURE 50.5
The Properties dialog box for an Outlook shortcut.

5. Use the Find Target button to locate the executable if it is not stored in the Office folder on your computer.
6. Click the OK button to save your changes.

Changing the Command Line for the Special Outlook Desktop Icon

When you install Outlook on a system, it places a special icon on your desktop. The icon isn't a shortcut and if you right-click it and choose Properties, you can quickly access the Mail applet from the Control Panel. The downside of this capability is that the command line used when you double-click the icon isn't readily available. It's deeply nestled in your machine's Registry at this location:

```
HKEY_CLASSES_ROOT\CLSID\{00020D75-0000-0000-C000-000000000046}\Shell\Open\Command
```

CAUTION

If you are uncomfortable modifying your machine's Registry, you might want to skip this section.

To change it, you need to use a Registry-editing tool. These instructions cover changing it with RegEdit.EXE because it should be on every Windows (95/98/NT) machine. They may not apply if you are using another tool.

1. Start RegEdit (click the Start button, choose Run, enter `REGEDIT.EXE`, and press the Enter button).
2. RegEdit presents the Registry in a hierarchical fashion. You can navigate to the key mentioned previously by expanding each of the branches in Windows Explorer fashion (click the plus signs) until you reach your destination.
3. When you have the Command Registry key highlighted in the left pane of RegEdit, you should see the (Default) value in the right pane with a data value showing the command line used to start Outlook.
4. Double-click the (Default) label in the right pane. Change the value in the Edit String dialog box that appears (see Figure 50.6). Click OK to save your changes.

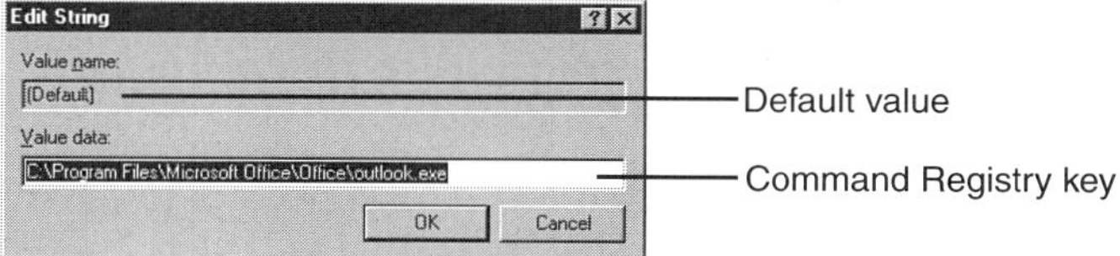

FIGURE 50.6
Locating and changing the command line in the Registry.

5. Close RegEdit.

Changing the Command Line That Internet Explorer Uses to Start Outlook

If you've chosen to make Outlook your default Internet email program, you can start it by choosing Go, Mail. Once again, the command line used in this situation is located in the Registry, albeit in a distinctly different location. You will find the value used here:

```
HKEY_LOCAL_MACHINE\Software\Clients\Mail\Microsoft Outlook\shell\open\command
```

You can use the same procedure detailed in the previous section to modify this command line.

Using a Command Line in the Start Menu's Run Command

The quickest way to start Outlook with a special command line is through the use of the Start menu's Run command. This is probably the way you'll want to start Outlook if you're going to be using a special debugging/repair command-line switch (discussed in the next section).

1. Click the Start button; choose Run.
2. Enter your command line in the Open field. The command line will consist of the full path to the Outlook.EXE file followed by any switches you might need. An example of a command line you might use in this scenario would be

   ```
   "C:\Program Files\Microsoft Office\Office\Outlook.EXE" /checkclient
   ```

3. Press the Enter key or click the OK button.

Command-Line Options

Now that you know all the places where you can find the options, you need to know what you can add to the command line to affect Outlook. The options fall into three categories: Appearance, Creation, and Debugging/Repair.

Appearance You can define the folder that Outlook displays at startup in the extensive Options dialog box. In the event you want to override this default by appending an Outlook URL to the command line, the URL uses this format:

```
Outlook:<Folder Name>
```

For example, the following command line causes Outlook to open, displaying the Contacts folder:

```
"C:\Program Files\Microsoft Office\Office\Outlook.EXE" Outlook:Contacts
```

NOTE If any of the folder names contain a space, you should surround the entire URL with quotation marks (") so that it is interpreted correctly.

There are other command-line switches that directly affect the Outlook interface. Table 50.2 lists these switches.

Table 50.2 Additional Display-Related Switches

Switch	Description
/folder	Suppresses display of the Folder List and/or the Outlook Bar
/nopreview	Disables the display and use of the Preview Pane
/recycle	Causes Outlook to reuse an existing window as opposed to opening a new one

NOTE In addition to the obvious use, the /nopreview switch can also come in handy if the first message in your Inbox causes problems when previewed.

Creation You can modify the command line used to start Outlook so that it doesn't open to the main Outlook window but to an empty item ready for use. The item is saved in the default folder for the item type. Table 50.3 lists the options available for use.

Table 50.3 Creation Switches

Switch	Description
/c IPM.Activity	Creates a journal entry
/c IPM.Appointment	Creates an appointment
/c IPM.Contact	Creates a contact

Switch	Description
/c IPM.Note	Creates an email item
/c IPM.Post	Creates a post in an Outlook folder
/c IPM.StickyNote	Creates a note
/a `filename`	When used in conjunction with the /c switches, attaches the specified file to the new item
/m `e-mail address`	Addresses the new item to the given address

Debugging/Repair Every now and then, things go wrong. There are a handful of command-line switches for Outlook that can help fix a number of those things. The biggest problem is knowing when to use which switch.

CAUTION

Be extremely careful when using any of the switches in this section. Many of them delete data, and others make Registry modifications.

- /CheckClient switch—This causes Outlook to prompt you if it is no longer set as the default client for contacts, email, and news. You may need to use this if you've installed another mail or news program and set it as the default, and then decide not to use it anymore.
- /CleanFreeBusy switch—This removes and regenerates the free/busy data for your calendar. You can use this if you find that your calendar has dates bolded that don't contain any appointments.
- /CleanReminders switch—This removes and regenerates the reminder information for your calendar folder. If you find that Outlook is displaying reminders for appointments that have long since passed, you might want to try using this switch.
- /CleanSchedPlus switch—Similar to the /CleanFreeBusy switch, this causes Outlook to delete any Schedule+ data associated with your account from the Exchange Server. Use this if you find that other users are viewing your free/busy information incorrectly or your network contains Schedule+ 1.0 users.
- /CleanViews switch—Removes any custom views you may have created and restores the default views. If you find that switching to different views of a folder produces errors or widely inaccurate results, you might want to use this switch.
- /RegServer switch—Re-creates the Registry entries associated with Outlook that are normally created only at install time. This might come in handy if you find that Registry entries are missing from a user's machine (perhaps due to permission problems) even though the installation procedure completed successfully.
- /ResetFolders switch—If you find that you're missing one of the Outlook default folders (Calendar, Contacts, Deleted Items, Drafts, Inbox, Journal, Notes, Outbox, Sent Items,

Tasks), use this switch. You could simply create a folder with a correct name but it wouldn't have the special properties that the regular default folders do (for example, reminders are generated only out of the special Calendar folder). This situation might occur whether you change message stores (you switch from using your Exchange Server mailbox to Personal Folders or you switch Personal Folder files) or you use the base Exchange Server client (EXCHNG32.EXE) to delete folders that you thought you didn't need.

- /UnRegServer switch—Removes all Registry keys associated with Outlook from your machine's Registry. This is typically used before using the /RegServer switch to cleanly register Outlook on a given computer.

CHAPTER 51

Installation and Integration Issues with Outlook

In this chapter

Changing Your Outlook Installation

If you originally installed Office 2000 without including some Outlook 2000 features, you can add these later. You can also remove Outlook features you don't need.

If, while you're working with Outlook, some capability that you need to use isn't available, it's possible that the required component hasn't been installed. You can use the steps described here to install the missing component.

To change your Outlook 2000 installation:

1. Start from the Windows desktop.
2. Insert your Office 2000 CD-ROM into the drive.
3. Choose Start in the Windows taskbar, move the pointer onto Settings, and choose Control Panel.
4. Double-click Add/Remove Programs and then, in the Add/Remove Programs Properties dialog box, choose Install. Choose Next in the first window that appears, and choose Finish in the second window. After a few seconds, the Maintenance Mode window shown in Figure 51.1 appears.

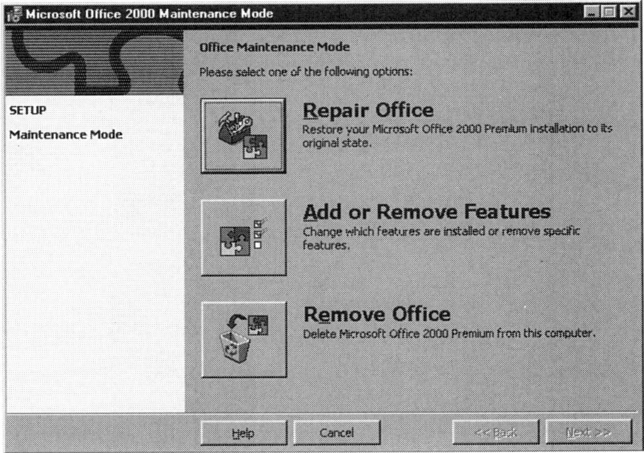

FIGURE 51.1
This is the window in which you can repair, change, or remove your Office installation.

5. Choose the button at the left of Add or Remove Features. The window shown in Figure 51.2 appears.
6. Click the + at the left of Microsoft Outlook for Windows to see a list of Outlook components, as shown in Figure 51.3.
7. To change a component's installation, to remove a component, or to install a component, choose the button at the left of that component's name to display a list of installation options, as shown in Figure 51.4.

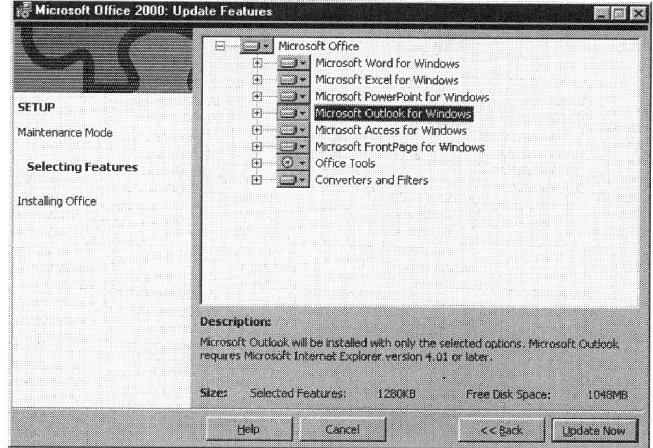

FIGURE 51.2
This window lists the principal components of Office 2000.

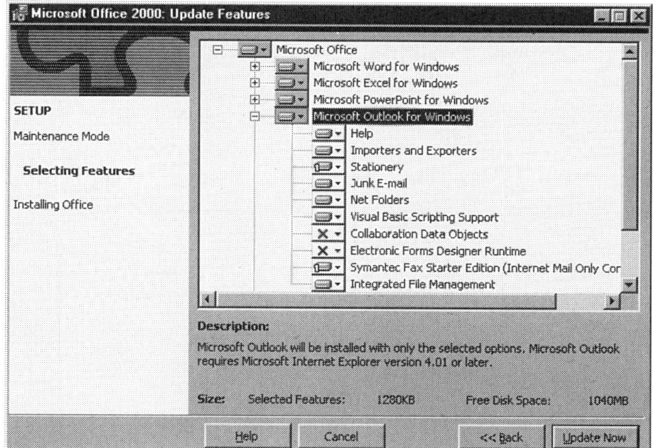

FIGURE 51.3
The icons at the left of each Outlook component indicate how that component is currently installed. Components not installed are marked with a red X.

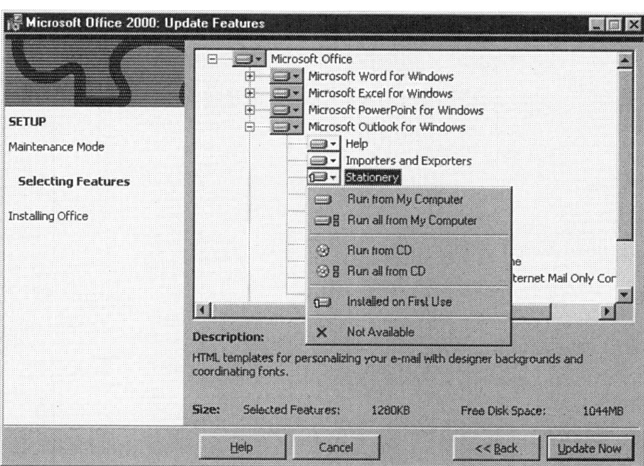

FIGURE 51.4
The available installation options vary according to which component you choose.

8. Select the installation option you want for the selected component. Repeat this step if you want to change the installation for other components.
9. Choose Update Now to update your Outlook configuration. Outlook reads the required files from your CD-ROM.

Running Outlook for the First Time

The first time you start Outlook, the initial Outlook 2000 Startup Wizard window appears as shown in Figure 51.5.

NOTE The procedure described here is what happens the first time you run Outlook 2000 if you have had a previous version of Outlook installed on your computer. The procedure is slightly different if you've not had a previous version of Outlook installed.

FIGURE 51.5
This is the first of a series of wizard windows that guide you through the process of configuring Outlook.

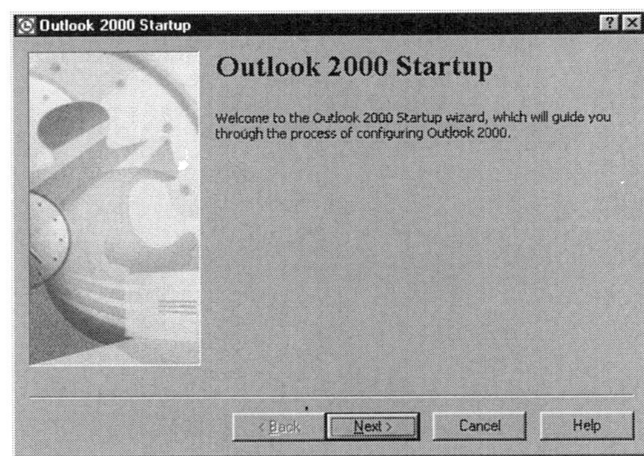

To configure Outlook:

1. With the first wizard window displayed, choose Next to display the second wizard window, shown in Figure 51.6.

FIGURE 51.6
This screen appears only if you had a previous version of Outlook installed on your computer.

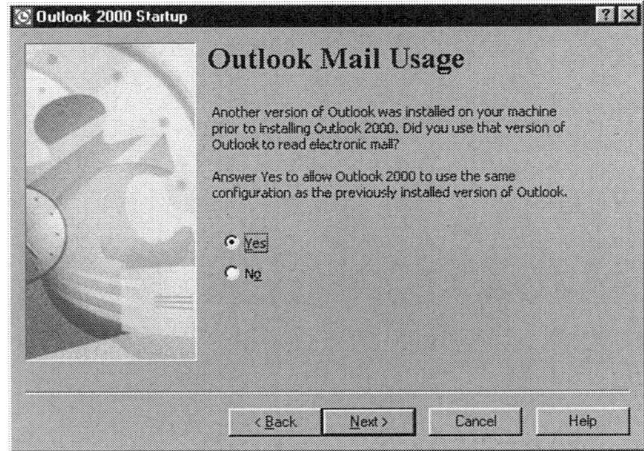

2. Choose Yes if you want to use the same Outlook configuration as before, or No if you want to select a configuration. If you want to see what configurations are available, choose No, and then choose Next to display the window shown in Figure 51.7.

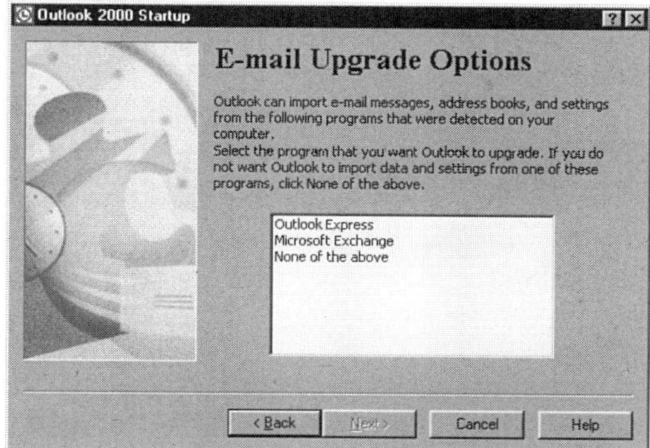

FIGURE 51.7
This dialog box lists email programs already available on your computer.

NOTE The email programs you see listed may be different from those shown here, depending on the email clients to which you have access.

3. If you want Outlook to import messages, address books, and settings from an email program you've been using previously, select that program from the list. Otherwise, select None of the Above. Choose Next to display the wizard window shown in Figure 51.8.

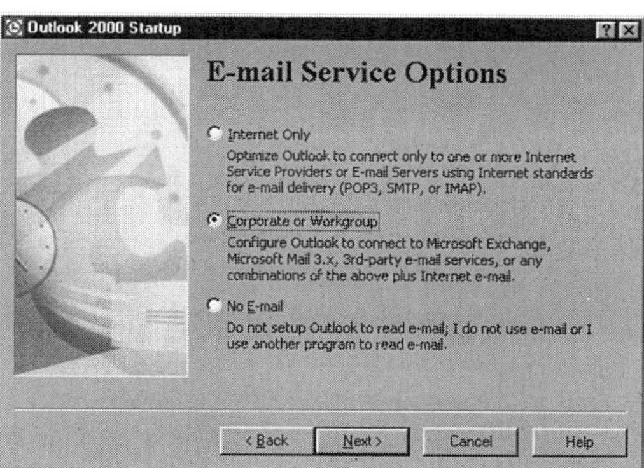

FIGURE 51.8
Use this dialog box to select which of the Outlook email service options you want to install.

4. Select Internet Only, Corporate or Workgroup, or No E-Mail. From here, the procedure depends on which service option you choose. The following step assumes you selected Internet Only. Choose Next to display the message shown in Figure 51.9.

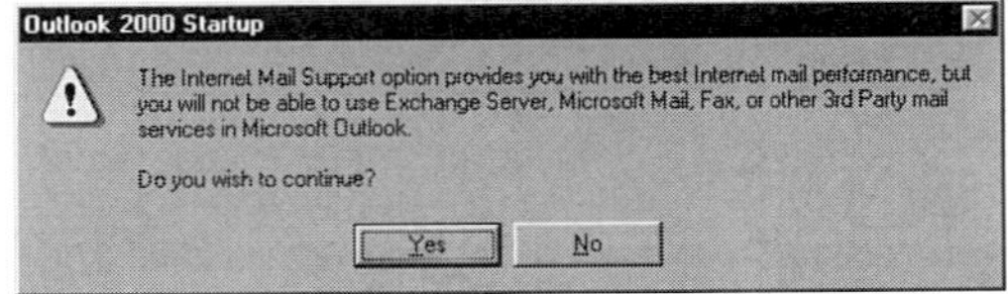

FIGURE 51.9
The message displayed here provides information about the service option you've selected.

5. Choose Yes to continue. If you don't have the Office CD-ROM inserted, a message box appears and asks you to insert it. The files required for the email service option you selected are read from the CD-ROM, and then Outlook opens.

Instead of Outlook opening, you may be asked to open an email account. This happens if you're running Outlook for the first time on a computer that hasn't previously had a version of Outlook installed and you've chosen to install the Internet Only E-Mail option. A wizard leads you through the process of creating an email account.

You may be asked to create some information services. This happens if you're running Outlook for the first time on a computer that hasn't previously had a version of Outlook installed and you chose to install the Corporate or Workgroup email option. A wizard leads you through the process of creating information services.

NOTE You'll also be asked to create an email account or some information services if the previous version of Outlook on your computer was installed with the No E-Mail option, and you are now installing Outlook 2000 with either the Internet Mail Only or Corporate or Workgroup options.

Switching to a Different Service Option

As explained previously, you can use Outlook 2000 (and Outlook 98) with one of three service options enabled: No E-Mail, Internet Mail Only (IMO), or Corporate/Workgroup (C/W). In Outlook 98, it wasn't easy to switch from one service option to another. In fact, you had to choose Add/Remove programs in the Windows Control Panel, choose Add New Components, and then install the new service option from the Office CD-ROM. Outlook 2000 corrects this problem by providing a way to switch easily between service options.

NOTE To find out which service option you currently have, display any Outlook Information viewer, and choose Help, About Microsoft Outlook. The second line of the About Microsoft Outlook dialog box contains the name of the current service option.

If several people share Outlook on the same computer, all of them have to use the same service option. If one person changes the service option, all the other people have to use Outlook with the new service option.

Switching from No E-Mail to Internet Mail Only

If you initially install the No E-Mail option, you can change to Internet Mail Only, but not directly to Corporate or Workgroup.

To switch from No E-Mail to Internet Mail Only:

1. With any Outlook Information viewer displayed, choose Tools, Accounts to display the Internet Accounts dialog box.
2. Use this dialog box to add an Internet account.

Outlook automatically changes to the Internet Mail Only option when you create an Internet account.

To switch back to No E-mail, remove all the Internet accounts.

Switching from Internet Mail Only to Corporate or Workgroup

If you have Outlook running with the Internet Mail Only option, you can switch to Corporate or Workgroup.

To switch from Internet Mail Only to Corporate or Workgroup:

1. With any Outlook Information viewer displayed, choose Tools, Options, and select the Mail Delivery tab to display the Options dialog box shown in Figure 51.10.

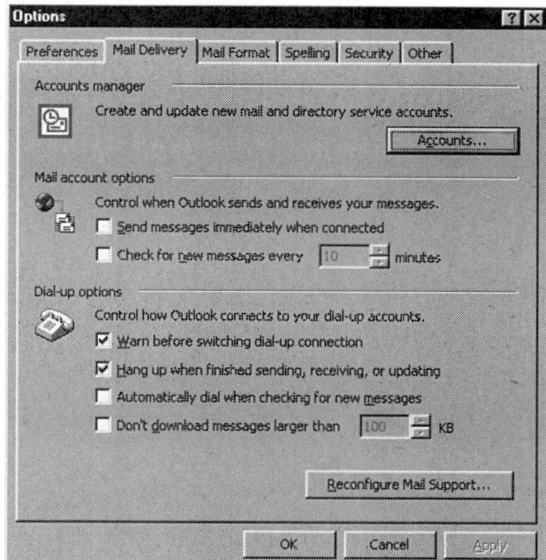

FIGURE 51.10
IMO Outlook displays this dialog box after you select the Mail Delivery tab.

2. Choose Reconfigure Mail Support to display the window shown in Figure 51.11.
3. Select Corporate or Workgroup; then choose Next to display the message shown in Figure 51.12.

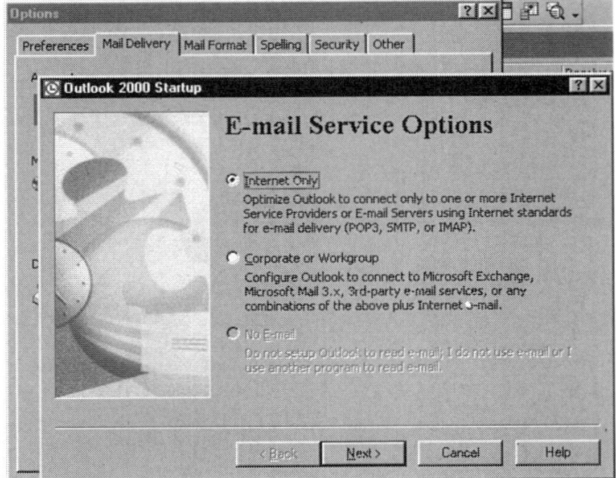

FIGURE 51.11
This window summarizes the capabilities of the Internet Mail Only and Corporate or Workgroup service options.

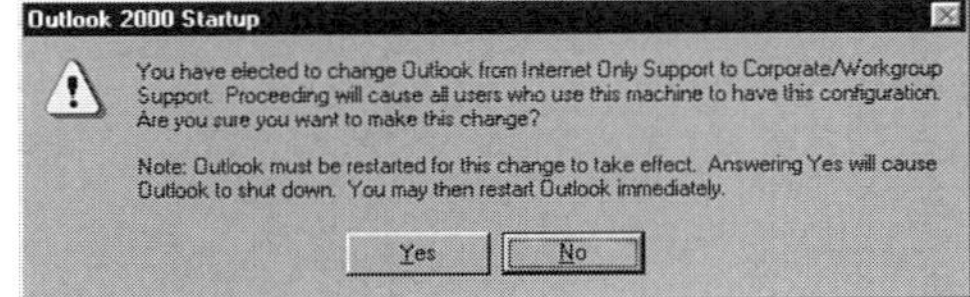

FIGURE 51.12
This message contains important information about the consequences of changing from Internet Mail Only to Corporate or Workgroup.

4. Choose Yes. Outlook closes and returns you to the Windows desktop.
5. Restart Outlook. You'll be told to insert the Office 2000 CD-ROM. A series of messages is displayed while the necessary files are loaded. After a few seconds, Outlook opens, this time with the Corporate or Workgroup service option enabled.

Switching from Corporate or Workgroup to Internet Mail Only

You can switch from Corporate or Workgroup to Internet Mail Only by implementing almost the same steps described in the preceding section. The principal differences are

- In step 1, select the Mail Services tab.
- In step 3, choose Internet Only.

Installing Add-Ins

When you install Outlook, you have access to many communication and information capabilities. Outlook comes with additional capabilities (known as add-ins) that you can install. In addition to the add-ins supplied with Outlook, more add-ins (some are called add-ons) are available from Microsoft and other suppliers.

Most add-ins are installed by the method described in the following steps. However, some add-ins are installed from the Control Panel in the same way as Windows applications.

To install an add-in:

1. With any Outlook Information viewer displayed, choose Tools, Options. Select the Other tab.
2. Choose Advanced Options, and then choose Add-In Manager to display the dialog box shown in Figure 51.13

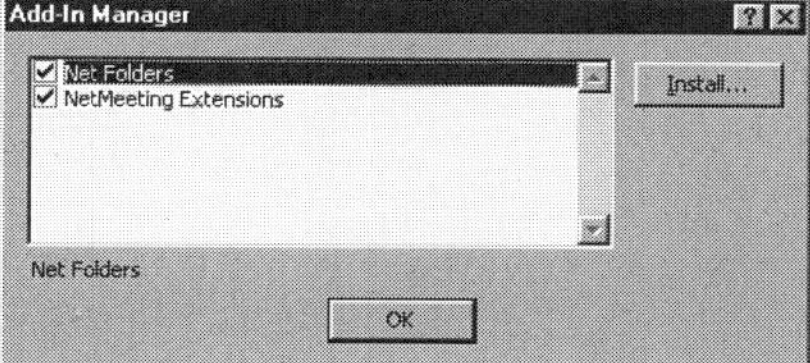

FIGURE 51.13
This dialog box lists the add-ins already installed.

NOTE The add-ins listed in this box are all installed. However, only those checked are enabled for use. You can disable an installed add-in by unchecking it.

3. Choose Install to display the dialog box shown in Figure 51.14.

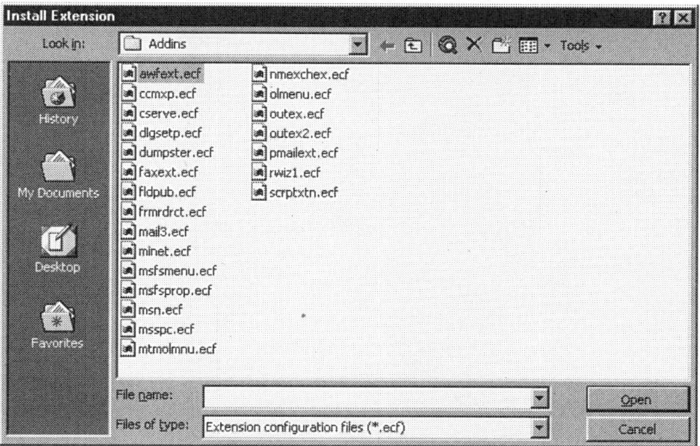

FIGURE 51.14
This dialog box lists add-ins available for installation.

NOTE The dialog box shown in Figure 51.14 lists the add-ins supplied with Outlook. If you want to install an add-in from another source, navigate to the folder that contains the add-in file.

4. Select the add-in you want to install, and choose Open to return to the Add-In Manager dialog box in which the new add-in is listed and checked.

The dialog box shown previously in Figure 51.14 lists available add-ins by filename. Table 51.1 relates filenames to the functions of add-ins.

Table 51.1 Add-In Filenames

Add-In	Filename
Delegate Access	dlgsetp.ecf
Exchange Extensions Commands	outex.ecf
Exchange Extensions Property Pages	outex2.ecf
NetMeeting Extensions	nmexchex.ecf
TeamStatus Form	olmenu.ecf
Rules Wizard	rwiz1.ecf
Mail 3.0 Extensions	mail3.ecf
Deleted Item Recovery	dumpster.ecf
Server Scripting	scrptxtn.ecf
Internet Mail	minet.ecf
(Corporate or Workgroup mode only)	
Net Folders	fldpub.ecf
Fax Extension	faxext.ecf
cc:Mail Menu Extension	ccmxp.ecf
Digital Security	etexch.ecf
Microsoft Fax	awfext.ecf
Microsoft Mail 3.x Menu Extensions	msfsmenu.ecf
Microsoft Mail 3.x Property Sheet Extensions	msfsprop.ecf
Schedule+	msspc.ecf
The Microsoft Network	msn.ecf
CompuServe Email	cserve.ecf
Windows CE Support	pmailext.ecf
Outlook Forms Redirector	frmrdrct.ecf

You can open Add-In (ECF) files with a standard text editor (such as Windows NotePad) to gather more information about them. Under no circumstances, however, should you modify ECF files. Doing so may cause an add-in to function incorrectly (if at all).

Also, be aware that installing an add-in with the Add-In Manager does not necessarily add the functions of the add-in to Outlook. Many Add-ins depend on other components (such as transports) without which they will not operate. An example of this is Exchange add-ins, which must have the Exchange Server information service installed and functioning.

Repairing Your Outlook Installation

Outlook shares certain self-repairing capabilities with other Office 2000 applications. When you open Outlook, the Windows Installer automatically checks to be sure essential files are present. If files are missing, the Installer reinstalls them with little or no user intervention (if you originally installed Outlook from a CD-ROM, you have to put that into the drive). In addition to checking files, the Installer also checks related Registry entries and, if necessary, repairs them.

You may occasionally run into the problem that Outlook starts but subsequently behaves abnormally. This can be due to such things as corrupted font files or missing templates. You can usually solve these kinds of problems by choosing Help, Detect and Repair. This utility scans noncritical files for discrepancies between their current and original states. In most cases, problems are corrected automatically.

CHAPTER 52

Integrating Outlook with Exchange Server

In this chapter

Outlook As a Client for Exchange

Outlook is Microsoft's premier client for Exchange server. Although Outlook can be used as a client for other email servers, Outlook offers its full capabilities as an Exchange client.

This chapter provides detailed information about using Outlook as a client for Exchange, explaining what Exchange is and what it can do. The chapter doesn't provide information about administering Exchange. Refer to the book *Special Edition Using Microsoft Exchange Server 5.5*, published by Que, for that information.

What Is Exchange?

Before going any further, I should point out that Microsoft has used the name Exchange for two completely different products. Windows 95 contained an application known as Exchange that was a mail client intended for use with Microsoft Mail. It was, in fact, the precursor of Outlook, which became available in Office 97. This Exchange is now known as Windows Messaging.

The other Exchange, the subject here, is a mail and collaboration server that became available in 1996.

Exchange is the heart of corporate messaging and collaboration systems and includes facilities for

- Transmitting email messages between computer users
- Connecting to other email systems including the Internet, Lotus Notes, Lotus cc:Mail, Microsoft Mail, and IBM PROFS
- Automatically responding to messages according to user-defined rules
- Recalling and replacing messages you've previously sent but haven't yet been read by recipients
- Providing a way for people to vote on issues and for the results of those votes to be tallied
- Enabling individual users to assign delegates
- Enabling users to work offline and from time-to-time to synchronize their information with that maintained on an Exchange server
- Acting as an information store that can be used to publish information
- Acting as an electronic bulletin board
- Organizing Web pages for a group to share
- Scheduling group activities, such as meetings
- Hosting online meetings
- Creating and distributing electronic forms

The preceding list is intended to give you an idea of the scope of Exchange's capabilities, and is by no means comprehensive.

NOTE The remaining pages of this chapter contain information about some of the topics in the previous list. For more complete information, refer to *Special Edition Using Microsoft Office 2000*, published by Que.

Exchange can be used as a messaging and collaboration system by groups of almost any size. It's available as part of Microsoft's Small Business Server package with licenses for only five people. At the other end of the spectrum, Exchange can be used by international enterprises with hundreds of thousands of employees.

Exchange runs under Windows NT Server and is, in many ways, integrated with Windows NT Server. For example, Exchange can be installed in such a way that each user can have a single password to log on to the server network and on to Exchange. Exchange can be set up to share user account information with Windows NT, thus simplifying an administrator's tasks. This integration is available with Windows 2000 Server, too.

Storing Information

Exchange saves information in what's known as information stores. There are three information stores: Public, Private, and Directory. Prior to version 5.5, each of these stores had a maximum capacity of 16GB (gigabytes). Although this is more than sufficient for small organizations, it is not adequate for large enterprises. In version 5.5, the maximum capacity of each store is 16,000GB.

Each user keeps email and other personal information in the Private store. An Exchange administrator can limit the amount of space available to each user. Shared information is kept in the Public store.

NOTE If you use Outlook as a client for Exchange, you can choose whether you want to save email messages and other information in the Exchange store or in an Outlook Personal Folders file (*.pst) on your computer's hard drive.

When a person sends a message to a number of people, Exchange saves that message only once, a technique known as *single-instance message storage*. The message remains in the store until the last recipient deletes it.

Sending and Receiving Email

You can send and receive email within the Exchange environment. You can also use Exchange to connect to other email environments.

With Outlook as your mail client, you can create messages and choose Send. As long as your computer is connected to the Exchange Server, your messages are immediately sent to the Exchange information store and, from there, to the recipients' inboxes. Similarly, messages sent to you arrive from the Exchange information store in your inbox.

You can use Exchange to send and receive email messages and other information by way of the Internet or an intranet. Exchange supports many Internet protocols, including HTML, HTTP, IMAP4, LDAP, NNTP, POP3, SMTP, S/MIME, and SSL.

▶ **See** "Improved Compatibility with Internet Standards," **p. 1336**

Because Exchange supports all the major Internet protocols, you can use Outlook and any other Internet email client to send and receive messages from your Exchange information store.

You can interchange email messages with users who use other messaging systems. The supported messaging system includes IBM PROFS, IBM SNADS, Lotus cc:Mail, and Lotus Notes.

Other Exchange Capabilities

The remainder of this chapter explains how you can use many of Exchange's capabilities when you're using Outlook as an Exchange client. These capabilities include

- Dealing with email automatically by creating rules
- Giving people delegate access to your Exchange account so that they can send and receive messages on your behalf
- Sharing your personal folders with other people
- Using Public Folders to publish information
- Accessing your Exchange account from a remote location
- Working with your Exchange account when you're offline
- Planning meetings automatically by sharing calendars among your colleagues

To use Outlook as a client for Exchange, you should have the Microsoft Exchange Server information service in your Outlook profile. The following sections explain how to add that service to your profile and how to set its properties.

Adding the Exchange Server Information Service

You add the Exchange Server information service to a profile in the same way that you add other information services. After you've added the service, you must close and restart Outlook before you can use it.

To add the Exchange Server information service to your profile, follow these steps:

1. With any Outlook Information viewer displayed, choose Tools, Services to display the dialog box shown in Figure 52.1.
2. Choose Add to display the Add Service to Profile dialog box, which lists available information services.

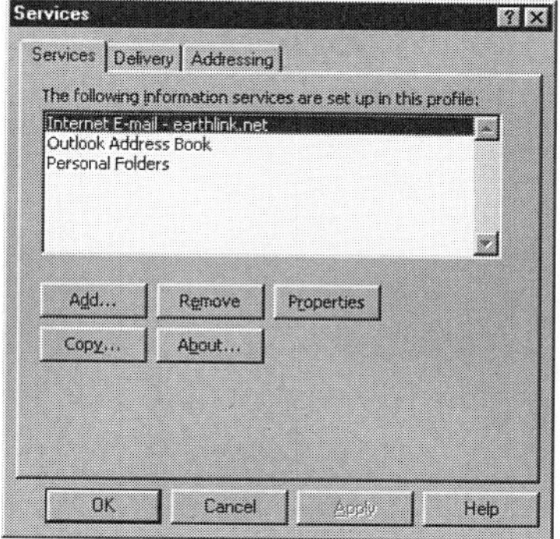

FIGURE 52.1
The Services dialog box lists the information services already in your profile.

3. Select Microsoft Exchange Server and choose OK. Outlook displays the Microsoft Exchange Server dialog box, shown in Figure 52.2.

NOTE If the Exchange Server information service is already in your profile, Outlook displays a message saying that you can't add Exchange Server a second time.

CAUTION

You may run into a problem if you have the Exchange Server information service in your profile and, after experiencing problems with connectivity to Exchange, decide to remove the service and then add it back into your profile.

To remove the service, choose Tools, Services, to display the Services dialog box. Select Microsoft Exchange Server in the list of services, and choose Remove. Outlook removes the service from the list.

At that point, you might be tempted to immediately add the service back into your profile. That won't work! Although the service isn't listed, it remains active until you close and restart Outlook. If you do try to add the Microsoft Exchange Server information service at this time, you'll find that you can't set the properties of the service you just added. If you attempt to set its properties, Outlook displays a message stating `Changes cannot be made while mail is running.`

The solution to this problem is to close (use File, Exit and Log Off) and restart Outlook after you've removed the service. With Outlook restarted, you can go ahead and add the service back into your profile and set its properties.

Setting the Properties

The Microsoft Exchange Server dialog box shown in Figure 52.2 is displayed when you choose OK in the Add Service to Profile dialog box to add the service to your profile. You can redisplay this dialog box by selecting the service in the Properties dialog box and then choosing Properties.

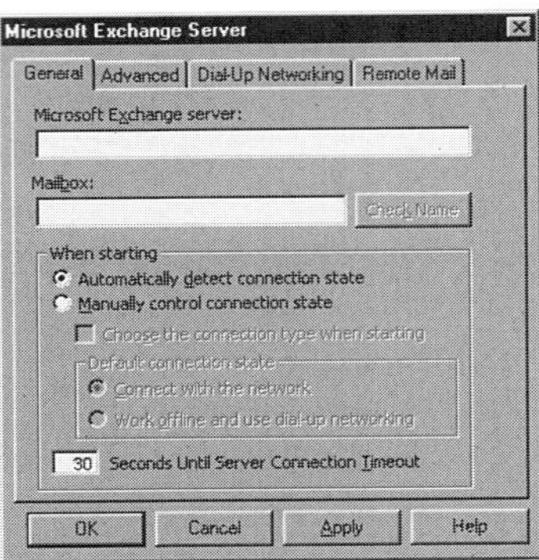

FIGURE 52.2
The Microsoft Exchange Server properties dialog box opens with the General tab selected.

Setting the General Properties

You can set the principal properties of the Exchange Server information service in the General tab.

NOTE If you're setting up Outlook as a client for Exchange on a local network, you'll probably be concerned only with the settings in the General tab.

While you're adding the Exchange Server information service to your profile, you have to provide the names of the Exchange server and your mailbox on that server. Subsequently, if you open the Microsoft Exchange Server dialog box, the Microsoft Exchange Server and Mailbox boxes are gray; you can't change the server or mailbox names. To change the server or mailbox names, you must remove the information service from your profile, close and restart Outlook, and add the information service into your profile again.

To identify your Exchange mailbox:

1. Enter the name of the Exchange server in the Microsoft Exchange Server box.
2. Enter the name of your Exchange mailbox in the Mailbox box. The Check Name button becomes enabled after you've entered the server and mailbox names.
3. Choose Check Name to verify the server and mailbox names. After a short delay, Outlook underlines these names to signify they are valid, and disables the Check Name button. If one or both of the server and mailbox names are not valid, Outlook displays a message that reads `The name could not be resolved`. If that happens, check with your Exchange administrator for the correct names to use.

NOTE You may see a message that reads `Network problems are preventing connection to the Microsoft Exchange Server computer`. This is a problem to be solved by the LAN or Exchange administrator.

Use the lower part of the General tab to specify what happens when Outlook starts.

If you're setting up Outlook on a desktop computer that's permanently connected to the server, you should select the default Automatically Detect Connection State.

If you're setting up Outlook on a laptop computer that's only sometimes connected to the server, you'll probably have two or more profiles.

- In the profile you use when the computer is connected to the server, select Automatically Detect Connection State.
- In the profile you use when you are out of the office, select Manually Control Connection State. In most cases, leave Choose the Connection Type When Starting unchecked and select Work Offline and Use Dial-Up Networking. If you select Choose the Connection Type When Starting, a dialog box is displayed when you start Outlook, asking whether you want to work offline or connect to your network.

The Seconds Until Server Connection Timeout box at the bottom of the dialog box is where you specify how long Outlook tries to connect to the server before telling you that a connection cannot be established. The default 30 seconds is usually more than enough for a local connection. However, if you're connecting from a remote location, particularly if you're using Dial-Up Networking, you may have to increase the default time significantly.

NOTE Refer to *Special Edition Using TCP/IP*, published by Que, for specific TCP/IP Dial-Up Networking information.

Setting the Advanced Properties

Select the Advanced tab to set advanced properties of the information service. The Advanced tab is shown in Figure 52.3.

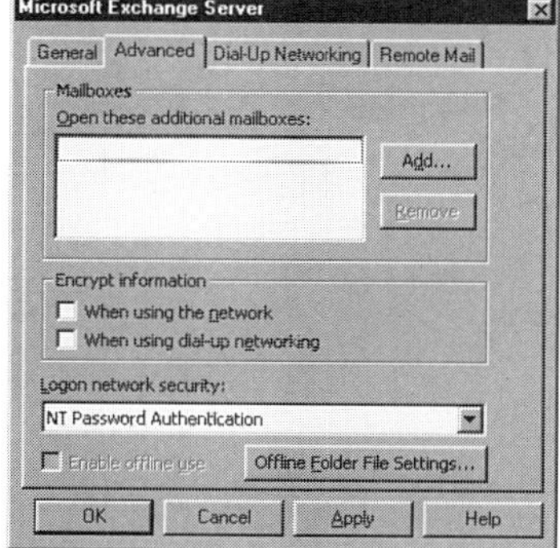

FIGURE 52.3
You can use the Advanced tab to set more properties.

The top section of the dialog box is where you can identify Exchange mailboxes (other than your own) that you want to access. The owners of those mailboxes must, of course, give you permission to access those mailboxes. In some circumstances, you might own more than one mailbox. In that case, you identify the principal one in the General tab and others in this tab.

▶ **See** "Sharing Your Folders," **p. 1408**

To identify an Exchange mailbox to which you have delegate access, enter the name of the mailbox in the Open These Additional Mailboxes box. After you've entered the mailbox name, choose Add. You can list as many mailboxes as you need in this way.

NOTE The Add button is not enabled if you selected Work Offline and Use Dial-Up Networking. Nor is it available if you didn't enter your mailbox name and chose Check Name in the General tab.

If you want to remove a mailbox from the list, select that mailbox and choose Remove.

By default, Outlook doesn't encrypt messages that you send to Exchange. If you want to encrypt messages, check one or both of the boxes in the Encrypt Information section of the dialog box.

As explained previously in this chapter, Exchange can be set up to share passwords with Windows NT Server. To specify how you want the Exchange Server information service to handle passwords, open the Logon Network Security drop-down list and select

- NT Password Authentication—Choose this if you want to log on to Exchange Server with the same password you use to log on to Windows NT Server.
- Distributed Password Authentication—Choose this if the server you're accessing makes use of Microsoft's Membership Directory Services.
- None—After you choose this, you'll be asked for a password when you open Outlook.

Check the Enable Offline Use box if you want to work offline and enable automatic offline synchronization.

Choose Offline Folder File Settings to display the Offline Folder File Settings dialog box. From here, you can specify your offline folder settings.

▶ **See** "Using Outlook Offline," **p. 1414**

Setting the Dial-Up Networking Properties

You need to use the Dial-Up Networking tab, shown in Figure 52.4, only if you're setting up Outlook to connect to Exchange by Dial-Up Networking.

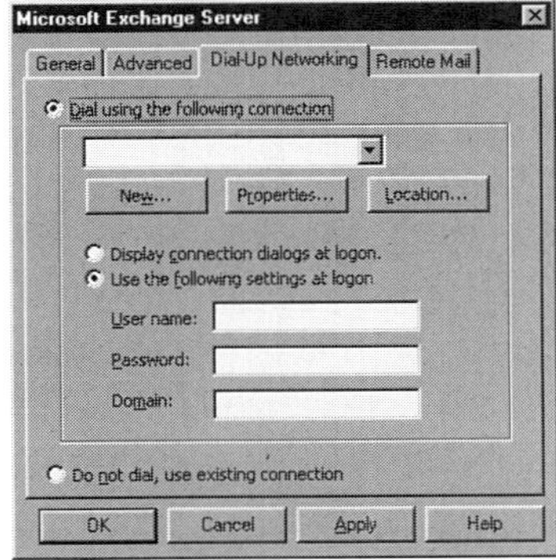

FIGURE 52.4
Use this tab to define how Outlook connects to Exchange by Dial-Up Networking.

Make sure Dial Using the Following Connection is selected, then open the drop-down list of available connections, and if the one you want to use is available, select it.

NOTE If you haven't previously set up the dial-up connection, you can use the New, Properties, and Locations buttons to set up a dial-up connection.

Enter your mailbox name in the User Name box, your password in the Password box, and your server domain name in the Domain box.

Setting Remote Mail Properties

You need to use the Mail Properties tab only if you're setting up Outlook to use remote mail.

▶ For information about setting up remote mail, **see** "Copying an Address Book into Your Remote Computer," **p. 1414**

Making the Information Service Available

After setting up properties in the General tab and any of the other three tabs that are appropriate, choose OK. Outlook displays a message telling you to close Outlook and restart it. Choose OK to close the message box, choose OK to close the Services dialog box, and then choose File, Exit and Log Off to close Outlook. The Microsoft Exchange Server information service is available the next time you start Outlook.

Setting Up Outlook As an Exchange Client

To use Outlook as an Exchange client, you must have C/W Outlook installed on your computer, have the Microsoft Exchange Server information service in your profile, have a LAN connection to a server on which Exchange Server is installed, and have an email account on that Exchange Server.

Selecting a Storage Location

If you use IMO Outlook, or C/W Outlook but not as a client for an Exchange server, Outlook stores your email and all other Outlook items in a Personal Folders file on your hard drive. However, if you use C/W Outlook as a client for an Exchange server, you can choose one of three places to store your email and other Outlook items:

- A Personal Folders file on your local hard drive
- The Exchange Server information store
- An Offline Folders file on your local hard drive

▶ For information about working with offline folders, **see** "Understanding Offline Folders," **p. 1410**

You should keep your Outlook items in the Exchange Server information store if you want to take advantage of Exchange Server's collaboration capabilities. If you and other Outlook users do that, you can easily share such information as Calendar and Contact items, and be able to replicate your offline folders with the information store. The downside of doing that is each time you work with Outlook items, you create traffic on the LAN. If you have a reliable, high-performance LAN, you should keep your Outlook items in the Exchange Server information store. Only consider saving Outlook items locally if you experience LAN problems.

NOTE The Exchange administrator usually decides where Outlook items are saved.

Finding Out Where Outlook Items Are Saved

You can easily see where Outlook items are stored. With any Outlook Information viewer displayed, choose View, Folder List to display the list of folders. If the only place you have available for saving Outlook items is the Exchange store, you'll see a list of folders such as that shown in Figure 52.5.

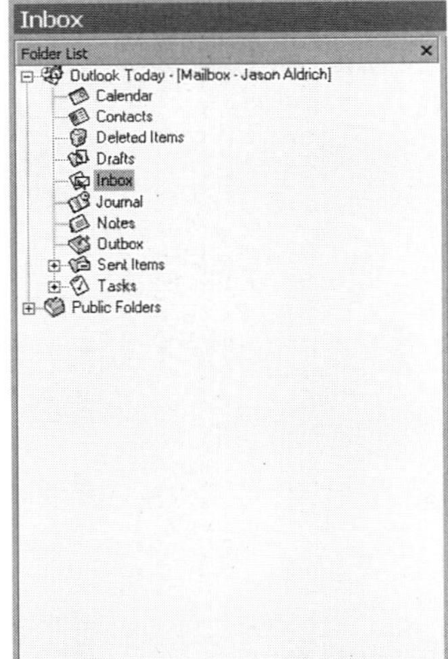

FIGURE 52.5 The top-level folder in this case is named Outlook Today – {mailbox – Jason Aldrich}. The word "mailbox" in this name indicates that your Outlook items are saved in an Exchange mailbox.

In this example, Jason Aldrich owns the mailbox.

NOTE This list shows two top-level folders. The one with the name that starts with the words "Outlook Today" contains your Outlook items. Public Folders is an area of the Exchange store you can use to share information with other people. See "Using Public Folders" later in this chapter.

If you have a mailbox on an Exchange server and a Personal Folders file in your local disk, the folder list contains an additional folder—Personal Folders.

In this case, you can select either your mailbox on the Exchange server or your Personal Folders file on your local disk as the place to save your Outlook items. Outlook can save items in one or the other.

The place where Outlook currently saves your Outlook items is indicated in two ways:

- By the image of a house superimposed over a top-level folder icon
- By the words "Outlook Today" at the beginning of a top-level folder's name

Changing Where Outlook Items Are Stored

Use these steps to change where Outlook saves items:

1. With any Outlook Information viewer displayed, choose Tools, Services to display the Services dialog box. Select the Delivery tab, shown in Figure 52.6.

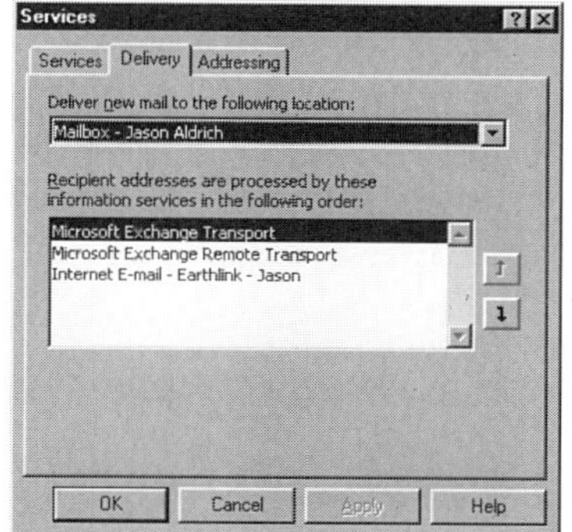

FIGURE 52.6
The Delivery tab shows where Outlook items are currently saved—the Exchange store in this case.

2. Open the Deliver New Mail to the Following Location drop-down list to display a list of available locations.

NOTE Although the name of the box refers specifically to mail, Outlook uses the same location for all items.

3. Select the location in which you want to save Outlook items. Select a location that has a name starting with "Mailbox" to save Outlook items in the Exchange store; select the name of a Personal Folders file to save Outlook items on your local hard drive.
4. Choose OK to close the dialog box. The new delivery location doesn't take effect until you choose File, Exit and Log Off to close Outlook, and then restart it.

TIP Outlook doesn't tell you that you must close and restart Outlook before the new delivery location takes effect. However, that step is necessary.

After you restart Outlook, the folder list contains a folder named "Mailbox – *[user's name]*."

If you want to use the Exchange server's store to save Outlook items, you must have that selected. The remainder of this chapter assumes that you're using the Exchange store.

Copying Items to the Mailbox Folder

If you have previously been using a Personal Folders file to save your Outlook items, you may want to copy those items to a Mailbox folder on Exchange Server.

You must display the items to be copied in a Table view.

To copy Outlook items from a Personal Folders file to a server Mailbox:

1. With any Table type of Outlook Information viewer displayed, choose View, Folder List.
2. If necessary, expand your Personal Folders file to display the names of the folders it contains. Also, if necessary, expand your Mailbox to display the folders it contains.
3. In the folder list, select the folder in your Personal Folders file from which you want to copy items.
4. Select one or more items. If you want to select all items in the folder, choose Edit, Select All.
5. Hold down Ctrl while you drag the selected item or items onto the folder in your Mailbox into which you want to copy items. If you want to move items from one folder to the other instead of copying them, hold down Shift while you drag.

Sending and Receiving Email

Sending and receiving email messages using Exchange Server as the mail server is almost the same as sending and receiving Internet email messages. One difference is that if your computer is directly connected to the server, you don't have to do anything to send messages from your Outbox to the server, nor do you have to do anything to collect messages waiting for you on the server. Outlook automatically sends messages you create to the server and saves copies of them in your Sent Items folder, and automatically collects messages waiting for you on the server and places them in your Inbox folder.

In addition to sending messages on your behalf, you can send messages on behalf of another person.

When you create messages to be sent to other people who have accounts on an Exchange server, you should normally use the Microsoft Outlook Rich Text mail format because that's the native format used by Exchange. By using this format, you can be sure recipients will see your messages exactly as you create them. However, for messages that go to people outside your Exchange environment who may not be using message clients that accept Rich Text Format, it's better to use Plain Text.

You might, under some circumstances, run into formatting problems if you send messages using the HTML format. Refer to the Microsoft Knowledge Base article Q183668, "HTML Formatting Not Retained on Exchange 5.5," for detailed information about this.

The remainder of this chapter describes messaging capabilities provided by Exchange Server that are in addition to the basic processes of sending and receiving messages.

Changing Delivery Options for Messages

You can set several delivery options for messages you send by way of Exchange Server.

Redirecting Replies

Normally, when you send a message and recipients reply to it, the replies are automatically sent to you. You can, however, request that replies to specific messages are automatically sent to someone else.

To redirect replies:

1. At any time while you're creating a message in the Message form, choose Options in the form's toolbar to display the Message Options dialog box, shown in Figure 52.7.

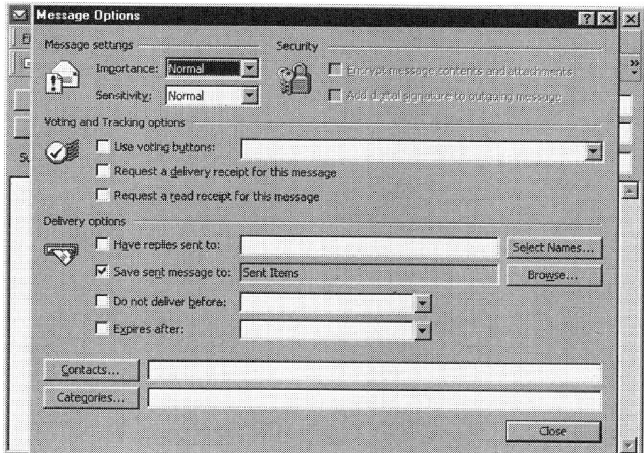

FIGURE 52.7
Use this dialog box to change the delivery options for a message.

2. In the Delivery Options section of the dialog box, check Have Replies Sent To. When you do so, your own name appears in the adjacent text box. The name is underlined to indicate the name is an alias for an email address.
3. If you know the email address of the person to whom you want replies to be sent, you can replace your own name with the email address of the person to whom you want replies to be sent. Otherwise, choose Select Names to display the Have Replies Sent To dialog box shown in Figure 52.8.

NOTE The Have Replies Sent To dialog box may be a little confusing. The Message Recipients box is actually where the name of the person who should receive replies to your message appears, not a list of the people who receive your messages.

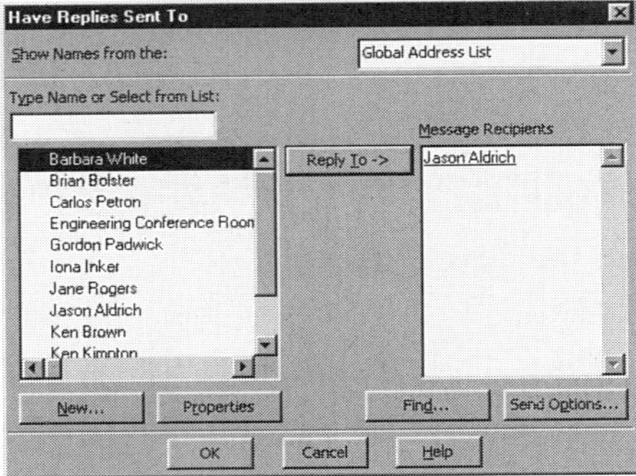

FIGURE 52.8
This dialog box initially shows your name in the Message Recipients box.

4. Delete your own name from the Message Recipients list.
5. In the list of names on the left, select the name of the person to whom you want replies to be directed. Then choose Reply To to copy that name into the Message Recipients list.
6. Choose OK to return to the Message Options dialog box that now shows the name of the person you selected in the Have Replies Sent To box.

The name you select in this manner applies only to the message you're currently creating.

NOTE If the person who receives messages has created a rule that generates automatic replies, the automatic reply is sent to you, not to the person you designate to receive replies.

When recipients receive a message in which replies have been redirected, they won't see anything unusual about the message. The message header contains the name of the sender as usual. However, when a user replies to the message, the reply will be addressed to the person designated in the Have Replies Sent To box in the original message.

Scheduling a Message for Later Delivery

In the Exchange messaging environment, you can create a message and mark it not to be delivered until a certain time and date. After you create the message and send it, Outlook sends it to Exchange in the normal way. Exchange holds the message until the date and time you specify and then sends it to the recipients.

To schedule a message for later delivery:

1. At any time while you're creating a message in the Message form, choose Options in the form's toolbar to display the Message Options dialog box, shown previously in Figure 52.7.
2. In the Delivery Options section of the dialog box, check Do Not Deliver Before. Outlook proposes tomorrow's date and 5:00 p.m.
3. You can edit the proposed date and time. Alternatively, click the button at the right end of the box to display a calendar in which you can select a date.

Outlook saves copies of messages that are set for delayed delivery in your Sent Items folder in the same way that it saves ordinary messages. You can see these messages listed in the Sent Items Information viewer. You can double-click a message in the Information viewer to display it in a Message form. The InfoBar near the top of the Message form contains the delayed delivery information.

Setting an Expiration Date and Time

You can set an expiration date and time for a message. After you do so, Exchange automatically deletes the message if the recipient hasn't opened it by the date and time you specify. The procedure for setting an expiration time and date is the same as that described in the preceding section. Instead of checking the Do Not Deliver Before box, check the Expires After box.

You can see the headers of messages you've sent that have an expiration date in your Sent Items Information viewer. You can double-click a message header to display it in a Message form. The InfoBar near the top of the form contains the expiration information.

Requesting Receipts

You can ask Outlook to send you two types of delivery receipts either for all messages you send or for individual messages. You can request delivery receipts for a specific message by checking boxes in the Message Options dialog box, shown previously in Figure 52.11.

To request a receipt when a message arrives in a recipient's Inbox, check Request a Delivery Receipt for This Message. To request a receipt when a recipient opens a message, check Request a Read Receipt for This Message.

The following steps describe how you request delivery receipts for all messages you send. These steps apply to delivery receipts, to responses you get from meeting requests you send, and from messages you send that include voting buttons.

To request delivery receipts for all messages:

1. With any Outlook Information viewer displayed, choose Tools, Options, and select the Preferences tab in the Options dialog box.
2. Choose E-Mail Options and then, in the E-Mail Options dialog box, choose Tracking Options to display the Tracking Options dialog box, shown in Figure 52.9.

Within your Exchange Server environment, tracking options work as explained here. If you're using Outlook as an Exchange client and are communicating with people who have other messaging environments, some of the choices you make here may not operate as you expect.

3. If you want to keep delivery receipts and other responses in a folder other than your Inbox folder, check After Processing, Move Receipts To. When you do that, Outlooks proposes to move receipts and responses to your Deleted Items folder. You can choose Browse to open the Select Folder dialog box, in which you can select any other Outlook folder (or create a new folder and select that folder).

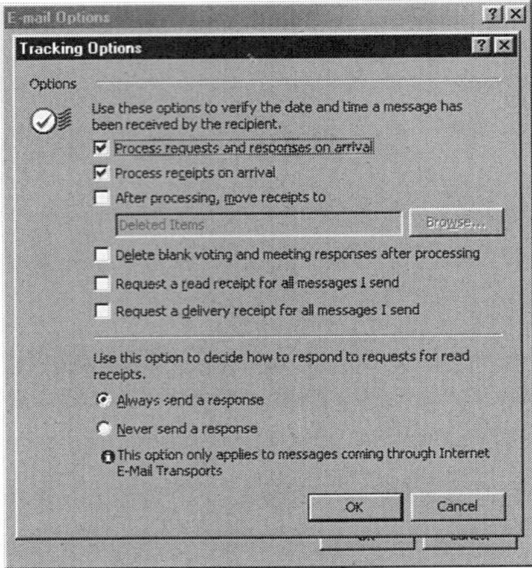

FIGURE 52.9
Use this dialog box to set tracking options that apply to all the messages you create.

4. If you want to delete voting and meeting responses that contain no text, check the Delete Blank Voting and Meeting Request Responses After Processing. By doing so, these responses are deleted from your Inbox (or other folder that you specified). Even though the response messages are deleted, those responses are still tallied.
5. To request a read receipt for all messages you send, check the Request a Read Receipt for All Messages I Send box.
6. To request a delivery receipt for all messages you send, check the Request a Delivery Receipt for All Messages I Send box.
7. Choose the Always Send a Response option button if you are willing to send responses to requests for read receipts. Alternatively, check the Never Send a Response if you don't want to respond to requests for read receipts. This choice applies only to responses requested by way of an Internet mail server.

After you've set receipt options that apply to all messages, you can use the Message form's Message Options dialog box (shown previously in Figure 52.7) to make other choices for individual messages.

After you send messages for which you request one or both receipts, Exchange automatically sends receipt messages to your Inbox.

When you receive a read receipt, all you know is that a recipient opened the message, or marked it as read. You have no guarantee the recipient actually read it. If you really want to know that a recipient has read the message, you should request the recipient to send an acknowledgment to you.

Tracking Message Receipts

If you send a message in which you have requested a delivery receipt, a read receipt, or both to several people, you can easily see a tally that shows which people have read your message.

To see a tally of people who have read your message:

1. With any Outlook Information viewer displayed, select the My Shortcuts section of the Outlook Bar and select Sent Items to display the Sent Items Information viewer.
2. In the Sent Items Information viewer, double-click the message for which you want to see the tally. Outlook displays a message form that now has two tabs. The Message tab is selected—it contains your original message.
3. Select the Tracking tab shown in Figure 52.10.

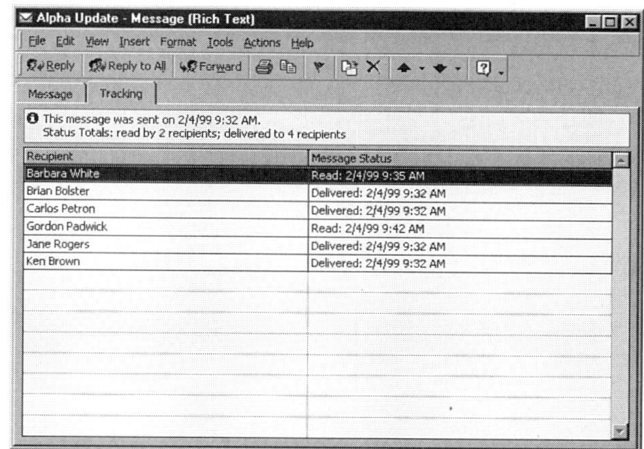

FIGURE 52.10
The tracking tab contains a table that lists the message recipients to whom you sent the original message and shows which of those recipients have read it. Notice the status totals at the top of the table.

4. If you want to print a copy of the response tally, open the form's File menu and choose Print.

You can arrange the list of recipients in alphabetical order by clicking the title at the top of the Recipients column. To send a copy of some or all rows in the list to someone else, select the rows you want to send, press Ctrl+C to copy the list into the Clipboard, create a new message, and press Ctrl+V to paste the selected rows into that message.

Recalling Messages

Subject to certain conditions, you can recall a message that you've previously sent. For a message recall to be successful:

- The recipient must have Outlook running.
- The recipient must be logged on to Exchange.
- The recipient must not have opened the message.
- The message must be in the recipient's Inbox folder.

It should be normal practice for all users to keep Outlook running (probably minimized) while their computers are turned on. If that happens, the first of these conditions is satisfied.

Normally, when a user logs on to Windows NT Server, that user is automatically logged on to Exchange Server. That satisfies the second condition.

The third condition is common sense. A recipient who has opened a message has probably read it, or at the least knows it's waiting to be read. You wouldn't want to open a message and subsequently find that somebody else has deleted it from your Inbox.

The last condition is the one that might give you trouble. Many users employ rules in Outlook or Exchange to place messages in specific folders other than their Inbox folders. Because of that, many of the messages you send are likely to be in folders other than Inbox folders on users' computers or in their Exchange stores.

The Power of Read Receipts

For Outlook on your computer to know whether a recipient has opened a message, you must have sent the message with a read receipt requested. If you sent the message you're trying to recall without requesting a read receipt, Outlook won't receive a read receipt even though the recipient has opened the message. As a result, Outlook will report `No recipients have reported reading the message` even though some may have done so. This will make you think that you can successfully recall the message when in fact you can't. For this reason, you should consider requesting a read receipt for all messages you send by way of Exchange. The disadvantage of requesting receipts is that it increases network traffic and also increases each Outlook user's storage requirements.

In general, because there's a strong possibility that you won't be able to recall messages, be careful what you send.

Knowing that message recall works only some of the time, here's how you attempt to recall a message.

To recall a message:

1. With any Outlook Information viewer displayed, select the My Shortcuts section of the Outlook Bar and choose Sent Items to display the Sent Items Information viewer.
2. Double-click the message you want to recall to display that message in the Message form.
3. Choose Actions, Recall This Message to display the dialog box shown in Figure 52.11.

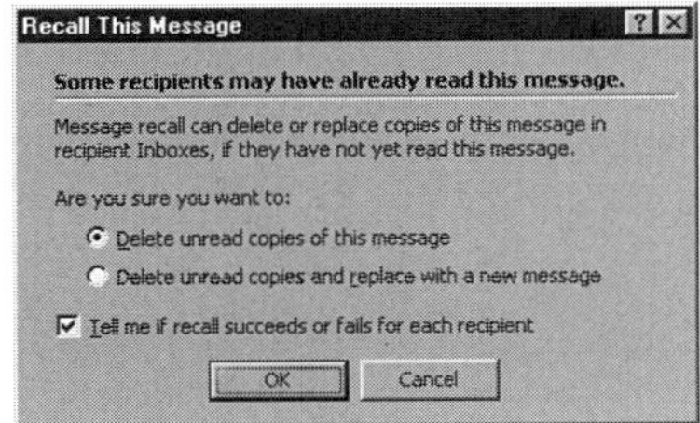

FIGURE 52.11
This dialog box warns you that you may not be able to recall the message from some recipients.

4. Choose the Delete Unread Copies of This Message option button and go to step 6. Alternatively, choose the Delete Unread Copies and Replace with a New Message option button and go to step 5.
5. Edit the original message that Outlook automatically displays in a Message form. Then choose Send in the form's toolbar to send the revised message. If the recall is successful, the revised message replaces the original message in the recipients' Inboxes.
6. Normally, leave the Tell Me If Recall Succeeds or Fails for Each Recipient box checked.

Within a short time, you should have messages in your Inbox telling you whether your recalls have succeeded or failed.

Using Server-Based Rules

If you use Outlook as a client for Exchange, you can set up rules that run on the server—rules that operate whether or not your computer is turned on—providing, of course, the server is up and running.

Using the Out of Office Assistant

You can use the Out of Office Assistant running on Exchange to process your email automatically, even when your computer is turned off. After you turn on the Out of Office Assistant, it automatically sends whatever reply you choose to senders. You can also set up the Out of Office Assistant to process rules you create. Of course, the Out of Office Assistant deals only with email you receive by way of Exchange. It doesn't, for example, know anything about Internet email that arrives directly to your computer.

To turn on the Out of Office Assistant:

1. With any Outlook Information viewer displayed, choose Tools, Out of Office Assistant to display the dialog box shown in Figure 52.12.

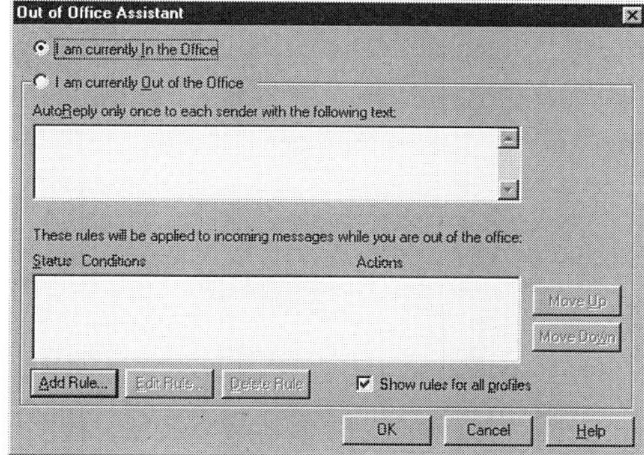

FIGURE 52.12
This dialog box opens with I Am Currently in the Office selected.

2. Choose I Am Currently out of the Office.
3. In the AutoReply Only Once to Each Sender box with the Following Text box, enter the message you want to be sent. Choose OK.

From now on, the message you entered in step 3 is automatically sent whenever the first message from each sender arrives in your Exchange store.

When you return to the office and are ready to respond to messages, open the Out of Office Assistant dialog box again and choose I Am Currently in the Office.

You can use the Out of Office Assistant to do much more than just send an automatic reply. With the Out of Office Assistant dialog box open, choose Add Rule to display the dialog box shown in Figure 52.13. You can use this dialog box to create several rules.

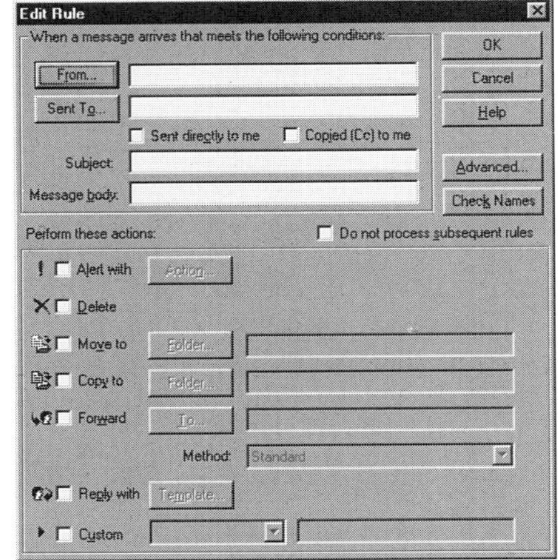

FIGURE 52.13
Use this dialog box to define a rule that runs on the server when a message arrives in your mailbox in the Exchange store.

The top section of the dialog box contains boxes in which you can define certain aspects of incoming messages. The rule is applied only if it satisfies all the criteria you define in these boxes. The bottom section of the dialog box is where you can define what the rule does.

You can make more precise definitions of the message to be acted on by choosing Advanced to display the Advanced options. Use this dialog box to specify additional criteria about messages to be responded to.

Running Outlook Rules on Exchange

When you've finished designing a rule using the Outlook Rules Wizard, choose Finish to save that rule. At that time, Outlook examines the rule to see if it can run on Exchange without access to your computer. If for some reason that's not possible—for example, if the rule involves saving a message in a folder on your computer's hard drive—Outlook displays a message stating `This rule is a client-only rule, and will process only if Outlook is running`. When you see that message you have no alternative but to choose OK. Outlook saves the rule and the wizard window lists the rule with the words "client only" after the rule's name.

If you create a rule that can be run on the server and doesn't need access to your computer, by default Outlook automatically saves that rule on the server instead of on your computer's hard disk. In that case, the rule's name is displayed in the wizard window without the words "client only" being added.

You know, therefore, that rule names displayed in the wizard window with the words "client only" appended refer to rules that operate only when Outlook is running on your computer; rule names without those words appended run on the server whether or not Outlook is running on your computer.

You can control whether Outlook saves rules on the server. To do so, choose Tools, Rules Wizard to open the Rules Wizard, and then choose Options to display the dialog box shown in Figure 52.14.

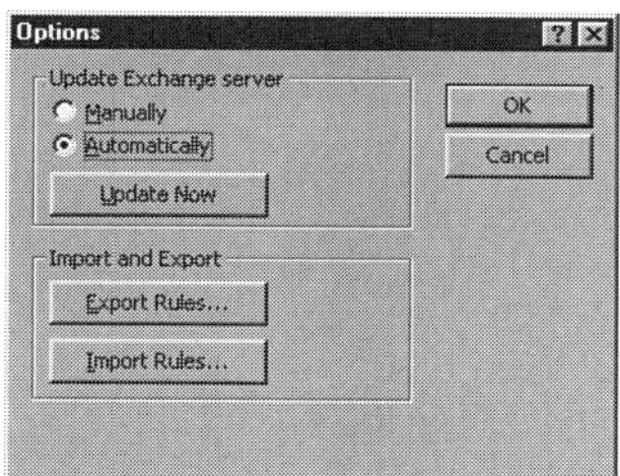

FIGURE 52.14
Use this dialog box to choose whether Outlook automatically saves new rules on the server.

By default, Automatically is selected in the Update Exchange Server section of this dialog box. If you want to manually control whether Outlook saves rules on the server, select Manually.

Outlook saves the Automatically or Manually selection from one Outlook session to the next. If you select Manually and subsequently exit from Outlook, that setting will be in effect the next time you start Outlook.

After you select Manually, Outlook saves rules on your computer. To move those rules that can run on the server from your computer to the server, choose Update Now in the Rules Wizard Options dialog box.

Using Web Services

If your Exchange Server administrator has set up and enabled Outlook Web Access on Exchange, you can create and access forms in HTML format from within Outlook. In this situation, the new command Web Form appears on Outlook's Actions menu. When you choose this command, you can choose a form that your default Web browser automatically opens.

NOTE You can find more information in books about Exchange Server, such as *Special Edition Using Microsoft Exchange Server 5.5*, published by Que.

Sharing Information

When you're using C/W Outlook as a client for an Exchange server, you can choose among three ways to share information with other people who have Exchange accounts:

- Delegate Access—To give someone permission to access your Outlook folders and act on your behalf. For example, designating delegate access is useful if you are a manager and need an assistant to act on your behalf while you're away.
- Shared Folders—To share information in your folders with many people in a workgroup.
- Public Folders—To make information available throughout a group or organization.

▶ If you want to designate another person to have delegate access to your folders, **see** "Giving Permission to Access to Your Folders," **p. 1408**

Using Public Folders

Public folders on the server are used to make information available to members of a group of any size. Common uses of Public Folders are to publish companywide information such as Employee Policy Manuals and corporate calendars.

NOTE The process of putting information into a Public Folder is known as *posting*.

You can use Public Folders for such purposes as

- Posting information for many people to see—Normally, one person has permission to post, edit, and delete information in a Public Folder of this type, and everyone has permission to read that information.
- Maintaining an unmoderated electronic bulletin board—Used in this way, a Public Folder is similar to an Internet newsgroup. Everyone has permission to post and read information. Normally, only one person has permission to delete information.
- Maintaining a moderated bulletin board—People offer items to a moderator who decides which items to post on the bulletin board. Only the moderator has post and delete permissions; everyone has read permission.
- Sharing Outlook items with other people—The people who own the items copy those items to a Public Folder and give specific people permission to read them.
- Sharing files created in other applications, such as documents created in Word, worksheets created in Excel, and databases created in Access—The people who own the files copy them to a Public Folder and give specific other people whatever permissions are appropriate.

Creating a Public Folder

Public folders are created within an existing Public Folder in the Exchange *store*. Exchange Server 5.5 provides up to 16 gigabytes of space for Public Folders; the Exchange administrator can limit the size of individual Public Folders. You must have permission to create a folder to create a folder within an existing Public Folder.

NOTE The Exchange Server administrator uses Exchange Server Administrator to control permissions for creating folders on the server. For information about this, I recommend *Special Edition Using Microsoft Exchange Server 5.5*, also published by Que.

This chapter assumes you have the permission required to create Public Folders. If that's not the case, ask your Exchange Server administrator to grant you the necessary permission.

To create a Public Folder:

1. With any Outlook Information viewer displayed, choose View, Folder List to display your folder list, such as the one shown in Figure 52.15.

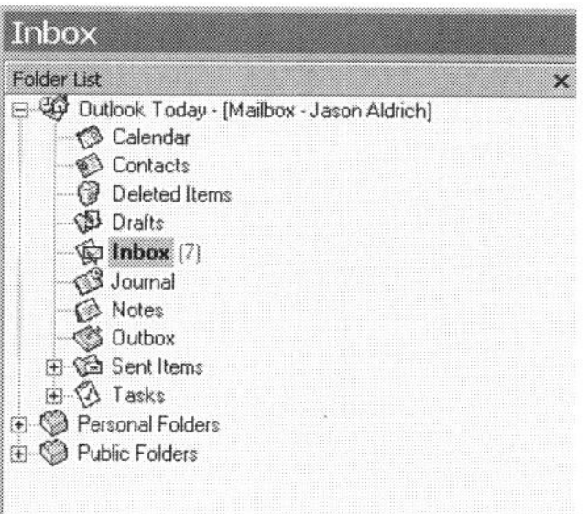

FIGURE 52.15
If you have the Microsoft Exchange Server information service in your profile, your folder list should contain a folder named Public Folders.

2. Expand the Public Folders folder and then expand the All Public Folders folder.

NOTE Your All Public Folders folder may be empty or may contain a long list of folders. The icon at the left of each folder name indicates the type of item that folder contains.

3. Right-click All Public Folders to display its context menu (be careful to right-click All Public Folders, not Public Folders). Choose New Folder in the context menu to display the New folder dialog box.
4. Enter a name for the new Public Folder in the Name box.
5. Unless you specifically intend to use the new folder for a particular type of Outlook item, leave Mail Items in the Folder Contains box. You can open the drop-down list and select another type of Outlook item.

NOTE Use Mail Items in the Folder Contains box if you're setting up a Public Folder to use for general information or as a bulletin board.

6. Because you started creating the new folder with All Public Folders selected in the folder list, Outlook proposes to save the new folder as a subfolder of All Public Folders. Don't change that, unless you want the new folder to be a subfolder under an existing folder.
7. Choose OK to finish creating the new folder.

8. Outlook asks if you want to add a shortcut to the new folder on the Outlook Bar. Choose Yes if you expect to access the Public Folder frequently; otherwise, choose No. The dialog box closes and the new folder is shown in the folder list as a subfolder of All Public Folders.

The name of the new Public Folder appears in your folder list in its correct alphabetical position.

Giving People Access to a Public Folder

After you create a Public Folder, you own it and control who has access to it. The only other person who can control access is the Exchange administrator. You can give access to individual people or to groups. Outlook gives you two ways to do this. You can give specific permissions to individuals or groups, or you can assign roles to individuals or groups. The available permissions are listed in Table 52.1; predefined roles are listed in Table 52.2.

Table 52.1 Available Permissions

Permission Types	Individual Permissions
Access	Create items, Read items, Edit own items, Edit all items, Create subfolders, Folder visible
Ownership	Folder owner, Folder contact
Delete	Delete own items, Delete all items

Table 52.2 Outlook's Predefined Roles

Role	Permissions
Author	Create, read, modify, and delete own items and files
Contributor	Read items; Submit items and files
Custom	Any combination of permissions
Editor	Create, read, modify, and delete all items and files
Non-Editing Author	Create and read items; Delete own items
Owner	Create, read, modify, and delete all items and files; Create subfolders; Set permissions for other people to access the folder
Publishing Author	Create and read items; Modify and delete own items; Create subfolders
Publishing Editor	Create, read, modify, and delete all items and files; Create subfolders
Reviewer	Read items

Examining the Default Permissions With a Public Folder (one that you own) for which you want to assign permissions visible in the folder list, right-click the name of that folder to display its context menu. In the context menu, choose Properties to display the folder's properties dialog box. Choose the Permissions tab to display the dialog box shown in Figure 52.16. The Properties dialog box has a Permissions tab only for the Public Folders you own.

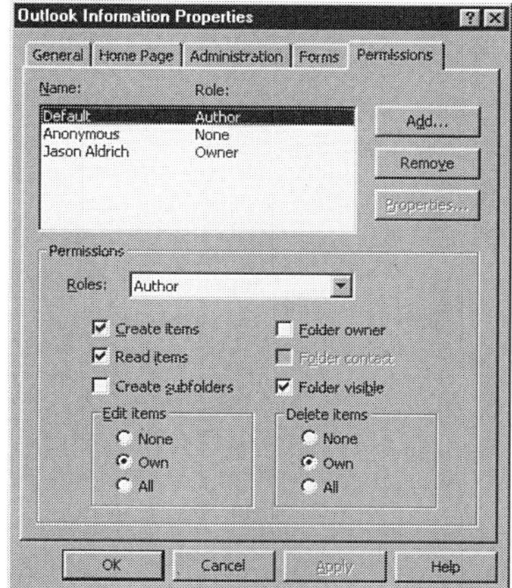

FIGURE 52.16
The dialog box opens with some names listed, each with a specific role.

NOTE After you right-click the name of a Public Folder that someone else created and, therefore, owns, the dialog box has a Summary tab instead of a Permissions tab. Choose the Summary tab to see, but not change, the permissions you have for that folder.

Outlook defines default permissions to three names: Default, Anonymous, and your own name.

- Default defines the permissions everyone who has an Exchange Server account gets unless you specifically give a person different permissions. Outlook assigns Author permissions to default users.
- Anonymous defines the permissions given to people who don't have an Exchange Server account but, if the server administrator allows, can log on to Exchange Server as Anonymous. The same permissions apply to people who log on as Anonymous by way of Outlook Web Access or an Active Server Page. Outlook assigns no permissions to anonymous users.

NOTE For information about Outlook Web Access, see *Special Edition Using Microsoft Exchange Server 5.5*, published by Que. For more information about Active Server Pages (ASP), see *Special Edition Using Microsoft FrontPage 2000*, also published by Que.

- Your own name defines the permissions you have as the owner of the Public Folder. Outlook assigns Owner permissions to the folder owner.

When the dialog box first appears, the first name in the list—Default—is selected. The Permissions section in the bottom part of the dialog box shows the permissions given to default users. You can select the other two names to see the permissions given to them.

For each name in the list of users, the Permissions section of the dialog box shows permissions in two ways. The Roles box shows permissions in terms of a predefined role. Below that are check boxes and option buttons that show the individual permissions associated with the role.

Changing People's Permissions You don't have to accept the default permissions Outlook assigns. For example, you may want to change the permissions for Default to None, so that only those people you specifically assign permissions to can access the Public Folder. If the Public Folder is intended to contain information available for everyone on the LAN to read, you should change the permissions for Anonymous to Read Items.

To change a person's or group's role:

1. Select the person or group in the list in the upper part of the dialog box.
2. Open the Roles drop-down list and select the role you want to assign. The role in the second column of the list of users changes to the role you selected. Also, the check boxes and option buttons below Roles change to show the individual permissions associated with the new role.

To assign specific permissions to a person or group:

1. Select the person or group in the list in the upper part of the dialog box.
2. Check the check boxes and select the option buttons in the lower part of the dialog box to assign specific permissions. If you select a combination of check boxes and option buttons that correspond to a predefined role, the name of that role appears in the Roles box. Otherwise, the Roles box contains the word Custom.

If you don't want a group, such as Anonymous, to see the Public Folder, remove the check mark from the Folder Visible box.

Adding Permissions You can add individuals and groups to the Permissions list.

To add permissions for a person or group:

1. In the Permissions tab of the Public Folder's Properties dialog box, choose Add to display the Add Users dialog box shown in Figure 52.17.
2. Choose the name of a person (or of several people) for whom you want to assign permissions.
3. Choose Add to move the selected names into the Add Users list, and then choose OK to return to the dialog box that shows the names you selected with the permissions you previously assigned to Default users.
4. Select the new users (you can select them individually or select any combination of them).

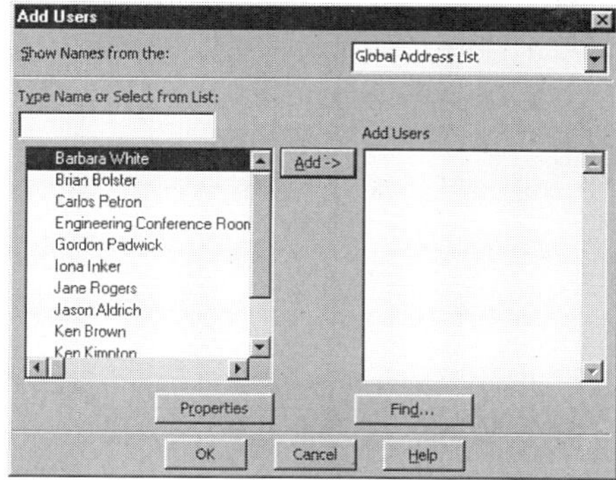

FIGURE 52.17
This dialog box opens showing a list of people who have accounts on the Exchange server.

5. Either assign a role to the new user (or users) or select the individual permissions you want them to have.

Withdrawing a User's Permissions To withdraw the permissions you've previously given for a user to access the Public Folder, select that user's name in the Permissions tab, and then choose Remove. Outlook immediately removes the user's name from the list of users.

Getting Information About a User To see information about a user, select that user's name in the list of users in the Permissions tab. Then choose Properties. Outlook displays the selected user's Properties dialog box. Use the five tabs in this dialog box to view information about the selected user.

Posting Information on a Public Folder

You can post Outlook items or files on a Public Folder for which you have Create Items permission. After you post an item in a Public Folder, other people who have permission to create items can respond to it. The chain of responses is known as a *conversation*. A conversation has a name that's the same as the subject of the message that started the conversation.

Posting a Message Posting information in a Public Folder is much like sending an email message.

To post information in a Public Folder:

1. Select the Public Folder into which you want to post information. If you have a shortcut icon for the Public Folder in your Outlook Bar, choose it. Otherwise, open your folder list and choose the Public Folder. Either way, Outlook displays an Information viewer that shows items already in the Public Folder.
2. Choose the New button at the left end of the viewer's Standard toolbar to display the Discussion form shown in Figure 52.18.
3. Enter a subject for the item in the Subject box and press Enter or Tab to move the insertion point into the large text box. The subject text appears as the name of the conversation in the header.
4. Enter text into the large box that occupies most of the form.

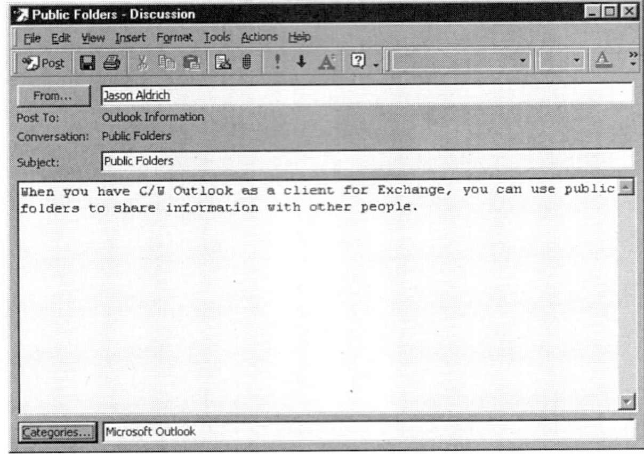

FIGURE 52.18
The Discussion form opens with the name of the Public Folder near the top. The form shown here is ready to post.

5. If you want your post to include insertions, choose Insert in the form's Standard toolbar and choose File (to insert a file), Item (to insert an Outlook item), or Object (to insert a Windows object).
6. Choose Categories to display the Categories dialog box, in which you can select one or more categories for the item.
7. Choose Post in the form's Standard toolbar to post your item in the Public Folder.

An item posted in this way appears in the Public Folder's Information viewer in much the same way as received email appears in the Inbox Information viewer. You, or anyone else who has access to the Public Folder, can double-click the posted items header in the viewer to see the item in the Discussion form.

TIP A Public Folder's Information viewer can be displayed with or without a Preview pane. Choose View, Preview Pane to display or hide the Preview pane.

Responding to a Post When you read something that another person has posted in a Public Folder, you may want to ask a question or add information; you can if you have permission to create items. Instead of creating a new post, you should reply to the existing one. In that way, you create a conversation in which your reply is linked to the original message, as subsequently described in this chapter.

NOTE You can use Public Folders as a conversation forum. See "Using a Public Folder As an Unmoderated Bulletin Board" later in this chapter.

Posting a File You can post a file created in an Office, or Office-compatible, application into a Public Folder.

To post an Office file into a Public Folder:

1. Open the file you want to post using the Office application in which the file was created.

2. Choose File, move the pointer onto Send To, and choose Exchange Folder. After a few moments' delay, a dialog box such as that shown in Figure 52.19 is displayed. Initially, only top-level folders are listed. You have to expand these folders to see individual folders.

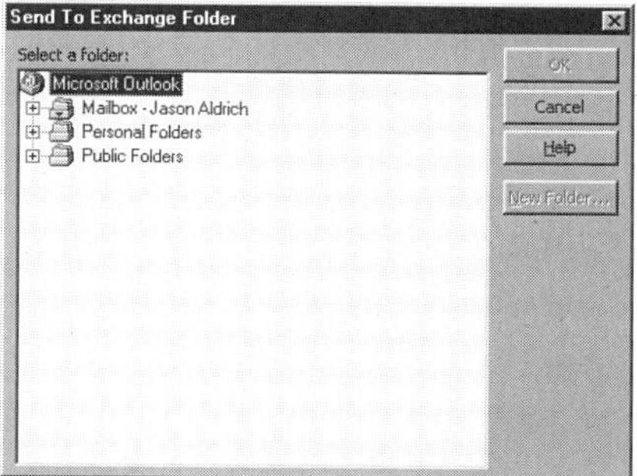

FIGURE 52.19
This dialog box initially lists the available, top-level folders.

NOTE The folders listed in this dialog box are those available on your computer as well as the folders on your Exchange Server.

3. Expand Public Folders, expand All Public Folders, and select the Public Folder into which you want to post the file.
4. Choose OK to post the file in the selected Public Folder.

After following these steps, you'll find the file available in the Public Folder's Information viewer. The symbols at the left of item names identify whether an item is a message or a file. If the item is a file, the item's name becomes the subject of the file.

Using a Public Folder As an Unmoderated Bulletin Board

You can use a Public Folder as a bulletin board, a community resource people can use to discuss whatever is on their minds. Anyone who has Create Item permission for the Public Folder can post items on the bulletin board and respond to items already posted there.

To use a Public Folder you've created in this way, you should probably set the Default role as Author. Having done that, anyone who has an Exchange account can post items in the folder, read whatever anyone else has posted, and respond to posted items. You might consider, however, whether you want to enable users to edit and delete items they've previously posted, both of which are permissions included in the Author role.

In the Permissions tab of the Public Folder's dialog box, you can change the Default permissions to include only Create and Read items. After you've done that, users can't change or delete items after they've posted them—more in the spirit of a bulletin board.

When a Public Folder is used as a bulletin board, users can post items onto that board. Other users see those items when they open the bulletin board Public Folder, and they can double-click the item header to see the item in full in the Discussion form, such as was previously shown in Figure 52.18.

NOTE If the text in the form is read-only, it's because the Public Folder's owner assigned Author permissions to other people. Author permissions enable a user to read items, to create new items, and to edit only the items that the user has created.

To respond to an item, after double-clicking the item header in the Public Folder's Information viewer to display the item in a Discussion form, choose Post Reply in the form's Standard toolbar. Now you see the original post with space above it for your response, as shown in Figure 52.20.

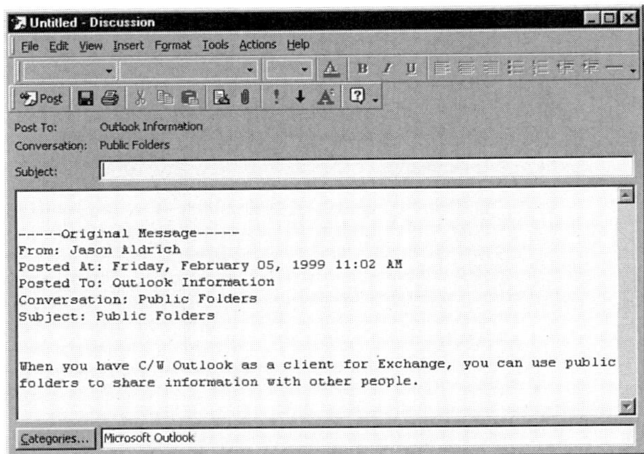

FIGURE 52.20
The form you use for a response already has the original post's subject as the name of the conversation, but the Subject box is empty. You should provide a subject for your response.

Responding to a post is much like replying to an email message. After completing your response, choose Post in the Discussion form's Standard toolbar to post the reply. After you've posted your response, you're left with the original post displayed in the Discussion form. Close that form when you've finished reading it.

Viewing a Conversation A Public Folder used as a bulletin board may contain many conversations, each started by someone who posts a message. Any number of people can respond to the original message; other people can respond to those responses. Before long, the bulletin board contains many conversations, each with several (perhaps many) responses.

You can group messages by conversation so that you can easily follow through a thread of messages. To do so, display the Public Folder's Information viewer, choose View, move the pointer onto Current View, and choose By Conversation Topic. Outlook displays conversation topics, initially with all of them collapsed so that you can't see the items within each conversation. Choose the + at the left of a conversation topic to expand that topic, as shown in Figure 52.21.

FIGURE 52.21
The By Conversation Topic view indents items to show their relationships.

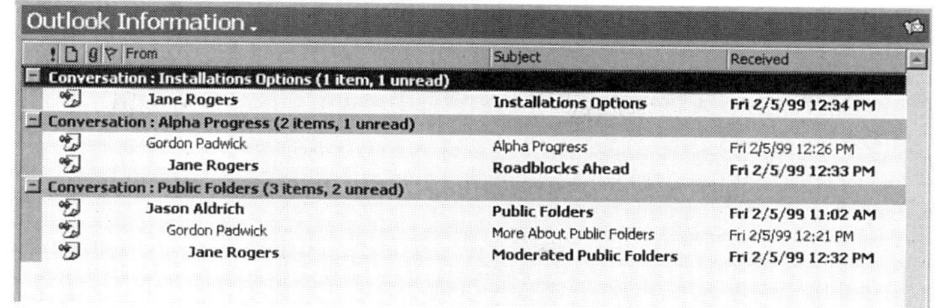

In this view, double-click any message to display it in the Discussion form.

Outlook 2000 offers a fast way to display message threads. If a message has been replied to, or is a reply to another message, you can click the InfoBar near the top of the Discussion form to display message threads.

Sending an Email Response to a Conversation Item People should normally respond to bulletin board messages on the bulletin board so that everyone can benefit from those responses. There are times, however, when you might want to send a private response to a person who posted a message. You can do so by sending email directly to that person.

Also, you might want to send a copy of a bulletin board message to someone who doesn't have access to the bulletin board. You can do so by using email.

To email a conversation item:

1. Display the Public Folder's Information viewer.
2. Select the conversation item you want to send by email.
3. Choose Reply in the viewer's toolbar if you want to send a reply to the person who posted the conversation item; alternatively, choose Forward if you want to send the item to someone. In either case, Outlook displays a Message form that contains the conversation item.
4. Proceed in the normal way to send the message.

Using a Public Folder As a Moderated Bulletin Board

A moderated bulletin board is one for which people can submit items for posting on the bulletin board to a moderator. The moderator decides whether to post those items.

To designate a Public Folder as a moderated bulletin board, you must be the owner of that Public Folder.

To create a moderated bulletin board:

1. In the folder list, right-click the name of a Public Folder for which you have Owner permission to display the folder's context menu.
2. Choose Properties to display the folder's Properties dialog box. Select the Administration tab to display the dialog box shown in Figure 52.22.

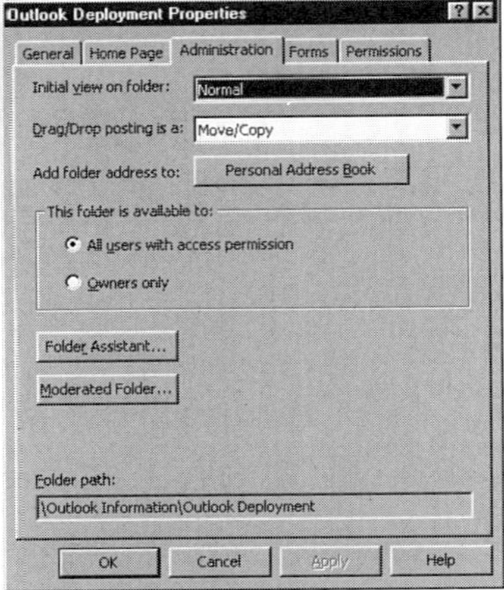

FIGURE 52.22
Choose Help at the bottom of this dialog box if you want to see information about what it contains.

3. Choose Moderated Folder to display the dialog box shown in Figure 52.23.

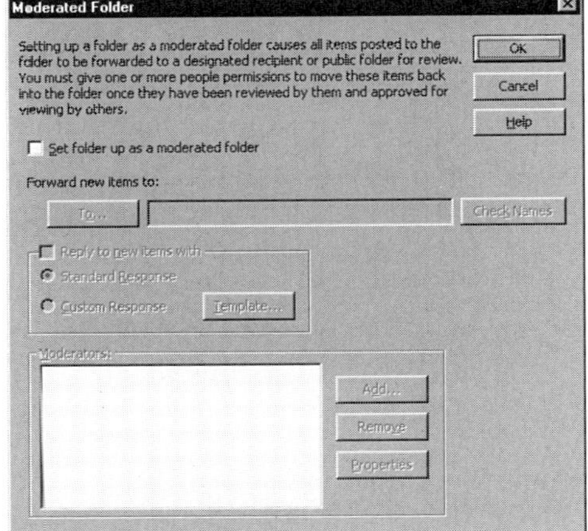

FIGURE 52.23
Read the text at the top of this dialog box to get a brief description of how moderated folders work.

4. Check Set Folder Up As a Moderated folder. When you do so, the boxes and buttons in the lower part of the dialog box become available.
5. Choose To… to display a dialog box in which you can select the name of a moderator to whom items submitted to the moderated folder will be forwarded for consideration.

NOTE The person you select here is who Outlook automatically sends submissions to, not necessarily the person who accepts or rejects submissions. The people who actually accept or reject submissions are selected in step 7. Instead of naming a person, you can name another Public Folder where submitted messages are to be saved for review by the moderators.

6. If you want Outlook to automatically reply to all submissions, check Reply to New Items With. To use Outlook's automatic response, accept the default Standard Response; otherwise, select Custom Response (in which case you must have a response previously saved as an Outlook template; choose Template to select that template).
7. Choose Add to select the Select Additional Moderators dialog box. Select one or more moderators and then choose OK. The names of the moderators you selected are displayed in the Moderators box at the bottom of the Moderated Folder dialog box.

After you've selected one or more moderators, all items submitted to the Public Folder are automatically forwarded to those moderators. Those moderators need to have Create Item permission to the Public Folder so that, if they approve items, they can post them in the folder.

Using Custom Forms Within Public Folders

By default, Public Folders offer the Post form, shown in the preceding sections of this chapter, for people to use when posting items. However, you can use Public Folders for many specialized purposes that require a Public Folder to offer a custom form.

▶ **See** "Creating and Using Custom Forms," **p. 1475**

After you've created a custom form, you can associate that form with a Public Folder. You must have Owner permission to do so.

To associate a custom form with a Public Folder:

1. Display your folder list and right-click the name of the Public Folder to which you want to associate a form.
2. Choose Properties in the Public Folder's context menu and select the General tab. By default, Public Folders use the Post form.
3. Open the When Posting to This Folder, Use drop-down box. Most likely, you'll see only Post and Forms listed. Choose Forms to display the dialog box shown in Figure 52.24.

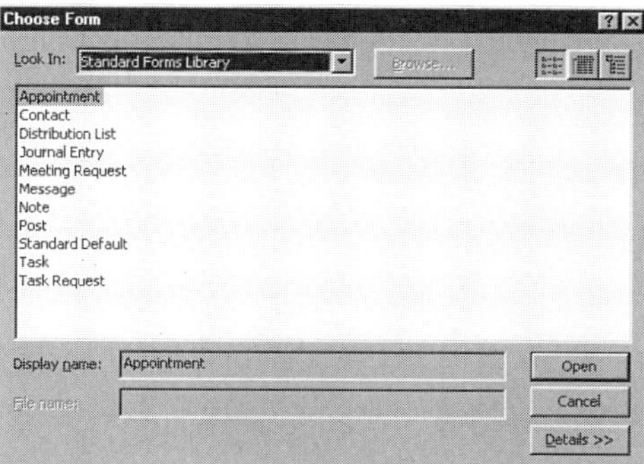

FIGURE 52.24
This dialog box opens showing a list of forms in the Outlook Standard Forms Library.

4. Open the Look In drop-down list and select the forms library in which you have saved the custom form (probably Personal Forms Library).
5. Select the form you want to associate with the Public Folder and choose Open to return to the Properties dialog box in which the name of the form you chose is shown.

Subsequently, when a person chooses New in the Public Folder's Information viewer toolbar, Outlook displays the form you specified.

Making a Public Folder Available Offline

Normally, Public Folders are available when your computer is connected to Exchange Server. However, there may be times when you need access to a Public Folder when you're working offline. The following procedure shows you how to do just that.

To make a Public Folder available offline:

1. Display your folder list.
2. Point onto the name of the folder you want to be able to use offline. Press the mouse button and drag the Public Folder onto the Favorites subfolder (under Public Folders). Now you have a copy of the Public Folder in your Favorites folder.
3. Expand Favorites and right-click the folder you just dragged into Favorites to display its context menu.
4. Choose Properties in the context menu to open the Properties dialog box. Select the Synchronization tab.
5. Select When Offline or Online.

When you work offline, any changes you make to the contents of your copy of the Public Folder don't affect the actual Public Folder on the server. Likewise, any changes other people make to the Public Folder on the server don't affect your offline copy. Later, when you're again online, you can synchronize your offline copy of the Public Folder with the actual Public Folder on the server. The synchronization process updates both folders so that each of them contains the most recent information.

▶ **See** "Setting Up Remote Mail," **p. 1418**

Creating Rules for a Public Folder

You can create rules for a Public Folder in a similar manner to creating rules in the Out of Office Assistant.

▶ **See** "Using the Out of Office Assistant," **p. 1391**

NOTE You must have Owner permission for a Public Folder to create rules for it.

To create rules for a Public Folder:

1. Display your folder list and right-click the name of a Public Folder to display its context menu.

2. Choose Properties in the context menu to display the Properties dialog box. Select the Administration tab, shown previously in Figure 52.22.
3. Choose Folder Assistant to display the Folder Assistant dialog box, which contains no rules initially.
4. Choose Add Rule to display the Edit Rule dialog box, shown in Figure 52.25, in which you can enter and select information to define a rule.

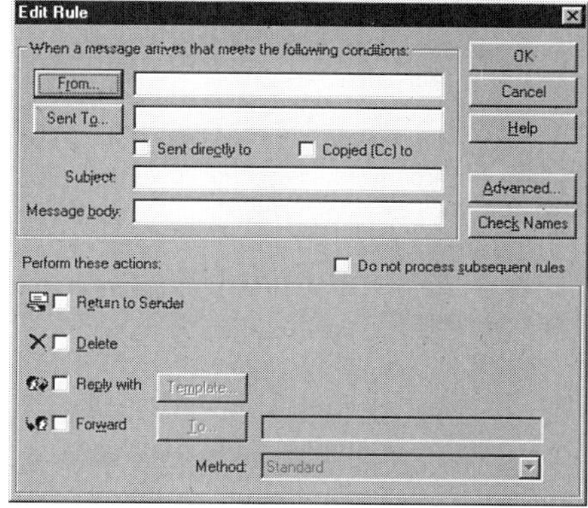

FIGURE 52.25
This dialog box provides facilities for you to specify the details of a rule for a Public Folder.

5. After you've defined the rule, choose OK to return to the Folder Assistant dialog box that lists the rule you created.

Using the Favorites Folder

The word "favorites" in the Outlook environment has two completely different meanings:

- The Favorites shortcut in the Other Shortcuts group in the Outlook Bar provides access to files, folders, and shortcuts (including URL shortcuts) in the Windows Favorites folder.
- Favorites in the folder list is an Outlook Public Folder that contains a subset of the Public Folders available in the Exchange store.

This section deals with the second meaning of the word.

The Exchange store in a large organization might contain hundreds, if not thousands, of Public Folders, only a few of which each person accesses regularly. To simplify access to frequently used Public Folders, each person can copy those Public Folders from the All Public Folders section of the folder list into the Favorites section.

To copy a Public Folder from the All Public Folders section to the Favorites section, drag the name of the Public Folder from one section to the other. After you've done that, you can access a Public Folder by selecting from the few folders listed in the Favorites section instead of from the many folders listed in the All Public Folders section.

As explained previously in this chapter, you can make Public Folders listed in the Favorites section of Public Folders available for offline use, something you can't do for Public Folders listed only in the All Public Folders section.

Sharing Your Folders

If you're using C/W Outlook as a client for Exchange and you save your Outlook items in the Exchange store, you can give other people access to your folders. You can't share folders in your Personal Folders file.

NOTE You can, of course, share your entire Personal Folders file within the Windows environment. When you do that, you have no control over sharing individual folders within the file.

Giving Permission to Access Your Folders

Sharing your own folders has much in common with sharing Public Folders. Most organizations use Public Folders to create a long-term resource available throughout a large group or even the entire enterprise. Individuals who want to share information with a few colleagues often prefer to share information in their own existing folders instead of taking the time to create a Public Folder. Although you need to have the appropriate permission from the Exchange Server administrator to create a Public Folder, you don't require any such permission to share your own folders.

To share a single Outlook folder:

1. Display your folder list and right-click the name of a folder you want to share to display its context menu.
2. Choose Properties to display the Properties dialog box. Select the Permissions tab.

NOTE The Permissions tab initially shows that Default users have None as their permissions, meaning that nobody has access to your folders.

3. To give someone access to your folders, choose Add to display the Add Users dialog box, shown previously in Figure 52.17, in which you can select the names of people who have accounts on Exchange to whom you want to grant access permission.
4. Select the names of one or more people whom you want to have access to your folder. Choose Add and then choose OK to return to the folder's Properties dialog box, which now shows the people's names you just selected. Each has the same role (None) as the Default.
5. Select one or more of the names you selected in the previous step.
6. To assign a role to the selected names, open the Roles drop-down list and select a role. Alternatively, check individual permissions and select option buttons. This is similar to granting permissions for a Public Folder, described previously in this chapter.

▶ **See** "Giving People Access to a Public Folder" **p. 1396**

Now, the people you selected have the permissions you assigned to access your folders. At any time you can return to this dialog box to change these permissions:

- You can select a person's name and then choose Remove to remove all the permissions you gave that person.
- You can select a person's name and then change the role or individual permissions you gave that person.

Accessing Another Person's Folders

After other people have granted you access to their folders in the Exchange store, you can open those folders.

To open another person's Outlook folders:

1. With any Outlook Information viewer displayed, choose File, move the pointer onto Open, and choose Other User's Folder to display the dialog box shown in Figure 52.26.

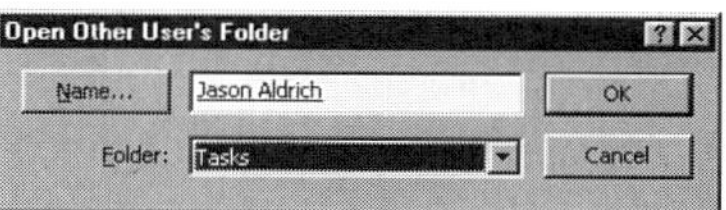

FIGURE 52.26
The dialog box is shown here with a user's name and one of that user's folders selected.

2. Choose Name to display the Select Name dialog box. Use that dialog box to select the name of the person who has granted you folder access.
3. Open the Folder drop-down list and select the folder to which you have been granted access.
4. Choose OK to display the folder.

Subject to the permissions the folder's owner granted, you can now work with the other person's folder.

When You're out of the Office

Some people use Outlook in more than one place. If you're like many people who work in an office, you probably do most of your Outlook work there; sometimes, perhaps often, you use Outlook at home.

If you travel on business, you probably take a laptop computer with you. You may use the same laptop with a connection to your server while you're in the office, or you may use a desktop computer that stays on your desk. You don't have a permanent connection to the server while you're traveling with your laptop.

In these and other circumstances, you need a way to use Outlook while you're not connected to the server, and you need a way to keep your Outlook data on two or more computers synchronized, to ensure that the same and most recent data is on all the computers.

Outlook offers several ways for you to solve these problems.

> **CAUTION**
>
> Setting up a computer to work remotely in the Exchange environment isn't simple. That's because Outlook has to deal with various configuration matters, not because Outlook is inherently difficult to use. If you work for a large enterprise, you will probably be issued with a laptop for your remote work, all set up and ready to go. Lucky you! If you have to set up a laptop by yourself for remote use, and you've never done it before, be prepared for some headaches.

The scenario considered here is that of a corporate environment in which desktop computers use a LAN on which Exchange Server is used as an email system. Individuals use C/W Outlook on their computers as clients for Exchange. To take advantage of the collaboration facilities available in Exchange, users save their Outlook items in the Exchange store.

Users who work away from the office use laptop computers on which C/W Outlook is installed and use an Offline Folders file to save Outlook items while the computers aren't connected to the server.

Understanding Offline Folders

An Offline Folders file is similar to a Personal Folders file. The file contains folders that are used to save Outlook items.

Personal Folders Versus Offline Folders

Although a Personal Folders file and an Offline Folders file are similar in that they both contain folders used to store Outlook items, there is a significant difference between the two. A Personal Folders file contains a set of Outlook folders that are independent of any other Outlook folders.

In contrast, an Offline Folders file contains Outlook folders that are closely related to Outlook folders in the Exchange store. When you create an Offline Folders file, that file contains a copy of the Outlook folders you have in your Exchange store. While you work with Outlook, you can synchronize the Outlook folders in your Offline Folders file with your Outlook folders in the Exchange store so that both contain the most recent data.

Personal Folders files have .pst as their filename extensions; Offline Folders files have .ost as their filename extensions.

When your laptop computer is connected to a LAN, you can synchronize the information in your Offline Folders file with information from your Exchange store. Then you can disconnect the computer from the LAN and work with Outlook while you're traveling or in a different location. Sometime later, when your computer is again connected to the LAN, you can synchronize your Offline Folders file with your Exchange store.

NOTE Synchronization is the process by which two sets of folders are compared and updated so that the most recent items are saved in both sets of folders.

Creating a Profile for Offline Use

If you're going to use your computer offline (not connected to Exchange), you must create a profile for that purpose. You should do that after you've created a profile for working with Outlook when your computer is connected to Exchange.

NOTE If you already have a profile for working online with Exchange, the offline profile you create automatically contains the folder structure in your online profile and the individual folders contain the Outlook items in your Exchange store.

To create a profile for offline use:

1. If Outlook is already running, choose File, Exit and Log Off to close Outlook.
2. Choose Start on the Windows taskbar, move the pointer onto Settings, and choose Control Panel.
3. In the Control Panel, double-click Mail (or Mail and Fax) to display the Properties dialog box.
4. Choose Show Profiles to display the Mail dialog box that contains a list of existing profiles.
5. Choose Add to display the Microsoft Outlook Setup Wizard. The wizard offers two information services you can include in a new profile—Microsoft Exchange Server and Internet E-Mail.
6. Check Microsoft Exchange Server; then choose Next to display the second wizard window.
7. Replace the suggested name with something more appropriate, such as Offline. Choose Next to display the third wizard window. Use this window to specify your Exchange server and the name of your mailbox on that server.
8. Enter the name of your server and the name of your mailbox. Choose Next to display the fourth wizard window. This is the window in which you let the profile know that you will be working offline.
9. The window asks `Do you travel with this computer?`. Choose Yes to indicate that you will be working offline. Choose Next to display the final wizard window.
10. Choose Finish to display the Mail dialog box shown in Figure 52.27. Don't close this dialog box yet.

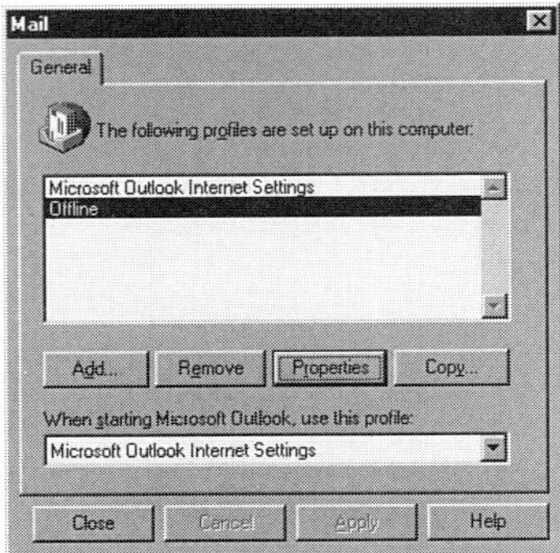

FIGURE 52.27
This dialog box lists the profiles available on your computer, including the one you just created.

Now you have to set the properties of the new profile, as explained in the next section.

If you intend to use the Internet for email while you're traveling, you should also add the Internet E-Mail information service to your profile. You should also make sure you have the TCP/IP protocol installed in Windows and that your computer is set up for Dial-Up Networking.

Creating an Offline Folders File

To create and use an Offline Folders file, you must have C/W Outlook installed on your computer and you must have created a profile for using Outlook offline, as explained in the preceding section.

The following steps continue from those in the preceding section.

To create an Offline Folders file:

1. After creating a profile for offline use, as described in the preceding section, select that profile in the Mail dialog box previously shown in Figure 52.27 and choose Properties to display the dialog box for that profile, as shown in Figure 52.28.

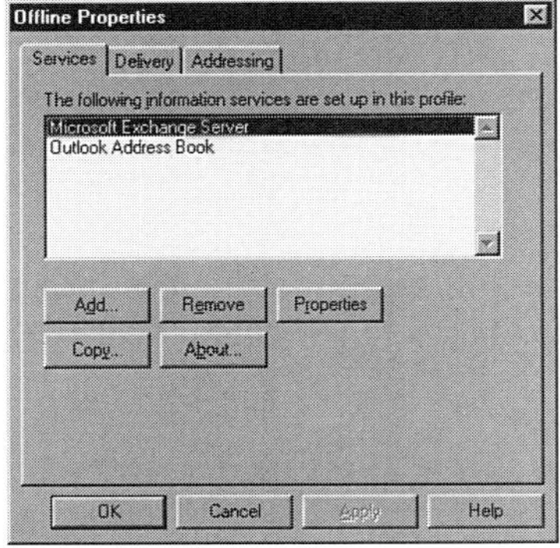

FIGURE 52.28
This dialog box opens with the Services tab selected, showing the information services in your profile.

2. Select the Microsoft Exchange Server information service and choose Properties to display the Properties dialog box. Select the Advanced tab, shown in Figure 52.29.

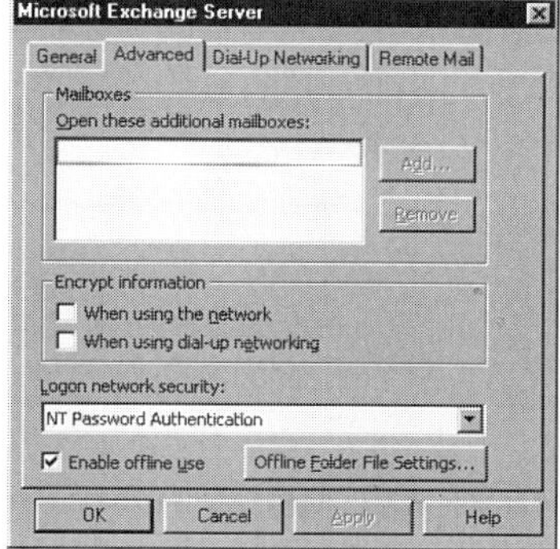

FIGURE 52.29
Use this dialog box to begin creating an Offline Folders file.

3. Choose Offline Folder File Settings to display the dialog box shown in Figure 52.30.

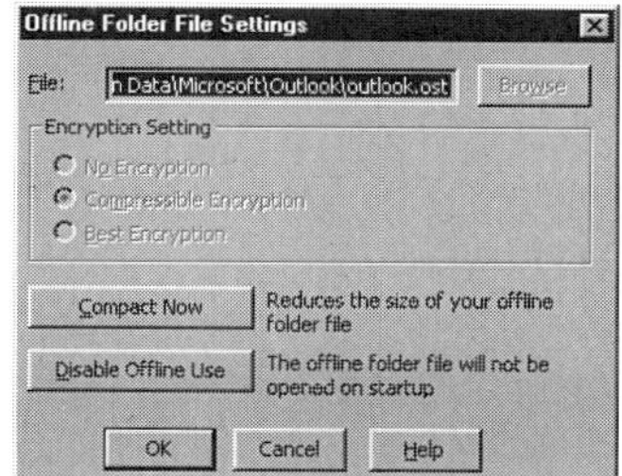

FIGURE 52.30
Windows proposes to create an Offline Folders file named outlook.ost.

4. Enter the full pathname for the Offline Folders file you want to use in the File box. Alternatively, choose Browse to navigate to a folder and enter a filename.

It's a good idea to replace the default filename with your own name or email account name. For example, if your email account name is kbrown, use kbrown.ost as the filename.

5. Choose the encryption setting you want to use.

NOTE You have to select an encryption setting at the time you create an Offline Folders file. You can't subsequently change the encryption setting.

6. Choose OK three times and then close the Control Panel.

After completing these steps, you have on your computer an Offline Folders file that contains a duplicate of the folders and Outlook items in your Exchange store.

The next time you open Outlook, you may see the Choose Profile dialog box. In that case, select the offline profile you just created.

If Outlook starts without displaying the Show Profile dialog box, you need to change Outlook's options so that this dialog box does appear. To do so, with any Information viewer displayed, choose Tools, Options to display the Options dialog box. Select the Mail Services tab and, in the Startup Settings section, select Prompt for a Profile to Be Used, and then choose OK to save that option. After doing that, when you start Outlook, you'll see the Choose Profile dialog box and be able to select the profile you want to use—either the one you use when your computer is connected to the server or the one you use offline.

Using Outlook Offline

After completing the steps described in the preceding two sections, you can unplug your computer from the network and use Outlook offline.

Start Outlook in the normal way. If, as suggested in the previous section, you set the Outlook option to Prompt for a Profile to Be Used, Outlook displays the Choose Profile dialog box. Open the drop-down list of profiles, select your offline profile, and choose OK. Outlook opens in the normal way.

To see that you have Outlook open with access to your Offline folder, you can choose View, Folder List to see a list of folders. Each of the folder icons has a superimposed box containing a plus sign to indicate that you're accessing offline folders.

From here, you can continue to work with Outlook in the normal way.

Copying an Address Book into Your Remote Computer

If you intend to send email while you're working remotely you need to have a list of email addresses available. One way you can do this is to copy the Global Address Book from your Exchange server into your remote computer.

With your remote computer connected to the LAN and with Outlook running under your offline profile, proceed as follows to copy the Global Address Book:

1. With any Outlook Information viewer displayed, choose Tools, move the pointer onto Synchronize, and choose Download Address Book. Outlook displays the dialog box shown in Figure 52.31.

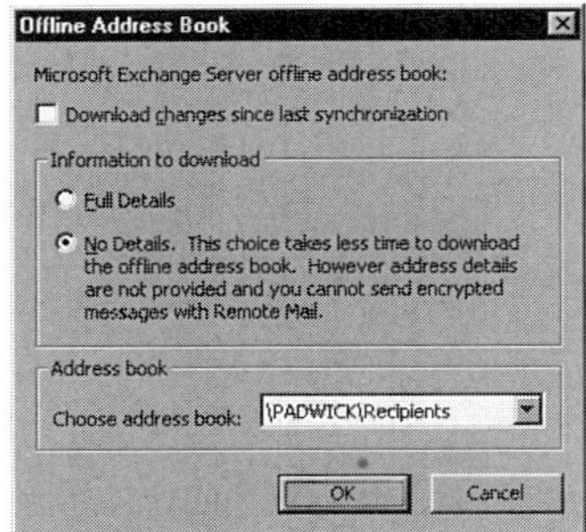

FIGURE 52.31
Use this dialog box to specify what you want to download.

2. The first time you copy the Global Address Book, uncheck Download Changes Since Last Synchronization. When you subsequently copy the Global Address Book, check this box.
3. In the Information to Be Downloaded section of the dialog box, you'll normally want to leave the default Full Details selected.
4. Open the Choose Address Book drop-down list and select the address book you want to download.
5. Choose OK to start downloading.

Synchronizing Your Offline Folders

The process of synchronizing your offline folders compares the contents of your folders in the Exchange store with the contents of your offline folders. If a later version of an item is in the Exchange store, that item is copied into the corresponding offline folder. If a later version of an item is in an offline folder, that item is copied into the corresponding folder in the Exchange store.

NOTE During synchronization, an item that's been deleted from an offline folder is deleted from the corresponding server folder. Likewise, any item that's been deleted from the server folder is deleted from the corresponding offline folder.

When you create an Offline Folders file on your remote computer, the items currently in your Exchange store are automatically copied into your offline folders. However, in the interval between setting up your remote computer and going on a trip, some of the items in your Exchange store will have changed, so you must synchronize to bring your offline folders up-to-date.

Manually Synchronizing Folders To synchronize your folders, start with any Outlook Information viewer displayed, open the Tools menu, move the pointer onto Synchronize, and choose All Folders, if you want to synchronize all folders. Alternatively, if you want to synchronize only the folder that the current Information viewer displays, choose This Folder.

Automatically Synchronizing Folders You can set up Outlook so that offline folders are automatically synchronized with corresponding folders in the Exchange store at certain times.

To configure automatic synchronization:

1. With any Outlook Information viewer displayed, choose Tools, Options to display the Options dialog box. Select the Mail Services tab, which provides facilities for setting automatic synchronization.
2. Check Enable Offline Access. When you do that, the check boxes within the Enable Offline Access section of the dialog box become available.
3. To automatically synchronize all offline folders whenever you exit from Outlook, check the first check box.

4. To automatically synchronize all offline folders while you're online, check the second check box and specify the number of minutes between each synchronization.
5. To automatically synchronize all offline folders while you're offline, check the third check box and specify the number of minutes between each synchronization.

NOTE After you check When Offline, Automatically Synchronize, Outlook attempts to make an online connection at the defined intervals. For this to happen successfully, you must have a physical connection to the server either by way of a network or Dial-Up Networking.

Choosing Offline Folder Settings

The Offline Folders file always contains the standard Outlook folders: Calendar, Contacts, Deleted Items, Drafts, Inbox, Journal, Notes, Outbox, Sent Items, and Tasks. If you have created custom folders in your Outlook store, you can choose whether you want to have these custom folders available when you're working remotely.

To make this choice, open the Tools menu from any Outlook Information viewer, move the pointer onto Synchronize, and choose Offline Folder Settings to display the dialog box shown in Figure 52.32.

FIGURE 52.32
Choose which folders you want to use offline.

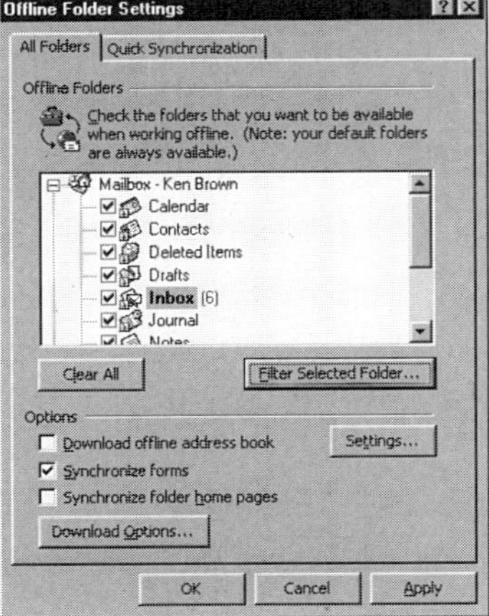

TIP You can also open this dialog box by choosing Offline Folder Settings in the Mail Services tab of the Options dialog box.

By default, all the standard Outlook folders are checked. If you uncheck one of these, Outlook displays a message saying this folder can't be unselected. If you want to work with custom folders, check those folders, and then choose OK.

To uncheck all checked custom folders, choose Clear All.

By default, synchronization involves all items in folders. If you want to filter items so that only those that satisfy specific criteria are synchronized, select a folder and choose Filter Selected Folder. When you do this, Outlook displays the dialog box shown in Figure 52.33.

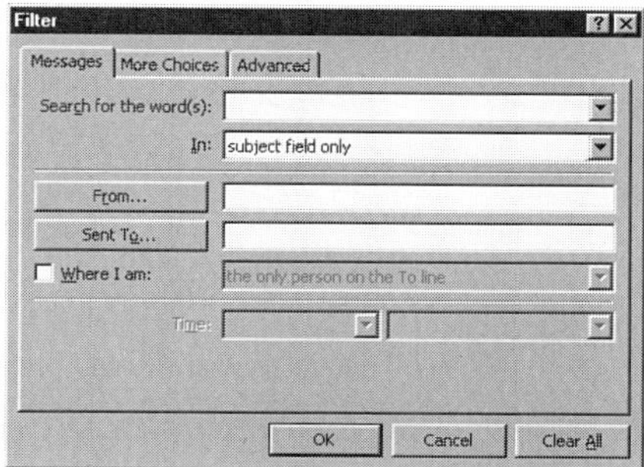

FIGURE 52.33
Use this dialog box to specify criteria for the items you want to synchronize.

Apart from the name in its title bar, the Filter dialog box works the same as Outlook's Advanced Find dialog box. Use this dialog box to define criteria for the items you want to synchronize.

Notice that the Filter dialog box has three tabs. You can define criteria in all three tabs. Initially, each tab contains no criteria. Items must satisfy criteria defined in all three tabs to be included in the synchronization process.

Using Public Folders Remotely

When you're working offline, you can't access Exchange Public Folders directly. You can, however, access copies of Public Folders that have been created in Exchange's Public Folders Favorites folder.

While you're working offline, you can access the Favorites folder that contains the information that existed the last time you synchronized. Any offline changes you make are copied to your Favorites folder in the Exchange store the next time you synchronize.

Connecting to Your Exchange Mailbox

Your Exchange Server administrator has probably set up Exchange Server so that remote users can connect by way of a dial-up connection. The details of this depend on how the dial-up connection at the server end is configured to maintain the necessary level of security. To connect to the server, you may have to provide one or more passwords. In some cases, after you have provided those passwords, you may be instructed to disconnect and wait for the server to call you back. All this is necessary to avoid the possibility of unauthorized people gaining access to your account on the server.

Your first step, then, is to ask the Exchange administrator for information about the connection procedure.

Then, you have to set up the Microsoft Exchange Server information service on your computer. Use the Dial-Up Networking and Remote Mail tabs to do so.

Setting Up Dial-Up Networking With any Outlook Information viewer displayed, choose Tools, Services to display the Services dialog box. In that dialog box, select the Microsoft Exchange Server information service, and then choose Properties. Select the Dial-Up Networking tab. Use this tab to define the dial-up connection to your Exchange Server.

If you have a permanent dial-up connection to the server, select Do Not Dial, Use Existing Connection (at the bottom of the dialog box).

Otherwise, accept the default Dial Using the Following Connection and proceed as follows.

To select a dial-up connection:

1. Open the drop-down list of existing dial-up connections and select the one you want to use.

NOTE If you haven't previously created a dial-up connection to the Exchange Server phone number, choose New to create a new connection.

If you want to check, or change, the properties of an existing connection, choose Properties. If you want to check, or change, the location from which you're calling, choose Location.

2. Enter your username for your Exchange account in the User Name box.
3. Enter your password for your Exchange account in the Password box.
4. Enter the name of the Windows NT domain in which your Exchange account is available in the Domain box.

Setting Up Remote Mail With any Outlook Information viewer displayed, choose Tools, Services to display the Services dialog box. In that dialog box, select the Microsoft Exchange Server information service, and then choose Properties. Select the Remote Mail tab, as shown in Figure 52.34.

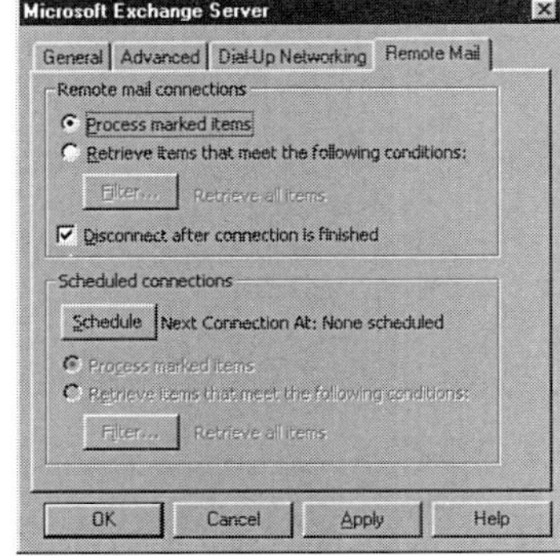

FIGURE 52.34
This is where you can specify how you want your remote computer to interact with your Exchange mailbox.

In the Remote Mail Connections section of the dialog box, you can choose

- Process Marked Items—After you do so and connect to your Exchange mailbox, you'll see a list of items waiting for your attention. You can select the items you see to have them transmitted to you.
- Retrieve Items That Meet the Following Conditions—After you do this, the Filter button becomes available. Choose this button to display the dialog box shown in Figure 52.35.

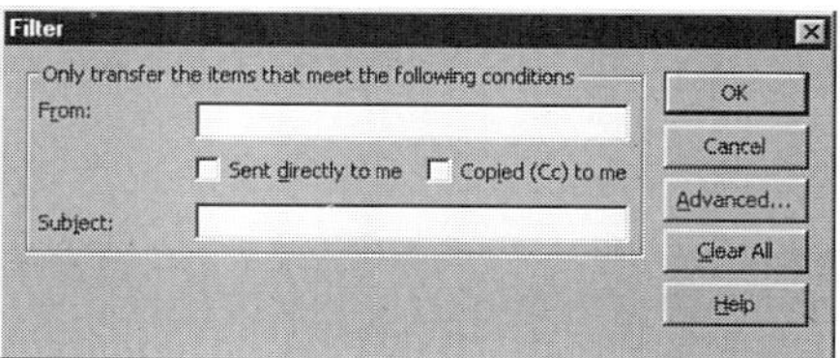

FIGURE 52.35 Use this dialog box to specify the mail items you want to receive.

In the Remote Mail Connections section in the Microsoft Exchange Server dialog box, you can leave Disconnect After Connection Is Finished checked if you want to disconnect automatically or uncheck it if you want to remain connected. With the Filter dialog box (shown in Figure 52.35) displayed, you can be even more selective by choosing Advanced to display the dialog box shown in Figure 52.36.

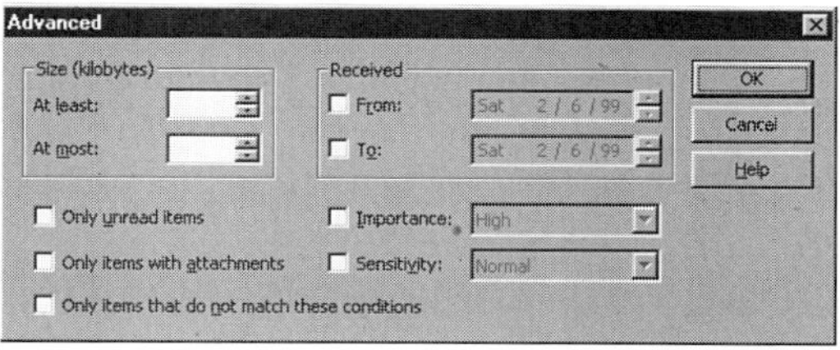

FIGURE 52.36 Here are more choices you can make to define which mail messages you want to receive.

You can use the Scheduled Connections section of the Remote Mail dialog box to select automatic connection to the Exchange server at specified times. To do so, choose Schedule to display the dialog box shown in Figure 52.37.

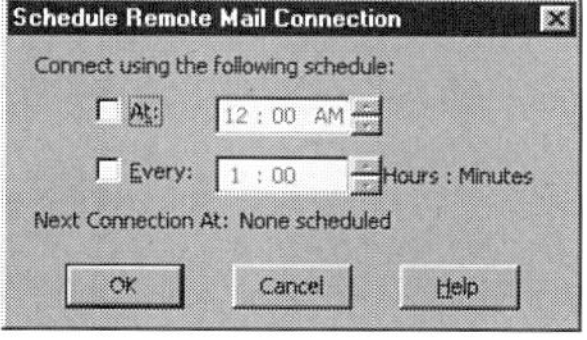

FIGURE 52.37 Use this dialog box to schedule the next connection to Exchange and the subsequent interval between connections.

You can use the two options buttons and the Filter button to further control which messages are transmitted from and to Exchange server.

When your remote computer connects to your Exchange server, it receives messages and has them waiting for you according to the criteria you've defined.

Any outgoing messages you create on your remote computer are saved in your Outbox until a connection to your Exchange server is established. When that happens, the messages in your Outbox are transmitted to your Outbox in the Exchange store and then processed as they would be if you had created those messages locally.

CHAPTER 53

Managing Email

In this chapter

Three Flavors of Outlook

If you think of Outlook as a neighborhood, then it's a quite diverse one. It's a *Personal Information Manager* (PIM) and more, although many users consider the main use of Outlook to be that of an email client. This one function of Outlook is also the one that seems to cause the most confusion for users, especially when it comes to getting Outlook configured properly. This chapter, however, shines some light on what can be the darkest corner of the Outlook "neighborhood."

To fully appreciate Outlook's mail features, a little history might be in order. Outlook 97's mail functionality evolved directly from that of the Microsoft Exchange email client (also known as Windows Messaging). It exclusively utilized the full MAPI *(Mail Application Programming Interface)* subsystem with its often-confusing combination of transport services (components that interface with your mail servers to send and receive mail) and address books.

After the release of Office 97 (which included Outlook 97), the next big product release from Microsoft was Internet Explorer 4. Part of the Internet Explorer 4 suite was an update to the Internet Mail and News client, now christened Outlook Express. Although the two products (Outlook 97 and Outlook Express) had little to do with each other, Microsoft wanted to create a family of messaging products all containing the word Outlook. This created a mass of confusion for Internet Explorer 4 users who later installed Outlook 97. Many had expected that Outlook 97 would be Outlook Express with PIM features. This led to a backlash against Outlook 97, with users complaining that a free email client was more powerful than one that they had to purchase.

In an effort to create wider acceptance of Outlook, Microsoft sought to meld the ease of use found in Outlook Express with the power of Outlook. The biggest problem with that goal is that some of the most desired Outlook Express features (such as the capability to easily choose which account will send a piece of mail) would require extensive reworking of the MAPI subsystem. Because Microsoft didn't want to take on this task yet, the decision was made to create two mail modes for Outlook 98—Corporate or Workgroup and Internet Mail Only. Additionally, a nonmail/PIM-only mode called, appropriately enough, No Email was included. Outlook 2000 builds on the same multimode foundation that was introduced with Outlook 98.

Corporate or Workgroup (CW) Mode

This email mode might be better named Classic or Full MAPI because it uses essentially the same mail setup as Outlook 97. CW mode utilizes the extended MAPI subsystem with its support for multiple transports that can support different mail systems (including Microsoft Exchange Server, Microsoft Mail, Lotus cc:Mail, and Internet Email) and other transports (pagers and faxes). Among the reasons you would want to use this mode are

- You need to access a server that's not an Internet-standard (POP3/SMTP or IMAP4) type.

NOTE Many non-Internet standard mail servers now offer users a way to use Internet standard mail clients to retrieve their mail. Frequently, this involves a loss in functionality. For example, with an Exchange Server, you lose the capability to access Public Folders if you use a POP3 (Post Office Protocol version 3) mail client to access your mailbox.

- You are using another program on your machine that requires Extended MAPI functionality. Corel WordPerfect is an example of such a program. Its address book is a MAPI address book that will not function if you attempt to use Outlook 2000's Internet Mail Only mode.
- You want to utilize the MS Fax service that you used with Exchange/Windows Messaging/Outlook 97. MS Fax is a MAPI transport that works only in CW mode.
- You want to have multiple users (or, potentially, a single user with a need for multiple configurations) utilize Outlook with different setups (transports, storage locations, and so on), but you don't want to use different operating system logins.
- You want to use the Remote Mail feature in Outlook. This feature gives you the capability to download all the message headers (showing who sent the item, the subject, and the size of the item).

Internet Mail Only (IMO) Mode

This mode also has a misleading name (you could very easily set up a CW mode profile that uses only Internet Email transports, making it an Internet Mail Only profile). It is also called Internet Only in some dialog boxes. The name is derived from the fact that the transport used in this mode is capable only of collecting and sending mail through Internet standard mail servers. Because many Outlook users also expect to be able to send faxes in addition to Internet email, Microsoft includes Symantec WinFax SE (Starter Edition) for use with this mode. Among the reasons you'd want to use this mode are

- You need to collect mail from an IMAP4 server. The IMO mode transport includes that capability. If you used CW mode, you'd need to acquire a third-party transport to do this because the Internet email service for use with CW mode can collect mail only from POP3 servers.
- You use Internet-standard servers only for mail and do little or no faxing. The Symantec WinFax SE module is best used for occasional faxing only. It lacks many of the functions of even a basic fax program such as MS Fax.
- You want (or need) the capability to easily and frequently choose which one of your Internet email accounts sends a particular message.
- You want to use the Internet Free-Busy feature. The capability to post your free-busy time to an Internet host (either an FTP or Web server) is available only in IMO mode.

NOTE The two modes of Outlook enable you to use Outlook with almost all kinds of email. One notable exception is America Online (AOL) mail. AOL doesn't utilize standard POP3/SMTP servers for mail (at least not as of the writing of this chapter), and it doesn't offer a MAPI transport for use in Corporate mode. AOL did have such a transport in beta testing for a short while, but it decided to cancel the testing and not release the software.

No Email Mode

Technically, this isn't a mail mode because it doesn't support the sending or receiving of mail or faxes. What it does is enable you to utilize Outlook as a PIM with no mail functions. It utilizes a small portion of the MAPI subsystem to support access to a Personal Folder file for storage of your data. Because it doesn't use the full MAPI subsystem, this mode also doesn't support the use of other MAPI transports or address books by other programs on your computer. The primary reason you would want to use this mode is if you already have an email package and just want to use the information management features of Outlook.

Configuring Outlook

Before configuring Outlook, you should gather a few pieces of information:

- The type of email server that you use—If you're going to be using Internet Mail Only mode, you should know whether you collect email from a POP3 or an IMAP server. If you're using Corporate mode, you'll need to know what type(s) of email server(s) you will be using. If you're not sure what type of server to which you need to connect, contact your Internet Service Provider or email administrator.
- The name(s) of the email server(s)—For Internet mail, you need to know the name of your incoming mail server and the name of your outgoing mail server. For most other types of email, only one server exists for both incoming and outgoing email items. In most cases, this is something like `smtp.yourserver.com`.
- Username and password—Most email servers require some sort of authentication before you can access your email. Your ISP or email system administrator will provide this information to you.

Another thing you'll want to do before configuring Outlook is to install your fax software.

The fax software for Internet Mail Only mode (WinFax SE) is an option in the Office 2000 setup, so it can be easily installed during the standard Office setup.

The fax software for Corporate mode isn't part of the Office 2000 setup. You have to install it separately. In Windows 95, you have to add the software from the Windows Setup tab of the Windows Control Panel's Add/Remove Programs applet. In Windows 98, run the AWFAX.exe program that's on the Windows 98 compact disc. For U.S. users, it's in the Tools\OldWin95\Message\US folder on the CD.

You don't need to choose a mode until the first time you run Outlook 2000, unlike the setup of Outlook 98 where you chose the mode you wanted during the initial setup phase. As with most things you can do in Outlook, multiple ways exist to go through the Outlook Startup Wizard. Next, I'll detail the way that gives you the most control over how things get configured.

To configure Outlook's mail mode, follow these steps:

1. Start Outlook.
2. When the Outlook 2000 Startup Wizard appears, click the Next button.
3. If you have other mail programs installed on your computer, the E-Mail Upgrade Options dialog box shown in Figure 53.1 appears. Click the None of the Above selection to highlight it, and then click the Next button.

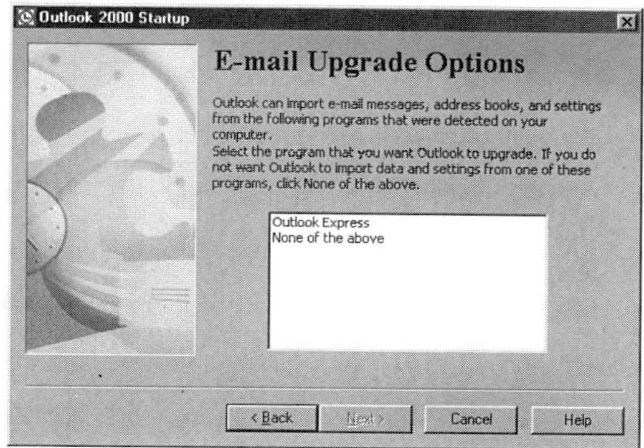

FIGURE 53.1
The E-Mail Upgrade Options dialog box enables you to move easily from your old email program to Outlook 2000.

NOTE If you select an option other than None of the Above, Outlook automatically makes a decision about which mail mode you want to use. Most of the time, this results in the choice of IMO mode. The only time that CW mode is chosen is if you choose to upgrade from either Microsoft Exchange or an earlier version of Outlook, and Outlook detects that the default MAPI profile on your system contains services other than Internet Mail and MS Fax. Outlook also attempts to import your data and settings from the program you chose.

4. In the E-Mail Service Options dialog box (see Figure 53.2), choose the mode you've decided to use. Click the Next button.

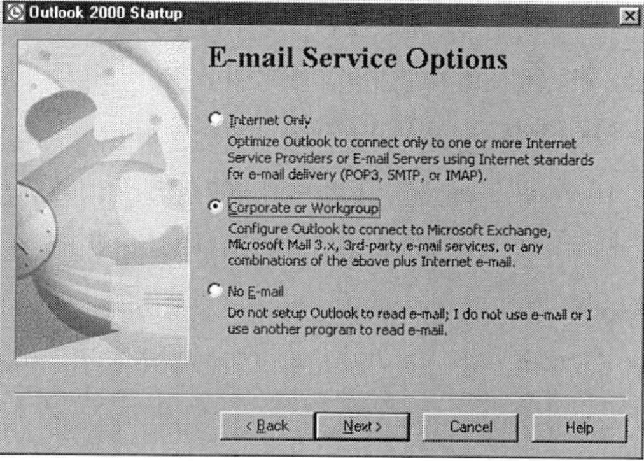

FIGURE 53.2
The E-Mail Service Options screen enables you to decide which mode you want Outlook 2000 to use.

After you've chosen a mode, the directions diverge based on the mode you've picked. We'll cover them mode for mode—skip to the section that discusses the mode you selected.

Configuring for the Internet Only Mode If you selected Internet Only in the E-Mail Service Options dialog box, the remainder of the Outlook startup procedures for this mode are detailed next:

1. A dialog box appears that warns you of the limitations of this mode. Because you should have considered them already based on the discussion earlier in this chapter, click the Yes button. The Internet Connection Wizard then starts the process of creating the first Internet mail account.
2. Enter the name you want to show as the From name on your emails. Click the Next button.
3. Enter the email address associated with the account. Click the Next button.
4. Choose your incoming mail server type (POP3 or IMAP) in the drop-down list. Enter the names of the incoming and outgoing mail servers in the fields provided. Click the Next button.

NOTE You must enter the name for both servers even if both the incoming and outgoing servers are the same.

5. Enter your account name and password. If you'd rather enter your password each time you check for mail, mark the Always Prompt for Password check box. Alternately, you can select the Log On Using Secure Password Authentication (SPA) option. The SPA option is used for special POP3 or IMAP servers that provide their own authentication scheme that veers from the Internet standard. SPA is used most notably by the Microsoft Network (MSN) and CompuServe in conjunction with their mail servers. Click the Next button.
6. Choose your connection type from the ones displayed. Click the Next button.
7. You have completed the setup for your first Internet email account. Click the Finish button on the Congratulations dialog box. Outlook now opens and displays the Inbox folder.

After Outlook is open, you can begin the configuration of the WinFax SE software. You must select Actions, New Fax Message to start the configuration because Outlook waits until you actually try to use the module to configure it.

1. The Symantec WinFax Starter Edition Setup Wizard appears. Click the Next button to continue past the Introduction dialog box.
2. In the User Information dialog box, complete the Name, Company, Fax Number, Voice Number, and Station Identifier fields. These fields will be used in fax cover pages. Click the Next button.
3. In the Address Information dialog box, complete the Address, City, Province/State, Country, and Post/Zip Code fields. Click the Next button.

4. If you want to automatically receive faxes, mark the Automatically Receive Fax check box and set the number of rings to wait before answering the phone. Click the Setup Modem button to configure your modem for faxing.
5. Highlight the modem you want to use for faxing in the Modem Properties dialog box. Click the Properties button. Click the Yes button in the Modem Properties dialog box that asks whether you want to run the Modem Configuration Wizard.
6. The Modem Configuration Wizard dialog box appears. Be sure that your modem is connected, turned on, and that it is not being used. Click the Next button.
7. The wizard queries the modem for its properties and settings. When it's complete, click the Next button to continue.
8. A message indicating that modem configuration has been successful appears. Click the Finish button to complete the wizard's task.
9. The Properties dialog box for your modem appears. Click the OK button to return to the Modem Properties dialog box.
10. Click the OK button in the Modem Properties dialog box to return to the Symantec WinFax Starter Edition Setup Wizard. Click the Next button in the wizard dialog box.
11. If you want to send a cover page along with your faxes, mark the Send Cover Page check box and choose a cover page type from the Template drop-down box. Click the Next button.
12. Click the Finish button in the dialog box that congratulates you for completing the Configuration Wizard.
13. If this is your first time through the WinFax SE configuration, you'll be prompted to register the software. You can either complete the wizard now or click the Skip button to complete the IMO mode setup. Outlook now opens and displays the Inbox folder.

Configuring for the Corporate/Workgroup Mode If you selected Corporate/Workgroup in the E-Mail Service Options dialog box, the remainder of the Outlook startup procedures for this mode are detailed next:

1. After selecting Corporate/Workgroup, the Inbox Setup Wizard dialog box appears. This enables you to set up which transport services you want to use with Outlook. You can choose to have the wizard configure most of your profile settings automatically, or you can manually configure your profile.

NOTE This section assumes that you are configuring your profile with the Internet Email service and MS Fax service. If you need to configure your profile for Exchange Server, see Chapter 52, "Integrating Outlook with Exchange Server."

2. Check the boxes in front of Internet E-Mail and Microsoft Fax in the Use the Following Information Services section of the dialog box. Click the Next button.
3. Pick the modem you want to use for faxing. Click the Next button.
4. Choose your fax auto-answer setting. If you plan on using Outlook only for outgoing faxes, select No. Otherwise, choose Yes and select the number of rings you want Outlook to wait before it answers the phone. Click the Next button.

5. Enter your name, choose your country from the Country drop-down list, and enter the phone number associated with your fax modem. Click the Next button. This finishes the initial setup for the fax transport.
6. Click the Setup Mail Account button to begin setting up your Internet Email service. A four-tabbed Mail Account Properties dialog box (shown in Figure 53.3) appears.

NOTE You will notice some major differences between setting up an Internet email service in CW mode and setting up an Internet mail account in IMO mode. For one thing, no wizard exists to assist you in setting up the CW mode service. Another obvious difference you'll notice is that many more fields and options are available in the CW Service Properties dialog box than the IMO Mode Wizard prompted you to enter. IMO mode accounts have most of the same options available that you find in CW mode services. The wizard shields you from many of them to reduce potential confusion. Later, this chapter shows you where you can access the Extended Properties dialog box for IMO mode accounts that contains the additional options.

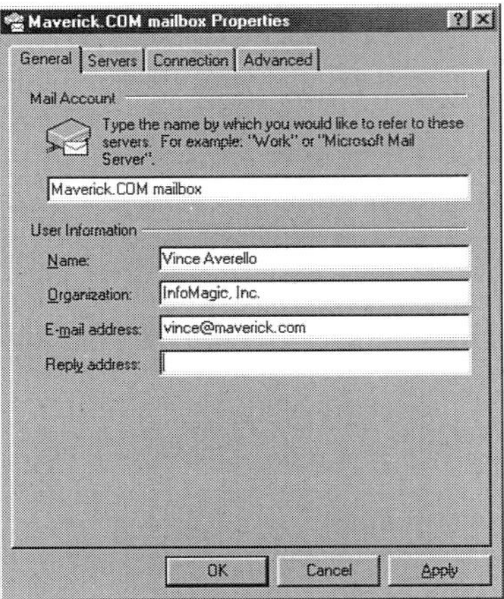

FIGURE 53.3
The Internet Email service Properties dialog box.

7. Enter a name for the service that you're setting up. Pick a name that has some meaning to you. Names such as `Main mail account` or `Ben's mail account` work well here.
8. In the Name field, enter the name you want to show as the From name on your emails.
9. Enter your company name (if applicable) in the Organization field. Your company name is also included in emails that you send via this service.
10. In the E-Mail Address field, enter the email address associated with the service.
11. If you want replies to mail items sent via this mail service to be returned to a different email address, enter that address in the Reply Address field.
12. Click the Servers tab.
13. Enter the names for your outgoing (SMTP) and incoming (POP3) mail servers.

NOTE You will notice that IMAP isn't mentioned on this dialog box. As discussed earlier, IMAP isn't supported by the CW mode Internet email service.

14. Enter your account name and password. If you'd rather enter your password each time you check for mail, mark the Always Prompt for Password check box. Alternatively, you can select the Log On Using Secure Password Authentication (SPA) option. The SPA option is used for special POP3 or IMAP servers that provide their own authentication scheme that veers from the Internet standard. SPA is used most notably by the Microsoft Network (MSN) and CompuServe in conjunction with their mail servers. Click the Next button.
15. If your SMTP server requires user authentication, mark the My Server Requires Authentication check box. Click the Settings button to complete the authentication details for the server. They are similar to the fields used for POP3 authentication.
16. Click the Connection tab.
17. Choose your connection type.

▶ **See** "Connection Types," **p. 1435**

18. Click the Advanced tab. You will see the dialog box shown in Figure 53.4 (although the dialog box name will be different, depending on the name of your account).

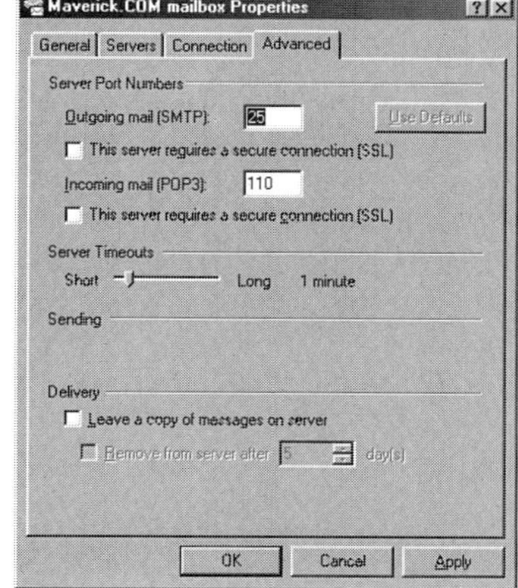

FIGURE 53.4
The less-frequently used options are grouped together on the Advanced tab.

NOTE You should leave the fields at their default values unless you have a very specific reason to change them. Later in this chapter, we'll discuss the ones that some users would typically want to change.

19. If you frequently encounter server timeout errors when accessing your mail servers, you might want to increase the timeout value by dragging the Server Timeout slider to the right.
20. If you want to leave a copy of your mail on the POP3 server (useful if you like to retrieve your mail from multiple locations), mark the Leave a Copy of Messages on Server check box. After that item is checked, you can also choose to leave the mail on the server only for a set number of days so that you don't have to manage the removal of items from the server.

NOTE A practical use for this feature is for checking your office mail while at home. You want to leave the messages on the server so that you can get them back in the office (where you can set Outlook to delete the messages from the mailbox).

21. After you made all the changes you need, click the Apply button, then click OK.
22. The Internet E-Mail Service Properties dialog box disappears and the Inbox Setup Wizard dialog box appears; click Next.
23. Enter a name for your Personal Folders file, or click browse to use a file selection dialog box to navigate to the location for the file. Click the Next button.
24. You'll be presented with a dialog box that summarizes your mail profile. Click the Finish button to terminate the Inbox Setup Wizard and start Outlook.

Creating and Managing Profiles

If you find the need for multiple users or configuration on a single machine, Outlook can handle it. As with the initial setup, this procedure varies based on which mail mode you've chosen.

Using Multiple Profiles in the Corporate/Workgroup Mode

One of the advantages of Corporate/Workgroup mode is that you can run Outlook with multiple configurations without having to use operating-system-level user profiles. This means that you can switch configurations without logging out, and then back into Windows. You might want to set up multiple profiles for a number of reasons. Here are a few of them:

- Multiple family members using the same machine want to keep their mail and data separate. Each family member could set up a profile with different Personal Folder files to hold his or her information.
- You want to connect to more than one Exchange Server. Because a profile can contain only a single Exchange Server service, you have to configure multiple profiles to accomplish your goal.

You can change profiles in one of two manners:

- One way to change profiles is by configuring Outlook to ask at startup which profile to use. You can find this option by choosing Tools, Options, and the Mail Services tab. Select the Prompt for a Profile to Be Used option. Be aware that only one MAPI profile can be active at any time on your computer. So even if you have the prompt option selected, Outlook will not prompt for a profile if one is already active (possibly because you have another instance of Outlook already active).
- The other way to choose a profile at startup time is to use the /profile command-line switch, followed by the name of the profile you want to use.

▶ **See** "Using Command-Line Switches to Control Outlook," **p. 1355**

The focal point for managing MAPI profiles is the Mail applet of the Control Panel. From there, you can create new profiles (using either the wizard interface we detailed earlier, or manually) or modify existing ones (no wizard exists for modifications, so it's a totally manual process).

Creating a New Profile From the Mail applet, click the Show Profiles button. The dialog box shown in Figure 53.5 displays all the MAPI profiles defined on your computer. Click the Add button to begin the addition process. Because we covered the wizard earlier in this chapter, we'll discuss the manual method next. We'll create a profile for use with Internet Mail.

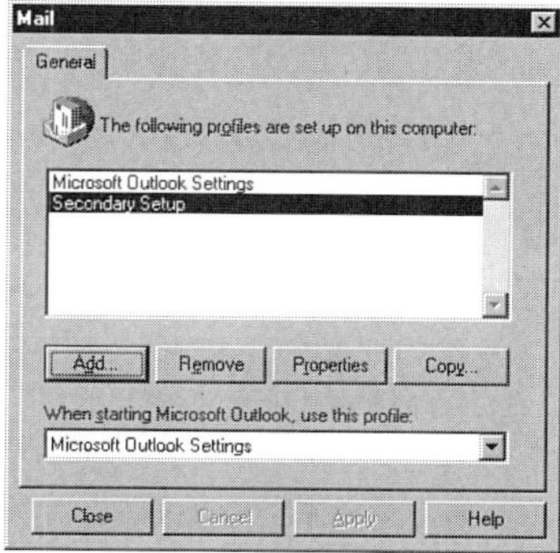

FIGURE 53.5
From here, you can control all your profiles.

To manually add a profile, follow these steps:

1. Choose the Manually Configure Information Services option. Then click the Next button.
2. Give the profile a name. It should define what it will be used for (but it doesn't necessarily have to have a meaning). Then click the Next button.
3. You are presented with an empty Profile dialog box. Click the Add button to add the first service to the new profile. The next thing you'll need is a place to keep your data (messages, calendar, and so on). If you're using an Exchange Server, you could use your server mailbox to hold your data. Because we're not configuring our profile to connect to one of those, we'll need to use something else. The other storage facility that Outlook allows for is a Personal Folder file. Choose Personal Folders from the Add Service to Profile dialog box that appears. Then click the OK button.
4. In the Create/Open Personal Folders File dialog box, select an existing PST (which stands for Personal STore) file or enter a new name. Then click the Open button.
5. In the Create Microsoft Personal Folders dialog box that appears, you can choose a descriptive name for this particular Personal Folder service. This comes in handy if you choose to have more than one Personal Folder service in a profile. You can then choose an encryption level to be used. This defaults to (and should be left at) Compressible Encryption. This setting gives you the best combination of space management and security. An extra level of security can be achieved by adding a password to the PST file, using the fields provided. You will be prompted to provide the password when the PST file is opened (which, in the case of the primary PST, is when you start Outlook). Click the OK button when you've finished with this dialog box.

6. Click the Add button and choose to add the Outlook Address Book service. This service enables you to see the electronic addresses (email and fax) of your contacts as an address book (in Outlook and Word). No configuration is needed for the service at this time, so it's added to the profile immediately.

NOTE Users of Windows Messaging, Exchange, and earlier versions of Outlook might notice that we didn't tell you to add the Personal Address Book service to the profile. The main reason you needed to use it in earlier versions of Outlook was that it was the most direct way to get support for distribution lists. Outlook 2000 adds support for distribution lists to the contact folder, so the Personal Address Book service is no longer necessary.

7. Click the Add button and choose to add the Internet E-Mail Service. The same Properties dialog box that we discussed in the Corporate/Workgroup setup section appears (refer to Figure 53.3). Follow steps 5 through 19 of that procedure to complete the service setup.
8. Click the Delivery tab to examine the options available there. In the Deliver New Mail to the Following Location drop-down list, you can configure which storage facility will hold your default Outlook special folders (in addition to being where mail will be delivered).

NOTE Many times only one item is shown in the drop-down list, but if you've got more than one Personal Folder service in your profile, or if you're using an Exchange Server in addition to Personal Folders, you will see additional items (your Exchange Server mailbox and any Personal Folders configured in the profile) in a drop-down list.

9. Also on this tab, you will find the way to configure which services will carry your mail items. It's not manifestly obvious from the title, but the section named Recipient Addresses Are Processed by These Information Services in the Following Order performs this important function. This comes into play when you have multiple services that can carry a particular type of mail (for example, two Internet E-Mail services or an Internet E-Mail service along with the Exchange Server service). The service listed higher up in the order will be the one to carry all mail of a particular type. The most troublesome type of mail in this regard is SMTP (in laymen's terms, Internet mail) because more than one type of service can transport it. The Internet E-Mail, Exchange Server, and MS Mail service are all capable of carrying that type of mail.
10. Click the Addressing tab to examine the options available there.
11. Click the OK button to complete the setup of your profile and return to the final screen of the Inbox Setup Wizard. Click the Finish button to return to the Mail Control Panel applet dialog box. Click the Close button to close the applet.

Modifying an Existing Profile When you initially open the Control Panel's Mail applet, shown in Figure 53.6, you see the services configured for use in your default profile. If you want to modify this profile, you can do that directly from here. If you want to modify another profile, click the Show Profiles button, choose a profile to modify, and then click the Properties button. This opens the profile for modification.

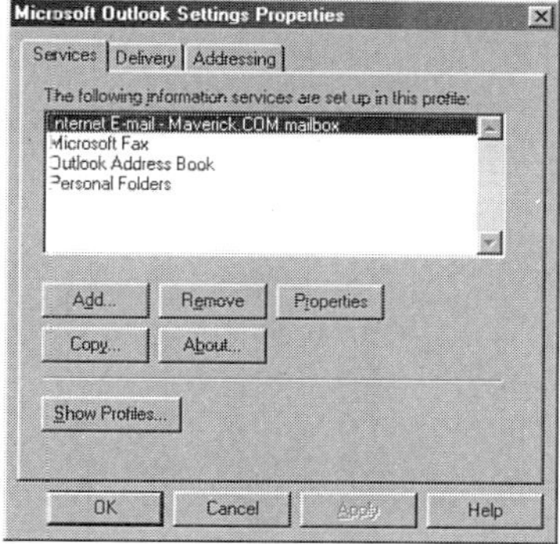

FIGURE 53.6
The Mail applet enables you to get at the "nitty-gritty" of your messaging profile and make any changes you need.

The main uses of the dialog box shown in Figure 53.6 are to add more services (transport, storage, or address book types), to remove services already in the profile, or to change the properties of an existing service. The services you would typically want to add are the Personal Folder service (to add support in a profile for another place to store your mail or other Outlook items) or the Internet E-Mail service (to add support for another POP3 mailbox either at the same ISP as your first or at a completely different ISP).

To add a service, simply click the Add button and choose the service to add from the list displayed. The Properties dialog box for that service appears, enabling you to configure it. To modify a service, highlight the name in the profile display and click the Properties button. That service's Properties dialog box is displayed and enables you to make changes to the service's setup parameters. You can perform some rather commonly requested changes by modifying a few of what some users consider well-hidden settings. Some of those modifications you might like to make include the following:

- If you want to change the sort order of the address book, highlight Outlook Address Book and click Properties. Choose either the First Last or File As order. The File As order gives you the most control because it utilizes the File As field in the contact record.
- If you think that your Personal Folder file has grown too large and you've emptied the Deleted Items folder, go to the Windows Control Panel, Mail applet (it's best to compact while Outlook isn't running). Highlight the Personal Folder service and click Properties. Click the Compact Now button. This begins the compact process. After the Compact Now dialog box clears, the process is complete. You might need to compact several times to achieve results. Be aware that any attachments to mail items are stored in the Personal Folder file, so this can add significant bulk to the file.
- If you decide that you want to move your Personal Folder file. This one is easier said than done. It's not as obvious as going into the properties of the Personal Folder service and changing the path. If you look at the properties in that service, you'll see that the path name is displayed, but it isn't modifiable. However, two ways exist to do it. Both procedures start with moving the Personal Folder file to its new location while Outlook

isn't running. The first method is to remove the Personal Folder service from your profile, and then add it again but direct it to the new location of the file. The second method is

1. Start Outlook. A message stating that the Personal Folder file could not be found is displayed. Click the OK button.
2. A file selection dialog box appears. Locate the Personal Folder file and click the Open button.
3. Close Outlook.

After you've changed your profile (either directly or indirectly), you should start Outlook once with the /ResetOutlookBar command line switch—to regenerate a default Outlook Bar—that you will have to customize again. The reason for this is that the shortcuts on the Outlook Bar contain the full path to the message store that they reference.

▶ **See** "Using Command-Line Switches to Control Outlook," **p. 1355**

Enabling Multiple User Support in Internet Mail Only Mode

When used in IMO mode, Outlook has no internal support for multiple setups or profiles as Corporate/Workgroup mode does. To enable multiple-user support in Internet Mail Only mode, you need to enable support for multiple-user profiles in your operating system. User profile support is automatic in Windows NT, but it's not automatically enabled in either Windows 95 or Windows 98.

NOTE It's quite important that you set up user profiles before configuring Outlook for Internet Mail Only mode. Otherwise, the parameters (mail accounts, Personal Folder File location, and so on) you used in creating the first user will be duplicated to every other user that logs in to the machine.

To enable profiles in Windows 95 or Windows 98, use these steps:

1. Open the Windows Control Panel.
2. Start the Passwords applet.
3. Click the User Profiles tab.
4. Choose the Users Can Customize Their Preferences and Desktop Settings option.
5. Click the OK button.
6. Restart your machine to put the changes into effect.

To create a new profile, you need to log in to Windows with a different username. When you start Outlook, you'll go through the Setup Wizard for your first Internet mail account.

NOTE Even though Internet Mail Only mode doesn't support MAPI profiles as does Corporate/Workgroup mode, it actually uses a profile of its own for each user. The static name of the profile is Microsoft Outlook Internet Settings. This is the reason that you have to create new users to have multiple setups using Internet Mail Only mode.

Modifying Your IMO Mode Configuration To modify your configuration while using IMO mode, open the Mail applet in the Windows Control Panel. The IMO mode Mail applet is much simpler than the CW mode version. This version of the Mail applet features only one tab, titled Mail. The applet enables you to add, change, or remove an account. If you click the Add button, you'll be led through the same Account Setup Wizard described in the Internet Only portion of the "Choosing a Mode" section of this chapter. To delete an account you no longer want to use, highlight it and click the Remove button. Click the Yes button in the confirmation dialog box to complete the removal process. To make changes to an existing account, highlight the account and click the Properties button. This displays a four-tabbed dialog box that enables you to change any of the parameters for the account.

▶ **See** "Using Multiple Files in the Corporate/Workgroup Mode," **p. 1430**

NOTE Actually, one configuration option exists that you can't change from the Properties dialog box. The incoming server type can be set only during account setup. If you need to change it, you must remove the account and set it up again (choosing the correct server type).

Changing Mail Modes

If, after using Outlook, you decide that you want to use the other mode, Microsoft has made it easier to switch than it was in Outlook 98. To switch modes, follow these steps:

1. Select Tools, Options.
2. If you're using Corporate/Workgroup mode, click the Mail Services tab; if you're using Internet Mail Only mode, click the Mail Delivery tab.
3. Click the Reconfigure Mail Support button.
4. Choose the mode you want to use in the Outlook 2000 Startup Wizard dialog box. Click the Next button.
5. A dialog box appears that warns you that all users on your machine will make the mode switch. Click the Yes button.
6. Outlook terminates automatically. Restart Outlook to continue the mode switch.
7. The Windows Installer starts to install the required components for the mode switch. You might be prompted to insert your install CD. When the installer is complete, Outlook opens, using the new mail mode.

Connection Types

In an effort to support as many users and situations as possible, Outlook enables you to utilize a variety of methods to connect to your mail server. Three methods can be used for your connection.

Local Area Network (LAN) Connections

Local Area Network (LAN) connections are designed for users who are directly connected, typically by Network Interface Cards (NIC), to the network that includes their mail server(s). This connection type can also be used by modem users. This apparent contradiction makes sense when you take into account that Windows (both Windows 95 and 98 and Windows NT) considers a dial-up network connection to be a LAN connection (albeit a very slow one). One good reason for choosing this connection type while using a modem is that Outlook doesn't attempt to manage (connect or disconnect) a LAN connection because it thinks that the connection is permanent. To make the appearance of a LAN complete, you should probably set up Internet autodialing on your machine. Windows NT normally asks the user to use a dial-up connection when no LAN connection exists. To accomplish this task under Windows 97 or 98 using Internet Explorer 5, follow these steps:

1. Open the Internet applet in the Windows Control Panel.
2. Click the Connection tab.
3. Check the Dial the Default Connection When Needed box

Using autodialing can be an issue if you need to use different dial-up connections for different accounts (where you might want Outlook to manage the connection).

Phone Line Connections

Phone line connections are the standard connection type for those who use Dial-Up Networking (DUN) to establish their link to the Internet (and mail server). The drop-down list on the Connection tab enables you to choose the DUN "connectoid" that will be used when Outlook connects to your mail server. This connection type is best used when you want Outlook to manage the dial-up connection. IMO mode especially features a variety of settings that control the connection state (select Tools, Options, Mail Delivery tab). CW mode has some settings on the Tools, Options, Internet E-Mail tab.

Manual Connections

This is the connection type to use when you want Outlook to be completely hands-off with regard to the connection. If you use a modem, you have to establish the connection before attempting to connect to your mail server.

Mail Formats

As further evidence of Outlook's spirit of diversity, it includes support for three formats in which to send your mail. The formats are Plain Text, Rich Text Format (RTF), and Hypertext Markup Language (HTML). Each format has a slightly different editor that enables you to take advantage of the features of the format.

Plain Text

This is the most simplistic format you can use to send mail. The format name says it all. When you use this format, your message will be composed entirely of simple text characters. Among its advantages are that virtually anyone capable of receiving email can read a Plain Text email message, and it produces the smallest message size (when compared to an identical message using either of the other formats).

This is also the best format to use when you're uncertain of your recipient's capabilities. It does little good if the lovely email you've so carefully crafted arrives in your recipient's mailbox as a mass of unintelligible gibberish. Of course, being the most simplistic format also means that it's the most limited. You can't change fonts, add color, or embed pictures in the body of the mail item (you can, however, attach files to the mail item). Because there's no capacity for formatting, the editor used for Plain Text emails is about as simplistic as the format itself.

Rich Text Format (RTF)

This was the first type of enriched format supported by Microsoft's mail programs (Microsoft Exchange, Windows Messaging, and Outlook). It fully supports font changes and effects. You can also embed OLE (Object Linking and Embedding) objects in mail items. This format also allows for the sending of other Outlook items, such as tasks, over the Internet to other Outlook users.

The biggest disadvantage to using RTF is that only Exchange, Windows Messaging, and Outlook (but not Outlook Express) can interpret it correctly. Other users will receive a Plain Text version of the mail item sent along with an attachment named `WinMail.dat`. Users inadvertently sending RTF messages to Internet mailing lists have been the cause of much conversation and frustration since the release of Windows 95 and Exchange. The editor used for RTF mail items includes support for all the features of RTF, including simple word processing elements such as bulleted lists and text alignment.

Hypertext Markup Language (HTML)

HTML was added to the Outlook line in Outlook 98 and continues as part of the product in Outlook 2000.

The editor used for HTML items has most of the formatting features of the RTF editor (except, notably, the omission of insertable OLE objects). One of the important configurable settings in this format is Send Pictures from the Internet (found on the Format menu while composing mail items, or you can set the default for this setting on the Mail Format tab of the Options dialog box while HTML is set as the mail format).

This enables you to reduce the size of your outgoing messages by not including an actual copy of an inserted picture in the mail item; instead, a hyperlink to the picture is inserted. The downside of using this option is that the recipient of your email must be connected to the Internet to fully view the content of your email. Otherwise, the recipient will see a broken image link in place of the graphic. Although Outlook's HTML editor is sufficient for most simple HTML messages, you might want to use another HTML editor to compose your masterpiece, and then use Outlook to send it. This can easily be accomplished by inserting the HTML code generated by the other editor directly into your mail messages. You can achieve this while composing an email by using these steps:

1. Choose Insert, File.
2. Select the Text Only option in the Insert File dialog box.
3. Use the Insert File dialog box to navigate to and select the HTML file you want to insert.

Using Microsoft Word As Your Email Editor

In addition to Outlook's internal editors, Outlook 2000 enables you to use Microsoft Word as your email editor. This brings with it all the power and features found in Word. Of course, along with that power comes the resource drain associated with running Word and Outlook at the same time. If your computer has 32MB of RAM or less, we recommend that you not use Word as your email editor. Also, new to Outlook 2000 is the capability to use Word to send HTML messages (previously, Word could be used only for Plain Text or RTF messages).

NOTE After you've designated Word as your email editor, you lose the capability to change your message format on-the-fly. You'll have to change the default format to match the format you want to use on a message-by-message basis.

Choosing Email Formats

Outlook enables you to choose a default format for outgoing emails, and it also enables you to switch formats for a single mail item on-the-fly. I'd recommend setting the default to Plain Text and switching to one of the other formats as needed. To set your default format, choose Tools, Options, and then click the Mail Format tab. Then choose the format in the Send in This Message Format drop-down list. You can also switch formats while composing an email by choosing one on the Format menu.

NOTE You can't switch formats directly from HTML or RTF to the other. You must choose Plain Text and then choose the format you want.

Contact Settings That Affect Mail Formats

You might find that you've send out a formatted piece of email (in either RTF or HTML) but your recipient gets the item in Plain Text. Outlook has contact settings that can determine whether someone gets your formatted item. The location of the setting, the setting's name, and the intent vary with the mode in which you are running Outlook (Corporate/Workgroup or Internet Mail Only).

For Corporate mode users:

1. Select the Contact folder (or other folder containing contact records) from the Outlook Bar or folder list.

2. Open a contact record.
3. Choose which of the three email addresses you want to view or modify from the E-Mail drop-down list on the contact form.
4. Right-click the email address and choose Properties from the context menu that appears.
5. Check or uncheck the Always Send to This Recipient in Microsoft Outlook Rich-Text Format (RTF) option.
6. Click the OK button to save changes to the email address properties.
7. Save the contact record.

For Internet Mail Only mode users:

1. Select the Contact folder (or other folder containing contact records) from the Outlook Bar or folder list.
2. Open a contact record.
3. Check or uncheck the Send Using Plain Text option.

NOTE Notice that the setting in this mode affects all the addresses associated with a contact, unlike Corporate mode where each address has its own format setting.

4. Save the contact record.

As you can see, each mode enables you to force one format (RTF) or another (Plain Text) on a contact, but you can't force a contact address to have all its mail sent in HTML.

Using the Rules Wizard

After you've configured Outlook to send and receive mail, you might find that your Inbox folder is getting crowded with mail. You might find yourself moving items into separate folders to keep related mail items together. For example, you want to keep all the mail you get from a friend in a special place. This can become quite a chore if you do it manually. Outlook provides a tool called the Rules Wizard, which can automate this task (and others like it) for you. The Rules Wizard can automatically perform the following actions on incoming messages:

- Move, copy, delete, forward, or print messages
- Reply to messages
- Display custom pop-up messages
- Play a sound
- Apply a scheduled action flag
- Assign a category
- Start an application
- Mark the item with an importance flag
- Perform a custom action

NOTE The last action, perform a custom action, can be particularly powerful. A custom action is an external module that can do a variety of functions (such as automatically marking an item as read). You can find a collection of them here:

`http://www.ornic.com`

`http://www.slipstick.com/exchange/gallery.htm`

Explaining every option available in the Rules Wizard might turn this book into a multivolume set. Because the basic rule setup is the same for most rules, I'll detail the setting up of a common rule (moving incoming messages from a recipient into a folder):

1. Open the Rules Wizard by selecting Tools, Rules Wizard.
2. Click the New button to define a new rule.
3. Select the Check Messages When They Arrive type in the Rules Wizard dialog box, as seen in Figure 53.7. Click the Next button.

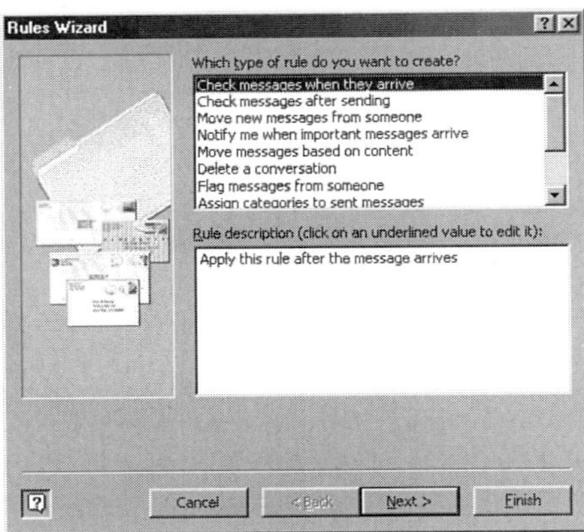

FIGURE 53.7
The Rules Wizard provides a way to automatically process messages.

4. Check the From People or Distribution condition box. In the Rules description box, click the underlined text People or Distribution List.
5. In the Rule Address dialog box, choose an address or addresses from your address book to use in this rule.
6. After you've returned to the Rules Wizard dialog box, click the Next button.
7. Check the Move It to the Specified Folder action. In the Rules Description box, click the underlined text Specified.
8. Choose a folder where you want the items moved. If you need to create a new folder, click the New button. Click the OK button to return to the Rules Wizard dialog box.
9. Check any exceptions you want to apply to this rule. For this particular example, simply click the Next button.

10. The Rules Wizard dialog box now displays the full rule and gives you the opportunity to name the rule. You can also enable or disable the rule from here. More important (and new to Outlook 2000), you can also run the rule on messages already in the folder you had selected when you started the Rules Wizard. Click Finish to return to the list of defined rules.

From the full list of defined rules, you can also run any of the rules by selecting a rule and clicking the Run Now button. When the Run Rules Now dialog box appears (as shown in Figure 53.8), you can select any of your defined rules to run, in which folders to run them, and on what kind of messages (all, read, or unread).

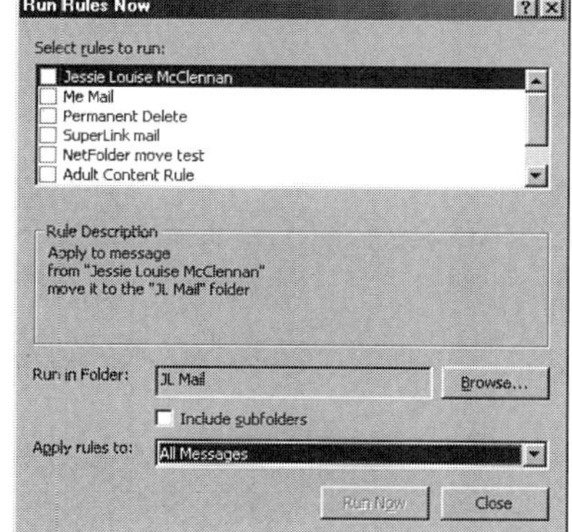

FIGURE 53.8
The Run Rules Now dialog box gives you a way to retroactively apply new rules.

CHAPTER 54

E-Mail Security

In this chapter

Security Concerns

If you use Outlook on a standalone computer to which only you have access and which doesn't have a modem, your concerns about security are that Outlook accurately saves the information you enter and returns that information when you need it—and that no one steals your computer.

You probably don't use Outlook like that. If you use Outlook on a standalone computer, you probably have a modem and use Outlook to send and receive e-mail by way of the Internet or another e-mail service. If you use Outlook on a networked computer, you can share information in many ways.

When you use Outlook on a computer that's connected either by phone line or LAN to other computers, several issues arise. These include the following:

- Can you be sure that information you want to keep private can't be accessed by other people?
- Can you be sure that information you want to share with other people is accessible only by those people with whom you want to share that information?
- When you send an e-mail message, can you be sure that message is received by the people to whom you addressed it—and only by them?
- When people receive a message from you, can you be sure the message hasn't been tampered with?
- When you receive an e-mail message, can you be sure that message was actually sent by the person from whom it appears to be sent?
- When you receive an e-mail message, can you be sure the message hasn't been tampered with?

These and other questions are addressed in this chapter.

Securing Your Computer

No such thing as absolute security exists. However, you can do a lot to make your security close to impenetrable. The degree to which you are willing to adopt these measures depends on the value of the information stored on your computer and on the information to which your computer has access.

Later in this chapter, you'll read about certificates. It's particularly important to secure your computer if you have a certificate. If your computer is not secure, it's possible that other people can obtain copies of your certificate and then pass themselves off as you.

▶ **See** "Sending Secure Messages over the Internet," **p. 1451**

Physically Securing Your Computer

By physically securing your computer, I mean preventing unauthorized people from gaining access to it. If you're using a desktop computer, that might mean keeping it in a vault that's as difficult to get into as a bank's strong room. In less-demanding situations, it's usually adequate to keep your computer in a room that's always locked when you're not there.

An alternative is to replace the hard drive in your computer with a removable hard drive. When you're finished working, you can remove the hard drive and either keep it with you or put it into a safe.

NOTE You can't protect your data by deleting files from your hard disk because deleting removes only an index entry that points to where the data is stored. You, or someone else, can easily recover deleted files. Even if you reformat your drive, sophisticated equipment might be able to retrieve information from the disk. If your hard disk contains sensitive information and it must be replaced, your best bet is to physically destroy the drive to ensure that your data cannot be retrieved by an intrepid snoop.

Laptop computers are a particular problem as far as security is concerned. Short of chaining the computer to your body, no way exists to eliminate the possibility of the computer being stolen with all your valuable data on its hard disk. If you use a laptop and have data that must not be accessible to other people, make sure you keep that data only on a removable disk. Keep that disk in your personal possession, not plugged into the computer.

Preventing Access to Your Computer

The preceding section addresses the issues of preventing people from gaining access to your computer. Those methods are probably too extreme in most environments. What do you do if you live in a cubicle to which many people have access while you're at lunch or in a meeting?

One possibility is to use a so-called screen saver. Although modern monitors don't seem to need any help to prevent ghost images being permanently registered on their screens, you can use a screen saver to blank out your screen while you're away from your computer. You, or someone else, can see the screen again only by entering a password.

Although a screen saver can prevent a casual intruder from using your computer, it won't deter a skilled hacker.

Windows NT, unlike Windows 95 and Windows 98 (which I'll refer to collectively as Windows 9x), has a more effective way of preventing access to your computer. Running under Windows NT, you can set up accounts that can be accessed only by entering a username and password. This is in contrast to Windows 9x, which uses a username and password only to determine a user's Windows settings. Someone wanting to access the data on your computer running Windows 9x can simply choose Cancel to sidestep the password prompt. Windows 9x will continue loading without a hitch, leaving your data vulnerable to prying eyes.

The password security offered by Windows NT is one of a number of very good reasons to use that operating system instead of Windows 9x. Combined with the use of the NT File System, it should stop most attempts to access your data without your permission.

Creating Private Outlook Items

When you create an Outlook item, you can mark that item as private. After doing so, the item is displayed just like any other Outlook item when you display Outlook items in an Information viewer. However, if someone else with whom you have shared your Outlook folder opens that folder, that person will see that the item exists but won't be able to see any information about it.

For example, if you allow your administrative assistant to have access to your Calendar, you can create an appointment and mark it private. Subsequently, your administrative assistant can see that you have blocked out time on your calendar but cannot see the details of that item.

NOTE In a Corporate/Workgroup (C/W) installation with Outlook used as a client for an Exchange server, you can allow a delegate to see items you've marked as private. To do so, choose Tools, Options, and select the Delegates tab. Select a delegate, and then choose Permissions. Check Delegate Can See My Private Items.

Controlling Access to Folders

Access to Outlook folders differs according to whether you're working with Outlook in either Internet Mail Only (IMO) mode or Corporate/Workgroup (C/W) mode.

Controlling Folder Access in Internet Mail Only Mode

If you're using Outlook in IMO mode, you have access only to the Outlook folders within the Personal Folders files on the computer you're using. You can access this folder in the same way you can access other Windows files.

Nothing prevents anyone who has access to your computer from copying a Personal Folders file. As mentioned previously in this chapter, if you use Windows NT or Windows 98, you can protect all your files by requiring a password to start the operating system.

When you install Outlook in IMO mode, a Personal Folders file with the name Outlook.pst is automatically created and has the standard Outlook folders. To examine the properties of the Personal Properties file, right-click Outlook Today in the Outlook Bar and choose Properties in the context menu to display the Personal Folders Properties dialog box. Choose Advanced to display the dialog box shown in Figure 54.1.

This dialog box shows the following:

- The Name—Personal Folders—by which the file is known, within Outlook. You can change that name from Personal Folders to something else.
- The Path of the file. You can't change that.
- The fact that Compressible Encryption is used to save Outlook items within the file. You can't change that.

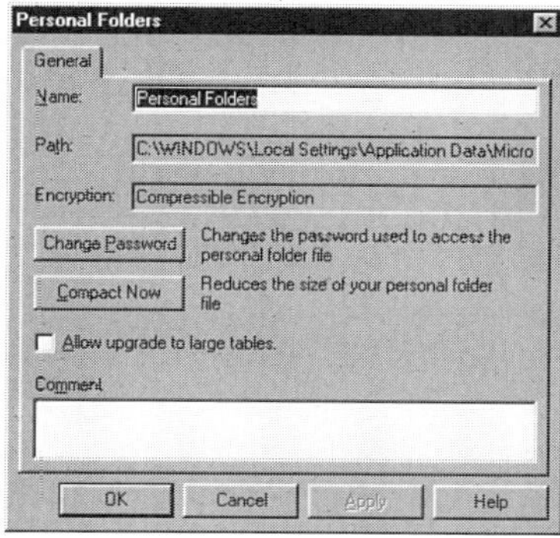

FIGURE 54.1
This dialog box displays information about your Personal Folders file.

NOTE Although you can't change the encryption for the existing Personal Folders file, you can create another Personal Folders file and set it to Best Encryption. You can designate the new file as your default personal store.

Initially, Outlook creates your Personal Folders file without a password. To provide protection for your Outlook items saved in your Personal Folders file, you can protect the file with a password.

To protect your Personal Folders file with a password, follow these steps:

1. In the Personal Folders dialog box, choose Change Password to display the dialog box shown in Figure 54.2.

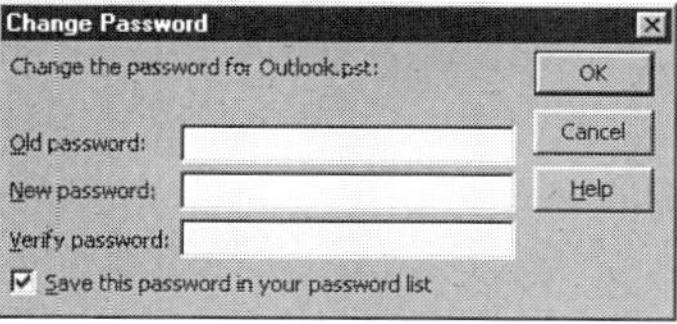

FIGURE 54.2
Use this dialog box to designate a password.

2. If you haven't previously designated a password for your Personal Folders file, leave the Old Password box empty. If you have previously password-protected your Personal Folders file, enter that password in the Old Password box.
3. Enter the new password in the New Password box. Outlook remembers the characters you enter but displays asterisks in the box.
4. Enter the new password again in the Verify Password box.

NOTE Outlook passwords are case sensitive. You must enter the same combination of uppercase and lowercase characters in both boxes. Later, when you use the password to gain access to your Outlook items, you must use the correct combination of uppercase and lowercase characters.

5. Leave the Save This Password in Your Password List box unchecked. Choose OK. If you enter the same characters in the New Password and Verify Password boxes, Outlook accepts the new password and closes the dialog box. If you don't enter the same characters in both boxes, Outlook tells you that both boxes must have the same content; you must correct that problem by reentering the password in both boxes.
6. Choose OK three times to close the dialog boxes.
7. Choose File, Exit to close Outlook.

The next time you start Outlook, you'll see the dialog box shown in Figure 54.3.

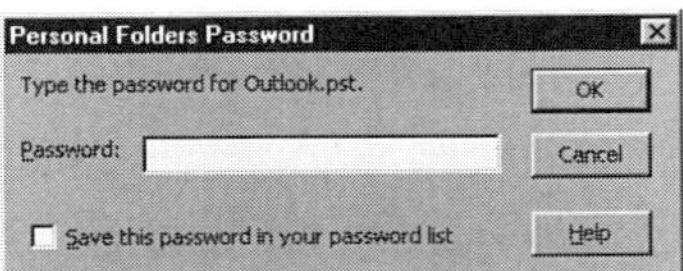

FIGURE 54.3
You must enter your password before Outlook will start.

NOTE If you enter the wrong password, Outlook displays a message about that. Choose OK to close the message box, and then enter the correct password.

If you click outside the Personal Folders Password dialog box, that dialog box disappears and Outlook appears to freeze. Click the Personal Folders Password button in the Windows taskbar to redisplay the Personal Folders Password dialog box.

Controlling Folder Access in Corporate/Workgroup mode

If you're using Outlook in C/W mode but not as a client for an Exchange server, the situation is much the same as for Outlook in IMO mode, described in the preceding section.

If you're using Outlook in C/W mode as a client for an Exchange server, you have access to any number of Personal Folders files and Offline Folders files on your local hard drive, and also to any number of sets of Outlook folders within Exchange server stores. You can control access to any folder that you own in the Exchange store—your own Outlook folders and public folders for which you have Owner permissions.

Setting Logon Security

Outlook provides password protection for access to mail servers. If you're concerned about other people reading e-mail addressed to you, you should set up your e-mail accounts so a password is required before Outlook will connect to a mail server. In many cases, you don't have any choice about this because most mail servers are set up to require a password.

Connecting to an Internet Mail Server

If you're running Outlook in IMO mode and you have an Internet e-mail account, you can set up Outlook so it automatically supplies your password when you attempt to connect to the server, or so you have to provide the password each time you attempt to connect. Having Outlook automatically supply the password is convenient, but it presents a security risk. If your computer is accessible to other people, it's generally better not to have Outlook automatically supply the password.

NOTE Internet e-mail servers normally use the same account name and password for receiving and sending mail. If you're accessing a server that requires (or allows) separate names and passwords for receiving and sending, refer to the information about outgoing mail servers later in this section.

To have Outlook automatically supply a password for access to an Internet mail server, follow these steps:

1. Choose Tools, Accounts to display the Internet Accounts dialog box. With the Mail tab selected, select the Internet account for which you want to supply a password, and then choose Properties and select the Servers tab, as shown in Figure 54.4. The dialog box name changes depending on the name of your account.

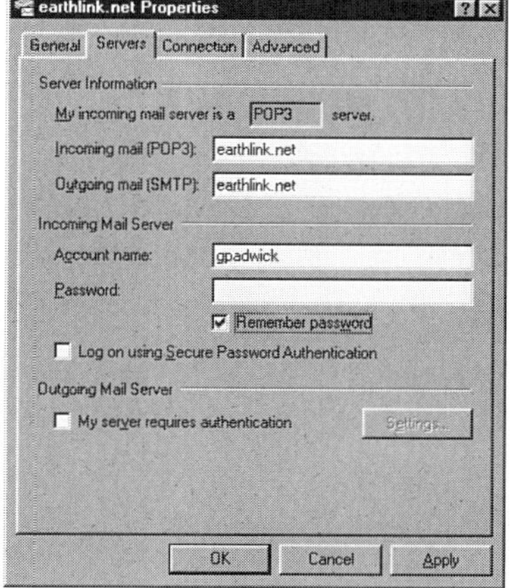

FIGURE 54.4
The Incoming Mail Server section of this dialog box is where you specify a password.

2. Enter your e-mail account password in the Password box.
3. Check Remember Password.
4. Choose OK to close the dialog box; then choose Close to close the Internet Accounts dialog box.

The next time you attempt to log on to your Internet e-mail server, you won't be asked for your name or password.

If you want the security protection provided by being asked for your password when you attempt to log on to your e-mail server, be sure Remember Password in the Properties dialog box shown in Figure 54.4 is not checked. After you do so, you'll see the dialog box shown in Figure 54.5 when you attempt to log on to your Internet account.

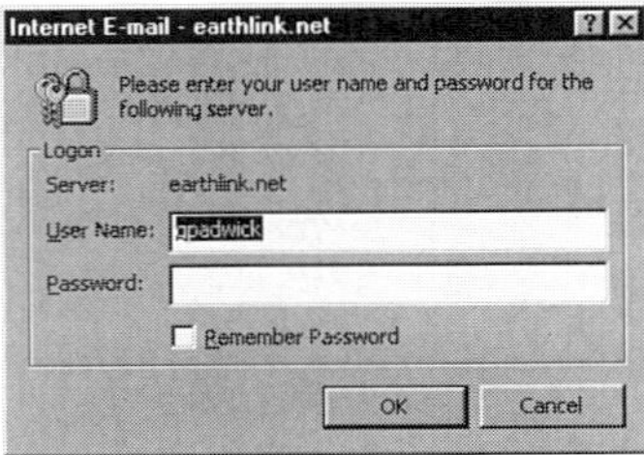

FIGURE 54.5
Enter your password in this dialog box to gain access to your Internet account.

NOTE If you access an Internet server that requires secure password authentication (such as the servers at MSN and CompuServe), select Log On Using Secure Password Authentication in the Properties dialog box, previously shown in Figure 54.4.

If your Internet service provider's outbound mail servers require you to log in before sending mail, you can also set up the Internet e-mail information service to prompt for that password before mail can be sent from the account. If you don't do that, anyone who has access to your computer can send a message that appears to recipients to be from you.

To require a password before Outlook will send Internet e-mail, check My Server Requires Authentication and then choose Settings to display the dialog box shown in Figure 54.6.

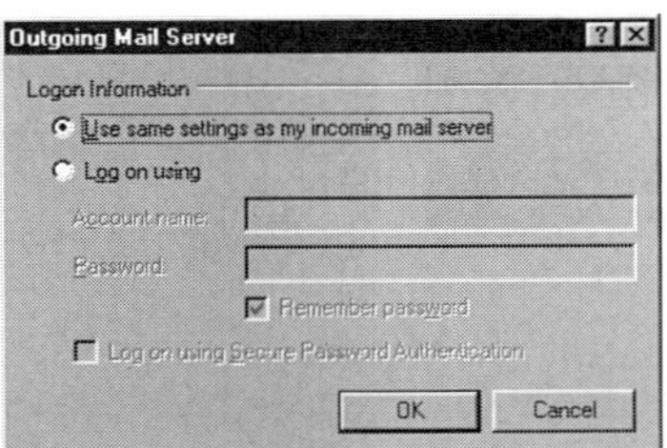

FIGURE 54.6
Make choices for outgoing e-mail in this dialog box in much the same way as you previously did for incoming e-mail.

NOTE If you're running Outlook in C/W mode, you set up an Internet e-mail account by adding an Internet e-mail information service to your profile. Do this in almost the same way as described previously for Outlook in IMO mode.

The only difference is the way you start. Choose Tools, Services to display the Services dialog box. In the Services tab, select an Internet e-mail information service, then choose Properties, and select the Servers tab shown previously in Figure 54.4.

Connecting to an Exchange Server

If you're using Outlook in C/W mode as a client for an Exchange server, when you start Outlook it automatically connects, by default, to Outlook folders in the Exchange store.

To require a password to access an Exchange server, follow these steps:

1. Choose Tools, Services to display the Services dialog box. Select the Microsoft Exchange Server information service and then choose Properties. Select the Advanced tab shown in Figure 54.7.

FIGURE 54.7
Use this dialog box to control access to the Exchange server.

NOTE By default, NT Password Authentication is displayed in the Logon Network Security box. This means that the same password you use to log on to your Windows NT server is used to log you on to your Exchange Server—convenient, but a possible security risk.

2. Open the drop-down Logon Network Security list and choose None.
3. Choose OK twice to close the dialog boxes. Choose File, Exit and Log Off to close Outlook.

The next time you start Outlook, you'll see the dialog box shown in Figure 54.8.

FIGURE 54.8
You must supply your Exchange password before Outlook will connect to the Exchange server.

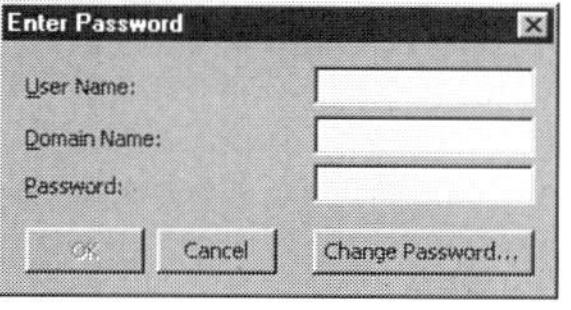

Sending Secure Messages over the Internet

Although the Internet is convenient to use, you might wonder how secure it is and what you can do to enhance the security of your Internet communications. For normal communications, the Internet seems to be at least as secure as postal mail. Whereas it's not unusual to hear about mail being stolen from postal mailboxes, it's rare to hear about e-mail messages being stolen.

NOTE This chapter covers only basic information about security over the Internet. For much more detailed information, consult books such as *Special Edition Using the Internet*, published by Que, *Using Microsoft Internet Explorer 5.0*, published by Que, and for comprehensive information on the subject, *Internet Security Professional Reference*, published by New Riders.

If the messages you send and receive contain confidential information, you should consider enhancing e-mail security by using a *certificate*. Outlook fully supports the use of certificates. Microsoft recommends VeriSign as a source of certificates; therefore, this chapter focuses on certificates issued by that company. VeriSign calls certificates *Digital IDs*.

NOTE Certificates rely on the *Secure Multipurpose Internet Mail Extensions* (S/MIME) protocol that Outlook supports. You can send secure e-mail messages to—and receive secure e-mail messages from—people who use Outlook or other e-mail programs that support S/MIME. E-mail programs that support S/MIME include Outlook, Outlook Express, Netscape Messenger, Worldtalk, Frontier, Pre-mail, Opensoft, Connectsoft, and Eudora.

For detailed information about using VeriSign Digital IDs with Outlook, refer to the article "Personal IDs for Outlook Users," available at `http://www.verisign.com/securemail/outlook98/outlook.html`

Understanding Certificates

A certificate serves two purposes: authentication and encryption.

- *Authentication* means that you can send messages to other people and those people can have a high level of confidence that the messages they receive really are from you and that those messages haven't been tampered with in any way. Authentication also means other people can send messages to you and you can have the same confidence that the messages you receive are really from the apparent senders and are the messages those people actually sent.
- *Encryption* is the process of converting plain text into an encoded form. If you have a certificate, you can encrypt your messages so that only a recipient who knows how to decrypt those messages can read them. Likewise, other people can send encrypted messages to you.

When you receive a certificate, you get two keys: your private key and your public key. The private key is just that—*private*. It's an entry in the Windows Registry on your computer that's protected by a password. Your private key is created on your computer and resides only there. It is not known to the organization or person who issued the certificate. Your private key is used to create digital signatures and to decrypt messages encrypted with the corresponding public key.

The public key, on the other hand, is a file you can make freely available to other people. You must provide your public key to people before they can send you encrypted messages. Your public key is used to encrypt messages that can be decrypted by your private key.

NOTE The private key and matching public key are sometimes referred to as a *key pair*.

After you've installed a certificate on your computer, you're ready to send secure mail. If you want to send encrypted mail to someone, you must have that person's public key.

- When you send a message secured by your certificate, a recipient who uses an e-mail program that supports S/MIME can verify that the message is really from you and hasn't been tampered with by anyone else.
- When people send you messages secured by their certificates, you can verify that the message is really from the apparent sender and hasn't been tampered with.
- To send an encrypted message a recipient can decrypt, you must have the recipient's public key in the Contact item for that recipient in your Contacts folder.
- For other people to send you encrypted messages you can decrypt, those people must have your public key.

Obtaining a Certificate

You can use Outlook to obtain a certificate from VeriSign, either a 60-day trial version at no cost, or on a subscription basis which, at the time this book was written, was available for $9.95 per year.

To get a certificate from VeriSign, you have to connect to VeriSign's Web site. You must, of course, have Outlook set up to connect to the Internet.

NOTE VeriSign uses the term *Digital ID* as a brand name for certificates.

To obtain a VeriSign Digital ID, follow these steps:

1. With any Outlook Information viewer displayed, choose Tools, Options and select the Security tab shown in Figure 54.9.

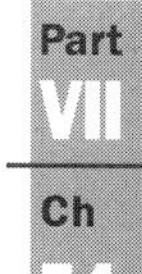

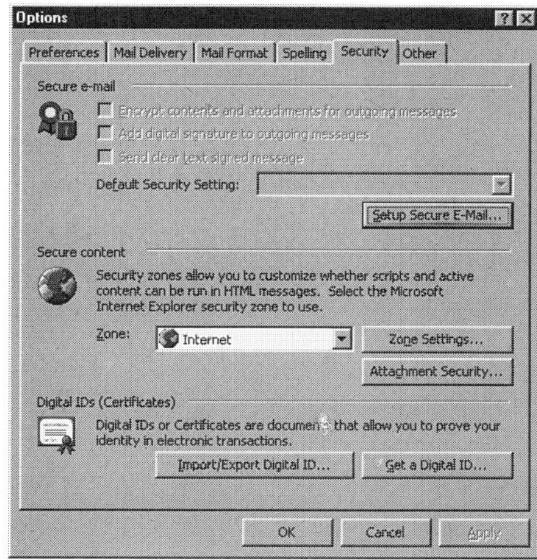

FIGURE 54.9
The Security tab provides access to Outlook's security options.

2. Choose Get a Digital ID. Outlook accesses your ISP and connects you to a Microsoft Web page discussing sources for certificates. Click the VeriSign link to connect to that site.

3. Follow the instructions there to apply for either an evaluation or an annual subscription to a Digital ID and for installing that Digital ID on your computer.

A short while after you apply for a Digital ID, you'll receive an e-mail message confirming that your application has been accepted and instructing you how to proceed. You must install the Digital ID on the same computer you used to apply for the Digital ID. As explained later in this chapter, you can move your Digital ID from one computer to another.

Setting the Security Level for Your Private Key

During the process of installing your private key, you'll be asked to select a security level. Three security levels are available:

- High—Choose this if you want to password-protect your private key. You'll be asked for the password each time you use your private key.
- Medium—Choose this if you don't want to password-protect your private key. Outlook displays a message each time you use your private key.
- Low—Choose this if you want to be able to use your private key without being asked for a password and without Outlook displaying a message.

Making a Backup Copy of Your Digital ID

You should make a backup copy of your Digital ID for two reasons:

- So that you can restore your Digital ID if it becomes corrupted on your hard disk
- So that you can move your Digital ID to another computer or hard disk

Normally, you should save a copy of your Digital ID on a floppy disk and keep that disk in a secure place.

To make a copy of your Digital ID, perform the following steps:

1. With any Outlook Information viewer displayed, choose Tools, Options to display the Options dialog box and select the Security tab, shown previously in Figure 54.9.
2. Choose Import/Export Digital ID to display the dialog box shown in Figure 54.10.
3. Select Export Your Digital ID to a File.
4. Choose Select to display a dialog box similar to that shown in Figure 54.11.
5. Select the Digital ID you want to save.
6. If you want to see information about the Digital ID, you can choose View Certificate. This step isn't required.
7. Choose OK to return to the Import/Export Security Information and Digital ID dialog box; in the Digital ID box, the name of the Digital ID you selected in Step 5 is now displayed.
8. Enter a full pathname for the exported file in the Export File box. Alternatively, you can choose Browse, navigate to a disk, and enter a name for the exported file.

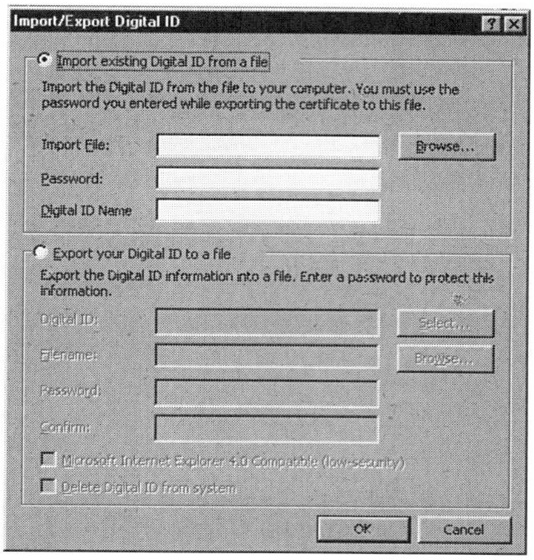

FIGURE 54.10
You can use this dialog box to import a previously saved Digital ID as well as to export the Digital ID on your computer.

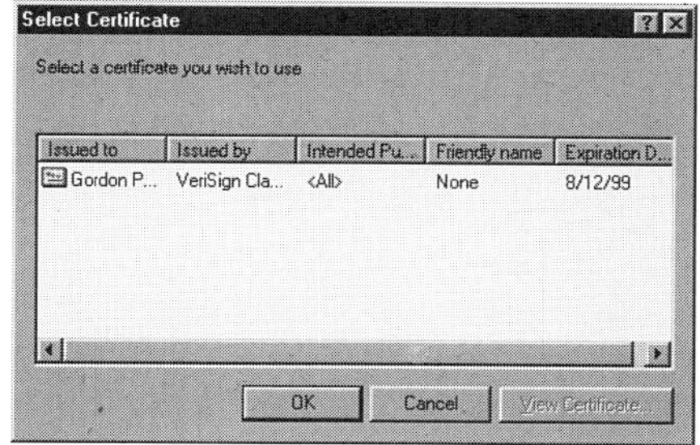

FIGURE 54.11
This dialog box lists information about your installed certificates.

9. Enter a password for the exported file into the Password box. Enter the password again into the Confirm box.
10. Unless you want your Digital ID to be compatible with the low-security protocol of Internet Explorer 4.0, leave the Microsoft Internet Explorer 4.0 Compatible box unchecked.
11. Choose OK to display the dialog box shown in Figure 54.12.

FIGURE 54.12
This dialog box states the security level of the private key you're about to export.

12. Choose OK to create the exported file. After a short delay, the Outlook Options dialog box reappears. Outlook saves the file with .pfx as its filename extension.

If someone else gains access to the backup copy of your Digital ID, that person could import your Digital ID onto another computer. For that reason, it's important to protect the backup file with a password and to keep the backup disk in a secure place.

Removing Your Digital ID from a Computer

When the time comes to replace your hard disk with another one, you must remember to remove your Digital ID from the old disk. Otherwise, if someone else inherits your old hard disk, that person also inherits your Digital ID. Likewise, if you replace your computer with a new one, remember to remove your Digital ID before you pass your old computer on to someone else.

To remove your Digital ID, follow the first seven steps in the preceding procedure. Then select Delete Digital ID from System and choose OK.

"Removing" doesn't really remove information from your hard disk—it just makes that information inaccessible by normal means. Techniques are available to recover information you may have removed.

In high-security environments, any disk that contains, or has contained, confidential information that's removed from a computer should be physically destroyed to avoid any possibility that a dedicated and talented hacker can recover the information.

Importing Your Digital ID from a Backup Disk

The process of importing your Digital ID from a backup disk in similar to the process of exporting your Digital ID.

To import your Digital ID, follow these steps:

1. With any Outlook Information viewer displayed, choose Tools, Options to display the Options dialog box and select the Security tab, shown previously in Figure 54.9.
2. Choose Import/Export Digital ID to display the dialog box previously shown in Figure 54.10.
3. Select Import Existing Digital ID from a File.
4. In the Import File box, enter the full pathname of the file you want to import. Alternatively, choose Browse, navigate to the disk that contains the file, select the file, and choose Open to return to the Import/Export Security Information and Digital ID dialog box, as shown in Figure 54.13.
5. In the Password box, enter the password of the saved file.
6. In the Digital ID Name box, enter the name by which you want Outlook to refer to your Digital ID. You can use any name, but your own name or mailbox name are appropriate.

FIGURE 54.13
The dialog box now contains the pathname of the file to be imported.

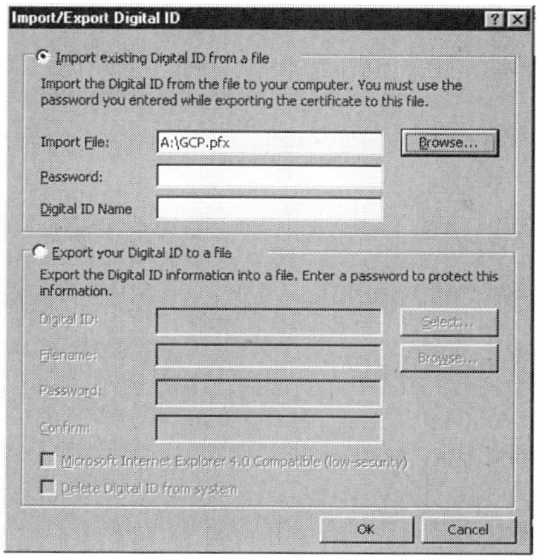

Import/Export Digital ID

Import existing Digital ID from a file

Import the Digital ID from the file to your computer. You must use the password you entered while exporting the certificate to this file.

Import File: A:\GCP.pfx Browse...

Password:

Digital ID Name

Export your Digital ID to a file

Export the Digital ID information into a file. Enter a password to protect this information.

Digital ID: Select...

Filename: Browse...

Password:

Confirm:

Microsoft Internet Explorer 4.0 Compatible (low-security)

Delete Digital ID from system

OK Cancel

Adding Digital ID Buttons to the Message Form's Toolbar

You can add two Digital ID buttons to the Message form's Standard toolbar. After doing so, you can readily see whether your digital signature and encryption are turned on or off, and also enable and disable those options.

To add Digital ID buttons to the Message form's Standard toolbar:

1. With the Inbox Information viewer displayed, choose New in the Standard toolbar to display the Message form.
2. Choose View, move the pointer to Toolbars, and choose Customize. Select the Commands tab, scroll down the Categories box, and select Standard, as shown in Figure 54.14.

FIGURE 54.14
The right box contains a list of commands in the Standard category.

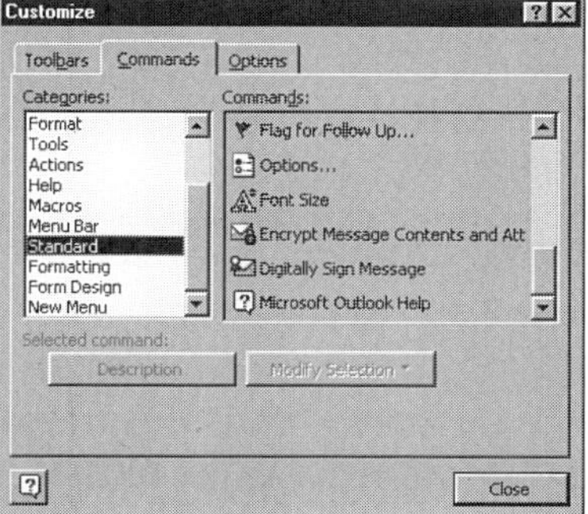

3. Scroll down to the bottom of the list of commands.
4. Drag the Encrypt Message Contents and Attachments command into the Message form's Standard toolbar, just to the right of the Office Assistant button.

5. Drag the Digitally Sign Message command into the Message form's Standard toolbar, just to the right of the Encrypt Message Contents and Attachments button.
6. Choose Close to close the Customize dialog box. The Message form's Standard toolbar now contains the two added buttons, as shown in Figure 54.15.

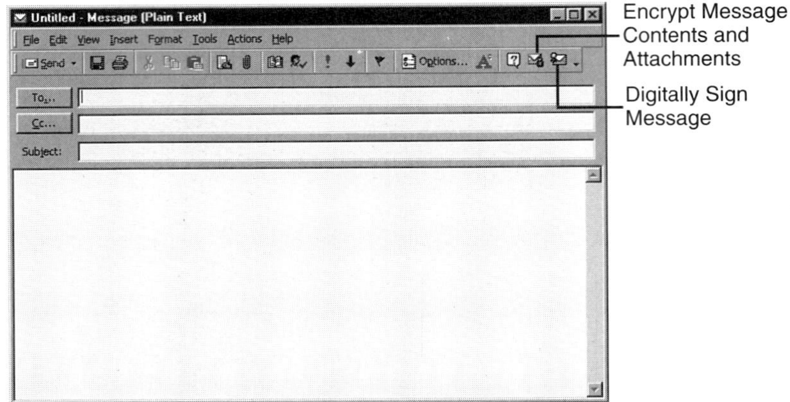

FIGURE 54.15
This is the Message form's Standard toolbar with the two Digital ID buttons added.

When encryption and digital signing are turned off, the two buttons have a normal, gray background. The buttons have a bright background and appear pressed when those options are enabled. Click a button to change from disabled to enabled and vice versa.

Sending and Receiving Digitally Signed Messages

You can set up Outlook so that the default is either to send all your messages with a digital signature or without a digital signature. Whichever you choose as the default, you can turn the digital signature off or on for each message.

Choosing Digital Signatures As the Default

If you expect to digitally sign most of the messages you send, you should set this as a default.

To set digital signing as the default, perform the following steps:

1. With an Outlook Information viewer displayed, choose Tools, Options to display the Options dialog box. Select the Security tab shown in Figure 54.16.
2. Check Add Digital Signature to Outgoing Messages.
3. If you want people who use e-mail applications that don't support S/MIME signatures to be able to read your messages, check Send Clear Text Signed Messages.

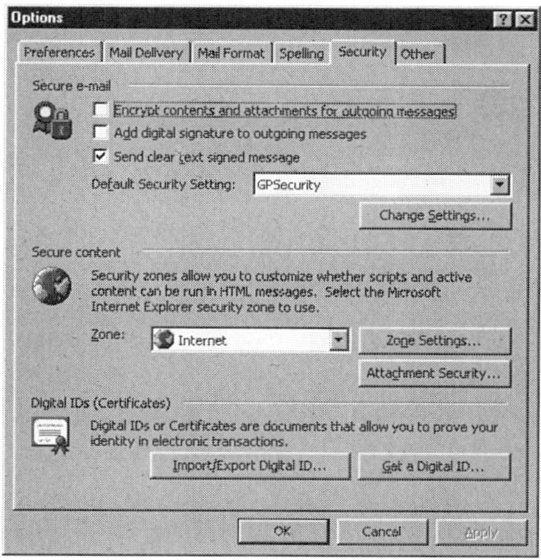

FIGURE 54.16
When you have a Digital ID installed, the Secure E-Mail section of this dialog box is enabled.

NOTE If you leave the Send Clear Text Signed Messages unchecked, only recipients who use an e-mail application that supports S/MIME signatures will be able to read your messages. Those people will also be able to verify that the message actually came from you and has not been tampered with.

If you check the Send Clear Text Signed Messages box, all recipients (whether they use an application that supports S/MIME or not) will be able to read your messages. Recipients who don't use an application that supports S/MIME won't be able to verify that the message actually came from you, nor can they be certain the message hasn't been tampered with.

Examining and Changing Security Settings

Your Digital ID has certain security settings. You can examine and change these settings by choosing Change Settings (in the Security tab of the Options dialog box) to display the dialog box shown in Figure 54.17.

FIGURE 54.17
You can use this dialog box to change your security settings and to create new settings.

To change the Digital ID settings:

1. If you want to change the default name of your security settings, edit the name in the Security Settings Name box.
2. The default Secure Message Format is S/MIME, which is what you want if you're going to send and receive secure mail by way of the Internet or an intranet.

NOTE If you're using Outlook in C/W mode as a client for an Exchange server and you will be using that messaging system, open the drop-down Secure Message Format list and select Exchange Server Security.

3. Leave Default Security Setting for This Secure Message Format checked to make the current security settings the default for the format shown in the Secure Message Format box.
4. Leave Default Security Setting for All Secure Messages checked to make the current security settings the default if you use Exchange and S/MIME.
5. If you want to create another security setting, choose New. Outlook removes the name in the Security Settings Name box. Enter a name for the new setting in that box and choose a Secure Message Format.
6. If you want to delete a security setting, select that setting and choose Delete.
7. By default, the Signing Certificate box contains the name of your Digital ID. If you have more than one Digital ID, choose Choose to open the Select a Certificate dialog box, in which you can select the certificate you want to use for signing messages in the current set of security settings.
8. Leave the Hash Algorithm as the default SHA-1.
9. By default, the Encryption Certificate box contains the name of your Digital ID. If you have more than one Digital ID, choose Choose to open the Select a Certificate dialog box, in which you can select the certificate you want to use for encrypting messages in the current security settings.
10. Leave the Encryption Algorithm as the default.

NOTE For an in-depth discussion of encryption and hashing algorithms, visit the RSA Labs FAQ: `http://www.rsa.com/rsalabs/faq/`

11. If you want to send your public key with messages, check the Send These Certificates with Signed Messages box. You should check this box if you want people to whom you send messages to be able to send you encrypted messages. This box is not available if you select Exchange Server Security as the Secure Message Format.

Creating New Security Settings

The preceding section assumes you need only one set of security settings. You can have more than one set.

Starting from the Security tab in the Options dialog box, choose Change Settings to display the Change Security Settings dialog box shown previously in Figure 54.16. In that dialog box, choose Create New to clear all the boxes. You can now follow the steps in the preceding procedure to name and select security settings for another set.

When you have two or more named sets of security settings, you can open the drop-down Security Settings Name list to select the set you want to use.

Deleting a Set of Security Settings

To delete a set of security settings, select that set, as explained in the preceding section, and then choose Delete Setting.

Sending a Digitally Signed Message

When you send a digitally signed message, that message contains your digital signature. The message recipient who uses an e-mail program that supports S/MIME can examine that signature to verify the message actually came from you. This works because only a computer on which your Digital ID is installed can send a message that contains your digital signature.

A digitally signed message contains the original message and an encrypted version of that message. When the message is received by a computer on which the e-mail program supports S/MIME, the original message and encrypted message are compared to make sure they are identical. Any difference between the two indicates that the message has been tampered with.

After you've set the default to send messages with a digital signature, create a message to be sent in the normal way. The Message form's Standard toolbar contains a button you can use to turn a digital signature on or off, as shown previously in Figure 54.15.

If you've set the default to send all messages with a digital signature, the Digitally Sign Message button has a bright background. To send the current message without a digital signature, click the button—the bright background disappears, signifying that the digital signature is turned off.

NOTE You can also enable and disable your digital signature by checking or unchecking the Add Digital Signature to Outgoing Message box in the Message Options dialog box.

If you've set the default to send all messages without a digital signature, the Digitally Sign Message button doesn't have a bright background. To send the current message with a digital signature, click the button—the bright background appears, signifying that the digital signature is turned on.

NOTE If you use the Microsoft Outlook Rich Text format to create a message and you send that message as a secure message using your S/MIME digital signature, Outlook automatically changes the message format to HTML to ensure the correct processing of your digital signature. As a result, some of the message formatting may be lost.

After you've sent a digitally signed message, you can see that message in your Sent Items folder. It is identified as a message that was sent with a digital signature by the red ribbon on the message symbol. Also, if you open the sent message in a Message form, the header contains the red ribbon.

Receiving Digitally Signed Messages

Some of the people to whom you send digitally signed messages may be using an e-mail program that supports S/MIME; others may not. Three possibilities exist:

- A recipient uses an e-mail application that supports S/MIME.
- A recipient uses an e-mail application that doesn't support S/MIME, and you haven't checked Send Clear Text Signed Message in the Security tab of the Options dialog box.
- A recipient uses an e-mail application that doesn't support S/MIME, and you have checked Send Clear Text Signed Message in the Security tab of the Options dialog box.

The preceding section described the Send Clear Test Signed Message option.

▶ **See** "Choosing Digital Signatures As the Default," **p. 1458**

Receiving a Digitally Signed Message on a Computer that Supports S/MIME The Inbox Information viewer initially displays the header for a secure message with a red ribbon superimposed on the message symbol. When you select the message header, the Preview Pane doesn't show the message if it has been encrypted (it contains the words "Encrypted or encoded items cannot be shown in the Preview Pane. Open the message to read it"). Messages that are signed yet not encrypted are shown in the Preview Pane with a red ribbon in the pane's header.

NOTE The Inbox Information viewer always indicates that received secure messages have an attachment. As explained previously, a secure message contains the original message and an encrypted version of that message. The attachment is actually the encrypted version of the message.

You can double-click the message to display it in the Message form, as shown in Figure 54.18.

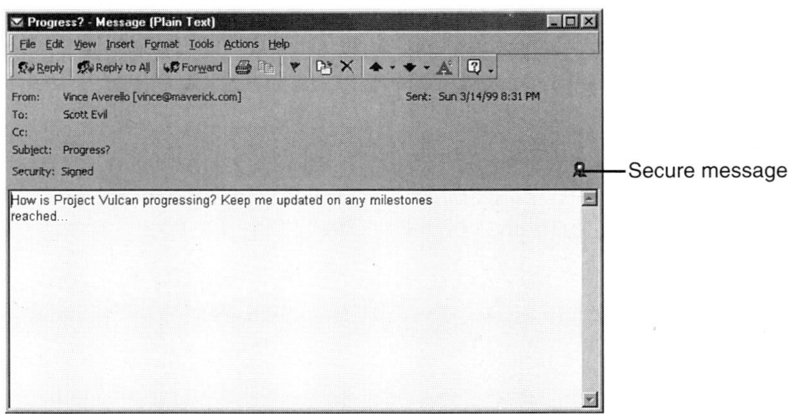

FIGURE 54.18
The ribbon (red on your screen) at the right side of the message header indicates the message is secure.

If you want to verify the identity of the sender, follow these steps:

To verify a sender's identity:

1. With the received message displayed in a Message form, choose File, Properties to display the Security Properties dialog box. Select the Security tab shown in Figure 54.19.

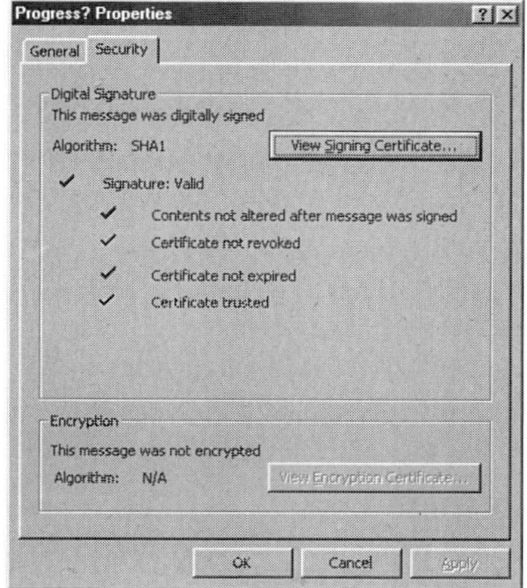

FIGURE 54.19
This dialog box confirms, or does not confirm, the authenticity of the message.

NOTE All five items in this dialog box should be checked if the message is fully authenticated.

2. To obtain more information about the sender, choose View Signing Certificate to display the View Certificate dialog box, in which you can examine information about the sender's Digital ID.

Receiving a Digitally Signed Message on a Computer That Does Not Support S/MIME

Two possibilities exist, depending on how the sender set up Outlook to send digitally signed messages.

- If the sender chose to send the message with Send Clear Text Signed Messages not enabled, recipients who use an e-mail program that does not support S/MIME are not able to read digitally signed messages.
- If the sender chose to send the message with Send Clear Text Signed Messages enabled, recipients who use an e-mail program that does not support S/MIME are able to read digitally signed messages, but are not able to verify the authenticity of those messages.

The Send Clear Text Signed Messages capability is described previously in this chapter.

▶ **See** "Choosing Digital Signatures As the Default," **p. 1458**

Sending and Receiving Encrypted Messages

Sending an encrypted message is much like sending a secure message. However, you must have a person's public key in your Contacts folder to send an encrypted message to that person. This is because the encryption is based on information in the recipient's Digital ID.

Getting Public Keys

You must have a person's public key to send a secure message. For example, if you want to send an encrypted message to John Aldrich, you must have John Aldrich's public key and add that key to the John Aldrich item in your Contacts folder. The following paragraphs explain how you obtain the public key and add that key to a Contact item.

Getting a Public Key from Another Person The easiest way to get another person's public key is to ask that person to send you a message that includes that public key. When you receive the message, proceed as follows.

To add a public key to an existing Contact item or create a new Contact item that contains a public key, perform these steps:

1. Double-click the message that contains the sender's public key to display that message in a Message form.
2. Right-click the sender's name in the Message form to display a context menu.
3. Choose Add to Contacts to display a Contact form that shows the sender's name and e-mail address. Select the Certificates tab shown in Figure 54.20.

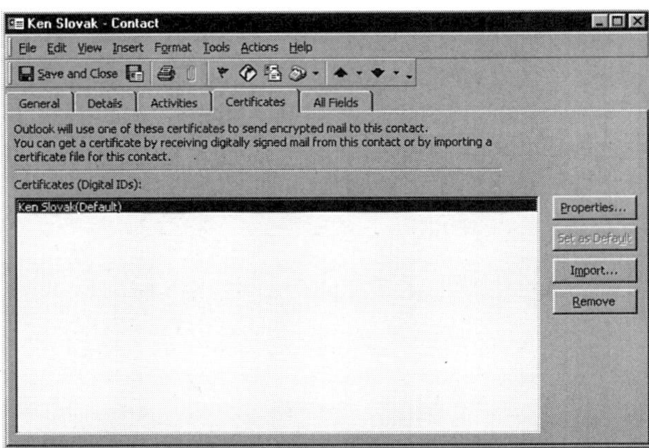

FIGURE 54.20
The Certificates tab contains the name of the sender's Digital ID.

4. Choose Save and Close to save the Contact item that contains the sender's public key.

After following these steps, you have the sender's public key, which you can use to send encrypted messages to that person.

Downloading a Public Key You can obtain public keys from the VeriSign Web page (`https://digitalid.verisign.com/services/client/index.htm`) shown in Figure 54.21.

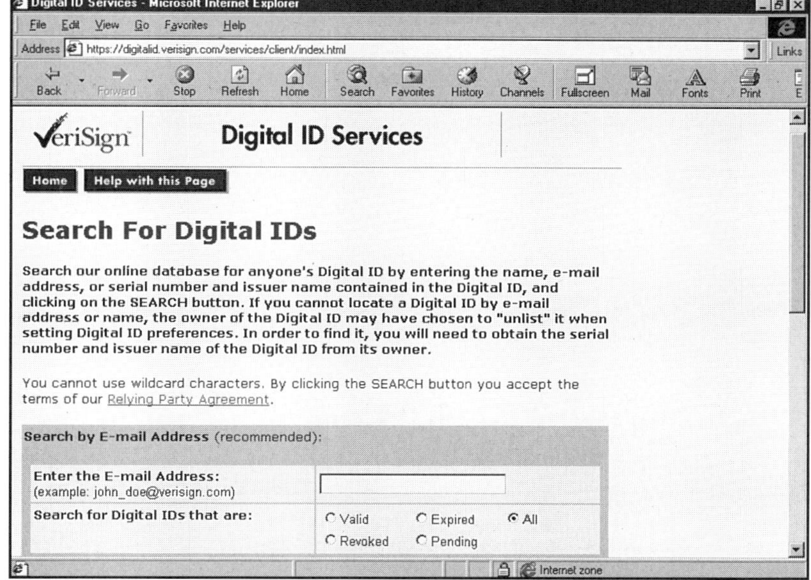

FIGURE 54.21
Use this page to specify the e-mail address of the person whose public key you need.

To download someone's public key:

1. Enter the person's e-mail address in the first box.
2. Choose Valid—only valid public keys are of any use to you.
3. Choose Search (not shown in the figure). After several seconds, the name of the person you're searching for is displayed.
4. Click the person's name to display a page that contains detailed information. Scroll to the bottom of that page and choose Download. The page shown in Figure 54.22 is displayed.
5. Open the Click Here to Choose drop-down list and select Someone Else's Digital ID for Microsoft IE (4.0 or Later)/Outlook Express/Outlook.
6. Choose Download This Certificate. The File Download dialog box proposes to Save This File to Disk, which is what you want to do. Choose OK to open the Save As dialog box.
7. Navigate to the folder in which you want to save the public key, change the File Name to the contact's name, and choose OK. A moment later, a Download Complete message appears. Choose OK.

You have to repeat these steps to obtain the public key for every person to whom you want to send encrypted messages.

The next step is to add the public key to a Contact item.

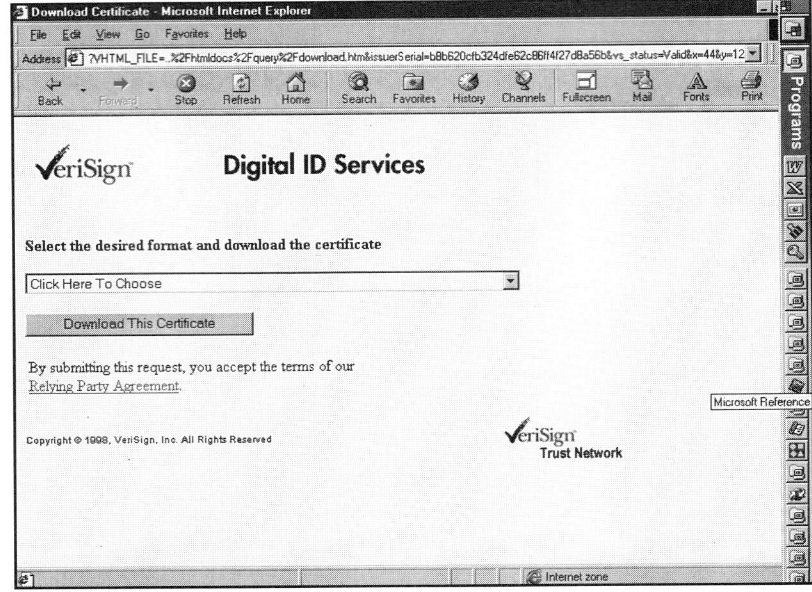

FIGURE 54.22
Be sure to select the format you need before downloading the public key.

To add a public key to a Contact item:

1. Open Outlook and choose Contacts in the Outlook Bar.
2. Locate the Contact item to which you want to add a public key.
3. Double-click the Contact item to open the item in a Contact form. Select the Certificates tab shown in Figure 54.23.

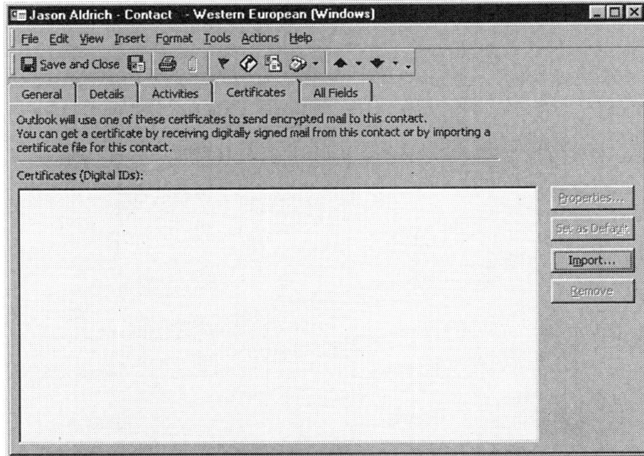

FIGURE 54.23
The Certificates (Digital IDs) box is initially empty.

4. Choose Import to display the Locate Security Profile dialog box.
5. Navigate to the folder in which you saved the public key you previously downloaded.

6. Select the public key for the contact and choose Open. The public key is now listed in the Certificates (Digital IDs) box, and the Properties button becomes available.
7. You can choose Properties to display information about the public key. This step is not required.
8. Choose Save and Close to save the Contact item.

Importing Public Keys from Outlook Express If, prior to using Outlook, you've been using Outlook Express to send secure messages, you have one or more public keys in your Outlook Express address book. When you import that address book into Outlook, public keys are not imported with the rest of the contact information. You have to import each public key separately.

To export a public key from Outlook Express:

1. In Outlook Express, choose Tools, Address Book.
2. Double-click the contact whose public key you want to export to display that contact's properties. Select the Digital IDs tab.

NOTE You can identify the contacts with Digital IDs by the small red ribbon shown as part of the icon in the address book.

3. Select the address whose public key you want to export, then select the public key, and choose Export.
4. Enter the full pathname for the file in which you want to save the exported public key; then choose Save. Outlook Express saves the file.

NOTE Outlook Express automatically provides the filename extension .cer.

After you've exported a public key from Outlook Express, use the procedure described previously in this chapter to add that public key to the appropriate Outlook Contact item.

Changing the Trust Status of a Public Key When you import someone's public key into that person's Contact item, that public key has a trust status associated with it. Ideally, you should be able to absolutely trust Digital IDs, but that isn't necessarily the case.

To trust a Digital ID, you must have complete confidence that

- The Digital ID was properly issued. This means that the issuing authority verified the identity of the person to whom the Digital ID was issued, never issues the same Digital ID to more than one person, and keeps Digital IDs completely confidential.
- The person to whom the Digital ID was issued makes sure no one else can obtain a copy of that Digital ID.

When a Digital ID is issued by a trusted certifying authority such as VeriSign, you can be sure that the Digital ID was properly issued. Only if the person to whom the Digital ID was issued installed it on a secure computer and, if a backup is made, that backup is kept in a secure place, can you be sure that the Digital ID can be trusted.

NOTE Individuals usually get their Digital IDs from a reliable certifying authority such as VeriSign. However, you may come across Digital IDs issued by individuals or organizations you don't necessarily trust.

Three trust status levels are available:

- Inherit Trust from Issuer—This, the default, provides the same trust status as the one associated with the organization or person who issued the person's Digital ID.
- Explicitly Trust This Certificate—This trust status says that you trust the source, irrespective of who issued the person's Digital ID.
- Explicitly Don't Trust This Certificate—This trust status says that you distrust the source, irrespective of who issued the person's Digital ID.

To examine or change the trust status of a public key after you've added it to a Contact item, follow these steps:

1. With the Contacts Information viewer displayed, double-click the contact to display it in a Contact form. Choose the Certificates tab and select the public key, as previously shown in Figure 54.23, although this time with one or more certificates listed.
2. Choose Properties to display the Certificate Properties dialog box. Select the Trust tab shown in Figure 54.24.

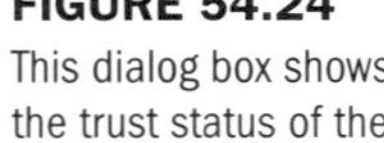

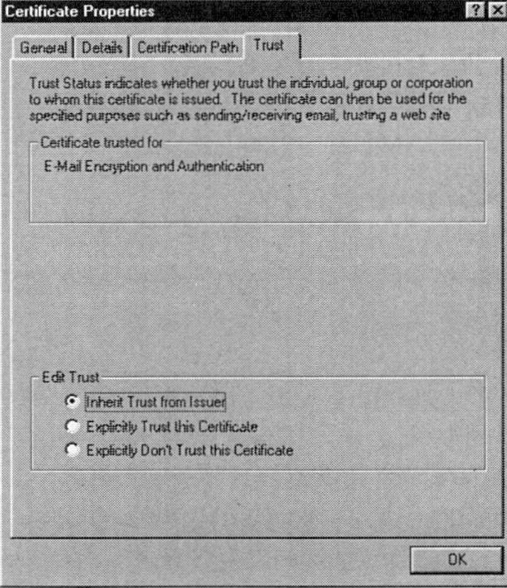

FIGURE 54.24
This dialog box shows the trust status of the Digital ID.

3. To change the trust status, choose the appropriate option button in the Edit Trust section near the bottom of the dialog box.

Sending an Encrypted Message

To send an encrypted message, create the message in the usual way. In the Message form, choose the Encrypt Message Contents and Attachments button on the Standard toolbar, shown previously in Figure 54.9, and then send the message in the normal way.

NOTE You can also enable or disable encryption by checking or unchecking the Encrypt Message Contents and Attachments button in the Message Options dialog box.

After you send an encrypted message, you can see that message in the Sent Items Information viewer. The message symbol is marked with the blue padlock to indicate it was sent as an encrypted message.

If you double-click the message to display it in a message form, Outlook displays a message telling you that it is using your private key to decrypt the message. Choose OK to proceed. The header in the Message form contains the blue padlock to indicate that the message was sent encrypted.

Receiving an Encrypted Message

When you receive an encrypted message, the message header appears in your Inbox Information viewer with a blue padlock symbol superimposed on the message icon. As is the case for secure messages received, the preview pane doesn't display the message. You can double-click the message to display it in the Message form; a blue padlock symbol at the right of the form's header indicates that the message was encrypted.

NOTE Encrypted messages can be decrypted only if you're using e-mail software, such as Outlook, that supports S/MIME.

Using Security Zones

Incoming e-mail messages and Web pages you access can contain scripts that run on your computer. Although most of these scripts are useful, some may either accidentally or deliberately damage files on your hard disk. By taking advantage of Security Zones, you can control what happens when you receive messages or access Web pages that contain scripts. By choosing an appropriate zone for each Web page you access, you can prevent potentially damaging content from being downloaded or receive a warning before potentially damaging content is downloaded.

You can choose from four zones:

- Local Intranet Zone—For sites on a local intranet that you trust.
- Trusted Sites Zone—For sites outside your local intranet that you trust.
- Internet Zone—For most Web sites.
- Restricted Sites Zone—For sites you don't trust.

By default, each zone has a security level assigned to it, as listed in Table 54.1.

Table 54.1 Default Security Levels for Zones

Zone	Security Level
Local Intranet Zone	Medium
Trusted Sites Zone	Low
Internet Zone	Medium
Restricted Sites Zone	High

You can change the security level for any zone.

The effect of each security level is defined in Table 54.2.

Table 54.2 Effects of Security Levels

Level	Effect
High	All potentially damaging content is not downloaded to your computer.
Medium	Outlook warns you before running any potentially damaging content.
Low	Outlook accepts potentially damaging content without giving you any warning.
Custom	It's up to you to specify how Outlook handles potentially damaging content.

You're probably wondering exactly what type of potentially damaging content security levels are concerned with and exactly what zones do about potentially damaging content.

The principal message content and other activities that security levels detect are

- ActiveX controls and plug-ins
- Downloading signed and unsigned ActiveX controls
- Initializing and scripting ActiveX controls not marked as safe
- Using active scripting
- Stored cookie acceptance
- Session cookie acceptance
- User authentication
- Downloading files and fonts
- Scripting Java applets
- Sending unencrypted form data
- Launching helper applications and files
- Installing items on the Windows desktop
- Dragging and dropping or copying and pasting files

Changing the Security Level for a Zone

You can change the security level for each zone to other than the default. For example, you may have complete confidence in your local intranet so that you want to change its security level to Low.

To change the security level of a zone, follow these steps:

1. In the Options dialog box, select the Security tab, shown previously in Figure 54.9.
2. Choose Zone Settings. Outlook displays a warning message about changing security settings. Choose OK to display the dialog box shown in Figure 54.25.

FIGURE 54.25
This is the dialog box you use to work with zones.

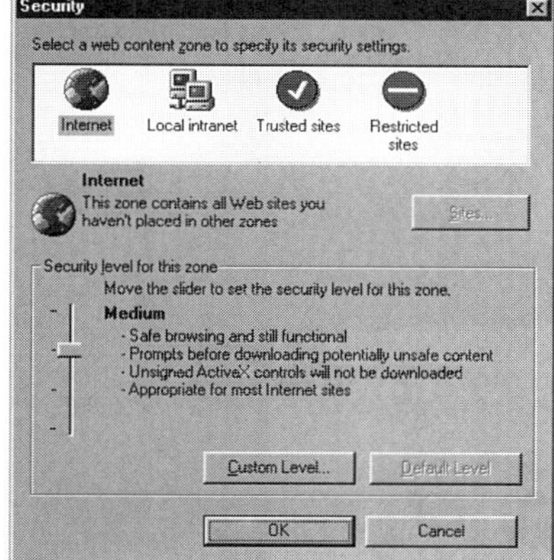

3. Select one of the four zones in the box at the top of the dialog box.
4. Move the slider at the left side of the box to set the security level for that zone.
5. To customize the security level, choose Custom Level to display the dialog box shown in Figure 54.26.

FIGURE 54.26
This is the beginning of a list of available security settings.

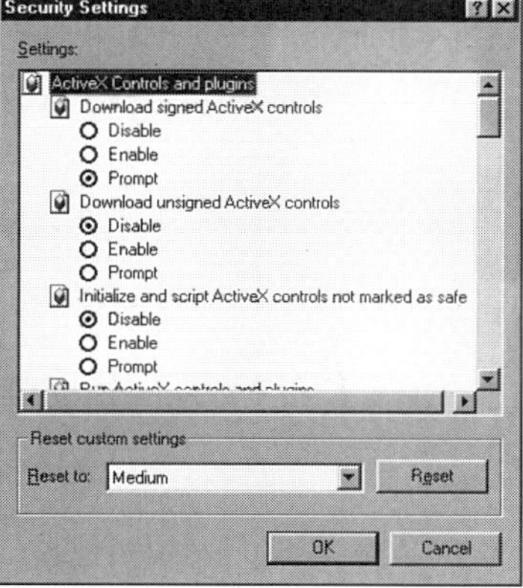

6. Select Disable, Enable, or Prompt for each security setting. Alternatively, you can open the Reset To drop-down list and select a preset combination.

NOTE To restore a zone's security level to the default, choose Default Level.

Assigning Web Sites to Zones

When you first start using Outlook, no Web sites are assigned to any zones. By default, Outlook assumes the use of the Internet Zone, so you are warned before Outlook runs any potentially damaging content.

Assigning Sites to the Local Intranet Zone You define what kind of sites you want to assign to the Local Intranet Zone. You can also assign sites that are outside your local intranet to this zone.

To assign types of intranet sites and sites outside your intranet to this zone, follow these steps:

1. In the Security dialog box, select Local Intranet.
2. Choose Sites to display the dialog box shown in Figure 54.27.

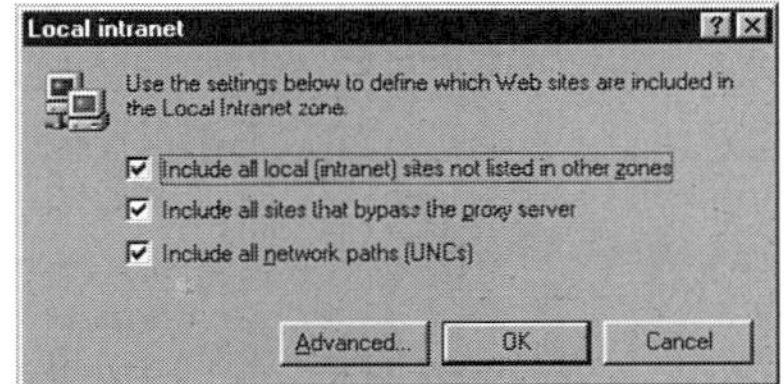

FIGURE 54.27
You can choose any combination of the check boxes in this dialog box.

3. By default, all three check boxes are checked. Uncheck any that are inappropriate.
4. Choose Advanced to display the dialog box shown in Figure 54.28.

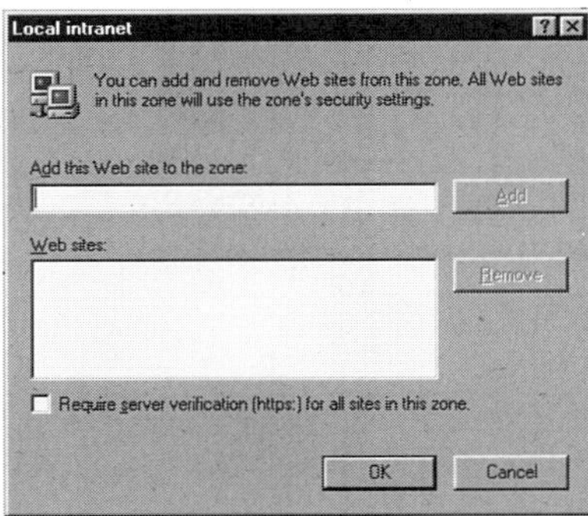

FIGURE 54.28
Use this dialog box to assign specific Web sites to the zone.

5. Enter the complete URL of a site into the Add This Web Site to the Zone box, and then choose Add. The URL you entered is added to the list of sites in the Web Sites box.
6. Repeat Step 5 to add more URLs.
7. For added security, check the Require Server Verification (https) for All Sites in This Zone. By doing that, Outlook will use the Local Intranet Zone for sites in the Web Sites box that are accessed by a secure server.

NOTE To remove a site, select that site in the Web Sites box, and then choose Remove.

Assigning Sites to the Trusted Sites Zone You can assign any Web site to the Trusted Sites Zone.

To assign outside sites to this zone, follow these steps:

1. In the Security dialog box, select Trusted Sites.
2. Choose Sites to display the Trusted Sites Zone dialog box similar to the one previously shown in Figure 54.28.
3. Enter a URL in the Add This Web Site to the Zone box, and then choose Add. The site is added to the list in the Web Sites box.
4. For added security, you can check Require Server Verification (https) for All Sites in This Zone. After you do so, Outlook will use the Trusted Sites Zone only for sites that are accessed by a secure server.

TIP You can't add specific sites to the Internet Zone. Outlook automatically assigns sites that aren't assigned to another zone to the Internet Zone. You can, however, assign sites to the Restricted Sites Zone in the same way that you add sites to the Trusted Sites Zone, as described previously.

CHAPTER 55

Creating and Using Custom Forms

In this chapter

Why Do You Need Custom Forms?

Outlook's standard forms comprise a complete Personal Information Manager (PIM) that includes all the functionality needed for many users. But Outlook is also a development environment that gives you the tools you need to create your own custom forms, based on the standard forms. This flexibility means that you are not tied down to the form design or data fields that Microsoft built into the Outlook standard forms. You can customize a copy of a standard form by adding a few custom fields or you can create an entirely new form.

You can even create a complete application consisting of several interlinked Outlook forms, and maybe a few Office UserForms (new to Outlook 2000). If you need to interact with other applications (such as Access or Word), you can use OLE Automation to link Outlook forms to data stored in other Office applications (or vice versa).

Reviewing Outlook's Built-In Forms

Unlike Word and Excel, which let developers create a new document or worksheet from scratch, the Outlook form designer restricts developers to creating customized forms based on one of the standard Outlook forms. In the Outlook interface, the available forms are displayed in the New Object drop-down list.

The order of forms in the drop-down list changes with the current Outlook folder. The default form for that folder is at the top of the list, and you can click the icon heading the list (just to the left of the word "New") to create a new instance of the default form without dropping down the list.

The standard forms available for selection in the interface are listed in Table 55.1, which lists the forms available for developers to customize, and their IPM message class (used to reference forms in VBS or VBA code). Some discrepancies exist between these lists. Although Appointments, Contacts, Tasks, and Task Requests have the same name throughout, the form called Mail Message in the interface is called just Message in the Forms Library, and its IPM class is Note.

The form called Note in the interface and the Forms Library has an IPM class of StickyNote, and the Post form in the Forms Library is not a selection in the New Object drop-down list in some folders.

The new NetFolder Conflict and NetFolder Invitation forms are not available from the drop-down menu, but they are available from the Choose Form dialog box (although not in the Design Form dialog box).

Finally, Office documents are not in the Forms Library, but they do have IPM message classes.

IPM Message Classes

The MessageClass property of an Outlook item is a string starting with IPM (Interpersonal Message). Each of the Outlook standard items in the interface has an equivalent MessageClass value, which you can use to determine what kind of object it is when iterating through items in a folder from VBS or VBA code.

When you create and publish a custom form, your form name is added on after the standard form name, indicating which standard form your form was based on. For example, if you create a custom form called "Sales Call" based on the Contact form, its MessageClass value will be "IPM.Contact.Sales Call." Piggybacking a custom form on the standard form allows the item to use the standard form in case a custom form is not available.

Table 55.1 Standard Outlook Form Types

Drop-Down List	Forms Library	IPM Class	Editable Pages
Contact	Contact	IPM.Contact	
Task	Task	IPM.Task	[None]
Task Request	Task Request	IPM.TaskRequest	[None]
Mail Message	Message	IPM.Note	Message
Appointment	Appointment	IPM.Appointment	[None]
Meeting Request	Meeting Request	IPM.Schedule.Meeting. Request	[None]
Distribution List	Distribution List	IPM.DistList	[None]
Journal Entry	Journal Entry	IPM.Activity	[None]
Note	Note	IPM.StickyNote	[None]
	Post	IPM.Post	Message
	Standard Default	IPM	Message
	NetFolder Conflict	IPM.Note.FolderPub. Conflict	[None]
	NetFolder Invitation	IPM.Note.FolderPub. NewSubscriber	[None]
Office Document		IPM.Document.Excel. Sheet.8	
		IPM.Document.Word. Document.8	
		IPM.Document.PowerPoint. Show.8	

Part VII Ch 55

The Task, Mail Message, Contact, and Appointment forms are the most useful to Outlook developers because they are the main forms users will need to work with. The Note form isn't customizable—you can't switch to Design view and add custom controls to it—but it is still of some use, because you can open a Note from code and fill in the text.

NOTE If you need help with Outlook forms, open Outlook Help, click the Contents tab, click the Advanced Customization book (it's near the bottom of the list), and then select one of the books under the Advanced Customization book.

In the following sections, you will learn the techniques you need to create a custom form, complete with controls.

Creating a New or Modified Form Based on a Built-In Outlook Form

When you create an Outlook form, you can't start with a blank form, as in Access. Every custom form must be based on one of the standard forms, so the first step in creating a custom form is to select one of the standard form types from the New submenu or select the form from the Standard Forms Library. Normally, one of the first two options is preferable because these choices are more convenient.

To select a form from the New submenu or the Standard Forms Library, follow these steps:

1. Choose File, New, Choose Form on the main Outlook toolbar.
2. Select the desired form from the list of standard forms, and click the Open button as shown in Figure 55.1.

NOTE If you're trying to create a new Post form and the Post form isn't available on the New submenu, select a mail item folder on the Outlook Bar or Folder List and choose the Post in This Folder command on the New submenu.

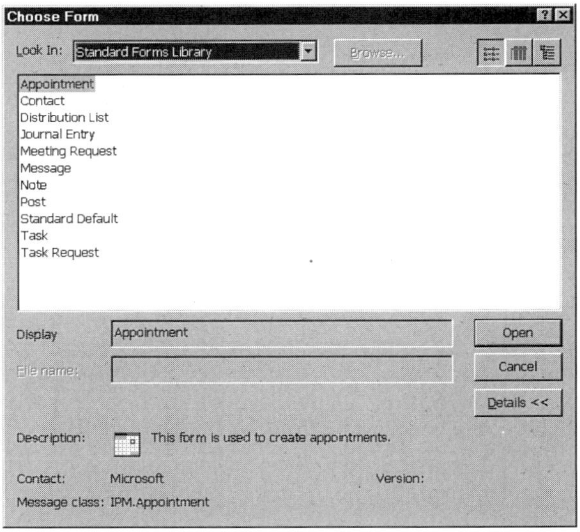

FIGURE 55.1
The Choose Form dialog box opens to the Standard Forms Library.

NOTE The Choose Form dialog box offers several choices of forms libraries. In addition to the Standard Forms Library, you can choose the Personal Forms Library (where your customized forms are stored), an Organizational Forms Library (if you are attached to a network), and a number of other selections. Click the Look In drop-down list to see your choices.

Understanding a Form's Anatomy

Unlike Visual Basic or Access forms, where data storage is completely separate from form design, Outlook form data and design are stored together in each item. In Outlook 97, form data and design were hard to separate—when you switched to Design view in a form, you would see whatever data you had entered onto that item. Then when you saved the form after making design changes, the data was saved along with the design, so if you made a new item from that saved form, it would have the item's data on it. You had to carefully strip out all the data before saving a form to avoid this problem.

Fortunately, this clumsy workaround is no longer necessary. You can now run a form from Design view by choosing Form, Run This Form to open a fresh instance of the form, which you can test by entering data as needed. When you close the form instance, none of the data is saved to the form design.

CAUTION

If you want to save a new custom form from a filled-in item, you still need to delete the data before publishing the form; otherwise, every new item you create from the form will have that data.

To streamline your form design work, you can add the Run This Form command to the Outlook toolbar, as described in the following steps:

1. Right-click the gray background area on the toolbar.
2. Select the Customize command from the shortcut menu, as shown in Figure 55.2.

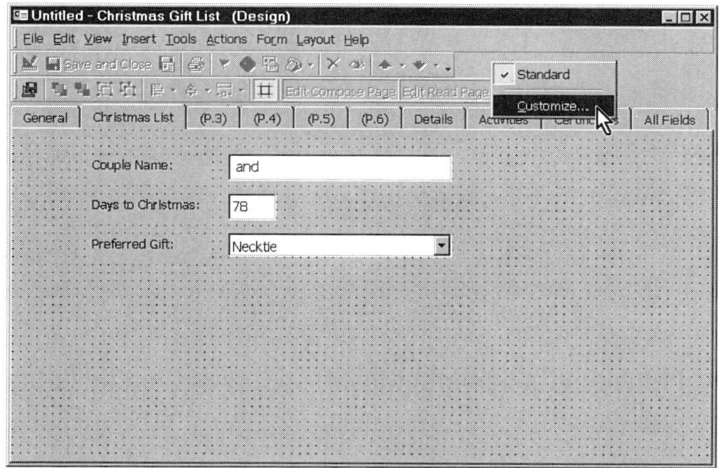

FIGURE 55.2
Customizing toolbars in Outlook forms is done in much the same way as customizing any Office toolbar.

3. In the Customize dialog box, select the Form category and then drag the Run This Form command to the toolbar.
4. Click the Modify Selection button, and select the Default Style selection.
5. Next, right-click the new blank toolbar button, select Change Button Image from the shortcut menu, and select an image for the button.
6. Close the Customize dialog box by clicking the Close button.

From the design point of view, an Outlook form is a container for controls. Most forms have a collection of pages—one or more of which are normally displayed in form view—while the others can be made visible to add more controls to the form. You cannot add a completely new page to a form; you can make only one of the existing extra pages visible.

NOTE The Note form is an exception. It is a single-page form, which does not allow any changes to its interface.

Table 55.1 (earlier in this chapter) lists the Outlook forms.

Controls are interface elements that can display data from the item's properties (called fields in the interface), or just add decorative or informative elements to the form. A control that displays data from a field is called a ***bound control***, and controls that do not display field data are ***unbound fields***. Some controls can be bound or unbound, although others cannot be bound to data, so they are always unbound controls.

Figure 55.3 shows the Toolbox floating toolbar, which is used to place controls on an Outlook form. The process of placing controls on a form is described in more detail in the Adding Controls to a Form section later in this chapter.

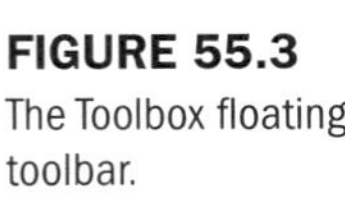

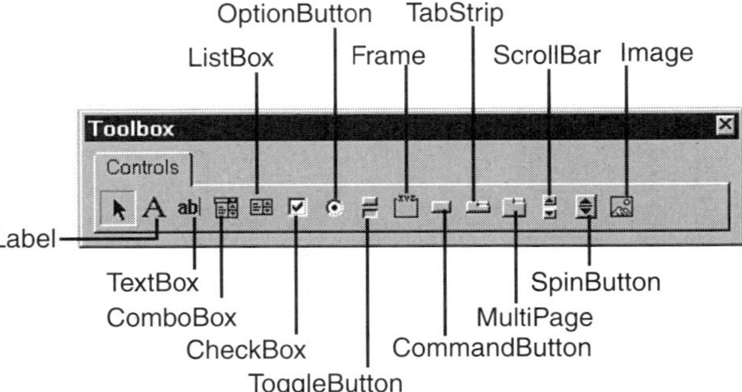

FIGURE 55.3
The Toolbox floating toolbar.

The most commonly used Built-In Outlook controls are described in the following sections.

Label Control

The *Label control* is used to display text on a form. Label controls cannot be bound to a data field. Labels are typically used either to describe an adjacent bound field (usually a text box), or to provide general information about a form, such as a caption for a group of controls.

TextBox Control

The *TextBox control* is probably the most frequently used of all the controls. A TextBox control can be (and usually is) bound to a data field, and is used to enter or modify data in the item. TextBoxes may be unbound, however; in that case, they are generally used to hold the results of a formula or calculation.

ComboBox Control

The *ComboBox control* enables the user to select a value from a drop-down list, or enter text into a text box field at the top of the list. This control may be bound to a field, in which case the selected entry is stored in the field. The entries available in a ComboBox control's drop-down list may be hard-coded into its properties sheet, or written to the control from VBS code.

ListBox Control

The *ListBox control*, like the ComboBox, displays a list of items for user choice. However, the ListBox's list is always displayed, and the user cannot enter a value that is not in the list. Because the ListBox control does not collapse into a single row when not in use, it takes up more room on a form than a ComboBox, and thus is not practical except for a small list.

ListBox controls can be bound or unbound, such as ComboBox controls. When a ListBox is bound to a field, the entries to display in its drop-down list are entered in the same way as for the ComboBox control.

CheckBox Control

A *CheckBox control* is used to display a Yes/No value. Although a CheckBox control need not be bound, it usually is, because an unbound CheckBox is not of much use. When checked, the CheckBox represents a Yes value; when unchecked, it represents a No value.

OptionButton Control

The *OptionButton control* is similar in function to the CheckBox control; instead of a check mark, the Yes value is displayed by a black center, and the No value by a white center.

ToggleButton Control

The *ToggleButton control* also functions as an interface for a Yes/No field; when the button appears to be pressed, it represents a Yes value, and when it appears to be raised, it represents a No value. ToggleButtons may be bound or unbound, but like CheckBoxes and OptionButtons, they are not of much use unless they are bound. The ToggleButton control is rarely used because it takes up more room than the CheckBox or OptionButton and its meaning is not as intuitive.

Frame Control

The *Frame control* cannot be bound to a field (unlike the Access Frame control); it is used to contain a group of other controls, usually CheckBoxes or OptionButtons, to indicate that they are alternate choices for an option. A group of CheckBoxes or OptionButtons within a Frame is often referred to as an Option Group. Unlike option groups in Access, you can save a text value to a control in an option group. Additionally, a Frame Control can be set to a very short height, in which case it is a Line control (see the "Creating a Line Control" sidebar later in this chapter).

CommandButton Control

The *Command Button control* cannot be bound to a field, and it needs a VBScript to be functional. When a Command Button is clicked, the attached VBScript runs to perform a specified action.

NOTE To learn more about using scripts with Command Button controls, see Chapter 43, "Enhancing Outlook Forms with Visual Basic Script Code," in *Special Edition Using Microsoft Outlook 2000*, published by Que.

Image Control

The *Image control* is used to display an image on a form. If it is bound, a separate image can be stored in the control for each record; an unbound Image control displays the same image on each record.

The remaining controls in the Toolbox (the TabStrip, MultiPage, ScrollBar, and SpinButton controls) are less commonly used because they require programming to make them useful. The MultiPage control is discussed in a later section in this chapter.

In addition to the standard Outlook controls, you can also add *ActiveX controls* to an Outlook form. However, there is no guarantee that an ActiveX control will have full functionality on an Outlook form. Additionally, if you are going to distribute your custom form to other users, they may not be able to use the form unless they have the same version of that ActiveX control installed. For this reason, it is best to avoid ActiveX controls except in an environment where the computer setup is standardized for all users, so you can be sure that all users have the necessary support files.

Creating a Custom Form Based on a Built-In Outlook Form

The first step in creating a custom form is to decide which of the Built-In Outlook forms you will use as the template for the form. (The available forms are listed in Table 55.1.) If the form you are designing doesn't really look like any of the standard forms, check the available built-in fields for each form to see which form type has the most useful collection of fields for your purposes.

NOTE Even if you create a form based on the Standard Default form, it is still based on one of the standard forms—the Mail Message form, message class IPM.Note.

You don't need to open a form of that type to check the available fields for a particular type of form; you can check the fields available for any type of form by following these steps:

1. Create a new Contact item, and switch to Design view.
2. Right-click a control, and select Properties from the shortcut menu.
3. Select the Properties sheet's Value tab, and then click the Choose Field button to open the list of available field groupings.
4. Select the group you want to examine from the list. Figure 55.4 shows the All Task Fields list.

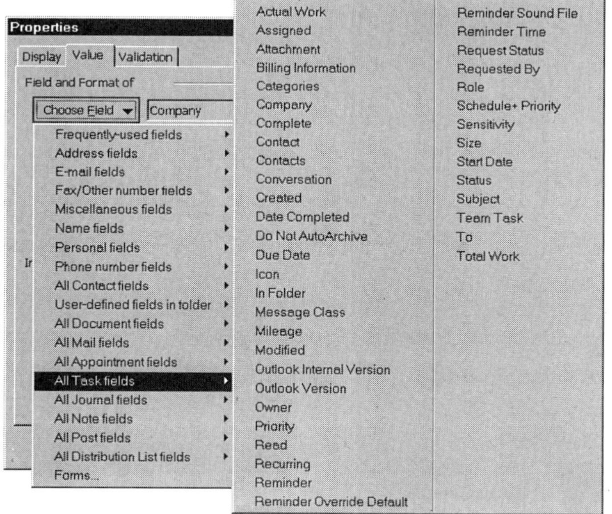

FIGURE 55.4
The All Task Fields list.

Part VII
Ch 55

TIP You can see an alphabetical list of all Outlook fields and their matching properties by opening the Help topic "Outlook Fields and Equivalent Properties."

CAUTION

It's true that you can open a list of fields belonging to another form type from a Contact form. However, if you select a field that's available only on another type of form, you will get the error message shown in Figure 55.5 when you try to bind a control to that field. (The same message appears if you try to drag an inappropriate field to a form from the Field Chooser palette.)

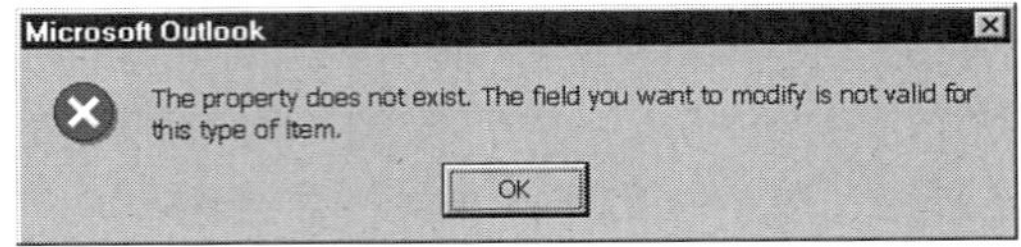

FIGURE 55.5
Error message resulting from trying to insert the Start Date Task field on a Contact form.

After deciding which set of fields best fits your needs, you can start customizing your form by selecting a new form from the New Object drop-down list.

Because the Contact form is the heart of an Outlook application—especially with the new Contact Linking features in Outlook 2000—the next section describes the creation of a custom Contact form in detail.

Customizing a Form

Start by opening a new form and then switch to Design view. The General page on the Contact form is editable, so delete the controls and graphics that you won't need. To delete a control, just click it and press the Delete button.

Next, add controls to the page as needed.

If you don't need any of the built-in controls on a form page that is normally displayed, you can hide that page by choosing Form, Display This Page (the check mark disappears). To make one of the extra pages (P.2 to P.6) visible, choose Form, Display This Page to check it, so the page will be visible.

Next, switch back to the General page and insert the built-in Spouse and Children fields, and a Family label. The fields are in the Name Fields group, so they can be dragged to the page from the Field Chooser after selecting that group (see Figure 55.6). (Note that the pointer changes into a little gray box with a plus sign attached to it while the field is being dragged.)

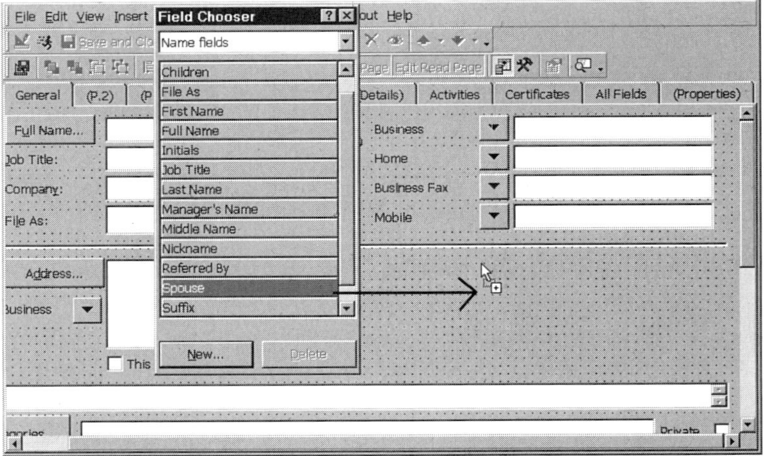

FIGURE 55.6
Dragging the Spouse field to a Contact form.

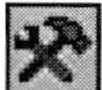

When you drag a text field to a form from the Field Chooser, it appears as a TextBox control with an attached Label control. After dragging the Children field to the form in a similar manner, the next step is to move the new fields down a bit, and then insert a Label control for the group title. Because Label controls aren't bound to fields, they can't be dragged from the Field Chooser. To insert a Label control, first click the Toolbox button on the toolbar to open the Control Toolbox, as shown in Figure 55.7.

FIGURE 55.7
Opening the Control Toolbox.

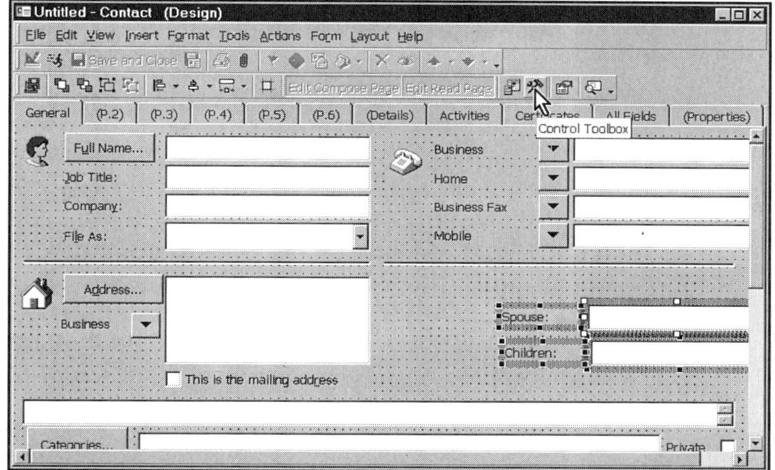

After clicking the Label tool in the Toolbox (it's the one with the large "A"), either click the form to insert a default-sized Label control, or click and drag a rectangle on the form to create a Label control of the desired size. You can change its caption directly in the control by double-clicking the original Label*n* text and replacing it with the text you want. Right-click the new Label control and open its Advanced Properties sheet to select a different font size and color.

You can modify the color properties from either the Properties sheet or the Advanced Properties sheet. Keep in mind, however, that the Advanced Properties sheet lets you see the foreground and background colors, although the Properties sheet just gives you a cryptic list of various Windows attributes to select from (such as Info Text and Inactive Caption).

NOTE Outlook controls have two properties sheets: The Properties sheet and the Advanced Properties sheet. Although many control properties appear in both sheets, some do not—for example, you can bind a control to a field only in the Properties sheet, although the WordWrap property is found only in the Advanced Properties sheet. To make things more confusing, some properties listed in the Advanced Properties sheet (such as ControlSource) are nonfunctional in Outlook.

To give the Label control a caption, start by right-clicking the new Label control and opening its Advanced Properties sheet from the shortcut menu.

Select the Caption property row. To enter the caption, type it into the box at the top of the Advanced Properties sheet and click the Apply button, as shown in Figure 55.8.

FIGURE 55.8

Entering a caption for the new Label control.

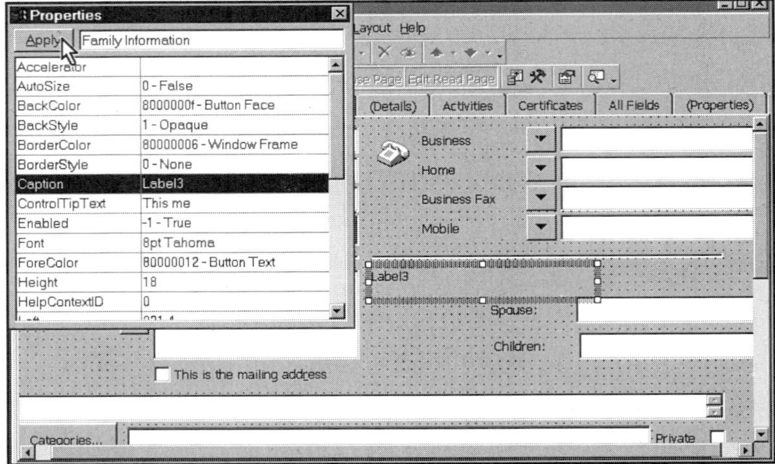

You can move quickly to another property in the Advanced Properties sheet by typing its first letter.

To align the control, select the TextAlign property and either double-click the property in the sheet, or select the desired alignment from the drop-down list at the top of the Advanced Properties sheet, as shown in Figure 55.9.

FIGURE 55.9

Changing the control's alignment.

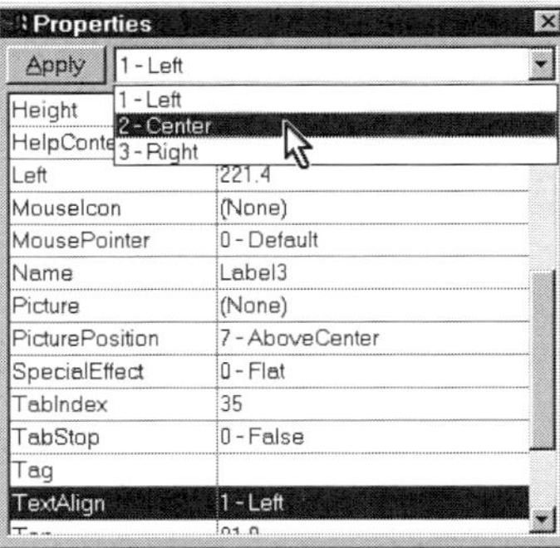

Next, select the Font property. To select a different font, click the Build button next to the current font name at the top of the Advanced Properties sheet (it's the one with the three dots), and select the desired font, size, and emphasis from the Font dialog box.

The BackColor and ForeColor properties are set from either a drop-down list with the same cryptic Windows components that are in the Properties sheet (see Figure 55.10), or a considerably more intuitive Color dialog box shown in Figure 55.11.

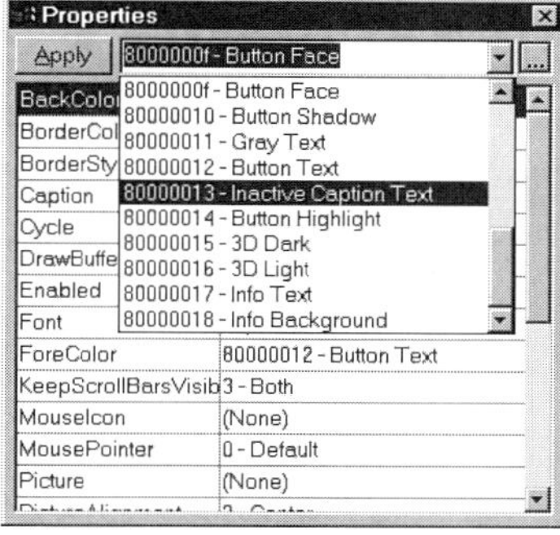

FIGURE 55.10
Selecting a BackColor value from the drop-down list.

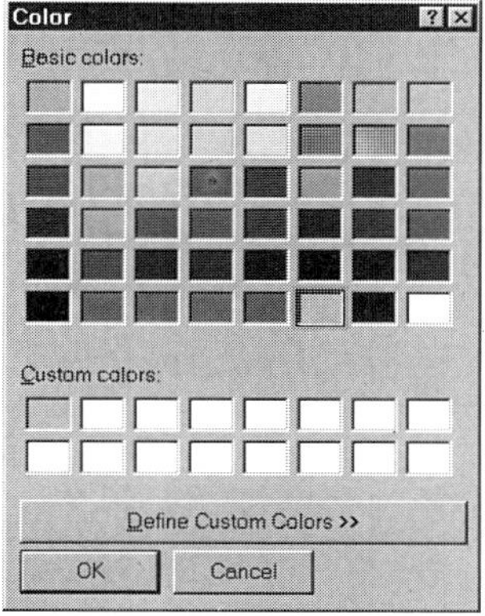

FIGURE 55.11
Selecting a color from the Color dialog box.

Adding Graphics to a Form

To add an image control, click the Image tool in the Toolbox (it's the last button on the right). Open the control's Advanced Properties sheet and select an image for its Picture property by clicking the Build button at the top of the sheet to open the Load Picture dialog box to select an appropriate image.

Office 2000 comes with an extensive collection of clip art, which you can use for images on Outlook forms. The default location for these files is C:\Program Files\Common Files\Microsoft Shared\Clipart. Additionally, if you have the Premium Edition of Office 2000, you will have many more images from which to choose.

You might find it more convenient to do any necessary editing or resizing of images in another program, such as Paintbrush, because Outlook offers only limited tools for manipulating images in Image controls. After resizing or editing an image, you can save it as a separate file, and then just select the edited file for your Image control.

Understanding the Control Properties Sheet

When you work with controls on a form, you need to set many of the control properties through the Properties sheet, accessible via a control's shortcut menu. Different types of controls have somewhat different selections on their Properties sheets. Most control Properties sheets have three pages—Display, Value, and Validation. However, depending on the control type, some of the properties on one or more pages of the Properties sheet may be disabled.

For example, all the properties on a Label control's Value and Validation pages are disabled, because a Label control is not bound to a field. Most of the properties on a CommandButton control's Value and Validation pages are disabled, because CommandButtons are not bound either, except for a few special cases. The Properties sheet for a Frame or Line control is more limited: It has just a single page, Display, with all properties enabled. However, you can adjust more of a Frame or Line control's properties by opening its Advanced Properties sheet.

Creating a Line Control

There is no Line control in the Control Toolbox, but you can see controls named Line*n* on the General page of the default Contact form. A Line control is just a very short Frame control, so to insert a Line control on a form, start by inserting a Frame control from the Control Toolbox.

Next, open the Advanced Properties sheet for the new Frame control and set its Height property to just a few points—2–4 points makes a chiseled line, and 1 point makes a thin solid line. You can adjust the appearance of the line further by changing the Special Effect and BorderStyle properties in the Advanced Properties sheet.

The following discussion deals with the Properties sheet for a TextBox, ComboBox, or ListBox control, which has the fullest selection of adjustable properties.

To open a control's Properties sheet, right-click the control and select Properties from its shortcut menu. Initially, the Properties sheet opens to the Display page, shown in Figure 55.12.

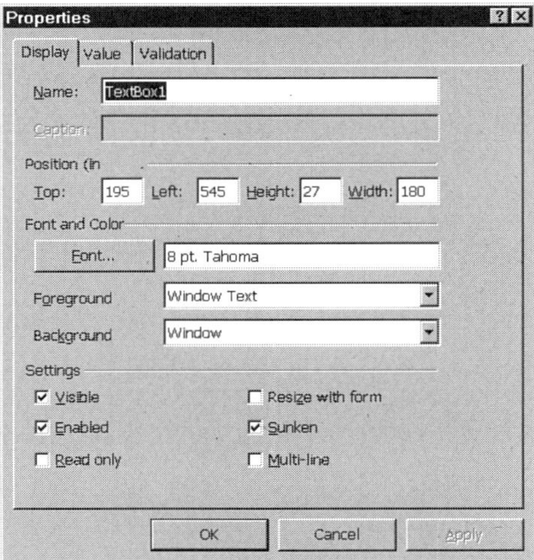

FIGURE 55.12
The Display page of a TextBox control's Properties sheet.

The first property shown on the Display page is the control's name—the default name is TextBox*n* for a TextBox control, and similar for other control types. You can leave the name as is, but if you are going to write any code that references the control, it is a good idea to give it a more descriptive name, possibly using an identifying prefix from Table 55.2, based on the Leszynski Naming Convention (LNC) for various dialects of Visual Basic.

Table 55.2 Suggested Control Name Prefixes

Control Type	Suggested Prefix
Label	lbl
TextBox	txt
ComboBox	cbo
ListBox	lst
CheckBox	chk
OptionButton	opt
ToggleButton	tgl
Frame	fra
Line	lin
CommandButton	cmd
TabStrip	tab
Image	img

The Caption property is grayed out for TextBox controls, but it can be filled in as desired for controls that have a visible caption, such as Label, CheckBox, and OptionButton controls.

The Position group has four controls used to set the control's position on the form. These properties set the control's Top, Left, Height, and Width in points (a point is 1/72 of an inch).

The Font button opens a standard Font dialog box where you can select a new font, size, and emphasis for the text displayed in the control.

Finally, the Settings group lets you adjust a miscellaneous selection of properties that affect either the control's appearance or functionality:

- Visible—The control is visible if this property is checked, and invisible if it is unchecked.
- Enabled—The control is enabled if this property is checked, and disabled if it is unchecked. Disabled controls appear grayed out and can't be used.
- Read Only—The control is read-only if this property is checked, and read/write if it is unchecked. Read-only controls look normal, but they can't be edited.

- Resize with Form—When checked, this property enables the control to be automatically resized when the form is resized; if unchecked, the control remains the same size when the form is resized. Many of the default controls on Outlook's built-in forms are resizable.
- Sunken—If this property is checked, the control has the Sunken special effect (this is the default setting for TextBox controls on the standard Outlook forms). If the property is unchecked, the control has the Flat special effect. (You can set more special effect properties from the control's Advanced Properties sheet.)
- Multi-Line—If this property is checked, the control takes multiple lines of text, using the Enter key to start a new line. This is especially useful for entering address data. If the property is unchecked, the control accepts only one line of data.

The Value page of a TextBox control's Properties sheet is shown in Figure 55.13. On this page, you can select a field for binding a control, as described in the next section. You can also select another property to use; however, the default Value property is almost always appropriate.

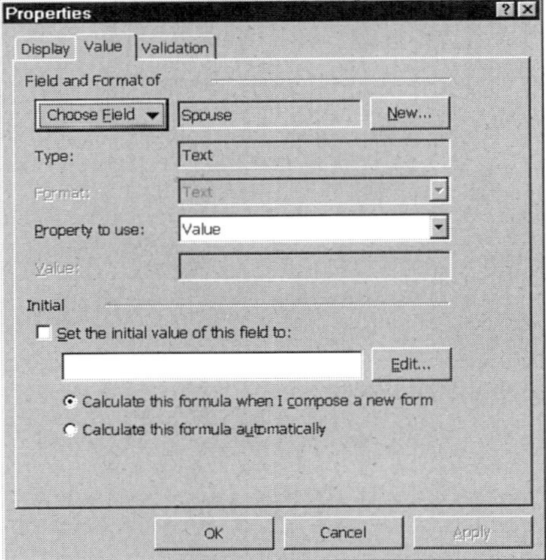

FIGURE 55.13
The Value page of a TextBox control's Properties sheet.

The read-only Type property indicates the data type of the field to which the control is bound. The Format and Value properties are disabled.

The Initial section of this page lets you enter an initial (default) value for the control; you can also use the Edit button to open a screen where you can create a Combination or Formula field. If you have entered a formula, you can use the two option buttons at the bottom of the page to determine whether the formula should be calculated automatically, or when a new form is created.

The Value page of a ComboBox or ListBox control (shown in Figure 55.14) is somewhat different; it has a List Type property where you can select two options for the drop-down list: Dropdown (the default) or Droplist. The combo box looks the same whichever list type you choose: The only difference is that a Droplist list type limits the user's choice to the items in the list, and a Dropdown list lets the user enter an item not in the list. (This choice is roughly equivalent to the Access Limit to List property.)

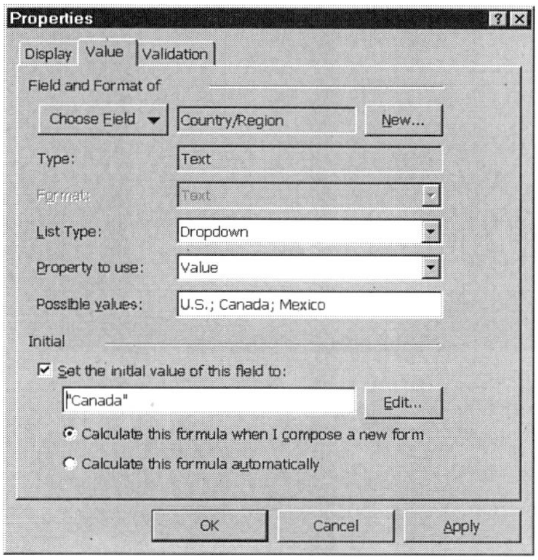

FIGURE 55.14
The Value page of a ComboBox control's properties sheet.

The Validation page is the final page of the Properties sheet; it is used to enter a rule for validating data entered into the control.

For example, you may want to ensure that an out-of-stock product is not shipped. To ensure that a form can't be saved with "Sprockets" entered into the Product field, enter the validation formula

```
<> "Sprockets"
```

and the validation text

```
"Sprockets are currently out of stock"
```

in the properties on the Validation page of a control, as shown in Figure 55.15.

Now, if you try to save and close a form with "Sprockets" entered into the Product field, you will get the error message shown in Figure 55.16, and you won't be able to save and close the form until you delete or change the text in the Product text box.

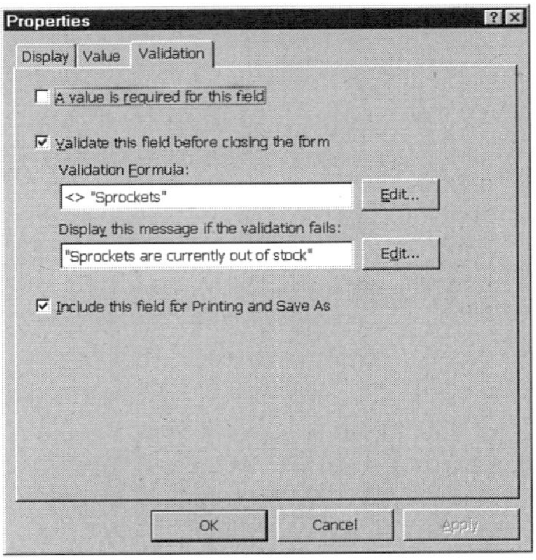

FIGURE 55.15
The Validation page of a TextBox control's Properties sheet.

FIGURE 55.16
An error message for a control with a validation rule.

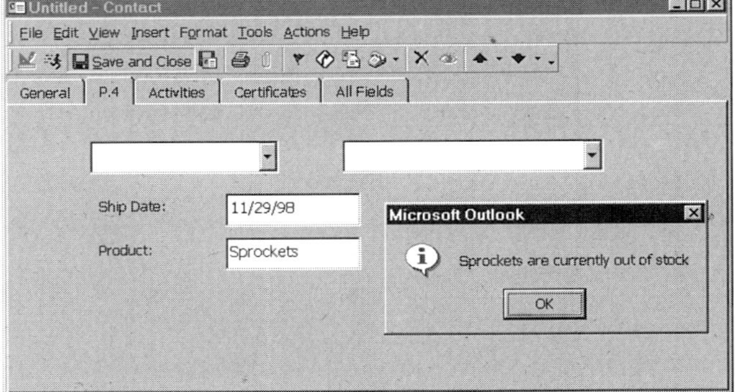

Associating Controls with Fields

In addition to dragging fields to a form from the Field Chooser, as described earlier in this chapter, you can also use the Control Toolbox to place a control of a specific type on a form, and then bind the control to a field. This technique is particularly useful when you want to associate a ComboBox or ListBox control with a field. You can bind a control to either a built-in Outlook field or a custom field you have created.

If you need to validate a field before saving the entire form, you can place a validation formula on the PropertyChange or CustomPropertyChange event of the form. For more information, see Chapter 43, "Enhancing Outlook Forms with Visual Basic Script Code" in *Special Edition Using Microsoft Outlook 2000*, published by Que.

To associate a control with a built-in field, click the Choose Field button on the Value page of a control's Properties sheet, and then select one of the field groups from the drop-down list, as shown in Figure 55.17.

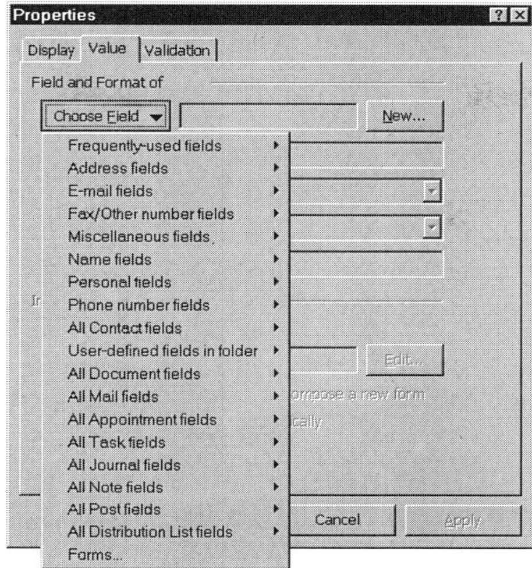

FIGURE 55.17
The list of field groups for binding a control to a field.

Select one of the field groups, and then select a field from the group. Figure 55.18 shows the control's Properties sheet with the Personal Home Page field selected from the Frequently Used Fields group.

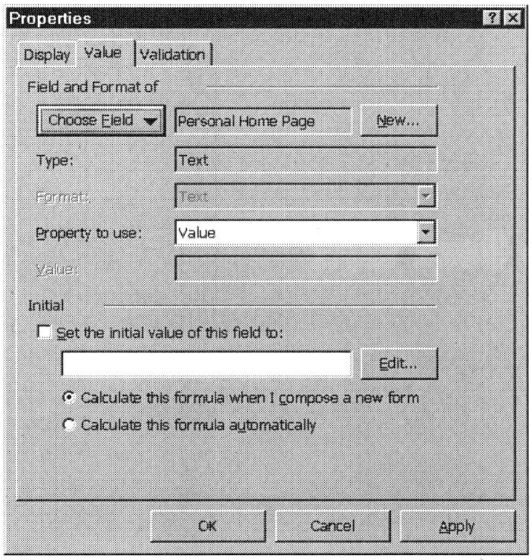

Properties
Display | Value | Validation
Field and Format of
Choose Field | Personal Home Page | New...
Type: Text
Format: Text
Property to use: Value
Value:
Initial
Set the initial value of this field to:
Edit...
Calculate this formula when I compose a new form
Calculate this formula automatically
OK | Cancel | Apply

FIGURE 55.18
A newly inserted TextBox control bound to the Personal Home Page field.

To bind a control to an already existing custom field in the item or folder, select the User-Defined Fields in Folder list, as shown in Figure 55.19.

You can also create a new field for a control on-the-fly by clicking the New button on the Value page of the properties sheet, and filling in the properties on the New Field dialog box.

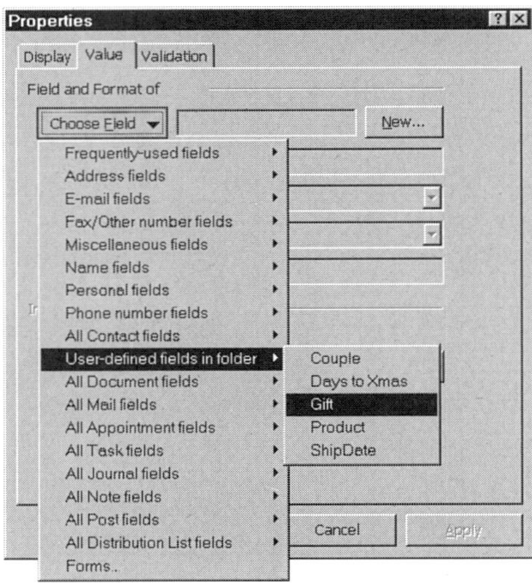

FIGURE 55.19
Selecting a user-defined field for a control value.

Arranging Controls

After you have placed some controls on a form, you will generally need to rearrange them. To move a control, click it to give it the focus (you will see little white squares—*sizing handles*—on each corner and the midpoint of each side), then hold the mouse button down, and drag the control to another location. To resize the control, click one of the sizing handles (the pointer changes into an arrow), and then stretch out the control in the direction of the arrow. You can resize a control horizontally, vertically, or diagonally.

Additionally, the Outlook form designer has a number of useful tools for this purpose.

Bring to Front/Send to Back Tools

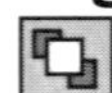

If you want to position a control underneath or on top of other controls—say an Image control as a background under an option group—you can use the Bring to Front or Send to Back tools. Select the control to be brought to the front (or sent to the back) and click the appropriate tool to move the control to the front (or back). The Bring to Front and Send to Back tools are the first two tools on the Design toolbar.

Group/Ungroup Tools

When you have a group of controls you want to treat as a unit, you can use the Group tool to create a semipermanent group. To group controls, either draw an imaginary rectangle enclosing a part of each, or click the first control, and then Shift+click the others. While all the controls are highlighted, click the Group tool to create the group, as shown in Figure 55.20.

To clear the group, select it and click the Ungroup button.

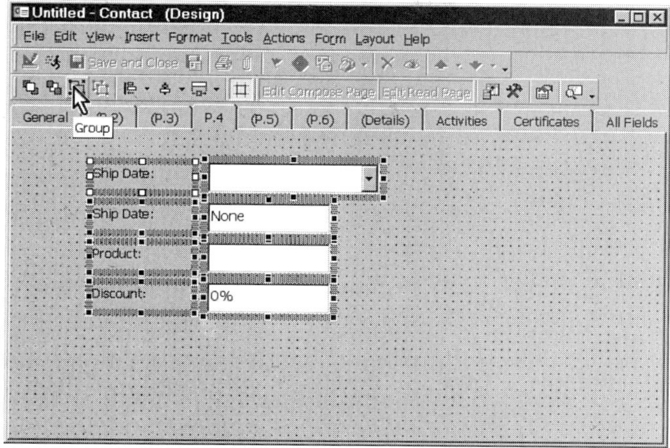

FIGURE 55.20
Grouping a set of controls.

Alignment Tools

To the right of the Ungroup tool on the Design toolbar, there are three drop-down lists offering choices of alignment tools. The Align drop-down list offers a choice of aligning the selected controls to the Left, Center, Right, Top, Middle, Bottom, or To Grid.

The Middle selection on the Align list is especially useful for aligning a TextBox control with its Label control, as shown in Figure 55.21.

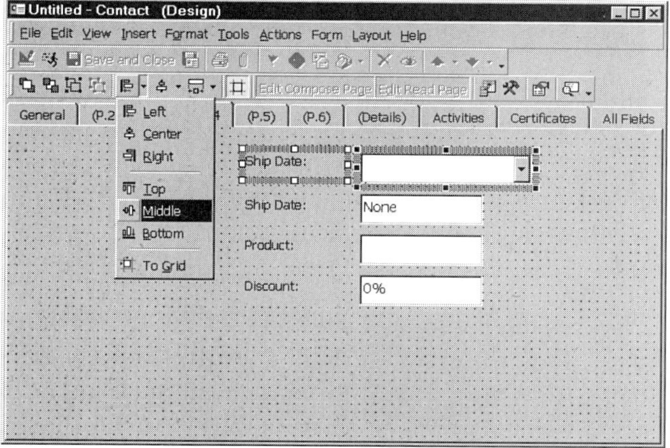

FIGURE 55.21
Aligning a TextBox control with its Label control.

The next drop-down list, the Center list, offers a choice of centering options—Horizontally and Vertically. Finally, the Make Same Size drop-down list lets you make a group of controls the same width, height, or both, as shown in Figure 55.22.

When you align controls using these tools, they are aligned relative to the dominant control.

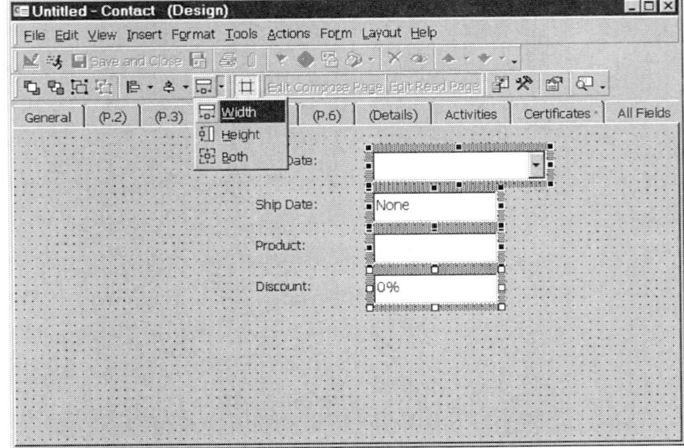

FIGURE 55.22
Making a group of controls the same width.

The Dominant Control for the Sizing and Grouping Commands

Some alignment and sizing operations for groups of controls make use of a *dominant control*—the control to which the other controls are aligned or sized. You can select a group of controls to resize or align by several methods. Each method results in a different control being the dominant control.

When you Shift+click to select controls, the first control selected is the dominant control. When you Ctrl+click to select controls, the last control selected is the dominant control, and when you draw a rectangle around a group of controls with the mouse pointer, the control nearest the pointer when you start drawing is the dominant control.

You can change the dominant control by Ctrl+clicking twice on a control; that control then becomes the dominant control. You can tell which control in a group is the dominant control by the color of its sizing handles; the dominant control's sizing handles are white, and the other controls have black handles (refer to Figure 55.21).

When you select a group of controls and place the pointer over the border of one of the controls in the group, the mouse pointer turns into a double-pointed arrow, as shown in Figure 55.23, indicating that you can move the group.

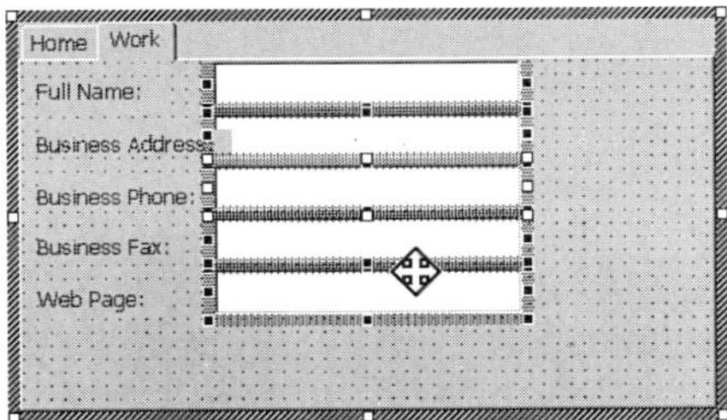

FIGURE 55.23
The Move Group pointer.

Figure 55.24 shows the Contact form after adding new controls, and resizing and aligning the controls.

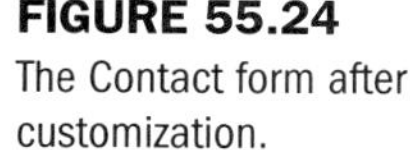

FIGURE 55.24
The Contact form after customization.

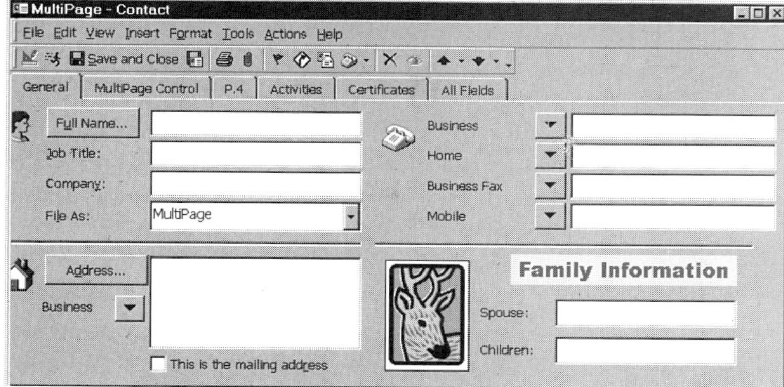

Using the TabStrip or MultiPage Control to Create a Multipage Form

Although each of the standard Outlook forms is itself a multipage tabbed form (although some only display a single page by default), if you need a more sophisticated interface for displaying complex data, you can add a TabStrip or MultiPage control to one of the form pages. These two controls look very similar, but they have somewhat different functionality.

The MultiPage control is intended for managing large amounts of data that can be sorted into several categories (but all belonging to one record). The TabStrip control, on the other hand, is intended to present different sets of data, possibly from different data sources, in a visual group. For other Office applications, such as Access, this is a real distinction; however, Outlook offers considerably less functionality for binding controls to diverse data sources, so there is little practical difference between these controls, except that the MultiPage control is easier to work with.

You can easily place different controls on each page of a MultiPage control, which makes this control an excellent interface for displaying several sets of related information in a compact form. The user clicks the tab to open the appropriate page of data.

To add a MultiPage control to an Outlook form page, click the MultiPage tool in the Control Toolbox and place the control on a form. Initially, a MultiPage control has two pages, called Page1 and Page2. To change the caption of a page, right-click the tab to open its shortcut menu, and select the Rename command, as shown in Figure 55.25.

Enter the Caption, Accelerator Key, and ControlTip Text information (only the Caption is required) in the Rename dialog box.

You can add, delete, or move pages as needed by selecting the Insert, Delete, or Move command from the MultiPage control's shortcut menu (right-click any page tab, or the gray area to the right of the tabs, to open this menu). If you have entered an Accelerator key for a page, that letter will be displayed with an underline. Setting accelerator keys lets the user activate a page by pressing Alt+*N*, where *N* represents the letter entered as the accelerator key for that page.

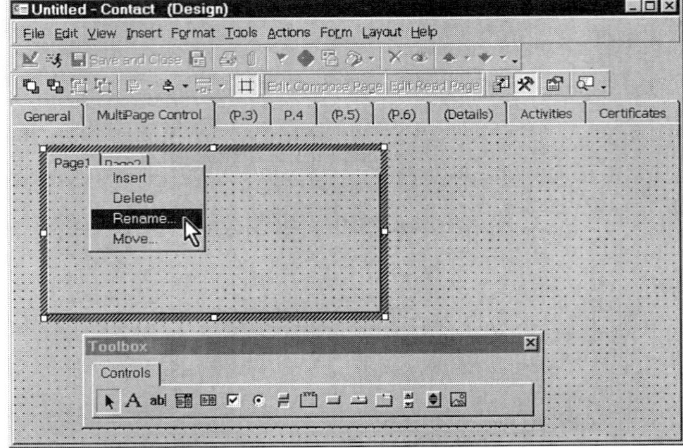

FIGURE 55.25
Renaming a page of a MultiPage control.

Figures 55.26 and 55.27 show the Work and Home tabs of MultiPage control, with the appropriate home or business fields displayed.

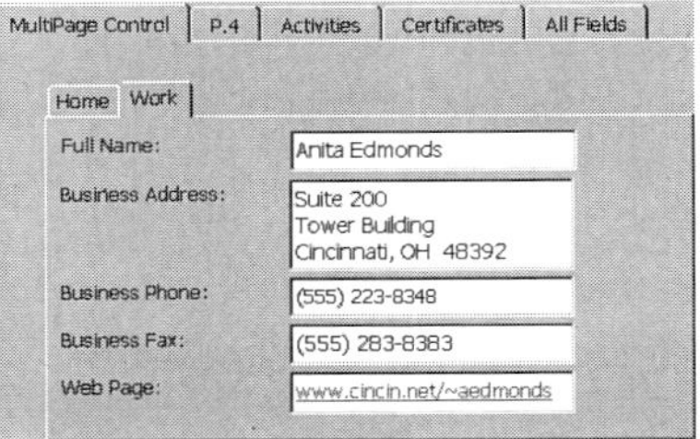

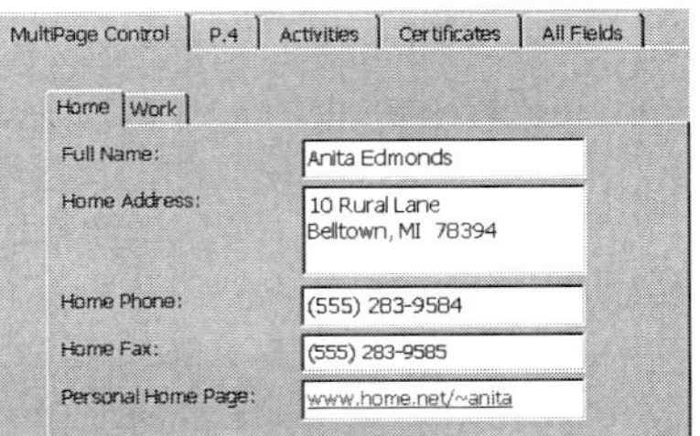

FIGURE 55.26
The Work address is shown first.

FIGURE 55.27
The Home address is shown next.

Creating a Form Based on an Office Document

In addition to creating a form based on one of the standard Outlook forms, you can also choose to create a form in an Outlook folder based on one of four Office document selections (Word document, Excel worksheet, Excel chart, and PowerPoint presentation). To create a form based on an Office document, select Office Document from the New Object menu.

The New Office Document dialog box opens with a choice of Excel Worksheet, Excel Chart, PowerPoint Presentation, or Word Document. Selecting one of these options opens a document of the indicated type, which is generally similar to a normal document created directly from the application, with a few extra features for interfacing with Outlook, and perhaps lacking a few standard features.

A number of differences exist between a regular Excel worksheet or chart, PowerPoint Presentation, or Word document and its Outlook Office Document counterpart. These differences will be discussed in detail for Excel worksheets; the menu differences are similar across the board, but there are some other application-specific differences which will be mentioned in the following sections.

The Excel Worksheet Office Document

When you select an Excel worksheet, a dialog box appears asking whether you want to post the document in the current Outlook folder, or send it to another user via email.

After choosing one of the options (the Post selection is the default), a new Excel worksheet opens, looking much like a regular worksheet. However, if you examine an Office document worksheet in comparison to a regular worksheet (see Figure 55.28), you should see some differences.

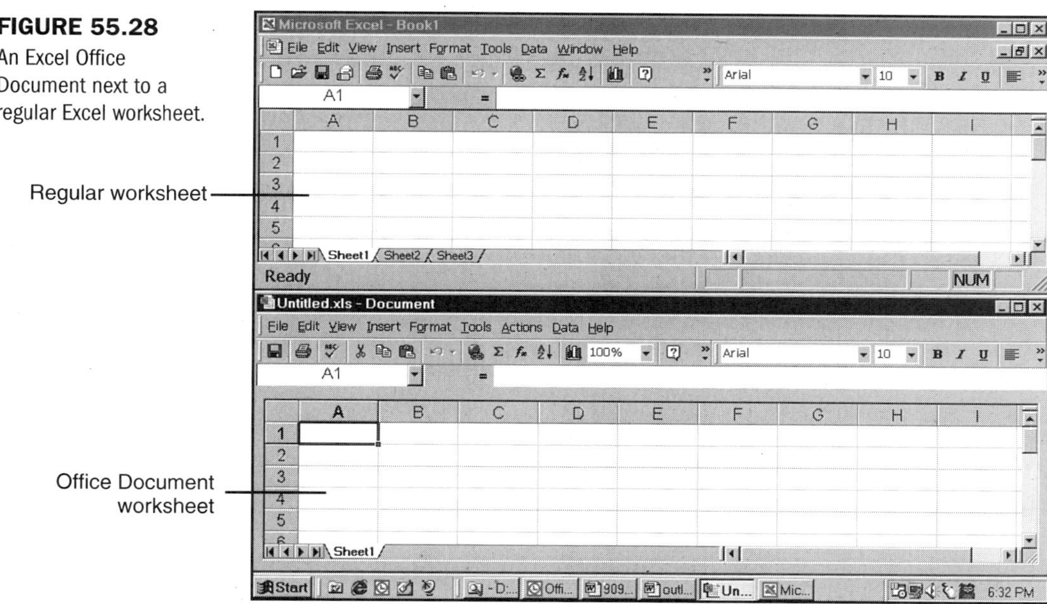

FIGURE 55.28
An Excel Office Document next to a regular Excel worksheet.

Table 55.3 lists the main interface differences between the two types of worksheets:

Table 55.3 Regular Excel Worksheet Versus Excel Office Document Worksheet

Regular Worksheet	Office Document Worksheet
MDI interface	SDI interface
Regular icon in Taskbar	Special icon in Taskbar
Has a Window menu	Has no Window menu
Has no Actions menu	Has an Actions menu
Has New, Open, and E-Mail tools on toolbar	Lacks New, Open, and E-Mail tools on toolbar

NOTE MDI (Multiple Document Interface) lets you open multiple documents in one program window. Word 97 had MDI, and Excel 2000 has MDI.

SDI (Single Document Interface) requires you to open a new instance of a program for each document. Word 2000 and Access 2000 have SDI.

Additionally, significant differences exist in the selections available on several of the menus of an Excel Office Document worksheet, as opposed to the corresponding menus in a regular worksheet.

NOTE The Insert, Format, Data, and Help menus are the same in both worksheets, and the Window menu is available only in the regular worksheet.

After entering the data you want in the Office Document worksheet, select the Post command from the File menu to save it to the Outlook folder, where its name (default: Untitled.xls) appears as the document's Subject.

The Excel Chart Office Document

The differences between Excel Chart Office Documents and regular Excel charts are similar to the differences between Excel worksheet Office Documents and regular Excel worksheets, so they will not be discussed in detail.

The PowerPoint Presentation Office Document

PowerPoint has a Single Document Interface, so PowerPoint Office Document presentations are similar to regular PowerPoint presentations in that respect. There are menu differences similar to the ones in Excel, however.

The Word Office Document

Word 2000 now has an SDI interface, so there is no difference between a regular Word document and an Office Document Word document in that respect. However, Word Office Documents have several extra toolbar buttons: Design This Form, Run This Form, and Post.

Clicking the Design This Form button opens a form vaguely similar to an Outlook form, with a blank Document page, a Properties page, and an Actions page. You can type text into the large white area on the Document page (and format it), and use the Properties and Actions pages as in an Outlook form. Clicking the Run This Form button returns you to the normal Word document view, and clicking the Post button posts the Word Office Document to the Outlook folder.

As with Excel documents, the default document title (Untitled.doc) becomes the Subject of the posted Word Office Document.

The menu differences for Word are generally similar to those in Excel.

Form Management

After you have customized a form, to use it again, you need to publish the form to a forms library. Outlook offers a number of options for publishing and saving custom forms, as described in the following sections.

Publishing a Form to a Forms Library

To conveniently reuse the custom form on your own computer, you need to publish the form to an appropriate forms library (Personal or Global). To publish a custom form to the Personal Forms Library (the usual choice):

1. Open the custom form and switch to Design view.
2. Delete any sample data entered into fields on the item that you don't want on the generic form.
3. Access the Tools menu, open the Forms submenu, and select Publish Form from the pop-out Forms submenu, (or click the Publish Form button on the toolbar).
4. The Publish Form As dialog box opens, where you can select the library for storing the form, as shown in Figure 55.29.
5. On the same dialog box, you can select the library for storing the form, enter the display name and form name for the custom form, and view (but not change) the message class.
6. Finally, click the Publish button to save the custom form to the selected Forms library.

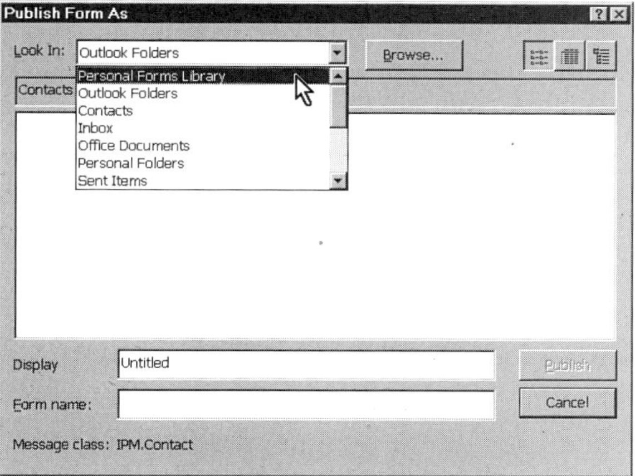

FIGURE 55.29
Selecting the Personal Forms Library for saving a custom form.

Using Custom Forms

After you have published a form, you can select it from the Personal Forms Library to make a new custom item based on the form. To view the list of available forms in the Personal Forms Library:

1. Choose File, New, Choose Form.

Alternatively, you can save a click by selecting Choose Form from the New Object list.

2. The Choose Forms dialog box opens with the Standard Forms Library as the default library selection.
3. Drop down the Look In list and select the Personal Forms Library.
4. Select the desired form from the Personal Forms Library list, and click the Open button.
5. A new form opens, based on the custom form, ready to enter data.

In addition to saving a form to the Personal (or Organizational) Forms Library, which makes it available on your local computer or the network to which your computer is attached, you have several other options for saving a form, as described in the following sections.

Saving a Form in a Folder

When you create a new instance of a form, either from a standard Outlook form or a custom form, after you click the Save and Close button, the form is saved as an item in the current folder, along with any data you have entered into it. For example, your Contacts folder contains the Contact items made from the standard Contact form by clicking the New Contact button, and possibly items made from a custom Contact form you have assigned to that folder, and similarly for the other folders.

NOTE *Saving* a form saves an individual instance of the form with a particular set of data in its fields. *Publishing* a form saves the form design to a forms library, where it can be used to create form instances based on its design.

Saving a Form As a Template

You can also save a form as a form template. An Outlook template is a separate file with an .oft extension (similar in functionality to the Word .dot template). Outlook templates are convenient for emailing to other users or saving to a disk for transfer to another computer. To save a form as a template, you can start with a new blank form created from a form in a forms library or you can use a form item (but be sure you clear it of unnecessary data before saving it).

To save a form template:

1. In either form or Design view, choose File, Save As.

   The Save As dialog box opens with a choice of several save types.
2. Select the Outlook Template (*.oft) save format, and click the Save button.

Saving a Form As a File

There are several other options for saving an item as a file. The Text Only (.txt) format saves the data in the item as unformatted text. The Rich Text Format (.rtf) option may be disappointing if you are expecting to see the saved form as it looks in Outlook. All you get is a text output of the data in the item, with minimal formatting, as shown in Figure 55.30.

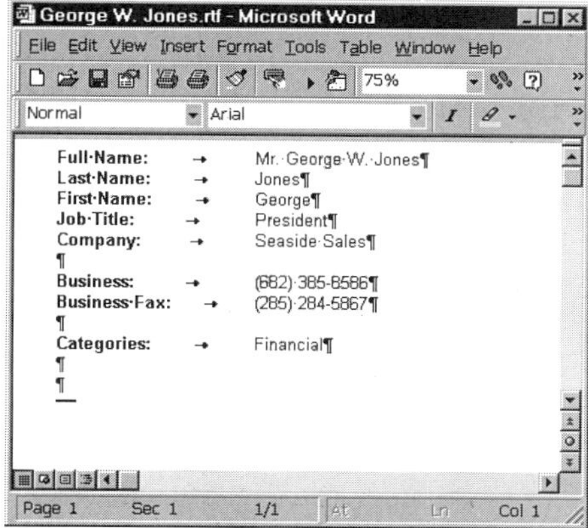

FIGURE 55.30
A Contact item saved in Rich Text Format.

The Message (.msg) format produces a file that can be opened directly by double-clicking; it opens as a standard Outlook item. This is a good choice for saving an individual item to send to another person or transfer to another computer on a disk. After opening a message format file, it can be saved to a folder in the user's Outlook folders tree.

The vcard (.vcf) option saves a contact in a special format that can be emailed and then easily added to the recipient's Contacts list. A vcard file cannot be opened directly, unlike a message file.

Distributing a Form

The Message and Template save options are useful for sending files to other users because they can be attached to mail messages and then opened on the recipient's computer. Additionally, you can send a vcard directly (without the need to save a contact in vcard format first) by selecting Forward as vCard from the Actions menu of a Contact item.

Form Libraries and Managing Forms

If you open the Forms Management dialog box from a folder's properties sheet, you can delete forms from a forms library, and copy and move forms to other folders. To open the Forms Management dialog box:

1. Choose Tools, Options to open the Options dialog box.
2. Click the Other tab, and then click the Advanced Options button.
3. In the Advanced Options dialog box, click the Custom Forms button.
4. On the Custom Forms dialog box, click the Manage Forms button.
5. The Forms Manager dialog box opens with two panes, one of them generally displaying your Organizational or Personal Forms Library (see Figure 55.31).

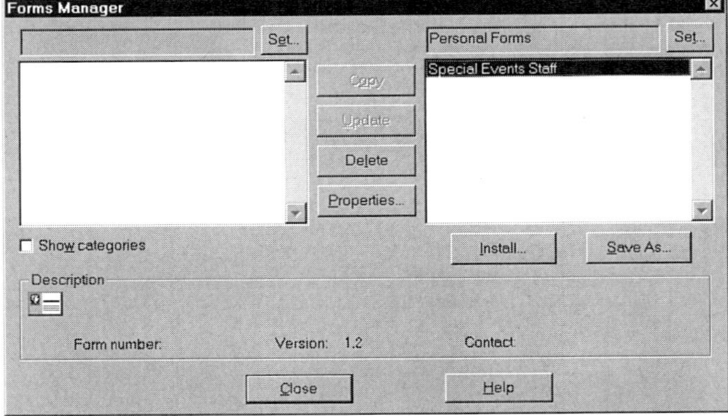

FIGURE 55.31
The Forms Manager dialog box, with the Personal Forms Library selected in the right pane

6. If you see the form you want to delete, just select it and press the Delete key.
7. Otherwise, you can locate the form by clicking the Set button over one of the panes to open the Set Library To dialog box.
8. You can either select a forms library in the Forms Library drop-down list with the Forms Library option selected (the default), or select an Outlook folder by clicking the Folder Forms Library option button and expanding the Personal (or Organizational) Folders tree, as shown in Figure 55.32.

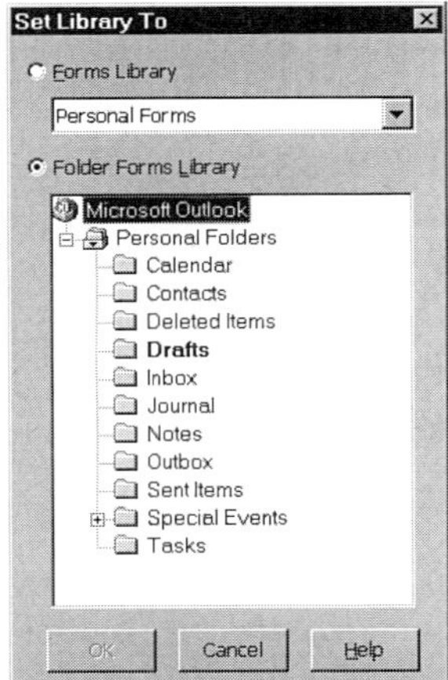

FIGURE 55.32
The Set Library To dialog box, with the Folder Forms Library option selected and the Outlook folder tree expanded.

9. After you locate the folder that contains the form you want to delete, click the OK button in the Set Library To dialog box to return to the Manage Forms dialog box.
10. You can now select the form to delete from the folder you opened, and click the Delete button to delete the form.

NOTE In the same Manage Forms dialog box, you can also copy a form from one folder to another, or from a folder to a library.

CAUTION

The Forms Manager dialog box is available only if you installed Outlook for Corporate/Workgroup E-Mail support; it is not available if you installed Outlook for Internet Mail Only.

Changing the Default Form Used by Contact Items

If you have created a custom Contact form and want to use it in place of the default Contact form for any contact items created in your Contacts folder, first save the custom form to your Personal Forms Library, and then select it as the form to use for the Contacts folder:

1. Right-click the Contacts icon in the Outlook bar (or the Contacts folder in the Folders List) and select Properties from the shortcut menu.

   The default Contact form is the selection in the When Posting to This Folder, Use drop-down list in the middle of the Properties sheet.
2. Select the Forms entry from the drop-down list.
3. Select the Personal Forms Library in the Look In list, and then select the custom contact form you want to use, and click the Open button.
4. Now the chosen custom Contact form will be used when you create a new Contact item in the Contacts folder.

CAUTION

Assigning a new form to a folder ensures that any new forms created in a folder will be based on the new form, but it does not change the form type of items already present in the folder. To do that, you need to write VBS code to change the message class of all forms in the folder. You can download a form with a VBS procedure to upgrade the message class of items in a folder from this site, `http://www.ulster.net/~hfeddema/CodeSamples.htm`.

If you just have a few items to change to another form, you can create a new contact with the *exact* same name and then save it. A dialog box pops up telling you that there is another contact with the same name and asking whether you want to use that data. Click OK to replace the old form with the new one. If you have numerous items to upgrade, however, you will need to write code to change them to another form.

Part VII
Ch 55

Sharing Custom Forms

If your computer is attached to a network running Exchange Server, you can share a custom form by saving it to the Organizational Forms Library instead of the Personal Forms Library. The Organizational Forms Library is available to all users on the network, so they can all use your form to make new items.

CHAPTER 56

Using VBA with Outlook 2000

In this chapter

VBA Versus VBScript

Outlook 2000, like earlier versions of Outlook, supports VBScript for creating code behind forms. However, in addition to VBScript, Outlook now hosts real Visual Basic for Applications (VBA) for creating applicationwide code—a significant advance in functionality for Outlook developers. You can write macros (procedures) in VBA, using applicationwide events such as the NewMail event, which lets you control Outlook without having to attach code to a specific form. Also, you can write code for custom toolbar buttons. Office standard UserForms (new to Outlook 2000, although you may know them from Word) are handy for creating enhanced dialog boxes for code.

NOTE To learn more about creating VBScript code for Outlook, see Chapter 43, "Enhancing Outlook Forms with Visual Basic Script Code," in *Special Edition Using Microsoft Outlook 2000*, published by Que.

See "Designing `UserForms`," **p. 170**

The VBA dialect of Visual Basic is considerably more powerful than the VBScript dialect, which is used to create code behind forms in Outlook. The main differences between the dialects are listed in Table 56.1.

VBScript (*Visual Basic Scripting Edition)* is a scripting language developed by Microsoft. VBScript is based on the Visual Basic programming language, but is much easier to learn. VBScript (much like JavaScript) enables Web authors to add interactive controls to Web pages.

Table 56.1 Differences Between the Current Versions of VBA and VBScript

Feature	VBA v. 6.0	VBScript v. 5.0
Environment	Runs within the Outlook application	Runs from an Outlook form
Host	Hosted by all Office applications (and some non-Office applications)	Hosted by Outlook, Internet Explorer, and some non-Office applications
Development Environment	Has the powerful VBE developer's environment	Has the limited Script Editor development environment
Object Browser	Has a full-featured Object Browser, listing objects for other applications as well as Outlook objects	Has a limited Object Browser, listing only Outlook objects

Feature	VBA v. 6.0	VBScript v. 5.0
Data Typing	Supports data typing for variables	Does not support data typing; all variables are of the Variant type
Named Constants	Supports named constants for function arguments and setting values	Does not support named constants for function arguments and setting values; numeric values must be used instead
Portability	Cannot be sent to another user with a form	Can be sent to another user with a form
Event Scope	Works with application-wide events, such as selecting a folder	Works only with form events, such as changing the value of a field on a form
Syntax	Uses different syntax for some settings	Uses different syntax for some settings

Additionally, VBA comes with a sophisticated development interface, the *Visual Basic Editor* (VBE), which gives developers a set of powerful tools for creating and debugging their code.

Using VBA to Create Applicationwide Outlook Code

In Outlook 2000, VBA code is used to respond to events at the application level and to events attached to many Outlook objects (Folders, Explorers, Inspectors, OutlookBarGroups, and others), as opposed to the limited number of form events and the single control event available for use in Outlook VBScript code. Using the VBE development environment discussed in the following sections, you can write VBA code to respond to an applicationwide event, such as the arrival of new mail, or to an event such as a user opening a new Explorer window.

Unlike VBScript code (which is attached to forms), VBA code can be run regardless of whether an item is open, making it much more flexible than VBScript, which runs only when the form to which it is attached is open.

As in other Office applications, VBA code resides in code modules located in VB projects, which also may contain UserForms (see the UserForms section later in this chapter). Outlook VBA projects belong to a particular Outlook user, so each user can have a customized Outlook environment. Samples of VBA code using applicationwide events will be given in later sections of this chapter.

A full discussion of using the VBA programming language is beyond the scope of this book; the following sections assume that the reader is generally familiar with Visual Basic programming from using VB or some dialect of VBA, such as Word or Excel VBA, or the older WordBasic or

AccessBasic dialects. Rather than attempt to teach you VBA, this chapter introduces some of the special features of VBA used in Outlook, with an emphasis on using VBA to add functionality to the Outlook interface.

NOTE For more information about VBA programming, see Chapters 5 and 6. Also, see *Special Edition Using Visual Basic 6*, published by Que.

The VBA Developer's Environment

The Visual Basic Editor (described in detail in the next section) is used to create and edit both code modules and UserForms in Outlook VBA projects. If you have worked with Word or Excel macros and procedures in previous versions of Office, or Access code in Office 2000, the VBE environment will be familiar to you. Office 2000 finally offers a standardized development environment for all its components (except Publisher), replacing the nonstandard (although equally powerful) Access developer's environment with the standard VBE window, and giving Outlook the VBE environment for applicationwide code, while leaving the limited Script Editor for working with VBScript code.

Outlook form events are available for use in VBScript code behind Outlook forms. On the application level, however, there are numerous other events, all new to Outlook 2000, which can be used in VBA procedures. The Outlook events are listed in Table 56.2.

Table 56.2 The Outlook Events

Event Name	Applies to Object(s)
*Activate	Explorer, Inspector
*AttachmentAdd	Items
*AttachmentRead	Items
*BeforeAttachmentSave	Items
*BeforeCheckNames	Items
*BeforeFolderSwitch	Explorer
*BeforeGroupAdd	OutlookBarGroups
*BeforeGroupRemove	OutlookBarGroups
*BeforeGroupSwitch	OutlookBarPane
*BeforeNavigate	OutlookBarPane
*BeforeShortcutAdd	OutlookBarShortcuts
*BeforeShortcutRemove	OutlookBarShortcuts
*BeforeViewSwitch	Explorer

Event Name	Applies to Object(s)
Close	Items
CustomAction	Items
CustomPropertyChange	Items
*Deactivate	Explorer, Inspector
*FolderAdd	Folders
*FolderChange	Folders
*FolderRemove	Folders
*FolderSwitch	Explorer
Forward	Items
*GroupAdd	OutlookBarGroups
*ItemAdd	Items
*ItemChange	Items
*ItemRemove	Items
*ItemSend	Application
*NewExplorer	Explorers
*NewInspector	Inspectors
*NewMail	Application
*OnError	SyncObject
Open	Items
*OptionsPagesAdd	Application, NameSpace
*Progress	SyncObject
PropertyChange	Items
*Quit	Application
Read	Items
*Reminder	Application
Reply	Items
ReplyAll	Items
*SelectionChange	Explorer

continues

Table 56.2 Continued

Event Name	Applies to Object(s)
Send	Items
*ShortcutAdd	OutlookBarShortcuts
*Startup	Application
*SyncEnd	SyncObject
*SyncStart	SyncObject
*ViewSwitch	Explorer
Write	Items

**New to Outlook 2000*

Understanding the VBE window

To create or edit Outlook VBA code, start by opening the VBE window by choosing Tools, Macro, Macros, and selecting the Visual Basic Editor command.

You can press Alt+F11 from the main Outlook window to open the VBE window quickly.

The Visual Basic Editor window opens, as shown in Figure 56.1. The VBE window is used to create (or delete) modules, to edit code in modules, and to create (or delete) UserForms. It contains a powerful Object Browser and debugging tools to aid you in figuring out problems with your code. You can also export your code to text files so that you can share it with other users.

NOTE The title bar of the VBE window says "Microsoft Visual Basic," but it is generally referred to as the VBE window.

The VBE window normally opens with three of its component windows (panes) visible: the Project Explorer, Properties Sheet, and Code Window. You can open a number of other windows as needed: the Object Browser, Immediate window, Locals window, Toolbox, UserForm window, and Watches window. All the VBE component windows can either be paned, or used as free-floating windows or toolbars, as you prefer. The VBE component windows are discussed in the following sections.

To convert a VBE component window from docked to free-floating, click its title bar and drag it to a new location. To dock a free-floating window, click and drag its title bar to the VBE window edge where you want to dock it.

Additionally, the VBE window has five toolbars; they are discussed later in this chapter.

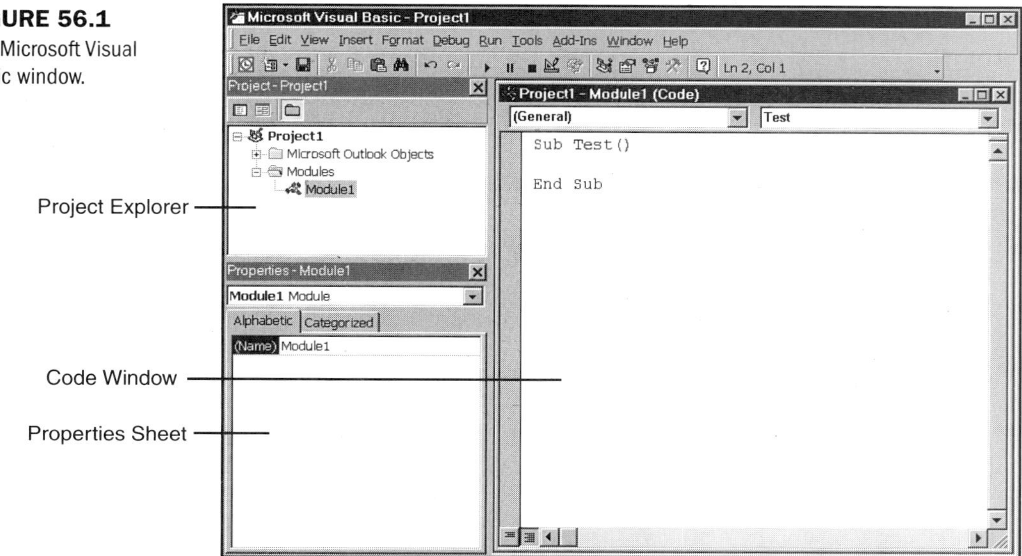

FIGURE 56.1
The Microsoft Visual Basic window.

Project Explorer

The Project Explorer window has a tree-type display, similar to the Windows Explorer. If you see only a Project*n* node with a plus sign to its left, indicating that this node is collapsed, you can expand it (to open up the branches) by clicking the plus sign, as shown in Figure 56.2.

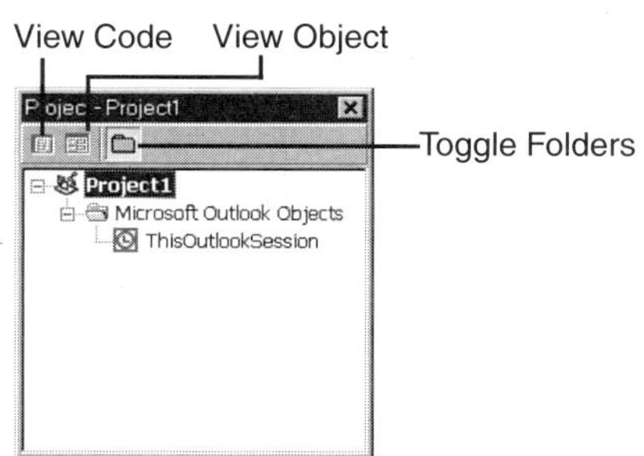

FIGURE 56.2
The Project Explorer window, in collapsed mode.

The Project Explorer window has its own toolbar, with three buttons:

View Code	Displays the Code window for the selected item
View Object	Displays the Object window for the selected Document or UserForm
Toggle Folders	Hides or shows object folders

If you have not created any code modules, the Project Explorer will initially have only one folder, Microsoft Outlook Objects, with just one object, ThisOutlookSession, under it, representing the current Outlook session, as shown in Figure 56.3. You can create a new module in the Project Explorer by opening the Insert Object menu on the Standard toolbar and selecting Module.

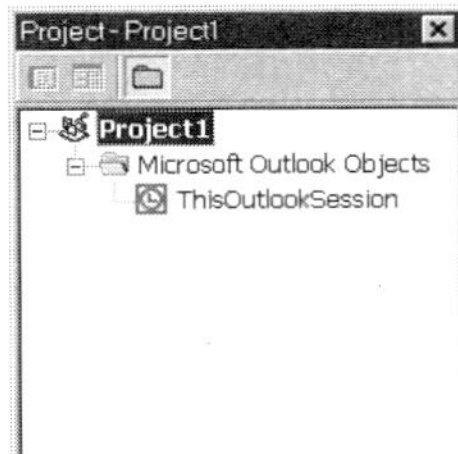

FIGURE 56.3
The Project Explorer window, in expanded mode.

NOTE You can also create a new module to contain your macros by selecting Macro from the Tools menu (see the Macros section for more details on this method). Whether you create a macro (procedure) from the Macro menu or from the VBE window, it ends up in a module you can view in the VBE window.

A new Code window opens to a blank module, as shown in Figure 56.4. Now the Project Explorer has a Modules folder, with the new module under it.

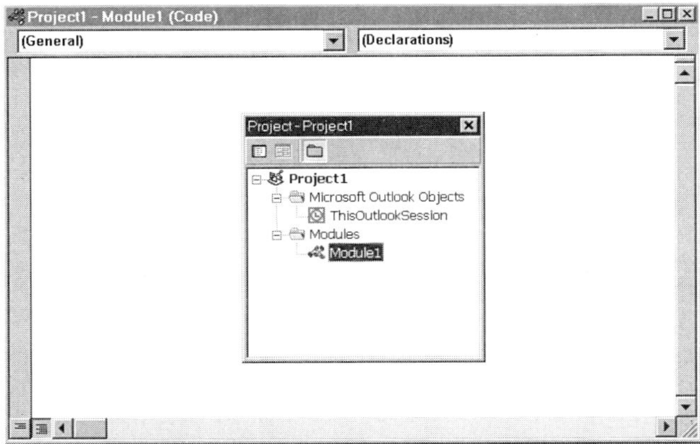

FIGURE 56.4
A newly created Code window.

You can create new UserForms in a similar manner. Select the UserForm selection from the New Object drop-down list on the Standard menu. As you create new objects, they are added to the Project Explorer tree. You can easily select the one you want to work on by selecting the item and pressing Enter, or by double-clicking it.

Properties Window

The Properties window (similar to the Advanced Properties sheet in the Outlook form design window) lists the design-time properties of the selected object. If you have selected multiple controls, the Properties window displays just the properties common to all the selected controls.

If the Properties window is not visible, you can display it by clicking the Properties Window button on the Standard toolbar.

You won't see many properties in the Properties Window when a module is highlighted (see Figure 56.5); this window is primarily used for UserForms and their controls.

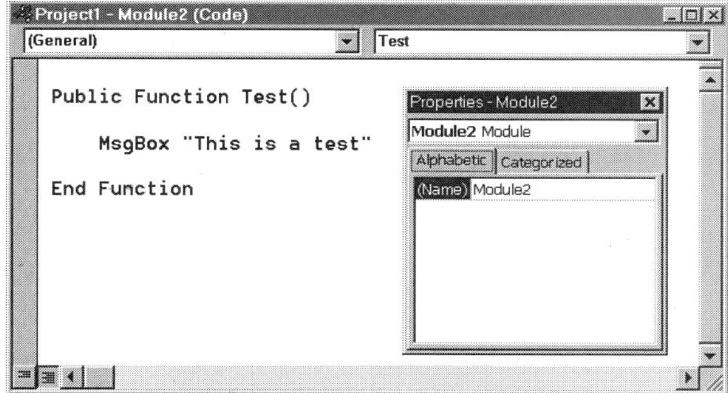

FIGURE 56.5
The Properties Window for a code module.

The Properties window has two tabs: If you select the Alphabetic tab, the properties are listed alphabetically in one long list. If you select the Categorized tab, the properties are categorized by property type.

Code Window

The Code window displays your code, with a variety of tools for editing, running, and debugging it. Each module opens in its own Code window (see Figure 56.6), and you can have multiple Code windows open at once. On the top of a Code window, there are two drop-down lists. The one on the left is the Object Box, where you can select objects associated with the form or other object the code belongs to.

The Procedures/Events Box (on the right) displays procedures and events in the module, so you can go directly to the one you want to work with. At the top of the list there is a (Declarations) selection, which takes you to the top of the module, where you can enter options, declare global variables, and create general procedures.

On top of the vertical scrollbar is a little Split Bar, which you can drag up and down to split the Code window into two portions, each displaying a separate portion of code.

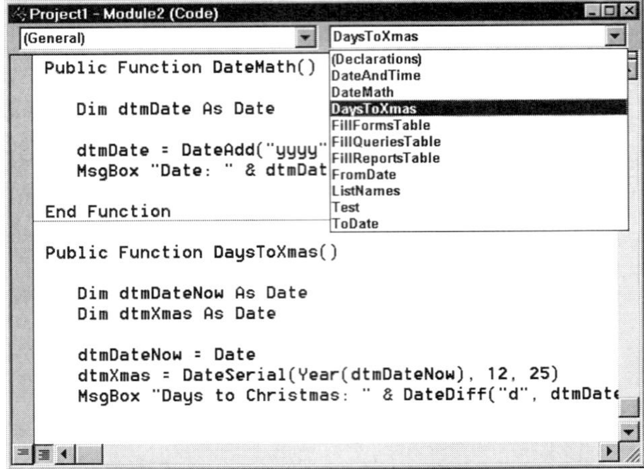

FIGURE 56.6 The Code window, with the Procedures/Events dialog box displayed.

In the bottom-right corner, there are two icons:

Procedure View	Displays one procedure at a time in the Code window
Full Module View	Displays all the code in the module

Object Browser

The VBA Object Browser (like the VBScript Object Browser) lets you examine Outlook objects and their properties, methods, and events. However, it also lets you inspect objects, properties, methods, and events belonging to other applications—a significant enhancement.

The two main components of the Object Browser window are the Classes list on the left side, where you can select a class to examine from the selected type library, and the Members list on the right, which shows the methods, properties, events, and constants for the selected class.

The Window Elements Project/Library dialog box (see Figure 56.7) lets you select the type library with the objects you want to examine, and the Search Text Box underneath it lets you enter a search string (click the Search button to run the search).

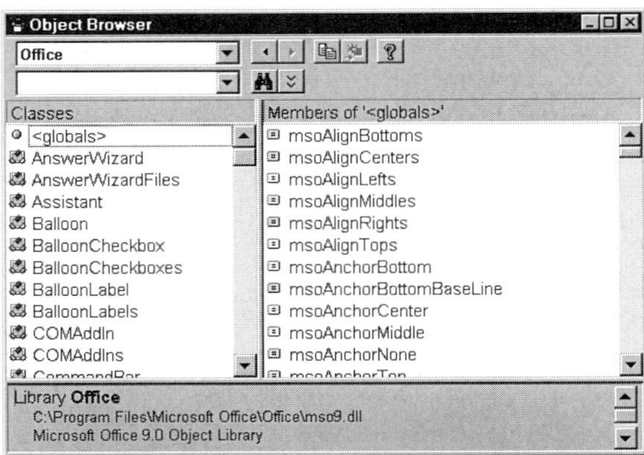

FIGURE 56.7 The Object Browser, with the Office type library selected.

The Object Browser's toolbar buttons are described in the following list:

- Go Back—Returns to previous selection in Classes and Members list.
- Go Forward—Repeats original selection in Classes and Members list.

- Copy to Clipboard—Copies current selection to the Windows Clipboard.

- View Definition—Moves the cursor to the place in the Code window where the selection in the Classes or Members list is defined.

- Help—Opens context-specific help for the selected item.

- Search—Starts searching for the text string in the Search box.

- Show/Hide Search—Opens or hides the Search Results pane, with the results of the current search.

If you want to examine the components of another Office application's object model, you need to set a reference to it. To set a reference to the Access type library, implement the following steps:

NOTE The selections you see in the References list may be called type libraries or object libraries–these terms are used interchangeably.

1. Open the VBE window, if it is not already open.
2. Choose Tools, References. The References dialog box opens, with the checked type libraries at the top.
3. If the Microsoft Access 9.0 Object Library selection is checked, you don't need to do anything; just close the dialog box.
4. If the Access selection is not checked, locate it in the list of type libraries and check it, as shown in Figure 56.8.
5. Click OK to close the References dialog box.
6. Press F2 to open the Object Browser, if it is not already open.
7. Select Access from the drop-down list of type libraries.

   The Access objects are listed in the Classes list, and their events, properties, and methods in the Members list, each with a distinctive icon, as listed in Figure 56.9.

NOTE For an illustration of the Object Browser icons, see Chapter 43, "Enhancing Outlook Forms with Visual Basic Script Code," in *Special Edition Using Microsoft Outlook 2000*, published by Que.

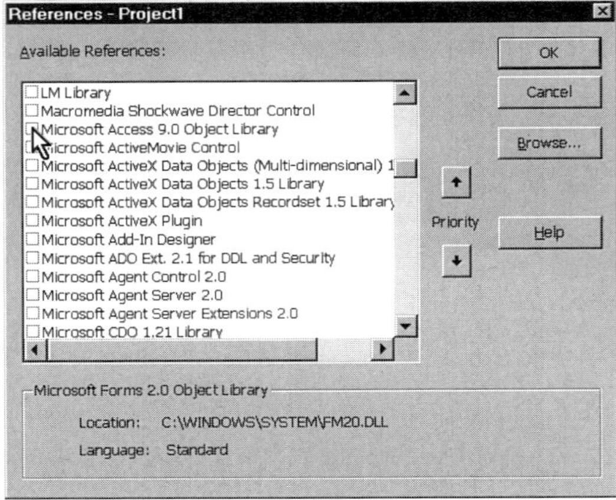

FIGURE 56.8
Opening the References window from the Access Visual Basic window

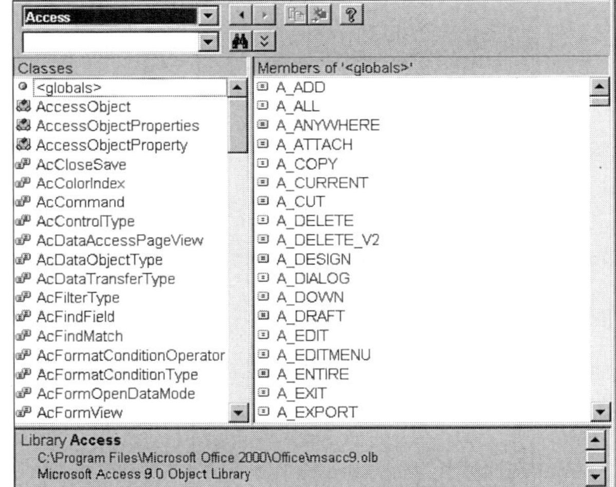

FIGURE 56.9
The Access object library.

Definitions of Terms

An *object* is an element of an application, such as an Outlook folder or task.

A *collection* is an object that contains one or more other objects, such as the Outlook Folders and Controls collections.

An *event* is an action recognized by an object, such as the Close event that occurs when closing an Outlook form.

A *method* is an action that an object can perform, such as the Save method for an Outlook item.

A *property* is an attribute defining one of an object's characteristics. In Outlook, each item has numerous properties, which are also called *fields*. The name and address controls on a Contact item are bound to various Outlook properties.

A *constant* is a fixed value used as an argument for a function or method, or for setting a value.

You can open the Help topic for a property, event, or method by right-clicking it and selecting Help from the context menu; or you can click the Help button on the Object Browser's toolbar.

Immediate Window

The Immediate Window (which you can open by pressing Ctrl+G, or by choosing View, Immediate Window) enables you to execute code directly by typing it into the window and pressing Enter. Although this can be handy, the major usefulness of the Immediate Window is for displaying the values of variables you use in code, by using the Debug.Print method.

Using Debug.Print to display the values of variables (as opposed to using message boxes) enables you to run your code all the way through, without interruption; if anything goes wrong, you can examine the variables in the Immediate window to see whether any of them contains inappropriate information. (This technique is used in several of the code listings later in this chapter.) Figure 56.10 shows the Immediate window displaying a variable (with explanatory text) from a function that calculates the days left until Christmas.

FIGURE 56.10
The Immediate window displaying the contents of a variable in a Code module.

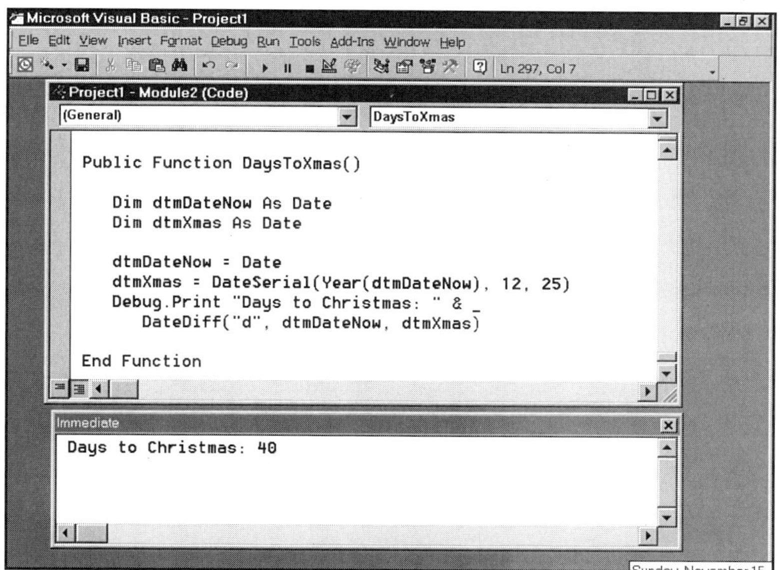

Locals Window, Watches Window

The Locals window and Watches window are used for advanced debugging, beyond the scope of this book.

UserForm Window

A UserForm window opens when you select UserForm from the Insert Object drop-down list on the Standard Outlook toolbar. UserForms (just as in Word) are standard Office forms on which you can place a variety of controls using the Toolbox (see the next section). UserForms are used to enter information, make selections, and run code—each UserForm has its own attached VBA code module, which you can edit in a Code window. However, UserForms can't be bound to data.

CAUTION

Office UserForms and Outlook forms are different types of objects; their interfaces and functionality differ significantly, so it isn't safe to assume that if you can do something in a UserForm, you can do it in an Outlook form, or vice versa.

To open a UserForm's code module, double-click its background.

Unlike regular Outlook forms, which are based on one of the standard Outlook item templates, UserForms have no built-in fields or controls; you have to populate them with controls of your choice. UserForms are convenient for use as enhanced dialog boxes to let users make choices or enter information needed in your code.

UserForms have their own set of special toolbars, which are discussed in the following sections.

Toolbox The Toolbox appears when you open a UserForm, as shown in Figure 56.11. It contains a set of standard Visual Basic controls, and possibly one or more ActiveX controls you have added to it.

FIGURE 56.11
A newly created UserForm with the Toolbox.

The Visual Basic controls most commonly used on UserForms are described in the following sections.

Label Control The Label control is used to display text on a UserForm. Labels are typically used either to describe an adjacent TextBox or ComboBox control, or to provide general information about a UserForm, such as a caption for a group of controls. Label controls can't be modified by the user.

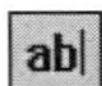

TextBox Control The TextBox control is used to enter or display data, which can be retrieved from code.

ComboBox Control The ComboBox control enables the user to select a value from a drop-down list, or to enter text into the box at the top of the list. You can add a list of predefined values for the ComboBox by entering them in the Possible Values field (separated by semicolons) on the Value tab of the control's Properties dialog box. You can also write values to the control's drop-down list from VBScript code, using an array.

ListBox Control The ListBox control, like the Combo Box, displays a list of items for user choice. However, the ListBox's list is always displayed, and the user can't enter a value that is not in the list. Because the ListBox control doesn't collapse into a single row when not in use, it takes up more room on a UserForm than a ComboBox, and thus is not practical unless the list is small.

CheckBox Control A CheckBox control is used to display a Yes/No value. When checked, the CheckBox represents a Yes value; when unchecked, it represents a No value.

OptionButton Control The OptionButton control is similar in function to the CheckBox control; instead of a check mark, the Yes value is displayed by a black center, and the No value by a white center.

ToggleButton Control The ToggleButton control also functions as an interface for a Yes/No field; when the button appears to be pressed, it represents a Yes value, and when it appears to be raised, it represents a No value. ToggleButtons are rarely used, because they take up more room than CheckBox or OptionButton controls, and their meaning is not as intuitive.

Frame Control The Frame control is used to contain a group of other controls, usually CheckBoxes or OptionButtons, to indicate that they are alternative choices for an option. A group of CheckBoxes or OptionButtons within a Frame is often referred to as an Option Group.

CommandButton Control The CommandButton control is used to run a Subprocedure, which runs when it is clicked.

Image Control The Image control is used to display an image on a UserForm.

Other Controls The remaining controls in the Toolbox (the TabStrip, MultiPage, ScrollBar, and SpinButton controls) are less commonly used because they require programming to make them useful.

ActiveX Controls In addition to the standard Visual Basic controls, you can also add ActiveX controls to a UserForm. As with adding ActiveX controls to an Outlook form, there is no guarantee that an ActiveX control will have full functionality on a UserForm.

UserForm Toolbar The UserForm Toolbar has a number of useful tools for working with controls on UserForms.

The tools on the UserForm toolbar work exactly like their counterparts on the Outlook Form Design toolbar.

VBE Standard Toolbar

The VBE Standard toolbar has a number of tools to help you work with code in modules.

The buttons work as follows:

- View Outlook—Switches back to the Outlook window.

- Insert Object—Drops down a list from which you can choose a new object to insert:

  UserForm

  Module

  Class Module

  Procedure

- Save—Saves the current project, including its component forms and modules.
- Cut—Cuts the selected object to the Clipboard.
- Copy—Copies the selected object to the Clipboard.
- Paste—Pastes the selected object from the Clipboard.
- Find—Opens the Find dialog box and searches for the text in the Find What box.
- Undo—Reverses the last edit action.
- Redo—Undoes the last Undo action.
- Run—Runs the current procedure or UserForm, or a macro if neither the Code window nor a UserForm is active.
- Break—Stops execution of code and switches to Break mode.
- Reset—Clears variables and resets the project.
- Design Mode—Toggles Design mode on and off.
- Project Explorer—Opens the Project Explorer.
- Properties Window—Opens the Properties Window.
- Object Browser—Opens the Object Browser.
- Toolbox—Opens the Toolbox.
- Office Assistant—Opens the Office Assistant (or Help, if you have turned the Office Assistant off).

Edit Toolbar

The Edit Toolbar contains some specialized buttons to aid you in working with code:

- List Properties/Methods—Opens a box that lists an object's properties and methods.
- List Constants—Opens a box that lists the constants for a property.
- Quick Info—Gives the syntax for a variable, function, method, or procedure.
- Parameter Info—Opens a pop-up dialog box listing the parameters for a function.
- Complete Word—Completes the word you are typing.
- Indent—Shifts the selected text to the next tab stop.

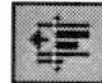

- Outdent—Shifts the selected text to the previous tab stop.

- Toggle Breakpoint—Toggles a breakpoint on or off on the current line of code.

- Comment Block—Adds the comment character to each line of highlighted code.

- Uncomment Block—Removes the comment character from each line of highlighted code.

- Toggle Bookmark—Toggles a bookmark on or off for the current line of code.

- Next Bookmark—Goes to the next bookmark.

- Previous Bookmark—Goes to the previous bookmark.

- Clear All Bookmarks—Clears all bookmarks.

NOTE The Edit Toolbar is enabled only when you have a Code window open.

Debug Toolbar

The Debug Toolbar is used when you are trying to figure out why your code isn't working as you intended.

See "Debugging Your Code," **p. 174**

Some of the buttons on the Debug Toolbar (Design Mode, Run, Break, Reset, Toggle, Breakpoint) are also on the Standard or Edit toolbars (see their descriptions in preceding sections); the others are used for advanced debugging purposes, beyond the scope of this book.

Macros

Outlook macros don't work like macros in Word or Excel. You can't record an Outlook macro; they are actually procedures in a VBA module, similar to the modules you create directly in the VBE window. All macros are procedures, but not all procedures are macros: In Outlook (and all other Office applications except Access), a macro is a subprocedure that doesn't accept arguments. All your Outlook macros are stored in a single module.

Although it isn't required—Outlook will just name the module containing macros Module*n*—I recommend naming the module "Modules" (or "basModules" if you use a naming convention) so that you will know which one it is when you look at the Project Explorer.

You can create a macro in the regular Outlook window by choosing Tools, Macro, Macros.

The Macros window opens (see Figure 56.12), enabling you to enter a name for the new macro, and click the Create button. The VBE window opens to a new module (or the module containing your existing macros, if this is not your first macro) containing a new subprocedure with the name you assigned to the macro, as shown in Figure 56.13.

FIGURE 56.12
The Macros window.

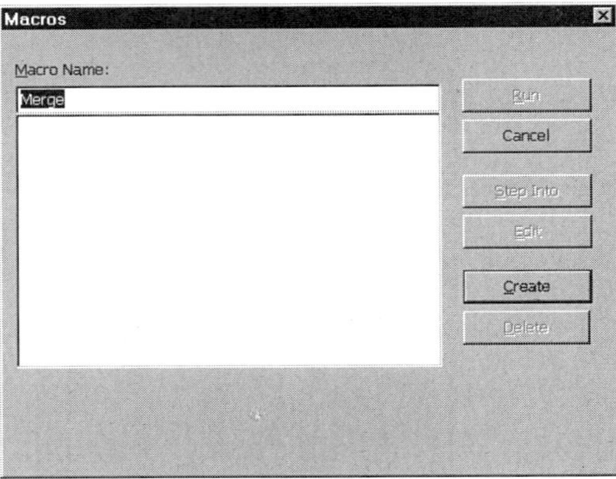

At this point, you are in the VBE window, and can continue working on the macro just as if you had started it from the VBE window, using the New Procedure button on the Standard toolbar.

NOTE After you have created a macro in an Outlook session, when you create additional macros, they will all be created in the same module. Procedures created in this module appear in the Macros dialog box; they are the only procedures available through the Macros dialog box.

FIGURE 56.13
The new macro as a subprocedure.

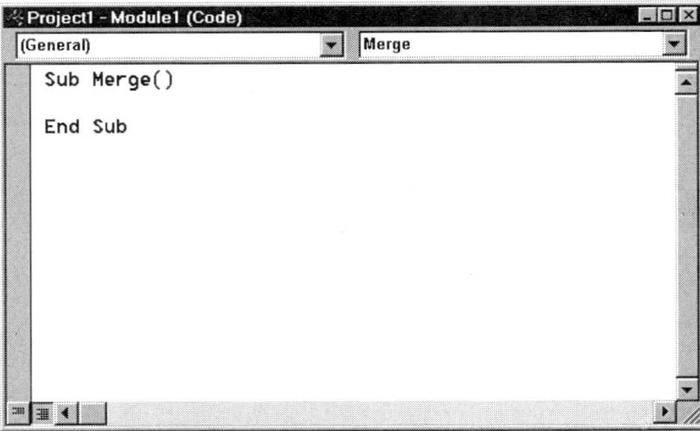

If you have created one or more macros, when you open the VBE window, you will see a dialog box reading, `ThisOutlookSession contains macros.` Choose whether you want macros enabled or disabled (see Figure 56.14). The virus warning message appears only the first time you open the VBE window in an Outlook session; if you close the VBE window and then reopen it (without closing down Outlook), it will not appear again.

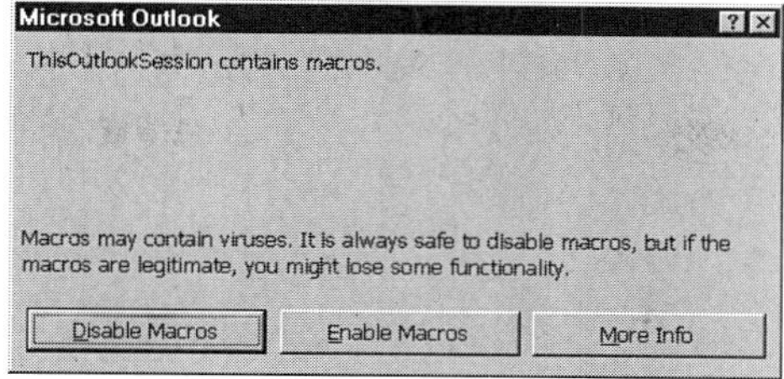

FIGURE 56.14 The Macro Virus Warning dialog box.

To turn off the session macro virus warning permanently, follow these steps:

1. Choose Tools, Macro, Security in the main Outlook window.

   The Security dialog box opens, as shown in Figure 56.15.
2. Choose from three security levels: High, Medium, and Low. Selecting Low turns off the warning permanently, but (as the text says) it is somewhat risky.

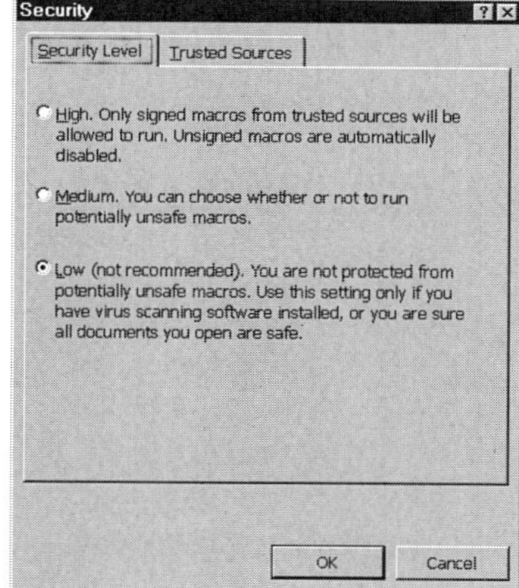

FIGURE 56.15 The Security dialog box.

> **CAUTION**
>
> The macro virus warning described previously is for the entire Outlook session; the form macro virus warning described in Chapter 55, "Creating and Using Custom Forms," can be turned off by publishing the form, as described in that chapter.

Programming Common Outlook Tasks with VBA

With the introduction of VBA to Outlook 2000, many exciting possibilities have opened up, enabling developers much greater control over the Outlook environment and Outlook events, both from within Outlook and from other Automation applications. The following sections will give you an idea of how you can use Outlook VBA code to make it easier to perform common tasks, or customize the Outlook interface.

Creating a Custom Toolbar Button to Print New Mail Messages

Since the earliest version of Outlook, users have wanted to be able to print new mail messages automatically. With Outlook 2000, it is easy to write a macro that prints all the unread mail messages in the Inbox, and (if desired) you can place a button to run the macro on your Outlook toolbar. To create such a macro, follow these steps:

1. From the Outlook window, press Alt+F8 to open the Macros dialog box.
2. Enter `PrintMail` as the macro name and click the Create button.

   The VBE window opens to the module containing your macros, with a code stub for the new macro, as shown in Figure 56.16.

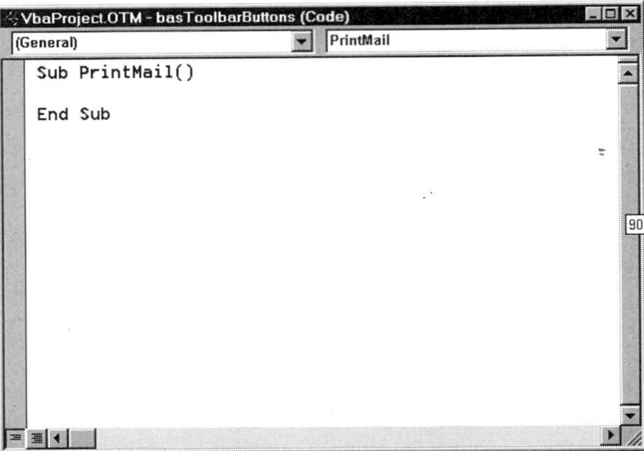

FIGURE 56.16
The new macro's code stub.

3. Start by declaring variables to reference the Outlook objects you need—the Outlook application itself, the NameSpace object, a Folder object for the Inbox, Items for the mail messages in the Inbox, and MailItem for each message. You can select the appropriate object types for each of these objects, using the Methods/Properties list that appears after you type "Outlook." (See the following code list for the complete procedure.)

```
Sub PrintMail()

   Dim objOutlook As Outlook.Application
   Dim fld As Outlook.MAPIFolder
   Dim nms As Outlook.NameSpace
   Dim itms As Outlook.Items
   Dim itm As MailItem

   Set objOutlook = CreateObject("Outlook.application")
   Set nms = objOutlook.GetNamespace("MAPI")
   Set fld = nms.GetDefaultFolder(olFolderInbox)
   Set itms = fld.Items

   For Each itm In itms
      If itm.UnRead = True Then
```

```
            itm.PrintOut
        End If
    Next itm

End Sub
```

4. Next, set references to the objects just dimensioned, using the Set keyword because these are object variables.
5. Use the For Each…Next construct to loop through the mail messages in the Inbox, checking each for the value of its Unread property, and printing the message `if Unread = True`.
6. To check that the macro works, run it from the Code window by clicking the Run button on the toolbar.
7. After verifying that the macro works (all unread mail messages should print), you can make a toolbar button for the macro.
8. Close the VBE window (you can't customize an Outlook toolbar while the VBE window—or any modal dialog box—is open).
9. Switch back to the Outlook window, if necessary.
10. Right-click the gray background of the Standard toolbar to display its context menu, and then click the Customize selection.
11. Select the Commands tab on the Customize dialog box, if it is not already selected.
12. Select the Macros category from the Categories list.
13. Drag the PrintMail macro from the Commands list to the toolbar, as shown in Figure 56.17.

FIGURE 56.17
Dragging the new macro to the toolbar.

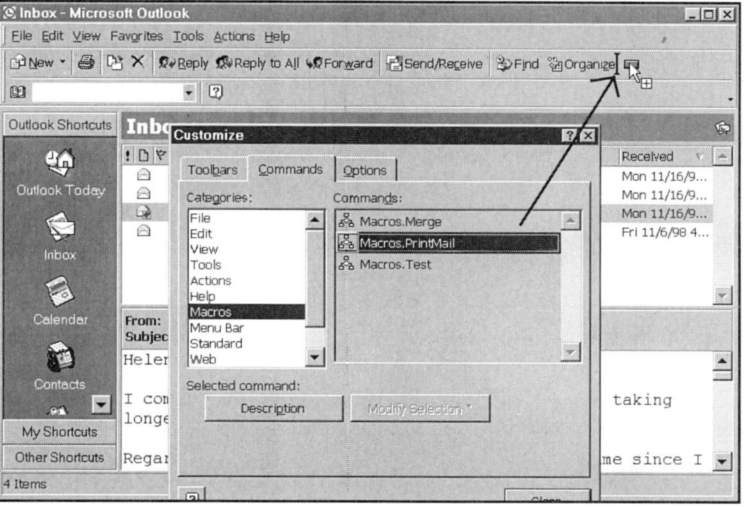

14. By default, the button will have a text label along with a macro icon. To change it to an icon-only button, click the Modify Selection button on the Customize dialog box and select Default Style from the menu.
15. Close the Customize dialog box by clicking its Close button.
16. Now the new PrintMail button appears on the Standard toolbar.

You don't have to leave the toolbar button's name as Macros.PrintMail (or even worse, Module*n*.PrintMail). To rename a toolbar button, open the Customize dialog as described previously, right-click the button, and rename it in the Name property of its menu.

Using the NewMail Event to Print New Mail Messages When Received

The previous section showed you how to create a toolbar button to print unread mail messages. But what if you want to fully automate this procedure so that every time you receive mail, the new mail messages print out automatically? You can do this by using the NewMail event, one of the new applicationwide events introduced in Outlook 2000. To write an event procedure for printing new mail messages when mail is received, follow these steps:

1. Open the VBE window by pressing Alt+F11 from the Outlook window.
2. If the Project Explorer is not visible, click the Project Explorer button on the toolbar to open it.
3. Open the Microsoft Outlook Objects folder and double-click the ThisOutlookSession selection under it to open its code module.
4. Select Application in the Object Box, and NewMail in the Procedures/Events Box in the Code window, to create a code stub for the NewMail event procedure, as shown in Figure 56.18.
5. Enter the code into the event procedure—the same code used for the preceding macro procedure will do; replace the line that sets the objOutlook variable with a line that dimensions the objOutlook variable as "Outlook.Application." (See the following code listing for the full procedure.)

```
Private Sub Application_NewMail()

   Dim fld As Outlook.MAPIFolder
   Dim nms As Outlook.NameSpace
   Dim itms As Outlook.Items
   Dim itm As Outlook.MailItem

   Set objOutlook = CreateObject("Outlook.application")
Set nms = objOutlook.GetNamespace("MAPI")
   Set fld = nms.GetDefaultFolder(olFolderInbox)
   Set itms = fld.Items

   For Each itm In itms
      If itm.UnRead = True Then
```

```
            itm.PrintOut
        End If
    Next itm

End Sub
```

Now every time you get new mail, the new mail messages will be printed automatically.

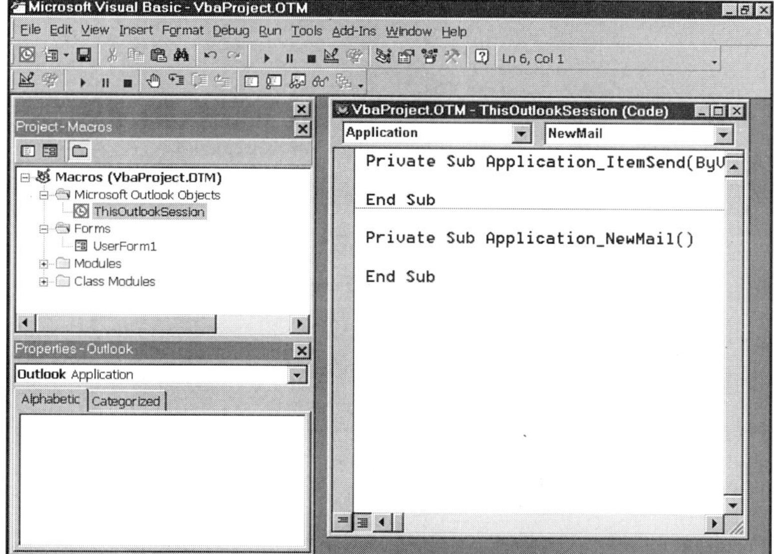

FIGURE 56.18
Creating an applicationwide event procedure.

Selecting Contacts for Mail Merge

In previous versions of Outlook, it was possible to merge an individual Outlook contact to a Word letter by using the limited built-in merge functionality, or by creating a custom contact form with a command button to run VBScript code to do the merge. You could also write Word VBA or Outlook VBScript code to merge all the contacts in a folder to a Word merge letter, or to merge just the contacts with a certain value in the Categories field.

With Outlook 2000, you can go a step further: With a UserForm, you can let users select as many contacts as they want from a multiselect ListBox control, and then merge the selected contacts only. This method lets you easily select the contacts you want to send a letter to, even though they don't have the same category. To create a UserForm with code to do a mail merge, follow these steps:

1. Open the VBE window by pressing Alt+F11 from the Outlook window.
2. Create a new UserForm by selecting UserForm from the Insert Object menu on the toolbar.
3. Open the Project Explorer and Properties Window (if they are not already open) by clicking their buttons on the toolbar.

4. Select the new UserForm in the Project Explorer, and double-click it to open the UserForm.
5. Highlight the default UserForm name in the Properties window and change it to frmMerge.
6. Similarly, give the form's Caption property the name "Merge." The renamed Name and Caption properties are shown in Figure 56.19.

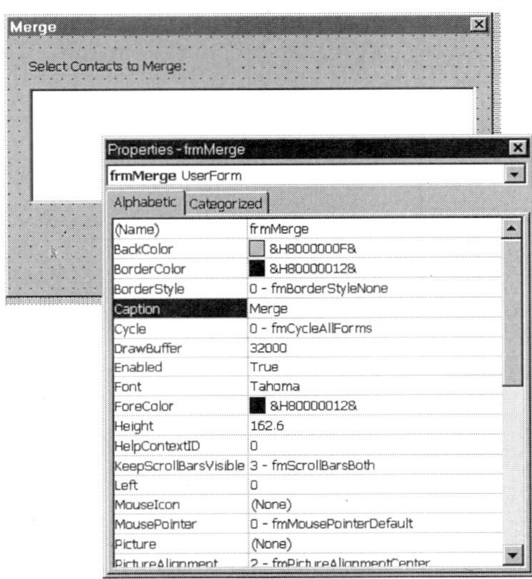

FIGURE 56.19
A UserForm's properties sheet.

7. Using the Toolbox, place a Label control, a ListBox control, and two CommandButton controls on the UserForm.
8. Select the ListBox control and make the following selections for some of its properties, to make it a multiselect ListBox with check boxes for selecting contacts:

Name	**lstMergeContacts**
ColumnWidths	72 pt;256 pt
ListStyle	1 - fmListStyleOption
MultiSelect	1 - fmMultiSelectMulti

9. Using the Properties window, change the Label control's caption to "Select Contacts to Merge:", and the CommandButtons' captions to "Merge" and "Cancel," and their names to "cmdMerge" and "cmdCancel."
10. Now open the UserForm's code module by double-clicking the form's background.
11. To fill the ListBox control with contact names, select the Initialize event from the Procedures/Events Box to create a code stub for the event.

12. Enter the code shown in the following code listing to fill the ListBox control (lstMergeContacts) with contact names, using a two-dimensional array filled from the contacts in your default Contacts folder.
13. The two CommandButtons on the UserForm run the Sub procedures listed in the following code listing—the Cancel button closes the form without doing anything, while the Merge button merges the selected contacts to a Word mail merge letter, and then closes the form.

```
Option Explicit

Dim objOutlook As Outlook.Application
Dim fld As Outlook.MAPIFolder
Dim nms As Outlook.NameSpace
Dim itms As Outlook.Items
Dim itm As Outlook.ContactItem
Dim i As Single
Dim j As Single
Dim lngContacts As Long

Private Sub UserForm_Initialize()

   Dim aryMerge()

   Set objOutlook = CreateObject("Outlook.application")
   Set nms = objOutlook.GetNamespace("MAPI")
   Set fld = nms.GetDefaultFolder(olFolderContacts)
   Set itms = fld.Items
   lngContacts = itms.Count
   Debug.Print "Number of contacts: " & lngContacts
   ReDim aryMerge(lngContacts - 1, 1)
   i = 0
   j = 0
   lstMergeContacts.ColumnCount = 2

   For Each itm In itms
      Debug.Print "Setting row " & i & ", column " & j
      aryMerge(i, j) = itm.FullName
      Debug.Print "Setting row " & i & ", column " & j + 1
      aryMerge(i, j + 1) = itm.BusinessAddress
      i = i + 1
   Next itm

   lstMergeContacts.List() = aryMerge

End Sub

Private Sub cmdCancel_Click()

   Unload FrmMerge

End Sub

Private Sub cmdMerge_Click()
```

```
   Dim lst As ListBox
   Dim objWord As Word.Application
   Dim strWordTemplate As String
   Dim prps As Object

   Set objOutlook = CreateObject("Outlook.application")
   Set objWord = CreateObject("Word.application")
   Set nms = objOutlook.GetNamespace("MAPI")
   Set fld = nms.GetDefaultFolder(olFolderContacts)
   Set itms = fld.Items
   Set lst = lstMergeContacts
   strWordTemplate = "C:\Windows\Application Data\Microsoft\Templates\Letter from
➥Outlook.dot"

   lngContacts = itms.Count

   For i = 0 To lngContacts - 1
      If lst.Selected(i) = True Then
         Debug.Print "Selected name: " & lst.List(i)
         'Open a new letter based on the selected template
         objWord.Documents.Add strWordTemplate

         'Write info from contact item to Word custom doc properties
         Set prps = objWord.ActiveDocument.CustomDocumentProperties
         prps.Item("FullName").Value = Nz(lst.List(i, 0))
         prps.Item("BusinessAddress").Value = Nz(lst.List(i, 1))

         'Update fields in Word document and activate it
         objWord.Selection.WholeStory
         objWord.Selection.Fields.Update
         objWord.Selection.HomeKey 6
         objWord.Visible = True
         objWord.Activate
      End If
   Next i

   Unload frmMerge

End Sub
```

14. Displaying the UserForm (so the user can select contacts to merge) takes a procedure in another module—for example, a macro in the Macros module.
15. Open the Macros module and create a new subprocedure, using the following code:

```
Sub Merge()


   Load frmMerge
   frmMerge.Show

End Sub
```

16. If desired, put the code that opens the UserForm on a toolbar button, as in the preceding NewMail example.

17. Now when you run the macro or click the button, the UserForm opens (see Figure 56.20), and you can check off the contacts to merge, and then click the Merge button to do the merge to Word.

FIGURE 56.20
Selecting contacts to merge from a UserForm.

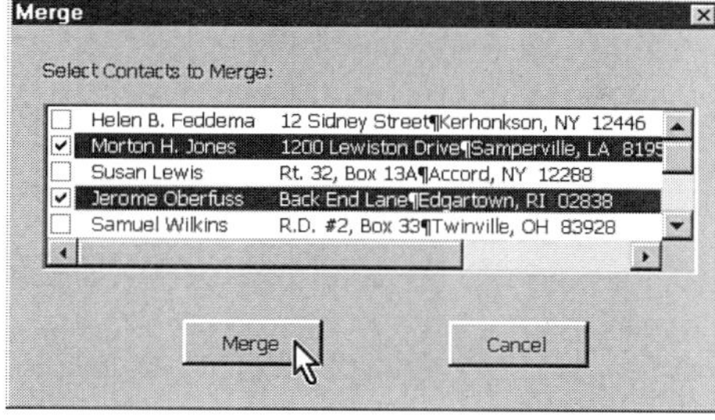

18. A new Word document is created from the template for each checked contact.

19. The Word template (located in the default User Templates folder) has two custom document properties: FullName and BusinessAddress, which are displayed in DocProperty fields in the letter. Figure 56.21 shows the custom document properties being created in the template's properties sheet, and Figure 56.22 shows the DocProperty fields in a document based on the template, which display the values in the properties.

FIGURE 56.21
Creating custom document properties for a Word document.

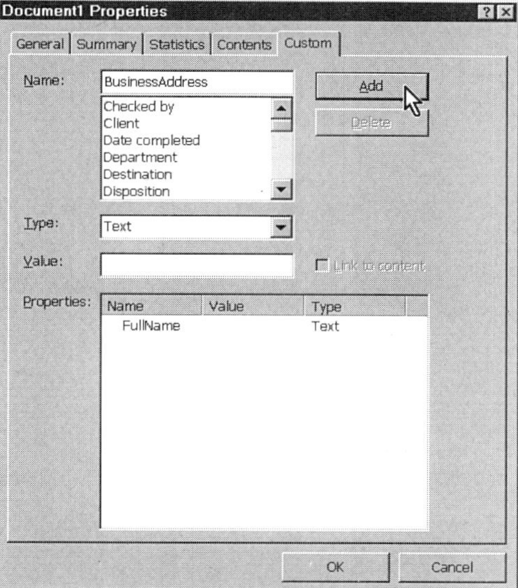

Part VII
Ch 56

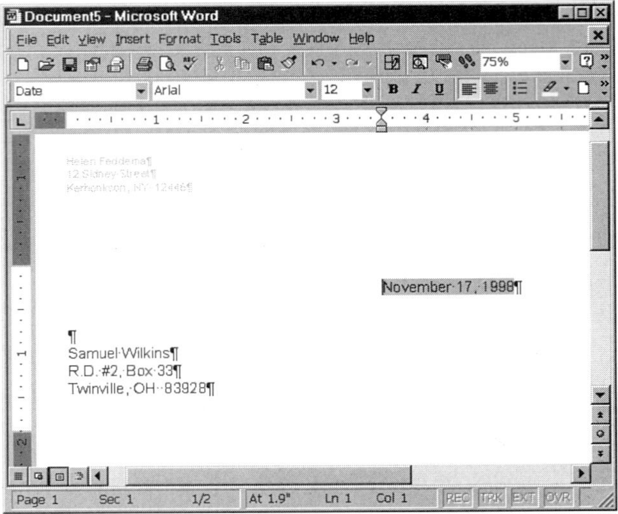

FIGURE 56.22
A Word document created from VBA code and filled with Outlook contact information.

Word custom document properties are located on the Custom page of a document's properties sheet, as previously shown in Figure 56.21. When creating custom document properties, it is advisable to avoid using the same names as built-in properties, to avoid confusing when referencing the properties.

NOTE You can't create an empty custom document property in Word; when you create a new text custom document property, save it with a space, or a zero, for a numeric property.

Using Word's Mail Merge Helper Image

You can borrow Word's Mail Merge Helper image for your Outlook Merge button by implementing the following steps:

1. Right-click the Outlook toolbar and select Customize from the menu.
2. Drag the new Merge button from the Macros list to the toolbar.
3. Leave the Customize dialog box open, and open a Word mail merge document.
4. Right-click the Word toolbar and select Customize from the menu.
5. Right-click the Mail Merge Helper toolbar button and select Copy Button Image.
6. Switch back to Outlook, right-click the Merge button, and select Paste Button Image.
7. Close the Outlook and Word Customize dialog boxes.
8. The Outlook Merge button now has the Mail Merge Helper image.

Buttons to Paste Boilerplate Text into Mail Messages

If you need more than a few signatures for your mail messages—in particular, if you want to be able to paste in paragraphs of boilerplate text—you can create one or more toolbar buttons to paste chunks of text into a mail message.

TIP If you have only a few selections, make a button for each. If you have several pieces of boilerplate text, it may be more practical to select the one you want to use from a ListBox or ComboBox control on a UserForm, using a technique similar to the one used in the last section to select a contact for a mail merge letter.

I have a Notepad document containing a collection of URLs I frequently need to paste into mail messages. To automate this process, I created a macro to run from a toolbar button. You can create such a macro by following these steps:

1. Open the VBE window by pressing Alt+F11 from the Outlook window.
2. Open the Macros module and create a new procedure—say, WebSites.
3. Enter the following code in the procedure:

```
Public Sub WebSites()

   Dim objOutlook As Outlook.Application
   Dim ins As Outlook.Inspector
   Dim itm As Outlook.MailItem
   Dim strText As String

   Set objOutlook = CreateObject("Outlook.application")
   Set ins = objOutlook.ActiveInspector
   Set itm = ins.CurrentItem

   'Add the text to the text already in the main Body field,
   'by concatenating it in chunks
   strText = itm.Body
   strText = strText & _
      "I recommend the following Web sites for Outlook and Exchange" & _
      vbCrLf & vbCrLf
   strText = strText & _
      "US East Outlook Developers Resource Center Code Samples page" & _
      vbCrLf
   strText = strText & _
      "http://www.outlook.useast.com/outlook/OutlookCodeExample.htm" & _
      vbCrLf & vbCrLf
   strText = strText & _
      "Slipstick Systems Exchange Center" & vbCrLf
   strText = strText & _
      "http://www.slipstick.com/exchange/index.htm" & vbCrLf & vbCrLf
   strText = strText & "WOPR Lounge" & vbCrLf
   strText = strText & "http://wopr.com" & vbCrLf & vbCrLf
   strText = strText & "Helen Feddema's Web Site" & vbCrLf
   strText = strText & "http://www.ulster.net/~hfeddema"

   'Write the text back to the Body field
   itm.Body = strText

End Sub
```

4. Save the module and make a toolbar button for the WebSites macro, as in the earlier examples.

5. Start writing a mail message. At the point where you want to insert the boilerplate text, click the WebSite toolbar button.
6. Alternatively, you can run a macro that has not been assigned to a toolbar button by choosing Tools, Macro, Macros to open the Macros dialog box.
7. Select the WebSites macro in the list of available macros, and click the Run button.
8. The text is pasted into the mail message.

The best place for a button (or several buttons) like this is in a New Message window's toolbar; this ensures that the focus remains in the Message window.

NOTE If the boilerplate text is pasted into a message with an automatic signature, the insertion point is placed after the signature. Also, the cursor is left positioned at the beginning of the inserted text.

CAUTION

Because of a "by design" feature of Outlook 2000 (some might call it a bug), pasting text from code into a mail message automatically converts it into a Rich Text message. If you want the message to be Plain Text or HTML, you can select another format from the message's Format menu.

CHAPTER 57

Sharing Outlook Data with Other Applications

In this chapter

Your data (contacts, calendar, and so on) are of limited use to you if you can use them only in Outlook. The full potential of Outlook is best realized when used in conjunction with the other components of the Office 2000 suite. There are a number of ways to get data into and out of the program. In this chapter, you will explore some of the basic ways to share your Outlook data with other programs and other people.

Using Outlook Contacts in Word

Before you can successfully share your contact data with Word 2000, you need to ensure that you have Outlook set up to share the contact addresses. Make sure that

- The Outlook Address Book service is in your profile (Corporate mode users only).
- Your Contact folder (or other folder containing contact items) is configured as an email address book.
- Address Book component of Word 2000 is installed.

NOTE To configure a contact folder for use as an address book, right-click the folder, choose Properties from the context menu that appears, click the Outlook Address Book tab, and then check the Show This Folder As an E-Mail Address Book box.

See "Choosing Email Formats," **p. 1438**

Addressing Envelopes Using Outlook Contacts

One of the more common ways to use your Outlook contact data is as the source for addresses on envelopes, labels, and letters. Word 2000 includes wizards that help you use contact addresses for each of those items. Each of the wizards can produce either a single item (be it an envelope, page of identical labels, or a letter) referencing an individual or a series of items—each featuring data from a different Outlook contact record. You can find them on the Letters & Faxes tab in the New Office Document dialog box that you can access from the New Office Document item on your Start Menu. The basic structure of the wizards is similar, so we'll examine only the Envelope Wizard in detail.

To create a single envelope using the Envelope Wizard, follow these steps:

1. Click File, New, and select the Letters & Faxes tab.
2. Double-click the Envelope Wizard icon.
3. The Envelope Wizard welcome screen appears giving two choices: Create One Envelope or Create Envelopes for a Mailing List. For purposes of this demonstration, I'll choose to create a single envelope label. The following section, "Creating Envelopes for Mass Mailings," discusses the second option in more detail.

4. Click the Address Book button above the Delivery Address field to choose an address book entry for use as an addressee (see Figure 57.1). Be sure you've installed the

Address Book component of Word so that the Address Book button will appear. The Select Name dialog box shows you the contents of each of your defined address books (which could include the Microsoft Exchange Personal Address Book, multiple contact folders, and others) from which you can pick a record. To change the address book that's being used for your addresses, choose an address book from the Show Names from The drop-down list.

NOTE If you're using Corporate Mode in Outlook and you choose to view the contents of one of your contact folders, notice that the dialog box enables you to choose the Mailing, Home, or Other address from a contact's record.

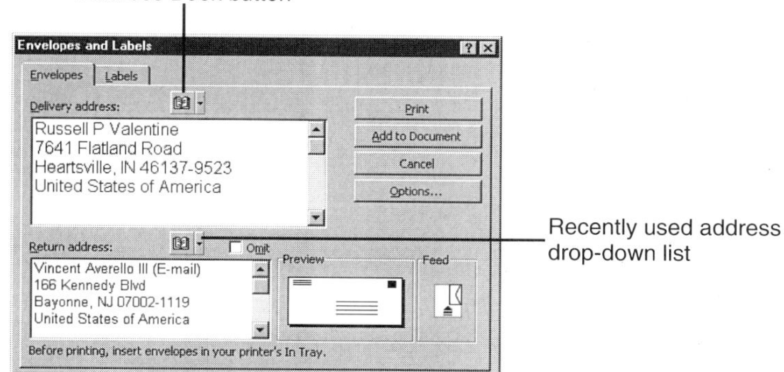

FIGURE 57.1
The Envelope Wizard enables you to print an envelope containing Outlook contact data quickly and easily.

5. Repeat the same action for the Return Address field. You can also click the drop-down arrow next to the Address Book icon to display a list of recently used addresses for you to choose.
6. Click the Options button to verify the settings for the envelope. These include size, font, address placement, and postal bar code options. Click OK to close the Envelope Options dialog box.
7. Click the Print button to output the formatted envelope to your printer.

NOTE If you've entered (or chosen) a return address different from the default return address, the Office Assistant queries you about saving it as the new default return address at this point. Default return address information is listed in Word (choose Tools, Options, User Information tab).

Creating Envelopes for Mass Mailings

You can also use the Envelope Wizard to create multiple envelopes. This use of the Envelope Wizard can come in handy if you're trying to send out mass mailings of any sort (advertisements, invoices, holiday cards). This is a nice complement to Word's mail-merge features, which enable you to quickly produce letters for mass mailings.

▶ **See** "Advanced Mail Merge Features," **p. 509**

To use the Envelope Wizard:

1. Start the Envelope Wizard as described earlier in "Addressing Envelopes Using Outlook Contacts."
2. Click the Create Envelopes for a Mailing List option in the wizard's welcome message. The Mail Merge Helper dialog box appears as shown in Figure 57.2.

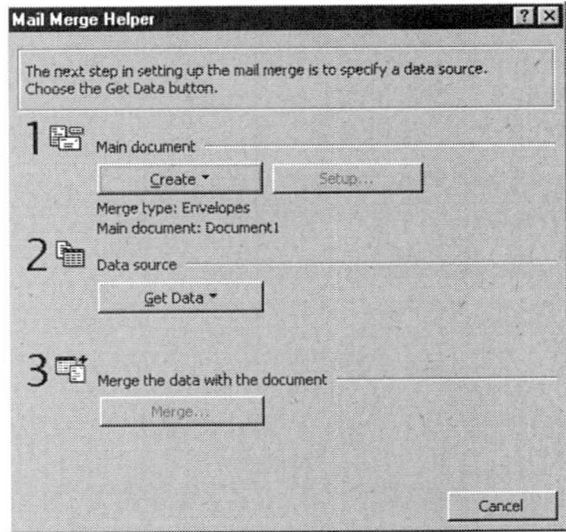

FIGURE 57.2
The Mail Merge Helper dialog box details all the steps needed to create a batch of envelopes.

3. Click the Get Data button and choose the Use Address Book option.
4. In the Use Address Book dialog box, choose Outlook Address Book.
5. Click the Set Up Main Document button when Word prompts you about the need to set up the envelope layout.
6. Set the envelope size and fonts in the Envelope Options dialog box. Click OK to save the options and display the Envelope Address dialog box, as shown in Figure 57.3.

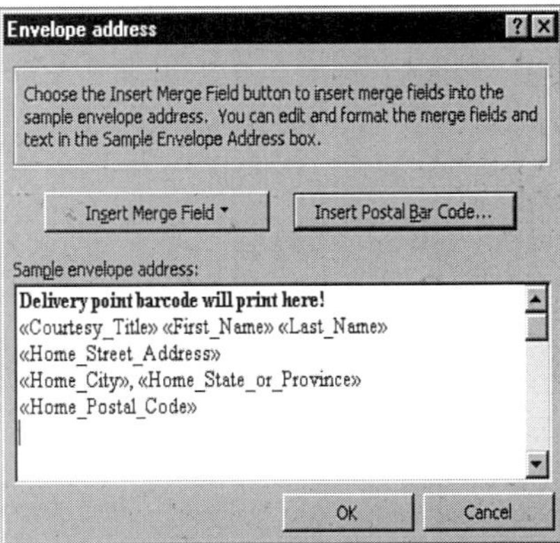

FIGURE 57.3
The Envelope Address dialog box enables you to lay out the recipient address to your liking.

7. Use the Insert Merge Field drop-down list to place markers for Outlook contact fields into the Sample Envelope Address field. Be sure to include proper punctuation

(including commas and spaces) between the field markers or the fields will be placed immediately next to each other, which is most likely not the result you want.

8. Click the Insert Postal Bar Code button to add a PostNet bar code to your label. You'll need to enter the zip code and street address field codes you're using into the Insert Postal Bar Code dialog box that appears. Click the OK button to close the dialog box and insert the bar code. The text `Delivery point barcode will print here!` appears.

NOTE You can use Postal Bar Codes (also known as PostNet Bar Codes) for any addresses in the United States for which you know the zip code. The bar code speeds the delivery of the item because a significant part of the address can be read by a machine so that the item is sorted automatically.

9. After you finish editing the sample, click the OK button to save the layout.
10. The Mail Merge dialog box (shown in Figure 57.3) appears again. Click the Merge button to display the Merge dialog box. You can narrow the number of contacts used in the merge (for example, filtering contacts based on state or Company Name) and set other options here. Click the Merge button to complete the process.

Importing and Exporting Whole Folders

Some of your data-sharing needs might fall outside the realm of simple Word data merges. For these needs, you can make use of Outlook's full-featured Import and Export Wizard (IEW). This wizard enables you to

- Export to The Timex Data Link Watch
- Export to a File
- Import Internet Mail Account Settings
- Import Internet Mail and Addresses
- Import from Another Program or File
- Import a vCalendar File
- Import a vCARD File

In this chapter, you learn about the Export to File and the Import from Another Program or File features of the wizard.

Exporting Outlook Folders to Files

While working with the Office suite, you might need to use your Outlook data in another program—such as generating a sales report in Excel or creating an Access database containing your contacts. You might also want to send the contents of one of your Outlook folders to another user. This is exactly where the IEW comes into play. You can export data directly to a file that can be used or imported by another application (see Figure 57.4).

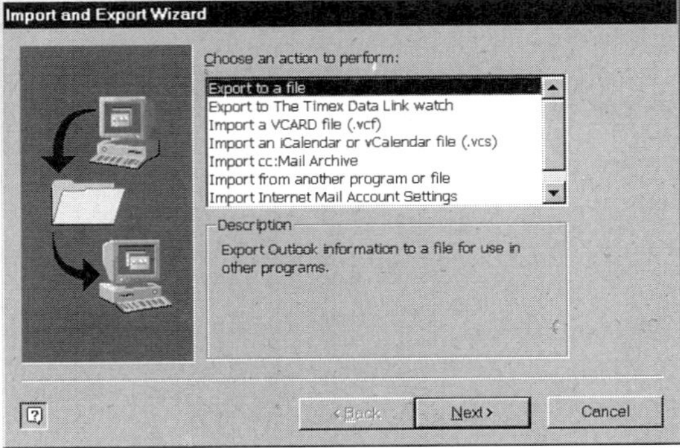

FIGURE 57.4
The Import and Export Wizard provides an easy way to get data into and out of Outlook.

To Export an Outlook folder, follow these steps:

1. To start the Import and Export Wizard (IEW), choose File, Import and Export. The Import and Export Wizard dialog box appears, as shown in Figure 57.4.
2. In the Choose an Action to Perform list, select Export to a File and click the Next button.
3. A list of possible file types appears, as shown in Figure 57.5. Pick an export file type and click the Next button.

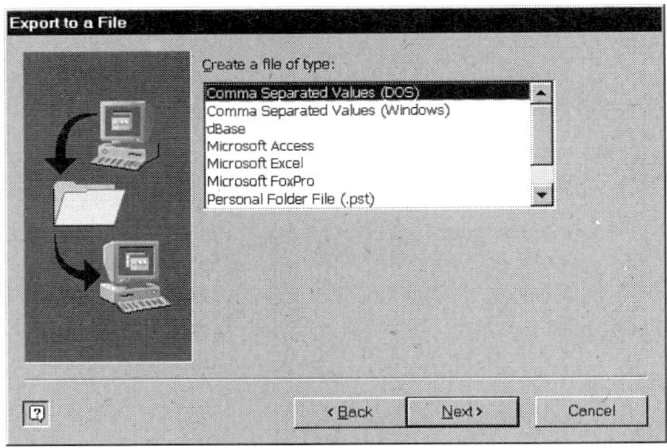

FIGURE 57.5
The Export to a File dialog box shows a list of exportable file types.

NOTE Some of the export file types displayed make their targets obvious (Microsoft Access, Microsoft Excel, dBASE, and Microsoft FoxPro). Others might require a little explanation. The comma-separated and tab-separated types are text files where each line of the file is a record and each field on a line is separated by a particular character (either a comma or a tab). The Personal Folder File type is the format used by Outlook to store its data when used without an Exchange Server. It's best used for moving folders of data from one Outlook installation to another or when backing up your Outlook email, contacts, and so on (something we highly recommend).

4. Choose the folder you want to export from the tree view, as shown in Figure 57.6. Then click the Next button. In this case, Inbox is selected. Of course, if you want to back up your Outlook data or copy it to a disk to install on another machine, you'll want to select Personal Folders, which backs up all your Outlook items.

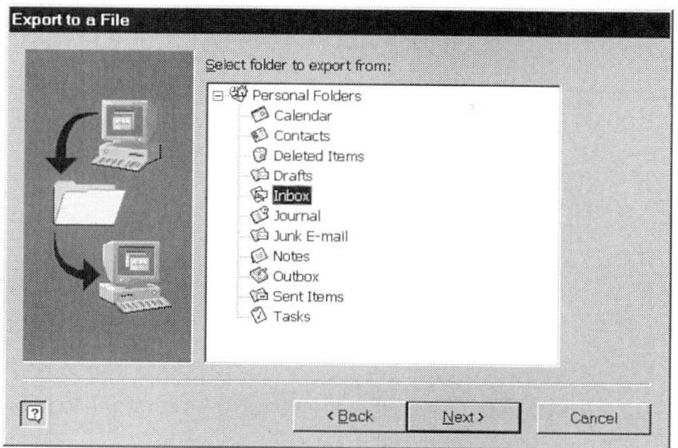

FIGURE 57.6
You can use the Outlook folder navigator to quickly choose a source from any of your connected message stores.

5. Either type a filename or click the Browse button to navigate to the location you want to use for your export file, and then enter its name. Click the Next button.
6. Click the Finish button to complete the export process.

The final dialog box in the wizard gives you the opportunity to either finish the process or set up a data map for the export to follow. A map is a list of the fields you want to export and what you want the fields to be named in the export file. You can access the field-mapping dialog box by clicking the Map Custom Fields button. The Map Custom Field dialog box enables you to drag and drop fields from the full list of available fields onto a list of fields to be exported.

In addition to exporting to files, the Import and Export Wizard can also export your schedule and contacts to a Timex Data Link watch.

Importing Data into Outlook Folders

So far, we've examined ways of getting data out of Outlook to use in other places. The day might come when someone gives you a file that needs to be brought into Outlook (possibly some names and addresses or other useful information). Outlook data sharing isn't a one-way street. Outlook can import from a variety of sources, including the following:

- Symantec ACT! 2.0 and 3.0
- NetManage ECCO 2.0, 3.0, and 4.0
- Lotus Organizer 1.0, 1.1, 2.1, 97
- Microsoft Access
- Microsoft Excel
- Microsoft FoxPro
- Microsoft Mail
- Microsoft Exchange Personal Address Book
- Microsoft Exchange Personal Folder File
- Microsoft Schedule Plus 1.0 and 7.0
- Starfish Sidekick 2.0 and 95

- dBASE
- Comma- and Tab-Separated Values Files

The import process is similar to the export process:

1. Start the Import and Export Wizard by choosing File, Import and Export.
2. Choose Import from Another Program or File and click the Next button.
3. Choose a file type or program from which to import and click the Next button.

NOTE You may notice that Outlook can import from more formats than it can export. Most of the additional formats are there to assist in migrating from other Personal Information Management (PIM) programs (Symantec's ACT!, Starfish's Sidekick, NetManage's ECCO, Lotus' Organizer, and Microsoft's own Schedule+). Some of these import filters (ECCO and Organizer) require that the program you're importing from still be installed correctly to perform the data import.

4. Either type a filename or click the Browse button to navigate to the file you want to use for your import. You can also choose how to deal with duplicate items. Outlook can normally detect duplicates successfully only if the data is being imported from a Personal Folder file (and not perfectly even then). Click the Next button.

NOTE Duplicate detection depends on the internal ID that each item gets when it's in a MAPI message store (such as a Personal Folder file). The biggest problem is that the ID changes when you export data from one Personal Folder file to another, which makes duplicate detection difficult.

5. Choose the folder into which you want to import the data from the tree view shown and click the Next button.
6. The final dialog box in the wizard gives you the opportunity to either finish the process or set up a data "map" for the import to follow.

▶ **See** "Importing Data into Outlook Folders," **p. 1543**

If you have trouble importing data, try this trick: Create a folder in Outlook of the same type you're trying to import. Add a single record to that folder, and then export it to a file using the same format you're trying to import. Open the file you just exported in a text editor to see what (and how) Outlook has exported the data. Use that knowledge to modify your import file.

Importing and Exporting Single Items via the Personal Data Interchange (PDI) Format Standard

Using the IEW might seem like a lot of work if all you want to do is send a single contact or appointment to another user. Also, you may want to share one of those records with a user of another PIM (Personal Information Manager) or mail program (such as the Netscape product line). Outlook 2000 provides the capability to save contacts and appointments in an Internet standard format. The formats are called *vCard* for contact information and *vCalendar* for appointment information. They're also known collectively as the *Personal Data Interchange (PDI) standard.*

TIP You can find detailed specifications for the PDI data formats at the Internet Mail Consortium Web site:

```
http://www.imc.org/pdi
```

Exporting Items in the PDI Format

Outlook supports the export of single items in PDI file formats directly from the contact and appointment data forms. This makes it very easy to utilize this increasingly important cross-platform format.

NOTE You might want to create a contact record for yourself so that you can make your own vCard. You can then use it as you might use a business card (for example, attach it to email items).

To export single items, follow these steps:

1. Open a contact or appointment record.
2. Choose File, Save As.
3. Change the Save As Type entry to either vCard Files or vCalendar Format (based on which item type you're trying to save).
4. Type a filename in the File Name field and click the Save button.

Importing Items in the PDI Format

As easy as saving items in PDI format is, importing them is even easier; it's little more than a point-and-click operation.

1. Double-click a file with either a . vcf (vCard) or .vcs (vCalendar) extension in either My Computer or Windows Explorer. If you receive the item in a mail message, open the mail message, right-click the item, and choose Open.
2. After the contact or appointment form opens, choose File, Copy to Folder.
3. Choose the folder into which you want to save the item from the tree view shown and click the OK button.

Synchronizing Outlook Installations Without an Exchange Server

Many users have a computer at home that they want to keep in sync with their office computers. One of the most-requested features since the release of Outlook 97 has been the capability to synchronize folders between two machines without the use of an Exchange Server. Microsoft has finally answered those pleas in Outlook 2000. It's a two-phase process by which you save a synchronization file on one machine and open it on the other machine. Because it's a file-based method, you don't need to have both machines connected to each other or to the same LAN. You can move the synchronization files around in a number of methods (mail message, floppy disk, zip disk, and so on).

Saving a Synchronization File

Outlook uses files to maintain synchronized data across multiple machines. The file contains the data that has changed on this machine since the last synchronization file creation.

To save a synchronization file, use these steps:

1. Choose Tools, Synchronize Other Computer. Then choose Save File. The Save Synchronization File dialog box appears.
2. Click the New button. The Synchronize Other Computer dialog box appears, as shown in Figure 57.7.
3. Enter a name for the machine you're using and a name for the destination computer; check the folders you want synchronized. These settings will be remembered for future synchronizations between these two machines. Click the OK button.

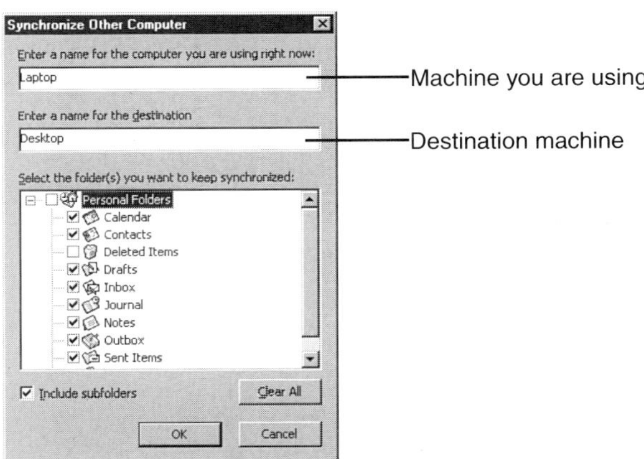

FIGURE 57.7
The Synchronize Other Computer dialog box enables you to synchronize Outlook data across multiple computers.

4. The Save Synchronization File dialog box appears. If you're satisfied with the filename chosen for the synchronization file, click the OK button. Otherwise, you can change the filename by typing a new name or by clicking the Browse button and using the Select a Folder or Existing File to Save In dialog box to pick a name.
5. Watch the Synchronizing Folders dialog box. It counts down the amount of time needed to write the synchronization file. Click the Details button to see more information about the process. When the file is completely written, click the Close button.

Opening a Synchronization File

To open the synchronization file on the destination machine, follow these steps:

1. Choose Tools, Synchronize Other Computer. Then choose Open File. The Open Synchronization File dialog box appears (see Figure 57.8).

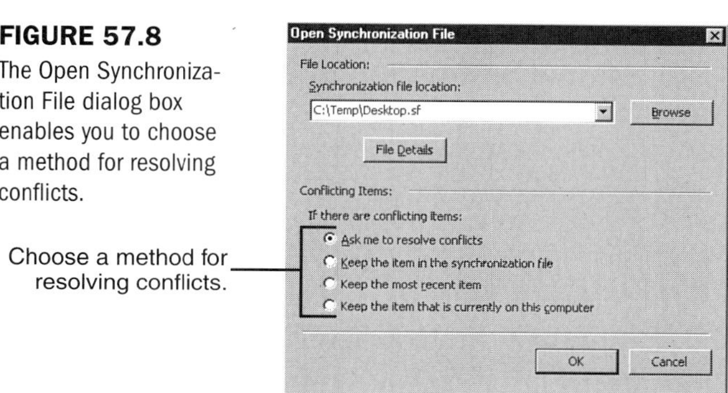

FIGURE 57.8
The Open Synchronization File dialog box enables you to choose a method for resolving conflicts.

2. Pick a method to deal with item conflicts.
3. If you're satisfied with the filename chosen for the synchronization file, click the OK button. Otherwise, you can change the filename by typing a new name or by clicking the Browse button and using the File Selection dialog box to select a name.
4. Watch the Synchronizing Folders dialog box. It counts down the amount of time needed to write the synchronization file. Click the Details button to see more information about the process. After the file is completely written, click the Close button.

PART VIII

Microsoft FrontPage

CHAPTER 58

Web Page Development

In this chapter

Developing Web Pages

With the introduction of Office 2000, Microsoft has come a long way in realizing its vision for the future of Web-site development and the internetwork.

You now can create Web pages by using virtually the same Web-integrated interface throughout the Office 2000 suite. The integration of applications in the suite—and their integration with the Web—is so strong that you can easily save Office documents into FrontPage Web sites, and share and collaborate information using browsers.

You can create Web pages in FrontPage just as easily as you create other Office documents and never even look at the HTML. You can create Web pages in Word and the other applications just as easily, and import them into your Web site.

For all but the simplest of formats, you can expect visual anomalies between application-generated HTML files and their actual interpretation and display through a browser.

For a good overview of W3C HTML compatibility issues, see `http://www.Webreference.com/dev/html4nsie/standards.html`.

The primary benefit of FrontPage is its WYSIWYG interface (Page view) for automating the development of sophisticated HTML documents—Web pages—and its Web-management tools for structuring and managing collections of pages into Web sites. FrontPage organizes all these documents and objects and provides additional programmability for packaging and delivering (publishing) Web sites to any type of Web server: Internet, intranet, or extranet. FrontPage also provides reports and tools for testing and exposing errors in your pages before you publish them. The fundamental tools for building Web pages are covered in this chapter, as are the following new features in FrontPage 2000:

- Integrated Editor and Explorer interface—No more switching views to manage and edit Web pages. Folders and Page views can be displayed simultaneously.
- Multiple Web sessions—Manage several sites at once. FrontPage opens a new window for each Web site and you can and drag and drop files among them.
- Compatibilities feature—You can more accurately design your site for specific browsers and versions, and include only features that you know will work.
- Reveal tags—See HTML tags and comments in WYSIWYG, as in Dreamweaver.
- Background spell checking—Just as in Word.
- Integrated theme designer and many new themes—More than 60 new themes provide instant designs throughout your Web site, or as a starting point for creating your own.
- Sitewide Cascading Style Sheets (CSS)—FrontPage now supports using style sheets applied to your entire Web site.
- Comprehensive Web reports—Run reports listing important Web-site information, such as slow pages, broken links, and recent files.

More advanced features for inserting pictures, video, forms, components, and databases into your Web pages are covered in Chapters 59, "Working with Images and Videos," and 60, "Creating Advanced Pages," of this book. Thorough information on "Creating, Publishing, and Managing Web Sites" and Office collaboration with FrontPage 2000 can be found on the CD.

Designing a Web site is more than adding pretty pictures to text scanned from a corporate brochure. The Web is a communications media all its own, with its own nuances and idiosyncrasies. These tools and their capabilities are powerful, and their implementation can be esoteric and complex. It can also be simple: A Wizard and templates for pages, frames, forms, style sheets, and Themes help you get started quickly and easily.

Hypertext Markup Language (HTML)

FrontPage automatically creates HTML code when you insert and format objects on a Web page in the WYSIWYG editor. You could use FrontPage as an HTML editor, but that would be missing the point: By using FrontPage, you really can create Web pages without ever knowing any more about HTTP and HTML than how to enter the URL address for a hyperlink.

Although you don't have to know HTML to develop Web pages with FrontPage, knowing the basics of HTML is essential for deciphering and troubleshooting your pages. Many excellent resources are available in print and on the Web that provide introductions to beginning and advanced HTML, as well as related scripts and languages such as DHTML, JavaScript, VBScript, XML, SQL, ASP, and other scripts that describe a page and its events (`www.hotwired.com`, `www.zndet.com`, and The Mining Company provide many overviews, tutorials, and examples, for starters). For the aficionado, there are many more resources for exploring the secrets of the evolution and future of HTML.

The quickest way to learn the page description language of HTML is by examining an HTML file:

```
<HTML>
<HEAD>
<meta http-equiv="Content-Language" content="en-us">
<meta http-equiv="Content-Type" content="text/html; charset=windows-1252">
<meta name="GENERATOR" content="Microsoft FrontPage 4.0">
<meta name="ProgId" content="FrontPage.Editor.Document">
<meta http-equiv="Description" content="This is an example HTML document with
➥metatags.">
<meta http-equiv="Keywords" content="HTML, example, metatags, metacontent">
<TITLE>Example HTML Document</TITLE>
<style fprolloverstyle>A:hover {color: red; font-weight: bold}
</style>
<bgsound src="indigo.wav" loop="3">
</HEAD>
<body bgcolor="#008000" link="#800000" alink="#FF00FF" topmargin="1"
➥leftmargin="1">
<p>"If you understand, things are as they are. If you don't understand, things
➥are as they are."</p>
<p>"If you understand, things are as they are.
If you don't understand, things are as they are."</p>
<p>"If you understand, <br>
things are as they are. <br>
If you don't understand, <br>
```

continues

continued

```
things are as they are." </p>
</BODY>
</HTML>
```

The header of this example file includes required <HTML>, <HEAD>, <TITLE>, and <BODY> tags, as well as metatags and a style tag.

The <HTML> and </HTML> tags define the beginning and end of an HTML document. Nested inside these tags are several basic components required in every HTML file.

<HEAD> and </HEAD> tags define the document's heading information, which must include a <TITLE>, and can include optional metatags, directions for background sound, styles, and more.

Nested inside the <HEAD> tags are the <TITLE> and </TITLE> tags. The text between these tags becomes the name of your Web page and appears in the header of a browser when the page is displayed. This title is also used by search engines to index your Web page. No other information between the <HEAD> tags is displayed in a browser.

Unlike other HTML tags, metatags are used to describe the content of a page. As the sheer volume of sites and pages on the Internet and corporate intranets continues to balloon, meta information is becoming increasingly vital to organizing and finding information.

The Description and Keywords metatags are particularly useful for maintaining searchability and visibility with search engines and indexes that support metatags, such as Infoseek. They are also used in larger intranets to more meaningfully manage and control content. FrontPage also inserts its own meta content in the head when you create a page. To get started with metatags, visit one of the many free metatag resources on the Web. Based on your responses to their questions, they will write metatag code you can insert inside the <HEAD> and <TITLE> tags in your document.

Style tags define formats for the text and other objects in the body of the page. In this example, the style tag specifies a format for a mouseover color change on hyperlinked text.

Nested within the <BODY> and </BODY> tags are the HTML tags and other scripts used to describe the page to the browser. The <BODY> tag itself can take several attributes, including background color, link colors, and margins:

```
<body bgcolor="#008000" link="#800000" alink="#FF00FF">
```

HTML documents are free-flowing, that is, spaces other than a single space between characters or words, including line breaks, are ignored when the browser interprets the HTML. In the main example, you can see how the <P> and </P> paragraph tags define paragraph breaks, and the <BR> tag defines line breaks. The first line of the text displays as one line when a user sees it in a browser, as does the second line. To make the line break within a paragraph, you insert a <BR> break tag (one of the few tags without a closing tag).

By using the mouse in Page Normal view, you can choose Insert, Break to force line breaks and create blank lines. When using the keyboard to enter text, Enter automatically inserts <p> and </p> paragraph tags into the HTML, and Shift+Enter inserts a <br> break tag.

Additional spaces are inserted between characters and words by using the spacebar in Normal view, which automatically inserts the HTML code (* *) to describe a nonbreaking space, as seen in the following code, which would place five spaces (two spaces and three nonbreaking spaces) between A and B:

```
<p>A     B</p>
```

The </BODY> closes the body, and the </HTML> tag closes the document, so the browser knows when to stop interpreting the page and its contents.

Navigating FrontPage

FrontPage 2000 is simpler and more powerful than before, facilitating the easy and rapid development of Web pages while being capable of extending its facilitation of sophisticated events and interactions.

The separate Editor and Explorer of prior FrontPage versions are now integrated, and you can display Folders and Page views in one window, making it much easier to quickly create and edit pages.

The HTML editor (HTML view) finally has HTML Preservation to meet the many objections levied at previous versions. You can import existing HTML and other scripting code into a page and retain the code's original formatting without the enforced reformatting and redundancy seen in earlier versions.

NOTE FrontPage no longer requires or includes Personal Web Server. The implication is that you can run local Web sites without the server. Otherwise, you must publish to a server or install server software on your computer.

Microsoft Personal Web Server (part of the Windows NT 4.0 options pack) is the Windows 95 and Windows NT Workstation version of Microsoft's Internet Information Server. For serving data to a corporate intranet, it includes both HTTP and FTP services and supports CGI scripting and customization through ISAPI.

Personal Web Server for Windows 95 is part of the Windows NT 4.0 Option Pack and is also intended for use with Windows 95. Select it separately at the beginning of the download process for Windows NT 4.0 Option Pack. Free downloads are available on the Internet, and additional information is available at `http://www.microsoft.com/Windows/ie/pws/default.htm`.

See "Modifying How the FrontPage Editor Displays and Reformats HTML," **p. CD147**

The Standard toolbar is a familiar component. The available text styles, fonts, and formats are shared throughout the Office system. You can edit, change views, change toolbars, and insert and format objects with their properties menus as you would in any other application.

Creating a new Web page is as easy as clicking the familiar New icon on the Standard toolbar. Just open a new page and the page appears in Page Normal view with the cursor ready to accept your commands. Type some text. Format the text. Insert a picture. Save as a filename. A new Web page is born.

Normal View

The WYSIWYG editor that is in Normal view (see Figure 58.1) accepts your text, images, objects, and directions, and FrontPage creates the HTML code seen in HTML view.

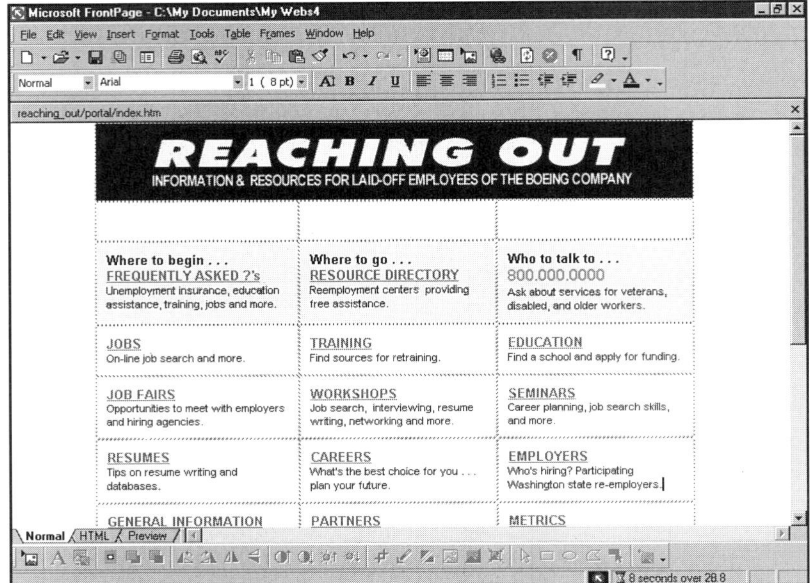

FIGURE 58.1
Create and edit your Web page in Normal view without ever seeing the HTML.

Although Normal view is more accurate than before, you can still expect variations between Normal, Preview, and the actual display of your page in a browser. Margins and spacing are still displayed slightly differently in the various browsers and their versions.

HTML View

As an HTML editor, FrontPage has never been great, but it is much improved.

Most of the menu functions insert HTML code directly into your page in both Normal and HTML view. You can insert images, components, forms, Java applets, and plug-ins directly into your HTML from the Insert menu. For example, place your cursor anywhere on a page and choose Insert, Form, Radio Button. A radio button appears in Normal view. The HTML code for a radio button is displayed in HTML view (see Figure 58.2).

The beauty of FrontPage is that you don't have to know HTML to build a page. It sure helps, however, especially when you have to decipher why your text isn't formatting correctly or your image won't appear. After editing the same page many times and reformatting in Normal view, you may find that your style tags get corrupted. If you move your pages and images around in your structure a lot, you can expect to find hyperlinks that need repair.

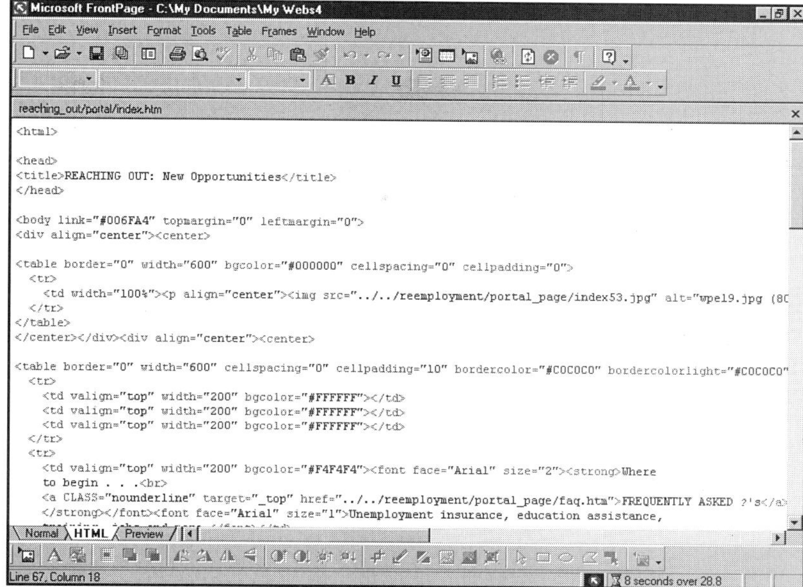

FIGURE 58.2
Use the HTML view to edit the code directly.

Although FrontPage provides a WYSIWYG editing environment that hides much of the HTML tags and structure from you, it is useful to understand the fundamentals of HTML.

To quickly find the HTML code for any object on your page, highlight the object in Normal view, and then click the HTML view tab. The code for the selected objects appears highlighted in the HTML view.

To view HTML tags in Normal view, choose View, Reveal Tags.

Preview View

The preview displays your page as it would be seen in Microsoft Internet Explorer, as seen in Figure 58.3. If you want to see how your page displays with other browsers, follow these steps:

1. Choose File, Preview in Browser. In the Preview in Browser dialog box (see Figure 58.3), select the browser you want to use to view the page.
2. Choose an alternative window size to see how your page formats for users with smaller screens.
3. Mark the Automatically Save Page check box to update your page before viewing it in an external browser.

HTML documents may not display exactly as you design them in Normal view. Users can override document formatting with their own browsers' format features. For instance, many users change the font size, which affects the text flow of your document.

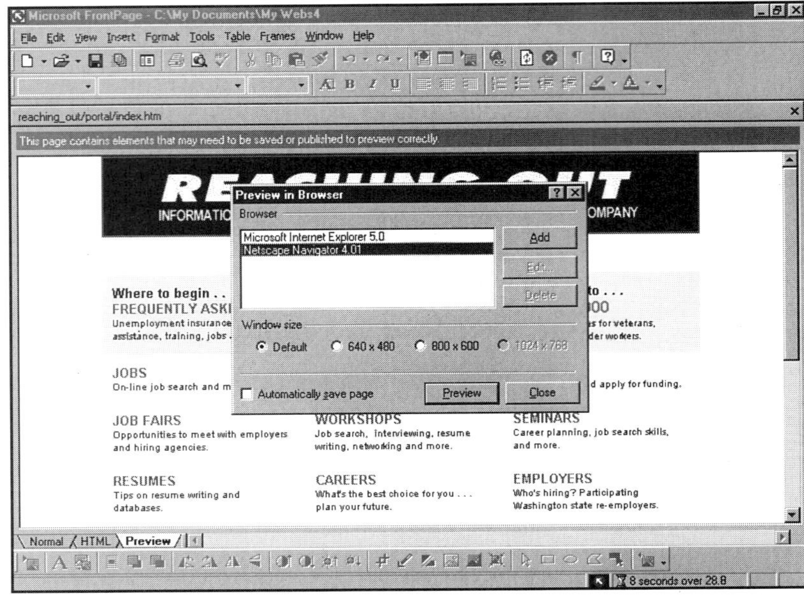

FIGURE 58.3
Preview replicates Internet Explorer 5. If you are developing for Netscape or other versions, choose File, Preview in Browser and select a browser to preview your page.

Folders, Reports, Navigation, Hyperlinks, and Tasks Managing your site is easier than ever. Folders, Reports, Navigation, Hyperlinks, and Tasks are the navigation tools and views used to create, manage, and troubleshoot the structure for your Web.

- Folders view looks and operates like Windows Explorer. Use the Folders icon to place Folders and the Editor in one integrated window making it easier to create and edit pages.
- You can manage your site more efficiently using Reports view with its 13 Web reports to help you find, diagnose, and fix potential problems.
- Navigation view helps you quickly develop a site structure and automate the development of menus (see the upcoming sidebar).
- Hyperlinks provide a visual reference for understanding the relationships of pages and links in your Web site.
- In each of these views, you can add tasks to files and assign these tasks to members of a workgroup. You can also create new tasks by choosing Edit, Tasks. The Task dialog box enables you to name, assign, describe, and prioritize a task. A log of tasks is managed in Tasks view.

Using Navigation View to Structure Your Web

Plan your Web site's navigational structure before you begin. Design a structure of links for users to find and access your pages quickly and efficiently.

By using Navigation view, you can build Web pages and their relationships in a graphical interface. Drag pages into the Navigation view from the Folder list, or create new pages directly in the view.

1. To create a new page, click the New Page button on the Standard toolbar.
2. FrontPage adds an icon for the new page to the Navigation view.
3. When the icon displays, click the page name twice to enter a new name.
4. Drag the icon to its location in your structure.
5. Add additional pages and arrange them.

Take a top-down approach when building your navigational structure. Start with the home page and use it as your main navigational page to the first level pages of your Web site. Use the main organizational units of your information as the first-level pages within your Web site. Then build out your site from there. When complete, every page in your Web site should be represented.

To apply this navigational layout to your pages, add a Top- or Left-Shared Border to every page, and insert the Navigation Bar component into the shared border. Used together, the Navigation view, Navigation Bar Component, and Shared Borders make a powerful combination to build and maintain the structure of your Web site.

▶ **See** "Navigation View," **p. CD139**

▶ **See** "Using Shared Borders," **p. 1580**

Before you implement a new navigational layout over an existing site, make a copy or backup of your current Web site, in case your changes create a Web site beyond repair.

For an easy backup, use FrontPage to Publish your Web to a local disk folder.

▶ **See** "Publishing Web Sites," **p. CD159**

Creating New Web Pages

FrontPage gives programmers and nonprogrammers an environment for rapidly developing Web pages that can be as simple or sophisticated as necessary. There are three fundamental ways to create pages in your FrontPage Web:

- Create a new page using the New Page icon on the Standard toolbar.
- Create a page with a wizard or template by choosing File, New, Page from the menu bar.
- Import files in Folders view.

New pages are handled the same as other documents in Office. You create a new page, do something to it, and save it as a name somewhere. There is really nothing new or different here other than the capability to create and save files with Web compatible extensions:

- .htm, .html, .shtml, .shtm, .scm, and .asp for Web pages
- .tm for FrontPage Templates
- .asp for Active Server Pages

- .htt for Hypertext Templates
- .css for Cascading Style Sheets

The default page extension is .htm. The other extensions are required to enable the functions of their pages.

Structuring pages using tables and frames, and the newer technologies for shared borders and themes are discussed in-depth later in this chapter.

Creating Pages Using the Wizard and Templates

Choose File, New, Page to view the New dialog box containing the Form Page Wizard and templates. A preview box in the dialog box helps you determine which type of Web page or form page to create.

Use the Frames Pages tab to select from various layouts using frames. The Style Sheets tab provides a variety of formats for applying Cascading Style Sheets to pages.

- The General Tab—Use this tab for creating pages and form pages. The Form Page Wizard walks you through the process of creating a form page. The available templates use tables to lay out the page. Separate template pages for Feedback, Confirmation, Guest Book, Search, and User Registration are provided. These templates for form pages and the Table of Contents include instructions for customizing the template in Page Normal view. Customize the template form pages to meet the needs of your site.

▶ **See** "Form Page Wizard," **p. 1638**

- The Frames Pages Tab—Frames Pages are multipage layouts that tell the browser how to divide the page into separate frames, and which pages to include in those frames. Each frame also has its own properties, such as background color and image, sound, borders, and more. FrontPage provides 10 templates for creating the fundamental frames-based layouts.
- The Style Sheets Tab—Style Sheets define portable Cascading Style Sheet formats that can be applied to multiple pages for consistency and greater productivity.

Importing Pages and Other Content into Web Sites and SubWebs

If you have already developed Web pages and other content outside of FrontPage, you can import that information into your Web site. The original HTML and scripts are maintained in the HTML editor.

Choose File, Import to display the Import dialog box. You can import individual files (such as documents), images, or style sheets; or you can import entire folders or other Web sites. After you select the files or folders, you can click Modify to change the destination location where the content will be imported.

Page Properties

Page properties define the appearance and action of the page itself. Colors, margins, transitions, alternative representations, and background sound are all specified in the Pages Properties dialog box:

1. Right-click the page and select Page Properties from the shortcut menu.
2. On the General tab, enter a title, target frame, and include a sound file if desired.
3. Use the Background tab to enter the location of a Background picture, and check the watermark box if you want the image to print when the user prints the page. You can enable mouseover effects, specify default colors, or inherit properties from the settings of another page.
4. Specify top and left from the Margins tab. If you want the margins to be 0, specify 0.
5. Use the Custom tab to include additional metatags describing your content in the HTML.
6. The Language tab enables you to mark, save, and reload the page by using any of the 15 supported languages.
7. Use the Workgroup tab to coordinate development activity with a team. In the Available categories box, select the categories to which this file belongs. Use the Assigned To box, and type or select the person or workgroup to whom you want to assign the file. Change the review status of a file. Withhold a file from being published by using the Exclude This File check box.

   In addition to the visual page properties of Themes and Shared Borders discussed elsewhere in this chapter, the Page Transition property (found on the Format menu) enables a variety of PowerPoint-like page-transition effects.

For additional page customization, choose Tools, Page Options. The dialog box that appears provides tabs for specifying general defaults for tags and spelling, HTML Source, Default Font, Color Coding, Compatibility, and Auto Thumbnail for all pages in the current Web site.

Inserting and Editing Text and Other Objects in a Page

Although you can use FrontPage 2000 to build simple pages and sites, its greater potential is exploiting the many features in Internet Explorer 5.0 and its integration with Office 2000 applications for developing sophisticated, enterprise intranets and extranets. FrontPage provides an impressive set of tools for inserting and formatting pages, text, images, objects, and events to create dynamic Web pages and interactive sites for users of Internet Explorer and Netscape browsers version 4.0 and later.

Inserting and editing text in FrontPage is similar to inserting and editing text in Microsoft Word. You use the same keystrokes to insert and delete text, or to cut, copy, and paste information. FrontPage shares the familiar spelling checker with the other Office applications, complete with wavy red lines highlighting potential errors. New in FrontPage 2000 is the Thesaurus. FrontPage also provides traditional horizontal lines and the capability to add and view comments in the HTML.

A powerful new feature of FrontPage 2000 is the capability to perform find-and-replace operations on all pages in your Web site. You also can find and replace text within the HTML tags of your Web pages—a valuable tool for those authors who need to perform global changes quickly, such as changing the background color of every page in a Web site.

In addition to inserting and formatting text, lines, and comments as discussed next, you can insert pictures, sound, components, objects, and scripts, such as DHTML, JavaScript, VBScript, applets, plug-ins, ActiveX controls, and databases.

HTML provides a simple tag, <HR> (horizontal rule), to create a horizontal line or rule across the browser page. Horizontal lines are mostly used to separate sections of your page.

To insert a horizontal line, position the cursor where you want the line and choose Insert, Horizontal Line. If you want to customize the line's appearance, right-click the line and choose Horizontal Line Properties. You can adjust the width, height, color, shading, and alignment of your horizontal rules.

Comments are hidden text that is not displayed within the browser window. To see the comments, a user must view the document's HTML source. In HTML, comment text is enclosed within `<!--` and `-->` tags.

Comments are useful for differentiating sections of code within the HTML of your document, and identifying specific components. For example, to define the beginning of a menu, you might use the comment `<!-- Navigation Links Go Here -->`.

Another use of comment tags is to disable HTML that you want to leave in your file. For example, when testing new code you could enclose the old code with comment tags `<!--` *`your code here`* `-->` and insert your new code in the HTML below it. After testing, you can remove the comment tags to revive the old code.

FrontPage also provides a way to create comments that are visible in Normal view. To insert a comment in Normal view, choose Insert, Comment. Type your comment in the Comment dialog box and click OK.

To view HTML comments in your document, choose View, Reveal Tags. This applies only to comments that are made directly in the HTML or that have been imported. Comments inserted with the Insert Comments tool are always visible in Normal view.

Formatting Text

In HTML, style tags define the format for text or objects contained within the tags. Using FrontPage, you can define styles in Normal or HTML view by applying formatting to the highlighted text or object, and FrontPage writes the code for you.

When you import text from other editors into FrontPage, the text arrives with the formatting it inherited from the original authoring application, which may appear corrupted in FrontPage. It is often more productive to remove all the formatting and redefine using FrontPage rather than attempt to edit it. To remove the formatting, select the text and choose Format, Remove Formatting.

Specifying Fonts, Sizes, Styles, and Colors

In FrontPage, the Formatting toolbar works similar to Word, with familiar tools for styles, fonts, sizes, alignment, and so on. Just select the text and choose a tool from the toolbar.

In HTML, the <FONT></FONT> tags are used to specify the typeface, size, and color of the enclosed text. A typical tag is shown here:

```
<font color="#008000" size="3" face="Adelaide">your text here</font>
```

Fonts Specifying fonts is simple if you stick to the basics. It can be tricky if you want to get clever (which is why fancy fonts are usually included as images). Not all users have the same fonts installed in their systems. If the font you specify is not available on a user's system, the browser will use the default fonts specified in its preferences. Several fonts are native to most operating systems and applications, including *Arial, Courier, Times New Roman,* and *Verdana.* New technologies for embedding fonts also can be explored, although they require additional coding in your HTML. A good place to begin exploring new font technologies is at `www.hotwired.com`.

Font Size In HTML, text sizes can be absolute (defined in points) or relative. Relative sizes are based on a 7-level system, where font size 1 is the smallest (about 8-point), 3 is normal (about 12-point), and 7 represents the largest (about 36-point).

Relative font sizes also are relative to the user's preferences defined in the browser. For example, if a user specifies the use of large-size fonts (using the Display dialog box selected from the Control Panel), normal text displays larger and all other font sizes scale proportionately.

Applying Styles to Text Like Microsoft Word, you can select text and choose the Bold, Italic, or Underline toolbar buttons to change the text's appearance. The Bold effect uses the <B></B> HTML tags, Italic uses <I></I>, and Underline uses <U></U>.

Normal Text The Normal style is the basic style for all paragraph text within your document. Normal text has no tags and accepts the default styles for the page.

Many additional font properties are available in the Font dialog box. Highlight your text, right-click, and choose Font from the shortcut menu. The Font dialog box provides access to many of the Cascading Style Sheet font properties, such as Small Caps, All Caps, Superscript, and Subscript, as well as character spacing.

If you are using Cascading Style Sheets, you can modify character spacing and position using the Character Spacing property tab. Choose expanded or condensed text, and position the text above or below the baseline. Use the preview to see how your adjustments affect the text.

Font Color To adjust the color of text, highlight the text and use the Font Color tool from the Formatting toolbar. Click the tool to specify the color of the tool. Click the arrow next to the tool to choose from several options:

- Automatic (default)
- Standard colors
- Document colors
- The color picker to select from the standard "Web-safe" Windows colors, or customize your own.
- If you are using a theme, you also can choose from the theme's color scheme.

You can choose a background color for text using the Highlight Color toolbar button. Using a Highlight Color requires browser support for Cascading Style Sheets.

Using Styles from Style Sheets

The default style sheet contains the following styles for formatting text:

- Normal
- Formatted
- Address
- Headings
- Numbered List
- Bulleted List
- Directory
- Menu List
- Defined Term
- Definition

To apply a style, highlight the text to be formatted and select a style from the style list.

HTML supports a rich set of attributes for lists and FrontPage makes it easy to customize them for your documents. You can also create multilevel lists and collapsible lists that respond to mouse clicks.

Formatted Text The Formatted style marks text that should appear in a monospaced font. This formatting honors multiple spaces within text, and can be used to align columns of text. HTML uses the <PRE> and </PRE> tags to achieve the effect seen in Figure 58.4.

HTML example:

```
<body>

<pre>1   2   3</pre>
<pre>   4   5   6</pre>
<pre>       7   8   9</pre>

</body>
```

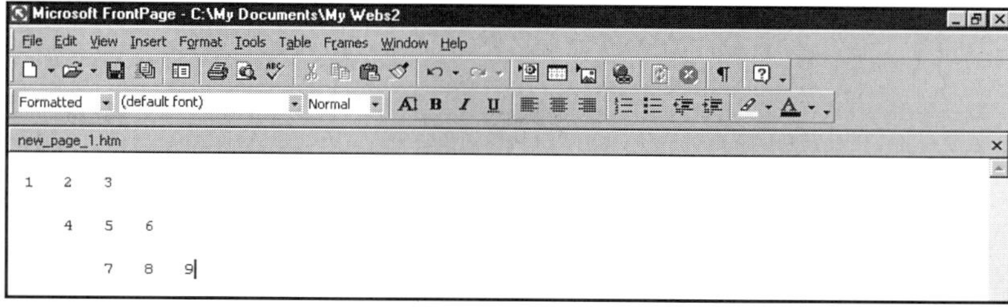

FIGURE 58.4
The Formatted style enables you to maintain monospaced formatting of characters and spaces.

Address The Address style seen in Figure 58.5 is used to identify text that defines your address information. The HTML tags for the Address style are <ADDRESS> and </ADDRESS>.

HTML example:

```
<body>

<address>
John and Mary Begonia
</address>
<address>
  1796 Elm Street
</address>
<address>
  North Little Mesa
</address>
<address>
  SD 62754
</address>
<address>
  USA
</address>

</body>
```

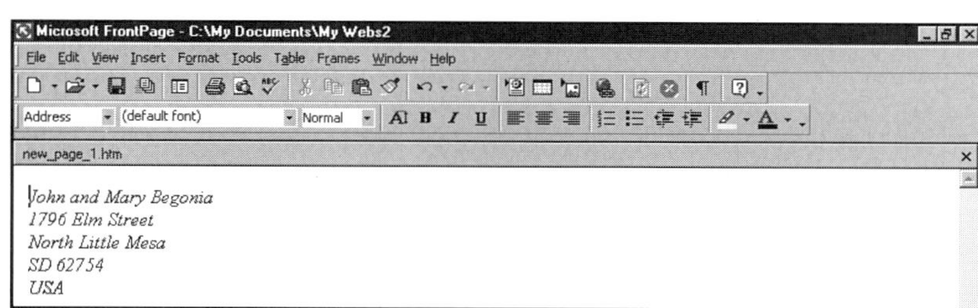

FIGURE 58.5
HTML provides a consistent convention for Address style.

Headings In HTML, there are six predefined heading levels, as seen in Figure 58.6. The first heading uses the <H1></H1> tags, the next uses <H2></H2>, and so on.

To apply a heading level, highlight the text to be formatted and choose a style from the Formatting toolbar.

HTML example:

```
<body>

<h1>Heading 1</h1>
<h2>Heading 2</h2>
<h3>Heading 3</h3>
<h4>Heading 4</h4>
<h5>Heading 5</h5>
<h6>Heading 6</h6>

</body>
```

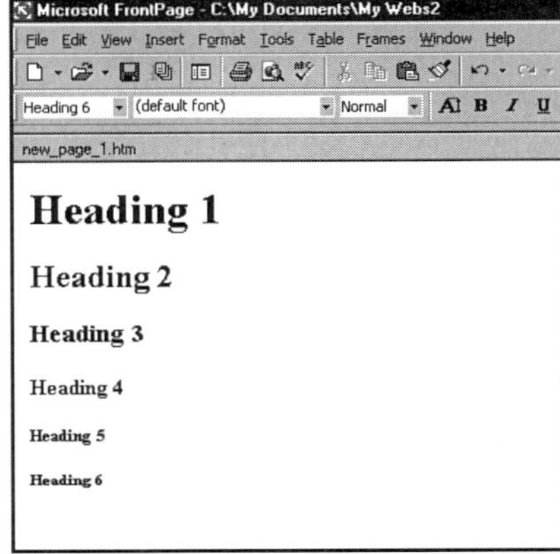

FIGURE 58.6
Six levels of headings are defined by the HTML style conventions.

Creating Numbered Lists Numbered lists begin with the <OL> tag and end with </OL>. Each list item within the numbered list is introduced by the <LI> tag. The <OL> tag can take additional attributes to change the counter appearance, such as <OL type="I"> for Roman Numerals.

To create a numbered list, enter the first item in the list and click the Numbering toolbar button. Then, press Enter at the end of each new list item. To stop the list, press Enter twice, or click the Numbering toolbar button again.

After you insert your numbered list, right-click the list in Normal view and choose List Properties to specify the type of numbering, as shown in Figure 58.7.

HTML example:

```
<body>

<ol type="I">
  <li>Apples</li>
  <li>Pears</li>
  <li>Oranges</li>
  <li>Pineapples</li>
</ol>

</body>
```

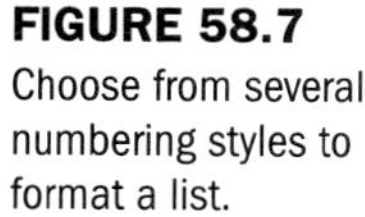

FIGURE 58.7
Choose from several numbering styles to format a list.

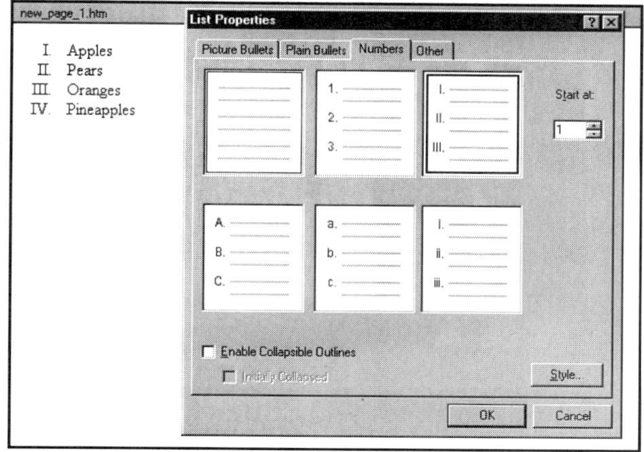

To change the number format for the specific item, right-click a list item and choose List Item Properties. You can also set the value—which is useful when you want to skip a number.

Creating Bulleted Lists To begin a bulleted list, enter the first item in the list and click the Bullets toolbar button. Then, press Enter at the end of each new list item. To stop the list, press Enter twice or click the Bullets toolbar button again.

In HTML, bulleted lists begin with the <UL> tag and end with </UL>. Like the numbered list, each item within the list is introduced by the <LI> tag. The <UL> tag can take additional attributes to change the bullet appearance, such as <UL type="square"> for square bullets, or you can define your own pictures to act as bullets.

To select a bullet style, right-click the list in Normal view and choose List Properties, as shown in Figure 58.8.

HTML example:

```
<body>

<ul>
  <li>Apples</li>
  <li>Pears</li>
  <li>Oranges</li>
  <li>Pineapples</li>
  <li> </li>
</ul>

</body>
```

To change the bullet style of an item, right-click a list item and choose List Item Properties from the shortcut menu.

Directory and Menu Lists HTML tags for Directory and Menu Lists are primarily useful for identifying types of lists within the HTML, but are rather archaic at this point. Their value has been surpassed by the many newer features for creating lists, menus, and tables of contents.

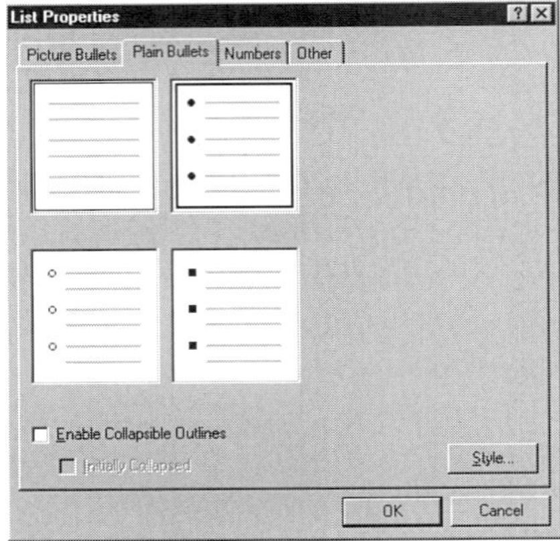

FIGURE 58.8
Choose from several bullet styles or specify an image or symbol from the Plain Bullets tab of the List Properties dialog box.

Definition Lists, Defined Terms, and Definitions A Definition List is similar to what you might see in a Glossary or Dictionary. The list is composed of individual terms and their definitions. In HTML, the <DL> and </DL> tags delimit a Definition List. The <DT> tag introduces each definition term, and the <DD> introduces the term's definition. Normally, browsers display the definition term flush left, and the accompanying definition indented below the term. If you want to add more paragraphs for a definition, use Shift+Enter to insert a line break.

Some browsers can display a Definition List in multiple columns, if the definitions are not too long. To request this behavior, right-click the list and choose List Properties. Click the Other property tab and check the Compact Layout check box.

Creating Multilevel Lists In FrontPage, you can create complex multilevel lists, complete with nested sublists using mixed bulleted and numbered styles. Wherever you want to insert a new list, nested within another, place the cursor there and type the first item of the sublist, and then click the Increase Indent toolbar button twice. Then click the appropriate toolbar button to choose numbered or bulleted list. You can also right-click the new sublist to choose a different number or bullet style.

When you have entered the last item of the sublist, press Enter twice. If you want to demote a list item to appear as a paragraph at the current or previous level, use the Decrease Indent toolbar button.

Creating Collapsible Lists Using FrontPage, you can create an interactive collapsible list that responds to mouse clicks to open and close the sublists. To create a collapsible list, first create a multilevel list as detailed in the previous section. Then, right-click an item in the list and choose List Properties from the shortcut menu. Check the Enable Collapsible Outlines check box. If you want the list to appear collapsed when it is first displayed, mark the Initially Collapsed check box. Pages with collapsible lists must be published to a Web site before you will be able to test your results.

Paragraphs and Line Breaks

HTML defines two simple tags for identifying paragraphs and forced line breaks:

- The <P> and </P> tags are used to enclose paragraphs, which browsers display with line breaks between them. When you press Enter in Normal view, FrontPage inserts these tags in the HTML.
- The <BR> tag (with no closing tag) forces a line break without an additional line space. Use Shift+Enter to enter a line break.

Paragraph properties for alignment, indenting, and spacing are controlled by selecting a paragraph and choosing Format, Paragraph. You also can right-click a paragraph and choose Paragraph from the shortcut menu to display the Paragraph Properties dialog box.

Similarly, you can change line break properties. In Normal view, select the line break, right-click, and choose Line Break Properties. You can include attributes to force the subsequent text to resume after the right, left, or both margins are clear. For example, use the clear attributes when text is juxtaposed beside an image, and you want the subsequent text to continue after the image's bottom border.

Indenting Text

To indent text as shown in Figure 58.9, position the cursor on the text and click the Increase Indent toolbar button. Alternatively, click the Decrease Indent toolbar button to shift the text back to the left.

The HTML <BLOCKQUOTE> tag indents the text, and the </BLOCKQUOTE> removes the indent. When you indent the text more than once, FrontPage nests the <BLOCKQUOTE> and </BLOCKQUOTE>.

HTML example:

```
<body>

<blockquote>
  <p><b><font face="Arial">This text has been indented once.</font></b></p>
  <blockquote>
    <p><b><font face="Arial">This text has been indented twice.</font></b></p>
    <blockquote>
      <p><b><font face="Arial">This text has been indented three times.</font></
➥b></p>
    </blockquote>
  </blockquote>
</blockquote>

</body>
```

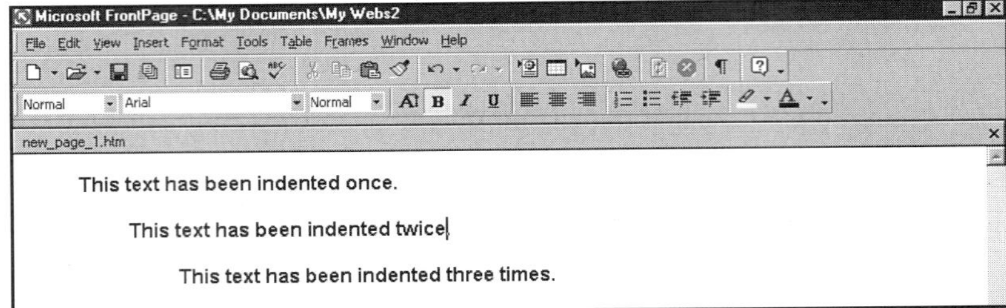

FIGURE 58.9
Refer to the HTML example to see how the <BLOCKQUOTE> and </BLOCKQUOTE> tags are nested to create indents.

Page Layout

Perhaps the most challenging and critical decision is defining a layout for your pages. Many design and compatibility factors must be considered when choosing a layout that will make your Web consistent, usable, navigable, and maintainable. You have many options from which to choose:

- Tables provide considerable flexibility for formatting pages and placing formats within the page format. They are the most universally compatible layout device, although they are not entirely compatible across browsers. Using tables, the entire page scrolls from one scrollbar. The page templates in the New Page dialog box offer many options for getting started with tables-based pages, which are the safest alternative for providing the greatest compatibility.
- Frames offer a powerful, complex, and potentially incompatible layout that enables you to include several pages within a single page. Each page has its own properties, and there are many additional properties for defining its frame. Only the currently active frame scrolls.
- Shared borders enable you to include objects, such as images, navigation bars, banners, forms, and other components within top, bottom, left, and right borders of the page, but the entire page shares the same properties and scrolls as one page. Shared Borders therefore act like cells to define areas of a page layout without using tables, and attempt to meet the many objections to frames, but are static compared to the properties available with frames.
- Style Sheets are template files that format text and objects and can be shared throughout your Web site.
- Themes are template files that provide visual formats that can be shared throughout your Web site.
- FrontPage also provides an Include Page feature that enables you to place and position another page within a page.

Users prefer a consistent layout when they browse from page to page within your site. Sites can appear complex and intimidating to new users, who will feel more comfortable if they can predict where the next link will go and what the page will look like.

Using Tables

Tables organize information into columns and rows. You can use tables to organize the layout of your entire page and insert tables within cells of other tables. Many successful Web sites, including the major search engines and portals, use tables to present a clean, professional, and organized look to their users while maintaining the maximum compatibility that can be achieved without avoiding page layout features altogether.

Creating Tables The procedures used for creating tables are similar to those in Word. You can employ various methods using the Insert Table icon on the Standard toolbar, the Table menu, or by displaying the Table toolbar.

- Use the Insert Table tool on the Standard toolbar to quickly build some rows and columns. Their sizes will be relative to the content you put in them.
- Use the Draw Table tool on the menu and toolbar to draw a cell of any size on the page.
- Convert selected text into a relative table by choosing Table, Convert, Text to Table.
- For more control, create with absolute sizing. Choose Table, Insert, Table and use the Insert Table dialog box to specify table properties for size, border, cell padding, and spacing.

In the Insert Table dialog box (see Figure 58.10), enter the number of rows and columns, and specify the width, height, and alignment of the table. You can always change these settings later.

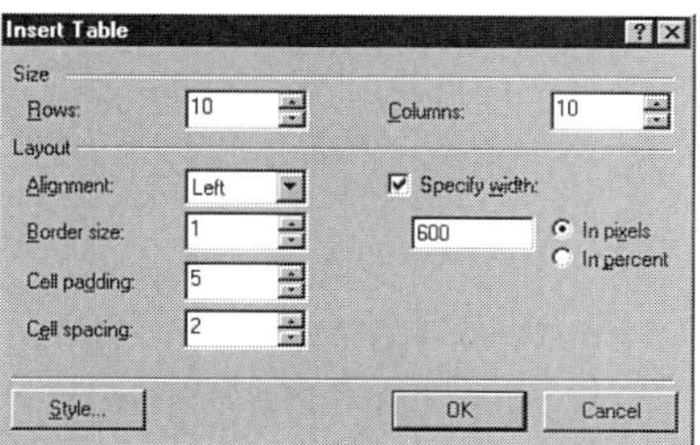

FIGURE 58.10
Use the Insert Table dialog box to insert a new table and define some of its properties.

If you want your table to have a border, specify a Border Size. Values are listed in pixels. Specify a "0" border size for no borders. The default for a new table in a new page is "1."

Use the Cell Padding value to specify the number of pixels that pad or act as a margin for the contents of each cell. The Cell Spacing value determines the distance in pixels between adjacent cells. If you are not sure what values to choose, accept the defaults. You can always change the settings later. Defaults change to the size specified in the last table you created—except for rows and columns, which always default to two each. FrontPage saves the other setting in a session for subsequent tables.

Table size can be relative or absolute. To specify the absolute width of your table, mark the Specify Width check box and enter the width. You can define the width as an absolute pixel size, or as a percentage of the current window width.

Relative size resizes the table to fit in the browser window. As a user changes the size of the browser window, the table will shrink or expand accordingly. Using the width percentage can be useful to maintain a margin around the table.

After a table has been created, you can specify additional properties by using the Tables Properties dialog box. Right-click the table and select Table Properties from the shortcut menu to specify a background color or image and border colors, as well as the other properties.

If you want text to flow around the table, right-click the table and choose Table Properties to Float the table to the right or left of adjacent text.

Editing Cell Contents To insert new text within a cell, click in the cell and type, paste, or drag and drop. You can add text, images, links, lists, and even other tables into table cells.

You can apply formatting and other styles to multiple cells at once. To select adjacent cells, click and drag over the contents of the cells. To select an entire column, move the mouse pointer to just above the column where the pointer turns into a down arrow. Click once to select the column, and drag to select adjacent columns. Similarly, you can select entire rows—move the mouse pointer to the left of the row until it changes to a right arrow. Click and drag to select more rows.

After you have selected the cells, you can apply formatting to their contents, such as font style and color, and background color. To clear contents from selected cells, press the Delete key.

Inserting Rows and Columns To insert a new row or column in your table, select an adjacent row and choose Table, Insert, Rows or Columns. Use the Insert Rows or Columns dialog box to specify the number of rows or columns to add, and where to insert them.

You can also right-click in any cell and choose Insert Row or Insert Column to quickly add a single row or column.

Alternatively, if you want to add a new row to the bottom of your table, click in the last cell on the bottom right and press the Tab key. FrontPage adds a new row automatically.

Inserting and Deleting Individual Table Cells Inserting and deleting cells is identical to an Excel worksheet. To insert a cell, click into the cell where you want a new cell to appear and choose Table, Insert, Cell. When you insert a cell, shift the cells of that row to the right.

You also can delete cells from your table, but the results can be unexpected. To delete a cell, select it and click Cut or the Delete Cell toolbar button. When you delete a cell, the cells to the right will move to the left, and you'll be left with a row that has fewer cells than the other rows in the table.

NOTE If you want to clear the cell's contents, select the data and press the Delete key. The cell remains, but the contents are removed. If you want to delete the cell, select the cell and Cut it.

Merging and Splitting Table Cells In Figure 58.11, cells have been merged to create a table with headers for the columns beneath.

To create cells that span multiple columns or rows, merge adjacent cells together. To merge cells, select them and click the Merge Cells toolbar button. If there is content in the cells, the content also is merged and separated by paragraph breaks.

You can also split cells into more cells. Select a cell, click the Split Cells toolbar button, and then choose how you want to split the cells. You must specify whether you want to split the cell into new columns or new rows.

If there is any content in the cell before the split, the content will remain in the topmost or leftmost cell after the split.

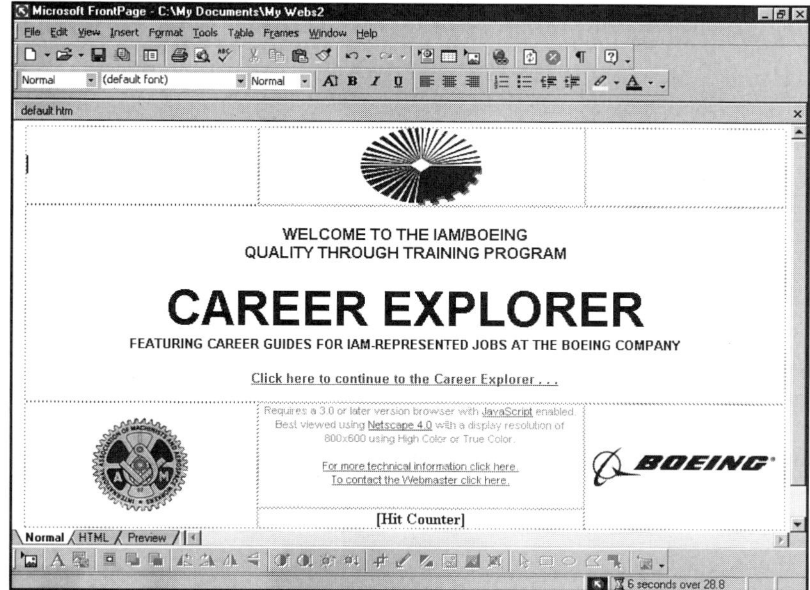

FIGURE 58.11
This example began as nine cells. Three cells in the middle were merged into one row, and the middle cell of the bottom has been split into two rows.

Adding Background Color and Images Right-click a table and choose Table Properties from the shortcut menu. In the Table Properties dialog box, you can control border and background colors, background images, and the alignment of content within the entire table and each of its cells (see Figure 58.12).

You can select a standard Background color, one from the current theme or document, or create your own.

To specify the border color of your table, the border width must be greater than zero. If you want a 3D-style, raised border, increase the width to a value higher than three and specify the light and dark border colors.

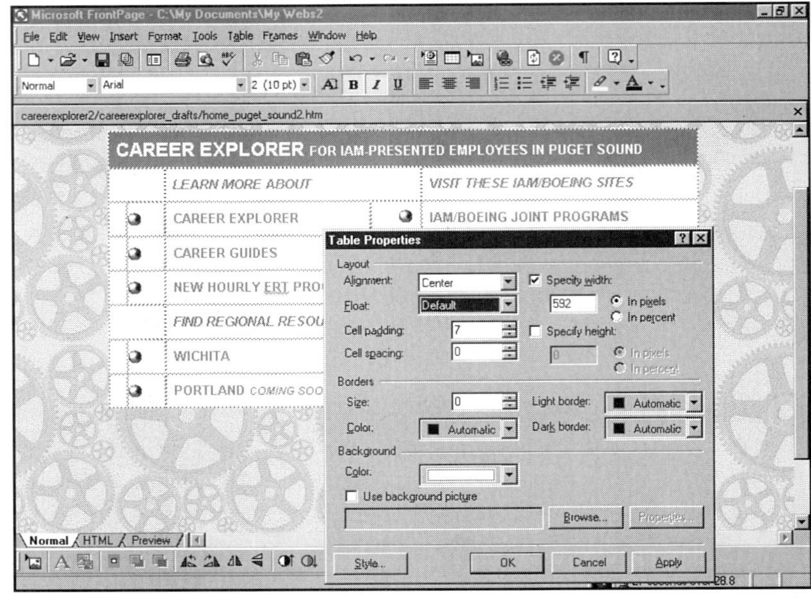

FIGURE 58.12
Use the Table Properties dialog box to control background color, image, and borders. In this figure, the background color is white and the borders are "0."

Right-click a cell or select multiple cells and choose Cell Properties (see Figure 58.13) to provide a background color or image for each cell or cells. Check the Use Background Picture check box and click Browse to locate the image to use.

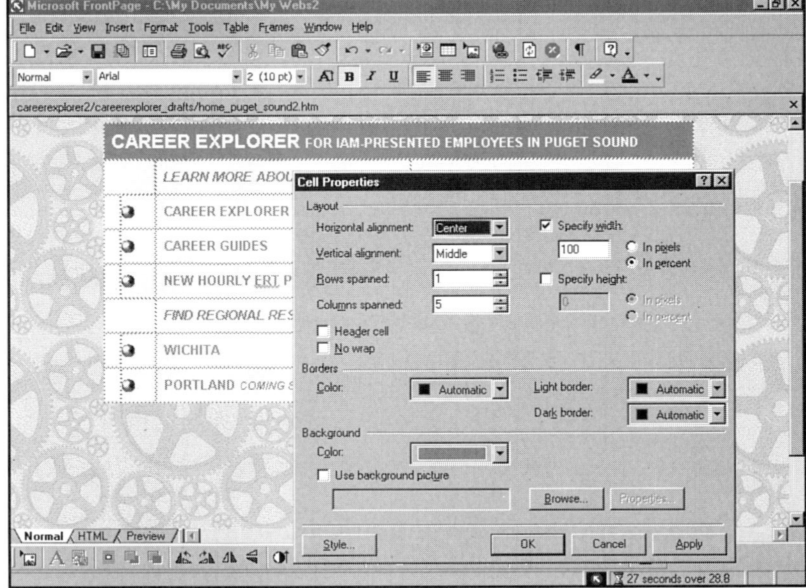

FIGURE 58.13
Use the Cell Properties dialog box to control cell color, images, and borders. In this figure, the background of the selected cell is blue.

TIP In some versions of Netscape, cells often won't display properly unless there is something in them, such as a nonbreaking space ($nbsp;).

Content Alignment in Tables and Cells You can specify how content is aligned within the entire table and within each cell. Right-click a cell and select Table Properties or Cell Properties from the shortcut menu, and then specify Horizontal Alignment and Vertical Alignment options.

Check the No Wrap check box to prevent the contents of the cell from line wrapping. If you want to declare specific cells as Header Cells, check the Header Cell check box. Browsers automatically display text in Header Cells as centered and bold.

Using Frames: The <Frameset> Tag

A Frames page is an HTML document that defines where and how pages are included in the frames page when it is displayed in the browser. Each frame within a frames page defines another page that loads in the defined frame and is displayed according to the frame's properties, including scrollbars, borders, and margins, when the frames page is displayed in the browser.

Frames have a role when you want to facilitate navigation through a Web site or application while maintaining a base context from which the user navigates. For example, in Figure 58.14, this frames page includes four navigational frames with menus for selecting links that display in the body frame that is the main focus of the page, and has a scrollbar. The surrounding frames and their menus provide a consistent context from which to navigate.

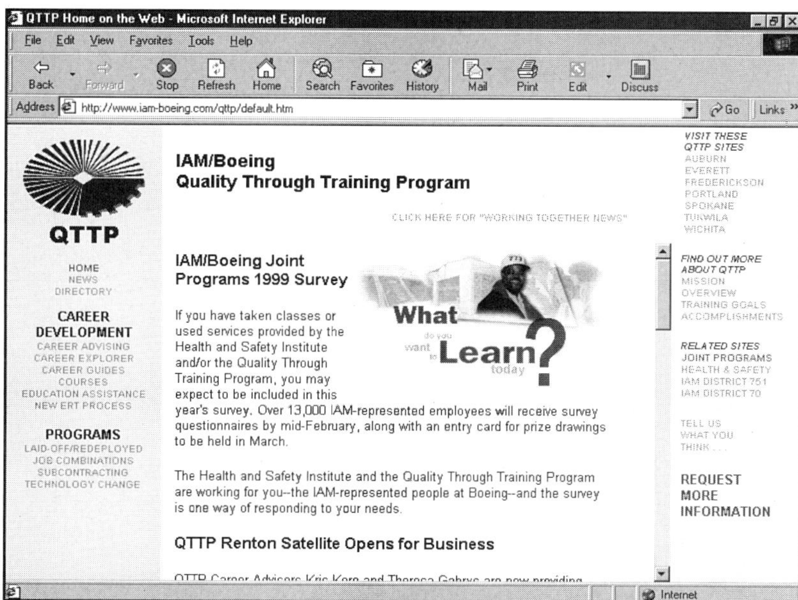

FIGURE 58.14
Use frames to divide a page into separate pages that can link to one another. In this example, the frames surrounding the larger body frame provide menus of links that display in the body.

Although frames pages can be more difficult to set up and manage, large sites can be more easily maintained. For example, if a frames page contains a page with a menu used with a hundred other frames pages, only the page with the menu needs to be updated with changes, instead of updating a menu on each of the hundred pages.

Although many programmers and designers shy away from forms as a matter of principle, forms can be employed for both greater efficiency of navigation and maintenance of a site. Even if their initial development can be more laborious, after developing just a few frames-based pages, even a novice can understand and control the forms' behavior.

Creating Frames To create a frame, choose File, New, Page and click the Frames Pages tab (see Figure 58.15). Browse through the available templates and use the preview to visualize the layout of the Frames. Find a layout that best fits your needs. If one doesn't match exactly, choose one that you can modify—you can later use tools to reshape your frames.

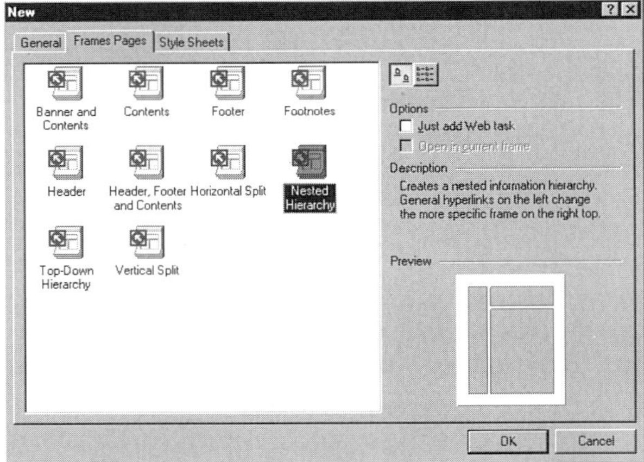

FIGURE 58.15
The Frames Pages tab shows the available templates.

When the Frames page is created from the template, FrontPage provides buttons in each frame to create a New Page or Set Initial Page from an existing page (see Figure 58.16). Also notice that when a frames page is opened, Page view displays additional tabs for No Frames and Frames Page HTML.

NOTE Browsers that don't support frames, such as Netscape Navigator 2, default to the No Frames file. Use the No Frames tab to link users to an alternative text-based version of your Web site.

When using frames pages, the HTML tab displays the code for the active frame's page. The Frames Page HTML tab displays the code for the frames page that defines the frames and their pages.

Click the New Page button to create a new blank page in the frame. Click Set Initial Page to browse for a page within your Web site. You can also use Set Initial Page to create a new page using templates.

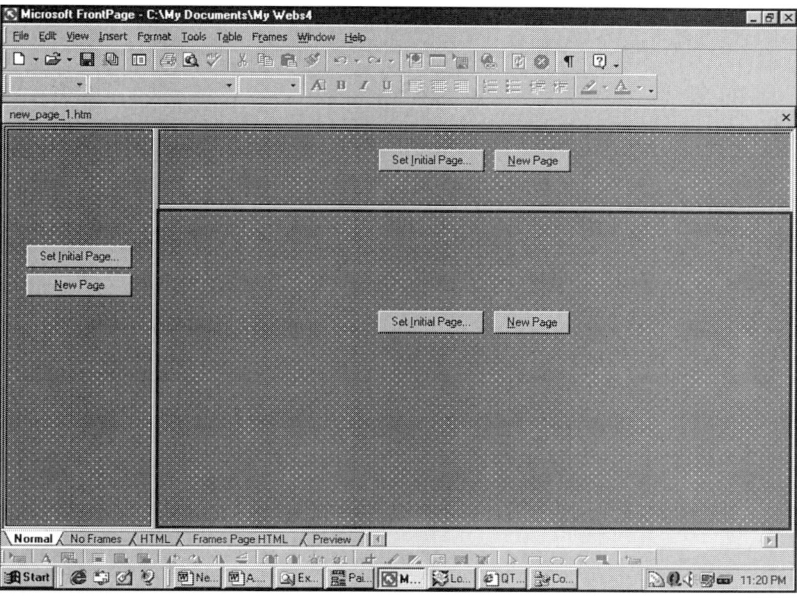

FIGURE 58.16
A frames page ready to be built.

Adjust the size of each frame by dragging the frame border. To remove a frame, select the frame and choose Frames, Delete Frame.

To create additional frames, choose Frames, Split Frame to divide a selected frame into rows or columns.

To define frame properties, right-click the frame and choose Frame Properties from the shortcut menu (see Figure 58.17).

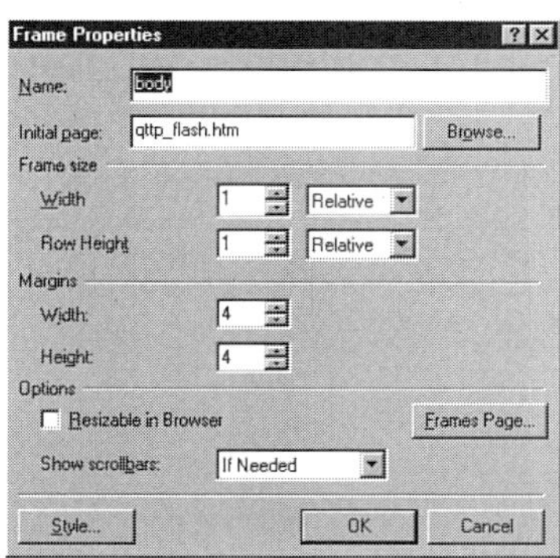

FIGURE 58.17
Use Frame Properties to define the appearance of a frame.

When defining the height and width of the frame, you can choose whether the value is a pixel size, a percentage of the browser window, or relative to the size of other frames on the page.

NOTE If other frames share the same column or row of the selected frame, adjusting the width or height of the selected frame adjusts the other frames in the column or row respectively.

You can also adjust the frame margins in pixel increments. If you want the user to be able to resize your frame, mark the Resizable in Browser check box. Additionally, you can choose whether the frame displays scrollbars only if needed, always, or never.

To edit the settings of the page that defines the set of frames, click the Frames Page button. In the Page dialog box, use the Frames tab to specify spacing between frames and whether to display borders, as shown in Figure 58.18.

TIP To make the frames in your frames page appear as one page, use the Frames Properties and Frames Page dialog boxes to define the same background color and disable the frame borders on each of the frames.

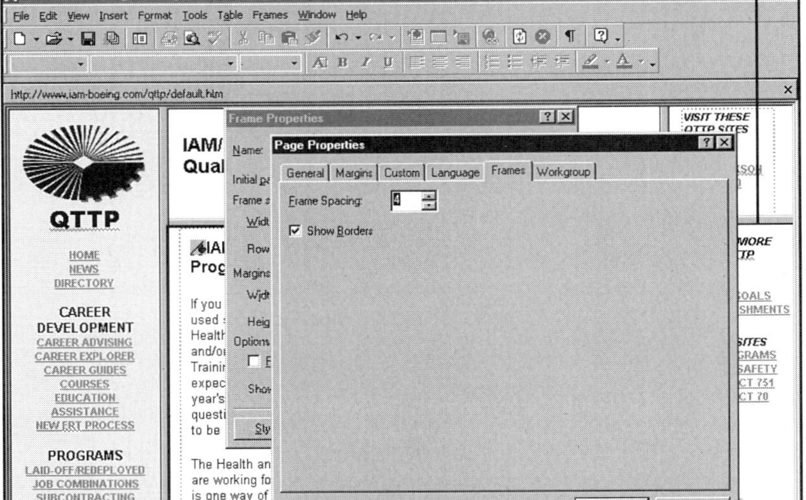

FIGURE 58.18
The spacing between frames can also be borders.

Targeting Hyperlinks to Frames When creating hyperlinks to pages in frames, specify a Target frame from the Create Hyperlink dialog box, as shown in Figure 58.19. If you do not specify a target frame for the hyperlink, the linked page loads within the frame from which it was selected.

FIGURE 58.19
Target links from frames to another frame, to refresh and display a new page in the current window, or to open a new browser window.

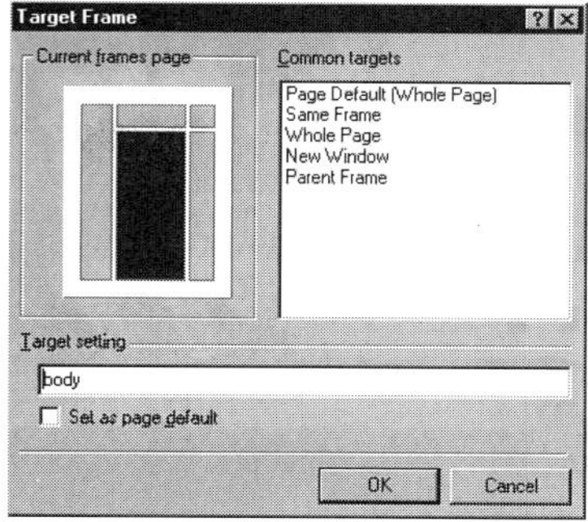

Frames and Search Indexes

Internet search engines such as Infoseek and HotBot do not index the frame content of individual frames within a frames page because the links to these pages aren't followed by search engine indexers. Only the frames page gets indexed. You must provide searchability for the content in the frames of your frames pages through the frames page. Give your frames page a title, description, and keywords that reference the content on your site's pages.

You can also take advantage of this to prevent indexing of pages in your site that do not need to be indexed. For example, if you are leading users through a stepped procedure, you want them to find the beginning of the process, not an isolated page.

You can also submit important pages to search engines individually to help assure that they get indexed. The use of metacontent can also improve your searchability.

Using Shared Borders

To solve the problems with frames and provide many of the same benefits, FrontPage provides Shared Borders. Using Shared Borders, you define the common information to appear at the top, left, right, or bottom of the page, and the Office Server Extensions add them to your pages when you save the pages to your Web site. You can place any kind of HTML information in these shared borders, including navigational buttons and banners.

Shared Borders provide an easy way to add and maintain the same content at the top, left, right or bottom of your Web pages. Shared Borders provide a powerful tool to keep a consistent layout for your Web pages, and make it a snap to maintain when you have a change to the shared content.

When you edit a page using Shared Borders, FrontPage displays the shared regions with dashed lines in Page view, as shown in Figure 58.20. You can edit the Shared Border contents as you do any other page. When you save the page, the Shared Border is saved as well, and all other pages that reference that border are updated.

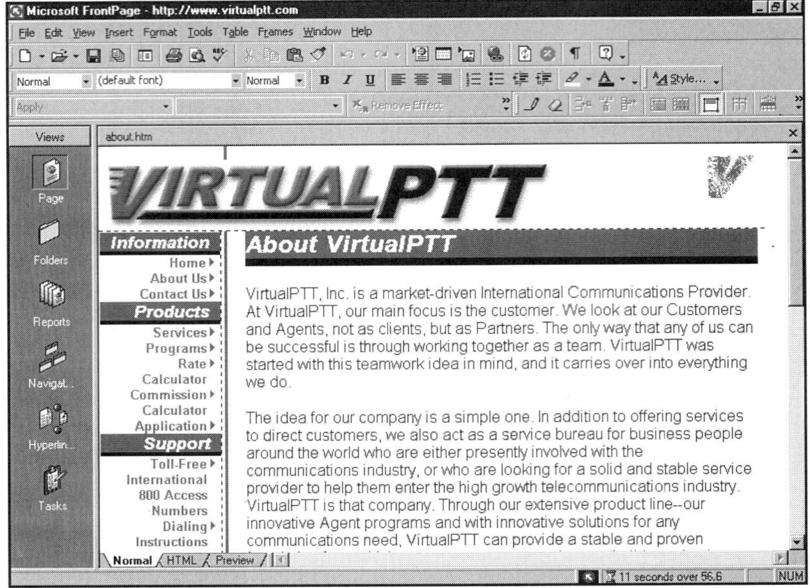

FIGURE 58.20
Use Shared Borders for an easy and powerful way to maintain the layout for your Web pages.

To accomplish this nifty feat of ingenuity, FrontPage uses the Office Server Extensions to include the content of your page and all the referenced Shared Borders into a pagewide HTML table. When you browse a page saved with Shared Borders, use the browser's View Source command to see how the Office Server Extensions performed their magic.

Shared Borders can be applied to individual pages, or to your Web site as a whole. Also, if you enable Shared Borders for your entire Web site, you can turn them off on a page-by-page basis.

To use Shared Borders, follow these steps:

1. Choose Format, Shared Borders to display the Shared Borders dialog box, as shown in Figure 58.21.
2. Click the All Pages radio button to apply the Shared Borders to your entire Web site.
3. Choose the Shared Borders you desire, such as Top, Left, Right, or Bottom. If you choose Top or Left, FrontPage can include Navigation Bars for you automatically.

▶ **See** "Using FrontPage Components," **p. 1651**

While editing a page, you can turn on or off individual Shared Borders in a similar fashion. Click the Current Page radio button and check or uncheck the borders you want to affect. If you want to restore a page to use the Shared Borders used for your entire Web site, mark the Reset Borders for Current Page to Web Default check box.

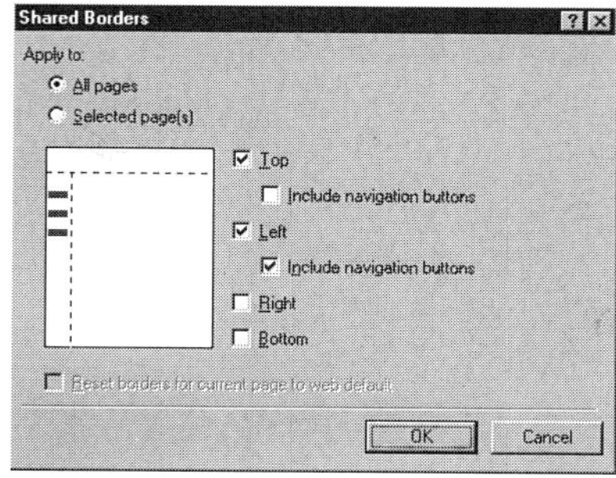

FIGURE 58.21
Choose from Top, Left, Right, or Bottom Shared Borders.

Using Style Sheets

HTML uses a specification called Cascading Style Sheets (CSS) to enable you to create and assign your own user-defined styles to document elements. In a collaborative environment, authors editing a page with a set style sheet can edit that page and then apply the new style to anything on the page.

Before you use Style Sheets, consider your Web site's audience. The first version of the CSS specification enables you to define rich formatting constructs, although the second version enables you to position elements more accurately on the page.

CSS Version 1 is supported by version 4 and later browsers, although CSS Version 2 will likely be supported only by version 5 browsers, such as Internet Explorer 5.0. Browsers that don't support CSS will default to other compatible formats, if also written in HTML, or to the browser defaults. If you are sure that your users will be able to use style sheets, choose Tools, Page Properties and click the Compatibility property sheet to enable the style sheet support within FrontPage.

FrontPage enables you to assign CSS styles to any page element. If you've wondered what those Style buttons do that you find on nearly every property dialog box, they enable you to define and assign CSS styles. You can create new styles of your own, or change the default style of standard HTML tags. For example, if you wanted all Heading Level 1 paragraphs to use bold, sans serif text, in a light color, shaded with a dark background, you can create a CSS style that applies to all H1 tags.

CSS Styles can be defined and applied to single elements within your Web page, to all like elements on the Web page, and to all like elements in your Web site. If you have the same style defined at multiple levels, the browser merges the definitions to give a composite style.

Styles Associated with a Single Element

As you edit your Web documents, you may find that you want to modify the appearance or position of an element on the page. If you know that your changes don't need to apply to other elements on the same page or the Web site, you can apply CSS-style attributes directly to the element. Styles applied to individual elements are known as *inline styles*.

To apply inline styles, you use the standard formatting dialog boxes, such as Font, Paragraph, Bullets and Numbering, Borders and Shading, and Position. Select the document element that you want to modify and select the appropriate choice from the Format menu. For example, choose Format, Font to modify the CSS text characteristics, such as capitalization and character spacing.

See "Choosing Compatibility for Your Web," **p. CD146**

Styles Embedded Within a Page

If you have styles that you want to apply to an entire Web page, create an embedded style sheet in the page. The styles you create in an embedded style sheet then become available in the Style toolbar drop-down list, so you can apply the same style to multiple elements on the same page. You can also apply your styles together with standard HTML styles to produce a combined effect.

Remember that embedded style sheets cannot be shared with other pages within your Web site. If you want to share styles with multiple pages, use an external style sheet. See "Styles Shared by Several Web Pages," later in this chapter.

Creating an Embedded Style Sheet To create an embedded style sheet, open the page in Normal view and choose Format, Style. The Style dialog box appears, as shown in Figure 58.22. In this dialog, box you can preview the available HTML styles, as well as any user-defined styles. Click the New button to create a new user-defined style.

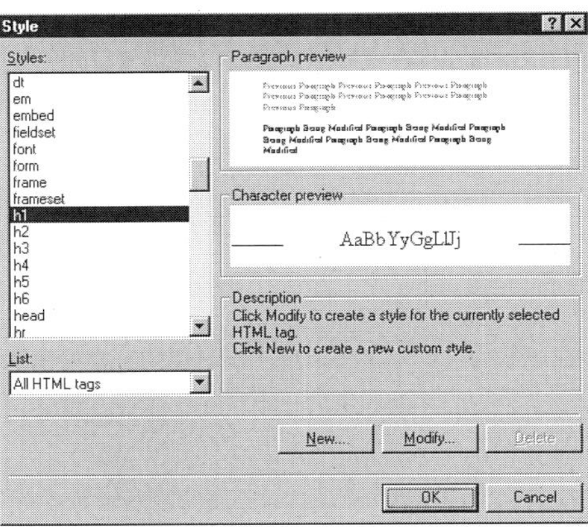

FIGURE 58.22
Use Cascading Style Sheets to change the appearance and position of your document elements.

In the New Style dialog box, as shown in Figure 58.23, type a name for your new style. Use a name that describes the style's purpose, rather than its appearance. For example, type "PressAnnouncement" rather than "ShadedWBlackBorder." This way, if you change the style's appearance later, your style name will stand the test of time.

Alternatively, you can choose one of the standard HTML styles and apply changes to it. Choose the HTML style and click Modify.

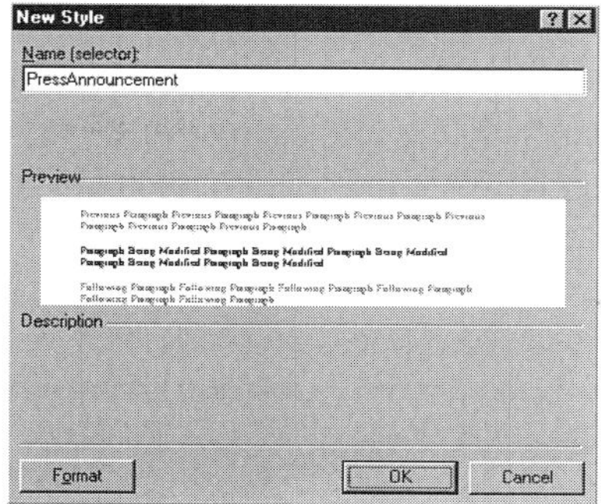

FIGURE 58.23
Name your styles for their purpose within your document.

To complete your format preferences for the style, click the Format button to reveal a menu of choices, as follows:

- Choose Font to adjust attributes associated with the text font, such as typeface, size, capitalization, superscript, and character spacing.
- Choose Paragraph to adjust the text alignment, indentation, line spacing, and word spacing.
- Choose Border to apply text borders, padding, foreground color, background shading color, and background textures.
- Choose Numbering to modify the bullet and numbering style, including picture bullets.
- Choose Position to set attributes such as text wrapping, absolute or relative positioning, and the z-order.

▶ **See** "Absolute Positioning and Layering," **p. 1616**

NOTE FrontPage enables you to include spaces in your style names, but they do not appear on their style list.

Applying Embedded Styles After you have defined your embedded styles, you can apply them to text within your Web document. Your new styles appear in the Style drop-down list on the toolbar, and are prefixed by a period. To apply one of your styles, select the text within your document and choose the Style name from the Style drop-down list.

If you want to quickly apply the style from one of your page elements to another element, use the Format Painter button on the toolbar. Select the source element, click the Format Painter toolbar button, and then select the element to which you want to apply the change. FrontPage assigns the styles to the element automatically.

To remove the effect of your style on the text, select one of the standard HTML styles, such as Normal.

Single-clicking the Format Painter button puts it only in "single-use" mode. After you paint that format once, the Format Painter turns off. Double-clicking the Format Painter makes it persistent...you can paint that format as many times as you want until you click the Format Painter again to turn it off.

Modifying Embedded Styles You can change the appearance of one of your embedded styles, or change the formatting for a standard HTML style. Choose Format, Style Figure and select the style from the list in the Styles dialog box (refer to Figure 58.22). Click Modify to display the Modify Style dialog box, as shown in Figure 58.24.

FIGURE 58.24
Modify your styles to meet changing requirements.

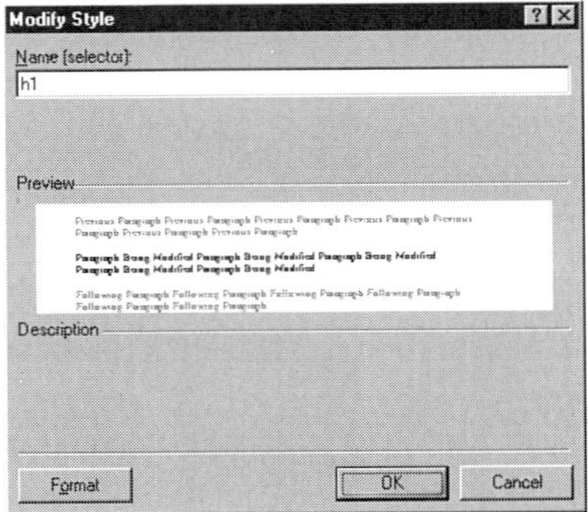

Modify the style using the same format choices as you did when you created the style (see "Creating an Embedded Style Sheet," earlier in this chapter).

To modify styles in an external style sheet, you must open the style sheet separately and modify them there. See "Modifying Styles in an External Style Sheet," later in this chapter.

Removing Embedded Styles If you no longer need a user-defined style, or the modifications made to a standard HTML style, you can delete it from the embedded style sheet. Choose Format, Style Figure and select the style from the list of styles. Click Delete to remove the style or the formatting changes.

NOTE When you remove an embedded style, FrontPage does not remove the style reference from the text elements where you applied the style. If you later add a style with the same name, those text elements inherit the new style's formatting.

To delete styles in an external style sheet, you must open the style sheet separately and delete them there. See "Deleting Styles from an External Style Sheet," later in this chapter.

Styles Shared by Several Web Pages

To share styles with several Web pages within your Web site, create an external style sheet and link the pages to the external style sheet.

As with embedded style sheets, styles you create in an external style sheet become available in the Style toolbar drop-down list, so you can apply the same style to multiple elements on the same page. You can also apply your styles together with standard HTML styles to produce a combined effect. If a page uses both an embedded and external style sheet, then the applied styles will have a combined effect in your Web document.

Creating an External Style Sheet To create an external style sheet, choose File, New, Page. In the New dialog box, click the Style Sheets tab (see Figure 58.25). Select each style sheet and read the description to find the style sheet that best matches your needs. If you do not find one, use the Normal Style sheet template to create a blank CSS file. External style sheets are saved in files with the .css extension.

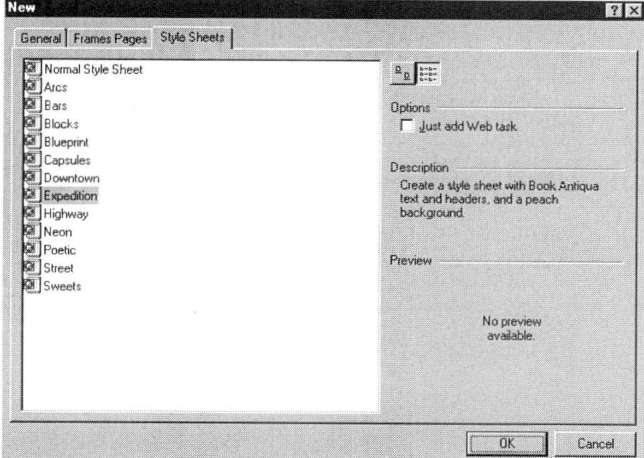

FIGURE 58.25
Choose from a number of Style Sheet templates.

With your external style sheet open in Page view, choose Format, Style to modify the standard HTML styles or to create your own. The Style dialog box appears, as shown in Figure 58.26. In this dialog box, you can preview the available HTML styles, as well as any user-defined styles.

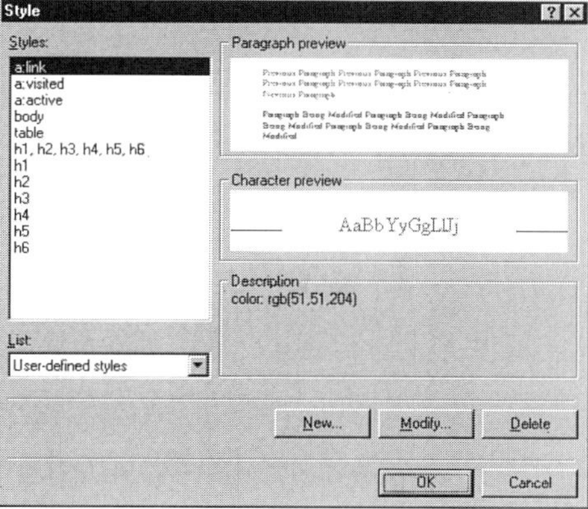

FIGURE 58.26
Use an external style sheet to apply styles to multiple Web pages in your Web site.

Choose one of the standard HTML styles and click Modify to apply changes to it. Or, click the New button to create a new user-defined style.

In the New Style dialog box, as shown in Figure 58.27, type a name for your new style. Use a name that describes the style's purpose, rather than its appearance. For example, type "JobPosting" rather than "BoldDoubleBorder." This way, if you change the style's appearance later, your style name can remain the same.

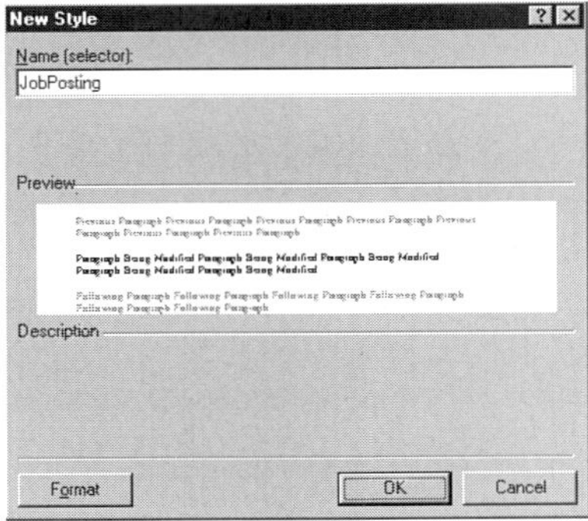

FIGURE 58.27
Choose meaningful names for your styles.

To complete your format preferences for the style, click the Format button to reveal a menu of choices, as described earlier in this chapter in the "Creating an Embedded Style Sheet" section.

Linking Pages to an External Style Sheet After you have created your external style sheet, you need to link it to the pages within your Web site. In Folder view, select the Web pages to which you want to link the style sheet and choose Format, Style Sheet Links. In the Link Style Sheet dialog box (shown in Figure 58.28), choose whether you want to link the style sheet to all pages within your Web site, or only the selected pages.

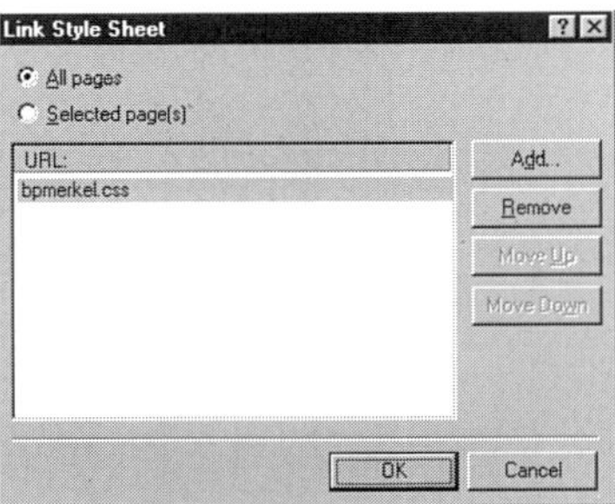

FIGURE 58.28
Link the external style sheet to your Web pages.

If you have other style sheets you want to link to your pages, click the Add button to add them to the list. To remove a style sheet from the list, select it and click the Remove button.

When you link multiple style sheets to a page, the order can affect how styles combine formatting. Use the Move Up and Move Down buttons to change the order. Contrary to intuition, the style sheet listed at the bottom of the list will have higher precedence than those above it.

Applying Styles from an External Style Sheet After you have defined your new styles, you can apply them to text within your Web documents. Your new styles appear in the Style drop-down list on the toolbar, and are prefixed by a period. To apply one of your styles, select the text within your document and choose the Style name from the Style drop-down list. You can also apply another HTML style to get the combined effect of both styles.

If you want to quickly apply the style of one of your page elements to another, use the Format Painter button on the toolbar. Select the source element, click the Format Painter toolbar button, and then select the element to which you want to apply the change. FrontPage assigns the styles to the element automatically.

To remove the effect of your style on the text, select one of the standard HTML styles, such as Normal.

Modifying Styles in an External Style Sheet In your external style sheet, you can modify the appearance of one of your styles, or change the formatting for a standard HTML style. Open your external style sheet in Page view and choose Format, Style (refer to Figure 58.26) and select the style from the list of styles. Click Modify to display the Modify Style dialog box, as shown in Figure 58.29.

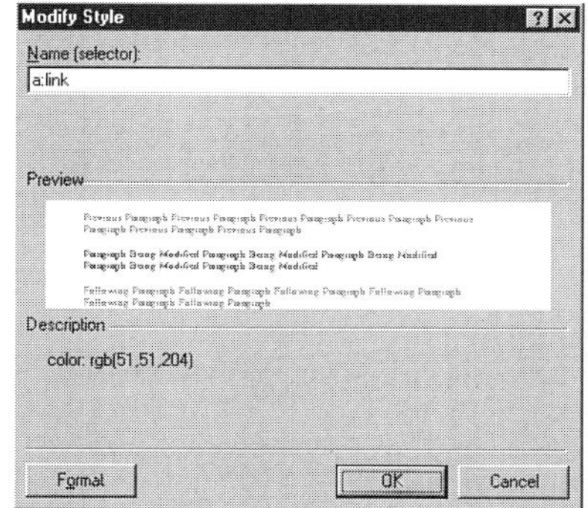

FIGURE 58.29
Modify your external style sheet styles and all pages that link to it will inherit the changes.

Modify the style using the same format choices as you did when you created the style (see "Creating an Embedded Style Sheet," earlier in this chapter).

Deleting Styles from an External Style Sheet If you no longer need a user-defined style, or your modification to a standard HTML style, you can delete it from the external style sheet. Open the external style sheet file in Page view and choose Format, Style (refer to Figure 58.29). Select the style you want to remove from the list of styles. Click Delete to remove the style.

NOTE When you remove a style from an external style sheet, FrontPage does not remove the references to the style from the text elements where you applied the style. If you later add a style with the same name, those text elements inherit the new style's formatting.

Applying Themes

Like all Office 2000 applications, you can leverage Themes to provide consistency and good looks to all the Web pages in your Web site. Office 2000 includes several Themes from which to choose—each Theme has its own personality, and all are designed by Microsoft's team of professional Web designers. *Themes* assemble styles, images, colors, and fonts together to provide one-stop shopping for a coordinated design for your Web pages.

To see the Themes available for your Web site, choose Format, Theme (see Figure 58.30). Browse through the list of Themes and view the samples to find one for your site. If you find that only a few Themes are available, you can install the complete set from your installation media. Office 2000 includes over 60 predesigned Themes.

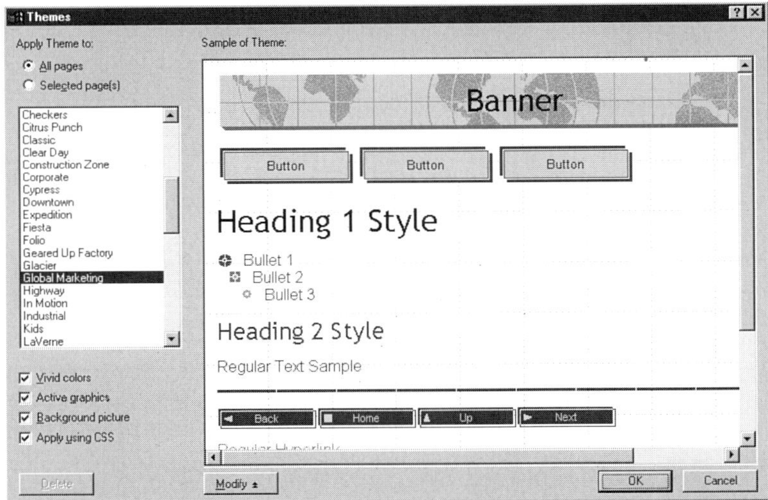

FIGURE 58.30
Choose from over 60 Themes to apply a consistent and coordinated design to your Web pages.

▶ **See** "Using FrontPage Components," **p. 1651**

Each Theme offers different variations. After you find a Theme that matches the general look for your Web site, choose between vivid colors, active graphics, and a background picture. Mark the Vivid Colors check box to use an alternative bright color scheme for the Theme. Mark the Active Graphics check box to use animated banners, bullets, and buttons that change when the user hovers his mouse pointer over them. If you want to use the Theme's background image, mark the Background Picture check box; otherwise, the background will be a solid color.

If you prefer not to use Cascading Style Sheets with your Web site, FrontPage can apply the Theme formatting directly within the HTML. Uncheck the Apply Using CSS option in this case. If the check box is not available, you need to select the compatibility options for your Web site.

▶ **See** "Choosing Compatibility for Your Web," **p. CD146**

You can apply a theme to selected pages, or to all the pages within your Web site. If you apply the Theme to your entire Web site, FrontPage remembers your selection and automatically assigns the Theme to new pages added to the Web site in the future. Click OK to apply the Theme.

Changing the Styles, Colors, and Images of a Theme

It is possible that none of the predesigned Themes implement the metaphor exactly as you have in mind for your Web site. Not to worry; you can pick a Theme and modify it to use your own preferred colors, graphics, or styles. You can then save the revised Theme under a new name, and apply it to your Web pages such as the standard predesigned Themes.

To create a custom Theme, choose Format, Theme and browse through the list of Themes. Choose the Theme that best approximates the look and feel that you want to achieve. This way, you will have to make fewer modifications to the colors, styles, or graphics.

Because graphics are the most time-consuming to re-create, find the Theme that suits your intended graphics look. It is easiest to alter the colors and styles first, and you can replace the graphics later.

With the best matching Theme selected, click the Modify button to reveal a row of customization buttons (see Figure 58.31).

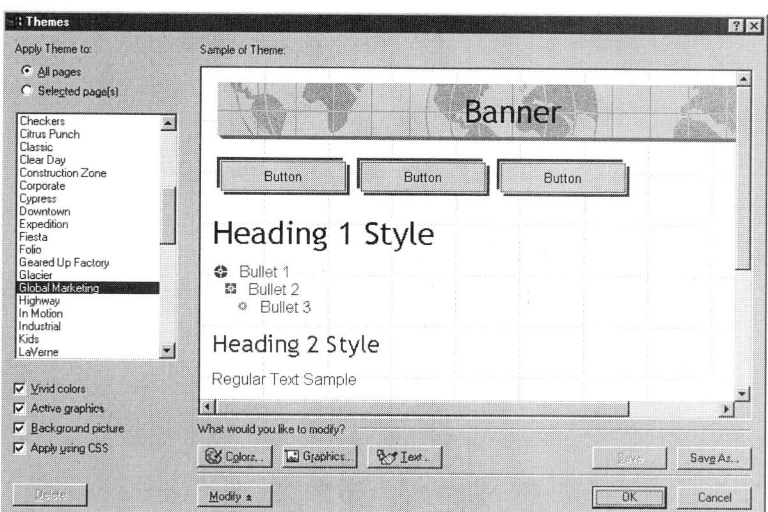

FIGURE 58.31
Use the Colors, Graphics, and Text buttons to customize your Theme.

Modifying Theme Colors Click the Colors button to modify the color scheme for your Theme. In the Modify Theme dialog box, you can choose from current Color Schemes (see Figure 58.32), or build your own coordinated scheme using the Color Wheel (see Figure 58.33). If you want to assign colors at the individual HTML element level, use the Custom tab (see Figure 58.34).

Remember that you can assign two color schemes to your theme, one color scheme to use normally, and the other when you choose Vivid Colors. Click OK after you have defined the color schemes for your new Theme.

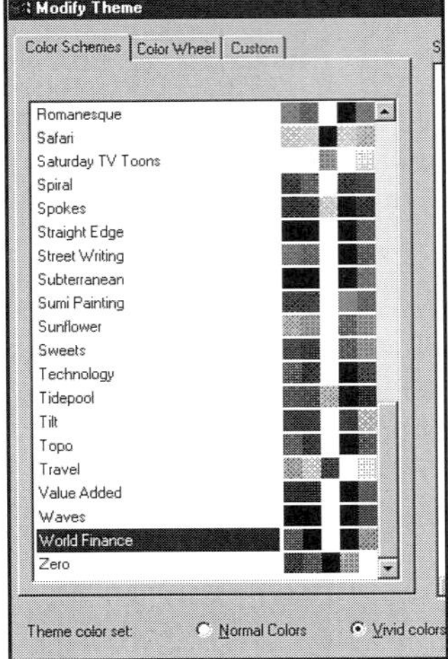

FIGURE 58.32
Choose from one of the coordinated Color Schemes for your new Theme.

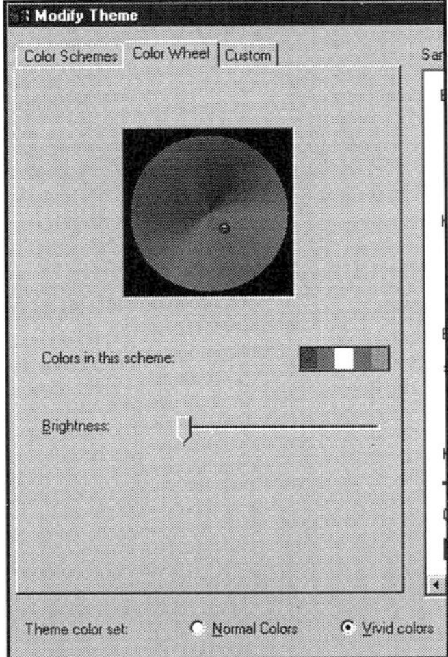

FIGURE 58.33
Use the color wheel to generate a new color scheme.

Modifying Theme Graphics Each FrontPage Theme includes 11 graphical elements to use for bullets, buttons, banners, the background, and horizontal rules. Also, each Theme uses two sets of these graphical elements—one set for normal graphics, and the other to apply when using active graphics. To modify the graphics for your Theme, choose Format, Theme and click Modify to display the row of customization buttons (refer to Figure 58.31). Click the Graphics button to display the Modify Theme dialog box. Click the Picture tab (see Figure 58.35) to modify the image elements to your Theme.

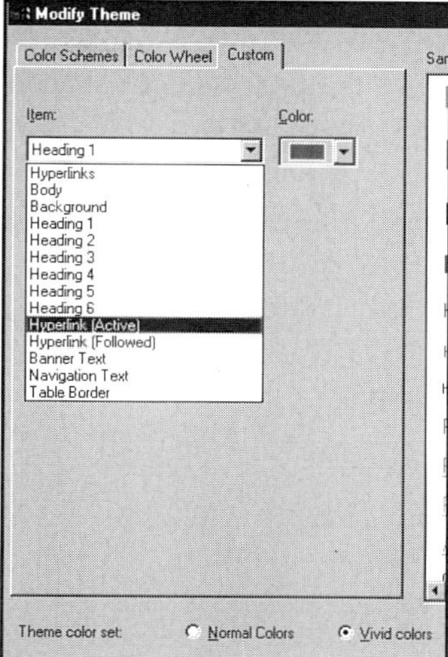

FIGURE 58.34
Assign your own custom colors to the HTML elements.

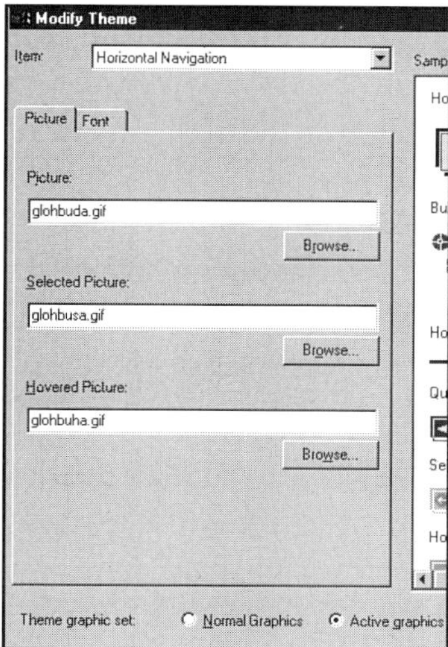

FIGURE 58.35
Use your own custom graphics for your Theme.

Choose the element you want to work on in the Item list, and for each picture listed in the Picture tab, click Browse to locate the image you want to use for that purpose. For instance, you need to select the first three levels of bullet images, and in Active graphics mode, you need three images for your navigational buttons:

- One when the button is not selected
- Another when a user hovers their mouse pointer over the button
- And yet another when the user clicks the button

Modifying the Style of Text on Your Graphics Most of the graphical elements can have their own text style. The text style is used when FrontPage creates the element for a specific page. For instance, when you use the Banner Component in graphics mode, FrontPage overlays the title of the page onto the banner image using your text style. This way, you can be assured that the banner text is consistent with the other text formatting of your Web site.

To modify the text formatting for the graphics for your Theme, choose Format, Theme and click Modify to display the row of customization buttons (refer to Figure 58.31). Click the Graphics button to display the Modify Theme dialog box. Click the Font tab (see Figure 58.36) to modify the text overlay elements to your Theme.

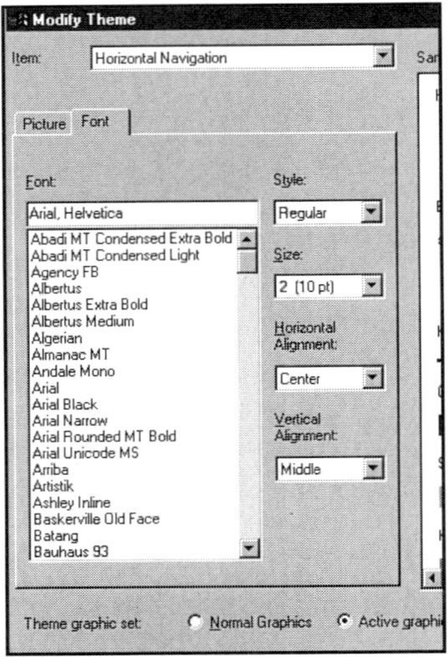

FIGURE 58.36
Define the text styles for your images to be consistent with the text formatting you use on your Web site.

Choose the graphical element from the Item option list at the top of the dialog box. Then select the font name from the Font list and choose a style, size, and horizontal and vertical alignments.

To maintain compatibility with Web browsers on multiple platforms, you can type additional font names, delimited by commas. When a browser cannot find the first font listed, it looks for the second and so on. Otherwise, it displays the default font, which is usually Times New Roman. Remember to make your font changes for both Normal and Active Graphics.

Modifying the Style of HTML Text of Your Document To modify the HTML text formatting of your documents for your Theme, choose Format, Theme and click Modify to display the row of customization buttons (refer to Figure 58.31). Click the Text button to display the Modify Theme dialog box, as shown in Figure 58.37. Choose the HTML text element from the Item option list at the top of the dialog box. Then select the font name from the Font list. Click the More Text Styles button to customize the CSS styles in your Theme.

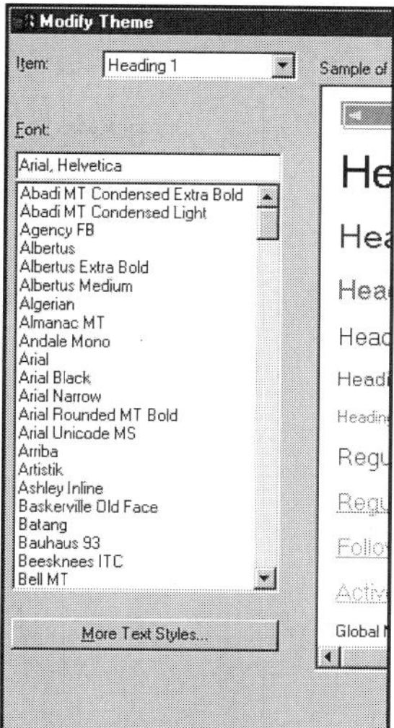

FIGURE 58.37
Define the text styles for consistent HTML text within your Web pages.

Creating Hyperlinks

The power behind the Web, the one feature that makes it the dynamic media it has become, is the capability to hyperlink text, pictures, and objects to pages, bookmarks, images, objects, and events virtually anywhere on the Web. Hyperlinks provide the interactive power to your Web pages, the capability to move from location to location almost seamlessly (depending on your Internet connection).

Links can target almost any type of object (file, image, email, video, presentation, spreadsheet, and so on) from almost any location (network, intranet, Internet). And they can link to executable programs on the server, such as Active Server Pages (ASPs) that return HTML responses.

The cursor turns into a hand whenever it "hovers" over a hyperlink or "hot spot" on a Web page. When you execute a link by clicking it or causing another event, such as a mouseover, it loads the target page into the browser, and into a target frame in a frames page.

Hyperlinks consist of a Web address or URL (Universal Resource Locator), and can include bookmarks and queries.

A bookmark is an additional location on a Web page that can be the target (destination) of a hyperlink. Bookmarks are useful for driving users directly to the content they seek on long pages, and you can create menus of hyperlinks to facilitate.

Relative and Absolute Links

An absolute link or URL—for example: `http://www.microsoft.com/frontpage/default.asp`—is used to target an address outside of the current Web site. Relative links are used to target addresses within the current Web site or subWeb.

An absolute link includes the following elements:

- The protocol used to access the destination (http://, ftp://, or file:///)
- The domain name or address (`www.microsoft.com`)
- The path to the resource on the host (`/frontpage/default.asp`)

A relative link provides only the path within the current Web site or subWeb, for example /frontpage/default.asp. Relative links provide the advantage of being easily portable from one Web or subWeb to another. Pages that remain in the same order relative to their root will maintain their links, whereas absolute links within the same Web have to be updated with new absolute addresses when pages are moved.

Creating Links to Other Pages

To create a link to another page

1. Open the page in Normal view.
2. Select the text or object from which to link.
3. Click the Hyperlink tool on the Standard toolbar. The Edit Hyperlink dialog box shown in Figure 58.38 lists the files and folders within your Web site.

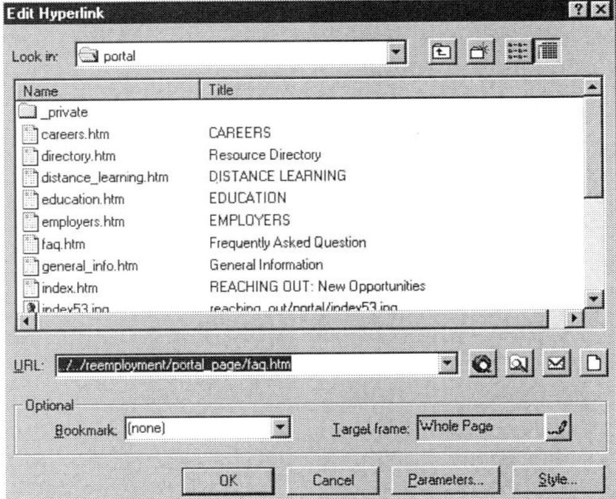

FIGURE 58.38
You can easily define relative links to other pages in your Web using the Hyperlink dialog box.

4. Define the URL. Enter an address in the URL box or select one from the list. Browse to another location on the Web, link to a Local File, or link to an Email Address.
5. To create a new address to a new page, click the New Page icon. Save the page with the name of the link you created. Using this technique, you can build a Web site page-by-page as your content grows.
6. If the target page has bookmarks listed, you can optionally select a bookmark.

7. You can also identify a Target Frame if the linked page is to be loaded into a frames page, or if you want it to display in a new page or window.
8. Click OK and the link is inserted into your HTML.

Using Bookmarks to Link to Locations Within a Page

Bookmarks define links to specific locations on a page. When you link to a bookmark on another page, it automatically scrolls that location to the top of its window or frame.

Bookmarks are placed after the page address in a hyperlink. For example, this link would display the location defined by *#new* on the products.htm page:

```
www.megacorp.com/products.htm#new
```

Often, heads and subheads are used as bookmarks, but you can bookmark any object or location on your page. To create a bookmark, follow these steps:

1. Highlight the text or place your cursor in the location to bookmark.
2. Choose Insert, Bookmark to display the Bookmark dialog box.
3. If you highlighted text to bookmark, the first word of the text appears in the Name box. If that name has already been used, the box is blank. Use the name offered or enter another unique name. If other bookmarks are on the page, they appear in the scrolling text box below the name. You can select a bookmark from this list and click Go To to see its location on the page (in which case the dialog box stays on top so you can go to other bookmarks) or you can click Clear to remove the bookmark (in which case the dialog box closes).
4. Click OK.

In Normal view, FrontPage displays bookmarked text with a dashed underline, as shown in Figure 58.39. Bookmarked locations are indicated by the bookmark icon, a little gray box with a little blue flag. To remove bookmarks, double-click the bookmark and click Clear on the Bookmarks dialog box. Also, when you remove a bookmarked text or object, its bookmark is removed.

You can link to bookmarks in the same page as well as other pages. For long pages with several sections, bookmarks can be used to create a table of contents or menu to the sections.

To create a new link to a bookmark, follow these steps:

1. Open the page in Normal view.
2. Select the text or object from which to link.
3. Click the Hyperlink tool on the Standard toolbar to display the Edit Hyperlink dialog box.
4. Select the destination page for the link.
5. Choose a Bookmark from the list of bookmarks for that page (see Figure 58.40).

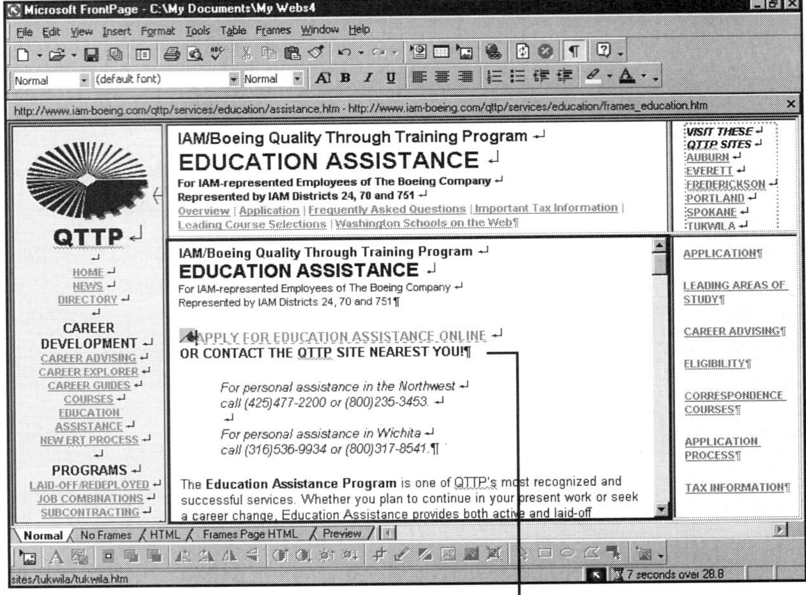

FIGURE 58.39
Bookmarks define specific text or locations on a page to which you can create hyperlinks.

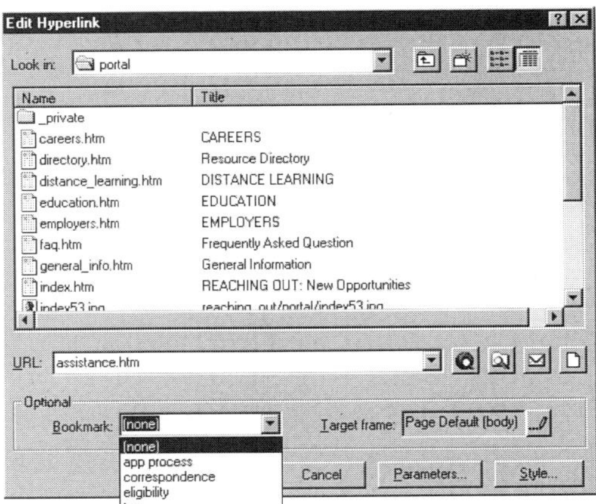

FIGURE 58.40
Select bookmarks from the list of bookmarks for the destination page.

Creating Links to Resources on the Internet

Link to files on other Web sites and FTP servers using the Uniform Resource Locator (URL) that defines the location of the destination file.

Use the Create Hyperlink dialog box. Type the full URL of the Internet resource or click the Use Your Web Browser to Select a Page or File button. If it is not already open, FrontPage launches your default Web browser. Navigate to the actual resource or file to which you want to link. When you have located the resource, close the browser and FrontPage captures the URL in the dialog box for you.

Creating Email Links

When a user clicks an email link, his or her email application opens and starts a new message addressed to the email recipient defined in the link.

To create an email link, use the Create Hyperlink dialog box. Click the Make a Hyperlink That Sends E-Mail button and type the email address in the Create E-Mail Hyperlink dialog box.

Links to email addresses will spawn a new message using the default mail program in the user's system using the Send To address from the Create E-Mail Hyperlink dialog box.

Removing Links

If you want to remove a link, right-click the link text and choose Hyperlink Properties. When the Edit Hyperlink dialog box appears, press Delete to clear the contents of the URL text box. To completely remove the hyperlink so the text will not appear as linked, select the *http://* reference that remains and delete it, too. Click OK and the link is removed.

67.18413 CH58

CHAPTER 59

Working with Images and Videos

In this chapter

The FrontPage Image and Video Tools

FrontPage provides a range of image and video tools so that you can be as simple and direct or as complex and creative as your imagination, time, and budget will allow. Visual elements can be added into the page as easily as copying and pasting an object or inserting a file. You also can create results that are clever and complex by scheduling the appearance of elements, creating animations, and using Dynamic HTML to trigger events.

When working with visual elements on the Web, the challenge is balancing quality and speed of delivery. You usually do not have control over many of the variables in the process. Servers, distance, connections (modem, network, router, server, and so on), PC configuration, display drivers, and monitors all impact how your pictures will be perceived. What you can control are your design and the properties of the images themselves: quantity, size, colors, and format.

As for design, keep your site simple and direct, especially at the higher levels of navigation. Images invariably slow the user's experience. There may be mountains of useful information to be found at your site, but if getting to that information is too painful, the user will abandon the site and move on. After a user has mined deep enough to find the information he seeks, he will be willing to invest time waiting to download more involved presentations. For example, you might provide a catalog of smaller thumbnail images that link to larger and more detailed images or video.

Image files themselves must be kept as small as possible without losing too much image quality: Even when working with small, compressed files, a page with many small files quickly adds up to a lengthy download. Nonetheless, you can make a site visually dynamic and appealing by meeting these challenges with the effective use of images combined with creative backgrounds, text, and dynamic effects.

Preparing Images and Videos for the Web

You must consider many factors when preparing images and videos for the Web. Compromises must be made, and judicious handling is required.

You must also consider the many types of Web environments that are now available. Each has different objectives and requires different solutions for the use of images:

- Corporate identity sites on the Internet have become sophisticated and usually combine high-quality design and images with a high level of ease-of-use. Many now are incorporating streaming video and live video feeds.
- E-commerce sites are often visually dynamic, with many small images linking to product presentations with larger images.
- Education and Distance Learning have taken to the Web for widespread distribution of courseware requiring sophisticated multimedia.
- Entertainment consolidators are streaming audio and video to broad audiences and selling catalogs of products.

- Intranets are controlled environments, with more speed and flexibility for higher-quality multimedia and data-intensive applications that favor content over design.
- Extranets and Virtual Private Networks (VPN) combine the cross-platform efficiencies of the Web to serve users outside the network through the Internet, and are excellent for maintaining communications with customers, sales forces, and vendors. They typically require more content-delivery and relationship building, with high service and security expectations.

If you are developing for a corporate intranet, you will want to know the prevalent platform and the current standard, and be able to anticipate what next year's standard will be.

If you are developing for a widespread retail consumer audience, you may want to develop a simple but graphically dynamic site with fast graphics that can be accessed by all browsers.

The best way to identify those solutions is to know your audience. Decisions regarding image editors, video processors, file formats, colors, resolution, and design are extremely important (and often esoteric). But profiling and understanding your audience, and the intent of your Web communication, are essential to informing those decisions.

Is the person viewing your site a novice using Windows 3.1 on a 486 with a 14-inch, 600×480 monitor and a 14Kbps modem, or a business user running Windows 98 on a Pentium III with a 17-inch, 1024×768 monitor and a 56Kbps modem? Their experiences with your design and graphics will be significantly different.

Knowing the speed and display characteristics of your audience's computers, and the ways your audience will use the site, can help you make decisions about the size, colors, and positioning of your graphic elements. That's why many developers play it safe and work with limited sets of forgiving colors, tables, and accurately positioned images.

The profile of your development computer is probably much different than your audience's computers. Maintain test computers to view the results your audience will experience using the lowest and highest common denominator configurations, and any extraordinary configurations, for which you are developing. For example, if your audience will be accessing your site on the Internet using a 28.8Kbps modem, test your site using a 28.8Kbps modem. If you expect that a significant share of your users will be using Macs, test your site on Macs as well as PCs.

Setting Browser Compatibility Options

While developing Web sites, it is important to remember that Web pages require browsers to be viewed and experienced. The combination of FrontPage 2000 and Internet Explorer 5 clearly provides opportunities for developing more highly dynamic user interfaces and greater interactivity between the browser and database applications. Putting these opportunities into practice, however, presents interesting and difficult challenges for mixed-browser environments. Internet Explorer and Netscape browsers, and their version 3 and 4 variations, each provide differing levels of support for some of the FrontPage features used for implementing and formatting images and videos, including ActiveX Controls, VBScript, Dynamic HTML, and Cascading Style Sheets. Web TV supports none of these.

Enterprises upgrading to Microsoft Office 2000 must absorb Internet Explorer 5 with compatible servers and server extensions to realize the promise of FrontPage 2000. The Office Server Extensions implement the sophisticated server-based automation required for the Office 2000 applications. The Front Page Server Extensions facilitate publishing your Web site to a server, and enable much of the advanced functionality that can be developed with FrontPage. However, many service providers and corporate environments discourage or prohibit the use of these extensions on their servers.

An extremely useful new Compatibility Properties facility helps prevent you from using FrontPage to create results that won't work without Internet Explorer browsers or the server extensions. To customize FrontPage compatibility, choose Tools, Page Options, and select the Compatibility tab in the Page Options dialog box. Select the browser, version, and server variables for which you are developing. FrontPage automatically disables tools and technologies that won't work with the browser and server formats you select (see Figure 59.1). When a tool or technology is disabled, it appears in gray on the menus and cannot be selected.

Compatibility properties established in the current Web site are applied to all Web pages in your FrontPage development environment. When you change these settings for one Web page, they are applied to all Web pages. Developing Web pages with different compatibility properties requires separate development systems.

You also can specify a custom set of tools to enable the development of your Web with features that will not work in some environments. Code for these features is usually ignored by other browsers. For example, if you use Cascading Style Sheets, the CSS features appear in Internet Explorer 3 and later and Netscape 4, but are ignored by Netscape 3. You can combine code for both conditions: CSS code that will be interpreted and used by Internet Explorer and Netscape 4, and JavaScript code that will provide similar functionality in Netscape 3, but which will be overridden by the CSS code and ignored by Internet Explorer.

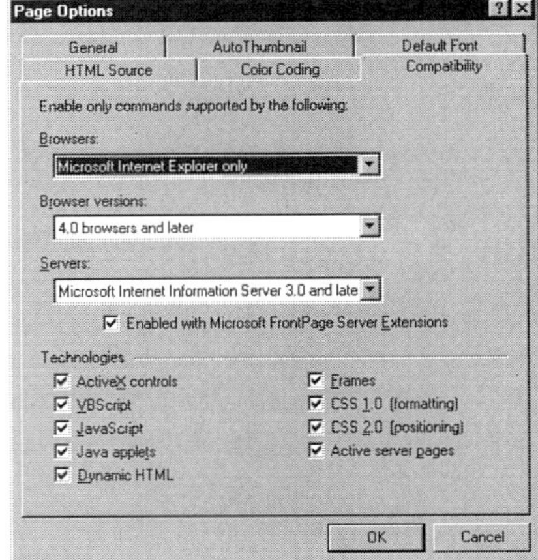

FIGURE 59.1
Establish compatibility properties before developing your Web page to prevent using features that won't work for your target browsers, and to help you create Web pages that your entire audience can use.

When implementing the advanced Internet Explorer features that require ActiveX Controls or server extensions, it will be difficult to satisfy both Internet Explorer and Netscape users. Knowing these parameters might lead you to develop separate sites for different types of users, browsers and/or connection speeds. You can manually insert browser detection into your HTML to direct different users to separate experiences as they enter your Web site. JavaScript for browser detection can be found at `http://www.Webreference.com/js/column6/browser.html`.

NOTE It is important to remember that visual elements cannot be experienced by the visually impaired, and events triggered by these elements also will not be experienced. This is often a consideration in larger corporations and organizations that serve diverse audiences. Therefore, you might consider maintaining alternate text-only presentations of your content.

File Format Considerations

The important issues when considering file formats are image quality, size, and speed of delivery. Quality is a function of resolution and file type. Speed is a function of file size, connection speed, and the display properties of the user's computer.

Although computer platforms and development languages are constantly evolving, and competing browsers and streaming video formats vie for position, two image file formats have emerged as consistent standards for the Web—GIFs and JPEGs. Meanwhile, the AVI video file format remains the one standard that can be viewed by virtually all users of Macintosh or Windows operating systems with their resident media players.

FrontPage 2000 forces you to use one of these three image file formats:

- GIFs—GIF images contain 8 bits and up to 256 colors. One color can be made transparent. Most clip art is provided in GIF format. GIFs also can be interlaced using Picture Properties to display the image with increasing detail while it is being loaded, which is useful for larger, slower loading GIFs.
- JPEGs—JPEGs are high-color, 24-bit images used for high-quality pictures and photos containing thousands or millions of colors. Files are kept small through what is known as "lossy" compression. As file compression increases and file size decreases, loss of resolution increases.

  JPEG conversion enables you to specify a Quality setting from 1 to 100. Higher quality reduces compression and increases file size. Lower quality increases compression and decreases file size. The Progressive Passes setting defines the number of passes a Web browser performs to "unfold" an image as it downloads.

  When you find a combination that works well for your site, stick with it for consistency among your images. For backgrounds, use JPEGs to achieve the highest compression and speed while maintaining as much quality as possible.

  JPEGs will look grainy and lose color value when viewed on 256-color displays. If your audience uses Windows Display settings of 256 colors, test your JPEGs at 256 colors, or use GIFs to maintain consistency for both 256-color and high-color displays.

- PNG—A new Microsoft file format that supports transparency, such as GIFs, for high-color images, such as JPEGs. However, the FrontPage Transparency tool does not work with PNGs, and requires a plug-in for Netscape browsers.

GIF files are considerably larger than the JPEG format. Figure 59.2 shows the same image captured in GIF and JPEG formats. The GIF image on the left is 87KB and requires about 46 seconds to download over a 28.8Kbps modem. The JPEG image on the right is 37KB and requires about 19 seconds to download.

FIGURE 59.2
The higher-quality JPEG image is less than half the file size of the GIF version of the same image and takes less than half the time to download.

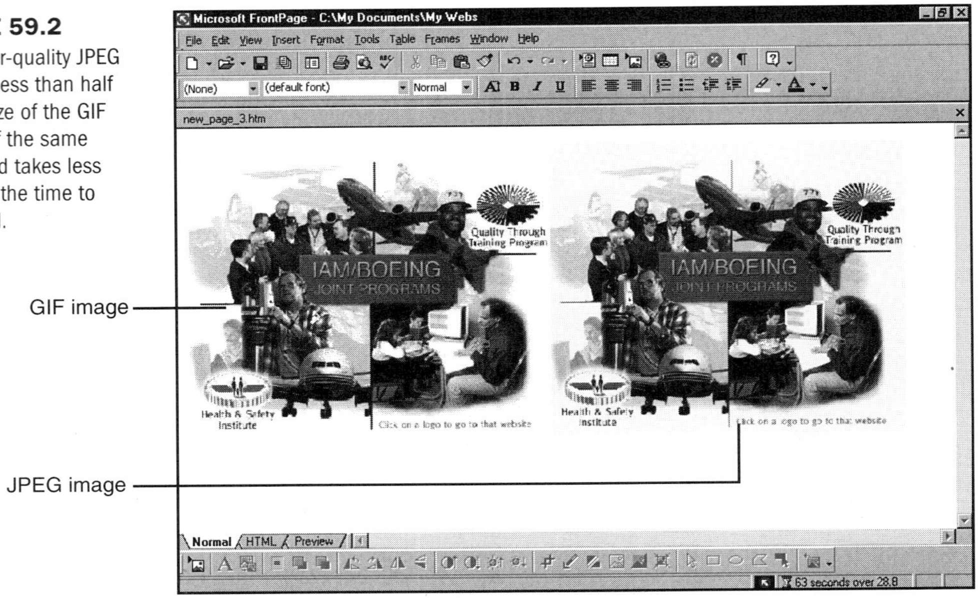

GIF image

JPEG image

Image files can come from many different sources: drawings, clip art, scanned images, and CD and Web-based photo libraries. Some are Web-ready. Others require conversion to compatible file formats to work well on the Web. Which format you choose depends on how the image will be used, and tradeoffs of quality, size, and speed.

For images with millions of colors, such as photos, JPEGs provide the best overall quality with the smallest and fastest file. For 256-color images, such as most buttons, horizontal rules, and clip art, GIFs typically provide higher quality and smaller file size. GIFs also are required for using the Transparency tool (discussed under "Manipulating Images") and for creating GIF animations (also discussed under "Manipulating Images," later in this chapter). Use the format most appropriate to optimize image appearance and functionality. Try to keep image file sizes as small as possible while maintaining enough clarity for your purpose.

With FrontPage 2000, you can quickly and easily use Picture Properties to convert GIF, PNG, and JPEG files to each of the other formats. Generally, you will be using an image editor to control the conversion of larger image files, such as Bitmaps or TIFFs, into GIFs and JPEGs, although FrontPage automatically converts these formats to GIFs and JPEGs when you save a page into which they have been inserted.

If you add an image to your page with a format other than GIF, JPEG, or PNG, FrontPage automatically converts the file to a GIF if it has 8 bits of color or less, or to a JPEG if it has more than 8 bits of color.

After you've created your pages and inserted your images, use View, Reports, Slow Pages to identify pages that download too slow and may contain image files that are too large.

Choosing an Image Editor

FrontPage offers some serious tools for manipulating your images, and the Office 2000 Premium Edition includes PhotoDraw for more advanced image editing. Hundreds of other products are available for working with images as well, from the simplicity of the Paint accessory to the sophistication of Adobe Photoshop. Many freeware and shareware products are available for GIF animation, banner ad creation, and image-file management.

Your choice of image editor is ultimately a tradeoff of image quality, tools, features, and cost. Although most image editors can convert the most commonly used image file formats into GIFs and JPEGs, not all editors produce the same quality image. Hundreds of resources are available on the Internet for learning more about image-file formats and editors. Just search for "Web graphics" using your favorite search engine. To search for free images to use on your site, try the Lycos Pictures and Sounds search engine at `http://www.lycos.com/picturethis/`.

Video Files and Players

When presenting videos, considerations of image size and file size become more critical than with other pictures, and must be balanced with speed and resolution. Many types of video file formats, players, and codecs are now available for interpreting video files, from the simplicity of basic AVI (Video for Windows) and QT (Apple QuickTime), to competing standards for streaming, live, and on-demand video: AFS (Windows Media), and RAM or RA (RealMedia).

When a video file is downloaded, it contains instructions to spawn a player with a codec that is compatible with its format. For example, when a QuickTime file is downloaded, it attempts to spawn a QuickTime player. If the QuickTime player is not available, it attempts to spawn another compatible player, such as Windows Media Player, which supports many codecs, including QuickTime. If the video file spawns Windows Media Player and the required QuickTime codec is not found, the player attempts to automatically download the codec and play the file.

Windows Media Player also automatically adjusts in several ways to accommodate the incoming video stream and provide maximum performance. Similarly, professional video production systems such as RealProducer Pro create a video file that dynamically scales to the user's bandwidth and adjusts the transmission rate as a user's connection changes due to network congestion.

If you have loaded multiple players into your system, you can specify which player to use for a specific file type. For example, if you have both a QuickTime player and a Windows Media Player loaded in your system, you can force QT files to play on the Windows Media Player instead of the QuickTime player. To associate a file, follow these steps:

1. Choose Start, Settings, and Folder Options.
2. Click the File Types tab.
3. Choose a file type from the scrollable list at the left and choose Edit to display the Edit File Type dialog box.
4. Click the Edit button to display the Editing Actions for Type: [file extension] dialog box.
5. Enter the full path to the application you want to associate with a particular file type. Click OK to close the dialog box.
6. Click Set As Default if you want Windows to always associate a particular extension with a particular application. Click Close.

Table 59.1 is a simplified overview of common video file types and extensions. Their compatible video players are indicated by an "X."

Table 59.1 Video File Types, File Extensions, and Player Compatibility

File Types	Windows RealVideo	Microsoft Streaming Media	QuickTime	MPEG	Animation and Video File
File Extensions	.avi	.asf	.mov	.m1v	.ram
		.asx	.qt	.mp2	.ra
				.mpa	.rm
				.mpe	.rmm
				.mpeg	
RealPlayer	X*		X*		X
Windows Media Player	X	X	X	X	X
QuickTime Movie Player			X	X	

* *Requires additional downloadable module.*

AVIs are usually smaller files of short duration that can be transmitted using standard Hypertext Transfer Protocol (HTTP). Anything longer than 30 seconds can take what seems forever to download over a modem.

Unlike AVI, which requires the entire file to download before the browser can begin playing that file, streaming video begins playing almost immediately.

Streaming technology compresses the media file and delivers the compressed data to a player. The streaming media player buffers the initial several seconds of data and then begins playing regardless of the length of the entire file. The file is delivered in small packets of data as requested, enabling the user to fast forward, rewind, or skip around in the file.

Streaming media is required to transmit video of any real duration, and to provide live video. Among its many uses are online training, corporate communications, customer and sales support, news and entertainment, and marketing.

Competing for the streaming media market are Microsoft and Real Media, which has over 40 million RealPlayer 5.0 and G2 players currently in use. Whereas Real Media is a proprietary technology for video production, servers, and broadcast, Microsoft hopes that by offering its Advanced Streaming Format (ASF) technology as an open system expected to work with tools from most multimedia vendors, it will become the standard.

Behind all these product names and file types lie technologies for video compression and decompression called codecs. A short discussion of codecs is provided in the accompanying sidebar.

ASF 1.0 works with Windows NT 4.0, Windows 95, and Internet Explorer 4.0 through NetShow.

ASF 2.0 works with Windows NT 5.0, Internet Explorer 5.0, and updates to Windows 98.

NOTE When delivering video, server traffic must be known and accommodated, just as audiences and their players must be known and accommodated. How many users will hit this video during peak traffic? Do you have the capacity? As the number and size of your videos increases, or the number of viewers increases, these issues become critical to overall performance of your server and your Web site. Although you can serve AVI and streaming video from your Web server, for greater reliability of delivery to larger audiences you will need to publish your video to specialized video servers.

Understanding Codecs

Codec stands for compressor/decompressor technology. When media is created, a codec is selected for compressing the content. When you play the content, the same or a compatible codec is employed. The quality, frame rate, and frame size you choose for your streaming media are largely determined by the codec you choose.

Microsoft claims Windows Media Player (formerly NetShow Services) is codec-independent and will choose from available codecs for the best one to fit the content. Most video technologies use proprietary codecs. For example, RealMedia files require a RealMedia codec.

To the average user, the issue of codecs is transparent. They click a link to a video, and it plays (if they have NetShow, Windows Media Player, QuickTime, or a similar player installed) or they are prompted to download a codec. For example, a RealMedia file prompts the user to download a RealPlayer if it is not present in the user's system, or a compatible player, such as Windows Media Player, if the user does not have a RealMedia codec installed. Similarly, RealPlayer requires additional modules (codecs) to play non-native formats such as AVI and QuickTime.

Image Color and Size Considerations

When using images, consider the color settings of your users' display. If the viewer is using 256 colors, your high-color image will lack resolution and appear distorted, whereas a 256-color GIF will appear the same on both 256-color and high-color displays. Most clip art and drawings are developed in 256 colors for maximum compatibility. Photos typically are scanned into Bitmaps or TIFFs using millions of colors and then converted into high-color JPEGs for compression.

- 256 colors—Microsoft seems to be calling them "Web-safe" colors, although only 216 basic colors are truly consistent. Generally speaking, the colors found in the color pickers in FrontPage are fairly accurate, whether they are from the basic "Web-safe" selection or a custom color. When creating images, you can use the eyedropper to make color selections that are saved as preferences in the color picker and can be used across applications. This can be useful for developing Web designs to match corporate or product colors used in document or presentation designs.
- High Color—Most newer PCs and monitors support the thousands of colors and higher resolution required by JPEGs and video for clarity. JPEGs and videos appear grainy on 256-color displays.
- Millions of colors—High resolution formats such as Bitmaps and TIFFs use millions of colors, and must be compressed into JPEG or PNG formats to retain quality with a smaller file size. If they are reduced to 256-color GIFs, the quality is more severely reduced while the file sizes remain large.

Inserting Pictures

FrontPage 2000 makes it easy to drag and drop an object into a Web Page (see Figure 59.3).

From Page Normal view, click the Folders button on the main toolbar. Then select a file from the directory structure, and place it in your page. You also can use Insert, Picture to insert any picture that has been imported to your Web site, or browse for a picture from any Web site or directory location. Images from other sources can be copied and pasted directly from the Clipboard into your page as well.

Inserting Images and Clip Art

Images are inserted from files and clip art, or scanned directly to your page. Inserting images is a simple process with innumerable and complex nuances. In the past, images could be either foreground or background objects. Now foreground objects can be positioned and layered with infinite variation.

Inserting Images and Clip Art As Foreground Objects Foreground objects can be any type of picture: images, animated GIFs, banner ads, clip art, or videos. Tables are also foreground objects, and pictures can be positioned and layered in their cells.

FIGURE 59.3
Drag and drop images from the Folder view into your Web page.

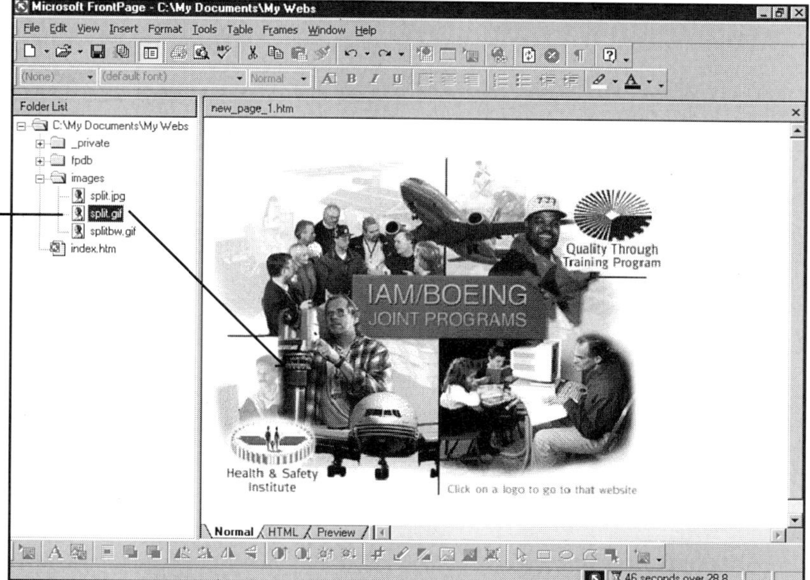

Before FrontPage 2000, images were usually put into tables to more accurately position their appearance on the page. Absolute Positioning (described later) could be achieved only through tedious manual coding of pixel positions and image sizes. Early attempts at layering also had to be meticulously hand-coded. Now you can easily layer images anywhere on the page, and positioning can be relative or absolute. Image objects can be aligned with one another and text can be automatically wrapped around an image, just as in Word.

To edit the Picture Properties of foreground objects, right-click a picture and then select Picture Properties from the shortcut menu. As shown in Figure 59.4, from the General tab of the Picture Properties dialog box you can specify the Picture source (which is useful when you want to replace a picture), the File type (which can be quickly converted to a GIF, JPEG, or PNG), an Alternative representation, and a Default hyperlink to a URL.

From the Appearance tab, you can further define the picture's Alignment, Spacing from other images and text, and Border (specify "0" for the image to appear with no border in Netscape). You can also resize the picture while automatically maintaining the aspect ratio of the original size, although this will not Resample and reduce the file size (see "Resample" under "Manipulating Images" later in this chapter).

If the picture is a video, use the Video tab to specify the appearance of the video player's controls, the repeat properties, and when to start playing the video, on File Open or on MouseOver.

FIGURE 59.4
Use the Picture Properties dialog box to specify the actions and appearance of foreground objects.

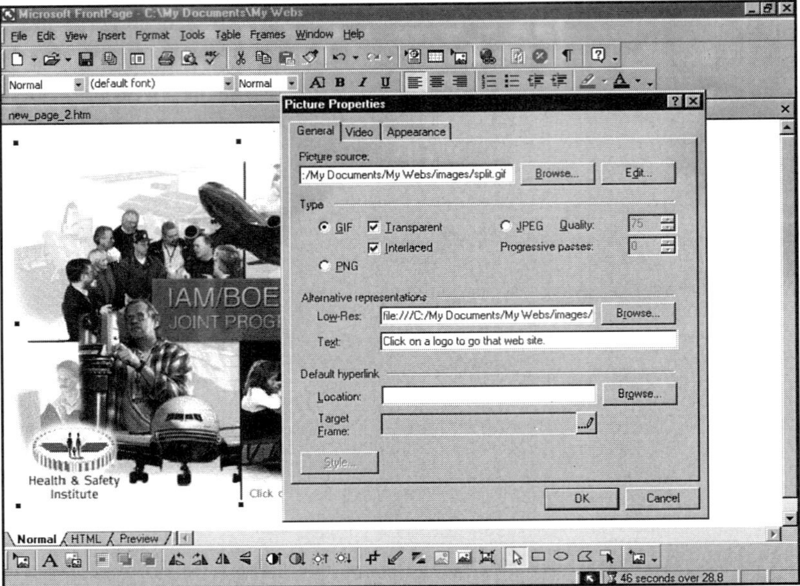

If the picture requires a lengthy download, you can display an alternative representation while it is loading. This alternative representation can be a Low-Res image or Text. The Low-Res alternative representation should be a fast-loading, low-resolution version of the same image that displays while the final version is downloading. This option does not reduce the amount of time the original picture takes to download, but provides a visual reference for the user while it is downloading. The Text message also appears when the user hovers the cursor over the image.

In a graphics program, create a low-resolution or black-and-white version of the picture and import it into your Web. Then identify that file in the Low-Res address on the General tab of the Picture Properties dialog box.

In Figure 59.5, the original color GIF image is 87KB and requires about 46 seconds to download at 28.8Kbps. The alternative representation is a low-resolution, black-and-white GIF that is only 30KB and takes about 16 seconds to download. The color image is shown in the top half of the picture loading over the black-and-white image in the bottom half of the picture.

Inserting Images and Clip Art As Background Objects Background images are often used for decorative effect, to provide a background pattern, a border, or to "watermark" a page. Use Format/Background to enter the image name or browse to select a background picture, and then select Watermark if you want it to appear in the background when a user prints it. In Figure 59.6, a small image of several gears has been used to create a seamless pattern with the appearance of many interconnected gears.

Color GIF downloading over black-and-white GIF.

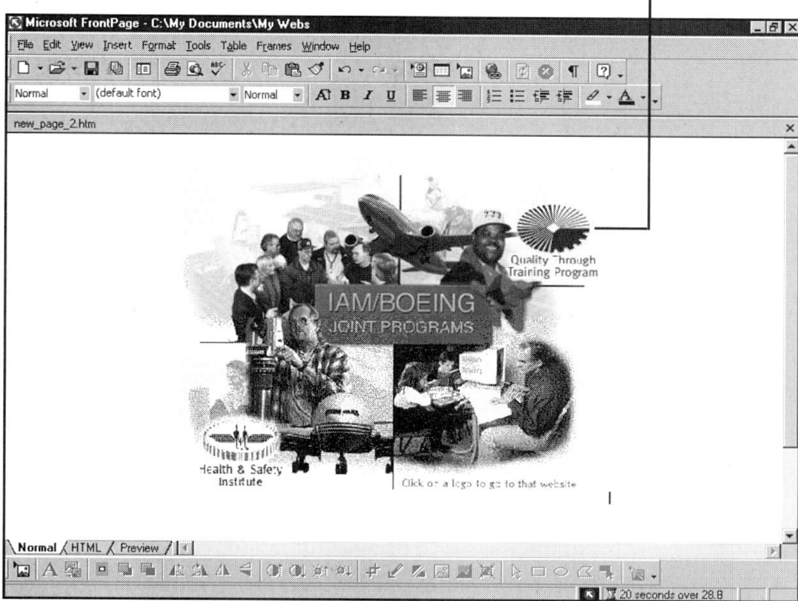

FIGURE 59.5
The black-and-white alternative representation loads in the user's browser first. While the color image is downloading over the alternative representation, it gives the appearance of "colorizing" the black-and-white image.

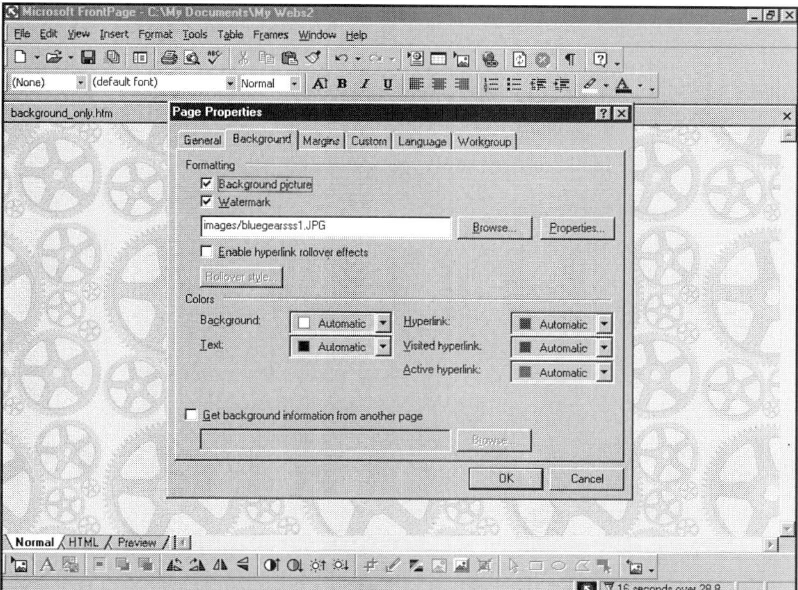

FIGURE 59.6
Background images repeat to fill the entire Web page.

Here again, file size is critical. Although you can use any file type for a background image, downloading the background image adds more time to downloading the entire page. Select a background color to appear while your background image is downloading.

When using background images, remember that the background image repeats itself to fill the entire height and width of your page. A background that looks good on your 800×600, 17-inch monitor could easily look silly on a laptop LCD running 1,024×768.

Tables can have their own background images and colors, and cells within tables can have their own background images and colors, which are layered, as text is, above the background.

The page in Figure 59.7 has multiple backgrounds in frames and tables, combining images and colors. The colored text buttons in the black menu on top look like Hover Buttons, but are images activated by mouseovers written in JavaScript. The gears pattern in the body of the page repeats in soft blue. The much darker blue of the original was brightened to a lighter blue by using the Brightness tool on the Picture toolbar.

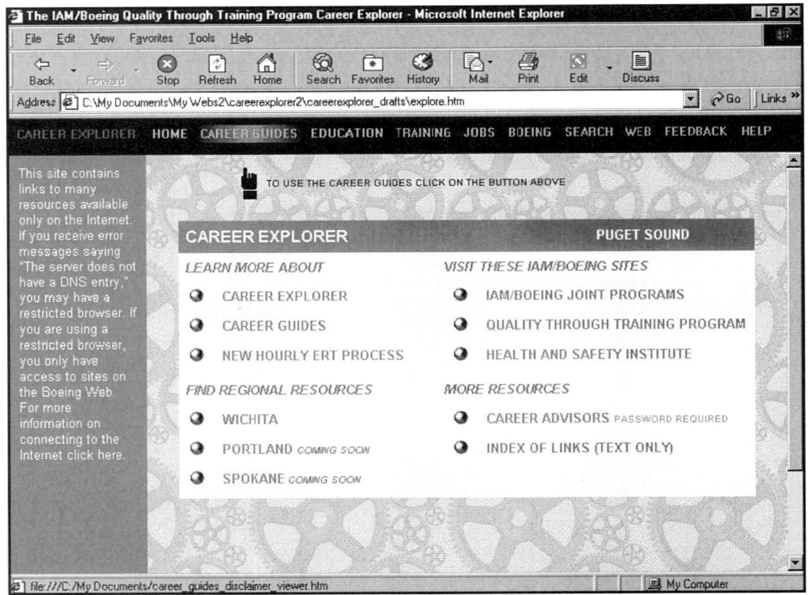

FIGURE 59.7
Use tables to combine a variety of elements and backgrounds over a background image on your page.

Two objects are in the foreground: an arrow and a table. The Table Properties have been set to a white background color, and No Borders has been selected to make the table structure transparent to the viewer. The type is contained in cells that have their own background colors. The images of the metal ball are in the foreground of their cells, hyperlinked to their topics.

A quick and easy way to prepare an image for background use is to insert the image into a new page and then alter the image using the FrontPage Picture tools. When you save the page, the Embedded file's dialog box prompts you to save the image. Save it to your Web with a new filename and then specify it as the background image by using Format, Background, Formatting, Background Picture.

Useful tools for preparing background images are the brightness, contrast, black and white, and washout tools.

Manipulating Images

FrontPage provides a powerful array of tools for manipulating images, including these new features in FrontPage 2000:

- Dynamic HTML can be easily applied to images and hotspots using Format, Dynamic HTML Events.
- Absolute Positioning provides precise placement of elements on the page with fairly accurate cross-browser compatibility.
- Content elements are layered using z-order in Absolute Positioning.
- Text boxes can be placed and positioned within images.
- Text wrapping around images is now automated.
- Auto Thumbnail settings provide an easy process for developing storefront catalogs and documentation—any application where collections of images are being collected and published.
- Estimated Download displays in the status bar the duration your page will take to download on a 28.8K modem.
- New templates and wizards make it easier to get started.

When you select an image, the Picture toolbar appears. The Picture toolbar in Figure 59.8 is usually found at the bottom of the FrontPage window, but you can drag and place it anywhere on the page.

Layering Text Boxes on Images

With FrontPage 2000, you now can easily layer text boxes over GIFs. Select an image, and then select the Text tool from the Picture toolbar. If the image is not already a GIF when you select it, FrontPage prompts you to allow it to convert the image to a GIF and reduce it to 256 colors. Type text into the box, and then select the text box and position it.

In Figure 59.9, a large JPEG image was sized smaller using AutoThumbnail, washed out, and beveled, and then a Text Box was applied over the image. The image in the figure is selected to show the boundaries of the image and the text box.

Auto Thumbnail and Bevel

To make a thumbnail of an image, select the image and then click the Auto Thumbnail tool. To set default properties for your thumbnails, including size, border, and bevel properties, choose Tools, Page Options, AutoThumbnail.

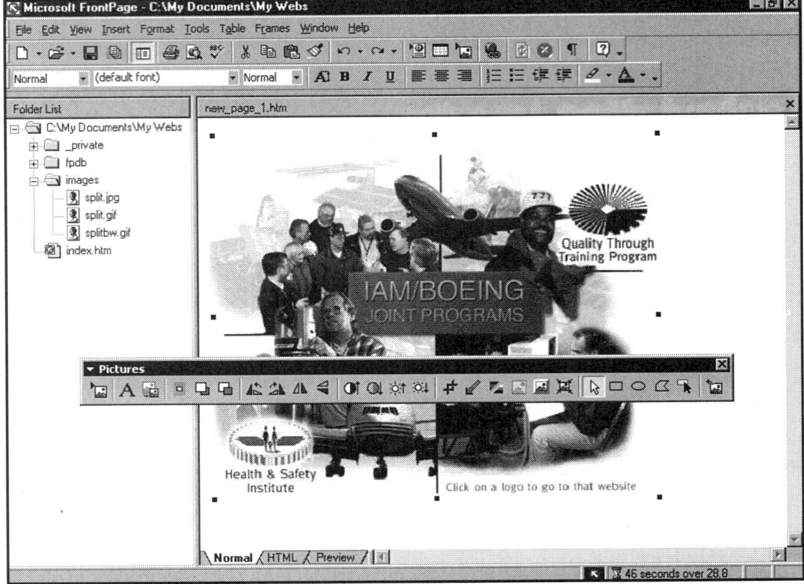

FIGURE 59.8
All the tools for manipulating images except formatting Dynamic HTML effects are found on the Picture toolbar.

FIGURE 59.9
A text box is easily layered and positioned over an image by using the Text tool.

FrontPage creates the thumbnail picture with a hyperlink to the original image in its original dimensions. When you change the size or border properties in the thumbnail's dialog box, they are retained and can be applied to subsequent images to create a consistent catalog of images.

You can add a beveled three-dimensional border to any picture and give it a raised appearance. Select an image and select Bevel on the Pictures toolbar. This works well to give thumbnails the appearance of buttons. In Figure 59.10 the original image on the left was transformed into the thumbnail image in the middle, which was then beveled.

This feature does not work with images smaller than the thumbnail-size properties, and will not capture hyperlinks, hotspots, or animations.

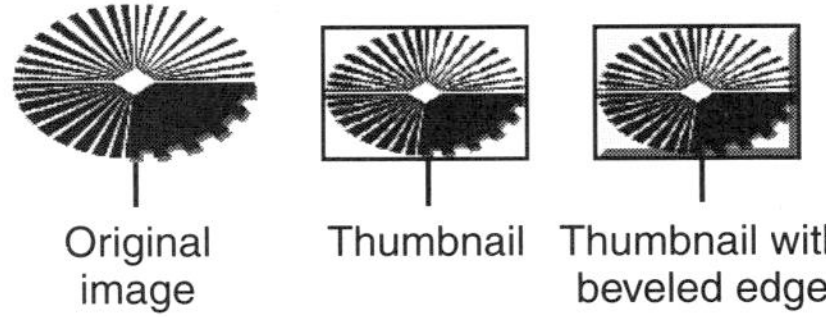

FIGURE 59.10
Creating thumbnails is an easy way to create buttons for your Web.

Absolute Positioning and Layering

Absolute Positioning can be manipulated to create striking effects. In Page Normal view, insert the images you want to position (their initial location is unimportant). Then select the image to be positioned, and select the Absolute Positioning icon from the Images toolbar. Place the image anywhere you want.

The position is recorded as measured by pixel from the top-left corner of its container, whether it's a page, frame, or cell in a table. After an image has been positioned, you can select it again and click the Absolute Positioning to undo, and the image reverts to its former position.

For more control, display the Positioning Toolbar using View, Toolbars, Positioning. You can drag the element to a new location or enter the Left (x-coordinate) and Top (y-coordinate) pixel coordinates in the Positioning toolbar.

You can also use the Positioning toolbar to layer images by specifying a Z-index value. The z-order is the element's position in the layers of the page. Positive values place elements in ascending order in front of the main text-flow layer (layer 0), and negative values place elements in descending order behind layer 0.

In Figure 59.11 the three logos have been positioned and then layered. The icon that was auto-thumbnailed is layer one, the large icon is layer 2, and the auto-thumbnailed and beveled icon is layer three.

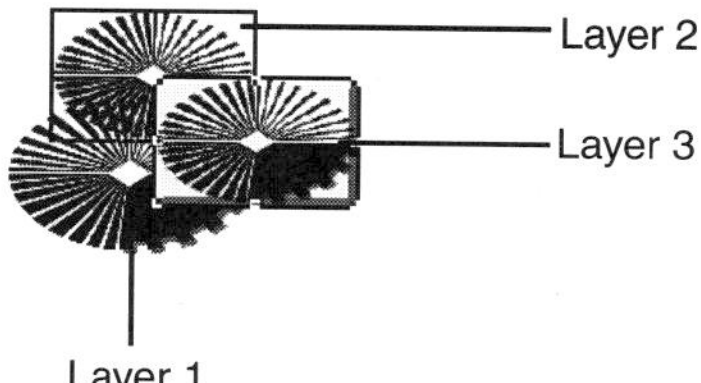

FIGURE 59.11
Combine Absolute Positioning and Layering to create dynamic visual impacts.

In Figure 59.12 two JPEG images were positioned and layered. The photographic JPEG was positioned and layered on top of the text, which is also a JPEG image. The photo was then resized to fit the outline of the bottom JPEG.

FIGURE 59.12
Images can be positioned and layered to give the appearance of a single image.

If several instances of the same image file are positioned on the page, any effect applied to one of the images will be applied to all instances of that image. To make a collage of the same image using Absolute Positioning, make as many copies of the image as you need in Folders view, giving each copy a unique name. Then insert the unique images into your page, and alter them individually.

CAUTION

Tags and nonprinting characters alter absolute positioning if they are displayed while you are positioning. Turn off Reveal Tags and Show All so that your page layout in Page Normal view will more closely match your browser view. Preview your results often, and test the results at all expected screen resolutions that your users will be viewing. Although an absolutely positioned element always appears at the same coordinates you specify, the final results may vary by browser and resolution.

Also, be aware that Dynamic HTML effects are unpredictable when used with absolute positioning. So many possible combinations of features and effects are available that you will have to verify your expected results through trial and error.

Flip and Rotate

Use the horizontal and vertical Flip tools to reverse images and create mirror images (see Figure 59.13). To create a mirror, make two file copies of an image and then flip one of the images.

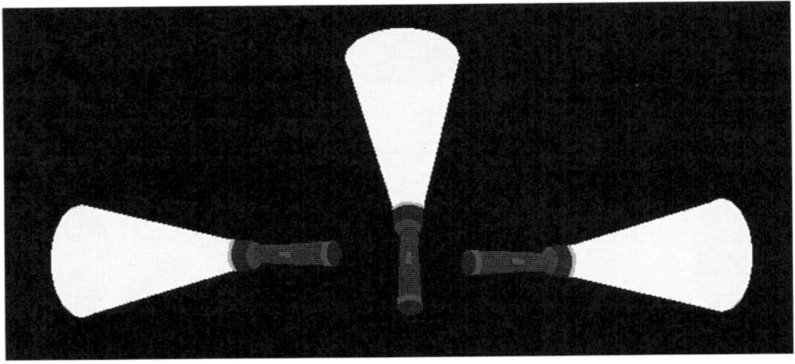

FIGURE 59.13
Flip and rotate copies of the same image to create interesting visual effects.

The Rotate icons work in 90% increments. Select the image and then click the left or right rotate icon to rotate the image to the desired position.

Black and White, Contrast, Brightness, and Washout

These effects are great for using the same image in several ways. You can convert a color image to black and white, or washout an image, much like adding a screen. Use Contrast to increase or decrease clarity. Use Brightness to make the image lighter or darker and heavier.

In Figure 59.14, an original and four copies of the image were pasted into the page. The top image is the dark original, which was brightened in the first copy, then converted to black and white in the second copy. In the third copy, contrast was added to the black-and-white image for greater clarity. The fourth copy demonstrates a washout of the original image.

FIGURE 59.14
Images can be altered directly in FrontPage for greater clarity and visual effect.

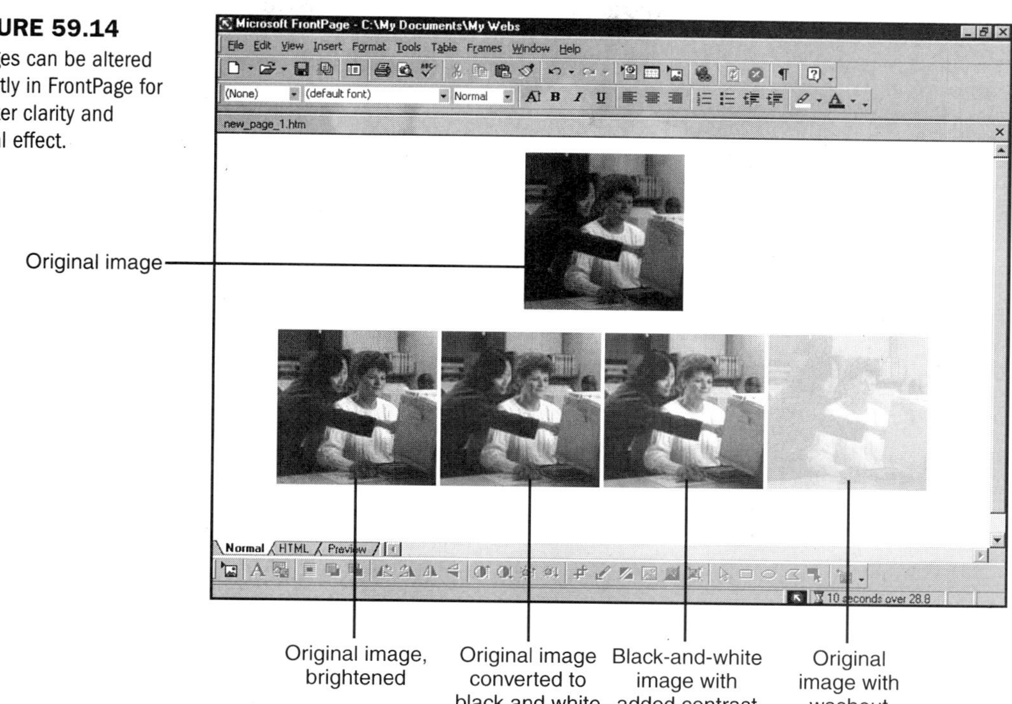

Cropping Images

To crop an image, select it and then select the Crop tool. A box is displayed over the image. Use the Crop cursor to drag the handles of the box to adjust your crop, or click between the outside of the box and inside of the picture frame and draw your own box. When you are satisfied with the position of the box, click Crop again to complete the crop.

In Figure 59.15 the larger JPEG image has been cropped to the area of the crop box. The smaller image shows the result of the crop.

Transparency (Set Transparent Color)

The Transparency tool requires that the selected image be in GIF format. If the image selected is a JPEG, FrontPage prompts you to convert it to a GIF.

Use the Transparency cursor to select the color you want to make transparent. This works well only on images with solid colors to make transparent, such as the white background behind most clip art.

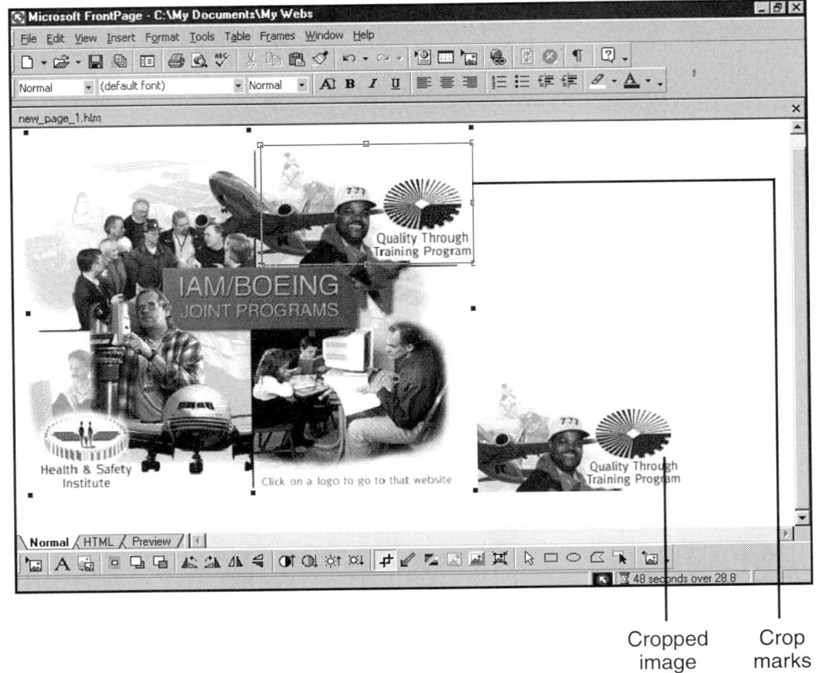

FIGURE 59.15
Images can be cropped directly in FrontPage to fit your design, focus on a highlight, or eliminate unnecessary portions of the image.

TIP After a GIF has been made transparent, you can use the Picture Properties to deselect the Transparent property, or use the Transparency tool to undo.

In Figure 59.16 two copies of a logo in GIF format have been pasted into two cells of a table. The table background is black, and the cell backgrounds are light blue. The dark blue logo on top has a white background, which was made transparent on the logo in the bottom cell.

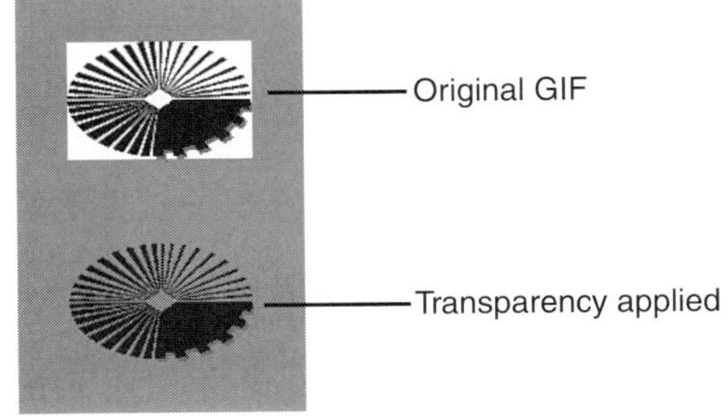

FIGURE 59.16
Use Transparency to apply images such as logos and clip art over a background color on your page.

Creating Hot Spots for Image Maps

You can easily apply hyperlinked hot spots to any area of an image to create an image map:

1. Select the image on which you want to create an image map.
2. From the Picture toolbar, select the type of hot-spot shape you want to create: rectangular, circular, or polygonal.
3. Draw the shape over the image.
4. The Create Hyperlink dialog box appears enabling you to specify a hyperlink from your Web; use your browser to surf for a page on the World Wide Web or your intranet. You can also specify a file on your computer or network, an email address, or create a new page and link.

After a hot spot has been created, just double-click a hot spot to respecify its hyperlink by using the Create Hyperlink dialog box. Figure 59.17 shows a large GIF with three rectangular hot spots outlined.

FIGURE 59.17
FrontPage makes easy work of creating hot spots for your image maps.

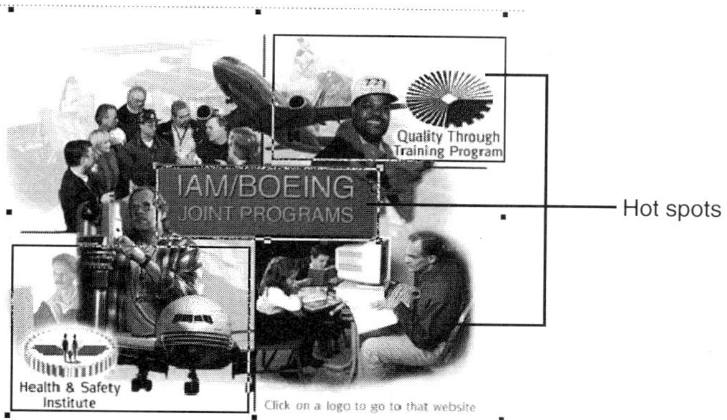

To more easily view hot-spot areas on an image, select the image and then select Highlight Hotspots on the Pictures Toolbar to view the hot spots only, as shown in Figure 59.18.

Resample and Restore

After an image has been resized, either manually or using the Picture Properties, it still retains its original file size. To reduce the file size for a picture that has been made smaller, select the picture and then select the Resample tool.

After an image has been altered, use the Restore tool to return it to its original size and properties.

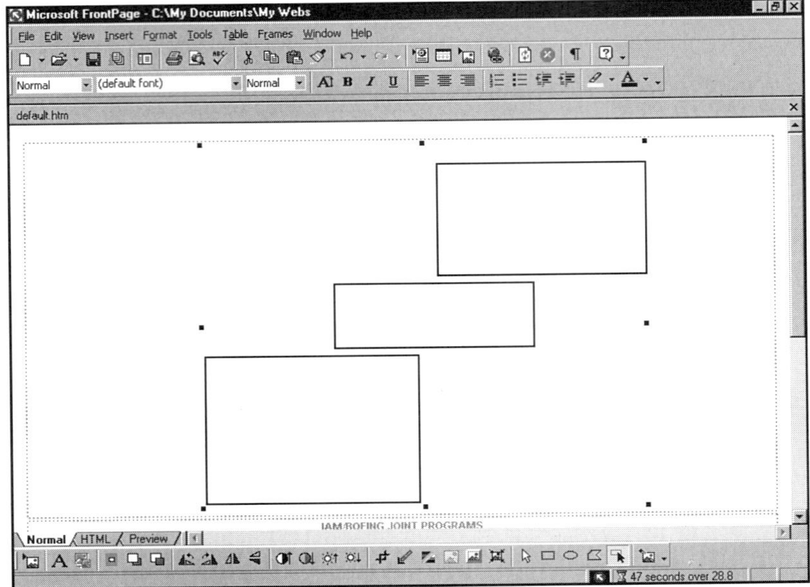

FIGURE 59.18
Use Highlight Hotspots to clearly identify the hot-spot areas of your image.

Animated Images

Whether used for grabbing attention, highlighting an illustration, showing off, or advertising, animations offer endless opportunities for creativity. Used wisely, they can be effective traffic generators; used poorly they can offend and insult your audience and send them away from your site.

GIF animations are series of images displayed at intervals that create the perception of motion. Advertisers and pornography sites have been leaders in GIF animation, developing simple, compelling images in motion that tantalize and motivate traffic to their sites.

In Figure 59.19, an animated GIF has been inserted into the page. It congregates 12 separate GIF files into one 156KB file, and displays a new image every few seconds. Because each image is small, they display quickly, giving the appearance of a seamless transition. The file loops continuously, and has been used on several pages within its Web. Figures 59.20 and 59.21 are two of the other 12 images in this GIF.

FIGURE 59.19
The total animated GIF file is 156KB, but each image is only about 13KB, so the first image appears quickly.

FIGURE 59.20
While the first image displays, the second image is downloading, and appears seamlessly, replacing the first after a specified time period.

FIGURE 59.21
The third image appears after the specified time period, and the images continue to revolve, each seamlessly replacing the previous.

You can also use Dynamic HTML (DHTML) to quickly and easily create animation-like effects with your images and just about anything else on your page, including animated GIFs. These effects are triggered by events, such as loading a page, or a mouseover. These effects work well with both Microsoft Internet Explorer and Netscape Navigator 4.0 and later, and degrade into static images for both version 3 browsers.

To apply DHTML effects to an object, perform the following steps:

1. Select the element to be animated.
2. Select Format from the main menu.
3. Select Dynamic HTML Effects to display the DHTML Effects toolbar. The toolbar can be positioned anywhere on the page.
4. In the On box, select the event that will trigger the animation, such as Click, Double Click, Mouse Over, or Page Load.
5. In the Apply box, select the type of animation effect to be used on occurrence of the type of event you selected in the On box.
6. In the Choose Settings box, select the settings for the effect selected in the Apply box. If you use an event such as mouseover, also specify an event such as mouseout.

TIP To highlight elements using DHTML animation, use the Highlight DHTML Effects tool on the DHTML Effects toolbar. To remove an effect, select the element and then click Remove Effect on the DHTML Effects toolbar. Use Format Painter on the Standard toolbar to copy effects from one page element to another.

CAUTION

Although you can and should combine multiple effects on the same element, such as separate effects for a page load: a mouseover and a click, combinations can be unpredictable and should be previewed in a browser.

Inserting Video

When used judiciously, video can be a powerful medium. For example, in an industrial application, you might provide real-world examples of a process or product in action for training purposes. Corporate communications from chief executives might be dispersed to employees via video. Live events can also be fed through your pages to remote viewers.

Adding video to your Web site requires planning. Production, development, data storage, and hosting all play a critical role. Size, quality, and speed must be balanced to produce an experience that will be effective, and remain within the constraints of your hosting environment and budget.

Know your audience and how they will benefit from the video. Plan how the video will interact with the users' other experiences on your site. As with using text and graphics, make sure it's the best way to present your information.

Identify the format you will use and which player or players your audience will need to view the video. Identify roles and responsibilities—producer, developer, server administration—and plan how much time and effort will need to be invested, and how that will impact your budget.

If you are just beginning, you might want to start small. Every second of video adds a substantial incremental cost to you and the user in bandwidth, time, and data storage. Test different formats to determine what will work best for development, hosting, and the user's site.

Microsoft provides several alternatives for playing videos, and third-party video players abound, with their own proprietary formats and controls. They can be just as easily incorporated into your page. Just be aware that the user must have a compatible player for the file format you provide.

▶ For more about playing video files, **see** "Video Files and Players," **p. 1606**

It's often good policy to inform users before they attempt to start a video whether it might require a unique or nonresident player, and provide a link to quickly and easily download the player. For example, many sites feature video clips in several formats, such as RealVideo and MPEG, and provide links to RealMedia to download the RealVideo player for free.

Inserting Video As a Picture

The simplest way to incorporate a video into your page is to choose Insert, Picture, Video and specify an AVI file just like any other image. The video file in Figure 59.22 was inserted this way. The file contains all the information it needs to spawn a compatible viewer, and it can be resized and restored just as any other image.

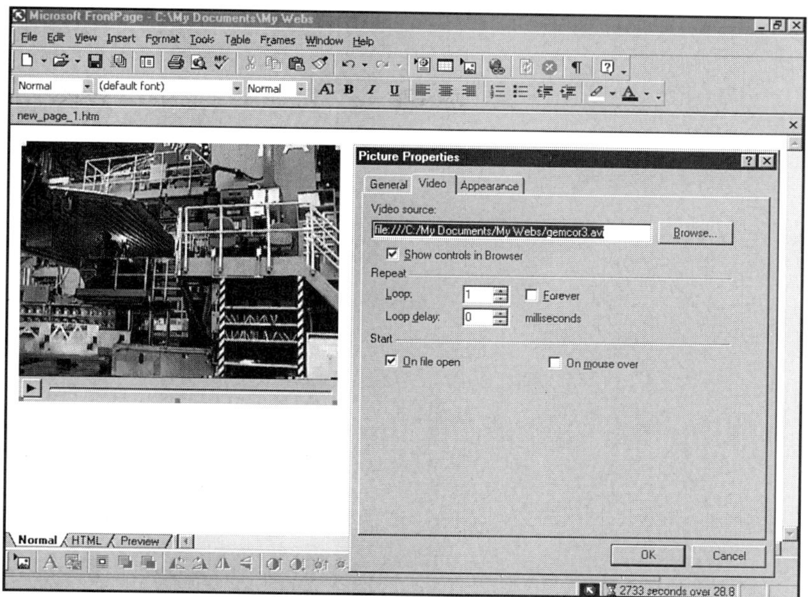

FIGURE 59.22
Discretion is required when using nonstreaming video: The 15-second, 5MB video represented here takes 45 minutes to download over a 28.8K modem.

Controlling Video Using ActiveX Controls

To incorporate streaming video into your Web site with FrontPage, you'll need to use ActiveX Controls. Microsoft provides a collection of ActiveX controls with FrontPage 2000. Control parameters can be customized or used as is, and you can create your own controls using various development tools, including the ActiveX Control Pad and Microsoft Visual InterDev.

ActiveX Controls are inserted into a Web page in Page Normal view by using Insert, Advanced, ActiveX Controls. When you insert a control, you are actually embedding a player in your page that is controlled by the properties you establish for the control. The list of available controls includes the following:

- ActiveMovie Control Object, Microsoft NetShow Player, and Windows Media Player ActiveX Controls—Insert an ActiveMovie Control from the ActiveX Controls list, and then right-click the video object and select ActiveX Control Properties from the shortcut menu, as shown in Figure 59.23. The Options dialog box provides Playback controls for audio volume and balance, repeat properties, and size. Advanced options are available for playing both RealMedia and Windows Media. The Object tag offers basic layout options, and you can provide an alternative representation while the player is downloading. The Parameters tag lists additional properties that can be adjusted to control the appearance and actions of the player. The NetShow and Windows Media Player controls operate in the same manner.

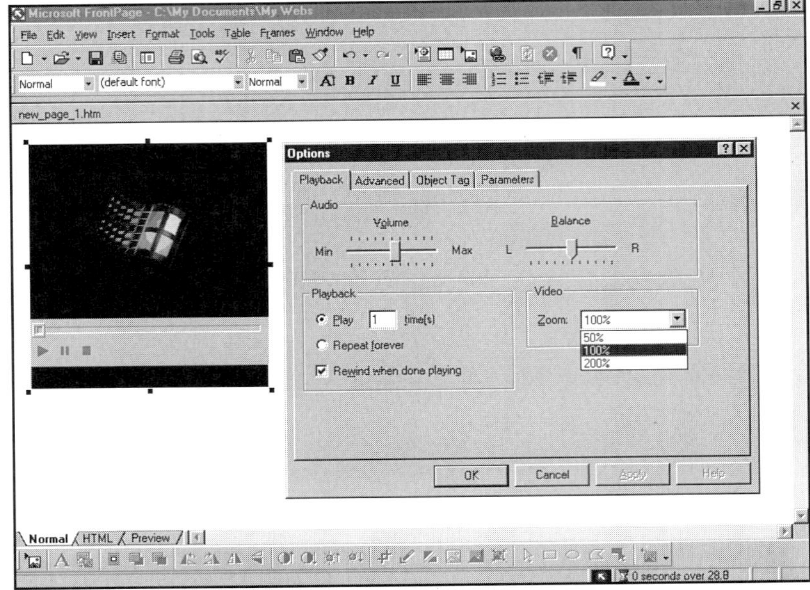

FIGURE 59.23
The ActiveX control properties for the ActiveMovie Control Object, Microsoft NetShow Player, and Windows Media Player provide the same basic functionality with different sets of customizable parameters.

- RealPlayer ActiveX Control Object—You might have to add this control from the Customize ActiveX Control List. The control shown in Figure 59.24 uses NetShow with RealMedia 4.0 Filter to play RealVideo files through the RealPlayer.

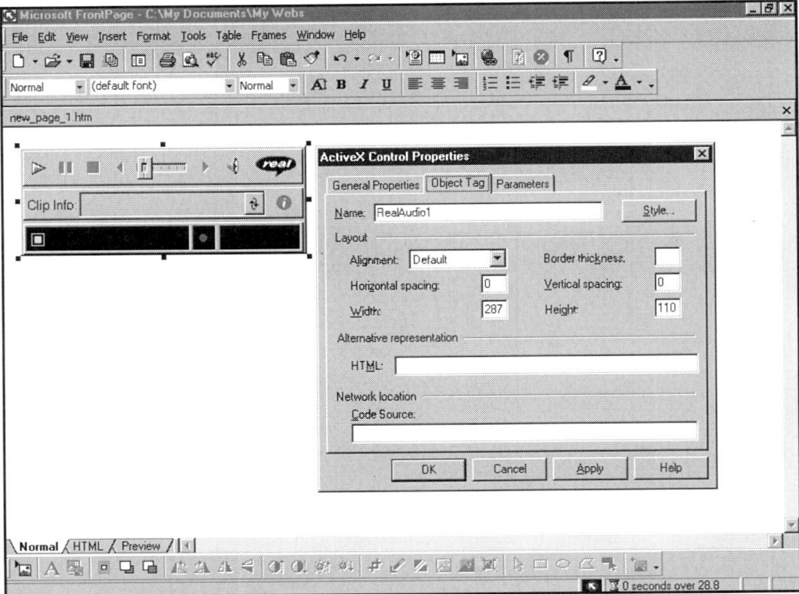

FIGURE 59.24
You can embed a RealPlayer control in your page, by using the RealPlayer ActiveX Control Object.

Using the *<OBJECT>* Tag to Add ActiveX Controls

ActiveX controls also can be coded into your HTML using the <OBJECT> tag. The <OBJECT> tag does not work with Netscape, which requires its own <EMBED> tag and a plug-in (Npdsplay.dll) to allow users of Netscape Navigator to enable ASF content on Netscape browsers. When you use both tags, each browser ignores the other's tag. The following HTML code provides an example of how you might use the <OBJECT> and <EMBED> tags to provide compatibility for both browsers:

```
<OBJECT ID="MediaPlayer" width=320 height=240
  classid="CLSID:22D6F312-B0F6-11D0-94AB-0080C74C7E95"
  codebase="http://activex.microsoft.com/activex/controls/mplayer/en/
➥nsmp2inf.cab#Version=,1,52,701"
  standby="Loading Microsoft Windows Media Player components..."
  type="application/x-oleobject">
  <PARAM name="FileName" value="mms://myserver/mypath/myfile.asf">
  <EMBED type="application/x-mplayer2"
    pluginspage="http://www.microsoft.com/Windows/Downloads/Contents/
➥Products/MediaPlayer/"
    SRC="mms://myserver/mypath/myfile.asf"
    name="MediaPlayer"
    width=320
    height=240>
  </EMBED>
</OBJECT>
```

CHAPTER 60

Creating Advanced Pages

In this chapter

Applying the Advanced Functionality of FrontPage 2000

If you are working in a comprehensive, integrated Microsoft Office environment, creating visually and operationally dynamic Web sites is much easier with FrontPage 2000. Many new and enhanced features in FrontPage 2000 exploit its further integration with Office.

If you are developing Web sites for a mixed browser/server environment, the issues are more complex. The power of using FrontPage advanced components and automated "programming without programming" features comes with a price. To use most of the advanced features of FrontPage, FrontPage Extensions must be maintained on the Web server. Some features also require Office 2000 server extensions and applications, such as Access, and some require that clients use Internet Explorer 5.

Microsoft, of course, offers many solutions, including server-based application distribution and a host of Web server systems. However, compromises must be made between investment in more powerful servers and network infrastructures, thereby allowing the organization to distribute thinner client PCs, or install thinner servers and ever more-bloated client PCs to absorb ever more-bloated code.

If your organization is using any browser but Internet Explorer, true interoperability of Web pages across browsers can be achieved only by programming with scripts: PERL, CGI, SQL, Visual Basic, JavaScript, XML, and so on. Nonetheless, FrontPage 2000 enables nonprogrammers to develop advanced functionality where before only capable programmers dared to venture.

Developing Webs for the Future (and the Past)

"Evolvability is about growing through change with as little damage as possible...it's about making things future-proof," said Tim Berners-Lee, director of the World Wide Web Consortium (W3C), philosophizing about Web design for the future.

Competing standards. Competing products. Competing philosophies, approaches, designs. The world of the Web, still in its infancy, is already complex, confusing, and challenging, ripe with opportunity for great success and grand failure.

The decisions you make today must stand the test of time. As computers get faster, tools get smarter, and the potential increases almost exponentially every changing season, how do you harness that potential for the power user with more advanced technology, while not excluding the novice or entry-level user?

In a world of haves and have nots, as the price of entry continues to decrease, so does the value of that entry as speed, capability, and potential increase for those who can afford it. How do you balance these issues with your own missions, goals, and abilities? There are no easy answers.

Organizations tasked to communicate and interact with diverse audiences have been forced to remain focused on the lowest common denominator, unable to take advantage of the many advances in functionality and development productivity offered by products such as FrontPage 2000. Tightly focused organizations serving the more affluent are able to leverage the technology for greater profit and pleasure.

Can Berners-Lee's idea be realized? As the Web industry evolves and expands, consolidates and spreads, only time will tell.

Adding Forms to Your FrontPage Web

A *form* is a collection of fields for gathering information. Users fill out a form by typing text in boxes, clicking radio (also called option) buttons and check boxes, and selecting options from drop-down menus. After a form is completed, submitted, and validated, the data is processed through a form handler that feeds the information to a database, email, or text file.

Using FrontPage, you can send the results to more than one destination. For example, you could send the results to a file to import into a sales database, and also send an email to alert marketing of the information that has been received. You also can use the Database Results Wizard to both feed database information to a form and feed information from a form to a database.

FrontPage provides form automation for the most common uses of forms on the Web:

- Collect contact information
- Receive information requests and feedback
- Receive ordering, shipping, and billing information
- Set up a guest book
- Provide Web site searching
- Provide password-protected access to a Web site

To get started quickly, choose File, New, Page, Form Page Wizard. Then select the types of questions to put in the form. Figure 60.1 demonstrates how the Information Request Form in the background was created using the Form Page Wizard. Form fields were selected using the check boxes.

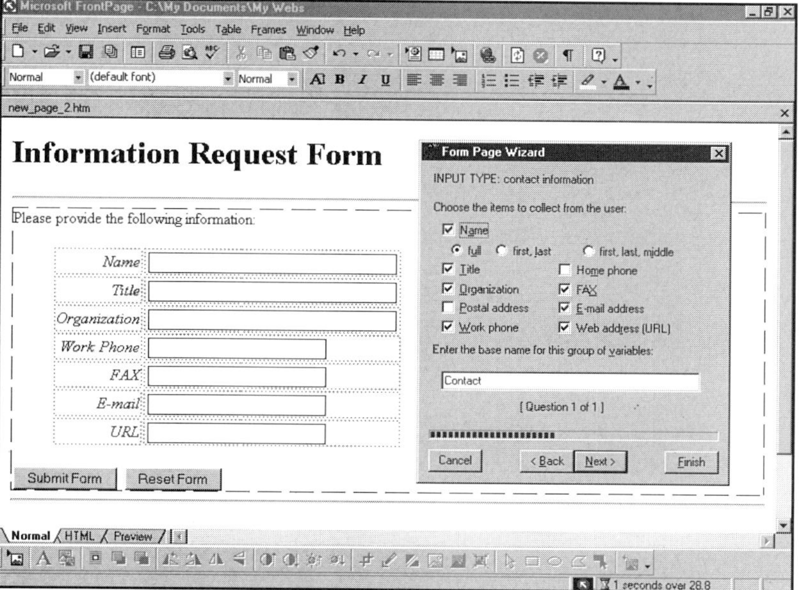

FIGURE 60.1
The Form Page Wizard guides you through the process of selecting and formatting form fields to be included in a new form page. The result of this dialog box is seen in the background.

To insert a new form on any new or existing page, choose Insert, Form, Form. You can create a form anywhere on a page outside of an existing form (you cannot create a form within a form), and place multiple forms on the same page. As seen in Figure 60.2, FrontPage outlines the form area with a dashed line and places Submit and Reset buttons inside the form.

The Submit button transfers the form results to a form handler, which processes and delivers the information to its destination. The Reset button restores the form to its default state and clears all entries so that users can abort or redo the form before it is submitted.

You can also start a new form by choosing Insert, Form, and selecting any of the form fields. To place additional form fields and buttons within the form, also choose Insert, Form, and select a form field.

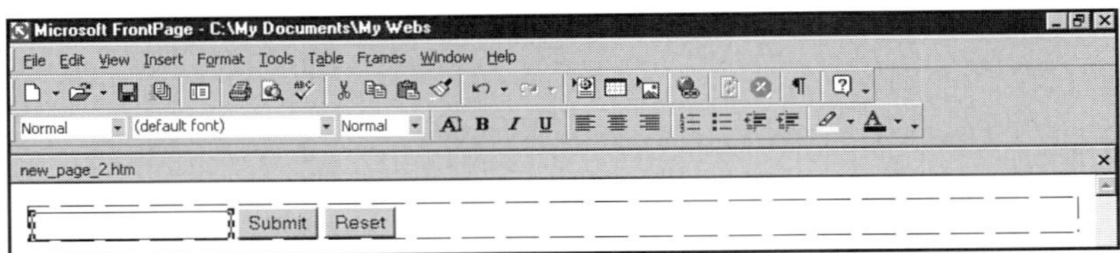

FIGURE 60.2
Create a new form anywhere on a page by choosing Insert, Form and selecting Form or a Form Field from the menu.

While inserting a form field, double-click the field to establish its properties and set validation rules for entry of the field by the user. This prevents freeform and potentially meaningless or useless entries in the field.

After a form has been completed and submitted by the user, a form handler validates the responses against the rules you have established for each field in the form. If entry errors or empty fields requiring an entry are found during validation, a default validation page is automatically displayed to inform the user which form fields need to be entered or corrected. You also can create your own validation pages.

- For more information and a discussion of each type of form field, **see** "Inserting and Validating Form Fields" **p. 1631**
- To learn how to create an optional confirmation page, **see** "Confirmation Form," **p. 1639**
- To learn more about saving form results, **see** "Saving and Sending Form Results," **p. 1644**

FrontPage provides several form handlers for saving the form results, and you can use scripts (PERL, CGI, and so on) to create your own custom form handlers. Form results are saved to a text file in the _private folder of your Web by default.

NOTE If you are using scripts to handle the form results, you must place form fields outside the outlined form area. To facilitate using form fields with scripts, you can disable automatic form functionality. Choose Tools, Page Options, and clear the Automatically Enclose Form Fields Within a Form check box on the General tab.

Inserting and Validating Form Fields

Form fields are placed on the page just like text. You can use tables, line breaks, cascading style sheets, and absolute positioning to format the style of the fields within the form.

Use text and images placed inside the form to provide labels, questions, definitions, and directions for visitors to use the form fields. Tables placed inside a form are useful for structuring your form and accurately positioning the text and form fields.

Each form field has different properties, and provides a different approach for gathering and validating information; sometimes more than one approach may work for your needs.

To set properties for a field, double-click the field to display the Form Field Properties dialog box. You can specify the length of a text box, whether an option is selected by default, and the choices in a drop-down menu, for example. To establish validation rules for the field, click the Validate button on the Form Field Properties dialog box.

Validation

Validation rules control the way data is entered in the form fields. Just double-click any form field, and then click the button to display the Validation Properties dialog box. Formats for entering information, such as dates, phone numbers, and zip codes, can be enforced to prevent errors and ensure usability of the data collected. The Display Name in the Validation Properties dialog box is used to identify the field on the validation page.

When the user submits the form, the entries are compared to the validation rules. If errors exist, a validation page is returned with directions for correcting those errors. An optional confirmation page can be displayed when all fields have been entered correctly and passed validation.

Decide which form fields to use based on how the visitor will use the form, and how the form fields will be validated.

- One-line and scrolling text boxes are used to require a formatted textual entry of characters, integers, numbers, and symbols.
- Radio (option) buttons can enforce selection of a single button, or force selection of one button of a group. Radio buttons can also be used for multiple choice, such as check boxes.
- Drop-down menus allow multiple selection from a group of choices and can enforce single or multiple selection from a group.
- Check boxes are used for single or multiple entries that are optional, and are not validated.

FrontPage provides a default validation results page linked to its form, or you can create your own validation page. To link your validation page with its form, perform these steps:

1. Right-click the form and select Form Properties from the shortcut menu.
2. Click Options.
3. Click the Confirmation Page tab.
4. Enter the address of your validation page in the URL of Validation Failure Page box (if you don't provide an address, the default validation page is used).

Make it as easy as possible for the visitor to navigate the form in a logical and efficient manner. Keep related form fields together to prevent unnecessary scrolling while the user completes the form, and use the Form Field Properties dialog box to specify a Tab Order for each form field so that a user can quickly tab through the form and bypass fields that don't require entries.

NOTE A new feature in Internet Explorer 5 offers auto-text entry while typing entries into Web forms. During your journey through Internet Explorer 5, it records your entries into the text fields. When it recognizes redundant entries, a dialog box appears that enables you to allow auto-text entry. If you choose auto-entry, Internet Explorer maintains scrolling menus of previously entered values. This is useful to reduce redundant data entry, but might also promote redundant entries when more unique results are desired.

One-Line Text Boxes

Use one-line text boxes to collect a small amount of text, such as a name, date, number, comment, or description. These text boxes can be any width. For entries requiring more than one line, use Scrolling Text Boxes.

Use validation to establish required formats for the entries:

1. Double-click the form.
2. Click the Validate button.
3. Enter a Display name. In Figure 60.3, the display name is Home Phone. This name will be used on the validation page to identify a missing entry for this field.
4. Specify the type of data (text, integer, or number). For example, to collect a telephone number, use the text data type to accept only digits and hyphens, and require a minimum data length of 12 characters to help ensure accuracy of the entry, as shown in Figure 60.3.

Use text labels to tell the user how to fill in the box. In the example of Figure 60.3, the instructions next to the Home Phone box are `Enter in 000-000-0000 format`.

To collect a nine-digit zip code, you could create two text boxes separated by a hyphen. Use the Text Box Properties dialog box to establish the width of each box in characters, and then use the Text Box Validation dialog box to require a minimum and maximum entry of five integers in the first text box and four integers in the second text box.

Radio Buttons

A single radio button (also called option buttons) can be used to require an entry, such as an "I agree" or other acknowledgment, before the form can be processed. A group of radio buttons can be used for multiple entries (instead of check boxes), or you can use validation to enforce the selection of one option from a group (see Figure 60.4).

To enforce a selection from a series of radio buttons, all associated buttons must be part of a group and have individual names. One of the buttons can be specified as Selected, or they can all be left Not selected. Providing a default selection can speed user entry, but can also lead to less meaningful or useful results if users accept the defaults.

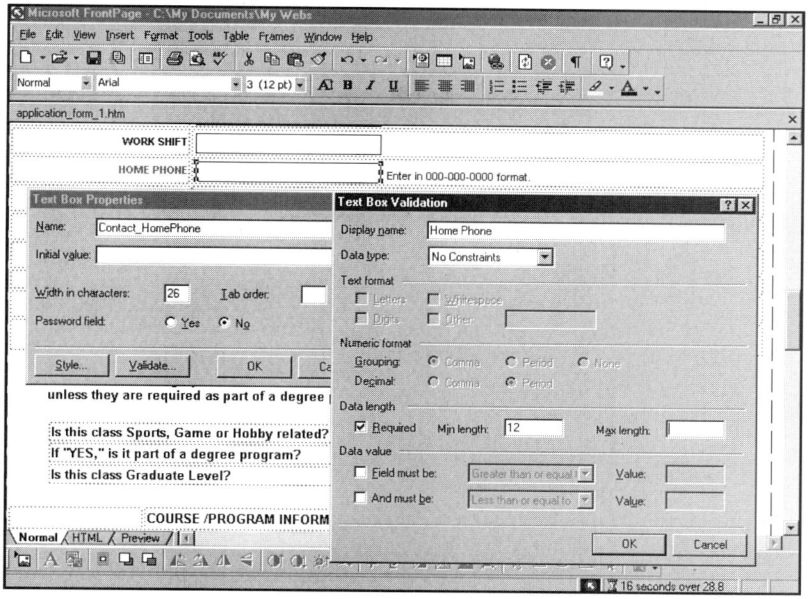

FIGURE 60.3
One-line text boxes are used to collect simple data, such as the user's name, email address, or phone number. The selected form field is shown with its Properties and Validation dialog boxes displayed.

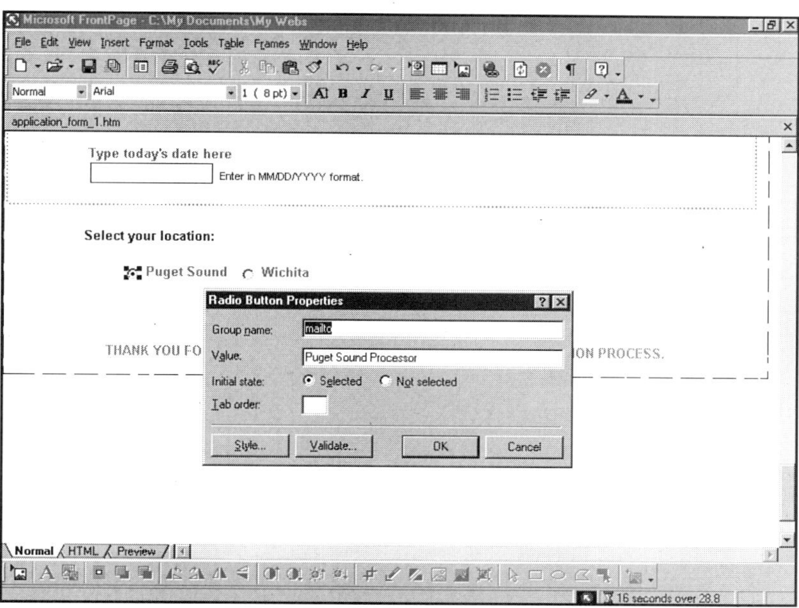

FIGURE 60.4
Use radio buttons to enforce the selection of one option from a group.

In Figure 60.4, for example, it is known that the greater majority of users will want to select Puget Sound, so the Puget Sound option button is Selected. If this information were not known, it would be better to leave both buttons Not Selected and force the user to make the appropriate choice.

A single radio button can be displayed unselected, and the user required to select that button before the form will process. In Figure 60.5, for example, the user must specifically select the radio button to agree with the statement "Do you agree to the policies stated above?"

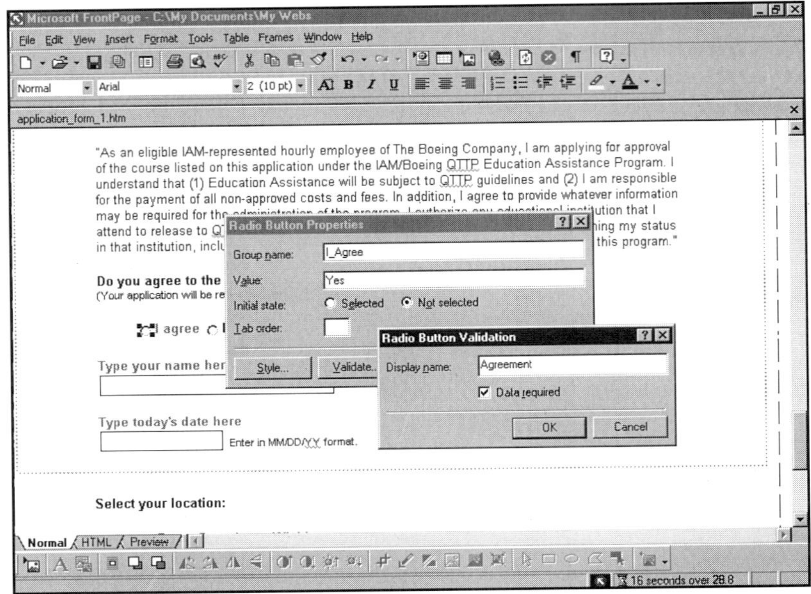

FIGURE 60.5
To force an explicit response to a single radio button, use validation to require an entry to provide a display name for the field on a validation page.

Scrolling Text Boxes

The scrolling text box collects multiple lines of text, such as longer comments and descriptions, and can be sized to accommodate any expected length of text. A scrollbar is provided to scroll through text entries larger than the size of the box, as shown in Figure 60.6. In this example, users are encouraged to enter a text message in addition to the information collected from other fields in the form.

Drop-Down Menus

Drop-down menus present a list of choices, similar to using radio buttons. The difference is that radio buttons are excellent when you have only a few choices to select from, or want all choices to be visible, although drop-down menus are better when long lists must be selected from. Drop-down menus also allow multiple selections, whereas radio button validation enforces one selection only.

To insert a drop-down menu, follow these steps:

1. Choose Insert, Form, Drop-Down Menu.
2. Double-click the form field. Figure 60.7 shows the Drop-Down Menu Properties dialog box.

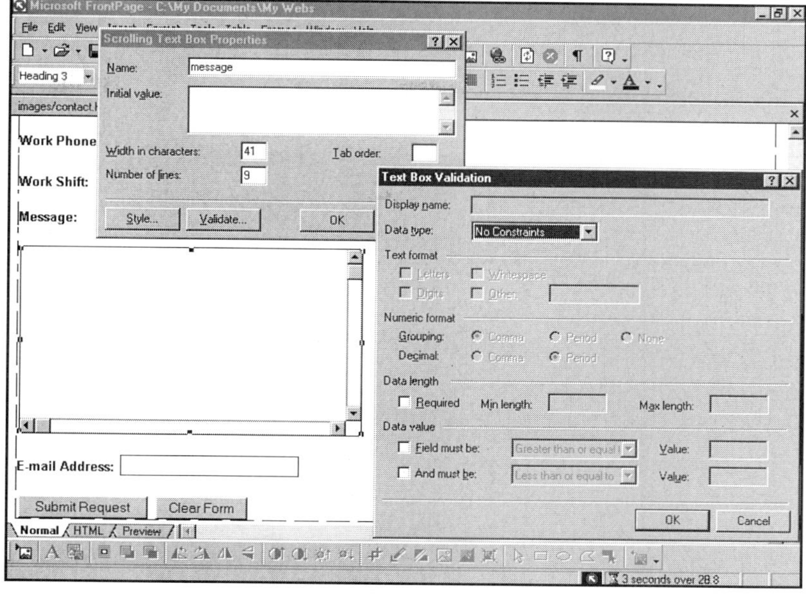

FIGURE 60.6

Scrolling text boxes are useful for collecting comments and descriptions from users, such as in a feedback form or guest book. Entry can be optional, or specific results can be required and validated using Text box validation.

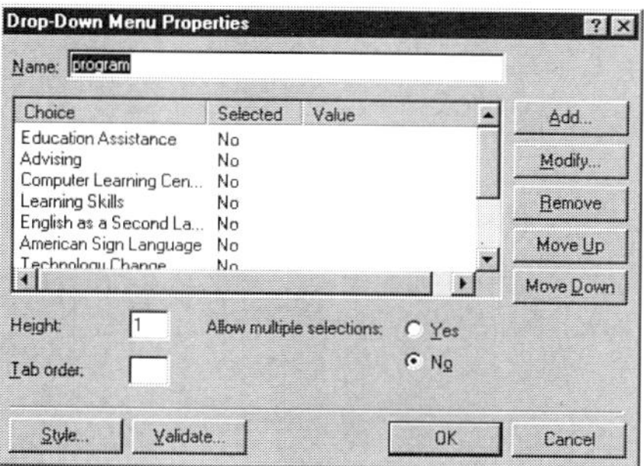

FIGURE 60.7

Use the Drop-Down Menu Properties dialog box to create menus with multiple selections.

3. Click the Validate button. To enforce a selection from a drop-down menu, set the minimum number of selections required in the Validation dialog box. You can force the user to select as many items as needed. You can also disallow the first menu item from being selected. This is useful if the first item is an instruction, such as "Select an item from the list below," or "Select three items."

Figure 60.8 shows the results as seen in Internet Explorer 5.

Check Boxes

Check boxes are another way to offer multiple choice, especially when it is advantageous to present the viewer all selections at once, as seen in Figure 60.9. An All of the Above check box could also be created.

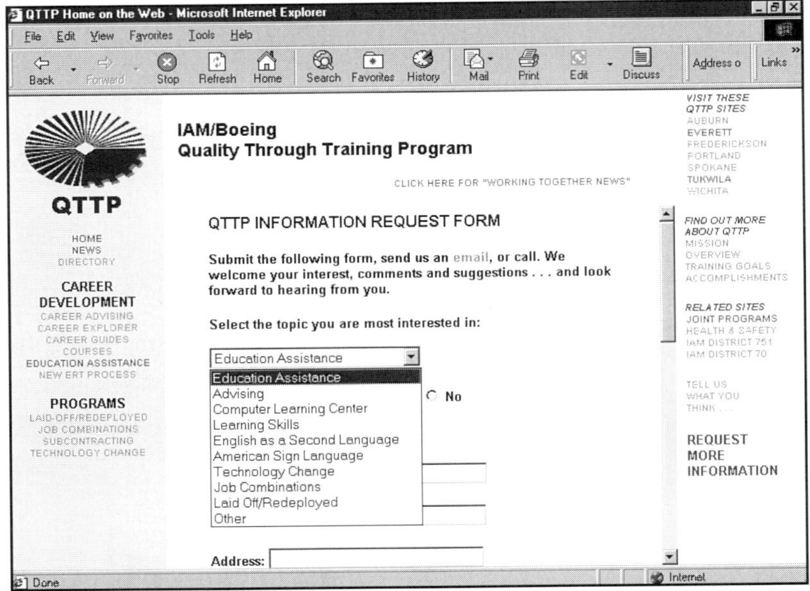

FIGURE 60.8
This drop-down menu enables users to request more information on selected areas of interest.

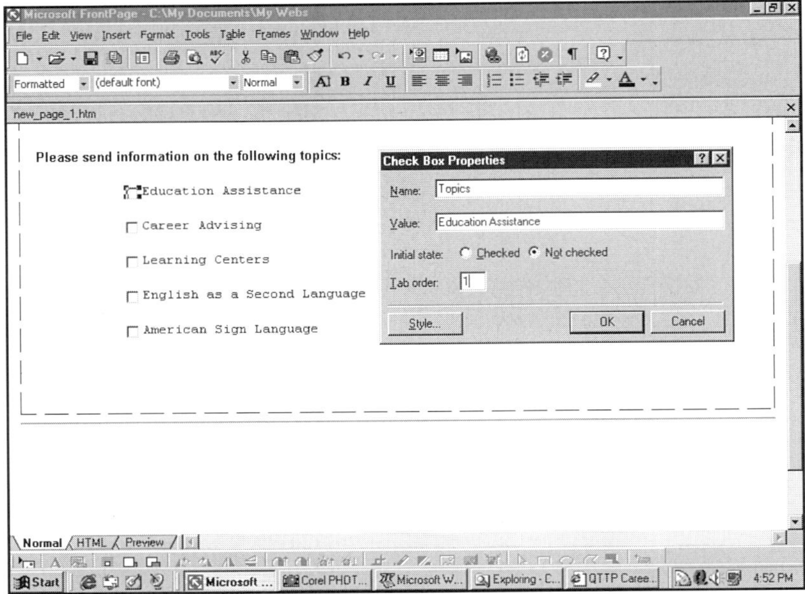

FIGURE 60.9
Check boxes are used to offer multiple choices.

Check boxes are either checked or unchecked, and are not validated. Use radio buttons to enforce a selection.

Push Buttons

Submit and Reset buttons are inserted by default when you begin a new form using the wizard or by choosing Insert, Form, Form. These buttons can be renamed, and their actions can be invoked by other means, such as picture or text links, but the action of the Submit button (which invokes the Post or Get action to process the form) must be invoked to process the form.

In Figure 60.10, the Submit button has been renamed Process, which invokes the Submit action.

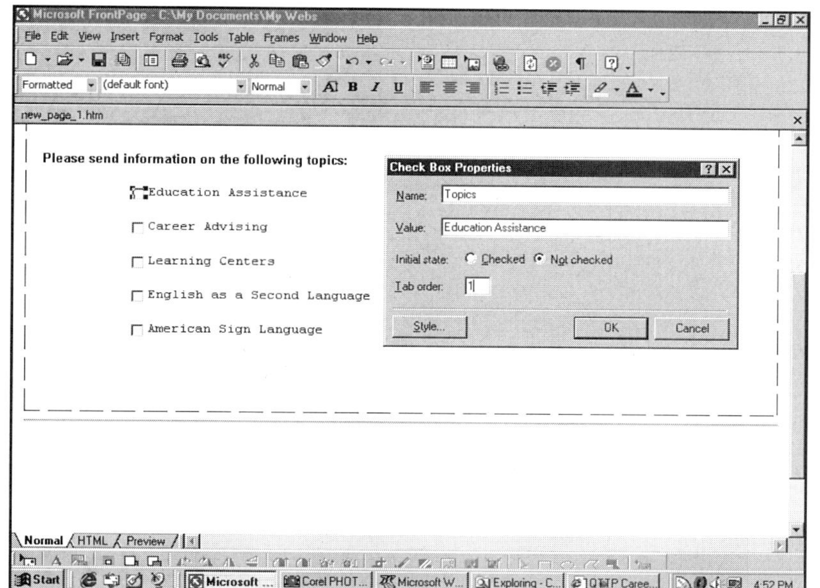

FIGURE 60.10
The Submit button can be renamed, but its action (Get or Post) must be invoked to process the form.

FrontPage Form Automation

FrontPage provides several automated functions to simplify developing what is actually a complex process for creating, handling, validating, and confirming forms.

The simplest way to develop a form is to use the Form Page Wizard to create a form page and take advantage of the default form handler and validation page associated with the form. This works for any form created using the Form Page Wizard as well as the Feedback Form, User Registration Form, Guest book, and Discussion Groups.

For more unique and sophisticated form processes, you can customize handling, validation, and confirmation using the Options for Saving Results of Form dialog box, the Validation Form template, and the Confirmation Form template. You can also create your own forms, custom form handlers, and validation and confirmation pages, and associate them with your forms.

▶ For more about saving form results, **see** "Saving and Sending Form Results," **p. 1644**

Form Page Wizard

This wizard is great for getting started with forms. Choose File, New, Page and select Form Page Wizard. The wizard guides you through the process of developing a page with commonly used forms and form fields. Select a form from the list of available forms, and then select from a list of commonly used fields to place in the form. After the form is created, you can manually customize the form to further meet your needs, or use the wizard again to further edit the form.

Forms created with the wizard are associated with a default validation form, and results are saved to a file located in the _private folder of your Web site by default. You also can create and associate confirmation pages with these forms.

▶ For more about confirmation pages, **see** "Confirmation Form," **p. 1639**

Feedback Form

Every Web site should have a form for gathering feedback from users. A convenient template for feedback forms is created by choosing File, New, Page, Feedback Form. Customize the form as required. By default, the form data is saved to a text file located in the _private folder in your Web site. The results also can be sent to an email account or a database using the Form Properties dialog box, as shown in Figure 60.11. Further parameters for file results, email results, confirmation pages, and fields to be saved can be established from the Options button, which displays the Options for Saving Form Results dialog box.

▶ For more about saving forms, **see** "Saving and Sending Form Results," **p. 1644**

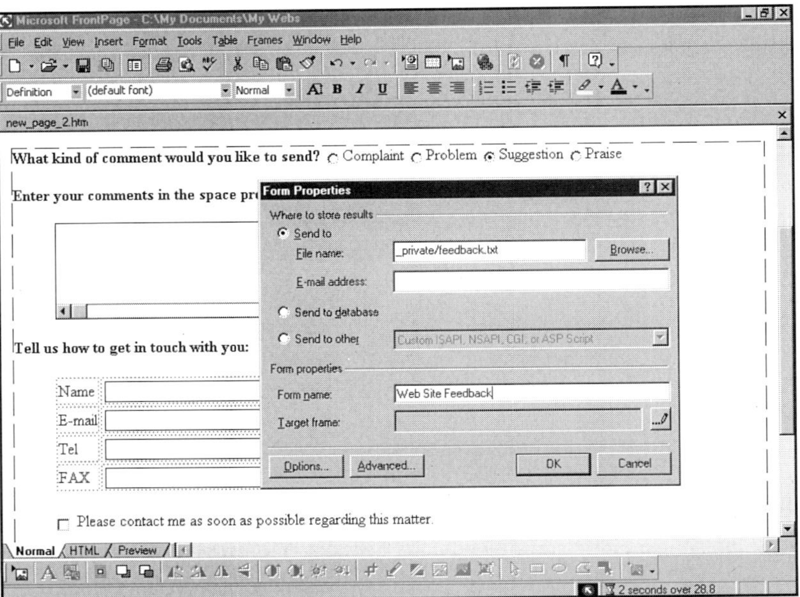

FIGURE 60.11
Use the Form Properties dialog box to specify a destination for the results of your feedback form.

Confirmation Form

After a user submits a form, it is good practice to display a page with a "thank-you" or other message to acknowledge receipt and give the user an opportunity to correct any errors. The FrontPage Confirmation Form creates the confirmation page template shown in Figure 60.12.

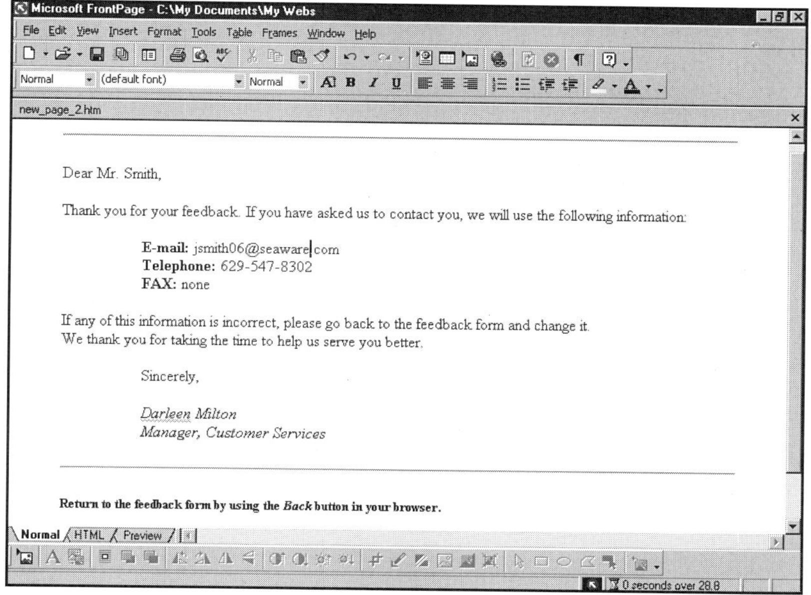

FIGURE 60.12
Confirmation pages provide the user an opportunity to review the information being submitted and return to the previous form to make corrections.

Unlike a validation page, a confirmation page is not provided by default. You can create your own confirmation pages just as you would any other pages in your Web site, or you can use the Confirmation Form as a template for your confirmation page and associate it with an input form. The contents of any of the form fields on an input form can be included in a confirmation page.

To enter a Form Field Component that displays the user's entry in a form field, perform these steps:

1. Place the cursor where you want to place the Form Field Component.
2. Choose Insert, Component, Confirmation Field.
3. In the Name of Form Field to Confirm box, enter the name of the field from which to display information, and then click OK.

The name of the field is displayed in brackets on the form, and this component can be placed in a salutation, a sentence, a list, or anywhere else in the confirmation page. When listing a series of entries, provide text to describe the entry just as you would for a form field in the input form. After publishing your Web site, the component displays the user's entry for that field when the confirmation form is displayed.

From this page the user can review the information being submitted. To make corrections, the browser's Back button is used to return to the form being submitted. The user can correct, resubmit, and review the results repeatedly until satisfied with the information being submitted.

The default confirmation page displays a sample list of field names from the feedback form. These Confirmation Field Components are identified by the names of the form fields being handled. Any of the form fields from Form Results, Registration Forms, or Discussion Groups, can be used as FrontPage Confirmation Field Components on the Confirmation Form to show users what they have submitted.

To insert field results, follow these steps:

1. Choose Insert, Components, Confirmation Field.
2. Enter the name of a field (use the name specified in Form Field Properties for the field) from the form being handled.
3. Repeat these steps to insert each additional form field component.

To link a form to its confirmation page, perform these steps:

1. Open the page containing your form.
2. Right-click the form (not a form field), and then select Form Properties from the shortcut menu.
3. Click Options.
4. Click the Confirmation page tab.
5. Enter the address of the confirmation page in the URL of Confirmation Page box as shown in Figure 60.13.
6. Save the form.

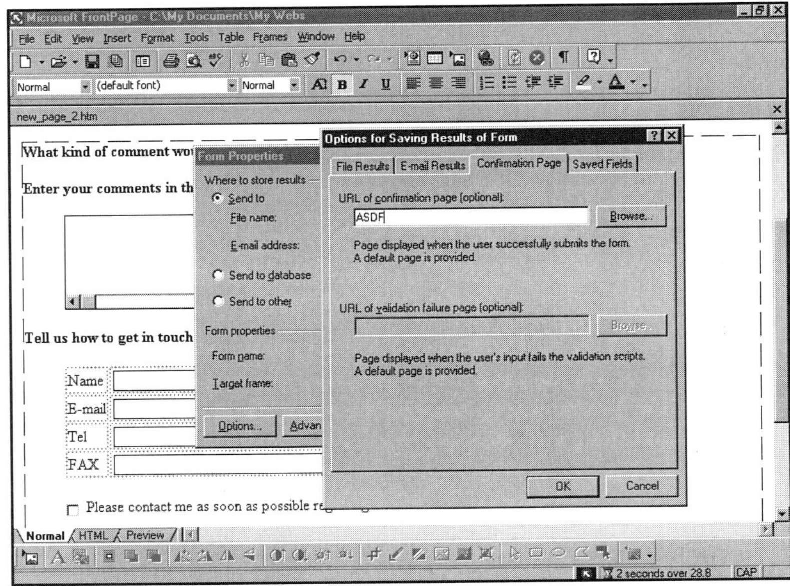

FIGURE 60.13
Link a custom confirmation page to its form using the Confirmation Page tab.

The confirmation form will not display until all fields have been entered according to the validation rules you establish for each field. If any field is entered incorrectly or a required field is not entered or checked when the user submits the form, a validation page is returned to the user. The validation page identifies the corrections to be made and gives the user an opportunity to return to the form to make those corrections.

A link should be provided on the confirmation page to enable the user to advance to another page after reviewing the results. When the user advances, the form handler sends the results to their destination.

Guest Book

Guest books are used to accumulate comments from visitors to your site. These comments are saved to the file guestlog.htm by default. This file is displayed when the guest book page is reloaded, and you can provide links to this file anywhere else on your site.

To capture comments in a different file, follow these steps:

1. Right-click the guest book form and select Form Properties from the shortcut menu.
2. Click Options.
3. Change the filename on the File Results tab.
4. Click OK, and then click OK again.
5. Right-click the hidden Include Page Properties component below the form. In Figure 60.14, the hidden Include component has been selected and is highlighted by the black bar.
6. Enter the filename of the Page to Include and click OK.

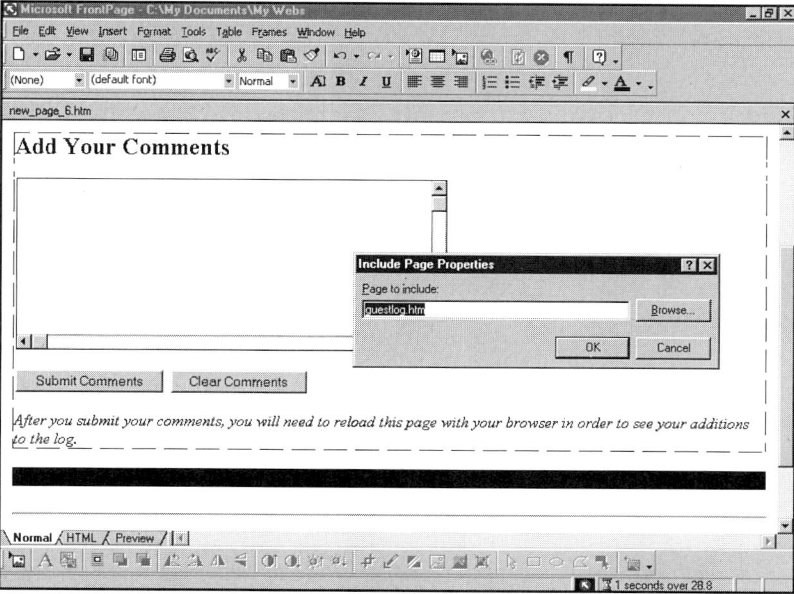

FIGURE 60.14
Visitors to your site can enter comments in a guest book and then view their comments with all other comments in the guest book when they reload the page. In this figure, a portion of the guest book form is displayed behind the Include Page Properties component.

Using the FrontPage form handler, you can save results to two files (and an email account). For example, you could save guest book comments to both an HTML file that can be viewed on your site and to a second comma-delimited file used to collect selected fields in a database.

User Registration Form

When you need to control access to a site or page, the User Registration Form provides simple password security. You can use the default form page, or place the registration form component on the page visitors will use to acquire entry to your restricted Web site or sub-Web. FrontPage Extensions are required, and the registration form must be saved in the root Web page of your site.

The form requires visitors to enter a username and password. The Registration Form Handler compares these entries to a list of authenticated users that you have established, and also logs the names of users who have entered. Notice that you can save results from the form in addition to the username and password. In this example, an email field is being captured. You can also capture the user's Username (which can be different from the registration username), Remote computer name, Browser type, and the date and time of entry using the Saved Fields tab of the Options for Registration Form Handler.

To create the form, perform the following steps:

1. Choose File, New, Page.
2. From the General tab, select User Registration. The form appears in Page Normal view as in Figure 60.15.

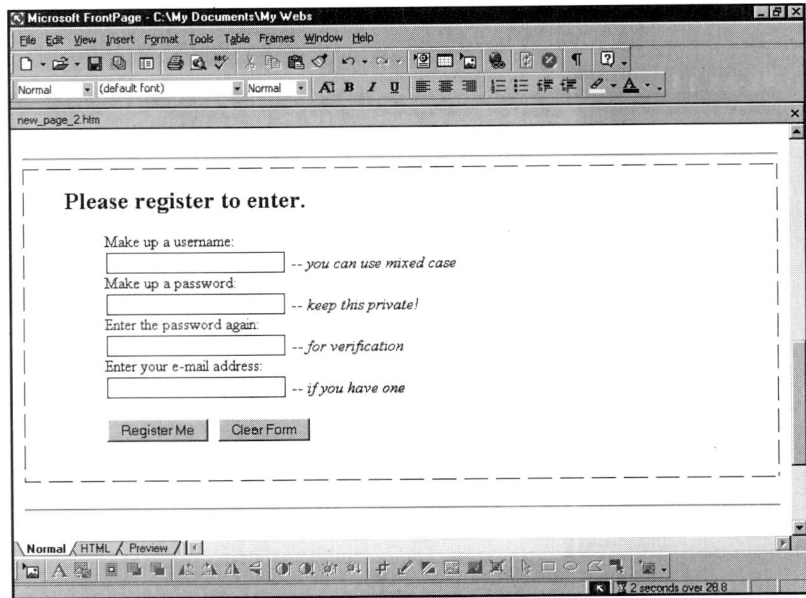

FIGURE 60.15
FrontPage provides a default User Registration Form and automatically assigns it to the Registration Form Handler.

3. Right-click the form and select Form Properties from the shortcut menu.
4. Click Options to display the Options for Registration Form Handler dialog box.
5. On the Registration tab, specify the following:

   The name of the Web site or sub-Web being entered.

   The Username fields (such as Name or FirstName, LastName).

   The Password field.

   The Password confirmation field.
6. Select or deselect the Require Secure Password check box. If the box is deselected, the handler only collects the username, and doesn't require a password.
7. Enter an optional URL of Registration Failure Page (similar to a validation page) to be displayed when there are errors in the username or password entries.
8. Select the File Results tab and provide destinations for saving the results.
9. Select the Saved Fields tab. In the example shown in Figure 60.16, a mail field is being captured. You could collect additional information by creating additional form fields on the User Registration Form. From this tab you can also capture the user's Username (which can be different from the registration username), Remote computer name, and Browser type, and format the date and time of entry.

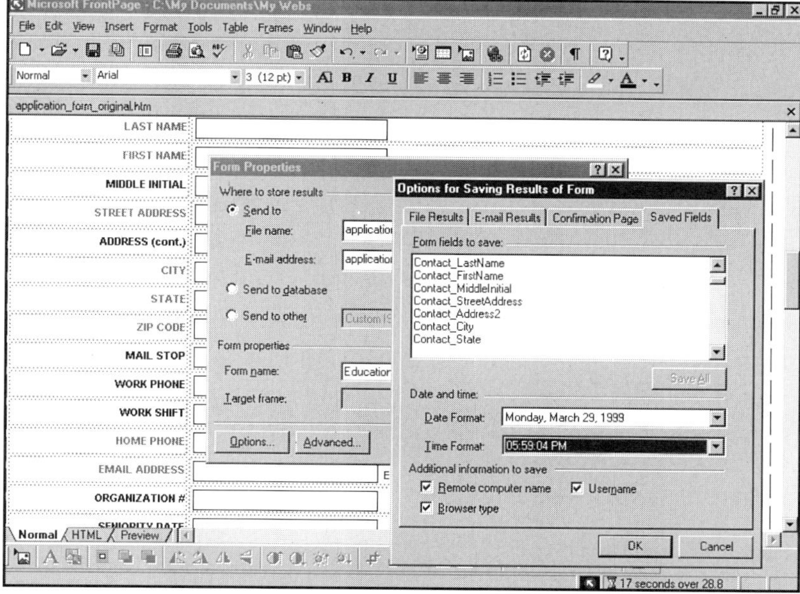

FIGURE 60.16
Select the Saved Fields tab.

Next, to implement password-protected security for entry to the Web site or sub-Web, perform the following steps:

1. Choose Tools, Security, Permissions, Settings.
2. Select Use Unique Permissions for this Web.

3. Choose Apply Users.
4. Select Only Registered Users Have Browser Access.
5. Add users under categories for Browse, Author, and Administer Access Permissions.
6. If your Web server supports a domain hierarchy, you can obtain a list from the server and select by domain or group. In the Names box select or type a username and add each user, and specify the type of access.

CAUTION

Registration provides restricted access only to your Web site. Self-registration is not allowed on Microsoft Web servers that use Windows NT accounts to establish Web permissions. Windows NT security and Microsoft Internet Information Services (IIS) do not allow registration through a Web browser. Other Web servers also may not allow self-registration.

Saving and Sending Form Results

FrontPage provides three form handlers: a Form handler, a Registration Form handler, and a Discussion Group form handler. When a form is created using the automated form development tools, FrontPage automatically assigns a form handler to the form. You can save results to files, email accounts, and databases, or designate custom scripts to process the form.

NOTE The FrontPage form handlers require FrontPage Server Extensions. You must use custom scripts (CGI, PERL, and so on) to process the forms through servers without the extensions.

To control the Form handler, use the Form Properties dialog box shown in Figure 60.17 to specify destinations and select options for saving and sending form results:

1. Right-click the form and select Form Properties from the shortcut menu.
2. Select an option button to specify Where to Store Results.
3. Enter an optional Form Name and Target Frame if desired.

In addition to selecting form fields to save, you can include the time, address, username, and Web browser of the user, as shown in Figure 60.18.

To specify the form results to be saved, follow this procedure:

1. Right-click the form and select Form Properties from the shortcut menu.
2. Click Options.
3. Click the Saved Fields tab.
4. The fields in the form appear in the Form Fields to Save list. Delete any fields that you do not want to include in the form results, or select All.

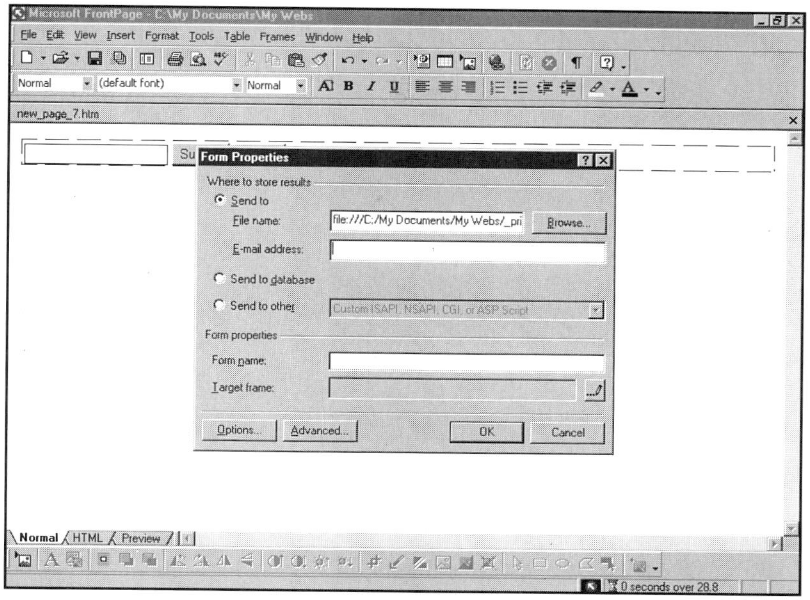

FIGURE 60.17
Use the Form Properties dialog box to handle form results.

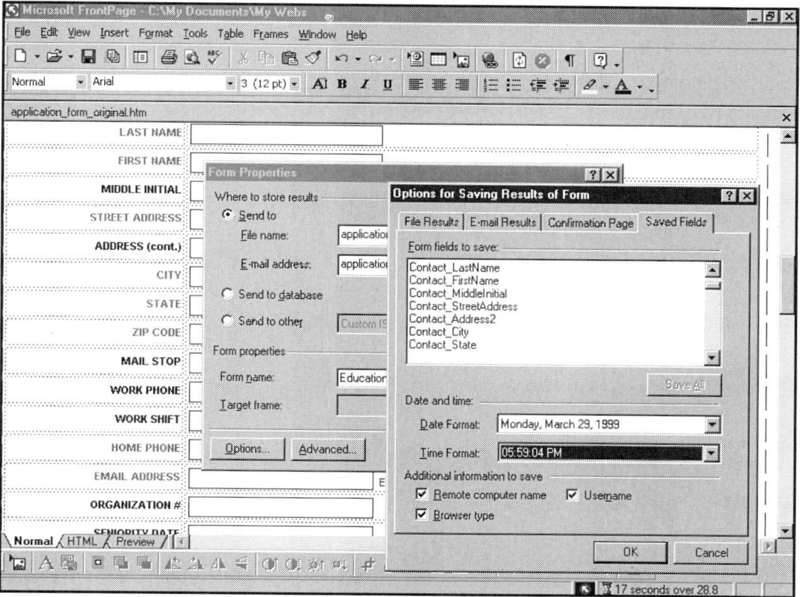

FIGURE 60.18
Use the Saved Fields tab on the Options for Saving Results of Form dialog box to select form fields and additional user information to save with the form results.

5. Then format the Date and Time, if desired.
6. Select any additional information you want to save with the form results:
   - Name or IP address of the visitor's computer
   - Username of the visitor
   - Web browser used by the visitor
7. Click OK, and then click OK again on the Form Properties dialog box.

The form handler sends results to a file by default, and results are appended to the file. This file can be formatted as text, HTML, and delimited for use with a database. The results from each submission of the form also can be sent as email in any of these formats. By saving results to an HTML file, you can display the results back to users, as you would with a guest book form.

The Registration Form and Discussion Group Handlers operate similarly and are controlled through their own separate dialog boxes. For example, right-click a registration form and choose Form Properties, Options to display the Options for Registration Form Handler dialog box.

Save Results to a Text or HTML File

The default form handler appends results to a file each time a user submits a form. By default, a text file is created in the _private directory, although it can be placed anywhere in your Web site.

The file format can be text, HTML, or a delimited file for import into a database, and the results of each transaction can be emailed in these formats. By saving the results to an HTML file, they can be viewed on the Web. You also can save the results to a second file, so you can save in two formats, and in an email, as shown in Figure 60.19.

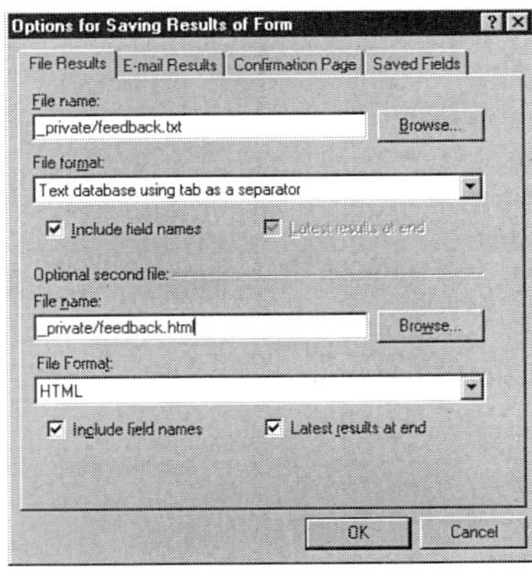

FIGURE 60.19
You can save form results to two files. In this example results are saved to a text file and an HTML file.

Use the Form Properties dialog box and Options to specify files and formats:

1. Right-click the form and select Form Properties.
2. Click Send To. The default address for the results file is displayed. You can specify another address, or click Browse to locate another file.

3. Click Options.
4. Select the File Results tab.
5. Specify the format of the text file and specify whether to include field names in the form results. You can also specify a second file to which to save results.

Send the Results to an Email

You can send form results as an email only, or to both an email and a file, as shown in Figure 60.20. The results can be in text, HTML, or delimited for databases.

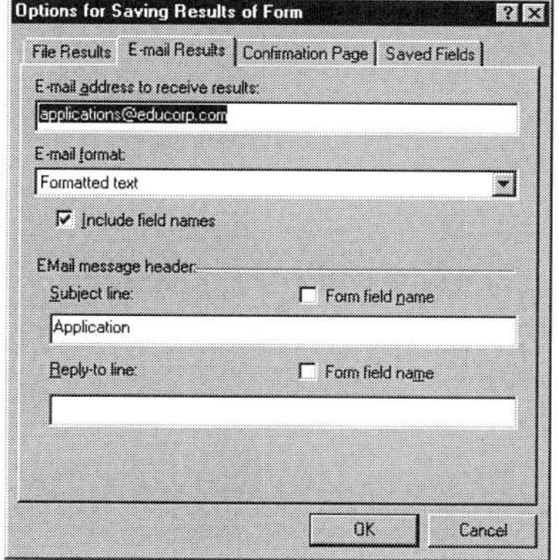

FIGURE 60.20
Use the E-Mail Results tab to format form results to be sent as email.

1. Right-click the form and select Form Properties from the shortcut menu.
2. Click Options.
3. Select the E-Mail Results tab.
4. In the Send to E-Mail address box, type the email address to which you want to send the form results.
5. Select the check box to Include Field Names in the results.
6. In the Subject line box, type a useful identification for the email. The default is "Form Results." You can identify a form field to be the subject line. Just type the name of the form field in the Subject line box. For example, you might choose the field named "Comments" from a comment form.
7. The Reply-To Line enables you to provide a return address. If your form contains a field to collect the site visitor's email address, you can use that address as the sender's return address. Select Form Field Name, and then in the Reply-To Line box, type the name of the form field.

NOTE This feature requires that FrontPage Server Extensions be correctly configured for email.

Save the Results to a Database

The form handler can save form results directly to any ODBC-compliant database. First, you must establish a database connection.

Use Tools, Web Settings, Database to create a new connection. If the database is on a Web or network server, you must establish a Data Source Name (DSN) using the ODBC Data Sources control panel.

When you import a database into your Web site, FrontPage creates the connection for you.

1. Select Folders view.
2. Import a database file into your Web site. The example in Figure 60.21 shows importing the sample database into the /fpdb directory used as the FrontPage default.

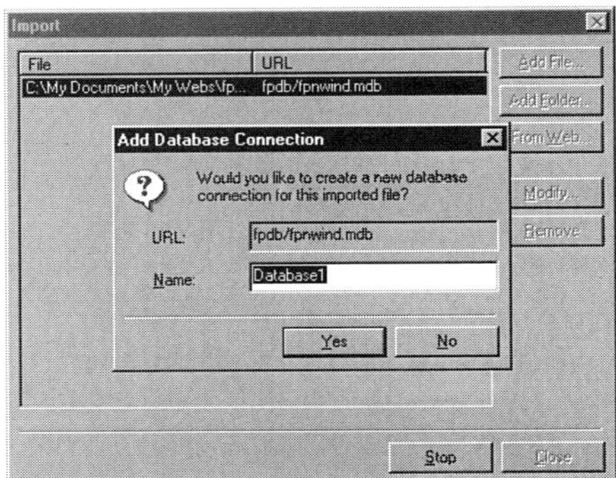

FIGURE 60.21
FrontPage creates a new database connection when you import a database file.

3. FrontPage prompts you to enter a name for the new database connection. Type in a name and click Yes to create the connection. The connection is contained in the global.asa file FrontPage creates in the root directory.
4. Select Page Normal view.
5. Right-click the form, and select Form Properties from the shortcut menu.
6. Select Send to Database.
7. Select Options.
8. On the Database Results tab, select the database connection you previously created.
9. Identify the database table for the form results in the Table to Hold Form Results box.
10. Click the Saved Fields tab.
11. For each of the fields in your form, specify the column of the table in which to save the data.
12. In the Form Fields to Save box, select a form field and then select Modify.
13. In the Save to Database Column box, columns from the table you specified are listed. Specify a column in which to save the form field data, and then select OK.

Repeat these steps for each form field.

Save Results to a New Access Database

If a database is not already created, FrontPage creates a new Access database table using the fields in your form to create columns. The default destination is the /fpdb folder.

1. Right-click the form, and then select Form Properties.
2. Select Send to database.
3. Click Options.
4. On the Database Results tab shown in Figure 60.22, select, add, or create a database connection. To create a new database connection, click Add Connection, then click Add, and enter a name for the new connection. Click OK, and then click OK again to return to the Database Results tab.

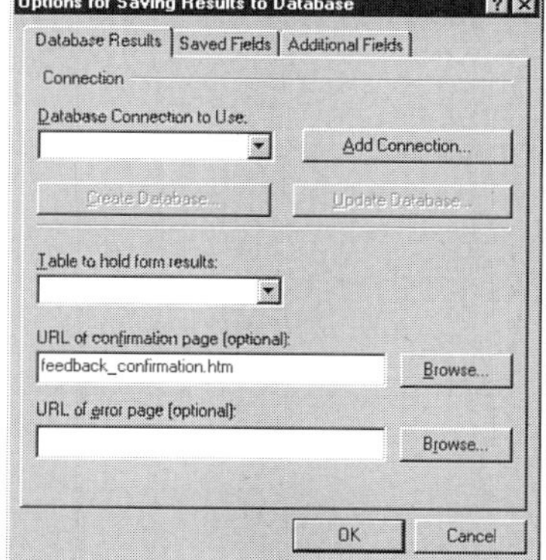

FIGURE 60.22
Create a new database from the Database Results tab on the Options for Saving Database Results to Database dialog box.

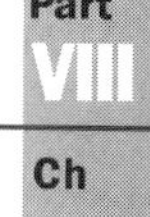

5. After you select a database connection, select a table in which to store the results.
6. Click Create Database. A message confirms the database has been created and provides the name and location in your Web site as shown in Figure 60.23.

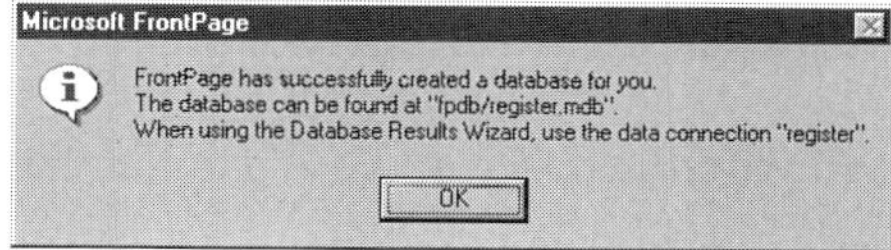

FIGURE 60.23
FrontPage creates a database and provides the name and location in your Web site.

The form page must have an Active Server Page (ASP) file extension (.asp) for the database connection to operate. If the extension of the form page is not already .asp, you are prompted to rename the page with an .asp extension when you save the file.

Save Form Results Using a Custom Form Handler

If you are not using FrontPage Extensions on your server, you can specify a custom script to handle your form results.

1. In Folders view, right-click the folder containing the script and then select Properties on the shortcut menu.
2. Select Allow Scripts to Be Run.
3. Clear the Allow Files to Be Browsed check box to prevent users from browsing the files in the folder, and then click OK.
4. Select Page Normal view.
5. Right-click the form and select Form Properties.
6. Select Send to Other, and then select the type of script: Custom ISAPI, NSAPI, CGI, or ASP from the drop-down list.
7. Select Options.
8. In the Action box, replace Submit with the URL of the custom script form handler (see Figure 60.24).

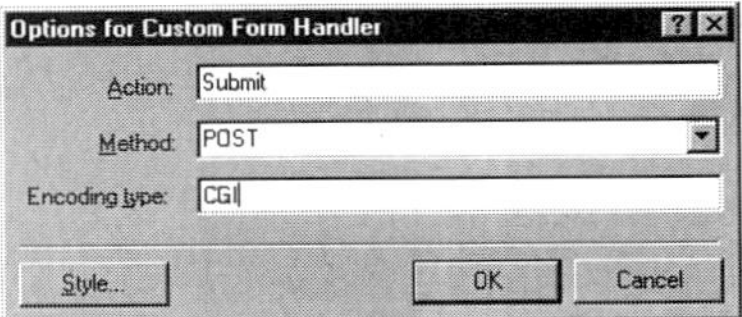

FIGURE 60.24
Use the Options for Custom Form Handler dialog box to specify the Action, Method, and type of script for the form handler.

9. In the Method box, select the method to be used for submitting the results to the form handler:
   - Get method encodes the form's name-value pairs in a server variable named QUERY_STRING.
   - Post method passes the name-value pair directly to the form handler.
10. Click OK, and then click OK again on the Form Properties dialog box.

If you leave the Encoding type box blank, the default encoding method is "*application/x-www-form-urlencoded*."

Using FrontPage Components

FrontPage components are ActiveX Controls that act as drag-and-drop objects on a Web page. FrontPage provides two ways to insert these objects, as a Component or an ActiveX Control. Either way, the component is inserted as an ActiveX Control with properties for alignment, spacing, border, and so on. You also can provide an alternative picture or text representation to replace the object while it is downloading or if the user is unable to download the file.

The components provided with FrontPage accomplish a variety of specialized tasks without programming, including text searches, discussion groups, feedback forms and hit counters.

Third-party components also are available, including snap-in tools and utilities that extend functionality, such as

- Java Applets
- ActiveX Controls
- Visual InterDev Design-Time Controls (DTCs)
- COM Components
- Browser plug-ins

Applications for these components include e-commerce shopping cart applications, streaming media players, and 3D graphics. You also can use FrontPage or Visual InterDev to create your own components. Visual InterDev Design-Time Controls and add-on programs can be used to further automate the creation and management of content across a Web site. Further programmability features in FrontPage include macros, Visual Basic Editor, and Microsoft Script Editor.

The FrontPage HTML editor itself supports HTML, DHTML, JavaScript, VBScript, Active Server Pages, and the rapidly proliferating XML. The Script Editor adds your scripting language code directly into FrontPage with automatic statement completion.

Inserting Office Spreadsheets, PivotTables, and Charts

In Office 2000, the Spreadsheet, Chart, and PivotTable Web components can be used to interact with Office functionality through the Internet Explorer. Through the browser, the user can edit and manipulate data from Excel, Chart, and Access, and return data to the original application.

Office Web Components are ActiveX controls that encapsulate discrete bits of Office functionality:

- The Spreadsheet component enables users to display information from Excel, enter text and numbers, create formulas, recalculate, sort, filter, and format.
- The Chart component provides automatic updates and interactive charts.
- The PivotTable dynamic views component enables users to browse, sort, filter, group, and total data from Access through the browser.

Banner Ad Manager

Harvesting traffic is not only a concern to commercial sites. Within large intranets, and even within large Web sites, banner ads can be an effective means to direct users to important information within the Web site.

The banner ad manager is a basic image animator, rotating a series of images at a specified interval. Choose Insert, Component, Banner Ad to display the Banner Ad Manager Properties dialog box. You can select a transition effect, duration, and the images to include in the ad. After a banner ad is created, it can be sized and absolutely positioned on the page, just like any other picture.

Unfortunately, you can specify only one link for all images in the ad. To rotate individual banner ads in the same space, use the Scheduled Picture component.

Hit Counter

FrontPage provides several basic counters. To include a counter in Page Normal view, go to Insert, Component, Hit Counter and select a folder containing counter images. You also can create custom counters. There are a few rules:

- Counter files must be GIF files with the numbers "0123456789".
- Each GIF image (number) must be evenly spaced.
- These files must be organized into a folder.
- The folder and GIF files must be imported into the Web site. Do not automatically import these pictures.
- Do not use transparent colors.
- Specify a size, any size.
- These counters require FrontPage Extensions on your server.

Hover Buttons

These buttons mimic Dynamic HTML events used to swap pictures on mouseovers. This enables you to quickly create visually dynamic buttons and menus of buttons without developing separate images and applying Dynamic HTML events to each image.

These are useful only if you are developing for a discrete environment where you know the display characteristics of the users' computers. Otherwise, their effects are easily sabotaged by users who have selected large fonts when you have used small fonts, or vice versa. Test the way these buttons display in several setups before committing to them in your design.

Marquees

Marquees are useful for streaming messages across your page, such as up-to-date news tickers or important messages you don't want the user to miss. Multiple marquees of varying sizes, colors, speeds, and directions can also be used to produce creative and visually dynamic effects. Mostly, marquees are obnoxious and hinder the user's experience of the page if the information they contain is not of high value. No new marquee properties have been provided with FrontPage 2000.

Include Page

This component includes the contents of another HTML file into the specified location on the current page. This is useful for repeatedly incorporating different types of elements as one component throughout your Web pages, rather than inserting each element separately on each page. Create a page with the elements you want grouped together and then include that page on any other page on which you want it to appear.

For example, you might want to display a consistent menu at the top of each page. This menu could be developed using text, images, and other objects on its own page, with its own page properties. The page containing the menu and all of its objects and properties can then be included on any other page by selecting the Include Page component from the destination page.

This is similar to using frames to include separate pages on a Web page. Using the Include Page component, however, you can insert pages on a page without requiring the user to have a frames-compatible browser.

Scheduled Picture

Whereas Banner Ads loop a defined series of images at one specified interval, Schedule Picture provides for a linear schedule of events, with each element having its own date and time. For example, if you include advertising on your site, you can establish locations that rotate pictures at specified times, replacing expired ads with new ads.

Categories

This new component requires both Office 2000 and FrontPage Extensions. When building large sites, you can plan ahead and develop a framework for defining categories that group different types of files, regardless of their location. When a file with a recognized category property is added to your Web site, the Categories component updates a list of links to all the files within that category.

In the future, additional tools should offer features that further support applications of this component for greater efficiencies in developing large Web applications for e-commerce, corporate intranets, and entertainment.

For example, you might have a news site that presents several categories of new information (local news, international news, business news, and sports) by date. Although the files are organized in your folders by date of their initial appearance, you could use categories to organize and present archives of links to these articles by category. The stories themselves might be in one folder, while associated images could be located in image folders, and consistent elements such as headers and menus in their own folders, all associated by the categories you defined and specified.

Use the Reports view to display Web files by category. Files are also identified by category within folders.

Search Form

A Search Form enables users to search your Web site just like a search engine searches the Web, using words, phrases, and Boolean operators. The form can be inserted on its own page, or on all pages in your Web site.

To use the Search Form component, FrontPage Server Extensions must be enabled. Choose Tools, Page Options, select the Compatibility tab, and check the Enabled with Microsoft FrontPage Server Extensions check box under Servers.

To insert the component, choose Insert, Component, Search Form. Using the Search Form Properties dialog box, you can customize the form size, add labels for instructions and buttons, and specify formats for the search results.

When you insert a Search Form component, FrontPage begins creating a text index of all words by page in your Web site, and all words from new pages when they are saved to the Web site. To complete a search, FrontPage checks the text index and returns a list of links to locations that match the search text. Searches are limited to the discrete Web site and sub-Web where the search form resides.

FrontPage adds new words to the text index only when you save a page. To refresh the list and delete words that have been removed from your Web site, choose Tools, Recalculate Hyperlinks.

Table of Contents

Use this component to automatically generate a table of contents based on the navigation structure of your Web site. You can create a table for the entire Web site, or for any starting point you specify to create tables that begin anywhere within the hierarchy of your Web site.

The table is refreshed whenever a page is saved to the Web site; you also can manually refresh the table by opening and saving the page containing the table of contents.

To create a table, go to Insert, Components, Table of Contents. In the Table of Contents Properties dialog box, specify the Page URL for Starting Point of Table, and a Heading Font Size or None. The Heading is the title of the starting page. Select Show Each Page Only Once if it has multiple hyperlinks to it and you don't want to display them all. To display pages that aren't hyperlinked, select Show Pages with No Incoming Links.

If the table is on the same page as the starting point, the URL for Starting Point is a hyperlink to the starting-point page.

Discussion Groups

A discussion group is an interactive area on your Web site that lets visitors discuss topics by reading, replying to, and posting new articles or topics. The Discussion Group Wizard creates a sub-Web within the current Web site that includes the following features:

- Table of contents with hyperlinks to discussion topics
- Search form to search articles by word or phrase
- Entry form to post an article
- Threaded replies for posting a new top-level topic or a reply to a current topic
- Confirmation page to confirm that an article has been posted
- Registration form to log in with password protection

To initiate a Discussion Group, choose File, New, Web, Discussion Group Wizard. Note that this wizard feature requires a Web server with FrontPage Extensions.

Querying Databases

The increased integration between FrontPage, Office, and Internet Explorer 5.0 means individuals and workgroups can collaborate more seamlessly and productively to develop database applications over the Web, and more users within an Internetwork will become potential content creators and users.

Integrating databases with the Web is never easy, but with the Office 2000 suite, Microsoft has come a long way in reducing, although not eliminating, the pain. The suite is Web-friendly everywhere; there's even a graphical Web editor included with Access. Information can be quickly and universally shared throughout an organization or published to the Internet, with far greater ease than ever before, while maintaining security at the network and application levels.

FrontPage 2000 provides numerous strategies for moving data to and from databases, and you can create and update a database almost as easily as creating a form. Forms and databases can be coordinated to acquire, analyze, and present data. You can incorporate database queries into your pages, and create Web pages that are updated as users enter the page or refresh it, customizing content based on profile information collected through the Web page from the user.

The database can be on the Web server, a data server, a network share, or almost any addressable Internetwork location. Theoretically, the database could be hosted on any Internetworked computer, including databases on extranets and virtual private networks. You can also combine disparate sources of data by creating an Access database composed of linked tables from other databases, such as dBASE, Paradox, or any ODBC-compatible database. You then can use Access and FrontPage tools to control the movement of data to and from a Web page. This also can simplify the collection and distribution of data from forms through Access to other databases.

FrontPage supports three types of database connections:

- File-based connection to a database in your Web site. FrontPage automatically creates a database connection when you import an Access database into your Web.
- System Data Source Name (System DSN) connection to a database on a Web server.
- Network connection to a database server, such as a SQL server.

If you plan to use a file-based connection to an Access database or other database, import it into your Web before creating a new database connection or running the Database Results Wizard. Later, you can modify the database using the wizard or the Database Results Properties dialog box.

A database connection specifies a name, location, and type of database. To establish a database connection, perform the following steps:

1. Choose Tools, Web Settings to display the Web Settings dialog box.
2. Select the Database tab.
3. Click the Add button.
4. Enter a name for the new connection as shown in Figure 60.25.

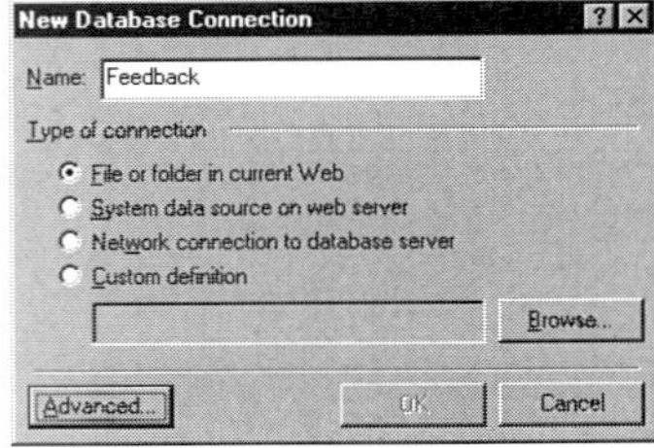

FIGURE 60.25
Use the New Database Connection dialog box to add a new connection.

5. Select a Type of connection:
   - File folder in current Web
   - System data source on Web server
   - Network connection to database server
   - Custom definition
6. Click OK.
7. Click Advanced to enter optional properties including username, password, timeouts, and custom parameters. Click OK.
8. Click OK on the New Database Connection dialog box.
9. Click OK on the Web settings dialog box.

After a database connection has been established, you can insert data into your page using the Database Results Wizard by following these steps:

1. Put the cursor on the page where you want to place the database.
2. Choose Insert, Database, Results to start the wizard.
3. Specify a database connection and click Next. Click New to create a new database connection from the Web Settings dialog box (see steps for creating a new database connection as stated previously). Sample databases and connections are provided to help familiarize you with the process (see Figure 60.26).

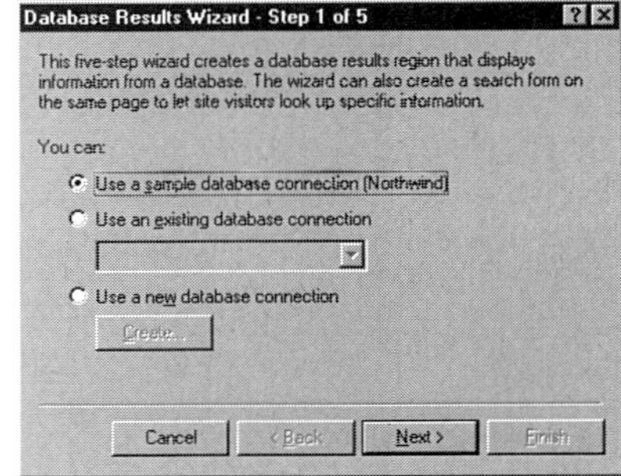

FIGURE 60.26
Select a sample database, existing database connection, or create a new database connection by using the Database Results Wizard.

4. Specify a record source from the database (see Figure 60.27) and click Next. You can also specify a custom SQL query from this dialog box.

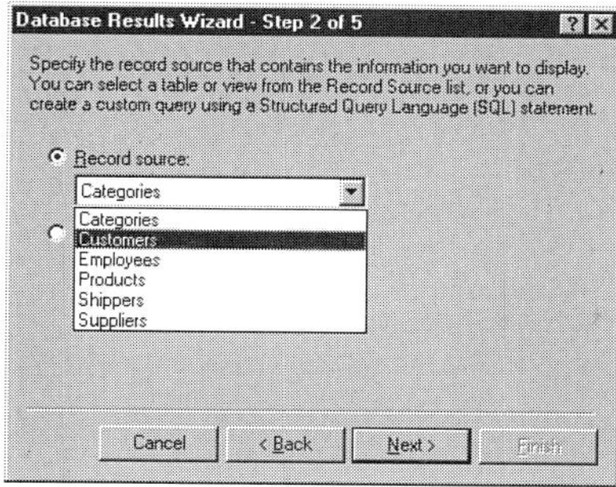

FIGURE 60.27
Choose the record source from the database.

5. Select the fields to be displayed (see Figure 60.28). Additional options are available to filter, limit, sort, set up a search form, and provide default values for the search form.

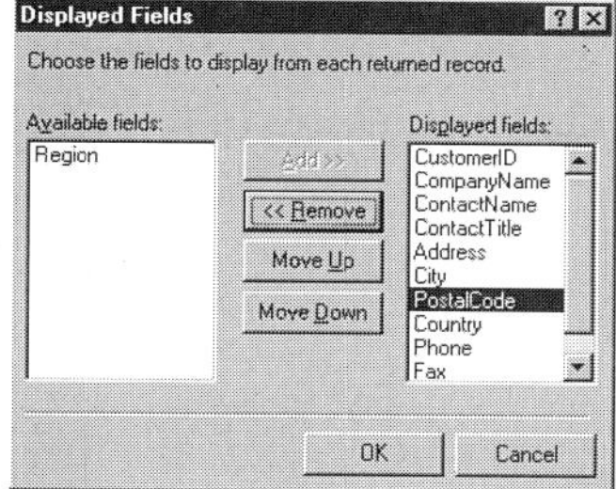

FIGURE 60.28
Choose the fields you want displayed from each returned record.

6. Select options for formatting how the results will be displayed (see Figure 60.29).

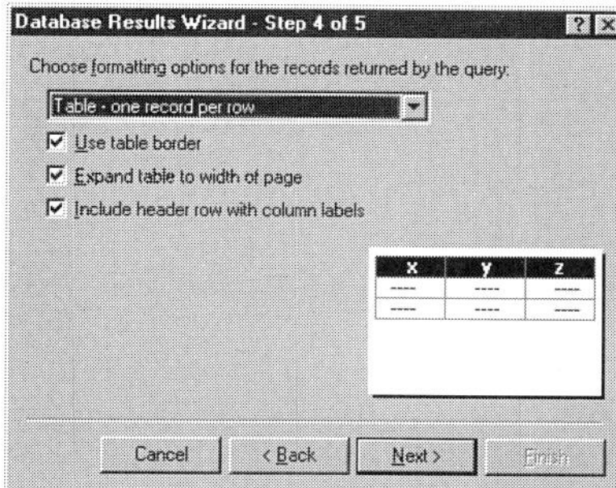

FIGURE 60.29
Choose the formatting for the records returned by your query.

7. Specify how many records will be returned. You can display all records in a single list on one page, or split records into smaller groups to be displayed on multiple pages. The example in Figure 60.30 displays five records per group.

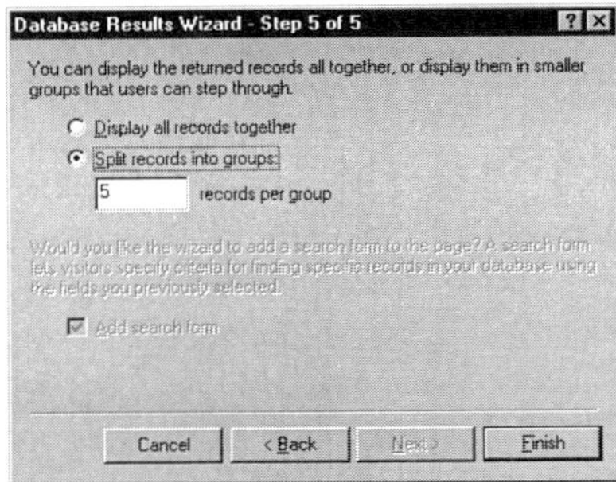

FIGURE 60.30
Specify how many records will be displayed on a page.

A format for the Database Results Region is inserted on the page, as shown in Figure 60.31. A page containing a Database Results Region must be designated an Active Server Page (ASP) and requires FrontPage Extensions. If the file extension of the page is not already .asp, just save the page with an .asp extension.

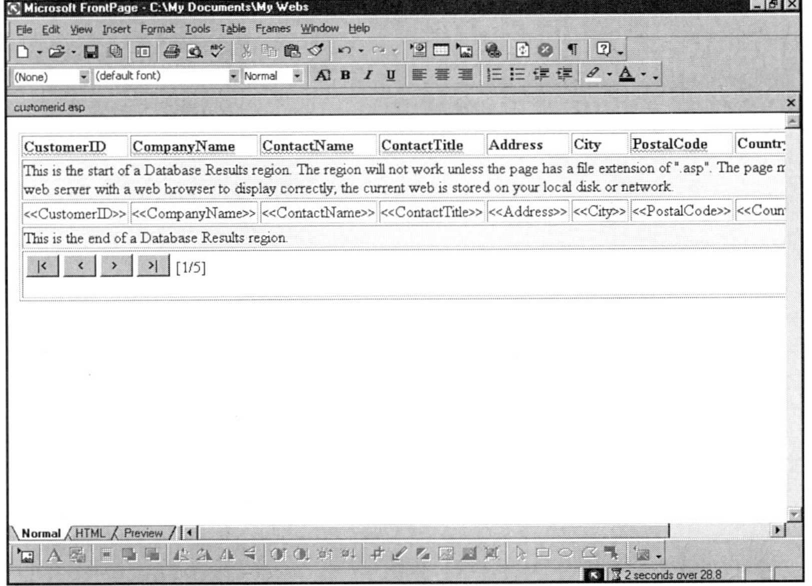

FIGURE 60.31
The Database Results Region defines how the database on your Web page will be populated after your Web site is published and the page is displayed.

Data Access Pages and Data Binding

Data Access Pages enable users to share and collaborate on Access databases over the Web. Data Access Pages are built using the Data Pages Designer in Access and delivered from an Access *.mdb file as HTML files and stored on a Web server. Users download them into Web pages where they can be edited through the browser and returned to the server. Fresh data can be returned from the database each time the page is reloaded, and the data can come from any ODBC-compliant source, including Access and SQL. This topic is discussed in Chapter 38, "Access and the Web."

Data Access Pages require the data-binding capabilities of Internet Explorer 5 or later. Compatible browsers must support data binding.

The Data Binding architecture enables you to sort, filter, and query data from a Web browser just as you can with other Office applications. You can embed a data source such as Data Access Pages on an HTML page that queries the Web server and/or database server where the data is located whenever the page is reloaded.

Although FrontPage provides many tools for the nonprogrammer to implement Access databases on the Web, developing robust databases applications and applications for mixed-browser environments requires considerable knowledge of programming for VBA, COM, ODBC, SQL, ASP, and so on.

The Microsoft Office 2000 Developer Strategy white paper provides a good overview of their vision for Visual Basic for Applications (VBA) and the Component Object Model (COM) as standards for delivering integrated, Web-compatible solutions that "automate Microsoft Office and contribute to achieving a true 'digital nervous system.'" The paper is found on this page:

`http://msdn.microsoft.com/library/backgrnd/html/msdn_odewhpp.htm`

For more information on data binding, visit these pages:

`http://msdn.microsoft.com/workshop/Author/databind/data_binding.asp`

`http://msdn.microsoft.com/workshop/author/databind/architecture.asp#ch_databind_architecture`

CHAPTER 61

Using Microsoft PhotoDraw

In this chapter

Introducing PhotoDraw

Realizing that business communications of all kinds (reports, presentations, Web pages, and so on) have more images in them than ever before, and that most Office users have not had formal training in the graphic arts, Microsoft decided to create an easy-to-use image-editing software program specifically for Office users. PhotoDraw, the newest addition to the Office lineup of applications, is the fruit of that labor. It makes quick work of creating and editing images, particularly images destined for Web sites. Although PhotoDraw won't rival most high-end imaging applications, such as Adobe Photoshop, its assortment of image-editing tools are welcome additions to the Office environment. These tools are especially helpful if you need to edit images and graphics for a Web site, because PhotoDraw works especially well with FrontPage. And if you need to create custom graphics for your PowerPoint presentations or your Publisher publications, you'll find that PhotoDraw is just the ticket.

Microsoft included many familiar Office interface elements in PhotoDraw, including floatable and dockable toolbars. Thus, the interface should look somewhat familiar, although as a savvy Office user, you'll notice right away that the overall PhotoDraw interface is a significant departure from that of the core Office applications. In this chapter, I'll introduce you to a number of these interface quirks, although you'll most likely discover and work your way around them with little trouble.

With PhotoDraw you can assemble and edit images in any of the following categories:

- Clip art
- Photographs, including clip stock images and scanned images
- Scanned images
- Text
- Images from other programs including popular draw and paint programs
- Images taken with digital cameras

PhotoDraw is not automatically installed when you install Office 2000. However, it is included in the Premium and Developer editions, so look for it on the other CDs in the pack and install it after you install the core Office applications.

You can also create text and simple line drawings by using the creation tools included in the program. After you've created these items, you can continue to refine and change their appearance by using the editing tools in the program.

After you have created or edited an image, you can save it in any one of a dozen or so file formats, including all the major file formats used for PC and Web graphics. If you are not sure what file format you should use, the Save for Use Wizard makes the decisions for you after asking a few questions about how you are going to use the images.

You can incorporate the edited and saved images into all the Office applications by taking a few simple steps. For example, you can use the same image in a presentation you are making in PowerPoint, in a written report in Word, or even as part of a Web-page design in FrontPage.

You are not restricted to using these images in Office applications, either. Because you can save your images in a variety of the standard file formats, you can give them to other people or use them yourself in many other applications.

The PhotoDraw Interface

Microsoft did some research into how business users create and edit images and found that most business people do not create their own images from scratch. That's because most people aren't the best artists on paper, let alone using a computer mouse!

Because Microsoft is right about how most people use image-editing programs, it is well worth the time to scan through the resources included with the program before you get started on a project. Look for images and fonts that fit the look you have in mind.

If you can't come up with ideas for your project or aren't sure what you want to do, look over the basic image ingredients that come with PhotoDraw. You might find images in the collections that start your creative juices flowing.

Here's a list of the materials and resources that come with PhotoDraw that you can use in your projects:

- 800 clip-art images
- 300 templates
- 500 background images
- 375 textures
- 75 edges
- 200 fonts

You can also use any of the clip art that comes with other Microsoft programs, such as Publisher, and clip-art and stock-image collections from other companies. In fact, when you insert a clip-art image in PhotoDraw, the program automatically presents images in the Publisher clip-art collection for you to browse through. If you select one of these images, the program prompts you to insert the Publisher CD into your drive so that it can access the proper image file.

Making Use of Built-In Templates and Graphics

Unless you have the time and inclination to create your own portfolio of design elements from scratch, use the tools and templates that come with PhotoDraw. Even if you don't like anything more than the shape of an image, using a preexisting image cuts down on your design time.

For example, the Web graphic templates include more than a dozen designs each for banners, circular buttons, connecting buttons, festive buttons, and rectangular ones. Start with one of these and customize it by changing the colors, the fonts, or the outline.

Always look through the image template possibilities for Web graphics before you start a new project. Choose a few you like and decide whether you want to use the templates that can be used in mixed or matched sets. If you decide which sets to use by looking before you start designing, you'll save time by narrowing your options up front.

After you have customized a few images, you can start your own collection of images for later use. After only a few projects, you will have your own library of images already customized for your regular use. This cuts down considerably on the amount of time you have to spend creating and editing images.

Keep It Simple

There's one design rule to keep in mind when creating images for use in business-related communications: *Keep it simple*. Keeping it simple means you spend less time at the computer. It also helps you to keep your focus on the content of your message instead of on creating overly ornate or busy images.

Experiment with a few of PhotoDraw's special effects that catch your eye as you move through the program or the tutorial. Learn how to use these special effects in several different ways. If you do this, you can make even a simple line of text look completely different within minutes.

Keep it simple means using the fewest possible special effects on your images and text. Use only one or two of the possibilities. Just because the program offers you many different possibilities doesn't mean you have to fit them all into one image or screen.

Creating Images and Text

Before you can edit an image in PhotoDraw, you must create a new PhotoDraw file by using the New command under the File pull-down menu. Icons of the blank templates (either pictures or labels) appear and you must select one of the templates to get started.

Each of the templates appears onscreen as a white rectangle or circle and carries with it the appropriate image dimensions. Select the template that most closely matches the intended use of the image. For example, if you want to create a mailing label, you would choose the shipping label template and the envelope template to create a business envelope design.

You insert text and images using the various options under the Insert pull-down menu. PhotoDraw is not a drawing or illustration program and therefore it doesn't have extensive drawing capabilities. You can use the tools of the program to create basic shapes, but if you want something more complex it's better to look for a preexisting image that has most of what you want already in it.

NOTE If you need to create professional-quality drawings, I recommend that you look into applications such as Adobe Illustrator, Adobe Freehand, or CorelDRAW. The Office suite does not have the tools to meet professional-quality requirements.

To use the image templates that come with PhotoDraw, click the New Template item on the File menu. The program comes with five sets of templates: Web graphics, business graphics, cards, designer edges, and designer clip art. Before you start creating your own images, it's a good idea to look through the items in these categories. You might find something that is 75% or 80% of what you're looking for.

When you select an image from the image templates, the program walks you through a series of possible editing steps and then reminds you to save your work. You can opt to use the steps as presented or choose your own effects.

After you've created the text or image or imported a preexisting image, you can move on to the editing process. This is where the real fun of using PhotoDraw begins. Using the wide variety of editing options in PhotoDraw, you can create entirely new-looking images from preexisting ones.

Editing Images and Text

You don't need to create your own images to use PhotoDraw because the software comes with so many ready-to-use images. You can also open and edit any image that has been saved in one of the following formats:

- BMP (Bitmap)
- CDR (CorelDRAW)
- CGM (Computer Graphics Metafile)
- DRW (Micrografx Designer/Draw)
- DXF (AutoCad format 2D)
- EMF (Enhanced Metafile)
- EPS (Encapsulated PostScript)
- FPX (Flashpix)
- GIF (Graphics Interchange Format)
- JPG (Joint Photographic Experts Group)
- MIC (Microsoft Image Composer)
- MIX (native file format for PictureIt! 99 and PhotoDraw)
- PCD (Kodak Photo CD)
- PCX (PC Paintbrush)
- PICT (Macintosh PICT, also known as PCT)
- PNG (Portable Network Graphics)
- PSD (native file format for Adobe Photoshop)
- TGA (Targa)
- TIF (Tagged Image File Format, also known as TIFF)
- WMF (Windows Metafile)
- WPG (WordPerfect Graphics)

To be able to open WPG files, you must install PhotoDraw with the WPG filter selected. If it wasn't installed when PhotoDraw was first installed, it won't appear on the list of files PhotoDraw can open and you must reinstall PhotoDraw.

Most of the time you will want to do more to an image than import it into PhotoDraw. You might want to make at least a minor edit to an image, such as changing its size or orientation. Sometimes you will want to make more extensive changes, such as cropping it or changing some of the colors.

If you are editing an image in PhotoDraw, you don't need to invest a lot of time and effort into making the edits. The program gives you many ready-to-use effects that you can apply in minutes. If you want to further customize the image, you can take a few more minutes and use the tools to make a radically different image.

Other ways to make images look different in PhotoDraw with a minimum amount of effort include

- Changing the colors in an existing image
- Flipping or rotating an image
- Cropping part of an image
- Combining existing images or parts of images for an entirely new look
- Adding text to an image
- Adding 3D special effects to existing images
- Applying one or more of the other special effects available in PhotoDraw

Any, or all, of these editing procedures can be used together to change the look of an image. But keep the design maxim mentioned previously firmly in mind when working with PhotoDraw. Edits are so easy to make and take so little time that you'll be tempted to try out quite a few of them. Keep in mind that you're trying to make the most effective image for your purposes, not the most artistic one, and you're trying to make the most of your time. So, make only the edits you absolutely must make.

With these skills under your belt, plus a little general information about using graphic design ideas and concepts for business communication, you can quickly turn out enough professional-looking images.

If you're interested in creating and editing images for use on a Web site, you'll also need to learn about how images can look in various browsers. PhotoDraw has done most of the hard work for you, so it's not a lot to learn. However, learning and using this information is crucial to turning out consistently professional-looking results for Web images.

Choosing Colors

Color is one of the most powerful aspects of any image, so you'll have to be careful when choosing the new colors for an image. For example, bold, powerful colors work best when you're communicating with younger adults.

To choose the colors for your project, start by scanning through the color selections in PhotoDraw by looking through the colors in the palettes that come with the programs. Choose a few complementary colors for your images and make note of where they appear on the palette.

Be sure to limit yourself to no more than six color choices because more than a handful of colors in your images is distracting to the reader.

By choosing the colors before you begin and limiting yourself to the ones you've selected, you will also be making sure that all the images you work on for a particular project will automatically coordinate. You'll be able to mix and match as you complete the design of the entire project and not have to rush back to PhotoDraw to correct colors at the last minute.

It is very important to know that, if you are creating Web graphics, you must use the colors in the Web-dithered or Web-solid palettes. There are only 216 colors that all Web browsers can display properly and, to make life much easier, Microsoft put all those colors on each of these two palettes (see Figure 61.1). By using only these two palettes, you prevent possible problems with image colors appearing differently with different Web browsers.

NOTE Placing dots of different colors very close together so that they appear to create a new color creates dithered colors.

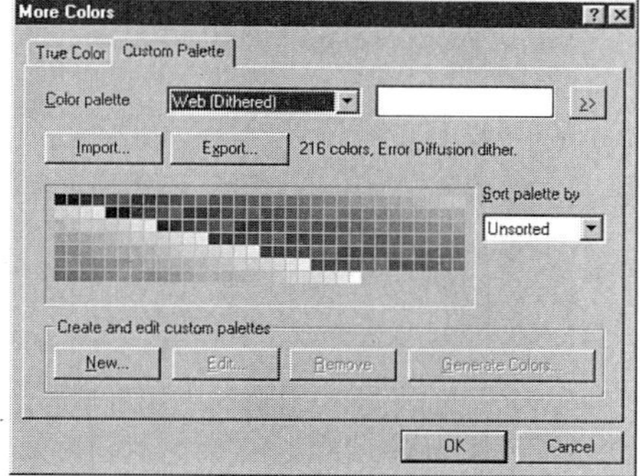

FIGURE 61.1
Web graphics must use colors from the Web-dithered or Web-solid palettes.

Use the Web-dithered palette for photographic images and images with subtle gradations in color. Use the Web-solid palette for images that are made up of solid colors or lines, such as simple cartoons. When in doubt, stick to the Web-dithered palette, which is the program's default setting.

You can also use colors in other PhotoDraw images by using the eyedropper tool that appears on the color palette window. Click the eyedropper and then click the part of the image where the color you want to copy appears. The color appears in the active color box on the window. The next time you use the fill tool, it will use this color.

Write down the RGB formula for a custom color and keep track of this information. That way, you can reproduce the color at any time by typing in the formula in the True Color palette window.

If you want to use specific colors for your images, such as the company's corporate or logo colors, you must first find out what the RGB formula is for each color. The *RGB formula* is the amount of Red, Green, and Blue in the color. With PhotoDraw, you can use only RGB and not any other color recipes, such as the CMYK model used for printing (see Figure 61.2). This, of course, is one of PhotoDraw's primary limitations.

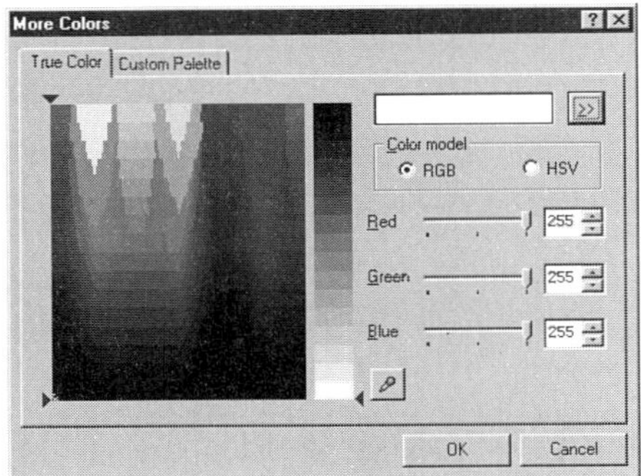

FIGURE 61.2
RGB is the only color recipe you can use in PhotoDraw.

After you have this information, you can create your own custom palette in PhotoDraw by creating a custom palette and typing the RGB formulas for each color. The software remembers these colors and makes them available whenever you need them. You can save up to 256 colors in one palette, plus you can export any palette in PhotoDraw for use in other Office applications.

To use a color in an image that is not in PhotoDraw's native file format, but for which the correct filters have been installed in PhotoDraw:

1. Open the image in PhotoDraw.
2. Sample the color by opening the Solid Color pane under the Fill portion of the Format menu.
3. Choose the Eyedropper tool and then click a specific color in the image that you want to use as the new fill.
4. The selected color appears in the active color box in PhotoDraw. You can then use that color to fill something else or to fill the entire image.

This is a good way to access your corporate colors in PhotoDraw; if the colors are accurate in PowerPoint, they will be accurate in PhotoDraw after you've imported them.

The eyedropper tool can also be used to copy colors from one PhotoDraw image to another by using the same procedure. So, you can color coordinate several pieces of clip art. Simply select a color that you like from one image and use it to fill portions of the others you've chosen.

Changing the Colors in an Existing Image

Changing the colors in an existing image is one of the fastest and most effective ways to make preexisting images look new. With PhotoDraw you can accomplish this task in only a few minutes if you're working with a single image.

The first place to start changing an image's colors is by using the Colorize tool on the Color Menu (available by choosing Format, Color and choosing the Colorize tool) (see Figure 61.3). When you select a color, the program blends that color into all the colors in the image—almost as if you laid a sheet of translucent colored paper over the image.

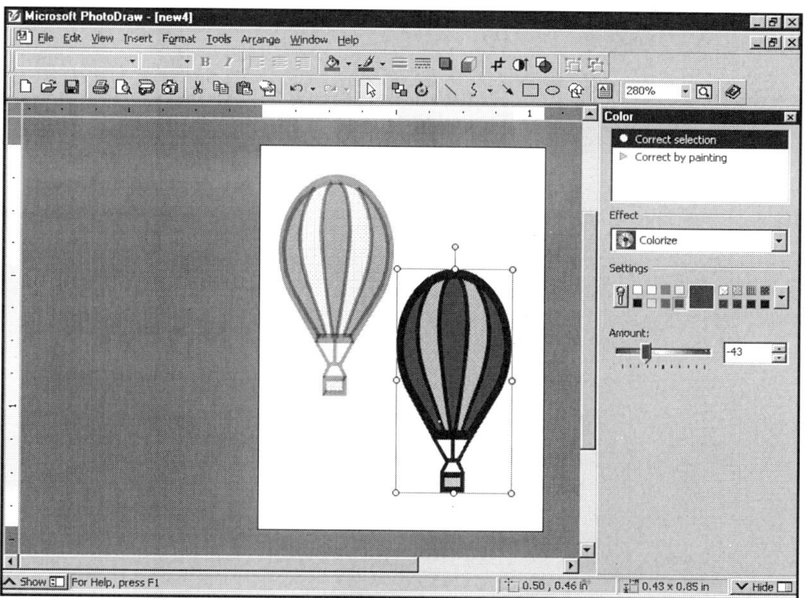

FIGURE 61.3
The Colorize tool was used to change the colors in the second image, which started out as a copy of the image on the upper left.

You can control the depth of the new color by adjusting the slider bar or typing in a percentage. You can also add several layers of color—meaning that you can keep adding colors and PhotoDraw blends the new one in with the existing ones. Experiment with various color combinations until you find something you like.

Another way to quickly change the colors in an image is to use the Outline tools, which are also accessible through the Color Menu. There are a variety of outline options, but they all work the same way by outlining the edges of the object with the effect you choose. They can be used to change the color of an object and can also change the overall look of the image (see Figure 61.4).

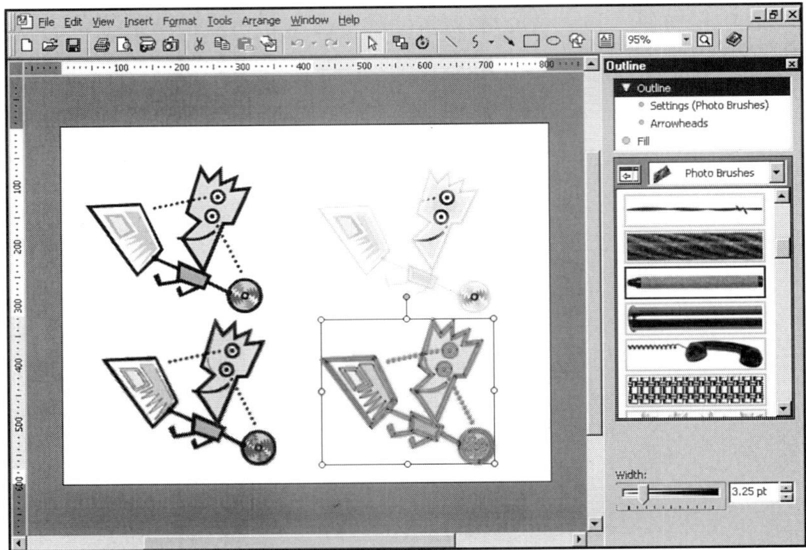

FIGURE 61.4
This simple shape changes color and appearance after one of the artistic brushes outline tools is applied to it.

Experiment with all the options to see the amazing range of different effects you can achieve. Even something as simple as changing the width of the outline can make a dramatic difference in how an image appears.

Once again, to keep things simple, only use one or two of the possible effects on your image. If you aren't happy with how something looks during the experimenting stage, use the Undo feature (Edit, Undo or Ctrl+Z) to take the image back to how it was before you applied the last edit.

The Fill tool (found in the Format menu) is very powerful because it allows you to fill the entire space in an image in a few steps. You select the image and then select the fill you want to apply and the program takes care of the rest (see Figure 61.5).

To fill in the background behind an image with a color or another image, draw a rectangle, and then fill the rectangle. To fill the rectangle, select it, open the Fill tools (Format, Fill, then select the kind of fill you want). The program fills the rectangle with the solid, gradient, texture, or picture fill you've chosen.

At this point, the filled rectangle is on top of and covering the first image. To move it to the background, use the Order command under the Arrange pull-down menu to send the background to the back of the first image where it belongs.

Before you create a background, however, take a minute to save the original image without a background. Doing so enables you to keep the original image separate so that you can use it for other projects without the background.

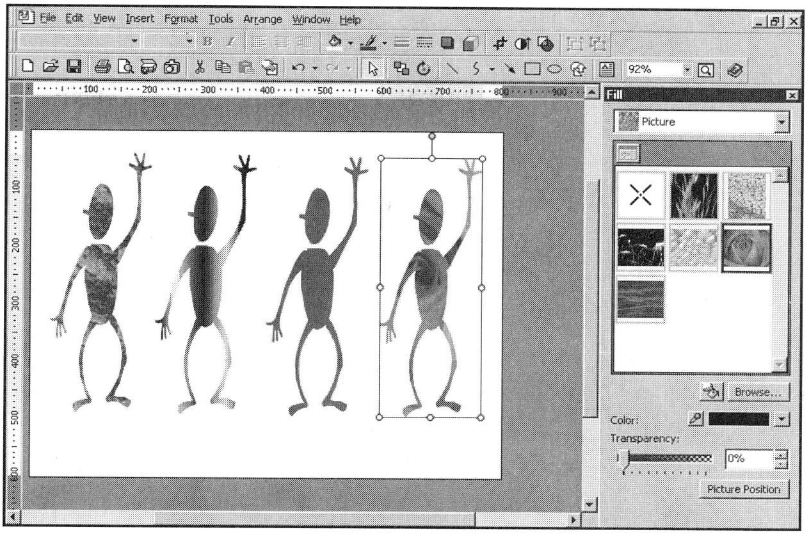

FIGURE 61.5
There are a variety of fill types in PhotoDraw, including solids and textures.

TIP To keep the foreground and background images together, use the Select All command under the Edit menu and then use the Group command under the Arrange menu. This selects all the elements of the image as one, allowing you to move the composite image around at will.

The Paint features in PhotoDraw give you many ways to change the look of an image, but they are not intended to help you change colors inside an image. Changing the colors inside an image by using the Fill and Colorize options is easier.

The paint features enable you to paint color and images, such as chains and ropes, over parts of an image with PhotoDraw's brush tools. The net effect is similar to that of taking a paintbrush or spray can and painting over parts of an image or layering objects over an existing one.

The Paint features are worth experimenting with if you often want to change the overall look of an image. The artistic and photobrushes are fun to use and enable you to create painted effects that are hard to match with other image-editing tools.

Unless you've got a steady hand and a practiced eye, changing the colors in an image this way can make your images look as if a graffiti artist has been at work. If that's the effect you're looking for, using the paint features is a great way to achieve it. If not, try all the other ways to change color first.

Rotating or Flipping an Image

It's hard to believe that something as simple as rotating or flipping an image can make a dramatic difference in how an image looks, but it's true. With PhotoDraw this image sleight of hand is even easier because the program contains 2D and 3D tools that help you make the most of this simple technique.

After you've flipped or rotated an image, experiment with a few different sizes for the new image. This quickly changes the look of the image even more.

To rotate a 2D image in PhotoDraw, click the Rotation Handle that appears at the top of the image when you select the image. Moving the handle left makes the image rotate to the left, moving it to the right rotates the image to the right. When you're happy with the effect, let go of the handle (see Figure 61.6).

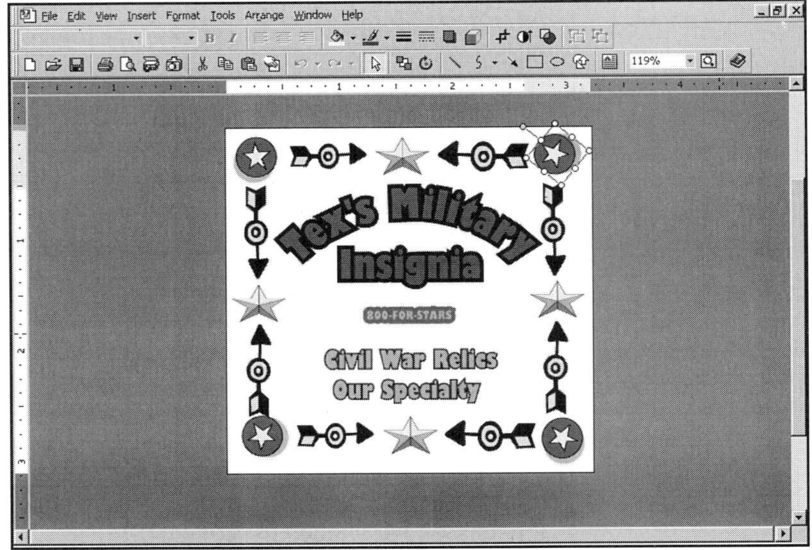

FIGURE 61.6
In this example, the star in the upper-right portion of the image is being rotated. Each of the stars was rotated to a different degree after the original star image was imported and copied.

To rotate a 3D image, select the image and then click 3D on the Effects menu. Click Rotate and Tilt; then enter values in the Rotation fields to change the rotation and tilt of the image. Nothing happens until you press Enter and then you will see the effects of your changes. If you don't like what you've created, use the Undo option under the Edit menu to eliminate the changes.

Flipping an image is even easier than rotating one. Click the image to select the image and choose Arrange, Flip. Decide which way you want to flip the image and have some fun. Flip it around until you're satisfied with the look.

CAUTION

Choose carefully the images you flip and rotate; look for ones with no obvious orientation. Images with obvious orientations such as building and office equipment look strange when their orientations are changed, so avoid doing so unless you want to make an artistic statement. Flipping images of people can produce obviously misleading results.

After you've rotated or flipped an image, you can create unusual looking frames, lines, or borders for the images by using the copy and paste commands under the Edit menu to duplicate the original image (see Figure 61.7). Or, you can cluster several copies of the image for an entirely different look.

FIGURE 61.7
In this example, part of the larger image was cropped away and the image of the clock was imported into the white area and then rotated.

Use the align functions under the Arrange Menu to help you line up the images for a dividing line or a border. You can also use the drawing tools to draw a rectangle or square to help you line up the images for a frame. Delete the rectangle or box after you've got all the images arranged to your liking.

Cropping Images

Some images, especially clip art, do not have to be *cropped* before they are used while others, such as photographs, benefit greatly from having extraneous portions removed. Even professionally taken photographs might have items in them that you do not want to use every time you use the image.

If you're talking about the president of your company and the only photograph of the president is a group shot of all the corporate executives, you might be able to crop the photograph to get a head and shoulders shot of the president. You might also want to use only foreground portions of an image and place the cropped image on a new background.

Cropping an image is also an effective way to restrict the viewer's focus to a particular part of an image. If you select an unexpected slice of the image, you can come up with some eye-catching special effects for an advertisement. Just be sure to get enough of the image so that the viewers can recognize what's in the slice.

PhotoDraw makes cropping images very easy—so easy it's like using cookie cutters. After you access the cropping tools under the Format menu, you can use any of the shapes that appear to cut out the part of the image you want to keep. Or, you can choose to throw away the part of the image inside the cropping shape.

There are more than 20 different cropping shapes for you to choose from, including normal geometric shapes such as circles and squares (see Figure 61.8). There are also more creative shapes such as starbursts, fish, and trees.

FIGURE 61.8
PhotoDraw gives you lots of cropping shapes to apply to an image so that you can cut away any portion of the image outside the cropping shape.

You can also crop an image by using the Cut options under the Format menu. It works the same way as cropping a picture in that you position the cutting shape over the original image. You can also draw freehand around the part of the image you want to cut out. After you've finished cutting, the rest of the image is deleted and you're left with the part you cut out, just as if you used a pair of scissors.

Before you cut or crop an image, save the original file in a separate folder under a new name. That way you always have the original, uncut image to go back to later if you need it for another project.

Combining Images and Parts of Images

Here's where you can have a lot of fun editing images. By putting different images together, you can create exciting new images. Use this technique to generate images that grab the viewers' attention or to create images that you wish a photographer had been able to generate.

Stay away from the sensationalist journalism style of image editing; don't combine parts of images or photographs that you know shouldn't go together, such as ones that create a false impression. Honesty in images is always the best policy.

To combine parts of an image for a collage effect (see Figure 61.9), open the image files that contain the original images, make your cuts and crops as needed and then open a new image file in PhotoDraw. Copy and paste the pieces into the new file and arrange the components until you've achieved the desired effect.

FIGURE 61.9
PhotoDraw gives you the ability to create collage images.

This technique is very effective when you combine it with a few of the other editing opportunities. For example, you could apply a photographic or stylistic fill to a clip-art image and use that as the background for your collage. Or, you could use a creatively cropped shape on a photographic image and then use the cropped image to make a frame for the collective image.

Use the Order functions under the Arrange Menu to put some of the images in the collage in front of some of the others.

Adding Text to an Image

Formatted text becomes an image itself after you've done some work on the text using the PhotoDraw text-formatting tools. Combining formatted text with one or more other images is a fast way to completely customize those images (see Figure 61.10).

After you've finished with these images, they make great image content for Web sites. You can add hyperlinks to any image to create image maps for your FrontPage Webs.

Adding text to an existing image in PhotoDraw is simple; open the files in PhotoDraw (including the one with the customized text) and copy and paste the text into the other image. Or, you can create the custom text in the image by using the Insert Text function on the Insert Menu.

You can even bend text in one of several shapes and format the text further by using the image-editing tools on a text portion of the image (see Figure 61.11). Sometimes modifying the text is the best way to improve the overall look of the image (see Figure 61.12).

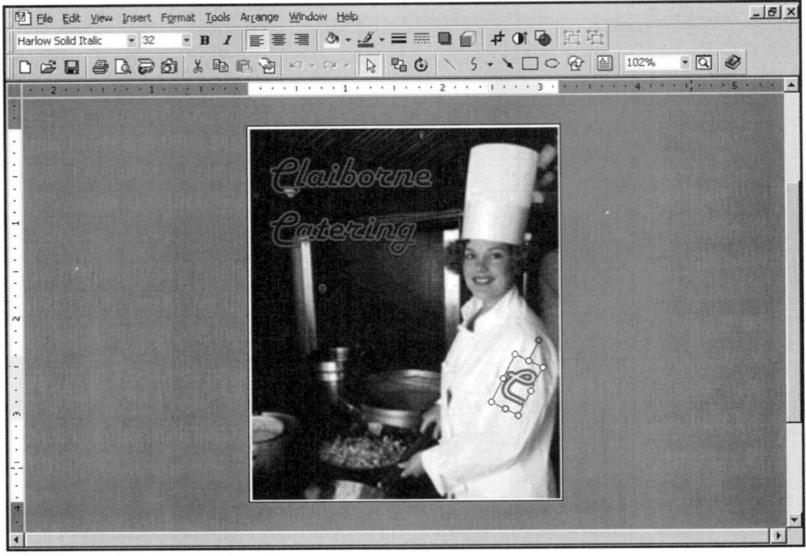

FIGURE 61.10
This image was created by combining text with an image. Text was placed at the top and on the sleeve of the chef.

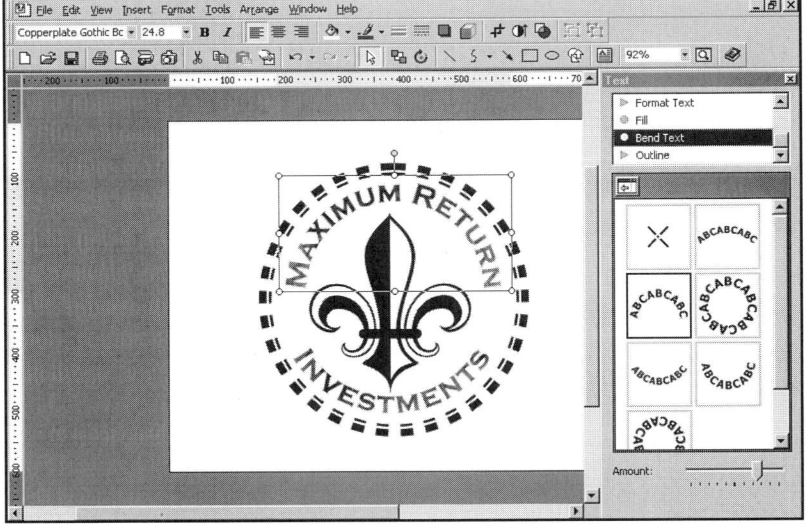

FIGURE 61.11
PhotoDraw lets you first add text and then curve it to make it fit inside a circle or around an object.

Whenever you add text to another text that doesn't have text in it, you have to decide which part of the resulting image you want to emphasize. If you don't take the time to make this decision, you might end up with an image that doesn't have the desired effect.

If you want the text to dominate, experiment with the size, font, and color of the text until it's the first thing you notice when you look at the image. If you want the other parts of the image to be more noticeable, make the text small and unobtrusive. If in doubt as to the final effect, create a few variations of the basic image and ask people to tell you which part of the image jumps out at them first.

FIGURE 61.12
PhotoDraw lets you outline all kinds of objects, including text. In this example, text is outlined to make it stand out more against the dark background.

TIP Even a single letter of text can customize an image. Use a font and color that are similar to your company's logo or letterhead and place the letter on top of a stock photographic image.

You don't have to take a lot of time when combining text and images. Even a line or two of text in an unexpected area can make people remember your message. For example, if you want people to remember a slogan such as "T.E.A.M. Together Everyone Achieves More," you could add that text to a stock image of a blackboard (see Figure 61.13). Doing so is far more effective and memorable for your employees than typing the slogan at the bottom of a screen or Web page.

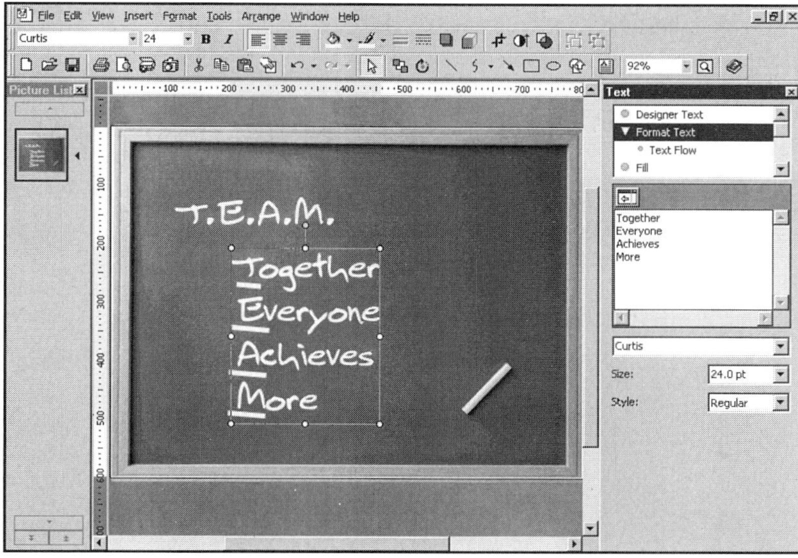

FIGURE 61.13
Adding text to a stock image can be a quick and easy way to make something memorable.

Adding 3D Effects

It used to be that adding a 3D effect to an image was something only graphic arts professionals with expensive computer equipment could do. It required lots of time, specialized software, and (sometimes) enough illustration experience to qualify the person as an engineer!

Thanks to the computing power of today's personal computer, 3D special effects are within reach of anyone with a late-model computer. You can use a program specifically created for 3D modeling—something you might consider if you want to create extraordinary effects or if you work with large, complex images.

You can use the 3D editing tools in PhotoDraw to turn out respectable-looking 3D images within a few minutes (see Figure 61.14). You'll have to be careful, especially when you first start using the 3D tools. PhotoDraw has so many special 3D effects that it is difficult to find the one perfect effect to apply to your image.

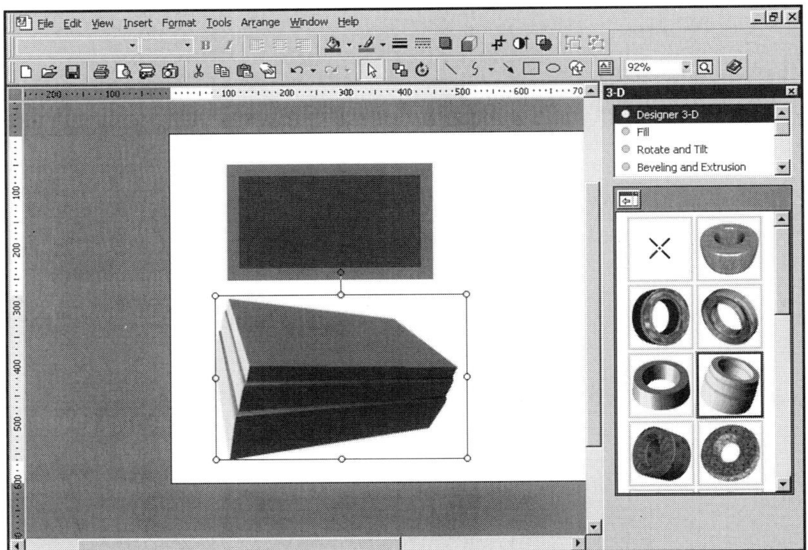

FIGURE 61.14
This square was converted into a 3D object in one step by selecting one of the 3D effects shown on the right.

The 3-D special effects can create very powerful images that can easily overwhelm a design. To help you figure out which 3D effect to use, take the time to think about how you intend to use the finished image. Make the 3D effect stronger if you want the 3D image to dominate the entire design. If you simply want to add a little dimension to an image that doesn't need to stand out, such as a Web page button, tone down the 3D effect considerably.

To apply a 3D effect to an image, select the object first and then select and apply a 3D effect from the Effects menu located on the Format pull-down menu. Doing so not only applies the 3D shape to the image, but also the colors of the 3D example shown in the gallery of options. The program also applies the effect only to the outline of the image.

TIP Remember you can apply 3D effects to any image, including clip art, scanned images, and stock photography.

There are several ways to apply a 3D effect to text. You can apply any of the effects in the 3D gallery or you can choose one of the 3D treatments that appears on the Designer Text portion of the text-formatting window. With either approach, PhotoDraw applies the color and format of the 3D effect shown, but it also applies the effect to each letter in the text.

The 3D effects on the gallery of 3D options are more extreme than those on the Designer Text palette, but be sure to try one or two treatments from both before making up your mind.

PhotoDraw puts so many exciting 3D features at your fingertips; therefore, it's worth taking the time to do the 3D portion of the tutorial. You can also explore the options on your own by drawing a simple, filled rectangle and picking a series of effects to apply.

Here is a summary of the ways PhotoDraw enables you to apply and modify 3D effects. All these modification options are available by selecting options in the 3D workpane. They can be applied after the initial 3D effect is applied:

- Modify the fill—You can replace the preset 3D fill with any of the fill options available, such as a solid color, an image, or a texture. Select the object and then click the Fill option in the 3D workpane to access the different fill options.
- Modify the shininess—You can change the shininess of any fill to make it brighter or darker. The shininess controls appear after you've clicked on the Fill option in the 3D workpane.
- Modify the bevel or edges—After you apply a 3D effect, you can change the appearance of the bevel or edges. To change the Bevel, click the Beveling and Extrusion option on the 3D workpane.
- Modify the lighting style—You can change the lighting style to make the image look lighter or darker or change the angle of a shadow. To change the lighting, click the Lighting option on the 3D workpane.
- Modify the rotation or tilt—Not only can you rotate the 3D image, but you can also change the amount of rotation up and down and side to side. To change the rotation or tilt, click the rotate and tilt option on the 3D workpane.

Although it's not specifically a 3D effect, you can also change the size of the object and its position on the page by selecting the position and size option on the same 3D workpane.

You can apply only one 3D effect from the galleries to an image, but afterwards you can modify the image in one or more of the ways listed previously. These effects can so dramatically change the way an image looks that it's also worth the time to experiment by using a simple filled object such as a square or circle.

TIP Changing the shininess of an object is a good way to change its overall appearance. Making it brighter is a good way to make the fill look more metallic. Making it darker makes it look more like a plastic material.

It won't take you long to figure out how to apply the different 3D effects and possible modifications. One thing that might not be immediately obvious is how to change the fill in the dimensional areas of a 3D object. After you know how to do it, the process makes sense and is easy to remember.

Here's how to change the fill on a 3D object: On the Fill list that comes up when you select the 3D style there are three fill placement options—one each for the face, bevel, and sides of an object. Choose the style of the fill you want and then click the Placement option. For the front of the object, choose Face; for the beveled edges, pick Bevel; and for the sides choose Sides. It's that simple.

Another way to give an image a 3D appearance is to put a shadow behind the image. In PhotoDraw adding a shadow to any image takes only a few minutes and you can choose from any of a dozen different shadow options.

Unless you have a very avant-garde-looking Web site, avoid using shadows on your Web-page elements. Shadows are real attention-getters and usually you want Web-page elements such as buttons and bars to serve as functional, background elements.

After you've created a shadow, you can edit it in several different ways. You can alter the degree of the shadow's transparency, soften the edges, and alter the angle of the shadow. You can even separate the shadow from the image and move the shadow around and away from the image (see Figure 61.15). The default color for the shadow is solid black, but you can change that to a shade of gray or any other color.

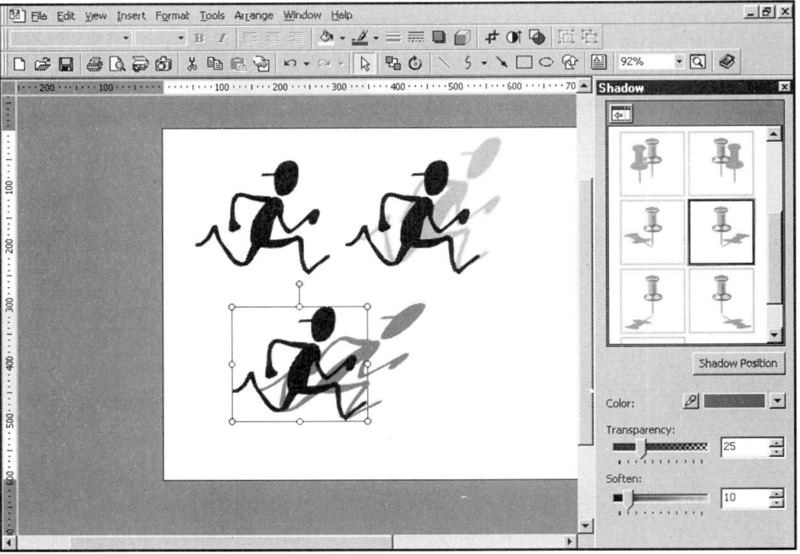

FIGURE 61.15
PhotoDraw makes it easy to add shadows to images. You have lots of shadow choices from which to choose.

Shadows are such evocative images and carry lots of subconscious meaning, so be careful how you use them in your images. Stick with PhotoDraw's default shadow settings unless you are focusing on making a design statement with your image.

Other Powerful Editing Options

Through its Designer Effects item on the Effects portion of the Format pull-down menu, PhotoDraw gives you hundreds of ways to change the look of an entire image. These special effects can be combined endlessly, giving you enough options for a lifetime of projects (see Figure 61.16).

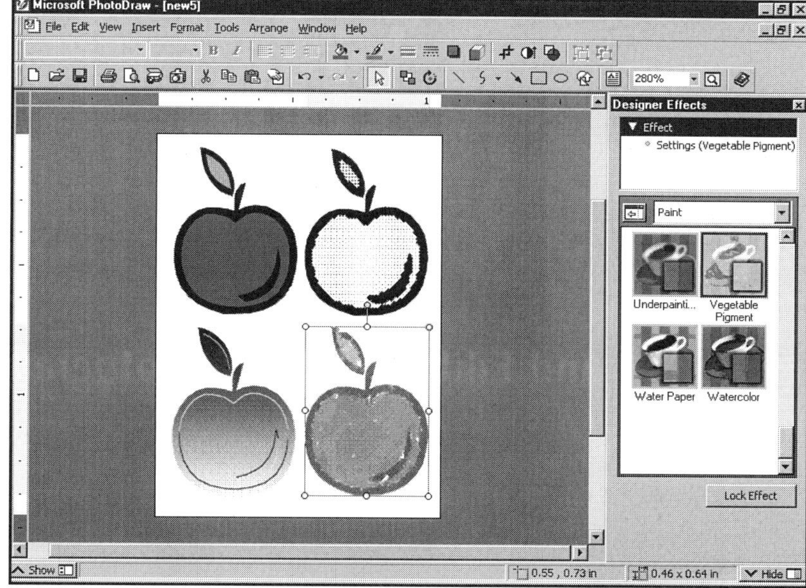

FIGURE 61.16
In this example, three different Designer Effects were used on copies of the original apple image.

Categories of special effects include crayon, markers, sketch, and stamp, as well as special artistic effects such as pointillist and watercolor. Each category contains dozens of related special effects and for each one a small thumbnail example is presented so you can browse.

TIP These designer effects are great for creating unusual Web-page elements such as buttons and banners. If you use them, you're guaranteed that no one else's Web site will look like yours.

To combine special effects, lock the first one you've selected by clicking the Lock Effect button after you've applied the effect. Click the button again after each new effect to lock the effect in before you try something else.

Other powerful special effects in PhotoDraw include Transparency, Fade Out, Blur and Sharpen, and Distort (see Figure 61.17). All these special effects do what their names imply, which might make them sound not so special. However, even simple effects can have powerful impact on images; take the time to investigate these various options and you'll find some potent editing capabilities.

FIGURE 61.17
One of the distortion effects was applied to this company logo to give it this bowed-out effect.

For example, you can use the Fade Out effect to make part, or all, of an image look as though it is fading away. You could use this effect to make part of a design less obvious than others or you could use the Transparency effect to make part of an image look translucent. Combine the two effects and you can turn a plain image into something hauntingly beautiful.

Correcting and Editing Digital Photographs

If you have a scan of a photograph that looks terrible (and it happens), don't despair. PhotoDraw has some image-correction tools that help you correct the most common problems with photographs, such as red eye and scratches (see Figure 61.18). You don't even have to be a photographic expert to use the tools.

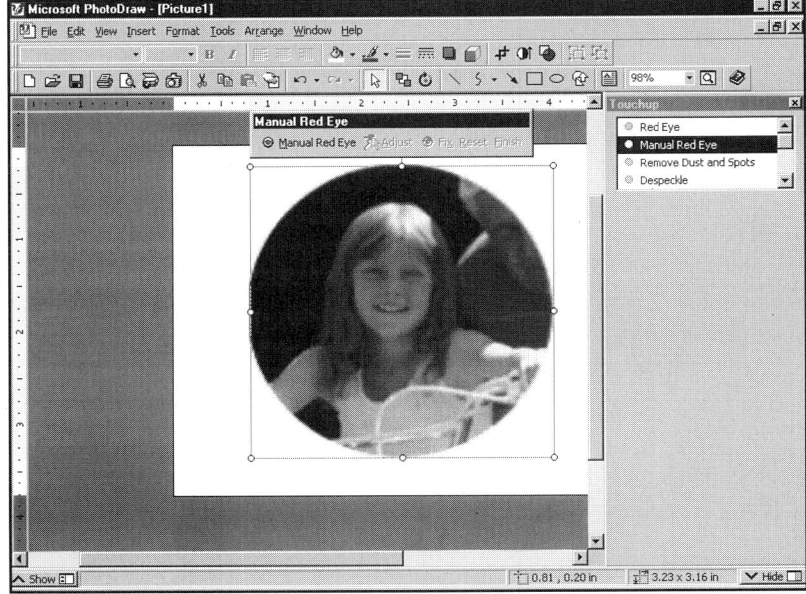

FIGURE 61.18
PhotoDraw lets you correct many problems in photographs—including red eye—that would be difficult, or impossible, to eliminate otherwise.

There are also color-correction tools that help correct color-related problems with images and tools to help adjust the focus of a photograph. Fair warning, though—as effective as these tools are, there are some photographs that are beyond help.

To save time when you use the color and focus tools, use the Automatic correction method first by clicking on the Automatic button for each option. Use the sliders on the options only if you don't like the Automatic feature results.

Saving and Managing Your Images

To keep the new images you've created in PhotoDraw, you'll have to save them before you leave the program. If you make it a habit to save your work periodically while you are still working on it, you'll have to spend less time redoing your edits in case of a computer error or power failure.

Saving your image before trying to print it is a very good idea, in case a problem occurs with the printer that in turn triggers a problem with PhotoDraw.

There are a number of file formats in which you can save PhotoDraw images, including MIX, the native PhotoDraw file format. Always save the image in MIX even if you save the image in another file format. That way, you always have the original image file to use if you want to make changes to the image later on.

Here is a list of the file formats, other than MIX, that you can use to save your PhotoDraw images:

- BMP (Bitmap)
- EMF (Enhanced Metafile)
- EPS (Encapsulated PostScript)
- GIF (Graphics Interchange Format)
- JPG (Joint Photographic Experts Group)
- PCX (native file format for PC Paintbrush)
- PNG (Portable Network Graphics)
- PSD (native file format for Adobe Photoshop)
- TGA (Targa)
- TIF (Tagged Image File Format, also known as TIFF)

The PCX file format is not automatically installed when you installed PhotoDraw. So, if you want to use the PCX format you must reinstall PhotoDraw with the PCX filter selected.

If you are going to use the image in a document that will be printed, the EPS, TIF, and PCX file formats are all commonly used file formats for printed documents. You can also readily use files saved in these formats in all the popular word processing programs (such as Microsoft Word and Corel WordPerfect), page layout programs (such as Adobe PageMaker and Quark XPress) and other image-editing programs (such as Ulead Systems' PhotoImpact and Adobe Photoshop).

If you haven't grouped the objects in your image into a single group and you want to use them that way, be sure to select the Save Image As a Group option when saving the file.

If you are going to use the image in a Web page or site, use the GIF or JPG formats as these are the two most commonly used file formats for Web graphics. These file formats can also be opened in other image-editing programs and imported into other software applications.

No matter which file format you choose, there are saving options associated with these formats that you should be aware of and change the default settings if necessary. For example, when saving a JPG file, two of the options include setting the amount of compression and whether to save the file as a color or grayscale image.

If you don't know that you must or should change the saving options settings, you can leave the default settings alone and hope for the best. A better idea is to check with whoever is going to use the file next to see whether they have any requirements or suggestions.

If you are going to handle these next steps yourself or you can't get this information, take advantage of PhotoDraw's Save for Use Wizard by clicking on the Save for Use In item on the File menu. After activated, the Wizard asks a series of questions about your plans for using the image and, depending upon your answers, saves the file in a PNG, TIF, GIF, or JPG format. If necessary, it also adjusts the default saving options according to your answers.

After you've created, edited, and saved a few images, it's time to start organizing them by adding them to the Clip Gallery in PhotoDraw (see Figure 61.19). The Gallery contains many different categories of images, such as People at Work and Science and Technology. You can also create your own categories.

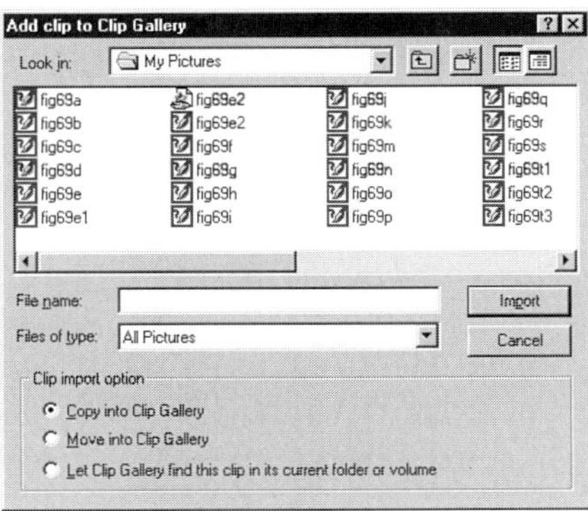

FIGURE 61.19
PhotoDraw comes with many categories of images, but you can always add your own.

To add clips to a new category, open the Gallery by clicking on Clip Art under the Insert menu and then clicking on Import Clips. To create a new category, click the New Category icon. Type the name of your category when prompted and then add images to the category by clicking the Import Clips icon at the top of the screen. Locate the clips you want to add on your hard disk or network.

You can add images to an existing category by opening that category first and then clicking the Import Clips icon to start the rest of the procedure. After you have located the folder that contains the image files, select the filename of the image (you can select multiple files). Then you click "Let Clip Gallery Find This Clip in Its Current Folder or Volume," which is under the Clip Import Option, and then click Import.

You add descriptions for each image by clicking on the Description Tab and type the descriptions. To assign categories, click the Categories Tab and select the categories in which you want the preview to appear. To add keywords, click the Keywords Tab and add keywords to make it possible to later find images that match particular keywords.

To make it easier for you or others to find your images later, add keywords to each image as you put it into a category. Use these keywords to search for the image.

Not only should you use a keyword when adding the file, you should also use the description and categories options to further organize your images. If you don't, it will be more difficult to find your images later.

Incorporating Images into Office Documents

One of the reasons for using PhotoDraw is because it is designed to work hand-in-hand with the other applications in the suite of Office products. You can import PhotoDraw images in their native format into other Office applications in one of three ways:

- Drag and drop the image from an open PhotoDraw file into an open Office file.
- Use the Insert command inside any Office application.
- Use the Copy command in PhotoDraw and the Paste command in the other application.

Most of the time you will be importing PhotoDraw images into only three Office applications: FrontPage, PowerPoint, and Word. You'll need to know some details about how to import images into each of these applications to work more efficiently with PhotoDraw images in these applications.

Unless you elect to drag and drop images from PhotoDraw into other applications, organize your images by copying them into a separate folder before opening the other Office applications.

If you saved your images in a collection inside PhotoDraw, you can access that collection within any Office application. This is the fastest and easiest way of bringing your completed images along with you into another program.

If you use PhotoDraw to edit images in the Gallery and then save the edited file, the revised image automatically shows up when you open the other Office application files that use that image. This also happens if you edit the file but don't save it into a Gallery and don't move it from the spot on the disk where it was when you created the other files.

Adding PhotoDraw Images to FrontPage Webs

Start the process of importing images from PhotoDraw by putting your FrontPage file in Page view and click the point where you want the picture to appear. If you saved your images in the clip-art gallery inside PhotoDraw, you can open the same clip-art gallery inside FrontPage by using the Picture/Clip Art selection under the Insert pull-down menu. You have to search for your images by the keywords you assigned when you added them, but they will be there.

Click the image to bring it into the FrontPage design you are working on. You can save the images in the Gallery as MIX files, but to properly use them on a Web site, you should save them as JPG or GIF files before you import them into your Web page-creation software.

As noted earlier, you can also use the copy and paste commands or drag and drop the image from an open PhotoDraw file into the open FrontPage file. If you have more than one file to move, the most efficient way to use the images is to add them to the Gallery in PhotoDraw before starting FrontPage.

If you forget to do this, FrontPage converts the files for you to either JPG or GIF when you save the pictures to the Web. Files with 256 or fewer colors are converted to GIF format and all other files are converted to JPG.

If you saved your files into any format other than MIX, JPG, or GIF, you might still be able to import them into FrontPage (see Figure 61.20). The program can import files in these formats: TIF, TGA, RAS, EPS, PCX, PNG, PCG, and WMF.

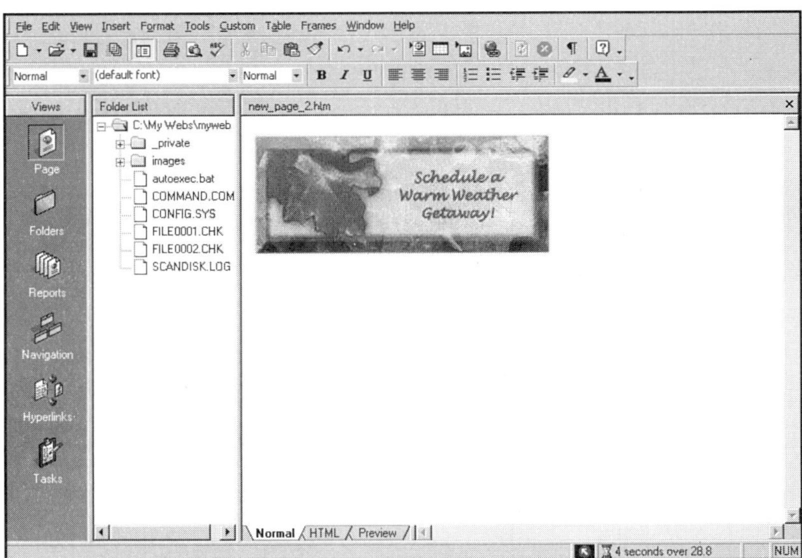

FIGURE 61.20
You can import images you've created or edited in PhotoDraw into FrontPage.

Adding PhotoDraw Images to PowerPoint Slides

If you are using a design template in PowerPoint, there are areas reserved for clip art on some of the templates. If you click one of these areas, the Office Clip Gallery automatically appears and you can select your image from the Gallery.

If you have not put them in the Gallery, you can access the files by using the Insert Picture option on the Insert pull-down menu instead of the Insert Clip Art option. To insert a PhotoDraw file when you are creating your presentation without using a template, you can still use the Insert Picture or Insert Clip Art options in the same way.

After you have imported the picture, you can use all but one of the image-editing features inside PowerPoint. If you want to recolor the image, you must return to PhotoDraw and complete the desired edits in that program.

Aside from MIX, you can import into PowerPoint any image files saved in these formats without installing a separate filter: EMF, GIF, JPG, PNG, BMP, RLE, DIB, and WMF. You can also install individual filters for more than a dozen other file formats including CDR, EPS, and TIF.

Adding PhotoDraw Images to Word Documents

Inserting a picture into a Word document is simple—all you need to do to start is open the document and click the point where you want to insert the image. You can use the Insert File or Insert Clip Art options on the Insert pull-down menu to access and import your images.

After you have inserted images, you can make minor edits to the image by clicking the image and using the options under the Object command on the Format pull-down menu. You can change the colors of the lines in the image as well as resize the image.

You can also make text flow around the object by clicking the object to open the picture toolbar and selecting the Text Flow Around icon. You can also access the Text Flow Around icon by clicking the object or picture and using the options under the Format Object or Format Picture commands under the Format pull-down menu (see Figure 61.21).

You can insert some graphic files directly into Word documents without having to first install a separate filter for EMF, JPG, PNG, BMP, RIE, DIG, GIF, and WMF files. To install filters for the other file formats that Word can accommodate, you must run the Setup program again and add the required graphics filters. Word comes with separate graphics filters for many graphic file formats including CDR, ENF, EPS, PCD, and PCX files.

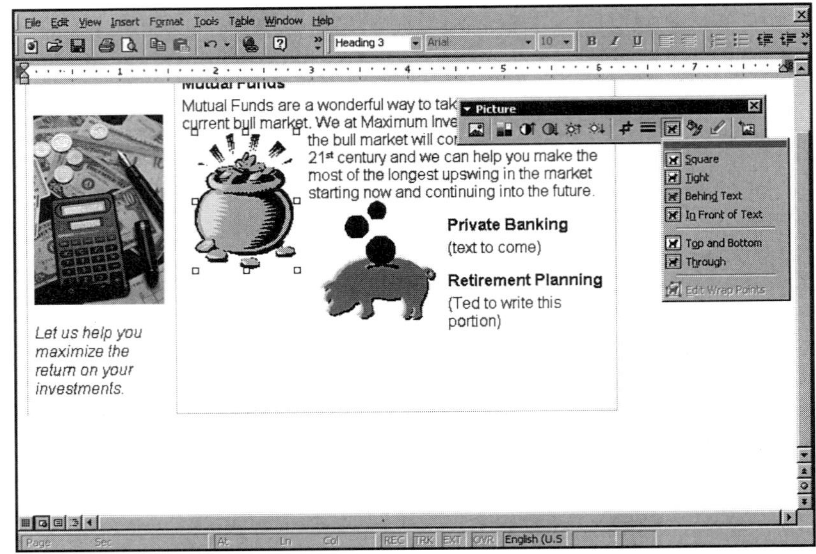

FIGURE 61.21
You can make text flow around objects in Word in several ways. Here the text is being made to flow around the objects by selecting one of the flow patterns shown on the right.

PART IX

Installing and Supporting Office 2000

CHAPTER 62

Installing Office 2000

In this chapter

Considerations Before Installing Office 2000

The issues associated with installing Office 2000 are numerous indeed. Choosing the optimal configurations and the most efficient deployment methods can be a daunting task. Whenever a piece of software as complex and powerful as Office 2000 is on the table, the dreaded planning phase becomes all too important.

This chapter focuses on hardware requirements, installation alternatives, and the tools you can use to install Office 2000. Although I do cover installing Office 2000 on a standalone PC, this chapter is geared toward the Office administrator who is charged with rolling out Office to a workgroup, or possibly the entire company.

Office 2000 uses the new Windows Installer, which gives you an incredible number of options when doing your enterprisewide installation. If you couple that with the capabilities of the Office 2000 Resource Kit and all its utilities and tools, the choices are almost mind-boggling.

One key feature of Office 2000 is its capability to "Install on First Use," which means the software isn't really distributed until the user actually does something that would require it. This can be done with Help files, templates, and sample documents, for example, or entire applications.

The task of installing the software is not overwhelming if you have a written roadmap of what you need to do. In the next few sections, we'll discuss some of your considerations and options. Some issues are pretty much "carved in stone" and others are strictly subjective. It's the strictly subjective issues that can make or break you. Be sure to check out all your options before you chart your course, and be sure you know what steps you intend to take to reach the installation's goals.

System Requirements

It would be great if a quick and simple answer existed to the systems requirements question, but the fact is it depends on how you intend to make Office 2000 available to your users that dictates the answer. You have options to locally install all or part of the suite on each computer, install the software on a distribution server, or install on a Terminal Server. The Office 2000 Resource Kit provides package descriptor files (PDF) for using Systems Management Server (SMS) as a vehicle for distributing the applications for local or shared access. Depending on which method(s) you choose, based on your network and the requirements of your users, the systems can be anything from handheld Windows CE devices to multiple processor behemoths.

Before starting your installation, it will behoove you to sit down with some paper and a few pencils and figure out the best way to implement Office 2000 in a manner that will best suit the end users, management, and administrators. One additional thought —this is not something you should do in a vacuum. As discussed (in depth) in the previous chapter, get some help and base your decisions on as many viewpoints as possible.

Individual PC Requirements

For the purpose of the next few sections, we'll assume you're going to do a local installation of the most typical components of Office 2000. This means all the applications, but without all the add-ons. Another consideration here is that the PC specifications we discuss assume original processor configurations, not a 386 that has a Pentium upgrade chip. Although these systems will see an improvement in performance, they typically will not perform at the same level as a standard Pentium, Pentium II, or Pentium III system.

Windows 95/98 System Requirements The Microsoft minimum configuration for an Office 2000 installation on a Windows 95/98 computer is

- 486/66 Processor
- 16MB RAM (although you'll suffer with anything less than 32MB; and all things considered, we don't recommend anything less than 64MB)
- 200MB free disk space (for Office 2000 only, not including the operating system)
- VGA or better video card/monitor
- CD-ROM drive

Please note that these are the Microsoft minimum system requirements for Office 2000. Experience tells us that a system with this configuration would likely perform so poorly as to be impractical for all but the most casual users.

NOTE I actually performed an installation on a Pentium 90MHz computer with 64MB RAM and a 1GB hard drive, and the performance, after the installation finally completed, was perfectly acceptable. I do have my doubts about the older P60 and P75 processors, though. The amount of RAM is another key issue here, and I believe this component is actually more important than the processor, at least for most of the Office 2000 applications. This P90 was in standalone mode, disconnected from the network, and had absolutely nothing to do but concentrate on Office 2000. It also didn't have to deal with mail or sharing data.

The bottom line is that rarely, if ever, do two machines, no matter how "identical," function the same. If you're close to the borderline on hardware, be sure to look at each machine to be sure it will support the user in the manner to which he or she is accustomed. Consider the following configuration as a standard for your Windows 95/98 business environment:

- Pentium 133 or later processor
- 64MB or more of RAM
- At least 1GB of free disk space (accounts for Office 2000 and locally created files)
- SVGA video adapter and monitor
- 24X or faster CD-ROM

This gives you some room to grow and enhances the environment for the user. Nothing is worse than having all the coolest applications and having them run like molasses in winter. Outlook, in particular, seems to have a huge appetite for system resources, but it matches that hunger with outstanding functionality. Just make sure it's well fed!

Windows NT 4.0 Workstation System Requirements The Microsoft minimum configuration for an Office 2000 installation on a Windows NT 4.0 Workstation computer is

- Windows NT 4.0 Service Pack 3 or later (NT 3.5x is not supported)
- 486/66 or later (a Pentium-based system is preferred)
- 16MB RAM (as with Windows 95/98 systems, you greatly increase system performance with more RAM)
- 200MB free disk space
- VGA or better video card/monitor
- CD-ROM
- At least 4MB of available space in the Registry

The minimum system requirements are the same for Windows NT 4.0 Workstation and Windows 98; however, NT likes its peripherals on the high end. At the low end of the scale, Windows 98 typically outperforms NT Workstation, but add a little horsepower and NT takes off and leaves 98 in the dust. This is going to become even more the case with Windows 2000 Professional (previously known as Windows NT Workstation). But speed isn't the only reason to use an operating system.

Microsoft has never been crazy about huge installations of Windows 95/98 in the business arena. They see Windows NT Workstation as the prime candidate for this implementation because of its reliability, security, and performance capabilities (support for multiple processors, New Technology File System (NTFS), and so on). It stands to reason, then, that it requires a little more consideration in the resource category, so the following is a premium configuration you might consider to take advantage of NT Workstation's Office capabilities:

- Pentium 233 or higher processor
- 128MB or more of RAM
- Sufficient SCSI disk space, multiple drives
- SVGA or better video card/monitor
- 24X or faster CD-ROM

Yes, this is more than you absolutely need to run the operating system and Office 2000, but NT Workstation will use these resources to their maximum potential, and you'll be ready to move to Windows 2000 Professional. Always assume the next generation of software/operating systems will rely on the most current technology and buy the most you can afford.

If you are really going to be putting Office 2000 through its paces, you should be looking at running a Pentium Pro 200 or faster, either by itself or in a dual-processor configuration. This would imply that you intend to use the Office 2000 products together in massive PowerPoint presentations, large Access database applications, significant Excel spreadsheets, or perhaps for the purpose of establishing your own Peer Web Services intranet site.

NOTE Of course, if you have the option of installing NT and Office 2000 on a Pentium II or Pentium III system, you'll be pleased with the boosted performance (to say the least).

Windows NT performs particularly well on SCSI hard drives, especially because they can be *striped* to span drives and access large data files simultaneously across those drives. This process is called disk *striping* and allows data to be striped across multiple drives in 64KB blocks. The effect of this is that a 3GB database striped across three SCSI drives reaps the benefits of three sets of read/write heads acting on the file simultaneously for a dramatic improvement in access time. Large databases, spreadsheets, slide presentations, or even documents can achieve significant reductions in the time between selection and display. Disk striping can be used with IDE drives with multiple controllers; however, the effect is not quite as dramatic.

So, does your user need all this processing power? Will very large files be created and stored on the PC? Will intranet hosting be provided through Peer Web Services? These are questions that you need to answer before deciding what hardware platform to run.

Be sure to give your users what they need, plus a little, but don't bankrupt the company by buying super computers for users who will use them as paperweights. The same is true of distributing Office 2000. If the only thing the user is going to do is create text documents, then just distribute Word 2000 and its components.

Understanding the Installation

The new Windows Installer makes use of several files to perform the installation. Although the most visible of these files, to the average user, is `SETUP.EXE`, it's actually just the butler, in a manner of speaking. Let's take a moment to examine the various files the installation process utilizes and see what each one does.

SETUP.EXE

`SETUP.EXE` is actually a *Bootstrap* program. What that means is that it runs a few checks and uses the information it obtains, in addition to any command-line options you've given it, and passes that on to the real installer—`MSIEXEC.EXE`. `SETUP.EXE` is shown in Figure 62.1.

When you run `SETUP.EXE` by inserting the CD, it checks to see whether the CD was inserted in response to a request by the Windows Installer—for example, if you attempted to use a feature that was set to Install on First Use. If the Windows Installer is already running, then `SETUP.EXE` quits to let the Installer do its job.

`SETUP` launches automatically if you have your Windows AutoPlay settings configured to detect the insertion of a CD. If you have intentionally disabled this feature, simply open Windows Explorer, navigate to your CD-ROM drive, and manually launch `SETUP.EXE`.

If you want `SETUP` to launch automatically (in either Windows 95 or 98), choose Settings from the Start menu and select Control Panel, System, and then select the Device Manager tab. Open the CD-ROM hardware class. Highlight your CD-ROM drive and click Properties. Click the Settings tab and select Auto Insert Notification. Click OK on both dialog boxes and restart your computer. When you reinsert the CD, it launches automatically.

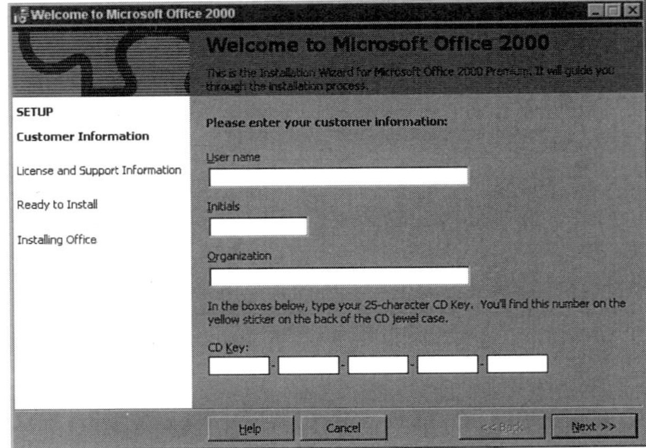

FIGURE 62.1
SETUP.EXE gets you started on the installation process.

If the Installer did not request the CD, SETUP.EXE then checks to see whether any of the major Office applications are installed as "Run from CD or Network" (more on that soon, too). If they are, SETUP.EXE quits because it expects that the Installer will soon request a file so that the application can be run.

If neither of those conditions is true, or if you run SETUP.EXE manually (from Start, Run or by double-clicking the file), it performs the next three steps:

- Checks to see whether the Windows Installer is already installed on this machine and if it is an older version than the one with Office 2000. If it doesn't exist or is an older version, SETUP.EXE installs or upgrades the Windows Installer for you.

NOTE If you're installing on a Windows NT machine, you have to be logged in with an account that has administrative permissions to the machine in order to install the Installer components.

- Checks to see whether Office is already installed. If it is, SETUP runs in Maintenance mode, which allows the user to add and remove features, uninstall Office, or repair the Office installation by reinstalling and/or reconfiguring the Office files and components.

Remember to think things through before you make changes. Making a decision to remove Word 2000 from a user's computer right before the user has a report due is not a good plan. Likewise, if a user is expecting to get a spreadsheet that describes how his or her salary is calculated, that user would be really upset to find you had removed Excel the night before.

- Runs the Windows Installer (MSIEXEC.EXE) to perform the installation.

MSIEXEC.EXE

This is the actual Windows Installer. It's not a good idea to run this program directly; instead, it is best to always let SETUP start it for you.

CAUTION

When Windows Installer is installed on a computer, it registers itself as the default program to run .msi files. It's a good idea to go to Windows Explorer and remove this association so that your users don't inadvertently run MSIEXEC by double-clicking an .msi file.

MSIEXEC.EXE will read the Installer Package file (.msi), apply any Transform file (.mst) specified, utilize any options provided to SETUP.EXE in the settings (.ini) file or on the command line, and perform the installation.

The Windows Installer will be used by all new Microsoft applications, including the upcoming Windows 2000 operating systems and BackOffice products.

Installer Package File (.MSI)

This file is basically a database that contains all the information needed for the Office 2000 installation. This includes system dependencies, folder paths, component files, Registry entries, and installation options.

The default Installer Package file for Office 2000 is INSTALL.MSI. One of the strengths of the new Windows Installer is that the Installer Package file is never edited. Any changes or options are implemented in the Transform file (see the following), the Settings file, or from the SETUP.EXE command line. Because you always have a base Installer Package file to work from, distributing multiple variations of the installation is much easier.

You can utilize different Installer Package files, if you want.

Transform Files (.MST)

These files are databases that are used to alter any of the installation options in the Installer Package file you're using. You can create a custom .mst file byusing the Custom Installation Wizard (see the folowing) and use it when you run SETUP to customize the setup options.

You can use the Transform file to have SETUP perform certain actions during the installation, such as

- Remove specific versions of previous Office applications (Word 95 or Excel 97, for example).
- You can specify if you want the user's existing profile information migrated, if you want the default profile used, or if you want to use an Office Application Settings Profile created by the Office Profile Wizard.
- Have SETUP add certain specific, non-Office files to the user's machine. These can be macros, batch files—even documents or templates.
- It can add any Registry entries you like to the user's machine.

Configuration Files (.INI)

These files are text files that contain instructions for SETUP to use. Basically, it's a way to present SETUP with a large number of command-line options in an easy-to-reuse manner.

NOTE Any settings you specify in this file override any conflicting settings that exist in the .msi file or that you've specified in the .mst file.

The default Configuration file is called `SETUP.INI`. You can either modify this file or create a new one. If you create a new `SETUP.INI` file, you'll need to specify the new file when running `SETUP`. To do this, add `/settings` *`[filename.ini]`* to the command-line option (*where* *`[filename.ini]`* is the name of the new configuration file).

Following are the configuration file components:

- MSI Section—This is where you can specify the filename of the MSI file you want to use. Only one key is in this section, `MSI=`, which you simply follow with the filename of the MSI file you want to use.
- MST Section—The same as the MSI section, except this section specifies the name of the .mst (Transform) file you want to use.

Don't forget to include the path to these files if they aren't in the same directory with `SETUP.EXE`!

- Options—In the options section, you specify properties that you don't want the user to have to input—things such as the CD Key, the Installation Language, or the UserName. For a more complete list of options, see the "Installation Options" section.
- Display—This section controls the user interface of the setup. Here you can select how much (or how little) you want the user to see as setup progresses. I'll detail the possible display settings in the "Installation Options" section.
- Logging—This section lets you specify the level of logging that you want the system to do during the installation. Logging options are covered in detail in the following section.

Office Profile Settings Files (.OPS)

Later, we'll discuss in greater depth how to use the Office Profile Wizard, but the result of that wizard is an .ops file that contains the user settings for that machine. This .ops file can be used to implement a standard set of user settings across an organization or department or to simply make a cleaner migration of a user from an old machine to a new one.

It is very important, however, before you go standardizing all the users' desktops with a profile, that they know what is happening. If you install Office 2000 and don't tell them about the change to a standard profile, watch out for flying debris. The perception will be that you "took their stuff away" and that is not a good thing. Work with the users and make sure they understand the benefits of a standard profile during the initial stages of installation.

OPC File

The OPC file is used by the Office Removal Wizard to identify Registry entries, INI file entries, files, and to start menu items that were installed or updated by previous versions of Office or

Office-related products. The OPC file also contains rules that describe which of these files or entries to remove, where they are located, and under what conditions they can be deleted.

Installation Options

In this section, we talk about the most common installation options available to you. Keep in mind that these can be used either as command-line switches for `SETUP.EXE` or as part of the Options section of the `SETUP.INI` file.

If conflicting settings exist, the Command-Line settings override the .ini file settings, which in turn, override the .mst file settings.

ALLUSERS

If you're installing on an NT Workstation and logged in with Administrator privilege, Office will be installed for all users of that workstation.

If you don't have Administrator privilege on your NT Workstation, `SETUP` installs Office only for the current user.

This option is ignored if you install Office on a Windows 95 or Windows 98 computer.

Syntax: `ALLUSERS="TRUE"`

COMPANYNAME

This setting enables you to specify the company name in advance so the user doesn't have to type it.

If you want the users to enter the company name the first time they try to run any Office application, *don't* use the `COMPANY` name option and *do* use the `NOCOMPANYNAME` option. (syntax `NOCOMPANYNAME="TRUE"`). This can be useful if you're running in an environment in which different users might need to specify different organization names—perhaps for branch offices or affiliates.

Syntax: `COMPANYNAME="ABC Corp."`

DONOTMIGRATEUSERSETTINGS

This instructs Office SETUP not to migrate the user settings from previous Office installs, if any. This defaults to true if an OPS file is in the .mst file. You might set this option to TRUE if you want to give users a fresh, clean installation with none of their previous settings or if you're using an .ops file to deploy Office with a standard set of User Settings.

If an OPS file is in the .mst file and you set this property to FALSE, the user's previous settings, if any, override the settings in the OPS file.

Syntax: `DONOTMIGRATEUSERSETTINGS="TRUE"`

INSTALLLANGUAGE

This is the language that SETUP uses to configure the user-dependent settings, such as text layout in Word and language auto-detection.

More than 40 languages are offered as of this writing. Table 62.1 lists a few of the most common ones. For a more complete list, look at the multipk.xls file in your Office 2000 Resource Kit.

Table 62.1 Installation Language Options

Language	Code Number
English	1033
Spanish	1034
Japanese	1041
French	1036
German	1031
Italian	1040

Syntax: `INSTALLLANGUAGE="1033"`

NOTE To change the language setup, simply change the Installation Language Options to the desired setting. For example, type `INSTALLLANGUAGE="1041"` if you want to set the language to Japanese.

INSTALLLOCATION

This setting enables you to change the directory where the Office program files will be installed. By default they will install to `C:\Program Files\Microsoft Office`.

NOTE If you use this setting on the command line or in the settings (.ini) file, you have to specify an absolute path (`"C:\etc"`). If you set this in the .mst file with the Office Custom Installation Wizard, you can use a relative path with a predefined folder.

Syntax: `INSTALLLOCATION="C:\office"`

REBOOT

This setting dictates how (or if) SETUP will reboot the user's computer. Four valid options exist:

- `OnlyIfNeeded`—This is the default setting. SETUP reboots the system only if system files currently being used need to be updated, or for other reasons.
- `Force`—This tells SETUP to always reboot the user's computer at the end of the installation.

- `Suppress`—This tells `SETUP` *not* to reboot to update system files that are in use. `SETUP` may still reboot for other reasons, however.
- `ReallySuppress`—A nominee for the most honest command-line switch, this tells `SETUP` not to reboot the machine under any circumstances.

If this is set in the .mst file, remember that you can override it on the command line. Simply clearing this value sets it to the default (`OnlyIfNeeded`), so a simple `REBOOT=""` on the command line resets this property to the default.

Syntax: `REBOOT="Force"`

TRANSFORMS

This tells `SETUP` where to look for the .mst file you're using to modify the installation parameters. You can use the absolute path (`C:\etc\install.mst`), a relative path (`\install\install.mst`), or even one with a variable in it (`%user%\install.mst`).

If you're setting this with the Settings (.ini) file, place this property in the `[MST]` section.

Syntax: `TRANSFORMS="C:\install.mst"`

USERNAME

This enables you to specify the username automatically so that the user is not prompted to enter it.

If you would like the users to be prompted for their name the first time they run any of the Office applications, do not set this property and do set the `NOUSERNAME` (Syntax: `NOUSERNAME="True"`) property.

Syntax: `USERNAME="Joe Smith"`

Controlling the Installation Interface

In the `[Display]` section of the settings (.ini) file, you can set two properties:

- How much you want the user to see
- Whether you want a message at the end to confirm that the installation was completed

To control the level of interface, simply add the `"DISPLAY="` property with one of the following values:

- `None`—No user interface at all. This runs the installation in "silent mode." You can also do this at the command line for `SETUP.EXE` by adding the `"/qn"` parameter.
- `Basic`—This displays only simple progress indicators and any errors that may occur. You can do this at the command line with the `"/qb"` parameter.

- `Reduced`—Full-progress indicators and errors are displayed, but installation does not interact with the user to prompt for information. You can set this at the command line with the `"/qr"` parameter.
- `Full`—This is the default; it displays all the normal dialog boxes, messages, and prompts. You can set this at the command line with the `"/qf"` parameter—although you don't have to unless you're overriding a conflicting setting elsewhere, because it's the default.

The other setting here is to display a completion message at the end of the installation. To do this, simply add the `CompletionNotice=` property to the `[DISPLAY]` section and set the value to `Yes.` (`"CompletionNotice=Yes"`).

You can do this from the command line by just adding a `+` to the end of whichever `/q` option you set, like this: `/qn+`.

NOTE You need to add the completion notice only to installs that you're running in either `Display=None` or `Display=Basic` mode. It appears by default on the Reduced or Full installs.

Setup Logging Options

`SETUP.EXE` and the Windows installer each keep separate log files of their activities. The two files have the same name except the Windows Installer's log file appends "_msiexec" to the end of the filename.

You can set three properties in the `[LOGGING]` section of the settings (.ini) file.

The `PATH=` property enables you to specify a path to store the created log files. You can use environment variables (`%USERNAME%`) in this path.

The `TEMPLATE=` property enables you to specify how you would like the filename of the log files. Add a `"(*)"` to insert a unique four-digit number in the filename. For example, `"SETUP(*).TXT"` creates log files called `SETUP0001.TXT` and `SETUP0001_msiexec.TXT`.

The `Type` property has several switches that control what information to include in the Windows Installer log file (the `SETUP.EXE` log file cannot be changed).

These `Type` property switches are

- `i`—Log information-only messages.
- `w`—Log warning messages.
- `e`—Log error messages, including fatal ones that terminate the installation process.
- `f`—Log a list of the files that are in use and need to be replaced.
- `a`—Log the start of action notification.
- `r`—Log the action data record, which contains action-specific information.
- `u`—Log the user-request messages.

- c—Log the initial User Interface parameters.
- m—Log any out-of-memory messages that occur.
- p—Record a list of the properties that are set with the Settings (.ini) file, .mst, and command line.
- v—Verbose. This includes all debug messages.
- *—Turns on all options except Verbose.
- +—Appends this log to an existing log file if one exists.

You can set these logging options from the command line by using the `/Loptions logfile` parameter. For example: `"/lieacm+ SETUP.TXT"`

Other Command-Line Options

A handful of other command-line options are available for `SETUP.EXE` to perform a variety of other useful tasks.

- `/i misfile`—This tells `SETUP` to use the specified .msi file to perform the setup. This file must be in the same folder as `SETUP.EXE`.
- `/a misfile`—This tells `SETUP` to perform an administrative installation of Office using the .msi file specified. As previously, the .msi file must be in the same folder with `SETUP.EXE`. You would use this to prepare a network installation point.
- `/foption misfile`—This tells `SETUP.EXE` to repair the Office installation using one of several parameters. The parameters are detailed in Table 62.2.
- `/X misfile`—Uninstalls Office. The .msi file must be in the same folder with `SETUP.EXE`.
- `/Settings [filename]`—Specifies a Settings file (.ini) for `SETUP.EXE` to use. `[filename]` represents the name of your custom .ini file.
- `/WAIT`—Tells `SETUP.EXE` to wait until the Windows Installer is finished with the installation before terminating. If this option is not set, `SETUP.EXE` will terminate before the installation is finished.

Table 62.2 Valid Repair Parameters

Parameter	What It Does
P	Reinstalls the file only if it's missing.
O	Reinstalls the file if it's missing or newer than the existing file.
E	Reinstalls if the file is missing or is equal in age, or newer than, the existing file.
D	Reinstalls if the file is missing or is a different version than the existing file.

continues

Table 62.2 Continued

Parameter	What It Does
C	Reinstalls a file if it's missing or if the checksum of that file doesn't match—indicating that it may be corrupt.
A	Reinstalls all files regardless of status.
U	Rewrites all required user Registry entries.
M	Rewrites all required local machine Registry entries.
S	Reinstalls all shortcuts, overwriting any existing shortcuts.
V	Runs from the source package and recaches the local package.

Understanding the Installation Options and Methods

Because of the new flexibility built into the Office Setup Wizard, most people will no longer choose to run the standard installation. This section details some of the key concepts regarding your Office 2000 installation.

Standard Installation

By clicking Install Now after entering your CD key and accepting the license agreement, the standard installation will be performed. The standard installation is just that—the most typical or common installation (as defined by your installer package files) containing the default options.

The advantage to this type of installation is that it is extremely easy and requires very little interaction with the user.

The disadvantages of using the default installer package file are that some useful features are installed in Install on First Use mode (discussed more in-depth as follows), and you really don't have a lot of choices in how the software is installed.

One variation on the standard installation is the Upgrade installation. The primary difference is that, by default, the Upgrade is going to install only applications that were previously installed. For example, if you had a previous version of Word installed, it will install Word 2000, but if you did not have a previous version of Word, it won't install it.

Custom Installation

This is the most useful of the installation modes in that it lets you view and control what's going to be installed and where.

The advantage is that for the medium-to-advanced user or administrator, this feature helps you to customize your installation by installing (or omitting) certain features and to control where files are installed (see Figure 62.2).

The disadvantage to this is that it requires considerably more involvement by the user in making and/or confirming selections.

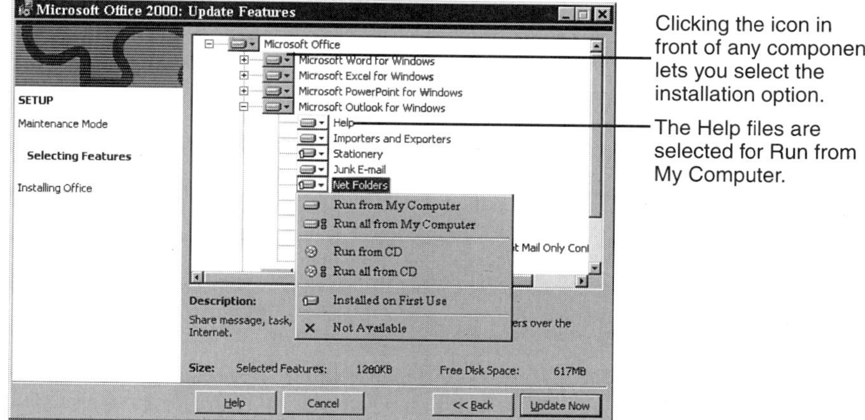

FIGURE 62.2
Custom installation enables you to select how you would like the components installed.

Run from My Computer

This tells the installer to install the files or components to your local hard drive for use by your system.

The advantage to this is that when you go to use those options, they are installed and ready to use. Also, they load as quickly as possible because they're stored locally.

The disadvantage to this is that the installation takes slightly longer, but more important, you use storage space on your drive to store these files. For example, a full installation of the Premium Edition of Office 2000 takes approximately 494MB of disk space.

Install on First Use

This is a clever new feature that tells Office 2000 that you don't want this feature or component installed now, but if and when you need it, the feature will be installed. The result is that the feature or component is added to your menus and toolbars as usual, but the files aren't actually copied to your drive until you attempt to use that feature.

The advantage to this is that it saves a little bit of install time and saves disk space from being taken up by features that you might not use.

The big disadvantage is that if and when you decide you do want to use the feature (for the first time), it must be installed—which means that you'll have to have access to your Office 2000 CD or your Network Installation Point. If you're in an airplane over the Pacific Ocean and you try to run a Install on First Use feature for the first time…you'd better have your Office 2000 CD handy or you will be out of luck.

There is also the minor inconvenience of having to wait a minute or more for the installation of that feature to complete before you can make use of it.

Run from CD/Run from Network

These two features are variations of each other. The basic idea is that rather than actually install the application or feature, it will be run from the installation CD or Network Installation Point.

NOTE Which of these options you have depends upon how you're doing your installation. If you're installing from CD, you'll have the Run from CD option. If you're installing from a Network share point, you'll have the Run from Network option.

The advantage to this is that you don't have to use disk space for rarely used features or components because they remain on the CD or Network Installation Point.

The disadvantage to this is that you have to either have the CD available or be connected to that Network Installation Point whenever you want to use these features. Another disadvantage is that even if you have those resources available, the feature executes more slowly than if it were loading from the local hard drive.

If you do an installation to Microsoft Terminal Server, you must specify Run from CD or Run from Network because they cannot install any of the features locally.

Running from the network is also a good idea if you have a lot of roaming users. By having the applications run from the network server instead of the local hard drive, you simplify your administration and deployment. Anywhere users travel, as long as they can access the server, they can access their applications; and by using Roaming Profiles, they can have their own custom settings.

Profiles

Profiles are one way to adjust the installation status of one or more Office 2000 components. Whenever a new profile is introduced, it has the potential to change everything about the way a user interfaces with any of the Office 2000 components, which is a double-edged sword. If you have more than one administrator, you need to be very careful to not undo what the other person spent hours doing. Flexibility is a great thing, as long as some coordination is involved.

Standalone PC Installations

The first choice for disseminating Office 2000 is individually, one computer at a time, with the CD gripped firmly in your fist. As you will be able to tell from the first couple of installs, this is a very time-consuming proposition. It typically takes an hour to an hour and a half for the installation to complete. If you have a large number of machines to install, you may see Office 2001 released before you finish with Office 2000!

The steps involved in doing this kind of installation are simple: If you want to do a standard installation, you simply insert the CD into the CD-ROM drive. Most machines automatically start the SETUP program, which launches the Windows Installer.

NOTE If you put the CD in your drive and it doesn't automatically launch the installer, chances are that you have AutoPlay disabled on that machine. If that happens, you can go to Windows Explorer, double-click to open the CD-ROM drive and double-click the SETUP program, or click Start, Run, <D:>\Setup (where D: is the drive letter of your CD-ROM drive).

After you are asked to provide some personal information (name, initials, organization), the CD-KEY for your Office 2000 CD, and confirm the license agreement, you are presented with a screen that asks if you want to Install Now (or Upgrade Now if you have a previous version of Office on this machine) or if you wish to do a custom installation.

Selecting Install Now (or Upgrade Now) will perform a standard installation with all the default options, unless you've specified custom options in your .mst, .ini, command line, or elsewhere. Among other things, it installs Internet Explorer 5 on your system, places all the Office 2000 files in the default location on the hard drive, and removes any previous versions of Office (although it will migrate your user settings).

If you expect to have multiple users sharing the same Windows 95/98 machine, install Office 2000 to the machine before you enable user profiles on the machine so that all users of that machine can use the Office Applications. If you set up the user profiles first, you'll have to set it up for each user so that all can access it.

For a small site with only a few machines receiving the Office 2000 installation, this may be an acceptable solution, and it may even be ultimately easier than taking the time to learn how to set up a mass installation. For a site with more than a few machines, however, better options exist.

Network Installations

Before you install Office 2000 in a network environment, take some time to look over your situation and decide which resources you're going to use. The first question you need to ask yourself is "What is a server?" The answer is "any device with resources you want to share." When I say resources, I may mean hard drives, printers, modems, or any number of other sharable resources. Now, how do you want to distribute this load? Do you have multiple servers available or are you going to have to make do with one or two? Are you going to implement a secure domain environment, or is your user base small and you're planning to stick to a workgroup (peer-to-peer) structure? First, let's take a look at the network environment and check out the potential functions of servers.

Workgroup

If you have less than 15 users, you might consider the workgroup environment. In this structure, each computer operating as a server contains its own accounts database for those users who can log on and use its resources. This environment is called a *peer-to-peer network* because sharing can occur between any two computers as long as user permissions support access. This structure works well for small companies that want to make do with existing computer resources. An NT Server, in this environment, is called a *standalone server* because no NT Domain is available to connect to.

No central administration of either accounts or resources exists, which could be a problem if the number of users and computers grows. In this scenario, Office 2000 would probably be installed locally in each computer and user data files would probably be stored on the NT standalone server, if it exists; otherwise, they would be stored on a selected peer server or the local hard drives.

Domain

In a larger organization, the NT servers become much more involved. The recommended structure here is called a *domain* and involves NT servers functioning in multiple roles for the purpose of centralizing security and resource administration. This is where the options for distributing Office 2000 really come into play.

Primary Domain Controller (PDC)

Atthe top of the heap in an NT domain is the *Primary Domain Controller (PDC)*. This server is responsible for maintaining the domain security accounts database as well as keeping track of published resources throughout the domain and enterprise and, in its spare time, validating users' authentication requests. For all practical purposes, the PDC is domain administration. If this server goes down, no new user or group accounts can be created, no account modifications made, no password or policy changes; in short, no administration.

Although the PDC "owns" the security accounts database, it allows *Backup Domain Controllers (BDC)* to keep copies so they can assist in the validation of users. Basically, when the PDC makes changes to the security accounts database, it notifies the BDCs of those changes. The BDC then "pulls" those changes from the PDC.

So why am I telling you all this? Just to show that perhaps the PDC is not the ideal candidate for distributing the software for Office 2000, acting as a network share point for shared applications, or playing the part of Terminal Server. The PDC is an integral part of domain administration with plenty of things to do without the added burden of Office 2000 issues. This is not to say, given the proper resources, the PDC could not support this, but if you have a choice, the PDC is probably not the ideal server for the job.

Backup Domain Controller (BDC)

The Backup Domain Controller (BDC) is another validation source for users—when a user tries to log on to a domain, it broadcasts its request and the first domain controller available validates them. It also has the potential to pick up for a failed PDC by being promoted to a PDC. Depending on the activity on your network, the BDC may actually be busier than the PDC, which implies the PDC may not always be the most powerful server on the network (it generally isn't, in fact). BDCs typically are placed either geographically or functionally throughout the domain or enterprise to accept user authentication requests. Because it has a copy of the security accounts database, it is quite capable of validating users, even if the PDC is offline. The BDC cannot, however, make any changes to the security accounts database without the PDC being online.

BDCs are also used by Systems Management Server (SMS) as Logon Servers for the purpose of distributing software and instructions to SMS client computers. Although PDCs can be designated as Logon Servers as well, it's less common than using the BDCs.

Now this sounds like a prime candidate for distributing Office 2000, right? Well, yes and no. Although SMS Logon Servers do distribute software, it's the SMS Client software that is installed on each SMS client machine. What the Logon Servers do, however, is point the client to distribution servers throughout the network where they can find applications software, such as Office 2000. After the SMS client finds a distribution server, depending on how the software is to be implemented, the SMS client will either cause the software to be installed on its local hard drive from the distribution server (distributed application) or establish pointers to the distribution server so it can pull the executables into memory when the user accesses that application (shared application). More on SMS later.

Member Servers

A server that is not a domain controller but is a member of a domain is called a *Member Server* (in contrast to a server that is installed in a workgroup being called a Standalone Server). These are the unsung heroes of the domain because they don't share in the glory of validating users. They simply provide file, print, application, and remote access services to the network. They go quietly about their business, especially when *Distributed File Services (DFS)* is being used. With DFS, the servers disappear completely into the background because the users and administrators see only a file structure spread across all servers on the network. No one sees the servers, only the file structure. That makes doing searches really easy for end users and for the administrators—and backups are a snap. This also makes data storage much simpler because all storage on the network now appears as a single-storage hierarchy.

A Member Server probably is the best choice for distribution servers. It doesn't have any administrative responsibilities, so it can focus totally on the software needs of the end users. What are your choices for distributing Office 2000, and how can you make use of each of these servers?

A Windows 9x (95 or 98) machine can be a member server of sorts, as well. With File and Printer Sharing enabled (through Control Panel, Network), you can allow some or all users on your network to access the hard drive, the CD-ROM, the printers, or even the floppy drive that is hosted by that Windows 9x machine. By setting the access control to User-Level, you can have your Windows 9x machine use your Domain as the repository for user accounts (thus maintaining some central control), and you can then share out your resources and assign permissions to accounts and/or groups in your domain. It goes without saying, by the way, that to use User-Level access control, you have to have a Windows NT Server or domain from which to get the account information.

If you don't have a Domain to provide the account information to a Windows 9x machine, you'll have to use Share-Level security—which enables you to set a password (you can leave it blank if you don't want any security on the resource) for access on each individual resource that you're sharing.

In some cases, this capability has been used to share CD-ROM drives across the network or to create storage areas for archived or little-used data. Keep in mind that this is not going to be as fast, secure, or efficient as using an NT Server for this task. It is a good way to get a little extra use out of a high-powered machine that's being used as a workstation, however.

Installation Options in a Network Environment

If you are deploying Office in a large organization, one of the most efficient methods of deploying Office is to first to do an Administrative installation of Office on a network server, make any organizationwide adjustments, and then have users run the setup from the administrative installation point.

NOTE Windows 2000 offers more installation options because the operating system has actually picked up some of the functionality of SMS. Windows 2000 actually lets you *publish* software, which gives the user the option of installing/upgrading to the published software. The administrator can also *assign* the software, meaning the software is installed regardless of whether the user wants it. ■

One of your first considerations as an Office 2000 administrator is which components to download to which clients. Office 2000 is very large, and it may be that you don't need to take up all that disk space on a client machine whose users will never use anything except Word. An important question to ask here is "Do I know enough about these users to make a determination about what software they are going to need?" If you don't know the answer, go ask someone. Don't guess.

Another potential pitfall to this installation process is in migrating the existing application settings from Office 97 or 95 into Office 2000. Nothing is wrong with this, as long as you have done some research and know that the previous version was installed properly (there's no sense in propagating a bad installation). Office 2000 evaluates the previous installation and conforms to the applications and options selected, and those may be exactly what the user needs—or not.

If you choose to use a tool such as SMS to deploy Office 2000, you can change anything about the installation you like, including removing it from the users' systems. The SMS Client is very obedient when it comes to changing the status of one or more components of any application.

After you've decided which server you're going to install to, which applications to install, and how you would like them installed, you're ready to proceed with the Administrative installation.

This option allows for customization of the installation to the point of a complete, unattended installation (Windows Installer). You simply complete the following steps:

1. Create a share point on any or all distribution servers by setting up a directory and share, on the server, where you will place the installation files.
2. Place the distribution files at that share point by doing an Administrative installation (`SETUP /a`) to the share point you just created.
3. Customize the installation by using the Custom Installation Wizard to create an .mst file.
4. Have the users map to the share and issue the setup command.

If your internal email application supports it, you can email a shortcut to your users so that they don't have to worry about the details of initiating an unattended installation.

The user provides as little or as much input as you specify by your customization.

This option can also be facilitated by Systems Management Server (SMS). SMS allows the administrator to create a *Package Descriptor File (PDF)* of software and setup instructions and place that package on distribution servers. The administrator then creates a *job* that directs the SMS Client software to connect to a distribution server and download the software, using whatever customization is specified in the PDF.

The user's part in all this is through an SMS interface called the *Package Command Manager*. It allows the user to

- `EXECUTE` the job and download the package
- `ARCHIVE` the job for later execution (the administrator can make the job mandatory, which will cause the job to run on a particular date regardless of user choice)
- Get `DETAILS` about the job and its related software

The end result is a clean transition for the users because they no longer have to know how to connect to a server, deal with setup issues, and so on. SMS takes care of all that through the Package Command Manager. This also allows for some fault tolerance because the Package Command Manager can actually load balance between the distribution servers, or discount servers, that aren't online.

The second option is to again establish network servers, but this time the goal is not to install the software across the network, but share it from a pool of servers. The users actually connect to the distribution server, pull the executables into their local memory, and run the application locally. Two advantages exist to doing this:

- Very little disk space is used on the user's computer.
- The administrator has only a limited number of installations to maintain.

In a solid, well-connected, high-bandwidth environment, the users won't notice a difference between having the software installed locally or on a network server.

One very appealing aspect to this type of installation is that it is by user and not by computer. That means that if a computer is shared by two or three people (for example, in shift work), each person would see different shared applications. If an application is not meant to be used by a particular user, the entry on the program menu or the program item simply wouldn't show up. This gives the administrator additional control over who gets what software.

All this has a downside. Because the users must use network resources each time they access an application, it could put quite a strain on the existing network. An example of this might be for Excel 2000. Many people think of this as just one application, but in fact, it consists of the main application as well as other smaller components, such as Microsoft Query. Each time users of a shared application need another "piece" of the parent application, they access the network and pull it into their computer's memory. Depending on how frequently this occurs (and what else is happening on the network that generates activity), it could cause a serious "traffic jam." These traffic jams, of course, cause complaints because the system performance degrades. It's your call, but check it out before you implement this solution.

SMS is again the best resource for setting up a shared installation. The administrator actually does an administrative installation for the application (`SETUP/A`) on each distribution server. A package is then created with the application instructions for each application to be shared (that is, one package for Word 2000 and one package for Excel 2000). Another package must also be created to display a program group and program item or program menu entry on the client computer. Because no installation is taking place on the user's computer, this is the only way for them to "see" an item to select. Jobs are then created to route the packages to the proper locations.

The user interface is provided by an SMS interface called *Program Group Control*, which supplies the users' desktops with any shared application entries available to them. Program Group Control checks a Network Application Database on the Logon Server for any shared applications available to the currently logged-on user, and then adds the appropriate icons or entries to the desktop. It also works with other SMS components to connect users to the appropriate distribution server when they access that application.

Installing Office in a Multinational Environment

Installing Office in a multinational organization is actually much simpler than it ever has been. Essentially, you take the steps you would take to deploy Office from a network (that is, perform an Administrative installation to a network share), and then you add the step of doing an administrative installation of the Office 2000 MultiLanguage Pack.

After you've done these administrative installs, you'll want to create customized setups for each location.

The easiest way to get the language settings you want is to install Office 2000 and the MultiLanguage Pack, from your network share, onto a test computer. Then choose Start, Programs, Office Tools, Microsoft Office Language Settings to select the language(s) that you want to use. Run the various Office applications, making any settings that you want the users to have, and finally, use the Office Profile Wizard (as described earlier) to save an .ops file containing these settings.

After you've created .ops files for the various language installations you'll want to do, you can use the Microsoft Office Custom Installation Wizard to create customized setups that utilize those OPS settings for your users; then simply have your users run `SETUP.EXE` with the proper Transform (.mst) files for their language or national installation.

For more details on this process, an excellent article, "How to Deploy Office in a Multinational Organization," is available in the Office Resource Kit.

Preparing to Install Office 2000

Before you install Office 2000, you need to take into account previous Office installations. Do your users have custom settings they'll want to preserve? Do you want to replace the previous installations, or do you want to try to install Office 2000 side-by-side with the previous installation? In this section, we'll examine some of those options.

Preserving Custom Settings When Upgrading

Office 2000 pays special attention to users' custom settings during the upgrade process. Any setting a user has changed from the default can be saved and brought across to the new Office 2000 environment. Examples of custom settings might include default file formats for saving files in the application to custom dictionaries for the spellchecker.

A consideration exists here, however, for a standardized installation. The Office Profile Wizard, included in the Office 2000 Resource Kit, makes it possible to set up a standard profile for your entire company. With all the new customizable features in Office 2000 applications, this makes training and Help desk functions much more manageable. Even though users can do their own customizing of the settings, they'll typically be much more comfortable if they can ask a coworker or administrator a question and know the answer pertains to their setup.

Removing Previous Versions of Office

The new Office Removal Wizard is another flexible tool included in the Office 2000 Resource Kit. Its functionality basically is that of `SETUP.EXE` but gives the administrator a significant boost in capabilities. You can specify, down to the file level, exactly what you want removed. This is beneficial if the files for the application you're removing have some impact on other applications.

Running the Office Removal Wizard interactively is a simple procedure. Choose the Start menu and select Office Tools, Microsoft Office 2000 Resource Kit Tools. When you start it, the wizard asks you which type of cleanup you would like to perform, and when you click Next, it searches for the appropriate files and then waits for you to confirm removal.

The three cleanup options are

- Remove Only the Files That I Absolutely Do Not Need—This option searches your system for files from older versions of Microsoft Office that are no longer being used, and then offers to remove them for you.
- Let Me Decide Which Microsoft Office Applications Will Be Removed—This searches your system for previous versions of Office and shows you a list of the files that can be removed. You can then select which files to remove and which to keep.
- Completely Remove All of My Old Microsoft Office Applications—This removes all old Office files, including any that you may still be using.

Regardless of which option you select, the Office Removal Wizard displays a list of the files to be removed, which you can save or print, and asks you to confirm that you want to remove them.

If you just want a list of which files are used by Microsoft Office, you can run the Office Removal Wizard, have it find the files to remove, save or print the resulting list, and then cancel the wizard before any files are removed.

Another way to run the Office Removal Wizard is one you may not have suspected: when you use the Office Custom Installation Wizard to tell SETUP to remove previous versions of Office Applications, SETUP is really using the Office Removal Wizard to perform that task.

Another interesting capability of the Office Removal Wizard is that it's not limited only to Office 2000. It can basically remove anything on the system. Again, this can be either a good thing or a bad thing if you don't plan properly and know the impact of removing a particular file or component. The wizard gives you a huge number of parameters you can work with to isolate and remove that pesky file that just won't go away, or that is hiding so completely you just can't find it. You can remove components, Registry entries, or individual files easily and quickly. A list of these parameters is included in the Office 2000 Resource Kit.

All this removing is done through the use of an *OPC* file (see Figure 62.3). This file contains the logic used to remove components of existing Office installations from the file structure, Registry, and so on. By changing the OPC file (carefully, I might add), you can control exactly how the wizard does its job. This file consists of two sections—the definitions section and the commands section. The definitions section controls the logic used to identify components or even specific files, and specifies which commands will be used to accomplish the removal. A default OPC file for Office 2000 is called `Offcln9.opc`. It is customizable, but I highly recommend that you save a copy of the original.

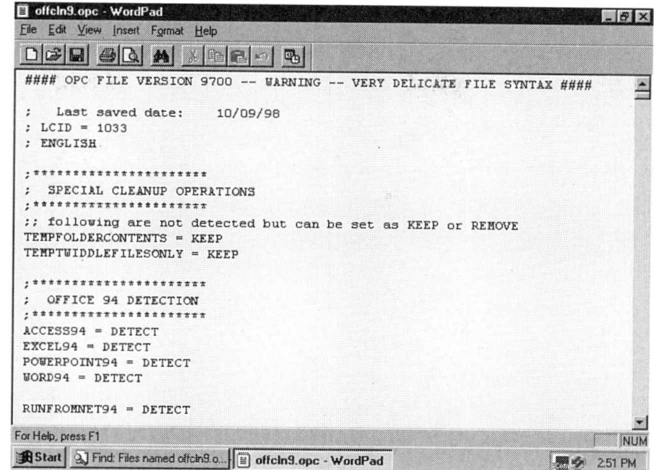

FIGURE 62.3
Example of the *OFFCLN9.OPC* file viewed through Notepad. If you've edited or created a custom .opc file, chances are you're going to want to run the Office Removal Wizard from the command line.

The syntax for using a custom .opc file from the command line is as follows:

```
Offcln9.exe MY.OPC
```

`Offcln9.exe` is the Office Removal Wizard and `MY.OPC` is the .opc file that you created or customized.

NOTE For more information on Office Removal Wizard and its command-line options, see the "Office Removal Wizard" document in the Microsoft Office 2000 Resource Kit.

Office Custom Installation Wizard (OCIW)

This tool replaces the Network Installation Wizard offered in the Office 97 Resource Kit. It is designed to create an Installer Transform file (.mst), which has the capability to temporarily alter the Windows Installer's Installer Package (MSI) database. Sounds confusing? You don't have to worry about it—just use the wizard.

The Custom Installation Wizard can be used on any application that uses the Windows Installer and can also utilize Office Profile Settings (OPS) files to preset user options in applications. You can even run the Internet Explorer Administration Kit from within the Custom Installation Wizard to customize Internet Explorer 5 installations.

TIP One of the best features of the OCIW is the capability to create multiple .mst files for different types of users. The Finance Department might have different application needs than the Sales Department, so the OCIW allows you to create a unique .mst file for each group of users.

To install the Office Custom Installation Wizard, insert the Office 2000 Resource Kit CD and run the `SETUP` application in the `\CIW` directory. This installs the OCIW, Office Profile Wizard, and Internet Explorer Administration Kit (IEAK).

Running the OCIW is a multiple-step process (the exact number of steps vary depending on what installation you're customizing). After acknowledging the welcome screen and pointing OCIW to the Installer Package File (.msi) that you plan to use, you have the option of creating a new .mst file or opening an existing one to edit.

As you step through the wizard, you are given options to set the default installation path, the organization name, to specify which components to install and how (Run from CD, Install on First Use, and so on) and even add additional, non-Office files such as templates or batch files.

If you're customizing the main Office 2000 installation, you will get a screen that allows you to Customize the Default Application settings. On this screen, you can specify an .ops file (captured by the Office Profile Wizard) with the user-application settings that you want applied to this installation.

NOTE If you specify an .ops file and/or any additional, non-Office files to install, copies of those files are placed in the actual .mst file. As you can imagine, this means your .mst file could grow quite large. Keep this in mind when planning your distribution method.

On one screen you are given the option to use the OCIW to have SETUP remove specific previous versions of Microsoft Office products, such as Excel 97 or PowerPoint 4, as part of the installation process.

You are also given the option to specify new Registry settings that you want to add to the system during installation. A nice feature of this screen is the Import button, which lets you import those Registry entries from a .reg file so that you don't have to type them in. This could be useful if you have a particular Registry subtree you want to add to your machines; you could set it up on one machine, export that subtree to a .reg file, and then import those into the OCIW.

When you have finished creating your .mst file, you should use the Transforms command line switch with SETUP.EXE like this:

```
setup.exe transforms="F:\install\office\sales.mst"
```

TIP For a seamless and quiet installation, add the "/qn+" switch to the end of your SETUP.EXE command line to run the setup in silent mode but with a confirmation message that displays when the installation completes. This way, the user doesn't have to watch the setup happen, or interact with it, and is notified when the process is finished. Note that if Office needs to reboot the machine after the installation completes, the confirmation message will not be displayed.

The administrator can also incorporate customized installations of Internet Explorer by using the Internet Explorer Administration Kit (IEAK). Figure 62.4 shows an example of this step in the Custom Installation Wizard.

The OCIW allows the administrator many opportunities to implement subtle changes in the installation without corrupting the standard installation.

FIGURE 62.4
The Custom Installation Wizard shows options to configure profiles and Internet Explorer 5.

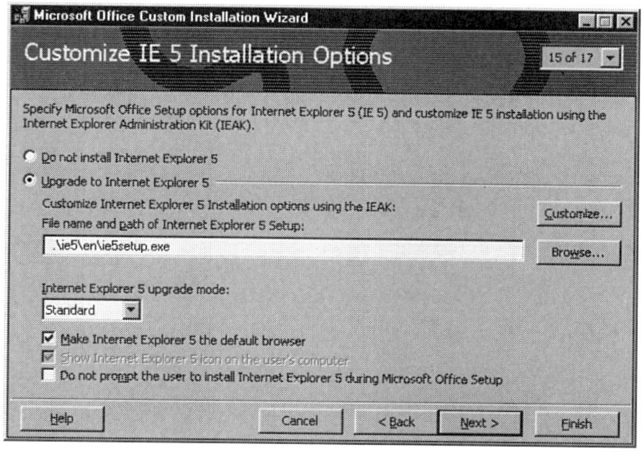

Office Profile Wizard (OPW)

This tool enables you to configure all the user-configurable settings for Office 2000 applications, take a snapshot of those changes, and save it in the form of a profile that can be distributed along with the product. This makes it very easy to try different settings yourself, to decide which ones are appropriate for a group of users, and to capture those settings.

To install the Office Profile Wizard, insert the Office Resource Kit CD and run SETUP.EXE from the root directory. If you've previously run the installation but did not install the Office Profile Wizard, you can add it with Add/Remove Features.

After it is installed, it can be run from the Start menu. Depending on which Start Menu group you installed it to, you should find it under that group and Microsoft Office 2000 Resource Kit Tools.

Using the Office Profile Wizard is about as easy as it can possibly be. The Wizard has only two steps and the first one is just a welcome screen. After you click past the Welcome screen, you're presented with the only two options in the program: Save Settings or Restore Settings.

Just specify the filename that you wish to save the settings to or restore settings from, click Finish, and your .ops file is created (or restored from).

The Office Profile Wizard can be helpful to you in several ways:

- To distribute a common collection of user settings to an entire department—Using the Office Custom Installation Wizard (OCIW), you can include an OPS file that you create with the Office Profile Wizard and have those settings automatically installed when Office is installed.
- To upgrade a user to a new machine—Rather than just install Office 2000 on the new machine and force the user to manually re-create settings, as we've had to do in the past, you can use the OPW to get a snapshot of the settings on the old machine, then install Office 2000 on the new machine with that .ops file, and all settings are migrated over.

- As a troubleshooting step—We've all had temporary employees who thought they were helping us out by "fixing" a bunch of settings on the machine on which they were working. By saving an OPS file while the machine is working properly, we can easily restore that OPS file to undo any damage that users intentionally or accidentally do to the settings.

Distributing Custom Installations for Organizations

If you're deploying Office 2000 across an organization, you will probably want to do some customized setup. Previous sections of this chapter introduced you to the tools for customizing setups—Office Custom Installation Wizard (OCIW), Settings (.ini) files, Office Profile Wizard and its .ops files, and so forth. The following section discusses techniques for distributing the custom installation you've created.

Creating Custom CDs to Distribute Office 2000

If you have the capability to burn your own CDs, you can create custom installation CDs that you can distribute to your various users and administrators.

> **CAUTION**
>
> Be very careful with your licensing issues here. You can't just start burning CD copies of Microsoft Office and passing them out to all users. Be sure that you are installing and using only the amount of software that you are licensed by Microsoft to use.

The first step to creating a custom CD is creating a Disk Image of the Office CD. This sounds a lot more intimidating than it really is; basically, all you're doing is copying the entire set of folders and files, without altering the hierarchy in any way, to a folder on a hard drive. Keep in mind that this requires upward of 566MB of free drive space to do.

After you've created this disk image, you can make any modifications you need to the Settings (.ini) file, add any Transform (.mst) file, and then burn that entire directory to a clean CD.

> **CAUTION**
>
> Don't modify anything other than the Settings and Transform files. SETUP expects to find certain files in certain places, and any unexpected change in the files or folders could cause SETUP to fail.

Just like that, you've created a customized Microsoft Office install CD.

Adding Office to an Existing Disk Image

Some of you will deploy Office as part of a larger upgrade and, toward that end, are already creating custom disk images that contain Windows and other files and applications.

Adding Office 2000 to that image is a simple process—you simply install it, with the options you want your users to have, onto the test computer before you create the disk image from that computer. When you create the disk image, Office 2000 is included in the image.

Terminal Server

Windows NT 4.0 Terminal Server Edition enables users to run Windows-based programs on computers that cannot run the latest versions of Windows. With Terminal Server, you can deploy Office 2000 on the server and have users run Office applications over the network.

Terminal Server provides a thin-client solution in which Windows-based programs are executed on the server and remotely displayed on the client. If your users have computers with limited disk space, memory, or processing speed, you can install Office to run in this environment.

Terminal Server represents a sort of step backward in how most people think of computers. Today, everyone expects to have all kinds of power right there on the desktop. It's almost an ego thing in the workplace—who's got the biggest computer on their desk.

Terminal Server returns to the theory that smaller is better. It supports what used to be called dumb terminals because very little processing actually takes place on the desktop. Terminal Server generates even the interface (desktop). Software doesn't run on the desktop computer, it runs on Terminal Server and the results of the processing are displayed to the desktop computer.

Sun Microsystems has been doing this for years. Microsoft simply saw a gap in their coverage. It may sound old-fashioned, but consider this—how would you like all the functionality of Office 2000, including significant document storage, on your palmtop or CE-based handheld computer? How would you like to be able to access huge amounts of processing power and storage capacity for use with Office 2000 applications from the remote keyboard and mouse in front of your television? These things are possible with Terminal Server because your "computer" is just acting as a front end to the true processor.

Office Server Extensions (OSEs)

Office Server Extensions offer the capability for users to make comments through any of the Office 2000 applications.

Office Server Extensions offer a way for users to have discussions through any application file included in Office 2000, including any HTML or Rich Text documents. The discussions are stored externally in either a SQL database or in the Office built-in database on the extension server.

The discussions can take place across a LAN or across the Internet using a Web browser and take the form of "anchors" in the document being discussed. This allows changes to the document without disrupting the discussions. The administrator can configure Autonavigate to enable the users to connect to a Web server and view their Web folders, which contain the discussions, as a series of HTML pages.

Support is provided for any capable Web browser, including the earlier versions of Internet Explorer and Netscape Navigator. The end result is that any of these browsers that support frames can see and take part in OSE document discussions.

The Office 2000 Resource Kit contains additional instructions for establishing and configuring an extension server, as well as how to take part in discussions, but I'll briefly explain how to install these features.

The OSE requires NT4 Server (or later) and Internet Information Server (IIS) 4.0 or later.

To run the OSE Setup program, insert the appropriate Office 2000 CD and run the `SETUP.EXE` program from the `\OSE` directory. The setup proceeds in two phases—specifying locations and configuring the OSE.

After you click Install, `SETUP` installs the Web pages and FrontPage Server Extensions. If you don't have SQL 6.5 (or later) installed on this server, `SETUP` also installs the built-in Office server database engine.

Specifying Locations

Unless you have a compelling reason (such as insufficient space) to do so, it's best to let the files install to their default locations. For the Start pages, the default location is the `\inetpub\wwwroot` directory. If you're already using that directory for an Internet or intranet site, you may want to specify a different directory for the Start pages.

If you do choose a different location for the Start pages, you'll need to run Internet Service Manager to define a virtual directory mapped to this new location.

Either way, the Start page for the end user is installed in the `\msoffice` subdirectory, and the one for the administrator is installed in the `\msoffice\msoadmin` subdirectory of the main directory that you've chosen for your Start pages.

OSE Configuration Wizard

Before the OSE can be started, the configuration settings have to be set; however, you can change any of them later if you wish, so don't worry if you're not sure how you want to configure the OSE now.

The first step of the Configuration Wizard asks for your name and organization. After you've entered that and accepted the license agreement, the wizard asks you for a location to install to and prompts you to Install Now.

When the file installation is complete, the last three steps of the wizard begin.

The first step relates to the database where the Web Discussions and Subscriptions will be stored. You're asked to provide a name for the database and a password for administration.

After you've completed that step, you're given the opportunity to specify who will participate in the Web Discussions and Subscriptions. If you've already mapped out your security intentions, you can set them now. If not, you can always accept the defaults and modify these settings later.

The final step asks you to specify a mail server for the OSE to send messages, such as subscription notifications, through. Specify an SMTP server for the OSE to use and click Finish.

Web Discussions

The Web Discussions component is part of the Office Server Extensions, so installing them simply requires installing the Office Server Extensions (OSE) and enabling (or leaving enabled) the Web Discussions Collaboration feature.

▶ **See** "Using Web Discussions," **p. 62**

Web Subscription and Notification

Like Web Discussions, installing Web Subscription and Notification requires only that you install the OSE and configure it to enable the Web Subscriptions feature.

▶ **See** "Using Web Subscriptions and Notifications," **p. 68**

International Support for Languages

International Support and Language Packs enable administrators to customize Office 2000 to allow users to access their programs in their native language. Even countries that are multilingual are supported. This translates to remote users profiles acting in a similar manner with a U.S. user traveling to France, yet seeing the desktop in English. These capabilities are allowed because of the modular structure of Office 2000. Regardless of the installation country, the executables stay essentially the same—only the language pack changes.

The Office 2000 Resource Kit contains options for installing more than 100 languages. Each language has varying capabilities for grammar and spell checking, but all are supported to some degree. The neat thing about this is that installation doesn't change; no matter what country you install in, the same steps are followed.

After the basic installation of Office 2000 has completed, the administrator applies the language pack and the applications are ready for users in their own language. Because of this "laid-on-top-of" approach, profiles still work and display a traveling user's desktop in his or her native language.

Office 2000 Multilanguage Packs for Travelers

Suppose you are an executive from a large global company and you travel to Zimbabwe, where the native language is Shona. Your notebook batteries just kicked up their little feet and died and there's not a Radio Shack in sight. You find the prongs on your power adapter were definitely configured for another part of the world.

Because your notebook is dead, you're forced to use a local machine. Unfortunately, you don't speak Shona. You sit down at a desktop-networked PC (loaded with Office 2000) and carefully type in your name and password where you think they should go (because the logon screen is in Shona). When you are authenticated and logon is complete, you have a completely English desktop.

This happens because your profile specifies you as an English user and it loads the appropriate language pack.

Roaming User Profiles

To make this mobile capability work, you should utilize Roaming User Profiles. Two steps exist to enabling roaming user profiles under Windows NT.

1. Create a profiles folder on an NT Server. Not only does this server not have to be your PDC, but it often shouldn't be. A member server is a good choice to handle this load. You can place the Profiles folder just about anywhere except in the %systemroot% folder on that server.
2. Set up the user to point to that profiles directory to get, store, and retrieve his or her profile. You do this by going into User Manager for Domains, selecting the user, going to Properties and Profiles, and pointing the account to the proper directory. A slight difference occurs, depending on the type of client (Win95 or WinNT) that the user has.
    - Windows NT: Set the User Profile Path to be the full path to the profiles directory you created.
    - Windows 95/98: Set the Home Directory to be the full path to the profiles directory you created. For example, `\\MyServer\Users\profiles`.

If your client machines are Windows NT, you are ready to go. If your client machines are Windows 95 or 98, however, you have an additional step or two to take.

- Windows 98—Go to Control Panel, Passwords, and click User Can Customize on the User Profiles tab.
- Windows 95—You first need to install Internet Explorer 4.0 (because it creates the Application Data folder and stores files there), and then follow the steps for Windows 98.

After you've done this, the next time the user logs on, that profile is retrieved from this directory; when the user logs off, an updated profile is saved to this directory.

Office Web Components

Office Web Components are a group of COM controls that enable you to publish databases, spreadsheets, and charts to an intranet or Internet site. Essentially, they then allow visitors to the data to interact with it as if they were using a browser-version of Excel or Access.

These components are completely programmable—you can provide users with custom, interactive, Web-based solutions.

The Office Web Components are part of the default Office 2000 installation.

▶ **See** "The Office Web Components," **p. 56**

SQL Server OLAP Services

Microsoft SQL Online Analytical Processing (OLAP) is now fully supported in Office 2000. This allows the users to access SQL data from Excel or Access without the performance penalties that previous solutions were stuck with. You can even use the OLAP Services in conjunction with Office Web Components to provide Web-based access to your SQL 7.0 data.

In an OLAP database, data is organized hierarchically and stored in cubes instead of tables. OLAP data is organized for querying and reporting instead of processing transactions.

OLAP cubes can either be server-based or file-based. Cubes are created using an OLAP Product, such as the Microsoft SQL Server OLAP Services (that comes with Office 2000), or using a third-party OLAP Product. After the cube is created, an OLAP Provider is needed to access the data in a cube. OLAP Providers contain the client software and the data source drivers. Excel includes an OLAP Provider that can access cubes created by the Microsoft OLAP Product (Microsoft SQL Server OLAP Services). This Provider can be used with two types of OLAP data sources: from a database on an OLAP server on a network and from an offline cube file.

If a third-party Product was used to create the cube, the third-party OLAP Provider must provide the client software and drivers necessary to access the cube data. Any third-party OLAP Provider must be Office compatible and comply with the OLE-DB for OLAP standards. OLAP cubes files have a .CUB extension.

▶ **See** "Using and Creating OLAP Cubes," **p. 749**

To install OLAP Services, insert the Microsoft SQL Server CD. If you don't have AutoRun enabled for the CD-ROM drive, manually run the `AUTORUN.EXE` on the CD.

When `SETUP` starts, click Install SQL Server 7.0 Components, and then select OLAP Services. The OLAP Server and Client Components are required; you can install the OLAP Manager and Sample Applications if you like.

CHAPTER 63

Configuring Office 2000

In this chapter

Office 2000 Planning

Office 2000 has many configuration options. Proper selection of those options ensures user and management satisfaction. Improper selection just as certainly ensures dissatisfaction on both sides. Planning is essential, but you probably can't do it alone. The end users can tell you what they want, and management representatives can tell you what you can afford. Keep in mind the "afford" aspect is not necessarily directly associated with dollars, although that is typically the bottom line. Additional bandwidth, speed, and add-ons all translate to bucks somewhere down the line.

The key here is knowing how your people work and what they need to accomplish. You need to evaluate what is going on now as well as what is expected in the future. If the end users are getting along just fine now, you want to be sure you don't take anything away from them—at least nothing you aren't replacing with something both you and they perceive as better. On the other hand, if management is putting out a lot of money to upgrade systems, software, and the network with the idea of increasing productivity or perhaps taking on a bunch of new functions, you need to know that as well.

Administration of any computer product or network can be difficult or rewarding, depending on how everything is set up and what tools you have chosen to work with. To easily administer Office 2000, you need to start with the installation of your operating system. Assuming you're operating in a Windows NT domain environment, here are some components that need to be in place:

- Proper transport protocol, correctly configured for your environment (TCP/IP, NWLink, NetBEUI, and so on)
- Adequate and appropriately placed domain controllers
- Required services installed and started appropriately (DHCP, WINS, Directory Replicator, and so on)
- Extensible naming conventions for users, groups, servers, share points, and so on
- Templates for consistently creating users and assigning them to global groups
- Global groups appropriately placed in local groups to establish permissions
- Appropriate trust relationships set up between domains, if you have multiple domains, forming a reasonable enterprise model
- Established enterprise maintenance functions set up and assigned (backups, and so on)

Setting up your Windows NT/Office 2000/BackOffice system is like building a house. You want your foundation completely solid and properly configured before you start building the walls. Think of the implications when building a house if the foundation wasn't dry or the shape of the foundation wasn't correct.

NOTE A complete discussion of installing and configuring Windows NT or BackOffice is well beyond the scope of an Office book. Several excellent Que books provide the information you need. I recommend

- *Special Edition Using Windows NT Workstation 4*
- *Special Edition Using Windows NT Server 4*
- *Special Edition Using Microsoft BackOffice, Second Edition—Volumes 1 and 2*

After Windows NT is properly set up and configured, you're ready to start planning how to deal with Office 2000. The following tools offered by Windows NT, Office 2000, and the *Office 2000 Resource Kit* will help you during all phases of this endeavor.

System Policies

Although they'll rarely admit it, users are more comfortable if they function in a controlled environment. They need to feel that they can do everything necessary to accomplish their work, but they also need to know they won't destroy anything, at least not unintentionally and/or permanently. Some users want to go exploring, and they should be able to, but not to the point of causing system problems.

This is a delicate balance. Establishing that balance typically involves a Windows NT tool called the System Policy Editor. This tool allows the administrator to control the user desktop settings, menu item access, and logon options. This can be accomplished at the "default" level, which would apply to all users and computers, or at the individual user, group, or computer level. Once again, if the end users have a hand in establishing their environment and understand why they aren't being allowed to perform a certain functions, they'll much more readily accept the whole situation.

One example of using the System Policies would be if you want to disable the user's ability to use the Visual Basic editor. Using the System Policy Editor, you disable the ALT+F11 shortcut key and disable the Tools, Macros, Visual Basic Editor menu item and shortcut.

Policies in Windows 95/98

Windows 9x (95 or 98) policies must be created on a Windows 9x computer and are named Config.pol. After you've created the policy file, it should be placed at the NETLOGON share point (WINNT\System32\Repl\Import\Scripts) of a Windows NT Server Domain Controller or the \Public directory of a NetWare server.

NOTE If you want to use User Policies on a Windows 95/98 machine, you must use the Passwords applet in Control Panel to enable User Profiles on that client. Just go to the User Profiles tab of the Passwords Applet and select Users Can Customize Their Preferences...

Otherwise, only the Computer policies (if any) will be applied.

To enable a Windows 9x computer to use Group Policies you must do the following:

1. Open the Control Panel, double-click Add/Remove Programs, click the Windows Setup tab, and then click Have Disk.
2. In the Install from Disk dialog box, click Browse and specify the \tools\reskit\netadmin\poledit directory of your Windows 98 CD or the \admin\apptools\poledit directory of your Windows 95 CD. (Be sure to use the version for the operating system you're using.)
3. Click OK and step through the dialog boxes.
4. When you get to the Have Disk dialog box, check Group Policies, and then click Install.

The install procedure makes the needed changes to your Registry and, importantly, place the Grouppol.dll file in your \Windows\System directory.

Policies in Windows NT

The tool you need to establish this environment is right at your fingertips with Office 2000 templates and the Windows NT 4 System Policy Editor.

You can affect basically two things with policy—the computer and the user. Users can be affected either individually, through their group memberships, or as a "default" user. When you establish computer policy, it overlays portions of the HKEY_LOCAL_MACHINE subtree in the Registry and when you establish user policy, it overlays portions of the HKEY_CURRENT_USER subtree.

▶ **See** "Working with the Registry" on the CD-ROM accompanying this book.

If policy is specifically created for a user in the System Policy Editor, that policy becomes their policy. If a user is not identified specifically and belongs to multiple groups that have policy assigned to them, a group order is established in the System Policy Editor (Options/Group Priority) with the highest priority group establishing the policy for that user (see Figure 63.1). The computer policy is always applied last, after any user policy. The order is important because the last thing applied becomes the effective policy, because it overlays whatever was in the Registry before. If a user isn't specified individually or in a group, and the Default User policy has been configured, the default user policy is applied to their process. The same is true for the computer.

In Windows NT 4, all policy is contained in a single file called Ntconfig.pol and that file is placed at the NETLOGON share point (that is, WINNT\SYSTEM32\REPL\IMPORT\SCRIPTS) on validating servers in the domain. Policy becomes effective when the user process finds an entry in that file for themselves and/or their computer during the logon process. It then follows that Directory Replication must be set up properly for the policies to be consistently applied. Directory Replication is a domain controller process that distributes scripts and policy from the Primary Domain Controller to the Backup Domain Controllers.

The *Office 2000 Resource Kit* includes an updated version of the System Policy Editor and sample policy templates for both Office 2000 as a whole and each individual application within the suite. Figure 63.2 shows the Default User Properties dialog box from the System Policy Editor.

FIGURE 63.1
The System Policy Editor displaying policy icons for an additional user, group, and computer.

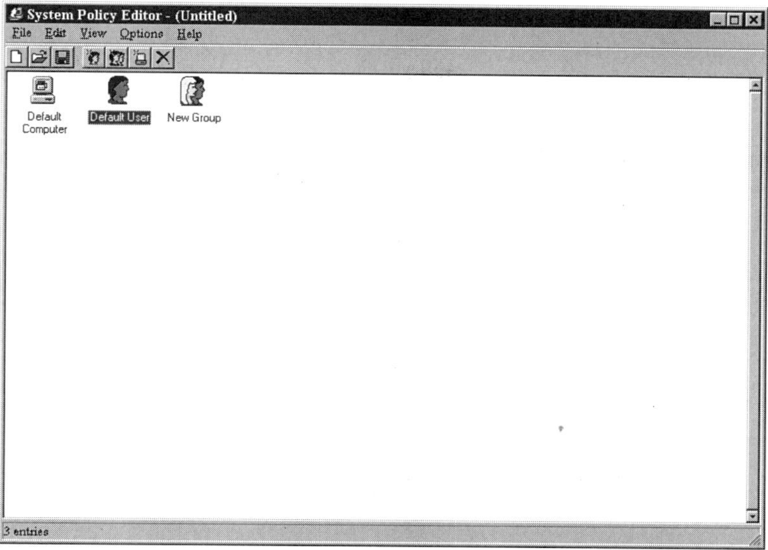

FIGURE 63.2
The System Policy Editor displaying a User Profile with the Office 2000 Template installed.

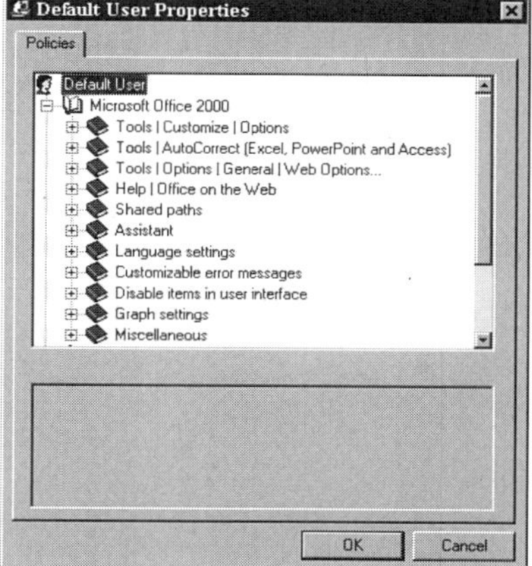

Policy Templates As you examine all the options available in the System Policy Editor, it's a little awesome to consider all the aspects of the user process you can impact. Even with all the options, there may still be some things you want to do but can't figure out how. Setting up a standard policy for your entire organization will benefit you greatly but it relies on good planning.

The purpose behind a template is to establish some standards and apply them over a significant portion of your network or installation. For the same reasons you may use templates to create users in Windows NT to standardize group memberships and resource access, you should consider using policy templates to assist in applying consistent, well-thought-out policy to those users. Of course, the first step is to identify groups of users that lend themselves to standardized policies. That may be the hardest part.

Typically, users can be grouped functionally, based on their workcenter's tasks, resource requirements, and the user's skill level.

NOTE When considering the skill level of your users, remember that some people use a computer because they must do so as part of their jobs. For these users, it can be preferable to set up system policies that prevent the user from inadvertently fouling the system. Conversely, there may be groups of "power users" that are completely comfortable with all aspects of computers and constantly search for new and better ways of doing their jobs. Sometimes, this type of intrepid user can cause problems because he or she continually tinkers with the system. These folks require a different—and more aggressive—type of containment.

Consider a typical office environment. Generally, you can group users by the tasks they need to complete as part of their jobs. Perhaps your contract division uses Word and Excel, but has no use for the Visual Basic Editor, Access, or FrontPage. Your sales force uses Word, and PowerPoint, but never touches Access. Your research department, on the other hand, uses Access every day. And everyone uses Outlook, but no one uses Publisher. As you consider the people in your company using Office, consider the tools they need and the tools they don't need.

It's helpful to create a chart that groups users in several broad categories. Try to keep your chart as simple and high level as you can. If you burrow too deeply, you'll end up with one person per group.

Next, you need to determine how people in each of these categories work and what level of complexity they'll be comfortable with. You need to do this for their entire Windows NT experience, but try to focus on the areas shown in the System Policy Editor; Control Panel, Desktop, Shell, System, Microsoft Office 2000, and so on. Keep in mind, you're still in "grouping" mode and trying to find common ground for a significant number of your users. If you intend to use an Office 2000 Resource Kit template (which is recommended), remember to invoke the template before you open any policies. Whether your users are all going to get the entire suite (or a subset of it) will dictate the template you use. Before you start asking questions, be sure to take a look at what you have to work with in the templates.

Now, after all this research, it's entirely possible to discover everyone could use the same policies. This is a wonderful thing because all you need to do is configure the Default User and Default Computer policies and you're done. Never overlook the simplest solution, even though it may be the hardest to identify.

NOTE As you go through the process of making the aforementioned determinations, be sure to document your progress. Don't just note those things that you actually do, but those things that were discarded, lessons learned, and so on. If you are using paper to record this information, be sure to transfer it to electronic media as soon as possible. This lets you organize it into a usable format and search for required information more easily.

There are people who absolutely hate documenting (hypothetically speaking, of course), but they have learned over the years that a few hours spent solidifying several weeks' worth of work can save considerable time and effort down the road. So consider taking a little "time hit" now and reaping the benefits later.

Configuring Internet Explorer

If you've ever looked through the property pages in Internet Explorer, you know how many options are available for this powerful tool. Many times the end users are totally lost in all the possibilities, so the Internet Explorer Administration Kit (IEAK) allows the administrator to customize Internet Explorer so that the end user doesn't have to worry about it. You can establish the connection type, phone book entries, telephony information, dialing prefixes, and so on.

This particular tool is handy for geographically dispersed organizations where different locations achieve Internet access through many different means. You can create a profile for each location and then implement those profiles with the Custom Installation Wizard. This, of course, assumes you have a good knowledge of what will be required at each site. The only thing worse than not having an automated profile all set up for the users is to have an incorrect profile setup that doesn't work. Coordination is a key ingredient to using this tool to your best advantage.

The Internet Explorer Administration Kit is composed of four basic parts, plus an extensive help file:

- Internet Explorer Customization Wizard—Helps you create customized Internet Explorer install packages.
- Internet Explorer Administration Kit Profile Manager—Lets you change user settings and restrictions automatically, after IE has already been installed.
- Connection Manager Administration Kit (CMAK)—Helps you customize and configure the Microsoft Connection Manager dialer. This wizard creates an .exe file that installs on your users' computers. When a user clicks the custom icon, a custom dialer dialog box (that you create) appears. If you're planning to use the IE Customization Wizard to create custom install packages, do this first so that you can include the CMAK .exe file in the custom install package for your users.
- IEAK Toolkit—This contains a variety of helpful files, such as the sample signup files and Internet Explorer Express Wizard. Look in the "Toolkit folder" of the IEAK program folder.

NOTE For more information on the IEAK and its operation, see the IEAK Help file in the Microsoft IEAK folder of your Start, Programs menu.

Among the settings you may want to control in Internet Explorer are the security settings. IE5 has four different settings you can choose from ranging from Low to High.

At the Low level of security, the user gets a minimal level of warnings and prompts. Virtually all Internet applications will execute, some of them without even prompting the user first. It probably goes without saying that it's not good policy to set this level of security on your general Internet access.

At the High level of security, you have the other extreme: Cookies are disabled and virtually no Internet applications will execute without considerable prompting and notification. This is the most secure way to browse, but also the most intrusive for the user.

In between these settings are the Medium and Medium-Low settings. Medium is generally considered the most reasonable setting for Internet browsing; it prompts where appropriate but still allows most of the Internet functionality. Unsigned Java applets are not downloaded, but otherwise the user is able to access most sites and features.

If none of these settings are exactly what you want, IE5 allows you to create a custom security setting by clicking the "Custom Setting" button. A dialog box appears in which you can select the level of functionality for everything from ActiveX to file downloads and even automatic logins.

Creating Custom Office 2000 Online Help Screens

Often users complain that the help articles are not easy for them to understand or don't seem to apply to their particular situation. It's a variation of Murphy's Law that the one thing you need help with will be the one thing that the help system doesn't cover. Well, with Office 2000, you can solve that problem by creating your own, customized, help articles. You can either write easier-to-understand help articles for problems already covered in the help system, or create entirely new articles to answer questions about specific functions or custom applications that you use in your environment. You could even create help articles to explain your workflow for example: "After finishing the purchase order form, it should be forwarded to the accounting department."

When a user has a question in Office 2000, similar to Office 97, they can consult the Office Assistant. When the user types in their question, the assistant provides your customized help response, just as it would directly from the master Office help database. This is a great opportunity to answer all those questions about where a print device is located, how to map a particular drive to a specified resource (not just the "how to map a drive" help, but directed at the resources on your network).

These custom help files are created using two basic tools: the Answer Wizard and an HTML editor. The Office Help system is basically a database with an Answer Wizard file, which is an index of keywords and pointers to the related articles. These articles are located on the local hard drive, a network drive, the World Wide Web, or even some combination of locations.

This tool has far-reaching implications. Imagine filling out a form in Access 2000 but not knowing whom to send the form to (they forgot to automate that part). The user could just invoke help and ask about the form, and it would tell them to send the form to "Stella" or whoever is appropriate. There is a small warning here, however. As you can see, your users could spend too much time just using the Answer Wizard, especially if you get too specific with your assistance. Try to keep it fairly general and provide answers to questions that will remain reasonably constant.

The Microsoft Answer Wizard Builder (see Figure 63.3) depends on Hypertext Markup Language (HTML) answer files. These can be created in either HTML or Compressed HTML (CHM) format. An HTML editing tool is included for this purpose in the Office 2000 Resource Kit. It's called the HTML Help Workshop. This tool lets you edit existing help or create your own new help.

NOTE To install the Answer Builder, go to the \ORK\PFILES\ORKTOOLS\TOOLBOX\TOOLS\ANSWIZ directory of your Office Resource Kit CD and run the Setup.exe program.

If you have an intranet Web server set up for your company, you can use HTML and direct the user to your Web site for the help files. The good side of this is that you have only one location to maintain and it's not taking any disk space from the clients. The only drawback to this method is that the user must have connectivity to get there. The alternative is to create the CHM files and install them locally on the client machine or on a network share.

Locating the files on the client's hard drive has pros and cons as well. The pros are that the client achieves an improvement in speed and there's no need for Internet/intranet connectivity. The cons are that you will be taking space on the client's hard drive and you'll have to have some sort of distribution method.

Locating the files on a network share solves the distribution and space problems but can result in a performance penalty because the clients have to access the servers for the Help files. This can also cause problems for roaming users (laptop users, for instance).

FIGURE 63.3
Microsoft Answer Wizard project creation screen.

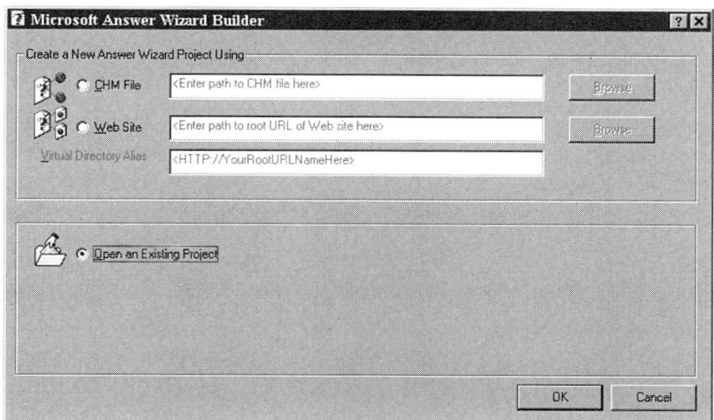

What basically happens is that the Answer Wizard Builder creates an Answer Wizard project (AWB) file that contains your HTML or CHM help topics. The Answer Wizard Builder then uses the AWB file to create an Answer Wizard (AW) file that acts as an index to the help system. When a user types in a question, that index is searched and points to potential help topics.

For more information on the exact mechanics of implementing this help enhancement, consult the Office 2000 Resource Kit. It contains the tools mentioned previously, as well as extensive text on how to perform these enhancements and sample scenarios to assist in planning your Help rollout.

Customizing Office 2000 Error and Alert Messages

A little less subtle tool allows you to customize the information contained in error messages. These custom error messages are also referred to as custom alerts and many, although not all, can be enhanced to include custom information. Additionally, you can selectively disable existing error messages.

It is important to note that you're really just customizing existing error messages by adding a button to the message to take the user to customized content. You aren't adding entirely new messages to events.

Creating and Editing Error Messages

An example might be a user who is attempting to delete a file when they have only read permission. The customized error message, instead of just saying "access denied" which is frustrating for a user, would have a button with text of your choosing (for example, "Push Me for More Information") and an associated Uniform Resource Locator (URL). The URL could take the user to a Web page on your intranet with further information about the error message, and possibly some alternatives or points of contact for additional actions.

Most error messages are blunt, and this is a way to make them more palatable and informative to the end users. Instead of leaving them frustrated, or dialing the help desk phone number, the Web document specified by the URL could provide a more detailed explanation. This might satisfy them and preclude the involvement of any administrative staff.

For certain, serious, error messages you might set up the custom error messages to allow the end user to click a button that begins an email message to the help desk to report the error.

The ideal way to implement these Custom Error Messages, if you have an Internet Information Server available, is to create custom Active Server Pages (ASPs) instead of static text pages. ASPs enable you to capture information about what generated the alert and even take appropriate action based on that information. If you choose this method, you'll need Microsoft Visual Basic Scripting Edition or a CGI-based scripting tool. Whatever tool you use will be used to create a script that will run on the server. That script processes things such as error message numbers, Global User Identification (GUID) numbers (the equivalent of computer object Social Security numbers), and so on and to return an ASP that contains information pertaining to the error or actions the user can take. You could even personalize the message for the user so that it refers to them by name.

What's a GUID?

A GUID is a Globally Unique Identifier. There are a number of ways of obtaining one, but the method that Microsoft uses is to use a generated number that is a combination of the date and time that the GUID was created and the MAC address of the network card (if any) in your computer. If there is no network card, then it just uses a default number to go along with the date and time stamp. Although it is possible that two machines would have the same GUID, it's not likely.

This number is generated by the Windows installer.

An Active Server Page (ASP) is used to embed applications and databases into HTML documents. They allow the programmer to create complex scripts and applets that will execute on the server side rather than being passed to the client and as such can be considerably more powerful and dynamic than standard HTML documents.

Disabling Specific Error Messages

You can, of course, disable Custom Error Messages either per message, per application, or across the whole system. Some of the already existing error message extensions rely on connections to the Internet. If you don't have those connections, you might consider turning those off. If you turn off a custom error message, the effect is to remove the custom button in the error message box. The message continues to function as designed. If you haven't deployed Office 2000 yet, you can disable the custom error messages by using the Office Custom Installation Wizard (OCIW) to ensure that none of the Registry settings that turn on the custom error messages are created.

The relevant Registry entries are

HKEY_CURRENT_USER\Software\Microsoft\Office\9.0\Common\General\ExtendableAlertDefaultBaseURL

HKEY_CURRENT_USER\Software\Microsoft\Office\9.0\Common\General\ExtendableAlertDefaultButtonText

You'll want to make certain that both of those entries are blank.

If you want to disable a specific custom Error Message, just remove the appropriate entry under

HKEY_CURRENT_USER\Software\Microsoft\Office\<*application*> \ExtendableAlerts

To disable all Custom Error messages for the specific application, remove ALL of the entries under that subkey.

If you have already deployed Office 2000, then you'll want to use a System Policy to disable the Custom Error Messages. To disable all messages, clear the BASE URL policy under the \\Default User\Microsoft Office 2000\Customizable Alerts section.

To disable a single message, go to the \\Default User\<*application*>\Customizable Alerts\List of alerts to Customize. Click the Show button in the "Settings" area, select the appropriate message Value, and remove it.

To remove all the Custom Error Messages for an application, you could follow the previous procedure and remove them all, but you'll find it easier to clear the "List of Alerts to Customize" check box in the \\Default User\<*application*>\Customizable Alerts section.

Travelling with Office 2000

Office 2000 really has gone out of its way to accommodate travelling users through roaming profiles and multilingual capabilities. Whether your users are accessing Office 2000 from a remote computer on the network, through a dial-in connection, or in an airport, their files and applications can follow them.

Roaming User Profiles

The foremost rule to keep in mind when setting up roaming user profiles is that they have to be available on servers that can be "seen" by the user's computer when travelling. When the client dials in from Timbuktu or uses their neighbor's computer 10 feet from their own, the server that validates them must have a reference to their profile and access to its location. Another consideration is that Windows NT and Windows 95/98 profiles are not compatible. This means that your user can't sit down at just any machine, regardless of operating system, and expect to have the profiles work correctly. More on that later.

Profiles in Office 2000 are no longer desktop settings. They enable a user to easily take files and folders along with them when they travel as well as their desktop and system settings. Actually, they can take the whole application along if they like.

Office 2000 implements roaming profiles by putting all user information about the application settings, preferences, and working files in a central location called the Application Data folder. This is generally WINNT\PROFILES*username* on Windows NT systems and WINDOWS\PROFILES*username* on Windows 95/98 systems.

Office 2000 also breaks from tradition in that it stores all the user settings in a single subtree (HKEY_LOCAL_USER) in the Registry. This further centralizes the profile information for easy "packing" when travelling or moving between machines in the local environment.

One significant issue to discuss here is the inability to switch between Windows NT and Windows 95/98 machines. Because these two operating systems are different in their structure and functionality, you need to set some guidelines for your roaming users. Your users cannot expect their Windows NT profile to be properly implemented on a Windows 95/98 platform. This is a limitation, but not an insurmountable one. If you deploy notebooks to your traveling users, those users will generally take their own notebook computers with them and you can just be sure they are running the same operating system there as they are on their desktop system. If they are going to be "borrowing" computers from their travel destination, they just have to be sure the computer they use is the same platform as their desktop system back home. Implementing this properly involves some knowledge of your organization. If you have all Windows 95/98 machines in the field, you probably don't want a user who's going to be travelling to those areas to have a Windows NT desktop.

The two basic steps to setting this up are

- Create a folder on an accessible server for the profile.
- Configure the user-profile portion of the user account through User Manager for Domains to point to that newly created folder.

NOTE Do not create the profile folder in the %systemroot% folder (\WINNT\PROFILES) on the server because this will cause the client to use their locally stored profiles instead of the roaming profiles. Select a different location such as \ROAMING\PROFILES.

When you edit the user's profile entry with User Manager for Domains, be sure to specify where the profile is located on the network (for example, \\MYSERVER\ROAMING\PROFILES). Be sure the server you specify will always be visible to the client from wherever they log on.

NOTE To use Roaming User Profiles, you'll need to have Windows NT Server 4.0 or 5.0, Novell NetWare version 3 or later, or some other server-type that supports roaming user profiles. Additionally, the server needs to support long filenames.

Windows NT clients are already ready to roam. User profiles are enabled by default, so after you configure the location of the profile in User Manager for Domains, they're ready to go. This is not the case with the Windows 95/98 platforms, although Windows 98 is "more ready" than Windows 95.

On Windows 98, you'll need to go into the Control Panel, access the Passwords applet, select the User Profiles tab, and click User Can Customize. That is all that's necessary to make Windows 98 ready to travel, because it's basically set up for roaming profiles anyway. You will, of course, need to set up the central location for the profile and specify that in the user's directory entry.

For Windows 95, you must also take the additional step of installing Internet Explorer 4.0. This installation basically brings the Windows 95 platform up to Windows 98 level as far as roaming profiles are concerned. After Internet Explorer 4.0 is installed, you follow the same steps as for Windows 98 to set up the profiles.

One of the most common uses for roaming profiles is for users who like to log in and work at home. Unfortunately, the type and configuration of users' home machines can vary widely and be difficult to accurately determine. If you plan to have them work from home, it's best to try to match their home and work configurations, at least in terms of operating system, as closely as possible. If you have a user who likes to work from home extensively, you might consider having them use a laptop computer as their primary workstation to simplify support and access issues.

Some of the issues that will come up for your international travelers have to do with code pages and languages. Code pages dictate the character set that's associated with the keys on the keyboard. It goes without saying that if you're trying to use a profile on a machine that has a different code page installed, it's not going to perform as expected. Languages can be troublesome because the user interface is going to display in the language set established for that machine. There is a way to get around that, at least with Windows 2000.

Windows 2000 Professional (previously Windows NT 5 Workstation) can be configured with a Multilingual User Interface (MUI) which can support all languages used throughout your enterprise. The user sets his preferred language in his profile, and then when he travels to another computer running Windows 2000, his profile goes right along with him in his native language. This is about the only way to get around the language barrier, if you have locations all over the world with the operating system installed for their native languages, and you have users who don't speak the language they need to use their computers.

▶ **See** "International Support for Languages," **p. 1721**

Supporting Office 2000

A number of resources are available for support of Microsoft Office 2000. The following sections point out a few that you may find useful.

Microsoft Support Newsgroups

Microsoft hosts support newsgroups for every product on their own news servers. These groups, although not staffed with Microsoft employees, typically are monitored by Microsoft MVP's (Most Valuable Professionals) who are volunteers that have been judged by Microsoft to have strong knowledge of the product and who volunteer their time to answer questions in the newsgroups.

To access these newsgroups, configure your newsreader (such as Outlook Express) to access the `msnews.Microsoft.com` news server. You will find a long list of newsgroups where you can post questions and read the questions and solutions of other users.

Microsoft Support on the Web

Microsoft offers a wealth of online content. The most obvious one can be found by clicking Help, Office on the Web from any Microsoft Office 2000 application. This takes you to the Office on the Web site that Microsoft maintains where you can read articles; download updates, add-ins, and patches; and follow links to Microsoft-recommended sites.

Other valuable Microsoft Support resources online include

- Technet: (`http://www.Microsoft.com/Technet/`)—This site is for administrators and power users and offers some excellent technical articles about Microsoft products.
- Microsoft Knowledge Base: (`http://support.microsoft.com/support/search/c.asp`)—The Microsoft Knowledge Base of problems, questions, and solutions. An excellent starting point for troubleshooting any Microsoft product.
- Microsoft Office Resource Kit: (`http://www.microsoft.com/office/ork/`)—An online place for more information, white-papers, and articles about Office 97 and 2000.

Third-Party Sites

Many more useful sites are available than we can possibly list here, so I'll just point out some of the highlights.

- Slipstick Systems: (`http://www.slipstick.com`)—Funny name, but outstanding resource for Microsoft Outlook and Exchange questions and information.
- Chip Pearson's Microsoft Excel Pages: (`http://home.gvi.net/~cpearson/excelmain.htm`)—When it comes to Excel, few are better than Chip Pearson.
- Woody's Office Watch: (`http://mcc.com.au/wow/`)—The weekly free e-newsletter that Woody Leonhard and his friends will send you is more than worth the time it takes to sign up. A must-read for any serious Office administrator.
- Inside Microsoft Access Journal: (`http://www.zdjournals.com/ima/`)—From Ziff-Davis, a site and a publication dedicated to Microsoft Access programming.

PART X

Appendixes

APPENDIX A

Applications Found in Each Office 2000 Edition

In this appendix

Office 2000 Editions—An Overview

Office 2000 is designed to take advantage of the increased popularity and use of the Internet and corporate intranets to share information. The software suite helps users streamline the way they work to collaborate with people and manage information. Because needs differ in both personal and business computing, Microsoft has made Microsoft Office 2000 available in five versions:

- Office 2000 Standard
- Office 2000 Small Business
- Office 2000 Professional
- Office 2000 Premium
- Office 2000 Developer

This book discusses the advanced topics in all the Office 2000 applications, with the exception of the Small Business Tools and some features unique to the Developer version.

Office 2000 Standard

Office 2000 Standard is suited for users who want the powerful document creation, analysis, and contact information features but who do not need to manage and track complex business information (for which Microsoft Access 2000 would be used).

Office 2000 Standard includes the following applications:

- Word 2000
- Excel 2000
- PowerPoint 2000
- Outlook 2000
- Internet Explorer

Office 2000 Small Business

Office 2000 Small Business offers the core set of tools to help manage and run a small business more effectively. Office 2000 Small Business provides productivity applications to improve the process of working with people and information; it also provides a rich set of business analysis and enhancement tools to help users make better business decisions and streamline business operations.

Office 2000 Small Business includes the following applications:

- Word 2000
- Excel 2000
- Outlook 2000

- Publisher 2000
- Small Business Tools
- Internet Explorer

Office 2000 Professional

Office 2000 Professional provides a complete set of tools that enables users to improve collaboration between colleagues and business associates. Office 2000 Professional includes Access 2000, which provides powerful information-tracking and analytical tools to extract valuable data from corporate databases.

Office 2000 Professional includes the following applications:

- Word 2000
- Excel 2000
- PowerPoint 2000
- Access 2000
- Outlook 2000
- Publisher 2000
- Internet Explorer

Office 2000 Premium

Office 2000 Premium includes all the applications found in Office Professional. It also includes FrontPage 2000 and PhotoDraw 2000. By adding these applications, Office 2000 Premium provides users with everything they need to create and manage great intranet (and extranet) sites, as well as easy-to-use tools for editing photo images and creating high-quality graphics. In addition, Office 2000 Premium streamlines the process of working with people and information, making it easier to create, publish, and analyze information on an intranet.

Office 2000 Premium includes the following applications:

- Word 2000
- Excel 2000
- PowerPoint 2000
- Access 2000
- Outlook 2000
- Publisher 2000
- FrontPage 2000
- PhotoDraw 2000
- Internet Explorer

Office 2000 Developer

Office 2000 Developer is designed for professional developers who build solutions with Microsoft Office. Office Developer includes all the applications found in Office 2000 Premium, as well as tools and documentation for building, managing, and deploying Office-based solutions.

- COM Add-In Designer—Enables developers to create and debug standalone VBA COM add-ins (DLLs) that can be used from multiple Office applications, all from within the VBA development environment.
- VBA Productivity Tools—Includes add-ins such as the Code Librarian, which provides a searchable database that makes it easy for development teams to share a wide range of reusable code. It also includes add-ins to automate code documentation, error-handling routines, and automatic string parsing, as well as other tools for enhancing productivity.
- Learning Materials and Programming Resources—The MSDN Library, hard-copy documentation, and prewritten code for standard routines for VBA and the Visual Studio development system are included in these tools.
- Visual Studio Templates and Code Samples—Provide a starting point for building COM add-ins and automating Microsoft Office externally.

APPENDIX B

Suggested References

In this appendix

Other Reference Books

This book presents information about each of the applications in the Premium Edition of Microsoft Office 2000. Que publishes a number of books focusing on Office as a whole and on each individual application within the suite. If you need more specialized information on any of the applications, I recommend that you check out the books I've recommended in the following sections. These books can be found at most bookstores or ordered via the Web from `www.amazon.com`.

Que's Platinum Edition Using Series

In addition to this book, there are two other key books in the Platinum Edition Using series that provide a tremendous amount of information. These books are written for experienced users:

- *Platinum Edition Using Windows 98*
- *Platinum Edition Using Microsoft Access 2000*

Que's Special Edition Using Series

The Special Edition Using series of books is written for experienced computer users and is geared for the intermediate-level user. Que offers an array of Special Edition Using Series books, covering Office 2000 and each of its applications. I suggest the following books for additional information:

- *Special Edition Using Microsoft Office 2000*
- *Special Edition Using Microsoft Word 2000*
- *Special Edition Using Microsoft Excel 2000*
- *Special Edition Using Microsoft Access 2000*
- *Special Edition Using Microsoft PowerPoint 2000*
- *Special Edition Using Microsoft Outlook 2000*
- *Special Edition Using Microsoft FrontPage 2000*
- *Special Edition Using Microsoft Publisher 2000*

Online References

A wealth of information is available online about Microsoft Office Applications. These resources include newsletters, Web sites, and newsgroups.

Online Newsletters

Woody Leonhard, a renowned Office expert and author, produces two newsletters deliverable directly to your email Inbox. They contain up-to-date information about new Microsoft releases (including service releases), really useful tips, and great "workarounds" for Microsoft Office features that don't work the way you want them to. The best thing about these newsletters is they are FREE (and Woody doesn't sell his mailing list).

- Woody's Office Watch (WOW)—This newsletter is distributed weekly.
- Woody's Windows Watch (WWW)—This newsletter is distributed biweekly.

You can subscribe to these newsletters by sending an email to `wow@wopr.com` or pointing your browser to `www.wopr.com/wow`.

In addition to Woody's newsletters, Microsoft produces a variety of newsletters. Among the most useful are

- Industry Solutions Newsletter—In this monthly newsletter, business customers learn about the latest and best software applications built on Microsoft products that will solve their information challenges in different lines of business.
- Microsoft Internet Dispatch—A monthly report on the latest offerings from the Home.Microsoft.Com and Internet Explorer Web sites. This report alerts you to exciting content and features as well as to product upgrades and Internet security developments.
- Microsoft Product Support Services News Watch—Keep current on top support issues received by Microsoft Product Support Services. Editions include

  BackOffice

  Developer Products

  Games, Reference & Kids' Products

  Office

  Windows and Internet Explorer
- Microsoft: This Week—A weekly newsletter highlighting Microsoft's top new products, contests, advice, tips, and free downloads.
- Office Enterprise Insider—A monthly newsletter for IT professionals who are evaluating, implementing, and deploying Microsoft Office.
- TechNet Flash—A biweekly newsletter for the Information Technology professional that brings you information and highlights on technology issues, trends, and events from Microsoft and its partners.

To subscribe to the Microsoft newsletters, point your browser to the Microsoft Web site (`www.microsoft.com`). Click Free Newsletters from the list of links. You have to fill out some profile information and then you are given the opportunity to subscribe to any or all of the newsletters.

Web Sites

You might want to add these Web sites to your favorites list:

- Microsoft Office Web site—`www.microsoft.com/office/`
- Microsoft Wish Web site—`www.microsoft.com/mswish/`
- Woody's Office Watch—`www.wopr.com`

You can also get to the Microsoft Wish site by clicking Write Us on the Microsoft Home or Microsoft Office Web site and choosing Send a Wish from the list of options. I have the Microsoft Wish site in my list of favorites and routinely send requests for features I want to see in the next release of a product. I believe in the "squeaky wheel" theory—the more frequently Microsoft sees a feature request, the more likely that it will be included in the next software release.

Newsgroups

A large number of Microsoft Public newsgroups are available to which you can subscribe. Some are application-specific and some are by topic. These newsgroups provide a forum where users can exchange information with one another. The newsgroups are organized by application; for example:

```
microsoft.public.access
microsoft.public.excel
microsoft.public.powerpoint
microsoft.public.win98
microsoft.public.word
```

Newsgroups that have just the application name can be used for any topic about that application. However, other newsgroups are available that address specific issues. For example, for Excel these are among the available newsgroups:

```
microsoft.public.excel.charting
microsoft.public.excel.links
microsoft.public.excel.printing
microsoft.public.excel.programming
microsoft.public.excel.worksheetfunctions
```

NOTE Some newsgroups are very active whereas others are not. To get an indication of the activity level in the newsgroups, display a newsgroup and look at the dates items were posted. If the dates are recent, then the newsgroup is active.

Many of the Microsoft Public newsgroups are monitored by kind-hearted volunteers who attempt to answer your questions and give advice.

To distinguish these volunteers from others who respond to your questions, Microsoft has a recognition program that designates the most active and accurate volunteers in the newsgroups. These are Microsoft MVPs (Most Valuable Professionals). Microsoft MVPs typically include their MVP designation after their name when they respond to newsgroup items. Several of the Microsoft MVPs have contributed to this book, including

- Vince Averello (Outlook MVP)
- Kyle Bryant (Desktop Systems and Internet Explorer MVP)
- Daryl Lucas (Word MVP)
- Ben Schorr (Outlook MVP)
- Herb Tyson (Word MVP)
- Gordon Padwick (Outlook MVP)

Index

Symbols

A

C

D

E

F

G

H

I

J

K

L

M

N

O

P

Q

R

S

T

U

V

W

X

Y-Z

Special Edition

Using

The One Source for Comprehensive Solutions™

The one-stop shop for serious users, *Special Edition Using* offers readers a thorough understanding of software and technologies. Intermediate to advanced users get detailed coverage that is clearly presented and to the point.

Other Special Edition Using Titles

Special Edition Using Windows 98
Ed Bott and Ron Person
0-7897-1488-4
$39.99

Special Edition Using Windows 95 Second Edition
Ron Person
0-7897-1381-0
$19.99

Special Edition Using Microsoft PowerPoint 2000
Patrice Rutledge
0-7897-1904-5
$39.99

Special Edition Using Microsoft Outlook 2000
Gordon Padwick
0-7897-1909-6
$39.99

Special Edition Using Microsoft FrontPage 2000
Dennis Jones
0-7897-1910-x
$39.99

Special Edition Using Microsoft Access 2000
Roger Jennings
0-7897-1606-2
$39.99

Special Edition Using VBA 2000
0-7897-1953-3
Coming summer 1999, $29.99

www.quecorp.com

Special Edition Using Microsoft Word 2000
Bill Camarda
0-7897-1852-9
$39.99

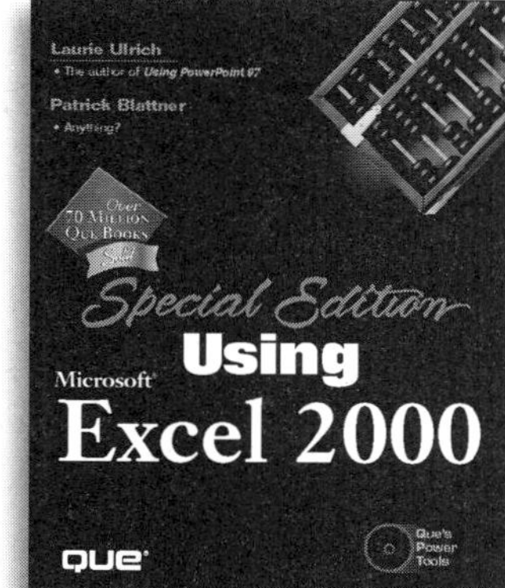

Special Edition Using Microsoft Excel 2000
Laurie Ulrich and Patrick Blattner
0-7897-1729-8
$39.99

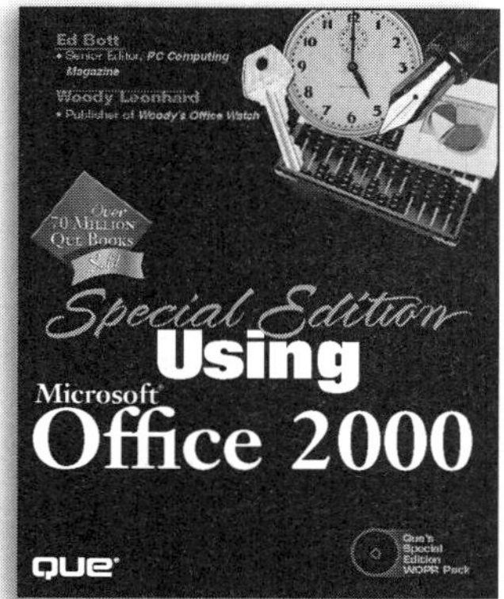

Special Edition Using Microsoft Office 2000
Ed Bott and Woody Leonhard
0-7897-1842-1
$39.99

All prices are subject to change.

Other Related Titles

Special Edition Using SQL Server 7
Steven Wynkoop
0-7897-1523-6
$39.99

Platinum Edition Using VB 6
Loren Eidahl
0-7897-1961-9
$49.99

Platinum Edition Using Windows 95 Second Edition
Ron Person
0-7897-1383-7
$60.00

Special Edition Using Visual InterDev 6
Steve Banick
0-7897-1549-x
$39.99

Special Edition Using Exchange Server 5.5
Spectrum Software
0-7897-1503-1
$39.99

Using the Windows 98 Registry
Jerry Honeycutt
0-7897-1658-5
$29.99

Microsoft Office 2000 Quick Reference
Nancy Warner
0-7897-1932-0
$9.99

Upgrading and Repairing PCs, 10th Anniversary Edition
Scott Mueller
0-7897-1636-4
$54.99

www.quecorp.com

Microsoft Office 2000 Administrator's Desk Reference
Bill Camarda
0-7897-1931-2
$49.99
Coming summer 1999

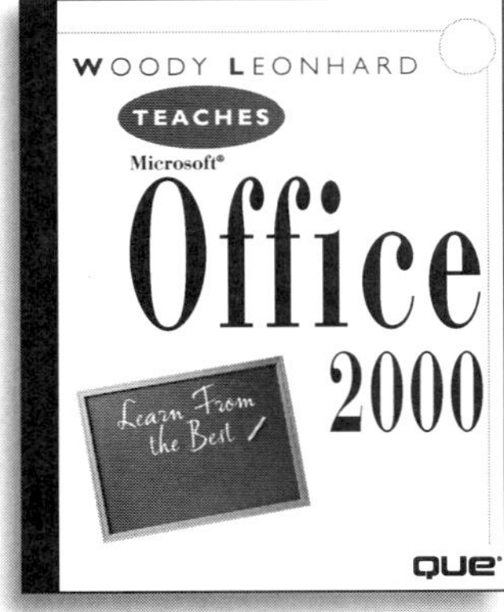

Woody Leonhard Teaches Microsoft Office2000
Woody Leonhard
0-7897-1871-5
$29.99

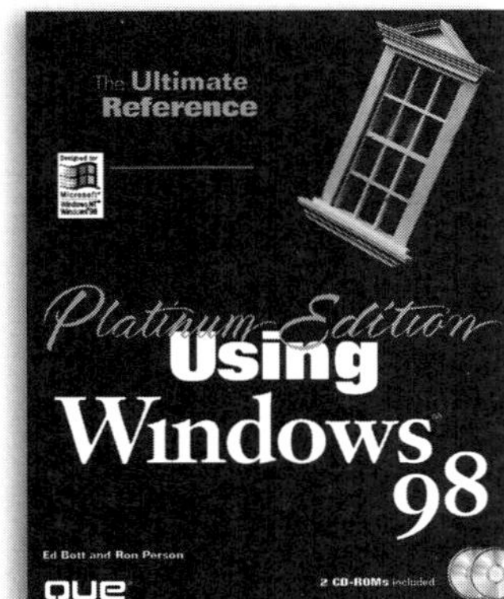

Platinum Edition Using Windows 98
Ed Bott and Ron Person
0-7897-1489-2
$49.99

All prices are subject to change.

SPECIAL OFFER

The OfficeReady™ templates you re using are just a selection from the 650 templates offered in the complete version of OfficeReady.

If you re enjoying the time-saving benefits of these professionally designed, ready-to-use templates, just imagine having templates for nearly every task you perform using Microsoft¤ Office.

It s easy. All of the additional templates are already located on *Que's Platinum Edition Pack.* You ll immediately be able to use them for all of the work you do using Microsoft Office. Even better, you ll have all 650 templates for only $19.95. That s 50% off the normal retail price!

Ordering is easy. Just call 1-(800) 385-2155. All of the additional templates are already located on your CD-ROM. You ll be issued a password to unlock the templates.

Designing documents in Microsoft Office can take up hours of your valuable time. Now, for only $19.95, you can save that time, and devote it to something that makes sense — like your business.

Offer subject to availability. Prices subject to change without notice.

Que's Platinum Edition Pack

By opening this package, you are agreeing to be bound by the following agreement:

Windows 95/98/NT4 CD Installation Instructions

1. Insert the CD-ROM disc into your CD-ROM drive.
2. From the Windows 95 desktop, double-click on the My Computer icon.
3. Double-click on the icon representing your CD-ROM drive.
4. Double-click on the icon titled START.EXE to run the installation program.

NOTE If Windows 95 or 98 is installed on your computer, and you have the AutoPlay feature enabled, the SETUP.EXE program starts automatically whenever you insert the disc into your CD-ROM drive.

CAUTION

Because of the new security model in Microsoft Office 2000, it is possible that the security settings in Office may prevent some of the applications on this CD-ROM from running. Many of these applications are based on macros in templates. Although all the macros and templates on this CD are virus-free, Office security settings may prevent them from running anyway. If your Office security settings are set to "High," unsigned macros will not run and you will not be given a prompt to change them. You can change this option by following the directions discussed in this book. If your company has "locked" your copy of Office to prevent you from changing this setting, you will need to contact your Office 2000 administrator where you work to change this setting to allow these to run.

Some of the macros have been signed with a digital certificate to authenticate the macro creator identity. With these, you may be prompted whether or not to run them and asked whether or not you "trust" the signer. You should accept the prompt to allow the template or macro to work correctly.